# J. W. McKENZIE

*Specialists in antiquarian, secondhand
cricket books, particularly
John Wisden's Cricketers' Almanack*

**BOOKS AND COLLECTIONS BOUGHT**

12 STONELEIGH PARK ROAD
EWELL, EPSOM, SURREY KT19 0QT
ENGLAND

CATALOGUES SENT ON REQUEST

TEL: 081-393 7700
FAX: 081-393 1694

129TH YEAR

# WISDEN

## CRICKETERS' ALMANACK

# 1992

EDITED BY GRAEME WRIGHT

PUBLISHED BY JOHN WISDEN & CO LTD

A COMPANY JOINTLY OWNED BY
GRAYS OF CAMBRIDGE (INTERNATIONAL) LIMITED
AND
BOWATER PLC

SOFT COVER EDITION £18.50                CASED EDITION £21.50

ISBN
Cased edition 0 947766 18 9
Soft cover edition 0 947766 19 7

John Wisden & Co Ltd
25 Down Road
Merrow
Guildford
Surrey
GU1 2PY

Computer typeset by Spottiswoode Ballantyne Ltd, Colchester
Printed in Great Britain by William Clowes Limited, Beccles

# PREFACE

There appears, on page 52 of this 129th edition of *Wisden*, a photograph of John Arlott at work, not as a broadcaster but as a writer, for that was his connection with the Almanack. From the 1950 *Wisden* to this one, apart from a gap of two years, he recorded as many as possible of the previous year's books and other publications. His copy for the books received in 1991 was delivered a matter of weeks before he died in December. An appreciation, written by Mike Brearley, for whom John had a special affection, appears early in this *Wisden*.

Readers will notice a change in the format of the schools section. The particular highlights of a school's season have been linked to the averages, to which extra information has been added, and a new feature is the list of teams beaten. Elsewhere, Gerald Howat, in the course of reviewing the MCC Schools Festival at Oxford and Lord's, has provided a thoughtful analysis of schools cricket today. To complement the inclusion of two girls' elevens – Denstone and Roedean – in the schools section, Teresa McLean has written on women in cricket. Other features contrast the personalities and techniques of Gordon Greenidge and Desmond Haynes, West Indies' opening batsmen from 1978 to 1991; celebrate the centenary of the Lancashire League; and enjoy some of the advertisements which appeared in the *Wisdens* of the late-Victorian and Edwardian years.

One of the pleasures of working on *Wisden* has been the willingness with which people in cricket give their help. Many are listed on the following page, and I am grateful also to those at Lord's, at both MCC and TCCB, and at the county clubs for their co-operation. To the county scorers and statisticians, who give their time to check scorecards and generally answer a number of queries throughout the season, my special thanks. I suspect I am less enthusiastic about the soul who, I gather, has persuaded the Pakistan and Hampshire fast bowler, Aqib Javed, that his first name should be spelt Aaqib, the player himself having requested a single *a* at the beginning of last season. He appears in this edition as Aqib Javed.

Finally, I would like to thank those who have been closely connected with the production of this Almanack. The presence of Harriet Monkhouse in the Wisden office has provided a statistical as well as an editorial strength; she has been responsible for much of the day-to-day routine which is so essential in a book such as *Wisden*. Meanwhile, Roy Smart, attending to the computer, and Gordon Burling, as a valued proofreader, played essential roles at either end of the production cycle. If Christine Forrest's workload lightened, it was only by a little, and her expertise in the final stages was once again invaluable, not least in the preparation of the Index. To these four, and to Peter Bather and Mike Smith at Spottiswoode Ballantyne, our typesetter, this edition owes much.

GRAEME WRIGHT

Eastcote
Middlesex

## LIST OF CONTRIBUTORS

The editor acknowledges with gratitude the assistance afforded in the preparation of the Almanack by the following:

Jonathan Agnew
Jack Arlidge (Sussex)
John Arlott (Books)
David Armstrong
Chris Aspin (Lancashire Leagues)
Philip Bailey
Mark Baldwin
Jack Bannister (Warwickshire)
June Bayliss
Brian Bearshaw (Lancashire)
Sir William Becher
Michael Berry
Scyld Berry
Edward Bevan (Glamorgan)
J. Watson Blair (Scotland)
Mike Brearley
Dick Brittenden
Robert Brooke (Births and Deaths)
Gordon Burling
C. R. Buttery (New Zealand)
John Callaghan (Yorkshire)
Terry Cooper (Middlesex)
Geoffrey Copinger
Ted Corbett
Tony Cozier (West Indies)
Brian Croudy
Jon Culley (Leicestershire)
Norman de Mesquita
Patrick Eagar
Paton Fenton (Oxford University)
David Field (Surrey)
Bill Frindall (Records)
Nigel Fuller (Essex)
Ghulam Mustafa Khan
G. S. Gordon
Benny Green
David Hallett (Cambridge University)
David Hardy (The Netherlands)
Peter Hargreaves (Denmark)
Bob Harragan (Welsh Schools)
Les Hatton
Frank Heydenrych (South Africa)
Eric Hill (Somerset)
Dr Grenville Holland (UAU)

Gerald Howat
Brian Hunt
Ken Ingman (ESCA)
Kate Jenkins
Ihithisham Kamardeen
Abid Ali Kazi (Pakistan)
John Kitchin (Obituaries)
Stephanie Lawrence
Alan Lee
Nick Lucy (Nottinghamshire)
Steven Lynch
John MacKinnon (Australia)
Teresa McLean
A. R. May
Allan Miller
John Minshull-Fogg
R. Mohan (India)
Chris Moore (Worcestershire)
Dudley Moore (Kent)
Graham Morris
Gerald Mortimer (Derbyshire)
David Munden
Brian Murgatroyd
Mike Neasom (Hampshire)
David Norrie
Lord Orr-Ewing
Francis Payne
Qamar Ahmed
Andrew Radd (Northamptonshire)
Rex Roberts
Peter Roebuck
Carol Salmon (Women's Cricket)
Geoffrey Saulez
Derek Scott (Ireland)
Roy Smart
Bill Smith
John Thicknesse
Stephen Thorpe
Sudhir Vaidya (India)
Gerry Vaidyasekera (Sri Lanka)
David Walsh (HMC Schools)
Geoffrey Wheeler (Gloucestershire)
Peter Wynne-Thomas

Thanks are accorded also to the following for checking the scorecards of first-class matches:
M. R. L. W. Ayers, L. Beaumont, G. R. Blackburn, Mrs C. Byatt, L. V. Chandler, W. Davies, B. T. Denning, J. Foley, V. H. Isaacs, B. H. Jenkins, D. Kendix, A. C. Kingston, D. A. Oldam, S. W. Tacey and R. D. Wilkinson.

5

# CONTENTS

# INDEX

Note: For reasons of space, certain entries which appear in alphabetical order in sections of the Almanack are not included in this index. These include names that appear in Test Cricketers, Births and Deaths of Cricketers, individual batting and bowling performances in the 1991 first-class season, and Oxford and Cambridge Blues.

*c.* = catches; *d.* = dismissals; *p'ship* = partnership; *r.* = runs; *w.* = wickets.
*Signifies not out or an unbroken partnership.*

*Index*

## J

Morgan, H. E. (Glam.):– 254 v Monmouth-shire, *271*.

Morkel, D. P. B. (SA):– 222 for 8th wkt, *154*.

Moroney, J. R. (Aust.):– 2 hundreds in same Test, *177, 229*.

Morris, A. R. (Aust.):– Test captain, *201, 231*; 12,614 r. (avge 53.67), *146*; 3,533 r. in Tests, *179*; 2,080 r. v England, *209*; 46 hundreds, *140*; 12 Test hundreds, *205, 229, 232, 237*; 2 hundreds in same Test, *177, 205*; 2 hundreds in match (2), *138*; 148 and 111 on début, *137*; 301 for 2nd wkt v England, *186*; Test p'ship record, *237*.

Morris, H. (Eng.):– 10,000 r., *278*; 2,000 r. since 1969 (1), *242*; 1st to 1,000 r. in 1991, *276*; 2 hundreds in match (2), *138*; Test p'ship record, *227*.

Morris, J. E. (Eng.):– 10,000 r., *278*.

Morrison, J. F. M. (NZ):– 1 Test hundred, *235*.

Mortimore, J. B. (Eng.):– All-round, *166*; 1,807 w., *164*.

Moss, A. E. (Cant.):– 10 w. in innings on début, *157*.

Moss, J. K. (Aust.):– 390* for 3rd wkt, *153*.

Motz, R. C. (NZ):– 100 w. in Tests, *189*.

Moxon, M. D. (Eng.):– Captain of York-shire, *630*; Hundred on début, *136*; 200 in 1991, *275*.

Mudassar Nazar (Pak.):– 4,114 r., *181*; 761 r. in series, *177*; 42 hundreds, *140*; 10 Test hundreds, *225, 253, 256*; Slowest Test hundred, *185*; Carrying bat in Test, *182*; Avge of 82.50 in English season, *143*; 111 w. in one-day ints, *267*; All-round in one-day ints, *268*; 451 for 3rd wkt, *151, 185, 257*; 389 for 1st wkt, *151*; Test p'ship records, *226, 253, 257, 260*.

Munaweera, S. (Colts):– 153 for 9th wkt, *155*.

Munir Shaukat (Faisalabad):– Wkt with 1st ball in f-c cricket, *1164*.

Munton, T. A. (Warwicks.):– 8 w. in innings, *277*.

Murdoch, W. L. (Aust. and Eng.):– Test captain, *200-1*; 2 Test hundreds, *205*; 321 v Victoria, *134*.

Murray, A. R. A. (SA):– 1 Test hundred, *242*; Test p'ship record, *242*.

Murray, D. A. (WI):– 10 d. in match, *168*; 9 d. in Test, *193*.

Murray, D. L. (WI):– Test captain, *231*; 189 d. in Tests, *194*; 24 d. in series, *193*; Test p'ship records, *233, 247, 249*.

Murray, J. T. (Eng.):– 1,025 r. and 104 d. in season, *166*; 1 Test hundred, *215*; Slow batting in Test, *184*; 1,527 d., *168*; 100 d. in season (2), *168*; 6 d. in Test innings, *193*; Test p'ship record, *217*.

Mushtaq Ali (Ind.):– 2 Test hundreds, *222, 247*.

Mushtaq Mohammad (Pak.):– Test captain, *238, 248, 252, 255*; Youngest Test player,

*198*; 31,091 r., *144*; 3,643 r. in Tests, *181*; 1,000 r. (15), *142*; 72 hundreds, *140*; 10 Test hundreds, *225, 239, 249, 253, 256*; 303* v Karachi Univ., *135*; All-round in Tests, *191*; 350 for 4th wkt v New Zealand, *153, 185, 253*; Test p'ship records, *226, 249, 253*.

Musleh-ud-Din (Pak. Rlwys):– Handled the ball, *155*.

Mycroft, W. (Derbys.):– 17 w. in match, *158*.

## N

Nadeem Yousuf (MCB):– 196* for 10th wkt, *155*.

Nadkarni, R. G. (Ind.):– 1 Test hundred, *223*; 10 w. or more in Test (1), *238*; Test p'ship records, *223, 251*.

Nagarwalla, N. D. (M'tra):– 245 for 9th wkt, *154*.

Nanan, R. (WI):– Test p'ship record, *249*.

Nash, G. (Lancs.):– 4 w. with consecutive balls, *159*.

Nash, M. A. (Glam.):– Fastest hundred in B & H Cup, *743*.

Nasim-ul-Ghani (Pak.):– Test début at 16, *198*; 1 Test hundred, *225*; Test p'ship record, *226*.

Nasir Valika (Kar. Whites):– Handled the ball, *155*.

National Association of Young Cricketers:– v MCC, *678*; v MCC Schools, *353-4*; v Australian Young Cricketers, *895*.

National Club Championship, *354-5*.

National Cricket Association:– *291*; Address, *1304*; England Amateur XI v Australian Young Cricketers, *893*; Young Cricketers v Combined Services, *354*.

National Power Awards, *546*.

National Village Championship, *356-7*.

NatWest Bank Trophy, *687-712*.

Nayudu, C. K. (Ind.):– Test captain, *221*; 11 sixes in innings, *149*.

Nayyar, R. (H. Pradesh):– Handled the ball, *156*.

Nazar Mohammad (Pak.):– 1 Test hundred, *256*; Carrying bat in Test, *182*.

Neale, P. A. (Worcs.):– Captain of Wor-cestershire, *613*.

Netherlands, The:– Cricket in, *1187-8*; Representative body, *1304*; Under-23 v Australian Young Cricketers, *893*.

Newham, W. (Eng.):– 344 for 7th wkt, *154*.

Newman, J. A. (Hants):– All-round, *166*; 2,032 w., *163, 164*; 100 w. (9), *162*.

Newport, P. J. (Eng.):– Test p'ship record, *227*.

New South Wales:– v Wellington, *1115-6*.

New Zealand:– B & H World Series Cup, *1168-78*; Domestic season 1990-91, *1141-9*; Highest individual Test innings, *175*; Highest Test innings, *196*; Leading batsmen in Tests, *180*; Leading bowlers in Tests, *189*; Lowest Test innings, *197*;

## U

# INDEX OF FILLERS

# NOTES BY THE EDITOR

Twelve months ago, as the Notes to the 1991 *Wisden* were being written, England failed to regain the Ashes in Australia, and were soon to embark on a series of embarrassing defeats in New Zealand. England's cricket, without a doubt, was in desperate straits. What a difference a year makes. Two Test wins over West Indies, and a drawn series, restored the confidence in English cricket which had been badly shaken by the events in Australia and New Zealand.

Although those victories were very much team efforts, they owed everything to individual performances, in particular to the batting of Graham Gooch, the captain, and Robin Smith. No-one, however, delighted more than the left-arm spinner, Philip Tufnell, whose own passage from doldrums to buoyancy encapsulated that of the England team. Tufnell turned the final Test against West Indies with a spell of slow bowling on the Saturday which will find its way into cricketing mythology – where it will be joined by his achievement in bowling England to an unlikely victory over New Zealand at Christchurch in January.

At the end of a decade which had seen Test cricket dominated by relentless fast bowling, evidence that a slow bowler, through flight and spin, could not only change the course of a Test match but also win one was not simply a welcome relief. It encouraged optimism for the future of the game. For too long, cricket has been crying out for genuine variety. Perhaps now the philosophy of bowling will change. "If I can't bowl you out, I'll knock you out" might become "Hit me if you dare", and the game will develop as a more fascinating contest. Yet in some quarters there are those, it seems, who think that the future belongs not to the spin bowler but to the man who paints logos on the outfield. In which case there might not be a place for the likes of P. C. R. Tufnell. With his short run-up, and with batsmen reluctant to hit him back over his head, one logo will be lost to the television cameras for overs on end. What price a logo in an age of spin, one wonders.

## Symbolism in the outfield

The logo on the outfield is a symbol. It is a symbol of the level to which English cricket has to go to earn a crust. Indeed, it brings to mind that tragic figure of Victorian melodrama: the mother who goes out on the street to support her family in hard times. (Not that the editor of *Wisden* is best placed to cast the first stone.) But it is a symbol, too, of the influence which the marketing committee has within the Test and County Cricket Board, and of the diminishing influence of those whose first concern is for the game of cricket itself. The periphery, one feels, has become more important than the middle.

Last summer's decision by the first-class counties to ignore the advice of the TCCB's cricket committee, with regard to the future of the Sunday League, and instead to take on board the plans of the marketing men, further illustrates the struggle for the soul of the game. For sound cricketing reasons – and perhaps for good commercial ones, too – the cricket committee advocated playing the Sunday League in two divisions of eight teams each, with a knockout stage to determine the season's champions. While cutting the number of 40-overs games – technically more damaging to playing standards than other forms of cricket – this would also have offered variety for spectators by freeing some Sundays for either 55-overs Benson and Hedges Cup matches or for Championship cricket. Instead the TCCB rejected these proposals, voting in favour of the existing format and also for teams to wear coloured clothing and play with a white ball against black sightscreens.

Somehow the marketing men and the counties – Kent, Leicestershire, Middlesex and Surrey excepted – got it badly wrong. For a start they were flying in the face of members' opinion; not that members' opinions worry committeemen much, until the members get their act together and vote them out of office. Replying to a questionnaire sent out prior to the Special Meeting of the TCCB in May last year, the majority of county members who replied gave an emphatic thumbs down to coloured clothing. So did Refuge Assurance, the sponsors of the Sunday League. They chose not to renew their contract. But even worse, no-one else wanted to sponsor the Board's colourful new package either.

This does raise a question. If members opposed coloured clothing, and sponsors didn't want it, for whom was it intended? Television? Only a small minority of potential viewers watch Sunday League cricket on television, now that the broadcasting rights reside with BSkyB, the satellite network. To realise how few of the game's supporters bother with BSkyB, one had only to hear the thunderous applause which greeted the announcement at Lord's, during the NatWest Bank Trophy final, that the BBC would again cover the Benson and Hedges Cup, as well as continuing to screen the NatWest and all international matches in England.

Money should not be the only determining factor when it comes to broadcasting rights. Cricket is not such a popular sport that audience figures can afford to be ignored, especially with cricket being played at fewer schools and young people being offered a whole range of alternative leisure activities. Cricket needs maximum exposure more than ever. Thousands of viewers in Britain will have watched the World Cup, perhaps hundreds of thousands. The fact that it would have been millions had the World Cup been shown on the BBC or ITV should be of concern to the TCCB. One feels it is not.

## The need for balance

This has little to do with cricket itself, after a year when it is cricket that deserves to be celebrated. But the way the game is administered is, I believe, a matter for debate. Given the place cricket has in national life, a balance must be struck between cricket, the game, and cricket, the business. The game will continue to be played, from summer to summer, on Saturdays and Sundays and long into weekday evenings; by men and women from all walks of life. But what this game is, and how it is played, is influenced by the business that is cricket. The proliferation of the limited-overs game in club, league and schools cricket since the advent of the Gillette Cup, 30 years ago, testifies to that.

The problem, as I see it, is the need to support the professional county game, with its playing and administrative staffs. Just as many newspapers and magazines cannot survive on buyers alone, needing advertising revenue to cover their costs, so county cricket is unable to exist only on those who watch the games. The county clubs require a healthy membership, but even then they need the revenue generated by marketing the game. The danger comes when the marketing men struggle to sell the product because its image no longer suits prospective sponsors. They then try to tailor it to suit the sponsor, rather as they might demand changes to a magazine's editorial approach or format in order to please advertisers, disregarding the fact that it was the editorial approach or the format which first attracted the magazine's readers. What often results then is a falling-off in readership until new readers are found who will accept the changed version. This is what is happening in cricket.

County cricket, unable to attract enough customers to pay its way, has come to depend on income from other sources. One of these, as of course it has been for some time, is the England team – through attendances at and broadcasting fees from Test matches and one-day internationals. In 1992, incidentally, there will be five of the latter, instead of three as has been the norm on a full tour. Because of the money it brings to the game, the England team has grown in importance in the last decade, to the extent that today its welfare is given priority. One consequence of this is that county members have had to put up with changes in long-established fixture arrangements. Championship games, for example, start on Friday rather than Saturday so that the England team can assemble a day earlier before Test matches. That may not sound like a great hardship. But coming in halfway through a game – as those who can watch only on Saturdays must now do – is not the same as being there on the first day. Decisions like this make members wonder if those who run cricket ever watch the game as the paying spectator does; or if they see it merely from inside a committee room, with its attendant attractions. Perhaps, on the other hand, the committeemen are looking out at the sparse crowd, then at the cost of running a county club, and are asking themselves what matters most.

More and more I prefer watching a day of county cricket to a day of Test match cricket. Nevertheless I can't help wondering what the rationale is for this April to September circuit that is so erratically supported; is at times no more than a meeting place for pensioners and a refuge for the truant. Benson and Hedges Cup games, played in April and May, often draw poor attendances, and the Sunday League is no longer the attraction it once was. Yet this summer, eighteen counties will endeavour to keep the show on the road and off the breadline. Why? Because it has always been thus? Because it is part of the fabric of English life? Or because no-one will stand back and say that the time has come to overhaul the professional game?

## Yet another working party

Last summer the TCCB set up a working party, under the chairmanship of M. P. Murray, the Middlesex chairman, to investigate the state of the first-class game in England. This could be interpreted as recognition of the need for change in the game, were it not for the fact that, only six years ago, the counties chose not to implement the major recommendations of the Palmer Report into the Standards of Play of English Cricket in Test and First-class County Cricket. Establishing working parties and commissions is an easy way of persuading people that something is being done, even when nothing is done as a result of them. The county chairmen who make the decisions at the TCCB meetings will, on past performance, vote for logos on the outfield ahead of any radical changes to the structure of county cricket. By changes I don't mean uncovering pitches for County Championship matches, four-day games only in the Championship, or even a more meaningful formula for Championship cricket; rather, I mean making changes which would provide a dynamic, viable circuit for the professional game in the 1990s and beyond.

## The counties concede their birthright

Such changes would almost certainly bring about the demise of some counties, but then it seems to me that county affiliation, with regard to players, becomes more nebulous every year. If the regulations governing the qualification and registration of players are anything to go by, the counties recognise this themselves. Up to 1991, a first-class county had first claim on a cricketer who qualified for it by birth, or one year's residence, or by his father having played regularly for that county. Not any more. Cricketers registered for a county, and cricketers under sixteen with "close cricketing connections" with a first-class county, may not be approached without that county's permission. All others are now open to offers from interested parties. Lord Harris must be turning in his grave at the prospect of cricketers flitting back and forth across the Forest Hill Road with impunity. The change in the regulations took me by surprise, for I thought the counties valued their locally produced players more than that.

## The status of Oxford and Cambridge cricket

Surely the time has come for the TCCB to examine the first-class status of cricket at Oxford and Cambridge Universities. The cricket played is not first-class; it is, as often as not, barely Second Eleven standard. I know there are those who defend the retention of first-class status for a number of reasons: tradition, the facilities at Oxford and Cambridge, and the advantage young cricketers have, being able to play against county cricketers at such nurseries. Yet more young cricketers, who will go on to county cricket, would benefit from an early introduction to first-class cricket if Durham University were accorded first-class status. That university has facilities for first-class cricket, and in county cricket today its alumni outnumber those of Oxford and Cambridge combined by two to one. For every Atherton or Crawley who remains in the public eye by playing his cricket at Fenner's or in The Parks, others of promise remain virtually out of sight for three years while they attend, say, Durham or Loughborough or Swansea.

This, however, is a side-issue to my main argument, which is that the cricket played by the majority of young men at Oxford and Cambridge does not merit first-class status. Occasionally a batsman shines, but the bowling has become embarrassingly weak. The International Cricket Council, while leaving it to the Test match countries to decide the status of their cricket, none the less reminds them that "the interest of first-class cricket will be served by ensuring that first-class status is *not* accorded to any match in which one or other of the teams taking part cannot on a strict interpretation of the definition be adjudged first-class".

## Investing in England's success

There are days at county games, too, when it is reasonable to ask if one is watching first-class cricket. But as often as not those players will prove their worth another day. The standard of county cricket, however, is no longer sufficiently high to allow players to move effortlessly from the county game to Test cricket. Test cricket today requires a different approach, and given the importance of the England team's success to the economy of the domestic game, the effort that now goes into preparing England teams should not be undervalued. It may be pragmatic, but it is purposeful and it is producing results. For that, English cricket owes more to Micky Stewart's vision and determination than is usually allowed. Five years ago he outlined what he saw as the problems of English cricket at international level, and he did not see answers to those problems within the county structure. His solution, if he could achieve it, was specialist preparation for players: something that would bridge the gap between county cricket and international cricket.

The benefit of such preparation was brought into focus by England's early success in the West Indies in 1990. Now, through the sponsorship of Whittingdale, a group of City investment managers, the senior England side and the A team are able to prepare thoroughly before going on tour. Prior to the winter's tours, for example, there were twice-weekly practice sessions at Lord's, The Oval, Headingley, Lilleshall and Cheltenham, as well as "teach-ins" with specialist coaches. Finally, the teams had four days at Lilleshall before setting off. In addition to the tourists, players on the fringe of selection were also invited to attend. The sponsorship, furthermore, has enabled the team managers to video players at practice, and to build up a dossier on their progress. It is the kind of thing much admired when other countries do it, yet there is a feeling in some circles that this extraordinary preparation should not be necessary for English cricketers. Well, it shouldn't be. It wouldn't be if the counties were willing to implement a county programme which would be a natural stepping-stone to international cricket.

## A challenge for Test cricket

If I put great stress on the international game, it is because there lies the future of cricket in terms of public perception. More than likely there will be too much of it – there already is – and both goose and golden egg will be consumed in the gluttony. How many years are left for Test cricket if crowds continue to decline, as they do in countries other than England? The return of South Africa to the international fold presents both an opportunity and a challenge. The opportunity lies in a population deprived of international cricket for twenty years. The challenge will be in sustaining an audience for Test cricket after the initial enthusiasm is satisfied. The new generation, unaccustomed to the gradual development of a Test match, may wonder what all the fuss was about. A one-day international under lights, on a warm evening flavoured by steaks cooking on a barbecue, may well be what they want. Cricket currently needs the variety that South Africa will bring, but as the new South Africans seek their place in the sun, they could also quicken the erosion of what one increasingly thinks of as traditional cricket.

It is said that support for cricket continues to fall away in the West Indies. This is worrying. The West Indies team is in a state of transition, with those young players coming through still to establish themselves. As more and more people in the Caribbean look towards the United States for interests and influence, cricket must produce new heroes and counter-attractions. World cricket cannot afford a second-best West Indies side. The one that is now breaking up has been one of the great attractions of the past decade, producing the fastest bowlers and some of the most breathtaking batsmen.

## ICC takes action on bouncers

It will be interesting to see how the West Indians react to the new ICC regulations concerning over-rates and short-pitched bowling, both of which have been integral to their game plan in their years at the top. They have not been so formidable in one-day cricket since the lawmakers clipped their wings. Personally, I do not like the restriction of one bouncer per over to one batsman. Not that I favour six an over, or even two. But this new limitation takes from the game a psychological element that made it intriguing. Now, as he wonders what the bowler will deliver after a bouncer, the batsman can be fairly sure that it won't be another bouncer, and I believe the game is poorer for that.

On the other hand it will be richer if batting is not confined entirely to the back foot. There was a stroke last summer, a straight drive by Botham on the front foot, which reminded me how beautiful the game can be. As long as cricket needs spectators, it has to provide entertainment; and something did have to be done to reduce the amount of short-pitched bowling, given the weakness of umpires to take the necessary action. It just seems a pity that it had to be by yet more legislation.

Similar regret can be expressed about the need for a Code of Conduct, details of which appear in the ICC section of this Almanack. There was never any reason for cricketers to behave like members of the House of Commons. Cricket should be a civilised game and a civilising one, and if that sounds high-falutin I make no apologies. What happened in India, during the final of the Duleep Trophy of 1990-91, when a bowler attacked a batsman with a stump, should never have happened in a game of cricket. The fact that the attack was not without provocation only intensifies the wrong. As for spectators in New Zealand aping Australian manners during a one-day international in Auckland . . . .

# A parting shot

Much has been written in recent years about the decline of cricket in schools. This does not necessarily mean that the game is losing interested young players, however, for the responsibility for their development has moved to other areas, such as local clubs and the county associations. There are good young cricketers in England, and it was encouraging to see how well the England Under-19 players fought back to level the series against their Australian counterparts, after being drubbed in the first "Test" at Leicester.

In some ways I am less concerned about the state of cricket in schools than I am about the state of education there, if the replies for the Almanack's schools section is any indication. Some 78 per cent of schools last year were unable to fill in the form correctly; in 32 per cent of the forms returned, there were numerical errors; almost seven per cent of the schools made mistakes in spelling the names of their opponents. In some instances, what passed for handwriting was beyond even the skill of our typesetter. This is not a new phenomenon, but that should be a worry more than a consolation. Reviewing the schools 30 years ago for *Wisden*, E. M. Wellings noted that some of the forms "reached the editor appearing more like jig-saw puzzles than cricket statistics. Most remarkable was the list which arranged its batsmen so that the number one found himself placed sixth, his average of 59 following others of 14, 15 and 17." That certainly sounds familiar. Given the restriction on space in the Almanack, I am tempted to include only those schools whose forms are 100 per cent correct. This may smack of élitism, but as most of the schools are of the fee-paying variety, such a charge will carry little weight.

# JOHN ARLOTT

## A LOVER OF CRICKET AND LIFE

### By MIKE BREARLEY

It is not an empty cliché to say of John Arlott that he was the voice of cricket. In his early days at the BBC, the house style was pukka, formal and, whenever possible, scripted. John brought the eye and tongue of a poet; the accent and timbre of a Hampshire grave-digger's son; and the courage to describe a whole scene, to give a rich game its setting. He knew cricket more in the way of the lover than of the critic, and as such tended to romanticise the performers.

His own disappointed aspirations as player (he appeared for Hampshire Club and Ground in 1937 as an opening batsman) never soured into envy or rancour. He saw professional cricketers, with few exceptions, as honest and likeable craftsmen in a worthy tradition. He regarded the invitation from the Cricketers' Association to be its first president, a post he held from 1968 to his death, as a great honour.

In his later years as a member of the Radio 3 Test match team – by which time the individuality and informality, which his own example among others had encouraged, had often descended to triviality and egocentricity – John gave the commentary a needed ballast of objectivity and seriousness.

John Arlott was born in Basingstoke in 1914. He was an only child in a happy family. Hating his sadistic headmaster, he left school at sixteen after failing the School Certificate "spectacularly". He worked in local government; then as a clerk in a mental hospital, calculating the amounts of each item of food needed daily by the wards.

In 1934 he joined the Southampton police force. He enjoyed his eleven years on the beat, but his interests were wider. He must have been an unusual policeman, composing poetry on quiet duties and writing programmes free-lance for the BBC. This led in 1945 to his first job with the BBC, as a staff producer. Soon the opportunity came to broadcast cricket. He toyed with the idea of modifying his country accent but, thankfully for him and the rest of us, was dissuaded. He started, too, his prolific cricket-writing career, which continued beyond his retirement in 1980 from radio and TV until his death.

In 1949, when he stopped off in Sicily on his way home from the MCC tour of South Africa, he was introduced to the local wines. Thus began yet another passion and career, on the fruit of the vine, and on the food, particularly cheeses, to be eaten with it. He always regretted that cricket is not played in the Latin countries.

John Arlott managed to combine qualities that do not often come together. He was both passionate and moderate in his opinions. He was a lover of tradition – policeman, cricketer, historian, collector – and a rebel against many authorities: he was outspoken in his antagonism to the regime in South Africa, and had little time for sports administrators, dismissing Lord's as feudal.

Among all else, he found the time and energy to stand as the Liberal candidate in two parliamentary elections in the 1950s. He regarded his part in bringing Basil D'Oliveira to England in 1960, to play in the Central Lancashire League, as one of the best things he did in his life. As a diplomat

[*Patrick Eagar*

and negotiator, he sometimes found that the need for restraint was tested by his sentiment and conviction, but he nevertheless steered the Cricketers' Association towards a constructive role in both the major divisive issues of the past twenty years – South Africa and Packer.

In his personal life, John suffered two untimely losses. On New Year's Eve of 1965 his eldest son, Jimmy, was killed at 21 in a motorbike accident. Then in March 1976 came the death at 42 of his much-loved second wife, Valerie.

His son's death changed John's vision; at a deep level he felt thereafter that there could not be any underlying meaning in life. The second loss increased his tendency to lugubriosity. The pleasures of life, of friendship, family, cricket, wine, food, poetry, were real enough, but even the best moments were tinged with an awareness of their inevitable ending. So a claret or an innings became "desperately" good, and those protruding eyes would fill with tears.

He became less healthy. Too much tobacco, wine and food left him with chronic bronchitis. He would emerge panting from his cellar at lunch-time, clutching armfuls of dusty bottles. He became overweight and less handsome. His move to Alderney in 1981 was in part motivated by the need for clean air, though living on a small island also satisfied some longing for solitude, for the rhythm of the sea and no doubt for much else.

Over the last two to three years, John suffered badly from the deterioration in his health, and needed constant care. This he received with steadfast love and patience from his third wife, Pat. Others, too, were tolerant and affectionate, moved by the hints of the person he had been and by the shell that he had almost become. Now he often demanded company and feared being alone. He was also afraid of dying, but the end came peacefully, in his sleep in the early morning on Saturday, December 14, 1991. Pat and his much loved sons, Tim and Robert, were with him in the house and had spent the previous evening at his bedside.

Until the last painful phase, despite the grief and the ill health, and despite the increasing tendency to monologue, John remained immensely generous and lovable. He was a marvellous raconteur, ranging brilliantly over past and present while from time to time shaking his head and hand as if to say: "But what does it all matter?"

And he *did* feel that cricket mattered not a jot in comparison, say, with the death of one person in the violence of Ulster. He acknowledged that cricket and wine and aquatints are in the last resort *marginal*, so, recognising this, he would in mid-flow subtly (with, as I say, this characteristic little demurring, self-dismissive, pushing-away gesture with his hand and fingers) undermine the importance of his story before embarking on another.

As to generosity, I think of it as a wide-ranging attitude of thought and of deed. His hospitality was rich. He liked strong foods, pâtés, smoked eel, meat, matured cheese; he was not bothered about delicacies much – sweets, salads, chocolates. I suppose you could call it a man's taste – with perhaps an apple pie permitted as a robust dessert. He was generous in thought, too, though he could be savage about those he found to be beyond the pale of decency and kindness.

He was generous with his time. In the company of friends, John never made one aware of his other commitments and anxieties; he wanted to talk over a meal and long beyond. I once sat down to Sunday lunch with John, his family and some friends at two o'clock, and we did not get up from the table until ten at night.

On leaving South Africa in 1949, John left blank the section marked "race" on a form provided by the immigration authorities. When an Afrikaner official insisted that the space had to be filled, John spat out: "I am a member of the *human* race."

*Much of this article first appeared in the* Sunday Times, *and is reproduced with the kind permission of the newspaper.*

[*Patrick Eagar*
Gordon Greenidge (*left*) and Desmond Haynes at The Oval after the Fifth Test between England and West Indies in 1984 – the summer of the "blackwash". Haynes won the Man of the Match award there, and Greenidge was named Player of the Series.

# BEGINNINGS ARE EVERYTHING

## A TRIBUTE TO GREENIDGE AND HAYNES

### By PETER ROEBUCK

As Joey "The Lips" Fagan said in *The Commitments*, "Beginnings are everything. Get a start and the rest is inevitable." So it is in cricket. Powerful teams are strong at top and bottom, in their head and their feet. Those early exchanges with bat and ball which so dictate the course of events must be won. Take early wickets, forge an effective opening stand, and the enemy is forever in retreat. And resistance, however heroic, seldom brings victory. As Sir Winston said after the valiant and celebrated withdrawal from Dunkirk, "We cannot afford many victories such as this".

Throughout their fifteen-year stint as cricket's outstanding team, West Indies have been superb and ruthless in their use of the new ball. At even a hint of grass, or freshness in the pitch, Clive Lloyd or Viv Richards chose to bowl first, confident that his august pace merchants would seize their opportunity. Already their names are legion, and it was these men, Roberts, Holding, Garner, Croft, Marshall, Ambrose and Patterson among them, whom opposing teams feared, for this was West Indies' most potent and irresistible weapon.

And yet this was but half the tale. Throughout their reign as world champions of Test cricket, the West Indians also fielded two of the game's most reliable opening pairs, Greenidge and Fredericks, Greenidge and Haynes. Their names trip off the tongue as smoothly as Laurel and Hardy, Simon and Garfunkel, or Astaire and Rogers; excellent in themselves, brilliant in combination. Time after time they gave their team a secure start, a start which allowed men such as Viv Richards, Clive Lloyd, Alvin Kallicharran and Richie Richardson to turn strength into domination.

Both pairs feature in the ranks of Test cricket's most productive opening partnerships. Including only those who put on at least 1,000 runs, and averaged 40.00, Fredericks and Greenidge lie eleventh in the list with an average of 57.73, and Haynes and Greenidge fourteenth with an average of 46.94. Hobbs and Sutcliffe top a list which also includes Hutton and Washbrook (seventh) and Simpson and Lawry (eighth). But in many respects Haynes and Greenidge have been the greatest pair of them all, because they walked out together in 89 games, far, far more than any rival partnership (Gavaskar and Chauhan worked in unison 36 times). In terms of longevity, fitness and consistency they are unrivalled.

It helped, of course, that they were so diverse in temperament and technique. Desmond Haynes emerged from his quarters in a back room of his mother's Barbados rum shop as a cheerful, extrovert man, alert to every situation, prepared to hit hard, high and, at first anyhow, to any quarter. To him cricket was a simple and spontaneous game, full of life and love and laughter. He could strike balls over cover, could run like a hare, and hook with a sudden, quick, wristy movement. On his feet he was light, and as he collected his runs he was smiling, charming, crisp and flamboyant.

In time Haynes changed, as men do when they begin to experience the barbs and the bouquets; and though still grinning he began to calculate, and to irritate. If he was just as much a dasher in manner, his performances told a different tale, one of a man now fully versed in the arts of life, a man with a position to protect, and to advance. At the crease he continued to move forward to play off his pads with characteristic Caribbean expertise, or to go back to drive through cover. He was, and is, a creative player, but as his batting gathered discipline, so he personally began to bubble not with the delight of spring, but with the moodiness of autumn.

As his career hardened, as he saw and knew more, Haynes turned from calypso, with its happy chants, to reggae, with its biting edge. Like his captain, Vivian Richards, in maturity he can entertain; and yet, now, a distance is felt, as if the entertainer were no longer as comfortable with himself or his audience. None the less he has continued to improve and stands as arguably the leading opening batsman in world cricket. Moreover his versatility is formidable, for he has scored hundreds on bowlers' pitches, on turning tracks, notably in Sydney, and in one-day matches. If no longer a cavalier, he remains a respected warrior.

Gordon Greenidge had never seemed straightforward: he rarely smiled, rather he lived within himself. His nature was not so much contrary as suspicious, to which trait was added a dangerous colleague, imagination. Born in the West Indies and raised in England, Greenidge had a foot in both camps and a tent in neither. Accordingly he was inclined to set a guard by his door with instructions to challenge all outsiders. "Who are you and what do you want?" Greenidge tried hard, perhaps too hard, to avoid being hurt, and he may have resented his more gregarious and greater contemporary, Vivian Richards. They learned to work together and to play their parts in a formidable team, yet were never as close as thunder and lightning, for all that they were thunder and lightning.

Technically Greenidge was a master, moving further forward and further back than any contemporary, square cutting with withering power or driving straight with bare-knuckle force. He could hook, too, and had a penchant for pick-up shots off his pads, strokes which often despatched the ball into the next parish. And while he could murder spin, it was not with the range of shots used by Haynes, but with the crushing brutality of a tank.

His weakness, apart from a brooding nature, lay in the very muscularity which sometimes destroyed bowling, and in an upbringing on English pitches which left him a less accomplished player on bouncy pitches. He did not score a first-class hundred in Australia until his final visit there, in 1988-89. Perhaps, too, he lacked touch, but no man can have everything.

In full flight, Greenidge was a glorious sight, and impossible to contain. So awesome was his power, so complete his authority, that once a bombardment was under way not a ball could be bowled to him. In this mood he was like an orator suddenly aroused with passion, devouring opposition with a tongue-lashing which was vivid, inspired and devastating. For hours, weeks, days, he seemed to wander along, holding his own in debate, giving no quarter, until in a moment it would all fit into place and a ferocious harangue would begin. At his best, unleashed, he was intimidating.

And now Greenidge is in retirement and the partnership with Haynes is broken. As a pair they put on fifty 26 times, 100 on twelve occasions and 200 four times. More significantly still, in 48 Tests won by West Indies in their time as praetorian gatemen, their average partnership was 48.83, while in eight games lost they averaged 29.87. Unsurprisingly their average was higher still – 49.57 – in drawn matches, a tribute to some docile pitches. They were, in some measure, unsung heroes, but they will be missed. As a pair they were distinguished, dependable and complementary in all forms of cricket. They performed their awkward task with authority and, sometimes, élan. Repeatedly they defied all manner of peril to cut a path through the foliage along which others might travel at their ease.

## C. G. GREENIDGE/D. L. HAYNES – OPENING STANDS

| Series | T | I | Unbr. | R | Highest stand | Avge | 100s | 50s | W | L | D |
|---|---|---|---|---|---|---|---|---|---|---|---|
| 1977-78 v Australia | 2 | 3 | 0 | 234 | 131 | 78.00 | 1 | 1 | 2 | 0 | 0 |
| 1979-80 in Australia | 3 | 6 | 1 | 197 | 68 | 39.40 | 0 | 1 | 2 | 0 | 1 |
| 1979-80 in New Zealand | 3 | 6 | 0 | 329 | 225 | 54.83 | 1 | 1 | 0 | 1 | 2 |
| 1980 in England | 5 | 6 | 0 | 169 | 83 | 28.16 | 0 | 1 | 1 | 0 | 4 |
| 1980-81 v England | 4 | 5 | 0 | 320 | 168 | 64.00 | 2 | 0 | 2 | 0 | 2 |
| 1981-82 in Australia | 2 | 4 | 0 | 85 | 37 | 21.25 | 0 | 0 | 1 | 0 | 1 |
| 1982-83 v India | 5 | 7 | 1 | 567 | 296 | 94.50 | 1 | 2 | 2 | 0 | 3 |
| 1983-84 in India | 6 | 10 | 0 | 291 | 50 | 29.10 | 0 | 1 | 3 | 0 | 3 |
| 1983-84 v Australia | 5 | 8 | 3 | 684 | 250* | 136.80 | 3 | 1 | 3 | 0 | 2 |
| 1984 in England | 5 | 8 | 0 | 295 | 106 | 36.87 | 1 | 2 | 5 | 0 | 0 |
| 1984-85 in Australia | 5 | 8 | 0 | 189 | 83 | 23.62 | 0 | 1 | 3 | 1 | 1 |
| 1984-85 v New Zealand | 4 | 7 | 2 | 220 | 82 | 44.00 | 0 | 2 | 2 | 0 | 2 |
| 1985-86 v England | 5 | 6 | 1 | 325 | 79* | 65.00 | 0 | 4 | 5 | 0 | 0 |
| 1986-87 in Pakistan | 3 | 5 | 0 | 116 | 49 | 23.20 | 0 | 0 | 1 | 1 | 1 |
| 1986-87 in New Zealand | 3 | 6 | 1 | 245 | 150 | 49.00 | 1 | 0 | 0 | 1 | 2 |
| 1987-88 in India | 3 | 6 | 0 | 247 | 114 | 41.16 | 1 | 2 | 1 | 3 | 0 |
| 1987-88 v Pakistan | 2 | 4 | 0 | 42 | 21 | 10.50 | 0 | 0 | 1 | 0 | 1 |
| 1988 in England | 3 | 5 | 0 | 247 | 131 | 49.40 | 1 | 1 | 2 | 0 | 1 |
| 1988-89 in Australia | 5 | 10 | 0 | 447 | 135 | 44.70 | 1 | 2 | 3 | 1 | 1 |
| 1988-89 v India | 4 | 7 | 0 | 221 | 84 | 31.57 | 0 | 1 | 3 | 0 | 1 |
| 1989-90 v England | 4 | 7 | 0 | 506 | 298 | 72.28 | 1 | 2 | 2 | 1 | 1 |
| 1990-91 in Pakistan | 3 | 5 | 0 | 91 | 47 | 18.20 | 0 | 0 | 1 | 1 | 1 |
| 1990-91 v Australia | 5 | 9 | 2 | 416 | 129 | 59.42 | 2 | 1 | 2 | 1 | 2 |
| | 89 | 148 | 11 | 6,483 | 298 | 47.32 | 16 | 26 | 48 | 8 | 33 |

* Signifies unbroken.

# LEADING OPENING PAIRS IN TESTS

(Qualification: 1,000 runs, average 40.00)

| | T | I | Unbr. | R | Avge | 100s | 50s | W | L | D | T |
|---|---|---|---|---|---|---|---|---|---|---|---|
| J. B. Hobbs/H. Sutcliffe (E) .......... | 25 | 38 | 1 | 3,249 | 87.81 | 15 | 10 | 12 | 5 | 8 | 0 |
| A. F. Rae/J. B. Stollmeyer (WI) ..... | 13 | 21 | 2 | 1,349 | 71.00 | 5 | 3 | 4 | 4 | 5 | 0 |
| G. A. Gooch/M. A. Atherton (E) ..... | 13 | 23 | 0 | 1,500 | 65.21 | 6 | 3 | 3 | 3 | 7 | 0 |
| J. H. Fingleton/W. A. Brown (A) ..... | 10 | 16 | 0 | 1,020 | 63.75 | 3 | 4 | 7 | 0 | 3 | 0 |
| J. B. Hobbs/W. Rhodes (E) ......... | 22 | 36 | 1 | 2,146 | 61.31 | 8 | 5 | 12 | 7 | 3 | 0 |
| Sadiq Mohammad/Majid Khan (P).... | 14 | 26 | 3 | 1,391 | 60.47 | 4 | 9 | 4 | 3 | 7 | 0 |
| L. Hutton/C. Washbrook (E) ........ | 28 | 51 | 3 | 2,880 | 60.00 | 8 | 13 | 7 | 9 | 12 | 0 |
| R. B. Simpson/W. M. Lawry (A) ..... | 34 | 62 | 2 | 3,596 | 59.93 | 9 | 18 | 9 | 8 | 17 | 0 |
| T. L. Goddard/E. J. Barlow (SA) .... | 18 | 34 | 2 | 1,806 | 56.43 | 6 | 11 | 4 | 3 | 11 | 0 |
| T. J. Franklin/J. G. Wright (NZ) .... | 16 | 28 | 0 | 1,543 | 55.10 | 5 | 5 | 3 | 3 | 10 | 0 |
| R. C. Fredericks/C. G. Greenidge (WI) | 16 | 31 | 2 | 1,593 | 54.93 | 5 | 5 | 7 | 5 | 4 | 0 |
| S. M. Gavaskar/C. P. S. Chauhan (I) . | 36 | 59 | 3 | 3,010 | 53.75 | 10 | 10 | 9 | 7 | 20 | 0 |
| J. H. Edrich/G. Boycott (E).......... | 21 | 35 | 3 | 1,672 | 52.25 | 6 | 8 | 7 | 3 | 11 | 0 |
| C. G. Greenidge/D. L. Haynes (WI).. | 89 | 148 | 11 | 6,483 | 47.32 | 16 | 26 | 48 | 8 | 33 | 0 |
| R. W. Barber/G. Boycott (E) ....... | 16 | 26 | 1 | 1,171 | 46.84 | 2 | 7 | 5 | 3 | 8 | 0 |
| G. R. Marsh/M. A. Taylor (A) ....... | 21 | 39 | 2 | 1,733 | 46.83 | 4 | 7 | 10 | 3 | 8 | 0 |
| D. C. Boon/G. R. Marsh (A)........ | 24 | 41 | 1 | 1,871 | 46.77 | 5 | 8 | 7 | 14 | 1 |
| K. R. Stackpole/W. M. Lawry (A) ... | 16 | 31 | 2 | 1,302 | 44.89 | 0 | 13 | 5 | 5 | 6 | 0 |
| S. M. Gavaskar/K. Srikkanth (I)...... | 23 | 34 | 0 | 1,469 | 43.20 | 3 | 9 | 4 | 3 | 15 | 1 |

*Note:* Figures to August 1991.

*Statistics compiled by Robert Brooke.*

# THE LANCASHIRE LEAGUE CELEBRATES ITS CENTENARY

By CHRIS ASPIN

When east Lancashire was full of cotton mills, you could sometimes see 78 tall black chimneys from the old wooden scorebox in the top corner of Church cricket ground. I counted them once, during the local holiday week. On other days, sharp-eyed spectators could discern about a dozen through the sooty haze, and it would surprise me if as many as that now rise above Accrington, Great Harwood and the distant brickfields of Clayton-le-Moors. The smoking mills, familiar for so long to spectators at Lancashire League matches, have gone. The Pennine air is refreshingly clean this centenary year, though it will probably be too sharp at times for the overseas professionals who have followed in the steps of Learie Constantine, Ray Lindwall, Everton Weekes, Clive Lloyd, Dennis Lillee, Viv Richards and a host of other immortals in order to play in what is widely regarded as the world's foremost league. The fourteen clubs have always insisted on keeping the game for local players – overseas amateurs regularly offer their services in vain – and have been rewarded with the loyal, often passionate, support of a numerous following. The aggregate attendance at the seven games on a Sunday usually exceeds that at Old Trafford.

There have been many times when I have wondered why cricket ever took root in these parts. Snow has more than once prevented play, and the sight and feel of cold Lancashire rain falling from a pewter sky is almost enough to put people off the game for ever. But on a sunny afternoon, with noble hills providing the backcloth to a keenly contested game involving two world-class professionals, there are few better cricketing occasions. Though Lancashire League clubs are often criticised for paying large fees for Test stars, few are likely to abandon a tradition which began with men like McDonald, Headley and Constantine during the inter-war years, and which now provides amateurs with a rare chance to pit their skills against the world's best. Long before the League was formed in 1892, clubs regularly engaged English professionals with first-class and Test experience. And for important matches they occasionally included three or four paid men, causing resentment among opponents who could afford only one or two. The control of professionalism was one of the stated aims of the Lancashire League. Two pros were allowed in the early years, but since 1900 the number has been one.

Many of the older clubs can trace their roots to the enthusiasm for cricket which was fired at public schools attended by the sons of mill owners and professional men. The Blackburn club, East Lancashire, is unusual in having been started by officers of the town's volunteer corps, and its stars included A. N. (Monkey) Hornby, the Lancashire and England player, who was a member of one of the county's oldest cotton families. Most of these players were batsmen. Professionals were engaged to coach and to bowl, with working men occasionally helping out in the nets. Some of the enthusiasts became good enough to be included in the teams, and by the time the League was formed, artisans were well represented both on the field and in the committee rooms.

Mills worked till noon on Saturdays well into this century; and to enable spectators to see a full match, wickets were pitched at two o'clock. Today, the starting time is 1.45 p.m., but since limited-overs cricket came in twenty years ago, there has been no fixed finishing time. As many games are now played on Sundays as on Saturdays. Sponsorship has become increasingly important, though bar takings and the renting of rooms provide most of the income. The current League sponsor is the Marsden Building Society, which took over in 1991 from the Matthew Brown brewery.

If I could choose one match from the thousands which have been played during the past 100 years, it would be that between Rawtenstall and Nelson in 1931. It brought into conflict the great Sidney Barnes, aged 59, but still a bowler without equal, and the young Learie Constantine, the cricketing phenomenon, who was the greatest single attraction any league has known. "Connie", as everyone called him, often said that the 96 he scored in front of a vast crowd that afternoon was the best innings he ever played. The duel with Barnes, who took seven for 68, was cricket at the very highest level and was remembered vividly long after the result of the match was forgotten. Nelson won by 72 runs. Constantine was professional for Nelson from 1929 to 1937, and in those nine seasons he gained seven championship medals. Against Accrington in 1934 he took all ten wickets for 10 runs.

Looking over the club records, one sees that bowlers had their best years in the early decades of the competition. One would certainly have liked to watch Sam Moss, the Manchester shoemaker, who burst into league cricket in the 1890s. In his first game as professional for Haslingden in 1896, he took five wickets in eight balls – all bowled – and for Bacup four years later he finished with 143 wickets at 8.2. Publicans throughout the district put up glass cases to display the stumps he broke, and those who saw Moss were in no doubt that they had never come across anyone faster. Nowadays batsmen have the upper hand, and the recent policy of rearranging games hit by the weather has helped them to score more runs than ever before. The Australian, Peter Sleep, professional for Rishton, and the Rawtenstall amateur, Peter Wood, both achieved Lancashire League aggregate records last season.

Over the years, the Lancashire League has provided Lancashire and England with many fine players. Eddie Paynter, who worked in the brickfields at Clayton-le-Moors and who played for Enfield at both the start and the end of his career, was one of the best known. After his performances for England during the Australian tour of 1932-33, the League presented him with a pair of silver candlesticks. Accrington have the distinction of nurturing David Lloyd and Graeme Fowler, two other left-handers who have played for their country, and many League players have gone to other counties. In 1939, five Bacup-born players were in the first-class game.

Nelson have won the Lancashire League championship eighteen times; East Lancashire and Burnley thirteen times each. During the past decade, Haslingden have gained most of the honours, winning the championship in six of the last nine seasons and being runners-up twice. The knockout competition for the Worsley Cup, started in 1919, has been won thirteen times by East Lancashire. To mark its centenary, the League has arranged a varied programme of events. MCC and Lancashire are sending sides to play Lancashire League elevens; and on July 9 the Pakistani tourists will be at Haslingden to take on the League Cricket Conference.

# THE MCC SCHOOLS FESTIVAL

## THE SCHOOLBOY CRICKETER IN 1991

### By GERALD HOWAT

In recent years, MCC has sponsored a week's Schools Festival in July, at Oxford and at Lord's, which brings together 44 young cricketers who are broadly representative of current schoolboy talent at the top. The editor of *Wisden* has asked for my thoughts on some of those who appeared in the 1991 Festival.

On the first two days there were two matches on nearby college grounds in Oxford. The Headmasters' Conference Schools selectors, under their chairman, David Walsh, picked 22 boys from their members for one match, while the selectors of the English Schools' Cricket Association, led by Hugh Cherry, called on 22 boys from their county affiliations, all of whom were still at school or at a VI Form College. On the third day the 44 boys were regrouped into four mixed sides, and a final trial took place on the fourth day on the Christ Church ground, involving 24 boys. Of those 24, eighteen appeared in at least one match at Lord's in the following three days.

In the Lord's games, the boys appeared as MCC Schools, playing, on successive days, MCC and the National Association of Young Cricketers, the latter representing uncontracted county players under the age of nineteen. On the third and final day at Lord's, the National Cricket Association fielded a side, drawn from both NAYC and the schoolboys who had played in the two earlier games, against the Combined Services.

In absolute terms the schoolboys who played at Lord's may not necessarily have been the best nation-wide, but they were undoubtedly the keenest. They really wanted to play, day after day, and their enthusiasm and commitment were clear. They had come straight from the end-of-term festivals, so much a feature nowadays of the school cricket calendar, and they would go on to play in national Under-19 matches, the Esso county knockout competition, and for county second elevens. The distinction may be made between these dedicated schoolboy cricketers, and those for whom the summer term is enough and who then look to other attractions in the holidays. No criticism is implied – they are just two different breeds. It is as well that the ambitious ones test their day-to-day vocation early, so that the call to professional cricket, if it comes, is rightly understood before it is answered.

The selectors faced a difficult task in deciding whom to invite. The HMC ones, relying on information from schools, had to balance facts and figures against the standard played on a school's particular "circuit". There are schools which, through diffidence or dilatoriness, do not submit names, and inevitably some potential candidates go unnoticed. The ESCA selectors had the advantage of a well-established structure which allows boys to advance through county age-groups. Despite some honourable exceptions, the evidence is gathering that the maintained sector of education at secondary level is contributing less than ever to cricket. Only two boys in the last 24 (both from a VI Form College) were prepared to give any credit to a state school for their cricket apprenticeship. Much has been written elsewhere on the nadir of cricket in state schools. Perhaps as the significance of 1992 is upon us, we are approaching the accepted European pattern in which sport has no part in state education. At the moment we, in the United Kingdom, lie uneasily between that position and that of the United States, where sport is a major school involvement.

All the boys in the last 24 at Oxford had one common area of experience – that of league cricket. Those who came from the HMC schools played it in the holidays and some of them, at day schools, in term time as well. For the others, it was their main source of cricket. League cricket has become the anvil on which so much talent is forged. The boys who play it have their game tempered in the heat of adult competitiveness, though one should not forget the huge number of matches ESCA arranges for schoolboys – upwards of 1,000 games at various age-levels in 1991.

Brief mention should be made of a few in the initial 44 who did not play at Lord's. Among the batsmen were Karl Thomas (Whitcliffe Mount), Gul Khan (who had such a successful season for Ipswich) and Paul Whitaker; among the bowlers, the slow left-armer, Philip Jacques (Millfield), and the off-spinner, Christopher Sketchley (Medina). Andrew Payne, an all-rounder who was unfit to bowl at Oxford, later batted courageously against the Australian Under-19 tourists at Worksop. Both batsmen and slow bowlers were much in evidence in the trials, and competition for the Lord's places was particularly keen in these areas.

Four opening batsmen went to Lord's and all may be said to have done themselves justice. Against MCC, Andrew Jones (Monmouth) made his second century of the week's cricket, an innings marked by assured technique and confident temperament. Scarcely a ball was in the air unless he intended it to be, and his driving and cutting were of a high order. His partner, Keith (K. A.) Parsons (Richard Huish, Taunton), proved a good back-foot player, strong outside the off stump in cutting and driving, and a good judge of the ball *not* to hit. He also bowled medium-paced away-swingers. Against NAYC, sixteen-year-old Robin Weston (Durham), who had made a very fine century in the Oxford trials, looked to have great potential, especially when he is stronger. The experience at Lord's will have been invaluable – he batted 195 minutes for his half-century – but he forced the later batsmen to have to look for runs. Later he made a fine century against Wales Under-19. In terms of his age, Weston performed extremely well and he has a prolific record of scoring runs since he was ten. As a former captain of England Under-14 and Under-15 he must be taken very seriously.

His elder brother, Philip, was one of four players who had taken part in the 1990 Festival but were absent in 1991 because of their selection for the England Under-18 team that went to Canada for the International Youth Tournament. The other three were Jeremy Snape (Denstone), Jason Laney (St John's, Marlborough) and Glen Chapple (West Craven High). Philip Weston, while still at Durham School, became a contracted Worcestershire player and he must top any list of the outstanding schoolboys of 1991, as he demonstrated by his batting in the Under-19 "Tests" for England against Australia. He was selected as captain of the England Under-19 side which toured Pakistan in the winter, but his acceptance of this honour provided an example of the hard decisions ambitious young cricketers may have to make. Going to Pakistan meant that Weston had to give up the place offered him at Keble College, Oxford. The matter received much press attention, with the balance of opinion feeling that Oxford's continuing claims to first-class status were not strengthened by such an attitude.

Robin Weston's opening partner against NAYC, Mark Harvey (Habergham High), was a good straight-driver, playing the better of his two innings at Lord's against the Combined Services. The other Parsons twin, Kevin (K.J.) (Richard Huish, Taunton), can also open, though he did not do so at Lord's. He is a strong leg-side player who responded to a run-chase and was one of the best fielders on show. He also batted well for ESCA against the Australian Under-19s.

Among the middle-order batsmen were Matthew Walker (King's, Rochester), a left-hander of considerable strength, capable of taking the game to the bowlers. He had the skill and power to find gaps in a defensive field and, among the many batsmen on display, he seemed to be particularly well equipped to read the demands of a situation. He also had an exceptional arm. Andrew Hall, awarded the captaincy at Lord's from among five captains used at Oxford and many more present there, had one especially good innings in the final Oxford trial. Mark Semmence (Hurstpierpoint) established his claim to Lord's by a sound half-century at Oxford and a very good school record. He was unluckily run out without facing a ball in the first match. At Oxford he had shown himself to be a good, defensive front-foot player, with a wide range of shots but some lack of confidence in displaying them. He has the technical equipment to prosper and the confidence will come. As a seam bowler he used his height well and will be more effective and faster when he has gained strength and weight. In the final Oxford trial he proved very economical, bowling several successive maiden overs.

No really quick bowler emerged, although two with some pace were Matthew Robinson (King's, Taunton) and Richard Ballinger (Millfield). Robinson commanded respect from the former first-class batsmen in the MCC side, dismissing Clive Radley with a brilliant caught and bowled. He made two fifties in the Oxford Festival and marked himself out as an all-rounder of genuine promise. Ballinger bowled a good line and length, and was one of the few who hit the stumps regularly. The Oxford pitches did not help him, but at Lord's he was brisk and lively, especially against the Combined Services. He has a good action but might consider shortening his run-up. Richard Yeabsley (Haberdashers' Aske's) was a right-arm medium-pace bowler who has played for Devon in the NatWest Bank Trophy; his natural ability was evident. Alastair Richardson (Oundle), who bowled fast-medium for NAYC against the Schools, is a tall player and has the physique to increase his pace.

James Hindson, a league cricketer from Caythorpe, was the pick of a variety of slow bowlers, possessing a natural left-arm action and a fluency of movement. In the MCC match, when the former Northamptonshire players, Duncan Wild and Peter Mills, put on more than 200, his return of 33 runs in eleven overs was by far the best. Jonathan Whittington (Eton), another slow left-armer, had good figures against NAYC and was the ablest of his kind from the HMC Schools.

Although no outstanding wicket-keeper emerged, there were three who had sound matches, with little to pick between them in ability. Nicholas Workman, who plays league cricket in the Midlands, and Kevin Sedgbeer (Taunton) had a match each for the Schools at Lord's, while Nicholas Harvey kept very well for NAYC against the Schools, as did Workman, later, against the Australian tourists. The ground fielding was excellent and some splendid catches were held.

Much of the cricket at Oxford and Lord's was a delight to watch because of the attitude of the players, who supported and encouraged each other so well, the positive batting and the amount of slow bowling. Rather more than half the overs bowled by any side at Lord's were by the spinners, and a lot of batsmen were ready to play strokes off the front foot with confidence. In the end, however, one has to accept that the batting was more mature than the bowling. Over the whole period of the Festival, eighteen sides went to the wicket – if one discounts the two adult teams of MCC and Combined Services – and an average of 5.94 wickets fell per innings, only one side being bowled out. In other words, results throughout the week were possible only because captains made declarations. In the three games at Lord's, the side which batted second won, certainly in two cases because the captains kept the game "open". With neither trophies nor pots of gold at stake, or even club reputations, no harm was done by generous declarations. Had the games had a mercenary or professional edge, the philosophy of each day would have been different.

I digress on the wider issue of schoolboy captaincy, which presents its own particular problems. In the representative matches, captains led sides whose players they barely knew and which included others, like themselves, who were current captains. Exceptional qualities of leadership and personality had to be matched to a technical and tactical awareness. Andrew Hall showed himself a competent and imaginative leader of the ESCA and MCC Schools XIs, and his natural leadership was readily accepted by his colleagues. North of the border, I saw Charles Breese (Glenalmond) lead the Scottish Wayfarers' Colts most competently against the much more experienced Scotland Under-19 side.

Within the confines of a short, busy and examination-dominated summer term, a school captain faces considerable personal pressures. Only in the closing games, often bunched into a Festival, may he feel he has the leisure to concentrate and experience to draw upon. "The Captain of the Eleven. What a post is his in the School-world! Almost as hard as the Doctor's", the master observed to Tom Brown in the immortal match at Rugby. It was a view echoed by a schoolmaster last summer, who called it "the most difficult job a schoolboy can do". Understandably, therefore, it is in captaincy that some weaknesses in the current school cricket scene may be most exposed. Far too many matches end in draws, and the result is predictable at an early stage. Both batting and fielding captains are at their most vulnerable in the first half of a one-day match. Declarations can be ill-timed, over-rates unduly slow (a matter of much concern), and field-placings simply "wait upon events".

The common error is to bat for too long – sometimes for two out of the three sessions of an all-day game. Bowlers can be dilatory in getting back to their marks quickly, while field-setting can be on the one hand inflexible and on the other impetuous: a rush to change because a bad ball has been duly punished. When the second side goes in to bat, it may face a target which is unrealistic or defensively regarded as unattainable. Both circumstances will produce a draw. At the heart of such a situation is the fear of losing. One may probe deeply: captains feel more secure if their side remains unbeaten, despite a paucity of actual victories; masters-in-charge can be equally sensitive, especially in relation to particular "key" fixtures. Even head-masters share some of the responsibility. Inexperienced captaincy is not the only explanation of so many drawn games. Reputations are not made, so the argument runs, by losing, and some schools feel accountable to governors, parents and old boys as much for sports results as for A-level ones.

Central to captaincy lies the decision of when to change from attack to defence or vice versa. This will come with experience, as will the remedying of some other faults I noticed in watching a lot of schools cricket last summer. There were batsmen who moved to the ball too early and who were ill-equipped for the high backlift they adopted. Better judging of a run is needed and the skill to look for quick singles. The pace of many a game simply needed increasing. There were too many chest-on bowlers and, one sensed, an insufficiency of thought about variety in each delivery. This may be related to what has gone on in the nets, where coaching so often concentrates on batsmen rather than bowlers.

What of the future of those extremely talented young cricketers who played at Lord's? Many years ago, *Wisden* listed the destinations – Oxford or Cambridge – of the leading public school cricketers of the day, and there seemed no more to be said. Not till Paul Gibb went to Essex did a "true-blue" (Cambridge) public school amateur become a professional cricketer. The best of the Oxbridge men played first-class cricket as amateurs, although, as the late Sir George Allen and many another would testify, it was difficult to earn a living and find time to play regularly. Today, players from the HMC schools have brief county careers, as professionals of course, before turning to business and the professions: Nigel Popplewell (Radley, Cambridge and Somerset) is a case in point. Others have a more extended professional career, such as Derek Pringle (Felsted, Cambridge, Essex and England). There were 82 such players on county staffs in 1991, 37 of whom had been capped.

The boys themselves, who have come thus far, have to think about their position. Counties are making approaches, and several boys have already made second eleven appearances for one or more counties. Parents in the wings at Oxford and Lord's could be seen seeking advice on what was best for their offspring from attendant schoolmasters, and even from this correspondent! Universities, whose cricketing hue is not necessarily blue, expressed interest in the balance between A-level grades expectant and runs and wickets accomplished. Nothing, these days, admits a simple answer as the young embark on further study and on careers. The cricket world pursues their talents through the MCC Festival, ESCA, the Development of Excellence programme and Cricket 2000; but cricket is but a part of the equation of life which they must work out for themselves.

[*David Munden*

South Africa put the seal on their return to international cricket, sanctioned by ICC in July, by making a first, historic visit to India. The ancient fortress at Gwalior provided a dramatic backdrop to the second of three one-day games.

ENGLAND'S VICTORIOUS TEAM AT HEADINGLEY

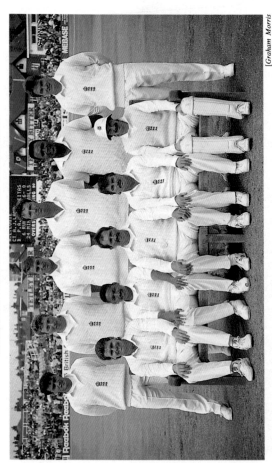

[Graham Morris

England's victory over West Indies at Headingley in the First Test of the 1991 series was their first at home since 1969. The winning team was: *Back row:* M. R. Ramprakash, M. A. Atherton, S. L. Watkin, D. R. Pringle, D. E. Malcolm, G. A. Hick. *Front row:* R. A. Smith, P. A. J. DeFreitas, G. A. Gooch (*captain*), A. J. Lamb, R. C. Russell.

THE 1991 WEST INDIAN TEAM IN ENGLAND

*[Graham Morris*

*Back row*: D. Waight (*physiotherapist*), C. L. Hooper, P. V. Simmons, C. A. Walsh, C. E. L. Ambrose, B. P. Patterson, H. A. G. Anthony, I. B. A. Allen, B. C. Lara, D. Williams, D. A. J. Holford (*assistant manager*). *Front row*: R. B. Richardson, D. L. Haynes, I. V. A. Richards (*captain*), L. R. Gibbs (*manager*), P. J. L. Dujon, A. L. Logie. *Absent*: C. G. Greenidge, C. B. Lambert.

THE 1991 SRI LANKAN TEAM IN ENGLAND

[*Patrick Eagar*

*Back row:* M. S. Atapattu, S. T. Jayasuriya, K. I. W. Wijegunawardene, C. P. H. Ramanayake, A. W. R. Madurasinghe, H. P. Tillekeratne, U. C. Hathurusinghe, R. S. Kaluwitharana, M. Muralitharan. *Front row:* F. S. Ahangama, R. S. Mahanama, R. J. Ratnayake, P. A. de Silva (*captain*), A. P. Gurusinha, S. D. Anurasiri, D. S. B. P. Kuruppu.

## A MOMENT OF SHAME

[*The Hindu*

This shameful incident, in which bowler Rashid Patel attacked batsman Raman Lamba with a stump, occurred in the 1991 final of India's Duleep Trophy tournament.

# AT THE PARTING OF THE WAY

[*David Munden*

Viv Richards is chaired from the field at Edgbaston, having won the Fourth Test for West Indies to ensure he would retire unbeaten as their captain in a Test series.

TWO FORMER ENGLAND CRICKETERS RETIRE

[*Patrick Eagar*

[*Patrick Eagar*

The early retirement in 1991 of Chris Smith, Hampshire's prolific opening batsman, and Paul Downton, the Middlesex wicket-keeper, robbed the county game of two popular cricketers. Downton played in 30 Tests for England and Smith eight.

# FIVE CRICKETERS OF THE YEAR

[*Patrick Eagar*

P. A. J. DeFreitas (Lancashire and England)

# FIVE CRICKETERS OF THE YEAR

[*David Munden*

Waqar Younis (Surrey)

FIVE CRICKETERS OF THE YEAR

[*Patrick Eagar*

R. B. Richardson (West Indies)

# FIVE CRICKETERS OF THE YEAR

[*Patrick Eagar*

A. A. Donald (Warwickshire)

# FIVE CRICKETERS OF THE YEAR

[*Patrick Eagar*

C. E. L. Ambrose (West Indies)

# FIVE CRICKETERS OF THE YEAR

## CURTLY AMBROSE

The spectre of the gangling Curtly Ambrose will undoubtedly haunt those batsmen unfortunate enough to confront him in England last season, when the 27-year-old Antiguan carried all before him, and single-handedly almost stilled the nascent Test career of Graeme Hick, a figure so thoroughly disenchanted before the series was complete that the selectors were forced to drop him. Ambrose has the ability to exert a debilitating psychological influence which so often precipitates a cluster of wickets after the initial breach has been made. It is no fun waiting in the wings, knowing your time is nigh. Hick, as an obvious example, often looked a sentenced man on his way to the crease, and this from a player who usually raced down the pavilion steps in expectation of the plunder to come.

No other explanation exists, either, for that telling passage off the first ball of the Fourth Test at Edgbaston, when Graham Gooch sparred at a widish loosener from Ambrose, only for Carl Hooper, uncharacteristically, to put the chance to grass. Surely no other bowler could have provoked such an involuntary response from the England captain. Ambrose accounted for Hick six times out of seven before England's new recruit was relieved of duty to undergo a very necessary period of recuperation outside the demanding environment of Test cricket. But in that he was not alone. Others before had had their profile reduced by the 6ft 7in marauder who was born on September 21, 1963 in Swetes, a village in the parched interior of Antigua.

CURTLY ELCONN LYNWALL AMBROSE grew up as a natural basketballer and considered migrating to the United States before starting cricket at seventeen, graduating from beach cricket and umpiring to the parish team. Andy Roberts was an early mentor, emphasising the psychological aspect of bowling and instilling a belief in Ambrose that he could join countrymen Baptiste, Ferris and Benjamin at the highest level. After an early foray in the West Indies regional competition in 1985-86, when four wickets cost 35 runs apiece, he left an indelible mark on the 1987-88 competition in establishing a record of 35 wickets at only 15.51 during his first full season, thereby erasing Winston Davis's previous tournament best of 33, which had stood since 1982-83. The West Indian selectors immediately pitched him into Test cricket that April, against Pakistan at Bourda, but it was an inauspicious début, coinciding with West Indies' first home defeat for a decade.

In 1986, at Viv Richards's instigation, Ambrose had summered in England, playing for Chester Boughton Hall in the Liverpool Competition, where he is remembered as an "inveterate late arriver, though he only lived across the road". The following year he moved to Heywood in the Central Lancashire League, in which he garnered 115 cheap wickets, and in 1988 he was back again, but this time as a member of the West Indian touring team. Extremely shy and retiring, and sometimes lugubrious in his formative years as a cricketer, he never enjoyed the tag of "pro" and has tended towards recluseness beneath the ubiquitous "Walkman". Yet he occasionally gives evidence of a rare humour. Once asked which was his favourite football team, he replied, "Crown Paints, man!"

If, as his name suggests, he is not quite a Lindwall in terms of the range of his bowling, he does have outright pace and he generates a disconcerting, steepling bounce from fuller-length deliveries. But while he was once no-balled for throwing, by the Trinidadian umpire, Clyde Cumberbatch, in the Leewards' first match of the 1987-88 Red Stripe Cup, against Trinidad & Tobago at Guaracara Park, Ambrose's action is unequivocally legal. His height and a slender, sinewy wrist contribute greatly to the final velocity, the wrist snapping forward at the instant of release to impart extra thrust to the ball's downward trajectory. Michael Holding had this vital asset, and Courtney Walsh's wrist action, too, has given rise to notions of illegal delivery. Never a great swinger of the ball, he compensates with a smooth, leggy run-up, fast arm action and accuracy. Like Joel Garner, he possesses a lethal yorker and a nasty bouncer, but his career-best eight for 45 against hapless England at Bridgetown in 1990 owed everything to the virtues of speed and straightness. Five victims were lbw, pinned to their stumps as Ambrose squared a series England had waged so gallantly until then.

Jeffrey Dujon's station has allowed him a unique insight into the relative merits of the phalanx of West Indies quicks over the years, and in his assessment Holding was undeniably the fastest, while Roberts, an introvert and a deep thinker, was capable of delivering two different bouncers with no discernible change in action. "Wonderful control was the essence, and the faster one shocked some very good batsmen", Dujon affirms. He reserves special affection, too, for the relatively inexperienced Ambrose, who he reckons has the credentials to take his place among the greats. "He is mature beyond his years, has pace, accuracy, heart and determination, plus, importantly, real pride in economical figures."

The crucial question now is for how long a spindly frame can withstand the rigours of Test-match bowling. Ambrose has spearheaded West Indies' attack for four years, and Richards, his captain, has already demanded a considerable work-load; yet his appetite for the game and that keen concern for the economy rate have remained undimmed. His consistency has become a byword since the 1988 tour of England, his first, which produced 22 Test wickets at 20.22. In Australia in 1988-89 he was the most outstanding performer with 26 wickets at 21.46, and last summer against England his 28 wickets cost 20 apiece. Moreover, he was arguably the essential difference between the two sides in what proved to be a zestful series.

Assuredly, not many batsmen will relish another confrontation, but they have at least been granted some respite. West Indies' next full series is not until the winter of 1992-93, in Australia, when "Amby" will be looking to improve on an outstanding Test record of 140 wickets at 23.14. By then, he will have entered the peak years for a bowler of his type, 28 to 32, still with only five years of international cricket behind him. It is an awesome prospect. – Stephen Thorpe.

## RICHIE RICHARDSON

For the West Indians on their 1991 tour of England, the satisfactions were not so numerous as usual. Carl Hooper developed a measure of consistency, and Curtly Ambrose was as accurate as fast hostility can be, but nobody made a great leap forward – nobody, that is, except their No. 3 batsman, Richie Richardson. As the season went on, and he finally adapted to English conditions, the Antiguan in a maroon sunhat progressed from cold to hot like the summer itself. And in the autumn Richardson's career could also be said to have reached fruition, when he was appointed to succeed Viv Richards as captain of West Indies.

Richardson arrived in England in May with two distinct reputations. One was for being the most brilliant hard-wicket batsman of the moment. Against Australia in the immediately preceding series, he had scored 182 at Bourda in Guyana during only 70 overs at the wicket. After Australia had been dismissed for a fairly safe total of 348 on the second afternoon, Richardson blazed away at a match-winning rate until the athleticism of Australia's fielders counted for nothing, and he continued the next morning. "It was like being in a trance," Richardson recalled, "and it was one of those rare occasions when it carried on overnight." Whatever it felt like, the innings not only won the match but also, by demoralising his opponents, the series.

On the other hand was Richardson's second reputation, for being no sort of soft-wicket player. He had never done anything of note in England; and until he had done something, he was going to be denied the accolade of world-class batsman. His chances were understandably few on his first tour in 1984, for Larry Gomes was preferred for his solidity and his experience of English conditions. But in 1988, even after several seasons in English and Welsh leagues, Richardson again had a lean time, before injury cost him his place in the last two Tests. In the thoughtful, open, yet undemonstrative way that is his style, he admits that he listened to too many people advising him to push forward to stifle seam movement. By last summer he had worked out that he could still play his blazing, bottom-handed square-drives and slashes, so long as he was patient and waited for the ball to reach him. The result was that he became the leading run-maker on either side in the series and emerged as a world-class batsman, the heir to Weekes, Worrell, Walcott, Kanhai, Sobers and Richards himself as a strokeplayer of the highest quality and entertainment.

Richardson's scores through the summer tell of his advance. He made 3, 13 and 41 in the one-day internationals. In the Tests he scored 29 (run out) and 68 (top score of the innings) at Headingley; 57 and 1 at Lord's; 43 and 52 not out in the nine-wicket victory at Trent Bridge; 104 and 0 in the seven-wicket victory at Edgbaston; and 20 and 121 at The Oval. Both of his centuries were of the grafting type, though in the Fifth Test he did spurt from 85 to 99 off four balls from David Lawrence. In fact, England had to be grateful that Richardson was never offered a match situation in which he could blaze away without restraint. The failure of Phil Simmons meant that the No. 3 never had the platforms which Gordon Greenidge and Desmond Haynes had customarily given him, and this made his advance the more creditable.

Bowlers who have been ferociously square-driven – according to Ian Chappell, Richardson at Bourda gave the finest exhibition of square-driving since Everton Weekes – might be surprised to learn that Richardson was a defensive batsman as a schoolboy. Born in Five Islands, Antigua, on January 12, 1962, RICHARD BENJAMIN RICHARDSON grew to be the captain of the first team at Ottos Comprehensive School, batted at No. 4 and never made a century. The circumstances, however, explain a lot: school matches in Antigua consisted of one day's play and two innings per side. In any event, he was noted by the coach, Guy Yearwood, who worked on further tightening his defence.

The strokes – those uninhibited strokes, in which he seems to throw the kitchen sink as well as everything else at the ball – were developed in the nets and in the middle, when Richardson, initially an opening batsman for the Leeward Islands, found that a succession of fast bowlers gave him few chances to score conventionally. He learnt to use the hook as a most productive stroke, especially on West Indian grounds with their short boundaries, but circumspectly. Yet he has never worn a helmet or a chest protector to date, like his strokeplaying predecessors of yore, but like Viv Richards alone among contemporary Test players.

However, there has been another quality in Richardson's cricket, in addition to his batting and the excitement which it can generate. On his Test début, against India in 1983-84, he hit his second ball into his pad, and after an orchestrated appeal by the close fielders, supported by much of Bombay, he was given out leg-before. It was a forlorn figure who walked back to the pavilion, not a petulant one; and ever after Richardson has been as sportsmanlike as any of his peers. While batting, or in the slips, he has not indulged in those marginal practices which have made a code of conduct necessary. "Fairness comes from within", says Richardson, whose upbringing was informed with his family's Christianity, and so far he has suited the action to the word.

When Richards broke a finger on the first day of the 1989-90 domestic season, Richardson took over the captaincy of the Leeward Islands until Richards's return, for the final game. By then, winning their first four matches, the Leewards had already claimed their first title in the history of the Red Stripe Cup, or the Shell Shield as it had previously been. Enjoying the responsibility after early nerves, Richardson was the leading run-scorer in the competition, with an aggregate of 421 runs at 70.16. And while he was fortunate to have two experienced bowlers in Ambrose (his room-mate on West Indian tours) and Eldine Baptiste, Leeward Islands teams had boasted greater talents in the past without translating their potential into victory.

It might have been politically expedient if Desmond Haynes, as a Barbadian, had taken over from Richards as the West Indian captain, if only as an interregnum between the two Antiguans. But the West Indian Board was sufficiently impressed by Richardson's attributes to invest in him, just as he has prudently invested for the future in a duty-free shop and a sports store in the Antiguan capital of St John's. By the age of 29 the man in the maroon sunhat had become an outstanding batsman. He also had it in him to become an outstanding leader. – Scyld Berry.

## PHILLIP DeFREITAS

England began their 1991 campaign against the West Indians in complete disarray. They had been badly beaten in the winter's Test series in Australia, a performance which produced from their captain, Graham Gooch, an uncharacteristic outburst in which he was highly critical of the character of several players. Now England faced the undisputed world champions of Test cricket, who had just beaten Australia in a highly charged, ill-tempered series. Viv Richards, who had never lost a Test series as West Indies' captain, was determined to win in what he declared would be his last one. And to make matters worse, Angus Fraser, England's most consistent seam bowler, had been ruled out for the summer because of injury.

No-one could have forecast the dramatic about-turn in England's attitude and performance which led to the series being squared, two matches apiece. And while Gooch must take much of the credit through his direct, uncompromising leadership and inspirational batting, the startling rise in stature of Phillip DeFreitas as England's principal bowler was also a major factor.

Overlooked as an original selection for the winter's tour of Australia, and put down instead for the A team's visit to Pakistan, DeFreitas was in determined mood when he boarded the plane for Australia shortly before Christmas to cover for the injured Gladstone Small. He impressed at Adelaide and Perth, taking four for 56 in 26.2 overs in Australia's first innings at Adelaide, and he returned home more certain than some of his team-mates of selection for the summer's series.

In the six Tests in 1991, DeFreitas took 30 wickets at an average of just 19.06, including career-best figures of seven for 70 against the Sri Lankans at Lord's in their solitary Test match. His contribution to England's morale-boosting victory over the West Indians in the opening Test, at Headingley, was match figures of eight for 93; and having reduced West Indies to 24 for three in the second innings of the Fourth Test, at Edgbaston, he came within a millimetre of immediately dismissing Richards, who went on to steer his team home and ensure that they could not lose the rubber. DeFreitas finished the series with 22 wickets at 20.77, his wickets only decimal points more expensive than those of Ambrose, and throughout it he had fielded breath-takingly. At Trent Bridge, in the Third Test, he registered his maiden Test half-century during a frantic, crowd-pleasing partnership of 58 with David Lawrence which resulted in the game going into the fifth day.

PHILLIP ANTHONY JASON DeFREITAS, more commonly referred to on the county circuit as "Daffy", was born at Scotts Head, Dominica, on February 18, 1966. His parents brought him to London ten years later, where he attended Willesden High School, along with his England and former Leicestershire colleague, Chris Lewis. A spell on the Lord's groundstaff confirmed that DeFreitas was a cricketer with rare potential, and Don Wilson, the MCC coach, recommended him to the then Leicestershire coach, Ken Higgs.

I remember his trial match well. Smarting at having been forced to play for Leicestershire's Second Eleven against MCC Young Professionals, having had a long stint on first-team duty, I had my spirits lifted immediately by the sight of Gordon Parsons being lofted into the ladies' toilets on the Milligan Road car park. The same willowy youth then drilled me for six over extra cover, and when he later bowled with genuine fire, he returned to London that evening with the ink still drying on a contract for the 1985 season. He made eight Championship appearances that year, his 21 wickets at 29.47 including an innings return of five for 39 against Lancashire on his début.

Given a regular place in 1986, he responded by taking 94 first-class wickets and scoring useful runs attractively in the lower order. His flamboyant maiden first-class century against Kent, made in 106 minutes with seventeen fours, came against an attack comprising Alderman, Dilley, Underwood and Ellison after Leicestershire were 43 for seven. Then, taking a leaf out of Alderman's book with regard to line and length, he took six for 21 in 10.4 overs as Kent were dismissed for 87. His prize was a place in that winter's touring party to Australia, where he played in four Tests as Mike Gatting's side retained the Ashes, and he was virtually ever-present as England swept the board in the two limited-overs tournaments.

It was on his return from Australia that relations with Leicestershire began to sour. With the benefit of hindsight, it is fair to say that some of his colleagues, myself included, expected too much of a 21-year-old who was still trying to come to terms with instant success, and with the dramatic transformation of his lifestyle which resulted from it. He appeared moody at times, and although he never failed to perform on the big occasion, DeFreitas did seem rather less enchanted with the more mundane atmosphere of the County Championship. Peter Willey returned the leadership of Leicestershire to David Gower for the 1988 season, but the impasse continued, and after a couple of well-documented confrontations, DeFreitas and Leicestershire parted company before the summer was through.

"I felt I was being knocked when I didn't perform", he has subsequently said. "Perhaps it was no bad thing at that age, but I felt I had to go, and the move to Lancashire was the best thing I could have done."

From my first encounter with him at Grace Road in 1984, DeFreitas has never looked anything but an international cricketer to me. Yet until last summer he had struggled to hold his place in the England team. I believe this was because the England hierarchy had failed to identify precisely what his role should be. Bristling with natural aggression on the field, and capable of bowling genuinely fast at times, he was looked on purely as a strike bowler in his early years, but he lacked the required control. A strike-rate of a wicket every 88 balls, at a cost of 42.31 each, bore little testimony to his undoubted ability. The fact that his greatest success came in limited-overs cricket, for which he was usually an automatic choice, served only to prove that he was at his most effective when bowling within himself.

In 1991, with accuracy paramount against the West Indians, DeFreitas took the opportunity to bowl regularly at that reduced pace. He moved the ball both ways off the seam, and he recaptured his ability to make the ball bounce from that whippy action of his, and he reaped the reward. He is now 26 years old, and appears contented and confident. It is my belief that his most productive cricket is still to come. – Jonathan Agnew.

## ALLAN DONALD

The time was October 1986, the place Bloemfontein, the occasion a pre-season celebratory dinner, given by their supporters, for the Orange Free State team. The players, a set of enthusiastic youngsters, were headed by Corrie van Zyl, then the best young fast bowler in South Africa. But Roger Prideaux, the former England, Sussex and Northamptonshire batsman, drew my attention to someone else. "That's the bowler I would take into county cricket", he said. "He's nearly twenty, and he has as much genuine potential to be fast as any bowler I've seen."

That bowler was ALLAN ANTHONY DONALD, born on October 20, 1966 in Bloemfontein, where he was educated at the Technical High School and went on to be selected for the South African Schools XI in 1984, as twelfth man, and 1985. He made his début for Orange Free State in 1985-86, against Transvaal at the Wanderers, having Jimmy Cook caught behind early on, and since then he has become one of the leading fast bowlers in world cricket. Arguably he is one of only two white bowlers, Australia's Craig McDermott being the other, who could have forced his way into a full-strength West Indies side in 1991.

Figures can be misleading or unrepresentative, but Donald's, compared with those of David Lawrence and Devon Malcolm to the end of the 1991 season, provide a telling story. A comparison with Curtly Ambrose's record is similarly revealing.

|  | M | W | Avge | 5W/i | 10W/m | Avge W/m | Balls/ wkt |
|---|---|---|---|---|---|---|---|
| C. E. L. Ambrose.... | 89 | 354 | 21.87 | 18 | 3 | 4.0 | 51 |
| A. A. Donald ....... | 126 | 450 | 23.09 | 24 | 3 | 3.6 | 47 |
| D. V. Lawrence ..... | 178 | 497 | 32.11 | 20 | 1 | 2.8 | 52 |
| D. E. Malcolm ...... | 108 | 341 | 31.00 | 8 | 1 | 3.2 | 54 |

The speed of Donald's advance, even among a breed of cricketer which reaches its peak sooner than most, is outstanding, particularly as he has had to overcome two major problems. The occasional advantage of bowling fast all year round is heavily outweighed by the strain imposed on his body, and Donald has received regular advice from both Warwickshire and Orange Free State about the need to conserve his talent. But while that is a problem common to most overseas bowlers who ply their trade in England, a bigger one for Donald was fighting his way through the maze of Warwickshire's contractual obligations to cricketers from abroad.

From 1987 to 1989, he shared the overseas slot at Edgbaston with the West Indian fast bowler, Tony Merrick, and in the first two seasons he managed only eighteen first-class games to Merrick's 30. Such was his glittering promise, however, that in 1989 he headed the national averages with 86 wickets at 16.25 apiece and played an important part in Warwickshire's success in the NatWest Bank Trophy. It came as no surprise when Warwickshire released Merrick at the end of the summer, and it appeared that all the arguments concerning overseas players had come to an end.

But not so. The county signed Tom Moody for 1990, with the intention of playing him in the Sunday League so that Donald would be spared the strain sometimes brought about by bowling off a shortened run-up. In the event, what happened helped to precipitate a crisis within the club which came close to ending Donald's career at Edgbaston. Injury, followed by loss of form and confidence, coincided with a magnificent series of Championship innings from Moody and led to Donald being resigned to the fact that the big Australian would be preferred to him for 1991. Happily, the Warwickshire committee decided in the South African's favour, not only on cricketing grounds but also on the ethical ones of honouring a long-term contract.

Last summer Donald repaid Warwickshire's faith in him by bowling them to the verge of the Britannic Assurance Championship title, taking 83 wickets at 19.68 to finish behind Waqar Younis in the national first-class averages. Until the last three weeks of the season, his captain, Andy Lloyd, rigidly restricted him to spells of no more than five or six overs, even when he was taking wickets. But Donald showed great reserves of stamina and courage by bowling unchanged for twenty overs in the final home game against Northamptonshire, despite a back injury, and his six for 69 in the second innings to win that game, and another six in the first innings at Taunton, took to eight his five-wicket returns in 1991. Only Waqar Younis exceeded that figure, and twice Donald finished with ten wickets in a match.

His physical attributes are there for all to see. A magnificent natural athlete, he has a not over-long run-up, which accelerates him into a high, balanced, slightly open action. Despite this openness, he still has that priceless ability to run the ball away from the right-handed batsman, both in the air and off the pitch. He bowls a fuller length than most fast men – a deliberate change of method in 1991 – which is why some 70 per cent of his wickets were either bowled, lbw or caught at the wicket. Occasional losses of rhythm, with their subsequent diminution of effectiveness, occurred less frequently last summer, and Donald's ability to cope with the pressure of international cricket brought him instant success in South Africa's historic week in India in November.

Bowlers capable of genuine speed rarely sustain fitness and form for more than a decade, and Donald is now halfway through that period. The best is yet to come; the question is, for how long? His physique and action should carry him through another five years – always provided that his commitments to Warwickshire, Orange Free State and now South Africa are treated sensibly by all parties. – Jack Bannister.

## WAQAR YOUNIS

By taking 113 wickets in 582 overs for Surrey in 1991, at a mere 14.65 apiece, and by carrying on his shoulders an otherwise moderate county attack, WAQAR YOUNIS announced himself as one of the finest contemporary bowlers and hinted that in time he may achieve the greatness which, it seems, has already been thrust upon him; with which, perhaps, he was born. In just eleven Tests for Pakistan before last summer he had taken 55 wickets, capturing five wickets in an innings five times. Moreover, he had provoked Martin Crowe, captain of New Zealand, into saying that he had never faced pace and swing bowling of such quality. What is more, he made him attach a grille to his helmet for the first time. Not even the West Indian fast bowlers had been able to do that. And this on Pakistani pitches, under a gruelling sun.

An astonishing number of Waqar's wickets have been clean bowled or have come from leg-before decisions, for his strength lies in a deadly combination of explosive pace and late swing, with which he has regularly been able to shatter the stumps or bruise the toes of apparently well-established batsmen. Waqar's sudden dismissal of Graeme Hick at Worcester last summer with one of his specials, an in-swinging yorker, was particularly memorable, for Hick, just 5 runs away from 150, was well and truly set fair. No modern bowler can have relied on the pitch less for help, and few have been as capable of changing the course of a game in a handful of overs. He took his wickets in 1991 despite generally slow pitches at The Oval, and despite the fact that county batsmen had been alerted to his most potent deliveries after encountering him in 1990, his first season. Surrey have long since been grateful for Ian Greig's haste in signing Waqar after a solitary net and a fulsome recommendation from Imran Khan.

Bounding in on a fast, long run, reminiscent of Malcolm Marshall in his pomp, Waqar is an immensely physical bowler. There is about him the aggression of an impassioned warrior. At delivery he jumps high, and, pulling his arm through rather in the manner of Andy Roberts, he hurls himself at the batsman, often finishing his follow-through just yards from his enemy and still breathing fire. However, Waqar is by temperament more docile than his Antiguan predecessor, besides which he is young yet and unversed in the subtleties of psychological warfare. Apart from pace and swing, his greatest assets are his stamina and a flexibility of body which allows him to bowl his fastest from the first delivery of every spell, no matter what the time of day or how many overs he has already bowled.

In his early overs he concentrates on an out-swinger delivered to a full length and interspersed only occasionally with bumpers, a weapon used solely as a reminder to batsmen not to plunge too glibly forward. Because he pitches to such a full length and bowls to an unrelentingly attacking field, Waqar can in his first spell be expensive, for he invites batsmen to drive, wanting wickets not maidens. Nor is his bowling yet mechanical. Rather it is raw, though never vulgar, and he searches constantly for the extremity of what he can do. Accordingly, he is sometimes inaccurate.

If wickets do not fall in this first spell, and occasionally they do not, his captain will rest him. But if batsmen do capitulate, Waqar will want to carry on, for he is strong and willing, and inclined to the fervour of a prep school bowler who regards giving lesser fry a chance as an indication of weakness. Conservation of energy is not for him, and nor is he reluctant to bowl to great batsmen; quite the contrary in both cases. But his later spells can be just as effective; more so even, for he finds control easier with the old ball and swings it even more, much to the consternation of Occidental batsmen, who whisper about Oriental tricks. In Pakistan, it is rumoured, bowlers have been taught to interfere with the ball by roughing up one side with bottle tops and the like, a tactic which produces prodigious swing confusingly against the shine.

For a time Waqar's ability to bowl searing in-swingers with a decrepit ball was thought to be due to this ruse. Umpires were on their guard in 1991 and ball checks were a regular occurrence at The Oval and elsewhere. Notwithstanding these, Waqar ran amok once more, silencing those critics and proving that he relied on such dubious tactics less, not more, than anybody else.

Beyond doubt Waqar is an outstanding bowler, probably the finest to emerge from Pakistan since Fazal Mahmood. And yet his emergence owed something to chance, for though he was born in Burewala in the Vehari area of the Punjab, breeding ground of so many courageous fighters, on November 16, 1971, he was raised in Sharjah, where his father was a contract worker. Returning to Pakistan in his adolescence, Waqar played in obscurity until, in 1988, he was noticed by Imran Khan while bowling in a televised local knockout game. As fate would have it, the Pakistan captain was convalescing in his bed in Lahore and had turned on his television set to while away a few hours. Watching this vibrant if erratic pace bowler and immediately detecting talent, Imran saw in him the means of meeting Pakistan's need for a fast bowler to support Wasim Akram. He took the seventeen-year-old under his wing, and played him in Sharjah and in the Nehru Cup in 1989-90 before giving him his Test début against India. He also included him in the team for Australia, where his surging pace made an impression.

Imran refined Waqar's run and action, taught him the fundamentals of swing, and so unleashed on the cricket world a bowler of exuberance and danger. A buzz spreads around the ground as Waqar removes his sweater, and a silence descends as he begins his charge to the crease. This is a bowler of brilliance and élan, a bowler as entertaining in his way as any batsman, as enthralling as any spinner, a bowler who could become, as Imran predicted, the greatest of them all. – Peter Roebuck.

# WOMEN IN CRICKET

## By TERESA McLEAN

"What is human life but a game of cricket?" asked the 3rd Duke of Dorset, fervent cricket fan and supporter of the Hambledon club, in a letter to "a circle of Ladies, his intimate Friends"[1] in 1777. "And if so, why should not the ladies play it as well as we?"

Unreliable though he was in most of his dealings with the female sex, the 3rd Duke was unfailingly generous towards women's cricket. He liked his women sporty and rangy, in the outdoor mode, and his support for women's cricket was only one of his many efforts to help women play the game, however much opposition they met.

At this early stage in the life of cricket there was little concerted opposition to women taking part in the game. The standard attitude was one of ignorance, with a vague predisposition to believe that cricket was, as W. G. Grace still considered it more than a century later, "not a game for women, and although the fair sex occasionally join in a picnic game, they are not constitutionally adapted for the sport!"[2]

Even so, eighteenth and early nineteenth century women's matches were popular as freakish amusements and attracted large crowds, married women v maidens being one of the favourites. On October 5, 1811, a *Times* reporter described a serious women's match at Newington, between a Hampshire XI and a Surrey XI, which lasted three days and was played for 500 guineas a side. It was won by Hampshire, by 15 notches (runs), and led to another match being fixed immediately, as there had been "some very excellent play, and much skill". Nevertheless, it was the burlesque element which appealed most to the public, and "a great concourse of people attended to witness this singular contention", which they would not have done had it not been so exotically singular.

Most women lacked the patronage, interest or incentive to play the game as the Newington ladies played it. Most kept busy in the tavern, preparing refreshments for the men on the field of play. Most preferred, or at least accepted, this state of affairs. However, female support sometimes extended beyond washing clothes and making tea. Women cricket writers have been a small and intermittent but talented minority since Mary Russell Mitford first published her article "The Cricket Match" in *The Lady's Magazine* in 1823, then again, with great success, in her book *Our Village* in 1824. Just over a century later Marjorie Pollard completed her career in an era of enthusiasm for cricket and for all women's sports by writing a regular cricket column for the *Morning Post* and *London Evening News*. There are one or two female correspondents today, enjoying being presented with press packs of ties and men's tee-shirts.

Before cricket writing had become as inflated an operation as it is now, the only way women who did not want to be tea ladies could participate actively in men's cricket was as teachers. John Willes of Kent, famous as the pioneer of round-arm bowling, is often said to have picked up the idea of this new "march-of-intellect system", radical and widely mistrusted all through his lifetime, from his sister. She is supposed to have started bowling round-arm

---

[1] *The Sporting Magazine*, April 1803.

[2] W. G. Grace, *Cricketing Reminiscences and Personal Recollections*, 1891.

when her voluminous skirt got in the way of her under-arm action. There is, however, no clear evidence for this, and Christina Willes, John Willes's daughter, knew nothing of it, though she took a lively interest in the game, as her cricketing aunt had before her. Martha Grace was an amazon among cricket enthusiasts, watching, coaching and commenting on her five sons' performances on the field of play. Three of them, E.M., G.F. and W.G., played for England in the first Test in England against Australia, at The Oval in 1880. The late nineteenth century was a high point of female efforts to improve men's cricket and a starting-point of serious women's cricket, played as a sport rather than being an amusing spectacle.

The White Heather Club, founded in 1887 and surviving until 1950, was the first women's cricket club, its members mostly Yorkshire ladies with enough money to pay their own expenses. Even after the Women's Cricket Association was founded in 1926, and women's cricket had enjoyed a flourishing decade in the 1930s, the game was still expensive for those taking part. It was no longer weird enough to attract big, curious crowds, nor well enough established to count as a major sport and so attract sponsors. It has, however, always had some distinguished male supporters, such as the 3rd Duke of Dorset, C. B. Fry, Frank Chester in the 1920s, and Jack Hayward, the outstanding patron of women's cricket in the 1970s. But a minor sport, with few women knowing anything about it, still less how to play it, is not a recipe for prosperity.

Cricket is fighting to keep going in boys' schools; it is almost non-existent in girls' schools. The WCA is, in the words of Cathy Mowat, its current chairman, "either staying static or holding its own, depending on how you look at it". The 1970s were high-profile years, with England's women under the captaincy of Rachael Heyhoe Flint and the patronage of Jack Hayward. Since then things have been quieter.

Women's cricket clubs have to inspire and teach their own juniors, although the National Cricket Association provides qualified coaches, and the Lord's Taverners provide some funds. And in the last 30 years or so, women's cricket has been given more institutional help. Women playing for Oxford and Cambridge – sometimes with more will than skill – are given only half-Blues, but Cyril Coote, the incomparable groundsman at Fenner's, gladly let women play there when I asked him, on behalf of Cambridge, in 1978. Similarly, women in the last 30 years have been allowed the use of the nets at Lord's and a growing share in the MCC coaching awards. Above all, England's women have been allowed the use of Lord's for Test matches since 1976, when Rachael Heyhoe Flint first persuaded MCC to let women tread the hallowed turf.

The WCA's relations with MCC remain friendly, and it looks likely that the next Women's World Cup will be played at Lord's in 1993, as long as the WCA's money-raising efforts can find the quarter-million pounds, or thereabouts, required. Every player had to pay her own passage on the 1991-92 tour of New Zealand, and as John Featherstone, the WCA's secretary, put it: "Playing at international level means finding money for flights, clothing and equipment, perhaps taking unpaid leave of absence, or even giving up one's job. However, the cricketers are all amateurs, playing for the love of the game and the pleasure they gain from it. Long may it continue."

Cricket is doing particularly well in Europe, where England retained the European Cup at Haarlem, in The Netherlands, in July 1991, against spirited opposition from Denmark, Ireland and the host country. However, England is the only country where first-class women's games are umpired by women, without payment. Women also umpire a few men's games in the Lancashire League, and in local and village matches, as I know from nerve-racking personal experience. The present, outstanding chairman of the Association of Cricket Umpires is a woman, Sheila Hill.

The last decade has seen the emergence of a new breed of cricket career woman, driven by different motives from Miss Hill, not interested in playing or in working without due payment. Derbyshire, Kent, Sussex and Nottinghamshire county clubs have women physiotherapists, chosen from the big female majority of physio students. Sheila Ball has been the physiotherapist at Trent Bridge since 1985 and has been well treated everywhere, after initial problems gaining entry into the Lord's Pavilion with her team for the 1985 NatWest final. Nottinghamshire are used to female physios; they started using them back in 1975, and they are proud of the excellent work Sheila does for them. "Oh yes, we're taking over these days", she told me cheerfully.

Women administrators in the upper echelons of men's cricket tend to provoke more unease. The game's administration is growing into a concourse of assorted secretaries, executives and managers, in which several women now occupy senior positions at several counties. Rose FitzGibbon was made the assistant secretary at Old Trafford in 1978, after starting as the principal private secretary. She is now the cricket secretary, which means, she told me with the weary humour of one who has to survive in this warren of titles, that one of her duties is to "deputise for the chief executive". She says she is accepted by everyone at the club, though it has taken time and she still feels that she, like most women in cricket administration, has been given prominence but not proper recognition.

Lancashire's members have traditionally been a conservative lot, but the debate at the AGM on December 9, 1989, on whether to admit women to full membership, won the club a brief flurry of improbable notoriety. The motion proposing that women be admitted was passed after one of the members, "Mr Keith Hull (otherwise known as Stephanie Lloyd) advised the Meeting that by a legal technicality he was the Club's first full female Member".[1] He had had a sex-change operation and so the club already had a woman member. After some noble discussion – including Mr John Treveloni's threat to alter his will if women were admitted to membership, and the Revd Malcolm Lorimer's support for "the preservation of tradition where it was worth preserving . . . If the Church of England could move towards women Priests, if Eastern Europe could make changes as had been seen in recent weeks then Lancashire CCC could also change" – full membership for women was finally accepted by the necessary two-thirds majority. The club now seems happy with the arrangement, after its uncertain start. The next step, said Rose FitzGibbon, is ladies on the committee and "maybe, in time, they will have a lady president".

Maybe. Rachael Heyhoe Flint stood for membership of MCC early in the summer of 1991 but was refused. Members at Surrey and Nottinghamshire feel they have benefited enormously from having women among their numbers and take a rather pitying view of MCC's members, who chose to see the issue in terms of defending their traditions and, not surprisingly, voted

---

[1] Minutes of Lancashire CCC Annual General Meeting, December 9, 1989.

for the defence. Lt-Col. John Stephenson, secretary of MCC, thinks that women will probably be admitted to membership in the end – possibly even before the end of the next century – but stresses that the decision lies with the members.

Diana Edulji, captain of the Indian women's team in England in 1986, took an angrier view of being banned from the Pavilion at Lord's when India's men were playing England there that summer. "I was shocked at the male chauvinism which has survived. I had to sit in the Tavern stand. The MCC should change their name to MCP."

Women's cricket is extremely popular in India, where it was taught, maybe even introduced, at Kottanam in 1913 by an Australian teacher, Ann Kelleve, who made it compulsory in the school she set up. Mrs Gandhi was a strong devotee of women's cricket and it is widely played. When Young England toured there in 1980-81, crowds of 20,000 to 25,000 attended the major matches in some centres. In Australia it has always had more of a pioneering spirit. The sex war is a hard-fought inheritance in Antipodean cricket, and it was a great achievement when Peggy Antonio, the great lady spin bowler from Victoria, was christened "Girl Grimmett" by the Australian press after taking six English wickets for 49 in the Third Test at Melbourne in 1934-35. She inspired Neville Cardus to ask: "Suppose one day the greatest slow left-handed bowler in England is discovered to be a woman, will any male selection committee at Lord's send her an invitation?"

The 3rd Duke of Dorset would laugh in his grave if a woman played for England, flourishing against the odds.

"Mind not, my dear ladies, the impertinent interrogatories of silly coxcombs, or the dreadful apprehensions of semi-men . . . Go on, and attach yourselves to the athletic."

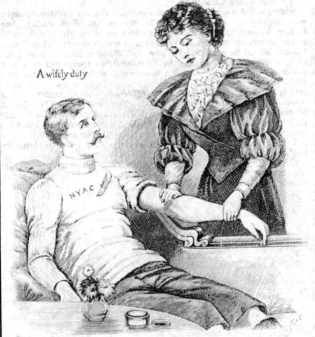

# PUSHING THE PRODUCT

## ADVERTISEMENTS IN WISDEN, 1864-1915

### By BENNY GREEN

Nobody knows precisely when John Wisden had the shrewd idea of accepting advertisements for his Almanack, but certainly by the fourth edition he was using a shameless, illustrated puff for the Catapulta, a primitive form of bowling machine built on the principles of archery. The operator released the ball from a concave bow by cranking a handle. In the 1867 edition, the identity of this mysterious operator is hidden behind the contraption's superstructure, and we catch no more than a glimpse of someone wearing a hat and sporting extravagant sideburns. The Catapulta cost £12, which represented two years' wages for a scullery-maid of the period, although no evidence exists of a scullery-maid ever purchasing one. But this sign that the Almanack was augmenting its income by selling space is misleading. The only customer John Wisden could find was himself; the Catapulta was his own patent. Indeed, even in the first edition of 1864, the back cover was a mere sandwich board for the contents of Wisden's shop in New Coventry Street, among which were Indian clubs, shrinkless flannels for "trowsers and jackets", Electro Registered belts and, symbolically, dumb-bells.

The introduction of advertising represents a smart recovery from a calamitous start. The inaugural edition of 1864 had been a disaster, although today it is the very absurdity of the contents which renders it irresistibly endearing. Like a great many editors then and since, John Wisden, once he had conceived the masterstroke of an annual about the game, had no faint idea what to put into it. The innocent researcher, turning back to that famous first edition, is amazed as well as amused to find there everything from the length of the chief British canals to a disquisition on the constitutional implications of the trial of Charles I. In retrospect, it is surprising that a man witty enough to have dismissed the Atlantic Ocean from his presence with, "What this pitch needs is ten minutes of the heavy roller", should have been so all at sea in a different sense when it came to his Almanack. But he was quick to see the error of his ways, and advertisements were an early sign that he meant business, literally.

At first the advertising concerned only the accoutrements of the game – bats and balls, pads and stumps, gloves and scorebooks. Slowly the range widened. The first signs came with the advent of other sports; puffs for golf balls and clubs, tennis balls and rackets, even offers of cheaply constructed tennis courts. Then followed boxing gloves, running shoes, horse boots, marquees and pavilions. At last the ads crept indoors, and readers were offered full-size billiard tables, a reminder to posterity that once upon a time people lived in houses with rooms spacious enough to accommodate such a luxury. But the insights into Victorian life really begin with the publication of ads quite unconnected with the sporting life.

A casual browse through the 1880s soon discloses home truths unlinked to cricket. In 1883 E. M. Reilly and Co., of Oxford Street, were defining the class structure in the plainest way. Mr Reilly sold sporting guns, and his tariff makes a definite distinction between Gentleman and Player; £7. 10s. for a

Naturalist's gun, but only £6. 10s. for a Keeper's gun. Two years later we find the implication that cricket fanciers must also be fishermen. Messrs Hardy's of Northumberland announced their new "Carry-All Fishing Basket", with compartments for "a sandwich, cane, flask, tackle, book", and then, apparently as an afterthought, "fish".

By 1889 it must have occurred to some bright spark that cricketers occasionally had wives, otherwise why would Neil's, purveyors of Infants' and Invalids' food, have placed an ad incorporating a small masterpiece in the art of euphemism: "Babies fed with it thrive equal to those nourished by the Mother. Mothers that take it nourish their Babies as well as themselves." This was the time when a white cashmere shirt could be had for half a guinea, and the firm of Epps was offering cocoa which was "not only comforting but grateful". The modern age, unfamiliar with cocoa even in its ungrateful state, can only wonder what Mr Epps had come up with.

In 1894 calligraphy entered the ring. To this day the curlicues of the Victorian age inspire awe, so it is no shock to discover that Joseph Collard, of Cranbourne Street, was offering a range of pen-nibs whose glories have long since been buried under a mountain of typewriters, biros and word processors: "The Waverly, Pickwick, Nile, Hindoo, Phaeton, Owl, Flying Scotchman, Flying Dutchman, Big J, Big Waverly, Commercial." A name like Collard was not likely to daunt the prospective buyer. Nor was that of Cox and Yeman, makers of billiard tables for the War Office and the Admiralty, with accessories for the far-flung outposts of Empire: "Tables and Lamps made expressly for India and Extreme Climates." But in the 1896 *Wisden* there appeared an ad suggesting that the epoch had not yet woken up to the fact that there are names and there are warnings, and that to use one when the other would be more appropriate is not good for business. The truss-maker who trumpeted in *Wisden* his range of "enemas, syringes, pessaries, rubber goods, &c." probably went to his grave without realising that the poor response lay in his name: Theodore Skull. At any rate, his entry soon disappeared from the pages of the Almanack.

It was the back cover of Mr Skull's edition which painted a more congenial portrait of the extra-sporting life. There we find a comely lady applying something called Exaino to the arm of a mustachioed young man, whose smug expression might suggest a long and intimate relationship with his nurse. To avoid any misunderstandings, the designers of the sketch appended the words, "A wifely duty", floating like a halo a few inches above the patient's brilliantined head. By now this style of huckstering was the social norm. Cadbury had pulled off the coup of the age by placing magazine ads showing Queen Victoria sitting in a railway carriage confronted by a cup of the company's cocoa. Bovril had responded by claiming that there were only two infallibles in this uncertain world, and backed the claim with a sketch of the Pope enjoying a cup of the product. *Wisden* never went to these lengths, but as the new century dawned, the advertising boom was certainly reflected in its pages. Long before then it had appointed an agency to handle applications for advertising space, and by the time Edward VII was crowned, *Wisden* was carrying two indexes — one for cricket, the other for advertising.

Symbolically, it was the edition heralding the new century which reflected this boom in business. The reader of the 1901 *Wisden* found himself bewildered by the profusion of choices. If disconcerted by the full page proclaiming the comforts of the Footballers' Hospital in Manchester, he could console himself with the thought that the Railway Passengers'

Assurance Co. (deputy chairman, Sir Spencer Ponsonby-Fane) was offering insurance against injuries sustained on the cricket field. And if all else failed, there was always Mr Weiss of Oxford Street, with his kindly offer of false knee-caps "made of finest plated steel wire, meshed so as to contract and expand with the movement of the knee . . .". Mr Weiss was nothing if not thorough, adding thoughtfully: "In ordering . . . state for which leg."

But how might a man mislay his own knee? Possibly through an excess of faith in Messrs Heath and George's Horizontal and Parallel Bars, illustrated with a man of ominously Pooteresque aspect straining to pull wire expanders before him, surely bringing the entire house down about his ears. Still, there was always the Footballers' Hospital, after which, having equipped himself with a false knee-cap out of the money supplied by Sir Spencer Ponsonby-Fane, he could enjoy a soapless, waterless, brushless shave with Euxesis, and then limp along to the Greek Stores in Cranbourne Street, where he could order 500 Egyptian cigarettes at seven shillings per hundred, with his name printed on each one at no extra cost.

By 1903 things were calming down a little, with the peace which passeth all understanding available at the Waterloo Hotel, "within ten minutes of the Oval Cricket Ground. Special terms to Cricket Teams . . . Telegraphic Address:– 'Tuffins Hotel'". But the Waterloo was hopelessly upstaged by the Horns Hotel, which was not only much closer to The Oval but also, according to its proprietor, a Mr Brinkley, possessed the "Best Kitchen in the South of London", dining-rooms which were "overlooking Kennington Park . . . Comfortable Smoking and Billiard Rooms . . . Wines of all best known Brands . . . Cigars of Choicest Crops . . . Iced Munich Spaten Beer on draught". Why, having stumbled on this paradisal watering-hole, bother to leave it for the cricket at all? Similar thoughts must have occurred to the clients of the Peru House Private Hotel in Woburn Place, haven of "Convenience, Quietude, Comfort, and Economy", where a man could find "Electric Light and Bells throughout", meat breakfasts and a telephone, all for 4s. 6d. a night.

A return to the Surrey connection was available with the offer of "Recordine", an "oilless disinfectant embrocation", with an impressive list of endorsers. Among these was Tom Richardson, dismissed elsewhere in the edition as "no longer great", but sought after eagerly enough when it came to Recordine. Poor Tom seems to have done everything with the stuff except drink it for breakfast. He used it for sprains and bruises, and in hot weather he rubbed himself all over with it, before the start of a game and again during the interval. He also claimed that after rubbing his feet with it, he felt cooler.

The claims of the salesmen became steadily more hysterical. In 1904 a very rash gentleman calling himself Professor Szalay, pushing something called Szalay's Developer, claimed that its use would "guarantee a big innings". Three years later we find two gents meeting in the labyrinth of a country house. Both are dressed in shirts of hideous aspect. The monocled one is saying to the mustachioed one: "*Mine* are not shrunk, as they are 'Viyella.'" It is not made clear what he is referring to. By 1911 Ivelcon had arrived on the market, a mysterious beverage which contained "many times more nutriment than beef tea", and which would "help you win the game". It is a sad comment on the vigilence of MCC that nobody had the wit to organise a match between the invincible users of Professor Szalay's Developer and the equally invincible swiggers of Ivelcon, each member of the winning side to

be awarded an Aermagna shirt, which claimed in 1914 to be "Noted for Durability, Absorbent and Hygienic".

It speaks volumes for *Wisden's* advertisers that their loyalty to the Almanack remained unshaken by the outbreak of the Great War, and the slamming of the door on a society which had enjoyed comparative peace for a hundred years. By the time the 1915 edition was in the better class of bookshop, the war had been raging for several bloody months. Yet the list of advertisers fills a complete page of the saddest of all editions of *Wisden*, the wartime edition obliged to array itself in the bright colours of peace, as though nothing had changed. There they all were, the endorsements for bats and balls and pads and gloves, for lawnmowers and marquees, horse boots and squash courts. And of them all, none is more powerfully evocative of a lost time than that on the inside cover, announcing the Sybaritic luxuries of Nevill's Turkish Baths, with outposts all over the town. Any doubts about the probity of the establishment were crushed once and for all with:

> Nevill's Turkish Baths are a live and up-to-date concern, the decoration of the bath rooms is tasteful, the attendance prompt and obliging, the shampooers capable and efficient; each establishment is in charge of a competent and experienced manager; the attendants are chosen from the best of their class, and can be relied on for knowledge of their work and readiness to assist the inexperienced bather. The supply of air is scientifically treated and arranged; it is filtered before entering the bath, heated by a scientific apparatus of considerable repute, while the system of ventilation ensures a rapid flow of fresh untainted air through the bathrooms.

Nevill's remained faithful to *Wisden* throughout the war, but by the 1919 edition only nine advertisers had survived. Like the rest of English life, they had been almost decimated.

No review of the concerns which spent money boosting their products in *Wisden* would be halfway complete without a mention of its two most memorable advertisers, the one which distinguished itself for artistic endeavour, the other for dogged commercialism in the face of evidence to the contrary. Dr J. Collis Browne must have been a man sorely harassed by the machinations of the scientists. Among the first of John Wisden's customers, the good doctor was pursued down the labyrinth of the century by the relentless advance of medical science. Each time curative discovery took a step forward, so the doctor deftly took a corresponding step back, covering his flanks as best he could with wonderfully impudent bombast like "Important Caution: The immense sale of this remedy has given rise to many unscrupulous imitations. Be careful to observe trade mark." But he must have known there could be only one ending to the dance.

The Chlorodyne ads first began to appear around the time of the Queen's first Jubilee; in the 1894 edition, only months before the discovery of X-rays, Dr Collis Browne was claiming that his potion was "the best remedy known for Coughs, Consumption, Bronchitis, and Asthma"; that it "checks and arrests . . . Diphtheria, Fever, Croup, Ague"; that it "acts like a charm in Diarrhoea" and was "the only specific in Cholera and Dysentery"; that it "cuts short attacks of Epilepsy, Hysteria, Palpitation, and Spasms", and was "the only palliative for Neuralgia, Rheumatism, Gout, Cancer, Toothache, Meningitis".

Slowly the retreat began. In 1903 Meningitis and Ague were dropped from the side and Colic was promoted. By 1913 the doctor had tactfully dropped Coughs, Consumption, Asthma, Diphtheria, Epilepsy and Cancer. Perhaps he was forewarned by the publication in 1911 of *Tono-Bungay*, H. G. Wells's brilliant exposition of the art of foisting on the public bottles of tonic which do them "only a little harm". But what finally brought about the surrender was neither science nor art, but the Great War. In the 1915 *Wisden*, Chlorodyne's tattered flag twitches weakly in the winds of war and is then seen no more.

The advertising campaign for Pears Soap was in complete contrast. Although it laid claims to its own indispensability, laughter was never very far away, and there was in addition a genuine attempt to vary the sales pitch from season to season. It was the Pears ads in *Wisden* which introduced to the great British sporting public the adjective "saponaceous" (meaning soapy). It was Pears again who conducted some of the earliest experiments in under-statement; one edition of the Almanack carries a full page which reads simply, "Pears". Among the choicer items in the history of Pears in *Wisden* are:

"100 Not Out. Centuries are not uncommon in Cricket, but in soap manufacture they are rare indeed. Pears Soap, however, is the Soap of Three Centuries. Invented in the 18th, holding the lead all through the nineteenth and more popular than ever in the 20th. They played cricket in top hats when Pears was young, and cricketers used it then as they do now, and for the same reason, because it is matchless for the complexion." (1895)

"Pears, soapmakers to the King, and holders of the only Grand Prix." (1902)

"A Wonderful Hit. When Cricket was 120 years younger . . . these were the days of 'big hits' in many directions, and the heaviest scorer in toilet soap invention was Pears . . . the World's Top Scorer in Toilet Soaps." (1911)

But Pears' finest hour had come in mid-Edwardian editions of the Almanack. In 1907 Sydney Pardon had shrewdly applied to *Punch* for permission to reproduce a cartoon by Harry Furniss. It shows a grime-encrusted beggar writing a letter, saying: "Two years ago I used your soap, *since when* I have used no other!" Furniss, who had been known to write choleric letters to *The Times* about the advertising hoardings displayed at Lord's, seems to have been happy enough about plugging soap. Probably he was reconciled to this climbdown because a far greater artist's work had been recruited in the same cause only a year before. The inside back cover of the Almanack had depicted a pair of Woosteresque toffs smiling at a hoarding which reads: "Apples Make Cider, but Pears make Soap." Perhaps the smiles are inspired less by the text than by the presence of a statuesque lady, straight out of Toulouse-Lautrec, who is smiling either at the hoarding or at the gentlemen. Underneath this charmingly ambiguous sketch, it says, "Specially drawn for Messrs Pears by the late Phil May". O, my Tuffins and my Euxesis long ago!

# TEST CRICKETERS

FULL LIST FROM 1877 TO AUGUST 27, 1991

These lists have been compiled on a home and abroad basis, appearances abroad being printed in *italics*.

**Abbreviations.** E: England. A: Australia. SA: South Africa. WI: West Indies. NZ: New Zealand. In: India. P: Pakistan. SL: Sri Lanka.

All appearances are placed in this order of seniority. Hence, any England cricketer playing against Australia in England has that achievement recorded first and the remainder of his appearances at home (if any) set down before passing to matches abroad. Although the distinction between amateur and professional was abolished in 1963, initials of English professionals before that date are still given in brackets. The figures immediately following each name represent the total number of appearances in *all* Tests.

Where the season embraces two different years, the first year is given; i.e. 1876 indicates 1876-77.

## ENGLAND

Number of Test cricketers: 552

Abel (R.) 13: v A 1888 (3) 1896 (3) 1902 (2); *v A 1891 (3); v SA 1888 (2)*
Absolom, C. A. 1: *v A 1878*
Agnew, J. P. 3: v A 1985 (1); v WI 1984 (1); v SL 1984 (1)
Allen (D. A.) 39: v A 1961 (4) 1964 (1); v SA 1960 (2); v WI 1963 (2) 1966 (1); v P 1962 (4); *v A 1962 (1) 1965 (4); v SA 1964 (4); v WI 1959 (5); v NZ 1961 (5); v P 1961 (3)*
Allen, G. O. B. 25: v A 1930 (1) 1934 (2); v WI 1933 (1); v NZ 1931 (3); v In 1936 (3); *v A 1932 (5) 1936 (5); v WI 1947 (3); v NZ 1932 (2)*
Allom, M. J. C. 5: *v SA 1930 (1); v NZ 1929 (4)*
Allott, P. J. W. 13: v A 1981 (1) 1985 (4); v WI 1984 (3); v In 1982 (2); v SL 1984 (1); *v In 1981 (1); v SL 1981 (1)*
Ames (L. E. G.) 47: v A 1934 (5) 1938 (2); v SA 1929 (1) 1935 (4); v WI 1933 (3); v NZ 1931 (3) 1937 (3); v In 1932 (1); *v A 1932 (5) 1936 (5); v SA 1938 (5); v WI 1929 (4) 1934 (4); v NZ 1932 (2)*
Amiss, D. L. 50: v A 1968 (1) 1975 (2) 1977 (2); v WI 1966 (1) 1973 (3) 1976 (1); v NZ 1973 (3); v In 1967 (2) 1971 (1) 1974 (3); v P 1967 (1) 1971 (3) 1974 (3); *v A 1974 (5) 1976 (1); v WI 1973 (5) v NZ 1974 (2); v In 1972 (3) 1976 (5); v P 1972 (3)*
Andrew (K. V.) 2: v WI 1963 (1); *v A 1954 (1)*
Appleyard (R.) 9: v A 1956 (1); v SA 1955 (1); v P 1954 (1); *v A 1954 (1); v NZ 1954 (2)*
Archer, A. G. 1: *v SA 1898*
Armitage (T.) 2: *v A 1876 (2)*
Arnold (E. G.) 10: v A 1905 (4); v SA 1907 (2); *v A 1903 (4)*
Arnold, G. G. 34: v A 1972 (3) 1975 (1); v WI 1973 (3); v NZ 1969 (1) 1973 (3); v In 1974 (2); v P 1967 (2) 1974 (3); *v A 1974 (4); v WI 1973 (3); v NZ 1974 (2); v In 1972 (4); v P 1972 (3)*
Arnold (J.) 1: v NZ 1931
Astill (W. E.) 9: *v SA 1927 (5); v WI 1929 (4)*
Atherton, M. A. 18: v A 1989 (2); v WI 1991 (5); v NZ 1990 (3); v In 1990 (3); *v A 1990 (5)*
Athey, C. W. J. 23: v A 1980 (1); v WI 1988 (1); v NZ 1986 (3); v In 1986 (2); v P 1987 (4); *v A 1986 (5) 1987 (1); v WI 1980 (1); v NZ 1987 (1); v P 1987 (3)*
Attewell (W.) 10: v A 1890 (1); *v A 1884 (5) 1887 (1) 1891 (3)*

Bailey, R. J. 4: v WI 1988 (1); *v WI 1989 (3)*
Bailey, T. E. 61: v A 1953 (5) 1956 (4); v SA 1951 (2) 1955 (5); v WI 1950 (2) 1957 (4); v NZ 1949 (4) 1958 (4); v P 1954 (3); *v A 1950 (4) 1954 (5) 1958 (5); v SA 1956 (5); v WI 1953 (5); v NZ 1950 (2) 1954 (2)*

Bairstow, D. L. 4: v A 1980 (1); v WI 1980 (1); v In 1979 (1); *v WI 1980 (1)*
Bakewell (A. H.) 6: v SA 1935 (2); v WI 1933 (1); v NZ 1931 (2); *v In 1933 (1)*
Balderstone J. C. 2: v WI 1976 (2)
Barber, R. W. 28: v A 1964 (1) 1968 (1); v SA 1960 (1) 1965 (3); v WI 1966 (2); v NZ 1965 (3); *v A 1965 (5); v SA 1964 (4); v In 1961 (5); v P 1961 (3)*
Barber (W.) 2: v SA 1935 (2)
Barlow, G. D. 3: v A 1977 (1); *v In 1976 (2)*
Barlow (R. G.) 17: v A 1882 (1) 1884 (3) 1886 (3); *v A 1881 (4) 1882 (4) 1886 (2)*
Barnes (S. F.) 27: v A 1902 (1) 1909 (3) 1912 (3); v SA 1912 (3); *v A 1901 (3) 1907 (5) 1911 (5); v SA 1913 (4)*
Barnes (W.) 21: v A 1880 (1) 1882 (1) 1884 (2) 1886 (2) 1888 (3) 1890 (2); *v A 1882 (4) 1884 (5) 1886 (1)*
Barnett (C. J.) 20: v A 1938 (3) 1948 (1); v SA 1947 (3); v WI 1933 (1); v NZ 1937 (3); v In 1936 (1); *v A 1936 (5); v In 1933 (3)*
Barnett, K. J. 4: v A 1989 (3); v SL 1988 (1)
Barratt (F.) 5: v A 1929 (1); *v NZ 1929 (3)*
Barrington (K. F.) 82: v A 1961 (5) 1964 (5) 1968 (3); v SA 1955 (2) 1960 (4) 1965 (3); v WI 1963 (5) 1966 (2); v NZ 1965 (2); v In 1959 (5) 1967 (3); *v P 1962 (4) 1967 (3); v A 1962 (5) 1965 (5); v SA 1964 (5); v WI 1959 (5) 1967 (5); v NZ 1962 (3); v In 1961 (5) 1963 (1); v P 1961 (2)*
Barton (V. A.) 1: *v SA 1891*
Bates (W.) 15: *v A 1881 (4) 1882 (4) 1884 (5) 1886 (2)*
Bean (G.) 3: *v A 1891 (3)*
Bedser (A. V.) 51: v A 1948 (5) 1953 (5); v SA 1947 (2) 1951 (5) 1955 (1); v WI 1950 (3); v NZ 1949 (2); v In 1946 (3) 1952 (4); v P 1954 (2); *v A 1946 (5) 1950 (5) 1954 (1); v SA 1948 (5); v NZ 1946 (1) 1950 (2)*
Benson, M. R. 1: v In 1986
Berry (R.) 2: v WI 1950 (2)
Bird M. C. 10: *v SA 1909 (5) 1913 (5)*
Birkenshaw J. 5: *v WI 1973 (2); v In 1972 (2); v P 1972 (1)*
Bligh, Hon. I. F. W. 4: *v A 1882 (4)*
Blythe (C.) 19: v A 1905 (1) 1909 (2); v SA 1907 (3); *v A 1901 (5) 1907 (1); v SA 1905 (5) 1909 (2)*
Board (J. H.) 6: v SA 1898 (2) 1905 (4)
Bolus, J. B. 7: v WI 1963 (2); *v In 1963 (5)*
Booth (M. W.) 2: v SA 1913 (2)
Bosanquet, B. J. T. 7: v A 1905 (3); *v A 1903 (4)*
Botham, I. T. 99: v A 1977 (2) 1980 (1) 1981 (6) 1985 (6) 1989 (3); v WI 1980 (5) 1984 (5) 1991 (1); v NZ 1978 (3) 1983 (4) 1986 (1); v In 1979 (4) 1982 (3); v P 1978 (3) 1982 (3) 1987 (5); v SL 1984 (1) 1991 (1); *v A 1978 (6) 1979 (3) 1982 (5) 1986 (4); v WI 1980 (4) 1985 (5); v NZ 1977 (3) 1983 (3); v In 1979 (1) 1981 (6); v P 1983 (1); v SL 1981 (1)*
Bowden, M. P. 2: *v SA 1888 (2)*
Bowes (W. E.) 15: v A 1934 (3) 1938 (2); v SA 1935 (4); v WI 1939 (2); v In 1932 (1) 1946 (1); *v A 1932 (1); v NZ 1932 (1)*
Bowley (E. H.) 5: v A 1929 (2); *v NZ 1929 (3)*
Boycott, G. 108: v A 1964 (4) 1968 (3) 1972 (2) 1977 (3) 1980 (1) 1981 (6); v SA 1965 (2); v WI 1966 (4) 1969 (3) 1973 (3) 1980 (5); v NZ 1965 (2) 1969 (3) 1973 (3) 1978 (2); v In 1967 (2) 1971 (1) 1974 (1) 1979 (4); v P 1967 (1) 1971 (2); *v A 1965 (5) 1970 (5) 1978 (6) 1979 (3); v SA 1964 (5); v WI 1967 (5) 1973 (5) 1980 (4); v NZ 1965 (2) 1977 (3); v In 1979 (1) 1981 (4); v P 1977 (3)*
Bradley, W. M. 2: v A 1899 (2)
Braund (L. C.) 23: v A 1902 (5); v SA 1907 (3); *v A 1901 (5) 1903 (5) 1907 (5)*
Brearley, J. M. 39: v A 1977 (5) 1981 (4); v WI 1976 (2); v NZ 1978 (3); v In 1979 (4); v P 1978 (3); *v A 1976 (1) 1978 (6) 1979 (3); v In 1976 (5) 1979 (1); v P 1977 (2)*
Brearley, W. 4: v A 1905 (2) 1909 (1); v SA 1912 (1)
Brennan, D. V. 2: v SA 1951 (2)
Briggs (John) 33: v A 1886 (3) 1888 (3) 1893 (2) 1896 (1) 1899 (1); *v A 1884 (5) 1886 (2) 1887 (1) 1891 (3) 1894 (5) 1897 (5); v SA 1888 (2)*
Broad, B. C. 25: v A 1989 (2); v WI 1984 (4) 1988 (2); v P 1987 (4); v SL 1984 (1); *v A 1986 (5) 1987 (1); v NZ 1987 (3); v P 1987 (3)*
Brockwell (W.) 7: v A 1893 (1) 1899 (1); *v A 1894 (5)*
Bromley-Davenport, H. R. 4: *v SA 1895 (3) 1898 (1)*
Brookes (D.) 1: *v WI 1947*
Brown (A.) 2: *v In 1961 (1); v P 1961 (1)*

Brown, D. J. 26: v A 1968 (4); v SA 1965 (2); v WI 1966 (1) 1969 (3); v NZ 1969 (1); v In 1967 (2): *v A 1965 (4); v WI 1967 (4); v NZ 1965 (2); v P 1968 (3)*

Brown, F. R. 22: v A 1953 (1); v SA 1951 (5); v WI 1950 (1); v NZ 1931 (2) 1937 (1) 1949 (2); v In 1932 (1); *v A 1950 (5); v NZ 1932 (2) 1950 (2)*

Brown, (G.) 7: v A 1921 (3); *v SA 1922 (4)*

Brown, (J. T.) 8: v A 1896 (2) 1899 (1); *v A 1894 (5)*

Buckenham, (C. P.) 4: *v SA 1909 (4)*

Butcher, A. R. 1: v In 1979

Butcher, R. O. 3: *v WI 1980 (3)*

Butler (H. J.) 2: v SA 1947 (1); *v WI 1947 (1)*

Butt (H. R.) 3: *v SA 1895 (3)*

Calthorpe, Hon. F. S. G. 4: *v WI 1929 (4)*

Capel, D. J. 15: v A 1989 (1); v WI 1988 (2); v P 1987 (1); *v A 1987 (1); v WI 1989 (4); v NZ 1987 (3); v P 1987 (3)*

Carr, A. W. 11: v A 1926 (4); v SA 1929 (2); *v SA 1922 (5)*

Carr, D. B. 2: *v In 1951 (2)*

Carr, D. W. 1: v A 1909

Cartwright, T. W. 5: v A 1964 (2); v SA 1965 (1); v NZ 1965 (1); *v SA 1964 (1)*

Chapman, A. P. F. 26: v A 1926 (4) 1930 (4); v SA 1924 (2); v WI 1928 (3); *v A 1924 (4) 1928 (4); v SA 1930 (5)*

Charlwood (H. R. J.) 2: *v A 1876 (2)*

Chatterton (W.) 1: *v SA 1891*

Childs, J. H. 2: v WI 1988 (2)

Christopherson, S. 1: v A 1884

Clark (E. W.) 8: v A 1934 (2); v SA 1929 (1); v WI 1933 (1); *v In 1933 (3)*

Clay, J. C. 1: v SA 1935

Close (D. B.) 22: v A 1961 (1); v SA 1955 (1); v WI 1957 (2) 1963 (5) 1966 (1) 1976 (3); v NZ 1949 (1); v In 1959 (1) 1967 (3); v P 1967 (3); *v A 1950 (1)*

Coldwell (L. J.) 7: v A 1964 (2); v P 1962 (2); *v A 1962 (2); v NZ 1962 (1)*

Compton (D. C. S.) 78: v A 1938 (4) 1948 (5) 1953 (5) 1956 (1); v SA 1947 (5) 1951 (4) 1955 (5); v WI 1939 (3) 1950 (1); v NZ 1937 (1) 1949 (4); v In 1946 (3) 1952 (2); v P 1954 (4); *v A 1946 (5) 1950 (4) 1954 (4); v SA 1948 (5) 1956 (5); v WI 1953 (5); v NZ 1946 (1) 1950 (2)*

Cook (C.) 1: v SA 1947

Cook, G. 7: v In 1982 (3); *v A 1982 (3); v SL 1981 (1)*

Cook, N. G. B. 15: v A 1989 (3); v WI 1984 (3); v NZ 1983 (2); *v NZ 1983 (1); v P 1983 (3) 1987 (3)*

Cope, G. A. 3: *v P 1977 (3)*

Copson (W. H.) 3: v SA 1947 (1); v WI 1939 (2)

Cornford (W. L.) 4: *v NZ 1929 (4)*

Cottam, R. M. H. 4: *v In 1972 (2); v P 1968 (2)*

Coventry, Hon. C. J. 2: *v SA 1888 (2)*

Cowans, N. G. 19: v A 1985 (1); v WI 1984 (1); v NZ 1983 (4); *v A 1982 (4); v NZ 1983 (2); v In 1984 (5); v P 1983 (2)*

Cowdrey, C. S. 6: v WI 1988 (1); *v In 1984 (5)*

Cowdrey, M. C. 114: v A 1956 (5) 1961 (4) 1964 (3) 1968 (4); v SA 1955 (1) 1960 (5) 1965 (3); v WI 1957 (5) 1963 (2) 1966 (4); v NZ 1958 (4) 1965 (3); v In 1959 (5); v P 1962 (4) 1967 (2) 1971 (1); *v A 1954 (5) 1958 (5) 1962 (5) 1965 (4) 1970 (3) 1974 (5); v SA 1956 (5); v WI 1959 (5) 1967 (5); v NZ 1954 (2) 1958 (2) 1962 (3) 1965 (3) 1970 (1); v In 1963 (3); v P 1968 (3)*

Coxon (A.) 1: v A 1948

Cranston, J. 1: v A 1890

Cranston, K. 8: v A 1948 (1); v SA 1947 (3); *v WI 1947 (4)*

Crapp (J. F.) 7: v A 1948 (3); *v SA 1948 (4)*

Crawford, J. N. 12: v SA 1907 (2); *v A 1907 (5); v SA 1905 (5)*

Curtis, T. S. 5: v A 1989 (3); v WI 1988 (2)

Cuttell (W. R.) 2: *v SA 1898 (2)*

Dawson, E. W. 5: *v SA 1927 (1); v NZ 1929 (4)*

Dean (H.) 3: v A 1912 (2); v SA 1912 (1)

DeFreitas, P. A. J. 26: v A 1989 (1); v WI 1988 (3) 1991 (5); v NZ 1990 (2); v P 1987 (1); v SL 1991 (1); *v A 1986 (4) 1990 (3); v WI 1989 (2); v NZ 1987 (2); v P 1987 (2)*

Denness, M. H. 28: v A 1975 (1); v NZ 1969 (1); v In 1974 (3); v P 1974 (3); *v A 1974 (5); v WI 1973 (5); v NZ 1974 (2); v In 1972 (5); v P 1972 (3)*

Denton (D.) 11: v A 1905 (1); *v SA 1905 (5) 1909 (5)*

Dewes, J. G. 5: v A 1948 (1); v WI 1950 (2); *v A 1950 (2)*

Dexter, E. R. 62: v A 1961 (5) 1964 (5) 1968 (2); v SA 1960 (5); v WI 1963 (5); v NZ 1958 (1) 1965 (2); v In 1959 (2); v P 1962 (5); *v A 1958 (2) 1962 (5); v SA 1964 (5); v WI 1959 (5); v NZ 1958 (2) 1962 (3); v In 1961 (5); v P 1961 (3)*

Dilley, G. R. 41: v A 1981 (3) 1989 (2); v WI 1980 (3) 1988 (4); v NZ 1983 (1) 1986 (2); v In 1986 (2); v P 1987 (4); *v A 1979 (2) 1986 (4) 1987 (1); v WI 1980 (4); v NZ 1987 (3); v In 1981 (4); v P 1983 (1) 1987 (1)*

Dipper (A. E.) 1: v A 1921

Doggart, G. H. G. 2: v WI 1950 (2)

D'Oliveira, B. L. 44: v A 1968 (2) 1972 (5); v WI 1966 (4) 1969 (5); v NZ 1969 (3); v In 1967 (2) 1971 (3); v P 1967 (3) 1971 (3); *v A 1970 (6); v WI 1967 (5); v NZ 1970 (2); v P 1968 (3)*

Dollery (H. E.) 4: v A 1948 (2); v SA 1947 (1); v WI 1950 (1)

Dolphin (A.) 1: *v A 1920*

Douglas, J. W. H. T. 23: v A 1912 (1) 1921 (5); v SA 1924 (1); *v A 1911 (5) 1920 (5) 1924 (1); v SA 1913 (5)*

Downton, P. R. 30: v A 1981 (1) 1985 (6); v WI 1984 (5) 1988 (3); v In 1986 (1); v SL 1984 (1); *v WI 1980 (3) 1985 (5); v In 1984 (5)*

Druce, N. F. 5: *v A 1897 (5)*

Ducat (A.) 1: v A 1921

Duckworth (G.) 24: v A 1930 (5); v SA 1924 (1) 1929 (4) 1935 (1); v WI 1928 (1); v In 1936 (3); *v A 1928 (5); v SA 1930 (3); v NZ 1932 (1)*

Duleepsinhji, K. S. 12: v A 1930 (4); v SA 1929 (1); v NZ 1931 (3); *v NZ 1929 (4)*

Durston (F. J.) 1: v A 1921

Edmonds, P. H. 51: v A 1975 (2) 1985 (5); v NZ 1978 (3) 1983 (2) 1986 (3); v In 1979 (4) 1982 (3) 1986 (2); v P 1978 (3) 1987 (5); *v A 1978 (1) 1986 (5); v WI 1985 (3); v NZ 1977 (3); v In 1984 (5); v P 1977 (2)*

Edrich, J. H. 77: v A 1964 (3) 1968 (5) 1972 (5) 1975 (4); v SA 1965 (1); v WI 1963 (3) 1966 (1) 1969 (3) 1976 (2); v NZ 1965 (1) 1969 (3); v In 1967 (2) 1971 (3) 1974 (3); v P 1971 (3) 1974 (3); *v A 1965 (5) 1970 (6) 1974 (4); v WI 1967 (5); v NZ 1965 (3) 1970 (2) 1974 (2); v In 1963 (2); v P 1968 (3)*

Edrich, W. J. 39: v A 1938 (4) 1948 (5) 1953 (3); v SA 1947 (4); v WI 1950 (2); v NZ 1949 (4); v In 1946 (1); v P 1954 (1); *v A 1946 (5) 1954 (4); v SA 1938 (5); v NZ 1946 (1)*

Elliott (H.) 4: v WI 1928 (1); *v SA 1927 (1); v In 1933 (2)*

Ellison, R. M. 11: v A 1985 (2); v WI 1984 (1); v In 1986 (1); v SL 1984 (1); *v WI 1985 (3); v In 1984 (3)*

Emburey, J. E. 60: v A 1980 (1) 1981 (4) 1985 (6) 1989 (3); v WI 1980 (3) 1988 (3); v NZ 1978 (1) 1986 (2); v In 1986 (3); v P 1987 (4); v SL 1988 (1); *v A 1978 (4) 1986 (5) 1987 (1); v WI 1980 (4) 1985 (4); v NZ 1987 (3); v In 1979 (1) 1981 (3); v P 1987 (3); v SL 1981 (1)*

Emmett (G. M.) 1: v A 1948

Emmett (T.) 7: *v A 1876 (2) 1878 (1) 1881 (4)*

Evans, A. J. 1: v A 1921

Evans (T. G.) 91: v A 1948 (5) 1953 (5) 1956 (5); v SA 1947 (5) 1951 (3) 1955 (5); v WI 1950 (3) 1957 (5); v NZ 1949 (4) 1958 (5); v In 1946 (1) 1952 (4) 1959 (2); v P 1954 (4); *v A 1946 (4) 1950 (5) 1954 (4) 1958 (3); v SA 1948 (3) 1956 (5); v WI 1947 (4) 1953 (4); v NZ 1946 (1) 1950 (2) 1954 (2)*

Fagg (A. E.) 5: v WI 1939 (1); v In 1936 (2); *v A 1936 (2)*

Fairbrother, N. H. 7: v NZ 1990 (3); v P 1987 (1); *v NZ 1987 (2); v P 1987 (1)*

Fane, F. L. 14: *v A 1907 (4); v SA 1905 (5) 1909 (5)*

Farnes, K. 15: v A 1934 (2) 1938 (4); *v A 1936 (2); v SA 1938 (5); v WI 1934 (2)*

Farrimond (W.) 4: v SA 1935 (1); *v SA 1930 (2); v WI 1934 (1)*

Fender, P. G. H. 13: v A 1921 (2); v SA 1924 (2) 1929 (1); *v A 1920 (3); v SA 1922 (5)*

Ferris, J. J. 1: *v SA 1891*

Fielder (A.) 6: *v A 1903 (2) 1907 (4)*

Fishlock (L. B.) 4: v In 1936 (2) 1946 (1); *v A 1946 (1)*

Flavell (J. A.) 4: v A 1961 (2) 1964 (2)

Fletcher, K. W. R. 59: v A 1968 (1) 1972 (1) 1975 (2); v WI 1973 (3); v NZ 1969 (2) 1973 (3); v In 1971 (2) 1974 (3); v P 1974 (3); *v A 1970 (5) 1974 (5) 1976 (1); v WI 1973 (4); v NZ 1970 (1) 1974 (2); v In 1972 (5) 1976 (3) 1981 (6); v P 1968 (3) 1972 (3); v SL 1981 (1)*

Flowers (W.) 8: v A 1893 (1); *v A 1884 (5) 1886 (2)*

Ford, F. G. J. 5: *v A 1894 (5)*

Foster, F. R. 11: v A 1912 (3); v SA 1912 (3); *v A 1911 (5)*

Foster, N. A. 28: v A 1985 (1) 1989 (3); v WI 1984 (1) 1988 (2); v NZ 1983 (1) 1986 (1); v In 1986 (1); v P 1987 (5); v SL 1988 (1); *v A 1987 (1); v WI 1985 (3); v NZ 1983 (2); v In 1984 (2); v P 1983 (2) 1987 (2)*

Foster, R. E. 8: v SA 1907 (3); *v A 1903 (5)*

Fothergill (A. J.) 2: *v SA 1888 (2)*

Fowler, G. 21: v WI 1984 (5); v NZ 1983 (2); v P 1982 (1); v SL 1984 (1); *v A 1982 (3); v NZ 1983 (2); v In 1984 (2); v P 1983 (2)*

Fraser, A. R. C. 11: v A 1989 (3); v In 1990 (3); *v A 1990 (3); v WI 1989 (2)*

Freeman (A. P.) 12: v SA 1929 (3); v WI 1928 (3); *v A 1924 (2); v SA 1927 (4)*

French, B. N. 16: v NZ 1986 (3); v In 1986 (2); v P 1987 (4); *v A 1987 (1); v NZ 1987 (3); v P 1987 (2)*

Fry, C. B. 26: v A 1899 (5) 1902 (3) 1905 (4) 1909 (3) 1912 (3); v SA 1907 (3) 1912 (3); *v SA 1895 (2)*

Gatting, M. W. 68: v A 1980 (1) 1981 (6) 1985 (6) 1989 (1); v WI 1980 (4) 1984 (1) 1988 (2); v NZ 1983 (2) 1986 (3); v In 1986 (3); v P 1982 (1) 1987 (5); *v A 1986 (5) 1987 (1); v WI 1980 (1) 1985 (1); v NZ 1977 (1) 1983 (2) 1987 (3); v In 1981 (5) 1984 (5); v P 1977 (1) 1983 (3) 1987 (3)*

Gay, L. H. 1: *v A 1894*

Geary (G.) 14: v A 1926 (2) 1930 (1) 1934 (2); v SA 1924 (1) 1929 (2); *v A 1928 (4); v SA 1927 (2)*

Gibb, P. A. 8: v In 1946 (2); *v A 1946 (1); v SA 1938 (5)*

Gifford, N. 15: v A 1964 (2) 1972 (3); v NZ 1973 (2); v In 1971 (2); v P 1971 (2); *v In 1972 (2); v P 1972 (2)*

Gilligan, A. E. R. 11: v SA 1924 (4); *v A 1924 (5); v SA 1922 (2)*

Gilligan, A. H. H. 4: *v NZ 1929 (4)*

Gimblett (H.) 3: v WI 1939 (1); v In 1936 (2)

Gladwin (C.) 8: v SA 1947 (2); v NZ 1949 (1); *v SA 1948 (5)*

Goddard (T. W.) 8: v A 1930 (1); v WI 1939 (1); v NZ 1937 (2); *v SA 1938 (3)*

Gooch, G. A. 91: v A 1975 (2) 1980 (1) 1981 (5) 1985 (6) 1989 (5); v WI 1980 (5) 1988 (5) 1991 (5); v NZ 1978 (3) 1986 (3) 1990 (3); v In 1979 (4) 1986 (3) 1990 (3); v P 1978 (2); v SL 1988 (1) 1991 (1); *v A 1978 (6) 1979 (2) 1990 (4); v WI 1980 (4) 1985 (5) 1989 (2); v In 1979 (1) 1981 (6); v P 1987 (3); v SL 1981 (1)*

Gover (A. R.) 4: v NZ 1937 (2); v In 1936 (1) 1946 (1)

Gower, D. I. 114: v A 1980 (1) 1981 (5) 1985 (6) 1989 (6); v WI 1980 (1) 1984 (5) 1988 (4); v NZ 1978 (3) 1983 (4) 1986 (3); v In 1979 (4) 1982 (3) 1986 (2) 1990 (3); v P 1978 (3) 1982 (3) 1987 (5); v SL 1984 (1); *v A 1978 (6) 1979 (3) 1982 (5) 1986 (5) 1990 (5); v WI 1980 (4) 1985 (5); v NZ 1983 (3); v In 1979 (1) 1981 (6) 1984 (5); v P 1983 (3); v SL 1981 (1)*

Grace, E. M. 1: v A 1880

Grace, G. F. 1: v A 1880

Grace, W. G. 22: v A 1880 (1) 1882 (1) 1884 (3) 1886 (3) 1888 (3) 1890 (2) 1893 (2) 1896 (3) 1899 (1); *v A 1891 (3)*

Graveney (T. W.) 79: v A 1953 (5) 1956 (2) 1968 (5); v SA 1951 (1) 1955 (5); v WI 1957 (4) 1966 (4) 1969 (1); v NZ 1958 (4); v In 1952 (4) 1967 (3); v P 1954 (3) 1962 (4) 1967 (3); *v A 1954 (2) 1958 (5) 1962 (3); v WI 1953 (5) 1967 (5); v NZ 1954 (2) 1958 (2); v In 1951 (4); v P 1968 (3)*

Greenough (T.) 4: v SA 1960 (1); v In 1959 (3)

Greenwood (A.) 2: *v A 1876 (2)*

Greig, A. W. 58: v A 1972 (5) 1975 (4) 1977 (5); v WI 1973 (3) 1976 (5); v NZ 1973 (3); v In 1974 (3); v P 1974 (3); *v A 1974 (6) 1976 (1); v WI 1973 (5); v NZ 1974 (2); v In 1972 (5) 1976 (5); v P 1972 (3)*

Greig, I. A. 2: v P 1982 (2)

Grieve, B. A. F. 2: *v SA 1888 (2)*

Griffith, S. C. 3: *v SA 1948 (2); v WI 1947 (1)*

Gunn (G.) 15: v A 1909 (1); *v A 1907 (5) 1911 (5); v WI 1929 (4)*

Gunn (J.) 6: v A 1905 (1); *v A 1901 (5)*

Gunn (W.) 11: v A 1888 (2) 1890 (2) 1893 (3) 1896 (1) 1899 (1); *v A 1886 (2)*

Haig, N. E. 5: v A 1921 (1); *v WI 1929 (4)*

Haigh (S.) 11: v A 1905 (2) 1909 (1) 1912 (1); *v SA 1898 (2) 1905 (5)*

Hallows (C.) 2: v A 1921 (1); v WI 1928 (1)

Hammond, W. R. 85: v A 1930 (5) 1934 (5) 1938 (4); v SA 1929 (4) 1935 (5); v WI 1928 (3) 1933 (3) 1939 (3); v NZ 1931 (3) 1937 (3); v In 1932 (1) 1936 (2) 1946 (3); *v A 1928 (5) 1932 (5) 1936 (5) 1946 (4); v SA 1927 (5) 1930 (5) 1938 (5); v WI 1934 (4); v NZ 1932 (2) 1946 (1)*

Hampshire, J. H. 8: v A 1972 (1) 1975 (1); v WI 1969 (2); *v A 1970 (2); v NZ 1970 (2)*

Hardinge (H. T. W.) 1: v A 1921

Hardstaff (J.) 5: *v A 1907 (5)*

Hardstaff (J. jun.) 23: v A 1938 (2) 1948 (1); v SA 1935 (1); v WI 1939 (3); v NZ 1937 (3); v In 1936 (2) 1946 (2); *v A 1936 (5) 1946 (1); v WI 1947 (3)*

Harris, Lord 4: v A 1880 (1) 1884 (2); *v A 1878 (1)*

Hartley, J. C. 2: *v SA 1905 (2)*

Hawke, Lord 5: *v SA 1895 (3) 1898 (2)*

Hayes (E. G.) 5: v A 1909 (1); v WI 1912 (1); *v SA 1905 (3)*

Hayes, F. C. 9: v WI 1973 (3) 1976 (2); *v WI 1973 (4)*

Hayward (T. W.) 35: v A 1896 (2) 1899 (5) 1902 (1) 1905 (5) 1909 (1); v SA 1907 (3); *v A 1897 (5) 1901 (5) 1903 (5); v SA 1895 (3)*

Hearne (A.) 1: *v SA 1891*

Hearne (F.) 2: *v SA 1888 (2)*

Hearne (G. G.) 1: *v SA 1891*

Hearne (J. T.) 12: v A 1896 (3) 1899 (3); *v A 1897 (5); v SA 1891 (1)*

Hearne (J. W.) 24: v A 1912 (3) 1921 (1) 1926 (1); v SA 1912 (2) 1924 (3); *v A 1911 (5) 1920 (2) 1924 (4); v SA 1913 (3)*

Hemmings, E. E. 16: v A 1989 (1); v NZ 1990 (3); v In 1990 (3); v P 1982 (2); *v A 1982 (3) 1987 (1) 1990 (1); v NZ 1987 (1); v P 1987 (1)*

Hendren (E. H.) 51: v A 1921 (2) 1926 (5) 1930 (2) 1934 (4); v SA 1924 (5) 1929 (4); v WI 1928 (1); *v A 1920 (5) 1924 (5) 1928 (5); v SA 1930 (5); v WI 1929 (4) 1934 (4)*

Hendrick, M. 30: v A 1977 (3) 1980 (1) 1981 (2); v WI 1976 (2) 1980 (2); v NZ 1978 (2); v In 1974 (3) 1979 (4); v P 1974 (2); *v A 1974 (2) 1978 (5); v NZ 1974 (1) 1977 (1)*

Heseltine, C. 2: v SA 1895 (2)

Hick, G. A. 4: v WI 1991 (4)

Higgs, K. 15: v A 1968 (1); v WI 1966 (5); v SA 1965 (1); v In 1967 (1); v P 1967 (3); *v A 1965 (1); v NZ 1965 (3)*

Hill (A.) 2: *v A 1876 (2)*

Hill, A. J. L. 3: *v SA 1895 (3)*

Hilton (M. J.) 4: v SA 1951 (1); v WI 1950 (1); *v In 1951 (2)*

Hirst (G. H.) 24: v A 1899 (1) 1902 (4) 1905 (3) 1909 (4); v SA 1907 (3); *v A 1897 (4) 1903 (5)*

Hitch (J. W.) 7: v A 1912 (1) 1921 (1); v SA 1912 (1); *v A 1911 (3) 1920 (1)*

Hobbs (J. B.) 61: v A 1909 (3) 1912 (3) 1921 (1) 1926 (5) 1930 (5); v SA 1912 (3) 1924 (4) 1929 (1); v WI 1928 (2); *v A 1907 (4) 1911 (5) 1920 (5) 1924 (5) 1928 (5); v SA 1909 (5) 1913 (5)*

Hobbs, R. N. S. 7: v In 1967 (3); v P 1967 (1) 1971 (1); *v WI 1967 (1); v P 1968 (1)*

Hollies (W. E.) 13: v A 1948 (1); v SA 1947 (3); v WI 1950 (2); v NZ 1949 (4); *v WI 1934 (3)*

Holmes, E. R. T. 5: v SA 1935 (1); *v WI 1934 (4)*

Holmes (P.) 7: v A 1921 (1); v In 1932 (1); *v SA 1927 (5)*

Hone, L. 1: *v A 1878*

Hopwood (J. L.) 2: v A 1934 (2)

Hornby, A. N. 3: v A 1882 (1) 1884 (1); *v A 1878 (1)*

Horton (M. J.) 2: v In 1959 (2)

Howard, N. D. 4: *v In 1951 (4)*

Howell (H.) 5: v A 1921 (1); v SA 1924 (1); *v A 1920 (3)*

Howorth (R.) 5: v SA 1947 (1); *v WI 1947 (4)*

Humphries (J.) 3: *v A 1907 (3)*

Hunter (J.) 5: *v A 1884 (5)*

Hussain, N. 3: *v WI 1989 (3)*

Hutchings, K. L. 7: v A 1909 (2); *v A 1907 (5)*

Hutton (L.) 79: v A 1938 (3) 1948 (4) 1953 (5); v SA 1947 (5) 1951 (5); v WI 1939 (3) 1950 (3); v NZ 1937 (3) 1949 (4); v In 1946 (3) 1952 (4); v P 1954 (2); *v A 1946 (5) 1950 (5) 1954 (5); v SA 1938 (4) 1948 (5); v WI 1947 (2) 1953 (5); v NZ 1950 (2) 1954 (2)*

Hutton, R. A. 5: v In 1971 (3); v P 1971 (2)

Iddon (J.) 5: v SA 1935 (1); *v WI 1934 (4)*

Igglesden, A. P. 1: v A 1989

Ikin (J. T.) 18 : v SA 1951 (3) 1955 (1); v In 1946 (2) 1952 (2); *v A 1946 (5); v NZ 1946 (1); v WI 1947 (4)*

Illingworth (R.) 61 : v A 1961 (2) 1968 (2) 1972 (5); v SA 1960 (4); v WI 1966 (2) 1969 (3) 1973 (3); v NZ 1958 (1) 1965 (1) 1969 (3) 1973 (3); v In 1959 (2) 1967 (3) 1971 (3); v P 1962 (1) 1967 (1) 1971 (3); *v A 1962 (2) 1970 (6); v WI 1959 (5); v NZ 1962 (3) 1970 (2)*

Illingworth, R. K. 2 : v WI 1991 (2)

Insole, D. J. 9 : v A 1956 (1); v SA 1955 (1); v WI 1950 (1) 1957 (1); *v SA 1956 (5)*

Jackman, R. D. 4 : v P 1982 (2); *v WI 1980 (2)*
Jackson, F. S. 20 : v A 1893 (2) 1896 (3) 1899 (5) 1902 (5) 1905 (5)
Jackson (H. L.) 2 : v A 1961 (1); v NZ 1949 (1)
Jameson, J. A. 4 : v In 1971 (2); *v WI 1973 (2)*
Jardine, D. R. 22 : v WI 1928 (2) 1933 (2); v NZ 1931 (3); v In 1932 (1); *v A 1928 (5) 1932 (5); v NZ 1932 (1); v In 1933 (3)*
Jarvis, P. W. 6 : v A 1989 (2); v WI 1988 (2); *v NZ 1987 (2)*
Jenkins (R. O.) 9 : v WI 1950 (2); v In 1952 (2); *v SA 1948 (5)*
Jessop, G. L. 18 : v A 1899 (1) 1902 (4) 1905 (1) 1909 (2); v SA 1907 (3) 1912 (2); *v A 1901 (3)*
Jones, A. O. 12 : v A 1899 (1) 1905 (2) 1909 (2); *v A 1901 (5) 1907 (2)*
Jones, I. J. 15 : v WI 1966 (2); *v A 1965 (4); v WI 1967 (5); v NZ 1965 (3); v In 1963 (1)*
Jupp (H.) 2 : *v A 1876 (2)*
Jupp, V. W. C. 8 : v A 1921 (2); v WI 1928 (2); *v SA 1922 (4)*

Keeton (W. W.) 2 : v A 1934 (1); v WI 1939 (1)
Kennedy (A. S.) 5 : *v SA 1922 (5)*
Kenyon (D.) 8 : v A 1953 (2); v SA 1955 (3); *v In 1951 (3)*
Killick, E. T. 2 : v SA 1929 (2)
Kilner (R.) 9 : v A 1926 (4); v SA 1924 (2); *v A 1924 (3)*
King (J. H.) 1 : v A 1909
Kinneir (S. P.) 1 : *v A 1911*
Knight (A. E.) 3 : *v A 1903 (3)*
Knight (B. R.) 29 : v A 1968 (2); v WI 1966 (1) 1969 (3); v NZ 1969 (2); v P 1962 (2); *v A 1962 (1) 1965 (2); v NZ 1962 (3) 1965 (2); v In 1961 (4) 1963 (5); v P 1961 (2)*
Knight, D. J. 2 : v A 1921 (2)
Knott, A. P. E. 95 : v A 1968 (5) 1972 (5) 1975 (4) 1977 (5) 1981 (2); v WI 1969 (3) 1973 (3) 1976 (5) 1980 (4); v NZ 1969 (3) 1973 (3); v In 1971 (3) 1974 (3); v P 1967 (2) 1971 (3) 1974 (3); *v A 1970 (6) 1974 (6) 1976 (1); v WI 1967 (2) 1973 (5); v NZ 1970 (1) 1974 (2); v In 1972 (5) 1976 (5); v P 1968 (3) 1972 (3)*
Knox, N. A. 2 : v SA 1907 (2)

Laker (J. C.) 46 : v A 1948 (3) 1953 (3) 1956 (5); v SA 1951 (2) 1955 (1); v WI 1950 (1) 1957 (4); v NZ 1949 (1) 1958 (4); v In 1952 (4); v P 1954 (1); *v A 1958 (4); v SA 1956 (5); v WI 1947 (4) 1953 (4)*
Lamb, A. J. 74 : v A 1985 (6) 1989 (1); v WI 1984 (5) 1988 (4) 1991 (4); v NZ 1983 (4) 1986 (1) 1990 (3); v In 1982 (3) 1986 (2) 1990 (3); v P 1982 (3); v SL 1984 (1) 1988 (1); *v A 1982 (5) 1986 (5) 1990 (3); v WI 1985 (5) 1989 (4); v NZ 1983 (3); v In 1984 (5); v P 1983 (3)*
Langridge (James) 8 : v SA 1935 (1); v WI 1933 (2); v In 1936 (1) 1946 (1); *v In 1933 (3)*
Larkins, W. 13 : v A 1981 (1); v WI 1980 (1); *v A 1979 (1) 1990 (3); v WI 1989 (4); v In 1979 (1)*
Larter (J. D. F.) 10 : v SA 1965 (2); v NZ 1965 (1); v P 1962 (1); *v NZ 1962 (3); v In 1963 (3)*
Larwood (H.) 21 : v A 1926 (2) 1930 (3); v SA 1929 (3); v WI 1928 (2); v NZ 1931 (1); *v A 1928 (5) 1932 (5)*
Lawrence, D. V. 4 : v WI 1991 (2); v SL 1988 (1) 1991 (1)
Leadbeater (E.) 2 : *v In 1951 (2)*
Lee (H. W.) 1 : *v SA 1930*
Lees (W. S.) 5 : *v SA 1905 (5)*
Legge G. B. 5 : *v SA 1927 (1); v NZ 1929 (4)*
Leslie, C. F. H. 4 : *v A 1882 (4)*
Lever, J. K. 21 : v A 1977 (3); v WI 1980 (1); v In 1979 (1) 1986 (1); *v A 1976 (1) 1978 (1) 1979 (1); v NZ 1977 (1); v In 1976 (5) 1979 (1) 1981 (2); v P 1977 (3)*
Lever, P. 17 : v A 1972 (1) 1975 (1); v In 1971 (1); v P 1971 (3); *v A 1970 (5) 1974 (2); v NZ 1970 (2) 1974 (2)*
Leveson Gower, H. D. G. 3 : *v SA 1909 (3)*
Levett, W. H. V. 1 : *v In 1933*

Lewis, A. R. 9: v NZ 1973 (1); *v In 1972* (5); *v P 1972* (3)

Lewis, C. C. 7: v WI 1991 (2); v NZ 1990 (1); v In 1990 (2) v SL 1991 (1); *v A 1990* (*1*)

Leyland (M.) 41: v A 1930 (3) 1934 (5) 1938 (1); v SA 1929 (5) 1935 (4); v WI 1928 (1) 1933 (1); v In 1936 (2); *v A 1928* (*1*) *1932* (5) *1936* (5); *v SA 1930* (5); *v WI 1934* (3)

Lilley (A. A.) 35: v A 1896 (3) 1899 (4) 1902 (5) 1905 (5) 1909 (5); v SA 1907 (3); *v A 1901* (5) *1903* (5)

Lillywhite (James jun.) 2: *v A 1876* (2)

Lloyd, D. 9: v In 1974 (2); v P 1974 (3); *v A 1974* (4)

Lloyd, T. A. 1: v WI 1984

Loader (P. J.) 13: v SA 1955 (1); v WI 1957 (2); v NZ 1958 (3); v P 1954 (1); *v A 1958* (2); *v SA 1956* (4)

Lock (G. A. R.) 49: v A 1953 (2) 1956 (4) 1961 (3); v SA 1955 (3); v WI 1957 (3) 1963 (3); v NZ 1958 (5); v In 1952 (2); v P 1962 (3); *v A 1958* (*4*); *v SA 1956* (*1*); *v WI 1953* (5) *1967* (2); *v NZ 1958* (2); *v In 1961* (5); *v P 1961* (2)

Lockwood (W. H.) 12: v A 1893 (2) 1899 (1) 1902 (4); *v A 1894* (5)

Lohmann (G. A.) 18: v A 1886 (3) 1888 (3) 1890 (2) 1896 (1); *v A 1886* (2) *1887* (*1*) *1891* (3); *v SA 1895* (3)

Lowson (F. A.) 7: v SA 1951 (2) 1955 (1); *v In 1951* (4)

Lucas, A. P. 5: v A 1880 (1) 1882 (1) 1884 (2); *v A 1878* (*1*)

Luckhurst, B. W. 21: v A 1972 (4); v WI 1973 (2); v In 1971 (3); v P 1971 (3); *v A 1970* (5) *1974* (2); *v NZ 1970* (2)

Lyttelton, Hon. A. 4: v A 1880 (1) 1882 (1) 1884 (2)


Macaulay (G. G.) 8: v A 1926 (1); v SA 1924 (1); v WI 1933 (2); *v SA 1922* (4)

MacBryan, J. C. W. 1: v SA 1924

McConnon (J. E.) 2: v P 1954 (2)

McGahey, C. P. 2: *v A 1901* (2)

MacGregor, G. 8: v A 1890 (2) 1893 (3); *v A 1891* (3)

McIntyre (A. J. W.) 3: v SA 1955 (1); v WI 1950 (1); *v A 1950* (*1*)

MacKinnon, F. A. 1: *v A 1878*

MacLaren, A. C. 35: v A 1896 (2) 1899 (4) 1902 (5) 1905 (4) 1909 (5); *v A 1894* (5) *1897* (5) *1901* (5)

McMaster, J. E. P. 1: *v SA 1888*

Makepeace (J. W. H.) 4: *v A 1920* (4)

Malcolm, D. E. 18: v A 1989 (1); v WI 1991 (2); v NZ 1990 (3); v In 1990 (3); *v A 1990* (5); *v WI 1989* (4)

Mann, F. G. 7: v NZ 1949 (2); *v SA 1948* (5)

Mann, F. T. 5: *v SA 1922* (5)

Marks, V. J. 6: v NZ 1983 (1); v P 1982 (1); *v NZ 1983* (*1*); *v P 1983* (3)

Marriott, C. S. 1: v WI 1933

Martin (F.) 2: v A 1890 (1); *v SA 1891* (*1*)

Martin, J. W. 1: v SA 1947

Mason, J. R. 5: *v A 1897* (5)

Matthews (A. D. G.) 1: v NZ 1937

May, P. B. H. 66: v A 1953 (2) 1956 (5) 1961 (4); v SA 1951 (2) 1955 (5); v WI 1957 (5); v NZ 1958 (5); v In 1952 (4) 1959 (3); v P 1954 (4); *v A 1954* (5) *1958* (5); *v SA 1956* (5); *v WI 1953* (5) *1959* (3); *v NZ 1954* (2) *1958* (2)

Maynard, M. P. 1: v WI 1988

Mead (C. P.) 17: v A 1921 (2); *v A 1911* (4) *1928* (*1*); *v SA 1913* (5) *1922* (5)

Mead (W.) 1: v A 1899

Midwinter (W. E.) 4: *v A 1881* (4)

Milburn, C. 9: v A 1968 (2); v WI 1966 (4); v In 1967 (1); v P 1967 (1); *v P 1968* (*1*)

Miller, A. M. 1: *v SA 1895*

Miller, G. 34: v A 1977 (2); v WI 1976 (1) 1984 (2); v NZ 1978 (2); v In 1979 (3) 1982 (1); v P 1978 (3) 1982 (1); *v A 1978* (6) *1979* (*1*) *1982* (5); *v WI 1980* (*1*); *v NZ 1977* (3); *v P 1977* (3)

Milligan, F. W. 2: *v SA 1898* (2)

Millman (G.) 6: v P 1962 (2); *v In 1961* (2); *v P 1961* (2)

Milton (C. A.) 6: v NZ 1958 (2); v In 1959 (2); *v A 1958* (2)

Mitchell (A.) 6: v SA 1935 (2); v In 1936 (1); *v In 1933* (3)

Mitchell, F. 2: *v SA 1898* (2)

Mitchell (T. B.) 5: v A 1934 (2); v SA 1935 (1); *v A 1932* (*1*); *v NZ 1932* (*1*)

Mitchell-Innes, N. S. 1: v SA 1935

Mold (A. W.) 3: v A 1893 (3)
Moon, L. J. 4: *v SA 1905 (4)*
Morley (F.) 4: v A 1880 (1); *v A 1882 (3)*
Morris, H. 3: v WI 1991 (2); v SL 1991 (1)
Morris, J. E. 3: v In 1990 (3)
Mortimore (J. B.) 9: v A 1964 (1); v In 1959 (2); *v A 1958 (1); v NZ 1958 (2); v In 1963 (3)*
Moss (A. E.) 9: v A 1956 (1); v SA 1960 (2); v In 1959 (3); *v WI 1953 (1) 1959 (2)*
Moxon, M. D. 10: v A 1989 (1); v WI 1988 (2); v NZ 1986 (2); v P 1987 (1); *v A 1987 (1); v NZ 1987 (3)*
Murdoch, W. L. 1: *v SA 1891*
Murray, J. T. 21: v A 1961 (5); v WI 1966 (1); v In 1967 (3); v P 1962 (3) 1967 (1); *v A 1962 (1); v SA 1964 (1); v NZ 1962 (1) 1965 (1); v In 1961 (3); v P 1961 (1)*

Newham (W.) 1: *v A 1887*
Newport, P. J. 3: v A 1989 (1); v SL 1988 (1); *v A 1990 (1)*
Nichols (M. S.) 14: v A 1930 (1); v SA 1935 (4); v WI 1933 (1) 1939 (1); *v NZ 1929 (4); v In 1933 (3)*

Oakman (A. S. M.) 2: v A 1956 (2)
O'Brien, Sir T. C. 5: v A 1884 (1) 1888 (1); *v SA 1895 (3)*
O'Connor (J.) 4: v SA 1929 (1); *v WI 1929 (3)*
Old, C. M. 46: v A 1975 (3) 1977 (2) 1980 (1) 1981 (2); v WI 1973 (1) 1976 (2) 1980 (1); v NZ 1973 (2) 1978 (1); v In 1974 (3); v P 1974 (3) 1978 (3); *v A 1974 (2) 1976 (1) 1978 (1); v WI 1973 (4) 1980 (1); v NZ 1974 (1) 1977 (2); v In 1972 (4) 1976 (4); v P 1972 (1) 1977 (1)*
Oldfield (N.) 1: v WI 1939

Padgett (D. E. V.) 2: v SA 1960 (2)
Paine (G. A. E.) 4: *v WI 1934 (4)*
Palairet, L. C. H. 2: v A 1902 (2)
Palmer, C. H. 1: *v WI 1953*
Palmer, K. E. 1: *v SA 1964*
Parfitt (P. H.) 37: v A 1964 (4) 1972 (3); v SA 1965 (2); v WI 1969 (1); v NZ 1965 (2); v P 1962 (5); *v A 1962 (2); v SA 1964 (5); v NZ 1962 (3) 1965 (3); v In 1961 (2) 1963 (3); v P 1961 (2)*
Parker (C. W. L.) 1: v A 1921
Parker, P. W. G. 1: v A 1981
Parkhouse (W. G. A.) 7: v WI 1950 (2); v In 1959 (2); *v A 1950 (2); v NZ 1950 (1)*
Parkin (C. H.) 10: v A 1921 (4); v SA 1924 (1); *v A 1920 (3)*
Parks (J. H.) 1: v NZ 1937
Parks (J. M.) 46: v A 1965 (5) 1965 (3); v WI 1963 (4) 1966 (4); v NZ 1965 (3); v P 1954 (1); *v A 1965 (5); v SA 1964 (5); v WI 1959 (1) 1967 (3); v NZ 1965 (2); v In 1963 (5)*
Pataudi sen., Nawab of, 3: v A 1934 (1); *v A 1932 (2)*
Paynter (E.) 20: v A 1938 (4); v WI 1939 (2); v NZ 1931 (1) 1937 (2); v In 1932 (1); *v A 1932 (3); v SA 1938 (5); v NZ 1932 (2)*
Peate (E.) 9: v A 1882 (1) 1884 (3) 1886 (1); *v A 1881 (4)*
Peebles, I. A. R. 13: v A 1930 (2); v NZ 1931 (3); *v SA 1927 (4) 1930 (4)*
Peel (R.) 20: v A 1888 (3) 1890 (1) 1893 (1) 1896 (1); *v A 1884 (5) 1887 (1) 1891 (3) 1894 (5)*
Penn, F. 1: v A 1880
Perks (R. T. D.) 2: v WI 1939 (1); *v SA 1938 (1)*
Philipson, (H.) 5: *v A 1891 (1) 1894 (4)*
Pigott, A. C. S. 1: *v NZ 1983*
Pilling (R.) 8: v A 1884 (1) 1886 (1) 1888 (1); *v A 1881 (4) 1887 (1)*
Place (W.) 3: *v WI 1947 (3)*
Pocock, P. I. 25: v A 1968 (1); v WI 1976 (2) 1984 (2); v SL 1984 (1); *v WI 1967 (2) 1973 (4); v In 1972 (4) 1984 (5); v P 1968 (1) 1972 (3)*
Pollard (R.) 4: v A 1948 (1); v In 1946 (1); *v NZ 1946 (1)*
Poole (C. J.) 3: *v In 1951 (3)*
Pope (G. H.) 1: v SA 1947
Pougher (A. D.) 1: *v SA 1891*
Price, J. S. E. 15: v A 1964 (2) 1972 (1); v In 1971 (3); v P 1971 (1); *v SA 1964 (4); v In 1963 (4)*
Price, W. F. F.) 1: v A 1938
Prideaux, R. M. 3: v A 1968 (1); *v P 1968 (2)*

Pringle, D. R. 25: v A 1989 (2); v WI 1984 (3) 1988 (4) 1991 (4); v NZ 1986 (1); v In 1982 (3) 1986 (3); v P 1982 (1); v SL 1988 (1); *v A 1982 (3)*

Pullar (G.) 28: v A 1961 (5); v SA 1960 (3); v In 1959 (3); v P 1962 (2); *v A 1962 (4); v WI 1959 (5); v In 1961 (3); v P 1961 (3)*

Quaife (W. G.) 7: v A 1899 (2); *v A 1901 (5)*

Radford, N. V. 3: v NZ 1986 (1); v In 1986 (1); *v NZ 1987 (1)*
Radley, C. T. 8: v NZ 1978 (3); v P 1978 (3); *v NZ 1977 (2)*
Ramprakash, M. R. 6: v WI 1991 (5); v SL 1991 (1)
Randall, D. W. 47: v A 1977 (5); v WI 1984 (1); v NZ 1983 (3); v In 1979 (3) 1982 (3); v P 1982 (3); *v A 1976 (1) 1978 (6) 1979 (2) 1982 (4); v NZ 1977 (3) 1983 (3); v In 1976 (4); v P 1977 (3) 1983 (3)*
Ranjitsinhji, K. S. 15: v A 1896 (3) 1899 (5) 1902 (3); *v A 1897 (5)*
Read, H. D. 1: v SA 1935
Read (J. M.) 17: v A 1882 (1) 1890 (2) 1893 (1); *v A 1884 (5) 1886 (2) 1887 (1) 1891 (3); v SA 1888 (2)*
Read, W. W. 18: v A 1884 (2) 1886 (3) 1888 (3) 1890 (2) 1893 (1); *v A 1882 (4) 1887 (1); v SA 1891 (1)*
Relf (A. E.) 13: v A 1909 (1); *v A 1903 (2); v SA 1905 (5) 1913 (5)*
Rhodes (H. J.) 2: v In 1959 (2)
Rhodes (W.) 58: v A 1899 (3) 1902 (5) 1905 (4) 1909 (4) 1912 (3) 1921 (1) 1926 (1); v SA 1912 (3); *v A 1903 (5) 1907 (5) 1911 (5) 1920 (5); v SA 1909 (5) 1913 (5); v WI 1929 (4)*
Richards, C. J. 8: v WI 1988 (2); v P 1987 (1); *v A 1986 (5)*
Richardson (D. W.) 1: v WI 1957
Richardson (P. E.) 34: v A 1956 (5); v WI 1957 (5) 1963 (1); v NZ 1958 (4); *v A 1958 (4); v SA 1956 (5); v NZ 1958 (2); v In 1961 (5); v P 1961 (3)*
Richardson (T.) 14: v A 1893 (1) 1896 (3); *v A 1894 (5) 1897 (5)*
Richmond (T. L.) 1: v A 1921
Ridgway (F.) 5: *v In 1951 (5)*
Robertson (J. D.) 11: v SA 1947 (1); v NZ 1949 (1); *v WI 1947 (4); v In 1951 (5)*
Robins, R. W. V. 19: v A 1930 (2); v SA 1929 (1) 1935 (3); v WI 1933 (2); v NZ 1931 (1) 1937 (3); v In 1932 (1) 1936 (2); *v A 1936 (4)*
Robinson, R. T. 29: v A 1985 (6) 1989 (2); v In 1986 (1); v P 1987 (5); v SL 1988 (1); *v A 1987 (1); v WI 1985 (4); v NZ 1987 (3); v In 1984 (5); v P 1987 (2)*
Roope, G. R. J. 21: v A 1975 (1) 1977 (2); v WI 1973 (1); v NZ 1973 (3) 1978 (1); v P 1978 (3); *v NZ 1977 (3); v In 1972 (2); v P 1972 (2) 1977 (3)*
Root (C. F.) 3: v A 1926 (3)
Rose, B. C. 9: v WI 1980 (3); *v WI 1980 (1); v NZ 1977 (2); v P 1977 (3)*
Royle, V. P. F. A. 1: *v A 1878*
Rumsey, F. E. 5: v A 1964 (1); v SA 1965 (1); v NZ 1965 (3)
Russell (A. C.) 10: v A 1921 (2); *v A 1920 (4); v SA 1922 (4)*
Russell, R. C. 25: v A 1989 (6); v WI 1991 (4); v NZ 1990 (3); v In 1990 (3); v SL 1988 (1) 1991 (1); *v A 1990 (3); v WI 1989 (4)*
Russell, W. E. 10: v SA 1965 (1); v WI 1966 (2); v P 1967 (1); *v A 1965 (1); v NZ 1965 (3); v In 1961 (1); v P 1961 (1)*

Sandham (A.) 14: v A 1921 (1); v SA 1924 (2); *v A 1924 (2); v SA 1922 (5); v WI 1929 (2)*
Schultz, S. S. 1: *v A 1878*
Scotton (W. H.) 15: v A 1884 (1) 1886 (3); *v A 1881 (4) 1884 (5) 1886 (2)*
Selby (J.) 6: *v A 1876 (2) 1881 (4)*
Selvey, M. W. W. 3: v WI 1976 (2); *v In 1976 (1)*
Shackleton (D.) 7: v SA 1951 (1); v WI 1950 (1) 1963 (4); *v In 1951 (1)*
Sharp (J.) 3: v A 1909 (3)
Sharpe (J. W.) 3: v A 1890 (1); *v A 1891 (2)*
Sharpe, P. J. 12: v A 1964 (2); v WI 1963 (3) 1969 (3); v NZ 1969 (3); *v In 1963 (1)*
Shaw (A.) 7: v A 1880 (1); *v A 1876 (2) 1881 (4)*
Sheppard, Rev. D. S. 22: v A 1956 (2); v WI 1950 (1) 1957 (2); v In 1952 (2); v P 1954 (2) 1962 (2); *v A 1950 (2) 1962 (5); v NZ 1950 (1) 1963 (3)*
Sherwin (M.) 3: v A 1888 (1); *v A 1886 (2)*
Shrewsbury (A.) 23: v A 1884 (3) 1886 (3) 1890 (3) 1893 (3); *v A 1881 (4) 1884 (5) 1886 (2) 1887 (1)*
Shuter, J. 1: v A 1888

Shuttleworth, K. 5: v P 1971 (1); *v A 1970 (2); v NZ 1970 (2)*

Sidebottom, A. 1: v A 1985

Simpson, R. T. 27: v A 1953 (3); v SA 1951 (3); v WI 1950 (3); v NZ 1949 (2); v In 1952 (2); v P 1954 (3); *v A 1950 (5) 1954 (1); v SA 1948 (1); v NZ 1950 (2) 1954 (2)*

Simpson-Hayward, G. H. 5: *v SA 1909 (5)*

Sims (J. M.) 4: v SA 1935 (1); v In 1936 (1); *v A 1936 (2)*

Sinfield (R. A.) 1: v A 1938

Slack, W. N. 3: v In 1986 (1); *v WI 1985 (2)*

Smailes (T. F.) 1: v In 1946

Small, G. C. 17: v A 1989 (1); v WI 1988 (1); v NZ 1986 (2) 1990 (3); *v A 1986 (2) 1990 (4); v WI 1989 (1)*

Smith, A. C. 6: *v A 1962 (4); v NZ 1962 (2)*

Smith, C. A. 1: *v SA 1888*

Smith (C. I. J.) 5: v NZ 1937 (1); *v WI 1934 (4)*

Smith, C. L. 8: v NZ 1983 (2); v In 1986 (1); *v NZ 1983 (2); v P 1983 (3)*

Smith (D.) 2: v SA 1935 (2)

Smith D. M. 2: *v WI 1985 (2)*

Smith (D. R.) 5: *v In 1961 (5)*

Smith (D. V.) 3: v WI 1957 (3)

Smith (E. J.) 11: v A 1912 (3); v SA 1912 (3); *v A 1911 (4); v SA 1913 (1)*

Smith (H.) 1: v WI 1928

Smith, M. J. K. 50: v A 1961 (1) 1972 (3); v SA 1960 (4) 1965 (3); v WI 1966 (1); v NZ 1958 (3) 1965 (3); v In 1959 (2); *v A 1965 (5); v SA 1964 (5); v WI 1959 (5); v NZ 1965 (3); v In 1961 (4) 1963 (5); v P 1961 (3)*

Smith, R. A. 28: v A 1989 (5); v WI 1988 (2) 1991 (4); v NZ 1990 (3); v In 1990 (3); v SL 1988 (1) 1991 (1); *v A 1990 (5); v WI 1989 (4)*

Smith (T. P. B.) 4: v In 1946 (1); *v A 1946 (2); v NZ 1946 (1)*

Smithson (G. A.) 2: *v WI 1947 (2)*

Snow, J. A. 49: v A 1968 (5) 1972 (5) 1975 (4); v SA 1965 (1); v WI 1966 (3) 1969 (3) 1973 (1) 1976 (3); v NZ 1965 (1) 1969 (2) 1973 (3); v In 1967 (3) 1971 (2); v P 1967 (1); *v A 1970 (6); v WI 1967 (4); v P 1968 (2)*

Southerton (J.) 2: *v A 1876 (2)*

Spooner, R. H. 10: v A 1905 (2) 1909 (2) 1912 (3); v SA 1912 (3)

Spooner (R. T.) 7: v SA 1955 (1); *v In 1951 (5); v WI 1953 (1)*

Stanyforth, R. T. 4: *v SA 1927 (4)*

Staples (S. J.) 3: *v SA 1927 (3)*

Statham (J. B.) 70: v A 1953 (1) 1956 (3) 1961 (4); v SA 1951 (2) 1955 (4) 1960 (5) 1965 (1); v WI 1957 (3) 1963 (2); v NZ 1958 (2); v In 1959 (3); v P 1954 (4) 1962 (3); *v A 1954 (5) 1958 (4) 1962 (5); v SA 1956 (4); v WI 1953 (4) 1959 (3); v NZ 1950 (1) 1954 (2); v In 1951 (5)*

Steel, A. G. 13: v A 1880 (1) 1882 (1) 1884 (3) 1886 (3) 1888 (1); *v A 1882 (4)*

Steele, D. S. 8: v A 1975 (3); v WI 1976 (5)

Stephenson, J. P. 1: v A 1989

Stevens, G. T. S. 10: v A 1926 (2); *v SA 1922 (1) 1927 (5); v WI 1929 (2)*

Stevenson, G. B. 2: *v WI 1980 (1); v In 1979 (1)*

Stewart, A. J. 14: v WI 1991 (1); v NZ 1990 (3); v SL 1991 (1); *v A 1990 (5); v WI 1989 (1)*

Stewart (M. J.) 8: v WI 1963 (4); v P 1962 (2); *v In 1963 (2)*

Stoddart, A. E. 16: v A 1893 (3) 1896 (2); *v A 1887 (1) 1891 (3) 1894 (5) 1897 (2)*

Storer (W.) 6: v A 1899 (1); *v A 1897 (5)*

Street (G. B.) 1: *v SA 1922*

Strudwick (H.) 28: v A 1921 (2) 1926 (5); v SA 1924 (1); *v A 1911 (1) 1920 (4) 1924 (5); v SA 1909 (5) 1913 (5)*

Studd, C. T. 5: v A 1882 (1); *v A 1882 (4)*

Studd, G. B. 4: *v A 1882 (4)*

Subba Row, R. 13: v A 1961 (5); v SA 1960 (4); v NZ 1958 (1); v In 1959 (1); *v WI 1959 (2)*

Sugg (F. H.) 2: v A 1888 (2)

Sutcliffe (H.) 54: v A 1926 (5) 1930 (4) 1934 (4); v SA 1924 (5) 1929 (5) 1935 (2); v WI 1928 (3) 1933 (2); v NZ 1931 (2); v In 1932 (1); *v A 1924 (5) 1928 (4) 1932 (5); v SA 1927 (5); v NZ 1932 (2)*

Swetman (R.) 11: v In 1959 (3); *v A 1958 (2); v WI 1959 (4); v NZ 1958 (2)*

Tate (F. W.) 1: v A 1902

Tate (M. W.) 39: v A 1926 (5) 1930 (5); v SA 1924 (5) 1929 (3) 1935 (1); v WI 1928 (3); v NZ 1931 (1); *v A 1924 (5) 1928 (5); v SA 1930 (5); v NZ 1932 (1)*

Tattersall (R.) 16: v A 1953 (1); v SA 1951 (5); v P 1954 (1); *v A 1950 (2); v NZ 1950 (2); v In 1951 (5)*

Tavaré, C. J. 31: v A 1981 (2) 1989 (1); v WI 1980 (2) 1984 (1); v NZ 1983 (4); v In 1982 (3); v P 1982 (3); v SL 1984 (1); *v A 1982 (5); v NZ 1983 (2); v In 1981 (6); v SL 1981 (1)*

Taylor (K.) 3: v A 1964 (1); v In 1959 (2)

Taylor, L. B. 2: v A 1985 (2)

Taylor, R. W. 57: v A 1981 (3); v NZ 1978 (3) 1983 (4); v In 1979 (3) 1982 (3); v P 1978 (3) 1982 (3); *v A 1978 (6) 1979 (3) 1982 (5); v NZ 1970 (1) 1977 (3) 1983 (3); v In 1979 (1) 1981 (6); v P 1977 (3) 1983 (3); v SL 1981 (1)*

Tennyson, Hon. L. H. 9: v A 1921 (4); *v SA 1913 (5)*

Terry, V. P. 2: v WI 1984 (2)

Thomas, J. G. 5: v NZ 1986 (1); *v WI 1985 (4)*

Thompson (G. J.) 6: v A 1909 (1); *v SA 1909 (5)*

Thomson, N. I. 5: *v SA 1964 (5)*

Titmus (F. J.) 53: v A 1962 (1) 1965 (3); v WI 1963 (4) 1966 (3); v NZ 1965 (3); v P 1962 (1) 1967 (2); *v A 1962 (5) 1965 (5) 1974 (4); v SA 1964 (5); v WI 1967 (2); v NZ 1962 (3); v In 1963 (5)*

Tolchard, R. W. 4: *v In 1976 (4)*

Townsend, C. L. 2: v A 1899 (2)

Townsend, D. C. H. 3: *v WI 1934 (3)*

Townsend (L. F.) 4: *v WI 1929 (1); v In 1933 (3)*

Tremlett (M. F.) 3: *v WI 1947 (3)*

Trott (A. E.) 2: *v SA 1898 (2)*

Trueman (F. S.) 67: v A 1953 (1) 1956 (2) 1961 (4) 1964 (4); v SA 1955 (1) 1960 (5); v WI 1957 (5) 1963 (5); v NZ 1958 (5) 1965 (2); v In 1952 (4) 1959 (5); v P 1962 (4); *v A 1958 (3) 1962 (5); v WI 1953 (3) 1959 (5); v NZ 1958 (2) 1962 (2)*

Tufnell, N. C. 1: *v SA 1909*

Tufnell, P. C. R. 6: v A 1991 (1); v SL 1991 (1); *v A 1990 (4)*

Turnbull, M. J. 9: v WI 1933 (2); v In 1936 (1); *v SA 1930 (5); v NZ 1929 (1)*

Tyldesley (E.) 14: v A 1921 (3) 1926 (1); v WI 1928 (3); *v A 1928 (1); v SA 1927 (5)*

Tyldesley (J. T.) 31: v A 1899 (2) 1902 (5) 1905 (5) 1909 (4); v SA 1907 (3); *v A 1901 (5) 1903 (5); v SA 1898 (2)*

Tyldesley (R. K.) 7: v A 1930 (2); v SA 1924 (4); *v A 1924 (1)*

Tylecote, E. F. S. 6: v A 1886 (2); *v A 1882 (4)*

Tyler (E. J.) 1: *v SA 1895*

Tyson (F. H.) 17: v A 1956 (1); v SA 1955 (2); v P 1954 (1); *v A 1954 (2) 1958 (2); v SA 1956 (2); v NZ 1954 (2) 1958 (2)*

Ulyett (G.) 25: v A 1882 (1) 1884 (3) 1886 (3) 1888 (2) 1890 (1); *v A 1876 (2) 1878 (1) 1881 (4) 1884 (5) 1887 (1); v SA 1888 (2)*

Underwood, D. L. 86: v A 1968 (4) 1972 (4) 1975 (4) 1977 (5); v WI 1966 (2) 1969 (2) 1973 (2) 1976 (5) 1980 (1); v NZ 1969 (3) 1973 (1); v In 1971 (1) 1974 (3); v P 1967 (2) 1971 (1) 1974 (3); *v A 1970 (5) 1974 (5) 1976 (1) 1979 (3); v WI 1973 (4); v NZ 1970 (2) 1974 (2); v In 1972 (4) 1976 (5) 1979 (1) 1981 (6); v P 1968 (3) 1972 (2); v SL 1981 (1)*

Valentine, B. H. 7: *v SA 1938 (5); v In 1933 (2)*

Verity (H.) 40: v A 1934 (5) 1938 (4); v SA 1935 (4); v WI 1933 (2) 1939 (1); v NZ 1931 (2) 1937 (1); v In 1936 (3); *v A 1932 (4) 1936 (5); v SA 1938 (5); v NZ 1932 (1); v In 1933 (3)*

Vernon, G. F. 1: *v A 1882*

Vine (J.) 2: *v A 1911 (2)*

Voce (W.) 27: v NZ 1931 (1) 1937 (1); v In 1932 (1) 1936 (1) 1946 (1); *v A 1932 (4) 1936 (5) 1946 (2); v SA 1930 (5); v WI 1929 (4); v NZ 1932 (2)*

Waddington (A.) 2: *v A 1920 (2)*

Wainwright (E.) 5: v A 1893 (1); *v A 1897 (4)*

Walker (P. M.) 3: v SA 1960 (3)

Walters, C. F. 11: v A 1934 (5); v WI 1933 (3); *v In 1933 (3)*

Ward, A. 5: v WI 1976 (1); v NZ 1969 (1); v P 1971 (1)

Ward (A.) 7: v A 1893 (2); *v A 1894 (5)*

Wardle (J. H.) 28: v A 1953 (3) 1956 (1); v SA 1951 (2) 1955 (3); v WI 1950 (1) 1957 (1); v P 1954 (4); *v A 1954 (4); v SA 1956 (4); v WI 1947 (1) 1953 (2); v NZ 1954 (2)*

Warner, P. F. 15: v A 1909 (1) 1912 (1); v SA 1912 (1); *v A 1903 (5); v SA 1898 (2) 1905 (5)*

Warr, J. J. 2: v A 1950 (2)
Warren (A. R.) 1: v A 1905
Washbrook (C.) 37: v A 1948 (4) 1956 (3); v SA 1947 (5); v WI 1950 (2); v NZ 1937 (1) 1949 (2); v In 1946 (3); *v A 1946 (5) 1950 (5); v SA 1948 (5); v NZ 1946 (1) 1950 (1)*
Watkin, S. L. 2: v WI 1991 (2)
Watkins (A. J.) 15: v A 1948 (1); v NZ 1949 (1); v In 1952 (3); *v SA 1948 (5); v In 1951 (5)*
Watson (W.) 23: v A 1953 (3) 1956 (2); v SA 1951 (5) 1955 (1); v NZ 1958 (2); v In 1952 (1); *v A 1958 (2); v WI 1953 (5); v NZ 1958 (2)*
Webbe, A. J. 1: *v A 1878*
Wellard (A. W.) 2: v A 1938 (1); v NZ 1937 (1)
Wharton (A.) 1: v NZ 1949
Whitaker, J. J. 1: *v A 1986*
White (D. W.) 2: v P 1961 (2)
White, J. C. 15: v A 1921 (1) 1930 (1); v SA 1929 (3); v WI 1928 (1); *v A 1928 (5); v SA 1930 (4)*
Whysall (W. W.) 4: v A 1930 (1); *v A 1924 (3)*
Wilkinson (L. L.) 3: *v SA 1938 (3)*
Willey, P. 26: v A 1980 (1) 1981 (4) 1985 (1); v WI 1976 (2) 1980 (5); v NZ 1986 (1); v In 1979 (1); *v A 1979 (3); v WI 1980 (4) 1985 (4)*
Williams, N. F. 1: v In 1990
Willis, R. G. D. 90: v A 1977 (5) 1981 (6); v WI 1973 (1) 1976 (2) 1980 (4) 1984 (3); v NZ 1978 (3) 1983 (4); v In 1974 (1) 1979 (3) 1982 (3); v P 1974 (1) 1978 (3) 1982 (2); *v A 1970 (4) 1974 (5) 1976 (1) 1978 (6) 1979 (3) 1982 (5); v WI 1973 (3); v NZ 1970 (1) 1977 (3) 1983 (3); v In 1976 (5) 1981 (5); v P 1977 (3) 1983 (1); v SL 1981 (1)*
Wilson, C. E. M. 2: *v SA 1898 (2)*
Wilson, D. 6: *v NZ 1970 (1); v In 1963 (5)*
Wilson, E. R. 1: *v A 1920*
Wood (A.) 4: v A 1938 (1); v WI 1939 (3)
Wood, B. 12: v A 1972 (1) 1975 (3); v WI 1976 (1); v P 1978 (1); *v NZ 1974 (2); v In 1972 (3); v P 1972 (1)*
Wood, G. E. C. 3: v SA 1924 (3)
Wood (H.) 4: v A 1888 (1); *v SA 1888 (2) 1891 (1)*
Wood (R.) 1: *v A 1886*
Woods S. M. J. 3: *v SA 1895 (3)*
Woolley (F. E.) 64: v A 1909 (1) 1912 (3) 1921 (5) 1926 (5) 1930 (2) 1934 (1); v SA 1912 (3) 1924 (5) 1929 (3); v WI 1928 (3); v NZ 1931 (1); v In 1932 (1); *v A 1911 (5) 1920 (5) 1924 (5); v SA 1909 (5) 1913 (5) 1922 (5); v NZ 1929 (4)*
Woolmer, R. A. 19: v A 1975 (2) 1977 (5) 1981 (2); v WI 1976 (5) 1980 (2); *v A 1976 (1); v In 1976 (2)*
Worthington (T. S.) 9: v In 1936 (2); *v A 1936 (3); v NZ 1929 (4)*
Wright, C. W. 3: *v SA 1895 (3)*
Wright (D. V. P.) 34: v A 1938 (3) 1948 (1); v SA 1947 (4); v WI 1939 (3) 1950 (1); v NZ 1949 (1); v In 1946 (2); *v A 1946 (5) 1950 (5); v SA 1938 (3) 1948 (3); v NZ 1946 (1) 1950 (2)*
Wyatt, R. E. S. 40: v A 1930 (1) 1934 (4); v SA 1929 (2) 1935 (5); v WI 1933 (2); v In 1936 (1); *v A 1932 (5) 1936 (2); v SA 1927 (5) 1930 (5); v WI 1929 (2) 1934 (4); v NZ 1932 (2)*
Wynyard, E. G. 3: v A 1896 (1); *v SA 1905 (2)*

Yardley, N. W. D. 20: v A 1948 (5); v SA 1947 (5); v WI 1950 (3); *v A 1946 (5); v SA 1938 (1); v NZ 1946 (1)*
Young (H. I.) 2: v A 1899 (2)
Young (J. A.) 8: v A 1948 (3); v SA 1947 (1); v NZ 1949 (2); *v SA 1948 (2)*
Young, R. A. 2: *v A 1907 (2)*


# AUSTRALIA

Number of Test cricketers: 349

a'Beckett, E. L. 4: v E 1928 (2); v SA 1931 (1); *v E 1930 (1)*
Alderman, T. M. 41: v E 1982 (1) 1990 (4); v WI 1981 (2) 1984 (3) 1988 (2); v NZ 1989 (1); v P 1981 (3) 1989 (2); v SL 1989 (2); *v E 1981 (6) 1989 (6); v WI 1983 (3) 1990 (1); v NZ 1981 (3) 1989 (1); v P 1982 (1)*
Alexander, G. 2: v E 1884 (1); *v E 1880 (1)*

Alexander, H. H. 1: v E 1932

Allan, F. E. 1: v E 1878

Allan, P. J. 1: v E 1965

Allen, R. C. 1: v E 1886

Andrews, T. J. E. 16: v E 1924 (3); *v E 1921 (5) 1926 (5); v SA 1921 (3)*

Archer, K. A. 5: v E 1950 (3); v WI 1951 (2)

Archer, R. G. 19: v E 1954 (4); v SA 1952 (1); *v E 1953 (3) 1956 (5); v WI 1954 (5); v P 1956 (1)*

Armstrong, W. W. 50: v E 1901 (4) 1903 (3) 1907 (5) 1911 (5) 1920 (5); v SA 1910 (5); *v E 1902 (5) 1905 (5) 1909 (5) 1921 (5); v SA 1902 (3)*

Badcock, C. L. 7: v E 1936 (3); *v E 1938 (4)*

Bannerman, A. C. 28: v E 1878 (1) 1881 (3) 1882 (4) 1884 (4) 1886 (1) 1887 (1) 1891 (3); *v E 1880 (1) 1882 (1) 1884 (3) 1888 (3) 1893 (3)*

Bannerman, C. 3: v E 1876 (2) 1878 (1)

Bardsley, W. 41: v E 1911 (4) 1920 (5) 1924 (3); v SA 1910 (5); *v E 1909 (5) 1912 (3) 1921 (5) 1926 (5); v SA 1912 (3) 1921 (3)*

Barnes, S. G. 13: v E 1946 (4); v In 1947 (3); *v E 1938 (1) 1948 (4); v NZ 1945 (1)*

Barnett, B. A. 4: *v E 1938 (4)*

Barrett, J. E. 2: *v E 1890 (2)*

Beard, G. R. 3: *v P 1979 (3)*

Benaud, J. 3: v P 1972 (2); *v WI 1972 (1)*

Benaud, R. 63: v E 1954 (5) 1958 (5) 1962 (5); v SA 1952 (4) 1963 (4); v WI 1951 (1) 1960 (5); *v E 1953 (3) 1956 (5) 1961 (4); v SA 1957 (5); v WI 1954 (5); v In 1956 (3) 1959 (5); v P 1956 (1) 1959 (3)*

Bennett, M. J. 3: v WI 1984 (2); *v E 1985 (1)*

Blackham, J. McC. 35: v E 1876 (2) 1878 (1) 1881 (4) 1882 (4) 1884 (4) 1886 (1) 1887 (1) 1891 (3) 1894 (1); *v E 1880 (1) 1882 (1) 1884 (3) 1886 (3) 1888 (3) 1890 (2) 1893 (3)*

Blackie, D. D. 3: v E 1928 (3)

Bonnor, G. J. 17: v E 1882 (4) 1884 (3); *v E 1880 (1) 1882 (1) 1884 (3) 1886 (2) 1888 (3)*

Boon, D. C. 58: v E 1986 (4) 1987 (1) 1990 (5); v WI 1984 (3) 1988 (5); v NZ 1985 (3) 1987 (3) 1989 (1); v In 1985 (3); v P 1989 (2); v SL 1987 (1) 1989 (2); *v E 1985 (4) 1989 (6); v WI 1990 (5); v NZ 1985 (3) 1989 (1); v In 1986 (3); v P 1988 (3)*

Booth, B. C. 29: v E 1962 (5) 1965 (3); v SA 1963 (4); v P 1964 (1); *v E 1961 (2) 1964 (5); v WI 1964 (3); v In 1964 (3); v P 1964 (1)*

Border, A. R. 125: v E 1978 (3) 1979 (3) 1982 (5) 1986 (5) 1987 (1) 1990 (5); v WI 1979 (3) 1981 (3) 1984 (5) 1988 (5); v NZ 1980 (3) 1985 (3) 1987 (3) 1989 (1); v In 1980 (3) 1985 (3); v P 1978 (2) 1981 (3) 1983 (5) 1989 (3); v SL 1987 (1) 1989 (2); *v E 1980 (1) 1981 (6) 1985 (6) 1989 (6); v WI 1983 (5) 1990 (5); v NZ 1981 (3) 1985 (3) 1989 (1); v In 1979 (6) 1986 (3); v P 1979 (3) 1982 (3) 1988 (3); v SL 1982 (1)*

Boyle, H. F. 12: v E 1878 (1) 1881 (4) 1882 (1) 1884 (1); *v E 1880 (1) 1882 (1) 1884 (3)*

Bradman, D. G. 52: v E 1928 (4) 1932 (4) 1936 (5) 1946 (5); v SA 1931 (5); v WI 1930 (5); v In 1947 (5); *v E 1930 (5) 1934 (5) 1938 (4) 1948 (5)*

Bright, R. J. 25: v E 1979 (1); v WI 1979 (1); v NZ 1985 (1); v In 1985 (3); *v E 1977 (3) 1980 (1) 1981 (3); v NZ 1985 (2); v In 1986 (3); v P 1979 (3) 1982 (2)*

Bromley, E. H. 2: v E 1932 (1); *v E 1934 (1)*

Brown, W. A. 22: v E 1936 (2); v In 1947 (3); *v E 1934 (5) 1938 (4) 1948 (2); v SA 1935 (5); v NZ 1945 (1)*

Bruce, W. 14: v E 1884 (2) 1891 (3) 1894 (4); *v E 1886 (2) 1893 (3)*

Burge, P. J. 42: v E 1954 (1) 1958 (1) 1962 (3) 1965 (4); v SA 1963 (5); v WI 1960 (2); *v E 1956 (3) 1961 (5) 1964 (5); v SA 1957 (1); v WI 1954 (1); v In 1956 (3) 1959 (2) 1964 (3); v P 1959 (2) 1964 (1)*

Burke, J. W. 24: v E 1950 (2) 1954 (2) 1958 (5); v WI 1951 (1); *v E 1956 (5); v SA 1957 (5); v In 1956 (3); v P 1956 (1)*

Burn, K. E. 2: *v E 1890 (2)*

Burton, F. J. 2: v E 1886 (1) 1887 (1)

Callaway, S. T. 3: v E 1891 (2) 1894 (1)

Callen, I. W. 1: v In 1977

Campbell, G. D. 4: v P 1989 (1); v SL 1989 (1); *v E 1989 (1); v NZ 1989 (1)*

Carkeek, W. 6: *v E 1912 (3); v SA 1912 (3)*

Carlson, P. H. 2: v E 1978 (2)

Carter, H. 28: v E 1907 (5) 1911 (5) 1920 (2); v SA 1910 (5); *v E 1909 (5) 1921 (4); v SA 1921 (2)*

Chappell, G. S. 87: v E 1970 (5) 1974 (6) 1976 (1) 1979 (3) 1982 (5); v WI 1975 (6) 1979 (3) 1981 (3); v NZ 1973 (3) 1980 (3); v In 1980 (3); *v E 1972 (5); v WI 1972 (5); v NZ 1973 (3) 1976 (2) 1981 (3); v P 1979 (3); v SL 1982 (1)*

Chappell, I. M. 75: v E 1965 (2) 1970 (6) 1974 (6) 1979 (2); v WI 1968 (5) 1975 (6) 1979 (1); v NZ 1973 (3); v In 1967 (4); v P 1964 (1) 1972 (3); *v E 1968 (5) 1972 (5) 1975 (4); v SA 1966 (5) 1969 (4); v WI 1972 (5); v NZ 1973 (3); v In 1969 (5)*

Chappell, T. M. 3: *v E 1981 (3)*

Charlton, P. C. 2: v E 1890 (2)

Chipperfield, A. G. 14: v E 1936 (3); *v E 1934 (5) 1938 (1); v SA 1935 (5)*

Clark, W. M. 10: v In 1977 (5); v P 1978 (1); *v WI 1977 (4)*

Colley, D. J. 3: *v E 1972 (3)*

Collins, H. L. 19: v E 1920 (5) 1924 (5); *v E 1921 (3) 1926 (3); v SA 1921 (3)*

Coningham, A. 1: v E 1894

Connolly, A. N. 29: v E 1965 (1) 1970 (1); v SA 1963 (3); v WI 1968 (5); v In 1967 (3); *v E 1968 (5); v SA 1969 (4); v In 1964 (2); 1969 (5)*

Cooper, B. B. 1: v E 1876

Cooper, W. H. 2: v E 1881 (1) 1884 (1)

Corling, G. E. 5: *v E 1964 (5)*

Cosier, G. J. 18: v E 1976 (1) 1978 (2); v WI 1975 (3); v In 1977 (4); v P 1976 (3); *v WI 1977 (3); v NZ 1976 (2)*

Cottam, W. J. 1: v E 1886

Cotter, A. 21: v E 1903 (2) 1907 (2) 1911 (4); v SA 1910 (5); *v E 1905 (3) 1909 (3)*

Coulthard, G. 1: v E 1881

Cowper, R. M. 27: v E 1965 (4); v In 1967 (4); v P 1964 (1); *v E 1964 (1) 1968 (4); v SA 1966 (5); v WI 1964 (5); v In 1964 (2); v P 1964 (1)*

Craig, I. D. 11: v SA 1952 (1); *v E 1956 (2); v SA 1957 (5); v In 1956 (2); v P 1956 (1)*

Crawford, W. P. A. 4: *v E 1956 (1); v In 1956 (3)*

Darling, J. 34: v E 1894 (5) 1897 (5) 1901 (3); *v E 1896 (3) 1899 (5) 1902 (5) 1905 (5); v SA 1902 (3)*

Darling, L. S. 12: v E 1932 (2) 1936 (1); *v E 1934 (4); v SA 1935 (5)*

Darling, W. M. 14: v E 1978 (4); v In 1977 (1); v P 1978 (1); *v WI 1977 (3); v In 1979 (5)*

Davidson, A. K. 44: v E 1954 (3) 1958 (5) 1962 (5); v WI 1960 (4); *v E 1953 (5) 1956 (2) 1961 (5); v SA 1957 (5); v In 1956 (1) 1959 (5); v P 1956 (1) 1959 (3)*

Davis, I. C. 15: v E 1976 (1); v NZ 1973 (3); v P 1976 (3); *v E 1977 (3); v NZ 1973 (3) 1976 (2)*

Davis, S. P. 1: *v NZ 1985*

De Courcy, J. H. 3: *v E 1953 (3)*

Dell, A. R. 2: v E 1970 (1); v NZ 1973 (1)

Dodemaide, A. I. C. 8: v E 1987 (1); v WI 1988 (2); v NZ 1987 (1); v SL 1987 (1); *v P 1988 (3)*

Donnan, H. 5: v E 1891 (2); *v E 1896 (3)*

Dooland, B. 3: v E 1946 (2); v In 1947 (1)

Duff, R. A. 22: v E 1901 (4) 1903 (5); *v E 1902 (5) 1905 (5); v SA 1902 (3)*

Duncan, J. R. F. 1: v E 1970

Dyer, G. C. 6: v E 1986 (1) 1987 (1); v NZ 1987 (3); v SL 1987 (1)

Dymock, G. 21: v E 1974 (1) 1978 (3) 1979 (3); v WI 1979 (2); v NZ 1973 (1); v P 1978 (1); *v NZ 1973 (2); v In 1979 (5); v P 1979 (3)*

Dyson, J. 30: v E 1982 (5); v WI 1981 (2) 1984 (3); v NZ 1980 (3); v In 1977 (3) 1980 (3); *v E 1981 (5); v NZ 1981 (3); v P 1982 (3)*

Eady, C. J. 2: v E 1901 (1); *v E 1896 (1)*

Eastwood, K. H. 1: v E 1970

Ebeling, H. I. 1: *v E 1934*

Edwards, J. D. 3: *v E 1888 (3)*

Edwards, R. 20: v E 1974 (5); v P 1972 (2); *v E 1972 (4) 1975 (4); v WI 1972 (5)*

Edwards, W. J. 3: v E 1974 (3)

Emery, S. H. 4: *v E 1912 (2); v SA 1912 (2)*

Evans, E. 6: v E 1881 (2) 1882 (1) 1884 (1); *v E 1886 (2)*

Fairfax, A. G. 10: v E 1928 (1); v WI 1930 (5); *v E 1930 (4)*

Favell, L. E. 19: v E 1954 (4) 1958 (2); v WI 1960 (4); *v WI 1954 (2); v In 1959 (4); v P 1959 (3)*

Ferris, J. J. 8: v E 1886 (2) 1887 (1); *v E 1888 (3) 1890 (2)*

Fingleton, J. H. 18: v E 1932 (3) 1936 (5); v SA 1931 (1); *v E 1938 (4); v SA 1935 (5)*

Fleetwood-Smith, L. O'B. 10: v E 1936 (3); *v E 1938 (4); v SA 1935 (3)*

Francis, B. C. 3: *v E 1972 (3)*

Freeman, E. W. 11: v WI 1968 (4); v In 1967 (2); *v E 1968 (2); v SA 1969 (2); v In 1969 (1)*

Freer, F. W. 1: v E 1946


Gannon, J. B. 3: v In 1977 (3)

Garrett, T. W. 19: v E 1876 (2) 1878 (1) 1881 (3) 1882 (3) 1884 (3) 1886 (2) 1887 (1); *v E 1882 (1) 1886 (3)*

Gaunt, R. A. 3: v SA 1963 (1); *v E 1961 (1); v SA 1957 (1)*

Gehrs, D. R. A. 6: v E 1903 (1); v SA 1910 (4); *v E 1905 (1)*

Giffen, G. 31: v E 1881 (3) 1882 (4) 1884 (3) 1891 (3) 1894 (5); *v E 1882 (1) 1884 (3) 1886 (3) 1893 (3) 1896 (3)*

Giffen, W. F. 3: v E 1886 (1) 1891 (2)

Gilbert, D. R. 9: v NZ 1985 (3); v In 1985 (2); *v E 1985 (1); v NZ 1985 (1); v In 1986 (2)*

Gilmour, G. J. 15: v E 1976 (1); v WI 1975 (5); v NZ 1973 (2); v P 1976 (3); *v E 1975 (1); v NZ 1973 (1) 1976 (2)*

Gleeson, J. W. 29: v E 1970 (5); v WI 1968 (5); v In 1967 (4); *v E 1968 (5) 1972 (3); v SA 1969 (4); v In 1969 (3)*

Graham, H. 6: v E 1894 (2); *v E 1893 (3) 1896 (1)*

Gregory, D. W. 3: v E 1876 (2) 1878 (1)

Gregory, E. J. 1: v E 1876

Gregory, J. M. 24: v E 1920 (5) 1924 (5) 1928 (1); *v E 1921 (5) 1926 (5); v SA 1921 (3)*

Gregory, R. G. 2: v E 1936 (2)

Gregory, S. E. 58: v E 1891 (1) 1894 (5) 1897 (5) 1901 (5) 1903 (4) 1907 (2) 1911 (1); *v E 1890 (2) 1893 (3) 1896 (3) 1899 (5) 1902 (5) 1905 (3) 1909 (5) 1912 (3); v SA 1902 (3) 1912 (3)*

Grimmett, C. V. 37: v E 1924 (1) 1928 (5) 1932 (5); v SA 1931 (5); v WI 1930 (5); *v E 1926 (3) 1930 (5) 1934 (5); v SA 1935 (5)*

Groube, T. U. 1: *v E 1880*

Grout, A. T. W. 51: v E 1958 (5) 1962 (2) 1965 (5); v SA 1963 (5); v WI 1960 (5); *v E 1961 (5) 1964 (5); v SA 1957 (5); v WI 1964 (5); v In 1959 (4) 1964 (1); v P 1959 (3) 1964 (1)*

Guest, C. E. J. 1: v E 1962


Hamence, R. A. 3: v E 1946 (1); v In 1947 (2)

Hammond, J. R. 5: *v WI 1972 (5)*

Harry, J. 1: v E 1894

Hartigan, R. J. 2: v E 1907 (2)

Hartkopf, A. E. V. 1: v E 1924

Harvey, M. R. 1: v E 1946

Harvey, R. N. 79: v E 1950 (5) 1954 (5) 1958 (5) 1962 (5); v SA 1952 (5); v WI 1951 (5) 1960 (4); v In 1947 (2); *v E 1948 (2) 1953 (5) 1956 (5) 1961 (5); v SA 1949 (5) 1957 (4); v WI 1954 (5); v In 1956 (3) 1959 (5); v P 1956 (1) 1959 (3)*

Hassett, A. L. 43: v E 1946 (5) 1950 (5); v SA 1952 (5); v WI 1951 (4); v In 1947 (4); *v E 1938 (4) 1948 (5) 1953 (5); v SA 1949 (5); v In 1947 (4)*

Hawke, N. J. N. 27: v E 1962 (1) 1965 (4); v SA 1963 (4); v In 1967 (1); v P 1964 (1); *v E 1964 (5) 1968 (2); v SA 1966 (2); v WI 1964 (5); v In 1964 (1); v P 1964 (1)*

Hazlitt, G. R. 9: v E 1907 (2) 1911 (1); *v E 1912 (3); v SA 1912 (3)*

Healy, I. A. 31: v E 1990 (5); v WI 1988 (5); v NZ 1989 (1); v P 1989 (3); v SL 1989 (2); *v E 1989 (6); v WI 1990 (5); v NZ 1989 (1); v P 1988 (3)*

Hendry, H. S. T. L. 11: v E 1924 (1) 1928 (4); *v E 1921 (4); v SA 1921 (2)*

Hibbert, P. A. 1: v In 1977

Higgs, J. D. 22: v E 1978 (5) 1979 (1); v WI 1979 (1); v NZ 1980 (3); v In 1980 (2); *v WI 1977 (4); v In 1979 (6)*

Hilditch, A. M. J. 18: v E 1978 (1); v WI 1984 (2); v NZ 1985 (1); v P 1978 (2); *v E 1985 (6); v In 1979 (6)*

Hill, C. 49: v E 1897 (5) 1901 (5) 1903 (5) 1907 (5) 1911 (5); v SA 1910 (5); *v E 1896 (3) 1899 (3) 1902 (5) 1905 (5); v SA 1902 (3)*

Hill, J. C. 3: *v E 1953 (2); v WI 1954 (1)*

Hoare, D. E. 1: v WI 1960

Hodges, J. H. 2: v E 1876 (2)

Hogan, T. G. 7: v P 1983 (1); *v WI 1983 (5); v SL 1982 (1)*

Hogg, R. M. 38: v E 1978 (6) 1982 (3); v WI 1979 (2) 1984 (4); v NZ 1980 (2); v In 1980 (2); v P 1978 (2) 1983 (4); *v E 1981 (2); v WI 1983 (4); v In 1979 (6); v SL 1982 (1)*

Hohns, T. V. 7: v WI 1988 (2); *v E 1989 (5)*

Hole, G. B. 18: v E 1950 (1) 1954 (3); v SA 1952 (4); v WI 1951 (5); *v E 1953 (5)*

Holland, R. G. 11: v WI 1984 (3); v NZ 1985 (3); v In 1985 (1); *v E 1985 (4)*

Hookes, D. W. 23: v E 1976 (1) 1982 (5); v WI 1979 (1); v NZ 1985 (2); v In 1985 (2); *v E 1977 (5); v WI 1983 (5); v P 1979 (1); v SL 1982 (1)*

Hopkins, A. J. Y. 20: v E 1901 (2) 1903 (5); *v E 1902 (5) 1905 (3) 1909 (2); v SA 1902 (3)*

Horan, T. P. 15: v E 1876 (1) 1878 (1) 1881 (4) 1882 (4) 1884 (4); *v E 1882 (1)*

Hordern, H. V. 7: v E 1911 (5); v SA 1910 (2)

Hornibrook, P. M. 6: v E 1928 (1); *v E 1930 (5)*

Howell, W. P. 18: v E 1897 (3) 1901 (4) 1903 (3); *v E 1899 (5) 1902 (1); v SA 1902 (2)*

Hughes, K. J. 70: v E 1978 (6) 1979 (3) 1982 (5); v WI 1979 (3) 1981 (3) 1984 (4); v NZ 1980 (3); v In 1977 (2) 1980 (3); v P 1978 (2) 1981 (3) 1983 (5); *v E 1977 (1) 1980 (1) 1981 (6); v WI 1983 (5); v NZ 1981 (3); v In 1979 (6); v P 1979 (3) 1982 (3)*

Hughes, M. G. 32: v E 1986 (1) 1990 (4); v WI 1988 (4); v NZ 1987 (1) 1989 (1); v In 1985 (1); v P 1989 (3); *v E 1989 (6); v WI 1990 (5)*

Hunt, W. A. 1: v SA 1931

Hurst, A. G. 12: v E 1978 (6); v NZ 1973 (1); v In 1977 (1); v P 1978 (2); *v In 1979 (2)*

Hurwood, A. 2: v WI 1930 (2)

Inverarity, R. J. 6: v WI 1968 (1); *v E 1968 (2) 1972 (3)*

Iredale, F. A. 14: v E 1894 (5) 1897 (4); *v E 1896 (2) 1899 (3)*

Ironmonger, H. 14: v E 1928 (2) 1932 (4); v SA 1931 (4); v WI 1930 (4)

Iverson, J. B. 5: v E 1950 (5)

Jackson, A. 8: v E 1928 (2); v WI 1930 (4); *v E 1930 (2)*

Jarman, B. N. 19: v E 1962 (3); v WI 1968 (4); v In 1967 (4); v P 1964 (1); *v E 1968 (4); v In 1959 (1); 1964 (2)*

Jarvis, A. H. 11: v E 1884 (3) 1894 (4); *v E 1886 (2) 1888 (2)*

Jenner, T. J. 9: v E 1970 (2) 1974 (2); v WI 1975 (1); *v WI 1972 (4)*

Jennings, C. B. 6: *v E 1912 (3); v SA 1912 (3)*

Johnson I. W. 45: v E 1946 (4) 1950 (5) 1954 (4); v SA 1952 (1); v WI 1951 (4); v In 1947 (4); *v E 1948 (4) 1956 (5); v SA 1949 (5); v WI 1954 (5); v NZ 1945 (1); v In 1956 (2); v P 1956 (1)*

Johnson, L. J. 1: v In 1947

Johnston W. A. 40: v E 1950 (5) 1954 (4); v SA 1952 (5); v WI 1951 (5); v In 1947 (4); *v E 1948 (5) 1953 (4); v SA 1949 (5); v WI 1954 (4)*

Jones, D. M. 44: v E 1986 (5) 1987 (1) 1990 (5); v WI 1988 (3); v NZ 1987 (3) 1989 (1); v P 1989 (3); v SL 1987 (1) 1989 (2); *v E 1989 (6); v WI 1983 (2) 1990 (5); v NZ 1989 (1); v In 1986 (3); v P 1988 (3)*

Jones, E. 19: v E 1894 (1) 1897 (5) 1901 (2); *v E 1896 (3) 1899 (5) 1902 (2); v SA 1902 (1)*

Jones, S. P. 12: v E 1881 (2) 1884 (4) 1886 (1) 1887 (1); *v E 1882 (1) 1886 (3)*

Joslin, L. R. 1: v In 1967

Kelleway, C. 26: v E 1911 (4) 1920 (5) 1924 (5) 1928 (1); v SA 1910 (5); *v E 1912 (3); v SA 1912 (3)*

Kelly, J. J. 36: v E 1897 (5) 1901 (5) 1903 (5); *v E 1896 (3) 1899 (5) 1902 (5) 1905 (5); v SA 1902 (3)*

Kelly, T. J. D. 2: v E 1876 (1) 1878 (1)

Kendall, T. 2: v E 1876 (2)

Kent, M. F. 3: *v E 1981 (3)*

Kerr, R. B. 2: v NZ 1985 (2)

Kippax, A. F. 22: v E 1924 (1) 1928 (5) 1932 (1); v SA 1931 (4); v WI 1930 (5); *v E 1930 (5) 1934 (1)*

Kline L. F. 13: v E 1958 (2); v WI 1960 (2); *v SA 1957 (5); v In 1959 (3); v P 1959 (1)*

Laird, B. M. 21: v E 1979 (2); v WI 1979 (3) 1981 (3); v P 1981 (3); *v E 1980 (1); v NZ 1981 (3); v P 1979 (3) 1982 (3)*

Langley, G. R. A. 26: v E 1954 (2); v SA 1952 (5); v WI 1951 (5); *v E 1953 (4) 1956 (3); v WI 1954 (4); v In 1956 (2); v P 1956 (1)*

Laughlin, T. J. 3: v E 1978 (1); *v WI 1977 (2)*

Laver, F. 15: v E 1901 (1) 1903 (1); *v E 1899 (4) 1905 (5) 1909 (4)*

Lawry, W. M. 67: v E 1962 (5) 1965 (5) 1970 (5); v SA 1963 (5); v WI 1968 (5); v In 1967 (4); v P 1964 (1); *v E 1961 (5) 1964 (5) 1968 (4); v SA 1966 (5) 1969 (4); v WI 1964 (5); v In 1964 (3) 1969 (5); v P 1964 (1)*

Lawson, G. F. 46: v E 1982 (5) 1986 (1); v WI 1981 (1) 1984 (5) 1988 (1); v NZ 1980 (1) 1985 (2) 1989 (1); v P 1983 (5); v SL 1989 (1); *v E 1981 (3) 1985 (6) 1989 (6); v WI 1983 (5); v P 1982 (3)*

Lee, P. K. 2: v E 1932 (1); v SA 1931 (1)

Lillee, D. K. 70: v E 1970 (2) 1974 (6) 1976 (1) 1979 (3) 1982 (1); v WI 1975 (5) 1979 (3) 1981 (3); v NZ 1980 (3); v In 1980 (3); v P 1972 (3) 1976 (3) 1981 (3) 1983 (5); *v E 1972 (5) 1975 (4) 1980 (1) 1981 (6); v WI 1972 (1); v NZ 1976 (2) 1981 (3); v P 1979 (3); v SL 1982 (1)*

Lindwall, R. R. 61: v E 1946 (4) 1950 (5) 1954 (4) 1958 (2); v SA 1952 (4); v WI 1951 (5); v In 1947 (5); *v E 1948 (5) 1953 (2) 1956 (4); v SA 1949 (4); v WI 1954 (5); v NZ 1945 (1); v In 1956 (3) 1959 (2); v P 1956 (1) 1959 (2)*

Love, H. S. B. 1: v E 1932

Loxton, S. J. E. 12: v E 1950 (3); v In 1947 (1); *v E 1948 (3); v SA 1949 (5)*

Lyons, J. J. 14: v E 1886 (1) 1891 (3) 1894 (3) 1897 (1); *v E 1888 (1) 1890 (2) 1893 (3)*


McAlister, P. A. 8: v E 1903 (2) 1907 (4); *v E 1909 (2)*

Macartney, C. G. 35: v E 1907 (5) 1911 (1) 1920 (2); v SA 1910 (4); *v E 1909 (5) 1912 (3) 1921 (5) 1926 (5); v SA 1912 (3) 1921 (2)*

McCabe, S. J. 39: v E 1932 (5) 1936 (5); v SA 1931 (5); v WI 1930 (5); *v E 1930 (5) 1934 (5) 1938 (4); v SA 1935 (5)*

McCool, C. L. 14: v E 1946 (5); v In 1947 (3); *v SA 1949 (5) v NZ 1945 (1)*

McCormick, E. L. 12: v E 1936 (4); *v E 1938 (3); v SA 1935 (5)*

McCosker, R. B. 25: v E 1974 (3) 1976 (1) 1979 (2); v WI 1975 (4) 1979 (1); v P 1976 (3); *v E 1975 (4) 1977 (5); v NZ 1976 (2)*

McDermott, C. J. 31: v E 1986 (1) 1987 (1) 1990 (2); v WI 1984 (2) 1988 (2); v NZ 1985 (2) 1987 (3); v In 1985 (2); v SL 1987 (1); *v E 1985 (6); v WI 1990 (5); v NZ 1985 (2); v In 1986 (2)*

McDonald, C. C. 47: v E 1954 (2) 1958 (5); v SA 1952 (5); v WI 1951 (1) 1960 (5); *v E 1956 (5) 1961 (3); v SA 1957 (5); v WI 1954 (5); v In 1956 (2) 1959 (5); v P 1956 (1) 1959 (3)*

McDonald, E. A. 11: v E 1920 (3); *v E 1921 (5); v SA 1921 (3)*

McDonnell, P. S. 19: v E 1881 (4) 1882 (3) 1884 (2) 1886 (2) 1887 (1); *v E 1880 (1) 1884 (3) 1888 (3)*

McIlwraith, J. 1: *v E 1886*

Mackay K. D. 37: v E 1958 (5) 1962 (3); v WI 1960 (5); *v E 1956 (3) 1961 (3); v SA 1957 (5); v In 1956 (3) 1959 (5); v P 1959 (3)*

McKenzie, G. D. 60: v E 1962 (5) 1965 (4) 1970 (3); v SA 1963 (5); v WI 1968 (5); v In 1967 (2); v P 1964 (1); *v E 1961 (3) 1964 (5) 1968 (5); v SA 1966 (5) 1969 (3); v WI 1964 (5); v In 1964 (3) 1969 (5); v P 1964 (1)*

McKibbin, T. R. 5: v E 1894 (1) 1897 (2); *v E 1896 (2)*

McLaren, J. W. 1: v E 1911

Maclean, J. A. 4: v E 1978 (4)

McLeod, C. E. 17: v E 1894 (1) 1897 (5) 1901 (2) 1903 (3); *v E 1899 (1) 1905 (5)*

McLeod, R. W. 6: v E 1891 (3); *v E 1893 (3)*

McShane, P. G. 3: v E 1884 (1) 1886 (1) 1887 (1)

Maddocks, L. V. 7: v E 1954 (3); *v E 1956 (2); v WI 1954 (1); v In 1956 (1)*

Maguire, J. N. 3: v P 1983 (1); *v WI 1983 (2)*

Mailey, A. A. 21: v E 1920 (5) 1924 (5); *v E 1921 (3) 1926 (5); v SA 1921 (3)*

Mallett, A. A. 38: v E 1970 (2) 1974 (5) 1979 (1); v WI 1968 (1) 1975 (6) 1979 (1); v NZ 1973 (3); v P 1972 (2); *v E 1968 (1) 1972 (2) 1975 (4) 1980 (1); v SA 1969 (1); v NZ 1973 (3); v In 1969 (5)*

Malone, M. F. 1: *v E 1977*

Mann, A. L. 4: v In 1977 (4)

Marr, A. P. 1: v E 1884

Marsh, G. R. 46: v E 1986 (5) 1987 (1) 1990 (5); v WI 1988 (5); v NZ 1987 (3); v In 1985 (3); v P 1989 (2); v SL 1987 (1); *v E 1989 (6); v WI 1990 (5); v NZ 1985 (3) 1989 (1); v In 1986 (3); v P 1988 (3)*

Marsh, R. W. 96: v E 1970 (6) 1974 (6) 1976 (1) 1979 (3) 1982 (5); v WI 1975 (6) 1979 (3) 1981 (3); v NZ 1973 (3) 1980 (3); v In 1980 (3); v P 1972 (3) 1976 (3) 1981 (3) 1983 (5); *v E 1972 (5) 1975 (4) 1977 (5) 1980 (1) 1981 (6); v WI 1972 (5); v NZ 1973 (3) 1976 (2) 1981 (3); v P 1979 (3) 1982 (3)*

Martin, J. W. 8: v SA 1963 (1); v WI 1960 (1); *v SA 1966 (1); v In 1964 (2); v P 1964 (1)*

Massie, H. H. 9: v E 1881 (4) 1882 (3) 1884 (1); *v E 1882 (1)*

Massie, R. A. L. 6: v P 1972 (2); *v E 1972 (4)*

Matthews, C. D. 3: v E 1986 (2); v WI 1988 (1)

Matthews, G. R. J. 28: v E 1986 (4) 1990 (5); v WI 1984 (1); v NZ 1985 (3); v In 1985 (3); v P 1983 (2); *v E 1985 (1); v WI 1983 (1) 1990 (2); v NZ 1985 (3); v In 1986 (3)*

Matthews, T. J. 8: v E 1911 (2); *v E 1912 (3); v SA 1912 (3)*

May, T. B. A. 7: v WI 1988 (5); v NZ 1987 (1); *v P 1988 (3)*

Mayne, E. R. 4: *v E 1912 (1); v SA 1912 (1) 1921 (2)*

Mayne, L. C. 6: *v SA 1969 (2); v WI 1964 (3); v In 1969 (1)*

Meckiff, I. 18: v E 1958 (4); v SA 1963 (1); v WI 1960 (2); *v SA 1957 (1); v In 1959 (5); v P 1959 (2)*

Meuleman, K. D. 1: *v NZ 1945*

Midwinter, W. E. 8: v E 1876 (2) 1882 (1) 1886 (2); *v E 1884 (3)*

Miller, K. R. 55: v E 1946 (5) 1950 (5) 1954 (4); v SA 1952 (4); v WI 1951 (5); v In 1947 (5); *v E 1948 (5) 1953 (5) 1956 (5); v SA 1949 (5); v WI 1954 (5); v NZ 1945 (1); v P 1956 (1)*

Minnett, R. B. 9: v E 1911 (5); *v E 1912 (1); v SA 1912 (3)*

Misson, F. M. 5: v WI 1960 (3); *v E 1961 (2)*

Moody, T. M. 4: v NZ 1989 (1); v P 1989 (1); v SL 1989 (1)

Moroney, J. R. 7: v E 1950 (1); v WI 1951 (1); *v SA 1949 (5)*

Morris, A. R. 46: v E 1946 (5) 1950 (5) 1954 (4); v SA 1952 (5); v WI 1951 (4); v In 1947 (4); *v E 1948 (5) 1953 (5); v SA 1949 (5); v WI 1954 (4)*

Morris, S. 1: v E 1884

Moses, H. 6: v E 1886 (2) 1887 (1) 1891 (2) 1894 (1)

Moss, J. K. 1: v P 1978

Moule, W. H. 1: *v E 1880*

Murdoch, W. L. 18: v E 1876 (1) 1878 (1) 1881 (4) 1882 (4) 1884 (1); *v E 1880 (1) 1882 (1) 1884 (3) 1890 (2)*

Musgrove, H. 1: v E 1884

Nagel, L. E. 1: v E 1932

Nash, L. J. 2: v E 1936 (1); v SA 1931 (1)

Nitschke, H. C. 2: v SA 1931 (2)

Noble, M. A. 42: v E 1897 (4) 1901 (5) 1903 (5) 1907 (5); *v E 1899 (5) 1902 (5) 1905 (5) 1909 (5); v SA 1902 (3)*

Noblet, G. 3: v SA 1952 (1); v WI 1951 (1); *v SA 1949 (1)*

Nothling, O. E. 1: v E 1928

O'Brien, L. P. J. 5: v E 1932 (2) 1936 (1); *v SA 1935 (2)*

O'Connor, J. D. A. 4: v E 1907 (3); *v E 1909 (1)*

O'Donnell, S. P. 6: v NZ 1985 (1); *v E 1985 (5)*

Ogilvie, A. D. 5: v In 1977 (2); *v WI 1977 (2)*

O'Keeffe, K. J. 24: v E 1970 (2) 1976 (1); v NZ 1973 (3); v P 1972 (2) 1976 (3); *v E 1977 (3); v WI 1972 (5); v NZ 1973 (3) 1976 (2)*

Oldfield, W. A. 54: v E 1920 (3) 1924 (5) 1928 (5) 1932 (4) 1936 (5); v SA 1931 (5); v WI 1930 (5); *v E 1921 (1) 1926 (5) 1930 (5) 1934 (5); v SA 1921 (1) 1935 (5)*

O'Neill, N. C. 42: v E 1958 (5) 1962 (5); v SA 1963 (4); v WI 1960 (5); *v E 1961 (5) 1964 (4); v WI 1964 (4); v In 1959 (5) 1964 (2); v P 1959 (3)*

O'Reilly, W. J. 27: v E 1932 (5) 1936 (5); v SA 1931 (2); *v E 1934 (5) 1938 (4); v SA 1935 (5); v NZ 1945 (1)*

Oxenham, R. K. 7: v E 1928 (3); v SA 1931 (1); v WI 1930 (3)

Palmer, G. E. 17: v E 1881 (4) 1882 (4) 1884 (2); *v E 1880 (1) 1884 (3) 1886 (3)*

Park, R. L. 1: v E 1920

Pascoe, L. S. 14: v E 1979 (2); v WI 1979 (1) 1981 (1); v NZ 1980 (3); v In 1980 (3); *v E 1977 (3) 1980 (1)*

Pellew, C. E. 10: v E 1920 (4); *v E 1921 (5); v SA 1921 (1)*

Phillips, W. B. 27: v WI 1984 (2); v NZ 1985 (3); v In 1985 (3); v P 1983 (5); *v E 1985 (6); v WI 1983 (5); v NZ 1985 (3)*

Philpott, P. I. 8: v E 1965 (3); *v WI 1964 (5)*

Ponsford, W. H. 29: v E 1924 (5) 1928 (2) 1932 (3); v SA 1931 (4); v WI 1930 (5); *v E 1926 (2) 1930 (4) 1934 (4)*

Pope, R. J. 1: v E 1884

Rackemann, C. G. 12: v E 1982 (1) 1990 (1); v WI 1984 (1); v NZ 1989 (1); v P 1983 (2) 1989 (3); v SL 1989 (1); *v WI 1983 (1); v NZ 1989 (1)*

Ransford, V. S. 20: v E 1907 (5) 1911 (5); v SA 1910 (5); *v E 1909 (5)*

Redpath, I. R. 66: v E 1965 (1) 1970 (6) 1974 (6); v SA 1963 (1); v WI 1968 (5) 1975 (6); v In 1967 (3); v P 1972 (3); *v E 1964 (5) 1968 (5); v SA 1966 (5) 1969 (4); v WI 1972 (5); v NZ 1973 (3); v In 1964 (2) 1969 (5); v P 1964 (1)*

Reedman, J. C. 1: v E 1894

Reid, B. A. 24: v E 1986 (5) 1990 (4); v NZ 1987 (2); v In 1985 (3); *v WI 1990 (2); v NZ 1985 (3); v In 1986 (2); v P 1988 (3)*

Renneberg, D. A. 8: v In 1967 (3); *v SA 1966 (5)*

Richardson, A. J. 9: v E 1924 (4); *v E 1926 (5)*

Richardson, V. Y. 19: v E 1924 (3) 1928 (2) 1932 (5); *v E 1930 (4); v SA 1935 (5)*

Rigg, K. E. 8: v E 1936 (3); v SA 1931 (4); v WI 1930 (1)

Ring, D. T. 13: v SA 1952 (5); v WI 1951 (5); v In 1947 (1); *v E 1948 (1) 1953 (1)*

Ritchie, G. M. 30: v E 1986 (4); v WI 1984 (1); v NZ 1985 (3); v In 1985 (2); *v E 1985 (6); v WI 1983 (5); v NZ 1985 (3); v In 1986 (3); v P 1982 (3)*

Rixon, S. J. 13: v WI 1984 (3); v In 1977 (5); *v WI 1977 (5)*

Robertson, W. R. 1: v E 1884

Robinson, R. D. 3: *v E 1977 (3)*

Robinson, R. H. 1: v E 1936

Rorke, G. F. 4: v E 1958 (2); *v In 1959 (2)*

Rutherford, J. W. 1: *v In 1956*

Ryder, J. 20: v E 1920 (5) 1924 (3) 1928 (5); *v E 1926 (4); v SA 1921 (3)*


Saggers, R. A. 6: *v E 1948 (1); v SA 1949 (5)*

Saunders, J. V. 14: v E 1901 (1) 1903 (2) 1907 (5); *v E 1902 (4); v SA 1902 (2)*

Scott, H. J. H. 8: v E 1884 (2); *v E 1884 (3) 1886 (3)*

Sellers, R. H. D. 1: *v In 1964*

Serjeant, C. S. 12: v In 1977 (4); *v E 1977 (3); v WI 1977 (5)*

Sheahan, A. P. 31: v E 1970 (2); v WI 1968 (5); v NZ 1973 (2); v In 1967 (4); v P 1972 (2); *v E 1968 (5) 1972 (2); v SA 1969 (4); v In 1969 (5)*

Shepherd, B. K. 9: v E 1962 (2); v SA 1963 (4); v P 1964 (1); *v WI 1964 (2)*

Sievers, M. W. 3: v E 1936 (3)

Simpson, R. B. 62: v E 1958 (1) 1962 (5) 1965 (3); v SA 1963 (5); v WI 1960 (5); v In 1967 (3) 1977 (5); v P 1964 (1); *v E 1961 (5) 1964 (5); v SA 1957 (5) 1966 (5); v WI 1964 (5) 1977 (5); v In 1964 (3); v P 1964 (1)*

Sincock, D. J. 3: v E 1965 (1); v P 1964 (1); *v WI 1964 (1)*

Slater, K. N. 1: v E 1958

Sleep, P. R. 14: v E 1986 (3) 1987 (1); v NZ 1987 (3); v P 1978 (1) 1989 (1); v SL 1989 (1); *v In 1979 (2); v P 1982 (1) 1988 (1)*

Slight, J. 1: *v E 1880*

Smith, D. B. M. 2: *v E 1912 (2)*

Smith, S. B. 3: *v WI 1983 (3)*

Spofforth, F. R. 18: v E 1876 (1) 1878 (1) 1881 (1) 1882 (4) 1884 (3) 1886 (1); *v E 1882 (1) 1884 (3) 1886 (3)*

Stackpole, K. R. 43: v E 1965 (2) 1970 (6); v WI 1968 (5); v NZ 1973 (3); v P 1972 (1); *v E 1972 (5); v SA 1966 (5) 1969 (4); v WI 1972 (4); v NZ 1973 (3); v In 1969 (5)*

Stevens, G. B. 4: *v In 1959 (2); v P 1959 (2)*


Taber, H. B. 16: v WI 1968 (1); *v E 1968 (1); v SA 1966 (5); 1969 (4); v In 1969 (5)*

Tallon, D. 21: v E 1946 (5) 1950 (5); v In 1947 (5); *v E 1948 (4) 1953 (1); v NZ 1945 (1)*

Taylor, J. M. 20: v E 1920 (5) 1924 (5); *v E 1921 (5) 1926 (3); v SA 1921 (2)*

Taylor, M. A. 25: v E 1990 (5); v WI 1988 (2); v NZ 1989 (1); v P 1989 (3); v SL 1989 (2); *v E 1989 (4); v WI 1990 (5); v NZ 1989 (1)*

Taylor, P. L. 11: v E 1986 (1) 1987 (1); v WI 1988 (2); v P 1989 (2); v SL 1987 (1); *v WI 1990 (1); v NZ 1989 (1); v P 1988 (2)*

Thomas, G. 8: v E 1965 (3); *v WI 1964 (5)*

Thompson, N. 2: v E 1876 (2)

Thoms, G. R. 1: v WI 1951

Thomson, A. L. 4: v E 1970 (4)

Thomson, J. R. 51: v E 1974 (5) 1979 (1) 1982 (4); v WI 1975 (6) 1979 (1) 1981 (2); v In 1977 (5); v P 1972 (1) 1976 (1) 1981 (3); *v E 1975 (4) 1977 (5) 1985 (2); v WI 1977 (5); v NZ 1981 (3); v P 1982 (3)*

Thurlow, H. M. 1: v SA 1931

Toohey, P. M. 15: v E 1978 (5) 1979 (1); v WI 1979 (1); v In 1977 (5); *v WI 1977 (3)*

Toshack, E. R. H. 12: v E 1946 (5); v In 1947 (2); *v E 1948 (4); v NZ 1945 (1)*

Travers, J. P. F. 1: v E 1901

Tribe, G. E. 3: v E 1946 (3)

Trott, A. E. 3: v E 1894 (3)

Trott, G. H. S. 24: v E 1891 (3) 1894 (5) 1897 (5); *v E 1888 (3) 1890 (2) 1893 (3) 1896 (3)*

Trumble, H. 32: v E 1894 (1) 1897 (5) 1901 (5) 1903 (4); *v E 1890 (2) 1893 (3) 1896 (3) 1899 (5) 1902 (3); v SA 1902 (1)*

Trumble, J. W. 7: v E 1884 (4); *v E 1886 (3)*

Trumper, V. T. 48: v E 1901 (5) 1903 (5) 1907 (5) 1911 (5); v SA 1910 (5); *v E 1899 (5) 1902 (5) 1905 (5) 1909 (5); v SA 1902 (3)*

Turner, A. 14: v WI 1975 (6); v P 1976 (3); *v E 1975 (3); v NZ 1976 (2)*

Turner, C. T. B. 17: v E 1886 (2) 1887 (1) 1891 (3) 1894 (3); *v E 1888 (3) 1890 (2) 1893 (3)*

Veivers, T. R. 21: v E 1965 (4); v SA 1963 (3); v P 1964 (1); *v E 1964 (5); v SA 1966 (4); v In 1964 (3); v P 1964 (1)*

Veletta, M. R. J. 8: v E 1987 (1); v WI 1988 (2); v NZ 1987 (3); v P 1989 (1); v SL 1987 (1)

Waite, M. G. 2: *v E 1938 (2)*

Walker, M. H. N. 34: v E 1974 (6); 1976 (1); v WI 1975 (3); v NZ 1973 (1); v P 1972 (2) 1976 (2); *v E 1975 (4); 1977 (5); v WI 1972 (5); v NZ 1973 (3) 1976 (2)*

Wall, T. W. 18: v E 1928 (1) 1932 (4); v SA 1931 (3); v WI 1930 (1); *v E 1930 (5) 1934 (4)*

Walters, F. H. 1: v E 1884

Walters, K. D. 74: v E 1965 (5) 1970 (6) 1974 (6) 1976 (1); v WI 1968 (4); v NZ 1973 (3) 1980 (3); v In 1967 (2) 1980 (3); v P 1972 (1) 1976 (3); *v E 1968 (5) 1972 (4) 1975 (4) 1977 (5); v SA 1969 (4); v WI 1972 (5); v NZ 1973 (3) 1976 (2); v In 1969 (5)*

Ward, F. A. 4: v E 1936 (3); *v E 1938 (1)*

Watkins, J. R. 1: v P 1972

Watson, G. D. 5: *v E 1972 (2); v SA 1966 (3)*

Watson, W. 4: v E 1954 (1); *v WI 1954 (3)*

Waugh, M. E. 7: v E 1990 (3); *v WI 1990 (5)*

Waugh, S. R. 44: v E 1986 (5) 1987 (1) 1990 (3); v WI 1988 (5); v NZ 1987 (3) 1989 (1); v In 1985 (2); v P 1989 (3); v SL 1987 (1) 1989 (2); *v E 1989 (6); v WI 1990 (2); v NZ 1985 (3) 1989 (1); v In 1986 (3); v P 1988 (3)*

Wellham, D. M. 6: v E 1986 (1); v WI 1981 (1); v P 1981 (2); *v E 1981 (1) 1985 (1)*

Wessels, K. C. 24: v E 1982 (4); v WI 1984 (5); v NZ 1985 (1); v P 1983 (5); *v E 1985 (6); v WI 1983 (2); v SL 1982 (1)*

Whatmore, D. F. 7: v P 1978 (2); *v In 1979 (5)*

Whitney, M. R. 6: v WI 1988 (1); v NZ 1987 (1); *v E 1981 (2); v WI 1990 (2)*

Whitty, W. J. 14: v E 1911 (2); v SA 1910 (5); *v E 1909 (1) 1912 (3); v SA 1912 (3)*

Wiener, J. M. 6: v E 1979 (2); v WI 1979 (2); *v P 1979 (2)*

Wilson, J. W. 1: *v In 1956*

Wood, G. M. 59: v E 1978 (6) 1982 (1); v WI 1981 (3) 1984 (5) 1988 (3); v NZ 1980 (3); v In 1977 (1) 1980 (3); v P 1978 (1) 1981 (3); *v E 1980 (1) 1981 (6) 1985 (5); v WI 1977 (5) 1983 (1); v NZ 1981 (3); v In 1979 (2); v P 1982 (3) 1988 (3); v SL 1982 (1)*

Woodcock, A. J. 1: v NZ 1973

Woodfull, W. M. 35: v E 1928 (5) 1932 (5); v SA 1931 (5); v WI 1930 (5); *v E 1926 (5) 1930 (5) 1934 (5)*

Woods, S. M. J. 3: *v E 1888 (3)*

Woolley, R. D. 2: *v WI 1983 (1); v SL 1982 (1)*

Worrall, J. 11: v E 1884 (1) 1887 (1) 1894 (1) 1897 (1); *v E 1888 (3) 1899 (4)*

Wright, K. J. 10: v E 1978 (2); v P 1978 (2); *v In 1979 (6)*

Yallop, G. N. 39: v E 1978 (6); v WI 1975 (3) 1984 (1); v In 1977 (1); v P 1978 (1) 1981 (1) 1983 (5); *v E 1980 (1) 1981 (6); v WI 1977 (4); v In 1979 (3); v SL 1982 (1)*

Yardley, B. 33: v E 1978 (4) 1982 (5); v WI 1981 (3); v In 1977 (1) 1980 (2); v P 1978 (1) 1981 (3); *v WI 1977 (5); v NZ 1981 (3); v In 1979 (3); v P 1982 (2); v SL 1982 (1)*

Zoehrer, T. J. 10: v E 1986 (4); *v NZ 1985 (3); v In 1986 (3)*

## SOUTH AFRICA

Number of Test cricketers: 235

Adcock, N. A. T. 26: v E 1956 (5); v A 1957 (5); v NZ 1953 (5) 1961 (2); *v E 1955 (4) 1960 (5)*
Anderson, J. H. 1: v A 1902
Ashley, W. H. 1: v E 1888


Bacher, A. 12: v A 1966 (5) 1969 (4); *v E 1965 (3)*
Balaskas, X. C. 9: v E 1930 (2) 1938 (1); v A 1935 (3); *v E 1935 (1); v NZ 1931 (2)*
Barlow, E. J. 30: v E 1964 (5); v A 1966 (5) 1969 (4); v NZ 1961 (5); *v E 1965 (3); v A 1963 (5); v NZ 1963 (3)*
Baumgartner, H. V. 1: v E 1913
Beaumont, R. 5: v E 1913 (2); *v E 1912 (1); v A 1912 (2)*
Begbie, D. W. 5: v E 1948 (3); v A 1949 (2)
Bell, A. J. 16: v E 1930 (3); *v E 1929 (3) 1935 (3); v A 1931 (5); v NZ 1931 (2)*
Bisset, M. 3: v E 1898 (2) 1909 (1)
Bissett, G. F. 4: v E 1927 (4)
Blanckenberg, J. M. 18: v E 1913 (5) 1922 (5); v A 1921 (3); *v E 1924 (5)*
Bland, K. C. 21: v E 1964 (5); v A 1966 (1); v NZ 1961 (5); *v E 1965 (3); v A 1963 (4); v NZ 1963 (3)*
Bock, E. G. 1: v A 1935
Bond, G. E. 1: v E 1938
Botten, J. T. 3: *v E 1965 (3)*
Brann, W. H. 3: v E 1922 (3)
Briscoe, A. W. 2: v E 1938 (1); v A 1935 (1)
Bromfield, H. D. 9: v E 1964 (3); v NZ 1961 (5); *v E 1965 (1)*
Brown, L. S. 2: *v A 1931 (1); v NZ 1931 (1)*
Burger, C. G. de V. 2: v A 1957 (2)
Burke, S. F. 2: v E 1964 (1); v NZ 1961 (1)
Buys, I. D. 1: v E 1922


Cameron, H. B. 26: v E 1927 (5) 1930 (5); *v E 1929 (4) 1935 (5); v A 1931 (5); v NZ 1931 (2)*
Campbell, T. 5: v E 1909 (4); *v E 1912 (1)*
Carlstein, P. R. 8: v A 1957 (1); *v E 1960 (5); v A 1963 (2)*
Carter, C. P. 10: v E 1913 (2); v A 1921 (3); *v E 1912 (2) 1924 (3)*
Catterall, R. H. 24: v E 1922 (5) 1927 (5) 1930 (4); *v E 1924 (5) 1929 (5)*
Chapman, H. W. 2: v E 1913 (1); v A 1921 (1)
Cheetham, J. E. 24: v E 1948 (1); v A 1949 (3); v NZ 1953 (5); *v E 1951 (5) 1955 (3); v A 1952 (5); v NZ 1952 (2)*
Chevalier, G. A. 1: v A 1969
Christy, J. A. J. 10: v E 1930 (1); *v E 1929 (2); v A 1931 (5); v NZ 1931 (2)*
Chubb, G. W. A. 5: *v E 1951 (5)*
Cochran, J. A. K. 1: v E 1930
Coen, S. K. 2: v E 1927 (2)
Commaille, J. M. M. 12: v E 1909 (5) 1927 (2); *v E 1924 (5)*
Conyngham, D. P. 1: v E 1922
Cook, F. J. 1: v E 1895
Cooper, A. H. C. 1: v E 1913
Cox, J. L. 3: v E 1913 (3)
Cripps, G. 1: v E 1891
Crisp, R. J. 9: v A 1935 (4); *v E 1935 (5)*
Curnow, S. H. 7: v E 1930 (3); *v A 1931 (4)*


Dalton, E. L. 15: v E 1930 (1) 1938 (4); v A 1935 (1); *v E 1929 (1) 1935 (4); v A 1931 (2); v NZ 1931 (2)*
Davies, E. Q. 5: v E 1938 (3); v A 1935 (2)
Dawson, O. C. 9: v E 1948 (4); *v E 1947 (5)*
Deane, H. G. 17: v E 1927 (5) 1930 (2); *v E 1924 (5) 1929 (5)*
Dixon, C. D. 1: v E 1913

Dower, R. R. 1: v E 1898
Draper, R. G. 2: v A 1949 (2)
Duckworth, C. A. R. 2: v E 1956 (2)
Dumbrill, R. 5: v A 1966 (2); *v E 1965 (3)*
Duminy, J. P. 3: v E 1927 (2); *v E 1929 (1)*
Dunell, O. R. 2: v E 1888 (2)
Du Preez, J. H. 2: v A 1966 (2)
Du Toit, J. F. 1: v E 1891
Dyer, D. V. 3: *v E 1947 (3)*

Elgie, M. K. 3: v NZ 1961 (3)
Endean, W. R. 28: v E 1956 (5); v A 1957 (5); v NZ 1953 (5); *v E 1951 (1) 1955 (5); v A 1952 (5); v NZ 1952 (2)*

Farrer, W. S. 6: v NZ 1961 (3); *v NZ 1963 (3)*
Faulkner, G. A. 25: v E 1905 (5) 1909 (5); *v E 1907 (3) 1912 (3) 1924 (1); v A 1910 (5) 1912 (3)*
Fellows-Smith, J. P. 4: *v E 1960 (4)*
Fichardt, C. G. 2: v E 1891 (1) 1895 (1)
Finlason, C. E. 1: v E 1888
Floquet, C. E. 1: v E 1909
Francis, H. H. 2: v E 1898 (2)
Francois, C. M. 5: v E 1922 (5)
Frank, C. N. 3: v A 1921 (3)
Frank, W. H. B. 1: v E 1895
Fuller, E. R. H. 7: v A 1957 (1); *v E 1955 (2); v A 1952 (2); v NZ 1952 (2)*
Fullerton, G. M. 7: v A 1949 (2); *v E 1947 (2) 1951 (3)*
Funston, K. J. 18: v E 1956 (3); v A 1957 (5); v NZ 1953 (3); *v A 1952 (5); v NZ 1952 (2)*

Gamsy, D. 2: v A 1969 (2)
Gleeson, R. A. 1: v E 1895
Glover, G. K. 1: v E 1895
Goddard, T. L. 41: v E 1956 (5) 1964 (5); v A 1957 (5) 1966 (5) 1969 (3); *v E 1955 (5) 1960 (5); v A 1963 (5); v NZ 1963 (3)*
Gordon, N. 5: v E 1938 (5)
Graham, R. 2: v E 1898 (2)
Grieveson, R. E. 2: v E 1938 (2)
Griffin, G. M. 2: *v E 1960 (2)*

Hall, A. E. 7: v E 1922 (4) 1927 (2) 1930 (1)
Hall, G. G. 1: v E 1964
Halliwell, E. A. 8: v E 1891 (1) 1895 (3) 1898 (1); v A 1902 (3)
Halse, C. G. 3: *v A 1963 (3)*
Hands, P. A. M. 7: v E 1913 (5); v A 1921 (1); *v E 1924 (1)*
Hands, R. H. M. 1: v E 1913
Hanley, M. A. 1: v E 1948
Harris, T. A. 3: v E 1948 (1); *v E 1947 (2)*
Hartigan, G. P. D. 5: v E 1913 (3); *v E 1912 (1); v A 1912 (1)*
Harvey, R. L. 2: v A 1935 (2)
Hathorn, C. M. H. 12: v E 1905 (5); v A 1902 (3); *v E 1907 (3); v A 1910 (1)*
Hearne, F. 4: v E 1891 (1) 1895 (3)
Hearne, G. A. L. 3: v E 1922 (2); *v E 1924 (1)*
Heine, P. S. 14: v E 1956 (5); v A 1957 (4); v NZ 1961 (1); *v E 1955 (4)*
Hime, C. F. W. 1: v E 1895
Hutchinson, P. 2: v E 1888 (2)

Ironside, D. E. J. 3: v NZ 1953 (3)
Irvine, B. L. 4: v A 1969 (4)

Johnson, C. L. 1: v E 1895

Keith, H. J. 8: v E 1956 (3); *v E 1955 (4); v A 1952 (1)*
Kempis, G. A. 1: v E 1888

Kotze, J. J. 3: v A 1902 (2); *v E 1907 (1)*
Kuys, F. 1: v E 1898


Lance, H. R. 13: v A 1966 (5) 1969 (3); v NZ 1961 (2); *v E 1965 (3)*
Langton, A. B. C. 15: v E 1938 (5); v A 1935 (5); *v E 1935 (5)*
Lawrence, G. B. 5: v NZ 1961 (5)
Le Roux, F. le S. 1: v E 1913
Lewis, P. T. 1: v E 1913
Lindsay, D. T. 19: v E 1964 (3); v A 1966 (5) 1969 (2); *v E 1965 (3); v A 1963 (3); v NZ 1963 (3)*
Lindsay, J. D. 3: *v E 1947 (3)*
Lindsay, N. V. 1: v A 1921
Ling, W. V. S. 6: v E 1922 (3); v A 1921 (3)
Llewellyn, C. B. 15: v E 1895 (1) 1898 (1); v A 1902 (3); *v E 1912 (3); v A 1910 (5) 1912 (2)*
Lundie, E. B. 1: v E 1913


Macaulay, M. J. 1: v E 1964
McCarthy, C. N. 15: v E 1948 (5); v A 1949 (5); *v E 1951 (5)*
McGlew, D. J. 34: v E 1956 (1); v A 1957 (5); v NZ 1953 (5) 1961 (5); *v E 1951 (2) 1955 (5) 1960 (5); v A 1952 (4); v NZ 1952 (2)*
McKinnon, A. H. 8: v E 1964 (2); v A 1966 (2); v NZ 1961 (1); *v E 1960 (1) 1965 (2)*
McLean, R. A. 40: v E 1956 (5) 1964 (2); v A 1957 (4); v NZ 1953 (4) 1961 (5); *v E 1951 (3) 1955 (5) 1960 (5); v A 1952 (5); v NZ 1952 (2)*
McMillan, Q. 13: v E 1930 (5); *v E 1929 (2); v A 1931 (4); v NZ 1931 (2)*
Mann, N. B. F. 19: v E 1948 (5); v A 1949 (5); *v E 1947 (5) 1951 (4)*
Mansell, P. N. F. 13: *v E 1951 (2) 1955 (4); v A 1952 (5); v NZ 1952 (2)*
Markham, L. A. 1: v E 1948
Marx, W. F. E. 3: v A 1921 (3)
Meintjes, D. J. 2: v E 1922 (2)
Melle, M. G. 7: v A 1949 (2); *v E 1951 (1); v A 1952 (4)*
Melville, A. 11: v E 1938 (5) 1948 (1); *v E 1947 (5)*
Middleton, J. 6: v E 1895 (2) 1898 (2); v A 1902 (2)
Mills, C. 1: v E 1891
Milton, W. H. 3: v E 1888 (2) 1891 (1)
Mitchell, B. 42: v E 1930 (5) 1938 (5) 1948 (5); v A 1935 (5); *v E 1929 (5) 1935 (5) 1947 (5); v A 1931 (5); v NZ 1931 (2)*
Mitchell, F. 3: *v E 1912 (1); v A 1912 (2)*
Morkel, D. P. B. 16: v E 1927 (5); *v E 1929 (5); v A 1931 (5); v NZ 1931 (1)*
Murray, A. R. A. 10: v NZ 1953 (4); *v A 1952 (4); v NZ 1952 (2)*


Nel, J. D. 6: v A 1949 (5) 1957 (1)
Newberry, C. 4: v E 1913 (4)
Newson, E. S. 3: v E 1930 (1) 1938 (2)
Nicholson, F. 4: v A 1935 (4)
Nicolson, J. F. W. 3: v E 1927 (3)
Norton, N. O. 1: v E 1909
Nourse, A. D. 34: v E 1938 (5) 1948 (5); v A 1935 (5) 1949 (5); *v E 1935 (4) 1947 (5) 1951 (5)*
Nourse, A. W. 45: v E 1905 (5) 1909 (5) 1913 (5) 1922 (5); v A 1902 (3) 1921 (3); *v E 1907 (3) 1912 (3) 1924 (5); v A 1910 (5) 1912 (3)*
Nupen, E. P. 17: v E 1922 (4) 1927 (5) 1930 (3); v A 1921 (2) 1935 (1); *v E 1924 (2)*


Ochse, A. E. 2: v E 1888 (2)
Ochse, A. L. 3: v E 1927 (1); *v E 1929 (2)*
O'Linn, S. 7: v NZ 1961 (2); *v E 1960 (5)*
Owen-Smith, H. G. 5: *v E 1929 (5)*


Palm, A. W. 1: v E 1927
Parker, G. M. 2: *v E 1924 (2)*
Parkin, D. C. 1: v E 1891
Partridge, J. T. 11: v E 1964 (3); *v A 1963 (5); v NZ 1963 (3)*
Pearse, O. C. 3: *v A 1910 (3)*
Pegler, S. J. 16: v E 1909 (1); *v E 1912 (3) 1924 (5); v A 1910 (4) 1912 (3)*
Pithey, A. J. 17: v E 1956 (3) 1964 (5); *v E 1960 (2); v A 1963 (4); v NZ 1963 (3)*

Pithey, D. B. 8: v E 1966 (2); *v A 1963 (3); v NZ 1963 (3)*
Plimsoll, J. B. 1: *v E 1947*
Pollock, P. M. 28: v E 1964 (5); v A 1966 (5) 1969 (4); v NZ 1961 (3); *v E 1965 (3); v A 1963 (5); v NZ 1963 (3)*
Pollock, R. G. 23: v E 1964 (5); v A 1966 (5) 1969 (4); *v E 1965 (3); v A 1963 (5); v NZ 1963 (1)*
Poore, R. M. 3: v E 1895 (3)
Pothecary, J. E. 3: *v E 1960 (3)*
Powell, A. W. 1: v E 1898
Prince, C. F. H. 1: v E 1898
Procter, M. J. 7: v A 1966 (3) 1969 (4)
Promnitz, H. L. E. 2: v E 1927 (2)

Quinn, N. A. 12: v E 1930 (1); *v E 1929 (4); v A 1931 (5); v NZ 1931 (2)*

Reid, N. 1: v A 1921
Richards, A. R. 1: v E 1895
Richards, B. A. 4: v A 1969 (4)
Richards, W. H. 1: v E 1888
Robertson, J. B. 3: v A 1935 (3)
Rose-Innes, A. 2: v E 1888 (2)
Routledge, T. W. 4: v E 1891 (1) 1895 (3)
Rowan, A. M. B. 15: v E 1948 (5); *v E 1947 (5) 1951 (5)*
Rowan, E. A. B. 26: v E 1938 (4) 1948 (4); v A 1935 (3); 1949 (5); *v E 1935 (5) 1951 (5)*
Rowe, G. A. 5: v E 1895 (2) 1898 (2); v A 1902 (1)

Samuelson, S. V. 1: v E 1909
Schwarz, R. O. 20: v E 1905 (5) 1909 (4); *v E 1907 (3) 1912 (1); v A 1910 (5) 1912 (2)*
Seccull, A. W. 1: v E 1895
Seymour, M. A. 7: v E 1964 (2); v A 1969 (1); *v A 1963 (4)*
Shalders, W. A. 12: v E 1898 (1) 1905 (5); v A 1902 (3); *v E 1907 (3)*
Shepstone, G. H. 2: v E 1895 (1) 1898 (1)
Sherwell, P. W. 13: v E 1905 (5); *v E 1907 (3); v A 1910 (5)*
Siedle, I. J. 18: v E 1927 (1) 1930 (5); v A 1935 (5); *v E 1929 (3) 1935 (4)*
Sinclair, J. H. 25: v E 1895 (3) 1898 (2) 1905 (5) 1909 (4); v A 1902 (3); *v E 1907 (3); v A 1910 (5)*
Smith, C. J. E. 3: v A 1902 (3)
Smith, F. W. 3: v E 1888 (2) 1895 (1)
Smith, V. I. 9: v A 1949 (3) 1957 (1); *v E 1947 (4) 1955 (1)*
Snooke, S. D. 1: *v E 1907*
Snooke, S. J. 26: v E 1905 (5) 1909 (5) 1922 (3); *v E 1907 (3) 1912 (3); v A 1910 (5) 1912 (2)*
Solomon, W. R. 1: v E 1898
Stewart, R. B. 1: v E 1888
Stricker, L. A. 13: v E 1909 (4); *v E 1912 (2); v A 1910 (5) 1912 (2)*
Susskind, M. J. 5: *v E 1924 (5)*

Taberer, H. M. 1: v A 1902
Tancred, A. B. 2: v E 1888 (2)
Tancred, L. J. 14: v E 1905 (5) 1913 (1); v A 1902 (3); *v E 1907 (1) 1912 (2); v A 1912 (2)*
Tancred, V. M. 1: v E 1898
Tapscott, G. L. 1: v E 1913
Tapscott, L. E. 2: v E 1922 (2)
Tayfield, H. J. 37: v E 1956 (5); v A 1949 (5) 1957 (5); v NZ 1953 (5); *v E 1955 (5) 1960 (5); v A 1952 (5); v NZ 1952 (2)*
Taylor, A. I. 1: v E 1956
Taylor, D. 2: v E 1913 (2)
Taylor, H. W. 42: v E 1913 (5) 1922 (5) 1927 (5) 1930 (4); v A 1921 (3); *v E 1912 (3) 1924 (5) 1929 (3); v A 1912 (3) 1931 (5); v NZ 1931 (1)*
Theunissen, N. H. G. de J. 1: v E 1888
Thornton, P. G. 1: v A 1902
Tomlinson, D. S. 1: *v E 1935*
Traicos, A. J. 3: v A 1969 (3)
Trimborn, P. H. J. 4: v A 1966 (3) 1969 (1)
Tuckett, L. 9: v E 1948 (4); *v E 1947 (5)*

Tuckett, L. R. 1: v E 1913
Twentyman-Jones, P. S. 1: v A 1902

van der Bijl, P. G. V. 5: v E 1938 (5)
Van der Merwe, E. A. 2: v A 1935 (1); *v E 1929 (1)*
Van der Merwe, P. L. 15: v E 1964 (2); v A 1966 (5); *v E 1965 (3); v A 1963 (3); v NZ 1963 (2)*
Van Ryneveld, C. B. 19: v E 1956 (5); v A 1957 (4); v NZ 1953 (5); *v E 1951 (5)*
Varnals, G. D. 3: v E 1964 (3)
Viljoen, K. G. 27: v E 1930 (3) 1938 (4) 1948 (2); v A 1935 (4); *v E 1935 (4) 1947 (5); v A 1931 (4); v NZ 1931 (1)*
Vincent, C. L. 25: v E 1927 (5) 1930 (5); *v E 1929 (4) 1935 (4); v A 1931 (5); v NZ 1931 (2)*
Vintcent, C. H. 3: v E 1888 (2) 1891 (1)
Vogler, A. E. E. 15: v E 1905 (5) 1909 (5); *v E 1907 (3); v A 1910 (2)*

Wade, H. F. 10: v A 1935 (5); *v E 1935 (5)*
Wade, W. W. 11: v E 1938 (3) 1948 (5); v A 1949 (3)
Waite, J. H. B. 50: v E 1956 (5); 1964 (2); v A 1957 (5); v NZ 1953 (5) 1961 (5); *v E 1951 (4) 1955 (5) 1960 (5); v A 1952 (5) 1963 (4); v NZ 1952 (2) 1963 (3)*
Walter, K. A. 2: v NZ 1961 (2)
Ward, T. A. 23: v E 1913 (5) 1922 (5); v A 1921 (3); *v E 1912 (2) 1924 (5); v A 1912 (3)*
Watkins, J. C. 15: v E 1956 (2); v A 1949 (3); v NZ 1953 (3); *v A 1952 (5); v NZ 1952 (2)*
Wesley, C. 3: *v E 1960 (3)*
Westcott, R. J. 5: v A 1957 (2); v NZ 1953 (3)
White, G. C. 17: v E 1905 (5) 1909 (4); *v E 1907 (3) 1912 (2); v A 1912 (3)*
Willoughby, J. T. I. 2: v E 1895 (2)
Wimble, C. S. 1: v E 1891
Winslow, P. L. 5: v A 1949 (2); *v E 1955 (3)*
Wynne, O. E. 6: v E 1948 (3); v A 1949 (3)

Zulch, J. W. 16: v E 1909 (5) 1913 (3); v A 1921 (3); *v A 1910 (5)*

# WEST INDIES

Number of Test cricketers: 198

Achong, E. 6: v E 1929 (1) 1934 (2); *v E 1933 (3)*
Alexander, F. C. M. 25: v E 1959 (5); v P 1957 (5); *v E 1957 (2); v A 1960 (5); v In 1958 (5); v P 1958 (3)*
Ali, Imtiaz 1: v In 1975
Ali, Inshan 12: v E 1973 (2); v A 1972 (3); v In 1970 (1); v P 1976 (1); v NZ 1971 (3); *v E 1973 (1); v A 1975 (1)*
Allan, D. W. 5: v A 1964 (1); v In 1961 (2); *v E 1966 (2)*
Allen, I. B. A. 2: *v E 1991 (2)*
Ambrose, C. E. L. 33: v E 1989 (3); v A 1990 (5); v In 1988 (4); v P 1987 (5); *v E 1988 (5) 1991 (5); v A 1988 (5); v P 1990 (3)*
Arthurton, K. L. T. 5: v In 1988 (4); *v E 1988 (1)*
Asgarali, N. 2: *v E 1957 (2)*
Atkinson, D. St E. 22: v E 1953 (4); v A 1954 (4); v P 1957 (1); *v E 1957 (2); v A 1951 (2); v NZ 1951 (1) 1955 (4); v In 1948 (4)*
Atkinson, E. St E. 8: v P 1957 (3); *v In 1958 (3); v P 1958 (2)*
Austin, R. A. 2: v A 1977 (2)

Bacchus, S. F. A. F. 19: v A 1977 (2); *v E 1980 (5); v A 1981 (2); v In 1978 (6); v P 1980 (4)*
Baichan, L. 3: *v A 1975 (1); v P 1974 (2)*
Baptiste, E. A. E. 10: v E 1989 (1); v A 1983 (3); *v E 1984 (5); v In 1983 (1)*
Barrett, A. G. 6: v E 1973 (2); v In 1970 (2); *v In 1974 (2)*
Barrow, I. 11: v E 1929 (1) 1934 (1); *v E 1933 (3) 1939 (1); v A 1930 (5)*
Bartlett, E. L. 5: *v E 1928 (1); v A 1930 (4)*
Benjamin, W. K. M. 8: v In 1988 (1); v P 1987 (3); *v E 1988 (3); v In 1987 (1)*
Best, C. A. 8: v E 1985 (3) 1989 (3); *v P 1990 (2)*

Betancourt, N. 1: v E 1929
Binns, A. P. 5: v A 1954 (1); v In 1952 (1); *v NZ 1955 (3)*
Birkett, L. S. 4: *v A 1930 (4)*
Bishop, I. R. 11: v E 1989 (4); v In 1988 (4); *v P 1990 (3)*
Boyce, K. D. 21: v E 1973 (4); v A 1972 (4); v In 1970 (1); *v E 1973 (3); v A 1975 (4); v In 1974 (3); v P 1974 (2)*
Browne, C. R. 4: v E 1929 (2); *v E 1928 (2)*
Butcher, B. F. 44: v E 1959 (2) 1967 (5); v A 1964 (5); *v E 1963 (5) 1966 (5) 1969 (3); v A 1968 (5); v NZ 1968 (3); v In 1958 (5) 1966 (3); v P 1958 (3)*
Butler, L. 1: v A 1954
Butts, C. G. 7: v NZ 1984 (1); *v NZ 1986 (1); v In 1987 (3); v P 1986 (3)*
Bynoe, M. R. 4: *v In 1966 (3); v P 1958 (1)*

Camacho, G. S. 11: v E 1967 (5); v In 1970 (2); *v E 1969 (2); v A 1968 (2)*
Cameron, F. J. 5: *v In 1948 (5)*
Cameron, J. H. 2: *v E 1939 (2)*
Carew, G. M. 4: v E 1934 (1) 1947 (2); *v In 1948 (1)*
Carew, M. C. 19: v E 1967 (1); v NZ 1971 (3); v In 1970 (3); *v E 1963 (2) 1966 (1) 1969 (1); v A 1968 (5); v NZ 1968 (3)*
Challenor, G. 3: *v E 1928 (3)*
Chang, H. S. 1: *v In 1978*
Christiani, C. M. 4: v E 1934 (4)
Christiani, R. J. 22: v E 1947 (4) 1953 (1); v In 1952 (2); *v E 1950 (4); v A 1951 (5); v NZ 1951 (1); v In 1948 (5)*
Clarke, C. B. 3: *v E 1939 (3)*
Clarke, S. T. 11: v A 1977 (1); *v A 1981 (1); v In 1978 (5); v P 1980 (4)*
Constantine, L. N. 18: v E 1929 (3) 1934 (3); *v E 1928 (3) 1933 (1) 1939 (3); v A 1930 (5)*
Croft, C. E. H. 27: v E 1980 (4); v A 1977 (2); v P 1976 (5); *v E 1980 (3); v A 1979 (3) 1981 (3); v NZ 1979 (3); v P 1980 (4)*

Da Costa, O. C. 5: v E 1929 (1) 1934 (1); *v E 1933 (3)*
Daniel, W. W. 10: v A 1983 (2); v In 1975 (1); *v E 1976 (4); v In 1983 (3)*
Davis, B. A. 4: v A 1964 (4)
Davis, C. A. 15: v A 1972 (2); v NZ 1971 (5); v In 1970 (4); *v E 1969 (3); v A 1968 (1)*
Davis, W. W. 15: v A 1983 (1); v NZ 1984 (2); v In 1982 (1); *v E 1984 (1); v In 1983 (6) 1987 (4)*
De Caires, F. I. 3: v E 1929 (3)
Depeiza, C. C. 5: v A 1954 (3); *v NZ 1955 (2)*
Dewdney, T. 9: v A 1954 (2); v P 1957 (3); *v E 1957 (1); v NZ 1955 (5)*
Dowe, U. G. 4: v A 1972 (1); v NZ 1971 (1); v In 1970 (2)
Dujon, P. J. L. 81: v E 1985 (4) 1989 (4); v A 1983 (5) 1990 (5); v NZ 1984 (4); v In 1982 (5) 1988 (4); *v P 1987 (3); v E 1984 (5) 1988 (5) 1991 (5); v A 1981 (3) 1984 (5) 1988 (5); v NZ 1986 (3); v In 1983 (6) 1987 (4); v P 1986 (3) 1990 (3)*

Edwards, R. M. 5: *v A 1968 (2); v NZ 1968 (3)*

Ferguson, W. 8: v E 1947 (4) 1953 (1); *v In 1948 (3)*
Fernandes, M. P. 2: v E 1929 (1); *v E 1928 (1)*
Findlay, T. M. 10: v A 1972 (1); v NZ 1971 (5); v In 1970 (2); *v E 1969 (2)*
Foster, M. L. C. 14: v E 1973 (1); v A 1972 (4) 1977 (1); v NZ 1971 (3); v In 1970 (2); v P 1976 (1); *v E 1969 (1) 1973 (1)*
Francis, G. N. 10: v E 1929 (1); *v E 1928 (3) 1933 (1); v A 1930 (5)*
Frederick, M. C. 1: v E 1953
Fredericks, R. C. 59: v E 1973 (5); v A 1972 (5); v NZ 1971 (5); v In 1970 (4) 1975 (4); *v E 1969 (5) 1973 (3) 1976 (5); v A 1968 (4) 1975 (6); v In 1974 (5); v NZ 1968 (3); v P 1974 (2)*
Fuller, R. L. 1: v E 1934
Furlonge, H. A. 3: v A 1954 (1); *v NZ 1955 (2)*

Ganteaume, A. G. 1: v E 1947
Garner, J. 58: v E 1980 (4) 1985 (5); v A 1977 (2) 1983 (5); v NZ 1984 (4); v In 1982 (4); v P 1976 (5); *v E 1980 (5) 1984 (5); v A 1979 (3) 1981 (3) 1984 (5); v NZ 1979 (3) 1986 (2); v P 1980 (3)*
Gaskin, B. B. M. 2: v E 1947 (2)

Gibbs, G. L. R. 1: v A 1954

Gibbs, L. R. 79: v E 1967 (5) 1973 (5); v A 1964 (5) 1972 (5); v NZ 1971 (2); v In 1961 (5) 1970 (1); v P 1957 (4); *v E 1963 (5) 1966 (5) 1969 (3) 1973 (3); v A 1960 (3) 1968 (5) 1975 (6); v NZ 1968 (3); v In 1958 (1) 1966 (3) 1974 (5); v P 1958 (3) 1974 (2)*

Gilchrist, R. 13: v P 1957 (5); *v E 1957 (4); v In 1958 (4)*

Gladstone, G. 1: v E 1929

Goddard, J. D. C. 27: v E 1947 (4); *v E 1950 (4) 1957 (5); v A 1951 (4); v NZ 1951 (2) 1955 (3); v In 1948 (5)*

Gomes, H. A. 60: v E 1980 (4) 1985 (5); v A 1977 (3) 1983 (2); v NZ 1984 (4); v In 1982 (5); *v E 1976 (2) 1984 (5); v A 1981 (3) 1984 (5); v NZ 1986 (3); v In 1978 (6) 1983 (6); v P 1980 (4) 1986 (3)*

Gomez, G. E. 29: v E 1947 (4) 1953 (4); v In 1952 (4); *v E 1939 (2) 1950 (4); v A 1951 (5); v NZ 1951 (1); v In 1948 (5)*

Grant, G. C. 12: v E 1934 (4); *v E 1933 (3); v A 1930 (5)*

Grant, R. S. 7: v E 1934 (4); *v E 1939 (3)*

Gray, A. H. 5: *v NZ 1986 (2); v P 1986 (3)*

Greenidge, A. E. 6: v A 1977 (2); *v In 1978 (4)*

Greenidge, C. G. 108: v E 1980 (4) 1985 (5) 1989 (4); v A 1977 (2) 1983 (5) 1990 (5); v NZ 1984 (4); v In 1982 (5) 1988 (4); v P 1976 (5) 1987 (3); *v E 1976 (5) 1980 (5) 1984 (5) 1988 (4); v A 1975 (2) 1979 (3) 1981 (2) 1984 (5) 1988 (5); v NZ 1979 (3) 1986 (3); v In 1974 (5) 1983 (6) 1987 (3); v P 1986 (3) 1990 (3)*

Greenidge, G. A. 5: v A 1972 (3); v NZ 1971 (2)

Grell, M. G. 1: v E 1929

Griffith, C. C. 28: v E 1959 (1) 1967 (4); v A 1964 (5); *v E 1963 (5) 1966 (5); v A 1968 (3); v NZ 1968 (2); v In 1966 (3)*

Griffith, H. C. 13: v E 1929 (3); *v E 1928 (3) 1933 (2); v A 1930 (5)*

Guillen, S. C. 5: *v A 1951 (3); v NZ 1951 (2)*


Hall, W. W. 48: v E 1959 (5) 1967 (4); v A 1964 (5); v In 1961 (5); *v E 1963 (5) 1966 (5); v A 1960 (5) 1968 (2); v NZ 1968 (1); v In 1958 (5) 1966 (3); v P 1958 (3)*

Harper, R. A. 24: v E 1985 (2); v A 1983 (4); v NZ 1984 (1); *v E 1984 (5) 1988 (3); v A 1984 (2) 1988 (1); v In 1983 (2) 1987 (1); v P 1986 (3)*

Haynes, D. L. 102: v E 1980 (4) 1985 (5) 1989 (4); v A 1977 (2) 1983 (5) 1990 (5); v NZ 1984 (4); v In 1982 (5) 1988 (4); v P 1987 (3); *v E 1980 (5) 1984 (5) 1988 (4) 1991 (5); v A 1979 (3) 1981 (3) 1984 (5) 1988 (5); v NZ 1979 (3) 1986 (3); v In 1983 (6) 1987 (4); v P 1980 (4) 1986 (3) 1990 (3)*

Headley, G. A. 22: v E 1929 (4) 1934 (4) 1947 (1) 1953 (1); *v E 1933 (3) 1939 (3); v A 1930 (5); v In 1948 (1)*

Headley, R. G. A. 2: *v E 1973 (2)*

Hendriks, J. L. 20: v A 1964 (4); v In 1961 (1); *v E 1966 (3) 1969 (1); v A 1968 (5); v NZ 1968 (3); v In 1966 (3)*

Hoad, E. L. G. 4: v E 1929 (1); *v E 1928 (1) 1933 (2)*

Holder, V. A. 40: v E 1973 (1); v A 1972 (3) 1977 (3); v NZ 1971 (4); v In 1970 (3) 1975 (1); v P 1976 (1); *v E 1969 (3) 1973 (2) 1976 (4); v A 1975 (3); v In 1974 (4) 1978 (6); v P 1974 (2)*

Holding, M. A. 60: v E 1980 (4) 1985 (4); v A 1983 (3); v NZ 1984 (3); v In 1975 (4) 1982 (5); *v E 1976 (4) 1980 (5) 1984 (4); v A 1975 (3) 1979 (3) 1981 (3) 1984 (3); v NZ 1979 (3) 1986 (1); v In 1983 (6)*

Holford, D. A. J. 24: v E 1967 (4); v NZ 1971 (5); v In 1970 (1) 1975 (2); v P 1976 (1); *v E 1966 (5); v A 1968 (2); v NZ 1968 (3); v In 1966 (1)*

Holt, J. K. 17: v E 1953 (5); v A 1954 (5); *v In 1958 (5); v P 1958 (2)*

Hooper, C. L. 32: v E 1989 (3); v A 1990 (3); v P 1987 (3); *v E 1988 (5) 1991 (5); v A 1988 (3); v In 1987 (3); v P 1990 (3)*

Howard, A. B. 1: v NZ 1971

Hunte, C. C. 44: v E 1959 (5); v A 1964 (5); v In 1961 (5); v P 1957 (5); *v E 1963 (5) 1966 (5); v A 1960 (5); v In 1958 (5) 1966 (3); v P 1958 (1)*

Hunte, E. A. C. 3: v E 1929 (3)

Hylton, L. G. 6: v E 1934 (4); *v E 1939 (2)*


Johnson, H. H. H. 3: v E 1947 (1); *v E 1950 (2)*

Johnson, T. F. 1: *v E 1939*

Jones, C. M. 4: v E 1929 (1) 1934 (3)

Jones, P. E. 9: v E 1947 (1); *v E 1950 (2); v A 1951 (1); v In 1948 (5)*

Julien, B. D. 24: v E 1973 (5); v In 1975 (4); v P 1976 (1); *v E 1973 (3) 1976 (2); v A 1975 (3); v In 1974 (4); v P 1974 (2)*

Jumadeen, R. R. 12: v A 1972 (1) 1977 (2); v NZ 1971 (1); v In 1975 (4); v P 1976 (1); *v E 1976 (1); v In 1978 (2)*

Kallicharran, A. I. 66: v E 1973 (5); v A 1972 (5) 1977 (5); v NZ 1971 (2); v In 1975 (4); v P 1976 (5); *v E 1973 (3) 1976 (3) 1980 (5); v A 1975 (6) 1979 (3); v NZ 1979 (3); v In 1974 (5) 1978 (6); v P 1974 (2) 1980 (4)*

Kanhai, R. B. 79: v E 1959 (5) 1967 (5) 1973 (5); v A 1964 (5) 1972 (5); v In 1961 (5) 1970 (5); v P 1957 (5); *v E 1957 (5) 1963 (5) 1966 (5) 1973 (3); v A 1960 (5) 1968 (5); v In 1958 (5) 1966 (3); v P 1958 (3)*

Kentish, E. S. M. 2: v E 1947 (1) 1953 (1)

King, C. L. 9: v P 1976 (1); *v E 1976 (3) 1980 (1); v A 1979 (1); v NZ 1979 (3)*

King, F. M. 14: v E 1953 (3); v A 1954 (4); v In 1952 (5); *v NZ 1955 (2)*

King, L. A. 2: v E 1967 (1); v In 1961 (1)

Lambert, C. B. 1: *v E 1991*

Lara, B. C. 1: *v P 1990*

Lashley, P. D. 4: *v E 1966 (2); v A 1960 (2)*

Legall, R. 4: v In 1952 (4)

Lewis, D. M. 3: v In 1970 (3)

Lloyd, C. H. 110: v E 1967 (5) 1973 (5) 1980 (4); v A 1972 (3) 1977 (2) 1983 (4); v NZ 1971 (2); v In 1970 (5) 1975 (4) 1982 (5); v P 1976 (5); *v E 1969 (3) 1973 (3) 1976 (5) 1980 (4) 1984 (5); v A 1968 (4) 1975 (6) 1979 (2) 1981 (3) 1984 (5); v NZ 1968 (3) 1979 (3); v In 1966 (3) 1974 (5) 1983 (6); v P 1974 (2) 1980 (4)*

Logie, A. L. 52: v E 1989 (3); v A 1983 (1) 1990 (5); v NZ 1984 (4); v In 1982 (5) 1988 (4); v P 1987 (3); *v E 1988 (5) 1991 (4); v A 1988 (5); v NZ 1986 (3); v In 1983 (3) 1987 (4); v P 1990 (3)*

McMorris, E. D. A. 13: v E 1959 (4); v In 1961 (4); v P 1957 (1); *v E 1963 (2) 1966 (2)*

McWatt, C. A. 6: v E 1953 (5); v A 1954 (1)

Madray, I. S. 2: v P 1957 (2)

Marshall, M. D. 81: v E 1980 (1) 1985 (5) 1989 (2); v A 1983 (4) 1990 (5); v NZ 1984 (4); v In 1982 (5) 1988 (3); v P 1987 (2); *v E 1980 (4) 1984 (4) 1988 (5) 1991 (5); v A 1984 (5) 1988 (5); v NZ 1986 (3); v In 1978 (3) 1983 (6); v P 1980 (4) 1986 (3) 1990 (3)*

Marshall, N. E. 1: v A 1954

Marshall, R. E. 4: *v A 1951 (2); v NZ 1951 (2)*

Martin, F. R. 9: v E 1929 (1); *v E 1928 (3); v A 1930 (5)*

Martindale, E. A. 10: v E 1934 (4); *v E 1933 (3) 1939 (3)*

Mattis, E. H. 4: v E 1980 (4)

Mendonca, I. L. 2: v In 1961 (2)

Merry, C. A. 2: *v E 1933 (2)*

Miller, R. 1: v In 1952

Moodie, G. H. 1: v E 1934

Moseley, E. A. 2: v E 1989 (2)

Murray, D. A. 19: v E 1980 (4); v A 1977 (5); *v A 1981 (2); v In 1978 (6); v P 1980 (4)*

Murray, D. L. 62: v E 1967 (5) 1973 (5); v A 1972 (4) 1977 (2); v In 1975 (4); v P 1976 (5); *v E 1963 (5) 1973 (3) 1976 (5) 1980 (5); v A 1975 (6) 1979 (3); v NZ 1979 (3); v In 1974 (5); v P 1974 (2)*

Nanan, R. 1: *v P 1980*

Neblett, J. M. 1: v E 1934

Noreiga, J. M. 4: v In 1970 (4)

Nunes, R. K. 4: v E 1929 (1); *v E 1928 (3)*

Nurse, S. M. 29: v E 1959 (1) 1967 (5); v A 1964 (4); v In 1961 (1); *v E 1966 (5); v A 1960 (3) 1968 (5); v NZ 1968 (3); v In 1966 (2)*

Padmore, A. L. 2: v In 1975 (1); *v E 1976 (1)*

Pairaudeau, B. H. 13: v E 1953 (2); v In 1952 (5): *v E 1957 (2); v NZ 1955 (4)*

Parry, D. R. 12: v A 1977 (5); *v NZ 1979 (3); v In 1978 (6)*

Passailaigue, C. C. 1: v E 1929

Patterson, B. P. 26: v E 1985 (5) 1989 (1); v A 1990 (5); v P 1987 (1); *v E 1988 (2) 1991 (3); v A 1988 (4); v In 1987 (4); v P 1986 (1)*

Payne, T. R. O. 1: v E 1985
Phillip, N. 9: v A 1977 (3); *v In 1978 (6)*
Pierre, L. R. 1: v E 1947

Rae, A. F. 15: v In 1952 (2); *v E 1950 (4)*; *v A 1951 (3)*; *v NZ 1951 (1)*; *v In 1948 (5)*
Ramadhin, S. 43: v E 1953 (5) 1959 (4); v A 1954 (4); v In 1952 (4); *v E 1950 (4) 1957 (5)*; *v A 1951 (5) 1960 (2)*; *v NZ 1951 (2) 1955 (4)*; *v In 1958 (2)*; *v P 1958 (2)*
Richards, I. V. A. 121: v E 1980 (4) 1985 (5) 1989 (3); v A 1977 (2) 1983 (5) 1990 (5); v NZ 1984 (4); v In 1975 (4) 1982 (5) 1988 (4); v P 1976 (5) 1987 (2); *v E 1976 (4) 1980 (5) 1984 (5) 1988 (5) 1991 (5)*; *v A 1975 (6) 1979 (3) 1981 (3) 1984 (5) 1988 (5)*; *v NZ 1986 (3)*; *v In 1974 (5) 1983 (6) 1987 (4)*; *v P 1974 (2) 1980 (4) 1986 (3)*
Richardson, R. B. 62: v E 1985 (5) 1989 (4); v A 1983 (5) 1990 (5); v NZ 1984 (4); v In 1988 (4); *v P 1987 (3)*; *v E 1988 (3) 1991 (5)*; *v A 1984 (5) 1988 (5)*; *v NZ 1986 (3)*; *v In 1983 (1) 1987 (4)*; *v P 1986 (3) 1990 (3)*
Rickards, K. R. 2: v E 1947 (1); *v A 1951 (1)*
Roach, C. A. 16: v E 1929 (4) 1934 (1); *v E 1928 (3) 1933 (3)*; *v A 1930 (3)*
Roberts, A. M. E. 47: v E 1973 (1) 1980 (3); v A 1977 (2); v In 1975 (2) 1982 (5); v P 1976 (5); *v E 1976 (5) 1980 (3)*; *v A 1975 (5) 1979 (3) 1981 (2)*; *v NZ 1979 (2)*; *v In 1974 (5) 1983 (2)*; *v P 1974 (2)*
Roberts, A. T. 1: *v NZ 1955*
Rodriguez, W. V. 5: v E 1967 (1); v A 1964 (1); v In 1961 (2); *v E 1963 (1)*
Rowe, L. G. 30: v E 1973 (5); v A 1972 (3); v NZ 1971 (4); v In 1975 (4); *v E 1976 (2)*; *v A 1975 (6) 1979 (3)*; *v NZ 1979 (3)*

St Hill, E. L. 2: v E 1929 (2)
St Hill, W. H. 3: v E 1929 (1); *v E 1928 (2)*
Scarlett, R. O. 3: v E 1959 (3)
Scott, A. P. H. 1: v In 1952
Scott, O. C. 8: v E 1929 (1); *v E 1928 (2); v A 1930 (5)*
Sealey, B. J. 1: *v E 1933*
Sealy, J. E. D. 11: v E 1929 (2) 1934 (4); *v E 1939 (3); v A 1930 (2)*
Shepherd, J. N. 5: v In 1970 (2); *v E 1969 (3)*
Shillingford, G. C. 7: v NZ 1971 (2); v In 1970 (3); *v E 1969 (2)*
Shillingford, I. T. 4: v A 1977 (1); v P 1976 (3)
Shivnarine, S. 8: v A 1977 (3); *v In 1978 (5)*
Simmons, P. V. 7: v P 1987 (1); *v E 1991 (5); v In 1987 (1)*
Singh, C. K. 2: v E 1959 (2)
Small, J. A. 3: v E 1929 (1); *v E 1928 (2)*
Small, M. A. 2: v A 1983 (1); *v E 1984 (1)*
Smith, C. W. 5: v In 1961 (1); *v A 1960 (4)*
Smith, O. G. 26: v A 1954 (4); v P 1957 (5); *v E 1957 (5); v NZ 1955 (4); v In 1958 (5); v P 1958 (3)*
Sobers, G. S. 93: v E 1953 (1) 1959 (5) 1967 (5) 1973 (4); v A 1954 (4) 1964 (5); v NZ 1971 (5); v In 1961 (5); 1970 (5); v P 1957 (5); *v E 1957 (5) 1963 (5) 1966 (5) 1969 (3) 1973 (3); v A 1960 (5) 1968 (5); v NZ 1955 (4) 1968 (3); v In 1958 (5) 1966 (3); v P 1958 (3)*
Solomon, J. S. 27: v E 1959 (2); v A 1964 (5); v In 1961 (5); *v E 1963 (3); v A 1960 (5); v In 1958 (4); v P 1958 (3)*
Stayers, S. C. 4: v In 1961 (4)
Stollmeyer, J. B. 32: v E 1947 (2) 1953 (5); v A 1954 (2); v In 1952 (5); *v E 1939 (3) 1950 (4); v A 1951 (5); v NZ 1951 (2); v In 1948 (4)*
Stollmeyer, V. H. 1: *v E 1939*

Taylor, J. 3: v P 1957 (1); *v In 1958 (1); v P 1958 (1)*
Trim, J. 4: v E 1947 (1); *v A 1951 (1); v In 1948 (2)*

Valentine, A. L. 36: v E 1953 (3); v A 1954 (3); v In 1952 (5) 1961 (2); v P 1957 (1); *v E 1950 (4) 1957 (2); v A 1951 (5) 1960 (5); v NZ 1951 (2) 1955 (4)*
Valentine, V. A. 2: *v E 1933 (2)*

Walcott, C. L. 44: v E 1947 (4) 1953 (5) 1959 (2); v A 1954 (5); v In 1952 (5); v P 1957 (4); *v E 1950 (4) 1957 (5); v A 1951 (3); v NZ 1951 (2); v In 1948 (5)*
Walcott, L. A. 1: v E 1929

Walsh, C. A. 50: v E 1985 (1) 1989 (3); v A 1990 (5); v NZ 1984 (1); v In 1988 (4); v P 1987 (3); *v E 1988 (5) 1991 (5); v A 1984 (5) 1988 (5); v NZ 1986 (3); v In 1987 (4); v P 1986 (3) 1990 (3)*

Watson, C. 7: v E 1959 (5); v In 1961 (1); *v A 1960 (1)*

Weekes, E. D. 48: v E 1947 (4) 1953 (4); v A 1954 (5) v In 1952 (5); v P 1957 (5); *v E 1950 (4) 1957 (5); v A 1951 (5); v NZ 1951 (2) 1955 (4); v In 1948 (5)*

Weekes, K. H. 2: *v E 1939 (2)*

White, W. A. 2: v A 1964 (2)

Wight, C. V. 2: v E 1929 (1); *v E 1928 (1)*

Wight, G. L. 1: v In 1952

Wiles, C. A. 1: *v E 1933*

Willett, E. T. 5: v A 1972 (3); *v In 1974 (2)*

Williams, A. B. 7: v A 1977 (3); *v In 1978 (4)*

Williams, E. A. V. 4: v E 1947 (3); *v E 1939 (1)*

Wishart, K. L. 1: v E 1934

Worrell, F. M. M. 51: v E 1947 (3) 1953 (4) 1959 (4); v A 1954 (4); v In 1952 (5) 1961 (5); *v E 1950 (4) 1957 (5) 1963 (5); v A 1951 (5) 1960 (5); v NZ 1951 (2)*


# NEW ZEALAND

Number of Test cricketers: 174

Alabaster, J. C. 21: v E 1962 (2); v WI 1955 (1); v In 1967 (4); *v E 1958 (2); v SA 1961 (5); v WI 1971 (2); v In 1955 (4); v P 1955 (1)*

Allcott, C. F. W. 6: v E 1929 (2); v SA 1931 (1); *v E 1931 (3)*

Anderson, R. W. 9: v E 1977 (3); *v E 1978 (3); v P 1976 (3)*

Anderson, W. M. 1: v A 1945

Andrews, B. 2: *v A 1973 (2)*


Badcock, F. T. 7: v E 1929 (3) 1932 (2); v SA 1931 (2)

Barber, R. T. 1: v WI 1955

Bartlett, G. A. 10: v E 1965 (2); v In 1967 (4); v P 1964 (1); *v SA 1961 (5)*

Barton, P. T. 7: v E 1962 (3); *v SA 1961 (4)*

Beard, D. D. 4: v WI 1951 (2) 1955 (2)

Beck, J. E. F. 8: v WI 1955 (4); *v SA 1953 (4)*

Bell, W. 2: *v SA 1953 (2)*

Bilby, G. P. 2: v E 1965 (2)

Blain, T. E. 3: *v E 1986 (1); v In 1988 (2)*

Blair, R. W. 19: v E 1954 (1) 1958 (2) 1962 (2); v SA 1952 (2) 1963 (3); v WI 1955 (1); *v E 1958 (3); v SA 1953 (4)*

Blunt, R. C. 9: v E 1929 (4); v SA 1931 (2); *v E 1931 (3)*

Bolton, B. A. 2: v E 1958 (2)

Boock, S. L. 30: v E 1977 (3) 1983 (2) 1987 (1); v WI 1979 (3) 1986 (2); v P 1978 (3) 1984 (2) 1988 (1); *v E 1978 (3); v A 1985 (1); v WI 1984 (3); v P 1984 (3); v SL 1983 (3)*

Bracewell, B. P. 6: v P 1978 (1) 1984 (1); *v E 1978 (3); v A 1980 (1)*

Bracewell, J. G. 41: v E 1987 (3); v A 1985 (2) 1989 (1); v WI 1986 (3); v In 1980 (1) 1989 (2); v P 1988 (2); *v E 1983 (4) 1986 (3) 1990 (3); v A 1980 (3) 1985 (2) 1987 (3); v WI 1984 (1); v In 1988 (3); v P 1984 (2); v SL 1983 (2) 1986 (1)*

Bradburn, G. E. 4: v SL 1990 (1); *v P 1990 (3)*

Bradburn, W. P. 2: v SA 1963 (2)

Brown, V. R. 2: *v A 1985 (2)*

Burgess, M. G. 50: v E 1970 (1) 1977 (3); v A 1973 (1) 1976 (2); v WI 1968 (2); v In 1967 (4) 1975 (3); v P 1972 (3) 1978 (3); *v E 1969 (2) 1973 (3) 1978 (3); v A 1980 (3); v WI 1971 (5); v In 1969 (3) 1976 (3); v P 1969 (3) 1976 (3)*

Burke, C. 1: v A 1945

Burtt, T. B. 10: v E 1946 (1) 1950 (2); v SA 1952 (1); v WI 1951 (2); *v E 1949 (4)*

Butterfield, L. A. 1: v A 1945


Cairns, B. L. 43: v E 1974 (1) 1977 (1) 1983 (3); v A 1976 (1) 1981 (3); v WI 1979 (3); v In 1975 (1) 1980 (3); v P 1978 (3) 1984 (3); v SL 1982 (2); *v E 1978 (2) 1983 (4); v A 1973 (1) 1980 (3) 1985 (1); v WI 1984 (2); v In 1976 (2); v P 1976 (2); v SL 1983 (2)*

Cairns, C. L. 2: v SL 1990 (1); *v A 1989 (1)*

Cameron, F. J. 19: v E 1962 (3); v SA 1963 (3); v P 1964 (3); *v E 1965 (2)*; *v SA 1961 (5)*; *v In 1964 (1)*; *v P 1964 (2)*

Cave, H. B. 19: v E 1954 (2); v WI 1955 (3); *v E 1949 (4) 1958 (2)*; *v In 1955 (5)*; *v P 1955 (3)*

Chapple, M. E. 14: v E 1954 (1) 1965 (1); v SA 1952 (1) 1963 (3); v WI 1955 (1); *v SA 1953 (5) 1961 (2)*

Chatfield, E. J. 43: v E 1974 (1) 1977 (1) 1983 (3) 1987 (3); v WI 1986 (3); v P 1984 (3) 1988 (2); v SL 1982 (2); *v E 1983 (3) 1986 (1)*; *v A 1985 (2) 1987 (2)*; *v In 1988 (3)*; *v P 1984 (1)*; *v SL 1983 (2) 1986 (1)*

Cleverley, D. C. 2: v SA 1931 (1); v A 1945 (1)

Collinge, R. O. 35: v E 1970 (2) 1974 (2) 1977 (3); v A 1973 (3); v In 1967 (2) 1975 (3); v P 1964 (3) 1972 (2); *v E 1965 (3) 1969 (1) 1973 (3) 1978 (1)*; *v In 1964 (2) 1976 (1)*; *v P 1964 (3) 1976 (2)*

Colquhoun, I. A. 2: v E 1954 (2)

Coney, J. V. 52: v E 1983 (3); v A 1973 (2) 1981 (3) 1985 (3); v WI 1979 (3) 1986 (3); v In 1980 (3); v P 1978 (3) 1984 (3); v SL 1982 (2); *v E 1983 (4) 1986 (3)*; *v A 1973 (2) 1980 (2) 1985 (3)*; *v WI 1984 (4)*; *v P 1984 (3)*; *v SL 1983 (3)*

Congdon, B. E. 61: v E 1965 (3) 1970 (2) 1974 (2) 1977 (3); v A 1973 (3) 1976 (2); v WI 1968 (3); v In 1967 (4) 1975 (3); v P 1964 (3) 1972 (3); *v E 1965 (3) 1969 (3) 1973 (3) 1978 (3)*; *v A 1973 (3)*; *v WI 1971 (5)*; *v In 1964 (3) 1969 (3)*; *v P 1964 (1) 1969 (3)*

Cowie, J. 9: v E 1946 (1); v A 1945 (1); *v E 1937 (3) 1949 (4)*

Cresswell, G. F. 3: v E 1950 (2); *v E 1949 (1)*

Cromb, I. B. 5: v SA 1931 (2); *v E 1931 (3)*

Crowe, J. J. 39: v E 1983 (3) 1987 (2); v A 1989 (1); v WI 1986 (3); v P 1984 (3) 1988 (2); v SL 1982 (2); *v E 1983 (2) 1986 (3)*; *v A 1985 (3) 1987 (3) 1989 (1)*; *v WI 1984 (4)*; *v P 1984 (3)*; *v SL 1983 (3) 1986 (1)*

Crowe, M. D. 56: v E 1983 (3) 1987 (3); v A 1981 (3) 1985 (3); v WI 1986 (3); v In 1989 (3); v P 1984 (3) 1988 (2); v SL 1990 (2); *v E 1983 (4) 1986 (3) 1990 (3)*; *v A 1985 (3) 1987 (3) 1989 (1)*; *v WI 1984 (4)*; *v P 1984 (3) 1990 (3)*; *v SL 1983 (3) 1986 (1)*

Cunis, R. S. 20: v E 1965 (3) 1970 (2); v SA 1963 (1); v WI 1968 (3); *v E 1969 (1)*; *v WI 1971 (5)*; *v In 1969 (3)*; *v P 1969 (2)*

D'Arcy, J. W. 5: *v E 1958 (5)*

Dempster, C. S. 10: v E 1929 (4) 1932 (2); v SA 1931 (2); *v E 1931 (2)*

Dempster, E. W. 5: v SA 1952 (1); *v E 1953 (4)*

Dick, A. E. 17: v E 1962 (3); v SA 1963 (2); v P 1964 (3); *v E 1965 (2)*; *v SA 1961 (5)*; *v P 1964 (3)*

Dickinson, G. R. 3: v E 1929 (2); v SA 1931 (1)

Donnelly, M. P. 7: *v E 1937 (3) 1949 (4)*

Dowling, G. T. 39: v E 1962 (3) 1970 (2); v In 1967 (4); v SA 1963 (1); v WI 1968 (3); v P 1964 (2); *v E 1965 (3) 1969 (3)*; *v SA 1961 (4)*; *v WI 1971 (2)*; *v In 1964 (4) 1969 (3)*; *v P 1964 (2) 1969 (3)*

Dunning, J. A. 4: v E 1932 (1); *v E 1937 (3)*

Edgar, B. A. 39: v E 1983 (3); v A 1981 (3) 1985 (3); v WI 1979 (3); v In 1980 (3); v P 1978 (3); v SL 1982 (2); *v E 1978 (3) 1983 (4) 1986 (3)*; *v A 1980 (3) 1985 (3)*; *v P 1984 (3)*

Edwards, G. N. 8: v E 1977 (1); v A 1976 (2); v In 1980 (3); *v E 1978 (2)*

Emery, R. W. G. 2: v WI 1951 (2)

Fisher, F. E. 1: v SA 1952

Foley, H. 1: v E 1929

Franklin, T. J. 21: v E 1987 (3); v A 1985 (1) 1989 (1); v In 1989 (3); v SL 1990 (1); *v E 1983 (1) 1990 (3)*; *v In 1988 (3)*; *v P 1990 (3)*

Freeman, D. L. 2: v E 1932 (2)

Gallichan, N. 1: *v E 1937*

Gedye, S. G. 4: v SA 1963 (3); v P 1964 (1)

Gillespie, S. R. 1: v A 1985

Gray, E. J. 10: *v E 1983 (2) 1986 (3)*; *v A 1987 (1)*; *v In 1988 (1)*; *v P 1984 (2)*; *v SL 1986 (1)*

Greatbatch, M. J. 19: v E 1987 (2); v A 1989 (1); v In 1989 (3); v P 1988 (1); v SL 1990 (2); *v E 1990 (3)*; *v A 1989 (1)*; *v In 1988 (3)*; *v P 1990 (3)*

Guillen, S. C. 3: v WI 1955 (3)

Guy, J. W. 12: v E 1958 (2); v WI 1955 (2); *v SA 1961 (2)*; *v In 1955 (5)*; *v P 1955 (1)*

Hadlee, D. R. 26: v E 1974 (2) 1977 (1); v A 1973 (3) 1976 (1); v In 1975 (3); v P 1972 (2); *v E 1969 (2) 1973 (3); v A 1973 (3); v In 1969 (3); v P 1969 (3)*

Hadlee, Sir R. J. 86: v E 1977 (3) 1983 (3) 1987 (1); v A 1973 (2) 1976 (2) 1981 (3) 1985 (3) 1989 (1); v WI 1979 (3) 1986 (3); v In 1975 (2) 1980 (3) 1989 (3); v P 1972 (1) 1978 (3) 1984 (3) 1988 (2); v SL 1982 (2); *v E 1973 (1) 1978 (3) 1983 (4) 1986 (3) 1990 (3); v A 1973 (3) 1980 (3) 1985 (3) 1987 (3); v WI 1984 (4); v In 1976 (3) 1988 (3); v P 1976 (3); v SL 1983 (3) 1986 (1)*

Hadlee, W. A. 11: v E 1946 (1) 1950 (2); v A 1945 (1); *v E 1937 (3) 1949 (4)*

Harford, N. S. 8: *v E 1958 (4); v In 1955 (2); v P 1955 (2)*

Harford, R. I. 3: v In 1967 (3)

Harris, P. G. Z. 9: v P 1964 (1); *v SA 1961 (5); v In 1955 (1); v P 1955 (2)*

Harris, R. M. 2: v E 1958 (2)

Hastings, B. F. 31: v E 1974 (2); v A 1973 (3); v WI 1968 (3); v In 1975 (1); v P 1972 (3); *v E 1969 (3) 1973 (3); v A 1973 (3); v WI 1971 (5); v In 1969 (2); v P 1969 (3)*

Hayes, J. A. 15: v E 1950 (2) 1954 (1); v WI 1951 (2); *v E 1958 (4); v In 1955 (5); v P 1955 (1)*

Henderson, M. 1: v E 1929

Horne, P. A. 4: v WI 1986 (1); *v A 1987 (1); v P 1990 (1); v SL 1986 (1)*

Hough, K. W. 2: v E 1958 (2)

Howarth, G. P. 47: v E 1974 (2) 1977 (3) 1983 (3); v A 1976 (2) 1981 (3); v WI 1979 (3); v In 1980 (3); v P 1978 (3) 1984 (3); v SL 1982 (2); *v E 1978 (3) 1983 (4); v A 1980 (2); v WI 1984 (4); v In 1976 (2); v P 1976 (2); v SL 1983 (3)*

Howarth, H. J. 30: v E 1970 (2) 1974 (2); v A 1973 (3) 1976 (2); v In 1975 (3); v P 1972 (3); *v E 1969 (3) 1973 (2); v WI 1971 (5); v In 1969 (3); v P 1969 (3)*

James, K. C. 11: v E 1929 (4) 1932 (2); v SA 1931 (2); *v E 1931 (3)*

Jarvis, T. W. 13: v E 1965 (1); v P 1972 (3); *v WI 1971 (4); v In 1964 (2); v P 1964 (3)*

Jones, A. H. 20: v E 1987 (1); v A 1989 (1); v In 1989 (3); v P 1988 (2); v SL 1990 (3); *v E 1990 (3); v A 1987 (3); v In 1988 (3); v SL 1986 (1)*

Kerr, J. L. 7: v E 1932 (2); v SA 1931 (1); *v E 1931 (2) 1937 (2)*

Kuggeleijn, C. M. 2: *v In 1988 (2)*

Lees, W. K. 21: v E 1977 (2); v A 1976 (1); v WI 1979 (3); v P 1978 (3); v SL 1982 (2); *v E 1983 (2); v A 1980 (2); v In 1976 (3); v P 1976 (3)*

Leggat, I. B. 1: *v SA 1953*

Leggat, J. G. 9: v E 1954 (1); v SA 1952 (1); v WI 1951 (1) 1955 (1); *v In 1955 (3); v P 1955 (2)*

Lissette, A. F. 2: v WI 1955 (2)

Lowry, T. C. 7: v E 1929 (4); *v E 1931 (3)*

MacGibbon, A. R. 26: v E 1950 (2) 1954 (2); v SA 1952 (1); v WI 1955 (3); *v E 1958 (5); v SA 1953 (5); v In 1955 (3); v P 1955 (3)*

McEwan, P. E. 4: v WI 1979 (1); *v A 1980 (2); v P 1984 (1)*

McGirr, H. M. 2: v E 1929 (2)

McGregor, S. N. 25: v E 1954 (2) 1958 (2); v SA 1963 (3); v WI 1955 (4); v P 1964 (2); *v SA 1961 (5); v In 1955 (4); v P 1955 (3)*

McLeod, E. G. 1: v E 1929

McMahon T. G. 5: v WI 1955 (1); *v In 1955 (3); v P 1955 (1)*

McRae, D. A. N. 1: v A 1945

Matheson, A. M. 2: v E 1929 (1); *v E 1931 (1)*

Meale, T. 2: *v E 1958 (2)*

Merritt, W. E. 6: v E 1929 (4); *v E 1931 (2)*

Meuli, E. M. 1: v SA 1952

Milburn, B. D. 3: v WI 1968 (3)

Miller, L. S. M. 13: v SA 1952 (2); v WI 1955 (3); *v E 1958 (4); v SA 1953 (4)*

Mills, J. E. 7: v E 1929 (3) 1932 (1); *v E 1931 (3)*

Moir, A. M. 17: v E 1950 (2) 1954 (2) 1958 (2); v SA 1952 (1); v WI 1951 (2) 1955 (1); *v E 1958 (2); v In 1955 (2); v P 1955 (3)*

Moloney, D. A. R. 3: *v E 1937 (3)*

Mooney, F. L. H. 14: v E 1950 (2); v SA 1952 (2); v WI 1951 (2); *v E 1949 (3); v SA 1953 (5)*

Morgan, R. W. 20: v E 1965 (2) 1970 (2); v WI 1968 (1); v P 1964 (2); *v E 1965 (3); v WI 1971 (3); v In 1964 (4); v P 1964 (3)*

Morrison, B. D. 1: v E 1962

Morrison, D. K. 22: v E 1987 (3); v A 1989 (1); v In 1989 (3); v P 1988 (1); v SL 1990 (3); *v E 1990 (3); v A 1987 (3) 1989 (1); v P 1990 (3)*

Morrison, J. F. M. 17: v E 1974 (2); v A 1973 (3) 1981 (3); v In 1975 (3); *v A 1973 (3); v In 1976 (1); v P 1976 (2)*

Motz, R. C. 32: v E 1962 (2) 1965 (3); v A 1973 (3); v WI 1968 (3); v In 1967 (4); v P 1964 (3); *v E 1965 (3) 1969 (3); v SA 1961 (5); v In 1964 (3); v P 1964 (1)*

Murray, B. A. G. 13: v E 1970 (1); v In 1967 (4); *v E 1969 (2); v In 1969 (3); v P 1969 (3)*

Newman J. 3: v E 1932 (2); v SA 1931 (1)

O'Sullivan, D. R. 11: v In 1975 (1); v P 1972 (1); *v A 1973 (3); v In 1976 (3); v P 1976 (3)*

Overton, G. W. F. 3: *v SA 1953* (3)

Page, M. L. 14: v E 1929 (4) 1932 (2); v SA 1931 (2); *v E 1931 (3) 1937 (3)*

Parker, J. M. 36: v E 1974 (2) 1977 (3); v A 1973 (3) 1976 (2); v WI 1979 (3); v In 1975 (3); v P 1972 (1) 1978 (2); *v E 1973 (3) 1978 (2); v A 1973 (3) 1980 (3); v In 1976 (3); v P 1976 (3)*

Parker, N. M. 3: *v In 1976 (2); v P 1976 (1)*

Parore, A. C. 1: *v E 1990*

Patel, D. N. 13: v WI 1986 (3); v P 1988 (1); v SL 1990 (2); *v A 1987 (3) 1989 (1); v P 1990 (3)*

Petherick, P. J. 6: v A 1976 (1); *v In 1976 (3); v P 1976 (2)*

Petrie, E. C. 14: v E 1958 (2) 1965 (3); *v E 1958 (5); v In 1955 (2); v P 1955 (2)*

Playle, W. R. 8: v E 1962 (3); *v E 1958 (5)*

Pollard, V. 32: v E 1965 (3) 1970 (1); v WI 1968 (3); v In 1967 (4); v P 1972 (1); *v E 1965 (3) 1969 (3) 1973 (3); v In 1964 (4) 1969 (1); v P 1964 (3) 1969 (3)*

Poore, M. B. 14: v E 1954 (1); v SA 1952 (1); *v SA 1953 (5); v In 1955 (4); v P 1955 (3)*

Priest, M. W. 1: *v E 1990*

Pringle, C. 5: v SL 1990 (2); *v P 1990 (3)*

Puna, N. 3: v E 1965 (3)

Rabone, G. O. 12: v E 1954 (2); v SA 1952 (1); v WI 1951 (2); *v E 1949 (4); v SA 1953 (3)*

Redmond, R. E. 1: v P 1972

Reid, J. F. 19: v A 1985 (3); v In 1980 (3); v P 1978 (1) 1984 (3); *v A 1985 (3); v P 1984 (3); v SL 1983 (3)*

Reid, J. R. 58: v E 1950 (2) 1954 (2) 1958 (2) 1962 (3); v SA 1952 (2) 1963 (3); v WI 1951 (2) 1955 (4); v P 1964 (3); *v E 1949 (2) 1958 (5) 1965 (3); v SA 1953 (5) 1961 (5); v In 1955 (5) 1964 (4); v P 1955 (3) 1964 (3)*

Roberts, A. D. G. 7: v In 1975 (2); *v In 1976 (3); v P 1976 (2)*

Roberts, A. W. 5: v E 1929 (1); v SA 1931 (1); *v E 1937 (2)*

Robertson, G. K. 1: v A 1985

Rowe, C. G. 1: v A 1945

Rutherford, K. R. 28: v E 1987 (2); v A 1985 (3) 1989 (1); v WI 1986 (2); v In 1989 (3); v SL 1990 (3); *v E 1986 (1) 1990 (2); v A 1987 (1); v WI 1984 (4); v In 1988 (2); v P 1990 (3); v SL 1986 (1)*

Scott, R. H. 1: v E 1946

Scott, V. J. 10: v E 1946 (1) 1950 (2); v A 1945 (1); v WI 1951 (2); *v E 1949 (4)*

Shrimpton, M. J. F. 10: v E 1962 (2) 1965 (3) 1970 (2); v SA 1963 (1); *v A 1973 (2)*

Sinclair, B. W. 21: v E 1962 (3) 1965 (3); v SA 1963 (3); v In 1967 (2); v P 1964 (2); *v E 1965 (3); v In 1964 (2); v P 1964 (3)*

Sinclair, I. M. 2: v WI 1955 (2)

Smith, F. B. 4: v E 1946 (1); v WI 1951 (1); *v E 1949 (2)*

Smith, H. D. 1: v E 1932

Smith, I. D. S. 61: v E 1983 (3) 1987 (3); v A 1981 (3) 1985 (3) 1989 (1); v WI 1986 (3); v In 1980 (3) 1989 (3); v P 1984 (3) 1988 (2); v SL 1990 (3); *v E 1983 (2) 1986 (2) 1990 (2); v A 1980 (1) 1985 (3) 1987 (3) 1989 (1); v WI 1984 (4); v In 1988 (3); v P 1984 (3) 1990 (3); v SL 1983 (3) 1986 (1)*

Snedden, C. A. 1: v E 1946

Snedden, M. C. 25: v E 1983 (1) 1987 (2); v A 1981 (3) 1989 (1); v WI 1986 (1); v In 1980 (3) 1989 (3); v SL 1982 (2); *v E 1983 (1) 1990 (3); v A 1985 (1) 1987 (1) 1989 (1); v In 1988 (1); v SL 1986 (1)*

Sparling, J. T. 11: v E 1958 (2) 1962 (1); v SA 1963 (2); *v E 1958 (3); v SA 1961 (3)*

Stirling, D. A. 6: *v E 1986 (2); v WI 1984 (1); v P 1984 (3)*

Sutcliffe, B. 42: v E 1946 (1) 1950 (2) 1954 (2) 1958 (2); v SA 1952 (2); v WI 1951 (2) 1955 (2); *v E 1949 (4) 1958 (4) 1965 (1); v SA 1953 (5); v In 1955 (5) 1964 (4); v P 1955 (3) 1964 (3)*

Taylor, B. R. 30: v E 1965 (1); v WI 1968 (3); v In 1967 (3); v P 1972 (3); *v E 1965 (2) 1969 (2) 1973 (3); v WI 1971 (4); v In 1964 (3) 1969 (2); v P 1964 (3) 1969 (1)*
Taylor, D. D. 3: v E 1946 (1); v WI 1955 (2)
Thomson, K. 2: v In 1967 (2)
Thomson, S. A. 3: v In 1989 (1); v SL 1990 (2)
Tindill, E. W. T. 5: v E 1946 (1); v A 1945 (1); *v E 1937 (3)*
Troup, G. B. 15: v E 1981 (2) 1985 (2); v WI 1979 (3); v In 1980 (2); v P 1978 (2); *v A 1980 (2); v WI 1984 (1); v In 1976 (1)*
Truscott, P. B. 1: v P 1964
Turner, G. M. 41: v E 1970 (2) 1974 (2); v A 1973 (3) 1976 (2); v WI 1968 (3); v In 1975 (3); v P 1972 (3); v SL 1982 (2); *v E 1969 (2) 1973 (3); v A 1973 (2); v WI 1971 (5); v In 1969 (3) 1976 (3); v P 1969 (1) 1976 (2)*

Vance, R. H. 4: v E 1987 (1); v P 1988 (2); *v A 1989 (1)*
Vivian, G. E. 5: *v WI 1971 (4); v In 1969 (1)*
Vivian, H. G. 7: v E 1932 (1); v SA 1931 (1); *v E 1931 (2) 1937 (3)*

Wadsworth, K. J. 33: v E 1970 (2) 1974 (2); v A 1973 (3); v In 1975 (3); v P 1972 (3); *v E 1969 (3) 1973 (3); v A 1973 (3); v WI 1971 (5); v In 1969 (3); v P 1969 (3)*
Wallace, W. M. 13: v E 1946 (1) 1950 (2); v A 1945 (1); v SA 1952 (2); *v E 1937 (3) 1949 (4)*
Ward, J. T. 8: v SA 1963 (1); v In 1967 (1); v P 1964 (1); *v E 1965 (1); v In 1964 (4)*
Watson, W. 9: v SL 1990 (3); *v E 1986 (2); v A 1989 (1); v P 1990 (3)*
Watt, L. 1: v E 1954
Webb, M. G. 3: v E 1970 (1); v A 1973 (1); *v WI 1971 (1)*
Webb, P. N. 2: v WI 1979 (2)
Weir, G. L. 11: v E 1929 (1) 1932 (2); v SA 1931 (2); *v E 1931 (3) 1937 (1)*
Whitelaw, P. E. 2: v E 1932 (2)
Wright, J. G. 74: v E 1977 (3) 1983 (3) 1987 (3); v A 1981 (3) 1985 (2) 1989 (1); v WI 1979 (3) 1986 (3); v In 1980 (3) 1989 (3); v P 1978 (3) 1984 (3) 1988 (2); v SL 1982 (2) 1990 (3); *v E 1978 (2) 1983 (3) 1986 (3) 1990 (3); v A 1980 (3) 1985 (3) 1987 (3) 1989 (1); v WI 1984 (4); v In 1988 (3); v P 1984 (3); v SL 1983 (3)*

Yuile, B. W. 17: v E 1962 (2); v WI 1968 (3); v In 1967 (1); v P 1964 (3); *v E 1965 (1); v In 1964 (3) 1969 (1); v P 1964 (1) 1969 (2)*

# INDIA

Number of Test cricketers: 192

Abid Ali, S. 29: v E 1972 (4); v A 1969 (1); v WI 1974 (2); v NZ 1969 (3); *v E 1971 (3) 1974 (3); v A 1967 (4); v WI 1970 (5); v NZ 1967 (4)*
Adhikari, H. R. 21: v E 1951 (3); v A 1956 (2); v WI 1948 (5) 1958 (1); v P 1952 (2); *v E 1952 (3); v A 1947 (5)*
Amarnath, L. 24: v E 1933 (3) 1951 (3); v WI 1948 (5); v P 1952 (5); *v E 1946 (3); v A 1947 (5)*
Amarnath, M. 69: v E 1976 (2) 1984 (5); v A 1969 (1) 1979 (1) 1986 (3); v WI 1978 (2) 1983 (3) 1987 (3); v NZ 1976 (3); v P 1983 (2) 1986 (5); v SL 1986 (2); *v E 1979 (2) 1986 (2); v A 1977 (5) 1985 (3); v WI 1975 (4) 1982 (5); v NZ 1975 (3); v P 1978 (3) 1982 (6) 1984 (2); v SL 1985 (2)*
Amarnath, S. 10: v E 1976 (2): *v WI 1975 (2); v NZ 1975 (3); v P 1978 (3)*
Amar Singh 7: v E 1933 (3); *v E 1932 (1) 1936 (3)*
Amir Elahi 1: *v A 1947*
Ankola, S. A. 1: *v P 1989*
Apte, A. L. 1: *v E 1959*
Apte, M. L. 7: v P 1952 (2); *v WI 1952 (5)*
Arshad Ayub 13: v WI 1987 (4); v NZ 1988 (3); *v WI 1988 (4); v P 1989 (2)*
Arun, B. 2: v SL 1986 (2)
Arun Lal 16: v WI 1987 (4); v NZ 1988 (3); v P 1986 (1); v SL 1982 (1); *v WI 1988 (4); v P 1982 (3)*
Azad, K. 7: v E 1981 (3); v WI 1983 (2); v P 1983 (1); *v NZ 1980 (1)*

Gupte, S. P. 36: v E 1951 (1) 1961 (2); v A 1956 (3); v WI 1958 (5); v NZ 1955 (5); v P 1952 (2) 1960 (3); *v E 1959 (5); v WI 1952 (5); v P 1954 (5)*
Gursharan Singh 1: *v NZ 1989*

Hafeez, A. 3: *v E 1946 (3)*
Hanumant Singh 14: v E 1963 (2); v A 1964 (3); v WI 1966 (2); v NZ 1964 (4) 1969 (1); *v E 1967 (2)*
Hardikar, M. S. 2: v WI 1958 (2)
Hazare, V. S. 30: v E 1951 (5); v WI 1948 (5); v P 1952 (3); *v E 1946 (3) 1952 (4); v A 1947 (5); v WI 1952 (5)*
Hindlekar, D. D. 4: *v E 1936 (1) 1946 (3)*
Hirwani, N. D. 14: v WI 1987 (1); v NZ 1988 (3); v SL 1990 (1); *v E 1990 (3); v WI 1988 (3); v NZ 1989 (3)*

Ibrahim, K. C. 4: v WI 1948 (4)
Indrajitsinhji, K. S. 4: v A 1964 (3); v NZ 1969 (1)
Irani, J. K. 2: *v A 1947 (2)*

Jahangir Khan, M. 4: *v E 1932 (1) 1936 (3)*
Jai, L. P. 1: v E 1933
Jaisimha, M. L. 39: v E 1961 (5) 1963 (5); v A 1959 (1) 1964 (3); v WI 1966 (2); v NZ 1964 (4) 1969 (1); v P 1960 (4); *v E 1959 (1); v A 1967 (2); v WI 1961 (4) 1970 (3); v NZ 1967 (4)*
Jamshedji, R. J. 1: v E 1933
Jayantilal, K. 1: *v WI 1970*
Joshi, P. G. 12: v E 1951 (2); v A 1959 (1); v WI 1958 (1); v P 1952 (1) 1960 (1); *v E 1959 (3); v WI 1952 (3)*

Kanitkar, H. S. 2: v WI 1974 (2)
Kapil Dev 110: v E 1979 (1) 1981 (6) 1984 (4); v A 1979 (6) 1986 (3); v WI 1978 (6) 1983 (6) 1987 (4); v NZ 1988 (3); v P 1979 (6) 1983 (3) 1986 (5); v SL 1982 (1) 1986 (3) 1990 (1); *v E 1979 (4) 1982 (3) 1986 (3) 1990 (3); v A 1980 (3) 1985 (3); v WI 1982 (5) 1988 (4); v NZ 1980 (3) 1989 (3); v P 1978 (3) 1982 (6) 1984 (2) 1989 (4); v SL 1985 (3)*
Kardar, A. H. (*see* Hafeez)
Kenny, R. B. 5: v A 1959 (4); v WI 1958 (1)
Kirmani, S. M. H. 88: v E 1976 (5) 1979 (1) 1981 (6) 1984 (5); v A 1979 (6); v WI 1978 (6) 1983 (6); v NZ 1976 (3); v P 1979 (6) 1983 (3); v SL 1982 (1); *v E 1982 (3); v A 1977 (5) 1980 (3) 1985 (3); v WI 1975 (4) 1982 (5); v NZ 1975 (3) 1980 (3); v P 1978 (3) 1982 (6) 1984 (2)*
Kischenchand, G. 5: v P 1952 (1); *v A 1947 (4)*
Kripal Singh, A. G. 14: v E 1961 (3) 1963 (2); v A 1956 (2) 1964 (1); v WI 1958 (1); v NZ 1955 (4); *v E 1959 (1)*
Krishnamurthy, P. 5: *v WI 1970 (5)*
Kulkarni, R. R. 3: v A 1986 (1); v P 1986 (2)
Kulkarni, U. N. 4: *v A 1967 (3); v NZ 1967 (1)*
Kumar, V. V. 2: v E 1961 (1); v P 1960 (1)
Kumble, A. 1: *v E 1990*
Kunderan, B. K. 18: v E 1961 (1) 1963 (5); v A 1959 (3); v WI 1966 (2); v NZ 1964 (1); v P 1960 (2); *v E 1967 (2); v WI 1961 (2)*

Lall Singh 1: *v E 1932*
Lamba, R. 4: v WI 1987 (1); v SL 1986 (3)

Madan Lal 39: v E 1976 (2) 1981 (6); v WI 1974 (2) 1983 (3); v NZ 1976 (1); v P 1983 (3); v SL 1982 (1); *v E 1974 (2) 1982 (3) 1986 (1); v A 1977 (2); v WI 1975 (4) 1982 (2); v NZ 1975 (3); v P 1982 (3) 1984 (1)*
Maka, E. S. 2: v P 1952 (1); *v WI 1952 (1)*
Malhotra, A. 7: v E 1981 (2) 1984 (1); v WI 1983 (3); *v E 1982 (1)*
Maninder Singh 34: v A 1986 (3); v WI 1983 (4) 1987 (3); v P 1986 (4); v SL 1986 (3); *v E 1986 (3); v WI 1982 (3); v P 1982 (5) 1984 (1) 1989 (3); v SL 1985 (2)*
Manjrekar, S. V. 16: v WI 1987 (1); v SL 1990 (1); *v E 1990 (3); v WI 1988 (4); v NZ 1989 (3); v P 1989 (4)*

Manjrekar, V. L. 55: v E 1951 (2) 1961 (5) 1963 (4); v A 1956 (3) 1964 (3); v WI 1958 (4); v NZ 1955 (5) 1964 (1); v P 1952 (3) 1960 (5); *v E 1952 (4) 1959 (2); v WI 1952 (4) 1961 (5); v P 1954 (5)*

Mankad, A. V. 22: v E 1976 (1); v A 1969 (5); v WI 1974 (1); v NZ 1969 (2) 1976 (3); *v E 1971 (3) 1974 (1); v A 1977 (3); v WI 1970 (3)*

Mankad, V. 44: v E 1951 (5); v A 1956 (3); v WI 1948 (5) 1958 (2); v NZ 1955 (4); v P 1952 (4); *v E 1946 (3) 1952 (3); v A 1947 (5); v WI 1952 (5); v P 1954 (5)*

Mansur Ali Khan (*see* Pataudi)

Mantri, M. K. 4: v E 1951 (1); *v E 1952 (2); v P 1954 (1)*

Meherhomji, K. R. 1: *v E 1936*

Mehra, V. L. 8: v E 1961 (1) 1963 (2); v NZ 1955 (2); *v WI 1961 (3)*

Merchant, V. M. 10: v E 1933 (3) 1951 (1); *v E 1936 (3) 1946 (3)*

Milkha Singh, A. G. 4: v E 1961 (1); v A 1959 (1); v P 1960 (2)

Modi, R. S. 10: v E 1951 (1); v WI 1948 (5); v P 1952 (1); *v E 1946 (3)*

More, K. S. 35: v A 1986 (2); v WI 1987 (4); v NZ 1988 (3); v P 1986 (5); v SL 1986 (3) 1990 (1); *v E 1986 (3) 1990 (3); v WI 1988 (4); v NZ 1989 (3); v P 1989 (4)*

Muddiah, V. M. 2: v A 1959 (1); v P 1960 (1)

Mushtaq Ali, S. 11: v E 1933 (2) 1951 (1); v WI 1948 (3); *v E 1936 (3) 1946 (2)*

Nadkarni, R. G. 41: v E 1961 (1) 1963 (5); v A 1959 (5) 1964 (3); v WI 1958 (4) 1966 (1); v NZ 1955 (1) 1964 (4); v P 1960 (4); *v E 1959 (4); v A 1967 (3); v WI 1961 (5); v NZ 1967 (4)*

Naik, S. S. 3: v WI 1974 (2); *v E 1974 (1)*

Naoomal Jeoomal 3: v E 1933 (2); *v E 1932 (1)*

Narasimha Rao, M. V. 4: v A 1979 (2); v WI 1978 (2)

Navle, J. G. 2: v E 1933 (1); *v E 1932 (1)*

Nayak, S. V. 2: *v E 1982 (2)*

Nayudu, C. K. 7: v E 1933 (3); *v E 1932 (1) 1936 (3)*

Nayudu, C. S. 11: v E 1933 (2) 1951 (1); *v E 1936 (2) 1946 (2); v A 1947 (4)*

Nazir Ali, S. 2: v E 1933 (1); *v E 1932 (1)*

Nissar, Mahomed 6: v E 1933 (2); *v E 1932 (1) 1936 (3)*

Nyalchand, S. 1: v P 1952

Pai, A. M. 1: v NZ 1969

Palia, P. E. 2: *v E 1932 (1) 1936 (1)*

Pandit, C. S. 3: v A 1986 (2); *v E 1986 (1)*

Parkar, G. A. 1: *v E 1982*

Parkar, R. D. 2: v E 1972 (2)

Parsana, D. D. 2: v WI 1978 (2)

Patankar, C. T. 1: v NZ 1955

Pataudi sen., Nawab of, 3: *v E 1946 (3)*

Pataudi jun., Nawab of (now Mansur Ali Khan) 46: v E 1961 (3) 1963 (5) 1972 (3); v A 1964 (3) 1969 (5); v WI 1966 (3) 1974 (4); v NZ 1964 (4) 1969 (3); *v E 1967 (3); v A 1967 (3); v WI 1961 (3); v NZ 1967 (4)*

Patel, B. P. 21: v E 1976 (5); v WI 1974 (3); v NZ 1976 (3); *v E 1974 (2); v A 1977 (2); v WI 1975 (3); v NZ 1975 (3)*

Patel, J. M. 7: v A 1956 (2) 1959 (3); v NZ 1955 (1); *v P 1954 (1)*

Patel, R. 1: v NZ 1988

Patiala, Yuvraj of, 1: v E 1933

Patil, S. M. 29: v E 1979 (1) 1981 (4) 1984 (2); v WI 1983 (2); v P 1979 (2) 1983 (3); v SL 1982 (1); *v E 1982 (2); v A 1980 (3); v NZ 1980 (3); v P 1982 (4) 1984 (2)*

Patil, S. R. 1: v NZ 1955

Phadkar, D. G. 31: v E 1951 (4); v A 1956 (1); v WI 1948 (4) 1958 (1); v NZ 1955 (4); v P 1952 (2); *v E 1952 (4); v A 1947 (4); v WI 1952 (4); v P 1954 (3)*

Prabhakar, M. 13: v E 1984 (2); v SL 1990 (1); *v E 1990 (3); v NZ 1989 (3); v P 1989 (4)*

Prasanna, E. A. S. 49: v E 1961 (1) 1972 (3) 1976 (4); v A 1969 (5); v WI 1966 (1) 1974 (5); v NZ 1969 (3); *v E 1967 (3) 1974 (2); v A 1967 (4) 1977 (4); v WI 1961 (1) 1970 (3) 1975 (1); v NZ 1967 (4) 1975 (3); v P 1978 (2)*

Punjabi, P. H. 5: *v P 1954 (5)*

Rai Singh, K. 1: *v A 1947*

Rajinder Pal 1: v E 1963

Rajindernath, V. 1: v P 1952

Rajput, L. S. 2: *v SL 1985 (2)*
Raju, S. L. V. 3: v SL 1990 (1); *v NZ 1989 (2)*
Raman, W. V. 6: v WI 1987 (1); v NZ 1988 (1); *v WI 1988 (1)*; *v NZ 1989 (3)*
Ramaswami, C. 2: *v E 1936 (2)*
Ramchand, G. S. 33: v A 1956 (3) 1959 (5); v WI 1958 (3); v NZ 1955 (5); v P 1952 (3); *v E 1952 (4); v WI 1952 (5); v P 1954 (5)*
Ramji, L. 1: v E 1933
Rangachary, C. R. 4: v WI 1948 (2); *v A 1947 (2)*
Rangnekar, K. M. 3: *v A 1947 (3)*
Ranjane, V. B. 7: v E 1961 (3) 1963 (1); v A 1964 (1); v WI 1958 (1); *v WI 1961 (1)*
Razdan, V. 2: *v P 1989 (2)*
Reddy, B. 4: *v E 1979 (4)*
Rege, M. R. 1: v WI 1948
Roy, A. 4: v A 1969 (2); v NZ 1969 (2)
Roy, Pankaj 43: v E 1951 (5); v A 1956 (3) 1959 (5); v WI 1958 (5); v NZ 1955 (5); v P 1952 (3) 1960 (1); *v E 1952 (4) 1959 (5); v WI 1952 (4); v P 1954 (5)*
Roy, Pranab 2: v E 1981 (2)

Sandhu, B. S. 8: v WI 1983 (1); *v WI 1982 (4); v P 1982 (3)*
Sardesai, D. N. 30: v E 1961 (1) 1963 (5) 1972 (1); v A 1964 (3) 1969 (1); v WI 1966 (2); v NZ 1964 (3); *v E 1967 (1) 1971 (3); v A 1967 (2); v WI 1961 (3) 1970 (5)*
Sarwate, C. T. 9: v E 1951 (1); v WI 1948 (2); *v E 1946 (1); v A 1947 (5)*
Saxena, R. C. 1: *v E 1967*
Sekar, T. A. P. 2: *v P 1982 (2)*
Sen, P. 14: v E 1951 (2); v WI 1948 (5); v P 1952 (2); *v E 1952 (2); v A 1947 (3)*
Sengupta, A. K. 1: v WI 1958
Sharma, Ajay 1: v WI 1987
Sharma, Chetan 23: v E 1984 (3); v A 1986 (2); v WI 1987 (3); v SL 1986 (2); *v E 1986 (3); v A 1985 (2); v WI 1988 (4); v P 1984 (2); v SL 1985 (3)*
Sharma, Gopal 5: v E 1984 (1); v P 1986 (2); v SL 1990 (1); *v SL 1985 (1)*
Sharma, P. 5: v E 1976 (2); v WI 1974 (2); *v WI 1975 (1)*
Sharma, Sanjeev 2: v NZ 1988 (1); *v E 1990 (1)*
Shastri, R. J. 73: v E 1981 (6) 1984 (5); v A 1986 (3); v WI 1983 (6) 1987 (4); v NZ 1988 (3); v P 1983 (2) 1986 (5); v SL 1986 (3) 1990 (1); *v E 1982 (3) 1986 (3) 1990 (3); v A 1985 (3); v WI 1982 (5) 1988 (4); v NZ 1980 (3); v P 1982 (2) 1984 (2) 1989 (4); v SL 1985 (3)*
Shinde, S. G. 7: v E 1951 (1); v WI 1948 (1); *v E 1946 (1) 1952 (2)*
Shodhan, R. H. 3: v P 1952 (1); *v WI 1952 (2)*
Shukla, R. C. 1: v SL 1982
Sidhu, N. S. 17: v WI 1983 (2); v NZ 1988 (3); *v E 1990 (3); v WI 1988 (4); v NZ 1989 (1); v P 1989 (4)*
Sivaramakrishnan, L. 9: v E 1984 (5); *v A 1985 (2); v WI 1982 (1); v SL 1985 (1)*
Sohoni, S. W. 4: v E 1951 (1); *v E 1946 (2); v A 1947 (1)*
Solkar, E. D. 27: v E 1972 (5) 1976 (1); v A 1969 (4); v WI 1974 (4); v NZ 1969 (2); *v E 1971 (3) 1974 (3); v WI 1970 (5) 1975 (1)*
Sood, M. M. 1: v A 1959
Srikkanth, K. 39: v E 1981 (4) 1984 (2); v A 1986 (3); v WI 1987 (4); v NZ 1988 (3); v P 1986 (5); v SL 1986 (3); *v E 1986 (3); v A 1985 (3); v P 1982 (2) 1989 (4); v SL 1985 (3)*
Srinivasan, T. E. 1: *v NZ 1980*
Subramanya, V. 9: v WI 1966 (2); v NZ 1964 (1); *v E 1967 (2); v A 1967 (2); v NZ 1967 (2)*
Sunderram, G. 2: v NZ 1955 (2)
Surendranath, R. 11: v A 1959 (2); v WI 1958 (2); v P 1960 (2); *v E 1959 (5)*
Surti, R. F. 26: v E 1963 (1); v A 1964 (2) 1969 (1); v WI 1966 (2); v NZ 1964 (1) 1969 (2); v P 1960 (2); *v E 1967 (2); v A 1967 (4); v WI 1961 (5); v NZ 1967 (4)*
Swamy, V. N. 1: v NZ 1955

Tamhane, N. S. 21: v A 1956 (3) 1959 (1); v WI 1958 (4); v NZ 1955 (4); v P 1960 (2); *v E 1959 (2); v P 1954 (5)*
Tarapore, K. K. 1: v WI 1948
Tendulkar, S. R. 11: v SL 1990 (1); *v E 1990 (3); v NZ 1989 (3); v P 1989 (4)*

Umrigar, P. R. 59: v E 1951 (5) 1961 (4); v A 1956 (3) 1959 (3); v WI 1948 (1) 1958 (5); v NZ 1955 (5); v P 1952 (5) 1960 (5); *v E 1952 (4) 1959 (4); v WI 1952 (5) 1961 (5); v P 1954 (5)*

Vengsarkar, D. B. 111: v E 1976 (1) 1979 (1) 1981 (6) 1984 (5); v A 1979 (6) 1986 (2); v WI 1978 (6) 1983 (5) 1987 (3); v NZ 1988 (3); v P 1979 (5) 1983 (1) 1986 (5); v SL 1982 (1) 1986 (3) 1990 (1); *v E 1979 (4) 1982 (3) 1986 (3) 1990 (3); v A 1977 (5) 1980 (3) 1985 (3); v WI 1975 (2) 1982 (5) 1988 (4); v NZ 1975 (3) 1980 (3) 1989 (2); v P 1978 (3) 1982 (6) 1984 (2); v SL 1985 (3)*

Venkataraghavan, S. 57: v E 1972 (2) 1976 (1); v A 1969 (5) 1979 (3); v WI 1966 (2) 1974 (2) 1978 (6); v NZ 1964 (4) 1969 (2) 1976 (3); v P 1983 (2); *v E 1967 (1) 1971 (3) 1974 (2) 1979 (4); v A 1977 (1); v WI 1970 (5) 1975 (3) 1982 (5); v NZ 1975 (1)*

Venkataramana, M. 1: *v WI 1988*

Viswanath, G. R. 91: v E 1972 (5) 1976 (5) 1979 (1) 1981 (6); v A 1969 (4) 1979 (6); v WI 1974 (5) 1978 (6); v NZ 1976 (3); v P 1979 (6); v SL 1982 (1); *v E 1971 (3) 1974 (3) 1979 (4) 1982 (3); v A 1977 (5) 1980 (3); v WI 1970 (3) 1975 (4); v NZ 1975 (3) 1980 (3); v P 1978 (3) 1982 (6)*

Viswanath, S. 3: *v SL 1985 (3)*

Vizianagram, Maharaj Kumar of, Sir Vijay A. 3: *v E 1936 (3)*

Wadekar, A. L. 37: v E 1972 (5); v A 1969 (5); v WI 1966 (2); v NZ 1969 (3); *v E 1967 (3) 1971 (3) 1974 (3); v A 1967 (4); v WI 1970 (5); v NZ 1967 (4)*

Wassan, A. S. 4: *v E 1990 (1); v NZ 1989 (3)*

Wazir Ali, S. 7: v E 1933 (3); *v E 1932 (1) 1936 (3)*

Yadav, N. S. 35: v E 1979 (1) 1981 (1) 1984 (4); v A 1979 (5) 1986 (3); v WI 1983 (3); v P 1979 (5) 1986 (4); v SL 1986 (2); *v A 1980 (2) 1985 (3); v NZ 1980 (1); v P 1984 (1)*

Yajurvindra Singh 4: v E 1976 (2); v A 1979 (1); *v E 1979 (1)*

Yashpal Sharma 37: v E 1979 (1) 1981 (2); v A 1979 (6); v WI 1983 (1); v P 1979 (6) 1983 (3); v SL 1982 (1); *v E 1979 (3) 1982 (3); v A 1980 (3); v WI 1982 (5); v NZ 1980 (1); v P 1982 (2)*

Yograj Singh 1: *v NZ 1980*

*Note: Hafeez, on going later to Oxford University, took his correct name, Kardar.*

# PAKISTAN

Number of Test cricketers: 121

Aamer Malik 13: v E 1987 (2); v A 1988 (1); v WI 1990 (1); v In 1989 (4); *v A 1989 (2); v WI 1987 (1); v NZ 1988 (2)*

Abdul Kadir 4: v A 1964 (1); *v A 1964 (1); v NZ 1964 (2)*

Abdul Qadir 67: v E 1977 (3) 1983 (3) 1987 (3); v A 1982 (3) 1988 (3); v WI 1980 (2) 1986 (3) 1990 (2); v NZ 1984 (3) 1990 (2); v In 1982 (5) 1984 (1) 1989 (4); v SL 1985 (3); *v E 1982 (3) 1987 (4); v A 1983 (5); v WI 1987 (3); v NZ 1984 (2) 1988 (2); v In 1979 (3) 1986 (3); v SL 1985 (2)*

Afaq Hussain 2: v E 1961 (1); *v A 1964 (1)*

Aftab Baloch 2: v WI 1974 (1); v NZ 1969 (1)

Aftab Gul 6: v E 1968 (2); v NZ 1969 (1); *v E 1971 (3)*

Agha Saadat Ali 1: v NZ 1955

Agha Zahid 1: v WI 1974

Akram Raza 2: v WI 1990 (1); v In 1989 (1)

Alim-ud-Din 25: v E 1961 (2); v A 1956 (1) 1959 (1); v WI 1958 (1); v NZ 1955 (3); v In 1954 (5); *v E 1954 (3) 1962 (3); v WI 1957 (5); v In 1960 (1)*

Amir Elahi 5: *v E 1952 (5)*

Anil Dalpat 9: v E 1983 (3); v NZ 1984 (3); *v NZ 1984 (3)*

Anwar Hussain 4: *v In 1952 (4)*

Anwar Khan 1: *v NZ 1978*

Aqib Javed 5: v NZ 1990 (3); *v A 1989 (1); v NZ 1988 (1)*

Arif Butt 3: *v A 1964 (1); v NZ 1964 (2)*

Ashraf Ali 8: v E 1987 (3); v In 1982 (2); v SL 1981 (2) 1985 (1)

Asif Iqbal 58: v E 1968 (3) 1972 (3); v A 1964 (1); v WI 1974 (2); v NZ 1964 (3) 1969 (3) 1976 (3); v In 1978 (3); *v E 1967 (3) 1971 (3) 1974 (3); v A 1964 (1) 1972 (3) 1976 (3) 1978 (2); v WI 1976 (5); v NZ 1964 (3) 1972 (3) 1978 (2); v In 1979 (6)*

Asif Masood 16: v E 1968 (2) 1972 (1); v WI 1974 (2); v NZ 1969 (1); *v E 1971 (3) 1974 (3); v A 1972 (3) 1976 (1)*

Asif Mujtaba 3: v E 1987 (1); v WI 1986 (2)

Azeem Hafeez 18: v E 1983 (2); v NZ 1984 (3); v In 1984 (2); *v A 1983 (5); v NZ 1984 (3); v In 1983 (3)*

Azhar Khan 1: v A 1979
Azmat Rana 1: v A 1979

Burki, J. 25: v E 1961 (3); v A 1964 (1); v NZ 1964 (3) 1969 (1); *v E 1962 (5) 1967 (3); v A 1964 (1); v NZ 1964 (3); v In 1960 (5)*

D'Souza, A. 6: v E 1961 (2); v WI 1958 (1); *v E 1962 (3)*

Ehtesham-ud-Din 5: v A 1979 (1); *v E 1982 (1); v In 1979 (3)*

Farooq Hamid 1: *v A 1964*
Farrukh Zaman 1: v NZ 1976
Fazal Mahmood 34: v E 1961 (1); v A 1956 (1) 1959 (2); v WI 1958 (3); v NZ 1955 (2); v In 1954 (4); *v E 1954 (4) 1962 (2); v WI 1957 (5); v In 1952 (5) 1960 (5)*

Ghazali, M. E. Z. 2: *v E 1954 (2)*
Ghulam Abbas 1: *v E 1967*
Gul Mahomed 1: v A 1956

Hanif Mohammad 55: v E 1961 (3) 1968 (3); v A 1956 (1) 1959 (3) 1964 (1); v WI 1958 (1); v NZ 1955 (3) 1964 (3) 1969 (1); v In 1954 (5); *v E 1954 (4) 1962 (5) 1967 (3); v A 1964 (1); v WI 1957 (5); v NZ 1964 (3); v In 1952 (5) 1960 (5)*
Haroon Rashid 23: v E 1977 (3); v A 1979 (2) 1982 (3); v In 1982 (1); v SL 1981 (2); *v E 1978 (3) 1982 (1); v A 1976 (1) 1978 (1); v WI 1976 (5); v NZ 1978 (1)*
Haseeb Ahsan 12: v E 1961 (2); v A 1959 (1); v WI 1958 (1); *v WI 1957 (3); v In 1960 (5)*

Ibadulla, K. 4: v A 1964 (1); *v E 1967 (2); v NZ 1964 (1)*
Ijaz Ahmed 19: v E 1987 (3); v A 1988 (3); v WI 1990 (3); *v E 1987 (4); v A 1989 (3); v WI 1987 (2); v In 1986 (1)*
Ijaz Butt 8: v A 1959 (2); v WI 1958 (3); *v E 1962 (3)*
Ijaz Faqih 5: v WI 1980 (1); *v A 1981 (1); v WI 1987 (2); v In 1986 (1)*
Imran Khan 85: v A 1979 (2) 1982 (3); v WI 1980 (4) 1986 (3) 1990 (3); v NZ 1976 (3); v In 1978 (3) 1982 (6) 1989 (4); v SL 1981 (1) 1985 (3); *v E 1971 (1) 1974 (3) 1982 (3) 1987 (5); v A 1976 (3) 1978 (2) 1981 (3) 1983 (2) 1989 (3); v WI 1976 (5) 1987 (3); v NZ 1978 (2) 1988 (2); v In 1979 (5) 1986 (5); v SL 1985 (3)*
Imtiaz Ahmed 41: v E 1961 (3); v A 1956 (1) 1959 (3); v WI 1958 (3); v NZ 1955 (3); v In 1954 (5); *v E 1954 (4) 1962 (4); v WI 1957 (5); v In 1952 (5) 1960 (5)*
Intikhab Alam 47: v E 1961 (2) 1968 (3) 1972 (3); v A 1959 (1) 1964 (1); v WI 1974 (2); v NZ 1964 (3) 1969 (3) 1976 (3); *v E 1962 (3) 1967 (3) 1971 (3) 1974 (3); v A 1964 (1) 1972 (3); v WI 1964 (3); v NZ 1964 (3); v In 1960 (3)*
Iqbal Qasim 50: v E 1977 (3) 1987 (3); v A 1979 (3) 1982 (2) 1988 (3); v WI 1980 (4); v NZ 1984 (3); v In 1978 (3) 1982 (2); v SL 1981 (3); *v E 1978 (3); v A 1976 (3) 1981 (2); v WI 1976 (2); v NZ 1984 (1); v In 1979 (6) 1983 (1) 1986 (3)*
Israr Ali 4: v A 1959 (2); *v In 1952 (2)*

Jalal-ud-Din 6: v A 1982 (1); v In 1982 (2) 1984 (2); v SL 1985 (1)
Javed Akhtar 1: *v E 1962*
Javed Miandad 109: v E 1977 (3) 1987 (3); v A 1979 (3) 1982 (3) 1988 (3); v WI 1980 (4) 1986 (3) 1990 (2); v NZ 1976 (3) 1984 (3) 1990 (3); v In 1978 (3) 1982 (6) 1984 (2) 1989 (4); v SL 1981 (3) 1985 (3); *v E 1978 (3) 1982 (3) 1987 (5); v A 1976 (3) 1981 (3) 1983 (5) 1989 (3); v WI 1976 (1) 1987 (3); v NZ 1978 (3) 1984 (3) 1988 (2); v In 1979 (6) 1983 (3) 1986 (4); v SL 1985 (3)*

Kardar, A. H. 23: v A 1956 (1); v NZ 1955 (3); v In 1954 (4); *v E 1954 (4); v WI 1957 (5); v In 1952 (5)*
Khalid Hassan 1: *v E 1954*
Khalid Wazir 2: *v E 1954 (2)*
Khan Mohammad 13: v A 1956 (1); v NZ 1955 (3); v In 1954 (4); *v E 1954 (2); v WI 1957 (2); v In 1952 (1)*

Liaqat Ali 5: v E 1977 (2); v WI 1974 (1); *v E 1978 (2)*

Mahmood Hussain 27: v E 1961 (1); v WI 1958 (3); v NZ 1955 (1); v In 1954 (5); *v E 1954 (2) 1962 (3); v WI 1957 (3); v In 1952 (4) 1960 (5)*

Majid Khan 63: v E 1968 (3) 1972 (3); v A 1964 (1) 1979 (3); v WI 1974 (2) 1980 (4); v NZ 1964 (3) 1976 (3); v In 1978 (3) 1982 (1); v SL 1981 (1); *v E 1967 (3) 1971 (2) 1974 (3) 1982 (1); v A 1972 (3) 1976 (2) 1981 (3); v WI 1976 (5); v NZ 1972 (3) 1978 (2); v In 1979 (6)*

Mansoor Akhtar 19: v A 1982 (3); v WI 1980 (2); v In 1982 (3); v SL 1981 (1); *v E 1982 (3) 1987 (5); v A 1981 (1) 1989 (1)*

Manzoor Elahi 4: v NZ 1984 (1); v In 1984 (1); *v In 1986 (2)*

Maqsood Ahmed 16: v NZ 1955 (2); v In 1954 (5); *v E 1954 (4); v In 1952 (5)*

Masood Anwar 1: v WI 1990

Mathias, Wallis 21: v E 1961 (1); v A 1956 (1) 1959 (2); v WI 1958 (3); v NZ 1955 (1); *v E 1962 (3); v WI 1957 (5); v In 1960 (5)*

Miran Bux 2: v In 1954 (2)

Mohammad Aslam 1: *v E 1954*

Mohammad Farooq 7: v NZ 1964 (3); *v E 1962 (2); v In 1960 (2)*

Mohammad Ilyas 10: v E 1968 (2); v NZ 1964 (3); *v E 1967 (1); v A 1964 (1); v NZ 1964 (3)*

Mohammad Munaf 4: v E 1961 (2); v A 1959 (2)

Mohammad Nazir 14: v E 1972 (1); v WI 1980 (4); v NZ 1969 (3); *v A 1983 (3); v In 1983 (3)*

Mohsin Kamal 7: v E 1983 (1); v SL 1985 (1); *v E 1987 (4); v SL 1985 (1)*

Mohsin Khan 48: v E 1977 (1) 1983 (3); v A 1982 (3); v WI 1986 (3); v NZ 1984 (2); v In 1982 (6) 1984 (2); v SL 1981 (2) 1985 (2); *v E 1978 (3) 1982 (3); v A 1978 (1) 1981 (2) 1983 (5); v NZ 1978 (1) 1984 (3); v In 1983 (3); v SL 1985 (3)*

Moin Khan 2: v WI 1990 (2)

Mudassar Nazar 76: v E 1977 (3) 1983 (1) 1987 (3); v A 1979 (3) 1982 (3) 1988 (3); v WI 1986 (2); v NZ 1984 (3); v In 1978 (2) 1982 (6) 1984 (2); v SL 1981 (1) 1985 (3); *v E 1978 (3) 1982 (3) 1987 (5); v A 1976 (1) 1978 (1) 1981 (3) 1983 (5); v WI 1987 (3); v NZ 1978 (1) 1984 (3) 1988 (2); v In 1979 (5) 1983 (3); v SL 1985 (3)*

Mufasir-ul-Haq 1: *v NZ 1964*

Munir Malik 3: v A 1959 (1); *v E 1962 (2)*

Mushtaq Ahmed 3: v WI 1990 (2); *v A 1989 (1)*

Mushtaq Mohammad 57: v E 1961 (3) 1968 (3) 1972 (3); v WI 1958 (1) 1974 (2); v NZ 1969 (2) 1976 (3); v In 1978 (3); *v E 1962 (5) 1967 (3) 1971 (3) 1974 (3); v A 1972 (3) 1976 (3) 1978 (2); v WI 1976 (5); v NZ 1972 (2) 1978 (3); v In 1960 (5)*

Nadeem Abbasi 3: v In 1989 (3)

Nadeem Ghauri 1: *v A 1989*

Nasim-ul-Ghani 29: v E 1961 (2); v A 1959 (2) 1964 (1); v WI 1958 (3); *v E 1962 (5) 1967 (2); v A 1964 (1) 1972 (1); v WI 1957 (5); v NZ 1964 (3); v In 1960 (4)*

Naushad Ali 6: v NZ 1964 (3); *v NZ 1964 (3)*

Naved Anjum 2: v NZ 1990 (1); v In 1989 (1)

Nazar Mohammad 5: *v In 1952 (5)*

Nazir Junior (*see* Mohammad Nazir)

Niaz Ahmed 2: v E 1968 (1); *v E 1967 (1)*

Pervez Sajjad 19: v E 1968 (1) 1972 (2); v A 1964 (1); v NZ 1964 (3) 1969 (3); *v E 1971 (3); v NZ 1964 (3) 1972 (3)*

Qasim Omar 26: v E 1983 (3); v WI 1986 (3); v NZ 1984 (2); v In 1984 (3); v SL 1985 (3); *v A 1983 (5); v NZ 1984 (3); v In 1983 (1); v SL 1985 (3)*

Ramiz Raja 36: v E 1983 (2) 1987 (3); v A 1988 (3); v WI 1986 (3) 1990 (2); v NZ 1990 (3); v In 1989 (4); v SL 1985 (1); *v E 1987 (2); v A 1989 (2); v WI 1987 (3); v In 1986 (5); v SL 1985 (3)*

Rashid Khan 4: v SL 1981 (2); *v A 1983 (1); v NZ 1984 (1)*

Rehman, S. F. 1: *v WI 1957*

Rizwan-uz-Zaman 11: v WI 1986 (1); v SL 1981 (2); *v A 1981 (1); v NZ 1988 (2); v In 1986 (5)*

Sadiq Mohammad 41: v E 1972 (3) 1977 (2); v WI 1974 (1) 1980 (3); v NZ 1969 (3) 1976 (3); v In 1978 (1); *v E 1971 (3) 1974 (3) 1978 (3); v A 1972 (3) 1976 (2); v WI 1976 (5); v NZ 1972 (3); v In 1979 (3)*

Saeed Ahmed 41: v E 1961 (3) 1968 (3); v A 1959 (3) 1964 (1); v WI 1958 (3); v NZ 1964 (3); *v E 1962 (5) 1967 (3) 1971 (1); v A 1964 (1) 1972 (2); v WI 1957 (5); v NZ 1964 (3); v In 1960 (5)*

Saeed Anwar 1: v WI 1990

Salah-ud-Din 5: v E 1968 (1); v NZ 1964 (3) 1969 (1)

Saleem Jaffer 12: v E 1987 (1); v A 1988 (2); v WI 1986 (1); v NZ 1990 (2); v In 1989 (1); *v WI 1987 (1); v NZ 1988 (2); v In 1986 (2)*

Salim Altaf 21: v E 1972 (3); v NZ 1969 (2); v In 1978 (1); *v E 1967 (2) 1971 (2); v A 1972 (3) 1976 (2); v WI 1976 (3); v NZ 1972 (3)*

Salim Malik 63: v E 1983 (3) 1987 (3); v A 1988 (3); v WI 1986 (1) 1990 (3); v NZ 1984 (3) 1990 (3); v In 1982 (6) 1984 (2) 1989 (4); v SL 1981 (2) 1985 (3); *v E 1987 (5); v A 1983 (3) 1989 (1); v WI 1987 (3); v NZ 1984 (3) 1988 (2); v In 1983 (2) 1986 (5); v SL 1985 (3)*

Salim Yousuf 32: v A 1988 (3); v WI 1986 (3) 1990 (1); v NZ 1990 (3); v In 1989 (1); v SL 1981 (1) 1985 (2); *v E 1987 (5); v A 1989 (3); v WI 1987 (3); v NZ 1988 (2); v In 1986 (5)*

Sarfraz Nawaz 55: v E 1968 (1) 1972 (2) 1977 (2) 1983 (2); v A 1979 (3); v WI 1974 (2) 1980 (2); v NZ 1976 (3); v In 1978 (3) 1982 (6); *v E 1974 (3) 1978 (2) 1982 (1); v A 1972 (2) 1976 (2) 1978 (2) 1981 (3) 1983 (2); v WI 1976 (4); v NZ 1972 (3) 1978 (3)*

Shafiq Ahmed 6: v E 1977 (3); v WI 1980 (2); *v E 1974 (1)*

Shafqat Rana 5: v E 1968 (2); v A 1964 (1); v NZ 1969 (2)

Shahid Israr 1: v NZ 1976

Shahid Mahboob 1: v In 1989

Shahid Mahmood 1: *v E 1962*

Shahid Saeed 1: v In 1989

Sharpe, D. 3: v A 1959 (3)

Shoaib Mohammad 35: v E 1983 (1) 1987 (1); v A 1988 (3); v WI 1990 (3); v NZ 1984 (1) 1990 (3); v In 1989 (4); v SL 1985 (1); *v E 1987 (4); v A 1989 (3); v WI 1987 (3); v NZ 1984 (1) 1988 (2); v In 1983 (2) 1986 (3)*

Shuja-ud-Din 19: v E 1961 (2); v WI 1980 (1); v NZ 1976 (1); v In 1978 (2) 1982 (1); *v E 1954 (3)*

Sikander Bakht 26: v E 1977 (2); v WI 1980 (1); v NZ 1976 (1); v In 1978 (2) 1982 (1); *v E 1978 (3) 1982 (2); v A 1978 (2) 1981 (3); v WI 1976 (1); v NZ 1978 (3); v In 1979 (5)*

Tahir Naqqash 15: v A 1982 (3); v In 1982 (2); v SL 1981 (1); *v E 1982 (2); v A 1983 (1); v NZ 1984 (1); v In 1983 (3)*

Talat Ali 10: v E 1972 (3); *v E 1978 (2); v A 1972 (1); v NZ 1972 (1) 1978 (3)*

Taslim Arif 6: v A 1979 (3); v WI 1980 (2); *v In 1979 (1)*

Tauseef Ahmed 33: v E 1983 (2) 1987 (2); v A 1979 (3) 1988 (3); v WI 1986 (3); v NZ 1984 (1) 1990 (2); v In 1984 (1); v SL 1981 (3) 1985 (1); *v E 1987 (2); v A 1989 (3); v NZ 1988 (1); v In 1986 (4); v SL 1985 (2)*

Waqar Hassan 21: v A 1956 (1) 1959 (1); v WI 1958 (3); v NZ 1955 (3); v In 1954 (5); *v E 1954 (4); v WI 1957 (1); v In 1952 (5)*

Waqar Younis 11: v WI 1990 (3); v NZ 1990 (3); v In 1989 (2); *v A 1989 (3)*

Wasim Akram 37: v E 1987 (2); v WI 1986 (2) 1990 (3); v NZ 1990 (2); v In 1989 (4); v SL 1985 (3); *v E 1987 (5); v A 1989 (3); v WI 1987 (3); v NZ 1984 (2); v In 1986 (5); v SL 1985 (3)*

Wasim Bari 81: v E 1968 (3) 1972 (3) 1977 (3); v A 1982 (3); v WI 1974 (2) 1980 (2); v NZ 1969 (3) 1976 (2); v In 1978 (3) 1982 (6); *v E 1967 (3) 1971 (3) 1974 (3) 1978 (3) 1982 (3); v A 1972 (3) 1976 (3) 1978 (2) 1981 (3) 1983 (5); v WI 1976 (5); v NZ 1972 (3) 1978 (3); v In 1979 (6) 1983 (3)*

Wasim Raja 57: v E 1972 (1) 1977 (3) 1983 (3); v A 1979 (3); v WI 1974 (2) 1980 (4); v NZ 1976 (1) 1984 (1); v In 1982 (1) 1984 (1); v SL 1981 (3); *v E 1974 (2) 1978 (3) 1982 (1); v A 1978 (1) 1981 (3) 1983 (2); v WI 1976 (5); v NZ 1972 (3) 1978 (3) 1984 (2); v In 1979 (6) 1983 (3)*

Wazir Mohammad 20: v A 1956 (1) 1959 (1); v WI 1958 (3); v NZ 1955 (2); v In 1954 (5); *v E 1954 (2); v WI 1957 (5); v In 1952 (1)*

Younis Ahmed 4: v NZ 1969 (2); *v In 1986 (2)*

Zaheer Abbas 78: v E 1972 (2) 1983 (3); v A 1979 (2) 1982 (3); v WI 1974 (2) 1980 (3); v NZ 1969 (1) 1976 (3) 1984 (3); v In 1978 (3) 1982 (6) 1984 (2); v SL 1981 (1) 1985 (2); *v E 1971 (3) 1974 (3) 1982 (3); v A 1972 (3) 1976 (3) 1978 (2) 1981 (2) 1983 (5); v WI 1976 (3); v NZ 1972 (3) 1978 (2) 1984 (2); v In 1979 (5) 1983 (3)*

Zahid Fazal 3: v WI 1990 (3)

Zakir Khan 2: v In 1989 (1); *v SL 1985 (1)*

Zulfiqar Ahmed 9: v A 1956 (1); v NZ 1955 (3); *v E 1954 (2); v In 1952 (3)*

Zulqarnain 3: *v SL 1985 (3)*

## SRI LANKA

Number of Test cricketers: 50

Ahangama, F. S. 3: v In 1985 (3)
Amalean, K. N. 2: v P 1985 (1); *v A 1987 (1)*
Amerasinghe, A. M. J. G. 2: v NZ 1983 (2)
Anurasiri, S. D. 5: v NZ 1986 (1); v P 1985 (2); *v E 1991 (1); v In 1986 (1)*
Atapattu, M. S. 1: *v In 1990*
de Alwis, R. G. 11: v A 1982 (1); v NZ 1983 (3); v P 1985 (2); *v A 1987 (1); v NZ 1982 (1); v In 1986 (3)*
de Mel, A. L. F. 17: v E 1981 (1); v A 1982 (1); v In 1985 (3); v P 1985 (3); *v E 1984 (1); v In 1982 (1) 1986 (1); v P 1981 (3) 1985 (3)*
de Silva, D. S. 12: v E 1981 (1); v A 1982 (1); v NZ 1983 (3); *v E 1984 (1); v NZ 1982 (2); v In 1982 (1); v P 1981 (3)*
de Silva, E. A. R. 10: v In 1985 (1); v P 1985 (1); *v A 1989 (2); v NZ 1990 (3); v NZ 1990 (3); v In 1986 (3)*
de Silva, G. R. A. 4: v E 1981 (1); *v In 1982 (1); v P 1981 (2)*
de Silva, P. A. 22: v In 1985 (3); v P 1985 (2); *v E 1984 (1) 1988 (1) 1991 (1); v A 1987 (1) 1989 (2); v NZ 1990 (3); v In 1986 (3) 1990 (1); v P 1985 (2)*
Dias, R. L. 20: v E 1981 (1); v A 1982 (1); v NZ 1983 (2) 1986 (1); v In 1985 (3); v P 1985 (1); *v E 1984 (1); v In 1982 (1) 1986 (3); v P 1981 (3) 1985 (3)*

Fernando, E. R. N. S. 5: v A 1982 (1); v NZ 1983 (2); *v NZ 1982 (2)*

Goonatillake, H. M. 5: v E 1981 (1); *v In 1982 (1); v P 1981 (3)*
Gunasekera, Y. 2: *v NZ 1982 (2)*
Guneratne, R. P. W. 1: v A 1982
Gurusinha, A. P. 14: v NZ 1986 (1); v P 1985 (2); *v E 1991 (1); v A 1989 (2); v NZ 1990 (3); v In 1986 (3) 1990 (1); v P 1985 (1)*

Hathurusinghe, U. C. 3: *v E 1991 (1); v NZ 1990 (2)*

Jayasekera, R. S. A. 1: *v P 1981*
Jayasuriya S. T. 3: *v E 1991 (1); v NZ 1990 (2)*
Jeganathan, S. 2: *v NZ 1982 (2)*
John, V. B. 6: v NZ 1983 (3); *v E 1984 (1); v NZ 1982 (2)*
Jurangpathy, B. R. 2: v In 1985 (1); *v In 1986 (1)*

Kaluperuma, L. W. 2: v E 1981 (1); *v P 1981 (1)*
Kaluperuma, S. M. S. 4: v NZ 1983 (3); *v A 1987 (1)*
Kuruppu, D. S. B. P. 4: v NZ 1986 (1); *v E 1988 (1) 1991 (1); v A 1987 (1)*
Kuruppuarachchi, A. K. 2: v NZ 1986 (1); v P 1985 (1)

Labrooy, G. F. 9: *v E 1988 (1); v A 1987 (1) 1989 (2); v NZ 1990 (3); v In 1986 (1) 1990 (1)*

Madugalle, R. S. 21: v E 1981 (1); v A 1982 (1); v NZ 1983 (3) 1986 (1); v In 1985 (3); *v E 1984 (1) 1988 (1); v A 1987 (1); v NZ 1982 (2); v In 1982 (1); v P 1981 (3) 1985 (3)*
Madurasinghe, A. W. R. 2: *v E 1988 (1); v In 1990 (1)*
Mahanama, R. S. 9: v NZ 1986 (1); v P 1985 (2); *v E 1991 (1); v A 1987 (1) 1989 (2); v NZ 1990 (1); v In 1990 (1)*
Mendis, L. R. D. 24: v E 1981 (1); v A 1982 (1); v NZ 1983 (3) 1986 (1); v In 1985 (3); v P 1985 (3); *v E 1984 (1) 1988 (1); v In 1982 (1) 1986 (3); v P 1981 (3) 1985 (3)*

Ramanayake, C. P. H. 8: *v E 1988 (1) 1991 (1); v A 1987 (1) 1989 (2); v NZ 1990 (3)*
Ranasinghe, A. N. 2: *v In 1982 (1); v P 1981 (1)*
Ranatunga, A. 30: v E 1981 (1); v A 1982 (1); v NZ 1983'(3) 1986 (1); v In 1985 (3); v P 1985 (3); *v E 1984 (1) 1988 (1); v A 1987 (1) 1989 (2); v NZ 1990 (3); v In 1982 (1) 1986 (3) 1990 (1); v P 1981 (2) 1985 (3)*
Ranatunga, D. 2: *v A 1989 (2)*

Ratnayake, R. J. 20: v A 1982 (1); v NZ 1983 (1) 1986 (1); v In 1985 (3); v P 1985 (1); *v E 1991 (1); v A 1989 (1); v NZ 1982 (2) 1990 (3); v In 1986 (2) 1990 (1); v P 1985 (3)*
Ratnayeke, J. R. 22: v NZ 1983 (2) 1986 (1); v P 1985 (3); *v E 1984 (1) 1988 (1); v A 1987 (1) 1989 (2); v NZ 1982 (2); v In 1982 (1) 1986 (3); v P 1981 (2) 1985 (3)*

Samarasekera, M. A. R. 3: *v E 1988 (1); v A 1989 (1); v In 1990 (1)*
Senanayake, C. P. 3: *v NZ 1990 (3)*
Silva, S. A. R. 9: v In 1985 (3); v P 1985 (1); *v E 1984 (1) 1988 (1); v NZ 1982 (1); v P 1985 (2)*

Tillekeratne, H. P. 6: *v E 1991 (1); v A 1989 (1); v NZ 1990 (3); v In 1990 (1)*

Warnapura, B. 4: v E 1981 (1); *v In 1982 (1); v P 1981 (2)*
Warnaweera, K. P. J. 3: v P 1985 (1); *v NZ 1990 (1); v In 1990 (1)*
Weerasinghe, C. D. U. S. 1: v In 1985
Wettimuny, M. D. 2: *v NZ 1982 (2)*
Wettimuny, S. 23: v E 1981 (1); v A 1982 (1); v NZ 1983 (3); v In 1985 (3); v P 1985 (3); *v E 1984 (1); v NZ 1982 (2); v In 1986 (3); v P 1981 (3) 1985 (3)*
Wickremasinghe, A. G. D. 1: *v A 1989*
Wijegunawardene, K. I. W. 1: *v E 1991*
Wijesuriya, R. G. C. E. 4: *v P 1981 (1) 1985 (3)*

## TWO COUNTRIES

Twelve cricketers have appeared for two countries in Test matches, namely:

Amir Elahi, *India and Pakistan.*
J. J. Ferris, *Australia and England.*
S. C. Guillen, *West Indies and NZ.*
Gul Mahomed, *India and Pakistan.*
F. Hearne, *England and South Africa.*
A. H. Kardar, *India and Pakistan.*

W. E. Midwinter, *England and Australia.*
F. Mitchell, *England and South Africa.*
W. L. Murdoch, *Australia and England.*
Nawab of Pataudi, sen., *England and India.*
A. E. Trott, *Australia and England.*
S. M. J. Woods, *Australia and England.*

## MOST TEST APPEARANCES FOR EACH COUNTRY

England: M. C. Cowdrey and
    D. I. Gower 114.
Australia: A. R. Border 125.
South Africa: J. H. B. Waite 50.
West Indies: I. V. A. Richards 121.

New Zealand: Sir R. J. Hadlee 86.
India: S. M. Gavaskar 125.
Pakistan: Javed Miandad 109.
Sri Lanka: A. Ranatunga 30.

## MOST TEST APPEARANCES AS CAPTAIN
## FOR EACH COUNTRY

England: P. B. H. May 41.
Australia: A. R. Border 62.
South Africa: H. W. Taylor 18.
West Indies: C. H. Lloyd 74.

New Zealand: J. R. Reid 34.
India: S. M. Gavaskar 47.
Pakistan: Imran Khan 45.
Sri Lanka: L. R. D. Mendis 19.

## ENGLAND v REST OF THE WORLD

The following were awarded England caps for playing against the Rest of the World in England in 1970, although the five matches played are now generally considered not to have rated as full Tests: D. L. Amiss (1), G. Boycott (2), D. J. Brown (2), M. C. Cowdrey (4), M. H. Denness (1), B. L. D'Oliveira (4), J. H. Edrich (2), K. W. R. Fletcher (4), A. W. Greig (3), R. Illingworth (5), A. Jones (1), A. P. E. Knott (5), P. Lever (1), B. W. Luckhurst (5), C. M. Old (2), P. J. Sharpe (1), K. Shuttleworth (1), J. A. Snow (5), D. L. Underwood (3), A. Ward (1), D. Wilson (2).

# CRICKET RECORDS

Amended by BILL FRINDALL to end of the 1991 season in England

Unless stated to be of a minor character, all records apply only to first-class cricket including some performances in the distant past which have always been recognised as of exceptional merit.

   \* Denotes not out or an unbroken partnership.

   (A), (SA), (WI), (NZ), (I), (P) or (SL) indicates either the nationality of the player, or the country in which the record was made.

## FIRST-CLASS RECORDS

### BATTING RECORDS

### BOWLING RECORDS

## ALL-ROUND RECORDS

## WICKET-KEEPING RECORDS

## FIELDING RECORDS

## TEAM RECORDS

# TEST MATCH RECORDS

## BATTING RECORDS

## BOWLING RECORDS

## ALL-ROUND RECORDS

## WICKET-KEEPING RECORDS

## FIELDING RECORDS

## TEAM RECORDS

## TEST SERIES

## LIMITED-OVERS INTERNATIONAL RECORDS

## MISCELLANEOUS

# FIRST-CLASS RECORDS

## BATTING RECORDS

### HIGHEST INDIVIDUAL SCORES

| | | | |
|---|---|---|---|
| 499 | Hanif Mohammad | Karachi v Bahawalpur at Karachi | 1958-59 |
| 452* | D. G. Bradman | NSW v Queensland at Sydney | 1929-30 |
| 443* | B. B. Nimbalkar | Maharashtra v Kathiawar at Poona | 1948-49 |
| 437 | W. H. Ponsford | Victoria v Queensland at Melbourne | 1927-28 |
| 429 | W. H. Ponsford | Victoria v Tasmania at Melbourne | 1922-23 |
| 428 | Aftab Baloch | Sind v Baluchistan at Karachi | 1973-74 |
| 424 | A. C. MacLaren | Lancashire v Somerset at Taunton | 1895 |
| 405* | G. A. Hick | Worcestershire v Somerset at Taunton | 1988 |
| 385 | B. Sutcliffe | Otago v Canterbury at Christchurch | 1952-53 |
| 383 | C. W. Gregory | NSW v Queensland at Brisbane | 1906-07 |
| 377 | S. V. Manjrekar | Bombay v Hyderabad at Bombay | 1990-91 |
| 369 | D. G. Bradman | South Australia v Tasmania at Adelaide | 1935-36 |
| 366 | N. H. Fairbrother | Lancashire v Surrey at The Oval | 1990 |
| 365* | C. Hill | South Australia v NSW at Adelaide | 1900-01 |
| 365* | G. S. Sobers | West Indies v Pakistan at Kingston | 1957-58 |
| 364 | L. Hutton | England v Australia at The Oval | 1938 |
| 359* | V. M. Merchant | Bombay v Maharashtra at Bombay | 1943-44 |
| 359 | R. B. Simpson | NSW v Queensland at Brisbane | 1963-64 |
| 357* | R. Abel | Surrey v Somerset at The Oval | 1899 |
| 357 | D. G. Bradman | South Australia v Victoria at Melbourne | 1935-36 |
| 356 | B. A. Richards | South Australia v Western Australia at Perth | 1970-71 |
| 355* | G. R. Marsh | Western Australia v South Australia at Perth | 1989-90 |
| 355 | B. Sutcliffe | Otago v Auckland at Dunedin | 1949-50 |
| 352 | W. H. Ponsford | Victoria v NSW at Melbourne | 1926-27 |
| 350 | Rashid Israr | Habib Bank v National Bank at Lahore | 1976-77 |
| 345 | C. G. Macartney | Australians v Nottinghamshire at Nottingham | 1921 |
| 344* | G. A. Headley | Jamaica v Lord Tennyson's XI at Kingston | 1931-32 |
| 344 | W. G. Grace | MCC v Kent at Canterbury | 1876 |
| 343* | P. A. Perrin | Essex v Derbyshire at Chesterfield | 1904 |
| 341 | G. H. Hirst | Yorkshire v Leicestershire at Leicester | 1905 |
| 340* | D. G. Bradman | NSW v Victoria at Sydney | 1928-29 |
| 340 | S. M. Gavaskar | Bombay v Bengal at Bombay | 1981-82 |
| 338* | R. C. Blunt | Otago v Canterbury at Christchurch | 1931-32 |
| 338 | W. W. Read | Surrey v Oxford University at The Oval | 1888 |
| 337* | Pervez Akhtar | Railways v Dera Ismail Khan at Lahore | 1964-65 |
| 337† | Hanif Mohammad | Pakistan v West Indies at Bridgetown | 1957-58 |
| 336* | W. R. Hammond | England v New Zealand at Auckland | 1932-33 |
| 336 | W. H. Ponsford | Victoria v South Australia at Melbourne | 1927-28 |
| 334 | D. G. Bradman | Australia v England at Leeds | 1930 |
| 333 | K. S. Duleepsinhji | Sussex v Northamptonshire at Hove | 1930 |
| 333 | G. A. Gooch | England v India at Lord's | 1990 |
| 332 | W. H. Ashdown | Kent v Essex at Brentwood | 1934 |
| 331* | J. D. Robertson | Middlesex v Worcestershire at Worcester | 1949 |
| 325* | H. L. Hendry | Victoria v New Zealanders at Melbourne | 1925-26 |
| 325 | A. Sandham | England v West Indies at Kingston | 1929-30 |
| 325 | C. L. Badcock | South Australia v Victoria at Adelaide | 1935-36 |
| 324 | J. B. Stollmeyer | Trinidad v British Guiana at Port-of-Spain | 1946-47 |
| 324 | Waheed Mirza | Karachi Whites v Quetta at Karachi | 1976-77 |
| 323 | A. L. Wadekar | Bombay v Mysore at Bombay | 1966-67 |
| 322 | E. Paynter | Lancashire v Sussex at Hove | 1937 |
| 322 | I. V. A. Richards | Somerset v Warwickshire at Taunton | 1985 |
| 321 | W. L. Murdoch | NSW v Victoria at Sydney | 1881-82 |
| 320 | R. Lamba | North Zone v West Zone at Bhilai | 1987-88 |
| 319 | Gul Mahomed | Baroda v Holkar at Baroda | 1946-47 |
| 318* | W. G. Grace | Gloucestershire v Yorkshire at Cheltenham | 1876 |

| | | | |
|---|---|---|---|
| 317 | W. R. Hammond | Gloucestershire v Nottinghamshire at Gloucester ... | 1936 |
| 317 | K. R. Rutherford | New Zealanders v D. B. Close's XI at Scarborough. | 1986 |
| 316* | J. B. Hobbs | Surrey v Middlesex at Lord's ................... | 1926 |
| 316* | V. S. Hazare | Maharashtra v Baroda at Poona ............... | 1939-40 |
| 316 | R. H. Moore | Hampshire v Warwickshire at Bournemouth...... | 1937 |
| 315* | T. W. Hayward | Surrey v Lancashire at The Oval .............. | 1898 |
| 315* | P. Holmes | Yorkshire v Middlesex at Lord's................ | 1925 |
| 315* | A. F. Kippax | NSW v Queensland at Sydney ................. | 1927-28 |
| 314* | C. L. Walcott | Barbados v Trinidad at Port-of-Spain .......... | 1945-46 |
| 313* | S. J. Cook | Somerset v Glamorgan at Cardiff .............. | 1990 |
| 313 | H. Sutcliffe | Yorkshire v Essex at Leyton .................. | 1932 |
| 313 | W. V. Raman | Tamil Nadu v Goa at Panaji .................. | 1988-89 |
| 312* | W. W. Keeton | Nottinghamshire v Middlesex at The Oval‡ ...... | 1939 |
| 312* | J. M. Brearley | MCC Under 25 v North Zone at Peshawar ...... | 1966-67 |
| 311* | G. M. Turner | Worcestershire v Warwickshire at Worcester ..... | 1982 |
| 311 | J. T. Brown | Yorkshire v Sussex at Sheffield ............... | 1897 |
| 311 | R. B. Simpson | Australia v England at Manchester ............ | 1964 |
| 311 | Javed Miandad | Karachi Whites v National Bank at Karachi ..... | 1974-75 |
| 310* | J. H. Edrich | England v New Zealand at Leeds .............. | 1965 |
| 310 | H. Gimblett | Somerset v Sussex at Eastbourne .............. | 1948 |
| 309 | V. S. Hazare | The Rest v Hindus at Bombay ................ | 1943-44 |
| 308* | F. M. M. Worrell | Barbados v Trinidad at Bridgetown ............ | 1943-44 |
| 307 | M. C. Cowdrey | MCC v South Australia at Adelaide ........... | 1962-63 |
| 307 | R. M. Cowper | Australia v England at Melbourne ............. | 1965-66 |
| 306* | A. Ducat | Surrey v Oxford University at The Oval ........ | 1919 |
| 306* | E. A. B. Rowan | Transvaal v Natal at Johannesburg ............ | 1939-40 |
| 306* | D. W. Hookes | South Australia v Tasmania at Adelaide ........ | 1986-87 |
| 305* | F. E. Woolley | MCC v Tasmania at Hobart ................... | 1911-12 |
| 305* | F. R. Foster | Warwickshire v Worcestershire at Dudley ....... | 1914 |
| 305* | W. H. Ashdown | Kent v Derbyshire at Dover .................. | 1935 |
| 304* | A. W. Nourse | Natal v Transvaal at Johannesburg ............ | 1919-20 |
| 304* | P. H. Tarilton | Barbados v Trinidad at Bridgetown ............ | 1919-20 |
| 304* | E. D. Weekes | West Indians v Cambridge University at Cambridge | 1950 |
| 304 | R. M. Poore | Hampshire v Somerset at Taunton ............. | 1899 |
| 304 | D. G. Bradman | Australia v England at Leeds ................. | 1934 |
| 303* | W. W. Armstrong | Australians v Somerset at Bath ............... | 1905 |
| 303* | Mushtaq Mohammad | Karachi Blues v Karachi University at Karachi .. | 1967-68 |
| 303* | Abdul Azeem | Hyderabad v Tamil Nadu at Hyderabad ........ | 1986-87 |
| 302* | P. Holmes | Yorkshire v Hampshire at Portsmouth.......... | 1920 |
| 302* | W. R. Hammond | Gloucestershire v Glamorgan at Bristol ........ | 1934 |
| 302* | Arjan Kripal Singh | Tamil Nadu v Goa at Panaji .................. | 1988-89 |
| 302 | W. R. Hammond | Gloucestershire v Glamorgan at Newport ....... | 1939 |
| 302 | L. G. Rowe | West Indies v England at Bridgetown .......... | 1973-74 |
| 301* | E. H. Hendren | Middlesex v Worcestershire at Dudley .......... | 1933 |
| 301 | W. G. Grace | Gloucestershire v Sussex at Bristol ............ | 1896 |
| 300* | V. T. Trumper | Australians v Sussex at Hove ................. | 1899 |
| 300* | F. B. Watson | Lancashire v Surrey at Manchester ............ | 1928 |
| 300* | Imtiaz Ahmed | PM's XI v Commonwealth XI at Bombay ....... | 1950-51 |
| 300 | J. T. Brown | Yorkshire v Derbyshire at Chesterfield ......... | 1898 |
| 300 | D. C. S. Compton | MCC v N. E. Transvaal at Benoni ............ | 1948-49 |
| 300 | R. Subba Row | Northamptonshire v Surrey at The Oval ........ | 1958 |

† *Hanif Mohammad batted for 16 hours 10 minutes – the longest innings in first-class cricket.*
‡ *Played at The Oval because Lord's was required for Eton v Harrow.*
*Note:* W. V. Raman (313) and Arjan Kripal Singh (302*) provide the only instance of two triple-hundreds in the same innings.

## HIGHEST FOR TEAMS

*For English Teams in Australia*

| | | | |
|---|---|---|---|
| 307 | M. C. Cowdrey | MCC v South Australia at Adelaide ........... | 1962-63 |
| 287 | R. E. Foster | England v Australia at Sydney ................ | 1903-04 |

*Against Australians in England*

| 364 | L. Hutton | England v Australia at The Oval | 1938 |
| 219 | A. Sandham | Surrey at The Oval (record for any county) | 1934 |

*For Australian Teams in England*

| 345 | C. G. Macartney | v Nottinghamshire at Nottingham | 1921 |
| 334 | D. G. Bradman | Australia v England at Leeds | 1930 |

*Against English Teams in Australia*

| 307 | R. M. Cowper | Australia v England at Melbourne | 1965-66 |
| 280 | A. J. Richardson | South Australia v MCC at Adelaide | 1922-23 |

*For Each First-Class County*

| Derbyshire | 274 | G. Davidson v Lancashire at Manchester | 1896 |
| Essex | 343* | P. A. Perrin v Derbyshire at Chesterfield | 1904 |
| Glamorgan | 287* | D. E. Davies v Gloucestershire at Newport | 1939 |
| Gloucestershire | 318* | W. G. Grace v Yorkshire at Cheltenham | 1876 |
| Hampshire | 316 | R. H. Moore v Warwickshire at Bournemouth | 1937 |
| Kent | 332 | W. H. Ashdown v Essex at Brentwood | 1934 |
| Lancashire | 424 | A. C. MacLaren v Somerset at Taunton | 1895 |
| Leicestershire | 252* | S. Coe v Northamptonshire at Leicester | 1914 |
| Middlesex | 331* | J. D. Robertson v Worcestershire at Worcester | 1949 |
| Northamptonshire | 300 | R. Subba Row v Surrey at The Oval | 1958 |
| Nottinghamshire | 312* | W. W. Keeton v Middlesex at The Oval† | 1939 |
| Somerset | 322 | I. V. A. Richards v Warwickshire at Taunton | 1985 |
| Surrey | 357* | R. Abel v Somerset at The Oval | 1899 |
| Sussex | 333 | K. S. Duleepsinhji v Northamptonshire at Hove | 1930 |
| Warwickshire | 305* | F. R. Foster v Worcestershire at Dudley | 1914 |
| Worcestershire | 405* | G. A. Hick v Somerset at Taunton | 1988 |
| Yorkshire | 341 | G. H. Hirst v Leicestershire at Leicester | 1905 |

† *Played at The Oval because Lord's was required for Eton v Harrow.*

## HUNDRED ON DEBUT IN BRITISH ISLES

(The following list does not include instances of players who have previously appeared in first-class cricket outside the British Isles or who performed the feat before 1946. Particulars of the latter are in *Wisdens* prior to 1984.)

| 114 | F. W. Stocks | Nottinghamshire v Kent at Nottingham | 1946 |
| 108 | A. Fairbairn | Middlesex v Somerset at Taunton | †‡1947 |
| 124 | P. Hearn | Kent v Warwickshire at Gillingham | 1947 |
| 215* | G. H. G. Doggart | Cambridge University v Lancashire at Cambridge | 1948 |
| 106 | J. R. Gill | Ireland v MCC at Dublin | 1948 |
| 107* | G. Barker | Essex v Canadians at Clacton | †1954 |
| 135 | J. K. E. Slack | Cambridge University v Middlesex at Cambridge | 1954 |
| 100* | E. A. Clark | Middlesex v Cambridge University at Cambridge | 1959 |
| 113 | G. J. Chidgey | Free Foresters v Cambridge U. at Cambridge | 1962 |
| 108 | D. R. Shepherd | Gloucestershire v Oxford University at Oxford | 1965 |
| 110* | A. J. Harvey-Walker | Derbyshire v Oxford University at Burton upon Trent | †1971 |
| 173 | J. Whitehouse | Warwickshire v Oxford University at Oxford | 1971 |
| 106 | J. B. Turner | Minor Counties v Pakistanis at Jesmond | 1974 |
| 112 | J. A. Claughton | Oxford University v Gloucestershire at Oxford | †1976 |
| 100* | A. W. Lilley | Essex v Nottinghamshire at Nottingham | †1978 |
| 146* | J. S. Johnson | Minor Counties v Indians at Wellington | 1979 |
| 110 | N. R. Taylor | Kent v Sri Lankans at Canterbury | 1979 |
| 146* | D. G. Aslett | Kent v Hampshire at Bournemouth | 1981 |
| 116 | M. D. Moxon | Yorkshire v Essex at Leeds | †1981 |
| 100 | D. A. Banks | Worcestershire v Oxford University at Oxford | 1983 |
| 122 | A. A. Metcalfe | Yorkshire v Nottinghamshire at Bradford | 1983 |
| 117* | K. T. Medlycott | } Surrey v Cambridge University at Banstead | §1984 |
| 101* | N. J. Falkner | | |
| 106 | A. C. Storie | Northamptonshire v Hampshire at Northampton | †1985 |
| 102 | M. P. Maynard | Glamorgan v Yorkshire at Swansea | 1985 |

| | | | |
|---|---|---|---|
| 117* R. J. Bartlett | Somerset v Oxford University at Oxford .......... | 1986 |
| 100* P. D. Bowler | Leicestershire v Hampshire at Leicester ........... | 1986 |
| 145  I. L. Philip | Scotland v Ireland at Glasgow ................. | 1986 |
| 114* D. J. Atkins | Surrey v Cambridge University at The Oval ........ | 1988 |
| 100  B. M. W. Patterson | Scotland v Ireland at Dumfries ................ | 1988 |
| 116* J. J. B. Lewis | Essex v Surrey at The Oval................... | 1990 |

† *In his second innings.*

‡ *A. Fairbairn (Middlesex) in 1947 scored hundreds in the second innings of his first two matches in first-class cricket: 108 as above, 110* Middlesex v Nottinghamshire at Nottingham.*

§ *The only instance in England of two players performing the feat in the same match.*

*Notes:* A number of players abroad have also made a hundred on a first appearance.

The highest innings on début was hit by W. F. E. Marx when he made 240 for Transvaal against Griqualand West at Johannesburg in 1920-21.

There are three instances of a cricketer making two separate hundreds on début: A. R. Morris, New South Wales, 148 and 111 against Queensland in 1940-41, N. J. Contractor, Gujarat, 152 and 102* against Baroda in 1952-53, and Aamer Malik, Lahore "A", 132* and 110* against Railways in 1979-80.

J. S. Solomon, British Guiana, scored a hundred in each of his first three innings in first-class cricket: 114* v Jamaica; 108 v Barbados in 1956-57; 121 v Pakistanis in 1957-58.

R. Watson-Smith, Border, scored 310 runs before he was dismissed in first-class cricket, including not-out centuries in his first two innings: 183* v Orange Free State and 125* v Griqualand West in 1969-70.

G. R. Viswanath and D. M. Wellham alone have scored a hundred on both their début in first-class cricket and in Test cricket. Viswanath scored 230 for Mysore v Andhra in 1967-68 and 137 for India v Australia in 1969-70. Wellham scored 100 for New South Wales v Victoria in 1980-81 and 103 for Australia v England in 1981.

## TWO DOUBLE-HUNDREDS IN A MATCH

| | | | |
|---|---|---|---|
| A. E. Fagg........ | 244 | 202* | Kent v Essex at Colchester ........... | 1938 |

## TRIPLE-HUNDRED AND HUNDRED IN A MATCH

| | | | |
|---|---|---|---|
| G. A. Gooch ...... | 333 | 123 | England v India at Lord's ............ | 1990 |

## DOUBLE-HUNDRED AND HUNDRED IN A MATCH

| | | | | |
|---|---|---|---|---|
| C. B. Fry ......... | 125 | 229 | Sussex v Surrey at Hove .............. | 1900 |
| W. W. Armstrong.. | 157* | 245 | Victoria v South Australia at Melbourne. | 1920-21 |
| H. T. W. Hardinge. | 207 | 102* | Kent v Surrey at Blackheath ......... | 1921 |
| C. P. Mead ....... | 113 | 224 | Hampshire v Sussex at Horsham ...... | 1921 |
| K. S. Duleepsinhji. | 115 | 246 | Sussex v Kent at Hastings ........... | 1929 |
| D. G. Bradman .... | 124 | 225 | Woodfull's XI v Ryder's XI at Sydney .. | 1929-30 |
| B. Sutcliffe....... | 243 | 100* | New Zealanders v Essex at Southend ... | 1949 |
| M. R. Hallam ..... | 210* | 157 | Leicestershire v Glamorgan at Leicester . | 1959 |
| M. R. Hallam ..... | 203* | 143* | Leicestershire v Sussex at Worthing .... | 1961 |
| Hanumant Singh ... | 109 | 213* | Rajasthan v Bombay at Bombay ...... | 1966-67 |
| Salah-ud-Din ..... | 256 | 102* | Karachi v East Pakistan at Karachi .... | 1968-69 |
| K. D. Walters ..... | 242 | 103 | Australia v West Indies at Sydney..... | 1968-69 |
| S. M. Gavaskar.... | 124 | 220 | India v West Indies at Port-of-Spain.... | 1970-71 |
| L. G. Rowe ....... | 214 | 100* | West Indies v New Zealand at Kingston . | 1971-72 |
| G. S. Chappell .... | 247* | 133 | Australia v New Zealand at Wellington . | 1973-74 |
| L. Baichan ........ | 216* | 102 | Berbice v Demerara at Georgetown .... | 1973-74 |
| Zaheer Abbas ..... | 216* | 156* | Gloucestershire v Surrey at The Oval ... | 1976 |
| Zaheer Abbas ..... | 230* | 104* | Gloucestershire v Kent at Canterbury... | 1976 |
| Zaheer Abbas ..... | 205* | 108* | Gloucestershire v Sussex at Cheltenham . | 1977 |
| Saadat Ali ........ | 141 | 222 | Income Tax v Multan at Multan ....... | 1977-78 |
| Talat Ali ......... | 214* | 104 | PIA v Punjab at Lahore ............. | 1978-79 |
| Shafiq Ahmed ..... | 129 | 217* | National Bank v MCB at Karachi ..... | 1978-79 |
| D. W. Randall .... | 209 | 146 | Nottinghamshire v Middlesex at Nottingham ...................... | 1979 |
| Zaheer Abbas ..... | 215* | 150* | Gloucestershire v Somerset at Bath ..... | 1981 |

| Qasim Omar | 210* | 110 | MCB v Lahore at Lahore | 1982-83 |
| A. I. Kallicharran | 200* | 117* | Warwickshire v Northamptonshire at Birmingham | 1984 |
| Rizwan-uz-Zaman | 139 | 217* | PIA v PACO at Lahore | 1989-90 |
| G. A. Hick | 252* | 100* | Worcestershire v Glamorgan at Abergavenny | 1990 |
| N. R. Taylor | 204 | 142 | Kent v Surrey at Canterbury | 1990 |
| N. R. Taylor | 111 | 203* | Kent v Sussex at Hove | 1991 |

## TWO SEPARATE HUNDREDS IN A MATCH

**Eight times:** Zaheer Abbas.

**Seven times:** W. R. Hammond.

**Six times:** J. B. Hobbs, G. M. Turner.

**Five times:** C. B. Fry.

**Four times:** D. G. Bradman, G. S. Chappell, J. H. Edrich, L. B. Fishlock, T. W. Graveney, C. G. Greenidge, H. T. W. Hardinge, E. H. Hendren, Javed Miandad, G. L. Jessop, P. A. Perrin, B. Sutcliffe, H. Sutcliffe.

**Three times:** L. E. G. Ames, G. Boycott, I. M. Chappell, D. C. S. Compton, S. J. Cook, M. C. Cowdrey, D. Denton, K. S. Duleepsinhji, R. E. Foster, C. Fredericks, S. M. Gavaskar, W. G. Grace, G. Gunn, M. R. Hallam, Hanif Mohammad, M. J. Harris, T. W. Hayward, V. S. Hazare, D. W. Hookes, L. Hutton, A. Jones, P. N. Kirsten, R. B. McCosker, P. B. H. May, C. P. Mead, Rizwan-uz-Zaman A. C. Russell, Sadiq Mohammad, J. T. Tyldesley.

**Twice:** Agha Zahid, Ali Zia, D. L. Amiss, C. W. J. Athey, L. Baichan, Basit Ali, A. R. Border, B. J. T. Bosanquet, R. J. Boyd-Moss, A. R. Butcher, C. C. Dacre, G. M. Emmett, A. E. Fagg, L. E. Favell, H. Gimblett, G. A. Gooch, C. Hallows, R. A. Hamence, A. L. Hassett, G. A. Headley, G. A. Hick, A. I. Kallicharran, J. H. King, A. F. Kippax, J. G. Langridge, H. W. Lee, E. Lester, C. B. Llewellyn, C. G. Macartney, C. A. Milton, A. R. Morris, H. Morris, P. H. Parfitt, Nawab of Pataudi jun., E. Paynter, C. Pinch, R. G. Pollock, R. M. Prideaux, Qasim Omar, W. Rhodes, B. A. Richards, I. V. A. Richards, R. T. Robinson, Pankaj Roy, Salim Malik, James Seymour, Shafiq Ahmad, R. B. Simpson, C. L. Smith, G. S. Sobers, M. A. Taylor, N. R. Taylor, E. Tyldesley, C. L. Walcott, K. C. Wessels, W. W. Whysall, G. N. Yallop.

*Notes:* W. Lambert scored 107 and 157 for Sussex v Epsom at Lord's in 1817 and it was not until W. G. Grace made 130 and 102* for South of the Thames v North of the Thames at Canterbury in 1868 that the feat was repeated.

T. W. Hayward (Surrey) set up a unique record in 1906 when in one week – six days – he hit four successive hundreds, 144 and 100 v Nottinghamshire at Nottingham and 143 and 125 v Leicestershire at Leicester.

L. G. Rowe is alone in scoring hundreds on his first appearance in Test cricket: 214 and 100* for West Indies v New Zealand at Kingston in 1971-72.

Zaheer Abbas (Gloucestershire) set a unique record in 1976 by twice scoring a double hundred and a hundred in the same match without being dismissed: 216* and 156* v Surrey at The Oval and 230* and 104* v Kent at Canterbury. In 1977 he achieved this feat for a third time, scoring 205* and 108* v Sussex at Cheltenham, and in 1981 for a fourth time, scoring 215* and 150* v Somerset at Bath.

M. R. Hallam (Leicestershire), opening the batting each time, achieved the following treble: 210* and 157 v Glamorgan at Leicester, 1959; 203* and 143* v Sussex at Worthing, 1961; 107* and 149* v Worcestershire at Leicester, 1965. In the last two matches he was on the field the whole time.

C. J. B. Wood, 107* and 117* for Leicestershire v Yorkshire at Bradford in 1911, and S. J. Cook, 120* and 131* for Somerset v Nottinghamshire at Nottingham in 1989, are alone in carrying their bats and scoring hundreds in each innings.

W. L. Foster, 140 and 172*, and R. E. Foster, 134 and 101*, for Worcestershire v Hampshire at Worcester in July 1899, were the first brothers each to score two separate hundreds in the same first-class match.

The brothers I. M. Chappell, 145 and 121, and G. S. Chappell, 247* and 133, for Australia v New Zealand at Wellington in 1973-74, became the first players on the same side each to score a hundred in each innings of a Test match.

G. Gunn, 183, and G. V. Gunn, 100*, for Nottinghamshire v Warwickshire at Birmingham in 1931, provide the only instance of father and son each hitting a century in the same innings of a first-class match.

## Most recent instances

*In 1990-91*

| | | | |
|---|---|---|---|
| V. G. Kambli | 126 | 127 | Bombay v Hyderabad at Bombay. |
| A. Kaypee | 152 | 173 | Haryana v Uttar Pradesh at Faridabad. |
| A. J. Lamb | 154 | 105 | England XI v Australian XI at Hobart. |
| S. G. Law | 142* | 105 | Queensland v Western Australia at Perth. |
| Mansoor Rana | 122 | 157* | ADBP v HBFC at Peshawar. |
| M. H. Parmar | 111* | 119 | Gujarat v Bombay at Bombay. |
| Salim Malik | 138 | 133 | Habib Bank v National Bank at Lahore. |
| S. M. Small | 115 | 126 | New South Wales v Wellington at North Sydney. |

*In 1991:* See Features of 1991.

## FOUR HUNDREDS OR MORE IN SUCCESSION

**Six in succession:** C. B. Fry 1901; D. G. Bradman 1938-39; M. J. Procter 1970-71.

**Five in succession:** E. D. Weekes 1955-56.

**Four in succession:** C. W. J. Athey 1987; M. Azharuddin 1984-85; M. G. Bevan 1990-91; A. R. Border 1985; D. G. Bradman 1931-32, 1948-49; D. C. S. Compton 1946-47; N. J. Contractor 1957-58; S. J. Cook 1989; K. S. Duleepsinhji 1931; C. B. Fry 1911; C. G. Greenidge 1986; W. R. Hammond 1936-37, 1945-46; H. T. W. Hardinge 1913; T. W. Hayward 1906; J. B. Hobbs 1920, 1925; D. W. Hookes 1976-77; P. N. Kirsten 1976-77; J. G. Langridge 1949; C. G. Macartney 1921; K. S. McEwan 1977; P. B. H. May 1956-57; V. M. Merchant 1941-42; A. Mitchell 1933; Nawab of Pataudi sen. 1931; L. G. Rowe 1971-72; Pankaj Roy 1962-63; Rizwan-uz-Zaman 1989-90; Sadiq Mohammad 1976; Saeed Ahmed 1961-62; H. Sutcliffe 1931, 1939; E. Tyldesley 1926; W. W. Whysall 1930; F. E. Woolley 1929; Zaheer Abbas 1970-71, 1982-83.

*Note:* The most fifties in consecutive innings is ten – by E. Tyldesley in 1926 and by D. G. Bradman in the 1947-48 and 1948 seasons.

## MOST HUNDREDS IN A SEASON

**Eighteen:** D. C. S. Compton in 1947. These included six hundreds against the South Africans in which matches his average was 84.78. His aggregate for the season was 3,816, also a record.

**Sixteen:** J. B. Hobbs in 1925, when aged 42, played 16 three-figure innings in first-class matches. It was during this season that he exceeded the number of hundreds obtained in first-class cricket by W. G. Grace.

**Fifteen:** W. R. Hammond in 1938.

**Fourteen:** H. Sutcliffe in 1932.

**Thirteen:** G. Boycott in 1971, D. G. Bradman in 1938, C. B. Fry in 1901, W. R. Hammond in 1933 and 1937, T. W. Hayward in 1906, E. H. Hendren in 1923, 1927 and 1928, C. P. Mead in 1928, and H. Sutcliffe in 1928 and 1931.

## MOST HUNDREDS IN A CAREER

### (35 or more)

| | *Hundreds* | | *100th* | | *Hundreds* | | *100th* |
|---|---|---|---|---|---|---|---|
| | *Total* | *Abroad* | *100* | | *Total* | *Abroad* | *100* |
| J. B. Hobbs | 197 | 22 | 1923 | D. G. Bradman | 117 | 41† | 1947-48 |
| E. H. Hendren | 170 | 19 | 1928-29 | I. V. A. Richards | 111 | 91† | 1988-89 |
| W. R. Hammond | 167 | 33 | 1935 | Zaheer Abbas | 108 | 70† | 1982-83 |
| C. P. Mead | 153 | 8 | 1927 | M. C. Cowdrey | 107 | 27 | 1973 |
| G. Boycott | 151 | 27 | 1977 | A. Sandham | 107 | 20 | 1935 |
| H. Sutcliffe | 149 | 14 | 1932 | T. W. Hayward | 104 | 4 | 1913 |
| F. E. Woolley | 145 | 10 | 1929 | J. H. Edrich | 103 | 13 | 1977 |
| L. Hutton | 129 | 24 | 1951 | G. M. Turner | 103 | 85† | 1982 |
| W. G. Grace | 126 | 1 | 1895 | L. E. G. Ames | 102 | 13 | 1950 |
| D. C. S. Compton | 123 | 31 | 1952 | D. L. Amiss | 102 | 15 | 1986 |
| T. W. Graveney | 122 | 31 | 1964 | E. Tyldesley | 102 | 8 | 1934 |

† *"Abroad" for D. G. Bradman is outside Australia; for Zaheer Abbas, outside Pakistan; for G. M. Turner, outside New Zealand; for I. V. A. Richards, outside the West Indies.*
  *E. H. Hendren, D. G. Bradman and I. V. A. Richards scored their 100th hundreds in Australia, Zaheer Abbas scored his in Pakistan. Zaheer Abbas and G. Boycott did so in Test matches.*

| | | |
|---|---|---|
| J. W. Hearne | 96 | W. Rhodes | 58 | L. G. Berry | 45 |
| C. B. Fry | 94 | L. B. Fishlock | 56 | J. M. Brearley | 45 |
| C. G. Greenidge | 92 | A. Jones | 56 | A. W. Carr | 45 |
| G. A. Gooch | 89 | C. A. Milton | 56 | D. L. Haynes | 45 |
| A. I. Kallicharran | 87 | J. G. Wright | 56 | C. Hill | 45 |
| W. J. Edrich | 86 | S. J. Cook | 55 | N. C. O'Neill | 45 |
| G. S. Sobers | 86 | C. Hallows | 55 | E. Paynter | 45 |
| J. T. Tyldesley | 86 | Hanif Mohammad | 55 | Rev. D. S. Sheppard | 45 |
| P. B. H. May | 85 | W. Watson | 55 | K. D. Walters | 45 |
| R. E. S. Wyatt | 85 | D. J. Insole | 54 | H. H. I. Gibbons | 44 |
| J. Hardstaff, jun. | 83 | W. W. Keeton | 54 | V. M. Merchant | 44 |
| R. B. Kanhai | 83 | D. B. Vengsarkar | 54 | A. Mitchell | 44 |
| S. M. Gavaskar | 81 | W. Bardsley | 53 | P. E. Richardson | 44 |
| M. Leyland | 80 | B. F. Davison | 53 | B. Sutcliffe | 44 |
| B. A. Richards | 80 | A. E. Dipper | 53 | C. J. Tavaré | 44 |
| C. H. Lloyd | 79 | G. L. Jessop | 53 | G. R. Viswanath | 44 |
| Javed Miandad | 78 | James Seymour | 53 | P. Willey | 44 |
| K. F. Barrington | 76 | Shafiq Ahmad | 53 | E. J. Barlow | 43 |
| J. G. Langridge | 76 | E. H. Bowley | 52 | B. L. D'Oliveira | 43 |
| C. Washbrook | 76 | D. B. Close | 52 | J. H. Hampshire | 43 |
| H. T. W. Hardinge | 75 | A. Ducat | 52 | A. F. Kippax | 43 |
| R. Abel | 74 | E. R. Dexter | 51 | J. W. H. Makepeace | 43 |
| G. S. Chappell | 74 | J. M. Parks | 51 | B. C. Broad | 42 |
| D. Kenyon | 74 | D. W. Randall | 51 | James Langridge | 42 |
| K. S. McEwan | 73 | W. W. Whysall | 51 | Mudassar Nazar | 42 |
| Majid Khan | 73 | G. Cox jun. | 50 | H. W. Parks | 42 |
| A. J. Lamb | 72 | H. E. Dollery | 50 | R. T. Robinson | 42 |
| Mushtaq Mohammad | 72 | K. S. Duleepsinhji | 50 | T. F. Shepherd | 42 |
| J. O'Connor | 72 | H. Gimblett | 50 | V. T. Trumper | 42 |
| W. G. Quaife | 72 | W. M. Lawry | 50 | M. J. Harris | 41 |
| K. S. Ranjitsinhji | 72 | Sadiq Mohammad | 50 | K. R. Miller | 41 |
| D. Brookes | 71 | F. B. Watson | 50 | A. D. Nourse | 41 |
| A. C. Russell | 71 | W. Larkins | 49 | P. W. G. Parker | 41 |
| D. Denton | 69 | C. G. Macartney | 49 | J. H. Parks | 41 |
| M. J. K. Smith | 69 | M. J. Stewart | 49 | R. M. Prideaux | 41 |
| R. E. Marshall | 68 | K. G. Suttle | 49 | G. Pullar | 41 |
| R. N. Harvey | 67 | P. R. Umrigar | 49 | W. E. Russell | 41 |
| P. Holmes | 67 | W. M. Woodfull | 49 | C. W. J. Athey | 40 |
| J. D. Robertson | 67 | C. J. Barnett | 48 | R. C. Fredericks | 40 |
| M. W. Gatting | 66 | D. I. Gower | 48 | J. Gunn | 40 |
| P. A. Perrin | 66 | W. Gunn | 48 | G. D. Mendis | 40 |
| R. G. Pollock | 64 | E. G. Hayes | 48 | M. J. Smith | 40 |
| R. T. Simpson | 64 | B. W. Luckhurst | 48 | C. L. Walcott | 40 |
| K. W. R. Fletcher | 63 | M. J. Procter | 48 | D. M. Young | 40 |
| G. Gunn | 62 | C. E. B. Rice | 48 | Arshad Pervez | 39 |
| A. R. Border | 61 | K. C. Wessels | 48 | W. H. Ashdown | 39 |
| V. S. Hazare | 60 | P. N. Kirsten | 47 | J. B. Bolus | 39 |
| G. A. Hick | 60 | A. C. MacLaren | 47 | W. A. Brown | 39 |
| G. H. Hirst | 60 | W. H. Ponsford | 47 | R. J. Gregory | 39 |
| R. B. Simpson | 60 | C. L. Smith | 47 | W. R. D. Payton | 39 |
| P. F. Warner | 60 | A. R. Butcher | 46 | J. R. Reid | 39 |
| I. M. Chappell | 59 | J. Iddon | 46 | F. M. M. Worrell | 39 |
| A. L. Hassett | 59 | A. R. Morris | 46 | M. R. Benson | 38 |
| A. Shrewsbury | 59 | C. T. Radley | 46 | F. L. Bowley | 38 |
| M. D. Crowe | 58 | Younis Ahmed | 46 | P. J. Burge | 38 |
| A. E. Fagg | 58 | W. W. Armstrong | 45 | J. F. Crapp | 38 |
| P. H. Parfitt | 58 | Asif Iqbal | 45 | D. Lloyd | 38 |

| | | | |
|---|---|---|
| V. L. Manjrekar ...... 38 | G. Cook............ 37 | I. T. Botham ......... 36 |
| A. W. Nourse ........ 38 | G. M. Emmett ...... 37 | E. Oldroyd........... 36 |
| N. Oldfield .......... 38 | H. W. Lee .......... 37 | W. Place ............ 36 |
| Rev. J. H. Parsons ... 38 | M. A. Noble ........ 37 | A. L. Wadekar ....... 36 |
| W. W. Read .......... 38 | B. P. Patel ......... 37 | E. D. Weekes ........ 36 |
| J. Sharp ............. 38 | H. S. Squires ....... 37 | C. S. Dempster ....... 35 |
| L. J. Todd .......... 38 | N. R. Taylor........ 37 | D. R. Jardine ........ 35 |
| J. Arnold ........... 37 | R. T. Virgin ........ 37 | T. E. Jesty .......... 35 |
| D. C. Boon ......... 37 | C. J. B. Wood ...... 37 | B. H. Valentine ...... 35 |
| G. Brown............ 37 | N. F. Armstrong ...... 36 | G. M. Wood ......... 35 |

## 3,000 RUNS IN A SEASON

| | Season | I | NO | R | HI | 100s | Avge |
|---|---|---|---|---|---|---|---|
| D. C. S. Compton .... | 1947 | 50 | 8 | 3,816 | 246 | 18 | 90.85 |
| W. J. Edrich ........ | 1947 | 52 | 8 | 3,539 | 267* | 12 | 80.43 |
| T. W. Hayward ...... | 1906 | 61 | 8 | 3,518 | 219 | 13 | 66.37 |
| L. Hutton ........... | 1949 | 56 | 6 | 3,429 | 269* | 12 | 68.58 |
| F. E. Woolley........ | 1928 | 59 | 4 | 3,352 | 198 | 12 | 60.94 |
| H. Sutcliffe.......... | 1932 | 52 | 7 | 3,336 | 313 | 14 | 74.13 |
| W. R. Hammond...... | 1933 | 54 | 5 | 3,323 | 264 | 13 | 67.81 |
| E. H. Hendren ....... | 1928 | 54 | 7 | 3,311 | 209* | 13 | 70.44 |
| R. Abel.............. | 1901 | 68 | 8 | 3,309 | 247 | 7 | 55.15 |
| W. R. Hammond...... | 1937 | 55 | 5 | 3,252 | 217 | 13 | 65.04 |
| M. J. K. Smith ...... | 1959 | 67 | 11 | 3,245 | 200* | 8 | 57.94 |
| E. H. Hendren ....... | 1933 | 65 | 9 | 3,186 | 301* | 11 | 56.89 |
| C. P. Mead ........ | 1921 | 52 | 6 | 3,179 | 280* | 10 | 69.10 |
| T. W. Hayward ...... | 1904 | 63 | 5 | 3,170 | 203 | 11 | 54.65 |
| K. S. Ranjitsinhji.... | 1899 | 58 | 8 | 3,159 | 197 | 8 | 63.18 |
| C. B. Fry ........... | 1901 | 43 | 3 | 3,147 | 244 | 13 | 78.67 |
| K. S. Ranjitsinhji.... | 1900 | 40 | 5 | 3,065 | 275 | 11 | 87.57 |
| L. E. G. Ames ....... | 1933 | 57 | 5 | 3,058 | 295 | 9 | 58.80 |
| J. T. Tyldesley ...... | 1901 | 60 | 5 | 3,041 | 221 | 9 | 55.29 |
| C. P. Mead ......... | 1928 | 50 | 10 | 3,027 | 180 | 13 | 75.67 |
| J. B. Hobbs ........ | 1925 | 48 | 5 | 3,024 | 266* | 16 | 70.32 |
| E. Tyldesley ........ | 1928 | 48 | 10 | 3,024 | 242 | 10 | 79.57 |
| W. E. Alley ........ | 1961 | 64 | 11 | 3,019 | 221* | 11 | 56.96 |
| W. R. Hammond..... | 1938 | 42 | 2 | 3,011 | 271 | 15 | 75.27 |
| E. H. Hendren ....... | 1923 | 51 | 12 | 3,010 | 200* | 13 | 77.17 |
| H. Sutcliffe.......... | 1931 | 42 | 11 | 3,006 | 230 | 13 | 96.96 |
| J. H. Parks.......... | 1937 | 63 | 4 | 3,003 | 168 | 11 | 50.89 |
| H. Sutcliffe.......... | 1928 | 44 | 5 | 3,002 | 228 | 13 | 76.97 |

*Notes:* W. G. Grace scored 2,739 runs in 1871 – the first batsman to reach 2,000 runs in a season. He made ten hundreds and twice exceeded 200, with an average of 78.25 in all first-class matches. At the time, the over consisted of four balls.

The highest aggregate in a season since the reduction of County Championship matches in 1969 is 2,755 by S. J. Cook (42 innings) in 1991.

## 2,000 RUNS IN A SEASON

### Since Reduction of Championship Matches in 1969

**Four times:** G. A. Gooch 2,746 (1990), 2,559 (1984), 2,324 (1988), 2,208 (1985).

**Three times:** D. L. Amiss 2,239 (1984), 2,110 (1976), 2,030 (1978); S. J. Cook 2,755 (1991), 2,608 (1990), 2,241 (1989); G. A. Hick 2,713 (1988), 2,347 (1990), 2,004 (1986); G. M. Turner 2,416 (1973), 2,379 (1970), 2,101 (1981).

**Twice:** G. Boycott 2,503 (1971), 2,051 (1970); J. H. Edrich 2,238 (1969), 2,031 (1971); M. W. Gatting 2,257 (1984), 2,057 (1991); A. I. Kallicharran 2,301 (1984), 2,120 (1982); Zaheer Abbas 2,554 (1976), 2,306 (1981).

**Once:** M. Azharuddin 2,016 (1991); J. B. Bolus 2,143 (1970); B. C. Broad 2,226 (1990); A. R. Butcher 2,116 (1990); C. G. Greenidge 2,035 (1986); M. J. Harris 2,238 (1971); D. L. Haynes 2,346 (1990); Javed Miandad 2,083 (1981); A. J. Lamb 2,049 (1981); K. S. McEwan 2,176 (1983); Majid Khan 2,074 (1972); A. A. Metcalfe 2,047 (1990); H. Morris 2,276 (1990); D. W. Randall 2,151 (1985); I. V. A. Richards 2,161 (1977); R. T. Robinson 2,032 (1984); C. L. Smith 2,000 (1985); R. T. Virgin 2,223 (1970); D. M. Ward 2,072 (1990); M. E. Waugh 2,072 (1990).

## 1,000 RUNS IN A SEASON MOST TIMES

(Includes Overseas Tours and Seasons)

**28 times:** W. G. Grace 2,000 (6); F. E. Woolley 3,000 (1), 2,000 (12).

**27 times:** M. C. Cowdrey 2,000 (2); C. P. Mead 3,000 (2), 2,000 (9).

**26 times:** G. Boycott 2,000 (3); J. B. Hobbs 3,000 (1), 2,000 (16).

**25 times:** E. H. Hendren 3,000 (3), 2,000 (12).

**24 times:** D. L. Amiss 2,000 (3); W. G. Quaife 2,000 (1); H. Sutcliffe 3,000 (3), 2,000 (12).

**23 times:** A. Jones.

**22 times:** T. W. Graveney 2,000 (7); W. R. Hammond 3,000 (3), 2,000 (9).

**21 times:** D. Denton 2,000 (5); J. H. Edrich 2,000 (6); W. Rhodes 2,000 (2).

**20 times:** D. B. Close; K. W. R. Fletcher; G. Gunn; T. W. Hayward 3,000 (2), 2,000 (8); James Langridge 2,000 (1); J. M. Parks 2,000 (3); A. Sandham 2,000 (8); M. J. K. Smith 3,000 (1), 2,000 (5); C. Washbrook 2,000 (2).

**19 times:** J. W. Hearne 2,000 (4); G. H. Hirst 2,000 (3); D. Kenyon 2,000 (7); E. Tyldesley 3,000 (1), 2,000 (5); J. T. Tyldesley 3,000 (1), 2,000 (4).

**18 times:** L. G. Berry 2,000 (1); H. T. W. Hardinge 2,000 (5); R. E. Marshall 2,000 (6); P. A. Perrin; G. M. Turner 2,000 (3); R. E. S. Wyatt 2,000 (5).

**17 times:** L. E. G. Ames 3,000 (1), 2,000 (5); T. E. Bailey 2,000 (1); D. Brookes 2,000 (6); D. C. S. Compton 3,000 (1), 2,000 (5); C. G. Greenidge 2,000 (1); L. Hutton 3,000 (1), 2,000 (8); J. G. Langridge 2,000 (11); M. Leyland 2,000 (3); K. G. Suttle 2,000 (1), Zaheer Abbas 2,000 (2).

**16 times:** D. G. Bradman 2,000 (4); D. E. Davies 2,000 (1); G. A. Gooch 2,000 (4); E. G. Hayes 2,000 (2); C. A. Milton 2,000 (1); J. O'Connor 2,000 (4); C. T. Radley; I. V. A. Richards 2,000 (1); James Seymour 2,000 (1).

**15 times:** G. Barker; K. F. Barrington 2,000 (3); E. H. Bowley 2,000 (4); M. H. Denness; A. E. Dipper 2,000 (5); H. E. Dollery 2,000 (2); W. J. Edrich 3,000 (1), 2,000 (8); J. H. Hampshire; P. Holmes 2,000 (7); Mushtaq Mohammad; R. B. Nicholls 2,000 (1); P. H. Parfitt 2,000 (3); W. G. A. Parkhouse 2,000 (1); B. A. Richards 2,000 (1); J. D. Robertson 2,000 (9); G. S. Sobers; M. J. Stewart 2,000 (1); C. J. Tavaré.

*Notes:* F. E. Woolley reached 1,000 runs in 28 consecutive seasons (1907-1938). C. P. Mead did so 27 seasons in succession (1906-1936).

Outside England, 1,000 runs in a season has been reached most times by D. G. Bradman (in 12 seasons in Australia).

Three batsmen have scored 1,000 runs in a season in each of four different countries: G. S. Sobers in West Indies, England, India and Australia; M. C. Cowdrey and G. Boycott in England, South Africa, West Indies and Australia.

## HIGHEST AGGREGATES OUTSIDE ENGLAND

| | Season | I | NO | R | HI | 100s | Avge |
|---|---|---|---|---|---|---|---|
| *In Australia* | | | | | | | |
| D. G. Bradman | 1928-29 | 24 | 6 | 1,690 | 340* | 7 | 93.88 |
| *In South Africa* | | | | | | | |
| J. R. Reid | 1961-62 | 30 | 2 | 1,915 | 203 | 7 | 68.39 |
| *In West Indies* | | | | | | | |
| E. H. Hendren | 1929-30 | 18 | 5 | 1,765 | 254* | 6 | 135.76 |
| *In New Zealand* | | | | | | | |
| M. D. Crowe | 1986-87 | 21 | 3 | 1,676 | 175* | 8 | 93.11 |
| *In India* | | | | | | | |
| C. G. Borde | 1964-65 | 28 | 3 | 1,604 | 168 | 6 | 64.16 |

| | Season | I | NO | R | HI | 100s | Avge |
|---|---|---|---|---|---|---|---|
| *In Pakistan* | | | | | | | |
| Saadat Ali . . . . . . . . . | 1983-84 | 27 | 1 | 1,649 | 208 | 4 | 63.42 |
| *In Sri Lanka* | | | | | | | |
| A. Ranatunga . . . . . . . . | 1985-86 | 16 | 2 | 739 | 135* | 3 | 52.78 |

*Note:* In more than one country, the following aggregates of over 2,000 runs have been recorded.

| | | | | | | | |
|---|---|---|---|---|---|---|---|
| M. Amarnath (P/I/WI) | 1982-83 | 34 | 6 | 2,234 | 207 | 9 | 79.78 |
| J. R. Reid (SA/A/NZ). | 1961-62 | 40 | 2 | 2,188 | 203 | 7 | 57.57 |
| S. M. Gavaskar (I/P) . | 1978-79 | 30 | 6 | 2,121 | 205 | 10 | 88.37 |
| R. B. Simpson | | | | | | | |
| (I/P/A/WI) . . . . . . . | 1964-65 | 34 | 4 | 2,063 | 201 | 8 | 68.76 |

## HIGHEST AVERAGES IN AN ENGLISH SEASON

### (Qualification: 12 innings)

| | Season | I | NO | R | HI | 100s | Avge |
|---|---|---|---|---|---|---|---|
| D. G. Bradman . . . . . | 1938 | 26 | 5 | 2,429 | 278 | 13 | 115.66 |
| G. Boycott . . . . . . . . . | 1979 | 20 | 5 | 1,538 | 175* | 6 | 102.53 |
| W. A. Johnston . . . . . . | 1953 | 17 | 16 | 102 | 28* | 0 | 102.00 |
| G. A. Gooch . . . . . . . . | 1990 | 30 | 3 | 2,746 | 333 | 12 | 101.70 |
| G. Boycott . . . . . . . . . | 1971 | 30 | 5 | 2,503 | 233 | 13 | 100.12 |
| D. G. Bradman . . . . . . | 1930 | 36 | 6 | 2,960 | 334 | 10 | 98.66 |
| H. Sutcliffe . . . . . . . . | 1931 | 42 | 11 | 3,006 | 230 | 13 | 96.96 |
| C. L. Hooper . . . . . . . | 1991 | 25 | 9 | 1,501 | 196 | 5 | 93.81 |
| R. M. Poore . . . . . . . . | 1899 | 21 | 4 | 1,551 | 304 | 7 | 91.23 |
| D. R. Jardine . . . . . . . | 1927 | 14 | 3 | 1,002 | 147 | 5 | 91.09 |
| D. C. S. Compton . . . . | 1947 | 50 | 8 | 3,816 | 246 | 18 | 90.85 |
| G. A. Hick . . . . . . . . . | 1990 | 35 | 9 | 2,347 | 252* | 8 | 90.26 |
| G. M. Turner . . . . . . . . | 1982 | 16 | 3 | 1,171 | 311* | 5 | 90.07 |
| D. G. Bradman . . . . . . | 1948 | 31 | 4 | 2,428 | 187 | 11 | 89.92 |
| T. M. Moody . . . . . . . | 1990 | 15 | 2 | 1,163 | 168 | 7 | 89.46 |
| D. M. Jones . . . . . . . . | 1989 | 20 | 3 | 1,510 | 248 | 5 | 88.82 |
| Zaheer Abbas . . . . . . . | 1981 | 36 | 10 | 2,306 | 215* | 10 | 88.69 |
| K. S. Ranjitsinhji . . . . . | 1900 | 40 | 5 | 3,065 | 275 | 11 | 87.57 |
| D. R. Jardine . . . . . . . | 1928 | 17 | 4 | 1,133 | 193 | 3 | 87.15 |
| W. R. Hammond . . . . . | 1946 | 26 | 5 | 1,783 | 214 | 7 | 84.90 |
| D. G. Bradman . . . . . . | 1934 | 27 | 3 | 2,020 | 304 | 7 | 84.16 |
| R. B. Kanhai . . . . . . . | 1975 | 22 | 9 | 1,073 | 178* | 3 | 82.53 |
| Mudassar Nazar . . . . . | 1982 | 16 | 6 | 825 | 211* | 4 | 82.50 |
| C. G. Greenidge . . . . . | 1984 | 16 | 3 | 1,069 | 223 | 4 | 82.23 |
| J. B. Hobbs . . . . . . . . | 1928 | 38 | 7 | 2,542 | 200* | 12 | 82.00 |
| C. B. Fry . . . . . . . . . . | 1903 | 40 | 7 | 2,683 | 234 | 9 | 81.30 |
| S. J. Cook . . . . . . . . . | 1991 | 42 | 8 | 2,755 | 210* | 11 | 81.02 |
| W. J. Edrich . . . . . . . . | 1947 | 52 | 8 | 3,539 | 267* | 12 | 80.43 |

## 25,000 RUNS IN A CAREER

Dates in italics denote the first half of an overseas season; i.e. *1945* denotes the 1945-46 season.

| | Career | R | I | NO | HI | 100s | Avge |
|---|---|---|---|---|---|---|---|
| J. B. Hobbs . . . . . . . . | 1905-34 | 61,237 | 1,315 | 106 | 316* | 197 | 50.65 |
| F. E. Woolley . . . . . . . | 1906-38 | 58,969 | 1,532 | 85 | 305* | 145 | 40.75 |
| E. H. Hendren . . . . . . . | 1907-38 | 57,611 | 1,300 | 166 | 301* | 170 | 50.80 |
| C. P. Mead . . . . . . . . | 1905-36 | 55,061 | 1,340 | 185 | 280* | 153 | 47.67 |
| W. G. Grace . . . . . . . . | 1865-1908 | 54,896 | 1,493 | 105 | 344 | 126 | 39.55 |
| W. R. Hammond . . . . | 1920-51 | 50,551 | 1,005 | 104 | 336* | 167 | 56.10 |

| | Career | R | I | NO | HI | 100s | Avge |
|---|---|---|---|---|---|---|---|
| H. Sutcliffe......... | 1919-45 | 50,138 | 1,088 | 123 | 313 | 149 | 51.95 |
| G. Boycott......... | 1962-86 | 48,426 | 1,014 | 162 | 261* | 151 | 56.83 |
| T. W. Graveney ..... | 1948-71 | 47,793 | 1,223 | 159 | 258 | 122 | 44.91 |
| T. W. Hayward...... | 1893-1914 | 43,551 | 1,138 | 96 | 315* | 104 | 41.79 |
| D. L. Amiss........ | 1960-87 | 43,423 | 1,139 | 126 | 262* | 102 | 42.86 |
| M. C. Cowdrey..... | 1950-76 | 42,719 | 1,130 | 134 | 307 | 107 | 42.89 |
| A. Sandham........ | 1911-37 | 41,284 | 1,000 | 79 | 325 | 107 | 44.82 |
| L. Hutton......... | 1934-60 | 40,140 | 814 | 91 | 364 | 129 | 55.51 |
| M. J. K. Smith ..... | 1951-75 | 39,832 | 1,091 | 139 | 204 | 69 | 41.84 |
| W. Rhodes........ | 1898-1930 | 39,802 | 1,528 | 237 | 267* | 58 | 30.83 |
| J. H. Edrich....... | 1956-78 | 39,790 | 979 | 104 | 310* | 103 | 45.47 |
| R. E. S. Wyatt..... | 1923-57 | 39,405 | 1,141 | 157 | 232 | 85 | 40.04 |
| D. C. S. Compton.... | 1936-64 | 38,942 | 839 | 88 | 300 | 123 | 51.85 |
| E. Tyldesley....... | 1909-36 | 38,874 | 961 | 106 | 256* | 102 | 45.46 |
| J. T. Tyldesley..... | 1895-1923 | 37,897 | 994 | 62 | 295* | 86 | 40.66 |
| K. W. R. Fletcher.... | 1962-88 | 37,665 | 1,167 | 170 | 228* | 63 | 37.77 |
| C. G. Greenidge ..... | 1970-91 | 37,330 | 888 | 75 | 273* | 92 | 45.91 |
| J. W. Hearne...... | 1909-36 | 37,252 | 1,025 | 116 | 285* | 96 | 40.98 |
| L. E. G. Ames...... | 1926-51 | 37,248 | 951 | 95 | 295 | 102 | 43.51 |
| D. Kenyon........ | 1946-67 | 37,002 | 1,159 | 59 | 259 | 74 | 33.63 |
| W. J. Edrich ...... | 1934-58 | 36,965 | 964 | 92 | 267* | 86 | 42.39 |
| J. M. Parks....... | 1949-76 | 36,719 | 1,227 | 172 | 205* | 51 | 34.76 |
| D. Denton........ | 1894-1920 | 36,479 | 1,163 | 70 | 221 | 69 | 33.37 |
| G. H. Hirst....... | 1891-1929 | 36,323 | 1,215 | 151 | 341 | 60 | 34.13 |
| A. Jones......... | 1957-83 | 36,049 | 1,168 | 72 | 204* | 56 | 32.89 |
| W. G. Quaife...... | 1894-1928 | 36,012 | 1,203 | 185 | 255* | 72 | 35.37 |
| R. E. Marshall...... | 1945-72 | 35,725 | 1,053 | 59 | 228* | 68 | 35.94 |
| G. Gunn........ | 1902-32 | 35,208 | 1,061 | 82 | 220 | 62 | 35.96 |
| D. B. Close....... | 1949-86 | 34,994 | 1,225 | 173 | 198 | 52 | 33.26 |
| Zaheer Abbas ..... | 1965-86 | 34,843 | 768 | 92 | 274 | 108 | 51.54 |
| J. G. Langridge..... | 1928-55 | 34,380 | 984 | 66 | 250* | 76 | 37.45 |
| G. M. Turner ..... | 1964-82 | 34,346 | 792 | 101 | 311* | 103 | 49.70 |
| I. V. A. Richards ... | 1971-91 | 34,255 | 741 | 56 | 322 | 111 | 50.00 |
| C. Washbrook..... | 1933-64 | 34,101 | 906 | 107 | 251* | 76 | 42.67 |
| G. A. Gooch ...... | 1973-91 | 33,897 | 777 | 62 | 333 | 89 | 47.40 |
| M. Leyland ...... | 1920-48 | 33,660 | 932 | 101 | 263 | 80 | 40.50 |
| H. T. W. Hardinge ... | 1902-33 | 33,519 | 1,021 | 103 | 263* | 75 | 36.51 |
| R. Abel ......... | 1881-1904 | 33,124 | 1,007 | 73 | 357* | 74 | 35.46 |
| A. I. Kallicharran .... | 1966-90 | 32,650 | 834 | 86 | 243* | 87 | 43.64 |
| C. A. Milton ...... | 1948-74 | 32,150 | 1,078 | 125 | 170 | 56 | 33.73 |
| J. D. Robertson..... | 1937-59 | 31,914 | 897 | 46 | 331* | 67 | 37.50 |
| J. Hardstaff, jun. .... | 1930-55 | 31,847 | 812 | 94 | 266 | 83 | 44.35 |
| James Langridge..... | 1924-53 | 31,716 | 1,058 | 157 | 167 | 42 | 35.20 |
| K. F. Barrington .... | 1953-68 | 31,714 | 831 | 136 | 256 | 76 | 45.63 |
| C. H. Lloyd ...... | 1963-86 | 31,232 | 730 | 96 | 242* | 79 | 49.26 |
| Mushtaq Mohammad . | 1956-85 | 31,091 | 843 | 104 | 303* | 72 | 42.07 |
| C. B. Fry......... | 1892-1921 | 30,886 | 658 | 43 | 258* | 94 | 50.22 |
| D. Brookes........ | 1934-59 | 30,874 | 925 | 70 | 257 | 71 | 36.10 |
| P. Holmes ........ | 1913-35 | 30,573 | 810 | 84 | 315* | 67 | 42.11 |
| R. T. Simpson ..... | 1944-63 | 30,546 | 852 | 55 | 259 | 64 | 38.32 |
| L. G. Berry ...... | 1924-51 | 30,225 | 1,056 | 57 | 232 | 45 | 30.25 |
| K. G. Suttle ...... | 1949-71 | 30,225 | 1,064 | 92 | 204* | 49 | 31.09 |
| P. A. Perrin ...... | 1896-1928 | 29,709 | 918 | 91 | 343* | 66 | 35.92 |
| P. F. Warner ...... | 1894-1929 | 29,028 | 875 | 75 | 244 | 60 | 36.28 |
| R. B. Kanhai...... | 1954-81 | 28,774 | 669 | 82 | 256 | 83 | 49.01 |
| J. O'Connor ...... | 1921-39 | 28,764 | 903 | 79 | 248 | 72 | 34.90 |
| T. E. Bailey ...... | 1945-67 | 28,641 | 1,072 | 215 | 205 | 28 | 33.42 |
| E. H. Bowley ..... | 1912-34 | 28,378 | 859 | 47 | 283 | 52 | 34.94 |
| B. A. Richards ..... | 1964-82 | 28,358 | 576 | 58 | 356 | 80 | 54.74 |
| G. S. Sobers....... | 1952-74 | 28,315 | 609 | 93 | 365* | 86 | 54.87 |
| A. E. Dipper ....... | 1908-32 | 28,075 | 865 | 69 | 252* | 53 | 35.27 |

| | Career | R | I | NO | HI | 100s | Avge |
|---|---|---|---|---|---|---|---|
| D. G. Bradman . . . . . . | *1927-48* | 28,067 | 338 | 43 | 452* | 117 | 95.14 |
| J. H. Hampshire . . . . . | 1961-84 | 28,059 | 924 | 112 | 183* | 43 | 34.55 |
| P. B. H. May . . . . . . . | 1948-63 | 27,592 | 618 | 77 | 285* | 85 | 51.00 |
| Javed Miandad . . . . . . | *1973-* | 27,468 | 598 | 90 | 311 | 78 | 54.07 |
| B. F. Davison . . . . . . | 1967-87 | 27,453 | 766 | 79 | 189 | 53 | 39.96 |
| Majid Khan . . . . . . . . | *1961-84* | 27,444 | 700 | 62 | 241 | 73 | 43.01 |
| A. C. Russell . . . . . . | 1908-30 | 27,358 | 717 | 59 | 273 | 71 | 41.57 |
| E. G. Hayes . . . . . . . | 1896-1926 | 27,318 | 896 | 48 | 276 | 48 | 32.21 |
| D. W. Randall . . . . . . | 1972-91 | 27,294 | 788 | 78 | 237 | 51 | 38.44 |
| A. E. Fagg . . . . . . . . | 1932-57 | 27,291 | 803 | 46 | 269* | 58 | 36.05 |
| James Seymour . . . . . . | 1900-26 | 27,237 | 911 | 62 | 218* | 53 | 32.08 |
| P. H. Parfitt . . . . . . . | 1956-*73* | 26,924 | 845 | 104 | 200* | 58 | 36.33 |
| G. L. Jessop . . . . . . . | 1894-1914 | 26,698 | 855 | 37 | 286 | 53 | 32.63 |
| D. E. Davies . . . . . . . | 1924-54 | 26,564 | 1,032 | 80 | 287* | 32 | 27.90 |
| M. W. Gatting . . . . . . | 1975-91 | 26,512 | 640 | 101 | 258 | 66 | 49.18 |
| A. Shrewsbury . . . . . . | 1875-1902 | 26,505 | 813 | 90 | 267 | 59 | 36.65 |
| M. J. Stewart . . . . . . | 1954-72 | 26,492 | 898 | 93 | 227* | 49 | 32.90 |
| A. J. Lamb . . . . . . . . | *1972-91* | 26,472 | 648 | 95 | 294 | 72 | 47.86 |
| C. T. Radley . . . . . . . | 1964-87 | 26,441 | 880 | 134 | 200 | 46 | 35.44 |
| K. S. McEwan . . . . . . | *1972-89* | 26,309 | 698 | 66 | 218 | 73 | 41.62 |
| Younis Ahmed . . . . . . | *1961-86* | 26,063 | 762 | 118 | 221* | 46 | 40.47 |
| P. E. Richardson . . . . . | 1949-65 | 26,055 | 794 | 41 | 185 | 44 | 34.60 |
| M. H. Denness . . . . . . | 1959-80 | 25,886 | 838 | 65 | 195 | 33 | 33.48 |
| S. M. Gavaskar . . . . . . | *1966-87* | 25,834 | 563 | 61 | 340 | 81 | 51.46 |
| J. W. H. Makepeace . . | 1906-30 | 25,799 | 778 | 66 | 203 | 43 | 36.23 |
| C. E. B. Rice . . . . . . . | *1969-90* | 25,797 | 746 | 121 | 246 | 48 | 41.27 |
| W. Gunn . . . . . . . . . . | 1880-1904 | 25,691 | 850 | 72 | 273 | 48 | 33.02 |
| W. Watson . . . . . . . . | 1939-64 | 25,670 | 753 | 109 | 257 | 55 | 39.86 |
| G. Brown . . . . . . . . . | 1908-33 | 25,649 | 1,012 | 52 | 232* | 37 | 26.71 |
| G. M. Emmett . . . . . . | 1936-59 | 25,602 | 865 | 50 | 188 | 37 | 31.41 |
| J. B. Bolus . . . . . . . . | 1956-75 | 25,598 | 833 | 81 | 202* | 39 | 34.03 |
| W. E. Russell . . . . . . | 1956-72 | 25,525 | 796 | 64 | 193 | 41 | 34.87 |
| C. J. Barnett . . . . . . . | 1927-*53* | 25,389 | 821 | 45 | 259 | 48 | 32.71 |
| L. B. Fishlock . . . . . . | 1931-52 | 25,376 | 699 | 54 | 253 | 56 | 39.34 |
| D. J. Insole . . . . . . . . | 1947-63 | 25,241 | 743 | 72 | 219* | 54 | 37.61 |
| J. M. Brearley . . . . . . | 1961-83 | 25,185 | 768 | 102 | 312* | 45 | 37.81 |
| J. Vine . . . . . . . . . . . | 1896-1922 | 25,171 | 920 | 79 | 202 | 34 | 29.92 |
| R. M. Prideaux . . . . . . | 1958-*74* | 25,136 | 808 | 75 | 202* | 41 | 34.29 |
| J. H. King . . . . . . . . | 1895-1926 | 25,122 | 988 | 69 | 227* | 34 | 27.33 |

*Note:* Some works of reference provide career figures which differ from those in this list, owing to the exclusion or inclusion of matches recognised or not recognised as first-class by *Wisden*. Those figures are:

| | Career | R | I | NO | HI | 100s | Avge |
|---|---|---|---|---|---|---|---|
| J. B. Hobbs . . . . . . . . | 1905-34 | 61,760 | 1,325 | 107 | 316* | 199 | 50.66 |
| F. E. Woolley . . . . . . | 1906-38 | 58,959 | 1,530 | 84 | 305* | 145 | 40.77 |
| W. G. Grace . . . . . . . | 1865-1908 | 54,211 | 1,478 | 104 | 344 | 124 | 39.45 |
| H. Sutcliffe . . . . . . . . | 1919-45 | 50,670 | 1,098 | 124 | 313 | 151 | 52.02 |
| W. Rhodes . . . . . . . . | 1898-1930 | 39,969 | 1,534 | 237 | 267* | 58 | 30.58 |
| D. Denton . . . . . . . . | 1894-1920 | 36,440 | 1,161 | 70 | 221 | 69 | 33.40 |
| G. H. Hirst . . . . . . . . | 1891-1929 | 36,356 | 1,217 | 152 | 341 | 60 | 34.13 |

## CAREER AVERAGE OVER 50

(Qualification: 10,000 runs)

| Avge | | Career | I | NO | R | HI | 100s |
|---|---|---|---|---|---|---|---|
| 95.14 | D. G. Bradman | *1927-48* | 338 | 43 | 28,067 | 452* | 117 |
| 71.22 | V. M. Merchant | *1929-51* | 229 | 43 | 13,248 | 359* | 44 |
| 65.18 | W. H. Ponsford | *1920-34* | 235 | 23 | 13,819 | 437 | 47 |

| Avge | | Career | I | NO | R | HI | 100s |
|---|---|---|---|---|---|---|---|
| 64.99 | W. M. Woodfull | 1921-34 | 245 | 39 | 13,388 | 284 | 49 |
| 59.38 | G. A. Hick | 1983-91 | 326 | 38 | 17,103 | 405* | 60 |
| 58.24 | A. L. Hassett | 1932-53 | 322 | 32 | 16,890 | 232 | 59 |
| 58.19 | V. S. Hazare | 1934-66 | 365 | 45 | 18,621 | 316* | 60 |
| 57.80 | M. D. Crowe | 1979-90 | 336 | 53 | 16,359 | 299 | 58 |
| 57.22 | A. F. Kippax | 1918-35 | 256 | 33 | 12,762 | 315* | 43 |
| 56.83 | G. Boycott | 1962-86 | 1,014 | 162 | 48,426 | 261* | 151 |
| 56.55 | C. L. Walcott | 1941-63 | 238 | 29 | 11,820 | 314* | 40 |
| 56.37 | K. S. Ranjitsinhji | 1893-1920 | 500 | 62 | 24,692 | 285* | 72 |
| 56.22 | R. B. Simpson | 1952-77 | 436 | 62 | 21,029 | 359 | 60 |
| 56.10 | W. R. Hammond | 1920-51 | 1,005 | 104 | 50,551 | 336* | 167 |
| 55.51 | L. Hutton | 1934-60 | 814 | 91 | 40,140 | 364 | 129 |
| 55.34 | E. D. Weekes | 1944-64 | 241 | 24 | 12,010 | 304* | 36 |
| 54.87 | G. S. Sobers | 1952-74 | 609 | 93 | 28,315 | 365* | 86 |
| 54.74 | B. A. Richards | 1964-82 | 576 | 58 | 28,358 | 356 | 80 |
| 54.67 | R. G. Pollock | 1960-86 | 437 | 54 | 20,940 | 274 | 64 |
| 54.24 | F. M. M. Worrell | 1941-64 | 326 | 49 | 15,025 | 308* | 39 |
| 54.07 | Javed Miandad | 1973-91 | 598 | 90 | 27,468 | 311 | 78 |
| 53.78 | R. M. Cowper | 1959-69 | 228 | 31 | 10,595 | 307 | 26 |
| 53.67 | A. R. Morris | 1940-63 | 250 | 15 | 12,614 | 290 | 46 |
| 53.35 | D. B. Vengsarkar | 1975-90 | 375 | 51 | 17,288 | 258* | 54 |
| 52.42 | A. R. Border | 1976-90 | 500 | 79 | 22,071 | 205 | 61 |
| 52.32 | Hanif Mohammad | 1951-75 | 371 | 45 | 17,059 | 499 | 55 |
| 52.27 | P. R. Umrigar | 1944-67 | 350 | 41 | 16,154 | 252* | 49 |
| 52.20 | G. S. Chappell | 1966-83 | 542 | 72 | 24,535 | 247* | 74 |
| 51.95 | H. Sutcliffe | 1919-45 | 1,088 | 123 | 50,138 | 313 | 149 |
| 51.85 | D. C. S. Compton | 1936-64 | 839 | 88 | 38,942 | 300 | 123 |
| 51.54 | Zaheer Abbas | 1965-86 | 768 | 92 | 34,843 | 274 | 108 |
| 51.53 | A. D. Nourse | 1931-52 | 269 | 27 | 12,472 | 260* | 41 |
| 51.46 | S. M. Gavaskar | 1966-87 | 563 | 61 | 25,834 | 340 | 81 |
| 51.44 | W. A. Brown | 1932-49 | 284 | 15 | 13,838 | 265* | 39 |
| 51.00 | P. B. H. May | 1948-63 | 618 | 77 | 27,592 | 285* | 85 |
| 50.95 | N. C. O'Neill | 1955-67 | 306 | 34 | 13,859 | 284 | 45 |
| 50.93 | R. N. Harvey | 1946-62 | 461 | 35 | 21,699 | 231* | 67 |
| 50.90 | W. M. Lawry | 1955-71 | 417 | 49 | 18,734 | 266 | 50 |
| 50.90 | A. V. Mankad | 1963-82 | 326 | 71 | 12,980 | 265 | 31 |
| 50.80 | E. H. Hendren | 1907-38 | 1,300 | 166 | 57,611 | 301* | 170 |
| 50.65 | J. B. Hobbs | 1905-34 | 1,315 | 106 | 61,237 | 316* | 197 |
| 50.22 | C. B. Fry | 1892-1921 | 658 | 43 | 30,886 | 258* | 94 |
| 50.01 | Shafiq Ahmad | 1967-90 | 449 | 58 | 19,555 | 217* | 53 |
| 50.00 | I. V. A. Richards | 1971-91 | 741 | 56 | 34,255 | 322 | 111 |

# FAST FIFTIES

| Minutes | | | |
|---|---|---|---|
| 11 | C. I. J. Smith (66) | Middlesex v Gloucestershire at Bristol | 1938 |
| 14 | S. J. Pegler (50) | South Africans v Tasmania at Launceston | 1910-11 |
| 14 | F. T. Mann (53) | Middlesex v Nottinghamshire at Lord's | 1921 |
| 14 | H. B. Cameron (56) | Transvaal v Orange Free State at Johannesburg | 1934-35 |
| 14 | C. I. J. Smith (52) | Middlesex v Kent at Maidstone | 1935 |

*Note:* The following fast fifties were scored in contrived circumstances when runs were given from full tosses and long hops to expedite a declaration: C. C. Inman (8 minutes), Leicestershire v Nottinghamshire at Nottingham, 1965; T. M. Moody (11 minutes), Warwickshire v Glamorgan at Swansea, 1990; M. P. Maynard (14 minutes), Glamorgan v Yorkshire at Cardiff, 1987.

## FASTEST HUNDREDS

*Minutes*

| | | | |
|---|---|---|---|
| 35 | P. G. H. Fender (113*) | Surrey v Northamptonshire at Northampton ... | 1920 |
| 40 | G. L. Jessop (101) | Gloucestershire v Yorkshire at Harrogate ..... | 1897 |
| 42 | G. L. Jessop (101) | Gentlemen of South v Players of South at Hastings............................... | 1907 |
| 43 | A. H. Hornby (106) | Lancashire v Somerset at Manchester .......... | 1905 |
| 43 | D. W. Hookes (107) | South Australia v Victoria at Adelaide........ | 1982-83 |
| 44 | R. N. S. Hobbs (100) | Essex v Australians at Chelmsford ........... | 1975 |

*Notes:* The fastest recorded hundred in terms of balls received was scored off 34 balls by D. W. Hookes (above).

Research of the scorebook has shown that P. G. H. Fender scored his hundred from between 40 and 46 balls. He contributed 113 to an unfinished sixth-wicket partnership of 171 in 42 minutes with H. A. Peach.

E. B. Alletson (Nottinghamshire) scored 189 out of 227 runs in 90 minutes against Sussex at Hove in 1911. It has been estimated that his last 139 runs took 37 minutes.

The following fast hundreds were scored in contrived circumstances when runs were given from full tosses and long hops to expedite a declaration: T. M. Moody (26 minutes), Warwickshire v Glamorgan at Swansea, 1990; S. J. O'Shaughnessy (35 minutes), Lancashire v Leicestershire at Manchester, 1983; C. M. Old (37 minutes), Yorkshire v Warwickshire at Birmingham, 1977; N. F. M. Popplewell (41 minutes), Somerset v Gloucestershire at Bath, 1983.

## FASTEST DOUBLE-HUNDREDS

*Minutes*

| | | | |
|---|---|---|---|
| 113 | R. J. Shastri (200*) | Bombay v Baroda at Bombay............... | 1984-85 |
| 120 | G. L. Jessop (286) | Gloucestershire v Sussex at Hove............ | 1903 |
| 120 | C. H. Lloyd (201*) | West Indians v Glamorgan at Swansea ....... | 1976 |
| 130 | G. L. Jessop (234) | Gloucestershire v Somerset at Bristol......... | 1905 |
| 131 | V. T. Trumper (293) | Australians v Canterbury at Christchurch ..... | 1913-14 |

## FASTEST TRIPLE-HUNDREDS

*Minutes*

| | | | |
|---|---|---|---|
| 181 | D. C. S. Compton (300) | MCC v N. E. Transvaal at Benoni .......... | 1948-49 |
| 205 | F. E. Woolley (305*) | MCC v Tasmania at Hobart................ | 1911-12 |
| 205 | C. G. Macartney (345) | Australians v Nottinghamshire at Nottingham . | 1921 |
| 213 | D. G. Bradman (369) | South Australia v Tasmania at Adelaide ...... | 1935-36 |

## 300 RUNS IN ONE DAY

| | | | |
|---|---|---|---|
| 345 | C. G. Macartney | Australians v Nottinghamshire at Nottingham........ | 1921 |
| 334 | W. H. Ponsford | Victoria v New South Wales at Melbourne........... | 1926-27 |
| 333 | K. S. Duleepsinhji | Sussex v Northamptonshire at Hove ............... | 1930 |
| 331* | J. D. Robertson | Middlesex v Worcestershire at Worcester .......... | 1949 |
| 325* | B. A. Richards | S. Australia v W. Australia at Perth .............. | 1970-71 |
| 322† | E. Paynter | Lancashire v Sussex at Hove .................... | 1937 |
| 322 | I. V. A. Richards | Somerset v Warwickshire at Taunton ............. | 1985 |
| 318 | C. W. Gregory | New South Wales v Queensland at Brisbane......... | 1906-07 |
| 317 | K. R. Rutherford | New Zealanders v D. B. Close's XI at Scarborough.... | 1986 |
| 316† | R. H. Moore | Hampshire v Warwickshire at Bournemouth........ | 1937 |
| 315* | R. C. Blunt | Otago v Canterbury at Christchurch .............. | 1931-32 |
| 312* | J. M. Brearley | MCC Under 25 v North Zone at Peshawar ......... | 1966-67 |
| 311* | G. M. Turner | Worcestershire v Warwickshire at Worcester ....... | 1982 |
| 311* | N. H. Fairbrother | Lancashire v Surrey at The Oval ................. | 1990 |
| 309* | D. G. Bradman | Australia v England at Leeds .................... | 1930 |
| 307* | W. H. Ashdown | Kent v Essex at Brentwood...................... | 1934 |
| 306* | A. Ducat | Surrey v Oxford University at The Oval ........... | 1919 |
| 305* | F. R. Foster | Warwickshire v Worcestershire at Dudley.......... | 1914 |

† *E. Paynter's 322 and R. H. Moore's 316 were scored on the same day: July 28, 1937.*

## 1,000 RUNS IN MAY

| | Runs | Avge |
|---|---|---|
| W. G. Grace, May 9 to May 30, 1895 (22 days): | | |
| 13, 103, 18, 25, 288, 52, 257, 73*, 18, 169 . . . . . . . . . . . . . . . . . . | 1,016 | 112.88 |
| Grace was within two months of completing his 47th year. | | |
| W. R. Hammond, May 7 to May 31, 1927 (25 days): | | |
| 27, 135, 108, 128, 17, 11, 99, 187, 4, 30, 83, 7, 192, 14 . . . . . . . . . | 1,042 | 74.42 |
| Hammond scored his 1,000th run on May 28, thus equalling Grace's record of 22 days. | | |
| C. Hallows, May 5 to May 31, 1928 (27 days): | | |
| 100, 101, 51*, 123, 101*, 22, 74, 104, 58, 34*, 232 . . . . . . . . . . . . . | 1,000 | 125.00 |

## 1,000 RUNS IN APRIL AND MAY

| | Runs | Avge |
|---|---|---|
| T. W. Hayward, April 16 to May 31, 1900: | | |
| 120*, 55, 108, 131*, 55, 193, 120, 5, 6, 3, 40, 146, 92 . . . . . . . . . . . | 1,074 | 97.63 |
| D. G. Bradman, April 30 to May 31, 1930: | | |
| 236, 185*, 78, 9, 48*, 66, 4, 44, 252*, 32, 47* . . . . . . . . . . . . . . . . | 1,001 | 143.00 |
| On April 30 Bradman scored 75 not out. | | |
| D. G. Bradman, April 30 to May 31, 1938: | | |
| 258, 58, 137, 278, 2, 143, 145*, 5, 30* . . . . . . . . . . . . . . . . . . . . . | 1,056 | 150.85 |
| Bradman scored 258 on April 30, and his 1,000th run on May 27. | | |
| W. J. Edrich, April 30 to May 31, 1938: | | |
| 104, 37, 115, 63, 20*, 182, 71, 31, 53*, 45, 15, 245, 0, 9, 20* . . . . . | 1,010 | 84.16 |
| Edrich scored 21 not out on April 30. All his runs were scored at Lord's. | | |
| G. M. Turner, April 24 to May 31, 1973: | | |
| 41, 151*, 143, 85, 7, 8, 17*, 81, 13, 53, 44, 153*, 3, 2, 66*, 30, 10*, 111 . . . . . . . . . . . . . . . . . . . . . . . . . . . . . . . . . . . . . . . . . . . . . . | 1,018 | 78.30 |
| G. A. Hick, April 17 to May 29, 1988: | | |
| 61, 37, 212, 86, 14, 405*, 8, 11, 6, 7, 172 . . . . . . . . . . . . . . . . . . . . . | 1,019 | 101.90 |
| Hick scored a record 410 runs in April, and his 1,000th run on May 28. | | |

## 1,000 RUNS IN TWO SEPARATE MONTHS

Only four batsmen, C. B. Fry, K. S. Ranjitsinhji, H. Sutcliffe and L. Hutton, have scored over 1,000 runs in each of two months in the same season. L. Hutton, by scoring 1,294 in June 1949, made more runs in a single month than anyone else. He also made 1,050 in August 1949.

## MOST RUNS SCORED OFF ONE OVER

*(All instances refer to six-ball overs)*

| | | | |
|---|---|---|---|
| 36 | G. S. Sobers | off M. A. Nash, Nottinghamshire v Glamorgan at Swansea (six sixes) . . . . . . . . . . . . . . . . . . . . . . . . . . . . . . . . . . . . . . . . . | 1968 |
| 36 | R. J. Shastri | off Tilak Raj, Bombay v Baroda at Bombay (six sixes) . . . | 1984-85 |
| 34 | E. B. Alletson | off E. H. Killick, Nottinghamshire v Sussex at Hove (46604446; including two no-balls) . . . . . . . . . . . . . . . . . . | 1911 |
| 34 | F. C. Hayes | off M. A. Nash, Lancashire v Glamorgan at Swansea (646666) . . . . . . . . . . . . . . . . . . . . . . . . . . . . . . . . . . . . . . . . | 1977 |
| 32 | I. T. Botham | off I. R. Snook, England XI v Central Districts at Palmerston North (466466) . . . . . . . . . . . . . . . . . . . . . . . . . . . . . . . . . | 1983-84 |
| 32 | C. C. Inman | off N. W. Hill, Leicestershire v Nottinghamshire at Nottingham (466466; full tosses were provided for him to hit) . . . . . . . . . . . . . . . . . . . . . . . . . . . . . . . . . . . . . . . . . . | 1965 |
| 32 | T. E. Jesty | off R. J. Boyd-Moss, Hampshire v Northamptonshire at Southampton (666662) . . . . . . . . . . . . . . . . . . . . . . . . . . . . | 1984 |
| 32 | P. W. G. Parker | off A. I. Kallicharran, Sussex v Warwickshire at Birmingham (466664) . . . . . . . . . . . . . . . . . . . . . . . . . . . . . . | 1982 |

| 32 | I. R. Redpath | off N. Rosendorff, Australians v Orange Free State at Bloemfontein (666644) | 1969-70 |
| 32 | C. C. Smart | off G. Hill, Glamorgan v Hampshire at Cardiff (664664) . | 1935 |
| 31 | M. H. Bowditch (1) and M. J. Procter (30) | off A. A. Mallett, Western Province v Australians at Cape Town (Procter hit five sixes) | 1969-70 |
| 31 | A. W. Wellard | off F. E. Woolley, Somerset v Kent at Wells (666661) | 1938 |
| 30 | I. T. Botham | off P. A. Smith, Somerset v Warwickshire at Taunton (4466460 including one no-ball) | 1982 |
| 30 | D. G. Bradman | off A. P. Freeman, Australians v England XI at Folkestone (466464) | 1934 |
| 30 | H. B. Cameron | off H. Verity, South Africans v Yorkshire at Sheffield (444666) | 1935 |
| 30 | G. A. Gooch | off S. R. Gorman, Essex v Cambridge U. at Cambridge (662664) | 1985 |
| 30 | A. J. Lamb | off A. I. Kallicharran, Northamptonshire v Warwickshire at Birmingham (662664) | 1982 |
| 30 | D. T. Lindsay | off W. T. Greensmith, South African Fezela XI v Essex at Chelmsford (066666 to win the match) | 1961 |
| 30 | Majid Khan | off R. C. Davis, Pakistanis v Glamorgan at Swansea (606666) | 1967 |
| 30 | M. P. Maynard | off K. Sharp, Glamorgan v Yorkshire at Cardiff (464466) (runs were offered to expedite a declaration) | 1987 |
| 30 | A. W. Wellard | off T. R. Armstrong, Somerset v Derbyshire at Wells (066666) | 1936 |
| 30 | D. Wilson | off R. N. S. Hobbs, Yorkshire v MCC at Scarborough (466266) | 1966 |
| 30 | P. L. Winslow | off J. T. Ikin, South Africans v Lancashire at Manchester (446646) | 1955 |
| 30 | Zaheer Abbas | off D. Breakwell, Gloucestershire v Somerset at Taunton (466626) | 1979 |
| 30 | T. M. Moody | off A. E. Tucker, Western Australia v NSW at Sydney (644646) | 1990-91 |

*Notes:* The greatest number of runs scored off an eight-ball over is 34 (40446664) by R. M. Edwards off M. C. Carew, Governor-General's XI v West Indians at Auckland, 1968-69.

In a Shell Trophy match against Canterbury at Christchurch in 1989-90, R. H. Vance (Wellington), acting on the instructions of his captain, deliberately conceded 77 runs in an over of full tosses which contained seventeen no-balls and, owing to the umpire's miscalculation, only five legitimate deliveries.

## MOST SIXES IN AN INNINGS

| 15 | J. R. Reid (296) | Wellington v N. Districts at Wellington | 1962-63 |
| 14 | Shakti Singh (128) | Himachal Pradesh v Haryana at Dharmsala | 1990-91 |
| 13 | Majid Khan (147*) | Pakistanis v Glamorgan at Swansea | 1967 |
| 13 | C. G. Greenidge (273*) | D. H. Robins' XI v Pakistanis at Eastbourne | 1974 |
| 13 | C. G. Greenidge (259) | Hampshire v Sussex at Southampton | 1975 |
| 13 | G. W. Humpage (254) | Warwickshire v Lancashire at Southport | 1982 |
| 13 | R. J. Shastri (200*) | Bombay v Baroda at Bombay | 1984-85 |
| 12 | Gulfraz Khan (207) | Railways v Universities at Lahore | 1976-77 |
| 12 | I. T. Botham (138*) | Somerset v Warwickshire at Birmingham | 1985 |
| 12 | R. A. Harper (234) | Northamptonshire v Gloucestershire at Northampton | 1986 |
| 12 | D. M. Jones (248) | Australians v Warwickshire at Birmingham | 1989 |
| 11 | C. K. Nayudu (153) | Hindus v MCC at Bombay | 1926-27 |
| 11 | C. J. Barnett (194) | Gloucestershire v Somerset at Bath | 1934 |
| 11 | R. Benaud (135) | Australians v T. N. Pearce's XI at Scarborough | 1953 |
| 11 | R. Bora (126) | Assam v Tripura at Gauhati | 1987-88 |
| 11 | G. A. Hick (405*) | Worcestershire v Somerset at Taunton | 1988 |

*Note:* W. J. Stewart (Warwickshire) hit seventeen sixes in the match v Lancashire, at Blackpool, 1959; ten in his first innings of 155 and seven in his second innings of 125.

## MOST SIXES IN A SEASON

| | | | | | |
|---|---|---|---|---|---|
| 80 | I. T. Botham | 1985 | 66 | A. W. Wellard | 1935 |

*Note:* A. W. Wellard hit 50 or more sixes in a season four times. His number of sixes in 1935 has in the past been given as 72, but later research has caused this to be adjusted.

## MOST BOUNDARIES IN AN INNINGS

| 68 | P. A. Perrin (343*) | Essex v Derbyshire at Chesterfield | 1904 |
|---|---|---|---|
| 65 | A. C. MacLaren (424) | Lancashire v Somerset at Taunton | 1895 |
| 64 | Hanif Mohammad (499) | Karachi v Bahawalpur at Karachi | 1958-59 |
| 57 | J. H. Edrich (310*) | England v New Zealand at Leeds | 1965 |
| 55 | C. W. Gregory (383) | NSW v Queensland at Brisbane | 1906-07 |
| 55 | G. R. Marsh (355*) | Western Australia v South Australia at Perth | 1989-90 |
| 54 | G. H. Hirst (341) | Yorkshire v Leicestershire at Leicester | 1905 |
| 54 | S. V. Manjrekar (377) | Bombay v Hyderabad at Bombay | 1990-91 |
| 53 | A. W. Nourse (304*) | Natal v Transvaal at Johannesburg | 1919-20 |
| 53 | K. R. Rutherford (317) | New Zealanders v D. B. Close's XI at Scarborough. | 1986 |
| 52 | N. H. Fairbrother (366) | Lancashire v Surrey at The Oval | 1990 |
| 51 | C. G. Macartney (345) | Australians v Nottinghamshire at Nottingham | 1921 |
| 51 | B. B. Nimbalkar (443*) | Maharashtra v Kathiawar at Poona | 1948-49 |
| 50 | D. G. Bradman (369) | South Australia v Tasmania at Adelaide | 1935-36 |
| 50 | A. Ducat (306*) | Surrey v Oxford University at The Oval | 1919 |
| 50 | J. R. Reid (296) | Wellington v N. Districts at Wellington | 1962-63 |
| 50 | I. V. A. Richards (322) | Somerset v Warwickshire at Taunton | 1985 |

*Note:* Boundaries include sixes.

## HIGHEST PARTNERSHIPS

| 577 | V. S. Hazare (288) and Gul Mahomed (319), fourth wicket, Baroda v Holkar at Baroda | 1946-47 |
|---|---|---|
| 574* | F. M. M. Worrell (255*) and C. L. Walcott (314*), fourth wicket, Barbados v Trinidad at Port-of-Spain | 1945-46 |
| 561 | Waheed Mirza (324) and Mansoor Akhtar (224*), first wicket, Karachi Whites v Quetta at Karachi | 1976-77 |
| 555 | P. Holmes (224*) and H. Sutcliffe (313), first wicket, Yorkshire v Essex at Leyton | 1932 |
| 554 | J. T. Brown (300) and J. Tunnicliffe (243), first wicket, Yorkshire v Derbyshire at Chesterfield | 1898 |
| 502* | F. M. M. Worrell (308*) and J. D. C. Goddard (218*), fourth wicket, Barbados v Trinidad at Bridgetown | 1943-44 |
| 490 | E. H. Bowley (283) and J. G. Langridge (195), first wicket, Sussex v Middlesex at Hove | 1933 |
| 487* | G. A. Headley (344*) and C. C. Passailaigue (261*), sixth wicket, Jamaica v Lord Tennyson's XI at Kingston | 1931-32 |
| 470 | A. I. Kallicharran (230*) and G. W. Humpage (254), fourth wicket, Warwickshire v Lancashire at Southport | 1982 |
| 467 | A. H. Jones (186) and M. D. Crowe (299), third wicket, New Zealand v Sri Lanka at Wellington | 1990-91 |
| 465* | J. A. Jameson (240*) and R. B. Kanhai (213*), second wicket, Warwickshire v Gloucestershire at Birmingham | 1974 |
| 464* | M. E. Waugh (229*) and S. R. Waugh (216)*, fifth wicket, New South Wales v Western Australia at Perth | 1990-91 |
| | *Includes 20 runs for no-balls under ACB playing conditions; under the Laws of Cricket, only 7 runs would have resulted from 10 no-balls bowled in this partnership.* | |
| 462* | D. W. Hookes (306*) and W. B. Phillips (213*), fourth wicket, South Australia v Tasmania at Adelaide | 1986-87 |
| 456 | W. H. Ponsford (248) and E. R. Mayne (209), first wicket, Victoria v Queensland at Melbourne | 1923-24 |
| 456 | Khalid Irtiza (290) and Aslam Ali (236), third wicket, United Bank v Multan at Karachi | 1975-76 |
| 455 | K. V. Bhandarkar (205) and B. B. Nimbalkar (443*), second wicket, Maharashtra v Kathiawar at Poona | 1948-49 |

| | | |
|---|---|---|
| 451 | D. G. Bradman (244) and W. H. Ponsford (266), second wicket, Australia v England, Fifth Test, at The Oval | 1934 |
| 451* | S. Desai (218*) and R. M. H. Binny (211*), first wicket, Karnataka v Kerala at Chickmagalur | 1977-78 |
| 451 | Mudassar Nazar (231) and Javed Miandad (280*), third wicket, Pakistan v India, Fourth Test, at Hyderabad | 1982-83 |

## PARTNERSHIPS FOR FIRST WICKET

| | | |
|---|---|---|
| 561 | Waheed Mirza and Mansoor Akhtar, Karachi Whites v Quetta at Karachi | 1976-77 |
| 555 | P. Holmes and H. Sutcliffe, Yorkshire v Essex at Leyton | 1932 |
| 554 | J. T. Brown and J. Tunnicliffe, Yorkshire v Derbyshire at Chesterfield | 1898 |
| 490 | E. H. Bowley and J. G. Langridge, Sussex v Middlesex at Hove | 1933 |
| 456 | E. R. Mayne and W. H. Ponsford, Victoria v Queensland at Melbourne | 1923-24 |
| 451* | S. Desai and R. M. H. Binny, Karnataka v Kerala at Chikmagalur | 1977-78 |
| 431 | M. R. J. Veletta and G. R. Marsh, Western Australia v South Australia at Perth | 1989-90 |
| 428 | J. B. Hobbs and A. Sandham, Surrey v Oxford University at The Oval | 1926 |
| 424 | J. F. W. Nicholson and I. J. Siedle, Natal v Orange Free State at Bloemfontein | 1926-27 |
| 421 | S. M. Gavaskar and G. A. Parkar, Bombay v Bengal at Bombay | 1981-82 |
| 418 | Kamal Najamuddin and Khalid Alvi, Karachi v Railways at Karachi | 1980-81 |
| 413 | V. Mankad and Pankaj Roy, India v New Zealand at Madras (world Test record) | 1955-56 |
| 405 | C. P. S. Chauhan and M. S. Gupte, Maharashtra v Vidarbha at Poona | 1972-73 |
| 395 | D. M. Young and R. B. Nicholls, Gloucestershire v Oxford University at Oxford | 1962 |
| 391 | A. O. Jones and A. Shrewsbury, Nottinghamshire v Gloucestershire at Bristol | 1899 |
| 390 | G. L. Wight and G. L. R. Gibbs, B. Guiana v Barbados at Georgetown | 1951-52 |
| 390 | B. Dudleston and J. F. Steele, Leicestershire v Derbyshire at Leicester | 1979 |
| 389 | Majid Khan and Shafiq Ahmed, Punjab A v Sind A at Karachi | 1974-75 |
| 389 | Mudassar Nazar and Mansoor Akhtar, United Bank v Rawalpindi at Lahore | 1981-82 |
| 388 | K. C. Wessels and R. B. Kerr, Queensland v Victoria at St Kilda, Melbourne | 1982-83 |
| 387 | G. M. Turner and T. W. Jarvis, New Zealand v West Indies at Georgetown | 1971-72 |
| 382 | R. B. Simpson and W. M. Lawry, Australia v West Indies at Bridgetown | 1964-65 |
| 380 | H. Whitehead and C. J. B. Wood, Leicestershire v Worcestershire at Worcester | 1906 |
| 379 | R. Abel and W. Brockwell, Surrey v Hampshire at The Oval | 1897 |
| 378 | J. T. Brown and J. Tunnicliffe, Yorkshire v Sussex at Sheffield | 1897 |
| 377* | N. F. Horner and Khalid Ibadulla, Warwickshire v Surrey at The Oval | 1960 |
| 375 | W. H. Ponsford and W. M. Woodfull, Victoria v New South Wales at Melbourne | 1926-27 |

## FIRST-WICKET HUNDREDS IN BOTH INNINGS

There have been three instances of two double-century opening stands in the same match: B. Sutcliffe and D. D. Taylor, 220 and 286 for Auckland v Canterbury at Auckland in 1948-49; P. R. Pollard and R. T. Robinson, 222 and 282 for Nottinghamshire v Kent at Nottingham in 1989; and G. A. Gooch and J. P. Stephenson, 227 and 220 for Essex v Northamptonshire at Northampton in 1990.

T. W. Hayward and J. B. Hobbs in 1907 accomplished a performance without parallel by scoring over 100 together for Surrey's first wicket four times in one week: 106 and 125 v Cambridge University at The Oval, and 147 and 105 v Middlesex at Lord's.

L. Hutton and C. Washbrook, in three consecutive Test match innings which they opened together for England v Australia in 1946-47, made 138 in the second innings at Melbourne, and 137 and 100 at Adelaide. They also opened with 168 and 129 at Leeds in 1948.

J. B. Hobbs and H. Sutcliffe, in three consecutive Test match innings which they opened together for England v Australia in 1924-25, made 157 and 110 at Sydney and 283 at Melbourne. On 26 occasions – 15 times in Test matches – Hobbs and Sutcliffe took part in a three-figure first-wicket partnership. Seven of these stands exceeded 200.

G. Boycott and J. H. Edrich, in three consecutive Test match innings which they opened together for England v Australia in 1970-71, made 161* in the second innings at Melbourne, and 107 and 103 at Adelaide.

In 1971 R. G. A. Headley and P. J. Stimpson of Worcestershire shared in first-wicket hundred partnerships on each of the first four occasions they opened the innings together: 125 and 147 v Northamptonshire at Worcester, 102 and 128* v Warwickshire at Birmingham.

J. B. Hobbs during his career, which extended from 1905 to 1934, helped to make 100 or more for the first wicket in first-class cricket 166 times – 15 of them in 1926, when in consecutive innings he helped to make 428, 182, 106 and 123 before a wicket fell. As many as 117 of the 166 stands were made for Surrey. In all first-class matches Hobbs and A. Sandham shared 66 first-wicket partnerships of 100 or more runs.

P. Holmes and H. Sutcliffe made 100 or more runs for the first wicket of Yorkshire on 69 occasions; J. B. Hobbs and A. Sandham for Surrey on 63 occasions; W. W. Keeton and C. B. Harris of Nottinghamshire on 46; T. W. Hayward and J. B. Hobbs of Surrey on 40; G. Gunn and W. W. Whysall of Nottinghamshire on 40; J. D. Robertson and S. M. Brown of Middlesex on 34; C. B. Fry and J. Vine of Sussex on 33; R. E. Marshall and J. R. Gray of Hampshire on 33; and D. E. Davies and A. H. Dyson of Glamorgan on 32.

J. Douglas and A. E. Stoddart in 1896 scored over 100 runs for the Middlesex first wicket three times within a fortnight. In 1901, J. Iremonger and A. O. Jones obtained over 100 for the Nottinghamshire first wicket four times within eight days, scoring 134 and 144* v Surrey at The Oval, 238 v Essex at Leyton, and 119 v Derbyshire at Welbeck.

J. W. Lee and F. S. Lee, brothers, for Somerset in 1934, scored over 100 runs thrice in succession in the County Championship.

W. G. Grace and A. E. Stoddart, in three consecutive innings against the Australians in 1893, made over 100 runs for each opening partnership.

C. Hallows and F. B. Watson, in consecutive innings for Lancashire in 1928, opened with 200, 202, 107, 118; reached three figures twelve times, 200 four times.

H. Sutcliffe, in the period 1919-1939 inclusive, shared in 145 first-wicket partnerships of 100 runs or more.

There were four first-wicket hundred partnerships in the match between Somerset and Cambridge University at Taunton in 1960. G. Atkinson and R. T. Virgin scored 172 and 112 for Somerset and R. M. Prideaux and A. R. Lewis 198 and 137 for Cambridge University.

# PARTNERSHIP RECORDS FOR ALL COUNTRIES

## Best First-Wicket Stands

| Pakistan | 561 | Waheed Mirza (324) and Mansoor Akhtar (224*), Karachi Whites v Quetta at Karachi | 1976-77 |
|---|---|---|---|
| English | 555 | P. Holmes (224*) and H. Sutcliffe (313), Yorkshire v Essex at Leyton | 1932 |
| Australian | 456 | W. H. Ponsford (248) and E. R. Mayne (209), Victoria v Queensland at Melbourne | 1923-24 |
| Indian | 451* | S. Desai (218*) and R. M. H. Binny (211*), Karnataka v Kerala at Chickmagalur | 1977-78 |
| South African | 424 | J. F. W. Nicolson (252*) and I. J. Siedle (174), Natal v Orange Free State at Bloemfontein | 1926-27 |
| West Indian | 390 | G. L. Wight (262*) and G. L. R. Gibbs (216), British Guiana v Barbados at Georgetown | 1951-52 |
| New Zealand | 387 | G. M. Turner (259) and T. W. Jarvis (182), New Zealand v West Indies at Georgetown | 1971-72 |
| Sri Lankan | 214 | D. Ranatunga (170) and A. A. W. Gunawardene (96), Sinhalese SC v Old Cambrians at Colombo | 1989-90 |

## Best Second-Wicket Stands

| English | 465* | J. A. Jameson (240*) and R. B. Kanhai (213*), Warwickshire v Gloucestershire at Birmingham | 1974 |
|---|---|---|---|
| Indian | 455 | K. V. Bhandarkar (205) and B. B. Nimbalkar (443*), Maharashtra v Kathiawar at Poona | 1948-49 |
| Australian | 451 | W. H. Ponsford (266) and D. G. Bradman (244), Australia v England at The Oval | 1934 |
| West Indian | 446 | C. C. Hunte (260) and G. S. Sobers (365*), West Indies v Pakistan at Kingston | 1957-58 |
| Pakistan | 426 | Arshad Pervez (220) and Mohsin Khan (220), Habib Bank v Income Tax Dept at Lahore | 1977-78 |
| New Zealand | 317 | R. T. Hart (167*) and P. S. Briasco (157), Central Districts v Canterbury at New Plymouth | 1983-84 |

| | | | |
|---|---|---|---|
| South African | . . 305 | S. K. Coen (165) and J. M. M Commaille (186), Orange Free State v Natal at Bloemfontein | 1926-27 |
| Sri Lankan | . . . . . 272 | U. N. K. Fernando (160) and S. Sooriyarachchi (148), Western Province (Suburbs) v Central Province at Colombo | 1990-91 |

## Best Third-Wicket Stands

| | | | |
|---|---|---|---|
| New Zealand | . . . 467 | A. H. Jones (186) and M. D. Crowe (299), New Zealand v Sri Lanka at Wellington | 1990-91 |
| Pakistan | . . . . . . 456 | Khalid Irtiza (290) and Aslam Ali (236), United Bank v Multan at Karachi | 1975-76 |
| West Indian | . . . 434 | J. B. Stollmeyer (324) and G. E. Gomez (190), Trinidad v British Guiana at Port-of-Spain | 1946-47 |
| English | . . . . . . . . 424* | W. J. Edrich (168*) and D. C. S. Compton (252*), Middlesex v Somerset at Lord's | 1948 |
| Indian | . . . . . . . . 410 | L. Amarnath (262) and R. S. Modi (156), India in England v The Rest at Calcutta | 1946-47 |
| Australian | . . . . . 390* | J. M. Wiener (221*) and J. K. Moss (200*), Victoria v Western Australia at St Kilda, Melbourne | 1981-82 |
| South African | . . 341 | E. J. Barlow (201) and R. G. Pollock (175), South Africa v Australia at Adelaide | 1963-64 |
| Sri Lankan | . . . . . 240 | U. N. K. Fernando (130) and A. Ranatunga (105), Sinhalese SC v Panadura at Panadura | 1990-91 |

## Best Fourth-Wicket Stands

| | | | |
|---|---|---|---|
| Indian | . . . . . . . . 577 | V. S. Hazare (288) and Gul Mahomed (319), Baroda v Holkar at Baroda | 1946-47 |
| West Indian | . . . . 574* | C. L. Walcott (314*) and F. M. M. Worrell (255*), Barbados v Trinidad at Port-of-Spain | 1945-46 |
| English | . . . . . . . . 470 | A. I. Kallicharran (230*) and G. W. Humpage (254), Warwickshire v Lancashire at Southport | 1982 |
| Australian | . . . . . 462* | D. W. Hookes (306*) and W. B. Phillips (213*), South Australia v Tasmania at Adelaide | 1986-87 |
| Pakistan | . . . . . . 350 | Mushtaq Mohammad (201) and Asif Iqbal (175), Pakistan v New Zealand at Dunedin | 1972-73 |
| South African | . . 342 | E. A. B. Rowan (196) and P. J. M. Gibb (203), Transvaal v N. E. Transvaal at Johannesburg | 1952-53 |
| New Zealand | . . . 324 | J. R. Reid (188*) and W. M. Wallace (197), New Zealanders v Cambridge University at Cambridge | 1949 |
| Sri Lankan | . . . . . 263 | P. A. de Silva (221*) and H. P. Tillekeratne (100), Sri Lankans v Hampshire at Southampton | 1990 |

## Best Fifth-Wicket Stands

| | | | |
|---|---|---|---|
| Australian | . . . . . 464* | M. E. Waugh (229*) and S. R. Waugh (216*), New South Wales v Western Australia at Perth | 1990-91 |
| English | . . . . . . . . 393 | E. G. Arnold (200*) and W. B. Burns (196), Worcestershire v Warwickshire at Birmingham | 1909 |
| Indian | . . . . . . . . 360 | U. M. Merchant (217) and M. N. Raiji (170), Bombay v Hyderabad at Bombay | 1947-48 |
| Pakistan | . . . . . . 355 | Altaf Shah (276) and Tariq Bashir (196), House Building Finance Corporation v Multan at Multan | 1976-77 |
| South African | . . 355 | A. J. Lamb (294) and J. J. Strydom (107), OFS v Eastern Province at Bloemfontein | 1987-88 |
| New Zealand | . . . 341 | G. R. Larsen (161) and E. B. McSweeney (205*), Wellington v Central Districts at Levin | 1987-88 |
| West Indian | . . . 335 | B. F. Butcher (151) and C. H. Lloyd (201*), West Indies v Glamorgan at Swansea | 1969 |
| Sri Lankan | . . . . . 194 | M. de Mel (107) and M. Jayasena (99), Panadura v Air Force at Panadura | 1989-90 |

*Note:* The Waugh twins achieved the first instance of brothers each scoring a double-hundred in the same first-class innings. Their partnership includes 20 runs for no-balls under ACB playing conditions. Under the Laws of Cricket, only 7 runs would have resulted from 10 no-balls bowled in this partnership.

## Best Sixth-Wicket Stands

| | | | |
|---|---|---|---|
| West Indian.... | 487* | G. A. Headley (344*) and C. C. Passailaigue (261*), Jamaica v Lord Tennyson's XI at Kingston | 1931-32 |
| Australian..... | 428 | M. A. Noble (284) and W. W. Armstrong (172*), Australians v Sussex at Hove | 1902 |
| English........ | 411 | R. M. Poore (304) and E. G. Wynyard (225), Hampshire v Somerset at Taunton | 1899 |
| Indian ........ | 371 | V. M. Merchant (359*) and R. S. Modi (168), Bombay v Maharashtra at Bombay | 1943-44 |
| Pakistan....... | 353 | Salah-ud-Din (256) and Zaheer Abbas (197), Karachi v East Pakistan at Karachi | 1968-69 |
| South African .. | 259 | S. A. Jones (209*) and O. Henry (125), Boland v Border at East London | 1987-88 |
| New Zealand... | 246* | J. J. Crowe (120*) and R. J. Hadlee (151*), New Zealand v Sri Lanka at Colombo (CCC) | 1986-87 |
| Sri Lankan..... | 217* | H. P. Tillekeratne (128*) and A. G. D. Wickremasinghe (103*), Sri Lanka B v Zimbabwe at Harare | 1987-88 |

## Best Seventh-Wicket Stands

| | | | |
|---|---|---|---|
| West Indian.... | 347 | D. St E. Atkinson (219) and C. C. Depeiza (122), West Indies v Australia at Bridgetown | 1954-55 |
| English........ | 344 | K. S. Ranjitsinhji (230) and W. Newham (153), Sussex v Essex at Leyton | 1902 |
| Australian ..... | 335 | C. W. Andrews (253) and E. C. Bensted (155), Queensland v New South Wales at Sydney | 1934-35 |
| Pakistan....... | 308 | Waqar Hassan (189) and Imtiaz Ahmed (209), Pakistan v New Zealand at Lahore | 1955-56 |
| South African . | 299 | B. Mitchell (159) and A. Melville (153), Transvaal v Griqualand West at Kimberley | 1946-47 |
| Indian ........ | 274 | K. C. Ibrahim (250) and K. M. Rangnekar (138), Bijapur XI v Bengal XI at Bombay | 1942-43 |
| New Zealand... | 265 | J. L. Powell (164) and N. Dorreen (105*), Canterbury v Otago at Christchurch | 1929-30 |
| Sri Lankan..... | 159 | R. S. Madugalle (88) and D. S. de Silva (76), Sri Lankans v Kent at Canterbury | 1979 |

## Best Eighth-Wicket Stands

| | | | |
|---|---|---|---|
| Australian ..... | 433 | A. Sims (184*) and V. T. Trumper (293), An Australian XI v Canterbury at Christchurch | 1913-14 |
| English........ | 292 | R. Peel (210*) and Lord Hawke (166), Yorkshire v Warwickshire at Birmingham | 1896 |
| West Indian.... | 255 | E. A. V. Williams (131*) and E. A. Martindale (134), Barbados v Trinidad at Bridgetown | 1935-36 |
| Pakistan....... | 240 | Gulfraz Khan (207) and Raja Sarfraz (102), Railways v Universities at Lahore | 1976-77 |
| Indian ........ | 236 | C. T. Sarwate (235) and R. P. Singh (88), Holkar v Delhi and District at Delhi | 1949-50 |
| South African . | 222 | D. P. B. Morkel (114) and S. S. L. Steyn (261*), Western Province v Border at Cape Town | 1929-30 |
| New Zealand... | 190* | J. E. Mills (104*) and C. F. W. Allcott (102*), New Zealanders v Civil Service at Chiswick | 1927 |
| Sri Lankan..... | 159 | D. S. de Silva (97) and A. L. F. de Mel (94), Sri Lankans v Gloucestershire at Bristol | 1981 |

## Best Ninth-Wicket Stands

| | | | |
|---|---|---|---|
| English........ | 283 | J. Chapman (165) and A. Warren (123), Derbyshire v Warwickshire at Blackwell | 1910 |
| Indian ........ | 245 | V. S. Hazare (316*) and N. D. Nagarwalla (98), Maharashtra v Baroda at Poona | 1939-40 |
| New Zealand... | 239 | H. B. Cave (118) and I. B. Leggat (142*), Central Districts v Otago at Dunedin | 1952-53 |

| Australian | ..... | 232 | C. Hill (365*) and E. Walkley (53), South Australia v New South Wales at Adelaide | 1900-01 |
| South African | .. | 221 | N. V. Lindsay (160*) and G. R. McCubbin (97), Transvaal v Rhodesia at Bulawayo | 1922-23 |
| Pakistan | ....... | 190 | Asif Iqbal (146) and Intikhab Alam (51), Pakistan v England at The Oval | 1967 |
| West Indian | .. | 161 | C. H. Lloyd (161*) and A. M. E. Roberts (68), West Indies v India at Calcutta | 1983-84 |
| Sri Lankan | ..... | 153 | R. Wickremaratne (134) and S. Munaweera (65), Colts CC v Singha SC at Colombo | 1989-90 |

## Best Tenth-Wicket Stands

| Australian | ..... | 307 | A. F. Kippax (260*), and J. E. H. Hooker (62), New South Wales v Victoria at Melbourne | 1928-29 |
| Indian | ........ | 249 | C. T. Sarwate (124*) and S. N. Banerjee (121), Indians v Surrey at The Oval | 1946 |
| English | ........ | 235 | F. E. Woolley (185) and A. Fielder (112*), Kent v Worcestershire at Stourbridge | 1909 |
| Pakistan | ....... | 196* | Nadim Yousuf (202*) and Maqsood Kundi (109*) Muslim Commercial Bank v National Bank at Lahore | 1981-82 |
| New Zealand | ... | 184 | R. C. Blunt (338*) and W. Hawkesworth (21), Otago v Canterbury at Christchurch | 1931-32 |
| South African | .. | 174 | H. R. Lance (168) and D. Mackay-Coghill (57*), Transvaal v Natal at Johannesburg | 1965-66 |
| West Indian | .. | 138 | E. L. G. Hoad (149*) and H. C. Griffith (84), West Indians v Sussex at Hove | 1933 |
| Sri Lankan | ..... | 134 | F. R. M. de S. Goonetilleke (60*) and G. R. A. de Silva (75), Sri Lanka v Tamil Nadu at Madras | 1976-77 |

*Note:* All the English record wicket partnerships were made in the County Championship.

## OUT HANDLED THE BALL

| J. Grundy | MCC v Kent at Lord's | 1857 |
| G. Bennett | Kent v Sussex at Hove | 1872 |
| W. H. Scotton | Smokers v Non-Smokers at East Melbourne | 1886-87 |
| C. W. Wright | Nottinghamshire v Gloucestershire at Bristol | 1893 |
| E. Jones | South Australia v Victoria at Melbourne | 1894-95 |
| A. W. Nourse | South Africans v Sussex at Hove | 1907 |
| E. T. Benson | MCC v Auckland at Auckland | 1929-30 |
| A. W. Gilbertson | Otago v Auckland at Auckland | 1952-53 |
| W. R. Endean | South Africa v England at Cape Town | 1956-57 |
| P. J. Burge | Queensland v New South Wales at Sydney | 1958-59 |
| Dildar Awan | Services v Lahore at Lahore | 1959-60 |
| Mahmood-ul-Hasan | Karachi University v Railways-Quetta at Karachi | 1960-61 |
| Ali Raza | Karachi Greens v Hyderabad at Karachi | 1961-62 |
| Mohammad Yusuf | Rawalpindi v Peshawar at Peshawar | 1962-63 |
| A. Rees | Glamorgan v Middlesex at Lord's | 1965 |
| Pervez Akhtar | Multan v Karachi Greens at Sahiwal | 1971-72 |
| Javed Mirza | Railways v Punjab at Lahore | 1972-73 |
| R. G. Pollock | Eastern Province v Western Province at Cape Town | 1973-74 |
| C. I. Dey | Northern Transvaal v Orange Free State at Bloemfontein | 1973-74 |
| Nasir Valika | Karachi Whites v National Bank at Karachi | 1974-75 |
| Haji Yousuf | National Bank v Railways at Lahore | 1974-75 |
| Masood-ul-Hasan | PIA v National Bank B at Lyallpur | 1975-76 |
| D. K. Pearse | Natal v Western Province at Cape Town | 1978-79 |
| A. M. J. Hilditch | Australia v Pakistan at Perth | 1978-79 |
| Musleh-ud-Din | Railways v Lahore at Lahore | 1979-80 |
| Jalal-ud-Din | IDBP v Habib Bank at Bahawalpur | 1981-82 |
| Mohsin Khan | Pakistan v Australia at Karachi | 1982-83 |
| D. L. Haynes | West Indies v India at Bombay | 1983-84 |
| K. Azad | Delhi v Punjab at Amritsar | 1983-84 |
| Athar A. Khan | Allied Bank v HBFC at Sialkot | 1983-84 |

| A. N. Pandya | Saurashtra v Baroda at Baroda | 1984-85 |
| G. N. Linton | Barbados v Windward Islands at Bridgetown | 1985-86 |
| R. B. Gartrell | Tasmania v Victoria at Melbourne | 1986-87 |
| R. Nayyar | Himachal Pradesh v Punjab at Una | 1988-89 |
| A. M. Kane | Vidarbha v Railways at Nagpur | 1989-90 |

## OUT OBSTRUCTING THE FIELD

| C. A. Absolom | Cambridge University v Surrey at The Oval | 1868 |
| T. Straw | Worcestershire v Warwickshire at Worcester | 1899 |
| T. Straw | Worcestershire v Warwickshire at Birmingham | 1901 |
| J. P. Whiteside | Leicestershire v Lancashire at Leicester | 1901 |
| L. Hutton | England v South Africa at The Oval | 1951 |
| J. A. Hayes | Canterbury v Central Districts at Christchurch | 1954-55 |
| D. D. Deshpande | Madhya Pradesh v Uttar Pradesh at Benares | 1956-57 |
| M. Mehra | Railways v Delhi at Delhi | 1959-60 |
| K. Ibadulla | Warwickshire v Hampshire at Coventry | 1963 |
| Qaiser Khan | Dera Ismail Khan v Railways at Lahore | 1964-65 |
| Ijaz Ahmed | Lahore Greens v Lahore Blues at Lahore | 1973-74 |
| Qasim Feroze | Bahawalpur v Universities at Lahore | 1974-75 |
| T. Quirk | Northern Transvaal v Border at East London | 1978-79 |
| Mahmood Rashid | United Bank v Muslim Commercial Bank at Bahawalpur | 1981-82 |
| Arshad Ali | Sukkur v Quetta at Quetta | 1983-84 |
| H. R. Wasu | Vidarbha v Rajasthan at Akola | 1984-85 |
| Khalid Javed | Railways v Lahore at Lahore | 1985-86 |
| C. Binduhewa | Singha SC v Sinhalese SC at Colombo | 1990-91 |

## OUT HIT THE BALL TWICE

| H. E. Bull | MCC v Oxford University at Lord's | 1864 |
| H. R. J. Charlwood | Sussex v Surrey at Hove | 1872 |
| R. G. Barlow | North v South at Lord's | 1878 |
| P. S. Wimble | Transvaal v Griqualand West at Kimberley | 1892-93 |
| G. B. Nicholls | Somerset v Gloucestershire at Bristol | 1896 |
| A. A. Lilley | Warwickshire v Yorkshire at Birmingham | 1897 |
| J. H. King | Leicestershire v Surrey at The Oval | 1906 |
| A. P. Binns | Jamaica v British Guiana at Georgetown | 1956-57 |
| K. Bhavanna | Andhra v Mysore at Guntur | 1963-64 |
| Zaheer Abbas | PIA A v Karachi Blues at Karachi | 1969-70 |
| Anwar Miandad | IDBP v United Bank at Lahore | 1979-80 |
| Anwar Iqbal | Hyderabad v Sukkur at Hyderabad | 1983-84 |
| Iqtidar Ali | Allied Bank v Muslim Commercial Bank at Lahore | 1983-84 |
| Aziz Malik | Lahore Division v Faisalabad at Sialkot | 1984-85 |
| Javed Mohammad | Multan v Karachi Whites at Sahiwal | 1986-87 |
| Shahid Pervez | Jammu and Kashmir v Punjab at Srinagar | 1986-87 |

# BOWLING RECORDS

## TEN WICKETS IN ONE INNINGS

| | O | M | R | | |
|---|---|---|---|---|---|
| E. Hinkly (Kent) | | | | v England at Lord's | 1848 |
| *J. Wisden (North) | | | | v South at Lord's | 1850 |
| V. E. Walker (England) | 43 | 17 | 74 | v Surrey at The Oval | 1859 |
| V. E. Walker (Middlesex) | 44.2 | 5 | 104 | v Lancashire at Manchester | 1865 |
| G. Wootton (All England) | 31.3 | 9 | 54 | v Yorkshire at Sheffield | 1865 |
| W. Hickton (Lancashire) | 36.2 | 19 | 46 | v Hampshire at Manchester | 1870 |
| S. E. Butler (Oxford) | 24.1 | 11 | 38 | v Cambridge at Lord's | 1871 |
| James Lillywhite (South) | 60.2 | 22 | 129 | v North at Canterbury | 1872 |
| A. Shaw (MCC) | 36.2 | 8 | 73 | v North at Lord's | 1874 |
| E. Barratt (Players) | 29 | 11 | 43 | v Australians at The Oval | 1878 |
| G. Giffen (Australian XI) | 26 | 10 | 66 | v The Rest at Sydney | 1883-84 |

| | O | M | R | | |
|---|---|---|---|---|---|
| W. G. Grace (MCC) | 36.2 | 17 | 49 | v Oxford University at Oxford ... | 1886 |
| G. Burton (Middlesex) | 52.3 | 25 | 59 | v Surrey at The Oval | 1888 |
| †A. E. Moss (Canterbury) | 21.3 | 10 | 28 | v Wellington at Christchurch .... | 1889-90 |
| S. M. J. Woods (Cambridge U.) | 31 | 6 | 69 | v Thornton's XI at Cambridge ... | 1890 |
| T. Richardson (Surrey) | 15.3 | 3 | 45 | v Essex at The Oval | 1894 |
| H. Pickett (Essex) | 27 | 11 | 32 | v Leicestershire at Leyton | 1895 |
| E. J. Tyler (Somerset) | 34.3 | 15 | 49 | v Surrey at Taunton | 1895 |
| W. P. Howell (Australians) | 23.2 | 14 | 28 | v Surrey at The Oval | 1899 |
| C. H. G. Bland (Sussex) | 25.2 | 10 | 48 | v Kent at Tonbridge | 1899 |
| J. Briggs (Lancashire) | 28.5 | 7 | 55 | v Worcestershire at Manchester . | 1900 |
| A. E. Trott (Middlesex) | 14.2 | 5 | 42 | v Somerset at Taunton | 1900 |
| F. Hinds (A. B. St Hill's XI) | 19.1 | 6 | 36 | v Trinidad at Port-of-Spain ..... | 1900-01 |
| A. Fielder (Players) | 24.5 | 1 | 90 | v Gentlemen at Lord's | 1906 |
| E. G. Dennett (Gloucestershire) | 19.4 | 7 | 40 | v Essex at Bristol | 1906 |
| A. E. E. Vogler (E. Province) | 12 | 2 | 26 | v Griqualand West at Johannesburg | 1906-07 |
| C. Blythe (Kent) | 16 | 7 | 30 | v Northamptonshire at Northampton | 1907 |
| A. Drake (Yorkshire) | 8.5 | 0 | 35 | v Somerset at Weston-s-Mare .... | 1914 |
| W. Bestwick (Derbyshire) | 19 | 2 | 40 | v Glamorgan at Cardiff | 1921 |
| A. A. Mailey (Australians) | 28.4 | 5 | 66 | v Gloucestershire at Cheltenham | 1921 |
| C. W. L. Parker (Glos.) | 40.3 | 13 | 79 | v Somerset at Bristol | 1921 |
| T. Rushby (Surrey) | 17.5 | 4 | 43 | v Somerset at Taunton | 1921 |
| J. C. White (Somerset) | 42.2 | 11 | 76 | v Worcestershire at Worcester ... | 1921 |
| G. C. Collins (Kent) | 19.3 | 4 | 65 | v Nottinghamshire at Dover .... | 1922 |
| H. Howell (Warwickshire) | 25.1 | 5 | 51 | v Yorkshire at Birmingham ..... | 1923 |
| A. S. Kennedy (Players) | 22.4 | 10 | 37 | v Gentlemen at The Oval ....... | 1927 |
| G. O. B. Allen (Middlesex) | 25.3 | 10 | 40 | v Lancashire at Lord's | 1929 |
| A. P. Freeman (Kent) | 42 | 9 | 131 | v Lancashire at Maidstone ...... | 1929 |
| G. Geary (Leicestershire) | 16.2 | 8 | 18 | v Glamorgan at Pontypridd ..... | 1929 |
| C. V. Grimmett (Australians) | 22.3 | 8 | 37 | v Yorkshire at Sheffield | 1930 |
| A. P. Freeman (Kent) | 30.4 | 8 | 53 | v Essex at Southend | 1930 |
| H. Verity (Yorkshire) | 18.4 | 6 | 36 | v Warwickshire at Leeds | 1931 |
| A. P. Freeman (Kent) | 36.1 | 9 | 79 | v Lancashire at Manchester ..... | 1931 |
| V. W. C. Jupp (Northants) | 39 | 6 | 127 | v Kent at Tunbridge Wells ..... | 1932 |
| H. Verity (Yorkshire) | 19.4 | 16 | 10 | v Nottinghamshire at Leeds ..... | 1932 |
| T. W. Wall (South Australia) | 12.4 | 2 | 36 | v New South Wales at Sydney ... | 1932-33 |
| T. B. Mitchell (Derbyshire) | 19.1 | 4 | 64 | v Leicestershire at Leicester ..... | 1935 |
| J. Mercer (Glamorgan) | 26 | 10 | 51 | v Worcestershire at Worcester ... | 1936 |
| T. W. Goddard (Glos.) | 28.4 | 4 | 113 | v Worcestershire at Cheltenham . | 1937 |
| T. F. Smailes (Yorkshire) | 17.1 | 5 | 47 | v Derbyshire at Sheffield | 1939 |
| E. A. Watts (Surrey) | 24.1 | 8 | 67 | v Warwickshire at Birmingham .. | 1939 |
| *W. E. Hollies (Warwickshire) | 20.4 | 4 | 49 | v Nottinghamshire at Birmingham | 1946 |
| J. M. Sims (East) | 18.4 | 2 | 90 | v West at Kingston | 1948 |
| T. E. Bailey (Essex) | 39.4 | 9 | 90 | v Lancashire at Clacton | 1949 |
| J. K. Graveney (Glos.) | 18.4 | 2 | 66 | v Derbyshire at Chesterfield ..... | 1949 |
| R. Berry (Lancashire) | 36.2 | 9 | 102 | v Worcestershire at Blackpool ... | 1953 |
| S. P. Gupte (President's XI) | 24.2 | 7 | 78 | v Combined XI at Bombay ...... | 1954-55 |
| J. C. Laker (Surrey) | 46 | 18 | 88 | v Australians at The Oval ...... | 1956 |
| J. C. Laker (England) | 51.2 | 23 | 53 | v Australia at Manchester ...... | 1956 |
| G. A. R. Lock (Surrey) | 29.1 | 18 | 54 | v Kent at Blackheath | 1956 |
| K. Smales (Nottinghamshire) | 41.3 | 20 | 66 | v Gloucestershire at Stroud ..... | 1956 |
| P. M. Chatterjee (Bengal) | 19 | 11 | 20 | v Assam at Jorhat | 1956-57 |
| J. D. Bannister (Warwickshire) | 23.3 | 11 | 41 | v Comb. Services at Birmingham | 1959 |
| A. J. G. Pearson (Cambridge University) | 30.3 | 8 | 78 | v Leicestershire at Loughborough | 1961 |
| N. I. Thomson (Sussex) | 34.2 | 19 | 49 | v Warwickshire at Worthing .... | 1964 |
| P. J. Allan (Queensland) | 15.6 | 3 | 61 | v Victoria at Melbourne ........ | 1965-66 |
| I. J. Brayshaw (W. Australia) | 17.6 | 4 | 44 | v Victoria at Perth | 1967-68 |

| | O | M | R | | |
|---|---|---|---|---|---|
| Shahid Mahmood (Karachi Whites) | 25 | 5 | 58 | v Khairpur at Karachi | 1969-70 |
| E. E. Hemmings (International XI) | 49.3 | 14 | 175 | v West Indies XI at Kingston | 1982-83 |
| P. Sunderam (Rajasthan) | 22 | 5 | 78 | v Vidarbha at Jodhpur | 1985-86 |
| S. T. Jefferies (W. Province) | 22.5 | 7 | 59 | v Orange Free State at Cape Town | 1987-88 |
| Imran Adil (Bahawalpur) | 22.5 | 3 | 92 | v Faisalabad at Faisalabad | 1989-90 |

* *J. Wisden and W. E. Hollies achieved the feat without the direct assistance of a fielder. Wisden's ten were all bowled; Hollies bowled seven and had three leg-before-wicket.*
† *On debut in first-class cricket.*

*Note:* The following instances were achieved in 12-a-side matches:

| | O | M | R | | |
|---|---|---|---|---|---|
| E. M. Grace (MCC) | 32.2 | 7 | 69 | v Gents of Kent at Canterbury | 1862 |
| W. G. Grace (MCC) | 46.1 | 15 | 92 | v Kent at Canterbury | 1873 |

## OUTSTANDING ANALYSES

| | O | M | R | W | | |
|---|---|---|---|---|---|---|
| H. Verity (Yorkshire) | 19.4 | 16 | 10 | 10 | v Nottinghamshire at Leeds | 1932 |
| G. Elliott (Victoria) | 19 | 17 | 2 | 9 | v Tasmania at Launceston | 1857-58 |
| Ahad Khan (Railways) | 6.3 | 4 | 7 | 9 | v Dera Ismail Khan at Lahore | 1964-65 |
| J. C. Laker (England) | 14 | 12 | 2 | 8 | v The Rest at Bradford | 1950 |
| D. Shackleton (Hampshire) | 11.1 | 7 | 4 | 8 | v Somerset at Weston-s-Mare | 1955 |
| E. Peate (Yorkshire) | 16 | 11 | 5 | 8 | v Surrey at Holbeck | 1883 |
| F. R. Spofforth (Australians) | 8.3 | 6 | 3 | 7 | v England XI at Birmingham | 1884 |
| W. A. Henderson (N.E. Transvaal) | 9.3 | 7 | 4 | 7 | v Orange Free State at Bloemfontein | 1937-38 |
| Rajinder Goel (Haryana) | 7 | 4 | 4 | 7 | v Jammu and Kashmir at Chandigarh | 1977-78 |
| V. I. Smith (South Africans) | 4.5 | 3 | 1 | 6 | v Derbyshire at Derby | 1947 |
| S. Coststick (Victoria) | 21.1 | 20 | 1 | 6 | v Tasmania at Melbourne | 1868-69 |
| Israr Ali (Bahawalpur) | 11 | 10 | 1 | 6 | v Dacca U. at Bahawalpur | 1957-58 |
| A. D. Pougher (MCC) | 3 | 3 | 0 | 5 | v Australians at Lord's | 1896 |
| G. R. Cox (Sussex) | 6 | 6 | 0 | 5 | v Somerset at Weston-s-Mare | 1921 |
| R. K. Tyldesley (Lancashire) | 5 | 5 | 0 | 5 | v Leicestershire at Manchester | 1924 |
| P. T. Mills (Gloucestershire) | 6.4 | 6 | 0 | 5 | v Somerset at Bristol | 1928 |

## MOST WICKETS IN A MATCH

| | | | |
|---|---|---|---|
| 19-90 | J. C. Laker | England v Australia at Manchester | 1956 |
| 17-48 | C. Blythe | Kent v Northamptonshire at Northampton | 1907 |
| 17-50 | C. T. B. Turner | Australians v England XI at Hastings | 1888 |
| 17-54 | W. P. Howell | Australians v Western Province at Cape Town | 1902-03 |
| 17-56 | C. W. L. Parker | Gloucestershire v Essex at Gloucester | 1925 |
| 17-67 | A. P. Freeman | Kent v Sussex at Hove | 1922 |
| 17-89 | W. G. Grace | Gloucestershire v Nottinghamshire at Cheltenham | 1877 |
| 17-89 | F. C. L. Matthews | Nottinghamshire v Northants at Nottingham | 1923 |
| 17-91 | H. Dean | Lancashire v Yorkshire at Liverpool | 1913 |
| 17-91 | H. Verity | Yorkshire v Essex at Leyton | 1933 |
| 17-92 | A. P. Freeman | Kent v Warwickshire at Folkestone | 1932 |
| 17-103 | W. Mycroft | Derbyshire v Hampshire at Southampton | 1876 |
| 17-106 | G. R. Cox | Sussex v Warwickshire at Horsham | 1926 |
| 17-106 | T. W. Goddard | Gloucestershire v Kent at Bristol | 1939 |
| 17-119 | W. Mead | Essex v Hampshire at Southampton | 1895 |
| 17-137 | W. Brearley | Lancashire v Somerset at Manchester | 1905 |
| 17-159 | S. F. Barnes | England v South Africa at Johannesburg | 1913-14 |
| 17-201 | G. Giffen | South Australia v Victoria at Adelaide | 1885-86 |
| 17-212 | J. C. Clay | Glamorgan v Worcestershire at Swansea | 1937 |

*Notes:* H. A. Arkwright took eighteen wickets for 96 runs in a 12-a-side match for Gentlemen of MCC v Gentlemen of Kent at Canterbury in 1861.

W. Mead took seventeen wickets for 205 runs for Essex v Australians at Leyton in 1893, the year before Essex were raised to first-class status.

F. P. Fenner took seventeen wickets for Cambridge Town Club v University of Cambridge at Cambridge in 1844.

## SIXTEEN OR MORE WICKETS IN A DAY

| | | | |
|---|---|---|---|
| 17-48 | C. Blythe | Kent v Northamptonshire at Northampton....... | 1907 |
| 17-91 | H. Verity | Yorkshire v Essex at Leyton.................. | 1933 |
| 17-106 | T. W. Goddard | Gloucestershire v Kent at Bristol............. | 1939 |
| 16-38 | T. Emmett | Yorkshire v Cambridgeshire at Hunslet......... | 1869 |
| 16-52 | J. Southerton | South v North at Lord's.................... | 1875 |
| 16-69 | T. G. Wass | Nottinghamshire v Lancashire at Liverpool..... | 1906 |
| 16-38 | A. E. E. Vogler | E. Province v Griqualand West at Johannesburg.. | 1906-07 |
| 16-103 | T. G. Wass | Nottinghamshire v Essex at Nottingham........ | 1908 |
| 16-83 | J. C. White | Somerset v Worcestershire at Bath............. | 1919 |

## FOUR WICKETS WITH CONSECUTIVE BALLS

| | | |
|---|---|---|
| J. Wells | Kent v Sussex at Brighton........................... | 1862 |
| G. Ulyett | Lord Harris's XI v New South Wales at Sydney........ | 1878-79 |
| G. Nash | Lancashire v Somerset at Manchester................. | 1882 |
| J. B. Hide | Sussex v MCC and Ground at Lord's.................. | 1890 |
| F. J. Shacklock | Nottinghamshire v Somerset at Nottingham ........... | 1893 |
| A. D. Downes | Otago v Auckland at Dunedin........................ | 1893-94 |
| F. Martin | MCC and Ground v Derbyshire at Lord's.............. | 1895 |
| A. W. Mold | Lancashire v Nottinghamshire at Nottingham.......... | 1895 |
| W. Brearley† | Lancashire v Somerset at Manchester................. | 1905 |
| S. Haigh | MCC v Army XI at Pretoria......................... | 1905-06 |
| A. E. Trott‡ | Middlesex v Somerset at Lord's...................... | 1907 |
| F. A. Tarrant | Middlesex v Gloucestershire at Bristol ............... | 1907 |
| A. Drake | Yorkshire v Derbyshire at Chesterfield ............... | 1914 |
| S. G. Smith | Northamptonshire v Warwickshire at Birmingham...... | 1914 |
| H. A. Peach | Surrey v Sussex at The Oval ........................ | 1924 |
| A. F. Borland | Natal v Griqualand West at Kimberley ............... | 1926-27 |
| J. E. H. Hooker† | New South Wales v Victoria at Sydney ............... | 1928-29 |
| R. K. Tyldesley† | Lancashire v Derbyshire at Derby ................... | 1929 |
| R. J. Crisp | Western Province v Griqualand West at Johannesburg .. | 1931-32 |
| R. J. Crisp | Western Province v Natal at Durban ................. | 1933-34 |
| A. R. Gover | Surrey v Worcestershire at Worcester................. | 1935 |
| W. H. Copson | Derbyshire v Warwickshire at Derby ................. | 1937 |
| W. A. Henderson | N.E. Transvaal v Orange Free State at Bloemfontein.... | 1937-38 |
| F. Ridgway | Kent v Derbyshire at Folkestone .................... | 1951 |
| A. K. Walker§ | Nottinghamshire v Leicestershire at Leicester .......... | 1956 |
| S. N. Mohol | President's XI v Combined XI at Poona ............... | 1965-66 |
| P. I. Pocock | Surrey v Sussex at Eastbourne ...................... | 1972 |
| S. S. Saini† | Delhi v Himachal Pradesh at Delhi .................. | 1988-89 |
| D. Dias | W. Province (Suburbs) v Central Province at Colombo .. | 1990-91 |

† *Not all in the same innings.*

‡ *Trott achieved another hat-trick in the same innings of this, his benefit match.*

§ *Walker dismissed Firth with the last ball of the first innings and Lester, Tompkin and Smithson with the first three balls of the second innings, a feat without parallel.*

*Notes:* In their match with England at The Oval in 1863, Surrey lost four wickets in the course of a four-ball over from G. Bennett.

Sussex lost five wickets in the course of the final (six-ball) over of their match with Surrey at Eastbourne in 1972. P. I. Pocock, who had taken three wickets in his previous over, captured four more, taking in all seven wickets with eleven balls, a feat unique in first-class matches. (The eighth wicket fell to a run-out.)

# HAT-TRICKS

## Double Hat-Trick

Besides Trott's performance, which is given in the preceding section, the following instances are recorded of players having performed the hat-trick twice in the same match, Rao doing so in the same innings.

| | | |
|---|---|---|
| A. Shaw | Nottinghamshire v Gloucestershire at Nottingham ...... | 1884 |
| T. J. Matthews | Australia v South Africa at Manchester ............... | 1912 |
| C. W. L. Parker | Gloucestershire v Middlesex at Bristol ............... | 1924 |
| R. O. Jenkins | Worcestershire v Surrey at Worcester ............... | 1949 |
| J. S. Rao | Services v Northern Punjab at Amritsar ............. | 1963-64 |
| Amin Lakhani | Combined XI v Indians at Multan .................. | 1978-79 |

## Five Wickets with Six Consecutive Balls

| | | |
|---|---|---|
| W. H. Copson | Derbyshire v Warwickshire at Derby ................ | 1937 |
| W. A. Henderson | NE Transvaal v Orange Free State at Bloemfontein ..... | 1937-38 |
| P. I. Pocock | Surrey v Sussex at Eastbourne ..................... | 1972 |

## Most Hat-Tricks

**Seven times:** D. V. P. Wright.
**Six times:** T. W. Goddard, C. W. L. Parker.
**Five times:** S. Haigh, V. W. C. Jupp, A. E. G. Rhodes, F. A. Tarrant.
**Four times:** R. G. Barlow, J. T. Hearne, J. C. Laker, G. A. R. Lock, G. G. Macaulay, T. J. Matthews, M. J. Procter, T. Richardson, F. R. Spofforth, F. S. Trueman.
**Three times:** W. M. Bradley, H. J. Butler, S. T. Clarke, W. H. Copson, R. J. Crisp, J. W. H. T. Douglas, J. A. Flavell, A. P. Freeman, G. Giffen, K. Higgs, A. Hill, W. A. Humphries, R. D. Jackman, R. O. Jenkins, A. S. Kennedy, W. H. Lockwood, E. A. McDonald, T. L. Pritchard, J. S. Rao, A. Shaw, J. B. Statham, M. W. Tate, H. Trumble, D. Wilson, G. A. Wilson.

## Unusual Hat-Tricks

| | | |
|---|---|---|
| All "Stumped": | by W. H. Brain off C. L. Townsend, Gloucestershire v Somerset at Cheltenham .................................. | 1893 |
| All "Caught": | by G. J. Thompson off S. G. Smith, Northamptonshire v Warwickshire at Birmingham ......................... | 1914 |
| | by C. de L. White off R. Beesly, Border v Griqualand West at Queenstown ........................................ | 1946-47 |
| | by G. O. Dawkes (wicket-keeper) off H. L. Jackson, Derbyshire v Worcestershire at Kidderminster ..................... | 1958 |
| All "LBW": | H. Fisher, Yorkshire v Somerset at Sheffield ........... | 1932 |
| | J. A. Flavell, Worcestershire v Lancashire at Manchester .... | 1963 |
| | M. J. Procter, Gloucestershire v Essex at Westcliff ......... | 1972 |
| | B. J. Ikin, Griqualand West v OFS at Kimberley .......... | 1973-74 |
| | M. J. Procter, Gloucestershire v Yorkshire at Cheltenham ... | 1979 |
| | Aamer Wasim, Zone C v Lahore at Lahore ............... | 1985-86 |

## Most recent instances

*In 1990-91*

| | |
|---|---|
| Aamer Hanif | Karachi Whites v Bahawalpur at Karachi. |
| I. B. A. Allen | Windward Islands v Trinidad & Tobago at Pointe-à-Pierre. |
| D. Dias | W. Province (Suburbs) v Central Province at Colombo. |
| Shahid Ali Khan | Combined Universities v PNSC at Lahore. |
| T. G. Shaw | Eastern Province v Boland at Robertson. |
| C. J. van Heerden | OFS v Natal at Bloemfontein. |
| V. Venkatram | Bihar v Tripura at Jamshedpur. |

*In 1991:* None.

## 200 WICKETS IN A SEASON

| | Season | O | M | R | W | Avge |
|---|---|---|---|---|---|---|
| A. P. Freeman | 1928 | 1,976.1 | 423 | 5,489 | 304 | 18.05 |
| A. P. Freeman | 1933 | 2,039 | 651 | 4,549 | 298 | 15.26 |
| T. Richardson | 1895‡ | 1,690.1 | 463 | 4,170 | 290 | 14.37 |
| C. T. B. Turner** | 1888† | 2,427.2 | 1,127 | 3,307 | 283 | 11.68 |
| A. P. Freeman | 1931 | 1,618 | 360 | 4,307 | 276 | 15.60 |
| A. P. Freeman | 1930 | 1,914.3 | 472 | 4,632 | 275 | 16.84 |
| T. Richardson | 1897‡ | 1,603.4 | 495 | 3,945 | 273 | 14.45 |
| A. P. Freeman | 1929 | 1,670.5 | 381 | 4,879 | 267 | 18.27 |
| W. Rhodes | 1900 | 1,553 | 455 | 3,606 | 261 | 13.81 |
| J. T. Hearne | 1896 | 2,003.1 | 818 | 3,670 | 257 | 14.28 |
| A. P. Freeman | 1932 | 1,565.5 | 404 | 4,149 | 253 | 16.39 |
| W. Rhodes | 1901 | 1,565 | 505 | 3,797 | 251 | 15.12 |
| T. W. Goddard | 1937 | 1,478.1 | 359 | 4,158 | 248 | 16.76 |
| W. C. Smith | 1910 | 1,423.3 | 420 | 3,225 | 247 | 13.05 |
| T. Richardson | 1896‡ | 1,656.2 | 526 | 4,015 | 246 | 16.32 |
| A. E. Trott | 1899‡ | 1,772.4 | 587 | 4,086 | 239 | 17.09 |
| T. W. Goddard | 1947 | 1,451.2 | 344 | 4,119 | 238 | 17.30 |
| M. W. Tate | 1925 | 1,694.3 | 472 | 3,415 | 228 | 14.97 |
| J. T. Hearne | 1898‡ | 1,802.2 | 781 | 3,120 | 222 | 14.05 |
| C. W. L. Parker | 1925 | 1,512.3 | 478 | 3,311 | 222 | 14.91 |
| G. A. Lohmann | 1890‡ | 1,759.1 | 737 | 2,998 | 220 | 13.62 |
| M. W. Tate | 1923 | 1,608.5 | 331 | 3,061 | 219 | 13.97 |
| C. F. Root | 1925 | 1,493.2 | 416 | 3,770 | 219 | 17.21 |
| C. W. L. Parker | 1931 | 1,320.4 | 386 | 3,125 | 219 | 14.26 |
| H. Verity | 1936 | 1,289.3 | 463 | 2,847 | 216 | 13.18 |
| G. A. R. Lock | 1955 | 1,408.4 | 497 | 3,109 | 216 | 14.39 |
| C. Blythe | 1909 | 1,273.5 | 343 | 3,128 | 215 | 14.54 |
| E. Peate | 1882† | 1,853.1 | 868 | 2,466 | 214 | 11.52 |
| A. W. Mold | 1895‡ | 1,629 | 598 | 3,400 | 213 | 15.96 |
| W. Rhodes | 1902 | 1,306.3 | 405 | 2,801 | 213 | 13.15 |
| C. W. L. Parker | 1926 | 1,739.5 | 556 | 3,920 | 213 | 18.40 |
| J. T. Hearne | 1893‡ | 1,741.4 | 667 | 3,492 | 212 | 16.47 |
| A. P. Freeman | 1935 | 1,503.2 | 320 | 4,562 | 212 | 21.51 |
| G. A. R. Lock | 1957 | 1,194.1 | 449 | 2,550 | 212 | 12.02 |
| A. E. Trott | 1900 | 1,547.1 | 363 | 4,923 | 211 | 23.33 |
| G. G. Macaulay | 1925 | 1,338.2 | 307 | 3,268 | 211 | 15.48 |
| H. Verity | 1935 | 1,279.2 | 453 | 3,032 | 211 | 14.36 |
| J. Southerton | 1870† | 1,876.5 | 709 | 3,074 | 210 | 14.63 |
| G. A. Lohmann | 1888† | 1,649.1 | 783 | 2,280 | 209 | 10.90 |
| C. H. Parkin | 1923 | 1,356.2 | 356 | 3,543 | 209 | 16.95 |
| G. H. Hirst | 1906 | 1,306.1 | 271 | 3,434 | 208 | 16.50 |
| F. R. Spofforth | 1884† | 1,577 | 653 | 2,654 | 207 | 12.82 |
| A. W. Mold | 1894‡ | 1,288.3 | 456 | 2,548 | 207 | 12.30 |
| C. W. L. Parker | 1922 | 1,294.5 | 445 | 2,712 | 206 | 13.16 |
| A. S. Kennedy | 1922 | 1,346.4 | 366 | 3,444 | 205 | 16.80 |
| M. W. Tate | 1924 | 1,469.5 | 465 | 2,818 | 205 | 13.74 |
| E. A. McDonald | 1925 | 1,249.4 | 282 | 3,828 | 205 | 18.67 |
| A. P. Freeman | 1934 | 1,744.4 | 440 | 4,753 | 205 | 23.18 |
| C. W. L. Parker | 1924 | 1,303.5 | 411 | 2,913 | 204 | 14.27 |
| G. A. Lohmann | 1889‡ | 1,614.1 | 646 | 2,714 | 202 | 13.43 |
| H. Verity | 1937 | 1,386.2 | 487 | 3,168 | 202 | 15.68 |
| A. Shaw | 1878† | 2,630 | 1,586 | 2,203 | 202 | 10.89 |
| E. G. Dennett | 1907 | 1,216.2 | 305 | 3,227 | 201 | 16.05 |
| A. R. Gover | 1937 | 1,219.4 | 191 | 3,816 | 201 | 18.98 |
| C. H. Parkin | 1924 | 1,162.5 | 357 | 2,735 | 200 | 13.67 |
| T. W. Goddard | 1935 | 1,553 | 384 | 4,073 | 200 | 20.36 |
| A. R. Gover | 1936 | 1,159.2 | 185 | 3,547 | 200 | 17.73 |
| T. W. Goddard | 1939§ | 819 | 139 | 2,973 | 200 | 14.86 |
| R. Appleyard | 1951 | 1,313.2 | 391 | 2,829 | 200 | 14.14 |

† *Indicates 4-ball overs;* ‡ *5-ball overs. All others were 6-ball overs except* § *8-ball overs.*
** *Exclusive of matches not reckoned as first-class.*

*Notes:* In four consecutive seasons (1928-31), A. P. Freeman took 1,122 wickets, and in eight consecutive seasons (1928-35), 2,090 wickets. In each of these eight seasons he took over 200 wickets.

T. Richardson took 1,005 wickets in four consecutive seasons (1894-97).

In 1896, J. T. Hearne took his 100th wicket as early as June 12. In 1931, C. W. L. Parker did the same and A. P. Freeman obtained his 100th wicket a day later.

The most wickets in a season since the reduction of Championship matches in 1969 is 134 by M. D. Marshall (822 overs) in 1982.

## 100 WICKETS IN A SEASON

### Since Reduction of Championship Matches in 1969

**Five times:** D. L. Underwood 110 (1978), 106 (1979), 106 (1983), 102 (1971), 101 (1969).

**Four times:** J. K. Lever 116 (1984), 106 (1978), 106 (1979), 106 (1983).

**Twice:** B. S. Bedi 112 (1974), 105 (1973); T. W. Cartwright 108 (1969), 104 (1971); N. A. Foster 105 (1986), 102 (1991); N. Gifford 105 (1970), 104 (1983); R. J. Hadlee 117 (1984), 105 (1981); P. G. Lee 112 (1975), 101 (1973); M. D. Marshall 134 (1982), 100 (1986); M. J. Procter 109 (1977), 108 (1969); N. V. Radford 109 (1987), 101 (1985); F. J. Titmus 105 (1970), 104 (1971).

**Once:** J. P. Agnew 101 (1987); I. T. Botham 100 (1978); K. E. Cooper 101 (1988); R. M. H. Cottam 109 (1969); D. R. Doshi 101 (1980); J. E. Emburey 103 (1983); L. R. Gibbs 131 (1971); R. N. S. Hobbs 102 (1970); Intikhab Alam 104 (1971); R. D. Jackman 121 (1980); A. M. E. Roberts 119 (1974); P. J. Sainsbury 107 (1971); Sarfraz Nawaz 101 (1975); M. W. W. Selvey 101 (1978); D. J. Shepherd 106 (1970); F. D. Stephenson 125 (1988); C. A. Walsh 118 (1986); Waqar Younis 113 (1991); D. Wilson 102 (1969).

## 100 WICKETS IN A SEASON MOST TIMES

### (Includes Overseas Tours and Seasons)

**23 times:** W. Rhodes 200 wkts (3).

**20 times:** D. Shackleton (In successive seasons – 1949 to 1968 inclusive).

**17 times:** A. P. Freeman 300 wkts (1), 200 wkts (7).

**16 times:** T. W. Goddard 200 wkts (4), C. W. L. Parker 200 wkts (5), R. T. D. Perks, F. J. Titmus.

**15 times:** J. T. Hearne 200 wkts (3), G. H. Hirst 200 wkts (1), A. S. Kennedy 200 wkts (1).

**14 times:** C. Blythe 200 wkts (1), W. E. Hollies, G. A. R. Lock 200 wkts (2), M. W. Tate 200 wkts (3), J. C White.

**13 times:** J. B. Statham.

**12 times:** J. Briggs, E. G. Dennett 200 wkts (1), C. Gladwin, D. J. Shepherd, N. I. Thomson, F. S. Trueman.

**11 times:** A. V. Bedser, G. Geary, S. Haigh, J. C. Laker, M. S. Nichols, A. E. Relf.

**10 times:** W. Attewell, W. G. Grace, R. Illingworth, H. L. Jackson, V. W. C. Jupp, G. G. Macaulay 200 wkts (1), W. Mead, T. B. Mitchell, T. Richardson 200 wkts (3), J. Southerton 200 wkts (1), R. K. Tyldesley, D. L. Underwood, J. H. Wardle, T. G. Wass, D. V. P. Wright.

**9 times:** W. E. Astill, T. E. Bailey, W. E. Bowes, C. Cook, R. Howorth, J. Mercer, A. W. Mold 200 wkts (2), J. A. Newman, C. F. Root 200 wkts (1), A. Shaw 200 wkts (1), H. Verity 200 wkts (3).

**8 times:** T. W. Cartwright, H. Dean, J. A. Flavell, A. R. Gover 200 wkts (2), H. Larwood, G. A. Lohmann 200 wkts (3), R. Peel, J. M. Sims, F. A. Tarrant, R. Tattersall, G. J. Thompson, G. E. Tribe, A. W. Wellard, F. E. Woolley, J. A. Young.

## 100 WICKETS IN A SEASON OUTSIDE ENGLAND

| W | | Season | Country | R | Avge |
|---|---|---|---|---|---|
| 116 | M. W. Tate . . . . . . . | 1926-27 | India/Ceylon | 1,599 | 13.78 |
| 107 | Ijaz Faqih . . . . . . . . | 1985-86 | Pakistan | 1,719 | 16.06 |
| 106 | C. T. B. Turner . . . . | 1887-88 | Australia | 1,441 | 13.59 |
| 106 | R. Benaud . . . . . . . | 1957-58 | South Africa | 2,056 | 19.39 |
| 104 | S. F. Barnes . . . . . . . | 1913-14 | South Africa | 1,117 | 10.74 |
| 104 | Sajjad Akbar . . . . . . | 1989-90 | Pakistan | 2,328 | 22.38 |
| 103 | Abdul Qadir . . . . . . | 1982-83 | Pakistan | 2,367 | 22.98 |

## 1,500 WICKETS IN A CAREER

Dates in italics denote the first half of an overseas season; i.e. *1970* denotes the 1970-71 season.

| | Career | W | R | Avge |
|---|---|---|---|---|
| W. Rhodes. . . . . . . . . . . . . . | 1898-1930 | 4,187 | 69,993 | 16.71 |
| A. P. Freeman . . . . . . . . . . | 1914-36 | 3,776 | 69,577 | 18.42 |
| C. W. L. Parker . . . . . . . . . | 1903-35 | 3,278 | 63,817 | 19.46 |
| J. T. Hearne . . . . . . . . . . . . | 1888-1923 | 3,061 | 54,352 | 17.75 |
| T. W. Goddard . . . . . . . . . . | 1922-52 | 2,979 | 59,116 | 19.84 |
| W. G. Grace . . . . . . . . . . . . | 1865-1908 | 2,876 | 51,545 | 17.92 |
| A. S. Kennedy . . . . . . . . . . | 1907-36 | 2,874 | 61,034 | 21.23 |
| D. Shackleton . . . . . . . . . . | 1948-69 | 2,857 | 53,303 | 18.65 |
| G. A. R. Lock. . . . . . . . . . . | 1946-*70* | 2,844 | 54,709 | 19.23 |
| F. J. Titmus . . . . . . . . . . . | 1949-82 | 2,830 | 63,313 | 22.37 |
| M. W. Tate . . . . . . . . . . . . | 1912-37 | 2,784 | 50,571 | 18.16 |
| G. H. Hirst . . . . . . . . . . . . | 1891-1929 | 2,739 | 51,282 | 18.72 |
| C. Blythe . . . . . . . . . . . . . . | 1899-1914 | 2,506 | 42,136 | 16.81 |
| D. L. Underwood . . . . . . . . | 1963-87 | 2,465 | 49,993 | 20.28 |
| W. E. Astill . . . . . . . . . . . . | 1906-39 | 2,431 | 57,783 | 23.76 |
| J. C. White . . . . . . . . . . . . | 1909-37 | 2,356 | 43,759 | 18.57 |
| W. E. Hollies . . . . . . . . . . | 1932-57 | 2,323 | 48,656 | 20.94 |
| F. S. Trueman . . . . . . . . . . | 1949-69 | 2,304 | 42,154 | 18.29 |
| J. B. Statham . . . . . . . . . . . | 1950-68 | 2,260 | 36,995 | 16.36 |
| R. T. D. Perks . . . . . . . . . . | 1930-55 | 2,233 | 53,770 | 24.07 |
| J. Briggs . . . . . . . . . . . . . . | 1879-1900 | 2,221 | 35,430 | 15.95 |
| D. J. Shepherd . . . . . . . . . . | 1950-72 | 2,218 | 47,302 | 21.32 |
| E. G. Dennett . . . . . . . . . . | 1903-26 | 2,147 | 42,571 | 19.82 |
| T. Richardson . . . . . . . . . . | 1892-1905 | 2,104 | 38,794 | 18.43 |
| T. E. Bailey. . . . . . . . . . . . | 1945-67 | 2,082 | 48,170 | 23.13 |
| R. Illingworth . . . . . . . . . . | 1951-83 | 2,072 | 42,023 | 20.28 |
| N. Gifford . . . . . . . . . . . . | 1960-88 | 2,068 | 48,731 | 23.56 |
| F. E. Woolley . . . . . . . . . . | 1906-38 | 2,068 | 41,066 | 19.85 |
| G. Geary . . . . . . . . . . . . . | 1912-38 | 2,063 | 41,339 | 20.03 |
| D. V. P. Wright . . . . . . . . . | 1932-57 | 2,056 | 49,307 | 23.98 |
| J. A. Newman . . . . . . . . . . | 1906-30 | 2,032 | 51,111 | 25.15 |
| †A. Shaw . . . . . . . . . . . . . | 1864-97 | 2,027 | 24,580 | 12.12 |
| S. Haigh . . . . . . . . . . . . . . | 1895-1913 | 2,012 | 32,091 | 15.94 |
| H. Verity . . . . . . . . . . . . . | 1930-39 | 1,956 | 29,146 | 14.90 |
| W. Attewell . . . . . . . . . . . | 1881-1900 | 1,950 | 29,896 | 15.33 |
| J. C. Laker . . . . . . . . . . . . | 1946-*64* | 1,944 | 35,791 | 18.41 |
| A. V. Bedser . . . . . . . . . . . | 1939-60 | 1,924 | 39,279 | 20.41 |
| W. Mead . . . . . . . . . . . . . | 1892-1913 | 1,916 | 36,388 | 18.99 |
| A. E. Relf . . . . . . . . . . . . . | 1900-21 | 1,897 | 39,724 | 20.94 |
| P. G. H. Fender . . . . . . . . . | 1910-36 | 1,894 | 47,458 | 25.05 |
| J. W. H. T. Douglas . . . . . . . | 1901-30 | 1,893 | 44,159 | 23.32 |
| J. H. Wardle . . . . . . . . . . . | 1946-67 | 1,846 | 35,027 | 18.97 |
| G. R. Cox . . . . . . . . . . . . . | 1895-1928 | 1,843 | 42,136 | 22.86 |
| G. A. Lohmann . . . . . . . . . | 1884-97 | 1,841 | 25,295 | 13.73 |
| J. W. Hearne. . . . . . . . . . . . | 1909-36 | 1,839 | 44,926 | 24.42 |
| G. G. Macaulay . . . . . . . . . | 1920-35 | 1,837 | 32,440 | 17.65 |

|  | Career | W | R | Avge |
|---|---|---|---|---|
| M. S. Nichols | 1924-39 | 1,833 | 39,666 | 21.63 |
| J. B. Mortimore | 1950-75 | 1,807 | 41,904 | 23.18 |
| C. Cook | 1946-64 | 1,782 | 36,578 | 20.52 |
| R. Peel | 1882-99 | 1,753 | 28,442 | 16.22 |
| H. L. Jackson | 1947-63 | 1,733 | 30,101 | 17.36 |
| J. K. Lever | 1967-89 | 1,722 | 41,772 | 24.25 |
| T. P. B. Smith | 1929-52 | 1,697 | 45,059 | 26.55 |
| J. Southerton | 1854-79 | 1,681 | 24,290 | 14.44 |
| A. E. Trott | 1892-1911 | 1,674 | 35,317 | 21.09 |
| A. W. Mold | 1889-1901 | 1,673 | 26,010 | 15.54 |
| T. G. Wass | 1896-1920 | 1,666 | 34,092 | 20.46 |
| V. W. C. Jupp | 1909-38 | 1,658 | 38,166 | 23.01 |
| C. Gladwin | 1939-58 | 1,653 | 30,265 | 18.30 |
| W. E. Bowes | 1928-47 | 1,639 | 27,470 | 16.76 |
| A. W. Wellard | 1927-50 | 1,614 | 39,302 | 24.35 |
| P. I. Pocock | 1964-86 | 1,607 | 42,648 | 26.53 |
| N. I. Thomson | 1952-72 | 1,597 | 32,867 | 20.58 |
| J. Mercer | 1919-47 | 1,591 | 37,210 | 23.38 |
| G. J. Thompson | 1897-1922 | 1,591 | 30,058 | 18.89 |
| J. M. Sims | 1929-53 | 1,581 | 39,401 | 24.92 |
| T. Emmett | 1866-88 | 1,571 | 21,314 | 13.56 |
| Intikhab Alam | 1957-82 | 1,571 | 43,474 | 27.67 |
| B. S. Bedi | 1961-81 | 1,560 | 33,843 | 21.69 |
| W. Voce | 1927-52 | 1,558 | 35,961 | 23.08 |
| A. R. Gover | 1928-48 | 1,555 | 36,753 | 23.63 |
| T. W. Cartwright | 1952-77 | 1,536 | 29,357 | 19.11 |
| K. Higgs | 1958-86 | 1,536 | 36,267 | 23.61 |
| James Langridge | 1924-53 | 1,530 | 34,524 | 22.56 |
| J. A. Flavell | 1949-67 | 1,529 | 32,847 | 21.48 |
| C. F. Root | 1910-33 | 1,512 | 31,933 | 21.11 |
| R. K. Tyldesley | 1919-35 | 1,509 | 25,980 | 17.21 |

† *The figures for A. Shaw exclude one wicket for which no analysis is available.*

*Note:* Some works of reference provide career figures which differ from those in this list, owing to the exclusion or inclusion of matches recognised or not recognised as first-class by *Wisden*. Those figures are:

|  | Career | W | R | Avge |
|---|---|---|---|---|
| W. Rhodes | 1898-1930 | 4,204 | 70,322 | 16.72 |
| W. G. Grace | 1865-1908 | 2,808 | 50,982 | 18.15 |
| G. H. Hirst | 1891-1929 | 2,742 | 51,372 | 18.73 |
| C. Blythe | 1899-1914 | 2,503 | 42,099 | 16.81 |
| E. G. Dennett | 1903-26 | 2,151 | 42,640 | 19.82 |
| F. E. Woolley | 1906-38 | 2,066 | 41,058 | 19.87 |
| J. A. Newman | 1906-30 | 2,054 | 51,397 | 25.03 |
| R. Peel | 1882-99 | 1,776 | 28,758 | 16.19 |

## ALL-ROUND RECORDS

### HUNDRED AND TEN WICKETS IN ONE INNINGS

V. E. Walker, England v Surrey at The Oval; 20\*, 108, ten for 74, and four for 17.  1859
W. G. Grace, MCC v Oxford University at Oxford; 104, two for 60, and ten for 49.  1886

*Note:* E. M. Grace, for MCC v Gentlemen of Kent in a 12-a-side match at Canterbury in 1862, scored 192\* and took five for 77 and ten for 69.

### TWO HUNDRED RUNS AND SIXTEEN WICKETS

G. Giffen, South Australia v Victoria at Adelaide; 271, nine for 96, and seven for 70.  1891-92

## HUNDRED IN EACH INNINGS AND FIVE WICKETS TWICE

G. H. Hirst, Yorkshire v Somerset at Bath; 111, 117*, six for 70, and five for 45.    1906

## HUNDRED IN EACH INNINGS AND TEN WICKETS

B. J. T. Bosanquet, Middlesex v Sussex at Lord's; 103, 100*, three for 75, and eight for 53 .................................................... 1905
F. D. Stephenson, Nottinghamshire v Yorkshire at Nottingham; 111, 117, four for 105, and seven for 117 ............................................ 1988

## HUNDRED AND HAT-TRICK

G. Giffen, Australians v Lancashire at Manchester; 13, 113, and six for 55 including hat-trick.................................................... 1884
W. E. Roller, Surrey v Sussex at The Oval; 204, four for 28 including hat-trick, and two for 16. (Unique instance of 200 and hat-trick.)....................... 1885
W. B. Burns, Worcestershire v Gloucestershire at Worcester; 102*, three for 56 including hat-trick, and two for 21.................................. 1913
V. W. C. Jupp, Sussex v Essex at Colchester; 102, six for 61 including hat-trick, and six for 78 .................................................... 1921
R. E. S. Wyatt, MCC v Ceylon at Colombo; 124 and five for 39 including hat-trick. 1926-27
L. N. Constantine, West Indians v Northamptonshire at Northampton; seven for 45 including hat-trick, 107 (five 6s), and six for 67........................ 1928
D. E. Davies, Glamorgan v Leicestershire at Leicester; 139, four for 27, and three for 31 including hat-trick .......................................... 1937
V. M. Merchant, Dr C. R. Pereira's XI v Sir Homi Mehta's XI at Bombay; 1, 142, three for 31 including hat-trick, and no wicket for 17.................. 1946-47
M. J. Procter, Gloucestershire v Essex at Westcliff-on-Sea; 51, 102, three for 43, and five for 30 including hat-trick (all lbw)............................. 1972
M. J. Procter, Gloucestershire v Leicestershire at Bristol; 122, no wkt for 32, and seven for 26 including hat-trick........................................ 1979

*Note:* W. G. Grace, for MCC v Kent in a 12-a-side match at Canterbury in 1874, scored 123 and took five for 82 and six for 47 including a hat-trick.

## SEASON DOUBLES

### 2,000 RUNS AND 200 WICKETS

1906      G. H. Hirst     2,385 runs and 208 wickets

### 3,000 RUNS AND 100 WICKETS

1937      J. H. Parks     3,003 runs and 101 wickets

### 2,000 RUNS AND 100 WICKETS

| | Season | R | W | | Season | R | W |
|---|---|---|---|---|---|---|---|
| W. G. Grace | 1873 | 2,139 | 106 | F. E. Woolley | 1914 | 2,272 | 125 |
| W. G. Grace | 1876 | 2,622 | 129 | J. W. Hearne | 1920 | 2,148 | 142 |
| C. L. Townsend | 1899 | 2,440 | 101 | V. W. C. Jupp | 1921 | 2,169 | 121 |
| G. L. Jessop | 1900 | 2,210 | 104 | F. E. Woolley | 1921 | 2,101 | 167 |
| G. H. Hirst | 1904 | 2,501 | 132 | F. E. Woolley | 1922 | 2,022 | 163 |
| G. H. Hirst | 1905 | 2,266 | 110 | F. E. Woolley | 1923 | 2,091 | 101 |
| W. Rhodes | 1909 | 2,094 | 141 | L. F. Townsend | 1933 | 2,268 | 100 |
| W. Rhodes | 1911 | 2,261 | 117 | D. E. Davies | 1937 | 2,012 | 103 |
| F. A. Tarrant | 1911 | 2,030 | 111 | James Langridge | 1937 | 2,082 | 101 |
| J. W. Hearne | 1913 | 2,036 | 124 | T. E. Bailey | 1959 | 2,011 | 100 |
| J. W. Hearne | 1914 | 2,116 | 123 | | | | |

## 1,000 RUNS AND 200 WICKETS

|              | Season | R     | W   |              | Season | R     | W   |
|--------------|--------|-------|-----|--------------|--------|-------|-----|
| A. E. Trott  | 1899   | 1,175 | 239 | M. W. Tate   | 1923   | 1,168 | 219 |
| A. E. Trott  | 1900   | 1,337 | 211 | M. W. Tate   | 1924   | 1,419 | 205 |
| A. S. Kennedy| 1922   | 1,129 | 205 | M. W. Tate   | 1925   | 1,290 | 228 |

## 1,000 RUNS AND 100 WICKETS

**Sixteen times:** W. Rhodes.

**Ten times:** V. W. C. Jupp.

**Eight times:** T. E. Bailey, W. G. Grace, M. S. Nichols, A. E. Relf, F. A. Tarrant, M. W. Tate†, F. J. Titmus, F. E. Woolley.

**Seven times:** G. E. Tribe.

**Six times:** P. G. H. Fender, R. Illingworth, James Langridge.

**Five times:** J. W. H. T. Douglas, J. W. Hearne, A. S. Kennedy, J. A. Newman.

**Four times:** E. G. Arnold, J. Gunn, R. Kilner, B. R. Knight.

**Three times:** W. W. Armstrong (Australians), L. C. Braund, G. Giffen (Australians), N. E. Haig, R. Howorth, C. B. Llewellyn, J. B. Mortimore, Ray Smith, S. G. Smith, L. F. Townsend, A. W. Wellard.

**Fourteen times:** G. H. Hirst.

**Nine times:** W. E. Astill.

† *M. W. Tate also scored 1,193 runs and took 116 wickets for MCC in first-class matches on the 1926-27 MCC tour of India and Ceylon.*

*Note:* R. J. Hadlee (1984) and F. D. Stephenson (1988) are the only players to perform the feat since the reduction of County Championship matches. A complete list of those performing the feat before then will be found on p. 202 of the 1982 *Wisden.*

## WICKET-KEEPERS' DOUBLE

|                    | Season | R     | D   |
|--------------------|--------|-------|-----|
| L. E. G. Ames      | 1928   | 1,919 | 122 |
| L. E. G. Ames      | 1929   | 1,795 | 128 |
| L. E. G. Ames      | 1932   | 2,482 | 104 |
| J. T. Murray       | 1957   | 1,025 | 104 |

## 20,000 RUNS AND 2,000 WICKETS IN A CAREER

|                 | Career  | R      | Avge  | W     | Avge  | 'Doubles' |
|-----------------|---------|--------|-------|-------|-------|-----------|
| W. E. Astill    | 1906-39 | 22,731 | 22.55 | 2,431 | 23.76 | 9         |
| T. E. Bailey    | 1945-67 | 28,642 | 33.42 | 2,082 | 23.13 | 8         |
| W. G. Grace     | 1865-1908 | 54,896 | 39.55 | 2,876 | 17.92 | 8       |
| G. H. Hirst     | 1891-1929 | 36,323 | 34.13 | 2,739 | 18.72 | 14      |
| R. Illingworth  | 1951-83 | 24,134 | 28.06 | 2,072 | 20.28 | 6         |
| W. Rhodes       | 1898-1930 | 39,802 | 30.83 | 4,187 | 16.71 | 16      |
| M. W. Tate      | 1912-37 | 21,717 | 25.01 | 2,784 | 18.16 | 8         |
| F. J. Titmus    | 1949-82 | 21,588 | 23.11 | 2,830 | 22.37 | 8         |
| F. E. Woolley   | 1906-38 | 58,969 | 40.75 | 2,068 | 19.85 | 8         |

## WICKET-KEEPING RECORDS

### MOST DISMISSALS IN AN INNINGS

| 8 (all ct)    | A. T. W. Grout  | Queensland v Western Australia at Brisbane | 1959-60 |
|---------------|-----------------|---------------------------------------------|---------|
| 8 (all ct)†   | D. E. East      | Essex v Somerset at Taunton                 | 1985    |
| 8 (all ct)    | S. A. Marsh‡    | Kent v Middlesex at Lord's                  | 1991    |
| 7 (4ct, 3st)  | E. J. Smith     | Warwickshire v Derbyshire at Birmingham     | 1926    |
| 7 (6ct, 1st)  | W. Farrimond    | Lancashire v Kent at Manchester             | 1930    |
| 7 (all ct)    | W. F. F. Price  | Middlesex v Yorkshire at Lord's             | 1937    |
| 7 (3ct, 4st)  | D. Tallon       | Queensland v Victoria at Brisbane           | 1938-39 |

| 7 (all ct) | R. A. Saggers | New South Wales v Combined XI at Brisbane .... | 1940-41 |
|---|---|---|---|
| 7 (1ct, 6st) | H. Yarnold | Worcestershire v Scotland at Dundee............ | 1951 |
| 7 (4ct, 3st) | J. Brown | Scotland v Ireland at Dublin................... | 1957 |
| 7 (6ct, 1st) | N. Kirsten | Border v Rhodesia at East London ............. | 1959-60 |
| 7 (all ct) | M. S. Smith | Natal v Border at East London ............... | 1959-60 |
| 7 (all ct) | K. V. Andrew | Northamptonshire v Lancashire at Manchester ... | 1962 |
| 7 (all ct) | A. Long | Surrey v Sussex at Hove .................... | 1964 |
| 7 (all ct) | R. M. Schofield | Central Districts v Wellington at Wellington ..... | 1964-65 |
| 7 (all ct) | R. W. Taylor | Derbyshire v Glamorgan at Derby ............. | 1966 |
| 7 (6ct, 1st) | H. B. Taber | New South Wales v South Australia at Adelaide .. | 1968-69 |
| 7 (6ct, 1st) | E. W. Jones | Glamorgan v Cambridge University at Cambridge. | 1970 |
| 7 (6ct, 1st) | S. Benjamin | Central Zone v North Zone at Bombay.......... | 1973-74 |
| 7 (all ct) | R. W. Taylor | Derbyshire v Yorkshire at Chesterfield .......... | 1975 |
| 7 (6ct, 1st) | Shahid Israr | Karachi Whites v Quetta at Karachi .......... | 1976-77 |
| 7 (4ct, 3st) | Wasim Bari | PIA v Sind at Lahore ....................... | 1977-78 |
| 7 (all ct) | J. A. Maclean | Queensland v Victoria at Melbourne ........... | 1977-78 |
| 7 (5ct, 2st) | Taslim Arif | National Bank v Punjab at Lahore ............. | 1978-79 |
| 7 (all ct) | Wasim Bari | Pakistan v New Zealand at Auckland .......... | 1978-79 |
| 7 (all ct) | R. W. Taylor | England v India at Bombay .................. | 1979-80 |
| 7 (all ct) | D. L. Bairstow | Yorkshire v Derbyshire at Scarborough ......... | 1982 |
| 7 (6ct, 1st) | R. B. Phillips | Queensland v New Zealanders at Bundaberg ..... | 1982-83 |
| 7 (3ct, 4st) | Masood Iqbal | Habib Bank v Lahore at Lahore ............... | 1982-83 |
| 7 (3ct, 4st) | Arif-ud-Din | United Bank v PACO at Sahiwal............... | 1983-84 |
| 7 (6ct, 1st) | R. J. East | OFS v Western Province B at Cape Town ....... | 1984-85 |
| 7 (all ct) | B. A. Young | Northern Districts v Canterbury at Christchurch .. | 1986-87 |
| 7 (all ct) | D. J. Richardson | Eastern Province v OFS at Bloemfontein ........ | 1988-89 |
| 7 (6ct, 1st) | Dildar Malik | Multan v Faisalabad at Sahiwal .............. | 1988-89 |
| 7 (all ct) | W. K. Hegg | Lancashire v Derbyshire at Chesterfield ........ | 1989 |
| 7 (all ct) | Imran Zia | Bahawalpur v Faisalabad at Faisalabad ......... | 1989-90 |
| 7 (all ct) | I. D. S. Smith | New Zealand v Sri Lanka at Hamilton ......... | 1990-91 |
| 7 (all ct) | J. F. Holyman | Tasmania v Western Australia at Hobart ....... | 1990-91 |
| 7 (all ct) | P. J. L. Radley | OFS v Western Province at Cape Town ........ | 1990-91 |
| 7 (all ct) | C. P. Metson | Glamorgan v Derbyshire at Chesterfield ........ | 1991 |

† *The first eight wickets to fall.*   ‡ *S. A. Marsh also scored 108\*.*

## WICKET-KEEPERS' HAT-TRICKS

W. H. Brain, Gloucestershire v Somerset at Cheltenham, 1893 – three stumpings off successive balls from C. L. Townsend.

G. O. Dawkes, Derbyshire v Worcestershire at Kidderminster, 1958 – three catches off successive balls from H. L. Jackson.

R. C. Russell, Gloucestershire v Surrey at The Oval, 1986 – three catches off successive balls from C. A. Walsh and D. V. Lawrence (2).

## MOST DISMISSALS IN A MATCH

| 12 (8ct, 4st) | E. Pooley | Surrey v Sussex at The Oval ................. | 1868 |
|---|---|---|---|
| 12 (9ct, 3st) | D. Tallon | Queensland v New South Wales at Sydney .... | 1938-39 |
| 12 (9ct, 3st) | H. B. Taber | New South Wales v South Australia at Adelaide. | 1968-69 |
| 11 (all ct) | A. Long | Surrey v Sussex at Hove .................... | 1964 |
| 11 (all ct) | R. W. Marsh | Western Australia v Victoria at Perth......... | 1975-76 |
| 11 (all ct) | D. L. Bairstow | Yorkshire v Derbyshire at Scarborough ........ | 1982 |
| 11 (all ct) | W. K. Hegg | Lancashire v Derbyshire at Chesterfield ........ | 1989 |
| 11 (all ct) | A. J. Stewart | Surrey v Leicestershire at Leicester ........... | 1989 |
| 11 (all ct) | T. J. Nielsen | South Australia v Western Australia at Perth .. | 1990-91 |
| 10 (5ct, 5st) | H. Phillips | Sussex v Surrey at The Oval ................. | 1872 |
| 10 (2ct, 8st) | E. Pooley | Surrey v Kent at The Oval................... | 1878 |
| 10 (9ct, 1st) | T. W. Oates | Nottinghamshire v Middlesex at Nottingham ... | 1906 |
| 10 (1ct, 9st) | F. H. Huish | Kent v Surrey at The Oval................... | 1911 |
| 10 (9ct, 1st) | J. C. Hubble | Kent v Gloucestershire at Cheltenham ........ | 1923 |

| 10 (8ct, 2st) | H. Elliott | Derbyshire v Lancashire at Manchester ....... | 1935 |
| 10 (7ct, 3st) | P. Corrall | Leicestershire v Sussex at Hove............. | 1936 |
| 10 (9ct, 1st) | R. A. Saggers | New South Wales v Combined XI at Brisbane . | 1940-41 |
| 10 (all ct) | A. E. Wilson | Gloucestershire v Hampshire at Portsmouth ... | 1953 |
| 10 (7ct, 3st) | B. N. Jarman | South Australia v New South Wales at Adelaide. | 1961-62 |
| 10 (all ct) | L. A. Johnson | Northamptonshire v Sussex at Worthing ....... | 1963 |
| 10 (all ct) | R. W. Taylor | Derbyshire v Hampshire at Chesterfield ....... | 1963 |
| 10 (8ct, 2st) | L. A. Johnson | Northamptonshire v Warwickshire at Birmingham | 1965 |
| 10 (9ct, 1st) | R. C. Jordon | Victoria v South Australia at Melbourne ...... | 1970-71 |
| 10 (all ct) | R. W. Marsh† | Western Australia v South Australia at Perth .. | 1976-77 |
| 10 (6ct, 4st) | Taslim Arif | National Bank v Punjab at Lahore ........... | 1978-79 |
| 10 (9ct, 1st) | Arif-ud-Din | United Bank v Karachi B at Karachi.......... | 1978-79 |
| 10 (all ct) | R. W. Taylor | England v India at Bombay................. | 1979-80 |
| 10 (all ct) | R. J. Parks | Hampshire v Derbyshire at Portsmouth ....... | 1981 |
| 10 (9ct, 1st) | A. Ghosh | Bihar v Assam at Bhagalpur ............... | 1981-82 |
| 10 (8ct, 2st) | Z. Parkar | Bombay v Maharashtra at Bombay........... | 1981-82 |
| 10 (all ct) | R. V. Jennings | Transvaal v Arosa Sri Lankans at Johannesburg | 1982-83 |
| 10 (9ct, 1st) | Kamal Najamuddin | Karachi v Lahore at Multan ............... | 1982-83 |
| 10 (all ct) | D. A. Murray | West Indies XI v South Africa at Port Elizabeth. | 1983-84 |
| 10 (7ct, 3st) | Azhar Abbas | Bahawalpur v Lahore City Greens at Bahawalpur | 1983-84 |
| 10 (7ct, 3st) | B. N. French | Nottinghamshire v Oxford University at Oxford. | 1984 |
| 10 (8ct, 2st) | R. J. Ryall | Western Province v Transvaal at Cape Town .. | 1984-85 |
| 10 (all ct) | S. J. Rixon | Australian XI v South Africa at Johannesburg . | 1985-86 |
| 10 (8ct, 2st) | Anil Dalpat | Karachi v United Bank at Lahore............ | 1985-86 |
| 10 (all ct) | R. V. Jennings | Transvaal v Northern Transvaal at Verwoerdburg | 1986-87 |
| 10 (all ct) | S. J. Rixon | Australian XI v South Africa at Johannesburg . | 1986-87 |
| 10 (all ct) | R. V. Jennings | Transvaal v Orange Free State at Johannesburg | 1986-87 |
| 10 (9ct, 1st) | C. J. Richards | Surrey v Sussex at Guildford ................ | 1987 |
| 10 (all ct) | C. W. Scott | Nottinghamshire v Derbyshire at Derby........ | 1988 |
| 10 (all ct) | D. J. Richardson | Eastern Province v OFS at Bloemfontein ...... | 1988-89 |
| 10 (all ct) | A. N. Aymes | Hampshire v Oxford University at Oxford ..... | 1989 |
| 10 (all ct) | L. R. Fernando | Moratuwa v Panadura at Moratuwa .......... | 1989-90 |
| 10 (all ct) | Imran Zia | Bahawalpur v Faisalabad at Faisalabad ....... | 1989-90 |
| 10 (9ct, 1st) | D. J. Richardson | Eastern Province v N. Transvaal at Verwoerdburg | 1989-90 |

† *R. W. Marsh also scored 104.*

## MOST DISMISSALS IN A SEASON

| 128 (79ct, 49st) | L. E. G. Ames | Kent..................... | 1929 |
| 122 (70ct, 52st) | L. E. G. Ames | Kent..................... | 1928 |
| 110 (63ct, 47st) | H. Yarnold | Worcestershire................... | 1949 |
| 107 (77ct, 30st) | G. Duckworth | Lancashire..................... | 1928 |
| 107 (96ct, 11st) | J. G. Binks | Yorkshire ..................... | 1960 |
| 104 (40ct, 64st) | L. E. G. Ames | Kent ...................... | 1932 |
| 104 (82ct, 22st) | J. T. Murray | Middlesex ..................... | 1957 |
| 102 (69ct, 33st) | F. H. Huish | Kent...................... | 1913 |
| 102 (95ct, 7st) | J. T. Murray | Middlesex ..................... | 1960 |
| 101 (62ct, 39st) | F. H. Huish | Kent...................... | 1911 |
| 101 (85ct, 16st) | R. Booth | Worcestershire .................. | 1960 |
| 100 (91ct, 9st) | R. Booth | Worcestershire .................. | 1964 |

## MOST DISMISSALS IN A CAREER

Dates in italics denote the first half of an overseas season; i.e. *1914* denotes the 1914-15 season.

| | Career | M | Ct | St | Total |
|---|---|---|---|---|---|
| R. W. Taylor ............ | 1960-88 .......... | 639 | 1,473 | 176 | 1,649 |
| J. T. Murray ............ | 1952-75 .......... | 635 | 1,270 | 257 | 1,527 |
| H. Strudwick............ | 1902-27 .......... | 675 | 1,242 | 255 | 1,497 |

| | Career | M | Ct | St | Total |
|---|---|---|---|---|---|
| A. P. E. Knott | 1964-85 | 511 | 1,211 | 133 | 1,344 |
| F. H. Huish | 1895-1914 | 497 | 933 | 377 | 1,310 |
| B. Taylor | 1949-73 | 572 | 1,083 | 211 | 1,294 |
| D. Hunter | 1889-1909 | 548 | 906 | 347 | 1,253 |
| H. R. Butt | 1890-1912 | 550 | 953 | 275 | 1,228 |
| J. H. Board | 1891-*1914* | 525 | 852 | 355 | 1,207 |
| H. Elliott | 1920-47 | 532 | 904 | 302 | 1,206 |
| J. M. Parks | 1949-76 | 739 | 1,088 | 93 | 1,181 |
| R. Booth | 1951-70 | 468 | 948 | 178 | 1,126 |
| L. E. G. Ames | 1926-51 | 593 | 703 | 418 | 1,121 |
| D. L. Bairstow | 1970-90 | 459 | 961 | 138 | 1,099 |
| G. Duckworth | 1923-47 | 504 | 753 | 343 | 1,096 |
| H. W. Stephenson | 1948-64 | 462 | 748 | 334 | 1,082 |
| J. G. Binks | 1955-75 | 502 | 895 | 176 | 1,071 |
| T. G. Evans | 1939-69 | 465 | 816 | 250 | 1,066 |
| A. Long | 1960-80 | 452 | 922 | 124 | 1,046 |
| G. O. Dawkes | 1937-61 | 482 | 895 | 148 | 1,043 |
| R. W. Tolchard | 1965-83 | 483 | 912 | 125 | 1,037 |
| W. L. Cornford | 1921-47 | 496 | 675 | 342 | 1,017 |

## FIELDING RECORDS

(Excluding wicket-keepers)

### Most Catches in an Innings

| | | | |
|---|---|---|---|
| 7 | M. J. Stewart | Surrey v Northamptonshire at Northampton | 1957 |
| 7 | A. S. Brown | Gloucestershire v Nottinghamshire at Nottingham | 1966 |

### Most Catches in a Match

| | | | |
|---|---|---|---|
| 10 | W. R. Hammond† | Gloucestershire v Surrey at Cheltenham | 1928 |
| 8 | W. B. Burns | Worcestershire v Yorkshire at Bradford | 1907 |
| 8 | A. H. Bakewell | Northamptonshire v Essex at Leyton | 1928 |
| 8 | W. R. Hammond | Gloucestershire v Worcestershire at Cheltenham | 1932 |
| 8 | K. J. Grieves | Lancashire v Sussex at Manchester | 1951 |
| 8 | C. A. Milton | Gloucestershire v Sussex at Hove | 1952 |
| 8 | G. A. R. Lock | Surrey v Warwickshire at The Oval | 1957 |
| 8 | J. M. Prodger | Kent v Gloucestershire at Cheltenham | 1961 |
| 8 | P. M. Walker | Glamorgan v Derbyshire at Swansea | 1970 |
| 8 | Javed Miandad | Habib Bank v Universities at Lahore | 1977-78 |
| 8 | Masood Anwar | Rawalpindi v Lahore Division at Rawalpindi | 1983-84 |

† *Hammond also scored a hundred in each innings.*

### Most Catches in a Season

| | | | | | | |
|---|---|---|---|---|---|---|
| 78 | W. R. Hammond | 1928 | | 65 | D. W. Richardson | 1961 |
| 77 | M. J. Stewart | 1957 | | 64 | K. F. Barrington | 1957 |
| 73 | P. M. Walker | 1961 | | 64 | G. A. R. Lock | 1957 |
| 71 | P. J. Sharpe | 1962 | | 63 | J. Tunnicliffe | 1896 |
| 70 | J. Tunnicliffe | 1901 | | 63 | J. Tunnicliffe | 1904 |
| 69 | J. G. Langridge | 1955 | | 63 | K. J. Grieves | 1950 |
| 69 | P. M. Walker | 1960 | | 63 | C. A. Milton | 1956 |
| 66 | J. Tunnicliffe | 1895 | | 61 | J. V. Wilson | 1955 |
| 65 | W. R. Hammond | 1925 | | 61 | M. J. Stewart | 1958 |
| 65 | P. M. Walker | 1959 | | | | |

*Note:* The most catches by a fielder since the reduction of County Championship matches in 1969 is 49 by C. J. Tavaré in 1979.

## Most Catches in a Career

Dates in italics denote the first half of an overseas season; i.e. *1970* denotes the 1970-71 season.

| | | | | |
|---|---|---|---|---|
| 1,018 | F. E. Woolley (1906-38) | | 784 | J. G. Langridge (1928-55) |
| 887 | W. G. Grace (1865-1908) | | 764 | W. Rhodes (1898-1930) |
| 830 | G. A. R. Lock (1946-*70*) | | 758 | C. A. Milton (1948-74) |
| 819 | W. R. Hammond (1920-51) | | 754 | E. H. Hendren (1907-38) |
| 813 | D. B. Close (1949-86) | | | |

# TEAM RECORDS

## HIGHEST TOTALS

| | | |
|---|---|---|
| 1,107 | Victoria v New South Wales at Melbourne .................. | 1926-27 |
| 1,059 | Victoria v Tasmania at Melbourne ......................... | 1922-23 |
| 951-7 dec. | Sind v Baluchistan at Karachi ............................ | 1973-74 |
| 918 | New South Wales v South Australia at Sydney ............. | 1900-01 |
| 912-8 dec. | Holkar v Mysore at Indore ............................... | 1945-46 |
| 910-6 dec. | Railways v Dera Ismail Khan at Lahore ................... | 1964-65 |
| 903-7 dec. | England v Australia at The Oval ......................... | 1938 |
| 887 | Yorkshire v Warwickshire at Birmingham.................. | 1896 |
| 863 | Lancashire v Surrey at The Oval.......................... | 1990 |
| 860-6 dec.† | Tamil Nadu v Goa at Panaji ............................. | 1988-89 |
| 849 | England v West Indies at Kingston ....................... | 1929-30 |
| 843 | Australians v Oxford and Cambridge Universities Past and Present at Portsmouth ..................................... | 1893 |

† *Tamil Nadu's final total of 912-6 dec. included 52 penalty runs from their opponents' failure to meet the required bowling rate by 13 overs.*

*Notes:* North Zone totalled 868 v West Zone at Bhilai in 1987-88. However, this included 68 penalty runs for West Zone's failure to meet the required bowling rate by 17 overs.

Bombay's total of 855-6 dec. v Hyderabad at Bombay in 1990-91 included 48 penalty runs (four overs).

## HIGHEST FOR EACH FIRST-CLASS COUNTY

| | | | |
|---|---|---|---|
| Derbyshire........ | 645 | v Hampshire at Derby .................... | 1898 |
| Essex............ | 761-6 | v Leicestershire at Chelmsford ........... | 1990 |
| Glamorgan........ | 587-8 | v Derbyshire at Cardiff .................. | 1951 |
| Gloucestershire .... | 653-6 | v Glamorgan at Bristol .................. | 1928 |
| Hampshire........ | 672-7 | v Somerset at Taunton................... | 1899 |
| Kent............. | 803-4 | v Essex at Brentwood.................... | 1934 |
| Lancashire ....... | 863 | v Surrey at The Oval .................... | 1990 |
| Leicestershire...... | 701-4 | v Worcestershire at Worcester............ | 1906 |
| Middlesex ........ | 642-3 | v Hampshire at Southampton ............. | 1923 |
| Northamptonshire.. | 636-6 | v Essex at Chelmsford ................... | 1990 |
| Nottinghamshire ... | 739-7 | v Leicestershire at Nottingham........... | 1903 |
| Somerset ......... | 675-9 | v Hampshire at Bath .................... | 1924 |
| Surrey........... | 811 | v Somerset at The Oval .................. | 1899 |
| Sussex ........... | 705-8 | v Surrey at Hastings..................... | 1902 |
| Warwickshire ..... | 657-6 | v Hampshire at Birmingham .............. | 1899 |
| Worcestershire..... | 633 | v Warwickshire at Worcester.............. | 1906 |
| Yorkshire......... | 887 | v Warwickshire at Birmingham ........... | 1896 |

## LOWEST TOTALS

| | | |
|---|---|---|
| 12 | Oxford University v MCC and Ground at Oxford | †1877 |
| 12 | Northamptonshire v Gloucestershire at Gloucester | 1907 |
| 13 | Auckland v Canterbury at Auckland | 1877-78 |
| 13 | Nottinghamshire v Yorkshire at Nottingham | 1901 |
| 14 | Surrey v Essex at Chelmsford | 1983 |
| 15 | MCC v Surrey at Lord's | 1839 |
| 15 | Victoria v MCC at Melbourne | †1903-04 |
| 15 | Northamptonshire v Yorkshire at Northampton | †1908 |
| 15 | Hampshire v Warwickshire at Birmingham | 1922 |
| | (Following on, Hampshire scored 521 and won by 155 runs.) | |
| 16 | MCC and Ground v Surrey at Lord's | 1872 |
| 16 | Derbyshire v Nottinghamshire at Nottingham | 1879 |
| 16 | Surrey v Nottinghamshire at The Oval | 1880 |
| 16 | Warwickshire v Kent at Tonbridge | 1913 |
| 16 | Trinidad v Barbados at Bridgetown | 1942-43 |
| 16 | Border v Natal at East London (first innings) | 1959-60 |
| 17 | Gentlemen of Kent v Gentlemen of England at Lord's | 1850 |
| 17 | Gloucestershire v Australians at Cheltenham | 1896 |
| 18 | The Bs v England at Lord's | 1831 |
| 18 | Kent v Sussex at Gravesend | †1867 |
| 18 | Tasmania v Victoria at Melbourne | 1868-69 |
| 18 | Australians v MCC and Ground at Lord's | †1896 |
| 18 | Border v Natal at East London (second innings) | 1959-60 |
| 19 | Sussex v Surrey at Godalming | 1830 |
| 19 | Sussex v Nottinghamshire at Hove | †1873 |
| 19 | MCC and Ground v Australians at Lord's | 1878 |
| 19 | Wellington v Nelson at Nelson | 1885-86 |

† *Signifies that one man was absent.*

*Note:* At Lord's in 1810, The Bs, with one man absent, were dismissed by England for 6.

## LOWEST TOTAL IN A MATCH

| | | |
|---|---|---|
| 34 | (16 and 18) Border v Natal at East London | 1959-60 |
| 42 | (27 and 15) Northamptonshire v Yorkshire at Northampton | 1908 |

*Note:* Northamptonshire batted one man short in each innings.

## LOWEST FOR EACH FIRST-CLASS COUNTY

| | | | |
|---|---|---|---|
| Derbyshire | 16 | v Nottinghamshire at Nottingham | 1879 |
| Essex | 30 | v Yorkshire at Leyton | 1901 |
| Glamorgan | 22 | v Lancashire at Liverpool | 1924 |
| Gloucestershire | 17 | v Australians at Cheltenham | 1896 |
| Hampshire | 15 | v Warwickshire at Birmingham | 1922 |
| Kent | 18 | v Sussex at Gravesend | 1867 |
| Lancashire | 25 | v Derbyshire at Manchester | 1871 |
| Leicestershire | 25 | v Kent at Leicester | 1912 |
| Middlesex | 20 | v MCC at Lord's | 1864 |
| Northamptonshire | 12 | v Gloucestershire at Gloucester | 1907 |
| Nottinghamshire | 13 | v Yorkshire at Nottingham | 1901 |
| Somerset | 25 | v Gloucestershire at Bristol | 1947 |
| Surrey | 14 | v Essex at Chelmsford | 1983 |
| Sussex | 19 | v Nottinghamshire at Hove | 1873 |
| Warwickshire | 16 | v Kent at Tonbridge | 1913 |
| Worcestershire | 24 | v Yorkshire at Huddersfield | 1903 |
| Yorkshire | 23 | v Hampshire at Middlesbrough | 1965 |

## HIGHEST MATCH AGGREGATES

| | | |
|---|---|---|
| 2,376 for 38 wickets | Maharashtra v Bombay at Poona...................... | 1948-49 |
| 2,078 for 40 wickets | Bombay v Holkar at Bombay........................ | 1944-45 |
| 1,981 for 35 wickets | England v South Africa at Durban ................... | 1938-39 |
| 1,929 for 39 wickets | New South Wales v South Australia at Sydney ......... | 1925-26 |
| 1,911 for 34 wickets | New South Wales v Victoria at Sydney............... | 1908-09 |
| 1,905 for 40 wickets | Otago v Wellington at Dunedin .................... | 1923-24 |

## In England

| | | |
|---|---|---|
| 1,723 for 31 wickets | England v Australia at Leeds....................... | 1948 |
| 1,650 for 19 wickets | Surrey v Lancashire at The Oval .................... | 1990 |
| 1,641 for 16 wickets | Glamorgan v Worcestershire at Abergavenny .......... | 1990 |
| 1,614 for 30 wickets | England v India at Manchester ..................... | 1990 |
| 1,603 for 28 wickets | England v India at Lord's.......................... | 1990 |
| 1,601 for 29 wickets | England v Australia at Lord's ...................... | 1930 |
| 1,578 for 37 wickets | Sussex v Kent at Hove ........................... | 1991 |
| 1,570 for 29 wickets | Essex v Kent at Chelmsford........................ | 1988 |
| 1,530 for 19 wickets | Essex v Leicestershire at Chelmsford................ | 1990 |
| 1,509 for 36 wickets | Somerset v Worcestershire at Taunton ............... | 1990 |
| 1,507 for 28 wickets | England v West Indies at The Oval .................. | 1976 |
| 1,502 for 28 wickets | MCC v New Zealanders at Lord's.................... | 1927 |

## LOWEST AGGREGATE IN A COMPLETED MATCH

105 for 31 wickets    MCC v Australians at Lord's ...................... 1878

*Note:* The lowest aggregate since 1900 is 158 for 22 wickets, Surrey v Worcestershire at The Oval, 1954.

## HIGHEST FOURTH-INNINGS TOTALS

(Unless otherwise stated, the side making the runs won the match.)

| | | |
|---|---|---|
| 654-5 | England v South Africa at Durban............................ | 1938-39 |
| | (After being set 696 to win. The match was left drawn on the tenth day.) | |
| 604 | Maharashtra v Bombay at Poona............................. | 1948-49 |
| | (After being set 959 to win.) | |
| 576-8 | Trinidad v Barbados at Port-of-Spain ...................... | 1945-46 |
| | (After being set 672 to win. Match drawn on fifth day.) | |
| 572 | New South Wales v South Australia at Sydney................. | 1907-08 |
| | (After being set 593 to win.) | |
| 529-9 | Combined XI v South Africans at Perth ..................... | 1963-64 |
| | (After being set 579 to win. Match drawn on fourth day.) | |
| 518 | Victoria v Queensland at Brisbane .......................... | 1926-27 |
| | (After being set 753 to win.) | |
| 507-7 | Cambridge University v MCC and Ground at Lord's ............ | 1896 |
| 502-6 | Middlesex v Nottinghamshire at Nottingham ................. | 1925 |
| | (Game won by an unfinished stand of 271; a county record.) | |
| 502-8 | Players v Gentlemen at Lord's ............................. | 1900 |
| 500-7 | South African Universities v Western Province at Stellenbosch ........ | 1978-79 |

## LARGEST VICTORIES

### Largest Innings Victories

| | | |
|---|---|---|
| Inns and 851 runs: | Railways (910-6 dec.) v Dera Ismail Khan (Lahore) ...... | 1964-65 |
| Inns and 666 runs: | Victoria (1,059) v Tasmania (Melbourne) .............. | 1922-23 |
| Inns and 656 runs: | Victoria (1,107) v New South Wales (Melbourne) ...... | 1926-27 |
| Inns and 605 runs: | New South Wales (918) v South Australia (Sydney)....... | 1900-01 |
| Inns and 579 runs: | England (903-7 dec.) v Australia (The Oval)........... | 1938 |
| Inns and 575 runs: | Sind (951-7 dec.) v Baluchistan (Karachi) ............ | 1973-74 |
| Inns and 527 runs: | New South Wales (713) v South Australia (Adelaide) ..... | 1908-09 |
| Inns and 517 runs: | Australians (675) v Nottinghamshire (Nottingham) ....... | 1921 |

### Largest Victories by Runs Margin

| | | |
|---|---|---|
| 685 runs: | New South Wales (235 and 761-8 dec.) v Queensland (Sydney)...... | 1929-30 |
| 675 runs: | England (521 and 342-8 dec.) v Australia (Brisbane) ...... | 1928-29 |
| 638 runs: | New South Wales (304 and 770) v South Australia (Adelaide) ...... | 1920-21 |
| 625 runs: | Sargodha (376 and 416) v Lahore Municipal Corporation (Faisalabad) | 1978-79 |
| 609 runs: | Muslim Commercial Bank (575 and 282-0 dec.) v WAPDA (Lahore). | 1977-78 |
| 573 runs: | Sinhalese SC (395-7 dec. and 350-2 dec.) v Sebastianites C and AC (63 and 109) at Colombo ..................................... | 1990-91 |
| 571 runs: | Victoria (304 and 649) v South Australia (Adelaide).............. | 1926-27 |
| 562 runs: | Australia (701 and 327) v England (The Oval) ............. | 1934 |

### Victory Without Losing a Wicket

| | |
|---|---|
| Lancashire (166-0 dec. and 66-0) beat Leicestershire by ten wickets (Manchester) | 1956 |
| Karachi A (277-0 dec.) beat Sind A by an innings and 77 runs (Karachi) ...... | 1957-58 |
| Railways (236-0 dec. and 16-0) beat Jammu and Kashmir by ten wickets (Srinagar) | 1960-61 |
| Karnataka (451-0 dec.) beat Kerala by an innings and 186 runs (Chikmagalur).. | 1977-78 |

## TIED MATCHES IN FIRST-CLASS CRICKET

There have been 38 tied matches since the First World War.

| | |
|---|---|
| Somerset v Sussex at Taunton ............................... (The last Sussex batsman was not allowed to bat under Law 45 [subsequently Law 17 and now Law 31].) | 1919 |
| Orange Free State v Eastern Province at Bloemfontein...................... (Eastern Province had two wickets to fall.) | 1925-26 |
| Essex v Somerset at Chelmsford ............................... (Although Essex had one man to go in, MCC ruled that the game should rank as a tie. The ninth wicket fell half a minute before time.) | 1926 |
| Gloucestershire v Australians at Bristol............................. | 1930 |
| Victoria v MCC at Melbourne ............................... (Victoria's third wicket fell to the last ball of the match when one run was needed to win.) | 1932-33 |
| Worcestershire v Somerset at Kidderminster ..................... | 1939 |
| Southern Punjab v Baroda at Patiala ........................... | 1945-46 |
| Essex v Northamptonshire at Ilford ............................ | 1947 |
| Hampshire v Lancashire at Bournemouth ....................... | 1947 |
| D. G. Bradman's XI v A. L. Hassett's XI at Melbourne .......... | 1948-49 |
| Hampshire v Kent at Southampton ............................ | 1950 |
| Sussex v Warwickshire at Hove .............................. | 1952 |
| Essex v Lancashire at Brentwood ............................. | 1952 |
| Northamptonshire v Middlesex at Peterborough .................. | 1953 |
| Yorkshire v Leicestershire at Huddersfield ..................... | 1954 |
| Sussex v Hampshire at Eastbourne ............................ | 1955 |
| Victoria v New South Wales at Melbourne ..................... | 1956-57 |
| T. N. Pearce's XI v New Zealanders at Scarborough ............. | 1958 |

| Essex v Gloucestershire at Leyton | 1959 |
| Australia v West Indies (First Test) at Brisbane | 1960-61 |
| Bahawalpur v Lahore B at Bahawalpur | 1961-62 |
| Hampshire v Middlesex at Portsmouth | 1967 |
| England XI v England Under-25 XI at Scarborough | 1968 |
| Yorkshire v Middlesex at Bradford | 1973 |
| Sussex v Essex at Hove | 1974 |
| South Australia v Queensland at Adelaide | 1976-77 |
| Central Districts v England XI at New Plymouth | 1977-78 |
| Victoria v New Zealanders at Melbourne | 1982-83 |
| Muslim Commercial Bank v Railways at Sialkot | 1983-84 |
| Sussex v Kent at Hastings | 1984 |
| Northamptonshire v Kent at Northampton | 1984 |
| Eastern Province B v Boland at Albany SC, Port Elizabeth | 1985-86 |
| Natal B v Eastern Province B at Pietermaritzburg | 1985-86 |
| India v Australia (First Test) at Madras | 1986-87 |
| Gloucestershire v Derbyshire at Bristol | 1987 |
| Bahawalpur v Peshawar at Bahawalpur | 1988-89 |
| Wellington v Canterbury at Wellington | 1988-89 |
| Sussex v Kent at Hove | 1991 |

*Sussex (436) scored the highest total to tie a first-class match.*

*Note*: Since 1948 a tie has been recognised only when the scores are level with all the wickets down in the fourth innings. This ruling applies to all grades of cricket, and in the case of a one-day match to the second innings, provided that the match has not been brought to a further conclusion.

## MATCHES BEGUN AND FINISHED ON FIRST DAY

*Since 1900. A fuller list may be found in the* Wisden *of 1981 and preceding editions.*

| Yorkshire v Worcestershire at Bradford, May 7 | 1900 |
| MCC and Ground v London County at Lord's, May 20 | 1903 |
| Transvaal v Orange Free State at Johannesburg, December 30 | 1906 |
| Middlesex v Gentlemen of Philadelphia at Lord's, July 20 | 1908 |
| Gloucestershire v Middlesex at Bristol, August 26 | 1909 |
| Eastern Province v Orange Free State at Port Elizabeth, December 26 | 1912 |
| Kent v Sussex at Tonbridge, June 21 | 1919 |
| Lancashire v Somerset at Manchester, May 21 | 1925 |
| Madras v Mysore at Madras, November 4 | 1934 |
| Ireland v New Zealanders at Dublin, September 11 | 1937 |
| Derbyshire v Somerset at Chesterfield, June 11 | 1947 |
| Lancashire v Sussex at Manchester, July 12 | 1950 |
| Surrey v Warwickshire at The Oval, May 16 | 1953 |
| Somerset v Lancashire at Bath, June 6 (H. T. F. Buse's benefit) | 1953 |
| Kent v Worcestershire at Tunbridge Wells, June 15 | 1960 |

# TEST MATCH RECORDS

## BATTING RECORDS

### HIGHEST INDIVIDUAL INNINGS

| 365* | G. S. Sobers | West Indies v Pakistan at Kingston | 1957-58 |
| 364 | L. Hutton | England v Australia at The Oval | 1938 |
| 337 | Hanif Mohammad | Pakistan v West Indies at Bridgetown | 1957-58 |
| 336* | W. R. Hammond | England v New Zealand at Auckland | 1932-33 |
| 334 | D. G. Bradman | Australia v England at Leeds | 1930 |
| 333 | G. A. Gooch | England v India at Lord's | 1990 |

| 325 | A. Sandham | England v West Indies at Kingston | 1929-30 |
|---|---|---|---|
| 311 | R. B. Simpson | Australia v England at Manchester | 1964 |
| 310* | J. H. Edrich | England v New Zealand at Leeds | 1965 |
| 307 | R. M. Cowper | Australia v England at Melbourne | 1965-66 |
| 304 | D. G. Bradman | Australia v England at Leeds | 1934 |
| 302 | L. G. Rowe | West Indies v England at Bridgetown | 1973-74 |
| 299* | D. G. Bradman | Australia v South Africa at Adelaide | 1931-32 |
| 299 | M. D. Crowe | New Zealand v Sri Lanka at Wellington | 1990-91 |
| 291 | I. V. A. Richards | West Indies v England at The Oval | 1976 |
| 287 | R. E. Foster | England v Australia at Sydney | 1903-04 |
| 285* | P. B. H. May | England v West Indies at Birmingham | 1957 |
| 280* | Javed Miandad | Pakistan v India at Hyderabad | 1982-83 |
| 278 | D. C. S. Compton | England v Pakistan at Nottingham | 1954 |
| 274 | R. G. Pollock | South Africa v Australia at Durban | 1969-70 |
| 274 | Zaheer Abbas | Pakistan v England at Birmingham | 1971 |
| 271 | Javed Miandad | Pakistan v New Zealand at Auckland | 1988-89 |
| 270* | G. A. Headley | West Indies v England at Kingston | 1934-35 |
| 270 | D. G. Bradman | Australia v England at Melbourne | 1936-37 |
| 268 | G. N. Yallop | Australia v Pakistan at Melbourne | 1983-84 |
| 267 | P. A. de Silva | Sri Lanka v New Zealand at Wellington | 1990-91 |
| 266 | W. H. Ponsford | Australia v England at The Oval | 1934 |
| 262* | D. L. Amiss | England v West Indies at Kingston | 1973-74 |
| 261 | F. M. M. Worrell | West Indies v England at Nottingham | 1950 |
| 260 | C. C. Hunte | West Indies v Pakistan at Kingston | 1957-58 |
| 260 | Javed Miandad | Pakistan v England at The Oval | 1987 |
| 259 | G. M. Turner | New Zealand v West Indies at Georgetown | 1971-72 |
| 258 | T. W. Graveney | England v West Indies at Nottingham | 1957 |
| 258 | S. M. Nurse | West Indies v New Zealand at Christchurch | 1968-69 |
| 256 | R. B. Kanhai | West Indies v India at Calcutta | 1958-59 |
| 256 | K. F. Barrington | England v Australia at Manchester | 1964 |
| 255* | D. J. McGlew | South Africa v New Zealand at Wellington | 1952-53 |
| 254 | D. G. Bradman | Australia v England at Lord's | 1930 |
| 251 | W. R. Hammond | England v Australia at Sydney | 1928-29 |
| 250 | K. D. Walters | Australia v New Zealand at Christchurch | 1976-77 |
| 250 | S. F. A. F. Bacchus | West Indies v India at Kanpur | 1978-79 |

**The highest individual innings for India is:**

| 236* | S. M. Gavaskar | India v West Indies at Madras | 1983-84 |
|---|---|---|---|

## HUNDRED ON TEST DEBUT

| C. Bannerman (165*) | Australia v England at Melbourne | 1876-77 |
|---|---|---|
| W. G. Grace (152) | England v Australia at The Oval | 1880 |
| H. Graham (107) | Australia v England at Lord's | 1893 |
| †K. S. Ranjitsinhji (154*) | England v Australia at Manchester | 1896 |
| †P. F. Warner (132*) | England v South Africa at Johannesburg | 1898-99 |
| †R. A. Duff (104) | Australia v England at Melbourne | 1901-02 |
| R. E. Foster (287) | England v Australia at Sydney | 1903-04 |
| G. Gunn (119) | England v Australia at Sydney | 1907-08 |
| †R. J. Hartigan (116) | Australia v England at Adelaide | 1907-08 |
| †H. L. Collins (104) | Australia v England at Sydney | 1920-21 |
| W. H. Ponsford (110) | Australia v England at Sydney | 1924-25 |
| A. A. Jackson (164) | Australia v England at Adelaide | 1928-29 |
| †G. A. Headley (176) | West Indies v England at Bridgetown | 1929-30 |
| J. E. Mills (117) | New Zealand v England at Wellington | 1929-30 |
| Nawab of Pataudi sen. (102) | England v Australia at Sydney | 1932-33 |
| B. H. Valentine (136) | England v India at Bombay | 1933-34 |
| †L. Amarnath (118) | India v England at Bombay | 1933-34 |
| †P. A. Gibb (106) | England v South Africa at Johannesburg | 1938-39 |

| | | |
|---|---|---|
| S. C. Griffith (140) . . . . . . . | England v West Indies at Port-of-Spain . . . . . . . | 1947-48 |
| A. G. Ganteaume (112) . . . | West Indies v England at Port-of-Spain . . . . . . . | 1947-48 |
| †J. W. Burke (101*) . . . . . . . | Australia v England at Adelaide . . . . . . . . . . . . | 1950-51 |
| P. B. H. May (138) . . . . . . . | England v South Africa at Leeds . . . . . . . . . . . . | 1951 |
| R. H. Shodhan (110) . . . . . . | India v Pakistan at Calcutta . . . . . . . . . . . . . . | 1952-53 |
| B. H. Pairaudeau (115) . . . . | West Indies v India at Port-of-Spain . . . . . . . . . | 1952-53 |
| †O. G. Smith (104) . . . . . . . | West Indies v Australia at Kingston . . . . . . . . . | 1954-55 |
| A. G. Kripal Singh (100*) . . | India v New Zealand at Hyderabad . . . . . . . . . | 1955-56 |
| C. C. Hunte (142) . . . . . . . | West Indies v Pakistan at Bridgetown . . . . . . . . | 1957-58 |
| C. A. Milton (104*) . . . . . . | England v New Zealand at Leeds . . . . . . . . . . . . | 1958 |
| †A. A. Baig (112) . . . . . . . . | India v England at Manchester . . . . . . . . . . . . . | 1959 |
| Hanumant Singh (105) . . . . | India v England at Delhi . . . . . . . . . . . . . . . . . | 1963-64 |
| Khalid Ibadulla (166) . . . . . | Pakistan v Australia at Karachi . . . . . . . . . . . . | 1964-65 |
| B. R. Taylor (105) . . . . . . . | New Zealand v India at Calcutta . . . . . . . . . . . | 1964-65 |
| K. D. Walters (155) . . . . . . | Australia v England at Brisbane . . . . . . . . . . . . | 1965-66 |
| J. H. Hampshire (107) . . . . | England v West Indies at Lord's . . . . . . . . . . . . | 1969 |
| †G. R. Viswanath (137) . . . . | India v Australia at Kanpur . . . . . . . . . . . . . . | 1969-70 |
| G. S. Chappell (108) . . . . . | Australia v England at Perth . . . . . . . . . . . . . . | 1970-71 |
| ‡L. G. Rowe (214, 100*) . . . | West Indies v New Zealand at Kingston . . . . . . . | 1971-72 |
| A. I. Kallicharran (100*) . . | West Indies v New Zealand at Georgetown . . . . . | 1971-72 |
| R. E. Redmond (107) . . . . . | New Zealand v Pakistan at Auckland . . . . . . . . | 1972-73 |
| †F. C. Hayes (106*) . . . . . . . | England v West Indies at The Oval . . . . . . . . . . | 1973 |
| †C. G. Greenidge (107) . . . . | West Indies v India at Bangalore . . . . . . . . . . . | 1974-75 |
| †L. Baichan (105*) . . . . . . . | West Indies v Pakistan at Lahore . . . . . . . . . . . | 1974-75 |
| G. J. Cosier (109) . . . . . . . | Australia v West Indies at Melbourne . . . . . . . . | 1975-76 |
| S. Amarnath (124) . . . . . . . | India v New Zealand at Auckland . . . . . . . . . . | 1975-76 |
| Javed Miandad (163) . . . . . | Pakistan v New Zealand at Lahore . . . . . . . . . . | 1976-77 |
| †A. B. Williams (100) . . . . . . | West Indies v Australia at Georgetown . . . . . . . | 1977-78 |
| †D. M. Wellham (103) . . . . . | Australia v England at The Oval . . . . . . . . . . . | 1981 |
| †Salim Malik (100*) . . . . . . . | Pakistan v Sri Lanka at Karachi . . . . . . . . . . . . | 1981-82 |
| K. C. Wessels (162) . . . . . . | Australia v England at Brisbane . . . . . . . . . . . . | 1982-83 |
| W. B. Phillips (159) . . . . . . | Australia v Pakistan at Perth . . . . . . . . . . . . . | 1983-84 |
| §M. Azharuddin (110) . . . . . | India v England at Calcutta . . . . . . . . . . . . . . . | 1984-85 |
| D. S. B. P. Kuruppu (201*) . | Sri Lanka v New Zealand at Colombo (CCC) . . | 1986-87 |
| †M. J. Greatbatch (107*) . . | New Zealand v England at Auckland . . . . . . . . | 1987-88 |
| M. E. Waugh (138) . . . . . . . | Australia v England at Adelaide . . . . . . . . . . . . | 1990-91 |

  † *In his second innings of the match.*
  ‡ *L. G. Rowe is the only batsman to score a hundred in each innings on début.*
  § *M. Azharuddin is the only batsman to score hundreds in each of his first three Tests.*

*Note:* L. Amarnath and S. Amarnath provide the only instance of a father and son scoring a hundred on début.

## 300 RUNS IN FIRST TEST

| | | | |
|---|---|---|---|
| 314 | L. G. Rowe (214, 100*) | West Indies v New Zealand at Kingston . . . . . . . | 1971-72 |
| 306 | R. E. Foster (287, 19) | England v Australia at Sydney . . . . . . . . . . . . . | 1903-04 |

## TWO SEPARATE HUNDREDS IN A TEST

  **Three times:** S. M. Gavaskar v West Indies (1970-71), v Pakistan (1978-79), v West Indies (1978-79).
  **Twice in one series:** C. L. Walcott v Australia (1954-55).
  **Twice:** H. Sutcliffe v Australia (1924-25), v South Africa (1929); G. A. Headley v England (1929-30 and 1939); G. S. Chappell v New Zealand (1973-74), v West Indies (1975-76); ‡A. R. Border v Pakistan (1979-80), v New Zealand (1985-86).

**Once:** W. Bardsley v England (1909); A. C. Russell v South Africa (1922-23); W. R. Hammond v Australia (1928-29); E. Paynter v South Africa (1938-39); D. C. S. Compton v Australia (1946-47); A. R. Morris v England (1946-47); A. Melville v England (1947); B. Mitchell v England (1947); D. G. Bradman v India (1947-48); V. S. Hazare v Australia (1947-48); E. D. Weekes v India (1948-49); J. Moroney v South Africa (1949-50); G. S. Sobers v Pakistan (1957-58); R. B. Kanhai v Australia (1960-61); Hanif Mohammad v England (1961-62); R. B. Simpson v Pakistan (1964-65); K. D. Walters v West Indies (1968-69); †L. G. Rowe v New Zealand (1971-72); I. M. Chappell v New Zealand (1973-74); G. M. Turner v Australia (1973-74); C. G. Greenidge v England (1976); G. P. Howarth v England (1977-78); L. R. D. Mendis v India (1982-83); Javed Miandad v New Zealand (1984-85); D. M. Jones v Pakistan (1989-90); G. A. Gooch v India (1990); A. H. Jones v Sri Lanka (1990-91); A. P. Gurusinha v New Zealand (1990-91).

† *L. G. Rowe's two hundreds were on his Test début.*

‡ *A. R. Border scored 150\* and 153 against Pakistan to become the first batsman to score 150 in each innings of a Test match.*

## TRIPLE-HUNDRED AND HUNDRED IN SAME TEST

†G. A. Gooch (England)     333 and 123 v India at Lord's . . . . . . . . . . . . . . . . . .    1990

† *G. A. Gooch became the first to score a hundred and a triple-hundred in the same first-class match.*

## DOUBLE-HUNDRED AND HUNDRED IN SAME TEST

| | | |
|---|---|---|
| K. D. Walters (Australia) | 242 and 103 v West Indies at Sydney . . . . . . . . . . . | 1968-69 |
| S. M. Gavaskar (India) | 124 and 220 v West Indies at Port-of-Spain . . . . . . . | 1970-71 |
| †L. G. Rowe (West Indies) | 214 and 100\* v New Zealand at Kingston . . . . . . . . | 1971-72 |
| G. S. Chappell (Australia) | 247\* and 133 v New Zealand at Wellington . . . . . . | 1973-74 |

† *On Test début.*

## MOST RUNS IN A SERIES

| | T | I | NO | R | HI | 100s | Avge | | |
|---|---|---|---|---|---|---|---|---|---|
| D. G. Bradman . . . | 5 | 7 | 0 | 974 | 334 | 4 | 139.14 | A v E | 1930 |
| W. R. Hammond . | 5 | 9 | 1 | 905 | 251 | 4 | 113.12 | E v A | 1928-29 |
| M. A. Taylor . . . . . | 6 | 11 | 1 | 839 | 219 | 2 | 83.90 | A v E | 1989 |
| R. N. Harvey . . . . | 5 | 9 | 0 | 834 | 205 | 4 | 92.66 | A v SA | 1952-53 |
| I. V. A. Richards . | 4 | 7 | 0 | 829 | 291 | 3 | 118.42 | WI v E | 1976 |
| C. L. Walcott . . . . | 5 | 10 | 0 | 827 | 155 | 5 | 82.70 | WI v A | 1954-55 |
| G. S. Sobers . . . . . . | 5 | 8 | 2 | 824 | 365\* | 3 | 137.33 | WI v P | 1957-58 |
| D. G. Bradman . . . | 5 | 9 | 0 | 810 | 270 | 3 | 90.00 | A v E | 1936-37 |
| D. G. Bradman . . . | 5 | 5 | 1 | 806 | 299\* | 4 | 201.50 | A v SA | 1931-32 |
| E. D. Weekes . . . . | 5 | 7 | 0 | 779 | 194 | 4 | 111.28 | WI v I | 1948-49 |
| †S. M. Gavaskar . . . | 4 | 8 | 3 | 774 | 220 | 4 | 154.80 | I v WI | 1970-71 |
| Mudassar Nazar . . | 6 | 8 | 2 | 761 | 231 | 4 | 126.83 | P v I | 1982-83 |
| D. G. Bradman . . . | 5 | 8 | 0 | 758 | 304 | 2 | 94.75 | A v E | 1934 |
| D. C. S. Compton . | 5 | 8 | 0 | 753 | 208 | 4 | 94.12 | E v SA | 1947 |
| ‡G. A. Gooch . . . . | 3 | 6 | 0 | 752 | 333 | 3 | 125.33 | E v I | 1990 |

† *Gavaskar's aggregate was achieved in his first Test series.*

‡ *G. A. Gooch is alone in scoring 1,000 runs in Test cricket during an English season with 1,058 runs in eleven innings against New Zealand and India in 1990.*

## 1,000 TEST RUNS IN A CALENDAR YEAR

| | T | I | NO | R | HI | 100s | Avge | Year |
|---|---|---|---|---|---|---|---|---|
| I. V. A. Richards (WI) . . . . . . . . | 11 | 19 | 0 | 1,710 | 291 | 7 | 90.00 | 1976 |
| S. M. Gavaskar (I) . . . . . . . . . . | 18 | 27 | 1 | 1,555 | 221 | 5 | 59.80 | 1979 |
| G. R. Viswanath (I) . . . . . . . . . | 17 | 26 | 3 | 1,388 | 179 | 5 | 60.34 | 1979 |
| R. B. Simpson (A) . . . . . . . . . . | 14 | 26 | 3 | 1,381 | 311 | 3 | 60.04 | 1964 |

| | T | I | NO | R | HI | 100s | Avge | Year |
|---|---|---|---|---|---|---|---|---|
| D. L. Amiss (E) ............. | 13 | 22 | 2 | 1,379 | 262* | 5 | 68.95 | 1974 |
| S. M. Gavaskar (I) ............ | 18 | 32 | 4 | 1,310 | 236* | 5 | 46.78 | 1983 |
| G. A. Gooch (E) ............. | 9 | 17 | 1 | 1,264 | 333 | 4 | 79.00 | 1990 |
| M. A. Taylor (A) ............. | 11 | 20 | 1 | 1,219 | 219 | 4 | 64.15 | 1989† |
| G. S. Sobers (WI) ............ | 7 | 12 | 3 | 1,193 | 365* | 5 | 132.55 | 1958 |
| D. B. Vengsarkar (I) .......... | 18 | 27 | 4 | 1,174 | 146* | 5 | 51.04 | 1979 |
| K. J. Hughes (A) ............. | 15 | 28 | 4 | 1,163 | 130* | 2 | 48.45 | 1979 |
| D. C. S. Compton (E) .......... | 9 | 15 | 1 | 1,159 | 208 | 6 | 82.78 | 1947 |
| C. G. Greenidge (WI) .......... | 14 | 22 | 4 | 1,149 | 223 | 4 | 63.83 | 1984 |
| A. R. Border (A) ............. | 11 | 20 | 3 | 1,099 | 196 | 4 | 64.64 | 1985 |
| D. M. Jones (A) ............. | 11 | 18 | 3 | 1,099 | 216 | 4 | 73.26 | 1989 |
| I. T. Botham (E) ............. | 14 | 22 | 0 | 1,095 | 208 | 3 | 49.77 | 1982 |
| K. W. R. Fletcher (E) ......... | 13 | 22 | 4 | 1,090 | 178 | 2 | 60.55 | 1973 |
| M. Amarnath (I) ............. | 14 | 24 | 1 | 1,077 | 120 | 4 | 46.82 | 1983 |
| A. R. Border (A) ............. | 14 | 27 | 3 | 1,073 | 162 | 3 | 44.70 | 1979 |
| C. Hill (A) ................. | 12 | 21 | 2 | 1,061 | 142 | 2 | 55.84 | 1902 |
| D. I. Gower (E) ............. | 14 | 25 | 2 | 1,061 | 114 | 1 | 46.13 | 1982 |
| D. I. Gower (E) ............. | 14 | 25 | 1 | 1,059 | 136 | 2 | 44.12 | 1986 |
| W. M. Lawry (A) ............. | 14 | 27 | 2 | 1,056 | 157 | 2 | 42.24 | 1964 |
| S. M. Gavaskar (I) ............ | 9 | 15 | 2 | 1,044 | 205 | 4 | 80.30 | 1978 |
| G. A. Gooch (E) ............. | 9 | 17 | 1 | 1,040 | 174 | 3 | 65.00 | 1991 |
| K. F. Barrington (E) .......... | 12 | 22 | 2 | 1,039 | 132* | 3 | 51.95 | 1963 |
| E. R. Dexter (E) ............. | 11 | 15 | 1 | 1,038 | 205 | 2 | 74.14 | 1962 |
| K. F. Barrington (E) .......... | 10 | 17 | 4 | 1,032 | 172 | 4 | 79.38 | 1961 |
| Mohsin Khan (P) ............. | 10 | 17 | 3 | 1,029 | 200 | 4 | 73.50 | 1982 |
| D. G. Bradman (A) ........... | 8 | 13 | 4 | 1,025 | 201 | 5 | 113.88 | 1948 |
| S. M. Gavaskar (I) ............ | 11 | 20 | 1 | 1,024 | 156 | 4 | 53.89 | 1976 |
| A. R. Border (A) ............. | 11 | 19 | 3 | 1,000 | 140 | 5 | 62.50 | 1986 |

† *The year of his début.*

*Notes:* The earliest date for completing 1,000 runs is May 3 by M. Amarnath in 1983.

D. G. Bradman (A) scored 1,005 runs in five consecutive Tests, all against England, in 1936-37 and 1938: 13, 270, 26, 212, 169, 51, 144*, 18, 102*.

## MOST RUNS IN A CAREER

(Qualification: 2,000 runs)

### ENGLAND

| | T | I | NO | R | HI | 100s | Avge |
|---|---|---|---|---|---|---|---|
| G. Boycott ........... | 108 | 193 | 23 | 8,114 | 246* | 22 | 47.72 |
| D. I. Gower ......... | 114 | 199 | 16 | 8,081 | 215 | 18 | 44.15 |
| M. C. Cowdrey ...... | 114 | 188 | 15 | 7,624 | 182 | 22 | 44.06 |
| W. R. Hammond ..... | 85 | 140 | 16 | 7,249 | 336* | 22 | 58.45 |
| G. A. Gooch ........ | 91 | 166 | 6 | 7,028 | 333 | 15 | 43.92 |
| L. Hutton .......... | 79 | 138 | 15 | 6,971 | 364 | 19 | 56.67 |
| K. F. Barrington ..... | 82 | 131 | 15 | 6,806 | 256 | 20 | 58.67 |
| D. C. S. Compton .... | 78 | 131 | 15 | 5,807 | 278 | 17 | 50.06 |
| J. B. Hobbs ......... | 61 | 102 | 7 | 5,410 | 211 | 15 | 56.94 |
| I. T. Botham ........ | 99 | 157 | 6 | 5,176 | 208 | 14 | 34.27 |
| J. H. Edrich ........ | 77 | 127 | 9 | 5,138 | 310* | 12 | 43.54 |
| T. W. Graveney ...... | 79 | 123 | 13 | 4,882 | 258 | 11 | 44.38 |
| H. Sutcliffe ......... | 54 | 84 | 9 | 4,555 | 194 | 16 | 60.73 |
| P. B. H. May ........ | 66 | 106 | 9 | 4,537 | 285* | 13 | 46.77 |
| E. R. Dexter ........ | 62 | 102 | 8 | 4,502 | 205 | 9 | 47.89 |
| A. P. E. Knott ...... | 95 | 149 | 15 | 4,389 | 135 | 5 | 32.75 |
| A. J. Lamb .......... | 74 | 131 | 10 | 4,264 | 139 | 13 | 35.23 |
| M. W. Gatting ...... | 68 | 117 | 14 | 3,870 | 207 | 9 | 37.57 |
| D. L. Amiss ......... | 50 | 88 | 10 | 3,612 | 262* | 11 | 46.30 |
| A. W. Greig ........ | 58 | 93 | 4 | 3,599 | 148 | 8 | 40.43 |
| E. H. Hendren ...... | 51 | 83 | 9 | 3,525 | 205* | 7 | 47.63 |

|  | T | I | NO | R | HI | 100s | Avge |
|---|---|---|---|---|---|---|---|
| F. E. Woolley........ | 64 | 98 | 7 | 3,283 | 154 | 5 | 36.07 |
| K. W. R. Fletcher .... | 59 | 96 | 14 | 3,272 | 216 | 7 | 39.90 |
| M. Leyland.......... | 41 | 65 | 5 | 2,764 | 187 | 9 | 46.06 |
| C. Washbrook ...... | 37 | 66 | 6 | 2,569 | 195 | 6 | 42.81 |
| B. L. D'Oliveira..... | 44 | 70 | 8 | 2,484 | 158 | 5 | 40.06 |
| D. W. Randall ..... | 47 | 79 | 5 | 2,470 | 174 | 7 | 33.37 |
| W. J. Edrich ....... | 39 | 63 | 2 | 2,440 | 219 | 6 | 40.00 |
| T. G. Evans ........ | 91 | 133 | 14 | 2,439 | 104 | 2 | 20.49 |
| L. E. G. Ames ...... | 47 | 72 | 12 | 2,434 | 149 | 8 | 40.56 |
| W. Rhodes ......... | 58 | 98 | 21 | 2,325 | 179 | 2 | 30.19 |
| T. E. Bailey ....... | 61 | 91 | 14 | 2,290 | 134* | 1 | 29.74 |
| M. J. K. Smith ..... | 50 | 78 | 6 | 2,278 | 121 | 3 | 31.63 |
| R. A. Smith ........ | 28 | 53 | 13 | 2,118 | 148* | 6 | 52.95 |
| P. E. Richardson ..... | 34 | 56 | 1 | 2,061 | 126 | 5 | 37.47 |

## AUSTRALIA

|  | T | I | NO | R | HI | 100s | Avge |
|---|---|---|---|---|---|---|---|
| A. R. Border ....... | 125 | 215 | 38 | 9,257 | 205 | 23 | 52.29 |
| G. S. Chappell ...... | 87 | 151 | 19 | 7,110 | 247* | 24 | 53.86 |
| D. G. Bradman ..... | 52 | 80 | 10 | 6,996 | 334 | 29 | 99.94 |
| R. N. Harvey ...... | 79 | 137 | 10 | 6,149 | 205 | 21 | 48.41 |
| K. D. Walters ..... | 74 | 125 | 14 | 5,357 | 250 | 15 | 48.26 |
| I. M. Chappell ..... | 75 | 136 | 10 | 5,345 | 196 | 14 | 42.42 |
| W. M. Lawry....... | 67 | 123 | 12 | 5,234 | 210 | 13 | 47.15 |
| R. B. Simpson ..... | 62 | 111 | 7 | 4,869 | 311 | 10 | 46.81 |
| I. R. Redpath....... | 66 | 120 | 11 | 4,737 | 171 | 8 | 43.45 |
| K. J. Hughes ...... | 70 | 124 | 6 | 4,415 | 213 | 9 | 37.41 |
| D. C. Boon.......... | 58 | 106 | 10 | 3,982 | 200 | 10 | 41.47 |
| R. W. Marsh ...... | 96 | 150 | 13 | 3,633 | 132 | 3 | 26.51 |
| A. R. Morris....... | 46 | 79 | 3 | 3,533 | 206 | 12 | 46.48 |
| C. Hill ........... | 49 | 89 | 2 | 3,412 | 191 | 7 | 39.21 |
| G. M. Wood ...... | 59 | 112 | 6 | 3,374 | 172 | 9 | 31.83 |
| V. T. Trumper ..... | 48 | 89 | 8 | 3,163 | 214* | 8 | 39.04 |
| C. C. McDonald .... | 47 | 83 | 4 | 3,107 | 170 | 5 | 39.32 |
| A. L. Hassett ...... | 43 | 69 | 3 | 3,073 | 198* | 10 | 46.56 |
| D. M. Jones ...... | 44 | 75 | 9 | 3,045 | 216 | 9 | 46.13 |
| K. R. Miller ...... | 55 | 87 | 7 | 2,958 | 147 | 7 | 36.97 |
| W. W. Armstrong .... | 50 | 84 | 10 | 2,863 | 159* | 6 | 38.68 |
| K. R. Stackpole .... | 43 | 80 | 5 | 2,807 | 207 | 7 | 37.42 |
| N. C. O'Neill...... | 42 | 69 | 8 | 2,779 | 181 | 6 | 45.55 |
| G. N. Yallop ...... | 39 | 70 | 3 | 2,756 | 268 | 8 | 41.13 |
| S. J. McCabe ...... | 39 | 62 | 5 | 2,748 | 232 | 6 | 48.21 |
| G. R. Marsh ...... | 46 | 85 | 6 | 2,669 | 138 | 4 | 33.78 |
| W. Bardsley ...... | 41 | 66 | 5 | 2,469 | 193* | 6 | 40.47 |
| W. M. Woodfull .... | 35 | 54 | 4 | 2,300 | 161 | 7 | 46.00 |
| P. J. Burge ....... | 42 | 68 | 8 | 2,290 | 181 | 4 | 38.16 |
| S. E. Gregory ...... | 58 | 100 | 7 | 2,282 | 201 | 4 | 24.53 |
| M. A. Taylor ..... | 25 | 46 | 3 | 2,272 | 219 | 7 | 52.83 |
| R. Benaud ........ | 63 | 97 | 7 | 2,201 | 122 | 3 | 24.45 |
| C. G. Macartney .... | 35 | 55 | 4 | 2,131 | 170 | 7 | 41.78 |
| W. H. Ponsford .... | 29 | 48 | 4 | 2,122 | 266 | 7 | 48.22 |
| S. R. Waugh ...... | 44 | 67 | 11 | 2,097 | 177* | 3 | 37.44 |
| R. M. Cowper ...... | 27 | 46 | 2 | 2,061 | 307 | 5 | 46.84 |

## SOUTH AFRICA

|  | T | I | NO | R | HI | 100s | Avge |
|---|---|---|---|---|---|---|---|
| B. Mitchell .......... | 42 | 80 | 9 | 3,471 | 189* | 8 | 48.88 |
| A. D. Nourse ........ | 34 | 62 | 7 | 2,960 | 231 | 9 | 53.81 |
| H. W. Taylor ........ | 42 | 76 | 4 | 2,936 | 176 | 7 | 40.77 |
| E. J. Barlow ......... | 30 | 57 | 2 | 2,516 | 201 | 6 | 45.74 |

|                       | T   | I   | NO  | R      | HI   | 100s | Avge  |
|-----------------------|-----|-----|-----|--------|------|------|-------|
| T. L. Goddard ....... | 41  | 78  | 5   | 2,516  | 112  | 1    | 34.46 |
| D. J. McGlew ....... | 34  | 64  | 6   | 2,440  | 255* | 7    | 42.06 |
| J. H. B. Waite ....... | 50  | 86  | 7   | 2,405  | 134  | 4    | 30.44 |
| R. G. Pollock ....... | 23  | 41  | 4   | 2,256  | 274  | 7    | 60.97 |
| A. W. Nourse ...... | 45  | 83  | 8   | 2,234  | 111  | 1    | 29.78 |
| R. A. McLean ...... | 40  | 73  | 3   | 2,120  | 142  | 5    | 30.28 |

## WEST INDIES

|                        | T   | I   | NO  | R      | HI   | 100s | Avge  |
|------------------------|-----|-----|-----|--------|------|------|-------|
| I. V. A. Richards..... | 121 | 182 | 12  | 8,540  | 291  | 24   | 50.23 |
| G. S. Sobers ......... | 93  | 160 | 21  | 8,032  | 365* | 26   | 57.78 |
| C. G. Greenidge .... | 108 | 185 | 16  | 7,558  | 226  | 19   | 44.72 |
| C. H. Lloyd ......... | 110 | 175 | 14  | 7,515  | 242* | 19   | 46.67 |
| D. L. Haynes ........ | 102 | 178 | 21  | 6,644  | 184  | 16   | 42.31 |
| R. B. Kanhai ........ | 79  | 137 | 6   | 6,227  | 256  | 15   | 47.53 |
| R. B. Richardson..... | 62  | 107 | 10  | 4,647  | 194  | 14   | 47.90 |
| E. D. Weekes ........ | 48  | 81  | 5   | 4,455  | 207  | 15   | 58.61 |
| A. I. Kallicharran ... | 66  | 109 | 10  | 4,399  | 187  | 12   | 44.43 |
| R. C. Fredericks ..... | 59  | 109 | 7   | 4,334  | 169  | 8    | 42.49 |
| F. M. M. Worrell .... | 51  | 87  | 9   | 3,860  | 261  | 9    | 49.48 |
| C. L. Walcott ....... | 44  | 74  | 7   | 3,798  | 220  | 15   | 56.68 |
| P. J. L. Dujon ....... | 81  | 115 | 11  | 3,322  | 139  | 5    | 31.94 |
| C. C. Hunte ......... | 44  | 78  | 6   | 3,245  | 260  | 8    | 45.06 |
| H. A. Gomes ........ | 60  | 91  | 11  | 3,171  | 143  | 9    | 39.63 |
| B. F. Butcher ....... | 44  | 78  | 6   | 3,104  | 209* | 7    | 43.11 |
| S. M. Nurse ......... | 29  | 54  | 1   | 2,523  | 258  | 6    | 47.60 |
| A. L. Logie.......... | 52  | 78  | 9   | 2,470  | 130  | 2    | 35.79 |
| G. A. Headley ....... | 22  | 40  | 4   | 2,190  | 270* | 10   | 60.83 |
| J. B. Stollmeyer ..... | 32  | 56  | 5   | 2,159  | 160  | 4    | 42.33 |
| L. G. Rowe ......... | 30  | 49  | 2   | 2,047  | 302  | 7    | 43.55 |

## NEW ZEALAND

|                       | T   | I   | NO  | R      | HI   | 100s | Avge  |
|-----------------------|-----|-----|-----|--------|------|------|-------|
| J. G. Wright ........ | 74  | 132 | 6   | 4,706  | 185  | 11   | 37.34 |
| M. D. Crowe ........ | 56  | 92  | 9   | 3,993  | 299  | 13   | 48.10 |
| B. E. Congdon ...... | 61  | 114 | 7   | 3,448  | 176  | 7    | 32.22 |
| J. R. Reid .......... | 58  | 108 | 5   | 3,428  | 142  | 6    | 33.28 |
| Sir R. J. Hadlee...... | 86  | 134 | 19  | 3,124  | 151* | 2    | 27.16 |
| G. M. Turner ....... | 41  | 73  | 6   | 2,991  | 259  | 7    | 44.64 |
| B. Sutcliffe ......... | 42  | 76  | 8   | 2,727  | 230* | 5    | 40.10 |
| M. G. Burgess ...... | 50  | 92  | 6   | 2,684  | 119* | 5    | 31.20 |
| J. V. Coney ........ | 52  | 85  | 14  | 2,668  | 174* | 3    | 37.57 |
| G. P. Howarth....... | 47  | 83  | 5   | 2,531  | 147  | 6    | 32.44 |
| G. T. Dowling ....... | 39  | 77  | 3   | 2,306  | 239  | 3    | 31.16 |

## INDIA

|                       | T   | I   | NO  | R      | HI   | 100s | Avge  |
|-----------------------|-----|-----|-----|--------|------|------|-------|
| S. M. Gavaskar ...... | 125 | 214 | 16  | 10,122 | 236* | 34   | 51.12 |
| D. B. Vengsarkar..... | 111 | 176 | 22  | 6,710  | 166  | 17   | 43.57 |
| G. R. Viswanath .... | 91  | 155 | 10  | 6,080  | 222  | 14   | 41.93 |
| Kapil Dev .......... | 110 | 159 | 13  | 4,525  | 163  | 7    | 30.99 |
| M. Amarnath........ | 69  | 113 | 10  | 4,378  | 138  | 11   | 42.50 |
| P. R. Umrigar ...... | 59  | 94  | 8   | 3,631  | 223  | 12   | 42.22 |
| R. J. Shastri ........ | 73  | 110 | 14  | 3,460  | 187  | 10   | 36.04 |

| | T | I | NO | R | HI | 100s | Avge |
|---|---|---|---|---|---|---|---|
| V. L. Manjrekar ..... | 55 | 92 | 10 | 3,208 | 189* | 7 | 39.12 |
| C. G. Borde ......... | 55 | 97 | 11 | 3,061 | 177* | 5 | 35.59 |
| M. Azharuddin ...... | 41 | 61 | 3 | 2,976 | 199 | 10 | 51.31 |
| Nawab of Pataudi jun. | 46 | 83 | 3 | 2,793 | 203* | 6 | 34.91 |
| S. M. H. Kirmani .... | 88 | 124 | 22 | 2,759 | 102 | 2 | 27.04 |
| F. M. Engineer ...... | 46 | 87 | 3 | 2,611 | 121 | 2 | 31.08 |
| Pankaj Roy ......... | 43 | 79 | 4 | 2,442 | 173 | 5 | 32.56 |
| V. S. Hazare ........ | 30 | 52 | 6 | 2,192 | 164* | 7 | 47.65 |
| A. L. Wadekar....... | 37 | 71 | 3 | 2,113 | 143 | 1 | 31.07 |
| V. Mankad.......... | 44 | 72 | 5 | 2,109 | 231 | 5 | 31.47 |
| C. P. S. Chauhan .... | 40 | 68 | 2 | 2,084 | 97 | 0 | 31.57 |
| M. L. Jaisimha ...... | 39 | 71 | 4 | 2,056 | 129 | 3 | 30.68 |
| D. N. Sardesai ....... | 30 | 55 | 4 | 2,001 | 212 | 5 | 39.23 |

## PAKISTAN

| | T | I | NO | R | HI | 100s | Avge |
|---|---|---|---|---|---|---|---|
| Javed Miandad ...... | 109 | 165 | 18 | 8,064 | 280* | 22 | 54.85 |
| Zaheer Abbas........ | 78 | 124 | 11 | 5,062 | 274 | 12 | 44.79 |
| Mudassar Nazar ..... | 76 | 116 | 8 | 4,114 | 231 | 10 | 38.09 |
| Majid Khan ......... | 63 | 106 | 5 | 3,931 | 167 | 8 | 38.92 |
| Hanif Mohammad .... | 55 | 97 | 8 | 3,915 | 337 | 12 | 43.98 |
| Imran Khan ......... | 85 | 123 | 24 | 3,692 | 136 | 6 | 37.29 |
| Mushtaq Mohammad . | 57 | 100 | 7 | 3,643 | 201 | 10 | 39.17 |
| Asif Iqbal........... | 58 | 99 | 7 | 3,575 | 175 | 11 | 38.85 |
| Salim Malik ......... | 63 | 90 | 16 | 3,146 | 119* | 8 | 42.51 |
| Saeed Ahmed ........ | 41 | 78 | 4 | 2,991 | 172 | 5 | 40.41 |
| Wasim Raja ......... | 57 | 92 | 14 | 2,821 | 125 | 4 | 36.16 |
| Mohsin Khan........ | 48 | 79 | 6 | 2,709 | 200 | 7 | 37.10 |
| Sadiq Mohammad ... | 41 | 74 | 2 | 2,579 | 166 | 5 | 35.81 |
| Shoaib Mohammad ... | 35 | 53 | 6 | 2,307 | 203* | 7 | 49.08 |
| Imtiaz Ahmed ....... | 41 | 72 | 1 | 2,079 | 209 | 3 | 29.28 |

SRI LANKA: The highest aggregate is 1,824, average 36.48, by A. Ranatunga in 30 Tests.

## HIGHEST AVERAGES

(Qualification: 20 innings)

| Avge | | T | I | NO | R | HI | 100s |
|---|---|---|---|---|---|---|---|
| 99.94 | D. G. Bradman (A) ....... | 52 | 80 | 10 | 6,996 | 334 | 29 |
| 60.97 | R. G. Pollock (SA) ....... | 23 | 41 | 4 | 2,256 | 274 | 7 |
| 60.83 | G. A. Headley (WI) ....... | 22 | 40 | 4 | 2,190 | 270* | 10 |
| 60.73 | H. Sutcliffe (E) ........... | 54 | 84 | 9 | 4,555 | 194 | 16 |
| 59.23 | E. Paynter (E)............. | 20 | 31 | 5 | 1,540 | 243 | 4 |
| 58.67 | K. F. Barrington (E) ...... | 82 | 131 | 15 | 6,806 | 256 | 20 |
| 58.61 | E. D. Weekes (WI) ....... | 48 | 81 | 5 | 4,455 | 207 | 15 |
| 58.45 | W. R. Hammond (E) ...... | 85 | 140 | 16 | 7,249 | 336* | 22 |
| 57.78 | G. S. Sobers (WI) ......... | 93 | 160 | 21 | 8,032 | 365* | 26 |
| 56.94 | J. B. Hobbs (E)........... | 61 | 102 | 7 | 5,410 | 211 | 15 |
| 56.68 | C. L. Walcott (WI) ....... | 44 | 74 | 7 | 3,798 | 220 | 15 |
| 56.67 | L. Hutton (E) ............ | 79 | 138 | 15 | 6,971 | 364 | 19 |
| 55.00 | E. Tyldesley (E) .......... | 14 | 20 | 2 | 990 | 122 | 3 |
| 54.93 | A. H. Jones (NZ) ......... | 20 | 36 | 5 | 1,703 | 186 | 5 |
| 54.85 | Javed Miandad (P)........ | 109 | 165 | 18 | 8,064 | 280* | 22 |
| 54.20 | C. A. Davis (WI) ......... | 15 | 29 | 5 | 1,301 | 183 | 4 |
| 53.94 | M. J. Greatbatch (NZ) .... | 14 | 21 | 4 | 917 | 146* | 2 |
| 53.86 | G. S. Chappell (A) ........ | 87 | 151 | 19 | 7,110 | 247* | 24 |

| Avge | | T | I | NO | R | HI | 100s |
|------|--|---|---|----|---|----|------|
| 53.81 | A. D. Nourse (SA) ........ | 34 | 62 | 7 | 2,960 | 231 | 9 |
| 52.95 | R. A. Smith (E) ......... | 28 | 53 | 13 | 2,118 | 148* | 6 |
| 52.83 | M. A. Taylor (A) ......... | 25 | 46 | 3 | 2,272 | 219 | 7 |
| 52.29 | A. R. Border (A)........... | 125 | 215 | 38 | 9,257 | 205 | 23 |
| 51.62 | J. Ryder (A) ........... | 20 | 32 | 5 | 1,394 | 201* | 3 |
| 51.31 | M. Azharuddin (I) ...... | 41 | 61 | 3 | 2,976 | 199 | 10 |
| 51.12 | S. M. Gavaskar (I) ....... | 125 | 214 | 16 | 10,122 | 236* | 34 |
| 50.23 | I. V. A. Richards (WI)..... | 121 | 182 | 12 | 8,540 | 291 | 24 |
| 50.06 | D. C. S. Compton (E) ..... | 78 | 131 | 15 | 5,807 | 278 | 17 |

## MOST HUNDREDS

| Total | | E | A | SA | WI | NZ | I | P | SL |
|-------|--|---|---|----|----|----|---|---|----|
| 34 | S. M. Gavaskar (I)............... | 4 | 8 | — | 13 | 2 | — | 5 | 2 |
| 29 | D. G. Bradman (A)............... | 19 | — | 4 | 2 | — | 4 | — | — |
| 26 | G. S. Sobers (WI)............... | 10 | 4 | — | — | 1 | 8 | 3 | — |
| 24 | G. S. Chappell (A)............... | 9 | — | — | 5 | 3 | 1 | 6 | 0 |
| 24 | I. V. A. Richards (WI) ...... | 8 | 5 | — | — | 1 | 8 | 2 | — |
| 23 | A. R. Border (A) ............... | 7 | — | — | 2 | 4 | 4 | 6 | 0 |
| 22 | W. R. Hammond (E) ......... | — | 9 | 6 | 1 | 4 | 2 | — | — |
| 22 | M. C. Cowdrey (E)............... | — | 5 | 3 | 6 | 2 | 3 | 3 | — |
| 22 | G. Boycott (E) ............... | — | 7 | 1 | 5 | 2 | 4 | 3 | — |
| 22 | Javed Miandad (P)............... | 1 | 6 | — | 2 | 7 | 5 | — | 1 |
| 21 | R. N. Harvey (A)............... | 6 | — | 8 | 3 | — | 4 | 0 | — |
| 20 | K. F. Barrington (E) ......... | — | 5 | 2 | 3 | 3 | 3 | 4 | — |

## CARRYING BAT THROUGH TEST INNINGS

*(Figures in brackets show side's total)*

| | | | |
|--|--|--|--|
| A. B. Tancred ...... | 26* (47) | South Africa v England at Cape Town .. | 1888-89 |
| J. E. Barrett ....... | 67* (176) | Australia v England at Lord's ........... | 1890 |
| R. Abel ............ | 132* (307) | England v Australia at Sydney ......... | 1891-92 |
| P. F. Warner ...... | 132* (237) | England v South Africa at Johannesburg . | 1898-99 |
| W. W. Armstrong ... | 159* (309) | Australia v South Africa at Johannesburg | 1902-03 |
| J. W. Zulch........ | 43* (103) | South Africa v England at Cape Town .. | 1909-10 |
| W. Bardsley ....... | 193* (383) | Australia v England at Lord's ........... | 1926 |
| W. M. Woodfull ... | 30* (66)‡ | Australia v England at Brisbane ........ | 1928-29 |
| W. M. Woodfull ... | 73* (193)† | Australia v England at Adelaide ........ | 1932-33 |
| W. A. Brown ...... | 206* (422) | Australia v England at Lord's ........... | 1938 |
| L. Hutton ........ | 202* (344) | England v West Indies at The Oval ..... | 1950 |
| L. Hutton ........ | 156* (272) | England v Australia at Adelaide ........ | 1950-51 |
| Nazar Mohammad ... | 124* (331) | Pakistan v India at Lucknow ........... | 1952-53 |
| F. M. M. Worrell ... | 191* (372) | West Indies v England at Nottingham ... | 1957 |
| T. L. Goddard ..... | 56* (99) | South Africa v Australia at Cape Town . | 1957-58 |
| D. J. McGlew...... | 127* (292) | South Africa v New Zealand at Durban . | 1961-62 |
| C. C. Hunte ....... | 60* (131) | West Indies v Australia at Port-of-Spain . | 1964-65 |
| G. M. Turner ..... | 43* (131) | New Zealand v England at Lord's ...... | 1969 |
| W. M. Lawry ..... | 49* (107) | Australia v India at Delhi ............. | 1969-70 |
| W. M. Lawry ..... | 60* (116)† | Australia v England at Sydney ......... | 1970-71 |
| G. M. Turner ..... | 223* (386) | New Zealand v West Indies at Kingston . | 1971-72 |
| I. R. Redpath ..... | 159* (346) | Australia v New Zealand at Auckland ... | 1973-74 |
| G. Boycott........ | 99* (215) | England v Australia at Perth ........... | 1979-80 |
| S. M. Gavaskar .... | 127* (286) | India v Pakistan at Faisalabad ......... | 1982-83 |
| Mudassar Nazar .... | 152* (323) | Pakistan v India at Lahore ........... | 1982-83 |
| S. Wettimuny ...... | 63* (144) | Sri Lanka v New Zealand at Christchurch | 1982-83 |

| D. C. Boon ........ | 58* (103) | Australia v New Zealand at Auckland ... | 1985-86 |
| D. L. Haynes ...... | 88* (211) | West Indies v Pakistan at Karachi ...... | 1986-87 |
| G. A. Gooch ...... | 154* (252) | England v West Indies at Leeds ........ | 1991 |
| D. L. Haynes ...... | 75* (176) | West Indies v England at The Oval ..... | 1991 |

† *One man absent.*     ‡ *Two men absent.*

*Notes:* G. M. Turner (223*) holds the record for the highest score by a player carrying his bat through a Test innings. He is also the youngest player to do so, being 22 years 63 days old when he first achieved the feat (1969).

G. A. Gooch (61.11%) holds the record for the highest percentage of a side's total by anyone carrying his bat throughout a Test innings.

Nazar Mohammad and Mudassar Nazar provide the only instance of a father and son carrying their bat through a Test innings.

D. L. Haynes (55 and 105) opened the batting and was last man out in each innings for West Indies v New Zealand at Dunedin, 1979-80.

## FASTEST FIFTIES

*Minutes*

| 28 | J. T. Brown ...... | England v Australia at Melbourne ........... | 1894-95 |
| 29 | S. A. Durani ...... | India v England at Kanpur ............. | 1963-64 |
| 30 | E. A. V. Williams.. | West Indies v England at Bridgetown ........ | 1947-48 |
| 30 | B. R. Taylor ...... | New Zealand v West Indies at Auckland ..... | 1968-69 |
| 33 | C. A. Roach ...... | West Indies v England at The Oval ........ | 1933 |
| 34 | C. R. Browne ..... | West Indies v England at Georgetown ........ | 1929-30 |

The fastest fifties in terms of balls received (where recorded) are:

*Balls*

| 30 | Kapil Dev ........ | India v Pakistan at Karachi (2nd Test) ....... | 1982-83 |
| 32 | I. T. Botham ...... | England v New Zealand at The Oval ......... | 1986 |
| 32 | I. V. A. Richards .. | West Indies v India at Kingston ........... | 1982-83 |
| 33 | R. C. Fredericks ... | West Indies v Australia at Perth............. | 1975-76 |
| 33 | Kapil Dev ........ | India v Pakistan at Karachi ............. | 1978-79 |
| 33 | Kapil Dev ........ | India v England at Manchester ........... | 1982 |
| 33 | I. V. A. Richards .. | West Indies v England at St John's .......... | 1985-86 |

## FASTEST HUNDREDS

*Minutes*

| 70 | J. M. Gregory ..... | Australia v South Africa at Johannesburg ..... | 1921-22 |
| 75 | G. L. Jessop ...... | England v Australia at The Oval ........... | 1902 |
| 78 | R. Benaud ...... | Australia v West Indies at Kingston ........ | 1954-55 |
| 80 | J. H. Sinclair...... | South Africa v Australia at Cape Town ..... | 1902-03 |
| 81 | I. V. A. Richards .. | West Indies v England at St John's ......... | 1985-86 |
| 86 | B. R. Taylor ...... | New Zealand v West Indies at Auckland ..... | 1968-69 |

The fastest hundreds in terms of balls received (where recorded) are:

*Balls*

| 56 | I. V. A. Richards .. | West Indies v England at St John's .......... | 1985-86 |
| 67 | J. M. Gregory ..... | Australia v South Africa at Johannesburg .... | 1921-22 |
| 71 | R. C. Fredericks ... | West Indies v Australia at Perth............. | 1975-76 |
| 74 | Kapil Dev ........ | India v Sri Lanka at Kanpur................ | 1986-87 |
| 76 | G. L. Jessop ...... | England v Australia at The Oval ........... | 1902 |
| 77 | Majid Khan........ | Pakistan v New Zealand at Karachi .......... | 1976-77 |

## FASTEST DOUBLE-HUNDREDS

**Minutes**

| | | | |
|---|---|---|---|
| 214 | D. G. Bradman.... | Australia v England at Leeds ................ | 1930 |
| 223 | S. J. McCabe ..... | Australia v England at Nottingham ......... | 1938 |
| 226 | V. T. Trumper .... | Australia v South Africa at Adelaide ......... | 1910-11 |
| 234 | D. G. Bradman.... | Australia v England at Lord's .............. | 1930 |
| 240 | W. R. Hammond .. | England v New Zealand at Auckland ....... | 1932-33 |
| 241 | S. E. Gregory ..... | Australia v England at Sydney ............. | 1894-95 |
| 245 | D. C. S. Compton.. | England v Pakistan at Nottingham.......... | 1954 |

The fastest double-hundreds in terms of balls received (where recorded) are:

**Balls**

| | | | |
|---|---|---|---|
| 220 | I. T. Botham ...... | England v India at The Oval................ | 1982 |
| 232 | C. G. Greenidge ... | West Indies v England at Lord's............ | 1984 |
| 240 | C. H. Lloyd ...... | West Indies v India at Bombay ............ | 1974-75 |
| 241 | Zaheer Abbas ..... | Pakistan v India at Lahore ............... | 1982-83 |
| 242 | D. G. Bradman.... | Australia v England at The Oval .......... | 1934 |
| 242 | I. V. A. Richards .. | West Indies v Australia at Melbourne ....... | 1984-85 |

## FASTEST TRIPLE-HUNDREDS

**Minutes**

| | | | |
|---|---|---|---|
| 288 | W. R. Hammond .. | England v New Zealand at Auckland ....... | 1932-33 |
| 336 | D. G. Bradman.... | Australia v England at Leeds .............. | 1930 |

## MOST RUNS IN A DAY BY A BATSMAN

| | | | |
|---|---|---|---|
| 309 | D. G. Bradman ....... | Australia v England at Leeds .............. | 1930 |
| 295 | W. R. Hammond....... | England v New Zealand at Auckland ....... | 1932-33 |
| 273 | D. C. S. Compton ..... | England v Pakistan at Nottingham.......... | 1954 |
| 271 | D. G. Bradman ....... | Australia v England at Leeds .............. | 1934 |

## SLOWEST INDIVIDUAL BATTING

| | | | |
|---|---|---|---|
| 2* in 80 minutes | C. E. H. Croft, West Indies v Australia at Brisbane...... | | 1979-80 |
| 3* in 100 minutes | J. T. Murray, England v Australia at Sydney ........... | | 1962-63 |
| 5 in 102 minutes | Nawab of Pataudi jun, India v England at Bombay ...... | | 1972-73 |
| 7 in 123 minutes | G. Miller, England v Australia at Melbourne ......... | | 1978-79 |
| 9 in 125 minutes | T. W. Jarvis, New Zealand v India at Madras ......... | | 1964-65 |
| 10* in 133 minutes | T. G. Evans, England v Australia at Adelaide ......... | | 1946-47 |
| 16* in 147 minutes | D. B. Vengsarkar, India v Pakistan at Kanpur ......... | | 1979-80 |
| 17* in 166 minutes | G. M. Ritchie, Australia v India at Sydney............. | | 1985-86 |
| 18 in 194 minutes | W. R. Playle, New Zealand v England at Leeds......... | | 1958 |
| 19 in 217 minutes | M. D. Crowe, New Zealand v Sri Lanka at Colombo (SSC) | | 1983-84 |
| 28* in 250 minutes | J. W. Burke, Australia v England at Brisbane.......... | | 1958-59 |
| 31 in 264 minutes | K. D. Mackay, Australia v England at Lord's .......... | | 1956 |
| 34* in 271 minutes | Younis Ahmed, Pakistan v India at Ahmedabad ........ | | 1986-87 |
| 35 in 332 minutes | C. J. Tavaré, England v India at Madras ............. | | 1981-82 |
| 55 in 336 minutes | B. A. Edgar, New Zealand v Australia at Wellington .... | | 1981-82 |
| 57 in 346 minutes | G. S. Camacho, West Indies v England at Bridgetown ... | | 1967-68 |
| 58 in 367 minutes | Ijaz Butt, Pakistan v Australia at Karachi ............ | | 1959-60 |
| 60 in 390 minutes | D. N. Sardesai, India v West Indies at Bridgetown ..... | | 1961-62 |
| 62 in 408 minutes | Ramiz Raja, Pakistan v West Indies at Karachi......... | | 1986-87 |
| 68 in 458 minutes | T. E. Bailey, England v Australia at Brisbane.......... | | 1958-59 |
| 99 in 505 minutes | M. L. Jaisimha, India v Pakistan at Kanpur ........... | | 1960-61 |
| 105 in 575 minutes | D. J. McGlew, South Africa v Australia at Durban ...... | | 1957-58 |
| 114 in 591 minutes | Mudassar Nazar, Pakistan v England at Lahore ........ | | 1977-78 |
| 120* in 609 minutes | J. J. Crowe, New Zealand v Sri Lanka, Colombo (CCC) . | | 1986-87 |
| 158 in 648 minutes | C. T. Radley, England v New Zealand at Auckland ..... | | 1977-78 |
| 163 in 720 minutes | Shoaib Mohammad, Pakistan v New Zealand at Wellington | | 1988-89 |
| 337 in 970 minutes | Hanif Mohammad, Pakistan v West Indies at Bridgetown. | | 1957-58 |

## SLOWEST HUNDREDS

| | | |
|---|---|---|
| 557 minutes | Mudassar Nazar, Pakistan v England at Lahore . . . . . . . . . . . . . | 1977-78 |
| 545 minutes | D. J. McGlew, South Africa v Australia at Durban . . . . . . . . . . | 1957-58 |
| 515 minutes | J. J. Crowe, New Zealand v Sri Lanka, Colombo (CCC) . . . . . . | 1986-87 |
| 488 minutes | P. E. Richardson, England v South Africa at Johannesburg . . . . | 1956-57 |

*Notes:* The slowest hundred for any Test in England is 458 minutes (329 balls) by K. W. R. Fletcher, England v Pakistan, The Oval, 1974.

The slowest double-hundred in a Test was scored in 777 minutes (548 balls) by D. S. B. P. Kuruppu for Sri Lanka v New Zealand at Colombo (CCC), 1986-87, on his début. It is also the slowest-ever first-class double-hundred.

## HIGHEST PARTNERSHIPS FOR EACH WICKET

| | | | | |
|---|---|---|---|---|
| 413 for 1st | V. Mankad (231)/Pankaj Roy (173) . . . . . . . | I v NZ | Madras | 1955-56 |
| 451 for 2nd | W. H. Ponsford (266)/D. G. Bradman (244) . | A v E | The Oval | 1934 |
| 467 for 3rd | A. H. Jones (186)/M. D. Crowe (299) . . . . . | NZ v SL | Wellington | 1990-91 |
| 411 for 4th | P. B. H. May (285*)/M. C. Cowdrey (154) . . | E v WI | Birmingham | 1957 |
| 405 for 5th | S. G. Barnes (234)/D. G. Bradman (234) . . . | A v E | Sydney | 1946-47 |
| 346 for 6th | J. H. W. Fingleton (136)/D. G. Bradman (270) | A v E | Melbourne | 1936-37 |
| 347 for 7th | D. St E. Atkinson (219)/C. C. Depeiza (122) | WI v A | Bridgetown | 1954-55 |
| 246 for 8th | L. E. G. Ames (137)/G. O. B. Allen (122) . . | E v NZ | Lord's | 1931 |
| 190 for 9th | Asif Iqbal (146)/Intikhab Alam (51) . . . . . . | P v E | The Oval | 1967 |
| 151 for 10th | B. F. Hastings (110)/R. O. Collinge (68*) . . . | NZ v P | Auckland | 1972-73 |

## PARTNERSHIPS OF 300 AND OVER

| | | | | |
|---|---|---|---|---|
| 467 for 3rd | A. H. Jones (186)/M. D. Crowe (299) . . . . . . . . | NZ v SL | Wellington | 1990-91 |
| 451 for 2nd | W. H. Ponsford (266)/D. G. Bradman (244) . . | A v E | The Oval | 1934 |
| 451 for 3rd | Mudassar Nazar (231)/Javed Miandad (280*) . . | P v I | Hyderabad | 1982-83 |
| 446 for 2nd | C. C. Hunte (260)/G. S. Sobers (365*) . . . . . . . | WI v P | Kingston | 1957-58 |
| 413 for 1st | V. Mankad (231)/Pankaj Roy (173) . . . . . . . | I v NZ | Madras | 1955-56 |
| 411 for 4th | P. B. H. May (285*)/M. C. Cowdrey (154) . . | E v WI | Birmingham | 1957 |
| 405 for 5th | S. G. Barnes (234)/D. G. Bradman (234) . . . | A v E | Sydney | 1946-47 |
| 399 for 4th | G. S. Sobers (226)/F. M. M. Worrell (197*) . . | WI v E | Bridgetown | 1959-60 |
| 397 for 3rd | Qasim Omar (206)/Javed Miandad (203*) . . . . | P v SL | Faisalabad | 1985-86 |
| 388 for 4th | W. H. Ponsford (181)/D. G. Bradman (304) . . | A v E | Leeds | 1934 |
| 387 for 1st | G. M. Turner (259)/T. W. Jarvis (182) . . . . . | NZ v WI | Georgetown | 1971-72 |
| 382 for 2nd | L. Hutton (364)/M. Leyland (187) . . . . . . . . | E v A | The Oval | 1938 |
| 382 for 1st | W. M. Lawry (210)/R. B. Simpson (201) . . . . | A v WI | Bridgetown | 1964-65 |
| 370 for 3rd | W. J. Edrich (189)/D. C. S. Compton (208) . . | E v SA | Lord's | 1947 |
| 369 for 2nd | J. H. Edrich (310*)/K. F. Barrington (163) . . | E v NZ | Leeds | 1965 |
| 359 for 1st | L. Hutton (158)/C. Washbrook (195) . . . . . . . | E v SA | Johannesburg | 1948-49 |
| 351 for 2nd | G. A. Gooch (196)/D. I. Gower (157) . . . . . . . | E v A | The Oval | 1985 |
| 350 for 4th | Mushtaq Mohammad (201)/Asif Iqbal (175) . . | P v NZ | Dunedin | 1972-73 |
| 347 for 7th | D. St E. Atkinson (219)/C. C. Depeiza (122) . . | WI v A | Bridgetown | 1954-55 |
| 346 for 6th | J. H. Fingleton (136)/D. G. Bradman (270) . . | A v E | Melbourne | 1936-37 |
| 344* for 2nd | S. M. Gavaskar (182*)/D. B. Vengsarkar (157*) | I v WI | Calcutta | 1978-79 |
| 341 for 3rd | E. J. Barlow (201)/R. G. Pollock (175) . . . . . | SA v A | Adelaide | 1963-64 |
| 338 for 3rd | E. D. Weekes (206)/F. M. M. Worrell (167) . . | WI v E | Port-of-Spain | 1953-54 |
| 336 for 4th | W. M. Lawry (151)/K. D. Walters (242) . . . . | A v WI | Sydney | 1968-69 |
| 331 for 2nd | R. T. Robinson (148)/D. I. Gower (215) . . . . | E v A | Birmingham | 1985 |
| 329 for 1st | G. R. Marsh (138)/M. A. Taylor (219) . . . . . | A v E | Nottingham | 1989 |
| 323 for 1st | J. B. Hobbs (178)/W. Rhodes (179) . . . . . . . | E v A | Melbourne | 1911-12 |
| 319 for 3rd | A. Melville (189)/A. D. Nourse (149) . . . . . . | SA v E | Nottingham | 1947 |
| 316† for 3rd | G. R. Viswanath (222)/Yashpal Sharma (140) . | I v E | Madras | 1981-82 |
| 308 for 7th | Waqar Hassan (189)/Imtiaz Ahmed (209) . . . . | P v NZ | Lahore | 1955-56 |

| | | | | | |
|---|---|---|---|---|---|
| 308 | for 3rd | R. B. Richardson (154)/I. V. A. Richards (178) | WI v A | St John's | 1983-84 |
| 308 | for 3rd | G. A. Gooch (333)/A. J. Lamb (139) ........ | E v I | Lord's | 1990 |
| 303 | for 3rd | I. V. A. Richards (232)/A. I. Kallicharran (97) . | WI v E | Nottingham | 1976 |
| 301 | for 2nd | A. R. Morris (182)/D. G. Bradman (173*) ..... | A v E | Leeds | 1948 |

† *415 runs were scored for this wicket in two separate partnerships: D. B. Vengsarkar retired hurt when he and Viswanath had added 99 runs.*

## BOWLING RECORDS

## MOST WICKETS IN AN INNINGS

| | | | |
|---|---|---|---|
| 10-53 | J. C. Laker ...... | England v Australia at Manchester.......... | 1956 |
| 9-28 | G. A. Lohmann ... | England v South Africa at Johannesburg ..... | 1895-96 |
| 9-37 | J. C. Laker ...... | England v Australia at Manchester.......... | 1956 |
| 9-52 | R. J. Hadlee ..... | New Zealand v Australia at Brisbane......... | 1985-86 |
| 9-56 | Abdul Qadir ..... | Pakistan v England at Lahore ............. | 1987-88 |
| 9-69 | J. M. Patel ...... | India v Australia at Kanpur .............. | 1959-60 |
| 9-83 | Kapil Dev ....... | India v West Indies at Ahmedabad ......... | 1983-84 |
| 9-86 | Sarfraz Nawaz .... | Pakistan v Australia at Melbourne .......... | 1978-79 |
| 9-95 | J. M. Noreiga .... | West Indies v India at Port-of-Spain ........ | 1970-71 |
| 9-102 | S. P. Gupte ...... | India v West Indies at Kanpur ............ | 1958-59 |
| 9-103 | S. F. Barnes ..... | England v South Africa at Johannesburg ..... | 1913-14 |
| 9-113 | H. J. Tayfield .... | South Africa v England at Johannesburg ..... | 1956-57 |
| 9-121 | A. A. Mailey ..... | Australia v England at Melbourne .......... | 1920-21 |
| 8-7 | G. A. Lohmann ... | England v South Africa at Port Elizabeth .... | 1895-96 |
| 8-11 | J. Briggs ....... | England v South Africa at Cape Town ....... | 1888-89 |
| 8-29 | S. F. Barnes ..... | England v South Africa at The Oval ........ | 1912 |
| 8-29 | C. E. H. Croft.... | West Indies v Pakistan at Port-of-Spain ..... | 1976-77 |
| 8-31 | F. Laver........ | Australia v England at Manchester.......... | 1909 |
| 8-31 | F. S. Trueman .... | England v India at Manchester ............ | 1952 |
| 8-34 | I. T. Botham ..... | England v Pakistan at Lord's ............. | 1978 |
| 8-35 | G. A. Lohmann ... | England v Australia at Sydney ............ | 1886-87 |
| 8-38 | L. R. Gibbs ...... | West Indies v India at Bridgetown ......... | 1961-62 |
| 8-43† | A. E. Trott ...... | Australia v England at Adelaide ........... | 1894-95 |
| 8-43 | H. Verity ....... | England v Australia at Lord's ............ | 1934 |
| 8-43 | R. G. D. Willis ... | England v Australia at Leeds ............. | 1981 |
| 8-45 | C. E. L. Ambrose .. | West Indies v England at Bridgetown ....... | 1989-90 |
| 8-51 | D. L. Underwood .. | England v Pakistan at Lord's ............. | 1974 |
| 8-52 | V. Mankad ...... | India v Pakistan at Delhi ............... | 1952-53 |
| 8-53 | G. B. Lawrence ... | South Africa v New Zealand at Johannesburg .. | 1961-62 |
| 8-53† | R. A. L. Massie ... | Australia v England at Lord's ............ | 1972 |
| 8-55 | V. Mankad ...... | India v England at Madras .............. | 1951-52 |
| 8-56 | S. F. Barnes...... | England v South Africa at Johannesburg ..... | 1913-14 |
| 8-58 | G. A. Lohmann ... | England v Australia at Sydney ............ | 1891-92 |
| 8-58 | Imran Khan ..... | Pakistan v Sri Lanka at Lahore ........... | 1981-82 |
| 8-59 | C. Blythe ....... | England v South Africa at Leeds .......... | 1907 |
| 8-59 | A. A. Mallett..... | Australia v Pakistan at Adelaide .......... | 1972-73 |
| 8-60 | Imran Khan ..... | Pakistan v India at Karachi ............. | 1982-83 |
| 8-61† | N. D. Hirwani .... | India v West Indies at Madras ........... | 1987-88 |
| 8-65 | H. Trumble ...... | Australia v England at The Oval .......... | 1902 |
| 8-68 | W. Rhodes....... | England v Australia at Melbourne .......... | 1903-04 |
| 8-69 | H. J. Tayfield .... | South Africa v England at Durban ......... | 1956-57 |
| 8-69 | Sikander Bakht ... | Pakistan v India at Delhi ............... | 1979-80 |
| 8-70 | S. J. Snooke ..... | South Africa v England at Johannesburg ..... | 1905-06 |
| 8-71 | G. D. McKenzie ... | Australia v West Indies at Melbourne ....... | 1968-69 |
| 8-72 | S. Venkataraghavan | India v New Zealand at Delhi ............ | 1964-65 |
| 8-75† | N. D. Hirwani .... | India v West Indies at Madras ........... | 1987-88 |
| 8-76 | E. A. S. Prasanna . | India v New Zealand at Auckland ......... | 1975-76 |
| 8-79 | B. S. Chandrasekhar | India v England at Delhi ............... | 1972-73 |
| 8-81 | L. C. Braund ..... | England v Australia at Melbourne .......... | 1903-04 |
| 8-83 | J. R. Ratnayeke ... | Sri Lanka v Pakistan at Sialkot .......... | 1985-86 |
| 8-84† | R. A. L. Massie ... | Australia v England at Lord's ............ | 1972 |
| 8-85 | Kapil Dev ....... | India v Pakistan at Lahore .............. | 1982-83 |
| 8-86 | A. W. Greig ...... | England v West Indies at Port-of-Spain ...... | 1973-74 |

| | | | |
|---|---|---|---|
| 8-87 | M. G. Hughes . . . . . | Australia v West Indies at Perth . . . . . . . . . . . . | 1988-89 |
| 8-92 | M. A. Holding . . . . . | West Indies v England at The Oval . . . . . . . . . | 1976 |
| 8-94 | T. Richardson . . . . . | England v Australia at Sydney . . . . . . . . . . . . . | 1897-98 |
| 8-97 | C. J. McDermott . . . | Australia v England at Perth . . . . . . . . . . . . . . | 1990-91 |
| 8-103 | I. T. Botham . . . . . | England v West Indies at Lord's . . . . . . . . . . . | 1984 |
| 8-104† | A. L. Valentine . . . . | West Indies v England at Manchester . . . . . . . | 1950 |
| 8-106 | Kapil Dev . . . . . . | India v Australia at Adelaide . . . . . . . . . . . . . | 1985-86 |
| 8-107 | B. J. T. Bosanquet . . | England v Australia at Nottingham . . . . . . . . | 1905 |
| 8-107 | N. A. Foster . . . . . . | England v Pakistan at Leeds . . . . . . . . . . . . . | 1987 |
| 8-112 | G. F. Lawson . . . . . | Australia v West Indies at Adelaide . . . . . . . . | 1984-85 |
| 8-126 | J. C. White . . . . . . | England v Australia at Adelaide . . . . . . . . . . | 1928-29 |
| 8-141 | C. J. McDermott . . . | Australia v England at Manchester . . . . . . . . | 1985 |
| 8-143 | M. H. N. Walker . . | Australia v England at Melbourne . . . . . . . . . . | 1974-75 |

† *On Test début.*

## OUTSTANDING ANALYSES

| | O | M | R | W | | |
|---|---|---|---|---|---|---|
| J. C. Laker (E) | 51.2 | 23 | 53 | 10 | v Australia at Manchester . . . . . | 1956 |
| G. A. Lohmann (E) | 14.2 | 6 | 28 | 9 | v South Africa at Johannesburg . . . | 1895-96 |
| J. C. Laker (E) | 16.4 | 4 | 37 | 9 | v Australia at Manchester . . . . . | 1956 |
| G. A. Lohmann (E) | 9.4 | 5 | 7 | 8 | v South Africa at Port Elizabeth | 1895-96 |
| J. Briggs (E) | 14.2 | 5 | 11 | 8 | v South Africa at Cape Town . . . | 1888-89 |
| J. Briggs (E) | 19.1 | 11 | 17 | 7 | v South Africa at Cape Town . . . | 1888-89 |
| M. A. Noble (A) | 7.4 | 2 | 17 | 7 | v England at Melbourne . . . . . . . | 1901-02 |
| W. Rhodes (E) | 11 | 3 | 17 | 7 | v Australia at Birmingham . . . . . | 1902 |
| A. E. R. Gilligan (E) | 6.3 | 4 | 7 | 6 | v South Africa at Birmingham . | 1924 |
| S. Haigh (E) | 11.4 | 6 | 11 | 6 | v South Africa at Cape Town . . . | 1898-99 |
| D. L. Underwood (E) | 11.6 | 7 | 12 | 6 | v New Zealand at Christchurch | 1970-71 |
| S. L. V. Raju (I) | 17.5 | 13 | 12 | 6 | v Sri Lanka at Chandigarh . . . . | 1990-91 |
| H. J. Tayfield (SA) | 14 | 7 | 13 | 6 | v New Zealand at Johannesburg. | 1953-54 |
| C. T. B. Turner (A) | 18 | 11 | 15 | 6 | v England at Sydney . . . . . . . . . | 1886-87 |
| M. H. N. Walker (A) | 16 | 8 | 15 | 6 | v Pakistan at Sydney . . . . . . . . . | 1972-73 |
| E. R. H. Toshack (A) | 2.3 | 1 | 2 | 5 | v India at Brisbane . . . . . . . . . . | 1947-48 |
| H. Ironmonger (A) | 7.2 | 5 | 6 | 5 | v South Africa at Melbourne . . . | 1931-32 |
| Pervez Sajjad (P) | 12 | 8 | 5 | 4 | v New Zealand at Rawalpindi. . | 1964-65 |
| K. Higgs (E) | 9 | 7 | 5 | 4 | v New Zealand at Christchurch . | 1965-66 |
| P. H. Edmonds (E) | 8 | 6 | 6 | 4 | v Pakistan at Lord's . . . . . . . . . | 1978 |
| J. C. White (E) | 6.3 | 2 | 7 | 4 | v Australia at Brisbane . . . . . . . | 1928-29 |
| J. H. Wardle (E) | 5 | 2 | 7 | 4 | v Australia at Manchester . . . . . | 1953 |
| R. Appleyard (E) | 6 | 3 | 7 | 4 | v New Zealand at Auckland . . . | 1954-55 |
| R. Benaud (A) | 3.4 | 3 | 0 | 3 | v India at Delhi · . . . . . . . . . . . . | 1959-60 |

## MOST WICKETS IN A MATCH

| | | | |
|---|---|---|---|
| 19-90 | J. C. Laker . . . . . . | England v Australia at Manchester . . . . . . . . . | 1956 |
| 17-159 | S. F. Barnes . . . . . . | England v South Africa at Johannesburg . . . . . . . | 1913-14 |
| 16-136† | N. D. Hirwani . . . . | India v West Indies at Madras . . . . . . . . . . . . . | 1987-88 |
| 16-137† | R. A. L. Massie . . . | Australia v England at Lord's . . . . . . . . . . . . . . | 1972 |
| 15-28 | J. Briggs . . . . . . . . | England v South Africa at Cape Town . . . . . . . | 1888-89 |
| 15-45 | G. A. Lohmann . . . . | England v South Africa at Port Elizabeth . . . . | 1895-96 |
| 15-99 | C. Blythe . . . . . . . . | England v South Africa at Leeds . . . . . . . . . . | 1907 |
| 15-104 | H. Verity . . . . . . . . | England v Australia at Lord's . . . . . . . . . . . . . | 1934 |
| 15-123 | R. J. Hadlee . . . . . | New Zealand v Australia at Brisbane . . . . . . . | 1985-86 |
| 15-124 | W. Rhodes . . . . . . . | England v Australia at Melbourne . . . . . . . . . . | 1903-04 |
| 14-90 | F. R. Spofforth . . . | Australia v England at The Oval . . . . . . . . . . | 1882 |
| 14-99 | A. V. Bedser . . . . . | England v Australia at Nottingham . . . . . . . . | 1953 |
| 14-102 | W. Bates . . . . . . . . | England v Australia at Melbourne . . . . . . . . . . | 1882-83 |
| 14-116 | Imran Khan . . . . . . | Pakistan v Sri Lanka at Lahore . . . . . . . . . . . | 1981-82 |
| 14-124 | J. M. Patel . . . . . . . | India v Australia at Kanpur . . . . . . . . . . . . . . | 1959-60 |
| 14-144 | S. F. Barnes . . . . . . | England v South Africa at Durban . . . . . . . . . | 1913-14 |
| 14-149 | M. A. Holding . . . . | West Indies v England at The Oval . . . . . . . . | 1976 |
| 14-199 | C. V. Grimmett . . . | Australia v South Africa at Adelaide . . . . . . . . | 1931-32 |

† *On Test début.*

*Notes:* The best for South Africa is 13-165 by H. J. Tayfield against Australia at Melbourne, 1952-53.

The best for Sri Lanka is 9-125 by R. J. Ratnayake against India at Colombo (PSS), 1985-86.

## MOST WICKETS IN A SERIES

|  | T | R | W | Avge |  |  |
|---|---|---|---|---|---|---|
| S. F. Barnes | 4 | 536 | 49 | 10.93 | England v South Africa. | 1913-14 |
| J. C. Laker | 5 | 442 | 46 | 9.60 | England v Australia.... | 1956 |
| C. V. Grimmett | 5 | 642 | 44 | 14.59 | Australia v South Africa | 1935-36 |
| T. M. Alderman | 6 | 893 | 42 | 21.26 | Australia v England.... | 1981 |
| R. M. Hogg | 6 | 527 | 41 | 12.85 | Australia v England.... | 1978-79 |
| T. M. Alderman | 6 | 712 | 41 | 17.36 | Australia v England.... | 1989 |
| Imran Khan | 6 | 558 | 40 | 13.95 | Pakistan v India | 1982-83 |
| A. V. Bedser | 5 | 682 | 39 | 17.48 | England v Australia.... | 1953 |
| D. K. Lillee | 6 | 870 | 39 | 22.30 | Australia v England.... | 1981 |
| M. W. Tate | 5 | 881 | 38 | 23.18 | England v Australia.... | 1924-25 |
| W. J. Whitty | 5 | 632 | 37 | 17.08 | Australia v South Africa | 1910-11 |
| H. J. Tayfield | 5 | 636 | 37 | 17.18 | South Africa v England. | 1956-57 |
| A. E. E. Vogler | 5 | 783 | 36 | 21.75 | South Africa v England. | 1909-10 |
| A. A. Mailey | 5 | 946 | 36 | 26.27 | Australia v England.... | 1920-21 |
| G. A. Lohmann | 3 | 203 | 35 | 5.80 | England v South Africa. | 1895-96 |
| B. S. Chandrasekhar | 5 | 662 | 35 | 18.91 | India v England | 1972-73 |
| M. D. Marshall | 5 | 443 | 35 | 12.65 | West Indies v England | 1988 |

## MOST WICKETS IN A CAREER

(Qualification: 100 wickets)

### ENGLAND

|  | T | Balls | R | W | Avge | 5W/i | 10W/m |
|---|---|---|---|---|---|---|---|
| I. T. Botham | 99 | 21,539 | 10,741 | 380 | 28.26 | 27 | 4 |
| R. G. D. Willis | 90 | 17,357 | 8,190 | 325 | 25.20 | 16 | — |
| F. S. Trueman | 67 | 15,178 | 6,625 | 307 | 21.57 | 17 | 3 |
| D. L. Underwood | 86 | 21,862 | 7,674 | 297 | 25.83 | 17 | 6 |
| J. B. Statham | 70 | 16,056 | 6,261 | 252 | 24.84 | 9 | 1 |
| A. V. Bedser | 51 | 15,918 | 5,876 | 236 | 24.89 | 15 | 5 |
| J. A. Snow | 49 | 12,021 | 5,387 | 202 | 26.66 | 8 | 1 |
| J. C. Laker | 46 | 12,027 | 4,101 | 193 | 21.24 | 9 | 3 |
| S. F. Barnes | 27 | 7,873 | 3,106 | 189 | 16.43 | 24 | 7 |
| G. A. R. Lock | 49 | 13,147 | 4,451 | 174 | 25.58 | 9 | 3 |
| M. W. Tate | 39 | 12,523 | 4,055 | 155 | 26.16 | 7 | 1 |
| F. J. Titmus | 53 | 15,118 | 4,931 | 153 | 32.22 | 7 | — |
| H. Verity | 40 | 11,173 | 3,510 | 144 | 24.37 | 5 | 2 |
| C. M. Old | 46 | 8,858 | 4,020 | 143 | 28.11 | 4 | — |
| A. W. Greig | 58 | 9,802 | 4,541 | 141 | 32.20 | 6 | 2 |
| G. R. Dilley | 41 | 8,192 | 4,107 | 138 | 29.76 | 6 | — |
| J. E. Emburey | 60 | 14,227 | 5,105 | 138 | 36.99 | 6 | — |
| T. E. Bailey | 61 | 9,712 | 3,856 | 132 | 29.21 | 5 | 1 |
| W. Rhodes | 58 | 8,231 | 3,425 | 127 | 26.96 | 6 | 1 |
| P. H. Edmonds | 51 | 12,028 | 4,273 | 125 | 34.18 | 2 | — |
| D. A. Allen | 39 | 11,297 | 3,779 | 122 | 30.97 | 4 | — |
| R. Illingworth | 61 | 11,934 | 3,807 | 122 | 31.20 | 3 | — |
| J. Briggs | 33 | 5,332 | 2,094 | 118 | 17.74 | 9 | 4 |
| G. G. Arnold | 34 | 7,650 | 3,254 | 115 | 28.29 | 6 | — |
| G. A. Lohmann | 18 | 3,821 | 1,205 | 112 | 10.75 | 9 | 5 |
| D. V. P. Wright | 34 | 8,135 | 4,224 | 108 | 39.11 | 6 | 1 |
| R. Peel | 20 | 5,216 | 1,715 | 102 | 16.81 | 6 | 2 |
| J. H. Wardle | 28 | 6,597 | 2,080 | 102 | 20.39 | 5 | 1 |
| C. Blythe | 19 | 4,546 | 1,863 | 100 | 18.63 | 9 | 4 |

## AUSTRALIA

|  | T | Balls | R | W | Avge | 5W/i | 10W/m |
|---|---|---|---|---|---|---|---|
| D. K. Lillee ......... | 70 | 18,467 | 8,493 | 355 | 23.92 | 23 | 7 |
| R. Benaud .......... | 63 | 19,108 | 6,704 | 248 | 27.03 | 16 | 1 |
| G. D. McKenzie ..... | 60 | 17,681 | 7,328 | 246 | 29.78 | 16 | 3 |
| R. R. Lindwall ..... | 61 | 13,650 | 5,251 | 228 | 23.03 | 12 | — |
| C. V. Grimmett ...... | 37 | 14,513 | 5,231 | 216 | 24.21 | 21 | 7 |
| J. R. Thomson ....... | 51 | 10,535 | 5,601 | 200 | 28.00 | 8 | — |
| A. K. Davidson ..... | 44 | 11,587 | 3,819 | 186 | 20.53 | 14 | 2 |
| G. F. Lawson ........ | 46 | 11,118 | 5,501 | 180 | 30.56 | 11 | 2 |
| K. R. Miller ......... | 55 | 10,461 | 3,906 | 170 | 22.97 | 7 | 1 |
| T. M. Alderman .... | 41 | 10,181 | 4,616 | 170 | 27.15 | 14 | 1 |
| W. A. Johnston ..... | 40 | 11,048 | 3,826 | 160 | 23.91 | 7 | — |
| W. J. O'Reilly ....... | 27 | 10,024 | 3,254 | 144 | 22.59 | 11 | 3 |
| H. Trumble ......... | 32 | 8,099 | 3,072 | 141 | 21.78 | 9 | 3 |
| M. H. N. Walker .... | 34 | 10,094 | 3,792 | 138 | 27.47 | 6 | — |
| A. A. Mallett ....... | 38 | 9,990 | 3,940 | 132 | 29.84 | 6 | 1 |
| B. Yardley .......... | 33 | 8,909 | 3,986 | 126 | 31.63 | 6 | 1 |
| R. M. Hogg ........ | 38 | 7,633 | 3,503 | 123 | 28.47 | 6 | 2 |
| M. G. Hughes ....... | 32 | 7,224 | 3,643 | 122 | 29.86 | 5 | 1 |
| C. J. McDermott .... | 31 | 6,770 | 3,659 | 122 | 29.99 | 6 | 1 |
| M. A. Noble ........ | 42 | 7,159 | 3,025 | 121 | 25.00 | 9 | 2 |
| I. W. Johnson ....... | 45 | 8,780 | 3,182 | 109 | 29.19 | 3 | — |
| G. Giffen .......... | 31 | 6,391 | 2,791 | 103 | 27.09 | 7 | 1 |
| A. N. Connolly ...... | 29 | 7,818 | 2,981 | 102 | 29.22 | 4 | — |
| C. T. B. Turner ...... | 17 | 5,179 | 1,670 | 101 | 16.53 | 11 | 2 |

## SOUTH AFRICA

|  | T | Balls | R | W | Avge | 5W/i | 10W/m |
|---|---|---|---|---|---|---|---|
| H. J. Tayfield ........ | 37 | 13,568 | 4,405 | 170 | 25.91 | 14 | 2 |
| T. L. Goddard ....... | 41 | 11,736 | 3,226 | 123 | 26.22 | 5 | — |
| P. M. Pollock ........ | 28 | 6,522 | 2,806 | 116 | 24.18 | 9 | 1 |
| N. A. T. Adcock ..... | 26 | 6,391 | 2,195 | 104 | 21.10 | 5 | — |

## WEST INDIES

|  | T | Balls | R | W | Avge | 5W/i | 10W/m |
|---|---|---|---|---|---|---|---|
| M. D. Marshall ...... | 81 | 17,584 | 7,876 | 376 | 20.94 | 22 | 4 |
| L. R. Gibbs ......... | 79 | 27,115 | 8,989 | 309 | 29.09 | 18 | 2 |
| J. Garner ........... | 58 | 13,169 | 5,433 | 259 | 20.97 | 7 | — |
| M. A. Holding ...... | 60 | 12,680 | 5,898 | 249 | 23.68 | 13 | 2 |
| G. S. Sobers ........ | 93 | 21,599 | 7,999 | 235 | 34.03 | 6 | — |
| A. M. E. Roberts..... | 47 | 11,136 | 5,174 | 202 | 25.61 | 11 | 2 |
| W. W. Hall ......... | 48 | 10,421 | 5,066 | 192 | 26.38 | 9 | 1 |
| C. A. Walsh ......... | 50 | 9,827 | 4,342 | 174 | 24.95 | 5 | 1 |
| S. Ramadhin ........ | 43 | 13,939 | 4,579 | 158 | 28.98 | 10 | 1 |
| C. E. L. Ambrose .... | 33 | 7,855 | 3,239 | 140 | 23.13 | 5 | 1 |
| A. L. Valentine ...... | 36 | 12,953 | 4,215 | 139 | 30.32 | 8 | 2 |
| C. E. H. Croft ....... | 27 | 6,165 | 2,913 | 125 | 23.30 | 3 | — |
| V. A. Holder ........ | 40 | 9,095 | 3,627 | 109 | 33.27 | 3 | — |

## NEW ZEALAND

| | T | Balls | R | W | Avge | 5W/i | 10W/m |
|---|---|---|---|---|---|---|---|
| Sir R. J. Hadlee . . . . . . | 86 | 21,918 | 9,611 | 431 | 22.29 | 36 | 9 |
| B. L. Cairns . . . . . . . | 43 | 10,628 | 4,280 | 130 | 32.92 | 6 | 1 |
| E. J. Chatfield . . . . . . | 43 | 10,360 | 3,958 | 123 | 32.17 | 3 | 1 |
| R. O. Collinge . . . . . . | 35 | 7,689 | 3,392 | 116 | 29.24 | 3 | — |
| B. R. Taylor . . . . . . . | 30 | 6,334 | 2,953 | 111 | 26.60 | 4 | — |
| J. G. Bracewell . . . . . | 41 | 8,403 | 3,653 | 102 | 35.81 | 4 | 1 |
| R. C. Motz . . . . . . . . | 32 | 7,034 | 3,148 | 100 | 31.48 | 5 | — |

## INDIA

| | T | Balls | R | W | Avge | 5W/i | 10W/m |
|---|---|---|---|---|---|---|---|
| Kapil Dev . . . . . . . . | 110 | 23,263 | 11,249 | 376 | 29.91 | 21 | 2 |
| B. S. Bedi . . . . . . . . | 67 | 21,364 | 7,637 | 266 | 28.71 | 14 | 1 |
| B. S. Chandrasekhar . . | 58 | 15,963 | 7,199 | 242 | 29.74 | 16 | 2 |
| E. A. S. Prasanna . . . . | 49 | 14,353 | 5,742 | 189 | 30.38 | 10 | 2 |
| V. Mankad . . . . . . . . | 44 | 14,686 | 5,236 | 162 | 32.32 | 8 | 2 |
| S. Venkataraghavan . . | 57 | 14,877 | 5,634 | 156 | 36.11 | 3 | 1 |
| S. P. Gupte . . . . . . . | 36 | 11,284 | 4,403 | 149 | 29.55 | 12 | 1 |
| R. J. Shastri . . . . . . . | 73 | 15,103 | 5,913 | 143 | 41.34 | 2 | — |
| D. R. Doshi . . . . . . . | 33 | 9,322 | 3,502 | 114 | 30.71 | 6 | — |
| K. D. Ghavri . . . . . . . | 39 | 7,042 | 3,656 | 109 | 33.54 | 4 | — |
| N. S. Yadav . . . . . . . | 35 | 8,349 | 3,580 | 102 | 35.09 | 3 | — |

## PAKISTAN

| | T | Balls | R | W | Avge | 5W/i | 10W/m |
|---|---|---|---|---|---|---|---|
| Imran Khan . . . . . . . . | 85 | 19,404 | 8,242 | 362 | 22.76 | 23 | 6 |
| Abdul Qadir . . . . . . . | 67 | 17,126 | 7,742 | 236 | 32.80 | 15 | 5 |
| Sarfraz Nawaz . . . . . . | 55 | 13,927 | 5,798 | 177 | 32.75 | 4 | 1 |
| Iqbal Qasim . . . . . . . | 50 | 13,019 | 4,807 | 171 | 28.11 | 8 | 2 |
| Wasim Akram . . . . . . | 37 | 8,126 | 3,427 | 142 | 24.13 | 9 | 2 |
| Fazal Mahmood . . . . . | 34 | 9,834 | 3,434 | 139 | 24.70 | 13 | 4 |
| Intikhab Alam . . . . . . | 47 | 10,474 | 4,494 | 125 | 35.95 | 5 | 2 |

SRI LANKA: The highest aggregate is 70 wickets, average 33.44, by R. J. Ratnayake in 20 Tests.

# WICKET WITH FIRST BALL IN TEST CRICKET

| | Batsman dismissed | | | |
|---|---|---|---|---|
| A. Coningham | A. C. MacLaren | A v E . . . . . . . | Melbourne . . . . . . | 1894-95 |
| W. M. Bradley | F. Laver | E v A . . . . . . . . | Manchester . . . . . | 1899 |
| E. G. Arnold | V. T. Trumper | E v A . . . . . . . . | Sydney . . . . . . . | 1903-04 |
| G. G. Macaulay | G. A. L. Hearne | E v SA . . . . . . | Cape Town . . . . . | 1922-23 |
| M. W. Tate | M. J. Susskind | E v SA . . . . . . | Birmingham . . . . . | 1924 |
| M. Henderson | E. W. Dawson | NZ v E . . . . . . | Christchurch . . . . | 1929-30 |
| H. D. Smith | E. Paynter | NZ v E . . . . . . | Christchurch . . . . | 1932-33 |
| T. F. Johnson | W. W. Keeton | WI v E . . . . . . | The Oval . . . . . . | 1939 |
| R. Howorth | D. V. Dyer | E v SA . . . . . . | The Oval . . . . . . | 1947 |
| Intikhab Alam | C. C. McDonald | P v A . . . . . . . | Karachi . . . . . . . | 1959-60 |
| R. K. Illingworth | P. V. Simmons | E v WI . . . . . . | Nottingham . . . . . | 1991 |

## HAT-TRICKS

| | | |
|---|---|---|
| F. R. Spofforth .... | Australia v England at Melbourne ................... | 1878-79 |
| W. Bates ......... | England v Australia at Melbourne .................. | 1882-83 |
| J. Briggs......... | England v Australia at Sydney ..................... | 1891-92 |
| G. A. Lohmann .... | England v South Africa at Port Elizabeth .......... | 1895-96 |
| J. T. Hearne ...... | England v Australia at Leeds ...................... | 1899 |
| H. Trumble ....... | Australia v England at Melbourne .................. | 1901-02 |
| H. Trumble ....... | Australia v England at Melbourne .................. | 1903-04 |
| T. J. Matthews† ...⎫<br>T. J. Matthews ....⎭ | Australia v South Africa at Manchester ............. | 1912 |
| M. J. C. Allom‡ ... | England v New Zealand at Christchurch ............. | 1929-30 |
| T. W. Goddard .... | England v South Africa at Johannesburg ............ | 1938-39 |
| P. J. Loader....... | England v West Indies at Leeds .................... | 1957 |
| L. F. Kline ....... | Australia v South Africa at Cape Town ............. | 1957-58 |
| W. W. Hall ....... | West Indies v Pakistan at Lahore ................... | 1958-59 |
| G. M. Griffin .... | South Africa v England at Lord's .................. | 1960 |
| L. R. Gibbs ...... | West Indies v Australia at Adelaide ................ | 1960-61 |
| P. J. Petherick‡ .... | New Zealand v Pakistan at Lahore .................. | 1976-77 |
| C. A. Walsh§ .... | West Indies v Australia at Brisbane ................ | 1988-89 |
| M. G. Hughes§ .... | Australia v West Indies at Perth ................... | 1988-89 |

*† T. J. Matthews did the hat-trick in each innings of the same match.*
*‡ On Test début.*
*§ Not all in the same innings.*

## FOUR WICKETS IN FIVE BALLS

| | | | |
|---|---|---|---|
| M. J. C. Allom .... | England v New Zealand at Christchurch .............. | | 1929-30 |
| | *On début, in his eighth over: W-WWW* | | |
| C. M. Old ........ | England v Pakistan at Birmingham .................. | | 1978 |
| | *Sequence interrupted by a no-ball: WW-WW* | | |
| Wasim Akram..... | Pakistan v West Indies at Lahore (WW-WW).......... | | 1990-91 |

## MOST BALLS BOWLED IN A TEST

S. Ramadhin (West Indies) sent down 774 balls in 129 overs against England at Birmingham, 1957. It was the most delivered by any bowler in a Test, beating H. Verity's 766 for England against South Africa at Durban, 1938-39. In this match Ramadhin also bowled the most balls (588) in any single first-class innings, including Tests.

It should be noted that six balls were bowled to the over in the Australia v England Test series of 1928-29 and 1932-33, when the eight-ball over was otherwise in force in Australia.

## ALL-ROUND RECORDS

## 100 RUNS AND FIVE WICKETS IN AN INNINGS

**England**

| | | | | | |
|---|---|---|---|---|---|
| A. W. Greig | 148 | 6-164 | v West Indies | Bridgetown | 1973-74 |
| I. T. Botham | 103 | 5-73 | v New Zealand | Christchurch | 1977-78 |
| I. T. Botham | 108 | 8-34 | v Pakistan | Lord's | 1978 |
| I. T. Botham | 114 | 6-58<br>7-48 | v India | Bombay | 1979-80 |
| I. T. Botham | 149* | 6-95 | v Australia | Leeds | 1981 |
| I. T. Botham | 138 | 5-59 | v New Zealand | Wellington | 1983-84 |

**Australia**

| | | | | | |
|---|---|---|---|---|---|
| C. Kelleway | 114 | 5-33 | v South Africa | Manchester | 1912 |
| J. M. Gregory | 100 | 7-69 | v England | Melbourne | 1920-21 |
| K. R. Miller | 109 | 6-107 | v West Indies | Kingston | 1954-55 |
| R. Benaud | 100 | 5-84 | v South Africa | Johannesburg | 1957-58 |

**South Africa**

| | | | | | |
|---|---|---|---|---|---|
| J. H. Sinclair | 106 | 6-26 | v England | Cape Town | 1898-99 |
| G. A. Faulkner | 123 | 5-120 | v England | Johannesburg | 1909-10 |

**West Indies**

| | | | | | |
|---|---|---|---|---|---|
| D. St E. Atkinson | 219 | 5-56 | v Australia | Bridgetown | 1954-55 |
| O. G. Smith | 100 | 5-90 | v India | Delhi | 1958-59 |
| G. S. Sobers | 104 | 5-63 | v India | Kingston | 1961-62 |
| G. S. Sobers | 174 | 5-41 | v England | Leeds | 1966 |

**New Zealand**

| | | | | | |
|---|---|---|---|---|---|
| B. R. Taylor† | 105 | 5-86 | v India | Calcutta | 1964-65 |

**India**

| | | | | | |
|---|---|---|---|---|---|
| V. Mankad | 184 | 5-196 | v England | Lord's | 1952 |
| P. R. Umrigar | 172* | 5-107 | v West Indies | Port-of-Spain | 1961-62 |

**Pakistan**

| | | | | | |
|---|---|---|---|---|---|
| Mushtaq Mohammad | 201 | 5-49 | v New Zealand | Dunedin | 1972-73 |
| Mushtaq Mohammad | 121 | 5-28 | v West Indies | Port-of-Spain | 1976-77 |
| Imran Khan | 117 | 6-98<br>5-82 } | v India | Faisalabad | 1982-83 |
| Wasim Akram | 123 | 5-100 | v Australia | Adelaide | 1989-90 |

† *On début.*

## 100 RUNS AND FIVE DISMISSALS IN AN INNINGS

| | | | | | |
|---|---|---|---|---|---|
| D. T. Lindsay | 182 | 6ct | SA v A | Johannesburg | 1966-67 |
| I. D. S. Smith | 113* | 4ct, 1st | NZ v E | Auckland | 1983-84 |
| S. A. R. Silva | 111 | 5ct | SL v I | Colombo (PSS) | 1985-86 |

## 100 RUNS AND TEN WICKETS IN A TEST

| | | | | | |
|---|---|---|---|---|---|
| A. K. Davidson | 44<br>80 | 5-135<br>6-87 } | A v WI | Brisbane | 1960-61 |
| I. T. Botham | 114 | 6-58<br>7-48 } | E v I | Bombay | 1979-80 |
| Imran Khan | 117 | 6-98<br>5-82 } | P v I | Faisalabad | 1982-83 |

## 1,000 RUNS AND 100 WICKETS IN A CAREER

| | Tests | Runs | Wkts | Tests for Double |
|---|---|---|---|---|
| **England** | | | | |
| T. E. Bailey | 61 | 2,290 | 132 | 47 |
| I. T. Botham | 99 | 5,176 | 380 | 21 |
| J. E. Emburey | 60 | 1,540 | 138 | 46 |
| A. W. Greig | 58 | 3,599 | 141 | 37 |
| R. Illingworth | 61 | 1,836 | 122 | 47 |
| W. Rhodes | 58 | 2,325 | 127 | 44 |
| M. W. Tate | 39 | 1,198 | 155 | 33 |
| F. J. Titmus | 53 | 1,449 | 153 | 40 |
| **Australia** | | | | |
| R. Benaud | 63 | 2,201 | 248 | 32 |
| A. K. Davidson | 44 | 1,328 | 186 | 34 |
| G. Giffen | 31 | 1,238 | 103 | 30 |
| I. W. Johnson | 45 | 1,000 | 109 | 45 |
| R. R. Lindwall | 61 | 1,502 | 228 | 38 |
| K. R. Miller | 55 | 2,958 | 170 | 33 |
| M. A. Noble | 42 | 1,997 | 121 | 27 |

| | Tests | Runs | Wkts | Tests for Double |
|---|---|---|---|---|
| **South Africa** | | | | |
| T. L. Goddard............ | 41 | 2,516 | 123 | 36 |
| **West Indies** | | | | |
| M. D. Marshall.......... | 81 | 1,810 | 376 | 49 |
| G. S. Sobers ............. | 93 | 8,032 | 235 | 48 |
| **New Zealand** | | | | |
| J. G. Bracewell .......... | 41 | 1,001 | 102 | 41 |
| Sir R. J. Hadlee .......... | 86 | 3,124 | 431 | 28 |
| **India** | | | | |
| Kapil Dev ............... | 110 | 4,525 | 376 | 25 |
| V. Mankad ............. | 44 | 2,109 | 162 | 23 |
| R. J. Shastri ............. | 73 | 3,460 | 143 | 44 |
| **Pakistan** | | | | |
| Abdul Qadir ............. | 67 | 1,029 | 236 | 62 |
| Imran Khan ............. | 85 | 3,692 | 362 | 30 |
| Intikhab Alam ........... | 47 | 1,493 | 125 | 41 |
| Sarfraz Nawaz ........... | 55 | 1,045 | 177 | 55 |

## 1,000 RUNS, 100 WICKETS AND 100 CATCHES

| | Tests | Runs | Wkts | Ct |
|---|---|---|---|---|
| I. T. Botham | 99 | 5,176 | 380 | 117 |
| G. S. Sobers | 93 | 8,032 | 235 | 109 |

## WICKET-KEEPING RECORDS

### Most Dismissals in an Innings

| | | | |
|---|---|---|---|
| 7 (all ct) | Wasim Bari ....... | Pakistan v New Zealand at Auckland ... | 1978-79 |
| 7 (all ct) | R. W. Taylor....... | England v India at Bombay............ | 1979-80 |
| 7 (all ct) | I. D. S. Smith ..... | New Zealand v Sri Lanka at Hamilton .. | 1990-91 |
| 6 (all ct) | A. T. W. Grout.... | Australia v South Africa at Johannesburg | 1957-58 |
| 6 (all ct) | D. T. Lindsay ..... | South Africa v Australia at Johannesburg | 1966-67 |
| 6 (all ct) | J. T. Murray ...... | England v India at Lord's ............. | 1967 |
| 6 (5ct, 1st) | S. M. H. Kirmani.. | India v New Zealand at Christchurch ... | 1975-76 |
| 6 (all ct) | R. W. Marsh...... | Australia v England at Brisbane ....... | 1982-83 |
| 6 (all ct) | S. A. R. Silva .... | Sri Lanka v India at Colombo (SSC) .... | 1985-86 |
| 6 (all ct) | R. C. Russell ..... | England v Australia at Melbourne ..... | 1990-91 |

*Note:* The most stumpings in an innings is 5 by K. S. More for India v West Indies at Madras in 1987-88.

### Most Dismissals in One Test

| | | | |
|---|---|---|---|
| 10 (all ct) | R. W. Taylor...... | England v India at Bombay............ | 1979-80 |
| 9 (8ct, 1st) | G. R. A. Langley .. | Australia v England at Lord's ......... | 1956 |
| 9 (all ct) | D. A. Murray ..... | West Indies v Australia at Melbourne ... | 1981-82 |
| 9 (all ct) | R. W. Marsh...... | Australia v England at Brisbane ........ | 1982-83 |
| 9 (all ct) | S. A. R. Silva .... | Sri Lanka v India at Colombo (SSC) .... | 1985-86 |
| 9 (8ct, 1st) | S. A. R. Silva .... | Sri Lanka v India at Colombo (PSS) .... | 1985-86 |
| 8 (all ct) | J. J. Kelly ....... | Australia v England at Sydney ........ | 1901-02 |
| 8 (6ct, 2st) | L. E. G. Ames .... | England v West Indies at The Oval ..... | 1933 |
| 8 (all ct) | G. R. A. Langley .. | Australia v West Indies at Kingston..... | 1954-55 |
| 8 (6ct, 2st) | A. T. W. Grout.... | Australia v Pakistan at Lahore ........ | 1959-60 |
| 8 (all ct) | A. T. W. Grout.... | Australia v England at Lord's .......... | 1961 |
| 8 (all ct) | J. M. Parks ....... | England v New Zealand at Christchurch . | 1965-66 |
| 8 (all ct) | D. T. Lindsay ..... | South Africa v Australia at Johannesburg | 1966-67 |
| 8 (7ct, 1st) | H. B. Taber....... | Australia v South Africa at Johannesburg | 1966-67 |
| 8 (all ct) | Wasim Bari ....... | Pakistan v England at Leeds .......... | 1971 |
| 8 (all ct) | R. W. Marsh...... | Australia v West Indies at Melbourne ... | 1975-76 |

| | | | |
|---|---|---|---|
| 8 (all ct) | R. W. Marsh . . . . . . | Australia v New Zealand at Christchurch | 1976-77 |
| 8 (7ct, 1st) | R. W. Marsh . . . . . . | Australia v India at Sydney . . . . . . . . . . . | 1980-81 |
| 8 (all ct) | W. K. Lees . . . . . . . | New Zealand v Sri Lanka at Wellington . | 1982-83 |
| 8 (all ct) | R. W. Marsh . . . . . . | Australia v England at Adelaide . . . . . . . . | 1982-83 |
| 8 (all ct) | I. D. S. Smith . . . . . | New Zealand v Sri Lanka at Hamilton . . | 1990-91 |

*Notes:* S. A. R. Silva made 18 dismissals in two successive Tests.

The most stumpings in a match is 6 by K. S. More for India v West Indies at Madras in 1987-88.

## Most Dismissals in a Series

*(Played in 5 Tests unless otherwise stated)*

| | | | |
|---|---|---|---|
| 28 (all ct) | R. W. Marsh . . . . . . | Australia v England . . . . . . . . . . . . . . . . | 1982-83 |
| 26 (23ct, 3st) | J. H. B. Waite . . . . | South Africa v New Zealand . . . . . . . . . . | 1961-62 |
| 26 (all ct) | R. W. Marsh . . . . . . | Australia v West Indies (6 Tests) . . . . . . | 1975-76 |
| 24 (22ct, 2st) | D. L. Murray . . . . . | West Indies v England . . . . . . . . . . . . . . | 1963 |
| 24 (all ct) | D. T. Lindsay . . . . . | South Africa v Australia . . . . . . . . . . . . . | 1966-67 |
| 24 (21ct, 3st) | A. P. E. Knott . . . . | England v Australia (6 Tests) . . . . . . . . . | 1970-71 |
| 24 (all ct) | I. A. Healy . . . . . . . | Australia v England . . . . . . . . . . . . . . . . | 1990-91 |
| 23 (16ct, 7st) | J. H. B. Waite . . . . | South Africa v New Zealand . . . . . . . . . . | 1953-54 |
| 23 (22ct, 1st) | F. C. M. Alexander . | West Indies v England . . . . . . . . . . . . . . | 1959-60 |
| 23 (20ct, 3st) | A. T. W. Grout . . . . | Australia v West Indies . . . . . . . . . . . . . | 1960-61 |
| 23 (21ct, 2st) | A. E. Dick . . . . . . . | New Zealand v South Africa . . . . . . . . . . | 1961-62 |
| 23 (21ct, 2st) | R. W. Marsh . . . . . . | Australia v England . . . . . . . . . . . . . . . . | 1972 |
| 23 (22ct, 1st) | A. P. E. Knott . . . . | England v Australia (6 Tests) . . . . . . . . . | 1974-75 |
| 23 (all ct) | R. W. Marsh . . . . . . | Australia v England (6 Tests) . . . . . . . . . | 1981 |
| 23 (all ct) | P. J. L. Dujon . . . . . | West Indies v Australia . . . . . . . . . . . . . | 1990-91 |
| 22 (all ct) | S. J. Rixon . . . . . . . | Australia v India . . . . . . . . . . . . . . . . . . | 1977-78 |
| 22 (21ct, 1st) | S. A. R. Silva . . . . | Sri Lanka v India (3 Tests) . . . . . . . . . . | 1985-86 |
| 21 (15ct, 6st) | H. Strudwick . . . . . | England v South Africa . . . . . . . . . . . . . | 1913-14 |
| 21 (13ct, 8st) | R. A. Saggers . . . . . | Australia v South Africa . . . . . . . . . . . . | 1949-50 |
| 21 (16ct, 5st) | G. R. A. Langley . . . | Australia v West Indies . . . . . . . . . . . . . | 1951-52 |
| 21 (20ct, 1st) | A. T. W. Grout . . . . | Australia v England . . . . . . . . . . . . . . . . | 1961 |
| 21 (all ct) | R. W. Marsh . . . . . . | Australia v Pakistan . . . . . . . . . . . . . . . | 1983-84 |
| 20 (16ct, 4st) | D. Tallon . . . . . . . . | Australia v England . . . . . . . . . . . . . . . . | 1946-47 |
| 20 (16ct, 4st) | G. R. A. Langley . . . | Australia v West Indies (4 Tests) . . . . . . | 1954-55 |
| 20 (18ct, 2st) | T. G. Evans . . . . . . | England v South Africa . . . . . . . . . . . . . | 1956-57 |
| 20 (17ct, 3st) | A. T. W. Grout . . . . | Australia v England . . . . . . . . . . . . . . . . | 1958-59 |
| 20 (19ct, 1st) | H. B. Taber . . . . . . | Australia v South Africa . . . . . . . . . . . . | 1966-67 |
| 20 (18ct, 2st) | R. W. Taylor . . . . . . | England v Australia (6 Tests) . . . . . . . . . | 1978-79 |
| 20 (19ct, 1st) | P. J. L. Dujon . . . . . | West Indies v Australia . . . . . . . . . . . . . | 1983-84 |
| 20 (19ct, 1st) | P. R. Downton . . . . . | England v Australia (6 Tests) . . . . . . . . . | 1985 |
| 20 (all ct) | P. J. L. Dujon . . . . . | West Indies v England . . . . . . . . . . . . . . | 1988 |

## Most Dismissals in a Career

| | *T* | *Ct* | *St* | *Total* |
|---|---|---|---|---|
| R. W. Marsh (Australia) . . . . . . . . . . . . . . . . . . . . | 96 | 343 | 12 | 355 |
| P. J. L. Dujon (West Indies) . . . . . . . . . . . . . . . . . | 81 | 267 | 5 | 272 |
| A. P. E. Knott (England) . . . . . . . . . . . . . . . . . . . | 95 | 250 | 19 | 269 |
| Wasim Bari (Pakistan) . . . . . . . . . . . . . . . . . . . . . | 81 | 201 | 27 | 228 |
| T. G. Evans (England) . . . . . . . . . . . . . . . . . . . . . | 91 | 173 | 46 | 219 |
| S. M. H. Kirmani (India) . . . . . . . . . . . . . . . . . . . | 88 | 160 | 38 | 198 |
| D. L. Murray (West Indies) . . . . . . . . . . . . . . . . . | 62 | 181 | 8 | 189 |
| A. T. W. Grout (Australia) . . . . . . . . . . . . . . . . . . | 51 | 163 | 24 | 187 |
| R. W. Taylor (England) . . . . . . . . . . . . . . . . . . . . | 57 | 167 | 7 | 174 |
| I. D. S. Smith (New Zealand) . . . . . . . . . . . . . . . . | 61 | 164 | 8 | 172 |
| J. H. B. Waite (South Africa) . . . . . . . . . . . . . . . . | 50 | 124 | 17 | 141 |
| W. A. Oldfield (Australia) . . . . . . . . . . . . . . . . . . | 54 | 78 | 52 | 130 |
| J. M. Parks (England) . . . . . . . . . . . . . . . . . . . . . | 46 | 103 | 11 | 114 |
| Salim Yousuf (Pakistan) . . . . . . . . . . . . . . . . . . . | 32 | 91 | 13 | 104 |

*Notes:* The records for P. J. L. Dujon and J. M. Parks each include two catches taken when not keeping wicket in two and three Tests respectively.

S. A. R. Silva (33ct, 1st) has made most dismissals for Sri Lanka.

## FIELDING RECORDS

(Excluding wicket-keepers)

### Most Catches in an Innings

| | | | |
|---|---|---|---|
| 5 | V. Y. Richardson . . . . | Australia v South Africa at Durban . . . . . . . . . . . | 1935-36 |
| 5 | Yajurvindra Singh . . . . | India v England at Bangalore . . . . . . . . . . . . . . . | 1976-77 |
| 5 | M. Azharuddin . . . . . . . | India v Pakistan at Karachi . . . . . . . . . . . . . . . . | 1989-90 |

### Most Catches in One Test

| | | | |
|---|---|---|---|
| 7 | G. S. Chappell . . . . . . . | Australia v England at Perth . . . . . . . . . . . . . . . | 1974-75 |
| 7 | Yajurvindra Singh . . . . | India v England at Bangalore . . . . . . . . . . . . . . | 1976-77 |
| 6 | A. Shrewsbury . . . . . . . | England v Australia at Sydney . . . . . . . . . . . . . | 1887-88 |
| 6 | A. E. E. Vogler . . . . . . . | South Africa v England at Durban . . . . . . . . . . . | 1909-10 |
| 6 | F. E. Woolley . . . . . . . | England v Australia at Sydney . . . . . . . . . . . . . | 1911-12 |
| 6 | J. M. Gregory . . . . . . . | Australia v England at Sydney . . . . . . . . . . . . . | 1920-21 |
| 6 | B. Mitchell . . . . . . . . . . | South Africa v Australia at Melbourne . . . . . . . . | 1931-32 |
| 6 | V. Y. Richardson . . . . . | Australia v South Africa at Durban . . . . . . . . . . . | 1935-36 |
| 6 | R. N. Harvey . . . . . . . . | Australia v England at Sydney . . . . . . . . . . . . . | 1962-63 |
| 6 | M. C. Cowdrey . . . . . . . | England v West Indies at Lord's . . . . . . . . . . . . | 1963 |
| 6 | E. D. Solkar . . . . . . . . | India v West Indies at Port-of-Spain . . . . . . . . . | 1970-71 |
| 6 | G. S. Sobers . . . . . . . . | West Indies v England at Leeds . . . . . . . . . . . . | 1973 |
| 6 | I. M. Chappell . . . . . . . | Australia v New Zealand at Adelaide . . . . . . . . . | 1973-74 |
| 6 | A. W. Greig . . . . . . . . | England v Pakistan at Leeds . . . . . . . . . . . . . . | 1974 |
| 6 | D. F. Whatmore . . . . . . | Australia v India at Kanpur . . . . . . . . . . . . . . | 1979-80 |
| 6 | A. J. Lamb . . . . . . . . . . | England v New Zealand at Lord's . . . . . . . . . . . | 1983 |

### Most Catches in a Series

| | | | |
|---|---|---|---|
| 15 | J. M. Gregory . . . . . . . | Australia v England . . . . . . . . . . . . . . . . . . . | 1920-21 |
| 14 | G. S. Chappell . . . . . . . | Australia v England (6 Tests) . . . . . . . . . . . . . | 1974-75 |
| 13 | R. B. Simpson . . . . . . . | Australia v South Africa . . . . . . . . . . . . . . . . | 1957-58 |
| 13 | R. B. Simpson . . . . . . . | Australia v West Indies . . . . . . . . . . . . . . . . | 1960-61 |

### Most Catches in a Career

| | | |
|---|---|---|
| A. R. Border (Australia) . . . . . . . | 130 in 125 matches |
| G. S. Chappell (Australia) . . . . . | 122 in  87 matches |
| I. V. A. Richards (West Indies) . . | 122 in 121 matches |
| M. C. Cowdrey (England) . . . . . . | 120 in 114 matches |
| I. T. Botham (England) . . . . . . . . | 117 in  99 matches |
| R. B. Simpson (Australia) . . . . . . | 110 in  62 matches |
| W. R. Hammond (England) . . . . | 110 in  85 matches |
| G. S. Sobers (West Indies) . . . . . | 109 in  93 matches |
| S. M. Gavaskar (India) . . . . . . . | 108 in 125 matches |
| I. M. Chappell (Australia) . . . . . | 105 in  75 matches |

## TEAM RECORDS

### HIGHEST INNINGS TOTALS

| | | |
|---|---|---|
| 903-7 dec. | England v Australia at The Oval . . . . . . . . . . . . . . . . . . . . . . . . . . | 1938 |
| 849 | England v West Indies at Kingston . . . . . . . . . . . . . . . . . . . . . . . | 1929-30 |
| 790-3 dec. | West Indies v Pakistan at Kingston . . . . . . . . . . . . . . . . . . . . . . | 1957-58 |
| 758-8 dec. | Australia v West Indies at Kingston . . . . . . . . . . . . . . . . . . . . . . . | 1954-55 |
| 729-6 dec. | Australia v England at Lord's . . . . . . . . . . . . . . . . . . . . . . . . . . | 1930 |
| 708 | Pakistan v England at The Oval . . . . . . . . . . . . . . . . . . . . . . . . . | 1987 |
| 701 | Australia v England at The Oval . . . . . . . . . . . . . . . . . . . . . . . . . | 1934 |
| 699-5 | Pakistan v India at Lahore . . . . . . . . . . . . . . . . . . . . . . . . . . . . | 1989-90 |
| 695 | Australia v England at The Oval . . . . . . . . . . . . . . . . . . . . . . . . . | 1930 |
| 687-8 dec. | West Indies v England at The Oval . . . . . . . . . . . . . . . . . . . . . . . | 1976 |

| | | |
|---|---|---|
| 681-8 dec. | West Indies v England at Port-of-Spain .......................... | 1953-54 |
| 676-7 | India v Sri Lanka at Kanpur.................................. | 1986-87 |
| 674-6 | Pakistan v India at Faisalabad ............................... | 1984-85 |
| 674 | Australia v India at Adelaide ................................ | 1947-48 |
| 671-4 | New Zealand v Sri Lanka at Wellington ........................ | 1990-91 |
| 668 | Australia v West Indies at Bridgetown ......................... | 1954-55 |
| 659-8 dec. | Australia v England at Sydney ............................... | 1946-47 |
| 658-8 dec. | England v Australia at Nottingham ............................ | 1938 |
| 657-8 dec. | Pakistan v West Indies at Bridgetown .......................... | 1957-58 |
| 656-8 dec. | Australia v England at Manchester............................ | 1964 |
| 654-5 | England v South Africa at Durban ............................ | 1938-39 |
| 653-4 dec. | England v India at Lord's .................................... | 1990 |
| 652-7 dec. | England v India at Madras ................................... | 1984-85 |
| 652-8 dec. | West Indies v England at Lord's............................... | 1973 |
| 652 | Pakistan v India at Faisalabad ............................... | 1982-83 |
| 650-6 dec. | Australia v West Indies at Bridgetown ......................... | 1964-65 |

**The highest innings for the countries not mentioned above are:**

| | | |
|---|---|---|
| 622-9 dec. | South Africa v Australia at Durban ........................... | 1969-70 |
| 497 | Sri Lanka v New Zealand at Wellington ........................ | 1990-91 |

## HIGHEST FOURTH-INNINGS TOTALS

### To win

| | | |
|---|---|---|
| 406-4 | India (needing 403) v West Indies at Port-of-Spain ................ | 1975-76 |
| 404-3 | Australia (needing 404) v England at Leeds ..................... | 1948 |
| 362-7 | Australia (needing 359) v West Indies at Georgetown ............. | 1977-78 |
| 348-5 | West Indies (needing 345) v New Zealand at Auckland ............ | 1968-69 |
| 344-1 | West Indies (needing 342) v England at Lord's.................... | 1984 |

### To tie

| | | |
|---|---|---|
| 347 | India v Australia at Madras................................... | 1986-87 |

### To draw

| | | |
|---|---|---|
| 654-5 | England (needing 696 to win) v South Africa at Durban ............ | 1938-39 |
| 429-8 | India (needing 438 to win) v England at The Oval................. | 1979 |
| 423-7 | South Africa (needing 451 to win) v England at The Oval ........... | 1947 |
| 408-5 | West Indies (needing 836 to win) v England at Kingston ............ | 1929-30 |

### To lose

| | | |
|---|---|---|
| 445 | India (lost by 47 runs) v Australia at Adelaide ................... | 1977-78 |
| 440 | New Zealand (lost by 38 runs) v England at Nottingham............ | 1973 |
| 417 | England (lost by 45 runs) v Australia at Melbourne ............... | 1976-77 |
| 411 | England (lost by 193 runs) v Australia at Sydney................. | 1924-25 |

## MOST RUNS IN A DAY (BOTH SIDES)

| | | |
|---|---|---|
| 588 | England (398-6), India (190-0) at Manchester (2nd day) ........... | 1936 |
| 522 | England (503-2), South Africa (19-0) at Lord's (2nd day) .......... | 1924 |
| 508 | England (221-2), South Africa (287-6) at The Oval (3rd day) ........ | 1935 |

## MOST RUNS IN A DAY (ONE SIDE)

| | | |
|---|---|---|
| 503 | England (503-2) v South Africa at Lord's (2nd day) .............. | 1924 |
| 494 | Australia (494-6) v South Africa at Sydney (1st day)............... | 1910-11 |
| 475 | Australia (475-2) v England at The Oval (1st day)................. | 1934 |
| 471 | England (471-8) v India at The Oval (1st day).................... | 1936 |
| 458 | Australia (458-3) v England at Leeds (1st day)................... | 1930 |
| 455 | Australia (455-1) v England at Leeds (2nd day) .................. | 1934 |

## MOST WICKETS IN A DAY

27  England (18-3 to 53 out and 62) v Australia (60) at Lord's (2nd day) ...... 1888
25  Australia (112 and 48-5) v England (61) at Melbourne (1st day) ......... 1901-02

## HIGHEST MATCH AGGREGATES

| Runs | Wkts | | | *Days played*† |
|------|------|---|---|------|
| 1,981 | 35 | South Africa v England at Durban .................... | 1938-39 | 10† |
| 1,815 | 34 | West Indies v England at Kingston ................. | 1929-30 | 9‡ |
| 1,764 | 39 | Australia v West Indies at Adelaide ................. | 1968-69 | 5 |
| 1,753 | 40 | Australia v England at Adelaide .................... | 1920-21 | 6 |
| 1,723 | 31 | England v Australia at Leeds ...................... | 1948 | 5 |
| 1,661 | 36 | West Indies v Australia at Bridgetown ............... | 1954-55 | 6 |

† *No play on one day.*       ‡ *No play on two days.*

## LOWEST INNINGS TOTALS

26  New Zealand v England at Auckland ............................... 1954-55
30  South Africa v England at Port Elizabeth ...................... 1895-96
30  South Africa v England at Birmingham ........................ 1924
35  South Africa v England at Cape Town ......................... 1898-99
36  Australia v England at Birmingham ........................... 1902
36  South Africa v Australia at Melbourne ......................... 1931-32
42  Australia v England at Sydney ............................... 1887-88
42  New Zealand v Australia at Wellington ........................ 1945-46
42† India v England at Lord's ................................... 1974
43  South Africa v England at Cape Town .......................... 1888-89
44  Australia v England at The Oval ............................. 1896
45  England v Australia at Sydney ............................... 1886-87
45  South Africa v Australia at Melbourne ......................... 1931-32
47  South Africa v England at Cape Town .......................... 1888-89
47  New Zealand v England at Lord's ............................. 1958

**The lowest innings for the countries not mentioned above are:**

53  West Indies v Pakistan at Faisalabad .......................... 1986-87
62  Pakistan v Australia at Perth ................................ 1981-82
82  Sri Lanka v India at Chandigarh ............................. 1990-91

† *Batted one man short.*

## FEWEST RUNS IN A FULL DAY'S PLAY

95  At Karachi, October 11, 1956. Australia 80 all out; Pakistan 15 for two (first day, 5½ hours).
104  At Karachi, December 8, 1959. Pakistan 0 for no wicket to 104 for five v Australia (fourth day, 5½ hours).
106  At Brisbane, December 9, 1958. England 92 for two to 198 all out v Australia (fourth day, 5 hours). *England were dismissed five minutes before the close of play, leaving no time for Australia to start their second innings.*
112  At Karachi, October 15, 1956. Australia 138 for six to 187 all out; Pakistan 63 for one (fourth day, 5½ hours).
115  At Karachi, September 19, 1988. Australia 116 for seven to 165 all out and 66 for five following on v Pakistan (fourth day, 5½ hours).
117  At Madras, October 19, 1956. India 117 for five v Australia (first day, 5½ hours).
117  At Colombo (SSC), March 21, 1984. New Zealand 6 for no wicket to 123 for four (fifth day, 5 hours, 47 minutes).

**In England**

151   At Lord's, August 26, 1978. England 175 for two to 289 all out; New Zealand 37 for seven
      (third day, 6 hours).
159   At Leeds, July 10, 1971. Pakistan 208 for four to 350 all out; England 17 for one (third day,
      6 hours).

## LOWEST MATCH AGGREGATES

(For a completed match)

| Runs | Wkts | | | Days played |
|------|------|---|---|---|
| 234 | 29 | Australia v South Africa at Melbourne | 1931-32 | 3† |
| 291 | 40 | England v Australia at Lord's | 1888 | 2 |
| 295 | 28 | New Zealand v Australia at Wellington | 1945-46 | 2 |
| 309 | 29 | West Indies v England at Bridgetown | 1934-35 | 3 |
| 323 | 30 | England v Australia at Manchester | 1888 | 2 |

† *No play on one day.*

## YOUNGEST TEST PLAYERS

| Years | Days | | | |
|-------|------|---|---|---|
| 15 | 124 | Mushtaq Mohammad | Pakistan v West Indies at Lahore | 1958-59 |
| 16 | 189 | Aqib Javed | Pakistan v New Zealand at Wellington | 1988-89 |
| 16 | 205 | S. R. Tendulkar | India v Pakistan at Karachi | 1989-90 |
| 16 | 221 | Aftab Baloch | Pakistan v New Zealand at Dacca | 1969-70 |
| 16 | 248 | Nasim-ul-Ghani | Pakistan v West Indies at Bridgetown | 1957-58 |
| 16 | 352 | Khalid Hassan | Pakistan v England at Nottingham | 1954 |
| 17 | 5 | Zahid Fazal | Pakistan v West Indies at Karachi | 1990-91 |
| 17 | 118 | L. Sivaramakrishnan | India v West Indies at St John's | 1982-83 |
| 17 | 122 | J. E. D. Sealy | West Indies v England at Bridgetown | 1929-30 |
| 17 | 189 | C. D. U. S. Weerasinghe | Sri Lanka v India at Colombo (PSS) | 1985-86 |
| 17 | 193 | Maninder Singh | India v Pakistan at Karachi | 1982-83 |
| 17 | 239 | I. D. Craig | Australia v South Africa at Melbourne | 1952-53 |
| 17 | 245 | G. S. Sobers | West Indies v England at Kingston | 1953-54 |
| 17 | 265 | V. L. Mehra | India v New Zealand at Bombay | 1955-56 |
| 17 | 300 | Hanif Mohammad | Pakistan v India at Delhi | 1952-53 |
| 17 | 341 | Intikhab Alam | Pakistan v Australia at Karachi | 1959-60 |
| 17 | 364 | Waqar Younis | Pakistan v India at Karachi | 1989-90 |

*Note:* The youngest Test players for countries not mentioned above are: England – D. B. Close,
18 years 149 days, v New Zealand at Manchester, 1949; New Zealand – D. L. Freeman, 18 years
197 days, v England at Christchurch, 1932-33; South Africa – A. E. Ochse, 19 years
1 day, v England at Port Elizabeth, 1888-89.

## OLDEST PLAYERS ON TEST DEBUT

| Years | Days | | | |
|-------|------|---|---|---|
| 49 | 119 | J. Southerton | England v Australia at Melbourne | 1876-77 |
| 47 | 284 | Miran Bux | Pakistan v India at Lahore | 1954-55 |
| 46 | 253 | D. D. Blackie | Australia v England at Sydney | 1928-29 |
| 46 | 237 | H. Ironmonger | Australia v England at Brisbane | 1928-29 |
| 42 | 242 | N. Betancourt | West Indies v England at Port-of-Spain | 1929-30 |
| 41 | 337 | E. R. Wilson | England v Australia at Sydney | 1920-21 |
| 41 | 27 | R. J. D. Jamshedji | India v England at Bombay | 1933-34 |

| Years | Days | | | |
|-------|------|---|---|---|
| 40 | 345 | C. A. Wiles . . . . . | West Indies v England at Manchester . . | 1933 |
| 40 | 216 | S. P. Kinneir . . . . | England v Australia at Sydney . . . . . . . . | 1911-12 |
| 40 | 110 | H. W. Lee . . . . . . | England v South Africa at Johannesburg | 1930-31 |
| 40 | 56 | G. W. A. Chubb. | South Africa v England at Nottingham . | 1951 |
| 40 | 37 | C. Ramaswami . . | India v England at Manchester . . . . . . . . | 1936 |

*Note:* The oldest Test player on début for New Zealand was H. M. McGirr, 38 years 101 days, v England at Auckland, 1929-30; for Sri Lanka, D. S. de Silva, 39 years 251 days, v England at Colombo (PSS), 1981-82.

## OLDEST TEST PLAYERS

(Age on final day of their last Test match)

| Years | Days | | | |
|-------|------|---|---|---|
| 52 | 165 | W. Rhodes. . . . . . . . . | England v West Indies at Kingston . . . | 1929-30 |
| 50 | 327 | H. Ironmonger . . . . . . | Australia v England at Sydney . . . . . . . | 1932-33 |
| 50 | 320 | W. G. Grace . . . . . . . | England v Australia at Nottingham . . | 1899 |
| 50 | 303 | G. Gunn . . . . . . . . . | England v West Indies at Kingston . . . | 1929-30 |
| 49 | 139 | J. Southerton . . . . . . . | England v Australia at Melbourne . . . . | 1876-77 |
| 47 | 302 | Miran Bux . . . . . . . . . | Pakistan v India at Peshawar . . . . . . | 1954-55 |
| 47 | 249 | J. B. Hobbs . . . . . . . . | England v Australia at The Oval . . . . . | 1930 |
| 47 | 87 | F. E. Woolley . . . . . . | England v Australia at The Oval . . . . . | 1934 |
| 46 | 309 | D. D. Blackie . . . . . . | Australia v England at Adelaide . . . . . | 1928-29 |
| 46 | 206 | A. W. Nourse . . . . . . . | South Africa v England at The Oval . . | 1924 |
| 46 | 202 | H. Strudwick . . . . . . . | England v Australia at The Oval . . . . . | 1926 |
| 46 | 41 | E. H. Hendren . . . . . . | England v West Indies at Kingston . . . | 1934-35 |
| 45 | 245 | G. O. B. Allen . . . . . . | England v West Indies at Kingston . . . | 1947-48 |
| 45 | 215 | P. Holmes . . . . . . . . . | England v India at Lord's . . . . . . . . | 1932 |
| 45 | 140 | D. B. Close . . . . . . . . | England v West Indies at Manchester . | 1976 |

## MOST TEST MATCH APPEARANCES

| For | Total | | E | A | SA | WI | NZ | I | P | SL |
|-----|-------|---|---|---|----|----|----|---|---|----|
| England | 114 | M. C. Cowdrey | — | 43 | 14 | 21 | 18 | 8 | 10 | — |
| | 114 | D. I. Gower | — | 42 | — | 19 | 13 | 24 | 14 | 2 |
| Australia | 125 | A. R. Border | 41 | — | — | 26 | 17 | 15 | 22 | 4 |
| South Africa | 50 | J. H. B. Waite | 21 | 14 | — | — | 15 | — | — | — |
| West Indies | 121 | I. V. A. Richards | 36 | 34 | — | — | 7 | 28 | 16 | — |
| New Zealand | 86 | Sir R. J. Hadlee | 21 | 23 | — | 10 | — | 14 | 12 | 6 |
| India | 125 | S. M. Gavaskar | 38 | 20 | — | 27 | 9 | — | 24 | 7 |
| Pakistan | 109 | Javed Miandad | 17 | 25 | — | 13 | 17 | 28 | — | 9 |
| Sri Lanka | 30 | A. Ranatunga | 3 | 4 | — | 7 | 8 | 8 | — | — |

## MOST CONSECUTIVE TEST APPEARANCES

| | | |
|---|---|---|
| 122 | A. R. Border (Australia) . . . . . . . | March 1979 to May 1991 |
| 106 | S. M. Gavaskar (India) . . . . . . . . | January 1975 to February 1987 |
| 87 | G. R. Viswanath (India) . . . . . . . | March 1971 to February 1983 |
| 85 | G. S. Sobers (West Indies) . . . . . . | April 1955 to April 1972 |
| 72 | D. L. Haynes (West Indies) . . . . . . | December 1979 to June 1988 |
| 71 | I. M. Chappell (Australia) . . . . . . | January 1966 to February 1976 |
| 66 | Kapil Dev (India) . . . . . . . . . . . . | October 1978 to December 1984 |
| 65 | I. T. Botham (England) . . . . . . . . | February 1978 to March 1984 |
| 65 | A. P. E. Knott (England). . . . . . . . | March 1971 to August 1977 |

**The most consecutive Test appearances for the countries not mentioned above are:**

| | | |
|---|---|---|
| 58† | J. R. Reid (New Zealand) . . . . . . | July 1949 to July 1965 |
| 53 | Javed Miandad (Pakistan) . . . . . . | December 1977 to January 1984 |
| 45† | A. W. Nourse (South Africa). . . . | October 1902 to August 1924 |
| 22 | A. Ranatunga (Sri Lanka) . . . . . . | April 1983 to December 1989 |

† *Indicates complete Test career.*

## SUMMARY OF ALL TEST MATCHES

To end of 1991 season in England

| | | Tests | E | A | SA | WI | NZ | I | P | SL | Tied | Drawn |
|---|---|---|---|---|---|---|---|---|---|---|---|---|
| **England** | v Australia | 274 | 88 | 104 | – | | | | | | – | 82 |
| | v South Africa | 102 | 46 | – | 18 | – | | | | | – | 38 |
| | v West Indies | 104 | 24 | – | – | 43 | – | | | | – | 37 |
| | v New Zealand | 69 | 31 | – | – | – | 4 | – | | | – | 34 |
| | v India | 78 | 31 | – | – | – | – | 11 | – | | – | 36 |
| | v Pakistan | 47 | 13 | – | – | – | – | – | 5 | – | – | 29 |
| | v Sri Lanka | 4 | 3 | – | – | – | – | – | – | 0 | – | 1 |
| **Australia** | v South Africa | 53 | – | 29 | 11 | – | – | – | – | – | – | 13 |
| | v West Indies | 72 | – | 29 | – | 24 | – | – | | | 1 | 18 |
| | v New Zealand | 26 | – | 10 | – | – | 6 | – | | | – | 10 |
| | v India | 45 | – | 20 | – | – | – | 8 | – | | 1 | 16 |
| | v Pakistan | 34 | – | 12 | – | – | – | – | 9 | – | – | 13 |
| | v Sri Lanka | 4 | – | 3 | – | – | – | – | – | 0 | – | 1 |
| **South Africa** | v New Zealand | 17 | – | – | 9 | – | 2 | – | – | – | – | 6 |
| **West Indies** | v New Zealand | 24 | – | – | – | 8 | 4 | – | | | – | 12 |
| | v India | 62 | – | – | – | 26 | – | 6 | – | | – | 30 |
| | v Pakistan | 28 | – | – | – | 10 | – | – | 7 | – | – | 11 |
| **New Zealand** | v India | 31 | – | – | – | – | 6 | 12 | – | | – | 13 |
| | v Pakistan | 32 | – | – | – | – | 3 | – | 13 | – | – | 16 |
| | v Sri Lanka | 9 | – | – | – | – | 4 | – | – | 0 | – | 5 |
| **India** | v Pakistan | 44 | – | – | – | – | – | 4 | 7 | – | – | 33 |
| | v Sri Lanka | 8 | – | – | – | – | – | 3 | – | 1 | – | 4 |
| **Pakistan** | v Sri Lanka | 9 | – | – | – | – | – | – | 5 | 1 | – | 3 |
| | | 1,176 | 236 | 207 | 38 | 111 | 29 | 44 | 46 | 2 | 2 | 461 |

| | Tests | Won | Lost | Drawn | Tied | Toss Won |
|---|---|---|---|---|---|---|
| England | 678 | 236 | 185 | 257 | – | 335 |
| Australia | 508 | 207 | 146 | 153 | 2 | 256 |
| South Africa | 172 | 38 | 77 | 57 | – | 80 |
| West Indies | 290 | 111 | 70 | 108 | 1 | 151 |
| New Zealand | 208 | 29 | 83 | 96 | – | 103 |
| India | 268 | 44 | 91 | 132 | 1 | 134 |
| Pakistan | 194 | 46 | 43 | 105 | – | 100 |
| Sri Lanka | 34 | 2 | 18 | 14 | – | 17 |

## ENGLAND v AUSTRALIA

*Captains*

| Season | England | | Australia | T | E | A | D |
|---|---|---|---|---|---|---|---|
| 1876-77 | James Lillywhite | | D. W. Gregory | 2 | 1 | 1 | 0 |
| 1878-79 | Lord Harris | | D. W. Gregory | 1 | 0 | 1 | 0 |
| 1880 | Lord Harris | | W. L. Murdoch | 1 | 1 | 0 | 0 |
| 1881-82 | A. Shaw | | W. L. Murdoch | 4 | 0 | 2 | 2 |
| 1882 | A. N. Hornby | | W. L. Murdoch | 1 | 0 | 1 | 0 |

## THE ASHES

| Season | England | Captains Australia | T | E | A | D | Held by |
|--------|---------|--------------------|---|---|---|---|---------|
| 1882-83 | Hon. Ivo Bligh | W. L. Murdoch | 4* | 2 | 2 | 0 | E |
| 1884 | Lord Harris[1] | W. L. Murdoch | 3 | 1 | 0 | 2 | E |
| 1884-85 | A. Shrewsbury | T. Horan[2] | 5 | 3 | 2 | 0 | E |
| 1886 | A. G. Steel | H. J. H. Scott | 3 | 3 | 0 | 0 | E |
| 1886-87 | A. Shrewsbury | P. S. McDonnell | 2 | 2 | 0 | 0 | E |
| 1887-88 | W. W. Read | P. S. McDonnell | 1 | 1 | 0 | 0 | E |
| 1888 | W. G. Grace[3] | P. S. McDonnell | 3 | 2 | 1 | 0 | E |
| 1890† | W. G. Grace | W. L. Murdoch | 2 | 2 | 0 | 0 | E |
| 1891-92 | W. G. Grace | J. McC. Blackham | 3 | 1 | 2 | 0 | A |
| 1893 | W. G. Grace[4] | J. McC. Blackham | 3 | 1 | 0 | 2 | A |
| 1894-95 | A. E. Stoddart | G. Giffen[5] | 5 | 3 | 2 | 0 | E |
| 1896 | W. G. Grace | G. H. S. Trott | 3 | 2 | 1 | 0 | E |
| 1897-98 | A. E. Stoddart[6] | G. H. S. Trott | 5 | 1 | 4 | 0 | A |
| 1899 | A. C. MacLaren[7] | J. Darling | 5 | 0 | 1 | 4 | A |
| 1901-02 | A. C. MacLaren | J. Darling[8] | 5 | 1 | 4 | 0 | A |
| 1902 | A. C. MacLaren | J. Darling | 5 | 1 | 2 | 2 | A |
| 1903-04 | P. F. Warner | M. A. Noble | 5 | 3 | 2 | 0 | E |
| 1905 | Hon. F. S. Jackson | J. Darling | 5 | 2 | 0 | 3 | E |
| 1907-08 | A. O. Jones[9] | M. A. Noble | 5 | 1 | 4 | 0 | A |
| 1909 | A. C. MacLaren | M. A. Noble | 5 | 1 | 2 | 2 | A |
| 1911-12 | J. W. H. T. Douglas | C. Hill | 5 | 4 | 1 | 0 | E |
| 1912 | C. B. Fry | S. E. Gregory | 3 | 1 | 0 | 2 | E |
| 1920-21 | J. W. H. T. Douglas | W. W. Armstrong | 5 | 0 | 5 | 0 | A |
| 1921 | Hon. L. H. Tennyson[10] | W. W. Armstrong | 5 | 0 | 3 | 2 | A |
| 1924-25 | A. E. R. Gilligan | H. L. Collins | 5 | 1 | 4 | 0 | A |
| 1926 | A. W. Carr[11] | H. L. Collins[12] | 5 | 1 | 0 | 4 | E |
| 1928-29 | A. P. F. Chapman[13] | J. Ryder | 5 | 4 | 1 | 0 | E |
| 1930 | A. P. F. Chapman[14] | W. M. Woodfull | 5 | 1 | 2 | 2 | A |
| 1932-33 | D. R. Jardine | W. M. Woodfull | 5 | 4 | 1 | 0 | E |
| 1934 | R. E. S. Wyatt[15] | W. M. Woodfull | 5 | 1 | 2 | 2 | A |
| 1936-37 | G. O. B. Allen | D. G. Bradman | 5 | 2 | 3 | 0 | A |
| 1938† | W. R. Hammond | D. G. Bradman | 4 | 1 | 1 | 2 | A |
| 1946-47 | W. R. Hammond[16] | D. G. Bradman | 5 | 0 | 3 | 2 | A |
| 1948 | N. W. D. Yardley | D. G. Bradman | 5 | 0 | 4 | 1 | A |
| 1950-51 | F. R. Brown | A. L. Hassett | 5 | 1 | 4 | 0 | A |
| 1953 | L. Hutton | A. L. Hassett | 5 | 1 | 0 | 4 | E |
| 1954-55 | L. Hutton | I. W. Johnson[17] | 5 | 3 | 1 | 1 | E |
| 1956 | P. B. H. May | I. W. Johnson | 5 | 2 | 1 | 2 | E |
| 1958-59 | P. B. H. May | R. Benaud | 5 | 0 | 4 | 1 | A |
| 1961 | P. B. H. May[18] | R. Benaud[19] | 5 | 1 | 2 | 2 | A |
| 1962-63 | E. R. Dexter | R. Benaud | 5 | 1 | 1 | 3 | A |
| 1964 | E. R. Dexter | R. B. Simpson | 5 | 0 | 1 | 4 | A |
| 1965-66 | M. J. K. Smith | R. B. Simpson[20] | 5 | 1 | 1 | 3 | A |
| 1968 | M. C. Cowdrey[21] | W. M. Lawry[22] | 5 | 1 | 1 | 3 | A |
| 1970-71† | R. Illingworth | W. M. Lawry[23] | 6 | 2 | 0 | 4 | E |
| 1972 | R. Illingworth | I. M. Chappell | 5 | 2 | 2 | 1 | E |
| 1974-75 | M. H. Denness[24] | I. M. Chappell | 6 | 1 | 4 | 1 | A |
| 1975 | A. W. Greig[25] | I. M. Chappell | 4 | 0 | 1 | 3 | A |
| 1976-77‡ | A. W. Greig | G. S. Chappell | 1 | 0 | 1 | 0 | — |
| 1977 | J. M. Brearley | G. S. Chappell | 5 | 3 | 0 | 2 | E |
| 1978-79 | J. M. Brearley | G. N. Yallop | 6 | 5 | 1 | 0 | E |
| 1979-80‡ | J. M. Brearley | G. S. Chappell | 3 | 0 | 3 | 0 | — |
| 1980‡ | I. T. Botham | G. S. Chappell | 1 | 0 | 0 | 1 | — |
| 1981 | J. M. Brearley[26] | K. J. Hughes | 6 | 3 | 1 | 2 | E |
| 1982-83 | R. G. D. Willis | G. S. Chappell | 5 | 1 | 2 | 2 | A |
| 1985 | D. I. Gower | A. R. Border | 6 | 3 | 1 | 2 | E |
| 1986-87 | M. W. Gatting | A. R. Border | 5 | 2 | 1 | 2 | E |
| 1987-88‡ | M. W. Gatting | A. R. Border | 1 | 0 | 0 | 1 | — |
| 1989 | D. I. Gower | A. R. Border | 6 | 0 | 4 | 2 | A |
| 1990-91 | G. A. Gooch[27] | A. R. Border | 5 | 0 | 3 | 2 | A |

| | | | T | E | A | D | |
|---|---|---|---|---|---|---|---|
| In Australia . . . . . . . . . . . . . . . . . . . . . . | | | 145 | 51 | 70 | 24 | |
| In England . . . . . . . . . . . . . . . . . . . . . . | | | 129 | 37 | 34 | 58 | |
| Totals . . . . . . . . . . . . . . . . . . . | | | 274 | 88 | 104 | 82 | |

\* *The Ashes were awarded in 1882-83 after a series of three matches which England won 2-1. A fourth unofficial match was played, each innings being played on a different pitch, and this was won by Australia.*

† *The matches at Manchester in 1890 and 1938 and at Melbourne (Third Test) in 1970-71 were abandoned without a ball being bowled and are excluded.*

‡ *The Ashes were not at stake in these series.*

Notes: The following deputised for the official touring captain or were appointed by the home authority for only a minor proportion of the series:

[1]A. N. Hornby (First). [2]W. L. Murdoch (First), H. H. Massie (Third), J. McC. Blackham (Fourth). [3]A. G. Steel (First). [4]A. E. Stoddart (First). [5]J. McC. Blackham (First). [6]A. C. MacLaren (First, Second and Fifth). [7]W. G. Grace (First). [8]H. Trumble (Fourth and Fifth). [9]F. L. Fane (First, Second and Third). [10]J. W. H. T. Douglas (First and Second). [11]A. P. F. Chapman (Fifth). [12]W. Bardsley (Third and Fourth). [13]J. C. White (Fifth). [14]R. E. S. Wyatt (Fifth). [15]C. F. Walters (First). [16]N. W. D. Yardley (Fifth). [17]A. R. Morris (Second). [18]M. C. Cowdrey (First and Second). [19]R. N. Harvey (Second). [20]B. C. Booth (First and Third). [21]T. W. Graveney (Fourth). [22]B. N. Jarman (Fourth). [23]I. M. Chappell (Seventh). [24]J. H. Edrich (Fourth). [25]M. H. Denness (First). [26]I. T. Botham (First and Second). [27]A. J. Lamb (First).

## HIGHEST INNINGS TOTALS

| | | |
|---|---|---|
| For England in England: 903-7 dec. at The Oval | | 1938 |
| in Australia: 636 at Sydney | | 1928-29 |
| | | |
| For Australia in England: 729-6 dec. at Lord's | | 1930 |
| in Australia: 659-8 dec. at Sydney | | 1946-47 |

## LOWEST INNINGS TOTALS

| | | |
|---|---|---|
| For England in England: 52 at The Oval | | 1948 |
| in Australia: 45 at Sydney | | 1886-87 |
| | | |
| For Australia in England: 36 at Birmingham | | 1902 |
| in Australia: 42 at Sydney | | 1887-88 |

## INDIVIDUAL HUNDREDS

### For England (196)

**R. Abel** (1)
132\*‡ Sydney ..... 1891-92
**L. E. G. Ames** (1)
120 Lord's ...... 1934
**M. A. Atherton** (1)
105 Sydney ..... 1990-91
**R. W. Barber** (1)
185 Sydney ..... 1965-66
**W. Barnes** (1)
134 Adelaide .... 1884-85
**C. J. Barnett** (2)
129 Adelaide .... 1936-37
126 Nottingham . 1938
**K. F. Barrington** (5)
132\* Adelaide .... 1962-63
101 Sydney ..... 1962-63
256 Manchester.. 1964

102 Adelaide .... 1965-66
115 Melbourne .. 1965-66
**I. T. Botham** (4)
119\* Melbourne .. 1979-80
149\* Leeds ...... 1981
118 Manchester.. 1981
138 Brisbane ... 1986-87
**G. Boycott** (7)
113 The Oval.... 1964
142\* Sydney .... 1970-71
119\* Adelaide .... 1970-71
107 Nottingham . 1977
191 Leeds ...... 1977
128\* Lord's ...... 1980
137 The Oval.... 1981
**L. C. Braund** (2)
103\* Adelaide .... 1901-02
102 Sydney ..... 1903-04

**J. Briggs** (1)
121 Melbourne .. 1884-85
**B. C. Broad** (4)
162 Perth....... 1986-87
116 Adelaide .... 1986-87
112 Melbourne .. 1986-87
139 Sydney ..... 1987-88
**J. T. Brown** (1)
140 Melbourne .. 1894-95
**A. P. F. Chapman** (1)
121 Lord's ...... 1930
**D. C. S. Compton** (5)
102† Nottingham . 1938
147
103\* } Adelaide .... 1946-47
184 Nottingham . 1948
145\* Manchester.. 1948

**M. C. Cowdrey (5)**

| | | |
|---|---|---|
| 102 | Melbourne | 1954-55 |
| 100* | Sydney | 1958-59 |
| 113 | Melbourne | 1962-63 |
| 104 | Melbourne | 1965-66 |
| 104 | Birmingham | 1968 |

**M. H. Denness (1)**

| | | |
|---|---|---|
| 188 | Melbourne | 1974-75 |

**E. R. Dexter (2)**

| | | |
|---|---|---|
| 180 | Birmingham | 1961 |
| 174 | Manchester | 1964 |

**B. L. D'Oliveira (2)**

| | | |
|---|---|---|
| 158 | The Oval | 1968 |
| 117 | Melbourne | 1970-71 |

**K. S. Duleepsinhji (1)**

| | | |
|---|---|---|
| 173† | Lord's | 1930 |

**J. H. Edrich (7)**

| | | |
|---|---|---|
| 120† | Lord's | 1964 |
| 109 | Melbourne | 1965-66 |
| 103 | Sydney | 1965-66 |
| 164 | The Oval | 1968 |
| 115* | Perth | 1970-71 |
| 130 | Adelaide | 1970-71 |
| 175 | Lord's | 1975 |

**W. J. Edrich (2)**

| | | |
|---|---|---|
| 119 | Sydney | 1946-47 |
| 111 | Leeds | 1948 |

**K. W. R. Fletcher (1)**

| | | |
|---|---|---|
| 146 | Melbourne | 1974-75 |

**R. E. Foster (1)**

| | | |
|---|---|---|
| 287† | Sydney | 1903-04 |

**C. B. Fry (1)**

| | | |
|---|---|---|
| 144 | The Oval | 1905 |

**M. W. Gatting (3)**

| | | |
|---|---|---|
| 160 | Manchester | 1985 |
| 100* | Birmingham | 1985 |
| 100 | Adelaide | 1986-87 |

**G. A. Gooch (2)**

| | | |
|---|---|---|
| 196 | The Oval | 1985 |
| 117 | Adelaide | 1990-91 |

**D. I. Gower (9)**

| | | |
|---|---|---|
| 102 | Perth | 1978-79 |
| 114 | Adelaide | 1982-83 |
| 166 | Nottingham | 1985 |
| 215 | Birmingham | 1985 |
| 157 | The Oval | 1985 |
| 136 | Perth | 1986-87 |
| 106 | Lord's | 1989 |
| 100 | Melbourne | 1990-91 |
| 123 | Sydney | 1990-91 |

**W. G. Grace (2)**

| | | |
|---|---|---|
| 152† | The Oval | 1880 |
| 170 | The Oval | 1886 |

**T. W. Graveney (1)**

| | | |
|---|---|---|
| 111 | Sydney | 1954-55 |

**A. W. Greig (1)**

| | | |
|---|---|---|
| 110 | Brisbane | 1974-75 |

**G. Gunn (2)**

| | | |
|---|---|---|
| 119† | Sydney | 1907-08 |
| 122* | Sydney | 1907-08 |

**W. Gunn (1)**

| | | |
|---|---|---|
| 102* | Manchester | 1893 |

**W. R. Hammond (9)**

| | | |
|---|---|---|
| 251 | Sydney | 1928-29 |
| 200 | Melbourne | 1928-29 |
| 119* ⎫ | Adelaide | 1928-29 |
| 177 ⎭ | | |
| 113 | Leeds | 1930 |
| 112 | Sydney | 1932-33 |
| 101 | Sydney | 1932-33 |
| 231* | Sydney | 1936-37 |
| 240 | Lord's | 1938 |

**J. Hardstaff jun. (1)**

| | | |
|---|---|---|
| 169* | The Oval | 1938 |

**T. W. Hayward (2)**

| | | |
|---|---|---|
| 130 | Manchester | 1899 |
| 137 | The Oval | 1899 |

**J. W. Hearne (1)**

| | | |
|---|---|---|
| 114 | Melbourne | 1911-12 |

**E. H. Hendren (3)**

| | | |
|---|---|---|
| 127* | Lord's | 1926 |
| 169 | Brisbane | 1928-29 |
| 132 | Manchester | 1934 |

**J. B. Hobbs (12)**

| | | |
|---|---|---|
| 126* | Melbourne | 1911-12 |
| 187 | Adelaide | 1911-12 |
| 178 | Melbourne | 1911-12 |
| 107 | Lord's | 1912 |
| 122 | Melbourne | 1920-21 |
| 123 | Adelaide | 1920-21 |
| 115 | Sydney | 1924-25 |
| 154 | Melbourne | 1924-25 |
| 119 | Adelaide | 1924-25 |
| 119 | Lord's | 1926 |
| 100 | The Oval | 1926 |
| 142 | Melbourne | 1928-29 |

**K. L. Hutchings (1)**

| | | |
|---|---|---|
| 126 | Melbourne | 1907-08 |

**L. Hutton (5)**

| | | |
|---|---|---|
| 100† | Nottingham | 1938 |
| 364 | The Oval | 1938 |
| 122* | Sydney | 1946-47 |
| 156*‡ | Adelaide | 1950-51 |
| 145 | Lord's | 1953 |

**Hon. F. S. Jackson (5)**

| | | |
|---|---|---|
| 103 | The Oval | 1893 |
| 118 | The Oval | 1899 |
| 128 | Manchester | 1902 |
| 144* | Leeds | 1905 |
| 113 | Manchester | 1905 |

**G. L. Jessop (1)**

| | | |
|---|---|---|
| 104 | The Oval | 1902 |

**A. P. E. Knott (2)**

| | | |
|---|---|---|
| 106* | Adelaide | 1974-75 |
| 135 | Nottingham | 1977 |

**A. J. Lamb (1)**

| | | |
|---|---|---|
| 125 | Leeds | 1989 |

**M. Leyland (7)**

| | | |
|---|---|---|
| 137† | Melbourne | 1928-29 |
| 109 | Lord's | 1934 |
| 153 | Manchester | 1934 |
| 110 | The Oval | 1934 |
| 126 | Brisbane | 1936-37 |
| 111* | Melbourne | 1936-37 |
| 187 | The Oval | 1938 |

**B. W. Luckhurst (2)**

| | | |
|---|---|---|
| 131 | Perth | 1970-71 |
| 109 | Melbourne | 1970-71 |

**A. C. MacLaren (5)**

| | | |
|---|---|---|
| 120 | Melbourne | 1894-95 |
| 109 | Sydney | 1897-98 |
| 124 | Adelaide | 1897-98 |
| 116 | Sydney | 1901-02 |
| 140 | Nottingham | 1905 |

**J. W. H. Makepeace (1)**

| | | |
|---|---|---|
| 117 | Melbourne | 1920-21 |

**P. B. H. May (3)**

| | | |
|---|---|---|
| 104 | Sydney | 1954-55 |
| 101 | Leeds | 1956 |
| 113 | Melbourne | 1958-59 |

**C. P. Mead (1)**

| | | |
|---|---|---|
| 182* | The Oval | 1921 |

**Nawab of Pataudi sen. (1)**

| | | |
|---|---|---|
| 102† | Sydney | 1932-33 |

**E. Paynter (1)**

| | | |
|---|---|---|
| 216* | Nottingham | 1938 |

**D. W. Randall (3)**

| | | |
|---|---|---|
| 174† | Melbourne | 1976-77 |
| 150 | Sydney | 1978-79 |
| 115 | Perth | 1982-83 |

**K. S. Ranjitsinhji (2)**

| | | |
|---|---|---|
| 154*† | Manchester | 1896 |
| 175 | Sydney | 1897-98 |

**W. W. Read (1)**

| | | |
|---|---|---|
| 117 | The Oval | 1884 |

**W. Rhodes (1)**

| | | |
|---|---|---|
| 179 | Melbourne | 1911-12 |

**C. J. Richards (1)**

| | | |
|---|---|---|
| 133 | Perth | 1986-87 |

**P. E. Richardson (1)**

| | | |
|---|---|---|
| 104 | Manchester | 1956 |

**R. T. Robinson (2)**

| | | |
|---|---|---|
| 175† | Leeds | 1985 |
| 148 | Birmingham | 1985 |

**A. C. Russell (3)**

| | | |
|---|---|---|
| 135* | Adelaide | 1920-21 |
| 101 | Manchester | 1921 |
| 102* | The Oval | 1921 |

**R. C. Russell (1)**

| | | |
|---|---|---|
| 128* | Manchester | 1989 |

**J. Sharp (1)**

| | | |
|---|---|---|
| 105 | The Oval | 1909 |

**Rev. D. S. Sheppard (2)**

| | | |
|---|---|---|
| 113 | Manchester | 1956 |
| 113 | Melbourne | 1962-63 |

**A. Shrewsbury (3)**

| | | |
|---|---|---|
| 105* | Melbourne | 1884-85 |
| 164 | Lord's | 1886 |
| 106 | Lord's | 1893 |

**R. T. Simpson (1)**

| | | |
|---|---|---|
| 156* | Melbourne | 1950-51 |

**R. A. Smith (2)**

| | | |
|---|---|---|
| 143 | Manchester | 1989 |
| 101 | Nottingham | 1989 |

**A. G. Steel (2)**

| | | |
|---|---|---|
| 135* | Sydney | 1882-83 |
| 148 | Lord's | 1884 |

**A. E. Stoddart** (2)
| | | |
|---|---|---|
| 134 | Adelaide .... | 1891-92 |
| 173 | Melbourne .. | 1894-95 |

**R. Subba Row** (2)
| | | |
|---|---|---|
| 112† | Birmingham .. | 1961 |
| 137 | The Oval .... | 1961 |

**H. Sutcliffe** (8)
| | | |
|---|---|---|
| 115‡ | Sydney ...... | 1924-25 |
| 176 | } Melbourne .. | 1924-25 |
| 127 | | 1924-25 |
| 143 | Melbourne .. | 1924-25 |
| 161 | The Oval .... | 1926 |

**J. T. Tyldesley** (3)
| | | |
|---|---|---|
| 138 | Birmingham .. | 1902 |
| 100 | Leeds ...... | 1905 |
| 112* | The Oval .... | 1905 |

**G. Ulyett** (1)
| | | |
|---|---|---|
| 149 | Melbourne .. | 1881-82 |

**A. Ward** (1)
| | | |
|---|---|---|
| 117 | Sydney ..... | 1894-95 |

**C. Washbrook** (2)
| | | |
|---|---|---|
| 112 | Melbourne .. | 1946-47 |
| 143 | Leeds ...... | 1948 |

**W. Watson** (1)
| | | |
|---|---|---|
| 109† | Lord's ...... | 1953 |

**F. E. Woolley** (2)
| | | |
|---|---|---|
| 133* | Sydney ..... | 1911-12 |
| 123 | Sydney ..... | 1924-25 |

**R. A. Woolmer** (3)
| | | |
|---|---|---|
| 149 | The Oval .... | 1975 |
| 120 | Lord's ...... | 1977 |
| 137 | Manchester.. | 1977 |

† *Signifies hundred on first appearance in England–Australia Tests.*
‡ *Carried his bat.*

*Note:* In consecutive innings in 1928-29, W. R. Hammond scored 251 at Sydney, 200 and 32 at Melbourne, and 119* and 177 at Adelaide.

### For Australia (214)

**W. W. Armstrong** (4)
| | | |
|---|---|---|
| 133* | Melbourne .. | 1907-08 |
| 158 | Sydney ..... | 1920-21 |
| 121 | Adelaide .... | 1920-21 |
| 123* | Melbourne .. | 1920-21 |

**C. L. Badcock** (1)
| | | |
|---|---|---|
| 118 | Melbourne .. | 1936-37 |

**C. Bannerman** (1)
| | | |
|---|---|---|
| 165*† | Melbourne .. | 1876-77 |

**W. Bardsley** (3)
| | | |
|---|---|---|
| 136 | } The Oval.... | 1909 |
| 130 | | 1909 |
| 193*‡ | Lord's ...... | 1926 |

**S. G. Barnes** (2)
| | | |
|---|---|---|
| 234 | Sydney ..... | 1946-47 |
| 141 | Lord's ...... | 1948 |

**G. J. Bonnor** (1)
| | | |
|---|---|---|
| 128 | Sydney ..... | 1884-85 |

**D. C. Boon** (3)
| | | |
|---|---|---|
| 103 | Adelaide .... | 1986-87 |
| 184* | Sydney ..... | 1987-88 |
| 121 | Adelaide .... | 1990-91 |

**B. C. Booth** (2)
| | | |
|---|---|---|
| 112 | Brisbane .... | 1962-63 |
| 103 | Melbourne .. | 1962-63 |

**A. R. Border** (7)
| | | |
|---|---|---|
| 115 | Perth ...... | 1979-80 |
| 123* | Manchester.. | 1981 |
| 106* | The Oval .... | 1981 |
| 196 | Lord's ...... | 1985 |
| 146* | Manchester.. | 1985 |
| 125 | Perth ...... | 1986-87 |
| 100* | Adelaide .... | 1986-87 |

**D. G. Bradman** (19)
| | | |
|---|---|---|
| 112 | Melbourne .. | 1928-29 |
| 123 | Melbourne .. | 1928-29 |
| 131 | Nottingham . | 1930 |
| 254 | Lord's ...... | 1930 |
| 334 | Leeds ...... | 1930 |
| 232 | The Oval .... | 1930 |
| 103* | Melbourne .. | 1932-33 |
| 304 | Leeds ...... | 1934 |
| 244 | The Oval .... | 1934 |
| 270 | Melbourne .. | 1936-37 |
| 212 | Adelaide .... | 1936-37 |
| 169 | Melbourne .. | 1936-37 |
| 144* | Nottingham . | 1938 |
| 102* | Lord's ...... | 1938 |
| 103 | Leeds ...... | 1938 |
| 187 | Brisbane .... | 1946-47 |
| 234 | Sydney ..... | 1946-47 |
| 138 | Nottingham . | 1948 |
| 173* | Leeds ...... | 1948 |

**W. A. Brown** (3)
| | | |
|---|---|---|
| 105 | Lord's ...... | 1934 |
| 133 | Nottingham . | 1938 |
| 206*‡ | Lord's ...... | 1938 |

**P. J. Burge** (4)
| | | |
|---|---|---|
| 181 | The Oval .... | 1961 |
| 103 | Sydney ..... | 1962-63 |
| 160 | Leeds ...... | 1964 |
| 120 | Melbourne .. | 1965-66 |

**J. W. Burke** (1)
| | | |
|---|---|---|
| 101*† | Adelaide .... | 1950-51 |

**G. S. Chappell** (9)
| | | |
|---|---|---|
| 108† | Perth ...... | 1970-71 |
| 131 | Lord's ...... | 1972 |
| 113 | The Oval .... | 1972 |
| 144 | Sydney ..... | 1974-75 |
| 102 | Melbourne .. | 1974-75 |
| 112 | Manchester.. | 1977 |
| 114 | Melbourne .. | 1979-80 |
| 117 | Perth ...... | 1982-83 |
| 115 | Adelaide .... | 1982-83 |

**I. M. Chappell** (4)
| | | |
|---|---|---|
| 111 | Melbourne .. | 1970-71 |
| 104 | Adelaide .... | 1970-71 |
| 118 | The Oval .... | 1972 |
| 192 | The Oval .... | 1975 |

**H. L. Collins** (3)
| | | |
|---|---|---|
| 104† | Sydney ..... | 1920-21 |
| 162 | Adelaide .... | 1920-21 |
| 114 | Sydney ..... | 1924-25 |

**R. M. Cowper** (1)
| | | |
|---|---|---|
| 307 | Melbourne .. | 1965-66 |

**J. Darling** (3)
| | | |
|---|---|---|
| 101 | Sydney ..... | 1897-98 |
| 178 | Adelaide .... | 1897-98 |
| 160 | Sydney ..... | 1897-98 |

**R. A. Duff** (2)
| | | |
|---|---|---|
| 104† | Melbourne .. | 1901-02 |
| 146 | The Oval .... | 1905 |

**J. Dyson** (1)
| | | |
|---|---|---|
| 102 | Leeds ...... | 1981 |

**R. Edwards** (2)
| | | |
|---|---|---|
| 170* | Nottingham . | 1972 |
| 115 | Perth ...... | 1974-75 |

**J. H. Fingleton** (2)
| | | |
|---|---|---|
| 100 | Brisbane .... | 1936-37 |
| 136 | Melbourne .. | 1936-37 |

**G. Giffen** (1)
| | | |
|---|---|---|
| 161 | Sydney ..... | 1894-95 |

**H. Graham** (2)
| | | |
|---|---|---|
| 107† | Lord's ...... | 1893 |
| 105 | Sydney ..... | 1894-95 |

**J. M. Gregory** (1)
| | | |
|---|---|---|
| 100 | Melbourne .. | 1920-21 |

**S. E. Gregory** (4)
| | | |
|---|---|---|
| 201 | Sydney ..... | 1894-95 |
| 103 | Lord's ...... | 1896 |
| 117 | The Oval .... | 1899 |
| 112 | Adelaide .... | 1903-04 |

**R. J. Hartigan** (1)
| | | |
|---|---|---|
| 116† | Adelaide .... | 1907-08 |

**R. N. Harvey** (6)
| | | |
|---|---|---|
| 112† | Leeds ...... | 1948 |
| 122 | Manchester.. | 1953 |
| 162 | Brisbane .... | 1954-55 |
| 167 | Melbourne .. | 1958-59 |
| 114 | Birmingham . | 1961 |
| 154 | Adelaide .... | 1962-63 |

**A. L. Hassett** (4)
| | | |
|---|---|---|
| 128 | Brisbane .... | 1946-47 |
| 137 | Nottingham . | 1948 |
| 115 | Nottingham . | 1953 |
| 104 | Lord's ...... | 1953 |

**H. S. T. L. Hendry** (1)
112   Sydney ..... 1928-29

**A. M. J. Hilditch** (1)
119   Leeds         1985

**C. Hill** (4)
188   Melbourne .. 1897-98
135   Lord's ...... 1899
119   Sheffield .... 1902
160   Adelaide .... 1907-08

**T. P. Horan** (1)
124   Melbourne .. 1881-82

**K. J. Hughes** (3)
129   Brisbane .... 1978-79
117   Lord's ...... 1980
137   Sydney ..... 1982-83

**F. A. Iredale** (2)
140   Adelaide .... 1894-95
108   Manchester.. 1896

**A. A. Jackson** (1)
164†  Adelaide .... 1928-29

**D. M. Jones** (3)
184*  Sydney ..... 1986-87
157   Birmingham . 1989
122   The Oval.... 1989

**C. Kelleway** (1)
147   Adelaide .... 1920-21

**A. F. Kippax** (1)
100   Melbourne .. 1928-29

**W. M. Lawry** (7)
130   Lord's ...... 1961
102   Manchester.. 1961
106   Manchester.. 1964
166   Brisbane .... 1965-66
119   Adelaide .... 1965-66
108   Melbourne .. 1965-66
135   The Oval.... 1968

**R. R. Lindwall** (1)
100   Melbourne .. 1946-47

**J. J. Lyons** (1)
134   Sydney ..... 1891-92

**C. G. Macartney** (5)
170   Sydney ..... 1920-21
115   Leeds ...... 1921
133*  Lord's ...... 1926
151   Leeds ...... 1926
109   Manchester.. 1926

**S. J. McCabe** (4)
187*  Sydney ..... 1932-33
137   Manchester.. 1934
112   Melbourne .. 1936-37
232   Nottingham . 1938

**C. L. McCool** (1)
104*  Melbourne .. 1946-47

**R. B. McCosker** (2)
127   The Oval.... 1975
107   Nottingham . 1977

**C. C. McDonald** (2)
170   Adelaide .... 1958-59
133   Melbourne .. 1958-59

**P. S. McDonnell** (3)
147   Sydney ..... 1881-82
103   The Oval.... 1884
124   Adelaide .... 1884-85

**C. E. McLeod** (1)
112   Melbourne .. 1897-98

**G. R. Marsh** (2)
110†  Brisbane .... 1986-87
138   Nottingham . 1989

**R. W. Marsh** (1)
110*  Melbourne .. 1976-77

**G. R. J. Matthews** (1)
128   Sydney ..... 1990-91

**K. R. Miller** (3)
141*  Adelaide .... 1946-47
145*  Sydney ..... 1950-51
109   Lord's ...... 1953

**A. R. Morris** (8)
155   Melbourne .. 1946-47
122   } Adelaide .... 1946-47
124*  }
105   Lord's ...... 1948
182   Leeds ...... 1948
196   The Oval.... 1948
206   Adelaide .... 1950-51
153   Brisbane .... 1954-55

**W. L. Murdoch** (2)
153*  The Oval.... 1880
211   The Oval.... 1884

**M. A. Noble** (1)
133   Sydney ..... 1903-04

**N. C. O'Neill** (2)
117   The Oval.... 1961
100   Adelaide .... 1962-63

**C. E. Pellew** (2)
116   Melbourne .. 1920-21
104   Adelaide .... 1920-21

**W. H. Ponsford** (5)
110†  Sydney ..... 1924-25
128   Melbourne .. 1924-25
110   The Oval.... 1930
181   Leeds ...... 1934
266   The Oval.... 1934

**V. S. Ransford** (1)
143*  Lord's ...... 1909

**I. R. Redpath** (2)
171   Perth....... 1970-71
105   Sydney ..... 1974-75

**A. J. Richardson** (1)
100   Leeds ...... 1926

**V. Y. Richardson** (1)
138   Melbourne .. 1924-25

**G. M. Ritchie** (1)
146   Nottingham . 1985

**J. Ryder** (2)
201*  Adelaide .... 1924-25
112   Melbourne .. 1928-29

**H. J. H. Scott** (1)
102   The Oval.... 1884

**R. B. Simpson** (2)
311   Manchester.. 1964
225   Adelaide .... 1965-66

**K. R. Stackpole** (3)
207   Brisbane .... 1970-71
136   Adelaide .... 1970-71
114   Nottingham . 1972

**J. M. Taylor** (1)
108   Sydney ..... 1924-25

**M. A. Taylor** (2)
136†  Leeds ...... 1989
219   Nottingham . 1989

**G. H. S. Trott** (1)
143   Lord's ...... 1896

**V. T. Trumper** (6)
135*  Lord's ...... 1899
104   Manchester.. 1902
185*  Sydney ..... 1903-04
113   Adelaide .... 1903-04
166   Sydney ..... 1907-08
113   Sydney ..... 1911-12

**K. D. Walters** (4)
155†  Brisbane .... 1965-66
115   Melbourne .. 1965-66
112   Brisbane .... 1970-71
103   Perth....... 1974-75

**M. E. Waugh** (1)
138†  Adelaide .... 1990-91

**S. R. Waugh** (2)
177*  Leeds ...... 1989
152*  Lord's ...... 1989

**D. M. Wellham** (1)
103†  The Oval.... 1981

**K. C. Wessels** (1)
162†  Brisbane .... 1982-83

**G. M. Wood** (3)
100   Melbourne .. 1978-79
112   Lord's ...... 1980
172   Nottingham . 1985

**W. M. Woodfull** (6)
141   Leeds ...... 1926
117   Manchester.. 1926
111   Sydney ..... 1928-29
107   Melbourne .. 1928-29
102   Melbourne .. 1928-29
155   Lord's ...... 1930

**G. N. Yallop** (3)
102†  Brisbane .... 1978-79
121   Sydney ..... 1978-79
114   Manchester.. 1981

---

† *Signifies hundred on first appearance in England–Australia Tests.*

‡ *Carried his bat.*

*Notes:* D. G. Bradman's scores in 1930 were 8 and 131 at Nottingham, 254 and 1 at Lord's, 334 at Leeds, 14 at Manchester, and 232 at The Oval.

D. G. Bradman scored a hundred in eight successive Tests against England in which he batted – three in 1936-37, three in 1938 and two in 1946-47. He was injured and unable to bat at The Oval in 1938.

W. H. Ponsford and K. D. Walters each hit hundreds in their first two Tests.

C. Bannerman and H. Graham each scored their maiden hundred in first-class cricket in their first Test.

No right-handed batsman has obtained two hundreds for Australia in a Test match against England, and no left-handed batsman in a Test against Australia.

H. Sutcliffe, in his first two games for England, scored 59 and 115 at Sydney and 176 and 127 at Melbourne in 1924-25. In the latter match, which lasted into the seventh day, he was on the field throughout except for 86 minutes, namely 27 hours and 52 minutes.

C. Hill made 98 and 97 at Adelaide in 1901-02, and F. E. Woolley 95 and 93 at Lord's in 1921.

H. Sutcliffe in 1924-25, C. G. Macartney in 1926 and A. R. Morris in 1946-47 made three hundreds in consecutive innings.

J. B. Hobbs and H. Sutcliffe shared eleven first-wicket three-figure partnerships.

L. Hutton and C. Washbrook twice made three-figure stands in each innings, at Adelaide in 1946-47 and at Leeds in 1948.

H. Sutcliffe, during his highest score of 194, v Australia in 1932-33, took part in three stands each exceeding 100, viz. 112 with R. E. S. Wyatt for the first wicket, 188 with W. R. Hammond for the second wicket, and 123 with the Nawab of Pataudi sen. for the third wicket. In 1903-04 R. E. Foster, in his historic innings of 287, added 192 for the fifth wicket with L. C. Braund, 115 for the ninth with A. E. Relf, and 130 for the tenth with W. Rhodes.

When L. Hutton scored 364 at The Oval in 1938 he added 382 for the second wicket with M. Leyland, 135 for the third wicket with W. R. Hammond and 215 for the sixth wicket with J. Hardstaff jun.

D. C. S. Compton and A. R. Morris at Adelaide in 1946-47 provided the first instance of a player on each side hitting two separate hundreds in a Test match.

G. S. and I. M. Chappell at The Oval in 1972 provide the first instance in Test matches of brothers each scoring hundreds in the same innings.

## RECORD PARTNERSHIPS FOR EACH WICKET

### For England

| | | |
|---|---|---|
| 323 for 1st | J. B. Hobbs and W. Rhodes at Melbourne ................. | 1911-12 |
| 382 for 2nd† | L. Hutton and M. Leyland at The Oval .................. | 1938 |
| 262 for 3rd | W. R. Hammond and D. R. Jardine at Adelaide .......... | 1928-29 |
| 222 for 4th | W. R. Hammond and E. Paynter at Lord's .............. | 1938 |
| 206 for 5th | E. Paynter and D. C. S. Compton at Nottingham ........ | 1938 |
| 215 for 6th { | L. Hutton and J. Hardstaff jun. at The Oval ............ | 1938 |
|  | G. Boycott and A. P. E. Knott at Nottingham .......... | 1977 |
| 143 for 7th | F. E. Woolley and J. Vine at Sydney .................. | 1911-12 |
| 124 for 8th | E. H. Hendren and H. Larwood at Brisbane ............ | 1928-29 |
| 151 for 9th | W. H. Scotton and W. W. Read at The Oval ............ | 1884 |
| 130 for 10th† | R. E. Foster and W. Rhodes at Sydney ................ | 1903-04 |

### For Australia

| | | |
|---|---|---|
| 329 for 1st | G. R. Marsh and M. A. Taylor at Nottingham .......... | 1989 |
| 451 for 2nd† | W. H. Ponsford and D. G. Bradman at The Oval ........ | 1934 |
| 276 for 3rd | D. G. Bradman and A. L. Hassett at Brisbane .......... | 1946-47 |
| 388 for 4th† | W. H. Ponsford and D. G. Bradman at Leeds .......... | 1934 |
| 405 for 5th†‡ | S. G. Barnes and D. G. Bradman at Sydney ............ | 1946-47 |
| 346 for 6th† | J. H. Fingleton and D. G. Bradman at Melbourne ...... | 1936-37 |
| 165 for 7th | C. Hill and H. Trumble at Melbourne ................ | 1897-98 |
| 243 for 8th† | R. J. Hartigan and C. Hill at Adelaide ................ | 1907-08 |
| 154 for 9th | S. E. Gregory and J. McC. Blackham at Sydney ........ | 1894-95 |
| 127 for 10th† | J. M. Taylor and A. A. Mailey at Sydney .............. | 1924-25 |

† *Denotes record partnership against all countries.*
‡ *Record fifth-wicket partnership in first-class cricket.*

## MOST RUNS IN A SERIES

| | | | |
|---|---|---|---|
| England in England ........ | 732 (average 81.33) | D. I. Gower........ | 1985 |
| England in Australia ........ | 905 (average 113.12) | W. R. Hammond .. | 1928-29 |
| Australia in England ........ | 974 (average 139.14) | D. G. Bradman .... | 1930 |
| Australia in Australia........ | 810 (average 90.00) | D. G. Bradman .... | 1936-37 |

## TEN WICKETS OR MORE IN A MATCH

### For England (37)

| | | |
|---|---|---|
| 13-163 (6-42, 7-121) | S. F. Barnes, Melbourne ................... | 1901-02 |
| 14-102 (7-28, 7-74) | W. Bates, Melbourne...................... | 1882-83 |
| 10-105 (5-46, 5-59) | A. V. Bedser, Melbourne.................. | 1950-51 |
| 14-99 (7-55, 7-44) | A. V. Bedser, Nottingham ................ | 1953 |
| 11-102 (6-44, 5-58) | C. Blythe, Birmingham ................... | 1909 |
| 11-176 (6-78, 5-98) | I. T. Botham, Perth ...................... | 1979-80 |
| 10-253 (6-125, 4-128) | I. T. Botham, The Oval ................... | 1981 |
| 11-74 (5-29, 6-45) | J. Briggs, Lord's ........................ | 1886 |
| 12-136 (6-49, 6-87) | J. Briggs, Adelaide ...................... | 1891-92 |
| 10-148 (5-34, 5-114) | J. Briggs, The Oval ..................... | 1893 |
| 10-104 (6-77, 4-27)† | R. M. Ellison, Birmingham ............... | 1985 |
| 10-179 (5-102, 5-77)† | K. Farnes, Nottingham ................... | 1934 |
| 10-60 (6-41, 4-19) | J. T. Hearne, The Oval ................... | 1896 |
| 11-113 (5-58, 6-55) | J. C. Laker, Leeds ...................... | 1956 |
| 19-90 (9-37, 10-53) | J. C. Laker, Manchester .................. | 1956 |
| 10-124 (5-96, 5-28) | H. Larwood, Sydney ..................... | 1932-33 |
| 11-76 (6-48, 5-28) | W. H. Lockwood, Manchester ............. | 1902 |
| 12-104 (7-36, 5-68) | G. A. Lohmann, The Oval ................ | 1886 |
| 10-87 (8-35, 2-52) | G. A. Lohmann, Sydney .................. | 1886-87 |
| 10-142 (8-58, 2-84) | G. A. Lohmann, Sydney .................. | 1891-92 |
| 12-102 (6-50, 6-52)† | F. Martin, The Oval ..................... | 1890 |
| 10-58 (5-18, 5-40) | R. Peel, Sydney ......................... | 1887-88 |
| 11-68 (7-31, 4-37) | R. Peel, Manchester ..................... | 1888 |
| 15-124 (7-56, 8-68) | W. Rhodes, Melbourne ................... | 1903-04 |
| 10-156 (5-49, 5-107)† | T. Richardson, Manchester ............... | 1893 |
| 11-173 (6-39, 5-134) | T. Richardson, Lord's .................... | 1896 |
| 13-244 (7-168, 6-76) | T. Richardson, Manchester ............... | 1896 |
| 10-204 (8-94, 2-110) | T. Richardson, Sydney ................... | 1897-98 |
| 11-228 (6-130, 5-98)† | M. W. Tate, Sydney ..................... | 1924-25 |
| 11-88 (5-58, 6-30) | F. S. Trueman, Leeds .................... | 1961 |
| 10-130 (4-45, 6-85) | F. H. Tyson, Sydney ..................... | 1954-55 |
| 10-82 (4-37, 6-45) | D. L. Underwood, Leeds .................. | 1972 |
| 11-215 (7-113, 4-102) | D. L. Underwood, Adelaide ............... | 1974-75 |
| 15-104 (7-61, 8-43) | H. Verity, Lord's ....................... | 1934 |
| 10-57 (6-41, 4-16) | W. Voce, Brisbane....................... | 1936-37 |
| 13-256 (5-130, 8-126) | J. C. White, Adelaide .................... | 1928-29 |
| 10-49 (5-29, 5-20) | F. E. Woolley, The Oval .................. | 1912 |

### For Australia (38)

| | | |
|---|---|---|
| 10-151 (5-107, 5-44) | T. M. Alderman, Leeds................... | 1989 |
| 10-239 (4-129, 6-110) | L. O'B. Fleetwood-Smith, Adelaide ........ | 1936-37 |
| 10-160 (4-88, 6-72) | G. Giffen, Sydney ....................... | 1891-92 |
| 11-82 (5-45, 6-37)† | C. V. Grimmett, Sydney .................. | 1924-25 |
| 10-201 (5-107, 5-94) | C. V. Grimmett, Nottingham .............. | 1930 |
| 10-122 (5-65, 5-57) | R. M. Hogg, Perth ...................... | 1978-79 |
| 10-66 (5-30, 5-36) | R. M. Hogg, Melbourne .................. | 1978-79 |
| 12-175 (5-85, 7-90)† | H. V. Hordern, Sydney ................... | 1911-12 |

| 10-161 (5-95, 5-66) | H. V. Hordern, Sydney | 1911-12 |
|---|---|---|
| 10-164 (7-88, 3-76) | E. Jones, Lord's | 1899 |
| 11-134 (6-47, 5-87) | G. F. Lawson, Brisbane | 1982-83 |
| 10-181 (5-58, 5-123) | D. K. Lillee, The Oval | 1972 |
| 11-165 (6-26, 5-139) | D. K. Lillee, Melbourne | 1976-77 |
| 11-138 (6-60, 5-78) | D. K. Lillee, Melbourne | 1979-80 |
| 11-159 (7-89, 4-70) | D. K. Lillee, The Oval | 1981 |
| 11-85 (7-58, 4-27) | C. G. Macartney, Leeds | 1909 |
| 11-157 (8-97, 3-60) | C. J. McDermott, Perth | 1990-91 |
| 10-302 (5-160, 5-142) | A. A. Mailey, Adelaide | 1920-21 |
| 13-236 (4-115, 9-121) | A. A. Mailey, Melbourne | 1920-21 |
| 16-137 (8-84, 8-53)† | R. A. L. Massie, Lord's | 1972 |
| 10-152 (5-72, 5-80) | K. R. Miller, Lord's | 1956 |
| 13-77 (7-17, 6-60) | M. A. Noble, Melbourne | 1901-02 |
| 11-103 (5-51, 6-52) | M. A. Noble, Sheffield | 1902 |
| 10-129 (5-63, 5-66) | W. J. O'Reilly, Melbourne | 1932-33 |
| 11-129 (4-75, 7-54) | W. J. O'Reilly, Nottingham | 1934 |
| 10-122 (5-66, 5-56) | W. J. O'Reilly, Leeds | 1938 |
| 11-165 (7-68, 4-97) | G. E. Palmer, Sydney | 1881-82 |
| 10-126 (7-65, 3-61) | G. E. Palmer, Melbourne | 1882-83 |
| 13-148 (6-97, 7-51) | B. A. Reid, Melbourne | 1990-91 |
| 13-110 (6-48, 7-62) | F. R. Spofforth, Melbourne | 1878-79 |
| 14-90 (7-46, 7-44) | F. R. Spofforth, The Oval | 1882 |
| 11-117 (4-73, 7-44) | F. R. Spofforth, Sydney | 1882-83 |
| 10-144 (4-54, 6-90) | F. R. Spofforth, Sydney | 1884-85 |
| 12-89 (6-59, 6-30) | H. Trumble, The Oval | 1896 |
| 10-128 (4-75, 6-53) | H. Trumble, Manchester | 1902 |
| 12-173 (8-65, 4-108) | H. Trumble, The Oval | 1902 |
| 12-87 (5-44, 7-43) | C. T. B. Turner, Sydney | 1887-88 |
| 10-63 (5-27, 5-36) | C. T. B. Turner, Lord's | 1888 |

† *Signifies ten wickets or more on first appearance in England–Australia Tests.*

*Note:* J. Briggs, J. C. Laker, T. Richardson in 1896, R. M. Hogg, A. A. Mailey, H. Trumble and C. T. B. Turner took ten wickets or more in successive Tests. J. Briggs was omitted, however, from the England team for the first Test match in 1893.

## MOST WICKETS IN A SERIES

| England in England | 46 (average 9.60) | J. C. Laker | 1956 |
|---|---|---|---|
| England in Australia | 38 (average 23.18) | M. W. Tate | 1924-25 |
| Australia in England | 42 (average 21.26) | T. M. Alderman (6 Tests) | 1981 |
| Australia in Australia | 41 (average 12.85) | R. M. Hogg (6 Tests) | 1978-79 |

## WICKET-KEEPING – MOST DISMISSALS

| | M | Ct | St | Total |
|---|---|---|---|---|
| †R. W. Marsh (Australia) | 42 | 141 | 7 | 148 |
| A. P. E. Knott (England) | 34 | 97 | 8 | 105 |
| †W. A. Oldfield (Australia) | 38 | 59 | 31 | 90 |
| A. A. Lilley (England) | 32 | 65 | 19 | 84 |
| A. T. W. Grout (Australia) | 22 | 69 | 7 | 76 |
| T. G. Evans (England) | 31 | 63 | 12 | 75 |

† *The number of catches by R. W. Marsh (141) and stumpings by W. A. Oldfield (31) are respective records in England–Australia Tests.*

## SCORERS OF OVER 2,000 RUNS

|  | T |  | I |  | NO |  | R |  | HI |  | Avge |
|---|---|---|---|---|---|---|---|---|---|---|---|
| D. G. Bradman | 37 | .. | 63 | .. | 7 | .. | 5,028 | .. | 334 | .. | 89.78 |
| J. B. Hobbs | 41 | .. | 71 | .. | 4 | .. | 3,636 | .. | 187 | .. | 54.26 |
| D. I. Gower | 42 | .. | 77 | .. | 4 | .. | 3,269 | .. | 215 | .. | 44.78 |
| A. R. Border | 41 | .. | 73 | .. | 18 | .. | 3,115 | .. | 196 | .. | 56.63 |
| G. Boycott | 38 | .. | 71 | .. | 9 | .. | 2,945 | .. | 191 | .. | 47.50 |
| W. R. Hammond | 33 | .. | 58 | .. | 3 | .. | 2,852 | .. | 251 | .. | 51.85 |
| H. Sutcliffe | 27 | .. | 46 | .. | 5 | .. | 2,741 | .. | 194 | .. | 66.85 |
| C. Hill | 41 | .. | 76 | .. | 1 | .. | 2,660 | .. | 188 | .. | 35.46 |
| J. H. Edrich | 32 | .. | 57 | .. | 3 | .. | 2,644 | .. | 175 | .. | 48.96 |
| G. S. Chappell | 35 | .. | 65 | .. | 8 | .. | 2,619 | .. | 144 | .. | 45.94 |
| M. C. Cowdrey | 43 | .. | 75 | .. | 4 | .. | 2,433 | .. | 113 | .. | 34.26 |
| L. Hutton | 27 | .. | 49 | .. | 6 | .. | 2,428 | .. | 364 | .. | 56.46 |
| R. N. Harvey | 37 | .. | 68 | .. | 5 | .. | 2,416 | .. | 167 | .. | 38.34 |
| V. T. Trumper | 40 | .. | 74 | .. | 5 | .. | 2,263 | .. | 185* | .. | 32.79 |
| W. M. Lawry | 29 | .. | 51 | .. | 5 | .. | 2,233 | .. | 166 | .. | 48.54 |
| S. E. Gregory | 52 | .. | 92 | .. | 7 | .. | 2,193 | .. | 201 | .. | 25.80 |
| W. W. Armstrong | 42 | .. | 71 | .. | 9 | .. | 2,172 | .. | 158 | .. | 35.03 |
| I. M. Chappell | 30 | .. | 56 | .. | 4 | .. | 2,138 | .. | 192 | .. | 41.11 |
| K. F. Barrington | 23 | .. | 39 | .. | 6 | .. | 2,111 | .. | 256 | .. | 63.96 |
| A. R. Morris | 24 | .. | 43 | .. | 2 | .. | 2,080 | .. | 206 | .. | 50.73 |

## BOWLERS WITH 100 WICKETS

|  | T |  | Balls |  | R |  | W |  | 5W/i |  | Avge |
|---|---|---|---|---|---|---|---|---|---|---|---|
| D. K. Lillee | 29 | .. | 8,516 | .. | 3,507 | .. | 167 | .. | 11 | .. | 21.00 |
| I. T. Botham | 36 | .. | 8,479 | .. | 4,093 | .. | 148 | .. | 9 | .. | 27.65 |
| H. Trumble | 31 | .. | 7,895 | .. | 2,945 | .. | 141 | .. | 9 | .. | 20.88 |
| R. G. D. Willis | 35 | .. | 7,294 | .. | 3,346 | .. | 128 | .. | 7 | .. | 26.14 |
| M. A. Noble | 39 | .. | 6,845 | .. | 2,860 | .. | 115 | .. | 9 | .. | 24.86 |
| R. R. Lindwall | 29 | .. | 6,728 | .. | 2,559 | .. | 114 | .. | 6 | .. | 22.44 |
| W. Rhodes | 41 | .. | 5,791 | .. | 2,616 | .. | 109 | .. | 6 | .. | 24.00 |
| S. F. Barnes | 20 | .. | 5,749 | .. | 2,288 | .. | 106 | .. | 12 | .. | 21.58 |
| C. V. Grimmett | 22 | .. | 9,224 | .. | 3,439 | .. | 106 | .. | 11 | .. | 32.44 |
| D. L. Underwood | 29 | .. | 8,000 | .. | 2,770 | .. | 105 | .. | 4 | .. | 26.38 |
| A. V. Bedser | 21 | .. | 7,065 | .. | 2,859 | .. | 104 | .. | 7 | .. | 27.49 |
| G. Giffen | 31 | .. | 6,325 | .. | 2,791 | .. | 103 | .. | 7 | .. | 27.09 |
| W. J. O'Reilly | 19 | .. | 7,864 | .. | 2,587 | .. | 102 | .. | 8 | .. | 25.36 |
| R. Peel | 20 | .. | 5,216 | .. | 1,715 | .. | 102 | .. | 6 | .. | 16.81 |
| C. T. B. Turner | 17 | .. | 5,195 | .. | 1,670 | .. | 101 | .. | 11 | .. | 16.53 |
| T. M. Alderman | 17 | .. | 4,717 | .. | 2,117 | .. | 100 | .. | 11 | .. | 21.17 |
| J. R. Thomson | 21 | .. | 4,951 | .. | 2,418 | .. | 100 | .. | 5 | .. | 24.18 |

## ENGLAND v SOUTH AFRICA

|  |  | Captains |  |  |  |  |  |
|---|---|---|---|---|---|---|---|
| Season | England |  | South Africa | T | E | SA | D |
| 1888-89 | C. A. Smith[1] | O. R. Dunell[2] | | 2 | 2 | 0 | 0 |
| 1891-92 | W. W. Read | W. H. Milton | | 1 | 1 | 0 | 0 |
| 1895-96 | Lord Hawke[3] | E. A. Halliwell[4] | | 3 | 3 | 0 | 0 |
| 1898-99 | Lord Hawke | M. Bisset | | 2 | 2 | 0 | 0 |
| 1905-06 | P. F. Warner | P. W. Sherwell | | 5 | 1 | 4 | 0 |
| 1907 | R. E. Foster | P. W. Sherwell | | 3 | 1 | 0 | 2 |
| 1909-10 | H. D. G. Leveson Gower[5] | S. J. Snooke | | 5 | 2 | 3 | 0 |
| 1912 | C. B. Fry | F. Mitchell[6] | | 3 | 3 | 0 | 0 |
| 1913-14 | J. W. H. T. Douglas | H. W. Taylor | | 5 | 4 | 0 | 1 |

Captains

| Season | England | South Africa | T | E | SA | D |
|---|---|---|---|---|---|---|
| 1922-23 | F. T. Mann | H. W. Taylor | 5 | 2 | 1 | 2 |
| 1924 | A. E. R. Gilligan[7] | H. W. Taylor | 5 | 3 | 0 | 2 |
| 1927-28 | R. T. Stanyforth[8] | H. G. Deane | 5 | 2 | 2 | 1 |
| 1929 | J. C. White[9] | H. G. Deane | 5 | 2 | 0 | 3 |
| 1930-31 | A. P. F. Chapman | H. G. Deane[10] | 5 | 0 | 1 | 4 |
| 1935 | R. E. S. Wyatt | H. F. Wade | 5 | 0 | 1 | 4 |
| 1938-39 | W. R. Hammond | A. Melville | 5 | 1 | 0 | 4 |
| 1947 | N. W. D. Yardley | A. Melville | 5 | 3 | 0 | 2 |
| 1948-49 | F. G. Mann | A. D. Nourse | 5 | 2 | 0 | 3 |
| 1951 | F. R. Brown | A. D. Nourse | 5 | 3 | 1 | 1 |
| 1955 | P. B. H. May | J. E. Cheetham[11] | 5 | 3 | 2 | 0 |
| 1956-57 | P. B. H. May | C. B. van Ryneveld[12] | 5 | 2 | 2 | 1 |
| 1960 | M. C. Cowdrey | D. J. McGlew | 5 | 3 | 0 | 2 |
| 1964-65 | M. J. K. Smith | T. L. Goddard | 5 | 1 | 0 | 4 |
| 1965 | M. J. K. Smith | P. L. van der Merwe | 3 | 0 | 1 | 2 |
| | In South Africa | | 58 | 25 | 13 | 20 |
| | In England | | 44 | 21 | 5 | 18 |
| | Totals | | 102 | 46 | 18 | 38 |

*Notes:* The following deputised for the official touring captain or were appointed by the home authority for only a minor proportion of the series:

[1]M. P. Bowden (Second). [2]W. H. Milton (Second). [3]Sir T. C. O'Brien (First). [4]A. R. Richards (Third). [5]F. L. Fane (Fourth and Fifth). [6]L. J. Tancred (Second and Third). [7]J. W. H. T. Douglas (Fourth). [8]G. T. S. Stevens (Fifth). [9]A. W. Carr (Fourth and Fifth). [10]E. P. Nupen (First), H. B. Cameron (Fourth and Fifth). [11]D. J. McGlew (Third and Fourth). [12]D. J. McGlew (Second).

## HIGHEST INNINGS TOTALS

For England in England: 554-8 dec. at Lord's .......................................... 1947
in South Africa: 654-5 at Durban ........................... 1938-39

For South Africa in England: 538 at Leeds ............................. 1951
in South Africa: 530 at Durban ................... 1938-39

## LOWEST INNINGS TOTALS

For England in England: 76 at Leeds ...................................... 1907
in South Africa: 92 at Cape Town ........................... 1898-99

For South Africa in England: 30 at Birmingham........................ 1924
in South Africa: 30 at Port Elizabeth .................... 1895-96

## INDIVIDUAL HUNDREDS

### For England (87)

| | | | |
|---|---|---|---|
| **R. Abel** (1) | | 113 | The Oval.... | 1947 |

**R. Abel** (1)
120　　Cape Town .. 1888-89
**L. E. G. Ames** (2)
148* The Oval.... 1935
115　　Cape Town .. 1938-39
**K. F. Barrington** (2)
148* Durban ..... 1964-65
121　 Johannesburg 1964-65

**G. Boycott** (1)
117　Pt Elizabeth . 1964-65
**L. C. Braund** (1)
104† Lord's ...... 1907
**D. C. S. Compton** (7)
163† Nottingham . 1947
208　Lord's ...... 1947
115　Manchester.. 1947

113　The Oval.... 1947
114　Johannesburg 1948-49
112　Nottingham . 1951
158　Manchester.. 1955
**M. C. Cowdrey** (3)
101　Cape Town .. 1956-57
155　The Oval.... 1960
105　Nottingham . 1965

**D. Denton (1)**
104 Johannesburg 1909-10

**E. R. Dexter (1)**
172 Johannesburg 1964-65

**J. W. H. T. Douglas (1)**
119† Durban 1913-14

**W. J. Edrich (3)**
219 Durban 1938-39
189 Lord's 1947
191 Manchester.. 1947

**F. L. Fane (1)**
143 Johannesburg 1905-06

**C. B. Fry (1)**
129 The Oval 1907

**P. A. Gibb (2)**
106† Johannesburg 1938-39
120 Durban 1938-39

**W. R. Hammond (6)**
138* Birmingham 1929
101* The Oval 1929
136* Durban 1930-31
181 Cape Town 1938-39
120 Durban 1938-39
140 Durban 1938-39

**T. W. Hayward (1)**
122 Johannesburg 1895-96

**E. H. Hendren (2)**
132 Leeds 1924
142 The Oval 1924

**A. J. L. Hill (1)**
124 Cape Town 1895-96

**J. B. Hobbs (2)**
187 Cape Town 1909-10
211 Lord's 1924

**L. Hutton (4)**
100 Leeds 1947
158 Johannesburg 1948-49
123 Johannesburg 1948-49
100 Leeds 1951

**D. J. Insole (1)**
110* Durban 1956-57

**M. Leyland (2)**
102 Lord's 1929
161 The Oval 1935

**F. G. Mann (1)**
136* Pt Elizabeth 1948-49

**P. B. H. May (3)**
138† Leeds 1951
112 Lord's 1955
117 Manchester.. 1955

**C. P. Mead (3)**
102 Johannesburg 1913-14
117 Pt Elizabeth 1913-14
181 Durban 1922-23

**P. H. Parfitt (1)**
122† Johannesburg 1964-65

**J. M. Parks (1)**
108* Durban 1964-65

**E. Paynter (3)**
117
100 }†Johannesburg 1938-39
243 Durban 1938-39

**G. Pullar (1)**
175 The Oval 1960

**W. Rhodes (1)**
152 Johannesburg 1913-14

**P. E. Richardson (1)**
117† Johannesburg 1956-57

**R. W. V. Robins (1)**
108 Manchester.. 1935

**A. C. Russell (2)**
140
111 }Durban 1922-23

**R. T. Simpson (1)**
137 Nottingham . 1951

**M. J. K. Smith (1)**
121 Cape Town .. 1964-65

**R. H. Spooner (1)**
119† Lord's 1912

**H. Sutcliffe (6)**
122 Lord's 1924
102 Johannesburg 1927-28
114 Birmingham 1929
100 Lord's 1929
104
109* }The Oval 1929

**M. W. Tate (1)**
100* Lord's 1929

**E. Tyldesley (2)**
122 Johannesburg 1927-28
100 Durban 1927-28

**J. T. Tyldesley (1)**
112 Cape Town .. 1898-99

**B. H. Valentine (1)**
112 Cape Town .. 1938-39

**P. F. Warner (1)**
132*†‡Johannesburg 1898-99

**C. Washbrook (1)**
195 Johannesburg 1948-49

**A. J. Watkins (1)**
111 Johannesburg 1948-49

**H. Wood (1)**
134* Cape Town .. 1891-92

**F. E. Woolley (3)**
115* Johannesburg 1922-23
134* Lord's 1924
154 Manchester 1929

**R. E. S. Wyatt (2)**
113 Manchester 1929
149 Nottingham . 1935

## For South Africa (58)

**E. J. Barlow (1)**
138 Cape Town .. 1964-65

**K. C. Bland (2)**
144* Johannesburg 1964-65
127 The Oval.... 1965

**R. H. Catterall (3)**
120 Birmingham . 1924
120 Lord's 1924
119 Durban 1927-28

**E. L. Dalton (2)**
117 The Oval .... 1935
102 Johannesburg 1938-39

**W. R. Endean (1)**
116* Leeds 1955

**G. A. Faulkner (1)**
123 Johannesburg 1909-10

**T. L. Goddard (1)**
112 Johannesburg 1964-65

**C. M. H. Hathorn (1)**
102 Johannesburg 1905-06

**D. J. McGlew (2)**
104* Manchester.. 1955
133 Leeds 1955

**R. A. McLean (3)**
142 Lord's 1955
100 Durban 1956-57
109 Manchester.. 1960

**A. Melville (4)**
103 Durban 1938-39
189
104* }Nottingham 1947
117 Lord's 1947

**B. Mitchell (7)**
123 Cape Town .. 1930-31
164* Lord's 1935
128 The Oval.... 1935
109 Durban 1938-39
120
189* }The Oval 1947
120 Cape Town .. 1948-49

**A. D. Nourse (7)**
120 Cape Town .. 1938-39
103 Durban 1938-39
149 Nottingham . 1947
115 Manchester.. 1947
112 Cape Town .. 1948-49
129* Johannesburg 1948-49
208 Nottingham . 1951

**H. G. Owen-Smith (1)**
129 Leeds 1929

**A. J. Pithey (1)**
154 Cape Town .. 1964-65

**R. G. Pollock (2)**
137 Pt Elizabeth . 1964-65
125 Nottingham . 1965

**E. A. B. Rowan (2)**
156* Johannesburg 1948-49
236 Leeds 1951

**P. W. Sherwell (1)**
115 Lord's 1907

| | | | | |
|---|---|---|---|---|
| **I. J. Siedle** (1) | 102 | Durban . . . . . | 1922-23 | **W. W. Wade** (1) |
| 141 Cape Town . . 1930-31 | 101 | Johannesburg | 1927-28 | 125 Pt Elizabeth . 1948-49 |
| **J. H. Sinclair** (1) | 121 | The Oval . . . . | 1929 | **J. H. B. Waite** (1) |
| 106 Cape Town . . 1898-99 | 117 | Cape Town . . | 1930-31 | 113 Manchester . . 1955 |
| **H. W. Taylor** (7) | **P. G. V. van der Bijl** (1) | | | **G. C. White** (2) |
| 109 Durban . . . . . 1913-14 | 125 | Durban . . . . . | 1938-39 | 147 Johannesburg 1905-06 |
| 176 Johannesburg 1922-23 | **K. G. Viljoen** (1) | | | 118 Durban . . . . . 1909-10 |
| 101 Johannesburg 1922-23 | 124 | Manchester . . | 1935 | **P. L. Winslow** (1) |
| | | | | 108 Manchester . . 1955 |

† *Signifies hundred on first appearance in England–South Africa Tests.*

‡ *P. F. Warner carried his bat through the second innings.*

*Notes:* The highest score by a South African batsman on début is 93* by A. W. Nourse at Johannesburg in 1905-06.

P. N. F. Mansell made 90 at Leeds in 1951, the best on début in England.

A. Melville's four hundreds were made in successive Test innings.

H. Wood scored the only hundred of his career in a Test match.

## RECORD PARTNERSHIP FOR EACH WICKET

### For England

| | | | |
|---|---|---|---|
| 359 | for 1st† | L. Hutton and C. Washbrook at Johannesburg . . . . . . . . . . . . . | 1948-49 |
| 280 | for 2nd | P. A. Gibb and W. J. Edrich at Durban . . . . . . . . . . . . . . . . . . . . | 1938-39 |
| 370 | for 3rd† | W. J. Edrich and D. C. S. Compton at Lord's . . . . . . . . . . . . . | 1947 |
| 197 | for 4th | W. R. Hammond and L. E. G. Ames at Cape Town . . . . . . . . . . | 1938-39 |
| 237 | for 5th | D. C. S. Compton and N. W. D. Yardley at Nottingham . . . . . . | 1947 |
| 206* | for 6th | K. F. Barrington and J. M. Parks at Durban . . . . . . . . . . . . . . . | 1964-65 |
| 115 | for 7th | M. C. Bird and J. W. H. T. Douglas at Durban . . . . . . . . . . . . | 1913-14 |
| 154 | for 8th | C. W. Wright and H. R. Bromley-Davenport at Johannesburg . . | 1895-96 |
| 71 | for 9th | H. Wood and J. T. Hearne at Cape Town . . . . . . . . . . . . . . . . . | 1891-92 |
| 92 | for 10th | A. C. Russell and A. E. R. Gilligan at Durban . . . . . . . . . . . . . | 1922-23 |

### For South Africa

| | | | |
|---|---|---|---|
| 260 | for 1st† | I. J. Siedle and B. Mitchell at Cape Town . . . . . . . . . . . . . . . . | 1930-31 |
| 198 | for 2nd† | E. A. B. Rowan and C. B. van Ryneveld at Leeds . . . . . . . . . . . | 1951 |
| 319 | for 3rd | A. Melville and A. D. Nourse at Nottingham . . . . . . . . . . . . . . . | 1947 |
| 214 | for 4th† | H. W. Taylor and H. G. Deane at The Oval . . . . . . . . . . . . . . . | 1929 |
| 157 | for 5th† | A. J. Pithey and J. H. B. Waite at Johannesburg . . . . . . . . . . . | 1964-65 |
| 171 | for 6th | J. H. B. Waite and P. L. Winslow at Manchester . . . . . . . . . . . | 1955 |
| 123 | for 7th | H. G. Deane and E. P. Nupen at Durban . . . . . . . . . . . . . . . . . | 1927-28 |
| 109* | for 8th | B. Mitchell and L. Tuckett at The Oval . . . . . . . . . . . . . . . . . . | 1947 |
| 137 | for 9th† | E. L. Dalton and A. B. C. Langton at The Oval . . . . . . . . . . . . | 1935 |
| 103 | for 10th† | H. G. Owen-Smith and A. J. Bell at Leeds . . . . . . . . . . . . . . . . | 1929 |

† *Denotes record partnership against all countries.*

## MOST RUNS IN A SERIES

| | | | |
|---|---|---|---|
| England in England . . . . . . . . | 753 (average 94.12) | D. C. S. Compton . . | 1947 |
| England in South Africa . . . . . | 653 (average 81.62) | E. Paynter . . . . . . . . . | 1938-39 |
| South Africa in England . . . . . | 621 (average 69.00) | A. D. Nourse . . . . . | 1947 |
| South Africa in South Africa . . | 582 (average 64.66) | H. W. Taylor . . . . . . | 1922-23 |

## TEN WICKETS OR MORE IN A MATCH

**For England** (23)

| | | |
|---|---|---|
| 11-110 (5-25, 6-85)† | S. F. Barnes, Lord's . . . . . . . . . . . . . . . . . . . . . . . . . . . | 1912 |
| 10-115 (6-52, 4-63) | S. F. Barnes, Leeds . . . . . . . . . . . . . . . . . . . . . . . . . . . . | 1912 |
| 13-57 (5-28, 8-29) | S. F. Barnes, The Oval . . . . . . . . . . . . . . . . . . . . . . . . . | 1912 |
| 10-105 (5-57, 5-48) | S. F. Barnes, Durban . . . . . . . . . . . . . . . . . . . . . . . . . . | 1913-14 |
| 17-159 (8-56, 9-103) | S. F. Barnes, Johannesburg . . . . . . . . . . . . . . . . . . . . | 1913-14 |
| 14-144 (7-56, 7-88) | S. F. Barnes, Durban . . . . . . . . . . . . . . . . . . . . . . . . . . | 1913-14 |
| 12-112 (7-58, 5-54) | A. V. Bedser, Manchester . . . . . . . . . . . . . . . . . . . . . . | 1951 |
| 11-118 (6-68, 5-50) | C. Blythe, Cape Town . . . . . . . . . . . . . . . . . . . . . . . . . | 1905-06 |
| 15-99 (8-59, 7-40) | C. Blythe, Leeds . . . . . . . . . . . . . . . . . . . . . . . . . . . . . . | 1907 |
| 10-104 (7-46, 3-58) | C. Blythe, Cape Town . . . . . . . . . . . . . . . . . . . . . . . . . | 1909-10 |
| 15-28 (7-17, 8-11) | J. Briggs, Cape Town . . . . . . . . . . . . . . . . . . . . . . . . . | 1888-89 |
| 13-91 (6-54, 7-37)† | J. J. Ferris, Cape Town . . . . . . . . . . . . . . . . . . . . . . . . | 1891-92 |
| 10-207 (7-115, 3-92) | A. P. Freeman, Leeds . . . . . . . . . . . . . . . . . . . . . . . . . | 1929 |
| 12-171 (7-71, 5-100) | A. P. Freeman, Manchester . . . . . . . . . . . . . . . . . . . . | 1929 |
| 12-130 (7-70, 5-60) | G. Geary, Johannesburg . . . . . . . . . . . . . . . . . . . . . . . | 1927-28 |
| 11-90 (6-7, 5-83) | A. E. R. Gilligan, Birmingham . . . . . . . . . . . . . . . . . . | 1924 |
| 10-119 (4-64, 6-55) | J. C. Laker, The Oval . . . . . . . . . . . . . . . . . . . . . . . . . | 1951 |
| 15-45 (7-38, 8-7)† | G. A. Lohmann, Port Elizabeth . . . . . . . . . . . . . . . . . | 1895-96 |
| 12-71 (9-28, 3-43) | G. A. Lohmann, Johannesburg . . . . . . . . . . . . . . . . . . | 1895-96 |
| 11-97 (6-63, 5-34) | J. B. Statham, Lord's . . . . . . . . . . . . . . . . . . . . . . . . . . | 1960 |
| 12-101 (7-52, 5-49) | R. Tattersall, Lord's . . . . . . . . . . . . . . . . . . . . . . . . . . | 1951 |
| 12-89 (5-53, 7-36) | J. H. Wardle, Cape Town . . . . . . . . . . . . . . . . . . . . . . | 1956-57 |
| 10-175 (5-95, 5-80) | D. V. P. Wright, Lord's . . . . . . . . . . . . . . . . . . . . . . . | 1947 |

**For South Africa** (6)

| | | |
|---|---|---|
| 11-112 (4-49, 7-63)† | A. E. Hall, Cape Town . . . . . . . . . . . . . . . . . . . . . . . . | 1922-23 |
| 11-150 (5-63, 6-87) | E. P. Nupen, Johannesburg . . . . . . . . . . . . . . . . . . . . . | 1930-31 |
| 10-87 (5-53, 5-34) | P. M. Pollock, Nottingham . . . . . . . . . . . . . . . . . . . . . | 1965 |
| 12-127 (4-57, 8-70) | S. J. Snooke, Johannesburg . . . . . . . . . . . . . . . . . . . . | 1905-06 |
| 13-192 (4-79, 9-113) | H. J. Tayfield, Johannesburg . . . . . . . . . . . . . . . . . . . | 1956-57 |
| 12-181 (5-87, 7-94) | A. E. E. Vogler, Johannesburg . . . . . . . . . . . . . . . . . . | 1909-10 |

† *Signifies ten wickets or more on first appearance in England–South Africa Tests.*

*Note:* S. F. Barnes took ten wickets or more in his first five Tests v South Africa and in six of his seven Tests v South Africa. A. P. Freeman and G. A. Lohmann took ten wickets or more in successive matches.

## MOST WICKETS IN A SERIES

| | | | |
|---|---|---|---|
| England in England . . . . . . . . | 34 (average 8.29) | S. F. Barnes . . . . . . . | 1912 |
| England in South Africa . . . . . | 49 (average 10.93) | S. F. Barnes . . . . . . . | 1913-14 |
| South Africa in England . . . . . | 26 (average 21.84) | H. J. Tayfield . . . . . . | 1955 |
| South Africa in England . . . . . | 26 (average 22.57) | N. A. T. Adcock . . . | 1960 |
| South Africa in South Africa . . | 37 (average 17.18) | H. J. Tayfield . . . . . . | 1956-57 |

## ENGLAND v WEST INDIES

| | *Captains* | | | | | |
|---|---|---|---|---|---|---|
| *Season* | *England* | *West Indies* | *T* | *E* | *WI* | *D* |
| 1928 | A. P. F. Chapman | R. K. Nunes | 3 | 3 | 0 | 0 |
| 1929-30 | Hon. F. S. G. Calthorpe | E. L. G. Hoad[1] | 4 | 1 | 1 | 2 |
| 1933 | D. R. Jardine[2] | G. C. Grant | 3 | 2 | 0 | 1 |
| 1934-35 | R. E. S. Wyatt | G. C. Grant | 4 | 1 | 2 | 1 |
| 1939 | W. R. Hammond | R. S. Grant | 3 | 1 | 0 | 2 |
| 1947-48 | G. O. B. Allen[3] | J. D. C. Goddard[4] | 4 | 0 | 2 | 2 |
| 1950 | N. W. D. Yardley[5] | J. D. C. Goddard | 4 | 1 | 3 | 0 |
| 1953-54 | L. Hutton | J. B. Stollmeyer | 5 | 2 | 2 | 1 |
| 1957 | P. B. H. May | J. D. C. Goddard | 5 | 3 | 0 | 2 |
| 1959-60 | P. B. H. May[6] | F. C. M. Alexander | 5 | 1 | 0 | 4 |

## THE WISDEN TROPHY

| | *Captains* | | | | | | |
|---|---|---|---|---|---|---|---|
| *Season* | *England* | *West Indies* | *T* | *E* | *WI* | *D* | *Held by* |
| 1963 | E. R. Dexter | F. M. M. Worrell | 5 | 1 | 3 | 1 | WI |
| 1966 | M. C. Cowdrey[7] | G. S. Sobers | 5 | 1 | 3 | 1 | WI |
| 1967-68 | M. C. Cowdrey | G. S. Sobers | 5 | 1 | 0 | 4 | E |
| 1969 | R. Illingworth | G. S. Sobers | 3 | 2 | 0 | 1 | E |
| 1973 | R. Illingworth | R. B. Kanhai | 3 | 0 | 2 | 1 | WI |
| 1973-74 | M. H. Denness | R. B. Kanhai | 5 | 1 | 1 | 3 | WI |
| 1976 | A. W. Greig | C. H. Lloyd | 5 | 0 | 3 | 2 | WI |
| 1980 | I. T. Botham | C. H. Lloyd[8] | 5 | 0 | 1 | 4 | WI |
| 1980-81† | I. T. Botham | C. H. Lloyd | 4 | 0 | 2 | 2 | WI |
| 1984 | D. I. Gower | C. H. Lloyd | 5 | 0 | 5 | 0 | WI |
| 1985-86 | D. I. Gower | I. V. A. Richards | 5 | 0 | 5 | 0 | WI |
| 1988 | J. E. Emburey[9] | I. V. A. Richards | 5 | 0 | 4 | 1 | WI |
| 1989-90‡ | G. A. Gooch[10] | I. V. A. Richards[11] | 4 | 1 | 2 | 1 | WI |
| 1991 | G. A. Gooch | I. V. A. Richards | 5 | 2 | 2 | 1 | WI |
| | In England ................ | | 59 | 16 | 26 | 17 | |
| | In West Indies ................ | | 45 | 8 | 17 | 20 | |
| | Totals ........................ | | 104 | 24 | 43 | 37 | |

† *The Second Test, at Georgetown, was cancelled owing to political pressure and is excluded.*
‡ *The Second Test, at Georgetown, was abandoned without a ball being bowled and is excluded.*

*Notes:* The following deputised for the official touring captain or were appointed by the home authority for only a minor proportion of the series:

[1]N. Betancourt (Second), M. P. Fernandes (Third), R. K. Nunes (Fourth). [2]R. E. S. Wyatt (Third). [3]K. Cranston (First). [4]G. A. Headley (First), G. E. Gomez (Second). [5]F. R. Brown (Fourth). [6]M. C. Cowdrey (Fourth and Fifth). [7]M. J. K. Smith (First), D. B. Close (Fifth). [8]I. V. A. Richards (Fifth). [9]M. W. Gatting (First), C. S. Cowdrey (Fourth), G. A. Gooch (Fifth). [10]A. J. Lamb (Fourth and Fifth). [11]D. L. Haynes (Third).

## HIGHEST INNINGS TOTALS

| | | |
|---|---|---|
| For England in England: 619-6 dec. at Nottingham | ...................... | 1957 |
| in West Indies: 849 at Kingston | ............................. | 1929-30 |
| For West Indies in England: 687-8 dec. at The Oval | ...................... | 1976 |
| in West Indies: 681-8 dec. at Port-of-Spain | ................. | 1953-54 |

## LOWEST INNINGS TOTALS

For England in England: 71 at Manchester .......................... 1976
         in West Indies: 103 at Kingston ......................... 1934-35

For West Indies in England: 86 at The Oval ...................... 1957
          in West Indies: 102 at Bridgetown .................... 1934-35

## INDIVIDUAL HUNDREDS

### For England (88)

**L. E. G. Ames (3)**
105   Port-of-Spain 1929-30
149   Kingston.... 1929-30
126   Kingston.... 1934-35
**D. L. Amiss (4)**
174   Port-of-Spain 1973-74
262*  Kingston.... 1973-74
118   Georgetown . 1973-74
203   The Oval.... 1976
**A. H. Bakewell (1)**
107†  The Oval.... 1933
**K. F. Barrington (3)**
128†  Bridgetown . 1959-60
121   Port-of-Spain 1959-60
143   Port-of-Spain 1967-68
**G. Boycott (5)**
116   Georgetown . 1967-68
128   Manchester.. 1969
106   Lord's...... 1969
112   Port-of-Spain 1973-74
104*  St John's.... 1980-81
**D. C. S. Compton (2)**
120†  Lord's...... 1939
133   Port-of-Spain 1953-54
**M. C. Cowdrey (6)**
154*  Birmingham . 1957
152   Lord's...... 1957
114   Kingston.... 1959-60
119   Port-of-Spain 1959-60
101   Kingston.... 1967-68
148   Port-of-Spain 1967-68
**E. R. Dexter (2)**
136*† Bridgetown . 1959-60
110   Georgetown . 1959-60
**J. H. Edrich (1)**
146   Bridgetown . 1967-68
**T. G. Evans (1)**
104   Manchester.. 1950
**K. W. R. Fletcher (1)**
129*  Bridgetown . 1973-74
**G. Fowler (1)**
106   Lord's...... 1984
**G. A. Gooch (5)**
123   Lord's...... 1980
116   Bridgetown .. 1980-81

153   Kingston.... 1980-81
146   Nottingham . 1988
154*‡ Leeds...... 1991
**D. I. Gower (1)**
154*  Kingston.... 1980-81
**T. W. Graveney (5)**
258   Nottingham . 1957
164   The Oval.... 1957
109   Nottingham . 1966
165   The Oval.... 1966
118   Port-of-Spain 1967-68
**A. W. Greig (3)**
148   Bridgetown . 1973-74
121   Georgetown . 1973-74
116   Leeds...... 1976
**S. C. Griffith (1)**
140†  Port-of-Spain 1947-48
**W. R. Hammond (1)**
138   The Oval.... 1939
**J. H. Hampshire (1)**
107†  Lord's...... 1969
**F. C. Hayes (1)**
106*† The Oval.... 1973
**E. H. Hendren (2)**
205*  Port-of-Spain 1929-30
123   Georgetown . 1929-30
**J. B. Hobbs (1)**
159   The Oval.... 1928
**L. Hutton (5)**
196†  Lord's...... 1939
165*  The Oval.... 1939
202*‡ The Oval.... 1950
169   Georgetown . 1953-54
205   Kingston.... 1953-54
**R. Illingworth (1)**
113   Lord's...... 1969
**D. R. Jardine (1)**
127   Manchester.. 1933
**A. P. E. Knott (1)**
116   Leeds...... 1976
**A. J. Lamb (6)**
110†  Lord's...... 1984
100   Leeds...... 1984

100*  Manchester.. 1984
113   Lord's...... 1988
132   Kingston.... 1989-90
119   Bridgetown . 1989-90
**P. B. H. May (3)**
135   Port-of-Spain 1953-54
285*  Birmingham . 1957
104   Nottingham . 1957
**C. Milburn (1)**
126*  Lord's...... 1966
**J. T. Murray (1)**
112†  The Oval.... 1966
**J. M. Parks (1)**
101*† Port-of-Spain 1959-60
**W. Place (1)**
107   Kingston.... 1947-48
**P. E. Richardson (2)**
126   Nottingham . 1957
107   The Oval.... 1957
**J. D. Robertson (1)**
133   Port-of-Spain 1947-48
**A. Sandham (2)**
152†  Bridgetown . 1929-30
325   Kingston.... 1929-30
**M. J. K. Smith (1)**
108   Port-of-Spain 1959-60
**R. A. Smith (2)**
148*  Lord's...... 1991
109   The Oval ... 1991
**D. S. Steele (1)**
106†  Nottingham . 1976
**R. Subba Row (1)**
100†  Georgetown . 1959-60
**E. Tyldesley (1)**
122†  Lord's...... 1928
**C. Washbrook (2)**
114†  Lord's...... 1950
102   Nottingham . 1950
**W. Watson (1)**
116†  Kingston.... 1953-54
**P. Willey (1)**
100*  The Oval.... 1980
102*  St John's.... 1980-81

## For West Indies (99)

| | | |
|---|---|---|
| **I. Barrow** (1) | | |
| 105 | Manchester.. | 1933 |
| **C. A. Best** (1) | | |
| 164 | Bridgetown.. | 1989-90 |
| **B. F. Butcher** (2) | | |
| 133 | Lord's ...... | 1963 |
| 209* | Nottingham . | 1966 |
| **G. M. Carew** (1) | | |
| 107 | Port-of-Spain | 1947-48 |
| **C. A. Davis** (1) | | |
| 103 | Lord's ...... | 1969 |
| **P. J. L. Dujon** (1) | | |
| 101 | Manchester.. | 1984 |
| **R. C. Fredericks** (3) | | |
| 150 | Birmingham . | 1973 |
| 138 | Lord's ...... | 1976 |
| 109 | Leeds ...... | 1976 |
| **A. G. Ganteaume** (1) | | |
| 112† | Port-of-Spain | 1947-48 |
| **H. A. Gomes** (2) | | |
| 143 | Birmingham . | 1984 |
| 104* | Leeds ...... | 1984 |
| **C. G. Greenidge** (7) | | |
| 134 | } Manchester.. | 1976 |
| 101 | | 1976 |
| 115 | Leeds ...... | 1976 |
| 214* | Lord's ...... | 1984 |
| 223 | Manchester.. | 1984 |
| 103 | Lord's ...... | 1988 |
| 149 | St John's.... | 1989-90 |
| **D. L. Haynes** (5) | | |
| 184 | Lord's ...... | 1980 |
| 125 | The Oval.... | 1984 |
| 131 | St John's.... | 1985-86 |
| 109 | Bridgetown.. | 1989-90 |
| 167 | St John's.... | 1989-90 |
| **G. A. Headley** (8) | | |
| 176† | Bridgetown.. | 1929-30 |
| 114 | } Georgetown . | 1929-30 |
| 112 | | 1929-30 |
| 223 | Kingston.... | 1929-30 |
| 169* | Manchester.. | 1933 |
| 270* | Kingston.... | 1934-35 |

| | | |
|---|---|---|
| 106 | } Lord's ...... | 1939 |
| 107 | | |
| **D. A. J. Holford** (1) | | |
| 105* | Lord's ...... | 1966 |
| **J. K. Holt** (1) | | |
| 166 | Bridgetown.. | 1953-54 |
| **C. L. Hooper** (1) | | |
| 111 | Lord's ...... | 1991 |
| **C. C. Hunte** (3) | | |
| 182 | Manchester.. | 1963 |
| 108* | The Oval.... | 1963 |
| 135 | Manchester.. | 1966 |
| **B. D. Julien** (1) | | |
| 121 | Lord's ...... | 1973 |
| **A. I. Kallicharran** (2) | | |
| 158 | Port-of-Spain | 1973-74 |
| 119 | Bridgetown.. | 1973-74 |
| **R. B. Kanhai** (5) | | |
| 110 | Port-of-Spain | 1959-60 |
| 104 | The Oval.... | 1966 |
| 153 | Port-of-Spain | 1966 |
| 150 | Georgetown . | 1967-68 |
| 157 | Lord's ...... | 1973 |
| **C. H. Lloyd** (5) | | |
| 118† | Port-of-Spain | 1967-68 |
| 113* | Bridgetown.. | 1967-68 |
| 132 | The Oval.... | 1973 |
| 101 | Manchester.. | 1980 |
| 100 | Bridgetown.. | 1980-81 |
| **S. M. Nurse** (2) | | |
| 137 | Leeds ...... | 1966 |
| 136 | Port-of-Spain | 1967-68 |
| **A. F. Rae** (2) | | |
| 106 | Lord's ...... | 1950 |
| 109 | The Oval.... | 1950 |
| **I. V. A. Richards** (8) | | |
| 232† | Nottingham . | 1976 |
| 135 | Manchester.. | 1976 |
| 291 | The Oval.... | 1976 |
| 145 | Lord's ...... | 1980 |
| 182* | Bridgetown.. | 1980-81 |
| 114 | St John's.... | 1980-81 |
| 117 | Birmingham . | 1984 |
| 110* | St John's.... | 1985-86 |

| | | |
|---|---|---|
| **R. B. Richardson** (4) | | |
| 102 | Port-of-Spain | 1985-86 |
| 160 | Bridgetown.. | 1985-86 |
| 104 | Birmingham . | 1991 |
| 121 | The Oval ... | 1991 |
| **C. A. Roach** (2) | | |
| 122 | Bridgetown.. | 1929-30 |
| 209 | Georgetown . | 1929-30 |
| **L. G. Rowe** (3) | | |
| 120 | Kingston.... | 1973-74 |
| 302 | Bridgetown.. | 1973-74 |
| 123 | Port-of-Spain | 1973-74 |
| **O. G. Smith** (2) | | |
| 161† | Birmingham . | 1957 |
| 168 | Nottingham . | 1957 |
| **G. S. Sobers** (10) | | |
| 226 | Bridgetown.. | 1959-60 |
| 147 | Kingston.... | 1959-60 |
| 145 | Georgetown . | 1959-60 |
| 102 | Leeds ...... | 1963 |
| 161 | Manchester.. | 1966 |
| 163* | Lord's ...... | 1966 |
| 174 | Leeds ...... | 1966 |
| 113* | Kingston.... | 1967-68 |
| 152 | Georgetown . | 1967-68 |
| 150* | Lord's ...... | 1973 |
| **C. L. Walcott** (4) | | |
| 168* | Lord's ...... | 1950 |
| 220 | Bridgetown.. | 1953-54 |
| 124 | Port-of-Spain | 1953-54 |
| 116 | Kingston.... | 1953-54 |
| **E. D. Weekes** (3) | | |
| 141 | Kingston.... | 1947-48 |
| 129 | Nottingham . | 1950 |
| 206 | Port-of-Spain | 1953-54 |
| **K. H. Weekes** (1) | | |
| 137 | The Oval.... | 1939 |
| **F. M. M. Worrell** (6) | | |
| 131* | Georgetown . | 1947-48 |
| 261 | Nottingham . | 1950 |
| 138 | The Oval.... | 1950 |
| 167 | Port-of-Spain | 1953-54 |
| 191*‡ | Nottingham . | 1957 |
| 197* | Bridgetown.. | 1959-60 |

† *Signifies hundred on first appearance in England–West Indies Tests. S. C. Griffith provides the only instance for England of a player hitting his maiden century in first-class cricket in his first Test.*
‡ *Carried his bat.*

## RECORD PARTNERSHIPS FOR EACH WICKET

### For England

| | | | |
|---|---|---|---|
| 212 | for 1st | C. Washbrook and R. T. Simpson at Nottingham ............ | 1950 |
| 266 | for 2nd | P. E. Richardson and T. W. Graveney at Nottingham........ | 1957 |
| 264 | for 3rd | L. Hutton and W. R. Hammond at The Oval ................ | 1939 |
| 411 | for 4th† | P. B. H. May and M. C. Cowdrey at Birmingham .......... | 1957 |
| 130* | for 5th | C. Milburn and T. W. Graveney at Lord's ................ | 1966 |

| | | | |
|---|---|---|---|
| 163 for 6th | A. W. Greig and A. P. E. Knott at Bridgetown | .............. | 1973-74 |
| 197 for 7th† | M. J. K. Smith and J. M. Parks at Port-of-Spain | ........... | 1959-60 |
| 217 for 8th | T. W. Graveney and J. T. Murray at The Oval | ............ | 1966 |
| 109 for 9th | G. A. R. Lock and P. I. Pocock at Georgetown | ............ | 1967-68 |
| 128 for 10th | K. Higgs and J. A. Snow at The Oval | .................... | 1966 |

### For West Indies

| | | | |
|---|---|---|---|
| 298 for 1st† | C. G. Greenidge and D. L. Haynes at St John's | ............. | 1989-90 |
| 287* for 2nd | C. G. Greenidge and H. A. Gomes at Lord's | ............ | 1984 |
| 338 for 3rd† | E. D. Weekes and F. M. M. Worrell at Port-of-Spain | ........ | 1953-54 |
| 399 for 4th† | G. S. Sobers and F. M. M. Worrell at Bridgetown | ........ | 1959-60 |
| 265 for 5th† | S. M. Nurse and G. S. Sobers at Leeds | ..................... | 1966 |
| 274* for 6th† | G. S. Sobers and D. A. J. Holford at Lord's | ............ | 1966 |
| 155* for 7th‡ | G. S. Sobers and B. D. Julien at Lord's | ............... | 1973 |
| 99 for 8th | C. A. McWatt and J. K. Holt at Georgetown | ........... | 1953-54 |
| 150 for 9th | E. A. E. Baptiste and M. A. Holding at Birmingham | ........ | 1984 |
| 67* for 10th | M. A. Holding and C. E. H. Croft at St John's | ............. | 1980-81 |

† *Denotes record partnership against all countries.*
‡ *231 runs were added for this wicket in two separate partnerships: G. S. Sobers retired ill and was replaced by K. D. Boyce when 155 had been added.*

## TEN WICKETS OR MORE IN A MATCH

### For England (11)

| | | | |
|---|---|---|---|
| 11-98 (7-44, 4-54) | T. E. Bailey, Lord's | ............................... | 1957 |
| 10-93 (5-54, 5-39) | A. P. Freeman, Manchester | .................... | 1928 |
| 13-156 (8-86, 5-70) | A. W. Greig, Port-of-Spain | ................... | 1973-74 |
| 11-48 (5-28, 6-20) | G. A. R. Lock, The Oval | ...................... | 1957 |
| 10-137 (4-60, 6-77) | D. E. Malcolm, Port-of-Spain | ............... | 1989-90 |
| 11-96 (5-37, 6-59)† | C. S. Marriott, The Oval | .................... | 1933 |
| 10-142 (4-82, 6-60) | J. A. Snow, Georgetown | ..................... | 1967-68 |
| 10-195 (5-105, 5-90)† | G. T. S. Stevens, Bridgetown | ............ | 1929-30 |
| 11-152 (6-100, 5-52) | F. S. Trueman, Lord's | ..................... | 1963 |
| 12-119 (5-75, 7-44) | F. S. Trueman, Birmingham | ................. | 1963 |
| 11-149 (4-79, 7-70) | W. Voce, Port-of-Spain | ..................... | 1929-30 |

### For West Indies (12)

| | | | |
|---|---|---|---|
| 10-127 (2-82, 8-45) | C. E. L. Ambrose, Bridgetown | ...................... | 1989-90 |
| 11-147 (5-70, 6-77)† | K. D. Boyce, The Oval | ..................... | 1973 |
| 11-229 (5-137, 6-92) | W. Ferguson, Port-of-Spain | ............... | 1947-48 |
| 11-157 (5-59, 6-98)† | L. R. Gibbs, Manchester | .................... | 1963 |
| 10-106 (5-37, 5-69) | L. R. Gibbs, Manchester | .................... | 1966 |
| 14-149 (8-92, 6-57) | M. A. Holding, The Oval | .................... | 1976 |
| 10-96 (5-41, 5-55)† | H. H. H. Johnson, Kingston | ............... | 1947-48 |
| 10-92 (6-32, 4-60) | M. D. Marshall, Lord's | ..................... | 1988 |
| 11-152 (5-66, 6-86) | S. Ramadhin, Lord's | ....................... | 1950 |
| 10-123 (5-60, 5-63) | A. M. E. Roberts, Lord's | ................... | 1976 |
| 11-204 (8-104, 3-100)† | A. L. Valentine, Manchester | ............. | 1950 |
| 10-160 (4-121, 6-39) | A. L. Valentine, The Oval | .................. | 1950 |

† *Signifies ten wickets or more on first appearance in England–West Indies Tests.*

*Note:* F. S. Trueman took ten wickets or more in successive matches.

# ENGLAND v NEW ZEALAND

### Captains

| Season | England | New Zealand | T | E | NZ | D |
|--------|---------|-------------|---|---|----|----|
| 1929-30 | A. H. H. Gilligan | T. C. Lowry | 4 | 1 | 0 | 3 |
| 1931 | D. R. Jardine | T. C. Lowry | 3 | 1 | 0 | 2 |
| 1932-33 | D. R. Jardine[1] | M. L. Page | 2 | 0 | 0 | 2 |
| 1937 | R. W. V. Robins | M. L. Page | 3 | 1 | 0 | 2 |
| 1946-47 | W. R. Hammond | W. A. Hadlee | 1 | 0 | 0 | 1 |
| 1949 | F. G. Mann[2] | W. A. Hadlee | 4 | 0 | 0 | 4 |
| 1950-51 | F. R. Brown | W. A. Hadlee | 2 | 1 | 0 | 1 |
| 1954-55 | L. Hutton | G. O. Rabone | 2 | 2 | 0 | 0 |
| 1958 | P. B. H. May | J. R. Reid | 5 | 4 | 0 | 1 |
| 1958-59 | P. B. H. May | J. R. Reid | 2 | 1 | 0 | 1 |
| 1962-63 | E. R. Dexter | J. R. Reid | 3 | 3 | 0 | 0 |
| 1965 | M. J. K. Smith | J. R. Reid | 3 | 3 | 0 | 0 |
| 1965-66 | M. J. K. Smith | B. W. Sinclair[3] | 3 | 0 | 0 | 3 |
| 1969 | R. Illingworth | G. T. Dowling | 3 | 2 | 0 | 1 |
| 1970-71 | R. Illingworth | G. T. Dowling | 2 | 1 | 0 | 1 |
| 1973 | R. Illingworth | B. E. Congdon | 3 | 2 | 0 | 1 |
| 1974-75 | M. H. Denness | B. E. Congdon | 2 | 1 | 0 | 1 |
| 1977-78 | G. Boycott | M. G. Burgess | 3 | 1 | 1 | 1 |
| 1978 | J. M. Brearley | M. G. Burgess | 3 | 3 | 0 | 0 |
| 1983 | R. G. D. Willis | G. P. Howarth | 4 | 3 | 1 | 0 |
| 1983-84 | R. G. D. Willis | G. P. Howarth | 3 | 0 | 1 | 2 |
| 1986 | M. W. Gatting | J. V. Coney | 3 | 0 | 1 | 2 |
| 1987-88 | M. W. Gatting | J. J. Crowe[4] | 3 | 0 | 0 | 3 |
| 1990 | G. A. Gooch | J. G. Wright | 3 | 1 | 0 | 2 |
| | In New Zealand | | 32 | 11 | 2 | 19 |
| | In England | | 37 | 20 | 2 | 15 |
| | Totals | | 69 | 31 | 4 | 34 |

*Notes:* The following deputised for the official touring captain or were appointed by the home authority for only a minor proportion of the series:
[1]R. E. S. Wyatt (Second). [2]F. R. Brown (Third and Fourth). [3]M. E. Chapple (First). [4]J. G. Wright (Third).

## HIGHEST INNINGS TOTALS

| | | |
|---|---|---|
| For England in England: 546-4 dec. at Leeds | | 1965 |
| in New Zealand: 593-6 dec. at Auckland | | 1974-75 |
| For New Zealand in England: 551-9 dec. at Lord's | | 1973 |
| in New Zealand: 537 at Wellington | | 1983-84 |

## LOWEST INNINGS TOTALS

| | | |
|---|---|---|
| For England in England: 158 at Birmingham | | 1990 |
| in New Zealand: 64 at Wellington | | 1977-78 |
| For New Zealand in England: 47 at Lord's | | 1958 |
| in New Zealand: 26 at Auckland | | 1954-55 |

## INDIVIDUAL HUNDREDS

### For England (71)

**G. O. B. Allen** (1)
122† Lord's . . . . . . 1931

**L. E. G. Ames** (2)
137† Lord's . . . . . . 1931
103 Christchurch. 1932-33

**D. L. Amiss** (2)
138*† Nottingham . 1973
164* Christchurch. 1974-75

**M. A. Atherton** (1)
151† Nottingham . 1990

**T. E. Bailey** (1)
134* Christchurch. 1950-51

**K. F. Barrington** (3)
126† Auckland . . . 1962-63
137 Birmingham . 1965
163 Leeds . . . . . . 1965

**I. T. Botham** (3)
103 Christchurch. 1977-78
103 Nottingham . 1983
138 Wellington . 1983-84

**E. H. Bowley** (1)
109 Auckland . . . 1929-30

**G. Boycott** (2)
115 Leeds . . . . . . 1973
131 Nottingham . 1978

**B. C. Broad** (1)
114† Christchurch. 1987-88

**D. C. S. Compton** (2)
114 Leeds . . . . . . 1949
116 Lord's . . . . . . 1949

**M. C. Cowdrey** (2)
128* Wellington . . 1962-63
119 Lord's . . . . . . 1965

**M. H. Denness** (1)
181 Auckland . . . 1974-75

**E. R. Dexter** (1)
141 Christchurch. 1958-59

**B. L. D'Oliveira** (1)
100 Christchurch. 1970-71

**K. S. Duleepsinhji** (2)
117 Auckland . . . 1929-30
109 The Oval . . . . 1931

**J. H. Edrich** (3)
310*† Leeds . . . . . . 1965
115 Lord's . . . . . . 1969
155 Nottingham . 1969

**W. J. Edrich** (1)
100 The Oval . . . . 1949

**K. W. R. Fletcher** (2)
178 Lord's . . . . . . 1973
216 Auckland . . . 1974-75

**G. Fowler** (1)
105† The Oval . . . . 1983

**M. W. Gatting** (1)
121 The Oval . . . . 1986

**G. A. Gooch** (2)
183 Lord's . . . . . . 1986
154 Birmingham . 1990

**D. I. Gower** (4)
111† The Oval . . . . 1978
112* Leeds . . . . . . 1983
108 Lord's . . . . . . 1983
131 The Oval . . . . 1986

**A. W. Greig** (1)
139† Nottingham . 1973

**W. R. Hammond** (4)
100* The Oval . . . . 1931
227 Christchurch. 1932-33
336* Auckland . . . 1932-33
140 Lord's . . . . . . 1937

**J. Hardstaff jun.** (2)
114† Lord's . . . . . . 1937
103 The Oval . . . . 1937

**L. Hutton** (3)
100 Manchester . . 1937
101 Leeds . . . . . . 1949
206 The Oval . . . . 1949

**B. R. Knight** (1)
125† Auckland . . . 1962-63

**A. P. E. Knott** (1)
101 Auckland . . . 1970-71

**A. J. Lamb** (2)
102*† The Oval . . . . 1983
137* Nottingham . 1983

**G. B. Legge** (1)
196 Auckland . . . 1929-30

**P. B. H. May** (3)
113* Leeds . . . . . . 1958
101 Manchester . . 1958
124* Auckland . . . 1958-59

**C. A. Milton** (1)
104*† Leeds . . . . . . 1958

**P. H. Parfitt** (1)
131*† Auckland . . . 1962-63

**C. T. Radley** (1)
158 Auckland . . . 1977-78

**D. W. Randall** (2)
164 Wellington . 1983-84
104 Auckland . . . 1983-84

**P. E. Richardson** (1)
100† Birmingham . 1958

**J. D. Robertson** (1)
121† Lord's . . . . . . 1949

**P. J. Sharpe** (1)
111 Nottingham . 1969

**R. T. Simpson** (1)
103† Manchester . . 1949

**H. Sutcliffe** (2)
117† The Oval . . . . 1931
109* Manchester . . 1931

**C. J. Tavaré** (1)
109† The Oval . . . . 1983

**C. Washbrook** (1)
103* Leeds . . . . . . 1949

### For New Zealand (34)

**J. G. Bracewell** (1)
110 Nottingham . 1986

**M. G. Burgess** (2)
104 Auckland . . . 1970-71
105 Lord's . . . . . . 1973

**J. V. Coney** (1)
174* Wellington . . 1983-84

**B. E. Congdon** (2)
104 Christchurch. 1965-66
176 Nottingham . 1973
175 Lord's . . . . . . 1973

**J. J. Crowe** (1)
128 Auckland . . . 1983-84

**M. D. Crowe** (3)
100 Wellington . . 1983-84
106 Lord's . . . . . . 1986
143 Wellington . 1987-88

**C. S. Dempster** (2)
136 Wellington . . 1929-30
120 Lord's . . . . . . 1931

**M. P. Donnelly** (1)
206 Lord's . . . . . . 1949

**T. J. Franklin** (1)
101 Lord's . . . . . . 1990

**M. J. Greatbatch** (1)
107*† Auckland . . . 1987-88

**W. A. Hadlee** (1)
116 Christchurch. 1946-47

**G. P. Howarth** (3)
122 ⎱
102 ⎰ Auckland . . . 1977-78
123 Lord's . . . . . . 1978

| | | |
|---|---|---|
| **J. E. Mills** (1) | **J. R. Reid** (1) | **B. Sutcliffe** (2) |
| 117† Wellington .. 1929-30 | 100   Christchurch. 1962-63 | 101   Manchester.. 1949 |
| **M. L. Page** (1) | **K. R. Rutherford** (1) | 116   Christchurch. 1950-51 |
| 104   Lord's ...... 1931 | 107* Wellington .. 1987-88 | **J. G. Wright** (3) |
| **J. M. Parker** (1) | **B. W. Sinclair** (1) | 130   Auckland ... 1983-84 |
| 121   Auckland ... 1974-75 | 114   Auckland ... 1965-66 | 119   The Oval.... 1986 |
| **V. Pollard** (2) | **I. D. S. Smith** (1) | 103   Auckland ... 1987-88 |
| 116   Nottingham . 1973 | 113* Auckland ... 1983-84 | |
| 105* Lord's ...... 1973 | | |

† *Signifies hundred on first appearance in England–New Zealand Tests.*

## RECORD PARTNERSHIPS FOR EACH WICKET

### For England

| | | | | |
|---|---|---|---|---|
| 223 | for 1st | G. Fowler and C. J. Tavaré at The Oval ................... | | 1983 |
| 369 | for 2nd | J. H. Edrich and K. F. Barrington at Leeds ............... | | 1965 |
| 245 | for 3rd | W. R. Hammond and J. Hardstaff jun. at Lord's ............. | | 1937 |
| 266 | for 4th | M. H. Denness and K. W. R. Fletcher at Auckland ...... | | 1974-75 |
| 242 | for 5th | W. R. Hammond and L. E. G. Ames at Christchurch ....... | | 1932-33 |
| 240 | for 6th† | P. H. Parfitt and B. R. Knight at Auckland ............. | | 1962-63 |
| 149 | for 7th | A. P. E. Knott and P. Lever at Auckland ................ | | 1970-71 |
| 246 | for 8th† | L. E. G. Ames and G. O. B. Allen at Lord's ............. | | 1931 |
| 163* | for 9th† | M. C. Cowdrey and A. C. Smith at Wellington ........... | | 1962-63 |
| 59 | for 10th | A. P. E. Knott and N. Gifford at Nottingham ............ | | 1973 |

### For New Zealand

| | | | | |
|---|---|---|---|---|
| 276 | for 1st | C. S. Dempster and J. E. Mills at Wellington .......... | | 1929-30 |
| 131 | for 2nd | B. Sutcliffe and J. R. Reid at Christchurch .............. | | 1950-51 |
| 210 | for 3rd | B. A. Edgar and M. D. Crowe at Lord's ................ | | 1986 |
| 155 | for 4th | M. D. Crowe and M. J. Greatbatch at Wellington ......... | | 1987-88 |
| 177 | for 5th | B. E. Congdon and V. Pollard at Nottingham ............ | | 1973 |
| 134 | for 6th | K. R. Rutherford and J. G. Bracewell at Wellington ...... | | 1987-88 |
| 104 | for 7th | B. Sutcliffe and V. Pollard at Birmingham .............. | | 1965 |
| 104 | for 8th | D. A. R. Moloney and A. W. Roberts at Lord's .......... | | 1937 |
| 118 | for 9th | J. V. Coney and B. L. Cairns at Wellington ............. | | 1983-84 |
| 57 | for 10th | F. L. H. Mooney and J. Cowie at Leeds................. | | 1949 |

† *Denotes record partnership against all countries.*

## TEN WICKETS OR MORE IN A MATCH

### For England (7)

| | | |
|---|---|---|
| 11-140 (6-101, 5-39) | I. T. Botham, Lord's.............................. | 1978 |
| 10-149 (5-98, 5-51) | A. W. Greig, Auckland ........................... | 1974-75 |
| 11-65 (4-14, 7-51) | G. A. R. Lock, Leeds............................. | 1958 |
| 11-84 (5-31, 6-53) | G. A. R. Lock, Christchurch ....................... | 1958-59 |
| 11-70 (4-38, 7-32)† | D. L. Underwood, Lord's.......................... | 1969 |
| 12-101 (6-41, 6-60) | D. L. Underwood, The Oval........................ | 1969 |
| 12-97 (6-12, 6-85) | D. L. Underwood, Christchurch .................... | 1970-71 |

### For New Zealand (4)

| | | |
|---|---|---|
| 10-144 (7-74, 3-70) | B. L. Cairns, Leeds.............................. | 1983 |
| 10-140 (4-73, 6-67) | J. Cowie, Manchester............................. | 1937 |
| 10-100 (4-74, 6-26) | R. J. Hadlee, Wellington .......................... | 1977-78 |
| 10-140 (6-80, 4-60) | R. J. Hadlee, Nottingham ......................... | 1986 |

† *Signifies ten wickets or more on first appearance in England–New Zealand Tests.*

*Note:* D. L. Underwood took twelve wickets in successive matches against New Zealand in 1969 and 1970-71.

## HAT-TRICK AND FOUR WICKETS IN FIVE BALLS

M. J. C. Allom, in his first Test match, v New Zealand at Christchurch in 1929-30, dismissed C. S. Dempster, T. C. Lowry, K. C. James, and F. T. Badcock to take four wickets in five balls (w-www).

## ENGLAND v INDIA

| | Captains | | | | | |
|---|---|---|---|---|---|---|
| *Season* | *England* | *India* | *T* | *E* | *I* | *D* |
| 1932 | D. R. Jardine | C. K. Nayudu | 1 | 1 | 0 | 0 |
| 1933-34 | D. R. Jardine | C. K. Nayudu | 3 | 2 | 0 | 1 |
| 1936 | G. O. B. Allen | Maharaj of Vizianagram | 3 | 2 | 0 | 1 |
| 1946 | W. R. Hammond | Nawab of Pataudi sen. | 3 | 1 | 0 | 2 |
| 1951-52 | N. D. Howard[1] | V. S. Hazare | 5 | 1 | 1 | 3 |
| 1952 | L. Hutton | V. S. Hazare | 4 | 3 | 0 | 1 |
| 1959 | P. B. H. May[2] | D. K. Gaekwad[3] | 5 | 5 | 0 | 0 |
| 1961-62 | E. R. Dexter | N. J. Contractor | 5 | 0 | 2 | 3 |
| 1963-64 | M. J. K. Smith | Nawab of Pataudi jun. | 5 | 0 | 0 | 5 |
| 1967 | D. B. Close | Nawab of Pataudi jun. | 3 | 3 | 0 | 0 |
| 1971 | R. Illingworth | A. L. Wadekar | 3 | 0 | 1 | 2 |
| 1972-73 | A. R. Lewis | A. L. Wadekar | 5 | 1 | 2 | 2 |
| 1974 | M. H. Denness | A. L. Wadekar | 3 | 3 | 0 | 0 |
| 1976-77 | A. W. Greig | B. S. Bedi | 5 | 3 | 1 | 1 |
| 1979 | J. M. Brearley | S. Venkataraghavan | 4 | 1 | 0 | 3 |
| 1979-80 | J. M. Brearley | G. R. Viswanath | 1 | 1 | 0 | 0 |
| 1981-82 | K. W. R. Fletcher | S. M. Gavaskar | 6 | 0 | 1 | 5 |
| 1982 | R. G. D. Willis | S. M. Gavaskar | 3 | 1 | 0 | 2 |
| 1984-85 | D. I. Gower | S. M. Gavaskar | 5 | 2 | 1 | 2 |
| 1986 | M. W. Gatting[4] | Kapil Dev | 3 | 0 | 2 | 1 |
| 1990 | G. A. Gooch | M. Azharuddin | 3 | 1 | 0 | 2 |
| | In England | | 38 | 21 | 3 | 14 |
| | In India | | 40 | 10 | 8 | 22 |
| | Totals | | 78 | 31 | 11 | 36 |

*Notes:* The 1932 Indian touring team was captained by the Maharaj of Porbandar but he did not play in the Test match.

The following deputised for the official touring captain or were appointed by the home authority for only a minor proportion of the series:

[1]D. B. Carr (Fifth). [2]M. C. Cowdrey (Fourth and Fifth). [3]Pankaj Roy (Second). [4]D. I. Gower (First).

## HIGHEST INNINGS TOTALS

| | |
|---|---|
| For England in England: 653-4 dec. at Lord's | 1990 |
| in India: 652-7 dec. at Madras | 1984-85 |
| For India in England: 606-9 dec. at The Oval | 1990 |
| in India: 553-8 dec. at Kanpur | 1984-85 |

## LOWEST INNINGS TOTALS

| | |
|---|---|
| For England in England: 101 at The Oval | 1971 |
| in India: 102 at Bombay | 1981-82 |
| For India in England: 42 at Lord's | 1974 |
| in India: 83 at Madras | 1976-77 |

## INDIVIDUAL HUNDREDS

### For England (70)

**D. L. Amiss (2)**
188  Lord's...... 1974
179  Delhi...... 1976-77
**M. A. Atherton (1)**
131  Manchester.. 1990
**K. F. Barrington (3)**
151*  Bombay ...... 1961-62
172  Kanpur.... 1961-62
113*  Delhi...... 1961-62
**I. T. Botham (5)**
137  Leeds ...... 1979
114  Bombay ... 1979-80
142  Kanpur .... 1981-82
128  Manchester.. 1982
208  The Oval ... 1982
**G. Boycott (4)**
246*†  Leeds ...... 1967
155  Birmingham . 1979
125  The Oval .... 1979
105  Delhi ...... 1981-82
**M. C. Cowdrey (3)**
160  Leeds ...... 1959
107  Calcutta ... 1963-64
151  Delhi ...... 1963-64
**M. H. Denness (2)**
118  Lord's ...... 1974
100  Birmingham . 1974
**E. R. Dexter (1)**
126*  Kanpur .... 1961-62
**B. L. D'Oliveira (1)**
109†  Leeds ...... 1967
**J. H. Edrich (1)**
100*  Manchester.. 1974
**T. G. Evans (1)**
104  Lord's ...... 1952
**K. W. R. Fletcher (2)**
113  Bombay .... 1972-73
123*  Manchester.. 1974

**G. Fowler (1)**
201  Madras .... 1984-85
**M. W. Gatting (3)**
136  Bombay .... 1984-85
207  Madras .... 1984-85
183*  Birmingham . 1986
**G. A. Gooch (5)**
127  Madras .... 1981-82
114  Lord's ...... 1986
333 }
123 } Lord's ...... 1990
116  Manchester.. 1990
**D. I. Gower (2)**
200*†  Birmingham . 1979
157*  The Oval ... 1990
**T. W. Graveney (2)**
175†  Bombay .... 1951-52
151  Lord's ...... 1967
**A. W. Greig (3)**
148  Bombay .... 1972-73
106  Lord's ...... 1974
103  Calcutta .... 1976-77
**W. R. Hammond (2)**
167  Manchester.. 1936
217  The Oval.... 1936
**J. Hardstaff jun. (1)**
205*  Lord's ...... 1946
**L. Hutton (2)**
150  Lord's ...... 1952
104  Manchester.. 1952
**R. Illingworth (1)**
107  Manchester.. 1971
**B. R. Knight (1)**
127  Kanpur ..... 1963-64

**A. J. Lamb (3)**
107  The Oval.... 1982
139  Lord's ...... 1990
109  Manchester.. 1990
**A. R. Lewis (1)**
125  Kanpur .... 1972-73
**D. Lloyd (1)**
214*  Birmingham . 1974
**B. W. Luckhurst (1)**
101  Manchester.. 1971
**P. B. H. May (1)**
106  Nottingham . 1959
**P. H. Parfitt (1)**
121  Kanpur .... 1963-64
**G. Pullar (2)**
131  Manchester.. 1959
119  Kanpur..... 1961-62
**D. W. Randall (1)**
126  Lord's ...... 1982
**R. T. Robinson (1)**
160  Delhi....... 1984-85
**D. S. Sheppard (1)**
119  The Oval ... 1952
**M. J. K. Smith (1)**
100†  Manchester.. 1959
**R. A. Smith (2)**
100*†  Lord's ...... 1990
121*  Manchester.. 1990
**C. J. Tavaré (1)**
149  Delhi ...... 1981-82
**B. H. Valentine (1)**
136†  Bombay .... 1933-34
**C. F. Walters (1)**
102  Madras .... 1933-34
**A. J. Watkins (1)**
137*†  Delhi....... 1951-52
**T. S. Worthington (1)**
128  The Oval.... 1936

### For India (56)

**L. Amarnath (1)**
118†  Bombay .... 1933-34
**M. Azharuddin (5)**
110†  Calcutta ... 1984-85
105  Madras .... 1984-85
122  Kanpur .... 1984-85
121  Lord's ...... 1990
179  Manchester.. 1990
**A. A. Baig (1)**
112†  Manchester.. 1959
**F. M. Engineer (1)**
121  Bombay .... 1972-73
**S. M. Gavaskar (4)**
101  Manchester... 1974
108  Bombay ... 1976-77

221  The Oval.... 1979
172  Bangalore ... 1981-82
**Hanumant Singh (1)**
105†  Delhi....... 1963-64
**V. S. Hazare (2)**
164*  Delhi...... 1951-52
155  Bombay .... 1951-52
**M. L. Jaisimha (2)**
127  Delhi....... 1961-62
129  Calcutta ... 1963-64
**Kapil Dev (2)**
116  Kanpur .... 1981-82
110  The Oval ... 1990
**S. M. H. Kirmani (1)**
102  Bombay .... 1984-85

**B. K. Kunderan (2)**
192  Madras .... 1963-64
100  Delhi....... 1963-64
**V. L. Manjrekar (3)**
133  Leeds ...... 1952
189*  Delhi...... 1961-62
108  Madras .... 1963-64
**V. Mankad (1)**
184  Lord's ...... 1952
**V. M. Merchant (3)**
114  Manchester.. 1936
128  The Oval ... 1946
154  Delhi....... 1951-52
**Mushtaq Ali (1)**
112  Manchester.. 1936

| | | | | | | |
|---|---|---|---|---|---|---|
| **R. G. Nadkarni** (1) | | **R. J. Shastri** (4) | | 157 | Lord's ...... | 1982 |
| 122* | Kanpur .... 1963-64 | 142 | Bombay ..... 1984-85 | 137 | Kanpur ..... 1984-85 |
| **Nawab of Pataudi jun.** (3) | | 111 | Calcutta .... 1984-85 | 126* | Lord's ...... | 1986 |
| 103 | Madras .... 1961-62 | 100 | Lord's ....... | 1990 | 102* | Leeds ...... | 1986 |
| 203* | Delhi ...... 1963-64 | 187 | The Oval ... | 1990 | **G. R. Viswanath** (4) | |
| 148 | Leeds ...... 1967 | **S. R. Tendulkar** (1) | | 113 | Bombay .... 1972-73 |
| **S. M. Patil** (1) | | 119* | Manchester.. | 1990 | 113 | Lord's ...... | 1979 |
| 129* | Manchester.. 1982 | **P. R. Umrigar** (3) | | 107 | Delhi....... 1981-82 |
| **D. G. Phadkar** (1) | | 130* | Madras ..... 1951-52 | 222 | Madras ..... 1981-82 |
| 115 | Calcutta .... 1951-52 | 118 | Manchester.. | 1959 | **Yashpal Sharma** (1) | |
| **Pankaj Roy** (2) | | 147* | Kanpur ..... 1961-62 | 140 | Madras ..... 1981-82 |
| 140 | Bombay .... 1951-52 | **D. B. Vengsarkar** (5) | | | | |
| 111 | Madras ..... 1951-52 | 103 | Lord's ...... | 1979 | | | |

† *Signifies hundred on first appearance in England–India Tests.*

*Notes:* G. A. Gooch's match aggregate of 456 (333 and 123) for England at Lord's in 1990 is the record in Test matches and provides the only instance of a batsman scoring a triple-hundred and a hundred in the same first-class match. His 333 is the highest innings in any match at Lord's.
 M. Azharuddin scored hundreds in each of his first three Tests.

## RECORD PARTNERSHIPS FOR EACH WICKET

### For England

| | | |
|---|---|---|
| 225 for 1st | G. A. Gooch and M. A. Atherton at Manchester .............. | 1990 |
| 241 for 2nd | G. Fowler and M. W. Gatting at Madras .................... | 1984-85 |
| 308 for 3rd | G. A. Gooch and A. J. Lamb at Lord's ..................... | 1990 |
| 266 for 4th | W. R. Hammond and T. S. Worthington at The Oval.......... | 1936 |
| 254 for 5th† | K. W. R. Fletcher and A. W. Greig at Bombay.............. | 1972-73 |
| 171 for 6th | I. T. Botham and R. W. Taylor at Bombay.................. | 1979-80 |
| 125 for 7th | D. W. Randall and P. H. Edmonds at Lord's................ | 1982 |
| 168 for 8th | R. Illingworth and P. Lever at Manchester................. | 1971 |
| 83 for 9th | K. W. R. Fletcher and N. Gifford at Madras ............... | 1972-73 |
| 70 for 10th | P. J. W. Allott and R. G. D. Willis at Lord's............... | 1982 |

### For India

| | | |
|---|---|---|
| 213 for 1st | S. M. Gavaskar and C. P. S. Chauhan at The Oval ......... | 1979 |
| 192 for 2nd | F. M. Engineer and A. L. Wadekar at Bombay ............. | 1972-73 |
| 316 for 3rd†‡ | G. R. Viswanath and Yashpal Sharma at Madras ........... | 1981-82 |
| 222 for 4th† | V. S. Hazare and V. L. Manjrekar at Leeds ............... | 1952 |
| 214 for 5th† | M. Azharuddin and R. J. Shastri at Calcutta ............... | 1984-85 |
| 130 for 6th | S. M. H. Kirmani and Kapil Dev at The Oval............... | 1982 |
| 235 for 7th† | R. J. Shastri and S. M. H. Kirmani at Bombay ............ | 1984-85 |
| 128 for 8th | R. J. Shastri and S. M. H. Kirmani at Delhi .............. | 1981-82 |
| 104 for 9th | R. J. Shastri and Madan Lal at Delhi .................... | 1981-82 |
| 51 for 10th { | R. G. Nadkarni and B. S. Chandrasekhar at Calcutta ........ | 1963-64 |
| | S. M. H. Kirmani and Chetan Sharma at Madras............. | 1984-85 |

† *Denotes record partnership against all countries.*

‡ *415 runs were added between the fall of the 2nd and 3rd wickets: D. B. Vengsarkar retired hurt when he and Viswanath had added 99 runs.*

## TEN WICKETS OR MORE IN A MATCH

### For England (7)

| | | |
|---|---|---|
| 10-78 (5-35, 5-43)† | G. O. B. Allen, Lord's ............................. | 1936 |
| 11-145 (7-49, 4-96)† | A. V. Bedser, Lord's ............................. | 1946 |
| 11-93 (4-41, 7-52) | A. V. Bedser, Manchester ........................ | 1946 |
| 13-106 (6-58, 7-48) | I. T. Botham, Bombay ........................... | 1979-80 |
| 11-163 (6-104, 5-59)† | N. A. Foster, Madras ............................ | 1984-85 |
| 10-70 (7-46, 3-24)† | J. K. Lever, Delhi .............................. | 1976-77 |
| 11-153 (7-49, 4-104) | H. Verity, Madras .............................. | 1933-34 |

### For India (4)

| | | |
|---|---|---|
| 10-177 (6-105, 4-72) | S. A. Durani, Madras ............................ | 1961-62 |
| 12-108 (8-55, 4-53) | V. Mankad, Madras .............................. | 1951-52 |
| 10-188 (4-130, 6-58) | Chetan Sharma, Birmingham ...................... | 1986 |
| 12-181 (6-64, 6-117)† | L. Sivaramakrishnan, Bombay ..................... | 1984-85 |

† *Signifies ten wickets or more on first appearance in England–India Tests.*

*Note:* A. V. Bedser took eleven wickets in a match in the first two Tests of his career.

## ENGLAND v PAKISTAN

| Season | England | Captains Pakistan | T | E | P | D |
|---|---|---|---|---|---|---|
| 1954 | L. Hutton[1] | A. H. Kardar | 4 | 1 | 1 | 2 |
| 1961-62 | E. R. Dexter | Imtiaz Ahmed | 3 | 1 | 0 | 2 |
| 1962 | E. R. Dexter[2] | Javed Burki | 5 | 4 | 0 | 1 |
| 1967 | D. B. Close | Hanif Mohammad | 3 | 2 | 0 | 1 |
| 1968-69 | M. C. Cowdrey | Saeed Ahmed | 3 | 0 | 0 | 3 |
| 1971 | R. Illingworth | Intikhab Alam | 3 | 1 | 0 | 2 |
| 1972-73 | A. R. Lewis | Majid Khan | 3 | 0 | 0 | 3 |
| 1974 | M. H. Denness | Intikhab Alam | 3 | 0 | 0 | 3 |
| 1977-78 | J. M. Brearley[3] | Wasim Bari | 3 | 0 | 0 | 3 |
| 1978 | J. M. Brearley | Wasim Bari | 3 | 2 | 0 | 1 |
| 1982 | R. G. D. Willis[4] | Imran Khan | 3 | 2 | 1 | 0 |
| 1983-84 | R. G. D. Willis[5] | Zaheer Abbas | 3 | 0 | 1 | 2 |
| 1987 | M. W. Gatting | Imran Khan | 5 | 0 | 1 | 4 |
| 1987-88 | M. W. Gatting | Javed Miandad | 3 | 0 | 1 | 2 |
| | In England ..................... | | 29 | 12 | 3 | 14 |
| | In Pakistan ..................... | | 18 | 1 | 2 | 15 |
| | Totals ........................ | | 47 | 13 | 5 | 29 |

*Notes:* The following deputised for the official touring captain or were appointed by the home authority for only a minor proportion of the series:
[1]D. S. Sheppard (Second and Third). [2]M. C. Cowdrey (Third). [3]G. Boycott (Third). [4]D. I. Gower (Second). [5]D. I. Gower (Second and Third).

## HIGHEST INNINGS TOTALS

| | | |
|---|---|---|
| For England in England: 558-6 dec. at Nottingham ...................... | | 1954 |
| in Pakistan: 546-8 dec. at Faisalabad ........................ | | 1983-84 |
| For Pakistan in England: 708 at The Oval ................................ | | 1987 |
| in Pakistan: 569-9 dec. at Hyderabad ...................... | | 1972-73 |

## LOWEST INNINGS TOTALS

For England in England: 130 at The Oval .................................... 1954
           in Pakistan: 130 at Lahore .................................... 1987-88

For Pakistan in England: 87 at Lord's .................................... 1954
           in Pakistan: 191 at Faisalabad .................................... 1987-88

## INDIVIDUAL HUNDREDS

### For England (41)

**D. L. Amiss** (3)
112  Lahore ..... 1972-73
158  Hyderabad .. 1972-73
183  The Oval .... 1974
**C. W. J. Athey** (1)
123  Lord's ...... 1987
**K. F. Barrington** (4)
139†  Lahore ..... 1961-62
148  Lord's ...... 1967
109*  Nottingham . 1967
142  The Oval .... 1967
**I. T. Botham** (2)
100†  Birmingham . 1978
108  Lord's ...... 1978
**G. Boycott** (3)
121*  Lord's ...... 1971
112  Leeds ...... 1971
100*  Hyderabad .. 1977-78
**B. C. Broad** (1)
116  Faisalabad . 1987-88
**D. C. S. Compton** (1)
278  Nottingham . 1954

**M. C. Cowdrey** (3)
159†  Birmingham . 1962
182  The Oval .... 1962
100  Lahore ..... 1968-69
**E. R. Dexter** (2)
205  Karachi .... 1961-62
172  The Oval .... 1962
**B. L. D'Oliveira** (1)
114*  Dacca ...... 1968-69
**K. W. R. Fletcher** (1)
122  The Oval .... 1974
**M. W. Gatting** (2)
124  Birmingham . 1987
150*  The Oval .... 1987
**D. I. Gower** (2)
152  Faisalabad . 1983-84
173*  Lahore ..... 1983-84
**T. W. Graveney** (3)
153  Lord's ...... 1962
114  Nottingham . 1962
105  Karachi .... 1968-69

**A. P. E. Knott** (1)
116  Birmingham . 1971
**B. W. Luckhurst** (1)
108*†  Birmingham . 1971
**C. Milburn** (1)
139  Karachi .... 1968-69
**P. H. Parfitt** (4)
111  Karachi .... 1961-62
101*  Birmingham . 1962
119  Leeds ...... 1962
101*  Nottingham . 1962
**G. Pullar** (1)
165  Dacca ..... 1961-62
**C. T. Radley** (1)
106†  Birmingham . 1978
**D. W. Randall** (1)
105  Birmingham . 1982
**R. T. Robinson** (1)
166†  Manchester . 1987
**R. T. Simpson** (1)
101  Nottingham . 1954

### For Pakistan (30)

**Alim-ud-Din** (1)
109  Karachi .... 1961-62
**Asif Iqbal** (3)
146  The Oval .... 1967
104*  Birmingham . 1971
102  Lahore ..... 1972-73
**Hanif Mohammad** (3)
111 
104 } Dacca ...... 1961-62
187*  Lord's ...... 1967
**Haroon Rashid** (2)
122†  Lahore ..... 1977-78
108  Hyderabad .. 1977-78
**Imran Khan** (1)
118  The Oval .... 1987

**Intikhab Alam** (1)
138  Hyderabad .. 1972-73
**Javed Burki** (3)
138†  Lahore ..... 1961-62
140  Dacca ..... 1961-62
101  Lord's ...... 1962
**Javed Miandad** (1)
260  The Oval .... 1987
**Mohsin Khan** (2)
200  Lord's ...... 1982
104  Lahore ..... 1983-84
**Mudassar Nazar** (3)
114†  Lahore ..... 1977-78
124  Birmingham . 1987
120  Lahore ..... 1987-88

**Mushtaq Mohammad** (3)
100*  Nottingham . 1962
100  Birmingham . 1971
157  Hyderabad .. 1972-73
**Nasim-ul Ghani** (1)
101  Lord's ...... 1962
**Sadiq Mohammad** (1)
119  Lahore ..... 1972-73
**Salim Malik** (2)
116  Faisalabad . 1983-84
102  The Oval .... 1987
**Wasim Raja** (1)
112  Faisalabad . 1983-84
**Zaheer Abbas** (2)
274†  Birmingham . 1971
240  The Oval .... 1974

† *Signifies hundred on first appearance in England–Pakistan Tests.*

*Note:* Three batsmen – Majid Khan, Mushtaq Mohammad and D. L. Amiss – were dismissed for 99 at Karachi, 1972-73: the only instance in Test matches.

## RECORD PARTNERSHIPS FOR EACH WICKET

### For England

| | | | |
|---|---|---|---|
| 198 | for 1st | G. Pullar and R. W. Barber at Dacca | 1961-62 |
| 248 | for 2nd | M. C. Cowdrey and E. R. Dexter at The Oval | 1962 |
| 201 | for 3rd | K. F. Barrington and T. W. Graveney at Lord's | 1967 |
| 188 | for 4th | E. R. Dexter and P. H. Parfitt at Karachi | 1961-62 |
| 192 | for 5th | D. C. S. Compton and T. E. Bailey at Nottingham | 1954 |
| 153* | for 6th | P. H. Parfitt and D. A. Allen at Birmingham | 1962 |
| 167 | for 7th | D. I. Gower and V. J. Marks at Faisalabad | 1983-84 |
| 99 | for 8th | P. H. Parfitt and D. A. Allen at Leeds | 1962 |
| 76 | for 9th | T. W. Graveney and F. S. Trueman at Lord's | 1962 |
| 79 | for 10th | R. W. Taylor and R. G. D. Willis at Birmingham | 1982 |

### For Pakistan

| | | | |
|---|---|---|---|
| 173 | for 1st | Mohsin Khan and Shoaib Mohammad at Lahore | 1983-84 |
| 291 | for 2nd† | Zaheer Abbas and Mushtaq Mohammad at Birmingham | 1971 |
| 180 | for 3rd | Mudassar Nazar and Haroon Rashid at Lahore | 1977-78 |
| 234 | for 4th | Javed Miandad and Salim Malik at The Oval | 1987 |
| 197 | for 5th | Javed Burki and Nasim-ul-Ghani at Lord's | 1962 |
| 145 | for 6th | Mushtaq Mohammad and Intikhab Alam at Hyderabad | 1972-73 |
| 89 | for 7th | Ijaz Ahmed and Salim Yousuf at The Oval | 1987 |
| 130 | for 8th† | Hanif Mohammad and Asif Iqbal at Lord's | 1967 |
| 190 | for 9th† | Asif Iqbal and Intikhab Alam at The Oval | 1967 |
| 62 | for 10th | Sarfraz Nawaz and Asif Masood at Leeds | 1974 |

*† Denotes record partnership against all countries.*

## TEN WICKETS OR MORE IN A MATCH

### For England (2)

| | | | |
|---|---|---|---|
| 11-83 (6-65, 5-18)† | N. G. B. Cook, Karachi | | 1983-84 |
| 13-71 (5-20, 8-51) | D. L. Underwood, Lord's | | 1974 |

### For Pakistan (6)

| | | | |
|---|---|---|---|
| 10-194 (5-84, 5-110) | Abdul Qadir, Lahore | | 1983-84 |
| 13-101 (9-56, 4-45) | Abdul Qadir, Lahore | | 1987-88 |
| 10-186 (5-88, 5-98) | Abdul Qadir, Karachi | | 1987-88 |
| 10-211 (7-96, 3-115) | Abdul Qadir, The Oval | | 1987 |
| 12-99 (6-53, 6-46) | Fazal Mahmood, The Oval | | 1954 |
| 10-77 (3-37, 7-40) | Imran Khan, Leeds | | 1987 |

*† Signifies ten wickets or more on first appearance in England–Pakistan Tests.*

## FOUR WICKETS IN FIVE BALLS

C. M. Old, v Pakistan at Birmingham in 1978, dismissed Wasim Raja, Wasim Bari, Iqbal Qasim and Sikander Bakht to take four wickets in five balls (ww-ww).

## ENGLAND v SRI LANKA

*Captains*

| Season | England | Sri Lanka | T | E | SL | D |
|--------|---------|-----------|---|---|----|----|
| 1981-82 | K. W. R. Fletcher | B. Warnapura | 1 | 1 | 0 | 0 |
| 1984 | D. I. Gower | L. R. D. Mendis | 1 | 0 | 0 | 1 |
| 1988 | G. A. Gooch | R. S. Madugalle | 1 | 1 | 0 | 0 |
| 1991 | G. A. Gooch | P. A. de Silva | 1 | 1 | 0 | 0 |
| | In England .................... | | 3 | 2 | 0 | 1 |
| | In Sri Lanka ................... | | 1 | 1 | 0 | 0 |
| | Totals........................ | | 4 | 3 | 0 | 1 |

## INNINGS TOTALS

Highest innings total for England: 429 at Lord's .................... 1988
for Sri Lanka: 491-7 dec. at Lord's .................... 1984

Lowest innings total for England: 223 at Colombo (PSS) .................... 1981-82
for Sri Lanka: 175 at Colombo (PSS) .................... 1981-82

## INDIVIDUAL HUNDREDS

### For England (3)

| | | |
|---|---|---|
| **G. A. Gooch** (1) | **A. J. Lamb** (1) | **A. J. Stewart** (1) |
| 174  Lord's ......  1991 | 107†  Lord's ......  1984 | 113*†  Lord's ......  1991 |

### For Sri Lanka (3)

| | | |
|---|---|---|
| **L. R. D. Mendis** (1) | **S. A. R. Silva** (1) | **S. Wettimuny** (1) |
| 111  Lord's ......  1984 | 102*†  Lord's ......  1984 | 190  Lord's ......  1984 |

† *Signifies hundred on first appearance in England–Sri Lanka Tests.*

## BEST BOWLING

Best bowling in an innings for England: 7-70 by P. A. J. DeFreitas at Lord's ... 1991
for Sri Lanka: 5-69 by R. J. Ratnayake at Lord's .... 1991

## RECORD PARTNERSHIPS FOR EACH WICKET

### For England

| | | |
|---|---|---|
| 78 for 1st | G. A. Gooch and H. Morris at Lord's .................... | 1991 |
| 139 for 2nd | G. A. Gooch and A. J. Stewart at Lord's .................... | 1991 |
| 105 for 3rd | G. A. Gooch and R. A. Smith at Lord's .................... | 1991 |
| 87 for 4th | K. J. Barnett and A. J. Lamb at Lord's .................... | 1988 |
| 40 for 5th | A. J. Stewart and I. T. Botham at Lord's .................... | 1991 |
| 87 for 6th | A. J. Lamb and R. M. Ellison at Lord's .................... | 1984 |
| 63 for 7th | A. J. Stewart and R. C. Russell at Lord's .................... | 1991 |
| 12 for 8th | A. J. Stewart and P. A. J. DeFreitas at Lord's .............. | 1991 |
| 37 for 9th | P. J. Newport and N. A. Foster at Lord's .................... | 1988 |
| 9 for 10th | N. A. Foster and D. V. Lawrence at Lord's ................. | 1988 |

**For Sri Lanka**

| | | |
|---|---|---|
| 50 for 1st | D. S. B. P. Kuruppu and U. C. Hathurusinghe at Lord's ... | 1991 |
| 83 for 2nd | B. Warnapura and R. L. Dias at Colombo (PSS) ......... | 1981-82 |
| 101 for 3rd | S. Wettimuny and R. L. Dias at Lord's ............... | 1984 |
| 148 for 4th | S. Wettimuny and A. Ranatunga at Lord's ............. | 1984 |
| 150 for 5th† | S. Wettimuny and L. R. D. Mendis at Lord's .......... | 1984 |
| 138 for 6th† | S. A. R. Silva and L. R. D. Mendis at Lord's ......... | 1984 |
| 74 for 7th | U. C. Hathurusinghe and R. J. Ratnayake at Lord's ...... | 1991 |
| 29 for 8th | R. J. Ratnayake and C. P. H. Ramanayake at Lord's ...... | 1991 |
| 12 for 9th | J. R. Ratnayeke and G. F. Labrooy at Lord's........... | 1988 |
| | C. P. H. Ramanayake and K. I. W. Wijegunawardene at Lord's | 1991 |
| 64 for 10th† | J. R. Ratnayeke and G. F. Labrooy at Lord's........... | 1988 |

† *Denotes record partnership against all countries.*

## ENGLAND v REST OF THE WORLD

In 1970, owing to the cancellation of the South African tour to England, a series of matches was arranged, with the trappings of a full Test series, between England and the Rest of the World. It was played for the Guinness Trophy.

The following players represented the Rest of the World: E. J. Barlow (5), F. M. Engineer (2), L. R. Gibbs (4), Intikhab Alam (5), R. B. Kanhai (5), C. H. Lloyd (5), G. D. McKenzie (3), D. L. Murray (3), Mushtaq Mohammad (2), P. M. Pollock (1), R. G. Pollock (5), M. J. Procter (5), B. A. Richards (5), G. S. Sobers (5).

A list of players who appeared for England in these matches may be found on page 129.

## AUSTRALIA v SOUTH AFRICA

*Captains*

| Season | Australia | South Africa | T | A | SA | D |
|---|---|---|---|---|---|---|
| 1902-03*S* | J. Darling | H. M. Taberer[1] | 3 | 2 | 0 | 1 |
| 1910-11*A* | C. Hill | P. W. Sherwell | 5 | 4 | 1 | 0 |
| 1912*E* | S. E. Gregory | F. Mitchell[2] | 3 | 2 | 0 | 1 |
| 1921-22*S* | H. L. Collins | H. W. Taylor | 3 | 1 | 0 | 2 |
| 1931-32*A* | W. M. Woodfull | H. B. Cameron | 5 | 5 | 0 | 0 |
| 1935-36*S* | V. Y. Richardson | H. F. Wade | 5 | 4 | 0 | 1 |
| 1949-50*S* | A. L. Hassett | A. D. Nourse | 5 | 4 | 0 | 1 |
| 1952-53*A* | A. L. Hassett | J. E. Cheetham | 5 | 2 | 2 | 1 |
| 1957-58*S* | I. D. Craig | C. B. van Ryneveld[3] | 5 | 3 | 0 | 2 |
| 1963-64*A* | R. B. Simpson[4] | T. L. Goddard | 5 | 1 | 1 | 3 |
| 1966-67*S* | R. B. Simpson | P. L. van der Merwe | 5 | 1 | 3 | 1 |
| 1969-70*S* | W. M. Lawry | A. Bacher | 4 | 0 | 4 | 0 |
| | In South Africa................... | | 30 | 15 | 7 | 8 |
| | In Australia .................... | | 20 | 12 | 4 | 4 |
| | In England .................... | | 3 | 2 | 0 | 1 |
| | Totals...................... | | 53 | 29 | 11 | 13 |

*S Played in South Africa. A Played in Australia. E Played in England.*

*Notes:* The following deputised for the official touring captain or were appointed by the home authority for only a minor proportion of the series:

[1]J. H. Anderson (Second), E. A. Halliwell (Third). [2]L. J. Tancred (Third). [3]D. J. McGlew (First). [4]R. Benaud (First).

## HIGHEST INNINGS TOTALS

| | | |
|---|---|---|
| For Australia in Australia: 578 at Melbourne.................... | | 1910-11 |
| in South Africa: 549-7 dec. at Port Elizabeth ................. | | 1949-50 |
| For South Africa in Australia: 595 at Adelaide .................... | | 1963-64 |
| in South Africa: 622-9 dec. at Durban ................... | | 1969-70 |

## LOWEST INNINGS TOTALS

For Australia in Australia: 153 at Melbourne.................................... 1931-32
            in South Africa: 75 at Durban ..................................... 1949-50

For South Africa in Australia: 36† at Melbourne ........................... 1931-32
              in South Africa: 85 at Johannesburg ...................... 1902-03

*† Scored 45 in the second innings giving the smallest aggregate of 81 (12 extras) in Test cricket.*

## INDIVIDUAL HUNDREDS

### For Australia (55)

**W. W. Armstrong** (2)
159*‡ Johannesburg 1902-03
132 Melbourne .. 1910-11
**W. Bardsley** (3)
132† Sydney ..... 1910-11
121 Manchester.. 1912
164 Lord's ...... 1912
**R. Benaud** (2)
122 Johannesburg 1957-58
100 Johannesburg 1957-58
**B. C. Booth** (2)
169† Brisbane .... 1963-64
102* Sydney ..... 1963-64
**D. G. Bradman** (4)
226† Brisbane .... 1931-32
112 Sydney ..... 1931-32
167 Melbourne .. 1931-32
299* Adelaide .... 1931-32
**W. A. Brown** (1)
121 Cape Town .. 1935-36
**J. W. Burke** (1)
189 Cape Town .. 1957-58
**A. G. Chipperfield** (1)
109† Durban ..... 1935-36
**H. L. Collins** (1)
203 Johannesburg 1921-22
**J. H. Fingleton** (3)
112 Cape Town .. 1935-36

108 Johannesburg 1935-36
118 Durban ..... 1935-36
**J. M. Gregory** (1)
119 Johannesburg 1921-22
**R. N. Harvey** (8)
178 Cape Town .. 1949-50
151* Durban ..... 1949-50
100 Johannesburg 1949-50
116 Pt Elizabeth 1949-50
190 Brisbane .... 1952-53
116 Adelaide .... 1952-53
205 Melbourne .. 1952-53
**A. L. Hassett** (3)
112† Johannesburg 1949-50
167 Pt Elizabeth 1949-50
163 Adelaide .... 1952-53
**C. Hill** (3)
142† Johannesburg 1902-03
191 Sydney ..... 1910-11
100 Melbourne .. 1910-11
**C. Kelleway** (2)
114 Manchester.. 1912
102 Lord's ...... 1912
**W. M. Lawry** (1)
157 Melbourne .. 1963-64
**S. J. E. Loxton** (1)
101† Johannesburg 1949-50

**C. G. Macartney** (2)
137 Sydney ..... 1910-11
116 Durban ..... 1921-22
**S. J. McCabe** (2)
149 Durban ..... 1935-36
189* Johannesburg 1935-36
**C. C. McDonald** (1)
154 Adelaide .... 1952-53
**J. Moroney** (1)
118 ⎫
101* ⎬ Johannesburg 1949-50
**A. R. Morris** (2)
111 Johannesburg 1949-50
157 Pt Elizabeth 1949-50
**K. E. Rigg** (1)
127† Sydney ..... 1931-32
**J. Ryder** (1)
142 Cape Town .. 1921-22
**R. B. Simpson** (1)
153 Cape Town .. 1966-67
**K. R. Stackpole** (1)
134 Cape Town .. 1966-67
**V. T. Trumper** (2)
159 Melbourne .. 1910-11
214* Adelaide .... 1910-11
**W. M. Woodfull** (1)
161 Melbourne .. 1931-32

### For South Africa (36)

**E. J. Barlow** (5)
114† Brisbane .... 1963-64
109 Melbourne .. 1963-64
201 Adelaide .... 1963-64
127 Cape Town .. 1969-70
110 Johannesburg 1969-70
**K. C. Bland** (1)
126 Sydney ..... 1963-64
**W. R. Endean** (1)
162* Melbourne .. 1952-53
**G. A. Faulkner** (3)
204 Melbourne .. 1910-11
115 Adelaide .... 1910-11
122* Manchester.. 1912
**C. N. Frank** (1)
152 Johannesburg 1921-22
**B. L. Irvine** (1)
102 Pt Elizabeth 1969-70

**D. T. Lindsay** (3)
182 Johannesburg 1966-67
137 Durban ..... 1966-67
131 Johannesburg 1966-67
**D. J. McGlew** (2)
108 Johannesburg 1957-58
105 Durban ..... 1957-58
**A. D. Nourse** (2)
231 Johannesburg 1935-36
114 Cape Town .. 1949-50
**A. W. Nourse** (1)
111 Johannesburg 1921-22
**R. G. Pollock** (5)
122 Sydney ..... 1963-64
175 Adelaide .... 1963-64
209 Cape Town .. 1966-67
105 Pt Elizabeth 1966-67
274 Durban ..... 1969-70

**B. A. Richards** (2)
140 Durban ..... 1969-70
126 Pt Elizabeth 1969-70
**E. A. B. Rowan** (1)
143 Durban ..... 1949-50
**J. H. Sinclair** (2)
101 Johannesburg 1902-03
104 Cape Town .. 1902-03
**S. J. Snooke** (1)
103 Adelaide .... 1910-11
**K. G. Viljoen** (1)
111 Melbourne .. 1931-32
**J. H. B. Waite** (2)
115 Johannesburg 1957-58
134 Durban ..... 1957-58
**J. W. Zulch** (2)
105 Adelaide .... 1910-11
150 Sydney ..... 1910-11

*† Signifies hundred on first appearance in Australia-South Africa Tests.*
*‡ Carried his bat.*

## RECORD PARTNERSHIPS FOR EACH WICKET

### For Australia

| | | |
|---|---|---|
| 233 for 1st | J. H. Fingleton and W. A. Brown at Cape Town .......... | 1935-36 |
| 275 for 2nd | C. C. McDonald and A. L. Hassett at Adelaide ........... | 1952-53 |
| 242 for 3rd | C. Kelleway and W. Bardsley at Lord's ................. | 1912 |
| 168 for 4th | R. N. Harvey and K. R. Miller at Sydney ............... | 1952-53 |
| 143 for 5th | W. W. Armstrong and V. T. Trumper at Melbourne .......... | 1910-11 |
| 107 for 6th | C. Kelleway and V. S. Ransford at Melbourne ............ | 1910-11 |
| 160 for 7th | R. Benaud and G. D. McKenzie at Sydney ............... | 1963-64 |
| 83 for 8th | A. G. Chipperfield and C. V. Grimmett at Durban .......... | 1935-36 |
| 78 for 9th { | D. G. Bradman and W. J. O'Reilly at Adelaide ........... | 1931-32 |
| | K. D. Mackay and I. Meckiff at Johannesburg ............ | 1957-58 |
| 82 for 10th | V. S. Ransford and W. J. Whitty at Melbourne ........... | 1910-11 |

### For South Africa

| | | |
|---|---|---|
| 176 for 1st | D. J. McGlew and T. L. Goddard at Johannesburg ......... | 1957-58 |
| 173 for 2nd | L. J. Tancred and C. B. Llewellyn at Johannesburg ........ | 1902-03 |
| 341 for 3rd† | E. J. Barlow and R. G. Pollock at Adelaide ............. | 1963-64 |
| 206 for 4th | C. N. Frank and A. W. Nourse at Johannesburg ........... | 1921-22 |
| 129 for 5th | J. H. B. Waite and W. R. Endean at Johannesburg ......... | 1957-58 |
| 200 for 6th† | R. G. Pollock and H. R. Lance at Durban ............... | 1969-70 |
| 221 for 7th | D. T. Lindsay and P. L. van der Merwe at Johannesburg ..... | 1966-67 |
| 124 for 8th† | A. W. Nourse and E. A. Halliwell at Johannesburg ......... | 1902-03 |
| 85 for 9th | R. G. Pollock and P. M. Pollock at Cape Town ........... | 1966-67 |
| 53 for 10th | L. A. Stricker and S. J. Pegler at Adelaide ............. | 1910-11 |

† *Denotes record partnership against all countries.*

## TEN WICKETS OR MORE IN A MATCH

### For Australia (5)

| | | |
|---|---|---|
| 14-199 (7-116, 7-83) | C. V. Grimmett, Adelaide ................... | 1931-32 |
| 10-88 (5-32, 5-56) | C. V. Grimmett, Cape Town ................. | 1935-36 |
| 10-110 (3-70, 7-40) | C. V. Grimmett, Johannesburg ............... | 1935-36 |
| 13-173 (7-100, 6-73) | C. V. Grimmett, Durban .................... | 1935-36 |
| 11-24 (5-6, 6-18) | H. Ironmonger, Melbourne .................. | 1931-32 |

### For South Africa (2)

| | | |
|---|---|---|
| 10-116 (5-43, 5-73) | C. B. Llewellyn, Johannesburg ............... | 1902-03 |
| 13-165 (6-84, 7-81) | H. J. Tayfield, Melbourne .................. | 1952-53 |

*Note:* C. V. Grimmett took ten wickets or more in three consecutive matches in 1935-36.

## AUSTRALIA v WEST INDIES

|  | Captains | | | | | | |
|---|---|---|---|---|---|---|---|
| Season | Australia | West Indies | T | A | WI | T | D |
| 1930-31*A* | W. M. Woodfull | G. C. Grant | 5 | 4 | 1 | 0 | 0 |
| 1951-52*A* | A. L. Hassett[1] | J. D. C. Goddard[2] | 5 | 4 | 1 | 0 | 0 |
| 1954-55*W* | I. W. Johnson | D. St E. Atkinson[3] | 5 | 3 | 0 | 0 | 2 |
| 1960-61*A* | R. Benaud | F. M. M. Worrell | 5 | 2 | 1 | 1 | 1 |

## THE FRANK WORRELL TROPHY

### Captains

| Season | Australia | West Indies | T | A | WI | T | D | Held by |
|--------|-----------|-------------|---|---|----|----|---|---------|
| 1964-65 W | R. B. Simpson | G. S. Sobers | 5 | 1 | 2 | 0 | 2 | WI |
| 1968-69 A | W. M. Lawry | G. S. Sobers | 5 | 3 | 1 | 0 | 1 | A |
| 1972-73 W | I. M. Chappell | R. B. Kanhai | 5 | 2 | 0 | 0 | 3 | A |
| 1975-76 A | G. S. Chappell | C. H. Lloyd | 6 | 5 | 1 | 0 | 0 | A |
| 1977-78 W | R. B. Simpson | A. I. Kallicharran[4] | 5 | 1 | 3 | 0 | 1 | WI |
| 1979-80 A | G. S. Chappell | C. H. Lloyd[5] | 3 | 0 | 2 | 0 | 1 | WI |
| 1981-82 A | G. S. Chappell | C. H. Lloyd | 3 | 1 | 1 | 0 | 1 | WI |
| 1983-84 W | K. J. Hughes | C. H. Lloyd[6] | 5 | 0 | 3 | 0 | 2 | WI |
| 1984-85 A | A. R. Border[7] | C. H. Lloyd | 5 | 1 | 3 | 0 | 1 | WI |
| 1988-89 A | A. R. Border | I. V. A. Richards | 5 | 1 | 3 | 0 | 1 | WI |
| 1990-91 W | A. R. Border | I. V. A. Richards | 5 | 1 | 2 | 0 | 2 | WI |

| | | | T | A | WI | T | D | |
|---|---|---|---|---|----|----|---|---|
| In Australia | | | 42 | 21 | 14 | 1 | 6 | |
| In West Indies | | | 30 | 8 | 10 | 0 | 12 | |
| Totals | | | 72 | 29 | 24 | 1 | 18 | |

*A Played in Australia.   W Played in West Indies.*

*Notes:* The following deputised for the official touring captain or were appointed by the home authority for only a minor proportion of the series:
[1]A. R. Morris (Third). [2]J. B. Stollmeyer (Fifth). [3]J. B. Stollmeyer (Second and Third). [4]C. H. Lloyd (First and Second). [5]D. L. Murray (First). [6]I. V. A. Richards (Second). [7]K. J. Hughes (First and Second).

## HIGHEST INNINGS TOTALS

| | | |
|---|---|---|
| For Australia in Australia: | 619 at Sydney | 1968-69 |
| in West Indies: | 758-8 dec. at Kingston | 1954-55 |

| | | |
|---|---|---|
| For West Indies in Australia: | 616 at Adelaide | 1968-69 |
| in West Indies: | 573 at Bridgetown | 1964-65 |

## LOWEST INNINGS TOTALS

| | | |
|---|---|---|
| For Australia in Australia: | 76 at Perth | 1984-85 |
| in West Indies: | 90 at Port-of-Spain | 1977-78 |

| | | |
|---|---|---|
| For West Indies in Australia: | 78 at Sydney | 1951-52 |
| in West Indies: | 109 at Georgetown | 1972-73 |

## INDIVIDUAL HUNDREDS

### For Australia (70)

**R. G. Archer** (1)
128   Kingston.... 1954-55
**R. Benaud** (1)
121   Kingston.... 1954-55
**D. C. Boon** (2)
149   Sydney ..... 1988-89
109*  Kingston.... 1990-91
**B. C. Booth** (1)
117   Port-of-Spain 1964-65
**A. R. Border** (2)
126   Adelaide .... 1981-82
100*  Port-of-Spain 1983-84
**D. G. Bradman** (2)
223   Brisbane .... 1930-31
152   Melbourne .. 1930-31

**G. S. Chappell** (5)
106   Bridgetown .. 1972-73
123 ⎫
109*⎭ ‡Brisbane ... 1975-76
182*  Sydney ..... 1975-76
124   Brisbane .... 1979-80
**I. M. Chappell** (5)
117†  Brisbane .... 1968-69
165   Melbourne .. 1968-69
106*  Bridgetown .. 1972-73
109   Georgetown .. 1972-73
156   Perth ...... 1975-76
**G. J. Cosier** (1)
109†  Melbourne .. 1975-76

**R. M. Cowper** (2)
143   Port-of-Spain 1964-65
102   Bridgetown .. 1964-65
**J. Dyson** (1)
127*† Sydney ..... 1981-82
**R. N. Harvey** (3)
133   Kingston.... 1954-55
133   Port-of-Spain 1954-55
204   Kingston.... 1954-55
**A. L. Hassett** (2)
132   Sydney ..... 1951-52
102   Melbourne .. 1951-52
**A. M. J. Hilditch** (1)
113†  Melbourne .. 1984-85

**K. J. Hughes** (2)

| 130*† | Brisbane | 1979-80 |
|---|---|---|
| 100* | Melbourne | 1981-82 |

**D. M. Jones** (1)

| 216 | Adelaide | 1988-89 |

**A. F. Kippax** (1)

| 146† | Adelaide | 1930-31 |

**W. M. Lawry** (4)

| 210 | Bridgetown | 1964-65 |
| 105 | Brisbane | 1968-69 |
| 205 | Melbourne | 1968-69 |
| 151 | Sydney | 1968-69 |

**R. R. Lindwall** (1)

| 118 | Bridgetown | 1954-55 |

**R. B. McCosker** (1)

| 109* | Melbourne | 1975-76 |

**C. C. McDonald** (2)

| 110 | Port-of-Spain | 1954-55 |
| 127 | Kingston | 1954-55 |

**K. R. Miller** (4)

| 129 | Sydney | 1951-52 |

| 147 | Kingston | 1954-55 |
|---|---|---|
| 137 | Bridgetown | 1954-55 |
| 109 | Kingston | 1954-55 |

**A. R. Morris** (1)

| 111 | Port-of-Spain | 1954-55 |

**N. C. O'Neill** (1)

| 181† | Brisbane | 1960-61 |

**W. B. Phillips** (1)

| 120 | Bridgetown | 1983-84 |

**W. H. Ponsford** (2)

| 183 | Sydney | 1930-31 |
| 109 | Sydney | 1930-31 |

**I. R. Redpath** (4)

| 132 | Sydney | 1968-69 |
| 102 | Melbourne | 1975-76 |
| 103 | Adelaide | 1975-76 |
| 101 | Melbourne | 1975-76 |

**C. S. Serjeant** (1)

| 124 | Georgetown | 1977-78 |

**R. B. Simpson** (1)

| 201 | Bridgetown | 1964-65 |

**K. R. Stackpole** (1)

| 142 | Kingston | 1972-73 |

**M. A. Taylor** (1)

| 144 | St John's | 1990-91 |

**P. M. Toohey** (1)

| 122 | Kingston | 1977-78 |

**A. Turner** (1)

| 136 | Adelaide | 1975-76 |

**K. D. Walters** (6)

| 118 | Sydney | 1968-69 |
| 110 | Adelaide | 1968-69 |
| 242 | } Sydney | 1968-69 |
| 103 | | |
| 102* | Bridgetown | 1972-73 |
| 112 | Port-of-Spain | 1972-73 |

**M. E. Waugh** (1)

| 139* | St John's | 1990-91 |

**K. C. Wessels** (1)

| 173 | Sydney | 1984-85 |

**G. M. Wood** (2)

| 126 | Georgetown | 1977-78 |
| 111 | Perth | 1988-89 |

## For West Indies (73)

**F. C. M. Alexander** (1)

| 108 | Sydney | 1960-61 |

**D. St E. Atkinson** (1)

| 219 | Bridgetown | 1954-55 |

**B. F. Butcher** (3)

| 117 | Port-of-Spain | 1964-65 |
| 101 | Sydney | 1968-69 |
| 118 | Adelaide | 1968-69 |

**C. C. Depeiza** (1)

| 122 | Bridgetown | 1954-55 |

**P. J. L. Dujon** (2)

| 130 | Port-of-Spain | 1983-84 |
| 139 | Perth | 1984-85 |

**M. L. C. Foster** (1)

| 125† | Kingston | 1972-73 |

**R. C. Fredericks** (1)

| 169 | Perth | 1975-76 |

**H. A. Gomes** (6)

| 101† | Georgetown | 1977-78 |
| 115 | Kingston | 1977-78 |
| 126 | Sydney | 1981-82 |
| 124* | Adelaide | 1981-82 |
| 127 | Perth | 1984-85 |
| 120* | Adelaide | 1984-85 |

**C. G. Greenidge** (4)

| 120* | Georgetown | 1983-84 |
| 127 | Kingston | 1983-84 |
| 104 | Adelaide | 1988-89 |
| 226 | Bridgetown | 1990-91 |

**D. L. Haynes** (5)

| 103* | Georgetown | 1983-84 |
| 145 | Bridgetown | 1983-84 |
| 100 | Perth | 1988-89 |

| 143 | Sydney | 1988-89 |
|---|---|---|
| 111 | Georgetown | 1990-91 |

**G. A. Headley** (2)

| 102* | Brisbane | 1930-31 |
| 105 | Sydney | 1930-31 |

**C. C. Hunte** (1)

| 110 | Melbourne | 1960-61 |

**A. I. Kallicharran** (4)

| 101 | Brisbane | 1975-76 |
| 127 | Port-of-Spain | 1977-78 |
| 126 | Kingston | 1977-78 |
| 106 | Adelaide | 1979-80 |

**R. B. Kanhai** (5)

| 117 | } Adelaide | 1960-61 |
| 115 | | |
| 129 | Bridgetown | 1964-65 |
| 121 | Port-of-Spain | 1964-65 |
| 105 | Bridgetown | 1972-73 |

**C. H. Lloyd** (6)

| 129† | Brisbane | 1968-69 |
| 178 | Georgetown | 1972-73 |
| 149 | Perth | 1975-76 |
| 102 | Melbourne | 1975-76 |
| 121 | Adelaide | 1979-80 |
| 114 | Brisbane | 1984-85 |

**F. R. Martin** (1)

| 123* | Sydney | 1930-31 |

**S. M. Nurse** (2)

| 201 | Bridgetown | 1964-65 |
| 137 | Sydney | 1968-69 |

**I. V. A. Richards** (5)

| 101 | Adelaide | 1975-76 |
| 140 | Brisbane | 1979-80 |

| 178 | St John's | 1983-84 |
|---|---|---|
| 208 | Melbourne | 1984-85 |
| 146 | Perth | 1988-89 |

**R. B. Richardson** (7)

| 131* | Bridgetown | 1983-84 |
| 154 | St John's | 1983-84 |
| 138 | Brisbane | 1984-85 |
| 122 | Melbourne | 1988-89 |
| 106 | Adelaide | 1988-89 |
| 104* | Kingston | 1990-91 |
| 182 | Georgetown | 1990-91 |

**L. G. Rowe** (1)

| 107 | Brisbane | 1975-76 |

**O. G. Smith** (1)

| 104† | Kingston | 1954-55 |

**G. S. Sobers** (4)

| 132 | Brisbane | 1960-61 |
| 168 | Sydney | 1960-61 |
| 110 | Adelaide | 1968-69 |
| 113 | Sydney | 1968-69 |

**J. B. Stollmeyer** (1)

| 104 | Sydney | 1951-52 |

**C. L. Walcott** (5)

| 108 | Kingston | 1954-55 |
| 126 | } Port-of-Spain | 1954-55 |
| 110 | | |
| 155 | } Kingston | 1954-55 |
| 110 | | |

**E. D. Weekes** (1)

| 139 | Port-of-Spain | 1954-55 |

**A. B. Williams** (1)

| 100† | Georgetown | 1977-78 |

**F. M. M. Worrell** (1)

| 108 | Melbourne | 1951-52 |

† *Signifies hundred on first appearance in Australia–West Indies Tests.*

‡ *G. S. Chappell is the only player to score hundreds in both innings of his first Test as captain.*

*Note:* F. C. M. Alexander and C. C. Depeiza scored the only hundreds of their careers in a Test match.

## RECORD PARTNERSHIPS FOR EACH WICKET

### For Australia

| | | | |
|---|---|---|---|
| 382 for 1st† | W. M. Lawry and R. B. Simpson at Bridgetown | .............. | 1964-65 |
| 298 for 2nd | W. M. Lawry and I. M. Chappell at Melbourne | .......... | 1968-69 |
| 295 for 3rd† | C. C. McDonald and R. N. Harvey at Kingston | .......... | 1954-55 |
| 336 for 4th | W. M. Lawry and K. D. Walters at Sydney | ................ | 1968-69 |
| 220 for 5th | K. R. Miller and R. G. Archer at Kingston | ............... | 1954-55 |
| 206 for 6th | K. R. Miller and R. G. Archer at Bridgetown | ........... | 1954-55 |
| 134 for 7th | A. K. Davidson and R. Benaud at Brisbane | ............... | 1960-61 |
| 137 for 8th | R. Benaud and I. W. Johnson at Kingston | ................ | 1954-55 |
| 114 for 9th | D. M. Jones and M. G. Hughes at Adelaide | ............... | 1988-89 |
| 97 for 10th | T. G. Hogan and R. M. Hogg at Georgetown | ............. | 1983-84 |

### For West Indies

| | | | |
|---|---|---|---|
| 250* for 1st | C. G. Greenidge and D. L. Haynes at Georgetown | ...... | 1983-84 |
| 297 for 2nd | D. L. Haynes and R. B. Richardson at Georgetown | ....... | 1990-91 |
| 308 for 3rd | R. B. Richardson and I. V. A. Richards at St John's | ......... | 1983-84 |
| 198 for 4th | L. G. Rowe and A. I. Kallicharran at Brisbane | ......... | 1975-76 |
| 210 for 5th | R. B. Kanhai and M. L. C. Foster at Kingston | ......... | 1972-73 |
| 165 for 6th | R. B. Kanhai and D. L. Murray at Bridgetown | ......... | 1972-73 |
| 347 for 7th†‡ | D. St E. Atkinson and C. C. Depeiza at Bridgetown | ......... | 1954-55 |
| 87 for 8th | P. J. L. Dujon and C. E. L. Ambrose at Port-of-Spain | ....... | 1990-91 |
| 122 for 9th | D. A. J. Holford and J. L. Hendriks at Adelaide | ........ | 1968-69 |
| 56 for 10th | J. Garner and C. E. H. Croft at Brisbane | ................. | 1979-80 |

† *Denotes record partnership against all countries.*
‡ *Record seventh-wicket partnership in first-class cricket.*

## TEN WICKETS OR MORE IN A MATCH

### For Australia (11)

| | | | |
|---|---|---|---|
| 11-96 (7-46, 4-50) | A. R. Border, Sydney | .......................... | 1988-89 |
| 11-222 (5-135, 6-87)† | A. K. Davidson, Brisbane | ...................... | 1960-61 |
| 11-183 (7-87, 4-96)† | C. V. Grimmett, Adelaide | ...................... | 1930-31 |
| 10-115 (6-72, 4-43) | N. J. N. Hawke, Georgetown | .................. | 1964-65 |
| 10-144 (6-54, 4-90) | R. G. Holland, Sydney | ........................ | 1984-85 |
| 13-217 (5-130, 8-87) | M. G. Hughes, Perth | ......................... | 1988-89 |
| 11-79 (7-23, 4-56) | H. Ironmonger, Melbourne | .................... | 1930-31 |
| 11-181 (8-112, 3-69) | G. F. Lawson, Adelaide | ....................... | 1984-85 |
| 10-127 (7-83, 3-44) | D. K. Lillee, Melbourne | ....................... | 1981-82 |
| 10-159 (8-71, 2-88) | G. D. McKenzie, Melbourne | .................. | 1968-69 |
| 10-185 (3-87, 7-98) | B. Yardley, Sydney | ........................... | 1981-82 |

### For West Indies (3)

| | | | |
|---|---|---|---|
| 10-113 (7-55, 3-58) | G. E. Gomez, Sydney | ......................... | 1951-52 |
| 11-107 (5-45, 6-62) | M. A. Holding, Melbourne | .................... | 1981-82 |
| 10-107 (5-69, 5-38) | M. D. Marshall, Adelaide | ..................... | 1984-85 |

† *Signifies ten wickets or more on first appearance in Australia–West Indies Tests.*

## AUSTRALIA v NEW ZEALAND

*Captains*

| Season | Australia | New Zealand | T | A | NZ | D |
|--------|-----------|-------------|---|---|----|----|
| 1945-46N | W. A. Brown | W. A. Hadlee | 1 | 1 | 0 | 0 |
| 1973-74A | I. M. Chappell | B. E. Congdon | 3 | 2 | 0 | 1 |
| 1973-74N | I. M. Chappell | B. E. Congdon | 3 | 1 | 1 | 1 |
| 1976-77N | G. S. Chappell | G. M. Turner | 2 | 1 | 0 | 1 |
| 1980-81A | G. S. Chappell | G. P. Howarth[1] | 3 | 2 | 0 | 1 |
| 1981-82N | G. S. Chappell | G. P. Howarth | 3 | 1 | 1 | 1 |

## TRANS-TASMAN TROPHY

*Captains*

| Season | Australia | New Zealand | T | A | NZ | D | Held by |
|--------|-----------|-------------|---|---|----|----|---------|
| 1985-86A | A. R. Border | J. V. Coney | 3 | 1 | 2 | 0 | NZ |
| 1985-86N | A. R. Border | J. V. Coney | 3 | 0 | 1 | 2 | NZ |
| 1987-88A | A. R. Border | J. J. Crowe | 3 | 1 | 0 | 2 | A |
| 1989-90A | A. R. Border | J. G. Wright | 1 | 0 | 0 | 1 | A |
| 1989-90N | A. R. Border | J. G. Wright | 1 | 0 | 1 | 0 | NZ |

|  |  |  |  |  |  |  |
|--|--|--|--|--|--|--|
| In Australia | 13 | 6 | 2 | 5 | | |
| In New Zealand | 13 | 4 | 4 | 5 | | |
| Totals | 26 | 10 | 6 | 10 | | |

*A Played in Australia.  N Played in New Zealand.*

*Note:* The following deputised for the official touring captain: [1]M. G. Burgess (Second).

### HIGHEST INNINGS TOTALS

For Australia in Australia: 521-9 dec. at Perth .......................... 1989-90
in New Zealand: 552 at Christchurch ...................... 1976-77

For New Zealand in Australia: 553-7 dec. at Brisbane .................. 1985-86
in New Zealand: 484 at Wellington .................. 1973-74

### LOWEST INNINGS TOTALS

For Australia in Australia: 162 at Sydney .......................... 1973-74
in New Zealand: 103 at Auckland .................... 1985-86

For New Zealand in Australia: 121 at Perth ...................... 1980-81
in New Zealand: 42 at Wellington ...................... 1945-46

### INDIVIDUAL HUNDREDS

**For Australia (23)**

**D. C. Boon** (2)
143   Brisbane .... 1987-88
200   Perth ....... 1989-90
**A. R. Border** (4)
152*  Brisbane .... 1985-86
140   }Christchurch. 1985-86
114*  
205   Adelaide .... 1987-88
**G. S. Chappell** (3)
247*  }Wellington .. 1973-74
133   
176   Christchurch. 1981-82

**I. M. Chappell** (2)
145   }Wellington .. 1973-74
121   
**G. J. Gilmour** (1)
101   Christchurch. 1976-77
**G. R. Marsh** (1)
118   Auckland ... 1985-86
**R. W. Marsh** (1)
132   Adelaide .... 1973-74
**G. R. J. Matthews** (2)
115†  Brisbane .... 1985-86
130   Wellington .. 1985-86

**I. R. Redpath** (1)
159*‡ Auckland ... 1973-74
**K. R. Stackpole** (1)
122†  Melbourne .. 1973-74
**K. D. Walters** (3)
104*  Auckland ... 1973-74
250   Christchurch. 1976-77
107   Melbourne .. 1980-81
**G. M. Wood** (2)
111†  Brisbane .... 1980-81
100   Auckland ... 1981-82

### For New Zealand (17)

**J. V. Coney** (1)
101* Wellington .. 1985-86

**B. E. Congdon** (2)
132 Wellington .. 1973-74
107* Christchurch . 1976-77

**M. D. Crowe** (3)
188 Brisbane .... 1985-86
137 Christchurch . 1985-86
137 Adelaide .... 1987-88

**B. A. Edgar** (1)
161 Auckland ... 1981-82

**M. J. Greatbatch** (1)
146*† Perth ....... 1989-90

**B. F. Hastings** (1)
101 Wellington .. 1973-74

**A. H. Jones** (1)
150 Adelaide .... 1987-88

**J. F. M. Morrison** (1)
117 Sydney ..... 1973-74

**J. M. Parker** (1)
108 Sydney ..... 1973-74

**J. F. Reid** (1)
108† Brisbane .... 1985-86

**G. M. Turner** (2)
101 ⎫
110*⎬ Christchurch . 1973-74

**J. G. Wright** (2)
141 Christchurch . 1981-82
117* Wellington .. 1989-90

† *Signifies hundred on first appearance in Australia–New Zealand Tests.*
‡ *Carried his bat.*

*Notes:* G. S. and I. M. Chappell at Wellington in 1973-74 provide the only instance in Test matches of brothers both scoring a hundred in each innings and in the same Test.

## RECORD PARTNERSHIPS FOR EACH WICKET

### For Australia

| | | | |
|---|---|---|---|
| 106 for 1st | B. M. Laird and G. M. Wood at Auckland ................. | 1981-82 |
| 168 for 2nd | G. R. Marsh and W. B. Phillips at Auckland................ | 1985-86 |
| 264 for 3rd | I. M. Chappell and G. S. Chappell at Wellington ........... | 1973-74 |
| 116 for 4th | A. R. Border and S. R. Waugh at Adelaide ................ | 1987-88 |
| 213 for 5th | G. M. Ritchie and G. R. J. Matthews at Wellington ........ | 1985-86 |
| 197 for 6th | A. R. Border and G. R. J. Matthews at Brisbane ........... | 1985-86 |
| 217 for 7th† | K. D. Walters and G. J. Gilmour at Christchurch........... | 1976-77 |
| 93 for 8th | G. J. Gilmour and K. J. O'Keeffe at Auckland ............ | 1976-77 |
| 61 for 9th | A. I. C. Dodemaide and C. J. McDermott at Melbourne .... | 1987-88 |
| 60 for 10th | K. D. Walters and J. D. Higgs at Melbourne............... | 1980-81 |

### For New Zealand

| | | |
|---|---|---|
| 107 for 1st | G. M. Turner and J. M. Parker at Auckland .............. | 1973-74 |
| 128* for 2nd | J. G. Wright and A. H. Jones at Wellington .............. | 1989-90 |
| 224 for 3rd | J. F. Reid and M. D. Crowe at Brisbane ................. | 1985-86 |
| 229 for 4th† | B. E. Congdon and B. F. Hastings at Wellington .......... | 1973-74 |
| 88 for 5th | J. V. Coney and M. G. Burgess at Perth................. | 1980-81 |
| 109 for 6th | K. R. Rutherford and J. V. Coney at Wellington .......... | 1985-86 |
| 132* for 7th | J. V. Coney and R. J. Hadlee at Wellington .............. | 1985-86 |
| 88* for 8th | M. J. Greatbatch and M. C. Snedden at Perth ............ | 1989-90 |
| 73 for 9th | H. J. Howarth and D. R. Hadlee at Christchurch .......... | 1976-77 |
| 124 for 10th | J. G. Bracewell and S. L. Boock at Sydney ............... | 1985-86 |

† *Denotes record partnership against all countries.*

## TEN WICKETS OR MORE IN A MATCH

### For Australia (2)

| | | |
|---|---|---|
| 10-174 (6-106, 4-68) | R. G. Holland, Sydney ......................... | 1985-86 |
| 11-123 (5-51, 6-72) | D. K. Lillee, Auckland.......................... | 1976-77 |

### For New Zealand (4)

| | | |
|---|---|---|
| 10-106 (4-74, 6-32) | J. G. Bracewell, Auckland ...................... | 1985-86 |
| 15-123 (9-52, 6-71) | R. J. Hadlee, Brisbane ......................... | 1985-86 |
| 11-155 (5-65, 6-90) | R. J. Hadlee, Perth............................ | 1985-86 |
| 10-176 (5-109, 5-67) | R. J. Hadlee, Melbourne ....................... | 1987-88 |

## AUSTRALIA v INDIA

*Captains*

| Season | Australia | India | T | A | I | T | D |
|--------|-----------|-------|---|---|---|---|---|
| 1947-48*A* | D. G. Bradman | L. Amarnath | 5 | 4 | 0 | 0 | 1 |
| 1956-57*I* | I. W. Johnson[1] | P. R. Umrigar | 3 | 2 | 0 | 0 | 1 |
| 1959-60*I* | R. Benaud | G. S. Ramchand | 5 | 2 | 1 | 0 | 2 |
| 1964-65*I* | R. B. Simpson | Nawab of Pataudi jun. | 3 | 1 | 1 | 0 | 1 |
| 1967-68*A* | R. B. Simpson[2] | Nawab of Pataudi jun.[3] | 4 | 4 | 0 | 0 | 0 |
| 1969-70*I* | W. M. Lawry | Nawab of Pataudi jun. | 5 | 3 | 1 | 0 | 1 |
| 1977-78*A* | R. B. Simpson | B. S. Bedi | 5 | 3 | 2 | 0 | 0 |
| 1979-80*I* | K. J. Hughes | S. M. Gavaskar | 6 | 0 | 2 | 0 | 4 |
| 1980-81*A* | G. S. Chappell | S. M. Gavaskar | 3 | 1 | 1 | 0 | 1 |
| 1985-86*A* | A. R. Border | Kapil Dev | 3 | 0 | 0 | 0 | 3 |
| 1986-87*I* | A. R. Border | Kapil Dev | 3 | 0 | 0 | 1 | 2 |
| | In Australia | | 20 | 12 | 3 | 0 | 5 |
| | In India | | 25 | 8 | 5 | 1 | 11 |
| | Totals | | 45 | 20 | 8 | 1 | 16 |

*A Played in Australia.　I Played in India.*

*Notes*: The following deputised for the official touring captain or were appointed by the home authority for only a minor proportion of the series:
[1]R. R. Lindwall (Second). [2]W. M. Lawry (Third and Fourth). [3]C. G. Borde (First).

### HIGHEST INNINGS TOTALS

For Australia in Australia: 674 at Adelaide .............................. 1947-48
　　　　　　　　in India: 574-7 dec. at Madras ........................ 1986-87

For India in Australia: 600-4 dec. at Sydney ............................ 1985-86
　　　　　　　in India: 517-5 dec. at Bombay .......................... 1986-87

### LOWEST INNINGS TOTALS

For Australia in Australia: 83 at Melbourne .............................. 1980-81
　　　　　　　　in India: 105 at Kanpur ............................... 1959-60

For India in Australia: 58 at Brisbane .................................. 1947-48
　　　　　　　in India: 135 at Delhi .................................. 1959-60

### INDIVIDUAL HUNDREDS

#### For Australia (45)

**S. G. Barnes** (1)
112　Adelaide .... 1947-48

**D. C. Boon** (3)
123†　Adelaide .... 1985-86
131　Sydney ..... 1985-86
122　Madras ..... 1986-87

**A. R. Border** (4)
162†　Madras ..... 1979-80
124　Melbourne .. 1980-81
163　Melbourne .. 1985-86
106　Madras ..... 1986-87

**D. G. Bradman** (4)
185†　Brisbane .... 1947-48
132 ⎫
127* ⎬ Melbourne .. 1947-48
201　Adelaide .... 1947-48

**J. W. Burke** (1)
161　Bombay .... 1956-57

**G. S. Chappell** (1)
204†　Sydney ..... 1980-81

**I. M. Chappell** (2)
151　Melbourne .. 1967-68
138　Delhi....... 1969-70

**R. M. Cowper** (2)
108　Adelaide .... 1967-68
165　Sydney ..... 1967-68

**L. E. Favell** (1)
101　Madras ..... 1959-60

**R. N. Harvey** (4)
153　Melbourne .. 1947-48
140　Bombay .... 1956-57
114　Delhi....... 1959-60

102　Bombay .... 1959-60

**A. L. Hassett** (1)
198*　Adelaide .... 1947-48

**K. J. Hughes** (2)
100　Madras ..... 1979-80
213　Adelaide .... 1980-81

**D. M. Jones** (1)
210†　Madras ..... 1986-87

**W. M. Lawry** (1)
100　Melbourne .. 1967-68

**A. L. Mann** (1)
105　Perth....... 1977-78

**G. R. Marsh** (1)
101　Bombay .... 1986-87

**G. R. J. Matthews** (1)
100*　Melbourne .. 1985-86

| A. R. Morris (1) | | |
|---|---|---|
| 100* | Melbourne .. | 1947-48 |

| N. C. O'Neill (2) | | |
|---|---|---|
| 163 | Bombay .... | 1959-60 |
| 113 | Calcutta .... | 1959-60 |

| G. M. Ritchie (1) | | |
|---|---|---|
| 128† | Adelaide .... | 1985-86 |

| A. P. Sheahan (1) | | |
|---|---|---|
| 114 | Kanpur ..... | 1969-70 |

| R. B. Simpson (4) | | |
|---|---|---|
| 103 | Adelaide .... | 1967-68 |
| 109 | Melbourne .. | 1967-68 |
| 176 | Perth ...... | 1977-78 |
| 100 | Adelaide .... | 1977-78 |

| K. R. Stackpole (1) | | |
|---|---|---|
| 103† | Bombay .... | 1969-70 |

| K. D. Walters (1) | | |
|---|---|---|
| 102 | Madras .... | 1969-70 |

| G. M. Wood (1) | | |
|---|---|---|
| 125 | Adelaide .... | 1980-81 |

| G. N. Yallop (2) | | |
|---|---|---|
| 121† | Adelaide .... | 1977-78 |
| 167 | Calcutta .... | 1979-80 |

### For India (31)

| M. Amarnath (2) | | |
|---|---|---|
| 100 | Perth ...... | 1977-78 |
| 138 | Sydney ..... | 1985-86 |

| N. J. Contractor (1) | | |
|---|---|---|
| 108 | Bombay .... | 1959-60 |

| S. M. Gavaskar (8) | | |
|---|---|---|
| 113† | Brisbane .... | 1977-78 |
| 127 | Perth ...... | 1977-78 |
| 118 | Melbourne .. | 1977-78 |
| 115 | Delhi ...... | 1979-80 |
| 123 | Bombay .... | 1979-80 |
| 166* | Adelaide .... | 1985-86 |
| 172 | Sydney ..... | 1985-86 |
| 103 | Bombay .... | 1986-87 |

| V. S. Hazare (2) | | |
|---|---|---|
| 116 | Adelaide .... | 1947-48 |
| 145 | | |

| M. L. Jaisimha (1) | | |
|---|---|---|
| 101 | Brisbane .... | 1967-68 |

| Kapil Dev (1) | | |
|---|---|---|
| 119 | Madras ..... | 1986-87 |

| S. M. H. Kirmani (1) | | |
|---|---|---|
| 101* | Bombay .... | 1979-80 |

| V. Mankad (2) | | |
|---|---|---|
| 116 | Melbourne .. | 1947-48 |
| 111 | Melbourne .. | 1947-48 |

| Nawab of Pataudi jun. (1) | | |
|---|---|---|
| 128*† | Madras .... | 1964-65 |

| S. M. Patil (1) | | |
|---|---|---|
| 174 | Adelaide .... | 1980-81 |

| D. G. Phadkar (1) | | |
|---|---|---|
| 123 | Adelaide .... | 1947-48 |

| G. S. Ramchand (1) | | |
|---|---|---|
| 109 | Bombay .... | 1956-57 |

| R. J. Shastri (1) | | |
|---|---|---|
| 121* | Bombay .... | 1986-87 |

| K. Srikkanth (1) | | |
|---|---|---|
| 116 | Sydney ..... | 1985-86 |

| D. B. Vengsarkar (2) | | |
|---|---|---|
| 112 | Bangalore ... | 1979-80 |
| 164* | Bombay .... | 1986-87 |

| G. R. Viswanath (4) | | |
|---|---|---|
| 137† | Kanpur ..... | 1969-70 |
| 161* | Bangalore ... | 1979-80 |
| 131 | Delhi ...... | 1979-80 |
| 114 | Melbourne .. | 1980-81 |

| Yashpal Sharma (1) | | |
|---|---|---|
| 100* | Delhi ...... | 1979-80 |

† *Signifies hundred on first appearance in Australia–India Tests.*

## RECORD PARTNERSHIPS FOR EACH WICKET

### For Australia

| | | | |
|---|---|---|---|
| 217 | for 1st | D. C. Boon and G. R. Marsh at Sydney .................. | 1985-86 |
| 236 | for 2nd | S. G. Barnes and D. G. Bradman at Adelaide .............. | 1947-48 |
| 222 | for 3rd | A. R. Border and K. J. Hughes at Madras ................ | 1979-80 |
| 178 | for 4th | D. M. Jones and A. R. Border at Madras ................ | 1986-87 |
| 223* | for 5th | A. R. Morris and D. G. Bradman at Melbourne ........... | 1947-48 |
| 151 | for 6th | T. R. Veivers and B. N. Jarman at Bombay .............. | 1964-65 |
| 66 | for 7th | G. R. J. Matthews and R. J. Bright at Melbourne ......... | 1985-86 |
| 73 | for 8th | T. R. Veivers and G. D. McKenzie at Madras ............. | 1964-65 |
| 87 | for 9th | I. W. Johnson and W. P. A. Crawford at Madras .......... | 1956-57 |
| 77 | for 10th | A. R. Border and D. R. Gilbert at Melbourne ............ | 1985-86 |

### For India

| | | | |
|---|---|---|---|
| 192 | for 1st | S. M. Gavaskar and C. P. S. Chauhan at Bombay .......... | 1979-80 |
| 224 | for 2nd | S. M. Gavaskar and M. Amarnath at Sydney .............. | 1985-86 |
| 159 | for 3rd | S. M. Gavaskar and G. R. Viswanath at Delhi ............ | 1979-80 |
| 159 | for 4th | D. B. Vengsarkar and G. R. Viswanath at Bangalore ....... | 1979-80 |
| 109 | for 5th | A. A. Baig and R. B. Kenny at Bombay ................. | 1959-60 |
| 298* | for 6th† | D. B. Vengsarkar and R. J. Shastri at Bombay ............ | 1986-87 |
| 132 | for 7th | V. S. Hazare and H. R. Adhikari at Adelaide ............. | 1947-48 |
| 127 | for 8th | S. M. H. Kirmani and K. D. Ghavri at Bombay ........... | 1979-80 |
| 57 | for 9th | S. M. H. Kirmani and K. D. Ghavri at Sydney ........... | 1980-81 |
| | | Kapil Dev and N. S. Yadav at Madras .................. | 1986-87 |
| 94 | for 10th | S. M. Gavaskar and N. S. Yadav at Adelaide ............. | 1985-86 |

† *Denotes record partnership against all countries.*

## TEN WICKETS OR MORE IN A MATCH

### For Australia (8)

| | | |
|---|---|---|
| 11-105 (6-52, 5-53) | R. Benaud, Calcutta .................................. | 1956-57 |
| 12-124 (5-31, 7-93) | A. K. Davidson, Kanpur ............................. | 1959-60 |
| 12-166 (5-99, 7-67) | G. Dymock, Kanpur ................................. | 1979-80 |
| 10-91 (6-58, 4-33)† | G. D. McKenzie, Madras ............................ | 1964-65 |
| 10-151 (7-66, 3-85) | G. D. McKenzie, Melbourne .......................... | 1967-68 |
| 10-144 (5-91, 5-53) | A. A. Mallett, Madras ............................... | 1969-70 |
| 10-249 (5-103, 5-146) | G. R. J. Matthews, Madras ........................... | 1986-87 |
| 11-31 (5-2, 6-29)† | E. R. H. Toshack, Brisbane ........................... | 1947-48 |

### For India (6)

| | | |
|---|---|---|
| 10-194 (5-89, 5-105) | B. S. Bedi, Perth .................................... | 1977-78 |
| 12-104 (6-52, 6-52) | B. S. Chandrasekhar, Melbourne ..................... | 1977-78 |
| 10-130 (7-49, 3-81) | Ghulam Ahmed, Calcutta ............................ | 1956-57 |
| 11-122 (5-31, 6-91) | R. G. Nadkarni, Madras ............................. | 1964-65 |
| 14-124 (9-69, 5-55) | J. M. Patel, Kanpur ................................. | 1959-60 |
| 10-174 (4-100, 6-74) | E. A. S. Prasanna, Madras ........................... | 1969-70 |

† *Signifies ten wickets or more on first appearance in Australia–India Tests.*

## AUSTRALIA v PAKISTAN

| Season | Australia | Captains<br>Pakistan | T | A | P | D |
|---|---|---|---|---|---|---|
| 1956-57 *P* | I. W. Johnson | A. H. Kardar | 1 | 0 | 1 | 0 |
| 1959-60 *P* | R. Benaud | Fazal Mahmood[1] | 3 | 2 | 0 | 1 |
| 1964-65 *P* | R. B. Simpson | Hanif Mohammad | 1 | 0 | 0 | 1 |
| 1964-65 *A* | R. B. Simpson | Hanif Mohammad | 1 | 0 | 0 | 1 |
| 1972-73 *A* | I. M. Chappell | Intikhab Alam | 3 | 3 | 0 | 0 |
| 1976-77 *A* | G. S. Chappell | Mushtaq Mohammad | 3 | 1 | 1 | 1 |
| 1978-79 *A* | G. N. Yallop[2] | Mushtaq Mohammad | 2 | 1 | 1 | 0 |
| 1979-80 *P* | G. S. Chappell | Javed Miandad | 3 | 0 | 1 | 2 |
| 1981-82 *A* | G. S. Chappell | Javed Miandad | 3 | 2 | 1 | 0 |
| 1982-83 *P* | K. J. Hughes | Imran Khan | 3 | 0 | 3 | 0 |
| 1983-84 *A* | K. J. Hughes | Imran Khan[3] | 5 | 2 | 0 | 3 |
| 1988-89 *P* | A. R. Border | Javed Miandad | 3 | 0 | 1 | 2 |
| 1989-90 *A* | A. R. Border | Imran Khan | 3 | 1 | 0 | 2 |
| | In Pakistan ..................... | | 14 | 2 | 6 | 6 |
| | In Australia .................... | | 20 | 10 | 3 | 7 |
| | Totals ........................ | | 34 | 12 | 9 | 13 |

*A Played in Australia. P Played in Pakistan.*

*Notes:* The following deputised for the official touring captain or were appointed by the home
authority for only a minor proportion of the series:
[1]Imtiaz Ahmed (Second). [2]K. J. Hughes (Second). [3]Zaheer Abbas (First, Second and Third).

## HIGHEST INNINGS TOTALS

| | | |
|---|---|---|
| For Australia in Australia: 585 at Adelaide ............................. | | 1972-73 |
|      in Pakistan: 617 at Faisalabad ............................. | | 1979-80 |
| | | |
| For Pakistan in Australia: 624 at Adelaide ............................. | | 1983-84 |
|     in Pakistan: 501-6 dec. at Faisalabad ....................... | | 1982-83 |

## LOWEST INNINGS TOTALS

For Australia in Australia: 125 at Melbourne.............................. 1981-82
................... in Pakistan: 80 at Karachi ................................. 1956-57

For Pakistan in Australia: 62 at Perth ................................. 1981-82
................... in Pakistan: 134 at Dacca .............................. 1959-60

## INDIVIDUAL HUNDREDS

### For Australia (37)

**J. Benaud** (1)
142 Melbourne .. 1972-73
**A. R. Border** (6)
105† Melbourne .. 1978-79
150* ⎫
153 ⎭ Lahore ..... 1979-80
118 Brisbane .... 1983-84
117* Adelaide .... 1983-84
113* Faisalabad .. 1988-89
**G. S. Chappell** (6)
116* Melbourne .. 1972-73
121 Melbourne .. 1976-77
235 Faisalabad .. 1979-80
201 Brisbane .... 1981-82
150* Brisbane .... 1983-84
182 Sydney ..... 1983-84
**I. M. Chappell** (1)
196 Adelaide .... 1972-73
**G. J. Cosier** (1)
168 Melbourne .. 1976-77

**I. C. Davis** (1)
105† Adelaide .... 1976-77
**K. J. Hughes** (2)
106 Perth ....... 1981-82
106 Adelaide .... 1983-84
**D. M. Jones** (2)
116 ⎫
121* ⎭ Adelaide .... 1989-90
**R. B. McCosker** (1)
105 Melbourne .. 1976-77
**R. W. Marsh** (1)
118† Adelaide .... 1972-73
**N. C. O'Neill** (1)
134 Lahore ...... 1959-60
**W. B. Phillips** (1)
159† Perth ....... 1983-84
**I. R. Redpath** (1)
135 Melbourne.. 1972-73

**G. M. Ritchie** (1)
106* Faisalabad .. 1982-83
**A. P. Sheahan** (1)
127 Melbourne .. 1972-73
**R. B. Simpson** (2)
153 ⎫
115 ⎭ †Karachi .... 1964-65
**M. A. Taylor** (2)
101† Melbourne .. 1989-90
101* Sydney ..... 1989-90
**K. D. Walters** (1)
107 Adelaide .... 1976-77
**K. C. Wessels** (1)
179 Adelaide .... 1983-84
**G. M. Wood** (1)
100 Melbourne .. 1981-82
**G. N. Yallop** (3)
172 Faisalabad .. 1979-80
141 Perth ....... 1983-84
268 Melbourne .. 1983-84

### For Pakistan (31)

**Asif Iqbal** (3)
152* Adelaide .... 1976-77
120 Sydney ..... 1976-77
134* Perth ....... 1978-79
**Hanif Mohammad** (2)
101* Karachi ..... 1959-60
104 Melbourne .. 1964-65
**Ijaz Ahmed** (2)
122 Faisalabad .. 1988-89
121 Melbourne .. 1989-90
**Imran Khan** (1)
136 Adelaide ....1989-90
**Javed Miandad** (6)
129* Perth ....... 1978-79
106* Faisalabad .. 1979-80
138 Lahore ...... 1982-83

131 Adelaide .... 1983-84
211 Karachi ..... 1988-89
107 Faisalabad .. 1988-89
**Khalid Ibadulla** (1)
166† Karachi ..... 1964-65
**Majid Khan** (3)
158 Melbourne .. 1972-73
108 Melbourne .. 1978-79
110* Lahore ...... 1979-80
**Mansoor Akhtar** (1)
111 Faisalabad .. 1982-83
**Mohsin Khan** (3)
135 Lahore ...... 1982-83
149 Adelaide .... 1983-84
152 Melbourne .. 1983-84

**Mushtaq Mohammad** (1)
121 Sydney ..... 1972-73
**Qasim Omar** (1)
113 Adelaide .... 1983-84
**Sadiq Mohammad** (2)
137 Melbourne .. 1972-73
105 Melbourne .. 1976-77
**Saeed Ahmed** (1)
166 Lahore ...... 1959-60
**Taslim Arif** (1)
210* Faisalabad .. 1979-80
**Wasim Akram** (1)
123 Adelaide .... 1989-90
**Zaheer Abbas** (2)
101 Adelaide .... 1976-77
126 Faisalabad .. 1982-83

† *Signifies hundred on first appearance in Australia–Pakistan Tests.*

## RECORD PARTNERSHIPS FOR EACH WICKET

### For Australia

| | | |
|---|---|---|
| 134 for 1st | I. C. Davis and A. Turner at Melbourne..................... | 1976-77 |
| 259 for 2nd | W. B. Phillips and G. N. Yallop at Perth................... | 1983-84 |
| 203 for 3rd | G. N. Yallop and K. J. Hughes at Melbourne .............. | 1983-84 |
| 217 for 4th | G. S. Chappell and G. N. Yallop at Faisalabad ............ | 1979-80 |
| 171 for 5th { | G. S. Chappell and G. J. Cosier at Melbourne............. | 1976-77 |
| | A. R. Border and G. S. Chappell at Brisbane.............. | 1983-84 |
| 139 for 6th | R. M. Cowper and T. R. Veivers at Melbourne ........... | 1964-65 |
| 185 for 7th | G. N. Yallop and G. R. J. Matthews at Melbourne ....... | 1983-84 |
| 117 for 8th | G. J. Cosier and K. J. O'Keeffe at Melbourne ............ | 1976-77 |
| 83 for 9th | J. R. Watkins and R. A. L. Massie at Sydney ............. | 1972-73 |
| 52 for 10th { | D. K. Lillee and M. H. N. Walker at Sydney .............. | 1976-77 |
| | G. F. Lawson and T. M. Alderman at Lahore ............. | 1982-83 |

### For Pakistan

| | | |
|---|---|---|
| 249 for 1st† | Khalid Ibadulla and Abdul Kadir at Karachi.............. | 1964-65 |
| 233 for 2nd | Mohsin Khan and Qasim Omar at Adelaide............... | 1983-84 |
| 223* for 3rd | Taslim Arif and Javed Miandad at Faisalabad............. | 1979-80 |
| 155 for 4th | Mansoor Akhtar and Zaheer Abbas at Faisalabad.......... | 1982-83 |
| 186 for 5th | Javed Miandad and Salim Malik at Adelaide .............. | 1983-84 |
| 191 for 6th | Imran Khan and Wasim Akram at Adelaide ............... | 1989-90 |
| 104 for 7th | Intikhab Alam and Wasim Bari at Adelaide ............... | 1972-73 |
| 111 for 8th | Majid Khan and Imran Khan at Lahore ................... | 1979-80 |
| 56 for 9th | Intikhab Alam and Afaq Hussain at Melbourne ........... | 1964-65 |
| 87 for 10th | Asif Iqbal and Iqbal Qasim at Adelaide .................. | 1976-77 |

† *Denotes record partnership against all countries.*

## TEN WICKETS OR MORE IN A MATCH

### For Australia (3)

| | | |
|---|---|---|
| 10-111 (7-87, 3-24)† | R. J. Bright, Karachi ................................... | 1979-80 |
| 10-135 (6-82, 4-53) | D. K. Lillee, Melbourne ................................ | 1976-77 |
| 11-118 (5-32, 6-86)† | C. G. Rackemann, Perth ................................ | 1983-84 |

### For Pakistan (6)

| | | |
|---|---|---|
| 11-218 (4-76, 7-142) | Abdul Qadir, Faisalabad ................................ | 1982-83 |
| 13-114 (6-34, 7-80)† | Fazal Mahmood, Karachi ............................... | 1956-57 |
| 12-165 (6-102, 6-63) | Imran Khan, Sydney.................................... | 1976-77 |
| 11-118 (4-69, 7-49) | Iqbal Qasim, Karachi .................................. | 1979-80 |
| 11-125 (2-39, 9-86) | Sarfraz Nawaz, Melbourne.............................. | 1978-79 |
| 11-160 (6-62, 5-98) | Wasim Akram, Melbourne.............................. | 1989-90 |

† *Signifies ten wickets or more on first appearance in Australia–Pakistan Tests.*

## AUSTRALIA v SRI LANKA

| Season | *Captains* Australia | Sri Lanka | T | A | SL | D |
|---|---|---|---|---|---|---|
| 1982-83*SL* | G. S. Chappell | L. R. D. Mendis | 1 | 1 | 0 | 0 |
| 1987-88*A* | A. R. Border | R. S. Madugalle | 1 | 1 | 0 | 0 |
| 1989-90*A* | A. R. Border | A. Ranatunga | 2 | 1 | 0 | 0 |
| | In Australia..................... | | 3 | 2 | 0 | 1 |
| | In Sri Lanka .................... | | 1 | 1 | 0 | 0 |
| | Totals........................... | | 4 | 3 | 0 | 1 |

*A Played in Australia.   SL Played in Sri Lanka.*

## INNINGS TOTALS

Highest innings total for Australia: 514-4 dec. at Kandy . . . . . . . . . . . . . . . . . . . . 1982-83
for Sri Lanka: 418 at Brisbane . . . . . . . . . . . . . . . . . . . . . . . 1989-90

Lowest innings total for Australia: 224 at Hobart . . . . . . . . . . . . . . . . . . . . . . . . . . 1989-90
for Sri Lanka: 153 at Perth . . . . . . . . . . . . . . . . . . . . . . . . . 1987-88

## INDIVIDUAL HUNDREDS

### For Australia (8)

| | | |
|---|---|---|
| **D. W. Hookes** (1) | **T. M. Moody** (1) | **S. R. Waugh** (1) |
| 143*† Kandy . . . . . . 1982-83 | 106† Brisbane . . . . 1989-90 | 134* Hobart . . . . . 1989-90 |
| **D. M. Jones** (2) | **M. A. Taylor** (2) | **K. C. Wessels** (1) |
| 102† Perth . . . . . . 1987-88 | 164† Brisbane . . . . 1989-90 | 141† Kandy . . . . . . 1982-83 |
| 118* Hobart . . . . . 1989-90 | 108 Hobart . . . . . 1989-90 | |

### For Sri Lanka (1)

**P. A. de Silva** (1)
167 Brisbane . . . . 1989-90

† *Signifies hundred on first appearance in Australia–Sri Lanka Tests.*

## BEST BOWLING

Best bowling in an innings for Australia: 5-66 by T. G. Hogan at Kandy . . . . . . . 1982-83
for Sri Lanka: 6-66 by R. J. Ratnayake at Hobart . . . 1989-90

## RECORD PARTNERSHIPS FOR EACH WICKET

### For Australia

| | | | |
|---|---|---|---|
| 120 | for 1st | G. R. Marsh and D. C. Boon at Perth . . . . . . . . . . . . . . . . . . . . . . . | 1987-88 |
| 170 | for 2nd | K. C. Wessels and G. N. Yallop at Kandy . . . . . . . . . . . . . . . . . | 1982-83 |
| 158 | for 3rd | T. M. Moody and A. R. Border at Brisbane . . . . . . . . . . . . . . . . | 1989-90 |
| 163 | for 4th | M. A. Taylor and A. R. Border at Hobart . . . . . . . . . . . . . . . . . | 1989-90 |
| 155* | for 5th | D. W. Hookes and A. R. Border at Kandy . . . . . . . . . . . . . . . . . | 1982-83 |
| 260* | for 6th | D. M. Jones and S. R. Waugh at Hobart . . . . . . . . . . . . . . . . . | 1989-90 |
| 51* | for 7th | I. A. Healy and M. G. Hughes at Brisbane . . . . . . . . . . . . . . . . | 1989-90 |
| 44 | for 8th | M. G. Hughes and G. F. Lawson at Brisbane . . . . . . . . . . . . . . | 1989-90 |
| 17 | for 9th | P. R. Sleep and G. D. Campbell at Hobart . . . . . . . . . . . . . . . . | 1989-90 |
| 28 | for 10th | C. G. Rackemann and T. M. Alderman at Brisbane . . . . . . . . . . | 1989-90 |

### For Sri Lanka

| | | | |
|---|---|---|---|
| 51 | for 1st | R. S. Mahanama and D. S. B. P. Kuruppu at Perth . . . . . . . . . . | 1987-88 |
| 70 | for 2nd | D. Ranatunga and A. P. Gurusinha at Brisbane . . . . . . . . . . . . . | 1989-90 |
| 61 | for 3rd | S. Wettimuny and R. J. Ratnayake at Kandy . . . . . . . . . . . . . . | 1982-83 |
| 128 | for 4th | R. S. Mahanama and P. A. de Silva at Hobart . . . . . . . . . . . . . . | 1989-90 |
| 96 | for 5th | L. R. D. Mendis and A. Ranatunga at Kandy . . . . . . . . . . . . . . | 1982-83 |
| 78 | for 6th | A. Ranatunga and D. S. de Silva at Kandy . . . . . . . . . . . . . . . | 1982-83 |
| 144 | for 7th† | P. A. de Silva and J. R. Ratnayeke at Brisbane . . . . . . . . . . . . . | 1989-90 |
| 33 | for 8th | A. Ranatunga and C. P. H. Ramanayake at Perth . . . . . . . . . . . | 1987-88 |
| 27 | for 9th | A. Ranatunga and R. G. de Alwis at Kandy . . . . . . . . . . . . . . . | 1982-83 |
| 27 | for 10th | P. A. de Silva and C. P. H. Ramanayake at Brisbane . . . . . . . . . | 1989-90 |

† *Denotes record partnership against all countries.*

## SOUTH AFRICA v NEW ZEALAND

| | Captains | | | | | |
|---|---|---|---|---|---|---|
| Season | South Africa | New Zealand | T | SA | NZ | D |
| 1931-32N | H. B. Cameron | M. L. Page | 2 | 2 | 0 | 0 |
| 1952-53N | J. E. Cheetham | W. M. Wallace | 2 | 1 | 0 | 1 |
| 1953-54S | J. E. Cheetham | G. O. Rabone[1] | 5 | 4 | 0 | 1 |
| 1961-62S | D. J. McGlew | J. R. Reid | 5 | 2 | 2 | 1 |
| 1963-64N | T. L. Goddard | J. R. Reid | 3 | 0 | 0 | 3 |
| | In New Zealand | | 7 | 3 | 0 | 4 |
| | In South Africa | | 10 | 6 | 2 | 2 |
| | Totals | | 17 | 9 | 2 | 6 |

*N Played in New Zealand. S Played in South Africa.*

*Note:* The following deputised for the official touring captain:
[1]B. Sutcliffe (Fourth and Fifth).

## HIGHEST INNINGS TOTALS

For South Africa in South Africa: 464 at Johannesburg . . . . . . . . . . . . . . . . . . . .  1961-62
             in New Zealand: 524-8 at Wellington . . . . . . . . . . . . . . . . . . .  1952-53

For New Zealand in South Africa: 505 at Cape Town . . . . . . . . . . . . . . . . . . . . .  1953-54
           in New Zealand: 364 at Wellington . . . . . . . . . . . . . . . . . . . . . . .  1931-32

## LOWEST INNINGS TOTALS

For South Africa in South Africa: 148 at Johannesburg . . . . . . . . . . . . . . . . . . .  1953-54
            in New Zealand: 223 at Dunedin . . . . . . . . . . . . . . . . . . . . . . . . . . .  1963-64

For New Zealand in South Africa: 79 at Johannesburg . . . . . . . . . . . . . . . . . . . .  1953-54
           in New Zealand: 138 at Dunedin . . . . . . . . . . . . . . . . . . . . . . . . . . .  1963-64

## INDIVIDUAL HUNDREDS

### For South Africa (11)

**X. C. Balaskas** (1)
122* Wellington . . 1931-32
**J. A. J. Christy** (1)
103† Christchurch . 1931-32
**W. R. Endean** (1)
116 Auckland . . . 1952-53
**D. J. McGlew** (3)
255*† Wellington . . 1952-53

127*‡ Durban . . . . . 1961-62
120 Johannesburg 1961-62
**R. A. McLean** (2)
101 Durban . . . . . 1953-54
113 Cape Town . 1961-62
**B. Mitchell** (1)
113† Christchurch. 1931-32

**A. R. A. Murray** (1)
109† Wellington . . 1952-53
**J. H. B. Waite** (1)
101 Johannesburg 1961-62

### For New Zealand (7)

**P. T. Barton** (1)
109 Pt Elizabeth . 1961-62
**P. G. Z. Harris** (1)
101 Cape Town . 1961-62
**G. O. Rabone** (1)
107 Durban . . . . . 1953-54

**J. R. Reid** (2)
135 Cape Town . 1953-54
142 Johannesburg 1961-62
**B. W. Sinclair** (1)
138 Auckland . . . 1963-64

**H. G. Vivian** (1)
100† Wellington . . 1931-32

† *Signifies hundred on first appearance in South Africa–New Zealand Tests.*
‡ *Carried his bat.*

## RECORD PARTNERSHIPS FOR EACH WICKET

### For South Africa

| | | |
|---|---|---|
| 196 for 1st | J. A. J. Christy and B. Mitchell at Christchurch | 1931-32 |
| 76 for 2nd | J. A. J. Christy and H. B. Cameron at Wellington | 1931-32 |
| 112 for 3rd | D. J. McGlew and R. A. McLean at Johannesburg | 1961-62 |
| 135 for 4th | K. J. Funston and R. A. McLean at Durban | 1953-54 |
| 130 for 5th | W. R. Endean and J. E. Cheetham at Auckland | 1952-53 |
| 83 for 6th | K. C. Bland and D. T. Lindsay at Auckland | 1963-64 |
| 246 for 7th† | D. J. McGlew and A. R. A. Murray at Wellington | 1952-53 |
| 95 for 8th | J. E. Cheetham and H. J. Tayfield at Cape Town | 1953-54 |
| 60 for 9th | P. M. Pollock and N. A. T. Adcock at Port Elizabeth | 1961-62 |
| 47 for 10th | D. J. McGlew and H. D. Bromfield at Port Elizabeth | 1961-62 |

### For New Zealand

| | | |
|---|---|---|
| 126 for 1st | G. O. Rabone and M. E. Chapple at Cape Town | 1953-54 |
| 51 for 2nd | W. P. Bradburn and B. W. Sinclair at Dunedin | 1963-64 |
| 94 for 3rd | M. B. Poore and B. Sutcliffe at Cape Town | 1953-54 |
| 171 for 4th | B. W. Sinclair and S. N. McGregor at Auckland | 1963-64 |
| 174 for 5th | J. R. Reid and J. E. F. Beck at Cape Town | 1953-54 |
| 100 for 6th | H. G. Vivian and F. T. Badcock at Wellington | 1931-32 |
| 84 for 7th | J. R. Reid and G. A. Bartlett at Johannesburg | 1961-62 |
| 73 for 8th | P. G. Z. Harris and G. A. Bartlett at Durban | 1961-62 |
| 69 for 9th | C. F. W. Allcott and I. B. Cromb at Wellington | 1931-32 |
| 49* for 10th | A. E. Dick and F. J. Cameron at Cape Town | 1961-62 |

† *Denotes record partnership against all countries.*

## TEN WICKETS OR MORE IN A MATCH

### For South Africa (1)

| | | |
|---|---|---|
| 11-196 (6-128, 5-68)† | S. F. Burke, Cape Town | 1961-62 |

† *Signifies ten wickets or more on first appearance in South Africa–New Zealand Tests.*

*Note:* The best match figures by a New Zealand bowler are 8-180 (4-61, 4-119), J. C. Alabaster at Cape Town, 1961-62.

## WEST INDIES v NEW ZEALAND

| Season | West Indies | Captains New Zealand | T | WI | NZ | D |
|---|---|---|---|---|---|---|
| 1951-52*N* | J. D. C. Goddard | B. Sutcliffe | 2 | 1 | 0 | 1 |
| 1955-56*N* | D. St E. Atkinson | J. R. Reid[1] | 4 | 3 | 1 | 0 |
| 1968-69*N* | G. S. Sobers | G. T. Dowling | 3 | 1 | 1 | 1 |
| 1971-72*W* | G. S. Sobers | G. T. Dowling[2] | 5 | 0 | 0 | 5 |
| 1979-80*N* | C. H. Lloyd | G. P. Howarth | 3 | 0 | 1 | 2 |
| 1984-85*W* | I. V. A. Richards | G. P. Howarth | 4 | 2 | 0 | 2 |
| 1986-87*N* | I. V. A. Richards | J. V. Coney | 3 | 1 | 1 | 1 |
| | In New Zealand | | 15 | 6 | 4 | 5 |
| | In West Indies | | 9 | 2 | 0 | 7 |
| | Totals | | 24 | 8 | 4 | 12 |

*N Played in New Zealand. W Played in West Indies.*

*Notes:* The following deputised for the official touring captain or were appointed by the home authority for only a minor proportion of the series:
[1]H. B. Cave (First). [2]B. E. Congdon (Third, Fourth and Fifth).

## HIGHEST INNINGS TOTALS

For West Indies in West Indies: 564-8 at Bridgetown . . . . . . . . . . . . . . . . . . . . . . .   1971-72
                in New Zealand: 546-6 dec. at Auckland . . . . . . . . . . . . . . . . .   1951-52

For New Zealand in West Indies: 543-3 dec. at Georgetown . . . . . . . . . . . . . . .   1971-72
                in New Zealand: 460 at Christchurch . . . . . . . . . . . . . . . . . . .   1979-80

## LOWEST INNINGS TOTALS

For West Indies in West Indies: 133 at Bridgetown . . . . . . . . . . . . . . . . . . . . . . . . .   1971-72
                in New Zealand: 77 at Auckland . . . . . . . . . . . . . . . . . . . . . . . .   1955-56

For New Zealand in West Indies: 94 at Bridgetown . . . . . . . . . . . . . . . . . . . . . . . .   1984-85
                in New Zealand: 74 at Dunedin . . . . . . . . . . . . . . . . . . . . . . . .   1955-56

## INDIVIDUAL HUNDREDS

### By West Indies (25)

**M. C. Carew** (1)
109†   Auckland . . . 1968-69
**C. A. Davis** (1)
183   Bridgetown . . 1971-72
**R. C. Fredericks** (1)
163   Kingston . . . . 1971-72
**C. G. Greenidge** (2)
100   Port-of-Spain   1984-85
213   Auckland . . . 1986-87
**D. L. Haynes** (3)
105†   Dunedin . . . . 1979-80
122   Christchurch . 1979-80
121   Wellington . . 1986-87
**A. I. Kallicharran** (2)
100*†   Georgetown . 1971-72

101   Port-of-Spain   1971-72
**C. L. King** (1)
100*   Christchurch . 1979-80
**S. M. Nurse** (2)
168†   Auckland . . . 1968-69
258   Christchurch . 1968-69
**I. V. A. Richards** (1)
105   Bridgetown . . 1984-85
**R. B. Richardson** (1)
185   Georgetown . 1984-85
**L. G. Rowe** (3)
214  ⎫
100*  ⎬†Kingston . . . 1971-72
100    Christchurch . 1979-80

**G. S. Sobers** (1)
142   Bridgetown . . 1971-72
**J. B. Stollmeyer** (1)
152   Auckland . . . 1951-52
**C. L. Walcott** (1)
115   Auckland . . . 1951-52
**E. D. Weekes** (3)
123   Dunedin . . . . 1955-56
103   Christchurch . 1955-56
156   Wellington . . 1955-56
**F. M. M. Worrell** (1)
100   Auckland . . . 1951-52

### By New Zealand (17)

**M. G. Burgess** (1)
101   Kingston . . . . 1971-72
**B. E. Congdon** (2)
166*   Port-of-Spain   1971-72
126   Bridgetown . . 1971-72
**J. J. Crowe** (1)
112   Kingston . . . . 1984-85
**M. D. Crowe** (3)
188   Georgetown . 1984-85
119   Wellington . . 1986-87

104   Auckland . . . 1986-87
**B. A. Edgar** (1)
127   Auckland . . . 1979-80
**R. J. Hadlee** (1)
103   Christchurch . 1979-80
**B. F. Hastings** (2)
117*   Christchurch . 1968-69
105   Bridgetown . . 1971-72
**G. P. Howarth** (1)
147   Christchurch . 1979-80

**T. W. Jarvis** (1)
182   Georgetown . 1971-72
**B. R. Taylor** (1)
124†   Auckland . . . 1968-69
**G. M. Turner** (2)
223*‡   Kingston . . . . 1971-72
259   Georgetown . 1971-72
**J. G. Wright** (1)
138   Wellington . . 1986-87

† Signifies hundred on first appearance in West Indies–New Zealand Tests.
‡ Carried his bat.

*Notes:* E. D. Weekes in 1955-56 made three hundreds in consecutive innings.
    L. G. Rowe and A. I. Kallicharran each scored hundreds in their first two innings in Test cricket, Rowe being the only batsman to do so in his first match.

## RECORD PARTNERSHIPS FOR EACH WICKET

### For West Indies

225 for 1st    C. G. Greenidge and D. L. Haynes at Christchurch . . . . . . . . . . .   1979-80
269 for 2nd    R. C. Fredericks and L. G. Rowe at Kingston . . . . . . . . . . . . . . .   1971-72
185 for 3rd    C. G. Greenidge and R. B. Richardson at Port-of-Spain . . . . . . .   1984-85
162 for 4th   ⎰ E. D. Weekes and O. G. Smith at Dunedin . . . . . . . . . . . . . . . . .   1955-56
              ⎱ C. G. Greenidge and A. I. Kallicharran at Christchurch . . . . . . .   1979-80

| | | |
|---|---|---|
| 189 for 5th | F. M. M. Worrell and C. L. Walcott at Auckland . . . . . . . . . . . . | 1951-52 |
| 254 for 6th | C. A. Davis and G. S. Sobers at Bridgetown . . . . . . . . . . . . . . . . | 1971-72 |
| 143 for 7th | D. St E. Atkinson and J. D. C. Goddard at Christchurch . . . . . . . | 1955-56 |
| 83 for 8th | I. V. A. Richards and M. D. Marshall at Bridgetown . . . . . . . . . | 1984-85 |
| 70 for 9th | M. D. Marshall and J. Garner at Bridgetown . . . . . . . . . . . . . . . . | 1984-85 |
| 31 for 10th | T. M. Findlay and G. C. Shillingford at Bridgetown . . . . . . . . . . | 1971-72 |

### For New Zealand

| | | |
|---|---|---|
| 387 for 1st† | G. M. Turner and T. W. Jarvis at Georgetown . . . . . . . . . . . . . . | 1971-72 |
| 210 for 2nd† | G. P. Howarth and J. J. Crowe at Kingston . . . . . . . . . . . . . . . . | 1984-85 |
| 241 for 3rd | J. G. Wright and M. D. Crowe at Wellington . . . . . . . . . . . . . . . | 1986-87 |
| 175 for 4th | B. E. Congdon and B. F. Hastings at Bridgetown . . . . . . . . . . . . | 1971-72 |
| 142 for 5th | M. D. Crowe and J. V. Coney at Georgetown . . . . . . . . . . . . . . | 1984-85 |
| 220 for 6th | G. M. Turner and K. J. Wadsworth at Kingston . . . . . . . . . . . . | 1971-72 |
| 143 for 7th | M. D. Crowe and I. D. S. Smith at Georgetown . . . . . . . . . . . . | 1984-85 |
| 136 for 8th† | B. E. Congdon and R. S. Cunis at Port-of-Spain . . . . . . . . . . . . | 1971-72 |
| 62* for 9th | V. Pollard and R. S. Cunis at Auckland . . . . . . . . . . . . . . . . . . | 1968-69 |
| 41 for 10th | B. E. Congdon and J. C. Alabaster at Port-of-Spain . . . . . . . . . . | 1971-72 |

† *Denotes record partnership against all countries.*

## TEN WICKETS OR MORE IN A MATCH

### For West Indies (1)

| | | |
|---|---|---|
| 11-120 (4-40, 7-80) | M. D. Marshall, Bridgetown . . . . . . . . . . . . . . . . . . . . . . . | 1984-85 |

### For New Zealand (3)

| | | |
|---|---|---|
| 10-124 (4-51, 6-73)† | E. J. Chatfield, Port-of-Spain . . . . . . . . . . . . . . . . . . . . . . | 1984-85 |
| 11-102 (5-34, 6-68)† | R. J. Hadlee, Dunedin . . . . . . . . . . . . . . . . . . . . . . . . . . . . | 1979-80 |
| 10-166 (4-71, 6-95) | G. B. Troup, Auckland . . . . . . . . . . . . . . . . . . . . . . . . . . . . | 1979-80 |

† *Signifies ten wickets or more on first appearance in West Indies–New Zealand Tests.*

## WEST INDIES v INDIA

### Captains

| Season | West Indies | India | T | WI | I | D |
|---|---|---|---|---|---|---|
| 1948-49*I* | J. D. C. Goddard | L. Amarnath | 5 | 1 | 0 | 4 |
| 1952-53*W* | J. B. Stollmeyer | V. S. Hazare | 5 | 1 | 0 | 4 |
| 1958-59*I* | F. C. M. Alexander | Ghulam Ahmed[1] | 5 | 3 | 0 | 2 |
| 1961-62*W* | F. M. M. Worrell | N. J. Contractor[2] | 5 | 5 | 0 | 0 |
| 1966-67*I* | G. S. Sobers | Nawab of Pataudi jun. | 3 | 2 | 0 | 1 |
| 1970-71*W* | G. S. Sobers | A. L. Wadekar | 5 | 0 | 1 | 4 |
| 1974-75*I* | C. H. Lloyd | Nawab of Pataudi jun.[3] | 5 | 3 | 2 | 0 |
| 1975-76*W* | C. H. Lloyd | B. S. Bedi | 4 | 2 | 1 | 1 |
| 1978-79*I* | A. I. Kallicharran | S. M. Gavaskar | 6 | 0 | 1 | 5 |
| 1982-83*W* | C. H. Lloyd | Kapil Dev | 5 | 2 | 0 | 3 |
| 1983-84*I* | C. H. Lloyd | Kapil Dev | 6 | 3 | 0 | 3 |
| 1987-88*I* | I. V. A. Richards | D. B. Vengsarkar[4] | 4 | 1 | 1 | 2 |
| 1988-89*W* | I. V. A. Richards | D. B. Vengsarkar | 4 | 3 | 0 | 1 |
| | In India . . . . . . . . . . . . . . . . . . . . . . | | 34 | 13 | 4 | 17 |
| | In West Indies . . . . . . . . . . . . . . . . . | | 28 | 13 | 2 | 13 |
| | Totals . . . . . . . . . . . . . . . . . . . . . . . . | | 62 | 26 | 6 | 30 |

*I Played in India. W Played in West Indies.*

*Notes:* The following deputised for the official touring captain or were appointed by the home authority for only a minor proportion of the series:
[1] P. R. Umrigar (First), V. Mankad (Fourth), H. R. Adhikari (Fifth). [2] Nawab of Pataudi jun. (Third, Fourth and Fifth). [3] S. Venkataraghavan (Second). [4] R. J. Shastri (Fourth).

## HIGHEST INNINGS TOTALS

For West Indies in West Indies: 631-8 dec. at Kingston ..................... 1961-62
in India: 644-8 dec. at Delhi ................................ 1958-59

For India in West Indies: 469-7 at Port-of-Spain ..................... 1982-83
in India: 644-7 dec. at Kanpur .............................. 1978-79

## LOWEST INNINGS TOTALS

For West Indies in West Indies: 214 at Port-of-Spain ..................... 1970-71
in India: 127 at Delhi ............................... 1987-88

For India in West Indies: 97† at Kingston ............................ 1975-76
in India: 75 at Delhi .................................. 1987-88

† *Five men absent hurt. The lowest with eleven men batting is 98 at Port-of-Spain, 1961-62.*

## INDIVIDUAL HUNDREDS

### For West Indies (76)

| | | |
|---|---|---|
| **S. F. A. F. Bacchus** (1) | **A. I. Kallicharran** (3) | **R. B. Richardson** (2) |
| 250 Kanpur .... 1978-79 | 124† Bangalore ... 1974-75 | 194 Georgetown . 1988-89 |
| **B. F. Butcher** (2) | 103* Port-of-Spain 1975-76 | 156 Kingston .. 1988-89 |
| 103 Calcutta .... 1958-59 | 187 Bombay .... 1978-79 | **O. G. Smith** (1) |
| 142 Madras ..... 1958-59 | **R. B. Kanhai** (4) | 100 Delhi ...... 1958-59 |
| **R. J. Christiani** (1) | 256 Calcutta .... 1958-59 | **G. S. Sobers** (8) |
| 107† Delhi ...... 1948-49 | 138 Kingston ... 1961-62 | 142*† Bombay .... 1958-59 |
| **C. A. Davis** (2) | 139 Port-of-Spain 1961-62 | 198 Kanpur .... 1958-59 |
| 125* Georgetown . 1970-71 | 158* Kingston ... 1970-71 | 106* Calcutta .... 1958-59 |
| 105 Port-of-Spain 1970-71 | **C. H. Lloyd** (7) | 153 Kingston ... 1961-62 |
| **P. J. L. Dujon** (1) | 163 Bangalore ... 1974-75 | 104 Kingston ... 1961-62 |
| 110 St John's .... 1982-83 | 242* Bombay .... 1974-75 | 108* Georgetown . 1970-71 |
| **R. C. Fredericks** (2) | 102 Bridgetown . 1975-76 | 178* Bridgetown . 1970-71 |
| 100 Calcutta .... 1974-75 | 143 Port-of-Spain 1982-83 | 132 Port-of-Spain 1970-71 |
| 104 Bombay .... 1974-75 | 106 St John's .... 1982-83 | **J. S. Solomon** (1) |
| **H. A. Gomes** (1) | 103 Delhi ...... 1983-84 | 100* Delhi ...... 1958-59 |
| 123 Port-of-Spain 1982-83 | 161* Calcutta .... 1983-84 | **J. B. Stollmeyer** (2) |
| **G. E. Gomez** (1) | **A. L. Logie** (2) | 160 Madras ..... 1948-49 |
| 101† Delhi ...... 1948-49 | 130 Bridgetown . 1982-83 | 104* Port-of-Spain 1952-53 |
| **C. G. Greenidge** (5) | 101 Calcutta .... 1987-88 | **C. L. Walcott** (4) |
| 107† Bangalore .. 1974-75 | **E. D. A. McMorris** (1) | 152† Delhi ...... 1948-49 |
| 154* St John's .. 1982-83 | 125† Kingston ... 1961-62 | 108 Calcutta .... 1948-49 |
| 194 Kanpur .... 1983-84 | **B. H. Pairaudeau** (1) | 125 Georgetown . 1952-53 |
| 141 Calcutta .... 1987-88 | 115† Port-of-Spain 1952-53 | 118 Kingston ... 1952-53 |
| 117 Bridgetown . 1988-89 | **A. F. Rae** (2) | **E. D. Weekes** (7) |
| **D. L. Haynes** (2) | 104 Bombay .... 1948-49 | 128† Delhi ...... 1948-49 |
| 136 St John's .. 1982-83 | 109 Madras ..... 1948-49 | 194 Bombay .... 1948-49 |
| 112* Bridgetown . 1988-89 | **I. V. A. Richards** (8) | 162 ⎫ |
| **J. K. Holt** (1) | 192* Delhi ...... 1974-75 | 101 ⎬ Calcutta ... 1948-49 |
| 123 Delhi ...... 1958-59 | 142 Bridgetown . 1975-76 | 207 Port-of-Spain 1952-53 |
| **C. L. Hooper** (1) | 130 Port-of-Spain 1975-76 | 161 Port-of-Spain 1952-53 |
| 100* Calcutta .... 1987-88 | 177 Port-of-Spain 1975-76 | 109 Kingston ... 1952-53 |
| **C. C. Hunte** (1) | 109 Georgetown . 1982-83 | **A. B. Williams** (1) |
| 101 Bombay .... 1966-67 | 120 Bombay .... 1983-84 | 111 Calcutta .... 1978-79 |
| | 109* Delhi ...... 1987-88 | **F. M. M. Worrell** (1) |
| | 110 Kingston ... 1988-89 | 237 Kingston ... 1952-53 |

## For India (55)

| | | | | | | | | |
|---|---|---|---|---|---|---|---|---|
| **H. R. Adhikari** (1) | | | 120 | Delhi | 1978-79 | **R. J. Shastri** (2) | | |
| 114*† | Delhi | 1948-49 | 147* | Georgetown | 1982-83 | 102 | St John's | 1982-83 |
| **M. Amarnath** (3) | | | 121 | Delhi | 1983-84 | 107 | Bridgetown | 1988-89 |
| 101* | Kanpur | 1978-79 | 236* | Madras | 1983-84 | **N. S. Sidhu** (1) | | |
| 117 | Port-of-Spain | 1982-83 | **V. S. Hazare** (2) | | | 116 | Kingston | 1988-89 |
| 116 | St John's | 1982-83 | 134* | Bombay | 1948-49 | **E. D. Solkar** (1) | | |
| **M. L. Apte** (1) | | | 122 | Bombay | 1948-49 | 102 | Bombay | 1974-75 |
| 163* | Port-of-Spain | 1952-53 | **Kapil Dev** (3) | | | **P. R. Umrigar** (3) | | |
| **C. G. Borde** (3) | | | 126* | Delhi | 1978-79 | 130 | Port-of-Spain | 1952-53 |
| 109 | Delhi | 1958-59 | 100* | Port-of-Spain | 1982-83 | 117 | Kingston | 1952-53 |
| 121 | Bombay | 1966-67 | 109 | Madras | 1987-88 | 172* | Port-of-Spain | 1961-62 |
| 125 | Madras | 1966-67 | **S. V. Manjrekar** (1) | | | **D. B. Vengsarkar** (6) | | |
| **S. A. Durani** (1) | | | 108 | Bridgetown | 1988-89 | 157* | Calcutta | 1978-79 |
| 104 | Port-of-Spain | 1961-62 | **V. L. Manjrekar** (1) | | | 109 | Delhi | 1978-79 |
| **F. M. Engineer** (1) | | | 118 | Kingston | 1952-53 | 159 | Delhi | 1983-84 |
| 109 | Madras | 1966-67 | **R. S. Modi** (1) | | | 100 | Bombay | 1983-84 |
| **A. D. Gaekwad** (1) | | | 112 | Bombay | 1948-49 | 102 | Delhi | 1987-88 |
| 102 | Kanpur | 1978-79 | **Mushtaq Ali** (1) | | | 102* | Calcutta | 1987-88 |
| **S. M. Gavaskar** (13) | | | 106† | Calcutta | 1948-49 | **G. R. Viswanath** (4) | | |
| 116 | Georgetown | 1970-71 | **B. P. Patel** (1) | | | 139 | Calcutta | 1974-75 |
| 117* | Bridgetown | 1970-71 | 115* | Port-of-Spain | 1975-76 | 112 | Port-of-Spain | 1975-76 |
| 124 | } Port-of-Spain | 1970-71 | **Pankaj Roy** (1) | | | 124 | Madras | 1978-79 |
| 220 | | | 150 | Kingston | 1952-53 | 179 | Kanpur | 1978-79 |
| 156 | Port-of-Spain | 1975-76 | **D. N. Sardesai** (3) | | | | | |
| 102 | Port-of-Spain | 1975-76 | 212 | Kingston | 1970-71 | | | |
| 205 | Bombay | 1978-79 | 112 | Port-of-Spain | 1970-71 | | | |
| 107 | } Calcutta | 1978-79 | 150 | Bridgetown | 1970-71 | | | |
| 182* | | | | | | | | |

† *Signifies hundred on first appearance in West Indies–India Tests.*

## RECORD PARTNERSHIPS FOR EACH WICKET

### For West Indies

| | | | |
|---|---|---|---|
| 296 | for 1st | C. G. Greenidge and D. L. Haynes at St John's | 1982-83 |
| 255 | for 2nd | E. D. A. McMorris and R. B. Kanhai at Kingston | 1961-62 |
| 220 | for 3rd | I. V. A. Richards and A. I. Kallicharran at Bridgetown | 1975-76 |
| 267 | for 4th | C. L. Walcott and G. E. Gomez at Delhi | 1948-49 |
| 219 | for 5th | E. D. Weekes and B. H. Pairaudeau at Port-of-Spain | 1952-53 |
| 250 | for 6th | C. H. Lloyd and D. L. Murray at Bombay | 1974-75 |
| 130 | for 7th | C. G. Greenidge and M. D. Marshall at Kanpur | 1983-84 |
| 124 | for 8th† | I. V. A. Richards and K. D. Boyce at Delhi | 1974-75 |
| 161 | for 9th† | C. H. Lloyd and A. M. E. Roberts at Calcutta | 1983-84 |
| 98* | for 10th† | F. M. M. Worrell and W. W. Hall at Port-of-Spain | 1961-62 |

### For India

| | | | |
|---|---|---|---|
| 153 | for 1st | S. M. Gavaskar and C. P. S. Chauhan at Bombay | 1978-79 |
| 344* | for 2nd† | S. M. Gavaskar and D. B. Vengsarkar at Calcutta | 1978-79 |
| 159 | for 3rd | M. Amarnath and G. R. Viswanath at Port-of-Spain | 1975-76 |
| 172 | for 4th | G. R. Viswanath and A. D. Gaekwad at Kanpur | 1978-79 |
| 204 | for 5th | S. M. Gavaskar and B. P. Patel at Port-of-Spain | 1975-76 |
| 170 | for 6th | S. M. Gavaskar and R. J. Shastri at Madras | 1983-84 |
| 186 | for 7th | D. N. Sardesai and E. D. Solkar at Bridgetown | 1970-71 |
| 107 | for 8th | Yashpal Sharma and B. S. Sandhu at Kingston | 1982-83 |
| 143* | for 9th | S. M. Gavaskar and S. M. H. Kirmani at Madras | 1983-84 |
| 62 | for 10th | D. N. Sardesai and B. S. Bedi at Bridgetown | 1970-71 |

† *Denotes record partnership against all countries.*

## TEN WICKETS OR MORE IN A MATCH

### For West Indies (4)

| | | |
|---|---|---|
| 11-126 (6-50, 5-76) | W. W. Hall, Kanpur ............................... | 1958-59 |
| 11-89 (5-34, 6-55) | M. D. Marshall, Port-of-Spain.................... | 1988-89 |
| 12-121 (7-64, 5-57) | A. M. E. Roberts, Madras ....................... | 1974-75 |
| 10-101 (6-62, 4-39) | C. A. Walsh, Kingston ........................... | 1988-89 |

### For India (4)

| | | |
|---|---|---|
| 11-235 (7-157, 4-78)† | B. S. Chandrasekhar, Bombay.................... | 1966-67 |
| 10-223 (9-102, 1-121) | S. P. Gupte, Kanpur ............................ | 1958-59 |
| 16-136 (8-61, 8-75)† | N. D. Hirwani, Madras .......................... | 1987-88 |
| 10-135 (1-52, 9-83) | Kapil Dev, Ahmedabad .......................... | 1983-84 |

† *Signifies ten wickets or more on first appearance in West Indies-India Tests.*

## WEST INDIES v PAKISTAN

### Captains

| Season | West Indies | Pakistan | T | WI | P | D |
|---|---|---|---|---|---|---|
| 1957-58*W* | F. C. M. Alexander | A. H. Kardar | 5 | 3 | 1 | 1 |
| 1958-59*P* | F. C. M. Alexander | Fazal Mahmood | 3 | 1 | 2 | 0 |
| 1974-75*P* | C. H. Lloyd | Intikhab Alam | 2 | 0 | 0 | 2 |
| 1976-77*W* | C. H. Lloyd | Mushtaq Mohammad | 5 | 2 | 1 | 2 |
| 1980-81*P* | C. H. Lloyd | Javed Miandad | 4 | 1 | 0 | 3 |
| 1986-87*P* | I. V. A. Richards | Imran Khan | 3 | 1 | 1 | 1 |
| 1987-88*W* | I. V. A. Richards[1] | Imran Khan | 3 | 1 | 1 | 1 |
| 1990-91*P* | D. L. Haynes | Imran Khan | 3 | 1 | 1 | 1 |
| In West Indies .................. | | | 13 | 6 | 3 | 4 |
| In Pakistan ..................... | | | 15 | 4 | 4 | 7 |
| Totals........................... | | | 28 | 10 | 7 | 11 |

*P Played in Pakistan. W Played in West Indies.*

*Note:* The following was appointed by the home authority for only a minor proportion of the series:

[1]C. G. Greenidge (First).

## HIGHEST INNINGS TOTALS

| | | |
|---|---|---|
| For West Indies in West Indies: 790-3 dec. at Kingston..................... | | 1957-58 |
| in Pakistan: 493 at Karachi................................. | | 1974-75 |
| For Pakistan in West Indies: 657-8 dec. at Bridgetown.................... | | 1957-58 |
| in Pakistan: 406-8 dec. at Karachi ......................... | | 1974-75 |

## LOWEST INNINGS TOTALS

| | | |
|---|---|---|
| For West Indies in West Indies: 154 at Port-of-Spain..................... | | 1976-77 |
| in Pakistan: 53 at Faisalabad ............................. | | 1986-87 |
| For Pakistan in West Indies: 106 at Bridgetown ........................ | | 1957-58 |
| in Pakistan: 77 at Lahore ................................. | | 1986-87 |

## INDIVIDUAL HUNDREDS

### For West Indies (21)

| | | |
|---|---|---|
| **. Baichan (1)** | **C. C. Hunte (3)** | **I. V. A. Richards (2)** |
| 05*† Lahore ..... 1974-75 | 142† Bridgetown .. 1957-58 | 120* Multan ..... 1980-81 |
| **. J. L. Dujon (1)** | 260 Kingston.... 1957-58 | 123 Port-of-Spain 1987-88 |
| 06* Port-of-Spain 1987-88 | 114 Georgetown . 1957-58 | **I. T. Shillingford (1)** |
| **. C. Fredericks (1)** | **B. D. Julien (1)** | 120 Georgetown . 1976-77 |
| 20 Port-of-Spain 1976-77 | 101 Karachi .... 1974-75 | **G. S. Sobers (3)** |
| **. G. Greenidge (1)** | **A. I. Kallicharran (1)** | 365* Kingston.... 1957-58 |
| 00 Kingston .... 1976-77 | 115 Karachi .... 1974-75 | 125 ⎱ Georgetown . 1957-58 |
| **. L. Haynes (1)** | **R. B. Kanhai (1)** | 109* ⎰ |
| 17 Karachi ..... 1990-91 | 217 Lahore ..... 1958-59 | **C. L. Walcott (1)** |
| **. L. Hooper (1)** | **C. H. Lloyd (1)** | 145 Georgetown . 1957-58 |
| 34 Lahore ..... 1990-91 | 157 Bridgetown.. 1976-77 | **E. D. Weekes (1)** |
| | | 197† Bridgetown . 1957-58 |

### For Pakistan (17)

| | | |
|---|---|---|
| **Asif Iqbal (1)** | **Javed Miandad (2)** | **Saeed Ahmed (1)** |
| 35 Kingston .... 1976-77 | 114 Georgetown . 1987-88 | 150 Georgetown . 1957-58 |
| **Hanif Mohammad (2)** | 102 Port-of-Spain 1987-88 | **Salim Malik (1)** |
| 37† Bridgetown .. 1957-58 | **Majid Khan (2)** | 102 Karachi .... 1990-91 |
| 03 Karachi .... 1958-59 | 100 Karachi .... 1974-75 | **Wasim Raja (2)** |
| **Imtiaz Ahmed (1)** | 167 Georgetown . 1976-77 | 107* Karachi .... 1974-75 |
| 22 Kingston.... 1957-58 | **Mushtaq Mohammad (2)** | 117* Bridgetown . 1976-77 |
| **Imran Khan (1)** | 123 Lahore ..... 1974-75 | **Wazir Mohammad (2)** |
| 23 Lahore ..... 1980-81 | 121 Port-of-Spain 1976-77 | 106 Kingston.... 1957-58 |
| | | 189 Port-of-Spain 1957-58 |

† *Signifies hundred on first appearance in West Indies–Pakistan Tests.*

## RECORD PARTNERSHIPS FOR EACH WICKET

### For West Indies

| | | |
|---|---|---|
| 182 for 1st | R. C. Fredericks and C. G. Greenidge at Kingston ........... | 1976-77 |
| 446 for 2nd† | C. C. Hunte and G. S. Sobers at Kingston ................. | 1957-58 |
| 162 for 3rd | R. B. Kanhai and G. S. Sobers at Lahore ................. | 1958-59 |
| 188* for 4th | G. S. Sobers and C. L. Walcott at Kingston .............. | 1957-58 |
| 185 for 5th | E. D. Weekes and O. G. Smith at Bridgetown ............. | 1957-58 |
| 151 for 6th | C. H. Lloyd and D. L. Murray at Bridgetown ............. | 1976-77 |
| 70 for 7th | C. H. Lloyd and J. Garner at Bridgetown ............... | 1976-77 |
| 50 for 8th | B. D. Julien and V. A. Holder at Karachi ............... | 1974-75 |
| 61* for 9th | P. J. L. Dujon and W. K. M. Benjamin at Bridgetown ...... | 1987-88 |
| 44 for 10th | R. Nanan and S. T. Clarke at Faisalabad ............... | 1980-81 |

### For Pakistan

| | | |
|---|---|---|
| 159 for 1st‡ | Majid Khan and Zaheer Abbas at Georgetown............ | 1976-77 |
| 178 for 2nd | Hanif Mohammad and Saeed Ahmed at Karachi ........... | 1958-59 |
| 169 for 3rd | Saeed Ahmed and Wazir Mohammad at Port-of-Spain ...... | 1957-58 |
| 174 for 4th | Shoaib Mohammad and Salim Malik at Karachi ........... | 1990-91 |
| 87 for 5th | Mushtaq Mohammad and Asif Iqbal at Kingston .......... | 1976-77 |
| 166 for 6th | Wazir Mohammad and A. H. Kardar at Kingston ......... | 1957-58 |
| 128 for 7th | Wasim Raja and Wasim Bari at Karachi ............... | 1974-75 |
| 94 for 8th | Salim Malik and Salim Yousuf at Port-of-Spain .......... | 1987-88 |
| 73 for 9th | Wasim Raja and Sarfraz Nawaz at Bridgetown .......... | 1976-77 |
| 133 for 10th† | Wasim Raja and Wasim Bari at Bridgetown ............ | 1976-77 |

† *Denotes record partnership against all countries.*
‡ *219 runs were added for this wicket in two separate partnerships: Sadiq Mohammad retired hurt and was replaced by Zaheer Abbas when 60 had been added. The highest partnership by two opening batsmen is 152 by Hanif Mohammad and Imtiaz Ahmed at Bridgetown, 1957-58.*

## TEN WICKETS OR MORE IN A MATCH

### For Pakistan (2)

12-100 (6-34, 6-66)   Fazal Mahmood, Dacca ........................... 1958-59
11-121 (7-80, 4-41)   Imran Khan, Georgetown ......................... 1987-88

*Note:* The best match figures by a West Indian bowler are 9-95 (8-29, 1-66) by C. E. H. Croft at Port-of-Spain, 1976-77.

## NEW ZEALAND v INDIA

| Season | New Zealand | *Captains* India | T | NZ | I | D |
|---|---|---|---|---|---|---|
| 1955-56 *I* | H. B. Cave | P. R. Umrigar[1] | 5 | 0 | 2 | 3 |
| 1964-65 *I* | J. R. Reid | Nawab of Pataudi jun. | 4 | 0 | 1 | 3 |
| 1967-68 *N* | G. T. Dowling[2] | Nawab of Pataudi jun. | 4 | 1 | 3 | 0 |
| 1969-70 *I* | G. T. Dowling | Nawab of Pataudi jun. | 3 | 1 | 1 | 1 |
| 1975-76 *N* | G. M. Turner | B. S. Bedi[3] | 3 | 1 | 1 | 1 |
| 1976-77 *I* | G. M. Turner | B. S. Bedi | 3 | 0 | 2 | 1 |
| 1980-81 *N* | G. P. Howarth | S. M. Gavaskar | 3 | 1 | 0 | 2 |
| 1988-89 *I* | J. G. Wright | D. B. Vengsarkar | 3 | 1 | 2 | 0 |
| 1989-90 *N* | J. G. Wright | M. Azharuddin | 3 | 1 | 0 | 2 |
| | In India .......................... | | 18 | 2 | 8 | 8 |
| | In New Zealand ................. | | 13 | 4 | 4 | 5 |
| | Totals ........................ | | 31 | 6 | 12 | 13 |

*I Played in India.   N Played in New Zealand.*

*Notes:* The following deputised for the official touring captain or were appointed by the home authority for a minor proportion of the series:
[1]Ghulam Ahmed (First). [2]B. W. Sinclair (First). [3]S. M. Gavaskar (First).

## HIGHEST INNINGS TOTALS

For New Zealand in New Zealand: 502 at Christchurch .................... 1967-68
              in India: 462-9 dec. at Calcutta ........................ 1964-65

For India in New Zealand: 482 at Auckland ........................... 1989-90
              in India: 537-3 dec. at Madras ......................... 1955-56

## LOWEST INNINGS TOTALS

For New Zealand in New Zealand: 100 at Wellington ..................... 1980-81
              in India: 124 at Hyderabad ........................... 1988-89

For India in New Zealand: 81 at Wellington ........................... 1975-76
              in India: 88 at Bombay .............................. 1964-65

## INDIVIDUAL HUNDREDS

### For New Zealand (21)

| | | |
|---|---|---|
| **M. D. Crowe** (1) | **J. M. Parker** (1) | 230* Delhi....... 1955-56 |
| 13 Auckland ... 1989-90 | 104 Bombay .... 1976-77 | 151* Calcutta .... 1964-65 |
| **G. T. Dowling** (3) | **J. F. Reid** (1) | **B. R. Taylor** (1) |
| 120 Bombay .... 1964-65 | 123* Christchurch. 1980-81 | 105† Calcutta .... 1964-65 |
| 143 Dunedin .... 1967-68 | **J. R. Reid** (2) | **G. M. Turner** (2) |
| 239 Christchurch. 1967-68 | 119* Delhi....... 1955-56 | 117 Christchurch. 1975-76 |
| **J. W. Guy** (1) | 120 Calcutta .... 1955-56 | 113 Kanpur..... 1976-77 |
| 102† Hyderabad .. 1955-56 | **I. D. S. Smith** (1) | **J. G. Wright** (3) |
| **G. P. Howarth** (1) | 173 Auckland ... 1989-90 | 110 Auckland ... 1980-81 |
| 137* Wellington .. 1980-81 | **B. Sutcliffe** (2) | 185 Christchurch. 1989-90 |
| **A. H. Jones** (1) | 137*† Hyderabad .. 1955-56 | 113* Napier ..... 1989-90 |
| 170* Auckland ... 1989-90 | | |

### For India (22)

| | | |
|---|---|---|
| **S. Amarnath** (1) | 177 Delhi....... 1955-56 | **D. N. Sardesai** (2) |
| 124† Auckland ... 1975-76 | 102* Madras .... 1964-65 | 200* Bombay .... 1964-65 |
| **M. Azharuddin** (1) | **V. Mankad** (2) | 106 Delhi....... 1964-65 |
| 192 Auckland ... 1989-90 | 223 Bombay .... 1955-56 | **N. S. Sidhu** (1) |
| **C. G. Borde** (1) | 231 Madras .... 1955-56 | 116† Bangalore .. 1988-89 |
| 109 Bombay .... 1964-65 | **Nawab of Pataudi jun.** (2) | **P. R. Umrigar** (1) |
| **S. M. Gavaskar** (2) | 153 Calcutta .... 1964-65 | 223† Hyderabad .. 1955-56 |
| 116† Auckland ... 1975-76 | 113 Delhi....... 1964-65 | **G. R. Viswanath** (1) |
| 119 Bombay .... 1976-77 | **G. S. Ramchand** (1) | 103* Kanpur .... 1976-77 |
| **A. G. Kripal Singh** (1) | 106* Calcutta .... 1955-56 | **A. L. Wadekar** (1) |
| 100*† Hyderabad .. 1955-56 | **Pankaj Roy** (2) | 143 Wellington .. 1967-68 |
| **V. L. Manjrekar** (3) | 100 Calcutta .... 1955-56 | |
| 118† Hyderabad .. 1955-56 | 173 Madras ..... 1955-56 | |

† *Signifies hundred on first appearance in New Zealand–India Tests. B. R. Taylor provides the only instance for New Zealand of a player scoring his maiden hundred in first-class cricket in his first Test.*

## RECORD PARTNERSHIPS FOR EACH WICKET

### For New Zealand

| | | |
|---|---|---|
| 149 for 1st | T. J. Franklin and J. G. Wright at Napier................... | 1989-90 |
| 155 for 2nd | G. T. Dowling and B. E. Congdon at Dunedin .............. | 1967-68 |
| 222* for 3rd | B. Sutcliffe and J. R. Reid at Delhi...................... | 1955-56 |
| 125 for 4th | J. G. Wright and M. J. Greatbatch at Christchurch......... | 1989-90 |
| 119 for 5th | G. T. Dowling and K. Thomson at Christchurch............ | 1967-68 |
| 87 for 6th | J. W. Guy and A. R. MacGibbon at Hyderabad............ | 1955-56 |
| 163 for 7th | B. Sutcliffe and B. R. Taylor at Calcutta................. | 1964-65 |
| 103 for 8th | R. J. Hadlee and I. D. S. Smith at Auckland.............. | 1989-90 |
| 136 for 9th† | I. D. S. Smith and M. C. Snedden at Auckland............ | 1989-90 |
| 61 for 10th | J. T. Ward and R. O. Collinge at Madras................. | 1964-65 |

### For India

| | | |
|---|---|---|
| 413 for 1st† | V. Mankad and Pankaj Roy at Madras.................... | 1955-56 |
| 204 for 2nd | S. M. Gavaskar and S. Amarnath at Auckland............. | 1975-76 |
| 238 for 3rd | P. R. Umrigar and V. L. Manjrekar at Hyderabad......... | 1955-56 |
| 171 for 4th | P. R. Umrigar and A. G. Kripal Singh at Hyderabad....... | 1955-56 |
| 127 for 5th | V. L. Manjrekar and G. S. Ramchand at Delhi............ | 1955-56 |
| 193* for 6th | D. N. Sardesai and Hanumant Singh at Bombay........... | 1964-65 |
| 128 for 7th | S. R. Tendulkar and K. S. More at Napier................ | 1989-90 |
| 143 for 8th† | R. G. Nadkarni and F. M. Engineer at Madras............ | 1964-65 |
| 105 for 9th { | S. M. H. Kirmani and B. S. Bedi at Bombay............. | 1976-77 |
| | S. M. H. Kirmani and N. S. Yadav at Auckland.......... | 1980-81 |
| 57 for 10th | R. B. Desai and B. S. Bedi at Dunedin.................. | 1967-68 |

† *Denotes record partnership against all countries.*

## TEN WICKETS OR MORE IN A MATCH

### For New Zealand (2)

| | | |
|---|---|---|
| 11-58 (4-35, 7-23) | R. J. Hadlee, Wellington ......................... | 1975-76 |
| 10-88 (6-49, 4-39) | R. J. Hadlee, Bombay .............................. | 1988-89 |

### For India (2)

| | | |
|---|---|---|
| 11-140 (3-64, 8-76) | E. A. S. Prasanna, Auckland...................... | 1975-76 |
| 12-152 (8-72, 4-80) | S. Venkataraghavan, Delhi ....................... | 1964-65 |

## NEW ZEALAND v PAKISTAN

| Season | New Zealand | *Captains* Pakistan | T | NZ | P | D |
|---|---|---|---|---|---|---|
| 1955-56*P* | H. B. Cave | A. H. Kardar | 3 | 0 | 2 | 1 |
| 1964-65*N* | J. R. Reid | Hanif Mohammad | 3 | 0 | 0 | 3 |
| 1964-65*P* | J. R. Reid | Hanif Mohammad | 3 | 0 | 2 | 1 |
| 1969-70*P* | G. T. Dowling | Intikhab Alam | 3 | 1 | 0 | 2 |
| 1972-73*N* | B. E. Congdon | Intikhab Alam | 3 | 0 | 1 | 2 |
| 1976-77*P* | G. M. Turner[1] | Mushtaq Mohammad | 3 | 0 | 2 | 1 |
| 1978-79*N* | M. G. Burgess | Mushtaq Mohammad | 3 | 0 | 1 | 2 |
| 1984-85*P* | J. V. Coney | Zaheer Abbas | 3 | 0 | 2 | 1 |
| 1984-85*N* | G. P. Howarth | Javed Miandad | 3 | 2 | 0 | 1 |
| 1988-89*N*†| J. G. Wright | Imran Khan | 2 | 0 | 0 | 2 |
| 1990-91*P* | M. D. Crowe | Javed Miandad | 3 | 0 | 3 | 0 |
| | In Pakistan ..................... | | 18 | 1 | 11 | 6 |
| | In New Zealand ................. | | 14 | 2 | 2 | 10 |
| | Totals........................ | | 32 | 3 | 13 | 16 |

*N Played in New Zealand.   P Played in Pakistan.*

   † *The First Test at Dunedin was abandoned without a ball being bowled and is excluded.*

*Note:* The following deputised for the official touring captain:

[1] J. M. Parker (Third).

## HIGHEST INNINGS TOTALS

| | |
|---|---|
| For New Zealand in New Zealand 492 at Wellington....................... | 1984-85 |
| in Pakistan: 482-6 dec. at Lahore ....................... | 1964-65 |
| For Pakistan in New Zealand: 616-5 dec. at Auckland..................... | 1988-89 |
| in Pakistan: 565-9 dec. at Karachi .................... | 1976-77 |

## LOWEST INNINGS TOTALS

| | |
|---|---|
| For New Zealand in New Zealand: 156 at Dunedin ..................... | 1972-73 |
| in Pakistan: 70 at Dacca .............................. | 1955-56 |
| For Pakistan in New Zealand: 169 at Auckland .......................... | 1984-85 |
| in Pakistan: 102 at Faisalabad ....................... | 1990-91 |

## INDIVIDUAL HUNDREDS

### For New Zealand (18)

| | | | |
|---|---|---|---|
| **M. G. Burgess (2)** | | **G. P. Howarth (1)** | **J. R. Reid (1)** |
| 119* Dacca ...... 1969-70 | | 114 Napier ..... 1978-79 | 128 Karachi .... 1964-65 |
| 111 Lahore ..... 1976-77 | | **W. K. Lees (1)** | **B. W. Sinclair (1)** |
| **J. V. Coney (1)** | | 152 Karachi ... 1976-77 | 130 Lahore ..... 1964-65 |
| 111* Dunedin .... 1984-85 | | **S. N. McGregor (1)** | **G. M. Turner (1)** |
| **M. D. Crowe (2)** | | 111 Lahore ..... 1955-56 | 110† Dacca ..... 1969-70 |
| 174 Wellington .. 1988-89 | | **R. E. Redmond (1)** | **J. G. Wright (1)** |
| 108* Lahore ..... 1990-91 | | 107† Auckland ... 1972-73 | 107 Karachi .... 1984-85 |
| **B. A. Edgar (1)** | | **J. F. Reid (1)** | |
| 129† Christchurch. 1978-79 | | 106 Hyderabad .. 1984-85 | |
| **B. F. Hastings (1)** | | 148 Wellington .. 1984-85 | |
| 110 Auckland ... 1972-73 | | 158* Auckland ... 1984-85 | |

### For Pakistan (33)

| | | | |
|---|---|---|---|
| **Asif Iqbal (3)** | 118 Wellington .. 1988-89 | **Sadiq Mohammad (2)** | |
| 175 Dunedin .... 1972-73 | 271 Auckland .... 1988-89 | 166 Wellington .. 1972-73 | |
| 166 Lahore ..... 1976-77 | **Majid Khan (3)** | 103* Hyderabad .. 1976-77 | |
| 104 Napier ..... 1978-79 | 110 Auckland ... 1972-73 | **Saeed Ahmed (1)** | |
| **Hanif Mohammad (3)** | 112 Karachi .... 1976-77 | 172 Karachi .... 1964-65 | |
| 103 Dacca ...... 1955-56 | 119* Napier ..... 1978-79 | **Salim Malik (1)** | |
| 100* Christchurch. 1964-65 | **Mohammad Ilyas (1)** | 119* Karachi .... 1984-85 | |
| 203* Lahore ..... 1964-65 | 126 Karachi .... 1964-65 | **Shoaib Mohammad (5)** | |
| **Imtiaz Ahmed (1)** | **Mudassar Nazar (1)** | 163 Wellington .. 1988-89 | |
| 209 Lahore ..... 1955-56 | 106 Hyderabad .. 1984-85 | 112 Auckland ... 1988-89 | |
| **Javed Miandad (7)** | **Mushtaq Mohammad (3)** | 203* Karachi .... 1990-91 | |
| 163† Lahore ..... 1976-77 | 201 Dunedin .... 1972-73 | 105 Lahore ..... 1990-91 | |
| 206 Karachi .... 1976-77 | 101 Hyderabad .. 1976-77 | 142 Faisalabad .. 1990-91 | |
| 160* Christchurch. 1978-79 | 107 Karachi .... 1976-77 | **Waqar Hassan (1)** | |
| 104 } Hyderabad .. 1984-85 | | 189 Lahore ..... 1955-56 | |
| 103 } | | **Zaheer Abbas (1)** | |
| | | 135 Auckland ... 1978-79 | |

† *Signifies hundred on first appearance in New Zealand–Pakistan Tests.*

*Notes:* Mushtaq and Sadiq Mohammad, at Hyderabad in 1976-77, provide the fourth instance in Test matches, after the Chappells (thrice), of brothers each scoring hundreds in the same innings.

Shoaib Mohammad scored his first four hundreds in this series in successive innings.

## RECORD PARTNERSHIPS FOR EACH WICKET

### For New Zealand

| | | |
|---|---|---|
| 159 for 1st | R. E. Redmond and G. M. Turner at Auckland .............. | 1972-73 |
| 195 for 2nd | J. G. Wright and G. P. Howarth at Napier................. | 1978-79 |
| 178 for 3rd | B. W. Sinclair and J. R. Reid at Lahore ................... | 1964-65 |
| 128 for 4th | B. F. Hastings and M. G. Burgess at Wellington .......... | 1972-73 |
| 183 for 5th† | M. G. Burgess and R. W. Anderson at Lahore ............. | 1976-77 |
| 145 for 6th | J. F. Reid and R. J. Hadlee at Wellington ............... | 1984-85 |
| 186 for 7th† | W. K. Lees and R. J. Hadlee at Karachi.................. | 1976-77 |
| 100 for 8th | B. W. Yuile and D. R. Hadlee at Karachi................. | 1969-70 |
| 96 for 9th | M. G. Burgess and R. S. Cunis at Dacca ................. | 1969-70 |
| 151 for 10th† | B. F. Hastings and R. O. Collinge at Auckland .......... | 1972-73 |

### For Pakistan

| | | |
|---|---|---|
| 172 for 1st | Ramiz Raja and Shoaib Mohammad at Karachi.............. | 1990-91 |
| 114 for 2nd | Mohammad Ilyas and Saeed Ahmed at Rawalpindi ........... | 1964-65 |
| 248 for 3rd | Shoaib Mohammad and Javed Miandad at Auckland.......... | 1988-89 |
| 350 for 4th† | Mushtaq Mohammad and Asif Iqbal at Dunedin ............ | 1972-73 |

| 281 for 5th† | Javed Miandad and Asif Iqbal at Lahore | 1976-77 |
| 217 for 6th† | Hanif Mohammad and Majid Khan at Lahore | 1964-65 |
| 308 for 7th† | Waqar Hassan and Imtiaz Ahmed at Lahore | 1955-56 |
| 89 for 8th | Anil Dalpat and Iqbal Qasim at Karachi | 1984-85 |
| 52 for 9th | Intikhab Alam and Arif Butt at Auckland | 1964-65 |
| 65 for 10th | Salah-ud-Din and Mohammad Farooq at Rawalpindi | 1964-65 |

† *Denotes record partnership against all countries.*

## TEN WICKETS OR MORE IN A MATCH

### For Pakistan (6)

| 10-182 (5-91, 5-91) | Intikhab Alam, Dacca | 1969-70 |
| 11-130 (7-52, 4-78) | Intikhab Alam, Dunedin | 1972-73 |
| 10-106 (3-20, 7-86) | Waqar Younis, Lahore | 1990-91 |
| 12-130 (7-76, 5-54) | Waqar Younis, Faisalabad | 1990-91 |
| 10-128 (5-56, 5-72) | Wasim Akram, Dunedin | 1984-85 |
| 11-79 (5-37, 6-42)† | Zulfiqar Ahmed, Karachi | 1955-56 |

### For New Zealand (1)

| 11-152 (7-52, 4-100) | C. Pringle, Faisalabad | 1990-91 |

† *Signifies ten wickets or more on first appearance in New Zealand–Pakistan Tests.*

## NEW ZEALAND v SRI LANKA

| | | Captains | | | | |
| --- | --- | --- | --- | --- | --- | --- |
| Season | New Zealand | Sri Lanka | T | NZ | SL | D |
| 1982-83*N* | G. P. Howarth | D. S. de Silva | 2 | 2 | 0 | 0 |
| 1983-84*S* | G. P. Howarth | L. R. D. Mendis | 3 | 2 | 0 | 1 |
| 1986-87*S*† | J. J. Crowe | L. R. D. Mendis | 1 | 0 | 0 | 1 |
| 1990-91*N* | M. D. Crowe[1] | A. Ranatunga | 3 | 0 | 0 | 3 |
| | In New Zealand | | 5 | 2 | 0 | 3 |
| | In Sri Lanka | | 4 | 2 | 0 | 2 |
| | Totals | | 9 | 4 | 0 | 5 |

*N Played in New Zealand. S Played in Sri Lanka.*

† *The Second and Third Tests were cancelled owing to civil disturbances.*

*Note:* The following was appointed by the home authority for only a minor proportion of the series:

[1]I. D. S. Smith (Third).

## HIGHEST INNINGS TOTALS

| For New Zealand in New Zealand: 671-4 at Wellington | 1990-91 |
| in Sri Lanka: 459 at Colombo (CCC) | 1983-84 |

| For Sri Lanka in New Zealand: 497 at Wellington | 1990-91 |
| in Sri Lanka: 397-9 dec. at Colombo (CCC) | 1986-87 |

## LOWEST INNINGS TOTALS

| For New Zealand in New Zealand: 174 at Wellington | 1990-91 |
| in Sri Lanka: 198 at Colombo (SSC) | 1983-84 |

| For Sri Lanka in New Zealand: 93 at Wellington | 1982-83 |
| in Sri Lanka: 97 at Kandy | 1983-84 |

## INDIVIDUAL HUNDREDS

### For New Zealand (8)

**J. J. Crowe** (1)
120* Colombo
 (CCC)...... 1986-87

**M. D. Crowe** (1)
299 Wellington .. 1990-91

**R. J. Hadlee** (1)
151* Colombo
 (CCC)...... 1986-87

**A. H. Jones** (3)
186 Wellington .. 1990-91
122 ⎫
100* ⎬ Hamilton ... 1990-91

**J. F. Reid** (1)
180 Colombo
 (CCC)...... 1983-84

**J. G. Wright** (1)
101 Hamilton ... 1990-91

### For Sri Lanka (6)

**P. A. de Silva** (2)
267† Wellington .. 1990-91
123 Auckland ... 1990-91

**R. L. Dias** (1)
108† Colombo
 (SSC) ...... 1983-84

**A. P. Gurusinha** (2)
119 ⎫
102 ⎬ Hamilton ... 1990-91

**D. S. B. P. Kuruppu** (1)
201*† Colombo
 (CCC)...... 1986-87

† *Signifies hundred on first appearance in New Zealand–Sri Lanka Tests.*

*Note:* A. P. Gurusinha and A. H. Jones at Hamilton in 1990-91 provided the second instance of a player on each side hitting two separate hundreds in a Test match.

## RECORD PARTNERSHIPS FOR EACH WICKET

### For New Zealand

| | | | |
|---|---|---|---|
| 161 for 1st | T. J. Franklin and J. G. Wright at Hamilton | ............... | 1990-91 |
| 76 for 2nd | J. G. Wright and A. H. Jones at Auckland | ............... | 1990-91 |
| 467 for 3rd‡‡ | A. H. Jones and M. D. Crowe at Wellington | ............... | 1990-91 |
| 82 for 4th | J. F. Reid and S. L. Boock at Colombo (CCC) | ........ | 1983-84 |
| 113 for 5th | A. H. Jones and S. A. Thomson at Hamilton | ........ | 1990-91 |
| 246* for 6th† | J. J. Crowe and R. J. Hadlee at Colombo (CCC) | ........ | 1986-87 |
| 30 for 7th ⎰ | R. J. Hadlee and I. D. S. Smith at Kandy | ............ | 1983-84 |
| ⎱ | R. J. Hadlee and J. J. Crowe at Kandy | ............ | 1983-84 |
| 79 for 8th | J. V. Coney and W. K. Lees at Christchurch | ........ | 1982-83 |
| 42 for 9th | W. K. Lees and M. C. Snedden at Christchurch | ........ | 1982-83 |
| 52 for 10th | W. K. Lees and E. J. Chatfield at Christchurch | ........ | 1982-83 |

### For Sri Lanka

| | | | |
|---|---|---|---|
| 95 for 1st | C. P. Senanayake and U. C. Hathurusinghe at Hamilton | ...... | 1990-91 |
| 57 for 2nd | S. M. S. Kaluperuma and R. S. Madugalle at Colombo (CCC) | . | 1983-84 |
| 159* for 3rd†[1] | S. Wettimuny and R. L. Dias at Colombo (SSC) | ........ | 1983-84 |
| 178 for 4th | P. A. de Silva and A. Ranatunga at Wellington | ........ | 1990-91 |
| 130 for 5th | R. S. Madugalle and D. S. de Silva at Wellington | ........ | 1982-83 |
| 109* for 6th[2] | R. S. Madugalle and A. Ranatunga at Colombo (CCC) | ........ | 1983-84 |
| 55 for 7th | A. P. Gurusinha and A. Ranatunga at Hamilton | ........ | 1990-91 |
| 52 for 8th | H. P. Tillekeratne and G. F. Labrooy at Auckland | ........ | 1990-91 |
| 31 for 9th ⎰ | G. F. Labrooy and R. J. Ratnayake at Auckland | ............ | 1990-91 |
| ⎱ | S. T. Jayasuriya and R. J. Ratnayake at Auckland | ............ | 1990-91 |
| 60 for 10th | V. B. John and M. J. G. Amerasinghe at Kandy | ............ | 1983-84 |

† *Denotes record partnership against all countries.*

‡ *Record third-wicket partnership in first-class cricket.*

[1] *163 runs were added for this wicket in two separate partnerships: S. Wettimuny retired hurt and was replaced by L. R. D. Mendis when 159 had been added.*

[2] *119 runs were added for this wicket in two separate partnerships: R. S. Madugalle retired hurt and was replaced by D. S. de Silva when 109 had been added.*

## TEN WICKETS OR MORE IN A MATCH

**For New Zealand** (1)

10-102 (5-73, 5-29)    R. J. Hadlee, Colombo (CCC) ...................... 1983-84

*Note:* The best match figures by a Sri Lankan bowler are 8-159 (5-86, 3-73), V. B. John at Kandy, 1983-84.

## INDIA v PAKISTAN

|  |  | *Captains* |  |  |  |  |
|---|---|---|---|---|---|---|
| *Season* | *India* | *Pakistan* | *T* | *I* | *P* | *D* |
| 1952-53*I* | L. Amarnath | A. H. Kardar | 5 | 2 | 1 | 2 |
| 1954-55*P* | V. Mankad | A. H. Kardar | 5 | 0 | 0 | 5 |
| 1960-61*I* | N. J. Contractor | Fazal Mahmood | 5 | 0 | 0 | 5 |
| 1978-79*P* | B. S. Bedi | Mushtaq Mohammad | 3 | 0 | 2 | 1 |
| 1979-80*I* | S. M. Gavaskar[1] | Asif Iqbal | 6 | 2 | 0 | 4 |
| 1982-83*P* | S. M. Gavaskar | Imran Khan | 6 | 0 | 3 | 3 |
| 1983-84*I* | Kapil Dev | Zaheer Abbas | 3 | 0 | 0 | 3 |
| 1984-85*P* | S. M. Gavaskar | Zaheer Abbas | 2 | 0 | 0 | 2 |
| 1986-87*I* | Kapil Dev | Imran Khan | 5 | 0 | 1 | 4 |
| 1989-90*P* | K. Srikkanth | Imran Khan | 4 | 0 | 0 | 4 |
|  | In India........................ | | 24 | 4 | 2 | 18 |
|  | In Pakistan ................... | | 20 | 0 | 5 | 15 |
|  | Totals........................ | | 44 | 4 | 7 | 33 |

*I Played in India.   P Played in Pakistan.*

*Note:* The following was appointed by the home authority for only a minor proportion of the series:
    [1]G. R. Viswanath (Sixth).

## HIGHEST INNINGS TOTALS

For India in India: 539-9 dec. at Madras ................................ 1960-61
         in Pakistan: 509 at Lahore .................................... 1989-90

For Pakistan in India: 487-9 dec. at Madras ......................... 1986-87
         in Pakistan: 699-5 at Lahore ............................. 1989-90

## LOWEST INNINGS TOTALS

For India in India: 106 at Lucknow ................................. 1952-53
         in Pakistan: 145 at Karachi ................................. 1954-55

For Pakistan in India: 116 at Bangalore .............................. 1986-87
         in Pakistan: 158 at Dacca ................................. 1954-55

## INDIVIDUAL HUNDREDS

### For India (31)

| | | | |
|---|---|---|---|
| **M. Amarnath (4)** | 166 Madras .... 1979-80 | **K. Srikkanth (1)** | |
| 109* Lahore .... 1982-83 | 127*‡ Faisalabad .. 1982-83 | 123 Madras .... 1986-87 | |
| 120 Lahore .... 1982-83 | 103* Bangalore ... 1983-84 | **P. R. Umrigar (5)** | |
| 103* Karachi .... 1982-83 | **V. S. Hazare (1)** | 102 Bombay ... 1952-53 | |
| 101* Lahore .... 1984-85 | 146* Bombay .... 1952-53 | 108 Peshawar ... 1954-55 | |
| **M. Azharuddin (3)** | **S. V. Manjrekar (2)** | 115 Kanpur .... 1960-61 | |
| 141 Calcutta .... 1986-87 | 113*† Karachi .... 1989-90 | 117 Madras .... 1960-61 | |
| 110 Jaipur .... 1986-87 | 218 Lahore .... 1989-90 | 112 Delhi ...... 1960-61 | |
| 109 Faisalabad .. 1989-90 | **S. M. Patil (1)** | **D. B. Vengsarkar (2)** | |
| **C. G. Borde (1)** | 127 Faisalabad .. 1984-85 | 146* Delhi ...... 1979-80 | |
| 177* Madras .... 1960-61 | **R. J. Shastri (3)** | 109 Ahmedabad . 1986-87 | |
| **A. D. Gaekwad (1)** | 128 Karachi .... 1982-83 | **G. R. Viswanath (1)** | |
| 201 Jullundur .. 1983-84 | 139 Faisalabad .. 1984-85 | 145† Faisalabad .. 1978-79 | |
| **S. M. Gavaskar (5)** | 125 Jaipur ...... 1986-87 | | |
| 111 ⎫ Karachi .... 1978-79 | **R. H. Shodhan (1)** | | |
| 137 ⎭ | 110† Calcutta .... 1952-53 | | |

### For Pakistan (41)

| | | | |
|---|---|---|---|
| **Aamer Malik (2)** | 126 Faisalabad .. 1982-83 | **Saeed Ahmed (2)** | |
| 117 Faisalabad .. 1989-90 | 280* Hyderabad .. 1982-83 | 121† Bombay .... 1960-61 | |
| 113 Lahore .... 1989-90 | 145 Lahore .... 1989-90 | 103 Madras .... 1960-61 | |
| **Alim-ud-Din (1)** | **Mohsin Khan (1)** | **Salim Malik (3)** | |
| 103* Karachi .... 1954-55 | 101*† Lahore .... 1982-83 | 107 Faisalabad .. 1982-83 | |
| **Asif Iqbal (1)** | **Mudassar Nazar (6)** | 102* Faisalabad .. 1984-85 | |
| 104† Faisalabad .. 1978-79 | 126 Bangalore ... 1979-80 | 102* Karachi .... 1989-90 | |
| **Hanif Mohammad (2)** | 119 Karachi .... 1982-83 | **Shoaib Mohammad (2)** | |
| 142 Bahawalpur . 1954-55 | 231 Hyderabad .. 1982-83 | 101 Madras .... 1986-87 | |
| 160 Bombay .... 1960-61 | 152*‡ Lahore .... 1982-83 | 203* Lahore .... 1989-90 | |
| **Ijaz Faqih (1)** | 152 Karachi .... 1982-83 | **Wasim Raja (1)** | |
| 105† Ahmedabad . 1986-87 | 199 Faisalabad .. 1984-85 | 125 Jullundur ... 1983-84 | |
| **Imtiaz Ahmed (1)** | **Mushtaq Mohammad (1)** | **Zaheer Abbas (6)** | |
| 135 Madras .... 1960-61 | 101 Delhi ...... 1960-61 | 176† Faisalabad .. 1978-79 | |
| **Imran Khan (3)** | **Nazar Mohammad (1)** | 235* Lahore .... 1978-79 | |
| 117 Faisalabad .. 1982-83 | 124*‡ Lucknow ... 1952-53 | 215 Lahore .... 1982-83 | |
| 135* Madras .... 1986-87 | **Qasim Omar (1)** | 186 Karachi .... 1982-83 | |
| 109* Karachi .... 1989-90 | 210 Faisalabad .. 1984-85 | 168 Faisalabad .. 1982-83 | |
| **Javed Miandad (5)** | **Ramiz Raja (1)** | 168* Lahore .... 1984-85 | |
| 154*† Faisalabad .. 1978-79 | 114 Jaipur ...... 1986-87 | | |
| 100 Karachi .... 1978-79 | | | |

† *Signifies hundred on first appearance in India–Pakistan Tests.*
‡ *Carried his bat.*

## RECORD PARTNERSHIPS FOR EACH WICKET

### For India

| | | |
|---|---|---|
| 200 for 1st | S. M. Gavaskar and K. Srikkanth at Madras ................ | 1986-87 |
| 135 for 2nd | N. S. Sidhu and S. V. Manjrekar at Karachi ................ | 1989-90 |
| 190 for 3rd | M. Amarnath and Yashpal Sharma at Lahore ................ | 1982-83 |
| 186 for 4th | S. V. Manjrekar and R. J. Shastri at Lahore ................ | 1989-90 |
| 200 for 5th | S. M. Patil and R. J. Shastri at Faisalabad ................ | 1984-85 |
| 143 for 6th | M. Azharuddin and Kapil Dev at Calcutta ................ | 1986-87 |
| 155 for 7th | R. M. H. Binny and Madan Lal at Bangalore ................ | 1983-84 |
| 122 for 8th | S. M. H. Kirmani and Madan Lal at Faisalabad ............ | 1982-83 |
| 149 for 9th† | P. G. Joshi and R. B. Desai at Bombay ................ | 1960-61 |
| 109 for 10th† | H. R. Adhikari and Ghulam Ahmed at Delhi ................ | 1952-53 |

**For Pakistan**

| | | |
|---|---|---|
| 162 for 1st | Hanif Mohammad and Imtiaz Ahmed at Madras . . . . . . . . . . . . | 1960-61 |
| 250 for 2nd | Mudassar Nazar and Qasim Omar at Faisalabad . . . . . . . . . . . | 1984-85 |
| 451 for 3rd† | Mudassar Nazar and Javed Miandad at Hyderabad . . . . . . . . . | 1982-83 |
| 287 for 4th | Javed Miandad and Zaheer Abbas at Faisalabad. . . . . . . . . . . | 1982-83 |
| 213 for 5th | Zaheer Abbas and Mudassar Nazar at Karachi . . . . . . . . . . . . | 1982-83 |
| 207 for 6th | Salim Malik and Imran Khan at Faisalabad. . . . . . . . . . . . . . | 1982-83 |
| 154 for 7th | Imran Khan and Ijaz Faqih at Ahmedabad . . . . . . . . . . . . . . | 1986-87 |
| 112 for 8th | Imran Khan and Wasim Akram at Madras . . . . . . . . . . . . . . | 1986-87 |
| 60 for 9th | Wasim Bari and Iqbal Qasim at Bangalore. . . . . . . . . . . . . . | 1979-80 |
| 104 for 10th | Zulfiqar Ahmed and Amir Elahi at Madras . . . . . . . . . . . . . | 1952-53 |

† *Denotes record partnership against all countries.*

## TEN WICKETS OR MORE IN A MATCH

### For India (3)

| | | |
|---|---|---|
| 11-146 (4-90, 7-56) | Kapil Dev, Madras. . . . . . . . . . . . . . . . . . . . . . . . . . . . | 1979-80 |
| 10-126 (7-27, 3-99) | Maninder Singh, Bangalore . . . . . . . . . . . . . . . . . . . . . | 1986-87 |
| 13-131 (8-52, 5-79)† | V. Mankad, Delhi. . . . . . . . . . . . . . . . . . . . . . . . . . . . | 1952-53 |

### For Pakistan (5)

| | | |
|---|---|---|
| 12-94 (5-52, 7-42) | Fazal Mahmood, Lucknow. . . . . . . . . . . . . . . . . . . . . . | 1952-53 |
| 11-79 (3-19, 8-60) | Imran Khan, Karachi. . . . . . . . . . . . . . . . . . . . . . . . . | 1982-83 |
| 11-180 (6-98, 5-82) | Imran Khan, Faisalabad. . . . . . . . . . . . . . . . . . . . . . . | 1982-83 |
| 10-175 (4-135, 6-40) | Iqbal Qasim, Bombay. . . . . . . . . . . . . . . . . . . . . . . . . | 1979-80 |
| 11-190 (8-69, 3-121) | Sikander Bakht, Delhi. . . . . . . . . . . . . . . . . . . . . . . . | 1979-80 |

† *Signifies ten wickets or more on first appearance in India–Pakistan Tests.*

## INDIA v SRI LANKA

| | | Captains | | | | |
|---|---|---|---|---|---|---|
| Season | India | | Sri Lanka | T | I | SL | D |
| 1982-83*I* | S. M. Gavaskar | | B. Warnapura | 1 | 0 | 0 | 1 |
| 1985-86*S* | Kapil Dev | | L. R. D. Mendis | 3 | 0 | 1 | 2 |
| 1986-87*I* | Kapil Dev | | L. R. D. Mendis | 3 | 2 | 0 | 1 |
| 1990-91*I* | M. Azharuddin | | A. Ranatunga | 1 | 1 | 0 | 0 |
| | In India . . . . . . . . . . . . . . | | | 5 | 3 | 0 | 2 |
| | In Sri Lanka . . . . . . . . . . . | | | 3 | 0 | 1 | 2 |
| | Totals. . . . . . . . . . . . . . . | | | 8 | 3 | 1 | 4 |

*I Played in India. S Played in Sri Lanka.*

## HIGHEST INNINGS TOTALS

| | |
|---|---|
| For India in India: 676-7 at Kanpur . . . . . . . . . . . . . . . . . . . . . . . . . . . . . . . . . . . . | 1986-87 |
| in Sri Lanka: 325-5 dec. at Kandy . . . . . . . . . . . . . . . . . . | 1985-86 |
| For Sri Lanka in India: 420 at Kanpur . . . . . . . . . . . . . . . . . . . . . . . . . . . . . . . . . . . | 1986-87 |
| in Sri Lanka: 385 at Colombo (PSS) . . . . . . . . . . . . . . . | 1985-86 |

## LOWEST INNINGS TOTALS

| | |
|---|---|
| For India in India: 288 at Chandigarh . . . . . . . . . . . . . . . . . . . . . . . . . . . . . . . . . . . . | 1990-91 |
| in Sri Lanka: 198 at Colombo (PSS) . . . . . . . . . . . . . . . | 1985-86 |
| For Sri Lanka in India: 82 at Chandigarh . . . . . . . . . . . . . . . . . . . . . . . . . . . . . . . . . . | 1990-91 |
| in Sri Lanka: 198 at Kandy . . . . . . . . . . . . . . . . . . . . . | 1985-86 |

## INDIVIDUAL HUNDREDS

### For India (9)

**M. Amarnath** (2)
116*  Kandy...... 1985-86
131   Nagpur..... 1986-87
**M. Azharuddin** (1)
199   Kanpur..... 1986-87

**S. M. Gavaskar** (2)
155†  Madras..... 1982-83
176   Kanpur..... 1986-87
**Kapil Dev** (1)
163   Kanpur..... 1986-87

**S. M. Patil** (1)
114*† Madras..... 1982-83
**D. B. Vengsarkar** (2)
153   Nagpur..... 1986-87
166   Cuttack..... 1986-87

### For Sri Lanka (7)

**R. L. Dias** (1)
106   Kandy...... 1985-86
**R. S. Madugalle** (1)
103   Colombo
     (SSC) ...... 1985-86
**L. R. D. Mendis** (3)
105 ⎫
105 ⎬ †Madras..... 1982-83
124   Kandy...... 1985-86

**A. Ranatunga** (1)
111   Colombo
     (SSC) ...... 1985-86
**S. A. R. Silva** (1)
111   Colombo
     (PSS)....... 1985-86

*† Signifies hundred on first appearance in India–Sri Lanka Tests.*

## RECORD PARTNERSHIPS FOR EACH WICKET

### For India

| | | | |
|---|---|---|---|
| 156 | for 1st | S. M. Gavaskar and Arun Lal at Madras ................ | 1982-83 |
| 173 | for 2nd | S. M. Gavaskar and D. B. Vengsarkar at Madras ............ | 1982-83 |
| 173 | for 3rd | M. Amarnath and D. B. Vengsarkar at Nagpur ............. | 1986-87 |
| 163 | for 4th | S. M. Gavaskar and M. Azharuddin at Kanpur ............. | 1986-87 |
| 78 | for 5th | M. Amarnath and M. Azharuddin at Kandy ............... | 1985-86 |
| 272 | for 6th | M. Azharuddin and Kapil Dev at Kanpur ................. | 1986-87 |
| 78* | for 7th | S. M. Patil and Madan Lal at Madras .................... | 1982-83 |
| 70 | for 8th | Kapil Dev and L. Sivaramakrishnan at Colombo (PSS)........ | 1985-86 |
| 16 | for 9th | S. M. Gavaskar and Gopal Sharma at Colombo (SSC) ....... | 1985-86 |
| 29 | for 10th | Kapil Dev and Chetan Sharma at Colombo (PSS) ........... | 1985-86 |

### For Sri Lanka

| | | | |
|---|---|---|---|
| 159 | for 1st† | S. Wettimuny and J. R. Ratnayeke at Kanpur .............. | 1986-87 |
| 95 | for 2nd | S. A. R. Silva and R. S. Madugalle at Colombo (PSS) ........ | 1985-86 |
| 153 | for 3rd | R. L. Dias and L. R. D. Mendis at Madras ............... | 1982-83 |
| 216 | for 4th | R. L. Dias and L. R. D. Mendis at Kandy ............... | 1985-86 |
| 144 | for 5th | R. S. Madugalle and A. Ranatunga at Colombo (SSC) ....... | 1985-86 |
| 89 | for 6th | L. R. D. Mendis and A. N. Ranasinghe at Madras .......... | 1982-83 |
| 77 | for 7th | R. S. Madugalle and D. S. de Silva at Madras ............. | 1982-83 |
| 40* | for 8th | P. A. de Silva and A. L. F. de Mel at Kandy .............. | 1985-86 |
| 60 | for 9th† | H. P. Tillekeratne and A. W. R. Madurasinghe at Chandigarh . | 1990-91 |
| 44 | for 10th | R. J. Ratnayake and E. A. R. de Silva at Nagpur ........... | 1986-87 |

*† Denotes record partnership against all countries.*

## TEN WICKETS OR MORE IN A MATCH

### For India (1)

10-107 (3-56, 7-51)    Maninder Singh, Nagpur ........................ 1986-87

*Note:* The best match figures by a Sri Lankan bowler are 9-125 (4-76, 5-49) by R. J. Ratnayake against India at Colombo (PSS), 1985-86.

## PAKISTAN v SRI LANKA

| | | *Captains* | | | | |
|---|---|---|---|---|---|---|
| *Season* | *Pakistan* | *Sri Lanka* | *T* | *P* | *SL* | *D* |
| 1981-82*P* | Javed Miandad | B. Warnapura[1] | 3 | 2 | 0 | 1 |
| 1985-86*P* | Javed Miandad | L. R. D. Mendis | 3 | 2 | 0 | 1 |
| 1985-86*S* | Imran Khan | L. R. D. Mendis | 3 | 1 | 1 | 1 |
| | In Pakistan | | 6 | 4 | 0 | 2 |
| | In Sri Lanka | | 3 | 1 | 1 | 1 |
| | Totals | | 9 | 5 | 1 | 3 |

*P Played in Pakistan.  S Played in Sri Lanka.*

*Note:* The following deputised for the official touring captain:
  [1]L. R. D. Mendis (Second).

## HIGHEST INNINGS TOTALS

| | | |
|---|---|---|
| For Pakistan in Pakistan: 555-3 at Faisalabad | | 1985-86 |
| in Sri Lanka: 318 at Colombo (PSS) | | 1985-86 |
| For Sri Lanka in Pakistan: 479 at Faisalabad | | 1985-86 |
| in Sri Lanka: 323-3 at Colombo (PSS) | | 1985-86 |

## LOWEST INNINGS TOTALS

| | | |
|---|---|---|
| For Pakistan in Pakistan: 259 at Sialkot | | 1985-86 |
| in Sri Lanka: 132 at Colombo (CCC) | | 1985-86 |
| For Sri Lanka in Pakistan: 149 at Karachi | | 1981-82 |
| in Sri Lanka: 101 at Kandy | | 1985-86 |

## INDIVIDUAL HUNDREDS

### For Pakistan (7)

**Haroon Rashid** (1)
153† Karachi .... 1981-82
**Javed Miandad** (1)
203* Faisalabad .. 1985-86
**Mohsin Khan** (1)
129 Lahore ..... 1981-82
**Qasim Omar** (1)
206† Faisalabad .. 1985-86

**Ramiz Raja** (1)
122 Colombo
      (PSS)....... 1985-86
**Salim Malik** (1)
100*† Karachi .... 1981-82
**Zaheer Abbas** (1)
134† Lahore ...... 1981-82

### For Sri Lanka (6)

**P. A. de Silva** (2)
122† Faisalabad .. 1985-86
105   Karachi .... 1985-86
**R. L. Dias** (1)
109   Lahore ..... 1981-82
**A. P. Gurusinha** (1)
116* Colombo
      (PSS)....... 1985-86

**A. Ranatunga** (1)
135* Colombo
      (PSS)....... 1985-86
**S. Wettimuny** (1)
157   Faisalabad .. 1981-82

*† Signifies hundred on first appearance in Pakistan–Sri Lanka Tests.*

## RECORD PARTNERSHIPS FOR EACH WICKET

### For Pakistan

| | | | |
|---|---|---|---|
| 98* | for 1st | Mudassar Nazar and Mohsin Khan at Karachi............... | 1985-86 |
| 151 | for 2nd | Mohsin Khan and Majid Khan at Lahore................... | 1981-82 |
| 397 | for 3rd | Qasim Omar and Javed Miandad at Faisalabad............. | 1985-86 |
| 162 | for 4th | Salim Malik and Javed Miandad at Karachi............... | 1981-82 |
| 102 | for 5th | Mudassar Nazar and Salim Malik at Kandy............... | 1985-86 |
| 100 | for 6th | Zaheer Abbas and Imran Khan at Lahore................. | 1981-82 |
| 104 | for 7th | Haroon Rashid and Tahir Naqqash at Karachi............. | 1981-82 |
| 29 | for 8th | { Ashraf Ali and Iqbal Qasim at Faisalabad ............... | 1981-82 |
| | | Salim Yousuf and Abdul Qadir at Sialkot ............... | 1985-86 |
| | | Salim Yousuf and Abdul Qadir at Karachi ............... | 1985-86 |
| 127 | for 9th | Haroon Rashid and Rashid Khan at Karachi .............. | 1981-82 |
| 48 | for 10th | Rashid Khan and Tauseef Ahmed at Faisalabad ............ | 1981-82 |

### For Sri Lanka

| | | | |
|---|---|---|---|
| 77 | for 1st | S. Wettimuny and H. M. Goonatillake at Faisalabad......... | 1981-82 |
| 217 | for 2nd† | S. Wettimuny and R. L. Dias at Faisalabad ............... | 1981-82 |
| 85 | for 3rd | S. Wettimuny and R. L. Dias at Faisalabad ............... | 1985-86 |
| 240* | for 4th† | A. P. Gurusinha and A. Ranatunga at Colombo (PSS) ...... | 1985-86 |
| 58 | for 5th | R. L. Dias and L. R. D. Mendis at Lahore ............... | 1981-82 |
| 121 | for 6th | A. Ranatunga and P. A. de Silva at Faisalabad ........... | 1985-86 |
| 66 | for 7th | P. A. de Silva and J. R. Ratnayeke at Faisalabad ......... | 1985-86 |
| 61 | for 8th† | R. S. Madugalle and D. S. de Silva at Faisalabad ......... | 1981-82 |
| 52 | for 9th | P. A. de Silva and R. J. Ratnayake at Faisalabad ......... | 1985-86 |
| 36 | for 10th | R. J. Ratnayake and R. G. C. E. Wijesuriya at Faisalabad..... | 1985-86 |

*† Denotes record partnership against all countries.*

## TEN WICKETS OR MORE IN A MATCH

### For Pakistan (1)

14-116 (8-58, 6-58)   Imran Khan, Lahore ............................. 1981-82

*Note:* The best match figures by a Sri Lankan bowler are 9-162 (4-103, 5-59), D. S. de Silva at Faisalabad, 1981-82.

## TEST MATCH GROUNDS

### In Chronological Sequence

| City and Ground | Date of First Test | Match |
|---|---|---|
| 1. Melbourne, Melbourne Cricket Ground | March 15, 1877 | Australia v England |
| 2. London, Kennington Oval | September 6, 1880 | England v Australia |
| 3. Sydney, Sydney Cricket Ground (No. 1) | February 17, 1882 | Australia v England |
| 4. Manchester, Old Trafford | July 11, 1884 | England v Australia |
| *This match was due to have started on July 10, but rain prevented any play.* | | |
| 5. London, Lord's | July 21, 1884 | England v Australia |
| 6. Adelaide, Adelaide Oval | December 12, 1884 | Australia v England |
| 7. Port Elizabeth, St George's Park | March 12, 1889 | South Africa v England |
| 8. Cape Town, Newlands | March 25, 1889 | South Africa v England |
| 9. Johannesburg, Old Wanderers* | March 2, 1896 | South Africa v England |
| 10. Nottingham, Trent Bridge | June 1, 1899 | England v Australia |
| 11. Leeds, Headingley | June 29, 1899 | England v Australia |
| 12. Birmingham, Edgbaston | May 29, 1902 | England v Australia |
| 13. Sheffield, Bramall Lane* | July 3, 1902 | England v Australia |
| 14. Durban, Lord's* | January 21, 1910 | South Africa v England |
| 15. Durban, Kingsmead | January 18, 1923 | South Africa v England |

| | City and Ground | Date of First Test | Match |
|---|---|---|---|
| 16. | Brisbane, Exhibition Ground* | November 30, 1928 | Australia v England |
| 17. | Christchurch, Lancaster Park | January 10, 1930 | New Zealand v England |
| 18. | Bridgetown, Kensington Oval | January 11, 1930 | West Indies v England |
| 19. | Wellington, Basin Reserve | January 24, 1930 | New Zealand v England |
| 20. | Port-of-Spain, Queen's Park Oval | February 1, 1930 | West Indies v England |
| 21. | Auckland, Eden Park | February 17, 1930 | New Zealand v England |

*This match was due to have started on February 14, but rain prevented any play on the first two days. February 16 was a Sunday.*

| | City and Ground | Date of First Test | Match |
|---|---|---|---|
| 22. | Georgetown, Bourda | February 21, 1930 | West Indies v England |
| 23. | Kingston, Sabina Park | April 3, 1930 | West Indies v England |
| 24. | Brisbane, Woolloongabba | November 27, 1931 | Australia v South Africa |
| 25. | Bombay, Gymkhana Ground* | December 15, 1933 | India v England |
| 26. | Calcutta, Eden Gardens | January 5, 1934 | India v England |
| 27. | Madras, Chepauk (Chidambaram Stadium) | February 10, 1934 | India v England |
| 28. | Delhi, Feroz Shah Kotla | November 10, 1948 | India v West Indies |
| 29. | Bombay, Brabourne Stadium* | December 9, 1948 | India v West Indies |
| 30. | Johannesburg, Ellis Park* | December 27, 1948 | South Africa v England |
| 31. | Kanpur, Green Park (Modi Stadium) | January 12, 1952 | India v England |
| 32. | Lucknow, University Ground* | October 25, 1952 | India v Pakistan |
| 33. | Dacca, Dacca Stadium* | January 1, 1955 | Pakistan v India |
| 34. | Bahawalpur, Dring Stadium | January 15, 1955 | Pakistan v India |
| 35. | Lahore, Lawrence Gardens (Bagh-i-Jinnah)* | January 29, 1955 | Pakistan v India |
| 36. | Peshawar, Services Club Ground | February 13, 1955 | Pakistan v India |
| 37. | Karachi, National Stadium | February 26, 1955 | Pakistan v India |
| 38. | Dunedin, Carisbrook | March 11, 1955 | New Zealand v England |
| 39. | Hyderabad, Fateh Maidan (Lal Bahadur Stadium) | November 19, 1955 | India v New Zealand |
| 40. | Madras, Corporation Stadium* | January 6, 1956 | India v New Zealand |
| 41. | Johannesburg, New Wanderers | December 24, 1956 | South Africa v England |
| 42. | Lahore, Gaddafi Stadium | November 21, 1959 | Pakistan v Australia |
| 43. | Rawalpindi, Pindi Club Ground | March 27, 1965 | Pakistan v New Zealand |
| 44. | Nagpur, Vidarbha Cricket Association Ground | October 3, 1969 | India v New Zealand |
| 45. | Perth, Western Australian Cricket Association Ground | December 11, 1970 | Australia v England |
| 46. | Hyderabad, Niaz Stadium | March 16, 1973 | Pakistan v England |
| 47. | Bangalore, Karnataka State Cricket Association Ground (Chinnaswamy Stadium) | November 22, 1974 | India v West Indies |
| 48. | Bombay, Wankhede Stadium | January 23, 1975 | India v West Indies |
| 49. | Faisalabad, Iqbal Stadium | October 16, 1978 | Pakistan v India |
| 50. | Napier, McLean Park | February 16, 1979 | New Zealand v Pakistan |
| 51. | Multan, Ibn-e-Qasim Bagh Stadium | December 30, 1980 | Pakistan v West Indies |
| 52. | St John's (Antigua), Recreation Ground | March 27, 1981 | West Indies v England |
| 53. | Colombo, P. Saravanamuttu Stadium | February 17, 1982 | Sri Lanka v England |
| 54. | Kandy, Asgiriya Stadium | April 22, 1983 | Sri Lanka v Australia |
| 55. | Jullundur, Burlton Park | September 24, 1983 | India v Pakistan |
| 56. | Ahmedabad, Gujarat Stadium | November 12, 1983 | India v West Indies |
| 57. | Colombo, Sinhalese Sports Club Ground | March 16, 1984 | Sri Lanka v New Zealand |
| 58. | Colombo, Colombo Cricket Club Ground | March 24, 1984 | Sri Lanka v New Zealand |
| 59. | Sialkot, Jinnah Stadium | October 27, 1985 | Pakistan v Sri Lanka |
| 60. | Cuttack, Barabati Stadium | January 4, 1987 | India v Sri Lanka |
| 61. | Jaipur, Sawai Mansingh Stadium | February 21, 1987 | India v Pakistan |
| 62. | Hobart, Bellerive Oval | December 16, 1989 | Australia v Sri Lanka |
| 63. | Chandigarh, Sector 16 Stadium | November 23, 1990 | India v Sri Lanka |
| 64. | Hamilton, Trust Bank Park (Seddon Park) | February 22, 1991 | New Zealand v Sri Lanka |

*\* Denotes no longer used for Test matches. In some instances the ground is no longer in existence.*

# FAMILIES IN TEST CRICKET

## FATHERS AND SONS

**England**

M. C. Cowdrey (114 Tests, 1954-55–1974-75) and C. S. Cowdrey (6 Tests, 1984-85–1988).
J. Hardstaff (5 Tests, 1907-08) and J. Hardstaff jun. (23 Tests, 1935–1948).
L. Hutton (79 Tests, 1937–1954-55) and R. A. Hutton (5 Tests, 1971).
F. T. Mann (5 Tests, 1922-23) and F. G. Mann (7 Tests, 1948-49–1949).
J. H. Parks (1 Test, 1937) and J. M. Parks (46 Tests, 1954–1967-68).
M. J. Stewart (8 Tests, 1962–1963-64) and A. J. Stewart (14 Tests, 1989-90–1991).
F. W. Tate (1 Test, 1902) and M. W. Tate (39 Tests, 1924–1935).
C. L. Townsend (2 Tests, 1899) and D. C. H. Townsend (3 Tests, 1934-35).

**Australia**

E. J. Gregory (1 Test, 1876-77) and S. E. Gregory (58 Tests, 1890–1912).

**South Africa**

F. Hearne (4 Tests, 1891-92–1895-96) and G. A. L. Hearne (3 Tests, 1922-23–1924).
  *F. Hearne also played 2 Tests for England in 1888-89.*
J. D. Lindsay (3 Tests, 1947) and D. T. Lindsay (19 Tests, 1963-64–1969-70).
A. W. Nourse (45 Tests, 1902-03–1924) and A. D. Nourse (34 Tests, 1935–1951).
L. R. Tuckett (1 Test, 1913-14) and L. Tuckett (9 Tests, 1947–1948-49).

**West Indies**

G. A. Headley (22 Tests, 1929-30–1953-54) and R. G. A. Headley (2 Tests, 1973).
O. C. Scott (8 Tests, 1928–1930-31) and A. P. H. Scott (1 Test, 1952-53).

**New Zealand**

W. M. Anderson (1 Test, 1945-46) and R. W. Anderson (9 Tests, 1976-77–1978).
W. P. Bradburn (2 Tests, 1963-64) and G. E. Bradburn (4 Tests, 1990-91).
B. L. Cairns (43 Tests, 1973-74–1985-86) and C. L. Cairns (2 Tests, 1989-90–1990-91).
W. A. Hadlee (11 Tests, 1937–1950-51) and D. R. Hadlee (26 Tests, 1969–1977-78); Sir R. J. Hadlee (86 Tests, 1972-73–1990).
H. G. Vivian (7 Tests, 1931–1937) and G. E. Vivian (5 Tests, 1964-65–1971-72).

**India**

L. Amarnath (24 Tests, 1933-34–1952-53) and M. Amarnath (69 Tests, 1969-70–1987-88); S. Amarnath (10 Tests, 1975-76–1978-79).
D. K. Gaekwad (11 Tests, 1952–1960-61) and A. D. Gaekwad (40 Tests, 1974-75–1984-85).
Nawab of Pataudi (Iftikhar Ali Khan) (3 Tests, 1946) and Nawab of Pataudi (Mansur Ali Khan) (46 Tests, 1961-62–1974-75).
  *Nawab of Pataudi sen. also played 3 Tests for England, 1932-33–1934.*
V. L. Manjrekar (55 Tests, 1951-52–1964-65) and S. V. Manjrekar (16 Tests, 1987-88–1990-91).
V. Mankad (44 Tests, 1946–1958-59) and A. V. Mankad (22 Tests, 1969-70–1977-78).
Pankaj Roy (43 Tests, 1951-52–1960-61) and Pranab Roy (2 Tests, 1981-82).

**India and Pakistan**

M. Jahangir Khan (4 Tests, 1932–1936) and Majid Khan (63 Tests, 1964-65–1982-83).
S. Wazir Ali (7 Tests, 1932–1936) and Khalid Wazir (2 Tests, 1954).

**Pakistan**

Hanif Mohammad (55 Tests, 1954–1969-70) and Shoaib Mohammad (35 Tests, 1983-84–1990-91).
Nazar Mohammad (5 Tests, 1952-53) and Mudassar Nazar (76 Tests, 1976-77–1988-89).

## GRANDFATHERS AND GRANDSONS

**Australia**

V. Y. Richardson (19 Tests, 1924-25–1935-36) and G. S. Chappell (87 Tests, 1970-71–1983-84); I. M. Chappell (75 Tests, 1964-65–1979-80); T. M. Chappell (3 Tests, 1981).

## GREAT-GRANDFATHER AND GREAT-GRANDSON

**Australia**
W. H. Cooper (2 Tests, 1881-82 and 1884-85) and A. P. Sheahan (31 Tests, 1967-68–1973-74).

## BROTHERS IN SAME TEST TEAM

**England**
E. M., G. F. and W. G. Grace: 1 Test, 1880.
C. T. and G. B. Studd: 4 Tests, 1882-83.
A. and G. G. Hearne: 1 Test, 1891-92.
  *F. Hearne, their brother, played in this match for South Africa.*
D. W. and P. E. Richardson: 1 Test, 1957.

**Australia**
E. J. and D. W. Gregory: 1 Test, 1876-77.
C. and A. C. Bannerman: 1 Test, 1878-79.
G. and W. F. Giffen: 2 Tests, 1891-92.
G. H. S. and A. E. Trott: 3 Tests, 1894-95.
I. M. and G. S. Chappell: 43 Tests, 1970-71–1979-80.
S. R. and M. E. Waugh: 2 Tests, 1990-91 – the first instance of twins appearing together.

**South Africa**
S. J. and S. D. Snooke: 1 Test, 1907.
D. and H. W. Taylor: 2 Tests, 1913-14.
R. H. M. and P. A. M. Hands: 1 Test, 1913-14.
E. A. B. and A. M. B. Rowan: 9 Tests, 1948-49–1951.
P. M. and R. G. Pollock: 23 Tests, 1963-64–1969-70.
A. J. and D. B. Pithey: 5 Tests, 1963-64.

**West Indies**
G. C. and R. S. Grant: 4 Tests, 1934-35.
J. B. and V. H. Stollmeyer: 1 Test, 1939.
D. St E. and E. St E. Atkinson: 1 Test, 1957-58.

**New Zealand**
J. J. and M. D. Crowe: 34 Tests, 1983–1989-90.
D. R. and R. J. Hadlee: 10 Tests, 1973–1977-78.
H. J. and G. P. Howarth: 4 Tests, 1974-75–1976-77.
J. M. and N. M. Parker: 3 Tests, 1976-77.
B. P. and J. G. Bracewell: 1 Test, 1980-81.

**India**
S. Wazir Ali and S. Nazir Ali: 2 Tests, 1932–1933-34.
L. Ramji and Amar Singh: 1 Test, 1933-34.
C. K. and C. S. Nayudu: 4 Tests, 1933-34–1936.
A. G. Kripal Singh and A. G. Milkha Singh: 1 Test, 1961-62.
S. and M. Amarnath: 8 Tests, 1975-76–1978-79.

**Pakistan**
Wazir and Hanif Mohammad: 18 Tests, 1952-53–1959-60.
Wazir and Mushtaq Mohammad: 1 Test, 1958-59.
Hanif and Mushtaq Mohammad: 19 Tests, 1960-61–1969-70.
Hanif, Mushtaq and Sadiq Mohammad: 1 Test, 1969-70.
Mushtaq and Sadiq Mohammad: 26 Tests, 1969-70–1978–79.
Wasim and Ramiz Raja: 2 Tests, 1983-84.

**Sri Lanka**
A. and D. Ranatunga: 2 Tests, 1989-90.
M. D. and S. Wettimuny: 2 Tests, 1982-83.

# LIMITED-OVERS INTERNATIONAL RECORDS

*Note:* Limited-overs international matches do not have first-class status.

## SUMMARY OF ALL LIMITED-OVERS INTERNATIONALS

To October 16, 1991

| | | *Matches* | *E* | *A* | *I* | *NZ* | *P* | *SL* | *WI* | *B* | *C* | *EA* | *Z* | *Tied* | *NR* |
|---|---|---|---|---|---|---|---|---|---|---|---|---|---|---|---|
| | | | | | | | *Won by* | | | | | | | | |
| **England** | v Australia | 51 | 24 | 25 | – | – | – | – | – | – | – | – | – | 1 | 1 |
| | v India | 22 | 12 | – | 10 | – | – | – | – | – | – | – | – | – | – |
| | v New Zealand | 36 | 17 | – | – | 16 | – | – | – | – | – | – | – | – | 3 |
| | v Pakistan | 29 | 19 | – | – | – | 10 | – | – | – | – | – | – | – | – |
| | v Sri Lanka | 8 | 7 | – | – | – | – | 1 | – | – | – | – | – | – | – |
| | v West Indies | 42 | 17 | – | – | – | – | – | 23 | – | – | – | – | – | 2 |
| | v Canada | 1 | 1 | – | – | – | – | – | – | – | 0 | – | – | – | – |
| | v East Africa | 1 | 1 | – | – | – | – | – | – | – | – | 0 | – | – | – |
| **Australia** | v India | 33 | – | 18 | 12 | – | – | – | – | – | – | – | – | – | 3 |
| | v New Zealand | 49 | – | 34 | – | 13 | – | – | – | – | – | – | – | – | 2 |
| | v Pakistan | 33 | – | 15 | – | – | 16 | – | – | – | – | – | – | – | 2 |
| | v Sri Lanka | 20 | – | 15 | – | – | – | 3 | – | – | – | – | – | – | 2 |
| | v West Indies | 58 | – | 21 | – | – | – | – | 36 | – | – | – | – | 1 | – |
| | v Bangladesh | 1 | – | 1 | – | – | – | – | – | 0 | – | – | – | – | – |
| | v Canada | 1 | – | 1 | – | – | – | – | – | – | 0 | – | – | – | – |
| | v Zimbabwe | 4 | – | 3 | – | – | – | – | – | – | – | – | – | 1 | – |
| **India** | v New Zealand | 28 | – | – | 16 | 12 | – | – | – | – | – | – | – | – | – |
| | v Pakistan | 34 | – | – | 10 | – | 22 | – | – | – | – | – | – | – | 2 |
| | v Sri Lanka | 25 | – | – | 17 | – | – | 7 | – | – | – | – | – | – | 1 |
| | v West Indies | 33 | – | – | 6 | – | – | – | 27 | – | – | – | – | – | – |
| | v Bangladesh | 2 | – | – | 2 | – | – | – | – | 0 | – | – | – | – | – |
| | v East Africa | 1 | – | – | 1 | – | – | – | – | – | – | 0 | – | – | – |
| | v Zimbabwe | 4 | – | – | 4 | – | – | – | – | – | – | – | 0 | – | – |
| **New Zealand** | v Pakistan | 23 | – | – | – | 11 | 11 | – | – | – | – | – | – | – | 1 |
| | v Sri Lanka | 22 | – | – | – | 18 | – | 4 | – | – | – | – | – | – | – |
| | v West Indies | 13 | – | – | – | 1 | – | – | 11 | – | – | – | – | – | 1 |
| | v Bangladesh | 1 | – | – | – | 1 | – | – | – | 0 | – | – | – | – | – |
| | v East Africa | 1 | – | – | – | 1 | – | – | – | – | – | 0 | – | – | – |
| | v Zimbabwe | 2 | – | – | – | 2 | – | – | – | – | – | – | 0 | – | – |
| **Pakistan** | v Sri Lanka | 30 | – | – | – | – | 23 | 6 | – | – | – | – | – | – | 1 |
| | v West Indies | 51 | – | – | – | – | 16 | – | 35 | – | – | – | – | – | – |
| | v Bangladesh | 2 | – | – | – | – | 2 | – | – | 0 | – | – | – | – | – |
| | v Canada | 1 | – | – | – | – | 1 | – | – | – | 0 | – | – | – | – |
| **Sri Lanka** | v West Indies | 11 | – | – | – | – | – | 1 | 10 | – | – | – | – | – | – |
| | v Bangladesh | 3 | – | – | – | – | – | 3 | – | 0 | – | – | – | – | – |
| **West Indies** | v Zimbabwe | 2 | – | – | – | – | – | – | 2 | – | – | – | 0 | – | – |
| | | 678 | 98 | 133 | 78 | 75 | 101 | 25 | 144 | 0 | 0 | 0 | 1 | 2 | 21 |

| | *Matches* | *Won* | *Lost* | *Tied* | *No Result* | *% Won (excl. NR)* |
|---|---|---|---|---|---|---|
| West Indies | 210 | 144 | 62 | 1 | 3 | 69.56 |
| Australia | 250 | 133 | 105 | 2 | 10 | 55.41 |
| England | 190 | 98 | 85 | 1 | 6 | 53.26 |
| Pakistan | 203 | 101 | 96 | – | 6 | 51.26 |
| New Zealand | 175 | 75 | 93 | – | 7 | 44.64 |
| India | 182 | 78 | 98 | – | 6 | 44.31 |
| Sri Lanka | 119 | 25 | 90 | – | 4 | 21.73 |
| Zimbabwe | 12 | 1 | 11 | – | – | 8.33 |
| Bangladesh | 9 | – | 9 | – | – | |
| Canada | 3 | – | 3 | – | – | |
| East Africa | 3 | – | 3 | – | – | |

## 3,500 OR MORE RUNS

| | M | I | NO | R | HI | 100s | Avge |
|---|---|---|---|---|---|---|---|
| D. L. Haynes (West Indies) . . . . . . . | 182 | 181 | 23 | 6,780 | 152* | 16 | 42.91 |
| I. V. A. Richards (West Indies) . . . . | 187 | 167 | 24 | 6,721 | 189* | 11 | 47.00 |
| Javed Miandad (Pakistan) . . . . . . . | 176 | 167 | 32 | 5,654 | 119* | 6 | 41.88 |
| A. R. Border (Australia) . . . . . . . . . | 223 | 208 | 30 | 5,620 | 127* | 3 | 31.57 |
| C. G. Greenidge (West Indies) . . . . | 128 | 127 | 13 | 5,134 | 133* | 11 | 45.03 |
| D. M. Jones (Australia) . . . . . . . . . | 115 | 113 | 21 | 4,576 | 145 | 7 | 49.73 |
| R. B. Richardson (West Indies) . . . . | 137 | 134 | 17 | 4,206 | 110 | 3 | 35.94 |
| G. R. Marsh (Australia) . . . . . . . . . | 102 | 101 | 6 | 3,924 | 126* | 9 | 41.30 |
| J. G. Wright (New Zealand) . . . . . . | 141 | 140 | 1 | 3,767 | 101 | 1 | 27.10 |
| A. J. Lamb (England) . . . . . . . . . . . . | 110 | 106 | 16 | 3,710 | 118 | 4 | 41.22 |
| G. A. Gooch (England) . . . . . . . . . . | 96 | 94 | 5 | 3,641 | 142 | 8 | 40.91 |
| K. Srikkanth (India) . . . . . . . . . . . . | 126 | 125 | 3 | 3,541 | 123 | 4 | 29.02 |
| D. B. Vengsarkar (India) . . . . . . . . | 128 | 120 | 19 | 3,508 | 105 | 1 | 34.73 |

*The leading aggregate for Sri Lanka is:*

| | | | | | | | |
|---|---|---|---|---|---|---|---|
| A. Ranatunga (Sri Lanka) . . . . . . . | 99 | 96 | 18 | 2,594 | 86* | 0 | 33.25 |

## HIGHEST INDIVIDUAL SCORE FOR EACH COUNTRY

| | | | |
|---|---|---|---|
| 189* | I. V. A. Richards | **West Indies** v England at Manchester . . . . . . . . . . . . . . . | 1984 |
| 175* | Kapil Dev | **India** v Zimbabwe at Tunbridge Wells . . . . . . . . . . . | 1983 |
| 171* | G. M. Turner | **New Zealand** v East Africa at Birmingham . . . . . . . | 1975 |
| 158 | D. I. Gower | **England** v New Zealand at Brisbane . . . . . . . . . . . . . | 1982-83 |
| 145 | D. M. Jones | **Australia** v England at Brisbane . . . . . . . . . . . . . . . . . | 1990-91 |
| 126* | Shoaib Mohammad | **Pakistan** v New Zealand at Wellington . . . . . . . . . . | 1988-89 |
| 121 | R. L. Dias | **Sri Lanka** v India at Bangalore . . . . . . . . . . . . . . . . | 1982-83 |

## SEVEN OR MORE HUNDREDS

| Total | | E | A | WI | NZ | I | P | SL | Others |
|---|---|---|---|---|---|---|---|---|---|
| 16 | D. L. Haynes (West Indies) . . . . . | 1 | 6 | – | 2 | 2 | 4 | 1 | 0 |
| 11 | C. G. Greenidge (West Indies) . . . | 0 | 1 | – | 3 | 3 | 2 | 1 | 1 |
| 11 | I. V. A. Richards (West Indies) . | 3 | 3 | – | 1 | 3 | 0 | 1 | 0 |
| 9 | G. R. Marsh (Australia) . . . . . . . | 1 | – | 2 | 2 | 3 | 1 | 0 | 0 |
| 8 | G. A. Gooch (England) . . . . . . . . | – | 4 | 1 | 1 | 1 | 1 | 0 | 0 |
| 7 | D. I. Gower (England) . . . . . . . . . | – | 2 | 0 | 3 | 0 | 1 | 1 | 0 |
| 7 | D. M. Jones (Australia) . . . . . . . | 3 | – | 0 | 2 | 0 | 1 | 1 | 0 |
| 7 | Zaheer Abbas (Pakistan) . . . . . . . | 0 | 2 | 0 | 1 | 3 | – | 1 | 0 |

## HIGHEST PARTNERSHIP FOR EACH WICKET

| | | | |
|---|---|---|---|
| 212 | for 1st | G. R. Marsh (104) and D. C. Boon (111), Australia v India at Jaipur | 1986-87 |
| 221 | for 2nd | C. G. Greenidge (115) and I. V. A. Richards (149), West Indies v India at Jamshedpur . . . . . . . . . . . . . . . . . . . . . . . . . . . . . . | 1983-84 |
| 224* | for 3rd | D. M. Jones (99*) and A. R. Border (118*), Australia v Sri Lanka at Adelaide . . . . . . . . . . . . . . . . . . . . . . . . . . . . . . . . . . . . . | 1984-85 |
| 173 | for 4th | D. M. Jones (121) and S. R. Waugh (82), Australia v Pakistan at Perth | 1986-87 |
| 152 | for 5th | I. V. A. Richards (98) and C. H. Lloyd (89*), West Indies v Sri Lanka at Brisbane . . . . . . . . . . . . . . . . . . . . . . . . . . . . . . . . . . . . | 1984-85 |
| 144 | for 6th | Imran Khan (102*) and Shahid Mahboob (77), Pakistan v Sri Lanka at Leeds . . . . . . . . . . . . . . . . . . . . . . . . . . . . . . . . . . . . . . . | 1983 |
| 115 | for 7th | P. J. L. Dujon (57*) and M. D. Marshall (66), West Indies v Pakistan at Gujranwala . . . . . . . . . . . . . . . . . . . . . . . . . . . . . . . . . . | 1986-87 |
| 117 | for 8th | D. L. Houghton (141) and I. P. Butchart (54), Zimbabwe v New Zealand at Hyderabad (India) . . . . . . . . . . . . . . . . . . . . . . | 1987-88 |
| 126* | for 9th | Kapil Dev (175*) and S. M. H. Kirmani (24*), India v Zimbabwe at Tunbridge Wells . . . . . . . . . . . . . . . . . . . . . . . . . . . . . . . . . | 1983 |
| 106* | for 10th | I. V. A. Richards (189*) and M. A. Holding (12*), West Indies v England at Manchester . . . . . . . . . . . . . . . . . . . . . . . . . . . . . | 1984 |

## 100 OR MORE WICKETS

| | M | Balls | R | W | BB | 4W/i | Avge |
|---|---|---|---|---|---|---|---|
| Kapil Dev (India) ........... | 163 | 8,225 | 5,150 | 197 | 5-43 | 3 | 26.14 |
| Imran Khan (Pakistan) ....... | 154 | 6,553 | 4,209 | 167 | 6-14 | 4 | 25.20 |
| R. J. Hadlee (New Zealand) .. | 115 | 6,182 | 3,407 | 158 | 5-25 | 6 | 21.56 |
| J. Garner (West Indies) ...... | 98 | 5,330 | 2,752 | 146 | 5-31 | 5 | 18.84 |
| M. A. Holding (West Indies) .. | 102 | 5,473 | 3,034 | 142 | 5-26 | 6 | 21.36 |
| M. D. Marshall (West Indies).. | 121 | 6,413 | 3,735 | 142 | 4-23 | 5 | 26.30 |
| E. J. Chatfield (New Zealand).. | 114 | 6,065 | 3,621 | 140 | 5-34 | 3 | 25.86 |
| Wasim Akram (Pakistan) ..... | 99 | 4,941 | 3,131 | 133 | 5-21 | 5 | 23.54 |
| Abdul Qadir (Pakistan) ..... | 102 | 4,996 | 3,364 | 131 | 5-44 | 6 | 25.67 |
| I. T. Botham (England) ....... | 99 | 5,335 | 3,556 | 122 | 4-45 | 2 | 29.14 |
| I. V. A. Richards (West Indies) | 187 | 5,644 | 4,228 | 118 | 6-41 | 3 | 35.83 |
| R. J. Shastri (India) .......... | 128 | 5,810 | 4,068 | 115 | 4-38 | 2 | 35.37 |
| M. C. Snedden (New Zealand) . | 93 | 4,519 | 3,235 | 114 | 4-34 | 1 | 28.37 |
| Mudassar Nazar (Pakistan) ... | 122 | 4,855 | 3,431 | 111 | 5-28 | 2 | 30.90 |
| C. A. Walsh (West Indies) .... | 96 | 5,115 | 3,326 | 108 | 5-1 | 5 | 30.79 |
| S. P. O'Donnell (Australia) ... | 85 | 4,248 | 3,028 | 107 | 5-13 | 6 | 28.29 |
| D. K. Lillee (Australia) ....... | 63 | 3,593 | 2,145 | 103 | 5-34 | 6 | 20.82 |
| C. J. McDermott (Australia).. | 70 | 3,783 | 2,773 | 103 | 5-44 | 4 | 26.92 |
| S. R. Waugh (Australia) ..... | 111 | 4,255 | 3,191 | 100 | 4-33 | 2 | 31.91 |

*The leading aggregate for Sri Lanka is:*

| | | | | | | | |
|---|---|---|---|---|---|---|---|
| J. R. Ratnayeke ............. | 78 | 3,573 | 2,865 | 85 | 4-23 | 1 | 33.70 |

## BEST BOWLING FOR EACH COUNTRY

| | | | |
|---|---|---|---|
| 7-51 | W. W. Davis | **West Indies** v Australia at Leeds ............. | 1983 |
| 6-14 | G. J. Gilmour | **Australia** v England at Leeds ................. | 1975 |
| 6-14 | Imran Khan | **Pakistan** v India at Sharjah ................. | 1984-85 |
| 5-20 | V. J. Marks | **England** v New Zealand at Wellington ...... | 1983-84 |
| 5-21 | Arshad Ayub | **India** v Pakistan at Dhaka ................. | 1988-89 |
| 5-23 | R. O. Collinge | **New Zealand** v India at Christchurch ...... | 1975-76 |
| 5-26 | S. H. U. Karnain | **Sri Lanka** v New Zealand at Moratuwa ........ | 1983-84 |

## HAT-TRICKS

| | | |
|---|---|---|
| Jalal-ud-Din | Pakistan v Australia at Hyderabad ................... | 1982-83 |
| B. A. Reid | Australia v New Zealand at Sydney .................. | 1985-86 |
| Chetan Sharma | India v New Zealand at Nagpur ..................... | 1987-88 |
| Wasim Akram | Pakistan v West Indies at Sharjah ................... | 1989-90 |
| Wasim Akram | Pakistan v Australia at Sharjah ..................... | 1989-90 |
| Kapil Dev | India v Sri Lanka at Calcutta ...................... | 1990-91 |

## MOST DISMISSALS IN A MATCH

| | | | |
|---|---|---|---|
| 5 (all ct) | R. W. Marsh ....... | Australia v England at Leeds .......... | 1981 |
| 5 (all ct) | R. G. de Alwis ..... | Sri Lanka v Australia at Colombo (PSS) . | 1982-83 |
| 5 (all ct) | S. M. H. Kirmani ... | India v Zimbabwe at Leicester ......... | 1983 |
| 5 (3ct, 2st) | S. Viswanath ....... | India v England at Sydney ............ | 1984-85 |
| 5 (3ct, 2st) | K. S. More ........ | India v New Zealand at Sharjah ....... | 1987-88 |
| 5 (all ct) | H. P. Tillekeratne ... | Sri Lanka v Pakistan at Sharjah ....... | 1990-91 |

## 50 OR MORE DISMISSALS

|  | M | Ct | St | Total |
|---|---|---|---|---|
| P. J. L. Dujon (West Indies).......... | 165 | 181 | 19 | 200 |
| R. W. Marsh (Australia).............. | 92 | 120 | 4 | 124 |
| Salim Yousuf (Pakistan) .............. | 86 | 81 | 22 | 103 |
| I. D. S. Smith (New Zealand)........ | 86 | 72 | 5 | 77 |
| I. A. Healy (Australia)............... | 53 | 61 | 8 | 69 |
| K. S. More (India).................. | 63 | 38 | 24 | 62 |
| Wasim Bari (Pakistan)............... | 51 | 52 | 10 | 62 |

## MOST CATCHES IN A MATCH

### (Excluding wicket-keepers)

| 4 | Salim Malik....... | Pakistan v New Zealand at Sialkot ............ | 1984-85 |
|---|---|---|---|
| 4 | S. M. Gavaskar.... | India v Pakistan at Sharjah ................. | 1984-85 |
| 4 | R. B. Richardson ... | West Indies v England at Birmingham.......... | 1991 |

*Note:* While fielding as substitute, J. G. Bracewell held 4 catches for New Zealand v Australia at Adelaide, 1980-81.

## 50 OR MORE CATCHES

|  | M | Ct |  | M | Ct |
|---|---|---|---|---|---|
| A. R. Border (A) | 223 | 102 | Kapil Dev (I) | 163 | 58 |
| I. V. A. Richards (WI) | 187 | 101 | M. D. Crowe (NZ) | 111 | 53 |
| Javed Miandad (P) | 176 | 60 | J. G. Wright (NZ) | 141 | 50 |

## ALL-ROUND

### 1,000 Runs and 100 Wickets

|  | M | R | W |
|---|---|---|---|
| I. T. Botham (England)............ | 99 | 1,738 | 122 |
| R. J. Hadlee (New Zealand)....... | 115 | 1,749 | 158 |
| Imran Khan (Pakistan) ............ | 154 | 3,255 | 167 |
| Kapil Dev (India) ................ | 163 | 3,132 | 197 |
| Mudassar Nazar (Pakistan) ....... | 122 | 2,654 | 111 |
| S. P. O'Donnell (Australia) ........ | 85 | 1,232 | 107 |
| I. V. A. Richards (West Indies) .... | 187 | 6,721 | 118 |
| R. J. Shastri (India)............... | 128 | 2,567 | 115 |
| S. R. Waugh (Australia) .......... | 111 | 2,295 | 100 |

### 1,000 Runs and 100 Dismissals

|  | M | R | D |
|---|---|---|---|
| P. J. L. Dujon (West Indies) ...... | 165 | 1,877 | 200 |
| R. W. Marsh (Australia).......... | 92 | 1,225 | 124 |

## HIGHEST INNINGS TOTALS

| 360-4 | (50 overs) | **West Indies** v Sri Lanka at Karachi ............... | 1987-88 |
|---|---|---|---|
| 338-4 | (50 overs) | **New Zealand** v Bangladesh at Sharjah .............. | 1989-90 |
| 338-5 | (60 overs) | **Pakistan** v Sri Lanka at Swansea .................. | 1983 |
| 334-4 | (60 overs) | **England** v India at Lord's ...................... | 1975 |
| 333-8 | (45 overs) | West Indies v India at Jamshedpur ................. | 1983-84 |
| 333-9 | (60 overs) | England v Sri Lanka at Taunton ................... | 1983 |
| 332-3 | (50 overs) | **Australia** v Sri Lanka at Sharjah.................. | 1989-90 |
| 330-6 | (60 overs) | Pakistan v Sri Lanka at Nottingham ............... | 1975 |

*Note:* The highest score by **India** is 299-4 (40 overs) v Sri Lanka at Bombay, 1986-87, and the highest by **Sri Lanka** is 289-7 (40 overs) v India at Bombay, 1986-87.

## HIGHEST TOTALS BATTING SECOND

### Winning

| | | | |
|---|---|---|---|
| 298-6 | (54.5 overs) | New Zealand v England at Leeds................ | 1990 |
| 297-6 | (48.5 overs) | New Zealand v England at Adelaide ............ | 1982-83 |

### Losing

| | | | |
|---|---|---|---|
| 289-7 | (40 overs) | Sri Lanka v India at Bombay ...................... | 1986-87 |
| 288-9 | (60 overs) | Sri Lanka v Pakistan at Swansea ................. | 1983 |

## HIGHEST MATCH AGGREGATES

| | | | |
|---|---|---|---|
| 626-14 | (120 overs) | Pakistan v Sri Lanka at Swansea ................. | 1983 |
| 619-19 | (118 overs) | England v Sri Lanka at Taunton................. | 1983 |
| 604-9 | (120 overs) | Australia v Sri Lanka at The Oval ............... | 1975 |
| 603-11 | (100 overs) | Pakistan v Sri Lanka at Adelaide ............... | 1989-90 |

## LOWEST INNINGS TOTALS

| | | | |
|---|---|---|---|
| 45 | (40.3 overs) | Canada v England at Manchester.................. | 1979 |
| 55 | (28.3 overs) | **Sri Lanka** v West Indies at Sharjah ............. | 1986-87 |
| 63 | (25.5 overs) | **India** v Australia at Sydney .................... | 1980-81 |
| 64 | (35.5 overs) | **New Zealand** v Pakistan at Sharjah ............. | 1985-86 |
| 70 | (25.2 overs) | **Australia** v England at Birmingham .............. | 1977 |
| 70 | (26.3 overs) | Australia v New Zealand at Adelaide ............. | 1985-86 |
| 74 | (29 overs) | New Zealand v Australia at Wellington ........... | 1981-82 |
| 74 | (31.1 overs) | New Zealand v Pakistan at Sharjah ............... | 1989-90 |
| 78 | (24.1 overs) | India v Sri Lanka at Kanpur.................... | 1986-87 |
| 79 | (34.2 overs) | India v Pakistan at Sialkot ..................... | 1978-79 |
| 85 | (47 overs) | **Pakistan** v England at Manchester ............... | 1978 |

*Notes:* This section does not take into account those matches in which the number of overs was reduced.

The lowest innings total by **England** is 93 (36.2 overs) v Australia at Leeds, 1975, and the lowest by **West Indies** is 111 (41.4 overs) v Pakistan at Melbourne, 1983-84.

## LARGEST VICTORIES

| | |
|---|---|
| 232 runs | Australia (323-2 in 50 overs) v Sri Lanka (91 in 35.5 overs) at Adelaide....................................... 1984-85 |
| 206 runs | New Zealand (276-7 in 50 overs) v Australia (70 in 26.3 overs) at Adelaide....................................... 1985-86 |
| 202 runs | England (334-4 in 60 overs) v India (132-3 in 60 overs) at Lord's .... 1975 |

**By ten wickets:** There have been seven instances of victory by ten wickets.

## TIED MATCHES

| | |
|---|---|
| West Indies 222-5 (50 overs), Australia 222-9 (50 overs) at Melbourne ......... | 1983-84 |
| England 226-5 (55 overs), Australia 226-8 (55 overs) at Nottingham ........... | 1989 |

## WORLD CUP FINALS

| | |
|---|---|
| 1975 (60 overs) | West Indies (291-8) beat Australia (274) by 17 runs at Lord's. |
| 1979 (60 overs) | West Indies (286-9) beat England (194) by 92 runs at Lord's. |
| 1983 (60 overs) | India (183) beat West Indies (140) by 43 runs at Lord's. |
| 1987 (50 overs) | Australia (253-5) beat England (246-8) by 7 runs at Calcutta. |

# MISCELLANEOUS

## LARGE ATTENDANCES

**Test Series**

| | | |
|---|---|---|
| 943,000 | Australia v England (5 Tests) .................... | 1936-37 |
| *In England* | | |
| 549,650 | England v Australia (5 Tests) .................... | 1953 |

**Test Match**

| | | |
|---|---|---|
| †350,534 | Australia v England, Melbourne (Third Test) ......... | 1936-37 |
| 325,000+ | India v England, Calcutta (Second Test) ............ | 1972-73 |
| *In England* | | |
| 158,000+ | England v Australia, Leeds (Fourth Test) ........... | 1948 |
| 137,915 | England v Australia, Lord's (Second Test) ........... | 1953 |

**Test Match Day**

| | | |
|---|---|---|
| 90,800 | Australia v West Indies, Melbourne (Fifth Test, 2nd day) ...... | 1960-61 |

**Other First-Class Matches in England**

| | | |
|---|---|---|
| 80,000+ | Surrey v Yorkshire, The Oval (3 days) ..................... | 1906 |
| 78,792 | Yorkshire v Lancashire, Leeds (3 days) ................... | 1904 |
| 76,617 | Lancashire v Yorkshire, Manchester (3 days) ............... | 1926 |

**One-day International**

| | | |
|---|---|---|
| 86,133‡ | Australia v West Indies, Melbourne ..................... | 1983-84 |

† *Although no official figures are available, the attendance at the Fourth Test between India and England at Calcutta, 1981-82, was thought to have exceeded this figure.*

‡ *It is estimated that a crowd of more than 90,000 attended the one-day international between India and Pakistan at Calcutta, 1986-87. However, this figure has not been confirmed.*

## LORD'S CRICKET GROUND

Lord's and the MCC were founded in 1787. The Club has enjoyed an uninterrupted career since that date, but there have been three grounds known as Lord's. The first (1787-1810) was situated where Dorset Square now is; the second (1809-13), at North Bank, had to be abandoned owing to the cutting of the Regent's Canal; and the third, opened in 1814, is the present one at St John's Wood. It was not until 1866 that the freehold of Lord's was secured by the MCC. The present pavilion was erected in 1890 at a cost of £21,000.

## HIGHEST INDIVIDUAL SCORES MADE AT LORD'S

| | | | |
|---|---|---|---|
| 333 | G. A. Gooch ....... | England v India .................... | 1990 |
| 316* | J. B. Hobbs ........ | Surrey v Middlesex .................... | 1926 |
| 315* | P. Holmes ......... | Yorkshire v Middlesex .................... | 1925 |
| 281* | W. H. Ponsford..... | Australians v MCC .................... | 1934 |
| 278 | W. Ward .......... | MCC v Norfolk (with E. H. Budd, T. Vigne and F. Ladbroke) .................... | 1820 |
| 278 | D. G. Bradman..... | Australians v MCC .................... | 1938 |
| 277* | E. H. Hendren ..... | Middlesex v Kent .................... | 1922 |

*Note:* The longest innings in a first-class match at Lord's was played by S. Wettimuny (636 minutes, 190 runs) for Sri Lanka v England, 1984.

## HIGHEST TOTALS OBTAINED AT LORD'S

**First-Class Matches**

| | | |
|---|---|---|
| 729-6 dec. | Australia v England . . . . . . . . . . . . . . . . . . . . . . | 1930 |
| 665 | West Indians v Middlesex . . . . . . . . . . . . . . . . . . | 1939 |
| 653-4 dec. | England v India . . . . . . . . . . . . . . . . . . . | 1990 |
| 652-8 dec. | West Indies v England . . . . . . . . . . . . . . . . . . . . . . | 1973 |
| 629 | England v India . . . . . . . . . . . . . . . . . . . | 1974 |
| 612-8 dec. | Middlesex v Nottinghamshire . . . . . . . . . . . . . . | 1921 |
| 610-5 dec. | Australians v Gentlemen . . . . . . . . . . . . . . . . . . | 1948 |
| 609-8 dec. | Cambridge University v MCC and Ground . . . . . . . . . . . . | 1913 |
| 608-7 dec. | Middlesex v Hampshire . . . . . . . . . . . . . . . . . . | 1919 |
| 607 | MCC and Ground v Cambridge University . . . . . . . . . . . . | 1902 |

**Minor Match**

| | | |
|---|---|---|
| 735-9 dec. | MCC and Ground v Wiltshire . . . . . . . . . . . . . . . . . . . . . . | 1888 |

## BIGGEST HIT AT LORD'S

The only known instance of a batsman hitting a ball over the present pavilion at Lord's occurred when A. E. Trott, appearing for MCC against Australians on July 31, August 1, 2, 1899, drove M. A. Noble so far and high that the ball struck a chimney pot and fell behind the building.

## HIGHEST SCORE IN A MINOR COUNTY MATCH

| | | | |
|---|---|---|---|
| 323* | F. E. Lacey | Hampshire v Norfolk at Southampton . . . . . . . . . . . | 1887 |

## HIGHEST SCORE IN MINOR COUNTIES CHAMPIONSHIP

| | | | |
|---|---|---|---|
| 282 | E. Garnett | Berkshire v Wiltshire at Reading . . . . . . . . . . . . . . . | 1908 |
| 254 | H. E. Morgan | Glamorgan v Monmouthshire at Cardiff . . . . . . . . . . | 1901 |
| 253* | G. J. Whittaker | Surrey II v Gloucestershire II at The Oval . . . . . . . | 1950 |
| 253 | A. Booth | Lancashire II v Lincolnshire at Grimsby . . . . . . . . . | 1950 |
| 252 | J. A. Deed | Kent II v Surrey II at The Oval (on début) . . . . . . . | 1924 |

## HIGHEST SCORE FOR ENGLISH PUBLIC SCHOOL

| | | | |
|---|---|---|---|
| 278 | J. L. Guise | Winchester v Eton at Eton . . . . . . . . . . . . . . . . . . | 1921 |

## HIGHEST SCORES IN OTHER MATCHES

| | | |
|---|---|---|
| 628* | A. E. J. Collins, Clark's House v North Town at Clifton College.<br>(A Junior House match. His innings of 6 hours 50 minutes was spread over four afternoons.) . . . . . . . . . . . . . . . . . . | 1899 |
| 566 | C. J. Eady, Break-o'-Day v Wellington at Hobart . . . . . . . . . . . . | 1901-02 |
| 515 | D. R. Havewalla, B.B. and C.I. Rly v St Xavier's at Bombay . . . . . . . . | 1933-34 |
| 506* | J. C. Sharp, Melbourne GS v Geelong College at Melbourne . . . . . . . | 1914-15 |
| 502* | Chaman Lal, Mehandra Coll., Patiala v Government Coll., Rupar at Patiala | 1956-57 |
| 485 | A. E. Stoddart, Hampstead v Stoics at Hampstead . . . . . . . . . . . | 1886 |
| 475* | Mohammad Iqbal, Muslim Model HS v Islamia HS, Sialkot at Lahore . . . | 1958-59 |
| 466* | G. T. S. Stevens, Beta v Lambda (University College School House match) at Neasden . . . . . . . . . . . . . . . . . . | 1919 |
| 459 | J. A. Prout, Wesley College v Geelong College at Geelong . . . . . . . . . . . | 1908-09 |

## HIGHEST PARTNERSHIP IN MINOR CRICKET

664* for 3rd   V. G. Kambli and S. R. Tendulkar, Sharadashram Vidyamandir
          School v St Xavier's High School at Bombay ...............   1987-88

## RECORD HIT

The Rev. W. Fellows, while at practice on the Christ Church ground at Oxford in 1856, drove a ball bowled by Charles Rogers 175 yards from hit to pitch.

## THROWING THE CRICKET BALL

140 yards 2 feet, Robert Percival, on the Durham Sands, Co. Durham Racecourse   c1882
140 yards 9 inches, Ross Mackenzie, at Toronto ............................   1872

*Notes:* W. F. Forbes, on March 16, 1876, threw 132 yards at the Eton College sports. He was then eighteen years of age.

Onochie Onuorah, on June 5, 1987, threw a $4\frac{3}{4}$oz ball 100 yards 1 foot $8\frac{1}{2}$ inches (91.94 metres) at The Abbey School, Westgate, sports. He was then thirteen years of age.

William Yardley, while a boy at Rugby, threw 100 yards with his right hand and 78 yards with his left .

Charles Arnold, of Cambridge, once threw 112 yards with the wind and 108 against.

W. H. Game, at The Oval in 1875, threw the ball 111 yards and then back the same distance. W. G. Grace threw 109 yards one way and back 105, and George Millyard 108 with the wind and 103 against. At The Oval in 1868, W. G. Grace made three successive throws of 116, 117 and 118 yards, and then threw back over 100 yards. D. G. Foster (Warwickshire) threw 133 yards, and in 1930 he made a Danish record with 120.1 metres – about 130 yards.

## DATES OF FORMATION OF COUNTY CLUBS NOW FIRST-CLASS

| County | First known county organisation | Present Club | |
| --- | --- | --- | --- |
| | | Original date | Reorganisation, if substantial |
| Derbyshire ........ | November 4, 1870 | November 4, 1870 | — |
| Durham ........... | January 24, 1874 | May 10, 1882 | — |
| Essex ............ | By May, 1790 | January 14, 1876 | — |
| Glamorgan ........ | 1863 | July 6, 1888 | — |
| Gloucestershire .... | November 3, 1863 | 1871 | — |
| Hampshire ........ | April 3, 1849 | August 12, 1863 | July, 1879 |
| Kent ............. | August 6, 1842 | March 1, 1859 | December 6, 1870 |
| Lancashire ........ | January 12, 1864 | January 12, 1864 | — |
| Leicestershire ...... | By August, 1820 | March 25, 1879 | — |
| Middlesex ........ | December 15, 1863 | February 2, 1864 | — |
| Northamptonshire ... | 1820 | 1820 | July 31, 1878 |
| Nottinghamshire .... | March/April, 1841 | March/April, 1841 | December 11, 1866 |
| Somerset ......... | October 15, 1864 | August 18, 1875 | — |
| Surrey ........... | August 22, 1845 | August 22, 1845 | — |
| Sussex ........... | June 16, 1836 | March 1, 1839 | August, 1857 |
| Warwickshire ...... | May, 1826 | 1882 | — |
| Worcestershire ..... | 1844 | March 5, 1865 | — |
| Yorkshire ......... | March 7, 1861 | January 8, 1863 | December 10, 1891 |

# DATES OF FORMATION OF CLUBS IN THE CURRENT MINOR COUNTIES CHAMPIONSHIP

| County | First known county organisation | Present Club |
|---|---|---|
| Bedfordshire | May, 1847 | November 3, 1899 |
| Berkshire | By May, 1841 | March 17, 1895 |
| Buckinghamshire | November, 1864 | January 15, 1891 |
| Cambridgeshire | March 13, 1844 | June 6, 1891 |
| Cheshire | 1819 | September 29, 1908 |
| Cornwall | 1813 | November 12, 1894 |
| Cumberland | January 2, 1884 | April 10, 1948 |
| Devon | 1824 | November 26, 1899 |
| Dorset | 1862 *or* 1871 | February 5, 1896 |
| Herefordshire | July 13, 1836 | January 9, 1991 |
| Hertfordshire | 1838 | March 8, 1876 |
| Lincolnshire | 1853 | September 28, 1906 |
| Norfolk | January 11, 1827 | October 14, 1876 |
| Northumberland | 1834 | December, 1895 |
| Oxfordshire | 1787 | December 14, 1921 |
| Shropshire | 1819 or 1829 | June 28, 1956 |
| Staffordshire | November 24, 1871 | November 24, 1871 |
| Suffolk | July 27, 1864 | August, 1932 |
| Wiltshire | February 24, 1881 | January, 1893 |

## CONSTITUTION OF COUNTY CHAMPIONSHIP

There are references in the sporting press to a champion county as early as 1825, but the list is not continuous and in some years only two counties contested the title. The earliest reference in any cricket publication is from 1864, and at this time there were eight leading counties who have come to be regarded as first-class from that date – Cambridgeshire, Hampshire, Kent, Middlesex, Nottinghamshire, Surrey, Sussex and Yorkshire. The newly formed Lancashire club began playing inter-county matches in 1865, Gloucestershire in 1870 and Derbyshire in 1871, and they are therefore regarded as first-class from these respective dates. Cambridgeshire dropped out after 1871, Hampshire, who had not played inter-county matches in certain seasons, after 1885, and Derbyshire after 1887. Somerset, who had played matches against the first-class counties since 1879, were regarded as first-class from 1882 to 1885, and were admitted formally to the Championship in 1891. In 1894, Derbyshire, Essex, Leicestershire and Warwickshire were granted first-class status, but did not compete in the Championship until 1895 when Hampshire returned. Worcestershire, Northamptonshire and Glamorgan were admitted to the Championship in 1899, 1905 and 1921 respectively and are regarded as first-class from these dates. An invitation in 1921 to Buckinghamshire to enter the Championship was declined, owing to the lack of necessary playing facilities, and an application by Devon in 1948 was unsuccessful. Durham were admitted to the Championship in 1992 and were granted first-class status prior to their pre-season tour of Zimbabwe.

## MOST COUNTY CHAMPIONSHIP APPEARANCES

| | | | |
|---|---|---|---|
| 763 | W. Rhodes | Yorkshire | 1898-1930 |
| 707 | F. E. Woolley | Kent | 1906-38 |
| 665 | C. P. Mead | Hampshire | 1906-36 |

## MOST CONSECUTIVE COUNTY CHAMPIONSHIP APPEARANCES

| | | | |
|---|---|---|---|
| 423 | K. G. Suttle | Sussex | 1954-69 |
| 412 | J. G. Binks | Yorkshire | 1955-69 |
| 399 | J. Vine | Sussex | 1899-1914 |
| 344 | E. H. Killick | Sussex | 1898-1912 |
| 326 | C. N. Woolley | Northamptonshire | 1913-31 |
| 305 | A. H. Dyson | Glamorgan | 1930-47 |
| 301 | B. Taylor | Essex | 1961-72 |

*Notes:* J. Vine made 417 consecutive appearances for Sussex in all first-class matches between July 1900 and September 1914.

J. G. Binks did not miss a Championship match for Yorkshire between making his début in June 1955 and retiring at the end of the 1969 season.

# FEATURES OF 1991

## Double-Hundreds (18)

| | | |
|---|---|---|
| M. Azharuddin | 212 | Derbyshire v Leicestershire at Leicester. |
| K. J. Barnett | 217 | Derbyshire v Nottinghamshire at Derby. |
| M. R. Benson | 257 | Kent v Hampshire at Southampton. |
| S. J. Cook (2) | 210* | Somerset v Northamptonshire at Northampton. |
| | 209* | Somerset v Sri Lankans at Taunton. |
| T. S. Curtis | 248 | Worcestershire v Somerset at Worcester. |
| D. B. D'Oliveira | 237 | Worcestershire v Oxford University at Oxford. |
| M. W. Gatting | 215* | Middlesex v Derbyshire at Lord's. |
| G. A. Gooch | 259 | Essex v Middlesex at Chelmsford. |
| M. P. Maynard (2) | 204 | Glamorgan v Nottinghamshire at Cardiff. |
| | 243 | Glamorgan v Hampshire at Southampton. |
| T. M. Moody | 210 | Worcestershire v Warwickshire at Worcester. |
| M. D. Moxon | 200 | Yorkshire v Essex at Colchester. |
| Salim Malik | 215 | Essex v Leicestershire at Ilford. |
| C. L. Smith | 200 | Hampshire v Oxford University at Oxford. |
| N. R. Taylor | 203* | Kent v Sussex at Hove. |
| T. R. Ward | 235* | Kent v Middlesex at Canterbury. |
| A. P. Wells | 253* | Sussex v Yorkshire at Middlesbrough. |

## Three Hundreds in Successive Innings

| | |
|---|---|
| N. H. Fairbrother (Lancashire) | 107*, 109 and 102*. |
| N. R. Taylor (Kent) | 101, 111 and 203*. |

## Hundred in Each Innings of a Match (7)

| | | | |
|---|---|---|---|
| A. R. Butcher | 129 | 104 | Glamorgan v Lancashire at Liverpool. |
| S. J. Cook | 197 | 115* | Somerset v Hampshire at Southampton. |
| N. H. Fairbrother | 109 | 102* | Lancashire v Somerset at Taunton. |
| M. P. Maynard | 129 | 126 | Glamorgan v Gloucestershire at Cheltenham. |
| C. L. Smith | 145 | 101 | Hampshire v Sussex at Hove. |
| N. R. Taylor | 111 | 203* | Kent v Sussex at Hove. |
| T. R. Ward | 110 | 109 | Kent v Glamorgan at Maidstone. |

## Fastest Hundred

### (For the Walter Lawrence Trophy)

I. D. Austin ........ 61 balls   Lancashire v Yorkshire at Scarborough.
In 68 minutes, including six sixes and thirteen fours, and while batting at No. 10. It was Austin's maiden first-class hundred.

## Hundred Before Lunch (5)

| | | |
|---|---|---|
| C. J. Adams | 108* | Derbyshire v Cambridge University at Cambridge (3rd day). |
| D. B. D'Oliveira | 157 | Worcestershire v Oxford University at Oxford (2nd day). |
| A. J. Lamb | 100* | Northamptonshire v Lancashire at Lytham (2nd day). |
| A. A. Metcalfe | 104* | Yorkshire v Lancashire at Manchester (3rd day). |
| P. R. Pollard | 108* | Nottinghamshire v Lancashire at Nottingham (1st day). |

## First to 1,000 Runs

H. Morris (Glamorgan) on June 20.

## First to 2,000 Runs

S. J. Cook (Somerset) on August 16 – for the third season in succession.

## Carrying Bat Through Completed Innings (8)

C. W. J. Athey (2)†    77*   Gloucestershire (186) v Somerset at Bristol.
                      103*   Gloucestershire (287) v Sussex at Hove.
D. J. Bicknell . . . . . . 145*   Surrey (268) v Essex at Chelmsford.
N. E. Briers . . . . . . . . 60*   Leicestershire (108) v Northamptonshire at Leicester.
T. S. Curtis . . . . . . . . 186*   Worcestershire (382) v Glamorgan at Cardiff.
G. A. Gooch . . . . . . . 154*   England (252) v West Indies (First Test) at Leeds.
D. L. Haynes. . . . . . .  75*   West Indies (176) v England (Fifth Test) At The Oval.
P. M. Roebuck . . . . .  91*   Somerset (224) v Middlesex at Taunton.

*† In successive innings.*

## First-Wicket Partnership of 100 in Each Innings

274   129   V. P. Terry/C. L. Smith, Hampshire v Sussex at Hove.
161   124   D. J. Bicknell/R. I. Alikhan, Surrey v Nottinghamshire at The Oval.

*Note:* Essex achieved first-wicket partnerships of 168* (G. A. Gooch/N. Shahid) and 118 (J. P. Stephenson/D. R. Pringle) v Cambridge University at Cambridge.

## Other Notable Partnerships

**First Wicket**
300†   N. R. Taylor/M. R. Benson, Kent v Derbyshire at Canterbury.

**Second Wicket**
265    P. R. Pollard/R. T. Robinson, Nottinghamshire v Derbyshire at Derby.
264*   T. S. Curtis/T. M. Moody, Worcestershire v Essex at Ilford.

**Third Wicket**
269    D. Byas/R. J. Blakey, Yorkshire v Oxford University at Oxford.
258    M. W. Gatting/K. R. Brown, Middlesex v Derbyshire at Lord's.
256    T. S. Curtis/D. A. Leatherdale, Worcestershire v Somerset at Worcester.

**Fourth Wicket**
314†   Salim Malik/N. Hussain, Essex v Surrey at The Oval.
287    G. A. Gooch/N. Hussain, Essex v Northamptonshire at Colchester.

**Fifth Wicket**
316†   N. Hussain/M. A. Garnham, Essex v Leicestershire at Leicester.
243    D. B. D'Oliveira/D. A. Leatherdale, Worcestershire v Oxford Univ. at Oxford.

**Seventh Wicket**
219*†  J. D. R. Benson/P. Whitticase, Leicestershire v Hampshire at Bournemouth.

**Eighth Wicket**
184†   S. J. Rhodes/S. R. Lampitt, Worcestershire v Derbyshire at Kidderminster.
178    A. P. Wells/B. T. P. Donelan, Sussex v Yorkshire at Middlesbrough.

**Tenth Wicket**
133    S. P. Titchard/I. D. Austin, Lancashire v Nottinghamshire at Manchester.

*\* Unbroken partnership.      † County record.*

## Twelve Wickets in a Match

D. J. Millns . . . . . . .  12-91  Leicestershire v Derbyshire at Derby.
Waqar Younis . . . . . .  12-92  Surrey v Hampshire at The Oval.

## Eight or More Wickets in an Innings

D. G. Cork . . . . . . . .  8-53†  Derbyshire v Essex at Derby.
N. A. Foster . . . . . .  8-99  Essex v Lancashire at Manchester.
D. R. Gilbert . . . . .  8-55  Gloucestershire v Kent at Canterbury.
D. J. Millns . . . . . . . .  9-37  Leicestershire v Derbyshire at Derby.
T. A. Munton . . . . .  8-89  Warwickshire v Middlesex at Birmingham.

† *Before lunch on the second day, his twentieth birthday.*

## First to 100 Wickets

Waqar Younis (Surrey) on September 4.

## Nine Wicket-Keeping Dismissals in a Match

S. A. Marsh  (9 ct) . . . . . .  Kent v Middlesex at Lord's.

## Six or More Wicket-Keeping Dismissals in an Innings

M. A. Garnham  (6 ct) . . . . . .  Essex v Warwickshire at Chelmsford.
S. A. Marsh (2)  (8 ct)† . . . . . .  Kent v Middlesex at Lord's.
  (6 ct) . . . . . .  Kent v Leicestershire at Leicester.
C. P. Metson (2)  (6 ct) . . . . . .  Glamorgan v Oxford Univ. at Oxford.
  (7 ct)‡ . . . . . .  Glamorgan v Derbyshire at Chesterfield.

† *Equalled world record, and a new county record.*  ‡ *County record.*

## Match Double (100 Runs and 10 Wickets)

K. T. Medlycott . . . .  2, 109; 5-36, 6-98  Surrey v Cambridge Univ. at Cambridge.

## 100 Runs and Eight Dismissals in an Innings

S. A. Marsh . . . . . . . .  108*; 8 ct  Kent v Middlesex at Lord's.

## No Byes Conceded in Total of 500 or More

N. D. Burns . . .  Somerset v Worcestershire (575-8 dec.) at Worcester.
S. A. Marsh . . . .  Kent v Essex (544) at Folkestone.
W. K. Hegg . . . .  Lancashire v Yorkshire (501-6 dec.) at Scarborough.

## Tied Match

Kent (381 and 408-7 dec.) v Sussex (353 and 436) at Hove.

## Highest Innings Totals

```
621 . . . . . . . .  Essex v Leicestershire at Leicester.
575-8 dec. . . .  Worcestershire v Somerset at Worcester.
572-7 dec. . . .  Derbyshire v Nottinghamshire at Derby (after following on).
566-6 dec. . . .  Essex v Middlesex at Chelmsford.
544 . . . . . . . .  Essex v Kent at Folkestone.
543-8 dec. . . .  Essex v Derbyshire at Chelmsford.
514-9 dec. . . .  Glamorgan v Gloucestershire at Abergavenny.
504 . . . . . . . .  Glamorgan v Hampshire at Southampton.
501-6 dec. . . .  Yorkshire v Lancashire at Scarborough.
```

## Highest Fourth-Innings Totals

```
436 . . . . . .  Sussex v Kent at Hove (the highest total to tie a first-class match – set 437).
403 . . . . . .  Somerset v Warwickshire at Taunton (set 409).
```

## Lowest Innings Totals

```
51 . . . . . .  Middlesex v Essex at Chelmsford.
68 . . . . . .  Northamptonshire v Nottinghamshire at Wellingborough School.
83 . . . . . .  Warwickshire v Kent at Tunbridge Wells.
83† . . . . . .  Somerset v Worcestershire at Worcester.
96 . . . . . .  Middlesex v Kent at Canterbury.
97 . . . . . .  Sri Lankans v Gloucestershire at Bristol.
99 . . . . . . .  Cambridge University v Glamorgan at Cambridge.
```

*† One man absent injured.*

## Lowest First-Class Total in Britain to Include Two Hundreds

```
258 . . . . . .  Hampshire v Derbyshire at Chesterfield (C. L. Smith 114, K. D. James 101).
```

## Match Aggregates of 1,400 Runs

*Runs-Wkts*
```
1,578-37 . . Sussex v Kent at Hove.
1,442-29 . . Yorkshire v Lancashire at Scarborough.
1,415-25 . . Hampshire v Somerset at Southampton.
1,415-28 . . West Indies XI v World XI at Scarborough.
```

## 50 Extras in an Innings

| | b | l-b | w | n-b | |
|---|---|---|---|---|---|
| 65 | 8 | 32 | 1 | 24 | Nottinghamshire v Derbyshire at Derby. |
| 56 | 14 | 22 | 1 | 19 | Northamptonshire v Warwickshire at Northampton. |
| 54 | 8 | 10 | 1 | 35 | England v West Indies at The Oval. |
| 52 | 9 | 8 | 1 | 34 | Gloucestershire v Sussex at Hove. |

## Career Aggregate Milestones†

```
20,000 runs . . . . . . .  G. D. Mendis
10,000 runs . . . . . . .  P. Johnson, J. W. Lloyds, H. Morris, J. E. Morris, R. J. Shastri,
                           A. J. Stewart, A. P. Wells, J. J. Whitaker.
 1,000 wickets . . . . . .  P. Carrick.
```

*† Achieved since September 1990.*

# FIRST-CLASS AVERAGES, 1991

## BATTING

(Qualification: 8 innings, average 10.00)

\* *Signifies not out.* † *Denotes a left-handed batsman.*

| | M | I | NO | R | HI | 100s | 50s | Avge |
|---|---|---|---|---|---|---|---|---|
| C. L. Hooper (*West Indians & West Indies XI*) | 16 | 25 | 9 | 1,501 | 196 | 5 | 8 | 93.81 |
| S. J. Cook (*Somerset*) | 24 | 42 | 8 | 2,755 | 210* | 11 | 8 | 81.02 |
| M. W. Gatting (*Middx*) | 22 | 39 | 11 | 2,057 | 215* | 8 | 6 | 73.46 |
| Salim Malik (*Essex*) | 24 | 36 | 9 | 1,972 | 215 | 6 | 8 | 73.03 |
| G. A. Gooch (*Essex*) | 20 | 31 | 4 | 1,911 | 259 | 6 | 6 | 70.77 |
| R. B. Richardson (*West Indians & West Indies XI*) | 15 | 26 | 5 | 1,403 | 135* | 6 | 6 | 66.81 |
| †P. C. L. Holloway (*Warwicks.*) | 6 | 9 | 5 | 263 | 89* | 0 | 2 | 65.75 |
| C. L. Smith (*Hants*) | 16 | 27 | 3 | 1,553 | 200 | 6 | 7 | 64.70 |
| T. M. Moody (*Worcs.*) | 22 | 34 | 4 | 1,887 | 210 | 6 | 9 | 62.90 |
| D. W. Randall (*Notts.*) | 22 | 34 | 9 | 1,567 | 143* | 5 | 5 | 62.68 |
| M. P. Maynard (*Glam.*) | 23 | 36 | 6 | 1,803 | 243 | 7 | 5 | 60.10 |
| A. P. Wells (*Sussex*) | 22 | 36 | 6 | 1,784 | 253* | 7 | 5 | 59.46 |
| M. Azharuddin (*Derbys.*) | 22 | 39 | 5 | 2,016 | 212 | 7 | 10 | 59.29 |
| †G. J. Turner (*OUCC*) | 8 | 8 | 2 | 349 | 101* | 1 | 2 | 58.16 |
| R. T. Robinson (*Notts.*) | 22 | 37 | 8 | 1,673 | 180 | 3 | 10 | 57.68 |
| N. R. Taylor (*Kent*) | 23 | 36 | 4 | 1,806 | 203* | 7 | 5 | 56.43 |
| N. Hussain (*Essex*) | 25 | 33 | 8 | 1,354 | 196 | 3 | 8 | 54.16 |
| R. A. Smith (*Hants*) | 16 | 30 | 4 | 1,397 | 148* | 3 | 11 | 53.73 |
| C. J. Tavaré (*Somerset*) | 23 | 37 | 7 | 1,601 | 183 | 5 | 7 | 53.36 |
| †H. Morris (*Glam.*) | 23 | 41 | 7 | 1,803 | 156* | 5 | 8 | 53.02 |
| †C. B. Lambert (*West Indians & West Indies XI*) | 7 | 13 | 2 | 551 | 116 | 1 | 4 | 50.09 |
| †B. C. Broad (*Notts.*) | 21 | 38 | 3 | 1,739 | 166 | 5 | 7 | 49.68 |
| †N. V. Knight (*Essex*) | 7 | 10 | 1 | 441 | 101* | 1 | 3 | 49.00 |
| P. Johnson (*Notts.*) | 23 | 37 | 7 | 1,454 | 124 | 3 | 11 | 48.46 |
| D. A. Reeve (*Warwicks.*) | 20 | 33 | 7 | 1,260 | 99* | 0 | 14 | 48.46 |
| R. J. Shastri (*Glam.*) | 22 | 32 | 9 | 1,108 | 133* | 2 | 7 | 48.17 |
| †M. R. Benson (*Kent*) | 20 | 30 | 2 | 1,329 | 257 | 4 | 6 | 47.46 |
| †D. J. Bicknell (*Surrey*) | 24 | 42 | 2 | 1,888 | 151 | 5 | 9 | 47.20 |
| †K. D. James (*Hants*) | 24 | 37 | 10 | 1,274 | 134* | 2 | 6 | 47.18 |
| A. Fordham (*Northants*) | 24 | 42 | 3 | 1,840 | 165 | 4 | 9 | 47.17 |
| J. P. Crawley (*CUCC & Lancs.*) | 12 | 20 | 2 | 849 | 130 | 1 | 8 | 47.16 |
| M. A. Garnham (*Essex*) | 25 | 29 | 8 | 986 | 123 | 3 | 5 | 46.95 |
| T. R. Ward (*Kent*) | 22 | 34 | 2 | 1,493 | 235* | 5 | 6 | 46.65 |
| M. D. Moxon (*Yorks.*) | 21 | 37 | 1 | 1,669 | 200 | 3 | 12 | 46.36 |
| †N. H. Fairbrother (*Lancs.*) | 19 | 29 | 6 | 1,064 | 121 | 5 | 3 | 46.26 |
| A. J. Wright (*Glos.*) | 25 | 41 | 6 | 1,596 | 120 | 3 | 10 | 45.60 |
| †A. R. Butcher (*Glam.*) | 23 | 39 | 2 | 1,677 | 147 | 4 | 13 | 45.32 |
| C. W. J. Athey (*Glos.*) | 25 | 40 | 6 | 1,522 | 127 | 5 | 9 | 44.76 |
| T. S. Curtis (*Worcs.*) | 25 | 40 | 3 | 1,653 | 248 | 3 | 9 | 44.67 |
| A. J. Stewart (*Surrey*) | 19 | 34 | 8 | 1,161 | 113* | 2 | 6 | 44.65 |
| †D. Byas (*Yorks.*) | 24 | 41 | 6 | 1,557 | 153 | 5 | 2 | 44.48 |
| R. J. Harden (*Somerset*) | 24 | 39 | 6 | 1,355 | 134 | 3 | 9 | 43.70 |
| I. T. Botham (*Worcs.*) | 13 | 21 | 3 | 785 | 161 | 2 | 4 | 43.61 |
| D. R. Pringle (*Essex*) | 19 | 21 | 7 | 607 | 78* | 0 | 4 | 43.35 |
| †D. M. Smith (*Sussex*) | 20 | 35 | 6 | 1,238 | 126* | 1 | 8 | 42.68 |
| A. M. Hooper (*CUCC*) | 7 | 12 | 1 | 458 | 125 | 1 | 2 | 41.63 |
| †G. P. Thorpe (*Surrey*) | 23 | 38 | 9 | 1,203 | 177 | 4 | 4 | 41.48 |
| A. Dale (*Glam.*) | 17 | 26 | 5 | 869 | 140 | 1 | 5 | 41.38 |

| | M | I | NO | R | HI | 100s | 50s | Avge |
|---|---|---|---|---|---|---|---|---|
| J. E. Morris (*Derbys.*) | 21 | 36 | 2 | 1,398 | 131 | 2 | 8 | 41.11 |
| M. A. Atherton (*Lancs.*) | 14 | 23 | 3 | 820 | 138 | 3 | 2 | 41.00 |
| A. R. Roberts (*Northants*) | 14 | 15 | 9 | 244 | 48 | 0 | 0 | 40.66 |
| D. M. Ward (*Surrey*) | 23 | 40 | 6 | 1,372 | 151 | 1 | 10 | 40.35 |
| M. P. Speight (*Sussex*) | 14 | 20 | 1 | 754 | 149 | 1 | 5 | 39.68 |
| R. J. Bailey (*Northants*) | 21 | 36 | 5 | 1,224 | 117 | 1 | 11 | 39.48 |
| G. R. Cowdrey (*Kent*) | 22 | 34 | 4 | 1,175 | 114 | 3 | 5 | 39.16 |
| N. E. Briers (*Leics.*) | 24 | 43 | 5 | 1,485 | 160 | 4 | 7 | 39.07 |
| S. P. Titchard (*Lancs.*) | 8 | 15 | 1 | 546 | 135 | 1 | 2 | 39.00 |
| V. P. Terry (*Hants*) | 20 | 35 | 3 | 1,244 | 171 | 2 | 7 | 38.87 |
| A. J. Lamb (*Northants*) | 19 | 30 | 2 | 1,081 | 194 | 3 | 5 | 38.60 |
| P. V. Simmons (*West Indies & West Indies XI*) | 15 | 28 | 1 | 1,031 | 136 | 3 | 4 | 38.18 |
| P. E. Robinson (*Yorks.*) | 24 | 41 | 7 | 1,293 | 189 | 2 | 8 | 38.02 |
| J. J. Whitaker (*Leics.*) | 23 | 37 | 3 | 1,289 | 105 | 1 | 8 | 37.91 |
| K. J. Barnett (*Derbys.*) | 24 | 39 | 2 | 1,399 | 217 | 2 | 9 | 37.81 |
| M. A. Roseberry (*Middx*) | 24 | 44 | 4 | 1,511 | 123* | 2 | 8 | 37.77 |
| B. F. Smith (*Leics.*) | 15 | 23 | 5 | 674 | 71 | 0 | 3 | 37.44 |
| J. P. Stephenson (*Essex*) | 25 | 41 | 3 | 1,421 | 116 | 3 | 8 | 37.39 |
| M. R. Ramprakash (*Middx*) | 21 | 36 | 4 | 1,174 | 119 | 2 | 7 | 36.68 |
| D. P. Ostler (*Warwicks.*) | 22 | 40 | 5 | 1,284 | 120* | 1 | 10 | 36.68 |
| G. D. Mendis (*Lancs.*) | 23 | 43 | 5 | 1,394 | 127* | 4 | 3 | 36.68 |
| W. Larkins (*Northants*) | 9 | 16 | 6 | 365 | 75 | 0 | 2 | 36.50 |
| N. J. Lenham (*Sussex*) | 19 | 33 | 3 | 1,091 | 193 | 3 | 4 | 36.36 |
| P. J. Prichard (*Essex*) | 24 | 38 | 7 | 1,124 | 190 | 1 | 6 | 36.25 |
| S. A. Kellett (*Yorks.*) | 24 | 40 | 5 | 1,266 | 125* | 2 | 8 | 36.17 |
| N. A. Stanley (*Northants*) | 8 | 13 | 0 | 470 | 132 | 1 | 2 | 36.15 |
| J. D. R. Benson (*Leics.*) | 9 | 12 | 1 | 393 | 133* | 1 | 1 | 35.72 |
| P. D. Bowler (*Derbys.*) | 24 | 44 | 3 | 1,458 | 104* | 2 | 11 | 35.56 |
| B. T. P. Donelan (*Sussex*) | 13 | 15 | 5 | 353 | 61 | 0 | 2 | 35.30 |
| S. J. Rhodes (*Worcs.*) | 24 | 33 | 6 | 942 | 90 | 0 | 8 | 34.88 |
| G. D. Rose (*Somerset*) | 15 | 20 | 3 | 590 | 106 | 2 | 2 | 34.70 |
| †D. I. Gower (*Hants*) | 23 | 38 | 5 | 1,142 | 80* | 0 | 8 | 34.60 |
| C. C. Lewis (*Leics.*) | 16 | 20 | 2 | 621 | 73 | 0 | 4 | 34.50 |
| K. M. Curran (*Northants*) | 21 | 31 | 7 | 828 | 89* | 0 | 6 | 34.50 |
| K. R. Brown (*Middx*) | 24 | 41 | 6 | 1,184 | 143* | 1 | 6 | 33.82 |
| S. A. Marsh (*Kent*) | 23 | 32 | 5 | 910 | 113* | 2 | 5 | 33.70 |
| A. N. Hayhurst (*Somerset*) | 19 | 32 | 5 | 910 | 172* | 3 | 1 | 33.70 |
| A. J. Moles (*Warwicks.*) | 22 | 39 | 2 | 1,246 | 133 | 1 | 10 | 33.67 |
| C. M. Wells (*Sussex*) | 14 | 21 | 6 | 503 | 76 | 0 | 3 | 33.53 |
| †P. R. Pollard (*Notts.*) | 23 | 41 | 3 | 1,255 | 145 | 2 | 7 | 33.02 |
| R. I. Alikhan (*Surrey*) | 19 | 34 | 2 | 1,055 | 96* | 1 | 8 | 32.96 |
| P. N. Hepworth (*Leics.*) | 23 | 38 | 4 | 1,119 | 115 | 2 | 4 | 32.91 |
| G. A. Hick (*Worcs.*) | 22 | 36 | 2 | 1,119 | 186 | 3 | 5 | 32.91 |
| W. K. Hegg (*Lancs.*) | 22 | 32 | 8 | 784 | 97 | 0 | 3 | 32.66 |
| †T. A. Lloyd (*Warwicks.*) | 21 | 35 | 2 | 1,076 | 97 | 0 | 10 | 32.60 |
| P. M. Roebuck (*Somerset*) | 17 | 29 | 3 | 833 | 101 | 1 | 5 | 32.03 |
| M. W. Alleyne (*Glos.*) | 25 | 40 | 5 | 1,121 | 165 | 1 | 6 | 32.02 |
| J. D. Ratcliffe (*Warwicks.*) | 17 | 31 | 1 | 953 | 94 | 0 | 8 | 31.76 |
| M. V. Fleming (*Kent*) | 20 | 32 | 3 | 917 | 116 | 2 | 6 | 31.62 |
| C. J. Adams (*Derbys.*) | 15 | 24 | 2 | 691 | 134 | 2 | 1 | 31.40 |
| †A. C. H. Seymour (*Essex*) | 10 | 18 | 1 | 533 | 157 | 1 | 3 | 31.35 |
| T. J. Boon (*Leics.*) | 22 | 40 | 2 | 1,185 | 108 | 2 | 6 | 31.18 |
| L. Potter (*Leics.*) | 24 | 37 | 4 | 1,027 | 89 | 0 | 7 | 31.12 |
| †N. D. Burns (*Somerset*) | 23 | 34 | 8 | 808 | 108 | 1 | 4 | 31.07 |
| P. Whitticase (*Leics.*) | 20 | 25 | 5 | 620 | 114* | 1 | 4 | 31.00 |
| S. R. Lampitt (*Worcs.*) | 22 | 23 | 6 | 523 | 93 | 0 | 4 | 30.76 |
| †G. Fowler (*Lancs.*) | 19 | 33 | 2 | 953 | 113 | 2 | 3 | 30.74 |
| M. C. J. Nicholas (*Hants*) | 22 | 37 | 10 | 826 | 107* | 1 | 5 | 30.59 |
| K. Greenfield (*Sussex*) | 9 | 14 | 1 | 394 | 127* | 2 | 1 | 30.30 |
| M. A. Crawley (*Notts.*) | 11 | 13 | 4 | 272 | 112 | 1 | 0 | 30.22 |

| | M | I | NO | R | HI | 100s | 50s | Avge |
|---|---|---|---|---|---|---|---|---|
| N. M. K. Smith (*Warwicks.*) .... | 5 | 9 | 2 | 209 | 70 | 0 | 2 | 29.85 |
| T. C. Middleton (*Hants*) ........ | 18 | 31 | 2 | 864 | 102 | 1 | 3 | 29.79 |
| G. D. Hodgson (*Glos.*) ........ | 23 | 39 | 2 | 1,101 | 105 | 1 | 7 | 29.75 |
| A. A. Metcalfe (*Yorks.*) ........ | 24 | 43 | 2 | 1,210 | 123 | 2 | 6 | 29.51 |
| D. Ripley (*Northants*) .......... | 20 | 25 | 9 | 467 | 53* | 0 | 1 | 29.18 |
| J. R. Ayling (*Hants*) .......... | 10 | 14 | 3 | 321 | 58 | 0 | 2 | 29.18 |
| M. A. Feltham (*Surrey*) ........ | 13 | 18 | 5 | 375 | 69* | 0 | 1 | 28.84 |
| S. P. James (*Glam.*) .......... | 11 | 19 | 3 | 461 | 70 | 0 | 2 | 28.81 |
| P. Carrick (*Yorks.*) .......... | 21 | 32 | 9 | 662 | 67 | 0 | 4 | 28.78 |
| A. I. C. Dodemaide (*Sussex*) .... | 20 | 30 | 9 | 602 | 100* | 1 | 1 | 28.66 |
| J. W. Hall (*Sussex*) .......... | 15 | 26 | 2 | 686 | 117* | 1 | 4 | 28.58 |
| P. Moores (*Sussex*) .......... | 23 | 28 | 3 | 714 | 102 | 1 | 6 | 28.56 |
| I. J. F. Hutchinson (*Middx*) .... | 14 | 24 | 1 | 656 | 125 | 2 | 2 | 28.52 |
| N. A. Foster (*Essex*) .......... | 22 | 22 | 4 | 513 | 107* | 1 | 1 | 28.50 |
| N. J. Speak (*Lancs.*) .......... | 18 | 33 | 3 | 844 | 153 | 1 | 2 | 28.13 |
| R. R. Montgomerie (*OUCC & Northants*) ................ | 9 | 13 | 2 | 309 | 88 | 0 | 4 | 28.09 |
| E. A. E. Baptiste (*Northants*) .... | 18 | 22 | 1 | 589 | 80 | 0 | 4 | 28.04 |
| A. N. Aymes (*Hants*) .......... | 24 | 30 | 7 | 644 | 53 | 0 | 2 | 28.00 |
| R. G. Williams (*Northants*) ...... | 8 | 11 | 3 | 224 | 101* | 1 | 0 | 28.00 |
| D. Gough (*Yorks.*) .......... | 13 | 14 | 3 | 307 | 72 | 0 | 2 | 27.90 |
| T. J. G. O'Gorman (*Derbys.*) .... | 25 | 44 | 4 | 1,116 | 148 | 2 | 4 | 27.90 |
| K. H. MacLeay (*Somerset*) ...... | 15 | 21 | 6 | 417 | 63 | 0 | 2 | 27.80 |
| *Wasim Akram (*Lancs.*) ........ | 14 | 19 | 2 | 471 | 122 | 1 | 1 | 27.70 |
| †J. W. Lloyds (*Glos.*) .......... | 24 | 35 | 6 | 803 | 71* | 0 | 8 | 27.68 |
| R. J. Turner (*CUCC & Somerset*) . | 9 | 13 | 4 | 249 | 69* | 0 | 1 | 27.66 |
| G. D. Lloyd (*Lancs.*) .......... | 18 | 30 | 0 | 829 | 96 | 0 | 6 | 27.63 |
| D. B. D'Oliveira (*Worcs.*) ...... | 17 | 24 | 2 | 586 | 237 | 1 | 1 | 26.63 |
| S. C. Goldsmith (*Derbys.*) ...... | 16 | 26 | 3 | 610 | 127 | 1 | 2 | 26.52 |
| Asif Din (*Warwicks.*) .......... | 15 | 27 | 1 | 685 | 140 | 2 | 1 | 26.34 |
| K. P. Evans (*Notts.*) .......... | 15 | 18 | 7 | 289 | 56* | 0 | 1 | 26.27 |
| †I. D. Austin (*Lancs.*) .......... | 12 | 16 | 4 | 315 | 101* | 1 | 1 | 26.25 |
| R. P. Lefebvre (*Somerset*) ...... | 16 | 18 | 4 | 366 | 100 | 1 | 1 | 26.14 |
| R. J. Blakey (*Yorks.*) .......... | 24 | 38 | 2 | 941 | 196 | 1 | 6 | 26.13 |
| †R. J. Scott (*Glos.*) .......... | 20 | 34 | 1 | 848 | 127 | 2 | 3 | 25.69 |
| D. J. Capel (*Northants*) ........ | 22 | 33 | 2 | 792 | 100 | 1 | 7 | 25.54 |
| C. M. Gupte (*OUCC*) .......... | 8 | 9 | 1 | 200 | 55* | 0 | 1 | 25.00 |
| G. B. T. Lovell (*OUCC*) ........ | 9 | 13 | 3 | 250 | 49 | 0 | 0 | 25.00 |
| K. T. Medlycott (*Surrey*) ...... | 19 | 27 | 2 | 624 | 109 | 1 | 4 | 24.96 |
| P. N. Weekes (*Middx*) .......... | 6 | 11 | 1 | 249 | 86 | 0 | 2 | 24.90 |
| P. A. Neale (*Worcs.*) .......... | 14 | 21 | 4 | 419 | 69* | 0 | 1 | 24.64 |
| †B. C. Lara (*West Indians & West Indies XI*) .......... | 9 | 14 | 0 | 344 | 93 | 0 | 3 | 24.57 |
| M. Watkinson (*Lancs.*) ........ | 21 | 35 | 4 | 758 | 114* | 1 | 3 | 24.45 |
| P. W. G. Parker (*Sussex*) ...... | 16 | 26 | 1 | 607 | 111 | 1 | 3 | 24.28 |
| G. Yates (*Lancs.*) .......... | 20 | 26 | 13 | 315 | 100* | 1 | 0 | 24.23 |
| P. Bent (*Worcs.*) .......... | 8 | 13 | 1 | 288 | 100* | 1 | 1 | 24.00 |
| C. M. Tolley (*Worcs.*) .......... | 8 | 10 | 4 | 144 | 36 | 0 | 0 | 24.00 |
| R. K. Illingworth (*Worcs.*) ...... | 22 | 29 | 7 | 524 | 56* | 0 | 1 | 23.81 |
| D. C. Sandiford (*OUCC*) ........ | 9 | 9 | 1 | 189 | 83 | 0 | 1 | 23.62 |
| C. P. Metson (*Glam.*) .......... | 24 | 26 | 3 | 543 | 84 | 0 | 2 | 23.60 |
| R. E. Morris (*OUCC*) .......... | 8 | 11 | 1 | 236 | 71 | 0 | 2 | 23.60 |
| J. A. North (*Sussex*) .......... | 7 | 8 | 1 | 163 | 63* | 0 | 1 | 23.28 |
| K. M. Krikken (*Derbys.*) ...... | 24 | 38 | 8 | 697 | 65 | 0 | 2 | 23.23 |
| †R. C. Russell (*Glos.*) .......... | 20 | 32 | 5 | 627 | 111 | 1 | 2 | 23.22 |
| P. A. Cottey (*Glam.*) .......... | 14 | 20 | 7 | 299 | 55 | 0 | 1 | 23.00 |
| P. J. Hartley (*Yorks.*) .......... | 20 | 24 | 10 | 322 | 50* | 0 | 1 | 23.00 |
| †S. G. Hinks (*Kent*) .......... | 9 | 14 | 2 | 275 | 61* | 0 | 1 | 22.91 |
| J. G. Thomas (*Northants*) ...... | 12 | 12 | 3 | 206 | 64 | 0 | 1 | 22.88 |
| I. A. Greig (*Surrey*) .......... | 20 | 31 | 4 | 610 | 72 | 0 | 3 | 22.59 |
| I. Smith (*Glam.*) .......... | 10 | 13 | 2 | 245 | 47 | 0 | 0 | 22.27 |

| | M | I | NO | R | HI | 100s | 50s | Avge |
|---|---|---|---|---|---|---|---|---|
| C. S. Pickles (*Yorks.*) | 11 | 16 | 3 | 284 | 51 | 0 | 2 | 21.84 |
| †R. M. Ellison (*Kent*) | 17 | 26 | 7 | 415 | 61* | 0 | 3 | 21.84 |
| M. D. Marshall (*West Indians & West Indies XI*) | 11 | 11 | 2 | 196 | 67 | 0 | 1 | 21.77 |
| J. E. Emburey (*Middx*) | 24 | 33 | 4 | 630 | 74 | 0 | 3 | 21.72 |
| †J. D. Fitton (*Lancs.*) | 8 | 11 | 1 | 217 | 60 | 0 | 1 | 21.70 |
| M. A. Lynch (*Surrey*) | 10 | 17 | 1 | 342 | 141* | 1 | 1 | 21.37 |
| T. D. Topley (*Essex*) | 20 | 19 | 4 | 320 | 50* | 0 | 2 | 21.33 |
| D. G. Cork (*Derbys.*) | 18 | 28 | 8 | 423 | 44 | 0 | 0 | 21.15 |
| F. D. Stephenson (*Notts.*) | 22 | 27 | 7 | 423 | 58 | 0 | 1 | 21.15 |
| †G. J. Lord (*Worcs.*) | 11 | 18 | 0 | 378 | 55 | 0 | 3 | 21.00 |
| P. A. J. DeFreitas (*Lancs.*) | 18 | 26 | 2 | 499 | 60 | 0 | 3 | 20.79 |
| P. J. Newport (*Worcs.*) | 25 | 26 | 9 | 353 | 48 | 0 | 0 | 20.76 |
| M. Keech (*Middx*) | 15 | 24 | 3 | 420 | 58* | 0 | 2 | 20.00 |
| †N. A. Felton (*Northants*) | 16 | 28 | 3 | 497 | 55 | 0 | 1 | 19.88 |
| A. E. Warner (*Derbys.*) | 17 | 24 | 3 | 410 | 53 | 0 | 2 | 19.52 |
| G. C. Holmes (*Glam.*) | 7 | 8 | 1 | 136 | 54 | 0 | 1 | 19.42 |
| †J. C. Pooley (*Middx*) | 12 | 21 | 0 | 407 | 88 | 0 | 2 | 19.38 |
| †D. J. Millns (*Leics.*) | 20 | 24 | 8 | 306 | 44 | 0 | 0 | 19.12 |
| A. C. S. Pigott (*Sussex*) | 19 | 22 | 5 | 320 | 65 | 0 | 1 | 18.82 |
| P. A. Smith (*Warwicks.*) | 14 | 23 | 1 | 411 | 68 | 0 | 2 | 18.68 |
| †J. J. E. Hardy (*Glos.*) | 10 | 15 | 2 | 242 | 52 | 0 | 1 | 18.61 |
| D. P. Hughes (*Lancs.*) | 8 | 9 | 3 | 111 | 51 | 0 | 1 | 18.50 |
| N. Shahid (*Essex*) | 8 | 9 | 1 | 147 | 51 | 0 | 1 | 18.37 |
| J. D. Batty (*Yorks.*) | 18 | 17 | 6 | 202 | 51 | 0 | 1 | 18.36 |
| M. J. McCague (*Kent*) | 8 | 10 | 2 | 142 | 29 | 0 | 0 | 17.75 |
| K. J. Piper (*Warwicks.*) | 16 | 23 | 3 | 349 | 55 | 0 | 1 | 17.45 |
| R. P. Davis (*Kent*) | 20 | 26 | 4 | 383 | 44 | 0 | 1 | 17.40 |
| M. P. Bicknell (*Surrey*) | 15 | 22 | 4 | 312 | 63 | 0 | 1 | 17.33 |
| D. V. Lawrence (*Glos.*) | 18 | 26 | 1 | 433 | 66 | 0 | 1 | 17.32 |
| †C. Penn (*Kent*) | 18 | 22 | 4 | 311 | 52 | 0 | 1 | 17.27 |
| R. J. Maru (*Hants*) | 22 | 26 | 3 | 392 | 61 | 0 | 1 | 17.04 |
| P. J. Martin (*Lancs.*) | 16 | 13 | 8 | 85 | 29 | 0 | 0 | 17.00 |
| S. W. Johnson (*CUCC*) | 7 | 8 | 3 | 85 | 20 | 0 | 0 | 17.00 |
| G. C. Small (*Warwicks.*) | 20 | 29 | 7 | 370 | 58 | 0 | 1 | 16.81 |
| M. J. Lowrey (*CUCC*) | 10 | 16 | 2 | 234 | 51 | 0 | 1 | 16.71 |
| P. Willey (*Leics.*) | 12 | 18 | 5 | 217 | 42* | 0 | 0 | 16.69 |
| M. Saxelby (*Notts.*) | 7 | 10 | 1 | 149 | 44 | 0 | 0 | 16.55 |
| N. F. Sargeant (*Surrey*) | 21 | 28 | 4 | 391 | 49 | 0 | 0 | 16.29 |
| B. N. French (*Notts.*) | 21 | 24 | 4 | 315 | 65 | 0 | 2 | 15.75 |
| N. V. Radford (*Worcs.*) | 17 | 16 | 6 | 157 | 45 | 0 | 0 | 15.70 |
| L. Tennant (*Leics.*) | 6 | 9 | 3 | 94 | 23* | 0 | 0 | 15.66 |
| †A. L. Penberthy (*Northants*) | 12 | 15 | 3 | 186 | 52 | 0 | 1 | 15.50 |
| †M. I. Gidley (*Leics.*) | 6 | 9 | 2 | 107 | 80 | 0 | 1 | 15.28 |
| R. I. Clitheroe (*CUCC*) | 10 | 17 | 2 | 228 | 36 | 0 | 0 | 15.20 |
| †J. H. Childs (*Essex*) | 22 | 15 | 7 | 120 | 41* | 0 | 0 | 15.00 |
| R. D. B. Croft (*Glam.*) | 25 | 27 | 4 | 345 | 50 | 0 | 1 | 15.00 |
| P. Farbrace (*Middx*) | 20 | 27 | 5 | 326 | 50 | 0 | 1 | 14.81 |
| Waqar Younis (*Surrey*) | 18 | 20 | 8 | 177 | 31 | 0 | 0 | 14.75 |
| N. F. Williams (*Middx*) | 18 | 27 | 3 | 351 | 77 | 0 | 1 | 14.62 |
| I. J. Turner (*Hants*) | 8 | 10 | 4 | 87 | 39* | 0 | 0 | 14.50 |
| I. D. K. Salisbury (*Sussex*) | 22 | 21 | 8 | 188 | 34 | 0 | 0 | 14.46 |
| D. R. Gilbert (*Glos.*) | 22 | 28 | 7 | 303 | 28* | 0 | 0 | 14.42 |
| D. W. Headley (*Middx*) | 12 | 15 | 1 | 202 | 76 | 0 | 1 | 14.42 |
| J. P. Arscott (*CUCC*) | 9 | 12 | 1 | 157 | 74 | 0 | 1 | 14.27 |
| J. N. Maguire (*Leics.*) | 24 | 24 | 7 | 237 | 44* | 0 | 0 | 13.94 |
| W. M. Noon (*Northants*) | 6 | 9 | 2 | 96 | 36 | 0 | 0 | 13.71 |
| R. W. Sladdin (*Derbys.*) | 8 | 9 | 4 | 68 | 18 | 0 | 0 | 13.60 |
| †A. M. Babington (*Glos.*) | 18 | 20 | 7 | 176 | 58 | 0 | 1 | 13.53 |
| N. A. Mallender (*Somerset*) | 13 | 11 | 3 | 108 | 19 | 0 | 0 | 13.50 |
| †P. A. Booth (*Warwicks.*) | 10 | 13 | 0 | 175 | 62 | 0 | 1 | 13.46 |

| | M | I | NO | R | HI | 100s | 50s | Avge |
|---|---|---|---|---|---|---|---|---|
| †H. R. Davies (*OUCC*) | 7 | 9 | 3 | 80 | 38 | 0 | 0 | 13.33 |
| T. A. Munton (*Warwicks.*) | 23 | 24 | 7 | 226 | 31 | 0 | 0 | 13.29 |
| T. H. C. Hancock (*Glos.*) | 5 | 9 | 2 | 93 | 51 | 0 | 1 | 13.28 |
| M. J. Morris (*CUCC*) | 9 | 13 | 0 | 171 | 60 | 0 | 1 | 13.15 |
| †R. A. Pick (*Notts.*) | 23 | 16 | 5 | 142 | 46 | 0 | 0 | 12.90 |
| C. W. Wilkinson (*Leics.*) | 14 | 13 | 2 | 138 | 41 | 0 | 0 | 12.54 |
| S. L. Watkin (*Glam.*) | 22 | 19 | 8 | 136 | 25* | 0 | 0 | 12.36 |
| M. J. Gerrard (*Glos.*) | 8 | 9 | 5 | 49 | 42 | 0 | 0 | 12.25 |
| T. A. Merrick (*Kent*) | 19 | 23 | 6 | 204 | 36 | 0 | 0 | 12.00 |
| E. E. Hemmings (*Notts.*) | 16 | 16 | 4 | 143 | 29* | 0 | 0 | 11.91 |
| M. C. J. Ball (*Glos.*) | 6 | 9 | 0 | 106 | 28 | 0 | 0 | 11.77 |
| P. C. R. Tufnell (*Middx*) | 22 | 24 | 6 | 210 | 34 | 0 | 0 | 11.66 |
| N. G. B. Cook (*Northants*) | 18 | 15 | 5 | 114 | 29 | 0 | 0 | 11.40 |
| H. R. J. Trump (*Somerset*) | 18 | 17 | 7 | 108 | 30* | 0 | 0 | 10.80 |
| S. J. Base (*Derbys.*) | 15 | 18 | 4 | 151 | 36 | 0 | 0 | 10.78 |
| †A. N. Jones (*Sussex*) | 23 | 18 | 6 | 128 | 28 | 0 | 0 | 10.66 |
| P. J. W. Allott (*Lancs.*) | 9 | 8 | 2 | 63 | 26 | 0 | 0 | 10.50 |
| N. G. Cowans (*Middx*) | 23 | 29 | 11 | 186 | 35 | 0 | 0 | 10.33 |
| R. D. Stemp (*Worcs.*) | 9 | 8 | 5 | 30 | 15* | 0 | 0 | 10.00 |

## BOWLING

(Qualification: 10 wickets in 10 innings)

† *Denotes a left-arm bowler.*

| | O | M | R | W | BB | 5W/i | Avge |
|---|---|---|---|---|---|---|---|
| Waqar Younis (*Surrey*) | 582 | 112 | 1,656 | 113 | 7-87 | 13 | 14.65 |
| A. A. Donald (*Warwicks.*) | 522.3 | 91 | 1,634 | 83 | 6-69 | 8 | 19.68 |
| N. A. Foster (*Essex*) | 757.2 | 185 | 2,138 | 102 | 8-99 | 7 | 20.96 |
| D. A. Reeve (*Warwicks.*) | 402.1 | 117 | 957 | 45 | 6-73 | 1 | 21.26 |
| G. R. Dilley (*Worcs.*) | 305.2 | 62 | 823 | 37 | 5-91 | 1 | 22.24 |
| †Wasim Akram (*Lancs.*) | 429.3 | 99 | 1,251 | 56 | 6-66 | 7 | 22.33 |
| †C. M. Tolley (*Worcs.*) | 161 | 39 | 413 | 18 | 4-69 | 0 | 22.94 |
| N. A. Mallender (*Somerset*) | 349.5 | 76 | 969 | 42 | 6-43 | 3 | 23.07 |
| †R. J. Shastri (*Glam.*) | 307.5 | 88 | 724 | 31 | 5-71 | 1 | 23.35 |
| J. P. Stephenson (*Essex*) | 106.4 | 19 | 399 | 17 | 4-30 | 0 | 23.47 |
| J. R. Ayling (*Hants*) | 211.1 | 49 | 595 | 25 | 4-47 | 0 | 23.80 |
| O. H. Mortensen (*Derbys.*) | 559.1 | 143 | 1,384 | 58 | 6-101 | 2 | 23.86 |
| D. V. Lawrence (*Glos.*) | 515.1 | 79 | 1,790 | 74 | 6-67 | 4 | 24.18 |
| P. A. J. DeFreitas (*Lancs.*) | 657.1 | 173 | 1,780 | 73 | 7-70 | 3 | 24.38 |
| I. T. Botham (*Worcs.*) | 351.1 | 73 | 1,077 | 44 | 7-54 | 3 | 24.47 |
| K. J. Barnett (*Derbys.*) | 211.1 | 47 | 496 | 20 | 6-28 | 1 | 24.80 |
| †R. D. Stemp (*Worcs.*) | 172.1 | 43 | 425 | 17 | 4-62 | 0 | 25.00 |
| K. M. Curran (*Northants*) | 436.2 | 110 | 1,204 | 48 | 5-60 | 1 | 25.08 |
| †P. C. R. Tufnell (*Middx*) | 903.4 | 254 | 2,219 | 88 | 7-116 | 7 | 25.21 |
| C. C. Lewis (*Leics.*) | 471.4 | 127 | 1,213 | 48 | 6-111 | 3 | 25.27 |
| C. Penn (*Kent*) | 429.4 | 82 | 1,323 | 52 | 5-43 | 3 | 25.44 |
| T. A. Munton (*Warwicks.*) | 693.1 | 184 | 1,863 | 73 | 8-89 | 5 | 25.52 |
| †D. G. Cork (*Derbys.*) | 494.3 | 84 | 1,460 | 57 | 8-53 | 1 | 25.61 |
| F. D. Stephenson (*Notts.*) | 719.1 | 158 | 2,010 | 78 | 5-27 | 4 | 25.76 |
| M. D. Marshall (*West Indians & West Indies XI*) | 282.1 | 57 | 782 | 30 | 4-33 | 0 | 26.06 |
| †C. W. Taylor (*Middx*) | 147 | 30 | 480 | 18 | 3-35 | 0 | 26.66 |
| C. L. Hooper (*West Indians & West Indies XI*) | 336.2 | 71 | 837 | 31 | 5-94 | 1 | 27.00 |
| A. P. Igglesden (*Kent*) | 471 | 94 | 1,351 | 50 | 5-36 | 1 | 27.02 |
| S. R. Barwick (*Glam.*) | 307.5 | 86 | 767 | 28 | 4-46 | 0 | 27.39 |
| P. M. Such (*Essex*) | 370.1 | 101 | 933 | 34 | 3-7 | 0 | 27.44 |

| | O | M | R | W | BB | 5W/i | Avge |
|---|---|---|---|---|---|---|---|
| †M. J. Gerrard (*Glos.*) | 131.5 | 21 | 415 | 15 | 6-40 | 1 | 27.66 |
| D. R. Pringle (*Essex*) | 533.5 | 146 | 1,308 | 47 | 5-70 | 2 | 27.82 |
| M. P. Bicknell (*Surrey*) | 470.5 | 118 | 1,256 | 45 | 7-52 | 1 | 27.91 |
| †P. Carrick (*Yorks.*) | 701.2 | 231 | 1,748 | 61 | 5-13 | 2 | 28.65 |
| M. Frost (*Glam.*) | 533.2 | 90 | 1,868 | 65 | 7-99 | 1 | 28.73 |
| E. A. E. Baptiste (*Northants*) | 529.2 | 122 | 1,443 | 50 | 7-95 | 3 | 28.86 |
| D. R. Gilbert (*Glos.*) | 648.5 | 135 | 1,865 | 64 | 8-55 | 1 | 29.14 |
| T. A. Merrick (*Kent*) | 539 | 101 | 1,787 | 61 | 7-99 | 1 | 29.29 |
| †J. H. Childs (*Essex*) | 751.1 | 248 | 1,907 | 65 | 6-61 | 4 | 29.33 |
| S. R. Lampitt (*Worcs.*) | 503.4 | 84 | 1,643 | 56 | 5-70 | 4 | 29.33 |
| S. L. Watkin (*Glam.*) | 728.5 | 155 | 2,175 | 74 | 6-55 | 4 | 29.39 |
| N. V. Radford (*Worcs.*) | 434.1 | 92 | 1,363 | 46 | 7-43 | 2 | 29.63 |
| J. A. North (*Sussex*) | 156.3 | 26 | 597 | 20 | 4-47 | 0 | 29.85 |
| G. C. Small (*Warwicks.*) | 498 | 126 | 1,347 | 45 | 4-36 | 0 | 29.93 |
| M. J. McCague (*Kent*) | 153.3 | 23 | 481 | 16 | 6-88 | 1 | 30.06 |
| A. I. C. Dodemaide (*Sussex*) | 579 | 116 | 1,637 | 54 | 5-130 | 1 | 30.31 |
| M. C. J. Ball (*Glos.*) | 186 | 36 | 582 | 19 | 5-128 | 1 | 30.63 |
| M. A. Feltham (*Surrey*) | 349 | 57 | 1,075 | 35 | 4-36 | 0 | 30.71 |
| R. A. Pick (*Notts.*) | 650.4 | 117 | 2,080 | 67 | 5-17 | 3 | 31.04 |
| D. J. Millns (*Leics.*) | 550.1 | 95 | 1,957 | 63 | 9-37 | 3 | 31.06 |
| Aqib Javed (*Hants*) | 510.1 | 84 | 1,656 | 53 | 6-91 | 3 | 31.24 |
| S. J. W. Andrew (*Essex*) | 399.3 | 74 | 1,352 | 43 | 4-38 | 0 | 31.44 |
| R. M. Ellison (*Kent*) | 484.1 | 102 | 1,480 | 47 | 7-33 | 2 | 31.48 |
| Salim Malik (*Essex*) | 118.2 | 10 | 473 | 15 | 3-26 | 0 | 31.53 |
| J. N. Maguire (*Leics.*) | 786 | 168 | 2,437 | 77 | 7-57 | 4 | 31.64 |
| †J. A. Afford (*Notts.*) | 670.3 | 207 | 1,817 | 57 | 4-44 | 0 | 31.87 |
| J. E. Emburey (*Middx*) | 899.3 | 246 | 2,170 | 68 | 7-71 | 1 | 31.91 |
| K. P. Evans (*Notts.*) | 425 | 89 | 1,278 | 40 | 5-52 | 2 | 31.95 |
| T. D. Topley (*Essex*) | 498.3 | 86 | 1,767 | 55 | 5-58 | 3 | 32.12 |
| P. J. Newport (*Worcs.*) | 712.4 | 138 | 2,140 | 66 | 4-27 | 0 | 32.42 |
| D. J. Foster (*Glam.*) | 223.5 | 35 | 814 | 25 | 6-84 | 1 | 32.56 |
| P. J. Bakker (*Hants*) | 239.3 | 65 | 655 | 20 | 4-66 | 0 | 32.75 |
| A. E. Warner (*Derbys.*) | 446.4 | 101 | 1,215 | 37 | 4-42 | 0 | 32.83 |
| †K. D. James (*Hants*) | 442.5 | 99 | 1,354 | 41 | 4-32 | 0 | 33.02 |
| P. N. Hepworth (*Leics.*) | 119.2 | 20 | 463 | 14 | 3-51 | 0 | 33.07 |
| J. G. Thomas (*Northants*) | 278.4 | 39 | 937 | 28 | 5-62 | 2 | 33.46 |
| A. N. Jones (*Sussex*) | 527.2 | 74 | 1,918 | 57 | 5-46 | 2 | 33.64 |
| S. C. Goldsmith (*Derbys.*) | 187 | 32 | 607 | 18 | 3-42 | 0 | 33.72 |
| †A. M. Smith (*Glos.*) | 310.2 | 55 | 983 | 29 | 4-41 | 0 | 33.89 |
| †J. P. Taylor (*Northants*) | 295.2 | 50 | 920 | 27 | 5-42 | 1 | 34.07 |
| N. G. Cowans (*Middx*) | 542.1 | 145 | 1,500 | 44 | 4-42 | 0 | 34.09 |
| B. T. P. Donelan (*Sussex*) | 426.3 | 112 | 1,162 | 34 | 6-62 | 2 | 34.17 |
| P. A. Smith (*Warwicks.*) | 157.1 | 31 | 513 | 15 | 5-28 | 1 | 34.20 |
| D. E. Malcolm (*Derbys.*) | 388.5 | 54 | 1,451 | 42 | 5-45 | 1 | 34.54 |
| †K. T. Medlycott (*Surrey*) | 510.4 | 115 | 1,703 | 49 | 6-98 | 2 | 34.75 |
| K. H. MacLeay (*Somerset*) | 284.3 | 54 | 872 | 25 | 3-40 | 0 | 34.88 |
| P. J. Hartley (*Yorks.*) | 522.3 | 100 | 1,751 | 50 | 6-151 | 3 | 35.02 |
| J. D. Batty (*Yorks.*) | 459.4 | 106 | 1,439 | 41 | 6-48 | 1 | 35.09 |
| †M. M. Patel (*Kent*) | 183.2 | 43 | 458 | 13 | 3-33 | 0 | 35.23 |
| †R. K. Illingworth (*Worcs.*) | 551.1 | 155 | 1,342 | 38 | 5-43 | 3 | 35.31 |
| A. M. Babington (*Glos.*) | 483.3 | 89 | 1,487 | 42 | 4-33 | 0 | 35.40 |
| N. F. Williams (*Middx*) | 524.5 | 99 | 1,668 | 47 | 5-89 | 1 | 35.48 |
| †N. G. B. Cook (*Northants*) | 336.3 | 79 | 994 | 28 | 4-74 | 0 | 35.50 |
| A. R. Roberts (*Northants*) | 331.5 | 72 | 1,032 | 29 | 6-72 | 1 | 35.58 |
| †R. W. Sladdin (*Derbys.*) | 368.5 | 101 | 965 | 27 | 5-186 | 1 | 35.74 |
| C. M. Wells (*Sussex*) | 230.4 | 62 | 644 | 18 | 7-42 | 1 | 35.77 |
| M. V. Fleming (*Kent*) | 214 | 46 | 573 | 16 | 3-28 | 0 | 35.81 |
| P. J. Martin (*Lancs.*) | 454.4 | 107 | 1,323 | 36 | 4-30 | 0 | 36.75 |
| P. J. W. Allott (*Lancs.*) | 192.1 | 49 | 516 | 14 | 4-56 | 0 | 36.85 |
| A. L. Penberthy (*Northants*) | 174.2 | 29 | 555 | 15 | 3-37 | 0 | 37.00 |

| | O | M | R | W | BB | 5W/i | Avge |
|---|---|---|---|---|---|---|---|
| S. J. Base (*Derbys.*) | 433.4 | 69 | 1,344 | 36 | 4-34 | 0 | 37.33 |
| E. E. Hemmings (*Notts.*) | 638.3 | 171 | 1,721 | 46 | 6-46 | 2 | 37.41 |
| R. J. Bailey (*Northants*) | 122.3 | 16 | 419 | 11 | 3-44 | 0 | 38.09 |
| S. D. Fletcher (*Yorks.*) | 238.1 | 45 | 765 | 20 | 6-70 | 1 | 38.25 |
| K. J. Shine (*Hants*) | 343.5 | 48 | 1,454 | 38 | 5-43 | 2 | 38.26 |
| †P. A. Booth (*Warwicks.*) | 226.1 | 47 | 690 | 18 | 4-103 | 0 | 38.33 |
| C. A. Connor (*Hants*) | 390 | 69 | 1,306 | 34 | 4-49 | 0 | 38.41 |
| A. C. S. Pigott (*Sussex*) | 444.2 | 98 | 1,402 | 36 | 5-37 | 1 | 38.94 |
| †D. A. Graveney (*Somerset*) | 708.2 | 153 | 2,160 | 55 | 7-105 | 2 | 39.27 |
| D. J. Capel (*Northants*) | 383.1 | 83 | 1,127 | 28 | 4-83 | 0 | 40.25 |
| R. J. Scott (*Glos.*) | 199 | 40 | 614 | 15 | 3-43 | 0 | 40.93 |
| M. Watkinson (*Lancs.*) | 629.2 | 115 | 2,173 | 53 | 4-45 | 0 | 41.00 |
| †R. J. Maru (*Hants*) | 625.1 | 178 | 1,641 | 40 | 5-128 | 1 | 41.02 |
| †R. P. Davis (*Kent*) | 513.2 | 142 | 1,531 | 37 | 4-81 | 0 | 41.37 |
| H. R. J. Trump (*Somerset*) | 637.2 | 111 | 2,113 | 51 | 6-48 | 4 | 41.43 |
| I. D. K. Salisbury (*Sussex*) | 638.2 | 148 | 2,001 | 48 | 5-40 | 1 | 41.68 |
| J. Boiling (*Surrey*) | 181.3 | 44 | 505 | 12 | 4-157 | 0 | 42.08 |
| M. A. Crawley (*Notts.*) | 176.5 | 53 | 463 | 11 | 3-21 | 0 | 42.09 |
| I. A. Greig (*Surrey*) | 165.3 | 34 | 426 | 10 | 3-30 | 0 | 42.60 |
| G. D. Rose (*Somerset*) | 323 | 53 | 1,075 | 25 | 4-77 | 0 | 43.00 |
| M. W. Alleyne (*Glos.*) | 144.1 | 27 | 474 | 11 | 3-35 | 0 | 43.09 |
| D. W. Headley (*Middx*) | 329.3 | 51 | 1,258 | 29 | 5-46 | 2 | 43.37 |
| C. W. Wilkinson (*Leics.*) | 315 | 64 | 1,009 | 23 | 4-59 | 0 | 43.86 |
| †I. J. Turner (*Hants*) | 238.5 | 65 | 637 | 14 | 4-28 | 0 | 45.50 |
| S. Bastien (*Glam.*) | 356.2 | 96 | 1,023 | 22 | 5-39 | 1 | 46.50 |
| A. J. Murphy (*Surrey*) | 546.4 | 118 | 1,667 | 35 | 5-63 | 1 | 47.62 |
| †L. Potter (*Leics.*) | 457.2 | 105 | 1,338 | 28 | 4-116 | 0 | 47.78 |
| J. W. Lloyds (*Glos.*) | 541.2 | 122 | 1,650 | 34 | 6-94 | 1 | 48.52 |
| G. A. Hick (*Worcs.*) | 151.4 | 34 | 492 | 10 | 5-42 | 1 | 49.20 |
| M. A. Robinson (*Yorks.*) | 416.1 | 85 | 1,241 | 25 | 3-43 | 0 | 49.64 |
| R. D. B. Croft (*Glam.*) | 704.2 | 168 | 1,930 | 38 | 5-62 | 1 | 50.78 |
| D. Gough (*Yorks.*) | 270 | 55 | 945 | 18 | 5-41 | 1 | 52.50 |
| J. C. Hallett (*Somerset*) | 178.3 | 31 | 637 | 12 | 3-154 | 0 | 53.08 |
| B. S. Wood (*OUCC*) | 187.5 | 34 | 665 | 12 | 2-24 | 0 | 55.41 |
| R. P. Lefebvre (*Somerset*) | 365 | 74 | 1,075 | 18 | 3-51 | 0 | 59.72 |
| G. Yates (*Lancs.*) | 591 | 117 | 1,914 | 31 | 3-39 | 0 | 61.74 |
| I. D. Austin (*Lancs.*) | 237.2 | 42 | 787 | 12 | 3-58 | 0 | 65.58 |
| J. D. Fitton (*Lancs.*) | 237.1 | 39 | 829 | 12 | 2-42 | 0 | 69.08 |
| A. N. Hayhurst (*Somerset*) | 205.3 | 32 | 780 | 11 | 2-42 | 0 | 70.90 |
| R. M. Pearson (*CUCC*) | 332 | 59 | 1,098 | 15 | 4-84 | 0 | 73.20 |

The following bowlers took ten wickets but bowled in fewer than ten innings:

| | O | M | R | W | BB | 5W/i | Avge |
|---|---|---|---|---|---|---|---|
| P. W. Jarvis (*Yorks.*) | 95 | 26 | 235 | 12 | 4-28 | 0 | 19.58 |
| M. A. Ealham (*Kent*) | 118.1 | 24 | 354 | 17 | 5-39 | 2 | 20.82 |
| †N. M. Kendrick (*Surrey*) | 105 | 26 | 262 | 12 | 5-54 | 2 | 21.83 |
| L. Tennant (*Leics.*) | 99 | 20 | 393 | 12 | 4-54 | 0 | 32.75 |
| †A. A. Barnett (*Middx*) | 107.4 | 23 | 329 | 10 | 4-119 | 0 | 32.90 |
| M. Jean-Jacques (*Derbys.*) | 141.3 | 26 | 496 | 12 | 4-54 | 0 | 41.33 |
| R. H. Macdonald (*OUCC*) | 157 | 49 | 457 | 10 | 3-66 | 0 | 45.70 |

# INDIVIDUAL SCORES OF 100 AND OVER

There were 315 three-figure innings in first-class cricket in 1991, 113 fewer than in 1990, but 67 more than in 1989. Of these, eighteen were double-hundreds, compared with 32 in 1990. The following list includes 248 hundreds hit in the County Championship, and 49 in other first-class games, but not the seventeen by the West Indian touring team, nor the one by the Sri Lankan touring team, which may be found in their respective sections.

*Signifies not out.*

**S. J. Cook (11)**
| | |
|---|---|
| 162* | Somerset v West Indians, Taunton |
| 152 | Somerset v Glam., Swansea |
| 107* | Somerset v Hants, Bath |
| 131 | Somerset v Lancs., Taunton |
| 193* | Somerset v Essex, Southend |
| 210* | Somerset v Northants, Northampton |
| 126 | Somerset v Kent, Taunton |
| 209* | Somerset v Sri Lankans, Taunton |
| 197 | |
| 115* } | Somerset v Hants, Southampton |
| 127 | Somerset v Warwicks., Taunton |

**M. W. Gatting (8)**
| | |
|---|---|
| 117* | Middx v Sussex, Hove |
| 180 | Middx v Somerset, Taunton |
| 138* | Middx v Essex, Lord's |
| 100* | Middx v Northants, Uxbridge |
| 143* | Middx v Notts., Lord's |
| 215* | Middx v Derbys., Lord's |
| 120 | Middx v Worcs., Worcester |
| 174 | Middx v Kent, Canterbury |

**M. Azharuddin (7)**
| | |
|---|---|
| 116* | Derbys. v Cambridge U., Cambridge |
| 154 | Derbys. v Glos., Gloucester |
| 100 | Derbys. v Warwicks., Birmingham |
| 110 | Derbys. v Middx, Lord's |
| 160* | Derbys. v Lancs., Derby |
| 129* | Derbys. v Notts., Nottingham |
| 212 | Derbys. v Leics., Leicester |

**M. P. Maynard (7)**
| | |
|---|---|
| 133* | Glam. v Somerset, Taunton |
| 127 | Glam. v Sussex, Cardiff |
| 204 | Glam. v Notts., Cardiff |
| 129 | |
| 126 } | Glam. v Glos., Cheltenham |
| 103* | Glam. v Surrey, The Oval |
| 243 | Glam. v Hants, Southampton |

**N. R. Taylor (7)**
| | |
|---|---|
| 146 | Kent v Derbys., Canterbury |
| 138* | Kent v West Indians, Canterbury |
| 150 | Kent v Leics., Leicester |
| 109 | Kent v Glos., Canterbury |
| 101 | Kent v Middx, Canterbury |
| 111 | |
| 203* } | Kent v Sussex, Hove |

**A. P. Wells (7)**
| | |
|---|---|
| 120 | Sussex v Middx, Lord's |
| 137 | Sussex v Middx, Hove |
| 153* | Sussex v Glam., Cardiff |
| 107 | Sussex v Kent, Tunbridge Wells |
| 159 | Sussex v Somerset, Hove |
| 253* | Sussex v Yorks., Middlesbrough |
| 162 | Sussex v Kent, Hove |

**G. A. Gooch (6)**
| | |
|---|---|
| 101* | Essex v Cambridge U., Cambridge |
| 154* | England v West Indies, Leeds |
| 106 | Essex v Middx, Lord's |
| 173 | Essex v Northants, Colchester |
| 174 | England v Sri Lanka, Lord's |
| 259 | Essex v Middx, Chelmsford |

**T. M. Moody (6)**
| | |
|---|---|
| 135 | Worcs. v Lancs., Worcester |
| 118 | Worcs. v Glam., Worcester |
| 181* | Worcs. v Essex, Ilford |
| 107 | Worcs. v Notts., Worcester |
| 210 | Worcs. v Warwicks., Worcester |
| 135 | Worcs. v Middx, Worcester |

**Salim Malik (6)**
| | |
|---|---|
| 173 | Essex v Kent, Folkestone |
| 163 | Essex v Glos., Bristol |
| 215 | Essex v Leics., Ilford |
| 185* | Essex v Surrey, The Oval |
| 102 | Essex v Somerset, Southend |
| 165 | Essex v Derbys., Chelmsford |

**C. L. Smith (6)**
| | |
|---|---|
| 200 | Hants v Oxford U., Oxford |
| 125 | Hants v Glos., Bristol |
| 145 | |
| 101 } | Hants v Sussex, Hove |
| 112 | Hants v Yorks., Southampton |
| 114 | Hants v Derbys., Chesterfield |

**C. W. J. Athey (5)**
| | |
|---|---|
| 127 | Glos. v Oxford U., Oxford |
| 120 | Glos. v Warwicks., Birmingham |
| 101 | Glos. v Derbys., Gloucester |
| 127 | Glos. v Lancs., Bristol |
| 103* | Glos. v Sussex, Hove |

**D. J. Bicknell** (5)

| | |
|---|---|
| 145* | Surrey v Essex, Chelmsford |
| 125 | Surrey v Notts., The Oval |
| 126 | Surrey v Sussex, Arundel |
| 151 | Surrey v Kent, Canterbury |
| 136 | Surrey v Hants, The Oval |

**B. C. Broad** (5)

| | |
|---|---|
| 166 | Notts. v Kent, Nottingham |
| 137* | Notts. v Surrey, The Oval |
| 162 | Notts. v Worcs., Worcester |
| 158 | Notts. v Sussex, Eastbourne |
| 131 | Notts. v Somerset, Nottingham |

**D. Byas** (5)

| | |
|---|---|
| 101 | Yorks. v Oxford U., Oxford |
| 135 | Yorks. v Derbys., Scarborough |
| 153 | Yorks. v Notts., Worksop |
| 122* | Yorks. v Leics., Leicester |
| 120 | Yorks. v Lancs., Scarborough |

**N. H. Fairbrother** (5)

| | |
|---|---|
| 121 | Lancs. v Warwicks., Birmingham |
| 109 | Lancs. v Worcs., Worcester |
| 107* | Lancs. v Glam., Liverpool |
| 109 | } Lancs. v Somerset, Taunton |
| 102* | |

**C. L. Hooper** (5)

| | |
|---|---|
| 164* | West Indies XI v World XI, Scarborough |

C. L. Hooper's four hundreds for the West Indian touring team may be found in that section.

**H. Morris** (5)

| | |
|---|---|
| 141 | Glam. v Somerset, Taunton |
| 132 | Glam. v Northants, Cardiff |
| 156* | Glam. v Sussex, Cardiff |
| 156* | Glam. v Yorks., Leeds |
| 131 | Glam. v Hants, Southampton |

**D. W. Randall** (5)

| | |
|---|---|
| 104 | Notts. v Leics., Nottingham |
| 112* | Notts. v Glam., Cardiff |
| 120 | Notts. v Lancs., Nottingham |
| 143* | Notts. v Derbys., Nottingham |
| 121 | Notts. v Middx, Nottingham |

**C. J. Tavaré** (5)

| | |
|---|---|
| 109* | Somerset v West Indians, Taunton |
| 162 | Somerset v Glam., Swansea |
| 134 | Somerset v Sussex, Hove |
| 100 | Somerset v Kent, Taunton |
| 183 | Somerset v Glos., Bristol |

**T. R. Ward** (5)

| | |
|---|---|
| 141 | Kent v Essex, Folkestone |
| 122 | Kent v Oxford U., Oxford |
| 110 | } Kent v Glam., Maidstone |
| 109 | |
| 235* | Kent v Middx, Canterbury |

**M. R. Benson** (4)

| | |
|---|---|
| 257 | Kent v Hants, Southampton |
| 160 | Kent v Derbys., Canterbury |
| 105 | Kent v Warwicks., Tunbridge Wells |
| 142 | Kent v Surrey, Canterbury |

**N. E. Briers** (4)

| | |
|---|---|
| 160 | Leics. v Notts., Nottingham |
| 104 | Leics. v Worcs., Worcester |
| 133 | Leics. v Northants, Leicester |
| 114 | Leics. v Yorks., Leicester |

**A. R. Butcher** (4)

| | |
|---|---|
| 102 | Glam. v Somerset, Swansea |
| 129 | } Glam. v Lancs., Liverpool |
| 104 | |
| 147 | Glam. v Glos., Abergavenny |

**A. Fordham** (4)

| | |
|---|---|
| 131 | Northants v Derbys., Derby |
| 105 | Northants v Derbys., Northampton |
| 116 | Northants v Leics., Leicester |
| 165 | Northants v Yorks., Northampton |

**G. D. Mendis** (4)

| | |
|---|---|
| 127* | Lancs. v Cambridge U., Cambridge |
| 113 | Lancs. v Warwicks., Birmingham |
| 119 | Lancs. v Warwicks., Manchester |
| 114 | Lancs. v Yorks., Scarborough |

**P. J. Prichard** (4)

| | |
|---|---|
| 190 | Essex v Northants, Northampton |
| 129 | Essex v Middx, Lord's |
| 122 | Essex v Kent, Southend |
| 128 | Essex v Yorks., Colchester |

**G. P. Thorpe** (4)

| | |
|---|---|
| 106* | Surrey v Glam., The Oval |
| 116* | Surrey v Northants, Northampton |
| 177 | Surrey v Sussex, The Oval |
| 117 | Surrey v Middx, Lord's |

**M. A. Atherton** (3)

| | |
|---|---|
| 138 | Lancs. v Cambridge U., Cambridge |
| 110 | Lancs. v Worcs., Worcester |
| 114* | Lancs. v Yorks., Manchester |

**G. R. Cowdrey** (3)

| | |
|---|---|
| 109* | Kent v Notts., Nottingham |
| 114 | Kent v Warwicks., Tunbridge Wells |
| 104 | Kent v West Indians, Canterbury |

**T. S. Curtis** (3)

| | |
|---|---|
| 120 | Worcs. v Lancs., Blackpool |
| 248 | Worcs. v Somerset, Worcester |
| 186* | Worcs. v Glam., Cardiff |

**M. A. Garnham** (3)

| | |
|---|---|
| 102* | Essex v Cambridge U., Cambridge |
| 117 | Essex v Derbys., Chelmsford |
| 123 | Essex v Leics., Leicester |

**R. J. Harden (3)**
134	Somerset v Derbys., Derby
100*	Somerset v Sri Lankans, Taunton
101	Somerset v Notts., Nottingham

**A. N. Hayhurst (3)**
116	Somerset v Derbys., Derby
172*	Somerset v Glos., Bath
100*	Somerset v Notts., Nottingham

**G. A. Hick (3)**
186	Worcs. v Sussex, Hove
141	Worcs. v Hants, Portsmouth
145	Worcs. v Surrey, Worcester

**N. Hussain (3)**
128	Essex v Surrey, The Oval
141	Essex v Northants, Colchester
196	Essex v Leics., Leicester

**P. Johnson (3)**
105	Notts. v Middx, Lord's
124	Notts. v Essex, Nottingham
114	Notts. v Lancs., Manchester

**A. J. Lamb (3)**
125	Northants v Lancs., Lytham
194	Northants v Surrey, Northampton
109	Northants v Yorks., Northampton

**N. J. Lenham (3)**
137	Sussex v Kent, Tunbridge Wells
106	Sussex v Somerset, Hove
193	Sussex v Leics., Hove

**M. D. Moxon (3)**
108	Yorks. v Northants, Leeds
200	Yorks. v Essex, Colchester
115	Yorks. v Lancs., Scarborough

**P. R. Pollard (3)**
100	Notts. v Hants, Nottingham
145	Notts. v Lancs., Nottingham
123	Notts. v Derbys., Derby

**R. T. Robinson (3)**
101	Notts. v Leics., Leicester
145	Notts. v Derbys., Derby
180*	Notts. v Worcs., Nottingham

**R. A. Smith (3)**
148*	England v West Indies, Lord's
109	England v West Indies, The Oval
107	Hants v Somerset, Southampton

**J. P. Stephenson (3)**
113*	Essex v Kent, Southend
116	Essex v Yorks., Colchester
113	Essex v Leics., Leicester

**A. J. Wright (3)**
100*	Glos. v Yorks., Sheffield
101*	Glos. v Surrey, Guildford
120	Glos. v Worcs., Cheltenham

**C. J. Adams (2)**
134	Derbys. v Cambridge U., Cambridge
112	Derbys. v Yorks., Chesterfield

**Asif Din (2)**
100	Warwicks. v Lancs., Manchester
140	Warwicks. v Leics., Leicester

**K. J. Barnett (2)**
122	Derbys. v Northants, Northampton
217	Derbys. v Notts., Derby

**T. J. Boon (2)**
108	Leics. v Cambridge U., Cambridge
102	Leics. v Yorks., Leicester

**I. T. Botham (2)**
104	Worcs. v Lancs., Worcester
161	Worcs. v West Indians, Worcester

**P. D. Bowler (2)**
104*	Derbys. v Lancs., Derby
104	Derbys. v Leics., Leicester

**M. V. Fleming (2)**
116	Kent v West Indians, Canterbury
113	Kent v Surrey, Canterbury

**G. Fowler (2)**
103*	Lancs. v Derbys., Manchester
113	Lancs. v Surrey, The Oval

**K. Greenfield (2)**
127*	Sussex v Cambridge U., Hove
104	Sussex v Sri Lankans, Hove

**P. N. Hepworth (2)**
115	Leics. v Cambridge U., Cambridge
115	Leics. v Essex, Leicester

**I. J. F. Hutchinson (2)**
125	Middx v Sussex, Hove
114	Middx v Glos., Bristol

**K. D. James (2)**
134*	Hants v Yorks., Southampton
101	Hants v Derbys., Chesterfield

**S. A. Kellett (2)**
109*	Yorks. v Sri Lankans, Leeds
125*	Yorks. v Derbys., Chesterfield

**S. A. Marsh (2)**
108*	Kent v Middx, Lord's
113*	Kent v Somerset, Taunton

**A. A. Metcalfe** (2)
113*   Yorks. v Lancs., Manchester
123    Yorks. v Glam., Leeds

**J. E. Morris** (2)
131    Derbys. v Cambridge U., Cambridge
122*   Derbys. v Glam., Chesterfield

**T. J. G. O'Gorman** (2)
148    Derbys. v Lancs., Manchester
108*   Derbys. v Notts., Derby

**M. R. Ramprakash** (2)
119    Middx v Sussex, Lord's
110    Middx v Notts., Nottingham

**P. E. Robinson** (2)
100    Yorks. v Sri Lankans, Leeds
189    Yorks. v Lancs., Scarborough

**G. D. Rose** (2)
105*   Somerset v Yorks., Taunton
106    Somerset v Glos., Bristol

**M. A. Roseberry** (2)
123*   Middx v Cambridge U., Cambridge
119*   Middx v Leics., Uxbridge

**R. J. Scott** (2)
127    Glos. v Worcs., Worcester
122    Glos. v Glam., Cheltenham

**R. J. Shastri** (2)
107    Glam. v Leics., Neath
133*   Glam. v Lancs., Liverpool

**D. M. Smith** (2)
126*   Sussex v Middx, Hove
100*   Sussex v Sri Lankans, Hove

**A. J. Stewart** (2)
109    Surrey v Glos., Guildford
113*   England v Sri Lanka, Lord's

**V. P. Terry** (2)
171    Hants v Sussex, Hove
124    Hants v Warwicks., Portsmouth

The following each played one three-figure innings:

M. W. Alleyne, 165, Glos. v Northants, Bristol; I. D. Austin, 101*, Lancs. v Yorks., Scarborough.

R. J. Bailey, 117, Northants v Somerset, Northampton; J. D. R. Benson, 133*, Leics. v Hants, Bournemouth; P. Bent, 100*, Worcs. v Lancs., Blackpool; R. J. Blakey, 196, Yorks. v Oxford U., Oxford; K. R. Brown, 143*, Middx v Notts., Nottingham; N. D. Burns, 108, Somerset v Notts., Nottingham.

D. J. Capel, 100, Northants v Cambridge U., Cambridge; J. P. Crawley, 130, Lancs. v Surrey, Manchester; M. A. Crawley, 112, Notts. v Oxford U., Oxford.

D. B. D'Oliveira, 237, Worcs. v Oxford U., Oxford; A. Dale, 140, Glam. v Glos., Abergavenny; A. I. C. Dodemaide, 100*, Sussex v Glam., Cardiff.

N. A. Foster, 107*, Essex v Sussex, Horsham.

S. C. Goldsmith, 127, Derbys. v Sussex, Derby.

J. W. Hall, 117*, Sussex v Somerset, Taunton; G. D. Hodgson, 105, Glos. v Oxford U., Oxford; A. M. Hooper, 125, Cambridge U. v Surrey, Cambridge.

T. E. Jesty, 122*, Lancs. v Oxford U., Oxford.

N. V. Knight, 101*, Essex v Lancs., Manchester.

D. A. Leatherdale, 157, Worcs. v Somerset, Worcester; R. P. Lefebvre, 100, Somerset v Worcs., Weston-super-Mare; M. A. Lynch, 141*, Surrey v Middx, The Oval.

S. V. Manjrekar, 154*, World XI v West Indies XI, Scarborough; K. T. Medlycott, 109, Surrey v Cambridge U., Cambridge; T. C. Middleton, 102, Hants v Somerset, Bath; A. J. Moles, 133, Warwicks. v Glos., Birmingham; P. Moores, 102, Sussex v Sri Lankans, Hove.

M. C. J. Nicholas, 107*, Hants v Notts., Nottingham.

D. P. Ostler, 120*, Warwicks. v Kent, Tunbridge Wells.

P. W. G. Parker, 111, Sussex v Kent, Hove; B. M. W. Patterson, 108, Scotland v Ireland, Dublin (Malahide); I. L. Philip, 116*, Scotland v Ireland, Dublin (Malahide).

P. M. Roebuck, 101, Somerset v Glam., Taunton; R. C. Russell, 111, Glos. v Hants, Bristol.

A. C. H. Seymour, 157, Essex v Glam., Cardiff; N. J. Speak, 153, Lancs. v Surrey, Manchester; M. P. Speight, 149, Sussex v Cambridge U., Hove; N. A. Stanley, 132, Northants v Lancs., Lytham.

S. P. Titchard, 135, Lancs. v Notts., Manchester; G. J. Turner, 101*, Oxford U. v Lancs., Oxford.

D. M. Ward, 151, Surrey v Lancs., Manchester; Wasim Akram, 122, Lancs. v Hants, Basingstoke; M. Watkinson, 114*, Lancs. v Surrey, The Oval; J. J. Whitaker, 105, Leics. v Essex, Leicester; P. Whitticase, 114*, Leics. v Hants, Bournemouth; R. G. Williams, 101*, Northants v Cambridge U., Cambridge.

G. Yates, 100*, Lancs. v Essex, Manchester.

# TEN WICKETS IN A MATCH

There were nineteen instances of bowlers taking ten or more wickets in a match in first-class cricket in 1991, six more than in 1990. The list includes seventeen in the County Championship and two in other first-class matches.

**Waqar Younis** (3)
11-122, Surrey v Lancs., The Oval; 11-136, Surrey v Hants, Bournemouth; 12-92, Surrey v Hants, The Oval.

**A. A. Donald** (2)
10-96, Warwicks. v Yorks., Leeds; 10-74, Warwicks. v Glam., Swansea.

**T. A. Munton** (2)
11-127, Warwicks. v Middx, Birmingham; 10-91, Warwicks. v Worcs., Birmingham.

The following each took ten wickets in a match on one occasion:

D. G. Cork, 10-78, Derbys. v Essex, Derby.
B. T. P. Donelan, 10-136, Sussex v Glos., Hove.
N. A. Foster, 10-122, Essex v Middx, Chelmsford; M. Frost, 11-143, Glam. v Glos., Cheltenham.
M. J. Gerrard, 10-60, Glos. v Sri Lankans, Bristol.
N. M. Kendrick, 10-174, Surrey v Lancs., Manchester.
D. V. Lawrence, 11-129, Glos. v Hants, Bristol.
K. T. Medlycott, 11-134, Surrey v Cambridge U., Cambridge; D. J. Millns, 12-91, Leics. v Derbys., Derby.
F. D. Stephenson, 10-88, Notts. v Northants, Wellingborough School.
P. C. R. Tufnell, 11-228, Middx v Hants, Lord's.
Wasim Akram, 11-129, Lancs. v Middx, Uxbridge.

# THE CRICKET COUNCIL

The Cricket Council, which was set up in 1968 and reconstituted in 1974 and 1983, acts as the governing body for cricket in the British Isles. It comprises the following, the officers listed being those for 1990-91.

*Chairman:* W. R. F. Chamberlain.
*Vice-Chairman:* J. D. Robson.
*8 Representatives of the Test and County Cricket Board:* W. R. F. Chamberlain, C. R. M. Atkinson, D. J. Insole, M. P. Murray, D. H. Newton, D. N. Perry, H. J. Pocock, F. M. Turner.
*5 Representatives of the National Cricket Association:* M. J. K. Smith, J. D. Robson, F. H. Elliott, E. K. Ingman, J. G. Overy.
*3 Representatives of the Marylebone Cricket Club:* The Rt Hon. The Lord Griffiths, G. H. G. Doggart, R. H. Burton.
*1 Representative (non-voting) of the Minor Counties Cricket Association:* J. E. O. Smith.
*1 Representative (non-voting) of the Irish Cricket Union:* D. Scott.
*1 Representative (non-voting) of the Scottish Cricket Union:* R. W. Barclay.

*Secretary:* A. C. Smith.

# THE TEST AND COUNTY CRICKET BOARD

The TCCB was set up in 1968 to be responsible for Test matches, official tours, and first-class and minor county competitions. It is composed of representatives of the eighteen first-class counties; Marylebone Cricket Club; Minor Counties Cricket Association; Oxford University Cricket Club, Cambridge University Cricket Club, the Irish Cricket Union and the Scottish Cricket Union.

## Officers 1990-91

*Chairman:* W. R. F. Chamberlain.

*Chairmen of Committees:* W. R. F. Chamberlain (Executive); D. B. Carr (Pitches); O. S. Wheatley (Cricket), D. J. Insole (International); P. R. Bromage (Discipline); M. P. Murray (Finance); B. G. K. Downing (Marketing); D. R. W. Silk (Registration); E. R. Dexter (England Committee); A. C. Smith (Appointment of Umpires); Revd M. D. Vockins (Second XI Competitions).

*Chief Executive:* A. C. Smith. *Cricket Secretary:* T. M. Lamb. *Administration Secretary:* A. S. Brown. *Accountant:* C. A. Barker. *Marketing Manager:* T. D. M. Blake. *Media Relations Manager:* P. W. Smith. *England Team Manager:* M. J. Stewart.

# THE NATIONAL CRICKET ASSOCIATION

With the setting up of the Cricket Council in 1968 it was necessary to form a separate organisation to represent the interests of all cricket below the first-class game, and it is the National Cricket Association that carries out this function. It comprises representatives from 51 county cricket associations and seventeen national cricketing organisations.

## Officers 1990-91

*President:* M. J. K. Smith.
*Chairman:* J. D. Robson.
*Vice-Chairman:* F. H. Elliott.

*Chief Executive:* K. V. Andrew.
*General Secretary:* B. J. Aspital.
*Hon. Treasurer:* D. W. Carter.

# THE WEST INDIANS IN ENGLAND, 1991

The West Indian tourists of 1991 were not so formidable as their predecessors of 1984, who won 5-0, or 1988, who won 4-0; and therefore their Test series against England was the more interesting and attractive. From the moment at Leeds when England showed that they could at last compete with West Indies on roughly equal terms, public interest increased, until many a Test match day was sold out. In all, the series grossed receipts of £4,776,229, including the first £1 million Test at The Oval, a record for a Test ground other than Lord's. In financial terms, at the very least, the TCCB's decision to invite West Indies back after only three years, so that the lucrative tours by Australia and West Indies should not follow one another, was justified to the full.

Some critics had forecast that spectators would not be attracted by the sight of four fast bowlers hurling down bouncers, and taking longer than six hours to bowl the mandatory minimum of 90 overs. But their judgment was a little too aesthetic. Once England, in the persons of Graham Gooch and Robin Smith, had stood up to the West Indian bowling, the country at large was enthralled by the conflict, however far it was from subtle. Gooch had first fortified his players on their tour of the Caribbean in early 1990, but it was a welcome change for the British public to see England in something other than headlong flight.

The series was made even more attractive for being staged in the best of spirit, without any of the bad blood which had sullied the Australians' visit to the West Indies earlier in the year. Viv Richards, backed by a firm and worldly-wise manager in Lance Gibbs, promised at the outset "a nice, peaceful tour", and Gooch made a full contribution to its fulfilment. Indeed, had the weather been less cold in the early part of the season – there can be no doubt that this, along with their feeling jaded after the series against Australia, contributed to the West Indians' slow start – the summer could have ranked among the vintage ones. Only once before had England shared a home series 2-2: in 1972, when their series against Australia had been a fluctuating, seesaw affair. This time England won the First Test, on the back of what was widely considered to be as fine a captain's innings as there has ever been, when Gooch carried his bat for 154. Then, after a draw at Lord's, they appeared to succumb gradually yet inexorably to the cumulative shellshock which had done for previous England teams. Surprise, surprise, therefore, when England retaliated in the Fifth Test to square the series, and at The Oval, too, where West Indies had not been beaten since 1966.

It had been thought that the one Test pitch with some life in it would favour the tourists. However, the West Indians gave the impression of relaxing a shade after their victory in the Fourth Test at Edgbaston, which ensured that their record of being unbeaten in a Test series extended back to 1980. England, for their part, went for a daringly chosen team at The Oval, and its eventual success reflected great credit on Ted Dexter, Micky Stewart and Gooch himself. They brought back Alec Stewart to keep wicket and to score runs on his home ground, though he had not kept in a first-class match since the winter tour of Australia; Ian Botham, after a two-year absence from Test cricket (he had played in the first one-day international, but pulled a hamstring); and Philip Tufnell, who had been disregarded all summer because of his "attitudinal problems" in Australia. Each of them played outstanding parts in England's victory, as did David Lawrence, who returned for his second match of the series and supplied the pace and enthusiasm which England had vainly wanted from Devon Malcolm. It was Botham's first victory in his twentieth Test against West Indies.

Compared with their immediate predecessors, the West Indians were virtually as strong as ever in their first-choice Test bowling of Curtly Ambrose, Patrick Patterson, Malcolm Marshall and Courtney Walsh. They had declined in their batting, however – the loss of Gordon Greenidge during the Old Trafford one-day international was insuperable – and in their close catching, both in the slips and at short leg, where Gus Logie stood too deep and was anything but the world's best fielder that he could claim to be in other positions. The effect which the four main West Indian bowlers had on Mike Atherton, Graeme Hick and Allan Lamb demonstrated that their inherent quality was as high as their predecessors'. Atherton, after being the pillar of England's 3-0 victory in the one-day series, either misjudged the line of off-stump balls, or received a debated leg-before decision, or steered with an open-faced bat to slips who had not been there in the limited-overs games. Hick never made the runs commensurate with the enormous reputation he had built up, except in the third Texaco Trophy international at Lord's. During the Test matches, his footwork – never fluent – froze into immobility; then, to counter the short ball, he experimented with a more open-chested stance. But above all the newly qualified Zimbabwean was too hesitant, introspective and focused on defence to assert himself. For all his technical limitations, Hick could still have made some runs, against the less than new ball, had he been the confident young batsman of 1988 who had played his strokes and scored 172 against the tourists at Worcester.

Ambrose removed Hick in six of his seven Test innings with short-pitched bowling which was awesome not simply in its speed but in its pinpoint precision. However, if an England batsman had the expertise to deal with bouncers, the West Indians seldom bothered to bowl them. The pitches were uniformly slow, although the one at The Oval did have some bounce, and suited the home side, which had not been the case in 1984 and 1988. Unmitigated accuracy had to be the plan, both for West Indies and for England, although the latter usually had only Phillip DeFreitas and Derek Pringle to implement it.

Since the 1988 tour, Ambrose had improved his control to the point where a batsman had to play almost every ball – and not with a scoring stroke, either. In fact, both of England's victories could easily have been defeats: if Ambrose had been fully fit on the last day at The Oval, when England were 80 for four in pursuit of 143; and if Richards, instead of rotating his bowlers as usual, had kept Ambrose going after lunch on the third day at Headingley, by when he had reduced England's second innings to 47 for three in his opening spell. Ambrose's rise to the status of a giant – with the mannerism of celebrating each wicket by whirling his arms upwards, like a flock of doves taking to the air – was offset by Marshall's decline since 1988. The speed to frighten was no longer there, and less of the out-swinger, too. That most of Marshall's wickets now came with the in-swinger was a tribute to the cleverness of his wristwork at the moment of delivery. It was also a criticism of the England management, for failing to prepare their players fully with video analysis of Marshall's action.

Like Ambrose, Patterson was consistently better than he had been in 1988, through becoming accuracy itself for a bowler of his extreme pace. But in the same way, his improvement was offset by the tiredness of Courtney Walsh, who never bowled waywardly but was not as incisive as he had been. Walsh's place was under no threat: Ian Bishop had to withdraw from the original party with a stress fracture of the lower vertebrae; Ezra Moseley was left behind, perhaps because he had toured South Africa as a "rebel", and neither Ian Allen nor Hamesh Anthony was ready for Test cricket. Anthony, however, had the makings of a Test all-rounder. At the start of the tour he was bowling from wide of the crease and angling the ball in, but he got closer to the stumps and made it run away by the end. Likewise, the batting of this young Antiguan became less leg-sided.

Against such fast bowling, Gooch and Smith batted with astonishing consistency – Gooch had one score in the series under 25 – and the utmost mental rigour. It would hardly be an exaggeration to say they both batted virtually as well as humanly possible, knowing exactly when to take the risk of counter-attacking. Mark Ramprakash was also able to survive, but without having the experience to judge when to play his strokes. And that was the sum total of England's specialist batting until the final Test, when Stewart made runs and Hugh Morris battled through his difficulties with the short ball to share a century opening stand. However, England's lower order made frequent contributions, a sign of high morale, as it had not done in 1984 and 1988. In particular, Pringle held up one end, and DeFreitas or Chris Lewis or even Lawrence took the attack to the fast bowlers, who were at times confounded by their assault.

Over the series England averaged 27 runs per wicket, while West Indies averaged 30, a figure down on previous visits when Greenidge and Desmond Haynes had launched the innings. England's lowest total was their 188 at Edgbaston, the one occasion when their batting was an outright failure. The tourists "bettered" that, in paucity, three times, and if Richie Richardson had not made his adjustment to English pitches for the first time, they might have been embarrassingly short of runs. Richardson waited for the ball to reach him, instead of throwing himself forward at it, as he had tried to do on his 1988 tour of England. More may be read about him, and Ambrose, in the section on Five Cricketers of the Year. Phil Simmons, who replaced Greenidge in the Test team, had a similar power of stroke, but not the masterful judgment in deciding which ball to leave. Moreover, he was all at sea against spin, falling to the first over from Hick at Lord's and the very first ball in Test cricket from Richard Illingworth at Trent Bridge. Clayton Lambert, on the other hand, showed some capacity for improvement, though he could have done with being given an opportunity before the age of 29. Called in from the North Yorkshire and South Durham league club of Blackhall when Greenidge's knee gave way, Lambert made 99 against Glamorgan and a century against Essex, only his second in first-class cricket outside his native Guyana.

For brief periods the senior batsmen, Richards and Haynes, batted as well as ever, before furnishing evidence for the belief that long innings are the domain of the younger player, and at The Oval Haynes carried his bat for the second time in Tests. Richards was as eye-catching and unpredictable as ever, but strokes at Headingley and Trent Bridge made him hang his own head; and at The Oval he had the match in his hands during the follow-on before one last, fatal lapse. Against those unforced errors, he threw himself forward in the Third Test to avoid being leg-before and built the first-innings lead that brought West Indies back into the series. In the Fourth as well, albeit after another shaky start, he settled the outcome with a blaze of his finest strokes and was carried shoulder-high from the field.

It was hard on Brian Lara, the Trinidadian left-hander, that he should have injured an ankle during practice at the Edgbaston Test, so that it was Lambert who replaced Logie at The Oval and made his début. Logie had torn knee ligaments. Although Lara did not make many runs in the county games, it was felt that he was more than ready for a run in Test cricket. Logie and Dujon had been the leading run-makers in the 1988 Tests, but Logie's 78 at Nottingham was their one substantial innings this time. The wicket-keeping of Dujon had not deteriorated, however, and in warding off the challenge of the no less accomplished David Williams, he was able to move into second place in the Test list of career dismissals.

The tourists hardly felt their lack of a specialist spinner, for Carl Hooper bowled plenty of his improving off-spin in the county games. Their failure to win more than three of them was largely a result of rain. And in any event, come rain or shine, the £50,000 jackpot offered by Tetley Bitter to the tourists for winning nine or more out of eleven county games was little more than a publicity stunt. Even Don Bradman's 1948 Australians did not win so high a proportion of their county games, with fifteen out of twenty.

Hooper's tour batting average of 85.46 was the highest by a West Indian in England, and he also provided the most exciting passage of play in the series, when he assailed Tufnell and Lawrence with his high-class strokeplay on the fourth morning at The Oval. Could a batsman from any other Test team have hit three sixes in the first twenty minutes of any day's play, let alone when his side was following on? The cricket played by the West Indians was not their most successful, but it was entertaining – as entertaining as modern cricket, based on fast bowling, can be.

In this context, a surprising feature of the summer was that while crowds flocked to the Tests, there was a decline in active support for the tourists from West Indians living in Britain. Various causes were put forward, such as the ban on taking musical instruments into grounds and so making the occasion into a carnival, or the high cost of tickets, which often had to be purchased months in advance. There was also a sociological explanation, that the West Indians lived mainly in Britain's inner cities, where cricket is hardly played; and another that England's Test team had come to include two or three players of West Indian origin. Whatever the reason, the tourists received less support than previously, and the Tests were less colourful and animated as a result. But this time at least, the quality of cricket made good the deficiency. – Scyld Berry.

## WEST INDIAN TOUR RESULTS

*Test matches* – Played 5: Won 2, Lost 2, Drawn 1.
*First-class matches* – Played 16: Won 5, Lost 2, Drawn 9.
*Wins* – England (2), Middlesex, Leicestershire, Kent.
*Losses* – England (2).
*Draws* – England, Worcestershire, Somerset, Derbyshire, Northamptonshire, Hampshire, Glamorgan, Gloucestershire, Essex.
*One-day internationals* – Played 3: Lost 3.
*Other non first-class matches* – Played 7: Won 3, Lost 1, Drawn 3. *Wins* – Gloucestershire, League Cricket Conference, Wales. *Loss* – Lavinia, Duchess of Norfolk's XI. *Draws* – Oxford & Cambridge Universities, Minor Counties, Ireland.

## TEST MATCH AVERAGES
### ENGLAND – BATTING

|  | T | I | NO | R | HI | 100s | Avge |
|---|---|---|---|---|---|---|---|
| R. A. Smith ........ | 4 | 7 | 2 | 416 | 148* | 2 | 83.20 |
| G. A. Gooch ........ | 5 | 9 | 1 | 480 | 154* | 1 | 60.00 |
| M. R. Ramprakash .. | 5 | 9 | 0 | 210 | 29 | 0 | 23.33 |
| P. A. J. DeFreitas ... | 5 | 8 | 1 | 134 | 55* | 0 | 19.14 |
| D. R. Pringle ...... | 4 | 7 | 0 | 128 | 45 | 0 | 18.28 |
| R. K. Illingworth ... | 2 | 4 | 2 | 31 | 13 | 0 | 15.50 |
| A. J. Lamb ........ | 4 | 7 | 0 | 88 | 29 | 0 | 12.57 |
| H. Morris .......... | 2 | 4 | 0 | 50 | 44 | 0 | 12.50 |
| G. A. Hick ........ | 4 | 7 | 0 | 75 | 43 | 0 | 10.71 |
| R. C. Russell ...... | 4 | 7 | 0 | 73 | 46 | 0 | 10.42 |
| M. A. Atherton ..... | 5 | 9 | 0 | 79 | 32 | 0 | 8.77 |

Played in two Tests: D. V. Lawrence 4, 34, 9; C. C. Lewis 13, 65, 47*; D. E. Malcolm 5*, 4, 0; S. L. Watkin 2, 0, 6. Played in one Test: I. T. Botham 31, 4*; A. J. Stewart 31, 38*; P. C. R. Tufnell 2.

*\* Signifies not out.*

### BOWLING

|  | O | M | R | W | BB | 5W/i | Avge |
|---|---|---|---|---|---|---|---|
| P. A. J. DeFreitas ... | 185.5 | 55 | 457 | 22 | 4-34 | 0 | 20.77 |
| P. C. R. Tufnell ... | 60.3 | 9 | 175 | 7 | 6-25 | 1 | 25.00 |
| D. R. Pringle ...... | 128.1 | 33 | 322 | 12 | 5-100 | 1 | 26.83 |
| S. L. Watkin ........ | 36 | 4 | 153 | 5 | 3-38 | 0 | 30.60 |
| C. C. Lewis ........ | 79 | 30 | 201 | 6 | 6-111 | 1 | 33.50 |
| D. V. Lawrence ..... | 78.1 | 7 | 350 | 10 | 5-106 | 1 | 35.00 |

Also bowled: I. T. Botham 27-8-67-3; G. A. Gooch 8-1-14-0; G. A. Hick 24-5-95-2; R. K. Illingworth 56.4-10-213-4; D. E. Malcolm 42.3-3-180-3.

### WEST INDIES – BATTING

|  | T | I | NO | R | HI | 100s | Avge |
|---|---|---|---|---|---|---|---|
| R. B. Richardson ... | 5 | 10 | 1 | 495 | 121 | 2 | 55.00 |
| I. V. A. Richards ... | 5 | 8 | 1 | 376 | 80 | 0 | 53.71 |
| D. L. Haynes ....... | 5 | 10 | 3 | 323 | 75* | 0 | 46.14 |
| C. L. Hooper ....... | 5 | 9 | 2 | 271 | 111 | 1 | 38.71 |
| A. L. Logie ........ | 4 | 5 | 0 | 120 | 78 | 0 | 24.00 |
| M. D. Marshall ..... | 5 | 7 | 1 | 116 | 67 | 0 | 19.33 |
| P. V. Simmons ..... | 5 | 10 | 0 | 181 | 38 | 0 | 18.10 |
| P. J. L. Dujon ..... | 5 | 7 | 0 | 89 | 33 | 0 | 12.71 |
| C. A. Walsh ....... | 5 | 7 | 0 | 66 | 18 | 0 | 9.42 |
| B. P. Patterson .... | 3 | 5 | 3 | 11 | 5* | 0 | 5.50 |
| C. E. L. Ambrose ... | 5 | 7 | 0 | 37 | 17 | 0 | 5.28 |

Played in two Tests: I. B. A. Allen 1*, 4*. Played in one Test: C. B. Lambert 39, 14.

*\* Signifies not out.*

## BOWLING

|  | O | M | R | W | BB | 5W/i | Avge |
|---|---|---|---|---|---|---|---|
| C. E. L. Ambrose ... | 249 | 68 | 560 | 28 | 6-52 | 2 | 20.00 |
| M. D. Marshall ..... | 172.1 | 36 | 442 | 20 | 4-33 | 0 | 22.10 |
| B. P. Patterson ...... | 117.3 | 20 | 389 | 13 | 5-81 | 1 | 29.92 |
| C. A. Walsh ........ | 187 | 42 | 493 | 15 | 4-64 | 0 | 32.86 |
| I. B. A. Allen ....... | 47 | 4 | 180 | 5 | 2-69 | 0 | 36.00 |

Also bowled: C. L. Hooper 64–13–137–2; C. B. Lambert 0.4–0–4–1; I. V. A. Richards 5–1–6–0; P. V. Simmons 3–0–7–0.

# WEST INDIAN TOUR AVERAGES – FIRST-CLASS MATCHES

## BATTING

|  | M | I | NO | R | HI | 100s | Avge |
|---|---|---|---|---|---|---|---|
| C. L. Hooper ........ | 15 | 23 | 8 | 1,282 | 196 | 4 | 85.46 |
| R. B. Richardson .... | 14 | 24 | 5 | 1,290 | 135* | 6 | 67.89 |
| I. V. A. Richards .... | 12 | 18 | 4 | 817 | 131 | 1 | 58.35 |
| C. B. Lambert ....... | 6 | 11 | 2 | 452 | 116 | 1 | 50.22 |
| D. L. Haynes ....... | 13 | 22 | 5 | 721 | 151 | 1 | 42.41 |
| P. J. L. Dujon ....... | 11 | 14 | 3 | 439 | 142* | 1 | 39.90 |
| P. V. Simmons ...... | 14 | 26 | 1 | 985 | 136 | 3 | 39.40 |
| B. C. Lara .......... | 8 | 12 | 0 | 341 | 93 | 0 | 28.41 |
| A. L. Logie ......... | 12 | 17 | 1 | 433 | 78 | 0 | 27.06 |
| C. G. Greenidge .... | 2 | 4 | 1 | 72 | 26 | 0 | 24.00 |
| M. D. Marshall ..... | 10 | 11 | 2 | 196 | 67 | 0 | 21.77 |
| D. Williams ......... | 6 | 5 | 1 | 83 | 35 | 0 | 20.75 |
| I. B. A. Allen ....... | 10 | 5 | 4 | 16 | 8 | 0 | 16.00 |
| H. A. G. Anthony ... | 11 | 8 | 3 | 76 | 33* | 0 | 15.20 |
| C. A. Walsh ........ | 11 | 8 | 1 | 66 | 18 | 0 | 9.42 |
| C. E. L. Ambrose .... | 10 | 8 | 1 | 53 | 17 | 0 | 7.57 |
| B. P. Patterson ...... | 11 | 5 | 3 | 11 | 5* | 0 | 5.50 |

* *Signifies not out.*

## BOWLING

|  | O | M | R | W | BB | 5W/i | Avge |
|---|---|---|---|---|---|---|---|
| C. E. L. Ambrose .... | 390 | 122 | 869 | 51 | 6-52 | 3 | 17.03 |
| M. D. Marshall ..... | 261.1 | 51 | 706 | 28 | 4-33 | 0 | 25.21 |
| C. L. Hooper ........ | 305 | 68 | 696 | 26 | 4-49 | 0 | 26.76 |
| B. P. Patterson ...... | 287.4 | 68 | 912 | 32 | 5-81 | 2 | 28.50 |
| C. A. Walsh ........ | 324.4 | 75 | 915 | 29 | 4-39 | 0 | 31.55 |
| H. A. G. Anthony ... | 223.3 | 30 | 878 | 26 | 3-28 | 0 | 33.76 |
| P. V. Simmons ...... | 74 | 16 | 263 | 6 | 2-34 | 0 | 43.83 |
| I. B. A. Allen ....... | 217.4 | 35 | 811 | 16 | 2-61 | 0 | 50.68 |

Also bowled: C. B. Lambert 1.4–1–4–1; B. C. Lara 8–1–36–0; I. V. A. Richards 47–9–161–2; R. B. Richardson 5–2–6–0.

## FIELDING

26 – D. Williams (23 ct, 3 st); 21 – P. J. L. Dujon; 19 – C. L. Hooper; 12 – R. B. Richardson; 10 – P. V. Simmons; 9 – B. C. Lara; 8 – I. B. A. Allen, I. V. A. Richards; 7 – H. A. G. Anthony, A. L. Logie; 4 – D. L. Haynes, C. B. Lambert, B. P. Patterson, Substitutes; 1 – C. E. L. Ambrose, C. G. Greenidge.

## HUNDREDS FOR WEST INDIANS

The following 22 three-figure innings were played for the West Indians, seventeen in first-class matches and five in non first-class matches.

**R. B. Richardson** (6)
- 135*   v Leics., Leicester
- 114   v Derbys., Derby
- 109   v Glam., Swansea
- 104   v England, Birmingham (Fourth Test)
- 119   v Glos., Bristol
- 121   v England, The Oval (Fifth Test)

**C. L. Hooper** (4)
- 123   v Somerset, Taunton
- 111   v England, Lord's (Second Test)
- 196   v Hants, Southampton
- 111*   v Glos., Bristol

**C. B. Lambert** (3)
- †101*   v League Cricket Conference, Trowbridge
- †105   v Ireland, Downpatrick
- 116   v Essex, Chelmsford

**P. V. Simmons** (3)
- 134   v Worcs., Worcester
- 136   v Middx, Lord's
- 107   v Kent, Canterbury

**D. L. Haynes** (2)
- †101   v Glos., Bristol
- 151   v Glos., Bristol

**P. J. L. Dujon** (1)
- 142*   v Essex, Chelmsford

**B. C. Lara** (1)
- †110   v Oxford & Camb. Univs, Oxford

**A. L. Logie** (1)
- †118   v Ireland, Downpatrick

**I. V. A. Richards** (1)
- 131   v Worcs., Worcester

*\* Signifies not out.*    † *Not first-class.*

*Note:* Those matches which follow which were not first-class are signified by the use of a dagger.

## †LAVINIA, DUCHESS OF NORFOLK'S XI v WEST INDIANS

At Arundel, May 12. Lavinia, Duchess of Norfolk's XI won by two wickets. Toss: Lavinia, Duchess of Norfolk's XI. Morris, whose 98 came from 97 balls and included thirteen fours and a six, set up the first victory for the Duchess's men for five years. He had been bowled by a Simmons no-ball when 26, but then added 60 in ten overs with his captain and Derbyshire colleague, Azharuddin. After his dismissal at 195, the tail hung on to win with fourteen balls to spare. Simmons and Logie dominated the West Indians' innings, in which Greenidge fell to Sussex off-spinner Donelan's first ball. A crowd of 9,000 watched the match, which was to be the West Indians' only defeat outside the Tests and one-day internationals; 32 extras conceded were a portent of limited-overs games to come.

### West Indians

| | |
|---|---|
| C. G. Greenidge c Azharuddin b Donelan . | 22 |
| P. V. Simmons c Azharuddin b Donelan . | 40 |
| R. B. Richardson b Bainbridge . . . . . . . | 5 |
| B. C. Lara b Donelan . . . . . . . . . . . . . . | 15 |
| C. L. Hooper c Krikken b Bainbridge . . | 1 |
| A. L. Logie c and b Bainbridge . . . . . . . | 61 |
| *I. V. A. Richards c Azharuddin b Barnett . | 17 |
| †P. J. L. Dujon not out . . . . . . . . . . . . . | 21 |
| H. A. G. Anthony c Butcher b Mortensen . | 4 |
| I. B. A. Allen not out . . . . . . . . . . . . . . | 2 |
| B 1, l-b 12, w 9, n-b 1 . . . . . . . | 23 |
| 1/33 2/45 3/76    (8 wkts, 50 overs) | 211 |
| 4/77 5/117 6/174 | |
| 7/186 8/208 | |

B. P. Patterson did not bat.

Bowling: Mortensen 10–1–32–1; Lever 10–3–33–0; Bainbridge 10–1–36–3; Donelan 10–1–41–3; Barnett 6–0–32–1; Azharuddin 4–0–24–0.

## Lavinia, Duchess of Norfolk's XI

| | | | | |
|---|---|---|---|---|
| K. J. Barnett c Dujon b Patterson | 12 | B. T. P. Donelan c Dujon b Patterson | | 1 |
| B. R. Hardie b Anthony | 18 | O. H. Mortensen not out | | 1 |
| J. E. Morris c Logie b Anthony | 98 | | | |
| *M. Azharuddin c Logie b Hooper | 21 | B 9, l-b 9, w 10, n-b 4 | | 32 |
| R. O. Butcher b Hooper | 0 | | | |
| T. J. G. O'Gorman b Allen | 13 | 1/33 2/74 3/134 | (8 wkts, 47.4 overs) | 212 |
| P. Bainbridge c Hooper b Richards | 9 | 4/134 5/185 6/195 | | |
| †K. M. Krikken not out | 7 | 7/205 8/206 | | |

J. K. Lever did not bat.

Bowling: Patterson 8–2–23–2; Allen 10–1–41–1; Anthony 10–1–56–2; Simmons 10–0–52–0; Hooper 6–1–13–2; Richardson 1–0–4–0; Richards 2.4–0–5–1.

Umpires: A. A. Jones and K. J. Lyons.

## †GLOUCESTERSHIRE v WEST INDIANS

At Bristol, May 14. West Indians won by six wickets. Toss: West Indians. Gloucestershire provided a useful work-out for the touring team before the Texaco Trophy games, without ever threatening an upset. Wright held Gloucestershire's innings together and faced 157 balls while compiling his unbeaten 78. Hooper's spin and drift caused problems until a timely effort from Lloyds, who made 45 in 44 balls out of an unbroken 74 with Wright in the last fourteen overs. Haynes quickly took control of the West Indians' reply. He dealt especially harshly with Lawrence, whose first six overs went for 36 runs, and while some West Indian batsmen struggled with their timing he stroked his way to a century in 123 balls, hitting sixteen fours and a five.

## Gloucestershire

| | | | | |
|---|---|---|---|---|
| R. J. Scott c Hooper b Ambrose | 2 | J. W. Lloyds not out | | 45 |
| C. W. J. Athey b Marshall | 9 | | | |
| *A. J. Wright not out | 78 | B 2, l-b 13, w 7, n-b 3 | | 25 |
| M. W. Alleyne b Hooper | 15 | | | |
| †R. C. Russell b Hooper | 21 | 1/3 2/28 3/65 | (5 wkts, 55 overs) | 206 |
| P. W. Romaines b Hooper | 11 | 4/110 5/132 | | |

D. V. Lawrence, D. R. Gilbert, A. M. Babington and S. N. Barnes did not bat.

Bowling: Ambrose 4–2–5–1; Allen 10–2–32–0; Marshall 11–4–32–1; Anthony 11–1–46–0; Simmons 8–0–40–0; Hooper 11–1–36–3.

## West Indians

| | | | | |
|---|---|---|---|---|
| P. V. Simmons c Russell b Babington | 2 | A. L. Logie not out | | 12 |
| *D. L. Haynes c Lloyds b Gilbert | 101 | | | |
| R. B. Richardson c Romaines b Alleyne | 25 | L-b 8, w 7, n-b 2 | | 17 |
| B. C. Lara c Russell b Lawrence | 30 | 1/11 2/82 | (4 wkts, 53 overs) | 209 |
| C. L. Hooper not out | 22 | 3/155 4/183 | | |

†D. Williams, C. E. L. Ambrose, M. D. Marshall, H. A. G. Anthony and I. B. A. Allen did not bat.

Bowling: Gilbert 11–0–36–1; Babington 11–4–26–1; Lawrence 11–2–47–1; Barnes 9–0–26–0; Alleyne 9–0–54–1; Lloyds 2–0–12–0.

Umpires: H. D. Bird and D. R. Shepherd.

## WORCESTERSHIRE v WEST INDIANS

At Worcester, May 15, 16, 17. Drawn. Toss: West Indians. Only Botham, at his belligerent best, could have upstaged Richards, who launched the tourists' first-class schedule with his 111th century, a majestic 131 from 153 balls. The West Indian captain hit three sixes and seventeen fours, and added 139 for the fourth wicket with Simmons, whose career-best 134 in nearly five hours included 22 fours. Rain and bad light restricted the second day to an hour and 50 minutes, but on the final morning Worcestershire were 60 for four, still needing 200 to avoid the follow-on, when Botham walked to the wicket, aware that his recall to the England team for the Texaco Trophy was to be announced at noon. He immediately set about the bowling and off 83 balls bludgeoned his first hundred against a West Indian team, reaching the fastest century of the season to date with a pulled six off Simmons. Of the 228 runs added after his arrival, he plundered 161 from 139 balls, with one six and 32 fours. It was vintage Botham. After only two first-class hundreds in four years, this was his second in eight days, and his highest score for Worcestershire.

*Close of play:* First day, West Indians 376-6 (C. L. Hooper 27*, H. A. G. Anthony 17*); Second day, Worcestershire 36-1 (T. S. Curtis 30*, G. A. Hick 4*).

### West Indians

| | | | |
|---|---|---|---|
| C. G. Greenidge c Lampitt b Botham | 26 | – not out | 12 |
| P. V. Simmons b Illingworth | 134 | – not out | 24 |
| R. B. Richardson c Moody b Botham | 6 | | |
| B. C. Lara b Newport | 26 | | |
| *I. V. A. Richards c Illingworth b Newport | 131 | | |
| C. L. Hooper c Illingworth b Dilley | 42 | | |
| †P. J. L. Dujon c Bevins b Dilley | 0 | | |
| H. A. G. Anthony not out | 33 | | |
| B 1, l-b 4, n-b 6 | 11 | | |

1/54 2/75 3/139 4/278      (7 wkts dec.) 409      (no wkt) 36
5/341 6/346 7/409

I. B. A. Allen, C. A. Walsh and B. P. Patterson did not bat.

Bowling: *First Innings*—Dilley 21.2-4-68-2; Botham 29-5-83-2; Newport 29-6-110-2; Lampitt 17-2-81-0; Illingworth 18-4-62-1. *Second Innings*—Dilley 3-2-3-0; Newport 8-2-20-0; Lampitt 5-3-13-0.

### Worcestershire

| | | | | |
|---|---|---|---|---|
| T. S. Curtis c Lara b Patterson | 30 | R. K. Illingworth b Walsh | 4 |
| G. J. Lord c Hooper b Patterson | 1 | †S. R. Bevins c Allen b Walsh | 6 |
| G. A. Hick b Allen | 11 | G. R. Dilley not out | 0 |
| T. M. Moody run out | 11 | | |
| *P. A. Neale run out | 34 | B 2, l-b 11, w 1, n-b 13 | 27 |
| I. T. Botham c Allen b Anthony | 161 | | |
| P. J. Newport c Greenidge b Patterson | 0 | 1/15 2/40 3/50 4/60 5/196 | 288 |
| S. R. Lampitt c Allen b Walsh | 3 | 6/222 7/245 8/272 9/288 | |

Bowling: Patterson 20-5-49-3; Allen 18-5-64-1; Anthony 13-1-63-1; Walsh 13.1-1-64-3; Simmons 5-1-35-0.

Umpires: J. H. Hampshire and K. E. Palmer.

## MIDDLESEX v WEST INDIANS

At Lord's, May 18, 19, 20. West Indians won by six wickets. Toss: Middlesex. After a rapid start in which the openers took 93 from 21 overs, the rest of the Middlesex innings had little substance. Patterson kept returning with deadly effect, although Ramprakash employed 225 minutes in useful rehearsal for his forthcoming Test career. On the second day, Simmons recorded his third hundred in successive first-class matches (the first was against the Australians in Barbados in April), each of which bettered his previous highest score. He played with charm and deceptive power in hitting 22 fours and a six in 188 balls. His captain, Richards, held himself back by design, but when Middlesex batted again, Gatting's hamstring strain prevented him from appearing until his team's cause was almost sunk. This probably determined the result. Middlesex had looked safe when they wiped 74 off the arrears, with Roseberry and Ramprakash playing well. But Walsh removed them both, and the steady erosion of wickets left the West Indians a target of 69 in seventeen overs. The early batsmen hurried to little effect, and it took Richards to show how a match should be won. In nine balls he hit Williams for five fours and then a six, and the West Indians were there with 5.3 overs to spare.

*Close of play*: First day, Middlesex 275; Second day, West Indians 354-6 (D. Williams 21*, I. V. A. Richards 23*).

## Middlesex

| | | | |
|---|---|---|---|
| I. J. F. Hutchinson c Williams b Anthony | 37 | – c Williams b Patterson | 20 |
| M. A. Roseberry c Hooper b Patterson | 45 | – lbw b Walsh | 23 |
| *M. W. Gatting c Anthony b Patterson | 5 | – (9) b Walsh | 5 |
| M. R. Ramprakash c Anthony b Patterson | 38 | – (3) c Richardson b Walsh | 21 |
| K. R. Brown c Richards b Patterson | 2 | – (4) lbw b Simmons | 7 |
| †P. R. Downton b Walsh | 23 | – (5) c Williams b Anthony | 21 |
| J. E. Emburey c Logie b Anthony | 29 | – (6) b Simmons | 10 |
| N. F. Williams run out | 5 | – (7) b Hooper | 21 |
| P. C. R. Tufnell not out | 14 | – (8) c Patterson b Anthony | 26 |
| S. P. Hughes c Williams b Patterson | 5 | – not out | 3 |
| N. G. Cowans b Walsh | 35 | – b Walsh | 1 |
| L-b 13, n-b 21 | 34 | B 4, l-b 7, n-b 8 | 19 |
| | **275** | | **177** |

1/93 2/101 3/102 4/108 5/147    1/35 2/74 3/81 4/81 5/96
6/189 7/210 8/222 9/227         6/133 7/155 8/160 9/175

*Bowling: First Innings*—Patterson 20-4-88-5; Marshall 11-1-31-0; Anthony 14-2-59-2; Walsh 15.5-3-63-2; Simmons 4-1-21-0. *Second Innings*—Patterson 13-4-29-1; Anthony 12-4-35-2; Marshall 6-1-17-0; Simmons 11-3-34-2; Walsh 15.1-4-39-4; Hooper 4-2-12-1.

## West Indians

| | | | |
|---|---|---|---|
| C. G. Greenidge c and b Williams | 26 | – b Cowans | 8 |
| P. V. Simmons c Roseberry b Emburey | 136 | – c Downton b Williams | 5 |
| R. B. Richardson c Downton b Cowans | 7 | – not out | 10 |
| C. L. Hooper c Gatting b Hutchinson | 42 | – c Brown b Cowans | 16 |
| A. L. Logie c and b Emburey | 60 | – c Emburey b Williams | 1 |
| M. D. Marshall c sub b Hughes | 19 | | |
| †D. Williams c Brown b Williams | 35 | | |
| *I. V. A. Richards c sub b Cowans | 28 | – (6) not out | 28 |
| H. A. G. Anthony b Cowans | 11 | | |
| C. A. Walsh not out | 0 | | |
| B 5, l-b 6, n-b 9 | 20 | L-b 4 | 4 |
| | **384** | | **72** |

1/88 2/111 3/210 4/234 5/285    (9 wkts dec.) 384    1/8 2/14 3/35 4/36    (4 wkts) 72
6/318 7/362 8/382 9/384

B. P. Patterson did not bat.

*Bowling: First Innings*—Cowans 21.5-11-37-3; Williams 24-7-82-2; Hughes 19-5-64-1; Emburey 22.4-4-84-2; Tufnell 21-3-67-0; Gatting 2.2-1-9-0; Hutchinson 6-0-18-1; Ramprakash 2-0-12-0. *Second Innings*—Cowans 6-0-26-2; Williams 5.3-1-42-2.

Umpires: M. J. Kitchen and R. Palmer.

## †ENGLAND v WEST INDIES

### First Texaco Trophy Match

At Birmingham, May 23, 24. England won by one wicket. Toss: England. Atherton's diligence in making the only fifty of the match, after winning a close run-out decision when he was 13, and West Indies' profligacy in conceding 43 extras provided the bulk of England's winning total. Returning to the international arena after 21 months, Botham made good use of muggy weather; he had Richardson caught at cover with his second ball and, putting behind him the disappointment of having Richards dropped at slip, went on to record his best bowling figures in 99 limited-overs internationals. Only an unbroken ninth-wicket stand of 52 in ten overs between Ambrose and Walsh took Richards's men past 127, their lowest one-day score against England. However, the total looked healthier when Gooch was out to his first legitimate ball. Hick, making his international début on his 25th birthday, looked nervous, and struck just one boundary in 49 balls before becoming the first of Richardson's four catches. Bad light ended play prematurely when England needed 76 from 28 overs, but they seemed to be coasting on a sunny Friday morning until Botham tore a hamstring and was out next ball. Thereafter, there was little resistance until his Worcestershire team-mate, Illingworth, arrived to partner Atherton. Both played sensibly to see off the front-line bowlers, and Illingworth square cut Hooper for four to bring England victory with 5.2 overs to spare.

*Man of the Match:* M. A. Atherton.    *Attendance:* 18,342; *receipts* £326,600.

*Close of play:* England 98-4 (27 overs) (M. A. Atherton 35*, I. T. Botham 1*).

## West Indies

| | | |
|---|---|---|
| C. G. Greenidge c Russell b Botham | 23 | |
| P. V. Simmons c Gooch b Lewis | 4 | |
| R. B. Richardson c Illingworth b Botham | 3 | |
| *I. V. A. Richards c Fairbrother b Gooch | 30 | |
| A. L. Logie c DeFreitas b Botham | 18 | |
| C. L. Hooper c Russell b Botham | 10 | |
| †P. J. L. Dujon c Lewis b Illingworth | 5 | |
| M. D. Marshall c Lewis b DeFreitas | 17 | |

C. E. L. Ambrose not out . . . . . . . . . . . 21
C. A. Walsh not out . . . . . . . . . . . . . . . . 29

B 1, l-b 5, w 6, n-b 1 . . . . . . . . . 13

1/8 (2) 2/16 (3)    (8 wkts, 55 overs) 173
3/48 (1) 4/78 (5)
5/84 (4) 6/98 (6)
7/103 (7) 8/121 (8)

B. P. Patterson did not bat.

Bowling: DeFreitas 11–3–22–1; Lewis 11–3–41–1; Pringle 7–0–22–0; Botham 11–2–45–4; Gooch 5–0–17–1; Illingworth 10–1–20–1.

## England

| | | |
|---|---|---|
| *G. A. Gooch lbw b Ambrose | 0 | |
| M. A. Atherton not out | 69 | |
| G. A. Hick c Richardson b Marshall | 14 | |
| A. J. Lamb b Hooper | 18 | |
| N. H. Fairbrother c Dujon b Hooper | 4 | |
| I. T. Botham lbw b Walsh | 8 | |
| D. R. Pringle c Richardson b Walsh | 1 | |
| †R. C. Russell c Dujon b Patterson | 1 | |
| P. A. J. DeFreitas c Richardson b Marshall | | |

C. C. Lewis c Richardson b Patterson . . 0
R. K. Illingworth not out . . . . . . . . . . 9

L-b 9, w 18, n-b 16 . . . . . . . . . 43

1/1 (1) 2/41 (3)    (9 wkts, 49.4 overs) 175
3/80 (4) 4/87 (5)
5/123 (6) 6/126 (7)
7/134 (8) 8/147 (9)
9/152 (10)

Bowling: Ambrose 11–2–34–1; Patterson 11–2–38–2; Marshall 11–1–32–2; Walsh 11–0–34–2; Simmons 3–0–10–0; Hooper 2.4–0–18–2.

Umpires: J. H. Hampshire and M. J. Kitchen.

## †ENGLAND v WEST INDIES

### Second Texaco Trophy Match

At Manchester, May 25. England won by 9 runs. Toss: West Indies. An excellent all-round performance by England won the Texaco Trophy with a match to spare. Again their opponents conceded too many extras – 40 – and they were also handicapped by the injury to Greenidge's knee while he was fielding; this was to end his tour. In cloudy conditions, Richards put England in, perhaps hoping for swing; but Gooch, who hit four fours, and Atherton (six fours) put on 156 in 38 overs, a record for England's first wicket against West Indies, and the foundation of their highest score against them. When they were out in successive overs, Lamb, with 62 in 50 balls and ten fours, added 102 in thirteen overs with Hick, and there was just time for Ramprakash, making his début in place of the injured Botham, to open his account. The tourists started uncertainly, but a stand of 121 in 25 overs between Richards, who hit two sixes and six fours in 84 balls, and Hooper maintained their interest. When Lewis removed them both, Logie and Marshall continued the chase until they fell in a miserly penultimate over from Pringle.

*Man of the Match*: A. J. Lamb.　　　*Attendance*: 18,487; *receipts* £320,376.

### England

| | | | |
|---|---|---|---|
| *G. A. Gooch b Hooper | 54 | M. R. Ramprakash not out | 6 |
| M. A. Atherton c sub (B. C. Lara) b Ambrose | 74 | B 4, l-b 16, w 14, n-b 6 | 40 |
| G. A. Hick b Ambrose | 29 | | |
| A. J. Lamb c Dujon b Patterson | 62 | 1/156 (1) 2/156 (2) (4 wkts, 55 overs) | 270 |
| N. H. Fairbrother not out | 5 | 3/258 (3) 4/260 (4) | |

C. C. Lewis, D. R. Pringle, †R. C. Russell, P. A. J. DeFreitas and R. K. Illingworth did not bat.

Bowling: Ambrose 11–3–36–2; Patterson 10–1–39–1; Walsh 11–0–56–0; Marshall 10–0–45–0; Simmons 4–0–30–0; Hooper 9–0–44–1.

### West Indies

| | | | |
|---|---|---|---|
| P. V. Simmons run out | 28 | C. E. L. Ambrose not out | 5 |
| †P. J. L. Dujon c DeFreitas b Lewis | 21 | C. A. Walsh not out | 1 |
| R. B. Richardson c Russell b Gooch | 13 | | |
| C. L. Hooper c sub (D. A. Reeve) b Lewis | 48 | L-b 4, w 10, n-b 3 | 17 |
| *I. V. A. Richards lbw b Lewis | 78 | 1/34 (2) 2/61 (1) (8 wkts, 55 overs) | 261 |
| A. L. Logie c Illingworth b Pringle | 24 | 3/69 (3) 4/190 (4) | |
| M. D. Marshall c and b Pringle | 22 | 5/208 (5) 6/250 (6) | |
| C. G. Greenidge run out | 4 | 7/250 (7) 8/256 (8) | |

B. P. Patterson did not bat.

Bowling: DeFreitas 11–3–50–0; Lewis 11–0–62–3; Pringle 11–2–52–2; Illingworth 11–1–42–0; Gooch 11–1–51–1.

Umpires: H. D. Bird and D. R. Shepherd.

## †ENGLAND v WEST INDIES

### Third Texaco Trophy Match

At Lord's, May 27. England won by seven wickets. Toss: England. A third-wicket stand of 213 in 31 overs between Fairbrother and Hick, a record for any wicket in one-day internationals in England, made light of a substantial target and gave the home side a clean sweep in the three-match series. England brought in Lawrence – their only player in the tournament without a first-class hundred – and newcomer Reeve for Lamb, who had bruised his instep at Manchester; for West Indies, Lara replaced Greenidge. The tourists recovered well from the early loss of both openers, Simmons to a fine catch off the inside edge by Russell, but only Logie reached 50. They looked to be 15 to 20 runs short of a winning total, until Gooch was brilliantly run out by Hooper from backward point and Atherton also departed by the fifteenth over. Hick and Fairbrother might have gone, too, before they settled, but the one went on to his first fifty and the other to his maiden hundred for England. They also won the hearts of a full house, including the Compton and Edrich stands, officially opened by D. C. S. Compton during lunch, by refusing an offer of bad light. After Fairbrother was dismissed, having struck two sixes, a five and ten fours in 109 balls, Hick hit his eighth four to achieve a comfortable victory.

*Man of the Match:* N. H. Fairbrother.   *Attendance:* 24,871; *receipts* £595,426.

*Men of the Series:* England – M. A. Atherton; West Indies – I. V. A. Richards.

## West Indies

| | | | |
|---|---|---|---|
| P. V. Simmons c Russell b DeFreitas | 5 | C. E. L. Ambrose not out | 6 |
| †P. J. L. Dujon b Lawrence | 0 | C. A. Walsh lbw b Lawrence | 0 |
| R. B. Richardson c DeFreitas | | B. P. Patterson not out | 2 |
| b Illingworth | 41 | | |
| B. C. Lara c and b Illingworth | 23 | | |
| *I. V. A. Richards c Illingworth | | B 1, l-b 9, w 14, n-b 5 | 29 |
| b DeFreitas | 37 | | |
| A. L. Logie c and b Gooch | 82 | (9 wkts, 55 overs) | 264 |
| C. L. Hooper c Fairbrother | | 1/8 (2)  2/8 (1) | |
| b Lawrence | 26 | 3/71 (3)  4/91 (4) | |
| M. D. Marshall c DeFreitas | | 5/164 (5)  6/227 (7) | |
| b Lawrence | 13 | 7/241 (6)  8/258 (8) | |
| | | 9/258 (10) | |

Bowling: Lawrence 11–1–67–4; DeFreitas 11–1–26–2; Reeve 11–1–43–0; Illingworth 11–1–53–2; Pringle 9–0–56–0; Gooch 2–0–9–1.

## England

| | | | |
|---|---|---|---|
| *G. A. Gooch run out | 11 | M. R. Ramprakash not out | 0 |
| M. A. Atherton c Dujon b Marshall | 25 | B 4, l-b 12, w 10, n-b 4 | 30 |
| G. A. Hick not out | 86 | | |
| N. H. Fairbrother c Richards | | 1/28 (1)  2/48 (2)   (3 wkts, 46.1 overs) | 265 |
| b Patterson | 113 | 3/261 (4) | |

D. A. Reeve, D. R. Pringle, †R. C. Russell, P. A. J. DeFreitas, R. K. Illingworth and D. V. Lawrence did not bat.

Bowling: Ambrose 8–0–31–0; Patterson 10–0–62–1; Marshall 11–1–49–1; Walsh 11–1–50–0; Hooper 4.1–0–36–0; Simmons 2–0–21–0.

Umpires: M. J. Kitchen and D. R. Shepherd.

## SOMERSET v WEST INDIANS

At Taunton, May 29, 30, 31. Drawn. Toss: West Indians. The tourists' shaky start against the New Zealand-born Caddick was redressed by a delightful effort from Lara, who hit eleven fours, and by Hooper's 123 from 188 deliveries, his first hundred in England, with nineteen fours. In overcast and chilly weather, only Cook found an answer to Ambrose and Marshall. He faced 258 balls in 340 minutes, hitting nineteen fours, and was unbeaten when Somerset declared 72 behind. A back injury forced Haynes to retire, Richardson led a rapid run-chase, hitting seven fours and two sixes in 126 balls, which left Somerset to get 336 in what became 66 overs. They were quickly reduced to 46 for four, but this time Tavaré held the innings together. He reached a splendid hundred, his 40th in first-class cricket, in 141 balls, and hit nineteen fours in all, but another flurry of wickets prompted caution. At 156 for eight, with twenty overs to go, Somerset were facing defeat; but Graveney held firm for sixteen overs, and the injured Lefebvre stayed with Tavaré for the final four, surviving a chance to Lara at slip from Hooper's penultimate ball.

*Close of play:* First day, Somerset 24-0 (S. J. Cook 11*, P. M. Roebuck 7*); Second day, West Indians 82-0 (P. V. Simmons 43*, R. B. Richardson 18*).

## West Indians

| | | | |
|---|---|---|---|
| P. V. Simmons b Graveney | 10 | – lbw b Caddick | 51 |
| *D. L. Haynes c Roebuck b Caddick | 1 | – retired hurt | 16 |
| R. B. Richardson c Cook b Caddick | 7 | – not out | 91 |
| B. C. Lara c and b Trump | 93 | – c Cook b Graveney | 50 |
| C. L. Hooper lbw b Hayhurst | 123 | – not out | 48 |
| A. L. Logie c Harden b Trump | 48 | | |
| M. D. Marshall c Harden b Hayhurst | 14 | | |
| †D. Williams not out | 14 | | |
| C. E. L. Ambrose not out | 16 | | |
| L-b 13, n-b 3 | 16 | L-b 2, w 2, n-b 3 | 7 |

1/7 2/21 3/71 4/158 5/265 (7 wkts dec.) 342  1/95 2/178 (2 wkts dec.) 263
6/298 7/313

H. A. G. Anthony and I. B. A. Allen did not bat.

*In the second innings D. L. Haynes retired hurt at 55.*

Bowling: *First Innings*—Caddick 20–2–85–2; Lefebvre 12–3–27–0; Hayhurst 10–2–42–2; MacLeay 11–3–32–0; Graveney 21–3–68–1; Trump 20–2–69–2; Roebuck 2–1–6–0. *Second Innings*—Caddick 12–0–68–1; Hayhurst 4–0–23–0; MacLeay 7–0–33–0; Graveney 14–2–51–1; Trump 14–0–86–0.

## Somerset

| | | | |
|---|---|---|---|
| S. J. Cook not out | 162 | – c Williams b Ambrose | 14 |
| P. M. Roebuck c Lara b Ambrose | 10 | – b Allen | 3 |
| A. N. Hayhurst lbw b Marshall | 22 | – b Ambrose | 5 |
| *C. J. Tavaré lbw b Ambrose | 10 | – not out | 109 |
| R. J. Harden c Williams b Marshall | 7 | – c Williams b Marshall | 14 |
| †N. D. Burns c Hooper b Anthony | 0 | – b Hooper | 14 |
| K. H. MacLeay b Simmons | 15 | – c Richardson b Allen | 14 |
| R. P. Lefebvre b Hooper | 5 | – (11) not out | 0 |
| H. R. J. Trump not out | 20 | – (8) c Allen b Hooper | 9 |
| A. R. Caddick (did not bat) | | – (9) lbw b Hooper | 0 |
| D. A. Graveney (did not bat) | | – (10) lbw b Anthony | 8 |
| B 2, l-b 1, n-b 16 | 19 | B 5, l-b 1, n-b 10 | 16 |

1/45 2/94 3/141 4/159 5/160 (7 wkts dec.) 270  1/16 2/20 3/26 (9 wkts) 198
6/199 7/214                                    4/46 5/109 6/131
                                               7/140 8/156 9/192

Bowling: *First Innings*—Ambrose 18–7–35–2; Allen 15.4–1–71–0; Marshall 15–4–35–2; Anthony 16–0–72–1; Hooper 16–1–38–1; Simmons 7–1–16–1. *Second Innings*—Ambrose 18–7–35–2; Allen 12–1–61–2; Marshall 8–0–35–1; Anthony 9–5–34–1; Hooper 19–7–27–3.

Umpires: B. Hassan and K. E. Palmer.

## LEICESTERSHIRE v WEST INDIANS

At Leicester, June 1, 2, 3. West Indians won by six wickets. Toss: Leicestershire. With Ambrose injured and Marshall resting, the West Indians looked some way short of their best in their final match before the First Test. Five catches went down before Leicestershire, sixteenth in the Championship, declared at a prosperous 355 for seven from 86 overs. Briers was missed twice before reaching 20 and Hepworth escaped at 12; Martyn, the Australian Under-19 captain, at Grace Road on a scholarship, was put down when 9, and Lewis, who took a heavy toll of Richards and Simmons in smashing nine fours and two sixes while scoring 72 from 65 balls, should have gone at 11. Drizzle put paid to almost half of a gloomy second day, in which Richardson helped himself to runs against an erratic Lewis, but Maguire bowled tightly. The West Indians galvanised themselves on the final day. After Martyn had impressed, hitting eight fours and a six in 60 not out from 81 balls, a brilliant unbeaten 135 (142 balls, fourteen fours, two sixes) from the flamboyant Richardson enabled the tourists to pass a target of 276 from 51 overs with seventeen balls to spare.

*Close of play:* First day, West Indians 20–1 (P. V. Simmons 9*, R. B. Richardson 6*); Second day, West Indians 216–7 (P. J. L. Dujon 9*, I. B. A. Allen 0*).

## Leicestershire

| | | | |
|---|---|---|---|
| T. J. Boon c Dujon b Patterson | 15 | – lbw b Anthony | 5 |
| *N. E. Briers c Allen b Anthony | 68 | – c Anthony b Allen | 9 |
| P. N. Hepworth c Logie b Simmons | 68 | – c Dujon b Anthony | 21 |
| D. R. Martyn c Richardson b Allen | 35 | – not out | 60 |
| L. Potter c Anthony b Richards | 53 | – lbw b Anthony | 2 |
| B. F. Smith c Simmons b Walsh | 13 | – not out | 29 |
| C. C. Lewis c Lara b Anthony | 72 | | |
| †P. A. Nixon not out | 9 | | |
| M. I. Gidley not out | 0 | | |
| B 1, l-b 8, w 7, n-b 6 | 22 | L-b 9, w 1 | 10 |

1/27 2/105 3/158 4/253 5/253   (7 wkts dec.) 355    1/14 2/27   (4 wkts dec.) 136
6/317 7/352      3/46 4/48

D. J. Millns and J. N. Maguire did not bat.

Bowling: *First Innings*—Patterson 20–4–75–1; Allen 16–3–65–1; Anthony 13–1–69–2; Walsh 19–5–60–1; Simmons 9–3–45–1; Richards 9–3–32–1. *Second Innings*—Patterson 11–7–15–0; Allen 11–3–46–1; Walsh 8–5–18–0; Anthony 8–3–28–3; Lara 2–0–14–0; Simmons 2–0–6–0.

## West Indians

| | | | |
|---|---|---|---|
| P. V. Simmons c Nixon b Maguire | 42 | – c Boon b Lewis | 0 |
| C. B. Lambert b Maguire | 4 | – c Hepworth b Maguire | 51 |
| R. B. Richardson lbw b Maguire | 63 | – not out | 135 |
| B. C. Lara c Nixon b Maguire | 3 | – c Gidley b Maguire | 26 |
| A. L. Logie c and b Lewis | 32 | – b Lewis | 10 |
| *I. V. A. Richards b Maguire | 45 | – not out | 39 |
| †P. J. L. Dujon not out | 9 | | |
| H. A. G. Anthony c Potter b Millns | 9 | | |
| I. B. A. Allen not out | 0 | | |
| L-b 1, n-b 8 | 9 | L-b 12, n-b 4 | 16 |

1/7 2/100 3/117 4/122 5/179   (7 wkts dec.) 216    1/0 2/121 3/166 4/183   (4 wkts) 277
6/207 7/216

C. A. Walsh and B. P. Patterson did not bat.

Bowling: *First Innings*—Lewis 19–5–60–1; Maguire 17–3–44–5; Potter 11–2–47–0; Millns 13.3–1–64–1. *Second Innings*—Lewis 15–0–63–2; Millns 14–1–78–0; Gidley 5–0–38–0; Maguire 14.1–0–86–2.

Umpires: B. J. Meyer and A. G. T. Whitehead.

## ENGLAND v WEST INDIES

### First Cornhill Test

At Leeds, June 6, 7, 8, 9, 10. England won by 115 runs. Toss: West Indies. England gained their first home victory over West Indies since 1969, when Illingworth's team also won at Headingley. In addition to Gooch, the outstanding batsman, and DeFreitas, the most successful bowler, they possessed a greater discipline in testing conditions, and this eventually enabled them to outplay their opponents, in their 100th encounter.

Gooch gloriously confirmed his standing on the international stage. His decisive, unbeaten 154 in the second innings was the product of seven and a half hours of careful application. Unyielding concentration carried him through three interruptions for rain on the fourth day, and mental toughness enabled him to survive a series of disasters at the other end. In 331 deliveries, England's captain collected eighteen fours and scored two thirds of his side's runs from the bat as they built on a lead of 25; and he became the first England opener to carry his bat through a completed innings since G. Boycott finished with 99 not out, in a total of 215, against Australia at Perth in 1979-80. Three other England batsmen had achieved the feat,

among them Sir Leonard Hutton, the only one previously to do so in England; coincidentally, West Indies were on the receiving end of his unbeaten double-hundred at The Oval in 1950. Gooch's innings also gave him a full set of Test hundreds on each of England's six international grounds.

Although no praise could be too lavish for Gooch, DeFreitas, too, took a prominent role. His match figures of eight for 93 rewarded admirable control and impressive accuracy. Inevitably, as 40 wickets fell for only 785 runs, the pitch attracted a good deal of comment, not all favourable, and batting was never comfortable. The ball moved off the seam and the bounce became a shade variable towards the end; but the damp weather played a part, and far too many batsmen got out to strokes which reflected anxiety about what the ball might do, rather than what it actually did. There was also, at times, some high-class bowling, notably from Ambrose, and three players were run out during the first two innings. As Gooch eventually demonstrated, it was possible to score runs with a sound technique. But it was not a pitch for the flamboyant strokeplayer, and West Indies lost largely because they failed to appreciate this point. Significantly, it was the tenth successive Test on the ground to produce a positive result.

England included three newcomers to Test cricket in Hick, Ramprakash and Watkin. The last-mentioned was initially cover for Pringle, who was concerned about a back strain, but when this cleared up Watkin played instead of Lewis, who had reported feeling ill shortly before the start. England also left out Illingworth, the left-arm spinner. Haynes overcame his earlier back trouble to open for West Indies, and his presence was all the more valuable in view of the long-term injury to his regular partner, Greenidge.

Influenced by the thick cloud cover and a misty atmosphere, Richards elected to put England in, and he had no cause for regret when his bowlers dismissed them for 198, England failing to reach 200 for the seventh time in nine innings at Headingley. The pattern of the first day was set by Atherton, recently appointed deputy to Gooch, when he was bowled playing back to Patterson. Hick was given a thorough testing in his first innings for his adopted country, and eventually got out aiming at a wide delivery, while Lamb also lacked conviction. Gooch, though not at his best, attacked Marshall, but was undone by a quicker delivery from him. Marshall looked the pick of the West Indian pace quartet before limping off with a hamstring strain and three of England's top five batsmen to his credit. The good impression made by Ramprakash, and Smith's readiness to wrest the initiative, gave England visions of a recovery, until Ambrose ran out Smith by a fraction with a superb throw from third man. His 54 was made from 88 balls, and he hit seven fours as well as gaining a five from overthrows.

The batsmen had to contend with poor light at times, with near darkness removing 26 overs from the schedule, and conditions remained much the same on the second day, when the tables were neatly turned. Pringle and DeFreitas bowled tightly to compensate for the wayward Malcolm, and Ramprakash excelled in the field. He dived acrobatically to his right in the covers to catch Simmons, and then swooped to throw down the stumps at the bowler's end as Hooper attempted an apparently reasonable single. Hick held two catches at second slip, and the third débutant, Watkin, could also celebrate, as he claimed Haynes's wicket with his fourteenth ball in Test cricket. The West Indian batsmen were not blameless, however; Richards's poor judgment in turning down a straightforward third run left Richardson stranded. Nor could he hold together the bottom half of the innings, being caught steering the fifth ball of the third day to slip. His 98-ball 73, containing two sixes and seven fours in just over two hours, was his highest Test score on the ground, but he must have been disappointed, none the less, by the manner of his dismissal.

Despite their unexpected first-innings lead, England plunged into crisis as Ambrose struck some crippling blows. Twice he was on a hat-trick, with Lamb and Smith departing first ball, and he picked up the first six wickets while the scoreboard lurched to 124. Mixing short-pitched bowling with accurate yorkers, Ambrose made full use of his 6ft 7in, and kept the ball around the line of the off stump. Though Hick may have been slightly unfortunate in being bowled off bat and pad, he never really established himself, but Ramprakash, sharing a fourth-wicket stand of 78 with his captain, again showed promise. When rain brought an early finish, England had a lead of only 168 with four wickets in hand. The support Gooch needed was to come from Pringle, who stood firm while 98 runs were added for the seventh wicket. The Essex all-rounder used his height and reach to get well forward, thus frustrating Ambrose, and occasionally he added a well-timed stroke off his legs for good measure. Richards may have erred in not using Marshall at the start of the day.

When Gooch finally ran out of partners, England had 277 runs at their backs, and West Indian anxiety was reflected in an extravagant cut by Simmons, who dragged the first ball from DeFreitas into his stumps. England could even afford a rare error by Ramprakash on the last day – he missed a very hard chance offered by Haynes – as West Indies crumbled under pressure. Richards sacrificed his wicket with a wild stroke against Watkin, and while Richardson played an innings of quality, hitting eleven fours in his 68 from 141 balls, the West Indian batsmen generally could not control their aggressive streak. Though Watkin bowled too many half-volleys, no-one had the self-discipline to wait for the less risky scoring opportunity. West Indies swished away their faint hopes as DeFreitas and Pringle nagged away at them, supported by good catching, and despite a flourish from Dujon, the long-awaited triumph came without undue alarm. – John Callaghan.

*Man of the Match:* G. A. Gooch.　　　　*Attendance:* 46,325; *receipts* £565,000.

*Close of play:* First day, England 174-7 (D. R. Pringle 6*, P. A. J. DeFreitas 13*); Second day, West Indies 166-8 (I. V. A. Richards 73*, C. A. Walsh 1*); Third day, England 143-6 (G. A. Gooch 82*, D. R. Pringle 10*); Fourth day, West Indies 11-1 (D. L. Haynes 3*, R. B. Richardson 8*).

## England

| | | | |
|---|---|---|---|
| *G. A. Gooch c Dujon b Marshall | 34 | – not out | 154 |
| M. A. Atherton c Dujon b Patterson | 2 | – c Dujon b Ambrose | 6 |
| G. A. Hick c Dujon b Walsh | 6 | – b Ambrose | 6 |
| A. J. Lamb c Hooper b Marshall | 11 | – c Hooper b Ambrose | 0 |
| M. R. Ramprakash c Hooper b Marshall | 27 | – c Dujon b Ambrose | 27 |
| R. A. Smith run out | 54 | – lbw b Ambrose | 0 |
| †R. C. Russell lbw b Patterson | 5 | – c Dujon b Ambrose | 4 |
| D. R. Pringle c Logie b Patterson | 16 | – c Dujon b Marshall | 27 |
| P. A. J. DeFreitas c Simmons b Ambrose | 15 | – lbw b Walsh | 3 |
| S. L. Watkin b Ambrose | 2 | – c Hooper b Marshall | 0 |
| D. E. Malcolm not out | 5 | – b Marshall | 4 |
| L-b 5, w 2, n-b 14 | 21 | B 4, l-b 9, w 1, n-b 7 | 21 |

1/13 (2) 2/45 (1) 3/45 (3) 4/64 (4)　198　　1/22 (2) 2/38 (3) 3/38 (4)　252
5/129 (5) 6/149 (6) 7/154 (7) 8/177 (9)　　　4/116 (5) 5/116 (6) 6/124 (7)
9/181 (10) 10/198 (8)　　　7/222 (8) 8/236 (9)
　　　9/238 (10) 10/252 (11)

*Bowling: First Innings*—Ambrose 26-8-49-2; Patterson 26.2-8-67-3; Walsh 14-7-31-1; Marshall 13-4-46-3. *Second Innings*—Ambrose 28-6-52-6; Patterson 15-1-52-0; Marshall 25-4-58-3; Walsh 30-5-61-1; Hooper 4-1-11-0; Richards 4-1-5-0.

## West Indies

| | | | |
|---|---|---|---|
| P. V. Simmons c Ramprakash b DeFreitas | 38 | – b DeFreitas | 0 |
| D. L. Haynes c Russell b Watkin | 7 | – c Smith b Pringle | 19 |
| R. B. Richardson run out | 29 | – c Lamb b DeFreitas | 68 |
| C. L. Hooper run out | 0 | – c Lamb b Watkin | 5 |
| *I. V. A. Richards c Lamb b Pringle | 73 | – c Gooch b Watkin | 3 |
| A. L. Logie c Lamb b DeFreitas | 6 | – c Gooch b Watkin | 3 |
| †P. J. L. Dujon c Ramprakash b Watkin | 6 | – lbw b DeFreitas | 33 |
| M. D. Marshall c Hick b Pringle | 0 | – lbw b Pringle | 1 |
| C. E. L. Ambrose c Hick b DeFreitas | 0 | – c Pringle b DeFreitas | 14 |
| C. A. Walsh c Gooch b DeFreitas | 3 | – c Atherton b Malcolm | 9 |
| B. P. Patterson not out | 5 | – not out | 0 |
| L-b 1, n-b 5 | 6 | L-b 1, n-b 6 | 7 |

1/36 (2) 2/54 (1) 3/58 (4) 4/102 (3)　173　　1/0 (1) 2/61 (2) 3/77 (4)　162
5/139 (6) 6/156 (7) 7/160 (8) 8/165 (9)　　　4/85 (5) 5/88 (6) 6/136 (3)
9/167 (5) 10/173 (10)　　　7/137 (8) 8/139 (7)
　　　9/162 (9) 10/162 (10)

*Bowling: First Innings*—Malcolm 14-0-69-0; DeFreitas 17.1-5-34-4; Watkin 14-2-55-2; Pringle 9-3-14-2. *Second Innings*—DeFreitas 21-4-59-4; Malcolm 6.4-0-26-1; Pringle 22-6-38-2; Watkin 7-0-38-3.

Umpires: H. D. Bird and D. R. Shepherd.

## DERBYSHIRE v WEST INDIANS

At Derby, June 12, 13, 14. Drawn. Toss: West Indians. In depressingly cold and blustery conditions, Richardson dominated the first day after Base had earned three lbw decisions. He reached his century from 190 balls, hit two sixes and twelve fours in his 114 (223 balls), and shared a stand of 164 with Hooper, whose all-round performance earned him the sponsor's Man of the Match award. The second morning was lost to the weather, and when Derbyshire batted, only Azharuddin and Adams were able to compile substantial innings. However, when Haynes declared a second time, after another partnership of over 150 from Hooper and Richardson, Bowler led Derbyshire's spirited attempt to score 257 in what became 50 overs. They were going well until Azharuddin was bowled, the first of seven wickets to fall in ten overs. With the West Indians' interest in victory reawakened, Barnett, who had retired earlier with back trouble, had to return to play out the last five balls from Hooper.

*Close of play:* First day, West Indians 261-5 dec.; Second day, West Indians 17-2 (B. C. Lara 9*, A. L. Logie 3*).

## West Indians

| | | | |
|---|---|---|---|
| C. B. Lambert lbw b Base | 5 | – lbw b Cork | 4 |
| *D. L. Haynes lbw b Base | 31 | – b Warner | 0 |
| R. B. Richardson c Warner b Folley | 114 | – (6) not out | 48 |
| B. C. Lara lbw b Base | 1 | – (3) lbw b Cork | 20 |
| C. L. Hooper c Cork b Base | 82 | – not out | 95 |
| A. L. Logie not out | 3 | – (4) b Warner | 9 |
| L-b 10, w 3, n-b 12 | 25 | B 1, l-b 10, n-b 12 | 23 |

1/23 2/82 3/84 4/248 5/261     (5 wkts dec.) 261    1/0 2/14 3/33    (4 wkts dec.) 199
                                                                       4/48

M. D. Marshall, †D. Williams, C. E. L. Ambrose, H. A. G. Anthony and I. B. A. Allen did not bat.

Bowling: *First Innings*—Base 22.4-7-44-4; Warner 17-3-52-0; Folley 11-2-67-1; Griffith 10-3-39-0; Cork 16-3-49-0. *Second Innings*—Cork 10-2-27-2; Warner 10-2-26-2; Base 9-1-19-0; Folley 10-0-52-0; Griffith 6-1-28-0; Bowler 5-0-36-0.

## Derbyshire

| | | | |
|---|---|---|---|
| *K. J. Barnett b Allen | 1 | – not out | 12 |
| P. D. Bowler c Lambert b Marshall | 13 | – c Lambert b Allen | 63 |
| T. J. G. O'Gorman b Ambrose | 4 | – c Haynes b Hooper | 23 |
| M. Azharuddin c Ambrose b Hooper | 72 | – b Anthony | 35 |
| C. J. Adams b Anthony | 55 | – run out | 3 |
| F. A. Griffith b Anthony | 6 | – (7) st Williams b Hooper | 4 |
| †K. M. Krikken c Richardson b Hooper | 6 | – (8) run out | 3 |
| D. G. Cork not out | 11 | – (9) c Williams b Hooper | 4 |
| A. E. Warner b Hooper | 7 | – (6) st Williams b Hooper | 9 |
| I. Folley (did not bat) | | – b Marshall | 0 |
| S. J. Base (did not bat) | | – not out | 9 |
| B 5, l-b 16, n-b 8 | 29 | L-b 15, n-b 5 | 20 |

1/5 2/10 3/51 4/135 5/171    (8 wkts dec.) 204    1/70 2/139 3/153    (9 wkts) 185
6/181 7/182 8/204                                            4/156 5/161 6/165
                                                                   7/172 8/173 9/185

*In the second innings K. J. Barnett, when 12, retired hurt at 22 and resumed at 185.*

Bowling: *First Innings*—Ambrose 11-3-26-1; Allen 11-3-35-1; Anthony 13-0-45-2; Marshall 8-1-27-1; Hooper 22.2-7-50-3. *Second Innings*—Ambrose 7-2-18-0; Allen 8-0-37-1; Hooper 16-4-49-4; Marshall 9-2-22-1; Anthony 9-0-42-1; Lara 1-0-2-0.

Umpires: B. J. Meyer and R. A. White.

## NORTHAMPTONSHIRE v WEST INDIANS

At Northampton, June 15, 16, 17. Drawn. Toss: West Indians. The miserable weather, which prevented a start until 3.35 p.m. on the second day, deprived the county of important revenue and the tourists of meaningful match practice in advance of the Second Test. To complete the sorry picture, the West Indians lost a key member of their attack when Patterson suffered a calf injury, after bowling just three balls in Northamptonshire's innings at the tail-end of the game. Haynes completed a stylish fifty – his first of the tour in a first-class match – but the county bowlers were understandably reluctant to over-exert themselves in such a meaningless contest.

*Close of play:* First day, No play; Second day, West Indians 87-1 (D. L. Haynes 52*, B. C. Lara 4*).

## West Indians

| | | | | |
|---|---|---|---|---|
| P. V. Simmons c Cook b Curran | 29 | H. A. G. Anthony b Cook | | 6 |
| D. L. Haynes c Ripley b Curran | 60 | I. B. A. Allen lbw b Cook | | 8 |
| B. C. Lara c Cook b Baptiste | 4 | B 1, l-b 4, n-b 1 | | 6 |
| A. L. Logie lbw b Curran | 19 | | | |
| †P. J. L. Dujon c Cook b Thomas | 82 | 1/74 2/95 3/95 | (8 wkts dec.) | 310 |
| *I. V. A. Richards c Lamb b Thomas | 47 | 4/136 5/232 6/269 | | |
| C. L. Hooper not out | 49 | 7/284 8/310 | | |

C. A. Walsh and B. P. Patterson did not bat.

Bowling: Thomas 15-1-87-2; Taylor 10-2-36-0; Cook 16.2-1-74-2; Baptiste 12-5-25-1; Curran 16-4-60-3; Capel 6-0-23-0.

## Northamptonshire

| | |
|---|---|
| A. Fordham not out | 34 |
| N. A. Felton b Anthony | 20 |
| R. J. Bailey not out | 1 |
| B 2, l-b 4, w 1, n-b 6 | 13 |

1/66                    (1 wkt dec.) 68

*A. J. Lamb, D. J. Capel, K. M. Curran, E. A. E. Baptiste, J. G. Thomas, †D. Ripley, N. G. B. Cook and J. P. Taylor did not bat.

Bowling: Patterson 0.3-0-2-0; Walsh 7.3-1-13-0; Allen 7-0-27-0; Lara 3-1-9-0; Anthony 2-1-11-1.

Umpires: J. C. Balderstone and B. Dudleston.

## ENGLAND v WEST INDIES

### Second Cornhill Test

At Lord's, June 20, 21, 22, 23, 24. Drawn. Toss: West Indies. There were times in this match when it seemed that England's victory at Headingley had been nothing but a deception, and that West Indies were about to resume their prolonged domination, possibly with a victory inside three days. That it did not happen owed almost everything to a vivid century by Smith. Given a full five days' cricket the match could have gone either way, but, not for the first time, the weather did not smile upon the traditional June week. Almost two days were lost, including the first scheduled Sunday of Test cricket at Lord's for nine years. Ticket-holders were refunded, an outgoing of £400,000 which the Test and County Cricket Board's insurance policy did not completely cover.

England selected an unchanged eleven, and so went into the match without a specialist slow bowler on a ground which usually calls for one. By the end, Gooch was admitting that this had been an error. West Indies introduced Allen for the injured Patterson, and on winning the toss they enjoyed an untroubled morning against some wayward England bowling, notably from Malcolm, who conceded almost 6 runs an over. However, when Gooch brought on Hick, his emergency spinner, for the last over before lunch, Simmons obligingly dabbed a catch to slip.

Haynes, becalmed, was out to a good diving catch by Russell half an hour after the interval, ut the only other wicket to fall before the close was that of Richardson, who had a rush of lood against Hick soon after tea. The final session belonged to Hooper and Richards. Hooper ad overcome a frail start against Hick, and the way Richards batted as he scored 50 from 63 alls – the luckless DeFreitas was hooked into the Tavern stand for six – the stage looked set or his final Test century at Lord's. But in the third over on Friday morning, after a 75-minute elay because of the weather, he was lbw to DeFreitas, and Logie was rapidly swept away by he same, fast-developing bowler. Although Hooper reached his first hundred against ngland, Pringle picked up four of the last five wickets as West Indies declined from an vernight 317 for three to 419 all out. Hooper's 111, from 202 balls in 4 hours 40 minutes, ontained fourteen fours and a six.

Any satisfaction England felt at their revival lasted only as long as it took Ambrose to pluck ut Atherton and Hick, without conceding a run, in his first four overs. Atherton played on, rying to withdraw his bat, and Hick gloved a lifter to third slip to end a short but tortured tay. When Ambrose was bowling, this looked a different game; and Marshall, not to be utdone, reduced England to 16 for three, thanks to a hapless shot from Lamb. Between them, therton, Hick and Lamb aggregated 37 runs in nine innings in the series. Gooch, whose urvival was far from untroubled, found a resolute partner in Ramprakash, but after more han an hour together they were both out to the second wave of fast bowlers. England stood recariously at 84 for five, 136 short of the initial task of avoiding the follow-on, and even on vhat was still a very good pitch, this seemed an unlikely mission.

The full house which gathered on Saturday morning must have done so with trepidation; it vas clearly possible that they would witness the end of the game. And they might have done o if Logie had held on to a sharp catch at short leg before Smith had added to his overnight 3. It was the last chance he would offer in an innings which bestrode the sunny day as few thers can have on the Lord's Saturday. He received appreciable support from Russell, Pringle nd DeFreitas, and when the last man, Malcolm, gave a fourth wicket to Ambrose, Smith vas undefeated at his highest Test score after almost seven hours of graphic concentration. Moreover, England were only 65 runs behind. Smith had faced 271 balls and he hit twenty ours in his 148 not out.

The lost Sunday virtually ruled out all chance of a result, and yet when bad light, followed by further rain, drew a veil over proceedings on Monday morning it was, unbelievably, England who had their noses in front. In the 4.5 overs between the start of play, on time in a ear-deserted ground, and the weather closing in again, DeFreitas and Malcolm had removed Simmons and Richardson to put a spring back in England's step. – Alan Lee.

*Man of the Match*: R. A. Smith.    *Attendance*: 106,232; *receipts* £1,805,213.

*Close of play*: First day, West Indies 317-3 (C. L. Hooper 87\*, I. V. A. Richards 60\*); Second day, England 110-5 (R. A. Smith 23\*, R. C. Russell 16\*); Third day, West Indies 0-0 P. V. Simmons 0\*, D. L. Haynes 0\*); Fourth day, No play.

## West Indies

| | | | |
|---|---|---|---|
| P. V. Simmons c Lamb b Hick | 33 | – lbw b DeFreitas | 2 |
| D. L. Haynes c Russell b Pringle | 60 | – not out | 4 |
| R. B. Richardson c DeFreitas b Hick | 57 | – c Hick b Malcolm | 1 |
| C. L. Hooper c Lamb b Pringle | 111 | – not out | 1 |
| \*I. V. A. Richards lbw b DeFreitas | 63 | | |
| A. L. Logie b DeFreitas | 5 | | |
| †P. J. L. Dujon c Lamb b Pringle | 20 | | |
| M. D. Marshall lbw b Pringle | 25 | | |
| C. E. L. Ambrose c and b Malcolm | 5 | | |
| C. A. Walsh c Atherton b Pringle | 10 | | |
| B. A. Allen not out | 1 | | |
| B 3, l-b 7, n-b 19 | 29 | L-b 2, n-b 2 | 4 |
| | 419 | (2 wkts) | 12 |

/90 (1) 2/102 (2) 3/198 (3) 4/322 (5)    1/9 (1) 2/10 (3)
5/332 (6) 6/366 (4) 7/382 (7) 8/402 (9)
9/410 (8) 10/419 (10)

Bowling: *First Innings*—DeFreitas 31-6-93-2; Malcolm 19-3-76-1; Watkin 15-2-60-0; Pringle 35.1-6-100-5; Hick 18-4-77-2; Gooch 2-0-3-0. *Second Innings*—DeFreitas 3-2-1-1; Malcolm 2.5-0-9-1.

## England

| | | |
|---|---|---|
| *G. A. Gooch b Walsh | 37 | P. A. J. DeFreitas c Dujon b Marshall . 2 |
| M. A. Atherton b Ambrose | 5 | S. L. Watkin b Ambrose |
| G. A. Hick c Richardson b Ambrose | 0 | D. E. Malcolm b Ambrose |
| A. J. Lamb c Haynes b Marshall | 1 | L-b 1, n-b 22 . . . . . . . . . . . 2 |
| M. R. Ramprakash c Richards b Allen . | 24 | |
| R. A. Smith not out . . . . . . . . . . . . | 148 | 1/5 (2) 2/6 (3) 3/16 (4) 4/60 (5)    35 |
| †R. C. Russell b Dujon b Hooper | 46 | 5/84 (1) 6/180 (7) 7/269 (8) |
| D. R. Pringle c Simmons b Allen . . . . . | 35 | 8/316 (9) 9/353 (10) 10/354 (11) |

Bowling: Ambrose 34–10–87–4; Marshall 30–4–78–2; Walsh 26–4–90–1; Allen 23–2–88–2 Hooper 5–2–10–1.

Umpires: B. J. Meyer and K. E. Palmer.

## †OXFORD & CAMBRIDGE UNIVERSITIES v WEST INDIANS

At Oxford, June 26, 27. Drawn. Toss: West Indians. To the disappointment of the Universities' supporters, Haynes chose to bat on rather than declare in a bid for a result on the second afternoon. Earlier their hopes had been raised when the tourists, batting with Graeme Turner's agreement to avoid fielding in the damp, were bowled out in 65.5 overs. Gerrans' four wickets included three for 13 as five batsmen departed for 17 runs in ten overs. On Anthony, who hit the off-spinner, Pearson, for four sixes, restored respectability to the total. In reply, the Universities sank to 36 for four, but they recovered on the second morning, saving the follow-on and losing only three more wickets before they declared in hopes of a finish. Instead, the West Indians opted for batting practice, and Lara hit 21 fours in his 93-ball hundred.

*Close of play:* First day, Oxford & Cambridge Universities 82-5 (M. J. Lowrey 1*, P. S. Gerrans 0*).

## West Indians

| | | | | |
|---|---|---|---|---|
| P. V. Simmons b Gerrans | 28 | – (2) c Crawley b G. J. Turner . . | 8 |
| C. B. Lambert c Crawley b Pearson | 49 | – (1) lbw b Oppenheimer | 14 |
| A. L. Logie c and b Gerrans | 18 | – c R. J. Turner b Jenkins | 7 |
| B. C. Lara b Pearson | 1 | – b Pearson | 11 |
| P. J. L. Dujon run out . . . . . . . . . . . . | 31 | | |
| *D. L. Haynes lbw b Gerrans | 1 | – (5) st R. J. Turner | |
| | | b G. J. Turner . | 46 |
| M. D. Marshall b Gerrans | 12 | | |
| †D. Williams lbw b Jenkins | 17 | – (6) c Gerrans b G. J. Turner . | 14 |
| H. A. G. Anthony not out | 50 | – (7) not out . . . . . . . . . . . . . . | 25 |
| I. B. A. Allen lbw b Jenkins | 8 | – (8) not out . . . . . . . . . . . . . . | 1 |
| C. A. Walsh b Oppenheimer | 3 | | |
| B 1, l-b 10, w 2, n-b 11 . . . . . . . . . . | 24 | B 2, l-b 9, w 3, n-b 6 . . . . | 20 |

| | | |
|---|---|---|
| 1/73 2/101 3/101 4/103 5/104 | 242 | 1/22 2/151 3/206    (6 wkts dec.) 379 |
| 6/118 7/161 8/192 9/210 | | 4/327 5/345 6/377 |

Bowling: *First Innings*—Jenkins 14–2–48–2; Oppenheimer 8.5–1–36–1; Gerrans 16–3–45–4; Pearson 24–5–85–2; G. J. Turner 3–1–17–0. *Second Innings*—Jenkins 13–2–76–1; Oppenheimer 9–1–62–1; Gerrans 11–2–59–0; G. J. Turner 19–0–91–3; Pearson 13–1–80–1.

## Oxford & Cambridge Universities

| | | | | |
|---|---|---|---|---|
| A. M. Hooper c Simmons b Anthony . . | 18 | R. M. Pearson not out . . . . . . . . . . . . . | 1 |
| R. E. Morris c Simmons b Allen | 1 | R. H. J. Jenkins st Williams b Lara . . . | 1 |
| J. P. Crawley b Walsh | 9 | J. M. E. Oppenheimer not out | |
| *G. J. Turner lbw b Marshall . . . . . . . . | 3 | L-b 3, n-b 12 . . . . . . . . . | 1 |
| †R. J. Turner retired hurt | 19 | | |
| D. B. Pfaff lbw b Anthony | 24 | 1/20 2/20 3/35    (8 wkts dec.) 17 |
| M. J. Lowrey lbw b Walsh | 22 | 4/36 5/76 6/125 |
| P. S. Gerrans c sub b Marshall | 31 | 7/143 8/171 |

*R. J. Turner retired hurt at 82.*

Bowling: Allen 13–3–38–1; Anthony 15–2–50–2; Walsh 12–7–28–2; Marshall 9–2–31–2; mmons 2–0–11–0; Lara 1–0–14–1.

Umpires: J. D. Bond and J. W. Holder.

## †LEAGUE CRICKET CONFERENCE v WEST INDIANS

t Trowbridge, June 28. West Indians won by nine wickets. Toss: West Indians. Lambert, ho had played for the Conference against the Indians at Sunderland the previous year, this me hit their bowlers for a 97-ball hundred, with ten fours and three sixes, and the West dians won with 24 overs to spare. When the League players had batted, after a helicopter as called in to dry the pitch, all four of the wickets to fall went to West Indians better known s batsmen.

## eague Cricket Conference

| | | | |
|---|---|---|---|
| I. Foley b Simmons | 36 | S. C. Wundke not out | 2 |
| J. Lampitt c Logie b Simmons | 22 | L-b 9, w 5, n-b 10 | 24 |
| J. Ingham not out | 48 | | |
| N. J. Heaton st Williams b Lara | 44 | 1/62 2/74 (4 wkts, 55 overs) 194 | |
| A. Harper c Hooper b Richards | 18 | 3/156 4/191 | |

. Macauley, K. W. McLeod, K. Ecclesharf, V. D. Walcott and B. L. Holmes did not bat.

Bowling: Marshall 5–0–15–0; Allen 5–2–7–0; Anthony 5–0–17–0; Simmons 11–0–44–2; looper 11–4–22–0; Lara 11–0–53–1; Richards 7–0–27–1.

## West Indians

| | |
|---|---|
| . V. Simmons c Lampitt b Holmes | 70 |
| . B. Lambert not out | 101 |
| . B. Richardson not out | 11 |
| B 1, l-b 6, w 1, n-b 5 | 13 |

/162          (1 wkt, 31 overs) 195

. C. Lara, C. L. Hooper, *I. V. A. Richards, A. L. Logie, M. D. Marshall, †D. Williams, H. A. G. Anthony and I. B. A. Allen did not bat.

Bowling: McLeod 5–0–32–0; Walcott 3–0–19–0; Harper 5–0–27–0; Ecclesharf 3–0–33–0; Vundke 8–0–42–0; Holmes 7–0–35–1.

Umpires: M. Lovell and J. Stokes.

## HAMPSHIRE v WEST INDIANS

At Southampton, June 29, 30, July 1. Drawn. Toss: Hampshire. A match of some controversy vas dominated by the two century-makers of the Lord's Test. The controversy flared on the rst afternoon when Smith's entertaining innings was cut short by a high full toss from Ambrose, which badly bruised his right forefinger. The England batsman had punished Ambrose mercilessly, with three overs costing 33 runs, but after batting on for fifteen minutes e retired, with one six and nine fours, to leave Hampshire effectively 134 for three. From that oint they faded gently away. Patterson had also been forced off the field by his recurring calf njury. Rain held up play on the second day, which Hooper graced with an innings of masterly air. He added 110 with Lara, and his fifth-wicket stand with Dujon was extended to 184 rom 40 overs when Hampshire opted for batting practice on the final morning. Hooper reached he last over before lunch needing 28 for a maiden double-century, but after he had hit the first ve balls of Udal's over for 2 (as Middleton missed a chance), 6, 6, 6 and 4, his attempt to mash the last for another boundary fell into Maru's hands at mid-on. In all, he had struck five ixes and eighteen fours in 315 minutes' batting for his highest score. Richards's declaration eft Hampshire to survive 57 overs.

*Close of play:* First day, West Indians 82-2 (D. L. Haynes 36*, B. C. Lara 9*); Second day, West Indians 358-4 (C. L. Hooper 149*, P. J. L. Dujon 47*).

## Hampshire

| | | | |
|---|---|---|---|
| V. P. Terry c Anthony b Patterson | 12 | – (2) c Dujon b Ambrose | |
| T. C. Middleton c Richardson b Walsh | 20 | – (1) not out | 7 |
| *M. C. J. Nicholas c Simmons b Hooper | 37 | – not out | 5 |
| R. A. Smith retired hurt | 62 | | |
| D. I. Gower b Hooper | 10 | | |
| K. D. James not out | 11 | | |
| †A. N. Aymes c Hooper b Walsh | 5 | | |
| R. J. Maru c Haynes b Ambrose | 23 | | |
| S. D. Udal c Hooper b Ambrose | 0 | | |
| C. A. Connor c Dujon b Ambrose | 0 | | |
| K. J. Shine c sub b Ambrose | 12 | | |
| B 4, l-b 2, n-b 4 | 10 | L-b 7, w 4, n-b 4 | 1 |

1/21 2/42 3/144 4/151 5/158        202    1/9                (1 wkt) 15.
6/186 7/186 8/190 9/202

*In the first innings R. A. Smith retired hurt at 134.*

Bowling: *First Innings*—Ambrose 19–7–70–4; Patterson 7–2–19–1; Walsh 18–7–41–2
Anthony 10–2–30–0; Hooper 24–10–36–2. *Second Innings*—Ambrose 12–5–22–1; Wals
13–3–22–0; Anthony 14–1–57–0; Richards 4–1–13–0; Hooper 12–1–28–0; Simmons 2–0–3–(

## West Indians

| | | | |
|---|---|---|---|
| P. V. Simmons c Nicholas b Shine | 0 | *I. V. A. Richards not out | 1 |
| D. L. Haynes b Connor | 44 | | |
| R. B. Richardson c Aymes b James | 33 | B 3, l-b 5, w 1, n-b 9 | 1 |
| B. C. Lara b Udal | 75 | | |
| C. L. Hooper c Maru b Udal | 196 | 1/7 2/67 3/102 | (6 wkts dec.) 44 |
| †P. J. L. Dujon c Aymes b Connor | 68 | 4/212 5/396 6/449 | |

H. A. G. Anthony, C. E. L. Ambrose, C. A. Walsh and B. P. Patterson did not bat.

Bowling: Shine 27–4–104–1; Connor 28–2–100–2; James 19–2–77–1; Udal 22–3–117–2
Maru 8–2–43–0.

Umpires: B. Dudleston and R. Julian.

## ENGLAND v WEST INDIES

### Third Cornhill Test

At Nottingham, July 4, 5, 6, 8, 9. West Indies won by nine wickets. Toss: England. England
out-of-form batting, camouflaged by Gooch's match-winning innings at Headingley, Smith
match-saving defiance at Lord's, and solid late-order support in both Tests, was exposed a
Trent Bridge as the tourists drew level in the series. The disappointment felt by England wa
all the more acute because they had made an ideal start on a placid pitch after Gooch had wo
an important toss, going to lunch on the first day with an unbeaten century opening stan
already posted. But that was England's best session of the match; Ambrose upset England'
calm in the first innings and induced panic in the second. West Indies, on the other hanc
batted sensibly throughout after England had threatened an early breakthrough.

England made one change from their squad at Lord's, Reeve of Warwickshire replacin
Watkin. However, another Glamorgan player, Morris, was later added as a precautio
because of concern about Atherton and Smith. Atherton's problem was a groin strain, whil
Smith was still feeling the effect of the Ambrose full toss which hit him on the right inde
finger during the tourists' game at Southampton. That was the finger which Walsh had broke
during the final Test, in Antigua, of the 1989-90 series. Botham was again ruled out o

ntention because of his continuing hamstring trouble. On the Monday between the Tests, 'alcolm recorded his best bowling of the season, five for 45 against the county leaders, arwickshire, but it was not enough to save his place after seventeen consecutive matches for ngland and 60 Test wickets in just over sixteen months. Instead Lawrence was recalled, early three years after winning his first cap, and Illingworth, twelfth man at Headingley and ord's, came in to make his début. West Indies stayed with their Lord's XI after Patterson iled to last the match against Hampshire.

Ambrose destroyed England's solid start in two bursts, after lunch and tea. Gooch and therton's sixth century opening stand in 22 innings also took the England captain to 2,000 ns against West Indies when he reached 58, a feat previously achieved by S. M. Gavaskar nd G. Boycott, but both openers went early in the afternoon session. And although England ere still in reasonable shape at tea, with the score 175 for three, Ambrose then removed amprakash and Hick, giving him figures of four for 30 from sixteen overs in his two spells nce lunch. Hick had remained for two and a half hours for his 43, but his immobility resulted his being hit twice on the helmet. Only Smith offered any meaningful resistance, but he ran ut of partners, as at Lord's, suggesting his talents were being wasted at No. 6. In his last three nnings against the tourists, for England and Hampshire, Smith had scored 274 runs without eing dismissed.

With Illingworth and Lawrence each supporting him for about an hour, Smith had at least elped England reach 300. But between an opening stand of 108, and the final two wickets dding 72, England had wasted a great opportunity of batting West Indies out of the game. he tourists did not make the same mistake, although they stumbled to 45 for three early on riday afternoon before Richardson, Richards and Logie dug in to make England toil. lingworth, in his first Test, had a mixed afternoon. On the stroke of lunch he became the eventh bowler, the first since December 1959, to take a wicket with his first ball in Test ricket, and late in the day he removed Richards when the West Indies captain looked set for century. Otherwise, the left-arm spinner bowled a negative leg-side line that frustrated the pectators even more than the batsmen. Nor was it effective; at one time Illingworth, like awrence, was going for 5 runs an over.

Richards departed with both umpires giving him out. Hampshire, at the bowler's end, gave im out bowled off his pads, while Kitchen answered the stumping appeal off Russell's pads n the affirmative. The television replay only added to the confusion, although Hampshire's ecision was the official verdict. Richards was unfortunately and unnecessarily jeered by the rowd for departing rather slowly, but his confusion was understandable, especially as Russell ad scurried to gather the ball after it had hit the stumps. And when Richards looked for the quare-leg umpire's decision, Kitchen was actually signalling from cover, where he had moved ecause of the sun.

Marshall was England's tormentor on Saturday as West Indies took a first-innings lead f 97, but the performance of the day belonged to the Trent Bridge groundstaff. A violent nunderstorm flooded the ground before play, but an immaculate mopping-up operation neant that only half an hour was lost. Although Logie went early on, Marshall found support rom the late order and kept England in the field until after tea. England knew those final wenty overs of batting would be crucial, and Marshall and Ambrose made them terminal vith the wickets of Atherton, Hick and Gooch before Lamb and Ramprakash stopped the ollapse for the day. England's score left them in no position to enjoy the only rest day of the eries; with seven wickets left, they trailed by 43 runs.

When England slumped to 115 for eight on Monday, their lead was only 18. But DeFreitas, llingworth and Lawrence then conspired to take the match into the final day, with the crowd esponding to the enterprising last-wicket stand which brought DeFreitas his maiden Test fty after 36 attempts and nearly five years. Lawrence showed that his batting, unlike his owling, had plenty of grace and style, and after his dismissal he wasted no time when he got he new ball in his hand, removing Simmons with his second delivery. The West Indians, eeding 115 for victory, closed at 20 for one, but Haynes and Richardson ensured there vere no further setbacks and levelled the series on the stroke of lunch on the final ay. – *David Norrie.*

*Man of the Match:* C. E. L. Ambrose. *Attendance:* 33,417; *receipts* £540,115.

*Close of play:* First day, England 269-8 (R. A. Smith 40*, R. K. Illingworth 13*); Second ay, West Indies 262-5 (A. L. Logie 72*, P. J. L. Dujon 3*); Third day, England 54-3 A. J. Lamb 25*, M. R. Ramprakash 7*); Fourth day, West Indies 20-1 (D. L. Haynes 8*, R. B. Richardson 10*).

## England

| | First Innings | | Second Innings | |
|---|---|---|---|---|
| *G. A. Gooch lbw b Marshall | 68 | b Ambrose | | 1 |
| M. A. Atherton lbw b Ambrose | 32 | b Marshall | | |
| G. A. Hick c Dujon b Ambrose | 43 | c Dujon b Ambrose | | |
| A. J. Lamb lbw b Ambrose | 13 | lbw b Marshall | | 2 |
| M. R. Ramprakash b Ambrose | 13 | c Dujon b Ambrose | | 2 |
| R. A. Smith not out | 64 | c Richards b Walsh | | 1 |
| †R. C. Russell c Logie b Allen | 3 | b Walsh | | |
| D. R. Pringle c sub (C. B. Lambert) b Allen | 0 | c Simmons b Walsh | | |
| P. A. J. DeFreitas b Walsh | 8 | not out | | 5 |
| R. K. Illingworth c Hooper b Ambrose | 13 | c Simmons b Walsh | | 1 |
| D. V. Lawrence c Allen b Marshall | 4 | c Hooper b Allen | | 3 |
| L-b 17, w 1, n-b 21 | 39 | L-b 14, w 3, n-b 4 | | 2 |
| | **300** | | | **21** |

1/108 (2) 2/113 (1) 3/138 (4) 4/186 (5)
5/192 (3) 6/212 (7) 7/217 (8)
8/228 (9) 9/270 (10) 10/300 (11)

1/4 (2) 2/8 (3) 3/25 (1)
4/67 (4) 5/100 (6) 6/106 (5)
7/106 (7) 8/115 (8)
9/153 (10) 10/211 (11)

Bowling: *First Innings*—Ambrose 34–7–74–5; Marshall 21.5–6–54–2; Walsh 24–4–75–1; Allen 17–0–69–2; Hooper 6–4–10–0; Richards 1–0–1–0. *Second Innings*—Ambrose 27–7–61–3; Marshall 21–6–49–2; Allen 7–2–23–1; Walsh 24–7–64–4.

## West Indies

| | | |
|---|---|---|
| P. V. Simmons b Illingworth | 12 | c Russell b Lawrence |
| D. L. Haynes c Smith b Lawrence | 18 | not out |
| R. B. Richardson b Lawrence | 43 | not out |
| C. L. Hooper c Russell b DeFreitas | 11 | |
| *I. V. A. Richards b Illingworth | 80 | |
| A. L. Logie c Ramprakash b DeFreitas | 78 | |
| †P. J. L. Dujon c Hick b Pringle | 19 | |
| M. D. Marshall c Illingworth b DeFreitas | 67 | |
| C. E. L. Ambrose b Illingworth | 17 | |
| C. A. Walsh lbw b Pringle | 12 | |
| I. B. A. Allen not out | 4 | |
| B 2, l-b 13, w 1, n-b 20 | 36 | N-b 5 |
| | **397** | **(1 wkt)** 11 |

1/32 (2) 2/32 (1) 3/45 (4) 4/118 (3)
5/239 (5) 6/272 (6) 7/324 (7) 8/358 (9)
9/392 (10) 10/397 (8)

1/1 (1)

Bowling: *First Innings*—DeFreitas 31.1–9–67–3; Lawrence 24–2–116–2; Illingworth 33–8–110–3; Pringle 25–6–71–2; Hick 5–0–18–0. *Second Innings*—DeFreitas 11–3–29–0; Lawrence 12.2–0–61–1; Pringle 7–2–20–0; Illingworth 2–0–5–0.

Umpires: J. H. Hampshire and M. J. Kitchen.

## †MINOR COUNTIES v WEST INDIANS

At Darlington, July 10, 11. Drawn. Toss: West Indians. Two tailenders scored fifties in remarkable unbroken partnership of 101 for Minor Counties' last wicket. When Taylor of Dorset joined Oxfordshire's Evans, 46 runs were needed to save the follow-on; but Taylor put together a maiden fifty, with six fours and a six in 81 balls, while Evans's innings included seven fours. Their stand reached the hundred mark in 25.2 overs – just over an hour. Of the other Minor Counties batsmen, only Roberts had much success against the tourists' bowling, which was profligate as ever with no-balls. On the first day Lara had impressed with thirteen fours in his 160-minute 82; Lambert's 50 included six fours and a six, and Anthony made his unbeaten 63 in 59 balls with twelve fours. Three of the West Indians' second-innings wickets fell in the first nine overs, but Simmons and Hooper batted on to the close.

*Close of play:* First day, Minor Counties 45-3 (M. J. Roberts 11*, S. J. Dean 0*).

## West Indians

| | | | |
|---|---|---|---|
| P. V. Simmons c Roberts b Greensword | 33 | – not out | 78 |
| C. B. Lambert c Greensword b Evans | 50 | – c Love b Taylor | 23 |
| R. B. Richardson st Fothergill b Evans | 29 | – c Fothergill b Arnold | 0 |
| B. C. Lara c Greensword b Arnold | 82 | – b Arnold | 13 |
| C. L. Hooper c Arnold b Plumb | 21 | – not out | 41 |
| †D. Williams run out | 3 | | |
| H. A. G. Anthony not out | 63 | | |
| I. B. A. Allen b Taylor | 1 | | |
| *I. V. A. Richards c Dean b Taylor | 4 | | |
| C. A. Walsh not out | 9 | | |
| L-b 2, w 1, n-b 2 | 5 | B 4, l-b 4 | 8 |

1/87 2/87 3/139 4/204 5/219  (8 wkts dec.) 300  1/34 2/39 3/55  (3 wkts) 163
5/223 7/235 8/282

B. P. Patterson did not bat.

Bowling: *First Innings*—Taylor 18–5–59–2; Arnold 19.5–1–69–1; Greensword 21–7–53–1; Evans 24–7–67–2; Plumb 12–2–50–1. *Second Innings*—Arnold 10–1–48–2; Taylor 8–2–43–1; Plumb 5–0–22–0; Evans 4–1–17–0; Brown 3–0–15–0; Love 3–0–10–0.

## Minor Counties

| | | | |
|---|---|---|---|
| G. K. Brown c Williams b Patterson | 10 | R. A. Evans not out | 50 |
| M. J. Roberts c Richards b Anthony | 63 | K. A. Arnold c Williams b Anthony | 9 |
| N. A. Folland c Lambert b Allen | 6 | N. R. Taylor not out | 52 |
| J. D. Love b Allen | 2 | B 5, l-b 2, w 7, n-b 22 | 36 |
| S. J. Dean b Patterson | 0 | | |
| S. G. Plumb c Williams b Anthony | 5 | 1/14 2/34 3/38 | (9 wkts dec.) 256 |
| *S. Greensword c Williams b Anthony | 10 | 4/68 5/87 6/111 | |
| †A. R. Fothergill c Richards b Anthony | 7 | 7/121 8/134 9/155 | |

Bowling: Patterson 10–2–49–2; Allen 11–0–32–2; Anthony 17–4–45–5; Lara 22.3–1–104–0; Hooper 8–2–15–0; Richards 2–1–4–0.

Umpires: G. A. Stickley and T. G. Wilson.

## †IRELAND v WEST INDIANS

At Downpatrick, July 13. Drawn. Toss: West Indians. Ireland's batsmen, led by their captain, Warke, reached the close without difficulty, though making no attempt to chase a target of 322 in 160 minutes. The West Indians had scored their runs in three and a half hours; after Simmons and Lara were out in one over, Lambert (thirteen fours, two sixes) shared a third-wicket stand of 181 with Logie (83 balls, fourteen fours, three sixes). Logie had scored 129 on his previous visit, to Dublin in 1984.

## West Indians

| | | | |
|---|---|---|---|
| P. V. Simmons c Thompson b Hoey | 50 | *D. L. Haynes not out | 14 |
| C. B. Lambert c Jackson b Lewis | 105 | B 1, l-b 2, n-b 1 | 4 |
| B. C. Lara c Cohen b Hoey | 4 | | |
| A. L. Logie retired | 118 | 1/94 2/98 | (4 wkts dec.) 321 |
| C. L. Hooper not out | 26 | 3/279 4/287 | |

†D. Williams, H. A. G. Anthony, C. A. Walsh, I. B. A. Allen and B. P. Patterson did not bat.

Bowling: Nelson 14–2–73–0; Thompson 12–1–74–0; Hoey 12–1–63–2; Lewis 15–2–78–1; Harrison 7–0–30–0.

## Ireland

| | | | |
|---|---|---|---|
| *S. J. S. Warke b Hooper | 44 | G. D. Harrison not out | 2 |
| M. F. Cohen c Simmons b Hooper | 17 | | |
| S. G. Smyth c Williams b Anthony | 18 | B 8, l-b 6, w 2, n-b 3 | 19 |
| D. A. Lewis not out | 41 | | |
| T. J. T. Patterson run out | 8 | 1/33 2/88 3/92 | (5 wkts) 165 |
| D. A. Vincent c Lara b Haynes | 16 | 4/115 5/156 | |

N. E. Thompson, †P. B. Jackson, C. J. Hoey and A. N. Nelson did not bat.

Bowling: Patterson 5–0–14–0; Allen 7–1–17–0; Hooper 17–6–52–2; Walsh 6–2–13–0; Anthony 8–3–28–1; Haynes 3–0–14–1; Lara 3–0–13–0.

Umpires: H. Henderson and M. A. C. Moore.

## †WALES v WEST INDIES

At Brecon, July 15. West Indies won by 204 runs. Toss: West Indies. The tourists scored their runs at well over one a ball, hitting 15 sixes and 33 fours. Their most prolific batsman was Hooper, whose 88 came from 43 balls with eight sixes (three of them in succession) and five fours; while batting with Richards (63 balls, five sixes, four fours), he plundered 22 of 25 runs taken off one over. It was a far cry from the West Indians' previous encounter with Wales, in 1928 at Llandudno, when they lost by eight wickets as the 55-year-old S. F. Barnes took twelve for 118. Shaw, the England Under-19 wicket-keeper, made a good impression, and Bishop was the most successful of the Welshmen when they batted. Williams was allowed to keep wicket as substitute for Dujon during Wales's innings.

## West Indies

| | | | |
|---|---|---|---|
| P. V. Simmons c Bishop b Smith | 64 | A. L. Logie not out | 2 |
| R. B. Richardson c Shaw b Griffiths | 22 | | |
| B. C. Lara st Shaw b Watkins | 82 | B 4, l-b 8, w 5 | 17 |
| *I. V. A. Richards c Griffiths b Edwards | 68 | | |
| C. L. Hooper st Shaw b Edwards | 88 | 1/52 2/137 3/196 | (6 wkts, 55 overs) 362 |
| †P. J. L. Dujon c Shaw b Griffiths | 19 | 4/299 5/352 6/362 | |

H. A. G. Anthony, I. B. A. Allen, M. D. Marshall and B. P. Patterson did not bat.

Bowling: Edwards 11–0–61–2; Griffiths 11–1–51–2; Lloyd 11–0–59–0; Smith 11–1–57–1; Watkins 8–0–74–1; Roberts 3–0–48–0.

## Wales

| | | | |
|---|---|---|---|
| S. G. Watkins c Dujon b Patterson | 3 | †A. D. Shaw c Richardson b Logie | 1 |
| T. C. Hughes b Patterson | 3 | A. Smith c sub b Richards | 0 |
| A. W. Harris c Logie b Lara | 4 | A. D. Griffith not out | 8 |
| J. B. Bishop c Richards b Hooper | 50 | B 4, l-b 2, w 5, n-b 4 | 15 |
| N. G. Roberts c Richards b Patterson | 16 | | |
| *A. C. Puddle b Marshall b Lara | 16 | 1/6 2/9 3/29 | (9 wkts, 55 overs) 158 |
| B. J. Lloyd st sub b Richards | 23 | 4/60 5/92 6/104 | |
| G. Edwards not out | 19 | 7/144 8/146 9/149 | |

Bowling: Patterson 7–2–17–3; Allen 7–3–6–0; Lara 11–4–29–2; Anthony 6–1–19–0; Richards 10–0–34–2; Hooper 11–2–27–1; Logie 3–0–20–1.

Umpires: S. W. Kuhlmann and J. Waite.

## GLAMORGAN v WEST INDIES

At Swansea, July 16, 17, 18. Drawn. Toss: Glamorgan. Rain on the final day, in which only 39.2 overs were bowled, averted the defeat that loomed over Glamorgan, who were trailing by 62 runs with seven second-innings wickets left. On the first day, the West Indian fast bowlers had threatened to dismiss them for a paltry first-innings total, but a partnership of 126 in 35 overs between Dale and Butcher, plus Metson's late flourish, earned them a respectable 252.

Richardson's century, containing a six and sixteen fours, Lambert's 99 and Hooper's 80 enabled the West Indians to declare 164 ahead, and by the end of the second day Ambrose had strengthened their position, dismissing Morris for 0 for the second time in the match. It was the opener's first pair in first-class cricket, and these were his first scoreless innings of the season. Glamorgan's promising young all-rounder, Dale, revived the home side with his second fifty of the game, and a stand of 73 in 28 overs with James. He had stood firm against the West Indian bowlers for a total of six hours in the match when the weather intervened.

*Close of play:* First day, West Indians 43-0 (C. B. Lambert 9*, D. L. Haynes 31*); Second day, Glamorgan 7-1 (S. P. James 1*, C. P. Metson 2*).

## Glamorgan

| | | |
|---|---|---|
| S. P. James c Williams b Patterson | 8 | – c Richardson b Ambrose ...... 24 |
| H. Morris c Lara b Ambrose | 0 | – c Williams b Ambrose ......... 0 |
| A. Dale c Richardson b Ambrose | 62 | – (4) not out ................. 51 |
| M. P. Maynard c Williams b Marshall | 8 | – (5) not out ................. 7 |
| P. A. Cottey c Richardson b Marshall | 8 | |
| *A. R. Butcher b Anthony | 94 | |
| R. D. B. Croft c Williams b Ambrose | 0 | |
| †C. P. Metson c and b Hooper | 27 | – (3) b Ambrose ............... 5 |
| S. L. Watkin c Williams b Ambrose | 5 | |
| S. R. Barwick c Williams b Ambrose | 0 | |
| M. Frost not out | 0 | |
| L-b 6, w 2, n-b 32 | 40 | B 8, l-b 3, w 1, n-b 3 .... 15 |

1/1 2/16 3/38 4/60 5/186     **252**    1/1 2/14 3/87     (3 wkts) **102**
6/191 7/217 8/243 9/252

Bowling: *First Innings*—Ambrose 22.1-6-56-5; Patterson 19-5-61-1; Marshall 10-2-34-2; Anthony 15-3-59-1; Hooper 17-4-36-1. *Second Innings*—Ambrose 12-6-14-3; Patterson 13-7-14-0; Anthony 9.2-2-30-0; Hooper 10-2-22-0; Lara 2-0-11-0.

## West Indians

| | |
|---|---|
| C. B. Lambert lbw b Barwick ....... 99 | M. D. Marshall not out ............. 46 |
| *D. L. Haynes b Watkin ............ 45 | H. A. G. Anthony not out ........... 4 |
| R. B. Richardson st Metson b Croft ...109 | L-b 6, w 2, n-b 5 ........... 13 |
| B. C. Lara c Maynard b Frost ....... 6 | |
| C. L. Hooper c Croft b Barwick .... 80 | 1/92 2/208 3/221    (7 wkts dec.) 416 |
| A. L. Logie b Dale ................ 8 | 4/280 5/297 |
| †D. Williams c Maynard b Dale ...... 6 | 6/323 7/408 |

C. E. L. Ambrose and B. P. Patterson did not bat.

Bowling: Watkin 23-7-86-1; Frost 19-1-111-1; Croft 37-8-116-1; Barwick 21-7-41-2; Dale 14-2-56-2.

Umpires: Dr D. Fawkner-Corbett and J. W. Holder.

## KENT v WEST INDIANS

At Canterbury, July 20, 21, 22. West Indians won by 4 runs. Toss: West Indians. Simmons, Logie and Hooper, who hit three sixes and one four in an over from Davis, were the major contributors to an entertaining display by the tourists on a day shortened by bad light, whereas Kent's reply relied almost completely on Taylor, who on his 32nd birthday hit eighteen boundaries in an unbeaten stay of five and a quarter hours. The West Indians' second innings got off to a good start, with Simmons racing to 50 in 34 balls, helped by eleven fours; he hit nineteen fours and a six in his 107 from 92 balls. Hooper reached 1,000 first-class runs for the tour, taking another four sixes off the luckless Davis in the course of his second half-century of the match, and the declaration set Kent 342 to win in 70 overs. The whole complexion of the match was changed by Cowdrey and Fleming, who put Kent well on the way to becoming the first county to beat the tourists. Their fourth-wicket stand had reached 192 in 34 overs by the time Fleming was bowled by Walsh for a career-best 116 from 109 balls, having hit three sixes and sixteen fours. But the momentum was lost as three more wickets fell in quick succession while Cowdrey remained in the 90s. Kent now needed 31 from six overs, and even though Cowdrey went at 327, his 104 having come from 172 balls with nine fours, they were within 5 runs of victory when Merrick was last out, with two balls remaining.

*Close of play:* First day, West Indians 310-7 (C. L. Hooper 61*, I. B. A. Allen 3*); Second day, West Indians 113-2 (P. V. Simmons 81*, A. L. Logie 4*).

## West Indians

| | | |
|---|---|---|
| P. V. Simmons c Ellison b Davis | 77 | – c and b Merrick .................. 107 |
| D. L. Haynes c Igglesden b Merrick | 4 | – c Marsh b Igglesden .............. 4 |
| B. C. Lara lbw b Ellison | 19 | – b Davis ......................... 18 |
| A. L. Logie c Marsh b Igglesden | 70 | – c Ellison b Merrick .............. 26 |
| *I. V. A. Richards c Marsh b Fleming | 29 | – c Marsh b Davis ................. 56 |
| C. L. Hooper not out | 61 | – not out ......................... 54 |
| †P. J. L. Dujon c Ward b Ellison | 22 | |
| H. A. G. Anthony b Fleming | 7 | – (7) not out ...................... 6 |
| I. B. A. Allen not out | 3 | |
| L-b 4, n-b 14 | 18 | L-b 4, w 2, n-b 1 ....... 7 |

1/20 2/79 3/147 4/207 5/213    (7 wkts. dec.) 310    1/29 2/106 3/145    (5 wkts. dec.) 278
6/270 7/281        4/174 5/263

C. A. Walsh and B. P. Patterson did not bat.

*Bowling: First Innings*—Merrick 12-1-48-1; Igglesden 14-6-20-1; Penn 10-2-46-0; Ellison 18-2-55-2; Davis 16-1-87-1; Fleming 17-3-50-2. *Second Innings*—Igglesden 8-2-43-1; Merrick 10-0-51-2; Penn 12-1-61-0; Davis 11-1-69-2; Ellison 9-1-50-0.

## Kent

| | | |
|---|---|---|
| T. R. Ward c Lara b Patterson | 0 | – c sub b Patterson ............... 2 |
| S. G. Hinks c Lara b Patterson | 8 | – c Richards b Hooper ............ 31 |
| N. R. Taylor not out ................. | 138 | – c Richards b Allen .............. 21 |
| G. R. Cowdrey c Patterson b Anthony | 7 | – c Lara b Patterson ............. 104 |
| M. V. Fleming c Allen b Walsh | 7 | – b Walsh ....................... 116 |
| *†S. A. Marsh b Patterson | 22 | – run out ......................... 8 |
| R. M. Ellison c Simmons b Allen | 14 | – b Anthony ...................... 4 |
| R. P. Davis c Hooper b Patterson | 27 | – (9) b Anthony .................. 10 |
| C. Penn c Lara b Anthony | 9 | – (8) c Lara b Anthony ............ 3 |
| T. A. Merrick (did not bat) | | – c Logie b Patterson ............. 6 |
| A. P. Igglesden (did not bat) | | – not out ......................... 1 |
| B 1, l-b 8, w 1, n-b 5 | 15 | B 9, l-b 18, w 3, n-b 1 .... 31 |

1/0 2/30 3/45 4/56 5/125    (8 wkts. dec.) 247    1/6 2/80 3/80 4/272 5/293    337
6/150 7/220 8/247        6/301 7/311 8/327 9/331

*Bowling: First Innings*—Patterson 20-4-70-4; Allen 19-5-57-1; Anthony 14.1-2-47-2; Walsh 12-1-45-1; Hooper 10-1-19-0. *Second Innings*—Patterson 9.4-2-57-3; Allen 8-2-24-1; Anthony 13-0-65-3; Walsh 16-3-57-1; Hooper 14-2-64-1; Richards 9-1-43-0.

Umpires: D. J. Constant and M. J. Harris.

## ENGLAND v WEST INDIES

### Fourth Cornhill Test

At Birmingham, July 25, 26, 27, 28. West Indies won by seven wickets. Toss: West Indies. It could be argued that this match, which gave West Indies a 2-1 lead in the series with one Test to go, was lost by England when their selection committee chose not to include Botham, even though his fitness was no longer in doubt and the previous Test, at Trent Bridge, had cried out for the inspiration of his *joie de vivre*. The Edgbaston pitch, which favoured seam throughout, would have been better suited to Botham's medium-pace swing than to his county colleague, Illingworth, a lesson which was driven home with brutal force on the fourth afternoon, when Richards ended the match with a straight six off the Worcestershire left-arm spinner.

Indeed, the first act of the game, after the start had been delayed 75 minutes by overnight rain, made the point clear. Richards won the toss and, after his customary trip back to the dressing-room for advice, asked England to bat. The opening ball from Ambrose, not one to waste time in looseners, seamed and rose a minimum distance outside off stump. Gooch dabbed at it, but Hooper at second slip, as astonished as the batsman, dropped a regulation catch in front of his face. From that moment, England's supporters had few moments of ease. Morris, in his first Test, having come in for the injured Smith, was caught for 3. And although Atherton batted stubbornly for an hour, England were 88 for three when Gooch, the only batsman to pass 30, was comprehensively bowled by Marshall. Hick held out for two and a half hours (104 balls) while making 19, and Ramprakash served up elegant defence for 110 minutes in accumulating 29. But the innings was extended into the second morning, and then by just eight minutes, only because 21 overs were lost to bad light and rain.

The West Indies openers set about building a winning total in their own way. Simmons hit five fours in a first-wicket stand of 52, and Haynes lingered two and a half hours in making 32. But the innings belonged to Richardson, whose 104, from 229 balls with thirteen fours, was his thirteenth century in Tests. Typically, he began hesitantly, for the untrustworthy pitch precluded the kind of strokes with which he bewildered the Australians four months earlier in Georgetown. Still, his defence throughout four and a half hours mocked those who thought he would never succeed in England, and his Man of the Match award was entirely justified.

His rival for that prize was England's Guyanan-born all-rounder, Lewis, who recorded his best performances in Tests with bat and ball. Recalled after satisfying the selectors that his pre-Test giddiness was no longer a problem, he clearly revelled in the conditions and the responsibility of the new ball. He had Logie caught second ball on the third day and Richardson 1 run later, to begin a haul of five for 12 in 62 balls. From 253 for four overnight, West Indies were all out for 292. By the close of play, however, England were just 52 runs ahead with eight wickets down, and the question was not who would win but when West Indies would do it.

This time England's batting had been undermined by Patterson, who had missed the previous two Tests with a calf injury. Once he seemed to be just a big, strong fast bowler, with a streak of venom; the added benefit of bowling at the stumps and, mostly, on a length had made him a formidable performer. Straightness removed Morris lbw, lift had Atherton caught, and a superb in-swinger bowled Gooch after two and a half hours of defiance. England were 5 for three when Hick played round a ball from Ambrose that cut in, and although Lamb and Ramprakash each batted an hour and threequarters to reach 25 apiece, Sunday dawned with the prospect of play ending by lunch, a dismal outlook for a large crowd relishing the sunshine.

Instead, a major stand developed between Pringle and Lewis. Pringle dropped anchor – for five hours in total – but Lewis, giving further proof of his maturity, struck boldly to reach his first Test fifty, with ten fours in all, before he was smartly caught in the covers for 65. His disappointment was obvious as he walked back to the dressing-room, but for the first time it was clear that this was an all-rounder who demanded an England place. By the time Pringle was out to a diving catch at mid-wicket by the speedy Logie, England had made 255, a lead of 151.

After the exhilaration of the morning's play, there was chatter of a repeat of the Botham miracle at Edgbaston ten years earlier against Australia. When Simmons, Haynes and Richardson were gone for 24, all to DeFreitas, that chatter was turning to a roar. But this time there was no Botham and no miracle. Hooper, with elegance, and Richards, with jaw-jutting determination and growing ferocity, put together 133 at a run a minute to ensure that Richards would end his career as West Indies' captain without losing a series. He was carried from the field on the shoulders of his team, and later confessed to a few tears. It had also been a noteworthy match for Dujon; when he caught Ramprakash in the second innings, he passed A. P. E. Knott's tally of 269 Test victims, and only R. W. Marsh, with 355, stood ahead. – Ted Corbett.

*Man of the Match:* R. B. Richardson.          *Attendance:* 59,917; *receipts* £852,868.

*Close of play:* First day, England 184-9 (P. A. J. DeFreitas 7*, R. K. Illingworth 0*); Second day, West Indies 253-4 (R. B. Richardson 103*, A. L. Logie 24*); Third day, England 156-8 (D. R. Pringle 26*, C. C. Lewis 7*).

## England

| | | | |
|---|---|---|---|
| *G. A. Gooch b Marshall | 45 | – b Patterson | 40 |
| H. Morris c Dujon b Patterson | 3 | – lbw b Patterson | 1 |
| M. A. Atherton lbw b Walsh | 16 | – c Hooper b Patterson | 1 |
| G. A. Hick c Richards b Ambrose | 19 | – b Ambrose | 1 |
| A. J. Lamb lbw b Marshall | 9 | – c Dujon b Walsh | 25 |
| M. R. Ramprakash c Logie b Walsh | 29 | – c Dujon b Marshall | 25 |
| †R. C. Russell c Richardson b Ambrose | 12 | – c Dujon b Patterson | 0 |
| D. R. Pringle b Ambrose | 2 | – c Logie b Marshall | 45 |
| P. A. J. DeFreitas c Richardson b Marshall | 10 | – b Patterson | 7 |
| C. C. Lewis lbw b Marshall | 13 | – c sub (C. B. Lambert) b Ambrose | 65 |
| R. K. Illingworth not out | 0 | – not out | 5 |
| B 4, l-b 3, n-b 23 | 30 | B 5, l-b 21, n-b 14 | 40 |

1/6 (2) 2/53 (3) 3/88 (1) 4/108 (5)     **188**    1/2 (2) 2/4 (3) 3/5 (4) 4/71 (5)     **255**
5/129 (4) 6/159 (7) 7/163 (8) 8/163 (6)     5/94 (1) 6/96 (7) 7/127 (6)
9/184 (10) 10/188 (9)                 8/144 (9) 9/236 (10) 10/255 (8)

Bowling: *First Innings*—Ambrose 23–6–64–3; Patterson 11–2–39–1; Walsh 21–6–43–2; Marshall 12.4–1–33–4; Hooper 3–2–2–0. *Second Innings*—Ambrose 33–16–42–2; Patterson 31–6–81–5; Marshall 19.4–3–53–2; Walsh 7–1–20–1; Simmons 3–0–7–0; Hooper 12–3–26–0.

## West Indies

| | | | |
|---|---|---|---|
| P. V. Simmons c Hick b Lewis | 28 | – lbw b DeFreitas | 16 |
| D. L. Haynes c Russell b DeFreitas | 32 | – c Hick b DeFreitas | 8 |
| R. B. Richardson lbw b Lewis | 104 | – c Hick b DeFreitas | 0 |
| C. L. Hooper b Illingworth | 31 | – not out | 55 |
| *I. V. A. Richards c Lewis b Pringle | 22 | – not out | 73 |
| A. L. Logie c Atherton b Lewis | 28 | | |
| †P. J. L. Dujon lbw b DeFreitas | 6 | | |
| M. D. Marshall not out | 6 | | |
| C. E. L. Ambrose c Hick b Lewis | 1 | | |
| C. A. Walsh c and b Lewis | 18 | | |
| B. P. Patterson b Lewis | 3 | | |
| L-b 7, n-b 6 | 13 | L-b 4, n-b 1 | 5 |

1/52 (1) 2/93 (2) 3/148 (4) 4/194 (5)     **292**    1/23 (2) 2/23 (3)       (3 wkts) **157**
5/257 (6) 6/258 (3) 7/266 (7) 8/267 (9)     3/24 (1)
9/285 (10) 10/292 (11)

Bowling: *First Innings*—DeFreitas 25.3–9–40–2; Lewis 35–10–111–6; Pringle 23–9–48–1; Illingworth 17–2–75–1; Gooch 6–1–11–0; Hick 1–1–0–0. *Second Innings*—DeFreitas 13–2–54–3; Lewis 16–7–45–0; Pringle 7–1–31–0; Illingworth 4.4–0–23–0.

Umpires: B. Dudleston and D. R. Shepherd.

## GLOUCESTERSHIRE v WEST INDIANS

At Bristol, July 31, August 1, 2. Drawn. Toss: West Indians. Haynes, whose form had disappointed since his one-day hundred at Nevil Road in May, returned to regain his best touch. He played a sparkling innings of 151, with seventeen fours and a six, against an attack which looked plain without Lawrence, absent for a minor foot operation. His fellow-centurion in a second-wicket stand of 240 in 61 overs was Richardson, who also hit seventeen fours and when 23 reached 1,000 first-class runs on the tour. A final flurry from Lambert and Logie added 54 in seven overs. Although the West Indians seldom appeared fully committed in the field, Gloucestershire recovered well from 116 for four, which was effectively for five as Hodgson had withdrawn overnight with a trapped nerve in his elbow. The follow-on was avoided, thanks to Alleyne, Russell and Lloyds, and with that accomplished, Lloyds provided some good, clean hitting before Wright declared. The West Indians increased their lead to 206 before the close, but the final day became something of an anticlimax after Hooper's fourth hundred of the summer (three sixes, nine fours) and Russell's first first-class wicket – Richardson stumped by Alleyne, to the very occasional bowler's evident delight. Faced with a token target of 359 in two sessions, Gloucestershire blocked out a match poorly supported by the Bristol public.

*Close of play:* First day, Gloucestershire 27-1 (G. D. Hodgson 6*, A. J. Wright 6*); Second day, West Indians 109-2 (P. V. Simmons 57*, C. L. Hooper 35*).

## West Indians

| | | |
|---|---|---|
| P. V. Simmons c Russell b Gilbert | 26 | – lbw b Babington ............ 72 |
| *D. L. Haynes c Athey b Lloyds | 151 | |
| R. B. Richardson st Russell b Scott | 119 | – (6) st Alleyne b Russell ..... 48 |
| C. B. Lambert not out | 30 | – (2) c Wright b Gilbert ....... 8 |
| A. L. Logie lbw b Babington | 27 | |
| †D. Williams (did not bat) | | – (3) lbw b Babington .......... 4 |
| C. L. Hooper (did not bat) | | – (4) not out ................. 111 |
| M. D. Marshall (did not bat) | | – (5) c Hancock b Smith ....... 1 |
| L-b 3, n-b 12 | 15 | L-b 8, n-b 9 .............. 17 |

1/56 2/296 3/314 4/368      (4 wkts dec.) 368    1/21 2/26 3/146    (5 wkts dec.) 261
                                                     4/149 5/261

H. A. G. Anthony, I. B. A. Allen and B. P. Patterson did not bat.

*Bowling: First Innings*—Gilbert 11–0–56–1; Babington 13.4–0–65–1; Smith 13–2–46–0; Scott 14–1–48–1; Lloyds 21–1–112–1; Alleyne 9–1–38–0. *Second Innings*—Gilbert 10.1–0–38–1; Babington 15–1–68–2; Smith 13–2–69–1; Lloyds 7–0–34–0; Alleyne 11–2–40–0; Russell 0.5–0–4–1.

## Gloucestershire

| | | |
|---|---|---|
| G. D. Hodgson retired hurt | 6 | |
| R. J. Scott c Williams b Marshall | 9 | – (1) c Simmons b Hooper ....... 19 |
| *A. J. Wright c Williams b Anthony | 12 | – (2) c Williams b Hooper ....... 60 |
| C. W. J. Athey st Williams b Hooper | 35 | – (3) retired hurt .......... 4 |
| M. W. Alleyne c and b Hooper | 68 | – (4) c Allen b Hooper ....... 26 |
| T. H. C. Hancock c Williams b Allen | 1 | – (5) not out .......... 7 |
| †R. C. Russell c Patterson b Hooper | 35 | – (6) run out .......... 2 |
| J. W. Lloyds not out | 71 | – (7) not out .......... 3 |
| D. R. Gilbert not out | 6 | |
| L-b 9, w 1, n-b 18 | 28 | L-b 8, n-b 3 .............. 11 |

1/11 2/47 3/107 4/116      (6 wkts dec.) 271    1/54 2/117 3/119    (4 wkts) 132
5/167 6/242                                                   4/123

A. M. Smith and A. M. Babington did not bat.

*In the first innings G. D. Hodgson retired hurt at 27. In the second innings C. W. J. Athey retired hurt at 68.*

*Bowling: First Innings*—Patterson 11–2–28–0; Allen 19–3–55–1; Marshall 16–2–57–1; Hooper 24.4–6–55–3; Anthony 17–0–67–1. *Second Innings*—Patterson 6–2–16–0; Allen 7–2–14–0; Hooper 23–5–43–3; Anthony 5–0–27–0; Marshall 6–2–6–0; Richardson 5–2–6–0; Simmons 8–3–12–0; Lambert 1–1–0–0.

Umpires: J. H. Harris and D. O. Oslear.

## ESSEX v WEST INDIANS

At Chelmsford, August 3, 4, 5. Drawn. Toss: West Indians. Left with the nigh-impossible target of 336 in 56 overs, Essex were content to settle for a draw, and the captains departed the field midway through the final hour. On the opening day Lambert, who reached three figures in 152 balls, provided most of the entertainment. In all, he hit 22 boundaries in just over three hours. Dujon, who helped him put on 132 for the second wicket, lasted two hours longer, and gathered 24 fours between periods of watchful defence. The West Indians declared at their overnight score, and after Essex had made an uncertain start, Seymour confirmed his promise, striking nine fours and a six in his 74. Gooch, dropping down in the order, gave the innings substance against an attack lacking its Test match venom. Lambert caught the eye again on the final day, hitting nine fours and two sixes in his unbeaten 82, but the lack of a more generous declaration proved a big disappointment for the crowd. The three days attracted a total of around 15,000 spectators, and income, including sponsorship, in excess of £70,000.

*Close of play:* First day, West Indians 367-4 (P. J. L. Dujon 142*, D. L. Haynes 23*); Second day, West Indians 60-4 (C. B. Lambert 0*, P. V. Simmons 0*).

## West Indians

| | | | |
|---|---|---|---|
| P. V. Simmons lbw b Pringle | 51 | – (6) c Gooch b Andrew | 40 |
| C. B. Lambert c and b Such | 116 | – (5) not out | 82 |
| P. J. L. Dujon not out | 142 | – (7) not out | 27 |
| †D. Williams c Andrew b Pringle | 24 | | |
| H. A. G. Anthony c Childs b Andrew | 0 | | |
| D. L. Haynes not out | 23 | – (1) c Hussain b Such | 19 |
| R. B. Richardson (did not bat) | – | (2) c Such b Andrew | 5 |
| *I. V. A. Richards (did not bat) | – | (3) lbw b Pringle | 23 |
| C. L. Hooper (did not bat) | – | (4) c Stephenson b Such | 12 |
| L-b 6, n-b 5 | 11 | B 2, l-b 2, n-b 5 | 9 |

1/93 2/225 3/296 4/299          (4 wkts dec.) 367          1/15 2/47 3/59          (5 wkts dec.) 217
                                                            4/60 5/151

C. E. L. Ambrose and I. B. A. Allen did not bat.

Bowling: *First Innings*—Andrew 19-1-90-1; Pringle 16-4-48-2; Gooch 13-4-46-0; Childs 19-8-64-0; Stephenson 10-2-37-0; Such 28-8-76-1. *Second Innings*—Andrew 14-1-51-2; Pringle 11-2-29-1; Such 14-3-56-2; Childs 15-5-51-0; Stephenson 6-0-26-0.

## Essex

| | | | |
|---|---|---|---|
| A. C. H. Seymour c Williams b Richards | 74 | – c Hooper b Ambrose | 5 |
| J. P. Stephenson c Simmons b Ambrose | 0 | – c and b Anthony | 33 |
| P. J. Prichard c Williams b Anthony | 5 | – c Hooper b Allen | 13 |
| Salim Malik b Simmons | 9 | | |
| N. Hussain c Williams b Simmons | 28 | – (4) c Williams b Anthony | 41 |
| *G. A. Gooch c Williams b Ambrose | 66 | – not out | 25 |
| †M. A. Garnham c Anthony b Hooper | 12 | – (5) not out | 8 |
| D. R. Pringle not out | 31 | | |
| S. J. W. Andrew c Simmons b Ambrose | 0 | | |
| J. H. Childs c Richards b Hooper | 1 | | |
| P. M. Such b Ambrose | 4 | | |
| L-b 4, w 1, n-b 14 | 19 | L-b 4, n-b 7 | 11 |

1/4 2/34 3/45 4/106 5/153          249          1/8 2/24 3/89 4/106          (4 wkts) 136
6/192 7/231 8/231 9/234

Bowling: *First Innings*—Ambrose 14.5-6-29-4; Allen 10-1-27-0; Simmons 23-4-84-2; Anthony 10-1-23-1; Richards 13-3-49-1; Hooper 12-1-33-2. *Second Innings*—Ambrose 7-5-4-1; Allen 9-2-48-1; Hooper 17-2-47-0; Richards 7-0-18-0; Anthony 7-2-15-2.

Umpires: G. I. Burgess and N. T. Plews.

# ENGLAND v WEST INDIES

## Fifth Cornhill Test

At The Oval, August 8, 9, 10, 11, 12. England won by five wickets. Toss: England. As if by calculation, Botham struck his only delivery of England's second innings to "Compton's corner" to complete the victory which secured a drawn series against West Indies for the first time since 1973-74. Compton's famous sweep for the Ashes triumph of 1953 had finished in the same spot, and in many ways this match was just as memorable in Oval Test history. Certainly it could hardly have had a more popular final scene to gladden English hearts, Botham, with his Comptonesque flair for the big occasion, sealing the win in his first Test appearance for two years. It was, moreover, his first taste of victory in twenty Tests against West Indies.

This was the *coup de grâce*, but notwithstanding Smith's hundred, it was the left-arm spinner, Tufnell, who played the key role in a result many thought beyond England, against opposition nearing their formidable best after wins at Nottingham and Birmingham. His six for 25 on a hot Saturday afternoon obliged West Indies to follow on for the first time against England in 22 years and 48 Tests, and presented his captain, Gooch, with a priceless equation of runs and time.

Richards, in his 121st Test and his 50th as captain, was leading West Indies for the last time. He was forced to forgo the services of Logie, who had a knee injury, and called in the Guyanese left-hander, Lambert, for his Test début. England opted for what was described as a "high risk strategy". They dropped Hick, Lamb, Russell and Illingworth, and in addition to Smith, his finger injury now healed, they recalled Tufnell, Botham (for his 98th Test) and Stewart as a batsman-wicket-keeper. The selection of Stewart ahead of Russell was widely criticised, but ultimately was justified. Pringle's tonsillitis ruled him out of the match.

Gooch, winning the toss, decided to have first use of a pitch containing its usual generous bounce. This was exploited fully by West Indies' fast bowlers on the first afternoon, after Gooch and Morris had fought their way to 82 by lunch. No Law was broken by Ambrose, Patterson and Walsh, but as the bouncer became a regular weapon, the spirit of the game was sorely tested at times. And the attack had the desired effect; England lost three wickets for 8 runs in 21 deliveries, with Morris out one ball after a lifter from Ambrose had broken the chinstrap on his helmet. Atherton faced just four balls, but Ramprakash once more battled against the pace, only to fall, for the seventh time in the series, in the 20s. However, Smith, reaching 50 for the twentieth time in Tests, and Stewart saw their team to the close at 231 for four, and next day Smith's valiant sixth Test hundred, his second of the series, enabled England to reach 400 against West Indies for the first time in fifteen years. His square cut was again profitable, and he hit thirteen fours in almost six hours (257 balls) at the wicket.

There were important contributions, too, from Stewart, Botham and Lewis in the late middle order, with Botham dismissed in a bizarre fashion. Attempting to hook Ambrose, he over-balanced and dislodged a bail with his right thigh as he tried to straddle the stumps. Equally unusual was the pause in play late on the second day while stewards cleared away a mass of torn paper from the outfield, emanating from the tiresome Mexican wave. West Indies closed at a comfortable 90 for one, with Haynes and Richardson relieved to have survived a chance each.

The third day belonged to Tufnell, when Richards might have been expected to take command on his farewell stage. From 158 for three, West Indies declined rapidly to 176 all out as Tufnell spun the ball generously in a devastating spell of six for 4 in 33 deliveries either side of lunch. It has to be said, though, that a rash of reckless strokes contributed to this collapse, which began when Lambert miscued Tufnell's first ball of the day to cover. Marshall cut to slip, Richards, Ambrose and Walsh gave their wickets away in one over, and in Tufnell's next over, Botham dived for his third catch to dismiss Patterson. Richards had held himself back because of a headache. Haynes, who carried his bat for the second time in Test cricket, faced 198 balls in four and threequarter hours, and he batted eight minutes under three hours (114 balls) when West Indies followed on 243 behind. England collected three more wickets by the close.

There were no easy pickings for Tufnell on the fourth day, however. Twice Hooper struck him for six during a magnificent display of strokemaking which illuminated the first hour. Then Richards, given a standing ovation to the wicket, put on 97 for the fifth wicket with Richardson to put his side ahead for the first time in the game. Richards began needing 20 runs to guarantee an average of 50 in Tests, and he had gone well past that when he drove Lawrence to mid-on. He left the Test arena to rapturous applause, stopping on the way to raise his bat and maroon cap to both sides of the ground in gracious acknowledgement. Richardson finally reached his hundred, a dedicated effort, after six and a half hours, and West Indies led by 113, with four wickets in hand, on Sunday evening.

Marshall lost his middle stump to DeFreitas's second ball on Monday, Ambrose was lbw off his fourth, and then Lawrence claimed five wickets in a Test innings for the first time when he removed Walsh and, finally, Richardson. Richardson had batted for just over seven and a half hours for his 121, in which time he faced 312 deliveries and hit a six and eleven fours. This left England to score 143 to level the series, with time no object. However, the West Indian fast bowlers backed Richards's pledge that England would have to fight for victory, and wickets fell too regularly for England's comfort. At 80 for four the cricket was tense, but Stewart's coolness and sure strokeplay saw England to the finishing line. With the scores level, Ramprakash was lbw to Lambert's third ball in Test cricket, bringing in Botham to conclude the match with a little under two hours remaining. – David Field.

*Man of the Match:* R. A. Smith.      *Attendance:* 70,926; *receipts* £1,013,033.

*Men of the Series:* England – G. A. Gooch; West Indies – C. E. L. Ambrose.

*Close of play:* First day, England 231-4 (R. A. Smith 54*, A. J. Stewart 19*); Second day, West Indies 90-1 (D. L. Haynes 46*, R. B. Richardson 20*); Third day, West Indies 152-3 (R. B. Richardson 39*, C. L. Hooper 11*); Fourth day, West Indies 356-6 (R. B. Richardson 108*, M. D. Marshall 17*).

## England

| | | | |
|---|---|---|---|
| *G. A. Gooch lbw b Ambrose | 60 | – lbw b Marshall | 29 |
| H. Morris c Lambert b Ambrose | 44 | – c Dujon b Patterson | 2 |
| M. A. Atherton c Hooper b Walsh | 0 | – c Hooper b Patterson | 13 |
| R. A. Smith lbw b Marshall | 109 | – c Patterson b Walsh | 26 |
| M. R. Ramprakash c Lambert b Hooper | 25 | – lbw b Lambert | 19 |
| †A. J. Stewart c Richardson b Patterson | 31 | – not out | 38 |
| I. T. Botham hit wkt b Ambrose | 31 | – not out | 4 |
| C. C. Lewis not out | 47 | | |
| P. A. J. DeFreitas c Dujon b Walsh | 7 | | |
| D. V. Lawrence c Richards b Walsh | 9 | | |
| P. C. R. Tufnell c Haynes b Patterson | 2 | | |
| B 8, l-b 10, w 1, n-b 35 | 54 | B 4, w 1, n-b 10 | 15 |

1/112 (2) 2/114 (3) 3/120 (1) 4/188 (5)     419     1/3 (2) 2/40 (3)     (5 wkts) 146
5/263 (6) 6/336 (4) 7/351 (7) 8/386 (9)              3/80 (1) 4/80 (4)
9/411 (10) 10/419 (11)                               5/142 (5)

Bowling: *First Innings*—Ambrose 36-8-83-3; Patterson 25.1-3-87-2; Walsh 32-5-91-3; Marshall 24-5-62-1; Hooper 34-1-78-1. *Second Innings*—Ambrose 8-0-48-0; Patterson 9-0-63-2; Marshall 5-3-9-1; Walsh 9-3-18-1; Lambert 0.4-0-4-1.

## West Indies

| | | | |
|---|---|---|---|
| P. V. Simmons lbw b Lawrence | 15 | – c Lewis b Botham | 36 |
| D. L. Haynes not out | 75 | – lbw b Lawrence | 43 |
| R. B. Richardson c Stewart b Botham | 20 | – (4) c Gooch b Lawrence | 121 |
| C. L. Hooper c Stewart b DeFreitas | 3 | – (5) c Gooch b Tufnell | 54 |
| C. B. Lambert c Ramprakash b Tufnell | 39 | – (3) lbw b Botham | 14 |
| †P. J. L. Dujon lbw b Lawrence | 0 | – (7) c Stewart b Lawrence | 5 |
| M. D. Marshall c Botham b Tufnell | 0 | – (8) b DeFreitas | 17 |
| *I. V. A. Richards c Stewart b Tufnell | 2 | – (6) c Morris b Lawrence | 60 |
| C. E. L. Ambrose c Botham b Tufnell | 0 | – lbw b DeFreitas | 0 |
| C. A. Walsh c Gooch b Tufnell | 0 | – lbw b Lawrence | 14 |
| B. P. Patterson c Botham b Tufnell | 2 | – not out | 1 |
| L-b 9, n-b 11 | 20 | B 7, l-b 5, w 2, n-b 6 | 20 |

1/52 (1) 2/95 (3) 3/98 (4) 4/158 (5)     176     1/53 (1) 2/71 (3) 3/125 (2)     385
5/160 (6) 6/161 (7) 7/172 (8) 8/172 (9)          4/208 (5) 5/305 (6) 6/311 (7)
9/172 (10) 10/176 (11)                           7/356 (8) 8/356 (9)
                                                 9/378 (10) 10/385 (4)

Bowling: *First Innings*—DeFreitas 13-6-38-1; Lawrence 16-1-67-2; Tufnell 14.3-3-25-6; Botham 11-4-27-1; Lewis 3-1-10-0. *Second Innings*—DeFreitas 20-9-42-2; Lawrence 25.5-4-106-5; Lewis 25-12-35-0; Tufnell 16-6-150-1; Botham 16-4-40-2.

Umpires: J. W. Holder and M. J. Kitchen.

# THE SRI LANKANS IN ENGLAND, 1991

The third visit to England in four years by a Sri Lankan team did little to alter the impression, given by their predecessors, of talented, natural cricketers lacking experience in competitive first-class cricket. Although in recent years Sri Lanka had allocated first-class status to its top level of club cricket, and had striven to develop a regional competition played over four days, the evidence offered by the tourists again suggested that, in attitude and application, the Sri Lankans in general had still to make the transition from weekend club cricketers to first-class cricketers.

On easy-paced pitches, against bowling offering some latitude outside the off stump, their batsmen delighted by the richness of their strokeplay. In their only win in seven first-class games on the tour, over Somerset, they successfully chased a target of 249 in 49 overs for the loss of only two wickets, with Aravinda de Silva, the captain, and the left-handed Sanath Jayasuriya scoring the last 83 runs in eight overs. But it was another matter entirely when the ball swung, seamed or turned, as it did at Worcester and Bristol, where the tourists suffered heavy defeats. On both occasions, flair and lack of discipline betrayed their generally sound techniques, which could have stood them in good stead.

Jayasuriya, who against Sussex scored the side's only hundred, and de Silva timed the ball exquisitely, as they showed in the Test match at Lord's. There, de Silva lit up the closing stages of the second day with a startling display of derring-do which, in its virtuosity, matched Hooper's batting for West Indies on the Sunday morning of The Oval Test. However, although it was a stunning catch by Lewis, in the gully, which dismissed de Silva first thing next morning, the situation called for something more temperate from the captain. He was leading a young side, with an average age between 24 and 25, and his players required a standard to emulate. Once or twice on the tour, too, they could have done with a reminder of the tenets of the game with regard to sportsmanship.

Chandika Hathurusinghe and Marvan Atapattu confirmed the impression they gave in 1990 of being well organised in defence, without this inhibiting their attacking strokes, and at Taunton Brendon Kuruppu demonstrated his ability to play either an attacking role or an adventurous one. Hashan Tillekeratne, the first-choice wicket-keeper, was forced to miss the early matches after injuring a finger when the deckchair on which he was sitting collapsed, and this gave twenty-year-old Romesh Kaluwitharana the opportunity to gain valuable experience. Tillekeratne batted for more than an hour in both innings of the Test match, having played himself into form at Hove.

The Sri Lankan bowling, always likely to be the weaker of their principal suits, excelled itself at Lord's by bowling out England for 282, which would have been less had Stewart, England's century-maker, not been dropped when he was 24. Rumesh Ratnayake, on his first Test match tour of England, and Sri Lanka's leading wicket-taker in Tests, stood out. With his slinging action he could generate deceptive pace, and in helpful conditions at Bristol he took eight of the twelve Gloucestershire wickets to fall. Both there and at Lord's he also struck the ball in a thrilling fashion. Champaka Ramanayake maintained a tidy line and length, and was a willing workhorse, but neither he nor Kapila Wijegunawardene possessed the firepower to do more than contain at the highest level. The length of Wijegunawardene's run-up, not to mention his name, was hardly commensurate with his pace.

The left-arm spinner, Don Anurasiri, gained his third tour of England on the strength of his bowling against England A in February and March, and if Ranjith Madurasinghe, the off-spinner, had been able to recapture his form of 1990, when he was the Sri Lankans' leading wicket-taker, the attack would have boasted an experienced and contrasting spin combination to support their faster bowlers. Another off-spinner, Muttiah Muralitharan, failed to take a first-class wicket on tour, finding the pitches generally unsympathetic to his slow turn. However, at nineteen he was very much a novice, with time to learn the skills of his trade – if he can get the opportunity in a side which seems more welcome for one-day internationals than for first-class cricket. Of Sri Lanka's 34 Tests, for example, Lord's was only their ninth since April 1987, when New Zealand's tour of the country was abandoned owing to the civil unrest there. In the same period, Sri Lanka had played 49 one-day internationals against the Test-playing countries, all of them, like the Tests, away from home.

Finding enough of the right cricket is a serious problem for Sri Lanka. Financially, a three-Test tour of England is doubtless considered unpractical, but in cricketing terms it should be essential if Sri Lanka is to be helped to maturity as a Test match country. The mistakes seen at Lord's would not, one hopes, have been repeated in a subsequent Test a week or two later. Lessons would have been learned and heeded, as perhaps they were when, soon after the tour, the former captain, Arjuna Ranatunga, was recalled to the national squad. Ranatunga had been stripped of the captaincy and left out of the side for England following an enquiry into his leadership on recent tours of India and New Zealand.

The touring team in England was managed by Chandra Schaffter, who played for Ceylon as a swing bowler in the 1950s, with the 1984 tourist, Mumtaz Yusuf, as assistant-manager and coach.

## SRI LANKAN TOUR RESULTS

*Test matches* – Played 1: Lost 1.
*First-class matches* – Played 7: Won 1, Lost 3, Drawn 3.
*Win* – Somerset.
*Losses* – England, Worcestershire, Gloucestershire.
*Draws* – Yorkshire, Derbyshire, Sussex.
*Non first-class matches* – Played 4: Won 3, Lost 1. *Wins* – England Amateur XI, Durham, England A. *Loss* – England A.

## SRI LANKAN AVERAGES – FIRST-CLASS MATCHES

### BATTING

| | M | I | NO | R | HI | 100s | Avge |
|---|---|---|---|---|---|---|---|
| S. T. Jayasuriya | 6 | 11 | 2 | 482 | 100* | 1 | 53.55 |
| R. J. Ratnayake | 4 | 5 | 1 | 193 | 68* | 0 | 48.25 |
| M. S. Atapattu | 5 | 6 | 2 | 132 | 52* | 0 | 33.00 |
| P. A. de Silva | 5 | 7 | 1 | 198 | 57* | 0 | 33.00 |
| D. S. B. P. Kuruppu | 7 | 12 | 0 | 389 | 86 | 0 | 32.41 |

| | M | I | NO | R | HI | 100s | Avge |
|---|---|---|---|---|---|---|---|
| U. C. Hathurusinghe ........ | 6 | 11 | 1 | 311 | 74* | 0 | 31.10 |
| H. P. Tillekeratne ........... | 5 | 6 | 1 | 155 | 80* | 0 | 31.00 |
| A. P. Gurusinha ............ | 6 | 10 | 0 | 292 | 98 | 0 | 29.20 |
| C. P. H. Ramanayake ....... | 6 | 8 | 2 | 152 | 41* | 0 | 25.33 |
| R. S. Mahanama ............ | 6 | 9 | 0 | 146 | 65 | 0 | 16.22 |
| R. S. Kaluwitharana ........ | 3 | 5 | 0 | 73 | 34 | 0 | 14.60 |
| A. W. R. Madurasinghe ..... | 3 | 4 | 2 | 28 | 17* | 0 | 14.00 |
| K. I. W. Wijegunawardene ... | 5 | 6 | 2 | 52 | 26 | 0 | 13.00 |
| M. Muralitharan ............ | 3 | 4 | 1 | 27 | 22* | 0 | 9.00 |
| S. D. Anurasiri ............. | 4 | 3 | 1 | 17 | 16 | 0 | 8.50 |
| F. S. Ahangama ............ | 3 | 4 | 1 | 7 | 7 | 0 | 2.33 |

*\* Signifies not out.*

## BOWLING

| | O | M | R | W | BB | 5W/i | Avge |
|---|---|---|---|---|---|---|---|
| R. J. Ratnayake ............. | 137.3 | 15 | 447 | 17 | 6-97 | 2 | 26.29 |
| K. I. W. Wijegunawardene ... | 124.3 | 14 | 537 | 15 | 4-97 | 0 | 35.80 |
| C. P. H. Ramanayake ....... | 166 | 29 | 594 | 12 | 3-83 | 0 | 49.50 |
| A. W. R. Madurasinghe ...... | 82 | 15 | 252 | 5 | 1-13 | 0 | 50.40 |
| S. D. Anurasiri ............. | 208.1 | 51 | 560 | 9 | 3-122 | 0 | 62.22 |

Also bowled: F. S. Ahangama 64–20–189–2; P. A. de Silva 9–2–27–0; A. P. Gurusinha 18–5–41–2; U. C. Hathurusinghe 39.3–10–110–3; S. T. Jayasuriya 12.5–2–53–0; M. Muralitharan 70.1–8–209–0.

## FIELDING

9 – H. P. Tillekeratne; 8 – R. S. Mahanama; 4 – P. A. de Silva, D. S. B. P. Kuruppu; 3 – R. J. Ratnayake; 2 – M. S. Atapattu, A. P. Gurusinha, U. C. Hathurusinghe, R. S. Kaluwitharana, M. Muralitharan; 1 – S. D. Anurasiri, A. W. R. Madurasinghe, C. P. H. Ramanayake, Substitute.

## HUNDRED FOR SRI LANKANS

The following three-figure innings was played for the Sri Lankans.

**S. T. Jayasuriya:** 100* v Sussex, Hove.

*\* Signifies not out.*

*Note:* Those matches which follow which were not first-class are signified by the use of a dagger.

## †ENGLAND AMATEUR XI v SRI LANKANS

At Wolverhampton, July 24. Sri Lankans won by five wickets, their target having been adjusted to 151 from 41 overs. Toss: England Amateur XI. A lunch-time shower reduced the match from 55 to 52 overs a side, and further rain cut another eleven overs from the Sri Lankans' innings, but they overhauled their revised target with three and a half overs to spare. Jayasuriya's fifty dominated the closing stages. He had earlier taken four wickets and three catches in the Amateurs' innings. Dean of Staffordshire hit twelve fours and a six in his 86, but after reaching 147 for the loss of only one wicket, his team lost the remaining nine for 44.

## England Amateur XI

| | | | |
|---|---|---|---|
| S. J. Dean c Kaluwitharana | | P. G. Roshier b Jayasuriya | 1 |
| b Madurasinghe | 86 | N. French st Kaluwitharana | |
| †S. N. V. Waterton c Jayasuriya | | b Jayasuriya | 4 |
| b Gurusinha | 19 | R. A. Evans c and b Jayasuriya | 5 |
| J. Wright c Jayasuriya b Muralitharan | 26 | K. A. Arnold not out | 6 |
| R. J. Leiper c Kuruppu | | L-b 7, w 2, n-b 9 | 18 |
| b Madurasinghe | 22 | | |
| M. Hussain b Muralitharan | 0 | 1/72 2/147 3/152 | (51.4 overs) 191 |
| *P. J. Garner c Gurusinha b Jayasuriya | 0 | 4/153 5/154 6/167 | |
| N. J. Archer lbw b Madurasinghe | 4 | 7/168 8/180 9/186 | |

Bowling: Ramanayake 7–1–23–0; Wijegunawardene 4–0–33–0; Hathurusinghe 3–0–10–0; Muralitharan 11–0–30–2; Gurusinha 5–1–23–1; Jayasuriya 10.4–1–39–4; Madurasinghe 11–3–26–3.

## Sri Lankans

| | | | |
|---|---|---|---|
| R. S. Mahanama c Dean b Evans | 26 | S. T. Jayasuriya not out | 57 |
| U. C. Hathurusinghe c Archer | | D. S. B. P. Kuruppu not out | 11 |
| b Garner | 28 | | |
| *A. P. Gurusinha c Dean b Garner | 9 | L-b 5, w 3, n-b 1 | 9 |
| M. S. Atapattu run out | 12 | | |
| K. I. W. Wijegunawardene c Leiper | | 1/54 2/68 3/71 | (5 wkts, 37.3 overs) 153 |
| b Evans | 1 | 4/74 5/107 | |

†R. S. Kaluwitharana, A. W. R. Madurasinghe, C. P. H. Ramanayake and M. Muralitharan did not bat.

Bowling: Arnold 9–1–38–0; Roshier 1.1–0–2–0; Archer 0.5–0–5–0; French 8–2–28–0; Hussain 6.3–1–18–0; Wright 3–0–9–0; Evans 6–1–31–2; Garner 3–0–17–2.

Umpires: T. Brown and R. Julian.

## †DURHAM v SRI LANKANS

At Hartlepool, July 26. Sri Lankans won by 72 runs. Toss: Durham. On a slow wicket Mahanama and Kuruppu opened with a stand of 123, but this was followed by a flurry of wickets as Kuruppu ran out Gurusinha and de Silva went to a catch at deep mid-wicket. Atapattu kept the second half of the innings together, regularly finding the boundary wide of third man. In reply Durham struggled; their biggest partnership was the sixth-wicket stand of 34 between Bainbridge and Cook, and after Bainbridge was caught at deep cover, the last four wickets fell for 21 runs. Jayasuriya was again the Sri Lankans' most successful bowler.

## Sri Lankans

| | | | |
|---|---|---|---|
| R. S. Mahanama c Cook b Briers | 67 | C. P. H. Ramanayake run out | 9 |
| D. S. B. P. Kuruppu lbw b Wood | 53 | A. W. R. Madurasinghe b Wood | 0 |
| A. P. Gurusinha run out | 1 | S. D. Anurasiri not out | 1 |
| *P. A. de Silva c Glendenen b Briers | 5 | | |
| S. T. Jayasuriya c Blenkiron | | B 1, l-b 9, w 5, n-b 3 | 18 |
| b Bainbridge | 2 | | |
| †R. S. Kaluwitharana run out | 2 | 1/123 2/126 3/132 | (9 wkts, 55 overs) 221 |
| M. S. Atapattu not out | 33 | 4/154 5/163 6/172 | |
| R. J. Ratnayake b Bainbridge | 10 | 7/205 8/220 9/220 | |

Bowling: S. J. E. Brown 11–1–50–0; Wood 11–3–31–2; Conn 11–1–36–0; Bainbridge 11–1–47–2; Briers 8–0–36–2; Blenkiron 3–0–11–0.

## Durham

| | | | |
|---|---|---|---|
| G. K. Brown c Kaluwitharana | | †A. R. Fothergill run out ............ | 2 |
|     b Ratnayake . | 3 | J. Wood c Mahanama b Jayasuriya .... | 8 |
| J. D. Glendenen c de Silva | | I. E. Conn run out ................. | 1 |
|     b Ramanayake . | 15 | S. J. E. Brown not out .............. | 0 |
| P. Burn c and b Anurasiri .......... | 10 | | |
| P. Bainbridge c Ramanayake | | | |
|     b Jayasuriya . | 62 | L-b 2, w 9, n-b 3 ........... | 14 |
| M. P. Briers b Anurasiri ............. | 12 | | |
| D. A. Blenkiron c Jayasuriya b de Silva . | 2 | 1/8 2/27 3/49 | (48.1 overs) 149 |
| *G. Cook st Kaluwitharana | | 4/78 5/94 6/128 | |
|     b Jayasuriya . | 20 | 7/136 8/138 9/147 | |

Bowling: Ratnayake 5–0–12–1; Ramanayake 7–2–16–1; Madurasinghe 10.1–3–34–0; Gurusinha 2–0–8–0; Anurasiri 11–0–35–2; de Silva 7–0–16–1; Jayasuriya 6–0–26–3.

Umpires: B. Hassan and N. T. Plews.

## YORKSHIRE v SRI LANKANS

At Leeds, July 27, 28, 29. Drawn. Toss: Yorkshire. With match practice the tourists' chief interest, and Yorkshire's bowling seriously depleted, there was little prospect of a positive finish on an easy-paced pitch. Anurasiri was accurate with his slow left-arm bowling, but Kellett batted solidly to reach what was then his highest score, rationing himself to five boundaries in his 82 from 204 balls. The more robust Robinson completed his hundred in 148 deliveries, having batted 189 minutes and hit two sixes and ten fours. Although the seventeen-year-old Broadhurst bowled with great enthusiasm when the Sri Lankans batted, they easily gained a substantial lead after losing Mahanama to Broadhurst's first ball. Gurusinha and Jayasuriya added 149 in 35 overs of rich strokeplay; though neither could reach three figures, the former occupied 258 minutes for his 98 and hit one six and ten fours in 210 balls, while Jayasuriya collected twelve fours in making 94. Coming in at No. 9, Ratnayake hit four sixes off Batty. As Yorkshire played out time, Kellett registered his maiden first-class century, an unbeaten 109 in 225 minutes and 204 balls, with twelve fours. The match was Sidebottom's only first-class appearance in his last season for Yorkshire.

*Close of play:* First day, Sri Lankans 1-1 (D. S. B. P. Kuruppu 0*, C. P. H. Ramanayake 0*); Second day, Sri Lankans 327-6 (M. S. Atapattu 36*, R. S. Kaluwitharana 27*).

## Yorkshire

| | | | |
|---|---|---|---|
| S. A. Kellett b Ratnayake .......... | 82 | – not out .......... | 109 |
| *A. A. Metcalfe c Kuruppu b Madurasinghe ... | 26 | – b Madurasinghe ............. | 35 |
| D. Byas lbw b Anurasiri ........... | 12 | – not out .......... | 31 |
| †R. J. Blakey c Mahanama b Anurasiri ....... | 6 | | |
| P. E. Robinson c Ratnayake b Ramanayake ... | 100 | | |
| A. P. Grayson lbw b Ratnayake ............ | 0 | | |
| J. D. Batty c and b Anurasiri .............. | 51 | | |
| A. Sidebottom not out ................. | 18 | | |
| M. Broadhurst b Ramanayake ............. | 1 | | |
|     B 2, l-b 4, n-b 12 ............ | 18 | L-b 3, n-b 6 ........... | 9 |

| | | |
|---|---|---|
| 1/67 2/88 3/108 4/168 5/176 | (8 wkts dec.) 314 | 1/102 (1 wkt dec.) 184 |
| 6/274 7/310 8/314 | | |

I. J. Houseman and M. A. Robinson did not bat.

Bowling: *First Innings*—Ratnayake 16–2–61–2; Ramanayake 6–1–23–2; Anurasiri 45–8–122–3; Madurasinghe 24–5–67–1; de Silva 9–2–27–0; Jayasuriya 1–0–8–0. *Second Innings*—Ratnayake 2–0–6–0; Ramanayake 13–2–36–0; Anurasiri 27–9–64–0; Madurasinghe 23–4–75–1.

## Sri Lankans

| | | | |
|---|---|---|---|
| R. S. Mahanama c Blakey | | M. S. Atapattu c Kellett | |
| b Broadhurst . | 0 | b M. A. Robinson . | 41 |
| D. S. B. P. Kuruppu lbw b Sidebottom . | 19 | †R. S. Kaluwitharana c Sidebottom | |
| C. P. H. Ramanayake c Blakey | | b Broadhurst . | 31 |
| b Broadhurst . | 25 | R. J. Ratnayake not out . | 68 |
| A. P. Gurusinha c Blakey b Houseman | 98 | A. W. R. Madurasinghe not out . | 17 |
| *P. A. de Silva c P. E. Robinson | | L-b 5, w 2, n-b 4 . | 11 |
| b Batty . | 18 | | |
| | | 1/0 2/32 3/62 4/94        (8 wkts dec.) 422 | |
| S. T. Jayasuriya c Kellett | | 5/243 6/276 7/335 8/347 | |
| b M. A. Robinson . | 94 | | |

S. D. Anurasiri did not bat.

Bowling: Broadhurst 19–2–69–3; M. A. Robinson 25–5–71–2; Sidebottom 11–4–26–1; Houseman 21–4–52–1; Batty 33–7–146–1; Grayson 20–6–53–0.

Umpires: H. D. Bird and A. A. Jones
(J. W. Holder deputised for H. D. Bird on 2nd and 3rd days).

## WORCESTERSHIRE v SRI LANKANS

At Worcester, July 30, 31, August 1. Worcestershire won by an innings and 24 runs. Toss: Sri Lankans. Even against a half-strength home team, in a match often halted by rain, the Sri Lankans could not stave off an emphatic defeat. Tolley's career-best four for 69, in his third first-class game of the season, helped to dismiss the tourists for 181, which Worcestershire almost doubled. Moody put some mediocre bowling to the sword, hitting fifteen fours in 71 balls, and Lampitt and Illingworth shared an unbroken stand of 111 for the eighth wicket. Immediately Tolley plunged the Sri Lankans into deeper embarrassment, dismissing both Hathurusinghe and Gurusinha for 0 in his first seven balls of the second innings. But after the Sri Lankans had lost half their wickets for 53, Jayasuriya, who hit 78 off 119 balls, and Kaluwitharana added 78. Their partnership was ended by Illingworth, who took the last five wickets for 7 runs in 71 balls. When Tolley dismissed Atapattu, he had doubled the number of wickets to his credit in the previous thirteen games of his first-class career.

*Close of play:* First day, Sri Lankans 115-7 (C. P. H. Ramanayake 0*); Second day, Worcestershire 290-7 (S. R. Lampitt 19*, R. K. Illingworth 18*).

## Sri Lankans

| | | | |
|---|---|---|---|
| D. S. B. P. Kuruppu c Illingworth b Newport . | 9 | – c Curtis b Newport . | 4 |
| U. C. Hathurusinghe c Tolley b Newport . | 0 | – c Rhodes b Tolley . | 0 |
| A. P. Gurusinha lbw b Tolley . | 44 | – c Rhodes b Tolley . | 0 |
| *P. A. de Silva b Tolley . | 26 | – c Rhodes b Newport . | 0 |
| S. T. Jayasuriya c Rhodes b Lampitt . | 20 | – c Moody b Illingworth . | 78 |
| M. S. Atapattu st Rhodes b Tolley . | 2 | – lbw b Tolley . | 2 |
| †R. S. Kaluwitharana lbw b Lampitt . | 0 | – c Haynes b Illingworth . | 34 |
| C. P. H. Ramanayake c Moody b Newport . | 8 | – lbw b Illingworth . | 4 |
| K. I. W. Wijegunawardene lbw b Illingworth . | 26 | – not out . | 6 |
| F. S. Ahangama c Moody b Tolley . | 7 | – c Haynes b Illingworth . | 0 |
| M. Muralitharan not out . | 22 | – c Rhodes b Illingworth . | 0 |
| L-b 4, n-b 13 . | 17 | B 1, l-b 6, n-b 3 . | 10 |

| | | |
|---|---|---|
| 1/1 2/41 3/82 4/107 5/115 | 181 | 1/0 2/4 3/6 4/30 5/53        154 |
| 6/115 7/115 8/133 9/147 | | 6/131 7/137 8/148 9/154 |

Bowling: *First Innings*—Newport 20–3–51–3; Tolley 29–8–69–4; Lampitt 15–3–50–2; Illingworth 3.4–0–7–1. *Second Innings*—Newport 14–2–49–2; Tolley 12–5–24–3; Lampitt 7–0–17–0; Illingworth 20.1–7–43–5; D'Oliveira 9–4–11–0; Moody 3–1–3–0.

## Worcestershire

| | | | | |
|---|---|---|---|---|
| *T. S. Curtis c Gurusinha b Ahangama. | 1 | †S. J. Rhodes c Muralitharan | | |
| P. Bent b Ramanayake | 3 | b Wijegunawardene . | 35 |
| T. M. Moody b Wijegunawardene | 86 | S. R. Lampitt not out | 50 |
| D. B. D'Oliveira | | R. K. Illingworth not out | 47 |
| lbw b Wijegunawardene . | 14 | L-b 17, n-b 24 | 41 |
| D. A. Leatherdale c Kaluwitharana | | | |
| b Wijegunawardene . | 66 | 1/2 2/15 3/80 4/124 (7 wkts dec.) 359 |
| G. R. Haynes run out | 16 | 5/170 6/217 7/248 | |

C. M. Tolley and P. J. Newport did not bat.

Bowling: Ramanayake 22–4–84–1; Ahangama 17–6–41–1; Wijegunawardene 19–2–112–4; Muralitharan 31–2–97–0; Gurusinha 2–0–8–0.

Umpires: D. J. Constant and R. C. Tolchard.

---

## DERBYSHIRE v SRI LANKANS

At Derby, August 2, 3, 5. Drawn. Toss: Derbyshire. An early finish because of rain came as a relief, after a match lacking in enterprise. The Sri Lankan bowling, on a slow pitch, was essentially negative and, in response to a poor performance at Worcester, their batsmen set out to have an extended net. Goldsmith, 98 at the end of the first day after batting for 83 overs, completed his maiden century from 283 balls with thirteen fours. It was also Derbyshire's first hundred against the Sri Lankans, and an entertaining 52 by Warner helped the county to their best total against them. Kuruppu batted almost 83 overs for 76, and Hathurusinghe occupied more than three hours in reaching 50, but the captain, de Silva, delayed his appearance, having aggravated an arm injury, and did not bat. The innings cried out for his enterprising strokeplay. In his third first-class match, Sladdin bowled 53 overs with impressive control, although no batsman tried to attack him.

*Close of play:* First day, Derbyshire 258-5 (S. C. Goldsmith 98*, E. McCray 31*); Second day, Sri Lankans 174-3 (U. C. Hathurusinghe 26*, C. P. H. Ramanayake 0*).

## Derbyshire

| | | | | |
|---|---|---|---|---|
| *K. J. Barnett c Tillekeratne | | E. McCray lbw b Ramanayake | 31 |
| b Wijegunawardene . | 68 | †B. J. M. Maher b Ratnayake | 5 |
| A. M. Brown c Kuruppu | | A. E. Warner c Atapattu | |
| b Ramanayake . | 3 | b Wijegunawardene . | 52 |
| C. J. Adams c Mahanama | | S. J. Base c Mahanama b Anurasiri | 6 |
| b Wijegunawardene . | 24 | R. W. Sladdin not out | 0 |
| T. J. G. O'Gorman c de Silva | | L-b 15, w 4, n-b 9 | 28 |
| b Ramanayake . | 1 | | |
| S. C. Goldsmith b Wijegunawardene . . . | 127 | 1/12 2/55 3/63 4/116 5/141 | 358 |
| D. G. Cork c Tillekeratne b Ratnayake | 13 | 6/260 7/272 8/323 9/354 | |

Bowling: Ratnayake 32–3–94–2; Ramanayake 24–6–84–3; Wijegunawardene 31.3–3–97–4; Anurasiri 35–14–62–1; Gurusinha 3–2–6–0.

## Sri Lankans

| | | | | |
|---|---|---|---|---|
| R. S. Mahanama lbw b Base | 14 | C. P. H. Ramanayake not out | 41 |
| D. S. B. P. Kuruppu c Barnett | | | |
| b Sladdin . | 76 | L-b 8, n-b 8 | 16 |
| A. P. Gurusinha b Goldsmith | 46 | | |
| U. C. Hathurusinghe not out | 74 | 1/28 2/92 3/166 (3 wkts) 267 |

*P. A. de Silva, M. S. Atapattu, R. J. Ratnayake, K. I. W. Wijegunawardene, †H. P. Tillekeratne and S. D. Anurasiri did not bat.

Bowling: Base 16–3–33–1; Warner 6–2–11–0; Sladdin 53–25–84–1; Cork 11–3–34–0; Goldsmith 13–4–31–1; McCray 17–6–34–0; Barnett 16–2–32–0.

Umpires: H. D. Bird and J. D. Bond.

## GLOUCESTERSHIRE v SRI LANKANS

At Bristol, August 6, 7. Gloucestershire won by eight wickets. Toss: Gloucestershire. Gloucestershire's first first-class win over a Test-standard touring side since they beat the Indians in 1979 was gained inside two days. The Sri Lankan batsmen were mostly found wanting for application on a well-grassed pitch, and heavy cloud cover on the first morning also helped the home bowlers when the tourists, from 44 without loss in the eighteenth over, lost ten wickets for 53 in the next sixteen. Gilbert and Gerrard, supported by some excellent close catching, met serious resistance only from Ratnayake, who hit Gilbert for four fours and a six off successive deliveries. He then led Sri Lankan efforts to bowl themselves back into the game, and Gloucestershire lost five wickets before going ahead. By that time, however, Alleyne was firing off some powerful strokes, and next morning he hit 21 in three overs. In their second innings, the Sri Lankans were again disconcerted by Gerrard's persistence and occasional steep bounce. The young left-armer took six for 40 for match figures of ten for 60, the best to date of his short first-class career, and Gloucestershire were left with a simple task.

*Close of play:* First day, Gloucestershire 166-9 (M. W. Alleyne 70*, M. J. Gerrard 0*).

### Sri Lankans

| | | | |
|---|---:|---|---:|
| R. S. Mahanama c Hancock b Gerrard | 26 | – c Russell b Gilbert | 0 |
| D. S. B. P. Kuruppu c Russell b Gilbert | 17 | – c Athey b Gilbert | 10 |
| †H. P. Tillekeratne c Ball b Gerrard | 9 | – (6) c Athey b Gerrard | 0 |
| U. C. Hathurusinghe b Gerrard | 0 | – c Wright b Gerrard | 11 |
| S. T. Jayasuriya lbw b Gilbert | 3 | – c Alleyne b Gerrard | 30 |
| *A. P. Gurusinha c Ball b Gerrard | 0 | – (3) b Ball | 36 |
| R. S. Kaluwitharana run out | 8 | – lbw b Gerrard | 0 |
| R. J. Ratnayake b Gilbert | 27 | – c Hunt b Gerrard | 29 |
| A. W. R. Madurasinghe c Russell b Babington | 4 | – not out | 6 |
| F. S. Ahangama not out | 0 | – c Alleyne b Gilbert | 0 |
| M. Muralitharan c Ball b Gilbert | 0 | – c Wright b Gerrard | 5 |
| L-b 3 | 3 | L-b 4, n-b 3 | 7 |
| | **97** | | **134** |

1/44 2/46 3/52 4/57 5/57         97    1/0 2/33 3/58 4/78 5/84       134
6/59 7/69 8/97 9/97                       6/94 7/105 8/127 9/127

Bowling: *First Innings*—Gilbert 12.3–1–53–4; Babington 10–4–15–1; Gerrard 10–2–20–4; Ball 1–0–6–0. *Second Innings*—Gilbert 13–4–23–3; Babington 4–0–17–0; Scott 10–1–21–0; Gerrard 15.1–2–40–6; Ball 7–2–29–1.

### Gloucestershire

| | | | |
|---|---:|---|---:|
| R. J. Scott c Hathurusinghe b Gurusinha | 8 | | |
| A. J. Hunt c Tillekeratne b Ratnayake | 3 | – c Mahanama b Ratnayake | 12 |
| *A. J. Wright lbw b Ratnayake | 47 | | |
| C. W. J. Athey c Kuruppu b Ratnayake | 6 | | |
| M. W. Alleyne b Ratnayake | 91 | – (4) not out | 10 |
| T. H. C. Hancock c Tillekeratne b Ahangama | 1 | – (3) c and b Ratnayake | 1 |
| †R. C. Russell lbw b Ratnayake | 2 | – (1) not out | 22 |
| M. C. J. Ball c Madurasinghe b Gurusinha | 1 | | |
| D. R. Gilbert c Kaluwitharana b Madurasinghe | 5 | | |
| A. M. Babington b Ratnayake | 0 | | |
| M. J. Gerrard not out | 0 | | |
| B 4, l-b 6, w 2, n-b 11 | 23 | L-b 1, n-b 2 | 3 |
| | **187** | | (2 wkts) **48** |

1/6 2/40 3/51 4/89 5/90         187    1/35 2/37            (2 wkts) 48
6/117 7/120 8/154 9/158

Bowling: *First Innings*—Ratnayake 26.3–2–97–6; Ahangama 22–8–51–1; Gurusinha 11–3–16–2; Madurasinghe 2–0–13–1. *Second Innings*—Ratnayake 8–0–29–2; Ahangama 6–3–12–0; Hathurusinghe 1.3–0–6–0.

Umpires: B. Leadbeater and G. A. Stickley.

## SOMERSET v SRI LANKANS

At Taunton, August 10, 11, 12. Sri Lankans won by eight wickets. Toss: Sri Lankans. The most dazzling display in this batsman's match earned the Sri Lankans their only first-class victory of the tour. On a slightly grassy pitch, Somerset's first innings had been built around a double-hundred by their acting-captain, Cook, who struck 30 fours in 243 balls, having survived a difficult chance to the wicket-keeper when 18. He had sound support from Townsend, while Harden, after a quiet start, reached 100 in 142 deliveries, with eleven fours and two sixes. The patient Kuruppu held the response together, taking 179 balls for his 86, and Ramanayake was 37 overs scoring 38. But it was a different story when the Sri Lankans batted a second time. After half the second day was lost to rain, two declarations on the third left the Sri Lankans to chase 249 in 49 overs, in perfect weather and with the pitch at its easiest. From the start Kuruppu blazed away. Missed when 27, he hit thirteen fours in his 77 from 89 balls, and with Hathurusinghe (102 balls) also striking out boldly, the Sri Lankans wanted 83 from fifteen overs when the second wicket fell. Their third-wicket pair, de Silva and Jayasuriya, required just eight of them to win the match. Jayasuriya immediately joined his captain in a rush of powerful and exotic strokes, and de Silva, dropped when 1, hit his last two deliveries for six, to go with an earlier six and four fours and to finish with 57 from only 38 balls.

*Close of play:* First day, Sri Lankans 59-1 (D. S. B. P. Kuruppu 39*, C. P. H. Ramanayake 0*); Second day, Sri Lankans 198-5 (M. S. Atapattu 5*, S. T. Jayasuriya 16*).

### Somerset

| | | |
|---|---|---|
| *S. J. Cook not out ..............209 | | |
| G. T. J. Townsend c Hathurusinghe | | |
|     b Wijegunawardene . 53 | | |
| N. J. Pringle c de Silva b Madurisinghe ....... 1 | – (1) c Mahanama | |
| |     b Wijegunawardene . 20 | |
| R. J. Harden not out ....................100 | | |
| G. W. White (did not bat) ................ | – (2) c Atapattu b Madurisinghe .. 42 | |
| M. N. Lathwell (did not bat) ............. | – (3) c sub b Wijegunawardene ... 16 | |
| †R. J. Turner (did not bat) .............. | – (4) not out ................. 18 | |
| G. D. Rose (did not bat) ................. | – (5) not out ................. 23 | |
| L-b 2, n-b 12 .................... 14 | B 1, l-b 5, n-b 1 ........ 7 | |

1/158 2/169       (2 wkts dec.) 377    1/39 2/81 3/86     (3 wkts dec.) 126

H. R. J. Trump, A. R. Caddick and D. Beal did not bat.

Bowling: *First Innings*—Ramanayake 14-3-65-0; Ahangama 14-3-59-0; Wijeguna-wardene 20-1-109-1; Hathurusinghe 8-0-43-0; Madurisinghe 23-4-64-1; Jayasuriya 4.5-0-35-0. *Second Innings*—Ramanayake 7-0-24-0; Ahangama 5-0-26-0; Wijegunawardene 10-1-35-2; Madurisinghe 10-2-33-1; Jayasuriya 1-0-2-0.

### Sri Lankans

| | | |
|---|---|---|
| D. S. B. P. Kuruppu c Turner b Caddick ...... 86 | – c Townsend b Lathwell ........ 77 | |
| U. C. Hathurusinghe b Rose ............... 19 | – c Turner b Beal .............. 67 | |
| C. P. H. Ramanayake c Turner b White ....... 38 | | |
| M. S. Atapattu not out ................ 33 | | |
| *P. A. de Silva c Beal b Trump .......... 21 | – (3) not out .................. 57 | |
| R. S. Mahanama lbw b Caddick ............. 0 | | |
| S. T. Jayasuriya b Beal ................ 33 | – (4) not out .................. 37 | |
| A. W. R. Madurisinghe c Caddick b Rose...... 1 | | |
| K. I. W. Wijegunawardene c Cook b Trump ... 10 | | |
| B 1, l-b 10, n-b 3 ................. 14 | B 5, l-b 4, n-b 2 ........ 11 | |

1/59 2/150 3/150 4/179 5/179    (8 wkts dec.) 255    1/135 2/166      (2 wkts) 249
6/219 7/240 8/255

†H. P. Tillekeratne and F. S. Ahangama did not bat.

Bowling: *First Innings*—Caddick 21-8-40-2; Beal 20-2-64-1; Trump 20.5-6-54-2; Rose 10-2-41-2; Lathwell 6-3-15-0; White 6-1-30-1. *Second Innings*—Caddick 11.5-3-58-0; Beal 7-1-47-1; Rose 6-0-28-0; Trump 12-1-78-0; Lathwell 5-0-29-1.

Umpires: J. H. Hampshire and P. B. Wight.

## †ENGLAND A v SRI LANKANS

At Manchester, August 14. England A won by 63 runs. Toss: England A. The Sri Lankan batsmen seemed unable to cope with English spin on a slow Old Trafford pitch. At one time they were 99 for eight, but a ninth-wicket stand of 53 between Mahanama and Wijegunawardene repaired some of the damage. Mahanama batted throughout the innings, falling to the very last ball after three and a half hours and 149 deliveries, only one of which he hit for four. Six of his colleagues were dismissed by spin, which Moxon introduced by the twelfth over; Illingworth struck in his second and third overs, while Such and Hick each claimed a wicket in his first. England A, too, had found batting difficult, scoring only 19 runs in their first ten overs, and hitting thirteen fours in the entire innings. Hick, seeking to revive his international reputation, drove one of them but was beaten by his thirteenth delivery, caught behind off a ball that straightened. Fairbrother provided the most entertainment, hitting strongly on the off side, though even he was restricted to three fours and a "six" which included four overthrows. He added 56 in eighteen overs with his captain, Moxon, and his fellow-Lancastrian, Watkinson, shared a final flourish of 52 in eight overs with Marsh, who scored at a run a ball.

### England A

| | | | |
|---|---|---|---|
| *M. D. Moxon run out | 49 | M. Watkinson not out | 25 |
| T. R. Ward b Ratnayake | 5 | †S. A. Marsh not out | 26 |
| G. A. Hick c Tillekeratne | | | |
| b Ramanayake | 5 | B 9, l-b 17, w 6, n-b 3 | 35 |
| N. H. Fairbrother | | | |
| c and b Madurasinghe | 66 | 1/16 2/35 3/121 (5 wkts, 55 overs) 243 |
| P. Johnson st Tillekeratne b Jayasuriya | 32 | 4/177 5/191 | |

D. G. Cork, R. K. Illingworth, R. A. Pick and P. M. Such did not bat.

Bowling: Ramanayake 8-3-22-1; Ratnayake 10-2-28-1; Wijegunawardene 7-0-39-0; Gurusinha 8-0-44-0; Madurasinghe 11-0-41-1; Jayasuriya 11-0-43-1.

### Sri Lankans

| | | | |
|---|---|---|---|
| R. S. Mahanama lbw b Watkinson | 73 | C. P. H. Ramanayake c Ward b Hick | 3 |
| D. S. B. P. Kuruppu run out | 3 | K. I. W. Wijegunawardene c Moxon | |
| A. P. Gurusinha c Moxon b Illingworth | 12 | b Pick | 27 |
| *P. A. de Silva c Marsh b Illingworth | 10 | A. W. R. Madurasinghe not out | 5 |
| S. T. Jayasuriya c Marsh b Watkinson | 4 | | |
| M. S. Atapattu c and b Such | 7 | L-b 17, w 12, n-b 4 | 33 |
| †H. P. Tillekeratne c Illingworth | | | |
| b Hick | 3 | 1/10 2/36 3/46 4/53 5/66 (55 overs) 180 |
| R. J. Ratnayake c Fairbrother b Such | 0 | 6/83 7/95 8/99 9/152 | |

Bowling: Pick 11-2-23-1; Cork 10-2-41-0; Illingworth 11-0-31-2; Watkinson 6-0-21-2; Such 11-1-29-2; Hick 6-1-18-2.

Umpires: J. H. Hampshire and D. O. Oslear.

## †ENGLAND A v SRI LANKANS

At Manchester, August 15. Sri Lankans won by three wickets. Toss: England A. The match was played on the same pitch as the day before, but this time it was the Sri Lankan spinners, bowling all but fifteen of the allotted 55 overs, who made best use of its dry, slow surface. Again boundaries were rare; Ward of Kent, whose 78 was the highest score of the match, hit four fours but ran 41 singles in 131 balls, before he fell to a running catch by Madurasinghe at long leg. Hick lost his leg stump as he moved across on his sixth ball, his first from Ratnayake.

Soon afterwards the bowler left the field after hurting his neck in a collision with Anurasiri, whereupon Tillekeratne metamorphosed into an off-spinner, while Kuruppu took the wicket-keeper's gloves. England A also resorted to an emergency fourth spinner, Watkinson, who swapped to off-breaks for his last nine overs, but the home team could not regain their grip of the previous day. The Sri Lankans needed 53 from the last ten overs, and Ratnayake, recovered from his mishap, joined Atapattu to knock them off inside eight overs.

## England A

| | | |
|---|---|---|
| T. R. Ward c Madurasinghe | | |
| b Anurasiri . | 78 | |
| *M. D. Moxon st Tillekeratne | | |
| b Anurasiri . | 32 | |
| G. A. Hick b Ratnayake | 1 | |
| N. Hussain c Tillekeratne b Anurasiri . | 22 | |
| P. Johnson c and b Jayasuriya | 22 | |

| | |
|---|---|
| M. Watkinson c Kuruppu b Anurasiri . . | 2 |
| †S. A. Marsh not out | 28 |
| R. K. Illingworth not out | 10 |
| B 4, l-b 5, w 3, n-b 5 | 17 |
| | |
| 1/66 2/72 3/121 (6 wkts, 55 overs) 212 |
| 4/168 5/173 6/175 |

P. J. Martin, R. A. Pick and P. M. Such did not bat.

Bowling: Ramanayake 8-1-31-0; Ratnayake 5-1-10-1; Gurusinha 2-0-11-0; Anurasiri 11-0-35-4; Madurasinghe 11-0-49-0; Jayasuriya 11-0-40-1; Tillekeratne 7-0-27-0.

## Sri Lankans

| | | |
|---|---|---|
| U. C. Hathurusinghe c Illingworth | | |
| b Such . | 33 | |
| D. S. B. P. Kuruppu c Moxon b Pick . . | 0 | |
| *A. P. Gurusinha c Marsh b Martin . . . | 10 | |
| R. S. Mahanama run out | 44 | |
| S. T. Jayasuriya c Johnson | | |
| b Watkinson . | 35 | |
| M. S. Atapattu not out | 41 | |

| | |
|---|---|
| †H. P. Tillekeratne c Moxon b Hick . . . | 5 |
| C. P. H. Ramanayake run out | 2 |
| R. J. Ratnayake not out | 26 |
| L-b 6, w 7, n-b 4 | 17 |
| | |
| 1/1 2/17 3/74 (7 wkts, 52.5 overs) 213 |
| 4/129 5/136 |
| 6/156 7/160 |

S. D. Anurasiri and A. W. R. Madurasinghe did not bat.

Bowling: Pick 6.5-0-31-1; Martin 6-1-18-1; Watkinson 11-2-35-1; Such 11-1-49-1; Illingworth 11-0-36-0; Hick 7-0-38-1.

Umpires: G. I. Burgess and R. Palmer.

## SUSSEX v SRI LANKANS

At Hove, August 17, 18, 19. Drawn. Toss: Sri Lankans. The tourists opted to bat out time rather than chase the sponsor's cash bonus, finishing 20 runs short of victory with two wickets in hand. Sussex struggled on the opening morning, slumping to 98 for five before the determined Moores came to the rescue with his first hundred of the season, which included ten boundaries. The promising North, who was to take six wickets in the match, hit a pleasant 41. The Sri Lankans, in particular Jayasuriya, made good use of a perfect batting strip. The left-hander faced 105 balls, hitting ten fours and four sixes in his not out 100, and shared an unbroken sixth-wicket stand of 140 with Atapattu before the declaration, 50 runs behind. Smith, who was dropped when 16, and the uncapped Greenfield both made hundreds before Sussex declared, leaving the Sri Lankans to score 275 in a minimum of 52 overs. It looked within their compass when openers Kuruppu and Hathurusinghe put on 83, and Tillekeratne gave evidence of his ability to maintain the chase with a brisk unbeaten 80 off 85 balls (one six, ten fours). But when Mahanama was fifth out at 228, the Sri Lankans put safety first, much to the crowd's disappointment.

*Close of play:* First day, Sussex 330-9 (I. D. K. Salisbury 9*, A. N. Jones 9*); Second day, Sussex 53-1 (K. Greenfield 34*, D. M. Smith 15*).

## Sussex

| | | | |
|---|---|---|---|
| N. J. Lenham c Gurusinha b Ramanayake | 61 | – lbw b Ramanayake | 2 |
| D. M. Smith lbw b Ramanayake | 8 | – (3) not out | 100 |
| K. Greenfield c Kuruppu b Wijegunawardene | 7 | – (2) run out | 104 |
| *A. P. Wells c Tillekeratne b Wijegunawardene. | 0 | – not out | 7 |
| M. P. Speight lbw b Hathurusinghe | 33 | | |
| C. M. Wells c Tillekeratne b Hathurusinghe | 0 | | |
| J. A. North c Tillekeratne b Wijegunawardene | 41 | | |
| †P. Moores c Tillekeratne b Wijegunawardene. | 102 | | |
| A. C. S. Pigott c Muralitharan b Ramanayake | 29 | | |
| I. D. K. Salisbury not out | 9 | | |
| A. N. Jones not out | 9 | | |
| B 3, l-b 12, w 5, n-b 11 | 31 | L-b 4, n-b 7 | 11 |

1/24 2/31 3/31 4/86 5/98     (9 wkts dec.) 330   1/2 2/196     (2 wkts dec.) 224
6/127 7/202 8/305 9/313

Bowling: *First Innings*—Ramanayake 22–4–83–3; Wijegunawardene 24–3–111–4; Gurusinha 2–0–11–0; Hathurusinghe 12–4–18–2; Muralitharan 19–4–43–0; Anurasiri 23–3–45–0; Jayasuriya 3–1–4–0. *Second Innings*—Ramanayake 14–2–34–1; Wijegunawardene 8–3–24–0; Muralitharan 20.1–2–69–0; Anurasiri 25–5–87–0; Jayasuriya 2–1–3–0; Hathurusinghe 1–0–3–0.

## Sri Lankans

| | | | |
|---|---|---|---|
| D. S. B. P. Kuruppu lbw b North | 6 | – lbw b North | 59 |
| U. C. Hathurusinghe run out | 18 | – b North | 31 |
| *A. P. Gurusinha c Moores b Jones | 29 | – c C. M. Wells b North | 1 |
| †H. P. Tillekeratne lbw b Salisbury | 30 | – (6) not out | 80 |
| R. S. Mahanama c Moores b North | 24 | – (4) lbw b Jones | 65 |
| S. T. Jayasuriya not out | 100 | – (7) lbw b Pigott | 10 |
| M. S. Atapattu not out | 52 | – (5) c Moores b North | 2 |
| K. I. W. Wijegunawardene (did not bat) | | – st Moores b Jones | 0 |
| C. P. H. Ramanayake (did not bat) | | – run out | 2 |
| S. D. Anurasiri (did not bat) | | – not out | 0 |
| B 4, l-b 7, w 2, n-b 8 | 21 | L-b 5 | 5 |

1/22 2/45 3/75 4/122 5/140     (5 wkts dec.) 280   1/83 2/92 3/97 4/109     (8 wkts) 255
                                                  5/228 6/249 7/252 8/254

M. Muralitharan did not bat.

Bowling: *First Innings*—Jones 11–4–30–1; Pigott 16–5–61–0; North 15.3–5–43–2; C. M. Wells 14–2–46–0; Salisbury 19–3–89–1. *Second Innings*—Jones 9–1–50–2; Pigott 12.5–1–48–1; North 12–1–47–4; Salisbury 14–1–75–0; Greenfield 6–0–30–0.

Umpires: M. J. Harris and K. J. Lyons.

## ENGLAND v SRI LANKA

### Cornhill Test Match

At Lord's, August 22, 23, 24, 26, 27. England won by 137 runs. Toss: England. After the excitement of England's victory over West Indies at The Oval, it was inevitable that this match should prove something of an anticlimax. The impression, certainly on the first day, was that England's batsmen found it difficult to concentrate against the gentler Sri Lankan attack, after all the ducking and weaving forced on them by Ambrose and company. Gooch, for instance, looked to be struggling with his timing after he decided to bat, and he fell to a smart return catch by Ramanayake just as he seemed to be getting to grips with the pitch. Similarly, Botham was beginning to suggest that the Sri Lankan bowling might be torn apart when he top-edged a hook, and Ramprakash, who had batted for so long against West Indies without getting past the twenties, stayed only five deliveries for his first Test duck. Stewart, retained as a batsman, was less than impressive early on and was dropped, hooking

Ratnayake, when 24; but he showed his class and determination by refusing to be put off when three wickets fell in four overs during the hour after lunch. He then survived the departure of Botham and Lewis, and was 76 when bad light brought an early finish after 74 overs, with England 229 for six.

Friday was one of those frustrating days when rain causes a number of interruptions without falling heavily enough to allow everyone to go home early. It also featured the curious incident of Stewart scoring a run while in the pavilion, when the umpires decreed that a shot for which he ran 3 had crossed the rope and was worth four. In the meantime, Russell had been dismissed at the "wrong" end. After a late start, 35 overs were bowled, during which Stewart completed his maiden Test hundred in 280 minutes and 222 balls (in all he hit fourteen fours in 240 balls), England were dismissed for 282, and Sri Lanka started their innings as though playing a 40-overs match. They quickly lost Kuruppu and Gurusinha, but their captain, de Silva, batted superbly during the last half-hour, striking seven fours in 42 from only 30 deliveries.

To take advantage of England's relatively poor total, de Silva needed to bat for most of the third morning. But, much to the disappointment of a goodish Saturday crowd, he was brilliantly caught in the gully by Lewis in the second over. Hathurusinghe remained watchful and stubborn among his cavalier colleagues, and he found a like-minded ally in Tillekeratne. The wicket-keeper stayed for an hour and a quarter, only to lob a simple catch to forward short leg ten minutes before lunch, which Sri Lanka took in some disarray at 148 for six. The early afternoon session was enlivened by the hitting of Ratnayake, who followed his five for 69 in England's innings with a half-century in only 51 balls, including seven fours. He was the first Sri Lankan to achieve this double in a Test, but soon afterwards he took a severe blow on the helmet from DeFreitas. Several balls later he became the fast bowler's fifth wicket in his best Test return of seven for 70. Sri Lanka were all out for 224, a deficit of 58.

Gooch and Morris quickly built on that lead, with the England captain looking more like his efficient, magisterial self than in the first innings. By the close he was 60 and had hit seven fours, one all run, off 115 balls. He completed a record sixth Test hundred at Lord's, and his first against Sri Lanka, on the fourth morning, and was eventually bowled by Anurasiri for 174 after plundering the bowling for nineteen fours in 252 balls. The arrival of Russell, rather than Ramprakash or Botham, when Gooch was out came as a surprise, and the England management's subsequent explanation – something about wanting the left-hander to cope with the rough outside the leg stump – was none too convincing.

England's declaration left Sri Lanka needing 423 with 132 overs remaining; realistically it was an improbable target, because no side had scored so many in the fourth innings for a Test victory. Sri Lanka started as though they meant to make a stab at it, and it took England 25 overs to make the initial breakthrough. Lewis, the fourth bowler used, had Kuruppu leg before with the score 50, and then the somewhat belated introduction of Tufnell quickly accounted for Hathurusinghe, who chipped the ball to short mid-on.

On the final day Sri Lanka needed 344 to win with eight wickets in hand. Tufnell opened the proceedings, and in his seventh over of the morning he bowled Gurusinha round his legs, deceived through the air while trying to sweep. Lawrence had the next success, although de Silva looked surprised to be given caught at the wicket for a stubborn 18. His batting had been in complete contrast to his first innings, but it was a game that seemed alien to him. When, just before lunch, Mahanama was taken at slip off Tufnell, half the side had gone for 159. Nevertheless Jayasuriya, who had struck six fours while compiling 30 from only 28 balls before the interval, continued to bat as though he thought Sri Lanka could win. He hurried on to 66 before he was caught behind off the 70th ball he faced, and after that it was simply a matter of time before England won. Had they not spilled three catches before lunch and two afterwards, the match might have been over much earlier. As it was, the new ball was taken and tea delayed, giving Sri Lanka a moral victory of sorts.

The victory that counted, however, went to England, when Tufnell had Anurasiri leg-before with the third ball after the eventual tea interval, leaving Ramanayake not out 34 after an hour and a half. The winning margin was a comfortable 137 runs with more than 28 overs to spare. Tufnell finished with his third five-wicket return in his sixth Test, and the crowd, better than expected for the final day, went home having had a reasonable day's entertainment. – Norman de Mesquita.

*Men of the Match:* England – A. J. Stewart; Sri Lanka – R. J. Ratnayake.

*Attendance:* 38,000; receipts £451,600.

*Close of play:* First day, England 229-6 (A. J. Stewart 76*, R. C. Russell 11*); Second day, Sri Lanka 75-2 (U. C. Hathurusinghe 19*, P. A. de Silva 42*); Third day, England 100-1 (G. A. Gooch 60*, A. J. Stewart 7*); Fourth day, Sri Lanka 79-2 (A. P. Gurusinha 16*, P. A. de Silva 7*).

## England

| | | | |
|---|---|---|---|
| *G. A. Gooch c and b Ramanayake | 38 | – b Anurasiri | 174 |
| H. Morris lbw b Ratnayake | 42 | – c Mahanama b Anurasiri | 23 |
| A. J. Stewart not out | 113 | – c de Silva b Anurasiri | 43 |
| R. A. Smith c Til{\l}ekeratne b Ratnayake | 4 | – not out | 63 |
| M. R. Ramprakash c Mahanama | | | |
| b Hathurusinghe | 0 | | |
| I. T. Botham c Mahanama b Ramanayake | 22 | | |
| C. C. Lewis c de Silva b Anurasiri | 11 | | |
| †R. C. Russell b Anurasiri | 17 | – (5) not out | 12 |
| P. A. J. DeFreitas b Ratnayake | 1 | | |
| D. V. Lawrence c and b Ratnayake | 3 | | |
| P. C. R. Tufnell lbw b Ratnayake | 0 | | |
| B 9, l-b 8, n-b 14 | 31 | B 15, l-b 23, w 1, n-b 10 | 49 |

1/70 (1) 2/114 (3) 3/119 (4) 4/120 (5)                    282          1/78 (2)                    (3 wkts dec.) 364
5/160 (6) 6/183 (7) 7/246 (8) 8/258 (9)                                 2/217 (3)
9/276 (10) 10/282 (11)                                                  3/322 (1)

Bowling: *First Innings*—Ratnayake 27–4–69–5; Ramanayake 24–5–75–2; Wijegunawardene 10–1–36–0; Hathurisinghe 17–6–40–1; Anurasiri 17–4–45–2. *Second Innings*—Ratnayake 26–4–91–0; Ramanayake 20–2–86–0; Wijegunawardene 2–0–13–0; Anurasiri 36.1–8–135–3; Jayasuriya 1–0–1–0.

## Sri Lanka

| | | | |
|---|---|---|---|
| D. S. B. P. Kuruppu b DeFreitas | 5 | – lbw b Lewis | 21 |
| U. C. Hathurusinghe c Tufnell b DeFreitas | 66 | – c Morris b Tufnell | 25 |
| A. P. Gurusinha lbw b DeFreitas | 4 | – b Tufnell | 34 |
| *P. A. de Silva c Lewis b DeFreitas | 42 | – c Russell b Lawrence | 18 |
| R. S. Mahanama c Russell b Botham | 2 | – c Botham b Tufnell | 15 |
| S. T. Jayasuriya c Smith b DeFreitas | 11 | – c Russell b Lewis | 66 |
| †H. P. Tilf{l}ekeratne c Morris b Lawrence | 20 | – b Tufnell | 16 |
| R. J. Ratnayake b DeFreitas | 52 | – c sub (I. D. K. Salisbury) | |
| | | b Lawrence | 17 |
| C. P. H. Ramanayake lbw b DeFreitas | 0 | – not out | 34 |
| K. I. W. Wijegunawardene not out | 6 | – c Botham b DeFreitas | 4 |
| S. D. Anurasiri b Lawrence | 1 | – lbw b Tufnell | 16 |
| L-b 15 | 15 | B 1, l-b 16, n-b 2 | 19 |

1/12 (1) 2/22 (3) 3/75 (4) 4/86 (5)                    224          1/50 (1) 2/50 (2) 3/111 (3)                    285
5/105 (6) 6/139 (7) 7/213 (8) 8/213 (9)                              4/119 (4) 5/159 (5) 6/212 (7)
9/220 (10) 10/224 (11)                                               7/212 (6) 8/241 (8)
                                                                    9/253 (10) 10/285 (11)

Bowling: *First Innings*—DeFreitas 26–8–70–7; Lawrence 15.1–3–61–2; Lewis 10–5–29–0; Botham 10–3–26–1; Tufnell 7–2–23–0. *Second Innings*—DeFreitas 22–8–45–1; Lawrence 23–7–83–2; Botham 6–2–15–0; Lewis 18–4–31–2; Tufnell 34.3–14–94–5.

Umpires: H. D. Bird and J. H. Hampshire.

# THE MARYLEBONE CRICKET CLUB, 1991

Much attention, particularly in the media, centred on the 204th Annual
General Meeting of MCC, held at Lord's, on May 1, 1991, with the
President, The Rt Hon. The Lord Griffiths, in the chair. The reasons for this
were two amendments, proposed by T. M. B. Rice and seconded by B. A.

344 *The Marylebone Cricket Club, 1991*

Johnston, which if passed would allow women as well as men to be eligible for membership and/or be elected as honorary life members. In the event the members present and those voting by post defeated the first amendment by 4,727 to 2,371. Although the second proposal, that women be eligible for election as honorary life members, received the support of 3,684 members, with 3,365 against, the majority of 319 fell short of the two-thirds majority required by the Rules of the Club. A resolution that the Annual Report and Accounts "should give a proper detailed financial statement which will demonstrate and reflect properly the extent to which members subsidise the activities of the TCCB from the revenue generated from Big Matches played at Lord's Cricket Ground" was withdrawn.

In his statement to members, the President drew attention to the proposal that subscriptions should be increased by 35 per cent, after three years without an increase, and the increase was subsequently approved by the meeting. The President reminded members that not only did membership give wonderful value in terms of watching cricket at Lord's, but also it provided an opportunity to put something back into the game through the Club's support of cricket at youth and grass-roots level.

This support was reflected in the Club's Accounts for 1990, which showed that contributions of £85,000 had been made to the National Coaching Scheme and The Cricket Foundation. In presenting the accounts, the chairman of the finance sub-committee, D. L. Hudd, reported a surplus for the year, after taxation, of £369,000, compared with a surplus of £240,000 in 1989. While income rose by 6.5 per cent, expenditure had risen by 17.6 per cent, with the cost of maintaining the facilities at Lord's continuing at a high level. In part this resulted from the need for additional safety measures because of the disruption caused by the building of the new Compton and Edrich Stands, while the seating problems arising from the building works led to increased administration costs. An expression of thanks was made to Gestetner PLC for their contribution towards the capital cost of the Gestetner Tour of Lord's.

The President named M. E. L. Melluish, a merchant banker, a member of MCC since 1956 and an experienced committeeman, to succeed him on October 1. As a right-hand opening batsman and wicket-keeper, Melluish captained Rossall in 1951, scoring a record aggregate of 913 runs at 70.23 for the school and appearing for the Public Schools at Lord's. He played three times for Cambridge at Lord's against Oxford, as captain in 1956, his final year, when he was invited to play for the Gentlemen against the Players in the 150th anniversary match. He subsequently played first-class cricket for Middlesex and MCC.

The President Designate had earlier been elected to serve on the committee from October 1, along with Field-Marshal The Lord Bramall, R. G. Gibbs and D. R. W. Silk, to replace M. J. K. Smith, D. G. Trelford, J. C. Woodcock and H. M. Wyndham, who were to retire by rotation as elected members on September 30.

The membership of the Club on December 31, 1990 was 19,237, made up of 17,053 full members, 1,933 associate members and 251 honorary members. These comprised the following: 10,417 full and 1,598 associate town members, 2,309 full and 257 associate country members, 3,400 at the over-65 rate, 84 full and 37 associate members at the under-25 rate, 281 full and 19 associate members at the special schoolmasters' rate, 513 full and 22 associate members on the abroad list, 49 life members, 8 life vice-presidents, 15 60-year life members, 40 honorary England cricketers and 188 honorary life members. Candidates awaiting election numbered 9,338. In 1990, 411 vacancies occurred, owing to 231 deaths, 123 resignations and 57 lapsed memberships.

## MCC v MIDDLESEX

At Lord's, April 16, 17, 18, 19. Drawn. Toss: MCC. Rain and hail brought an end to the match after 49 balls on the final day. On the previous day only 26 overs had been possible between showers. Hick excepted, the MCC side was the winter's England A team, with Pick the sole survivor of the originally selected MCC seam attack. Newport, Ilott and Bicknell (Ilott's replacement) all withdrew because of side strains, while Gatting, the champion's captain, had a strained hamstring. His absence gave Hutchinson an outing for Middlesex, and he took his chance well in a three-hour partnership with Roseberry that added 151. Both were dismissed by Thorpe in the space of five overs. Of the MCC bowlers, Munton was economy personified on the first morning, conceding just 18 runs in ten overs before lunch, and on the second day Pick bowled a hostile, accurate spell with the new ball. Rhodes gave another tidy display behind the stumps, and on the second evening his Worcestershire colleague, Hick, raced to 57 not out from 57 balls, having hit four of his eleven boundaries in his first nineteen deliveries. Once or twice, however, he was hit glancing blows on the body by Williams, and Thorpe's movement into position, as well as his timing, was altogether more reassuring. So, too, was Tufnell's flight and turn.

*Close of play*: First day, Middlesex 266-4 (K. R. Brown 27*, P. R. Downton 13*); Second day, MCC 171-3 (G. A. Hick 57*, N. Hussain 11*); Third day, MCC 218-4 (N. Hussain 35*, G. P. Thorpe 19*).

## Middlesex

| | | | |
|---|---|---|---|
| M. A. Roseberry lbw b Thorpe ....... 98 | N. F. Williams run out ............. 29 |
| J. C. Pooley b Munton ............. 17 | D. W. Headley b Pick .............. 0 |
| I. J. F. Hutchinson c Morris b Thorpe . 70 | P. C. R. Tufnell c Hussain b Munton .. 34 |
| M. R. Ramprakash b Rhodes | N. G. Cowans not out............. 4 |
| b Illingworth . 28 | B 2, l-b 12, n-b 3 .......... 17 |
| K. R. Brown c Hick b Pick ......... 44 | |
| †P. R. Downton c Fairbrother b Watkin 32 | 1/38 2/189 3/202 4/246 5/292 377 |
| *J. E. Emburey c Bicknell b Watkin ... 4 | 6/308 7/317 8/318 9/373 |

Bowling: Pick 27-4-95-2; Watkin 30-7-88-2; Munton 31.1-7-68-2; Thorpe 15-2-48-2; Illingworth 22-2-46-1; Hick 4-0-18-0.

## MCC

| | | | |
|---|---|---|---|
| D. J. Bicknell c Headley b Williams ... 44 | G. P. Thorpe not out................ 37 |
| *H. Morris c Roseberry b Williams .... 44 | |
| G. A. Hick c Downton b Cowans ... 58 | L-b 7, n-b 8 ........ 15 |
| N. H. Fairbrother b Headley ........ 5 | |
| N. Hussain not out ................. 47 | 1/78 2/124 3/145 4/180 (4 wkts) 250 |

†S. J. Rhodes, R. K. Illingworth, T. A. Munton, R. A. Pick and S. L. Watkin did not bat.

Bowling: Cowans 16-6-38-1; Williams 18-2-70-2; Headley 20.1-7-78-1; Emburey 11-4-38-0; Tufnell 13-7-15-0; Ramprakash 1-0-4-0.

Umpires: D. J. Constant and A. G. T. Whitehead.

†At Lord's, May 7. Drawn. Toss: MCC. MCC 264 for four dec. (R. P. Merriman 62, D. L. Bairstow 48, R. O. Butcher 87, G. W. Humpage 50); MCC Young Cricketers 202 for eight (I. A. Kidd 85, C. J. Rogers 40; R. P. Gofton four for 48).

At Oxford, May 8, 9, 10. MCC drew with OXFORD UNIVERSITY (See Oxford University section).

At Cambridge, June 10, 11, 12. MCC lost to CAMBRIDGE UNIVERSITY by an innings and 52 runs (See Cambridge University section).

At Richmond, June 12. MCC beat CLUB CRICKET CONFERENCE by 49 runs (See Other Matches, 1991).

At Durham, June 13, 14. MCC drew with DURHAM UNIVERSITY (See Other Matches, 1991).

At Arundel, July 7. MCC beat LAVINIA, DUCHESS OF NORFOLK'S XI by eight wickets (See Other Matches, 1991).

At Gloucester, July 10. MCC drew with NATIONAL ASSOCIATION OF YOUNG CRICKETERS (See Other Matches, 1991).

## †MCC v MCC SCHOOLS

At Lord's, July 16. MCC Schools won by six wickets. Toss: MCC Schools. MCC set the Schools a fairly stiff target, which was achieved largely through the batting of Jones, of Monmouth School, whose fine unbeaten century was marked by both technique and temperament. After the medium-paced Robinson had taken two early MCC wickets, Wild and Mills put on an unbroken 205 for the third wicket, both batsmen being severe on anything short. Wild's century, containing a six and nineteen fours, came immediately after lunch. Ballinger had bowled an accurate line and length, while Hindson and Whittington, the spinners, both had good spells. Jones and Parsons gave the Schools a sound start, scoring freely off the seam bowlers, but the introduction of Knight, the former captain of Surrey, and a headmaster, brought scholarly respect. He and Allbrook, one of the Schools' selectors, restrained the scoring. However, Walker, a powerful left-hander, joined Jones in a third-wicket partnership of 75, and after Semmence was sadly run out without facing a ball, victory was achieved with two overs to spare.

## MCC

M. S. A. McEvoy c Sedgbeer b Robinson ... 1
J. P. C. Mills not out ................. 86
C. T. Radley c and b Robinson ....... 7
D. J. Wild not out ..................117
    B 5 ...................... 5

1/1 2/11         (2 wkts dec.) 216

R. D. V. Knight, *J. R. T. Barclay, †H. L. Jenner, C. Hodgkins, D. B. M. Fox, M. E. Allbrook and D. R. Doshi did not bat.

Bowling: Ballinger 10-3-43-0; Robinson 7-0-49-2; Hindson 11-3-33-0; Yeabsley 11-2-47-0; Whittington 9-3-39-0.

## MCC Schools

| | |
|---|---|
| A. J. Jones (*Monmouth*) not out . . . . . . .103 | M. F. D. Robinson (*King's, Taunton*) |
| K. A. Parsons (*Richard Huish*) | not out . 8 |
| lbw b Allbrook . 32 | |
| A. J. Hall (*Marple Hall*) c Knight | B 2, l-b 6, n-b 2 . . . . . . . . . . . . 10 |
| b Allbrook . 22 | |
| M. J. Walker (*King's, Rochester*) b Doshi 42 | 1/76 2/128 3/203      (4 wkts) 217 |
| M. J. Semmence (*Hurstpierpoint*) run out  0 | 4/204 |

R. S. Yeabsley (*Haberdashers' Aske's*), †K. G. Sedgbeer (*Taunton*), J. Hindson (*Toothill, Notts.*), J. M. S. Whittington (*Eton*) and R. T. Ballinger (*Millfield*) did not bat.

Bowling: Fox 4–0–19–0; Hodgkins 9–2–39–0; Knight 7–1–24–0; Allbrook 18–4–69–2; Doshi 16.4–1–58–1.

Umpires: T. H. Duckett and V. H. Earwicker.

At Birmingham, July 18. MCC lost to MIDLANDS CLUB CRICKET CONFERENCE by seven wickets (See Other Matches, 1991).

†At Lord's, July 22, 23. Drawn. Toss: MCC. MCC 237 for three dec. (M. S. A. McEvoy 46, M. J. Roberts 39, A. Needham 73 not out, R. D. V. Knight 52 not out) and 171 (M. S. A. McEvoy 30, G. Morgan 39; C. J. Hoey five for 48); Ireland 190 for three dec. (S. J. S. Warke 85, M. F. Cohen 60, D. A. Vincent 35) and 67 for three (S. J. S. Warke 35).

At Glasgow, August 20, 21, 22. MCC lost to SCOTLAND by an innings and 37 runs (See Other Matches, 1991).

†At High Wycombe, August 27, 28, 29. Drawn. Toss: Wales. Wales 191 (D. L. Hemp 68; P. J. Mir three for 26, J. Simmons four for 20) and 454 for four (A. W. Harris 63, D. L. Hemp 258 not out, G. Gibbons 101 not out); MCC 440 (A. J. Goldsmith 95, N. G. Folland 30, J. D. Love 79, S. D. Weale 61, J. Simmons 86; A. Ikram six for 131).

At Uxbridge, September 2. MCC drew with COMBINED SERVICES (See Other Matches, 1991).

## MCC HONORARY ENGLAND CRICKETERS

| | | |
|---|---|---|
| C. J. Barnett | T. W. Graveney, OBE | G. Pullar |
| H. Larwood | G. A. R. Lock | F. J. Titmus, MBE |
| D. C. S. Compton, CBE | D. A. Allen | D. J. Brown |
| D. V. P. Wright | R. W. Barber | M. H. Denness |
| T. G. Evans, CBE | E. R. Dexter | J. M. Brearley, OBE |
| C. Washbrook, CBE | P. H. Parfitt | R. W. Taylor, MBE |
| A. V. Bedser, CBE | F. H. Tyson | R. G. D. Willis, MBE |
| P. B. H. May, CBE | M. C. Cowdrey, CBE | J. H. Edrich, MBE |
| W. Watson | J. T. Murray, MBE | A. P. E. Knott |
| P. E. Richardson | J. M. Parks | C. M. Old |
| T. E. Bailey | D. B. Close, CBE | J. A. Snow |
| M. J. K. Smith, OBE | B. L. D'Oliveira, OBE | D. L. Amiss, MBE |
| J. B. Statham, CBE | R. Illingworth, CBE | K. W. R. Fletcher, OBE |
| F. S. Trueman, OBE | | |

# OTHER MATCHES AT LORD'S, 1991

May 27. Third Texaco Trophy match. ENGLAND beat WEST INDIES by seven wickets (See West Indian tour section).

### †ETON v HARROW

June 8. Eton won by three wickets. Toss: Eton. At 7.20 p.m., with three balls to spare, Eton completed a second successive win over Harrow. The principal architect was Morgan, who came in after Hawkins had reduced Eton to 45 for three, and batted 129 minutes (106 balls, four fours), only to be bowled in the final over. Ssennyamantono ran a bye to level the scores, and Lane hit the next ball for four. Harrow had struggled against Amies when asked to bat. After thirteen overs they were 30 for three, and could have lost another at 45 when Preece was "caught" off a Whittington no-ball. But Hill (166 minutes, 130 balls) and Preece stayed together for 34.2 overs to build Harrow's biggest stand of 62. Though Danby hit three fours in 24 balls, no-one else prospered against the tidy Ssennyamantono and Whittington, who bowled one continuous spell of slow left-arm for 24.3 overs. Three hours seemed ample to score 143, but Wagg fell first ball, and was soon followed by Strickland. Dunning and Larken steadied the innings, and then Morgan and Sellar, whose nose had been broken as he fielded at short leg, added 51 in 61 minutes. Hawkins returned to remove Sellar and Whittington, but Morgan continued to accumulate steadily.

## Harrow

| | | |
|---|---|---|
| M. A. Holyoake c Ssennyamantono b Amies | . | 3 |
| C. G. Hill c Larken b Amies | | 54 |
| C. E. Williams b Amies | | 5 |
| *S. M. Guillebaud b Lewis | | 3 |
| R. J. Preece lbw b Amies | | 23 |
| C. B. J. Danby c Larken b Whittington | | 19 |
| †H. D. Duncan c Lane b Lewis | | 4 |
| J. G. Fleming b Whittington | | 12 |

| | | |
|---|---|---|
| M. M. J. Hawkins st Lane b Ssennyamantono | . | 5 |
| R. E. Sexton c Morgan b Whittington | . . | 0 |
| R. A. H. Peasgood not out | | 4 |
| B 2, l-b 2, w 3, n-b 3 | | 10 |
| | | — |
| 1/5 2/13 3/30 4/92 5/99 | | 142 |
| 6/118 7/119 8/138 9/138 | | |

Bowling: Lewis 14–3–34–2; Amies 13–4–33–4; Ssennyamantono 15–6–30–1; Whittington 24.3–7–41–3.

## Eton

| | | |
|---|---|---|
| R. M. Wagg b Hawkins | | 0 |
| G. L. Dunning c Preece b Sexton | | 29 |
| S. C. E. Strickland c Danby b Hawkins | | 2 |
| J. J. S. Larken b Hawkins | | 25 |
| P. G. Morgan b Peasgood | | 45 |
| W. R. G. Sellar c Duncan b Hawkins | . . | 18 |
| *J. M. S. Whittington b Hawkins | | 2 |

| | | |
|---|---|---|
| †O. J. M. Lane not out | | 12 |
| B. K. Ssennyamantono not out | | 0 |
| B 3, l-b 6, w 3, n-b 1 | | 13 |
| | | — |
| 1/0 2/2 3/45 4/69 | | (7 wkts) 146 |
| 5/120 6/124 7/141 | | |

G. H. B. Lewis and E. J. M. Amies did not bat.

Bowling: Hawkins 22–4–50–5; Peasgood 14.3–2–37–1; Sexton 8–2–29–1; Williams 1–0–6–0; Fleming 8–2–15–0.

Umpires: P. Adams and D. J. Dennis.

## ETON v HARROW, RESULTS AND HUNDREDS

Of the 156 matches played Eton have won 52, Harrow 44 and 60 have been drawn. This is the generally published record, but Harrow men object strongly to the first game in 1805 being treated as a regular contest between the two schools, contending that it is no more correct to count that one than the fixture of 1857 which has been rejected.

The matches played during the war years 1915-18 and 1940-45 are not reckoned as belonging to the regular series.

Results since 1950:

| | | | |
|---|---|---|---|
| 1950 | Drawn | 1971 | Drawn |
| 1951 | Drawn | 1972 | Drawn |
| 1952 | Harrow won by seven wickets | 1973 | Drawn |
| 1953 | Eton won by ten wickets | 1974 | Harrow won by eight wickets |
| 1954 | Harrow won by nine wickets | 1975 | Harrow won by an innings and 151 runs |
| 1955 | Eton won by 38 runs | | |
| 1956 | Drawn | 1976 | Drawn |
| 1957 | Drawn | 1977 | Eton won by six wickets |
| 1958 | Drawn | 1978 | Drawn |
| 1959 | Drawn | 1979 | Drawn |
| 1960 | Harrow won by 124 runs | 1980 | Drawn |
| 1961 | Harrow won by an innings and 12 runs | 1981 | Drawn |
| | | 1982 | Drawn |
| 1962 | Drawn | 1983 | Drawn |
| 1963 | Drawn | 1984 | Drawn |
| 1964 | Eton won by eight wickets | 1985 | Eton won by 3 runs |
| 1965 | Harrow won by 48 runs | 1986 | Drawn |
| 1966 | Drawn | 1987 | Drawn |
| 1967 | Drawn | 1988 | Drawn |
| 1968 | Harrow won by seven wickets | 1989 | Drawn |
| 1969 | Drawn | 1990 | Eton won by seven wickets |
| 1970 | Eton won by 97 runs | 1991 | Eton won by three wickets |

Forty-five three-figure innings have been played in matches between these two schools. Those since 1918:

| | | | | | | | |
|---|---|---|---|---|---|---|---|
| 161* | M. K. Fosh | 1975 Harrow | | 106 | D. M. Smith | 1966 Eton |
| 159 | E. W. Dawson | 1923 Eton | | 104 | R. Pulbrook | 1932 Harrow |
| 158 | I. S. Akers-Douglas | 1928 Eton | | 103 | L. G. Crawley | 1921 Harrow |
| 153 | N. S. Hotchkin | 1931 Eton | | 103 | T. Hare | 1947 Eton |
| 151 | R. M. Tindall | 1976 Harrow | | 102* | P. H. Stewart-Brown | 1923 Harrow |
| 135 | J. C. Atkinson-Clark | 1930 Eton | | 102 | R. V. C. Robins | 1953 Eton |
| 115 | E. Crutchley | 1939 Harrow | | 100 | R. H. Cobbold | 1923 Eton |
| 112 | A. W. Allen | 1931 Eton | | 100* | P. V. F. Cazalet | 1926 Eton |
| 112* | T. M. H. James | 1978 Harrow | | 100 | A. N. A. Boyd | 1934 Eton |
| 111 | R. A. A. Holt | 1937 Harrow | | 100* | P. M. Studd | 1935 Harrow |
| 109 | K. F. H. Hale | 1929 Eton | | 100 | S. D. D. Sainsbury | 1947 Eton |
| 109 | N. S. Hotchkin | 1932 Eton | | 100 | M. J. J. Faber | 1968 Eton |
| 107 | W. N. Coles | 1946 Eton | | | | |

*\* Signifies not out.*

In 1904, D. C. Boles of Eton, making 183, set a record for the match, beating the 152 obtained for Eton in 1841 by Emilius Bayley, afterwards the Rev. Sir John Robert Laurie Emilius Bayley Laurie. M. C. Bird, Harrow, in 1907, scored 100 not out and 131, the only batsman who has made two 100s in the match. N. S. Hotchkin, Eton, played the following innings: 1931, 153; 1932, 109 and 96; 1933, 88 and 12.

June 20, 21, 22, 23, 24. Second Cornhill Test. ENGLAND drew with WEST INDIES (See West Indian tour section).

## OXFORD UNIVERSITY v CAMBRIDGE UNIVERSITY

July 2, 3, 4. Drawn. Toss: Cambridge University. Rain on the first two days, and Cambridge cautious cricket throughout, spoiled the 146th University Match as a meaningful contest. Onl three Oxford men batted, with Montgomerie reaching 50 twice on the final day. The openin day's play, stopped by rain at 3.35 p.m., centred on a second-wicket partnership of 160 in 46. overs between Hooper and Crawley, the former showing an encouraging willingness to h through the covers and the latter confirming his reputation, but with studied defence rathe than attacking strokes. Three consecutive fours off Turner's off-breaks just before lunch from a cover drive, a sweep and a squarish cut – provided a rare sighting of Crawley's talent though like Hooper he hit seven fours in his half-century. Hooper's came in 100 balls Crawley's in 114, and if Crawley had survived for another eight minutes these two might hav put Cambridge in a commanding position on the second day. Instead, after play got unde way at 2.30 p.m., Hooper went twenty minutes without scoring before he was out, havin batted 225 minutes (188 balls) in all, and Turner took 77 balls for his 27. When Oxford' Turner dismissed Lowrey, Pearson and Arscott in his fifth, sixth and seventh overs, an Macdonald took the last two wickets, also in consecutive overs, Cambridge had relinquishe the initiative.

Oxford tried to keep the match alive by declaring 134 runs in arrears after putting on 145 i 133 minutes, Morris hitting a six over cover and ten fours in his 71 (103 balls). Montgomeri reached 50 in 122 balls. But Cambridge stalled. Crawley used up 144 minutes for his not ou 59, hitting eight fours in 106 balls, and Oxford's target was finally set at 281 in two hours When the last hour was called they were 68 for one from eighteen overs, and not surprisingl they were content to call it a day soon after Montgomerie, with three fours off Arscott' immolation, had reached his second half-century in 65 balls (six fours). The bowling of neithe side was particularly memorable, and Gerrans, an Australian approaching medium pace delivered twelve no-balls in each Cambridge innings.

*Close of play:* First day, Cambridge University 175-2 (A. M. Hooper 89*, R. J. Turner 1*) Second day, Oxford University 49-0 (R. R. Montgomerie 25*, R. E. Morris 19*).

## Cambridge University

| | | | | |
|---|---|---|---|---|
| A. M. Hooper (*Latymer Upper and St John's*) c Lovell b Gerrans | 89 | – b Wood | | 4 |
| R. I. Clitheroe (*Monmouth and Christ's*) c Lovell b Wood | 6 | – c Sandiford b Gerrans | | 0 |
| J. P. Crawley (*Manchester GS and Trinity*) b Wood | 66 | – not out | | 59 |
| *†R. J. Turner (*Millfield and Magdalene*) lbw b Oppenheimer | 27 | – lbw b Wood | | 0 |
| M. J. Morris (*Cherwell and Pembroke*) c Lovell b Gerrans | 6 | – b Oppenheimer | | 27 |
| M. J. Lowrey (*Radley and Homerton*) c Morris b Turner | 25 | – lbw b Macdonald | | 10 |
| J. P. Arscott (*Tonbridge and Magdalene*) c Pfaff b Turner | 14 | – run out | | 10 |
| R. M. Pearson (*Batley GS and St John's*) c Montgomerie b Turner | 0 | – c Sandiford b Gerrans | | 10 |
| R. H. J. Jenkins (*Oundle and Downing*) c Sandiford b Macdonald | 9 | – not out | | 17 |
| S. W. Johnson (*Royal GS, Newcastle and Magdalene*) c Gupte b Macdonald | 7 | | | |
| R. B. Waller (*Radley and Trinity*) not out | 6 | | | |
| B 1, l-b 11, w 1, n-b 11 | 24 | L-b 5, w 3, n-b 11 | | 19 |

1/12 2/172 3/182 4/198 5/228     279    1/5 2/10 3/20    (7 wkts dec.) 146
6/253 7/253 8/256 9/267               4/72 5/81
                              6/111 7/126

Bowling: *First Innings*—Macdonald 24.2–6–73–2; Wood 21–7–41–2; Turner 8–2–32–3 Gerrans 23–5–73–2; Oppenheimer 19–4–48–1. *Second Innings*—Wood 7–2–24–2; Gerrans 13–1–65–2; Oppenheimer 4–2–11–1; Macdonald 8–3–16–1; Turner 8–1–25–0.

## Oxford University

| | | |
|---|---|---|
| R. R. Montgomerie (*Rugby and Worcester*) | | |
| not out...... | 50 – not out ...... | 53 |
| R. E. Morris (*Dyffryn Conwy, Llanrwst and Oriel*) | | |
| c Arscott b Waller ...... | 71 – c Arscott b Jenkins ...... | 18 |
| G. B. T. Lovell (*Sydney C. of E. GS, Sydney U.* | | |
| *and Exeter*) not out...... | 15 – not out ...... | 30 |
| B 6, l-b 2, n-b 1 ...... 9 | B 3, l-b 2, w 1, n-b 1 .... | 7 |

| | | |
|---|---|---|
| 1/125 | (1 wkt dec.) 145   1/30 | (1 wkt) 108 |

\*G. J. Turner (*St Stithian's, Cape Town U. and St Anne's*), D. B. Pfaff (*Hilton College, Cape Town U. and Keble*), C. M. Gupte (*John Lyon and Pembroke*), P. S. Gerrans (*Daramalau Coll., Aust. Nat. U. and Worcester*), †D. C. Sandiford (*Bolton GS and St Edmund Hall*), R. H. Macdonald (*Rondebosch Boys' HS, Cape Town U., Durham U. and Keble*), J. M. E. Oppenheimer (*Harrow and Christ Church*) and B. S. Wood (*Batley GS and Worcester*) did not bat.

Bowling: *First Innings*—Johnson 12–2–47–0; Jenkins 10–2–29–0; Waller 9.5–2–33–1; Pearson 8–1–28–0. *Second Innings*—Johnson 3–0–25–0; Jenkins 8–0–25–1; Pearson 11–2–24–0; Waller 4–0–16–0; Arscott 1–0–13–0.

Umpires: J. C. Balderstone and K. J. Lyons.

## OXFORD v CAMBRIDGE, RESULTS AND HUNDREDS

The University match dates back to 1827. Altogether there have been 146 official matches, Cambridge winning 54 and Oxford 46, with 46 drawn. The 1988 match was abandoned without a ball bowled. Results since 1950:

| | | | |
|---|---|---|---|
| 1950 | Drawn | 1972 | Cambridge won by an innings and 25 runs |
| 1951 | Oxford won by 21 runs | 1973 | Drawn |
| 1952 | Drawn | 1974 | Drawn |
| 1953 | Cambridge won by two wickets | 1975 | Drawn |
| 1954 | Drawn | 1976 | Oxford won by ten wickets |
| 1955 | Drawn | 1977 | Drawn |
| 1956 | Drawn | 1978 | Drawn |
| 1957 | Cambridge won by an innings and 186 runs | 1979 | Cambridge won by an innings and 52 runs |
| 1958 | Cambridge won by 99 runs | 1980 | Drawn |
| 1959 | Oxford won by 85 runs | 1981 | Drawn |
| 1960 | Drawn | 1982 | Cambridge won by seven wickets |
| 1961 | Drawn | 1983 | Drawn |
| 1962 | Drawn | 1984 | Oxford won by five wickets |
| 1963 | Drawn | 1985 | Drawn |
| 1964 | Drawn | 1986 | Cambridge won by five wickets |
| 1965 | Drawn | 1987 | Drawn |
| 1966 | Oxford won by an innings and 9 runs | 1988 | Abandoned |
| 1967 | Drawn | 1989 | Drawn |
| 1968 | Drawn | 1990 | Drawn |
| 1969 | Drawn | 1991 | Drawn |
| 1970 | Drawn | | |
| 1971 | Drawn | | |

Ninety-three three-figure innings have been played in the University matches. For those scored before 1919 see 1940 *Wisden*. Those subsequent to 1919 include the seven highest:

| | | | | | | |
|---|---|---|---|---|---|---|
| 238* | Nawab of Pataudi, sen. | 1931 Oxford | | 121 | J. N. Grover | 1937 Oxford |
| 211 | G. Goonesena | 1957 Cam. | | 119 | J. M. Brearley | 1964 Cam. |
| 201* | M. J. K. Smith | 1954 Oxford | | 118 | H. Ashton | 1921 Cam. |
| 201 | A. Ratcliffe | 1931 Cam. | | 118 | D. R. W. Silk | 1954 Cam. |
| 200 | Majid Khan | 1970 Cam. | | 117 | M. J. K. Smith | 1956 Oxford |
| 193 | D. C. H. Townsend | 1934 Oxford | | 116* | D. R. W. Silk | 1953 Cam. |
| 174 | P. A. C. Bail | 1986 Cam. | | 116 | M. C. Cowdrey | 1953 Oxford |
| 170 | M. Howell | 1919 Oxford | | 115 | A. W. Allen | 1934 Cam. |
| 167 | B. W. Hone | 1932 Oxford | | 114* | D. R. Owen-Thomas | 1972 Cam. |
| 158 | P. M. Roebuck | 1975 Cam. | | 114 | J. F. Pretlove | 1955 Cam. |
| 157 | D. R. Wilcox | 1932 Cam. | | 113* | J. M. Brearley | 1962 Cam. |
| 155 | F. S. Goldstein | 1968 Oxford | | 113 | E. R. T. Holmes | 1927 Oxford |
| 149 | J. T. Morgan | 1929 Cam. | | 112* | E. D. Fursdon | 1975 Oxford |
| 149 | G. J. Toogood | 1985 Oxford | | 111* | G. W. Cook | 1957 Cam. |
| 146 | R. O'Brien | 1956 Cam. | | 109 | C. H. Taylor | 1923 Oxford |
| 146 | D. R. Owen-Thomas | 1971 Cam. | | 109 | G. J. Toogood | 1984 Oxford |
| 145* | H. E. Webb | 1948 Oxford | | 108 | F. G. H. Chalk | 1934 Oxford |
| 145 | D. P. Toft | 1967 Oxford | | 106 | Nawab of Pataudi, sen. | 1929 Oxford |
| 142 | M. P. Donnelly | 1946 Oxford | | 105 | E. J. Craig | 1961 Cam. |
| 140 | M. A. Crawley | 1987 Oxford | | 104* | D. A. Thorne | 1986 Oxford |
| 139 | R. J. Boyd-Moss | 1983 Cam. | | 104 | H. J. Enthoven | 1924 Cam. |
| 136 | E. T. Killick | 1930 Cam. | | 104 | M. J. K. Smith | 1955 Oxford |
| 135 | H. A. Pawson | 1947 Oxford | | 103* | A. R. Lewis | 1962 Cam. |
| 131 | Nawab of Pataudi, jun. | 1960 Oxford | | 103* | D. R. Pringle | 1979 Cam. |
| 129 | H. J. Enthoven | 1925 Cam. | | 102* | A. P. F. Chapman | 1922 Cam. |
| 128* | A. J. T. Miller | 1984 Oxford | | 101* | R. W. V. Robins | 1928 Cam. |
| 127 | D. S. Sheppard | 1952 Cam. | | 101 | N. W. D. Yardley | 1937 Cam. |
| 124 | A. K. Judd | 1927 Cam. | | 100* | M. Manasseh | 1964 Oxford |
| 124 | A. Ratcliffe | 1932 Cam. | | 100 | P. J. Dickinson | 1939 Cam. |
| 124 | R. J. Boyd-Moss | 1983 Cam. | | 100 | N. J. Cosh | 1967 Cam. |
| 122 | P. A. Gibb | 1938 Cam. | | 100 | R. J. Boyd-Moss | 1982 Cam. |

*\* Signifies not out.*

## Highest Totals

| | | | | | |
|---|---|---|---|---|---|
| 503 | Oxford | 1900 | 432-9 | Cambridge | 1936 |
| 457 | Oxford | 1947 | 431 | Cambridge | 1932 |
| 453-8 | Oxford | 1931 | 425 | Cambridge | 1938 |

## Lowest Totals

| | | | | | |
|---|---|---|---|---|---|
| 32 | Oxford | 1878 | 42 | Oxford | 1890 |
| 39 | Cambridge | 1858 | 47 | Cambridge | 1838 |

*Notes:* A. P. F. Chapman and M. P. Donnelly enjoy the following distinction: Chapman scored a century at Lord's in the University match (102*, 1922); for Gentlemen v Players (160, 1922), (108, 1926); and for England v Australia (121, 1930). Donnelly scored a century at Lord's in the University match (142, 1946); for Gentlemen v Players (162*, 1947); and for New Zealand v England (206, 1949).

A. Ratcliffe's 201 for Cambridge in 1931 remained a record for the match for only one day, being beaten by the Nawab of Pataudi's 238* for Oxford next day.

M. J. K. Smith (Oxford) and R. J. Boyd-Moss (Cambridge) are the only players who have scored three hundreds. Smith scored 201* in 1954, 104 in 1955, and 117 in 1956; Boyd-Moss scored 100 in 1982 and 139 and 124 in 1983. His aggregate of 489 surpassed Smith's previous record of 477.

The following players have scored two hundreds: W. Yardley (Cambridge) 100 in 1870 and 130 in 1872; H. J. Enthoven (Cambridge) 104 in 1924 and 129 in 1925; Nawab of Pataudi (Oxford) 106 in 1929 and 238* in 1931; A. Ratcliffe (Cambridge) 201 in 1931 and 124 in 1932; D. R. W. Silk (Cambridge) 116* in 1953 and 118 in 1954; J. M. Brearley (Cambridge) 113* in 1962 and 119 in 1964; D. R. Owen-Thomas (Cambridge) 146 in 1971 and 114* in 1972; G. J. Toogood (Oxford) 109 in 1984 and 149 in 1985.

F. C. Cobden, in the Oxford v Cambridge match in 1870, performed the hat-trick by taking the last three wickets and won an extraordinary game for Cambridge by 2 runs. The feat is without parallel in first-class cricket. Other hat-tricks, all for Cambridge, have been credited to A. G. Steel (1879), P. H. Morton (1880), J. F. Ireland (1911), and R. G. H. Lowe (1926).

S. E. Butler, in the 1871 match, took all the wickets in the Cambridge first innings. The feat is unique in University matches. He bowled 24.1 overs. In the follow-on he took five wickets for 57, giving him match figures of fifteen for 95 runs.

The best all-round performances in the history of the match have come from P. R. Le Couteur, who scored 160 and took eleven Cambridge wickets for 66 runs in 1910, and G. J. Toogood, who in 1985 scored 149 and took ten Cambridge wickets for 93.

D. W. Jarrett (Oxford 1975, Cambridge 1976), S. M. Wookey (Cambridge 1975-76, Oxford 1978) and G. Pathmanathan (Oxford 1975-78, Cambridge 1983) are alone in gaining cricket Blues for both Universities.

July 13, 14. Benson and Hedges Cup final. WORCESTERSHIRE beat LANCASHIRE by 65 runs (See Benson and Hedges Cup section).

July 16. MCC SCHOOLS beat MCC by six wickets (See MCC section).

## †MCC SCHOOLS v NATIONAL ASSOCIATION OF YOUNG CRICKETERS

At Lord's, July 17. National Association of Young Cricketers won by three wickets. Toss: National Association of Young Cricketers. NAYC won the match in an exciting finish after a flurry of runs from Harrison and Foster. In order to give several more boys the experience of playing at Lord's, the selectors made three changes from the MCC Schools' side of the previous day, while four others of the schoolboys who had taken part in the MCC Oxford trials the previous weekend were included in the NAYC XI. The sixteen-year-old Weston gained valuable experience from his 195 minutes at the wicket and indicated great potential, while an early cover drive by Harvey gave a glimpse of his real ability. Both, however, took too long over their century opening partnership. Later batsmen were forced to look for runs and were the victims of Harrison's well-controlled off-spin. NAYC's reply began equally slowly and it was left to Harrison, a minor county player for Buckinghamshire, to take advantage of the attacking fields which the Schools set, almost to the end. Both wicket-keepers, Workman and Nick Harvey, had a good match, conceding a bye between them in almost 400 runs and taking the spinners well.

## MCC Schools

| | |
|---|---|
| R. M. S. Weston (*Durham*) c and b Harrison . 55 | M. J. Semmence (*Hurstpierpoint*) lbw b Harrison . 1 |
| M. E. Harvey (*Habergham HS*) b Harrison . 75 | J. E. Hindson (*Toothill, Notts.*) b Peirce . 7 |
| M. J. Walker (*King's, Rochester*) c Harvey b Harrison . 10 | †N. J. Workman (*King Edward VI, Stourbridge*) not out . 2 |
| *A. J. Hall (*Marple Hall*) b Peirce . 13 | B 1, l-b 9, n-b 7 . 17 |
| K. J. Parsons (*Richard Huish*) not out . 15 | |
| M. F. D. Robinson (*King's, Taunton*) st Harvey b Harrison . 2 | 1/127 2/143 3/162 (7 wkts dec.) 197 4/168 5/173 6/177 7/184 |

J. M. S. Whittington (*Eton*) and R. J. Ballinger (*Millfield*) did not bat.

Bowling: Ridgway 9-2-38-0; Foster 12-3-33-0; Harrison 26-9-60-5; Richardson 8-3-26-0; Peirce 9-1-30-2.

## National Association of Young Cricketers

| | |
|---|---|
| *J. M. A. Inglis (*Warwicks.*) | M. J. Foster (*Yorks.*) st Workman |
| c Robinson b Hindson . 46 | b Hindson . 24 |
| H. Morgan (*Devon*) b Whittington . . . . . 40 | D. Maddy (*Leics.*) c Weston |
| M. T. E. Peirce (*Sussex*) c Walker | b Hindson . 4 |
| b Hindson . 10 | A. W. Richardson (*Derbys.*) not out . . . . 4 |
| K. A. Parsons (*Somerset*) | |
| lbw b Whittington . 20 | N-b 4 . . . . . . . . . . . . . . . . . . . . . 4 |
| J. C. Harrison (*Bucks.*) not out . . . . . . . . 34 | |
| G. Evison (*Lincs.*) c Parsons | 1/65 2/84 3/108 4/127        (7 wkts) 201 |
| b Whittington . 15 | 5/164 6/191 7/197 |

P. F. Ridgway (*Staffs.*) and †N. Harvey (*Berks.*) did not bat.

Bowling: Ballinger 7–0–21–0; Robinson 6.1–1–18–0; Hindson 19–3–84–4; Semmence 6–2–25–0; Whittington 10–2–53–3.

Umpires: H. Cohen and A. R. Smith.

The National Cricket Association selected the following to play for NCA Young Cricketers against Combined Services: *J. M. A. Inglis (Warwicks.), M. E. Harvey (Lancs.), M. J. Walker (Kent), A. J. Hall (Cheshire), K. A. Parsons (Somerset), M. J. Foster (Yorks.), M. F. D. Robinson (Somerset), J. C. Harrison (Bucks.), R. J. Ballinger (Middx), J. E. Hindson (Notts.) and †N. J. Workman (Worcs.).

†July 18. NCA Young Cricketers won by four wickets. Toss: NCA Young Cricketers. Combined Services 175 for five (35 overs) (2nd Lt R. J. Greatorex 31, SAC A. Jones 88 not out); NCA Young Cricketers 178 for six (34.1 overs) (M. E. Harvey 32, M. J. Foster 42 not out).

August 6. AUSTRALIA YOUNG CRICKETERS beat ENGLAND YOUNG CRICKETERS by 9 runs (See Australian Young Cricketers tour section).

August 22, 23, 24, 26, 27. Cornhill Test. ENGLAND beat SRI LANKA by 137 runs.

August 29. Holt Cup Knockout final. STAFFORDSHIRE beat DEVON by four wickets (See Minor Counties section).

## †TEDDINGTON v WALSALL

### National Club Championship Final

August 30. Teddington won by 20 runs. Toss: Teddington. The London club's second Club Championship title in three years owed much to the all-round effort of Munday. Having top-scored with 57, he captured four wickets for 30 in seven overs of slow left-arm bowling at a time when Walsall were beginning to recover, through Gouldstone and Archer, from the earlier breakthrough effected by Barrett. Mackintosh, formerly of Nottinghamshire and Surrey, hurried his side to victory by taking the last two wickets with successive balls.

## Teddington

| | | | |
|---|---|---|---|
| G. Morgan c Mackelworth b Mayer | 40 | †R. S. Luddington lbw b Mayer | 0 |
| W. A. Donald b Nicholls | 9 | G. A. R. Harris not out | 4 |
| *A. J. T. Miller b Smith | 50 | | |
| S. L. Munday b Bryan | 57 | B 1, l-b 23, w 5, n-b 2 | 31 |
| T. I. Macmillan b Mayer | 5 | | |
| K. S. Mackintosh b Bryan | 3 | 1/44 2/55 3/156 (8 wkts, 45 overs) | 217 |
| J. C. Barrett b Mayer | 9 | 4/172 5/177 6/201 | |
| S. D. Weale not out | 9 | 7/211 8/211 | |

M. I. W. Russell did not bat.

Bowling: Bryan 9–0–58–2; Smith 9–1–30–1; Mayer 9–0–32–4; Nicholls 9–1–35–1; Dyer 9–0–38–0.

## Walsall

| | | | |
|---|---|---|---|
| S. J. Dean b Barrett | 47 | A. P. Bryan b Mackintosh | 5 |
| P. R. Oliver st Luddington b Barrett | 51 | D. G. Nicholls not out | 3 |
| W. Law c Miller b Barrett | 6 | J. Mayer b Mackintosh | 0 |
| M. R. Gouldstone b Munday | 26 | B 2, l-b 6, w 2, n-b 1 | 11 |
| N. J. Archer lbw b Munday | 44 | | |
| †A. N. Mackelworth b Munday | 1 | 1/78 2/96 3/109 (43.4 overs) | 197 |
| G. Smith c and b Munday | 0 | 4/170 5/182 6/182 | |
| *R. J. Dyer b Mackintosh | 3 | 7/189 8/189 9/197 | |

Bowling: Harris 5–0–13–0; Russell 5–0–27–0; Mackintosh 8.4–0–55–3; Weale 9–1–31–0; Barrett 9–2–33–3; Munday 7–0–30–4.

Umpires: Wg Cdr J. M. Mullaney and M. Rice.

## NATIONAL CLUB CHAMPIONSHIP WINNERS 1969-91

1969 HAMPSTEAD beat Pocklington Pixies by 14 runs.
1970 CHELTENHAM beat Stockport by three wickets.
1971 BLACKHEATH beat Ealing by eight wickets.
1972 SCARBOROUGH beat Brentham by six wickets.
1973 WOLVERHAMPTON beat The Mote by five wickets.
1974 SUNBURY beat Tunbridge Wells by seven wickets.
1975 YORK beat Blackpool by six wickets.
1976 SCARBOROUGH beat Dulwich by five wickets.
1977 SOUTHGATE beat Bowdon by six wickets.
1978 CHELTENHAM beat Bishop's Stortford by 15 runs.
1979 SCARBOROUGH beat Reading by two wickets.
1980 MOSELEY beat Gosport Borough by four wickets.
1981 SCARBOROUGH beat Blackheath by 57 runs.
1982 SCARBOROUGH beat Finchley by 4 runs.
1983 SHREWSBURY beat Hastings and St Leonards Priory by 2 runs.
1984 OLD HILL beat Bishop's Stortford by five wickets.
1985 OLD HILL beat Reading by nine wickets.
1986 STOURBRIDGE beat Weston-super-Mare by four wickets.
1987 OLD HILL beat Teddington by five wickets.
1988 ENFIELD beat Wolverhampton by nine wickets.
1989 TEDDINGTON beat Old Hill by 11 runs.
1990 BLACKPOOL beat Cheam by three wickets.
1991 TEDDINGTON beat Walsall by 20 runs.

*From 1969 to 1975, the Championship was contested for the D. H. Robins Trophy, from 1976 to 1982 for the John Haig Trophy, from 1983 to 1986 for the William Younger Cup, and from 1987 to 1990 for the Cockspur Cup.*

## †HAROME v ST FAGANS

### National Village Championship Final

August 31. St Fagans won by 17 runs. Toss: St Fagans. In spite of the proximity of the pitch to the Tavern boundary, it was the slow bowlers who held the key on a cloudless summer day. When the faster bowlers were recalled, as inevitably they had to be, batsmen found runs much easier to come by. St Fagans, choosing to bat first, looked on course for a good total to defend when they were 84 for one in the 25th over. However, Bowes and Dowson conceded just 53 runs in their eighteen overs, reducing St Fagans to 124 for six, and only brave hitting and good running by Mitchell and Rosser, including 19 runs off the last over, took the Welsh side to 169. Harome struggled against Lawlor and Hardwick, the St Fagans spinners introduced early on by Needham, but with 90 runs required off the last ten overs, Strickland set about the bowling. He hit three sixes off Makinson in an over costing 22 runs before being yorked by nineteen-year-old Sylvester, who capped his top score and two steepling catches by taking four for 17 with his off-spinners as St Fagans won the Village Championship for the third time, to match Troon's record.

*Man of the Match:* J. P. G. Sylvester.

### St Fagans

| | | | |
|---|---|---|---|
| *P. J. E. Needham b C. A. Marwood | 9 | †P. Mitchell not out | 24 |
| K. M. Bell run out | 35 | A. W. Rosser not out | 21 |
| J. P. G. Sylvester b Bowes | 38 | B 5, l-b 7, w 4, n-b 1 | 17 |
| R. H. Davies b Dowson | 9 | | |
| M. Powell c D. Collier b Bowes | 3 | 1/15 2/84 3/98 (6 wkts, 40 overs) 169 |
| P. R. Williams st D. Collier b Dowson | 13 | 4/107 5/110 6/124 | |

P. D. Makinson, P. J. Lawlor and P. G. Hardwick did not bat.

Bowling: Otterburn 9–1–45–0; C. A. Marwood 9–1–28–1; P. S. Collier 4–0–31–0; Bowes 9–1–31–2; Dowson 9–1–22–2.

### Harome

| | | | |
|---|---|---|---|
| P. S. Collier c Sylvester b Lawlor | 8 | C. A. Ellis not out | 1 |
| T. W. Marwood c Sylvester b Makinson | 33 | J. Greenlay st Mitchell b Sylvester | 0 |
| B. L. Dowson c Rosser b Hardwick | 5 | | |
| †D. Collier b Hardwick | 16 | L-b 10, w 6, n-b 1 | 17 |
| C. A. Marwood c Williams b Sylvester | 30 | | |
| G. Strickland b Sylvester | 30 | 1/12 2/41 3/51 (9 wkts, 40 overs) 152 |
| J. P. Marwood c Makinson b Sylvester | 7 | 4/80 5/126 6/139 | |
| A. S. Bowes run out | 5 | 7/151 8/151 9/152 | |

*I. J. Otterburn did not bat.

Bowling: Makinson 9–1–61–1; Rosser 8–2–17–0; Lawlor 9–3–23–1; Hardwick 9–2–24–2; Sylvester 5–0–17–4.

Umpires: J. F. Jarvis and G. Penberthy.

### VILLAGE CHAMPIONSHIP WINNERS 1972-91

1972 TROON (Cornwall) beat Astwood Bank (Worcestershire) by seven wickets.
1973 TROON (Cornwall) beat Gowerton (Glamorgan) by 12 runs.
1974 BOMARSUND (Northumberland) beat Collingham (Nottinghamshire) by three wickets.
1975 GOWERTON (Glamorgan) beat Isleham (Cambridgeshire) by six wickets.
1976 TROON (Cornwall) beat Sessay (Yorkshire) by 18 runs.
1977 COOKLEY (Worcestershire) beat Lindal Moor (Cumbria) by 28 runs.
1978 LINTON PARK (Kent) beat Toft (Cheshire) by four wickets.
1979 EAST BIERLEY (Yorkshire) beat Ynysygerwn (Glamorgan) by 92 runs.

1980 MARCHWIEL (Clwyd) beat Longparish (Hampshire) by 79 runs.
1981 ST FAGANS (Glamorgan) beat Broad Oak (Yorkshire) by 22 runs.
1982 ST FAGANS (Glamorgan) beat Collingham (Nottinghamshire) by six wickets.
1983 QUARNDON (Derbyshire) beat Troon (Cornwall) by eight wickets.
1984 MARCHWIEL (Clwyd) beat Hursley Park (Hampshire) by 8 runs.
1985 FREUCHIE (Fife) beat Rowledge (Surrey) by virtue of fewer wickets lost with the
     scores level.
1986 FORGE VALLEY (Yorkshire) beat Ynysygerwn (Glamorgan) by 5 runs.
1987 LONGPARISH (Hampshire) beat Treeton Welfare (Yorkshire) by 76 runs.
1988 GOATACRE (Wiltshire) beat Himley (West Midlands) by four wickets.
1989 TOFT (Cheshire) beat Hambledon (Hampshire) by six wickets.
1990 GOATACRE (Wiltshire) beat Dunstall (Staffordshire) by 50 runs.
1991 ST FAGANS (Glamorgan) beat Harome (Yorkshire) by 17 runs.

*From 1972 to 1977, the Village Championship was sponsored by John Haig Ltd, in 1978 and
1990 to 1991 by The Cricketer, from 1979 to 1984 by Samuel Whitbread and Co. Ltd, and 1986 to
1989 by Hydro Fertilizers. There was no sponsor in 1985.*

September 7. NatWest Bank Trophy final. HAMPSHIRE beat SURREY by four wickets
(See NatWest Bank Trophy section).

---

# STATUS OF MATCHES IN THE UK

## (a) Automatic First-Class Matches

The following matches of three or more days' duration should automatically be considered
first-class:

   (i) County Championship matches.
   (ii) Official representative tourist matches from Full Member Countries, unless
        specifically excluded.
   (iii) MCC v any First-Class County.
   (iv) Oxford v Cambridge and either University against First-Class Counties.
   (v) Scotland v Ireland.

## (b) Excluded from First-Class Status

The following matches of three or more days' duration should not normally be accorded
first-class status:

   (i) County "friendly" matches.
   (ii) Matches played by Scotland or Ireland, other than their annual match against each
        other.
   (iii) Unofficial tourist matches, unless circumstances are exceptional.
   (iv) MCC v Oxford/Cambridge.
   (v) Matches involving privately raised teams, unless included officially in a touring team's
       itinerary.

## (c) Consideration of Doubtful Status

Matches played by unofficial touring teams of exceptional ability can be considered in
advance and decisions taken accordingly.
Certain other matches comprising 22 recognised first-class cricketers might also be
considered in advance.

# BRITANNIC ASSURANCE
# COUNTY CHAMPIONSHIP, 1991

Before the season began, the consensus of opinion was that the main contenders for the 1991 Britannic Assurance Championship would be the reigning champions, Middlesex, Essex and Worcestershire, with Lancashire and perhaps Surrey and Hampshire worthy of interest. In the event, only Essex really came up to expectation, going on to win the title for the fifth time as the season reached a gripping climax. Middlesex, a shadow of the team that took the title in 1990, never got going and finished in fifteenth place, the most dramatic decline by a champion county in the history of the Championship. Lancashire fell away after being in second place on June 24, with four wins from eight games. They then dropped their pilot in favour of a cabin boy and managed only two more wins, while Worcestershire were never in contention after spending the first half of the season among the backmarkers.

The frontrunners for most of the summer were Warwickshire. Fifth in 1990, when they had the bowling but lacked the batting to win the Championship, they headed the table in 1991 from May 28 until August 26, albeit benefiting from having played one and sometimes two more games than their closest rivals. But for a hiccup in August, when they went four games without a win while Essex was closing a gap of 51 points, the Championship could well have been theirs. Indeed, in five of the previous six Championships their eleven wins would have been enough to gain the title. As it was, Essex also won eleven games, and the thirteen points which put them in front of Warwickshire came from bonus points.

However, it was experience as well as bonus points that stood Essex in good stead in the final weeks. As Warwickshire stumbled, winning just three of their last seven games, Essex in the same period won six of their last nine, all the time putting Warwickshire under unaccustomed pressure. Even

## BRITANNIC ASSURANCE CHAMPIONSHIP

| | | | | | Bonus points | | |
|---|---|---|---|---|---|---|---|
| *Win = 16 points* | Played | Won | Lost | Tied | Drawn | Batting | Bowling | Points |
| 1 – Essex (2) . . . . . . . . . . . . | 22 | 11 | 5 | 0 | 6 | 69 | 67 | 312 |
| 2 – Warwickshire (5) . . . . | 22 | 11 | 4 | 0 | 7 | 58 | 65 | 299 |
| 3 – Derbyshire (12) . . . . . . | 22 | 9 | 5 | 0 | 8 | 46 | 68 | 258 |
| 4 – Nottinghamshire (13) . | 22 | 7 | 5 | 0 | 10 | 64 | 69 | 245 |
| 5 – Surrey (9) . . . . . . . . . . | 22 | 8 | 6 | 0 | 8 | 47 | 66 | 241 |
| 6 – Kent (16) . . . . . . . . . . . | 22 | 6 | 3 | 1 | 12 | 50 | 55 | 209 |
| 6 – Worcestershire (4) . . . | 22 | 6 | 4 | 0 | 12 | 54 | 59 | 209 |
| 8 – Lancashire (6) . . . . . . . | 22 | 6 | 9 | 0 | 7 | 60 | 49 | 205 |
| 9 – Hampshire (3) . . . . . . . | 22 | 5 | 7 | 0 | 10 | 57 | 56 | 193 |
| 10 – Northamptonshire (11) | 22 | 5 | 6 | 0 | 11 | 55 | 54 | 189 |
| 11 – Sussex (17) . . . . . . . . . | 22 | 4 | 3 | 1 | 14 | 57 | 60 | 189 |
| 12 – Glamorgan (8) . . . . . . | 22 | 5 | 5 | 0 | 12 | 50 | 57 | 187 |
| 13 – Gloucestershire (13) . . | 22 | 5 | 10 | 0 | 7 | 42 | 53 | 175 |
| 14 – Yorkshire (10) . . . . . . | 22 | 4 | 6 | 0 | 12 | 58 | 37 | 159 |
| 15 – Middlesex (1) . . . . . . . | 22 | 3 | 9 | 0 | 10 | 48 | 63 | 159 |
| 16 – Leicestershire (7) . . . . | 22 | 3 | 8 | 0 | 11 | 46 | 53 | 147 |
| 17 – Somerset (15) . . . . . . . | 22 | 2 | 5 | 0 | 15 | 66 | 45 | 143 |

*1990 positions are shown in brackets.*

though Warwickshire finished strongly, making good use of their four-day programme, they were by then relying on Essex to falter. With Gooch firmly in control, and the Essex batsmen and bowlers banking bonus points as well as winning matches, this was more in hope than expectation. Essex had the look of champions; Warwickshire looked like a team that might win the Championship.

By the halfway stage, the Championship race had seemed wide open. After eleven games, Warwickshire had 139 points, with five wins, while Essex (134 points), Derbyshire (125 points), Lancashire (119 points) and Surrey (115 points) all had four wins from their first eleven games. Nottinghamshire, in eighth place with three wins and 112 points after completing half their programme, made ground quickly in the second half of the summer; by early August they were sharing second place with Surrey, when defeat at Derby pushed Essex out of the top three for the only time in 1991. Neither Nottinghamshire nor Surrey could sustain their challenge, however, and Derbyshire, winning four of their last seven games, held on to third place from the middle of August.

# REGULATIONS FOR BRITANNIC ASSURANCE CHAMPIONSHIP

(As applied in 1991)

## 1. Prizemoney

| | |
|---|---|
| First (Essex) | £44,000 |
| Second (Warwickshire) | £22,000 |
| Third (Derbyshire) | £12,750 |
| Fourth (Nottinghamshire) | £6,500 |
| Fifth (Surrey) | £3,250 |
| Winner of each match | £250 |
| Championship Player of the Year (N. A. Foster) | £1,000 |
| County of the Month | £1,000 |
| Player of the Month | £300 |

## 2. Scoring of Points

(*a*) For a win, sixteen points, plus any points scored in the first innings.

(*b*) In a tie, each side to score eight points, plus any points scored in the first innings.

(*c*) If the scores are equal in a drawn match, the side batting in the fourth innings to score eight points, plus any points scored in the first innings.

(*d*) **First-innings points** (awarded only for performances *in the first 100 overs* of each first innings and retained whatever the result of the match).

    (i) A maximum of four batting points to be available as under:
        150 to 199 runs – 1 point; 200 to 249 runs – 2 points; 250 to 299 runs – 3 points; 300 runs or over – 4 points.

    (ii) A maximum of four bowling points to be available as under:
        3 to 4 wickets taken – 1 point; 5 to 6 wickets taken – 2 points; 7 to 8 wickets taken – 3 points; 9 to 10 wickets taken – 4 points.

(*e*) If play starts when less than eight hours' playing time remains and a one-innings match is played, no first-innings points shall be scored. The side winning on the one innings to score twelve points.

(*f*) A county which is adjudged to have prepared a pitch unsuitable for first-class cricket shall be liable to have 25 points deducted from its aggregate of points.

(*g*) The side which has the highest aggregate of points gained at the end of the season shall be the Champion County. Should any sides in the Championship table be equal on points the side with most wins will have priority.

### 3. Hours of Play

1st, 2nd [3rd] days ...   11.00 a.m. to 6.30 p.m. or after 110 overs, whichever is the later.
(For Sunday play, the home county may decide to play from 12 noon to 7.30 p.m.)

Final day . . . . . . . . . .   11.00 a.m. to 6.00 p.m. or after 102 overs, whichever is the later.

*Note:* The hours of play, including intervals, were brought forward by half an hour for matches in September.

(*a*) If play is suspended (including any interval between innings) the minimum number of overs to be bowled in a day to be reduced by one over for each $3\frac{1}{2}$ minutes or part thereof of such suspension or suspensions in aggregate.

(*b*) If at 5.00 p.m. on the final day, nineteen overs or less remain to be bowled, the umpires shall indicate that play shall continue until a minimum of a further twenty overs has been bowled, or until 6.00 p.m., whichever is the later. Play may cease on the final day at any time between 5.30 p.m. and 6.00 p.m. by mutual agreement of the captains. Should an innings end between 4.50 p.m. and 5.00 p.m., the time at the end of the ten-minute interval to replace 5.00 p.m.

(*c*) The captains may agree or, in the event of disagreement, the umpires may decide to play 30 minutes (or minimum ten overs) extra time at the end of the first and/or second day's play (and/or the third day of four) if, in their opinion, it would bring about a definite result on that day. In the event of the possibility of a finish disappearing before the full period has expired, the whole period must be played out. Any time so claimed does not affect the timing for cessation of play on the final day.

(*d*) If an innings ends during the course of an over, that part shall count as a full over so far as the minimum number of overs per day is concerned.

(*e*) If play is suspended for the day in the middle of an over, that over must be completed next day in addition to the minimum overs required that day.

*Intervals*

Lunch: 1.15 p.m. to 1.55 p.m. (1st, 2nd [3rd] days), 2.15 p.m. to 2.55 p.m. on Sundays when play commences at 12 noon
1.00 p.m. to 1.40 p.m. (final day)
In the event of lunch being taken early because of a stoppage caused by weather or bad light (Law 16.2), the interval shall be limited to 40 minutes.

Tea: 4.10 p.m. to 4.30 p.m. (1st, 2nd [3rd] days), 5.10 p.m. to 5.30 p.m. on Sundays when play commences at 12 noon; or when 40 overs remain to be bowled, whichever is the later.
3.40 p.m. to 4.00 p.m. (final day), or when 40 overs remain to be bowled, whichever is the later.

### 4. Substitutes

Law 2.1 will apply, but in addition:

A substitute shall be allowed as of right in the event of a cricketer currently playing in a Championship match being required to join the England team for a Test match (or one-day international). Such a substitute may be permitted to bat or bowl in that match, subject to the approval of the TCCB. The player who is substituted may not take further part in the match, even though he might not be required by England. If batting at the time, the player substituted shall be retired "not out" and his substitute may be permitted to bat later in that innings subject to the approval of the TCCB.

The opposing captain shall have no right of objection to any player acting as substitute in the field, nor as to where he shall field. However, no substitute may act as wicket-keeper.

No substitute may take the field until the player for whom he is to substitute has been absent from the field for five consecutive complete overs, with the exception that if a fieldsman sustains an obvious, serious injury, a substitute shall be allowed immediately. If a player leaves the field during an over, the remainder of that over shall not count in the calculation of five complete overs.

## 5. Fieldsman Leaving the Field

No fieldsman shall leave the field or return during a session of play without the consent of the umpire at the bowler's end. The umpire's consent is also necessary if a substitute is required for a fieldsman at the start of play or when his side returns to the field after an interval.

If a member of the fielding side does not take the field at the start of play, leaves the field, or fails to return after an interval and is absent longer than fifteen minutes, he shall not bowl in that innings after his return until he has been on the field for at least the length of playing time for which he was absent; nor shall he be permitted to bat unless or until, in the aggregate, he has returned to the field and/or his side's innings has been in progress for at least the length of playing time for which he was absent or, if earlier, when his side has lost five wickets. The restrictions shall not apply if he has been absent for exceptional and acceptable reasons (other than injury or illness) and consent for a substitute has been granted by the opposing captain.

## 6. New ball

The captain of the fielding side shall have the choice of taking the new ball after 100 overs have been bowled with the old one.

## 7. Covering of Pitches and Bowler's Run-up

The whole pitch shall be covered:

(a) The night before a match and, if necessary, until the first ball is bowled.

(b) On each night of a match and, if necessary, throughout any rest days.

(c) In the event of play being suspended because of bad light or rain, during the hours of play.

The bowler's run-up shall be covered to a distance of at least ten yards, with a width of four yards.

## 8. Declarations

Law 14 will apply, but, in addition, a captain may also forfeit his first innings, subject to the provisions set out in Law 14.2. If, owing to weather conditions, the match has not started when fewer than eight hours of playing time remain, the first innings of each side shall automatically be forfeited and a one-innings match played.

# CHAMPION COUNTY SINCE 1864

*Note:* The earliest county champions were decided usually by the fewest matches lost, but in 1888 an unofficial points system was introduced. In 1890, the Championship was constituted officially. From 1977 to 1983 it was sponsored by Schweppes, and since 1984 by Britannic Assurance.

| | | | | | |
|---|---|---|---|---|---|
| 1864 | Surrey | 1880 | Nottinghamshire | 1896 | Yorkshire |
| 1865 | Nottinghamshire | 1881 | Lancashire | 1897 | Lancashire |
| 1866 | Middlesex | 1882 | Nottinghamshire | 1898 | Yorkshire |
| 1867 | Yorkshire | | Lancashire | 1899 | Surrey |
| 1868 | Nottinghamshire | 1883 | Nottinghamshire | 1900 | Yorkshire |
| 1869 | Nottinghamshire | 1884 | Nottinghamshire | 1901 | Yorkshire |
| | Yorkshire | 1885 | Nottinghamshire | 1902 | Yorkshire |
| 1870 | Yorkshire | 1886 | Nottinghamshire | 1903 | Middlesex |
| 1871 | Nottinghamshire | 1887 | Surrey | 1904 | Lancashire |
| 1872 | Nottinghamshire | 1888 | Surrey | 1905 | Yorkshire |
| 1873 | Gloucestershire | | Surrey | 1906 | Kent |
| | Nottinghamshire | 1889 | Lancashire | 1907 | Nottinghamshire |
| 1874 | Gloucestershire | | Nottinghamshire | 1908 | Yorkshire |
| 1875 | Nottinghamshire | 1890 | Surrey | 1909 | Kent |
| 1876 | Gloucestershire | 1891 | Surrey | 1910 | Kent |
| 1877 | Gloucestershire | 1892 | Surrey | 1911 | Warwickshire |
| 1878 | Undecided | 1893 | Yorkshire | 1912 | Yorkshire |
| 1879 | Nottinghamshire | 1894 | Surrey | 1913 | Kent |
| | Lancashire | 1895 | Surrey | 1914 | Surrey |

| 1919 | Yorkshire | 1949 { | Middlesex | 1971 | Surrey |
|------|-----------|--------|-----------|------|--------|
| 1920 | Middlesex | | Yorkshire | 1972 | Warwickshire |
| 1921 | Middlesex | 1950 { | Lancashire | 1973 | Hampshire |
| 1922 | Yorkshire | | Surrey | 1974 | Worcestershire |
| 1923 | Yorkshire | 1951 | Warwickshire | 1975 | Leicestershire |
| 1924 | Yorkshire | 1952 | Surrey | 1976 | Middlesex |
| 1925 | Yorkshire | 1953 | Surrey | 1977 { | Middlesex |
| 1926 | Lancashire | 1954 | Surrey | | Kent |
| 1927 | Lancashire | 1955 | Surrey | 1978 | Kent |
| 1928 | Lancashire | 1956 | Surrey | 1979 | Essex |
| 1929 | Nottinghamshire | 1957 | Surrey | 1980 | Middlesex |
| 1930 | Lancashire | 1958 | Surrey | 1981 | Nottinghamshire |
| 1931 | Yorkshire | 1959 | Yorkshire | 1982 | Middlesex |
| 1932 | Yorkshire | 1960 | Yorkshire | 1983 | Essex |
| 1933 | Yorkshire | 1961 | Hampshire | 1984 | Essex |
| 1934 | Lancashire | 1962 | Yorkshire | 1985 | Middlesex |
| 1935 | Yorkshire | 1963 | Yorkshire | 1986 | Essex |
| 1936 | Derbyshire | 1964 | Worcestershire | 1987 | Nottinghamshire |
| 1937 | Yorkshire | 1965 | Worcestershire | 1988 | Worcestershire |
| 1938 | Yorkshire | 1966 | Yorkshire | 1989 | Worcestershire |
| 1939 | Yorkshire | 1967 | Yorkshire | 1990 | Middlesex |
| 1946 | Yorkshire | 1968 | Yorkshire | 1991 | Essex |
| 1947 | Middlesex | 1969 | Glamorgan | | |
| 1948 | Glamorgan | 1970 | Kent | | |

*Notes:* The title has been won outright as follows: Yorkshire 31 times, Surrey 18, Nottinghamshire 14, Middlesex 10, Lancashire 8, Kent 6, Essex 5, Worcestershire 5, Gloucestershire 3, Warwickshire 3, Glamorgan 2, Hampshire 2, Derbyshire 1, Leicestershire 1.

Eight times the title has been shared as follows: Nottinghamshire 5, Lancashire 4, Middlesex 2, Surrey 2, Yorkshire 2, Gloucestershire 1, Kent 1.

The earliest date the Championship has been won in any season since it was expanded in 1895 was August 12, 1910, by Kent.

## BRITANNIC ASSURANCE CHAMPIONSHIP
## STATISTICS FOR 1991

| | For | | | Against | | |
|---|---|---|---|---|---|---|
| County | Runs | Wickets | Avge | Runs | Wickets | Avge |
| Derbyshire | 9,944 | 320 | 31.07 | 10,180 | 316 | 32.21 |
| Essex | 10,093 | 224 | 45.05 | 9,876 | 335 | 29.48 |
| Glamorgan | 9,465 | 246 | 38.47 | 9,462 | 273 | 34.65 |
| Gloucestershire | 8,887 | 316 | 28.12 | 9,220 | 274 | 33.64 |
| Hampshire | 9,490 | 281 | 33.77 | 9,535 | 264 | 36.11 |
| Kent | 9,697 | 286 | 33.90 | 9,061 | 305 | 29.70 |
| Lancashire | 9,819 | 306 | 32.08 | 10,224 | 254 | 40.25 |
| Leicestershire | 9,351 | 303 | 30.86 | 9,164 | 253 | 36.22 |
| Middlesex | 9,144 | 302 | 30.27 | 10,206 | 303 | 33.68 |
| Northamptonshire | 9,342 | 289 | 32.32 | 9,381 | 270 | 34.74 |
| Nottinghamshire | 9,832 | 256 | 38.40 | 10,795 | 322 | 33.52 |
| Somerset | 10,195 | 253 | 40.29 | 10,694 | 268 | 39.90 |
| Surrey | 9,746 | 312 | 31.23 | 9,279 | 314 | 29.55 |
| Sussex | 9,359 | 278 | 33.66 | 9,749 | 272 | 35.84 |
| Warwickshire | 9,562 | 311 | 30.74 | 8,739 | 308 | 28.37 |
| Worcestershire | 9,627 | 275 | 35.00 | 9,005 | 290 | 31.05 |
| Yorkshire | 9,652 | 296 | 32.60 | 8,635 | 233 | 37.06 |
| | 163,205 | 4,854 | 33.62 | 163,205 | 4,854 | 33.62 |

## COUNTY CHAMPIONSHIP – MATCH RESULTS, 1864-1991

| County | Years of Play | Played | Won | Lost | Tied | Drawn |
|---|---|---|---|---|---|---|
| Derbyshire | 1871-87; 1895-1991 | 2,134 | 526 | 774 | 1 | 833 |
| Essex | 1895-1991 | 2,097 | 596 | 601 | 5 | 895 |
| Glamorgan | 1921-1991 | 1,631 | 351 | 559 | 0 | 721 |
| Gloucestershire | 1870-1991 | 2,372 | 699 | 877 | 2 | 794 |
| Hampshire | 1864-85; 1895-1991 | 2,206 | 577 | 759 | 4 | 866 |
| Kent | 1864-1991 | 2,494 | 901 | 754 | 5 | 834 |
| Lancashire | 1865-1991 | 2,572 | 957 | 526 | 3 | 1,086 |
| Leicestershire | 1895-1991 | 2,064 | 444 | 769 | 1 | 850 |
| Middlesex | 1864-1991 | 2,274 | 845 | 579 | 5 | 845 |
| Northamptonshire | 1905-1991 | 1,831 | 434 | 649 | 3 | 745 |
| Nottinghamshire | 1864-1991 | 2,403 | 730 | 629 | 0 | 1,044 |
| Somerset | 1882-85; 1891-1991 | 2,104 | 487 | 856 | 3 | 758 |
| Surrey | 1864-1991 | 2,651 | 1,050 | 580 | 4 | 1,017 |
| Sussex | 1864-1991 | 2,543 | 706 | 873 | 6 | 958 |
| Warwickshire | 1895-1991 | 2,078 | 546 | 607 | 1 | 924 |
| Worcestershire | 1899-1991 | 2,019 | 499 | 707 | 1 | 812 |
| Yorkshire | 1864-1991 | 2,672 | 1,198 | 447 | 2 | 1,025 |
| Cambridgeshire | 1864-69; 1871 | 19 | 8 | 8 | 0 | 3 |
| | | 19,082 | 11,554 | 11,554 | 23 | 7,505 |

*Notes:* Matches abandoned without a ball bowled are wholly excluded.

Counties participated in the years shown, except that there were no matches in the years 1915-18 and 1940-45; Hampshire did not play inter-county matches in 1868-69, 1871-74 and 1879; Worcestershire did not take part in the Championship in 1919.

## COUNTY CHAMPIONSHIP – FINAL POSITIONS, 1890-1991

| | Derbyshire | Essex | Glamorgan | Gloucestershire | Hampshire | Kent | Lancashire | Leicestershire | Middlesex | Northamptonshire | Nottinghamshire | Somerset | Surrey | Sussex | Warwickshire | Worcestershire | Yorkshire |
|---|---|---|---|---|---|---|---|---|---|---|---|---|---|---|---|---|---|
| 1890 | — | — | — | 6 | — | 3 | 2 | — | 7 | — | 5 | — | 1 | 8 | — | — | 3 |
| 1891 | — | — | — | 9 | — | 5 | 2 | — | 3 | — | 4 | 5 | 1 | 7 | — | — | 8 |
| 1892 | — | — | — | 7 | — | 7 | 4 | — | 5 | — | 2 | 3 | 1 | 9 | — | — | 6 |
| 1893 | — | — | — | 9 | — | 4 | 2 | — | 3 | — | 6 | 8 | 5 | 7 | — | — | 1 |
| 1894 | — | — | — | 9 | — | 4 | 4 | — | 3 | — | 7 | 6 | 1 | 8 | — | — | 2 |
| 1895 | 5 | 9 | — | 4 | 10 | 14 | 2 | 12 | 6 | — | 12 | 8 | 1 | 11 | 6 | — | 3 |
| 1896 | 7 | 5 | — | 10 | 8 | 9 | 2 | 13 | 3 | — | 6 | 11 | 4 | 14 | 12 | — | 1 |
| 1897 | 14 | 3 | — | 5 | 9 | 12 | 1 | 13 | 8 | — | 10 | 11 | 2 | 6 | 7 | — | 4 |
| 1898 | 9 | 5 | — | 3 | 12 | 7 | 6 | 13 | 2 | — | 8 | 13 | 4 | 9 | 9 | — | 1 |
| 1899 | 15 | 6 | — | 9 | 10 | 8 | 4 | 13 | 2 | — | 10 | 13 | 1 | 5 | 7 | 12 | 3 |
| 1900 | 13 | 10 | — | 7 | 15 | 3 | 2 | 14 | 7 | — | 5 | 11 | 7 | 3 | 6 | 12 | 1 |
| 1901 | 15 | 10 | — | 14 | 7 | 7 | 3 | 12 | 2 | — | 9 | 12 | 6 | 4 | 5 | 11 | 1 |
| 1902 | 10 | 13 | — | 14 | 15 | 7 | 5 | 11 | 12 | — | 3 | 7 | 4 | 2 | 6 | 9 | 1 |
| 1903 | 12 | 8 | — | 13 | 14 | 8 | 4 | 14 | 1 | — | 5 | 10 | 11 | 2 | 7 | 6 | 3 |
| 1904 | 10 | 14 | — | 9 | 15 | 3 | 1 | 7 | 4 | — | 5 | 12 | 11 | 6 | 7 | 13 | 2 |
| 1905 | 14 | 12 | — | 8 | 16 | 6 | 2 | 5 | 11 | 13 | 10 | 15 | 4 | 3 | 7 | 8 | 1 |
| 1906 | 16 | 7 | — | 9 | 8 | 1 | 4 | 15 | 11 | 11 | 5 | 13 | 3 | 10 | 6 | 14 | 2 |
| 1907 | 16 | 7 | — | 10 | 12 | 8 | 6 | 11 | 5 | 15 | 1 | 14 | 4 | 13 | 9 | 2 | 2 |
| 1908 | 14 | 11 | — | 10 | 9 | 2 | 7 | 13 | 4 | 15 | 8 | 16 | 3 | 5 | 12 | 6 | 1 |
| 1909 | 15 | 14 | — | 16 | 8 | 1 | 2 | 13 | 6 | 7 | 10 | 11 | 5 | 4 | 12 | 8 | 3 |

| | Derbyshire | Essex | Glamorgan | Gloucestershire | Hampshire | Kent | Lancashire | Leicestershire | Middlesex | Northamptonshire | Nottinghamshire | Somerset | Surrey | Sussex | Warwickshire | Worcestershire | Yorkshire |
|---|---|---|---|---|---|---|---|---|---|---|---|---|---|---|---|---|---|
| 1910 | 15 | 11 | — | 12 | 6 | 1 | 4 | 10 | 3 | 9 | 5 | 16 | 2 | 7 | 14 | 13 | 8 |
| 1911 | 14 | 6 | — | 12 | 11 | 2 | 4 | 15 | 3 | 10 | 8 | 16 | 5 | 13 | 1 | 9 | 7 |
| 1912 | 12 | 15 | — | 11 | 6 | 3 | 4 | 13 | 5 | 2 | 8 | 14 | 7 | 10 | 9 | 16 | 1 |
| 1913 | 13 | 15 | — | 9 | 10 | 1 | 8 | 14 | 6 | 4 | 5 | 16 | 3 | 11 | 7 | 12 | 2 |
| 1914 | 12 | 8 | — | 16 | 5 | 3 | 11 | 13 | 2 | 9 | 10 | 15 | 1 | 6 | 7 | 14 | 4 |
| 1919 | 9 | 14 | — | 8 | 7 | 2 | 5 | 9 | 13 | 12 | 3 | 5 | 4 | 11 | 15 | — | 1 |
| 1920 | 16 | 9 | — | 8 | 11 | 5 | 2 | 13 | 1 | 14 | 7 | 10 | 3 | 6 | 12 | 15 | 4 |
| 1921 | 12 | 15 | 17 | 7 | 6 | 4 | 5 | 11 | 1 | 13 | 8 | 10 | 2 | 9 | 16 | 14 | 3 |
| 1922 | 11 | 8 | 16 | 13 | 6 | 4 | 5 | 14 | 7 | 15 | 2 | 10 | 3 | 9 | 12 | 17 | 1 |
| 1923 | 10 | 13 | 16 | 11 | 7 | 5 | 3 | 14 | 8 | 17 | 2 | 9 | 4 | 6 | 12 | 15 | 1 |
| 1924 | 17 | 15 | 13 | 6 | 12 | 5 | 4 | 11 | 2 | 16 | 6 | 8 | 3 | 10 | 9 | 14 | 1 |
| 1925 | 14 | 7 | 17 | 10 | 9 | 5 | 3 | 12 | 6 | 11 | 4 | 15 | 2 | 13 | 8 | 16 | 1 |
| 1926 | 11 | 9 | 8 | 15 | 7 | 3 | 1 | 13 | 6 | 16 | 4 | 14 | 5 | 10 | 12 | 17 | 2 |
| 1927 | 5 | 8 | 15 | 12 | 13 | 4 | 1 | 7 | 9 | 16 | 2 | 14 | 6 | 10 | 11 | 17 | 3 |
| 1928 | 10 | 16 | 15 | 5 | 12 | 2 | 1 | 9 | 8 | 13 | 3 | 14 | 6 | 7 | 11 | 17 | 4 |
| 1929 | 7 | 12 | 17 | 4 | 11 | 8 | 2 | 9 | 6 | 13 | 1 | 15 | 10 | 4 | 14 | 16 | 2 |
| 1930 | 9 | 6 | 11 | 2 | 13 | 5 | 1 | 12 | 16 | 17 | 4 | 13 | 8 | 7 | 15 | 10 | 3 |
| 1931 | 7 | 10 | 15 | 2 | 12 | 3 | 6 | 16 | 11 | 17 | 5 | 13 | 8 | 4 | 9 | 14 | 1 |
| 1932 | 10 | 14 | 15 | 13 | 8 | 3 | 6 | 12 | 10 | 16 | 4 | 7 | 5 | 2 | 9 | 17 | 1 |
| 1933 | 6 | 4 | 16 | 10 | 14 | 3 | 5 | 17 | 12 | 13 | 8 | 11 | 9 | 2 | 7 | 15 | 1 |
| 1934 | 3 | 8 | 13 | 7 | 14 | 5 | 1 | 12 | 10 | 17 | 9 | 15 | 11 | 2 | 4 | 16 | 5 |
| 1935 | 2 | 9 | 13 | 15 | 16 | 10 | 4 | 6 | 3 | 17 | 5 | 14 | 11 | 7 | 8 | 12 | 1 |
| 1936 | 1 | 9 | 16 | 4 | 10 | 8 | 11 | 15 | 2 | 17 | 5 | 7 | 6 | 14 | 13 | 12 | 3 |
| 1937 | 3 | 6 | 7 | 4 | 14 | 12 | 9 | 16 | 2 | 17 | 10 | 13 | 8 | 5 | 11 | 15 | 1 |
| 1938 | 5 | 6 | 16 | 10 | 14 | 9 | 4 | 15 | 2 | 17 | 12 | 7 | 3 | 8 | 13 | 11 | 1 |
| 1939 | 9 | 4 | 13 | 3 | 15 | 5 | 6 | 17 | 2 | 16 | 12 | 4 | 8 | 10 | 11 | 7 | 1 |
| 1946 | 15 | 8 | 6 | 5 | 10 | 6 | 3 | 11 | 2 | 16 | 13 | 4 | 11 | 17 | 14 | 8 | 1 |
| 1947 | 5 | 11 | 9 | 2 | 16 | 4 | 3 | 14 | 1 | 17 | 11 | 11 | 6 | 9 | 15 | 7 | 7 |
| 1948 | 6 | 13 | 1 | 8 | 9 | 15 | 5 | 11 | 3 | 17 | 14 | 12 | 2 | 16 | 7 | 10 | 4 |
| 1949 | 15 | 9 | 8 | 7 | 16 | 13 | 11 | 17 | 1 | 6 | 11 | 9 | 5 | 13 | 4 | 3 | 1 |
| 1950 | 5 | 17 | 11 | 7 | 12 | 9 | 1 | 16 | 14 | 10 | 15 | 7 | 1 | 13 | 4 | 6 | 3 |
| 1951 | 11 | 8 | 5 | 12 | 9 | 16 | 3 | 15 | 7 | 13 | 17 | 14 | 6 | 10 | 1 | 4 | 2 |
| 1952 | 4 | 10 | 7 | 9 | 12 | 15 | 3 | 6 | 5 | 8 | 16 | 17 | 1 | 13 | 10 | 14 | 2 |
| 1953 | 6 | 12 | 10 | 6 | 14 | 6 | 3 | 5 | 11 | 8 | 16 | 17 | 1 | 2 | 9 | 15 | 12 |
| 1954 | 3 | 15 | 4 | 13 | 14 | 11 | 10 | 16 | 7 | 7 | 5 | 17 | 1 | 9 | 6 | 11 | 2 |
| 1955 | 8 | 14 | 16 | 12 | 3 | 13 | 9 | 6 | 5 | 7 | 11 | 17 | 1 | 4 | 9 | 15 | 2 |
| 1956 | 12 | 11 | 13 | 3 | 6 | 16 | 2 | 17 | 5 | 4 | 8 | 15 | 1 | 9 | 14 | 9 | 7 |
| 1957 | 4 | 5 | 9 | 12 | 13 | 14 | 6 | 17 | 7 | 2 | 15 | 8 | 1 | 9 | 11 | 16 | 3 |
| 1958 | 5 | 6 | 15 | 14 | 2 | 8 | 7 | 12 | 10 | 4 | 17 | 3 | 1 | 13 | 16 | 9 | 11 |
| 1959 | 7 | 9 | 6 | 2 | 8 | 13 | 5 | 16 | 10 | 11 | 17 | 12 | 3 | 15 | 4 | 14 | 1 |
| 1960 | 5 | 6 | 11 | 8 | 12 | 10 | 2 | 17 | 9 | 16 | 14 | 7 | 4 | 3 | 15 | 13 | 1 |
| 1961 | 7 | 6 | 14 | 5 | 1 | 11 | 13 | 9 | 3 | 16 | 17 | 10 | 15 | 8 | 12 | 4 | 2 |
| 1962 | 7 | 9 | 14 | 4 | 10 | 11 | 16 | 17 | 13 | 8 | 15 | 6 | 5 | 2 | 3 | 2 | 1 |
| 1963 | 17 | 12 | 2 | 8 | 10 | 13 | 15 | 16 | 6 | 7 | 9 | 3 | 11 | 4 | 4 | 14 | 1 |
| 1964 | 12 | 10 | 11 | 17 | 12 | 7 | 14 | 6 | 3 | 15 | 8 | 4 | 9 | 9 | 2 | 1 | 5 |
| 1965 | 9 | 15 | 3 | 10 | 12 | 5 | 13 | 14 | 6 | 2 | 17 | 7 | 8 | 16 | 11 | 1 | 4 |
| 1966 | 9 | 16 | 14 | 15 | 11 | 4 | 12 | 8 | 12 | 5 | 17 | 3 | 7 | 10 | 6 | 2 | 1 |
| 1967 | 6 | 15 | 14 | 17 | 12 | 2 | 11 | 2 | 7 | 9 | 15 | 8 | 4 | 13 | 10 | 5 | 1 |
| 1968 | 8 | 14 | 3 | 16 | 5 | 2 | 6 | 9 | 10 | 4 | 12 | 15 | 17 | 17 | 7 | 11 | 1 |
| 1969 | 16 | 6 | 1 | 2 | 5 | 10 | 15 | 11 | 14 | 9 | 8 | 17 | 3 | 7 | 4 | 12 | 13 |
| 1970 | 7 | 12 | 2 | 17 | 10 | 1 | 3 | 15 | 16 | 14 | 11 | 13 | 5 | 9 | 7 | 6 | 4 |
| 1971 | 17 | 10 | 16 | 8 | 9 | 4 | 3 | 5 | 6 | 14 | 12 | 7 | 1 | 11 | 2 | 15 | 13 |
| 1972 | 17 | 5 | 13 | 3 | 9 | 2 | 15 | 6 | 8 | 4 | 14 | 11 | 12 | 16 | 1 | 7 | 10 |

| | Derbyshire | Essex | Glamorgan | Gloucestershire | Hampshire | Kent | Lancashire | Leicestershire | Middlesex | Northamptonshire | Nottinghamshire | Somerset | Surrey | Sussex | Warwickshire | Worcestershire | Yorkshire |
|---|---|---|---|---|---|---|---|---|---|---|---|---|---|---|---|---|---|
| 1973 | 16 | 8 | 11 | 5 | 1 | 4 | 12 | 9 | 13 | 3 | 17 | 10 | 2 | 15 | 7 | 6 | 14 |
| 1974 | 17 | 12 | 16 | 14 | 2 | 10 | 8 | 4 | 6 | 3 | 15 | 5 | 7 | 13 | 9 | 1 | 11 |
| 1975 | 15 | 7 | 9 | 16 | 3 | 5 | 4 | 1 | 11 | 8 | 13 | 12 | 6 | 17 | 14 | 10 | 2 |
| 1976 | 15 | 6 | 17 | 3 | 12 | 14 | 16 | 4 | 1 | 2 | 13 | 7 | 9 | 10 | 5 | 11 | 8 |
| 1977 | 7 | 6 | 14 | 3 | 11 | 1 | 16 | 5 | 1 | 9 | 17 | 4 | 14 | 8 | 10 | 13 | 12 |
| 1978 | 14 | 2 | 13 | 10 | 8 | 1 | 12 | 6 | 3 | 17 | 7 | 5 | 16 | 9 | 11 | 15 | 4 |
| 1979 | 16 | 1 | 17 | 10 | 12 | 5 | 13 | 6 | 14 | 11 | 9 | 8 | 3 | 4 | 15 | 2 | 7 |
| 1980 | 9 | 8 | 13 | 7 | 17 | 16 | 15 | 10 | 1 | 12 | 3 | 5 | 2 | 4 | 14 | 11 | 6 |
| 1981 | 12 | 5 | 14 | 13 | 7 | 9 | 16 | 8 | 4 | 15 | 1 | 3 | 6 | 2 | 17 | 11 | 10 |
| 1982 | 11 | 7 | 16 | 15 | 3 | 13 | 12 | 2 | 1 | 9 | 4 | 6 | 5 | 8 | 17 | 14 | 10 |
| 1983 | 9 | 1 | 15 | 12 | 3 | 7 | 12 | 4 | 2 | 6 | 14 | 10 | 8 | 11 | 5 | 16 | 17 |
| 1984 | 12 | 1 | 13 | 17 | 15 | 5 | 16 | 4 | 3 | 11 | 2 | 7 | 8 | 6 | 9 | 10 | 14 |
| 1985 | 13 | 4 | 12 | 3 | 2 | 9 | 14 | 16 | 1 | 10 | 8 | 17 | 6 | 7 | 15 | 5 | 11 |
| 1986 | 11 | 1 | 17 | 2 | 6 | 8 | 15 | 7 | 12 | 9 | 4 | 16 | 3 | 14 | 12 | 5 | 10 |
| 1987 | 6 | 12 | 13 | 10 | 5 | 14 | 2 | 3 | 16 | 7 | 1 | 11 | 4 | 17 | 15 | 9 | 8 |
| 1988 | 14 | 3 | 17 | 10 | 15 | 2 | 9 | 8 | 7 | 12 | 5 | 11 | 4 | 16 | 6 | 1 | 13 |
| 1989 | 6 | 2 | 17 | 9 | 6 | 15 | 4 | 13 | 3 | 5 | 11 | 14 | 12 | 10 | 8 | 1 | 16 |
| 1990 | 12 | 2 | 8 | 13 | 3 | 16 | 6 | 7 | 1 | 11 | 13 | 15 | 9 | 17 | 5 | 4 | 10 |
| 1991 | 3 | 1 | 12 | 13 | 9 | 8 | 16 | 15 | 10 | 14 | 4 | 17 | 5 | 11 | 2 | 6 | 14 |

*Note:* From 1969 onwards, positions have been given in accordance with the Championship regulations which state that "Should *any* sides in the table be equal on points the side with most wins will have priority".

## COUNTY CAPS AWARDED IN 1991

| | |
|---|---|
| Derbyshire ........ | M. Azharuddin. |
| Essex ............. | Salim Malik, P. M. Such. |
| Glamorgan ........ | M. Frost. |
| Hampshire ........ | J. R. Ayling, A. N. Aymes. |
| Leicestershire ...... | D. J. Millns. |
| Northamptonshire .. | J. G. Thomas. |
| Somerset .......... | R. P. Lefebvre. |
| Surrey ............ | G. P. Thorpe. |
| Sussex ............ | I. D. K. Salisbury, M. P. Speight. |
| Warwickshire ...... | D. P. Ostler. |
| Worcestershire ..... | T. M. Moody. |
| Yorkshire ......... | D. Byas. |

*No caps were awarded by Gloucestershire, Kent, Lancashire, Middlesex or Nottinghamshire.*

# DERBYSHIRE

*President:* Rear Admiral Sir David Haslam
*Chairman:* C. N. Middleton
*Chairman, Cricket Committee:* B. Holling
*Chief Executive:* R. J. Lark
　　County Ground, Nottingham Road, Derby
　　DE2 6DA (Telephone: 0332-383211)
*Captain:* K. J. Barnett
*Coach:* P. E. Russell

Derbyshire went into the last month of the season with a chance of winning the Britannic Assurance Championship, a new experience for Kim Barnett, who equalled G. R. Jackson's record of nine years as the county's captain. Their challenge foundered against the superior all-round quality of Essex at Chelmsford, but Derbyshire's season ended with a rosy glow as they recovered to beat Yorkshire at Chesterfield. Queen's Park was a picture, and an unlikely victory enabled Derbyshire to finish third, a feat they had not achieved since 1954 when G. L. Willatt, currently the club's vice-chairman, was captain. Nine Championship victories was Derbyshire's best tally since they won ten (out of 28) in 1961; and for the first time since 1971, five batsmen scored 1,000 runs.

The Championship success, coupled with the emergence of Dominic Cork and Richard Sladdin to strengthen the bowling, gave further substance to Barnett's belief that Derbyshire could be a significant force in the 1990s. They surprised themselves by doing well in the longer game, but after the exhilaration of the Refuge Assurance League title the previous year, their one-day season was soon in tatters. It finally collapsed at Bishop's Stortford, where Derbyshire became the first team, beating Oxfordshire by a short head, to be eliminated from the NatWest Bank Trophy in a bowling contest. After winning their first two Sunday League games, they lost the next eight to make retention of the trophy impossible.

Mohammad Azharuddin, engaged in place of Ian Bishop, gave enormous pleasure and became only the second batsman to score 2,000 runs in a season for Derbyshire. The weather was against him in the early weeks, and was still bleak when he scored his first Championship hundred at Gloucester. There were times when he threw away good positions, at Northampton and Lord's for example, but his range of strokes, his elegance, and his charm, on and off the field, made his one-year stay a summer to treasure. It is hard to imagine anybody batting better than Azharuddin did in his 212 at Leicester, and it was unfortunate that illness kept him out of the last match, when he had a chance to attack two Derbyshire records. He was 149 short of D. B. Carr's 2,165 runs in 1959 and one away from P. N. Kirsten's eight hundreds in 1982.

Although he missed only one Championship match, Barnett was frequently hampered by back trouble. In cold or damp weather, this reduced him to a trundle in the field. And it became worse if he bowled, which he did to great effect by taking six Glamorgan wickets for 28 at

Chesterfield, in the first of four consecutive Championship victories. Barnett was maturing as a captain, and he illustrated his determination in a match-saving 217 against Nottinghamshire at Derby. In that match he and Peter Bowler shared their fourteenth first-class century opening partnership, a county record, and one which emphasised Bowler's contribution since he was engaged from Leicestershire in 1988. He has been a model of steadiness. However, John Morris, so elated when he was chosen to tour Australia, returned aware that he was further than ever from the England team, and it showed in an uneven season. Tim O'Gorman, his law studies completed, edged past 1,000 runs in his first full season, and Chris Adams might have done the same had Steve Goldsmith not forced his way into the team with some important innings.

O'Gorman and Adams were two of the five young players Barnett asserted he would not exchange for any in the country. Karl Krikken, for his batting as well as his wicket-keeping, was another; he looked unorthodox but handled cleanly and moved quickly. His predecessor, Bernie Maher, continued to do an excellent job with the Second Eleven. The two others cherished by Barnett were the bowlers, Cork and Sladdin.

Devon Malcolm was troubled by a shoulder injury, after returning from Australia mentally and physically exhausted. He played in only half the Championship games and was dropped by England after two Tests. Derbyshire's chairman, Chris Middleton, was fined £750 by the Test and County Cricket Board for criticism of Micky Stewart's private, but well-publicised, coaching session with Malcolm, and as a result he resigned from the TCCB discipline committee. While Middleton's comments were immoderate, two important issues were raised. It seemed unreasonable to fine a man who devoted time and effort to cricket but derived no income from it; and the TCCB was unduly, if perhaps understandably, sensitive to comments about the stewardship of Stewart and Ted Dexter.

With Malcolm having to be nursed, and most of the seam bowlers over 30, Cork's development was as timely as it was welcome. He celebrated his twentieth birthday in spectacular style, taking eight for 53 against Essex at Derby. Though conditions were helpful, his performance that day earned the approval of Neil Foster, the Essex acting-captain, and Derbyshire's players and opponents alike were impressed by Cork's ability and attitude. He was an important member of the England Young Cricketers team in 1990, when he made two first-class appearances, and in 1991 he burst into county cricket with 57 wickets, a batting average of more than 20 and some high-class fielding. He was named Young Player of the Year by the Cricketers' Association and picked, along with Malcolm, for the England A tour.

Barnett's policy of keeping his bowlers fresh by resting them helped to preserve Ole Mortensen's position as the most respected of his type in the Championship. Allan Warner's effectiveness increased with experience, and Barnett believed that Simon Base was developing in the same way. The appearance of Sladdin, a left-arm spinner not only capable of bowling long spells but delighted to do so, gave an extra dimension to Derbyshire's attack, and more than compensated for Ian Folley's inability to recapture his best Lancashire form. Sladdin sent down 68 overs in Essex's innings at Chelmsford and showed an excellent temperament. – Gerald Mortimer.

368

DERBYSHIRE 1991

[*Bill Smith*

*Back row*: R. W. Sladdin, F. A. Griffith, E. McCray, D. G. Cork, T. J. G. O'Gorman, C. J. Adams, I. Folley, A. M. Brown. *Middle row*: S. W. Tacey (*scorer*), K. M. Krikken, S. C. Goldsmith, M. Jean-Jacques, S. J. Base, P. D. Bowler, B. Roberts, A. E. Warner. *Front row*: O. H. Mortensen, J. E. Morris, R. J. Lark (*chief executive*), K. J. Barnett (*captain*), P. E. Russell (*coach*), D. E. Malcolm, B. J. M. Maher. *Inset*: M. Azharuddin.

## DERBYSHIRE RESULTS

*All first-class matches – Played 25: Won 9, Lost 5, Drawn 11.*

*County Championship matches – Played 22: Won 9, Lost 5, Drawn 8.*

*Bonus points – Batting 46, Bowling 68.*

*Competition placings – Britannic Assurance County Championship, 3rd;*
*NatWest Bank Trophy, 1st round; Benson and Hedges Cup, 3rd in Group A;*
*Refuge Assurance League, 15th equal.*

## BRITANNIC ASSURANCE CHAMPIONSHIP AVERAGES

### BATTING

| | Birthplace | M | I | NO | R | HI | Avge |
|---|---|---|---|---|---|---|---|
| ‡M. Azharuddin . . . . . | Hyderabad, India | 20 | 35 | 3 | 1,773 | 212 | 55.40 |
| ‡J. E. Morris . . . . . . . | Crewe | 20 | 35 | 2 | 1,267 | 122* | 38.39 |
| ‡K. J. Barnett . . . . . . . | Stoke-on-Trent | 21 | 36 | 1 | 1,318 | 217 | 37.65 |
| ‡P. D. Bowler . . . . . . | Plymouth | 22 | 40 | 3 | 1,270 | 104* | 34.32 |
| T. J. G. O'Gorman . . | Woking | 22 | 39 | 4 | 1,060 | 148 | 30.28 |
| C. J. Adams . . . . . . . | Whitwell | 12 | 19 | 2 | 436 | 112 | 25.64 |
| K. M. Krikken . . . . . | Bolton | 22 | 35 | 8 | 677 | 65 | 25.07 |
| S. C. Goldsmith . . . . | Ashford, Kent | 15 | 25 | 3 | 483 | 73* | 21.95 |
| D. G. Cork . . . . . . . | Newcastle-under-Lyme | 16 | 25 | 7 | 395 | 44 | 21.94 |
| ‡A. E. Warner . . . . . | Birmingham | 14 | 20 | 3 | 289 | 46 | 17.00 |
| R. W. Sladdin . . . . . | Halifax | 7 | 8 | 3 | 68 | 18 | 13.60 |
| ‡S. J. Base . . . . . . . . | Maidstone | 13 | 16 | 3 | 136 | 36 | 10.46 |
| ‡D. E. Malcolm . . . . . | Kingston, Jamaica | 11 | 14 | 2 | 84 | 18 | 7.00 |
| I. Folley . . . . . . . . . | Burnley | 3 | 4 | 1 | 20 | 17* | 6.66 |
| M. Jean-Jacques . . . . | Soufrière, Dominica | 4 | 6 | 1 | 33 | 28 | 6.60 |
| ‡O. H. Mortensen . . . | Vejle, Denmark | 18 | 16 | 9 | 32 | 8 | 4.57 |

Also batted: F. A. Griffith (*Whipps Cross, London*) (1 match) 1; E. McCray (*Altrincham*)
(1 match) 37.

*\* Signifies not out.      ‡ Denotes county cap.*

The following played a total of fourteen three-figure innings for Derbyshire in County
Championship matches – M. Azharuddin 6, K. J. Barnett 2, P. D. Bowler 2, T. J. G.
O'Gorman 2, C. J. Adams 1, J. E. Morris 1.

### BOWLING

| | O | M | R | W | BB | 5W/i | Avge |
|---|---|---|---|---|---|---|---|
| O. H. Mortensen . . . . . . | 535.1 | 138 | 1,339 | 58 | 6-101 | 2 | 23.08 |
| K. J. Barnett . . . . . . . . . | 162.1 | 33 | 393 | 17 | 6-28 | 1 | 23.11 |
| D. G. Cork . . . . . . . . . | 457.3 | 76 | 1,350 | 55 | 8-53 | 1 | 24.54 |
| D. E. Malcolm . . . . . . . . | 346.2 | 51 | 1,271 | 39 | 5-45 | 1 | 32.58 |
| R. W. Sladdin . . . . . . . | 315.5 | 76 | 881 | 26 | 5-186 | 1 | 33.88 |
| S. C. Goldsmith . . . . . . . | 174 | 28 | 576 | 17 | 3-42 | 0 | 33.88 |
| A. E. Warner . . . . . . . . | 390.4 | 92 | 1,066 | 31 | 4-42 | 0 | 34.38 |
| S. J. Base . . . . . . . . . . . | 386 | 58 | 1,248 | 31 | 4-34 | 0 | 40.25 |

Also bowled: C. J. Adams 12.4–1–48–5; M. Azharuddin 63.4–9–211–3; P. D. Bowler
104–18–412–9; I. Folley 106–12–350–2; F. A. Griffith 15–2–58–2; M. Jean-Jacques
113.4–18–437–9; J. E. Morris 2–0–30–0; E. McCray 25–10–53–0; T. J. G. O'Gorman
15–0–59–1.

**Wicket-keeper:** K. M. Krikken 55 ct, 3 st.

**Leading Fielders:** M. Azharuddin 23, K. J. Barnett 23, T. J. G. O'Gorman 21, C. J. Adams 15,
P. D. Bowler 15.

## DERBYSHIRE v NORTHAMPTONSHIRE

At Derby, April 27, 29, 30, May 1. Drawn. Derbyshire 1 pt, Northamptonshire 4 pts. Toss: Derbyshire. Northamptonshire's Fordham, reaching three figures from 151 balls, became the first player to score a century in the 1991 Britannic Assurance Championship, and in all he batted for 225 minutes, faced 209 balls and hit nineteen fours. He shared a second-wicket stand of 160 with Bailey but, considering that Northamptonshire had such a prosperous first day, the bat was beaten remarkably often. No play was possible on the three remaining days because of the poor weather.

*Close of play:* First day, Northamptonshire 347-4 (A. J. Lamb 74\*, R. G. Williams 11\*); Second day, No play; Third day, No play.

### Northamptonshire

| | | | |
|---|---|---|---|
| A. Fordham c Krikken b Mortensen . . .131 | | R. G. Williams not out . . . . . . . . . . . . . | 11 |
| N. A. Felton c Bowler b Base . . . . . . . . | 9 | | |
| R. J. Bailey lbw b Azharuddin . . . . . . . | 83 | L-b 4, w 3, n-b 16 . . . . . . . . . | 23 |
| \*A. J. Lamb not out . . . . . . . . . . . . . . . | 74 | | |
| D. J. Capel lbw b Jean-Jacques . . . . . . . | 16 | 1/47 2/207 3/274 4/314 | (4 wkts) 347 |

N. G. B. Cook, E. A. E. Baptiste, †D. Ripley, J. G. Thomas and J. P. Taylor did not bat.

Bonus points – Northamptonshire 4, Derbyshire 1 (Score at 100 overs: 311-3).

Bowling: Mortensen 22-6-62-1; Jean-Jacques 28-5-81-1; Base 29-5-88-1; Warner 22-5-60-0; Azharuddin 14-1-52-1.

### Derbyshire

\*K. J. Barnett, P. D. Bowler, J. E. Morris, M. Azharuddin, M. Jean-Jacques, T. J. G. O'Gorman, C. J. Adams, †K. M. Krikken, A. E. Warner, O. H. Mortensen and S. J. Base.

Umpires: D. J. Constant and K. E. Palmer.

At Cambridge, May 9, 10, 11. DERBYSHIRE drew with CAMBRIDGE UNIVERSITY.

At Manchester, May 16, 17, 18, 20. DERBYSHIRE drew with LANCASHIRE.

## DERBYSHIRE v SOMERSET

At Derby, May 22, 23, 24. Drawn. Derbyshire 4 pts, Somerset 7 pts. Toss: Somerset. Hayhurst and Harden scored centuries and shared a fourth-wicket partnership of 187 against an unusually full ration of slow bowling on the opening day. Derbyshire sent down 120 overs and still had twenty minutes of batting after Tavaré's declaration. Hayhurst reached his century from 242 balls with his thirteenth four, and Harden, who went on to the best score of his career, reached his from 175 balls, including nine fours. Derbyshire's impetuous batting resulted in their following on next day, but Bowler and Morris suggested better things from the second innings with an opening stand of 110. This was followed by more purpose further down the order, and to win Somerset eventually had to score 157 from 22 overs. While they hit out bravely in poor light, Mortensen bowled so splendidly that until Roebuck came in at the fall of the seventh wicket, there was an outside chance of a Derbyshire victory.

*Close of play:* First day, Derbyshire 21-0 (P. D. Bowler 11\*, J. E. Morris 8\*); Second day, Derbyshire 127-2 (J. E. Morris 57\*, I. Folley 0\*).

## Somerset

| | | | | | | |
|---|---|---|---|---|---|---|
| S. J. Cook c Krikken b Mortensen | 10 | – b Mortensen | 7 |
| P. M. Roebuck c Krikken b Warner | 0 | – (9) not out | 8 |
| A. N. Hayhurst b Azharuddin | 116 | – (2) b Mortensen | 12 |
| *C. J. Tavaré c Krikken b Jean-Jacques | 13 | – (3) c Krikken b Mortensen | 26 |
| R. J. Harden c O'Gorman b Folley | 134 | – (4) c Adams b Jean-Jacques | 23 |
| †N. D. Burns lbw b Barnett | 0 | – (8) not out | 7 |
| K. H. MacLeay not out | 26 | – (6) b Mortensen | 11 |
| G. D. Rose run out | 37 | – (5) run out | 32 |
| R. P. Lefebvre not out | 12 | – (7) c Azharuddin b Jean-Jacques | 8 |
| B 4, l-b 6, n-b 15 | 25 | L-b 10 | 10 |

1/8 2/20 3/65 4/252 5/253    (7 wkts dec.) 373    1/12 2/27 3/68 4/73    (7 wkts) 144
6/306 7/358      5/107 6/127 7/127

D. A. Graveney and N. A. Mallender did not bat.

Bonus points – Somerset 3, Derbyshire 2 (Score at 100 overs: 285-5).

Bowling: *First Innings*—Mortensen 21–8–36–1; Warner 20–0–68–1; Jean-Jacques 18–1–62–1; Folley 26–2–107–1; Barnett 22–2–54–1; Azharuddin 13–2–36–1. *Second Innings*—Mortensen 11–0–47–4; Jean-Jacques 10.5–0–87–2.

## Derbyshire

| | | | | | | |
|---|---|---|---|---|---|---|
| P. D. Bowler lbw b MacLeay | 13 | – c Harden b Graveney | 59 |
| J. E. Morris c Tavaré b MacLeay | 43 | – c Lefebvre b Graveney | 91 |
| T. J. G. O'Gorman c Tavaré b Lefebvre | 23 | – lbw b Roebuck | 7 |
| M. Azharuddin b Lefebvre | 10 | – (5) b Roebuck | 37 |
| C. J. Adams c Lefebvre b Rose | 15 | – (6) c Burns b Graveney | 37 |
| *K. J. Barnett c Rose b Lefebvre | 1 | – (7) c Lefebvre b Rose | 21 |
| †K. M. Krikken not out | 46 | – (8) not out | 30 |
| A. E. Warner lbw b Mallender | 31 | – (10) b Roebuck | 1 |
| I. Folley lbw b Mallender | 0 | – (4) c Tavaré b Mallender | 3 |
| M. Jean-Jacques b MacLeay | 28 | – (9) c Tavaré b Graveney | 2 |
| O. H. Mortensen c Burns b Mallender | 1 | – c Harden b Graveney | 1 |
| L-b 5, n-b 6 | 11 | B 11, l-b 3, n-b 4 | 18 |

1/62 2/65 3/90 4/105 5/107      222    1/110 2/123 3/131 4/198 5/210    307
6/113 7/156 8/156 9/221      6/249 7/285 8/293 9/294

Bonus points – Derbyshire 2, Somerset 4.

Bowling: *First Innings*—Mallender 17.3–3–52–3; Rose 11–1–43–1; MacLeay 12–2–40–3; Lefebvre 15–5–51–3; Graveney 11–3–31–0. *Second Innings*—Mallender 16–4–37–1; MacLeay 16–4–60–0; Lefebvre 14–3–42–0; Graveney 44.3–21–68–5; Rose 17–6–44–1; Hayhurst 4–2–5–0; Roebuck 27–12–37–3.

Umpires: B. Dudleston and D. R. Shepherd.

At Canterbury, May 25, 27, 28. DERBYSHIRE lost to KENT by 208 runs.

At Northampton, May 31, June 1, 3. DERBYSHIRE drew with NORTHAMPTONSHIRE.

### DERBYSHIRE v GLAMORGAN

At Chesterfield, June 7, 8, 10. Derbyshire won by 108 runs. Derbyshire 23 pts, Glamorgan 5 pts. Toss: Derbyshire. Derbyshire had it in their minds that the Queen's Park pitch would not last, although it did, and set about some wayward bowling from Foster and Frost in a hectic first innings, which began with 80 coming from twelve overs. Metson's seven catches equalled E. W. Jones's Glamorgan record – set against Cambridge University in 1970, and including a stumping – for dismissals in an innings. Mortensen and Warner were particularly effective on the second day as Derbyshire gained a lead of 75, which Barnett and Morris set about improving before rain stopped play. On the third morning Morris completed a superb century from 83 balls to equal Botham's span for Worcestershire against the West Indians as the fastest of the season to date. In all, Morris hit seven sixes and nine fours and enabled Barnett to set Glamorgan a target of 301 in a minimum of 83 overs. Butcher and Morris shared a stand of 105, but then ten wickets fell while 87 were added as Barnett, despite a painful back injury, bowled out Glamorgan with high-class leg-spin for the best figures of his career. His six for 28 included a spell of five for 9 in 65 balls, and Derbyshire recorded their first Championship win of the season with almost seven overs to spare.

*Close of play:* First day, Glamorgan 55-0 (A. R. Butcher 23*, H. Morris 30*); Second day, Derbyshire 97-1 (K. J. Barnett 49*, J. E. Morris 25*).

## Derbyshire

| | | | | |
|---|---|---|---|---|
| *K. J. Barnett c Metson b Barwick | 38 | – c Morris b Barwick | 63 |
| P. D. Bowler c Metson b Frost | 38 | – c and b Foster | 15 |
| J. E. Morris c Metson b Barwick | 0 | – not out | 122 |
| M. Azharuddin c Metson b Frost | 43 | – c Foster b Smith | 9 |
| T. J. G. O'Gorman c Metson b Frost | 15 | – (6) not out | 2 |
| C. J. Adams c Smith b Barwick | 13 | | |
| †K. M. Krikken c Metson b Foster | 40 | | |
| D. G. Cork not out | 34 | | |
| A. E. Warner c Morris b Foster | 19 | – (5) run out | 3 |
| S. J. Base c Metson b Warner | 0 | | |
| O. H. Mortensen c Morris b Frost | 7 | | |
| L-b 1, n-b 11 | 12 | L-b 6, n-b 5 | 11 |

1/80 2/80 3/80 4/96 5/123          259     1/49 2/148     (4 wkts dec.) 225
6/180 7/210 8/231 9/241                     3/193 4/199

Bonus points – Derbyshire 3, Glamorgan 4.

Bowling: *First Innings*—Frost 16–2–84–4; Foster 15–0–102–2; Barwick 22–5–61–4; Dale 3–0–11–0. *Second Innings*—Frost 11–1–72–0; Barwick 13–0–53–1; Dale 6–2–30–0; Foster 6–0–27–1; Smith 3–0–37–1.

## Glamorgan

| | | | | |
|---|---|---|---|---|
| *A. R. Butcher c Cork b Base | 32 | – c Bowler b Cork | 71 |
| H. Morris c Base b Warner | 50 | – b Warner | 51 |
| M. P. Maynard c Krikken b Warner | 8 | – (4) lbw b Cork | 8 |
| R. J. Shastri c Krikken b Warner | 2 | – (8) c Morris b Barnett | 1 |
| I. Smith c Krikken b Base | 4 | – b Barnett | 7 |
| A. Dale c Krikken b Warner | 12 | – (3) c O'Gorman b Barnett | 13 |
| R. D. B. Croft c O'Gorman b Mortensen | 0 | – (6) c Krikken b Cork | 5 |
| †C. P. Metson c Adams b Cork | 34 | – (7) b Barnett | 7 |
| S. R. Barwick b Mortensen | 13 | – c Adams b Barnett | 0 |
| D. J. Foster c Bowler b Mortensen | 0 | – not out | 13 |
| M. Frost not out | 8 | – c Morris b Barnett | 0 |
| L-b 9, w 1, n-b 11 | 21 | B 6, w 3, n-b 7 | 16 |

1/75 2/85 3/95 4/105 5/127          184     1/105 2/133 3/145 4/158 5/161     192
6/127 7/127 8/172 9/172                     6/169 7/177 8/178 9/183

Bonus points – Glamorgan 1, Derbyshire 4.

Bowling: *First Innings*—Mortensen 21–7–40–3; Cork 11.3–1–37–1; Base 15–0–56–2; Warner 24–10–42–4. *Second Innings*—Cork 24–7–59–3; Mortensen 4–1–9–0; Base 16–2–54–0; Warner 13–3–36–1; Barnett 19.1–7–28–6.

Umpires: J. H. Hampshire and B. J. Meyer.

At Derby, June 12, 13, 14. DERBYSHIRE drew with WEST INDIANS (See West Indian tour section).

At Gloucester, June 18, 19, 20. DERBYSHIRE beat GLOUCESTERSHIRE by six wickets.

## DERBYSHIRE v SURREY

At Derby, June 21, 22, 24. Derbyshire won by three wickets. Derbyshire 20 pts, Surrey 1 pt. Toss: Derbyshire. After the first 140 minutes had been lost, Mortensen bowled extremely well and received good support from Base against irresolute Surrey batting to put Derbyshire in the driving seat. However, only eleven balls were sent down on the second day, so Morris, captaining Derbyshire for the first time, and Greig reached an agreement. Yet even this appeared to have been ruined when rain cost a further 26 overs after lunch on the third day, leaving Derbyshire to chase 242 in what became 42 overs. They required 153 from the last twenty overs, and 99 from the final ten, but Azharuddin and Goldsmith, in his first Championship match of the season, batted magnificently. Medlycott came in for heavy punishment, but it was a legitimate gamble for Greig to keep the spinner on. Azharuddin scored 63 from 47 balls, hitting two sixes and nine fours, while Goldsmith's unbeaten 73 came from 40 balls, including a six and ten fours, and Derbyshire won with four balls to spare.

*Close of play:* First day, Derbyshire 71-2 (P. D. Bowler 22*, M. Azharuddin 25*); Second day, Derbyshire 80-3 (P. D. Bowler 30*, C. J. Adams 0*).

## Surrey

| | | | |
|---|---|---|---|
| D. J. Bicknell c O'Gorman b Mortensen | 9 | – lbw b Goldsmith | 5 |
| R. I. Alikhan c Cork b Base | 3 | – lbw b Adams | 15 |
| A. J. Stewart lbw b Mortensen | 5 | – retired hurt | 10 |
| D. M. Ward run out | 26 | – not out | 94 |
| G. P. Thorpe c O'Gorman b Base | 3 | – c Bowler b Griffith | 1 |
| *I. A. Greig lbw b Cork | 5 | – c Goldsmith b O'Gorman | 27 |
| K. T. Medlycott c Bowler b Griffith | 18 | | |
| †N. F. Sargeant c Bowler b Base | 4 | | |
| M. P. Bicknell not out | 34 | – (7) not out | 24 |
| Waqar Younis c Morris b Mortensen | 17 | | |
| A. J. Murphy b Mortensen | 7 | | |
| L-b 3, w 1, n-b 2 | 6 | B 2, l-b 6 | 8 |
| | **137** | (4 wkts dec.) | **184** |

1/6 2/11 3/22 4/32 5/53 6/68 7/75 8/82 9/115    137    1/10 2/44 3/51 4/117    (4 wkts dec.) 184

Bonus points – Derbyshire 4.

*In the second innings A. J. Stewart retired hurt at 27.*

Bowling: *First Innings*—Mortensen 13.5-3-43-4; Base 15-0-60-3; Cork 9-2-15-1; Griffith 7-0-16-1. *Second Innings*—Goldsmith 11-3-41-1; Adams 6-0-19-1; Bowler 9-2-27-0; Griffith 8-2-42-1; Morris 2-0-30-0; O'Gorman 3-0-17-1.

## Derbyshire

| | | | |
|---|---|---|---|
| P. D. Bowler not out | 30 | – lbw b M. P. Bicknell | 27 |
| *J. E. Morris lbw b Waqar Younis | 14 | – b Waqar Younis | 12 |
| T. J. G. O'Gorman b Murphy | 2 | – b M. P. Bicknell | 38 |
| M. Azharuddin b Waqar Younis | 26 | – lbw b Waqar Younis | 63 |
| C. J. Adams not out | 0 | – lbw b Medlycott | 11 |
| S. C. Goldsmith (did not bat) | | – not out | 73 |
| †K. M. Krikken (did not bat) | | – lbw b Medlycott | 13 |
| F. A. Griffith (did not bat) | | – b Waqar Younis | 1 |
| D. G. Cork (did not bat) | | – not out | 0 |
| B 4, l-b 4 | 8 | B 1, l-b 3 | 4 |
| | (3 wkts dec.) **80** | (7 wkts) | **242** |

1/23 2/26 3/73    (3 wkts dec.) 80    1/26 2/57 3/92 4/115 5/171 6/234 7/241    (7 wkts) 242

S. J. Base and O. H. Mortensen did not bat.

Bonus point – Surrey 1.

Bowling: *First Innings*—Waqar Younis 7–2–11–2; M. P. Bicknell 8–0–32–0; Murphy 8.5–1–29–1. *Second Innings*—M. P. Bicknell 11–3–35–2; Waqar Younis 13.2–1–66–3; Murphy 6–0–35–0; Medlycott 11–0–102–2.

Umpires: D. J. Constant and R. Julian.

At Birmingham, June 28, 29, July 1. DERBYSHIRE beat WARWICKSHIRE by 173 runs.

## DERBYSHIRE v SUSSEX

At Derby, July 5, 6, 8. Drawn. Derbyshire 6 pts, Sussex 7 pts. Toss: Sussex. Cork, whose arrival in the Derbyshire team had coincided with four consecutive Championship wins for the first time since 1977, twice improved his best figures, with four wickets in each innings. He helped his county work through Sussex, solid after an explosive start by Smith (39 balls), but Base, having trouble with his front foot, managed a twelve-ball over and conceded ten no-balls in the first four overs. Steamy conditions, after a violent thunderstorm had delayed the start of the second day, were much to the liking of Wells, who returned his best figures of seven for 42 in Derbyshire's reply. Morris batted fluently, but Wells took the last five wickets for 17 in 32 balls. After further interruption because of rain, Parker offered Derbyshire a steep target, 243 in what would have been 44 overs. Azharuddin became the first Derbyshire player to reach 1,000 runs for the season, but Sussex were the likelier winners when Salisbury took three wickets in six overs. However, the young leg-spinner was then withdrawn from the attack, and after Pigott had focused the umpires' attention on the poor light with a chest-high full toss to Cork, the match came to an early end.

*Close of play:* First day, Derbyshire 31-1 (P. D. Bowler 7*, T. J. G. O'Gorman 16*); Second day, Sussex 39-1 (N. J. Lenham 13*, I. D. K. Salisbury 5*).

## Sussex

| | | | |
|---|---|---|---|
| N. J. Lenham c Cork b Base | 48 | – c Krikken b Cork | 13 |
| D. M. Smith c Krikken b Malcolm | 43 | – lbw b Malcolm | 16 |
| J. W. Hall lbw b Cork | 2 | – (4) b Cork | 8 |
| *P. W. G. Parker c Base b Warner | 7 | – (5) c Azharuddin b Cork | 20 |
| M. P. Speight c Barnett b Malcolm | 60 | – (6) c O'Gorman b Cork | 56 |
| C. M. Wells b Cork | 38 | – (7) not out | 14 |
| A. I. C. Dodemaide c Barnett b Malcolm | 2 | – (8) not out | 9 |
| †P. Moores c Azharuddin b Goldsmith | 19 | | |
| A. C. S. Pigott not out | 29 | | |
| I. D. K. Salisbury c Krikken b Cork | 9 | – (3) b Goldsmith | 34 |
| A. N. Jones c Warner b Cork | 6 | | |
| B 1, l-b 9, w 3, n-b 13 | 26 | L-b 5, w 2, n-b 6 | 13 |

1/69 2/76 3/93 4/157 5/195       289     1/30 2/42 3/57     (6 wkts dec.) 183
6/197 7/242 8/254 9/279                       4/88 5/136 6/166

Bonus points – Sussex 3, Derbyshire 4.

Bowling: *First Innings*—Malcolm 20–3–79–3; Base 17–1–58–1; Cork 20.1–2–66–4; Warner 16–5–32–1; Barnett 2–0–9–0; Goldsmith 15–6–35–1. *Second Innings*—Malcolm 10–3–29–1; Base 15–2–34–0; Barnett 1–0–3–0; Cork 11–2–25–4; Goldsmith 7–0–41–1; Bowler 4–0–46–0.

## Derbyshire

| | | | |
|---|---|---|---|
| *K. J. Barnett c Moores b Pigott | 8 | – c Moores b Jones | 3 |
| P. D. Bowler c Lenham b Wells | 38 | – lbw b Dodemaide | 7 |
| T. J. G. O'Gorman b Wells | 32 | – (5) c Moores b Salisbury | 19 |
| M. Azharuddin c Moores b Jones | 1 | – c Parker b Salisbury | 59 |
| J. E. Morris c Salisbury b Wells | 76 | – (3) c Pigott b Jones | 14 |
| S. C. Goldsmith lbw b Jones | 35 | – lbw b Salisbury | 6 |
| †K. M. Krikken c and b Wells | 18 | – not out | 27 |
| D. G. Cork lbw b Wells | 13 | – not out | 6 |
| A. E. Warner c Hall b Wells | 6 | | |
| S. J. Base not out | 0 | | |
| D. E. Malcolm c Salisbury b Wells | 0 | | |
| W 1, n-b 2 | 3 | L-b 1, w 1, n-b 1 | 3 |
| | **230** | **(6 wkts)** | **144** |

1/10 2/79 3/80 4/84 5/171    1/8 2/20 3/28
6/202 7/220 8/226 9/230    4/86 5/98 6/116

Bonus points – Derbyshire 2, Sussex 4.

*Bowling: First Innings*—Jones 15–2–67–2; Dodemaide 16–3–59–0; Pigott 21–2–62–1; Wells 20.4–8–42–7. *Second Innings*—Jones 8–1–36–2; Dodemaide 6–0–21–1; Pigott 7.5–0–36–0; Wells 8–2–33–0; Salisbury 6–1–17–3.

Umpires: J. W. Holder and B. Leadbeater.

At Scarborough, July 16, 17, 18. DERBYSHIRE drew with YORKSHIRE.

At Kidderminster, July 19, 20, 22. DERBYSHIRE drew with WORCESTERSHIRE.

## DERBYSHIRE v HAMPSHIRE

At Chesterfield, July 23, 24, 25. Hampshire won by 94 runs. Hampshire 19 pts, Derbyshire 4 pts. Toss: Hampshire. Hampshire batted over two days, both severely disrupted by rain, and their first-innings 258 was the lowest completed innings in first-class cricket to contain two centuries. This distinction was previously held by Lancashire, with 271 (W. Place 102, B. J. Howard 106) against Northamptonshire at Old Trafford in 1947. After eighteen overs in the 90s, Smith reached his century from 206 balls, with fifteen fours, while James completed his with a six and also hit thirteen fours in facing 228 balls. They shared a second-wicket partnership of 202, then nine wickets fell while 39 runs were added. In order to give themselves a chance of victory, Derbyshire forfeited their first innings, and following a further delay on the third morning, they set out to attain a target of 288 in a minimum of 90 overs on a poor pitch. Their efforts were hampered when Barnett was forced to retire with a groin injury, and although he tried to return, he was unable to continue. Turner bowled particularly well to help Hampshire to their first Championship victory of the season.

*Close of play:* First day, Hampshire 151-1 (C. L. Smith 92*, K. D. James 48*); Second day, Hampshire 29-2 (C. L. Smith 16*, D. I. Gower 0*).

## Hampshire

| | | | |
|---|---|---|---|
| T. C. Middleton run out | 3 | – c Krikken b Goldsmith | 11 |
| C. L. Smith c Krikken b Malcolm | 114 | – not out | 16 |
| K. D. James lbw b Mortensen | 101 | – c Barnett b Sladdin | 1 |
| D. I. Gower hit wkt b Malcolm | 3 | – not out | 0 |
| *M. C. J. Nicholas c Azharuddin b Mortensen | 2 | | |
| J. R. Ayling run out | 1 | | |
| †A. N. Aymes c Cork b Mortensen | 5 | | |
| R. J. Maru b Cork | 4 | | |
| I. J. Turner not out | 6 | | |
| C. A. Connor c Bowler b Cork | 0 | | |
| K. J. Shine c Azharuddin b Mortensen | 14 | | |
| L-b 5, n-b 14 | 19 | N-b 1 | 1 |
| | **258** | **(2 wkts dec.)** | **29** |

1/17 2/219 3/235 4/235 5/238    1/28 2/29
6/239 7/245 8/256 9/257

Bonus points – Hampshire 3, Derbyshire 4.

Bowling: *First Innings*—Malcolm 22–2–84–2; Mortensen 28.2–6–50–4; Cork 26–6–53–2; Goldsmith 6–1–22–0; Sladdin 13–2–44–0. *Second Innings*—Sladdin 8–3–18–1; Goldsmith 7.4–0–11–1.

## Derbyshire

*Derbyshire forfeited their first innings.*

| | | | |
|---|---|---|---|
| *K. J. Barnett retired hurt | 74 | D. E. Malcolm c Nicholas b Turner | 5 |
| P. D. Bowler c Aymes b Connor | 0 | R. W. Sladdin lbw b James | 4 |
| J. E. Morris b Maru | 35 | O. H. Mortensen not out | 0 |
| M. Azharuddin c Middleton b Maru | 0 | | |
| T. J. G. O'Gorman c Aymes b Turner | 42 | B 7, l-b 4, w 2, n-b 9 | 22 |
| S. C. Goldsmith c sub b Turner | 10 | | |
| †K. M. Krikken c Middleton b Turner | 1 | 1/16  2/88  3/88  4/177  5/179 | 193 |
| D. G. Cork b James | 0 | 6/181  7/182  8/193  9/193 | |

*K. J. Barnett, when 74, retired hurt at 160, resumed at 181 and retired again at 182-6.*

Bowling: Shine 4–0–34–0; Connor 7–1–22–1; Ayling 10–1–38–0; Maru 22–10–48–2; Turner 16–10–28–4; James 6–1–12–2.

Umpires: D. O. Oslear and K. E. Palmer.

At Derby, August 2, 3, 5. DERBYSHIRE drew with SRI LANKANS (See Sri Lankan tour section).

## DERBYSHIRE v ESSEX

At Derby, August 6, 7, 8. Derbyshire won by 199 runs. Derbyshire 21 pts, Essex 4 pts. Toss: Essex. Derbyshire's first Championship victory over Essex since 1967 owed much to brilliant bowling by Cork, who on his twentieth birthday took eight for 53 on the second morning. Not since W. H. Copson's eight for 11 against Warwickshire at Derby in 1937 had a Derbyshire bowler taken eight wickets in a first session. After a delayed start to the match, Derbyshire went for their strokes on a pitch which helped the seam bowlers, and their innings would have been shorter had Essex not dropped six catches. Cork, splendidly supported by Mortensen, gave Derbyshire a lead of 56, which Barnett and Bowler consolidated with their eleventh century opening partnership, equalling the county record held by two pairs: D. Smith and A. E. Alderman, and A. Hamer and C. Lee. Derbyshire's domination continued into the final day, when Essex were set 375 in a minimum of 95 overs. Base captured the important wickets of Salim Malik and Stephenson, Malcolm bowled one of his fastest spells of the season, and Derbyshire won before tea with more than 50 overs to spare.

*Close of play:* First day, Essex 30-0 (A. C. H. Seymour 20*, J. P. Stephenson 8*); Second day, Derbyshire 301-5 (S. C. Goldsmith 52*, C. J. Adams 14*).

## Derbyshire

| | | | |
|---|---|---|---|
| *K. J. Barnett b Foster | 16 | b Stephenson | 91 |
| P. D. Bowler c Knight b Andrew | 6 | c Salim Malik b Andrew | 56 |
| J. E. Morris c Garnham b Topley | 35 | c Salim Malik b Andrew | 36 |
| T. J. G. O'Gorman b Topley | 25 | c Prichard b Stephenson | 28 |
| S. C. Goldsmith c Garnham b Andrew | 3 | not out | 60 |
| C. J. Adams c and b Topley | 37 | (7) c Garnham b Andrew | 17 |
| †K. M. Krikken b Foster | 9 | (8) run out | 3 |
| D. G. Cork c Garnham b Topley | 3 | | |
| S. J. Base c Childs b Topley | 11 | (6) c Hussain b Stephenson | 3 |
| D. E. Malcolm c Seymour b Foster | 10 | | |
| O. H. Mortensen not out | 2 | | |
| L-b 11, w 2, n-b 10 | 23 | B 4, l-b 3, w 4, n-b 13 | 24 |

| | | | |
|---|---|---|---|
| 1/18  2/35  3/81  4/95  5/112 | 180 | 1/145  2/193  3/203  (7 wkts dec.) | 318 |
| 6/150  7/150  8/154  9/173 | | 4/262  5/275  6/308 | |
| | | 7/318 | |

Bonus points – Derbyshire 1, Essex 4.

Bowling: *First Innings*—Foster 14–2–57–3; Andrew 14–4–33–2; Topley 17.2–1–79–5. *Second Innings*—Foster 9–1–41–0; Andrew 17.3–2–71–3; Topley 14–0–65–0; Childs 17–6–48–0; Stephenson 23–2–86–3.

## Essex

| | | | |
|---|---|---|---|
| A. C. H. Seymour c Barnett b Cork | 22 | – c Barnett b Cork | 0 |
| J. P. Stephenson lbw b Cork | 14 | – c Krikken b Base | 35 |
| P. J. Prichard c Adams b Mortensen | 20 | – c O'Gorman b Mortensen | 11 |
| Salim Malik c Krikken b Cork | 15 | – c O'Gorman b Base | 27 |
| N. Hussain lbw b Mortensen | 0 | – c Goldsmith b Base | 12 |
| N. V. Knight b Cork | 4 | – c Krikken b Malcolm | 24 |
| †M. A. Garnham c Krikken b Cork | 15 | – b Malcolm | 0 |
| *N. A. Foster c Base b Cork | 19 | – (9) c Krikken b Malcolm | 24 |
| T. D. Topley c Krikken b Cork | 11 | – (8) lbw b Cork | 9 |
| S. J. W. Andrew c Base b Cork | 0 | – not out | 2 |
| J. H. Childs not out | 1 | – b Malcolm | 19 |
| N-b 3 | 3 | L-b 2, w 2, n-b 8 | 12 |

1/37 2/46 3/74 4/74 5/75     124    1/3 2/16 3/54 4/91 5/94   175
6/79 7/107 8/117 9/117            6/103 7/119 8/154 9/154

Bonus points – Derbyshire 4.

Bowling: *First Innings*—Malcolm 4–0–18–0; Mortensen 20–3–53–2; Cork 16.1–2–53–8. *Second Innings*—Mortensen 8–2–30–1; Cork 8–2–25–2; Base 14–3–34–3; Malcolm 14.2–1–84–4.

Umpires: R. A. White and P. B. Wight.

At Lord's, August 9, 10, 12. DERBYSHIRE lost to MIDDLESEX by 2 runs.

## DERBYSHIRE v LANCASHIRE

At Derby, August 16, 17, 19. Derbyshire won by five wickets. Derbyshire 23 pts, Lancashire 5 pts. Toss: Lancashire. On a slow pitch, Lancashire made faltering progress, but Lloyd, dropped in the slips when he had made 6, steered them to a reasonable total, hitting nine boundaries in his 85. Bowler and Azharuddin shared an unbroken partnership of 240 on the second day, with India's captain dominant. Bowler's first century of the summer came in 305 minutes, while Azharuddin's unbeaten 160 was made from 185 balls, with 22 boundaries. There was some tedious manipulation on the third morning, although Adams suggested he may become a more regular bowler, and eventually Fairbrother set Derbyshire to score 291 in what would have been 67 overs. Barnett and Bowler, both missed in the slips early on, gave them a good start with their twelfth century opening stand together, during which Bowler passed 1,000 runs for the season. Azharuddin, hitting nine fours in 52 balls, batted superbly until he inexplicably ran himself out, whereupon Adams and Krikken added 52 in five overs to win the game with two overs in hand, and move Derbyshire into third place.

*Close of play*: First day, Derbyshire 16-1 (P. D. Bowler 4*, S. J. Base 6*); Second day, Lancashire 81-2 (N. J. Speak 26*, N. H. Fairbrother 4*).

## Lancashire

| | | | |
|---|---|---|---|
| G. D. Mendis c Azharuddin b Mortensen | 65 | – b Cork | 12 |
| N. J. Speak lbw b Base | 32 | – c and b Sladdin | 39 |
| M. A. Atherton c O'Gorman b Sladdin | 14 | – b Base | 32 |
| *N. H. Fairbrother c Krikken b Mortensen | 33 | – c Base b Adams | 72 |
| G. D. Lloyd st Krikken b Sladdin | 85 | – lbw b Adams | 4 |
| M. Watkinson c Barnett b Goldsmith | 25 | – lbw b Adams | 3 |
| P. A. J. DeFreitas st Krikken b Goldsmith | 35 | – c Sladdin b Bowler | 17 |
| †W. K. Hegg c Azharuddin b Sladdin | 30 | – not out | 37 |
| G. Yates not out | 4 | – b Adams | 7 |
| P. J. Martin (did not bat) | | – not out | 6 |
| B 4, l-b 6, n-b 14 | 24 | B 2, l-b 11, n-b 1 | 14 |

1/64 2/118 3/158 4/163 5/217      (8 wkts dec.) 347      1/12 2/73 3/115      (8 wkts dec.) 243
6/286 7/336 8/347                                       4/126 5/144 6/180
                                                        7/219 8/227

P. J. W. Allott did not bat.

Bonus points – Lancashire 4, Derbyshire 3.

Bowling: *First Innings*—Mortensen 18–4–48–2; Cork 20–2–59–0; Base 20–2–97–1; Sladdin 27.3–6–93–3; Goldsmith 13–2–40–2. *Second Innings*—Cork 6–1–31–1; Mortensen 12–2–35–0; Base 10–2–24–1; Sladdin 15–7–23–1; Adams 6.4–1–29–4; O'Gorman 12–0–42–0; Bowler 7–1–46–1.

## Derbyshire

| | | | |
|---|---|---|---|
| *K. J. Barnett b DeFreitas | 5 | – c Yates b Allott | 52 |
| P. D. Bowler not out | 104 | – lbw b Allott | 62 |
| S. J. Base c Hegg b Allott | 22 | | |
| T. J. G. O'Gorman b DeFreitas | 2 | – (3) c Hegg b Martin | 24 |
| M. Azharuddin not out | 160 | – (4) run out | 67 |
| S. C. Goldsmith (did not bat) | | – (5) c Allott b Martin | 20 |
| C. J. Adams (did not bat) | | – (6) not out | 29 |
| †K. M. Krikken (did not bat) | | – (7) not out | 17 |
| L-b 3, w 1, n-b 3 | 7 | B 10, l-b 8, w 2 | 20 |

1/6 2/51 3/60              (3 wkts dec.) 300      1/110 2/118 3/177      (5 wkts) 291
                                                 4/237 5/239

D. G. Cork, O. H. Mortensen and R. W. Sladdin did not bat.

Bonus points – Derbyshire 4, Lancashire 1.

Bowling: *First Innings*—DeFreitas 22–8–62–2; Martin 22.3–5–78–0; Allott 15–3–39–1; Watkinson 11–1–46–0; Yates 16–2–72–0. *Second Innings*—DeFreitas 17–3–58–0; Martin 17–2–102–2; Allott 18–6–39–2; Watkinson 5–1–21–0; Yates 8–0–53–0.

Umpires: D. J. Constant and J. H. Harris.

## DERBYSHIRE v LEICESTERSHIRE

At Derby, August 20, 21. Leicestershire won by an innings and 131 runs. Leicestershire 23 pts, Derbyshire 3 pts. Toss: Leicestershire. Leicestershire, and Millns in particular, took control on a green pitch, totally different from the one Derbyshire had prepared for the previous match, although it did nothing extravagant. Millns, bowling fast to an excellent length, made marvellously effective use of the conditions to take nine for 37, the best return in English cricket since D. L. Underwood's nine for 32 for Kent against Surrey at The Oval in 1978. It was Leicestershire's best in the Championship since F. Geary's ten for 18 against Glamorgan in 1929, and their best in first-class matches since J. Cotton took nine for 29 against the Indians at Leicester in 1967. Derbyshire's bowlers found no similar response, and Whitticase fell only 7 runs short of his second century as Leicestershire built a lead of 275. Lacking the resolve to battle it out, Derbyshire were beaten in two days. Millns finished with match figures of twelve for 91, Wilkinson returned the best of his career in the second innings, and Whitticase capped a successful match by collecting eight catches.

*Close of play*: First day, Leicestershire 160-5 (B. F. Smith 13*, P. Whitticase 6*).

## Derbyshire

| | | | |
|---|---|---|---|
| *K. J. Barnett b Mills | 20 | c Whitticase b Wilkinson | 26 |
| P. D. Bowler b Mills | 0 | c Whitticase b Maguire | 5 |
| T. J. G. O'Gorman c Potter b Mills | 6 | c Whitticase b Mills | 13 |
| C. J. Adams c Whitticase b Wilkinson | 44 | lbw b Mills | 0 |
| M. Azharuddin c Whitticase b Mills | 3 | lbw b Maguire | 26 |
| S. C. Goldsmith lbw b Mills | 0 | run out | 20 |
| †K. M. Krikken b Mills | 0 | c Boon b Wilkinson | 24 |
| D. G. Cork c Whitticase b Mills | 25 | b Wilkinson | 8 |
| A. E. Warner b Mills | 10 | c Whitticase b Wilkinson | 8 |
| D. E. Malcolm not out | 5 | c Whitticase b Mills | 4 |
| O. H. Mortensen b Mills | 0 | not out | 0 |
| L-b 3, n-b 1 | 4 | L-b 1, w 3, n-b 6 | 10 |

1/1 2/24 3/39 4/43 5/45           117    1/19 2/45 3/45 4/47 5/91    144
6/57 7/99 8/109 9/113                    6/100 7/119 8/131 9/136

Bonus points – Leicestershire 4.

Bowling: *First Innings*—Mills 18.3-4-37-9; Maguire 13-2-37-0; Wilkinson 9-1-34-1; Potter 1-0-1-0; Benson 1-0-5-0. *Second Innings*—Mills 13-0-54-3; Maguire 12-3-30-2; Wilkinson 14-0-59-4.

## Leicestershire

| | | | |
|---|---|---|---|
| T. J. Boon c Azharuddin b Warner | 35 | J. D. R. Benson c Adams b Cork | 19 |
| *N. E. Briers b Malcolm | 0 | D. J. Mills c Krikken b Goldsmith | 17 |
| P. N. Hepworth b Cork | 18 | C. W. Wilkinson not out | 31 |
| J. J. Whitaker c O'Gorman | | J. N. Maguire c O'Gorman b Barnett | 26 |
|                b Mortensen | 47 | B 5, l-b 17, w 3, n-b 5 | 30 |
| L. Potter b Malcolm | 25 | | |
| B. F. Smith c Adams b Cork | 51 | 1/3 2/49 3/67 4/125 5/151 | 392 |
| †P. Whitticase b Warner | 93 | 6/234 7/284 8/314 9/341 | |

Bonus points – Leicestershire 3, Derbyshire 3 (Score at 100 overs: 291-7).

Bowling: Malcolm 32-5-117-2; Mortensen 28-8-59-1; Cork 25-8-62-3; Warner 29-3-99-2; Goldsmith 9-1-31-1; Barnett 1.4-0-2-1.

Umpires: D. J. Constant and J. H. Harris.

At Nottingham, August 23, 24, 26. DERBYSHIRE beat NOTTINGHAMSHIRE by four wickets.

At Leicester, August 28, 29, 30, 31. DERBYSHIRE beat LEICESTERSHIRE by 195 runs.

At Chelmsford, September 3, 4, 5, 6. DERBYSHIRE lost to ESSEX by an innings and 72 runs.

## DERBYSHIRE v NOTTINGHAMSHIRE

At Derby, September 10, 11, 12, 13. Drawn. Derbyshire 3 pts, Nottinghamshire 8 pts. Toss: Derbyshire. A green pitch, which prompted both captains to play without a recognised spin bowler, proved to have no life, and Pollard and Robinson shared a partnership of 265 in 73 overs. Pollard reached his century from 239 balls, hitting sixteen fours, while Robinson's came from 220 balls and included twelve fours. Mortensen withdrew from the attack with an infection after the first morning, and the 65 extras were the most conceded by Derbyshire. Base was no-balled seventeen times in thirteen overs. Inappropriate strokes hurried Derbyshire into trouble, and at one stage they lost five wickets for 10 runs in 26 balls. Robinson enforced the follow-on, but Barnett batted throughout the third day and into the fourth, for 7 hours 36 minutes, to save the game and keep Nottinghamshire pinned back in fifth place. He shared a century opening partnership with Bowler, their fourteenth together, and added 174 with Azharuddin for the third wicket, in which time Azharuddin became only the second player, after D. B. Carr in 1959, to score 2,000 runs in a season for Derbyshire. Barnett faced 399 balls and hit 35 fours in his 217, the second double-century of his career, and O'Gorman completed his second Championship century of the summer, from 215 balls with seventeen fours, before Barnett declared. Derbyshire's 572 for seven was their highest score against Nottinghamshire, and the aggregate of 777 was the highest in their history.

*Close of play*: First day, Nottinghamshire 376-5 (M. A. Crawley 4*, M. Saxelby 7*); Second day, Derbyshire 205; Third day, Derbyshire 354-2 (K. J. Barnett 178*, M. Azharuddin 87*).

## Nottinghamshire

| | | | |
|---|---|---|---|
| B. C. Broad c Azharuddin b Cork | 14 | – c Krikken b Base | 4 |
| P. R. Pollard c Barnett b Bowler | 123 | – not out | 35 |
| *R. T. Robinson b Base | 145 | – not out | 31 |
| P. Johnson c Barnett b Bowler | 0 | | |
| D. W. Randall c Krikken b Cork | 27 | | |
| M. A. Crawley lbw b Base | 4 | | |
| M. Saxelby lbw b Base | 13 | | |
| F. D. Stephenson c Base b Cork | 45 | | |
| †B. N. French c O'Gorman b Base | 3 | | |
| V. J. P. Broadley lbw b Cork | 6 | | |
| R. A. Pick not out | 3 | | |
| B 8, l-b 32, w 1, n-b 24 | 65 | L-b 1, n-b 6 | 7 |
| | **448** | 1/5     (1 wkt) | **77** |

1/36 2/301 3/301 4/350 5/364
6/379 7/410 8/424 9/435

Bonus points – Nottinghamshire 4, Derbyshire 1 (Score at 100 overs: 316-3).

Bowling: *First Innings*—Mortensen 11–6–21–0; Base 32–2–128–4; Warner 18–9–23–0; Cork 34–9–91–4; Goldsmith 15–2–39–0; Bowler 21–5–58–2; Azharuddin 13–2–48–0. *Second Innings*—Mortensen 6–2–14–0; Base 10–1–35–1; Cork 3–0–12–0; Warner 3–2–4–0; Azharuddin 5–1–11–0.

## Derbyshire

| | | | |
|---|---|---|---|
| *K. J. Barnett c Broad b Stephenson | 19 | – c Randall b Crawley | 217 |
| P. D. Bowler c French b Saxelby | 65 | – c French b Stephenson | 45 |
| J. E. Morris c Randall b Crawley | 39 | – run out | 28 |
| M. Azharuddin c French b Saxelby | 9 | – c Crawley b Broadley | 87 |
| T. J. G. O'Gorman not out | 34 | – not out | 108 |
| S. C. Goldsmith lbw b Saxelby | 0 | – b Pollard | 6 |
| †K. M. Krikken c French b Pick | 3 | – c Crawley b French | 1 |
| D. G. Cork c Randall b Pick | 0 | – c Pollard b Randall | 44 |
| A. E. Warner lbw b Crawley | 7 | – not out | 1 |
| S. J. Base c and b Crawley | 1 | | |
| O. H. Mortensen b Stephenson | 8 | | |
| B 8, l-b 2, n-b 10 | 20 | B 4, l-b 11, w 2, n-b 11 | 28 |
| | **205** | 1/130 2/180 3/354  (7 wkts dec.) | **572** |

1/41 2/117 3/144 4/151 5/151                    4/437 5/452
6/154 7/154 8/199 9/193                            6/463 7/549

Bonus points – Derbyshire 2, Nottinghamshire 4.

Bowling: *First Innings*—Pick 15–3–53–2; Stephenson 19.5–1–61–2; Broadley 6–1–19–0; Saxelby 13–1–41–3; Crawley 13–7–21–3. *Second Innings*—Stephenson 34–7–112–1; Pick 19–2–69–0; Broadley 26–5–92–1; Saxelby 25–4–110–0; Crawley 35–15–63–1; Pollard 20–8–46–1; French 13–4–37–1; Randall 4–0–19–1; Robinson 3–0–9–0.

Umpires: J. W. Holder and D. O. Oslear.

## DERBYSHIRE v YORKSHIRE

At Chesterfield, September 17, 18, 19, 20. Derbyshire won by 40 runs. Derbyshire 18 pts, Yorkshire 7 pts. Toss: Derbyshire. After being outplayed for two days, Derbyshire came back to record the victory they needed to finish third in the Championship, their best position since 1954. Jarvis, who had morning figures of 9–3–8–3 in his first competitive match since May, and Carrick were assisted by erratic Derbyshire batting. But Yorkshire did not make the most of their opportunity, despite Kellett's maiden Championship century, which he reached from 224 balls with ten fours. They lost their last five wickets while adding just 27, and when Derbyshire batted again Adams was dropped three times. Adams completed his century from 226 balls, with his thirteenth four, and he, Bowler and O'Gorman put Derbyshire back in the game. Yorkshire needed 191 to win, but a fine spell by Base, who took three for 1 in 28 balls, and excellent fielding reduced them to 36 for six on the final morning. Although Gough and Hartley batted with sensible aggression, they were unable to effect a recovery.

*Close of play:* First day, Yorkshire 91-2 (M. D. Moxon 36*, S. A. Kellett 10*); Second day, Derbyshire 123-3 (C. J. Adams 50*, R. W. Sladdin 0*); Third day, Yorkshire 8-0 (M. D. Moxon 6*, A. A. Metcalfe 2*).

### Derbyshire

| | | | | |
|---|---|---|---:|---:|
| *K. J. Barnett c Blakey b Jarvis | | 2 | – c Byas b Jarvis | 12 |
| P. D. Bowler c Byas b Hartley | | 0 | – c Moxon b Carrick | 54 |
| J. E. Morris c Batty b Gough | | 13 | – c Moxon b Jarvis | 0 |
| C. J. Adams b Jarvis | | 40 | – st Blakey b Carrick | 112 |
| T. J. G. O'Gorman c Blakey b Carrick | | 0 | – (6) c Hartley b Batty | 74 |
| S. C. Goldsmith lbw b Carrick | | 1 | – (7) b Jarvis | 30 |
| †K. M. Krikken c Blakey b Jarvis | | 0 | – (8) c Robinson b Batty | 0 |
| D. G. Cork not out | | 40 | – (9) b Batty | 9 |
| A. E. Warner c Kellett b Hartley | | 25 | – (10) not out | 33 |
| S. J. Base c Blakey b Jarvis | | 7 | – (11) c Kellett b Carrick | 4 |
| R. W. Sladdin lbw b Carrick | | 7 | – (5) lbw b Batty | 12 |
| L-b 4, w 1, n-b 4 | | 9 | B 12, l-b 15, n-b 7 | 34 |
| | | **144** | | **374** |

1/2 2/2 3/42 4/55 5/61        1/32 2/32 3/123 4/165 5/246
6/61 7/61 8/113 9/131        6/315 7/321 8/325 9/359

*Bonus points – Yorkshire 4.*

Bowling: *First Innings*—Jarvis 16–4–28–4; Hartley 14–3–45–2; Gough 9–2–31–1; Carrick 22.2–11–36–3. *Second Innings*—Jarvis 29–8–71–3; Hartley 19–3–57–0; Gough 12–1–53–0; Carrick 45.3–22–75–3; Batty 37–11–91–4.

### Yorkshire

| | | | | |
|---|---|---|---:|---:|
| *M. D. Moxon c and b Warner | | 50 | – c Krikken b Base | 13 |
| A. A. Metcalfe c Bowler b Cork | | 28 | – c Krikken b Warner | 4 |
| D. Byas lbw b Cork | | 6 | – b Base | 0 |
| S. A. Kellett not out | | 125 | – c Bowler b Sladdin | 26 |
| P. E. Robinson c Krikken b Warner | | 12 | – c Bowler b Base | 0 |
| †R. J. Blakey c Base b Cork | | 7 | – run out | 2 |
| P. Carrick run out | | 50 | – c Barnett b Base | 1 |
| D. Gough c Barnett b Bowler | | 0 | – c Base b Sladdin | 27 |
| P. J. Hartley c Sladdin b Bowler | | 5 | – not out | 34 |
| P. W. Jarvis b Bowler | | 2 | – b Warner | 22 |
| J. D. Batty b Warner | | 12 | – c Adams b Sladdin | 14 |
| L-b 9, n-b 22 | | 31 | B 2, l-b 4, n-b 1 | 7 |
| | | **328** | | **150** |

1/53 2/70 3/138 4/164 5/199        1/11 2/12 3/19 4/19 5/30
6/301 7/301 8/309 9/315        6/36 7/75 8/84 9/131

*Bonus points – Yorkshire 3, Derbyshire 2 (Score at 100 overs: 271-5).*

Bowling: *First Innings*—Cork 25–2–83–3; Base 22–2–65–0; Warner 27.1–8–52–3; Sladdin 22.4–53–0; Goldsmith 8–2–25–0; Bowler 14–1–41–3. *Second Innings*—Cork 13–1–31–0; Base 17–6–34–4; Warner 17–4–52–2; Sladdin 13–4–27–3.

Umpires: K. J. Lyons and D. O. Oslear.

# DURHAM

*Patrons:* Sir Donald Bradman and A. W. Austin
*President:* I. D. Caller
*Chairman:* J. D. Robson
*Director of Cricket:* G. Cook
*Chief Executive:* M. E. Gear
  McEwan's Indoor Centre, Mercantile Road,
  Rainton Bridge, Houghton-le-Spring
  DH4 5PH (Telephone: 091-512 0178)
*Captain:* D. A. Graveney

In 1992, 71 years after Glamorgan's introduction, Durham join the Britannic Assurance Championship and become the eighteenth first-class county. Their promotion ends a long association with the Minor Counties Championship, which they left as joint record-holders, with nine titles, and so it is appropriate to look back before assessing the exciting challenge that lies ahead.

Although games were played earlier by a team calling themselves Durham County Gentlemen, the first known organisation of a Durham County side was on January 24, 1874, and it was the demise of this club which led to the formation of the present Durham County Cricket Club on May 23, 1882. At a meeting in the Three Tuns Hotel, Durham City, called by the officers and committee of the long-established South Shields club, with J. M. Horsley of Darlington in the chair, it was agreed that "a county club for Durham be formed", and Sir Hedworth Williamson of Whitburn was invited to become the president. T. E. Main of North Durham CC was appointed honorary secretary and treasurer.

However, if it had not been for the efforts of R. H. (Harry) Mallett, a prominent MCC member, Durham may not have survived. Fixtures were difficult to arrange in those early days, and twice, in 1896 and 1898, Durham were forced to withdraw from the Second-Class Counties Competition and revert to playing friendly matches. This despite the fact that in 1895, the inaugural season of the new competition, Durham had shared first place with Norfolk in the closest of contests.

After that initial triumph in 1895, Durham won the title again in 1900 and 1901, giving them three wins in their first five seasons in the competition. But while they sought to establish a strong team, built mainly around league professionals, it was not until 1926 and 1930 that further titles were won. These represented a considerable achievement, for the Depression had hit Durham hard, and pit closures affected the leagues badly as players left the area in search of work. Prior to the First World War, Durham's best bowler was Alf Morris, from West Hartlepool, a medium-fast swing bowler who took 651 county wickets in 94 games from 1905 to 1914. Edgar "Tegger" Elliot, an England rugby international from Sunderland, was the top batsman with 5,384 runs.

Despite having many fine players, Durham went 46 years without further success. But for a decade from 1976 they dominated minor counties cricket, winning the championship in 1976, 1980, 1981 and

1984, and finishing runners-up in 1977, 1978 and 1979. During this period they played 65 championship matches without defeat, beating the previous record, 44, set by Surrey Second Eleven in the 1950s, and their record looks likely to stand for years. Leading players of this time were Neil Riddell, who scored 8,694 runs in 218 appearances – both county records – and all-rounder Steve Greensword, who scored 7,802 runs and took 427 wickets before moving to Northumberland in 1991.

In 1973, Durham made history by becoming the first minor county to beat a first-class county in the Gillette Cup when they beat Yorkshire at Harrogate, and in 1985 they became the first to defeat first-class opposition twice when they beat Derbyshire in the NatWest Trophy. Last summer, though losing to Glamorgan at Darlington, they became the first "minnow" to score 300 runs in an innings in this competition.

No fewer than 120 players – at the last count – born in County Durham have played first-class cricket. Among them are Test players such as A. E. Stoddart, Cec Parkin, David Townsend, Dick Spooner, Jim McConnon, Colin Milburn, Bob Willis and Peter Willey, as well as Roger Blunt of New Zealand and James Middleton, who appeared for South Africa after being bought out of the British army by the Cape Town club. Admittance to the first-class ranks now makes it possible for Durham-born cricketers to appear for England while wearing the colours of their own county.

Durham formally applied to the TCCB for first-class status on November 4, 1990, and at the Board's Winter Meeting their thoroughly professional application was accepted for the 1992 season. Subsequently, at their Annual General Meeting in March 1991, the old Durham club was dissolved and a limited company established, with six directors, since increased to eight. Remarkably, until then the county club had had only three secretaries since 1882, with Jack Iley, who died in June last year, having held the post from 1946 until March 1991.

Durham's plans for the future are ambitious. A splendid new stadium is to be built at Chester-le-Street's Riverside Park, and not only is it hoped that this will be ready for the 1995 season but also that it will eventually be up to Test match standard. In the meantime, Durham will use six grounds: the Racecourse, at Durham University; Feethams in Darlington; Grangefield Road, Stockton-on-Tees; Park Drive, Hartlepool; Eastwood Gardens, home of Gateshead Fell CC; and Ropery Lane, Chester-le-Street. Durham's director of cricket, Geoff Cook, has assembled a squad of 22 full-time professionals with a mixture of experience and untried youth; David Graveney leads established names such as Ian Botham, Australia's Dean Jones, Wayne Larkins, Paul Parker, Phil Bainbridge and Simon Hughes, along with several former minor counties players and six teenagers who eagerly await their chance. Whatever the season brings, the Dunelmians will hope to do better than Glamorgan, who, after winning their first County Championship match, finished bottom of the table in 1921.

Durham's squad is: D. A. Graveney (captain), P. Bainbridge, P. J. Berry, D. A. Blenkiron, I. T. Botham, M. P. Briers, G. K. Brown, S. J. E. Brown, J. A. Daley, A. R. Fothergill, J. D. Glendenen, P. W. Henderson, S. P. Hughes, S. Hutton, D. M. Jones, W. Larkins, S. M. McEwan, P. W. G. Parker, C. W. Scott, I. Smith, J. Wighan and J. Wood. – *Brian Hunt.*

384

# ESSEX

*President:* T. N. Pearce
*Chairman:* D. J. Insole
*Chairman, Cricket Committee:* G. J. Saville
*Secretary/General Manager:* P. J. Edwards
County Ground, New Writtle Street,
Chelmsford CM2 0PG
(Telephone: 0245-252420)
*Captain:* G. A. Gooch

Six victories in their last seven matches carried Essex to their fifth County Championship title in thirteen years, a success which spoke as much for the depth and quality of the playing staff as for their staying power. Graham Gooch and Derek Pringle missed almost half the season on duty with England, while Mark Ilott, the left-arm seamer of whom much was expected, failed to appear in the Championship because of a stress fracture of the back. With the young middle-order batsman, Nadeem Shahid, also absent for the final two months after breaking his finger, Essex had plenty of obstacles to overcome. However, the Championship triumph contrasted sharply with their fate in other competitions. They suffered a humiliating home defeat by nine wickets at the hands of Worcestershire in the semi-final of the Benson and Hedges Cup, were knocked out of the NatWest Bank Trophy by Surrey, after surrendering a winning position, and could manage only sixth place in the Refuge Assurance League. In this, though, they were dealt a severe blow by the weather, which prevented a positive result in four of their first nine games.

The surge started in early August at Trent Bridge, when the county were 51 points behind the Championship leaders, Warwickshire, albeit with two games in hand. With Gooch and Pringle missing, they were in danger of following on at 112 for seven. But not only did they avoid that threat, they fought back magnificently to beat Nottinghamshire by three wickets. That was the first of their six victories on the home straight, with one stutter at Colchester when they lost to Yorkshire by 3 runs.

Neil Foster was undoubtedly the key figure. He himself admitted to "dodgy knees", and for the last three seasons he had not been alone in wondering whether he could stand up to an arduous campaign. Yet still he managed to conquer the pain and destroy opponents with fast bowling of the highest class. His consistency left Essex members relieved that he was banned from Test cricket for his venture to South Africa early in 1990. Foster's reward was a haul of 102 first-class wickets; it was the second time he had reached three figures. On seven occasions he claimed five or more in an innings, including his best ever figures, eight for 99 against Lancashire, and fittingly he played the major role in the title-clinching victory over Middlesex, taking ten for 122 in the match. During a season in which he underlined his usefulness with the bat in a career-best unbeaten 107 against Sussex, Foster also proved an astute captain in Gooch's absence, with thoughtful field placings and challenging declarations.

Salim Malik was another outstanding success. Signed as a replacement for Mark Waugh, the Pakistani confirmed that he was one of the game's most gifted batsmen, with nearly 2,000 runs for a first-class average of just over 73. Exquisite timing, rather than explosive power, was the secret of his bountiful harvest, in which he reaped six hundreds, five over 150. Gooch scored 1,911 runs for Essex and England with his usual ease and authority, emphasising why many critics regarded him as the world's foremost contemporary batsman. His top score of 259 was the highest innings of the season, and a record for Essex against Middlesex. John Stephenson, Paul Prichard and Nasser Hussain all topped 1,000 without any difficulty, and Hussain rewrote county history in two record stands. The first, with Salim Malik, produced 314 for the fourth wicket against Surrey at The Oval in July, and two months later Hussain added 316 with wicket-keeper Mike Garnham for the fifth wicket against Leicestershire. At Leicester Garnham scored his second successive Championship hundred, one week after making his maiden one, against Derbyshire.

Pringle continued to confound and infuriate. Hardly a year had passed without his international career being written off, but the all-rounder announced yet another comeback with his praiseworthy contributions in the early Tests, before flu ruled him out at The Oval. Yet a mere four fifties and 47 wickets hardly did justice to his talent. Don Topley, the medium-pace bowler whose future with Essex seemed uncertain twelve months earlier, swept doubts aside with 55 first-class victims, while the veteran left-arm spinner, John Childs, who was 40 in August, brought all his guile and experience to bear, particularly in the second half of the summer when conditions best suited his craft. Off-spinner Peter Such, though he made less impact, was rewarded for his encouraging progress with a county cap, and Steve Andrew picked up useful wickets, albeit sometimes expensively.

Of the youngsters, 21-year-old Nicholas Knight impressed most, when a combination of injuries and Test calls summoned him to the first team. A tall, elegant left-hander, he seized his chance to score 388 runs in the Championship at an average of 48.50, with an unbeaten, match-winning hundred against Lancashire at Old Trafford the highlight. Though he had much to learn, and many more innings to play to be judged properly, first impressions suggested the technique and temperament to carve out a successful career. Ironically, Knight's progress contributed to Adam Seymour's move to Worcestershire. Another left-hander, Seymour underlined his potential with a maiden hundred against Glamorgan, opening in place of Gooch, but Essex, though prepared to re-engage him, agreed his interests might be better served elsewhere.

The county also released an old stalwart in David East. Capped in 1982, the dapper wicket-keeper was a key player in the glory years of the 1980s, until a serious finger fracture early in 1989 cost him his place. Always popular and widely respected, he claimed 533 victims, scored 4,553 runs, including four hundreds, and stole the headlines in 1985 when he took eight catches in an innings against Somerset at Taunton, equalling the world record. Another retirement was that of physiotherapist Ray Cole, who had served Essex nobly for fifteen years. – Nigel Fuller.

ESSEX 1991

*Back row*: M. A. Garnham, N. Hussain, K. A. Butler, J. J. B. Lewis, R. J. Rollins, A. C. Richards, C. A. Miller, N. Shahid, G. W. Ecclestone, A. C. H. Seymour. *Middle row*: Salim Malik, J. P. Stephenson, P. M. Such, M. C. Ilott, D. J. P. Boden, S. J. W. Andrew, A. G. J. Fraser, W. G. Lovell, N. V. Knight, R. Cole (*physiotherapist*). *Front row*: K. W. R. Fletcher, J. H. Childs, P. J. Prichard, D. R. Pringle, G. A. Gooch (*captain*), D. E. East, N. A. Foster, T. D. Topley.

[*Bill Smith*]

## ESSEX RESULTS

*All first-class matches – Played 25: Won 12, Lost 5, Drawn 8.*

*County Championship matches – Played 22: Won 11, Lost 5, Drawn 6.*

*Bonus points – Batting 69, Bowling 67.*

*Competition placings – Britannic Assurance County Championship, winners;*
*NatWest Bank Trophy, q-f; Benson and Hedges Cup, s-f;*
*Refuge Assurance League, 6th.*

# BRITANNIC ASSURANCE CHAMPIONSHIP AVERAGES

## BATTING

| | Birthplace | M | I | NO | R | HI | Avge |
|---|---|---|---|---|---|---|---|
| ‡Salim Malik | Lahore, Pakistan | 22 | 33 | 9 | 1,891 | 215 | 78.79 |
| ‡G. A. Gooch | Leytonstone | 11 | 16 | 1 | 996 | 259 | 66.40 |
| ‡D. R. Pringle | Nairobi, Kenya | 12 | 11 | 6 | 328 | 78* | 65.60 |
| ‡N. Hussain | Madras, India | 21 | 29 | 7 | 1,233 | 196 | 56.04 |
| N. V. Knight | Watford | 6 | 9 | 1 | 388 | 101* | 48.50 |
| ‡M. A. Garnham | Johannesburg, SA | 22 | 25 | 6 | 831 | 123 | 43.73 |
| P. J. Prichard | Billericay | 21 | 33 | 5 | 1,031 | 190 | 36.82 |
| ‡J. P. Stephenson | Stebbing | 22 | 36 | 2 | 1,234 | 116 | 36.29 |
| A. C. H. Seymour | Royston | 9 | 16 | 1 | 454 | 157 | 30.26 |
| ‡N. A. Foster | Colchester | 20 | 20 | 4 | 474 | 107* | 29.62 |
| ‡P. M. Such | Helensburgh | 11 | 5 | 4 | 27 | 23* | 27.00 |
| T. D. Topley | Canterbury | 19 | 19 | 4 | 320 | 50* | 21.33 |
| ‡J. H. Childs | Plymouth | 20 | 13 | 6 | 111 | 41* | 15.85 |
| N. Shahid | Karachi, Pakistan | 7 | 8 | 1 | 64 | 22* | 9.14 |
| S. J. W. Andrew | London | 14 | 8 | 2 | 30 | 13 | 5.00 |

Also batted: A. G. J. Fraser (*Edgware*) (3 matches) 52*, 23; J. J. B. Lewis (*Isleworth*) (1 match) 48.

\* *Signifies not out.*   ‡ *Denotes county cap.*

The following played a total of 24 three-figure innings for Essex in County Championship matches – Salim Malik 6, P. J. Prichard 4, G. A. Gooch 3, N. Hussain 3, J. P. Stephenson 3, M. A. Garnham 2, N. A. Foster 1, N. V. Knight 1, A. C. H. Seymour 1.

## BOWLING

| | O | M | R | W | BB | 5W/i | Avge |
|---|---|---|---|---|---|---|---|
| N. A. Foster | 693.5 | 163 | 2,000 | 91 | 8-99 | 7 | 21.97 |
| J. P. Stephenson | 77.4 | 14 | 296 | 12 | 3-20 | 0 | 24.66 |
| J. H. Childs | 667.1 | 218 | 1,702 | 58 | 6-61 | 4 | 29.34 |
| D. R. Pringle | 359.4 | 96 | 887 | 30 | 5-70 | 1 | 29.56 |
| S. J. W. Andrew | 366.3 | 72 | 1,211 | 40 | 4-38 | 0 | 30.27 |
| Salim Malik | 118.2 | 10 | 473 | 15 | 3-26 | 0 | 31.53 |
| P. M. Such | 290 | 75 | 743 | 23 | 3-23 | 0 | 32.30 |
| T. D. Topley | 484.3 | 83 | 1,720 | 53 | 5-58 | 3 | 32.45 |

Also bowled: A. G. J. Fraser 19-5-44-0; M. A. Garnham 4-0-39-0; G. A. Gooch 42.1-17-155-4; N. Hussain 8.3-0-50-0; N. V. Knight 5-0-32-0; P. J. Prichard 13.3-0-158-1; A. C. H. Seymour 4-0-27-0.

**Wicket-keeper:** M. A. Garnham 58 ct.

**Leading Fielders:** N. Hussain 34, Salim Malik 22, P. J. Prichard 17.

At Cambridge, April 19, 20, 22. ESSEX beat CAMBRIDGE UNIVERSITY by 350 runs.

## ESSEX v SURREY

At Chelmsford, April 27, 29, 30, May 1. Drawn. Essex 6 pts, Surrey 4 pts. Toss: Essex. The last two days were lost to the weather after Darren Bicknell had performed impressively to hold Surrey's first innings together. Displaying great concentration and application while carrying his bat, he hit nineteen boundaries in his 145, which spanned five and threequarter hours (314 balls). His colleagues, however, struggled against a seam attack in which Topley showed a welcome return to form. Although Gooch went cheaply, a resolute effort from Stephenson, two hours of occupation from night-watchman Topley, and a compact innings from Prichard redressed the balance before the weather had the last word.

*Close of play:* First day, Essex 21-1 (J. P. Stephenson 9*, T. D. Topley 1*); Second day, Essex 211-4 (P. J. Prichard 45*, N. Hussain 9*); Third day, No play.

### Surrey

| | | |
|---|---|---|
| D. J. Bicknell not out .............145 | M. P. Bicknell c Garnham b Topley ... | 6 |
| M. A. Lynch lbw b Pringle .......... 11 | A. J. Murphy lbw b Foster .......... | 2 |
| A. J. Stewart c Hussain b Pringle .... 19 | A. G. Robson b Andrew ............. | 0 |
| D. M. Ward c Garnham b Topley .... 30 | | |
| G. P. Thorpe c Garnham b Topley .... 0 | B 3, l-b 4, w 4, n-b 18 ....... | 29 |
| J. D. Robinson c Pringle b Foster ..... 15 | | — |
| *I. A. Greig c Gooch b Topley ....... 0 | 1/17 2/61 3/120 4/124 5/166 | 268 |
| †N. F. Sargeant lbw b Topley ........ 11 | 6/178 7/214 8/228 9/252 | |

Bonus points – Surrey 3, Essex 4.

Bowling: Foster 23–4–61–2; Pringle 29–6–74–2; Andrew 19–2–55–1; Topley 23–3–71–5.

### Essex

| | | |
|---|---|---|
| *G. A. Gooch c Sargeant b Murphy ... 3 | N. Hussain not out ................. | 19 |
| J. P. Stephenson c Lynch b Greig ..... 85 | | |
| T. D. Topley c Lynch b M. P. Bicknell .. 29 | B 4, l-b 17, w 6, n-b 3 ....... | 30 |
| P. J. Prichard not out ............. 45 | | — |
| Salim Malik lbw b Greig ............ 0 | 1/11 2/111 3/185 4/187 (4 wkts) | 211 |

N. Shahid, D. R. Pringle, †M. A. Garnham, N. A. Foster and S. J. W. Andrew did not bat.

Bonus points – Essex 2, Surrey 1.

Bowling: M. P. Bicknell 24–7–44–1; Murphy 25–5–57–1; Robson 15–4–31–0; Robinson 2–0–15–0; Thorpe 5–0–18–0; Greig 7–2–25–2.

Umpires: K. J. Lyons and P. B. Wight.

At Northampton, May 9, 10, 11, 13. ESSEX beat NORTHAMPTONSHIRE by eight wickets.

At Folkestone, May 16, 17, 18, 20. ESSEX drew with KENT.

## ESSEX v WARWICKSHIRE

At Chelmsford, May 22, 23, 24. Essex won by nine wickets. Essex 23 pts, Warwickshire 5 pts. Toss: Essex. Victory was achieved with fourteen balls to spare after Essex had found themselves chasing a target of 93 in fifteen overs. The final flourish came at the expense of Reeve who, earlier in the day, heard he was to join England's Texaco Trophy squad because of injuries in the international side. A career-best 94 not out from Ostler, including fourteen boundaries, led Warwickshire to respectability in the first innings after Foster's hostility had undone the top order, but none of their batsmen offered much resistance second time round. Andrew proved to be the main thorn after Foster had made an early breakthrough. Stephenson, whose 79 took 262 minutes to compile, was the Essex sheet-anchor, while Hussain provided the entertainment with a half-century in just over an hour.

*Close of play:* First day, Essex 17-0 (J. P. Stephenson 7*, N. Shahid 9*); Second day, Warwickshire 18-1 (Asif Din 7*, T. A. Munton 0*).

## Warwickshire

| | | | |
|---|---:|---|---:|
| A. J. Moles lbw b Foster | 23 | – c Garnham b Foster | 6 |
| Asif Din c Hussain b Andrew | 10 | – c Hussain b Foster | 20 |
| *T. A. Lloyd b Foster | 10 | – (4) c Garnham b Andrew | 22 |
| P. A. Smith c Lewis b Foster | 43 | – (5) lbw b Topley | 2 |
| D. A. Reeve b Foster | 4 | – (6) b Andrew | 20 |
| D. P. Ostler not out | 94 | – (7) c Garnham b Andrew | 7 |
| †K. J. Piper run out | 4 | – (8) c Garnham b Andrew | 11 |
| G. C. Small c Shahid b Childs | 1 | – (9) c Garnham b Foster | 11 |
| T. A. Munton c Salim Malik b Foster | 14 | – (3) c Garnham b Topley | 10 |
| A. R. K. Pierson lbw b Topley | 1 | – not out | 14 |
| A. A. Donald run out | 12 | – run out | 4 |
| L-b 6, n-b 15 | 21 | B 4, l-b 11, w 5, n-b 15 | 35 |

1/22 2/49 3/52 4/58 5/142      237    1/8 2/47 3/57 4/65 5/98    162
6/146 7/164 8/193 9/199                  6/110 7/111 8/125 9/151

Bonus points – Warwickshire 2, Essex 4 (Score at 100 overs: 235-9).

Bowling: *First Innings*—Foster 28-3-80-5; Andrew 23-5-47-1; Topley 19-6-60-1; Childs 26-15-35-1; Salim Malik 2-0-3-0; Stephenson 3.1-0-6-0. *Second Innings*—Foster 26.4-8-49-3; Andrew 21-9-38-4; Topley 23-6-60-2.

## Essex

| | | | |
|---|---:|---|---:|
| J. P. Stephenson c Piper b Munton | 79 | – not out | 40 |
| N. Shahid c and b Donald | 11 | | |
| P. J. Prichard c Piper b Donald | 5 | – not out | 12 |
| Salim Malik c and b Munton | 21 | – (2) c Piper b Small | 26 |
| N. Hussain b Reeve | 55 | | |
| J. J. B. Lewis lbw b Pierson | 48 | | |
| †M. A. Garnham not out | 46 | | |
| *N. A. Foster c Asif Din b Pierson | 2 | | |
| T. D. Topley c Piper b Donald | 4 | | |
| S. J. W. Andrew c Reeve b Pierson | 7 | | |
| B 8, l-b 13, w 1, n-b 7 | 29 | B 10, l-b 2, w 3 | 15 |

1/34 2/41 3/66 4/143 5/210    (9 wkts. dec.) 307    1/44      (1 wkt) 93
6/281 7/287 8/300 9/307

J. H. Childs did not bat.

Bonus points – Essex 3, Warwickshire 3 (Score at 100 overs: 288-7).

Bowling: *First Innings*—Donald 19-3-52-3; Munton 24-6-75-2; Small 17-5-34-0; Reeve 25-6-58-1; Pierson 14-1-45-3; Smith 8-0-22-0. *Second Innings*—Donald 6-0-27-0; Small 6-0-41-1; Reeve 0.4-0-13-0.

Umpires: D. O. Oslear and N. T. Plews.

At Bristol, May 31, June 1. ESSEX beat GLOUCESTERSHIRE by an innings and 124 runs.

## ESSEX v LEICESTERSHIRE

At Ilford, June 4, 5, 6. Drawn. Essex 8 pts, Leicestershire 7 pts. Toss: Essex. Rain had the final say, ending the prospects of an exciting finish. The last twenty overs had begun with Leicestershire requiring 92, with five wickets remaining, but only nine balls were bowled and both counties had to settle for a draw. The highlight of a competitive match was a magnificent 215 from Salim Malik, the highest score of his career, which contained 31 fours, came off 296 balls in 314 minutes, and included 104 runs between lunch and tea. It was an innings full of exquisite driving and timing, and he followed it up with another fine effort when Essex batted a second time. Maguire displayed admirable reserves of stamina and control in claiming six wickets on the opening day, while on the second Potter put together an entertaining 85, in just under two hours, to bring some sparkle to an otherwise drab Leicestershire reply.

*Close of play:* First day, Leicestershire 30-0 (T. J. Boon 16*, N. E. Briers 12*); Second day, Essex 50-2 (P. J. Prichard 16*, Salim Malik 12*).

## Essex

| | | | |
|---|---|---|---|
| J. P. Stephenson lbw b Millns | 24 | – lbw b Maguire | 16 |
| N. Shahid c Whitticase b Maguire | 0 | – c Boon b Millns | 4 |
| P. J. Prichard c Potter b Maguire | 10 | – c and b Potter | 50 |
| Salim Malik run out | 215 | – c Hepworth b Potter | 74 |
| N. Hussain b Maguire | 9 | – not out | 38 |
| †M. A. Garnham b Smith | 63 | – not out | 12 |
| *N. A. Foster c Whitticase b Maguire | 8 | | |
| T. D. Topley c and b Millns | 2 | | |
| S. J. W. Andrew b Maguire | 1 | | |
| J. H. Childs lbw b Maguire | 0 | | |
| P. M. Such not out | 0 | | |
| L-b 7, w 1, n-b 15 | 23 | B 1, n-b 8 | 9 |

1/0 2/21 3/103 4/117 5/286      355     1/14 2/26 3/127    (4 wkts dec.) 203
6/323 7/336 8/347 9/347                 4/178

Bonus points – Essex 4, Leicestershire 4.

Bowling: *First Innings*—Millns 18-2-73-2; Maguire 29.5-8-85-6; Wilkinson 17-1-96-0; Potter 21-1-66-0; Willey 5-1-23-0; Smith 1-0-5-1. *Second Innings*—Millns 10-0-49-1; Maguire 21-4-72-1; Potter 13-0-63-2; Wilkinson 2-0-18-0.

## Leicestershire

| | | | |
|---|---|---|---|
| T. J. Boon c Shahid b Topley | 66 | – c Shahid b Topley | 42 |
| *N. E. Briers c Garnham b Topley | 23 | – b Andrew | 23 |
| P. N. Hepworth lbw b Foster | 12 | – lbw b Topley | 7 |
| J. J. Whitaker lbw b Foster | 0 | – c Stephenson b Andrew | 12 |
| L. Potter c Garnham b Andrew | 85 | – c Foster b Childs | 37 |
| B. F. Smith lbw b Childs | 20 | – not out | 41 |
| P. Willey c Shahid b Topley | 11 | – not out | 3 |
| †P. Whitticase c Garnham b Andrew | 21 | | |
| D. J. Millns not out | 23 | | |
| C. W. Wilkinson lbw b Topley | 0 | | |
| J. N. Maguire c Shahid b Topley | 21 | | |
| L-b 2, n-b 12 | 14 | B 1, l-b 2, w 1, n-b 4 | 8 |

1/54 2/85 3/85 4/126 5/195      296     1/59 2/70 3/89     (5 wkts) 173
6/216 7/242 8/270 9/270                 4/94 5/162

Bonus points – Leicestershire 3, Essex 4.

Bowling: *First Innings*—Foster 24-9-42-2; Andrew 17-2-63-2; Such 12-2-55-0; Topley 18-3-58-5; Childs 26-6-76-1. *Second Innings*—Foster 13-2-53-0; Andrew 12-3-55-2; Topley 11-3-33-2; Childs 7.3-1-21-1; Such 4-1-8-0.

Umpires: D. O. Oslear and A. G. T. Whitehead.

## ESSEX v WORCESTERSHIRE

At Ilford, June 7, 8, 10. Drawn. Essex 6 pts, Worcestershire 7 pts. Toss: Worcestershire. Following an absorbing first two days, the third proved a huge disappointment and bordered on the farcical. Neither captain seemed willing to make victory his priority. First Foster decided to continue the Essex innings on the final day, even though his last pair were together; in the event they failed to add to the overnight total. Then Neale did not declare Worcestershire's second innings until tea, which left Essex with the impossible target of 361 in a minimum of 29 overs. Essex used an assortment of nine bowlers, many just tossing the ball up, to try to persuade Neale into an earlier declaration, but it was all to no avail. Moody's response was to amass 181 not out from 166 deliveries, with the help of six sixes and 23 fours, but just over 100 of his runs came when the bowling was of a frivolous nature. In Worcestershire's first innings, Lord (245 minutes), Rhodes and Lampitt compiled attractive half-centuries, while Seymour, with his first Championship fifty, and Garnham pursued a positive approach when Essex replied. Radford's six wickets brought him his best figures for two seasons.

*Close of play:* First day, Worcestershire 239-7 (S. J. Rhodes 29*, P. J. Newport 10*); Second day, Essex 255-9 (M. A. Garnham 68*, J. H. Childs 2*).

## Worcestershire

| | | | | |
|---|---|---|---|---|
| T. S. Curtis lbw b Foster | 2 | – not out | 68 |
| G. J. Lord c Stephenson b Topley | 85 | – c Prichard b Foster | 0 |
| T. M. Moody b Andrew | 10 | – not out | 181 |
| D. B. D'Oliveira c Andrew b Topley | 25 | | |
| *P. A. Neale b Foster | 28 | | |
| M. J. Weston c Garnham b Topley | 5 | | |
| †S. J. Rhodes b Childs | 64 | | |
| R. K. Illingworth b Salim Malik | 19 | | |
| P. J. Newport c Hussain b Foster | 12 | | |
| S. R. Lampitt not out | 58 | | |
| N. V. Radford not out | 7 | | |
| B 6, l-b 7, w 5, n-b 17 | 35 | L-b 3, n-b 13 | 16 |

1/3 2/19 3/92 4/141 5/149     (9 wkts dec.) 350    1/1      (1 wkt dec.) 265
6/182 7/229 8/248 9/331

Bonus points – Worcestershire 3, Essex 3 (Score at 100 overs: 293-8).

Bowling: *First Innings*—Andrew 28-6-86-1; Foster 36.4-8-102-3; Topley 21-4-77-3; Childs 16-6-44-1; Stephenson 4-2-9-0; Salim Malik 4-1-19-1. *Second Innings*—Foster 6-2-27-1; Topley 11-1-44-0; Childs 13-3-33-0; Andrew 5-0-32-0; Salim Malik 2-0-11-0; Prichard 5-0-52-0; Stephenson 4-0-27-0; Seymour 4-0-27-0; Hussain 3-0-9-0.

## Essex

| | | | | |
|---|---|---|---|---|
| J. P. Stephenson lbw b Radford | 0 | – b Radford | 4 |
| A. C. H. Seymour c D'Oliveira b Lampitt | 67 | – lbw b Radford | 3 |
| P. J. Prichard c Rhodes b Newport | 9 | – (6) not out | 0 |
| Salim Malik c Moody b Radford | 37 | | |
| N. Hussain c Moody b Radford | 8 | | |
| N. Shahid c D'Oliveira b Lampitt | 15 | – (3) not out | 22 |
| †M. A. Garnham lbw b Radford | 68 | | |
| *N. A. Foster c Moody b Newport | 32 | – (5) c D'Oliveira b Illingworth | 6 |
| T. D. Topley lbw b Radford | 3 | – (4) c Rhodes b Radford | 7 |
| S. J. W. Andrew b Radford | 0 | | |
| J. H. Childs not out | 2 | | |
| B 4, l-b 4, w 1, n-b 5 | 14 | L-b 2 | 2 |

1/0 2/11 3/69 4/95 5/142      255    1/4 2/7 3/15 4/44    (4 wkts) 44
6/145 7/215 8/234 9/246

Bonus points – Essex 3, Worcestershire 4.

Bowling: *First Innings*—Radford 21.2–4–76–6; Newport 24–2–76–2; Illingworth 23–5–51–0; Lampitt 14–3–44–2. *Second Innings*—Radford 7–1–19–3; Lampitt 4–1–6–0; Illingworth 7–6–1–1; Newport 4–1–16–0.

Umpires: D. O. Oslear and A. G. T. Whitehead.

At Horsham, June 21, 22, 24. ESSEX drew with SUSSEX.

At Lord's, June 28, 29, July 1. ESSEX beat MIDDLESEX by 113 runs.

## ESSEX v HAMPSHIRE

At Chelmsford, July 2, 3, 4. Drawn. Essex 5 pts, Hampshire 4 pts. Toss: Hampshire. In a thrilling finish Essex, having been set a target of 300 in a minimum of 54 overs, were 11 runs short of victory with their last pair together. Topley, who struck an unbeaten 33 from eleven balls, was responsible for the home county's getting so close after Salim Malik and Hussain set them on the way with half-centuries. Foster's fire and accuracy brought him his best figures of the season to date as Hampshire were made to fight for runs in their first innings, and later he opened up a rain-interrupted match by declaring so close after Salim Malik and Hussain set them on the way with half-centuries. Foster's fire and accuracy brought him his best figures of the season to date as Hampshire were made to fight for runs in their first innings, and later he opened up a rain-interrupted match by declaring 68 runs in arrears. Smith batted with purpose when the visitors went in again, as did Gower before retiring with a groin injury immediately after reaching fifty with a four off Garnham. Essex had put on their wicket-keeper and Prichard to provide easy runs and hasten a declaration.

*Close of play:* First day, Hampshire 114-3 (V. P. Terry 11*, D. I. Gower 19*); Second day, Hampshire 16-3 (C. L. Smith 6*, V. P. Terry 4*).

## Hampshire

| | | | | |
|---|---|---|---|---|
| T. C. Middleton c Garnham b Topley | 31 | – | lbw b Andrew | 3 |
| C. L. Smith c Hussain b Childs | 44 | – | c sub b Salim Malik | 93 |
| *M. C. J. Nicholas c Topley b Foster | 1 | – | (4) c Topley b Foster | 0 |
| V. P. Terry lbw b Foster | 14 | – | (5) c Garnham b Topley | 12 |
| D. I. Gower c Salim Malik b Foster | 23 | – | (6) retired hurt | 52 |
| K. D. James lbw b Topley | 51 | – | (7) c Salim Malik b Prichard | 45 |
| †A. N. Aymes c Prichard b Andrew | 17 | – | (8) not out | 20 |
| R. J. Maru c Andrew b Foster | 14 | – | (3) c Garnham b Foster | 0 |
| C. A. Connor b Topley | 5 | | | |
| K. J. Shine c Stephenson b Foster | 0 | | | |
| Aqib Javed not out | 0 | | | |
| L-b 8, n-b 12 | 20 | | L-b 1, n-b 5 | 6 |

1/82 2/84 3/89 4/119 5/125     220    1/9 2/12 3/12    (6 wkts dec.) 231
6/166 7/207 8/220 9/220             4/41 5/159 6/231

Bonus points – Hampshire 2, Essex 4.

*In the second innings D. I. Gower retired hurt at 183.*

Bowling: *First Innings*—Foster 23–8–45–5; Andrew 17–4–41–1; Topley 18.1–3–59–3; Childs 17–7–34–1; Fraser 14.5–5–31–0; Stephenson 2–1–2–0. *Second Innings*—Foster 13–3–38–2; Andrew 3–1–8–1; Topley 11–4–38–1; Childs 9–2–37–0; Salim Malik 8–0–42–1; Garnham 4–0–39–0; Prichard 3.3–0–28–1.

## Essex

| | | | | |
|---|---|---|---|---|
| J. P. Stephenson c Aymes b Aqib Javed | 17 | – b Aqib Javed | 5 |
| A. C. H. Seymour run out | 50 | – c Maru b James | 23 |
| P. J. Prichard c Shine b James | 3 | – (4) c Aymes b Connor | 38 |
| Salim Malik c Maru b Connor | 12 | – (3) c Smith b Aqib Javed | 66 |
| N. Hussain not out | 29 | – c Middleton b Shine | 52 |
| †M. A. Garnham b Shine | 8 | – c Terry b Aqib Javed | 14 |
| *N. A. Foster not out | 12 | – c and b Maru | 10 |
| A. G. J. Fraser (did not bat) | | – b Shine | 23 |
| T. D. Topley (did not bat) | | – not out | 33 |
| J. H. Childs (did not bat) | | – c Terry b Shine | 3 |
| S. J. W. Andrew (did not bat) | | – not out | 6 |
| B 1, l-b 3, w 2, n-b 15 | 21 | B 9, l-b 4, w 1, n-b 2 | 16 |

1/36 2/60 3/80 4/127 5/140  (5 wkts dec.) 152  1/26 2/45 3/117  (9 wkts) 289
4/178 5/198 6/213
7/237 8/252 9/268

Bonus points – Essex 1, Hampshire 2.

Bowling: *First Innings*—Aqib Javed 12.2-0-54-1; Shine 9-3-34-1; James 12-4-36-1; Connor 9-3-24-1. *Second Innings*—Aqib Javed 17-3-64-3; Shine 12-0-68-3; James 5-0-20-1; Maru 18-0-101-1; Connor 5-0-23-1.

Umpires: H. D. Bird and R. Julian.

At The Oval, July 5, 6, 8. ESSEX lost to SURREY by five wickets.

## ESSEX v KENT

At Southend, July 16, 17, 18. Kent won by 112 runs. Kent 20 pts, Essex 6 pts. Toss: Essex. Chasing a target of 313 in a minimum of 52 overs, Essex never looked like getting near it, and suffered their second Championship defeat of the summer, having gone down to Surrey in their previous match after setting a generous target. As they threw the bat with abandon, Igglesden reaped the major reward. Marsh, hitting ten fours and a six while scoring 83 from 81 deliveries, was the pick of Kent's batsmen on the first day, and Penn, with eleven fours, provided an entertaining fifty in 36 balls on the second morning to put the visitors in a strong position. Stephenson's first century of the summer and Prichard's third dominated Essex's reply, the pair adding 216 for the second wicket on an easy-paced pitch following Gooch's early departure. However, rain washed out the morning session on the final day, and when play began at two o'clock, Essex offered the visitors easy runs. Ward and Benson responded by adding a further 159 to their overnight score in 10.1 overs from Gooch and Prichard before the declaration.

*Close of play:* First day, Kent 303-8 (C. Penn 8*, M. J. McCague 1*); Second day, Kent 24-0 (T. R. Ward 10*, M. R. Benson 11*).

## Kent

| | | | |
|---|---|---|---|
| T. R. Ward c Gooch b Pringle | 53 | – not out | 88 |
| *M. R. Benson lbw b Foster | 0 | – not out | 92 |
| N. R. Taylor lbw b Topley | 50 | | |
| G. R. Cowdrey c Hussain b Andrew | 67 | | |
| S. G. Hinks c Hussain b Andrew | 8 | | |
| M. V. Fleming c Topley b Andrew | 4 | | |
| †S. A. Marsh c Garnham b Andrew | 83 | | |
| R. P. Davis c Garnham b Childs | 7 | | |
| C. Penn b Childs | 52 | | |
| M. J. McCague b Pringle | 16 | | |
| A. P. Igglesden not out | 12 | | |
| B 6, l-b 8, w 1, n-b 13 | 28 | L-b 1, n-b 2 | 3 |

1/1 2/86 3/139 4/171 5/175  380  (no wkt dec.) 183
6/267 7/294 8/294 9/358

Bonus points – Kent 4, Essex 3 (Score at 100 overs: 303-8).

Bowling: *First Innings*—Foster 17–2–58–1; Andrew 28–5–104–4; Pringle 27–7–74–2; Topley 22–5–64–1; Childs 19.3–5–66–2. *Second Innings*—Andrew 3–1–7–0; Pringle 3–1–4–0; Childs 5–2–4–0; Salim Malik 4–1–8–0; Gooch 5.1–0–81–0; Prichard 5–0–78–0.

## Essex

| | | | | | |
|---|---|---|---|---|---|
| *G. A. Gooch lbw b Igglesden | 0 | – c Marsh b Fleming | 27 |
| J. P. Stephenson not out | 113 | – c Taylor b Igglesden | 19 |
| P. J. Prichard c Ward b Davis | 122 | – c Marsh b Fleming | 14 |
| Salim Malik not out | 8 | – c Benson b Penn | 51 |
| N. Hussain (did not bat) | | – lbw b Igglesden | 0 |
| †M. A. Garnham (did not bat) | | – c Marsh b Igglesden | 16 |
| D. R. Pringle (did not bat) | | – c Benson b Davis | 27 |
| T. D. Topley (did not bat) | | – run out | 5 |
| N. A. Foster (did not bat) | | – c Ward b Davis | 33 |
| S. J. W. Andrew (did not bat) | | – b Igglesden | 1 |
| J. H. Childs (did not bat) | | – not out | 0 |
| L-b 3, w 1, n-b 4 | 8 | B 1, l-b 5, n-b 1 | 7 |

1/17 2/233                    (2 wkts dec.) 251    1/44 2/61 3/67 4/75 5/101    200
                                                   6/156 7/160 8/193 9/200

Bonus points – Essex 3.

Bowling: *First Innings*—McCague 11–1–47–0; Igglesden 15–4–35–1; Davis 28–5–97–1; Penn 8–1–36–0; Fleming 11.3–1–27–0; Cowdrey 2–1–6–0. *Second Innings*—McCague 3–0–25–0; Igglesden 13.3–1–36–4; Fleming 8–0–45–2; Davis 9–0–70–2; Penn 6–1–18–1.

Umpires: J. D. Bond and K. E. Palmer.

## ESSEX v SOMERSET

At Southend, July 19, 20, 22. Essex won by 136 runs. Essex 22 pts, Somerset 4 pts. Toss: Somerset. Although Gooch's declaration, leaving Somerset to score 262 in 73 overs, seemed on the generous side, the visitors never posed a threat and folded embarrassingly. A succession of poor strokes and a lack of application led to their demise; the last five wickets fell for the addition of 4 runs from Hallett, the No. 11 batsman. Salim Malik's fifth Championship hundred, arriving from 147 balls, was the highlight of the Essex innings, while Gooch and Hussain also batted attractively. Gooch and Stephenson provided a platform with 140 for the first wicket, and Malik and Hussain hurried Essex to four batting points in a fourth-wicket partnership of 180. Somerset's reply was built around Cook, who batted throughout the second day, receiving 376 balls and hitting 27 fours. Gooch led the home side's quest for quick runs on the final day, 56 of his runs coming in boundaries as he posted 97 from 89 deliveries.

*Close of play:* First day, Essex 413-6 (D. R. Pringle 25*, T. D. Topley 16*); Second day, Somerset 308-5 (S. J. Cook 193*, N. D. Burns 13*).

## Essex

| | | | | | |
|---|---|---|---|---|---|
| *G. A. Gooch c and b Hallett | 79 | – c Harden b Hayhurst | 97 |
| J. P. Stephenson run out | 70 | – c Trump b Beal | 11 |
| P. J. Prichard b Hallett | 0 | – lbw b MacLeay | 8 |
| Salim Malik c Tavaré b Lefebvre | 102 | – not out | 35 |
| N. Hussain c Hallett b MacLeay | 88 | – not out | 0 |
| †M. A. Garnham b MacLeay | 14 | | |
| D. R. Pringle not out | 25 | | |
| T. D. Topley not out | 16 | | |
| B 1, l-b 12, w 2, n-b 4 | 19 | B 2, l-b 1, n-b 2 | 5 |

1/140 2/146 3/171 4/351    (6 wkts dec.) 413    1/64 2/99 3/149    (3 wkts dec.) 156
5/357 6/380

S. J. W. Andrew, J. H. Childs and P. M. Such did not bat.

Bonus points – Essex 4, Somerset 1 (Score at 100 overs: 331-3).

Bowling: *First Innings*—Hallett 20–2–52–2; Beal 15–1–75–0; MacLeay 22–4–72–2; Lefebvre 17–1–72–1; Trump 29–1–102–0; Roebuck 8–0–25–0; Hayhurst 1–0–2–0. *Second Innings*—Hallett 6–0–36–0; Beal 8–2–37–1; MacLeay 7–1–32–1; Lefebvre 5–0–30–0; Trump 1.1–0–9–0; Hayhurst 1–0–9–1.

## Somerset

| | | | | |
|---|---|---|---|---|
| S. J. Cook not out | 193 | – c Prichard b Childs | 21 |
| P. M. Roebuck c Garnham b Childs | 38 | – b Andrew | 11 |
| A. N. Hayhurst c Garnham b Childs | 11 | – (5) c Gooch b Such | 0 |
| *C. J. Tavaré c Hussain b Such | 0 | – (3) b Stephenson | 20 |
| R. J. Harden lbw b Such | 20 | – (4) b Such | 45 |
| K. H. MacLeay c Topley b Childs | 6 | – c Salim Malik b Such | 7 |
| †N. D. Burns not out | 13 | – b Childs | 4 |
| R. P. Lefebvre (did not bat) | | – c Hussain b Childs | 0 |
| D. Beal (did not bat) | | – b Childs | 0 |
| H. R. J. Trump (did not bat) | | – not out | 0 |
| J. C. Hallett (did not bat) | | – lbw b Childs | 4 |
| L-b 4, w 1, n-b 22 | 27 | B 3, l-b 3, n-b 7 | 13 |

1/128 2/169 3/174 4/216 5/262     (5 wkts dec.) 308     1/24 2/37 3/92 4/95 5/112    125
                                                                6/121 7/121 8/121 9/121

Bonus points – Somerset 3, Essex 2 (Score at 100 overs: 266-5).

Bowling: *First Innings*—Andrew 13–0–65–0; Pringle 18–2–55–0; Childs 39–16–66–3; Topley 5–0–26–0; Such 26–7–46–2; Salim Malik 13–1–46–0. *Second Innings*—Pringle 9–1–40–0; Andrew 5–1–11–1; Childs 17.4–8–20–5; Topley 2–0–17–0; Such 15–7–23–3; Stephenson 4–2–8–1.

Umpires: J. D. Bond and K. E. Palmer.

At Cardiff, July 23, 24, 25. ESSEX lost to GLAMORGAN by four wickets.

At Chelmsford, August 3, 4, 5. ESSEX drew with WEST INDIANS (See West Indian tour section).

At Derby, August 6, 7, 8. ESSEX lost to DERBYSHIRE by 199 runs.

At Nottingham, August 9, 10, 12. ESSEX beat NOTTINGHAMSHIRE by three wickets.

## ESSEX v NORTHAMPTONSHIRE

At Colchester, August 16, 17, 19. Essex won by an innings and 12 runs. Essex 24 pts, Northamptonshire 3 pts. Toss: Essex. The Essex spinners captured seventeen wickets on a pitch which provided substantial turn and was scrutinised by Harry Brind, the TCCB's Inspector of Pitches, before the start of the final day's play. His visit came after the umpires had contacted Lord's, stating that they considered the pitch to be "poor", as opposed to "unfit". Gooch certainly found it to his liking on the opening day, hitting 24 fours and two sixes in his 173 from 243 deliveries, and so did Hussain, whose 141 from 276 balls contained eighteen fours and a six. These two shared a partnership of 287 after Capel had picked up three early wickets. Next day Childs returned his best figures of the season as Northamptonshire were forced to follow on 231 in arrears, and they would have been beaten in two days had Essex accepted all their chances. Gooch claimed the extra half-hour, but the Essex bowlers were unable to remove the final pair, and victory had to wait until early on Monday.

*Close of play:* First day, Essex 403-8 (N. A. Foster 41*, J. H. Childs 7*); Second day, Northamptonshire 202-9 (A. R. Roberts 3*, N. G. B. Cook 10*).

## Essex

| | | | |
|---|---|---|---|
| *G. A. Gooch c Capel b Roberts | 173 | T. D. Topley c Williams b Bailey | 7 |
| J. P. Stephenson c Ripley b Capel | 0 | J. H. Childs not out | 7 |
| P. J. Prichard b Capel | 2 | | |
| Salim Malik c Bailey b Capel | 0 | B 1, l-b 10 | 11 |
| N. Hussain c Lamb b Williams | 141 | | |
| †M. A. Garnham b Curran | 16 | 1/15 2/21 3/21     (8 wkts dec.) 403 |
| D. R. Pringle c Lamb b Roberts | 5 | 4/308 5/333 6/347 |
| N. A. Foster not out | 41 | 7/368 8/385 |

P. M. Such did not bat.

Bonus points – Essex 4, Northamptonshire 2 (Score at 100 overs: 358-6).

Bowling: Capel 14-3-40-3; Baptiste 23-7-61-0; Curran 16-2-44-1; Cook 18.1-2-65-0; Williams 10.5-1-51-1; Roberts 21-0-107-2; Bailey 7-1-24-1.

## Northamptonshire

| | | | |
|---|---|---|---|
| A. Fordham c Garnham b Childs | 29 | c Topley b Pringle | 18 |
| *A. J. Lamb c Stephenson b Topley | 9 | c Garnham b Pringle | 4 |
| R. J. Bailey c Prichard b Such | 21 | c Hussain b Salim Malik | 56 |
| N. A. Stanley c Prichard b Childs | 0 | b Such | 23 |
| D. J. Capel c Prichard b Such | 0 | c Salim Malik b Childs | 0 |
| K. M. Curran c Hussain b Childs | 11 | c Prichard b Such | 8 |
| E. A. E. Baptiste b Childs | 42 | lbw b Salim Malik | 28 |
| R. G. Williams c Stephenson b Such | 19 | c Hussain b Such | 17 |
| †D. Ripley b Childs | 17 | c Garnham b Salim Malik | 15 |
| A. R. Roberts not out | 12 | not out | 17 |
| N. G. B. Cook lbw b Childs | 0 | c Salim Malik b Childs | 11 |
| B 4, l-b 6, n-b 2 | 12 | B 15, l-b 4, n-b 3 | 22 |

1/28 2/51 3/51 4/54 5/67             172    1/16 2/31 3/76 4/77 5/110             219
6/81 7/141 8/141 9/172                       6/151 7/158 8/186 9/190

Bonus points – Northamptonshire 1, Essex 4.

Bowling: *First Innings*—Foster 8-3-21-0; Pringle 10-3-14-0; Topley 7-2-20-1; Childs 20.1-6-61-6; Such 19-4-46-3. *Second Innings*—Foster 7-3-17-0; Pringle 7-1-26-2; Childs 23.3-5-77-2; Such 16-4-54-3; Salim Malik 8-2-26-3.

Umpires: R. Julian and R. C. Tolchard.

## ESSEX v YORKSHIRE

At Colchester, August 20, 21, 22. Yorkshire won by 3 runs. Yorkshire 21 pts, Essex 5 pts. Toss: Yorkshire. An absorbing contest ended with Yorkshire clinching victory from the second ball of the final over, after Essex had been set 319 in 68 overs. The home side had appeared to be coasting to victory at 293 for five, but they lost their last five wickets for 22 runs in 7.2 overs. Their problems started when Stephenson was lbw to Batty 3 runs short of his second century of the match; after that, Batty and his fellow-spinner, Carrick, took control. Yorkshire's captain, Moxon, dominated the opening day, with more than half his runs coming in boundaries (one six and 26 fours). His double-hundred was the highest score by a Yorkshire player at Castle Park, beating Sir Leonard Hutton's 156 in 1950, but he was unable to add to it, falling to the first ball he received on the second day. Stephenson, who plundered five sixes off Batty, as well as hitting ten fours, and Prichard (nineteen fours) spent the afternoon putting Yorkshire to the sword in a partnership of 246, and Foster declared as soon as Essex gained their fourth bonus point. Moxon again batted fluently and then set up the thrilling finish with the third declaration of the match. Knight's 60 in the run-chase was his first Championship half-century.

*Close of play:* First day, Yorkshire 363-4 (M. D. Moxon 200*, R. J. Blakey 45*); Second day, Yorkshire 6-1 (M. D. Moxon 2*).

## Yorkshire

| | | | |
|---|---|---|---|
| *M. D. Moxon c Garnham b Foster | 200 | – c and b Topley | 66 |
| A. A. Metcalfe c Garnham b Foster | 22 | – c Seymour b Topley | 4 |
| D. Byas c Garnham b Such | 25 | – c Seymour b Topley | 7 |
| S. A. Kellett c Garnham b Salim Malik | 58 | – lbw b Childs | 41 |
| P. E. Robinson lbw b Salim Malik | 0 | – not out | 35 |
| †R. J. Blakey c Knight b Topley | 56 | – not out | 4 |
| C. S. Pickles lbw b Topley | 0 | | |
| P. Carrick c Knight b Stephenson | 28 | | |
| P. J. Hartley not out | 33 | | |
| J. D. Batty c Prichard b Stephenson | 5 | | |
| L-b 9, w 2, n-b 8 | 19 | B 8, l-b 5, n-b 2 | 15 |

1/50 2/90 3/255 4/262 5/364     (9 wkts dec.) 446    1/6 2/20     (4 wkts dec.) 172
6/365 7/380 8/436 9/446                    3/100 4/162

M. A. Robinson did not bat.

Bonus points – Yorkshire 4, Essex 1 (Score at 100 overs: 312-4).

Bowling: *First Innings*—Foster 30-7-97-2; Topley 21-3-86-2; Stephenson 5.1-1-19-2; Childs 36-11-86-0; Such 14-1-52-1; Salim Malik 23-0-97-2. *Second Innings*—Foster 11-2-46-0; Topley 16-3-47-3; Stephenson 2-0-24-0; Childs 10-1-42-1.

## Essex

| | | | |
|---|---|---|---|
| A. C. H. Seymour c Kellett b Carrick | 27 | – c Moxon b Hartley | 9 |
| J. P. Stephenson c Metcalfe b M. A. Robinson | 116 | – lbw b Batty | 97 |
| P. J. Prichard c Byas b M. A. Robinson | 128 | – b M. A. Robinson | 8 |
| Salim Malik not out | 11 | – c Kellett b Batty | 56 |
| N. Hussain not out | 1 | – st Blakey b Carrick | 5 |
| N. V. Knight (did not bat) | | – c Metcalfe b Carrick | 60 |
| †M. A. Garnham (did not bat) | | – c M. A. Robinson b Carrick | 68 |
| *N. A. Foster (did not bat) | | – b Batty | 4 |
| T. D. Topley (did not bat) | | – c sub b Batty | 3 |
| J. H. Childs (did not bat) | | – c Batty b Carrick | 1 |
| P. M. Such (did not bat) | | – not out | 0 |
| L-b 16, n-b 1 | 17 | B 2, l-b 2 | 4 |

1/34 2/280 3/289       (3 wkts dec.) 300    1/12 2/31 3/102 4/107 5/205     315
                                       6/293 7/303 8/311 9/314

Bonus points – Essex 4, Yorkshire 1.

Bowling: *First Innings*—M. A. Robinson 17-7-36-2; Hartley 10-1-34-0; Carrick 32-12-89-1; Batty 22-4-104-0; Pickles 6-1-21-0. *Second Innings*—Hartley 6-0-52-1; Pickles 4-0-19-0; Carrick 25.2-1-92-4; M. A. Robinson 11-1-62-1; Batty 21-0-86-4.

Umpires: R. Julian and R. C. Tolchard.

At Manchester, August 23, 24, 26. ESSEX beat LANCASHIRE by eight wickets.

## ESSEX v DERBYSHIRE

At Chelmsford, September 3, 4, 5, 6. Essex won by an innings and 72 runs. Essex 23 pts, Derbyshire 4 pts. Toss: Derbyshire. Victory over third-placed Derbyshire took Essex to the top of the Championship table well before lunch on the final day. Derbyshire's failure to take advantage of winning the toss meant they were always having to struggle, and only Barnett saved them from embarrassment. He was out 1 run short of joining the ranks of those with hundreds against all the other first-class counties, just as he was when seeking the same landmark at Southend three years earlier. The Essex reply was one of consolidation, the aim being that they would not need to bat again. Salim Malik passed 150 for the fifth time in the season, gathering 22 boundaries, and Garnham, with the first Championship century of his career, and Pringle pushed Derbyshire back to the point of no return. Sladdin, Derbyshire's left-arm spinner, toiled manfully through 68 overs to collect five wickets, but his effort was merely hinting at what the admirable Childs would achieve in spinning Essex to an emphatic win.

*Close of play*: First day, Essex 19-0 (G. A. Gooch 14*, J. P. Stephenson 3*); Second day, Essex 323-5 (Salim Malik 138*, M. A. Garnham 16*); Third day, Derbyshire 142-7 (K. M. Krikken 13*, A. E. Warner 0*).

## Derbyshire

| | | | |
|---|---|---|---|
| *K. J. Barnett c Hussain b Childs | 99 | – b Foster | 0 |
| P. D. Bowler run out | 1 | – c Pringle b Foster | 9 |
| J. E. Morris c Knight b Foster | 0 | – b Childs | 42 |
| M. Azharuddin c Hussain b Gooch | 13 | – c Hussain b Childs | 12 |
| T. J. G. O'Gorman c Prichard b Gooch | 7 | – c Hussain b Childs | 16 |
| S. C. Goldsmith lbw b Childs | 18 | – c Salim Malik b Childs | 37 |
| †K. M. Krikken lbw b Foster | 19 | – c Garnham b Salim Malik | 56 |
| D. G. Cork c Knight b Foster | 30 | – c Garnham b Childs | 0 |
| A. E. Warner c Prichard b Salim Malik | 25 | – c Foster b Childs | 28 |
| R. W. Sladdin not out | 8 | – lbw b Salim Malik | 18 |
| O. H. Mortensen c and b Salim Malik | 0 | – not out | 5 |
| L-b 6, n-b 5 | 11 | B 3, l-b 5, n-b 9 | 17 |
| | **231** | | **240** |

1/10 2/10 3/39 4/47 5/94            1/0 2/26 3/56 4/82 5/122
6/143 7/179 8/200 9/231            6/131 7/141 8/193 9/233

Bonus points – Derbyshire 2, Essex 4.

Bowling: *First Innings*—Foster 24-6-69-3; Pringle 14-2-44-0; Gooch 7-3-16-2; Childs 25-11-45-2; Such 19-3-30-0; Salim Malik 5.5-0-21-2. *Second Innings*—Foster 15-5-39-2; Pringle 5-1-20-0; Childs 34-12-68-6; Such 18-5-57-0; Salim Malik 10.3-0-48-2.

## Essex

| | | | |
|---|---|---|---|
| *G. A. Gooch c Morris b Cork | 44 | N. A. Foster c O'Gorman | |
| J. P. Stephenson lbw b Mortensen | 14 | b Azharuddin | 6 |
| P. J. Prichard b Sladdin | 27 | | |
| Salim Malik c and b Sladdin | 165 | B 11, l-b 14, n-b 4 | 29 |
| N. Hussain c Barnett b Sladdin | 35 | | |
| N. V. Knight b Sladdin | 28 | 1/53 2/80 3/116 | (8 wkts dec.) 543 |
| †M. A. Garnham b Sladdin | 117 | 4/180 5/248 6/367 | |
| D. R. Pringle not out | 78 | 7/536 8/543 | |

J. H. Childs and P. M. Such did not bat.

Bonus points – Essex 3, Derbyshire 2 (Score at 100 overs: 250-5).

Bowling: Mortensen 36-13-73-1; Cork 21-6-44-1; Warner 27-3-87-0; Sladdin 68-13-186-5; Bowler 28-6-93-0; Azharuddin 10.4-2-35-1.

Umpires: B. Dudleston and B. Hassan.

At Leicester, September 10, 11, 12, 13. ESSEX beat LEICESTERSHIRE by nine wickets.

## ESSEX v MIDDLESEX

At Chelmsford, September 17, 18, 19. Essex won by an innings and 208 runs. Essex 24 pts, Middlesex 1 pt. Toss: Essex. Essex secured their fifth Championship title in thirteen seasons shortly after lunch on the third day, when Foster removed Headley to claim his sixth wicket of the innings and tenth of the match. The outcome of the game was never in serious doubt after Middlesex, put in, had capitulated on a pitch that was green but never venomous. The 1990 champions surrendered for the lowest Championship total of the season in 24.3 overs, after which Gooch, at his majestic best, compiled the highest score by an Essex player against Middlesex. He banished any thoughts that the pitch was to blame for Middlesex's poor performance with a double-century before the close, and next day he went on to 259, made in 405 minutes, from 380 deliveries, with 37 fours and two sixes. Salim Malik, Hussain and Knight all supported their captain in major stands, and by the time Gooch declared Middlesex faced the massive task of scoring 515, or batting for more than seven sessions, to avoid an innings defeat. They never threatened to stave off that ignominy, despite the resistance of Roseberry and Brown, who held out in a partnership of 122 before Pringle removed both of them in the space of nine balls.

*Close of play*: First day, Essex 385-3 (G. A. Gooch 202*, N. Hussain 50*); Second day, Middlesex 171-3 (M. A. Roseberry 70*, K. R. Brown 38*).

## Middlesex

| | | | | |
|---|---|---|---|---|
| M. A. Roseberry b Pringle | 2 | – c Gooch b Pringle | 99 |
| M. Keech hit wkt b Foster | 3 | – c Garnham b Foster | 0 |
| *M. W. Gatting lbw b Pringle | 0 | – c Gooch b Foster | 35 |
| M. R. Ramprakash c Pringle b Foster | 0 | – b Foster | 19 |
| K. R. Brown c Gooch b Foster | 4 | – c Hussain b Pringle | 59 |
| P. N. Weekes run out | 5 | – b Andrew | 0 |
| J. E. Emburey lbw b Pringle | 1 | – lbw b Topley | 37 |
| N. F. Williams c Hussain b Andrew | 23 | – c Topley b Pringle | 6 |
| D. W. Headley c Garnham b Foster | 1 | – (10) c Salim Malik b Foster | 22 |
| †P. Farbrace not out | 12 | – (9) c Topley b Foster | 8 |
| N. G. Cowans c Hussain b Andrew | 0 | – not out | 8 |
| L-b 5, n-b 9 | | | 14 |

1/5 2/5 3/5 4/5 5/13 6/15   **51**   1/5 2/63 3/91 4/213 5/222   **307**
7/15 8/26 9/51                6/225 7/262 8/268 9/278

Bonus points – Essex 4.

Bowling: *First Innings*—Foster 11–6–18–4; Pringle 12–3–25–3; Andrew 1.3–0–8–2. *Second Innings*—Foster 30.4–4–104–6; Pringle 20–9–38–2; Andrew 13–1–48–1; Topley 19–5–70–1; Stephenson 5–1–10–0; Salim Malik 7–0–32–0.

## Essex

| | | | |
|---|---|---|---|
| *G. A. Gooch c Weekes b Williams | ..259 | †M. A. Garnham not out | 24 |
| J. P. Stephenson lbw b Headley | 18 | D. R. Pringle not out | 14 |
| P. J. Prichard lbw b Williams | 11 | B 14, l-b 11, w 2, n-b 15 | 42 |
| Salim Malik c Brown b Headley | 80 | | |
| N. Hussain c Farbrace b Cowans | 57 | 1/37 2/74 3/256   (6 wkts dec.) 566 |
| N. V. Knight c Farbrace b Weekes | 61 | 4/395 5/494 6/539 |

N. A. Foster, T. D. Topley and S. J. W. Andrew did not bat.

Bonus points – Essex 4, Middlesex 1 (Score at 100 overs: 440-4).

Bowling: Williams 30–7–140–2; Cowans 26–7–70–1; Headley 30–3–153–2; Gatting 16–0–62–0; Emburey 14–0–87–0; Weekes 4–0–21–1; Roseberry 3–0–8–0.

Umpires: B. Hassan and N. T. Plews.

# BRITANNIC ASSURANCE CHALLENGE

## †ESSEX v VICTORIA

At Chelmsford, September 22. Victoria won by 59 runs. Toss: Victoria. O'Donnell, the visiting captain, was the star of this 50-overs match between the 1991 county champions and the holders of the Sheffield Shield. His 71 not out, from 45 balls, included three sixes and five fours, and with Jones he added 120 in the last thirteen overs of Victoria's innings. Jones's unbeaten 86 came from 101 deliveries, and Ramshaw batted attractively for 71 to give the Australian champions a good start. Essex never recovered from losing Gooch to the fourth ball of their innings, despite a fluent half-century from Pringle. Hughes did most of the damage, and the Australians went off with the sponsor's cheque for £4,000.

*Man of the Match*: S. P. O'Donnell.

## Victoria

| | | | | |
|---|---|---|---|---|
| D. J. Ramshaw b Pringle | 71 | *S. P. O'Donnell not out | 71 |
| W. N. Phillips run out | 23 | B 1, l-b 11, w 3, n-b 3 | 18 |
| D. M. Jones not out | 86 | | |
| D. S. Lehmann c Andrew b Pringle | 5 | 1/56 2/148 3/154 (3 wkts, 50 overs) | 274 |

G. R. Parker, A. I. C. Dodemaide, M. G. Hughes, †D. S. Berry, D. W. Fleming and P. W. Jackson did not bat.

Bowling: Andrew 10–0–74–0; Pringle 10–0–50–2; Topley 10–0–46–0; Such 10–1–41–0; Gooch 8–0–36–0; Stephenson 2–0–15–0.

## Essex

| | | | | |
|---|---|---|---|---|
| *G. A. Gooch c Berry b Hughes | 0 | T. D. Topley b Hughes | 17 |
| J. P. Stephenson b Jackson | 49 | S. J. W. Andrew not out | 4 |
| P. J. Prichard c Lehmann b Hughes | 12 | P. M. Such b Hughes | 0 |
| N. Hussain c Berry b Dodemaide | 36 | B 1, l-b 9, w 2, n-b 1 | 13 |
| D. R. Pringle c Lehmann b Hughes | 51 | | |
| N. V. Knight b Jackson | 10 | 1/0 2/44 3/102 (48.5 overs) | 215 |
| †M. A. Garnham c and b Fleming | 23 | 4/108 5/130 6/163 | |
| J. J. B. Lewis lbw b Fleming | 0 | 7/163 8/205 9/213 | |

Bowling: Hughes 9.5–1–41–5; Fleming 10–0–40–2; Dodemaide 10–0–40–1; O'Donnell 9–0–39–0; Jackson 10–0–45–2.

Umpires: D. J. Constant and A. A. Jones.

## ESSEX v VICTORIA

At Chelmsford, September 23, 24, 25, 26. Drawn. Toss: Essex. Rain, which restricted the second day's play to just under an hour, washed out this Britannic Assurance Challenge match half an hour after lunch on the fourth afternoon and saved Victoria from a heavy defeat. Forced to follow on 175 behind, the visitors were all at sea against the spin of Childs and Such in helpful conditions. Hughes, with a valiant 60 not out, provided determined resistance in Victoria's first innings, and he was again unbeaten when the match was abandoned. On the final morning, Foster claimed his 100th first-class wicket of the season, for the second time in his career, when he dismissed Fleming. But it was not such a happy match for Pringle, who had batted well for his 68 to give Essex a useful total. Taking the catch which gave Foster his 98th wicket, at the start of Victoria's first innings, he suffered a double fracture of his left index finger. The rain proved costly to Essex in financial terms, for the winners were due to receive £12,000. Instead, with the match drawn, both sides finished with £2,500 each.

*Man of the Match:* J. H. Childs.

*Close of play:* First day, Essex 199-5 (N. V. Knight 51*, M. A. Garnham 18*); Second day, Essex 248-7 (D. R. Pringle 12*, N. A. Foster 19*); Third day, Victoria 157-8 (M. G. Hughes 54*, D. W. Fleming 8*).

## Essex

| | | | | |
|---|---|---|---|---|
| *G. A. Gooch c Berry b Fleming | 31 | N. A. Foster st Berry b Jackson | 37 |
| J. P. Stephenson b Dodemaide | 54 | J. H. Childs not out | 8 |
| P. J. Prichard lbw b O'Donnell | 2 | | |
| N. Hussain c and b Dodemaide | 5 | B 10, l-b 9, w 4, n-b 4 | 27 |
| N. V. Knight run out | 53 | | |
| J. J. B. Lewis b Jackson | 25 | 1/61 2/80 3/96 (9 wkts dec.) | 343 |
| †M. A. Garnham lbw b Fleming | 33 | 4/103 5/159 6/206 | |
| D. R. Pringle lbw b Hughes | 68 | 7/217 8/277 9/343 | |

P. M. Such did not bat.

Bowling: Hughes 30.3–7–85–1; Fleming 25–5–88–2; O'Donnell 13–6–47–1; Dodemaide 24–6–54–2; Jackson 18–11–50–2.

## Victoria

| | | | | |
|---|---|---|---|---|
| D. J. Ramshaw lbw b Childs | 11 | – c Garnham b Foster | 0 |
| W. N. Phillips c Pringle b Foster | 2 | – lbw b Stephenson | 11 |
| D. M. Jones c Gooch b Childs | 25 | – c Hussain b Such | 9 |
| D. S. Lehmann c Hussain b Such | 15 | – lbw b Childs | 8 |
| *S. P. O'Donnell c Prichard b Such | 12 | – b Childs | 5 |
| G. R. Parker b Childs | 0 | – lbw b Childs | 1 |
| A. I. C. Dodemaide lbw b Foster | 21 | – b Such | 0 |
| M. G. Hughes not out | 60 | – not out | 12 |
| †D. S. Berry c Prichard b Childs | 1 | – lbw b Such | 4 |
| D. W. Fleming c Garnham b Foster | 8 | | |
| P. W. Jackson c Gooch b Foster | 4 | | |
| L-b 9 | 9 | B 5, l-b 1 | 6 |

1/3 2/39 3/48 4/70 5/71       168     1/8 2/14 3/29 4/33     (8 wkts) 56
6/71 7/136 8/137 9/158               5/37 6/40 7/40 8/56

Bowling: *First Innings*—Foster 33.3–12–63–4; Pringle 3–3–0–0; Childs 43–15–71–4; Such 17–7–25–2. *Second Innings*—Foster 4–1–14–1; Stephenson 4–1–10–1; Childs 7–2–19–3; Such 6.1–2–7–3.

Umpires: R. Julian and K. E. Palmer.

## OVERS BOWLED AND RUNS SCORED IN THE BRITANNIC ASSURANCE CHAMPIONSHIP, 1991

| | Over-rate per hour | Run-rate/ 100 balls |
|---|---|---|
| Derbyshire (3) | 19.0050 | 55.5841 |
| Essex (1) | 18.8305 | 61.6479 |
| Glamorgan (12) | 19.1390 | 53.0401 |
| Gloucestershire (13) | 18.7623 | 48.5729 |
| Hampshire (9) | 18.5905 | 51.9459 |
| Kent (6=) | 18.0398* | 52.9399 |
| Lancashire (8) | 18.6654 | 53.2311 |
| Leicestershire (16) | 18.0887* | 48.8099 |
| Middlesex (15) | 18.7941 | 51.7429 |
| Northamptonshire (10) | 18.7237 | 53.7082 |
| Nottinghamshire (4) | 18.6786 | 54.8753 |
| Somerset (17) | 18.7124 | 51.4374 |
| Surrey (5) | 18.6190 | 52.7975 |
| Sussex (11) | 18.5832 | 49.8880 |
| Warwickshire (2) | 17.7747† | 50.7349 |
| Worcestershire (6=) | 18.5601 | 54.3192 |
| Yorkshire (14) | 18.6598 | 49.4315 |
| | | |
| 1991 average rate | 18.6015 | 52.6298 |
| 1990 average rate | 18.1260 | 55.5025 |
| 1989 average rate | 18.3621 | 50.6788 |
| 1988 average rate | 18.9202 | 43.9340 |
| 1987 average rate | 18.64 | 51.79 |
| 1986 average rate | 18.49 | 52.22 |
| 1985 average rate | 18.43 | 52.61 |

*1991 Championship positions are shown in brackets.*
* £4,000 fine.    † £6,000 fine.

# GLAMORGAN

*Patron:* HRH The Prince of Wales
*President:* W. Wooller
*Chairman:* A. R. Lewis
*Chairman, Cricket Committee:* A. R. Lewis
*Secretary:* G. R. Stone
  Sophia Gardens, Cardiff CF1 9XR
  (Telephone: 0222-343478)
*Captain:* A. R. Butcher
*Senior Coach:* A. Jones

Glamorgan maintained their improvement of 1990, again winning five Championship matches, despite dropping four places to twelfth in the Britannic Assurance table. Significantly, they played themselves into winning positions in four other games, and victory in only two of those would have been enough to lift them to sixth. In the space of a fortnight they were thwarted by the Northamptonshire tailenders, a dropped caught-and-bowled chance cost them the match against Sussex, and rain ended play at Worcester with Hugh Morris and Matthew Maynard in control. Another opportunity was lost at Cheltenham in July, when Gloucestershire hung on with nine second-innings wickets down.

Their form in the limited-overs competitions was more disappointing, and provided further evidence of Glamorgan's long-standing failure to adapt to the needs of one-day cricket. The county did not qualify for the knockout rounds of the Benson and Hedges Cup and would have struggled to beat the Minor Counties had Ravi Shastri not contributed a timely century. They finished next to bottom in the Refuge Assurance League, and although hopes were raised in the NatWest Bank Trophy by their second-round success against Worcestershire, the thousands of supporters who travelled to Northampton were frustrated by another sub-standard performance. Glamorgan were well on course for a target of 255 after Alan Butcher and Morris had opened with 85, but two self-inflicted run-outs in the middle order precipitated a collapse and defeat by 26 runs.

Without Viv Richards, whose inspiration and seven hundreds in 1990 had revived Glamorgan's fortunes after more than a decade of mediocrity, many predicted an indifferent year. But Maynard showed the benefits of Richards's guidance by scoring 1,803 runs at 60.10 in his best season yet. It was the form everyone knew him capable of, but which previously his youthful impetuosity had prevented him delivering. He struck two double-centuries, the first against Nottinghamshire at Cardiff and the second against Hampshire, in the final game of the season, which brought Glamorgan's fifth Championship win. His 243 at Southampton was only 44 runs short of the county record, and allied to these notable innings were a century from 75 balls against Surrey, and two hundreds in the same match against Gloucestershire, on a bouncy pitch at Cheltenham. In addition, Maynard had been instrumental in Glamorgan's first Championship victory, over Somerset, when he scored 85 and 133 not out. Daren Foster, eager to impress against his former colleagues, dismissed Jimmy Cook twice and collected nine wickets in that match.

Consistency was the hallmark of Glamorgan's batting, with four batsmen reaching 1,000 runs and three of them going on to pass 1,500. The left-handed opening combination of Butcher and Morris again flourished, with Morris receiving recognition from the England selectors and playing in three of the summer's Tests. Butcher had another splendid season, his value reflected in four Championship hundreds and twelve fifties, and his only England cap, gained in 1979, was a continuing indictment of the selectors' disregard for an opening batsman of genuine quality. The emergence of Adrian Dale at No. 3 was a considerable boost, for this position had not been adequately occupied for several years. The young all-rounder, having been promoted against Worcestershire in the NatWest game, responded by scoring 86, to be named Man of the Match; and having been dismissed for 99 against Warwickshire, he achieved his maiden Championship hundred in the following match, against Gloucestershire. Tony Cottey, although given numerous chances, failed to establish himself, but Steve James played some important innings. He was set to learn his trade in the middle order, the intention being that he would eventually succeed Butcher as opener.

Steve Watkin and Mark Frost were the most successful bowlers, and both were rewarded for their whole-hearted effort and resilience: Watkin played twice for England against West Indies, while Frost was awarded his county cap at the end of August. Watkin's 728.5 overs were surpassed by only five other bowlers, and he was Glamorgan's leading wicket-taker for the third year running with 74 first-class victims. The county would also have benefited had Shastri consistently bowled as well as he did in his last four Championship matches, in which he took 23 wickets at a low cost.

The Indian left-arm spinner had returned at the start of the season having lost all confidence in his bowling, and it took weeks of practice with Don Shepherd, the county's bowling coach, before he could pitch on a length, let alone take wickets. Robert Croft, who promised much in 1990, had a moderate season, his 38 wickets captured at a high cost, and he was capable of far more than the 345 runs he accumulated in the lower middle order. The national selectors, though, recognised his undoubted ability, and a tour of the Caribbean with England A during the winter offered him further opportunities for development. Less fortunate was Colin Metson, who dismissed 76 batsmen, six more than any of his rivals in 1991 and the most by a Glamorgan wicket-keeper for 21 years. His omission from the winter touring teams was a huge disappointment for the player, club and supporters.

Geoff Holmes, a Glamorgan all-rounder for fourteen years, was forced to retire through injury at the end of his benefit year, and Simon Dennis, a trier and at times an effective left-arm seamer, also left, having been troubled by a persistent back injury. Shastri, Glamorgan's overseas player since 1987, was another departure, but it was expected that Richards would fulfil the second season of a three-year contract – as well as provide further inspiration for the Welsh county. – Edward Bevan.

404

GLAMORGAN 1991

[Bill Smith]

*Back row*: P. A. Cottey, M. J. Cann, R. D. B. Croft, S. Kirnon, D. L. Hemp, S. P. James, D. J. Foster, A. Dale, M. Davies, G. Lewis (*2nd XI scorer*). *Middle row*: B. T. Denning (*1st XI scorer*), D. Conway (*physiotherapist*), M. L. Roberts, S. J. Dennis, M. Frost, I. Smith, S. Bastien, D. J. Shepherd (*assistant coach*), G. R. Stone (*secretary*). *Front row*: A. Jones (*senior coach*), C. P. Metson, M. P. Maynard, A. R. Butcher (*captain*), S. R. Barwick, G. C. Holmes, J. Derrick, J. F. Steele (*2nd XI captain*). *Insets*: H. Morris, S. L. Watkin.

# GLAMORGAN RESULTS

*All first-class matches – Played 25: Won 6, Lost 5, Drawn 14.*

*County Championship matches – Played 22: Won 5, Lost 5, Drawn 12.*

*Bonus points – Batting 50, Bowling 57.*

*Competition placings – Britannic Assurance County Championship, 12th;
NatWest Bank Trophy, q-f; Benson and Hedges Cup, 4th in Group D;
Refuge Assurance League, 15th equal.*

## BRITANNIC ASSURANCE CHAMPIONSHIP AVERAGES

### BATTING

|  | Birthplace | M | I | NO | R | HI | Avge |
|---|---|---|---|---|---|---|---|
| ‡H. Morris . . . . . . . . . | Cardiff | 17 | 30 | 7 | 1,601 | 156* | 69.60 |
| ‡M. P. Maynard . . . . . | Oldham | 20 | 32 | 5 | 1,766 | 243 | 65.40 |
| ‡R. J. Shastri . . . . . . . | Bombay | 21 | 31 | 8 | 1,056 | 133* | 45.91 |
| ‡A. R. Butcher . . . . . . | Croydon | 21 | 37 | 1 | 1,558 | 147 | 43.27 |
| A. Dale . . . . . . . . . . | Germiston, SA | 15 | 23 | 3 | 711 | 140 | 35.55 |
| S. P. James . . . . . . . | Lydney | 10 | 17 | 3 | 429 | 70 | 30.64 |
| ‡C. P. Metson . . . . . . | Goffs Oak | 22 | 24 | 3 | 511 | 84 | 24.33 |
| P. A. Cottey . . . . . . | Swansea | 11 | 16 | 5 | 259 | 55 | 23.54 |
| I. Smith . . . . . . . . . . | Chopwell | 8 | 11 | 2 | 196 | 39 | 21.77 |
| ‡G. C. Holmes . . . . . . | Newcastle-upon-Tyne | 6 | 8 | 1 | 136 | 54 | 19.42 |
| ‡S. L. Watkin . . . . . . | Maesteg | 18 | 15 | 8 | 123 | 25* | 17.57 |
| R. D. B. Croft . . . . . | Morriston | 22 | 25 | 4 | 331 | 50 | 15.76 |
| S. Bastien . . . . . . . . | Stepney, London | 11 | 6 | 3 | 26 | 22* | 8.66 |
| ‡S. R. Barwick . . . . . | Neath | 11 | 9 | 1 | 64 | 24* | 8.00 |
| D. J. Foster . . . . . . . | Tottenham, London | 8 | 9 | 3 | 35 | 13* | 5.83 |
| ‡M. Frost . . . . . . . . . | Barking | 18 | 11 | 4 | 19 | 8* | 2.71 |

Also batted: M. J. Cann (*Cardiff*) 29*; S. J. Dennis (*Scarborough*) (1 match) 0, 3;
D. L. Hemp (*Bermuda*) (1 match) 8, 4*.

\* *Signifies not out.* ‡ *Denotes county cap.*

The following played a total of nineteen three-figure innings for Glamorgan in County
Championship matches – M. P. Maynard 7, H. Morris 5, A. R. Butcher 4, R. J. Shastri 2,
A. Dale 1.

### BOWLING

|  | O | M | R | W | BB | 5W/i | Avge |
|---|---|---|---|---|---|---|---|
| R. J. Shastri . . . . . . . . . | 288.5 | 80 | 704 | 27 | 5-71 | 1 | 26.07 |
| S. R. Barwick . . . . . . . | 286.5 | 79 | 726 | 26 | 4-46 | 0 | 27.92 |
| S. L. Watkin . . . . . . . | 639.5 | 137 | 1,848 | 66 | 6-55 | 4 | 28.00 |
| M. Frost . . . . . . . . . . . . | 497.2 | 84 | 1,728 | 61 | 7-99 | 1 | 28.32 |
| D. J. Foster . . . . . . . . . | 210.5 | 34 | 753 | 24 | 6-84 | 1 | 31.37 |
| R. D. B. Croft . . . . . . . | 646.2 | 151 | 1,777 | 34 | 5-62 | 1 | 52.26 |
| S. Bastien . . . . . . . . . . . | 329.2 | 86 | 946 | 17 | 5-39 | 1 | 55.64 |

Also bowled: A. R. Butcher 2–1–1–0; M. J. Cann 8–0–37–0; A. Dale 106.1–22–380–7;
S. J. Dennis 12–1–49–0; M. P. Maynard 4.5–0–34–0; I. Smith 36.1–7–132–3.

**Wicket-keeper:** C. P. Metson 67 ct, 2 st.

**Leading Fielder:** M. P. Maynard 14.

At Oxford, April 17, 18, 19. GLAMORGAN drew with OXFORD UNIVERSITY.

At Leicester, April 27, 29, 30, May 1. GLAMORGAN drew with LEICESTERSHIRE.

At Taunton, May 9, 10, 11, 13. GLAMORGAN beat SOMERSET by 180 runs.

## GLAMORGAN v WARWICKSHIRE

At Swansea, May 16, 17, 18, 20. Warwickshire won by six wickets. Warwickshire 23 pts, Glamorgan 5 pts. Toss: Glamorgan. Donald, Warwickshire's South African fast bowler, took advantage of a suspect St Helen's pitch to return match figures of ten for 74 and quash any hopes of Glamorgan winning their first home game of the season. Holmes, with a four-and-a-half-hour fifty in the first innings, was the only major contributor to a modest total, and Warwickshire's 83-run lead was crucial as the pitch deteriorated. Off-spinner Croft had career-best figures of five for 62, taking three wickets for 7 runs in eighteen balls, and he was one of the few batsmen to figure as Glamorgan succumbed again to Donald in the second innings. Had he and Metson, who made his first Championship fifty for four years, not put together a partnership of 71 in eighteen overs, Warwickshire's task would have been easier than the 121 runs they required for victory. Harry Brind, the TCCB Inspector of Pitches, was summoned to the ground on the final day, and although confirming that the pitch was inadequate, he accepted the groundsman's explanation, so sparing Glamorgan the indignity of having 25 points deducted.

*Close of play:* First day, Glamorgan 149-6 (G. C. Holmes 42*, C. P. Metson 24*); Second day, Warwickshire 252-9 (G. C. Small 29*, A. A. Donald 1*); Third day, Warwickshire 58-1 (A. J. Moles 23*, T. A. Munton 1*).

### Glamorgan

| | | | |
|---|---:|---|---:|
| *A. R. Butcher lbw b Donald | 8 | – c sub b Booth | 12 |
| H. Morris lbw b Reeve | 11 | – lbw b Donald | 6 |
| S. P. James c Piper b Small | 5 | – b Donald | 14 |
| R. J. Shastri c Piper b Reeve | 5 | – c Smith b Small | 31 |
| G. C. Holmes c Piper b Donald | 54 | – lbw b Donald | 1 |
| I. Smith b Reeve | 28 | – c Smith b Booth | 29 |
| R. D. B. Croft lbw b Munton | 10 | – c sub b Munton | 31 |
| †C. P. Metson lbw b Donald | 28 | – c Booth b Donald | 57 |
| S. J. Dennis c Piper b Donald | 0 | – c Small b Booth | 3 |
| S. L. Watkin not out | 1 | – not out | 2 |
| D. J. Foster c Munton b Small | 0 | – b Donald | 0 |
| B 1, l-b 10, w 4, n-b 8 | 23 | B 5, l-b 7, n-b 5 | 17 |
| | **173** | | **203** |

1/20 2/29 3/33 4/42 5/80         1/13 2/29 3/53 4/55 5/84
6/108 7/154 8/158 9/173       6/116 7/187 8/200 9/203

Bonus points – Glamorgan 1, Warwickshire 4.

Bowling: *First Innings*—Donald 17.5–5–38–5; Munton 24–8–43–1; Small 17–4–35–1; Reeve 24–11–30–3; Smith 6–0–16–0. *Second Innings*—Donald 14.4–2–36–5; Small 15–6–34–1; Munton 22–9–41–1; Booth 27–5–71–3; Smith 2–0–9–0.

## Warwickshire

| | | | |
|---|---|---|---|
| A. J. Moles st Metson b Croft | 55 | – c Morris b Croft | 45 |
| Asif Din c Butcher b Watkin | 15 | – c James b Watkin | 29 |
| P. A. Smith c Metson b Watkin | 37 | – (5) run out | 6 |
| *T. A. Lloyd c and b Croft | 29 | | |
| D. A. Reeve c Metson b Foster | 1 | | |
| D. P. Ostler b Croft | 10 | – (4) not out | 12 |
| †K. J. Piper c Smith b Croft | 21 | – (6) not out | 5 |
| P. A. Booth c Metson b Croft | 18 | | |
| G. C. Small c Holmes b Watkin | 31 | | |
| T. A. Munton c Smith b Foster | 6 | – (3) c Morris b Shastri | 6 |
| A. A. Donald not out | 2 | | |
| L-b 19, w 3, n-b 9 | 31 | B 4, l-b 6, n-b 8 | 18 |
| | **256** | (4 wkts) | **121** |

1/27 2/82 3/135 4/157 5/167
6/171 7/205 8/215 9/241    1/54 2/80 3/100 4/106

Bonus points – Warwickshire 3, Glamorgan 4.

*In the first innings T. A. Lloyd, when 28, retired hurt at 118 and resumed at 167.*

Bowling: *First Innings*—Foster 19-2-73-2; Watkin 19.4-7-53-3; Dennis 12-1-49-0; Croft 24-5-62-5. *Second Innings*—Watkin 14-3-31-1; Foster 2-0-17-0; Croft 16.2-4-38-1; Shastri 12-3-25-1.

Umpires: A. G. T. Whitehead and P. B. Wight.

## GLAMORGAN v NORTHAMPTONSHIRE

At Cardiff, May 22, 23, 24. Drawn. Glamorgan 7 pts, Northamptonshire 3 pts. Toss: Glamorgan. Glamorgan, in control for most of the game, were denied their second Championship win of the season by the Northamptonshire tailenders, in particular Ripley and Roberts, who defended stubbornly for the final fifteen overs. In Northamptonshire's first innings this same pair had added 55 for the ninth wicket. Glamorgan led by 112 on the first innings after Morris had scored his second Championship century of the season, including sixteen fours, and Bastien had taken five wickets with a splendid display of controlled seam bowling. Butcher and Morris set up the declaration with an opening partnership of 149, whereupon Watkin raised Welsh hopes with two wickets before lunch. A stand of 94 between Bailey and Capel redressed the balance, but Glamorgan fought back by taking three quick wickets after tea. However, Ripley, assisted by Noon and then Roberts, saved Northamptonshire, with Roberts, a young leg-spinner, belying his position as a No. 10 batsman.

*Close of play:* First day, Glamorgan 299-8 (S. L. Watkin 5*, S. Bastien 0*); Second day, Glamorgan 100-0 (A. R. Butcher 67*, H. Morris 28*).

## Glamorgan

| | | | |
|---|---|---|---|
| *A. R. Butcher lbw b Taylor | 2 | – c Capel b Penberthy | 96 |
| H. Morris run out | 132 | – not out | 88 |
| S. P. James lbw b Penberthy | 15 | – not out | 11 |
| R. J. Shastri lbw b Bailey | 50 | | |
| G. C. Holmes c Thomas b Penberthy | 21 | | |
| I. Smith run out | 13 | | |
| R. D. B. Croft b Bailey | 16 | | |
| †C. P. Metson lbw b Bailey | 24 | | |
| S. L. Watkin not out | 5 | | |
| S. Bastien not out | 0 | | |
| B 5, l-b 15, w 1 | 21 | B 2, l-b 5, n-b 1 | 8 |
| (8 wkts dec.) | **299** | (1 wkt dec.) | **203** |

1/6 2/58 3/158 4/219 5/247
6/253 7/286 8/299    1/149

D. J. Foster did not bat.

Bonus points – Glamorgan 3, Northamptonshire 2 (Score at 100 overs: 258-6).

Bowling: *First Innings*—Taylor 14-2-37-1; Thomas 21-3-61-0; Penberthy 17-5-37-2; Capel 22-8-27-0; Roberts 16-2-56-0; Bailey 23-5-61-3. *Second Innings*—Thomas 9-0-44-0; Taylor 14-2-49-0; Capel 7-2-21-0; Penberthy 12-0-49-1; Bailey 6-0-33-0.

## Northamptonshire

| | | | |
|---|---|---|---|
| A. Fordham c Metson b Watkin | 13 | – lbw b Watkin | 3 |
| N. A. Felton b Bastien | 13 | – b Watkin | 3 |
| *R. J. Bailey c Butcher b Bastien | 5 | – c Metson b Foster | 61 |
| D. J. Capel b Foster | 41 | – b Croft | 56 |
| K. M. Curran lbw b Watkin | 0 | – c James b Watkin | 11 |
| A. L. Penberthy c Metson b Bastien | 7 | – b Watkin | 0 |
| J. G. Thomas lbw b Foster | 2 | – c Metson b Watkin | 0 |
| †D. Ripley c Metson b Bastien | 49 | – not out | 32 |
| W. M. Noon c Metson b Bastien | 10 | – lbw b Watkin | 0 |
| A. R. Roberts not out | 17 | – not out | 13 |
| J. P. Taylor b Watkin | 2 | | |
| B 6, l-b 14, w 1, n-b 7 | 28 | B 9, l-b 3, w 1, n-b 5 | 18 |

1/17 2/24 3/61 4/69 5/83          187     1/6 2/7 3/101 4/129     (8 wkts) 199
6/96 7/105 8/129 9/184                      5/143 6/143
                                     7/164 8/170

Bonus points – Northamptonshire 1, Glamorgan 4.

Bowling: *First Innings*—Watkin 20.4–6–30–3; Foster 21–5–53–2; Bastien 22–8–39–5; Croft 13–3–35–0; Smith 4–0–10–0. *Second Innings*—Watkin 25.5–6–55–6; Bastien 24–7–66–0; Foster 11–2–23–1; Shastri 3–0–16–0; Croft 12–5–25–1; Butcher 1–1–0–0; Smith 2–1–2–0.

Umpires: J. D. Bond and A. A. Jones.

## GLAMORGAN v SUSSEX

At Cardiff, May 25, 27, 28. Drawn. Glamorgan 7 pts, Sussex 3 pts. Toss: Sussex. Glamorgan were again denied victory by resolute batting, but a dropped catch almost certainly lost them another sixteen points. Sussex, 90 for five on the final morning, would have been in deeper trouble had Croft held on to a return catch from century-maker Wells when he had scored 34. Instead, Wells went on to an undefeated 153, with a six and fifteen fours, and to share an unbeaten, match-saving partnership of 222 in 73 overs with Dodemaide, who reached his century in the last over. Glamorgan had earlier gained a first-innings lead of 132, thanks to an excellent partnership of 202 in only 38 overs between Morris and Maynard. Accelerating after tea on the second day, they put on 88 in ten overs, which enabled Butcher to declare earlier than expected and to claim the important wicket of Smith before the close. Smith's half-century on the opening day was his fifth in his last seven first-class innings, while Parker narrowly missed a hundred in his second Championship match of the summer.

*Close of play:* First day, Glamorgan 9-0 (A. R. Butcher 6*, H. Morris 3*); Second day, Sussex 18-1 (J. W. Hall 7*, B. T. P. Donelan 10*).

## Sussex

| | | | |
|---|---|---|---|
| D. M. Smith b Frost | 61 | – lbw b Frost | 0 |
| J. W. Hall c Metson b Watkin | 3 | – c Metson b Frost | 7 |
| N. J. Lenham c Morris b Croft | 21 | – (4) b Bastien | 11 |
| A. P. Wells b Croft | 0 | – (5) not out | 153 |
| *P. W. G. Parker b Bastien | 95 | – (6) b Croft | 9 |
| A. I. C. Dodemaide c Metson b Smith | 12 | – (7) not out | 100 |
| †P. Moores b Frost | 28 | | |
| I. D. K. Salisbury lbw b Frost | 0 | | |
| B. T. P. Donelan b Bastien | 17 | – (3) b Watkin | 22 |
| R. A. Bunting not out | 2 | | |
| A. N. Jones c Shastri b Watkin | 3 | | |
| B 3, l-b 6, w 2, n-b 2 | 21 | B 1, l-b 5, n-b 4 | 10 |

1/12 2/71 3/71 4/114 5/154      263     1/1 2/26 3/32     (5 wkts) 312
6/205 7/205 8/257 9/258                       4/53 5/90

Bonus points – Sussex 3, Glamorgan 3 (Score at 100 overs: 257-8).

Bowling: *First Innings*—Watkin 20–2–52–2; Frost 20–4–45–3; Bastien 24–6–49–2; Croft 34–12–93–2; Smith 5–3–7–1. *Second Innings*—Watkin 21–5–59–1; Frost 23–3–75–2; Bastien 23–11–40–1; Croft 25–3–103–1; Smith 7.1–1–28–0; Butcher 1–0–1–0.

## Glamorgan

| | | | |
|---|---|---|---|
| A. R. Butcher c Smith b Salisbury | ... 52 | I. Smith not out | ................... 12 |
| M. Morris not out | ...........156 | | |
| R. J. Shastri b Bunting | ............. 26 | B 11, l-b 6, w 1, n-b 4 | ...... 22 |
| M. P. Maynard c Moores b Jones | .....127 | | |
| G. C. Holmes lbw b Jones | .......... 0 | 1/102 2/170 3/372 4/376    (4 wkts dec.) 395 |

R. D. B. Croft, †C. P. Metson, S. L. Watkin, S. Bastien and M. Frost did not bat.

Bonus points – Glamorgan 4 (Score at 100 overs: 321-2).

Bowling: Dodemaide 21–4–57–0; Jones 24-2-92–2; Salisbury 30–9–85–1; Donelan 23–3–78–0; Bunting 16-2-66–1.

Umpires: J. D. Bond and A. A. Jones.

At Worcester, May 31, June 1, 3. GLAMORGAN drew with WORCESTERSHIRE.

## GLAMORGAN v SOMERSET

At Swansea, June 4, 5, 6. Drawn. Glamorgan 1 pt, Somerset 4 pts. Toss: Somerset. On a benign St Helen's pitch, quite unlike the one reported by the umpires in May, Somerset built a commanding first-innings total. Cook, who the previous year had plundered the Glamorgan bowling with an innings of 313 not out at Cardiff, scored 152 from 260 balls, with 21 fours, and added 242 for the third wicket with his captain, Tavaré, whose 162 came from 243 balls and contained 25 fours. The second day was washed out, and as a result of the captains' conferring at the start of the last day, Glamorgan were eventually left with the stiff task of scoring 366 in 90 overs. Despite an excellent start from Morris and Butcher, who put on 183 for the first wicket, the middle order faltered, although Maynard struck a brisk 39. Butcher hit seven fours in his 186-ball innings of 102. Glamorgan required 122 from the final twenty overs, but when they lost three wickets for 19 runs they called off the chase.

*Close of play*: First day, Somerset 422-5 (N. D. Burns 62*, K. H. MacLeay 8*); Second day, No play.

## Somerset

| | | | |
|---|---|---|---|
| S. J. Cook b Frost | ...................152 | K. H. MacLeay not out | ............. 8 |
| P. M. Roebuck c Butcher b Frost | ..... 7 | | |
| A. N. Hayhurst c Metson b Barwick | .. 1 | B 4, l-b 5, w 1, n-b 5 | ........ 15 |
| *C. J. Tavaré c Maynard b Barwick | ...162 | | |
| R. J. Harden c Cann b Croft | ......... 15 | 1/40 2/41 3/283    (5 wkts dec.) 422 |
| †N. D. Burns not out | .............. 62 | 4/303 5/372 |

G. D. Rose, H. R. J. Trump, N. A. Mallender and D. A. Graveney did not bat.

Bonus points – Somerset 4, Glamorgan 1 (Score at 100 overs: 370-4).

Bowling: Frost 16–0–81–2; Bastien 25-2-113–0; Barwick 30–5–85-2; Smith 3–1–7–0; Croft 28–6–90–1; Cann 8-0-37-0.

*Somerset forfeited their second innings.*

## Glamorgan

| | | | |
|---|---|---|---|
| I. Smith not out | ..................... 33 | – (6) run out | ............ 11 |
| †C. P. Metson not out | ............ 21 | – (7) c Tavaré b Rose | ........... 0 |
| *A. R. Butcher (did not bat) | ................ | – (1) c Mallender b MacLeay | ....102 |
| H. Morris (did not bat) | ................... | – (2) lbw b MacLeay | .... 84 |
| R. J. Shastri (did not bat) | .............. | – (3) c Tavaré b Mallender | .... 8 |
| M. P. Maynard (did not bat) | ............... | – (4) c Tavaré b Rose | .... 39 |
| M. J. Cann (did not bat) | .................. | – (5) not out | .... 29 |
| R. D. B. Croft (did not bat) | ............... | – not out | ........... 4 |
| B 1, l-b 2 | ..................... 3 | B 2, l-b 10, w 1, n-b 14 .. 27 |
| | (no wkt dec.) 57 | 1/183 2/209 3/230    (6 wkts) 304 |
| | | 4/279 5/298 6/298 |

S. R. Barwick, S. Bastien and M. Frost did not bat.

Bowling: *First Innings*—Harden 4.5–0–28–0; Cook 4–0–26–0. *Second Innings*—Mallende
14–3–42–1; Rose 11–1–31–2; Hayhurst 13–2–49–0; MacLeay 17–0–71–2; Trump 9–3–24–0
Graveney 18–4–53–0; Roebuck 7–0–22–0.

Umpires: J. W. Holder and K. E. Palmer.

At Chesterfield, June 7, 8, 10. GLAMORGAN lost to DERBYSHIRE by 108 runs.

# GLAMORGAN v MIDDLESEX

At Cardiff, June 14, 15, 17. Glamorgan won by 129 runs. Glamorgan 19 pts, Middlesex 3 pts
Toss: Glamorgan. Glamorgan's win was their first at Sophia Gardens for four years, and their
first over Middlesex in the County Championship since 1969. Their late-order batsmen ha
ensured a useful first-innings total, with Croft and Metson making solid contributions, bu
rain on the second day changed the course of the match dramatically. Gatting, anxious to
record Middlesex's first win of the season, declared 227 runs behind, and Butcher responde
by striking a rapid half-century before the close. His declaration on the last morning, and
delayed start because of rain, left Middlesex needing 341 to win from a minimum of 98 overs
Gatting and Emburey added 74 for the fifth wicket, but when Emburey was adjudged leg
before to Frost, the lower order had no answer to Glamorgan's accurate pace attack. Gatting
however, was immovable and struck eleven fours in a determined 96 not out from 22
deliveries. Without his contribution, Middlesex would have been in a sorry state.
*Close of play:* First day, Glamorgan 238-6 (R. D. B. Croft 40\*, C. P. Metson 4\*); Second
day, Glamorgan 113-2 (R. J. Shastri 25\*, M. P. Maynard 9\*).

## Glamorgan

| | | | | |
|---|---|---|---|---|
| \*A. R. Butcher c Roseberry b Cowans | 31 | – c Sylvester b Brown | | 5? |
| H. Morris c Emburey b Tufnell | 48 | – b Tufnell | | 1? |
| R. J. Shastri c Emburey b Cowans | 33 | – not out | | 2? |
| M. P. Maynard c Farbrace b Tufnell | 0 | – not out | | ? |
| P. A. Cottey c Williams b Cowans | 24 | | | |
| A. Dale c Farbrace b Cowans | 34 | | | |
| R. D. B. Croft c Emburey b Williams | 50 | | | |
| †C. P. Metson b Tufnell | 49 | | | |
| S. L. Watkin not out | 13 | | | |
| B 5, l-b 7, w 1, n-b 18 | 31 | B 5, l-b 1, n-b 1 | | ? |

1/51 2/101 3/101 4/145 5/150     (8 wkts dec.) 313    1/64 2/92     (2 wkts dec.) 113
6/227 7/269 8/313

S. R. Barwick and M. Frost did not bat.

Bonus points – Glamorgan 3, Middlesex 3 (Score at 100 overs: 272-7).

Bowling: *First Innings*—Williams 26–6–79–1; Sylvester 15–2–80–0; Cowans 19–8–42–4
Tufnell 36.3–13–76–3; Emburey 10–2–24–0. *Second Innings*—Sylvester 5–0–18–0; Cowan
4–0–16–0; Emburey 5–0–31–0; Tufnell 7–0–25–1; Brown 3–0–17–1.

## Middlesex

| | | | | |
|---|---|---|---|---|
| I. J. F. Hutchinson c Metson b Frost | 9 | – c Metson b Frost | | ? |
| M. A. Roseberry not out | 40 | – lbw b Barwick | | 3? |
| \*M. W. Gatting b Watkin | 13 | – not out | | 9? |
| M. R. Ramprakash not out | 16 | – c Metson b Barwick | | ? |
| K. R. Brown (did not bat) | | – c Butcher b Frost | | 1? |
| J. E. Emburey (did not bat) | | – lbw b Frost | | 4? |
| N. F. Williams (did not bat) | | – c Cottey b Frost | | ? |
| †P. Farbrace (did not bat) | | – run out | | ? |
| P. C. R. Tufnell (did not bat) | | – c Maynard b Barwick | | ? |
| N. G. Cowans (did not bat) | | – b Barwick | | ? |
| S. A. Sylvester (did not bat) | | – c Metson b Watkin | | ? |
| L-b 7, n-b 1 | 8 | B 1, l-b 8, n-b 1 | | 1? |

1/30 2/52               (2 wkts dec.) 86     1/15 2/62 3/62 4/82 5/156     21?
                                             6/158 7/181 8/198 9/198

Bowling: *First Innings*—Watkin 13–4–35–1; Frost 9–3–24–1; Barwick 12–6–20–0. *Second Innings*—Watkin 25.5–3–82–1; Frost 21–6–55–4; Barwick 24–8–49–4; Dale 4–1–6–0; Croft 5–2–10–0.

Umpires: D. J. Constant and K. J. Lyons.

At Cambridge, June 18, 19, 20. GLAMORGAN beat CAMBRIDGE UNIVERSITY by 181 runs.

## GLAMORGAN v LEICESTERSHIRE

At Neath, June 21, 22, 23. Drawn. Glamorgan 3 pts, Leicestershire 2 pts. Toss: Glamorgan. When Glamorgan play at The Gnoll, the game is often ruined by the weather, and the 1991 fixture was no exception. There was no play after lunch on the second day. On the first day Shastri took five and a half hours to reach his first Championship hundred of the season, hitting eleven fours, but while scoring was difficult on a slow pitch on which the ball kept low, Maynard enlivened the proceedings by hitting 61 from 67 balls, 46 of his runs coming in boundaries. Leicestershire also found scoring difficult, and had lost Briers and Hepworth before the rain set in.

*Close of play:* First day, Glamorgan 291-7 (R. J. Shastri 101*, S. Bastien 8*); Second day, Leicestershire 46-2 (T. J. Boon 18*, J. J. Whitaker 2*).

### Glamorgan

| | | | |
|---|---|---|---|
| *A. R. Butcher c Boon b Maguire | 15 | S. Bastien not out | 22 |
| H. Morris c Whitticase b Wilkinson | 35 | S. R. Barwick not out | 24 |
| R. J. Shastri c Briers b Wilkinson | 107 | | |
| M. P. Maynard c and b Wilkinson | 61 | L-b 4, w 2, n-b 6 | 12 |
| P. A. Cottey c sub b Lewis | 7 | | |
| A. Dale c Whitticase b Wilkinson | 15 | (8 wkts dec.) 337 | |
| R. D. B. Croft b Maguire | 25 | | |
| †C. P. Metson c Briers b Potter | 14 | | |

1/36 2/79 3/156
4/168 5/195 6/252
7/281 8/307

M. Frost did not bat.

Bonus points – Glamorgan 3, Leicestershire 2 (Score at 100 overs: 256-6).

Bowling: Lewis 33–8–90–1; Maguire 35–11–77–2; Millns 8–1–14–0; Wilkinson 31–9–106–4; Potter 13–1–46–1.

### Leicestershire

| | |
|---|---|
| T. J. Boon not out | 18 |
| *N. E. Briers b Frost | 4 |
| P. N. Hepworth b Bastien | 21 |
| J. J. Whitaker not out | 2 |
| N-b 1 | 1 |

1/12 2/39        (2 wkts) 46

L. Potter, B. F. Smith, C. C. Lewis, †P. Whitticase, D. J. Millns, C. W. Wilkinson and J. N. Maguire did not bat.

Bowling: Frost 10–4–20–1; Barwick 6–3–9–0; Bastien 8–2–17–1; Croft 1–1–0–0.

Umpires: G. I. Burgess and D. R. Shepherd.

At Liverpool, June 28, 29, July 1. GLAMORGAN drew with LANCASHIRE.

## GLAMORGAN v NOTTINGHAMSHIRE

At Cardiff, July 2, 3, 4. Nottinghamshire won by eight wickets. Nottinghamshire 22 pts, Glamorgan 5 pts. Toss: Glamorgan. Despite a maiden double-hundred from Maynard, Nottinghamshire continued their impressive form by inflicting on Glamorgan their third Championship defeat of the season. The home county, without Morris, who was on stand-by for England at Trent Bridge, were soon in trouble on the first morning against the hostile bowling of Pick and Stephenson. Apart from Cottey, no-one looked capable of the gritty innings needed to master the Nottinghamshire attack. Watkin restricted the visitors' first-innings lead to 67 by taking the last three wickets for no runs in six balls, and in doing so robbed Robinson of the chance to reach three figures; but Glamorgan were soon in trouble again. However, Maynard now played an innings of rare quality, striking two sixes and 28 fours in scoring 204 from 226 balls, and Butcher was able to set Nottinghamshire a challenging target of 274 in a minimum of 73 overs. Broad and Pollard gave them a positive start, whereupon Randall, with a fluent, undefeated century, and Johnson hurried them to victory with fourteen overs remaining.

*Close of play:* First day, Nottinghamshire 124-3 (R. T. Robinson 33*, D. W. Randall 20*). Second day, Glamorgan 211-3 (M. P. Maynard 143*, P. A. Cottey 4*).

### Glamorgan

| | | | |
|---|---:|---|---:|
| *A. R. Butcher b Stephenson | 37 | – c Afford b Stephenson | 0 |
| S. P. James lbw b Pick | 1 | – lbw b Pick | 42 |
| R. J. Shastri lbw b Pick | 0 | – c Stephenson b Afford | 7 |
| M. P. Maynard c Pick b Stephenson | 2 | – c Hemmings b Crawley | 204 |
| P. A. Cottey lbw b Pick | 46 | – c Pollard b Crawley | 55 |
| A. Dale st French b Afford | 25 | – b Afford | 13 |
| R. D. B. Croft c Pollard b Stephenson | 0 | – not out | 1 |
| †C. P. Metson run out | 4 | | |
| S. L. Watkin b Stephenson | 15 | | |
| S. R. Barwick c French b Afford | 0 | | |
| M. Frost not out | 2 | | |
| L-b 5, w 4, n-b 10 | 19 | B 4, l-b 6, n-b 7 | 17 |

1/8 2/8 3/24 4/49 5/114      151     1/3 2/15 3/167     (6 wkts dec.) 340
6/117 7/127 8/132 9/133                4/301 5/332 6/340

Bonus points – Glamorgan 1, Nottinghamshire 4.

Bowling: *First Innings*—Pick 18-4-54-3; Stephenson 13.3-3-40-4; Hemmings 11-5-19-0; Crawley 3-0-13-0; Afford 13-6-20-2. *Second Innings*—Pick 17-6-60-1; Stephenson 16-4-66-1; Afford 27-9-67-2; Hemmings 14-2-65-0; Crawley 18.3-3-72-2.

### Nottinghamshire

| | | | |
|---|---:|---|---:|
| B. C. Broad c and b Croft | 34 | – c Barwick b Frost | 36 |
| P. R. Pollard c Cottey b Frost | 26 | – lbw b Barwick | 33 |
| *R. T. Robinson not out | 91 | | |
| P. Johnson run out | 8 | – not out | 77 |
| D. W. Randall lbw b Watkin | 20 | – (3) not out | 112 |
| M. A. Crawley c Cottey b Watkin | 5 | | |
| F. D. Stephenson b Barwick | 22 | | |
| †B. N. French b Barwick | 3 | | |
| E. E. Hemmings b Watkin | 4 | | |
| R. A. Pick c Metson b Watkin | 0 | | |
| J. A. Afford lbw b Watkin | 0 | | |
| N-b 5 | 5 | B 4, l-b 7, w 1, n-b 6 | 18 |

1/57 2/68 3/84 4/126 5/134      218     1/58 2/101        (2 wkts) 276
6/195 7/204 8/218 9/218

Bonus points – Nottinghamshire 2, Glamorgan 4.

Bowling: *First Innings*—Watkin 22.5-3-59-5; Frost 15-0-58-1; Croft 41-11-89-1; Barwick 14-8-12-2. *Second Innings*—Watkin 12-0-47-0; Frost 9-0-59-1; Barwick 15-3-67-1; Croft 15-1-65-0; Shastri 8-0-27-0.

Umpires: D. O. Oslear and R. C. Tolchard.

At Maidstone, July 5, 6, 8. GLAMORGAN drew with KENT.

At Swansea, July 16, 17, 18. GLAMORGAN drew with WEST INDIANS (See West Indian tour section).

At Cheltenham, July 19, 20, 22. GLAMORGAN drew with GLOUCESTERSHIRE.

## GLAMORGAN v ESSEX

At Cardiff, July 23, 24, 25. Glamorgan won by four wickets. Glamorgan 16 pts, Essex 3 pts. Toss: Glamorgan. Glamorgan achieved their third Championship win of the season, and their second at Cardiff, when Essex set them 271 in 68 overs after rain had allowed only 43 overs on the first day and no more than 6.2 on the second. It was a generous target, especially as Essex were without Gooch and Pringle, on Test duty, and Foster, who was absent through injury. The highlight of Essex's innings was a career-best 157 from Seymour, who compiled his maiden first-class century, and an opening partnership of 206 with Stephenson, over three days in between stoppages. He hit fifteen fours in an innings of four and a half hours. Both sides forfeited innings, and Glamorgan were given a rousing start by Butcher, who scored 61, including eight boundaries, in an opening partnership of 90 with James before treading on his stumps. In contrast to James, who went 51 minutes before scoring, Maynard raced to 24 with six boundaries, and when he was eventually out for 38, Shastri guided Glamorgan to victory with an over and a half remaining. He was tied down early on by Childs's accuracy, and reprieved when Garnham missed a stumping chance, but he played an authoritative innings, hitting eight fours and receiving valuable support from Cottey, Croft and Metson.

*Close of play:* First day, Essex 113-0 (A. C. H. Seymour 69\*, J. P. Stephenson 38\*); Second day, Essex 133-0 (A. C. H. Seymour 77\*, J. P. Stephenson 50\*).

### Essex

| | | |
|---|---|---|
| A. C. H. Seymour b Croft | | 157 |
| J. P. Stephenson b Frost | | 76 |
| *P. J. Prichard not out | | 22 |
| N. Hussain not out | | 6 |
| L-b 5, w 1, n-b 3 | | 9 |

1/206 2/258 (2 wkts dec.) 270

Salim Malik, N. Shahid, †M. A. Garnham, T. D. Topley, A. G. J. Fraser, S. J. W. Andrew and J. H. Childs did not bat.

Bonus points – Essex 3.

Bowling: Watkin 23-3-75-0; Frost 17-1-58-1; Bastien 22-6-63-0; Croft 10.1-2-23-1; Dale 10-1-46-0.

*Essex forfeited their second innings.*

### Glamorgan

*Glamorgan forfeited their first innings.*

| | | |
|---|---|---|
| *A. R. Butcher hit wkt b Stephenson | | 61 |
| S. P. James c Topley b Stephenson | | 16 |
| A. Dale c Hussain b Andrew | | 9 |
| M. P. Maynard c and b Childs | | 38 |
| R. J. Shastri not out | | 70 |
| P. A. Cottey b Childs | | 20 |
| R. D. B. Croft c Salim Malik b Andrew | | 10 |
| †C. P. Metson not out | | 19 |
| B 6, l-b 5, w 1, n-b 16 | | 28 |

1/90 2/94 3/143 (6 wkts) 271
4/150 5/199 6/224

S. L. Watkin, S. Bastien and M. Frost did not bat.

Bowling: Andrew 22.3-3-90-2; Topley 17-1-50-0; Stephenson 9-2-50-2; Childs 18-5-70-2.

Umpires: J. C. Balderstone and A. A. Jones.

At The Oval, July 26, 27, 29. GLAMORGAN drew with SURREY.

# GLAMORGAN v HAMPSHIRE

At Swansea, August 9, 10, 12. Hampshire won by 172 runs. Hampshire 18 pts, Glamorgan 4 pts. Toss: Glamorgan. Having been set 317 from a minimum of 78 overs, Glamorgan never looked like achieving their target against Hampshire bowlers who fully exploited a grassy pitch. The Glamorgan seamers had had their own opportunity on the rain-interrupted first day, when Hampshire were put in, but the eventual margin of victory reflected their inaccuracy, as well as their inability to capitalise on conditions which assisted swing bowling. Gower, with eight fours in a cultured 47 from 68 deliveries, and a career-best 39 not out by Turner helped Hampshire reach a respectable 216 for nine in the 67.3 overs of play. When the second day fell victim to the rain, Hampshire added a further 100 runs on the final morning, following an agreement between the captains. Glamorgan needed Butcher to lay the foundations of victory, but he was out to the fifth ball of the innings, and Maynard also went cheaply. Glamorgan were soon 84 for five, and only Shastri, who remained unbeaten looked capable of coping with an attack in which Shine shone.

*Close of play:* First day, Hampshire 216-9 (I. J. Turner 39*, K. J. Shine 0*); Second day, No play.

## Hampshire

| | | |
|---|---|---|
| T. C. Middleton c Maynard b Barwick | 20 | |
| C. L. Smith c James b Foster | 0 – not out | 49 |
| K. D. James c Shastri b Watkin | 32 | |
| D. I. Gower c Dale b Foster | 47 | |
| *M. C. J. Nicholas c Metson b Watkin | 4 – (1) not out | 50 |
| R. M. F. Cox b Frost | 26 | |
| †A. N. Aymes c Butcher b Watkin | 13 | |
| T. M. Tremlett c Metson b Frost | 2 | |
| I. J. Turner not out | 39 | |
| C. A. Connor lbw b Frost | 12 | |
| K. J. Shine not out | 0 | |
| B 9, l-b 9, n-b 3 | 21 | N-b 1 ............ 1 |

1/0 2/57 3/75 4/80 5/136      (9 wkts dec.) 216      (no wkt dec.) 100
6/144 7/146 8/181 9/215

Bonus points – Hampshire 2, Glamorgan 4.

Bowling: *First Innings*—Watkin 24–11–57–3; Foster 12.3–5–39–2; Frost 15–2–56–3; Barwick 16–3–46–1. *Second Innings*—Dale 6–2–17–0; Croft 10–1–49–0; Maynard 4.5–0–34–0.

## Glamorgan

*Glamorgan forfeited their first innings.*

| | | | |
|---|---|---|---|
| *A. R. Butcher c Connor b Shine | 1 | D. J. Foster c Cox b Shine | 0 |
| S. P. James lbw b Tremlett | 20 | M. Frost b Shine | 6 |
| A. Dale c Aymes b James | 18 | S. R. Barwick c Aymes b James | 3 |
| M. P. Maynard c Middleton b James | 4 | | |
| R. J. Shastri not out | 44 | B 4, l-b 1, w 4, n-b 8 | 17 |
| R. D. B. Croft c Turner b Shine | 16 | | |
| †C. P. Metson c Aymes b Connor | 10 | 1/2 2/39 3/55 4/57 5/84 | 144 |
| S. L. Watkin c Aymes b Shine | 5 | 6/105 7/118 8/118 9/128 | |

Bowling: Shine 16–1–58–5; Connor 12–5–15–1; Tremlett 10–3–39–1; James 13–5–27–3.

Umpires: D. J. Constant and R. C. Tolchard.

At Leeds, August 16, 17, 19. GLAMORGAN drew with YORKSHIRE.

At Birmingham, August 20, 21, 22. GLAMORGAN drew with WARWICKSHIRE.

## GLAMORGAN v GLOUCESTERSHIRE

At Abergavenny, August 28, 29, 30, 31. Glamorgan won by nine wickets. Glamorgan 23 pts, Gloucestershire 4 pts. Toss: Glamorgan. Glamorgan's fourth Championship win of the season was built on their equalling the highest total at the Pen-y-Pound ground – Worcestershire's 514 for four declared the previous season. Butcher and Morris gave them a formidable start of 197, with the captain hitting a six and 21 fours in his third Championship century at Abergavenny in successive years since 1989. Morris, when 19, became the youngest player to score 10,000 runs for the county. Later, after three wickets had fallen for 2 runs, Dale, who hit eighteen fours and his first Championship hundred, put on 172 with James for the fifth wicket. Despite the efforts of Lloyds and Lawrence, whose career-best 66 from 52 balls contained 56 runs in boundaries, Gloucestershire failed by 8 runs to avoid the follow-on. Batting again they were soon in trouble at 46 for four, but Wright batted for five and a half hours and, supported by Russell and Alleyne, ensured that his side would not lose by an innings. Lawrence hit another six fours in his 44, and eventually Glamorgan had to score 153 from 51 overs. An unbroken partnership of 123 between Morris and Dale saw them there with 13.3 overs in hand.

*Close of play:* First day, Glamorgan 368-4 (A. Dale 79*, S. P. James 42*); Second day, Gloucestershire 184-4 (A. J. Wright 63*, R. C. Russell 13*); Third day, Gloucestershire 153-5 (A. J. Wright 47*, R. C. Russell 34*).

### Glamorgan

| | | | | |
|---|---|---|---|---|
| *A. R. Butcher c and b Gilbert | 147 | – c Russell b Babington | 20 |
| H. Morris c Russell b Lawrence | 85 | – not out | 50 |
| A. Dale run out | 140 | – not out | 80 |
| M. P. Maynard c and b Babington | 2 | | |
| R. J. Shastri lbw b Babington | 0 | | |
| S. P. James b Ball | 66 | | |
| R. D. B. Croft c Russell b Scott | 14 | | |
| †C. P. Metson not out | 26 | | |
| S. L. Watkin run out | 4 | | |
| S. Bastien st Russell b Ball | 2 | | |
| B 4, l-b 10, n-b 14 | 28 | B 1, l-b 1, n-b 1 | 3 |

1/197 2/254 3/256 4/256 5/428   (9 wkts dec.) 514    1/30       (1 wkt) 153
6/477 7/478 8/494 9/514

M. Frost did not bat.

Bonus points – Glamorgan 4, Gloucestershire 1 (Score at 100 overs: 335-4).

Bowling: *First Innings*—Lawrence 21–2–63–1; Gilbert 23–2–85–1; Babington 32–3–120–2; Ball 36.3–7–109–2; Scott 19–4–59–1; Lloyds 8–0–28–0; Alleyne 12–4–33–0; Athey 2–0–3–0. *Second Innings*—Lawrence 5–0–23–0; Babington 4–0–13–1; Ball 7–1–29–0; Gilbert 9–1–31–0; Lloyds 7–2–24–0; Athey 5–0–27–0; Wright 0.3–0–4–0.

## Gloucestershire

| | | | |
|---|---|---|---|
| G. D. Hodgson c Metson b Croft | 38 | – lbw b Watkin | 4 |
| R. J. Scott lbw b Bastien | 21 | – (3) c Metson b Dale | 10 |
| *A. J. Wright c James b Shastri | 89 | – (4) c Maynard b Frost | 83 |
| C. W. J. Athey c Morris b Shastri | 2 | – (5) lbw b Dale | 0 |
| M. W. Alleyne c Metson b Frost | 40 | – (6) c Butcher b Shastri | 33 |
| †R. C. Russell run out | 15 | – (7) st Metson b Croft | 39 |
| J. W. Lloyds c and b Croft | 5 | – (2) c Metson b Shastri | 12 |
| M. C. J. Ball c Morris b Shastri | 0 | – c Maynard b Shastri | 23 |
| D. V. Lawrence c Metson b Frost | 66 | – b Watkin | 44 |
| D. R. Gilbert b Shastri | 2 | – not out | 16 |
| A. M. Babington not out | 14 | – c Butcher b Frost | 24 |
| L-b 8, n-b 12 | 20 | B 4, l-b 10, n-b 7 | 21 |

1/51 2/69 3/72 4/148 5/216       357     1/17 2/17 3/46 4/46 5/106     309
6/221 7/223 8/296 9/309             6/178 7/211 8/268 9/268

Bonus points – Gloucestershire 3, Glamorgan 3 (Score at 100 overs: 298-8).

Bowling: *First Innings*—Watkin 24–7–51–0; Frost 21–5–82–2; Bastien 17–4–76–1; Croft 23.1–4–66–2; Shastri 38–13–74–4. *Second Innings*—Frost 11.4–3–30–2; Bastien 3–0–13–0; Watkin 16–3–73–2; Shastri 42–20–73–3; Dale 7–2–33–2; Croft 31–9–73–1.

Umpires: K. E. Palmer and A. G. T. Whitehead.

## GLAMORGAN v WORCESTERSHIRE

At Cardiff, September 10, 11, 12, 13. Worcestershire won by ten wickets. Worcestershire 23 pts, Glamorgan 3 pts. Toss: Worcestershire. A resounding defeat on the final morning provided a disappointing end to Glamorgan's programme of home games, but once Curtis had batted throughout the Worcestershire innings, unbeaten after nine hours, the visitors dominated the game. By the third day the pitch had become responsive to spin, and apart from Butcher, Dale and James, none of the Glamorgan batsmen could come to terms with the combination of Hick's off-breaks and the slow left-arm spin of Stemp. Glamorgan had been made to follow on after collapsing in the first innings to the swing and seam bowling of Radford and Newport, with the last five wickets falling for 32 runs on the third morning. There were hopes of a second-innings recovery when Butcher and Dale added 103 for the second wicket, but when they departed, only James's rearguard action prevented defeat in three days. As it was, Worcestershire needed just one over, from Hick, on the fourth morning to finish off the Glamorgan innings, and 40 minutes' batting to achieve their sixth Championship win of the season.

*Close of play:* First day, Worcestershire 282-6 (T. S. Curtis 136*, R. K. Illingworth 22*); Second day, Glamorgan 135-5 (S. P. James 28*, R. D. B. Croft 5*); Third day, Glamorgan 247-9 (M. Frost 2*, D. J. Foster 8*).

## Worcestershire

| | | | |
|---|---|---|---|
| *T. S. Curtis not out | 186 | | |
| C. M. Tolley b Frost | 15 | – not out | 4 |
| G. A. Hick c Metson b Frost | 4 | | |
| D. A. Leatherdale c Metson b Barwick | 24 | | |
| D. B. D'Oliveira c Morris b Barwick | 2 | | |
| †S. J. Rhodes c Metson b Frost | 19 | – (1) not out | 33 |
| S. R. Lampitt b Barwick | 31 | | |
| R. K. Illingworth c Morris b Shastri | 44 | | |
| P. J. Newport c Metson b Shastri | 0 | | |
| N. V. Radford c Maynard b Croft | 20 | | |
| R. D. Stemp c Metson b Shastri | 3 | | |
| B 1, l-b 9, w 3, n-b 21 | 34 | N-b 1 | 1 |

1/25 2/29 3/90 4/97 5/135      382      (no wkt) 38
6/210 7/322 8/324 9/379

Bonus points – Worcestershire 3, Glamorgan 2 (Score at 100 overs: 257-6).

Bowling: *First Innings*—Frost 29–4–72–3; Foster 22–0–99–0; Barwick 33–7–68–3; Dale 8–3–24–0; Shastri 42–13–63–3; Croft 22–6–46–1. *Second Innings*—Frost 3–1–6–0; Barwick 2–1–2–0; Shastri 3.5–0–21–0; Croft 3–1–9–0.

## Glamorgan

| | | |
|---|---|---|
| *A. R. Butcher c Rhodes b Lampitt | 61 | – c Rhodes b Hick ............ 93 |
| H. Morris c D'Oliveira b Newport | 2 | – c Rhodes b Lampitt .......... 7 |
| A. Dale c Rhodes b Radford | 12 | – c Rhodes b Stemp ........... 46 |
| M. P. Maynard b Radford | 0 | – c Illingworth b Hick ........ 21 |
| R. J. Shastri b Tolley | 10 | – c Curtis b Stemp ............ 1 |
| S. P. James not out | 47 | – b Stemp.................... 30 |
| R. D. B. Croft lbw b Newport | 9 | – b Hick .................... 4 |
| †C. P. Metson c Curtis b Newport | 0 | – b Stemp................... 10 |
| S. R. Barwick b Radford | 2 | – c Newport b Hick ........... 5 |
| D. J. Foster b Radford | 0 | – (11) c Lampitt b Hick ....... 12 |
| M. Frost b Newport | 0 | – (10) not out ............... 2 |
| B 10, l-b 5, w 2, n-b 7 | 24 | B 4, l-b 4, w 4, n-b 8 .... 20 |

1/5 2/31 3/31 4/79 5/120                        167        1/22 2/125 3/166 4/167 5/187        251
5/143 7/153 8/160 9/160                                    6/212 7/224 8/231 9/238

Bonus points – Glamorgan 1, Worcestershire 4.

Bowling: *First Innings*—Radford 18–8–29–4; Newport 22–3–44–4; Tolley 13–3–29–1; Lampitt 5–0–36–1; Illingworth 9–4–8–0; Stemp 5–2–6–0. *Second Innings*—Radford 3–0–16–0; Newport 9–1–27–0; Lampitt 10–0–39–1; Tolley 7–0–30–0; Illingworth 8–1–15–0; Stemp 37–11–74–4; Hick 29–11–42–5.

Umpires: R. Palmer and A. G. T. Whitehead.

At Southampton, September 17, 18, 19, 20. GLAMORGAN beat HAMPSHIRE by seven wickets.

## COUNTY BENEFITS AWARDED FOR 1992

| | | | |
|---|---|---|---|
| Derbyshire | K. J. Barnett. | Middlesex | Middlesex Youth Development. |
| Essex | D. R. Pringle. | Northamptonshire | Target 2000. |
| Gloucestershire | C. A. Walsh. | Nottinghamshire | R. T. Robinson. |
| Hampshire | R. J. Parks. | Surrey | I. A. Greig. |
| Kent | N. R. Taylor. | Warwickshire | G. C. Small. |
| Lancashire | D. P. Hughes. | Yorkshire | S. N. Hartley. |

*No benefit was awarded by Glamorgan, Leicestershire, Somerset, Sussex or Worcestershire.*

# GLOUCESTERSHIRE

*Patron:* HRH The Princess of Wales
*President:* F. J. Twisleton
*Chairman:* R. W. Rossiter
*Secretary:* P. G. M. August
   Phoenix County Ground, Nevil Road,
   Bristol BS7 9EJ (Telephone: 0272-245216)
*Captain:* A. J. Wright
*Senior Coach:* 1991 – E. J. Barlow
*Assistant Coach:* A. W. Stovold
*Youth Coach:* G. G. M. Wiltshire

Gloucestershire confounded the pessimists among their supporters – as well as those bookmakers and professional pundits who consigned them to bottom place in the Britannic Assurance Championship before a ball was bowled – by winning one more game than in 1990, while holding on to thirteenth place. Halfway through the programme, in fact, Gloucestershire were fifth, but suspicions that this would prove deceptive were eventually confirmed. As the season wore on, the team fell away so badly that the last five games were lost, some by embarrassingly wide margins.

During this unhappy sequence, it was announced that Eddie Barlow, the senior coach, would not be returning from South Africa for the final year of his three-year contract. Barlow cited pressures of business at his vineyard in Orange Free State, saying that he was "bitterly disappointed" that he could not finish rebuilding the team. "We have gone a long way towards getting things rolling. We have players in the England side and we are doing more things right than wrong. We pulled through a difficult time last year and some fine young players are being brought on", he commented. It was too early to pass final judgment, but it seems fair to point out that Jack Russell and David Lawrence were capped by England before Barlow's arrival, and Gloucestershire's sixteenth place in the Second Eleven Championship hardly suggested a wealth of young talent.

At first, it seemed that the loss of Curran, Graveney, Bainbridge and Walsh from the 1990 side might be overcome painlessly. Richard Scott, from Hampshire, the new opening partner for Dean Hodgson, began with a hundred against Worcestershire, and the next four-day match, against Hampshire, was won convincingly with Lawrence, at his fastest, taking eleven wickets. But then reality intervened, in the shape of two-day defeats by Warwickshire and Essex. It was greatly to the credit of Tony Wright, the captain, that spirits did not flag. He conjured a win over Leicestershire, in a match reduced to one innings by forfeits, with only one capped bowler in the side, and there were also victories against Hampshire, Northamptonshire and Lancashire. However, the Lancashire game was the only one affording maximum bonus points.

The batting was Gloucestershire's main problem. Flimsy, brittle and even abject were among descriptions applied, and the county's total of batting points was comfortably the lowest in the competition. Bill Athey scored four of only eleven Gloucestershire hundreds in the Championship, and Wright, emerging from his trough of 1990, hit three. Wright was obviously happier at No. 3 than opening, though he was usually at the crease with the ball still new, and his batting had a reassuringly solid air. Athey's reliability was such as to be taken for granted, and his wicket remained the one most highly prized by opponents. Towards the end of the season he moved up the order to open, and he carried his bat in successive innings, against Somerset and Sussex.

Some players showed a great propensity for not bothering the scorers. Mark Alleyne headed this league table with seven noughts; Scott got five, Richard Williams, the reserve wicket-keeper, four and Jonathan Hardy four in ten innings. Hardy was unable to force his way into the side for long, which was a pity, for at his best he would have been a great asset. When going well, 23-year-old Alleyne was good to watch, and again he made the county's highest score of the season, 165 against Northamptonshire. Paul Romaines was recalled for the well-attended Cheltenham festival without making a mark, while Tim Hancock, a young batsman from Oxfordshire, played five first-class games, with an encouraging fifty against Sussex.

When Lawrence was free of England calls – and it was one of the pleasures of the summer to see him win a greater public through his Test match endeavours – Gloucestershire had a useful attack. David Gilbert, the Australian replacement for Courtney Walsh, was more a workhorse than a match-winner, despite an eight-wicket return against Kent, but he took 55 Championship wickets in twenty games none the less. Andy Babington, from Sussex, was a tireless worker with a happy knack of breaking partnerships, and in the first half of the season Mike Smith, a left-armer who had played for Combined Universities, skidded the ball through at a lively pace. Martin Gerrard, a more powerfully built exponent of the same style, who arrived from Bristol club cricket, showed the ability to make the ball bounce and leave the batsman.

Martyn Ball, a young off-spinner who was highly regarded several seasons earlier, re-emerged in the closing weeks and took sixteen wickets in three matches. Generally, however, the off-spin was left to Jeremy Lloyds, who also contributed some useful batting and held his share of blinding catches at slip. But there was no left-arm spinner to provide variety, and this, along with a top-class opening batsman, was an urgent need for the future. Although Hodgson usually made a start, and reached 50 seven times, he never went on to a Championship hundred, while Scott, who gave the ball a good thump when established, looked better suited to the middle order.

Gloucestershire's limited-overs record was again disappointing. They failed to reach the knockout stages of the Benson and Hedges Cup, although they won two group matches and lost to Derbyshire only because their opponents had fewer wickets down with the scores tied. In the NatWest Bank Trophy they fell at the second hurdle, and they rarely scored quickly enough to pose a threat in the Refuge Assurance League.

At the end of the season Romaines returned to his native Durham, to become marketing director for the Championship newcomers, and Stuart Barnes, Robert Bell and Edward Milburn were also released. The return of Walsh was expected to strengthen the side, but reinforcements were also required for Gloucestershire to take the field with any real hope of winning trophies. – Geoffrey Wheeler.

420

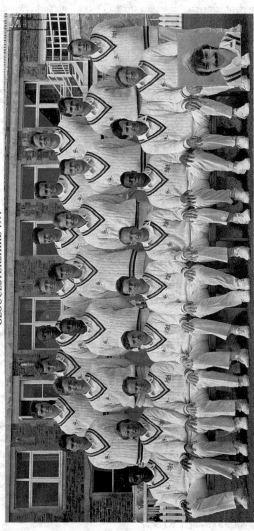

GLOUCESTERSHIRE 1991

*Back row:* T. H. C. Hancock, R. C. J. Williams, R. C. Williams, M. C. J. Ball, A. J. Hunt, A. M. Smith, R. J. Scott. *Middle row:* G. D. Hodgson, S. N. Barnes, H. F. Irving, R. M. Bell, J. J. E. Hardy, A. M. Babington, E. T. Milburn, G. G. M. Wiltshire (*youth coach*). *Front row:* M. W. Alleyne, J. W. Lloyds, A. W. Stovold (*assistant coach*), P. W. Romaines, A. J. Wright (*captain*), C. W. J. Athey, D. V. Lawrence, D. R. Gilbert, E. J. Barlow (*senior coach*). *Inset:* R. C. Russell.

[*Bill Smith*]

## GLOUCESTERSHIRE RESULTS

*All first-class matches – Played 25: Won 6, Lost 10, Drawn 9.*

*County Championship matches – Played 22: Won 5, Lost 10, Drawn 7.*

*Bonus points – Batting 42, Bowling 53.*

*Competition placings – Britannic Assurance County Championship, 13th;
NatWest Bank Trophy, 2nd round; Benson and Hedges Cup, 4th in Group A;
Refuge Assurance League, 12th equal.*

## BRITANNIC ASSURANCE CHAMPIONSHIP AVERAGES

### BATTING

|  | Birthplace | M | I | NO | R | HI | Avge |
|---|---|---|---|---|---|---|---|
| ‡A. J. Wright ....... | Stevenage | 22 | 38 | 6 | 1,477 | 120 | 46.15 |
| ‡C. W. J. Athey ..... | Middlesbrough | 22 | 36 | 5 | 1,350 | 127 | 43.54 |
| ‡R. C. Russell ...... | Stroud | 12 | 19 | 3 | 464 | 111 | 29.00 |
| ‡M. W. Alleyne ..... | Tottenham, London | 22 | 35 | 3 | 921 | 165 | 28.78 |
| G. D. Hodgson ..... | Carlisle | 21 | 37 | 1 | 990 | 89 | 27.50 |
| R. J. Scott ......... | Bournemouth | 17 | 30 | 1 | 763 | 127 | 26.31 |
| ‡J. W. Lloyds ...... | Penang, Malaya | 22 | 33 | 4 | 729 | 69 | 25.13 |
| T. H. C. Hancock .. | Reading | 3 | 5 | 1 | 83 | 51 | 20.75 |
| J. J. E. Hardy ..... | Nakaru, Kenya | 10 | 15 | 2 | 242 | 52 | 18.61 |
| ‡D. V. Lawrence .... | Gloucester | 15 | 22 | 1 | 383 | 66 | 18.23 |
| A. M. Babington ... | London | 15 | 19 | 7 | 176 | 58 | 14.66 |
| D. R. Gilbert ...... | Sydney, Australia | 20 | 26 | 6 | 292 | 28* | 14.60 |
| M. C. J. Ball ...... | Bristol | 5 | 8 | 0 | 105 | 28 | 13.12 |
| M. J. Gerrard ..... | Bristol | 7 | 8 | 4 | 49 | 42 | 12.25 |
| R. C. J. Williams .. | Bristol | 10 | 12 | 2 | 95 | 55* | 9.50 |
| ‡P. W. Romaines .... | Bishop Auckland | 3 | 5 | 0 | 35 | 28 | 7.00 |
| A. M. Smith ....... | Dewsbury | 13 | 13 | 2 | 60 | 22 | 5.45 |

Also batted: J. M. de la Pena (*London*) (2 matches) 1*, 0; R. C. Williams (*Camberwell, London*) (1 match) 0, 13.

*\* Signifies not out.  ‡ Denotes county cap.*

The following played a total of eleven three-figure innings for Gloucestershire in County Championship matches – C. W. J. Athey 4, A. J. Wright 3, R. J. Scott 2, M. W. Alleyne 1, R. C. Russell 1.

### BOWLING

|  | O | M | R | W | BB | 5W/i | Avge |
|---|---|---|---|---|---|---|---|
| D. V. Lawrence ....... | 398.5 | 62 | 1,296 | 60 | 6-67 | 3 | 21.60 |
| M. C. J. Ball ......... | 178 | 34 | 547 | 18 | 5-128 | 1 | 30.38 |
| D. R. Gilbert ........ | 602.2 | 129 | 1,695 | 55 | 8-55 | 1 | 30.81 |
| A. M. Smith ......... | 284.2 | 51 | 868 | 28 | 4-41 | 0 | 31.00 |
| M. W. Alleyne ....... | 118.1 | 23 | 381 | 11 | 3-35 | 0 | 34.63 |
| A. M. Babington ...... | 428.2 | 80 | 1,300 | 35 | 4-33 | 0 | 37.14 |
| R. J. Scott .......... | 175 | 38 | 545 | 14 | 3-43 | 0 | 38.92 |
| J. W. Lloyds ......... | 510.2 | 121 | 1,493 | 33 | 6-94 | 1 | 45.24 |

Also bowled: C. W. J. Athey 60-8-179-2; J. M. de la Pena 25-0-138-3; M. J. Gerrard 106.4-17-355-5; R. C. Russell 0.3-0-10-0; R. C. Williams 26-4-81-1; A. J. Wright 0.3-0-4-0.

**Wicket-keepers:** R. C. Russell 36 ct, 3 st; R. C. J. Williams 18 ct, 3 st.

**Leading Fielders:** J. W. Lloyds 21, A. J. Wright 16, C. W. J. Athey 15.

At Worcester, April 27, 28, 29, 30. GLOUCESTERSHIRE drew with WORCESTER-SHIRE.

## GLOUCESTERSHIRE v HAMPSHIRE

At Bristol, May 9, 10, 11, 13. Gloucestershire won by eight wickets. Gloucestershire 21 pts, Hampshire 6 pts. Toss: Gloucestershire. Lawrence, with his first ten-wicket return, and Russell were key figures in a surprise victory for Gloucestershire. Hampshire, put in on a pitch showing signs of damp, were again indebted to Chris Smith, who batted for 387 minutes and hit sixteen fours in compiling his fourth three-figure score of the season in all cricket. He and Maru added 126 runs for the seventh wicket in 43 overs, and when James reduced Gloucestershire to 82 for four next day, Hampshire's total looked adequate. With Bakker unfit to bowl, however, they were unable to press home their advantage. Russell completed the fourth century of his career on the third morning, with Babington clinging on for ten overs to see him there. By the close of the third day Hampshire were struggling. Lawrence again bowled with great heart and hostility, and Gilbert cut short Robin Smith's attempt to revive their fortunes. Gloucestershire had two full sessions in which to make 159, and after the early loss of Scott and Hodgson, Wright and Athey slowly gained control.

*Close of play:* First day, Gloucestershire 4-0 (G. D. Hodgson 4*, R. J. Scott 0*); Second day, Gloucestershire 313-8 (R. C. Russell 75*, A. M. Smith 0*); Third day, Hampshire 157-6 (K. D. James 14*, R. J. Maru 2*).

### Hampshire

| | | |
|---|---|---|
| V. P. Terry c Wright b Lawrence | 18 | – c Russell b Lawrence ......... 5 |
| C. L. Smith b Lawrence | 125 | – b Babington ......... 24 |
| D. I. Gower c Russell b Babington | 14 | – c Wright b Lawrence ......... 3 |
| R. A. Smith b Lawrence | 31 | – lbw b Gilbert ......... 74 |
| *M. C. J. Nicholas c Athey b Lawrence | 9 | – c Lloyds b Lawrence ......... 31 |
| K. D. James lbw b Lawrence | 3 | – c Lloyds b Babington ......... 34 |
| †A. N. Aymes b Gilbert | 17 | – lbw b Lawrence ......... 1 |
| R. J. Maru c Russell b Lawrence | 61 | – c Russell b Gilbert ......... 31 |
| C. A. Connor b Gilbert | 1 | – lbw b Gilbert ......... 4 |
| P. J. Bakker b Gilbert | 0 | – not out ......... 6 |
| Aqib Javed not out | 4 | – c Gilbert b Lawrence ......... 0 |
| B 4, l-b 7, w 2, n-b 4 | 17 | L-b 1, n-b 4 ......... 5 |
| | **300** | **218** |

1/41 2/57 3/117 4/132 5/137     300     1/22 2/26 3/57 4/112 5/147     218
6/169 7/295 8/296 9/296                     6/150 7/202 8/208 9/213

Bonus points – Hampshire 3, Gloucestershire 2 (Score at 100 overs: 282-6).

Bowling: *First Innings*—Gilbert 24.4–5–57–3; Lawrence 25–4–77–6; Babington 19–1–70–1; Smith 21–7–50–0; Lloyds 9–2–15–0; Scott 4–1–17–0; Athey 3–0–3–0. *Second Innings*—Gilbert 32–11–51–3; Lawrence 27.1–6–52–5; Babington 25–8–53–2; Lloyds 21–8–39–0; Smith 10–3–22–0.

### Gloucestershire

| | | |
|---|---|---|
| G. D. Hodgson lbw b James | 26 | – c sub b Aqib Javed ......... 8 |
| R. J. Scott b James | 29 | – c Aymes b Aqib Javed ......... 0 |
| *A. J. Wright c Aymes b James | 15 | – not out ......... 61 |
| C. W. J. Athey c Aymes b Maru | 9 | – not out ......... 65 |
| M. W. Alleyne c Aymes b Maru | 79 | |
| J. W. Lloyds c Terry b Aqib Javed | 48 | |
| †R. C. Russell b Maru | 111 | |
| D. V. Lawrence b Aqib Javed | 0 | |
| D. R. Gilbert b James | 20 | |
| A. M. Smith b Aqib Javed | 3 | |
| A. M. Babington not out | 0 | |
| B 3, l-b 10, w 1, n-b 6 | 20 | B 4, l-b 12, w 1, n-b 8 ... 25 |
| | **360** | **(2 wkts) 159** |

1/58 2/67 3/82 4/82 5/168     360     1/5 2/16     (2 wkts) 159
6/265 7/268 8/313 9/328

Bonus points – Gloucestershire 3, Hampshire 3 (Score at 100 overs: 290-7).

Bowling: *First Innings*—Aqib Javed 29-4-95-3; Connor 26-6-70-0; James 23-6-72-4; Maru 37.5-14-95-3; Nicholas 5-1-15-0. *Second Innings*—Aqib Javed 12-3-16-2; Bakker 15-7-20-0; Connor 8-1-41-0; James 9-4-24-0; Maru 8-1-30-0; Nicholas 3.5-1-12-0.

Umpires: D. J. Constant and B. J. Meyer.

At Bristol, May 14. GLOUCESTERSHIRE lost to WEST INDIANS by six wickets (See West Indian tour section).

At Oxford, May 15, 16, 17. GLOUCESTERSHIRE drew with OXFORD UNIVERSITY.

At Sheffield, May 22, 23, 24. GLOUCESTERSHIRE drew with YORKSHIRE.

At Birmingham, May 25, 27. GLOUCESTERSHIRE lost to WARWICKSHIRE by nine wickets.

## GLOUCESTERSHIRE v ESSEX

At Bristol, May 31, June 1. Essex won by an innings and 124 runs. Essex 24 pts, Gloucestershire 3 pts. Toss: Essex. Gloucestershire's second successive two-day defeat looked inevitable when they were bowled out in less than three hours in conditions ideal for swing and seam bowling. Lawrence spared no effort trying to bowl his side back into the game, finding a perfect yorker for Gooch, while de la Pena, a schoolboy from Cheltenham, marked his début at the age of eighteen by dismissing Prichard. On Saturday, the second day, Salim Malik did much as he liked in the course of century partnerships with Foster and Topley. Fine, wristy strokeplay brought him 23 fours in a stay of just under four hours (174 balls), and when he eventually fell to Lawrence, Essex were 315 ahead. Although Alleyne and Lloyds fought hard to counter the effects of some fragile batting, Essex fielded and bowled in an ebullient style which brooked no argument.

*Close of play:* First day, Essex 232-6 (Salim Malik 45*, N. A. Foster 13*).

## Gloucestershire

| | | | | | |
|---|---|---|---|---|---|
| G. D. Hodgson b Foster | | 3 | – c Hussain b Childs | | 40 |
| R. J. Scott lbw b Andrew | | 13 | – lbw b Foster | | 15 |
| *A. J. Wright c Salim Malik b Pringle | | 22 | – c Topley b Andrew | | 8 |
| C. W. J. Athey c Salim Malik b Pringle | | 10 | – lbw b Andrew | | 4 |
| M. W. Alleyne b Topley | | 17 | – c Garnham b Foster | | 46 |
| †R. C. Russell c Hussain b Topley | | 26 | – c Foster b Andrew | | 3 |
| J. W. Lloyds c Garnham b Andrew | | 4 | – c Garnham b Foster | | 56 |
| D. V. Lawrence c Garnham b Andrew | | 3 | – c sub b Foster | | 10 |
| A. M. Smith lbw b Topley | | 9 | – b Foster | | 4 |
| J. M. de la Pena not out | | 1 | – b Topley | | 0 |
| A. M. Babington b Topley | | 0 | – not out | | 0 |
| B 1, l-b 2, n-b 7 | | 10 | W 1, n-b 4 | | 5 |

1/16 2/21 3/43 4/66 5/77         118     1/35 2/51 3/55 4/75 5/84       191
6/84 7/90 8/113 9/118                        6/159 7/171 8/177 9/191

Bonus points – Essex 4.

Bowling: *First Innings*—Foster 13-9-13-1; Andrew 15-2-51-3; Topley 10.4-0-34-4; Pringle 9-2-17-2. *Second Innings*—Foster 16-4-54-5; Andrew 14-2-51-3; Pringle 5-3-4-0; Childs 9-2-47-1; Topley 7.2-1-35-1.

## Essex

| | | | | |
|---|---|---|---|---|
| *G. A. Gooch b Lawrence | 1 | N. A. Foster run out | 39 |
| J. P. Stephenson c Lloyds b Smith | 38 | T. D. Topley not out | 50 |
| P. J. Prichard c Russell b de la Pena | 10 | | |
| N. Hussain c Russell b Lawrence | 67 | L-b 13, n-b 14 | 27 |
| †M. A. Garnham b Babington | 14 | | |
| D. R. Pringle lbw b Lawrence | 24 | 1/4 2/53 3/60 4/92 | (8 wkts dec.) 433 |
| Salim Malik c Wright b Lawrence | 163 | 5/152 6/174 7/309 8/433 | |

S. J. W. Andrew and J. H. Childs did not bat.

Bonus points – Essex 4, Gloucestershire 3 (Score at 100 overs: 412-7).

Bowling: Lawrence 27.2–4–111–4; Babington 28–3–101–1; Smith 21–2–68–1; de la Pena 12–0–69–1; Alleyne 4–0–21–0; Lloyds 7–1–35–0; Athey 3–0–15–0.

Umpires: J. W. Holder and R. Palmer.

## GLOUCESTERSHIRE v MIDDLESEX

At Bristol, June 4, 5, 6. Drawn. Gloucestershire 4 pts, Middlesex 6 pts. Toss: Middlesex. Although much time was made up during a remarkable pre-lunch session on the third day, the loss of the second day to rain prevented a definite result. Had Gloucestershire's slip catching been of the highest standard, Middlesex might have been dismissed cheaply on the opening day. Hutchinson, missed when 9, battled away for five hours (245 balls, thirteen fours) for his second century of the season, but only Roseberry and Taylor afforded him much support. Gloucestershire struggled in turn as Emburey flighted and drifted the ball skilfully, and when they resumed on the final morning Tufnell benefited as quick runs were sought. He claimed Gloucestershire's six remaining wickets in less than an hour at a cost of 16 runs and finished with career-best figures of six for 34. When Lawrence and Gilbert then reduced Middlesex to 26 for four, ten wickets had fallen while 78 runs were scored. However, Gatting, on his 34th birthday, restored order in company with Emburey, and the batsmen gained ascendancy for the first time in the match. When Middlesex declared, Gloucestershire showed no interest in making 251 in a minimum of 41 overs.

*Close of play:* First day, Gloucestershire 79-4 (M. W. Alleyne 18*, R. C. J. Williams 0*); Second day, No play.

## Middlesex

| | | | | |
|---|---|---|---|---|
| I. J. F. Hutchinson c Babington b Scott | 114 | – c Scott b Lawrence | 0 |
| M. A. Roseberry c Hodgson b Babington | 17 | – c Babington b Gilbert | 7 |
| *M. W. Gatting c Athey b Gilbert | 15 | – not out | 68 |
| K. R. Brown b Gilbert | 3 | – c Williams b Gilbert | 2 |
| M. Keech b Lawrence | 8 | – c Williams b Lawrence | 2 |
| J. E. Emburey c Williams b Lawrence | 6 | – run out | 74 |
| †P. Farbrace b Babington | 5 | – not out | 0 |
| A. R. C. Fraser b Gilbert | 0 | | |
| P. C. R. Tufnell c Williams b Babington | 4 | | |
| C. W. Taylor b Williams b Lawrence | 11 | | |
| N. G. Cowans not out | 0 | | |
| L-b 15, w 1, n-b 10 | 26 | B 1, l-b 12, w 1, n-b 5 | 19 |

| | | |
|---|---|---|
| 1/56 2/77 3/85 4/112 5/125 | 209 | 1/0 2/10 3/19 | (5 wkts dec.) 172 |
| 6/142 7/148 8/157 9/209 | | 4/26 5/171 | |

Bonus points – Middlesex 2, Gloucestershire 4.

Bowling: *First Innings*—Lawrence 17.2–4–44–3; Babington 21–4–56–3; Gilbert 21–2–49–3; Athey 3–0–8–0; Scott 9–1–29–1; Lloyds 4–1–8–0. *Second Innings*—Lawrence 9–0–35–2; Gilbert 10–4–22–2; Babington 6–1–32–0; Scott 3–0–14–0; Lloyds 7–0–26–0; Alleyne 4–0–30–0.

## Gloucestershire

| | | |
|---|---|---|
| G. D. Hodgson lbw b Emburey | 16 – not out | 15 |
| R. J. Scott b Emburey | 14 – c Fraser b Taylor | 0 |
| *A. J. Wright lbw b Fraser | 9 – not out | 35 |
| C. W. J. Athey c Hutchinson b Emburey | 19 | |
| M. W. Alleyne st Farbrace b Tufnell | 25 | |
| †R. C. J. Williams c Brown b Tufnell | 0 | |
| J. J. E. Hardy c Brown b Tufnell | 15 | |
| J. W. Lloyds c and b Tufnell | 2 | |
| D. V. Lawrence b Tufnell | 8 | |
| D. R. Gilbert c Taylor b Tufnell | 14 | |
| A. M. Babington not out | 1 | |
| L-b 8 | 8 | B 4, l-b 3, w 1 ........ 8 |

| | | | |
|---|---|---|---|
| | **131** | 1/1 | **(1 wkt) 58** |

1/29 2/30 3/44 4/73 5/82
6/87 7/89 8/101 9/118

Bonus points – Middlesex 4.

Bowling: *First Innings*—Taylor 6–1–15–0; Cowans 4–1–10–0; Emburey 20–7–50–3; Fraser 5–0–14–1; Tufnell 14.3–3–34–6. *Second Innings*—Taylor 3–2–1–1; Fraser 4–2–6–0; Emburey 11–4–11–0; Tufnell 13–2–19–0; Keech 7–4–9–0; Roseberry 2–0–5–0.

Umpires: B. J. Meyer and R. Palmer.

At Southampton, June 7, 8, 10. GLOUCESTERSHIRE beat HAMPSHIRE by six wickets.

## GLOUCESTERSHIRE v NOTTINGHAMSHIRE

At Gloucester, June 14, 15, 17. Drawn. Gloucestershire 3 pts, Nottinghamshire 4 pts. Toss: Gloucestershire. Both captains did their best to make up for the loss of the second day, but it proved impossible to obtain a definite result. Only Athey of the specialist batsmen successfully came to terms with a slow pitch on the opening day, and Gloucestershire would have earned their second batting point but for Lawrence's breezy 41 from 55 balls. Gilbert then put in a fine spell to leave Nottinghamshire 64 for four at the close. Robinson declared at this score when the match resumed, and Wright reciprocated at lunch, setting a target of 281 in a minimum of 67 overs. Lawrence struck with his first and fourth deliveries, and at 35 for four Nottinghamshire were in danger of defeat. However, Babington, having just dismissed Broad, had to go off with a groin strain, and Randall and Crawley had regained the initiative with a partnership worth 130 in 34 overs when the game was given up. With Randall needing no more than 103 balls for his 85, and Crawley playing in composed style, they might well have set up a victory had further showers not caused the loss of another eleven overs.

*Close of play:* First day, Nottinghamshire 64-4 (D. W. Randall 9*, K. P. Evans 2*); Second day, No play.

## Gloucestershire

| | | |
|---|---|---|
| G. D. Hodgson c Crawley b Stephenson | 11 – (2) b Afford | 57 |
| J. J. E. Hardy lbw b Pick | 10 – (1) c Johnson b Afford | 31 |
| *A. J. Wright c French b Pick | 34 – not out | 45 |
| C. W. J. Athey c French b Afford | 63 | |
| M. W. Alleyne lbw b Stephenson | 1 | |
| J. W. Lloyds c Pollard b Crawley | 18 – (4) not out | 3 |
| †R. C. Russell b Afford | 5 | |
| D. V. Lawrence b Pick | 41 | |
| D. R. Gilbert c Afford b Pick | 8 | |
| A. M. Smith c Evans b Stephenson | 2 | |
| A. M. Babington not out | 0 | |
| L-b 3, w 1, n-b 4 | 8 | L-b 3, n-b 4 ........ 7 |

| | | | |
|---|---|---|---|
| | **201** | 1/56 2/121 | **(2 wkts dec.) 143** |

1/21 2/25 3/105 4/108 5/143
6/143 7/148 8/170 9/177

Bonus points – Gloucestershire 2, Nottinghamshire 4.

Bowling: *First Innings*—Pick 20.4–4–61–4; Stephenson 19–6–51–3; Evans 10–0–39–0; Afford 13–6–32–2; Crawley 4–1–15–1. *Second Innings*—Stephenson 6–4–10–0; Pick 6–1–22–0; Afford 12–0–48–2; Evans 7–0–35–0; Crawley 4–0–25–0.

## Nottinghamshire

| | | | |
|---|---|---|---|
| B. C. Broad lbw b Gilbert | 19 | – lbw b Babington | 16 |
| P. R. Pollard lbw b Lawrence | 3 | – lbw b Lawrence | 0 |
| *R. T. Robinson b Gilbert | 28 | – c Wright b Lawrence | 0 |
| P. Johnson c Russell b Gilbert | 0 | – lbw b Gilbert | 6 |
| D. W. Randall not out | 9 | – not out | 85 |
| K. P. Evans not out | 2 | | |
| M. A. Crawley (did not bat) | | – (6) not out | 49 |
| N-b 3 | 3 | L-b 4, w 5 | 9 |

1/5 2/45 3/45 4/62　　　　　　(4 wkts dec.) 64　　1/0 2/0 3/14 4/35　　　(4 wkts) 165

F. D. Stephenson, †B. N. French, R. A. Pick and J. A. Afford did not bat.

Bonus point – Gloucestershire 1.

Bowling: *First Innings*—Lawrence 7–1–18–1; Gilbert 11–4–18–3; Babington 3–0–13–0; Lloyds 6–1–15–0. *Second Innings*—Gilbert 9.4–1–20–1; Lawrence 10–0–37–2; Babington 4.2–3–5–1; Smith 8–0–30–0; Lloyds 11–0–62–0; Athey 2–0–7–0.

Umpires: B. Leadbeater and N. T. Plews.

## GLOUCESTERSHIRE v DERBYSHIRE

At Gloucester, June 18, 19, 20. Derbyshire won by six wickets. Derbyshire 24 pts, Gloucestershire 3 pts. Toss: Gloucestershire. Azharuddin, irked by the absence of his name from the leading first-class averages, put matters right by scoring his first Championship century, and it proved a match-winning innings. By the time Gerrard, on his début, took the wicket of Morris in his first over, Azharuddin was established and playing his way into form. He and O'Gorman added 211 for the fourth wicket, and once past his century India's captain delighted with the ease and timing of his strokeplay. In all he hit a six and 21 fours from 229 balls. McCray, a newcomer from Cheshire, played well for 37 before the declaration. With the exception of Lloyds, Gloucestershire batted poorly, and made to follow on they had lost six second-innings wickets by lunch on the third day. Derbyshire were held up, however, by an admirable stand of 104 for the eighth wicket between Athey and wicket-keeper Williams. Athey fell the ball after reaching his century from 180 balls, having hit fourteen fours, but Williams went on to his first Championship fifty.

*Close of play:* First day, Derbyshire 287–5 (K. J. Barnett 4*, K. M. Krikken 16*); Second day, Gloucestershire 45–1 (G. D. Hodgson 17*, A. J. Wright 11*).

## Derbyshire

| | | | |
|---|---|---|---|
| P. D. Bowler c Lloyds b Gilbert | 0 | – b Smith | 24 |
| C. J. Adams b Smith | 0 | – b Smith | 6 |
| J. E. Morris c R. C. J. Williams b Gerrard | 30 | – run out | 31 |
| M. Azharuddin st R. C. J. Williams b Lloyds | 154 | – not out | 31 |
| T. J. G. O'Gorman c Athey b R. C. Williams | 73 | – st R. C. J. Williams b Smith | 3 |
| *K. J. Barnett b Smith | 20 | | |
| †K. M. Krikken c Alleyne b Lloyds | 23 | – (6) not out | 1 |
| E. McCray b Smith | 37 | | |
| D. G. Cork not out | 27 | | |
| L-b 8, w 3, n-b 6 | 17 | L-b 2, n-b 1 | 3 |

1/0 2/0 3/55 4/266 5/266　　　(8 wkts dec.) 381　　1/25 2/25 3/50 4/59　　(4 wkts) 68
6/298 7/328 8/381

A. E. Warner and O. H. Mortensen did not bat.

Bonus points – Derbyshire 4, Gloucestershire 2 (Score at 100 overs: 306–6).

Bowling: *First Innings*—Gilbert 24–3–84–1; Smith 19.5–5–71–3; Gerrard 13–4–46–1; R. C. Williams 26–4–81–1; Lloyds 32–11–81–2; Athey 4–1–10–0. *Second Innings*—Gilbert 8–1–31–0; Smith 9.4–1–21–3; Gerrard 2–0–14–0.

## Gloucestershire

| | | | | |
|---|---|---|---|---|
| J. J. E. Hardy c Barnett b Warner | 0 | – (2) lbw b Mortensen | 13 |
| †R. C. J. Williams c Azharuddin b Warner | 8 | – (9) not out | 55 |
| *A. J. Wright c Adams b Warner | 13 | – c Krikken b Cork | 20 |
| C. W. J. Athey c Krikken b Mortensen | 11 | – b Cork | 101 |
| M. W. Alleyne c Adams b Cork | 18 | – c and b Mortensen | 4 |
| J. W. Lloyds c McCray b Barnett | 69 | – c Krikken b Mortensen | 7 |
| R. C. Williams lbw b Cork | 0 | – (8) c Bowler b Barnett | 13 |
| G. D. Hodgson b Barnett | 12 | – (1) lbw b Mortensen | 22 |
| D. R. Gilbert c Krikken b Barnett | 13 | – (7) lbw b Cork | 15 |
| A. M. Smith lbw b Cork | 0 | – lbw b Barnett | 15 |
| M. J. Gerrard not out | 3 | – b Warner | 0 |
| L-b 1, n-b 7 | 8 | B 5, l-b 12, n-b 11 | 28 |

|  |  |  |
|---|---|---|
| 1/7 2/14 3/33 4/33 5/69 | 155 | 1/20 2/52 3/63 4/71 5/86 | 293 |
| 6/69 7/109 8/151 9/151 | | 6/120 7/154 8/258 9/291 | |

Bonus points – Gloucestershire 1, Derbyshire 4.

Bowling: *First Innings*—Mortensen 17–6–28–1; Warner 15–2–35–3; McCray 15–5–41–0; Cork 11–1–36–3; Barnett 9.3–2–14–3. *Second Innings*—Mortensen 25–3–66–4; Warner 15.4–3–53–1; McCray 10–5–12–0; Barnett 24–8–36–2; Cork 25–1–101–3; Bowler 3–1–8–0.

Umpires: B. Leadbeater and N. T. Plews.

At Bath, June 21, 22, 24. GLOUCESTERSHIRE drew with SOMERSET.

At Luton, June 28, 29, July 1. GLOUCESTERSHIRE beat NORTHAMPTONSHIRE by three wickets.

At Hinckley, July 2, 3, 4. GLOUCESTERSHIRE beat LEICESTERSHIRE by 36 runs.

At Taunton, July 7. SOMERSET v GLOUCESTERSHIRE. Abandoned.

At Guildford, July 16, 17, 18. GLOUCESTERSHIRE lost to SURREY by two wickets.

## GLOUCESTERSHIRE v GLAMORGAN

At Cheltenham, July 19, 20, 22. Drawn. Gloucestershire 4 pts, Glamorgan 6 pts. Toss: Gloucestershire. This match would have been notable for Maynard's two glorious centuries even before its tense final day when, against the odds, Gloucestershire saved it. After Glamorgan had been put in on a pitch which started damp, Maynard's clean striking repulsed the threat of Lawrence, who had taken three wickets in four overs. When Lawrence dropped short he was pulled and hooked with certainty, and the other bowlers were treated even more dismissively. Maynard hit 23 fours and a six in his 129, made in three hours, and with Croft he put on 146 in 32 overs for the sixth wicket. Watkin and Frost made short work of the Gloucestershire first innings, which allowed Maynard to entertain the Saturday crowd with a second-innings display bordering on the nonchalant. His hundred came in 90 minutes from 83 balls, equalling the fastest of the season to date. Botham and Derbyshire's Morris had also reached three figures off 83 balls. Batting again, Gloucestershire lost two wickets in the first over, and were 123 for five when Russell joined Scott on the third morning. Scott, hooking and cutting powerfully, hit three sixes and sixteen fours before he was caught in the gully after a stay of 257 minutes, and when Lloyds batted freely an improbable home victory came briefly into view. However, Frost removed Lloyds and Lawrence with successive deliveries, which left Russell, who batted for more than five hours, to guide his side to the draw. Frost, whose return of seven for 99 was a career best, had three balls at the last man, Smith, who survived them.

*Close of play:* First day, Gloucestershire 114-7 (J. W. Lloyds 4*, D. V. Lawrence 6*); Second day, Gloucestershire 87-2 (R. J. Scott 48*, C. W. J. Athey 33*).

## Glamorgan

| | | |
|---|---:|---|
| *A. R. Butcher c Hodgson b Lawrence | 0 | – b Gilbert ... 12 |
| H. Morris lbw b Lawrence | 6 | – c Russell b Alleyne ... 84 |
| A. Dale c Scott b Lawrence | 4 | – c Russell b Lawrence ... 0 |
| M. P. Maynard c Russell b Lloyds | 129 | – c Athey b Lawrence ... 126 |
| R. J. Shastri c Wright b Smith | 22 | – c Hodgson b Smith ... 4 |
| P. A. Cottey lbw b Smith | 0 | – not out ... 37 |
| R. D. B. Croft run out | 44 | – c Russell b Alleyne ... 0 |
| †C. P. Metson c Lawrence b Lloyds | 5 | – b Gilbert ... 16 |
| S. L. Watkin c Russell b Lawrence | 15 | – not out ... 5 |
| S. R. Barwick st Russell b Lloyds | 12 | |
| M. Frost not out | 0 | |
| L-b 6, w 3, n-b 1 | 10 | L-b 7, w 2, n-b 1 ... 10 |

1/0 2/10 3/13 4/57 5/57 　　　　　　　　　　247　 1/26 2/31 3/204　　(7 wkts dec.) 294
6/203 7/213 8/233 9/245 　　　　　　　　　　　　　 4/213 5/242
　　　　　　　　　　　　　　　　　　　　　　　　 6/243 7/283

Bonus points – Glamorgan 2, Gloucestershire 4.

Bowling: *First Innings*—Lawrence 18-3-62-4; Gilbert 14-5-37-0; Smith 15-2-56-2; Scott 4-0-32-0; Lloyds 9-4-27-3; Alleyne 6-0-27-0. *Second Innings*—Lawrence 12-2-38-2; Gilbert 16-2-45-2; Smith 15-1-71-1; Alleyne 11.3-0-48-2; Lloyds 13-3-56-0; Athey 2-0-10-0; Scott 2-0-19-0.

## Gloucestershire

| | | |
|---|---:|---|
| G. D. Hodgson c Shastri b Frost | 29 | – c Metson b Frost ... 0 |
| R. J. Scott lbw b Frost | 0 | – c Maynard b Frost ... 122 |
| *A. J. Wright lbw b Watkin | 0 | – (5) c Metson b Watkin ... 4 |
| C. W. J. Athey c Maynard b Croft | 21 | – c Cottey b Barwick ... 37 |
| M. W. Alleyne c Dale b Frost | 2 | – (6) c Metson b Frost ... 4 |
| P. W. Romaines c Dale b Watkin | 28 | – (3) c Metson b Frost ... 0 |
| †R. C. Russell c Metson b Watkin | 21 | – not out ... 79 |
| J. W. Lloyds c Cottey b Watkin | 24 | – c Metson b Frost ... 61 |
| D. V. Lawrence c Metson b Frost | 6 | – c Maynard b Frost ... 0 |
| A. M. Smith c Morris b Watkin | 1 | – (11) not out ... 0 |
| D. R. Gilbert not out | 2 | – (10) lbw b Frost ... 17 |
| B 2, l-b 4 | 6 | B 7, l-b 9, w 3, n-b 3 ... 22 |

1/4 2/7 3/52 4/52 5/61 　　　　　　　　　　140　 1/1 2/1 3/100　　　(9 wkts) 346
6/91 7/108 8/114 9/127 　　　　　　　　　　　　　 4/117 5/123 6/197
　　　　　　　　　　　　　　　　　　　　　　　　 7/307 8/307 9/346

Bonus points – Glamorgan 4.

Bowling: *First Innings*—Watkin 17.4-3-49-5; Frost 15.4-4-44-4; Barwick 8-4-9-0; Dale 3-0-9-0; Croft 8-3-23-1. *Second Innings*—Frost 29-7-99-7; Watkin 35-9-89-1; Barwick 26-10-67-1; Croft 24-10-45-0; Shastri 16-5-30-0.

Umpires: G. I. Burgess and P. B. Wight.

## GLOUCESTERSHIRE v SUSSEX

At Cheltenham, July 23, 24, 25. Drawn. Gloucestershire 3 pts, Sussex 4 pts. Toss: Sussex. Although there were only five sessions of play, the match was not short of incident. Athey picked up 5 of his 10 runs when he was missed by Parker at slip and the ball struck the fielding side's helmet, placed behind the wicket-keeper; and there were 6 leg-byes from a single delivery when, after the ball had been returned to him, Moores had a shy at the stumps at the bowler's end and the ball ran to the boundary. Hodgson and Wright gave Gloucestershire a sound foundation, but Jones and Dodemaide carried all before them as seven wickets fell in nineteen overs. However, extraordinary hitting by Babington against his former county brought him a maiden half-century; his 58 from 30 balls contained five sixes and three fours, and with Gilbert he added 78 for the ninth wicket in eight overs. Rain washed out the second day and prevented a start on the third until 1.45 p.m., when the captains agreed to play even though the ground was not really fit. Innings having been forfeited, Sussex had 70 overs in which to score 284, and with the bowlers gaining plenty of bounce they looked set for defeat at 111 for seven. Smith, batting at No. 8 because of a strained back, and Donelan saved the game; Smith's 65 runs comprised sixteen fours and a single.

*Close of play:* First day, Gloucestershire 283; Second day, No play.

### Gloucestershire

| | | | |
|---|---|---|---|
| G. D. Hodgson b Dodemaide | 46 | D. R. Gilbert not out | 28 |
| R. J. Scott c Speight b Dodemaide | 18 | A. M. Babington c Lenham b Jones | 58 |
| *A. J. Wright c Moores b Jones | 70 | M. J. Gerrard c Moores b Jones | 2 |
| C. W. J. Athey c Lenham b Dodemaide | 10 | | |
| M. W. Alleyne b Jones | 0 | L-b 19, w 1, n-b 14 | 34 |
| P. W. Romaines c Moores b Jones | 4 | | |
| J. W. Lloyds c Speight b Dodemaide | 8 | 1/25 2/142 3/165 4/170 5/170 | 283 |
| †R. C. J. Williams c Smith b Dodemaide | 5 | 6/178 7/190 8/190 9/268 | |

Bonus points – Gloucestershire 3, Sussex 4.

Bowling: Jones 23–3–84–5; Dodemaide 33–3–130–5; Pigott 7–3–13–0; Lenham 4–0–14–0; Salisbury 2–0–8–0; Donelan 10–5–15–0.

*Gloucestershire forfeited their second innings.*

### Sussex

*Sussex forfeited their first innings.*

| | | | |
|---|---|---|---|
| N. J. Lenham c Alleyne b Gilbert | 46 | D. M. Smith not out | 65 |
| †P. Moores c Scott b Babington | 6 | B. T. P. Donelan not out | 28 |
| *P. W. G. Parker c Babington b Gerrard | 13 | | |
| A. P. Wells c Hodgson b Gerrard | 7 | B 1, l-b 3, w 1, n-b 2 | 7 |
| M. P. Speight c Wright b Gilbert | 26 | | |
| A. I. C. Dodemaide lbw b Gilbert | 0 | 1/14 2/40 3/51 4/97 | (7 wkts) 199 |
| A. C. S. Pigott b Lloyds | 1 | 5/98 6/99 7/111 | |

I. D. K. Salisbury and A. N. Jones did not bat.

Bowling: Gilbert 28.4–5–78–3; Babington 17–3–66–1; Gerrard 10–3–25–2; Lloyds 14–6–26–1.

Umpires: G. I. Burgess and P. B. Wight.

## GLOUCESTERSHIRE v WORCESTERSHIRE

At Cheltenham, July 26, 27, 29. Worcestershire won by 108 runs. Worcestershire 24 pts, Gloucestershire 6 pts. Toss: Gloucestershire. Those among the first-day crowd who had been drawn by the prospect of watching Botham play his first innings on the College ground were not disappointed. After some early miscues, he located the middle of the bat and struck twelve fours and a six in his 74 from 83 balls. There was also a solid effort from Curtis, a brisk 79 from D'Oliveira (two sixes, ten fours), and a late onslaught by Newport. Wright ensured that Gloucestershire would avoid following on by keeping the hostile Dilley at bay, and his 120, from 179 balls, included nineteen fours and a six. However, only Alleyne gave him much support, and there was time for Moody, who had held three good slip catches, to provide fine entertainment for the Saturday crowd. His 80, containing twelve fours, was rich in aggressive strokes. Worcestershire sought quick runs on the third morning, and a target of 317 from 85 overs was offered. Hodgson and Wright played with such certainty while adding 112 that a score of 146 for two at tea hinted at an exciting finish. But Dilley, with the young left-arm spinner, Stemp, as his ally, exposed the frailty of the home batting and the last eight wickets melted away in thirteen overs.

*Close of play:* First day, Gloucestershire 13-0 (G. D. Hodgson 3*, R. J. Scott 10*); Second day, Worcestershire 145-3 (D. B. D'Oliveira 6*, G. R. Dilley 4*).

## Worcestershire

| | | | |
|---|---:|---|---:|
| T. S. Curtis c Lloyds b Gilbert | 65 | – c Wright b Gilbert | 6 |
| P. Bent c Williams b Gilbert | 9 | – c Williams b Gilbert | 42 |
| T. M. Moody c Athey b Scott | 31 | – c Romaines b Alleyne | 80 |
| D. B. D'Oliveira b Lawrence | 79 | – c Lloyds b Gilbert | 11 |
| *P. A. Neale c Lloyds b Scott | 0 | – (7) c Gerrard b Gilbert | 6 |
| I. T. Botham c Gilbert b Lloyds | 74 | – b Lawrence | 0 |
| †S. J. Rhodes c Lloyds b Alleyne | 2 | – (8) c Wright b Lawrence | 10 |
| S. R. Lampitt b Lloyds | 12 | – (6) b Lawrence | 21 |
| P. J. Newport c Athey b Lawrence | 48 | – (10) not out | 24 |
| G. R. Dilley lbw b Gilbert | 0 | – (5) b Lawrence | 14 |
| R. D. Stemp not out | 3 | – not out | 0 |
| L-b 8, w 1, n-b 1 | 10 | L-b 8, n-b 2 | 10 |
| | **333** | (9 wkts dec.) | **224** |

1/30 2/76 3/168 4/177 5/211
6/227 7/253 8/294 9/303

1/7 2/120 3/140
4/160 5/160 6/166
7/167 8/181 9/216

Bonus points – Worcestershire 4, Gloucestershire 4 (Score at 100 overs: 330-9).

Bowling: *First Innings*—Lawrence 19.1-2-60-2; Gilbert 24-7-72-3; Gerrard 19-4-72-0; Scott 17-4-39-2; Lloyds 14-4-48-2; Alleyne 9-1-34-1. *Second Innings*—Lawrence 16-1-80-4; Gilbert 21-6-59-4; Gerrard 7-0-21-0; Lloyds 5-1-25-0; Scott 4-0-16-0; Alleyne 6-2-15-1.

## Gloucestershire

| | | | |
|---|---:|---|---:|
| G. D. Hodgson c Moody b Botham | 12 | – c Moody b Lampitt | 71 |
| R. J. Scott b Dilley | 10 | – c D'Oliveira b Dilley | 6 |
| *A. J. Wright c Botham b Dilley | 120 | – c D'Oliveira b Dilley | 52 |
| C. W. J. Athey c Moody b Dilley | 2 | – c Rhodes b Stemp | 15 |
| M. W. Alleyne b Lampitt | 44 | – lbw b Dilley | 5 |
| P. W. Romaines c Moody b Dilley | 3 | – c Dilley b Stemp | 0 |
| J. W. Lloyds b Lampitt | 19 | – c Moody b Dilley | 21 |
| †R. C. J. Williams c Neale b Botham | 2 | – (9) run out | 0 |
| D. V. Lawrence c Rhodes b Botham | 1 | – (8) c Rhodes b Stemp | 17 |
| D. R. Gilbert c Neale b Newport | 17 | – c Moody b Stemp | 2 |
| M. J. Gerrard not out | 0 | – not out | 0 |
| L-b 6, n-b 5 | 11 | B 1, l-b 3, n-b 15 | 19 |
| | **241** | | **208** |

1/21 2/31 3/47 4/111 5/140
6/169 7/182 8/192 9/236

1/12 2/124 3/149 4/159 5/161
6/186 7/188 8/199 9/208

Bonus points – Gloucestershire 2, Worcestershire 4.

Bowling: *First Innings*—Dilley 15.3-7-45-4; Newport 14-4-44-1; Botham 21-3-74-3; Lampitt 18-2-72-2. *Second Innings*—Dilley 16-1-39-4; Botham 6-1-21-0; Stemp 28-6-85-4; Newport 7-2-24-0; Lampitt 9-1-35-1.

Umpires: J. D. Bond and D. J. Constant.

At Bristol, July 31, August 1, 2. GLOUCESTERSHIRE drew with WEST INDIANS (See West Indian tour section).

At Bristol, August 6, 7. GLOUCESTERSHIRE beat SRI LANKANS by eight wickets
(See Sri Lankan tour section).

## GLOUCESTERSHIRE v LANCASHIRE

At Bristol, August 9, 10, 12. Gloucestershire won by an innings and 98 runs. Gloucestershire
24 pts, Lancashire 1 pt. Toss: Lancashire. For a team with, statistically at least, a chance of
finishing in the first three in the Championship, Lancashire gave a lack-lustre display, and
Gloucestershire seized on their visitors' shortcomings to gain their fifth Championship win,
picking up maximum bonus points for the first time in 1991. With Fairbrother absent, though
he played in the Sunday match, Lancashire failed to spark in their first innings. Gloucestershire, in contrast, lost only Russell, a volunteer opener, before taking the lead, and they were 35
ahead when Wright mistimed an attempted sweep against Watkinson's off-spin. Athey, who
ensured that a match-winning advantage was obtained, took well over five hours for a century
which included only eight fours, and in all he faced 311 deliveries (eleven fours). Alleyne was
much more positive, hitting eighteen fours in an entertaining 90. Ball's rehabilitation was
advanced by more unconvincing batting in Lancashire's second innings, and the young off-
spinner finished with match figures of eight for 95, easily the best of his career.

*Close of play:* First day, Gloucestershire 101-1 (C. W. J. Athey 35\*, A. J. Wright 40\*);
Second day, Lancashire 35-1 (G. D. Mendis 24\*, G. D. Lloyd 7\*).

### Lancashire

| | | | | |
|---|---|---|---|---|
| G. D. Mendis c Wright b Gilbert | 18 | – c Lloyds b Gilbert | | 44 |
| G. Fowler c and b Ball | 23 | – run out | | 4 |
| G. D. Lloyd c Russell b Babington | 20 | – c Russell b Babington | | 8 |
| N. J. Speak b Ball | 29 | – c Russell b Ball | | 16 |
| S. P. Titchard c and b Ball | 20 | – (7) c Hancock b Gerrard | | 20 |
| M. Watkinson c Lloyds b Gilbert | 9 | – (5) c Alleyne b Ball | | 0 |
| Wasim Akram c Ball b Babington | 7 | – (8) b Gilbert | | 13 |
| †W. K. Hegg c Russell b Babington | 13 | – (6) c Hancock b Ball | | 16 |
| G. Yates c Ball b Babington | 3 | – not out | | 15 |
| *P. J. W. Allott c Athey b Ball | 4 | – c Gerrard b Babington | | 26 |
| P. J. Martin not out | 1 | – c Alleyne b Ball | | 0 |
| L-b 4 | 4 | L-b 3 | | 3 |
| | **151** | | | **165** |

1/22 2/49 3/90 4/99 5/110
6/130 7/130 8/146 9/149

1/14 2/47 3/75 4/75 5/80
6/96 7/116 8/131 9/165

Bonus points – Lancashire 1, Gloucestershire 4.

Bowling: *First Innings*—Gilbert 14-2-46-2; Babington 19-5-33-4; Gerrard 9-2-19-0;
Alleyne 7-3-9-0; Ball 16.3-4-40-4. *Second Innings*—Gilbert 22-6-44-2; Babington 13-2-40-2;
Ball 23.1-6-55-4; Lloyds 2-0-2-0; Gerrard 7-0-21-1.

### Gloucestershire

| | | | |
|---|---|---|---|
| C. W. J. Athey b Martin | 127 | M. C. J. Ball c sub b Watkinson | 8 |
| †R. C. Russell c Titchard b Wasim Akram | 15 | A. M. Babington c Hegg b Watkinson | 22 |
| *A. J. Wright c Hegg b Watkinson | 85 | B 6, l-b 12, n-b 8 | 26 |
| M. W. Alleyne c sub b Martin | 90 | | |
| J. J. E. Hardy c sub b Martin | 12 | 1/31 2/186 3/322 | (8 wkts dec.) 414 |
| J. W. Lloyds c Watkinson b Martin | 12 | 4/352 5/356 6/365 | |
| T. H. C. Hancock not out | 17 | 7/381 8/414 | |

D. R. Gilbert and M. J. Gerrard did not bat.

Bonus points – Gloucestershire 4 (Score at 100 overs: 322-2).

Bowling: Wasim Akram 11.2-3-36-1; Martin 34.4-11-97-4; Allott 23-8-39-0; Yates
25-2-84-0; Watkinson 30-3-140-3.

Umpires: B. Hassan and D. R. Shepherd.

At Canterbury, August 20, 21, 22. GLOUCESTERSHIRE lost to KENT by one wicket.

At Abergavenny, August 28, 29, 30, 31. GLOUCESTERSHIRE lost to GLAMORGAN by
nine wickets.

## GLOUCESTERSHIRE v NORTHAMPTONSHIRE

At Bristol, September 3, 4, 5, 6. Northamptonshire won by five wickets. Northamptonshire 22 pts, Gloucestershire 7 pts. Toss: Northamptonshire. Saved from the threat of the follow-on by Roberts and Noon, their eighth-wicket pair, Northamptonshire carried through their recovery so effectively that they went on to a comprehensive victory. Gloucestershire, with a first-innings lead of 125, were strongly placed at 103 for two in their second innings, with Wright and Athey going well. But Wright was run out attempting a second run to Curran on the boundary, and the innings fell away sharply. Athey was brilliantly caught by Capel at mid-wicket. As Northamptonshire set out to score 313 for victory, Fordham, who had held their first innings together, again played soundly and attractively before falling for a second time in the nineties. He added 127 in 36 overs with Lamb, whose dashing 82 came from 124 balls, and when they were out, Capel and Stanley took Northamptonshire closer to their target with solid batting. In Gloucestershire's first innings, Alleyne had picked up a stuttering start with 165 in 219 minutes, many of his 26 fours coming from drives and cuts which left the off-side fieldsmen helpless.

*Close of play:* First day, Gloucestershire 314-5 (M. W. Alleyne 108*, J. W. Lloyds 52*); Second day, Northamptonshire 287-8 (A. R. Roberts 37*, A. Walker 0*); Third day, Northamptonshire 57-0 (A. Fordham 30*, R. J. Bailey 23*).

### Gloucestershire

| | | | |
|---|---|---|---|
| G. D. Hodgson b Walker | 15 | – b Capel | 1 |
| R. J. Scott c Noon b Walker | 11 | – b Curran | 8 |
| *A. J. Wright c Larkins b Capel | 42 | – run out | 52 |
| C. W. J. Athey b Roberts b Capel | 54 | – c Capel b Curran | 86 |
| M. W. Alleyne c Lamb b Walker | 165 | – c Lamb b Roberts | 0 |
| †R. C. Russell lbw b Baptiste | 12 | – b Roberts | 0 |
| J. W. Lloyds c Larkins b Capel | 59 | – c Noon b Baptiste | 13 |
| M. C. J. Ball c Baptiste b Capel | 8 | – c Noon b Roberts | 12 |
| D. V. Lawrence b Curran | 24 | – b Curran | 4 |
| D. R. Gilbert not out | 7 | – b Curran | 2 |
| A. M. Babington c Curran b Baptiste | 17 | – not out | 4 |
| B 3, l-b 12, w 1, n-b 6 | 22 | B 2, l-b 3 | 5 |

1/27 2/30 3/123 4/134 5/153　　　　　436　　1/9 2/9 3/103 4/113 5/115　　　187
6/334 7/352 8/387 9/417　　　　　　　　　　6/148 7/173 8/179 9/182

Bonus points – Gloucestershire 3, Northamptonshire 2 (Score at 100 overs: 279-5).

Bowling: *First Innings*—Capel 30-8-83-4; Curran 32-3-115-1; Walker 26-5-84-3; Baptiste 31.5-11-67-2; Roberts 11-3-41-0; Bailey 8-0-31-0. *Second Innings*—Curran 20.1-1-52-4; Capel 8-2-20-1; Baptiste 13-2-36-1; Walker 10-1-26-0; Roberts 19-3-48-3.

### Northamptonshire

| | | | |
|---|---|---|---|
| A. Fordham c Athey b Lawrence | 96 | – c and b Scott | 90 |
| R. J. Bailey b Babington | 9 | – st Russell b Lloyds | 28 |
| *A. J. Lamb lbw b Babington | 16 | – c Russell b Lloyds | 82 |
| N. A. Stanley lbw b Gilbert | 27 | – c Russell b Lawrence | 30 |
| D. J. Capel c Athey b Ball | 1 | – c Athey b Lawrence | 43 |
| K. M. Curran c Babington b Ball | 11 | – not out | 19 |
| E. A. E. Baptiste lbw b Lawrence | 29 | | |
| A. R. Roberts c Lloyds b Lawrence | 48 | | |
| †W. M. Noon c Russell b Lloyds | 36 | | |
| A. Walker c Lloyds b Lawrence | 13 | | |
| W. Larkins not out | 0 | – (7) not out | 4 |
| B 4, l-b 11, n-b 10 | 25 | B 3, l-b 10, n-b 6 | 19 |

1/32 2/60 3/99 4/104 5/122　　　　　311　　1/62 2/189 3/211　　(5 wkts) 315
6/183 7/210 8/287 9/310　　　　　　　　　　4/281 5/289

Bonus points – Northamptonshire 4, Gloucestershire 4.

Bowling: *First Innings*—Lawrence 24-4-64-4; Gilbert 16-4-48-1; Babington 13-3-59-2; Ball 21-3-95-2; Scott 5-0-10-0; Lloyds 12-4-20-1. *Second Innings*—Lawrence 14.5-1-65-2; Gilbert 17-3-45-0; Babington 19-5-32-0; Lloyds 27-6-86-2; Ball 10-0-50-0; Alleyne 4-1-9-0; Scott 3-0-15-1.

Umpires: K. J. Lyons and D. R. Shepherd.

## GLOUCESTERSHIRE v SOMERSET

At Bristol, September 10, 11, 12. Somerset won by nine wickets. Somerset 23 pts, Gloucestershire 5 pts. Toss: Gloucestershire. Somerset's second victory of the season lifted them, temporarily, off the bottom of the Championship table. Much of the credit for it was due to Tavaré, whose 183, occupying fifteen minutes short of eight hours, provided the home batsmen with an object lesson in the requirements of four-day cricket. It had seemed that Somerset would have to struggle for any sort of lead when four wickets fell for 93, but MacLeay helped his captain stabilise the innings, and Rose was a robust partner in the decisive sixth-wicket partnership of 207. There were fourteen fours in Rose's second Championship century, while Tavaré hit nineteen boundaries in his highest score of the season. No blame could be attached to Athey for Gloucestershire's fourth successive defeat. Having moved up to open, he put them in a useful position in the first innings, only for the last eight wickets to fall for 101 runs. In the second, he carried his bat and saved the innings defeat in a last-wicket stand of 56 with Gerrard. Trump, Somerset's off-spinner, had a spell of three wickets in four balls during Gloucestershire's deflating second-innings display, and he finished with five wickets to hurry his side to victory with a day to spare.

*Close of play:* First day, Somerset 40-0 (S. J. Cook 21*, N. D. Burns 15*); Second day, Somerset 263-5 (C. J. Tavaré 122*, G. D. Rose 39*).

### Gloucestershire

| | | | | |
|---|---|---|---|---|
| G. D. Hodgson c Burns b MacLeay | 29 | – c Burns b Mallender | 6 |
| C. W. J. Athey c Rose b MacLeay | 90 | – not out | 77 |
| *A. J. Wright lbw b Mallender | 16 | – c Rose b Mallender | 11 |
| M. W. Alleyne lbw b Hallett | 47 | – c and b Trump | 4 |
| J. W. Lloyds c Cook b Rose | 3 | – lbw b Lefebvre | 23 |
| T. H. C. Hancock c Tavaré b Mallender | 12 | – c Burns b Lefebvre | 0 |
| †R. C. Russell run out | 0 | – c MacLeay b Trump | 8 |
| D. V. Lawrence c Tavaré b Hallett | 30 | – c and b Trump | 0 |
| D. R. Gilbert c Bartlett b Rose | 28 | – c Harden b Trump | 0 |
| A. M. Babington c Burns b Lefebvre | 1 | – b Mallender | 0 |
| M. J. Gerrard not out | 2 | – c Harden b Trump | 42 |
| L-b 9, n-b 7 | 16 | L-b 2, n-b 13 | 15 |
| | **274** | | **186** |

1/87 2/133 3/173 4/178 5/202    1/15 2/53 3/68 4/111 5/111
6/202 7/242 8/245 9/248    6/128 7/128 8/128 9/130

Bonus points – Gloucestershire 3, Somerset 4.

Bowling: *First Innings*—Mallender 20–6–44–2; Hallett 19–2–71–2; Lefebvre 21–4–64–1; Rose 20·5–46–2; MacLeay 12–4–28–2; Trump 7–4–12–0. *Second Innings*—Mallender 16–2–60–3; Hallett 5–0–23–0; Lefebvre 7–1–20–2; Trump 22·3–5–64–5; Rose 7–1–17–0.

### Somerset

| | | | | |
|---|---|---|---|---|
| S. J. Cook c Wright b Lawrence | 21 | – lbw b Babington | 16 |
| †N. D. Burns c Russell b Gilbert | 37 | – not out | 6 |
| R. J. Harden c Hancock b Babington | 1 | – not out | 1 |
| *C. J. Tavaré lbw b Lawrence | 183 | | |
| R. J. Bartlett c Alleyne b Lloyds | 1 | | |
| K. H. MacLeay b Gilbert | 31 | | |
| G. D. Rose c Hancock b Lloyds | 106 | | |
| R. P. Lefebvre c Russell b Lawrence | 13 | | |
| N. A. Mallender not out | 13 | | |
| H. R. J. Trump c Hancock b Lloyds | 0 | | |
| J. C. Hallett c Russell b Gilbert | 15 | | |
| L-b 14, w 1, n-b 5 | 20 | | |
| | **441** | 1/17 | **(1 wkt) 23** |

1/41 2/42 3/80 4/93 5/174    441    1/17    (1 wkt) 23
6/381 7/401 8/411 9/412

Bonus points – Somerset 3, Gloucestershire 2 (Score at 100 overs: 263-5).

Bowling: *First Innings*—Lawrence 31–4–106–3; Gilbert 25·1–5–78–3; Babington 24–10–55–1; Gerrard 16–1–64–0; Lloyds 46–12–106–3; Alleyne 8–3–18–0. *Second Innings*—Gerrard 2·4–1–14–0; Babington 2–0–9–1.

Umpires: A. A. Jones and B. J. Meyer.

At Hove, September 17, 18, 19, 20. GLOUCESTERSHIRE lost to SUSSEX by 139 runs.

# HAMPSHIRE

*President:* W. J. Weld
*Chairman:* D. Rich
*Chairman, Cricket Committee:* J. R. Gray
*Chief Executive:* A. F. Baker
    Northlands Road, Southampton SO9 2TY
    (Telephone: 0703-333788)
*Captain:* M. C. J. Nicholas
*Coach:* T. M. Tremlett

Winning the NatWest Bank Trophy at Lord's made the summer of 1991 one of fond memories for Hampshire supporters. Few would have contested their right to a moment in the limelight on September 7; the route to their first appearance in the final of the most prestigious one-day competition could scarcely have been more difficult.

When the draw was made, few were optimistic. A potential second-round meeting with Lancashire, the holders, looked daunting ten months off, and even more so on the day. By then, Hampshire had not won a first-class match, and their campaign in the Refuge Assurance League had foundered after a promising start. Lancashire, meanwhile, headed the Sunday League and were booked for the Benson and Hedges Cup final two days later. In the event, victory was comparatively easy. Lancashire's powerful batting was restricted by tight bowling and eager fielding, and Robin Smith and David Gower batted with dismissive arrogance to provide an eight-wicket win. The third round was a similar story; Nottinghamshire were contained, and beaten by seven wickets.

For the fourth year in succession, Hampshire were in the semi-finals, and their destination was Edgbaston, where the Warwickshire seam attack had reigned supreme in the County Championship. But what had seemed a tricky hurdle proved the easiest to negotiate. Again Hampshire's bowling was tight and their fielding keen, setting up victory by nine wickets with ten overs to spare.

The build-up to Lord's was hardly propitious. Chris Smith, the centre-piece of their batting, had retired as the Edgbaston win was celebrated, to become marketing manager of the Western Australian Cricket Association, and a quirk of the fixture list took Hampshire to The Oval to face their fellow finalists, Surrey, immediately before the encounter at Lord's. The Championship match lasted until noon on the third of four days; Waqar Younis destroyed their batting – and kept their captain, Mark Nicholas, out of the final by breaking the little finger of his left hand. But while Surrey inevitably went to Lord's as favourites, once again the odds were mocked, and by the same formula. Hampshire's bowling and fielding restricted their opponents to 240, and the scourge of Waqar Younis, who had taken 23 wickets in the summer's two Championship meetings, was denied. In the end it was perilously close. Two balls remained when Jon Ayling hit the winning boundary, after Tony Middleton's solid foundation had filled the gap left by Chris Smith, and Robin Smith had provided much-needed acceleration. Nicholas's disappointment at having to sit out the match as a spectator was softened by the knowledge that Hampshire had established an enviable record: victory in both their Lord's finals. Moreover, this was the third major prize they had won since he succeeded N. E. J. Pocock in 1985, and now only the County Championship eluded him.

Yet the triumph for teamwork perhaps clouded assessment of the overall tenor of the summer. Did it constitute success, or was it a smokescreen hiding a season of under-achievement? A dispassionate assessment suggested the latter.

The Benson and Hedges Cup had looked promising when the first three matches were won convincingly, but the prize of a home quarter-final was dissipated at Leeds, where Hampshire's much-vaunted batting was routed for 50, and the road to Lord's ended at Chelmsford. The Refuge Assurance League was a disaster. Two wins in the opening three fixtures were encouraging, but after beating Kent on May 12, Hampshire did not win again until August 25, by which time they were well adrift at the bottom of the table.

For many, though, the Championship is the benchmark for a season's achievement, and in that Hampshire performed fitfully, dropping six places. Their first win was delayed until Derbyshire's collapse in a run-chase at Chesterfield in late July, although two months earlier, when Surrey won at Bournemouth, four results were possible with two balls remaining, and in the next game, at Trent Bridge, Hampshire looked to be winning until a brief interruption for rain derailed them. The victory at Chesterfield was the first of five in seven matches, which ultimately ensured mid-table security. Whether that was enough, allied to the NatWest Bank Trophy, to sustain a verdict of success was a moot point.

It was also a summer of hung verdicts for individuals. Only two batsmen really matched potential with achievement: the brothers Smith. Chris provided the steely core of the batting, and by the time he retired he had scored 1,553 first-class runs at 64.70. Robin's contribution was inevitably curtailed, first by his recovery from surgery and then by England's demands, but he finished just short of 1,000 runs in his eleven matches for the county. Otherwise only Kevan James could winter with complete satisfaction, after reaching 1,000 runs for the first time. He also reinforced his value with 41 first-class wickets, a figure exceeded only by Aqib Javed, the eighteen-year-old Pakistani who stood in for Malcolm Marshall and suggested a profitable future. Paul Terry scored his near-inevitable 1,200 runs, while Gower was Gower: perennial but all too often unfulfilled promise. This time he did top 1,000 runs, but in two summers he had managed only one Championship century.

Not surprisingly, shorn of Marshall's cutting edge, Hampshire bowled only one side out twice in a match – Surrey at The Oval. Yet apart from Aqib Javed and James, it was in the bowling that perhaps the greatest bonus of the summer was gained, with the progress of Kevin Shine. His figures – 38 wickets at 38.26 – were not sensational, but the fact that he remained fit enough to appear in sixteen first-class matches, seven more than his aggregate for the previous two seasons, held hope for the future. Further encouragement came from the off-spinner, Shaun Udal. Although a persistent groin injury restricted him to a single first-class game, Udal was a major contributor in the NatWest campaign. – Mike Neasom.

436

HAMPSHIRE 1991

[Bill Smith]

Back row: N. R. Taylor, R. S. M. Morris, S. D. Udal, I. J. Turner, K. J. Shine, M. J. Thursfield, D. P. J. Flint, R. M. F. Cox. Middle row: T. M. Tremlett (coach), A. N. Aymes, Aqib Javed, K. D. James, P. J. Bakker, J. R. Ayling, T. C. Middleton, C. A. Connor, P. J. Sainsbury (coach). Front row: R. J. Maru, D. I. Gower, V. P. Terry, M. C. J. Nicholas (captain), C. L. Smith, R. J. Parks, R. A. Smith, J. R. Wood.

## HAMPSHIRE RESULTS

*All first-class matches – Played 24: Won 5, Lost 7, Drawn 12.*

*County Championship matches – Played 22: Won 5, Lost 7, Drawn 10.*

*Bonus points – Batting 57, Bowling 56.*

*Competition placings – Britannic Assurance County Championship, 9th;*
*NatWest Bank Trophy, winners; Benson and Hedges Cup, q-f;*
*Refuge Assurance League, 17th.*

## BRITANNIC ASSURANCE CHAMPIONSHIP AVERAGES

### BATTING

|  | Birthplace | M | I | NO | R | HI | Avge |
|---|---|---|---|---|---|---|---|
| ‡C. L. Smith | Durban, SA | 15 | 26 | 3 | 1,353 | 145 | 58.82 |
| ‡K. D. James | Lambeth, London | 22 | 35 | 9 | 1,216 | 134* | 46.76 |
| ‡R. A. Smith | Durban, SA | 10 | 20 | 0 | 852 | 107 | 42.60 |
| ‡V. P. Terry | Osnabruck, WG | 18 | 32 | 2 | 1,226 | 171 | 40.86 |
| ‡D. I. Gower | Tunbridge Wells | 22 | 37 | 5 | 1,132 | 80* | 35.37 |
| ‡M. C. J. Nicholas | London | 20 | 34 | 9 | 723 | 107* | 28.92 |
| ‡T. C. Middleton | Winchester | 16 | 28 | 1 | 766 | 102 | 28.37 |
| ‡A. N. Aymes | Southampton | 22 | 28 | 6 | 587 | 53 | 26.68 |
| ‡J. R. Ayling | Portsmouth | 9 | 13 | 2 | 269 | 58 | 24.45 |
| ‡R. J. Maru | Nairobi, Kenya | 20 | 25 | 3 | 369 | 61 | 16.77 |
| I. J. Turner | Denmead | 8 | 10 | 4 | 87 | 39* | 14.50 |
| ‡C. A. Connor | The Valley, Anguilla | 14 | 15 | 0 | 148 | 30 | 9.86 |
| K. J. Shine | Bracknell | 15 | 17 | 8 | 80 | 25 | 8.88 |
| Aqib Javed | Sheikhupura, Pakistan | 17 | 12 | 8 | 25 | 15* | 6.25 |
| ‡P. J. Bakker | Vlaardingen, Netherlands | 9 | 6 | 2 | 17 | 6* | 4.25 |

Also batted: R. M. F. Cox (*Guildford*) (2 matches) 15, 26; ‡T. M. Tremlett (*Wellington, Somerset*) (1 match) 2; J. R. Wood (*Winchester*) (2 matches) 25, 0.

* *Signifies not out.*   ‡ *Denotes county cap.*

The following played a total of twelve three-figure innings for Hampshire in County Championship matches – C. L. Smith 5, K. D. James 2, V. P. Terry 2, T. C. Middleton 1, M. C. J. Nicholas 1, R. A. Smith 1.

### BOWLING

|  | O | M | R | W | BB | 5W/i | Avge |
|---|---|---|---|---|---|---|---|
| J. R. Ayling | 185.5 | 36 | 555 | 21 | 4-47 | 0 | 26.42 |
| Aqib Javed | 485.1 | 81 | 1,586 | 53 | 6-91 | 3 | 29.92 |
| K. D. James | 396.5 | 85 | 1,219 | 37 | 4-32 | 0 | 32.94 |
| P. J. Bakker | 209.3 | 52 | 595 | 18 | 4-66 | 0 | 33.05 |
| K. J. Shine | 316.5 | 44 | 1,350 | 37 | 5-43 | 2 | 36.48 |
| C. A. Connor | 331 | 58 | 1,128 | 29 | 4-49 | 0 | 38.89 |
| R. J. Maru | 570.1 | 159 | 1,534 | 34 | 5-128 | 1 | 45.11 |
| I. J. Turner | 238.5 | 65 | 637 | 14 | 4-28 | 0 | 45.50 |

Also bowled: D. I. Gower 0.1–0–4–0; T. C. Middleton 12–2–77–3; M. C. J. Nicholas 67.5–6–288–4; C. L. Smith 19–3–63–0; R. A. Smith 18–3–97–3; T. M. Tremlett 10–3–39–1; J. R. Wood 6–0–17–0.

**Wicket-keeper:** A. N. Aymes 45 ct, 2 st.

**Leading Fielders:** R. J. Maru 29, V. P. Terry 23.

At Oxford, April 13, 15, 16. HAMPSHIRE drew with OXFORD UNIVERSITY.

## HAMPSHIRE v KENT

At Southampton, April 27, 28, 29, 30. Drawn. Hampshire 1 pt, Kent 5 pts. Toss: Kent. A match cut short by rain was dominated by Benson, whose 257 eclipsed by some way his previous highest score of 162, also against Hampshire. On a typically bland Southampton pitch, the Kent captain offered only a single chance, a catch at the wicket off Nicholas when he was 161. His century came off 164 deliveries and contained eleven fours, and his second hundred took 186 balls with another fourteen boundaries. By the time he was seventh out he had batted for almost eight and threequarter hours, faced 421 balls and hit 32 fours, having shared a 224-run partnership for the fourth wicket with Chris Cowdrey. Hampshire, left with 22 overs to negotiate at the end of the second day, lost the top four of their order to Merrick, but the weather, claiming the remaining two days, robbed Kent of the opportunity of turning their strong advantage into victory.

*Close of play:* First day, Kent 197-3 (M. R. Benson 104*, C. S. Cowdrey 37*); Second day, Hampshire 88-4 (M. C. J. Nicholas 5*); Third day, No play.

### Kent

| | | | |
|---|---|---|---|
| N. R. Taylor lbw b Bakker | 3 | T. A. Merrick not out | 9 |
| *M. R. Benson c Nicholas b Bakker | 257 | A. P. Igglesden c Bakker b Ayling | 7 |
| T. R. Ward c Aymes b Aqib Javed | 35 | †S. A. Marsh absent injured | |
| G. R. Cowdrey c Gower b Maru | 0 | | |
| C. S. Cowdrey c Maru b Nicholas | 97 | B 10, l-b 10, w 3, n-b 13 | 36 |
| R. M. Ellison lbw b Bakker | 1 | | |
| R. P. Davis b Aqib Javed | 0 | 1/10 2/98 3/101 4/325 5/343 | 482 |
| C. Penn c Middleton b Bakker | 37 | 6/346 7/455 8/464 9/482 | |

Bonus points – Kent 4, Hampshire 1 (Score at 100 overs: 318-3).

Bowling: Aqib Javed 33-6-103-2; Bakker 32-5-95-4; Maru 31-8-86-1; James 17-5-59-0; Ayling 22.4-3-64-1; Wood 6-0-17-0; Nicholas 8-0-38-1.

### Hampshire

| | | | |
|---|---|---|---|
| T. C. Middleton c G. R. Cowdrey b Merrick | 15 | *M. C. J. Nicholas not out | 5 |
| C. L. Smith c Taylor b Merrick | 19 | B 6, l-b 5, n-b 2 | 13 |
| D. I. Gower c Benson b Merrick | 11 | | |
| J. R. Wood b Merrick | 25 | 1/40 2/52 3/57 4/88        (4 wkts) | 88 |

J. R. Ayling, K. D. James, †A. N. Aymes, R. J. Maru, P. J. Bakker and Aqib Javed did not bat.

Bonus point – Kent 1.

Bowling: Merrick 11-3-37-4; Igglesden 8-0-34-0; Penn 3-0-6-0.

Umpires: J. H. Harris and N. T. Plews.

At Bristol, May 9, 10, 11, 13. HAMPSHIRE lost to GLOUCESTERSHIRE by eight wickets.

At Hove, May 16, 17, 18, 20. HAMPSHIRE drew with SUSSEX.

## HAMPSHIRE v SURREY

At Bournemouth, May 25, 27, 28. Surrey won by one wicket. Surrey 22 pts, Hampshire 7 pts. Toss: Surrey. A match as bleak as the chilling conditions came dramatically to life in the last twenty overs, with Surrey squeezing victory off the last ball – delivered in the twilight at 6.45 p.m. following a fourteen-minute over by the left-arm spinner, Maru. Until then the sparse crowd had seen the game neutered by a depressingly slow pitch on which few batsmen played with any assurance. Waqar Younis claimed six wickets in Hampshire's laboured first innings, and another five before Nicholas set Surrey a target of 256 at just under 5 runs an over. At tea Surrey had lost two wickets in reducing this to 172 off a minimum of 33 overs; from the last twenty they needed 114 with six wickets in hand, and by the thirteenth Greig and Thorpe had it down to 30. Two wickets in an over by Connor swung the match Hampshire's way, and after Surrey had taken 17 from two overs, the recalled Maru removed Thorpe and Martin Bicknell in his first over. Surrey now needed 13 off two overs. Five singles came in the first; the first three balls of the second brought 6 runs, but then Sargeant fell to Maru's diving return catch. However, Murphy, the incoming batsman, immediately hit a single, and Younis won the match off the last ball.

*Close of play:* First day, Surrey 31-0 (D. J. Bicknell 19*, R. I. Alikhan 7*); Second day, Hampshire 93-3 (R. A. Smith 7*, R. J. Maru 0*).

### Hampshire

| | | |
|---|---|---|
| V. P. Terry c Sargeant b Waqar Younis | 8 | – c Sargeant b Waqar Younis .... 17 |
| C. L. Smith c Ward b Waqar Younis | 55 | – c Sargeant b Waqar Younis .... 47 |
| *M. C. J. Nicholas c Sargeant b Waqar Younis. | 0 | – lbw b Waqar Younis .......... 14 |
| R. A. Smith c Lynch b Thorpe | 33 | – c Medlycott b Waqar Younis .. 29 |
| D. I. Gower b Murphy | 29 | – (6) lbw b Waqar Younis ....... 3 |
| K. D. James c Sargeant b Waqar Younis | 29 | – (7) not out ................... 39 |
| †A. N. Aymes b Greig | 53 | – (8) not out ................... 23 |
| R. J. Maru b Waqar Younis | 36 | – (5) c Lynch b Murphy ........ 23 |
| C. A. Connor c sub b Murphy | 12 | |
| P. J. Bakker b Waqar Younis | 0 | |
| Aqib Javed not out | 1 | |
| B 6, l-b 17, w 1, n-b 1 | 25 | B 2, l-b 8, w 3, n-b 1 .... 14 |

1/8 2/8 3/85 4/110 5/141       281     1/56 2/85 3/90    (6 wkts dec.) 209
6/211 7/258 8/279 9/279            4/136 5/140 6/144

Bonus points – Hampshire 3, Surrey 4.

Bowling: *First Innings*—Waqar Younis 19-5-66-6; M. P. Bicknell 15-10-23-0; Murphy 25.4-8-56-2; Greig 22.3-4-47-1; Thorpe 9-1-38-1; Medlycott 8.3-3-28-0. *Second Innings*—Waqar Younis 30-5-70-5; Murphy 41.5-12-103-1; Greig 13-2-26-0.

### Surrey

| | | |
|---|---|---|
| D. J. Bicknell b Connor | 48 | – b Bakker ...................... 0 |
| R. I. Alikhan b Bakker | 13 | – c R. A. Smith b Aqib Javed ... 53 |
| D. M. Ward c Maru b James | 22 | – lbw b Bakker ................. 18 |
| M. A. Lynch c R. A. Smith b Connor | 0 | – c Nicholas b Connor .......... 30 |
| G. P. Thorpe b Connor | 25 | – c Gower b Maru ............... 58 |
| K. T. Medlycott c R. A. Smith b James | 45 | – (7) b Connor ................. 0 |
| *I. A. Greig c R. A. Smith b Connor | 4 | – (6) c and b Connor ........... 61 |
| †N. F. Sargeant lbw b Aqib Javed | 4 | – c and b Maru ................. 17 |
| M. P. Bicknell b Aqib Javed | 18 | – c C. L. Smith b Maru ......... 0 |
| Waqar Younis not out | 16 | – not out ...................... 4 |
| A. J. Murphy c Terry b Aqib Javed | 9 | – not out ...................... 1 |
| B 5, l-b 16, n-b 10 | 31 | B 3, l-b 8, w 1, n-b 2 .... 14 |

1/57 2/81 3/86 4/95 5/166       235     1/0 2/32 3/102      (9 wkts) 256
6/175 7/175 8/196 9/197            4/115 5/226 6/226
                                          7/243 8/243 9/254

Bonus points – Surrey 2, Hampshire 4.

Bowling: *First Innings*—Aqib Javed 20.4-1-72-3; Bakker 18-4-48-1; Maru 2-1-1-0; Connor 16-2-49-4; James 15-4-44-2. *Second Innings*—Bakker 13-1-56-2; Aqib Javed 17-3-73-1; Maru 14-2-65-3; James 4-0-10-0; Connor 12-1-41-3.

Umpires: B. Hassan and A. G. T. Whitehead.

At Nottingham, May 31, June 1, 3. HAMPSHIRE drew with NOTTINGHAMSHIRE.

## HAMPSHIRE v LANCASHIRE

At Basingstoke, June 4, 5, 6. Lancashire won by 128 runs. Lancashire 20 pts, Hampshire 4 pts.
Toss: Lancashire. A remarkable all-round performance by Wasim Akram gave Lancashire
victory in a rain-affected match. Lancashire, struggling on a damp pitch, would have been 151
for six had Wasim been dismissed off a stumping chance when he was 16. Instead he survived
to launch a brutal assault, in company with Hegg, which lifted Lancashire to 250 before Hegg
was out for 69, with 58 of his runs coming in boundaries. Wasim was ninth out for 122, which
included two sixes and fifteen fours off 165 deliveries. Rain washed out much of the second
day, and after negotiations between the captains, Hampshire were eventually challenged to
score 350 in 74 overs. It was never realistic, but halfway through the last twenty overs they at
least seemed safe from defeat. However, Watkinson, bowling his off-spinners, flicked away
James's off bail to make Hampshire 212 for six, whereupon Wasim swept away the last four
wickets in nine balls without conceding a run.

*Close of play:* First day, Hampshire 8-0 (T. C. Middleton 1*, C. L. Smith 5*); Second day,
Hampshire 66-1 (T. C. Middleton 25*, M. C. J. Nicholas 14*).

## Lancashire

| | | | |
|---|---|---|---|
| G. D. Mendis c Maru b Aqib Javed | 13 | – (2) not out | 39 |
| G. Fowler c Terry b Aqib Javed | 57 | – (1) not out | 40 |
| G. D. Lloyd lbw b James | 8 | | |
| N. H. Fairbrother c Gower b James | 25 | | |
| M. Watkinson lbw b Bakker | 6 | | |
| Wasim Akram c James b Bakker | 122 | | |
| †W. K. Hegg c and b Maru | 69 | | |
| I. D. Austin b Bakker | 2 | | |
| G. Yates run out | 15 | | |
| *D. P. Hughes c Nicholas b Bakker | 4 | | |
| P. J. Martin not out | 1 | | |
| L-b 3, n-b 7 | 10 | L-b 1, n-b 3 | 4 |

1/35 2/56 3/90 4/106 5/115      332         (no wkt dec.) 83
6/250 7/277 8/325 9/331

Bonus points – Lancashire 4, Hampshire 4.

Bowling: *First Innings*—Bakker 21.2–7–66–4; Aqib Javed 18–4–67–2; Connor 11–1–56–0;
James 14–3–50–2; Maru 27–8–69–1; Nicholas 5–0–21–0. *Second Innings*—Connor 9–1–40–0;
James 7–1–18–0; Maru 5–2–8–0; Nicholas 3–0–13–0; Smith 1–0–3–0.

## Hampshire

| | | | |
|---|---|---|---|
| T. C. Middleton not out | 25 | – c Hegg b Wasim Akram | 16 |
| C. L. Smith c Hegg b Watkinson | 22 | – c Martin b Watkinson | 51 |
| *M. C. J. Nicholas not out | 14 | – (6) lbw b Wasim Akram | 19 |
| †A. N. Aymes (did not bat) | | – (3) run out | 33 |
| V. P. Terry (did not bat) | | – (4) b Martin | 52 |
| D. I. Gower (did not bat) | | – (5) c Fairbrother b Austin | 14 |
| K. D. James (did not bat) | | – b Watkinson | 14 |
| R. J. Maru (did not bat) | | – not out | 5 |
| C. A. Connor (did not bat) | | – b Wasim Akram | 0 |
| P. J. Bakker (did not bat) | | – lbw b Wasim Akram | 0 |
| Aqib Javed (did not bat) | | – b Wasim Akram | 0 |
| B 2, n-b 3 | 5 | B 8, l-b 4, n-b 5 | 17 |

1/36              (1 wkt dec.) 66    1/55 2/83 3/149 4/171 5/179      221
                                      6/212 7/217 8/221 9/221

Bowling: *First Innings*—Wasim Akram 8-4-10-0; Martin 7-1-20-0; Austin 8-2-23-0; Watkinson 7-3-11-1. *Second Innings*—Wasim Akram 20.4-3-48-5; Martin 19-5-60-1; Watkinson 16-3-48-2; Austin 11-4-26-1; Yates 6-1-27-0.

Umpires: B. Dudleston and R. Julian.

## HAMPSHIRE v GLOUCESTERSHIRE

At Southampton, June 7, 8, 10. Gloucestershire won by six wickets. Gloucestershire 19 pts, Hampshire 3 pts. Toss: Gloucestershire. Another rain-ruined match ended in victory for the visitors with three balls to spare after both sides had forfeited an innings. Hampshire's first innings had been halted after 27 overs on the opening day, and again on the second afternoon, and when play resumed on the final afternoon acting-captain Smith gave Gloucestershire a minimum of 50 overs in which to chase 257 for victory. Hampshire's total owed much to the in-form Smith, who reached 50 for the sixth time in twelve Championship innings. Gloucestershire began in a rush, Hodgson and Hardy putting on 99 in 25 overs, and when Lloyds joined Hodgson they added 100 in twelve overs, with Lloyds hitting 67 off 51 deliveries, including a six and ten fours. After that their win was almost a formality.
*Close of play*: First day, Hampshire 78-0 (T. C. Middleton 23*, C. L. Smith 46*); Second day, Hampshire 256-8 (A. N. Aymes 38*, P. J. Bakker 6*).

### Hampshire

| | | | |
|---|---|---|---|
| T. C. Middleton c Wright b Lawrence | 27 | K. J. Shine lbw b Smith | 0 |
| *C. L. Smith c Williams b Gilbert | 61 | P. J. Bakker not out | 6 |
| K. D. James c Babington b Smith | 14 | | |
| V. P. Terry lbw b Babington | 19 | B 5, l-b 19, n-b 4 | 28 |
| D. I. Gower c Lloyds b Gilbert | 28 | | |
| R. M. F. Cox c Hodgson b Babington | 15 | 1/85 2/104 3/131 (8 wkts dec.) 256 |
| †A. N. Aymes not out | 38 | 4/145 5/172 6/190 |
| R. J. Maru c Williams b Smith | 20 | 7/241 8/241 |

Aqib Javed did not bat.

Bonus points – Hampshire 3, Gloucestershire 3.

Bowling: Gilbert 17-5-46-2; Lawrence 17-5-38-1; Smith 23-8-54-3; Babington 18-1-69-2; Lloyds 10-3-25-0.

*Hampshire forfeited their second innings.*

### Gloucestershire

*Gloucestershire forfeited their first innings.*

| | | | |
|---|---|---|---|
| G. D. Hodgson run out | 89 | M. W. Alleyne not out | 3 |
| J. J. E. Hardy b Shine | 52 | | |
| J. W. Lloyds run out | 67 | B 6, l-b 5, w 1, n-b 7 | 19 |
| *A. J. Wright c Aymes b Maru | 17 | | |
| C. W. J. Athey not out | 10 | 1/99 2/199 3/235 4/249 (4 wkts) 257 |

D. R. Gilbert, †R. C. J. Williams, D. V. Lawrence, A. M. Smith and A. M. Babington did not bat.

Bowling: Aqib Javed 10-0-47-0; Shine 13-0-67-1; Bakker 9-2-54-0; Maru 12.3-0-48-1; James 5-0-30-0.

Umpires: B. Dudleston and R. Julian.

At Bath, June 18, 19, 20. HAMPSHIRE drew with SOMERSET.

At Northampton, June 21, 22, 23. HAMPSHIRE drew with NORTHAMPTONSHIRE.

At Southampton, June 29, 30, July 1. HAMPSHIRE drew with WEST INDIANS (See West Indian tour section).

At Chelmsford, July 2, 3, 4. HAMPSHIRE drew with ESSEX.

## HAMPSHIRE v YORKSHIRE

At Southampton, July 5, 6, 8. Drawn. Hampshire 7 pts, Yorkshire 4 pts. Toss: Hampshire. Heavy rain washed out the final day's play and frustrated the enterprise of Yorkshire's captain, Moxon, who had laid down his challenge by declaring their first innings on the second evening as soon as the follow-on had been avoided. Until then Hampshire had enjoyed one of their most productive games of the season. Smith hit his fourth Championship century of 1991, and James produced his highest score for two years. During his innings of 3 hours 23 minutes (167 balls) – his 40th first-class hundred for Hampshire – Smith completed 1,000 Championship runs for the season and hit five sixes and twelve fours, including a six to reach three figures. Yorkshire hit back as Hartley claimed three wickets in six balls, but James and Aymes added 119 and James and Maru another 103 in fifteen overs. James's unbeaten 134 included three sixes and eighteen fours in three hours seventeen minutes. Yorkshire's top order, except for Moxon, struggled against the pace of Aqib Javed and the spin of Maru and Turner, but Kellett and Gough rebuilt the innings with a stand of 56 for the seventh wicket. A flourish from Hartley ended Hampshire's fading hopes of enforcing the follow-on.

*Close of play:* First day, Hampshire 417-7 (K. D. James 134*); Second day, Hampshire 8-0 (V. P. Terry 6*, C. L. Smith 2*).

### Hampshire

| | | |
|---|---|---|
| V. P. Terry c Robinson b Fletcher | 13 | – not out ............... 6 |
| C. L. Smith c Robinson b Hartley | 112 | – not out ............... 2 |
| *M. C. J. Nicholas c Moxon b Hartley | 16 | |
| D. I. Gower c Carrick b Hartley | 49 | |
| J. R. Wood lbw b Hartley | 0 | |
| K. D. James not out | 134 | |
| †A. N. Aymes c Hartley b Carrick | 34 | |
| R. J. Maru b Gough | 36 | |
| B 7, l-b 12, w 2, n-b 2 | 23 | |

1/29 2/82 3/194 4/194 5/195          (7 wkts. dec.) 417          (no wkt) 8
6/314 7/417

I. J. Turner, K. J. Shine and Aqib Javed did not bat.

Bonus points – Hampshire 4, Yorkshire 2 (Score at 100 overs: 351-6).

Bowling: *First Innings*—Hartley 21-4-82-4; Fletcher 20-5-57-1; Carrick 34-6-109-1; Gough 18-0-86-1; Batty 17-1-64-0. *Second Innings*—Hartley 3-1-3-0; Fletcher 2-1-5-0.

### Yorkshire

| | | |
|---|---|---|
| *M. D. Moxon c Aymes b Aqib Javed | 68 | P. J. Hartley b Turner ............ 26 |
| A. A. Metcalfe c Aymes b James | 6 | J. D. Batty not out ............... 0 |
| D. Byas c and b Turner | 27 | |
| †R. J. Blakey c Maru b Aqib Javed | 4 | |
| P. E. Robinson c Aymes b Maru | 25 | B 1, l-b 5, w 2, n-b 10 ...... 18 |
| S. A. Kellett not out | 56 | |
| P. Carrick c Aymes b Maru | 6 | 1/47 2/109 3/118          (8 wkts. dec.) 268 |
| D. Gough c Maru b Turner | 32 | 4/122 5/159 6/173 |
| | | 7/229 8/265 |

S. D. Fletcher did not bat.

Bonus points – Yorkshire 2, Hampshire 3 (Score at 100 overs: 246-7).

Bowling: Shine 11-2-41-0; Aqib Javed 20.1-4-55-2; Maru 34-9-79-2; James 8-1-20-1; Turner 32-9-67-3; Smith 1-1-0-0.

Umpires: K. J. Lyons and D. R. Shepherd.

## HAMPSHIRE v WORCESTERSHIRE

At Portsmouth, July 16, 17, 18. Drawn. Hampshire 8 pts, Worcestershire 4 pts. Toss: Worcestershire. The weather was the decisive factor in Hampshire missing out on their first Championship win of the season. Rain claimed 60 overs on the final day, and Worcestershire, only 16 runs ahead with five second-innings wickets remaining when play got under way at 3.30 p.m., made good their escape. On the first day Hampshire had made Neale regret his decision to field. By lunch they were 175 for one, with Terry having hit fifteen fours in scoring 87 from 102 balls. Smith's 87, slightly slower, contained twelve fours and a six, and Gower kept up the entertainment with eleven boundaries in his 77. Aqib Javed had two Worcestershire wickets by the close, and next day Shine forced the visitors to follow on, 255 in arrears, with a career-best return of five for 43. Three of his wickets came in six deliveries. However, Hick made a mockery of his Test form when Worcestershire batted again, scoring an immaculate 141 from 171 balls, with 23 fours, and adding 143 with Neale for the fourth wicket. His dismissal by Shine shortly before the end of the day held out the promise of that elusive win for Hampshire, but it was not to be.

*Close of play:* First day, Worcestershire 12-2 (T. S. Curtis 7*, G. A. Hick 0*); Second day, Worcestershire 271-5 (I. T. Botham 25*, G. R. Dilley 1*).

### Hampshire

| | | | | |
|---|---|---|---|---|
| V. P. Terry c Rhodes b Dilley | 87 | C. A. Connor c Newport b Botham | 18 | |
| C. L. Smith b Dilley | 87 | K. J. Shine b Illingworth | 1 | |
| *M. C. J. Nicholas c Hick b Newport | 9 | Aqib Javed not out | 1 | |
| D. I. Gower c sub b Hick | 77 | | | |
| K. D. James c Moody b Botham | 84 | L-b 7, w 2, n-b 6 | 15 | |
| J. R. Ayling c Rhodes b Dilley | 3 | | | |
| †A. N. Aymes run out | 10 | 1/172 2/179 3/212 4/289 5/309 | | 419 |
| R. J. Maru c Rhodes b Botham | 27 | 6/360 7/376 8/404 9/413 | | |

Bonus points – Hampshire 4, Worcestershire 3 (Score at 100 overs: 379-7).

Bowling: Dilley 21-7-50-3; Radford 16-1-72-0; Botham 11.5-2-51-3; Newport 10-0-60-1; Illingworth 26-2-94-1; Hick 19-2-85-1.

### Worcestershire

| | | | |
|---|---|---|---|
| T. S. Curtis c Maru b Shine | 53 | – c Gower b Shine | 6 |
| G. J. Lord c Aymes b Aqib Javed | 2 | – c Nicholas b Aqib Javed | 0 |
| R. K. Illingworth b Aqib Javed | 0 | | |
| G. A. Hick b Connor | 15 | – (3) c Terry b Shine | 141 |
| T. M. Moody c Terry b Shine | 10 | – (4) c Maru b Ayling | 25 |
| *P. A. Neale c Maru b Ayling | 15 | – (5) c Gower b Shine | 49 |
| I. T. Botham c Terry b Shine | 26 | – (6) c Aymes b Shine | 42 |
| †S. J. Rhodes c Maru b Shine | 0 | – not out | 46 |
| P. J. Newport c sub b Connor | 12 | | |
| N. V. Radford not out | 6 | | |
| G. R. Dilley b Shine | 0 | – (7) not out | 15 |
| L-b 1, w 2, n-b 22 | 25 | L-b 11, w 1, n-b 24 | 36 |

| | | | |
|---|---|---|---|
| 1/9 2/12 3/47 4/74 5/102 | 164 | 1/5 2/8 3/84 | (6 wkts) 360 |
| 6/138 7/138 8/144 9/164 | | 4/227 5/270 6/291 | |

Bonus points – Worcestershire 1, Hampshire 4.

Bowling: *First Innings*—Aqib Javed 13-1-37-2; Maru 1-0-4-0; Shine 11.5-2-43-5; Connor 14-3-46-2; James 4-1-5-0; Ayling 5-2-28-1. *Second Innings*—Aqib Javed 16-2-69-1; Shine 17-2-91-4; Maru 21-7-44-0; Ayling 15-2-52-1; Connor 8-0-39-0; James 11-1-54-0.

Umpires: J. H. Harris and A. G. T. Whitehead.

## HAMPSHIRE v WARWICKSHIRE

At Portsmouth, July 19, 20, 22. Warwickshire won by three wickets. Warwickshire 21 pts, Hampshire 7 pts. Toss: Hampshire. Terry's 124 in five hours eighteen minutes, containing eleven boundaries, was a masterpiece of application on a pitch that favoured the Warwickshire seam bowlers. However, he lacked support, apart from Gower (58 balls) and Ayling, and after Donald had forced Ayling to retire hurt, Hampshire lost their last six wickets for 11 runs. Hampshire's seam bowlers, spearheaded by Aqib Javed, earned their side a lead of 74, but before the second day was over Reeve and Donald had countered by bowling Hampshire out a second time, leaving the Championship leaders requiring 251 for victory. Once again Ratcliffe was the only Warwickshire batsman to play with any comfort, and at 175 for six the odds appeared to favour Hampshire. However, Piper, ignoring a fractured right thumb, batted with considerable courage and saw Warwickshire to victory.

*Close of play:* First day, Warwickshire 74-2 (J. D. Ratcliffe 45*, D. P. Ostler 11*); Second day, Warwickshire 12-0 (A. J. Moles 1*, J. D. Ratcliffe 10*).

### Hampshire

| | | | | |
|---|---|---|---|---|
| V. P. Terry lbw b Reeve | 124 | – c Ratcliffe b Munton | 18 |
| *M. C. J. Nicholas lbw b Small | 0 | – c Piper b Donald | 5 |
| K. D. James c Reeve b Munton | 7 | – c Piper b Reeve | 0 |
| R. A. Smith c Asif Din b Munton | 19 | – (7) c Piper b Reeve | 0 |
| D. I. Gower c Piper b Donald | 43 | – (4) c Moles b Donald | 18 |
| J. R. Ayling not out | 42 | – c Donald b Reeve | 16 |
| †A. N. Aymes c and b Reeve | 4 | – (5) c Ostler b Small | 35 |
| R. J. Maru c Ratcliffe b Reeve | 2 | – c Ostler b Reeve | 6 |
| C. A. Connor b Reeve | 4 | – run out | 17 |
| K. J. Shine c Piper b Small | 1 | – b Donald | 0 |
| Aqib Javed c Ostler b Small | 0 | – not out | 2 |
| B 1, l-b 6, w 4, n-b 5 | 16 | B 16, l-b 9, w 12, n-b 3 | 40 |
| | **265** | | **176** |

1/2 2/21 3/67 4/128 5/254         1/25 2/41 3/78 4/80 5/127
6/256 7/258 8/263 9/263           6/144 7/144 8/166 9/167

*Bonus points – Hampshire 3, Warwickshire 4.*

*In the first innings J. R. Ayling, when 40, retired hurt at 232 and resumed at 263-9.*

Bowling: *First Innings*—Donald 13.5-1-41-1; Small 17.1-4-45-3; Munton 22-3-80-2; Reeve 22-7-46-4; Smith 8-0-38-0; Asif Din 3-1-8-0. *Second Innings*—Donald 15.4-4-32-3; Small 16-3-50-1; Munton 8-1-28-1; Smith 2-0-14-0; Reeve 15-5-27-4.

### Warwickshire

| | | | | |
|---|---|---|---|---|
| A. J. Moles b Shine | 1 | – c Maru b James | 15 |
| J. D. Ratcliffe lbw b Aqib Javed | 52 | – c Gower b Shine | 77 |
| *T. A. Lloyd lbw b Aqib Javed | 11 | – c Nicholas b Connor | 12 |
| D. P. Ostler lbw b Aqib Javed | 20 | – c Aymes b Ayling | 12 |
| D. A. Reeve c Terry b James | 3 | – lbw b Ayling | 4 |
| Asif Din c Terry b Ayling | 19 | – c James b Ayling | 13 |
| P. A. Smith c Maru b James | 7 | – c Aymes b Shine | 27 |
| †K. J. Piper c Aymes b Ayling | 6 | – not out | 31 |
| G. C. Small c Aymes b Ayling | 17 | – not out | 12 |
| T. A. Munton c Maru b Shine | 14 | | |
| A. A. Donald not out | 8 | | |
| B 1, l-b 15, n-b 17 | 33 | B 4, l-b 14, w 6, n-b 16 | 40 |
| | **191** | (7 wkts) | **251** |

1/17 2/29 3/97 4/101 5/110         1/68 2/115 3/128 4/141   (7 wkts) 251
6/134 7/145 8/159 9/183            5/152 6/175 7/219

*Bonus points – Warwickshire 1, Hampshire 4.*

Bowling: *First Innings*—Aqib Javed 13-5-18-3; Shine 16-1-63-2; Connor 9-3-32-0; James 12-3-39-2; Ayling 10.1-2-23-3. *Second Innings*—Aqib Javed 6-2-23-0; Shine 22-3-68-2; Ayling 20-4-47-3; Connor 18-1-59-1; Maru 4-3-3-0; James 10.5-1-33-1.

Umpires: J. H. Harris and A. G. T. Whitehead.

At Chesterfield, July 23, 24, 25. HAMPSHIRE beat DERBYSHIRE by 94 runs.

At Lord's, August 2, 3, 5. HAMPSHIRE beat MIDDLESEX by five wickets.

At Canterbury, August 6, 7, 8. HAMPSHIRE drew with KENT.

At Swansea, August 9, 10, 12. HAMPSHIRE beat GLAMORGAN by 172 runs.

## HAMPSHIRE v LEICESTERSHIRE

At Bournemouth, August 16, 17, 19. Hampshire won by two wickets. Hampshire 21 pts, Leicestershire 6 pts. Toss: Leicestershire. Successive boundaries by Shine off the fourth and fifth balls of the final over, bowled by Lewis, brought Hampshire victory after a fascinating match. Leicestershire, having chosen to bat first, were in danger of being dismissed cheaply when Lewis was sixth out at 175 in the 55th over, but a county seventh-wicket record of 219 unbroken by Benson and Whitticase carried them to a declaration at 394 off 100 overs. Benson's hundred, containing 21 fours, was his first in the Championship, while Whitticase reached his maiden first-class hundred from 127 balls and hit eighteen fours in all. Smith excepted, Hampshire's reply was pedestrian. James lingered three and threequarter hours over his 45; Nicholas took three hours for 73, including eleven fours. It needed Nicholas's declaration to keep the match alive, and when Leicestershire reciprocated, Hampshire's target was 283 in a minimum of 66 overs. At 187 for five, needing 96 from sixteen overs, they appeared out of contention; but James and Aymes produced a partnership of 85 in fourteen overs before James, who hit two successive sixes off Millns, was caught 14 runs short of reaching 1,000 in a summer for the first time. Connor and Aymes were run out off the first and third balls of the last over, bringing Shine to the wicket to hit the winning runs.

*Close of play*: First day, Hampshire 13-1 (T. C. Middleton 2*, I. J. Turner 1*); Second day, Leicestershire 24-1 (N. E. Briers 7*, P. N. Hepworth 0*).

## Leicestershire

| | | | |
|---|---|---|---|
| T. J. Boon run out | 53 | – c Nicholas b Shine | 12 |
| *N. E. Briers c Aymes b Aqib Javed | 8 | – not out | 80 |
| P. N. Hepworth c Middleton b James | 4 | – not out | 43 |
| J. J. Whitaker c Aymes b Turner | 10 | | |
| L. Potter lbw b James | 14 | | |
| J. D. R. Benson not out | 133 | | |
| C. C. Lewis c Middleton b Turner | 34 | | |
| †P. Whitticase not out | 114 | | |
| B 8, l-b 3, n-b 13 | 24 | B 7, l-b 3, n-b 5 | 15 |

1/14 2/31 3/65 4/97 5/97 6/175    (6 wkts dec.) 394    1/23      (1 wkt dec.) 150

D. J. Millns, C. W. Wilkinson and J. N. Maguire did not bat.

Bonus points – Leicestershire 4, Hampshire 2.

Bowling: *First Innings*—Aqib Javed 16–2–72–1; Connor 17–4–62–0; Shine 15–2–66–0; James 17–4–56–2; Turner 25–7–69–2; Nicholas 6–0–36–0; Smith 4–1–22–0. *Second Innings*—Aqib Javed 11–3–22–0; Shine 11–1–46–1; Turner 13–3–32–0; Connor 9–0–34–0; James 3–1–6–0.

## Hampshire

| | | | | |
|---|---|---|---|---|
| T. C. Middleton c Benson b Lewis | 22 | – (2) lbw b Lewis | 20 |
| V. P. Terry lbw b Millns | 10 | – (1) lbw b Maguire | 79 |
| I. J. Turner c Whitticase b Millns | 1 | – (9) not out | 1 |
| K. D. James c Wilkinson b Maguire | 45 | – (6) c Briers b Millns | 72 |
| R. A. Smith c Wilkinson b Potter | 61 | – (4) c Wilkinson b Potter | 39 |
| D. I. Gower c Lewis b Potter | 11 | – (3) c Potter b Millns | 16 |
| *M. C. J. Nicholas not out | 73 | – (5) b Maguire | 9 |
| †A. N. Aymes not out | 32 | – (7) run out | 29 |
| C. A. Connor (did not bat) | | – (8) run out | 1 |
| K. J. Shine (did not bat) | | – not out | 8 |
| W 2, n-b 5 | 7 | B 3, l-b 4, w 1, n-b 3 | 11 |

1/12 2/18 3/41 4/130      (6 wkts dec.) 262    1/59 2/83 3/156 4/166    (8 wkts) 285
5/150 6/178                                    5/187 6/272 7/275 8/277

Aqib Javed did not bat.

Bonus points – Hampshire 3, Leicestershire 2 (Score at 100 overs: 256-6).

Bowling: *First Innings*—Lewis 20-7-42-1; Millns 19-6-48-2; Maguire 27-7-52-1; Wilkinson 13-1-51-0; Potter 19-1-59-2; Hepworth 3-2-1-0; Benson 2-0-9-0. *Second Innings*—Millns 11-1-65-2; Lewis 16.5-1-72-1; Maguire 19-3-65-2; Potter 14-2-56-1; Hepworth 5-1-20-0.

Umpires: N. T. Plews and R. A. White.


## HAMPSHIRE v SUSSEX

At Bournemouth, August 20, 21, 22. Drawn. Hampshire 7 pts, Sussex 4 pts. Toss: Hampshire. Sussex, challenged to score 306 in a minimum of 72 overs, still needed 269 from 51 overs, with eight wickets in hand, when bad light and rain claimed the final afternoon. It was a match when the ball generally dominated the bat. James and Gower worked hard to put together a century partnership for the third wicket in each innings, and Nicholas grafted his way past 50 on the opening day. Sussex found batting even more difficult, with acting-captain Wells offering the only positive resistance to Aqib Javed, whose third five-wicket return of the summer helped Hampshire to a lead of 99.

*Close of play:* First day, Hampshire 297-9 (K. J. Shine 16*, Aqib Javed 0*); Second day, Hampshire 85-2 (K. D. James 1*, D. I. Gower 2*).


## Hampshire

| | | | | |
|---|---|---|---|---|
| T. C. Middleton c Speight b Jones | 6 | – c Moores b Pigott | 36 |
| V. P. Terry c Greenfield b Jones | 4 | – c Greenfield b Pigott | 42 |
| K. D. James c Smith b Donelan | 68 | – not out | 50 |
| D. I. Gower c Lenham b Dodemaide | 51 | – b North | 58 |
| *M. C. J. Nicholas c Pigott b Dodemaide | 55 | – not out | 10 |
| J. R. Ayling c Moores b Pigott | 13 | | |
| †A. N. Aymes lbw b North | 15 | | |
| R. J. Maru c Greenfield b Donelan | 34 | | |
| I. J. Turner b Jones | 6 | | |
| K. J. Shine not out | 16 | | |
| Aqib Javed not out | 0 | | |
| B 5, l-b 4, w 1, n-b 19 | 29 | L-b 6, w 2, n-b 2 | 10 |

1/7 2/10 3/120 4/150 5/184      (9 wkts dec.) 297    1/76 2/83 3/185    (3 wkts dec.) 206
6/222 7/253 8/274 9/297

Bonus points – Hampshire 3, Sussex 3 (Score at 100 overs: 258-7).

Bowling: *First Innings*—Jones 18-6-46-3; Dodemaide 28-4-71-2; Pigott 15-3-34-1; North 20-6-55-1; Donelan 29-10-82-2. *Second Innings*—Jones 10-1-37-0; Dodemaide 14-1-47-0; Pigott 18-5-51-2; Donelan 18-2-47-0; North 4-0-18-1.

## Sussex

| | | | |
|---|---|---|---|
| N. J. Lenham c Terry b Aqib Javed | 8 | – c Turner b Shine | 1 |
| D. M. Smith c Middleton b Aqib Javed | 10 | – not out | 16 |
| K. Greenfield lbw b Ayling | 22 | – lbw b Aqib Javed | 0 |
| *A. P. Wells c Aymes b Aqib Javed | 76 | – not out | 18 |
| M. P. Speight c Terry b Maru | 8 | | |
| J. A. North c Maru b Turner | 22 | | |
| A. I. C. Dodemaide c Terry b Aqib Javed | 12 | | |
| †P. Moores run out | 1 | | |
| A. C. S. Pigott c Ayling b Turner | 10 | | |
| B. T. P. Donelan not out | 7 | | |
| A. N. Jones b Aqib Javed | 7 | | |
| L-b 9, n-b 6 | 15 | L-b 2 | 2 |

1/13 2/26 3/69 4/104 5/147       198    1/3 2/6        (2 wkts) 37
6/165 7/166 8/175 9/187

Bonus points – Sussex 1, Hampshire 4.

Bowling: *First Innings*—Aqib Javed 15–4–47–5; Shine 5–0–32–0; James 6–2–12–0; Ayling 9–2–27–1; Maru 20–8–38–1; Turner 22–9–33–2. *Second Innings*—Aqib Javed 8–4–11–1; Shine 7–2–19–1; Turner 4–1–3–0; Maru 2–0–2–0.

Umpires: N. T. Plews and R. A. White.

## HAMPSHIRE v SOMERSET

At Southampton, August 28, 29, 30, 31. Hampshire won by two wickets. Hampshire 21 pts, Somerset 6 pts. Toss: Somerset. An excellent four-day contest on a typically bland Southampton pitch ended with Hampshire edging home in an exciting finish. It was a match dominated by Cook, who hit hundreds in both innings, his ninth and tenth of the summer, to equal W. E. Alley's Somerset record of ten hundreds in a season, set in 1961. In the first innings he scored a chanceless 197 off 309 balls, with 28 fours, sharing a third-wicket partnership of 162 with Tavaré. Terry, Smith and Gower, whose 89-ball 73 took him past his 1,000 runs for the season without a single century, produced a positive response for Hampshire, and when Nicholas declared 142 behind, early on the third afternoon, Cook provided another masterpiece of timing and placement. He went to his record-equalling hundred from 171 balls, having hit seventeen fours, and was unbeaten on 115 at the close. However, he was unwell overnight and unable to continue, and after four overs on the final morning Tavaré set Hampshire a target of 370 in a minimum of 95 overs. They lost three wickets for 98, but Smith, needing only 93 balls for his first hundred of the summer for Hampshire, and hitting two sixes and thirteen fours in his 107, took them to 243 for five. Nicholas played his part magnificently, remaining unbeaten for 90, and helped by a massive six from Shine off Graveney and a dropped catch in the deep, Hampshire scrambled to victory with eleven balls to spare.

Close of play: First day, Somerset 331-4 (I. Fletcher 25*, N. D. Burns 5*); Second day, Hampshire 194-2 (V. P. Terry 85*, R. A. Smith 56*); Third day, Somerset 218-2 (S. J. Cook 115*, C. J. Tavaré 10*).

## Somerset

| | | | |
|---|---|---|---|
| S. J. Cook c Aymes b James | 197 | – retired ill | 115 |
| G. T. J. Townsend c James b Shine | 29 | – c Smith b Turner | 18 |
| R. J. Harden c Aymes b Maru | 0 | – c Gower b Maru | 62 |
| *C. J. Tavaré c Middleton b Shine | 66 | – not out | 15 |
| I. Fletcher c Aymes b Aqib Javed | 56 | – not out | 2 |
| †N. D. Burns not out | 61 | | |
| G. D. Rose c Smith b Turner | 20 | | |
| R. P. Lefebvre run out | 12 | | |
| H. R. J. Trump not out | 16 | | |
| B 4, l-b 6, n-b 13 | 23 | B 4, l-b 3, n-b 8 | 15 |

1/91 2/105 3/267 4/320 5/380   (7 wkts dec.) 480   1/74 2/199   (2 wkts dec.) 227
6/428 7/447

A. P. van Troost and D. A. Graveney did not bat.

Bonus points – Somerset 4, Hampshire 1 (Score at 100 overs: 320-4).

*In the second innings S. J. Cook retired ill at 218.*

Bowling: *First Innings*—Aqib Javed 24–1–102–1; Shine 22–2–91–2; James 28–6–67–1; Turner 34–6–114–1; Maru 40–17–78–1; Nicholas 4–0–18–0. *Second Innings*—Shine 8–2–17–0; Aqib Javed 11–2–54–0; Turner 23–7–70–1; James 7–2–17–0; Maru 20–3–62–1.

## Hampshire

| | | | |
|---|---|---|---|
| V. P. Terry c Burns b Trump | 86 | – c and b Trump | 31 |
| T. C. Middleton c Townsend b Trump | 24 | – b Trump | 49 |
| K. D. James c Tavaré b Trump | 25 | – c and b Graveney | 10 |
| R. A. Smith st Burns b Trump | 81 | – c Graveney b Lefebvre | 107 |
| D. I. Gower b Cook b Trump | 73 | – c Burns b Graveney | 15 |
| *M. C. J. Nicholas not out | 27 | – not out | 90 |
| †A. N. Aymes c Townsend b Trump | 13 | – b Graveney | 33 |
| R. J. Maru c Cook b Rose | 1 | – b Graveney | 3 |
| I. J. Turner c Burns b Rose | 0 | – run out | 3 |
| K. J. Shine not out | 0 | – not out | 16 |
| L-b 3, n-b 5 | 8 | L-b 8, w 4, n-b 1 | 13 |

1/47 2/99 3/201 4/253 5/314     (8 wkts dec.) 338    1/75 2/94 3/98 4/160    (8 wkts) 370
6/336 7/338 8/338                                  5/243 6/316 7/326 8/333

Aqib Javed did not bat.

Bonus points – Hampshire 4, Somerset 2 (Score at 100 overs: 314-5).

Bowling: *First Innings*—van Troost 18–5–42–0; Rose 20–3–78–2; Lefebvre 23–5–52–0; Trump 43–11–121–6; Harden 3–0–11–0; Graveney 7–1–31–0. *Second Innings*—van Troost 8–0–28–0; Rose 11–0–32–0; Lefebvre 12–1–29–1; Trump 33–3–132–2; Graveney 30.1–3–141–4.

Umpires: A. A. Jones and D. R. Shepherd.

At The Oval, September 3, 4, 5. HAMPSHIRE lost to SURREY by 171 runs.

## HAMPSHIRE v GLAMORGAN

At Southampton, September 17, 18, 19, 20. Glamorgan won by seven wickets. Glamorgan 24 pts, Hampshire 6 pts. Toss: Hampshire. Hampshire were in end-of-term mood in the aftermath of their NatWest Bank Trophy triumph and failed to make the most of another excellent Southampton batting pitch. Gower's 59 from 58 balls, spiced with nine fours and a six, was delightful, and James and Aymes were steady; but only Terry, with twelve fours in his 81, did himself full justice. Any satisfaction Hampshire had at gaining maximum batting points quickly evaporated as first Morris and then Maynard destroyed their bowling. Morris hit a pugnacious 131, which included two sixes and seventeen fours, and Maynard unveiled his full range of strokes in a career-best 243. He put on 154 in 35 overs with Croft for the sixth wicket, to which Croft supplied 35, and Maynard's powerful display, with shots to all parts of the ground, contained 32 fours and six sixes. Glamorgan led by 174, and again only Terry showed the necessary application as Croft bowled the visitors into a winning position. Eventually they required 150, with 83 overs available, and Butcher and Dale made certain they got them without undue alarms.

*Close of play:* First day, Glamorgan 53-0 (S. P. James 17*, H. Morris 26*); Second day, Glamorgan 484-6 (M. P. Maynard 238*, C. P. Metson 9*); Third day, Hampshire 271-8 (I. J. Turner 11*).

## Hampshire

| | | | |
|---|---|---|---|
| V. P. Terry c Metson b Frost | 81 | – b Croft | 70 |
| T. C. Middleton c Morris b Watkin | 8 | – b Watkin | 43 |
| K. D. James c Maynard b Croft | 49 | – b Foster | 43 |
| R. A. Smith b Croft | 14 | – b Croft | 29 |
| *D. I. Gower c James b Foster | 59 | – b Croft | 38 |
| J. R. Ayling c Maynard b Watkin | 5 | – c Croft b Watkin | 28 |
| †A. N. Aymes c Maynard b Watkin | 46 | – b Croft | 0 |
| R. J. Maru c Metson b Frost | 19 | – c and b Foster | 1 |
| I. J. Turner lbw b Frost | 3 | – not out | 28 |
| C. A. Connor run out | 30 | – b Frost | 30 |
| K. J. Shine not out | 3 | – b Watkin | 3 |
| L-b 3, w 1, n-b 9 | 13 | L-b 8, n-b 2 | 10 |

1/22 2/140 3/153 4/185 5/196     330     1/118 2/120 3/153 4/224 5/234   323
6/236 7/288 8/293 9/315                  6/235 7/236 8/271 9/320

Bonus points – Hampshire 4, Glamorgan 4.

Bowling: *First Innings*—Frost 22.3–4–89–3; Watkin 26–5–70–3; Foster 13–0–62–1; Dale 5–0–17–0; Croft 22–2–89–2. *Second Innings*—Frost 17–3–47–1; Watkin 30.2–6–92–3; Foster 14–3–36–2; Croft 43–9–119–4; Dale 8–1–21–0.

## Glamorgan

| | | | |
|---|---|---|---|
| S. P. James c Smith b James | 31 | – (2) c James b Maru | 22 |
| H. Morris c Smith b Maru | 131 | | |
| A. Dale c and b Maru | 3 | – not out | 47 |
| M. P. Maynard c Maru b Connor | 243 | – c James b Smith | 18 |
| *A. R. Butcher c Aymes b Connor | 1 | – (1) b Smith | 58 |
| D. L. Hemp b Maru | 8 | – (5) not out | 4 |
| R. D. B. Croft c and b James | 35 | | |
| †C. P. Metson lbw b Maru | 19 | | |
| S. L. Watkin c Aymes b Connor | 0 | | |
| M. Frost c Ayling b Maru | 1 | | |
| D. J. Foster not out | 4 | | |
| B 1, l-b 11, w 1, n-b 15 | 28 | W 1, n-b 2 | 3 |

1/108 2/134 3/227 4/242 5/265     504     1/50 2/110 3/144     (3 wkts) 152
6/419 7/489 8/489 9/499

Bonus points – Glamorgan 4, Hampshire 2 (Score at 100 overs: 354-5).

Bowling: *First Innings*—Shine 24–8–84–0; Connor 24–7–49–3; Ayling 11–3–44–0; Turner 24–3–109–0; James 17–5–78–2; Maru 38.3–7–128–5. *Second Innings*—Shine 4–0–16–0; Connor 5–1–9–0; Turner 18–4–48–0; James 3–0–10–0; Maru 10–3–28–1; Ayling 5–1–17–0; Smith 5–1–20–2; Gower 0.1–0–4–0.

Umpires: R. Palmer and P. B. Wight
(For the final session of the 3rd day and all of the 4th, first T. M. Tremlett and then J. N. Lark, standing at square leg, deputised for P. B. Wight).

# KENT

*Patron:* HRH The Duke of Kent
*President:* 1991 – P. G. Foster
     1992 – D. S. Kemp
*Chairman:* P. H. Edgley
*Chairman, Cricket Committee:*
 A. J. P. Woodhouse
*Secretary:* S. T. W. Anderson
 St Lawrence Ground, Old Dover Road,
 Canterbury CT1 3NZ
 (Telephone: 0227-456886)
*Captain:* M. R. Benson
*Cricket Administrator:* B. W. Luckhurst
*Coach:* D. H. Foster

"Marked improvement" would be a fair end-of-season report on Kent, still chasing their first major trophy since 1978. Under new management on and off the field, they kept their supporters' interest alive throughout, particularly in the Britannic Assurance Championship, where they made their boldest showing for several years, apart from their runners-up season of 1988. Having finished sixteenth in 1990, Kent had to climb, which they did by ten places, and they looked capable of playing a much bigger role in the Championship than they finally did. Certainly the influence of the coach, Daryl Foster, aiming to reproduce his success with Western Australia, was apparent, and the new captain, Mark Benson, enjoyed a fine summer, both with the bat and as a leader. Foster's immediate objective was to instil a competitive attitude, and this was forthcoming. Kent's first-class results proved that, as well as becoming likelier winners, they were not easy losers.

The period of transition was set to continue, with five players not retained at the end of the season. Three were recognised first-team players: Tony Merrick, the Antiguan fast bowler, Simon Hinks and the former captain, Chris Cowdrey. The news of Cowdrey's release came in August, one year exactly after he resigned the captaincy, and he did not appear again for the county. Troubled by injury during the season, he had played mainly in limited-overs cricket. It was sad that his departure should be so abrupt after fifteen years with Kent, but he followed in a line of senior players no longer required, for whatever reason. In another break with the past, his father, Colin Cowdrey, had resigned as one of the club's trustees, thus conceding his place on the general committee.

Despite the interest generated by their Championship revival, Kent were not so successful in one-day cricket. They duly qualified for the Benson and Hedges quarter-finals, but progressed no further; in the NatWest Bank Trophy they accounted for Cambridgeshire, only to fall at the next hurdle, to Surrey at The Oval. Inconsistency was their prime failing in the Refuge Assurance League, in which they made a poor start and did not win a match until the end of May. In July, however, they put together a winning run, prompting thoughts of a place in the Refuge Assurance Cup, but those hopes were eclipsed by four defeats in August. Benson and Neil Taylor were their leading Sunday run-getters, well supported by Trevor Ward, Matthew Fleming and Graham Cowdrey.

The Championship was a different story. From the start the team's promise in all departments was apparent, with Benson scoring 257 in the first match and 96 in the second, when Kent beat Surrey by an innings. It was an important victory, for it proved to the players that they could bowl out the opposition twice. For most of the summer, Kent relied on pace and seam, and the policy reaped rewards. Alan Igglesden, Merrick, Chris Penn and Richard Ellison between them captured more than 200 wickets, and it was Igglesden and Penn who bowled the side to victory in the first game of the Maidstone Week, against Northamptonshire.

That was an important week for a batsman, too. Ward, recently promoted to open, responded with a hundred in each innings in the next match, against Glamorgan, and he blossomed to register his first double-century, an unbeaten 235 against Middlesex at Canterbury, by the end of the season. It had been a profitable move for both county and player, and Ward was summoned to open for England A against the Sri Lankans in Manchester. Another Kent player who took part in those one-day games was Steve Marsh, and his recognition was equally well earned. Competitive by nature, Marsh scored 910 first-class runs, and his consistency behind the stumps was highlighted by his achievement against Middlesex at Lord's, where he held eight catches in an innings to equal the world record. Demonstrating his all-round ability, he hit a hundred in the same match.

A tremendous finish against the West Indians saw Kent lose by only 4 runs, the closest the tourists came to defeat in a county match, and by the start of Canterbury Week Kent were poised to have their say in the Championship. Two draws, and a defeat by Leicestershire at Grace Road, put their chances in perspective, but in late August they defeated Gloucestershire in a thrilling match by one wicket and beat Middlesex, whose second innings, shattered by the Kent pace and seam attack, mustered only 96. The county's leading run-scorer, Taylor, dominated this late phase; five of his seven first-class hundreds came in four consecutive matches, culminating in 111 and an unbeaten 203 in the tie with Sussex at Hove. This was Kent's second tie of the summer, having finished level with Essex in the Sunday League in May.

The last three matches featured Mark Ealham, son of Alan, the county's former captain now in charge of youth coaching. He displayed his father's hard-hitting batting and superb fielding, plus a useful-looking brand of medium pace. Having waited so long for a sustained chance in the Championship, he seized it eagerly, taking five wickets for the first time at Hove and repeating the feat in the final game, against Leicestershire. He could look forward to a longer run in the next season.

In 1992 Kent also have the exciting prospect of the West Indian Test player, Carl Hooper. Throughout the summer, and indeed at Canterbury, where he scored two unbeaten fifties for the tourists, he showed how valuable his batting would be. In addition, his off-spin bowling promised to answer one of Kent's deficiencies for some seasons, and his specialist slip fielding was a welcome asset for a team whose most obvious weakness was its catching, particularly in that area. For many years the start of a new season had been based on hope. The evidence of 1991, plus the acquisition of Hooper, suggested that Kent's expectations should have a surer foundation in 1992. – Dudley Moore.

452

KENT 1991

[*Bill Smith*]

*Back row*: N. W. Preston, M. T. Brimson, D. P. Fulton, T. N. Wren, N. J. Llong, G. J. Kersey. *Middle row*: J. Foley (*scorer*), D. H. Foster (*coach*), J. I. Longley, M. A. Ealham, R. P. Davis, D. J. M. Kelleher, M. V. Fleming, V. J. Wells, M. C. Dobson, T. A. Merrick, A. G. E. Ealham (*director of youth coaching*). *Front row*: G. R. Cowdrey, C. Penn, N. R. Taylor, S. A. Marsh, M. R. Benson (*captain*), C. S. Cowdrey, R. M. Ellison, S. G. Hinks, A. P. Igglesden, T. R. Ward. *Inset*: M. M. Patel.

## KENT RESULTS

*All first-class matches – Played 24: Won 6, Lost 4, Tied 1, Drawn 13.*

*County Championship matches – Played 22: Won 6, Lost 3, Tied 1, Drawn 12.*

*Bonus points – Batting 50, Bowling 55.*

*Competition placings – Britannic Assurance County Championship, 6th equal;
NatWest Bank Trophy, 2nd round; Benson and Hedges Cup, q-f;
Refuge Assurance League, 10th.*

## BRITANNIC ASSURANCE CHAMPIONSHIP AVERAGES

### BATTING

| | Birthplace | M | I | NO | R | HI | Avge |
|---|---|---|---|---|---|---|---|
| ‡N. R. Taylor . . . . . . . | Orpington | 22 | 34 | 3 | 1,647 | 203* | 53.12 |
| ‡M. R. Benson . . . . . . | Shoreham | 20 | 30 | 2 | 1,329 | 257 | 47.46 |
| ‡T. R. Ward . . . . . . . | Farningham | 20 | 31 | 2 | 1,369 | 235* | 47.20 |
| ‡C. S. Cowdrey . . . . . | Farnborough, Kent | 3 | 4 | 0 | 154 | 97 | 38.50 |
| ‡G. R. Cowdrey . . . . . | Farnborough, Kent | 21 | 32 | 4 | 1,064 | 114 | 38.00 |
| ‡S. A. Marsh . . . . . . | Westminster, London | 21 | 29 | 5 | 823 | 113* | 34.29 |
| ‡M. V. Fleming . . . . . | Macclesfield | 18 | 29 | 3 | 734 | 113 | 28.23 |
| ‡S. G. Hinks . . . . . . . | Northfleet | 8 | 12 | 2 | 236 | 61* | 23.60 |
| ‡R. M. Ellison . . . . . . | Ashford, Kent | 16 | 24 | 7 | 397 | 61* | 23.35 |
| M. A. Ealham . . . . . | Willesborough | 3 | 5 | 0 | 96 | 36 | 19.20 |
| ‡C. Penn . . . . . . . . . . | Dover | 17 | 20 | 4 | 299 | 52 | 18.68 |
| ‡R. P. Davis . . . . . . . | Margate | 18 | 23 | 4 | 338 | 44 | 17.78 |
| M. J. McCague . . . . . | Larne, N. Ireland | 8 | 10 | 2 | 142 | 29 | 17.75 |
| M. M. Patel . . . . . . . | Bombay, India | 5 | 7 | 2 | 76 | 43 | 15.20 |
| N. J. Llong . . . . . . . . | Ashford, Kent | 3 | 6 | 2 | 54 | 42* | 13.50 |
| T. A. Merrick . . . . . . | St John's, Antigua | 18 | 22 | 6 | 198 | 36 | 12.37 |
| ‡A. P. Igglesden . . . . . | Farnborough, Kent | 18 | 16 | 3 | 100 | 16* | 7.69 |

Also batted: G. J. Kersey (*Plumstead, London*) (1 match) 27*; V. J. Wells (*Dartford*)
(2 matches) 1, 28, 0.

*\* Signifies not out.*  ‡ *Denotes county cap.*

The following played a total of nineteen three-figure innings for Kent in County
Championship matches – N. R. Taylor 6, M. R. Benson 4, T. R. Ward 4, G. R. Cowdrey 2,
S. A. Marsh 2, M. V. Fleming 1.

### BOWLING

| | O | M | R | W | BB | 5W/i | Avge |
|---|---|---|---|---|---|---|---|
| M. A. Ealham . . . . . . . . | 98.1 | 20 | 274 | 15 | 5-39 | 2 | 18.26 |
| C. Penn . . . . . . . . . . . . . | 407.4 | 79 | 1,216 | 52 | 5-43 | 3 | 23.38 |
| A. P. Igglesden . . . . . . . | 449 | 86 | 1,288 | 48 | 5-36 | 1 | 26.83 |
| T. A. Merrick . . . . . . . . | 517 | 100 | 1,688 | 58 | 7-99 | 1 | 29.10 |
| M. J. McCague . . . . . . . | 153.3 | 23 | 481 | 16 | 6-88 | 1 | 30.06 |
| R. M. Ellison . . . . . . . . | 457.1 | 99 | 1,375 | 45 | 7-33 | 2 | 30.55 |
| M. M. Patel . . . . . . . . . | 183.2 | 43 | 458 | 13 | 3-33 | 0 | 35.23 |
| R. P. Davis . . . . . . . . . | 455.2 | 126 | 1,325 | 32 | 4-81 | 0 | 41.40 |
| M. V. Fleming . . . . . . . . | 184 | 41 | 498 | 12 | 3-28 | 0 | 41.50 |

Also bowled: M. R. Benson 13-0-44-0; G. R. Cowdrey 2-1-6-0; N. J. Llong 5-1-28-0;
S. A. Marsh 5-0-28-0; N. R. Taylor 3-0-26-0; T. R. Ward 17-4-40-1.

**Wicket-keepers:** S. A. Marsh 61 ct, 4 st; G. J. Kersey 5 ct.

**Leading Fielders:** R. P. Davis 22, G. R. Cowdrey 17.

At Southampton, April 27, 28, 29, 30. KENT drew with HAMPSHIRE.

At The Oval, May 9, 10, 11, 13. KENT beat SURREY by an innings and 3 runs.

## KENT v ESSEX

At Folkestone, May 16, 17, 18, 20. Drawn. Kent 5 pts, Essex 5 pts. Toss: Kent. On a curtailed opening day Kent were sustained by an unbroken partnership of 182 between Benson and Ward, who reached his hundred (out of 161) off 144 balls, having batted for 158 minutes and hit one six and fourteen fours. But this good work was dissipated on the second day as the last eight wickets went in 23 overs for 49 runs. Essex shrugged off the early loss of Gooch with an innings dominated by Salim Malik, whose career-best 173, off 300 balls, included eighteen fours in a stay of 390 minutes. Hussain shared in the best stand of the innings, 150 off 38 overs for the fifth wicket, and Garnham and Foster added 73 off nineteen for the eighth. Kent in their second innings were in early trouble, and with Ward suffering from a damaged shoulder they welcomed the recovery afforded by Cowdrey and Hinks. When Essex threatened to take control again, they were denied for 43 overs by a battling partnership between Marsh and Davis.

*Close of play:* First day, Kent 240-1 (M. R. Benson 88\*, T. R. Ward 113\*); Second day, Essex 172-3 (Salim Malik 61\*, T. D. Topley 2\*); Third day, Kent 0-0 (S. G. Hinks 0\*, M. R. Benson 0\*).

### Kent

| | | | | |
|---|---|---|---|---|
| N. R. Taylor c Garnham b Pringle | 26 | – (3) b Pringle | | 4 |
| \*M. R. Benson c Hussain b Topley | 88 | – lbw b Foster | | 3 |
| T. R. Ward lbw b Salim Malik | 141 | | | |
| G. R. Cowdrey c Foster b Salim Malik | 32 | – c Garnham b Such | | 36 |
| S. G. Hinks c Salim Malik b Pringle | 6 | – (1) b Such | | 40 |
| R. M. Ellison lbw b Foster | 0 | – (5) b Pringle | | 7 |
| †S. A. Marsh b Topley | 18 | – (6) run out | | 36 |
| R. P. Davis b Gooch | 5 | – (7) c Hussain b Foster | | 30 |
| C. Penn not out | 2 | – (8) not out | | 2 |
| T. A. Merrick b Gooch | 8 | – (9) not out | | 4 |
| A. P. Igglesden b Topley | 1 | | | |
| B 1, l-b 7, w 3, n-b 7 | 18 | L-b 6, w 2, n-b 4 | | 12 |
| | 345 | | (7 wkts) | 174 |

1/58 2/242 3/296 4/305 5/307
6/309 7/334 8/334 9/342

1/5 2/11 3/77 4/88
5/106 6/152 7/165

Bonus points – Kent 4, Essex 1 (Score at 100 overs: 307-4).

Bowling: *First Innings*—Foster 26-4-98-1; Pringle 28-9-56-2; Topley 32-7-98-3; Childs 9-2-28-0; Gooch 12-5-21-2; Such 9-3-20-0; Stephenson 1-0-3-0; Salim Malik 3-0-13-2. *Second Innings*—Foster 24-7-57-2; Pringle 20-9-25-2; Topley 9-4-16-0; Childs 24-12-34-0; Such 24-15-19-2; Salim Malik 10-3-17-0.

### Essex

| | | | | |
|---|---|---|---|---|
| \*G. A. Gooch lbw b Merrick | 7 | N. A. Foster c Hinks b Davis | | 38 |
| J. P. Stephenson c Marsh b Ellison | 45 | J. H. Childs b Merrick | | 15 |
| P. J. Prichard run out | 53 | P. M. Such not out | | 23 |
| Salim Malik c Cowdrey b Ellison | 173 | | | |
| T. D. Topley run out | 37 | L-b 12, n-b 7 | | 19 |
| N. Hussain c Igglesden b Ellison | 72 | | | |
| D. R. Pringle lbw b Ellison | 5 | 1/12 2/78 3/169 4/233 5/383 | | 544 |
| †M. A. Garnham c Benson b Igglesden | 57 | 6/393 7/419 8/492 9/499 | | |

Bonus points – Essex 4, Kent 1 (Score at 100 overs: 301-4).

Bowling: Merrick 34-6-109-2; Igglesden 37-7-113-1; Penn 25-2-99-0; Ellison 42-8-125-4; Davis 21-5-86-1.

Umpires: B. Dudleston and A. A. Jones.

At Nottingham, May 22, 23, 24. KENT drew with NOTTINGHAMSHIRE.

## KENT v DERBYSHIRE

At Canterbury, May 25, 27, 28. Kent won by 208 runs. Kent 22 pts, Derbyshire 6 pts. Toss: Kent. Kent struggled against the Derbyshire pace and seam attack, with Base, born in Kent, cutting into the middle order with a spell of four for 27 in 10.3 overs. Derbyshire began badly but were held together by Barnett, who reached 53 out of 75 in 66 minutes, scoring his runs off 65 balls with eight spanking fours. Merrick's pace and the left-arm spin of Davis brought about a Derbyshire collapse on Monday – the last six wickets fell for 51 runs in seventeen overs – after which Taylor and Benson put Kent on top with a county record opening stand of 300. The previous record, 283 between A. E. Fagg and P. R. Sunnucks against Essex at Colchester, had stood since 1938. Benson scored his 160 off 220 balls in 254 minutes, with two sixes and seventeen fours, while Taylor hit a six and eighteen fours in his 146 from 226 balls in 284 minutes. Given 90 overs in which to score 376, Derbyshire never recovered from another poor start. Penn took three for 12 in 33 balls, and Davis again played a prominent part as Derbyshire were dismissed by mid-afternoon.

*Close of play:* First day, Derbyshire 95-4 (K. J. Barnett 68*, T. J. G. O'Gorman 2*); Second day, Kent 326-1 (N. R. Taylor 144*, G. R. Cowdrey 9*).

### Kent

| | | | |
|---|---|---|---|
| N. R. Taylor b Jean-Jacques | 24 | – c O'Gorman b Base | 146 |
| *M. R. Benson lbw b Malcolm | 14 | – c Base b Malcolm | 160 |
| G. R. Cowdrey c Adams b Jean-Jacques | 8 | – not out | 37 |
| M. V. Fleming lbw b Base | 33 | – hit wkt b Malcolm | 10 |
| N. J. Llong c Krikken b Base | 11 | – not out | 1 |
| R. M. Ellison c Azharuddin b Base | 16 | | |
| †S. A. Marsh b Base | 3 | | |
| R. P. Davis c Adams b Jean-Jacques | 27 | | |
| C. Penn c Barnett b Malcolm | 19 | | |
| T. A. Merrick not out | 13 | | |
| A. P. Igglesden c Adams b Jean-Jacques | 1 | | |
| B 4, l-b 10, w 2, n-b 20 | 36 | L-b 5, w 3, n-b 10 | 18 |

1/37 2/47 3/49 4/82 5/109         205     1/300 2/328 3/370  (3 wkts dec.) 372
6/121 7/126 8/181 9/198

Bonus points – Kent 2, Derbyshire 4.

Bowling: *First Innings*—Malcolm 23–3–54–2; Jean-Jacques 18.5–5–54–4; Base 16–4–43–4; Folley 20–4–40–0. *Second Innings*—Malcolm 21.5–2–87–2; Base 21–2–109–1; Folley 20–2–70–0; Jean-Jacques 9–1–54–0; Barnett 10–1–47–0.

### Derbyshire

| | | | |
|---|---|---|---|
| *K. J. Barnett c Cowdrey b Merrick | 85 | – c Igglesden b Merrick | 0 |
| P. D. Bowler run out | 1 | – b Merrick | 24 |
| J. E. Morris b Merrick | 10 | – c Llong b Penn | 17 |
| M. Azharuddin c Ellison b Penn | 12 | – b Penn | 47 |
| I. Folley c Marsh b Penn | 0 | – (9) not out | 17 |
| T. J. G. O'Gorman c Merrick | 36 | – (5) c Davis b Penn | 7 |
| C. J. Adams c Merrick b Davis | 26 | – b Davis | 11 |
| †K. M. Krikken c Marsh b Merrick | 1 | – (6) c and b Davis | 18 |
| M. Jean-Jacques b Davis | 0 | – (8) lbw b Merrick | 3 |
| S. J. Base not out | 19 | – st Marsh b Davis | 0 |
| D. E. Malcolm c Marsh b Davis | 2 | – c Davis b Igglesden | 18 |
| B 1, l-b 3, n-b 6 | 10 | B 1, n-b 4 | 5 |

1/14 2/34 3/87 4/87 5/151        202     1/0 2/27 3/78 4/94 5/103    167
6/151 7/153 8/162 9/195                  6/122 7/127 8/147 9/147

Bonus points – Derbyshire 2, Kent 4.

Bowling: *First Innings*—Merrick 18–3–55–4; Igglesden 9–0–50–0; Ellison 3–0–17–0; Penn 12–0–48–2; Davis 17.1–10–28–3. *Second Innings*—Merrick 13–2–60–3; Igglesden 6.5–0–22–1; Penn 12–1–31–3; Davis 17–4–53–3.

Umpires: J. W. Holder and N. T. Plews.

At Lord's, May 31, June 1, 3. KENT drew with MIDDLESEX.

## KENT v WARWICKSHIRE

At Tunbridge Wells, June 4, 5, 6. Drawn. Kent 8 pts, Warwickshire 4 pts. Toss: Kent. Warwickshire, bowled out for 83 on the second day and made to follow on, achieved a comfortable draw through the sterling batting of twenty-year-old Ostler. His 120 not out, a maiden first-class century, was scored off 202 balls and contained eighteen fours; he had put on 180 with Reeve for the fifth wicket when stumps were drawn for the last time. Earlier, Moles and Lloyd had eased Warwickshire towards a safer position with 130 for the second wicket. A career-best seven for 33 by Ellison had undone the Championship front-runners in the first innings. On the opening day Kent had been rescued by hundreds from Benson and Cowdrey, who shared a third-wicket stand of 169 in 50 overs. Benson reached three figures off 152 balls in 198 minutes (one six, sixteen fours), with his second fifty coming from only 39 deliveries, while Cowdrey hit fifteen fours in a stay of 345 minutes. Reeve then snapped up five wickets for 27 in 41 balls, and his final figures, six for 73, were his best for Warwickshire.

*Close of play:* First day, Warwickshire 4-0 (A. J. Moles 3*, J. D. Ratcliffe 1*); Second day, Warwickshire 106-1 (A. J. Moles 24*, T. A. Lloyd 38*).

### Kent

| | | | | |
|---|---|---|---|---|
| N. R. Taylor b Donald | 4 | M. J. McCague c Piper b Smith | 18 |
| *M. R. Benson run out | 105 | T. A. Merrick not out | 25 |
| T. R. Ward lbw b Small | 5 | A. P. Igglesden c Lloyd b Reeve | 10 |
| G. R. Cowdrey lbw b Reeve | 114 | | |
| M. V. Fleming c Ratcliffe b Reeve | 42 | B 4, l-b 15, n-b 1 | 20 |
| R. M. Ellison c Piper b Reeve | 0 | | |
| †S. A. Marsh b Reeve | 0 | 1/4 2/9 3/178 4/265 5/269 | 352 |
| R. P. Davis c Piper b Reeve | 9 | 6/282 7/293 8/313 9/319 | |

Bonus points – Kent 4, Warwickshire 4 (Score at 100 overs: 351-9).

Bowling: Donald 9–1–22–1; Small 22–3–68–1; Reeve 26.4–9–73–6; Munton 20–3–66–0; Booth 11–0–60–0; Smith 11–2–38–1; Moles 1–0–6–0.

### Warwickshire

| | | | |
|---|---|---|---|
| A. J. Moles c Marsh b Merrick | 3 | – lbw b Igglesden | 48 |
| J. D. Ratcliffe c Davis b Ellison | 13 | – c Igglesden b McCague | 33 |
| *T. A. Lloyd run out | 34 | – c Davis b Igglesden | 97 |
| D. P. Ostler lbw b Ellison | 7 | – not out | 120 |
| P. A. Smith lbw b Ellison | 7 | – c Davis b Igglesden | 2 |
| D. A. Reeve c Fleming b Ellison | 7 | – not out | 66 |
| †K. J. Piper lbw b Ellison | 0 | | |
| P. A. Booth lbw b Ellison | 0 | | |
| G. C. Small c McCague b Ellison | 5 | | |
| T. A. Munton b Merrick | 6 | | |
| A. A. Donald not out | 0 | | |
| W 1 | 1 | B 2, l-b 10, w 9, n-b 2 | 23 |

| | | |
|---|---|---|
| 1/4 2/23 3/35 4/65 5/65 | 83 | 1/48 2/178 3/203 4/209   (4 wkts) 389 |
| 6/65 7/71 8/76 9/83 | | |

Bonus points – Kent 4.

Bowling: *First Innings*—Merrick 13.1–5–14–2; Igglesden 6–3–13–0; Ellison 14–3–33–7; McCague 7–1–23–0. *Second Innings*—Merrick 15–4–42–0; Igglesden 29–6–69–3; McCague 22–3–51–1; Ellison 24–5–72–0; Davis 30–11–86–0; Fleming 9–1–27–0; Marsh 5–0–28–0; Benson 1–0–2–0.

Umpires: D. J. Constant and B. Hassan.

## KENT v SUSSEX

At Tunbridge Wells, June 7, 8, 10. Drawn. Kent 4 pts, Sussex 8 pts. Toss: Kent. Five stoppages for rain on the final day spoiled what could have been an exciting natural climax. As it was, a contrived declaration by Parker, and Kent's chase for victory kept the game alive, with both teams happy to stay on the field despite poor light and steady drizzle. Salisbury was working his way through the tail and finished with five for 40 as Kent, set 224 in a minimum of 40 overs, ended on 180 with two wickets in hand. Benson, having put Sussex in, had time to reflect on his decision while Lenham (263 balls, nineteen fours) and Alan Wells (185 balls, one six, twelve fours) were sharing a third-wicket stand of 235 in 62 overs. Lenham batted 303 minutes for his highest score. Apart from Taylor at the beginning, and Marsh and Davis near the end, Kent struggled against a Sussex pace and seam attack which was backed up by some impressive catching in the slips.

*Close of play:* First day, Sussex 253-2 (N. J. Lenham 117*, A. P. Wells 76*); Second day, Kent 220.

## Sussex

| | | | |
|---|---|---|---|
| D. M. Smith c Davis b Igglesden | 48 | – b McCague | 17 |
| J. W. Hall c Marsh b Igglesden | 5 | – c Davis b McCague | 11 |
| N. J. Lenham c Fleming b Igglesden | 137 | – lbw b Igglesden | 1 |
| A. P. Wells c Benson b Igglesden | 107 | – c Davis b Igglesden | 0 |
| *P. W. G. Parker c Fleming b Davis | 20 | – c Marsh b McCague | 8 |
| C. M. Wells c Taylor b Davis | 3 | – not out | 30 |
| †P. Moores not out | 1 | | |
| A. I. C. Dodemaide (did not bat) | | – (7) not out | 37 |
| B 4, l-b 4 | 8 | L-b 10 | 10 |

1/26 2/70 3/305 4/312 5/328     (6 wkts dec.) 329     1/33 2/34 3/34     (5 wkts dec.) 114
6/329     4/40 5/51

A. C. S. Pigott, I. D. K. Salisbury and A. N. Jones did not bat.

Bonus points – Sussex 4, Kent 2.

Bowling: *First Innings*—Merrick 8–0–36–0; Igglesden 24–4–68–4; Ellison 20–5–72–0; McCague 10–1–44–0; Fleming 18–7–39–0; Davis 19.3–3–62–2. *Second Innings*—Igglesden 14–5–22–2; McCague 13–1–38–3; Benson 4–0–18–0; Taylor 3–0–26–0.

## Kent

| | | | |
|---|---|---|---|
| N. R. Taylor c Moores b Pigott | 52 | – c Parker b C. M. Wells | 58 |
| *M. R. Benson c Lenham b Dodemaide | 4 | – c Smith b Jones | 8 |
| T. R. Ward b C. M. Wells | 13 | – c Parker b Jones | 2 |
| G. R. Cowdrey c Pigott b Jones | 41 | – c Hall b Salisbury | 41 |
| M. V. Fleming c Dodemaide b Jones | 0 | – c Moores b Salisbury | 4 |
| R. M. Ellison c Moores b Pigott | 4 | – (7) not out | 23 |
| †S. A. Marsh b Pigott | 50 | – (6) c Smith b Salisbury | 26 |
| R. P. Davis c Moores b Dodemaide | 44 | – c Lenham b Salisbury | 6 |
| M. J. McCague c A. P. Wells b Pigott | 2 | – (10) not out | 0 |
| T. A. Merrick b C. M. Wells | 10 | – (9) lbw b Salisbury | 1 |
| A. P. Igglesden not out | 16 | | |
| L-b 7, w 2 | 9 | L-b 7, w 4 | 11 |

1/8 2/38 3/84 4/84 5/91     220     1/29 2/31 3/106 4/121     (8 wkts) 180
6/92 7/168 8/170 9/186     5/126 6/165
7/176 8/179

Bonus points – Kent 2, Sussex 4.

Bowling: *First Innings*—Jones 17–1–41–2; Dodemaide 14.3–6–25–2; Pigott 22–5–75–4; C. M. Wells 23–7–48–2; Salisbury 12–5–24–0. *Second Innings*—Jones 9–0–56–2; Dodemaide 8–1–27–0; Pigott 5–0–25–0; C. M. Wells 7–0–25–1; Salisbury 10.5–1–40–5.

Umpires: D. J. Constant and B. Hassan.

At Harrogate, June 14, 15, 17. KENT drew with YORKSHIRE.

At Oxford, June 18, 19, 20. KENT drew with OXFORD UNIVERSITY.

At Manchester, June 21, 22, 24. KENT lost to LANCASHIRE by 59 runs.

## KENT v NORTHAMPTONSHIRE

At Maidstone, July 2, 3, 4. Kent won by 120 runs. Kent 17 pts, Northamptonshire 4 pts. Toss: Northamptonshire. Kent, put in to bat, struggled against the pace of their former player, Baptiste, who had taken four wickets before the weather put paid to the first day's play after 34 overs. It was mid-afternoon next day before Kent resumed their innings, and apart from Benson, taking 128 balls for his not out 50, they fared no better. With so much time lost, Bailey, Northamptonshire's acting-captain, attempted to achieve a definite result by forfeiting his side's first innings, and when Kent declared at 115 for five, the visitors were left to score 274 to win in a minimum of 76 overs. They lost Felton and Bailey in Igglesden's first two overs, and both he and Penn reaped deserved success for their hostile, accurate seam bowling. Capel, though feeling unwell, provided Northamptonshire's only real resistance in a stay of 77 minutes, hitting nine fours before edging Igglesden to slip. Kent completed a comfortable victory with 27 overs to spare.

*Close of play:* First day, Kent 89-5 (M. R. Benson 27*, S. A. Marsh 3*); Second day, Kent 34-2 (M. J. McCague 5*, N. R. Taylor 0*).

### Kent

| | | | |
|---|---:|---|---:|
| T. R. Ward c Ripley b Baptiste | 31 | – c Bailey b Cook | 18 |
| S. G. Hinks c Curran b Thomas | 1 | – c Curran b Taylor | 7 |
| N. R. Taylor b Baptiste | 18 | – (4) c Capel b Taylor | 26 |
| G. R. Cowdrey lbw b Baptiste | 2 | – (5) not out | 36 |
| *M. R. Benson not out | 50 | – (6) c Taylor b Cook | 1 |
| M. V. Fleming c Ripley b Baptiste | 3 | – (7) not out | 15 |
| †S. A. Marsh b Baptiste | 14 | | |
| C. Penn lbw b Thomas | 1 | | |
| M. J. McCague c Cook b Baptiste | 10 | – (3) b Taylor | 7 |
| T. A. Merrick b Cook | 18 | | |
| A. P. Igglesden lbw b Cook | 0 | | |
| L-b 8, w 2 | 10 | L-b 3, w 1, n-b 1 | 5 |
| | **158** | (5 wkts dec.) | **115** |

1/19 2/44 3/48 4/73 5/81
6/108 7/111 8/126 9/158

1/23 2/32 3/38
4/84 5/85

Bonus points – Kent 1, Northamptonshire 4.

Bowling: *First Innings*—Thomas 11–3–35–2; Taylor 10–0–28–0; Baptiste 26–5–57–6; Curran 12–2–26–0; Cook 1–0–4–2. *Second Innings*—Taylor 18–3–45–3; Thomas 11–1–38–0; Cook 8–2–29–2; Roberts 1–1–0–0.

### Northamptonshire

*Northamptonshire forfeited their first innings.*

| | | | |
|---|---:|---|---:|
| A. Fordham c Hinks b Penn | 38 | †D. Ripley c Marsh b Igglesden | 7 |
| N. A. Felton b Igglesden | 0 | N. G. B. Cook c Taylor b Penn | 2 |
| *R. J. Bailey c Marsh b Igglesden | 1 | J. P. Taylor not out | 0 |
| A. R. Roberts lbw b Penn | 11 | | |
| K. M. Curran b Penn | 11 | B 4, l-b 5, n-b 2 | 11 |
| E. A. E. Baptiste c Fleming b Penn | 2 | | |
| D. J. Capel c Taylor b Igglesden | 56 | 1/2 2/4 3/31 4/60 5/70 | **153** |
| J. G. Thomas c Merrick b Igglesden | 10 | 6/72 7/111 8/142 9/147 | |

Bowling: Merrick 13–3–39–0; Igglesden 17–8–36–5; Penn 12–2–43–5; McCague 7–1–26–0.

Umpires: G. I. Burgess and R. Palmer.

## KENT v GLAMORGAN

At Maidstone, July 5, 6, 8. Drawn. Kent 8 pts, Glamorgan 6 pts. Toss: Kent. Ward dominated the Kent batting, becoming the sixteenth player in the county's history to score a hundred in each innings. In the first, he reached 100, out of 175, off 122 balls in 148 minutes, and went on to 110, including a six and seventeen fours. Taylor helped him add 184 in a stand of 45 overs, but Glamorgan fought back well in the afternoon, with Croft's off-spin commanding respect in a long spell. Glamorgan's first-innings deficit would have been worse but for a defiant innings by Metson. Having come in as night-watchman, he batted for four hours, hitting ten fours and putting on 98 for the fourth wicket with Maynard, whose punishing strokes raised his half-century in 67 balls. Ward cruised to his second century of the match off 141 balls, in 143 minutes, and hit fifteen fours in his 109 from 146 deliveries. But by the time he reached his hundred on Monday, the weather had already made its presence felt. There was no play before lunch, and further rain ended Glamorgan's attempt to score 269 in a minimum of 61 overs.

*Close of play:* First day, Glamorgan 16-1 (H. Morris 3*, C. P. Metson 0*); Second day, Kent 129-0 (T. R. Ward 85*, S. G. Hinks 37*).

## Kent

| | | | |
|---|---|---|---|
| T. R. Ward c Butcher b Bastien | 110 | – c Metson b Frost | 109 |
| S. G. Hinks c Croft b Watkin | 5 | – not out | 55 |
| N. R. Taylor b Bastien | 77 | | |
| G. R. Cowdrey not out | 55 | | |
| *M. R. Benson c Metson b Croft | 5 | | |
| M. V. Fleming c Metson b Bastien | 4 | – (3) not out | 1 |
| †S. A. Marsh c Maynard b Croft | 0 | | |
| C. Penn c Shastri b Frost | 21 | | |
| M. J. McCague run out | 28 | | |
| T. A. Merrick lbw b Watkin | 5 | | |
| A. P. Igglesden b Croft | 2 | | |
| L-b 8, n-b 14 | 22 | L-b 5, w 1, n-b 4 | 10 |

1/13 2/197 3/209 4/222 5/227          334          1/167          (1 wkt dec.) 175
6/228 7/255 8/310 9/327

Bonus points – Kent 4, Glamorgan 4.

Bowling: *First Innings*—Watkin 16–2–76–2; Frost 15–2–65–1; Bastien 25–7–73–3; Croft 39.4–8–97–3; Dale 3–0–15–0. *Second Innings*—Watkin 19–1–63–0; Frost 7.2–0–52–1; Bastien 6–1–27–0; Croft 12–3–26–0; Shastri 4–2–2–0.

## Glamorgan

| | | | |
|---|---|---|---|
| *A. R. Butcher c Fleming b Igglesden | 12 | – c Hinks b Penn | 13 |
| H. Morris c Marsh b McCague | 40 | – c Marsh b Merrick | 11 |
| †C. P. Metson b Fleming | 84 | | |
| R. J. Shastri c Penn b McCague | 4 | | |
| M. P. Maynard b Penn | 59 | – (4) c Fleming b Merrick | 16 |
| P. A. Cottey c Fleming b Penn | 4 | – (3) c Marsh b Merrick | 16 |
| A. Dale c Marsh b McCague | 9 | – (5) not out | 23 |
| R. D. B. Croft b Fleming | 9 | – (6) not out | 15 |
| S. L. Watkin not out | 7 | | |
| S. Bastien run out | 1 | | |
| M. Frost lbw b Fleming | 0 | | |
| B 2, l-b 8, w 4, n-b 6 | 20 | W 2, n-b 7 | 9 |

1/16 2/73 3/83 4/181 5/209          241          1/16 2/32 3/42 4/72          (4 wkts) 103
6/216 7/222 8/236 9/241

Bonus points – Glamorgan 2, Kent 4.

Bowling: *First Innings*—Merrick 11–1–39–0; Igglesden 16–3–64–1; Penn 16–4–46–2; McCague 14–1–36–3; Ward 1–0–6–0; Fleming 18.1–5–40–3. *Second Innings*—Igglesden 5–0–23–0; Merrick 12–3–26–3; Penn 11–0–49–1; McCague 1.2–0–5–0.

Umpires: G. I. Burgess and R. Palmer.

At Southend, July 16, 17, 18. KENT beat ESSEX by 112 runs.

At Canterbury, July 20, 21, 22. KENT lost to WEST INDIANS by 4 runs (See West Indian tour section).

At Worcester, July 23, 24, 25. KENT drew with WORCESTERSHIRE.

At Taunton, July 26, 27, 29. KENT drew with SOMERSET.

## KENT v SURREY

At Canterbury, August 2, 3, 5. Drawn. Kent 8 pts, Surrey 5 pts. Toss: Kent. The first day was notable for the consistent, full-throttle fast bowling of Waqar Younis and the contrasting centuries by Benson and Fleming, who added 178 off 33 overs for the fifth wicket. Benson batted for 5 hours 23 minutes, hitting only eight fours in his 142, whereas Fleming's 113 was a more dashing affair, requiring 109 balls in just over two hours. He hit one six and seventeen fours before Younis cut short his and Kent's innings with four wickets for 1 run in seven balls. Surrey, losing their last seven wickets for 30 runs in seven overs, collapsed as spectacularly but did much better when they followed on. Bicknell batted for two minutes under six hours, hitting eighteen fours in an innings that saved the game for his side. In the end it was Kent, with 32 overs in which to score 206, who were hanging on for the draw, having lost five wickets for 7 runs in eleven overs.

*Close of play:* First day, Surrey 23-0 (D. J. Bicknell 19\*, R. I. Alikhan 2\*); Second day, Surrey 142-2 (D. J. Bicknell 78\*, N. F. Sargeant 1\*).

### Kent

| | | | |
|---|---|---|---|
| T. R. Ward b Waqar Younis | 6 | – c Bicknell b Murphy | 26 |
| *M. R. Benson b Medlycott | 142 | | |
| N. R. Taylor c Stewart b Waqar Younis | 5 | – c Greig b Medlycott | 35 |
| G. R. Cowdrey c Sargeant b Feltham | 40 | – b Feltham | 15 |
| S. G. Hinks lbw b Feltham | 5 | – (2) c Bicknell b Murphy | 9 |
| M. V. Fleming c Greig b Waqar Younis | 113 | – (5) c Murphy b Medlycott | 3 |
| †S. A. Marsh not out | 20 | – (6) b Waqar Younis | 3 |
| R. M. Ellison b Waqar Younis | 0 | – (7) not out | 5 |
| C. Penn b Waqar Younis | 0 | – (8) lbw b Waqar Younis | 0 |
| T. A. Merrick b Waqar Younis | 4 | – (9) not out | 4 |
| A. P. Igglesden c Greig b Medlycott | 5 | | |
| B 8, l-b 8, w 2 | 18 | L-b 3 | 3 |

1/8 2/22 3/129 4/137 5/315      358    1/10 2/62 3/87 4/90      (7 wkts) 103
6/327 7/327 8/327 9/333                    5/94 6/94 7/94

Bonus points – Kent 4, Surrey 4.

Bowling: *First Innings*—Waqar Younis 29-3-72-6; Murphy 11-4-35-0; Feltham 26-11-64-2; Medlycott 21.4-1-119-2; Greig 3-0-11-0; Stewart 2-0-12-0; Thorpe 4-0-29-0. *Second Innings*—Waqar Younis 12-7-26-2; Murphy 7-1-41-2; Feltham 4-0-15-1; Medlycott 8.5-4-18-2.

## Surrey

| | | | |
|---|---|---|---|
| D. J. Bicknell c Fleming b Ellison | 41 | – c and b Ellison | 151 |
| R. I. Alikhan c Hinks b Fleming | 30 | – b Penn | 20 |
| A. J. Stewart c Marsh b Ellison | 10 | – lbw b Ellison | 32 |
| D. M. Ward c Marsh b Penn | 53 | – (5) c sub b Merrick | 35 |
| G. P. Thorpe b Igglesden | 7 | – (6) c Cowdrey b Igglesden | 25 |
| *I. A. Greig not out | 8 | – (7) b Ellison | 22 |
| K. T. Medlycott c Taylor b Penn | 4 | – (8) b Igglesden | 24 |
| M. A. Feltham run out | – | – (9) not out | 10 |
| †N. F. Sargeant b Igglesden | 0 | – (4) c Cowdrey b Ward | 34 |
| Waqar Younis c Cowdrey b Penn | 8 | – c Hinks b Merrick | 9 |
| A. J. Murphy b Penn | 7 | – b Merrick | 0 |
| B 2, l-b 1, w 1, n-b 6 | 10 | L-b 8, w 1, n-b 14 | 23 |

1/65 2/75 3/120 4/148 5/149    178    1/48 2/138 3/249 4/253 5/306    385
6/154 7/157 8/157 9/166                 6/325 7/346 8/372 9/385

Bonus points – Surrey 1, Kent 4.

*Bowling: First Innings*—Merrick 12–4–33–0; Igglesden 16–2–51–2; Penn 15–4–36–4; Ellison 7–0–43–2; Fleming 3–0–12–1. *Second Innings*—Merrick 25.3–3–86–3; Igglesden 26–6–81–2; Ellison 35–9–102–3; Penn 26.9–9–70–1; Ward 7–1–20–1; Fleming 11–7–18–0.

Umpires: R. Julian and K. J. Lyons.

## KENT v HAMPSHIRE

At Canterbury, August 6, 7, 8. Drawn. Kent 7 pts, Hampshire 6 pts. Toss: Kent. On the opening day the home side's batting improved the farther it progressed. Half the side had been dismissed for 121 by the 48th over before Marsh and Ellison added 115 in 39 overs. Marsh batted 139 minutes for his 73, which contained one five and seven fours. Hampshire struggled to come to terms with the pace of Merrick and had every reason to be grateful to Middleton, who played an important sheet-anchor role for four and a quarter hours. Kent found runs easier to come by in their second innings, especially when Smith and Middleton treated them to 69 runs off eight overs, and when the declaration came, Hampshire were given a target of 253 in 60 overs. They were never on the right course, and there was every possibility of defeat when they were 131 for seven in the 43rd over. Aymes and Maru calmly and resolutely averted it with a stand of 65 off seventeen overs.

*Close of play:* First day, Hampshire 19-1 (V. P. Terry 6*, R. J. Maru 2*); Second day, Kent 8-0 (T. R. Ward 4*, V. J. Wells 4*).

## Kent

| | | | |
|---|---|---|---|
| T. R. Ward c Aymes b Shine | 65 | – c Nicholas b Connor | 50 |
| V. J. Wells c Middleton b Shine | 1 | – c Ayling b James | 28 |
| N. R. Taylor b Connor | 24 | – not out | 59 |
| G. R. Cowdrey c Terry b Shine | 16 | – b James | 12 |
| M. V. Fleming lbw b Ayling | 12 | – b Middleton | 23 |
| *†S. A. Marsh c Gower b Ayling | 73 | – st Aymes b Middleton | 2 |
| R. M. Ellison not out | 61 | – not out | 19 |
| R. P. Davis c Gower b Connor | 27 | | |
| C. Penn run out | 3 | | |
| T. A. Merrick lbw b Connor | 0 | | |
| A. P. Igglesden run out | 1 | | |
| L-b 1, w 1, n-b 5 | 7 | B 1, l-b 8, n-b 1 | 10 |

1/10 2/76 3/104 4/121 5/121    290    1/74 2/86 3/108    (5 wkts dec.) 203
6/236 7/282 8/287 9/287            4/154 5/164

Bonus points – Kent 3, Hampshire 4.

Bowling: *First Innings*—Shine 18–3–75–3; Connor 22–5–57–3; James 13–2–35–0; Ayling 22–1–64–2; Maru 24.3–6–58–0. *Second Innings*—Shine 6–1–23–0; Connor 10–1–39–1; James 12–0–44–2; Ayling 3–2–1–0; Nicholas 4–0–18–0; Smith 4–0–28–0; Middleton 4–0–41–2.

## Hampshire

| | | |
|---|---|---|
| V. P. Terry c Davis b Ellison | 26 | – b Merrick ............................ 7 |
| C. L. Smith c Marsh b Merrick | 10 | – (5) c Taylor b Davis .......... 2 |
| R. J. Maru c Fleming b Igglesden | 10 | – (9) not out .......................... 21 |
| T. C. Middleton st Marsh b Davis | 66 | – (2) c Marsh b Davis .......... 26 |
| D. I. Gower c Marsh b Merrick | 36 | – (4) c Ward b Davis .......... 40 |
| K. D. James b Merrick | 7 | – (3) c Marsh b Penn .......... 15 |
| *M. C. J. Nicholas lbw b Fleming | 33 | – (6) run out ........................ 15 |
| J. R. Ayling c Marsh b Fleming | 19 | – (7) c Wells b Ellison .......... 17 |
| †A. N. Aymes c Marsh b Merrick | 8 | – (8) not out ........................ 48 |
| C. A. Connor b Davis | 7 | |
| K. J. Shine not out | 2 | |
| B 5, l-b 3, w 2, n-b 7 | 17 | L-b 1, n-b 4 ............ 5 |

1/17 2/36 3/69 4/123 5/137              241        1/10 2/43 3/55 4/77    (7 wkts) 196
6/187 7/215 8/221 9/238                            5/92 6/116 7/131

Bonus points – Hampshire 2, Kent 4.

Bowling: *First Innings*—Merrick 22.5–2–67–4; Igglesden 17–3–43–1; Ellison 16–0–47–1; Penn 13–2–33–0; Davis 10–4–25–2; Fleming 8–0–18–2. *Second Innings*—Merrick 17–2–54–1; Igglesden 6–1–10–0; Penn 8–0–32–1; Fleming 9–2–24–0; Davis 15.4–4–62–3; Ellison 4–0–13–1.

Umpires: J. C. Balderstone and K. J. Lyons.

At Leicester, August 9, 10, 12. KENT lost to LEICESTERSHIRE by five wickets.

## KENT v GLOUCESTERSHIRE

At Canterbury, August 20, 21, 22. Kent won by one wicket. Kent 20 pts, Gloucestershire 5 pts. Toss: Gloucestershire. Seventeen wickets fell on the first day, and yet at lunch Gloucestershire had looked comfortably placed at 107 for one. Afterwards, they lost nine wickets for 75 runs as first Patel's accurate left-arm spin accounted for their middle order, and then Igglesden came back to take the last four wickets. Athey batted through 28 overs for his 22. When Kent replied, Ward was out to the first ball from Gilbert, who in his next over forced Taylor to retire with a bruised thumb. Pace and movement off the pitch brought the Australian six wickets for 33 by the close – his first four came at a cost of 8 runs – and next morning he finished with career-best figures as Kent made their lowest total of the season. Gloucestershire were again in trouble in their second innings, losing five wickets for 60 runs before an unbroken eighth-wicket stand of 56 in thirteen overs, between Lloyds and Gilbert, enabled Wright to leave Kent with the last day in which to score 309. Although Taylor gave them a strong foundation in a stay of three and a half hours, hitting fifteen fours in his fourth hundred of the summer, the target began to look too much for Kent. However, the lower order sparked effectively, Merrick's six off Ball brought the margin down to 5 runs, and the last pair squeezed home with four balls to spare.

*Close of play:* First day, Kent 62-7 (C. Penn 13*, T. A. Merrick 2*); Second day, Gloucestershire 233-7 (J. W. Lloyds 67*, D. R. Gilbert 2*).

## Gloucestershire

| | | | |
|---|---|---|---|
| G. D. Hodgson c Marsh b Patel | 60 | – b Merrick | 26 |
| R. J. Scott b Merrick | 17 | – c Marsh b Penn | 30 |
| *A. J. Wright c Cowdrey b Merrick | 47 | – c Marsh b Davis | 45 |
| C. W. J. Athey c Marsh b Igglesden | 22 | – lbw b Igglesden | 13 |
| M. W. Alleyne c Ward b Penn | 0 | – lbw b Igglesden | 0 |
| J. W. Lloyds b Patel | 8 | – not out | 67 |
| †R. C. J. Williams b Patel | 0 | – c Penn b Igglesden | 4 |
| M. C. J. Ball c Marsh b Igglesden | 15 | – b Patel | 11 |
| D. R. Gilbert not out | 4 | – not out | 22 |
| A. M. Babington c Cowdrey b Igglesden | 0 | | |
| M. J. Gerrard b Igglesden | 0 | | |
| B 3, l-b 2, n-b 4 | 9 | B 5, l-b 4, n-b 6 | 15 |
| | **182** | (7 wkts dec.) | **233** |

1/23 2/124 3/136 4/142 5/153　　　　182　　　1/49 2/91 3/117　　(7 wkts dec.) 233
6/153 7/171 8/182 9/182　　　　　　　　　　　4/119 5/121
　　　　　　　　　　　　　　　　　　　　　　6/148 7/177

Bonus points – Gloucestershire 1, Kent 4.

Bowling: *First Innings*—Merrick 16–5–41–2; Igglesden 15.3–2–46–4; Penn 18–3–41–1; Davis 9–2–16–0; Patel 22–9–33–3. *Second Innings*—Merrick 20–4–85–1; Igglesden 19–1–47–3; Davis 26–6–57–1; Penn 6–1–10–1; Patel 12–3–25–1.

## Kent

| | | | |
|---|---|---|---|
| T. R. Ward c Williams b Gilbert | 0 | – c and b Ball | 48 |
| *M. R. Benson c Williams b Babington | 6 | – b Gilbert | 2 |
| N. R. Taylor not out | 17 | – c Wright b Ball | 109 |
| G. R. Cowdrey b Gilbert | 6 | – lbw b Babington | 12 |
| M. V. Fleming lbw b Gilbert | 0 | – c Williams b Babington | 0 |
| †S. A. Marsh c Athey b Gilbert | 30 | – c Williams b Gerrard | 36 |
| R. P. Davis lbw b Gilbert | 0 | – not out | 37 |
| C. Penn c Athey b Gilbert | 16 | – b Ball | 35 |
| M. M. Patel b Gilbert | 4 | – b Ball | 3 |
| T. A. Merrick lbw b Gilbert | 12 | – c Athey b Ball | 18 |
| A. P. Igglesden c Gilbert b Ball | 13 | – not out | 0 |
| L-b 2, n-b 1 | 3 | B 2, l-b 4, n-b 3 | 9 |
| | **107** | (9 wkts) | **309** |

1/0 2/12 3/12 4/21 5/21　　　　　107　　　1/11 2/117 3/152　　(9 wkts) 309
6/56 7/60 8/75 9/80　　　　　　　　　　　4/152 5/198 6/217
　　　　　　　　　　　　　　　　　　　　7/276 8/286 9/308

Bonus points – Gloucestershire 4.

*In the first innings N. R. Taylor, when 0, retired hurt at 1 and resumed at 75.*

Bowling: *First Innings*—Gilbert 22–5–55–8; Babington 10–2–25–1; Ball 17.5–7–25–1. *Second Innings*—Gilbert 21.2–3–50–1; Babington 24–6–68–2; Gerrard 13–2–35–1; Ball 42–5–128–5; Scott 4–0–22–0.

Umpires: B. Hassan and K. J. Lyons.

## KENT v MIDDLESEX

At Canterbury, August 28, 29, 30, 31. Kent won by 208 runs. Kent 21 pts, Middlesex 7 pts. Toss: Middlesex. Put in, and struggled, mainly against the pace of Headley. Middlesex, too, were in some difficulty but were revived by Ramprakash and Gatting, who added 219 off 68 overs for the sixth wicket. Gatting, who on the first day had broken the little finger on his left hand, batted for five hours five minutes (288 balls) and hit one six and 23 fours in his eighth Championship hundred of the season; Ramprakash's 87 contained ten fours. When Kent batted again, Ward and Taylor set up the innings with a partnership of 226, after which Ward and Cowdrey added 134. Taylor hit ten fours in making 101 from 187 balls, but he was overshadowed by Ward, whose first double-hundred, from 399 balls, featured a six and 29 fours.

Middlesex's eventual target was 305 off 69 overs. But with Gatting, who by now had also suffered a scalded chest, unable to bat until No. 7, Middlesex never promised to approach it. This second injury to Gatting had occurred at lunch on the third day, when a waitress spilled a pot of tea over him. Ellison had an opening spell of four for 29 in 10.3 overs to pave the way for a resounding Middlesex collapse, and as Kent ran out easy winners, Penn finished with match figures of nine for 149.

*Close of play:* First day, Middlesex 31-2 (M. A. Roseberry 17*, M. R. Ramprakash 0*); Second day, Middlesex 342-8 (D. W. Headley 3*, P. C. R. Tufnell 0*); Third day, Kent 287-2 (T. R. Ward 140*, G. R. Cowdrey 6*).

## Kent

| | | | |
|---|---|---|---|
| T. R. Ward c Farbrace b Cowans | 51 | – not out | 235 |
| *M. R. Benson lbw b Headley | 8 | – c Pooley b Tufnell | 20 |
| N. R. Taylor c Farbrace b Headley | 17 | – c sub b Williams | 101 |
| G. R. Cowdrey c Farbrace b Headley | 38 | – c Farbrace b Tufnell | 46 |
| M. V. Fleming b Headley | 30 | – not out | 23 |
| †S. A. Marsh c Emburey b Williams | 5 | | |
| M. A. Ealham c Farbrace b Williams | 34 | | |
| R. M. Ellison b Headley | 33 | | |
| R. P. Davis not out | 15 | | |
| C. Penn lbw b Williams | 0 | | |
| A. P. Igglesden c Headley b Emburey | 11 | | |
| B 5, l-b 4, n-b 7 | 16 | B 8, l-b 8, n-b 9 | 25 |

1/24 2/64 3/108 4/145 5/162　　　　258　　1/39 2/265 3/399　　(3 wkts dec.) 450
6/162 7/231 8/232 9/232

Bonus points – Kent 3, Middlesex 4.

Bowling: *First Innings*—Cowans 15-3-42-1; Williams 23-5-52-3; Headley 24-5-100-5; Tufnell 16-6-31-0; Gatting 8-4-13-0; Emburey 6.5-1-11-1. *Second Innings*—Cowans 22-3-78-0; Williams 22-0-87-1; Headley 19-1-112-0; Tufnell 30-9-70-2; Emburey 21-4-53-0; Weekes 12-1-34-0.

## Middlesex

| | | | |
|---|---|---|---|
| M. A. Roseberry c Ellison b Penn | 18 | – c Ellison b Ealham | 5 |
| J. C. Pooley c Marsh b Igglesden | 11 | – c Marsh b Ellison | 14 |
| †P. Farbrace lbw b Penn | 0 | – (6) lbw b Ellison | 0 |
| M. R. Ramprakash lbw b Ellison | 87 | – (3) c sub b Ellison | 5 |
| P. N. Weekes c Davis b Ellison | 4 | – (4) c Marsh b Ealham | 2 |
| J. E. Emburey lbw b Ealham | 20 | – (5) c Marsh b Ellison | 11 |
| *M. W. Gatting c Davis b Ealham | 174 | – c Ealham b Penn | 9 |
| N. F. Williams b Penn | 1 | – c Ward b Penn | 5 |
| D. W. Headley b Penn | 26 | – b Penn | 14 |
| P. C. R. Tufnell not out | 31 | – c Marsh b Penn | 4 |
| N. G. Cowans lbw b Penn | 5 | – not out | 23 |
| B 1, l-b 12, n-b 14 | 27 | L-b 1, n-b 3 | 4 |

1/27 2/28 3/33 4/39 5/87　　　　404　　1/19 2/21 3/28 4/28 5/30　　96
6/306 7/311 8/342 9/393　　　　　　　6/45 7/53 8/61 9/71

Bonus points – Middlesex 3, Kent 2 (Score at 100 overs: 290-5).

Bowling: *First Innings*—Igglesden 5.1-1-12-1; Penn 39.5-11-105-5; Ealham 18.5-4-47-2; Ellison 35-9-88-2; Fleming 17-3-65-0; Davis 17-1-74-0. *Second Innings*—Penn 11-3-44-4; Ellison 18-5-40-4; Ealham 8-3-11-2.

Umpires: B. Hassan and R. Palmer.

At Hove, September 3, 4, 5, 6. KENT tied with SUSSEX.

## KENT v LEICESTERSHIRE

At Canterbury, September 17, 18, 19, 20. Leicestershire won by 90 runs. Leicestershire 22 pts, Kent 5 pts. Toss: Leicestershire. Batting collapses were a feature of Leicestershire's third win of the season – their second over Kent – which lifted them off bottom place on the Championship table. The 10.30 a.m. start helped the bowlers on the first morning, when Ellison in particular was in his element, but as the conditions improved after lunch Hepworth restored the Leicestershire innings, adding 120 for the seventh wicket with Parsons and batting for just over five hours. Kent fared better early in their innings but faded faster as Maguire took four wickets for 7 runs in 6.1 overs. Taylor was three hours over his half-century, but Marsh's 69, including ten boundaries, enlivened a grey day and kept Kent in touch. Solid batting in the second innings extended Leicestershire's lead to 302 with five wickets in hand, but as they looked for quick runs before the close, Ealham took four wickets in twelve balls. Kent, with all of the last day in which to score 306, were 119 for five at lunch. The pitch, dry and worn, was helping Potter and Hepworth turn the ball, and Leicestershire's victory was simply a matter of patience and time.

*Close of play:* First day, Leicestershire 258-9 (D. J. Millns 11*, J. N. Maguire 4*); Second day, Leicestershire 10-0 (T. J. Boon 10*, N. E. Briers 0*); Third day, Kent 14-0 (T. R. Ward 7*, M. R. Benson 7*).

## Leicestershire

| | | | |
|---|---|---|---|
| T. J. Boon c Benson b Ellison | 10 | – c Ealham b Davis | 50 |
| *N. E. Briers c Ward b Ellison | 0 | – b Penn | 20 |
| J. J. Whitaker b Penn | 15 | – c and b Davis | 58 |
| B. F. Smith lbw b Ealham | 6 | – (7) c Marsh b Ealham | 24 |
| L. Potter c Davis b Ellison | 0 | – (4) c and b Davis | 42 |
| P. N. Hepworth c Benson b Penn | 97 | – (5) run out | 30 |
| †P. Whitticase c Ealham b Penn | 27 | – (8) c Davis b Ealham | 9 |
| G. J. Parsons c Patel b Penn | 63 | – (6) c Marsh b Ealham | 5 |
| D. J. Millns not out | 20 | – b Ealham | 3 |
| C. W. Wilkinson c Llong b Penn | 2 | – not out | 2 |
| J. N. Maguire c Davis b Ellison | 17 | – b Ealham | 1 |
| B 2, l-b 9, w 1, n-b 12 | 24 | B 2, l-b 9, n-b 4 | 15 |
| | **281** | | **259** |

1/1 2/28 3/28 4/31 5/38    1/72 2/87 3/156 4/193 5/209
6/109 7/229 8/243 9/247    6/242 7/248 8/252 9/257

Bonus points – Leicestershire 2, Kent 3 (Score at 100 overs: 244-8).

Bowling: *First Innings*—Penn 39–1–90–5; Ellison 31.2–3–93–4; Ealham 11–1–32–1; Patel 16–8–13–0; Davis 15–7–28–0; Fleming 5–0–14–0. *Second Innings*—Penn 20–6–45–1; Ellison 9–4–20–0; Patel 21–6–55–0; Davis 29–13–58–3; Ealham 23.2–5–65–5; Fleming 2–0–5–0.

## Kent

| | | | |
|---|---|---|---|
| T. R. Ward c Boon b Millns | 38 | – c Whitaker b Wilkinson | 13 |
| *M. R. Benson b Millns | 8 | – c Whitticase b Maguire | 34 |
| N. R. Taylor c and b Maguire | 59 | – c and b Maguire | 32 |
| M. V. Fleming c Potter b Maguire | 19 | – c Millns b Hepworth | 4 |
| N. J. Llong b Maguire | 0 | – c Boon b Hepworth | 0 |
| †S. A. Marsh c Hepworth b Millns | 69 | – b Potter | 17 |
| M. A. Ealham c Hepworth b Maguire | 0 | – c Whitticase b Potter | 36 |
| R. M. Ellison b Millns | 13 | – (11) c Maguire b Hepworth | 23 |
| R. P. Davis lbw b Millns | 0 | – (8) c Maguire b Potter | 7 |
| C. Penn c Whitaker b Wilkinson | 2 | – (9) lbw b Maguire | 27 |
| M. M. Patel not out | 0 | – (10) not out | 18 |
| L-b 8, n-b 5 | 13 | B 8, l-b 5, w 1, n-b 4 | 18 |
| | **221** | | **229** |

1/9 2/93 3/125 4/125 5/140    1/28 2/79 3/92 4/92 5/92
6/142 7/172 8/186 9/189    6/124 7/132 8/183 9/185

Bonus points – Kent 2, Leicestershire 4.

Bowling: *First Innings*—Millns 21.5–7–65–5; Wilkinson 15–2–43–1; Maguire 16–6–39–4; Parsons 14–4–27–0; Hepworth 3–1–3–0; Potter 11–4–36–0. *Second Innings*—Millns 18–3–61–0; Maguire 17–3–59–3; Wilkinson 7–1–13–1; Hepworth 12.2–2–51–3; Potter 15–3–32–3.

Umpires: G. I. Burgess and B. Dudleston.

# LANCASHIRE

*Patron:* HM The Queen
*President:* A. J. Leggat
*Chairman:* R. Bennett
*Chief Executive:* J. M. Bower
*Cricket Secretary:* Miss R. B. FitzGibbon
  County Cricket Ground, Old Trafford,
  Manchester M16 0PX
  (Telephone: 061-848 7021)
*Captain:* 1991 – D. P. Hughes
        1992 – N. H. Fairbrother
*Manager/Coach:* J. A. Ormrod

Despite reaching the final of the Benson and Hedges Cup and finishing runners-up in the Refuge Assurance League, Lancashire had their worst season since 1986, in a summer of two distinct halves. On July 11, they stood fourth in the Britannic Assurance Championship, 47 points behind the leaders with two games in hand, and headed the Refuge Assurance League; they were unbeaten in limited-overs cricket since April 21. On July 12, they were knocked out of the NatWest Bank Trophy by Hampshire, in the second round, and two days later they lost the Benson and Hedges Cup to Worcestershire.

Little went right after that. Lancashire won only two, and lost seven, of their remaining twelve Championship matches, to finish eighth, and their nerve failed on the run-in to the Sunday League as they were beaten in two of their last three home games. It was significant that David Hughes, whose appointment as captain in 1987 had signalled the advent of the county's best cricket for more than a decade, played his last matches in the weekend following the Benson and Hedges defeat. He had not appeared in the final, to enable Lancashire to include an extra batsman, and he handed over the captaincy for the rest of the season to Neil Fairbrother, who was confirmed in the post for 1992 before the last Championship match.

The Championship campaign began quietly. Lancashire were in their fifth game, at the start of June, before their first victory. This heralded their best period of the summer, with four successive wins carrying them into second place in the table. The key player was Wasim Akram, who claimed eight wickets against Sussex, destroyed Hampshire's and Leicestershire's second innings in contrived finishes – he also scored a hundred against Hampshire – and took six Kent wickets after a double forfeiture. In July, when Middlesex were beaten at Uxbridge, he took eleven wickets and hit a half-century in a brilliant all-round performance. But that was Lancashire's only victory from their eighth match to their 22nd, when they rounded off the season with a one-wicket win over Surrey. Injury restricted Wasim to only one appearance in the last eight games, six of which were lost, although he was fit enough to play in the remainder of the Refuge Assurance League.

Lancashire went into their last six Championship matches 70 points behind the leaders, Warwickshire, with two games in hand. It was a huge gap, but they had not forgotten 1987, when at the same stage they were

62 points behind Nottinghamshire, having played the same number of games, and finished only four points adrift. Then, Lancashire won all six matches to collect 125 points; this time they won only one and took 47. They could point to injury and the loss of Mike Atherton and Phillip DeFreitas to the Test team. But Championship-winning sides usually have to overcome such problems.

Atherton was suffering from a back problem which required an operation near the end of the summer, and he was limited to eight Championship matches in which he scored 603 runs for an average of 60.30. DeFreitas's outstanding England bowling was not reproduced for Lancashire, for whom he took 39 Championship wickets with only two five-wicket returns. On paper Wasim Akram and DeFreitas formed the strongest opening attack in the country; in practice they played together only six times in the Championship. In consequence, Peter Martin had a long run, and although he won no matches his control and pace impressed. Ian Austin played more than half the season but performed moderately in the Championship, the highlight coming against Yorkshire in the penultimate match when, batting at No. 10, he scored a maiden hundred in 61 balls, the fastest of the season. In the Refuge Assurance League he set a county record of 28 wickets over the summer.

Only two players, Gehan Mendis and Fairbrother, reached 1,000 runs, with Mendis maintaining his consistent aggregate of at least 1,350 runs in each of his six seasons with the club. Although it was Fairbrother's eighth successive year topping 1,000, he was probably dissatisfied with the later half of his season. He scored five centuries in the first half, plus one for England's one-day team, but in his seven matches after Hughes withdrew he managed only 251 runs, reaching 50 just once.

Throughout, Lancashire's batting lacked consistency; twelve players scored first-class hundreds, but only four more than once. It was disappointing that Graham Lloyd and Nick Speak did not make more of their chances. Lloyd failed to score a century at all, and Speak had to wait until the final match, when his 153 against Surrey was the highest innings for Lancashire in 1991. Graeme Fowler, in his benefit year, failed to reach 1,000 runs, despite missing only four Championship games, but in the closing stages Steve Titchard, aged 23, and nineteen-year-old John Crawley both hit maiden hundreds. Warren Hegg had another good year behind the stumps, as well as his best as a batsman, and was rewarded with a second England A tour.

The county sorely needed an experienced spinner. They missed Atherton's leg-spin because of his injury, while their off-spinners, Yates, who was given an extended run, and Fitton, both struggled. Mike Watkinson, who scored 758 first-class runs and took 53 wickets, was forced to abandon medium pace for off-breaks several times, and looked the pick of Lancashire's slow bowlers. During the close season the club signed Middlesex's under-employed slow left-armer, Alex Barnett, and engaged the Transvaal fast bowler, Steven Jack, as their overseas player in Wasim Akram's absence with his national side.

After granting women full membership in 1990, Lancashire made history in May by appointing Rose FitzGibbon as their cricket secretary to replace Chris Hassell, who had moved to Yorkshire as chief executive. Miss FitzGibbon became the first woman to hold such a post in county cricket. – Brian Bearshaw.

468

LANCASHIRE 1991

[Bill Smith]

Back row: J. E. R. Gallian, T. M. Orrell, G. Yates, M. A. Sharp, R. C. Irani, N. A. Derbyshire, N. J. Speak, J. D. Fitton, G. D. Lloyd.
Middle row: L. G. Brown (physiotherapist), J. A. Ormrod (manager/coach), I. D. Austin, W. K. Hegg, S. P. Titchard, P. J. Martin, J. Stanworth, T. E. Jesty, J. S. Savage (coach), W. Davies (scorer). Front row: G. D. Mendis, Wasim Akram, G. Fowler, P. J. W. Allott, D. P. Hughes (captain), N. H. Fairbrother, M. A. Atherton, P. A. J. DeFreitas, M. Watkinson. Inset: J. P. Crawley.

## LANCASHIRE RESULTS

*All first-class matches – Played 24 : Won 7, Lost 9, Drawn 8.*

*County Championship matches – Played 22 : Won 6, Lost 9, Drawn 7.*

*Bonus points – Batting 60, Bowling 49.*

*Competition placings – Britannic Assurance County Championship, 8th ;
NatWest Bank Trophy, 2nd round ; Benson and Hedges Cup, finalists ;
Refuge Assurance League, 2nd ; Refuge Assurance Cup, finalists.*

## BRITANNIC ASSURANCE CHAMPIONSHIP AVERAGES

### BATTING

|  | Birthplace | M | I | NO | R | HI | Avge |
|---|---|---|---|---|---|---|---|
| ‡M. A. Atherton .... | Manchester | 8 | 13 | 3 | 603 | 114* | 60.30 |
| J. P. Crawley ..... | Maldon | 2 | 4 | 0 | 230 | 130 | 57.50 |
| ‡N. H. Fairbrother .. | Warrington | 17 | 26 | 5 | 1,011 | 121 | 48.14 |
| S. P. Titchard ...... | Warrington | 7 | 13 | 1 | 464 | 135 | 38.66 |
| ‡G. D. Mendis ...... | Colombo, Ceylon | 22 | 41 | 4 | 1,223 | 119 | 33.05 |
| ‡W. K. Hegg ....... | Whitefield | 21 | 31 | 7 | 758 | 97 | 31.58 |
| ‡G. Fowler ......... | Accrington | 18 | 31 | 2 | 865 | 113 | 29.82 |
| N. J. Speak ....... | Manchester | 17 | 31 | 2 | 806 | 153 | 27.79 |
| ‡Wasim Akram...... | Lahore, Pakistan | 14 | 19 | 1 | 471 | 122 | 27.70 |
| ‡I. D. Austin ....... | Haslingden | 12 | 16 | 4 | 315 | 101* | 26.25 |
| G. D. Lloyd ....... | Accrington | 17 | 28 | 0 | 720 | 96 | 25.71 |
| G. Yates .......... | Ashton-under-Lyne | 18 | 24 | 12 | 292 | 100* | 24.33 |
| ‡M. Watkinson .... | Westhoughton | 20 | 33 | 3 | 713 | 114* | 23.76 |
| J. D. Fitton........ | Littleborough | 6 | 10 | 1 | 201 | 60 | 22.33 |
| ‡P. A. J. DeFreitas .. | Scotts Head, Dominica | 11 | 16 | 1 | 325 | 60 | 21.66 |
| ‡D. P. Hughes ..... | Newton-le-Willows | 8 | 9 | 3 | 111 | 51 | 18.50 |
| P. J. Martin ....... | Accrington | 15 | 13 | 8 | 85 | 29 | 17.00 |
| ‡P. J. W. Allott ..... | Altrincham | 8 | 8 | 2 | 63 | 26 | 10.50 |

‡J. Stanworth (*Oldham*) (1 match) did not bat.

* *Signifies not out.*   ‡ *Denotes county cap.*

The following played a total of nineteen three-figure innings for Lancashire in County
Championship matches – N. H. Fairbrother 5, G. D. Mendis 3, M. A. Atherton 2, G. Fowler
2, I. D. Austin 1, J. P. Crawley 1, N. J. Speak 1, S. P. Titchard 1, Wasim Akram 1,
M. Watkinson 1, G. Yates 1.

### BOWLING

|  | O | M | R | W | BB | 5W/i | Avge |
|---|---|---|---|---|---|---|---|
| Wasim Akram ........ | 429.3 | 99 | 1,251 | 56 | 6-66 | 7 | 22.33 |
| P. A. J. DeFreitas..... | 394.2 | 95 | 1,127 | 39 | 6-88 | 2 | 28.89 |
| P. J. Martin........ | 422.4 | 99 | 1,262 | 33 | 4-30 | 0 | 38.24 |
| P. J. W. Allott........ | 173.1 | 43 | 489 | 12 | 4-56 | 0 | 40.75 |
| M. Watkinson ........ | 603.2 | 106 | 2,116 | 51 | 4-45 | 0 | 41.49 |
| I. D. Austin ......... | 237.2 | 42 | 787 | 12 | 3-58 | 0 | 65.58 |
| G. Yates............. | 529.4 | 97 | 1,770 | 26 | 3-47 | 0 | 68.07 |

Also bowled: J. D. Fitton 187.1–30–691–8; G. Fowler 7–0–41–1; D. P. Hughes
85.2–21–245–5; G. D. Lloyd 10–0–57–1; N. J. Speak 0.1–0–0–1.

**Wicket-keepers:** W. K. Hegg 39 ct, 3 st; J. P. Crawley 2 ct; J. Stanworth 1 ct, 1 st.

**Leading Fielder:** N. H. Fairbrother 18.

At Cambridge, April 13, 14, 15. LANCASHIRE drew with CAMBRIDGE UNIVERSITY.

At Birmingham, April 27, 29, 30, May 1. LANCASHIRE drew with WARWICKSHIRE.

At Worcester, May 9, 10, 11, 13. LANCASHIRE drew with WORCESTERSHIRE.

## LANCASHIRE v DERBYSHIRE

At Manchester, May 16, 17, 18, 20. Drawn. Lancashire 4 pts, Derbyshire 8 pts. Toss: Lancashire. After only eleven overs had been possible on the first two days because of rain and bad light, Derbyshire decided to press on for victory without resorting to a concocted finish. They dismissed Lancashire inside 53 overs, mainly through a fine spell of seam bowling by Mortensen, who bowled unchanged throughout the morning session on the third day. O'Gorman then batted beautifully, hitting two sixes and twenty fours in a career-best 148 (219 balls) and sharing in partnerships of 108 with Azharuddin and 116 with Morris, who was batting down the order after injuring his back. Derbyshire declared 176 ahead, and Lancashire lost two early wickets before Fowler, hitting thirteen boundaries in the 33rd century of his career, and Atherton batted out time with an unbroken stand of 167.

*Close of play:* First day, No play; Second day, Lancashire 27-3 (M. A. Atherton 5*, G. D. Lloyd 0*); Third day, Derbyshire 195-4 (T. J. G. O'Gorman 86*, K. M. Krikken 10*).

## Lancashire

| | | | | |
|---|---|---|---|---|
| G. D. Mendis c Base b Malcolm | 7 | – c Adams b Mortensen | 1 | |
| G. Fowler b Malcolm | 10 | – not out | 103 | |
| N. J. Speak c Bowler b Mortensen | 0 | – c Krikken b Malcolm | 3 | |
| M. A. Atherton b Mortensen | 16 | – not out | 62 | |
| G. D. Lloyd c Barnett b Malcolm | 20 | | | |
| Wasim Akram b Base | 15 | | | |
| P. A. J. DeFreitas c and b Mortensen | 26 | | | |
| †W. K. Hegg c O'Gorman b Mortensen | 13 | | | |
| G. Yates not out | 19 | | | |
| I. D. Austin b Warner | 12 | | | |
| *P. J. W. Allott c Krikken b Warner | 9 | | | |
| B 1, l-b 10, w 1, n-b 2 | 14 | L-b 6, n-b 1 | 7 | |

1/11 2/12 3/26 4/58 5/74  161    1/6 2/9        (2 wkts) 176
6/88 7/109 8/125 9/143

Bonus points – Lancashire 1, Derbyshire 4.

Bowling: *First Innings*—Mortensen 23-5-46-4; Malcolm 16-2-47-3; Base 10-2-37-1; Warner 3.5-0-20-2. *Second Innings*—Mortensen 9-4-19-1; Malcolm 12-3-38-1; Base 10-0-28-0; Warner 10-2-28-0; Barnett 11-2-28-0; Azharuddin 8-1-29-0.

## Derbyshire

| | | | |
|---|---|---|---|
| *K. J. Barnett c Fowler b DeFreitas | 15 | A. E. Warner b Yates | 0 |
| P. D. Bowler c Hegg b DeFreitas | 1 | S. J. Base not out | 15 |
| T. J. G. O'Gorman b Yates | 148 | B 1, l-b 7, w 2, n-b 14 | 24 |
| M. Azharuddin c Speak b Allott | 53 | | |
| C. J. Adams b Yates | 18 | 1/10 2/25 3/133     (8 wkts dec.) 337 |
| †K. M. Krikken lbw b Wasim Akram | 10 | 4/162 5/201 6/317 |
| J. E. Morris c Atherton b Allott | 53 | 7/318 8/337 |

D. E. Malcolm and O. H. Mortensen did not bat.

Bonus points – Derbyshire 4, Lancashire 3.

Bowling: Wasim Akram 22-3-90-1; DeFreitas 16-2-74-2; Austin 4-0-36-0; Allott 15-0-60-2; Yates 18.2-2-69-3.

Umpires: R. Julian and K. J. Lyons.

At The Oval, May 22, 23, 24. LANCASHIRE lost to SURREY by eight wickets.

## LANCASHIRE v SUSSEX

At Manchester, May 31, June 1, 3. Lancashire won by seven wickets. Lancashire 24 pts, Sussex 5 pts. Toss: Lancashire. Lancashire's depth of batting, with the first nine batsmen all getting into double figures, carried them to a first-innings lead of 192. Hegg, night-watchman from the opening day, led the assault on the Sussex bowling, and DeFreitas continued it by hitting 60 in 57 balls, with two sixes and eight fours. For the eighth wicket, he and Wasim Akram added 92 from seventeen overs. Bunting followed his Championship-best innings of 51 not out, in a last-wicket stand of 74 with Jones in the Sussex first innings, by taking the last three Lancashire wickets in six balls. Wasim took four wickets in each innings, and Watkinson turned from medium pace to bowl 21 overs of off-spin for four wickets in the Sussex second innings. Lancashire raced against the threat of rain to record their first Championship victory with nine overs to spare.

*Close of play:* First day, Lancashire 124-3 (M. A. Atherton 37*, W. K. Hegg 5*); Second day, Sussex 96-2 (J. W. Hall 47*, I. D. K. Salisbury 5*).

### Sussex

| | | | |
|---|---|---|---|
| D. M. Smith c Yates b Watkinson | 40 | – (7) b Wasim Akram | 2 |
| J. W. Hall lbw b Wasim Akram | 4 | – b Watkinson | 92 |
| N. J. Lenham b Wasim Akram | 0 | – (1) c Hegg b DeFreitas | 18 |
| A. P. Wells c Hughes b Watkinson | 6 | – (5) b Watkinson | 40 |
| *P. W. G. Parker lbw b DeFreitas | 11 | – (3) c Mendis b Yates | 17 |
| A. I. C. Dodemaide lbw b Yates | 20 | – (8) c Hegg b Wasim Akram | 0 |
| †P. Moores c Watkinson b Wasim Akram | 33 | – (6) lbw b Watkinson | 51 |
| A. C. S. Pigott b Wasim Akram | 1 | – (9) c Yates b Watkinson | 4 |
| I. D. K. Salisbury b Yates | 0 | – (4) c Fairbrother b Wasim Akram | 17 |
| R. A. Bunting not out | 51 | – not out | 14 |
| A. N. Jones c Wasim Akram b DeFreitas | 28 | – b Wasim Akram | 1 |
| B 5, l-b 3, w 3, n-b 4 | 15 | B 18, l-b 4, w 5, n-b 7 | 34 |
| | **209** | | **290** |

1/15 2/15 3/32 4/65 5/73     209  1/41 2/86 3/127 4/187 5/217  290
6/125 7/125 8/126 9/135        6/254 7/254 8/265 9/278

Bonus points – Sussex 2, Lancashire 4.

Bowling: *First Innings*—Wasim Akram 26-6-76-4; DeFreitas 12.2-5-21-2; Watkinson 18-3-64-2; Yates 12-1-40-2. *Second Innings*—Wasim Akram 38.4-11-86-4; DeFreitas 18-6-42-1; Watkinson 30-6-95-4; Yates 24-5-45-1.

### Lancashire

| | | | |
|---|---|---|---|
| G. D. Mendis b Dodemaide | 13 | – b Jones | 39 |
| G. Fowler c Smith b Pigott | 32 | – b Salisbury | 36 |
| M. A. Atherton c Moores b Jones | 39 | | |
| N. H. Fairbrother c Moores b Bunting | 22 | – not out | 7 |
| †W. K. Hegg b Pigott | 86 | | |
| G. D. Lloyd lbw b Jones | 45 | – (3) c Moores b Salisbury | 8 |
| M. Watkinson lbw b Salisbury | 41 | – (5) not out | 2 |
| Wasim Akram c Moores b Bunting | 37 | | |
| P. A. J. DeFreitas b Bunting | 60 | | |
| *D. P. Hughes b Bunting | 1 | | |
| G. Yates not out | 1 | | |
| B 3, l-b 16, w 5 | 24 | B 1, l-b 6 | 7 |
| | **401** | | **(3 wkts) 99** |

1/13 2/67 3/110 4/127 5/225   401  1/74 2/80 3/97  (3 wkts) 99
6/284 7/306 8/398 9/398

Bonus points – Lancashire 4, Sussex 3 (Score at 100 overs: 339-7).

Bowling: *First Innings*—Jones 26–4–86–2; Dodemaide 5.2–1–21–1; Bunting 19.2–3–99–4;
Pigott 23–3–88–2; Salisbury 36–11–88–1. *Second Innings*—Jones 10–0–38–1; Pigott 6–0–38–0;
Salisbury 4.5–1–15–2; Bunting 1–0–1–0.

Umpires: J. C. Balderstone and J. D. Bond.

At Basingstoke, June 4, 5, 6. LANCASHIRE beat HAMPSHIRE by 128 runs.

At Oxford, June 7, 8, 10. LANCASHIRE beat OXFORD UNIVERSITY by five wickets.

At Leicester, June 18, 19, 20. LANCASHIRE beat LEICESTERSHIRE by 115 runs.

## LANCASHIRE v KENT

At Manchester, June 21, 22, 24. Lancashire won by 59 runs. Lancashire 20 pts, Kent 4 pts.
Toss: Kent. Only 84 overs were possible on the first two days, leading to a double forfeiture of
innings on the last morning and a victory target for Kent of 321 in 87 overs. They reached 123
for the loss of only Ward before Wasim Akram burst through with five wickets for 16 in ten
overs and his first six-wicket return for Lancashire since April 1989. Ellison threatened to
deny Lancashire in rapidly deteriorating light, but Austin clinched the victory by yorking
Igglesden with eight balls remaining. In the Lancashire innings, Watkinson hit ten fours in
scoring 52 from 54 balls.

*Close of play:* First day, Lancashire 152-4 (N. J. Speak 23*, M. Watkinson 33*); Second
day, Lancashire 288-9 (D. P. Hughes 10*, P. J. Martin 4*).

## Lancashire

| | | | |
|---|---|---|---|
| G. D. Mendis c Fleming b Igglesden .. | 5 | I. D. Austin c and b Penn ........... | 7 |
| G. Fowler c Marsh b Igglesden ....... | 27 | *D. P. Hughes not out .............. | 25 |
| G. D. Lloyd b Igglesden ............ | 32 | P. J. Martin not out ............... | 21 |
| N. H. Fairbrother c Ward b Merrick .. | 24 | L-b 12, n-b 4 .............. | 16 |
| N. J. Speak c Davis b Merrick ....... | 24 | | |
| M. Watkinson c Ward b Merrick ..... | 52 | 1/11  2/70  3/79 | (9 wkts dec.) 320 |
| Wasim Akram c Ward b Ellison ...... | 42 | 4/103  5/153  6/186 | |
| †W. K. Hegg c Ellison b Penn ....... | 45 | 7/253  8/270  9/280 | |

Bonus points – Lancashire 4, Kent 4 (Score at 100 overs: 319-9).

Bowling: Merrick 23–6–88–3; Igglesden 25–3–75–3; Ellison 15–4–47–1; Penn 21–6–62–2;
Davis 1–0–4–0; Ward 8–3–8–0; Benson 8–0–24–0.

*Lancashire forfeited their second innings.*

## Kent

*Kent forfeited their first innings.*

| | | | |
|---|---|---|---|
| T. R. Ward c Speak b Martin ........ | 37 | C. Penn c Lloyd b Austin ........... | 12 |
| *M. R. Benson c Watkinson | | R. M. Ellison not out .............. | 19 |
|     b Wasim Akram . | 52 | T. A. Merrick c Austin b Wasim Akram | 1 |
| N. R. Taylor c Lloyd b Wasim Akram . | 33 | A. P. Igglesden b Austin ........... | 1 |
| G. R. Cowdrey b Hegg b Wasim Akram | 2 | | |
| M. V. Fleming c Fairbrother | | L-b 2, w 2, n-b 11 ......... | 15 |
|     b Wasim Akram . | 64 | | |
| †S. A. Marsh c Hegg b Austin ....... | 3 | 1/49  2/123  3/125  4/153  5/158 | 261 |
| R. P. Davis c Hegg b Wasim Akram .. | 19 | 6/224  7/224  8/245  9/255 | |

Bowling: Wasim Akram 29–7–86–6; Martin 22–4–79–1; Watkinson 14–4–36–0; Austin
20.4–4–58–3.

Umpires: D. O. Oslear and P. B. Wight.

## LANCASHIRE v GLAMORGAN

At Liverpool, June 28, 29, July 1. Drawn. Lancashire 4 pts, Glamorgan 6 pts. Toss: Lancashire. Two excellent hundreds by Butcher on another perfect Aigburth pitch were the highlights of a match ruined by rain on the final day. He hit 22 fours in the first innings and a six and eleven fours in the second. Shastri scored his second century in successive innings, Maynard hit 89 in 139 balls, and Glamorgan completed an impressive opening day by taking two wickets in the closing five overs. Fairbrother declared 141 behind, having hit his third century of the summer, containing fifteen fours, and Glamorgan's declaration on the final morning, after they had totalled 630 for five wickets in the match, left Lancashire to score 379 in 75 overs. Heavy rain soon forced the chase to be abandoned.

*Close of play:* First day, Lancashire 16-2 (G. D. Mendis 4*, M. A. Atherton 0*); Second day, Glamorgan 118-1 (A. R. Butcher 72*, R. J. Shastri 16*).

## Glamorgan

| | | | |
|---|---|---|---|
| *A. R. Butcher c and b Yates | 129 | – c Watkinson b DeFreitas | 104 |
| H. Morris lbw b Watkinson | 35 | – c Hegg b DeFreitas | 28 |
| R. J. Shastri not out | 133 | – not out | 58 |
| M. P. Maynard c Atherton b Austin | 89 | – not out | 43 |
| P. A. Cottey not out | 2 | | |
| L-b 1, n-b 4 | 5 | L-b 4 | 4 |

1/70 2/327 3/383          (3 wkts dec.) 393     1/59 2/176      (2 wkts dec.) 237

A. Dale, R. D. B. Croft, †C. P. Metson, S. L. Watkin, S. R. Barwick and S. Bastien did not bat.

Bonus points – Glamorgan 4, Lancashire 1 (Score at 100 overs: 392-3).

*In the first innings A. R. Butcher, when 94, retired hurt at 182 and resumed at 327.*

Bowling: *First Innings*—DeFreitas 18-3-71-0; Martin 16-2-55-0; Watkinson 20-1-84-1; Yates 24-1-109-1; Austin 23-2-73-1. *Second Innings*—DeFreitas 23-1-78-2; Martin 16-1-57-0; Yates 13-1-66-0; Austin 7-0-24-0; Watkinson 1-0-8-0.

## Lancashire

| | | | |
|---|---|---|---|
| G. D. Mendis c Bastien b Watkin | 15 | – not out | 18 |
| G. Fowler c Metson b Bastien | 4 | | |
| †W. K. Hegg c Dale b Watkin | 6 | – (5) not out | 11 |
| M. A. Atherton c Metson b Croft | 43 | | |
| *N. H. Fairbrother not out | 107 | | |
| N. J. Speak b Dale | 38 | – (2) c Metson b Watkin | 17 |
| M. Watkinson not out | 20 | – (3) b Watkin | 21 |
| P. A. J. DeFreitas (did not bat) | | – (4) c Croft b Bastien | 12 |
| L-b 10, w 1, n-b 8 | 19 | N-b 1 | 1 |

1/9 2/16 3/38 4/118 5/212    (5 wkts dec.) 252    1/20 2/50 3/63      (3 wkts) 80

G. Yates, I. D. Austin and P. J. Martin did not bat.

Bonus points – Lancashire 3, Glamorgan 2.

Bowling: *First Innings*—Watkin 18-3-71-2; Bastien 16-5-55-1; Barwick 16-3-45-0; Croft 22-8-34-1; Shastri 3-0-11-0; Dale 4.1-1-26-1. *Second Innings*—Watkin 9-0-40-2; Bastien 8-0-40-1.

Umpires: J. D. Bond and N. T. Plews.

At Taunton, July 2, 3, 4. LANCASHIRE lost to SOMERSET by four wickets.

At Nottingham, July 16, 17, 18. LANCASHIRE lost to NOTTINGHAMSHIRE by an innings and 34 runs.

At Uxbridge, July 19, 20, 22. LANCASHIRE beat MIDDLESEX by six wickets.

## LANCASHIRE v WARWICKSHIRE

At Manchester, July 23, 24, 25. Drawn. Lancashire 7 pts, Warwickshire 3 pts. Toss: Warwickshire. This clash between two of the top three teams in the Championship table was doomed to a draw after only sixteen overs had been possible on the opening day. Warwickshire were understandably happy to maintain their sizeable points lead at the top, and there was never any question of a contrived finish. Asif Din took advantage of escapes at 2, 40 and 64 to record his first Championship hundred for three years and share in a fourth-wicket recovery stand of 180 with Reeve. Mendis's century in 187 balls ended a lean spell stretching over nearly three months, and his opening partnership of 214 in 68 overs with Lloyd was the best of the season for Lancashire. Wasim Akram, who was removed from the Lancashire attack by umpire Plews for persistent intimidatory bowling on the second day, was fined £1,000 by the club the following day.

*Close of play:* First day, Warwickshire 16-2 (Asif Din 1*, D. P. Ostler 0*); Second day, Lancashire 56-0 (G. D. Mendis 21*, G. D. Lloyd 26*).

### Warwickshire

| | | |
|---|---|---|
| A. J. Moles lbw b Martin | 9 | |
| J. D. Ratcliffe c Allott b Martin | 0 – (1) not out | 51 |
| Asif Din c Titchard b Watkinson | 100 | |
| D. P. Ostler lbw b Martin | 9 – (2) c Stanworth b Watkinson | 32 |
| *D. A. Reeve b Wasim Akram | 88 – (3) not out | 12 |
| P. A. Smith b Yates | 24 | |
| †P. C. L. Holloway not out | 26 | |
| G. C. Small c Mendis b Yates | 0 | |
| T. A. Munton c Martin b Watkinson | 3 | |
| A. A. Donald st Stanworth b Watkinson | 1 | |
| A. R. K. Pierson not out | 3 | |
| B 3, l-b 4, n-b 26 | 33 | B 4, n-b 2    6 |

1/4 2/16 3/35 4/215 5/251    (9 wkts dec.) 296    1/66    (1 wkt) 101
6/258 7/263 8/285 9/292

Bonus points – Warwickshire 3, Lancashire 4.

Bowling: *First Innings*—Wasim Akram 24.5–4–86–1; Martin 20–9–40–3; Allott 17.1–7–45–0; Watkinson 19–2–58–3; Yates 19–5–60–2. *Second Innings*—Yates 18–9–36–0; Watkinson 18–4–61–1.

### Lancashire

| | |
|---|---|
| G. D. Mendis c Ratcliffe b Pierson | 119 |
| G. D. Lloyd c Holloway b Asif Din | 96 |
| S. P. Titchard not out | 15 |
| *N. H. Fairbrother not out | 6 |
| L-b 10, n-b 4 | 14 |

1/214 2/243    (2 wkts dec.) 250

G. Fowler, M. Watkinson, Wasim Akram, G. Yates, P. J. W. Allott, P. J. Martin and †J. Stanworth did not bat.

Bonus points – Lancashire 3.

Bowling: Donald 14–1–50–0; Small 8–2–18–0; Reeve 12–2–29–0; Munton 14–4–34–0; Pierson 16–0–67–1; Asif Din 17–6–42–1.

Umpires: R. Palmer and N. T. Plews.

## LANCASHIRE v YORKSHIRE

At Manchester, August 2, 3, 5. Drawn. Lancashire 7 pts, Yorkshire 7 pts. Toss: Lancashire. Rain ruined the promise of an interesting finish after Lancashire had been set to score 281 runs at about 4 an over. Yorkshire had recovered well after losing two wickets in the first over of the match, Kellett scoring a Championship-best 81, with 60 of his runs coming from boundaries, and sharing in a century partnership with Pickles. The second day was dominated by Atherton, who held Lancashire's innings together for four and a half hours, and Carrick, whose fourth wicket, that of DeFreitas, was his 1,000th in 22 seasons of first-class cricket. Lloyd, on the other hand, claimed his first wicket on the final morning, when Metcalfe took advantage of the declaration bowling to record his first century of the season.

*Close of play:* First day, Lancashire 33-2 (W. K. Hegg 11*, M. A. Atherton 2*); Second day, Yorkshire 35-0 (M. D. Moxon 22*, A. A. Metcalfe 9*).

## Yorkshire

| | | | |
|---|---|---|---|
| *M. D. Moxon c Hegg b Wasim Akram | 0 | – c Atherton b DeFreitas | 30 |
| A. A. Metcalfe c Wasim Akram b DeFreitas | 30 | – not out | 113 |
| D. Byas c Atherton b Wasim Akram | 0 | – run out | 26 |
| †R. J. Blakey c Fairbrother b DeFreitas | 9 | – c Yates b Lloyd | 7 |
| P. E. Robinson b Martin | 58 | – c Hegg b Fowler | 44 |
| S. A. Kellett b Watkinson | 81 | – not out | 1 |
| C. S. Pickles c Martin b Wasim Akram | 50 | | |
| P. Carrick c Watkinson b Yates | 26 | | |
| D. Gough b Wasim Akram | 9 | | |
| P. J. Hartley not out | 6 | | |
| M. A. Robinson b Wasim Akram | 4 | | |
| B 2, l-b 8, w 6, n-b 29 | 45 | B 7, l-b 7, w 1, n-b 2 | 17 |

1/0 2/1 3/16 4/93 5/139      318    1/49 2/107    (4 wkts dec.) 238
6/241 7/286 8/306 9/306             3/132 4/229

Bonus points – Yorkshire 4, Lancashire 4.

Bowling: *First Innings*—Wasim Akram 22.2–1–91–5; DeFreitas 19–2–66–2; Martin 18–5–41–1; Watkinson 27–1–93–1; Yates 11–3–17–1. *Second Innings*—Wasim Akram 5–2–9–0; DeFreitas 9.3–2–23–1; Martin 1–0–1–0; Yates 19–0–88–0; Watkinson 2.3–1–5–0; Fowler 7–0–41–1; Lloyd 10–0–57–1.

## Lancashire

| | | | |
|---|---|---|---|
| G. D. Mendis lbw b M. A. Robinson | 10 | – not out | 59 |
| G. Fowler c Byas b M. A. Robinson | 9 | – c Moxon b Hartley | 4 |
| †W. K. Hegg c Blakey b Hartley | 19 | | |
| M. A. Atherton not out | 114 | – (3) not out | 37 |
| *N. H. Fairbrother c Gough b M. A. Robinson | 32 | | |
| G. D. Lloyd c Blakey b Carrick | 31 | | |
| M. Watkinson b Carrick | 21 | | |
| Wasim Akram c M. A. Robinson b Carrick | 14 | | |
| P. A. J. DeFreitas b Carrick | 5 | | |
| G. Yates not out | 10 | | |
| B 3, l-b 2, n-b 6 | 11 | B 2, l-b 2, w 1 | 5 |

1/18 2/21 3/52 4/109 5/175    (8 wkts dec.) 276    1/29        (1 wkt) 105
6/218 7/239 8/253

P. J. Martin did not bat.

Bonus points – Lancashire 3, Yorkshire 3.

Bowling: *First Innings*—Hartley 17–2–72–1; M. A. Robinson 14–4–43–3; Gough 13–2–51–0; Carrick 30–11–75–4; Pickles 9–0–30–0. *Second Innings*—Hartley 9–2–28–1; M. A. Robinson 5–0–34–0; Gough 4–0–23–0; Carrick 5–1–12–0; Pickles 2–0–4–0.

Umpires: A. A. Jones and A. G. T. Whitehead.

## LANCASHIRE v NORTHAMPTONSHIRE

At Lytham, August 6, 7, 8. Northamptonshire won by 53 runs. Northamptonshire 21 pts, Lancashire 2 pts. Toss: Northamptonshire. Only 24 overs were possible on the opening day, but in that time Stanley went halfway towards his maiden century. Next morning Lamb hit a hundred before lunch, and together he and Stanley put on 236 for the third wicket. Stanley hit 21 fours in his 132, while Lamb's hundred, his first in a poor season, contained two sixes and thirteen fours and followed his being dropped by England three days earlier. Lancashire lost three wickets in the 23 overs left to them on the second day, and after Northamptonshire forfeited their second innings they were given a stiff victory target of 351. They had at least 95 overs in which to get them but were hardly in the hunt as Roberts, Northamptonshire's twenty-year-old leg-break bowler, registered his best figures in the Championship.

*Close of play:* First day, Northamptonshire 88-2 (N. A. Stanley 51*, A. J. Lamb 17*); Second day, Lancashire 80-3 (G. Yates 15*, N. H. Fairbrother 6*).

### Northamptonshire

| | | | |
|---|---|---|---|
| A. Fordham c Allott b Martin | 10 | E. A. E. Baptiste st Hegg b Fitton | 14 |
| W. Larkins lbw b Allott | 10 | †D. Ripley not out | 6 |
| N. A. Stanley b Austin | 132 | B 13, l-b 8, w 5 | 26 |
| *A. J. Lamb c Hegg b Martin | 125 | | |
| A. L. Penberthy c and b Yates | 38 | 1/18 2/20 3/256 | (6 wkts dec.) 450 |
| K. M. Curran not out | 89 | 4/286 5/382 6/409 | |

A. R. Roberts, N. G. B. Cook and J. P. Taylor did not bat.

Bonus points – Northamptonshire 4, Lancashire 2 (Score at 100 overs: 409-6).

Bowling: Martin 24-2-87-2; Allott 21-3-84-1; Austin 20-4-63-1; Yates 25-4-89-1; Fitton 22-1-106-1.

*Northamptonshire forfeited their second innings.*

### Lancashire

| | | | |
|---|---|---|---|
| G. D. Mendis b Taylor | 4 | – c Ripley b Cook | 19 |
| G. Fowler lbw b Lamb | 24 | – c Lamb b Curran | 24 |
| G. D. Lloyd lbw b Lamb | 28 | – c Fordham b Roberts | 79 |
| G. Yates not out | 28 | – (9) c Curran b Roberts | 0 |
| *N. H. Fairbrother not out | 13 | – (4) c Ripley b Taylor | 38 |
| N. J. Speak (did not bat) | – | (5) b Roberts | 13 |
| †W. K. Hegg (did not bat) | – | (6) c Baptiste b Curran | 37 |
| I. D. Austin (did not bat) | – | (7) c Curran b Roberts | 0 |
| J. D. Fitton (did not bat) | – | (8) c Fordham b Roberts | 60 |
| P. J. W. Allott (did not bat) | – | b Roberts | 6 |
| P. J. Martin (did not bat) | – | not out | 5 |
| B 1, l-b 1, n-b 1 | 3 | B 5, l-b 8, n-b 3 | 16 |

1/4 2/55 3/74　　　　　(3 wkts dec.) 100　　1/37 2/47 3/141 4/178 5/185　　297
6/193 7/269 8/281 9/286

Bonus point – Northamptonshire 1.

Bowling: *First Innings*—Taylor 8-0-33-1; Baptiste 7-1-15-0; Cook 2-0-3-0; Roberts 2-2-0-0; Fordham 4-0-18-0; Lamb 3.4-0-29-2. *Second Innings*—Taylor 17-5-54-1; Baptiste 11-4-30-0; Cook 22-8-79-1; Curran 15-3-49-2; Roberts 23.3-7-72-6.

Umpires: A. A. Jones and A. G. T. Whitehead.

At Bristol, August 9, 10, 12. LANCASHIRE lost to GLOUCESTERSHIRE by an innings and 98 runs.

At Derby, August 16, 17, 19. LANCASHIRE lost to DERBYSHIRE by five wickets.

## LANCASHIRE v WORCESTERSHIRE

At Blackpool, August 20, 21, 22. Drawn. Lancashire 5 pts, Worcestershire 6 pts. Toss: Worcestershire. After losing three wickets, including those of Hick and Moody, for 27 runs, Worcestershire spent the rest of the opening day in recovery. Lancashire, too, were made to work for their runs and were kept in touch by the last three wickets adding 98. Yates struck two sixes and four fours in making his unbeaten 29 from 36 deliveries. Curtis and Bent recorded their first hundreds of the season, and equalled the record opening stand of 225 for Worcestershire against Lancashire before Curtis declared and left Lancashire 59 overs in which to score 272. They were well on course through a fifth-wicket partnership of 82 in eleven overs between Lloyd and Watkinson, but with only 11 runs wanted from three overs, rain denied them their first win for a month.

*Close of play*: First day, Worcestershire 261; Second day, Worcestershire 78-0 (T. S. Curtis 49\*, P. Bent 23\*).

### Worcestershire

| | | | | |
|---|---|---|---|---|
| *T. S. Curtis c and b Austin | 32 | – c Austin b Fitton | | 120 |
| P. Bent lbw b Martin | 3 | – not out | | 100 |
| G. A. Hick c Hegg b Watkinson | 12 | – not out | | 15 |
| T. M. Moody c Mendis b Martin | 1 | | | |
| D. B. D'Oliveira b Yates | 30 | | | |
| S. R. Lampitt b Martin | 25 | | | |
| †S. J. Rhodes lbw b Martin | 48 | | | |
| R. K. Illingworth run out | 29 | | | |
| C. M. Tolley b Yates | 36 | | | |
| P. J. Newport not out | 22 | | | |
| N. V. Radford b Austin | 11 | | | |
| L-b 9, n-b 3 | 12 | L-b 10, w 5, n-b 1 | | 16 |

1/7 2/20 3/27 4/56 5/107     261    1/225      (1 wkt dec.) 251
6/113 7/160 8/215 9/238

Bonus points – Worcestershire 2, Lancashire 3 (Score at 100 overs: 222-8).

Bowling: *First Innings*—Martin 20–7–30–4; Watkinson 24–3–81–1; Austin 19.3–4–39–2; Yates 27–10–39–2; Fitton 25–11–63–0. *Second Innings*—Martin 9–4–14–0; Watkinson 17–4–48–0; Fitton 16.5–1–74–1; Yates 19–4–67–0; Austin 6–0–38–0.

### Lancashire

| | | | | |
|---|---|---|---|---|
| G. D. Mendis lbw b Tolley | 47 | – c D'Oliveira b Tolley | | 47 |
| G. Fowler c D'Oliveira b Tolley | 12 | – c Curtis b Radford | | 19 |
| N. J. Speak b Lampitt | 10 | – c Rhodes b Illingworth | | 45 |
| *N. H. Fairbrother lbw b Illingworth | 44 | – c Moody b Tolley | | 0 |
| G. D. Lloyd c Moody b Illingworth | 19 | – b Illingworth | | 58 |
| M. Watkinson c Moody b Illingworth | 0 | – run out | | 51 |
| †W. K. Hegg b D'Oliveira | 10 | – (8) not out | | 21 |
| J. D. Fitton c Bent b Hick | 1 | – (9) not out | | 9 |
| I. D. Austin lbw b Illingworth | 43 | – (7) run out | | 0 |
| G. Yates not out | 29 | | | |
| P. J. Martin c Hick b Illingworth | 17 | | | |
| L-b 7, w 1, n-b 1 | 9 | B 4, l-b 5, w 1, n-b 1 | | 11 |

1/42 2/75 3/81 4/123 5/129     241    1/25 2/101 3/101 4/124   (7 wkts) 261
6/140 7/143 8/186 9/199                  5/206 6/209 7/243

Bonus points – Lancashire 2, Worcestershire 4.

Bowling: *First Innings*—Newport 6–0–32–0; Radford 12–5–21–0; Tolley 15–6–30–2; Lampitt 14–4–33–1; Illingworth 21.1–6–49–5; Hick 7–1–33–1; D'Oliveira 9–1–36–1. *Second Innings*—Newport 7–1–19–0; Radford 6–2–24–1; Lampitt 5–1–21–0; Tolley 7–0–27–2; Illingworth 19–3–82–2; Hick 6–1–47–0; D'Oliveira 6–0–32–0.

Umpires: B. Dudleston and J. W. Holder.

## LANCASHIRE v ESSEX

At Manchester, August 23, 24, 26. Essex won by eight wickets. Essex 21 pts, Lancashire 3 pts.
Toss: Lancashire. Knight, 21, in only his fourth Championship match, played the major role
in the win which took Essex to the top of the Championship table. Hitting nine boundaries in
his unbeaten hundred, from 168 deliveries, he shared in a partnership of 140 with Stephenson
and an unbroken one of 120 with Salim Malik to bring Essex victory with three balls to spare.
A generous declaration had left them 67 overs in which to score 270. A career-best bowling
return for Foster, and his declaration 96 runs behind on the second afternoon, had made up for
many of the 76 overs lost through rain on the first two days. Hussain batted brightly on a pitch
which provided awkward bounce at one end, and which resulted in Mendis and Salim Malik
both being hit on the hand while batting and having to retire hurt. Yates, who went in as
night-watchman on the second day, led the way to Lancashire's declaration, hitting a six and
twelve fours in the second century of his career. Some friendly bowling by Hussain and
Knight helped him score the second fifty from 57 balls.
  *Close of play*: First day, Lancashire 175-5 (W. K. Hegg 21\*, J. D. Fitton 20\*); Second day,
Lancashire 14-1 (G. Fowler 6\*, G. Yates 3\*).

### Lancashire

| | | |
|---|---|---|
| G. D. Mendis c Garnham b Pringle | 49 | – (4) not out ................... 30 |
| G. Fowler c Topley b Foster | 43 | – (1) b Such ..................... 26 |
| N. J. Speak b Foster | 15 | – (2) lbw b Pringle ............. 2 |
| *N. H. Fairbrother c Garnham b Topley | 1 | |
| G. D. Lloyd c Childs b Foster | 3 | |
| M. Watkinson b Foster | 20 | |
| †W. K. Hegg c and b Foster | 30 | |
| J. D. Fitton c Stephenson b Foster | 36 | |
| I. D. Austin not out | 25 | |
| G. Yates c Salim Malik b Foster | 6 | – (3) not out ...................100 |
| P. J. Martin c Topley b Foster | 0 | |
| L-b 7, w 1, n-b 10 | 18 | B 8, l-b 1, n-b 6 ........ 15 |

1/71 2/106 3/106 4/123 5/139                246          1/2 2/77        (2 wkts dec.) 173
6/206 7/209 8/213 9/238

Bonus points – Lancashire 2, Essex 4.

*In the first innings G. D. Mendis, when 44, retired hurt at 98 and resumed at 206.*

  Bowling: *First Innings*—Foster 34.4-9-99-8; Pringle 22-9-44-1; Topley 14-5-60-1; Childs
6-0-25-0; Salim Malik 2-0-11-0. *Second Innings*—Foster 10-4-16-0; Pringle 11-2-24-1;
Topley 5-1-27-0; Such 9-3-14-1; Childs 5-2-10-0; Hussain 5.3-0-41-0; Knight 5-0-32-0.

### Essex

| | | |
|---|---|---|
| A. C. H. Seymour c Fairbrother b Watkinson | 28 | – c Hegg b Watkinson .......... 12 |
| J. P. Stephenson lbw b Martin | 5 | – c Watkinson b Fitton ........ 85 |
| N. V. Knight c Hegg b Fitton | 37 | – not out ......................101 |
| Salim Malik retired hurt | 11 | – not out ...................... 70 |
| N. Hussain not out | 65 | |
| †M. A. Garnham not out | 0 | |
| L-b 3, n-b 1 | 4 | B 1, l-b 3, n-b 1 ........ 5 |

1/17 2/49 3/149            (3 wkts dec.) 150    1/13 2/153          (2 wkts) 273

D. R. Pringle, *N. A. Foster, T. D. Topley, J. H. Childs and P. M. Such did not bat.

Bonus points – Essex 1, Lancashire 1.

*In the first innings Salim Malik retired hurt at 60.*

  Bowling: *First Innings*—Martin 13-4-47-1; Watkinson 16-5-49-1; Austin 11-4-24-0;
Yates 5.3-1-20-0; Fitton 3-0-7-1. *Second Innings*—Martin 11-2-34-0; Watkinson
15-1-65-1; Austin 19.3-3-80-0; Yates 9-2-48-0; Fitton 12-2-42-1.

Umpires: B. Dudleston and J. W. Holder.

## LANCASHIRE v NOTTINGHAMSHIRE

At Manchester, August 28, 29, 30, 31. Nottinghamshire won by three wickets. Nottinghamshire 22 pts, Lancashire 6 pts. Toss: Lancashire. An enterprising fourth-wicket partnership of 158 between Johnson and French was the highlight of a fine victory by Nottinghamshire. Lancashire's batting had been carried through both innings by Titchard, 23 years old and playing in only his fifth Championship match. He was 75 when the ninth wicket fell in the first innings, but Austin shared in a partnership of 133 which enabled Titchard to reach his maiden century after batting for more than five hours (278 balls) and hitting fifteen fours. Following an opening century stand between Broad and Pollard, Nottinghamshire's first innings collapsed against Watkinson's off-spin and DeFreitas's pace. And when Nottinghamshire lost three second-innings wickets in the final session of the third day, in their pursuit of 359 in 146 overs, Lancashire looked on course for victory. Instead Johnson, who batted for three hours and hit fourteen boundaries in his 114, led Nottinghamshire to a Championship double over Lancashire in 1991.

*Close of play:* First day, Lancashire 284-9 (S. P. Titchard 115*, I. D. Austin 43*); Second day, Nottinghamshire 212; Third day, Nottinghamshire 102-3 (P. Johnson 16*, B. N. French 0*).

### Lancashire

| | | | |
|---|---|---|---|
| G. D. Mendis b Pick | 7 | – b Stephenson | 0 |
| N. J. Speak b Pick | 9 | – c French b Pick | 11 |
| G. D. Lloyd b Saxelby | 25 | – c Stephenson b Hemmings | 22 |
| *N. H. Fairbrother c Randall b Pick | 0 | – c Robinson b Hemmings | 12 |
| S. P. Titchard c French b Pick | 135 | – c French b Pick | 77 |
| M. Watkinson c French b Afford | 20 | – c Johnson b Afford | 27 |
| P. A. J. DeFreitas c Pollard b Afford | 2 | – b Hemmings | 16 |
| †W. K. Hegg c French b Hemmings | 33 | – c Randall b Hemmings | 40 |
| J. D. Fitton c Robinson b Afford | 4 | – lbw b Pick | 1 |
| G. Yates c Johnson b Afford | 0 | – not out | 11 |
| I. D. Austin not out | 61 | – lbw b Hemmings | 2 |
| B 6, l-b 12, n-b 9 | 27 | B 11, l-b 8, w 1, n-b 5 | 25 |
| | **326** | | **244** |

1/11 2/26 3/33 4/67 5/111 6/135 7/178 8/193 9/193    **326**

1/2 2/21 3/54 4/54 5/93 6/120 7/218 8/223 9/239    **244**

Bonus points – Lancashire 2, Nottinghamshire 4 (Score at 100 overs: 243-9).

Bowling: *First Innings*—Stephenson 23.4–62–0; Pick 22.3–3–75–4; Saxelby 5–2–17–1; Afford 36–11–78–4; Hemmings 37–16–76–1. *Second Innings*—Stephenson 12–0–55–1; Pick 11–1–37–3; Afford 20–5–58–1; Hemmings 23.1–3–75–5.

### Nottinghamshire

| | | | |
|---|---|---|---|
| B. C. Broad c Fairbrother b Fitton | 54 | – lbw b DeFreitas | 10 |
| P. R. Pollard c Austin b Yates | 43 | – lbw b Austin | 12 |
| *R. T. Robinson lbw b DeFreitas | 44 | – not out | 59 |
| D. W. Randall c Speak b Watkinson | 0 | – b Watkinson | 39 |
| P. Johnson c Lloyd b Yates | 11 | – lbw b DeFreitas | 114 |
| M. Saxelby c Lloyd b Watkinson | 5 | – (7) lbw b DeFreitas | 1 |
| F. D. Stephenson b DeFreitas | 24 | – (8) b DeFreitas | 6 |
| †B. N. French b DeFreitas | 6 | – (6) c Hegg b DeFreitas | 65 |
| E. E. Hemmings b Watkinson | 6 | – not out | 29 |
| R. A. Pick c Lloyd b Watkinson | 1 | | |
| J. A. Afford not out | 0 | | |
| B 4, l-b 10, n-b 4 | 18 | B 8, l-b 15, n-b 1 | 24 |
| | **212** | **(7 wkts)** | **359** |

1/102 2/124 3/133 4/154 5/173 6/173 7/199 8/208 9/211    **212**

1/12 2/35 3/101 4/259 5/278 6/280 7/296    **(7 wkts) 359**

Bonus points – Nottinghamshire 2, Lancashire 4.

*In the second innings R. T. Robinson, when 19, retired hurt at 63 and resumed at 259.*

Bowling: *First Innings*—DeFreitas 25–8–44–3; Watkinson 23.1–7–55–4; Austin 4–1–15–0; Fitton 17–3–37–1; Yates 25–5–47–2. *Second Innings*—DeFreitas 38–12–71–5; Watkinson 49.3–11–165–1; Austin 9–3–21–1; Yates 9–0–40–0; Fitton 10–0–39–0.

Umpires: J. D. Bond and R. A. White.

At Scarborough, September 3, 4, 5, 6. LANCASHIRE lost to YORKSHIRE by 48 runs.

## LANCASHIRE v SURREY

At Manchester, September 17, 18, 19, 20. Lancashire won by one wicket. Lancashire 23 pts, Surrey 2 pts. Toss: Lancashire. Lancashire ended a run of six defeats in seven matches by securing their only win since July 22. In a tense finish Lancashire, who had needed 181 in 64 overs, were steered through by Hegg as the last two wickets put on 42 runs. In their first innings Crawley hit a maiden century, in under three hours with fifteen fours, in his third Championship match, and Speak registered the highest individual score by a Lancashire player in 1991. Surrey followed on 264 behind but fought back spiritedly from 199 for five in their second innings. Ward, dropped at 3 and 51, scored his only hundred of the season in an innings of 202 balls (one six, 22 fours) as the last five wickets put on 245 runs. Kendrick's second five-wicket return of the match, and the best figures of his career, put Surrey in sight of a remarkable win before Hegg saw Lancashire home.

*Close of play:* First day, Lancashire 222-1 (N. J. Speak 83*, J. P. Crawley 114*); Second day, Surrey 110-2 (J. D. Robinson 54*, A. J. Stewart 13*); Third day, Surrey 312-6 (D. M. Ward 115*, M. P. Bicknell 0*).

## Lancashire

| | | | | |
|---|---|---|---|---|
| G. D. Mendis c Ward b Robinson | 19 | – b Murphy | | 26 |
| N. J. Speak c and b Boiling | 153 | – c Stewart b Murphy | | 34 |
| J. P. Crawley lbw b Boiling | 130 | – lbw b Kendrick | | 15 |
| G. D. Lloyd st Sargeant b Kendrick | 2 | – (5) c and b Kendrick | | 15 |
| S. P. Titchard b Kendrick | 1 | – (4) c Stewart b Kendrick | | 17 |
| *M. Watkinson lbw b Boiling | 21 | – c M. P. Bicknell b Kendrick | | 5 |
| P. A. J. DeFreitas c Boiling b Kendrick | 8 | – lbw b Kendrick | | 0 |
| †W. K. Hegg c and b Boiling | 97 | – not out | | 36 |
| I. D. Austin lbw b Kendrick | 3 | – b Boiling | | 7 |
| J. D. Fitton c Ward b Kendrick | 5 | – run out | | 15 |
| P. J. Martin not out | 0 | – not out | | 3 |
| B 8, l-b 7, w 4, n-b 5 | 24 | B 4, l-b 5, n-b 1 | | 10 |

1/32 2/243 3/246 4/252 5/283      463    1/14 2/61 3/92      (9 wkts) 181
6/294 7/408 8/423 9/463             4/103 5/115 6/115
                                      7/130 8/139 9/170

Bonus points – Lancashire 3, Surrey 1 (Score at 100 overs: 252-4).

Bowling: *First Innings*—M. P. Bicknell 22-4-72-0; Murphy 14-2-65-0; Robinson 6-1-18-1; Boiling 53.2-17-157-4; Kendrick 53-16-120-5; Lynch 6-1-16-0. *Second Innings*—M. P. Bicknell 4-0-20-0; Murphy 9-1-38-2; Kendrick 23-3-54-5; Boiling 17-1-60-1.

## Surrey

| | | | | |
|---|---|---|---|---|
| D. J. Bicknell b Martin | 18 | – c Hegg b DeFreitas | | 3 |
| J. D. Robinson c Lloyd b Watkinson | 79 | – b Fitton | | 50 |
| G. P. Thorpe c Hegg b Martin | 11 | – b Martin | | 34 |
| *A. J. Stewart c Hegg b DeFreitas | 14 | – b Watkinson | | 28 |
| D. M. Ward c Hegg b DeFreitas | 0 | – b Martin | | 151 |
| M. A. Lynch c Hegg b Martin | 30 | – run out | | 49 |
| †N. F. Sargeant lbw b Watkinson | 10 | – lbw b Fitton | | 49 |
| M. P. Bicknell c Crawley b Watkinson | 0 | – b Austin | | 63 |
| N. M. Kendrick c Crawley b Martin | 17 | – c Crawley b DeFreitas | | 24 |
| J. Boiling lbw b Watkinson | 1 | – c Crawley b DeFreitas | | 1 |
| A. J. Murphy not out | 0 | – not out | | 1 |
| B 5, l-b 6, n-b 8 | 19 | B 2, l-b 10, w 1, n-b 2 | | 15 |

1/79 2/95 3/111 4/111 5/171      199    1/14 2/77 3/98 4/151 5/199      444
6/171 7/174 8/191 9/193               6/312 7/380 8/428 9/434

Bonus points – Surrey 1, Lancashire 4.

Bowling: *First Innings*—DeFreitas 16-6-45-2; Martin 21.3-4-57-4; Austin 2-0-15-0; Fitton 7-1-26-0; Watkinson 18-4-45-4. *Second Innings*—DeFreitas 27-1-82-3; Austin 10.4-1-47-1; Watkinson 30-3-145-1; Martin 19-3-69-2; Fitton 23-5-89-2.

Umpires: J. W. Holder and B. Leadbeater.

# LEICESTERSHIRE

*President:* C. H. Palmer
*Chairman:* J. M. Josephs
*Chairman, Cricket Committee:* P. R. Haywood
*Chief Executive:* F. M. Turner
 County Cricket Ground, Grace Road,
 Leicester LE2 8AD
 (Telephone: 0533-831880/832128)
*Captain:* N. E. Briers
*Cricket Manager:* 1991 – R. B. Simpson
       1992 – J. Birkenshaw
*Coach:* 1991 – J. Birkenshaw

The 1991 season was a deeply disappointing one for Leicestershire, and troubles on the field were compounded by the county's worst performance off it. After decades of modest surpluses and occasional small losses, various factors conspired to plunge the club into serious deficit. Falling membership, a sharp drop in commercial revenue owing to the recession, and a hefty wage bill destroyed the prospect of running at a profit. Indeed, the county braced itself for a loss of more than £100,000, and plans to build a £400,000 indoor cricket school had to be shelved.

Against this grim backcloth, a modest measure of success on the field would have provided some relief, and after finishing seventh in the Britannic Assurance Championship in 1990, Leicestershire believed progress was possible. Moreover, they had a double ration of top coaching expertise, Jack Birkenshaw having joined forces with the Australian coach, Bob Simpson. Instead the side continued to struggle, with poor results in the one-day competitions and such a nose-dive in the Championship that only the defeat of Kent on the last day of the season averted the ignominy of the wooden spoon.

The county had to wait until August to open their Championship account, when Kent, who provided their last success nearly twelve months before, were beaten at Grace Road. Subsequently, they gained an innings victory away to the title aspirants, Derbyshire, after Millns had produced the startling figures of nine for 37, the best bowling of the season. But Derbyshire won the return emphatically the following week, when the dominant individual was Mohammad Azharuddin, with a superb 212, and Essex were convincing winners at Grace Road as they pursued the title. Even so, Leicestershire ended in relatively encouraging form, with the last eight Championship fixtures yielding three wins and two close-run encounters with Yorkshire and Hampshire.

A lean year had not been difficult to predict. The departure of Phillip DeFreitas and David Gower in successive seasons had been followed in 1990 by the retirement from county cricket of three international fast bowlers, Jon Agnew, Les Taylor and Winston Benjamin. Another, George Ferris, had already been released. But even taking these losses into account, Leicestershire's struggle to compete was hard to accept. With Simpson's talent supplemented by the solid experience of Birkenshaw, it had been hoped that the remaining players could be blended into a unit capable of upholding the county's honour.

Simpson returned to Australia a week before the end of the season, having completed his two-year contract as cricket manager. His supporters credited him with bringing a professional discipline to the dressing-room, in contrast to the easy-going atmosphere under Gower's captaincy. They also believed that Simpson's ideas enabled the club to focus more sharply on its recruitment policy. But tangible evidence of his success was not easy to identify. Probably his appointment should be written off as a mistake, though whether it could have been avoided is open to debate. In 1989, after a long period in which tensions were rarely submerged, the side cried out for firm leadership. Appointing a manager to reinforce the authority of the new captain, Nigel Briers, looked the right course to take. However, the talents that guided Australia to their Ashes triumph in 1989 did not translate to running an English county side, certainly not one in transition like Leicestershire.

Time will tell whether Birkenshaw, with recent management experience at Somerset and a deeper knowledge of the county game, can do better. His chances have not been helped by the financial crisis, for the emphasis on economy has already put top-quality recruits beyond his budget. Concentrating on uncovering young talent is a longer-term strategy, so the immediate requirement is to maximise the available resources, improving the performances of players yet to achieve their potential and of those who have recently under-achieved. In the first category are Peter Hepworth, Ben Smith and David Millns, who did enough in 1991 to suggest their promise. Given a long-overdue run in the first team, Hepworth responded with more than 1,000 first-class runs, including centuries against Cambridge University and Essex, a standard Smith should not be long in matching. Millns, a bowler of genuine pace, left all previous form behind in taking 63 first-class wickets.

Of the more established players, Nigel Briers had another good year at the top of the batting order, and James Whitaker emerged from a lean spell mid-season to finish on a high note. But Tim Boon and Laurie Potter both fell a little short of their best, while Justin Benson, after recovering from a knee injury, both impressed and frustrated. Wicketkeeper Phil Whitticase achieved a well-deserved maiden hundred, and almost collected another in the next match. Sadly, Peter Willey lost his form, and then his place, midway through his 26th season in first-class cricket, and he was released halfway through a two-year contract.

The biggest weakness was the bowling, which suffered from Alan Mullally's continuing lack of fitness – he appeared in only two Championship matches – and the absences, through injury or England calls, of Chris Lewis. The England all-rounder later added to the personnel problems by moving to Nottinghamshire. Consequently, with Gordon Parsons severely restricted by a shoulder operation, and Craig Wilkinson discovering the gulf between Australian grade cricket and the English county game, Leicestershire owed a considerable debt to the Australian fast-medium bowler, John Maguire, for his 786 overs and 77 first-class wickets (101 in all cricket). The team was still glaringly deficient in spin, though Hepworth showed some promise with his off-breaks and Potter gamely bowled slow left-arm. Finding a quality spinner, preferably a left-armer, looked essential, though it was by no means the only headache facing Leicestershire, at one of the lowest points in their 113 years. – Jon Culley.

LEICESTERSHIRE 1991

[*Roger Wootton*

*Back row*: D. R. Martyn, C. W. Wilkinson, P. A. Nixon, M. I. Gidley, I. F. Plender, A. Roseberry, B. F. Smith. *Middle row*: R. Stenner (*physiotherapist*), P. N. Hepworth, R. A. Cobb, L. Potter, J. D. R. Benson, A. D. Mullally, D. J. Millns, J. N. Maguire, L. Tennant, P. Whitticase, G. R. Blackburn (*scorer*). *Front row*: G. J. Parsons, J. Birkenshaw (*coach*), J. M. Josephs (*chairman*), N. E. Briers (*captain*), C. H. Palmer (*president*), J. J. Whitaker, F. M. Turner (*chief executive*), T. J. Boon, P. Willey. *Inset*: C. C. Lewis.

## LEICESTERSHIRE RESULTS

*All first-class matches – Played 24: Won 3, Lost 9, Drawn 12.*

*County Championship matches – Played 22: Won 3, Lost 8, Drawn 11.*

*Bonus points – Batting 46, Bowling 53.*

*Competition placings – Britannic Assurance County Championship, 16th;
NatWest Bank Trophy, 2nd round; Benson and Hedges Cup, 4th in Group C;
Refuge Assurance League, 14th.*

# BRITANNIC ASSURANCE CHAMPIONSHIP AVERAGES

## BATTING

| | Birthplace | M | I | NO | R | HI | Avge |
|---|---|---|---|---|---|---|---|
| ‡N. E. Briers | Leicester | 22 | 40 | 5 | 1,358 | 160 | 38.80 |
| ‡J. J. Whitaker | Skipton | 22 | 36 | 3 | 1,242 | 105 | 37.63 |
| J. D. R. Benson | Dublin, Ireland | 9 | 12 | 1 | 393 | 133* | 35.72 |
| B. F. Smith | Corby | 13 | 20 | 3 | 585 | 71 | 34.41 |
| ‡P. Whitticase | Solihull | 19 | 25 | 5 | 620 | 114* | 31.00 |
| ‡T. J. Boon | Doncaster | 20 | 37 | 2 | 1,057 | 102 | 30.20 |
| P. N. Hepworth | Ackworth | 21 | 35 | 4 | 915 | 115 | 29.51 |
| ‡C. C. Lewis | Georgetown, Guyana | 12 | 15 | 1 | 413 | 73 | 29.50 |
| ‡L. Potter | Bexleyheath | 22 | 34 | 3 | 899 | 89 | 29.00 |
| ‡G. J. Parsons | Slough | 2 | 4 | 1 | 78 | 63 | 26.00 |
| ‡D. J. Millns | Clipstone | 19 | 24 | 8 | 306 | 44 | 19.12 |
| ‡P. Willey | Sedgefield | 12 | 18 | 5 | 217 | 42* | 16.69 |
| L. Tennant | Walsall | 5 | 9 | 3 | 94 | 23* | 15.66 |
| M. I. Gidley | Leicester | 4 | 8 | 1 | 107 | 80 | 15.28 |
| J. N. Maguire | Murwillumbah, Australia | 22 | 24 | 7 | 237 | 44* | 13.94 |
| C. W. Wilkinson | Wardle | 13 | 13 | 2 | 138 | 41 | 12.54 |

Also batted: P. A. Nixon (*Carlisle*) (3 matches) 31, 5, 9. A. D. Mullally (*Southend-on-Sea*) (2 matches) did not bat.

* *Signifies not out.*   ‡ *Denotes county cap.*

The following played a total of nine three-figure innings for Leicestershire in County Championship matches – N. E. Briers 4, J. D. R. Benson 1, T. J. Boon 1, P. N. Hepworth 1, J. J. Whitaker 1, P. Whitticase 1.

## BOWLING

| | O | M | R | W | BB | 5W/i | Avge |
|---|---|---|---|---|---|---|---|
| C. C. Lewis | 330.4 | 83 | 829 | 37 | 5-35 | 2 | 22.40 |
| D. J. Millns | 522.4 | 93 | 1,815 | 62 | 9-37 | 3 | 29.27 |
| P. N. Hepworth | 102.2 | 20 | 404 | 13 | 3-51 | 0 | 31.07 |
| J. N. Maguire | 730.5 | 160 | 2,222 | 69 | 7-57 | 3 | 32.20 |
| L. Potter | 418.2 | 93 | 1,237 | 26 | 4-116 | 0 | 47.57 |
| C. W. Wilkinson | 293 | 56 | 974 | 20 | 4-59 | 0 | 48.70 |

Also bowled: J. D. R. Benson 35.1–7–145–1; T. J. Boon 10–3–21–1; M. I. Gidley 79.4–18–241–3; A. D. Mullally 37.4–10–99–1; G. J. Parsons 40–10–116–3; B. F. Smith 7–0–71–1; L. Tennant 69–12–296–5; J. J. Whitaker 1–0–14–0; P. Willey 157.4–36–441–5.

**Wicket-keepers:** P. Whitticase 42 ct, 2 st; P. A. Nixon 6 ct, 1 st; J. D. R. Benson 1 ct; P. N. Hepworth 1 ct.

**Leading Fielders:** L. Potter 17, N. E. Briers 16, P. N. Hepworth 16.

## LEICESTERSHIRE v GLAMORGAN

At Leicester, April 27, 29, 30, May 1. Drawn. Leicestershire 4 pts, Glamorgan 1 pt. Toss: Glamorgan. Lewis, recovered from a stress fracture of the back, which had been diagnosed in December while he was with England in Australia, made a promising return. Without extending himself fully, he was the main architect of Glamorgan's collapse on the opening day; on a slow, straw-coloured pitch, only Maynard, batting two hours, and Smith applied themselves. The visitors were without Butcher, their captain, who was injured. Maguire, the former Australian Test bowler, made a tidy Championship début, and Briers and Hepworth had strengthened Leicestershire's position by the close. But after a full first day the match was ruined by the weather. The second and final days were completely washed out, and only seventeen overs were possible on the third.

*Close of play:* First day, Leicestershire 77-0 (P. N. Hepworth 29*, N. E. Briers 42*); Second day, No play; Third day, Glamorgan 31-0 (H. Morris 15*, P. A. Cottey 16*).

## Glamorgan

| | | |
|---|---|---|
| *H. Morris b Lewis | 11 | – not out ........ 15 |
| P. A. Cottey c Whitticase b Lewis | 3 | – not out ........ 16 |
| R. J. Shastri c Whitticase b Millns | 0 | |
| M. P. Maynard c Lewis b Millns | 41 | |
| G. C. Holmes c Whitticase b Lewis | 18 | |
| I. Smith lbw b Maguire | 39 | |
| R. D. B. Croft c Willey b Lewis | 15 | |
| †C. P. Metson c Benson b Lewis | 0 | |
| S. L. Watkin not out | 13 | |
| S. R. Barwick c Briers b Maguire | 5 | |
| M. Frost lbw b Millns | 0 | |
| L-b 9, w 1, n-b 6 | 16 | |

1/9 2/10 3/23 4/79 5/79             161                  (no wkt) 31
6/104 7/104 8/145 9/157

Bonus points – Glamorgan 1, Leicestershire 4.

Bowling: *First Innings*—Lewis 22–7–35–5; Millns 11.5–2–41–3; Maguire 15–6–35–2; Mullally 16–6–40–0; Potter 2–1–1–0. *Second Innings*—Lewis 4–0–8–0; Millns 6–0–15–0; Maguire 5–4–4–0; Mullally 2–1–4–0.

## Leicestershire

| | |
|---|---|
| P. N. Hepworth not out | 29 |
| *N. E. Briers not out | 42 |
| L-b 5, w 1 | 6 |

(no wkt dec.) 77

J. J. Whitaker, P. Willey, L. Potter, C. C. Lewis, J. D. R. Benson, †P. Whitticase, D. J. Millns, J. N. Maguire and A. D. Mullally did not bat.

Bowling: Watkin 14–2–29–0; Frost 10–2–16–0; Barwick 9–4–12–0; Croft 8–3–9–0; Shastri 2–0–6–0.

Umpires: H. D. Bird and J. D. Bond.

At Nottingham, May 9, 10, 11, 13. LEICESTERSHIRE lost to NOTTINGHAMSHIRE by seven wickets.

At Northampton, May 16, 17, 18, 20. LEICESTERSHIRE drew with NORTHAMPTON-SHIRE.

At Cambridge, May 22, 23, 24. LEICESTERSHIRE drew with CAMBRIDGE UNIVERSITY.

## LEICESTERSHIRE v NOTTINGHAMSHIRE

At Leicester, May 25, 27, 28. Drawn. Leicestershire 5 pts, Nottinghamshire 8 pts. Toss: Nottinghamshire. On a pitch of erratic bounce, on the higher part of the square, Whitaker's 65 off 136 balls provided the fabric of Leicestershire's first innings. Both he and Boon were struck on the hands, but Whitaker survived to hit eleven fours and to partner Potter in a fourth-wicket stand worth 107 in 34 overs. Smith was dropped three times close to the wicket before bad light ended the opening day after 88 overs. On the second morning Nottinghamshire soon lost Pollard, who retired suffering from mild shingles. But despite lack-lustre bowling, Broad (66 balls, nine fours), Randall and Saxelby prospered in partnership with Robinson, whose first century of the season spanned more than four hours and included twelve fours. Potter, Hepworth and Smith saved Leicestershire's second innings, but Nottinghamshire must have been disappointed to finish 12 runs short, with four wickets in hand, after earning themselves a target of 206 in 40 overs. Broad, having hit 91 off 113 balls, was caught and bowled off a full toss with 19 required from two overs.

*Close of play:* First day, Leicestershire 257-7 (B. F. Smith 39*, L. Tennant 7*); Second day, Leicestershire 28-2 (N. E. Briers 17*, P. N. Hepworth 3*).

### Leicestershire

| | | | |
|---|---|---|---|
| T. J. Boon c Evans b Afford | 30 | – run out | 5 |
| *N. E. Briers c Pick b Evans | 14 | – b Stephenson | 21 |
| P. N. Hepworth b Evans | 21 | – (4) c Johnson b Afford | 56 |
| J. J. Whitaker c French b Pick | 65 | – (5) c French b Evans | 14 |
| L. Potter lbw b Evans | 44 | – (6) lbw b Afford | 64 |
| B. F. Smith c Randall b Pick | 43 | – (7) c French b Pick | 43 |
| P. Willey c Afford b Pick | 2 | – (8) lbw b Afford | 6 |
| †P. Whitticase c Evans b Afford | 1 | – (9) lbw b Pick | 1 |
| L. Tennant b Pick | 12 | – (10) not out | 8 |
| D. J. Millns not out | 5 | – (3) c Robinson b Stephenson | 0 |
| J. N. Maguire b Pick | 0 | – b Stephenson | 0 |
| B 8, l-b 19, w 1, n-b 8 | 36 | L-b 8, n-b 9 | 17 |

1/32 2/75 3/85 4/192 5/225        270    1/9 2/14 3/39 4/74 5/139      235
6/237 7/248 8/266 9/267                6/193 7/219 8/223 9/225

Bonus points – Leicestershire 3, Nottinghamshire 4.

Bowling: *First Innings*—Stephenson 17–8–33–0; Pick 23.4–6–66–5; Evans 19–4–72–3; Afford 30–17–48–2; Saxelby 5–1–24–0. *Second Innings*—Pick 20–0–66–2; Stephenson 19.5–4–53–3; Evans 15–3–42–1; Afford 13.5–46–3; Saxelby 4–0–20–0.

### Nottinghamshire

| | | | |
|---|---|---|---|
| B. C. Broad c Briers b Maguire | 51 | – c and b Maguire | 91 |
| P. R. Pollard retired ill | 7 | – b Maguire | 33 |
| *R. T. Robinson c and b Maguire | 101 | – (5) c Briers b Millns | 1 |
| P. Johnson c Hepworth b Tennant | 24 | – (3) c Potter b Maguire | 20 |
| D. W. Randall c Whitticase b Potter | 45 | – (4) b Millns | 35 |
| M. Saxelby c and b Hepworth | 44 | – (8) not out | 3 |
| K. P. Evans not out | 6 | | |
| F. D. Stephenson not out | 16 | – (7) not out | 3 |
| †B. N. French (did not bat) | | – (6) c Whitticase b Millns | 0 |
| L-b 1, n-b 5 | 6 | B 1, l-b 5, w 1, n-b 1 | 8 |

1/72 2/115 3/187 4/278 5/278  (5 wkts. dec.) 300    1/68 2/98 3/164    (6 wkts) 194
                                     4/177 5/177 6/187

R. A. Pick and J. A. Afford did not bat.

Bonus points – Nottinghamshire 4, Leicestershire 2.

*In the first innings P. R. Pollard retired ill at 18.*

Bowling: *First Innings*—Millns 17–4–69–0; Maguire 28.5–3–105–2; Tennant 7–0–40–1; Willey 11–2–40–0; Potter 18–7–37–1; Hepworth 1–0–8–1. *Second Innings*—Maguire 20–0–90–3; Millns 16–1–70–3; Willey 4–0–28–0.

Umpires: G. I. Burgess and R. Julian.

At Leicester, June 1, 2, 3. LEICESTERSHIRE lost to WEST INDIANS by six wickets (See West Indian tour section).

At Ilford, June 4, 5, 6. LEICESTERSHIRE drew with ESSEX.

At Uxbridge, June 7, 8, 10. LEICESTERSHIRE drew with MIDDLESEX.

## LEICESTERSHIRE v SURREY

At Leicester, June 14, 15, 17. Drawn. Leicestershire 2 pts, Surrey 4 pts. Toss: Surrey. Waqar Younis dominated the first session after the home side had been put in, taking four wickets as Leicestershire slumped to 107 for five. He bowled Boon and Whitaker with his renowned yorker, and he would have dismissed Lewis after lunch had Thorpe held a chance in the slips. Lewis, 8 when he escaped, went on to strike eight fours; Younis, though weary, returned later to bowl Millns and complete his fifth five-wicket haul in four matches. After rain had washed out the second day, Surrey declared 142 runs behind, to which Leicestershire responded by setting a target of 276 from what transpired to be 62 overs. Bicknell and Ward batted handsomely, and Surrey looked like winning at 209 for three with ten overs left. However, Ward, who had twice hit Potter's left-arm spin for six, was caught on the mid-wicket boundary attempting something similar against Maguire and, with 32 wanted off four overs, Lewis came back to take three wickets in two overs. Consequently, Leicestershire ended as close to victory – two wickets as opposed to 15 runs – as their opponents.

*Close of play:* First day, Surrey 90-1 (R. I. Alikhan 28*, A. J. Stewart 17*); Second day, No play.

### Leicestershire

| | | | | |
|---|---|---|---|---|
| T. J. Boon b Waqar Younis | 9 | – b Medlycott | 13 |
| *N. E. Briers c Stewart b Murphy | 31 | – c Sargeant b Medlycott | 30 |
| P. N. Hepworth c Sargeant b Waqar Younis | 0 | – b Murphy | 30 |
| J. J. Whitaker b Waqar Younis | 44 | – not out | 43 |
| L. Potter c Bicknell b Waqar Younis | 10 | – not out | 14 |
| B. F. Smith c Sargeant b Feltham | 24 | | |
| C. C. Lewis st Sargeant b Medlycott | 46 | | |
| P. Willey c Sargeant b Feltham | 18 | | |
| †P. Whitticase not out | 32 | | |
| D. J. Millns b Waqar Younis | 3 | | |
| J. N. Maguire c and b Feltham | 5 | | |
| L-b 6, n-b 4 | 10 | L-b 3 | 3 |

1/30 2/36 3/63 4/100 5/107          232   1/27 2/66 3/112   (3 wkts dec.) 133
6/165 7/183 8/207 9/227

Bonus points – Leicestershire 2, Surrey 4.

Bowling: *First Innings*—Waqar Younis 16–3–57–5; Murphy 21–6–67–1; Feltham 27–5–91–3; Medlycott 6–2–11–1. *Second Innings*—Murphy 17.5–1–53–1; Waqar Younis 3–0–9–0; Medlycott 20–6–46–2; Feltham 6–0–22–0.

## Surrey

| | | | | |
|---|---|---|---|---|
| D. J. Bicknell c Hepworth b Millns | 38 | – b Lewis | 86 |
| R. I. Alikhan not out | 28 | – c Hepworth b Millns | 35 |
| A. J. Stewart not out | 17 | – c Whitticase b Potter | 13 |
| D. M. Ward (did not bat) | | – c Smith b Maguire | 60 |
| G. P. Thorpe (did not bat) | | – c Whitticase b Millns | 24 |
| *I. A. Greig (did not bat) | | – not out | 27 |
| K. T. Medlycott (did not bat) | | – b Lewis | 3 |
| M. A. Feltham (did not bat) | | – c Potter b Lewis | 2 |
| †N. F. Sargeant (did not bat) | | – c Briers b Lewis | 0 |
| Waqar Younis (did not bat) | | – not out | 2 |
| L-b 7 | 7 | B 1, l-b 5, w 1, n-b 2 | 9 |

1/60                                   (1 wkt dec.) 90    1/71 2/96 3/181 4/224    (8 wkts) 261
                                                          5/226 6/245 7/255 8/255

A. J. Murphy did not bat.

Bowling: *First Innings*—Lewis 9–3–17–0; Maguire 9–3–22–0; Willey 11–5–19–0; Millns 10–4–25–1; Potter 1–1–0–0. *Second Innings*—Lewis 14–3–45–4; Maguire 12–2–45–1; Willey 14–2–50–0; Millns 5–0–43–2; Potter 17–1–72–1.

Umpires: J. W. Holder and R. Julian.

## LEICESTERSHIRE v LANCASHIRE

At Leicester, June 18, 19, 20. Lancashire won by 115 runs. Lancashire 18 pts, Leicestershire 4 pts. Toss: Leicestershire. Bad weather was again a factor. On the first day Lancashire, 39 for three, left the field in steady rain at 11.50 a.m., after Speak had denied Lewis a hat-trick; resuming at 5.30 p.m., they recovered to 84 for four from 23 overs, with Mendis having been dropped on the boundary by Lewis when hooking Millns. No play was possible until after lunch on the second day. Lancashire continued recklessly but were rescued by Hughes (104 balls), who compiled the 53rd half-century of his first-class career and helped Austin put on 88 for the ninth wicket. With the terms of a run-chase tacitly agreed, Leicestershire declared at 34 for one overnight, only for Lancashire to make an untidy job of completing their part of the bargain. Losing six wickets before reaching the required 81, they needed a sacrificial over of Smith's occasional medium pace, from which Wasim Akram struck five consecutive fours. Five wickets by Wasim then turned the match Lancashire's way as Leicestershire, their target 274 in 72 overs, collapsed to 119 for nine with nineteen overs left. However, defied by Whitticase and Maguire, Lancashire had only fifteen balls to spare when they completed an unconvincing victory.

*Close of play:* First day, Lancashire 84-4 (G. D. Mendis 34*, W. K. Hegg 0*); Second day, Leicestershire 34-1 (N. E. Briers 21*, P. N. Hepworth 0*).

## Lancashire

| | | | | |
|---|---|---|---|---|
| G. D. Mendis b Millns | 37 | – c and b Maguire | 26 |
| G. Fowler run out | 23 | – c Lewis b Millns | 5 |
| G. D. Lloyd lbw b Lewis | 0 | – c Potter b Maguire | 13 |
| N. H. Fairbrother lbw b Lewis | 0 | – b Millns | 7 |
| N. J. Speak c Whitticase b Lewis | 26 | – lbw b Maguire | 0 |
| †W. K. Hegg c Briers b Lewis | 23 | – (8) not out | 4 |
| M. Watkinson c Hepworth b Millns | 12 | – (6) c Whitaker b Millns | 6 |
| Wasim Akram c Potter b Lewis | 0 | – (7) not out | 20 |
| I. D. Austin c Potter b Willey | 43 | | |
| *D. P. Hughes c Briers b Willey | 51 | | |
| P. J. Martin not out | 2 | | |
| L-b 1, w 1, n-b 7 | 9 | | |

1/35 2/39 3/39 4/83 5/87                 226    1/24 2/32 3/51    (6 wkts dec.) 81
6/121 7/125 8/125 9/213                          4/51 5/53 6/57

Bonus points – Lancashire 2, Leicestershire 4.

Bowling: *First Innings*—Lewis 27–8–60–5; Millns 25–3–99–2; Maguire 15–2–51–0; Willey 4–0–15–2. *Second Innings*—Lewis 5–3–3–0; Millns 14.3–4–45–3; Maguire 9–5–13–3; Smith 1–0–20–0.

## Leicestershire

| | | | |
|---|---|---|---|
| T. J. Boon c Fairbrother b Wasim Akram | 7 | – c Fairbrother b Wasim Akram . | 0 |
| *N. E. Briers not out | 21 | – c Fairbrother b Martin | 7 |
| P. N. Hepworth not out | 0 | – c Fairbrother b Wasim Akram . | 25 |
| J. J. Whitaker (did not bat) | | – c Martin b Austin | 28 |
| L. Potter (did not bat) | | – c Hughes b Wasim Akram | 10 |
| B. F. Smith (did not bat) | | – c Speak b Watkinson | 13 |
| C. C. Lewis (did not bat) | | – lbw b Wasim Akram | 9 |
| P. Willey (did not bat) | | – c Mendis b Watkinson | 0 |
| †P. Whitticase (did not bat) | | – not out | 51 |
| D. J. Millns (did not bat) | | – b Wasim Akram | 3 |
| J. N. Maguire (did not bat) | | – b Watkinson | 5 |
| L-b 4, n-b 2 | 6 | B 3, l-b 2, n-b 2 | 7 |

| | | |
|---|---|---|
| 1/21 | (1 wkt dec.) 34 | 1/6 2/8 3/58 4/64 5/85 158 |
| | | 6/95 7/95 8/103 9/119 |

Bowling: *First Innings*—Wasim Akram 6.2–3–7–1; Martin 6–1–23–0. *Second Innings*—Wasim Akram 26–8–61–5; Martin 12–4–17–1; Watkinson 22.3–9–47–3; Austin 9–1–28–1.

Umpires: J. W. Holder and R. Julian.

At Neath, June 21, 22, 23. LEICESTERSHIRE drew with GLAMORGAN.

At Worcester, June 28, 29, July 1. LEICESTERSHIRE drew with WORCESTERSHIRE.

## LEICESTERSHIRE v GLOUCESTERSHIRE

At Hinckley, July 2, 3, 4. Gloucestershire won by 36 runs. Gloucestershire 19 pts, Leicestershire 1 pt. Toss: Gloucestershire. Missed catches proved costly for Leicestershire after the visitors had elected to bat first on a sluggish pitch. Scott, Wright, Athey and Alleyne all contributed half-centuries, but three of them were dropped – Wright when he had made just 2 – and Athey survived a stumping chance off Potter. Extensive use of spinners permitted 122 overs to be bowled on the first day. The second day was lost after an overnight storm proved too much for the club ground's covers, but a declaration and two forfeitures revived the game and left Leicestershire to score 308 to win in a full day. Despite the absence of Lawrence, Gilbert and Babington, Gloucestershire achieved a workmanlike victory by dismissing the home side with eighteen overs to spare, although not before Lewis made a bold attempt to lead Leicestershire home from the unpromising position of 102 for five. At 252 for seven Leicestershire needed only 56 with 23 overs left, but an excellent catch in the gully by the Gloucestershire substitute, M. C. J. Ball, removed Lewis for 73, and with him went Leicestershire's hopes. Briers, the Leicestershire captain, was making his 300th first-class appearance.

*Close of play:* First day, Gloucestershire 307-6 (J. W. Lloyds 6*, R. C. J. Williams 5*); Second day, No play.

## Gloucestershire

| | | | |
|---|---|---|---|
| G. D. Hodgson c Hepworth b Lewis | 7 | J. W. Lloyds not out | 6 |
| R. J. Scott run out | 51 | †R. C. J. Williams not out | 5 |
| *A. J. Wright st Nixon b Potter | 63 | B 5, l-b 13, w 1, n-b 14 | 33 |
| C. W. J. Athey lbw b Maguire | 52 | | |
| M. W. Alleyne c Nixon b Willey | 55 | 1/25 2/133 3/155 (6 wkts dec.) 307 |
| J. J. E. Hardy b Hepworth | 35 | 4/231 5/272 6/300 |

A. M. Smith, J. M. de la Pena and M. J. Gerrard did not bat.

Bonus points – Gloucestershire 3, Leicestershire 1 (Score at 100 overs: 250-4).

Bowling: Lewis 15–3–36–1; Maguire 24–5–75–1; Wilkinson 19–4–41–0; Willey 37–10–87–1; Potter 18–8–31–1; Hepworth 9–5–19–1.

*Gloucestershire forfeited their second innings.*

## Leicestershire

*Leicestershire forfeited their first innings.*

| | | | | |
|---|---|---|---|---|
| T. J. Boon c Lloyds b Smith | 2 | †P. A. Nixon b Smith | | 31 |
| *N. E. Briers c Lloyds b de la Pena | 14 | C. W. Wilkinson c Wright b Smith | | 10 |
| P. N. Hepworth c Lloyds b Scott | 35 | J. N. Maguire not out | | 2 |
| J. J. Whitaker b Scott | 30 | | | |
| L. Potter c Wright b Lloyds | 1 | B 5, l-b 3, w 4, n-b 26 | | 38 |
| B. F. Smith c Hodgson b Lloyds | 29 | | | — |
| C. C. Lewis c sub b Smith | 73 | 1/8 2/59 3/91 4/100 5/102 | | 271 |
| P. Willey c Williams b de la Pena | 6 | 6/147 7/162 8/252 9/262 | | |

Bowling: Smith 17.1–3–41–4; de la Pena 13–0–69–2; Gerrard 8–0–24–0; Lloyds 35–9–93–2; Scott 15–1–36–2.

Umpires: A. A. Jones and N. T. Plews.

## LEICESTERSHIRE v NORTHAMPTONSHIRE

At Leicester, July 5, 6, 8. Drawn. Leicestershire 3 pts, Northamptonshire 8 pts. Toss: Northamptonshire. After a solid start was wrecked by Maguire, who took three wickets for 5 runs in the space of 26 balls, Northamptonshire recovered well, owing much to a highly responsible innings from Fordham. His 116, off 261 balls, occupied five hours, in which time he hit fifteen boundaries and shared a stand of 147 for the fourth wicket with Curran. Leicestershire's attack lacked Lewis, who was prevented from bowling by a back injury but was picked for his batting. In the eight overs left of the first day, following Bailey's declaration, Leicestershire lost four wickets for 19 runs. Briers survived this debacle, however, and batted throughout the second day, first carrying his bat for 60 through a paltry first innings of 108 and then remaining unbeaten with 75 at the close after Leicestershire followed on. He was helped by Whitaker's aggressive 74 in a second-wicket stand of 136, and his partnership of 107 in 36 overs with Smith on the rain-interrupted final day was enough to earn his side a draw. When he was sixth out, on the stroke of tea, Briers had batted 6 hours 21 minutes and faced 326 balls for his 133, which included thirteen fours.

*Close of play:* First day, Leicestershire 19-4 (N. E. Briers 12*); Second day, Leicestershire 177-5 (N. E. Briers 75*).

## Northamptonshire

| | | | | |
|---|---|---|---|---|
| A. Fordham lbw b Maguire | 116 | †D. Ripley c Nixon b Millns | | 0 |
| N. A. Felton c Nixon b Maguire | 28 | A. R. Roberts not out | | 6 |
| *R. J. Bailey b Maguire | 0 | B 2, l-b 6, w 2, n-b 4 | | 14 |
| D. J. Capel c Nixon b Maguire | 7 | | | — |
| K. M. Curran b Millns | 67 | 1/64 2/64 3/74 | (7 wkts dec.) | 300 |
| E. A. E. Baptiste c Nixon b Millns | 40 | 4/221 5/248 | | |
| J. G. Thomas not out | 22 | 6/277 7/277 | | |

N. G. B. Cook and J. P. Taylor did not bat.

Bonus points – Northamptonshire 4, Leicestershire 3.

Bowling: Millns 19–4–70–3; Maguire 23–5–57–4; Wilkinson 13–3–33–0; Willey 29–6–79–0; Potter 15–1–53–0.

## Leicestershire

| | | | |
|---|---|---|---|
| T. J. Boon c Cook b Thomas | 0 | – c Capel b Thomas | 5 |
| *N. E. Briers not out | 60 | – c Capel b Curran | 133 |
| D. J. Millns c Felton b Taylor | 0 | – (9) not out | 31 |
| J. J. Whitaker c Baptiste b Taylor | 0 | – (3) b Roberts | 74 |
| L. Potter c Ripley b Thomas | 4 | – (4) c Bailey b Roberts | 0 |
| C. C. Lewis c Felton b Thomas | 8 | – (5) lbw b Baptiste | 3 |
| B. F. Smith lbw b Cook | 12 | – c Ripley b Curran | 47 |
| P. Willey c Ripley b Baptiste | 9 | – not out | 19 |
| †P. A. Nixon c Ripley b Baptiste | 5 | – (6) lbw b Bailey | 9 |
| C. W. Wilkinson lbw b Cook | 0 | | |
| J. N. Maguire c Bailey b Baptiste | 4 | | |
| L-b 1, w 1, n-b 4 | 6 | B 4, l-b 10, n-b 6 | 20 |

| | | | |
|---|---|---|---|
| 1/6 2/14 3/14 4/19 5/41 | 108 | 1/12 2/148 3/150 | (7 wkts dec.) 341 |
| 6/61 7/94 8/100 9/101 | | 4/163 5/177 | |
| | | 6/284 7/289 | |

Bonus points – Northamptonshire 4.

Bowling: *First Innings*—Taylor 11–0–37–2; Thomas 9–4–21–3; Baptiste 10.3–4–37–3; Cook 9–3–12–2. *Second Innings*—Baptiste 30–9–66–1; Thomas 24–1–64–1; Taylor 11–1–54–0; Curran 13–4–38–2; Roberts 24–10–42–2; Cook 21–9–33–0; Capel 8–3–21–0; Bailey 4–2–9–1.

Umpires: A. A. Jones and N. T. Plews.

At Hove, July 19, 20, 22. LEICESTERSHIRE lost to SUSSEX by 5 runs.

## LEICESTERSHIRE v WARWICKSHIRE

At Leicester, July 26, 27, 28. Warwickshire won by an innings and 44 runs. Warwickshire 24 pts, Leicestershire 3 pts. Toss: Leicestershire. Munton, born in Melton Mowbray, reminded Leicestershire of the talent they had been unable to accommodate when they rejected him as a nineteen-year-old in 1984. He swung the ball prodigiously as Warwickshire, top of the Championship table, bowled out the home side, anchored to the bottom, for 161. On a dry, slow pitch no batsman found the going easy, but after Millns had removed the Warwickshire openers, Ratcliffe and Moles, in a useful opening spell, Ostler and Reeve built a promising position with a fourth-wicket stand of 83. Ostler perished in the second over of the second day, but Asif Din provided ample compensation with a marvellous innings of 140 off 162 balls, scored in three and a quarter hours. With Holloway, the reserve wicket-keeper, he added 137 for the sixth wicket, and he made Leicestershire suffer for the paucity of their bowling reserves by hitting twenty fours and a six. Holloway was 11 runs short of a maiden first-class century when Lloyd declared 288 in front, and on the final day Munton improved his match figures to nine for 78 as Leicestershire's second innings mustered 244, of which 52 came in eleven overs for the last wicket. Earlier, Hepworth resisted for 59 overs for 32 runs. The pace of Donald was also a factor in Warwickshire's victory, and their slip fielding was admirable as the gulf between top and bottom was harshly illustrated.

*Close of play:* First day, Warwickshire 133-3 (D. P. Ostler 65*, D. A. Reeve 35*); Second day, Leicestershire 90-3 (P. N. Hepworth 14*, P. Whitticase 0*).

## Leicestershire

| | | | |
|---|---|---|---|
| T. J. Boon c Holloway b Donald | 18 | – b Munton | 41 |
| *N. E. Briers c Holloway b Munton | 33 | – c Holloway b Small | 3 |
| P. N. Hepworth run out | 15 | – c Ostler b Donald | 32 |
| J. J. Whitaker b Munton | 23 | – b Donald | 12 |
| L. Potter c Holloway b Small | 8 | – (6) c Reeve b Small | 44 |
| J. D. R. Benson c Lloyd b Munton | 11 | – (7) c Moles b Munton | 8 |
| M. I. Gidley c Asif Din b Munton | 10 | – (8) c Ostler b Munton | 1 |
| †P. Whitticase lbw b Munton | 2 | – (5) b Donald | 17 |
| D. J. Millns b Donald | 6 | – not out | 24 |
| L. Tennant not out | 11 | – b Munton | 0 |
| J. N. Maguire b Donald | 2 | – c Pierson b Donald | 18 |
| B 9, l-b 5, w 1, n-b 7 | 22 | B 19, l-b 21, w 1, n-b 3 | 44 |

| | | | |
|---|---|---|---|
| 1/28 2/59 3/80 4/111 5/123 | 161 | 1/20 2/65 3/88 4/114 5/165 | 244 |
| 6/127 7/138 8/146 9/149 | | 6/184 7/186 8/192 9/192 | |

Bonus points – Leicestershire 1, Warwickshire 4.

Bowling: *First Innings*—Donald 13–0–64–3; Small 13–4–34–1; Reeve 7–4–7–0; Munton 24–10–32–5; Asif Din 4–0–10–0. *Second Innings*—Donald 24–7–59–4; Small 16–3–52–2; Reeve 6–3–9–0; Munton 20–4–46–4; Pierson 15–4–38–0.

## Warwickshire

| | | | | |
|---|---|---|---|---|
| A. J. Moles c Hepworth b Millns | 5 | A. R. K. Pierson c Boon b Benson | 35 |
| J. D. Ratcliffe b Millns | 7 | A. A. Donald not out | 1 |
| *T. A. Lloyd c Whitticase b Tennant | 20 | | |
| D. P. Ostler c Briers b Millns | 65 | L-b 3, w 2, n-b 1 | 6 |
| D. A. Reeve c Whitticase b Potter | 67 | | |
| Asif Din c Gidley b Maguire | 140 | 1/7 2/24 3/50 | (8 wkts dec.) 449 |
| †P. C. L. Holloway not out | 89 | 4/133 5/217 6/354 | |
| G. C. Small st Whitticase b Gidley | 14 | 7/375 8/445 | |

T. A. Munton did not bat.

Bonus points – Warwickshire 4, Leicestershire 2 (Score at 100 overs: 321-5).

Bowling: Millns 27–5–106–3; Maguire 24–6–85–1; Tennant 21–3–82–1; Gidley 23–1–79–1; Benson 7–3–18–1; Potter 16–3–58–1; Hepworth 3–0–18–0.

Umpires: B. J. Meyer and D. O. Oslear.

At Weston-super-Mare, August 2, 3, 5. LEICESTERSHIRE drew with SOMERSET.

## LEICESTERSHIRE v YORKSHIRE

At Leicester, August 6, 7, 8. Drawn. Leicestershire 5 pts. Toss: Yorkshire. Moxon's decision to put Leicestershire in looked sensible enough: there was a green tinge to the pitch, conditions were damp (32 overs of the first session were lost), and Leicestershire were without a Championship win. However, Briers and Boon denied Yorkshire for 76 overs with a stand of 219 for the first wicket before Boon, who had made 102 off 216 balls with ten fours, chipped to mid-wicket. Rain and poor light restricted play to 43.4 overs on the second day, but the contest was rescued by some manoeuvring on the last morning, as a result of which Yorkshire were set a target of 313 in 80 overs. This became academic as the visitors collapsed to 53 for six, all the wickets falling to Millns, whose fierce pace brought him career-best figures. A Leicestershire victory was prevented, however, by an excellent, unbeaten innings of 122 from Byas, who shared a critical partnership of 155 for the seventh wicket with Carrick. This frustrated Leicestershire into the ninth over of the last twenty, and when Leicestershire had nine overs in which to get the last two wickets, Batty helped Byas secure the draw. Yorkshire's task was made easier by the absence of Mullally, Leicestershire's left-arm seamer, who in only his second first-class appearance of the season had broken down with a recurrence of back trouble.

*Close of play:* First day, Leicestershire 225-1 (N. E. Briers 108*, J. J. Whitaker 5*); Second day, Yorkshire 74-3 (D. Byas 32*, P. E. Robinson 7*).

## Leicestershire

| | | |
|---|---|---|
| T. J. Boon c Kellett b M. A. Robinson | 102 – not out | 29 |
| *N. E. Briers b Blakey b Hartley | 114 – not out | 51 |
| J. J. Whitaker not out | 31 | |
| P. N. Hepworth not out | 40 | |
| L-b 6, n-b 7 | 13 | L-b 3, n-b 3 ........... 6 |

1/219 2/234       (2 wkts dec.) 300       (no wkt dec.) 86

L. Potter, J. D. R. Benson, †P. Whitticase, D. J. Millns, J. N. Maguire, A. D. Mullally and C. W. Wilkinson did not bat.

Bonus points – Leicestershire 4.

Bowling: *First Innings*—Hartley 24-3-78-1; M. A. Robinson 24-6-59-1; Pickles 13-2-45-0; Carrick 22-3-58-0; Batty 17-4-54-0. *Second Innings*—Hartley 3-1-7-0; M. A. Robinson 4-1-11-0; Pickles 2-0-9-0; Kellett 2-0-3-0; P. E. Robinson 5-0-30-0; Metcalfe 3-0-23-0.

## Yorkshire

| | | |
|---|---|---|
| *M. D. Moxon c Whitticase b Mullally | 22 – c Hepworth b Millns | 12 |
| A. A. Metcalfe c Potter b Millns | 0 – lbw b Millns | 2 |
| D. Byas not out | 32 – not out | 122 |
| †R. J. Blakey c Whitaker b Maguire | 8 – c Whitaker b Millns | 2 |
| P. E. Robinson not out | 7 – c Briers b Millns | 9 |
| S. A. Kellett (did not bat) | – b Millns | 3 |
| C. S. Pickles (did not bat) | – c Potter b Millns | 0 |
| P. Carrick (did not bat) | – c Benson b Hepworth | 61 |
| P. J. Hartley (did not bat) | – b Hepworth | 2 |
| J. D. Batty (did not bat) | – not out | 4 |
| L-b 3, n-b 2 | 5 | B 1, l-b 5, w 4, n-b 5 ..... 17 |

1/7 2/38 3/64     (3 wkts dec.) 74     1/7 2/19 3/21 4/49     (8 wkts) 234
                                               5/53 6/53 7/208 8/214

M. A. Robinson did not bat.

Bonus point – Leicestershire 1.

Bowling: *First Innings*—Millns 9-1-33-1; Mullally 10.4-1-35-1; Maguire 3-1-3-1. *Second Innings*—Mullally 9-2-20-0; Millns 22-6-59-6; Maguire 14-2-53-0; Wilkinson 12-3-35-0; Potter 7-1-20-0; Benson 4-1-9-0; Hepworth 11-3-29-2; Boon 1-0-1-0.

Umpires: J. D. Bond and D. O. Oslear.

## LEICESTERSHIRE v KENT

At Leicester, August 9, 10, 12. Leicestershire won by five wickets. Leicestershire 23 pts, Kent 3 pts. Toss: Leicestershire. After nineteen Championship games without a win, Leicestershire renewed acquaintance with the side they had last beaten. They must have been disappointed not to have made more of Briers's decision to bat first, for while there were runs from all the recognised batsmen, bar Hepworth, none went on to make anything substantial. McCague took the last three wickets in four balls to finish with career-best figures, and Marsh was rewarded for a tidy performance behind the stumps with half-a-dozen catches. Kent lost two wickets in Maguire's second over and never recovered, slumping to 35 for seven before Ellison, McCague and Patel restored a modicum of respectability, the last-named pair adding 50 in eight overs for the ninth wicket. Maguire's dismissal of Patel, for a career-best 43, gave him county-best figures of seven for 57. Asked to follow on, Kent performed rather better, Taylor and Cowdrey putting on 217 for the second wicket before Taylor, who had just completed a splendid 150 with 23 fours in five hours, was caught at long-off. Cowdrey fell 10 short of a century, but Kent's recovery was convincing enough for Leicestershire to resort to feeding them runs to encourage the declaration. This gave the home side a target of 252 from a minimum of 55 overs. Although the pitch was now offering help to the spinners, Briers and Boon put on 111 before Davis claimed Briers as the first of four victims. Boon soon followed, but Whitaker hammered a breathtaking 70 off 74 balls, including twelve fours, and Leicestershire won their first Championship match of the season with nine balls to spare.

*Close of play:* First day, Kent 2-2 (R. P. Davis 1\*, N. R. Taylor 0\*); Second day, Kent 211-1 (N. R. Taylor 112\*, G. R. Cowdrey 51\*).

## Leicestershire

| | | |
|---|---|---|
| T. J. Boon c Marsh b Merrick | 63 | – c and b Davis | 47 |
| \*N. E. Briers c Marsh b McCague | 29 | – st Marsh b Davis | 66 |
| P. N. Hepworth c Marsh b McCague | 8 | | |
| J. J. Whitaker c Marsh b McCague | 36 | – (3) c Cowdrey b Davis | 70 |
| L. Potter c Ellison b Patel | 61 | – (4) c Fleming b Davis | 37 |
| J. D. R. Benson b Davis | 31 | – (5) lbw b Patel | 5 |
| B. F. Smith lbw b Patel | 27 | – (6) not out | 19 |
| †P. Whitticase not out | 2 | | |
| D. J. Millns c Marsh b McCague | 11 | – (7) not out | 6 |
| C. W. Wilkinson c Marsh b McCague | 0 | | |
| J. N. Maguire b McCague | 0 | | |
| L-b 4, n-b 10 | 14 | L-b 1, w 1, n-b 2 | 4 |

1/69 2/87 3/132 4/145 5/218     282     1/111 2/120 3/212     (5 wkts) 254
6/269 7/269 8/282 9/282            4/222 5/240

Bonus points – Leicestershire 3, Kent 3 (Score at 100 overs: 281-7).

Bowling: *First Innings*—Merrick 21-4-43-1; McCague 26-4-88-6; Ellison 19-2-53-0; Davis 25-6-70-1; Patel 3-2-4-2; Fleming 7-0-20-0. *Second Innings*—Merrick 7-0-32-0; McCague 1-0-4-0; Ellison 9-1-37-0; Patel 23-2-93-1; Davis 19.3-2-81-4; Ward 1-0-6-0.

## Kent

| | | |
|---|---|---|
| T. R. Ward lbw b Maguire | 1 | – c Briers b Wilkinson | 41 |
| R. P. Davis c Potter b Millns | 6 | | |
| V. J. Wells b Maguire | 0 | | |
| N. R. Taylor lbw b Maguire | 18 | – (2) c Millns b Potter | 150 |
| G. R. Cowdrey lbw b Millns | 4 | – (3) c Hepworth b Wilkinson | 90 |
| M. V. Fleming c Benson b Maguire | 0 | – (4) c Whitaker b Boon | 58 |
| \*†S. A. Marsh b Maguire | 1 | – (5) not out | 39 |
| R. M. Ellison c Hepworth b Maguire | 13 | – (6) not out | 7 |
| M. J. McCague c Millns b Potter | 29 | | |
| M. M. Patel c Smith b Maguire | 43 | | |
| T. A. Merrick not out | 6 | | |
| B 1, l-b 6, w 1, n-b 1 | 9 | L-b 10, w 3, n-b 5 | 18 |

1/1 2/1 3/27 4/33 5/34     130     1/70 2/287     (4 wkts dec.) 403
6/34 7/35 8/57 9/107            3/302 4/376

Bonus points – Leicestershire 4.

Bowling: *First Innings*—Millns 19-7-27-2; Maguire 18.2-6-57-7; Wilkinson 5-1-23-0; Potter 5-2-16-1. *Second Innings*—Millns 15-1-61-0; Maguire 19-2-85-0; Wilkinson 18-2-52-2; Potter 37-9-90-1; Benson 5.1-1-22-0; Hepworth 5-0-13-0; Smith 4-0-45-0; Boon 4-0-11-1; Whitaker 1-0-14-0.

Umpires: J. D. Bond and D. O. Oslear.

At Bournemouth, August 16, 17, 19. LEICESTERSHIRE lost to HAMPSHIRE by two wickets.

At Derby, August 20, 21. LEICESTERSHIRE beat DERBYSHIRE by an innings and 131 runs.

## LEICESTERSHIRE v DERBYSHIRE

At Leicester, August 28, 29, 30, 31. Derbyshire won by 195 runs. Derbyshire 23 pts, Leicestershire 6 pts. Toss: Derbyshire. Having inflicted a heavy defeat on Derbyshire a week earlier, Leicestershire must have felt they could do so again when the visitors, still outside candidates for the Championship, were 79 for six on the opening day. Millns had been the destroyer at Derby; this time Maguire, moving the ball off the seam, did the damage, taking four wickets for no runs in fourteen balls as Derbyshire reeled from 58 for one to 60 for five. However, Bowler, facing his former county, saved Derbyshire with a five-and-a-half-hour century, and when it was Leicestershire's turn to get out of trouble, it needed a career-best 80 from off-spinner Gidley to rescue them from 53 for six. The last wicket put on 96, with Maguire's 44 not out in two and a quarter hours being his best for Leicestershire. The third day belonged to Azharuddin, who played one of the summer's best innings, a captivating 212 off 230 balls, of which the second hundred came off only 66 deliveries. His four-and-threequarter-hour innings produced three sixes and 29 fours, as well as century partnerships with O'Gorman, Barnett and Krikken, and it enabled the Derbyshire captain to declare and leave the home side to make 487 in 90 minutes plus the whole of the final day. They began badly, losing two wickets before the close, but Whitaker put on 61 with Boon and 89 with Potter before being caught at slip, attempting to drive Sladdin's left-arm spin. When Potter went in a similar way, 64 runs later, Leicestershire lost four wickets for no runs – three of them to Bowler in eleven balls – and Derbyshire went on to win before tea.

*Close of play:* First day, Leicestershire 12-2 (N. E. Briers 6*, P. N. Hepworth 6*); Second day, Derbyshire 78-2 (T. J. G. O'Gorman 7*, M. Azharuddin 20*); Third day, Leicestershire 51-2 (T. J. Boon 20*, J. J. Whitaker 18*).

### Derbyshire

| | | | | |
|---|---|---|---|---|
| *K. J. Barnett c Whitaker b Millns | 1 | – (6) c Potter b Hepworth | 36 |
| P. D. Bowler lbw b Wilkinson | 104 | – (1) c Potter b Wilkinson | 26 |
| J. E. Morris c Briers b Maguire | 37 | – (2) b Maguire | 17 |
| M. Azharuddin c Whitticase b Maguire | 0 | – c Maguire b Parsons | 212 |
| T. J. G. O'Gorman c Whitaker b Maguire | 0 | – (3) c Whitticase b Wilkinson | 33 |
| S. C. Goldsmith c Whitticase b Maguire | 0 | – (5) c Boon b Potter | 9 |
| †K. M. Krikken c Whitticase b Parsons | 9 | – c Boon b Gidley | 65 |
| D. G. Cork c Whitaker b Wilkinson | 28 | – not out | 22 |
| A. E. Warner c Hepworth b Parsons | 46 | – c Millns b Hepworth | 6 |
| S. J. Base b Maguire | 36 | – c Wilkinson b Gidley | 8 |
| R. W. Sladdin not out | 4 | | |
| B 4, l-b 5 | 9 | B 1, l-b 6, w 1, n-b 5 | 13 |

1/2 2/58 3/58 4/60 5/60      **274**    1/39 2/51 3/152    (9 wkts dec.) **447**
6/79 7/127 8/206 9/251                 4/175 5/288 6/396
                                  7/421 8/439 9/447

Bonus points – Derbyshire 3, Leicestershire 4 (Score at 100 overs: 274-9).

Bowling: *First Innings*—Millns 24–5–63–1; Maguire 23.2–4–67–5; Wilkinson 26–5–59–2; Parsons 16–5–44–2; Potter 11–2–32–0. *Second Innings*—Millns 15–1–68–0; Parsons 10–1–45–1; Wilkinson 20–2–81–2; Maguire 20–5–62–1; Gidley 11.4–0–58–2; Potter 20–3–69–1; Hepworth 8–1–57–2.

### Leicestershire

| | | | | |
|---|---|---|---|---|
| T. J. Boon c Krikken b Cork | 0 | – c Krikken b Warner | 40 |
| *N. E. Briers c Azharuddin b Warner | 10 | – c Barnett b Cork | 3 |
| G. J. Parsons lbw b Cork | 0 | – (8) not out | 10 |
| P. N. Hepworth c Barnett b Base | 22 | – (3) c Barnett b Warner | 7 |
| J. J. Whitaker c Krikken b Warner | 12 | – (4) c Azharuddin b Sladdin | 85 |
| L. Potter lbw b Barnett | 24 | – (5) c Morris b Sladdin | 64 |
| †P. Whitticase c Krikken b Base | 0 | – (6) c Azharuddin b Bowler | 33 |
| M. I. Gidley c Barnett b Sladdin | 80 | – (7) c Azharuddin b Bowler | 0 |
| D. J. Millns c and b Sladdin | 12 | – b Bowler | 0 |
| C. W. Wilkinson c Base b Barnett | 6 | – c Base b Sladdin | 22 |
| J. N. Maguire not out | 44 | – run out | 20 |
| B 4, l-b 11, n-b 10 | 25 | W 1, n-b 6 | 7 |

1/0 2/0 3/28 4/43 5/53      **235**    1/11 2/23 3/84 4/173 5/237    **291**
6/53 7/111 8/130 9/139                 6/237 7/237 8/237 9/263

Bonus points – Leicestershire 2, Derbyshire 4.

Bowling: *First Innings*—Cork 18–3–38–2; Warner 21–5–76–2; Base 15–7–28–2; Barnett 27–5–49–2; Sladdin 17.1–4–29–2. *Second Innings*—Cork 20–3–74–1; Base 22–7–54–0; Warner 17–5–55–2; Sladdin 30.4–11–60–3; Goldsmith 4–1–7–0; Bowler 11–2–41–3.

Umpires: J. C. Balderstone and G. I. Burgess.

## LEICESTERSHIRE v ESSEX

At Leicester, September 10, 11, 12, 13. Essex won by nine wickets. Essex 24 pts, Leicestershire 5 pts. Toss: Essex. Aware that the Championship pennant would be theirs with victory here if Warwickshire failed to beat Northamptonshire at Edgbaston, Essex gambled on the frailty of Leicestershire's batting and chose to bowl first. The decision seemed the right one as Foster, in a hostile opening spell, claimed four wickets for 14 in nine overs. But Essex were then stopped in their tracks by two Yorkshiremen, Hepworth and Whitaker, who combined in a 204-run partnership for the fifth wicket. Both made centuries, Whitaker hitting eighteen fours in his 105 and Hepworth 21 in his maiden Championship hundred, an innings which confirmed his emergence as a highly talented batsman after being dropped down the order from No. 3 to No. 6. The Essex reply, however, was even more impressive, launched by an opening partnership of 189 in 40 overs between Gooch (eleven fours) and Stephenson (two sixes, seventeen fours). Hussain and Garnham pressed on with 316 for the fifth wicket, a county record, and Essex established a first-innings lead of 268 soon after lunch on the third day. Hussain's 196 contained a six and 28 fours, while Garnham's second hundred in consecutive innings was a career best. Whitaker batted well again as Leicestershire fought to stay in contention, failing by 17 runs to become the first Leicestershire batsman for 26 years to score centuries in both innings. But once Essex had broken his gallant fourth-wicket stand of 112 with Potter, Leicestershire lost their next six wickets for 86 runs. Essex, left to score just 23, won handsomely early on the final afternoon.

*Close of play:* First day, Leicestershire 353; Second day, Essex 405-4 (N. Hussain 107*, M. A. Garnham 66*); Third day, Leicestershire 203-3 (J. J. Whitaker 82*, L. Potter 45*).

## Leicestershire

| | | | | |
|---|---|---|---|---|
| T. J. Boon c Prichard b Foster | 12 | – c Hussain b Childs | 15 |
| *N. E. Briers c Gooch b Foster | 3 | – c Garnham b Foster | 22 |
| J. J. Whitaker c sub b Topley | 105 | – c Prichard b Childs | 83 |
| J. D. R. Benson c Gooch b Foster | 0 | – c Hussain b Childs | 16 |
| L. Potter lbw b Foster | 0 | – c Gooch b Pringle | 45 |
| P. N. Hepworth b Foster | 115 | – lbw b Such | 17 |
| C. C. Lewis c Gooch b Topley | 49 | – c Hussain b Foster | 17 |
| M. I. Gidley run out | 6 | – c Such b Childs | 5 |
| †P. Whitticase c Childs b Pringle | 10 | – not out | 21 |
| D. J. Millns c Foster b Topley | 28 | – c Hussain b Such | 0 |
| J. N. Maguire not out | 9 | – lbw b Foster | 16 |
| L-b 6, w 1, n-b 9 | 16 | B 16, l-b 11, n-b 6 | 33 |
| | **353** | | **290** |

1/5 2/18 3/27 4/27 5/231          353          1/38 2/54 3/92 4/204 5/208          290
6/271 7/299 8/304 9/337                          6/226 7/239 8/254 9/254

Bonus points – Leicestershire 4, Essex 4 (Score at 100 overs: 349-9).

Bowling: *First Innings*—Foster 27–7–86–5; Pringle 25.4–5–78–1; Topley 18–1–91–3; Gooch 7–2–29–0; Childs 15–7–24–0; Such 10–1–21–0; Salim Malik 3–1–18–0; Stephenson 1–1–0–0. *Second Innings*—Foster 22.5–3–71–3; Pringle 14–5–22–1; Topley 3–0–6–0; Childs 39–16–82–4; Such 15–3–53–2; Salim Malik 5–0–29–0.

## Essex

| | | |
|---|---|---|
| *G. A. Gooch lbw b Lewis | 68 – not out | 18 |
| J. P. Stephenson c Whitaker b Maguire | 113 – b Hepworth | 5 |
| P. J. Prichard c Benson b Lewis | 9 – not out | 2 |
| Salim Malik lbw b Lewis | 16 | |
| N. Hussain c sub b Maguire | 196 | |
| †M. A. Garnham c Hepworth b Potter | 123 | |
| D. R. Pringle not out | 45 | |
| N. A. Foster c Gidley b Potter | 3 | |
| T. D. Topley c Gidley b Potter | 7 | |
| J. H. Childs c Benson b Maguire | 9 | |
| P. M. Such b Potter | 2 | |
| B 8, l-b 15, w 5, n-b 2 | 30 | B 2, l-b 1 ............. 3 |

1/189 2/209 3/223 4/232 5/548          621       1/14          (1 wkt) 28
6/560 7/567 8/586 9/614

Bonus points – Essex 4, Leicestershire 1 (Score at 100 overs: 403-4).

Bowling: *First Innings*—Millns 17-1-96-0; Lewis 35-6-101-3; Maguire 41-5-157-3; Potter 31.5-5-116-4; Gidley 18-5-56-0; Hepworth 6-0-30-0; Benson 6-0-42-0. *Second Innings*—Potter 4.3-2-13-0; Hepworth 4-1-12-1.

Umpires: M. J. Kitchen and K. E. Palmer.

At Canterbury, September 17, 18, 19, 20. LEICESTERSHIRE beat KENT by 90 runs.

---

## FIELDING IN 1991

### (Qualification: 20 dismissals)

| | | | | |
|---|---|---|---|---|
| 76 | C. P. Metson (73 ct, 3 st) | | 26 | †G. A. Hick |
| 70 | *S. A. Marsh (66 ct, 4 st) | | 25 | K. J. Barnett |
| 62 | B. N. French (54 ct, 8 st) | | 25 | J. E. Emburey |
| 62 | M. A. Garnham (all ct) | | 25 | Salim Malik |
| 62 | P. Moores (56 ct, 6 st) | | 24 | M. Azharuddin |
| 62 | S. J. Rhodes (54 ct, 8 st) | | 24 | †A. J. Stewart |
| 61 | K. M. Krikken (58 ct, 3 st) | | 24 | V. P. Terry |
| 54 | P. Farbrace (46 ct, 8 st) | | 23 | R. P. Davis |
| 54 | N. F. Sargeant (46 ct, 8 st) | | 22 | G. A. Gooch |
| 53 | A. N. Aymes (51 ct, 2 st) | | 21 | D. Byas |
| 52 | R. C. Russell (48 ct, 4 st) | | 21 | D. B. D'Oliveira |
| 48 | K. J. Piper (all ct) | | 21 | R. J. Harden |
| 47 | P. Whitticase (44 ct, 3 st) | | 21 | A. J. Lamb |
| 46 | W. K. Hegg (43 ct, 3 st) | | 21 | J. W. Lloyds |
| 45 | R. J. Blakey (40 ct, 5 st) | | 21 | T. J. G. O'Gorman |
| 43 | N. D. Burns (35 ct, 8 st) | | 21 | P. R. Pollard |
| 43 | D. Ripley (41 ct, 2 st) | | 21 | L. Potter |
| 38 | N. Hussain | | 21 | R. C. J. Williams (18 ct, 3 st) |
| 36 | †K. R. Brown | | 20 | C. L. Hooper |
| 36 | T. M. Moody | | 20 | D. P. Ostler |
| 31 | R. J. Maru | | 20 | P. E. Robinson |
| 27 | D. Williams (24 ct, 3 st) | | 20 | C. J. Tavaré |

* *S. A. Marsh took one catch in the field.*
  † *K. R. Brown took one catch, G. A. Hick three catches and A. J. Stewart twelve catches as wicket-keeper.*

# MIDDLESEX

*Patron:* HRH The Duke of Edinburgh
*President:* D. C. S. Compton
*Chairman:* M. P. Murray
*Chairman, Cricket Committee:* R. A. Gale
*Secretary:* J. Hardstaff
   Lord's Cricket Ground, St John's Wood,
   London NW8 8QN (Telephone: 071-289 1300)
*Captain:* M. W. Gatting
*Coach:* D. Bennett

Mike Gatting did his best to galvanise Middlesex with dynamic batting and enterprising captaincy as a nightmare of a season wore remorselessly on. Nothing worked until August, when his team achieved a victory, over Derbyshire, so late that it was almost an afterthought. With the resumption of the four-day games at the end of the month there were two more wins, but the last match saw the abject surrender of their title to Essex, who dismissed them for 51 in 24.3 overs at Chelmsford. A final position of fifteenth was the worst decline by a previous season's winner in Championship history, though in 1986 they sank from first to twelfth, and they had set the existing record with their plunge from joint-champions to fourteenth in 1950.

As the draws and defeats tumbled over each other, and the limited-overs competitions failed to provide any compensation, the toast was "absent friends". Many counties overcome the loss of key players through injury, unavailability or Test calls, but Middlesex were handicapped by all three, which intensified the impact of Desmond Haynes's absence with the West Indian tourists, the only one they could have anticipated. The county had been reluctant to recruit a temporary overseas player, arguing that in any case there was nobody appropriate, and as a result Gatting was left with the burden of being principal batsman, often surrounded by near novices.

Angus Fraser's hip injury restricted him to fewer than 40 overs (in which he underlined his value with six wickets), Ricardo Ellcock dropped out after four first-class matches with back problems, and prolonged injuries to Simon Hughes and the promising Dean Headley further depleted the struggling pace attack. But the saddest note of a sorry season was struck by Paul Downton's sudden retirement, brought about by the after-effects of his eye injury in 1990. It robbed the county of not only a fine wicket-keeper but also an ideal No. 6 batsman and team man.

In addition to these losses, Mark Ramprakash was called up by England at the start of the international summer, and in August the selectors recalled Philip Tufnell. It could be argued that a county like Middlesex, with six Championships in fifteen years, should have had the resources to overcome such depredations. This time, though, the reserves, and in some cases the understudies for the reserves, could not deliver. Ironically, this may have been a by-product of the successes of 1990; there had been little opportunity for such players when the top five batsmen played throughout the Championship and the main bowlers did not require prolonged reinforcement. Gatting also believed that the standard of Second Eleven cricket had dropped since his youth, and that newer players had not been hardened by competing regularly against opponents with long first-team experience. He pointed to the disappointing returns of Ian Hutchinson, Jason Pooley and Matthew Keech when they tried to reproduce their Second Eleven form – though Hutchinson did make two hundreds early on.

When it was made public that Haynes would not be replaced, many asked: "How do you make up 2,036 runs?" The question was rhetorical, but the answer was provided rather neatly; in the Championship the three main openers scored 2,049 between them. But only Mike Roseberry, with 1,222 of those, could be satisfied with his efforts. Further down the order, Keith Brown had a tougher time than in the previous season, when he thrived on batsmen's pitches against a flat-seamed ball, often after the higher order had already taken heavy toll of the bowling.

Gatting took out his increasing irritation on opposing attacks, and in reaching 2,000 runs in the Championship for the first time he topped his already towering standards of the previous decade. Afflicted by hamstring and back trouble, he sometimes chose to bat down the order, to give others extra responsibility, but all too often he found himself trailing in to repair the wreckage.

In the past, Middlesex had managed to survive when their batting was shaky because the bowlers could be relied on to make up the shortcomings. That did not happen in 1991. The demands of the pace attack fell squarely on Norman Cowans and Neil Williams, and it was not surprising that Cowans flagged so much that he did not take more than one wicket per innings after July 22. Not until September, when their spin claimed 30 of the 40 wickets in Middlesex's two late victories, did John Emburey and Tufnell settle into their previous year's role as a match-winning pair.

As early as the second game there was a hint that the Championship campaign might not run smoothly. Sussex, bottom of the table in 1990, had the assurance to outplay Middlesex by ten wickets with a day to spare. But the disastrous course of the summer was determined in eight matches between mid-June and the start of August. The six defeats in this spell were by substantial margins – 129 runs, 113 runs, 93 runs, six wickets, four wickets and five wickets. Middlesex either set targets, and saw them achieved, or were given a run-chase, and lost. During the season Gatting declared behind on the first innings six times. "It was maddeningly frustrating", he said. "We ended up setting ridiculous targets, because either you have a game of cricket or you don't, and I would rather play a meaningful game."

In the Benson and Hedges Cup, Middlesex subsided to the bottom of a strong group after beating Somerset, who later knocked them out of the NatWest Bank Trophy in the second round. (On a first-round trip to Ireland, Middlesex had symbolically lost the Championship pennant.) The Refuge Assurance League provided a familiar story. Early progress raised hopes at the halfway mark of reaching the Refuge Assurance Cup. But that minute compensation proved an illusion, and eleventh place emphasised yet again that 40-overs cricket was not really Middlesex's game, in good seasons or in bad. – *Terry Cooper*.

500

MIDDLESEX 1991

[Bill Smith]

Back row: R. J. Sims, T. A. Radford, R. M. Ellcock, J. C. Pooley, P. N. Weekes, M. Keech, A. Habib. Middle row: H. P. Sharp (scorer), D. Bennett (coach), P. Farbrace, C. W. Taylor, A. A. Barnett, M. R. Ramprakash, M. A. Roseberry, I. J. F. Hutchinson, D. W. Headley, S. Shephard (physiotherapist), A. Jones (2nd XI scorer): Front row: N. F. Williams, P. C. R. Tufnell, N. G. Cowans, J. E. Emburey, M. W. Gatting (captain), P. R. Downton, K. R. Brown, A. R. C. Fraser.

# MIDDLESEX RESULTS

*All first-class matches – Played 25: Won 3, Lost 10, Drawn 12.*

*County Championship matches – Played 22: Won 3, Lost 9, Drawn 10.*

*Bonus points – Batting 48, Bowling 63.*

*Competition placings – Britannic Assurance County Championship, 15th;*
*NatWest Bank Trophy, 2nd round; Benson and Hedges Cup, 5th in Group B;*
*Refuge Assurance League, 11th.*

## BRITANNIC ASSURANCE CHAMPIONSHIP AVERAGES

### BATTING

|  | *Birthplace* | *M* | *I* | *NO* | *R* | *HI* | *Avge* |
|---|---|---|---|---|---|---|---|
| ‡M. W. Gatting ..... | *Kingsbury* | 21 | 37 | 11 | 2,044 | 215* | 78.61 |
| ‡M. R. Ramprakash . | *Bushey* | 12 | 22 | 4 | 877 | 119 | 48.72 |
| ‡K. R. Brown ....... | *Edmonton* | 21 | 36 | 6 | 1,069 | 143* | 35.63 |
| ‡M. A. Roseberry .. | *Houghton-le-Spring* | 21 | 40 | 3 | 1,222 | 119* | 33.02 |
| P. N. Weekes ..... | *Hackney, London* | 6 | 11 | 1 | 249 | 86 | 24.90 |
| I. J. F. Hutchinson.. | *Welshpool* | 11 | 20 | 1 | 437 | 125 | 23.00 |
| ‡J. E. Emburey...... | *Peckham* | 21 | 29 | 3 | 586 | 74 | 22.53 |
| J. C. Pooley ....... | *Hammersmith, London* | 11 | 20 | 0 | 390 | 88 | 19.50 |
| M. Keech ......... | *Hampstead* | 14 | 22 | 2 | 362 | 58* | 18.10 |
| D. W. Headley .... | *Norton, Stourbridge* | 11 | 14 | 1 | 202 | 76 | 15.53 |
| P. Farbrace........ | *Ash, Kent* | 19 | 26 | 5 | 317 | 50 | 15.09 |
| ‡N. F. Williams .... | *Hope Well, St Vincent* | 16 | 24 | 3 | 296 | 77 | 14.09 |
| C. W. Taylor ..... | *Banbury* | 7 | 5 | 0 | 59 | 21 | 11.80 |
| ‡N. G. Cowans ..... | *Enfield St Mary, Jamaica* | 20 | 26 | 10 | 146 | 23* | 9.12 |
| ‡P. C. R. Tufnell ... | *Barnet* | 17 | 18 | 4 | 120 | 31* | 8.57 |

Also batted: A. A. Barnett (*Malaga, Spain*) (2 matches) 1*, 11*; ‡P. R. Downton (*Farnborough, Kent*) (3 matches) 51*, 38, 24*; R. M. Ellcock (*Bridgetown, Barbados*) (3 matches) 26*; ‡A. R. C. Fraser (*Billinge*) (2 matches) 12, 0; ‡S. P. Hughes (*Kingston-upon-Thames*) (3 matches) 1, 0*, 2; S. A. Sylvester (*Chalfont St Giles*) (1 match) 0.

*\* Signifies not out.* *‡ Denotes county cap.*

The following played a total of fourteen three-figure innings for Middlesex in County Championship matches – M. W. Gatting 8, I. J. F. Hutchinson 2, M. R. Ramprakash 2, K. R. Brown 1, M. A. Roseberry 1.

### BOWLING

|  | *O* | *M* | *R* | *W* | *BB* | *5W/i* | *Avge* |
|---|---|---|---|---|---|---|---|
| P. C. R. Tufnell ...... | 733.4 | 199 | 1,818 | 70 | 7-116 | 5 | 25.97 |
| C. W. Taylor ......... | 147 | 30 | 480 | 18 | 3-35 | 0 | 26.66 |
| J. E. Emburey........ | 848.5 | 228 | 2,031 | 64 | 7-71 | 1 | 31.73 |
| A. A. Barnett........ | 107.4 | 23 | 329 | 10 | 4-119 | 0 | 32.90 |
| N. F. Williams ...... | 477.2 | 89 | 1,474 | 41 | 5-89 | 1 | 35.95 |
| N. G. Cowans ....... | 485.2 | 121 | 1,370 | 34 | 4-42 | 0 | 40.29 |
| D. W. Headley ...... | 309.2 | 44 | 1,180 | 28 | 5-46 | 2 | 42.14 |

Also bowled: K. R. Brown 3–0–17–1; R. M. Ellcock 50–9–189–7; P. Farbrace 4.1–0–64–1; A. R. C. Fraser 39.5–12–91–6; M. W. Gatting 28–4–90–0; S. P. Hughes 70.5–14–270–5; I. J. F. Hutchinson 6–0–11–0; M. Keech 11–6–16–0; M. R. Ramprakash 5–1–25–1; M. A. Roseberry 9–1–36–0; S. A. Sylvester 20–2–98–0; P. N. Weekes 56.4–12–188–7.

**Wicket-keepers:** P. Farbrace 44 ct, 8 st; P. R. Downton 8 ct, 1 st; K. R. Brown 1 ct.

**Leading Fielders:** K. R. Brown 32, J. E. Emburey 21, M. A. Roseberry 16.

At Lord's, April 16, 17, 18, 19. MIDDLESEX drew with MCC.

## MIDDLESEX v YORKSHIRE

At Lord's, April 27, 29, 30, May 1. Drawn. Middlesex 1 pt, Yorkshire 3 pts. Toss: Yorkshire. Blakey, batting for 288 minutes and hitting fourteen fours, held Yorkshire's innings together. Headley marked his Championship début with a wicket first ball, and he repeatedly had batsmen mistiming the moving ball. It was a satisfying, five-wicket start. Only fifteen overs were possible after the opening day, with the match to all intents and purposes ending at noon on the second day. By then, however, there had already been evidence that Middlesex's top batting would prove a worry to them as the season developed.

*Close of play*: First day, Yorkshire 250-9 (P. W. Jarvis 18*, M. A. Robinson 4*); Second day, Middlesex 41-3 (M. W. Gatting 25*, K. R. Brown 12*); Third day, No play.

### Yorkshire

| | | |
|---|---|---|
| *M. D. Moxon b Cowans | 15 | P. J. Hartley b Headley ............ 1 |
| A. A. Metcalfe c Downton b Headley | 18 | J. D. Batty c Cowans b Taylor ....... 0 |
| D. Byas c Downton b Headley | 32 | M. A. Robinson c Brown b Headley ... 8 |
| †R. J. Blakey c Downton b Headley | 97 | |
| P. E. Robinson c Downton b Tufnell | 10 | B 1, l-b 11, n-b 2 .......... 14 |
| S. A. Kellett run out | 42 | |
| P. Carrick c Gatting b Emburey | 0 | 1/26 2/38 3/125 4/141 5/224      259 |
| P. W. Jarvis not out | 22 | 6/225 7/227 8/229 9/240 |

Bonus points – Yorkshire 2, Middlesex 1 (Score at 100 overs: 208-4).

Bowling: Cowans 18-3-44-1; Taylor 20-2-57-1; Headley 18-5-46-5; Emburey 32-13-55-1; Tufnell 27-10-45-1.

### Middlesex

| | | |
|---|---|---|
| I. J. F. Hutchinson lbw b Jarvis | 1 | K. R. Brown not out .............. 12 |
| J. C. Pooley c Blakey b M. A. Robinson | 3 | |
| *M. W. Gatting not out | 25 | — |
| M. R. Ramprakash lbw b Jarvis | 0 | 1/4 2/4 3/4            (3 wkts) 41 |

†P. R. Downton, J. E. Emburey, D. W. Headley, C. W. Taylor, P. C. R. Tufnell and N. G. Cowans did not bat.

Bonus point – Yorkshire 1.

Bowling: Jarvis 6-1-25-2; M. A. Robinson 6-2-16-1; Hartley 1-1-0-0.

Umpires: B. Hassan and A. A. Jones.

## MIDDLESEX v SUSSEX

At Lord's, May 9, 10, 11. Sussex won by ten wickets. Sussex 24 pts, Middlesex 4 pts. Toss: Sussex. After an even first day, Sussex won handsomely with a day to spare. Pigott began a match in which he played an influential role with an early strike, and after Ramprakash, watchful for nearly four hours, Brown and Downton had effected repairs, he quickly rounded up the tail. Smith, hitting the ball with great force, put the batsmen on top for the first time: 82 runs came from the first fourteen overs on the second day, and his stand of 130 with Wells for the third wicket required only 28 overs. Even so, the Sussex innings was ebbing at 209 for six when Pigott joined Wells, and he played with rare assurance in a match-turning partnership of 122. Pigott then took two wickets to finish this day's work, and although Ramprakash on the third day provided an artistic defiance which featured fifteen fours, and outlasted Wells's five-hour innings for Sussex, there was no way back for Middlesex. Moores, promoted to open because of Smith's back injury, was commanding as Sussex raced to victory, hitting fifteen fours in his unbeaten 86.

*Close of play*: First day, Sussex 87-2 (D. M. Smith 38*, A. P. Wells 14*); Second day, Middlesex 46-3 (M. R. Ramprakash 19*, K. R. Brown 15*).

## Middlesex

| | | |
|---|---|---|
| I. J. F. Hutchinson c Moores b Pigott | 5 | – c Moores b Jones | 3 |
| M. A. Roseberry b Jones | 18 | – c Greenfield b Pigott | 0 |
| *M. W. Gatting c Salisbury b Pigott | 19 | – b Pigott | 4 |
| M. R. Ramprakash c Moores b Giddins | 65 | – c Greenfield b Pigott | 119 |
| K. R. Brown lbw b North | 30 | – lbw b North | 19 |
| †P. R. Downton not out | 51 | – c Greenfield b North | 38 |
| J. E. Emburey c Salisbury b Pigott | 14 | – c Moores b Jones | 17 |
| N. F. Williams lbw b North | 0 | – lbw b Pigott | 28 |
| D. W. Headley c Greenfield b Pigott | 2 | – (10) c Moores b Jones | 3 |
| P. C. R. Tufnell b Pigott | 0 | – (9) not out | 8 |
| N. G. Cowans b North | 5 | – c Hall b Jones | 2 |
| B 1, l-b 9, w 5, n-b 3 | 18 | B 3, l-b 10, w 2 | 15 |
| | **227** | | **256** |

1/7 2/37 3/45 4/98 5/183     227     1/2 2/8 3/10 4/60 5/137
6/212 7/213 8/218 9/218     6/194 7/242 8/243 9/254

Bonus points – Middlesex 2, Sussex 4.

Bowling: *First Innings*—Jones 14-3-48-1; Pigott 19-7-37-5; Giddins 14-1-43-1; North 18.3-3-65-3; Salisbury 9-1-24-0. *Second Innings*—Jones 21.4-5-65-4; Pigott 21-5-52-4; Giddins 16-2-49-0; Salisbury 16-6-22-0; North 16-3-55-2.

## Sussex

| | | |
|---|---|---|
| D. M. Smith c Downton b Emburey | 90 | |
| J. W. Hall lbw b Headley | 18 | – (1) not out | 18 |
| K. Greenfield run out | 5 | |
| *A. P. Wells c Hutchinson b Headley | 120 | |
| M. P. Speight c Downton b Emburey | 5 | |
| J. A. North c Brown b Emburey | 0 | |
| †P. Moores c Gatting b Williams | 8 | – (2) not out | 86 |
| A. C. S. Pigott b Cowans | 65 | |
| I. D. K. Salisbury c Downton b Williams | 19 | |
| A. N. Jones b Williams | 6 | |
| E. S. H. Giddins not out | 14 | |
| B 2, l-b 2, n-b 22 | 26 | L-b 4, w 1 | 5 |
| | **376** | | **(no wkt) 109** |

1/38 2/56 3/186 4/195 5/195     376     (no wkt) 109
6/209 7/331 8/337 9/346

Bonus points – Sussex 4, Middlesex 2 (Score at 100 overs: 317-6).

Bowling: *First Innings*—Cowans 25-11-86-1; Williams 29.3-4-91-3; Headley 25-2-96-2; Emburey 32-10-64-3; Tufnell 10-0-35-0. *Second Innings*—Cowans 6-1-25-0; Williams 6-1-20-0; Headley 3-0-19-0; Tufnell 6.4-1-31-0; Emburey 4-2-10-0.

Umpires: D. O. Oslear and K. E. Palmer.

At Cambridge, May 15, 16, 17. MIDDLESEX drew with CAMBRIDGE UNIVERSITY.

At Lord's, May 18, 19, 20. MIDDLESEX lost to WEST INDIANS by six wickets (See West Indian tour section).

At Hove, May 22, 23, 24. MIDDLESEX drew with SUSSEX.

At Taunton, May 25, 27, 28. MIDDLESEX drew with SOMERSET.

## MIDDLESEX v KENT

At Lord's, May 31, June 1, 3. Drawn. Middlesex 5 pts, Kent 5 pts. Toss: Middlesex. Marsh dominated the game in a way that would have been a highlight even for his distinguished predecessors as Kent's wicket-keeper, first equalling the world record of eight catches in an innings – jointly held by A. T. W. Grout and D. E. East – and then hitting the fourth century of his career. He took one more catch in Middlesex's second innings before Ellison began hitting the stumps, instead of finding the edge. As Fraser marked his first Championship appearance of the summer with four cheap wickets, it was evident that swing, especially, and movement off the pitch would dictate the play. Marsh took six of his catches on the first day, and after his name had entered the record books he was only one yard away from heading the list: the last catch went to the substitute fielder, M. V. Fleming, at first slip. Kent were poorly placed at 137 for five in their second innings, but Marsh and Ellison combined to add 145. Marsh batted for five hours and hit thirteen fours. Kent set an unrealistic target of 343 in 62 overs, and Ellison was involved in every wicket as Middlesex struggled to avoid defeat.

*Close of play:* First day, Middlesex 93-7 (K. R. Brown 13*, C. W. Taylor 0*); Second day, Kent 234-5 (R. M. Ellison 35*, S. A. Marsh 57*).

### Kent

| | | | |
|---|---|---|---|
| N. R. Taylor c Gatting b Taylor | 46 | – c Hutchinson b Embury | 64 |
| *M. R. Benson run out | 9 | – c Fraser b Taylor | 1 |
| T. R. Ward c Embury b Taylor | 12 | – lbw b Taylor | 4 |
| G. R. Cowdrey c Farbrace b Fraser | 25 | – lbw b Taylor | 20 |
| C. S. Cowdrey lbw b Fraser | 6 | – c Gatting b Fraser | 38 |
| R. M. Ellison c Farbrace b Fraser | 7 | – c Brown b Embury | 60 |
| †S. A. Marsh c Gatting b Taylor | 6 | – not out | 108 |
| R. P. Davis c Farbrace b Hughes | 6 | – lbw b Williams | 5 |
| C. Penn not out | 10 | | |
| M. J. McCague c Hutchinson b Hughes | 11 | – (9) not out | 21 |
| T. A. Merrick c Farbrace b Fraser | 4 | | |
| B 8, l-b 4, n-b 6 | 18 | B 3, l-b 12, n-b 9 | 24 |

1/15 2/59 3/76 4/87 5/95                        160    1/9 2/23 3/81        (7 wkts dec.) 345
6/111 7/133 8/135 9/152                                4/118 5/137
                                                       6/282 7/305

Bonus points – Kent 1, Middlesex 4.

Bowling: *First Innings*—Hughes 12-2-46-2; Fraser 15.5-9-24-4; Williams 13-3-39-0; Taylor 13-4-35-3; Embury 1-0-4-0. *Second Innings*—Taylor 20-4-61-3; Fraser 15-1-47-1; Hughes 24-4-95-0; Williams 27-3-66-1; Embury 29-7-60-2; Hutchinson 1-0-1-0.

### Middlesex

| | | | |
|---|---|---|---|
| I. J. F. Hutchinson c Marsh b Penn | 22 | – c Marsh b Ellison | 1 |
| M. A. Roseberry c Marsh b Merrick | 2 | – b Ellison | 16 |
| *M. W. Gatting b McCague | 34 | – b Ellison | 32 |
| M. R. Ramprakash c Marsh b Ellison | 1 | – c G. R. Cowdrey b Ellison | 0 |
| K. R. Brown not out | 47 | – not out | 76 |
| J. E. Embury c Taylor b Ellison | 5 | – b Ellison | 16 |
| N. F. Williams c Marsh b Ellison | 0 | – c Ellison b McCague | 8 |
| †P. Farbrace c Marsh b Merrick | 0 | – not out | 7 |
| C. W. Taylor c Marsh b Merrick | 21 | | |
| A. R. C. Fraser c Marsh b Ellison | 12 | | |
| S. P. Hughes c sub b Davis | 1 | | |
| B 8, l-b 4, n-b 6 | 18 | L-b 6, w 3, n-b 2 | 11 |

1/10 2/46 3/69 4/79 5/92                        163    1/7 2/36 3/36        (6 wkts) 164
6/92 7/93 8/129 9/148                                 4/89 5/128 6/143

Bonus points – Middlesex 1, Kent 4.

Bowling: *First Innings*—McCague 9.1-4-21-1; Merrick 18-4-61-3; Davis 3.4-0-11-1; Penn 5-0-19-1; Ellison 23-9-79-4. *Second Innings*—Merrick 15.3-3-38-0; Ellison 27-3-77-5; Davis 13-4-25-0; McCague 7-0-18-1.

Umpires: B. Dudleston and P. B. Wight.

At Bristol, June 4, 5, 6. MIDDLESEX drew with GLOUCESTERSHIRE.

## MIDDLESEX v LEICESTERSHIRE

At Uxbridge, June 7, 8, 10. Drawn. Middlesex 7 pts, Leicestershire 5 pts. Toss: Middlesex. Two early wickets supported Gatting's decision to put Leicestershire in, but the visitors' middle order supplied a string of useful scores on a cold, overcast day. Smith reached his maiden first-class fifty, with a six over third man, in 79 balls. Roseberry, eliminating risky shots, held the Middlesex innings together, and he was into his sixth hour at the crease when he passed 100; even on this fast-scoring ground he had hit only six fours. With Ellcock and Taylor injured, Emburey opened the Middlesex bowling on the second evening, but he resumed his normal craft on the final day, when Leicestershire yielded gradually to the home side's spin attack. Emburey had one spell of 69 balls with no run coming from the bat, and Tufnell took five wickets for 21 runs in 47 balls. By then, though, breaks for rain had militated against a win. Middlesex's notional target was 232 at more than 7 runs an over, and 180 from the final twenty overs was regarded as impossible.

*Close of play:* First day, Middlesex 4-0 (I. J. F. Hutchinson 0*, M. A. Roseberry 2*); Second day, Leicestershire 47-0 (T. J. Boon 22*, N. E. Briers 21*).

### Leicestershire

| | | | |
|---|---|---|---|
| T. J. Boon c Farbrace b Ellcock | 11 | – c Roseberry b Tufnell | 33 |
| *N. E. Briers b Taylor | 0 | – c Brown b Emburey | 50 |
| P. N. Hepworth c Emburey b Williams | 32 | – b Emburey | 8 |
| J. J. Whitaker c Emburey b Williams | 35 | – (7) b Tufnell | 16 |
| L. Potter c Hutchinson b Emburey | 41 | – (4) c and b Emburey | 2 |
| B. F. Smith c Brown b Tufnell | 54 | – (5) st Farbrace b Tufnell | 17 |
| P. Willey not out | 42 | – (6) st Farbrace b Tufnell | 26 |
| †P. Whitticase c Williams b Taylor | 9 | – c Farbrace b Tufnell | 0 |
| D. J. Millns c Roseberry b Tufnell | 44 | – b Tufnell | 10 |
| C. W. Wilkinson c Brown b Williams | 0 | – c Hutchinson b Emburey | 8 |
| J. N. Maguire c Gatting b Williams | 2 | – not out | 1 |
| B 1, l-b 5, w 5, n-b 10 | 21 | B 6, l-b 7, w 3, n-b 5 | 21 |
| | **291** | | **192** |

1/6 2/18 3/72 4/99 5/149     291     1/70 2/99 3/100 4/103 5/144     192
6/209 7/224 8/285 9/285              6/159 7/160 8/179 9/186

Bonus points – Leicestershire 3, Middlesex 4.

Bowling: *First Innings*—Ellcock 7-3-22-1; Taylor 16-1-84-2; Williams 22.4-3-79-4; Emburey 14-3-43-1; Tufnell 22-5-57-2. *Second Innings*—Emburey 37.5-17-59-4; Williams 11-1-31-0; Tufnell 36-6-82-6; Keech 2-0-7-0.

### Middlesex

| | | | |
|---|---|---|---|
| I. J. F. Hutchinson c Whitticase b Maguire | 12 | – not out | 29 |
| M. A. Roseberry not out | 119 | – not out | 44 |
| *M. W. Gatting c Willey b Wilkinson | 6 | | |
| K. R. Brown lbw b Millns | 30 | | |
| M. Keech c Millns b Willey | 16 | | |
| J. E. Emburey lbw b Millns | 24 | | |
| N. F. Williams not out | 19 | | |
| B 6, l-b 3, n-b 17 | 26 | L-b 1, n-b 2 | 3 |
| | **252** | | **76** |

1/52 2/64 3/106 4/146 5/200     (5 wkts dec.) 252     (no wkt) 76

†P. Farbrace, C. W. Taylor, P. C. R. Tufnell and R. M. Ellcock did not bat.

Bonus points – Middlesex 3, Leicestershire 2.

Bowling: *First Innings*—Millns 21-1-95-2; Maguire 29-8-70-1; Wilkinson 25-8-41-1; Willey 17.4-6-37-1. *Second Innings*—Millns 7-1-18-0; Maguire 4-0-15-0; Hepworth 4-1-20-0; Willey 6-1-11-0; Wilkinson 2-0-10-0; Smith 1-0-1-0.

Umpires: M. J. Kitchen and R. C. Tolchard.

At Cardiff, June 14, 15, 17. MIDDLESEX lost to GLAMORGAN by 129 runs.

At Sheffield, June 21, 22, 24. MIDDLESEX drew with YORKSHIRE.

## MIDDLESEX v ESSEX

At Lord's, June 28, 29, July 1. Essex won by 113 runs. Essex 20 pts, Middlesex 5 pts. Toss: Essex. Middlesex took four wickets in the first session, only for Prichard and Garnham to bat with growing fluency through the rest of a rain-hit day. Prichard's hundred contained seventeen fours, and on the second morning Garnham all but doubled his score with significant ease. The afternoon brought cheer to the Middlesex watchers, with Gatting and Ramprakash adding 163 in 29 overs. Gatting battered the pace bowlers and dealt with the spinners with his usual authority. He hit seventeen fours and four sixes, and had faced 176 balls by the time he declared 49 runs in arrears. There was more class batting as Gooch was made to work for his first 45 runs, but the loss of the morning session on Monday led to his being fed the runs which provided his century; his last 61 runs came from fifteen scoring shots. The target set Middlesex was 251 in 66 overs, but with Gatting unable to bat until No. 8, because of back trouble, the day belonged to the Essex fast bowlers. Foster was hostile and straight, Pringle took three wickets in nine deliveries, and Andrew swept aside the last three batsmen in the space of six.

*Close of play:* First day, Essex 237-4 (P. J. Prichard 113*, M. A. Garnham 46*); Second day, Essex 86-2 (G. A. Gooch 45*, J. H. Childs 0*).

### Essex

| | | |
|---|---|---|
| *G. A. Gooch c Farbrace b Williams | 47 | – c Roseberry b Farbrace ..........106 |
| J. P. Stephenson c Farbrace b Cowans | 2 | – c Hughes b Tufnell ............... 38 |
| P. J. Prichard c Hutchinson b Cowans | 129 | – b Tufnell ........................ 0 |
| Salim Malik c Emburey b Tufnell | 8 | – (5) not out ...................... 12 |
| N. Hussain c and b Tufnell | 0 | |
| †M. A. Garnham not out | 91 | |
| D. R. Pringle not out | 0 | |
| J. H. Childs (did not bat) | | – (4) not out ...................... 41 |
| B 4, l-b 10, n-b 12 | 26 | L-b 3, w 1 .................... 4 |

1/7 2/88 3/113 4/117 5/291      (5 wkts dec.) 303     1/84 2/84 3/185     (3 wkts dec.) 201

N. A. Foster, S. J. W. Andrew and P. M. Such did not bat.

Bonus points – Essex 4, Middlesex 2.

Bowling: *First Innings*—Cowans 23–6–61–2; Williams 28.4–7–89–1; Hughes 12–1–71–0; Emburey 8–0–33–0; Tufnell 14–5–35–2. *Second Innings*—Cowans 7–2–29–0; Williams 3.1–2–4–0; Hughes 3.5–0–13–0; Emburey 9–2–50–0; Tufnell 6–2–16–2; Hutchinson 1–0–1–0; Roseberry 2–0–21–0; Farbrace 4.1–0–64–1.

### Middlesex

| | | |
|---|---|---|
| I. J. F. Hutchinson c Gooch b Foster | 4 | – c Salim Malik b Foster ......... 3 |
| M. A. Roseberry lbw b Stephenson | 24 | – lbw b Foster .................... 19 |
| *M. W. Gatting not out | 138 | – (8) not out ..................... 11 |
| M. R. Ramprakash not out | 70 | – (3) lbw b Foster ............... 12 |
| K. R. Brown (did not bat) | | – (4) c Foster b Pringle.......... 23 |
| J. E. Emburey (did not bat) | | – (5) lbw b Pringle .............. 46 |
| †P. Farbrace (did not bat) | | – (6) c Garnham b Foster ......... 4 |
| N. F. Williams (did not bat) | | – (7) c Garnham b Pringle........ 0 |
| S. P. Hughes (did not bat) | | – c Hussain b Andrew ............ 2 |
| P. C. R. Tufnell (did not bat) | | – c Garnham b Andrew ........... 4 |
| N. G. Cowans (did not bat) | | – c and b Andrew ............... 0 |
| B 4, l-b 6, n-b 8 | 18 | L-b 6, n-b 7 ................ 13 |

1/14 2/91       (2 wkts dec.) 254     1/11 2/38 3/45 4/107 5/114     137
                                            6/114 7/122 8/131 9/136

Bonus points – Middlesex 3.

Bowling: *First Innings*—Foster 14.2–1–62–1; Andrew 18–6–71–0; Pringle 13–2–44–0; Stephenson 6–2–16–1; Such 5–0–22–0; Childs 5–0–29–0. *Second Innings*—Foster 16–6–36–4; Andrew 14–4–30–3; Pringle 14–5–38–3; Childs 8–2–27–0.

Umpires: J. C. Balderstone and D. R. Shepherd.

At Birmingham, July 2, 3, 4. MIDDLESEX lost to WARWICKSHIRE by 93 runs.

## MIDDLESEX v NORTHAMPTONSHIRE

At Uxbridge, July 16, 17, 18. Drawn. Middlesex 7 pts, Northamptonshire 5 pts. Toss: Northamptonshire. Fordham's confident driving was the mainspring in Northamptonshire's start, which brought 100 up in 27 overs. Later, batting became much harder work against Emburey and Tufnell, and the run-rate was torpid. Ripley organised a useful total on the second morning. Cook was on the point of mastering the Middlesex batsmen when Gatting, batting down the order because of a cold, dismissively put the Northamptonshire spinners in their place. He hit Roberts for three fours and a six in one over, and hammered 16 off one of Cook's; his unbeaten century needed only 89 balls, and included fifteen fours and two sixes. When Northamptonshire batted a second time, Tufnell was on after one over, and his two wickets before the close increased the chances of a good finish. Instead, rain prevented any play on the final day.

*Close of play:* First day, Northamptonshire 286-8 (D. Ripley 2*, A. R. Roberts 4*); Second day, Northamptonshire 43-2 (R. J. Bailey 20*, A. J. Lamb 12*).

## Northamptonshire

| | | | | |
|---|---|---|---|---|
| A. Fordham c Pooley b Cowans | 85 | – c Emburey b Tufnell | 4 |
| N. A. Felton c Farbrace b Ramprakash | 55 | – c Brown b Tufnell | 6 |
| R. J. Bailey c Farbrace b Cowans | 51 | – not out | 20 |
| *A. J. Lamb st Farbrace b Tufnell | 1 | – not out | 12 |
| D. J. Capel c Farbrace b Tufnell | 36 | | |
| K. M. Curran lbw b Emburey | 32 | | |
| E. A. E. Baptiste c and b Tufnell | 3 | | |
| R. G. Williams b Tufnell | 0 | | |
| †D. Ripley not out | 43 | | |
| A. R. Roberts c Tufnell b Emburey | 10 | | |
| N. G. B. Cook b Cowans | 14 | | |
| B 1, l-b 11, n-b 6 | 18 | N-b 1 | 1 |

1/128 2/167 3/174 4/222 5/256      348    1/10 2/21       (2 wkts) 43
6/276 7/280 8/280 9/308

Bonus points – Northamptonshire 3, Middlesex 3 (Score at 100 overs: 284-8).

Bowling: *First Innings*—Cowans 19.2–5–57–3; Headley 15–2–74–0; Emburey 49–14–110–2; Tufnell 39–8–95–4; Ramprakash 1–1–0–1. *Second Innings*—Cowans 1–0–1–0; Tufnell 7–2–21–2; Emburey 7–1–21–0.

## Middlesex

| | | |
|---|---|---|
| M. A. Roseberry lbw b Cook | 47 | J. E. Emburey not out ............... 16 |
| J. C. Pooley c Ripley b Cook | 20 | |
| M. R. Ramprakash c Felton b Cook | 25 | B 5, l-b 5, n-b 1 ........... 11 |
| K. R. Brown c Ripley b Baptiste | 53 | |
| M. Keech c Baptiste b Williams | 31 | 1/49 2/89 3/102    (5 wkts dec.) 303 |
| *M. W. Gatting not out | 100 | 4/163 5/214 |

†P. Farbrace, D. W. Headley, P. C. R. Tufnell and N. G. Cowans did not bat.

Bonus points – Middlesex 4, Northamptonshire 2.

Bowling: Capel 5–0–19–0; Curran 6–0–21–0; Cook 30–4–120–3; Baptiste 19–4–43–1; Roberts 6–2–26–0; Williams 16.4–1–64–1.

Umpires: J. C. Balderstone and R. C. Tolchard.

## MIDDLESEX v LANCASHIRE

At Uxbridge, July 19, 20, 22. Lancashire won by six wickets. Lancashire 22 pts, Middlesex 5 pts. Toss: Middlesex. Some life in the pitch had Middlesex in trouble from the start against Wasim Akram. Roseberry toiled for three and a half hours over 63, but Gatting, still feeling the effects of a cold, scored his 41 at a run a ball, and Farbrace and Tufnell batted bravely at the end. In Lancashire's reply, Atherton was happy to bat for almost five hours, and Fairbrother played one of his rare, restrained innings as they added 129 for the third wicket in 48 overs. Almost throughout they were confronted by spin bowling, but whereas it was spin that wrapped up the Lancashire innings, Emburey taking three wickets in seven balls, it was Wasim Akram's in-swinging yorkers which cut through Middlesex's second innings. Roseberry again batted defiantly and Ramprakash worked hard before Wasim's incursions, but they betrayed their efforts with careless dismissals. Lancashire, left to get 142 in 36 overs, had plenty of aggressive batsmen to help them to victory, and it was appropriate that Wasim Akram, having taken eleven wickets in the match for 129, was there at the finish to hit the winning boundary. Afterwards it was revealed that the umpires had criticised Lancashire's general conduct on the field, without naming any player.

*Close of play:* First day, Lancashire 57-1 (G. D. Mendis 41*, M. A. Atherton 9*); Second day, Middlesex 23-0 (M. A. Roseberry 16*, J. C. Pooley 2*).

## Middlesex

| | | |
|---|---|---|
| M. A. Roseberry lbw b Wasim Akram | 63 | – run out ........ 65 |
| J. C. Pooley c Watkinson b Wasim Akram | 5 | – c Yates b Martin ........ 5 |
| M. R. Ramprakash c Fairbrother b Martin | 5 | – lbw b Watkinson ........ 56 |
| K. R. Brown c Hegg b Martin | 2 | – lbw b Wasim Akram ........ 16 |
| M. Keech b Wasim Akram | 35 | – lbw b Wasim Akram ........ 3 |
| *M. W. Gatting b Yates | 41 | – lbw b Wasim Akram ........ 27 |
| J. E. Emburey b Wasim Akram | 4 | – b Wasim Akram ........ 19 |
| †P. Farbrace c Mendis b Hughes | 42 | – lbw b Wasim Akram ........ 5 |
| N. F. Williams lbw b Wasim Akram | 0 | – not out ........ 1 |
| P. C. R. Tufnell not out | 24 | – c Atherton b Watkinson ........ 0 |
| N. G. Cowans c Wasim Akram b Hughes | 6 | – b Wasim Akram ........ |
| B 7, l-b 7, n-b 9 | 23 | B 1, l-b 10, n-b 12 ........ 23 |
| | **250** | **220** |

1/7 2/15 3/19 4/79 5/136    1/43 2/88 3/132 4/132 5/144
6/151 7/174 8/176 9/244    6/176 7/207 8/214 9/219

Bonus points – Middlesex 3, Lancashire 4.

Bowling: *First Innings*—Wasim Akram 22-4-63-5; Martin 22-5-65-2; Watkinson 9-0-41-0; Yates 20-6-60-1; Hughes 3.2-1-7-2. *Second Innings*—Wasim Akram 17.2-3-66-6; Martin 15-4-43-1; Yates 11-0-42-0; Watkinson 14-3-40-2; Hughes 14-7-18-0.

## Lancashire

| | | |
|---|---|---|
| G. D. Mendis lbw b Cowans | 43 | – b Cowans ........ 2 |
| G. Fowler b Cowans | 2 | – b Cowans ........ 34 |
| M. A. Atherton c Farbrace b Tufnell | 91 | – c Pooley b Tufnell ........ 35 |
| N. H. Fairbrother c Pooley b Cowans | 53 | |
| N. J. Speak lbw b Williams | 11 | – (4) not out ........ 25 |
| M. Watkinson c Cowans b Emburey | 35 | – (5) c Farbrace b Emburey ........ 21 |
| Wasim Akram st Farbrace b Tufnell | 63 | – (6) not out ........ 15 |
| †W. K. Hegg c Gatting b Emburey | 5 | |
| G. Yates not out | 0 | |
| *D. P. Hughes b Emburey | 0 | |
| P. J. Martin lbw b Emburey | 0 | |
| B 14, l-b 5, w 1, n-b 6 | 26 | B 9, l-b 2, w 1, n-b 1 ........ 13 |
| | **329** | **(4 wkts) 145** |

1/18 2/68 3/197 4/215 5/215    1/8 2/74 3/100 4/129
6/303 7/329 8/329 9/329

Bonus points – Lancashire 2, Middlesex 2 (Score at 100 overs: 227-5).

Bowling: *First Innings*—Williams 22-3-60-1; Cowans 24-7-51-3; Tufnell 44-16-94-2; Emburey 39.2-11-96-4; Ramprakash 1-0-9-0. *Second Innings*—Cowans 10-1-35-2; Williams 4-0-18-0; Tufnell 8-1-32-1; Emburey 11.1-0-49-1.

Umpires: J. C. Balderstone and R. C. Tolchard.

## MIDDLESEX v NOTTINGHAMSHIRE

At Lord's, July 26, 27, 29. Nottinghamshire won by four wickets. Nottinghamshire 22 pts, Middlesex 5 pts. Toss: Middlesex. The Middlesex top-order batting was in no state to cope with Stephenson in his testing opening spell, and the contributions from the middle order were insufficient. However, Williams kept Middlesex in the game with his two wickets and spectacular run-out of Pollard on the first evening, and when he took two more wickets next day, Nottinghamshire urgently needed French's unbeaten half-century to gain a first-innings lead. Pooley reached 50 for the first time in a first-class match, and Gatting powered on in typical fashion, scoring 143 not out from 208 balls with nineteen fours. He and Keech put on 121 in 26 overs before the declaration gave Nottinghamshire 66 overs in which to score 282. Tufnell was ill, and when Williams hurt his knee, Nottinghamshire's prospects brightened. Pollard and Robinson laid a sound basis, and the match was won by an exquisite century from Johnson which contained almost every shot. He hit seventeen fours and scored his runs from 111 deliveries. The closing stages saw Stephenson strike Emburey into the Middlesex dressing-room after the penultimate over had begun with 17 runs wanted.

*Close of play:* First day, Nottinghamshire 83-3 (D. W. Randall 21*, P. Johnson 8*); Second day, Middlesex 173-2 (M. W. Gatting 71*, K. R. Brown 25*).

### Middlesex

| | | | |
|---|---:|---|---:|
| M. A. Roseberry c Pollard b Stephenson | 2 | – c French b Stephenson | 4 |
| J. C. Pooley lbw b Stephenson | 11 | – c Evans b Field-Buss | 58 |
| *M. W. Gatting lbw b Stephenson | 5 | – not out | 143 |
| K. R. Brown c Pollard b Evans | 38 | – c French b Pick | 42 |
| M. Keech c Broad b Stephenson | 32 | – not out | 58 |
| J. E. Emburey c French b Pick | 34 | | |
| †P. Farbrace c Broad b Pick | 20 | | |
| N. F. Williams c Pollard b Hemmings | 9 | | |
| D. W. Headley not out | 19 | | |
| P. C. R. Tufnell c Robinson b Hemmings | 1 | | |
| N. G. Cowans b Evans | 9 | | |
| B 4, l-b 3, n-b 7 | 14 | L-b 17, n-b 8 | 25 |
| | **194** | (3 wkts dec.) | **330** |

1/2 2/8 3/44 4/85 5/113          194       1/12 2/116 3/209   (3 wkts dec.) 330
6/144 7/163 8/163 9/170

Bonus points – Middlesex 1, Nottinghamshire 4.

Bowling: *First Innings*—Stephenson 20.2–5–59–4; Pick 19–4–54–2; Evans 20.5–7–44–2; Hemmings 16–4–30–2. *Second Innings*—Stephenson 22–5–71–1; Pick 17–3–76–1; Evans 16.4–2–69–0; Hemmings 4–2–24–0; Field-Buss 18–3–73–1.

### Nottinghamshire

| | | | |
|---|---:|---|---:|
| B. C. Broad b Williams | 14 | – c Brown b Williams | 3 |
| P. R. Pollard run out | 11 | – c Headley b Emburey | 42 |
| *R. T. Robinson c Farbrace b Williams | 20 | – b Cowans | 62 |
| D. W. Randall c Farbrace b Williams | 34 | – c Brown b Emburey | 8 |
| P. Johnson c Williams b Headley | 34 | – c Emburey b Headley | 105 |
| K. P. Evans c Farbrace b Williams | 0 | – not out | 28 |
| †B. N. French not out | 58 | – run out | 2 |
| F. D. Stephenson b Emburey | 14 | – not out | 11 |
| M. G. Field-Buss c Farbrace b Cowans | 25 | | |
| E. E. Hemmings lbw b Williams | 5 | | |
| R. A. Pick c Gatting b Headley | 5 | | |
| L-b 8, w 1, n-b 14 | 23 | B 7, l-b 8, w 1, n-b 7 | 23 |
| | **243** | (6 wkts) | **284** |

1/17 2/49 3/49 4/121 5/126     243     1/7 2/71 3/101   (6 wkts) 284
6/126 7/151 8/225 9/234                4/195 5/262 6/264

Bonus points – Nottinghamshire 2, Middlesex 4.

Bowling: *First Innings*—Cowans 23–11–38–1; Williams 29–7–89–5; Headley 24.2–5–61–2; Emburey 12–6–22–1; Tufnell 10–3–25–0. *Second Innings*—Cowans 13–0–59–1; Williams 11–2–42–1; Emburey 25–6–86–2; Headley 16.1–0–82–1.

Umpires: A. G. T. Whitehead and P. B. Wight.

## MIDDLESEX v HAMPSHIRE

At Lord's, August 2, 3, 5. Hampshire won by five wickets. Hampshire 23 pts, Middlesex 6 pts.
Toss: Hampshire. Middlesex recovered well from the loss of Pooley and Gatting in Shine's
second over. On the second day, Tufnell virtually monopolised the Nursery End, his turn and
variations of flight earning him career-best figures of seven for 116. But when he wearied,
Ayling and Aymes forced Hampshire into a lead. Headley, the Middlesex night-watchman,
was one of those to benefit as Hampshire's occasional bowlers gave away 91 runs off
seventeen overs, but he deserved his highest first-class score. Hampshire, for their part, won a
target of 243 in a minimum of 50 overs. It was expecting a lot of Tufnell to match his first-
innings standards of control and penetration, especially as the pitch had become slower;
besides, once he had disposed of the Hampshire openers he was confronted by Gower and
Smith, who added 97 in 94 balls. The dismissal of Smith and Nicholas in the 49th over, with
another six to be bowled, was little more than a hiccup, and Hampshire went on to win with
two balls to spare.

*Close of play:* First day, Hampshire 54-1 (T. C. Middleton 19*, K. D. James 9*);
Second day, Middlesex 71-1 (J. C. Pooley 23*, D. W. Headley 4*).

## Middlesex

| | | | |
|---|---|---|---|
| M. A. Roseberry c Middleton b James | 47 | – c Terry b Connor | 38 |
| J. C. Pooley b Shine | 4 | – c Aymes b Connor | 27 |
| *M. W. Gatting b Shine | 0 | – (4) b Smith | 85 |
| M. R. Ramprakash c Gower b James | 79 | – (5) not out | 28 |
| K. R. Brown c James b Connor | 53 | – (6) not out | 6 |
| M. Keech c Shine b James | 0 | | |
| †P. Farbrace c Middleton b Connor | 1 | | |
| D. W. Headley c Aymes b James | 26 | – (3) st Aymes b Middleton | 76 |
| C. W. Taylor c Maru b Ayling | 11 | | |
| P. C. R. Tufnell c Maru b Ayling | 17 | | |
| N. G. Cowans not out | 4 | | |
| B 3, l-b 5, n-b 9 | 17 | L-b 7, w 3, n-b 4 | 14 |

1/6 2/6 3/103 4/178 5/178      259      1/58 2/76      (4 wkts dec.) 274
6/190 7/209 8/225 9/255               3/205 4/255

Bonus points – Middlesex 3, Hampshire 4.

Bowling: *First Innings*—Shine 15-3-70-2; Connor 18-3-61-2; Ayling 20.2-6-52-2; Maru
15-3-36-0; James 13-0-32-4. *Second Innings*—Connor 11-1-61-2; Shine 11-0-48-0; Maru
17-5-42-0; Ayling 2-0-8-0; James 8-3-17-0; Smith 9-1-55-1; Middleton 8-2-36-1.

## Hampshire

| | | | |
|---|---|---|---|
| T. C. Middleton c Gatting b Tufnell | 23 | – (2) c Farbrace b Tufnell | 32 |
| V. P. Terry c Farbrace b Tufnell | 25 | – (1) c Farbrace b Connor | 39 |
| K. D. James c Brown b Tufnell | 36 | – (6) c Taylor b Headley | 7 |
| R. A. Smith st Farbrace b Tufnell | 55 | – c Ramprakash b Tufnell | 57 |
| D. I. Gower c Headley b Tufnell | 40 | – (3) not out | 80 |
| *M. C. J. Nicholas c Gatting b Tufnell | 4 | – (5) b Tufnell | 0 |
| J. R. Ayling c Roseberry b Taylor | 58 | – not out | 10 |
| †A. N. Aymes b Cowans | 31 | | |
| R. J. Maru c Farbrace b Taylor | 0 | | |
| C. A. Connor b Tufnell | 7 | | |
| K. J. Shine not out | 4 | | |
| B 1, l-b 5, w 1, n-b 1 | 8 | B 8, l-b 9, w 2, n-b 2 | 21 |

1/36 2/73 3/99 4/173 5/187      291      1/53 2/114 3/211      (5 wkts) 246
6/192 7/260 8/260 9/275               4/211 5/234

Bonus points – Hampshire 3, Middlesex 3 (Score at 100 overs: 260-7).

Bowling: *First Innings*—Cowans 20-7-43-1; Headley 18-3-45-0; Taylor 26-9-65-2;
Tufnell 48-13-116-7; Ramprakash 3-0-16-0. *Second Innings*—Headley 14-0-50-1; Cowans
10-2-47-0; Tufnell 24.4-1-112-4; Taylor 6-1-20-0.

Umpires: B. Leadbeater and K. E. Palmer.

## MIDDLESEX v DERBYSHIRE

At Lord's, August 9, 10, 12. Middlesex won by 2 runs. Middlesex 22 pts, Derbyshire 3 pts. Toss: Middlesex. The foundation of Middlesex's first Championship win of the summer was the support which the other batsmen gave Gatting, who inevitably provided the major innings. Sharing big stands with Pooley, whose 88 was a career best, and Brown, in a third-wicket alliance of 258 which bowled along at 4.7 an over, Gatting went 1 run better than Middlesex's previous individual best against Derbyshire – 214 not out by D. C. S. Compton at Lord's in 1939. Gatting hit 28 fours in his unbeaten 215, made from 273 balls in 5 hours 40 minutes. The second day was equally fascinating as Azharuddin took on the Middlesex spinners and, with 110 from 177 balls (thirteen fours), eased Derbyshire towards the follow-on mark. Morris, battling against a mild attack of viral meningitis, made sure his skilful innings was not in vain. Embury and Barnett bowled 48 overs in tandem, and Barnett, in only his second Championship appearance, delivered 44 unchanged. On the final morning, Middlesex looked for runs and eventually set a target of 286 in a minimum of 60 overs. Bowler and Azharuddin seemed to be winning the match for Derbyshire, and after a middle-order collapse against the spinners, Krikken kept them on course, so that 10 were wanted from the last over. He hit Barnett for six, but the young left-armer then had him caught at mid-wicket. With 3 runs now needed from three balls, Morris was caught on the Grand Stand boundary off the first of them.

*Close of play:* First day, Middlesex 454-3 dec.; Second day, Derbyshire 315-6 (K. M. Krikken 40*, J. E. Morris 45*).

## Middlesex

| | | | | |
|---|---|---|---|---|
| M. A. Roseberry lbw b Base | 28 | – b Goldsmith | | 15 |
| J. C. Pooley c and b Cork | 88 | – b Mortensen | | 29 |
| *M. W. Gatting not out | 215 | – (6) retired hurt | | 2 |
| K. R. Brown c Azharuddin b Cork | 96 | – (3) c Azharuddin b Goldsmith | | 25 |
| M. Keech (did not bat) | | – (4) b Goldsmith | | 0 |
| †P. Farbrace (did not bat) | | – (5) st Krikken b Base | | 50 |
| N. G. Cowans (did not bat) | | – not out | | 16 |
| A. A. Barnett (did not bat) | | – not out | | 1 |
| B 1, l-b 16, w 2, n-b 8 | 27 | B 2, l-b 3, w 1, n-b 2 | | 8 |

1/58 2/196 3/454    (3 wkts dec.) 454    1/30 2/75 3/75    (5 wkts dec.) 146
                                          4/75 5/136

J. E. Embury, D. W. Headley and C. W. Taylor did not bat.

Bonus points – Middlesex 4 (Score at 100 overs: 412-2).

*In the second innings M. W. Gatting retired hurt at 111.*

Bowling: *First Innings*—Malcolm 18-0-95-0; Mortensen 20-2-50-0; Base 21-1-80-1; Cork 16.4-2-61-2; Goldsmith 24-1-102-0; Barnett 10-0-49-0. *Second Innings*—Cork 8-2-25-0; Goldsmith 16.2-0-62-3; Mortensen 7-2-12-1; Base 5-2-11-1; Bowler 2-0-31-0.

## Derbyshire

| | | | | |
|---|---|---|---|---|
| *K. J. Barnett c Brown b Cowans | 4 | – c Brown b Cowans | | 13 |
| P. D. Bowler c Gatting b Embury | 63 | – run out | | 89 |
| T. J. G. O'Gorman c Farbrace b Taylor | 16 | – c Roseberry b Embury | | 38 |
| M. Azharuddin c Embury b Barnett | 110 | – c Keech b Embury | | 72 |
| S. C. Goldsmith b Barnett | 1 | – (6) c Roseberry b Barnett | | 6 |
| †K. M. Krikken not out | 40 | – (7) c Brown b Barnett | | 27 |
| D. G. Cork lbw b Barnett | 18 | – (8) st Farbrace b Barnett | | 11 |
| J. E. Morris not out | 45 | – (11) c Roseberry b Barnett | | 0 |
| D. E. Malcolm (did not bat) | | – (5) b Embury | | 4 |
| S. J. Base (did not bat) | | – (9) c and b Embury | | 0 |
| O. H. Mortensen (did not bat) | | – (10) not out | | 7 |
| B 8, l-b 6, n-b 4 | 18 | B 5, l-b 5, n-b 6 | | 16 |

1/10 2/37 3/175 4/178    (6 wkts dec.) 315    1/36 2/110 3/213 4/219 5/236    283
5/218 6/246                                   6/241 7/260 8/261 9/283

Bonus points – Derbyshire 3, Middlesex 2 (Score at 100 overs: 261-6).

Bowling: *First Innings*—Cowans 12–3–35–1; Taylor 8–1–55–1; Headley 12–2–42–0; Emburey 39–19–52–1; Barnett 46–13–117–3. *Second Innings*—Cowans 10–4–35–1; Headley 6–1–23–0; Barnett 23.4–2–119–4; Emburey 26–1–96–4.

Umpires: R. Palmer and R. A. White.

At The Oval, August 20, 21, 22. MIDDLESEX drew with SURREY.

At Worcester, August 23, 24, 26. MIDDLESEX drew with WORCESTERSHIRE.

At Canterbury, August 28, 29, 30, 31. MIDDLESEX lost to KENT by 208 runs.

At Nottingham, September 3, 4, 5, 6. MIDDLESEX beat NOTTINGHAMSHIRE by 248 runs.

## MIDDLESEX v SURREY

At Lord's, September 10, 11, 12, 13. Middlesex won by 60 runs. Middlesex 22 pts, Surrey 6 pts. Toss: Middlesex. Surrey's bowlers did not take a wicket until Middlesex were past 100, but Waqar Younis, bowling his customary perfect line, more than made amends as the innings disintegrated. He beat Gatting with sheer pace. Surrey's second-wicket pair also provided what substance there was to their innings, and after Williams had disposed of Darren Bicknell and Ward in the same over, the pitch revealed its true nature as the spinners exerted a grip. Thorpe, though, found regular opportunities to drive, and his fighting display, which brought him 117 runs from 261 balls, contained eighteen fours. At 129 for seven on the third day, only 118 ahead, Middlesex looked beaten. But the game turned when Waqar, who had taken four wickets in a 34-ball spell either side of lunch, went off with a strained leg. This gave Williams and Farbrace just enough scope to set Surrey an awkward target, which looked much more difficult when Middlesex claimed four wickets in the final session. On the last day Lynch ran himself out early on, and the lower-order batsmen were no match for Tufnell and the sharply turning ball.

*Close of play:* First day, Surrey 65-1 (D. J. Bicknell 38\*, G. P. Thorpe 22\*); Second day, Surrey 235; Third day, Surrey 69-4 (M. A. Lynch 9\*, N. M. Kendrick 0\*).

## Middlesex

| | | | |
|---|---|---|---|
| M. A. Roseberry b Waqar Younis | 53 | – b Waqar Younis | 62 |
| D. W. Headley run out | 2 | – c Thorpe b M. P. Bicknell | 7 |
| M. R. Ramprakash lbw b M. P. Bicknell | 85 | – c Sargeant b Feltham | 12 |
| \*M. W. Gatting b Waqar Younis | 8 | – b Waqar Younis | 29 |
| K. R. Brown b Waqar Younis | 34 | – c Sargeant b Waqar Younis | 5 |
| P. N. Weekes c Greig b Boiling | 0 | – c Sargeant b M. P. Bicknell | 6 |
| J. E. Emburey c Lynch b M. P. Bicknell | 6 | – c Thorpe b Waqar Younis | 2 |
| N. F. Williams c Lynch b M. P. Bicknell | 18 | – lbw b Kendrick | 26 |
| †P. Farbrace lbw b Waqar Younis | 0 | – b Kendrick | 26 |
| P. C. R. Tufnell b Waqar Younis | 1 | – b M. P. Bicknell | 1 |
| N. G. Cowans not out | 6 | – not out | 0 |
| L-b 8, n-b 3 | 11 | B 5, l-b 6 | 11 |
| | **224** | | **187** |

1/6 2/123 3/151 4/157 5/163     224     1/10 2/37 3/101 4/107 5/126     187
6/190 7/208 8/208 9/218                 6/128 7/129 8/174 9/187

Bonus points – Middlesex 2, Surrey 4.

Bowling: *First Innings*—Waqar Younis 17.3–3–53–5; M. P. Bicknell 20–4–62–3; Feltham 14–2–48–0; Kendrick 11–3–34–0; Boiling 12–3–19–1. *Second Innings*—Waqar Younis 16–3–42–4; M. P. Bicknell 21.4–7–33–3; Feltham 6–0–21–1; Kendrick 18–4–54–2; Boiling 13–5–26–0.

## Surrey

| | | | |
|---|---|---|---|
| D. J. Bicknell c Emburey b Williams | 41 | – lbw b Williams | 6 |
| †N. F. Sargeant lbw b Williams | 2 | – b Tufnell | 19 |
| G. P. Thorpe c and b Emburey | 117 | – b Cowans | 4 |
| D. M. Ward b Williams | 0 | – b Emburey | 23 |
| M. A. Lynch run out | 0 | – run out | 12 |
| *I. A. Greig lbw b Tufnell | 24 | – (7) c Emburey b Tufnell | 4 |
| M. A. Feltham c sub b Emburey | 25 | – (8) b Emburey | 15 |
| M. P. Bicknell b Emburey | 5 | – (9) c Brown b Tufnell | 1 |
| N. M. Kendrick not out | 6 | – (6) c Brown b Tufnell | 11 |
| Waqar Younis b Emburey | 0 | – b Tufnell | 0 |
| J. Boiling c Brown b Tufnell | 3 | – not out | 0 |
| L-b 8, n-b 4 | 12 | B 2, l-b 15, n-b 4 | 21 |

1/13 2/90 3/90 4/99 5/161        235     1/16 2/25 3/43 4/69 5/79       116
6/201 7/219 8/224 9/224                6/94 7/109 8/113 9/113

Bonus points – Surrey 2, Middlesex 4.

Bowling: *First Innings*—Williams 21–7–52–3; Cowans 11–5–28–0; Emburey 26–8–25–4; Tufnell 21.3–5–52–2; Headley 19–4–70–0. *Second Innings*—Williams 13–4–25–1; Cowans 6–2–10–1; Headley 2–0–6–0; Tufnell 19–11–17–5; Emburey 23.4–8–41–2.

Umpires: D. R. Shepherd and R. A. White.

At Chelmsford, September 17, 18, 19. MIDDLESEX lost to ESSEX by an innings and 208 runs.

---

# YOUNG CRICKETER OF THE YEAR

*(Elected by the Cricket Writers Club)*

| | | | |
|---|---|---|---|
| 1950 | R. Tattersall | 1972 | D. R. Owen-Thomas |
| 1951 | P. B. H. May | 1973 | M. Hendrick |
| 1952 | F. S. Trueman | 1974 | P. H. Edmonds |
| 1953 | M. C. Cowdrey | 1975 | A. Kennedy |
| 1954 | P. J. Loader | 1976 | G. Miller |
| 1955 | K. F. Barrington | 1977 | I. T. Botham |
| 1956 | B. Taylor | 1978 | D. I. Gower |
| 1957 | M. J. Stewart | 1979 | P. W. G. Parker |
| 1958 | A. C. D. Ingleby-Mackenzie | 1980 | G. R. Dilley |
| 1959 | G. Pullar | 1981 | M. W. Gatting |
| 1960 | D. A. Allen | 1982 | N. G. Cowans |
| 1961 | P. H. Parfitt | 1983 | N. A. Foster |
| 1962 | P. J. Sharpe | 1984 | R. J. Bailey |
| 1963 | G. Boycott | 1985 | D. V. Lawrence |
| 1964 | J. M. Brearley | 1986 | A. A. Metcalfe / J. J. Whitaker |
| 1965 | A. P. E. Knott | | |
| 1966 | D. L. Underwood | 1987 | R. J. Blakey |
| 1967 | A. W. Greig | 1988 | M. P. Maynard |
| 1968 | R. M. H. Cottam | 1989 | N. Hussain |
| 1969 | A. Ward | 1990 | M. A. Atherton |
| 1970 | C. M. Old | 1991 | M. R. Ramprakash |
| 1971 | J. Whitehouse | | |

An additional award, in memory of Norman Preston, Editor of *Wisden* from 1952 to 1980, was made to C. W. J. Athey in 1980.

# NORTHAMPTONSHIRE

*Patron:* The Earl of Dalkeith
*President:* W. R. F. Chamberlain
*Chairman:* L. A. Wilson
*Chairman, Cricket Committee:* A. P. Arnold
*Chief Executive:* S. P. Coverdale
  County Ground, Wantage Road,
  Northampton NN1 4TJ
  (Telephone: 0604-32917)
*Captain:* A. J. Lamb
*Director of Cricket:* M. J. Procter
*Coach:* R. M. Carter
*Cricket Development Officer:* B. L. Reynolds

Northamptonshire's strong finish to the season, coinciding with the omission of Allan Lamb from the England team and his subsequent return to form, ensured a limited improvement in their overall showing, compared with 1990. Going into August with a single Britannic Assurance Championship victory to their credit, the side rallied by winning four of the last seven matches to claim tenth position in the table, a rise of one place. In those games Lamb scored 670 runs from ten innings, including centuries against Lancashire, Surrey and Yorkshire.

Expectations were always higher in the one-day competitions, but the revival of Northamptonshire's fortunes in the Refuge Assurance League, in which they moved up from seventeenth to third, their best ever finish, was remarkable. However, the subsequent Refuge Assurance Cup semi-final took them for the third time in the summer to Old Trafford, where they had never won a limited-overs game in twelve attempts since 1973, and that unhappy record was extended as they succumbed by four wickets. Lancashire had won their earlier encounters in the Sunday League and the quarter-finals of the Benson and Hedges Cup.

As in the previous year, the NatWest Bank Trophy engendered conflicting emotions. After Northamptonshire had reached the last four with commendable efficiency, their run ended at The Oval. This single performance encapsulated the best and worst aspects of the team, who apparently had the match within their grasp more than once, only to hand back the advantage to Surrey each time.

Again, the captain's appearances were limited by international commitments. Lamb played in the first four Tests against West Indies until a barren spell with the bat, unprecedented in his fourteen English seasons, cost him his place. His handling of the Northamptonshire team attracted criticism on occasions, but he was nevertheless reappointed for a fourth season in charge, in line with the strong recommendation of Mike Procter, the director of cricket. Procter himself was breaking new ground at the club. His role continued to evolve throughout the season, but despite his all-embracing title he was, in effect, first-team manager. And within a few weeks he had already encountered a depressingly familiar occurrence at Northampton – an injury crisis.

Nevertheless there was reason to look to the future with confidence. The flowering of Alan Fordham as an opening batsman of national repute caused much satisfaction, as did the emergence of Andy Roberts and Paul Taylor. Neil Stanley returned from serious injury to record a maiden Championship century, a sharp, competitive edge was provided by the new recruit, Kevin Curran, and there were encouraging signs of development from the younger generation, under the guidance of the chief coach, Bob Carter.

Fordham enjoyed a magnificent season, and of England-qualified players only Gatting, Gooch and Darren Bicknell exceeded his tally of 1,840 first-class runs. He also weighed in with 980 runs in one-day games, winning four match awards, and he was voted Player of the Year by both club and supporters. Robert Bailey's achievements were less spectacular, but he still topped 2,000 runs in all competitions, and earned praise for his thoughtful captaincy when Lamb was away. Sidelined for two months with a broken thumb, Wayne Larkins shone in the later Refuge League matches. But at the end of a season which saw him become only the fourth player to complete 20,000 runs in a first-class career for Northamptonshire, he chose to end his 23-year association with the club and headed north to join Geoff Cook at Durham.

Northamptonshire went into 1991 with a proliferation of seam-bowling all-rounders, who experienced varying degrees of success. Curran's first summer at Wantage Road brought him an impressive return of 828 runs and 48 wickets in first-class games, and Eldine Baptiste, knowing his engagement was for one year only, made many friends around the county with his wholehearted approach. In contrast, it was a season to forget for David Capel, while the promising Tony Penberthy needs a more clearly defined function within the side if his considerable ability is to be harnessed properly.

Alan Walker, like Stanley, fought back from a severe back problem with great tenacity and was an invaluable member of the attack on Sundays, along with the left-armer, Taylor. Discarded by Derbyshire in 1987, Taylor rebuilt his career in the professional game and proved a shrewd signing, although his season, like that of Greg Thomas, was unfortunately cut short by injury. It came as little surprise when Thomas announced his retirement in the autumn.

Question marks also appeared over the long-term fitness of Richard Williams and Nick Cook, both plagued by knee trouble. However, their absences left the way clear for Roberts, the twenty-year-old leg-spinner, to establish himself, and he was undoubtedly Northamptonshire's most improved player. His 29 wickets – including a match-winning six for 72 against Lancashire at Lytham – and several resolute batting displays bore witness to his all-round skill and cheerful determination.

The Monday afternoon in July 1980 when Jim Watts lifted the Benson and Hedges Cup, Northamptonshire's most recent honour, is a fond but ever more distant memory. Partly by accident and partly by design, the club has embarked on the necessary task of constructing a side with an outlook unclouded by the failures of the past decade. The raw material would seem to be there, not least in the five youngsters on the staff selected for England Under-19 teams during 1991. However, with such thoughts of rejuvenation in the air, it was poignant that 1991 should see the deaths of F. R. Brown, captain from 1949 to 1953, and the former secretary, Ken Turner – arguably the two men most influential in raising and maintaining Northamptonshire's status on the post-war county scene. – Andrew Radd.

NORTHAMPTONSHIRE 1991

[Bill Smith]

*Back row:* W. M. Noon, R. R. Montgomerie, M. B. Loye, A. L. Penberthy, K. Bird, N. A. Stanley, J. G. Hughes, J. P. Taylor, R. J. Warren, A. R. Roberts. *Middle row:* R. Norman (*physiotherapist*), A. Fordham, A. Walker, D. B. K. Page, K. M. Curran, J. G. Thomas, E. A. E. Baptiste, D. Ripley, N. A. Felton, R. M. Carter (*coach*). *Front row:* R. G. Williams, N. G. B. Cook, R. J. Bailey, A. J. Lamb (*captain*), M. J. Procter (*director of cricket*), W. Larkins, D. J. Capel.

# NORTHAMPTONSHIRE RESULTS

*All first-class matches – Played 24: Won 5, Lost 6, Drawn 13.*

*County Championship matches – Played 22: Won 5, Lost 6, Drawn 11.*

*Bonus points – Batting 55, Bowling 54.*

*Competition placings – Britannic Assurance County Championship, 10th;*
*NatWest Bank Trophy, s-f; Benson and Hedges Cup, q-f;*
*Refuge Assurance League, 3rd; Refuge Assurance Cup, s-f.*

## BRITANNIC ASSURANCE CHAMPIONSHIP AVERAGES

### BATTING

| | Birthplace | M | I | NO | R | HI | Avge |
|---|---|---|---|---|---|---|---|
| ‡A. J. Lamb . . . . . . . | Langebaanweg, SA | 14 | 23 | 2 | 993 | 194 | 47.28 |
| ‡A. Fordham . . . . . . | Bedford | 22 | 40 | 2 | 1,725 | 165 | 45.39 |
| A. R. Roberts . . . . . | Kettering | 14 | 15 | 9 | 244 | 48 | 40.66 |
| ‡R. J. Bailey . . . . . . . | Biddulph | 19 | 34 | 4 | 1,202 | 117 | 40.06 |
| ‡W. Larkins . . . . . . . | Roxton | 9 | 16 | 6 | 365 | 75 | 36.50 |
| N. A. Stanley . . . . . | Bedford | 8 | 13 | 0 | 470 | 132 | 36.15 |
| K. M. Curran . . . . . | Rusape, S. Rhodesia | 19 | 30 | 7 | 749 | 89* | 32.56 |
| E. A. E. Baptiste . . . | Liberta, Antigua | 17 | 22 | 1 | 589 | 80 | 28.04 |
| ‡D. Ripley . . . . . . . . . | Leeds | 18 | 24 | 8 | 429 | 53* | 26.81 |
| ‡D. J. Capel . . . . . . . | Northampton | 20 | 32 | 2 | 692 | 71 | 23.06 |
| ‡J. G. Thomas . . . . . | Trebanos | 10 | 13 | 2 | 206 | 64 | 22.88 |
| ‡N. A. Felton . . . . . . | Guildford | 14 | 25 | 2 | 439 | 55 | 19.08 |
| ‡R. G. Williams . . . . | Bangor | 7 | 10 | 2 | 123 | 35 | 15.37 |
| A. L. Penberthy . . . . | Troon | 11 | 14 | 2 | 184 | 52 | 15.33 |
| W. M. Noon . . . . . . | Grimsby | 6 | 9 | 2 | 96 | 36 | 13.71 |
| ‡A. Walker . . . . . . . . | Emley | 4 | 4 | 1 | 35 | 13 | 11.66 |
| ‡N. G. B. Cook . . . . . | Leicester | 16 | 15 | 5 | 114 | 29 | 11.40 |
| J. P. Taylor . . . . . . . | Ashby-de-la-Zouch | 11 | 11 | 4 | 22 | 5* | 3.14 |

Also batted: M. B. Loye (*Northampton*) (1 match) 3*; R. R. Montgomerie (*Rugby*) (1 match) 2, 7. J. G. Hughes (*Wellingborough*) (1 match) did not bat.

* *Signifies not out.* ‡ *Denotes county cap.*

The following played a total of nine three-figure innings for Northamptonshire in County Championship matches – A. Fordham 4, A. J. Lamb 3, R. J. Bailey 1, N. A. Stanley 1.

### BOWLING

| | O | M | R | W | BB | 5W/i | Avge |
|---|---|---|---|---|---|---|---|
| K. M. Curran . . . . . . . . | 410.2 | 101 | 1,128 | 45 | 5-60 | 1 | 25.06 |
| E. A. E. Baptiste . . . . . . | 517.2 | 117 | 1,418 | 49 | 7-95 | 3 | 28.93 |
| J. P. Taylor . . . . . . . . . | 267.2 | 45 | 828 | 24 | 5-42 | 1 | 34.50 |
| J. G. Thomas . . . . . . . . | 248.4 | 33 | 829 | 24 | 5-62 | 2 | 34.54 |
| A. R. Roberts . . . . . . . . | 331.5 | 72 | 1,032 | 29 | 6-72 | 1 | 35.58 |
| R. J. Bailey . . . . . . . . . | 118.3 | 16 | 409 | 11 | 3-44 | 0 | 37.18 |
| N. G. B. Cook . . . . . . . . | 305.1 | 70 | 895 | 24 | 4-74 | 0 | 37.29 |
| D. J. Capel . . . . . . . . | 373.1 | 82 | 1,099 | 28 | 4-83 | 0 | 39.25 |
| A. L. Penberthy . . . . . . | 163.4 | 26 | 531 | 13 | 3-37 | 0 | 40.84 |

Also bowled: N. A. Felton 6-0-66-0; A. Fordham 13-0-78-1; J. G. Hughes 12-1-43-1; A. J. Lamb 3.4-0-29-2; W. Larkins 6-4-2-0; N. A. Stanley 10-2-19-0; A. Walker 103-20-296-6; R. G. Williams 87.3-17-256-4.

**Wicket-keepers:** D. Ripley 37 ct, 2 st; W. M. Noon 11 ct.

**Leading Fielder:** A. J. Lamb 13.

At Cambridge, April 16, 17, 18. NORTHAMPTONSHIRE drew with CAMBRIDGE UNIVERSITY.

At Derby, April 27, 29, 30, May 1. NORTHAMPTONSHIRE drew with DERBYSHIRE.

## NORTHAMPTONSHIRE v ESSEX

At Northampton, May 9, 10, 11, 13. Essex won by eight wickets. Essex 23 pts, Northamptonshire 6 pts. Toss: Northamptonshire. Pringle's all-round contribution proved decisive in securing a comfortable victory for Essex 40 minutes into the final day. Northamptonshire began solidly on a slow pitch, Fordham and Bailey adding 145, but Pringle's spell of five for 34 in 41 balls disposed of the middle order, and it was left to Ripley and Thomas to ensure maximum batting points. Essex struggled in turn, with half the side out for 170, only for Prichard and Pringle to recapture the initiative with a 166-run partnership in 40 overs. Prichard batted for just over five and a half hours for his 190 (261 balls), which contained a six and 24 fours. The home team were unlucky to lose Cook and Baptiste through injury, and they began their second innings 151 behind. Application was clearly called for, but it was not forthcoming as several of the leading batsmen failed to capitalise on good starts. Childs, removing Bailey, Lamb and Capel, virtually settled the result, and he and Foster shared the second-innings bowling honours.

*Close of play:* First day, Essex 13-0 (G. A. Gooch 8*, J. P. Stephenson 5*); Second day, Essex 428-7 (N. A. Foster 53*, T. D. Topley 2*); Third day, Essex 25-1 (G. A. Gooch 19*, D. R. Pringle 4*).

## Northamptonshire

| | | | |
|---|---|---|---|
| A. Fordham c Garnham b Pringle | 90 | – lbw b Pringle | 47 |
| N. A. Felton b Foster | 0 | – c Garnham b Foster | 5 |
| R. J. Bailey lbw b Pringle | 57 | – c Hussain b Childs | 30 |
| *A. J. Lamb lbw b Pringle | 24 | – c Salim Malik b Childs | 61 |
| D. J. Capel c Foster b Pringle | 22 | – c Garnham b Childs | 0 |
| W. Larkins b Pringle | 0 | – c Salim Malik b Foster | 27 |
| E. A. E. Baptiste c Prichard b Topley | 28 | – c Pringle b Foster | 24 |
| †D. Ripley c Garnham b Salim Malik | 30 | – b Childs | 15 |
| J. G. Thomas c Foster b Salim Malik | 43 | – c Hussain b Such | 11 |
| N. G. B. Cook not out | 12 | – not out | 6 |
| J. P. Taylor not out | 5 | – lbw b Such | 0 |
| B 1, l-b 13, w 1, n-b 2 | 17 | B 2, l-b 17, w 1, n-b 2 | 22 |

1/3 2/148 3/163 4/198 5/204 (9 wkts dec.) 328   1/29 2/79 3/111 4/113 5/184   248
6/221 7/241 8/297 9/319   6/190 7/220 8/230 9/248

Bonus points – Northamptonshire 4, Essex 3 (Score at 100 overs: 301-8).

Bowling: *First Innings*—Foster 20-3-78-1; Pringle 29-6-70-5; Topley 17-1-63-1; Childs 13-5-32-0; Gooch 11-7-8-0; Such 12-2-37-0; Salim Malik 6-1-26-2. *Second Innings*—Foster 17-5-44-3; Pringle 15-3-51-1; Topley 16-2-54-0; Childs 30-12-69-4; Such 5-1-8-2; Salim Malik 1-0-3-0.

## Essex

| | | | |
|---|---|---|---|
| *G. A. Gooch c and b Baptiste | 45 | – c Ripley b Taylor | 22 |
| J. P. Stephenson c Taylor b Thomas | 11 | – c Ripley b Thomas | 1 |
| P. J. Prichard c Ripley b Thomas | 190 | | |
| Salim Malik b Baptiste | 24 | – not out | 37 |
| N. Hussain c Ripley b Capel | 17 | | |
| †M. A. Garnham c Ripley b Capel | 1 | | |
| D. R. Pringle st Ripley b Bailey | 68 | – (3) not out | 37 |
| N. A. Foster c Ripley b Thomas | 63 | | |
| T. D. Topley lbw b Thomas | 30 | | |
| J. H. Childs lbw b Thomas | 0 | | |
| P. M. Such not out | 2 | | |
| B 10, l-b 18 | 28 | L-b 1 | 1 |

1/34 2/94 3/142 4/164 5/170    479    1/20 2/28    (2 wkts) 98
6/336 7/392 8/474 9/474

Bonus points – Essex 4, Northamptonshire 2 (Score at 100 overs: 370-6).

Bowling: *First Innings*—Taylor 34-8-101-0; Thomas 33.5-2-146-5; Capel 22-2-73-2; Baptiste 14-4-59-2; Bailey 19-1-72-1. *Second Innings*—Taylor 8-1-43-1; Thomas 7-1-25-1; Capel 2-0-19-0; Bailey 1.1-0-10-0.

Umpires: J. D. Bond and J. H. Hampshire.

## NORTHAMPTONSHIRE v LEICESTERSHIRE

At Northampton, May 16, 17, 18, 20. Drawn. Northamptonshire 5 pts, Leicestershire 2 pts. Toss: Northamptonshire. Much excellent cricket was played on a pitch of lively pace which offered batsmen and bowlers alike every opportunity to show their skills. Only 44 overs were possible on the first two days because of rain, but on the third Thomas – four for 15 in 33 balls – had Leicestershire in trouble until Whitticase counter-attacked with a career-best 73. Northamptonshire replied positively. Larkins, when he had scored 21, became only the fourth batsman, following D. Brookes, J. E. Timms and G. Cook, to complete 20,000 first-class runs for the county, but his pleasure was short-lived. A lifting ball from Millns broke his right thumb. Capel was at his fluent best, moving effortlessly to 58 off 36 deliveries, and after Bailey's enterprising declaration the visitors established a lead of 172 going into the final day. They continued to make good progress, thanks to Whitaker (166 minutes, 136 balls, nineteen fours), and Northamptonshire were left to score 295 in 64 overs. Given a bright start by Fordham and Felton, the home side subsequently ran into difficulties against Maguire, and it took 8.4 overs of grim defence from Thomas and the injured Williams to save the match.

*Close of play:* First day, Leicestershire 85-2 (T. J. Boon 39*, J. J. Whitaker 13*); Second day, Leicestershire 108-2 (T. J. Boon 49*, J. J. Whitaker 26*); Third day, Leicestershire 83-3 (J. J. Whitaker 30*, L. Potter 3*).

## Leicestershire

| | | | |
|---|---|---|---|
| T. J. Boon c Cook b Thomas | 49 | – lbw b Taylor | 20 |
| *N. E. Briers b Thomas | 8 | – c Cook b Taylor | 2 |
| P. N. Hepworth lbw b Williams | 15 | – lbw b Taylor | 23 |
| J. J. Whitaker c Capel b Thomas | 33 | – b Taylor | 99 |
| L. Potter c Ripley b Taylor | 10 | – c Bailey b Taylor | 22 |
| P. Willey c Fordham b Thomas | 0 | – c Penberthy b Capel | 26 |
| C. C. Lewis lbw b Thomas | 12 | – not out | 8 |
| †P. Whitticase c Felton b Taylor | 73 | | |
| L. Tennant c Larkins b Taylor | 12 | | |
| D. J. Millns c Ripley b Williams | 14 | | |
| J. N. Maguire not out | 0 | | |
| B 5, l-b 8, n-b 1 | 14 | L-b 4, n-b 1 | 5 |

1/27 2/52 3/112 4/119 5/119    240    1/14 2/42 3/63    (6 wkts dec.) 205
6/135 7/153 8/175 9/240               4/123 5/194 6/205

Bonus points – Leicestershire 2, Northamptonshire 4.

Bowling: *First Innings*—Thomas 26.4–6–62–5; Taylor 31–5–72–3; Penberthy 4.2–1–10–0; Cook 10–1–38–0; Williams 12.4–3–29–2; Capel 9–2–26–0. *Second Innings*—Thomas 9–1–44–0; Taylor 14.4–2–42–5; Capel 12–5–28–1; Penberthy 10–1–43–0; Cook 2–1–2–0; Williams 0.2–0–3–0; Bailey 10.4–0–39–0.

## Northamptonshire

| | | | |
|---|---|---|---|
| A. Fordham lbw b Lewis | 1 | – c Willey b Millns | 42 |
| W. Larkins retired hurt | 39 | | |
| *R. J. Bailey c Millns b Lewis | 7 | – c Briers b Maguire | 32 |
| N. A. Felton not out | 31 | – (2) c Whitaker b Millns | 25 |
| D. J. Capel not out | 58 | – (4) c Whitaker b Maguire | 10 |
| A. L. Penberthy (did not bat) | | – (5) lbw b Maguire | 0 |
| †D. Ripley (did not bat) | | – (6) c Whitticase b Potter | 20 |
| J. G. Thomas (did not bat) | | – (7) not out | 36 |
| J. P. Taylor (did not bat) | | – (8) c Willey b Potter | 3 |
| N. G. B. Cook (did not bat) | | – (9) c Whitticase b Maguire | 0 |
| R. G. Williams (did not bat) | | – (10) not out | 4 |
| L-b 2, n-b 13 | 15 | B 4, l-b 5, w 1, n-b 11 | 21 |

1/2 2/14          (2 wkts dec.) 151     1/71 2/90 3/100 4/100    (8 wkts) 193
                                              5/127 6/166
                                              7/186 8/187

Bonus point – Northamptonshire 1.

*In the first innings W. Larkins retired hurt at 73.*

Bowling: *First Innings*—Lewis 8–1–38–2; Millns 10–1–45–0; Maguire 10–1–42–0; Tennant 2–0–24–0. *Second Innings*—Lewis 16–3–41–0; Millns 12–1–45–2; Maguire 21–4–69–4; Willey 1–0–4–0; Tennant 4–1–9–0; Potter 9–8–14–2; Hepworth 1–0–2–0.

Umpires: J. C. Balderstone and J. H. Harris.

At Cardiff, May 22, 23, 24. NORTHAMPTONSHIRE drew with GLAMORGAN.

At Leeds, May 25, 27, 28. NORTHAMPTONSHIRE drew with YORKSHIRE.

## NORTHAMPTONSHIRE v DERBYSHIRE

At Northampton, May 31, June 1, 3. Drawn. Northamptonshire 6 pts, Derbyshire 5 pts. Toss: Derbyshire. A well-judged declaration by Lamb, an outstanding innings of 122 from Barnett (272 minutes, 224 balls, one six, ten fours), and the willingness of the players to stay on the field in steady rain during the closing stages all contributed to an exciting finish. Set 309 to win in 80 overs, Derbyshire were put on course by Barnett and Azharuddin, who added 93, and Krikken gave his captain excellent support in a sixth-wicket stand of 75 in sixteen overs. Barnett's departure then, with 38 still needed, left the remaining batsmen with just too much to do, although they kept up the chase until the last over, from Cook, which Mortensen safely negotiated to gain a draw. The game's early exchanges were dominated by the bowlers. Northamptonshire rallied from 83 for six thanks to Capel, Thomas and Ripley; then Morris held the visitors' batting together after Thomas had made inroads with the new ball. Building on a lead of 59, the home side were indebted to Fordham, who survived five chances in 192 minutes (171 balls, sixteen fours), and Lamb was able to close the innings 40 minutes before lunch on the final day.

*Close of play:* First day, Northamptonshire 248; Second day, Northamptonshire 181-2 (R. J. Bailey 33*, J. G. Thomas 0*).

## Northamptonshire

| | | | |
|---|---|---|---|
| A. Fordham c Krikken b Malcolm | 4 | – c Base b Malcolm | 105 |
| N. A. Felton c Krikken b Mortensen | 15 | – c Krikken b Mortensen | 37 |
| R. J. Bailey c Azharuddin b Mortensen | 7 | – c Barnett b Malcolm | 56 |
| *A. J. Lamb c Adams b Mortensen | 8 | – (5) c Base b Malcolm | 9 |
| D. J. Capel c Azharuddin b Jean-Jacques | 70 | – (6) c and b Mortensen | 13 |
| K. M. Curran c Adams b Mortensen | 6 | – (7) run out | 9 |
| A. L. Penberthy c Krikken b Mortensen | 0 | – (8) not out | 1 |
| J. G. Thomas b Malcolm | 64 | – (4) c Mortensen b Malcolm | 9 |
| †D. Ripley not out | 53 | – not out | 0 |
| A. Walker c O'Gorman b Malcolm | 8 | | |
| N. G. B. Cook c Krikken b Malcolm | 4 | | |
| L-b 8, w 1 | 9 | L-b 8, w 1, n-b 1 | 10 |

| | | |
|---|---|---|
| 1/14 2/23 3/28 4/39 5/77 | 248 | 1/79 2/180 3/194    (7 wkts dec.) 249 |
| 6/83 7/147 8/200 9/226 | | 4/216 5/235 |
| | | 6/245 7/247 |

Bonus points – Northamptonshire 2, Derbyshire 4.

Bowling: *First Innings*—Malcolm 23.5-3-76-4; Mortensen 21-5-57-5; Base 22-2-57-0; Jean-Jacques 18-5-50-1. *Second Innings*—Malcolm 23.5-3-99-4; Mortensen 24-6-59-2; Base 12-3-34-0; Jean-Jacques 11-1-49-0.

## Derbyshire

| | | | |
|---|---|---|---|
| *K. J. Barnett c Lamb b Thomas | 11 | – c Fordham b Cook | 122 |
| P. D. Bowler c Ripley b Thomas | 0 | – c Ripley b Walker | 28 |
| J. E. Morris c Walker b Curran | 87 | – c Lamb b Curran | 4 |
| M. Azharuddin lbw b Walker | 2 | – b Cook | 55 |
| T. J. G. O'Gorman c Ripley b Thomas | 4 | – c Ripley b Capel | 14 |
| C. J. Adams lbw b Capel | 18 | – c Lamb b Cook | 2 |
| †K. M. Krikken c Felton b Curran | 37 | – st Ripley b Cook | 46 |
| M. Jean-Jacques c Cook b Thomas | 0 | – (10) not out | 0 |
| S. J. Base c Ripley b Curran | 8 | – c Walker b Curran | 2 |
| D. E. Malcolm b Curran | 6 | – (8) c Penberthy b Curran | 5 |
| O. H. Mortensen not out | 1 | – not out | 0 |
| B 4, l-b 10, w 1 | 15 | B 3, l-b 9 | 12 |

| | | |
|---|---|---|
| 1/1 2/20 3/27 4/42 5/95 | 189 | 1/60 2/67 3/160    (9 wkts) 290 |
| 6/154 7/157 8/170 9/176 | | 4/189 5/196 6/271 |
| | | 7/281 8/288 9/290 |

Bonus points – Derbyshire 1, Northamptonshire 4.

Bowling: *First Innings*—Thomas 17-3-62-4; Walker 13-2-42-1; Capel 8-2-30-1; Curran 13.1-1-39-4; Penberthy 1-0-2-0. *Second Innings*—Thomas 8-0-44-0; Walker 13-4-27-1; Curran 19-3-68-3; Penberthy 6-1-18-0; Capel 13-1-47-1; Cook 21-3-74-4.

Umpires: K. J. Lyons and R. A. White.

## NORTHAMPTONSHIRE v WORCESTERSHIRE

At Northampton, June 4, 5, 6. Northamptonshire won by six wickets. Northamptonshire 20 pts, Worcestershire 4 pts. Toss: Northamptonshire. Northamptonshire's first Championship victory of the season, and their first win in a first-class match at Northampton since August 1989, was a personal triumph for Bailey, who led a depleted side astutely and contributed two fine innings. Already beset by injury problems, Northamptonshire suffered another blow when Thomas pulled out shortly before the start. Loye, an eighteen-year-old batsman, was rushed down from the Second Eleven's match at Old Trafford to make his first-class début. With Curtis and Lord laying the foundation and Moody in sparkling form, hitting a six and nine fours, Worcestershire looked set for a formidable total until Penberthy claimed three wickets in fourteen balls to tilt the balance at the end of the first day. The visitors' advantage was restored next morning by Rhodes, but when rain intervened, any hope of a positive result was left in the hands of the two captains. An exchange of declarations gave Northamptonshire a target of 271 in 70 overs, and this generous challenge was taken up by Fordham and Felton, whose century opening stand paved the way for Bailey. Batting for 143 minutes, and partnered first by Curran and then by Ripley, he shouldered his responsibility splendidly. His unbeaten 95, containing eleven fours, came from just 119 deliveries and saw Northamptonshire home with ten balls to spare.

*Close of play:* First day, Worcestershire 236-6 (S. J. Rhodes 4\*, P. J. Newport 0\*); Second day, Northamptonshire 134-3 (R. J. Bailey 48\*, K. M. Curran 7\*).

## Worcestershire

| | | |
|---|---:|---|
| T. S. Curtis c Ripley b Curran | 52 | – c Loye b Cook .......... 30 |
| G. J. Lord c Curran b Walker | 55 | – c Ripley b Curran ......... 38 |
| T. M. Moody c Fordham b Curran | 71 | – not out .............. 14 |
| D. B. D'Oliveira c Ripley b Penberthy | 33 | – run out ............... 0 |
| *P. A. Neale c Roberts b Penberthy | 7 | – not out .............. 4 |
| M. J. Weston b Penberthy | 9 | |
| †S. J. Rhodes not out | 56 | |
| P. J. Newport c Roberts b Curran | 15 | |
| S. R. Lampitt not out | 18 | |
| B 1, l-b 9, w 1 | 11 | B 1, l-b 1, w 5 ......... 7 |

1/92 2/154 3/193 4/222 5/223      (7 wkts dec.) 327    1/74 2/74 3/75     (3 wkts dec.) 93
6/236 7/263

N. V. Radford and R. D. Stemp did not bat.

Bonus points – Worcestershire 3, Northamptonshire 3 (Score at 100 overs: 278-7).

Bowling: *First Innings*—Walker 20-4-62-1; Penberthy 30-7-97-3; Curran 22-11-45-3; Capel 5-1-17-0; Cook 15-4-53-0; Roberts 16-5-43-0. *Second Innings*—Walker 6-2-20-0; Penberthy 6-0-27-0; Cook 5-0-26-1; Curran 4-2-4-1; Fordham 1-0-14-0.

## Northamptonshire

| | | |
|---|---:|---|
| A. Fordham c Rhodes b Radford | 13 | – c Rhodes b Lampitt .......... 60 |
| N. A. Felton lbw b Newport | 40 | – c and b Newport ............ 47 |
| *R. J. Bailey c Moody b Radford | 50 | – not out ................ 95 |
| D. J. Capel b Newport | 16 | – c Rhodes b Weston ........... 1 |
| K. M. Curran not out | 17 | – c Radford b Lampitt .......... 32 |
| M. B. Loye not out | 3 | |
| †D. Ripley (did not bat) | | – (6) not out ............... 27 |
| L-b 7, n-b 4 | 11 | L-b 6, n-b 3 ............ 9 |

1/41 2/81 3/123 4/141      (4 wkts dec.) 150    1/106 2/128      (4 wkts) 271
                                   3/129 4/199

A. L. Penberthy, A. R. Roberts, A. Walker and N. G. B. Cook did not bat.

Bonus points – Northamptonshire 1, Worcestershire 1.

Bowling: *First Innings*—Radford 12.1-1-61-2; Newport 18-3-49-2; Lampitt 13-2-33-0. *Second Innings*—Radford 12-0-53-0; Newport 20.2-1-77-1; Lampitt 19-1-74-2; Stemp 12-3-34-0; Weston 5-1-27-1.

Umpires: K. J. Lyons and R. A. White.

At Northampton, June 15, 16, 17. NORTHAMPTONSHIRE drew with WEST INDIANS (See West Indian tour section).

## NORTHAMPTONSHIRE v HAMPSHIRE

At Northampton, June 21, 22, 23. Drawn. Northamptonshire 5 pts, Hampshire 6 pts. Toss: Hampshire. The good intentions of the captains counted for nothing in the end as rain had the decisive say. Northamptonshire's hectic first innings, more akin to a limited-overs contest, was notable for a hard-hitting fifth-wicket stand of 60 in eleven overs between Capel (93 balls, twelve fours) and Baptiste (78 balls, eleven fours), and for the testing fast bowling of Aqib Javed. Hampshire's reply owed much to Smith, who completed the 61 runs he required to become the second batsman to reach 1,000 first-class runs for the season. A torrential downpour on the second afternoon prompted the visitors to declare 58 behind, and Northamptonshire had extended their lead to 127 by the close. It promised to be an interesting last day, but only four overs could be bowled before the rain returned, and the match was abandoned at lunch.

*Close of play:* First day, Hampshire 57-0 (T. C. Middleton 16*, C. L. Smith 34*); Second day, Northamptonshire 69-0 (A. Fordham 37*, N. A. Felton 27*).

### Northamptonshire

| | | | | |
|---|---|---|---:|---:|
| A. Fordham c Gower b Aqib Javed | 13 | – not out | | 40 |
| N. A. Felton b Aqib Javed | 1 | – not out | | 38 |
| *R. J. Bailey c Terry b Aqib Javed | 37 | | | |
| D. J. Capel c Smith b Maru | 71 | | | |
| K. M. Curran c Maru b Shine | 31 | | | |
| E. A. E. Baptiste run out | 60 | | | |
| J. G. Thomas b Maru | 8 | | | |
| †D. Ripley b Aqib Javed | 13 | | | |
| A. L. Penberthy c Maru b Aqib Javed | 3 | | | |
| J. P. Taylor b Maru | 3 | | | |
| N. G. B. Cook not out | 1 | | | |
| L-b 4, w 4, n-b 12 | 20 | L-b 4, n-b 1 | | 5 |
| | **261** | **(no wkt)** | | **83** |

1/2 2/35 3/89 4/141 5/201
6/211 7/248 8/249 9/259

Bonus points – Northamptonshire 3, Hampshire 4.

Bowling: *First Innings*—Aqib Javed 20-4-49-5; Bakker 15-4-35-0; Shine 10-0-66-1; James 12-1-59-0; Maru 16.5-5-48-3. *Second Innings*—Aqib Javed 7-0-27-0; Bakker 6-0-20-0; Maru 6-1-19-0; Shine 5-3-13-0.

### Hampshire

| | | | | |
|---|---|---:|---|---:|
| T. C. Middleton c Thomas b Baptiste | 25 | †A. N. Aymes not out | | 10 |
| C. L. Smith c Ripley b Baptiste | 85 | R. J. Maru not out | | 0 |
| *M. C. J. Nicholas c Ripley b Taylor | 1 | B 1, l-b 16, n-b 3 | | 20 |
| V. P. Terry c Bailey b Penberthy | 22 | | | |
| D. I. Gower run out | 22 | 1/85 2/86 3/142 | **(6 wkts dec.)** | **203** |
| K. D. James b Baptiste | 18 | 4/171 5/172 6/199 | | |

K. J. Shine, P. J. Bakker and Aqib Javed did not bat.

Bonus points – Hampshire 2, Northamptonshire 2.

Bowling: Thomas 13-3-37-0; Taylor 13-4-27-1; Curran 13-3-36-0; Baptiste 18-5-49-3; Penberthy 10.2-0-37-1.

Umpires: B. Hassan and B. Leadbeater.

## NORTHAMPTONSHIRE v GLOUCESTERSHIRE

At Luton, June 28, 29, July 1. Gloucestershire won by three wickets. Gloucestershire 21 pts, Northamptonshire 5 pts. Toss: Gloucestershire. Heavy rain prior to the match left the Wardown Park pitch damp, and this gave Lawrence every encouragement in a hostile ten-over opening spell which brought him five wickets at a cost of 25 runs. Bailey, Baptiste and

Ripley engineered Northamptonshire's partial recovery before a thunderstorm caused the loss of half the first day's overs. The next day saw a protracted struggle for a first-innings lead, with Athey setting the tone by scoring 33 in 42 overs. Northamptonshire eventually gained a 21-run advantage, which they built upon in purposeful fashion against some skilful off-spin bowling from Lloyds, who obtained appreciable turn. Mindful of this, Lamb left Gloucestershire with effectively 70 overs in which to make 221, but surprisingly he did not use his own spinners in tandem until Scott and Hodgson had taken their side some way down the road to victory with an opening stand of 90. Roberts's leg-breaks transformed the situation, and at 164 for seven Gloucestershire were in danger of defeat. However, Russell and Lawrence added 59 in eleven overs and the target was reached with three overs remaining.

*Close of play:* First day, Northamptonshire 150-7 (D. Ripley 21*, A. R. Roberts 1*); Second day, Northamptonshire 8-0 (A. Fordham 4*, N. A. Felton 3*).

## Northamptonshire

| | | | | |
|---|---|---|---|---|
| A. Fordham lbw b Lawrence | 1 | – c Alleyne b Lloyds | 24 |
| N. A. Felton lbw b Lawrence | 0 | – c and b Lloyds | 4 |
| R. J. Bailey lbw b Smith | 57 | – c Lawrence b Lloyds | 30 |
| *A. J. Lamb c Russell b Lawrence | 3 | – b Lloyds | 51 |
| D. J. Capel b Lawrence | 5 | – c sub b Lloyds | 5 |
| K. M. Curran c Russell b Lawrence | 5 | – not out | 22 |
| E. A. E. Baptiste c Russell b Gilbert | 51 | – c Scott b Lloyds | 44 |
| †D. Ripley c Alleyne b Lawrence | 34 | – not out | 8 |
| A. R. Roberts not out | 18 | | |
| N. G. B. Cook b Lloyds | 6 | | |
| J. P. Taylor c Russell b Lloyds | 0 | | |
| L-b 2, w 1, n-b 5 | 8 | B 3, l-b 5, n-b 3 | 11 |

1/1 2/4 3/12 4/22 5/32              188     1/11 2/50 3/109     (6 wkts dec.) 199
6/99 7/141 8/172 9/180                      4/114 5/123 6/181

Bonus points – Northamptonshire 1, Gloucestershire 4.

Bowling: *First Innings*—Lawrence 27.2-8-67-6; Gilbert 15.4-3-43-1; Smith 14-3-41-1; Lloyds 17-6-35-2; Scott 2-2-0-0. *Second Innings*—Lawrence 2-2-0-0; Smith 2-0-8-0; Scott 9-1-50-0; Lloyds 21-4-94-6; Athey 12-6-29-0; Russell 0.3-0-10-0.

## Gloucestershire

| | | | | |
|---|---|---|---|---|
| G. D. Hodgson c Ripley b Taylor | 1 | – lbw b Cook | 60 |
| J. J. E. Hardy lbw b Curran | 0 | – (6) c and b Roberts | 12 |
| *A. J. Wright b Baptiste | 14 | – c Curran b Roberts | 20 |
| C. W. J. Athey c Capel b Taylor | 33 | – c Fordham b Roberts | 17 |
| J. W. Lloyds c Taylor b Curran | 26 | – (8) c Ripley b Baptiste | 1 |
| M. W. Alleyne b Curran | 22 | – (5) c Lamb b Roberts | 0 |
| R. J. Scott c Curran b Capel | 17 | – (2) c and b Baptiste | 50 |
| †R. C. Russell not out | 34 | – (7) not out | 20 |
| D. V. Lawrence c Baptiste b Cook | 2 | – not out | 36 |
| A. M. Smith c Ripley b Capel | 1 | | |
| D. R. Gilbert c Ripley b Taylor | 3 | | |
| L-b 11, w 3 | 14 | B 1, l-b 6 | 7 |

1/1 2/7 3/37 4/74 5/95              167     1/90 2/127 3/139 4/144     (7 wkts) 223
6/125 7/127 8/145 9/146                     5/162 6/163 7/164

Bonus points – Gloucestershire 1, Northamptonshire 4.

Bowling: *First Innings*—Taylor 18.5-7-31-3; Curran 17-9-23-3; Cook 19-4-34-1; Baptiste 15-5-34-1; Capel 9-2-34-2. *Second Innings*—Taylor 5-1-37-0; Curran 7-3-16-0; Cook 14-0-42-1; Baptiste 17-2-58-2; Roberts 24-8-63-4.

Umpires: J. H. Harris and R. A. White.

At Maidstone, July 2, 3, 4. NORTHAMPTONSHIRE lost to KENT by 120 runs.

At Leicester, July 5, 6, 8. NORTHAMPTONSHIRE drew with LEICESTERSHIRE.

At Uxbridge, July 16, 17, 18. NORTHAMPTONSHIRE drew with MIDDLESEX.

## NORTHAMPTONSHIRE v NOTTINGHAMSHIRE

At Wellingborough School, July 19, 20. Nottinghamshire won by an innings and 1 run. Nottinghamshire 24 pts, Northamptonshire 7 pts. Toss: Nottinghamshire. Nottinghamshire's remarkable victory, achieved with a full day to spare, owed much to a fine all-round performance from Pick and some irresolute Northamptonshire batting. Pick could do no wrong on the dramatic second day. His side had just edged ahead on first innings (thanks to Johnson's 81 in 218 minutes, with a six and eleven fours) when he was joined at the crease by Crawley, who had retired the previous evening with a broken right thumb. The injured opener lent brave support as Pick played a most valuable innings, and they added 55 to secure maximum batting points and a lead of 69. Moreover, their stand tilted the psychological balance markedly back in Nottinghamshire's favour, and Northamptonshire began their second innings knowing that a difficult last session awaited them on a pitch showing signs of wear. Their worst fears were realised; Pick snatched four wickets for 5 runs in twenty balls, and also held a sharp catch in the gully to dismiss Lamb off the equally hostile Stephenson. From 20 for seven there was no way back for Northamptonshire, and although Curran held firm, the tail was swept away. Nottinghamshire won with seven deliveries left in the extra half-hour.

*Close of play:* First day, Nottinghamshire 44-0 (P. R. Pollard 27*, R. T. Robinson 15*).

## Northamptonshire

| | | | | |
|---|---|---|---|---|
| A. Fordham b Stephenson | 12 | – lbw b Pick | 9 |
| N. A. Felton c Pollard b Pick | 0 | – c sub b Pick | 1 |
| R. J. Bailey c Robinson b Pick | 57 | – b Stephenson | 2 |
| *A. J. Lamb lbw b Evans | 33 | – c Pick b Stephenson | 2 |
| D. J. Capel c Johnson b Evans | 0 | – c French b Pick | 0 |
| K. M. Curran b Stephenson | 18 | – not out | 20 |
| E. A. E. Baptiste b Stephenson | 80 | – b Stephenson | 3 |
| R. G. Williams b Stephenson | 12 | – c Evans b Pick | 0 |
| †D. Ripley b Pick | 8 | – (10) b Stephenson | 6 |
| N. G. B. Cook not out | 15 | – (9) b Stephenson | 4 |
| J. P. Taylor lbw b Stephenson | 4 | – b Pick | 2 |
| B 1, l-b 12, n-b 1 | 14 | B 14, l-b 5 | 19 |

1/12 2/12 3/56 4/60 5/90       253      1/9 2/12 3/12 4/14 5/14      68
6/155 7/181 8/219 9/249               6/19 7/20 8/39 9/57

Bonus points – Northamptonshire 3, Nottinghamshire 4.

Bowling: *First Innings*—Stephenson 22.4–7–61–5; Pick 24–6–74–3; Evans 21–5–65–2; Afford 8–2–19–0; Crawley 8–3–15–0; Hemmings 3–0–6–0. *Second Innings*—Stephenson 12–2–27–5; Pick 8.5–2–17–5; Evans 3–1–5–0.

## Nottinghamshire

| | | | |
|---|---|---|---|
| P. R. Pollard c Cook b Capel | 52 | E. E. Hemmings b Cook | 10 |
| M. A. Crawley not out | 17 | R. A. Pick c Bailey b Taylor | 46 |
| *R. T. Robinson lbw b Taylor | 43 | J. A. Afford lbw b Curran | 0 |
| P. Johnson b Cook | 81 | | |
| D. W. Randall lbw b Curran | 45 | B 6, l-b 16, w 1, n-b 1 | 24 |
| K. P. Evans c and b Curran | 1 | | |
| †B. N. French b Curran | 2 | 1/87 2/127 3/213 4/215 5/217 | 322 |
| F. D. Stephenson b Ripley b Curran | 1 | 6/227 7/250 8/266 9/267 | |

Bonus points – Nottinghamshire 4, Northamptonshire 4 (Score at 100 overs: 311-9).

*M. A. Crawley, when 0, retired hurt at 8 and resumed at 267.*

Bowling: Taylor 19.5–2–68–2; Baptiste 29–4–81–0; Cook 20–6–51–2; Williams 1–0–6–0; Capel 13–4–34–1; Curran 24–6–60–5.

Umpires: H. D. Bird and B. J. Meyer.

## NORTHAMPTONSHIRE v SOMERSET

At Northampton, July 23, 24, 25. Drawn. Somerset 5 pts. Toss: Northamptonshire.
Somerset's Cook dominated the early stages of the match with a chanceless innings,
displaying his crisp and well-organised strokeplay to best advantage. His 210 not out was the
highest score by a Somerset batsman against Northamptonshire, beating B. C. Rose's 205 at
Weston-super-Mare in 1977, and he hit 27 fours in his 383-minute stay, facing 343 balls.
Northamptonshire, with the exception of Fordham, struggled in reply, but rain on the second
afternoon prompted an agreement between the two captains which, after reciprocal declarations, left the home side needing 330 in a minimum of 80 overs. Fordham shone again,
and together with Bailey (266 minutes, 231 balls, seven fours) laid a solid foundation with 138
for the second wicket. However, Graveney dismissed them both, and also Larkins, to force
a reappraisal of the situation. Curran's belligerent 60 off 58 deliveries kept the challenge
going, and 13 runs were required from the last over, bowled by van Troost in his second
Championship game. The Dutch teenager conceded just 4 – including two wides – while three
wickets fell, and it was left to Cook to block the final ball and deny Somerset victory at the
end of an absorbing session.

*Close of play:* First day, Somerset 266-2 (S. J. Cook 173*, C. J. Tavaré 22*); Second day,
Northamptonshire 137-4 dec.

### Somerset

| | | |
|---|---|---|
| S. J. Cook not out | .210 | |
| P. M. Roebuck c Ripley b Baptiste | 32 | |
| A. N. Hayhurst b Cook | 29 | – (1) c Capel b Fordham ........ 23 |
| *C. J. Tavaré not out | 65 | |
| R. J. Harden (did not bat) | | – (2) not out................ 59 |
| †N. D. Burns (did not bat) | | – (3) run out .............. 11 |
| K. H. MacLeay (did not bat) | | – (4) not out............ 21 |
| L-b 6, w 4, n-b 2 | 12 | L-b 1, w 2, n-b 1 ....... 4 |

1/135 2/230                 (2 wkts dec.) 348   1/36 2/57        (2 wkts dec.) 118

R. P. Lefebvre, J. C. Hallett, D. A. Graveney and A. P. van Troost did not bat.

Bonus points – Somerset 4 (Score at 100 overs: 309-2).

Bowling: *First Innings*—Thomas 22-2-89-0; Baptiste 26-3-99-1; Capel 17-3-41-0;
Curran 10-1-39-0; Cook 16-6-42-1; Williams 17-7-32-0. *Second Innings*—Curran 3-2-5-0;
Baptiste 3-1-4-0; Fordham 6-0-42-1; Felton 6-0-66-0.

### Northamptonshire

| | | |
|---|---|---|
| A. Fordham b Lefebvre | 73 | – c Burns b Graveney.......... 84 |
| N. A. Felton c and b Hallett | 4 | – b Hallett ................. 2 |
| *R. J. Bailey c van Troost b Harden | 40 | – st Burns b Graveney ........117 |
| W. Larkins not out | 4 | – c Hayhurst b Graveney ... 19 |
| D. J. Capel b Lefebvre | 15 | – c sub b Hayhurst ......... 0 |
| K. M. Curran (did not bat) | | – run out ................. 60 |
| E. A. E. Baptiste (did not bat) | | – run out ................ 18 |
| R. G. Williams (did not bat) | | – b van Troost............ 3 |
| J. G. Thomas (did not bat) | | – not out ............... 1 |
| †D. Ripley (did not bat) | | – b van Troost........... 0 |
| N. G. B. Cook (did not bat) | | – not out ............ 0 |
| W 1 | 1 | B 3, l-b 11, w 2, n-b 1 ..... 17 |

1/22 2/103 3/119 4/137     (4 wkts dec.) 137   1/10 2/148 3/208     (9 wkts) 321
                                               4/209 5/259 6/307
                                               7/317 8/320 9/321

Bonus point – Somerset 1.

Bowling: *First Innings*—Hallett 8-4-14-1; van Troost 9-2-24-0; Hayhurst 6-1-25-0; Lefebvre 10.4-3-39-2; Graveney 6-1-22-0; Harden 3-0-13-1. *Second Innings*—Hallett 9-4-20-1; van Troost 12-1-52-2; Lefebvre 18-4-58-0; Graveney 28-1-111-3; MacLeay 7-1-33-0; Hayhurst 12-1-33-1.

Umpires: H. D. Bird and B. J. Meyer.

At Eastbourne, August 2, 3, 5. NORTHAMPTONSHIRE drew with SUSSEX.

At Lytham, August 6, 7, 8. NORTHAMPTONSHIRE beat LANCASHIRE by 53 runs.

## NORTHAMPTONSHIRE v WARWICKSHIRE

At Northampton, August 9, 10, 12. Drawn. Northamptonshire 6 pts, Warwickshire 8 pts. Toss: Northamptonshire. After suffering two successive defeats, Warwickshire were keen to re-establish their Championship credentials. But once their bid to enforce the follow-on was thwarted, the match was allowed to die, with neither captain making any effort to revive it. Lamb's decision to bowl first looked like paying dividends until Asif Din (204 minutes, twelve fours) and Reeve added 134 for the fifth wicket, and Warwickshire's recovery was completed in spectacular fashion by Smith and Holloway, whose 108-run partnership occupied only sixteen overs. The aim, to dismiss Northamptonshire twice, was clear enough, but Warwickshire were held up first by Fordham and Stanley, and then by Lamb and Penberthy. None of them, however, upgraded a promising start into an innings of real substance, and when bad light halted play on the second evening, the home side still required 18 from their last pair to make Warwickshire bat next. That task was accomplished on Monday with the aid of some wayward bowling which presented 15 of the necessary runs in extras, including three lots of four byes down the leg side. A declaration at that point might have maintained Warwickshire's interest, but instead Cook and Roberts carried their stand to 85 – a figure not exceeded for the county's tenth wicket since 1936. The travesty of cricket that followed reflected little credit on either side.

*Close of play:* First day, Warwickshire 377-6 (N. M. K. Smith 55*, P. C. L. Holloway 35*); Second day, Northamptonshire 293-9 (A. R. Roberts 3*, N. G. B. Cook 2*).

## Warwickshire

| | | | |
|---|---|---|---|
| A. J. Moles c Larkins b Curran | 71 | – not out | 57 |
| J. D. Ratcliffe c Stanley b Capel | 21 | – lbw b Capel | 12 |
| *T. A. Lloyd c Lamb b Curran | 26 | | |
| D. P. Ostler b Curran | 1 | – (3) b Roberts | 65 |
| D. A. Reeve b Baptiste | 65 | | |
| Asif Din b Cook | 92 | – (4) not out | 17 |
| N. M. K. Smith c Penberthy b Capel | 70 | | |
| †P. C. L. Holloway not out | 74 | | |
| J. E. Benjamin lbw b Capel | 0 | | |
| T. A. Munton not out | 17 | | |
| B 6, l-b 13, w 3, n-b 1 | 23 | B 5, l-b 3 | 8 |

1/55 2/119 3/124 4/125 5/259     (8 wkts dec.) 460     1/19 2/117     (2 wkts dec.) 159
6/300 7/408 8/413

A. A. Donald did not bat.

Bonus points – Warwickshire 4, Northamptonshire 2 (Score at 100 overs: 324-6).

Bowling: *First Innings*—Capel 24-0-109-3; Baptiste 30-2-118-1; Penberthy 5-1-16-0; Curran 27-8-57-3; Roberts 6-1-49-0; Cook 29-5-92-1. *Second Innings*—Capel 5-0-21-1; Baptiste 5-0-12-0; Roberts 20-5-44-1; Penberthy 10-3-21-0; Cook 9-3-31-0; Stanley 9-2-16-0; Larkins 6-4-2-0; Fordham 2-0-4-0.

## Northamptonshire

| | | |
|---|---|---|
| A. Fordham c Ostler b Donald | 66 | – not out ............ 44 |
| W. Larkins b Benjamin | 3 | – not out ............ 28 |
| N. A. Stanley c Holloway b Munton | 62 | |
| *A. J. Lamb b Benjamin b Smith | 35 | |
| D. J. Capel b Munton | 0 | |
| A. L. Penberthy c Moles b Munton | 52 | |
| K. M. Curran b Reeve | 9 | |
| E. A. E. Baptiste lbw b Donald | 21 | |
| †D. Ripley c and b Munton | 5 | |
| A. R. Roberts not out | 36 | |
| N. G. B. Cook c Asif Din b Benjamin | 29 | |
| B 14, l-b 22, w 1, n-b 19 | 56 | W 1 .................... 1 |

1/4  2/121  3/161  4/161  5/216          374          (no wkt) 73
6/233  7/278  8/278  9/289

Bonus points – Northamptonshire 4, Warwickshire 4 (Score at 100 overs: 323-9).

Bowling: *First Innings*—Donald 26–3–82–2; Benjamin 21.4–4–66–2; Munton 30–7–85–4;
Smith 14–3–50–1; Reeve 17–5–55–1. *Second Innings*—Moles 10–1–30–0; Asif Din 9–1–20–0;
Ratcliffe 3–1–14–0; Smith 5–3–2–0; Ostler 2–1–7–0.

Umpires: G. I. Burgess and B. Leadbeater.

At Colchester, August 16, 17, 19. NORTHAMPTONSHIRE lost to ESSEX by an innings
and 12 runs.

## NORTHAMPTONSHIRE v SURREY

At Northampton, August 23, 24, 26. Northamptonshire won by 138 runs. Northamptonshire
21 pts, Surrey 4 pts. Toss: Northamptonshire. Lamb made up for the 61 overs lost on a
frustrating first day which saw play interrupted on seven occasions by rain. Taking full
advantage of the absence, through injury, of Waqar Younis, he batted for six hours, facing 289
balls for his 194 and hitting 31 fours. At 146, Lamb became the ninth batsman to reach 15,000
first-class runs for the county, but his innings ended in a curious fashion when Montgomerie, a
Championship débutant, was run out while acting as runner for his captain, who had suffered
a pelvic strain. Medlycott, leading Surrey after Greig had omitted himself from the side,
declared 251 behind, and a farcical period of "run-feeding" enabled Northamptonshire to set
a target of 357 in a minimum of 96 overs. Alone of the Surrey batsmen, Thorpe came to terms
with the home attack, remaining unbeaten for four and a quarter hours and hitting sixteen
fours in his 116 from 200 balls. The Northamptonshire bowling was intelligently handled by
the acting-captain, Bailey, who himself broke two stubborn partnerships, dismissing
Robinson and Feltham, and claimed the last wicket 70 minutes from time.
    *Close of play:* First day, Northamptonshire 121-5 (A. J. Lamb 61*, A. R. Roberts 2*);
Second day, Northamptonshire 77-3 (R. J. Bailey 29*, W. M. Noon 0*).

## Northamptonshire

| | | |
|---|---|---|
| R. R. Montgomerie lbw b M. P. Bicknell | 2 | – lbw b Alikhan ............ 7 |
| A. Fordham c Sargeant b Murphy | 28 | – b Alikhan ............ 25 |
| R. J. Bailey b Murphy | 4 | – not out ............ 37 |
| *A. J. Lamb run out | 194 | |
| N. A. Stanley lbw b Robinson | 18 | – (4) c Murphy b D. J. Bicknell .. 16 |
| D. J. Capel c Sargeant b M. P. Bicknell | 1 | |
| A. R. Roberts c Sargeant b Feltham | 11 | |
| K. M. Curran b M. P. Bicknell | 52 | – (6) not out .................... 6 |
| E. A. E. Baptiste not out | 63 | |
| A. L. Penberthy c Ward b Medlycott | 0 | |
| †W. M. Noon not out | 8 | – (5) c Sargeant b D. J. Bicknell .. 14 |
| L-b 18, n-b 2 | 20 | |

1/10  2/15  3/61  4/102  5/109          (9 wkts dec.) 401          1/9  2/44          (4 wkts dec.) 105
6/147  7/282  8/377  9/381                                        3/63  4/99

Bonus points – Northamptonshire 4, Surrey 3 (Score at 100 overs: 322-7).

Bowling: *First Innings*—M. P. Bicknell 33–8–92–3; Murphy 27–4–103–2; Feltham 27.1–5–68–1; Robinson 13–1–58–1; Medlycott 13–1–62–1. *Second Innings*—D. J. Bicknell 5.3–0–62–2; Alikhan 5–0–43–2.

## Surrey

| | | | |
|---|---|---|---|
| D. J. Bicknell c Baptiste b Penberthy | 40 | – c Penberthy b Capel | 4 |
| R. I. Alikhan c Montgomerie b Penberthy | 37 | – c Montgomerie b Baptiste | 1 |
| G. P. Thorpe not out | 51 | – not out | 116 |
| D. M. Ward c Roberts b Penberthy | 5 | – c Noon b Curran | 28 |
| M. A. Lynch b Roberts | 14 | – lbw b Curran | 1 |
| J. D. Robinson not out | 0 | – lbw b Bailey | 22 |
| *K. T. Medlycott (did not bat) | | – c Stanley b Curran | 4 |
| M. A. Feltham (did not bat) | | – b Bailey | 16 |
| †N. F. Sargeant (did not bat) | | – c Noon b Roberts | 5 |
| M. P. Bicknell (did not bat) | | – c and b Roberts | 0 |
| A. J. Murphy (did not bat) | | – c Fordham b Bailey | 0 |
| B 1, l-b 2 | 3 | B 11, l-b 9, w 1 | 21 |

1/72 2/85 3/98 4/149     (4 wkts dec.) 150    1/10 2/16 3/56 4/58 5/126    218
                                                   6/136 7/186 8/213 9/217

Bonus points – Surrey 1, Northamptonshire 1.

Bowling: *First Innings*—Curran 6–0–37–0; Capel 7–0–29–0; Penberthy 8–0–37–3; Roberts 8–0–41–1; Bailey 1.1–0–3–0. *Second Innings*—Capel 11–4–26–1; Baptiste 11–4–22–1; Roberts 25–9–73–2; Curran 11–5–26–3; Bailey 12.3–2–44–3; Penberthy 4–1–4–0; Stanley 1–0–3–0.

Umpires: B. Leadbeater and K. J. Lyons.

## NORTHAMPTONSHIRE v YORKSHIRE

At Northampton, August 28, 29, 30, 31. Northamptonshire won by nine wickets. Northamptonshire 22 pts, Yorkshire 3 pts. Toss: Northamptonshire. Northamptonshire secured their third Championship victory in August shortly after tea on the final afternoon, having outplayed Yorkshire in all departments. The visitors gained just two batting points from a dour performance, enlivened later by Carrick, who hit ten boundaries, and it took Northamptonshire only 78 overs to match their total. Fordham (354 minutes, 271 balls, two sixes, twenty fours) and Lamb (151 minutes, 155 balls, one six, seventeen fours) were in sparkling form. They added 173 in 42 overs, and Capel, passing 50 for the first time in first-class cricket since July 4, and Penberthy cemented the home side's strong position. Facing a deficit of 182, Yorkshire put up a brave display, only for two minor collapses to leave them facing defeat at the end of the third day, just 18 runs ahead with half their wickets gone. Gough's maiden half-century, featuring crisp pulling and driving, and another stubborn innings from Carrick prolonged the match, but Baptiste was always a threat and he returned his best figures since joining Northamptonshire. Fordham, whose 44 runs came off 43 balls, Larkins and Bailey duly completed the win.

*Close of play*: First day, Yorkshire 267-6 (P. Carrick 60*, D. Gough 12*); Second day, Northamptonshire 354-4 (A. Fordham 137*, D. J. Capel 28*); Third day, Yorkshire 200-5 (D. Gough 8*, R. J. Blakey 4*).

## Yorkshire

| | | | |
|---|---|---|---|
| *M. D. Moxon lbw b Baptiste | 12 | – b Baptiste | 55 |
| A. A. Metcalfe lbw b Baptiste | 66 | – lbw b Baptiste | 42 |
| D. Byas c Roberts b Penberthy | 8 | – b Roberts | 38 |
| S. A. Kellett run out | 36 | – c and b Bailey | 3 |
| P. E. Robinson lbw b Roberts | 30 | – c Lamb b Baptiste | 34 |
| †R. J. Blakey b Roberts | 19 | – (7) c Noon b Baptiste | 20 |
| P. Carrick lbw b Capel | 67 | – (8) not out | 29 |
| D. Gough c Noon b Curran | 22 | – (6) c Stanley b Baptiste | 72 |
| P. J. Hartley not out | 19 | – c Stanley b Roberts | 4 |
| S. D. Fletcher c Fordham b Curran | 5 | – c Bailey b Baptiste | 5 |
| M. A. Robinson c Capel | 3 | – b Baptiste | 0 |
| B 4, l-b 20, n-b 4 | 28 | B 5, l-b 15, n-b 3 | 23 |

1/51 2/66 3/130 4/165 5/188    315    1/98 2/99 3/102 4/187 5/187    325
6/211 7/284 8/284 9/303                                       6/237 7/298 8/312 9/325

Bonus points – Yorkshire 2, Northamptonshire 2 (Score at 100 overs: 229-6).

Bowling: *First Innings*—Capel 38.1–10–99–2; Curran 25–9–51–2; Baptiste 31–12–64–2; Penberthy 5–1–16–1; Roberts 20–6–40–2; Bailey 7–0–21–0. *Second Innings*—Capel 15–4–46–0; Curran 16–4–55–0; Roberts 29–4–90–2; Baptiste 32–5–95–7; Bailey 8–4–19–1.

## Northamptonshire

| | | | |
|---|---|---|---|
| A. Fordham c Fletcher b Hartley | 165 | – c Hartley b M. A. Robinson | 44 |
| W. Larkins c Blakey b Hartley | 5 | – not out | 62 |
| R. J. Bailey c P. E. Robinson b Fletcher | 12 | – not out | 31 |
| *A. J. Lamb c Blakey b Hartley | 109 | | |
| N. A. Stanley lbw b Hartley | 34 | | |
| D. J. Capel c Blakey b Hartley | 66 | | |
| K. M. Curran c M. A. Robinson b Gough | 2 | | |
| E. A. E. Baptiste lbw b Hartley | 5 | | |
| A. L. Penberthy c Fletcher b Carrick | 41 | | |
| A. R. Roberts c Moxon b M. A. Robinson | 9 | | |
| †W. M. Noon not out | 10 | | |
| B 4, l-b 23, w 2, n-b 10 | 39 | L-b 6, n-b 1 | 7 |

1/5 2/43 3/216 4/302 5/402      497    1/79      (1 wkt) 144
6/427 7/429 8/433 9/452

Bonus points – Northamptonshire 4, Yorkshire 1 (Score at 100 overs: 396-4).

Bowling: *First Innings*—Hartley 38–6–151–6; Gough 30–7–87–1; Fletcher 11–0–78–1; M. A. Robinson 27–6–58–1; Carrick 31.4–6–96–1. *Second Innings*—Hartley 4–0–27–0; Gough 4–0–29–0; M. A. Robinson 7–0–27–1; Fletcher 10–1–34–0; Carrick 8.4–1–21–0.

Umpires: B. Dudleston and J. H. Harris.

At Bristol, September 3, 4, 5, 6. NORTHAMPTONSHIRE beat GLOUCESTERSHIRE by five wickets.

At Birmingham, September 10, 11, 12, 13. NORTHAMPTONSHIRE lost to WARWICK-SHIRE by three wickets.

# NOTTINGHAMSHIRE

*President:* R. T. Simpson
*Chairman:* C. W. Gillott
*Chairman, Cricket Committee:* A. Wheelhouse
*General Manager/Secretary:* B. Robson
   County Cricket Ground, Trent Bridge,
   Nottingham NG2 6AG
   (Telephone: 0602-821525)
*Captain:* R. T. Robinson
*Cricket Manager:* J. D. Birch

Nottinghamshire swept aside the seeds of doubt in 1991 and demonstrated a fierce determination to remain at the forefront of English
cricket. Drawing fresh impetus from their vigorous new team manager,
John Birch, they captured their first Sunday League title, and finished a
creditable fourth in the Britannic Assurance Championship. The county
crowned a heartening year by signing two of the world's most exciting
young all-rounders, Chris Lewis of England and the New Zealander,
Chris Cairns. Such a vivid upturn in fortunes dispersed the memory of
the gloom that descended on Trent Bridge in late 1990, when seven of the
last eleven Championship games ended in defeat.

Indeed, the glow of satisfaction was slightly dimmed only by a feeling
that even greater heights could have been scaled. There was some
disappointment that Nottinghamshire did not mount a stronger challenge in the Championship, and they made an early exit from the
Benson and Hedges Cup after two hair's-breadth defeats. But overall the
revival reflected a wealth of talent, and reinforced Birch's confidence
on succeeding Ken Taylor in 1990.

Not content with managing one of the best sides in the country, Birch
wanted Nottinghamshire to be the best. That ambitious philosophy was
underlined by his no-nonsense approach to replacing the West Indian all-
rounder, Franklyn Stephenson, with Cairns, and his success in the hotly
contested race to sign Lewis. These acquisitions gave him seven players
with Test caps, and three more with England A status. Assuming that
Lewis's promising Test career continues to develop, Nottinghamshire
believe they have capable support for him and Cairns in Andy Pick,
Keith Evans and Kevin Cooper. Indeed, it was their lack of seam-
bowling depth, exposed by injuries, which proved to be the major
stumbling-block in the 1991 Championship campaign. The biggest blow
was the loss of the dependable Cooper for almost all season to a double
stress fracture of the spine, which required major surgery. The county's
Refuge Assurance League triumph was all the more commendable in the
absence of this economic seamer, but with much depending on them,
Stephenson, Pick and Evans rose to the task admirably.

Although fitness had not been Stephenson's strongest point in the
previous two seasons, he never missed a match in the 1991 Championship, and 78 wickets made him Nottinghamshire's leading wicket-taker
for the fourth successive year since his arrival at Trent Bridge. His
departure and subsequent move to Sussex were a surprise, but Nottinghamshire had offered him only a one-year contract because they were

anxious that Cairns, whom they had given an opening in county cricket in 1988 and 1989, should not slip from their grasp. Stephenson's record speaks for itself: 349 first-class wickets in four seasons, with an illustrious double of 1,018 runs and 125 wickets in the first year. It was a hard act to follow.

In completing a full season without injury, Pick dispelled fears that his body could not withstand the strain and illustrated his growing confidence since his tour with England A. He claimed 67 first-class wickets. The restoration of seam-bowling resources in 1992 could reduce opportunities for the spinners, Eddie Hemmings and Andy Afford, to operate in tandem, but together they bowled more than 1,300 overs in 1991. Left-armer Afford enjoyed a more productive summer than in 1990, while 42-year-old Hemmings soldiered on despite niggling fitness troubles.

The batting proved as strong as it looked on paper. Once again Chris Broad was the leading run-scorer, and all five of the principal batsmen passed 1,000 runs comfortably. The return to full fitness of Derek Randall, after a hernia operation, and the re-emergence of Paul Pollard were prime reasons for the turnaround since the previous season. Randall, an improbable 40, was back to his flamboyant best in the Championship, and thrived as an opener in the Sunday League. He and Broad shared three century stands and five more over 50 in this.

Pollard, who had reached 50 only once in 1990, repaid the faith shown in him by establishing himself as Broad's regular partner in the Championship. Tim Robinson benefited, both as leader and as run-maker, from Birch easing the weight on his shoulders. The second trophy of his term in charge gave him, and many of his senior colleagues, a full set of winners' medals. His vice-captain, Paul Johnson, responded to his new responsibility by showing even greater consistency, and this was recognised by his selection for England A, reviving hopes for the Test career that once seemed likely.

The all-round talent at Trent Bridge, to be supplemented by Lewis and Cairns, included Mark Crawley, who settled in well despite his season being interrupted by a broken thumb. Mark Saxelby played a vital role in the Refuge League success, and Evans demonstrated his claims to be considered a useful lower-order batsman as well as a front-line bowler. Such strengths should make Nottinghamshire an even more formidable unit in the limited-overs competitions than in 1991, which they began with a nine-wicket win in the Sunday League over Lancashire, who emerged as their closest rivals. Nottinghamshire suffered only three Sunday defeats along the way, and another nine-wicket victory, over title-holders Derbyshire, in the final match was a fitting climax.

In contrast, Nottinghamshire performed below par in the quarter-finals of the NatWest Bank Trophy at Southampton, where they went down by seven wickets to Hampshire, and a disastrous collapse to Graeme Hick's occasional off-spin knocked them out of the Refuge Assurance Cup. Defeats by 4 runs at Southampton and by 1 run at Cardiff robbed them of a quarter-final place in the Benson and Hedges Cup, and further opportunities were missed in the Championship. Dropped catches denied them at least three victories early on. Long-term prospects looked healthy, however, particularly as the Second Eleven brought home another trophy after beating Surrey in the Bain Clarkson final at The Oval. – Nick Lucy.

NOTTINGHAMSHIRE 1991

[*Roger Wootton*

*Back row*: P. R. Pollard, M. A. Crawley, M. Saxelby, R. T. Bates, G. W. Mike, W. A. Dessaur, S. M. Brogan. *Middle row*: G. Stringfellow (*2nd XI scorer*), G. F. Archer, C. W. Scott, D. J. R. Martindale, K. P. Evans, J. A. Afford, M. Newell, M. G. Field-Buss, J. Hodgson, S. Ball (*physiotherapist*), L. Beaumont (*scorer*). *Front row*: K. E. Cooper, F. D. Stephenson, D. W. Randall, E. E. Hemmings, R. T. Robinson (*captain*), J. D. Birch (*cricket manager*), P. Johnson, B. C. Broad, B. N. French, K. Saxelby. *Inset*: R. A. Pick.

# NOTTINGHAMSHIRE RESULTS

*All first-class matches – Played 23: Won 7, Lost 5, Drawn 11.*

*County Championship matches – Played 22: Won 7, Lost 5, Drawn 10.*

*Bonus points – Batting 64, Bowling 69.*

*Competition placings – Britannic Assurance County Championship, 4th;
NatWest Bank Trophy, q-f; Benson and Hedges Cup, 3rd in Group D;
Refuge Assurance League, winners; Refuge Assurance Cup, s-f.*

## BRITANNIC ASSURANCE CHAMPIONSHIP AVERAGES

### BATTING

| | Birthplace | M | I | NO | R | HI | Avge |
|---|---|---|---|---|---|---|---|
| ‡D. W. Randall ..... | Retford | 22 | 34 | 9 | 1,567 | 143* | 62.68 |
| ‡R. T. Robinson..... | Sutton-in-Ashfield | 22 | 37 | 8 | 1,673 | 180 | 57.68 |
| ‡B. C. Broad....... | Bristol | 21 | 38 | 3 | 1,739 | 166 | 49.68 |
| ‡P. Johnson ....... | Newark | 22 | 36 | 6 | 1,357 | 124 | 45.23 |
| P. R. Pollard...... | Nottingham | 22 | 40 | 3 | 1,235 | 145 | 33.37 |
| ‡K. P. Evans ...... | Calverton | 14 | 17 | 7 | 276 | 56* | 27.60 |
| ‡F. D. Stephenson .. | St James, Barbados | 22 | 27 | 7 | 423 | 58 | 21.15 |
| M. A. Crawley ..... | Newton-le-Willows | 10 | 12 | 4 | 160 | 49* | 20.00 |
| M. Saxelby ....... | Worksop | 6 | 9 | 1 | 136 | 44 | 17.00 |
| ‡B. N. French ..... | Warsop | 21 | 24 | 4 | 315 | 65 | 15.75 |
| ‡R. A. Pick....... | Nottingham | 21 | 16 | 5 | 142 | 46 | 12.90 |
| ‡E. E. Hemmings.... | Leamington Spa | 16 | 16 | 4 | 143 | 29* | 11.91 |
| J. A. Afford ...... | Crowland | 18 | 12 | 4 | 42 | 13 | 5.25 |

Also batted: V. J. P. Broadley (*Sutton-in-Ashfield*) (1 match) 6; M. G. Field-Buss (*Mtarfa, Malta*) (2 matches) 25, 16. ‡K. E. Cooper (*Hucknall*) (1 match) and ‡C. W. Scott (*Thorpe-on-the-Hill*) (1 match) did not bat.

\* *Signifies not out.*     ‡ *Denotes county cap.*

The following played a total of nineteen three-figure innings for Nottinghamshire in County Championship matches – B. C. Broad 5, D. W. Randall 5, P. Johnson 3, P. R. Pollard 3, R. T. Robinson 3.

### BOWLING

| | O | M | R | W | BB | 5W/i | Avge |
|---|---|---|---|---|---|---|---|
| F. D. Stephenson...... | 719.1 | 158 | 2,010 | 78 | 5-27 | 4 | 25.76 |
| R. A. Pick........... | 623.4 | 113 | 1,985 | 65 | 5-17 | 3 | 30.53 |
| J. A. Afford ........ | 670.3 | 207 | 1,817 | 57 | 4-44 | 0 | 31.87 |
| K. P. Evans.......... | 425 | 89 | 1,278 | 40 | 5-52 | 2 | 31.95 |
| E. E. Hemmings....... | 638.3 | 171 | 1,721 | 46 | 6-46 | 2 | 37.41 |
| M. A. Crawley........ | 176.5 | 53 | 463 | 11 | 3-21 | 0 | 42.09 |

Also bowled: V. J. P. Broadley 32–6–111–1; K. E. Cooper 17–3–54–1; M. G. Field-Buss 53–11–187–1; B. N. French 14–4–48–1; P. Johnson 12.2–1–62–2; P. R. Pollard 23.5–8–75–1; D. W. Randall 4–0–19–1; R. T. Robinson 8–0–39–1; M. Saxelby 97.2–17–423–4.

**Wicket-keepers:** B. N. French 54 ct, 8 st; C. W. Scott 3 ct.

**Leading Fielders:** P. R. Pollard 21, R. T. Robinson 18, D. W. Randall 15.

At Oxford, April 27, 29, 30. NOTTINGHAMSHIRE drew with OXFORD UNIVERSITY.

## NOTTINGHAMSHIRE v LEICESTERSHIRE

At Nottingham, May 9, 10, 11, 13. Nottinghamshire won by seven wickets. Nottinghamshire 24 pts, Leicestershire 5 pts. Toss: Leicestershire. Pick and Evans soon had the visitors on the defensive, the fifth wicket falling with just 60 on the board, but Willey proved obdurate, remaining 37 overs for his 24, and Millns embarrassed his former county by helping add 65 for the last wicket. In contrast, Nottinghamshire made a sound start, and after four wickets had gone for 29, Randall and the later batsmen provided a lead of 159. Randall faced 222 deliveries and hit two sixes and ten fours in a stay of more than four hours. Leicestershire prospered on the third day, with Briers (fourteen fours) and Whitaker (one six, fourteen fours) adding 190 for the third wicket, but from 282 for two they tumbled to 325 all out. This left Nottinghamshire ample time in which to score 167 for victory, and Johnson and Robinson accomplished this soon after lunch on the last day.

*Close of play:* First day, Nottinghamshire 133-4 (P. Johnson 2*, D. W. Randall 0*); Second day, Leicestershire 50-1 (N. E. Briers 38*, P. N. Hepworth 6*); Third day, Nottinghamshire 4-2 (B. C. Broad 1*).

### Leicestershire

| | | | |
|---|---|---|---|
| T. J. Boon c French b Pick | 3 | – b Stephenson | 2 |
| *N. E. Briers b Stephenson | 22 | – c Pollard b Stephenson | 160 |
| P. N. Hepworth b Pick | 0 | – c Robinson b Pick | 37 |
| J. J. Whitaker c Johnson b Evans | 15 | – c Pollard b Evans | 86 |
| L. Potter c French b Evans | 6 | – c Pick b Evans | 0 |
| P. Willey c Afford b Evans | 24 | – c Broad b Evans | 0 |
| †P. Whitticase b Evans | 9 | – c French b Stephenson | 0 |
| L. Tennant c Pollard b Stephenson | 13 | – lbw b Pick | 8 |
| C. W. Wilkinson b Evans | 41 | – b Evans | 16 |
| D. J. Millns not out | 26 | – not out | 0 |
| J. N. Maguire lbw b Stephenson | 33 | – c Randall b Pick | 0 |
| B 2, l-b 11, w 4, n-b 11 | 28 | B 6, l-b 3, w 1, n-b 6 | 16 |

1/3 2/9 3/42 4/53 5/60          **220**    1/14 2/92 3/282 4/282 5/300    **325**
6/73 7/95 8/153 9/155                        6/300 7/302 8/319 9/325

Bonus points – Leicestershire 2, Nottinghamshire 4.

Bowling: *First Innings*—Stephenson 20.4-6-52-3; Pick 19-5-75-2; Evans 21-5-52-5; Hemmings 6-1-20-0; Afford 3-1-8-0. *Second Innings*—Stephenson 27-11-33-3; Pick 22.1-2-89-3; Evans 29-8-83-4; Hemmings 25-6-56-0; Afford 23-6-55-0.

### Nottinghamshire

| | | | |
|---|---|---|---|
| B. C. Broad c Whitticase b Maguire | 67 | – c Briers b Hepworth | 29 |
| P. R. Pollard c Whitticase b Tennant | 45 | – lbw b Millns | 0 |
| *R. T. Robinson c Millns b Tennant | 13 | – (4) not out | 68 |
| R. A. Pick c Whitticase b Maguire | 0 | | |
| P. Johnson c Whitticase b Wilkinson | 37 | – not out | 57 |
| D. W. Randall c Briers b Millns | 104 | | |
| K. P. Evans c Hepworth b Tennant | 22 | | |
| F. D. Stephenson c Whitticase b Wilkinson | 28 | | |
| †B. N. French c Potter b Maguire | 9 | – (3) run out | 1 |
| E. E. Hemmings not out | 15 | | |
| J. A. Afford c Wilkinson b Maguire | 13 | | |
| B 2, l-b 10, w 5, n-b 9 | 26 | L-b 6, n-b 6 | 12 |

1/103 2/121 3/128 4/132 5/198    **379**    1/1 2/4 3/43    (3 wkts) **167**
6/245 7/296 8/332 9/352

Bonus points – Nottinghamshire 4, Leicestershire 3 (Score at 100 overs: 316-7).

Bowling: *First Innings*—Millns 31-6-86-1; Maguire 30.3-5-92-4; Wilkinson 22-5-80-2; Willey 7-1-15-0; Tennant 19-3-65-3; Potter 10-0-29-0. *Second Innings*—Millns 11-3-23-1; Maguire 8-1-34-0; Hepworth 8-0-31-1; Tennant 6-2-22-0; Potter 12-2-34-0; Wilkinson 2-0-17-0.

Umpires: B. Dudleston and N. T. Plews.

At Leeds, May 16, 17, 18, 20. NOTTINGHAMSHIRE drew with YORKSHIRE.

## NOTTINGHAMSHIRE v KENT

At Nottingham, May 22, 23, 24. Drawn. Nottinghamshire 7 pts, Kent 5 pts. Toss: Nottinghamshire. Kent began the match a player short, as Davis was obliged to return home unexpectedly and his replacement, Llong, did not arrive in time. Broad batted convincingly from the start, reaching 50 from 52 balls, and he gave no chances in his 166, which contained 27 fours and lasted 330 minutes. His partnership for the second wicket with Robinson was worth 214. On the second day Hinks, injured while batting, retired but resumed later with a runner to support Cowdrey on his way to his unbeaten century (two sixes, fifteen fours). Randall's 64 came off 69 balls as Nottinghamshire raced to set a target on the last day, but Kent never looked likely to reach 264 off 59 overs. With wickets falling, they were content to bat out time.

*Close of play:* First day, Kent 10-1 (S. G. Hinks 6*, C. Penn 1*); Second day, Nottinghamshire 17-1 (P. R. Pollard 9*, R. T. Robinson 8*).

## Nottinghamshire

| | | |
|---|---|---|
| B. C. Broad c Marsh b Merrick | 166 | – c Marsh b Merrick .......... 0 |
| P. R. Pollard c Marsh b Igglesden | 16 | – c Fleming b Ellison .......... 48 |
| *R. T. Robinson c Marsh b Penn | 85 | – c Marsh b Merrick .......... 16 |
| D. W. Randall c Taylor b Ellison | 12 | – (5) not out .......... 64 |
| P. Johnson not out | 38 | – (4) c Merrick b Penn .......... 65 |
| F. D. Stephenson c Penn b Ellison | 1 | – c Taylor b Penn .......... 2 |
| †B. N. French c Taylor b Fleming | 12 | – run out .......... 1 |
| E. E. Hemmings (did not bat) | | – c Llong b Penn .......... 8 |
| R. A. Pick (did not bat) | | – not out .......... 11 |
| L-b 9, w 3, n-b 3 | 15 | L-b 1, w 1, n-b 1 .......... 3 |

1/36 2/250 3/289 4/303    (6 wkts dec.) 345    1/0 2/46 3/126    (7 wkts dec.) 218
5/304 6/345                                     4/132 5/146
                                                6/149 7/180

K. E. Cooper and J. A. Afford did not bat.

Bonus points – Nottinghamshire 4, Kent 2.

Bowling: *First Innings*—Merrick 19-1-78-1; Igglesden 18-5-60-1; Ellison 24-8-85-2; Penn 17-1-63-1; Fleming 17.2-5-38-1; Llong 3-1-12-0. *Second Innings*—Merrick 17-3-67-2; Igglesden 11-1-48-0; Ellison 5-0-22-1; Penn 13-0-64-3; Llong 2-0-16-0.

## Kent

| | | |
|---|---|---|
| S. G. Hinks not out | 61 | |
| *M. R. Benson lbw b Pick | 0 | – c sub b Pick .......... 6 |
| C. Penn c sub b Cooper | 13 | – (8) not out .......... 8 |
| N. R. Taylor c Broad b Afford | 45 | – (1) b Pick .......... 0 |
| G. R. Cowdrey not out | 109 | – (3) c French b Afford .......... 36 |
| M. V. Fleming c Pollard b Hemmings | 40 | – (4) c Hemmings b Afford .......... 27 |
| N. J. Llong c French b Hemmings | | – not out .......... 42 |
| R. M. Ellison run out | 5 | – (7) c Randall b Afford .......... 13 |
| †S. A. Marsh lbw b Hemmings | 10 | – (6) st French b Afford .......... 11 |
| T. A. Merrick c Broad b Hemmings | 4 | |
| B 4, l-b 2, w 1, n-b 6 | 13 | B 4, l-b 2, n-b 6 .......... 12 |

1/3 2/30 3/144 4/215 5/215    (8 wkts dec.) 300    1/1 2/12 3/70    (6 wkts) 155
6/223 7/240 8/276                                  4/89 5/113 6/138

A. P. Igglesden did not bat.

Bonus points – Kent 3, Nottinghamshire 3 (Score at 100 overs: 276-8).

*In the first innings S. G. Hinks, when 58, retired hurt at 97 and resumed at 276.*

Bowling: *First Innings*—Stephenson 16.2-4-44-0; Pick 19-5-44-1; Hemmings 29-9-70-4; Cooper 17-3-54-1; Afford 25-6-82-1. *Second Innings*—Stephenson 12-3-26-0; Pick 11.3-1-48-2; Hemmings 16-6-31-0; Afford 19-8-44-4.

Umpires: H. D. Bird and R. A. White.

t Leicester, May 25, 27, 28. NOTTINGHAMSHIRE drew with LEICESTERSHIRE.

## NOTTINGHAMSHIRE v HAMPSHIRE

At Nottingham, May 31, June 1, 3. Drawn. Nottinghamshire 4 pts, Hampshire 6 pts. Toss: Nottinghamshire. The weather was miserable for the opening day, and the cricket was similar until bad light ended play early. On a slow wicket the home side made runs at 2.5 per over, and Pollard's 100, containing thirteen boundaries, occupied five hours and 252 deliveries. Hampshire made slightly faster progress on the second day, with Nicholas hitting 107 (fifteen fours) off 191 balls before declaring. On the last morning Nottinghamshire were given easy runs, and Hampshire were eventually set 260 off 57 overs. Middleton and Robin Smith both batted well to put Hampshire on course, and Smith and Gower (34 balls) added 76 in eleven overs. But rain robbed Hampshire of four overs, and when Gower was out the chase was abandoned.

*Close of play:* First day, Nottinghamshire 238-7 (B. N. French 0*, E. E. Hemmings 1*); second day, Nottinghamshire 15-1 (B. C. Broad 4*, R. T. Robinson 7*).

## Nottinghamshire

| | | | |
|---|---|---|---|
| B. C. Broad c Gower b Aqib Javed | 5 | – b James | 59 |
| P. R. Pollard c Bakker b Aqib Javed | 100 | – c Aymes b Aqib Javed | 0 |
| R. T. Robinson c Gower b Aqib Javed | 48 | – not out | 95 |
| P. Johnson b Connor | 16 | – lbw b James | 0 |
| D. W. Randall c Aymes b Aqib Javed | 13 | – not out | 48 |
| K. P. Evans lbw b Aqib Javed | 16 | | |
| F. D. Stephenson c Aymes b Maru | 22 | | |
| *B. N. French b Bakker | 21 | | |
| E. E. Hemmings b Aqib Javed | 25 | | |
| R. A. Pick b Bakker | 4 | | |
| M. A. Afford not out | 0 | | |
| B 6, l-b 8, w 1, n-b 4 | 19 | B 1, l-b 2, w 7, n-b 9 | 19 |

1/5 2/127 3/162 4/181 5/194 289    1/2 2/116 3/118    (3 wkts dec.) 221
6/237 7/237 8/275 9/285

Bonus points – Nottinghamshire 3, Hampshire 3 (Score at 100 overs: 275-7).

Bowling: *First Innings*—Bakker 21.1-10-42-2; Aqib Javed 30-6-91-6; Connor 20-5-62-1; James 10-4-28-0; Maru 24-7-52-1. *Second Innings*—Aqib Javed 8-1-32-1; Bakker 3-2-23-0; James 12-2-27-2; Maru 17-4-58-0; Nicholas 10-0-47-0; C. L. Smith 10-0-31-0.

## Hampshire

| | | | |
|---|---|---|---|
| T. C. Middleton lbw b Pick | 26 | – st French b Hemmings | 63 |
| C. L. Smith b Stephenson | 22 | – c French b Stephenson | 0 |
| *M. C. J. Nicholas not out | 107 | – b Hemmings | 29 |
| R. A. Smith c Pollard b Evans | 46 | – b Evans | 60 |
| D. I. Gower c Johnson b Stephenson | 10 | – c Evans b Stephenson | 44 |
| K. D. James not out | 21 | – not out | 2 |
| L-b 9, n-b 10 | 19 | B 1, l-b 14, w 1, n-b 4 | 20 |

1/40 2/81 3/151 4/175    (4 wkts dec.) 251    1/1 2/67 3/136    (5 wkts) 218
4/212 5/218

†A. N. Aymes, R. J. Maru, C. A. Connor, P. J. Bakker and Aqib Javed did not bat.

Bonus points – Hampshire 3, Nottinghamshire 1.

Bowling: *First Innings*—Stephenson 17-6-23-2; Pick 13-2-43-1; Evans 12-4-21-1; Hemmings 25-5-75-0; Afford 16.5-2-80-0. *Second Innings*—Stephenson 12-1-57-2; Evans 13.2-1-72-36-1; Afford 9-0-51-0; Hemmings 16-2-59-2.

Umpires: M. J. Kitchen and N. T. Plews.

At The Oval, June 4, 5, 6. NOTTINGHAMSHIRE drew with SURREY.

At Gloucester, June 14, 15, 17. NOTTINGHAMSHIRE drew with GLOUCESTERSHIRE.

At Worcester, June 18, 19, 20. NOTTINGHAMSHIRE lost to WORCESTERSHIRE by one wicket.

## NOTTINGHAMSHIRE v WARWICKSHIRE

At Nottingham, June 21, 22, 24. Drawn. Nottinghamshire 3 pts, Warwickshire 3 pts. Toss Nottinghamshire. Rain prevented any play on the opening day until mid-afternoon, when Robinson invited Warwickshire to bat. Progress was pedestrian, and further rain meant that only 49 overs were bowled. On Saturday, however, Reeve put some punch into the match, and Munton helped him add 61 for the ninth wicket. Nottinghamshire were disadvantaged by Stephenson's inability to bowl because of injury. On the last day Robinson declared at the overnight total, Warwickshire forfeited their second innings, and Nottinghamshire set out to make 298 in 102 overs. Once rain at lunch had reduced the available overs by nineteen, the game meandered to an inevitable draw.

*Close of play:* First day, Warwickshire 102-1 (A. J. Moles 41*, K. J. Piper 3*); Second day, Nottinghamshire 37-0 (B. C. Broad 28*, P. R. Pollard 8*).

### Warwickshire

| | | | | |
|---|---|---|---|---|
| A. J. Moles c Crawley b Evans | 57 | P. A. Booth lbw b Afford | | 12 |
| J. D. Ratcliffe lbw b Crawley | 47 | T. A. Munton c Robinson b Pick | | 25 |
| †K. J. Piper c Johnson b Crawley | 55 | A. A. Donald b Crawley | | 5 |
| *T. A. Lloyd run out | 4 | | | |
| D. P. Ostler lbw b Afford | 14 | B 2, l-b 25, n-b 7 | | 34 |
| D. A. Reeve not out | 70 | | | |
| P. A. Smith st French b Afford | 7 | 1/99 2/171 3/177 4/184 5/210 | | 334 |
| G. C. Small b Afford | 4 | 6/232 7/236 8/258 9/319 | | |

Bonus points – Warwickshire 3, Nottinghamshire 3 (Score at 100 overs: 253-7).

Bowling: Stephenson 7-3-17-0; Pick 30-5-77-1; Afford 29-6-65-4; Evans 29-7-91-1; Crawley 23.2-7-57-3.

*Warwickshire forfeited their second innings.*

### Nottinghamshire

| | | | |
|---|---|---|---|
| B. C. Broad not out | 28 | – c Piper b Small | 8 |
| P. R. Pollard not out | 8 | – b Booth | 38 |
| *R. T. Robinson (did not bat) | | – b Booth | 39 |
| P. Johnson (did not bat) | | – c Munton b Donald | 12 |
| D. W. Randall (did not bat) | | – c Piper b Booth | 21 |
| M. A. Crawley (did not bat) | | – not out | 22 |
| K. P. Evans (did not bat) | | – not out | 17 |
| N-b 1 | 1 | L-b 8, w 4, n-b 3 | 15 |

(no wkt dec.) 37    1/17 2/74 3/88    (5 wkts) 172
4/112 5/123

F. D. Stephenson, †B. N. French, R. A. Pick and J. A. Afford did not bat.

Bowling: *First Innings*—Donald 2-1-1-0; Munton 6-2-12-0; Smith 6-2-10-0; Booth 2-0-8-0; Lloyd 1-0-6-0. *Second Innings*—Donald 17-5-31-1; Small 9-3-14-1; Munton 12-5-26-0; Reeve 9-3-21-0; Booth 23-7-47-3; Smith 9-3-20-0; Moles 1-0-5-0.

Umpires: J. D. Bond and M. J. Kitchen.

At Cardiff, July 2, 3, 4. NOTTINGHAMSHIRE beat GLAMORGAN by eight wickets.

## NOTTINGHAMSHIRE v LANCASHIRE

At Nottingham, July 16, 17, 18. Nottinghamshire won by an innings and 34 runs. Nottinghamshire 24 pts, Lancashire 5 pts. Toss: Nottinghamshire. Although Broad and Robinson were dismissed cheaply by Wasim Akram, Pollard was unimpressed and, scoring all round the wicket, he reached his hundred, off 104 balls, nineteen minutes before lunch. By this time Nottinghamshire were 185 for two. With Johnson, Pollard added 159 for the third wicket, and later Randall carried on from where his two young colleagues left off. The former England cricketer completed his 49th first-class hundred and had hit a six and sixteen fours when he ran himself out. Pollard hit 24 boundaries in his highest Championship score. On the second day, Lancashire made steady progress until Robinson brought on Hemmings and Afford, who removed the last seven batsmen for 41 runs. The follow-on was enforced, and although Fowler was run out, runs came steadily for Lancashire until Pick bowled Mendis. At lunch the visitors were 144 for two, but they lost Speak, Fairbrother and Watkinson in the first three overs afterwards as Hemmings embarked on his best return of the summer.

*Close of play:* First day, Lancashire 13-0 (G. D. Mendis 8*, G. Fowler 3*); Second day, Lancashire 82-1 (G. D. Mendis 28*, N. J. Speak 12*).

## Nottinghamshire

| | | | | |
|---|---|---|---|---|
| B. C. Broad c Titchard | | | | |
| b Wasim Akram | . 12 | †B. N. French c Watkinson | | |
| P. R. Pollard b DeFreitas | 145 | b Wasim Akram | . 26 |
| *R. T. Robinson c Hegg | | E. E. Hemmings b Wasim Akram | . . . . . 0 |
| b Wasim Akram | . 2 | R. A. Pick not out | . . . . . 20 |
| P. Johnson c Hegg b Wasim Akram | . . . 71 | J. A. Afford run out | . . . . . . . . . . . . . . . 1 |
| O. W. Randall run out | . . . . . . . . . . . . . . 120 | B 14, l-b 8, n-b 7 | 29 |
| M. A. Crawley c Hegg b Watkinson | . . . 0 | | |
| F. D. Stephenson lbw b Watkinson | . . . 0 | 1/33 2/61 3/220 4/265 5/266 | 426 |
| | | 6/266 7/341 8/341 9/425 | |

Bonus points – Nottinghamshire 4, Lancashire 4.

Bowling: Wasim Akram 29–5–117–5; DeFreitas 13–4–55–1; Watkinson 12–2–67–2; Yates 34.4–6–137–0; Hughes 9–3–28–0.

## Lancashire

| | | | |
|---|---|---|---|
| G. D. Mendis c Robinson b Stephenson | 29 | – b Pick | 50 |
| G. Fowler c French b Stephenson | 22 | – run out | 34 |
| N. J. Speak c sub b Pick | 0 | – c Robinson b Afford | 38 |
| N. H. Fairbrother c Pollard b Hemmings | 54 | – b Hemmings | 10 |
| S. P. Titchard c Pollard b Afford | 46 | – b Hemmings | 23 |
| M. Watkinson c French b Afford | 18 | – b Hemmings | 0 |
| Wasim Akram c French b Afford | 1 | – c Robinson b Afford | 18 |
| P. A. J. DeFreitas b Hemmings | 8 | – b Hemmings | 3 |
| †W. K. Hegg st French b Afford | 0 | – c Randall b Hemmings | 1 |
| *D. P. Hughes not out | 1 | – b Hemmings | 4 |
| G. Yates c French b Afford | 1 | – not out | 0 |
| B 6, l-b 4, w 1, n-b 2 | 13 | B 7, l-b 7, n-b 4 | 18 |

| | | | |
|---|---|---|---|
| 1/46 2/53 3/55 4/152 5/168 | 193 | 1/63 2/133 3/144 4/144 5/144 | 199 |
| 6/169 7/179 8/184 9/191 | | 6/185 7/191 8/193 9/194 | |

Bonus points – Lancashire 1, Nottinghamshire 4.

Bowling: *First Innings*—Stephenson 18–4–56–2; Pick 14–4–31–1; Hemmings 29–13–50–3; Afford 15.3–2–46–4. *Second Innings*—Stephenson 9–2–32–0; Pick 13–4–44–1; Afford 40–18–62–2; Hemmings 35.2–20–46–6; Crawley 4–3–1–0.

Umpires: D. J. Constant and D. R. Shepherd.

At Wellingborough School, July 19, 20. NOTTINGHAMSHIRE beat NORTHAMPTON-SHIRE by an innings and 1 run.

## NOTTINGHAMSHIRE v YORKSHIRE

At Worksop, July 23, 24, 25. Yorkshire won by 111 runs. Yorkshire 20 pts, Nottinghamshire 4 pts. Toss: Yorkshire. Moxon, having decided to bat, lost his wicket to the first ball of the match, but Yorkshire reached 50 without further mishap before the rain, which had threatened, forced the players in. The rest of the day was marred by showers, and with 54 overs bowled, bad light put paid to any more play. On the second day Byas reached a career-best 153, with twenty fours and four sixes, having added 133 for the sixth wicket in 30 overs with Carrick, but in reply Nottinghamshire had faced only 9.5 overs before rain again curtailed play. Robinson declared first thing next morning, and after Moxon and Metcalfe had put on 50, Nottinghamshire were left with a minimum of 88 overs in which to make 332. Broad and Pollard began confidently enough, but Batty found the wicket taking spin and dismissed Broad. When Robinson was foolishly run out, this left Randall alone who could cope with the turning ball. The lower-order batsmen were too confused to launch a counter-attack, and, with Batty enjoying his best figures, Yorkshire won by a handsome margin.

*Close of play:* First day, Yorkshire 124-3 (D. Byas 61*, P. E. Robinson 1*); Second day, Nottinghamshire 32-1 (B. C. Broad 24*, R. T. Robinson 0*).

### Yorkshire

| | | | |
|---|---|---|---|
| *M. D. Moxon c French b Stephenson | 0 | – not out | 25 |
| A. A. Metcalfe c Robinson b Pick | 29 | – not out | 20 |
| D. Byas c Robinson b Evans | 153 | | |
| †R. J. Blakey c French b Evans | 19 | | |
| P. E. Robinson c Randall b Stephenson | 3 | | |
| S. A. Kellett c Pollard b Stephenson | 9 | | |
| P. Carrick c French b Evans | 63 | | |
| P. J. Hartley not out | 7 | | |
| J. D. Batty c Pick b Evans | 3 | | |
| S. D. Fletcher lbw b Hemmings | 2 | | |
| M. A. Robinson lbw b Hemmings | 0 | | |
| L-b 17, n-b 8 | 25 | L-b 5 | 5 |

1/0 2/54 3/118 4/142 5/156          313          (no wkt dec.) 50
6/289 7/304 8/310 9/313

Bonus points – Yorkshire 4, Nottinghamshire 4.

*Bowling: First Innings*—Stephenson 19-3-57-3; Pick 20-4-50-1; Evans 18-4-56-4; Hemmings 35-10-102-2; Afford 8-2-31-0. *Second Innings*—Stephenson 4-0-19-0; Pick 5-1-17-0; Evans 2-1-9-0.

### Nottinghamshire

| | | | |
|---|---|---|---|
| B. C. Broad not out | 24 | – c Metcalfe b Batty | 54 |
| P. R. Pollard c Blakey b M. A. Robinson | 8 | – b Hartley | 35 |
| *R. T. Robinson not out | 0 | – (4) run out | 0 |
| D. W. Randall (did not bat) | | – (3) c Carrick b Batty | 65 |
| P. Johnson (did not bat) | | – c P. E. Robinson b Batty | 13 |
| K. P. Evans (did not bat) | | – c Blakey b Batty | 6 |
| F. D. Stephenson (did not bat) | | – c Metcalfe b Carrick | 10 |
| †B. N. French (did not bat) | | – c Kellett b Batty | 11 |
| E. E. Hemmings (did not bat) | | – c P. E. Robinson b Batty | 13 |
| R. A. Pick (did not bat) | | – c P. E. Robinson b Carrick | 4 |
| J. A. Afford (did not bat) | | – not out | 0 |
| | | L-b 2, n-b 7 | 9 |

1/24          (1 wkt dec.) 32          1/73 2/92 3/92 4/127 5/143          220
6/154 7/199 8/215 9/220

*Bowling: First Innings*—Hartley 5-1-15-0; M. A. Robinson 4.5-1-17-1. *Second Innings*—Hartley 18-1-75-1; M. A. Robinson 11-0-42-0; Fletcher 3-0-16-0; Carrick 15-6-37-2; Batty 23.5-11-48-6.

Umpires: J. H. Hampshire and R. A. White.

At Lord's, July 26, 27, 29. NOTTINGHAMSHIRE beat MIDDLESEX by four wickets.

At Eastbourne, August 6, 7, 8. NOTTINGHAMSHIRE drew with SUSSEX.

## NOTTINGHAMSHIRE v ESSEX

At Nottingham, August 9, 10, 12. Essex won by three wickets. Essex 22 pts, Nottinghamshire 7 pts. Toss: Nottinghamshire. A sound opening stand by Broad and Pollard was largely wasted when both Robinson and Randall went cheaply. Fortunately Johnson was in excellent form, and with the aid of Evans he added 90 for the fifth wicket. Johnson's hundred came off 146 balls, and in all he faced 146 balls and hit two sixes and thirteen fours. Pick helped him put on 53 for the ninth wicket, and was soon bowling an extremely hostile spell in which Stephenson was all at sea. Struck by a ball from Pick, he retired hurt with 4. On the second day Essex looked in danger of following on until Knight, Topley and the tail saw them to safety. Fast accurate seam bowling by Foster, who took four wickets in 21 balls, meant that Nottinghamshire were unable to capitalise on their first-innings lead, and eventually Essex required 291 off a minimum of 71 overs. The game remained evenly balanced up to the final hour, when Salim Malik and Hussain set about the Nottinghamshire bowlers, and Knight played another responsible innings. Essex's victory took them back into second place in the Championship and pushed Nottinghamshire down to third.

*Close of play:* First day, Essex 38-0 (A. C. H. Seymour 13*, P. J. Prichard 17*); Second day, Nottinghamshire 118-5 (D. W. Randall 44*, F. D. Stephenson 13*).

### Nottinghamshire

| | | | |
|---|---|---|---|
| B. C. Broad c Salim Malik b Topley | 36 | – b Foster | 10 |
| P. R. Pollard lbw b Foster | 56 | – c Garnham b Foster | 16 |
| *R. T. Robinson b Topley | 6 | – c Garnham b Foster | 0 |
| D. W. Randall c Hussain b Childs | 6 | – c Garnham b Foster | 44 |
| P. Johnson c Andrew b Childs | 124 | – c Salim Malik b Foster | 0 |
| K. P. Evans lbw b Foster | 32 | – c Foster b Childs | 22 |
| F. D. Stephenson lbw b Foster | 0 | – b Stephenson | 58 |
| †B. N. French c Garnham b Foster | 2 | – c Seymour b Stephenson | 35 |
| E. E. Hemmings c Topley b Andrew | 2 | – b Topley | 1 |
| R. A. Pick b Topley | 14 | – not out | 5 |
| J. A. Afford not out | 4 | – c Seymour b Stephenson | 3 |
| L-b 2, w 2, n-b 8 | 12 | B 2, l-b 3, w 2, n-b 14 | 21 |
| | **294** | | **215** |

1/66 2/95 3/102 4/110 5/200     294
6/200 7/209 8/221 9/274

1/23 2/24 3/36 4/36 5/73     215
6/123 7/202 8/205 9/207

Bonus points – Nottinghamshire 3, Essex 4.

Bowling: *First Innings*—Foster 19-1-58-4; Andrew 14-0-65-1; Topley 22-4-92-3; Childs 22.5-1-77-2. *Second Innings*—Foster 23-2-56-5; Andrew 13-4-37-0; Topley 19-2-72-1; Childs 8-1-25-1; Stephenson 5.2-0-20-3.

### Essex

| | | | |
|---|---|---|---|
| A. C. H. Seymour run out | 13 | – c Stephenson b Evans | 19 |
| J. P. Stephenson c French b Evans | 4 | – c French b Evans | 14 |
| P. J. Prichard c Robinson b Evans | 25 | – lbw b Evans | 38 |
| Salim Malik b Evans | 18 | – b Pick | 74 |
| N. Hussain c French b Evans | 13 | – st French b Afford | 64 |
| N. V. Knight c French b Hemmings | 31 | – c French b Stephenson | 42 |
| †M. A. Garnham c Robinson b Evans | 6 | – c Johnson b Stephenson | 9 |
| *N. A. Foster c Robinson b Stephenson | 12 | – not out | 15 |
| T. D. Topley b Stephenson | 50 | – not out | 0 |
| S. J. W. Andrew run out | 13 | | |
| J. H. Childs not out | 13 | | |
| B 3, l-b 8, w 1, n-b 9 | 21 | B 4, l-b 10, n-b 4 | 18 |
| | **219** | (7 wkts) | **293** |

1/39 2/47 3/48 4/79 5/80     219
6/95 7/112 8/155 9/195

1/28 2/51 3/122 4/182    (7 wkts) 293
5/258 6/273 7/285

Bonus points – Essex 2, Nottinghamshire 4.

*In the first innings J. P. Stephenson, when 4, retired hurt at 18 and resumed at 47.*

Bowling: *First Innings*—Stephenson 22.2–7–46–2; Pick 28–5–62–0; Hemmings 5–1–16–1
Evans 24–5–66–5; Afford 8–3–18–0. *Second Innings*—Stephenson 19.2–0–90–2; Pick
12–2–40–1; Evans 12–2–51–3; Afford 11–1–44–1; Hemmings 13–1–54–0.

Umpires: J. H. Harris and K. E. Palmer.

## NOTTINGHAMSHIRE v SOMERSET

At Nottingham, August 16, 17, 19. Drawn. Nottinghamshire 5 pts, Somerset 6 pts. Toss:
Somerset. The visitors made slow progress for much of the first day until Harden and Burns
joined forces. In twenty overs after tea the total rose from 202 to 300. Harden completed a
well-made century, with three sixes and nine fours, only to fall to Stephenson shortly before
the close, and on Saturday morning Burns had time to reach three figures before Tavaré
declared. On the opening day Cook had become, for the third year in succession, the first to
score 2,000 first-class runs in the season. The Nottinghamshire innings was a team effort, and
Robinson closed it as soon as four batting points were secured. Tavaré judged his second
declaration with care, continuing for two overs after lunch and at the same time allowing
Hayhurst his hundred. Johnson kept wicket while French bowled. Nottinghamshire's target
was 322 off a minimum of 58 overs, and Broad set the pace, hitting twelve fours in his 131 and
in the process completing hundreds against all seventeen first-class counties. He had scored
one against Nottinghamshire when he was playing for Gloucestershire. Randall continued to
chase the target, but 12 runs were required off the last over and this proved too much.
*Close of play*: First day, Somerset 349–5 (N. D. Burns 87*, G. D. Rose 7*); Second day,
Somerset 4–1 (S. J. Cook 2*, A. N. Hayhurst 1*).

## Somerset

| | | | |
|---|---|---|---|
| S. J. Cook c Pick b Stephenson | 43 | – lbw b Pick | 2 |
| G. T. J. Townsend b Stephenson | 20 | – c French b Pick | 1 |
| A. N. Hayhurst c Stephenson b Afford | 33 | – not out | 100 |
| *C. J. Tavaré c Johnson b Evans | 47 | – lbw b Evans | 50 |
| R. J. Harden c French b Stephenson | 101 | – b Johnson | 38 |
| †N. D. Burns b Evans | 108 | – not out | 19 |
| G. D. Rose c French b Stephenson | 31 | | |
| I. G. Swallow not out | 8 | | |
| H. R. J. Trump c Robinson b Evans | 1 | | |
| B 1, l-b 5, n-b 8 | 14 | B 1, l-b 3, n-b 1 | 5 |

1/54 2/65 3/149 4/149 5/327     (8 wkts dec.) 406     1/3 2/4                    (4 wkts dec.) 215
6/381 7/404 8/406                                                        3/92 4/156

D. A. Graveney and J. C. Hallett did not bat.

Bonus points – Somerset 4, Nottinghamshire 1 (Score at 100 overs: 323-4).

Bowling: *First Innings*—Stephenson 28–6–73–4; Pick 16–1–79–0; Evans 37.1–10–105–3;
Hemmings 24–6–81–0; Afford 21–8–62–1. *Second Innings*—Pick 8–2–24–2; Stephenson
7–2–23–0; Afford 13–3–64–0; Evans 6–1–24–1; Johnson 8–0–36–1; Pollard 3.5–0–29–0;
French 1–0–11–0.

## Nottinghamshire

| | | | |
|---|---|---|---|
| B. C. Broad b Graveney | 37 | – c Swallow b Hallett | 131 |
| P. R. Pollard lbw b Trump | 63 | – c Rose b Graveney | 25 |
| *R. T. Robinson c and b Trump | 49 | – lbw b Hayhurst | 44 |
| D. W. Randall c Swallow b Hayhurst | 13 | – (5) not out | 73 |
| P. Johnson not out | 71 | – (4) run out | 19 |
| K. P. Evans c Hallett b Swallow | 14 | – (8) b Hallett | 7 |
| F. D. Stephenson b Graveney | 44 | – (6) run out | 9 |
| †B. N. French not out | 0 | – (7) b Trump | 0 |
| E. E. Hemmings (did not bat) | | – not out | 0 |
| B 2, l-b 1, w 2, n-b 4 | 9 | B 1, l-b 5, w 1, n-b 2 | 9 |

1/60 2/153 3/158 4/182     (6 wkts dec.) 300     1/54 2/132 3/158 4/259     (7 wkts) 317
5/226 6/299                                                 5/286 6/286 7/311

R. A. Pick and J. A. Afford did not bat.

Bonus points – Nottinghamshire 4, Somerset 2.

Bowling: *First Innings*—Rose 14–2–51–0; Hallett 12–1–44–0; Hayhurst 14–2–48–1; Graveney 13–1–46–2; Trump 16–2–41–2; Swallow 12.1–1–67–1. *Second Innings*—Rose 5–0–28–0; Hallett 9–0–50–2; Trump 18–2–87–1; Graveney 15–0–60–1; Swallow 12–1–49–0; Hayhurst 8–0–37–1.

Umpires: J. H. Hampshire and P. B. Wight.

## NOTTINGHAMSHIRE v DERBYSHIRE

At Nottingham, August 23, 24, 26. Derbyshire won by four wickets. Derbyshire 23 pts, Nottinghamshire 5 pts. Toss: Nottinghamshire. The Nottinghamshire batsmen seemed sluggish on a docile pitch against some moderate bowling, and with rain curtailing the playing time, the first day was altogether a dull affair. Saturday, however, was enlivened by the cultured batting of the Indian Test cricketer, Azharuddin, who in two and a half hours hit three sixes and twelve fours while making 129 from 141 balls. Barnett declared immediately 300 was reached – in 30 overs less than the home side had taken – and for once both Nottinghamshire openers failed. Randall helped Robinson add 113 for the third wicket by stumps, and on Monday he completed his 50th first-class hundred. He was still at the crease, having hit two sixes and fifteen fours in his 143, when Robinson declared and left Derbyshire with 79 overs in which to score 303. Barnett and Bowler (two sixes, eight fours) placed their side in a strong position, Azharuddin again found few terrors in the bowling, and Derbyshire hit the final 7 runs off the last over. Nottinghamshire's chances of taking the Championship title all but vanished with this defeat.

*Close of play*: First day, Nottinghamshire 284-7 (B. N. French 6*, M. G. Field-Buss 7*); Second day, Nottinghamshire 126-2 (R. T. Robinson 56*, D. W. Randall 54*).

## Nottinghamshire

| | | | | | |
|---|---|---|---|---|---|
| B. C. Broad c Krikken b Mortensen | 36 | – c Krikken b Mortensen | 5 |
| P. R. Pollard b Mortensen | 7 | – b Warner | 2 |
| *R. T. Robinson c Krikken b Sladdin | 53 | – c Folley b Sladdin | 67 |
| D. W. Randall b Sladdin | 76 | – not out | 143 |
| P. Johnson c Azharuddin b Sladdin | 58 | – c Sladdin b Goldsmith | 33 |
| M. Saxelby c Barnett b Warner | 9 | – c Barnett b Sladdin | 28 |
| F. D. Stephenson c and b Folley | 24 | – not out | 10 |
| †B. N. French not out | 9 | | |
| M. G. Field-Buss b Sladdin | 16 | | |
| R. A. Pick not out | 0 | | |
| B 3, l-b 7, n-b 2 | 12 | B 5, l-b 3, w 1, n-b 5 | 14 |

| | | |
|---|---|---|
| 1/23 2/48 3/174 4/177 5/204 | (8 wkts dec.) 300 | 1/6 2/13 3/146 (5 wkts dec.) 302 |
| 6/253 7/273 8/296 | | 4/210 5/288 |

J. A. Afford did not bat.

Bonus points – Nottinghamshire 4, Derbyshire 3.

Bowling: *First Innings*—Mortensen 23–3–63–2; Warner 13–4–49–1; Sladdin 42.3–10–118–4; Folley 21–3–60–1. *Second Innings*—Mortensen 11–2–34–1; Warner 11–2–32–1; Sladdin 25–1–118–2; Folley 19–1–73–0; Goldsmith 7–0–37–1.

## Derbyshire

| | | | | | |
|---|---|---|---|---|---|
| *K. J. Barnett c Randall b Stephenson | 32 | – c Field-Buss b Afford | 65 |
| P. D. Bowler b Pick | 10 | – c and b Pick | 99 |
| J. E. Morris c Broad b Stephenson | 63 | – c French b Afford | 0 |
| M. Azharuddin not out | 129 | – b Stephenson | 72 |
| T. J. G. O'Gorman not out | 51 | – c and b Afford | 0 |
| S. C. Goldsmith (did not bat) | | – not out | 29 |
| A. E. Warner (did not bat) | | – b Stephenson | 5 |
| †K. M. Krikken (did not bat) | | – not out | 5 |
| B 2, l-b 8, w 2, n-b 3 | 15 | B 5, l-b 20, n-b 3 | 28 |

| | | |
|---|---|---|
| 1/22 2/110 3/117 | (3 wkts dec.) 300 | 1/103 2/103 3/217 (6 wkts) 303 |
| | | 4/222 5/275 6/282 |

R. W. Sladdin, O. H. Mortensen and I. Folley did not bat.

Bonus points – Derbyshire 4, Nottinghamshire 1.

Bowling: *First Innings*—Stephenson 10–0–44–2; Pick 12–2–41–1; Saxelby 11–1–54–0; Afford 23–4–96–0; Field-Buss 14–1–55–0. *Second Innings*—Stephenson 17–1–62–2; Pick 11.5–1–50–1; Afford 26–4–104–3; Field-Buss 21–7–59–0; Saxelby 3–1–3–0.

Umpires: M. J. Kitchen and P. B. Wight.

At Manchester, August 28, 29, 30, 31. NOTTINGHAMSHIRE beat LANCASHIRE by three wickets.

## NOTTINGHAMSHIRE v MIDDLESEX

At Nottingham, September 3, 4, 5, 6. Middlesex won by 248 runs. Middlesex 22 pts, Nottinghamshire 4 pts. Toss: Middlesex. Pick gave his side a splendid start, but Ramprakash and Gatting soon had the measure of the bowling in their third-wicket stand of 156. Gatting was severe on anything loose; Ramprakash took more care, remaining for four and a half hours. Brown, however, stayed and stayed, remaining unbeaten with 143 after 330 minutes. Nottinghamshire seemed in no hurry, with Randall alone showing any sense of urgency as he raced to 50 in 48 minutes, and the 100 overs brought only 275 runs. Nottinghamshire finished 109 runs in arrears, and Middlesex built up a formidable lead before Gatting declared, leaving Nottinghamshire with the last day in which to make 351. They were 74 for two at lunch, with Randall and Robinson apparently established, but after the interval no-one played the spin of Tufnell competently. The sweep was the downfall of several batsmen, and the last eight Nottinghamshire wickets fell for 28 runs in 50 minutes. Tufnell returned excellent figures, but marred his performance by some gauche behaviour.

*Close of play:* First day, Middlesex 334-5 (K. R. Brown 81*, J. E. Emburey 2*); Second day, Nottinghamshire 207-3 (D. W. Randall 67*, P. Johnson 30*); Third day, Middlesex 241-6 (M. R. Ramprakash 83*, N. G. Cowans 9*).

## Middlesex

| | | | | |
|---|---:|---|---|---:|
| M. A. Roseberry b Pick | 9 | – c Crawley b Afford | | 56 |
| J. C. Pooley c French b Pick | 2 | – st French b Hemmings | | 36 |
| M. R. Ramprakash c Randall b Hemmings | 110 | – not out | | 83 |
| *M. W. Gatting c Afford b Pick | 91 | – lbw b Hemmings | | 14 |
| K. R. Brown not out | 143 | – b Hemmings | | 3 |
| P. N. Weekes c French b Pick | 31 | – c French b Afford | | 10 |
| J. E. Emburey run out | 21 | – lbw b Afford | | 7 |
| N. F. Williams b Afford | 7 | | | |
| †P. Farbrace c Johnson b Hemmings | 3 | | | |
| P. C. R. Tufnell c Crawley b Afford | 6 | | | |
| N. G. Cowans b Pick | 19 | – (8) not out | | 9 |
| B 5, l-b 5, n-b 3 | 13 | B 5, l-b 15, n-b 3 | | 23 |

1/4 2/40 3/196 4/244 5/327  455  1/85 2/119 3/144 (6 wkts dec.) 241
6/369 7/404 8/407 9/426  4/156 5/183 6/217

Bonus points – Middlesex 3, Nottinghamshire 1 (Score at 100 overs: 298-4).

Bowling: *First Innings*—Stephenson 27–7–50–0; Pick 31–7–86–5; Crawley 17–2–64–0; Hemmings 40–3–144–2; Afford 38–5–101–2. *Second Innings*—Stephenson 7–1–18–0; Pick 5–1–19–0; Hemmings 27–2–98–3; Afford 26–7–86–3.

# Nottinghamshire

| | | | |
|---|---|---|---|
| B. C. Broad b Tufnell | 45 | – c Tufnell b Emburey | 4 |
| P. R. Pollard b Emburey | 26 | – b Tufnell | 18 |
| *R. T. Robinson st Farbrace b Tufnell | 34 | – c Brown b Emburey | 20 |
| D. W. Randall c Weekes b Emburey | 121 | – b Emburey | 25 |
| P. Johnson c Tufnell b Williams | 52 | – b Tufnell | 0 |
| M. A. Crawley b Williams | 0 | – c Brown b Emburey | 0 |
| F. D. Stephenson c Cowans b Tufnell | 0 | – not out | 19 |
| †B. N. French c Brown b Emburey | 3 | – b Tufnell | 0 |
| E. E. Hemmings not out | 23 | – b Tufnell | 2 |
| R. A. Pick c Pooley b Emburey | 14 | – b Tufnell | 1 |
| J. A. Afford c Ramprakash b Tufnell | 12 | – run out | 0 |
| L-b 10, n-b 6 | 16 | L-b 13 | 13 |
| | **346** | | **102** |

1/45 2/102 3/145 4/247 5/253    1/21 2/27 3/75 4/78 5/78
6/254 7/271 8/311 9/332           6/78 7/84 8/88 9/98

Bonus points – Nottinghamshire 3, Middlesex 3 (Score at 100 overs: 275-7).

Bowling: *First Innings*—Williams 17–3–47–2; Cowans 11–0–38–0; Emburey 36–3–90–4; Tufnell 46.3–13–137–4; Weekes 5–1–24–0. *Second Innings*—Cowans 6–3–13–0; Williams 3–1–4–0; Emburey 21–9–38–4; Tufnell 18.3–4–30–5; Weekes 1–0–4–0.

Umpires: H. D. Bird and J. H. Hampshire.

At Derby, September 10, 11, 12, 13. NOTTINGHAMSHIRE drew with DERBYSHIRE.

## NOTTINGHAMSHIRE v WORCESTERSHIRE

At Nottingham, September 17, 18, 19. Nottinghamshire won by an innings and 70 runs. Nottinghamshire 24 pts, Worcestershire 2 pts. Toss: Nottinghamshire. Worcestershire fielded an eleven lacking Moody, Botham and Dilley and, despite the presence of Hick, were found wanting. Robinson batted with confidence throughout most of the first day; by the close he had been at the wicket for five and a half hours without a mistake, and by the time he was dismissed on the second day he had hit 23 fours in his 180. When Worcestershire batted, Stephenson bowled well in what was to be his final appearance for Nottinghamshire, and the spinners dealt with the middle order before the West Indian all-rounder brushed aside the tail on the third morning. In previous seasons, Illingworth and Newport, the overnight batsmen, had rescued Worcestershire from the Nottinghamshire attack, but this time they failed and Robinson was able to enforce the follow-on. Afford and Hemmings again brooked few arguments, only Hick being capable of making runs, and Stephenson administered the *coup de grâce* as Nottinghamshire won with a day to spare.

*Close of play:* First day, Nottinghamshire 342-5 (R. T. Robinson 165*, F. D. Stephenson 12*); Second day, Worcestershire 167-7 (R. K. Illingworth 16*, P. J. Newport 0*).

## Nottinghamshire

| | | | |
|---|---|---|---|
| B. C. Broad lbw b Newport | 38 | E. E. Hemmings c and b Lampitt | 0 |
| P. R. Pollard c Leatherdale b Lampitt | 10 | R. A. Pick lbw b Illingworth | 14 |
| *R. T. Robinson c Rhodes b Lampitt | 180 | J. A. Afford b Newport | 9 |
| D. W. Randall lbw b Lampitt | 39 | | |
| P. Johnson b Illingworth | 57 | B 2, l-b 7, w 2, n-b 5 | 16 |
| M. A. Crawley c Rhodes b Radford | 4 | | |
| F. D. Stephenson c D'Oliveira b Lampitt | 19 | 1/42 2/60 3/155 4/277 5/312 | **428** |
| †B. N. French not out | 36 | 6/355 7/377 8/381 9/417 | |

Bonus points – Nottinghamshire 4, Worcestershire 1 (Score at 100 overs: 308-4).

Bowling: Radford 27–3–83–1; Newport 29.3–7–83–2; Lampitt 30–6–86–5; Illingworth 30–8–71–2; Stemp 17–3–57–0; Hick 9–0–39–0.

## Worcestershire

| | | | |
|---|---|---|---|
| *T. S. Curtis lbw b Stephenson | 31 | – lbw b Hemmings | 27 |
| W. P. C. Weston lbw b Stephenson | 8 | – c French b Pick | 15 |
| G. A. Hick c and b Crawley | 17 | – c Crawley b Afford | 63 |
| D. A. Leatherdale run out | 31 | – b Hemmings | 7 |
| D. B. D'Oliveira lbw b Hemmings | 33 | – c and b Hemmings | 17 |
| †S. J. Rhodes c French b Afford | 5 | – c Johnson b Afford | 0 |
| S. R. Lampitt c French b Afford | 17 | – lbw b Afford | 3 |
| R. K. Illingworth c Crawley b Stephenson | 20 | – not out | 9 |
| P. J. Newport lbw b Stephenson | 8 | – run out | 4 |
| N. V. Radford b Stephenson | 1 | – c Crawley b Stephenson | 4 |
| R. D. Stemp not out | 1 | – b Stephenson | 8 |
| B 3, l-b 6, n-b 3 | 12 | L-b 9, w 1, n-b 7 | 17 |
| | **184** | | **174** |

1/30 2/59 3/59 4/118 5/126          1/31 2/74 3/91 4/113 5/114
6/138 7/166 8/182 9/183             6/142 7/155 8/160 9/164

Bonus points – Worcestershire 1, Nottinghamshire 4.

Bowling: *First Innings*—Pick 5–1–16–0; Stephenson 19.3–4–63–5; Crawley 11–1–24–1; Afford 25–14–28–2; Hemmings 20–3–44–1. *Second Innings*—Stephenson 15.4–5–26–2; Pick 8–1–19–1; Crawley 4–2–16–0; Hemmings 26–4–81–3; Afford 13–5–23–3.

Umpires: J. C. Balderstone and J. D. Bond.

---

## THE NATIONAL POWER 6-HIT AWARDS, 1991

Carl Hooper, who toured England in 1991 with the West Indians, won the major prize of £2,000 for the most sixes hit in those matches which qualified for the National Power 6-Hit Award. A sum of £2,000 also went to the West Indies Cricket Board of Control, as part of the National Power sponsorship. In addition to the major award, quarterly awards of £1,000 each were available. In order to qualify for the National Power Awards, sixes had to be hit in the Britannic Assurance Championship and Challenge match, Cornhill Test matches, and other first-class matches played by MCC and the West Indian and Sri Lankan touring teams. The National Power Award was run with the co-operation of *Wisden Cricket Monthly*.

**Quarterly Awards** (£1,000)
April 16–June 6 . . . . . . . 6 – I. V. A. Richards (West Indians)
June 7–July 4 . . . . . . . 11 – C. L. Hooper (West Indians) and T. M. Moody (Worcestershire)
July 5–August 8 . . . . . . 13 – C. L. Hooper (West Indians)
August 9–September 26 14 – J. P. Stephenson (Essex)

**1991 Award** (£2,000)
28 – C. L. Hooper (West Indians)
27 – M. P. Maynard (Glamorgan) and T. M. Moody (Worcestershire)
20 – J. P. Stephenson (Essex)
19 – P. Johnson (Nottinghamshire)
17 – M. V. Fleming (Kent)
16 – K. D. James (Hampshire)
15 – I. V. A. Richards (West Indians)
14 – D. A. Reeve (Warwickshire), P. E. Robinson (Yorkshire) and A. J. Wright (Gloucestershire)
13 – G. D. Rose (Somerset), R. J. Scott (Gloucestershire) and Wasim Akram (Lancashire)

**Previous 6-Hit Winners**
1986 – I. T. Botham (Somerset) 34; 1987 – M. P. Maynard (Glamorgan) 30; 1988 – G. A. Hick (Worcestershire) 40; 1989 – G. A. Hick (Worcestershire) 29; 1990 – I. V. A. Richards (Glamorgan) 40.

# SOMERSET

*President:* J. Luff
*Chairman:* R. Parsons
*Chairman, Cricket Committee:* R. E. Marshall
*Chief Executive:* P. W. Anderson
  The County Ground, St James's Street,
  Taunton TA1 1JT
  (Telephone: 0823-272946)
*Captain:* C. J. Tavaré
*Coach:* P. J. Robinson

Too few wins, too many farewells, and the officially acknowledged prospect of heavy financial loss made 1991 another season for Somerset to forget. There were, none the less, some remarkable individual performances, almost inevitably dominated by the South African opener, Jimmy Cook, who was in his third and final season for the county Recording only two Britannic Assurance Championship victories, though there were seven near-misses, Somerset finished bottom of the table. They registered the highest but one number of batting points, and the lowest but one number of bowling points. However, it may be appropriate to remind the county's supporters that the last time they were seventeenth, in 1985, Viv Richards, Joel Garner and Ian Botham played in a total of 45 Championship matches.

Although Benson and Hedges Cup hopes soon died – Somerset did not qualify for a quarter-final place – victories in the first four Refuge Assurance League matches raised hopes, and while these were to be extinguished in July, late wins over two counties seeking prizemoney were encouraging. The most heartening campaign was fought in the NatWest Bank Trophy, in which a good second-round victory over Middlesex led to a heroic quarter-final performance from Andy Hayhurst. His five for 60 and unbeaten 91 brought a weakened Somerset, missing Neil Mallender and Ken MacLeay, within a whisker of triumph over much-fancied Warwickshire. The final Championship game, against the same opponents, ended in defeat, but only after a memorable fight in which Somerset scored 403 in the last innings to lose by 5 runs.

The paucity of bowling points could partly be explained by the fact that, in contrast to 1990, the fitness record of the seam bowlers was very poor. Adrian Jones, who had returned to Sussex, was certainly missed. Mallender began and ended strongly, but missed nine Championship matches in mid-season, and Graham Rose, MacLeay and Roland Lefebvre were also absent for lengthy spells, during which Jeremy Hallett showed his worth. In his one season for the county David Graveney, who was often carrying injuries, did a splendid job, collecting the biggest haul of 55 first-class wickets at 39.27 with his slow left-arm bowling. His advice and presence markedly improved the contribution of off-spinner Harvey Trump, who took 51 wickets at 41.43. At the end of the summer, Graveney left to captain Durham, with Somerset's best wishes.

Bowling hopes for 1992 revolved around the same group, plus New Zealand-born Andrew Caddick and the tall, quick Dutchman, Adrianus van Troost. These two helped the Second Eleven to a welcome third position in their Championship, and the 6ft 5in Caddick's 96 wickets, at an average of 12.84, suggested an interesting prospect. If an overseas bowler could be found, and fitness levels improved, a much more formidable attack would be available to support what should still be a strong batting line-up.

Certainly in 1991 the batting, centred around Cook, the captain, Chris Tavaré, Richard Harden and Peter Roebuck, rarely faltered. Regrettably, Roebuck announced his retirement in August. Despite three excellent hundreds, Hayhurst found run-getting more difficult in his second year with Somerset, but Rose and Lefebvre made maiden centuries, and Burns produced some useful innings later in the season. MacLeay, the Wiltshire-born Western Australian, showed he could bat, and he bowled to good effect in limited-overs games. As the year wore on, Ricky Bartlett, once again, Mark Lathwell, Gareth Townsend and Ian Fletcher all revealed the bright promise of the county's younger batsmen.

Somerset will assuredly need these men, and more, in the future. The year was clouded by the death of the president, Colin Atkinson, by the premature retirement of Roebuck, and by Cook's return to South Africa. Each, in his own way, made contributions of great importance to the county.

Cook's remarkable three seasons demand expansion. He was 35 years old when he arrived in 1989, eight days younger than another notable opener, Graham Gooch. In all his matches for Somerset he compiled 10,639 runs at an average of 62.21, including 7,604 in first-class games at 72.41, with 28 hundreds. Three of these came against the New Zealand, West Indian and Sri Lankan touring teams, while the rest were divided between all the counties except Yorkshire (against whom his highest score was 85 not out) and Derbyshire (where his best was 85). Twice he made two centuries in a match, and on the first occasion, at Trent Bridge in 1989, he carried his bat through two completed innings, the first time this had been achieved since 1911. Ironically, Somerset lost both matches. In curious contrast, he had a new experience in 1991; he was out twice first ball, to Chris Lewis and Neal Radford.

In the Refuge Assurance League Cook made 2,004 runs at 46.60, including 902 in 1990, then a record, and scored seven hundreds. The Benson and Hedges Cup brought him 854 runs at 53.37, with one hundred, and the NatWest Bank Trophy 177 at 25.28 – it was the only major competition in which he did not reach three figures. He never missed a match, was invariably lively in the field, always put the team's needs first, and established a superb reputation for chivalry and modesty. For all these reasons Jimmy Cook will be fondly remembered by friend and foe, and many were glad on the November day in 1991 when he stepped on to the field at Calcutta, India to represent South Africa in recognised international competition for the first time. – Eric Hill.

SOMERSET 1991

[*Bill Smith*]

*Back row*: G. W. White, H. R. J. Trump, A. N. Hayhurst, I. G. Swallow, R. J. Bartlett. *Middle row*: N. J. Pringle, A. C. Cottam, D. Beal, K. H. MacLeay, A. R. Caddick, D. A. Graveney, M. W. Cleal, R. P. Lefebvre, G. T. J. Townsend, I. Fletcher, M. N. Lathwell. *Front row*: G. D. Rose, N. D. Burns, S. J. Cook, C. J. Tavaré (*captain*), R. Parsons (*chairman*), P. J. Robinson (*coach*), P. M. Roebuck, N. A. Mallender, R. J. Harden. *Insets*: R. J. Turner, J. C. Hallett.

## SOMERSET RESULTS

*All first-class matches – Played 24: Won 2, Lost 6, Drawn 16.*

*County Championship matches – Played 22: Won 2, Lost 5, Drawn 15.*

*Bonus points – Batting 66, Bowling 45.*

*Competition placings – Britannic Assurance County Championship, 17th;*
*NatWest Bank Trophy, q-f; Benson and Hedges Cup, 3rd in Group B;*
*Refuge Assurance League, 8th equal.*

# BRITANNIC ASSURANCE CHAMPIONSHIP AVERAGES

## BATTING

| | *Birthplace* | *M* | *I* | *NO* | *R* | *HI* | *Avge* |
|---|---|---|---|---|---|---|---|
| ‡S. J. Cook . . . . . . . . | *Johannesburg, SA* | 22 | 39 | 6 | 2,370 | 210* | 71.81 |
| ‡C. J. Tavaré . . . . . . . . | *Orpington* | 22 | 35 | 6 | 1,482 | 183 | 51.10 |
| ‡R. J. Harden . . . . . . . | *Bridgwater* | 22 | 36 | 7 | 1,242 | 134 | 42.82 |
| ‡A. N. Hayhurst . . . . | *Manchester* | 18 | 30 | 5 | 883 | 172* | 35.32 |
| ‡P. M. Roebuck . . . . . | *Oxford* | 16 | 27 | 3 | 820 | 101 | 34.16 |
| I. G. Swallow . . . . . . | *Barnsley* | 4 | 5 | 3 | 67 | 41* | 33.50 |
| ‡G. D. Rose . . . . . . . . | *Tottenham, London* | 14 | 19 | 2 | 567 | 106 | 33.35 |
| ‡N. D. Burns . . . . . . . | *Chelmsford* | 22 | 32 | 8 | 794 | 108 | 33.08 |
| K. H. MacLeay . . . . . | *Bradford-on-Avon* | 14 | 19 | 6 | 388 | 63 | 29.84 |
| R. J. Bartlett . . . . . . | *Ash Priors* | 5 | 7 | 1 | 177 | 71 | 29.50 |
| ‡R. P. Lefebvre . . . . | *Rotterdam, Netherlands* | 15 | 16 | 3 | 361 | 100 | 27.76 |
| G. T. J. Townsend . . | *Tiverton* | 2 | 4 | 0 | 68 | 29 | 17.00 |
| ‡N. A. Mallender . . . . | *Kirk Sandall* | 13 | 11 | 3 | 108 | 19 | 13.50 |
| H. R. J. Trump . . . . . | *Taunton* | 16 | 15 | 6 | 79 | 30* | 8.77 |
| J. C. Hallett . . . . . . | *Yeovil* | 8 | 5 | 1 | 35 | 15 | 8.75 |
| D. A. Graveney . . . . | *Bristol* | 20 | 13 | 7 | 51 | 17 | 8.50 |

Also batted: D. Beal (*Butleigh*) (2 matches) 1, 0; I. Fletcher (*Sawbridgeworth*) (1 match) 56, 2*; M. N. Lathwell (*Bletchley*) (1 match) 4, 43; N. J. Pringle (*Weymouth*) (1 match) 7, 17; A. P. van Troost (*Schiedam, Netherlands*) (4 matches) 0*.

*\* Signifies not out.  ‡ Denotes county cap.*

The following played a total of 23 three-figure innings for Somerset in County Championship matches – S. J. Cook 9, C. J. Tavaré 4, A. N. Hayhurst 3, R. J. Harden 2, G. D. Rose 2, N. D. Burns 1, R. P. Lefebvre 1, P. M. Roebuck 1.

## BOWLING

| | *O* | *M* | *R* | *W* | *BB* | *5W/i* | *Avge* |
|---|---|---|---|---|---|---|---|
| N. A. Mallender . . . . . . | 349.5 | 76 | 969 | 42 | 6-43 | 3 | 23.07 |
| K. H. MacLeay . . . . . . . | 266.3 | 51 | 807 | 25 | 3-40 | 0 | 32.28 |
| D. A. Graveney . . . . . . . | 673.2 | 148 | 2,041 | 53 | 7-105 | 2 | 38.50 |
| H. R. J. Trump . . . . . . . | 570.3 | 102 | 1,826 | 47 | 6-48 | 4 | 38.85 |
| G. D. Rose . . . . . . . . . . | 307 | 51 | 1,006 | 23 | 4-77 | 0 | 43.73 |
| J. C. Hallett . . . . . . . . . | 178.3 | 31 | 637 | 12 | 3-154 | 0 | 53.08 |
| R. P. Lefebvre . . . . . . . . | 353 | 71 | 1,048 | 18 | 3-51 | 0 | 58.22 |

Also bowled: D. Beal 44-3-209-1; S. J. Cook 4-0-26-0; R. J. Harden 23.5-0-122-3; A. N. Hayhurst 191.3-30-715-9; M. N. Lathwell 17-6-55-0; P. M. Roebuck 128-32-309-9; I. G. Swallow 100.1-16-354-8; A. P. van Troost 86.4-12-267-6.

**Wicket-keeper:** N. D. Burns 35 ct, 8 st.

**Leading Fielders:** C. J. Tavaré 20, R. J. Harden 19.

## SOMERSET v SUSSEX

At Taunton, April 27, 29, 30, May 1. Drawn. Somerset 4 pts, Sussex 8 pts. Toss: Somerset. In conditions which helped swing bowling, the varied and businesslike Sussex attack kept the home side's batting in check. Cook's fifty came from 109 balls. Rain washed out the next two days, and the loss of the first hour of the final day, allied to a bitter northerly gale, prompted Sussex to go for batting points, rather than consider a contrived finish. Hall, reaching a steady hundred in 275 balls (eleven fours), anchored the innings, and with Moores hitting a lively 69 from 73 balls, the fourth batting point was obtained just before the overs ran out.

*Close of play:* First day, Sussex 33-0 (D. M. Smith 14*, J. W. Hall 11*); Second day, No play; Third day, No play.

### Somerset

| | | | |
|---|---|---|---|
| S. J. Cook b Pigott | 57 | I. G. Swallow c Greenfield b Pigott | 4 |
| P. M. Roebuck c Smith b Jones | 18 | N. A. Mallender lbw b North | 15 |
| A. N. Hayhurst c Hall b Salisbury | 32 | D. A. Graveney not out | 4 |
| *C. J. Tavaré c Moores b North | 25 | | |
| R. J. Harden c Moores b North | 19 | L-b 8, w 4, n-b 7 | 19 |
| †N. D. Burns c Smith b Donelan | 7 | | |
| G. D. Rose c Salisbury b Donelan | 13 | 1/51 2/103 3/123 4/152 5/167 | 229 |
| R. P. Lefebvre c Greenfield b Pigott | 16 | 6/175 7/193 8/207 9/210 | |

Bonus points – Somerset 2, Sussex 4.

Bowling: Jones 13-2-28-1; Pigott 21-6-36-3; North 15.3-2-54-3; Salisbury 23-7-64-1; Donelan 16-4-39-2.

### Sussex

| | | | |
|---|---|---|---|
| D. M. Smith b Swallow | 53 | A. C. S. Pigott not out | 5 |
| J. W. Hall not out | 117 | | |
| *P. W. G. Parker c Burns b Swallow | 11 | L-b 10, w 1, n-b 16 | 27 |
| A. P. Wells b Swallow | 3 | | |
| J. A. North c Harden b Mallender | 15 | 1/120 2/147 3/153 (5 wkts) 300 | |
| †P. Moores c Swallow b Rose | 69 | 4/193 5/290 | |

K. Greenfield, I. D. K. Salisbury, A. N. Jones and B. T. P. Donelan did not bat.

Bonus points – Sussex 4, Somerset 2.

Bowling: Mallender 16-3-33-1; Rose 19-2-90-1; Graveney 5-5-0-0; Swallow 20-3-43-3; Lefebvre 15-2-50-0; Roebuck 17-3-54-0; Hayhurst 3-0-20-0.

Umpires: J. C. Balderstone and A. G. T. Whitehead.

## SOMERSET v GLAMORGAN

At Taunton, May 9, 10, 11, 13. Glamorgan won by 180 runs. Glamorgan 22 pts, Somerset 6 pts. Toss: Glamorgan. A patient innings by Morris (473 minutes, 382 balls), with good support from Shastri early on and later from Maynard, put Glamorgan in a strong position. Maynard hit three sixes and ten fours in scoring 85 from 137 balls. Somerset struggled throughout against their former fast bowler, Foster, who produced career-best figures, and they were indebted to Roebuck (210 balls) and Harden (114 balls) for their small deficit. Batting again, Glamorgan found runs came readily, especially to Maynard, who disregarded a broken finger as he raced to an unbeaten 133 from 162 balls. Somerset, set to get 368 in 89 overs, faltered once more against Foster, and only Roebuck's fighting 64 from 125 balls held the innings together. However, good close catching brought a dramatic slump against Watkin and Frost before the last-wicket pair, Swallow and Graveney, kept Glamorgan waiting for sixteen overs as they added 53, the best partnership of the innings.

*Close of play:* First day, Glamorgan 269-6 (H. Morris 108*, C. P. Metson 8*); Second day, Somerset 259-6 (N. A. Mallender 5*, G. D. Rose 8*); Third day, Glamorgan 294-3 (M. P. Maynard 98*, G. C. Holmes 8*).

# Glamorgan

| | | | |
|---|---|---|---|
| *A. R. Butcher lbw b Mallender | 12 | – c Cook b Swallow | 65 |
| H. Morris c Tavaré b Graveney | 141 | – c Rose b Graveney | 39 |
| R. J. Shastri b Swallow | 37 | – c Harden b Graveney | 68 |
| M. P. Maynard c Lefebvre b Graveney | 85 | – not out | 133 |
| G. C. Holmes c Harden b Graveney | 2 | – not out | 25 |
| I. Smith lbw b Rose | 6 | | |
| R. D. B. Croft c Harden b Graveney | 2 | | |
| †C. P. Metson c Tavaré b Rose | 24 | | |
| S. L. Watkin not out | 25 | | |
| D. J. Foster not out | 6 | | |
| L-b 6, w 5, n-b 2 | 13 | B 5, l-b 7, n-b 6 | 18 |

1/20 2/94 3/235 4/237 5/244    (8 wkts dec.) 353    1/88 2/131 3/278   (3 wkts dec.) 348
6/250 7/309 8/330

M. Frost did not bat.

Bonus points – Glamorgan 3, Somerset 2 (Score at 100 overs: 251-6).

Bowling: *First Innings*—Mallender 29-7-58-1; Rose 29-5-89-2; Lefebvre 26-10-51-0; Graveney 29-7-89-4; Swallow 17-5-47-1; Roebuck 7-2-13-0. *Second Innings*—Mallender 21-5-75-0; Rose 9-0-28-0; Graveney 31-8-110-2; Lefebvre 14-2-49-0; Swallow 13-1-62-1; Roebuck 7-1-12-0.

# Somerset

| | | | |
|---|---|---|---|
| S. J. Cook c Metson b Foster | 15 | – (2) b Foster | 20 |
| P. M. Roebuck c Smith b Foster | 101 | – (1) c Butcher b Foster | 64 |
| R. J. Harden b Foster | 73 | – c Smith b Foster | 26 |
| *C. J. Tavaré c Metson b Frost | 8 | – b Watkin | 9 |
| R. J. Bartlett c Metson b Foster | 32 | – lbw b Frost | 0 |
| †N. D. Burns b Foster | 6 | – c Croft b Frost | 0 |
| N. A. Mallender c Metson b Watkin | 19 | – (10) c Metson b Watkin | 4 |
| G. D. Rose lbw b Frost | 24 | – (7) c Smith b Watkin | 2 |
| R. P. Lefebvre c Metson b Watkin | 39 | – (8) c Metson b Watkin | 1 |
| I. G. Swallow b Foster | 1 | – (9) not out | 41 |
| D. A. Graveney not out | 0 | – c Metson b Watkin | 17 |
| L-b 8, w 1, n-b 7 | 16 | W 1, n-b 2 | 3 |

1/26 2/155 3/189 4/227 5/246      334    1/34 2/85 3/104 4/105 5/105    187
6/249 7/284 8/333 9/334                  6/114 7/124 8/124 9/134

Bonus points – Somerset 4, Glamorgan 3 (Score at 100 overs: 325-7).

Bowling: *First Innings*—Foster 28.2-3-84-6; Watkin 32-5-120-2; Frost 21-3-56-2; Croft 23-3-66-0. *Second Innings*—Foster 21-6-63-3; Watkin 20.3-5-63-5; Frost 15-0-52-2; Shastri 1-0-5-0; Croft 3-2-4-0.

Umpires: R. Julian and M. J. Kitchen.

At Derby, May 22, 23, 24. SOMERSET drew with DERBYSHIRE.


## SOMERSET v MIDDLESEX

At Taunton, May 25, 27, 28. Drawn. Somerset 4 pts, Middlesex 8 pts. Toss: Somerset. The Middlesex seam bowlers held sway on a greenish pitch in cloudy weather on the opening day, and while Roebuck carried his bat for the fourth time in his career, his 91 coming off 267 balls, the only other innings of significance was Cook's brisk 45. Somerset claimed two quick wickets that evening, but on Monday, in easier conditions, Gatting completely dominated the bowling. His 180, in five hours two minutes, came from 262 balls and contained 27 fours; he raced to his third fifty off 39 balls. Brown compiled a steady half-century, Keech a maiden one, and there was some entertaining hitting from the tail as Middlesex stretched their lead to 203. Cook (175 balls) and Roebuck fashioned Somerset's escape with a steadfast opening stand of 145 in 61 overs, mainly against the spinners, and later Harden was able to open out, reaching 50 in 88 balls.

*Close of play:* First day, Middlesex 42-2 (M. W. Gatting 15*, K. R. Brown 13*); Second day, Somerset 31-0 (S. J. Cook 12*, P. M. Roebuck 14*).

## Somerset

| | | | | |
|---|---|---|---|---|
| S. J. Cook c Farbrace b Ellcock | 45 | – c Farbrace b Emburey | 89 |
| P. M. Roebuck not out | 91 | – c Brown b Tufnell | 49 |
| A. N. Hayhurst c Emburey b Ellcock | 0 | – lbw b Ellcock | 26 |
| *C. J. Tavaré c Farbrace b Williams | 22 | – c Hutchinson b Emburey | 18 |
| R. J. Harden c Farbrace b Williams | 0 | – not out | 58 |
| †N. D. Burns c Farbrace b Ellcock | 6 | – c Farbrace b Ellcock | 0 |
| K. H. MacLeay c Brown b Tufnell | 19 | – not out | 9 |
| G. D. Rose c Emburey b Tufnell | 17 | | |
| N. A. Mallender c Farbrace b Williams | 6 | | |
| H. R. J. Trump c Keech b Ellcock | 5 | | |
| D. A. Graveney c Hutchinson b Williams | 1 | | |
| B 4, w 1, n-b 7 | 12 | B 4, l-b 5, w 1, n-b 10 | 20 |
| | **224** | (5 wkts) | **269** |

1/64 2/64 3/123 4/123 5/135    1/145 2/156 3/187
6/161 7/183 8/201 9/223    4/227 5/231

Bonus points – Somerset 2, Middlesex 4.

Bowling: *First Innings*—Ellcock 14-1-60-4; Cowans 14-2-47-0; Williams 20.2-5-46-4; Emburey 18-5-32-0; Tufnell 22-8-35-2. *Second Innings*—Ellcock 11-1-50-2; Williams 1-0-2-0; Emburey 49-22-66-2; Tufnell 48-13-108-1; Cowans 10-0-32-0; Roseberry 2-1-2-0; Keech 1-1-0-0.

## Middlesex

| | | | |
|---|---|---|---|
| I. J. F. Hutchinson c Burns b Mallender | 2 | P. C. R. Tufnell c Hayhurst b Graveney | 9 |
| M. A. Roseberry c Graveney b Rose | 7 | R. M. Ellcock not out | 26 |
| *M. W. Gatting lbw b Roebuck | 180 | N. G. Cowans c Rose b MacLeay | 20 |
| K. R. Brown c Hayhurst b Mallender | 53 | | |
| M. Keech run out | 51 | B 1, l-b 7, w 1, n-b 6 | 15 |
| J. E. Emburey lbw b Trump | 17 | | |
| N. F. Williams lbw b Mallender | 41 | 1/3 2/11 3/142 4/304 5/305 | **427** |
| †P. Farbrace b Trump | 6 | 6/338 7/344 8/361 9/404 | |

Bonus points – Middlesex 4, Somerset 2 (Score at 100 overs: 318-5).

Bowling: Mallender 21-2-82-3; Rose 5-1-14-1; Hayhurst 12-3-34-0; MacLeay 19.2-3-54-1; Trump 26-2-113-2; Graveney 34-4-111-1; Roebuck 6-2-11-1.

Umpires: J. H. Harris and B. J. Meyer.

At Taunton, May 29, 30, 31. SOMERSET drew with WEST INDIANS (See West Indian tour section).

At Swansea, June 4, 5, 6. SOMERSET drew with GLAMORGAN.

At Birmingham, June 7, 8, 10. SOMERSET drew with WARWICKSHIRE.

## SOMERSET v HAMPSHIRE

At Bath, June 18, 19, 20. Drawn. Somerset 4 pts, Hampshire 2 pts. Toss: Hampshire. On a slow pitch runs generally came grudgingly on the first day, only Terry and Gower (158 balls) making much progress. Mallender took three wickets with the second new ball in the second over of the second day, but James, who hit two sixes and seven fours in 75 not out, from 156 balls, masterminded 52 from the last wicket. Cook, given a life at 17, led Somerset's response in his smooth style with an unbeaten hundred in 197 balls, including eleven fours, and after Tavaré had declared 91 behind, Middleton underwrote the Hampshire second innings with 102 from 194 balls. The final equation offered Somerset the task of scoring 318 in 215 minutes, a minimum of 61 overs, but attempts to attack the seam bowlers quickly put them out of contention. Three quick wickets to Nicholas left Somerset eight wickets down with six overs remaining, but Burns lasted until the penultimate over, and Trump and Graveney held firm until the end.

*Close of play:* First day, Hampshire 221-5 (K. D. James 31*, A. N. Aymes 3*); Second day, Hampshire 61-0 (T. C. Middleton 27*, C. L. Smith 32*).

### Hampshire

| | | |
|---|---|---|
| T. C. Middleton c Burns b Lefebvre | 35 | – b Trump ..................... 102 |
| C. L. Smith b Lefebvre | 2 | – c Burns b MacLeay ........... 65 |
| *M. C. J. Nicholas b MacLeay | 23 | – c Cook b Trump ............. 28 |
| V. P. Terry c Trump b Hayhurst | 43 | – not out .................... 10 |
| D. I. Gower c Harden b Graveney | 69 | – not out .................... 18 |
| K. D. James not out | 75 | |
| †A. N. Aymes c Burns b Mallender | 3 | |
| R. J. Maru b Mallender | 2 | |
| I. J. Turner lbw b Mallender | 0 | |
| P. J. Bakker lbw b Mallender | 5 | |
| Aqib Javed not out | 15 | |
| L-b 8, n-b 11 | 19 | B 1, l-b 1, n-b 1 ........ 3 |

1/7 2/44 3/88 4/145 5/210       (9 wkts dec.) 291    1/114 2/196 3/200    (3 wkts dec.) 226
6/221 7/223 8/223 9/239

Bonus points – Hampshire 2, Somerset 2 (Score at 100 overs: 211-5).

Bowling: *First Innings*—Mallender 30–10–68–4; Lefebvre 31–8–66–2; Graveney 21–5–49–1; MacLeay 16–5–30–1; Trump 16–3–40–0; Hayhurst 9–1–30–1. *Second Innings*—Mallender 5–2–11–0; Lefebvre 4–1–12–0; Hayhurst 10–1–45–0; MacLeay 10–3–17–1; Graveney 23–4–70–0; Trump 13–1–69–2.

### Somerset

| | | |
|---|---|---|
| S. J. Cook not out | 107 | – b Bakker .................... 17 |
| P. M. Roebuck lbw b Aqib Javed | 4 | – b Aqib Javed ................ 12 |
| A. N. Hayhurst b Aqib Javed | 32 | – c Terry b James ............. 12 |
| *C. J. Tavaré not out | 49 | – c Aymes b Turner ........... 27 |
| R. J. Harden (did not bat) | – | – c Middleton b Maru ......... 13 |
| †N. D. Burns (did not bat) | – | – c Aymes b Aqib Javed ....... 49 |
| K. H. MacLeay (did not bat) | – | – c Aymes b Nicholas .......... 8 |
| R. P. Lefebvre (did not bat) | – | – b Nicholas .................. 4 |
| N. A. Mallender (did not bat) | – | – b Nicholas .................. 0 |
| H. R. J. Trump (did not bat) | – | – not out .................... 0 |
| D. A. Graveney (did not bat) | – | – not out .................... 0 |
| L-b 1, n-b 7 | 8 | L-b 7, n-b 11 ............ 18 |

1/8 2/87         (2 wkts dec.) 200    1/26 2/30 3/48          (9 wkts) 160
4/79 5/93 6/121
7/134 8/152 9/159

Bonus points – Somerset 2.

Bowling: *First Innings*—Aqib Javed 12–1–39–2; Bakker 11–2–35–0; Turner 15.5–5–0–47–0; James 9–3–18–0; Maru 15–1–60–0. *Second Innings*—Aqib Javed 13–2–50–2; Bakker 6–0–17–1; Maru 19–9–22–1; James 6–0–21–1; Turner 12–6–17–1; Smith 3–2–1–0; Nicholas 9–3–25–3.

Umpires: D. R. Shepherd and A. G. T. Whitehead.

## SOMERSET v GLOUCESTERSHIRE

At Bath, June 21, 22, 24. Drawn. Somerset 6 pts, Gloucestershire 3 pts. Toss: Gloucestershire. The rain which washed out the last day prevented Somerset from capitalising on their good work of the first two days. Mallender, finding some movement in the air and from a generally slow pitch, undermined Gloucestershire with an opening burst of three for 9 in 21 balls. They were saved from rout by Hodgson's defiance through 122 balls, Alleyne's 47 from 90 balls, which contained eight fours, and Scott's unbeaten 34. Lawrence's pace initially threatened Somerset, but a splendidly disciplined career-best 172 not out by Hayhurst put them in a commanding position. Hayhurst batted for seven hours eight minutes (346 balls) and hit 22 fours; he was well supported by Harden as they put on 106 in 52 overs for the fourth wicket, and after that he and Burns added a crisp 101 in twenty overs, mainly against the second new ball.

*Close of play:* First day, Somerset 64-2 (A. N. Hayhurst 41*, C. J. Tavaré 1*); Second day, Somerset 311-6 (A. N. Hayhurst 172*, R. P. Lefebvre 5*).

### Gloucestershire

| | | | |
|---|---|---|---|
| G. D. Hodgson lbw b MacLeay | 30 | D. V. Lawrence c Tavaré b Trump | 19 |
| J. J. E. Hardy lbw b Mallender | 9 | D. R. Gilbert c Burns b Mallender | 7 |
| *A. J. Wright c Burns b Mallender | 0 | A. M. Smith lbw b Mallender | 0 |
| C. W. J. Athey lbw b Mallender | 10 | | |
| M. W. Alleyne b Mallender | 47 | L-b 8, w 2, n-b 7 | 17 |
| J. W. Lloyds c Graveney b MacLeay | 2 | | |
| R. J. Scott not out | 34 | 1/18 2/18 3/39 4/94 5/106 | 183 |
| †R. C. J. Williams b Trump | 8 | 6/113 7/135 8/171 9/183 | |

Bonus points – Gloucestershire 1, Somerset 4.

Bowling: Mallender 17–2–43–6; Lefebvre 15–3–52–0; MacLeay 20–5–48–2; Hayhurst 9–5–11–0; Graveney 3–1–6–0; Trump 8–2–15–2.

### Somerset

| | | | |
|---|---|---|---|
| S. J. Cook c Athey b Lawrence | 0 | †N. D. Burns c Williams b Lawrence | 39 |
| P. M. Roebuck lbw b Smith | 15 | R. P. Lefebvre not out | 5 |
| A. N. Hayhurst not out | 172 | B 4, l-b 10, w 2, n-b 6 | 22 |
| *C. J. Tavaré lbw b Lawrence | 4 | | |
| R. J. Harden c Williams b Scott | 49 | 1/2 2/54 3/73 4/179 | (6 wkts) 311 |
| K. H. MacLeay b Lloyds | 5 | 5/193 6/294 | |

N. A. Mallender, H. R. J. Trump and D. A. Graveney did not bat.

Bonus points – Somerset 2, Gloucestershire 2 (Score at 100 overs: 220-5).

Bowling: Lawrence 23–5–69–3; Gilbert 10–2–27–0; Smith 28–9–53–1; Scott 27–10–67–1; Athey 5–0–12–0; Lloyds 27–5–69–1.

Umpires: R. C. Tolchard and A. G. T. Whitehead.

At The Oval, June 28, 29, July 1. SOMERSET drew with SURREY.

## SOMERSET v LANCASHIRE

At Taunton, July 2, 3, 4. Somerset won by four wickets. Somerset 22 pts, Lancashire 5 pts. Toss: Lancashire. Lancashire's first innings was brought to life by Fairbrother, whose 109, containing fifteen fours and a six, required just 135 balls and was backed by steady half-centuries from Speak and Titchard, the latter making his Championship début. Wasim Akram hit four sixes in a flurry, but a toe injury stopped him bowling more than three overs. A typical Cook century (196 balls, seventeen fours) had support from Hayhurst and Roebuck, but Roebuck's 183-ball 46, and the 50 overs occupied while they added 120 for the second wicket, ran counter to Somerset's pursuit of bonus points. Tavaré opened up the game by declaring 58 behind, but the loss of two early wickets put Lancashire on the defensive. Fairbrother, who survived chances when 45 and 94, received 258 balls for his second century of the match, hitting eleven fours this time, and only the introduction of Harden got Lancashire's score moving quickly. Somerset's eventual target of 294 in 188 minutes was a stiff one. After 104 in 30 overs from Cook and Roebuck, and a lively 57-ball 50 by Tavaré, they needed 150 from the final twenty overs. MacLeay hit four sixes in his 27-ball stay, Burns did well, and when Hayhurst joined Lefebvre, the requirement was 46 from the last five overs. Amid much excitement they took Somerset to their first Championship win of the season with two balls to spare.

*Close of play:* First day, Somerset 39-0 (S. J. Cook 27*, A. N. Hayhurst 10*); Second day, Lancashire 67-2 (N. J. Speak 45*, N. H. Fairbrother 19*).

### Lancashire

| | | | | |
|---|---|---|---|---|
| G. D. Mendis c and b Trump | 31 | – b Lefebvre | | 1 |
| G. Fowler c and b MacLeay | 14 | – lbw b Mallender | | 0 |
| N. J. Speak c Harden b MacLeay | 56 | – c Graveney b Lefebvre | | 49 |
| N. H. Fairbrother c MacLeay b Roebuck | 109 | – not out | | 102 |
| S. P. Titchard c Burns b Lefebvre | 53 | – b Lefebvre | | 0 |
| M. Watkinson c Harden b Trump | 13 | – (7) c Graveney b Harden | | 30 |
| Wasim Akram b Trump | 39 | – (8) lbw b Harden | | 2 |
| †W. K. Hegg not out | 0 | – (6) c Burns b MacLeay | | 17 |
| G. Yates lbw b Lefebvre | 0 | – not out | | 27 |
| B 4, l-b 1, w 2, n-b 4 | 11 | B 4, l-b 1, n-b 2 | | 7 |

1/24 2/66 3/177 4/233 5/276    (8 wkts dec.) 326    1/1 2/2 3/76 4/82    (7 wkts dec.) 235
6/326 7/326 8/326                                       5/129 6/180 7/182

*D. P. Hughes and P. J. Martin did not bat.

Bonus points – Lancashire 4, Somerset 3.

Bowling: *First Innings*—Mallender 15–3–42–0; Lefebvre 13.2–3–48–2; MacLeay 18–5–42–2; Hayhurst 8–0–39–0; Trump 15–2–47–3; Graveney 16–4–61–0; Roebuck 13–1–42–1. *Second Innings*—Mallender 3–0–6–1; Lefebvre 16–1–54–3; MacLeay 17–5–39–1; Trump 28–8–45–0; Roebuck 11–3–16–0; Hayhurst 2–2–0–0; Harden 13–0–70–2.

### Somerset

| | | | | |
|---|---|---|---|---|
| S. J. Cook c Speak b Watkinson | 131 | – st Hegg b Hughes | | 61 |
| A. N. Hayhurst c Titchard b Martin | 29 | – (8) not out | | 22 |
| P. M. Roebuck c Hegg b Hughes | 46 | – (2) c Titchard b Yates | | 52 |
| R. J. Harden not out | 29 | – c Titchard b Yates | | 12 |
| †N. D. Burns not out | 27 | – c Fairbrother b Watkinson | | 25 |
| *C. J. Tavaré (did not bat) | | – (3) run out | | 50 |
| K. H. MacLeay (did not bat) | | – (6) c and b Yates | | 36 |
| R. P. Lefebvre (did not bat) | | – (7) not out | | 23 |
| L-b 4, w 1, n-b 1 | 6 | B 6, l-b 5, w 1, n-b 1 | | 13 |

1/86 2/206 3/216            (3 wkts dec.) 268    1/104 2/124 3/144          (6 wkts) 294
                                            4/197 5/238 6/248

N. A. Mallender, H. R. J. Trump and D. A. Graveney did not bat.

Bonus points – Somerset 3, Lancashire 1.

Bowling: *First Innings*—Wasim Akram 3–1–7–0; Martin 13–0–42–1; Watkinson 21–3–70–1; Yates 26–8–59–0; Hughes 32–3–86–1. *Second Innings*—Martin 7–2–25–0; Watkinson 11–0–85–1; Hughes 19–4–90–1; Yates 23.4–3–83–3.

Umpires: D. J. Constant and B. Dudleston.

At Taunton, July 7. SOMERSET v GLOUCESTERSHIRE. Abandoned.


At Hove, July 16, 17, 18. SOMERSET drew with SUSSEX.


At Southend, July 19, 20, 22. SOMERSET lost to ESSEX by 136 runs.


At Northampton, July 23, 24, 25. SOMERSET drew with NORTHAMPTONSHIRE.


## SOMERSET v KENT

At Taunton, July 26, 27, 29. Drawn. Somerset 6 pts, Kent 4 pts. Toss: Kent. On a dry pitch offering occasional turn, Graveney, taking four wickets in his first eight overs, arrested Kent's promising start. However, Hinks and Fleming began a recovery and Marsh, undefeated with 113 from 193 balls, completed it. Cook (264 balls, thirteen fours), Harden and Tavaré established Somerset's reply on Saturday, and van Troost and Graveney had Kent in some difficulty at 47 for four 40 minutes into the final day. A vigorous 72-ball fifty from Fleming, and a steady effort by Benson, averted a crisis, and Benson was able to challenge Somerset to score 244 in two hours plus twenty overs. Tavaré, given excellent help by Harden and Burns, took them close with an exciting century before being run out in the penultimate over off the 133rd ball he faced. With 11 needed from the last over, Graveney hit a boundary, managed 4 leg-byes and then was caught in the deep. Trump, needing 3 to win off the last ball, swung hard but could achieve only a leg-bye.

*Close of play*: First day, Kent 315-9 (S. A. Marsh 113\*, A. P. Igglesden 11\*); Second day, Kent 16-1 (M. R. Benson 10\*, N. R. Taylor 5\*).

### Kent

| | | |
|---|---|---|
| T. R. Ward b Graveney | 31 | – c Cook b van Troost ............ 0 |
| *M. R. Benson c and b Graveney | 29 | – b Trump .................... 76 |
| N. R. Taylor c Burns b Graveney | 0 | – lbw b Graveney ............ 23 |
| G. R. Cowdrey b Graveney | 9 | – lbw b van Troost ............ 0 |
| S. G. Hinks c Burns b van Troost | 39 | – c Cook b Graveney ............ 0 |
| M. V. Fleming b Rose | 54 | – run out .................... 59 |
| †S. A. Marsh not out | 113 | – not out .................... 28 |
| R. P. Davis lbw b Graveney | 10 | – (9) not out ................ 13 |
| M. M. Patel c Pringle b Graveney | 0 | |
| T. A. Merrick lbw b Trump | 5 | – (8) b Trump ................ 2 |
| A. P. Igglesden c Tavaré b Graveney | 15 | |
| B 3, l-b 9, n-b 2 | 14 | B 4, l-b 4, w 1, n-b 2 .... 11 |

1/54 2/56 3/63 4/83 5/134                319           1/1 2/45 3/46   (7 wkts dec.) 212
6/195 7/251 8/275 9/284                               4/47 5/138
                                                      6/174 7/180

Bonus points – Kent 3, Somerset 3 (Score at 100 overs: 284-8).

Bowling: *First Innings*—van Troost 16–3–41–1; Rose 11–1–52–1; MacLeay 2.1–1–5–0; Graveney 41–10–105–7; Trump 38.5–9–87–1; Hayhurst 5–1–17–0. *Second Innings*—van Troost 11–1–25–2; Trump 22–5–91–2; Graveney 23.4–4–88–2.

## Somerset

| | | | |
|---|---|---|---|
| S. J. Cook lbw b Patel | 126 | – c Marsh b Igglesden | 10 |
| A. N. Hayhurst lbw b Merrick | 1 | – c Fleming b Merrick | 5 |
| R. J. Harden b Merrick | 54 | – b Merrick | 57 |
| *C. J. Tavaré c Cowdrey b Davis | 72 | – run out | 100 |
| N. J. Pringle st Marsh b Davis | 7 | – b Patel | 17 |
| †N. D. Burns c Taylor b Patel | 6 | – b Igglesden | 27 |
| G. D. Rose c and b Davis | 3 | – b Davis | 0 |
| K. H. MacLeay not out | 2 | – run out | 10 |
| H. R. J. Trump (did not bat) | | – not out | 1 |
| D. A. Graveney (did not bat) | | – c Patel b Igglesden | 4 |
| A. P. van Troost (did not bat) | | – not out | 0 |
| B 8, l-b 9 | 17 | B 2, l-b 9 | 11 |

1/5 2/131 3/238 4/255 5/282 (7 wkts dec.) 288
6/282 7/288

1/15 2/15 3/121 (9 wkts) 242
4/158 5/210 6/210
7/233 8/233 9/241

Bonus points – Somerset 3, Kent 1 (Score at 100 overs: 272-4).

Bowling: *First Innings*—Merrick 14–2–60–2; Igglesden 13–1–51–0; Patel 34–7–75–2; Davis 38.5–15–67–3; Fleming 8–0–18–0. *Second Innings*—Merrick 16–2–73–2; Igglesden 10–0–45–4; Davis 13–2–52–0; Patel 19–1–61–1.

Umpires: J. H. Harris and R. Julian.

## SOMERSET v LEICESTERSHIRE

At Weston-super-Mare, August 2, 3, 5. Drawn. Somerset 5 pts, Leicestershire 5 pts. Toss: Leicestershire. On a slow, slightly variable pitch, Leicestershire were sustained by Boon (173 balls) and Hepworth before a Trump-inspired slump left them 162 for seven. Benson and Whiticase, the latter scoring 52 from 115 balls, led a determined recovery; for Somerset, Trump finished with a career-best six for 107. Lewis had Somerset 29 for three early next day, but solid batting by Harden and Hayhurst, adding 94 in 41 overs, left the game interestingly balanced by the close. After Roebuck's remarkable spell of three for 10 on the final day, Leicestershire needed a lively stand of 74 between Potter and Lewis to help them set a target of 270 in a minimum of 53 overs. Lewis hit three sixes and four fours in making 43 from 41 deliveries, and when Leicestershire took the field he was quickly in action again, sending Cook back first ball. A 22-over delay for rain early in the Somerset innings upset the calculations, however, and Hayhurst and Tavaré had little option but to play out the remaining 23 overs.

*Close of play:* First day, Somerset 13-2 (S. J. Cook 5*, R. J. Harden 3*); Second day, Leicestershire 38-0 (T. J. Boon 26*, N. E. Briers 9*).

## Leicestershire

| | | | |
|---|---|---|---|
| T. J. Boon c Roebuck b Trump | 61 | – lbw b Roebuck | 40 |
| *N. E. Briers c Trump b Rose | 2 | – c and b Graveney | 46 |
| P. N. Hepworth b Graveney | 30 | – c Harden b Graveney | 4 |
| J. J. Whitaker b Trump | 5 | – b Roebuck | 16 |
| L. Potter b Trump | 22 | – not out | 43 |
| J. D. R. Benson lbw b Hallett | 49 | – st Burns b Roebuck | 14 |
| C. C. Lewis c Cook b Trump | 7 | – b Swallow | 43 |
| M. I. Gidley lbw b Trump | 1 | – (9) not out | 4 |
| †P. Whiticase c Harden b Trump | 52 | – (8) c Hayhurst b Swallow | 9 |
| D. J. Millns lbw b Rose | 4 | | |
| J. N. Maguire not out | 0 | | |
| B 4, l-b 2, w 1, n-b 4 | 11 | B 4, l-b 7, n-b 2 | 13 |

1/3 2/77 3/92 4/119 5/134 263
6/146 7/162 8/210 9/259

1/83 2/90 3/107 (7 wkts dec.) 232
4/118 5/134
6/208 7/222

Bonus points – Leicestershire 2, Somerset 3 (Score at 100 overs: 234-8).

Bowling: *First Innings*—Rose 16–6–24–2; Hallett 13–5–29–1; Trump 33–7–107–6; Hayhurst 5–0–17–0; Graveney 25–9–39–1; Swallow 17–3–41–0. *Second Innings*—Rose 3–0–7–0; Hallett 2–0–6–0; Graveney 20–5–71–2; Trump 18–3–82–0; Swallow 9–2–45–2; Roebuck 8–4–10–3.

## Somerset

| | | |
|---|---:|---:|
| S. J. Cook c Whitticase b Lewis | 10 | – c Whitticase b Lewis .......... 0 |
| P. M. Roebuck c Millns b Lewis | 4 | – b Potter .................... 14 |
| H. R. J. Trump lbw b Lewis | 0 | |
| R. J. Harden c Hepworth b Millns | 64 | |
| A. N. Hayhurst st Whitticase b Potter | 71 | – (3) not out ................. 26 |
| *C. J. Tavaré c Whitticase b Potter | 17 | – (4) not out ................. 20 |
| †N. D. Burns not out | 29 | |
| G. D. Rose c Whitaker b Millns | 14 | |
| I. G. Swallow not out | 13 | |
| L-b 3, w 1 | 4 | W 1 .................... 1 |

1/5 2/6 3/29 4/123 5/164 　　(7 wkts dec.) 226 　　1/0 2/27 　　　　(2 wkts) 61
6/181 7/204

J. C. Hallett and D. A. Graveney did not bat.

Bonus points – Somerset 2, Leicestershire 3 (Score at 100 overs: 205-7).

Bowling: *First Innings*—Lewis 14–6–22–3; Maguire 23–5–62–0; Millns 19–6–43–2; Gidley 18–8–33–0; Potter 31–11–52–2; Hepworth 2–0–11–0. *Second Innings*—Lewis 4–2–10–1; Maguire 4–2–5–0; Potter 9–5–13–1; Millns 2–1–4–0; Gidley 9–4–15–0; Boon 5–3–9–0; Hepworth 3–1–5–0.

Umpires: B. Hassan and B. J. Meyer.

## SOMERSET v WORCESTERSHIRE

At Weston-super-Mare, August 6, 7, 8. Drawn. Somerset 6 pts, Worcestershire 5 pts. Toss: Somerset. Rain either side of lunch and the attentions of the Worcestershire seam bowlers on a slightly grassy pitch gave the Somerset innings an uncertain start. However, Burns, with 96 from 239 balls, and Lefebvre put them in a good position with a decisive stand of 164 in 56 overs. Lefebvre, after a most unpromising start, completed an entertaining century from 182 balls, hitting fourteen fours, but in doing so he damaged a hamstring and was unable to bowl more than five overs. Worcestershire's innings followed a similar pattern to Somerset's, with Moody's powerful 77, off 116 balls, and the crisp efforts of Rhodes and Radford assured them of three batting points before Curtis declared in arrears. Somerset were in trouble at 86 for five, but somewhat curiously the main attack was then withdrawn, and Harden and Rose were encouraged to put on 88 in sixteen overs. The outcome was a target for Worcestershire of 265 in what became 69 overs. Curtis and Bent provided an ideal start with 110 in 37 overs, but as the chase developed Graveney and Trump, the latter improving his best figures, took advantage of the batsmen's indiscretions. Worcestershire did not give up until the fall of their ninth wicket, whereupon the last pair battled through the final four overs to earn a draw.

*Close of play:* First day, Somerset 251-6 (N. D. Burns 59*, R. P. Lefebvre 64*); Second day, Worcestershire 250-6 dec.

## Somerset

| | | |
|---|---:|---:|
| S. J. Cook c Moody b Lampitt | 37 | – c Rhodes b Illingworth ........ 38 |
| P. M. Roebuck lbw b Newport | 11 | – b Radford .................... 6 |
| A. N. Hayhurst lbw b Radford | 40 | – lbw b Stemp .................. 13 |
| *C. J. Tavaré c D'Oliveira b Lampitt | 10 | – st Rhodes b Stemp ............ 0 |
| R. J. Harden c Hick b Radford | 0 | – not out ...................... 74 |
| †N. D. Burns c Hick b Stemp | 96 | – run out ...................... 0 |
| G. D. Rose lbw b Newport | 12 | – not out ...................... 24 |
| R. P. Lefebvre st Rhodes b Illingworth | 100 | |
| H. R. J. Trump not out | 12 | |
| B 3, l-b 7, w 1, n-b 11 | 22 | L-b 4, n-b 4 .................. 8 |

1/25 2/83 3/97 4/98 5/113 　　(8 wkts dec.) 340 　　1/27 2/60 3/68 　　(5 wkts dec.) 174
6/158 7/322 8/340 　　　　　　　　　　　　　　　　4/82 5/86

J. C. Hallett and D. A. Graveney did not bat.

Bonus points – Somerset 4, Worcestershire 2 (Score at 100 overs: 310-6).

Bowling: *First Innings*—Radford 28–4–105–2; Newport 30–3–90–2; Lampitt 22–2–70–2; Illingworth 19–7–37–1; Hick 1–1–0–0; Stemp 10.1–2–28–1. *Second Innings*—Radford 5–0–25–1; Newport 6–2–25–0; Lampitt 3–0–8–0; Illingworth 6–2–7–1; Stemp 7–0–23–2; D'Oliveira 5–3–10–0; Moody 3–1–6–0; Curtis 5–1–31–0; Bent 3–1–5–0; Rhodes 1–0–30–0.

## Worcestershire

| | | | | |
|---|---|---|---|---|
| *T. S. Curtis c Cook b Rose | 7 | – | lbw b Trump | 55 |
| P. Bent lbw b Hayhurst | 39 | – | st Burns b Graveney | 65 |
| G. A. Hick b Rose | 10 | – | c Harden b Trump | 24 |
| T. M. Moody c Burns b Graveney | 77 | – | lbw b Trump | 12 |
| D. B. D'Oliveira c Tavaré b Graveney | 9 | – | st Burns b Trump | 9 |
| †S. J. Rhodes not out | 53 | – | c Tavaré b Graveney | 26 |
| R. K. Illingworth run out | 24 | – | (8) st Burns b Trump | 9 |
| N. V. Radford not out | 32 | – | (7) b Trump | 0 |
| S. R. Lampitt (did not bat) | | – | st Burns b Graveney | 7 |
| P. J. Newport (did not bat) | | – | not out | 8 |
| R. D. Stemp (did not bat) | | – | not out | 0 |
| B 1, l-b 3, n-b 3 | 7 | | L-b 16, n-b 1 | 17 |

1/26 2/46 3/101 4/118     (6 wkts dec.) 250    1/110 2/149 3/171    (9 wkts) 232
5/155 6/192                                      4/176 5/191 6/191
                                                    7/215 8/219 9/232

Bonus points – Worcestershire 3, Somerset 2.

Bowling: *First Innings*—Rose 14–2–58–2; Hallett 11–2–36–0; Lefebvre 5–3–11–0; Graveney 21–3–54–2; Hayhurst 7–1–18–1; Trump 19–2–69–0. *Second Innings*—Rose 6–2–15–0; Hallett 9–1–34–0; Hayhurst 4–1–15–0; Graveney 29–5–87–3; Trump 16–2–48–6; Roebuck 5–1–17–0.

Umpires: B. Hassan and B. J. Meyer.

At Taunton, August 10, 11, 12. SOMERSET lost to SRI LANKANS by eight wickets (See Sri Lankan tour section).

At Nottingham, August 16, 17, 19. SOMERSET drew with NOTTINGHAMSHIRE.

## SOMERSET v YORKSHIRE

At Taunton, August 23, 24, 26. Drawn. Somerset 6 pts, Yorkshire 6 pts. Toss: Yorkshire. After 36 overs had been lost to rain, Cook led Somerset's steady retort to being put in on a greenish, slightly variable pitch. They faltered for a time against the left-arm spin of Carrick, but were put back on course by Bartlett's 71 from 103 balls and, more dramatically, by Rose's maiden first-class century, from 114 balls with seven sixes and seven fours. Carrick was hit for a four and three sixes off consecutive balls by the big-hitting all-rounder. Yorkshire's batting lacked urgency, Byas facing 175 balls for his 79, and it was again up to Cook, with his not out 85 from 125 balls, to get the game into the position from which Yorkshire were set to score 311 in what became 64 overs. Moxon's 121-ball 91 and his opening partnership of 148 in 38 overs with Metcalfe gave them a promising start, but then Graveney, bowling over the wicket into the rough, took three wickets in fourteen deliveries. A run-out and two wickets by Trump put Yorkshire in some danger, but Byas and Carrick saw them through the last thirteen overs.

*Close of play:* First day, Somerset 264-6 (R. J. Bartlett 52*, G. D. Rose 21*); Second day, Yorkshire 219-5 (P. E. Robinson 22*, C. S. Pickles 0*).

## Somerset

| | | | |
|---|---|---|---|
| S. J. Cook lbw b Gough | 79 | – not out | 85 |
| P. M. Roebuck c Blakey b Pickles | 31 | – c Byas b M. A. Robinson | 2 |
| A. N. Hayhurst lbw b M. A. Robinson | 21 | – retired hurt | 9 |
| *C. J. Tavaré c Metcalfe b Carrick | 27 | – c Batty b Pickles | 18 |
| R. J. Harden lbw b Carrick | 13 | – not out | 24 |
| R. J. Bartlett c Blakey b Carrick | 71 | | |
| †N. D. Burns b Carrick | 0 | | |
| G. D. Rose not out | 105 | | |
| H. R. J. Trump lbw b Gough | 0 | | |
| D. A. Graveney b Gough | 7 | | |
| J. C. Hallett not out | 1 | | |
| B 4, l-b 12, n-b 7 | 23 | B 3, l-b 3, w 1, n-b 6 | 13 |

1/66 2/124 3/147 4/169 5/208          (9 wkts dec.) 378          1/20 2/86          (2 wkts dec.) 151
6/212 7/295 8/296 9/358

Bonus points – Somerset 4, Yorkshire 4.

*In the second innings A. N. Hayhurst retired hurt at 45.*

Bowling: *First Innings*—M. A. Robinson 16–2–77–1; Gough 27–6–99–3; Pickles 17–3–43–1; Kellett 2–0–4–0; Carrick 30.5–5–111–4; Batty 6–1–28–0. *Second Innings*—Gough 8–1–25–0; M. A. Robinson 10–1–40–1; Pickles 8–0–36–1; Carrick 8–1–24–0; Batty 3–0–20–0.

## Yorkshire

| | | | |
|---|---|---|---|
| *M. D. Moxon c Tavaré b Rose | 34 | – c Tavaré b Graveney | 91 |
| A. A. Metcalfe lbw b Rose | 6 | – c Burns b Graveney | 62 |
| D. Byas c Cook b Trump | 79 | – not out | 27 |
| S. A. Kellett c Burns b Graveney | 67 | – c and b Graveney | 1 |
| P. E. Robinson not out | 22 | – run out | 4 |
| †R. J. Blakey c and b Trump | 7 | – b Trump | 1 |
| C. S. Pickles not out | 0 | – c Harden b Trump | 0 |
| P. Carrick (did not bat) | – | – not out | 11 |
| L-b 2, w 1, n-b 1 | 4 | B 3, l-b 3, n-b 3 | 9 |

1/33 2/42 3/190 4/195 5/208          (5 wkts dec.) 219          1/148 2/161 3/165          (6 wkts) 206
                                                            4/174 5/183 6/190

D. Gough, J. D. Batty and M. A. Robinson did not bat.

Bonus points – Yorkshire 2, Somerset 2.

Bowling: *First Innings*—Hallett 13–3–42–0; Hayhurst 10–1–35–0; Graveney 26–9–58–1; Rose 13–3–29–2; Trump 24–7–53–2. *Second Innings*—Rose 5–0–28–0; Hallett 6–1–26–0; Trump 24–5–71–2; Hayhurst 3–0–10–0; Graveney 22–4–61–3; Roebuck 3–2–4–0.

Umpires: J. C. Balderstone and N. T. Plews.

At Southampton, August 28, 29, 30, 31. SOMERSET lost to HAMPSHIRE by two wickets.

At Worcester, September 3, 4, 5. SOMERSET lost to WORCESTERSHIRE by an innings and 142 runs.

At Bristol, September 10, 11, 12. SOMERSET beat GLOUCESTERSHIRE by nine wickets.

## SOMERSET v WARWICKSHIRE

At Taunton, September 17, 18, 19, 20. Warwickshire won by 5 runs. Warwickshire 23 pts, Somerset 6 pts. Toss: Warwickshire. A splendid match, played in beautiful weather on an ideal pitch, was decided with eleven balls left. Three brisk half-centuries set up the Warwickshire innings, and after a mid-innings slump against Mallender, Booth's half-century, from 77 balls, restored the momentum. Cook, completing his record eleventh century of the season for Somerset in 181 balls, firmly corrected the home side's early slide, with Bartlett and MacLeay (92 balls) contributing usefully. Ratcliffe again launched Warwickshire's innings soundly, with 84 from 121 balls, and Ostler reinforced the good impression he made on the opening day. Somerset's target was 409 in a minimum of 122 overs, and Cook, Harden (155 balls) and Tavaré (175 balls) gave the chase its early pace. However, Booth, bowling slow left-arm over the wicket, slowed the scoring and also took the important wickets of Cook and Tavaré. MacLeay and Rose, with 55 from 51 balls, picked up the challenge, but Booth had the final say, bowling Trump and, in the penultimate over, ending the determined last-wicket stand of 16 between Mallender and Graveney.

*Close of play:* First day, Warwickshire 316-7 (K. J. Piper 20*, P. A. Booth 30*); Second day, Somerset 289; Third day, Somerset 60-1 (S. J. Cook 26*, R. J. Harden 26*).

## Warwickshire

| | | | |
|---|---|---|---|
| A. J. Moles c Bartlett b Graveney | 26 | – c Trump b Rose | 1 |
| J. D. Ratcliffe c MacLeay b Mallender | 61 | – c Rose b Trump | 84 |
| *T. A. Lloyd c Trump b Graveney | 69 | – c Cook b Graveney | 18 |
| D. P. Ostler c Tavaré b Trump | 79 | – b Rose | 58 |
| D. A. Reeve lbw b Mallender | 11 | – c Lefebvre b Rose | 57 |
| Asif Din b Mallender | 11 | – b Mallender | 34 |
| N. M. K. Smith lbw b Mallender | 2 | – b Mallender | 1 |
| †K. J. Piper c Burns b Mallender | 35 | – b Rose | 30 |
| P. A. Booth c Rose b Trump | 62 | – c Cook b Graveney | 0 |
| T. A. Munton not out | 6 | – not out | 12 |
| A. A. Donald b Mallender | 4 | – not out | 8 |
| L-b 4, n-b 6 | 10 | B 2, l-b 14, w 1, n-b 1 | 18 |

1/74 2/95 3/225 4/249 5/255     376    1/11 2/46 3/161   (9 wkts dec.) 321
6/257 7/270 8/362 9/365            4/175 5/241 6/243
                                     7/278 8/285 9/309

Bonus points – Warwickshire 3, Somerset 3 (Score at 100 overs: 281-7).

Bowling: *First Innings*—Mallender 28.2-7-68-6; Rose 18-2-70-0; Trump 32-10-95-2; Graveney 26-6-73-2; Lefebvre 12-4-27-0; MacLeay 7-0-39-0. *Second Innings*—Mallender 16-4-55-2; Rose 20-3-77-4; Graveney 24-3-79-2; Trump 19-2-69-1; Lefebvre 8-0-25-0.

## Somerset

| | | | |
|---|---|---|---|
| S. J. Cook c Piper b Booth | 127 | – c Ratcliffe b Booth | 40 |
| †N. D. Burns b Donald | 5 | – b Donald | 0 |
| R. J. Harden b Booth | 5 | – c Reeve b Smith | 68 |
| *C. J. Tavaré lbw b Munton | 0 | – b Booth | 85 |
| R. J. Bartlett lbw b Reeve | 38 | – c Ostler b Reeve | 35 |
| K. H. MacLeay c Ostler b Donald | 63 | – c Piper b Reeve | 47 |
| G. D. Rose c Ostler b Donald | 10 | – c Piper b Munton | 55 |
| R. P. Lefebvre b Donald | 6 | – c Ratcliffe b Smith | 15 |
| N. A. Mallender b Donald | 6 | – not out | 13 |
| H. R. J. Trump b Donald | 8 | – b Booth | 4 |
| D. A. Graveney not out | 2 | – b Booth | 8 |
| B 4, l-b 8, n-b 7 | 19 | B 14, l-b 13, n-b 6 | 33 |

1/18 2/46 3/51 4/117 5/243     289    1/3 2/89 3/132 4/224 5/290   403
6/251 7/257 8/275 9/280           6/320 7/362 8/382 9/387

Bonus points – Somerset 3, Warwickshire 4.

Bowling: *First Innings*—Donald 20.2-2-84-6; Munton 20-5-52-1; Booth 27-6-76-2; Smith 11-2-38-0; Reeve 6-1-27-1. *Second Innings*—Donald 23-4-95-1; Munton 18-5-57-1; Smith 28-6-79-2; Booth 43.1-10-103-4; Asif Din 1-0-6-0; Reeve 13-1-36-2.

Umpires: D. R. Shepherd and R. C. Tolchard.

# SURREY

*Patron:* HM The Queen
*President:* 1991 – B. Coleman
              1992 – W. D. Wickson
*Chairman:* D. H. Newton
*Chairman, Cricket Committee:* J. A. Fulford
*Secretary:* D. G. Seward
    The Oval, London SE11 5SS
    (Telephone: 071-582 6660)
*Captain:* 1991 – I. A. Greig
          1992 – A. J. Stewart
*County Coach:* G. G. Arnold
*Assistant County Coach:* C. E. Waller

It is doubtful whether anyone has bowled faster or straighter in an English season than Waqar Younis did for Surrey in 1991. Contrary to modern practice among quick bowlers, the bouncer had a minimal place in his armoury; stumps were hit and pads thumped regularly to earn the young Pakistani a rich harvest of 151 wickets in all competitions, with an astonishing two-thirds of his victims bowled or lbw. Feet and ankles were constantly in danger of bruising, or worse, from Waqar's wicked full-length deliveries, which Surrey will sorely miss in 1992, when Pakistan require his services on their tour of England.

Surrey's coach, Geoff Arnold, could think of no fast bowler in the world he rated more highly. "He's unique: he has greater ability to swing the ball late, and at a faster pace – not to mention landing it in the blockhole – than anyone I've seen", he explained. A total of 113 batsmen fell Waqar's way, at a cost of 14.36 each, in the Britannic Assurance Championship, in which he picked up thirteen returns of five wickets or more. He was most effective with the shiny-rough contrast of the older ball, and he comfortably headed the national averages. On occasions he also displayed some explosive batting, as at Guildford, where his 31 from nineteen balls set up a last-over victory against Yorkshire, and in the NatWest Bank Trophy quarter-final at The Oval, where his eighteen-ball 26 helped Surrey reach a total which Essex could not match.

The county's support bowling often spluttered, however, and they had to settle for fifth place in the Championship – four up on 1990, but a disappointment after they had shared second position in early August. Surrey fell away at the end of the season, losing both their last Championship matches after being beaten by Hampshire in the final of the NatWest Bank Trophy, their first appearance in a Lord's showpiece since 1982. Still, had Lancashire not pipped them by a single wicket on the final day of the Championship season, Surrey's prizemoney of £3,250 would have been doubled.

The injury-troubled Martin Bicknell, who had toured Australia with England in the winter, failed to reach 50 wickets, while Tony Murphy's 35 came at an expensive 47.62 apiece – though earlier in the season he was Surrey's most effective one-day bowler. The left-arm spinner, Keith Medlycott, after suffering a disastrous loss of control and confidence in Sri Lanka with England A, constantly wrestled with his action without fully mastering it. This was doubly unfortunate because pitches at The Oval were a shade slower and more conducive to spin than normal, something which made Waqar Younis's achievements all the more remarkable.

Darren Bicknell was the most consistent of the batsmen, with five hundreds in his 1,888 first-class runs, and Graham Thorpe's season finished with a flourish: he scored three hundreds in five innings, the second a career-best 177 against Sussex, and 93 in the NatWest final to convince any doubters of the temperament and ability which the selectors acknowledged with his third successive England A tour. The Bicknell brothers were also selected to join him on the trip to the West Indies. David Ward, one of the band of ten to make 2,000 runs in the previous summer, was way short of that outstanding feat in 1991, while Alec Stewart, though regaining his England place for the last two Tests of the summer and making his first Test hundred, failed to score 1,000 runs in the Championship. The lower output at the crease was reflected in the batting points column of the Championship table, where Surrey returned the meagre total of 47, marginally better than Derbyshire and Leicestershire (46) and Gloucestershire (42).

Surrey had no real voice in the Benson and Hedges Cup, in which they won only one group match; nor did they put on their Sunday best for the Refuge Assurance League, in which seven wins earned them joint eighth place. But they were a potent force in the NatWest until the final, when a four-wicket defeat was the penalty for batting too slowly in the first half of their innings. It was also a rare moment when Waqar Younis did not rise to the occasion. They had won a thrilling semi-final against Northamptonshire after Martin Bicknell's unbeaten 66 had rescued an innings in ruins at 91 for six, and Waqar had collected five wickets in four deadly spells, the last of them going into a second day because of the deteriorating light on the first evening. Their closest shave, however, was in the first round at The Oval against the would-be giant-killers of Oxfordshire. When rain prevented a result in two attempts to play a match, the players had to move down to the indoor nets. There, the first-class county were saved from embarrassment by Murphy, who hit the stumps twice in the bowl-out – the cricketing equivalent of football's penalty shoot-out – for Surrey to win 3-2.

During the season the captain, Ian Greig, decided to step down after five years in charge, to allow Stewart to emulate his father, M. J. Stewart, who captained Surrey for ten seasons from 1963. Greig's knee problems had restricted his bowling, which in turn upset the balance of the side, although he was retained on the staff and awarded a benefit. At the end of July, HM The Queen, accompanied by HRH The Duke of Edinburgh, officially opened the £3 million multi-purpose Ken Barrington Centre, during the NatWest Trophy quarter-final against Essex. It was Her Majesty's first visit to The Oval since 1955, when she saw a Surrey team including Barrington play the touring South Africans. – David Field.

566

SURREY 1991

[*Bill Smith*]

*Back row*: M. A. Butcher, A. G. Robson, J. Boiling, N. H. Peters, A. J. Hollioake, A. W. Smith, N. F. Sargeant. *Middle row*: M. R.L. W. Ayers (*scorer*), G. G. Arnold (*county coach*), A. D. Brown, A. J. Murphy, R. I. Alikhan, P. D. Atkins, J. D. Robinson, N. M. Kendrick, C. E. Waller (*assistant county coach*), J. Deary (*physiotherapist*). *Front row*: Waqar Younis, D. M. Ward, M. P. Bicknell, A. J. Stewart, I. A. Greig (*captain*), M. A. Lynch, K. T. Medlycott, C. K. Bullen, M. A. Feltham. *Insets*: D. J. Bicknell, G. P. Thorpe.

## SURREY RESULTS

*All first-class matches – Played 23: Won 9, Lost 6, Drawn 8.*

*County Championship matches – Played 22: Won 8, Lost 6, Drawn 8.*

*Bonus points – Batting 47, Bowling 66.*

*Competition placings – Britannic Assurance County Championship, 5th;*
*NatWest Bank Trophy, finalists; Benson and Hedges Cup, 4th in Group B;*
*Refuge Assurance League, 8th equal.*

## BRITANNIC ASSURANCE CHAMPIONSHIP AVERAGES

### BATTING

| | Birthplace | M | I | NO | R | HI | Avge |
|---|---|---|---|---|---|---|---|
| ‡D. J. Bicknell | Guildford | 22 | 40 | 2 | 1,762 | 151 | 46.36 |
| ‡G. P. Thorpe | Farnham | 21 | 35 | 7 | 1,164 | 177 | 41.57 |
| ‡D. M. Ward | Croydon | 22 | 38 | 5 | 1,304 | 151 | 39.51 |
| ‡A. J. Stewart | Merton | 17 | 30 | 6 | 936 | 109 | 39.00 |
| J. D. Robinson | Epsom | 4 | 6 | 1 | 186 | 79 | 37.20 |
| R. I. Alikhan | Westminster | 18 | 33 | 2 | 963 | 96* | 31.06 |
| ‡M. A. Feltham | St John's Wood | 12 | 16 | 4 | 327 | 69* | 27.25 |
| ‡I. A. Greig | Queenstown, SA | 19 | 29 | 4 | 593 | 72 | 23.72 |
| ‡K. T. Medlycott | Whitechapel | 18 | 25 | 2 | 513 | 66 | 22.30 |
| ‡M. A. Lynch | Georgetown, BG | 10 | 17 | 1 | 342 | 141* | 21.37 |
| N. M. Kendrick | Bromley | 2 | 4 | 1 | 58 | 24 | 19.33 |
| ‡M. P. Bicknell | Guildford | 15 | 22 | 4 | 312 | 63 | 17.33 |
| N. F. Sargeant | Hammersmith, London | 20 | 27 | 4 | 362 | 49 | 15.73 |
| ‡Waqar Younis | Vehari, Pakistan | 17 | 20 | 8 | 177 | 31 | 14.75 |
| A. J. Murphy | Manchester | 19 | 20 | 8 | 71 | 18 | 5.91 |
| J. Boiling | New Delhi, India | 4 | 7 | 1 | 22 | 16 | 3.66 |

Also batted: A. G. Robson (*East Boldon*) (2 matches) 0, 0, 3.

*\* Signifies not out.    ‡ Denotes county cap.*

The following played a total of twelve three-figure innings for Surrey in County Championship matches – D. J. Bicknell 5, G. P. Thorpe 4, M. A. Lynch 1, A. J. Stewart 1, D. M. Ward 1.

### BOWLING

| | O | M | R | W | BB | 5W/i | Avge |
|---|---|---|---|---|---|---|---|
| Waqar Younis | 570.1 | 109 | 1,623 | 113 | 7-87 | 13 | 14.36 |
| N. M. Kendrick | 105 | 26 | 262 | 12 | 5-54 | 2 | 21.83 |
| M. P. Bicknell | 470.5 | 118 | 1,256 | 45 | 7-52 | 1 | 27.91 |
| M. A. Feltham | 328 | 56 | 996 | 35 | 4-36 | 0 | 28.45 |
| K. T. Medlycott | 458.5 | 98 | 1,569 | 38 | 4-56 | 0 | 41.28 |
| A. J. Murphy | 546.4 | 118 | 1,667 | 35 | 5-63 | 1 | 47.62 |

Also bowled: R. I. Alikhan 5–0–43–2; D. J. Bicknell 5.3–0–62–2; J. Boiling 149.1–37–420–9; I. A. Greig 154.2–31–398–9; M. A. Lynch 9–1–29–0; J. D. Robinson 28–3–110–2; A. G. Robson 39–14–103–1; N. F. Sargeant 5–0–88–1; A. J. Stewart 7–0–34–0; G. P. Thorpe 39–5–157–1; D. M. Ward 7.5–0–66–2.

**Wicket-keepers:** N. F. Sargeant 43 ct, 5 st; A. J. Stewart 8 ct.

**Leading Fielder:** M. A. Lynch 13.

At Chelmsford, April 27, 29, 30, May 1. SURREY drew with ESSEX.

## SURREY v KENT

At The Oval, May 9, 10, 11, 13. Kent won by an innings and 3 runs. Kent 22 pts, Surrey 3 pts. Toss: Kent. Surrey, made to follow on, were beaten with some ease twenty minutes before lunch on the fourth day. Kent had dominated the match from the first day, when Benson, dropped at slip when 27, continued his fine early-season form with 96 from 245 balls. Graham Cowdrey, who added 141 in 63 overs with his captain, batted four hours for his 58, and a half-century from Ellison pushed Kent towards 400 on the second day. By its close Surrey were in some difficulty, paying the price for a rash of irresponsible batting from their early order, and when next day they lost their first three wickets for 48 after following on, there was no conceivable escape route. The effectiveness of the Kent seam bowling was highlighted by the failure of any Surrey batsman to reach 50.

*Close of play:* First day, Kent 249-5 (R. M. Ellison 21*, R. P. Davis 14*); Second day, Surrey 153-7 (N. F. Sargeant 4*, M. P. Bicknell 12*); Third day, Surrey 147-6 (I. A. Greig 24*, N. F. Sargeant 6*).

### Kent

| | | | |
|---|---:|---|---:|
| N. R. Taylor lbw b M. P. Bicknell | 8 | †G. J. Kersey not out | 27 |
| *M. R. Benson b Murphy | 96 | T. A. Merrick c Sargeant b Medlycott | 36 |
| T. R. Ward c Sargeant b Robson | 17 | A. P. Igglesden b Medlycott | 5 |
| G. R. Cowdrey b Murphy | 58 | | |
| C. S. Cowdrey c Medlycott b Murphy | 13 | B 2, l-b 27, w 1, n-b 5 | 35 |
| R. M. Ellison b Medlycott | 50 | | |
| R. P. Davis c Thorpe b M. P. Bicknell | 36 | 1/24 2/50 3/191 4/206 5/211 | 420 |
| C. Penn c Alikhan b Medlycott | 39 | 6/303 7/309 8/352 9/406 | |

Bonus points – Kent 2, Surrey 2 (Score at 100 overs: 231-5).

Bowling: M. P. Bicknell 45–16–95–2; Murphy 46–20–98–3; Robson 24–10–72–1; Medlycott 38.3–13–103–4; Greig 10–3–23–0.

### Surrey

| | | | |
|---|---:|---|---:|
| D. J. Bicknell c Kersey b Merrick | 13 | – c Kersey b Merrick | 0 |
| R. I. Alikhan c Ellison b Penn | 29 | – b Davis | 31 |
| A. J. Stewart b Igglesden | 7 | – b Ellison | 12 |
| D. M. Ward c G. R. Cowdrey b Ellison | 40 | – c G. R. Cowdrey b Igglesden | 23 |
| G. P. Thorpe c Kersey b Penn | 6 | – c G. R. Cowdrey b Penn | 40 |
| *I. A. Greig c Taylor b Igglesden | 25 | – c Benson b Igglesden | 44 |
| K. T. Medlycott c C. S. Cowdrey b Penn | 4 | – lbw b Penn | 1 |
| †N. F. Sargeant not out | 24 | – not out | 23 |
| M. P. Bicknell c Penn b Merrick | 16 | – lbw b Penn | 12 |
| A. G. Robson c Kersey b Igglesden | 0 | – b Merrick | 3 |
| A. J. Murphy c Kersey b Penn | 11 | – c Davis b Penn | 18 |
| B 8, l-b 4, w 2, n-b 6 | 20 | B 4, l-b 5, w 2, n-b 4 | 15 |
| | | | |
| 1/17 2/34 3/83 4/103 5/104 | 195 | 1/0 2/21 3/48 4/107 5/113 | 222 |
| 6/118 7/135 8/165 9/166 | | 6/120 7/167 8/191 9/199 | |

Bonus points – Surrey 1, Kent 4.

Bowling: *First Innings*—Merrick 21–7–51–2; Igglesden 26–5–59–3; Penn 17.1–2–48–4; Ellison 12–8–25–1. *Second Innings*—Merrick 23–7–59–2; Igglesden 21–10–31–2; Davis 18–10–26–1; Penn 22.4–4–50–4; Ellison 15–3–47–1.

Umpires: H. D. Bird and R. Palmer.

At Cambridge, May 18, 20, 21. SURREY beat CAMBRIDGE UNIVERSITY by 38 runs.

## SURREY v LANCASHIRE

At The Oval, May 22, 23, 24. Surrey won by eight wickets. Surrey 24 pts, Lancashire 6 pts. Toss: Lancashire. In May 1990, Lancashire amassed 863 at The Oval in a match remarkable for its clutch of records. This time they came up against the pace of Waqar Younis, who was not on the Surrey staff when Lancashire visited twelve months earlier, and his eleven wickets for 122 in the match earned Surrey a comfortable win, despite two Lancashire hundreds. In Lancashire's first innings, Fowler batted nearly five hours for 113 (two sixes, ten fours) of their 254. Surrey's first innings was a mixture of solid and spectacular batting: Alikhan, Stewart and Medlycott all passed 60 in contrasting styles to provide a lead of 107. And when Waqar Younis produced another outstanding analysis, six for 65, only Watkinson, reaching his third Championship century from 114 balls, offered worthy opposition. His unbeaten 114, coming from 154 deliveries, contained fifteen fours and a six. Surrey, needing 127 in a minimum of 41 overs, won with time to spare thanks to Stewart's unbeaten 67 off 65 balls (one six, eleven fours).

*Close of play:* First day, Surrey 39-1 (R. I. Alikhan 13\*, A. J. Stewart 15\*); Second day, Lancashire 15-2 (G. D. Mendis 8\*, N. J. Speak 2\*).

### Lancashire

| | | | |
|---|---|---|---|
| G. D. Mendis c Alikhan b Waqar Younis | 15 | – b Waqar Younis | 8 |
| G. Fowler b Feltham | 113 | – c Stewart b Waqar Younis | 5 |
| G. D. Lloyd c Sargeant b Feltham | 0 | – (5) b Waqar Younis | 20 |
| N. J. Speak c Boiling b Waqar Younis | 6 | – c Sargeant b Waqar Younis | 6 |
| M. Watkinson b Waqar Younis | 55 | – (6) not out | 114 |
| Wasim Akram c and b Boiling | 19 | – (7) c Alikhan b Feltham | 3 |
| †W. K. Hegg c Sargeant b Medlycott | 3 | – (8) c D. J. Bicknell b Waqar Younis | 27 |
| I. D. Austin b Waqar Younis | 6 | – (3) c Stewart b M. P. Bicknell | 0 |
| *D. P. Hughes not out | 20 | – c Stewart b Waqar Younis | 5 |
| G. Yates b Waqar Younis | 0 | – b Medlycott | 12 |
| P. J. W. Allott c Waqar Younis b Feltham | 0 | – c Alikhan b M. P. Bicknell | 10 |
| B 1, l-b 11, n-b 5 | 17 | B 12, l-b 8, w 1, n-b 2 | 23 |
| | 254 | | 233 |

1/27 2/33 3/44 4/135 5/165 6/212 7/228 8/242 9/243     254

1/6 2/7 3/19 4/22 5/56 6/65 7/150 8/176 9/206     233

Bonus points – Lancashire 3, Surrey 4.

Bowling: *First Innings*—M. P. Bicknell 16–2–45–0; Waqar Younis 19–3–57–5; Feltham 16.3–0–64–3; Greig 7–2–13–0; Medlycott 9–2–19–1; Boiling 13–2–44–1. *Second Innings*—M. P. Bicknell 17.2–8–58–2; Waqar Younis 25–9–65–6; Feltham 13–2–58–1; Medlycott 7–3–17–1; Boiling 6–0–15–0.

### Surrey

| | | | |
|---|---|---|---|
| D. J. Bicknell lbw b Allott | 7 | – c Hegg b Watkinson | 4 |
| R. I. Alikhan c Hughes b Yates | 67 | – c Speak b Yates | 26 |
| A. J. Stewart c Hughes b Watkinson | 62 | – not out | 67 |
| D. M. Ward c Speak b Yates | 43 | – not out | 17 |
| *I. A. Greig c Hegg b Wasim Akram | 21 | | |
| K. T. Medlycott c Mendis b Watkinson | 66 | | |
| M. A. Feltham b Yates | 20 | | |
| N. F. Sargeant b Austin | 10 | | |
| M. P. Bicknell c Lloyd b Hughes | 30 | | |
| J. Boiling lbw b Watkinson | 1 | | |
| Waqar Younis not out | 9 | | |
| B 5, l-b 4, n-b 16 | 25 | B 3, l-b 3, w 1, n-b 6 | 13 |
| | 361 | (2 wkts) | 127 |

1/24 2/122 3/167 4/203 5/220 6/265 7/293 8/325 9/327     361

1/13 2/94     (2 wkts) 127

Bonus points – Surrey 4, Lancashire 3 (Score at 100 overs: 316-7).

Bowling: *First Innings*—Wasim Akram 29–9–84–1; Allott 13–5–35–1; Watkinson 25–4–82–3; Austin 13–2–40–1; Yates 25–6–95–3; Hughes 8–3–16–1. *Second Innings*—Wasim Akram 9–1–37–0; Watkinson 6–0–37–1; Yates 6.3–0–27–1; Austin 4–0–20–0.

Umpires: R. Palmer and A. G. T. Whitehead.

At Bournemouth, May 25, 27, 28. SURREY beat HAMPSHIRE by one wicket.

## SURREY v NOTTINGHAMSHIRE

At The Oval, June 4, 5, 6. Drawn. Surrey 4 pts, Nottinghamshire 4 pts. Toss: Nottinghamshire. A lifeless pitch and stoppages for bad light and rain left both captains with minimal latitude to push for victory. After Surrey were put in, Bicknell and Alikhan gave them a sound start with a stand of 161, Bicknell going on to a chanceless century, while from 12.30 p.m. until the close of play Hemmings's off-spin was a constant feature of the Nottinghamshire attack. Surrey declared immediately on achieving a fourth batting point, eight balls into the second morning, whereupon Broad's unbeaten hundred provided the substance of a largely colourless Nottinghamshire reply which meandered along at less than 3 runs an over. The bland surface diluted Waqar Younis's pace, and he finished wicketless when Nottinghamshire declared 52 behind on the final day. Bicknell added 81 to his first-innings hundred, and Alikhan was denied a century by Greig's declaration, which left Nottinghamshire to make 274 in 38 overs. They had hardly started when bad light sent the players off for the last time.

*Close of play:* First day, Surrey 290-3 (D. M. Ward 48\*, G. P. Thorpe 11\*); Second day, Nottinghamshire 241-2 (B. C. Broad 129\*, P. Johnson 7\*).

### Surrey

| | | | |
|---|---:|---|---:|
| D. J. Bicknell b Stephenson b Hemmings | 125 | – c Scott b Hemmings | 81 |
| R. I. Alikhan c Scott b Evans | 69 | – not out | 96 |
| A. J. Stewart c Scott b Evans | 30 | – not out | 37 |
| D. M. Ward not out | 52 | | |
| G. P. Thorpe not out | 19 | | |
| L-b 5, w 1, n-b 1 | 7 | L-b 7 | 7 |

1/161  2/203  3/233          (3 wkts dec.) 302     1/124          (1 wkt dec.) 221

*I. A. Greig, K. T. Medlycott, M. A. Feltham, †N. F. Sargeant, Waqar Younis and A. J. Murphy did not bat.

Bonus points – Surrey 4, Nottinghamshire 1.

Bowling: *First Innings*—Stephenson 18-4-51-0; Evans 26-5-71-2; Saxelby 9.2-2-49-0; Hemmings 37-8-109-1; Crawley 7-2-17-0. *Second Innings*—Stephenson 6-2-8-0; Evans 13-2-34-0; Saxelby 16-1-96-0; Crawley 21-6-47-0; Hemmings 21-9-29-1.

### Nottinghamshire

| | | | |
|---|---:|---|---:|
| B. C. Broad not out | 137 | | |
| P. R. Pollard b Feltham | 62 | – c Sargeant b Waqar Younis | 1 |
| M. A. Crawley lbw b Medlycott | 22 | – (1) not out | 20 |
| P. Johnson not out | 8 | | |
| *R. T. Robinson (did not bat) | | – (3) not out | 6 |
| B 4, l-b 1, w 6, n-b 10 | 21 | N-b 6 | 6 |

1/154  2/227          (2 wkts dec.) 250     1/15          (1 wkt) 33

D. W. Randall, K. P. Evans, F. D. Stephenson, †C. W. Scott, M. Saxelby and E. E. Hemmings did not bat.

Bonus points – Nottinghamshire 3.

Bowling: *First Innings*—Waqar Younis 17-4-54-0; Murphy 19.3-5-56-0; Feltham 15-1-42-1; Medlycott 34-6-84-1; Greig 3-1-9-0. *Second Innings*—Waqar Younis 3.3-0-12-1; Murphy 3-0-21-0.

Umpires: G. I. Burgess and J. H. Harris.

At Leicester, June 14, 15, 17. SURREY drew with LEICESTERSHIRE.

At Derby, June 21, 22, 24. SURREY lost to DERBYSHIRE by three wickets.

## SURREY v SOMERSET

At The Oval, June 28, 29, July 1. Drawn. Surrey 3 pts, Somerset 4 pts. Toss: Surrey. Surrey, pursuing a target of 357 in a minimum of 57 overs, were obliged to opt for survival in a rain-ruined match of two forfeitures. The first day was lost to the weather and the last did not start until 2.15 p.m. When they had Somerset 152 for five, Surrey held the upper hand, but Lefebvre's career-best 93 from 117 balls (two sixes, seven fours) turned a potentially moderate total into a good one. Although Surrey's initial response to Somerset's declaration was to seek batting points, Greig subsequently forfeited their first innings, and Somerset reciprocated. When five Surrey wickets went for 37, the visitors must have entertained thoughts of victory, but Ward and Medlycott added 98 in 27 overs, and when Ward was caught at long-on, Sargeant grittily saw Surrey to safety.

*Close of play:* First day, No play; Second day, Somerset 356-8 (N. A. Mallender 12*, D. A. Graveney 0*).

## Somerset

| | | | | |
|---|---|---|---|---|
| S. J. Cook b Murphy | 41 | K. H. MacLeay c Ward b Medlycott | 57 |
| P. M. Roebuck c Thorpe | | R. P. Lefebvre c Murphy b Medlycott | 93 |
| b Waqar Younis | 47 | N. A. Mallender not out | 12 |
| A. N. Hayhurst c Thorpe | | D. A. Graveney not out | 0 |
| b M. P. Bicknell | 9 | | |
| *C. J. Tavaré c M. P. Bicknell | | B 2, l-b 11, w 1, n-b 13 | 27 |
| b Murphy | 18 | | |
| R. J. Harden b M. P. Bicknell | 13 | 1/60 2/79 3/121 (8 wkts dec.) 356 |
| †N. D. Burns c Sargeant | | 4/123 5/152 6/210 |
| b M. P. Bicknell | 39 | 7/291 8/356 |

A. P. van Troost did not bat.

Bonus points – Somerset 4, Surrey 3 (Score at 100 overs: 313-7).

Bowling: Waqar Younis 21-1-86-1; M. P. Bicknell 28-2-56-3; Murphy 27-4-82-2; Greig 9-3-20-0; Medlycott 25-2-97-2.

*Somerset forfeited their second innings.*

## Surrey

*Surrey forfeited their first innings.*

| | | | | |
|---|---|---|---|---|
| D. J. Bicknell b van Troost | 15 | †N. F. Sargeant not out | 16 |
| R. I. Alikhan c Burns b Mallender | 6 | M. P. Bicknell not out | 1 |
| A. J. Stewart c Harden b Mallender | 3 | | |
| D. M. Ward c sub b Graveney | 71 | B 1, l-b 2, w 1, n-b 2 | 6 |
| G. P. Thorpe c Graveney b MacLeay | 2 | | |
| *I. A. Greig c Roebuck b MacLeay | 0 | 1/21 2/25 3/27 4/37 (7 wkts) 172 |
| K. T. Medlycott c Lefebvre b Graveney | 52 | 5/37 6/135 7/161 |

Waqar Younis and A. J. Murphy did not bat.

Bowling: Mallender 11-2-44-2; van Troost 12.4-0-55-1; Graveney 17-4-30-2; MacLeay 11-2-25-2; Lefebvre 2-0-8-0; Roebuck 3-1-7-0.

Umpires: H. D. Bird and B. Leadbeater.

At Arundel, July 2, 3, 4. SURREY drew with SUSSEX.

## SURREY v ESSEX

At The Oval, July 5, 6, 8. Surrey won by five wickets. Surrey 21 pts, Essex 7 pts. Toss: Essex. Stewart won the match for Surrey in the grandest manner with two sixes off Childs in the final over. That brace of blows brought victory with a ball to spare and lifted Stewart to 83 not out, his highest first-class score of the season to date. But defeat must have been especially deflating for Salim Malik and Hussain who, on the first day, had put on 314, a record for the Essex fourth wicket, after Martin Bicknell had taken three for 4 in seventeen balls. Malik, dropped by Greig at slip when 26, hit 23 fours in his 185 not out from 295 balls, and Hussain seventeen in 128 from 243. Acting-captain Foster capped an outstanding day for Essex by dismissing Darren Bicknell before the close. Next day Ward fell 2 runs short of a hundred and Surrey, prised out by Childs's left-arm spin, ably supported by Such's off-breaks, finished a single short of 300. Malik's exciting strokeplay brought him an unbeaten 59 before Foster set Surrey a generous target of 225 in 59 overs. Despite half-centuries from Darren Bicknell and Ward, they were off the required rate until Stewart's daring swung the game their way.

*Close of play:* First day, Surrey 13-1 (R. I. Alikhan 5*, N. F. Sargeant 8*); Second day, Essex 22-1 (J. P. Stephenson 8*, T. D. Topley 7*).

## Essex

| | | | |
|---|---|---|---|
| J. P. Stephenson c Sargeant b M. P. Bicknell | 0 | – (2) c Ward b Murphy | 18 |
| A. C. H. Seymour c Sargeant b M. P. Bicknell | 5 | – (9) not out | 10 |
| P. J. Prichard b M. P. Bicknell | 3 | – (4) c Thorpe b M. P. Bicknell | 14 |
| Salim Malik not out | 185 | – (5) not out | 59 |
| N. Hussain b Murphy | 128 | – (6) c Sargeant b Murphy | 36 |
| N. Shahid lbw b Murphy | 0 | – (8) run out | 12 |
| †M. A. Garnham not out | 2 | – (1) b Murphy | 6 |
| *N. A. Foster (did not bat) | | – (7) b Murphy | 0 |
| T. D. Topley (did not bat) | | – (3) b Murphy | 17 |
| B 7, l-b 7, n-b 1 | 15 | L-b 9, w 4 | 13 |

1/0 2/8 3/9 4/323 5/323       (5 wkts dec.) 338    1/11 2/34 3/50       (7 wkts dec.) 185
                                                   4/87 5/145
                                                   6/145 7/160

P. M. Such and J. H. Childs did not bat.

Bonus points – Essex 4, Surrey 2.

Bowling: *First Innings*—M. P. Bicknell 17-3-53-3; Murphy 18-5-52-2; Feltham 18-3-69-0; Medlycott 30-5-89-0; Greig 11-1-43-0; Thorpe 5-0-18-0. *Second Innings*—M. P. Bicknell 16-2-53-1; Murphy 19-2-63-5; Medlycott 10-3-40-0; Thorpe 3-0-20-0.

## Surrey

| | | | |
|---|---|---|---|
| D. J. Bicknell c Garnham b Foster | 0 | – lbw b Such | 54 |
| R. I. Alikhan b Topley | 20 | – c Prichard b Childs | 8 |
| †N. F. Sargeant lbw b Foster | 14 | | |
| A. J. Stewart c Seymour b Childs | 33 | – (3) not out | 83 |
| D. M. Ward c Prichard b Childs | 98 | – (4) lbw b Such | 54 |
| G. P. Thorpe b Such | 28 | – (5) b Childs | 2 |
| *I. A. Greig lbw b Childs | 20 | – (6) c Salim Malik b Childs | 9 |
| K. T. Medlycott c Prichard b Such | 20 | – (7) not out | 0 |
| M. A. Feltham b Childs | 28 | | |
| M. P. Bicknell c Hussain b Childs | 23 | | |
| A. J. Murphy not out | 1 | | |
| B 3, l-b 11 | 14 | B 8, l-b 12 | 20 |

1/4 2/28 3/44 4/83 5/174       299    1/30 2/89 3/185       (5 wkts) 230
6/202 7/241 8/249 9/298              4/188 5/218

Bonus points – Surrey 3, Essex 3 (Score at 100 overs: 279-8).

Bowling: *First Innings*—Foster 18-6-52-2; Topley 12-2-34-1; Childs 43.1-12-112-5; Such 34-8-87-2. *Second Innings*—Foster 4-0-17-0; Childs 25.5-7-85-3; Such 24-5-91-2; Salim Malik 1-0-3-0; Topley 4-0-14-0.

Umpires: R. Julian and B. J. Meyer.

## SURREY v GLOUCESTERSHIRE

At Guildford, July 16, 17, 18. Surrey won by two wickets. Surrey 22 pts, Gloucestershire 4 pts. Toss: Gloucestershire. Waqar Younis imposed his authority on the match at the start, claiming seven for 87 in Gloucestershire's first innings, and was involved at the end, helping Surrey to victory when they needed 7 runs off the final ten balls. Gloucestershire failed to build on a painstaking opening stand of 105 between Hodgson (132 balls) and Scott, both of whom fell to Waqar Younis in the space of five balls just after lunch. Indeed, it took the resolve of the tailenders to get the captain, Wright, 58 not out at the end of a rain-interrupted day, to his second century of the summer. He hit twelve fours and a six. Surrey were buoyed by a stand of 174, their best of the season to date, between the fortunate Bicknell, dropped three times at slip, and Stewart, who reached his first hundred since May the previous year. Stewart's 109 contained thirteen fours, while Bicknell hit fourteen in his 95. Surrey declared 54 runs behind, and on the final day Gloucestershire were encouraged to get the equation right for a declaration. Thirteen overs from Ward and Sargeant, the wicket-keeper, produced 154 runs. This farce left Surrey to make 252 in a minimum of 49 overs, and Ward's 80 from 113 balls was chiefly responsible for their reaching the target with two balls to spare.

*Close of play:* First day, Gloucestershire 225-7 (A. J. Wright 58*, D. R. Gilbert 9*); Second day, Gloucestershire 33-0 (G. D. Hodgson 21*, R. J. Scott 12*).

## Gloucestershire

| | | | |
|---|---|---|---|
| G. D. Hodgson b Waqar Younis | 34 | – c Alikhan b Ward | 21 |
| R. J. Scott b Waqar Younis | 63 | – c Medlycott b Ward | 47 |
| *A. J. Wright not out | 101 | – c Ward b Sargeant | 29 |
| C. W. J. Athey b Medlycott | 19 | – not out | 62 |
| M. W. Alleyne b Murphy | 1 | – not out | 37 |
| †R. C. Russell b Waqar Younis | 0 | | |
| J. W. Lloyds lbw b Waqar Younis | 10 | | |
| D. V. Lawrence b Waqar Younis | 19 | | |
| D. R. Gilbert b Waqar Younis | 15 | | |
| M. C. J. Ball b Waqar Younis | 28 | | |
| B 9, l-b 4, n-b 1 | 14 | L-b 1 | 1 |

1/105 2/108 3/117 4/118 5/130 (9 wkts dec.) 304    1/34 2/91 3/126 (3 wkts dec.) 197
6/160 7/190 8/246 9/304

A. M. Smith did not bat.

Bonus points – Gloucestershire 3, Surrey 3 (Score at 100 overs: 251-8).

*In the first innings C. W. J. Athey, when 2, retired hurt at 115 and resumed at 130.*

Bowling: *First Innings*—Waqar Younis 31.5-6-87-7; Murphy 35-4-108-1; Robinson 7-1-19-0; Greig 16.5-5-25-0; Thorpe 2-0-5-0; Medlycott 16-4-47-1. *Second Innings*—Waqar Younis 4-0-15-0; Murphy 6-3-14-0; Medlycott 2-0-4-0; Ward 7.5-0-66-2; Sargeant 5-0-88-1; Stewart 2-0-9-0.

## Surrey

| | | | |
|---|---|---|---|
| D. J. Bicknell c Russell b Lloyds | 95 | – c Russell b Lawrence | 10 |
| R. I. Alikhan lbw b Lawrence | 4 | – c Russell b Smith | 70 |
| A. J. Stewart b Lloyds | 109 | – run out | 1 |
| D. M. Ward not out | 40 | – c Russell b Smith | 80 |
| G. P. Thorpe not out | 0 | – c Russell b Smith | 33 |
| J. D. Robinson (did not bat) | | – b Lawrence | 20 |
| *I. A. Greig (did not bat) | | – not out | 23 |
| K. T. Medlycott (did not bat) | | – c Athey b Lawrence | 0 |
| †N. F. Sargeant (did not bat) | | – c Russell b Smith | 1 |
| Waqar Younis (did not bat) | | – not out | 2 |
| L-b 1, n-b 1 | 2 | B 3, l-b 6, n-b 3 | 12 |

1/8 2/182 3/245 (3 wkts dec.) 250    1/22 2/25 3/168 4/175 (8 wkts) 252
5/223 6/235 7/242 8/245

A. J. Murphy did not bat.

Bonus points – Surrey 3, Gloucestershire 1.

Bowling: *First Innings*—Lawrence 10-1-42-1; Gilbert 16-4-64-0; Ball 4-1-16-0; Lloyds 27.2-8-67-2; Smith 7-0-30-0; Scott 7-1-22-0; Athey 3-0-8-0. *Second Innings*—Lawrence 12.4-1-51-3; Gilbert 11-1-60-0; Lloyds 11-1-58-0; Smith 15-0-70-4; Scott 1-0-4-0.

Umpires: D. O. Oslear and R. A. White.

## SURREY v YORKSHIRE

At Guildford, July 19, 20, 22. Surrey won by one wicket. Surrey 22 pts. Yorkshire 2 pts. Toss: Surrey. Waqar Younis transformed the game with a typically devastating spell of fast bowling and, less predictably, struck 31 in nineteen balls to ensure Surrey's second victory of the Guildford week with two balls to spare. Waqar was not so effective on a slow pitch on the first day as Yorkshire were sustained by Moxon's four-hour stay, and by 74 from Robinson which included three sixes and eight fours. An opening stand of 150 between Bicknell, with thirteen fours in his 80, and Alikhan, followed by a bristling half-century in 53 balls from acting-captain Stewart, kept the game open, and when Surrey captured three Yorkshire wickets before the close, an absorbing final day was in prospect. Moxon batted with authority until lunch, but lost his middle stump as Waqar Younis embarked on a spell of 4.3–1–8–5 in the afternoon. Surrey, with 58 overs in which to score 193, found Yorkshire a tougher proposition than they might have expected, and when 54 were required off the last six overs, with two Surrey wickets remaining, the visitors seemed the more likely winners. However, Waqar and Medlycott added 52, with the Pakistan fast bowler striking a six in the final over to go with his four fours, and Murphy swept his first delivery for 2 runs to win the match.

*Close of play:* First day, Yorkshire 256-8 (P. J. Hartley 14*, J. D. Batty 0*); Second day, Yorkshire 42-3 (M. D. Moxon 18*, J. D. Batty 0*).

## Yorkshire

| | | | |
|---|--:|---|--:|
| *M. D. Moxon c Alikhan b Medlycott | 73 | – b Waqar Younis | 68 |
| A. A. Metcalfe c Medlycott b Feltham | 6 | – b Murphy | 2 |
| D. Byas c Bicknell b Feltham | 33 | – lbw b Waqar Younis | 0 |
| †R. J. Blakey b Waqar Younis | 11 | – c Alikhan b Medlycott | 17 |
| P. E. Robinson b Feltham | 74 | – c and b Medlycott | 17 |
| S. A. Kellett b Waqar Younis | 6 | – (7) lbw b Waqar Younis | 13 |
| C. S. Pickles b Murphy | 1 | – (8) c Bicknell b Waqar Younis | 2 |
| P. Carrick c Bicknell b Medlycott | 18 | – (9) b Waqar Younis | 7 |
| P. J. Hartley not out | 35 | – (10) b Waqar Younis | 0 |
| J. D. Batty b Murphy | 4 | – (6) c Feltham b Murphy | 12 |
| S. D. Fletcher c Alikhan b Feltham | 6 | – not out | 9 |
| B 1, l-b 9, n-b 12 | 22 | B 2, l-b 2, n-b 2 | 6 |

1/17 2/106 3/135 4/135 5/164      289     1/6 2/9 3/38 4/57 5/106      153
6/170 7/208 8/255 9/268                  6/133 7/135 8/136 9/136

Bonus points – Yorkshire 2, Surrey 3 (Score at 100 overs: 217-7).

*In the second innings R. J. Blakey, when 3, retired hurt at 15 and resumed at 57.*

Bowling: *First Innings*—Waqar Younis 28–8–54–2; Murphy 28–6–66–2; Feltham 34.2–10–64–4; Thorpe 8–4–8–0; Medlycott 24–5–87–2. *Second Innings*—Waqar Younis 22.3–3–40–6; Murphy 11–1–30–2; Medlycott 17–2–59–2; Feltham 6–1–20–0.

## Surrey

| | | | |
|---|--:|---|--:|
| D. J. Bicknell c Robinson b Carrick | 80 | – c Robinson b Hartley | 11 |
| R. I. Alikhan c Pickles b Batty | 86 | – c Byas b Carrick | 21 |
| *A. J. Stewart not out | 53 | – c and b Batty | 36 |
| D. M. Ward not out | 18 | – c Blakey b Fletcher | 3 |
| G. P. Thorpe (did not bat) | | – c Carrick b Batty | 22 |
| M. A. Lynch (did not bat) | | – c Moxon b Carrick | 13 |
| K. T. Medlycott (did not bat) | | – not out | 30 |
| M. A. Feltham (did not bat) | | – run out | 6 |
| †N. F. Sargeant (did not bat) | | – c Kellett b Batty | 3 |
| Waqar Younis (did not bat) | | – c Batty b Carrick | 31 |
| A. J. Murphy (did not bat) | | – not out | 2 |
| L-b 4, w 2, n-b 7 | 13 | B 6, l-b 6, w 1, n-b 2 | 15 |

1/150 2/228      (2 wkts dec.) 250     1/35 2/49 3/68      (9 wkts) 193
                                      4/94 5/115 6/123
                                      7/130 8/139 9/191

Bonus points – Surrey 3.

Bowling: *First Innings*—Hartley 13–4–56–0; Fletcher 10–0–44–0; Pickles 10–1–35–0; Carrick 25–5–44–1; Batty 16.4–0–67–1. *Second Innings*—Hartley 9–1–33–1; Fletcher 9–3–31–1; Carrick 22.4–5–56–3; Batty 15–2–48–3; Pickles 2–0–13–0.

Umpires: D. O. Oslear and R. A. White.

## SURREY v GLAMORGAN

At The Oval, July 26, 27, 29. Drawn. Surrey 6 pts, Glamorgan 7 pts. Toss: Glamorgan. Surrey missed a good chance to gain ground in the Championship when they failed by 32 runs to beat Glamorgan, for whom Maynard struck the fastest century of the season to date, in 75 balls and 93 minutes with five sixes and nine fours. Maynard's aggressive instincts were apparent in the first innings, when a punishing 75 flowed from his bat. For the third match in succession, Surrey declared in arrears as soon as they had their third batting point. Thorpe's unbeaten 74, containing ten boundaries, underpinned the effort. With Waqar Younis an absentee from the Surrey attack in Glamorgan's second innings, Butcher and Maynard capitalised, with Maynard fairly racing to his third Championship hundred in five innings before Surrey were set a target of 320 in 69 overs. Although Ward and Thorpe added 135 for the fourth wicket in 30 overs, Surrey found scoring 74 from the last ten overs beyond them. For a moment it looked as if Barwick, bowling off-cutters, and Shastri might win the match for Glamorgan, but Thorpe, with his first Championship hundred since 1989, precluded this possibility. During the match, Greig announced that he was to relinquish the Surrey captaincy at the end of the season, after five years in charge.

*Close of play:* First day, Surrey 2-1 (R. I. Alikhan 2*, N. F. Sargeant 0*); Second day, Glamorgan 78-0 (A. R. Butcher 59*, S. P. James 18*).

### Glamorgan

| | | | |
|---|---|---|---|
| *A. R. Butcher c Sargeant b Murphy | 15 | – st Sargeant b Medlycott | 68 |
| S. P. James run out | 70 | – lbw b Feltham | 24 |
| A. Dale b Waqar Younis | 89 | – c Sargeant b Greig | 20 |
| M. P. Maynard c sub b Feltham | 75 | – not out | 103 |
| R. J. Shastri b Waqar Younis | 38 | | |
| P. A. Cottey lbw b Waqar Younis | 1 | – (5) st Sargeant b Medlycott | 17 |
| R. D. B. Croft c Stewart b Medlycott | 10 | – (6) not out | 11 |
| †C. P. Metson lbw b Medlycott | 5 | | |
| S. L. Watkin b Waqar Younis | 3 | | |
| S. Bastien not out | 0 | | |
| B 8, l-b 4, w 1, n-b 2 | 15 | L-b 2, n-b 3 | 5 |

1/23 2/177 3/212 4/275 5/292     (9 wkts dec.) 321     1/87 2/97     (4 wkts dec.) 248
6/303 7/308 8/321 9/321     3/146 4/207

S. R. Barwick did not bat.

Bonus points – Glamorgan 4, Surrey 3 (Score at 100 overs: 321-8).

Bowling: *First Innings*—Waqar Younis 26–6–75–4; Murphy 10–2–33–1; Feltham 25–5–58–1; Greig 13–2–38–0; Medlycott 26.1–2–105–2. *Second Innings*—Feltham 20–2–77–1; Greig 9–0–49–1; Medlycott 24–7–100–2; Thorpe 1–0–10–0; Stewart 2–0–10–0.

### Surrey

| | | | |
|---|---|---|---|
| D. J. Bicknell c Cottey b Watkin | 0 | – c Cottey b Dale | 18 |
| R. I. Alikhan c Croft b Barwick | 40 | – b Shastri | 25 |
| †N. F. Sargeant lbw b Dale | 32 | – (10) not out | 3 |
| A. J. Stewart c Cottey b Barwick | 34 | – (3) run out | 29 |
| D. M. Ward b Barwick | 5 | – (4) lbw b Barwick | 71 |
| G. P. Thorpe not out | 74 | – (5) not out | 106 |
| *I. A. Greig c Metson b Barwick | 0 | – (6) lbw b Barwick | 0 |
| K. T. Medlycott b Bastien | 5 | – (7) b Shastri | 28 |
| M. A. Feltham not out | 38 | – (8) c Shastri b Barwick | 3 |
| Waqar Younis (did not bat) | | – (9) c James b Shastri | 0 |
| B 4, l-b 10, n-b 4 | 18 | B 2, l-b 3 | 5 |

1/0 2/63 3/106 4/114 5/121     (7 wkts dec.) 250     1/29 2/70 3/76 4/211     (8 wkts) 288
6/145 7/158     5/217 6/270 7/279 8/279

A. J. Murphy did not bat.

Bonus points – Surrey 3, Glamorgan 3.

Bowling: *First Innings*—Watkin 10–4–14–1; Bastien 23.2–6–74–1; Barwick 23–8–46–4; Dale 19–6–63–1; Croft 20–6–39–0. *Second Innings*—Barwick 17.5–1–75–3; Dale 5–0–19–1; Shastri 23–2–78–3; Croft 23–2–111–0.

Umpires: J. H. Hampshire and M. J. Kitchen.

At Canterbury, August 2, 3, 5. SURREY drew with KENT.

At Birmingham, August 6, 7, 8. SURREY beat WARWICKSHIRE by 67 runs.

At Worcester, August 16, 17, 19. SURREY lost to WORCESTERSHIRE by three wickets.

## SURREY v MIDDLESEX

At The Oval, August 20, 21, 22. Drawn. Surrey 7 pts, Middlesex 5 pts. Toss: Surrey. Lynch's first century in more than a year held the Surrey innings together on a pitch receptive enough to spin for Emburey and Barnett to be bowling together within the first hour. Unbeaten at the close, after four and threequarter hours, Lynch hit a six and fifteen fours in his 141, and with Medlycott had added 154 for the sixth wicket. Waqar Younis, nursed through four spells because of a viral infection, repeatedly checked Middlesex on the second day and finished with five wickets for the tenth time in the season. Gatting went to 50 off 66 balls, hitting seven boundaries, but it was Weekes, in only his fourth first-class innings, who saw the visitors to within 3 runs of maximum batting points in a stay of four hours. Gatting offered Surrey no favours on the final day, and in the end Middlesex were left with 50 overs in which to score 253. Roseberry gave them a good start with 51 from 63 balls, including three sixes, against a Surrey attack that was initially missing Waqar Younis. By the time bad light and then rain brought the match to an early end, a draw was looking the likeliest result.

*Close of play*: First day, Surrey 341-9 (M. A. Lynch 141\*, A. J. Murphy 2\*); Second day, Surrey 25-0 (D. J. Bicknell 13\*, N. F. Sargeant 7\*).

## Surrey

| | | | |
|---|---|---|---|
| D. J. Bicknell b Barnett | 33 | – b Cowans | 22 |
| †N. F. Sargeant c Weekes b Barnett | 37 | – b Headley | 19 |
| G. P. Thorpe c Emburey b Barnett | 0 | – c Roseberry b Emburey | 40 |
| D. M. Ward c Brown b Emburey | 9 | – c Roseberry b Emburey | 43 |
| M. A. Lynch not out | 141 | – lbw b Emburey | 0 |
| \*I. A. Greig c and b Weekes | 9 | – c Gatting b Headley | 4 |
| K. T. Medlycott c Pooley b Headley | 59 | – b Weekes | 40 |
| M. P. Bicknell c Roseberry b Headley | 24 | – c Keech b Headley | 1 |
| Waqar Younis c Keech b Cowans | 4 | – b Headley | 0 |
| J. Boiling b Headley | 0 | – c Roseberry b Weekes | 16 |
| A. J. Murphy not out | 2 | – not out | 7 |
| B 8, l-b 6, w 4, n-b 5 | 23 | B 4, l-b 7, n-b 5 | 16 |

1/72 2/72 3/85 4/95 5/129　　(9 wkts dec.) 341　　1/41 2/59 3/125 4/130 5/135　208
6/283 7/319 8/325 9/334　　　　　　　　　　　　6/148 7/159 8/159 9/191

Bonus points – Surrey 3, Middlesex 2 (Score at 100 overs: 267-5).

Bowling: *First Innings*—Headley 18–2–65–3; Cowans 19–3–65–1; Emburey 31–4–79–1; Barnett 36–7–88–3; Weekes 10–4–30–1. *Second Innings*—Headley 21–3–69–4; Cowans 12–1–27–1; Emburey 21–0–78–3; Barnett 2–1–5–0; Weekes 5.4–1–18–2.

## Middlesex

| | | | |
|---|---|---|---|
| M. A. Roseberry lbw b Waqar Younis | 2 | – c and b Medlycott | 51 |
| J. C. Pooley b Boiling | 20 | – lbw b Murphy | 1 |
| *M. W. Gatting c Boiling b Medlycott | 50 | – not out | 40 |
| K. R. Brown c Sargeant b Waqar Younis | 30 | – not out | 8 |
| M. Keech c Sargeant b M. P. Bicknell | 18 | | |
| P. N. Weekes st Sargeant b Boiling | 86 | | |
| J. E. Emburey c Waqar Younis b Medlycott | 59 | | |
| †P. Farbrace b Waqar Younis | 3 | | |
| D. W. Headley c Sargeant b Waqar Younis | 4 | | |
| N. G. Cowans b Waqar Younis | 0 | | |
| A. A. Barnett not out | 11 | | |
| B 4, l-b 7, w 1, n-b 2 | 14 | B 1 | 1 |

1/6 2/38 3/96 4/123 5/131         297     1/10 2/85       (2 wkts) 101
6/262 7/266 8/276 9/284

Bonus points – Middlesex 3, Surrey 4.

Bowling: *First Innings*—Waqar Younis 24-6-61-5; M. P. Bicknell 20-4-56-1; Murphy 9-3-21-0; Boiling 23.5-6-58-2; Medlycott 20-3-90-2. *Second Innings*—M. P. Bicknell 6-0-25-0; Murphy 4-2-2-1; Medlycott 9-3-24-1; Boiling 11-3-41-0; Waqar Younis 3.3-1-8-0.

Umpires: G. I. Burgess and A. A. Jones.

At Northampton, August 23, 24, 26. SURREY lost to NORTHAMPTONSHIRE by 138 runs.

## SURREY v SUSSEX

At The Oval, August 28, 29, 30. Surrey won by an innings and 128 runs. Surrey 24 pts, Sussex 3 pts. Toss: Sussex. Martin Bicknell's Championship-best return swept his side to victory soon after lunch on the third day of this four-day match. He had taken the three wickets to fall the previous evening, and on Friday morning he took another four in two hours of sustained hostility. Donelan batted with a night-watchman's resolve for more than an hour at the start, and Dodemaide and Pigott held Surrey up for 80 minutes while they added 57 runs at the end. Otherwise Sussex were even less convincing than in their first innings, prised open by Feltham and finished off with three wickets in eight balls by Waqar Younis. Only Moores (82 balls) and Dodemaide offered significant resistance in between, with 78 in 99 minutes for the sixth wicket. Surrey's batting was dominated by Thorpe's career-best 177, from 262 balls, an innings marked by the cover drives and square cuts which brought virtually all of his 28 fours. His second hundred in successive innings, it was an impressive performance on a pitch of occasionally uncertain bounce and sufficiently tinged with green to persuade Sussex to bowl first on it. Not even two stoppages on the opening day – the first of almost an hour when an underground pipe sprang a leak and flooded part of the ground, the second for poor light when Thorpe was 10 runs from his century – could disturb the young left-hander's progress.

*Close of play:* First day, Surrey 311-3 (G. P. Thorpe 153*, A. J. Stewart 42*); Second day, Sussex 26-3 (B. T. P. Donelan 11*, A. N. Jones 0*).

## Surrey

| | | |
|---|---|---|
| D. J. Bicknell b North | 36 | M. A. Feltham c Lenham b Dodemaide 37 |
| R. I. Alikhan c Moores b Pigott | 11 | M. P. Bicknell b North | 26 |
| G. P. Thorpe b Dodemaide | 177 | Waqar Younis not out | 3 |
| D. M. Ward lbw b Donelan | 44 | | |
| †A. J. Stewart c Smith b Donelan | 47 | B 9, l-b 9, w 3, n-b 14 | 35 |
| M. A. Lynch b Donelan | 0 | | |
| *I. A. Greig c Moores b Dodemaide | 25 | 1/54 2/54 3/200 4/340 5/340 | 445 |
| K. T. Medlycott c Wells b Pigott | 4 | 6/353 7/374 8/374 9/440 | |

Bonus points – Surrey 4, Sussex 2 (Score at 100 overs: 357-6).

Bowling: Jones 21-1-83-0; Dodemaide 32.3-6-104-3; North 23-4-107-2; Pigott 21-4-69-2; Donelan 30-9-64-3.

## Sussex

| | | | |
|---|---|---|---|
| N. J. Lenham retired hurt | 2 | – absent injured | |
| D. M. Smith c D. J. Bicknell b M. P. Bicknell | 10 | – c Lynch b M. P. Bicknell | 0 |
| K. Greenfield c Thorpe b Feltham | 21 | – c D. J. Bicknell b M. P. Bicknell | 8 |
| *A. P. Wells c sub b Feltham | 28 | – (6) c Stewart b M. P. Bicknell | 3 |
| R. Hanley c Lynch b Feltham | 19 | – (7) c Stewart b M. P. Bicknell | 0 |
| J. A. North b Waqar Younis | 0 | – (8) lbw b M. P. Bicknell | 48 |
| A. I. C. Dodemaide c Waqar Younis | | | |
|     b M. P. Bicknell | 23 | – (9) run out | 48 |
| †P. Moores lbw b Waqar Younis | 54 | – (1) c Ward b M. P. Bicknell | 7 |
| A. C. S. Pigott c Stewart b Waqar Younis | 0 | – (10) not out | 18 |
| B. T. P. Donelan c Stewart b Waqar Younis | 4 | – (4) b Feltham | 36 |
| A. N. Jones not out | 4 | – (5) b M. P. Bicknell | 19 |
| B 6, n-b 4 | 10 | B 2, l-b 1 | 3 |

1/23 2/39 3/72 4/73 5/89         175      1/7 2/15 3/26 4/58 5/72     142
6/167 7/167 8/171 9/175                 6/74 7/74 8/85 9/142

Bonus points – Sussex 1, Surrey 4.

*In the first innings N. J. Lenham retired hurt at 11.*

Bowling: *First Innings*—Waqar Younis 17–2–54–4; M. P. Bicknell 14.1–5–35–2; Feltham 16–2–63–3; Thorpe 2–0–11–0; Medlycott 5–1–8–0. *Second Innings*—Waqar Younis 15–2–51–0; M. P. Bicknell 23–5–52–7; Feltham 11–1–36–1; Medlycott 1–1–0–0.

Umpires: N. T. Plews and R. C. Tolchard.

## SURREY v HAMPSHIRE

At The Oval, September 3, 4, 5. Surrey won by 171 runs. Surrey 23 pts, Hampshire 4 pts. Toss: Hampshire. Surrey's second successive victory with more than a day to spare was overshadowed by the injury to the Hampshire captain, Nicholas, which kept him from playing in the NatWest Bank Trophy final between these two sides on the coming Saturday. Fending off a delivery from Waqar Younis, which he picked up late, Nicholas broke the little finger on his left hand and displaced the knuckle. Waqar Younis was in devastating form, capturing six wickets in both Hampshire innings; and when Gower was caught behind in the second, he became the first bowler since 1988 to take 100 wickets in a season. The pitch was not an easy one for batsmen, and Surrey owed a great deal to Bicknell's fifth Championship hundred of the summer, and to Lynch's 51 from 74 balls as these two put on 98 in twenty overs for the fifth wicket. Bicknell's first fifty took 98 balls, his second 57, and when he was ninth out, having hit a six and seventeen fours in his 136, he had batted for five and a quarter hours (242 balls). Ayling bowled well for Hampshire, and saved them from following on with top score in their first innings, but nothing could stand between Waqar Younis and the win which kept Surrey in fourth place in the Championship.

*Close of play:* First day, Hampshire 86-7 (J. R. Ayling 10*, R. J. Maru 0*); Second day, Hampshire 84-5 (K. D. James 26*, M. C. J. Nicholas 13*).

## Surrey

| | | | |
|---|---|---|---|
| D. J. Bicknell b Aqib Javed | 136 | – c Terry b Aqib Javed | 54 |
| R. I. Alikhan lbw b James | 11 | – lbw b James | 11 |
| G. P. Thorpe c Smith b Ayling | 0 | – c Terry b Aqib Javed | 8 |
| D. M. Ward c Aymes b Ayling | 0 | – c Terry b Ayling | 1 |
| †A. J. Stewart c Smith b Maru | 8 | – lbw b Aqib Javed | 3 |
| M. A. Lynch c Terry b Shine | 51 | – b Shine | 0 |
| *I. A. Greig c Middleton b Ayling | 5 | – c Maru b Shine | 25 |
| K. T. Medlycott c Maru b Ayling | 0 | – c James b Shine | 24 |
| M. A. Feltham c Smith b Maru | 20 | – c Aymes b Ayling | 27 |
| Waqar Younis not out | 1 | – not out | 0 |
| A. J. Murphy b Maru | 0 | – c Maru b Ayling | |
| B 9, l-b 2, w 2, n-b 13 | 26 | B 10, l-b 3, w 1, n-b 9 | 23 |

1/30 2/48 3/49 4/79 5/177     258     1/51 2/77 3/92 4/92 5/92     187
6/198 7/198 8/257 9/257             6/107 7/113 8/147 9/187

Bonus points – Surrey 3, Hampshire 4.

Bowling: *First Innings*—Shine 14–2–65–1; Aqib Javed 22–5–51–1; James 11–2–37–1; Ayling 13–2–47–4; Maru 20–7–47–3. *Second Innings*—Aqib Javed 23–6–50–3; Shine 10–1–52–3; Ayling 17.4–5–43–3; James 8–3–22–1; Maru 3–1–7–0.

## Hampshire

| | | |
|---|---|---|
| V. P. Terry c Bicknell b Waqar Younis | 30 – | c Lynch b Waqar Younis . . . . . . 2 |
| T. C. Middleton c Lynch b Waqar Younis | 6 – | b Murphy . . . . . . . . . . . . . . . . . . 3 |
| K. D. James lbw b Waqar Younis | 1 – | not out . . . . . . . . . . . . . . . . . . 42 |
| R. A. Smith b Feltham | 12 – | c Stewart b Greig . . . . . . . . . . 21 |
| D. I. Gower lbw b Waqar Younis | 7 – | c Stewart b Waqar Younis . . . . 3 |
| *M. C. J. Nicholas c Lynch b Feltham | 4 – | (7) retired hurt . . . . . . . . . . . 13 |
| J. R. Ayling b Waqar Younis | 34 – | (8) b Waqar Younis . . . . . . . . . 23 |
| †A. N. Aymes c Stewart b Feltham | 9 – | (9) c Greig b Waqar Younis . . . . 4 |
| R. J. Maru c Stewart b Feltham | 7 – | (6) c Ward b Feltham . . . . . . . . 6 |
| K. J. Shine b Waqar Younis | 1 – | b Waqar Younis . . . . . . . . . . . . 25 |
| Aqib Javed not out | 0 – | b Waqar Younis . . . . . . . . . . . . 2 |
| B 4, l-b 1, n-b 3 . . . . . . . . . . . . . . . . . . | 8 | B 5, l-b 3, n-b 3 . . . . . . . . . . 11 |

| | | | |
|---|---|---|---|
| 1/27 2/33 3/48 4/56 5/60 | | 119 | 1/3 2/18 3/52 4/57 5/66 155 |
| 6/68 7/86 8/117 9/119 | | | 6/111 7/115 8/149 9/155 |

Bonus points – Surrey 4.

*In the second innings M. C. J. Nicholas retired hurt at 87.*

Bowling: *First Innings*—Waqar Younis 13.2–2–45–6; Murphy 9–0–33–0; Feltham 12–2–36–4. *Second Innings*—Murphy 18–2–67–1; Waqar Younis 16.4–3–47–6; Feltham 6–1–11–1; Greig 4–1–4–1; Medlycott 4–2–5–0; Lynch 3–0–13–0.

Umpires: J. H. Harris and R. C. Tolchard.

At Lord's, September 10, 11, 12, 13. SURREY lost to MIDDLESEX by 60 runs.

At Manchester, September 17, 18, 19, 20. SURREY lost to LANCASHIRE by one wicket.

# SUSSEX

*President:* The Duke of Richmond and Gordon
*Chairman:* A. M. Caffyn
*Secretary:* N. Bett
  County Ground, Eaton Road,
  Hove BN3 3AN
  (Telephone: 0273-732161)
*Captain:* 1991 – P. W. G. Parker
       1992 – A. P. Wells
*Coach:* N. Gifford

Sussex's rise to eleventh place in the Britannic Assurance Championship, after finishing bottom twice in the previous four years, came as welcome encouragement. Coach Norman Gifford was convinced that, despite improvements in most areas, the players had yet to reach their full capabilities, especially in the Championship, and that their disappointing one-day record did not do them justice. Sussex failed to make the last eight in either the Benson and Hedges Cup or the NatWest Bank Trophy, and progressed from thirteenth to joint twelfth in the Refuge Assurance League. The former England spinner believed that his team were one of the best fielding sides in the country, and that the county had one of the strongest youth policies. "In the past few years we've placed a great deal of emphasis on developing Sussex-bred players. We have a talented crop of youngsters, and several have come through the ranks of the Second Eleven", he observed.

When the curtain came down on the season, it marked the end of an era for Paul Parker. He had been asked to give up the captaincy, which he had held for four seasons, by the committee, and although they had hoped he would stay at Hove as a player, after seventeen years with Sussex he chose to break new ground and signed for the Championship newcomers, Durham. Handicapped by injury, Parker was unable to complete 1,000 runs in any of his last three seasons, but his immense contribution to the club was fairly measured by his county career record of 15,150 runs, at an average of 35.48, scored in 494 innings. There were 37 centuries, a feat bettered by only ten other players, and he set a Sussex record for hundreds in the Sunday League. He also held 204 catches for the county in first-class cricket, and his brilliance in the covers saved countless runs. On leaving, Parker expressed the belief that Sussex were well on the way to winning a trophy within two years. "I've worked very hard to build a side, and there is a good spread of talent in a balanced squad", he said. "I would have liked to have carried on for at least another year, but with nothing to show on the mantelpiece, the club felt it was time for a change."

Early in the season another former captain, Ian Gould, was released to lead Middlesex's Second Eleven, and towards the end of the summer the committee also decided not to retain the Australian all-rounder, Tony Dodemaide, for a fourth year. It was a difficult choice, as he was considered a splendid team man and a dedicated professional. In his three seasons after being asked to follow Imran Khan, Dodemaide scored 2,265 first-class runs and took 178 wickets; but his 1991 return of 52 wickets, and 581 runs compared with 1,001 the previous year, did not meet expectations. Sussex wasted no time in approaching Franklyn Stephenson, newly departed from Nottinghamshire, as a replacement.

The club did not have to look far for their sixteenth post-war captain, with Alan Wells becoming only the fourth of that number born in the county, after James Langridge, Robin Marlar and Jim Parks. He took over the job at the height of his powers; his 1,784 first-class runs represented his most successful season since his début in 1981, and it was the sixth time he had reached four figures. His splendid unbeaten 253 against Yorkshire at Middlesbrough was the ninth-highest score by a Sussex player in the Championship, and it emphasised that, but for his Test ban after playing in South Africa, he would be pushing for an England place. Wells grew in stature as he led the team in Parker's absence, and two of Sussex's four first-class wins came with him at the helm.

Apart from Wells, only the openers, Neil Lenham and David Smith, topped 1,000 runs, and somewhat disappointingly eight players fell into the band between 300 and 750. Smith, troubled by a thumb injury the previous year, made two hundreds and eight other fifties, failing to reach double figures only nine times, while Lenham scored consistently until another finger injury cut short his season at the end of August. Jamie Hall, who hit 1,140 runs in twenty first-class games in 1990, managed 686 from fifteen in his second season, and there was also limited success for Martin Speight who, once he had secured his place, compiled 754 runs in fourteen matches, with a century against Cambridge University and five other scores over fifty. Wicket-keeper Peter Moores enjoyed his best season with the bat, hitting 714 runs, and his 56 catches and six stumpings were also a personal record. The new captain's brother, Colin Wells, pulled a hamstring while training after a hernia operation, and then suffered a poisoned arm, all of which restricted him to 503 runs and only eighteen wickets.

Adrian Jones, back with Sussex after four seasons with Somerset, missed only one first-class match and was the leading wicket-taker with 57 victims. But Tony Pigott struggled for his best form in his benefit year; 36 wickets was his lowest return in a full season. Leg-spinner Ian Salisbury, rewarded like Speight with a county cap, and chosen for his second England A tour, formed an effective partnership with the off-spinner, Bradleigh Donelan. They shared 82 first-class wickets, and Donelan underlined his potential with match figures of ten for 136 in the end-of-season victory over Gloucestershire. He also proved his worth with the bat, scoring 353 runs at 35.30.

Though attendances during the Eastbourne Week were lower than they had hoped, Sussex felt that the match at Arundel Castle was an even greater success than the inaugural fixture in 1990. The club's financial position continued to improve, with a pre-tax profit of £77,334, and members were delighted to hear that, for the first time in many years, Sussex were not borrowing from the bank. – Jack Arlidge.

SUSSEX 1991

[Bill Smith]

Back row: M. P. Speight, J. A. North, A. R. Hansford, P. W. Threlfall, E. S. H. Giddins, J. W. Hall, R. Hanley, C. C. Remy. Middle row: L. V. Chandler (1st XI scorer), C. P. Cale (assistant coach), N. Gifford (coach), N. J. Lenham, I. D. K. Salisbury, K. Greenfield, P. Moores, A. I. C. Dodemaide, R. A. Bunting, A. N. Jones, B. T. P. Donelan, I. C. Waring (assistant coach), F. Ketley (2nd XI scorer). Front row: J. W. Dean, A. P. Wells, C. M. Wells, I. J. Gould, P. W. G. Parker (captain), A. C. S. Pigott, D. M. Smith, A. R. Cornford.

## SUSSEX RESULTS

*All first-class matches – Played 24: Won 4, Lost 3, Tied 1, Drawn 16.*

*County Championship matches – Played 22: Won 4, Lost 3, Tied 1, Drawn 14.*

*Bonus points – Batting 57, Bowling 60.*

*Competition placings – Britannic Assurance County Championship, 11th;*
*NatWest Bank Trophy, 2nd round; Benson and Hedges Cup, 3rd in Group C;*
*Refuge Assurance League, 12th equal.*

# BRITANNIC ASSURANCE CHAMPIONSHIP AVERAGES

## BATTING

| | Birthplace | M | I | NO | R | HI | Avge |
|---|---|---|---|---|---|---|---|
| R. A. Bunting . . . . . | East Winch | 3 | 4 | 3 | 106 | 51* | 106.00 |
| ‡A. P. Wells . . . . . . . | Newhaven | 21 | 34 | 5 | 1,777 | 253* | 61.27 |
| ‡D. M. Smith . . . . . . | Balham, London | 19 | 33 | 5 | 1,130 | 126* | 40.35 |
| ‡N. J. Lenham . . . . . | Worthing | 18 | 31 | 3 | 1,028 | 193 | 36.71 |
| B. T. P. Donelan . . . | Park Royal, London | 12 | 15 | 5 | 353 | 61 | 35.30 |
| ‡M. P. Speight . . . . . | Walsall | 12 | 18 | 1 | 572 | 89 | 33.64 |
| ‡C. M. Wells . . . . . . | Newhaven | 12 | 19 | 5 | 451 | 76 | 32.21 |
| ‡A. I. C. Dodemaide . | Melbourne, Australia | 19 | 28 | 9 | 581 | 100* | 30.57 |
| J. W. Hall . . . . . . . . | Chichester | 14 | 25 | 2 | 685 | 117* | 29.78 |
| ‡P. Moores . . . . . . . | Macclesfield | 22 | 27 | 3 | 612 | 86* | 25.50 |
| ‡P. W. G. Parker . . . | Bulawayo, S. Rhodesia | 16 | 26 | 1 | 607 | 111 | 24.28 |
| J. A. North . . . . . . . | Slindon | 5 | 7 | 1 | 122 | 63* | 20.33 |
| ‡A. C. S. Pigott . . . . | London | 18 | 21 | 5 | 291 | 65 | 18.18 |
| K. Greenfield . . . . . | Brighton | 7 | 11 | 0 | 156 | 64 | 14.18 |
| ‡I. D. K. Salisbury . . | Northampton | 20 | 20 | 7 | 179 | 34 | 13.76 |
| ‡A. N. Jones . . . . . . . | Woking | 21 | 17 | 5 | 119 | 28 | 9.91 |

Also batted: E. S. H. Giddins (*Eastbourne*) (2 matches) 14*; R. Hanley (*Tonbridge*) (1 match) 19, 0.

* *Signifies not out.* ‡ *Denotes county cap.*

The following played a total of fourteen three-figure innings for Sussex in County Championship matches – A. P. Wells 7, N. J. Lenham 3, A. I. C. Dodemaide 1, J. W. Hall 1, P. W. G. Parker 1, D. M. Smith 1.

## BOWLING

| | O | M | R | W | BB | 5W/i | Avge |
|---|---|---|---|---|---|---|---|
| A. I. C. Dodemaide . . . | 555 | 110 | 1,583 | 52 | 5-130 | 1 | 30.44 |
| C. M. Wells . . . . . . . . . | 216.4 | 60 | 598 | 18 | 7-42 | 1 | 33.22 |
| B. T. P. Donelan . . . . . | 426.3 | 112 | 1,162 | 34 | 6-62 | 2 | 34.17 |
| A. N. Jones . . . . . . . . . | 502.2 | 68 | 1,829 | 53 | 5-46 | 2 | 34.50 |
| J. A. North . . . . . . . . . | 129 | 34 | 507 | 14 | 3-54 | 0 | 36.21 |
| A. C. S. Pigott . . . . . . . | 415.3 | 92 | 1,293 | 35 | 5-37 | 1 | 36.94 |
| I. D. K. Salisbury . . . . . | 605.2 | 144 | 1,837 | 47 | 5-40 | 1 | 39.08 |

Also bowled: R. A. Bunting 62.2–7–260–8; E. S. H. Giddins 56.2–6–186–2; N. J. Lenham 29–5–79–2; P. W. G. Parker 2–0–10–0; D. M. Smith 2–0–15–0; A. P. Wells 8–1–21–1.

**Wicket-keeper:** P. Moores 53 ct, 5 st.

**Leading Fielder:** K. Greenfield 15.

At Taunton, April 27, 29, 30, May 1. SUSSEX drew with SOMERSET.

At Lord's, May 9, 10, 11. SUSSEX beat MIDDLESEX by ten wickets.

## SUSSEX v HAMPSHIRE

At Hove, May 16, 17, 18, 20. Drawn. Sussex 4 pts, Hampshire 7 pts. Toss: Sussex. Chris Smith scored two hundreds and his opening partner, Terry, hit 171 and 55 as Hampshire's batsmen dominated the Sussex bowling on an easy-paced pitch. However, a draw always looked the likely outcome when 82 overs were lost to rain and bad light. Smith, with 22 fours in his 145, reached 1,000 runs in all cricket in 1991 when 135, while Terry, in imperious form, hit 26 fours. Having helped the elder Smith put on 274 in 82 overs, Terry then added 110 with Robin Smith for the second wicket. Needing 312 to avoid the follow-on, Sussex responded in style. Smith and Hall put on 157 for the first wicket, and North gave hint of a bright future with a maiden first-class fifty before Parker declared 111 runs behind on the third day. Terry and Smith again gave Hampshire a good start, and after Salisbury, benefiting from some slow turn, had dismissed Terry, Smith went on to 101, with fourteen fours. Sussex, left to score 315 in a minimum of 61 overs, were never really in the hunt once Bakker had struck two early blows. It was left to Wells, confirming his return to form with an unbeaten 83, to steer Sussex to safety.

*Close of play:* First day, Hampshire 298-1 (V. P. Terry 130\*, R. A. Smith 16\*); Second day, Sussex 130-0 (D. M. Smith 69\*, J. W. Hall 47\*); Third day, Hampshire 54-0 (V. P. Terry 28\*, C. L. Smith 23\*).

## Hampshire

| | | |
|---|---|---|
| V. P. Terry c and b North .................171 | – c sub b Salisbury ............ 55 |
| C. L. Smith c Salisbury b Pigott ..........145 | – lbw b Giddins ..............101 |
| R. A. Smith c Jones b North ..............68 | – c Hall b Salisbury ........... 16 |
| D. I. Gower c Moores b Salisbury ..........15 | – not out .................... 13 |
| *M. C. J. Nicholas b Salisbury ............23 | |
| K. D. James not out ....................17 | – (5) not out ................. 6 |
| L-b 20, w 2 ...........22 | B 7, l-b 4, n-b 1 ........ 12 |

1/274 2/384 3/417 4/421 5/461 (5 wkts dec.) 461    1/129 2/167 3/193 (3 wkts dec.) 203

†A. N. Aymes, R. J. Maru, C. A. Connor, P. J. Bakker and Aqib Javed did not bat.

Bonus points – Hampshire 4 (Score at 100 overs: 344-1).

*Bowling: First Innings*—Jones 21-3-64-0; Giddins 19-3-65-0; North 22-2-114-2; Pigott 25-5-77-1; Salisbury 37.4-9-107-2; Lenham 5-0-14-0. *Second Innings*—Jones 12.5-3-42-0; Pigott 9-2-36-0; North 10-0-39-0; Salisbury 11.4-4-46-2; Giddins 7.2-0-29-1.

## Sussex

| | | |
|---|---|---|
| D. M. Smith c Aymes b Bakker ............82 | – c Terry b Bakker ............. 5 |
| J. W. Hall lbw b Bakker .................65 | – c Connor b Maru ............. 40 |
| N. J. Lenham b Connor ..................35 | – c Aymes b Bakker ............ 8 |
| *A. P. Wells c R. A. Smith b Maru .........49 | – not out .................... 83 |
| K. Greenfield c Terry b Connor ............1 | – c Maru b Connor ............. 0 |
| J. A. North not out .....................63 | – b Maru .................... 22 |
| †P. Moores b James .....................16 | |
| A. C. S. Pigott c Maru b James ............0 | – (7) not out ................. 13 |
| I. D. K. Salisbury not out ................10 | |
| B 2, l-b 13, w 2, n-b 12 .......29 | L-b 7, w 1, n-b 3 ....... 11 |

1/157 2/168 3/239 4/242 5/267 (7 wkts dec.) 350    1/5 2/17 3/94 (5 wkts) 182
6/297 7/297                                         4/116 5/157

A. N. Jones and E. S. H. Giddins did not bat.

Bonus points – Sussex 4, Hampshire 3.

*Bowling: First Innings*—Aqib Javed 20-1-79-0; Bakker 21-7-52-2; Connor 19-2-88-2; James 23-5-61-2; Nicholas 8-0-40-0; Maru 8-1-15-1. *Second Innings*—Aqib Javed 8-1-17-0; Bakker 13-1-32-2; James 3-0-19-0; Connor 12-1-49-1; Maru 17-6-53-2; Nicholas 2-1-5-0.

Umpires: H. D. Bird and R. C. Tolchard.

## SUSSEX v MIDDLESEX

At Hove, May 22, 23, 24. Drawn. Sussex 5 pts, Middlesex 5 pts. Toss: Sussex. Inspired bowling on the final day by Emburey, whose seven wickets included a spell of five for 4 in 38 balls, seemed to have turned the match Middlesex's way. But Bunting and Donelan, joining forces when Sussex's lead was only 179, added 64 for the last wicket in cavalier style to confirm that it was poor batsmanship, rather than the vagaries of the pitch, which had put Sussex in a parlous position. Middlesex, left to score 244 in a minimum of 36 overs, had a chance while Gatting was there; without him they fell behind the rate, despite some lusty blows from Keech. Downton, who announced his retirement during the game, following the eye injury he sustained in 1990, remained unbeaten and at the end was clapped off by both sets of players, entering the pavilion to a standing ovation. On the opening day Wells had made 137, with 25 fours, adding 217 for the third wicket with Smith, whose undefeated 126 contained a six and nineteen fours. There were two centuries in Middlesex's first innings as well, with Hutchinson (22 fours) and Gatting (nineteen fours) putting on 175 for the second wicket.

*Close of play:* First day, Middlesex 9-0 (I. J. F. Hutchinson 4*, M. A. Roseberry 5*); Second day, Sussex 50-0 (N. J. Lenham 25*, J. W. Hall 20*).

### Sussex

| | | | | |
|---|---|---|---|---|
| D. M. Smith not out | 126 | – (7) run out | | 28 |
| J. W. Hall b Cowans | 3 | – lbw b Tufnell | | 41 |
| N. J. Lenham c Brown b Williams | 11 | – (1) st Downton b Emburey | | 32 |
| *A. P. Wells c Downton b Cowans | 137 | – c and b Emburey | | 2 |
| M. P. Speight c Cowans b Emburey | 40 | – (3) c Hutchinson b Emburey | | 0 |
| A. I. C. Dodemaide (did not bat) | | – (5) c Roseberry b Emburey | | 3 |
| †P. Moores (did not bat) | | – (6) c Brown b Emburey | | 9 |
| A. C. S. Pigott (did not bat) | | – c Tufnell b Emburey | | 6 |
| I. D. K. Salisbury (did not bat) | | – c Hutchinson b Emburey | | 5 |
| B. T. P. Donelan (did not bat) | | – not out | | 27 |
| R. A. Bunting (did not bat) | | – c Brown b Tufnell | | 39 |
| B 5, l-b 7, w 1, n-b 10 | 23 | L-b 6, n-b 5 | | 11 |

1/8 2/35 3/252 4/340     (4 wkts dec.) 340     1/67 2/67 3/73 4/77 5/87    203
6/107 7/122 8/132 9/139

Bonus points – Sussex 4, Middlesex 1.

Bowling: *First Innings*—Ellcock 9-3-28-0; Cowans 13-3-39-2; Williams 18-4-65-1; Emburey 25-7-76-1; Tufnell 30-8-111-0; Hutchinson 4-0-9-0. *Second Innings*—Ellcock 9-1-29-0; Cowans 4-1-8-0; Emburey 37-11-71-7; Williams 5-0-20-0; Tufnell 30-9-69-2; Keech 1-1-0-0.

### Middlesex

| | | | | |
|---|---|---|---|---|
| I. J. F. Hutchinson lbw b Bunting | 125 | – lbw b Dodemaide | | 46 |
| M. A. Roseberry c Wells b Dodemaide | 25 | – c Dodemaide b Bunting | | 47 |
| *M. W. Gatting not out | 117 | – run out | | 31 |
| K. R. Brown lbw b Pigott | 28 | – lbw b Bunting | | 3 |
| M. Keech not out | 0 | – st Moores b Salisbury | | 27 |
| †P. R. Downton (did not bat) | | – not out | | 24 |
| N. G. Cowans (did not bat) | | – b Donelan | | 0 |
| J. E. Emburey (did not bat) | | – not out | | 5 |
| B 2, n-b 3 | 5 | B 2, l-b 2, w 1, n-b 3 | | 8 |

1/67 2/242 3/298     (3 wkts dec.) 300     1/73 2/128 3/133   (6 wkts) 191
4/133 5/180 6/181

N. F. Williams, P. C. R. Tufnell and R. M. Ellcock did not bat.

Bonus points – Middlesex 4, Sussex 1.

Bowling: *First Innings*—Pigott 23-11-48-1; Dodemaide 19-3-63-1; Bunting 18-2-60-1; Salisbury 12-1-62-0; Donelan 16.1-5-54-0; Lenham 3-0-11-0. *Second Innings*—Pigott 4-1-11-0; Dodemaide 9-1-30-1; Bunting 8-0-34-2; Salisbury 12-1-62-1; Donelan 12-1-50-1.

Umpires: B. Hassan and J. W. Holder.

At Cardiff, May 25, 27, 28. SUSSEX drew with GLAMORGAN.

At Manchester, May 31, June 1, 3. SUSSEX lost to LANCASHIRE by seven wickets.

At Tunbridge Wells, June 7, 8, 10. SUSSEX drew with KENT.

## SUSSEX v WORCESTERSHIRE

At Hove, June 14, 15, 17. Drawn. Sussex 1 pt, Worcestershire 4 pts. Toss: Sussex. Worcestershire were in the driving seat for much of the game, but the loss of two sessions to rain on a gloomy second day ultimately cost them the chance of recording their first Championship win. Hick, returning to form in glorious style, dominated the opening day with his first hundred of the season, a chanceless 186 in four and a half hours (244 balls) with 23 fours and two sixes. It was the highest innings by a Worcestershire batsman against Sussex. Rhodes, promoted to open, helped Hick add 154 for the second wicket, after which Hick and Moody plundered 164 off 32 overs. Two declarations on the final day helped make up for time lost to the weather and left Sussex needing 356 to win in a minimum of 79 overs. Newport's three wickets, including the Wells brothers' with consecutive deliveries, had Sussex 70 for five, but Parker steered them to safety with a gritty, unbeaten 56, made in more than three hours. Dodemaide supported him for 42 overs, and Worcestershire, their ambition frustrated, acknowledged the draw halfway through the final hour.

*Close of play:* First day, Worcestershire 410-5 (D. B. D'Oliveira 12*, R. K. Illingworth 1*); Second day, Sussex 131-1 (D. M. Smith 67*, N. J. Lenham 4*).

## Worcestershire

| | | |
|---|---|---|
| T. S. Curtis c Dodemaide b Salisbury | 24 | – not out .......................... 33 |
| †S. J. Rhodes b Pigott ........................ | 77 | – c Hall b A. P. Wells ............. 10 |
| G. A. Hick b Dodemaide ..................... | 186 | – not out ......................... 28 |
| T. M. Moody c Moores b Dodemaide ......... | 73 | |
| *P. A. Neale b Pigott ........................ | 28 | |
| D. B. D'Oliveira not out ..................... | 12 | |
| R. K. Illingworth not out .................... | 1 | |
| L-b 3, n-b 6 ...................... | 9 | B 1, l-b 4 ............. 5 |

1/46 2/200 3/364 4/373 5/409　　(5 wkts dec.) 410　1/19　　(1 wkt dec.) 76

S. R. Lampitt, P. J. Newport, N. V. Radford and G. R. Dilley did not bat.

Bonus points – Worcestershire 4, Sussex 1 (Score at 100 overs: 373-4).

Bowling: *First Innings*—Jones 18-4-48-0; Dodemaide 21-7-45-2; C. M. Wells 17-3-77-0; Pigott 20-5-69-2; Salisbury 35-5-168-1. *Second Innings*—A. P. Wells 8-1-21-1; Lenham 8-0-25-0; Parker 2-0-10-0; Smith 2-0-15-0.

## Sussex

| | | |
|---|---|---|
| D. M. Smith not out ........................ | 67 | – c Rhodes b Dilley ............. 5 |
| J. W. Hall lbw b Illingworth ................ | 55 | – c Rhodes b Radford ........... 7 |
| N. J. Lenham not out ....................... | 4 | – c Hick b Newport ............. 21 |
| A. P. Wells (did not bat) .................... | | – c Hick b Newport ............. 20 |
| *P. W. G. Parker (did not bat) .............. | | – not out ......................... 56 |
| C. M. Wells (did not bat) ................... | | – lbw b Newport ................. 0 |
| A. I. C. Dodemaide (did not bat) ............ | | – not out ......................... 35 |
| B 2, l-b 1, n-b 2 ............... | 5 | L-b 3, n-b 9 ............. 12 |

1/124　　(1 wkt dec.) 131　1/8 2/30 3/44　　(5 wkts) 156
　　　　　　　　　　　　　　　　4/70 5/70

†P. Moores, A. C. S. Pigott, I. D. K. Salisbury and A. N. Jones did not bat.

Bowling: *First Innings*—Dilley 12–4–32–0; Radford 9–3–22–0; Lampitt 6–1–24–0; Illingworth 12–5–32–1; Newport 5–0–18–0. *Second Innings*—Dilley 12–2–25–1; Radford 14–5–32–1; Newport 18–7–32–3; Lampitt 12–3–31–0; Illingworth 16–8–21–0; Hick 3–1–8–0; Moody 2–1–4–0; D'Oliveira 1–1–0–0.

Umpires: H. D. Bird and J. H. Harris.

At Coventry, June 18, 19, 20. SUSSEX lost to WARWICKSHIRE by 98 runs.

## SUSSEX v ESSEX

At Horsham, June 21, 22, 24. Drawn. Sussex 4 pts, Essex 7 pts. Toss: Sussex. Although 176 overs were lost to the weather, including all of the third day, what play there was provided plenty of entertainment for a good crowd at this most picturesque of venues. For once, Parker's decision to field first appeared vindicated when Jones, bowling with venom, took two early wickets and Essex collapsed to 73 for five. However, Foster, captaining the visitors, rescued them with 107 not out off 129 balls, hitting fourteen fours and two huge, straight sixes. Fraser, formerly of Middlesex, and making his first-class début for Essex, provided solid support with an unbeaten half-century in an eighth-wicket stand of 130 in 31 overs, and Essex declared having gained maximum batting points. Lenham held Sussex's top order together with 60, but at 131 for seven, on a pitch giving all the bowlers some encouragement, they were in danger of having to follow on. Dodemaide and Pigott made sure that threat was avoided.

*Close of play:* First day, Essex 153-6 (M. A. Garnham 41*, N. A. Foster 17*); Second day, Sussex 176-8 (A. I. C. Dodemaide 27*, I. D. K. Salisbury 0*).

## Essex

| | | | | |
|---|---|---|---|---|
| J. P. Stephenson c Parker b Jones | 2 | *N. A. Foster not out | 107 |
| A. C. H. Seymour lbw b Jones | 9 | A. G. J. Fraser not out | 52 |
| P. J. Prichard c Lenham b C. M. Wells | 13 | | |
| Salim Malik c A. P. Wells b Pigott | 40 | L-b 10, w 2, n-b 7 | 19 |
| N. Hussain c Moores b Dodemaide | 20 | | |
| N. Shahid c Moores b Pigott | 0 | 1/6 2/17 3/43 (7 wkts dec.) | 303 |
| †M. A. Garnham b Dodemaide | 41 | 4/73 5/73 | |
| | | 6/109 7/173 | |

S. J. W. Andrew and J. H. Childs did not bat.

Bonus points – Essex 4, Sussex 3.

Bowling: Jones 18–0–110–2; Dodemaide 21.3–7–43–2; C. M. Wells 15–5–37–1; Pigott 16–3–61–2; Salisbury 12–4–42–0.

## Sussex

| | | | | |
|---|---|---|---|---|
| N. J. Lenham c Foster b Childs | 60 | †P. Moores b Childs | 10 |
| J. W. Hall c Stephenson b Andrew | 9 | A. C. S. Pigott c Seymour b Childs | 26 |
| *P. W. G. Parker b Andrew | 2 | I. D. K. Salisbury not out | 0 |
| A. P. Wells lbw b Foster | 26 | L-b 1, n-b 2 | 3 |
| M. P. Speight c Childs b Foster | 6 | | |
| C. M. Wells c Garnham b Childs | 7 | 1/42 2/48 3/99 4/99 (8 wkts) | 176 |
| A. I. C. Dodemaide not out | 27 | 5/112 6/112 7/131 8/175 | |

A. N. Jones did not bat.

Bonus points – Sussex 1, Essex 3.

Bowling: Foster 19–4–39–2; Andrew 16–5–44–2; Fraser 5–0–13–0; Stephenson 3–0–16–0; Childs 25–9–63–4.

Umpires: H. D. Bird and A. A. Jones.

## SUSSEX v CAMBRIDGE UNIVERSITY

At Hove, June 29, 30, July 1. Drawn. Toss: Sussex. Cambridge, in their last outing before the University Match, never looked like repeating their win in 1990. First Speight and Greenfield put Sussex in a strong position after Jenkins, celebrating his 21st birthday, had given Cambridge an early fillip by bowling Hall; and then rain set in to wash out the second and third days. Speight hit his career-best 149, out of a second-wicket stand of 237, from 164 balls with 24 fours and a six. Greenfield was more circumspect, but he eventually moved into three figures, hitting nine fours and a six, while adding exactly 100 with Wells. Although the students' bowling looked distinctly ordinary, the same could not be said of Jones and Threlfall's opening burst. Threlfall took the prized wicket of Crawley to reduce the visitors to 19 for three, but it was all academic. By lunchtime on Sunday the ground was under water.

*Close of play:* First day, Cambridge University 19-3 (R. I. Clitheroe 8*, R. J. Turner 0*); Second day, No play.

### Sussex

| | | |
|---|---|---|
| *K. Greenfield not out | ............. | 127 |
| J. W. Hall b Jenkins | ................. | 1 |
| †M. P. Speight b Lowrey | ........... | 149 |
| C. M. Wells not out | ................ | 52 |
| B 2, l-b 6, n-b 3 | ............ | 11 |

1/3 2/240          (2 wkts dec.) 340

R. Hanley, J. A. North, I. D. K. Salisbury, B. T. P. Donelan, R. A. Bunting, A. N. Jones and P. W. Threlfall did not bat.

Bowling: Jenkins 18-3-71-1; Bush 13-0-59-0; Waller 21-4-92-0; Pearson 13-1-35-0; Lowrey 17-1-58-1; Hooper 4-0-17-0.

### Cambridge University

| | | | |
|---|---|---|---|
| A. M. Hooper c Bunting b Jones | ...... 6 | *†R. J. Turner not out | ............. 0 |
| R. I. Clitheroe not out | ............. 8 | N-b 2 | ................ 2 |
| R. H. J. Jenkins b Threlfall | .... 3 | | |
| J. P. Crawley c Speight b Threlfall | .... 0 | 1/15 2/18 3/19 | (3 wkts) 19 |

M. J. Morris, M. J. Lowrey, J. P. Arscott, R. M. Pearson, D. J. Bush and R. B. Waller did not bat.

Bowling: Jones 5-1-9-1; Threlfall 4-1-10-2.

Umpires: R. Palmer and G. A. Stickley.

## SUSSEX v SURREY

At Arundel, July 2, 3, 4. Drawn. Sussex 3 pts, Surrey 7 pts. Toss: Surrey. Surrey controlled an absorbing tussle from start to finish, and Sussex were just 26 runs ahead with one wicket in hand when Greig gave up his bid for victory with four overs left. Surrey's bowlers, led by Waqar Younis, had exploited some first-day moisture, and a Sussex score of 216 reflected accurately the way the visitors' attack had performed. The game swung even more Surrey's way when Parker dropped a straightforward slip catch off Darren Bicknell before he had scored. It was to prove a costly miss, for Bicknell went on to make 126, with seventeen fours, putting on 147 for the first wicket with Alikhan. Stewart and Thorpe maintained the brisk momentum, and Greig was able to declare at the start of the final day, 177 ahead. Smith and Alan Wells, who made a priceless 77, added 72 for the third wicket as Sussex set out to save the match.

*Close of play:* First day, Surrey 45-0 (D. J. Bicknell 27*, R. I. Alikhan 17*); Second day, Surrey 393-7 (G. P. Thorpe 56*, M. P. Bicknell 7*).

## Sussex

| | | | |
|---|---|---|---|
| N. J. Lenham b M. P. Bicknell | 15 | – b Waqar Younis | 5 |
| D. M. Smith b Greig | 29 | – c Greig b Medlycott | 46 |
| *P. W. G. Parker lbw b Waqar Younis | 26 | – c Sargeant b Waqar Younis | 4 |
| A. P. Wells c Stewart b M. P. Bicknell | 20 | – b Medlycott | 77 |
| M. P. Speight c Stewart b Greig | 42 | – c Sargeant b M. P. Bicknell | 15 |
| C. M. Wells c Stewart b Greig | 4 | – c Alikhan b Medlycott | 1 |
| A. I. C. Dodemaide c Sargeant b Murphy | 1 | – b Waqar Younis | 2 |
| †P. Moores b Waqar Younis | 8 | – lbw b Greig | 14 |
| A. C. S. Pigott lbw b Waqar Younis | 26 | – not out | 12 |
| I. D. K. Salisbury c Sargeant b M. P. Bicknell | 17 | – b Medlycott | 4 |
| A. N. Jones not out | 14 | – not out | 0 |
| B 2, l-b 8, n-b 4 | 14 | B 8, l-b 7, w 2, n-b 6 | 23 |

| | | |
|---|---|---|
| 1/15 2/71 3/71 4/133 5/144 | 216 | 1/12 2/22 3/94 (9 wkts) 203 |
| 6/145 7/151 8/162 9/200 | | 4/116 5/134 6/143 |
| | | 7/186 8/190 9/198 |

Bonus points – Sussex 2, Surrey 4.

Bowling: *First Innings*—Waqar Younis 23-2-69-3; M. P. Bicknell 24.3-9-57-3; Murphy 20-3-50-1; Greig 12-3-30-3. *Second Innings*—Waqar Younis 19-2-42-3; M. P. Bicknell 19-6-30-1; Murphy 11-2-34-0; Medlycott 38-14-56-4; Greig 10-1-23-1; Stewart 1-0-3-0.

## Surrey

| | | | |
|---|---|---|---|
| D. J. Bicknell c Salisbury b Jones | 126 | †N. F. Sargeant st Moores b Salisbury | 4 |
| R. I. Alikhan lbw b Dodemaide | 58 | M. P. Bicknell not out | 7 |
| A. J. Stewart c Moores b Salisbury | 71 | | |
| D. M. Ward c Moores b Jones | 7 | B 3, l-b 10, w 3, n-b 1 | 17 |
| G. P. Thorpe not out | 56 | | |
| *I. A. Greig lbw b Dodemaide | 27 | 1/147 2/233 3/242 (7 wkts dec.) 393 |
| K. T. Medlycott c C. M. Wells | | 4/278 5/337 |
| b Dodemaide | 20 | 6/363 7/369 |

Waqar Younis and A. J. Murphy did not bat.

Bonus points – Surrey 3, Sussex 1 (Score at 100 overs: 279-4).

Bowling: Dodemaide 35-7-108-3; Jones 29-2-94-2; Pigott 21-4-77-0; C. M. Wells 16-7-39-0; Lenham 3-1-10-0; Salisbury 24-10-52-2.

Umpires: J. H. Harris and D. R. Shepherd.

At Derby, July 5, 6, 8. SUSSEX drew with DERBYSHIRE.

## SUSSEX v SOMERSET

At Hove, July 16, 17, 18. Drawn. Sussex 8 pts, Somerset 5 pts. Toss: Sussex. Batsmen dominated on another true Hove pitch, but rain on the final day ruined the prospect of an interesting finish. Tavaré led the way after Somerset had been put in, cracking 23 boundaries and a six in an entertaining 134 as the visitors piled up 324. But on the second day Lenham (sixteen fours) and Alan Wells launched a counter-offensive to put Sussex in control, adding 162 in 48 overs for the third wicket. Wells and Speight then took 127 from 22 overs off a desperately poor attack, and Roebuck's occasional slow bowling accounted for Wells when he was 3 runs short of a new career best. His 159 included 22 fours and a six. Sadly these efforts came to nothing. Nearly four hours were lost on the final day, when Cook completed a 37-ball fifty and hit ten fours in an innings of 66 before Lenham dismissed him. Lenham then caught and bowled Hayhurst in the same over.

*Close of play:* First day, Sussex 16-0 (N. J. Lenham 14*, D. M. Smith 2*); Second day, Somerset 43-0 (S. J. Cook 32*, P. M. Roebuck 9*).

## Somerset

| | | | |
|---|---|---|---|
| S. J. Cook c Lenham b Dodemaide | 30 | – c Moores b Lenham | 66 |
| P. M. Roebuck c Moores b Jones | 22 | – c Smith b Salisbury | 55 |
| A. N. Hayhurst lbw b Dodemaide | 12 | – c and b Lenham | 0 |
| *C. J. Tavaré c Parker b Dodemaide | 134 | | |
| R. J. Harden run out | 34 | – (4) not out | 27 |
| K. H. MacLeay b Dodemaide | 20 | – (5) not out | 2 |
| †N. D. Burns run out | 6 | | |
| R. P. Lefebvre b Salisbury | 14 | | |
| D. Beal lbw b Salisbury | 1 | | |
| H. R. J. Trump not out | 30 | | |
| D. A. Graveney not out | 7 | | |
| L-b 12, n-b 2 | 14 | L-b 11, n-b 3 | 14 |

1/49 2/65 3/88 4/195 5/251     (9 wkts dec.) 324     1/121 2/125 3/139     (3 wkts) 164
6/264 7/273 8/274 9/293

Bonus points – Somerset 4, Sussex 4 (Score at 100 overs: 304-9).

Bowling: *First Innings*—Jones 17–2–73–1; Dodemaide 28–6–90–4; Pigott 14–4–50–0; C. M. Wells 20–6–56–0; Salisbury 25–12–43–2. *Second Innings*—Jones 12–0–66–0; Dodemaide 8–1–46–0; Salisbury 16–7–22–1; C. M. Wells 6–1–14–0; Lenham 6–4–5–2.

## Sussex

| | | | |
|---|---|---|---|
| N. J. Lenham c Cook b MacLeay | 106 | A. I. C. Dodemaide not out | 27 |
| D. M. Smith c Burns b Hayhurst | 38 | †P. Moores not out | 17 |
| *P. W. G. Parker c Burns b MacLeay | 7 | L-b 9, n-b 4 | 13 |
| A. P. Wells b Roebuck | 159 | | |
| M. P. Speight c Harden b Hayhurst | 67 | 1/75 2/86 3/248     (6 wkts dec.) 446 | |
| C. M. Wells c Roebuck b MacLeay | 12 | 4/375 5/394 6/404 | |

A. C. S. Pigott, I. D. K. Salisbury and A. N. Jones did not bat.

Bonus points – Sussex 4, Somerset 1 (Score at 100 overs: 388-4).

Bowling: Beal 21–0–97–0; Lefebvre 19–2–55–0; MacLeay 23–3–83–3; Hayhurst 12–2–67–2; Graveney 14–4–38–0; Trump 15–0–58–0; Roebuck 6–0–39–1.

Umpires: B. Hassan and K. J. Lyons.

## SUSSEX v LEICESTERSHIRE

At Hove, July 19, 20, 22. Sussex won by 5 runs. Sussex 23 pts, Leicestershire 4 pts. Toss: Sussex. Sussex clinched their second Championship win of the season in thrilling fashion when off-spinner Donelan bowled Tennant with the penultimate ball. The success of Donelan, who took six for 92, and Salisbury (four for 92) fully justified Parker's decision to play both spinners on a pitch that offered generous turn on the final day. As Leicestershire chased a reasonable target of 248 in a minimum of 58 overs, Hepworth and Briers put on 94 for their first wicket, and after four wickets had gone for 105 the obdurate Benson brought them back into contention. But the task of scoring 14 off the final over proved beyond the last-wicket pair. Earlier in the game Lenham, enjoying a prolific summer, had fallen just 7 runs short of a double-century, but his personal-best 193, which included 26 fours, was still the highest in the Championship by a Sussex batsman for seven years. Lewis bowled with great heart for the visitors, and Potter batted bravely to ensure they avoided the follow-on.

*Close of play:* First day, Sussex 313-4 (N. J. Lenham 183*, C. M. Wells 12*); Second day, Leicestershire 286-8 (P. Willey 14*, L. Tennant 23*).

## Sussex

| | | | |
|---|---|---|---|
| N. J. Lenham b Maguire | 193 | – c Benson b Lewis | 4 |
| D. M. Smith c Benson b Lewis | 3 | – c sub b Hepworth | 50 |
| *P. W. G. Parker c Willey b Lewis | 33 | – c Lewis b Hepworth | 55 |
| A. P. Wells c Benson b Lewis | 12 | – not out | 33 |
| M. P. Speight c Smith b Maguire | 64 | – b Potter | 18 |
| C. M. Wells not out | 31 | – not out | 14 |
| A. I. C. Dodemaide not out | 12 | | |
| L-b 6 | 6 | L-b 5 | 5 |

1/9 2/74 3/100 4/269 5/342     (5 wkts dec.) 354    1/6 2/110     (4 wkts dec.) 179
3/119 4/148

†P. Moores, B. T. P. Donelan, I. D. K. Salisbury and A. N. Jones did not bat.

Bonus points – Sussex 4, Leicestershire 1 (Score at 100 overs: 322-4).

Bowling: *First Innings*—Lewis 35–5–106–3; Maguire 35–10–85–2; Tennant 10–3–54–0; Potter 17–5–51–0; Benson 10–2–40–0; Hepworth 2–0–12–0. *Second Innings*—Lewis 8.5–3–24–1; Maguire 9–2–40–0; Hepworth 12–2–62–2; Potter 11–1–48–1.

## Leicestershire

| | | | |
|---|---|---|---|
| P. N. Hepworth c Lenham b Jones | 7 | – lbw b Salisbury | 56 |
| *N. E. Briers lbw b Salisbury | 29 | – st Moores b Salisbury | 41 |
| J. J. Whitaker c Smith b Jones | 0 | – b Donelan | 5 |
| L. Potter c A. P. Wells b Donelan | 89 | – b Donelan | 0 |
| B. F. Smith b Donelan | 17 | – c Dodemaide b Donelan | 19 |
| J. D. R. Benson b Salisbury | 45 | – b Donelan | 62 |
| C. C. Lewis c Parker b Salisbury | 15 | – c sub b Donelan | 21 |
| P. Willey not out | 14 | – c and b Salisbury | 11 |
| †P. Whitticase c Speight b Dodemaide | 29 | – c Smith b Salisbury | 5 |
| L. Tennant not out | 23 | – b Donelan | 7 |
| J. N. Maguire (did not bat) | | – not out | 11 |
| B 4, l-b 7, n-b 7 | 18 | L-b 1, w 3 | 4 |

1/13 2/16 3/78 4/111 5/184     (8 wkts dec.) 286    1/94 2/103 3/105 4/105 5/149    242
6/213 7/219 8/255                                       6/192 7/206 8/224 9/228

Bonus points – Leicestershire 3, Sussex 3 (Score at 100 overs: 264-8).

Bowling: *First Innings*—Jones 9–2–20–2; Dodemaide 14–3–29–1; Salisbury 45–8–130–3; Donelan 39–14–96–2. *Second Innings*—Jones 5–2–23–0; Dodemaide 8–0–34–0; Salisbury 27–4–92–4; Donelan 27.5–1–92–6.

Umpires: B. Hassan and K. J. Lyons.

At Cheltenham, July 23, 24, 25. SUSSEX drew with GLOUCESTERSHIRE.

## SUSSEX v NORTHAMPTONSHIRE

At Eastbourne, August 2, 3, 5. Drawn. Sussex 7 pts, Northamptonshire 3 pts. Toss: Sussex. A somewhat mundane match came to life only on the final afternoon, when Ripley and Taylor had to survive two testing overs at the end to deny Sussex an unlikely victory. On a pitch that gave some assistance to the bowlers, Lenham and Smith put on 142 for Sussex's first wicket before Baptiste struck six wickets in thirteen balls. It was left to Speight, whose 89 included four sixes and nine fours, to revive the innings. On Saturday, Northamptonshire found batting a difficult proposition, and of the top-order batsmen only Larkins made much impression. Jones bowled with great fire to provide extra entertainment for the Sussex supporter holding his wedding reception in a marquee on the boundary, and there was a time when it looked as if Northamptonshire might have to follow on. Ripley and Williams avoided that possibility, and on the final day Sussex struggled to force the pace before eventually setting Northamptonshire a target of 262 in 72 overs. Larkins and Stanley added 53 in 24 overs, and after Dodemaide dismissed them both, Northamptonshire were kept in check by Donelan and Salisbury, who in 31 overs of contrasting spin together almost won the match.

*Close of play:* First day, Sussex 296-8 (B. T. P. Donelan 5*, I. D. K. Salisbury 2*);
Second day, Sussex 30-1 (D. M. Smith 17*, P. W. G. Parker 7*).

## Sussex

| | | | |
|---|---|---|---|
| N. J. Lenham c Penberthy b Baptiste | 75 | – b Taylor | 6 |
| D. M. Smith c and b Baptiste | 67 | – lbw b Baptiste | 39 |
| *P. W. G. Parker b Baptiste | 6 | – c and b Baptiste | 18 |
| A. P. Wells lbw b Baptiste | 0 | – c Taylor b Baptiste | 11 |
| M. P. Speight c Penberthy b Cook | 89 | – b Penberthy | 22 |
| C. M. Wells c Lamb b Curran | 12 | – not out | 20 |
| A. I. C. Dodemaide b Cook | 28 | – c Ripley b Baptiste | 1 |
| †P. Moores b Cook | 7 | – run out | 5 |
| B. T. P. Donelan not out | 17 | – b Curran | 2 |
| I. D. K. Salisbury not out | 10 | – c Larkins b Curran | 0 |
| A. N. Jones (did not bat) | | – not out | 7 |
| B 2, l-b 4 | 6 | L-b 6 | 6 |

1/142 2/145 3/145 4/166 5/212     (8 wkts dec.) 317     1/8 2/64 3/69     (9 wkts dec.) 137
6/266 7/285 8/290                                           4/90 5/103 6/104
                                                      7/117 8/126 9/126

Bonus points – Sussex 3, Northamptonshire 2 (Score at 100 overs: 254-5).

Bowling: *First Innings*—Taylor 9–1–37–0; Baptiste 30–8–79–4; Cook 31–7–74–3; Curran 14–5–33–1; Williams 26–4–66–0. *Second Innings*—Taylor 11–1–33–1; Baptiste 19–2–64–4; Cook 3–2–1–0; Williams 3–1–5–0; Penberthy 4–0–9–1; Curran 4–1–19–2.

## Northamptonshire

| | | | |
|---|---|---|---|
| A. Fordham b Jones | 0 | – b Dodemaide | 14 |
| W. Larkins b C. M. Wells | 34 | – c and b Dodemaide | 45 |
| N. A. Stanley b Dodemaide | 6 | – c and b Dodemaide | 36 |
| *A. J. Lamb c A. P. Wells b Salisbury | 13 | – c Salisbury b Donelan | 32 |
| K. M. Curran c Smith b Jones | 24 | – b Salisbury | 34 |
| A. L. Penberthy b Jones | 26 | – (8) c Moores b Donelan | 8 |
| E. A. E. Baptiste b Salisbury | 8 | – (6) c Donelan b Salisbury | 14 |
| R. G. Williams b Donelan | 22 | – (7) st Moores b Salisbury | 35 |
| †D. Ripley b Donelan | 22 | – not out | 11 |
| N. G. B. Cook c A. P. Wells b Salisbury | 10 | | |
| J. P. Taylor not out | 3 | – (10) not out | 0 |
| B 11, l-b 5, n-b 9 | 25 | B 1, l-b 10, n-b 3 | 14 |

1/0 2/21 3/59 4/61 5/108            193     1/24 2/77 3/110 4/158     (8 wkts) 243
6/126 7/126 8/162 9/179                        5/182 6/210 7/221 8/242

Bonus points – Northamptonshire 1, Sussex 4.

Bowling: *First Innings*—Jones 12–3–36–3; Dodemaide 23–4–52–1; Salisbury 21–6–35–3; C. M. Wells 9–2–19–1; Donelan 19.3–8–35–2. *Second Innings*—Jones 4–0–19–0; Dodemaide 20–7–45–3; C. M. Wells 6–1–22–0; Donelan 26–0–80–2; Salisbury 15.5–0–66–3.

Umpires: R. Palmer and D. R. Shepherd.

## SUSSEX v NOTTINGHAMSHIRE

At Eastbourne, August 6, 7, 8. Drawn. Sussex 3 pts, Nottinghamshire 8 pts. Toss: Nottinghamshire. An imperious innings by Broad put Nottinghamshire in the driving seat, but Sussex battled bravely throughout the final day to deny their visitors a fifth Championship win in six games. Broad's fourth Championship hundred brought back memories of halcyon days at The Saffrons when the pitches were always considered a bowlers' graveyard. Batting for a shade under six hours he hit sixteen crisp boundaries, driving and pulling superbly, and in 62 overs with Robinson he added 192 for the second wicket. Sussex needed 254 to avoid the follow-on, but only Lenham, staying for four and a half hours, displayed the necessary application. The other batsmen showed far more resolution second time around. Smith took almost three hours for his 46, and a stand of 102 in 39 overs between Wells and Speight, whose patient 37 was somewhat out of character, was just what Sussex required. Nottinghamshire agreed to the draw with sixteen overs remaining.

*Close of play:* First day, Nottinghamshire 356-4 (P. Johnson 33*, K. P. Evans 22*); Second day, Sussex 239-9 (I. D. K. Salisbury 19*, A. N. Jones 7*).

## Nottinghamshire

| | | | |
|---|---|---|---|
| B. C. Broad c Salisbury b Dodemaide . .158 | †B. N. French c Moores b Dodemaide . | 10 |
| P. R. Pollard c Moores b Pigott . . . . . . . 13 | | |
| *R. T. Robinson b Jones . . . . . . . . . . . 95 | L-b 10, n-b 2 . . . . . . . . . . . . . . | 12 |
| D. W. Randall b Salisbury . . . . . . . . . 26 | | |
| P. Johnson b Dodemaide . . . . . . . . . . 52 | 1/34 2/226 3/269     (7 wkts dec.) 403 |
| K. P. Evans c Moores b Pigott . . . . . . 37 | 4/321 5/393 |
| F. D. Stephenson not out . . . . . . . . . . 0 | 6/393 7/403 |

E. E. Hemmings, R. A. Pick and J. A. Afford did not bat.

Bonus points – Nottinghamshire 4, Sussex 1 (Score at 100 overs: 335-4).

Bowling: Jones 13-2-32-1; Dodemaide 25-5-71-3; Pigott 24-5-66-2; Salisbury 32-1-118-1; Donelan 28-3-106-0.

## Sussex

| | | |
|---|---|---|
| N. J. Lenham c Robinson b Stephenson . . . . . . . 85 | – c Robinson b Afford . . . . . . . . . . . | 26 |
| D. M. Smith b Stephenson . . . . . . . . . . . . . . . . . . 10 | – c Randall b Afford . . . . . . . . . . . . . | 46 |
| *P. W. G. Parker b Hemmings . . . . . . . . . . . . . . . 24 | – c Randall b Afford . . . . . . . . . . . . . | 2 |
| A. P. Wells c Pollard b Hemmings . . . . . . . . . . 6 | – run out . . . . . . . . . . . . . . . . . . . . | 73 |
| M. P. Speight c French b Afford . . . . . . . . . . . . 10 | – not out . . . . . . . . . . . . . . . . . . . . | 37 |
| A. I. C. Dodemaide lbw b Afford . . . . . . . . . . . . 2 | – not out . . . . . . . . . . . . . . . . . . . . | 0 |
| †P. Moores c Pollard b Hemmings . . . . . . . . . . 12 | | |
| A. C. S. Pigott c and b Afford . . . . . . . . . . . . . . 12 | | |
| B. T. P. Donelan st French b Afford . . . . . . . . 32 | | |
| I. D. K. Salisbury not out . . . . . . . . . . . . . . . . . 19 | | |
| A. N. Jones c French b Stephenson . . . . . . . . . . 9 | | |
| B 7, l-b 9, n-b 4 . . . . . . . . . . . . . . . . . . . 20 | L-b 8, n-b 1 . . . . . . . . . . . . | 9 |

| | | |
|---|---|---|
| 1/24 2/86 3/96 4/111 5/121 | 241 | 1/58 2/66 3/91 4/193     (4 wkts) 193 |
| 6/134 7/147 8/193 9/212 | | |

Bonus points – Sussex 2, Nottinghamshire 4 (Score at 100 overs: 235-9).

Bowling: *First Innings*—Stephenson 16.3-5-26-3; Pick 6-1-20-0; Evans 8-2-22-0; Hemmings 35-12-88-3; Afford 37-15-69-4. *Second Innings*—Stephenson 11-0-29-0; Pick 6-2-17-0; Hemmings 34-10-77-0; Afford 35-17-50-3; Evans 7-2-12-0.

Umpires: R. Palmer and D. R. Shepherd.

At Middlesbrough, August 9, 10, 12. SUSSEX beat YORKSHIRE by an innings and 24 runs.

At Hove, August 17, 18, 19. SUSSEX drew with SRI LANKANS (See Sri Lankan tour section).

At Bournemouth, August 20, 21, 22. SUSSEX drew with HAMPSHIRE.

At The Oval, August 28, 29, 30. SUSSEX lost to SURREY by an innings and 128 runs.

## SUSSEX v KENT

At Hove, September 3, 4, 5, 6. Tied. Sussex 16 pts, Kent 14 pts. Toss: Kent. A magnificent match ended in a thrilling tie with four balls left after 1,578 runs had been scored. It was the second such result between these old rivals in seven years, there being a similar outcome to their game at Hastings in 1984. Sussex scored more than 400 runs in the fourth innings for the first time since 1935, and went into the final over with the scores level and their last pair at the wicket. The non-striker, Salisbury, was almost run out off Patel's first delivery, and Pigott edged the next ball to Cowdrey at slip to bring a memorable contest to a fitting conclusion. That Sussex came so close to victory was due to Parker's 111 and Alan Wells's 162, his seventh Championship century of the season, which included twenty fours and a six and was made in 196 balls. Parker's return to form gave Sussex the perfect start and brought the captain his only first-class hundred of the summer. However, Merrick, bowling superbly on a batsman's pitch, took three wickets in ten balls, including the Wells brothers, and Sussex lost their last seven wickets for 65 runs. The previous day, Kent's Taylor had followed up his first-innings century with a masterful, unbeaten 203, the second time in successive seasons he had completed this match double. He hit fourteen fours and a six in his first innings, sharing with Fleming (three sixes, nine fours) a fourth-wicket partnership of 138 in 26 overs. Taylor's range of strokes and superb timing were a delight, and he scored almost half his side's runs in the second innings, hitting 28 fours and a six in a shade over five and a half hours (267 balls). His seventh hundred of the season, it was also his fifth in seven Championship innings.

*Close of play:* First day, Sussex 19-1 (J. W. Hall 0*, B. T. P. Donelan 10*); Second day, Sussex 345-9 (A. I. C. Dodemaide 21*, A. N. Jones 2*); Third day, Sussex 34-0 (P. W. G. Parker 18*, J. W. Hall 13*).

### Kent

| | | | |
|---|---|---|---|
| T. R. Ward c Greenfield b Salisbury | 51 | – c Donelan b Dodemaide | 38 |
| *M. R. Benson c Moores b Dodemaide | 48 | – c Moores b Dodemaide | 5 |
| N. R. Taylor lbw b Dodemaide | 111 | – not out | 203 |
| G. R. Cowdrey c Greenfield b Dodemaide | 4 | – run out | 78 |
| M. V. Fleming c Hall b Pigott | 69 | – c Pigott b Salisbury | 20 |
| †S. A. Marsh c Greenfield b Salisbury | 19 | – lbw b Dodemaide | 0 |
| M. A. Ealham st Moores b Donelan | 26 | – b Dodemaide | 0 |
| R. M. Ellison not out | 17 | – c Moores b Salisbury | 1 |
| R. P. Davis lbw b Salisbury | 0 | – not out | 29 |
| T. A. Merrick c Greenfield b Salisbury | 6 | | |
| M. M. Patel lbw b Pigott | 8 | | |
| B 2, l-b 6, w 1, n-b 13 | 22 | B 4, l-b 16, w 3, n-b 11 | 34 |

1/91 2/123 3/139 4/277 5/309          381          1/30 2/53 3/259    (7 wkts dec.) 408
6/321 7/348 8/349 9/356                            4/288 5/309
                                                   6/309 7/310

Bonus points – Kent 4, Sussex 4 (Score at 100 overs: 380-9).

Bowling: *First Innings*—Jones 9-0-57-0; Dodemaide 24-4-64-3; Pigott 14.4-0-56-2; C. M. Wells 12-3-43-0; Donelan 14-3-52-1; Salisbury 27-6-101-4. *Second Innings*—Dodemaide 22-3-87-4; Jones 10-1-64-0; Salisbury 21-3-102-2; Pigott 13-3-44-0; C. M. Wells 7-1-30-0; Donelan 21-4-61-0.

### Sussex

| | | | |
|---|---|---|---|
| †P. Moores b Merrick | 8 | – (7) lbw b Merrick | 0 |
| J. W. Hall c Cowdrey b Ealham | 41 | – b Merrick | 52 |
| B. T. P. Donelan b Davis | 61 | – (9) run out | 2 |
| K. Greenfield c Davis b Ealham | 22 | – (3) c Cowdrey b Merrick | 0 |
| A. P. Wells c Fleming b Patel | 74 | – (4) b Merrick | 162 |
| *P. W. G. Parker c Marsh b Ealham | 2 | – (1) lbw b Merrick | 111 |
| C. M. Wells b Merrick | 76 | – (5) lbw b Merrick | 34 |
| A. I. C. Dodemaide not out | 23 | – (6) c Benson b Patel | 25 |
| A. C. S. Pigott b Ealham | 5 | – (8) c Cowdrey b Patel | 26 |
| I. D. K. Salisbury b Ealham | 0 | – (11) not out | 1 |
| A. N. Jones b Ellison | 8 | – (10) b Merrick | 1 |
| B 6, l-b 5, w 6, n-b 16 | 33 | L-b 12, w 1, n-b 9 | 22 |

1/8 2/103 3/143 4/157 5/165          353          1/146 2/146 3/254 4/371 5/378          436
6/255 7/331 8/340 9/342                            6/378 7/428 8/430 9/434

Bonus points – Sussex 4, Kent 2 (Score at 100 overs: 310-6).

Bowling: *First Innings*—Merrick 24–8–81–2; Ellison 22.5–8–68–1; Fleming 15–3–51–0; Davis 25–5–72–1; Ealham 21–6–39–5; Patel 10–2–31–1. *Second Innings*—Merrick 27–1–99–7; Ellison 15–0–59–0; Patel 23.2–3–68–2; Ealham 16–1–80–0; Davis 32–5–109–0; Fleming 2–0–9–0.

Umpires: M. J. Kitchen and R. A. White.

## SUSSEX v GLOUCESTERSHIRE

At Hove, September 17, 18, 19, 20. Sussex won by 139 runs. Sussex 21 pts, Gloucestershire 4 pts. Toss: Sussex. Sussex ended the season with a resounding victory, and it was appropriate that Dodemaide, in his last match for the county, made the decisive breakthrough. Gloucestershire had been asked to score 314 in a minimum of 72 overs, and their last-wicket pair, Wright and Babington, the former Sussex bowler, had only four overs to negotiate when Parker, also making his farewell appearance, tossed the ball to Dodemaide. The Australian all-rounder promptly induced Babington to fend a rising delivery into the slips. Although Dodemaide took this crucial last wicket, it was off-spinner Donelan, with a career-best six for 62, who put Gloucestershire on the slide to their fifth successive Championship defeat. As in the previous match Donelan also proved his worth with the bat, adding 52 for the ninth wicket with Salisbury in the second innings to enable Parker to make a challenging declaration. Batting was often a difficult proposition, and in the first innings Sussex were grateful to Dodemaide, whose 72 came off 221 balls, Colin Wells, Greenfield and Moores. Athey, with an obdurate 103 off 350 balls in 405 minutes, carried his bat for the second innings in succession and held Gloucestershire's reply together. But he was dismissed cheaply in their second innings, and after that only Wright did anything to halt Sussex's victory march.

*Close of play:* First day, Sussex 315-7 (P. Moores 51*); Second day, Gloucestershire 158-5 (C. W. J. Athey 60*, T. H. C. Hancock 18*); Third day, Sussex 142-5 (A. I. C. Dodemaide 14*, P. Moores 36*).

## Sussex

| | | | |
|---|---|---|---|
| *P. W. G. Parker c Lloyds b Babington | 3 | – b Lloyds | 24 |
| J. W. Hall lbw b Babington | 25 | – c Wright b Lloyds | 17 |
| K. Greenfield b Scott | 64 | – c Lloyds b Gilbert | 13 |
| A. P. Wells lbw b Scott | 7 | – c Lloyds b Gilbert | 1 |
| C. M. Wells b Alleyne | 64 | – c Russell b Lloyds | 25 |
| A. I. C. Dodemaide lbw b Gilbert | 72 | – b Scott | 22 |
| †P. Moores lbw b Scott | 69 | – b Scott | 51 |
| B. T. P. Donelan c and b Lawrence | 9 | – not out | 30 |
| A. C. S. Pigott c Lloyds b Alleyne | 30 | – c Lawrence b Scott | 0 |
| I. D. K. Salisbury not out | 0 | – not out | 31 |
| A. N. Jones c sub b Alleyne | 1 | | |
| L-b 15, w 1, n-b 11 | 27 | B 3, l-b 7, n-b 5 | 15 |

1/6 2/94 3/104 4/104 5/218  
6/287 7/315 8/370 9/370     **371**     1/40 2/53 3/58     (8 wkts dec.) **229**  
4/79 5/91 6/162  
7/173 8/177

Bonus points – Sussex 3, Gloucestershire 2 (Score at 100 overs: 276-5).

Bowling: *First Innings*—Lawrence 11–1–44–1; Babington 22–0–83–2; Gilbert 32–8–73–1; Lloyds 22–5–60–0; Scott 25–8–51–3; Alleyne 23.2–8–45–3. *Second Innings*—Gilbert 17–6–37–2; Babington 15–6–41–0; Lloyds 33–8–98–3; Scott 15–5–43–3.

## Gloucestershire

| | | | | |
|---|---|---|---|---|
| G. D. Hodgson b Jones | 3 | – b Donelan | 16 |
| C. W. J. Athey not out | 103 | – c Moores b Dodemaide | 12 |
| *A. J. Wright b C. M. Wells | 31 | – not out | 68 |
| R. J. Scott b Donelan | 8 | – c Parker b Salisbury | 11 |
| M. W. Alleyne c Hall b Donelan | 0 | – b Donelan | 12 |
| J. W. Lloyds b Donelan | 4 | – c Greenfield b Donelan | 0 |
| T. H. C. Hancock b C. M. Wells | 51 | – c Moores b Salisbury | 3 |
| †R. C. Russell c Greenfield b Donelan | 11 | – b Donelan | 1 |
| D. V. Lawrence b Jones | 22 | – b Donelan | 8 |
| D. R. Gilbert lbw b Jones | 0 | – b Donelan | 8 |
| A. M. Babington b Dodemaide | 2 | – c Pigott b Dodemaide | 11 |
| B 9, l-b 8, w 1, n-b 34 | 52 | B 4, l-b 7, n-b 13 | 24 |

1/5 2/85 3/96 4/96 5/112        287     1/30 2/31 3/65 4/88 5/88     174
6/218 7/241 8/278 9/278                 6/100 7/101 8/118 9/143

Bonus points – Gloucestershire 2, Sussex 2 (Score at 100 overs: 229-6).

Bowling: *First Innings*—Jones 19-1-68-3; Dodemaide 18.5-4-34-1; Pigott 4-2-7-0; C. M. Wells 22-8-37-2; Donelan 30-8-74-4; Salisbury 24-8-50-0. *Second Innings*—Jones 12-5-22-0; Dodemaide 13.2-5-17-2; Donelan 27-13-62-6; Salisbury 24-4-62-2.

Umpires: J. H. Harris and M. J. Kitchen.

---

## UMPIRES FOR 1992

### FIRST-CLASS UMPIRES

V. A. Holder and G. I. Stickley have been promoted from the Reserve list of umpires to the first-class list for 1992, where they will be joined by G. Sharp, the former Northamptonshire wicket-keeper. Another former Northamptonshire player, P. Willey, who retired in 1991 after eight seasons with Leicestershire, joined the Reserve list, along with P. Adams, from the Minor Counties list, and A. Clarkson, the former Yorkshire and Somerset batsman. B. Hassan and K. J. Lyons, who were on the first-class list in 1991, have taken up positions at Nottinghamshire and Worcestershire respectively. The full list is: J. C. Balderstone, H. D. Bird, J. D. Bond, G. I. Burgess, D. J. Constant, B. Dudleston, J. H. Hampshire, J. H. Harris, J. W. Holder, V. A. Holder, A. A. Jones, R. Julian, M. J. Kitchen, B. Leadbeater, B. J. Meyer, D. O. Oslear, K. E. Palmer, R. Palmer, N. T. Plews, G. Sharp, D. R. Shepherd, G. I. Stickley, R. C. Tolchard, R. A. White, A. G. T. Whitehead and P. B. Wight. *Reserves*: P. Adams, A. Clarkson, Dr D. Fawkner-Corbett, M. J. Harris and P. Willey.

*Note*: The panel of umpires for the Test matches and one-day internationals was not available at the time *Wisden* went to press.

### MINOR COUNTIES UMPIRES

P. Adams, N. P. Atkins, R. Bell, K. Bray, P. Brown, R. K. Curtis, J. B. Foulkes, P. Gray, D. J. Halfyard, R. F. Harriott, M. A. Johnson, B. Knight, S. W. Kuhlmann, G. I. McLean, T. G. A. Morley, D. Norton, M. K. Reed, K. S. Shenton, C. Smith, C. T. Spencer, J. Stobart, D. S. Thompsett, R. Walker, T. V. Wilkins and T. G. Wilson. *Reserves*: D. L. Burden, K. Coburn, H. Cohen, H. W. Cook, R. M. Davison, R. F. Elliott, A. G. Forster, K. Hopley, M. P. Moran, W. Morgan, B. J. Orton, C. T. Puckett, G. B. Smith, J. M. Tythcott, J. Waite, T. J. White, B. H. Willey and R. Wood.

# WARWICKSHIRE

*President:* The Earl of Aylesford
*Chairman:* M. J. K. Smith
*Chairman, Cricket Committee:* D. L. Amiss
*Secretary:* D. M. W. Heath
 County Ground, Edgbaston,
 Birmingham B5 7QU
 (Telephone: 021-446 4422)
*Captain:* T. A. Lloyd
*Director of Coaching:* R. A. Woolmer

Warwickshire ended one of their most successful campaigns in 87 Championship seasons as runners-up for the third time. Nevertheless Andy Lloyd and his players were disappointed that, after leading the table from May 28 to August 26, and winning as many games as champions Essex, they were still thirteen points adrift. Their eleven wins would have won five Championships out of the previous six. However, although Warwickshire finished in style with successive wins at home over Worcestershire and Northamptonshire, and away at Taunton, their earlier loss of momentum in August had proved fatal to their hopes of winning a fourth Championship title.

It says much for the spirit of the side, and Lloyd's leadership, that they pushed Essex's stronger all-round squad to the last match. Warwickshire could also be proud that, in ten of their wins, they dismissed their opponents twice. In the other, when rain forced a declaration and a forfeited innings at Coventry, they bowled Sussex out on the final day. None of their victories, therefore, depended on the other side declaring and setting a target, and there could be little doubt that, in Allan Donald, Tim Munton, Gladstone Small and Dermot Reeve, they possessed the strongest fast-bowling attack in English cricket. None the less Warwickshire's success was not, as some would have it, built on over-helpful pitches at Edgbaston, even if the under-prepared strip for the penultimate home game against Worcestershire, when 32 wickets fell on the first two days, prompted much criticism. Five of their wins were in Birmingham, and one at Coventry, but the others were away from home at Leeds, Swansea, Portsmouth, Leicester and Taunton.

The season was a personal triumph for Donald and Lloyd, after both had featured in the storm which bedevilled the club during the winter. Some members had been highly critical of Lloyd, and of the committee's decision to retain Donald as their overseas player at the expense of the Australian batsman, Tom Moody. The South African responded with the best fast bowling of his career in the first part of the season. Of the regular county bowlers, only he and Surrey's Waqar Younis secured their wickets at under 20 runs apiece, and his 83 wickets at a strike-rate of one every 37.77 balls suggested that he would have been an automatic selection for any Test country, even West Indies. Munton bowled 662 overs in the Championship, as well as almost 200 in one-day games, and he was unlucky not to be selected for the Edgbaston Test, where conditions would have suited him so well. After an indifferent start, Small bowled somewhere near his best in the second half of the season.

The spin department was almost irrelevant, bowling well under 500 overs for 32 wickets in all Championship matches. A quarter of these came in the final game at Taunton, where Lloyd was saved by only 6 runs from paying the penalty for breaking up the four-man pace unit which had maintained the title challenge, omitting Small and playing both Paul Booth and Neil Smith. Their combined match figures of eight for 296, with Somerset reaching 403 on the final day, hardly justified the experiment.

Any top side needs at least one all-rounder, and Reeve's contribution, maximising every bit of his considerable talent, cannot be overstated. A medium-pace bowler of great variety, astutely mixing out-swing with cut and an excellent slower delivery, he took his 45 wickets at 21.26 each, an average bettered among regular Championship bowlers only by Waqar Younis and Donald. As for his batting, not only were his 1,260 runs scored at an average of 48.46, but he had the invaluable ability to organise the lower-middle and lower orders. His talent for improvising and his determination never to let things drift turned him into one of the most effective all-rounders in county cricket.

In a batting order that managed only four hundreds all season, but 63 more fifties, none impressed more than Dominic Ostler and Jason Ratcliffe. The leading run-scorer, Ostler was deservedly awarded his county cap after a splendid, disciplined innings helped Warwickshire beat Worcestershire, and his 1,284 runs at 36.68 underlined the astuteness of Lloyd's decision to promote this hard-hitting bat to No. 4. His only weakness was a tendency to play too much "inside to out" towards the off side. Ratcliffe played several important innings, notably at Portsmouth, and reached fifty eight times. Andy Moles was less productive than in 1990, but made a good number of solid contributions, while Lloyd scored rapidly at No. 3, with no consideration but the best interests of his side. Asif Din – despite scoring two of the county's hundreds – and Paul Smith, who was affected by serious injuries, had disappointing seasons. Keith Piper made considerable progress behind the stumps, and his batting average of 17.45 did him scant justice. His fighting qualities with the bat played a crucial part in the hard-fought wins over Hampshire at Portsmouth, after a painful blow to his thumb, and Northamptonshire.

The players were better organised in limited-overs cricket than the previous year, a tribute to the new director of coaching, Bob Woolmer. Warwickshire finished fifth in the Refuge Assurance League, two points behind Worcestershire, who tied their game at Edgbaston thanks to Piper's misapprehension that his side had won on fewer wickets lost. In the NatWest Bank Trophy, they swept to the semi-final with home wins over Yorkshire, Hertfordshire and Somerset, only to lose – again at Edgbaston – by an embarrassing margin of nine wickets to Hampshire. Batting failures cost them that match, as they had the Benson and Hedges quarter-final against Yorkshire at Headingley.

Following a winter of discontent, the newly elected club chairman, M. J. K. Smith, and Dennis Amiss, chairman of cricket, could look back with satisfaction on a season which restored harmony off the field, and signalled that Warwickshire were genuine contenders for honours on it. – Jack Bannister.

WARWICKSHIRE 1991

[*Roger Wootton*

*Back row*: K. J. Piper, R. G. Twose, G. Smith, T. L. Penney, G. M. Charlesworth, S. J. Green, M. Burns, O. S. Chagar, G. Welch, I. G. S. Steer.
*Middle row*: S. J. Nottingham (*physiotherapist*), S. J. Rouse (*assistant coach*), J. E. Benjamin, D. P. Ostler, Wasim Khan, A. R. K. Pierson,
T. A. Munton, J. D. Ratcliffe, B. C. Usher, N. M. K. Smith, P. A. Booth, D. M. W. Heath (*secretary*). *Front row*: R. N. Abberley (*coach*),
G. C. Small, A. J. Moles, R. A. Woolmer (*director of coaching*), T. A. Lloyd (*captain*), M. J. K. Smith (*chairman*), D. A. Reeve, Asif Din,
P. A. Smith, A. A. Donald. *Inset*: P. C. L. Holloway.

## WARWICKSHIRE RESULTS

*All first-class matches – Played 22; Won 11, Lost 4, Drawn 7.*

*County Championship matches – Played 22; Won 11, Lost 4, Drawn 7.*

*Bonus points – Batting 58, Bowling 65.*

*Competition placings – Britannic Assurance County Championship, 2nd;
NatWest Bank Trophy, s-f; Benson and Hedges Cup, q-f;
Refuge Assurance League, 5th.*

## BRITANNIC ASSURANCE CHAMPIONSHIP AVERAGES

### BATTING

|  | Birthplace | M | I | NO | R | HI | Avge |
|---|---|---|---|---|---|---|---|
| P. C. L. Holloway .. | *Helston* | 6 | 9 | 5 | 263 | 89* | 65.75 |
| ‡D. A. Reeve ...... | *Kowloon, Hong Kong* | 20 | 33 | 7 | 1,260 | 99* | 48.46 |
| ‡D. P. Ostler....... | *Solihull* | 22 | 40 | 5 | 1,284 | 120* | 36.68 |
| ‡A. J. Moles ....... | *Solihull* | 22 | 39 | 2 | 1,246 | 133 | 33.67 |
| ‡T. A. Lloyd ....... | *Oswestry* | 21 | 35 | 2 | 1,076 | 97 | 32.60 |
| J. D. Ratcliffe .... | *Solihull* | 17 | 31 | 1 | 953 | 94 | 31.76 |
| N. M. K. Smith ... | *Birmingham* | 5 | 9 | 2 | 209 | 70 | 29.85 |
| A. R. K. Pierson ... | *Enfield* | 5 | 6 | 4 | 55 | 35 | 27.50 |
| ‡Asif Din........ | *Kampala, Uganda* | 15 | 27 | 1 | 685 | 140 | 26.34 |
| ‡P. A. Smith........ | *Jesmond* | 14 | 23 | 1 | 411 | 68 | 18.68 |
| K. J. Piper ....... | *Leicester* | 16 | 23 | 3 | 349 | 55 | 17.45 |
| ‡G. C. Small ....... | *St George, Barbados* | 20 | 29 | 7 | 370 | 58 | 16.81 |
| P. A. Booth....... | *Huddersfield* | 10 | 13 | 0 | 175 | 62 | 13.46 |
| ‡T. A. Munton ..... | *Melton Mowbray* | 22 | 24 | 7 | 226 | 31 | 13.29 |
| ‡A. A. Donald ..... | *Bloemfontein, SA* | 21 | 21 | 9 | 96 | 18 | 8.00 |
| J. E. Benjamin ..... | *Christ Church, St Kitts* | 3 | 4 | 0 | 12 | 11 | 3.00 |

Also batted: S. J. Green (*Bloxwich*) (1 match) 77*; R. G. Twose (*Torquay*) (2 matches) 41, 1*.

* *Signifies not out.*   ‡ *Denotes county cap.*

The following played a total of four three-figure innings for Warwickshire in County Championship matches – Asif Din 2, A. J. Moles 1, D. P. Ostler 1.

### BOWLING

|  | O | M | R | W | BB | 5W/i | Avge |
|---|---|---|---|---|---|---|---|
| A. A. Donald......... | 522.3 | 91 | 1,634 | 83 | 6-69 | 8 | 19.68 |
| D. A. Reeve.......... | 402.1 | 117 | 957 | 45 | 6-73 | 1 | 21.26 |
| T. A. Munton ....... | 662 | 177 | 1,795 | 71 | 8-89 | 5 | 25.28 |
| G. C. Small ......... | 498 | 126 | 1,347 | 45 | 4-36 | 0 | 29.93 |
| P. A. Smith ......... | 157.1 | 31 | 513 | 15 | 5-28 | 1 | 34.20 |
| P. A. Booth .......... | 226.1 | 47 | 690 | 18 | 4-103 | 0 | 38.33 |

Also bowled: Asif Din 53–9–206–2; J. E. Benjamin 76.4–11–257–7; T. A. Lloyd 16–13–26–0; A. J. Moles 33–13–65–1; D. P. Ostler 2–1–7–0; A. R. K. Pierson 73–11–279–4; J. D. Ratcliffe 3–1–14–0; N. M. K. Smith 111–32–321–8; R. G. Twose 9–0–27–1.

**Wicket-keepers:** K. J. Piper 48 ct; P. C. L. Holloway 9 ct; Asif Din 2 ct.

**Leading Fielders:** D. P. Ostler 20, J. D. Ratcliffe 15.

## WARWICKSHIRE v LANCASHIRE

At Birmingham, April 27, 29, 30, May 1. Drawn. Warwickshire 2 pts, Lancashire 7 pts. Toss: Lancashire. With fourteen and a half hours lost to the weather, including all of the second day, there was little chance of anything being at stake other than bonus points. There were 48 overs on the third day and just 18.1 on the fourth. Lancashire's innings was given a platform by Mendis and took off when Fairbrother came to the wicket. Whereas Mendis took 232 deliveries for his 113 (thirteen fours), Fairbrother's 121 required only 129. He hit a six and 22 other boundaries, including four in succession off Munton, and such was the left-hander's dominance after tea that Speak contributed no more than 18 runs to their century partnership in sixteen overs for the fourth wicket. After this display, Warwickshire's reply was disappointing, even allowing for the unpleasant conditions.

*Close of play:* First day, Lancashire 377-5 (N. J. Speak 37*); Second day, No play; Third day, Warwickshire 123-3 (P. A. Smith 27*, D. A. Reeve 0*).

### Lancashire

| | | | | |
|---|---|---|---|---|
| G. D. Mendis lbw b Smith | 113 | M. Watkinson b Small | | 30 |
| G. Fowler c Moles b Small | 35 | B 13, l-b 11, w 1, n-b 6 | | 31 |
| M. A. Atherton c Ostler b Moles | 10 | | | |
| *N. H. Fairbrother c Small b Reeve | 121 | 1/111 2/150 3/224 | (5 wkts dec.) | 377 |
| N. J. Speak not out | 37 | 4/324 5/377 | | |

Wasim Akram, P. A. J. DeFreitas, †W. K. Hegg, G. Yates and P. J. W. Allott did not bat.

Bonus points – Lancashire 4, Warwickshire 1 (Score at 100 overs: 340-4).

Bowling: Donald 17–2–58–0; Small 21–5–67–2; Munton 20–3–83–0; Reeve 19–6–42–1; Pierson 15–5–49–0; Moles 8–2–14–1; Smith 10–1–40–1.

### Warwickshire

| | | | | |
|---|---|---|---|---|
| A. J. Moles c Fairbrother b Yates | 51 | G. C. Small b Speak | | 2 |
| Asif Din c Hegg b Allott | 15 | | | |
| *T. A. Lloyd c Wasim Akram b Yates | 19 | B 3, l-b 11, w 1, n-b 5 | | 20 |
| P. A. Smith c and b Wasim Akram | 27 | | | |
| D. A. Reeve not out | 20 | 1/25 2/62 3/119 | (7 wkts) | 169 |
| D. P. Ostler b Yates | 9 | 4/123 5/148 | | |
| †K. J. Piper lbw b DeFreitas | 6 | 6/165 7/169 | | |

A. R. K. Pierson, A. A. Donald and T. A. Munton did not bat.

Bonus points – Warwickshire 1, Lancashire 3.

Bowling: Wasim Akram 14–3–33–1; DeFreitas 22–8–45–1; Allott 8–1–30–1; Yates 22–6–47–3; Speak 0.1–0–0–1.

Umpires: J. H. Hampshire and B. Leadbeater.

At Leeds, May 9, 10, 11, 13. **WARWICKSHIRE** beat **YORKSHIRE** by 30 runs.

At Swansea, May 16, 17, 18, 20. **WARWICKSHIRE** beat **GLAMORGAN** by six wickets.

At Chelmsford, May 22, 23, 24. **WARWICKSHIRE** lost to **ESSEX** by nine wickets.

## WARWICKSHIRE v GLOUCESTERSHIRE

At Birmingham, May 25, 27. Warwickshire won by nine wickets. Warwickshire 24 pts, Gloucestershire 4 pts. Toss: Gloucestershire. The first-ball dismissal of Asif Din hardly seemed propitious for Warwickshire, yet by the end of the second day they had taken maximum points from a convincing win. Gloucestershire, having inserted the home team on a slow, seaming pitch, had every reason to rue the lives given to Moles and Lloyd in the first hour. They put on 82 for the second wicket, and Moles went on to register Warwickshire's first Championship hundred of the season, batting for almost five and a half hours and hitting fifteen fours in his 133 (300 balls). Gloucestershire struck back late in the day by dismissing the last five batsmen for 12 runs in 22 balls, but this collapse was eclipsed by their own batting on the Monday. Eighteen wickets fell in 97 overs. Smith and Small did the damage in the first innings, but after Donald had undone the second innings with five wickets in fifteen balls, Athey counter-attacked marvellously, hitting two sixes and twenty fours in 120 from 172 balls. He and Smith added 104 for the ninth wicket before Warwickshire's Smith came back to earn himself career-best match figures of nine for 56.

*Close of play:* First day, Gloucestershire 18-2 (G. D. Hodgson 2*, A. J. Wright 4*).

## Warwickshire

| | | |
|---|---|---|
| A. J. Moles b Alleyne | 133 – (2) not out | 2 |
| Asif Din b Babington | 0 – (1) b Smith | 4 |
| *T. A. Lloyd c Williams b Smith | 38 | |
| P. A. Smith lbw b Smith | 1 | |
| D. P. Ostler b Smith | 42 – (3) not out | 6 |
| R. G. Twose c Alleyne b Lloyds | 41 | |
| †K. J. Piper b Athey | 29 | |
| P. A. Booth run out | 4 | |
| G. C. Small c and b Alleyne | 3 | |
| T. A. Munton c Scott b Alleyne | 3 | |
| A. A. Donald not out | 2 | |
| B 1, l-b 16, w 2, n-b 3 | 22　　　L-b 3, n-b 2 | 5 |

1/0 2/82 3/92 4/171 5/250　　　　　　318　1/6　　　　　　(1 wkt) 17
6/306 7/310 8/313 9/313

Bonus points – Warwickshire 4, Gloucestershire 4.

Bowling: *First Innings*—Gilbert 19-5-64-0; Babington 18-4-47-1; Smith 27-5-71-3; Athey 9-0-29-1; Lloyds 15-0-55-1; Alleyne 9.2-1-35-3. *Second Innings*—Babington 4-0-11-0; Smith 3.4-1-3-1.

## Gloucestershire

| | | |
|---|---|---|
| G. D. Hodgson c Donald b Smith | 27 – c Piper b Donald | 16 |
| R. J. Scott c Booth b Small | 0 – lbw b Smith | 0 |
| †R. C. J. Williams c Munton b Small | 8 – (8) b Donald | 0 |
| *A. J. Wright b Munton | 24 – (3) c Piper b Smith | 2 |
| C. W. J. Athey c Piper b Donald | 6 – (4) c Piper b Smith | 120 |
| M. W. Alleyne c Piper b Small | 23 – (5) c Piper b Donald | 0 |
| J. J. E. Hardy lbw b Smith | 0 – (6) lbw b Donald | 0 |
| J. W. Lloyds not out | 22 – (7) lbw b Donald | 0 |
| D. R. Gilbert c Asif Din b Smith | 7 – c Booth b Munton | 19 |
| A. M. Smith c Piper b Smith | 0 – lbw b Smith | 22 |
| A. M. Babington c Lloyd b Smith | 8 – not out | 1 |
| L-b 7, n-b 2 | 9　　　L-b 16, n-b 4 | 20 |

1/4 2/12 3/64 4/66 5/85　　　　　　134　1/4 2/8 3/47 4/49 5/49　　　　200
6/96 7/96 8/121 9/122　　　　　　　　　6/50 7/50 8/75 9/179

Bonus points – Warwickshire 4.

Bowling: *First Innings*—Donald 13-6-27-1; Small 15-5-46-3; Smith 12.4-3-28-5; Munton 10-3-25-1; Lloyd 2-2-0-0; Booth 2-1-1-0. *Second Innings*—Small 10-2-34-0; Smith 8.3-2-28-4; Donald 10-3-33-5; Munton 14-3-51-1; Booth 9-0-38-0.

Umpires: J. C. Balderstone and B. Dudleston.

## WARWICKSHIRE v YORKSHIRE

At Birmingham, May 31, June 1, 3. Warwickshire won by 39 runs. Warwickshire 24 pts, Yorkshire 5 pts. Toss: Yorkshire. Warwickshire strengthened their position at the top of the Championship table with their fourth win of the season, and their second over Yorkshire in three weeks. Reeve's unbeaten 99, off 160 deliveries, featured a six and eleven fours, and his ninth-wicket partnership of 97 with Munton gave his side an advantage which was reinforced over the next two days by penetrative fast bowling and inspirational catching. Donald's first-ball dismissal cost Reeve the chance of a century, but the South African fast bowler showed his true value on the second day when, with four wickets in thirteen balls, he fired out the Yorkshire lower order. By the close, Moles and Ratcliffe had extended Warwickshire's lead to 251 with sure strokeplay against some indifferent bowling, and Lloyd's declaration on Monday left Yorkshire to score 308 from 87 overs, subsequently reduced by rain to 78 overs. Munton, unable to bowl in the first innings because of injury, returned after a weekend's rest to claim match-winning figures of six for 53 with a splendid display of sustained seam and swing bowling. Robinson's 93 off 121 deliveries (one six, twelve fours) kept his side in the game, and at the end Hartley resumed with an injured hand in an attempt to force a draw. But it was to no avail; Warwickshire won with 21 balls to spare.

*Close of play:* First day, Warwickshire 354; Second day, Warwickshire 114-0 (A. J. Moles 60*, J. D. Ratcliffe 43*).

## Warwickshire

| | | | | |
|---|---|---|---|---|
| A. J. Moles b Fletcher | 17 | – b Carrick | | 73 |
| J. D. Ratcliffe c Byas b M. A. Robinson | 68 | – c P. E. Robinson b Carrick | | 44 |
| *T. A. Lloyd c Byas b Fletcher | 2 | – not out | | 13 |
| D. P. Ostler c Blakey b Fletcher | 77 | – c Metcalfe b Carrick | | 7 |
| P. A. Smith c Byas b Gough | 11 | – not out | | 9 |
| D. A. Reeve not out | 99 | | | |
| †K. J. Piper c Kellett b Fletcher | 19 | | | |
| P. A. Booth b Hartley | 7 | | | |
| G. C. Small lbw b Hartley | 0 | | | |
| T. A. Munton b Fletcher | 28 | | | |
| A. A. Donald b Fletcher | 0 | | | |
| B 4, l-b 14, w 2, n-b 6 | 26 | B 4, l-b 12, w 2, n-b 6 | | 24 |

1/37 2/48 3/132 4/178 5/199     354     1/118 2/139 3/147   (3 wkts dec.) 170
6/237 7/257 8/257 9/354

Bonus points – Warwickshire 4, Yorkshire 3 (Score at 100 overs: 309-8).

Bowling: *First Innings*—Hartley 23–3–82–2; M. A. Robinson 28–6–70–1; Fletcher 27–6–70–6; Gough 20–3–85–1; Carrick 9–2–22–0; Byas 2–0–7–0. *Second Innings*—Hartley 9–1–36–0; M. A. Robinson 9–0–35–0; Fletcher 4–0–27–0; Gough 6–1–24–0; Carrick 10–1–32–3.

## Yorkshire

| | | | | |
|---|---|---|---|---|
| *M. D. Moxon c Moles b Booth | 37 | – c Ratcliffe b Munton | | 27 |
| A. A. Metcalfe c Donald b Booth | 44 | – c Piper b Munton | | 26 |
| D. Byas c Small b Reeve | 33 | – b Donald | | 49 |
| †R. J. Blakey c Reeve b Smith | 5 | – b Munton | | 0 |
| P. E. Robinson b Small | 16 | – c Moles b Munton | | 93 |
| S. A. Kellett c Piper b Donald | 30 | – c Ratcliffe b Reeve | | 0 |
| P. Carrick b Small | 0 | – c Small b Smith | | 8 |
| D. Gough b Donald | 24 | – c Booth b Munton | | 25 |
| P. J. Hartley c Piper b Donald | 0 | – not out | | 14 |
| S. D. Fletcher not out | 4 | – c Ratcliffe b Donald | | 8 |
| M. A. Robinson b Donald | 0 | – c Donald b Munton | | 0 |
| B 6, l-b 14, w 2, n-b 2 | 24 | L-b 14, n-b 4 | | 18 |

1/89 2/94 3/111 4/141 5/150     217     1/47 2/74 3/74 4/160 5/165    268
6/150 7/201 8/201 9/217            6/179 7/236 8/257 9/260

Bonus points – Yorkshire 2, Warwickshire 4.

*In the second innings P. J. Hartley, when 14, retired hurt at 259 and resumed at 260.*

Bowling: *First Innings*—Donald 12.3–4–28–4; Small 19–8–34–2; Smith 13–6–29–1; Reeve 17–5–44–1; Booth 19–5–62–2. *Second Innings*—Donald 13.3–3–47–2; Small 12–2–33–0; Munton 21–3–53–6; Booth 12–0–62–0; Smith 9–0–37–1; Reeve 7–1–22–1.

Umpires: J. H. Hampshire and A. A. Jones.

At Tunbridge Wells, June 4, 5, 6. WARWICKSHIRE drew with KENT.

## WARWICKSHIRE v SOMERSET

At Birmingham, June 7, 8, 10. Drawn. Warwickshire 5 pts, Somerset 3 pts. Toss: Somerset. Bad light at the start, and some six hours of rain on the second and third days, conspired against the attempts of the players to achieve a result. The most telling loss was that of almost two hours after Somerset had been set a target of 271 from a minimum of 69 overs. Even so, there was no excuse for the travesty of cricket which occurred in the final stages. As Warwickshire used Lloyd and Moles to improve their over-rate, Somerset's response was just four scoring strokes from their 24 overs. Earlier in the day Lloyd had confirmed his return to form with his second half-century of the match, from 40 deliveries. In the first innings there were also half-centuries from Ostler, Reeve (123 balls) and Green, with the last two adding 152 in 29 overs for the fifth wicket. Green, in his first Championship match for two years, hit two sixes and ten fours in his unbeaten 77 from 77 deliveries, his maiden first-class fifty. In Somerset's reply, Donald gave Roebuck a torrid time early on before retiring with torn stomach muscles, but after Cook and Roebuck had given their side an accomplished start, the weather dictated the course the game would take.

*Close of play:* First day, Warwickshire 359-5 (S. J. Green 77*, R. G. Twose 1*); Second day, Somerset 182-2 (S. J. Cook 80*, R. J. Harden 10*).

### Warwickshire

| | | | |
|---|---|---|---|
| A. J. Moles c Burns b MacLeay | 16 | – c Harden b Mallender | 16 |
| J. D. Ratcliffe c Bartlett b Hayhurst | 29 | – c Burns b Lefebvre | 0 |
| *T. A. Lloyd c Hayhurst b Graveney | 62 | – not out | 53 |
| D. P. Ostler c Burns b Graveney | 59 | – b MacLeay | 40 |
| D. A. Reeve c MacLeay b Graveney | 82 | – not out | 9 |
| S. J. Green not out | 77 | | |
| R. G. Twose not out | 1 | | |
| B 10, l-b 15, w 6, n-b 2 | 33 | L-b 7, n-b 2 | 9 |

1/41 2/59 3/172 4/205 5/357  (5 wkts dec.) 359  1/5 2/26 3/116  (3 wkts dec.) 121

†K. J. Piper, G. C. Small, T. A. Munton and A. A. Donald did not bat.

Bonus points – Warwickshire 4, Somerset 1 (Score at 100 overs: 316-4).

Bowling: *First Innings*—Mallender 16–4–29–0; Lefebvre 26–5–57–0; MacLeay 27–3–67–1; Hayhurst 14–3–67–1; Graveney 23–1–114–3. *Second Innings*—Mallender 6–0–40–1; Lefebvre 4–0–26–1; Hayhurst 5–0–26–0; MacLeay 3–0–22–1.

### Somerset

| | | | |
|---|---|---|---|
| S. J. Cook not out | 94 | – run out | 8 |
| P. M. Roebuck c Piper b Munton | 60 | – not out | 20 |
| A. N. Hayhurst c Piper b Reeve | 18 | – b Small | 8 |
| R. J. Harden lbw b Twose | 20 | | |
| R. J. Bartlett not out | 0 | | |
| *C. J. Tavaré (did not bat) | | – (4) not out | 13 |
| B 5, l-b 12, n-b 1 | 18 | B 1 | 1 |

1/140 2/167 3/206  (3 wkts dec.) 210  1/15 2/36  (2 wkts) 50

†N. D. Burns, K. H. MacLeay, R. P. Lefebvre, N. A. Mallender and D. A. Graveney did not bat.

Bonus points – Somerset 2, Warwickshire 1.

Bowling: *First Innings*—Donald 8–3–20–0; Small 10–2–27–0; Munton 22–5–52–1; Reeve 22.3–5–67–1; Twose 9–0–27–1. *Second Innings*—Small 6–0–26–1; Munton 5–0–13–0; Lloyd 11–11–0–0; Moles 13–10–10–0; Reeve 2–2–0–0.

Umpires: K. J. Lyons and R. Palmer.

## WARWICKSHIRE v SUSSEX

At Coventry, June 18, 19, 20. Warwickshire won by 98 runs. Warwickshire 19 pts, Sussex 4 pts. Toss: Sussex. With rain permitting no more than 28.2 overs on the first day and 34.4 on the second, it took negotiations in the pavilion to obtain a result. The target for Sussex was 256 from a minimum of 70 overs, and if this represented something of a gamble by Lloyd, given the proximity of the boundaries at the Binley Road ground, it gave him a good return. Sussex, after losing Smith to the first ball of the innings, collapsed against the hostile fast bowling of Donald and Small and were bowled out in 47.3 overs. Wicket-keeper Piper took five catches, one off an inside edge to dismiss Lenham and another down the leg side off Alan Wells's glance being fine efforts. The win, Warwickshire's fifth, extended their lead in the Championship to 34 points, and was the first in which they had not taken all twenty wickets. In their own innings, Lloyd set the pace with a sparkling 83 from 90 deliveries, his twelve fours including five in one over off Jones. Reeve was particularly strong off his legs in reaching 50 from 49 balls, and Piper also made a significant contribution.

*Close of play:* First day, Warwickshire 47-1 (A. J. Moles 21*, T. A. Lloyd 14*); Second day, Warwickshire 225-6 (K. J. Piper 19*, G. C. Small 0*).

## Warwickshire

| | | | |
|---|---:|---|---:|
| A. J. Moles b C. M. Wells | 28 | P. A. Booth c Moores b Jones | 2 |
| J. D. Ratcliffe run out | 10 | T. A. Munton not out | 5 |
| *T. A. Lloyd c Parker b C. M. Wells | 83 | A. A. Donald b Jones | 4 |
| D. P. Ostler b C. M. Wells | 9 | | |
| D. A. Reeve b Dodemaide | 56 | L-b 9 | 9 |
| P. A. Smith lbw b Dodemaide | 11 | | |
| †K. J. Piper b Jones | 41 | 1/27 2/99 3/111 4/154 5/187 | 283 |
| G. C. Small c Dodemaide b Pigott | 25 | 6/224 7/268 8/274 9/275 | |

Bonus points – Warwickshire 3, Sussex 4.

Bowling: Jones 21–2–97–3; Dodemaide 22–4–60–2; Pigott 21–4–75–1; C. M. Wells 13–3–42–3.

*Warwickshire forfeited their second innings.*

## Sussex

| | | | |
|---|---:|---|---:|
| D. M. Smith not out | 7 | b Donald | 0 |
| J. W. Hall b Donald | 0 | c Piper b Donald | 17 |
| N. J. Lenham not out | 16 | c Piper b Small | 20 |
| A. P. Wells (did not bat) | – | c Piper b Small | 11 |
| *P. W. G. Parker (did not bat) | – | b Donald | 23 |
| C. M. Wells (did not bat) | – | c Piper b Reeve | 24 |
| A. I. C. Dodemaide (did not bat) | – | c Munton b Donald | 27 |
| †P. Moores (did not bat) | – | c Donald b Small | 14 |
| A. C. S. Pigott (did not bat) | – | c Piper b Donald | 0 |
| I. D. K. Salisbury (did not bat) | – | b Small | 0 |
| A. N. Jones (did not bat) | – | not out | 4 |
| B 4, l-b 1 | 5 | B 9, l-b 3, w 1, n-b 2 | 15 |
| 1/5 | (1 wkt dec.) 28 | 1/0 2/21 3/41 4/52 5/85 | 157 |
| | | 6/103 7/129 8/137 9/150 | |

Bowling: *First Innings*—Donald 4–1–8–1; Small 5–2–7–0; Smith 4–2–6–0; Reeve 2–1–2–0. *Second Innings*—Donald 15–3–48–5; Small 11.3–3–36–4; Smith 5–1–15–0; Munton 10–2–36–0; Reeve 6–3–10–1.

Umpires: G. I. Burgess and J. H. Hampshire.

At Nottingham, June 21, 22, 24. WARWICKSHIRE drew with NOTTINGHAMSHIRE.

## WARWICKSHIRE v DERBYSHIRE

At Birmingham, June 28, 29, July 1. Derbyshire won by 173 runs. Derbyshire 23 pts, Warwickshire 7 pts. Toss: Warwickshire. Derbyshire's fourth Championship win of the season – all in successive matches since early June – lifted them to third place in the table, 25 points behind the home team with two games in hand. The defeat was Warwickshire's second. A demanding declaration had asked them to score 310 off a minimum of 59 overs, but the loss of the first four wickets to Malcolm and Mortensen for 29 runs inside half an hour left them with no option but to try to avoid defeat. With Malcolm showing a welcome return to form and winning a personal duel with Reeve, top-scorer for Warwickshire in both innings, even this was beyond them. The Championship leaders lost their last three wickets in eleven balls. The pitch was typically slow-paced, but only Azharuddin and Morris, for the visitors, and Reeve were able to play with any freedom. Azharuddin's first-innings hundred, off 110 balls, was a brilliant exhibition, including sixteen fours. Without it, Munton and Small, who shared nine wickets, would have bowled Warwickshire into the ascendancy. Morris was unlucky to be run out for 99 in Derbyshire's second innings, but his batting, together with another dazzling performance from Azharuddin, established an advantage for the visitors which Malcolm reinforced with his only five-wicket return of the summer.

*Close of play*: First day, Warwickshire 86-3 (A. J. Moles 27*, K. J. Piper 1*); Second day, Derbyshire 159-3 (J. E. Morris 82*, S. C. Goldsmith 17*).

## Derbyshire

| | | | | |
|---|---|---|---|---|
| *K. J. Barnett lbw b Munton | 12 | – c Reeve b Donald | | 0 |
| P. D. Bowler c Munton b Small | 40 | – run out | | 2 |
| J. E. Morris c Donald b Munton | 24 | – run out | | 99 |
| M. Azharuddin c Piper b Munton | 100 | – (6) c Small b Booth | | 73 |
| T. J. G. O'Gorman c Munton b Small | 5 | – (4) lbw b Donald | | 37 |
| S. C. Goldsmith b Small | 49 | – (5) lbw b Reeve | | 19 |
| †K. M. Krikken b Reeve | 13 | – lbw b Munton | | 14 |
| D. G. Cork lbw b Munton | 0 | – c Piper b Munton | | 13 |
| A. E. Warner c Piper b Munton | 0 | – not out | | 13 |
| D. E. Malcolm b Small | 15 | | | |
| O. H. Mortensen not out | 0 | | | |
| N-b 2 | 2 | B 9, l-b 5, w 9, n-b 6 | | 29 |

1/18 2/56 3/112 4/130 5/208          260          1/0 2/3 3/91     (8 wkts dec.) 299
6/242 7/243 8/245 9/249                              4/175 5/199 6/245
                                                     7/279 8/299

Bonus points – Derbyshire 3, Warwickshire 4.

Bowling: *First Innings*—Donald 10-0-53-0; Small 17.2-4-36-4; Munton 21-3-77-5; Reeve 20-3-55-1; Booth 1-1-0-0; Smith 5-0-39-0. *Second Innings*—Donald 16-4-51-2; Small 14-2-51-0; Munton 13.5-1-60-2; Reeve 15-3-25-1; Booth 24-6-81-1; Smith 4-0-17-0.

## Warwickshire

| | | | | |
|---|---|---|---|---|
| A. J. Moles c Krikken b Warner | 40 | – c Krikken b Malcolm | | 1 |
| J. D. Ratcliffe c O'Gorman b Cork | 15 | – c Azharuddin b Malcolm | | 3 |
| *T. A. Lloyd c Bowler b Mortensen | 20 | – c Krikken b Mortensen | | 16 |
| D. P. Ostler lbw b Mortensen | 0 | – c O'Gorman b Mortensen | | 0 |
| †K. J. Piper c Krikken b Cork | 9 | – (7) lbw b Cork | | 1 |
| D. A. Reeve b Goldsmith | 66 | – (5) c Barnett b Malcolm | | 66 |
| P. A. Smith lbw b Mortensen | 5 | – (6) c Morris b Warner | | 13 |
| G. C. Small c Krikken b Malcolm | 19 | – lbw b Barnett | | 7 |
| P. A. Booth run out | 29 | – (10) c Azharuddin b Malcolm | | 0 |
| T. A. Munton lbw b Goldsmith | 3 | – (9) c Bowler b Malcolm | | 5 |
| A. A. Donald not out | 0 | – not out | | 0 |
| L-b 11, w 1, n-b 23 | 35 | B 4, l-b 14, n-b 6 | | 24 |

1/35 2/69 3/84 4/100 5/134          250          1/2 2/21 3/21 4/29 5/72          136
6/146 7/214 8/220 9/240                              6/75 7/124 8/136 9/136

Bonus points – Warwickshire 3, Derbyshire 4.

Bowling: *First Innings*—Malcolm 27-8-86-1; Warner 20-5-35-1; Cork 22-1-64-2; Mortensen 20-7-36-3; Goldsmith 6-1-18-2. *Second Innings*—Malcolm 13-2-45-5; Mortensen 6-0-33-2; Warner 8-4-13-1; Cork 7-1-20-1; Barnett 5.3-3-7-1.

Umpires: B. J. Meyer and K. E. Palmer.

## WARWICKSHIRE v MIDDLESEX

At Birmingham, July 2, 3, 4. Warwickshire won by 93 runs. Warwickshire 22 pts, Middlesex 6 pts. Toss: Warwickshire. A slow, seaming pitch was exploited so well by the Warwickshire attack that Middlesex were beaten more easily than had seemed likely on the first two days. Neither side found batting straightforward, and on the opening day the home side were grateful for Paul Smith's patient, almost chanceless 68 from 172 balls. He hit eleven boundaries, mostly with drives through the off side, and helped Warwickshire recover from 106 for six to 230. On the second day, Munton bowled superbly to take a career-best eight for 89 in an unchanged spell of 30.2 overs, underlining both his stamina and his skill. His figures would have been even better had it not been for Williams's violent, counter-attacking 77, which included four sixes off Munton and eight fours in 67 deliveries. There was more exhilarating batting as Lloyd scored 82 off 90 deliveries in pursuit of the declaration that ultimately left Middlesex to score 268 from 72 overs. They never looked like approaching it, and although Brown batted determinedly through 34 overs, they were bowled out with 22 balls remaining. Munton took his match figures to eleven for 127, and there were three wickets apiece for Small and Donald.

*Close of play:* First day, Middlesex 21-0 (I. J. F. Hutchinson 2*, M. A. Roseberry 12*); Second day, Warwickshire 158-1 (J. D. Ratcliffe 51*, T. A. Lloyd 71*).

### Warwickshire

| | | | |
|---|---|---|---|
| A. J. Moles c Brown b Cowans | 38 | – c Cowans b Williams | 27 |
| J. D. Ratcliffe c Farbrace b Taylor | 5 | – c Emburey b Taylor | 94 |
| *T. A. Lloyd c Farbrace b Taylor | 14 | – c Roseberry b Tufnell | 82 |
| D. P. Ostler b Emburey | 17 | – not out | 48 |
| Asif Din c Brown b Williams | 11 | – c Pooley b Taylor | 3 |
| P. A. Smith c Roseberry b Cowans | 68 | – lbw b Taylor | 0 |
| †K. J. Piper c Brown b Cowans | 4 | | |
| G. C. Small c Brown b Williams | 24 | – (7) not out | 3 |
| P. A. Booth b Williams | 14 | | |
| T. A. Munton not out | 8 | | |
| A. A. Donald b Cowans | 4 | | |
| B 3, l-b 3, w 5, n-b 12 | 23 | L-b 13, w 2, n-b 2 | 17 |

1/14 2/36 3/63 4/87 5/98       230    1/54 2/189 3/248    (5 wkts dec.) 274
6/106 7/166 8/194 9/219                     4/254 5/267

Bonus points – Warwickshire 2, Middlesex 4.

Bowling: *First Innings*—Cowans 18-5-44-4; Taylor 17-3-44-2; Williams 25-4-73-3; Tufnell 15-4-26-0; Emburey 21-8-37-1. *Second Innings*—Cowans 18-2-59-0; Williams 7-0-42-1; Taylor 12-2-43-3; Emburey 13-0-56-0; Tufnell 17-3-61-1.

### Middlesex

| | | | |
|---|---|---|---|
| I. J. F. Hutchinson c Piper b Munton | 5 | – lbw b Small | 30 |
| M. A. Roseberry c Ostler b Munton | 27 | – lbw b Munton | 15 |
| K. R. Brown c Donald b Munton | 12 | – (4) b Donald | 47 |
| J. C. Pooley c Booth b Small | 18 | – (3) c Asif Din b Munton | 2 |
| M. Keech lbw b Munton | 26 | – c Ratcliffe b Donald | 11 |
| *J. E. Emburey lbw b Munton | 0 | – c Asif Din b Small | 13 |
| †P. Farbrace b Munton | 24 | – not out | 11 |
| N. F. Williams c Moles b Munton | 77 | – c Lloyd b Booth | 3 |
| C. W. Taylor c Ostler b Booth | 4 | – c Ostler b Small | 12 |
| P. C. R. Tufnell c Ostler b Munton | 0 | – lbw b Munton | 2 |
| N. G. Cowans not out | 3 | – b Donald | 4 |
| B 12, l-b 25, n-b 4 | 41 | B 11, l-b 7, n-b 6 | 24 |

1/25 2/56 3/57 4/106 5/110      237    1/49 2/50 3/55 4/88 5/120    174
6/133 7/157 8/201 9/208                 6/146 7/157 8/164 9/170

Bonus points – Middlesex 2, Warwickshire 4.

*In the second innings P. Farbrace, when 11, retired hurt at 142 and resumed at 164.*

Bowling: *First Innings*—Donald 15–4–43–0; Small 21–8–47–1; Munton 30.2–14–89–8; Smith 2–1–6–0; Booth 4–0–15–1. *Second Innings*—Donald 16.2–1–46–3; Munton 22–4–38–3; Small 15–5–23–3; Booth 15–2–49–1.

Umpires: B. J. Meyer and K. E. Palmer.

At Portsmouth, July 19, 20, 22. WARWICKSHIRE beat HAMPSHIRE by three wickets.

At Manchester, July 23, 24, 25. WARWICKSHIRE drew with LANCASHIRE.

At Leicester, July 26, 27, 28. WARWICKSHIRE beat LEICESTERSHIRE by an innings and 44 runs.

At Worcester, August 2, 3, 5. WARWICKSHIRE lost to WORCESTERSHIRE by an innings and 33 runs.

## WARWICKSHIRE v SURREY

At Birmingham, August 6, 7, 8. Surrey won by 67 runs. Surrey 22 pts, Warwickshire 5 pts. Toss: Warwickshire. Waqar Younis, in typically irresistible form, exposed Warwickshire's long-standing batting frailties and, with match figures of nine for 97 from 40 overs, played a significant role in Surrey's advance of three places into second in the Championship table, 50 points behind Warwickshire with two games in hand. Only Moles, and Neil Smith in the second innings, played the fastest bowler in county cricket with any degree of composure. Waqar received splendid support from Feltham, who took seven wickets in the match at little cost after rescuing his side on the first day from an unpromising position at 78 for five. He faced 152 deliveries for his unbeaten 69, hit eleven fours, and gained Surrey a control which they never relinquished. Warwickshire did not have Donald to counter Waqar's influence, and his absence told on the third afternoon when Darren Bicknell and Greig, with ten fours in his 52 from 57 balls, were adding 83 as the Surrey captain looked to set a challenging declaration. Warwickshire, with 56 overs in which to score 235, made a good start and at tea had reached 62 for one from sixteen overs. It was a different story afterwards, and they were well beaten with almost five overs remaining.

*Close of play:* First day, Warwickshire 35-1 (A. J. Moles 17*, T. A. Lloyd 15*); Second day, Surrey 32-3 (D. J. Bicknell 14*, G. P. Thorpe 0*).

## Surrey

| | | | | | |
|---|---|---|---|---|---|
| D. J. Bicknell c Munton b Small | 18 | – not out | 75 |
| R. I. Alikhan c Piper b Munton | 9 | – c Ostler b Benjamin | 0 |
| M. A. Lynch lbw b Reeve | 10 | – c Ostler b Small | 1 |
| D. M. Ward lbw b Reeve | 11 | – c Munton b Small | 14 |
| G. P. Thorpe b Reeve | 6 | – lbw b Benjamin | 17 |
| *I. A. Greig lbw b Munton | 22 | – b Smith | 52 |
| M. A. Feltham not out | 69 | – not out | 14 |
| †N. F. Sargeant c Reeve b Munton | 7 | | |
| M. P. Bicknell c Munton b Benjamin | 11 | | |
| Waqar Younis b Benjamin | 22 | | |
| A. J. Murphy b Reeve | 0 | | |
| B 1, l-b 11, w 1, n-b 8 | 21 | B 2, l-b 11, w 6, n-b 3 | 22 |

| | | | |
|---|---|---|---|
| 1/27 2/33 3/49 4/50 5/78 | 206 | 1/2 2/7 3/32 | (5 wkts dec.) 195 |
| 6/110 7/118 8/146 9/186 | | 4/89 5/172 | |

Bonus points – Surrey 2, Warwickshire 4.

Bowling: *First Innings*—Small 14–4–38–1; Benjamin 22–3–62–2; Munton 19–8–40–3; Reeve 28–9–54–4. *Second Innings*—Small 19–7–26–2; Benjamin 19–4–64–2; Munton 17–7–46–0; Reeve 4–1–23–0; Smith 3–2–3–1; Lloyd 2–0–20–0.

# Warwickshire

| | | | |
|---|---|---|---|
| A. J. Moles b Feltham | 59 | – b Feltham | 37 |
| J. D. Ratcliffe b Waqar Younis | 1 | – b Waqar Younis | 9 |
| *T. A. Lloyd c Sargeant b Waqar Younis | 15 | – lbw b M. P. Bicknell | 17 |
| D. P. Ostler b Murphy | 27 | – run out | 25 |
| Asif Din b Feltham | 5 | – (6) b Feltham | 2 |
| D. A. Reeve lbw b Waqar Younis | 25 | – (5) c Sargeant b Feltham | 7 |
| N. M. K. Smith b Waqar Younis | 5 | – not out | 40 |
| †K. J. Piper lbw b Waqar Younis | 5 | – c Lynch b Waqar Younis | 2 |
| G. C. Small c M. P. Bicknell b Feltham | 8 | – b Waqar Younis | 6 |
| J. E. Benjamin c and b Feltham | 1 | – (11) c Lynch b M. P. Bicknell | 11 |
| T. A. Munton not out | 1 | – (10) b Waqar Younis | 4 |
| B 2, l-b 7, w 3, n-b 3 | 15 | L-b 3, n-b 4 | 7 |

1/3 2/35 3/96 4/109 5/134                167    1/17 2/63 3/63 4/97 5/97              167
6/139 7/151 8/161 9/166                         6/107 7/117 8/137 9/145

Bonus points – Warwickshire 1, Surrey 4.

Bowling: *First Innings*—Waqar Younis 22–4–47–5; M. P. Bicknell 14–4–38–0; Murphy 14–4–32–1; Feltham 14–1–41–4. *Second Innings*—Waqar Younis 18–5–50–4; M. P. Bicknell 15.1–3–56–2; Murphy 7–2–30–0; Feltham 11–2–28–3.

Umpires: B. Dudleston and R. C. Tolchard.

At Northampton, August 9, 10, 12. WARWICKSHIRE drew with NORTHAMPTON-SHIRE.

## WARWICKSHIRE v GLAMORGAN

At Birmingham, August 20, 21, 22. Drawn. Warwickshire 6 pts, Glamorgan 7 pts. Toss: Warwickshire. With neither pace attack able to make an impression on a slow pitch, batsmen had their most comfortable match at Edgbaston since the season began. Eight players topped fifty in the first three innings, all of which ended in declarations. Lloyd hit sixteen boundaries in top-scoring for Warwickshire and Dale twelve in his Championship-best 99, while Shastri had a solid all-round game, taking nine wickets and scoring 119 runs without being dismissed. Small, however, redressed the balance when Glamorgan set out to chase a target of 259 in 50 overs, sending back Butcher, Dale and Maynard in a sensational second over. But as James and Shastri were rebuilding the innings, rain frustratingly robbed Warwickshire of the possibility of registering their first win for more than three weeks.

*Close of play:* First day, Glamorgan 30-1 (A. R. Butcher 16*, C. P. Metson 6*); Second day, Warwickshire 55-2 (Asif Din 12*, D. P. Ostler 10*).

# Warwickshire

| | | | |
|---|---|---|---|
| A. J. Moles c Metson b Dale | 65 | – c Metson b Watkin | 10 |
| P. A. Smith c Shastri b Dale | 50 | – b Frost | 16 |
| *T. A. Lloyd b Shastri | 86 | – (8) c Butcher b Shastri | 0 |
| D. P. Ostler c James b Shastri | 35 | – b Shastri | 56 |
| D. A. Reeve c Croft b Shastri | 40 | – not out | 55 |
| Asif Din c Dale b Watkin | 45 | – (3) c Maynard b Shastri | 27 |
| N. M. K. Smith c James b Shastri | 6 | – (6) lbw b Shastri | 17 |
| †P. C. L. Holloway not out | 4 | – (7) b Shastri | 0 |
| G. C. Small c Metson b Watkin | 4 | – not out | 45 |
| B 2, l-b 19, n-b 2 | 23 | B 6, l-b 12, n-b 2 | 20 |

1/85 2/207 3/223 4/259 5/338        (8 wkts dec.) 358    1/21 2/38 3/106      (7 wkts dec.) 246
6/344 7/354 8/358                                         4/125 5/149
                                                          6/155 7/155

T. A. Munton and A. A. Donald did not bat.

Bonus points – Warwickshire 4, Glamorgan 3.

Bowling: *First Innings*—Watkin 14.5–3–68–2; Frost 12–3–35–0; Bastien 20–6–61–0; Dale 15–3–43–2; Croft 17–6–57–0; Shastri 17–2–73–4. *Second Innings*—Frost 12–0–75–1; Bastien 9–3–18–0; Shastri 22–8–71–5; Watkin 18–5–46–1; Croft 6–2–18–0.

## Glamorgan

| | | | | |
|---|---|---|---|---|
| *A. R. Butcher b Donald | 61 | – b Small | | 1 |
| S. P. James c Moles b Munton | 4 | – not out | | 11 |
| †C. P. Metson lbw b Donald | 47 | | | |
| A. Dale b P. A. Smith | 99 | – (3) lbw b Small | | 0 |
| M. P. Maynard lbw b N. M. K. Smith | 24 | – (4) c Ostler b Small | | 0 |
| R. J. Shastri not out | 80 | – (5) not out | | 39 |
| P. A. Cottey not out | 2 | | | |
| B 10, l-b 7, w 4, n-b 8 | 29 | B 1, l-b 1, w 1 | | 3 |

1/24 2/118 3/134 4/185 5/323     (5 wkts dec.) 346     1/2 2/2 3/2     (3 wkts) 54

R. D. B. Croft, S. L. Watkin, M. Frost and S. Bastien did not bat.

Bonus points – Glamorgan 4, Warwickshire 2.

Bowling: *First Innings*—Donald 23–3–68–2; Small 15–7–25–0; Munton 16.1–6–38–1; N. M. K. Smith 21–8–68–1; P. A. Smith 12–3–55–1; Asif Din 12–1–75–0. *Second Innings*—Small 9–2–24–3; Munton 7–4–18–0; N. M. K. Smith 1–1–0–0; Donald 1–0–2–0; Asif Din 1–0–8–0.

Umpires: J. C. Balderstone and B. Leadbeater.

## WARWICKSHIRE v WORCESTERSHIRE

At Birmingham, August 28, 29, 30. Warwickshire won by four wickets. Warwickshire 20 pts, Worcestershire 5 pts. Toss: Worcestershire. Needing to score 211 to win on a controversial pitch which was marked "poor" by the umpires, Warwickshire produced their most solid batting of the season to secure the victory they needed to maintain their title challenge. Seventeen wickets fell on the first day, and evidence of the unpredictability of a pitch that was dry, cracked and irregularly grassed came in the second over when Hick was lbw first ball to a shooter from just short of a length. Only Moody's long reach could counter the inconsistent bounce, and his 91, with eleven boundaries, was all that stood between Worcestershire and a disastrous total. The big Australian was well supported in contrasting ways by Botham (27 balls, five fours) and Tolley, in stands of 38 and 56 respectively, before Munton bowled him to complete figures of seven for 59. Warwickshire fared no better, being bundled out in 57.4 overs, whereupon Worcestershire's acting-captain, Curtis, made sure that a first-innings lead of 40 would not be wasted. His watchful innings of 77, in four hours from 180 balls, all but carried his side out of reach, but a wild stroke from Botham precipitated a collapse in which the last five wickets fell for 14 runs. Reeve, pressed into service despite being considered unfit to bowl, took three wickets in nine deliveries without conceding a run. This left Warwickshire requiring the highest total of the match to win, but by now the pitch had eased slightly as it became slower and their ambition was achieved. The match, over in under two and a half days, produced an over-rate of fourteen per hour.

*Close of play:* First day, Warwickshire 120-7 (Asif Din 26*, T. A. Munton 1*); Second day, Warwickshire 108-2 (A. J. Moles 56*, T. A. Lloyd 0*).

## Worcestershire

| | | | | |
|---|---|---|---|---|
| *T. S. Curtis lbw b Munton | 11 | – c Munton b Reeve | | 77 |
| P. Bent c Holloway b Small | 1 | – b Munton | | 20 |
| G. A. Hick lbw b Small | 0 | – c and b Donald | | 13 |
| T. M. Moody b Munton | 91 | – c Ratcliffe b Donald | | 3 |
| D. B. D'Oliveira c Reeve b Munton | 0 | – c Lloyd b Small | | 1 |
| †S. J. Rhodes lbw b Munton | 4 | – b Benjamin | | 17 |
| I. T. Botham b Munton | 24 | – b Munton | | 1 |
| R. K. Illingworth c Ostler b Munton | 3 | – c Ratcliffe b Reeve | | 4 |
| C. M. Tolley c Lloyd b Munton | 7 | – c Holloway b Reeve | | 0 |
| P. J. Newport c Lloyd b Small | 12 | – not out | | 0 |
| N. V. Radford not out | 0 | – lbw b Reeve | | 0 |
| B 5, l-b 3, n-b 5 | 13 | B 9, l-b 7, w 7, n-b 4 | | 27 |

1/6 2/6 3/39 4/39 5/45     166     1/49 2/70 3/83 4/85 5/118     170
6/83 7/89 8/145 9/166                 6/156 7/168 8/169 9/170

Bonus points – Worcestershire 1, Warwickshire 4.

Bowling: *First Innings*—Donald 13–1–51–0; Small 11–4–20–3; Munton 18.3–2–59–7; Benjamin 6–0–28–0. *Second Innings*—Donald 10–0–27–2; Small 15–2–45–1; Munton 19–6–32–3; Benjamin 8–0–37–1; Reeve 5–3–13–3.

## Warwickshire

| | | | |
|---|---|---|---|
| A. J. Moles c Rhodes b Botham | 26 | – c Rhodes b Newport | 56 |
| J. D. Ratcliffe b Botham | 22 | – c and b Tolley | 25 |
| *T. A. Lloyd lbw b Tolley | 7 | – (4) c Illingworth b Newport | 13 |
| D. P. Ostler c D'Oliveira b Botham | 7 | – (5) b Newport | 41 |
| D. A. Reeve c Radford b Botham | 13 | – (6) st Rhodes b Illingworth | 29 |
| Asif Din c Hick b Radford | 26 | – (3) lbw b Radford | 23 |
| †P. C. L. Holloway c Rhodes b Radford | 6 | – not out | 7 |
| G. C. Small c Bent b Newport | 0 | – not out | 4 |
| T. A. Munton not out | 5 | | |
| J. E. Benjamin lbw b Newport | 0 | | |
| A. A. Donald b Newport | 0 | | |
| B 2, l-b 7, n-b 5 | 14 | B 1, l-b 13, n-b 2 | 16 |

| | | |
|---|---|---|
| 1/41 2/50 3/64 4/65 5/90 | 126 | 1/60 2/106 3/112   (6 wkts) 214 |
| 6/119 7/119 8/124 9/126 | | 4/127 5/197 6/203 |

Bonus points – Worcestershire 4.

Bowling: *First Innings*—Radford 14–9–14–2; Newport 15.4–3–36–3; Botham 17–2–50–4; Tolley 10–3–14–1; Illingworth 1–0–3–0. *Second Innings*—Radford 20–4–54–1; Newport 19–1–51–3; Botham 27–8–52–0; Illingworth 9–4–22–1; Tolley 7–2–21–1.

Umpires: R. Julian and P. B. Wight.

## WARWICKSHIRE v NORTHAMPTONSHIRE

At Birmingham, September 10, 11, 12, 13. Warwickshire won by three wickets. Warwickshire 22 pts, Northamptonshire 7 pts. Toss: Warwickshire. Warwickshire's tenth win of the season ensured that they would finish no lower than second in the Championship. Played on a good pitch, the match produced a thrilling final day and was a splendid advertisement for four-day cricket, with 1,143 runs, 34 wickets and the winning hit coming with four balls remaining. Bad light cost 55 overs on the second and third days. Northamptonshire, after being put in, held the advantage for the first two and a half days. Larkins (one six, thirteen fours), Lamb (one six, twelve fours) and Curran (twelve fours) all topped 70 with entertaining batting, and for some time the home side faced the prospect of following on. Smith and Small took them past that mark in an unbroken partnership of 67 which allowed Lloyd to declare 99 runs behind, gambling that either his bowlers would dismiss Northamptonshire cheaply or his batsmen would chase an offered target on the fourth day. Thanks to a magnificent effort by Donald, overcoming the back strain which had forced his retirement on the first day, the visitors were bowled out for 196. He swung and seamed the ball at great pace, and it was a spectacular return to top form after a quiet August. Needing 296 in 98 overs, Warwickshire reached 144 for one through the fast-improving Ratcliffe and Lloyd before a series of poor strokes reduced them to 159 for four, and then 242 for six. Reeve batted well against some probing leg-spin, delivered from around the wicket, by Roberts, and when he was bowled for 64, Piper and Small batted sensibly to secure the win. Needing 26 off ten overs, and then 15 off three, they were helped by 5 byes in Roberts's penultimate over when the ball struck the fielding helmet.

*Close of play:* First day, Northamptonshire 364-9 (A. R. Roberts 15*, A. Walker 0*); Second day, Warwickshire 143-3 (D. P. Ostler 46*, D. A. Reeve 13*); Third day, Northamptonshire 195-9 (W. M. Noon 13*, A. Walker 7*).

## Northamptonshire

| | | | |
|---|---|---|---|
| A. Fordham c Piper b Donald | 6 | – c Munton b Donald | 16 |
| W. Larkins b Munton | 75 | – c Moles b Donald | 10 |
| R. J. Bailey b Donald | 49 | – c Piper b Small | 4 |
| *A. J. Lamb b Donald | 74 | – b Donald | 22 |
| N. A. Stanley b Smith | 32 | – c Asif Din b Reeve | 54 |
| D. J. Capel b Smith | 2 | – b Small | 3 |
| K. M. Curran c Piper b Small | 71 | – b Donald | 39 |
| E. A. E. Baptiste lbw b Smith | 12 | – b Donald | 0 |
| A. R. Roberts not out | 20 | – c Ratcliffe b Reeve | 7 |
| †W. M. Noon c Lloyd b Reeve | 5 | – lbw b Donald | 13 |
| A. Walker c Piper b Reeve | 6 | – not out | 8 |
| B 9, l-b 7, n-b 7 | 23 | B 16, l-b 1, w 1, n-b 2 | 20 |

1/14 2/114 3/141 4/207 5/211     375     1/16 2/28 3/56 4/57 5/64     196
6/288 7/325 8/350 9/363     6/139 7/139 8/170 9/182

Bonus points – Northamptonshire 4, Warwickshire 3 (Score at 100 overs: 348-7).

Bowling: *First Innings*—Donald 15.4–2–55–3; Small 23–3–83–1; Munton 29–9–99–1; Reeve 28.2–7–72–2; Smith 19–4–50–3. *Second Innings*—Donald 20.4–2–69–6; Small 15–1–69–2; Smith 9–3–31–0; Reeve 8–3–10–2.

## Warwickshire

| | | | |
|---|---|---|---|
| A. J. Moles lbw b Baptiste | 18 | – b Capel | 8 |
| J. D. Ratcliffe c Larkins b Baptiste | 6 | – c Noon b Roberts | 70 |
| *T. A. Lloyd c Capel b Curran | 53 | – c Noon b Baptiste | 61 |
| D. P. Ostler b Baptiste | 68 | – c Noon b Baptiste | 13 |
| D. A. Reeve c Noon b Baptiste | 24 | – b Roberts | 64 |
| Asif Din b Curran | 6 | – c Bailey b Roberts | 15 |
| N. M. K. Smith not out | 50 | – run out | 18 |
| †K. J. Piper c Lamb b Baptiste | 1 | – not out | 23 |
| G. C. Small not out | 31 | – not out | 7 |
| B 5, l-b 14 | 19 | B 7, l-b 10 | 17 |

1/19 2/36 3/104 4/173 5/186     (7 wkts dec.) 276     1/38 2/144 3/144 4/159     (7 wkts) 296
6/196 7/209     5/210 6/242 7/270

T. A. Munton and A. A. Donald did not bat.

Bonus points – Warwickshire 3, Northamptonshire 3 (Score at 100 overs: 270-7).

Bowling: *First Innings*—Curran 33.1–8–78–2; Capel 19–6–49–0; Baptiste 34–8–95–5; Walker 15–2–35–0. *Second Innings*—Curran 10–1–27–0; Capel 21–5–63–1; Baptiste 29–5–73–2; Roberts 37.2–0–116–3.

Umpires: H. D. Bird and G. I. Burgess.

At Taunton, September 17, 18, 19, 20. WARWICKSHIRE beat SOMERSET by 5 runs.

# WORCESTERSHIRE

*Patron:* The Duke of Westminster
*President:* G. H. Chesterton
*Chairman:* C. D. Fearnley
*Chairman, Cricket Committee:* M. G. Jones
*Secretary:* The Revd Michael Vockins
   County Ground, New Road, Worcester
   WR2 4QQ (Telephone: 0905-748474)
*Captain:* 1991 – P. A. Neale
         1992 – T. S. Curtis
*Coach:* 1991 – B. L. D'Oliveira
     1992 – K. J. Lyons

Worcestershire were the only county to win two trophies in 1991; yet there was no denying that they could have done better. Victory by 65 runs over Lancashire in the Benson and Hedges Cup finally ended the hoodoo surrounding six defeats in a Lord's final, and the county triumphed again, by 7 runs, against the same opponents to win the Refuge Assurance Cup at Old Trafford. But rain hampered them in the early summer, wiping out nearly a quarter of scheduled play in their first six Britannic Assurance Championship matches, and their eventual joint sixth place in the table, with only six wins, was a disappointment.

The Refuge Assurance Cup final was Ian Botham's farewell appearance for Worcestershire, and it was no coincidence that his five years at New Road were the most successful in the county's history, with two Championships and two Refuge Assurance League titles before 1991. Ironically, Botham left for Durham after re-establishing himself as England's all-rounder in his best season for Worcestershire. As the West Indians arrived, he nudged the selectors with a Championship century against Lancashire, and he celebrated his call-up for the Texaco Trophy series with his first hundred against a West Indian team, reaching 100 in 83 balls and going on to 161, his highest score for the county. Later in the year he returned career-best Championship figures of seven for 54 against Warwickshire, and he also won the Gold Award after taking three for 11 against Essex in their Benson and Hedges semi-final.

Botham's early release inevitably dismayed some members, as did the announcement in August that the captain, Phil Neale, had been asked to stand down in favour of Tim Curtis for 1992. Neale had led Worcestershire for ten seasons and openly wanted to continue. But with the long-serving coach, Basil D'Oliveira, retiring and his replacement, Kevin Lyons, already lined up, the cricket committee judged it best to make the change ahead of schedule. Neale's frustration intensified when a broken thumb ended his season seven weeks early.

The player with greatest cause for satisfaction was Tom Moody, who started where he had left off the previous year at Warwickshire. The 6ft 6½in Australian earned both the supporters' nomination as Player of the Year and the Dick Lygon award for outstanding service – the first time this prize had gone to a newcomer at New Road. In all cricket Moody scored 3,274 runs and hit twelve hundreds: six in the Championship, four in the Refuge Assurance League and two in the Benson and Hedges Cup.

He hit a career-best 210 against Warwickshire, and by the time he left to join an Australian XI in Zimbabwe, thus missing three Championship games, he had scored 1,887 first-class runs at an average of 62.90.

In the Sunday League he became the first player to score four hundreds in a season, and beat Jimmy Cook's record aggregate of 1990 with 917 runs at 70.53. He and his opening partner, Curtis, each scored 50 or more nine times, equalling the competition record, and they put on 1,158 runs together, including six opening stands of more than 100, both new standards for the Sunday League. Moody's 160 against Kent was a county record in the competition, and after adding 323 runs in May he reached 500 on June 2, the earliest date for this feat and the day he was capped. His Sunday League aggregate reached 1,000 in 24 innings, improving by one innings B. A. Richards's achievement. He set another Worcestershire record with 382 runs in the Benson and Hedges Cup, while his aggregate of 1,378 in the three major limited-overs competitions was the highest in an English season.

What might Worcestershire have achieved had Graeme Hick carried on his own rich vein of form? After struggling to adjust to the pace and bounce of Australian wickets as he wintered in Queensland, Hick gave his long-awaited international career an early boost with his unbeaten 86 against West Indies in the Lord's one-day international. But his first four Tests yielded just 75 runs in seven innings, and this inevitably undermined his form for Worcestershire, for whom he scored only 986 first-class runs at a modest average, by his standards, of 37.92. In better moments his 186 at Hove beat D. Kenyon's record for Worcestershire against Sussex, and he won the Gold Award in the Benson and Hedges final, with 88 runs and three vital catches.

Richard Illingworth also played in the Texaco Trophy, before bowling himself into history as the eleventh man to take a wicket with his first ball in Test cricket. But his 26 Championship wickets were disappointing after 71 the year before. Philip Newport was the leading wicket-taker with 66, while all-rounder Stuart Lampitt's 56 confirmed his progress. Neal Radford took seven Bedfordshire wickets for 19 in the NatWest Bank Trophy, the best analysis by any Worcestershire bowler in limited-overs cricket, and the injury-prone Graham Dilley bowled well for his 37 wickets in only eleven matches.

Worcestershire's highest score of the season was Curtis's career-best 248 against Somerset, and in the next match he took an unbeaten 186 off Glamorgan. But again he lacked a reliable opening partner; the club have high hopes of the Young England captain, Philip Weston, and in the meantime have signed Adam Seymour from Essex. Two other candidates, Gordon Lord and Paul Bent, departed at the end of the season, and Steve Herzberg, Robert Gofton and, at his own request, Steve McEwan were also not retained.

Wicket-keeper Steve Rhodes enjoyed his best season with the bat, scoring 942 first-class runs, and his maiden limited-overs hundred won him the match award in the Refuge Assurance Cup final. However, he was named only as stand-by for England's winter tours. Of the younger brigade, David Leatherdale underlined his potential with a sparkling 157, his maiden century, against Somerset in the final home game, and Richard Stemp, a left-arm spinner, proved a more than capable deputy for Illingworth. – Chris Moore.

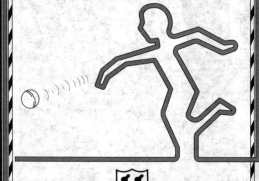

WORCESTERSHIRE 1991

[*Jim Ballard*]

*Back row*: G. R. Haynes, S. R. Bevins, D. A. Leatherdale, R. D. Stemp, P. Bent, T. M. Moody, A. Wylie, S. Herzberg, C. M. Tolley, R. P. Gofton, M. S. Scott. *Front row*: B. L. D'Oliveira (*coach*), S. R. Lampitt, I. T. Botham, P. J. Newport, S. J. Rhodes, N. V. Radford, T. S. Curtis, P. A. Neale (*captain*), D. B. D'Oliveira, G. A. Hick, R. K. Illingworth, M. J. Weston, G. R. Dilley, S. M. McEwan, G. J. Lord.

## WORCESTERSHIRE RESULTS

*All first-class matches – Played 25; Won 8, Lost 4, Drawn 13.*

*County Championship matches – Played 22; Won 6, Lost 4, Drawn 12.*

*Bonus points – Batting 54, Bowling 59.*

*Competition placings – Britannic Assurance County Championship, 6th equal;
NatWest Bank Trophy, 2nd round; Benson and Hedges Cup, winners;
Refuge Assurance League, 4th; Refuge Assurance Cup, winners.*

## BRITANNIC ASSURANCE CHAMPIONSHIP AVERAGES

### BATTING

| | Birthplace | M | I | NO | R | HI | Avge |
|---|---|---|---|---|---|---|---|
| ‡T. M. Moody | *Adelaide, Australia* | 19 | 31 | 4 | 1,770 | 210 | 65.55 |
| D. A. Leatherdale | *Bradford* | 3 | 4 | 0 | 219 | 157 | 54.75 |
| ‡T. S. Curtis | *Chislehurst* | 22 | 37 | 3 | 1,555 | 248 | 45.73 |
| ‡G. A. Hick | *Salisbury, Rhodesia* | 16 | 27 | 2 | 975 | 186 | 39.00 |
| ‡I. T. Botham | *Heswall* | 10 | 17 | 2 | 567 | 104 | 37.80 |
| ‡S. J. Rhodes | *Bradford* | 22 | 32 | 6 | 907 | 90 | 34.88 |
| ‡S. R. Lampitt | *Wolverhampton* | 19 | 20 | 5 | 447 | 93 | 29.80 |
| P. Bent | *Worcester* | 7 | 12 | 1 | 285 | 100* | 25.90 |
| ‡P. A. Neale | *Scunthorpe* | 13 | 20 | 4 | 385 | 69* | 24.06 |
| ‡R. K. Illingworth | *Bradford* | 17 | 23 | 4 | 442 | 56* | 23.26 |
| C. M. Tolley | *Kidderminster* | 6 | 9 | 3 | 137 | 36 | 22.83 |
| ‡P. J. Newport | *High Wycombe* | 22 | 24 | 9 | 340 | 48 | 22.66 |
| ‡G. J. Lord | *Birmingham* | 9 | 16 | 0 | 356 | 85 | 22.25 |
| ‡D. B. D'Oliveira | *Cape Town, SA* | 15 | 22 | 2 | 335 | 79 | 16.75 |
| ‡N. V. Radford | *Luanshya, N. Rhodesia* | 17 | 16 | 6 | 157 | 45 | 15.70 |
| R. D. Stemp | *Erdington* | 8 | 8 | 5 | 30 | 15* | 10.00 |
| ‡G. R. Dilley | *Dartford* | 10 | 10 | 4 | 37 | 15* | 6.16 |

Also batted: G. R. Haynes (*Stourbridge*) (3 matches) 13*, 16, 6; M. J. Weston (*Worcester*) (2 matches) 9, 5; W. P. C. Weston (*Durham*) (2 matches) 5, 8, 15.

\* *Signifies not out.* ‡ *Denotes county cap.*

The following played a total of fifteen three-figure innings for Worcestershire in County Championship matches – T. M. Moody 6, T. S. Curtis 3, G. A. Hick 3, P. Bent 1, I. T. Botham 1, D. A. Leatherdale 1.

### BOWLING

| | O | M | R | W | BB | 5W/i | Avge |
|---|---|---|---|---|---|---|---|
| G. R. Dilley | 281 | 56 | 752 | 35 | 5-91 | 1 | 21.48 |
| I. T. Botham | 279.1 | 55 | 886 | 38 | 7-54 | 3 | 23.31 |
| R. D. Stemp | 141.1 | 30 | 382 | 15 | 4-62 | 0 | 25.46 |
| C. M. Tolley | 105 | 21 | 292 | 11 | 3-40 | 0 | 26.54 |
| N. V. Radford | 434.1 | 92 | 1,363 | 46 | 7-43 | 2 | 29.63 |
| S. R. Lampitt | 422.4 | 74 | 1,358 | 45 | 5-70 | 3 | 30.17 |
| P. J. Newport | 609.4 | 115 | 1,840 | 54 | 4-44 | 0 | 34.07 |
| R. K. Illingworth | 430.4 | 132 | 971 | 26 | 5-49 | 2 | 37.34 |

Also bowled: P. Bent 3–1–5–0; T. S. Curtis 21–2–95–0; D. B. D'Oliveira 31–7–116–1; G. R. Haynes 19.2–2–82–0; G. A. Hick 123.4–29–379–8; T. M. Moody 8.4–3–25–0; P. A. Neale 17.5–1–86–1; S. J. Rhodes 1–0–30–0; M. J. Weston 5–1–27–1.

**Wicket-keepers:** S. J. Rhodes 48 ct, 7 st; G. A. Hick 3 ct.

**Leading Fielders:** T. M. Moody 29, D. B. D'Oliveira 21.

## WORCESTERSHIRE v GLOUCESTERSHIRE

At Worcester, April 27, 28, 29, 30. Drawn. Worcestershire 5 pts, Gloucestershire 5 pts. Toss: Gloucestershire. Rain, which prevented any play on the final two days, robbed Moody of the chance of a hundred on his Championship début for Worcestershire, a week after he had made 160 against Kent in the Sunday League on his first appearance for them. However, a similar feat had been achieved on the opening day, when the left-handed Scott, formerly of Hampshire, marked his first-class début for Gloucestershire with his maiden Championship century. He hit one six and eighteen fours altogether, having shared a first-wicket stand of 179 with Hodgson. Botham announced prior to the start that he was "getting fed up with people writing me off". As if to prove the point, he completed his first five-wicket Championship return for 21 months on the second morning, and followed up with seven boundaries in an unbeaten 39 off 50 balls before bad light forced a halt.

*Close of play:* First day, Gloucestershire 325-5 (C. W. J. Athey 22*, R. C. Russell 36*); Second day, Worcestershire 255-4 (T. M. Moody 82*, I. T. Botham 39*); Third day, No play.

### Gloucestershire

| | | | |
|---|---:|---|---:|
| G. D. Hodgson c Rhodes b Newport | 65 | D. R. Gilbert c Curtis b Botham | 16 |
| R. J. Scott st Rhodes b Radford | 127 | A. M. Smith not out | 3 |
| *A. J. Wright c Hick b Radford | 30 | A. M. Babington c Lord b Botham | 13 |
| C. W. J. Athey c Botham b Lampitt | 56 | | |
| M. W. Alleyne lbw b Radford | 2 | B 5, l-b 16, w 6, n-b 20 | 47 |
| J. W. Lloyds lbw b Botham | 4 | | |
| †R. C. Russell b Botham | 64 | 1/179 2/247 3/247 4/249 5/260 | 450 |
| D. V. Lawrence c Moody b Lampitt | 23 | 6/385 7/413 8/426 9/430 | |

Bonus points – Gloucestershire 4, Worcestershire 2 (Score at 100 overs: 301-5).

Bowling: Radford 28-2-94-2; Newport 25-2-85-1; Lampitt 34-10-75-2; Botham 34.2-8-125-5; Illingworth 14-4-40-0; Hick 6-2-10-0.

### Worcestershire

| | | | |
|---|---:|---|---:|
| T. S. Curtis lbw b Babington | 49 | I. T. Botham not out | 39 |
| G. J. Lord b Gilbert | 29 | | |
| G. A. Hick b Babington | 14 | L-b 8, n-b 5 | 13 |
| T. M. Moody not out | 82 | | |
| *P. A. Neale lbw b Babington | 29 | 1/77 2/91 3/103 4/167        (4 wkts) | 255 |

†S. J. Rhodes, R. K. Illingworth, P. J. Newport, S. R. Lampitt and N. V. Radford did not bat.

Bonus points – Worcestershire 3, Gloucestershire 1.

Bowling: Lawrence 12-1-50-0; Gilbert 15.1-2-78-1; Babington 20-4-55-3; Smith 7-1-34-0; Lloyds 10-0-30-0.

Umpires: G. I. Burgess and D. R. Shepherd.

## WORCESTERSHIRE v LANCASHIRE

At Worcester, May 9, 10, 11, 13. Drawn. Worcestershire 4 pts, Lancashire 6 pts. Toss: Worcestershire. Victory slipped from Worcestershire's grasp in a dramatic conclusion to a compelling contest. From Hegg's miscued pull off Botham, Dilley dropped an apparently easy catch at mid-on, and just three balls later rain rescued Lancashire's last-wicket pair with 13.4 overs remaining. The presence of the England manager and chairman of selectors brought out the best in Botham, whose first Championship century for Worcestershire at New Road, containing one six and thirteen fours off 115 balls, led the home side's recovery from 44 for four on the opening day. However, his four-wicket return could not prevent Lancashire from acquiring a lead of 74, thanks to contrasting centuries from Atherton and acting-captain Fairbrother. They added 189 for the third wicket, but after both were out at 326, the remaining six Lancashire wickets could manage only 77 more runs. Worcestershire began the final day 48 runs ahead with just five wickets in hand, but one of them was Moody's. Resuming at 70 not out, the big Australian duly completed his first Championship century for the county – his fourth of the summer in all matches – and added 105 for the seventh wicket with Illingworth. Moody batted for just over four and a half hours and hit sixteen fours, and Lancashire were eventually left a target of 199 in 49 overs. They were always fighting a rearguard action after losing three wickets when the score was 21, and had struggled to 144 for nine before Dilley spilled what would have been the winning catch in the 35th over.

*Close of play:* First day, Worcestershire 309-8 (S. J. Rhodes 62*, C. M. Tolley 9*); Second day, Lancashire 205-2 (M. A. Atherton 68*, N. H. Fairbrother 32*); Third day, Worcestershire 122-5 (T. M. Moody 70*, S. J. Rhodes 6*).

## Worcestershire

| | | | |
|---|---|---|---|
| T. S. Curtis c Fairbrother b Watkinson | 15 | – c Fairbrother b DeFreitas | 15 |
| G. J. Lord c Hegg b DeFreitas | 12 | – lbw b DeFreitas | 0 |
| G. A. Hick lbw b DeFreitas | 57 | – b DeFreitas | 0 |
| T. M. Moody lbw b Watkinson | 0 | – c Hegg b DeFreitas | 135 |
| *P. A. Neale lbw b Allott | 4 | – c Allott b DeFreitas | 11 |
| I. T. Botham c Lloyd b Wasim Akram | 104 | – c Lloyd b Wasim Akram | 9 |
| †S. J. Rhodes lbw b Allott | 67 | – c Hegg b Wasim Akram | 6 |
| R. K. Illingworth c Hegg b Allott | 34 | – not out | 56 |
| P. J. Newport c Fairbrother b Allott | 5 | – c sub b Wasim Akram | 3 |
| C. M. Tolley not out | 18 | – c Fairbrother b Wasim Akram | 18 |
| G. R. Dilley c Atherton b DeFreitas | 0 | – c Fairbrother b DeFreitas | 0 |
| B 5, l-b 6, n-b 2 | 13 | B 1, l-b 8, w 3, n-b 7 | 19 |
| | 329 | | 272 |

1/24 2/36 3/36 4/44 5/150 6/221 7/291 8/297 9/329      329

1/3 2/3 3/45 4/91 5/108 6/122 7/227 8/230 9/270      272

Bonus points – Worcestershire 3, Lancashire 2 (Score at 100 overs: 291-6).

Bowling: *First Innings*—Wasim Akram 30-9-69-1; DeFreitas 30.4-10-91-3; Watkinson 11.4-6-22-2; Allott 28-9-56-4; Yates 23-3-80-0. *Second Innings*—DeFreitas 31.5-6-88-6; Wasim Akram 36-9-89-4; Allott 15-1-62-0; Yates 5-1-24-0.

## Lancashire

| | | | |
|---|---|---|---|
| G. D. Mendis c Curtis b Dilley | 9 | – c Moody b Newport | 14 |
| G. Fowler lbw b Botham | 80 | – run out | 1 |
| M. A. Atherton c Neale b Botham | 110 | – c Neale b Dilley | 0 |
| *N. H. Fairbrother c Dilley b Tolley | 109 | – (6) c Hick b Dilley | 10 |
| G. D. Lloyd c sub b Dilley | 24 | – (4) c Hick b Dilley | 1 |
| M. Watkinson b Dilley | 12 | – (8) b Newport | 6 |
| Wasim Akram c Hick b Dilley | 17 | – c Lord b Newport | 24 |
| P. A. J. DeFreitas b Botham | 12 | – (5) b Newport | 47 |
| †W. K. Hegg c Moody b Dilley | 0 | – not out | 27 |
| G. Yates b Botham | 4 | – lbw b Botham | 0 |
| P. J. W. Allott not out | | – not out | 5 |
| B 1, l-b 10, w 1, n-b 11 | 23 | B 5, l-b 5, n-b 3 | 13 |
| | 403 | (9 wkts) | 148 |

1/40 2/137 3/326 4/326 5/341 6/375 7/396 8/396 9/396      403

1/21 2/21 3/21 4/36 5/74 6/88 7/98 8/125 9/125      (9 wkts) 148

Bonus points – Lancashire 4, Worcestershire 1 (Score at 100 overs: 330-4).

Bowling: *First Innings*—Dilley 36-8-91-5; Newport 36-8-106-0; Botham 31.1-4-105-4; Tolley 12-0-45-1; Illingworth 16-3-45-0. *Second Innings*—Dilley 14.2-2-64-3; Newport 17-3-58-4; Botham 4-1-16-1.

Umpires: B. Hassan and P. B. Wight.

At Worcester, May 15, 16, 17. WORCESTERSHIRE drew with WEST INDIANS (See West Indian tour section).

At Oxford, May 25, 27, 28. WORCESTERSHIRE beat OXFORD UNIVERSITY by an innings and 122 runs.

## WORCESTERSHIRE v GLAMORGAN

At Worcester, May 31, June 1, 3. Drawn. Worcestershire 6 pts, Glamorgan 5 pts. Toss: Worcestershire. For the fourth successive first-class game at New Road, rain prevented a result. Glamorgan were in the driving-seat at 154 for two, requiring 114 from the last 28 overs, when the weather intervened. With both attacks exploiting a lively pitch on the first two days, the batsmen required grit, as exemplified by Curtis throughout 70 overs, or some good fortune. Hick, whose 50 from 108 balls included ten boundaries, was dropped when he was 10. On the second day Shastri, using his height to control the lifting ball, underwrote Glamorgan's reply for more than three and a half hours, hitting eleven fours in his unbeaten 84 (172 balls) to take the visitors to within 27 runs of Worcestershire. No-one else scored more than 17. Before the close, Moody, out second ball in the first innings, reached 50 off 72 balls, and on the final morning he completed his seventh century of the summer; his second in the Championship. His 118, off 195 balls, contained a six and fifteen fours. The declaration set Glamorgan to score 268 in 72 overs, and Morris and Maynard (39 balls) had put on 83 in fifteen overs for the third wicket when the rain cut short their progress.

*Close of play:* First day, Glamorgan 34-2 (R. J. Shastri 6*, C. P. Metson 0*); Second day, Worcestershire 137-4 (T. M. Moody 80*, S. J. Rhodes 19*).

## Worcestershire

| | | | |
|---|---|---|---|
| T. S. Curtis lbw b Frost | 70 | – lbw b Watkin | 14 |
| G. J. Lord c Metson b Frost | 0 | – lbw b Croft | 8 |
| G. A. Hick c Watkin b Smith | 50 | – c Morris b Frost | 0 |
| T. M. Moody c Butcher b Watkin | 0 | – lbw b Watkin | 118 |
| *P. A. Neale b Bastien | 12 | – lbw b Frost | 7 |
| †S. J. Rhodes lbw b Watkin | 5 | – not out | 66 |
| R. K. Illingworth b Frost | 26 | – lbw b Frost | 13 |
| P. J. Newport c Frost b Watkin | 16 | – not out | 2 |
| S. R. Lampitt c Smith b Watkin | 19 | | |
| N. V. Radford c Watkin b Frost | 0 | | |
| G. R. Dilley not out | 0 | | |
| L-b 6, n-b 1 | 7 | B 2, l-b 8, n-b 2 | 12 |

1/6 2/87 3/90 4/110 5/123      205      1/19 2/20 3/39     (6 wkts dec.) 240
6/165 7/168 8/199 9/205                4/57 5/194 6/236

Bonus points – Worcestershire 2, Glamorgan 4.

Bowling: *First Innings*—Watkin 24-10-40-4; Frost 29.5-10-67-4; Bastien 26-6-51-1; Smith 12-1-41-1. *Second Innings*—Watkin 25-8-61-2; Frost 24-4-87-3; Bastien 28-6-71-0; Croft 5-0-11-1.

## Glamorgan

| | | | |
|---|---|---|---|
| *A. R. Butcher lbw b Dilley | 17 | – lbw b Dilley | 5 |
| H. Morris b Radford | 8 | – not out | 74 |
| R. J. Shastri not out | 84 | – c Hick b Lampitt | 28 |
| †C. P. Metson c Rhodes b Radford | 8 | | |
| M. P. Maynard c Illingworth b Dilley | 5 | – (4) not out | 33 |
| G. C. Holmes lbw b Lampitt | 15 | | |
| I. Smith c Curtis b Newport | 14 | | |
| R. D. B. Croft c Moody b Newport | 3 | | |
| S. L. Watkin c Moody b Lampitt | 10 | | |
| S. Bastien c Curtis b Dilley | 1 | | |
| M. Frost c Moody b Dilley | 0 | | |
| B 4, l-b 3, n-b 6 | 13 | L-b 7, n-b 7 | 14 |

1/22 2/28 3/42 4/47 5/99      178      1/11 2/71         (2 wkts) 154
6/130 7/138 8/161 9/176

Bonus points – Glamorgan 1, Worcestershire 4.

Bowling: *First Innings*—Dilley 19.3–2–60–4; Radford 10–1–42–2; Lampitt 20–5–37–2; Newport 11–2–32–2. *Second Innings*—Dilley 10–1–31–1; Radford 12–1–45–0; Newport 9.3–1–31–0; Lampitt 11–3–38–1; Illingworth 1–0–2–0.

Umpires: G. I. Burgess and B. Leadbeater.

At Northampton, June 4, 5, 6. WORCESTERSHIRE lost to NORTHAMPTONSHIRE by six wickets.

At Ilford, June 7, 8, 10. WORCESTERSHIRE drew with ESSEX.

At Hove, June 14, 15, 17. WORCESTERSHIRE drew with SUSSEX.

## WORCESTERSHIRE v NOTTINGHAMSHIRE

At Worcester, June 18, 19, 20. Worcestershire won by one wicket. Worcestershire 20 pts, Nottinghamshire 6 pts. Toss: Nottinghamshire. Worcestershire, set to score 311 in 87 overs, achieved their first Championship win of the season, with eleven balls to spare, after Lampitt and Stemp, the last-wicket pair, had added 24. The result, however, would have gone the other way had Stemp not been dropped off a return catch by Stephenson with 3 runs still required. Next over Lampitt made the winning hit to reach a richly deserved half-century. Worcestershire were again indebted to Moody, who was denied his second hundred of the match by the diving Randall's one-handed catch at extra-cover. Moody had hit fourteen fours in his 96. His first-innings hundred, off 128 balls between lunch and tea on the second day, after Worcestershire had lost both openers without a run on the board, had enabled the two captains to agree on an equation to contrive a finish, 40 overs having been lost to rain on the opening day. Neale declared 113 runs behind, and then collected his first first-class wicket for fifteen years when Worcestershire turned to their occasional bowlers. Broad needed 64 to win the race to 1,000 runs, following his 162 in the first innings (332 minutes, seventeen fours), but he fell to Lampitt before he had a chance to feed on the easy pickings.

*Close of play:* First day, Nottinghamshire 187–5 (B. C. Broad 108*); Second day, Nottinghamshire 112–2 (R. T. Robinson 33*, D. W. Randall 13*).

## Nottinghamshire

| | | | | |
|---|---|---|---|---|
| B. C. Broad c and b Dilley | 162 | – c Rhodes b Lampitt | 8 |
| P. R. Pollard c Moody b Lampitt | 18 | – c Moody b Neale | 13 |
| *R. T. Robinson lbw b Lampitt | 12 | – not out | 89 |
| P. Johnson c Rhodes b Lampitt | 22 | – retired hurt | 34 |
| D. W. Randall c Rhodes b Radford | 9 | – not out | 42 |
| M. A. Crawley run out | 11 | | |
| K. P. Evans not out | 56 | | |
| F. D. Stephenson c Moody b Dilley | 11 | | |
| L-b 3, w 2, n-b 7 | 12 | L-b 9, w 2 | 11 |

1/45 2/69 3/121 4/142 5/187     (7 wkts. dec.) 313    1/14 2/27     (2 wkts. dec.) 197
6/289 7/313

†B. N. French, R. A. Pick and J. A. Afford did not bat.

Bonus points – Nottinghamshire 4, Worcestershire 2 (Score at 100 overs: 305-6).

*In the second innings P. Johnson retired hurt at 89.*

Bowling: *First Innings*—Dilley 19.2–1–46–2; Radford 13–5–20–1; Lampitt 29–6–97–3; Newport 25–5–79–0; Stemp 4–0–13–0; Haynes 12–1–55–0. *Second Innings*—Dilley 4–0–12–0; Lampitt 4–0–14–1; Neale 16.5–1–81–1; Haynes 6–0–27–0; Curtis 12–0–50–0; Moody 2–1–4–0.

## Worcestershire

| | | | |
|---|---|---|---|
| T. S. Curtis b Stephenson | 0 | c Afford b Stephenson | 0 |
| †S. J. Rhodes c French b Pick | 0 | c Crawley b Stephenson | 17 |
| T. M. Moody c Broad b Robinson | 107 | c Randall b Evans | 96 |
| D. B. D'Oliveira c and b Stephenson | 26 | c French b Pick | 25 |
| *P. A. Neale not out | 46 | c French b Afford | 18 |
| S. R. Lampitt c Crawley b Johnson | 1 | not out | 50 |
| G. R. Haynes not out | 13 | b Stephenson | 16 |
| P. J. Newport (did not bat) | | c Crawley b Stephenson | 48 |
| N. V. Radford (did not bat) | | lbw b Stephenson | 2 |
| G. R. Dilley (did not bat) | | c and b Afford | 2 |
| R. D. Stemp (did not bat) | | not out | 15 |
| B 2, l-b 2, w 1, n-b 2 | 7 | B 4, l-b 10, n-b 8 | 22 |

1/0 2/0 3/72 4/148 5/149          (5 wkts dec.) 200          1/0 2/56 3/108          (9 wkts) 311
                                                              4/164 5/166 6/198
                                                              7/275 8/278 9/287

Bonus points – Worcestershire 2, Nottinghamshire 2.

Bowling: *First Innings*—Stephenson 12–4–16–2; Pick 8–0–36–1; Evans 8–0–37–0; Afford 6–1–38–0; Crawley 4–1–13–0; Robinson 5–0–30–1; Johnson 4.2–1–26–1. *Second Innings*—Stephenson 25–2–74–5; Pick 18–2–60–1; Evans 14–0–69–1; Afford 28.1–8–94–2.

Umpires: D. J. Constant and M. J. Kitchen.


## WORCESTERSHIRE v LEICESTERSHIRE

At Worcester, June 28, 29, July 1. Drawn. Worcestershire 4 pts, Leicestershire 5 pts. Toss: Worcestershire. Despite having all their big guns to hand, Worcestershire made no attempt to chase a target of 310 in a minimum of 61 overs on a slow wicket not conducive to strokeplay. Not that Smith and Lewis had found its lack of pace inhibiting on the first evening, when they added 102 for Leicestershire's sixth wicket in 22 overs. Neale, having rescued Worcestershire from 82 for five on the second day with his top score of the season, 69 not out, declared 105 behind with 30 overs of the day remaining. But Boon and Briers stayed together until the close, and on Monday Briers went on to complete his second Championship century of the summer, off 178 balls with eleven fours. However, the final two sessions proved to be of academic interest only. Lord and Curtis took 29 overs to put on 90 for the first wicket, and it was something of a relief that when stumps were drawn with fourteen overs remaining.
*Close of play:* First day, Worcestershire 6-0 (T. S. Curtis 0*, G. J. Lord 6*); Second day, Leicestershire 73-0 (T. J. Boon 23*, N. E. Briers 47*).


## Leicestershire

| | | | |
|---|---|---|---|
| T. J. Boon c Neale b Newport | 76 | lbw b Radford | 38 |
| *N. E. Briers c Rhodes b Lampitt | 29 | lbw b Botham | 104 |
| P. N. Hepworth c Rhodes b Newport | 19 | | |
| J. J. Whitaker c Curtis b Newport | 10 | (3) lbw b Botham | 23 |
| L. Potter c Rhodes b Lampitt | 15 | (4) not out | 16 |
| B. F. Smith c Lampitt b Newport | 71 | (5) not out | 8 |
| C. C. Lewis lbw b Botham | 68 | | |
| P. Willey not out | 0 | | |
| B 3, l-b 9, n-b 5 | 17 | L-b 13, n-b 2 | 15 |

1/69 2/124 3/144 4/145 5/199          (7 wkts dec.) 305          1/119 2/173 3/188          (3 wkts dec.) 204
6/301 7/305

†P. A. Nixon, C. W. Wilkinson and J. N. Maguire did not bat.

Bonus points – Leicestershire 3, Worcestershire 2 (Score at 100 overs: 278-5).

Bowling: *First Innings*—Radford 17–5–48–0; Newport 18.2–2–70–4; Botham 17–4–59–1; Lampitt 19–5–42–2; Illingworth 30–14–64–0; Hick 2–0–10–0. *Second Innings*—Radford 19–6–55–1; Newport 20–6–48–0; Lampitt 16–0–40–0; Illingworth 4–1–10–0; Botham 7–2–26–2; Neale 1–0–5–0; Moody 0.4–0–7–0.

## Worcestershire

| | | | |
|---|---|---|---|
| T. S. Curtis c Nixon b Maguire | 0 | – lbw b Lewis | 47 |
| G. J. Lord c Potter b Willey | 43 | – b Maguire | 64 |
| G. A. Hick lbw b Maguire | 0 | – b Lewis | 24 |
| T. M. Moody c Willey b Lewis | 25 | – c Wilkinson b Lewis | 13 |
| *P. A. Neale not out | 69 | – (6) not out | 0 |
| I. T. Botham lbw b Lewis | 8 | – (5) not out | 3 |
| †S. J. Rhodes lbw b Lewis | 36 | | |
| R. K. Illingworth not out | 17 | | |
| L-b 2 | 2 | B 4, l-b 7 | 11 |

1/7 2/7 3/68 4/70       (6 wkts dec.) 200     1/90 2/134 3/154     (4 wkts) 162
5/82 6/164                                         4/161

S. R. Lampitt, P. J. Newport and N. V. Radford did not bat.

Bonus points – Worcestershire 2, Leicestershire 2.

Bowling: *First Innings*—Lewis 25–10–40–3; Maguire 24–7–61–2; Wilkinson 16–7–49–0; Willey 8–2–19–1; Potter 9–3–29–0. *Second Innings*—Lewis 19–4–39–3; Maguire 20–2–65–1; Wilkinson 5–1–33–0; Willey 3–0–14–0.

Umpires: J. H. Hampshire and K. J. Lyons.

At Leeds, July 2, 3, 4. WORCESTERSHIRE lost to YORKSHIRE by 115 runs.

At Portsmouth, July 16, 17, 18. WORCESTERSHIRE drew with HAMPSHIRE.

## WORCESTERSHIRE v DERBYSHIRE

At Kidderminster, July 19, 20, 22. Drawn. Worcestershire 5 pts, Derbyshire 8 pts. Toss: Derbyshire. A county record eighth-wicket partnership of 184 between Rhodes and Lampitt saved Worcestershire from defeat after they had been forced to follow on for the second time in successive games. With an early finish on the cards, spectators were charged a nominal 50p entrance fee for the final day: Worcestershire were still 44 runs adrift, with six second-innings wickets standing. However, Rhodes and Lampitt ensured a full day's play by steering them from 163 for seven, a lead of just 9, to 347, beating on the way the eighth-wicket record of 177 unbroken, which Illingworth set with Hick at Taunton in 1988, when Hick made his quadruple-century. The last two wickets added a further 77 runs as Worcestershire posted their highest Championship total of the season to date. On the opening day, Derbyshire had batted enterprisingly on a dry pitch of variable bounce and had their fourth bonus point safely banked in the 79th over. The early impetus was provided by Barnett, who hit fourteen fours in his 80, and Morris, whose 97 included seventeen boundaries and took him past 1,000 runs for the season. It might have been different had Morris been caught in the slips by Botham off a difficult chance before he had scored, or Barnett held by Hick, also at slip, when he was 38.

*Close of play:* First day, Worcestershire 0-0 (T. S. Curtis 0*, G. J. Lord 0*); Second day, Worcestershire 110-4 (P. A. Neale 20*, R. K. Illingworth 12*).

## Derbyshire

| | | | |
|---|---|---|---|
| *K. J. Barnett lbw b Botham | 80 | | |
| P. D. Bowler c Hick b Lampitt | 2 | – (3) not out | 2 |
| J. E. Morris b Illingworth | 97 | | |
| M. Azharuddin c Rhodes b Newport | 25 | | |
| T. J. G. O'Gorman c Radford b Illingworth | 78 | | |
| S. C. Goldsmith c and b Illingworth | 10 | | |
| †K. M. Krikken c Lampitt b Newport | 32 | | |
| D. G. Cork st Rhodes b Illingworth | 15 | – (1) not out | 15 |
| A. E. Warner c Botham b Illingworth | 15 | | |
| D. E. Malcolm c Rhodes b Radford | 0 | – (2) c Radford b Illingworth | 4 |
| O. H. Mortensen not out | 0 | | |
| L-b 9, w 1, n-b 8 | 18 | | |

1/9 2/122 3/180 4/222 5/263       372   1/9       (1 wkt) 21
6/327 7/339 8/362 9/362

Bonus points – Derbyshire 4, Worcestershire 3 (Score at 100 overs: 362-7).

Bowling: *First Innings*—Radford 18-5-61-1; Lampitt 13-1-82-1; Newport 19-3-80-2; Botham 22-3-76-1; Illingworth 33.3-10-64-5. *Second Innings*—Illingworth 5-3-7-1; Curtis 4-1-14-0.

## Worcestershire

| | | | |
|---|---|---|---|
| T. S. Curtis lbw b Cork | 32 | – lbw b Mortensen | 14 |
| G. J. Lord c Krikken b Malcolm | 3 | – b Mortensen | 17 |
| G. A. Hick c Krikken b Cork | 24 | – run out | 3 |
| T. M. Moody c O'Gorman b Warner | 51 | – c O'Gorman b Goldsmith | 29 |
| *P. A. Neale b Cork | 0 | – c Bowler b Mortensen | 42 |
| I. T. Botham c Cork b Warner | 5 | – (7) b Mortensen | 17 |
| †S. J. Rhodes c Krikken b Warner | 15 | – (8) c Morris b Mortensen | 90 |
| R. K. Illingworth c Warner b Malcolm | 31 | – (6) c Azharuddin b Mortensen | 21 |
| S. R. Lampitt not out | 17 | – b Cork | 93 |
| P. J. Newport c Krikken b Mortensen | 6 | – not out | 18 |
| N. V. Radford lbw b Malcolm | 19 | – c Bowler b Barnett | 45 |
| L-b 8, w 1, n-b 6 | 15 | B 4, l-b 15, w 3, n-b 13 | 35 |

1/9 2/48 3/93 4/93 5/120      218   1/36 2/37 3/56 4/85 5/143   424
6/126 7/171 8/178 9/197            6/150 7/163 8/347 9/361

Bonus points – Worcestershire 2, Derbyshire 4.

Bowling: *First Innings*—Malcolm 16.3-3-57-3; Mortensen 17-8-29-1; Cork 14-1-49-3; Warner 20-2-75-3. *Second Innings*—Mortensen 31-9-101-6; Malcolm 26-3-90-0; Warner 20-6-40-0; Cork 24-5-84-1; Goldsmith 8-1-23-1; Barnett 15.2-2-46-1; Bowler 5-0-21-0.

Umpires: M. J. Kitchen and B. Leadbeater.

## WORCESTERSHIRE v KENT

At Worcester, July 23, 24, 25. Drawn. Toss: Worcestershire. Rain restricted play to just fourteen overs on the first day and six on the second. The final day was washed out altogether. Worcestershire recalled Bent, almost a year to the day since his previous Championship appearance, but he fell to Merrick's fourth delivery without scoring.

*Close of play:* First day, Worcestershire 55-1 (T. S. Curtis 27*, T. M. Moody 26*); Second day, Worcestershire 64-2 (T. M. Moody 30*, D. B. D'Oliveira 3*).

## Worcestershire

| | |
|---|---|
| T. S. Curtis c Hinks b Merrick | 27 |
| P. Bent c Marsh b Merrick | 0 |
| T. M. Moody not out | 30 |
| D. B. D'Oliveira not out | 3 |
| L-b 4 | 4 |

1/5 2/58         (2 wkts) 64

*P. A. Neale, G. R. Haynes, †S. J. Rhodes, S. R. Lampitt, P. J. Newport, G. R. Dilley and
R. D. Stemp did not bat.

Bowling: Merrick 10–2–35–2; Igglesden 6–0–11–0; Penn 4–1–14–0.

## Kent

*M. R. Benson, T. R. Ward, N. R. Taylor, G. R. Cowdrey, S. G. Hinks, †S. A. Marsh,
M. V. Fleming, C. Penn, R. P. Davis, T. A. Merrick and A. P. Igglesden.

Umpires: M. J. Kitchen and B. Leadbeater.

At Cheltenham, July 26, 27, 29. WORCESTERSHIRE beat GLOUCESTERSHIRE by
108 runs.

At Worcester, July 30, 31, August 1. WORCESTERSHIRE beat SRI LANKANS by an
innings and 24 runs (See Sri Lankan tour section).

## WORCESTERSHIRE v WARWICKSHIRE

At Worcester, August 2, 3, 5. Worcestershire won by an innings and 33 runs. Worcestershire
23 pts, Warwickshire 6 pts. Toss: Worcestershire. Botham celebrated his recall to the England
side for the Fifth Test against West Indies with his best Championship return, seven for 54,
on the last day. Warwickshire, needing 156 to avoid an innings defeat, slumped from 46
without loss to 52 for five in nineteen balls either side of lunch, and with Botham taking seven
of their last nine wickets for 35 runs in eleven overs of swing bowling, the Championship
leaders were well beaten. But it was Moody's career-best 210 on the opening day that
Warwickshire found hardest to digest. Promoted to open the innings in a reshuffled order
from which the injured captain, Neale, was missing, their former player cut loose with an
awesome display of controlled power to compile his first double-century in England, off 249
balls. Altogether he faced 256 balls, hit three sixes and 28 fours, and added 186 in 33 overs for
the fifth wicket with Botham, who contributed 81 off 105 deliveries. In addition to surviving a
stumping chance off Pierson when 61 and a slip catch to Munton at 159, Moody was beaten
repeatedly early on by the luckless Donald. Warwickshire appeared well set to avoid the
follow-on when Ostler and Reeve were adding 116 for the fourth wicket, but they failed by
7 runs after losing their last seven wickets for 104. Reeve batted for four and a half hours for
his 97, the tenth time in fifteen championship innings he had passed 50 without going on to three figures.
*Close of play:* First day, Warwickshire 36–0 (A. J. Moles 9*, J. D. Ratcliffe 20*); Second
day, Warwickshire 298.

## Worcestershire

| | | | |
|---|---|---|---|
| *T. S. Curtis c Ostler b Donald | 10 | P. J. Newport not out | 26 |
| T. M. Moody c Asif Din b Reeve | 210 | N. V. Radford not out | 10 |
| G. A. Hick b Donald | 4 | | |
| D. B. D'Oliveira run out | 10 | B 10, l-b 11, w 5, n-b 8 | 34 |
| †S. J. Rhodes c Ostler b Reeve | 48 | | |
| I. T. Botham c Donald b Asif Din | 81 | 1/17 2/25 3/46    (8 wkts dec.) 454 |
| S. R. Lampitt lbw b Reeve | 0 | 4/190 5/376 6/376 |
| R. K. Illingworth c Holloway b Munton | 21 | 7/414 8/431 |

G. R. Dilley did not bat.

Bonus points – Worcestershire 4, Warwickshire 3.

Bowling: Donald 17–3–90–2; Small 18–3–72–0; Reeve 21–3–67–3; Munton 23–4–87–1; Pierson 13–1–80–0; Asif Din 6–0–37–1.

## Warwickshire

| | | |
|---|---|---|
| A. J. Moles b Dilley | 9 | – lbw b Dilley .......... 21 |
| J. D. Ratcliffe b Newport | 48 | – c Hick b Botham ...... 28 |
| Asif Din c Moody b Radford | 0 | – (6) b Botham ......... 3 |
| D. P. Ostler b Newport | 55 | – b Botham ............ 0 |
| D. A. Reeve st Rhodes b Illingworth | 97 | – b Dilley ............. 0 |
| *T. A. Lloyd c D'Oliveira b Newport | 0 | – (3) lbw b Botham .... 1 |
| †P. C. L. Holloway c Botham b Radford | 16 | – c Rhodes b Botham .... 41 |
| G. C. Small lbw b Botham | 6 | – c D'Oliveira b Botham . 13 |
| T. A. Munton c Botham b Dilley | 12 | – lbw b Botham ........ 0 |
| A. A. Donald c Rhodes b Dilley | 18 | – b Newport ........... 12 |
| A. R. K. Pierson not out | 2 | – not out ............. 0 |
| B 1, l-b 13, w 1, n-b 20 | 35 | L-b 2, w 1, n-b 1 ...... 4 |

1/47 2/48 3/78 4/194 5/194       298    1/46 2/51 3/51 4/52 5/52    123
6/228 7/240 8/268 9/292             6/67 7/93 8/95 9/119

Bonus points – Warwickshire 3, Worcestershire 3 (Score at 100 overs: 271-8).

Bowling: *First Innings*—Dilley 27.2–7–56–3; Radford 20–4–55–2; Illingworth 14–2–32–1; Botham 20–5–43–1; Newport 21–2–59–3; Lampitt 9–0–38–0; D'Oliveira 1–0–1–0. *Second Innings*—Dilley 12–3–23–2; Radford 6–0–18–0; Botham 18–5–54–7; Newport 5.2–1–26–1.

Umpires: J. W. Holder and R. C. Tolchard.

At Weston-super-Mare, August 6, 7, 8. WORCESTERSHIRE drew with SOMERSET.

## WORCESTERSHIRE v SURREY

At Worcester, August 16, 17, 19. Worcestershire won by three wickets. Worcestershire 24 pts, Surrey 5 pts. Toss: Surrey. Hick, back to his best, won a personal battle against Waqar Younis with a match-winning 85 from 68 balls as Worcestershire pulled off a spectacular triumph to dent Surrey's Championship ambitions. Surrey themselves had a chance of victory after Waqar had yorked Moody, D'Oliveira and Botham in ten deliveries to leave the home side, needing 145 off 29 overs, 92 for five after fourteen. But Hick, who reached 50 off 28 balls, found an able ally in Rhodes, who saw Worcestershire home with eleven balls to spare. Botham, with his third five-wicket return of the summer, was instrumental in Surrey's first-day collapse, and on the second day he hit 61 off 42 balls as Worcestershire amassed a lead of 216 on the back of a second-wicket stand of 232 in 67 overs between Curtis (220 balls) and Hick. Hick reached his third Championship century of the season off 167 balls, and hit a six and twenty fours in his 145 from 211 balls. Surrey, 84 runs in arrears at the start of the final morning, looked to be saving the game as Greig and Medlycott were adding 108 for the seventh wicket. But a brilliant, one-handed catch by Rhodes, to dismiss Greig, opened the door for Worcestershire.

Close of play: First day, Worcestershire 137-1 (T. S. Curtis 65*, G. A. Hick 59*); Second day, Surrey 132-2 (D. J. Bicknell 67*, N. F. Sargeant 2*).

## Surrey

| | | | |
|---|---|---|---|
| O. J. Bicknell c D'Oliveira b Lampitt | 35 | – lbw b Dilley | 79 |
| R. I. Alikhan c Rhodes b Botham | 30 | – b Newport | 0 |
| A. J. Stewart c Curtis b Dilley | 9 | – c D'Oliveira b Lampitt | 57 |
| D. M. Ward lbw b Botham | 14 | – (5) c Botham b Lampitt | 1 |
| G. P. Thorpe lbw b Illingworth | 22 | – (6) c Curtis b Illingworth | 30 |
| *I. A. Greig not out | 38 | – (7) c Rhodes b Lampitt | 72 |
| K. T. Medlycott c D'Oliveira b Illingworth | 4 | – (8) c D'Oliveira b Lampitt | 57 |
| †N. F. Sargeant c D'Oliveira b Botham | 3 | – (4) c Moody b Dilley | 11 |
| M. P. Bicknell c Lampitt b Botham | 0 | – b Botham | 10 |
| Waqar Younis c D'Oliveira b Illingworth | 15 | – c Newport b Lampitt | 7 |
| A. J. Murphy c Curtis b Botham | 1 | – not out | 2 |
| L-b 3, w 2, n-b 9 | 14 | B 12, l-b 10, n-b 12 | 34 |

1/59 2/79 3/91 4/123 5/123     185     1/14 2/124 3/147 4/153 5/172     360
6/131 7/142 8/142 9/169     6/229 7/337 8/351 9/351

Bonus points – Surrey 1, Worcestershire 4.

Bowling: *First Innings*—Dilley 14–4–30–1; Newport 12–4–30–0; Lampitt 9–3–25–1; Botham 20.5–4–67–5; Illingworth 13–5–30–3. *Second Innings*—Dilley 25–5–87–2; Newport 19–4–64–1; Botham 15–3–40–1; Illingworth 26–8–39–1; Lampitt 18.4–3–70–5; Hick 10–1–30–0; D'Oliveira 4–2–8–0.

## Worcestershire

| | | | |
|---|---|---|---|
| *T. S. Curtis c Sargeant b Waqar Younis | 98 | – c Stewart b M. P. Bicknell | 8 |
| P. Bent b Waqar Younis | 5 | – c Sargeant b M. P. Bicknell | 0 |
| G. A. Hick b Waqar Younis | 145 | – c Greig b Medlycott | 85 |
| T. M. Moody c Murphy b M. P. Bicknell | 37 | – b Waqar Younis | 17 |
| D. B. D'Oliveira b Waqar Younis | 0 | – b Waqar Younis | 1 |
| †S. J. Rhodes c Sargeant b M. P. Bicknell | 12 | – (7) not out | 23 |
| I. T. Botham c Thorpe b Medlycott | 61 | – (6) b Waqar Younis | 0 |
| R. K. Illingworth lbw b M. P. Bicknell | 9 | – c Sargeant b Medlycott | 0 |
| S. R. Lampitt b M. P. Bicknell | 3 | – not out | 5 |
| P. J. Newport not out | 2 | | |
| G. R. Dilley not out | 5 | | |
| B 1, l-b 20, w 2, n-b 1 | 24 | L-b 5, n-b 1 | 6 |

1/15 2/247 3/266 4/303 5/303     (9 wkts dec.) 401     1/8 2/25 3/82 4/90     (7 wkts) 145
6/352 7/382 8/394 9/396     5/92 6/137 7/137

Bonus points – Worcestershire 4, Surrey 4.

Bowling: *First Innings*—Waqar Younis 24–5–78–4; M. P. Bicknell 33–5–104–4; Murphy 18–3–91–0; Greig 4–1–12–0; Medlycott 21–3–95–1. *Second Innings*—Waqar Younis 14–3–56–3; M. P. Bicknell 4–1–30–2; Medlycott 9.1–0–54–2.

Umpires: B. Dudleston and D. O. Oslear.

At Blackpool, August 20, 21, 22. WORCESTERSHIRE drew with LANCASHIRE.

## WORCESTERSHIRE v MIDDLESEX

At Worcester, August 23, 24, 26. Drawn. Worcestershire 7 pts, Middlesex 5 pts. Toss: Middlesex. Worcestershire missed out on the opportunity of a fourth win in six Championship games by dropping five catches on the final day. Gatting, put down at third slip by Moody off Newport when 12, went on to compile his seventh century of the season, off 156 balls with sixteen fours, to save the game for his side. Surprisingly, Gatting had elected to bat first on a pitch dampened by overnight rain, and against a four-pronged pace attack, with Rhodes taking five catches behind the stumps, Middlesex were hustled out between the showers in 62.5 overs. Tolley confirmed his promise with his best Championship figures, while for

Middlesex, 22-year-old Weekes provided the only prolonged resistance with an unbeaten 57 after being dropped by Radford off Lampitt at 3. Worcestershire lost their first six wickets for 114, but Moody and Lampitt regained control with a stand of 126. Moody's sixth Championship hundred of the summer contained three sixes and nine fours, and he hit three more sixes before falling for 135, made in 212 minutes. When Middlesex lost three wickets in the first eight overs on the final morning, they were still 33 runs in arrears. But Weekes, who was dropped three times, rode his luck in a stand of 109 with Gatting, who then found a staunch defender in Emburey. Together they added a match-saving 64 for the sixth wicket.

*Close of play:* First day, Worcestershire 13-1 (T. S. Curtis 2*, R. K. Illingworth 8*); Second day, Middlesex 44-0 (M. A. Roseberry 15*, J. C. Pooley 22*).

## Middlesex

| | | | | |
|---|---|---|---|---|
| M. A. Roseberry c Rhodes b Lampitt | 36 | – c Moody b Newport | 15 |
| J. C. Pooley c Rhodes b Newport | 8 | – lbw b Radford | 28 |
| *M. W. Gatting b Lampitt | 9 | – b Hick | 120 |
| K. R. Brown c Moody b Radford | 26 | – c Moody b Newport | 1 |
| M. Keech c Bent b Tolley | 1 | – (6) b Radford | 4 |
| P. N. Weekes not out | 57 | – (5) c Rhodes b Radford | 48 |
| J. E. Emburey c Rhodes b Radford | 4 | – not out | 55 |
| †P. Farbrace c Curtis b Tolley | 18 | – lbw b Newport | 11 |
| N. F. Williams b Tolley | 15 | – run out | 0 |
| D. W. Headley c Rhodes b Lampitt | 0 | – b Newport | 0 |
| N. G. Cowans c Rhodes b Lampitt | 0 | – not out | 2 |
| B 6, l-b 1, n-b 8 | 15 | B 3, l-b 11, w 2, n-b 4 | 20 |

1/13 2/38 3/64 4/67 5/112　　　　　189　　　1/51 2/53 3/64　　(9 wkts dec.) 304
6/128 7/156 8/184 9/189　　　　　　　　　　4/173 5/179 6/243
　　　　　　　　　　　　　　　　　　　　　　7/277 8/278 9/280

Bonus points – Middlesex 1, Worcestershire 4.

Bowling: *First Innings*—Newport 14-3-35-1; Radford 13-2-45-2; Tolley 19-4-40-3; Lampitt 15.5-2-53-4; Illingworth 1-0-9-0. *Second Innings*—Newport 27-11-51-4; Tolley 7-1-37-0; Illingworth 39-10-90-0; Hick 14-4-33-1; D'Oliveira 5-0-29-0; Moody 1-0-4-0.

## Worcestershire

| | | | | |
|---|---|---|---|---|
| *T. S. Curtis b Weekes | 22 | C. M. Tolley c Farbrace b Headley | 14 |
| P. Bent b Cowans | 1 | P. J. Newport c Williams b Headley | 4 |
| R. K. Illingworth c Farbrace b Williams | 16 | N. V. Radford not out | 0 |
| G. A. Hick c Gatting b Emburey | 30 | | |
| T. M. Moody c Pooley b Headley | 135 | L-b 12, w 1, n-b 6 | 19 |
| D. B. D'Oliveira c Headley b Weekes | 10 | | |
| †S. J. Rhodes lbw b Emburey | 0 | 1/3 2/25 3/71 4/93 5/111 | 286 |
| S. R. Lampitt c and b Weekes | 35 | 6/114 7/240 8/281 9/281 | |

Bonus points – Worcestershire 3, Middlesex 4.

Bowling: Cowans 11-2-23-1; Headley 24.5-6-67-3; Williams 12-3-36-1; Gatting 4-0-15-0; Emburey 28-4-76-2; Weekes 19-5-57-3.

Umpires: A. A. Jones and D. O. Oslear.

At Birmingham, August 28, 29, 30. WORCESTERSHIRE lost to WARWICKSHIRE by four wickets.

## WORCESTERSHIRE v SOMERSET

At Worcester, September 3, 4, 5. Worcestershire won by an innings and 142 runs. Worcestershire 24 pts, Somerset 1 pt. Toss: Somerset. Worcestershire claimed the extra half-hour to complete their fifth Championship win of the season without need of the fourth day. Tavaré's decision to field first, influenced by a haze and the 10.30 a.m. start, was rewarded with the early wickets of the Worcestershire newcomer, Weston, and Hick. But a third-wicket stand of 256 in 67 overs between Curtis and Leatherdale provided the platform for a mammoth total. Leatherdale, in his first Championship appearance of the season, proved a capable replacement for Moody; he reached his maiden first-class century off 141 deliveries, and altogether he hit four sixes and 22 fours. Curtis, 135 not out overnight, displayed monumental concentration in an innings two minutes short of ten hours. Having reached his first-ever double-century off 452 balls, he went on to score 248 from 501 balls, with 27 fours. Those who questioned his decision to delay the declaration until 2.40 p.m. on the second afternoon soon had their answer. Cook was bowled first ball, for only the second time in his career, and Radford, buoyed by this success, went on to finish with seven wickets in 15.4 overs as Somerset were skittled out for 83. When they followed on, Cook and Burns put on 101 for the first wicket, and there was further resistance from Tavaré, Lathwell, making his Championship début, and Rose. But it only delayed the inevitable.

*Close of play:* First day, Worcestershire 378-3 (T. S. Curtis 135*, S. J. Rhodes 57*); Second day, Somerset 33-0 (S. J. Cook 15*, N. D. Burns 18*).

## Worcestershire

| | | |
|---|---|---|
| *T. S. Curtis c Burns b Hallett......248 | C. M. Tolley not out ............... | 24 |
| W. P. C. Weston c Burns b Mallender . 5 | P. J. Newport not out ............. | 1 |
| G. A. Hick lbw b Mallender ......... 11 | | |
| D. A. Leatherdale b Mallender ......157 | L-b 15, w 1, n-b 9.......... | 25 |
| †S. J. Rhodes c Burns b Mallender ... 58 | | |
| S. R. Lampitt b Mallender .......... 4 | 1/7 2/25 3/281 | (8 wkts. dec.) 575 |
| G. R. Haynes c Burns b Hallett ...... 6 | 4/388 5/399 6/416 | |
| R. K. Illingworth c Burns b Hallett.... 36 | 7/516 8/561 | |

N. V. Radford did not bat.

Bonus points – Worcestershire 4, Somerset 1 (Score at 100 overs: 337-3).

Bowling: Mallender 32-7-80-5; Rose 23-5-55-0; Hallett 36.3-6-154-3; Hayhurst 14.3-1-56-0; Lathwell 17-6-55-0; Trump 25-1-75-0; Graveney 27-8-85-0.

## Somerset

| | | | |
|---|---|---|---|
| S. J. Cook b Radford ................ | 0 | – lbw b Lampitt .............. | 50 |
| †N. D. Burns c Hick b Newport ....... | 11 | – lbw b Lampitt .............. | 88 |
| R. J. Harden lbw b Radford .......... | 3 | – c Rhodes b Lampitt ......... | 8 |
| *C. J. Tavaré not out ............... | 39 | – c Curtis b Lampitt .......... | 59 |
| M. N. Lathwell lbw b Radford ........ | 4 | – c Hick b Newport ........... | 43 |
| G. D. Rose c Leatherdale b Radford.... | 4 | – c Hick b Lampitt ........... | 58 |
| N. A. Mallender lbw b Radford ....... | 6 | – c Tolley b Newport ......... | 14 |
| H. R. J. Trump lbw b Radford ........ | 2 | – run out ................... | 0 |
| D. A. Graveney c Rhodes b Newport ... | 1 | –(10) not out ............... | 0 |
| J. C. Hallett c Rhodes b Radford ...... | 11 | – (9) c Curtis b Radford....... | 4 |
| A. N. Hayhurst absent injured ........ | | – absent injured | |
| N-b 2 ....................... | 2 | B 5, l-b 8, w 3, n-b 10 ... | 26 |
| | — | | — |
| 1/0 2/8 3/22 4/29 5/37 | 83 | 1/101 2/114 3/211 4/225 5/280 | 350 |
| 6/57 7/59 8/68 9/83 | | 6/326 7/326 8/344 9/350 | |

Bonus points – Worcestershire 4.

Bowling: *First Innings*—Radford 15.4-3-43-7; Newport 15-3-40-2. *Second Innings*—Radford 24-6-85-1; Newport 26-9-67-2; Illingworth 28-11-46-0; Lampitt 20.1-4-78-5; Hick 17.4-5-42-0; Tolley 8-2-19-0; Haynes 1.2-1-0-0.

Umpires: J. W. Holder and R. Julian.

At Cardiff, September 10, 11, 12, 13. WORCESTERSHIRE beat GLAMORGAN by ten wickets.

At Nottingham, September 17, 18, 19. WORCESTERSHIRE lost to NOTTINGHAM-SHIRE by an innings and 70 runs.

# YORKSHIRE

*Patron:* HRH The Duchess of Kent
*President:* Sir Lawrence Byford
*Chairman:* Sir Lawrence Byford
*Chairman, Cricket Committee:* D. B. Close
*Chief Executive:* C. D. Hassell
   Headingley Cricket Ground, Leeds LS6 3BU
   (Telephone: 0532-787394)
*Captain:* M. D. Moxon
*Director of Cricket:* S. Oldham

Yorkshire were in such disarray by the end of June that the general committee, under the decisive leadership of their new president and chairman, Sir Lawrence Byford, broke with the tradition of relying exclusively on players from within the county. The majority view was that defeat by Warwickshire in the first round of the NatWest Bank Trophy had effectively ended their season – they were then bottom of the Championship table and could only hope for Sunday League success; the outcome was that on July 10 the committee agreed to employ an overseas player. And with remarkable speed and efficiency, the county announced on July 19 the signing of the Australian fast bowler, Craig McDermott, for 1992.

It proved to be a fairly painless process, with members generally accepting that Yorkshire cricket was in a desperate state. Spelling out the harsh financial facts, Sir Lawrence indicated that the club were facing a £100,000 loss on the year and that membership had declined by 3,000 since their last trophy in 1987. The threat of bankruptcy clouded the future, with little prospect of any improvement until things took a turn for the better on the field. Additionally, the players and the cricket manager, Steve Oldham, were very much in favour of recruiting outside help.

In the subsequent search for economies, Oldham was given a new role as director of cricket, which took him away from the first team's activities, while Stuart Fletcher and the Second Eleven captain, Neil Hartley, were released. Veteran all-rounder Arnie Sidebottom retired, after one first-class appearance against the Sri Lankans and eight in one-day matches, as did the uncapped Chris Shaw, and Phil Robinson, having failed to settle long-standing differences with the management, declined the offer of a new contract. Off-spinner Phil Berry was allowed to join Durham.

Yorkshire slipped from tenth to fourteenth in the Britannic Assurance Championship and were seventh in the Refuge Assurance League, compared to joint sixth in 1990. After a wretched start in the 40-overs competition, losing their first four games, they had the satisfaction of six successive victories, a club record, and of winning nine out of ten matches before falling away again to miss qualifying for the Refuge Assurance Cup. However, the highlight of the summer was the convincing run of wins in the Benson and Hedges Cup, and notably the dismissal of a strong Hampshire batting line-up for 50. But in the semi-finals, erratic bowling and a spectacular batting collapse undermined their challenge to Lancashire.

Remarkably, Yorkshire gained their four Championship victories by dismissing the opposition in a run-chase, but a more telling statistic revealed that they had the lowest number of bowling bonus points, their 37 being eight below those of bottom-placed Somerset. They were massively handicapped by injury to Paul Jarvis, who broke down with hamstring trouble in late May and did not return to first-class cricket until the final fixture with Derbyshire. In his absence, the seam bowling carried little penetration, although Peter Hartley occasionally achieved a degree of hostility.

Mark Robinson, returning to his native county from Northamptonshire, was a disappointment, and spent a long spell in the second team working on his run-up. Fletcher took only twenty first-class wickets and failed to make much of an impression, although he did capture a useful eighteen in the Sunday League. There was little success for Darren Gough, but he finished with something of a flourish to keep alive hopes that he would develop into an all-rounder of substance.

In the circumstances, Phil Carrick, who claimed his 1,000th first-class wicket in the Old Trafford Roses match, carried a heavy responsibility. The slow left-armer easily headed the averages for the regular bowlers, was the leading wicket-taker, and at times held the whole operation together. Left out of the Sunday side as a matter of policy in the early stages, he forced his way back and bowled as well as at any time in his career. He also chipped in with useful runs, and went into the 1992 season needing 13 more to complete 10,000 first-class runs in his career. Jeremy Batty, the twenty-year-old off-spinner, made important progress as Yorkshire successfully, if belatedly, adopted the policy of playing two slow bowlers at all levels, and he looked one of the brightest prospects for the future.

With such slender resources at his disposal, Martyn Moxon faced a difficult job as captain, but he remained both optimistic and positive, always ready to risk defeat in the search for victory. Much the most accomplished batsman, he enjoyed his most prolific summer with 1,669 Championship runs. David Byas, promoted to No. 3, responded by reaching 1,000 for the first time, fully deserving his cap and finally ending doubts over his consistency. After scoring heavily in 1990, Ashley Metcalfe did not live up to expectations, Robinson was also variable, while Simon Kellett, although compiling his maiden first-class century at the expense of the Sri Lankans, and hitting a Championship first at Chesterfield, made too many unforced errors. Richard Blakey, unfortunately, showed only fleeting glimpses of his best form, and moved down the order to No. 6 in an attempt to cope with the double demands of being both wicket-keeper and batsman. There remained some danger that he would fall between two stools.

For the first time since 1966, the county had five batsmen with 1,000 first-class runs. Yet they always looked vulnerable in anything approaching testing conditions. In general, what the team lacked was the old-fashioned Yorkshire quality of hard-nosed professionalism, and that was a matter requiring serious attention from a cricket committee which appeared to have become too distant from the players. – John Callaghan.

632

YORKSHIRE 1991

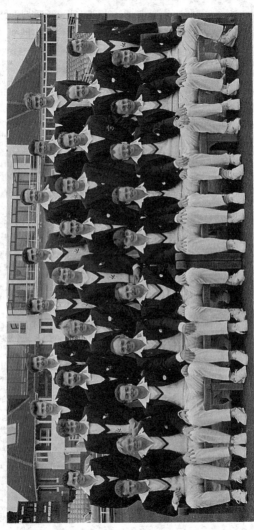

*Back row*: I. J. Houseman, P. J. Berry, C. White, M. A. Robinson, C. S. Pickles, D. Gough, M. J. Doidge. *Middle row*: W. P. Morton (*physiotherapist*), S. A. Kellett, C. Shaw, S. D. Fletcher, D. Byas, P. J. Hartley, A. P. Grayson, J. D. Batty, P. E. Robinson, M. K. Bore (*Academy coach*). *Front row*: P. W. Jarvis, D. E. V. Padgett (*coach*), K. Sharp, P. Carrick, S. Oldham (*manager*), M. D. Moxon (*captain*), A. A. Metcalfe, A. Sidebottom, S. N. Hartley, R. J. Blakey.

[*Jim Ballard*]

## YORKSHIRE RESULTS

*All first-class matches – Played 24: Won 4, Lost 6, Drawn 14.*

*County Championship matches – Played 22: Won 4, Lost 6, Drawn 12.*

*Bonus points – Batting 58, Bowling 37.*

*Competition placings – Britannic Assurance County Championship, 14th;*
*NatWest Bank Trophy, 1st round; Benson and Hedges Cup, s-f;*
*Refuge Assurance League, 7th.*

## BRITANNIC ASSURANCE CHAMPIONSHIP AVERAGES

### BATTING

| | Birthplace | M | I | NO | R | HI | Avge |
|---|---|---|---|---|---|---|---|
| ‡M. D. Moxon | Barnsley | 21 | 37 | 1 | 1,669 | 200 | 46.36 |
| ‡D. Byas | Kilham | 22 | 37 | 4 | 1,413 | 153 | 42.81 |
| ‡P. W. Jarvis | Redcar | 4 | 5 | 2 | 114 | 37* | 38.00 |
| ‡P. E. Robinson | Keighley | 22 | 38 | 6 | 1,136 | 189 | 35.50 |
| S. A. Kellett | Mirfield | 22 | 36 | 4 | 992 | 125* | 31.00 |
| ‡P. Carrick | Armley | 21 | 32 | 9 | 662 | 67 | 28.78 |
| ‡A. A. Metcalfe | Horsforth | 22 | 39 | 2 | 1,060 | 123 | 28.64 |
| D. Gough | Barnsley | 12 | 14 | 3 | 307 | 72 | 27.90 |
| ‡P. J. Hartley | Keighley | 20 | 24 | 10 | 322 | 50* | 23.00 |
| C. S. Pickles | Mirfield | 11 | 16 | 3 | 284 | 51 | 21.84 |
| ‡R. J. Blakey | Huddersfield | 22 | 36 | 2 | 739 | 97 | 21.73 |
| J. D. Batty | Bradford | 16 | 16 | 6 | 151 | 31 | 15.10 |
| ‡S. D. Fletcher | Keighley | 12 | 11 | 2 | 48 | 9* | 5.33 |
| M. A. Robinson | Hull | 15 | 13 | 4 | 17 | 8 | 1.88 |

*\* Signifies not out.    ‡ Denotes county cap.*

The following played a total of eleven three-figure innings for Yorkshire in County Championship matches – D. Byas 4, M. D. Moxon 3, A. A. Metcalfe 2, S. A. Kellett 1, P. E. Robinson 1.

### BOWLING

| | O | M | R | W | BB | 5W/i | Avge |
|---|---|---|---|---|---|---|---|
| P. W. Jarvis | 95 | 26 | 235 | 12 | 4-28 | 0 | 19.58 |
| P. Carrick | 701.2 | 231 | 1,748 | 61 | 5-13 | 2 | 28.65 |
| J. D. Batty | 399.4 | 91 | 1,230 | 37 | 6-48 | 1 | 33.24 |
| P. J. Hartley | 522.3 | 100 | 1,751 | 50 | 6-151 | 3 | 35.02 |
| S. D. Fletcher | 230.1 | 45 | 738 | 20 | 6-70 | 1 | 36.90 |
| M. A. Robinson | 377.1 | 78 | 1,126 | 23 | 3-43 | 0 | 48.95 |
| D. Gough | 252 | 52 | 890 | 16 | 5-41 | 1 | 55.62 |

Also bowled: D. Byas 2-0-7-0; S. A. Kellett 4-0-7-0; A. A. Metcalfe 3-0-23-0; M. D. Moxon 11-2-27-2; C. S. Pickles 138-19-468-6; P. E. Robinson 10-1-49-0.

**Wicket-keeper:** R. J. Blakey 35 ct, 4 st.

**Leading Fielders:** D. Byas 20, P. E. Robinson 19, S. A. Kellett 17, M. D. Moxon 17.

At Lord's, April 27, 29, 30, May 1. YORKSHIRE drew with MIDDLESEX.

## YORKSHIRE v WARWICKSHIRE

At Leeds, May 9, 10, 11, 13. Warwickshire won by 30 runs. Warwickshire 23 pts, Yorkshire 5 pts. Toss: Warwickshire. Scoring was never easy on a low, seaming pitch and, despite a solid half-century from Lloyd, Warwickshire were struggling at 167 for eight. Small, however, adopted a positive attitude, hitting two sixes and four fours in his 103-ball 58, and Munton also punished any bowling errors. Donald's extra pace subsequently proved the decisive factor for Warwickshire. Batsmen, forced to play back, became vulnerable to the uneven bounce. Metcalfe managed only three boundaries in making 52 from 144 deliveries in Yorkshire's reply, and Moles, with 73 from 190 balls, and with the patience to wait for the bad ball, was the only player to prosper in Warwickshire's second innings. Yorkshire had plenty of time in which to make 260 for victory, but never looked likely to prolong their resistance over a sufficient period. Moxon worked hard for more than three hours before being caught off a ball which lifted sharply, and only an eighth-wicket stand of 42 in twelve overs between Carrick and Hartley threatened Warwickshire. Donald finished with match figures of ten for 96, and fifteen of the 40 wickets fell to lbw decisions, believed to be a record for a Championship match in Yorkshire.

*Close of play:* First day, Yorkshire 6-0 (M. D. Moxon 5*, A. A. Metcalfe 1*); Second day, Warwickshire 73-3 (A. J. Moles 39*, D. A. Reeve 10*); Third day, Yorkshire 178-7 (P. Carrick 24*, P. J. Hartley 0*).

### Warwickshire

| | | | | |
|---|---:|---|---|---:|
| A. J. Moles c Blakey b Hartley | 0 | – lbw b Hartley | | 73 |
| J. D. Ratcliffe c P. E. Robinson b Fletcher | 13 | – lbw b M. A. Robinson | | 5 |
| *T. A. Lloyd c Byas b M. A. Robinson | 56 | – c P. E. Robinson b Pickles | | 15 |
| P. A. Smith lbw b Fletcher | 38 | – c Metcalfe b Pickles | | 0 |
| D. A. Reeve c Kellett b Fletcher | 5 | – b Hartley | | 24 |
| D. P. Ostler c Blakey b Hartley | 28 | – c Moxon b Carrick | | 1 |
| †K. J. Piper b Fletcher | 8 | – b Hartley | | 3 |
| P. A. Booth run out | 10 | – lbw b Fletcher | | 17 |
| G. C. Small c Moxon b Hartley | 58 | – not out | | 10 |
| T. A. Munton b Moxon | 31 | – c Byas b Carrick | | 2 |
| A. A. Donald not out | 11 | – lbw b Carrick | | 0 |
| B 2, l-b 2, w 2, n-b 4 | 10 | L-b 4, w 2 | | 6 |

1/3 2/50 3/101 4/119 5/122       268     1/22 2/59 3/59 4/122 5/123      156
6/132 7/161 8/167 9/230                        6/123 7/134 8/153 9/156

Bonus points – Warwickshire 3, Yorkshire 4 (Score at 100 overs: 251-9).

*Bowling: First Innings*—Hartley 24.1-9-47-3; M. A. Robinson 18-6-40-1; Pickles 18-2-59-0; Fletcher 28-8-70-4; Carrick 9-1-31-0; Moxon 7-1-17-1. *Second Innings*—Hartley 20.5-5-53-3; M. A. Robinson 18.4-4-42-1; Fletcher 11-3-36-1; Carrick 17.5-10-13-3; Pickles 4-1-8-2.

### Yorkshire

| | | | | |
|---|---:|---|---|---:|
| *M. D. Moxon c Moles b Donald | 14 | – c Lloyd b Donald | | 57 |
| A. A. Metcalfe lbw b Munton | 52 | – b Piper b Donald | | 1 |
| D. Byas lbw b Reeve | 44 | – lbw b Smith | | 7 |
| †R. J. Blakey c Ratcliffe b Donald | 2 | – lbw b Reeve | | 9 |
| P. E. Robinson b Donald | 0 | – lbw b Munton | | 33 |
| S. A. Kellett lbw b Munton | 8 | – b Donald | | 17 |
| C. S. Pickles b Munton | 10 | – lbw b Booth | | 0 |
| P. Carrick not out | 13 | – lbw b Donald | | 36 |
| P. J. Hartley c Munton b Donald | 0 | – c Reeve b Munton | | 21 |
| S. D. Fletcher c Lloyd b Munton | 1 | – lbw b Donald | | 5 |
| M. A. Robinson lbw b Donald | 0 | – not out | | 0 |
| B 9, l-b 4, w 3, n-b 5 | 21 | B 6, l-b 21, w 6, n-b 9 | | 42 |

1/18 2/100 3/104 4/112 5/123       165     1/12 2/35 3/57 4/108 5/151      229
6/132 7/148 8/156 9/161                        6/152 7/173 8/215 9/228

Bonus points – Yorkshire 1, Warwickshire 4.

Bowling: *First Innings*—Donald 14.3–2–42–5; Munton 30–11–57–4; Small 13–4–27–0; Smith 10–3–20–0; Reeve 5–1–6–1. *Second Innings*—Donald 22–5–54–5; Munton 30.1–7–65–2; Small 13–4–26–0; Smith 10–2–26–1; Booth 7–4–17–1; Reeve 9–4–14–1.

Umpires: J. C. Balderstone and R. A. White.

## YORKSHIRE v NOTTINGHAMSHIRE

At Leeds, May 16, 17, 18, 20. Drawn. Yorkshire 5 pts, Nottinghamshire 6 pts. Toss: Nottinghamshire. Yorkshire, put in on a pitch allowing some movement off the seam, were unsettled by Stephenson, who claimed three for 20 in his opening six overs. Robinson and Kellett held the innings together, adding 78 in 30 overs for the fifth wicket, and Carrick and Jarvis contributed another 64 in fourteen as the latter struck 31 from 38 balls. Broad, missed on 68 twice, led a careful Nottinghamshire reply with 86 from 130 deliveries, having initially raced to his fifty from 56 balls. Given a lead of 47, Yorkshire pressed on, although with a day lost, time was against them. Robinson again batted positively to make an unbeaten 53 from 108 balls, with a six and four fours. Moxon had limited room for manoeuvre, but he set a target of 235 in 49 overs. Broad and Pollard responded by putting on 69 in nineteen overs, but the innings gradually lost momentum in the face of a steady spell by Carrick, who exerted control with his slow left-arm bowling at a critical stage.

*Close of play:* First day, No play; Second day, Yorkshire 231-7 (P. Carrick 35*, P. J. Hartley 10*); Third day, Yorkshire 50-0 (M. D. Moxon 16*, A. A. Metcalfe 28*).

### Yorkshire

| | | |
|---|---|---|
| *M. D. Moxon b Stephenson | 2 | – c French b Hemmings ............ 36 |
| A. A. Metcalfe lbw b Stephenson | 22 | – lbw b Pick ............ 28 |
| D. Byas lbw b Stephenson | 4 | – lbw b Hemmings ............ 23 |
| †R. J. Blakey lbw b Pick | 11 | – c Pollard b Evans ............ 1 |
| P. E. Robinson c French b Hemmings | 57 | – not out ............ 53 |
| S. A. Kellett lbw b Hemmings | 41 | – c Pollard b Hemmings ...... 0 |
| P. Carrick c Broad b Pick | 47 | – not out ............ 20 |
| P. W. Jarvis b Hemmings | 31 | |
| P. J. Hartley c French b Stephenson | 24 | |
| S. D. Fletcher c Hemmings b Pick | 1 | |
| M. A. Robinson not out | 0 | |
| L-b 10, w 6, n-b 4 | 20 | B 1, l-b 15, w 1, n-b 9 ... 26 |

| | | |
|---|---|---|
| 1/3 2/17 3/40 4/59 5/137 | 260 | 1/55 2/89 3/96 (5 wkts dec.) 187 |
| 6/148 7/212 8/254 9/260 | | 4/118 5/120 |

Bonus points – Yorkshire 3, Nottinghamshire 4.

Bowling: *First Innings*—Stephenson 24–3–84–4; Pick 25.3–5–76–3; Evans 20–4–44–0; Hemmings 10–2–37–3; Saxelby 6–4–9–0. *Second Innings*—Stephenson 15–5–50–0; Pick 15–2–38–1; Hemmings 22–6–59–3; Evans 13–3–24–1.

### Nottinghamshire

| | | |
|---|---|---|
| B. C. Broad lbw b Hartley | 86 | – c Blakey b Jarvis ............ 48 |
| P. R. Pollard c Kellett b Hartley | 2 | – lbw b M. A. Robinson ........ 40 |
| *R. T. Robinson c P. E. Robinson b Fletcher | 25 | – (4) c Kellett b M. A. Robinson . 2 |
| P. Johnson lbw b Hartley | 31 | – (3) c Byas b Carrick ......... 7 |
| D. W. Randall not out | 37 | – b Carrick ............ 7 |
| M. Saxelby b Carrick | 17 | – lbw b Jarvis ............ 16 |
| K. P. Evans not out | 7 | – not out ............ 3 |
| F. D. Stephenson (did not bat) | | – not out ............ 24 |
| L-b 7, n-b 1 | 8 | B 2, w 1, n-b 1 ......... 4 |

| | | |
|---|---|---|
| 1/12 2/97 3/143 4/146 5/186 | (5 wkts dec.) 213 | 1/69 2/82 3/91 (6 wkts) 151 |
| | | 4/108 5/108 6/126 |

†B. N. French, E. E. Hemmings and R. A. Pick did not bat.

Bonus points – Nottinghamshire 2, Yorkshire 2.

Bowling: *First Innings*—Jarvis 15–3–37–0; Hartley 14–2–46–3; M. A. Robinson 17–3–42–0; Carrick 15–6–28–1; Fletcher 15–2–53–1. *Second Innings*—Jarvis 15–6–49–2; Hartley 6–0–27–0; M. A. Robinson 9–0–30–2; Fletcher 3–0–15–0; Carrick 15–7–28–2.

Umpires: J. D. Bond and B. Leadbeater.

## YORKSHIRE v GLOUCESTERSHIRE

At Sheffield, May 22, 23, 24. Drawn. Yorkshire 4 pts, Gloucestershire 4 pts. Toss: Yorkshire. Despite a sound start, Yorkshire scored too slowly on an easy-paced pitch, wasting the advantage given them by a second-wicket stand of 121 in 47 overs between Moxon and Byas. The latter's 87 used up 220 balls and included only eight fours. After Moxon had prolonged his side's first innings into the second day, Gloucestershire were equally cautious, only just managing a third batting point in the 100th over. Wright, missed when 5, 17 and 19, reached his century in 354 minutes from 288 deliveries, having hit one six and eight fours. But with his declaration, 115 behind, the tempo changed significantly. Moxon and Metcalfe took 100 runs from 25 overs, without any noticeable assistance from the bowlers, and Gloucestershire's target amounted to 235 in a minimum of 57 overs. Once off-spinner Batty had claimed three wickets for no runs in eight balls, however, Gloucestershire understandably concentrated on survival. Alleyne, making the most of escapes at 23 and 35, compiled a studious half-century and stood firm with Hardy for 24 overs.

*Close of play*: First day, Yorkshire 315-5 (S. A. Kellett 20*, P. W. Jarvis 6*); Second day, Gloucestershire 212-3 (A. J. Wright 72*, M. W. Alleyne 35*).

### Yorkshire

| | | | |
|---|---|---|---|
| *M. D. Moxon c Wright b Athey | 65 | – st Williams b Lloyds | 55 |
| A. A. Metcalfe b Smith | 15 | – c Alleyne b Lloyds | 47 |
| D. Byas c Hodgson b Alleyne | 87 | | |
| †R. J. Blakey lbw b Babington | 55 | | |
| P. E. Robinson c Gilbert b Babington | 31 | – (3) not out | 6 |
| S. A. Kellett lbw b Gilbert | 26 | | |
| P. W. Jarvis not out | 37 | | |
| D. Gough c Babington b Gilbert | 26 | | |
| B 14, l-b 13, w 1, n-b 18 | 46 | L-b 9, n-b 2 | 11 |

1/23 2/144 3/240 4/272 5/297    (7 wkts dec.) 388     1/100 2/119     (2 wkts dec.) 119
6/326 7/388

P. J. Hartley, J. D. Batty and M. A. Robinson did not bat.

Bonus points – Yorkshire 3, Gloucestershire 1 (Score at 100 overs: 278-4).

Bowling: *First Innings*—Gilbert 30–6–80–2; Babington 39–3–121–2; Smith 19–2–55–1; Lloyds 20–6–48–0; Alleyne 12–0–39–1; Athey 7–1–18–1. *Second Innings*—Gilbert 6–0–18–0; Babington 9–3–23–0; Lloyds 8–0–32–2; Smith 2–0–19–0; Alleyne 2–0–18–0.

### Gloucestershire

| | | | |
|---|---|---|---|
| G. D. Hodgson c Blakey b Batty | 54 | – b Batty | 20 |
| R. J. Scott c Gough b Jarvis | 17 | – c and b M. A. Robinson | 14 |
| *A. J. Wright not out | 100 | – lbw b Batty | 0 |
| C. W. J. Athey lbw b Gough | 12 | – c Kellett b Batty | 0 |
| M. W. Alleyne c Byas b Batty | 40 | – not out | 55 |
| J. J. E. Hardy not out | 21 | – not out | 32 |
| B 20, l-b 5, w 2, n-b 2 | 29 | B 2, l-b 1, w 1, n-b 1 | 5 |

1/35 2/124 3/144 4/223    (4 wkts dec.) 273     1/32 2/34 3/34 4/44     (4 wkts) 126

J. W. Lloyds, †R. C. J. Williams, D. R. Gilbert, A. M. Smith and A. M. Babington did not bat.

Bonus points – Gloucestershire 3, Yorkshire 1 (Score at 100 overs: 250-4).

Bowling: *First Innings*—Hartley 14.4–3–45–0; Jarvis 14–4–25–1; Gough 23–6–54–1; Batty 37–8–95–2; M. A. Robinson 12–2–24–0; P. E. Robinson 2–0–5–0. *Second Innings*—Hartley 7–1–18–0; Gough 9–2–28–0; M. A. Robinson 10–3–19–1; Batty 18–5–44–3; P. E. Robinson 3–1–14–0.

Umpires: R. C. Tolchard and P. B. Wight.

## YORKSHIRE v NORTHAMPTONSHIRE

At Leeds, May 25, 27, 28. Drawn. Yorkshire 4 pts, Northamptonshire 6 pts. Toss: Yorkshire. A weakened Northamptonshire attack reduced Yorkshire to 169 for five on a typical Headingley pitch allowing movement off the seam. Moxon made 108 in four hours from 198 balls, hitting seventeen fours, but Kellett, stiffening the late order, reached 53 from 143 deliveries without hitting a boundary. Northamptonshire batted very slowly in reply. Bailey and Capel put on 95 in 34 overs, with the former needing 151 balls for 50 and the latter 104 for his unbeaten 69. Without recourse to the ridiculous, Northamptonshire allowed Yorkshire to reach a position from which a target could be set, the final equation being 266 in 60 overs. Although Fordham set off at a gallop, Northamptonshire were never on course for victory. Carrick achieved some slow turn to pose problems, and Curran, resisting for 35 overs, had to work hard to prevent a total collapse. Carrick and Hartley both took two wickets with successive deliveries, and Roberts must have been desperately close to lbw as he foiled Hartley's attempt to complete a hat-trick. However, he then defended his way through the last eight overs with some style.

*Close of play:* First day, Northamptonshire 8-0 (A. Fordham 2*, N. A. Felton 5*); Second day, Yorkshire 3-0 (M. D. Moxon 1*, A. A. Metcalfe 2*).

## Yorkshire

| | | | |
|---|---:|---|---:|
| *M. D. Moxon c Ripley b Curran | 108 | – b Capel | 42 |
| A. A. Metcalfe c Ripley b Capel | 27 | – b Roberts | 53 |
| D. Byas b Penberthy | 5 | – not out | 40 |
| †R. J. Blakey c Curran b Hughes | 3 | | |
| P. E. Robinson lbw b Capel | 5 | – (4) lbw b Curran | 21 |
| S. A. Kellett lbw b Bailey | 53 | – (5) c Thomas b Curran | 5 |
| P. Carrick lbw b Thomas | 23 | – (6) not out | 31 |
| P. J. Hartley b Thomas | 0 | | |
| J. D. Batty c Curran b Thomas | 31 | | |
| S. D. Fletcher lbw b Capel | 2 | | |
| M. A. Robinson not out | 1 | | |
| B 1, l-b 16, w 2 | 19 | B 3, l-b 4 | 7 |
| | 277 | (4 wkts dec.) | 199 |

1/68 2/87 3/101 4/124 5/169
6/210 7/210 8/256 9/267

1/92 2/100
3/139 4/151

Bonus points – Yorkshire 3, Northamptonshire 4 (Score at 100 overs: 272-9).

Bowling: *First Innings*—Thomas 21.1–3–48–3; Penberthy 15–3–54–1; Roberts 17–4–36–0; Capel 21–5–45–3; Curran 11–3–24–1; Hughes 12–1–43–1; Bailey 4–0–10–1. *Second Innings*—Thomas 6–0–9–0; Penberthy 7–0–32–0; Capel 8–0–32–1; Roberts 6–0–45–1; Bailey 7–1–33–0; Curran 6.5–1–41–2.

## Northamptonshire

| | | | |
|---|---:|---|---:|
| A. Fordham c Metcalfe b Fletcher | 33 | – b Hartley | 33 |
| N. A. Felton c Batty b Moxon | 43 | – c Metcalfe b Carrick | 32 |
| *R. J. Bailey b Fletcher | 50 | – c Blakey b M. A. Robinson | 6 |
| D. J. Capel not out | 69 | – lbw b Carrick | 9 |
| K. M. Curran c Moxon b Batty | 1 | – not out | 28 |
| A. L. Penberthy not out | 2 | – c P. E. Robinson b Carrick | 4 |
| J. G. Thomas (did not bat) | | – c Kellett b Carrick | 0 |
| †D. Ripley (did not bat) | | – b Hartley | 8 |
| W. M. Noon (did not bat) | | – b Hartley | 0 |
| A. R. Roberts (did not bat) | | – not out | 9 |
| L-b 7, w 1, n-b 5 | 13 | L-b 5, n-b 4 | 9 |
| | | | |
| | 211 | (8 wkts) | 138 |

1/68 2/100 3/195 4/198          (4 wkts dec.) 211
1/49 2/68 3/82 4/89      (8 wkts) 138
5/101 6/101 7/124 8/124

J. G. Hughes did not bat.

Bonus points – Northamptonshire 2, Yorkshire 1.

Bowling: *First Innings*—Fletcher 19.3–3–41–2; Hartley 16–5–35–0; Carrick 18–5–36–0; M. A. Robinson 12–2–29–0; Moxon 4–1–10–1; Batty 16–2–53–1. *Second Innings*—Hartley 16.5–5–34–3; Fletcher 5–0–28–0; M. A. Robinson 9–2–28–1; Carrick 19–9–25–4; Batty 10–4–18–0.

Umpires: R. C. Tolchard and P. B. Wight.

At Birmingham, May 31, June 1, 3. YORKSHIRE lost to WARWICKSHIRE by 39 runs.

At Oxford, June 4, 5, 6. YORKSHIRE drew with OXFORD UNIVERSITY.

## YORKSHIRE v KENT

At Harrogate, June 14, 15, 17. Drawn. Yorkshire 1 pt, Kent 2 pts. Toss: Yorkshire. Moxon's 90 from 165 balls included fifteen fours, but Fleming's three-wicket burst, which robbed the Yorkshire captain of a possible century, emphasised the sporting nature of the pitch. Rain cut the first day to 73 overs and, getting under the covers, prevented any further play.

*Close of play:* First day, Yorkshire 196-5 (R. J. Blakey 30*, P. Carrick 12*); Second day, No play.

### Yorkshire

| | | | | |
|---|---|---|---|---|
| *M. D. Moxon b Fleming | 90 | P. Carrick not out | | 12 |
| A. A. Metcalfe c Penn b McCague | 10 | | | |
| D. Byas c Taylor b Ellison | 36 | B 2, l-b 7, w 2, n-b 2 | | 13 |
| †R. J. Blakey not out | 30 | | | — |
| P. E. Robinson lbw b Fleming | 0 | 1/18 2/105 3/158 | (5 wkts) | 196 |
| S. A. Kellett c Marsh b Fleming | 5 | 4/158 5/169 | | |

D. Gough, J. D. Batty, C. S. Pickles and S. D. Fletcher did not bat.

Bonus points – Yorkshire 1, Kent 2.

Bowling: Igglesden 14–4–33–0; McCague 22–6–55–1; Davis 3–2–6–0; Ellison 12–2–51–1; Penn 7–2–14–0; Fleming 15–7–28–3.

### Kent

N. R. Taylor, *M. R. Benson, T. R. Ward, G. R. Cowdrey, M. V. Fleming, R. M. Ellison, †S. A. Marsh, R. P. Davis, M. J. McCague, C. Penn and A. P. Igglesden.

Umpires: J. D. Bond and G. I. Burgess.

## YORKSHIRE v MIDDLESEX

At Sheffield, June 21, 22, 24. Drawn. Yorkshire 4 pts, Middlesex 2 pts. Toss: Middlesex. Put in on an easy-paced pitch, Yorkshire batted steadily, helped later on by Middlesex missing Robinson on 16 and Pickles on 14. Gatting was happy to declare behind, to make up time lost to the weather on the first day, and Middlesex gained a clear advantage by reducing Yorkshire to 41 for five on the third morning. However, Pickles survived a shaky start to launch a counter-attack, going to 51 from 83 deliveries (seven fours) and adding 55 in sixteen overs with Carrick. Metcalfe's declaration left Middlesex to make 277 in what became 69 overs. Gatting kept them in touch with 82 from 121 balls, hitting fifteen fours, but when Hartley took three wickets for 1 run in eighteen balls, Middlesex were left to fight a rearguard action. Hughes and Tufnell, their last pair, held out for 37 balls to ensure a draw.

*Close of play:* First day, Yorkshire 117-1 (A. A. Metcalfe 58*, D. Byas 37*); Second day, Yorkshire 26-2 (S. A. Kellett 14*, J. D. Batty 6*).

## Yorkshire

| | | | |
|---|---|---|---|
| S. A. Kellett c Brown b Williams | 13 | – b Tufnell | 18 |
| *A. A. Metcalfe lbw b Cowans | 61 | – c and b Hughes | 3 |
| D. Byas lbw b Tufnell | 49 | – c Roseberry b Emburey | 2 |
| †R. J. Blakey c Hutchinson b Hughes | 44 | – (5) b Embury | 21 |
| P. E. Robinson c Farbrace b Hughes | 33 | – (6) lbw b Tufnell | 0 |
| C. S. Pickles not out | 22 | – (7) lbw b Embury | 51 |
| P. Carrick not out | 13 | – (8) not out | 12 |
| J. D. Batty (did not bat) | | – (4) c Farbrace b Williams | 10 |
| D. Gough (did not bat) | | – not out | 2 |
| L-b 7, n-b 8 | 15 | B 4, l-b 5, n-b 2 | 11 |

1/30 2/133 3/133 4/207 5/212     (5 wkts dec.) 250    1/4 2/16 3/30     (7 wkts dec.) 130
4/39 5/41
6/73 7/128

P. J. Hartley and S. D. Fletcher did not bat.

Bonus points – Yorkshire 3, Middlesex 2.

Bowling: *First Innings*—Williams 18–3–53–1; Cowans 16–5–30–1; Emburey 23–7–54–0; Tufnell 26.5–9–62–1; Hughes 14–3–44–2. *Second Innings*—Cowans 5–2–3–0; Hughes 5–4–1–1; Williams 9–1–23–1; Tufnell 20–6–59–2; Emburey 13–2–35–3.

## Middlesex

| | | | |
|---|---|---|---|
| I. J. F. Hutchinson c Blakey b Pickles | 21 | – c Blakey b Hartley | 0 |
| M. A. Roseberry c Fletcher b Gough | 12 | – c Byas b Pickles | 29 |
| K. R. Brown run out | 0 | – (4) lbw b Hartley | 30 |
| M. Keech c and b Batty | 30 | – (5) b Batty | 9 |
| †P. Farbrace not out | 36 | – (9) c Blakey b Hartley | 11 |
| N. F. Williams not out | 0 | – (7) c Kellett b Carrick | 5 |
| *M. W. Gatting (did not bat) | | – (3) b Hartley | 82 |
| J. E. Emburey (did not bat) | | – (6) lbw b Hartley | 1 |
| N. G. Cowans (did not bat) | | – (8) c Blakey b Carrick | 5 |
| S. P. Hughes (did not bat) | | – not out | 0 |
| P. C. R. Tufnell (did not bat) | | – not out | 1 |
| L-b 2, n-b 3 | 5 | L-b 2, n-b 2 | 4 |

1/32 2/37 3/38 4/104     (4 wkts dec.) 104    1/0 2/63 3/136     (9 wkts) 177
4/146 5/148 6/160
7/160 8/176 9/176

Bonus point – Yorkshire 1.

Bowling: *First Innings*—Hartley 8–1–27–0; Gough 7–4–13–1; Fletcher 4–1–12–0; Pickles 5–0–18–1; Carrick 7–3–19–0; Batty 6–3–13–1. *Second Innings*—Hartley 18–8–32–5; Gough 6–0–26–0; Pickles 10.4–4–24–1; Fletcher 14–3–32–0; Carrick 12–7–32–2; Batty 9–2–29–1.

Umpires: J. H. Hampshire and J. W. Holder.

# YORKSHIRE v WORCESTERSHIRE

At Leeds, July 2, 3, 4. Yorkshire won by 115 runs. Yorkshire 19 pts, Worcestershire 3 pts. Toss: Yorkshire. On a pitch offering some movement off the seam, Yorkshire had to work hard for their runs. Newport, removing both openers in the space of four balls, caused problems, but Blakey and Robinson established the innings with a fourth-wicket partnership worth 85 in 28 overs. Heavy rain cut 69 and 78 overs out of the first and second days respectively, and after Yorkshire had declared, both sides forfeited an innings. This left Worcestershire with a minimum of 78 overs, but some lively bowling by Hartley and Fletcher undermined their position in the space of fifteen overs. Botham, ignoring the defensive possibilities, thrashed 57 from 39 balls with five fours and four sixes, taking 22 in one over from Hartley. Carrick had him caught at long-off, however, and the left-arm spinner went on to take the next four wickets as well, breaking a determined stand of 75 in 24 overs between Lampitt and Newport in the process.

*Close of play:* First day, Yorkshire 114-2 (D. Byas 30*, R. J. Blakey 34*); Second day, Yorkshire 202-3 (R. J. Blakey 73*, P. E. Robinson 34*).

## Yorkshire

| | | | | |
|---|---|---|---|---|
| *M. D. Moxon b Newport | 26 | D. Gough c D'Oliveira b Stemp | 2 |
| A. A. Metcalfe lbw b Newport | 13 | P. J. Hartley not out | 0 |
| D. Byas lbw b Lampitt | 37 | | |
| †R. J. Blakey c D'Oliveira b Stemp | 79 | L-b 8, n-b 16 | 24 |
| P. E. Robinson c Botham b Stemp | 57 | | |
| S. A. Kellett not out | 36 | 1/41 2/42 3/138 (8 wkts dec.) 291 |
| C. S. Pickles lbw b Newport | 4 | 4/223 5/243 6/248 | |
| P. Carrick st Rhodes b Stemp | 13 | 7/277 8/279 | |

S. D. Fletcher did not bat.

Bonus points – Yorkshire 3, Worcestershire 3.

Bowling: Dilley 23–2–61–0; Lampitt 20–5–57–1; Newport 25–5–76–3; Botham 7–0–27–0; Stemp 21–3–62–4.

*Yorkshire forfeited their second innings.*

## Worcestershire

*Worcestershire forfeited their first innings.*

| | | | | |
|---|---|---|---|---|
| T. S. Curtis c and b Fletcher | 1 | P. J. Newport c Byas b Carrick | 44 |
| G. J. Lord lbw b Hartley | 0 | G. R. Dilley not out | 1 |
| T. M. Moody c Byas b Hartley | 6 | R. D. Stemp b Carrick | 0 |
| D. B. D'Oliveira c Blakey b Fletcher | 7 | | |
| *P. A. Neale lbw b Hartley | 10 | B 8, l-b 10 | 18 |
| I. T. Botham c Fletcher b Carrick | 57 | | |
| †S. J. Rhodes c Pickles b Carrick | 4 | 1/1 2/1 3/7 4/20 5/24 | 176 |
| S. R. Lampitt c Moxon b Carrick | 28 | 6/92 7/96 8/171 9/176 | |

Bowling: Hartley 16–4–70–3; Fletcher 16–5–36–2; Carrick 8.5–5–13–5; Gough 10–7–14–0; Pickles 5–0–25–0.

Umpires: B. Hassan and J. W. Holder.

At Southampton, July 5, 6, 8. YORKSHIRE drew with HAMPSHIRE.

## YORKSHIRE v DERBYSHIRE

At Scarborough, July 16, 17, 18. Drawn. Yorkshire 8 pts, Derbyshire 5 pts. Toss: Derbyshire. Barnett's decision to field first brought no reward on a very slow pitch of low bounce. Byas, despite being hit on the helmet by Malcolm and having his cheek cut, marked the awarding of his county cap with a career-best 135, made from 238 balls and including twenty fours. He and Blakey added 150 in 46 overs, and Yorkshire batted on into the second day, thrashing a dispirited attack which included, on his début, a Halifax-born left-arm spinner, Sladdin. Derbyshire made a solid reply, but spinners Carrick and Batty maintained a frustrating pressure which brought about a number of errors. Bowler, whose 73 came from 161 deliveries and included a six and eleven fours, was brilliantly run out by Batty, who hit the stumps while on his knees some 35 yards away at cover. Following on, Derbyshire were propped up by Morris, who survived a difficult chance to the wicket-keeper, Blakey, when 11 and went on to resist for more than two hours. Krikken defended stoutly through 34 overs to deny Yorkshire victory, while Sladdin kept him company during the last twelve.

*Close of play:* First day, Yorkshire 353-7 (S. A. Kellett 32*, P. J. Hartley 22*); Second day, Derbyshire 241-9 (D. E. Malcolm 6*, O. H. Mortensen 0*).

## Yorkshire

| | | | |
|---|---|---|---|
| *M. D. Moxon c O'Gorman b Mortensen | 44 | P. J. Hartley not out | 50 |
| A. A. Metcalfe lbw b Malcolm | 8 | J. D. Batty not out | 27 |
| D. Byas lbw b Goldsmith | 135 | | |
| †R. J. Blakey b Goldsmith | 90 | B 8, l-b 11, w 1, n-b 3 | 23 |
| P. E. Robinson c Cork b Sladdin | 2 | | |
| S. A. Kellett b Malcolm | 36 | 1/13 2/128 3/278 (8 wkts dec.) | 418 |
| P. Carrick c Barnett b Goldsmith | 2 | 4/293 5/293 6/305 | |
| D. Gough b Sladdin | 1 | 7/318 8/373 | |

S. D. Fletcher did not bat.

Bonus points – Yorkshire 4, Derbyshire 3 (Score at 100 overs: 318-7).

Bowling: Malcolm 23–5–86–2; Cork 19–3–52–0; Mortensen 21–5–86–1; Sladdin 34–11–112–2; Barnett 4–1–21–0; Goldsmith 17–7–42–3.

## Derbyshire

| | | | |
|---|---|---|---|
| *K. J. Barnett b Hartley | 33 | – c Blakey b Carrick | 22 |
| P. D. Bowler run out | 73 | – c Moxon b Carrick | 48 |
| J. E. Morris c Metcalfe b Carrick | 25 | – c Moxon b Carrick | 59 |
| M. Azharuddin c Metcalfe b Gough | 1 | – c Moxon b Carrick | 0 |
| T. J. G. O'Gorman c Kellett b Batty | 0 | – c Robinson b Batty | 0 |
| S. C. Goldsmith c Blakey b Carrick | 37 | – c Robinson b Batty | 4 |
| †K. M. Krikken c Byas b Batty | 13 | – not out | 16 |
| D. G. Cork c Blakey b Hartley | 26 | – c Moxon b Batty | 8 |
| R. W. Sladdin c Byas b Carrick | 7 | – not out | 8 |
| D. E. Malcolm not out | 6 | | |
| O. H. Mortensen lbw b Fletcher | 0 | | |
| B 9, l-b 9, n-b 3 | 21 | B 4, l-b 3, w 4 | 11 |

| | | |
|---|---|---|
| 1/54 2/101 3/102 4/115 5/154 | 242 | 1/48 2/105 3/105 4/106 (7 wkts) 176 |
| 6/191 7/196 8/224 9/239 | | 5/138 6/138 7/165 |

Bonus points – Derbyshire 2, Yorkshire 4.

Bowling: *First Innings*—Hartley 22–6–72–2; Fletcher 12.4–2–33–1; Carrick 30–14–50–2; Gough 7–1–25–1; Batty 22–10–44–3. *Second Innings*—Hartley 9–3–14–0; Fletcher 6–2–20–0; Carrick 43–28–48–4; Gough 4–0–17–0; Batty 35.2–14–70–3.

Umpires: H. D. Bird and J. H. Hampshire.

At Guildford, July 19, 20, 22. YORKSHIRE lost to SURREY by one wicket.

At Worksop, July 23, 24, 25. YORKSHIRE beat NOTTINGHAMSHIRE by 111 runs.

At Leeds, July 27, 28, 29. YORKSHIRE drew with SRI LANKANS (See Sri Lankan tour section).

At Manchester, August 2, 3, 5. YORKSHIRE drew with LANCASHIRE.

At Leicester, August 6, 7, 8. YORKSHIRE drew with LEICESTERSHIRE.

## YORKSHIRE v SUSSEX

At Middlesbrough, August 9, 10, 12. Sussex won by an innings and 24 runs. Sussex 24 pts. Yorkshire 5 pts. Toss: Yorkshire. Yorkshire had every reason to regret their decision to bat first on a pitch offering extra bounce at the Green Lane end. But for five missed catches in the first innings – Kellett was given several lives – they would have been routed. Sussex, in turn, were in trouble at 40 for four and then 144 for six, but their acting-captain, Alan Wells, went on to make the highest score on the ground, and also the biggest individual innings for his county at Yorkshire's expense, beating the 234 by C. B. Fry at Bradford in 1903. Wells's unbeaten 253, made in 406 minutes from 324 balls, included three sixes and 27 fours. His eighth-wicket stand of 178 in 44 overs with Donelan was also a record against Yorkshire, replacing the 172 put on by W. E. Astill and A. E. R. Gilligan for MCC at Scarborough in 1923. Much of the Yorkshire seam bowling was erratic, only the admirable Carrick exerting any control with his slow left-arm spin in the later stages of the Sussex innings. Facing a deficit of 195, Yorkshire lost Moxon in the first over of their second innings. And after Metcalfe and Byas had threatened prolonged resistance, Donelan found some slow turn to confound the batsmen, while Jones made the ball lift and move off the seam. Under constant pressure, Yorkshire collapsed in some confusion.

*Close of play:* First day, Sussex 53-4 (A. P. Wells 14*, C. M. Wells 10*); Second day, Sussex 356-7 (A. P. Wells 198*, B. T. P. Donelan 39*).

### Yorkshire

| | | | |
|---|---|---|---|
| *M. D. Moxon lbw b Jones | 33 | – c sub b Jones | 0 |
| A. A. Metcalfe c Moores b Dodemaide | 1 | – c and b Donelan | 36 |
| D. Byas c Moores b Jones | 8 | – c Moores b Donelan | 46 |
| S. A. Kellett c sub b Jones | 66 | – b Jones | 8 |
| P. E. Robinson c Speight b Jones | 8 | – lbw b Salisbury | 10 |
| †R. J. Blakey c Moores b C. M. Wells | 33 | – run out | 0 |
| C. S. Pickles c Salisbury b Dodemaide | 48 | – c Moores b Dodemaide | 33 |
| P. Carrick c Moores b Jones | 2 | – c Salisbury b Donelan | 14 |
| P. J. Hartley c Moores b Dodemaide | 17 | – c Moores b Jones | 10 |
| J. D. Batty c Smith b Dodemaide | 5 | – not out | 1 |
| M. A. Robinson not out | 1 | – lbw b Jones | 0 |
| B 4, l-b 8, n-b 7 | 19 | B 2, l-b 9, n-b 2 | 13 |
| | 241 | | 171 |

1/8 2/27 3/82 4/95 5/161          241          1/0 2/76 3/90 4/100 5/100          171
6/191 7/203 8/229 9/240                         6/121 7/146 8/170 9/171

Bonus points – Yorkshire 2, Sussex 4.

Bowling: *First Innings*—Jones 18-3–46–5; Dodemaide 24–2–67–4; C. M. Wells 11–2–30–1; Donelan 13–4–32–0; Salisbury 19–5–54–0. *Second Innings*—Jones 12.5–2–41–4; Dodemaide 21–8–36–1; Salisbury 12–4–36–1; Donelan 27–15–43–3; C. M. Wells 4–1–4–0.

### Sussex

| | | |
|---|---|---|
| N. J. Lenham c Blakey b Hartley | 0 | J. W. Hall c Moxon b Carrick | 28 |
| †P. Moores c P. E. Robinson b M. A. Robinson | 9 | B. T. P. Donelan run out | 59 |
| D. M. Smith b M. A. Robinson | 11 | I. D. K. Salisbury st Blakey b Carrick | 3 |
| *A. P. Wells not out | 253 | A. N. Jones c Kellett b Carrick | 1 |
| M. P. Speight c P. E. Robinson b Hartley | 7 | | |
| C. M. Wells c Kellett b Carrick | 42 | B 1, l-b 6, w 1, n-b 4 | 12 |
| A. I. C. Dodemaide c P. E. Robinson b Carrick | 11 | | 436 |

1/0 2/20 3/33 4/40 5/124
6/144 7/225 8/403 9/434

Bonus points – Sussex 4, Yorkshire 3 (Score at 100 overs: 309-7).

Bowling: Hartley 30–3–128–2; M. A. Robinson 29–3–118–2; Pickles 14–3–51–0; Carrick 40–10–103–5; Batty 8–2–29–0.

Umpires: B. Dudleston and A. G. T. Whitehead.

## YORKSHIRE v GLAMORGAN

At Leeds, August 16, 17, 19. Drawn. Yorkshire 5 pts, Glamorgan 5 pts. Toss: Yorkshire. This game was staged on the Test pitch, which lacked pace and allowed a little slow turn. Moxon and Metcalfe completed Yorkshire's best opening stand of the season, and the latter's 123, in which he hit two sixes and thirteen fours, used up 251 balls in 297 minutes. When 8, Metcalfe completed 9,000 first-class runs for Yorkshire. Foster bowled without luck, while Watkin overcame a shaky start to keep Yorkshire's rate in reasonable check. Glamorgan also made comfortable progress, with Morris becoming the first batsman to make a hundred at Headingley for them. His unbeaten 156 also equalled the highest individual total for his county against Yorkshire, matching the effort by Alan Jones at Middlesbrough in 1976. Rain caused several delays on the last day, when Yorkshire, given a lead of 74, slumped to 99 for eight in the face of some accurate slow bowling by Croft and Shastri. However, the danger of defeat receded as Pickles and Batty brought about a revival, and Glamorgan were finally set to make 218 in a minimum of 39 overs. Yorkshire were expected to bowl rather more than that, but the weather soon closed in and ended the contest.

*Close of play:* First day, Yorkshire 354-5 (P. E. Robinson 30*, C. S. Pickles 26*); Second day, Glamorgan 327-4 (H. Morris 156*, P. A. Cottey 9*).

## Yorkshire

| | | | |
|---|---|---|---|
| *M. D. Moxon c Shastri b Watkin | 80 | – (8) b Shastri | 0 |
| A. A. Metcalfe lbw b Foster | 123 | – lbw b Frost | 26 |
| D. Byas c Metson b Frost | 32 | – c Shastri b Croft | 20 |
| S. A. Kellett b Croft | 34 | – (1) b Foster | 16 |
| P. E. Robinson b Watkin | 51 | – (4) c and b Croft | 8 |
| †R. J. Blakey c Dale b Croft | 3 | – (5) c Dale b Shastri | 3 |
| C. S. Pickles c Butcher b Watkin | 28 | – (6) not out | 34 |
| P. Carrick c Butcher b Shastri | 9 | – (7) c Cottey b Shastri | 1 |
| P. J. Hartley not out | 8 | – c Metson b Croft | 6 |
| J. D. Batty not out | 4 | – not out | 19 |
| L-b 15, n-b 14 | 29 | B 4, l-b 3, n-b 3 | 10 |

1/156 2/245 3/277 4/305 5/315    (8 wkts dec.) 401    1/27 2/57 3/73    (8 wkts dec.) 143
6/358 7/380 8/396                        4/75 5/77 6/88
                                         7/88 8/99

M. A. Robinson did not bat.

Bonus points – Yorkshire 4, Glamorgan 1 (Score at 100 overs: 307-4).

Bowling: *First Innings*—Watkin 18.4–2–64–3; Frost 16–3–55–1; Shastri 38–5–111–1; Foster 20–7–48–1; Croft 37–5–108–2. *Second Innings*—Watkin 10–1–34–0; Foster 6–1–27–1; Frost 5–0–12–1; Croft 19–3–45–3; Shastri 14–7–18–3.

## Glamorgan

| | | | |
|---|---|---|---|
| *A. R. Butcher b Batty | 79 | – not out | 7 |
| H. Morris not out | 156 | – not out | 2 |
| A. Dale b Batty | 0 | | |
| M. P. Maynard c Blakey b Batty | 21 | | |
| R. J. Shastri c Byas b Batty | 41 | | |
| P. A. Cottey not out | 9 | | |
| B 12, l-b 4, n-b 5 | 21 | | |

1/164 2/164 3/194 4/262      (4 wkts dec.) 327               (no wkt) 9

R. D. B. Croft, †C. P. Metson, S. L. Watkin, M. Frost and D. J. Foster did not bat.

Bonus points – Glamorgan 4, Yorkshire 1 (Score at 100 overs: 303-4).

Bowling: *First Innings*—M. A. Robinson 16–6–42–0; Hartley 12–4–26–0; Carrick 35–9–97–0; Pickles 9–2–28–0; Batty 35–4–118–4. *Second Innings*—Hartley 3–0–8–0; M. A. Robinson 2.2–2–1–0.

Umpires: K. E. Palmer and R. Palmer.

At Colchester, August 20, 21, 22. YORKSHIRE beat ESSEX by 3 runs.


At Taunton, August 23, 24, 26. YORKSHIRE drew with SOMERSET.


At Northampton, August 28, 29, 30, 31. YORKSHIRE lost to NORTHAMPTONSHIRE by nine wickets.


## YORKSHIRE v LANCASHIRE

At Scarborough, September 3, 4, 5, 6. Yorkshire won by 48 runs. Yorkshire 21 pts, Lancashire 5 pts. Toss: Yorkshire. A lively new-ball spell by DeFreitas and Martin had Yorkshire in some trouble, but Lancashire crucially missed Byas, on 1, in the slips. Byas and Phil Robinson, who edged Martin just over the slips when 26, subsequently made the most of an easy-paced pitch with a partnership of 233 in 70 overs. Byas collected his runs from 241 deliveries, hitting one six and twenty fours, while Robinson's career-best 189 occupied 378 minutes (317 balls) and included one six and 27 fours. Yorkshire's total was their highest since 1953, when they compiled 525 for four declared against Somerset at Leeds. Lancashire scored readily in turn, led by Mendis, who was dropped by Carrick off Mark Robinson when 66. All their front-line batsmen established themselves, with Crawley reaching 50 in his first Championship innings, but the persistent Hartley always commanded respect. Moxon and Phil Robinson ensured that Yorkshire made the most of a substantial first-innings lead, adding 145 for the fourth wicket, and Lancashire were set a target of 343 in a minimum of 80 overs. Some poor batting in the face of a hostile burst by Gough, who claimed five wickets for the first time, left the Lancashire innings in ruins before DeFreitas inspired some resistance. Given a life by Carrick off his own bowling before scoring, DeFreitas slammed 50 in 28 balls, plundering 28 from one over by the left-arm spinner, and when he was out, Austin took over, hitting the fastest century of the season, in 68 minutes from 61 balls. It was, moreover, his maiden first-class hundred. Austin struck six sixes and thirteen fours, and after putting on 83 in eleven overs with Fitton for the ninth wicket, he added another 82 from thirteen with Martin for the last. By this time Yorkshire were looking distinctly worried, and they were relieved when Hartley brought the entertainment to an end.

*Close of play:* First day, Yorkshire 359-4 (P. E. Robinson 176*, R. J. Blakey 31*); Second day, Lancashire 217-2 (J. P. Crawley 23*, J. D. Fitton 5*); Third day, Yorkshire 163-3 (M. D. Moxon 83*, P. E. Robinson 43*).

## Yorkshire

| | | | |
|---|---|---|---|
| *M. D. Moxon c Hegg b DeFreitas | 4 | – c Titchard b Watkinson | 115 |
| A. A. Metcalfe c Crawley b DeFreitas | 2 | – lbw b DeFreitas | 2 |
| D. Byas c Lloyd b Martin | 120 | – c Crawley b Watkinson | 21 |
| S. A. Kellett c Hegg b Martin | 7 | – c Mendis b Fitton | 5 |
| P. E. Robinson lbw b Martin | 189 | – not out | 79 |
| †R. J. Blakey c Crawley b Watkinson | 59 | – st Hegg b Watkinson | 1 |
| P. Carrick not out | 36 | – lbw b Watkinson | 5 |
| D. Gough not out | 60 | – not out | 5 |
| L-b 17, w 1, n-b 6 | 24 | L-b 11, n-b 2 | 13 |

1/4 2/7 3/18 4/251                    (6 wkts dec.) 501      1/12 2/50 3/79      (6 wkts dec.) 244
5/381 6/426                                                          4/224 5/231 6/237

P. J. Hartley, J. D. Batty and M. A. Robinson did not bat.

Bonus points – Yorkshire 4, Lancashire 1 (Score at 100 overs: 309-4).

Bowling: *First Innings*—DeFreitas 30-5-104-2; Martin 32-11-71-3; Austin 30-6-97-0; Watkinson 37-7-117-1; Fitton 21.5-3-95-0. *Second Innings*—DeFreitas 6-3-7-1; Martin 5-1-8-0; Fitton 29.3-3-113-1; Watkinson 23-1-85-4; Austin 6-1-20-0.

## Lancashire

| | | | | |
|---|---|---|---|---|
| G. D. Mendis c Blakey b M. A. Robinson | 114 | – lbw b Gough | | 6 |
| N. J. Speak lbw b Hartley | 73 | – lbw b Gough | | 11 |
| J. P. Crawley lbw b Hartley | 52 | – c Gough b Carrick | | 13 |
| J. D. Fitton c Byas b Hartley | 33 | – (9) st Blakey b Batty | | 34 |
| G. D. Lloyd b Gough | 51 | – (4) lbw b Gough | | 3 |
| S. P. Titchard b Hartley | 35 | – (5) lbw b Carrick | | 22 |
| *M. Watkinson lbw b Hartley | 0 | – (6) c Blakey b Gough | | 17 |
| P. A. J. DeFreitas not out | 24 | – (7) c Metcalfe b Carrick | | 50 |
| I. D. Austin not out | 3 | – (10) not out | | 101 |
| †W. K. Hegg (did not bat) | | – (8) c Blakey b Gough | | 2 |
| P. J. Martin (did not bat) | | – c Moxon b Hartley | | 29 |
| L-b 10, n-b 8 | 18 | L-b 4, n-b 2 | | 6 |

1/180 2/211 3/273 4/288 5/356     (7 wkts dec.) 403     1/18 2/19 3/23 4/48 5/67     294
6/356 7/383                                            6/95 7/99 8/129 9/212

Bonus points – Lancashire 4, Yorkshire 1 (Score at 100 overs: 305-4).

Bowling: *First Innings*—Hartley 27-2-100-5; Gough 17-3-79-1; M. A. Robinson 31-8-84-1; Carrick 32-15-52-0; Batty 17.5-2-78-0. *Second Innings*—Hartley 12.5-1-36-1; Gough 18-6-41-5; Carrick 23-3-184-3; Batty 7-1-29-1.

Umpires: B. J. Meyer and D. O. Oslear.


At Scarborough, September 7. YORKSHIRE lost to THE YORKSHIREMEN by three wickets (See Other Matches, 1991).


At Scarborough, September 8. YORKSHIRE lost to WORLD XI by 34 runs (See Other Matches, 1991).


At Chesterfield, September 17, 18, 19, 20. YORKSHIRE lost to DERBYSHIRE by 40 runs.


## HONOURS' LIST, 1991

In 1991, the following were decorated for their services to cricket:
*New Year's Honours:* G. A. Gooch (England) OBE, B. A. Johnston (services to broadcasting and cricket) CBE, R. Subba Row CBE.
*Queen's Birthday Honours:* C. Washbrook (England) CBE, D. J. Wiley (services to umpiring) BEM.

OXFORD UNIVERSITY 1991

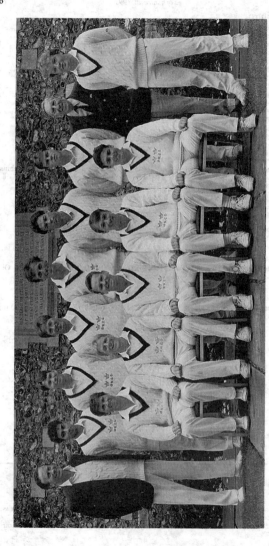

*Back row*: L. J. Lenham (*coach*), C. M. Gupte, R. R. Montgomerie, J. M. E. Oppenheimer, R. M. Macdonald, P. S. Gerrans, B. S. Wood, P. Gordon (*scorer*), H. R. Davies. *Front row*: D. B. Pfaff, R. E. Morris, G. J. Turner (*captain*), G. B. T. Lovell, D. C. Sandiford.

[*Bill Smith*

# THE UNIVERSITIES IN 1991

## OXFORD

*President:* M. J. K. Smith (St Edmund Hall)
*Hon. Treasurer:* Dr S. R. Porter (Nuffield College)

*Captain:* G. J. Turner (St Stithian's, University of Cape Town and St Anne's)
*Secretary:* M. J. Russell (Medina HS, Isle of Wight, and Pembroke)

*Captain for 1992:* G. B. T. Lovell (Sydney C. of E. GS, University of Sydney and Exeter)
*Secretary:* R. R. Montgomerie (Rugby and Worcester)

There was never any chance of Oxford University repeating their feat of 1990, when they were unbeaten in first-class cricket. The team was strong in batting, but with the departure of Mark Crawley and Willem van der Merwe, two outstanding all-rounders, and with only four Blues in residence, it was always going to be a difficult season for the new captain, Graeme Turner.

A captain relies on a nucleus of experienced players to build a side, but of Turner's fellow-Blues David Hagan was picked for only one match, Phil Gerrans missed much of the season, preparing for his Finals, and Russell Morris struggled to find the form of the previous year. The opening match featured no fewer than seven Freshmen making first-class débuts, an unprecedented number. Although several of them showed commendable skill with the bat on occasions, notably the South African left-hander, David Pfaff, Richard Montgomerie of Northamptonshire Second Eleven, Geoff Lovell, the first recipient of the Bradman Scholarship for Australian student cricketers, and Chinmay Gupte, an MCC Young Player of the Year, it was Turner who provided the backbone of the innings. He hit Oxford's only century, an unbeaten 101 against Lancashire, after coming close with 94 against Glamorgan and 99 against Worcestershire. There was some irony in the fact that his two highest scores coincided with the only defeats.

Bitterly cold weather early in the season and long periods of rain did not help concentration, or the build-up to the University Match, but as in the previous year the batting was stronger than the bowling. Rob Macdonald, who had a successful season with Durham University in 1990, was the pick of the seamers. He was well supported by Yorkshire-born Ben Wood, who improved as the season progressed and was invited by his county to attend nets once the season was over at The Parks. A broken toe caused Macdonald to miss two matches, thus leaving the way open for fellow-South African Jon Oppenheimer's return late in the season. In the event Turner picked all three for Lord's – Oppenheimer as cover for Macdonald in case he broke down – and off-spinner Henry Davies was the player omitted. Davies shared the slow bowling with Turner, but with the head groundsman, Richard Sula, again producing excellent batting pitches, none of the regular bowlers took his wickets at fewer than 45 runs apiece. As usual the county batsmen made the most of the conditions; Chris Smith hit 200 in 258 balls for Hampshire in the first match, but he was outdone by Damian D'Oliveira of Worcestershire, who scored 237 from a mere 219.

Witnessing Turner's problems leading the University did not deter Lovell from accepting the captaincy for 1992. He expected to have the majority of the 1991 side available, plus Alastair Storie, an opening batsman who has played for Northamptonshire, Warwickshire and Scotland, and an intake of promising Australians. Lovell must have been disappointed, however, that Worcestershire's talented all-rounder, Philip Weston, chose to lead an England Young Cricketers side to Pakistan, rather than take up residence at Keble College. He would have been an asset at The Parks. – Paton Fenton.

## OXFORD UNIVERSITY RESULTS

*First-class matches – Played 9: Lost 2, Drawn 7.*

## FIRST-CLASS AVERAGES

### BATTING AND FIELDING

| | Birthplace | M | I | NO | R | HI | Avge | Ct/St |
|---|---|---|---|---|---|---|---|---|
| G. J. Turner | Bulawayo, Rhodesia | 8 | 8 | 2 | 349 | 101* | 58.16 | 1 |
| D. B. Pfaff | Cape Town, SA | 8 | 7 | 2 | 231 | 50 | 46.20 | 4 |
| R. R. Montgomerie | Rugby | 8 | 11 | 2 | 300 | 88 | 33.33 | 7 |
| C. M. Gupte | Poona, India | 8 | 9 | 1 | 200 | 55* | 25.00 | 2 |
| G. B. T. Lovell | Sydney, Australia | 9 | 13 | 3 | 250 | 49 | 25.00 | 5 |
| D. C. Sandiford | Bolton | 9 | 9 | 1 | 189 | 83 | 23.62 | 11/1 |
| R. E. Morris | St Asaph | 8 | 11 | 1 | 236 | 71 | 23.60 | 3 |
| M. J. Russell | Lincoln | 3 | 6 | 0 | 91 | 30 | 15.16 | 0 |
| R. H. Macdonald | Cape Town, SA | 7 | 6 | 3 | 41 | 20 | 13.66 | 0 |
| H. R. Davies | Camberwell, London | 7 | 9 | 0 | 80 | 38 | 13.33 | 0 |
| J. G. Morris | Nottingham | 3 | 5 | 0 | 63 | 28 | 12.60 | 3 |
| B. S. Wood | Dewsbury | 9 | 6 | 1 | 8 | 6 | 1.60 | 0 |

Also batted: P. S. Gerrans (*Melbourne, Australia*) (3 matches) 17*, 14, 4; C. D. Jones (*Maidstone*) (1 match), 4, 23; J. M. E. Oppenheimer (*Johannesburg, SA*) (5 matches) 0* (1 ct); S. N. Warley (*Sittingbourne*) (2 matches) 3, 11, 1 (1 ct). D. A. Hagan (*Wide Open*) (1 match) did not bat.

*\* Signifies not out.*

G. J. Turner played the only three-figure innings for Oxford University.

### BOWLING

| | O | M | R | W | BB | 5W/i | Avge |
|---|---|---|---|---|---|---|---|
| R. H. Macdonald | 157 | 49 | 457 | 10 | 3-66 | 0 | 45.70 |
| J. M. E. Oppenheimer | 107 | 19 | 385 | 8 | 2-51 | 0 | 48.12 |
| B. S. Wood | 187.5 | 34 | 665 | 12 | 2-24 | 0 | 55.41 |
| P. S. Gerrans | 77.3 | 12 | 308 | 5 | 2-65 | 0 | 61.60 |
| G. J. Turner | 169 | 36 | 564 | 9 | 3-32 | 0 | 62.66 |

Also bowled: H. R. Davies 107.1–16–476–4; C. M. Gupte 24.1–3–120–3; G. B. T. Lovell 32–3–141–1; R. E. Morris 24–3–129–2; D. B. Pfaff 2–0–6–0; M. J. Russell 8–2–31–4.

†At Oxford, April 12. Middlesex won by 117 runs. Toss: Middlesex. Middlesex 230 for five (55 overs) (M. A. Roseberry 123; G. J. Turner three for 76); Oxford University 113 for six (55 overs) (D. B. Pfaff 52).

## OXFORD UNIVERSITY v HAMPSHIRE

At Oxford, April 13, 15, 16. Drawn. Toss: Oxford University. With seven Freshmen making first-class débuts, Oxford gained an honourable draw in a match dominated by Hampshire's opening batsman, Smith. Dropped when he was 45, after Hampshire had lost two wickets for 36 (effectively three with Terry injured), Smith completed the first double-century of the season in 279 minutes, hitting seven sixes and 25 fours. It was his third hundred in successive games against Oxford. He put on 106 with James, and personally scored 122 out of 149 added with Ayling. Needing 222 to avoid an innings defeat, the University occupied the crease throughout the third day, despite a shaky start, and at 238 for eight, with five overs remaining, Nicholas settled for a draw. Montgomerie and Lovell put on 103 for the third wicket, and after Pfaff, Oxford's top scorer on the first day, had contributed 50, Davies and Macdonald frustrated Hampshire by playing out seven of the last twelve overs.

*Close of play:* First day, Hampshire 20-0 (C. L. Smith 14*, T. C. Middleton 2*); Second day, Oxford University 10-1 (R. R. Montgomerie 3*, D. C. Sandiford 6*).

## Oxford University

| | | | |
|---|---|---|---|
| R. E. Morris lbw b James | 5 | – (7) lbw b Bakker | 0 |
| R. R. Montgomerie c Middleton b James | 10 | – (1) lbw b Bakker | 88 |
| C. M. Gupte c Aymes b Maru | 15 | – (2) b Connor | 0 |
| G. B. T. Lovell c Terry b Ayling | 18 | – c Maru b Ayling | 41 |
| *G. J. Turner lbw b Ayling | 9 | – c Aymes b James | 11 |
| D. B. Pfaff not out | 48 | – lbw b Maru | 50 |
| M. J. Russell c Aymes b Maru | 13 | – (8) c James b Maru | 0 |
| †D. C. Sandiford c Nicholas b Maru | 0 | – (3) b Connor | 10 |
| H. R. Davies c Aymes b Connor | 0 | – not out | 19 |
| R. H. Macdonald c Smith b Maru | 20 | – not out | 5 |
| B. S. Wood b Ayling | 0 | | |
| L-b 4, n-b 5 | 9 | B 4, l-b 7, n-b 3 | 14 |

1/9 2/21 3/39 4/58 5/63       147    1/2 2/19 3/122 4/145    (8 wkts) 238
6/105 7/107 8/114 9/147               5/171 6/171 7/172 8/225

Bowling: *First Innings*—Aqib Javed 11-1-27-0; Bakker 12-7-18-0; James 13-6-25-2; Connor 15-4-40-1; Maru 18-8-17-4; Ayling 12.2-5-16-3. *Second Innings*—Aqib Javed 14-2-43-0; Connor 16-5-38-2; James 14-6-33-1; Bakker 18-6-42-2; Ayling 13-8-24-1; Maru 29-9-47-2.

## Hampshire

| | | | |
|---|---|---|---|
| V. P. Terry retired hurt | 4 | K. D. James c and b Turner | 47 |
| C. L. Smith b Turner | 200 | J. R. Ayling not out | 52 |
| T. C. Middleton c Sandiford | | †A. N. Aymes not out | 52 |
|      b Macdonald | 2 | L-b 4, n-b 1 | 5 |
| *M. C. J. Nicholas c Montgomerie | | | |
|      b Macdonald | 7 | 1/20 2/36 3/142 4/291 | (4 wkts dec.) 369 |

R. J. Maru, P. J. Bakker, Aqib Javed and C. A. Connor did not bat.

*V. P. Terry retired hurt at 18.*

Bowling: Macdonald 30-10-81-2; Wood 12-3-41-0; Turner 31-7-105-2; Davies 17.1-2-78-0; Lovell 8-2-36-0; Gupte 5-1-24-0.

Umpires: J. H. Hampshire and R. C. Tolchard.

## OXFORD UNIVERSITY v GLAMORGAN

At Oxford, April 17, 18, 19. Drawn. Toss: Oxford University. Oxford's second first-class match was ruined by rain, which resulted in nearly twelve hours of play being lost, and a wind so bitterly cold that the umpires rang the TCCB for guidance on whether to play. The University lost their first six wickets for 86 after electing to bat, but Glamorgan were held up by Turner and Sandiford, who put on 105 for the seventh wicket. Turner hit a career-best 94 before becoming one of six victims for wicket-keeper Metson, who equalled the Glamorgan record for catches behind the wicket for the fourth time.

*Close of play:* First day, Oxford University 186-6 (G. J. Turner 74\*, D. C. Sandiford 28\*);
Second day, Glamorgan 34-0 (A. R. Butcher 25\*, P. A. Cottey 9\*).

## Oxford University

| | | | | |
|---|---|---|---|---|
| R. E. Morris c Maynard b Bastien | 30 | H. R. Davies c Metson b Frost | | 0 |
| R. R. Montgomerie lbw b Dennis | 0 | R. H. Macdonald c Metson b Dennis | | 4 |
| C. M. Gupte c Metson b Bastien | 1 | B. S. Wood not out | | 2 |
| G. B. T. Lovell lbw b Foster | 17 | | | |
| \*G. J. Turner c Metson b Dennis | 94 | B 1, l-b 3, w 1, n-b 14 | | 19 |
| D. B. Pfaff c Metson b Smith | 16 | | | |
| S. N. Warley c Metson b Frost | 3 | 1/3 2/18 3/51 4/58 5/83 | | 218 |
| †D. C. Sandiford lbw b Frost | 32 | 6/86 7/191 8/196 9/215 | | |

Bowling: Frost 17-5-29-3; Dennis 17.3-7-31-3; Bastien 14-5-40-2; Foster 13-1-61-1; Smith 6-1-24-1; Croft 15-7-29-0.

## Glamorgan

| | |
|---|---|
| \*A. R. Butcher not out | 25 |
| P. A. Cottey not out | 9 |
| | |
| **(no wkt) 34** | |

G. C. Holmes, M. P. Maynard, S. J. Dennis, I. Smith, R. D. B. Croft, †C. P. Metson, S. Bastien, D. J. Foster and M. Frost did not bat.

Bowling: Macdonald 4.4-1-15-0; Wood 4-0-19-0.

*Umpires: J. H. Hampshire and R. C. Tolchard.*

# OXFORD UNIVERSITY v NOTTINGHAMSHIRE

At Oxford, April 27, 29, 30. Drawn. Toss: Nottinghamshire. Nottinghamshire took full advantage of a perfect pitch at The Parks to score 368 for five, but rain prevented any play on the second and third days. After Oppenheimer had taken a wicket with his first ball, Crawley, who captained Oxford in 1990, and Newell added 166 for the second wicket. Crawley hit 112, with fifteen fours, on his first-class début for the county, and Newell 91, while late in the day Johnson flayed Oxford's tiring bowlers for an unbeaten 97.

*Close of play:* First day, Nottinghamshire 368-5 (P. Johnson 97\*, D. J. R. Martindale 4\*); Second day, No play.

## Nottinghamshire

| | | | | |
|---|---|---|---|---|
| P. R. Pollard lbw b Oppenheimer | 20 | K. P. Evans c Sandiford b Lovell | | 13 |
| M. Newell lbw b Turner | 91 | D. J. R. Martindale not out | | 4 |
| M. A. Crawley c Montgomerie | | B 11, l-b 1, w 6 | | 18 |
| b Gupte | 112 | | | |
| \*P. Johnson not out | 97 | 1/40 2/206 3/257 | (5 wkts) | 368 |
| M. Saxelby c Sandiford b Gupte | 13 | 4/285 5/348 | | |

†C. W. Scott, M. G. Field-Buss, R. A. Pick and J. A. Afford did not bat.

Bowling: Macdonald 23-8-55-0; Wood 19-3-74-0; Oppenheimer 19-2-75-1; Turner 29-6-92-1; Pfaff 2-0-6-0; Gupte 9-1-41-2; Lovell 4-0-13-1.

## Oxford University

R. E. Morris, R. R. Montgomerie, C. M. Gupte, G. B. T. Lovell, \*G. J. Turner, D. B. Pfaff, D. A. Hagan, †D. C. Sandiford, J. M. E. Oppenheimer, R. H. Macdonald and B. S. Wood.

*Umpires: R. Julian and G. A. Stickley.*

†At Oxford, May 1. Oxford University v Club Cricket Conference Over-25. Abandoned.

†At Oxford, May 3. Berkshire won by nine wickets. Toss: Oxford University. Oxford University 163 (R. R. Montgomerie 46, C. D. Jones 43 not out); Berkshire 164 for one (D. A. Shaw 61 not out, D. J. M. Mercer 82 not out).

†At Oxford, May 6. Buckinghamshire won by eight wickets. Toss: Buckinghamshire. Oxford University 140; Buckinghamshire 143 for two (A. R. Harwood 46, T. J. A. Scriven 60 not out).

†At Oxford, May 8, 9, 10. Drawn. Toss: MCC. MCC 241 for nine dec. (A. J. T. Miller 51, H. T. Tunnicliffe 60; R. H. Macdonald four for 54) and 313 for nine dec. (J. E. M. Nicholson 34, A. J. T. Miller 135 not out, T. K. Marriott 41; R. H. Macdonald three for 117, H. R. Davies four for 64); Oxford University 287 for four dec. (R. E. Morris 61, G. B. T. Lovell 94, D. B. Pfaff 63) and 166 for three (G. B. T. Lovell 52, D. A. Hagan 42 not out).

†At Oxford, May 13. Oxfordshire won by 62 runs. Toss: Oxfordshire. Oxfordshire 222 for six (50 overs) (S. N. V. Waterton 63, M. Cannons 32, G. P. Savin 30; M. J. Russell three for 74); Oxford University 160 for nine (50 overs) (R. E. Morris 50, D. B. Pfaff 34; J. S. Hartley three for 18).

†At Oxford, May 14. Loughborough University won by 1 run. Toss: Loughborough University. Loughborough University 210 for nine (50 overs) (N. V. Knight 102, K. Blackburn 30 not out); Oxford University 209 (50 overs) (C. D. Jones 31, G. J. Turner 34, R. H. Macdonald 38; K. Blackburn six for 50).

## OXFORD UNIVERSITY v GLOUCESTERSHIRE

At Oxford, May 15, 16, 17. Drawn. Toss: Oxford University. Although Athey and Hodgson scored centuries, Gloucestershire made heavy weather of it after being put in. They batted all day for 300 from 112 overs – at lunch they were only 69 – with all three wickets falling to Macdonald, and Turner's off-breaks conceding a mere 36 runs in 27 overs. Oxford lost Montgomerie and Morris for 18 on the second day, when only 182 minutes' play was possible because of rain, but Gupte, who completed a maiden fifty, and Lovell, narrowly missing his, added 99 for the third wicket. The University were 122 for three at the close, but persistent drizzle prevented any play on the last day.

*Close of play:* First day, Gloucestershire 300-3 (M. W. Alleyne 5*, S. N. Barnes 0*); Second day, Oxford University 122-3 (C. M. Gupte 55*, G. J. Turner 1*).

### Gloucestershire

| | |
|---|---|
| G. D. Hodgson c Montgomerie b Macdonald .105 | S. N. Barnes not out ............... 0 |
| R. J. Scott c Sandiford b Macdonald ... 49 | B 3, l-b 6, w 3, n-b 2 ........ 14 |
| C. W. J. Athey c Gupte b Macdonald .127 | |
| M. W. Alleyne not out ............. 5 | 1/97 2/277 3/298 (3 wkts dec.) 300 |

*A. J. Wright, J. W. Lloyds, †R. C. Russell, E. T. Milburn, R. M. H. Bell and A. M. Babington did not bat.

Bowling: Macdonald 23–9–66–3; Wood 13–1–53–0; Turner 27–12–36–0; Oppenheimer 19–6–33–0; Davies 22–3–70–0; Gupte 2–0–22–0; Lovell 6–0–11–0.

### Oxford University

| | |
|---|---|
| R. R. Montgomerie lbw b Babington ... 8 | *G. J. Turner not out ............... 1 |
| R. E. Morris lbw b Babington ........ 6 | L-b 3 .................... 3 |
| C. M. Gupte not out ............... 55 | |
| G. B. T. Lovell c Hodgson b Babington 49 | 1/9 2/18 3/117 (3 wkts) 122 |

D. B. Pfaff, †D. C. Sandiford, H. R. Davies, R. H. Macdonald, J. M. E. Oppenheimer and B. S. Wood did not bat.

Bowling: Babington 12.3–4–22–3; Barnes 12–4–23–0; Bell 5–2–9–0; Milburn 7–1–29–0; Lloyds 3–0–11–0; Alleyne 6–1–15–0; Athey 6–2–10–0.

Umpires: D. J. Constant and Dr D. Fawkner-Corbett.

†At Oxford, May 20. Oxford University won by 47 runs. Toss: Oxford University. Oxford University 243 for three (55 overs) (R. E. Morris 69, S. N. Warley 84 not out, G. B. T. Lovell 43); Royal Navy 196 (55 overs) (P. Barsby 60, A. Quinlan 53; G. B. T. Lovell five for 24).

†At Oxford, May 22. Wiltshire won by six wickets. Toss: Oxford University. Oxford University 204 (49.4 overs) (C. M. Gupte 54, J. G. Morris 38; G. Sheppard four for 22, A. Webb three for 41); Wiltshire 205 for four (43 overs) (D. R. Parry 71 not out, S. M. Perrin 36 not out).

# OXFORD UNIVERSITY v WORCESTERSHIRE

At Oxford, May 25, 27, 28. Worcestershire won by an innings and 122 runs. Toss: Oxford University. The University suffered their first defeat since June of 1989. They never recovered from losing Montgomerie and Gupte to Newport in the first over, and despite a fifth-wicket partnership of 65 in twelve overs between Pfaff and Turner, the innings closed at 119. Worcestershire's massive 490 for eight declared – with only 7 extras – was based on a magnificent partnership from D'Oliveira and Leatherdale, who coming together at 177 for four put on 243. D'Oliveira went on to 237, his highest score, from 219 balls in 217 minutes, hitting seven sixes and 31 fours. In the second morning's assault he made 157 in 95 minutes, and Worcestershire added 259 before lunch. Oxford did better in their second attempt, when they needed 371 to avoid an innings defeat. But though their captain, Turner, made a career-best 99, with solid support from Russell and Davies, the task was well beyond them.

*Close of play:* First day, Worcestershire 201-4 (D. B. D'Oliveira 80*, D. A. Leatherdale 11*); Second day, Oxford University 96-4 (G. J. Turner 29*, D. B. Pfaff 3*).

## Oxford University

| | | | |
|---|---|---|---|
| R. R. Montgomerie lbw b Newport | 0 | – c Bevins b Newport | 10 |
| J. G. Morris c Leatherdale b Newport | 15 | – (3) b Moody | 28 |
| C. M. Gupte c Moody b Newport | 0 | – (2) b Lampitt | 15 |
| G. B. T. Lovell c Bevins b Newport | 8 | – c Moody b Lampitt | 7 |
| *G. J. Turner b Lampitt | 24 | – c Moody b Lampitt | 99 |
| D. B. Pfaff c Bevins b Stemp | 46 | – run out | 11 |
| M. J. Russell lbw b Lampitt | 25 | – b Curtis | 0 |
| †D. C. Sandiford b Stemp | 1 | – c Leatherdale b Curtis | 0 |
| H. R. Davies not out | 6 | – c Weston b Lampitt | 38 |
| R. H. Macdonald b Lampitt | 8 | – not out | 3 |
| B. S. Wood b Lampitt | 0 | – c Bevins b Lampitt | 0 |
| B 5, l-b 4, n-b 2 | 11 | B 7, l-b 1, w 1, n-b 4 | 13 |

1/0 2/1 3/18 4/28 5/93             119    1/15 2/38 3/53 4/88 5/115       249
6/93 7/100 8/106 9/119                          6/174 7/176 8/225 9/249

Bowling: *First Innings*—Newport 11-3-27-4; Tolley 6-2-10-0; Weston 7-1-25-0; Lampitt 10-0-39-4; Stemp 7-1-9-2. *Second Innings*—Newport 21-7-43-1; Lampitt 27-2-85-5; Tolley 9-3-18-0; Stemp 24-12-34-0; D'Oliveira 11-5-19-0; Moody 15-7-19-1; Leatherdale 2-0-6-0; Curtis 7-1-17-2.

## Worcestershire

| | | | |
|---|---|---|---|
| *T. S. Curtis st Sandiford b Davies | 67 | S. R. Lampitt lbw b Wood | 23 |
| G. J. Lord c Morris b Macdonald | 21 | C. M. Tolley not out | 7 |
| T. M. Moody c Pfaff b Turner | 20 | B 1, l-b 4, w 1, n-b 1 | 7 |
| D. B. D'Oliveira c Lovell b Turner | 237 | | |
| M. J. Weston c Montgomerie b Davies | 1 | 1/40 2/66 3/163    (8 wkts. dec.) 490 |
| D. A. Leatherdale c Pfaff b Wood | 94 | 4/177 5/420 6/460 |
| P. J. Newport c Sandiford b Macdonald | 13 | 7/460 8/490 |

†S. R. Bevins and R. D. Stemp did not bat.

Bowling: Macdonald 30-8-103-2; Wood 19.5-3-79-2; Turner 23-2-106-2; Davies 30-5-144-2; Lovell 7-0-53-0.

Umpires: R. Palmer and R. A. White.

## OXFORD UNIVERSITY v YORKSHIRE

At Oxford, June 4, 5, 6. Drawn. Toss: Yorkshire. On a good batting strip Blakey and Byas launched a spectacular rescue, adding 269 after Yorkshire-born Wood had dismissed Metcalfe and Kellett, the county openers, in three balls. Blakey hit 196, with 21 fours, and Byas 101, and Robinson and Grayson continued with an unbroken stand of 42 before Metcalfe declared at 405 for four. Oxford's impressive reply was spearheaded by wicket-keeper Sandiford, who went in as night-watchman late on the first day. He added 84 with Montgomerie and 78 with Gupte, reaching a career-best 83 on the third day after two sessions were lost to weather on the second. Though the University faltered after reaching 241 with only five wickets lost, Pfaff saw them safely past the follow-on in the course of his punishing not out 40 from 48 balls. There was no longer any possibility of a result, so Turner declared, allowing Yorkshire's openers the opportunity of some useful practice in the time remaining.

*Close of play:* First day, Oxford University 32-1 (R. R. Montgomerie 20*, D. C. Sandiford 8*); Second day, Oxford University 135-2 (D. C. Sandiford 59*, C. M. Gupte 13*).

### Yorkshire

| | | | | | |
|---|---|---|---|---|---|
| S. A. Kellett lbw b Wood | 20 | – c Lovell b Gupte | | | 63 |
| *A. A. Metcalfe c Pfaff b Wood | 27 | – lbw b Davies | | | 62 |
| D. Byas c and b R. E. Morris | 101 | – (4) not out | | | 0 |
| †R. J. Blakey b R. E. Morris | 196 | | | | |
| P. E. Robinson not out | 35 | – (3) c Montgomerie b Davies | | | 22 |
| A. P. Grayson not out | 18 | | | | |
| L-b 3, w 4, n-b 1 | 8 | B 5, l-b 2, n-b 4 | | | 11 |

1/42 2/49 3/318 4/363     (4 wkts dec.) 405     1/115 2/158 3/158     (3 wkts) 158

D. Gough, J. D. Batty, M. Broadhurst, S. D. Fletcher and M. A. Robinson did not bat.

Bowling: *First Innings*—Macdonald 14-4-48-0; Wood 27-5-85-2; Turner 22-3-91-0; Davies 12-2-68-0; Lovell 7-1-28-0; R. E. Morris 17-3-82-2. *Second Innings*—Wood 11-2-37-0; Turner 8-1-16-0; Davies 14-2-46-2; Gupte 8.1-1-33-1; R. E. Morris 3-0-19-0.

### Oxford University

| | | | | |
|---|---|---|---|---|
| R. R. Montgomerie c Byas b Batty | 54 | H. R. Davies lbw b Batty | | 1 |
| R. E. Morris c Blakey b Broadhurst | 2 | B. S. Wood st Blakey b Batty | | 6 |
| †D. C. Sandiford b Broadhurst | 83 | R. H. Macdonald not out | | 1 |
| C. M. Gupte c Blakey b Gough | 48 | B 6, l-b 1, n-b 13 | | 20 |
| G. B. T. Lovell lbw b Broadhurst | 2 | | | |
| *G. J. Turner c and b Grayson | 10 | 1/9 2/93 3/171 | (9 wkts dec.) | 267 |
| D. B. Pfaff not out | 40 | 4/175 5/198 6/241 | | |
| J. G. Morris b Gough | 0 | 7/245 8/246 9/266 | | |

Bowling: Fletcher 8-0-27-0; Broadhurst 19-5-61-3; Gough 18-3-55-2; M. A. Robinson 14-2-44-0; Batty 27-8-63-3; Grayson 7-4-3-1; Byas 7-2-7-0.

Umpires: N. T. Plews and G. A. Stickley.

## OXFORD UNIVERSITY v LANCASHIRE

At Oxford, June 7, 8, 10. Lancashire won by five wickets. Toss: Oxford University. An unbeaten 122 by Jesty, in his only first-class game of the season, steered the county to victory in a match kept alive by three declarations. Play did not get under way until four o'clock on the first day. Set to score 255 in 195 minutes, Lancashire reached their target with nine balls to spare, but at 159 for five, with sixteen overs left, Oxford had high hopes of a rare win. They disappeared when Jesty was joined by Irani, to hit off the 96 runs required at more than 6 an over. Earlier, Turner had scored the University's only first-class century of 1991, hitting sixteen fours in 227 minutes, and he declared undefeated on 101 with his side 222 for seven. Lancashire closed their first innings before the start of the final day, and Oxford declared a second time at 113 for two when heavy rain stopped play. Turner expected a lengthy hold-up, but in the event the conditions quickly improved and little playing time was lost.

*Close of play:* First day, Oxford University 56-4 (C. M. Gupte 11*, G. J. Turner 1*); Second day, Lancashire 81-2 (N. J. Speak 30*, T. E. Jesty 4*).

## Oxford University

| | | | |
|---|---|---|---|
| R. R. Montgomerie c Titchard b Yates | 24 | – c Speak b Martin | 3 |
| R. E. Morris lbw b Sharp | 15 | – not out | 50 |
| C. M. Gupte run out | 23 | – c Martin b Yates | 43 |
| G. B. T. Lovell lbw b Martin | 1 | – not out | 16 |
| †D. C. Sandiford b Fitton | 0 | | |
| *G. J. Turner not out | 101 | | |
| D. B. Pfaff c Stanworth b Martin | 20 | | |
| H. R. Davies c Yates b Fitton | 4 | | |
| P. S. Gerrans not out | 17 | | |
| B 4, l-b 3, n-b 10 | 17 | L-b 1 | 1 |

1/28 2/50 3/51 4/54 5/110        (7 wkts dec.) 222   1/8 2/84        (2 wkts dec.) 113
6/159 7/182

J. M. E. Oppenheimer and B. S. Wood did not bat.

Bowling: *First Innings*—Martin 24–6–47–2; Sharp 15–7–21–1; Irani 19–3–50–0; Yates 22–6–55–1; Fitton 19–6–42–2. *Second Innings*—Martin 8–2–14–1; Irani 13.2–2–32–0; Yates 14–5–26–1; Fitton 10–1–34–0; Ward 2–0–6–0.

## Lancashire

| | | | |
|---|---|---|---|
| N. J. Speak not out | 30 | – c Sandiford b Oppenheimer | 8 |
| T. M. Orrell b Wood | 5 | – lbw b Oppenheimer | 16 |
| S. P. Titchard run out | 39 | – b Gerrans | 43 |
| T. E. Jesty not out | 4 | – not out | 122 |
| J. D. Fitton (did not bat) | | – c Montgomerie b Wood | 16 |
| G. Yates (did not bat) | | – c Sandiford b Turner | 12 |
| R. C. Irani (did not bat) | | – not out | 31 |
| B 1, l-b 1, n-b 1 | 3 | B 2, l-b 3, w 1, n-b 1 | 7 |

1/6 2/72        (2 wkts dec.) 81   1/11 2/46 3/86        (5 wkts) 255
                                   4/125 5/159

P. J. Martin, *†J. Stanworth, M. A. Sharp and M. J. P. Ward did not bat.

Bowling: *First Innings*—Oppenheimer 10–1–35–0; Wood 6–0–23–1; Gerrans 7–2–21–0. *Second Innings*—Oppenheimer 15–1–85–2; Wood 12–2–52–1; Gerrans 15.3–2–52–1; Turner 13–2–61–1.

Umpires: A. A. Jones and K. E. Palmer.

†At Oxford, June 13, 14. Drawn. Toss: Oxford University. Oxford University 156 for dec. (R. E. Morris 64) and 203 for three dec. (R. D. Oliphant-Callum 55, S. N. Warley 116); Harlequins 125 for two dec. (J. J. Rogers 58 not out, B. Macnamara 30) and 213 for nine (B. Macnamara 87, P. D. Lunn 35, A. Tucker 34).

## OXFORD UNIVERSITY v KENT

At Oxford, June 18, 19, 20. Drawn. Toss: Kent. Lacking five regulars, including their captain, Turner, the University did well to fend off defeat in the last first-class match of the season at The Parks. Morris and Russell started well with 75 after Kent's declaration left Oxford needing 342 in 288 minutes; but when two collapses left them 83 for four and then 139 for seven, the county looked set to win. They were thwarted by Sandiford and Davies, who played out the last twenty overs. In the first innings Oxford's weak attack was heavily punished by Ward and Fleming, who shared an opening stand of 96, and Wells and Marsh completed fifties before the latter declared at 344 for seven. Ward reached 100 in 114 balls, hitting thirteen fours and two sixes. In reply the University were dismissed for 132, with Wren and Kelleher sharing six wickets, but the follow-on was not enforced, permitting the final day's reprieve.

*Close of play:* First day, Kent 183-2 (T. R. Ward 101*, V. J. Wells 9*); Second day, Kent 20-0 (M. C. Dobson 5*, M. A. Ealham 10*).

# Kent

| | |
|---|---|
| T. R. Ward c Warley b Wood | 122 |
| M. V. Fleming c R. E. Morris b Oppenheimer | 60 |
| N. J. Llong c and b Oppenheimer | 9 |
| V. J. Wells c J. G. Morris b Russell | 58 |
| *S. A. Marsh b Russell | 57 |
| M. C. Dobson not out | 13 – (1) c Sandiford b Wood ....... 50 |
| D. J. M. Kelleher b Russell | 10 – (3) not out ............... 29 |
| R. P. Davis lbw b Russell | 8 |
| M. A. Ealham not out | 2 – (2) c J. G. Morris b Oppenheimer 37 |
| B 2, l-b 1, n-b 2 | 5    B 1, l-b 8, w 4 ......... 13 |

1/96 2/152 3/215 4/285 5/314     (7 wkts dec.) 344   1/57 2/129    (2 wkts dec.) 129
6/325 7/341

†G. J. Kersey and T. N. Wren did not bat.

Bowling: *First Innings*—Oppenheimer 10-1-51-2; Wood 23-4-77-1; Gerrans 17-2-84-0; Davies 12-2-70-0; R. E. Morris 4-0-28-0; Russell 8-2-31-4. *Second Innings*—Oppenheimer 11-2-47-1; Wood 13-2-60-1; Gerrans 2-0-13-0.

## Oxford University

| | |
|---|---|
| *R. E. Morris c Llong b Kelleher | 2 – c Kersey b Wells ............ 37 |
| M. J. Russell c Davis b Kelleher | 23 – b Wells ................ 30 |
| G. B. T. Lovell c Dobson b Kelleher | 17 – c Kersey b Wren .......... 29 |
| S. N. Warley lbw b Ealham | 11 – c Marsh b Davis ........... 1 |
| J. G. Morris b Wren | 19 – b Wells ................ 1 |
| C. D. Jones lbw b Ealham | 4 – b Fleming .............. 23 |
| P. S. Gerrans b Wells | 14 – b Fleming .............. 4 |
| †D. C. Sandiford b Wren | 28 – not out ............... 35 |
| H. R. Davies b Davis | 0 – not out ............... 12 |
| J. M. E. Oppenheimer not out | 0 |
| B. S. Wood b Wren | 0 |
| L-b 3, w 1, n-b 10 | 14    B 1, l-b 4, w 1, n-b 10 ... 16 |

1/7 2/40 3/58 4/63 5/68            132   1/75 2/76 3/77 4/83    (7 wkts) 188
6/89 7/131 8/132 9/132                   5/131 6/138 7/139

Bowling: *First Innings*—Wren 7.3-2-14-3; Kelleher 16-3-25-3; Ealham 10-2-38-2; Wells 10-3-24-1; Davis 11-2-28-1. *Second Innings*—Wren 12-1-34-1; Kelleher 10-2-22-0; Davis 20-12-22-1; Ealham 10-2-42-0; Fleming 13-2-25-2; Wells 12.4-5-21-3; Dobson 8-1-17-0.

Umpires: Dr D. Fawkner-Corbett and J. H. Harris.

†At Oxford, June 22, 23, 25. Drawn. Toss: Oxford University. Oxford University 258 for six dec. (R. E. Morris 74, C. M. Gupte 77, G. B. T. Lovell 58; P. Cattrail four for 25) and 60 for two dec. (R. R. Montgomerie 38 not out); Free Foresters 32 for one dec. and 160 for four (R. D. Oliphant-Callum 56 not out).

†At Uxbridge, June 30. Oxford University won by 24 runs. Toss: Oxford University. Oxford University 219 for seven (40 overs) (G. J. Turner 57); Combined Services 195 for eight (40 overs) (SAC R. Beeston 43, Flt Lt A. P. Laws 50 not out).

At Lord's, July 2, 3, 4. OXFORD UNIVERSITY drew with CAMBRIDGE UNIVERSITY (See Other Matches at Lord's, 1991).

CAMBRIDGE UNIVERSITY 1991

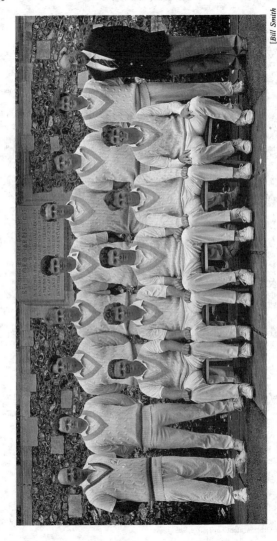

[Bill Smith]

*Back row*: G. J. Saville (*coach*), R. I. Clitheroe, R. H. J. Jenkins, J. P. Crawley, R. M. Pearson, D. J. Bush, R. B. Waller, J. P. Arscott, R. May (*scorer*).
*Front row*: A. M. Hooper, M. J. Lowrey, R. J. Turner (*captain*), M. J. Morris, S. W. Johnson.

# CAMBRIDGE

*President:* Professor A. D. Buckingham (Pembroke)

*Captain:* R. J. Turner (Millfield and Magdalene)
*Secretary:* M. J. Morris (Cherwell and Pembroke)

*Captain for 1992:* J. P. Crawley (Manchester GS and Downing)
*Secretary:* J. P. Arscott (Tonbridge and Magdalene)

Despite the arrival of two talented Freshmen and the continued presence of several Seniors, Cambridge University again found their matches against the first-class counties unequal contests. Indeed, they also struggled in several of their non first-class fixtures, the match against MCC being a notable exception.

Bowling was once more a particular problem, despite the availability of the previous season's opening attack. It was a difficulty only partially eased by the advent of Richard Pearson, an off-spinner from Batley Grammar School. He bore the brunt of the bowling on improving Fenner's pitches, and while his figures did not always do justice to his efforts, he impressed several counties, even when the weather was cold and the pitches slow. Northamptonshire moved swiftly to offer him a summer's contract.

The prime recruit was John Crawley, the latest talented youngster to emerge from Manchester Grammar School's cricket academy. Like Mike Atherton before him, Crawley arrived with an established reputation, built on his performances for England Young Cricketers, whom he had captained in New Zealand, and Lancashire. An innings of 83, against Lancashire, on his first-class début for the University – after he had scored a century against Loughborough in his first game for Cambridge – raised expectations; probably too many. That remained his highest first-class score of the term.

Crawley took on extra responsibilities in only his second first-class match. He was handed the captaincy when Robert Turner broke his thumb batting against Northamptonshire and was out of action for a month. The injury also prevented Turner from leading the Combined Universities in the Benson and Hedges zonal matches. He was missed both as captain and batsman by Cambridge, although his duties as wicket-keeper were expertly looked after by Roger Clitheroe, who was already in the side as an opening batsman. The biggest batting bonus was the form of Tony Hooper, a graduate student who won his Blue as an undergraduate four years earlier. He had not played regularly since, but he blossomed to score the University's only first-class century of the term – against Surrey, an innings which brought a brief glimpse of a possible victory. He followed that with 92 in the next match, against Leicestershire, and 89 against Oxford at Lord's.

Despite the difficulties experienced playing the counties, spirits remained high, for which much of the credit should go to Graham Saville, the coach, whose advice and very presence greatly benefited student players. If there is criticism, it has to be of some county captains who treated the fixtures as net practice, without any pretence of making a match. This was evident when county sides batted to tea on the third day before making token declarations. By contrast, Turner was often ready for an optimistic gamble. The Surrey match was a notable example of a game Cambridge could easily have saved, had their captain not insisted on a victory chase. That, at least, did him credit. Unfortunately he did not have the ammunition to back his aspirations, a fact most apparent in the rain-affected match against Oxford at Lord's. – David Hallett.

## CAMBRIDGE UNIVERSITY RESULTS

*First-class matches – Played 10: Lost 3, Drawn 7.*

## FIRST-CLASS AVERAGES

### BATTING AND FIELDING

|  | Birthplace | M | I | NO | R | HI | Avge | Ct/St |
|---|---|---|---|---|---|---|---|---|
| J. P. Crawley .. | Maldon | 10 | 16 | 2 | 619 | 83 | 44.21 | 6 |
| A. M. Hooper.. | Perivale | 7 | 12 | 1 | 458 | 125 | 41.63 | 0 |
| R. J. Turner ... | Malvern | 8 | 12 | 3 | 231 | 69* | 25.66 | 9/1 |
| S. W. Johnson . | Newcastle-upon-Tyne | 7 | 8 | 3 | 85 | 20 | 17.00 | 3 |
| M. J. Lowrey .. | Hampstead | 10 | 16 | 2 | 234 | 51 | 16.71 | 2 |
| R. I. Clitheroe . | Radcliffe | 10 | 17 | 2 | 228 | 36 | 15.20 | 2 |
| J. P. Arscott ... | Tooting | 9 | 12 | 1 | 157 | 74 | 14.27 | 7 |
| G. E. Thwaites . | Brighton | 3 | 5 | 0 | 68 | 32 | 13.60 | 2 |
| M. J. Morris ... | Melbourne, Australia | 9 | 13 | 0 | 171 | 60 | 13.15 | 2 |
| R. B. Waller ... | London | 5 | 4 | 3 | 12 | 6* | 12.00 | 1 |
| D. J. Bush..... | Solihull | 7 | 7 | 2 | 58 | 24* | 11.60 | 3 |
| R. H. J. Jenkins | Leicester | 6 | 8 | 1 | 64 | 20 | 9.14 | 2 |
| R. A. Pyman ... | Changi, Singapore | 2 | 4 | 1 | 20 | 8* | 6.66 | 1 |
| R. M. Pearson.. | Batley | 10 | 12 | 1 | 70 | 21 | 6.36 | 2 |
| G. W. Jones ... | Birmingham | 3 | 5 | 1 | 19 | 13* | 4.75 | 0 |

Also batted: D. C. Cotton (*Bletchley*) (1 match) 0*, 0; N. C. W. Fenton (*Bradford*) (1 match) 7*; R. J. Lyons (*Johannesburg, SA*) (1 match) 20, 18; J. N. Viljoen (*Wepener, SA*) (1 match) 1*.

* *Signifies not out.*

A. M. Hooper played the only three-figure innings for Cambridge University.

### BOWLING

|  | O | M | R | W | BB | 5W/i | Avge |
|---|---|---|---|---|---|---|---|
| J. P. Arscott ... | 48 | 4 | 252 | 7 | 1-17 | 0 | 36.00 |
| R. B. Waller ... | 85.2 | 16 | 363 | 7 | 3-31 | 0 | 51.85 |
| M. J. Lowrey .. | 136 | 17 | 496 | 9 | 3-31 | 0 | 55.11 |
| R. M. Pearson.. | 332 | 59 | 1,098 | 15 | 4-84 | 0 | 73.20 |
| R. H. J. Jenkins | 150 | 20 | 514 | 7 | 2-46 | 0 | 73.42 |
| D. J. Bush..... | 131.3 | 22 | 540 | 6 | 1-14 | 0 | 90.00 |

Also bowled: D. C. Cotton 21–4–85–1; J. P. Crawley 2–0–14–0; N. C. W. Fenton 25–5–95–0; A. M. Hooper 43–6–187–2; S. W. Johnson 131.1–17–608–3; R. J. Lyons 4–0–26–1; M. J. Morris 3–1–15–0; R. A. Pyman 65–15–216–4; J. N. Viljoen 22–2–99–1.

†At Cambridge, April 10. Loughborough University won by three wickets. Toss: Loughborough University. Cambridge University 224 for five (55 overs) (J. P. Crawley 128); Loughborough University 225 for seven (52.5 overs) (N. V. Knight 124 not out, K. Blackburn 35, S. Sheppherd 34).

†At Cambridge, April 11. Loughborough University won by 35 runs. Toss: Loughborough University. Loughborough University 215 for seven (55 overs) (I. Fletcher 40, A. McConky 42, D. Jones 30, P. J. Rendell 38; R. M. Pearson three for 39, R. J. Lyons three for 29); Cambridge University 180 (54 overs) (R. I. Clitheroe 44; K. Blackburn three for 24, M. J. M. Gore three for 32).

## CAMBRIDGE UNIVERSITY v LANCASHIRE

At Cambridge, April 13, 14, 15. Drawn. Toss: Lancashire. Atherton dominated the first day of the season when, on the ground he had graced as an undergraduate, he batted almost four hours for 138. It was the earliest date for a first-class century, beating by a day the previous record of T. W. Hayward, for Surrey against London County in 1903. His hundred included fifteen fours from 197 balls, and he added six more fours and a six from his remaining 30 deliveries before becoming one of three victims for Pearson, a promising Freshman off-spinner. Crawley's Cambridge début against his county was marked by a patient 256-minute innings of 83, with eight fours. After Lancashire had chosen not to enforce the follow-on, Mendis reached 100 in 175 minutes from 153 balls, hitting fourteen fours and a six, but even so Lancashire's acting-captain, Fairbrother, waited until tea before declaring. By then his team led by 447. The University lost three wickets in the final 90 minutes.

*Close of play:* First day, Lancashire 443-7 (W. K. Hegg 26*, G. Yates 11*); Second day, Cambridge University 251.

### Lancashire

| | | |
|---|---|---|
| G. D. Mendis c Turner b Arscott | 44 | – not out .................127 |
| G. Fowler c Arscott b Bush | 63 | – c Crawley b Lowrey............25 |
| M. A. Atherton st Turner b Pearson | 138 | |
| *N. H. Fairbrother c Bush b Waller | 23 | – (3) retired hurt ...........25 |
| G. D. Lloyd c Morris b Johnson | 70 | – (4) c Turner b Bush .........39 |
| M. Watkinson b Pearson | 10 | – (5) not out .............35 |
| P. A. J. DeFreitas b Pearson | 39 | |
| †W. K. Hegg not out | 26 | |
| G. Yates not out | 11 | |
| B 8, l-b 9, w 1, n-b 1 | 19 | B 1, n-b 3 ............4 |

1/84 2/133 3/173 4/307 5/328    (7 wkts dec.) 443    1/99 2/200    (2 wkts dec.) 255
6/377 7/414

J. D. Fitton and P. J. W. Allott did not bat.

*In the second innings N. H. Fairbrother retired hurt at 142.*

Bowling: *First Innings*—Bush 22-7-78-1; Waller 18-1-84-1; Johnson 24-3-88-1; Arscott 12-2-44-1; Pearson 38-6-124-3; Lowrey 1-0-8-0. *Second Innings*—Bush 11-0-45-1; Waller 6-2-23-0; Pearson 24-5-76-0; Lowrey 6-1-38-0; Johnson 6-1-38-0; Arscott 2-0-5-0.

### Cambridge University

| | | |
|---|---|---|
| G. W. Jones c Hegg b Allott | 1 | – c Hegg b DeFreitas ..........0 |
| R. I. Clitheroe c Lloyd b DeFreitas | 8 | – not out ...............22 |
| J. P. Crawley b Watkinson | 83 | – b Allott .............30 |
| *†R. J. Turner lbw b DeFreitas | 43 | |
| M. J. Lowrey c Fowler b DeFreitas | 43 | – not out ..............2 |
| M. J. Morris c Hegg b Watkinson | 0 | – (4) c Allott b Fitton .........0 |
| J. P. Arscott not out | 35 | |
| R. M. Pearson c Mendis b Yates | 2 | |
| R. B. Waller c Allott b Fitton | 2 | |
| S. W. Johnson c DeFreitas b Yates | 14 | |
| D. J. Bush c Hegg b Yates | 5 | |
| B 4, l-b 11 | 15 | B 4 ...............4 |

1/7 2/21 3/103 4/189 5/189    251    1/2 2/48 3/54    (3 wkts) 58
6/193 7/212 8/215 9/242

Bowling: *First Innings*—DeFreitas 23-5-62-3; Allott 15-5-23-1; Watkinson 22-7-52-2; Fitton 19-1-60-1; Yates 17.2-7-39-3. *Second Innings*—DeFreitas 6-2-19-1; Watkinson 4-2-5-0; Yates 8-2-24-0; Allott 4-1-4-1; Fitton 2-1-2-1.

Umpires: G. I. Burgess and M. J. Kitchen.

## CAMBRIDGE UNIVERSITY v NORTHAMPTONSHIRE

At Cambridge, April 16, 17, 18. Drawn. Toss: Cambridge University. A typically aggressive effort from Fordham set the tone for Northamptonshire's innings on a bitterly cold day. There was some early success for the University bowlers, but Capel hit seventeen fours and a six in a hundred from 84 balls in 106 minutes; and after his dismissal Williams, with fourteen fours and a six in a 149-ball century, and Curran took the total to 400. Once more Pearson was the main bowler employed and, despite conceding over 100 runs in an innings for the second successive match, he impressed Northamptonshire enough to be offered a contract. Cambridge lost early wickets, and when Turner, their captain, retired with a broken thumb after fending off a rising delivery from Thomas, they were effectively 56 for five. Although Crawley and Lowrey offered some resistance, Cambridge again failed to avoid the follow-on. However, Northamptonshire did not enforce it, and with no play possible on the final day their bowlers were not required to examine the Cambridge batting a second time.

*Close of play*: First day, Cambridge University 23-3 (R. H. J. Jenkins 8\*); Second day, Northamptonshire 66-0 (D. Ripley 38\*, N. A. Felton 26\*).

### Northamptonshire

| | | | | |
|---|---|---|---|---|
| A. Fordham c Waller b Arscott | 81 | | | |
| N. A. Felton c Clitheroe b Waller | 12 | – not out | | 26 |
| \*R. J. Bailey c Crawley b Jenkins | 21 | | | |
| D. J. Capel c Crawley b Pearson | 100 | | | |
| R. G. Williams not out | 101 | | | |
| K. M. Curran b Lowrey | 79 | | | |
| A. L. Penberthy not out | 2 | | | |
| †D. Ripley (did not bat) | | – (1) not out | | 38 |
| B 5, l-b 2, w 1 | 8 | L-b 2 | | 2 |

1/48 2/107 3/139 4/267 5/400    (5 wkts dec.) 404    (no wkt) 66

J. G. Thomas, J. P. Taylor and N. G. B. Cook did not bat.

Bowling: *First Innings*—Jenkins 19-3-71-1; Johnson 15.1-2-76-0; Waller 11-1-75-1; Arscott 3-0-26-1; Pearson 24-2-115-1; Lowrey 7-1-34-1. *Second Innings*—Jenkins 8-0-17-0; Johnson 5-0-42-0; Pearson 2-0-5-0.

### Cambridge University

| | | | | |
|---|---|---|---|---|
| G. W. Jones c Ripley b Taylor | 5 | J. P. Arscott c Ripley b Thomas | | 12 |
| R. I. Clitheroe b Cook | 8 | S. W. Johnson b Penberthy | | 20 |
| R. H. J. Jenkins c Cook b Thomas | 20 | R. B. Waller not out | | 4 |
| R. M. Pearson b Taylor | 0 | | | |
| J. P. Crawley c Ripley b Taylor | 39 | B 7, l-b 7, n-b 1 | | 15 |
| \*†R. J. Turner retired hurt | 0 | | | |
| M. J. Lowrey b Penberthy | 51 | 1/9 2/23 3/23 4/54 5/88 | | 174 |
| M. J. Morris lbw b Cook | 0 | 6/106 7/129 8/169 9/174 | | |

*R. J. Turner retired hurt at 56.*

Bowling: Taylor 18-3-56-3; Thomas 15-5-21-2; Cook 15-8-25-2; Williams 4-2-3-0; Penberthy 10.4-3-24-2; Capel 4-1-5-0; Curran 10-5-16-0; Bailey 4-0-10-0.

Umpires: G. I. Burgess and M. J. Kitchen.

## CAMBRIDGE UNIVERSITY v ESSEX

At Cambridge, April 19, 20, 22. Essex won by 350 runs. Toss: Cambridge University. Gooch launched his season with an unbeaten century, scored in 122 minutes off 110 balls with a six and sixteen fours before he detected the slightest of pulled calf muscles. It was another extremely cold day. However, his retirement brought little relief for the University, as all the Essex batsmen comfortably played themselves in. The home team were afforded no such luxury, with Foster heading a strong county attack on a day when there were several stoppages for hail. Waiving their right to enforce the follow-on, Essex picked up from where they had left off on the previous evening, with Stephenson and Pringle enjoying a century opening partnership. And by lunch on Monday, Garnham had contributed his maiden hundred for Essex; in 137 minutes, off 119 balls, he hit a six and twelve fours. Gooch declared then with a lead of 504, leaving the University to bat through two sessions to avoid a heavy defeat. Only Crawley, with a cultured fifty, made any progress before becoming one of four victims in sixteen balls for Stephenson, and Cambridge were dismissed inside 54 overs.

*Close of play:* First day, Cambridge University 22-1 (R. I. Clitheroe 3*); Second day, Essex 134-1 (J. P. Stephenson 71*, M. A. Garnham 8*).

## Essex

| | | | |
|---|---|---|---|
| *G. A. Gooch retired hurt | .101 | | |
| N. Shahid c Johnson b Lyons | 83 | | |
| P. J. Prichard not out | 55 | – (6) not out | 18 |
| Salim Malik b Arscott | 40 | – c Johnson b Pearson | 32 |
| J. P. Stephenson not out | 16 | – (1) c Jenkins b Bush | 84 |
| D. R. Pringle (did not bat) | | – (2) b Arscott | 52 |
| †M. A. Garnham (did not bat) | | – (3) not out | .102 |
| N. A. Foster (did not bat) | | – (5) c sub b Pearson | 2 |
| B 8, l-b 5, w 1, n-b 2 | 16 | L-b 1, w 1, n-b 6 | 8 |

| | | | |
|---|---|---|---|
| 1/209 2/282 | (2 wkts. dec.) 311 | 1/118 2/166 | (4 wkts dec.) 298 |
| | | 3/231 4/239 | |

T. D. Topley, M. C. Ilott and P. M. Such did not bat.

*G. A. Gooch retired hurt at 168.*

Bowling: *First Innings*—Jenkins 16–1–61–0; Bush 9–1–42–0; Pearson 18–3–77–0; Johnson 8–0–33–0; Lowrey 7–0–42–0; Lyons 4–0–26–1; Arscott 6–1–17–1. *Second Innings*—Jenkins 14–1–53–0; Bush 13–1–66–1; Pearson 23–5–88–2; Johnson 12–2–69–0; Arscott 4–0–21–1.

## Cambridge University

| | | | |
|---|---|---|---|
| G. E. Thwaites b Foster | 19 | – c Garnham b Pringle | 6 |
| †R. I. Clitheroe c Gooch b Ilott | 13 | – c Pringle b Ilott | 4 |
| *J. P. Crawley c Garnham b Topley | 39 | – c Pringle b Stephenson | 54 |
| M. J. Lowrey lbw b Pringle | 0 | – c Shahid b Such | 9 |
| R. J. Lyons c Gooch b Foster | 20 | – c Salim Malik b Stephenson | 18 |
| M. J. Morris b Topley | 2 | – c Salim Malik b Foster | 15 |
| J. P. Arscott c Salim Malik b Foster | 0 | – lbw b Stephenson | 0 |
| R. H. J. Jenkins b Foster | 5 | – lbw b Stephenson | 0 |
| R. M. Pearson b Such | 0 | – c Pringle b Foster | 15 |
| S. W. Johnson not out | 4 | – not out | 18 |
| D. J. Bush c Topley b Such | 0 | – b Ilott | 3 |
| B 1, l-b 1, n-b 1 | 3 | B 4, l-b 5, n-b 3 | 12 |

| | | | |
|---|---|---|---|
| 1/22 2/52 3/55 4/88 5/90 | 105 | 1/9 2/25 3/44 4/88 5/95 | 154 |
| 6/91 7/100 8/101 9/105 | | 6/99 7/99 8/119 9/134 | |

Bowling: *First Innings*—Foster 17–7–29–4; Ilott 12–4–32–1; Pringle 7–1–18–1; Topley 7–1–19–2; Such 5–3–5–2. *Second Innings*—Ilott 9.4–3–30–2; Pringle 9–7–4–1; Such 10–3–21–1; Topley 7–2–28–0; Foster 9–2–32–2; Stephenson 9–2–30–4.

Umpires: H. D. Bird and R. A. White.

†At Cambridge, May 5. Hertfordshire won by two wickets. Toss: Hertfordshire. Cambridge University 158 for nine (50 overs) (J. P. Crawley 47, M. J. Lowrey 30); Hertfordshire 161 for eight (50 overs) (R. M. Pearson three for 20).

†At Cambridge, May 6. Hertfordshire won by 60 runs. Toss: Hertfordshire. Hertfordshire 204 for seven (50 overs) (N. R. C. MacLaurin 61, M. James 30; R. B. Waller three for 43, A. M. Hooper three for 29); Cambridge University 144 for eight (50 overs) (M. J. Lowrey 59 not out, S. W. Johnson 37; D. M. Smith three for 25, A. Needham three for 6).

## CAMBRIDGE UNIVERSITY v DERBYSHIRE

At Cambridge, May 9, 10, 11. Drawn. Toss: Cambridge University. Derbyshire occupied the first day, scoring 431 from 107 overs, and much of the last. During a 200-run stand with Bowler for the second wicket in their first innings, Morris passed 100 in 147 minutes from 140 balls, and in all he hit eight sixes and eleven fours. Azharuddin followed with his first hundred for the county, from 126 balls in 148 minutes, hitting a six and ten fours off friendly bowling. Although Crawley, their best batsman, failed to score, the University replied with great commitment and found runs right through the order. The best batting came from Thwaites and Arscott, with the latter lasting three hours for 74, his maiden fifty. When Derbyshire declined to enforce the follow-on, Adams took the opportunity to score a career-best 134, reaching 100 in 130 minutes and 133 balls (nineteen fours). Pearson, again bearing the brunt of the work, collected four more wickets as the county extended their batting practice until tea on the third day.

*Close of play:* First day, Derbyshire 431-4 (M. Azharuddin 116\*, B. Roberts 36\*); Second day, Derbyshire 29-0 (P. D. Bowler 15\*, C. J. Adams 9\*).

### Derbyshire

| | | | |
|---|---|---|---|
| P. D. Bowler c Clitheroe b Hooper | 81 | – c Arscott b Viljoen | 31 |
| T. J. G. O'Gorman b Johnson | 14 | – (4) c Pearson b Lowrey | 14 |
| J. E. Morris c Arscott b Pearson | 131 | | |
| M. Azharuddin | 116 | – (9) not out | 20 |
| C. J. Adams c Clitheroe b Arscott | 39 | – (2) c Bush b Pearson | 134 |
| B. Roberts not out | 36 | – (8) not out | 44 |
| †K. M. Krikken (did not bat) | | – (3) c Thwaites b Pearson | 11 |
| M. Jean-Jacques (did not bat) | | – (5) b Pearson | 2 |
| O. H. Mortensen (did not bat) | | – (6) b Pearson | 0 |
| A. E. Warner (did not bat) | | – (7) c Lowrey b Arscott | 53 |
| B 6, l-b 1, w 1, n-b 6 | 14 | B 5, l-b 10, n-b 1 | 16 |

1/20 2/220 3/230 4/361      (4 wkts dec.) 431     1/65 2/165 3/192    (7 wkts dec.) 325
                                                            4/200 5/202
                                                            6/204 7/286

\*K. J. Barnett did not bat.

Bowling: *First Innings*—Johnson 17-1-66-1; Bush 16-4-53-0; Viljoen 11-0-65-0; Pearson 32-7-92-1; Arscott 11-1-52-1; Lowrey 15-1-61-0; Hooper 5-1-35-1. *Second Innings*—Johnson 8-3-25-0; Bush 7-1-44-0; Pearson 27-2-84-4; Viljoen 11-2-34-1; Hooper 5-2-15-0; Lowrey 14-1-46-1; Arscott 6-0-42-1; Morris 3-1-15-0; Crawley 1-0-5-0.

### Cambridge University

| | | | |
|---|---|---|---|
| A. M. Hooper c Roberts b Warner | 21 | – not out | 48 |
| †R. I. Clitheroe lbw b Jean-Jacques | 36 | – c Krikken b Adams | 7 |
| \*J. P. Crawley c Barnett b Warner | 0 | | |
| M. J. Lowrey c Mortensen b Warner | 2 | – (3) not out | 4 |
| M. J. Morris c Morris b Barnett | 17 | | |
| G. E. Thwaites c Krikken b Warner | 32 | | |
| J. P. Arscott c Azharuddin b Jean-Jacques | 74 | | |
| S. W. Johnson lbw b Barnett | 18 | | |
| R. M. Pearson lbw b Barnett | 21 | | |
| D. J. Bush c Krikken b Jean-Jacques | 13 | | |
| J. N. Viljoen not out | 1 | | |
| B 4, l-b 11, n-b 8 | 23 | N-b 1 | 1 |

1/40 2/40 3/44 4/82 5/88           258     1/41              (1 wkt) 60
6/140 7/174 8/230 9/252

Bowling: *First Innings*—Mortensen 16-1-37-0; Warner 23-2-60-4; Jean-Jacques 17.5-6-34-3; Barnett 33-12-71-3; Azharuddin 23-9-41-0. *Second Innings*—Mortensen 8-4-8-0; Jean-Jacques 10-2-25-0; Adams 7-2-11-1; Bowler 5-2-16-0.

Umpires: J. W. Holder and A. G. T. Whitehead.

†At Cambridge, May 12. Cryptics won by one wicket. Toss: Cambridge University. Cambridge University 216 for eight dec. (R. I. Clitheroe 52, M. J. Lowrey 33, M. E. D. Jarrett 31, G. W. Jones 57; A. J. Buzza three for 43); Cryptics 217 for nine (D. C. Elstone 38, J. A. Claughton 91, P. Nolan 40; R. H. J. Jenkins three for 45, A. M. Hooper four for 23).

†At Cambridge, May 14. Cambridge University won by 15 runs. Toss: Cambridge University. Cambridge University 202 for seven (55 overs) (J. P. Crawley 55, J. P. Arscott 35 not out; D. M. Cousins three for 41); Cambridgeshire 187 (53.2 overs) (R. A. Milne 61, D. P. Norman 48; M. J. Lowrey seven for 41).

## CAMBRIDGE UNIVERSITY v MIDDLESEX

At Cambridge, May 15, 16, 17. Drawn. Toss: Middlesex. Hutchinson and Roseberry batted without any alarms in an opening partnership of 164, but Ramprakash missed out, being bowled third ball by Pearson. Roseberry went on to complete his hundred from 215 balls in 228 minutes, hitting thirteen fours and two sixes, and Emburey declared with more than an hour of the evening session remaining. However, rain prevented Cambridge from starting their innings until noon on the second day. Then, between further showers, they lost their first five wickets for 38 before Turner, recovered from his injury, joined Crawley to share Cambridge's first hundred partnership of the term. More than three hours were lost to the weather in all, but after declarations by both captains the University were set a fourth-innings target of 248 in three and a half hours. Tufnell made sure that this remained beyond them, and with eight wickets down they were happy to bat out time.

*Close of play:* First day, Middlesex 280-3 dec. (M. A. Roseberry 123*, M. Keech 12*); Second day, Cambridge University 67-5 (J. P. Crawley 34*, R. J. Turner 15*).

## Middlesex

| | | | | |
|---|---|---|---|---|
| I. J. F. Hutchinson b Arscott | 92 | | | |
| M. A. Roseberry not out | 123 | | | |
| M. R. Ramprakash b Pearson | 0 | | | |
| K. R. Brown c Morris b Bush | 34 | – (1) c Crawley b Pearson | 28 |
| M. Keech not out | 12 | – (2) lbw b Jenkins | 46 |
| †P. Farbrace (did not bat) | | – (3) c Johnson b Jenkins | 9 |
| P. C. R. Tufnell (did not bat) | | – (4) not out | 14 |
| *J. E. Emburey (did not bat) | | – (5) not out | 1 |
| B 8, l-b 4, w 6, n-b 1 | 19 | B 4, l-b 2, n-b 2 | 8 |

1/164 2/165 3/257       (3 wkts dec.) 280     1/79 2/79 3/98       (3 wkts dec.) 106

R. M. Ellcock, S. P. Hughes and N. G. Cowans did not bat.

Bowling: *First Innings*—Johnson 7–2–37–0; Jenkins 19–6–39–0; Bush 15.3–5–52–1; Pearson 20–2–56–1; Hooper 8–2–28–0; Arscott 3–0–32–1; Lowrey 10–0–24–0. *Second Innings*—Johnson 5–0–28–0; Jenkins 14–1–46–2; Hooper 3–1–16–0; Pearson 6–2–10–1.

## Cambridge University

| | | | | |
|---|---|---|---|---|
| A. M. Hooper c Emburey b Cowans | 2 | – b Ellcock | 0 |
| †R. I. Clitheroe b Cowans | 6 | – c Farbrace b Cowans | 4 |
| J. P. Crawley not out | 52 | – c and b Tufnell | 43 |
| M. J. Lowrey c Roseberry b Cowans | 0 | – (5) c Hutchinson b Tufnell | 9 |
| M. J. Morris c Hutchinson b Tufnell | 2 | – (6) c Hutchinson b Emburey | 0 |
| J. P. Arscott c Farbrace b Tufnell | 2 | – (7) c Emburey b Tufnell | 1 |
| *R. J. Turner not out | 69 | – (4) c Ellcock b Emburey | 38 |
| R. H. J. Jenkins (did not bat) | | – c Brown b Tufnell | 10 |
| R. M. Pearson (did not bat) | | – not out | 4 |
| S. W. Johnson (did not bat) | | – not out | 4 |
| L-b 2, n-b 4 | 6 | B 4, l-b 2, n-b 2 | 8 |

1/7 2/12 3/16 4/20 5/38     (5 wkts dec.) 139     1/0 2/4 3/83 4/87       (8 wkts) 121
                                                       5/87 6/90 7/108 8/113

D. J. Bush did not bat.

Bowling: *First Innings*—Cowans 8–4–10–3; Ellcock 7–3–11–0; Tufnell 13–6–13–2; Hughes 10–4–29–0; Ramprakash 2–0–11–0; Keech 3–0–20–0; Roseberry 5–0–27–0; Brown 2.5–1–16–0. *Second Innings*—Ellcock 5–3–4–1; Cowans 5–3–19–1; Hughes 8–2–25–0; Emburey 17–10–17–2; Ramprakash 9–2–36–0; Tufnell 21–14–14–4.

Umpires: B. J. Meyer and H. J. Rhodes.

## CAMBRIDGE UNIVERSITY v SURREY

At Cambridge, May 18, 20, 21. Surrey won by 38 runs. Toss: Surrey. Spin decided a fluctuating encounter which was won with one ball to spare. For the fourth time in four matches, county openers shared a century stand against the University three bowlers. But Cambridge hit back when Lowrey, their second-string off-spinner, claimed three wickets for 1 run late in the day. Surrey declared overnight, and the University replied with their best batting of the term to date. Building on an opening partnership of 77, Crawley took them to 165 for two before Medlycott and Boiling exploited a turning pitch to take the next eight wickets for 70. Medlycott then followed with a 150-ball hundred, hitting fourteen fours in 171 minutes. A challenging declaration by Greig, a former Cambridge captain, set the University to chase 273 in what became 73 overs, and their hopes were raised by Hooper's maiden century. He batted 216 minutes and faced 194 balls, with a six, a five and fifteen fours in his 125, and he shared a second-wicket stand of 109 in 82 minutes with Crawley. However, Medlycott crowned a successful game with another six wickets, finishing with eleven for the match, as he and Bullen bowled Surrey to an exciting victory.

*Close of play:* First day, Surrey 255-5 (G. P. Thorpe 1*, M. A. Feltham 0*); Second day, Surrey 85-2 (N. F. Sargeant 28*, K. T. Medlycott 36*).

## Surrey

| | | | |
|---|---|---|---|
| D. J. Bicknell c Arscott b Pyman | 82 | | |
| R. I. Alikhan c Crawley b Pyman | 92 | | |
| D. M. Ward c Pyman b Lowrey | 66 | – (7) not out | 2 |
| G. P. Thorpe not out | 1 | – (2) lbw b Bush | 1 |
| *I. A. Greig c Crawley b Lowrey | 0 | – (1) c Thwaites b Cotton | 17 |
| K. T. Medlycott c Arscott b Lowrey | 2 | – (4) c Turner b Pearson | 109 |
| M. A. Feltham not out | 0 | – (5) c Turner b Pearson | 48 |
| †N. F. Sargeant (did not bat) | | – (3) b Pyman | 29 |
| C. K. Bullen (did not bat) | | – (6) not out | 37 |
| B 3, l-b 7, w 2 | 12 | B 5, l-b 2, w 1, n-b 1 | 9 |

1/125 2/246 3/252 4/252 5/254      (5 wkts dec.) 255    1/20 2/20 3/94      (5 wkts dec.) 252
                                              4/172 5/230

J. Boiling and Waqar Younis did not bat.

Bowling: *First Innings*—Bush 8–1–38–0; Cotton 13–4–42–0; Pearson 20–7–46–0; Pyman 28–9–74–2; Lowrey 18–6–31–3; Hooper 5–0–14–0. *Second Innings*—Bush 6–2–14–1; Cotton 8–0–43–1; Pearson 19–2–73–2; Pyman 13–2–52–1; Lowrey 15–3–63–0.

## Cambridge University

| | | | |
|---|---|---|---|
| A. M. Hooper c Sargeant b Thorpe | 47 | – c Alikhan b Medlycott | 125 |
| R. I. Clitheroe c Bullen b Greig | 34 | – lbw b Medlycott | 6 |
| J. P. Crawley st Sargeant b Boiling | 69 | – c Ward b Bullen | 56 |
| *†R. J. Turner c Bullen b Medlycott | 35 | – c Boiling b Bullen | 3 |
| M. J. Lowrey c Feltham b Medlycott | 2 | – c Bullen b Medlycott | 21 |
| G. E. Thwaites b Medlycott | 7 | – st Sargeant b Bullen | 4 |
| J. P. Arscott lbw b Medlycott | 1 | – (8) c Bullen b Pearson | 3 |
| R. A. Pyman c Sargeant b Boiling | 6 | – (9) c sub b Medlycott | 0 |
| R. M. Pearson st Sargeant b Boiling | 3 | – (7) c sub b Bullen | 1 |
| D. J. Bush c Waqar Younis b Medlycott | 11 | – not out | 2 |
| D. C. Cotton not out | 0 | – c Sargeant b Medlycott | 0 |
| B 9, l-b 7, n-b 4 | 20 | B 7, l-b 2, w 1, n-b 3 | 13 |

1/77 2/93 3/165 4/173 5/195        235    1/37 2/146 3/162 4/195 5/202        234
6/199 7/216 8/217 9/232                        6/222 7/229 8/230 9/234

Bowling: *First Innings*—Waqar Younis 9–3–28–0; Feltham 13–1–57–0; Thorpe 10–3–37–1; Greig 7–2–22–1; Medlycott 25–11–36–5; Boiling 18.2–4–39–3. *Second Innings*—Waqar Younis 2.5–0–5–0; Feltham 8–0–22–0; Greig 4.1–1–6–0; Medlycott 26.5–6–98–6; Boiling 14–3–46–0; Bullen 17–2–48–4.

Umpires: H. J. Rhodes and D. R. Shepherd.

## CAMBRIDGE UNIVERSITY v LEICESTERSHIRE

At Cambridge, May 22, 23, 24. Drawn. Toss: Cambridge University. Electing to bat for the first time in the season, the University were rewarded when Clitheroe, Morris (with a maiden fifty) and Lowrey enabled them to pass 200 before the rare luxury of a declaration. Leicestershire replied with hundreds from Boon (222 minutes, 186 balls, fifteen fours) and Hepworth, who reached three figures for the first time by hitting his 128th delivery for one of his two sixes; he also hit twelve fours in 156 minutes. All the county players had useful practice as Leicestershire batted right through the second day, and when rain prevented any play on the final morning, Cambridge survived the last two sessions after losing two quick wickets. Hooper and Morris rescued the innings by adding 68 at 6 an over for the third wicket, and Hooper was unfortunate not to complete his second hundred of the term.

*Close of play:* First day, Leicestershire 19-0 (T. J. Boon 12\*, N. E. Briers 7\*); Second day, Leicestershire 452-4 (L. Potter 73\*, B. F. Smith 47\*).

### Cambridge University

| | | | |
|---|---|---|---|
| A. M. Hooper c Boon b Tennant | 10 | – c Briers b Potter | 92 |
| R. I. Clitheroe b Wilkinson | 35 | – c Whitticase b Tennant | 0 |
| J. P. Crawley c Whitticase b Maguire | 7 | – lbw b Tennant | 0 |
| M. J. Morris c Hepworth b Tennant | 60 | – b Tennant | 22 |
| \*†R. J. Turner c Boon b Potter | 10 | – c Briers b Wilkinson | 4 |
| M. J. Lowrey c Potter b Wilkinson | 32 | – c Potter b Gidley | 30 |
| G. W. Jones c Potter b Tennant | 0 | – not out | 13 |
| R. A. Pyman c Briers b Tennant | 6 | – not out | 8 |
| R. M. Pearson st Whitticase b Hepworth | 13 | | |
| D. J. Bush not out | 24 | | |
| N. C. W. Fenton not out | 7 | | |
| B 5, l-b 11, w 2, n-b 6 | 24 | B 3, l-b 1, n-b 13 | 17 |

1/21 2/40 3/74 4/96 5/157 (9 wkts dec.) 228
6/157 7/172 8/189 9/218

1/10 2/10 3/78 (6 wkts) 186
4/95 5/147 6/177

Bowling: *First Innings*—Tennant 22–7–54–4; Maguire 17–4–38–1; Wilkinson 15–5–26–2; Smith 5–1–20–0; Potter 13–4–27–1; Hepworth 13–0–36–1; Gidley 4–1–11–0. *Second Innings*—Maguire 7–1–47–0; Tennant 8–1–43–3; Gidley 19–10–33–1; Wilkinson 7–3–9–1; Potter 15–6–27–1; Hepworth 4–0–23–0; Smith 1–1–0–0.

### Leicestershire

| | | | |
|---|---|---|---|
| T. J. Boon c Bush b Pyman | 108 | B. F. Smith not out | 47 |
| \*N. E. Briers c Turner b Bush | 50 | B 3, l-b 9 | 12 |
| P. N. Hepworth b Lowrey | 115 | | |
| J. J. Whitaker c and b Lowrey | 47 | 1/91 2/232 (4 wkts dec.) 452 |
| L. Potter not out | 73 | 3/295 4/358 |

M. I. Gidley, †P. Whitticase, L. Tennant, J. N. Maguire and C. W. Wilkinson did not bat.

Bowling: Fenton 25–5–95–0; Pyman 24–4–90–1; Pearson 28–6–103–0; Bush 11–0–49–1; Lowrey 14–1–62–2; Hooper 5–0–32–0; Crawley 1–0–9–0.

Umpires: Dr D. Fawkner-Corbett and B. Leadbeater.

†At Cambridge, June 9. Free Foresters won by 3 runs. Toss: Free Foresters. Free Foresters 187 for five dec. (N. J. Richardson 52, C. J. C. Rowe 84; R. H. J. Jenkins three for 38); Cambridge University 184 (A. M. Hooper 46, R. I. Clitheroe 49; R. A. Pyman four for 81, C. J. C. Rowe three for 38).

†At Cambridge, June 10, 11, 12. Cambridge University won by an innings and 52 runs. Toss: MCC. MCC 170 (P. J. Mir 52; S. W. Johnson four for 46, R. H. J. Jenkins three for 40) and 206 (P. G. Wakefield 55, P. J. Mir 72; R. H. J. Jenkins four for 50, R. M. Pearson three for 35); Cambridge University 428 for two dec. (A. M. Hooper 60, R. I. Clitheroe 35, J. P. Crawley 200 not out, R. J. Turner 106 not out).

†At Cambridge, June 13, 14, 15. Drawn. Toss: Cambridge University. Cambridge University 265 for five dec. (R. I. Clitheroe 36, M. J. Morris 122, J. P. Arscott 81) and 187 for four (R. I. Clitheroe 37, J. P. Crawley 80, M. J. Lowrey 32 not out); Combined Services 248 for three dec. (Capt. J. W. S. Cotterill 102 not out, SAC A. Jones 102 not out; R. H. J. Jenkins three for 36).

†At Cambridge, June 17. Club Cricket Conference Under-25 won by six wickets. Toss: Club Cricket Conference Under-25. Cambridge University 157 (49.5 overs) (R. I. Clitheroe 34, M. J. Lowrey 35; R. O'Sullivan three for 28, D. Beynon four for 35); Club Cricket Conference Under-25 160 for four (48.4 overs) (A. C. Churchill 42 not out; R. B. Waller three for 43).

## CAMBRIDGE UNIVERSITY v GLAMORGAN

At Cambridge, June 18, 19, 20. Glamorgan won by 181 runs. Toss: Cambridge University. Turner's bold move in forfeiting an innings to make up for time lost to rain cruelly misfired, when Cambridge were later dismissed in 52 overs for their lowest completed total of 1991. Much of the first and second days had been washed out, but before the showers Glamorgan prospered through Shastri and Smith. The county declared when the rains ceased, and the University's forfeit allowed Hugh Morris, on reaching 17, to become the first batsman to score 1,000 first-class runs in the season. Another declaration set Cambridge 281 to win in 163 minutes plus twenty overs, but on a rain-affected pitch the question was whether they could avoid defeat. The answer was no. Shastri picked up four cheap wickets as Cambridge lost their last five for 3 runs.

*Close of play:* First day, Glamorgan 141-3 (R. J. Shastri 52*, P. A. Cottey 2*); Second day, No play.

## Glamorgan

| | | | | |
|---|---|---|---|---|
| M. P. Maynard b Jenkins | 21 | – b Waller | | 1 |
| *H. Morris c Turner b Johnson | 10 | – c Pearson b Hooper | | 33 |
| R. J. Shastri not out | 52 | | | |
| I. Smith c Jenkins b Waller | 47 | – c Turner b Waller | | 2 |
| P. A. Cottey not out | 2 | – (3) c Turner b Waller | | 21 |
| A. Dale (did not bat) | | – (5) not out | | 45 |
| R. D. B. Croft (did not bat) | | – (6) c Turner b Jenkins | | 14 |
| J. Derrick (did not bat) | | – (7) not out | | 12 |
| B 5, l-b 3, n-b 1 | 9 | B 4, w 3, n-b 4 | | 11 |

| | | |
|---|---|---|
| 1/20 2/40 3/128 | (3 wkts dec.) 141 | 1/2 2/40 3/51 (5 wkts dec.) 139 |
| | | 4/77 5/104 |

†M. L. Roberts, S. J. Dennis and S. Bastien did not bat.

Bowling: *First Innings*—Johnson 9–1–34–1; Jenkins 15–3–55–1; Pearson 11–5–35–0; Waller 4.3–2–9–1. *Second Innings*—Jenkins 9–0–47–1; Waller 11–4–31–3; Hooper 8–0–30–1; Pearson 8–1–27–0.

# Cambridge University

*Cambridge University forfeited their first innings.*

| | | | |
|---|---|---|---|
| A. M. Hooper c Shastri b Bastien | 14 | R. M. Pearson c Roberts b Shastri | 1 |
| R. I. Clitheroe c Maynard b Shastri | 31 | R. H. J. Jenkins lbw b Croft | 0 |
| J. P. Crawley c Dale b Croft | 22 | S. W. Johnson st Roberts b Shastri | 0 |
| *†R. J. Turner c Derrick b Bastien | 2 | R. B. Waller not out | 0 |
| M. J. Morris lbw b Croft | 20 | | — |
| M. J. Lowrey c Croft b Bastien | 4 | 1/20 2/56 3/68 4/73 5/79 | 99 |
| J. P. Arscott st Roberts b Shastri | 5 | 6/96 7/98 8/99 9/99 | |

Bowling: Bastien 13–5–37–3; Dennis 7–1–18–0; Shastri 19–8–20–4; Derrick 7–3–16–0; Croft 6–2–8–3.

Umpires: V. A. Holder and P. B. Wight.

†At Cambridge, June 21. Essex Second Eleven won by four wickets. Toss: Cambridge University. Cambridge University 214 for seven (55 overs) (A. M. Hooper 58, J. P. Crawley 61, M. J. Morris 52); Essex Second Eleven 215 for six (54.5 overs) (K. A. Butler 64, J. J. B. Lewis 59 not out, A. C. Churchill 30).

†At Cambridge, June 23. Drawn. Toss: Quidnuncs. Quidnuncs 70 for one (P. A. C. Bail 37 not out) v Cambridge University.

At Hove, June 29, 30, July 1. CAMBRIDGE UNIVERSITY drew with SUSSEX.

At Lord's, July 2, 3, 4. CAMBRIDGE UNIVERSITY drew with OXFORD UNIVERSITY (See Other Matches at Lord's, 1991).

# OXFORD AND CAMBRIDGE BLUES

From 1946 to 1991, and some others

A full list of Blues from 1837 may be found in all *Wisdens* published between 1923 and 1939. Between 1948 and 1972 the list was confined to all those who had won Blues after 1880, plus some of "special interest for personal or family reasons". Between 1972 and 1982 the list was restricted to those who had won Blues since 1919. Such adjustments have been necessary owing to the exigencies of space.

## OXFORD

Aamer Hameed (Central Model HS and Punjab U.) 1979

Abell, G. E. B. (Marlborough) 1924, 1926-27

Allan, J. M. (Edinburgh Academy) 1953-56

Allerton, J. W. O. (Stowe) 1969

Allison, D. F. (Greenmore Coll.) 1970

Almaer, S. A. (Ilford County HS) 1988-89

Altham, H. S. (Repton) 1911-12

Arenhold, J. A. (Diocesan Coll., SA) 1954

Baig, A. A. (Aliya and Osmania U., India) 1959-62

Baig, M. A. (Osmania U., India) 1962-64

Bailey, J. A. (Christ's Hospital) (Capt. in 1958) 1956-58

Barber, A. T. (Shrewsbury) (Capt. in 1929) 1927-29

Barker, A. H. (Charterhouse) 1964-65, 1967

Bartlett, J. H. (Chichester) 1946, 1951

Beech, A. R. (John XXIII Coll., Perth and Univ. of Western Australia) 1987

Bettington, R. H. B. (The King's School, Parramatta) (Capt. in 1923) 1920-23

Bird, W. S. (Malvern) (Capt. in 1906) 1904-06

Birrell, H. B. (St Andrews, SA) 1953-54

Blake, P. D. S. (Eton) (Capt. in 1952) 1950-52

Bloy, N. C. F. (Dover) 1946-47

Boobbyer, B. (Uppingham) 1949-52

Bosanquet, B. J. T. (Eton) 1898-1900

Botton, N. D. (King Edward's, Bath) 1974

Bowman, R. C. (Fettes) 1957

Brettell, D. N. (Cheltenham) 1977

Bristowe, W. R. (Charterhouse) 1984-85

Brooks, R. A. (Quintin and Bristol U.) 1967

Brown, M. E. O. (Diocesan Coll. and Univ. of Cape Town) 1988

Burchnall, R. L. (Winchester) 1970-71

Burki, J. (St Mary's, Rawalpindi and Punjab U.) 1958-60

Burton, M. St J. W. (Umtali HS, Rhodesia and Rhodes U.) (Capt. in 1970) 1969-71

Bury, T. E. O. (Charterhouse) 1980

Bush, J. E. (Magdalen Coll. Sch.) 1952

Campbell, A. N. (Berkhamsted) 1970

Campbell, I. P. (Canford) 1949-50

Campbell, I. P. F. (Repton) (Capt. in 1913) 1911-13

Cantlay, C. P. T. (Radley) 1975

Carr, D. B. (Repton) (Capt. in 1950) 1949-51

Carr, J. D. (Repton) 1983-85

Carroll, P. R. (Newington Coll. and Sydney U.) 1971

Chalk, F. G. H. (Uppingham) (Capt. in 1934) 1931-34

Chesterton, G. H. (Malvern) 1949

Claughton, J. A. (King Edward's, Birmingham) (Capt. in 1978) 1976-79

Clements, S. M. (Ipswich) (Capt. in 1979) 1976, 1979

Clube, S. V. M. (St John's, Leatherhead) 1956

Cope, J. E. B. (St John's, Leatherhead) 1986-87

Corlett, S. C. (Worksop) 1971-72

Corran, A. J. (Gresham's) 1958-60

Coutts, I. D. F. (Dulwich) 1952

Cowan, R. S. (Lewes Priory CS) 1980-82

Cowdrey, M. C. (Tonbridge) (Capt. in 1954) 1952-54

Coxon, A. J. (Harrow CS) 1952

Crawley, A. M. (Harrow) 1927-30

Crawley, M. A. (Manchester GS) (Capt. in 1989) 1987-90

Crutchley, G. E. V. (Harrow) 1912

Cullinan, M. R. (Hilton Coll., SA) 1983-84

Curtis, D. M. (Falcon Coll., Harare and Cape Town U.) 1990

Curtis, I. J. (Whitgift) 1980, 1982

Cushing, V. G. B. (KCS Wimbledon) 1973

Cuthbertson, J. L. (Rugby) 1962-63

Davidson, W. W. (Brighton) 1947-48

Davis, F. J. (Blundell's) 1963

Dawson, T. A. J. (Mill Hill) 1986

Delisle, G. P. S. (Stonyhurst) 1955-56

de Saram, F. C. (Royal Coll., Colombo) 1934-35

Divecha, R. V. (Podar HS and Bombay U.) 1950-51

Dixon, E. J. H. (St Edward's, Oxford) (Capt. in 1939) 1937-39

Donnelly, M. P. (New Plymouth BHS and Canterbury U., NZ) (Capt. in 1947) 1946-47

Potter, I. C. (King's, Canterbury) 1961-62
Potts, H. J. (Stand GS) 1950
Price, V. R. (Bishop's Stortford) (Capt. in 1921) 1919-22
Pycroft, J. (Bath) 1836

Quinlan, J. D. (Sherborne) 1985

Rawlinson, H. T. (Eton) 1983-84
Raybould, J. G. (Leeds GS) 1959
Reynolds, G. D. (Wellington Coll.) 1988-89
Ridge, S. P. (Dr Challenor's GS) 1982
Ridley, G. N. S. (Milton HS, Rhodesia) (Capt. in 1967) 1965-68
Ridley, R. M. (Clifton) 1968-70
Robertson-Glasgow, R. C. (Charterhouse) 1920-23
Robinson, G. A. (Preston Cath. Coll.) 1971
Robinson, H. B. O. (North Shore Coll., Vancouver) 1947-48
Rogers, J. J. (Sedbergh) 1979-81
Ross, C. J. (Wanganui CS and Wellington U., NZ) (Capt. in 1980) 1978-80
Rudd, C. R. D. (Eton) 1949
Rumbold, J. S. (St Andrew's Coll., NZ) 1946
Rutnagur, R. S. (Westminster) 1985-86
Rydon, R. A. (Sherborne) 1986

Sabine, P. N. B. (Marlborough) 1963
Sale, R. (Repton) 1910
Sale, R. (Repton) 1939, 1946
Salvi, N. V. (Rossall) 1986
Sanderson, J. F. W. (Westminster) 1980
Sandiford, D. C. (Bolton GS) 1991
Sardesai, R. D. (St Xavier's Coll., Bombay and Univ. of Bombay) 1987
Saunders, C. J. (Lancing) 1964
Savage, R. Le Q. (Marlborough) 1976-78
Sayer, D. M. (Maidstone GS) 1958-60
Scott, M. D. (Winchester) 1957
Singleton, A. P. (Shrewsbury) (Capt. in 1937) 1934-37
Siviter, K. (Liverpool) 1976
Smith, A. C. (King Edward's, Birmingham) (Capt. in 1959-60) 1958-60
Smith, G. O. (Charterhouse) 1895-96
Smith, M. J. K. (Stamford) (Capt. in 1956) 1954-56
Stallibrass, M. J. D. (Lancing) 1974
Stevens, G. T. S. (UCS) (Capt. in 1922) 1920-23
Sutcliffe, S. P. (King George V GS, Southport) 1980-81
Sutton, M. A. (Ampleforth) 1946
Sygrove, M. R. (Lutterworth GS) 1988

Tavaré, C. J. (Sevenoaks) 1975-77
Taylor, C. H. (Westminster) 1923-26
Taylor, T. J. (Stockport GS) 1981-82
Thackeray, P. R. (St Edward's, Oxford and Exeter U.) 1974
Thomas, R. J. A. (Radley) 1965
Thorne, D. A. (Bablake) (Capt. in 1986) 1984-86

Toft, D. P. (Tonbridge) 1966-67
Toogood, G. J. (N. Bromsgrove HS) (Capt. in 1983) 1982-85
Tooley, C. D. M. (St Dunstan's) (Capt. in 1987) 1985-87
Topham, R. D. N. (Shrewsbury and Australian National U., Canberra) 1976
Travers, B. H. (Sydney U.) 1946, 1948
Trevelyan, R. W. D. (Marlborough) 1990
Turner, G. J. (St Stithian's and Cape Town U.) (Capt. in 1991) 1990-91
Twining, R. H. (Eton) (Capt. in 1912) 1910-13

van der Bijl, P. G. (Diocesan Coll., SA) 1932
van der Merwe, W. M. (Grey, OFS U. and Cape Town U.) 1990
Van Ryneveld, C. B. (Diocesan Coll., SA) (Capt. in 1949) 1948-50
Varey, J. G. (Birkenhead) 1982-83

Wagstaffe, M. C. (Rossall and Exeter U.) 1972
Walford, M. M. (Rugby) 1936, 1938
Walker, D. F. (Uppingham) (Capt. in 1935) 1933-35
Waller, G. de W. (Hurstpierpoint) 1974
Walsh, D. R. (Marlborough) 1967-69
Walshe, A. P. (Milton HS, Rhodesia) 1953, 1955-56
Walton, A. C. (Radley) (Capt. in 1957) 1955-57
Ward, J. M. (Newcastle-under-Lyme HS) 1971-73
Warner, P. F. (Rugby) 1895-96
Watson, A. G. M. (St Lawrence) 1965-66, 1968
Weale, S. D. (Westminster City) 1987-88, 1990
Webb, H. E. (Winchester) 1948
Webbe, A. J. (Harrow) (Capt. in 1877-78) 1875-78
Wellings, E. M. (Cheltenham) 1929, 1931
Westley, S. A. (Lancaster RGS) 1968-69
Wheatley, G. A. (Uppingham) 1946
Whitcombe, P. A. (Winchester) 1947-49
Whitcombe, P. J. (Worcester RGS) 1951-52
Wiley, W. G. A. (Diocesan Coll., SA) 1952
Williams, C. C. P. (Westminster) (Capt. in 1955) 1953-55
Wilson, P. R. B. (Milton HS, Rhodesia and Cape Town U.) 1968, 1970
Wilson, R. W. (Warwick) 1957
Wingfield Digby, A. R. (Sherborne) 1971, 1975-77
Winn, C. E. (KCS, Wimbledon) 1948-51
Wood, B. S. (Batley GS) 1991
Woodcock, R. G. (Worcester RGS) 1957-58
Wookey, S. M. (Malvern and Cambridge U.) 1978
Wordsworth, Chas. (Harrow) (Capt. both years, first Oxford Capt.) 1827, 1829
Worsley, D. R. (Bolton) (Capt. in 1964) 1961-64
Wrigley, M. H. (Harrow) 1949

# CAMBRIDGE

Acfield, D. L. (Brentwood) 1967-68

Aers, D. R. (Tonbridge) 1967

Ahluwalia, M. S. (Latymer Upper) 1986

Aird, R. (Eton) 1923

Alban, M. T. (Sedbergh) 1989

Alexander, F. C. M. (Wolmer's Coll., Jamaica) 1952-53

Allbrook, M. E. (Tonbridge) 1975-78

Allen, G. O. B. (Eton) 1922-23

Allom, M. J. C. (Wellington) 1927-28

Andrew, C. R. (Barnard Castle) (Capt. in 1985) 1984-85

Arscott, J. P. (Tonbridge) 1991

Ashton, C. T. (Winchester) (Capt. in 1923) 1921-23

Ashton, G. (Winchester) (Capt. in 1921) 1919-21

Ashton, H. (Winchester) (Capt. in 1922) 1920-22

Atherton, M. A. (Manchester GS) (Capt. in 1988-89) 1987-89

Atkins, G. (Dr Challenor's GS) 1960

Atkinson, J. C. M. (Millfield) (Capt. in 1990) 1988-90

Aworth, C. J. (Tiffin) (Capt. in 1975) 1973-75

Bail, P. A. C. (Millfield) 1986-88

Bailey, T. E. (Dulwich) 1947-48

Baker, R. K. (Brentwood) 1973-74

Bannister, C. S. (Caterham) 1976

Barber, R. W. (Ruthin) 1956-57

Barford, M. T. (Eastbourne) 1970-71

Barrington, W. E. J. (Lancing) 1982

Bartlett, H. T. (Dulwich) (Capt. in 1936) 1934-36

Bate, R. (Haberdashers' Aske's) 1988

Beaumont, D. J. (West Bridgford GS and Bramshill Coll.) 1978

Benke, A. F. (Cheltenham) 1962

Bennett, B. W. P. (Welbeck and RMA Sandhurst) 1979

Bennett, C. T. (Harrow) (Capt. in 1925) 1923, 1925

Bernard, J. R. (Clifton) 1958-60

Bhatia, A. N. (Doon School, India) 1969

Bligh, Hon. Ivo F. W. (Lord Darnley) (Eton) (Capt. in 1881) 1878-81

Blofeld, H. C. (Eton) 1959

Bodkin, P. E. (Bradfield) (Capt. in 1946) 1946

Boyd-Moss, R. J. (Bedford) 1980-83

Brearley, J. M. (City of London) (Capt. in 1963-64) 1961-64

Breddy, M. N. (Cheltenham GS) 1984

Brodie, B. N. (Union HS, SA) 1960

Brodrick, P. D. (Royal GS, Newcastle) 1961

Bromley, R. C. (Christ's Coll. and Canterbury U., NZ) 1970

Brooker, M. E. W. (Lancaster RGS and Burnley GS) 1976

Brown, A. D. (Clacton HS) 1986

Brown, F. R. (The Leys) 1930-31

Browne, D. W. (Stamford) 1986

Burnett, A. C. (Lancing) 1949

Burnley, I. D. (Queen Elizabeth, Darlington) 1984

Bush, D. J. (King Edward VI, Fiveways) 1989

Bushby, M. H. (Dulwich) (Capt. in 1954) 1952-54

Buzza, A. J. (Redruth CS) 1989-90

Calthorpe, Hon. F. S. G. (Repton) 1912-14, 1919

Cameron, J. H. (Taunton) 1935-37

Cangley, B. G. M. (Felsted) 1947

Carling, P. G. (Kingston GS) 1968, 1970

Chambers, R. E. J. (Forest) 1966

Chapman, A. P. F. (Oakham and Uppingham) 1920-22

Clitheroe, R. I. (Monmouth) 1991

Close, P. A. (Haileybury) 1965

Cobden, F. C. (Harrow) 1870-72

Cockett, J. A. (Aldenham) 1951

Coghlan, T. B. L. (Rugby) 1960

Conradi, E. R. (Oundle) 1946

Cook, G. W. (Dulwich) 1957-58

Cooper, N. H. C. (St Brendan's, Bristol and East Anglia U.) 1979

Cosh, N. J. (Dulwich) 1966-68

Cotterell, T. A. (Downside) 1983-85

Cottrell, G. A. (Kingston GS) (Capt. in 1968) 1966-68

Cottrell, P. R. (Chislehurst and Sidcup GS) 1979

Coverdale, S. P. (St Peter's, York) 1974-77

Craig, E. J. (Charterhouse) 1961-63

Crawford, N. C. (Shrewsbury) 1979-80

Crawley, E. (Harrow) 1887-89

Crawley, J. P. (Manchester GS) 1991

Crawley, L. G. (Harrow) 1923-25

Croft, P. D. (Gresham's) 1955

Crookes, D. V. (Michaelhouse, SA) 1953

Curtis, T. S. (Worcester RGS) 1983

Daniell, J. (Clifton) 1899-1901

Daniels, D. M. (Rutlish) 1964-65

Datta, P. B. (Asutosh Coll., Calcutta) 1947

Davies, A. G. (Birkenhead) 1984-85

Davies, J. G. W. (Tonbridge) 1933-34

Davidson, J. E. (Penglais) 1985-86

Dawson, E. W. (Eton) (Capt. in 1927) 1924-27

Day, S. H. (Malvern) (Capt. in 1901) 1899-1902

Dewes, A. R. (Dulwich) 1978

Dewes, J. G. (Aldenham) 1948-50

Dexter, E. R. (Radley) (Capt. in 1958) 1956-58

Dickinson, D. C. (Clifton) 1953

Doggart, A. G. (Bishop's Stortford) 1921-22

Doggart, G. H. G. (Winchester) (Capt. in 1950) 1948-50

Doggart, S. J. G. (Winchester) 1980-83

Douglas-Pennant, S. (Eton) 1959

Duleepsinhji, K. S. (Cheltenham) 1925-26, 1928

Edmonds, P. H. (Gilbert Rennie HS, Lusaka, Skinner's and Cranbrook) (Capt. in 1973) 1971-73

Edwards, T. D. W. (Sherborne) 1981

Elgood, B. C. (Bradfield) 1948

Ellison, C. C. (Tonbridge) 1982-83, 1985-86

Enthoven, H. J. (Harrow) (Capt. in 1926) 1923-26

Estcourt, N. S. D. (Plumtree, Southern Rhodesia) 1954

Falcon, M. (Harrow) (Capt. in 1910) 1908-11

Farnes, K. (Royal Liberty School, Romford) 1931-33

Fell, D. J. (John Lyon) 1985-87

Fenton, N. C. W. (Rugby) 1988

Field, M. N. (Bablake) 1974

Fitzgerald, J. F. (St Brendan's, Bristol) 1968

Ford, A. F. J. (Repton) 1878-81

Ford, F. G. J. (Repton) (Capt. in 1889) 1887-90

Ford, W. J. (Repton) 1873

Fosh, M. K. (Harrow) 1977-78

Gardiner, S. J. (St Andrew's, Bloemfontein) 1978

Garlick, P. L. (Sherborne) 1984

Gibb, P. A. (St Edward's, Oxford) 1935-38

Gibson, C. H. (Eton) 1920-21

Gilligan, A. E. R. (Dulwich) 1919-20

Goldie, C. F. E. (St Paul's) 1981-82

Golding, A. K. (Colchester GS) 1986

Goodfellow, A. (Marlborough) 1961-62

Goonesena, G. (Royal Coll., Colombo) (Capt. in 1957) 1954-57

Gorman, S. R. (St Peter's, York) 1985, 1987

Grace, W. G., jun. (Clifton) 1895-96

Grant, G. C. (Trinidad) 1929-30

Grant, R. S. (Trinidad) 1933

Green, D. J. (Burton GS) (Capt. in 1959) 1957-59

Greig, I. A. (Queen's Coll., SA) (Capt. in 1979) 1977-79

Grierson, H. (Bedford HS) 1911

Grimes, A. D. H. (Tonbridge) 1984

Griffith, M. G. (Marlborough) 1963-65

Griffith, S. C. (Dulwich) 1935

Griffiths, W. H. (Charterhouse) 1946-48

Hadley, R. J. (Sanfields CS) 1971-73

Hall, J. E. (Ardingly) 1969

Hall, P. J. (Geelong) 1949

Harvey, J. R. W. (Marlborough) 1965

Hawke, Hon. M. B. (Eton) (Capt. in 1885) 1882-83, 1885

Hayes, P. J. (Brighton) 1974-75, 1977

Hays, D. L. (Highgate) 1966, 1968

Hayward, W. I. D. (St Peter's Coll., Adelaide) 1950-51, 1953

Haywood, D. C. (Nottingham HS) 1968

Hazelrigg, A. G. (Eton) (Capt. in 1932) 1930-32

Heap, R. (Ipswich) 1989-90

Heath, S. D. (King Edward's, Birmingham) 1988

Henderson, S. P. (Downside and Durham U.) (Capt. in 1983) 1982-83

Hewitt, S. G. P. (Bradford GS) 1983

Hignell, A. J. (Denstone) (Capt. in 1977-78) 1975-78

Hobson, B. S. (Taunton) 1946

Hodgson, K. I. (Oundle) 1981-83

Hodson, R. P. (QEGS, Wakefield) 1972-73

Holliday, D. C. (Oundle) 1979-81

Hooper, A. M. (Latymer Upper) 1987, 1991

Howat, M. G. (Abingdon) 1977, 1980

Howland, C. B. (Dulwich) (Capt. in 1960) 1958-60

Hughes, G. (Cardiff HS) 1965

Human, J. H. (Repton) (Capt. in 1934) 1932-34

Hurd, A. (Chigwell) 1958-60

Hutton, R. A. (Repton) 1962-64

Huxter, R. J. A. (Magdalen Coll. Sch.) 1981

Insole, D. J. (Monoux, Walthamstow) (Capt. in 1949) 1947-49

Jackson, E. J. W. (Winchester) 1974-76

Jackson, F. S. (Harrow) (Capt. in 1892-93) 1890-93

Jahangir Khan (Lahore), 1933-36

James, R. M. (St John's, Leatherhead) 1956-58

James, S. P. (Monmouth) 1989-90

Jameson, T. E. N. (Taunton and Durham U.) 1970

Jarrett, D. W. (Wellington and Oxford U.) 1976

Jefferson, R. I. (Winchester) 1961

Jenkins, R. H. J. (Oundle) 1990-91

Jenner, Herbert (Eton) (Capt. in 1827, First Cambridge Capt.) 1827

Jessop, G. L. (Cheltenham GS) (Capt. in 1899) 1896-99

Johnson, P. D. (Nottingham HS) 1970-72

Johnson, S. W. (Royal GS, Newcastle) 1990-91

Jones, A. O. (Bedford Modern) 1893

Jorden, A. M. (Monmouth) (Capt. in 1969-70) 1968-70

Kelland, P. A. (Repton) 1950

Kemp-Welch, G. D. (Charterhouse) (Capt. in 1931) 1929-31

Kendall, M. P. (Gillingham GS) 1972

Kenny, C. J. M. (Ampleforth) 1952

Kerslake, R. C. (Kingswood) 1963-64

Killick, E. T. (St Paul's) 1928-30

Kirby, D. (St Peter's, York) (Capt. in 1961) 1959-61

Kirkman, M. C. (Dulwich) 1963
Knight, R. D. V. (Dulwich) 1967-70
Knightley-Smith, W. (Highgate) 1953

Lacey, F. E. (Sherborne) 1882
Lacy-Scott, D. G. (Marlborough) 1946
Lea, A. E. (High Arcal GS) 1984-86
Lewis, A. R. (Neath GS) (Capt. in 1962) 1960-62
Lewis, L. K. (Taunton) 1953
Littlewood, D. J. (Enfield GS) 1978
Lowrey, M. J. (Radley) 1990-91
Lowry, T. C. (Christ's College, NZ) (Capt. in 1924) 1923-24
Lumsden, V. R. (Munro College, Jamaica) 1953-55
Lyttelton, 4th Lord (Eton) 1838
Lyttelton, Hon. Alfred (Eton) (Capt. in 1879) 1876-79
Lyttelton, Hon. C. F. (Eton) 1908-09
Lyttelton, Hon. C. G. (Lord Cobham) (Eton) 1861-64
Lyttelton, Hon. Edward (Eton) (Capt. in 1878) 1875-78
Lyttelton, Hon. G. W. S. (Eton) 1866-67

McAdam, K. P. W. J. (Prince of Wales, Nairobi and Millfield) 1965-66
MacBryan, J. C. W. (Exeter) 1920
McCarthy, C. N. (Maritzburg Coll., SA) 1952
McDowall, J. I. (Rugby) 1969
MacGregor, G. (Uppingham) (Capt. in 1891) 1888-91
McLachlan, A. A. (St Peter's, Adelaide) 1964-65
McLachlan, I. M. (St Peter's, Adelaide) 1957-58
Majid Khan (Aitchison Coll., Lahore and Punjab U.) (Capt. in 1971-72) 1970-72
Malalasekera, V. P. (Royal Coll., Colombo) 1966-67
Mann, E. W. (Harrow) (Capt. in 1905) 1903-05
Mann, F. G. (Eton) 1938-39
Mann, F. T. (Malvern) 1909-11
Marlar, R. G. (Harrow) (Capt. in 1953) 1951-53
Marriott, C. S. (St Columba's) 1920-21
Mathews, K. P. A. (Felsted) 1951
May, P. B. H. (Charterhouse) 1950-52
Melluish, M. E. L. (Rossall) (Capt. in 1956) 1954-56
Meyer, R. J. O. (Haileybury) 1924-26
Middleton, M. R. (Harrow) 1987
Miller, M. E. (Prince Henry GS, Hohne, WG) 1963
Mills, J. M. (Oundle) (Capt. in 1948) 1946-48
Mills, J. P. C. (Oundle) (Capt. in 1982) 1979-82
Mischler, N. M. (St Paul's) 1946-47
Mitchell, F. (St Peter's, York) (Capt. in 1896) 1894-97

Morgan, J. T. (Charterhouse) (Capt. in 1930) 1928-30
Morgan, M. N. (Marlborough) 1954
Morris, M. J. (Cherwell) 1990-91
Morris, R. J. (Blundell's) 1949
Morrison, J. S. F. (Charterhouse) (Capt. in 1919) 1912, 1914, 1919
Moses, G. H. (Ystalyfera GS) 1974
Moylan, A. C. D. (Clifton) 1977
Mubarak, A. M. (Royal Coll., Colombo and Sri Lanka U.) 1978-80
Murray, D. L. (Queen's RC, Trinidad) (Capt. in 1966) 1965-66
Murrills, T. J. (The Leys) (Capt. in 1976) 1973-74, 1976

Nevin, M. R. S. (Winchester) 1969
Norris, D. W. W. (Harrow) 1967-68
Noyes, S. J. (Royal GS, High Wycombe) 1988

O'Brien, R. P. (Wellington) 1955-56
Odendaal, A. (Queen's Coll. and Stellenbosch U., SA) 1980
Owen-Thomas, D. R. (KCS, Wimbledon) 1969-72

Palfreman, A. B. (Nottingham HS) 1966
Palmer, R. W. M. (Bedford) 1982
Parker, G. (Crypt, Gloucester) (Capt. in 1935) 1934-35
Parker, P. W. G. (Collyer's GS) 1976-78
Parsons, A. B. D. (Brighton) 1954-55
Pathmanathan, Q. (Royal Coll., Colombo, Sri Lanka U. and Oxford U.) 1983
Paull, R. K. (Millfield) 1967
Payne, M. W. (Wellington) (Capt. in 1907) 1904-07
Pearman, H. (King Alfred's and St Andrew's U.) 1969
Pearson, A. J. G. (Downside) 1961-63
Pearson, R. M. (Batley GS) 1991
Peck, I. G. (Bedford) (Capt. in 1980-81) 1980-81
Pepper, J. (The Leys) 1946-48
Perry, J. N. (Ampleforth) 1987-88
Pieris, P. I. (St Thomas's, Colombo) 1957-58
Pointer, G. A. (St Dunstan's) 1987-88
Pollock, A. J. (Shrewsbury) (Capt. in 1984) 1982-84
Ponniah, C. E. M. (St Thomas's, Colombo) 1967-69
Ponsonby, Hon. F. G. B. (Lord Bessborough) (Harrow) 1836
Popplewell, N. F. M. (Radley) 1977-79
Popplewell, O. B. (Charterhouse) 1949-51
Pretlove, J. F. (Alleyn's) 1954-56
Price, D. G. (Haberdashers' Aske's) (Capt. in 1986-87) 1984-87
Prideaux, R. M. (Tonbridge) 1958-60
Pringle, D. R. (Felsted) (Capt. in 1982, when he did not play v Oxford owing to Test selection) 1979-81
Pritchard, G. C. (King's, Canterbury) 1964

Pryer, B. J. K. (City of London) 1948
Pyemont, C. P. (Marlborough) 1967
Pyman, R. A. (Harrow) 1989-90

Ranjitsinhji, K. S. (Rajkumar Coll., India) 1893
Ratcliffe, A. (Rydal) 1930-32
Reddy, N. S. K. (Doon School, India) 1959-61
Rimell, A. G. J. (Charterhouse) 1949-50
Robins, R. W. V. (Highgate) 1926-28
Roebuck, P. G. P. (Millfield) 1984-85
Roebuck, P. M. (Millfield) 1975-77
Roopnaraine, R. (Queen's RC, BG) 1965-66
Rose, M. H. (Pocklington) 1963-64
Ross, N. P. G. (Marlborough) 1969
Roundell, J. (Winchester) 1973
Russell, D. P. (West Park GS, St Helens) 1974-75
Russell, S. G. (Tiffin) (Capt. in 1967) 1965-67
Russom, N. (Huish's GS) 1980-81

Scott, A. M. G. (Seaford Head) 1985-87
Seabrook, F. J. (Haileybury) (Capt. in 1928) 1926-28
Seager, C. P. (Peterhouse, Rhodesia) 1971
Selvey, M. W. W. W. (Battersea GS and Manchester U.) 1971
Sheppard, D. S. (Sherborne) (Capt. in 1952) 1950-52
Short, R. L. (Denstone) 1969
Shufflebotham, D. H. (Neath GS) 1989-90
Shuttleworth, G. M. (Blackburn GS) 1946-48
Silk, D. R. W. (Christ's Hospital) (Capt. in 1955) 1953-55
Singh, S. (Khalsa Coll. and Punjab U.) 1955-59
Sinker, N. D. (Winchester) 1966
Slack, J. K. E. (UCS) 1954
Smith, C. S. (William Hulme's GS) 1954-57
Smith, D. J. (Stockport GS) 1955-56
Smyth, R. I. (Sedbergh) 1973-75
Snowden, W. (Merchant Taylors', Crosby) (Capt. in 1974) 1972-75
Spencer, J. (Brighton and Hove GS) 1970-72
Steele, H. K. (King's Coll., NZ) 1971-72
Stevenson, M. H. (Rydal) 1949-52
Studd, C. T. (Eton) (Capt. in 1883) 1880-83
Studd, G. B. (Eton) (Capt. in 1882) 1879-82
Studd, J. E. K. (Eton) (Capt. in 1884) 1881-84
Studd, P. M. (Harrow) (Capt. in 1939) 1937-39
Studd, R. A. (Eton) 1895

Subba Row, R. (Whitgift) 1951-53
Surridge, D. (Richard Hale and Southampton U.) 1979
Swift, B. T. (St Peter's, Adelaide) 1957

Taylor, C. R. V. (Birkenhead) 1971-73
Thomson, R. H. (Bexhill) 1961-62
Thwaites, I. G. (Eastbourne) 1964
Tindall, M. (Harrow) (Capt. in 1937) 1935-37
Tordoff, G. G. (Normanton GS) 1952
Trapnell, B. M. W. (UCS) 1946
Tremellen, J. M. (Bradfield) 1987-88
Turnbull, M. J. (Downside) (Capt. in 1929) 1926, 1928-29
Turner, R. J. (Millfield) (Capt. in 1991) 1988-91

Urquhart, J. R. (King Edward VI School, Chelmsford) 1948

Valentine, B. H. (Repton) 1929
Varey, D. W. (Birkenhead) 1982-83

Wait, O. J. (Dulwich) 1949, 1951
Waller, R. B. (Radley) 1991
Warr, J. J. (Ealing County GS) (Capt. in 1951) 1949-52
Watts, H. E. (Downside) 1947
Webster, W. H. (Highgate) 1932
Weedon, M. J. H. (Harrow) 1962
Wells, T. U. (King's Coll., NZ) 1950
Wheatley, O. S. (King Edward's, Birmingham) 1957-58
Wheelhouse, A. (Nottingham HS) 1959
White, R. C. (Hilton Coll., SA) (Capt. in 1965) 1962-65
Wilcox, D. R. (Dulwich) (Capt. in 1933) 1931-33
Wilenkin, B. C. G. (Harrow) 1956
Wilkin, C. L. A. (St Kitts GS) 1970
Willard, M. J. L. (Judd) 1959-61
Willatt, G. L. (Repton) (Capt. in 1947) 1946-47
Willatt, J. M. G. (Repton) 1989
Windows, A. R. (Clifton) 1962-64
Wood, G. E. C. (Cheltenham) (Capt. in 1920) 1914, 1919-20
Wookey, S. M. (Malvern) 1975-76
Wooller, W. (Rydal) 1935-36
Wright, S. (Mill Hill) 1973

Yardley, N. W. D. (St Peter's, York) (Capt. in 1938) 1935-38
Young, R. A. (Repton) (Capt. in 1908) 1905-08

# OTHER MATCHES, 1991

## TILCON TROPHY

### †DURHAM v LEICESTERSHIRE

At Harrogate, June 11. Durham beat Leicestershire 2-1 in a bowling contest, Ijaz Ahmed breaking the deadlock by hitting the single stump with the 78th ball of the competition. Rain ended the original match, which was delayed until 3.00 p.m., shortened to 33 overs a side, and abandoned at 5.48 p.m. Leicestershire were 16 for two in 6.1 overs, replying to Durham's 163 for four. The minor county's captain, Cook, scored 43 and Bainbridge, formerly of Gloucestershire, contributed an unbeaten 48.

### †SURREY v WARWICKSHIRE

At Harrogate, June 12. Surrey won by 1 run. Toss: Warwickshire. Two occasional bowlers returned their best bowling figures for their counties in any competition: Warwickshire captain Lloyd and Robinson of Surrey, who removed the top four batsmen to set up a tight victory over the Tilcon Trophy holders.

### Surrey

| | | | | | |
|---|---|---|---|---|---|
| D. J. Bicknell lbw b Small | 8 | | M. A. Feltham not out | | 32 |
| R. I. Alikhan c Munton b Small | 7 | | J. Boiling not out | | 11 |
| M. A. Lynch c Burns b Small | 2 | | | | |
| D. M. Ward b Munton | 16 | | B 4, l-b 12, w 13, n-b 3 | | 32 |
| G. P. Thorpe c Green b Booth | 44 | | | | |
| *†A. J. Stewart lbw b Lloyd | 61 | | 1/11 2/17 3/20 | (8 wkts, 55 overs) | 221 |
| J. D. Robinson c Green b Lloyd | 3 | | 4/55 5/156 6/159 | | |
| K. T. Medlycott lbw b Lloyd | 5 | | 7/165 8/166 | | |

A. J. Murphy did not bat.

Bowling: Small 7-1-16-3; Smith 9-0-24-0; Reeve 9-2-29-0; Munton 7-0-41-1; Booth 11-1-43-1; Lloyd 11-0-47-3; Twose 1-0-5-0.

### Warwickshire

| | | | | | |
|---|---|---|---|---|---|
| J. D. Ratcliffe b Robinson | 42 | | P. A. Booth b Feltham | | 0 |
| R. G. Twose lbw b Robinson | 16 | | T. A. Munton not out | | 13 |
| S. J. Green c Stewart b Robinson | 0 | | G. Smith not out | | 1 |
| D. P. Ostler b Robinson | 0 | | L-b 4, w 8 | | 12 |
| D. A. Reeve st Stewart b Medlycott | 48 | | | | |
| †M. Burns run out | 27 | | 1/53 2/53 3/61 | (9 wkts, 55 overs) | 220 |
| *T. A. Lloyd c Ward b Murphy | 46 | | 4/67 5/129 6/155 | | |
| G. C. Small c Boiling b Feltham | 15 | | 7/193 8/193 9/218 | | |

Bowling: Feltham 11-1-33-2; Murphy 10-1-48-1; Thorpe 2-0-17-0; Robinson 11-1-28-4; Boiling 11-0-35-0; Medlycott 10-1-55-1.

Umpires: J. D. Bond and G. I. Burgess.

## FINAL

### †DURHAM v SURREY

At Harrogate, June 13. Surrey won by 78 runs. Toss: Durham. Rain delayed the start until 3.13 p.m. and restricted the sides to 32 overs each. The match was dominated by Darren Bicknell, who beat the Tilcon Trophy record innings of 134, by Zaheer Abbas for Gloucestershire in 1979. His stand of 155 with Ward also surpassed the record of 151 set by Cook, now captain of Durham, and A. J. Lamb for Northamptonshire in 1981. Cook's hundred saved Durham from complete embarrassment.

## Surrey

| | | |
|---|---|---|
| D. J. Bicknell not out .............149 | *I. A. Greig not out ................ | 3 |
| J. D. Robinson c Cook b Brown ...... 0 | | |
| †A. J. Stewart c Briers b Wood ...... 0 | B 8, l-b 6, w 3 ........ | 17 |
| M. A. Lynch b Wood ............. 1 | | |
| D. M. Ward c Bainbridge b Brown .... 51 | 1/12 2/13 3/23    (5 wkts, 32 overs) 242 | |
| G. P. Thorpe b Day .............. 21 | 4/178 5/236 | |

K. T. Medlycott, M. A. Feltham, J. Boiling and M. P. Bicknell did not bat.

Bowling: Brown 7–1–53–2; Wood 6–1–28–2; Bainbridge 6–0–44–0; Day 6–0–46–1; Heseltine 7–0–57–0.

## Durham

| | | |
|---|---|---|
| *G. Cook c Lynch b Ward ..........101 | J. Wood b Boiling ................ | 2 |
| G. J. Weeks b Feltham ............. 1 | P. A. W. Heseltine c Boiling b Robinson | 2 |
| N. G. Nicholson c Stewart | S. J. E. Brown not out.............. | 10 |
| b M. P. Bicknell. 0 | B 6, l-b 5, w 10.......... | 21 |
| D. A. Blenkiron b M. P. Bicknell ..... 6 | | |
| P. Bainbridge st Stewart b Medlycott .. 7 | 1/4 2/9 3/20    (9 wkts, 32 overs) 164 | |
| M. P. Briers run out ................ 1 | 4/42 5/44 6/68 | |
| †A. R. Fothergill c and b Boiling...... 13 | 7/78 8/95 9/164 | |

A. C. Day did not bat.

Bowling: M. P. Bicknell 6–0–24–2; Feltham 4–1–9–1; Medlycott 7–0–29–1; Boiling 7–1–29–2; Robinson 4–0–31–1; D. J. Bicknell 3–0–23–0; Ward 1–0–8–1.

Umpires: J. D. Bond and G. I. Burgess.

†At Richmond, June 12. MCC won by 49 runs. Toss: MCC. MCC 214 for five dec. (J. A. Waterhouse 33, N. Gilbert 50, D. J. Wild 51, C. T. Radley 35 not out; J. H. Jones three for 63); Club Cricket Conference 165 (G. E. Loveday 76; W. G. Merry four for 38, S. Welch four for 32).

†At Durham, June 13, 14. Drawn. Toss: MCC. MCC 226 for four dec. (R. M. O. Cooke 51, K. C. Williams 35, S. P. Henderson 68 not out) and 218 for six dec. (K. C. Williams 129, G. T. E. Monkhouse 32); Durham University 177 for three dec. (J. I. Longley 76 not out, S. C. Ecclestone 50 not out) and 261 for six (R. S. M. Morris 100, C. L. Keey 35, J. I. Longley 50, S. C. Ecclestone 33 not out).

## IRELAND v SCOTLAND

At Malahide, June 22, 23, 24. Ireland won by 95 runs. Toss: Scotland. Malahide, eight miles north of Dublin, was a new first-class venue and the pitch was a very fair one. None the less Ireland, put in, batted slowly throughout the opening day, with the feature of their innings being the stand of 141 for the fifth wicket between Patterson and Harrison. They were overshadowed, however, by Scotland's opening pair, who broke all records against Ireland for any wicket. Philip's 116 not out was his third century against Ireland, and Patterson's 108 his second; neither gave a chance as they put on 236 in 61 overs, and Patterson's run-out was the likeliest way they would be parted. With it, Scotland declared, 48 runs behind, but Ireland again laboured. Their declaration, when it came, left Scotland to score 282 in something like 55 overs, and it seemed then that neither side had a chance of victory. However, having scored 102 for three in 103 minutes, the Scots lost their way, and by the time their thoughts turned to defence, it was too late. When Hoey, a leg-spinner, bowled Duthie around his legs, ten balls remained and Ireland had beaten Scotland for the first time since 1983, levelling the 70-match series at nineteen wins each. Both captains had agreed to extend the hours of play to make up time lost to rain on all three days, and Warke, Ireland's captain, with 110 runs in the match, increased his first-class aggregate to 815 – all against Scotland – for an average of 50.93.

*Close of play:* First day, Ireland 284-6 (T. J. T. Patterson 73*, N. E. Thompson 21*); Second day, Ireland 84-0 (S. J. S. Warke 43*, M. F. Cohen 31*).

## Ireland

| | | | |
|---|---|---|---|
| *S. J. S. Warke c Haggo b Cowan | 32 | – lbw b Cowan | 78 |
| M. F. Cohen c Salmond b Goram | 4 | – b Goram | 44 |
| M. P. Rea c Govan b Duthie | 27 | – c and b Cowan | 12 |
| D. A. Lewis run out | 14 | – st Haggo b Henry | 44 |
| T. J. T. Patterson not out | 73 | – c Swan b Cowan | 3 |
| G. D. Harrison b Cowan | 77 | – c Duthie b Govan | 21 |
| S. G. Smyth c Philip b Duthie | 14 | – not out | 7 |
| N. E. Thompson not out | 21 | – run out | 0 |
| C. J. Hoey (did not bat) | – | – not out | 1 |
| B 9, l-b 6, w 3, n-b 4 | 22 | L-b 21, w 1, n-b 1 | 23 |

| | | |
|---|---|---|
| 1/26 2/56 3/84 4/89 | (6 wkts dec.) 284 | 1/115 2/140 3/147 (7 wkts dec.) 233 |
| 5/230 6/255 | | 4/157 5/216 |
| | | 6/230 7/230 |

†K. R. Bailey and A. N. Nelson did not bat.

Bowling: *First Innings*—Cowan 31–8–92–2; Duthie 30–9–80–2; Goram 7–1–16–1; Henry 21–7–42–0; Govan 11–2–29–0; Russell 5–2–10–0. *Second Innings*—Cowan 22–5–41–3; Duthie 17–6–35–0; Goram 16–5–46–1; Henry 20–6–43–1; Govan 13–3–47–1.

## Scotland

| | | | |
|---|---|---|---|
| I. L. Philip not out | 116 | – c and b Nelson | 7 |
| B. M. W. Patterson run out | 108 | – c Bailey b Nelson | 6 |
| R. G. Swan (did not bat) | – | – lbw b Nelson | 15 |
| G. Salmond (did not bat) | – | – c Harrison b Lewis | 66 |
| A. B. Russell (did not bat) | – | – run out | 16 |
| A. L. Goram (did not bat) | – | – st Bailey b Harrison | 5 |
| *O. Henry (did not bat) | – | – b Hoey | 22 |
| †D. J. Haggo (did not bat) | – | – lbw b Nelson | 25 |
| J. W. Govan (did not bat) | – | – lbw b Hoey | 1 |
| P. G. Duthie (did not bat) | – | – b Hoey | 0 |
| D. Cowan (did not bat) | – | – not out | 2 |
| B 5, l-b 3, w 1, n-b 3 | 12 | B 14, l-b 6, n-b 1 | 21 |

| | | |
|---|---|---|
| 1/236 | (1 wkt dec.) 236 | 1/7 2/16 3/40 4/102 5/114 186 |
| | | 6/128 7/156 8/176 9/180 |

Bowling: *First Innings*—Nelson 13–2–49–0; Thompson 11.3–1–52–0; Harrison 18–5–50–0; Hoey 12–1–47–0; Lewis 6–0–23–0; Smyth 1–0–7–0. *Second Innings*—Nelson 14–4–30–4; Thompson 8–5–15–0; Hoey 13.2–6–38–3; Harrison 8–1–43–1; Lewis 10–1–40–1.

Umpires: L. Hogan and R. MacClancy.

†At Arundel, July 7. MCC won by eight wickets. Toss: Lavinia, Duchess of Norfolk's XI. Lavinia, Duchess of Norfolk's XI 187 (J. A. North 66, G. S. Clinton 65; G. R. Black five for 29); MCC 188 for two (C. T. Radley 79 not out, R. O. Butcher 60 not out).

†At The King's School, Gloucester, July 10. Drawn. Toss: MCC. MCC 241 for four dec. (B. C. Broad 73, J. C. P. Meadows 103 not out, M. J. Kilborn 36; J. E. Hindson three for 73); National Association of Young Cricketers 219 for nine (M. J. Foster 58; D. B. D'Oliveira five for 60).

†At Kings Heath, Birmingham, July 18. Midlands Club Cricket Conference won by seven wickets. Toss: MCC. MCC 151 (H. Cartwright 76; T. Heap three for 20, M. Higham three for 65, N. Ingram four for 22); Midlands Club Cricket Conference 155 for three (R. Cox 61, L. Roll 38).

†At Usk, July 24, 25, 26. Drawn. Wales 251 (S. W. Evans 53; C. J. Hoey six for 82) and 207 for six dec. (S. W. Evans 106; A. R. Dunlop four for 50); Ireland 243 (S. J. S. Warke 58, D. A. Vincent 43, P. McCrum 63; B. J. Lloyd four for 58, A. Ikram four for 77) and 102 for four (M. F. Cohen 46).

## HERITAGE HOMES FESTIVAL

### †ENGLAND XI v REST OF THE WORLD XI

At Jesmond, July 31. England XI won by five wickets. Toss: Rest of the World XI. Manjrekar hit ten fours and a six in his 128-ball innings, and Morris took 42 from 32 balls, but both were outshone by Lewis's unbeaten 89 (66 balls, 71 minutes) as he put on 115 with Blakey. Fresh from his successes in the Fourth Test, Lewis lifted three sixes into Osborne Avenue and one into All Saints cemetery, as well as hitting ten fours. Jesmond's eleventh international festival was sponsored by Heritage Homes.

*Man of the Match:* C. C. Lewis.

### Rest of the World XI

| | | | |
|---|---|---|---|
| Mudassar Nazar c Blakey b Salisbury . . | 31 | Wasim Akram b Allott . . . . . . . . . . . . | 7 |
| S. V. Manjrekar c Blakey b Allott . . . . . | 100 | P. R. Sleep not out . . . . . . . . . . . . . . . | 12 |
| S. R. Tendulkar c Salisbury b Embury . | 54 | B 4, l-b 2, w 6, n-b 1 . . . . . . . . | 13 |
| *M. Azharuddin c Moxon b Embury . . | 6 | | |
| Ijaz Ahmed b Allott . . . . . . . . . . . . . . | 46 | 1/72 2/166 3/190    (6 wkts, 55 overs) 283 |
| †J. C. Adams not out . . . . . . . . . . . . . . | 14 | 4/248 5/251 6/259 | |

P. R. Reiffel, A. I. C. Dodemaide and I. R. Bishop did not bat.

Bowling: Malcolm 11–0–61–0; Lewis 11–1–40–0; Salisbury 11–1–72–1; Allott 11–2–47–3; Embury 11–1–57–2.

### England XI

| | | | |
|---|---|---|---|
| K. J. Barnett b Dodemaide . . . . . . . . . . | 49 | C. C. Lewis not out . . . . . . . . . . . . . . | 89 |
| M. D. Moxon c Ijaz Ahmed | | †R. J. Blakey not out . . . . . . . . . . . . . | 21 |
| b Wasim Akram . | 5 | | |
| M. A. Atherton b Sleep . . . . . . . . . . . . | 31 | L-b 16, w 5, n-b 8 . . . . . . . . . | 29 |
| N. H. Fairbrother c Azharuddin | | | |
| b Dodemaide . | 21 | 1/26 2/92 3/103    (5 wkts, 45.1 overs) 287 |
| J. E. Morris c Adams b Reiffel . . . . . . | 42 | 4/119 5/172 | |

*J. E. Embury, P. J. W. Allott, I. D. K. Salisbury and D. E. Malcolm did not bat.

Bowling: Bishop 8–0–60–0; Wasim Akram 8.1–2–21–1; Dodemaide 9–1–66–2; Reiffel 9–0–59–1; Sleep 11–1–65–1.

Umpires: S. Levison and G. I. McLean.

### †ENGLAND XI v REST OF THE WORLD XI

At Jesmond, August 1. Rest of the World XI won by four wickets. Toss: England XI. Tendulkar and Azharuddin set up victory with thirteen overs to spare through their stand of 153 in 21 overs, after the Rest of the World had been 45 for three. Now eighteen years old, Tendulkar scored his 102 from 86 balls with twelve fours and four sixes.

*Man of the Match:* S. R. Tendulkar.

## England XI

| | | | | |
|---|---|---|---|---|
| K. J. Barnett b Dodemaide | 26 | P. J. W. Allott run out | 0 | |
| M. D. Moxon st Adams b Sleep | 40 | I. D. K. Salisbury b Bishop | 5 | |
| M. A. Atherton b Reiffel | 41 | D. E. Malcolm not out | 0 | |
| N. H. Fairbrother c Adams b Reiffel | 0 | B 8, l-b 5, w 3, n-b 7 | 23 | |
| J. E. Morris b Wasim Akram | 107 | | | |
| C. C. Lewis c Azharuddin b Bishop | 12 | 1/62 2/88 3/93 | (53.2 overs) 284 | |
| †R. J. Blakey c Dodemaide b Reiffel | 25 | 4/154 5/186 6/251 | | |
| *J. E. Emburey b Bishop | 5 | 7/259 8/260 9/283 | | |

Bowling: Bishop 10.2–0–38–3; Wasim Akram 10–2–49–1; Sleep 11–0–48–1; Dodemaide 11–2–60–1; Reiffel 9–0–61–3; Mudassar Nazar 2–0–15–0.

## Rest of the World XI

| | | | | |
|---|---|---|---|---|
| Mudassar Nazar c Blakey b Malcolm | 12 | †J. C. Adams not out | 28 | |
| S. V. Manjrekar c Blakey b Malcolm | 14 | A. I. C. Dodemaide not out | 6 | |
| Wasim Akram c Morris b Lewis | 6 | B 4, l-b 7, w 10, n-b 2 | 23 | |
| S. R. Tendulkar c Emburey b Malcolm | 102 | | | |
| *M. Azharuddin c Allott b Lewis | 56 | 1/24 2/34 3/45 | (6 wkts, 42 overs) 286 | |
| Ijaz Ahmed c Fairbrother b Salisbury | 39 | 4/198 5/219 6/270 | | |

P. R. Reiffel, P. R. Sleep and I. R. Bishop did not bat.

Bowling: Malcolm 9–0–61–3; Lewis 11–0–52–2; Allott 6–0–39–0; Salisbury 8–0–75–1; Emburey 8–1–48–0.

Umpires: S. Levison and G. I. McLean.

†At Titwood, Glasgow, August 20, 21, 22. Scotland won by an innings and 37 runs. Toss: MCC. MCC 257 (P. J. E. Needham 66, P. J. Mir 84, S. P. Henderson 37; D. Cowan three for 45, J. W. Govan four for 92) and 243 (P. J. E. Needham 46, P. J. Mir 55, R. J. Robinson 43, K. C. Williams 35; D. Cowan four for 64, O. Henry three for 50); Scotland 537 for five dec. (I. L. Philip 234, A. C. Storie 106, B. M. W. Patterson 38, O. Henry 102 not out, Extras 52; J. Paul three for 124).

†At Llanelli, August 26. Rest of the World XI won by 8 runs. Rest of the World XI 207 for three (40 overs) (S. R. Tendulkar 54, Javed Miandad 52 not out, C. L. Hooper 47 not out); Glamorgan 199 (39.1 overs) (M. P. Maynard 68, I. Smith 39).

# WORLD XI v WEST INDIES XI

At Scarborough, August 28, 29, 30. Drawn. Toss: West Indies XI. The pitch favoured the batsmen to such an extent that a positive result was out of the question, particularly as both sides competed keenly. The match produced 26 sixes and 187 fours, as well as two fives – a total of 215 boundaries. Hooper, with 164 from 160 balls, and Manjrekar, whose 154 used up the same number of deliveries, took the individual honours with high-quality unbeaten innings full of glorious strokes. Handicapped by injuries to his front-line bowlers, Greenidge delayed his declaration until he felt satisfied that the World XI's target, 411 in 200 minutes, was well beyond them.

*Close of play:* First day, World XI 49-1 (S. V. Manjrekar 28*, S. R. Tendulkar 13*); Second day, West Indies XI 216-5 (R. B. Richardson 90*, C. G. Greenidge 1*).

## West Indies XI

| | | | |
|---|---|---|---|
| P. V. Simmons c Javed Miandad b Wassan | 24 | – c sub b Kapil Dev | 22 |
| C. B. Lambert c Madan Lal b Maninder Singh | 80 | – c Morrison b Kapil Dev | 19 |
| R. B. Richardson c Mudassar Nazar b Morrison | 15 | – c Wassan b Maninder Singh | 98 |
| B. C. Lara lbw b Morrison | 2 | – (6) st Sleep b Maninder Singh | 1 |
| R. W. Staple b Maninder Singh | 40 | – (4) c Kapil Dev b Wassan | 56 |
| C. L. Hooper not out | 164 | – (8) c Morrison b Wassan | 55 |
| *C. G. Greenidge c and b Madan Lal | 14 | – not out | 55 |
| R. A. Harper not out | 63 | – (9) not out | 24 |
| †D. Williams (did not bat) | | – (5) c Sleep b Wassan | 19 |
| B 2, l-b 11, w 1, n-b 7 | 21 | B 2, l-b 3, n-b 8 | 13 |

1/49 2/84 3/95 4/152      (6 wkts dec.) 423      1/30 2/62 3/182      (7 wkts dec.) 362
5/188 6/232                                       4/206 5/207 6/230
                                                  7/319

M. D. Marshall and I. R. Bishop did not bat.

*Bowling: First Innings*—Davis 14-5-32-0; Wassan 22-3-106-1; Morrison 14-2-82-2; Maninder Singh 20-2-122-2; Kapil Dev 6-0-23-0; Madan Lal 6-0-25-1; Tendulkar 2-0-20-0. *Second Innings*—Kapil Dev 7-0-42-2; Davis 6-0-47-0; Wassan 27-1-114-3; Morrison 3-0-31-0; Maninder Singh 24-3-86-2; Madan Lal 3-0-22-0; Tendulkar 2-0-15-0.

## World XI

| | | | |
|---|---|---|---|
| *Mudassar Nazar c Hooper b Marshall | 3 | | |
| S. V. Manjrekar c Williams b Bishop | 45 | – (1) not out | 154 |
| S. R. Tendulkar c Simmons b Hooper | 61 | – c Richardson b Simmons | 14 |
| Javed Miandad c Greenidge b Hooper | 88 | – c sub b Lambert | 22 |
| †P. R. Sleep c Staple b Harper | 37 | – c Greenidge b Lambert | 13 |
| Kapil Dev c Lambert b Marshall | 22 | – (7) not out | 5 |
| Madan Lal c Simmons b Hooper | 9 | – (6) c Richardson b Greenidge | 16 |
| W. W. Davis not out | 54 | | |
| A. S. Wassan b Bishop | 23 | – (2) c sub b Simmons | 10 |
| Maninder Singh c Simmons b Hooper | 0 | | |
| D. K. Morrison c Staple b Hooper | 1 | | |
| B 13, l-b 13, w 1, n-b 5 | 32 | B 7, l-b 7, w 2, n-b 5 | 21 |

1/4 2/74 3/146 4/230                 375      1/34 2/89 3/145      (5 wkts) 255
5/276 6/292 7/292 8/349 9/360                 4/169 5/250

*Bowling: First Innings*—Marshall 21-6-76-2; Simmons 13-2-44-0; Hooper 16.2-1-94-5; Bishop 17-3-58-2; Harper 17-1-77-1. *Second Innings*—Simmons 13-4-39-2; Staple 8-1-56-0; Hooper 15-2-47-0; Lambert 10-2-33-2; Lara 3-0-23-0; Richardson 5-0-36-0; Greenidge 2-0-7-1.

Umpires: B. Leadbeater and D. O. Oslear.


# JOSHUA TETLEY SCARBOROUGH FESTIVAL TROPHY

## †DURHAM v ESSEX

At Scarborough, August 31. Essex won by 154 runs. Toss: Durham. The first over of Durham's innings lasted fourteen balls, as Andrew bowled seven wides and a no-ball, but he recovered to take four wickets.

*Man of the Match*: S. J. E. Brown.

## Essex

| | | | | |
|---|---|---|---|---|
| G. A. Gooch c Fothergill b S. J. E. Brown | 0 | M. A. Garnham not out | 5 |
| J. P. Stephenson c and b Henderson | 107 | | |
| *P. J. Prichard b S. J. E. Brown | 1 | L-b 4, w 3, n-b 2 | 9 |
| Salim Malik c Glendenen b Lovell | 108 | | |
| N. Hussain not out | 81 | 1/1 2/3 3/185 (5 wkts, 50 overs) | 323 |
| N. V. Knight b S. J. E. Brown | 12 | 4/278 5/303 | |

†D. E. East, T. D. Topley, P. M. Such and S. J. W. Andrew did not bat.

Bowling: Wood 10–1–66–0; S. J. E. Brown 10–1–29–3; Lovell 10–0–72–1; Conn 10–1–80–0; Henderson 10–0–72–1.

## Durham

| | | | | |
|---|---|---|---|---|
| J. D. Glendenen c Knight b Andrew | 0 | J. Wood c Knight b Such | 30 |
| S. Hutton run out | 0 | I. E. Conn c East b Andrew | 18 |
| G. K. Brown c East b Andrew | 7 | S. J. E. Brown c East b Stephenson | 0 |
| D. J. Lovell c East b Gooch | 32 | L-b 7, w 21, n-b 4 | 32 |
| D. A. Blenkiron c Prichard b Andrew | 0 | | |
| *G. Cook not out | 48 | 1/8 2/17 3/32 (40.2 overs) | 169 |
| P. W. Henderson run out | 1 | 4/34 5/74 6/83 | |
| †A. R. Fothergill lbw b Such | 1 | 7/89 8/127 9/167 | |

Bowling: Andrew 10–0–41–4; Topley 6–1–15–0; Gooch 8–0–34–1; Such 10–1–33–2; Stephenson 6.2–0–39–1.

*Umpires: B. Leadbeater and D. O. Oslear.*

---

## †YORKSHIRE v DERBYSHIRE

At Scarborough, September 1. Yorkshire won by four wickets. Toss: Derbyshire. O'Gorman hit ten fours and one six in his 93 from 114 balls. In Yorkshire's reply, Moxon and Metcalfe's 110-run opening stand took them twenty overs. The match was Sidebottom's last for Yorkshire.

*Man of the Match:* C. S. Pickles.

### Derbyshire

| | | | | |
|---|---|---|---|---|
| P. D. Bowler lbw b Sidebottom | 6 | *K. J. Barnett b Pickles | 10 |
| C. J. Adams b Pickles | 30 | E. McCray c Metcalfe b Pickles | 0 |
| J. E. Morris b Carrick | 16 | R. W. Sladdin not out | 1 |
| T. J. G. O'Gorman b Hartley | 93 | W 5, n-b 4 | 9 |
| S. C. Goldsmith run out | 21 | | |
| †K. M. Krikken b Pickles | 26 | 1/12 2/54 3/60 (9 wkts, 50 overs) | 237 |
| S. J. Base not out | 17 | 4/137 5/194 6/210 | |
| D. G. Cork c Robinson b Pickles | 8 | 7/219 8/230 9/231 | |

Bowling: Sidebottom 5–0–26–1; Hartley 9–0–45–1; Carrick 10–1–39–1; Pickles 10–1–50–5; Batty 10–0–55–0; Kellett 6–1–22–0.

### Yorkshire

| | | | | |
|---|---|---|---|---|
| *M. D. Moxon c Barnett b Sladdin | 63 | C. S. Pickles not out | 10 |
| A. A. Metcalfe c Barnett b Sladdin | 61 | P. Carrick not out | 9 |
| †R. J. Blakey c Krikken b Cork | 31 | L-b 6, w 5, n-b 3 | 14 |
| D. Byas st Krikken b Bowler | 35 | | |
| P. E. Robinson c Adams b Base | 5 | 1/110 2/143 3/184 (6 wkts, 49.1 overs) | 241 |
| S. A. Kellett b Base | 13 | 4/202 5/215 6/225 | |

P. J. Hartley, A. Sidebottom and J. D. Batty did not bat.

Bowling: Cork 10–0–43–1; Base 9.1–1–40–2; Goldsmith 7–0–53–0; Sladdin 10–0–45–2; McCray 10–1–42–0; Bowler 3–1–12–1.

*Umpires: B. Leadbeater and D. O. Oslear.*

# FINAL

## †YORKSHIRE v ESSEX

At Scarborough, September 2. Yorkshire won by five wickets. Toss: Yorkshire. Stephenson struck four fours and two sixes in 82 balls, and after Essex had later lost three quick wickets to Batty, Garnham put the finishing touches to their recovery by hitting 21 from the last over. Byas's 64 included seven fours and a six in 69 balls, and he added 76 in eleven overs with Robinson (36 balls).

*Man of the Match*: D. Byas.

### Essex

| | | | |
|---|---|---|---|
| G. A. Gooch c Blakey b Gough | 22 | T. D. Topley run out | 18 |
| J. P. Stephenson c Blakey b Gough | 57 | P. M. Such not out | 0 |
| *P. J. Prichard b Batty | 42 | L-b 9, w 7, n-b 4 | 20 |
| N. Hussain c Moxon b Batty | 16 | | — |
| N. V. Knight c P. E. Robinson b Batty | 0 | 1/38 2/105 3/151 (7 wkts, 50 overs) 242 | |
| †M. A. Garnham not out | 61 | 4/151 5/154 | |
| D. E. East lbw b Pickles | 6 | 6/174 7/236 | |

W. G. Lovell and S. J. W. Andrew did not bat.

Bowling: Hartley 8–0–50–0; M. A. Robinson 10–1–21–0; Gough 10–0–46–2; Pickles 10–1–57–1; Batty 10–2–35–3; Kellett 2–0–24–0.

### Yorkshire

| | | | |
|---|---|---|---|
| *M. D. Moxon c Gooch b Lovell | 32 | C. S. Pickles not out | 10 |
| A. A. Metcalfe c Garnham b Topley | 21 | | |
| †R. J. Blakey c East b Such | 42 | B 4, l-b 13, w 5, n-b 1 | 23 |
| D. Byas run out | 64 | | — |
| P. E. Robinson c Such b Stephenson | 41 | 1/34 2/79 3/141 (5 wkts, 49.1 overs) 243 | |
| S. A. Kellett not out | 10 | 4/217 5/217 | |

P. J. Hartley, D. Gough, J. D. Batty and M. A. Robinson did not bat.

Bowling: Topley 7–2–24–1; Andrew 8.1–0–47–0; Lovell 9–0–38–1; Gooch 5–0–21–0; Such 10–0–53–1; Stephenson 10–0–43–1.

Umpires: B. Leadbeater and D. O. Oslear.

---

†At RAF Uxbridge, September 2. Drawn. Toss: MCC. MCC 292 for four dec. (N. A. Felton 45, H. Cartwright 76, D. C. Briance 78 not out, C. D. M. Tooley 39); Combined Services 208 for seven (2nd Lt R. J. Greatorex 109, SAC A. Jones 37; A. T. Crouch four for 43).

# SEEBOARD TROPHY

## †SUSSEX v KENT

At Hove, September 7. Sussex won by one wicket. Toss: Kent. Donelan's match-winning 45 was his highest score in limited-overs games for Sussex.

*Man of the Match*: B. T. P. Donelan.

## Kent

| | | | | | |
|---|---|---|---|---|---|
| T. R. Ward run out | 2 | R. P. Davis c Donelan b Greenfield | 7 |
| M. A. Ealham run out | 12 | R. M. Ellison not out | 0 |
| J. I. Longley run out | 40 | M. M. Patel b Donelan | 1 |
| N. J. Llong c and b Bunting | 3 | B 2, l-b 4, w 6, n-b 3 | 15 |
| G. R. Cowdrey c Moores b Pigott | 25 | | |
| M. V. Fleming c Pigott b Salisbury | 8 | 1/14 2/16 3/30 | (34.2 overs) 117 |
| †S. A. Marsh b Pigott | 3 | 4/74 5/83 6/88 | |
| *M. R. Benson b Salisbury | 1 | 7/99 8/114 9/114 | |

Bowling: Dodemaide 5–0–12–0; Bunting 6–0–20–1; Pigott 7–0–18–2; Salisbury 10–1–45–2; Donelan 5.2–1–14–1; Greenfield 1–0–2–1.

## Sussex

| | | | | | |
|---|---|---|---|---|---|
| *P. W. G. Parker c Benson b Patel | 1 | B. T. P. Donelan not out | 45 |
| J. W. Hall c Davis b Ealham | 2 | I. D. K. Salisbury c Cowdrey b Fleming | 15 |
| K. Greenfield b Ealham | 5 | R. A. Bunting not out | 2 |
| C. M. Wells lbw b Ealham | 3 | L-b 6, w 2, n-b 1 | 9 |
| †P. Moores b Llong | 25 | | |
| A. I. C. Dodemaide b Davis | 12 | 1/1 2/10 3/11 | (9 wkts, 46.4 overs) 121 |
| A. P. Wells c Marsh b Davis | 2 | 4/16 5/51 6/53 | |
| A. C. S. Pigott run out | 0 | 7/53 8/62 9/115 | |

Bowling: Ealham 10–1–32–3; Patel 10–5–13–1; Llong 10–1–23–1; Davis 10–5–13–2; Fleming 5–0–27–1; Ellison 1.4–0–7–0.

Umpires: R. C. Tolchard and R. A. White.

## †GLOUCESTERSHIRE v SOMERSET

At Hove, September 8. Gloucestershire won by 27 runs. Toss: Gloucestershire. Alleyne hit ten fours as he and Wright (seven fours) put on 132 in 25 overs. Bartlett struck four fours and a six in Somerset's reply, but it was too late for them to overcome a disastrous start.

*Man of the Match:* M. W. Alleyne.

## Gloucestershire

| | | | | | |
|---|---|---|---|---|---|
| R. J. Scott c Cook b Mallender | 12 | M. C. J. Ball not out | 4 |
| M. W. Alleyne b Trump | 77 | A. M. Babington c Bartlett b MacLeay | 6 |
| *A. J. Wright c Mallender b Trump | 57 | M. J. Gerrard run out | 0 |
| J. W. Lloyds b Lefebvre | 26 | B 8, w 3, n-b 5 | 16 |
| R. I. Dawson st Burns b Trump | 4 | | |
| †R. C. Russell run out | 15 | 1/18 2/150 3/160 | (50 overs) 246 |
| T. H. C. Hancock c and b Lefebvre | 23 | 4/166 5/197 6/220 | |
| R. C. Williams b Lefebvre | 6 | 7/233 8/238 9/246 | |

Bowling: Mallender 6–2–17–1; Beal 8–0–43–0; Lefebvre 7–0–31–3; Hallett 10–0–59–0; Trump 10–0–41–3; MacLeay 9–0–47–1.

## Somerset

| | | | | | |
|---|---|---|---|---|---|
| *S. J. Cook b Babington | 0 | H. R. J. Trump not out | 18 |
| G. T. J. Townsend c Lloyds b Babington | 4 | D. Beal run out | 4 |
| R. J. Harden run out | 31 | J. C. Hallett not out | 3 |
| R. J. Bartlett c Williams b Lloyds | 67 | L-b 13, w 6, n-b 7 | 26 |
| K. H. MacLeay c Russell b Gerrard | 29 | | |
| †N. D. Burns c Ball b Babington | 2 | 1/2 2/5 3/53 | (9 wkts, 50 overs) 219 |
| R. P. Lefebvre run out | 0 | 4/124 5/164 6/167 | |
| N. A. Mallender b Gerrard | 6 | 7/189 8/190 9/210 | |

Bowling: Babington 10–3–36–3; Gerrard 9–0–18–2; Ball 7–0–38–0; Williams 6–1–19–0; Lloyds 10–0–46–1; Scott 4–0–24–0; Alleyne 4–0–25–0.

Umpires: R. C. Tolchard and R. A. White.

# FINAL

## †SUSSEX v GLOUCESTERSHIRE

At Hove, September 9. Sussex won on scoring-rate. Toss: Gloucestershire. Three days after Sussex's tie with Kent in the County Championship, they produced an identical total to Gloucestershire's, but won the Seeboard Trophy by virtue of having scored 70 in their first twenty overs, to Gloucestershire's 63. After 30 overs both had scored 109 for three.

*Man of the Match*: P. Moores.

### Gloucestershire

| | | |
|---|---|---|
| M. W. Alleyne c Moores b Bunting | 1 | A. M. Smith run out .......... 1 |
| R. J. Scott c Pigott b Bunting | 1 | A. M. Babington not out ........ 1 |
| †R. C. Russell c Hall b Dodemaide | 74 | |
| T. H. C. Hancock st Moores b Salisbury | 59 | B 1, l-b 3, w 7, n-b 5 ........ 16 |
| R. I. Dawson st Moores b Greenfield | 34 | |
| J. W. Lloyds run out | 15 | 1/3 2/4 3/108 (9 wkts, 50 overs) 221 |
| *A. J. Wright b Pigott | 3 | 4/166 5/195 6/200 |
| R. C. Williams run out | 16 | 7/208 8/219 9/221 |

M. J. Gerrard did not bat.

Bowling: Dodemaide 10–0–30–1; Bunting 6–0–20–2; Donelan 10–0–41–0; Pigott 10–1–50–1; Salisbury 7–0–32–1; Greenfield 7–0–44–1.

### Sussex

| | | |
|---|---|---|
| *P. W. G. Parker b Smith | 14 | B. T. P. Donelan b Lloyds ........ 24 |
| J. W. Hall c Russell b Smith | 24 | I. D. K. Salisbury not out ........ 6 |
| K. Greenfield b Gerrard | 26 | R. A. Bunting not out .......... 1 |
| A. P. Wells run out | 13 | B 1, l-b 11, w 8, n-b 11 ...... 31 |
| C. M. Wells run out | 15 | |
| †P. Moores c Gerrard b Smith | 66 | 1/27 2/54 3/85 (9 wkts, 50 overs) 221 |
| A. I. C. Dodemaide c Alleyne b Williams | 1 | 4/112 5/118 6/119 |
| A. C. S. Pigott lbw b Williams | 0 | 7/119 8/205 9/219 |

Bowling: Babington 10–0–31–0; Gerrard 9–0–38–1; Smith 10–0–38–3; Lloyds 10–1–46–1; Williams 6–0–29–2; Alleyne 5–0–27–0.

Umpires: R. C. Tolchard and R. A. White.

---

†At Scarborough, September 7. The Yorkshiremen won by three wickets. Toss: The Yorkshiremen. Yorkshire 223 for seven (50 overs) (M. D. Moxon 34, A. A. Metcalfe 67; C. W. J. Athey three for 23); The Yorkshiremen 224 for seven (50 overs) (C. W. J. Athey 76, S. J. Rhodes 56).

---

†At Scarborough, September 8. World XI won by 34 runs. Toss: World XI. World XI 221 for six (50 overs) (C. L. Hooper 30, G. E. Bradburn 51, S. J. Rhodes 55; D. Gough three for 33); Yorkshire 187 (45 overs) (A. A. Metcalfe 42, D. Byas 59; P. J. Newport three for 29, C. L. Hooper three for 12).

---

†At Durham University, September 16. Durham won by eight wickets after their target had been revised to 157 in 29 overs. Toss: Victoria. Victoria 232 for three (43 overs) (W. N. Phillips 72, W. G. Ayres 50, D. S. Lehmann 55 not out); Durham 157 for two (26.1 overs) (J. D. Glendenen 69 not out, S. Hutton 55). The match was initially reduced to 43 overs a side by rain.

## BRITANNIC ASSURANCE INVITATION

### †DURHAM v VICTORIA

At Durham University, September 17, 18, 19. Drawn. Toss: Victoria. Over three days 1,278 runs were scored, including five centuries, for the loss of nineteen wickets. Jones hit nineteen fours and four sixes in 146 balls on the day that he signed for Durham, and put on 233 runs in 47 overs with Ramshaw (fifteen fours, one six). Their captain, O'Donnell, scored his runs from 46 balls, with 22 fours and a six. Jones and Ramshaw also shared the wicket-keeper's duties, as D. S. Berry was injured before the match. Victoria's second innings featured a stand of 199 between Parker (fourteen fours, one six) and Lehmann (undefeated in 115 balls, with 22 fours and a six). But the highest score of the game came from Durham's Glendenen. In 227 balls he hit 32 fours, becoming only the second Durham player to register a double-century, and the first for 85 years. However, his team could not maintain the momentum in their final innings before achieving first-class status, as six wickets fell to Jackson, the left-arm spinner.

*Close of play:* First day, Durham 90-0 (G. K. Brown 34*, J. D. Glendenen 47*); Second day, Victoria 153-2 (G. R. Parker 37*, D. S. Lehmann 11*).

### Victoria

| | | | |
|---|---|---|---|
| †D. J. Ramshaw c G. K. Brown b Bainbridge | . .110 | – (2) c Cook b Cooper | 49 |
| W. N. Phillips lbw b Bainbridge | 9 | – (1) c Cook b Wood | 50 |
| †D. M. Jones c Scott b Wood | 144 | – (5) not out | 1 |
| D. S. Lehmann c G. K. Brown b Cooper | 56 | – not out | 137 |
| *S. P. O'Donnell b S. J. E. Brown | 60 | | |
| G. R. Parker not out | 0 | – (3) st Scott b Bainbridge | 104 |
| B 4, l-b 14, w 1, n-b 4 | 23 | B 2, l-b 2, n-b 5 | 9 |

1/26 2/259 3/288 4/402 5/402    (5 wkts dec.) 402    1/80 2/124 3/323    (3 wkts dec.) 350

W. G. Ayres, M. G. Hughes, J. A. Sutherland, D. W. Fleming and P. W. Jackson did not bat.

Bowling: *First Innings*—S. J. E. Brown 17-6-48-1; Wood 15-1-70-1; Bainbridge 21-7-83-2; Cooper 11.2-2-67-1; Briers 13-1-89-0; Lovell 6-0-27-0. *Second Innings*—S. J. E. Brown 13-1-55-0; Wood 15-0-70-1; Briers 8-0-34-0; Cooper 25-3-112-1; Blenkiron 8-0-32-0; Bainbridge 8-2-43-1.

### Durham

| | | | |
|---|---|---|---|
| G. K. Brown lbw b Hughes | 49 | – c Phillips b Hughes | 5 |
| J. D. Glendenen not out | 200 | – st Ramshaw b Jackson | 28 |
| D. J. Lovell b Jackson | 33 | – c Hughes b Fleming | 7 |
| P. Bainbridge c Ayres b Jackson | 21 | – st Ramshaw b Jackson | 44 |
| M. P. Briers not out | 34 | – c Ayres b Jackson | 12 |
| D. A. Blenkiron (did not bat) | | – st Ramshaw b Jackson | 11 |
| †C. W. Scott (did not bat) | | – not out | 17 |
| *G. Cook (did not bat) | | – c Fleming b Jackson | 8 |
| S. J. Cooper (did not bat) | | – lbw b Jackson | 0 |
| J. Wood (did not bat) | | – not out | 21 |
| B 2, l-b 7, w 1, n-b 7 | 17 | B 6, l-b 7, n-b 6 | 19 |

1/122 2/210 3/258    (3 wkts dec.) 354    1/25 2/39 3/89    (8 wkts) 172
4/112 5/117 6/133
7/145 8/148

S. J. E. Brown did not bat.

Bowling: *First Innings*—Hughes 15-2-68-1; Fleming 16.1-0-57-0; O'Donnell 14-1-66-0; Sutherland 13-2-54-0; Jackson 24-4-100-2. *Second Innings*—Hughes 10-0-34-1; Fleming 11-2-30-1; Sutherland 10-4-19-0; Jackson 25-10-53-6; O'Donnell 7-3-14-0; Jones 9-4-9-0.

Umpires: J. Stobart and A. G. T. Whitehead.

# NATWEST BANK TROPHY, 1991

Hampshire, one of only two counties who had never appeared in the final of the 60-overs competition, reached Lord's at the 29th attempt and went on to win the NatWest Bank Trophy, beating Surrey in an exciting, fluctuating finish by four wickets, with two balls to spare. Their win left Leicestershire as the only county still to play in the final, and one of three, with Glamorgan and Worcestershire, not to have won either the Gillette Cup or the NatWest Bank Trophy.

In addition to the trophy, held for a year, Hampshire won £26,500 in prizemoney, while Surrey received £13,000. The losing semi-finalists, Northamptonshire and Warwickshire, each received £6,500, and the losing quarter-finalists, Essex, Glamorgan, Nottinghamshire and Somerset, £3,250 each. The total prizemoney for the competition in 1991, including the Man of the Match awards, was £70,850, an increase of £6,350 over 1990.

During 1991, Graham Gooch of Essex and Hampshire's Chris Smith each won his eighth Man of the Match award, joining C. H. Lloyd (Lancashire) as the leading award winners. In addition, Gooch became the first player to total 2,000 runs in the competition, and Smith increased his record of hundreds to seven. Smith did not play in the final, having taken up an appointment in Perth, Western Australia, soon after Hampshire's semi-final win. The prizemoney for the Man of the Match awards was: first round, £125 each; second round, £150 each; quarter-finals, £250 each; semi-finals, £300 each; final, £550.

## FIRST ROUND

## BEDFORDSHIRE v WORCESTERSHIRE

At Bedford, June 26. Worcestershire won by eight wickets. Toss: Worcestershire. Play did not begin until 5.15 p.m., after an RAF helicopter had been hired to fan the pitch and Worcestershire had sent for more conventional drying aids from New Road. Nevertheless the match was over within three hours as Radford returned the best figures from a Worcestershire bowler in the competition; only four players of any county had done better. He took his seven wickets in one uninterrupted spell of twelve overs.

*Man of the Match*: N. V. Radford.

## Bedfordshire

| | | | | |
|---|---|---|---|---|
| M. R. Gouldstone lbw b Radford | 2 | P. D. Thomas c and b Illingworth | 4 |
| R. Swann lbw b Radford | 7 | B. C. Banks not out | 12 |
| P. D. B. Hoare c Moody b Dilley | 0 | †G. D. Sandford lbw b Lampitt | 0 |
| N. G. Folland b Radford | 10 | B 1, l-b 7, w 5, n-b 1 | 14 |
| R. Ashton c Hick b Radford | 1 | | |
| S. O. L. Davis b Radford | 14 | 1/4 2/10 3/14 (30 overs) | 66 |
| A. Dean b Radford | 0 | 4/22 5/30 6/30 | |
| *J. R. Wake c D'Oliveira b Radford | 2 | 7/45 8/46 9/65 | |

Bowling: Dilley 6–2–12–1; Radford 12–4–19–7; Hick 5–2–11–0; Illingworth 4–1–12–1; Lampitt 3–1–4–1.

## Worcestershire

| | | |
|---|---|---|
| T. M. Moody not out | .............. | 42 |
| †S. J. Rhodes c Wake b Dean | ........ | 10 |
| G. A. Hick b Dean | ................. | 0 |
| D. B. D'Oliveira not out | ............. | 10 |
| L-b 4, w 2, n-b 1 | ........... | 7 |

1/45 2/53            (2 wkts, 12.5 overs) 69

T. S. Curtis, *P. A. Neale, S. R. Lampitt, R. K. Illingworth, P. J. Newport, N. V. Radford and G. R. Dilley did not bat.

Bowling: Banks 2–0–8–0; Ashton 2–0–25–0; Dean 4.5–0–20–2; Swann 4–0–12–0.

Umpires: K. J. Lyons and T. C. Wilson.

## BERKSHIRE v HAMPSHIRE

At Reading, June 26, 27. Hampshire won by ten wickets. Toss: Hampshire. The match could not begin until after 4.00 p.m. on the second day, and was reduced to 22 overs a side.
*Man of the Match:* S. D. Udal

## Berkshire

| | | | | | |
|---|---|---|---|---|---|
| M. G. Lickley c C. L. Smith | | | P. J. Oxley run out | ............... | 18 |
| b Aqib Javed | . | 13 | D. A. Shaw not out | ................. | 1 |
| G. E. Loveday lbw b Connor | ........ | 14 | B 1, l-b 5, w 4, n-b 2 | ........ | 12 |
| G. T. Headley b Udal | ............... | 12 | | | |
| D. J. M. Mercer c Aqib Javed b Udal | . | 11 | 1/18 2/42 3/48 | (5 wkts, 22 overs) | 90 |
| *M. L. Simmons not out | ............. | 9 | 4/61 5/88 | | |

M. G. Stear, †M. E. Stevens, P. J. Lewington and J. H. Jones did not bat.

Bowling: Bakker 4–1–15–0; Aqib Javed 5–1–21–1; James 2–0–14–0; Connor 4–0–11–1; Udal 5–0–14–2; Nicholas 2–0–9–0.

## Hampshire

| | | |
|---|---|---|
| V. P. Terry not out | ................. | 42 |
| R. A. Smith not out | ................. | 43 |
| B 1, l-b 1, w 5, n-b 1 | ........ | 8 |

(no wkt, 20.2 overs) 93

*M. C. J. Nicholas, C. L. Smith, D. I. Gower, K. D. James, C. A. Connor, †A. N. Aymes, S. D. Udal, P. J. Bakker and Aqib Javed did not bat.

Bowling: Jones 3–0–9–0; Stear 3–0–11–0; Headley 4–0–19–0; Lewington 5–0–26–0; Shaw 3.2–0–17–0; Lickley 2–0–9–0.

Umpires: D. Dennis and P. B. Wight.

## DEVON v ESSEX

At Exmouth, June 26. Essex won by eight wickets. Toss: Essex. Folland's award-winning fifty came from 112 balls, with six fours, and his team-mate, Tierney, struck Childs for two sixes, two fours and a two in one over; but Pringle had already crushed Devon's hopes with three wickets in nine balls. Replying, Gooch hit eight fours and Stephenson, with his highest score in the competition, seven fours and a six. Prichard scored the last 15 runs from four balls.
*Man of the Match:* N. A. Folland.

And we're keen to see England's cricket back at the top.

That's why, apart from the NatWest Trophy, we support the NatWest Indoor Cricket Competition, the National Coaching Scheme, the Ken Barrington Under-13 Cup and Kwik-Cricket.

We're also active in other sports, the Arts and Community events. We're proud to be involved, and we aim to stay that way.

National Westminster Bank plc. Registered Office 41 Lothbury, EC2P 2BP.

### Devon

| | | | |
|---|---|---|---|
| *J. H. Edwards lbw b Foster | 0 | †C. S. Pritchard lbw b Childs | 0 |
| K. G. Rice c Salim Malik b Such | 15 | M. J. Record not out | 8 |
| N. A. Folland lbw b Gooch | 55 | M. C. Woodman c Salim Malik b Childs | 8 |
| A. J. Pugh lbw b Such | 0 | B 1, l-b 8, w 5, n-b 5 | 19 |
| R. I. Dawson c Garnham b Pringle | 13 | | |
| K. Donohue c Garnham b Pringle | 4 | 1/0 2/48 3/49 | (57.4 overs) 149 |
| T. W. Ward lbw b Pringle | 1 | 4/92 5/94 6/99 | |
| J. K. Tierney c Hussain b Topley | 26 | 7/99 8/128 9/128 | |

Bowling: Foster 8–4–17–1; Pringle 10–2–21–3; Such 12–1–29–2; Childs 11.4–4–43–2; Topley 11–3–21–1; Gooch 5–1–9–1.

### Essex

| | | | |
|---|---|---|---|
| *G. A. Gooch c Folland b Donohue | 57 | | |
| J. P. Stephenson c Folland b Donohue | 57 | | |
| P. J. Prichard not out | 27 | | |
| Salim Malik not out | 6 | | |
| L-b 2, n-b 1 | 3 | | |

1/108 2/119     (2 wkts, 44.4 overs) 150

N. Hussain, D. R. Pringle, †M. A. Garnham, N. A. Foster, T. D. Topley, J. H. Childs and P. M. Such did not bat.

Bowling: Donohue 12–3–34–2; Woodman 10–4–24–0; Ward 10.4–4–35–0; Record 6–0–32–0; Tierney 6–0–23–0.

Umpires: A. A. Jones and G. A. Stickley.

## DORSET v LANCASHIRE

At Bournemouth, June 26. Lancashire won by five wickets. Toss: Lancashire. Dorset's experience – they fielded seven former first-class players – showed as they reached 63 with only one wicket down, and later reduced the trophy-holders to 20 for two. Fairbrother, hitting five fours and adding 83 with Atherton, steered his team to victory.
*Man of the Match:* N. H. Fairbrother.

### Dorset

| | | | |
|---|---|---|---|
| G. S. Calway c Hegg b Martin | 12 | A. Willows c Hegg b Wasim Akram | 13 |
| J. A. Claughton b Austin | 29 | N. R. Taylor run out | 10 |
| J. M. H. Graham-Brown c Hughes b Watkinson | 18 | J. H. Shackleton not out | 0 |
| J. R. Hall c DeFreitas b Martin | 14 | L-b 8, w 6, n-b 1 | 15 |
| †G. D. Reynolds run out | 22 | | |
| *V. B. Lewis c Hughes b Watkinson | 4 | 1/25 2/63 3/67 | (59.3 overs) 147 |
| R. A. Pyman c Hughes b Wasim Akram | 1 | 4/105 5/110 6/111 | |
| S. Sawney c Mendis b Wasim Akram | 8 | 7/113 8/134 9/147 | |

Bowling: DeFreitas 12–3–24–0; Martin 12–2–19–2; Austin 12–1–46–1; Wasim Akram 11.3–2–40–3; Watkinson 12–7–10–2.

### Lancashire

| | | | |
|---|---|---|---|
| G. Fowler c Calway b Taylor | 9 | P. A. J. DeFreitas not out | 6 |
| G. D. Mendis b Taylor | 5 | | |
| M. A. Atherton run out | 38 | L-b 4, w 3, n-b 2 | 9 |
| N. H. Fairbrother c Claughton b Calway | 68 | | |
| M. Watkinson c Lewis b Hall | 5 | 1/7 2/20 3/103 | (5 wkts, 52.2 overs) 151 |
| Wasim Akram not out | 11 | 4/114 5/143 | |

†W. K. Hegg, *D. P. Hughes, I. D. Austin and P. J. Martin did not bat.

Bowling: Shackleton 12–5–16–0; Taylor 12–2–25–2; Calway 10–3–34–1; Pyman 12–2–41–0; Hall 4–0–16–1; Sawney 2.2–0–15–0.

Umpires: M. A. Johnson and R. Palmer.

## DURHAM v GLAMORGAN

At Darlington, June 26. Glamorgan won by 40 runs. Toss: Durham. Glamorgan's total was their highest in any limited-overs cricket – the last ten overs yielded 128 runs – and Morris and Maynard set a competition record for the third wicket, their unbeaten 259 in 35 overs eclipsing the 209 by P. Willey and D. I. Gower for Leicestershire against Ireland at Leicester in 1986. Morris's century was his third in the first round in successive years, and Maynard, having reached three figures for the first time in the competition, raced to his third 50 off eighteen balls. In all he faced 103 deliveries and hit seven sixes and twelve fours. Durham, appearing in the competition for the last time as a minor county, passed the minor county record of 261 for eight, also against Glamorgan, by Dorset in Swansea the previous year. Glendenen, another making his first NatWest hundred, hit four sixes and seven fours in his 133 balls, and added 103 in eighteen overs with Blenkiron.

*Man of the Match:* M. P. Maynard.

### Glamorgan

| | |
|---|---|
| *A. R. Butcher c Fothergill b Brown... | 17 |
| H. Morris not out ................. | 126 |
| R. J. Shastri c Fothergill b Heseltine... | 26 |
| M. P. Maynard not out ............. | 151 |
| B 3, l-b 11, w 11 ........... | 25 |

1/27 2/86            (2 wkts, 60 overs) 345

I. Smith, A. Dale, J. Derrick, †C. P. Metson, S. L. Watkin, S. R. Barwick and M. Frost did not bat.

Bowling: Brown 12–1–73–1; Wood 10–0–82–0; Bainbridge 12–0–42–0; Ijaz Ahmed 11–0–79–0; Heseltine 12–1–37–1; Patel 3–0–18–0.

### Durham

| | | | |
|---|---|---|---|
| *G. Cook c Smith b Frost | 13 | J. Wood b Smith | 1 |
| J. D. Glendenen c Frost b Watkin | 109 | S. J. E. Brown not out | 7 |
| P. Burn c Morris b Watkin | 2 | P. A. W. Heseltine not out | 5 |
| Ijaz Ahmed lbw b Barwick | 10 | L-b 13, w 8, n-b 5 | 26 |
| P. Bainbridge run out | 27 | | |
| D. A. Blenkiron c Frost b Derrick | 56 | 1/17 2/24 3/47 (9 wkts, 60 overs) 305 | | |
| A. S. Patel c Dale b Smith | 25 | 4/119 5/222 6/249 | | |
| †A. R. Fothergill c Shastri b Smith | 24 | 7/276 8/292 9/294 | | |

Bowling: Watkin 12–1–41–2; Frost 12–2–45–1; Barwick 9–0–51–1; Derrick 12–0–59–1; Dale 6–0–36–0; Smith 9–0–60–3.

Umpires: B. Hassan and D. O. Oslear.

## GLOUCESTERSHIRE v NORFOLK

At Bristol, June 26, 27. Gloucestershire won by 153 runs. Toss: Norfolk. Rain prolonged Gloucestershire's innings into the second day. Lawrence, who took his first two wickets for 8 runs, and then later claimed three for 4 in seventeen balls, and Scott both returned their best bowling figures in the competition. Close of play: Gloucestershire 174-5 (50 overs) (C. W. J. Athey 18*, R. J. Scott 4*).

*Man of the Match:* D. V. Lawrence.

### Gloucestershire

| | | | |
|---|---|---|---|
| G. D. Hodgson b Belmont | 7 | †R. C. Russell c Ellis b Thomas | 23 |
| J. J. E. Hardy run out | 70 | D. V. Lawrence not out | 2 |
| *A. J. Wright c Stamp b Plumb | 56 | B 1, l-b 10, w 3 | 14 |
| C. W. J. Athey not out | 47 | | |
| M. W. Alleyne run out | 3 | 1/15 2/133 3/152 (7 wkts, 60 overs) 237 | | |
| J. W. Lloyds b Ellis | 4 | 4/158 5/165 | | |
| R. J. Scott c Stamp b Ellis | 11 | 6/183 7/234 | | |

A. M. Smith and A. M. Babington did not bat.

Bowling: Ellis 12–4–33–2; Belmont 12–2–53–1; Thomas 12–0–58–1; Kingshott 12–0–46–0; Plumb 12–0–36–1.

## Norfolk

| | | | |
|---|---|---|---|
| C. J. Rogers b Lawrence | 2 | R. Kingshott not out | 4 |
| *D. R. Thomas b Lawrence | 2 | †D. E. Mattocks b Lawrence | 1 |
| D. M. Stamp c Russell b Scott | 6 | M. T. Ellis st Russell b Scott | 0 |
| R. J. Finney c Hodgson b Scott | 27 | B 2, l-b 9, w 3, n-b 7 | 21 |
| S. G. Plumb c Russell b Smith | 11 | | |
| S. B. Dixon b Lawrence | 0 | 1/4 2/14 3/47 | (33.2 overs) 84 |
| R. J. Belmont hit wkt b Lawrence | 9 | 4/61 5/62 6/67 | |
| D. G. Savage lbw b Scott | 1 | 7/77 8/77 9/78 | |

*D. M. Stamp, when 0, retired hurt at 4-1 and resumed at 47.*

Bowling: Lawrence 9–0–17–5; Babington 6–0–17–0; Scott 10.2–3–22–4; Smith 6–1–14–1; Lloyds 2–0–3–0.

Umpires: D. J. Halfyard and R. Julian.


## HERTFORDSHIRE v DERBYSHIRE

At Bishop's Stortford, June 26, 27. Hertfordshire won 2-1 in a bowling contest, after the match was abandoned. Rain prevented any play, and at 4.15 p.m. on the second day the "bowl out" was used for the first time in this competition to achieve a result. Five players from each team were required to bowl two deliveries each at a wicket (three stumps) on the Hertfordshire pitch. Derbyshire bowled first, and Goldsmith scored the only hit, with their ninth delivery; Hertfordshire's former Middlesex players, Needham and Merry, then won the match for the minor county with four deliveries to spare. Afterwards Barnett, the Derbyshire captain, called for the TCCB to amend its regulations, rather than resort to this method again.

The bowlers in the deciding contest were: Derbyshire – O. H. Mortensen, A. E. Warner, F. A. Griffith, S. J. Base and S. C. Goldsmith; Hertfordshire – A. Needham, J. D. Carr and W. G. Merry.


## IRELAND v MIDDLESEX

At Castle Avenue, Dublin, June 26, 27. Middlesex won by 45 runs. Toss: Ireland. All the Middlesex players except wicket-keeper Farbrace were given a chance to show off their bowling as Ireland struggled on a slow pitch with little bounce. Of more concern to Middlesex was the whereabouts of their County Championship pennant, which went missing during the match. Close of play: Ireland 75-4 (35 overs) (T. J. T. Patterson 1*, G. D. Harrison 0*).

*Man of the Match: D. A. Lewis.*

## Middlesex

| | | | |
|---|---|---|---|
| I. J. F. Hutchinson c Patterson b Thompson | 23 | †P. Farbrace not out | 13 |
| M. A. Roseberry c Harrison b McCrum | 6 | N. F. Williams c Cohen b McCrum | 6 |
| *M. W. Gatting c Patterson b Lewis | 65 | S. P. Hughes not out | 0 |
| M. R. Ramprakash c Warke b Lewis | 32 | L-b 9, w 5 | 14 |
| K. R. Brown c Rea b McCrum | 49 | | |
| J. E. Emburey b Nelson | 1 | 1/12 2/44 3/121 | (9 wkts, 60 overs) 216 |
| N. G. Cowans lbw b Lewis | 0 | 4/160 5/165 6/166 | |
| P. N. Weekes lbw b Lewis | 7 | 7/184 8/196 9/212 | |

Bowling: McCrum 10–1–31–3; Nelson 11–3–39–1; Thompson 12–3–30–1; Hoey 12–3–33–0; Harrison 5–0–27–0; Lewis 10–0–47–4.

# Ireland

| | | | | |
|---|---|---|---|---|
| *S. J. S. Warke c Hutchinson b Cowans | 3 | †K. R. Bailey b Ramprakash | | 0 |
| M. F. Cohen run out | 26 | P. McCrum st Farbrace b Gatting | | 16 |
| M. P. Rea c Farbrace b Williams | 3 | A. N. Nelson not out | | 8 |
| D. A. Lewis c Roseberry b Weekes | 25 | | | |
| T. J. T. Patterson c Hutchinson b Hughes | 5 | B 5, l-b 10, w 19, n-b 2 | | 36 |
| G. D. Harrison c Williams | | | | |
|           b Ramprakash | 9 | 1/18 2/21 3/73 | (9 wkts, 60 overs) | 171 |
| N. E. Thompson c Cowans b Hughes | 14 | 4/73 5/85 6/114 | | |
| C. J. Hoey not out | 26 | 7/115 8/116 9/163 | | |

Bowling: Cowans 6–1–10–1; Williams 6–2–11–1; Weekes 12–1–30–1; Emburey 12–7–13–0; Ramprakash 7–1–15–2; Hughes 11–2–24–2; Hutchinson 2–0–17–0; Roseberry 2–0–20–0; Brown 1–0–8–0; Gatting 1–0–8–1.

Umpires: J. C. Balderstone and D. R. Shepherd.

## KENT v CAMBRIDGESHIRE

At Canterbury, June 26. Kent won by six wickets. Toss: Kent. Igglesden's figures, his best in the 60-overs competition, were improved on by Cambridgeshire's Ajaz Akhtar, of Teesside Polytechnic.

*Man of the Match:* Ajaz Akhtar.

# Cambridgeshire

| | | | | |
|---|---|---|---|---|
| R. A. Milne c Marsh b Igglesden | 0 | †M. W. C. Olley not out | | 20 |
| *N. T. Gadsby b Merrick | 15 | M. G. Stephenson lbw b Igglesden | | 2 |
| R. P. Merriman c Igglesden b Penn | 0 | K. O. Thomas c Marsh b Igglesden | | 2 |
| N. J. Adams c and b Davis | 44 | L-b 9, w 4 | | 13 |
| D. P. Norman b Merrick | 2 | | | |
| A. M. Cade c and b Merrick | 0 | 1/2 2/3 3/36 | (44.2 overs) | 107 |
| Ajaz Akhtar lbw b Fleming | 2 | 4/48 5/58 6/76 | | |
| S. Turner c C. S. Cowdrey b Igglesden | 7 | 7/76 8/93 9/101 | | |

Bowling: Penn 9–4–14–1; Igglesden 9.2–1–29–4; Merrick 12–3–27–3; Davis 9–2–22–1; Fleming 5–1–6–1.

# Kent

| | | | | |
|---|---|---|---|---|
| T. R. Ward c Stephenson b Ajaz Akhtar | 20 | M. V. Fleming not out | | 35 |
| *M. R. Benson b Ajaz Akhtar | 21 | L-b 4, w 3, n-b 1 | | 8 |
| N. R. Taylor c Olley b Ajaz Akhtar | 2 | | | |
| G. R. Cowdrey not out | 25 | 1/43 2/46 | (4 wkts, 35.4 overs) | 111 |
| C. S. Cowdrey b Ajaz Akhtar | 0 | 3/55 4/59 | | |

†S. A. Marsh, R. P. Davis, T. A. Merrick, A. P. Igglesden and C. Penn did not bat.

Bowling: Thomas 4–0–22–0; Turner 12–3–23–0; Ajaz Akhtar 12–6–28–4; Stephenson 5.4–4–19–0; Adams 2–0–15–0.

Umpires: P. Adams and D. J. Constant.

## LEICESTERSHIRE v SHROPSHIRE

At Leicester, June 26. Leicestershire won by seven wickets. Toss: Leicestershire. Boon's innings was his highest in the competition.

*Man of the Match:* T. J. Boon.

## Shropshire

| | |
|---|---|
| *J. Foster c Whitticase b Wilkinson ... 10 | A. S. Barnard not out ............... 17 |
| J. B. R. Jones c Lewis b Millns ....... 1 | A. P. Pridgeon b Lewis............. 4 |
| J. Abrahams run out ................ 53 | G. Edmunds not out ................ 3 |
| T. Parton c Boon b Lewis............ 17 | L-b 5, w 6, n-b 1 ............ 12 |
| A. N. Johnson c Lewis b Wilkinson .. 20 | |
| †J. R. Weaver c Whitticase b Wilkinson 6 | 1/2 2/38 3/84 (9 wkts, 60 overs) 152 |
| A. B. Byram b Millns ............... 0 | 4/89 5/117 6/117 |
| P. B. Wormald b Lewis.............. 9 | 7/120 8/132 9/142 |

Bowling: Lewis 12-2-28-3; Millns 12-4-27-2; Maguire 12-0-49-0; Wilkinson 12-5-16-3; Willey 12-3-27-0.

## Leicestershire

| | |
|---|---|
| T. J. Boon not out ................. 76 | L. Potter not out ................. 25 |
| *N. E. Briers run out .............. 9 | L-b 1 ..................... 1 |
| J. J. Whitaker c Abrahams b Wormald . 39 | |
| P. Willey c Abrahams b Byram ....... 6 | 1/12 2/84 3/95 (3 wkts, 56.5 overs) 156 |

C. C. Lewis, B. F. Smith, †P. Whitticase, C. W. Wilkinson, D. J. Millns and J. N. Maguire did not bat.

Bowling: Pridgeon 10.5-7-21-0; Barnard 12-5-26-0; Edmunds 12-0-40-0; Abrahams 8-0-25-0; Wormald 8-1-18-1; Byram 6-0-25-1.

Umpires: B. Leadbeater and H. J. Rhodes.

# NOTTINGHAMSHIRE v LINCOLNSHIRE

At Nottingham, June 26. Nottinghamshire won by 134 runs, Lincolnshire having forfeited the balance of their innings. Toss: Lincolnshire. The minor county chose to concede the match, rather than return for a second day with only two wickets standing. Crawley's performances with bat and ball were his best in any of the limited-overs competitions; he added 146 in 22 overs with Robinson for the fourth wicket.

*Man of the Match:* M. A. Crawley.

## Nottinghamshire

| | |
|---|---|
| B. C. Broad b McKeown ............ 14 | M. Saxelby not out ................. 6 |
| D. W. Randall c and b Storer ........ 25 | L-b 9, w 6 ............. 15 |
| *R. T. Robinson c Fell b McKeown ...124 | |
| P. Johnson b McKeown ............. 48 | 1/20 2/64 (4 wkts, 60 overs) 306 |
| M. A. Crawley not out ............. 74 | 3/138 4/284 |

†B. N. French, F. D. Stephenson, R. A. Pick, E. E. Hemmings and J. A. Afford did not bat.

Bowling: McKeown 12-0-52-3; Christmas 12-2-80-0; Jelfs 9-1-51-0; Storer 5-0-17-1; Marshall 12-0-48-0; Fell 10-0-49-0.

## Lincolnshire

| | |
|---|---|
| P. J. Heseltine c French b Stephenson . 2 | P. D. McKeown not out ............. 1 |
| D. B. Storer c Robinson b Crawley ... 28 | †N. P. Dobbs not out .............. 0 |
| S. N. Warman b Crawley ........... 28 | |
| *J. D. Love c French b Crawley ...... 24 | L-b 6, w 15 ............. 21 |
| M. A. Fell c French b Saxelby....... 39 | |
| N. J. C. Gandon lbw b Crawley ...... 0 | 1/2 2/59 3/78 (8 wkts, 50.4 overs) 172 |
| A. C. Jelfs b Hemmings ........... 25 | 4/105 5/105 6/157 |
| D. A. Christmas c and b Saxelby...... 4 | 7/167 8/171 |

D. A. Marshall did not bat.

*Lincolnshire forfeited the balance of their innings.*

Bowling: Stephenson 5-0-10-1; Pick 6-2-10-0; Hemmings 9-1-40-1; Saxelby 6.4-0-42-2; Crawley 12-1-26-4; Afford 12-2-38-0.

Umpires: H. D. Bird and Dr D. Fawkner-Corbett.

## SCOTLAND v SUSSEX

At Myreside, Edinburgh, June 26. Sussex won by 72 runs. Toss: Scotland. Lenham reached his highest score in the 60-overs competition before being bowled by Goram, making a final appearance for Scotland before taking up his new position as goalkeeper for Rangers Football Club.

*Man of the Match:* N. J. Lenham.

### Sussex

| | | | | |
|---|---|---|---|---|
| N. J. Lenham b Goram | 66 | †P. Moores c Philip b Moir | 26 |
| D. M. Smith lbw b Duthie | 40 | I. D. K. Salisbury st Haggo b Russell | 4 |
| M. P. Speight c Haggo b Reifer | 20 | A. N. Jones not out | 0 |
| *P. W. G. Parker c Henry b Goram | 12 | B 3, l-b 3, w 6, n-b 4 | 16 |
| C. M. Wells c Goram b Henry | 0 | | |
| A. P. Wells st Haggo b Duthie | 8 | 1/78 2/126 3/142 (9 wkts, 60 overs) | 231 |
| A. C. S. Pigott c Haggo b Russell | 7 | 4/154 5/156 6/163 | |
| A. I. C. Dodemaide not out | 32 | 7/170 8/211 9/219 | |

Bowling: Moir 11-1-47-1; Reifer 8-0-40-1; Duthie 12-2-42-2; Goram 12-1-42-2; Henry 12-2-34-1; Russell 5-0-20-2.

### Scotland

| | | | | |
|---|---|---|---|---|
| I. L. Philip lbw b Dodemaide | 9 | P. G. Duthie c Moores b Pigott | 19 |
| B. M. W. Patterson lbw b Dodemaide | 4 | †D. J. Haggo c Parker b Pigott | 1 |
| G. N. Reifer lbw b C. M. Wells | 13 | J. D. Moir not out | 11 |
| R. G. Swan b C. M. Wells | 45 | L-b 15, w 8 | 23 |
| G. Salmond lbw b Lenham | 1 | | |
| *O. Henry b Lenham | 12 | 1/12 2/28 3/49 (54.5 overs) | 159 |
| A. B. Russell b Salisbury | 0 | 4/52 5/68 6/71 | |
| A. L. Goram c Parker b C. M. Wells | 21 | 7/114 8/128 9/131 | |

Bowling: Jones 5-0-30-0; Dodemaide 10-3-12-2; Pigott 7.5-1-25-2; Lenham 11-1-25-2; C. M. Wells 12-3-16-3; Salisbury 9-0-36-1.

Umpires: G. I. Burgess and B. Dudleston.

## SOMERSET v BUCKINGHAMSHIRE

At Bath, June 26. Somerset won by six wickets. Toss: Buckinghamshire.

*Man of the Match:* P. M. Roebuck.

### Buckinghamshire

| | | | | |
|---|---|---|---|---|
| A. R. Harwood c Graveney b Mallender | 4 | T. J. Barry not out | 30 |
| M. J. Roberts c Harden b Hayhurst | 21 | †D. J. Goldsmith not out | 2 |
| T. J. A. Scriven lbw b Mallender | 0 | | |
| S. Burrow c Lefebvre b MacLeay | 12 | B 9, l-b 10, w 3, n-b 1 | 23 |
| B. S. Percy c Burns b Lefebvre | 13 | | |
| *N. G. Hames c Graveney | 11 | 1/7 2/7 3/41 (8 wkts, 60 overs) | 159 |
| G. R. Black b MacLeay | 11 | 4/47 5/66 6/86 | |
| P. G. Roshier c Roebuck b Mallender | 32 | 7/103 8/153 | |

C. D. Booden did not bat.

Bowling: Mallender 12-4-23-3; Lefebvre 12-5-30-1; MacLeay 12-0-35-2; Hayhurst 12-2-28-1; Graveney 12-4-24-1.

## Somerset

| | | | |
|---|---|---|---|
| S. J. Cook b Roshier | 35 | †N. D. Burns not out | 5 |
| P. M. Roebuck not out | 63 | B 1, l-b 3, w 4 | 8 |
| A. N. Hayhurst c Hames b Burrow | 5 | | |
| *C. J. Tavaré c Black b Scriven | 25 | (4 wkts, 48.4 overs) | 161 |
| R. J. Harden b Percy | 20 | 1/52 2/70 | |
| | | 3/113 4/149 | |

K. H. MacLeay, R. P. Lefebvre, N. A. Mallender, G. D. Rose and D. A. Graveney did not bat.

Bowling: Roshier 12–1–40–1; Black 7–0–30–0; Burrow 9–2–18–1; Booden 9.4–2–35–0; Scriven 8–1–32–1; Percy 3–2–2–1.

Umpires: R. C. Tolchard and R. A. White.

## STAFFORDSHIRE v NORTHAMPTONSHIRE

At Stone, June 26. Northamptonshire won by 152 runs. Toss: Staffordshire. Bailey, who played for Staffordshire in 1980, faced 160 balls, hitting five fours and eight sixes (five off the bowling of Spiers). It was his maiden hundred, and the highest innings played for Northamptonshire, in the NatWest Bank Trophy, as well as his highest score in any limited-overs competition. He shared 104-run partnerships with Fordham for the second wicket and Lamb for the third, and he was not out until the penultimate ball of the innings. When Staffordshire replied, Baptiste took three wickets for 3 runs in nine balls.

*Man of the Match*: R. J. Bailey.

## Northamptonshire

| | | | |
|---|---|---|---|
| A. Fordham b Newman | 56 | E. A. E. Baptiste not out | 0 |
| N. A. Felton c Dean b Hackett | 11 | | |
| R. J. Bailey c Cartledge b Hackett | 145 | L-b 7, w 6 | 13 |
| *A. J. Lamb run out | 31 | | |
| D. J. Capel b Hackett | 1 | 1/26 2/130 3/234 (5 wkts, 60 overs) | 260 |
| K. M. Curran not out | 3 | 4/246 5/259 | |

†D. Ripley, A. Walker, N. G. B. Cook and J. P. Taylor did not bat.

Bowling: Newman 12–3–29–1; Hackett 12–0–45–3; Williams 12–0–41–0; Dutton 12–0–54–0; Spiers 10–1–65–0; Addison 2–0–19–0.

## Staffordshire

| | | | |
|---|---|---|---|
| S. J. Dean c Cook b Taylor | 0 | R. A. Spiers not out | 13 |
| D. Cartledge b Walker | 4 | G. D. Williams c Cook b Bailey | 7 |
| J. P. Addison b Taylor | 11 | N. P. Hackett lbw b Fordham | 0 |
| D. A. Banks b Baptiste | 3 | B 4, l-b 7, w 5 | 16 |
| *N. J. Archer c Ripley b Baptiste | 14 | | |
| A. J. Dutton lbw b Baptiste | 12 | 1/0 2/15 3/17 (43.3 overs) | 108 |
| P. G. Newman b Cook | 28 | 4/31 5/54 6/59 | |
| †M. I. Humphries lbw b Baptiste | 0 | 7/61 8/87 9/104 | |

Bowling: Taylor 8–0–11–2; Walker 8–2–18–1; Baptiste 12–1–27–4; Cook 12–0–35–1; Bailey 2–0–3–1; Fordham 1.3–0–3–1.

Umpires: J. H. Hampshire and V. A. Holder.

## SURREY v OXFORDSHIRE

At The Oval, June 26, 27. Surrey won 3–2 in a bowling contest, after two successive matches had been abandoned. As at Bishop's Stortford, the teams had to resort to bowling at a set of stumps, this time indoors in the Ken Barrington Sports Hall. Waqar Younis scored one hit, with his first delivery, and with the last two balls Murphy won the game for Surrey. Curtis and Laudat had one hit each for the minor county. In the first game Surrey, put in, were

42 for one from 32.2 overs overnight, with D. J. Bicknell 68 not out and A. J. Stewart 15 not out. When a new, twenty-overs-a-side match began at 3.15 p.m. on the second day, Oxfordshire were asked to bat and scored 91 for six; Surrey were 39 for three from 5.4 overs when the rain returned.

The bowlers in the deciding contest were: Oxfordshire – P. J. Garner, R. A. Evans, I. J. Curtis, S. V. Laudat and D. A. Hale. Surrey – Waqar Younis, M. A. Lynch, M. P. Bicknell, J. Boiling and A. J. Murphy.

## WARWICKSHIRE v YORKSHIRE

At Birmingham, June 26. Warwickshire won by seven wickets. Toss: Yorkshire. Despite bowling eight wides and two no-balls, Donald returned his best figures in the competition against a first-class county. In four matches against Yorkshire in 1991 he had taken 23 wickets for 233 runs in 82.3 overs.

*Man of the Match*: A. A. Donald.

### Yorkshire

| | | | | |
|---|---|---|---|---|
| *M. D. Moxon lbw b Donald | 2 | P. J. Hartley not out | | 6 |
| A. A. Metcalfe c Reeve b Munton | 8 | J. D. Batty c Piper b Small | | 4 |
| D. Byas b Donald | 2 | S. D. Fletcher c Piper b Reeve | | 9 |
| †R. J. Blakey b Donald | 0 | L-b 9, w 14, n-b 3 | | 26 |
| P. E. Robinson c Reeve b Small | 40 | | | |
| C. S. Pickles b Donald | 12 | 1/5 2/16 3/16 | (45.1 overs) | 123 |
| P. Carrick c Munton b Small | 12 | 4/42 5/83 6/88 | | |
| D. Gough b Smith | 2 | 7/102 8/102 9/107 | | |

Bowling: Donald 9-2-16-4; Small 12-5-28-3; Munton 8-1-21-1; Reeve 6.1-0-17-1; Smith 10-1-32-1.

### Warwickshire

| | | | | |
|---|---|---|---|---|
| A. J. Moles c Pickles b Batty | 30 | P. A. Smith not out | | 2 |
| J. D. Ratcliffe run out | 26 | B 2, l-b 5, w 7, n-b 11 | | 25 |
| D. P. Ostler not out | 34 | | | |
| D. A. Reeve c Moxon b Pickles | 7 | 1/65 2/96 3/110 | (3 wkts, 43.3 overs) | 124 |

*T. A. Lloyd, †K. J. Piper, G. C. Small, P. A. Booth, T. A. Munton and A. A. Donald did not bat.

Bowling: Hartley 8-1-19-0; Fletcher 5-0-15-0; Pickles 10.3-2-30-1; Gough 8-2-18-0; Carrick 6-1-18-0; Batty 6-2-17-1.

Umpires: M. J. Kitchen and N. T. Plews.

## SECOND ROUND

## GLOUCESTERSHIRE v NOTTINGHAMSHIRE

At Bristol, July 11, 12. Nottinghamshire won by three wickets. Toss: Nottinghamshire. Hemmings hit the winning run from the last ball to earn his side a place in the quarter-finals. Yet when rain had interrupted Nottinghamshire's innings at 180 for three in the 52nd over, there was the possibility of Gloucestershire going through on faster overall scoring-rate, even though they had been 150 for three at the same stage. Happily for Nottinghamshire, who had played the better cricket for much of the game, play resumed and, after some panicky moments, they scrambled home. Gloucestershire's innings took shape around a century partnership in 27 overs between Athey and Alleyne, after an uncertain start had seen the home county 50 for three in the 25th over. Rain prevented a start to Nottinghamshire's reply until the second day, when Broad and Randall put them on the right path with 83 by the 25th over.

*Man of the Match*: C. W. J. Athey.

## Gloucestershire

| | | | |
|---|---|---|---|
| J. J. E. Hardy b Hemmings | 23 | J. W. Lloyds not out | 13 |
| R. J. Scott c French b Pick | 0 | D. V. Lawrence not out | 5 |
| *A. J. Wright c French b Afford | 11 | B 1, l-b 12, w 8, n-b 2 | 23 |
| C. W. J. Athey c French b Pick | 76 | | |
| M. W. Alleyne c and b Pick | 45 | 1/14 2/37 3/50 (6 wkts, 60 overs) 221 | |
| †R. C. Russell c French b Stephenson | 25 | 4/172 5/179 6/212 | |

D. R. Gilbert, A. M. Smith and M. J. Gerrard did not bat.

Bowling: Stephenson 12–0–46–1; Pick 12–1–41–3; Evans 12–2–51–0; Hemmings 12–2–27–1; Afford 11–3–40–1; Crawley 1–0–3–0.

## Nottinghamshire

| | | | |
|---|---|---|---|
| B. C. Broad c Russell b Gilbert | 38 | †B. N. French c and b Gilbert | 1 |
| D. W. Randall c Russell b Scott | 46 | E. E. Hemmings not out | 17 |
| *R. T. Robinson c Lloyds b Scott | 48 | B 1, l-b 5, w 7, n-b 3 | 16 |
| P. Johnson c Russell b Lawrence | 18 | | |
| M. A. Crawley not out | 35 | 1/83 2/104 3/137 (7 wkts, 60 overs) 222 | |
| F. D. Stephenson lbw b Lawrence | 1 | 4/180 5/183 | |
| K. P. Evans c Lloyds b Smith | 2 | 6/187 7/192 | |

J. A. Afford and R. A. Pick did not bat.

Bowling: Gilbert 12–0–41–2; Smith 10–1–49–1; Gerrard 2–0–10–0; Lawrence 12–3–48–2; Lloyds 12–1–36–0; Scott 12–0–32–2.

Umpires: J. W. Holder and N. T. Plews.

# HAMPSHIRE v LANCASHIRE

At Southampton, July 11, 12. Hampshire won by eight wickets. Toss: Hampshire. Holders Lancashire went out of the NatWest Bank Trophy with an inept bowling performance which allowed the home side to win with 6.1 overs to spare. Hampshire, resuming on the second morning at 151 for two (R. A. Smith 20*, D. I. Gower 10*), needed another 111 from 22 overs for victory, and Smith (90 balls) and Gower (63 balls) hurried them there at 7 runs an over. Before bad light had stopped play the previous evening, Chris Smith, with ten boundaries in his 66, and Terry had given them an ideal start. Lancashire's openers also laid a good foundation, casting doubt on Nicholas's decision to field first, but their last eight wickets fell for 71 runs in thirteen overs. Lancashire's defeat was their first in seventeen limited-overs games in 1991, and ended a run of nineteen unbeaten games in this competition and the Benson and Hedges Cup. Next day Worcestershire beat them in the final of the Benson and Hedges Cup.

*Man of the Match:* R. A. Smith.

## Lancashire

| | | | |
|---|---|---|---|
| G. D. Mendis lbw b Udal | 50 | I. D. Austin c Maru b Aqib Javed | 2 |
| G. Fowler b Udal | 71 | *D. P. Hughes not out | 5 |
| G. D. Lloyd c Aymes b Connor | 39 | P. J. W. Allott c Ayling b Connor | 2 |
| N. H. Fairbrother c Udal b Connor | 24 | L-b 6, w 6, n-b 2 | 14 |
| M. Watkinson c Aqib Javed b Udal | 7 | | |
| Wasim Akram c Connor b Ayling | 29 | 1/111 2/138 3/190 (59.1 overs) 261 | |
| P. A. J. DeFreitas c Terry b Connor | 11 | 4/199 5/205 6/232 | |
| †W. K. Hegg run out | 7 | 7/247 8/254 9/258 | |

Bowling: Aqib Javed 12–0–53–1; Connor 11.1–0–61–4; Maru 12–2–37–0; Ayling 12–0–57–1; Udal 12–0–47–3.

# Hampshire

| | |
|---|---|
| V. P. Terry c Hegg b Watkinson | 47 |
| C. L. Smith c Hegg b Wasim Akram | 66 |
| R. A. Smith not out | 79 |
| D. I. Gower not out | 54 |
| L-b 4, w 9, n-b 3 | 16 |

1/87 2/133        (2 wkts, 53.5 overs) 262

*M. C. J. Nicholas, J. R. Ayling, †A. N. Aymes, R. J. Maru, S. D. Udal, Aqib Javed and C. A. Connor did not bat.

Bowling: Allott 12–3–48–0; DeFreitas 10–2–38–0; Wasim Akram 12–0–46–1; Austin 9–0–59–0; Watkinson 10–0–62–1; Hughes 0.5–0–5–0.

Umpires: B. Hassan and D. R. Shepherd.

# NORTHAMPTONSHIRE v LEICESTERSHIRE

At Northampton, July 11. Northamptonshire won by nine wickets. Toss: Northamptonshire. Leicestershire's 255 never looked enough in good batting conditions once Fordham got going, and Northamptonshire won handsomely with 13.1 overs in hand. Baptiste and Williams, the off-spinner, bowled with tight control for the home side, and it took a century stand between Whitaker (135 balls, eleven fours) and Potter to rally Leicestershire. Fordham and Felton inspired Northamptonshire's reply with an early assault on Mills, putting on 162 for the first wicket, and Fordham then added 97 with Bailey as he went on to 132 not out from 134 balls. Dropped three times, between 77 and 89, Fordham hit three sixes – two off Maguire in the penultimate over – and twelve fours.

*Man of the Match:* A. Fordham.

# Leicestershire

| | | | |
|---|---|---|---|
| T. J. Boon run out | 14 | P. Willey b Baptiste | 28 |
| *N. E. Briers c Ripley b Baptiste | 29 | | |
| J. J. Whitaker not out | 94 | B 1, l-b 13, w 6, n-b 1 | 21 |
| C. C. Lewis c Felton b Baptiste | 6 | | |
| L. Potter b Taylor | 57 | 1/49 2/55 3/73        (6 wkts, 60 overs) 255 |
| B. F. Smith c Williams b Taylor | 6 | 4/194 5/208 6/255 | |

†P. Whitticase, C. W. Wilkinson, D. J. Mills and J. N. Maguire did not bat.

Bowling: Walker 10–0–40–0; Taylor 10–1–50–2; Baptiste 11–3–45–3; Curran 12–1–58–0; Williams 12–2–24–0; Capel 5–0–24–0.

# Northamptonshire

| | |
|---|---|
| A. Fordham not out | 132 |
| N. A. Felton b Potter | 54 |
| R. J. Bailey not out | 48 |
| B 4, l-b 11, w 8, n-b 2 | 25 |

1/162        (1 wkt, 46.5 overs) 259

*A. J. Lamb, D. J. Capel, K. M. Curran, E. A. E. Baptiste, R. G. Williams, †D. Ripley, A. Walker and J. P. Taylor did not bat.

Bowling: Lewis 9–0–32–0; Mills 9–0–60–0; Maguire 11–1–45–0; Willey 7–0–29–0; Wilkinson 4.5–0–46–0; Potter 6–1–32–1.

Umpires: H. D. Bird and K. J. Lyons.

## SOMERSET v MIDDLESEX

At Taunton, July 11, 12. Somerset won by 10 runs. Toss: Somerset. On a slow and uneven
pitch, Somerset recovered from the early loss of Cook through a second-wicket stand of 74
between Roebuck and Hayhurst (107 balls). Later, Tavaré (80 balls) and Harden batted
enterprisingly while adding 72 in twelve overs. A thunderstorm interrupted the Somerset
innings and took the match into a second day, which began with Middlesex placed
promisingly at 92 for one from 27 overs (M. A. Roseberry 43\*, M. W. Gatting 18\*). However,
they lost Roseberry in the 29th over, the first of three run-outs, and only Gatting and
Ramprakash, adding 44 in ten overs, made much headway. Gatting (114 balls) remained a
threat until he was eighth out, but scoring 23 from the last thirteen balls proved beyond
Headley and Cowans, the tenth-wicket pair.

*Man of the Match:* M. W. Gatting.

### Somerset

| | | | | |
|---|---|---|---|---|
| S. J. Cook b Cowans | 7 | D. Beal run out | | 0 |
| P. M. Roebuck c Brown b Tufnell | 31 | H. R. J. Trump run out | | 1 |
| A. N. Hayhurst c Roseberry b Emburey | 58 | | | |
| \*C. J. Tavaré b Cowans | 59 | L-b 6, w 1, n-b 7 | | 14 |
| R. J. Harden c Gatting b Cowans | 39 | | | |
| K. H. MacLeay not out | 25 | 1/10 2/84 3/124 | (9 wkts, 60 overs) | 252 |
| R. P. Lefebvre c Gatting b Cowans | 13 | 4/196 5/215 6/238 | | |
| †N. D. Burns b Emburey | 5 | 7/243 8/243 9/252 | | |
| D. A. Graveney did not bat. | | | | |

Bowling: Cowans 12–0–51–4; Williams 6–0–32–0; Headley 12–0–51–0; Tufnell 12–2–29–1;
Emburey 12–0–52–2; Ramprakash 6–0–31–0.

### Middlesex

| | | | | |
|---|---|---|---|---|
| I. J. F. Hutchinson lbw b Graveney | 17 | D. W. Headley not out | | 11 |
| M. A. Roseberry run out | 44 | P. C. R. Tufnell c b Roebuck | | 8 |
| \*M. W. Gatting b Lefebvre | 85 | N. G. Cowans b Hayhurst | | 10 |
| M. R. Ramprakash lbw b Hayhurst | 25 | B 2, l-b 15, w 5 | | 22 |
| K. R. Brown b MacLeay | 8 | | | |
| J. E. Emburey run out | 2 | 1/46 2/97 3/141 | (59.3 overs) | 242 |
| †P. Farbrace run out | 7 | 4/177 5/182 6/195 | | |
| N. F. Williams c MacLeay b Lefebvre | 3 | 7/209 8/215 9/230 | | |

Bowling: Lefebvre 12–1–32–2; Beal 2–0–12–0; MacLeay 12–1–32–1; Hayhurst
11.3–1–49–2; Graveney 7–1–24–1; Trump 6–0–33–0; Roebuck 9–0–43–1.

Umpires: A. A. Jones and R. Julian.

## SURREY v KENT

At The Oval, July 11. Surrey won by seven wickets. Toss: Kent. Kent looked set for a big total
when they were 100 for one in the 23rd over. However, the return of Waqar Younis changed
the course of their innings. Ward, who earlier had cut and hooked Younis for two breathtaking boundaries in an over realising 15 runs, was bowled, and Cowdrey lasted two balls,
both of them bringing lbw appeals. Robinson, called on to bowl because Martin Bicknell had
injured his shoulder fielding off his own bowling, produced a steady spell which restricted
Kent to 192 for seven after 49 overs. But Penn and McCague added 36 for the ninth wicket to
set Surrey a target of just over 4 an over. They had 58 on the board before losing Darren
Bicknell in the eleventh over, and Stewart maintained the momentum with his unbeaten 76
from 93 balls. He hit ten fours, while Surrey's Ward had a six and five fours in his even-time
fifty.

*Man of the Match:* J. D. Robinson.

## Kent

| | | | |
|---|---|---|---|
| T. R. Ward b Waqar Younis | 55 | C. Penn not out | 20 |
| *M. R. Benson c Boiling b Murphy | 14 | M. J. McCague run out | 9 |
| N. R. Taylor c Stewart b Robinson | 44 | T. A. Merrick lbw b Waqar Younis | 0 |
| G. R. Cowdrey lbw b Waqar Younis | 0 | B 1, l-b 21, w 7, n-b 2 | 31 |
| S. G. Hinks b Boiling | 34 | | |
| M. V. Fleming b Robinson | 21 | 1/33 2/100 3/100 | (57.2 overs) 245 |
| †S. A. Marsh c Stewart b Feltham | 15 | 4/147 5/163 6/188 | |
| R. P. Davis lbw b Robinson | 2 | 7/192 8/208 9/244 | |

Bowling: Waqar Younis 10.2-2-51-3; M. P. Bicknell 3.5-1-9-0; Murphy 9-2-27-1; Thorpe 0.1-0-0-0; Feltham 10-1-46-1; Boiling 12-1-44-1; Robinson 12-2-46-3.

## Surrey

| | | | |
|---|---|---|---|
| D. J. Bicknell c Merrick b Davis | 27 | G. P. Thorpe not out | 20 |
| M. A. Lynch run out | 48 | L-b 9, w 7, n-b 7 | 23 |
| *†A. J. Stewart not out | 76 | | |
| D. M. Ward c Marsh b Penn | 55 | 1/58 2/106 3/191 | (3 wkts, 47.2 overs) 249 |

J. D. Robinson, M. A. Feltham, M. P. Bicknell, J. Boiling, Waqar Younis and A. J. Murphy did not bat.

Bowling: Merrick 9-1-47-0; McCague 7-0-47-0; Davis 11-2-34-1; Penn 9-0-55-1; Fleming 7.2-0-38-0; Cowdrey 4-0-19-0.

Umpires: K. E. Palmer and R. C. Tolchard.

## SUSSEX v ESSEX

At Hove, July 11. Essex won by four wickets. Toss: Sussex. Essex turned in a match-winning performance in the field. Prichard's running catch on the mid-wicket boundary to dismiss Lenham set the standard, and Hussain caught the eye later on with his direct hit from point to run out Speight. He followed that with a superb catch at gully to send back Moores. Smith gave the home side a good start with 62 from 86 balls, and Speight and Alan Wells added 80 in seventeen overs to hint at a more challenging total than Sussex's eventual 254. Jones troubled the Essex batsmen with his opening burst, but Gooch was resolute. His partnership of 142 in 29 overs with Hussain (eleven fours) took the match from Sussex, despite some shaky moments following the Essex captain's dismissal for 95 (146 balls) with 43 runs still needed. When 74, Gooch became the leading run-scorer in the 60-overs competition, moving ahead of D. L. Amiss (1,950 runs).

*Man of the Match: G. A. Gooch.*

## Sussex

| | | | |
|---|---|---|---|
| N. J. Lenham c Prichard b Such | 19 | A. C. S. Pigott b Topley | 0 |
| D. M. Smith c Salim Malik b Topley | 62 | I. D. K. Salisbury not out | 14 |
| M. P. Speight run out | 48 | | |
| *A. P. Wells c Shahid b Foster | 40 | L-b 3, w 3, n-b 6 | 12 |
| P. W. G. Parker c and b Pringle | 17 | | |
| C. M. Wells c Salim Malik b Pringle | 11 | 1/76 2/97 3/177 | (8 wkts, 60 overs) 254 |
| A. I. C. Dodemaide not out | 27 | 4/183 5/204 6/213 | |
| †P. Moores c Hussain b Topley | 4 | 7/224 8/224 | |

A. N. Jones did not bat.

Bowling: Foster 12-0-53-1; Pringle 12-1-54-2; Such 12-0-36-1; Topley 12-1-38-3; Salim Malik 6-0-34-0; Stephenson 1-0-8-0; Gooch 5-0-28-0.

## Essex

| | | | | |
|---|---|---|---|---|
| *G. A. Gooch c Dodemaide b Lenham | 95 | †M. A. Garnham not out | | 12 |
| J. P. Stephenson b Jones | 1 | N. A. Foster not out | | 10 |
| P. J. Prichard c Moores b Jones | 0 | L-b 3, w 11, n-b 1 | | 15 |
| Salim Malik b C. M. Wells | 23 | | | |
| N. Hussain c Smith b Pigott | 97 | 1/19 2/27 3/70 | (6 wkts, 58 overs) | 255 |
| D. R. Pringle b Salisbury | 2 | 4/212 5/219 6/238 | | |

N. Shahid, T. D. Topley and P. M. Such did not bat.

Bowling: Jones 7–0–46–2; Dodemaide 11–0–52–0; Pigott 12–0–40–1; C. M. Wells 9–0–39–1; Salisbury 12–1–40–1; Lenham 7–0–35–1.

Umpires: D. J. Constant and P. B. Wight.

## WARWICKSHIRE v HERTFORDSHIRE

At Birmingham, July 11. Warwickshire won by ten wickets. Toss: Hertfordshire. Hertfordshire, 56 for six at lunch, owed their eventual total to Ligertwood's unbeaten 37 – he and Smith, a former Warwickshire player, added 57 for the seventh wicket – and to the profligacy of Warwickshire's bowlers. They bowled 33 wides and five no-balls, while three dropped catches added to an impression of complacency in the field. Warwickshire's victory was achieved in good time, with the players staying out in heavy rain rather than return the next day.

*Man of the Match:* J. D. Ratcliffe.

## Hertfordshire

| | | | | |
|---|---|---|---|---|
| J. D. Carr run out | 14 | D. M. Smith b Reeve | | 15 |
| N. P. G. Wright c Piper b Small | 6 | W. G. Merry not out | | 7 |
| B. G. Evans c Munton b Reeve | 7 | L-b 5, w 33, n-b 2 | | 40 |
| M. F. Voss c and b Smith | 2 | | | |
| N. R. C. MacLaurin c Piper b Donald | 3 | 1/20 2/33 3/35 | (7 wkts, 60 overs) | 135 |
| A. Needham lbw b Smith | 4 | 4/38 5/43 | | |
| †D. G. C. Ligertwood not out | 37 | 6/56 7/113 | | |

*D. Surridge and G. A. R. Harris did not bat.

Bowling: Donald 12–1–40–1; Small 12–4–25–1; Munton 12–2–22–0; Reeve 12–5–19–2; Smith 12–2–24–2.

## Warwickshire

| | | |
|---|---|---|
| A. J. Moles not out | | 62 |
| J. D. Ratcliffe not out | | 68 |
| L-b 6, w 2 | | 8 |

(no wkt, 36.4 overs) 138

*T. A. Lloyd, D. P. Ostler, D. A. Reeve, P. A. Smith, Asif Din, †K. J. Piper, A. A. Donald, T. A. Munton and G. C. Small did not bat.

Bowling: Harris 4–1–17–0; Surridge 4–1–15–0; Needham 12–4–25–0; Merry 5–1–18–0; Carr 6–0–13–0; Smith 3–0–15–0; MacLaurin 2–0–20–0; Wright 0.4–0–9–0.

Umpires: J. D. Bond and D. O. Oslear.

## WORCESTERSHIRE v GLAMORGAN

At Worcester, July 11, 12. Glamorgan won by seven wickets. Toss: Worcestershire. Glamorgan's excellent all-round display sent Worcestershire to Lord's for the weekend's Benson and Hedges Cup final without the confidence-boosting win they were looking for. Moody's threatening start (37 from 46 balls) came to nothing, and Croft began his admirably economical spell of off-spin bowling by having Hick caught at cover from his fourth delivery. Glamorgan were 19 for one after 6.2 overs when rain stopped play (H. Morris 12*, A. Dale 4*), and next day the second-wicket pair extended their partnership to 108 from 34 overs. Dale (nine fours) then put on 92 with Maynard, whose 78 not out from 59 balls put the victory beyond doubt.

*Man of the Match:* A. Dale.

### Worcestershire

| | | | | |
|---|---|---|---|---|
| T. S. Curtis run out | 34 | S. R. Lampitt run out | | 7 |
| T. M. Moody c Metson b Barwick | 37 | N. V. Radford not out | | 15 |
| G. A. Hick c Dale b Croft | 10 | G. R. Dilley not out | | 7 |
| D. B. D'Oliveira c Frost b Dale | 13 | B 1, l-b 8, w 5 | | 14 |
| *P. A. Neale b Croft | 8 | | | |
| I. T. Botham c Butcher b Barwick | 27 | 1/56 2/88 3/91 | (9 wkts, 60 overs) | 223 |
| †S. J. Rhodes c Butcher b Frost | 41 | 4/107 5/115 6/153 | | |
| R. K. Illingworth run out | 10 | 7/166 8/181 9/203 | | |

Bowling: Watkin 12–1–35–0; Frost 12–0–58–1; Barwick 12–0–51–2; Dale 12–1–42–1; Croft 12–0–28–2.

### Glamorgan

| | | | | |
|---|---|---|---|---|
| *A. R. Butcher c and b Dilley | 0 | P. A. Cottey not out | | 3 |
| H. Morris c and b Illingworth | 40 | L-b 7, w 6, n-b 4 | | 17 |
| A. Dale c Botham b Lampitt | 86 | | | |
| M. P. Maynard not out | 78 | 1/8 2/116 3/208 | (3 wkts, 53.4 overs) | 224 |

I. Smith, R. D. B. Croft, †C. P. Metson, S. L. Watkin, S. R. Barwick and M. Frost did not bat.

Bowling: Dilley 12–1–35–1; Radford 10–0–35–0; Botham 10–0–39–0; Lampitt 9.4–0–61–1; Illingworth 12–1–47–1.

Umpires: G. I. Burgess and B. J. Meyer.

## QUARTER-FINALS

## HAMPSHIRE v NOTTINGHAMSHIRE

At Southampton, July 31. Hampshire won by seven wickets. Toss: Hampshire. Broad and Randall put Nottinghamshire on course for a big total, but after the left-hander was lbw to Maru in the eighteenth over, and Robinson was caught behind off Aqib Javed, the visitors relied too heavily on Randall. When he was bowled by Aqib, one of three wickets in a spell costing the Pakistani fast bowler 15 runs, Nottinghamshire could manage only 54 from the last ten overs. Hampshire's reply was dominated by the Smith brothers and overshadowed by the controversial dismissal of Terry, run out when he collided accidentally with the bowler, Evans, and could not make his ground before Hemmings's throw from mid-on hit the stumps. The incident brought Nicholas, Hampshire's captain, on to the pitch for discussions with the umpires and his opposite number, Robinson, but the decision stood. However, it also brought Robin Smith to the wicket, and in a partnership of 114 with his older brother he reached his fifty from 53 balls, and finished with 67 from 85. On his dismissal, Hampshire required 98 from seventeen overs, and Chris Smith, with nine fours in his seventh NatWest hundred, saw them safely to their fourth successive semi-final.

*Man of the Match:* C. L. Smith.

## Nottinghamshire

| | | | | |
|---|---|---|---|---|
| B. C. Broad lbw b Maru | 31 | †B. N. French c Terry b Connor | | 7 |
| D. W. Randall b Aqib Javed | 95 | E. E. Hemmings not out | | 5 |
| *R. T. Robinson c Aymes b Aqib Javed | 25 | R. A. Pick not out | | 0 |
| P. Johnson c Maru b Connor | 0 | | | |
| P. R. Pollard lbw b Connor | 6 | L-b 8, w 11, n-b 1 | | 20 |
| M. Saxelby b Ayling | 36 | | | |
| K. P. Evans c Aymes b Aqib Javed | 20 | 1/64 2/129 3/140 | (9 wkts, 60 overs) | 252 |
| F. D. Stephenson c Nicholas | | 4/156 5/198 6/218 | | |
| b Aqib Javed | 7 | 7/230 8/238 9/247 | | |

Bowling: Aqib Javed 12–0–51–4; Connor 12–0–42–3; Ayling 12–0–55–1; Maru 12–0–42–1; Udal 12–0–54–0.

## Hampshire

| | | | | |
|---|---|---|---|---|
| V. P. Terry run out | 26 | *M. C. J. Nicholas not out | | 24 |
| C. L. Smith not out | 105 | L-b 3, w 8, n-b 1 | | 12 |
| R. A. Smith b Pick | 67 | | | |
| D. I. Gower c Evans b Saxelby | 19 | 1/41 2/155 3/205 | (3 wkts, 59 overs) | 253 |

J. R. Ayling, †A. N. Aymes, R. J. Maru, S. D. Udal, C. A. Connor and Aqib Javed did not bat.

Bowling: Stephenson 12–0–43–0; Pick 12–1–60–1; Evans 11–1–31–0; Saxelby 12–1–48–1; Hemmings 12–0–68–0.

Umpires: J. C. Balderstone and R. Palmer.

# NORTHAMPTONSHIRE v GLAMORGAN

At Northampton, July 31. Northamptonshire won by 26 runs. Toss: Glamorgan. Glamorgan squandered an excellent chance of victory when Dale and Maynard, having played themselves in, departed in successive overs after attempting unnecessarily sharp singles to the substitute fielder, N. A. Felton, who hit the stumps with direct throws each time. Up to then, the visitors had looked the more likely winners. On a good batting pitch, but with an outfield slowed by overnight rain, Northamptonshire were never allowed to cut loose; and when Glamorgan replied, there was a solid opening stand between Morris and Butcher before Maynard, in outstanding form, began to strike the ball handsomely. Even after his dismissal, Glamorgan were still in a position to mount a serious challenge. But Shastri was unable to accelerate, and this put too much pressure on the batsmen at the other end, who were not up to the task. The highlights of Northamptonshire's innings were another polished performance from Fordham, which earned him a second Man of the Match award in consecutive rounds, and the wicket-keeping of Metson, who held brilliant catches to account for Capel and Baptiste.

*Man of the Match:* A. Fordham.

## Northamptonshire

| | | | | |
|---|---|---|---|---|
| A. Fordham c Watkin b Shastri | 71 | R. G. Williams run out | | 6 |
| W. Larkins lbw b Watkin | 8 | †D. Ripley not out | | 10 |
| R. J. Bailey c Shastri b Barwick | 55 | B 1, l-b 13, w 7, n-b 1 | | 22 |
| *A. J. Lamb b Shastri | 29 | | | |
| D. J. Capel c Metson b Barwick | 0 | 1/30 2/127 3/171 | (7 wkts, 60 overs) | 254 |
| K. M. Curran not out | 36 | 4/171 5/183 | | |
| E. A. E. Baptiste c Metson b Watkin | 17 | 6/221 7/233 | | |

A. Walker and J. P. Taylor did not bat.

Bowling: Watkin 12–0–40–2; Frost 7–0–34–0; Barwick 12–0–51–2; Dale 12–1–37–0; Croft 5–0–18–0; Shastri 12–0–60–2.

## Glamorgan

| | | |
|---|---|---|
| *A. R. Butcher c Williams b Baptiste .. | 70 | |
| H. Morris c and b Baptiste........... | 37 | |
| A. Dale run out ..................... | 15 | |
| M. P. Maynard not out............... | 27 | |
| R. J. Shastri run out ................ | 25 | |
| P. A. Cottey c and b Taylor.......... | 10 | |
| R. D. B. Croft c Lamb b Curran ...... | 13 | |
| †C. P. Metson b Walker............... | 9 | |

| | | |
|---|---|---|
| S. L. Watkin not out ................ | 5 | |
| S. R. Barwick lbw b Taylor ......... | 3 | |
| M. Frost b Walker .................. | 3 | |
| L-b 2, w 6, n-b 3 ........... | 11 | |
| | | |
| 1/85 2/117 3/151 | (60 overs) 228 | |
| 4/156 5/170 6/194 | | |
| 7/216 8/217 9/221 | | |

Bowling: Taylor 12–2–34–2; Walker 12–1–39–2; Baptiste 12–0–51–2; Curran 12–0–61–1; Williams 12–1–41–0.

Umpires: J. D. Bond and J. W. Holder.

## SURREY v ESSEX

At The Oval, July 31. Surrey won by 31 runs. Toss: Essex. Her Majesty The Queen visited The Oval, after an absence of 36 years, to open the £3 million Ken Barrington Sports Centre, and was introduced to the teams between innings. On either side of this presentation, Waqar Younis, first with the bat and later with the ball, engineered victory for the hosts. Coming in with Surrey 209 for seven, he struck a crucial 26 runs off eighteen balls, including two sixes; and when Essex, with four wickets in hand, were looking to score 56 from the last eight overs, he came back to remove Garnham and Seymour in one over with his fierce pace and late swing. Gooch and Stephenson had safely negotiated his new-ball thrust, and as their partnership approached 100 Surrey's score appeared increasingly vulnerable. However, Gooch was caught, trying to run a swinging delivery to third man, Stephenson was sensationally caught by Lynch, diving to his left at short extra-cover, and a pin-point throw by Martin Bicknell, coming in from deep square leg, ran out Salim Malik to leave Essex 175 for five. Their last five wickets were swept away in 38 balls. Surrey had been in some trouble when four middle-order wickets fell for 25, including three in seventeen balls, but Ward's assertive 62 off 74 deliveries kept them in contention, and Waqar Younis's late surge, mostly at Foster's expense, lifted them to a useful total.

*Man of the Match:* Waqar Younis.

## Surrey

| | | |
|---|---|---|
| D. J. Bicknell lbw b Topley .......... | 28 | |
| J. D. Robinson b Such............... | 47 | |
| †A. J. Stewart b Gooch............... | 35 | |
| D. M. Ward c and b Foster .......... | 62 | |
| G. P. Thorpe c Garnham b Gooch .... | 2 | |
| M. A. Lynch lbw b Such ............ | 6 | |
| *I. A. Greig c Hussain b Topley ...... | 20 | |
| M. P. Bicknell c Seymour b Pringle.... | 4 | |

| | | |
|---|---|---|
| Waqar Younis c Hussain b Foster ..... | 26 | |
| J. Boiling lbw b Pringle ............. | 7 | |
| A. J. Murphy not out ............... | 0 | |
| B 1, l-b 4, w 9, n-b 2 ........ | 16 | |
| | | |
| 1/55 2/118 3/118 | (59.5 overs) 253 | |
| 4/121 5/143 6/193 | | |
| 7/209 8/222 9/243 | | |

Bowling: Foster 11.5–2–57–2; Pringle 12–0–52–2; Topley 11–2–44–2; Stephenson 5–0–28–0; Such 12–1–37–2; Gooch 8–2–30–2.

## Essex

| | | |
|---|---|---|
| *G. A. Gooch c Stewart b Waqar Younis | 50 | |
| J. P. Stephenson c Lynch | | |
| b M. P. Bicknell . | 59 | |
| P. J. Prichard c Boiling b M. P. Bicknell | 11 | |
| Salim Malik run out ................ | 26 | |
| N. Hussain b Murphy ............... | 3 | |
| D. R. Pringle lbw b Waqar Younis .... | 19 | |
| N. A. Foster c Lynch b Robinson ..... | 9 | |
| †M. A. Garnham c Stewart | | |
| b Waqar Younis . | 9 | |

| | | |
|---|---|---|
| A. C. H. Seymour | | |
| lbw b Waqar Younis . | 0 | |
| T. D. Topley run out ................ | 7 | |
| P. M. Such not out ................. | 0 | |
| L-b 11, w 4 ............ | 15 | |
| | | |
| 1/92 2/121 3/132 | (56.1 overs) 222 | |
| 4/172 5/175 6/185 | | |
| 7/198 8/198 9/222 | | |

Bowling: M. P. Bicknell 12–0–49–2; Waqar Younis 10.1–1–37–4; Murphy 10–3–30–1; Robinson 12–1–48–1; Boiling 12–0–47–0.

Umpires: J. H. Hampshire and R. A. White.

## WARWICKSHIRE v SOMERSET

At Birmingham, July 31. Warwickshire won by 5 runs. Toss: Somerset. Somerset fought back well in a game which twice seemed to be slipping away from them, and on each occasion it was Hayhurst who brought them back into contention with competition-best performances. When Warwickshire were 191 for four with eight overs left, Hayhurst put a poor first spell behind him to take five wickets in 27 balls and restrict them to 229. Lloyd batted well for his 78, off 122 deliveries, but too many of his partners were out to poor strokes. Small rocked Somerset by removing Cook and Roebuck, but Hayhurst, with 91 not out from 118 balls, took them to within one hit of a victory which, at 157 for seven, looked out of the question. He was well supported by Lefebvre in an unbroken eighth-wicket stand of 67, but they found the task of scoring 15 from the last over too demanding. Hayhurst's six off Reeve's last delivery was no more than a final, defiant flourish. Reeve underlined his value as a bowler by holding his nerve in his two of the last four overs.

*Man of the Match:* A. N. Hayhurst.

### Warwickshire

| | | | |
|---|---:|---|---:|
| A. J. Moles c Tavaré b Lefebvre | 13 | G. C. Small c and b Hayhurst | 3 |
| Asif Din c Tavaré b Lefebvre | 17 | T. A. Munton lbw b Lefebvre | 1 |
| *T. A. Lloyd c Burns b Hayhurst | 78 | A. A. Donald not out | 2 |
| D. P. Ostler c Tavaré b Graveney | 10 | L-b 8, w 3, n-b 3 | 14 |
| D. A. Reeve run out | 25 | | |
| N. M. K. Smith b Hayhurst | 38 | 1/33 2/34 3/72 | (60 overs) 229 |
| P. A. Smith b Hayhurst | 26 | 4/131 5/191 6/200 | |
| †P. C. L. Holloway lbw b Hayhurst | 2 | 7/208 8/212 9/219 | |

Bowling: Rose 7–0–40–0; Hallett 12–1–31–0; Lefebvre 12–1–27–3; Hayhurst 12–1–60–5; Graveney 12–0–44–1; Roebuck 5–0–19–0.

### Somerset

| | | | |
|---|---:|---|---:|
| S. J. Cook c Holloway b Small | 14 | G. D. Rose run out | 3 |
| P. M. Roebuck c Reeve b Small | 5 | R. P. Lefebvre not out | 21 |
| R. J. Harden c Holloway b Munton | 10 | | |
| *C. J. Tavaré st Holloway | | B 1, l-b 5, w 12, n-b 2 | 20 |
| b N. M. K. Smith | 43 | | |
| A. N. Hayhurst not out | 91 | 1/21 2/35 3/41 | (7 wkts, 60 overs) 224 |
| M. N. Lathwell c Moles b Munton | 16 | 4/113 5/137 | |
| †N. D. Burns c Reeve b Donald | 1 | 6/152 7/157 | |

D. A. Graveney and J. C. Hallett did not bat.

Bowling: Donald 12–1–35–1; Small 12–2–26–2; Munton 12–3–42–2; Reeve 12–1–54–0; P. A. Smith 7–0–41–0; N. M. K. Smith 5–0–20–1.

Umpires: K. J. Lyons and B. J. Meyer.

## SEMI-FINALS

### SURREY v NORTHAMPTONSHIRE

At The Oval, August 14, 15. Surrey won by 7 runs. Toss: Surrey. The slow over-rate of both sides was the underlying cause of a crowd of more than 10,000 being deprived of a pulsating finish on the first day, and angry spectators, justified in expecting the tie to finish in one day, loudly let their feelings be known when, with the light deteriorating, Lamb, the Northamptonshire captain, called his batsmen off at 7.34 p.m. Northamptonshire, 187 for eight after 54 overs (K. M. Curran 38*, A. Walker 3*), needed another 22 runs to reach their second successive NatWest final. Earlier in the day Northamptonshire had bowled only 56 overs in the allotted time, and Surrey were several overs in arrears when play was called off. Once again Waqar Younis conjured a win for Surrey, his five wickets including the dismissal of Curran with his first ball on the second morning. However, Martin Bicknell, whose second crucial run-out in successive rounds settled the issue – a 25-yard throw to dismiss Walker – must have been a contender for the Man of the Match award. His 66 not out, a one-day best, lifted Surrey from 124 for seven to 208. At 164 for five Northamptonshire were still favourites, but Younis bowled Baptiste and Williams with fearsome straight deliveries to swing the tie towards Surrey.

*Man of the Match:* Waqar Younis.

## Surrey

| | | | |
|---|---|---|---|
| D. J. Bicknell run out | 21 | J. Boiling c Williams b Capel | 22 |
| J. D. Robinson c Ripley b Taylor | 0 | Waqar Younis b Walker | 4 |
| †A. J. Stewart c Larkins b Williams | 34 | A. J. Murphy not out | 1 |
| D. M. Ward b Capel | 34 | B 4, l-b 6, w 13 | 23 |
| G. P. Thorpe c Larkins b Taylor | 23 | | |
| M. A. Lynch lbw b Capel | 2 | 1/8 2/56 3/70 | (9 wkts, 60 overs) 208 |
| *I. A. Greig lbw b Williams | 8 | 4/70 5/72 6/91 | |
| M. P. Bicknell not out | 66 | 7/124 8/186 9/194 | |

Bowling: Walker 12–3–32–1; Taylor 12–3–37–2; Curran 8–2–21–0; Baptiste 7–0–48–0; Capel 9–0–26–3; Williams 12–1–34–2.

## Northamptonshire

| | | | |
|---|---|---|---|
| A. Fordham b Boiling | 29 | †D. Ripley b M. P. Bicknell | 3 |
| W. Larkins c Thorpe b Boiling | 31 | A. Walker run out | 11 |
| R. J. Bailey c Stewart b Waqar Younis | 5 | J. P. Taylor not out | 3 |
| *A. J. Lamb c Boiling b M. P. Bicknell | 24 | L-b 6, w 9, n-b 1 | 16 |
| D. J. Capel lbw b Waqar Younis | 6 | | |
| K. M. Curran c Lynch b Waqar Younis | 38 | 1/68 2/73 3/78 | (59.2 overs) 201 |
| E. A. E. Baptiste b Waqar Younis | 34 | 4/91 5/113 6/124 | |
| R. G. Williams b Waqar Younis | 1 | 7/166 8/174 9/187 | |

Bowling: Waqar Younis 12–2–40–5; M. P. Bicknell 12–0–45–2; Murphy 9.2–0–45–0; Robinson 4–1–15–0; Boiling 12–2–22–2; Lynch 10–1–28–0.

Umpires: B. Dudleston and J. H. Harris.

## WARWICKSHIRE v HAMPSHIRE

At Birmingham, August 14. Hampshire won by nine wickets. Toss: Warwickshire. Warwickshire's poor form of August resulted in a disappointingly one-sided game after the home side lost their last nine wickets for 106 and failed to bat out their full quota of overs. Only Asif Din and Reeve offered any resistance to a keen but far from devastating Hampshire attack, in which the combined spin of Udal and Maru played an essential role; their 24 overs cost just 50 runs. Hampshire's strong batting line-up was left with a comparatively easy task. Terry and Robin Smith tore the much vaunted Warwickshire bowling to pieces, and a crowd of 14,000 watched Hampshire win with embarrassing ease to qualify for their first 60-overs final, having lost seven previous semi-finals.

*Man of the Match:* V. P. Terry.

## Warwickshire

| | | | |
|---|---|---|---|
| A. J. Moles c Terry b Connor | 4 | G. C. Small c Aymes b Connor | 2 |
| Asif Din c Aymes b Maru | 44 | T. A. Munton b Aqib Javed | 5 |
| *T. A. Lloyd st Aymes b Udal | 18 | A. A. Donald c Nicholas b Aqib Javed | 1 |
| D. P. Ostler c Terry b James | 3 | B 1, l-b 8, w 6, n-b 8 | 23 |
| D. A. Reeve not out | 57 | | |
| N. M. K. Smith c Udal b Maru | 0 | 1/17 2/66 3/77 | (58.5 overs) 172 |
| P. A. Smith c Aymes b Connor | 14 | 4/94 5/96 6/124 | |
| †K. J. Piper c and b Connor | 1 | 7/128 8/134 9/170 | |

Bowling: Aqib Javed 11.5–1–34–2; Connor 12–2–29–4; James 11–0–50–1; Udal 12–3–30–1; Maru 12–5–20–2.

## Hampshire

| | |
|---|---|
| V. P. Terry not out | 62 |
| C. L. Smith c Reeve b N. M. K. Smith | 23 |
| R. A. Smith not out | 64 |
| B 6, l-b 11, w 5, n-b 2 | 24 |

1/63    (1 wkt, 50 overs) 173

D. I. Gower, *M. C. J. Nicholas, K. D. James, †A. N. Aymes, S. D. Udal, R. J. Maru, C. A. Connor and Aqib Javed did not bat.

Bowling: Donald 9–0–41–0; Small 9–2–32–0; Munton 9–1–26–0; Reeve 5.4–1–11–0; N. M. K. Smith 8–1–17–1; Asif Din 3–0–10–0; P. A. Smith 6.2–0–19–0.

Umpires: B. Leadbeater and A. G. T. Whitehead.

# FINAL

# HAMPSHIRE v SURREY

At Lord's, September 7. Hampshire won by four wickets. Toss: Hampshire. Smith was an undisputed choice by M. C. Cowdrey as Man of the Match, but Hampshire were equally indebted to Middleton and Ayling for the victory, with two balls to spare, which won them the NatWest Bank Trophy for the first time. Middleton, whose 78 came from 143 balls, saw off the early threat of Waqar Younis; and when the Pakistan fast bowler came back to complete his overs in fading light, Ayling proved equal to the task of getting Hampshire home. Smith, in his 78 from 94 balls, unleashed a series of powerful strokes; of his seven fours, a drive through extra-cover off Younis, late in the day, was a shot of the highest class. The 58th over of Hampshire's innings was the crucial one, bringing 14 runs after Hampshire had begun it needing 24 runs for victory – and ending with the dismissal of Smith. Ayling, who joined Smith when Gower and James were out in the 51st and 52nd overs, cracked Murphy high over gully for six and somehow got the ball past Greig at mid-on for four. However, there was jubilation for Surrey when Murphy, gathering a rebound off the stumps, threw down the wicket at the far end to run out the striker, Smith. Aymes was also run out, off the second ball of the last over, but two balls later Ayling won the match when he turned Martin Bicknell backward of square for four. His unbeaten 18 came off 26 balls, and adding 38 in six overs with Smith, he had helped put Hampshire back on course.

There was little in the pitch on a clear, sunny morning to assist the bowlers. But Surrey, put in, made a slow start against accurate bowling supported by some brilliant fielding. Gower, Terry and Smith were outstanding, and Gower led Hampshire well in the absence of Nicholas, whose little finger on his left hand had been broken two days earlier by Waqar Younis in a Championship match at The Oval. Surrey received an early setback when Robinson was struck on the helmet in the third over, and retired hurt, and they lost Darren Bicknell in the fifteenth over, bowled by Ayling. This meant that Stewart (123 balls, eight fours) and Thorpe (121 balls, ten fours) had to consolidate before eventually picking up the run-rate. At the halfway point Surrey had just 68 runs on the board. However, the left-handed Thorpe batted impressively, and Ward's 43 from 48 deliveries late in the innings almost put the game out of Hampshire's reach.

*Man of the Match:* R. A. Smith.    *Attendance:* 22,000 (excl. members); *receipts* £595,000.

## Surrey

| | | | |
|---|---|---|---|
| D. J. Bicknell b Ayling | 13 | *I. A. Greig not out | 7 |
| J. D. Robinson not out | 3 | B 2, l-b 4, w 3, n-b 1 | 10 |
| †A. J. Stewart b Ayling | 61 | | |
| G. P. Thorpe c James b Connor | 93 | 1/25 (1) 2/139 (3)    (5 wkts, 60 overs) 240 |
| D. M. Ward c Maru b Connor | 43 | 3/203 (4) 4/222 (5) |
| M. A. Lynch c Ayling b Connor | 10 | 5/233 (6) |

M. P. Bicknell, J. Boiling, Waqar Younis and A. J. Murphy did not bat.

J. D. Robinson, when 2, retired hurt at 5 and resumed at 233.

Bowling: Aqib Javed 12–2–54–0; Connor 12–4–39–3; Ayling 12–0–39–2; James 9–3–33–0; Maru 6–0–23–0; Udal 9–0–46–0.

## Hampshire

| | | | |
|---|---|---|---|
| V. P. Terry run out | 32 | R. J. Maru not out | 1 |
| T. C. Middleton b Murphy | 78 | | |
| R. A. Smith run out | 78 | L-b 17, w 5, n-b 3 | 25 |
| *D. I. Gower lbw b Waqar Younis | 9 | | |
| K. D. James c Stewart b M. P. Bicknell | 0 | 1/90 (1) 2/160 (2)    (6 wkts, 59.4 overs) 243 | |
| J. R. Ayling not out | 18 | 3/192 (4) 4/193 (5) | |
| †A. N. Aymes run out | 2 | 5/231 (3) 6/238 (7) | |

S. D. Udal, C. A. Connor and Aqib Javed did not bat.

Bowling: Waqar Younis 12–0–43–1; M. P. Bicknell 11.4–1–32–1; Murphy 12–0–56–1; Robinson 12–0–43–0; Boiling 12–1–52–0.

Umpires: M. J. Kitchen and K. E. Palmer.


# NATWEST BANK TROPHY RECORDS

### (Including Gillette Cup, 1963-80)

## Batting

**Highest individual scores:** 206, A. I. Kallicharran, Warwickshire v Oxfordshire, Birmingham, 1984; 177, C. G. Greenidge, Hampshire v Glamorgan, Southampton, 1975; 172*, G. A. Hick, Worcestershire v Devon, Worcester, 1987; 165*, V. P. Terry, Hampshire v Berkshire, Southampton, 1985; 162*, C. J. Tavaré, Somerset v Devon, Torquay, 1990; 159, C. L. Smith, Hampshire v Cheshire, Chester, 1989; 158, G. D. Barlow, Middlesex v Lancashire, Lord's, 1984; 158, Zaheer Abbas, Gloucestershire v Leicestershire, Leicester, 1983; 156, D. I. Gower, Leicestershire v Derbyshire, Leicester, 1984; 155, J. J. Whitaker, Leicestershire v Wiltshire, Swindon, 1984; 154*, H. Morris, Glamorgan v Staffordshire, Cardiff, 1989; 154, P. Willey, Leicestershire v Hampshire, Leicester, 1987; 153, A. Hill, Derbyshire v Cornwall, Derby, 1986; 151*, M. P. Maynard, Glamorgan v Durham, Darlington, 1991. (93 hundreds were scored in the Gillette Cup; 105 hundreds have been scored in the NatWest Bank Trophy.)

**Most runs:** 2,022, G. A. Gooch; 1,950, D. L. Amiss.

**Fastest hundred:** G. D. Rose off 36 balls, Somerset v Devon, Torquay, 1990.

**Most hundreds:** 7, C. L. Smith; 5, D. I. Gower and G. M. Turner.

**Highest innings totals** (off 60 overs): 413 for four, Somerset v Devon, Torquay, 1990; 404 for three, Worcestershire v Devon, Worcester, 1987; 392 for five, Warwickshire v Oxfordshire, Birmingham, 1984; 386 for five, Essex v Wiltshire, Chelmsford, 1988; 372 for five, Lancashire v Gloucestershire, Manchester, 1990; 371 for four, Hampshire v Glamorgan, Southampton, 1975; 365 for three, Derbyshire v Cornwall, Derby, 1986; 360 for two, Northamptonshire v Staffordshire, Northampton, 1990; 359 for four, Kent v Dorset, Canterbury, 1989; 354 for seven, Leicestershire v Wiltshire, Swindon, 1984; 349 for six, Lancashire v Gloucestershire, Bristol, 1984; 345 for two, Glamorgan v Durham, Darlington, 1991; 341 for six, Leicestershire v Hampshire, Leicester, 1987; 339 for four, Hampshire v Berkshire, Southampton, 1985; 336 for five, Worcestershire v Cumberland, Worcester, 1988; 336 for seven, Warwickshire v Hertfordshire, St Albans, 1990; 330 for four, Somerset v Glamorgan, Cardiff, 1978. *In the final:* 317 for four, Yorkshire v Surrey, 1965.

**Highest innings total by a minor county:** 305 for nine, Durham v Glamorgan, Darlington, 1991.

**Highest innings by a side batting first and losing:** 307 for six (60 overs), Essex v Hampshire, Chelmsford, 1990. *In the final:* 242 for eight (60 overs), Lancashire v Sussex, 1986.

**Highest totals by a side batting second:** 326 for nine (60 overs), Hampshire v Leicestershire, Leicester, 1987; 307 for five (60 overs), Hampshire v Essex, Chelmsford, 1990; 306 for six (59.3 overs), Gloucestershire v Leicestershire, Leicester, 1983; 305 for nine (60 overs), Durham v Glamorgan, Darlington, 1991; 298 (59 overs), Lancashire v Worcestershire, Manchester, 1985; 297 for four (57.1 overs), Somerset v Warwickshire, Taunton, 1978; 296 for four (58 overs), Kent v Surrey, Canterbury, 1985; 290 for seven (59.3 overs), Yorkshire v Worcestershire, Leeds, 1982; 287 for six (59 overs), Warwickshire v Glamorgan, Birmingham, 1976; 287 (60 overs), Essex v Somerset, Taunton, 1978; 282 for nine (60 overs), Leicestershire v Gloucestershire, Leicester, 1975. *In the final:* 279 for five (60 overs), Nottinghamshire v Essex, 1985.

**Highest total by a side batting second and winning:** 307 for five (60 overs), Hampshire v Essex, Chelmsford, 1990. *In the final:* 243 for three (58.2 overs), Sussex v Lancashire, 1986; 243 for six (59.4 overs), Hampshire v Surrey, 1991.

**Highest total by a side batting second and losing:** 326 for nine (60 overs), Hampshire v Leicestershire, Leicester, 1987.

**Lowest innings in the final at Lord's:** 118 (60 overs), Lancashire v Kent, 1974.

**Lowest completed innings totals:** 39 (26.4 overs), Ireland v Sussex, Hove, 1985; 41 (20 overs), Cambridgeshire v Buckinghamshire, Cambridge, 1972; 41 (19.4 overs), Middlesex v Essex, Westcliff, 1972; 41 (36.1 overs), Shropshire v Essex, Wellington, 1974.

**Lowest total by a side batting first and winning:** 98 (56.2 overs), Worcestershire v Durham, Chester-le-Street, 1968.

**Shortest innings:** 10.1 overs (60 for one), Worcestershire v Lancashire, Worcester, 1963.

*Matches re-arranged on a reduced number of overs are excluded from the above.*

**Record partnerships for each wicket**

| | | | |
|---|---|---|---|
| 242* | for 1st | M. D. Moxon and A. A. Metcalfe, Yorkshire v Warwickshire at Leeds | 1990 |
| 286 | for 2nd | I. S. Anderson and A. Hill, Derbyshire v Cornwall at Derby . . . . . . | 1986 |
| 259* | for 3rd | H. Morris and M. P. Maynard, Glamorgan v Durham at Darlington | 1991 |
| 234* | for 4th | D. Lloyd and C. H. Lloyd, Lancashire v Gloucestershire at Manchester | 1978 |
| 166 | for 5th | M. A. Lynch and G. R. J. Roope, Surrey v Durham at The Oval . . | 1982 |
| 105 | for 6th | G. S. Sobers and R. A. White, Nottinghamshire v Worcestershire at Worcester . . . . . . . . . . . . . . . . . . . . . . . . . . . . . . . . . . . . . . . . . | 1974 |
| 160* | for 7th | C. J. Richards and I. R. Payne, Surrey v Lincolnshire at Sleaford . . | 1983 |
| 83 | for 8th | S. N. V. Waterton and D. A. Hale, Oxfordshire v Gloucestershire at Oxford . . . . . . . . . . . . . . . . . . . . . . . . . . . . . . . . . . . . . . . . . . . | 1989 |
| 87 | for 9th | M. A. Nash and A. E. Cordle, Glamorgan v Lincolnshire at Swansea | 1974 |
| 81 | for 10th | S. Turner and R. E. East, Essex v Yorkshire at Leeds . . . . . . . . . . . | 1982 |

## Bowling

**Most wickets:** 81, G. G. Arnold; 79, J. Simmons.

**Hat-tricks (7):** J. D. F. Larter, Northamptonshire v Sussex, Northampton, 1963; D. A. D. Sydenham, Surrey v Cheshire, Hoylake, 1964; R. N. S. Hobbs, Essex v Middlesex, Lord's, 1968; N. M. McVicker, Warwickshire v Lincolnshire, Birmingham, 1971; G. S. le Roux, Sussex v Ireland, Hove, 1985; M. Jean-Jacques, Derbyshire v Nottinghamshire, Derby, 1987; J. F. M. O'Brien, Cheshire v Derbyshire, Chester, 1988.

**Four wickets in five balls:** D. A. D. Sydenham, Surrey v Cheshire, Hoylake, 1964.

**Best bowling** (12 overs unless stated): eight for 21 (10.1 overs), M. A. Holding, Derbyshire v Sussex, Hove, 1988; eight for 31 (11.1 overs), D. L. Underwood, Kent v Scotland, Edinburgh, 1987; seven for 15, A. L. Dixon, Kent v Surrey, The Oval, 1967; seven for 15 (9.3 overs), R. P. Lefebvre, Somerset v Devon, Torquay, 1990; seven for 19, N. V. Radford, Worcestershire v Bedfordshire, Bedford, 1991; seven for 30, P. J. Sainsbury, Hampshire v Norfolk, Southampton, 1965; seven for 32, S. P. Davis, Durham v Lancashire, Chester-le-Street, 1983; seven for 33, R. D. Jackman, Surrey v Yorkshire, Harrogate, 1970; seven for 37, N. A. Mallender, Northamptonshire v Worcestershire, Northampton, 1984.

**Most economical analysis:** 12–9–3–1, J. Simmons, Lancashire v Suffolk, Bury St Edmunds, 1985.

**Most expensive analysis:** 12–0–106–2, D. A. Gallop, Oxfordshire v Warwickshire, Birmingham, 1984.

## Wicket-keeping and Fielding

**Most dismissals:** 66 (58 ct, 8 st), R. W. Taylor; 65 (59 ct, 6 st), A. P. E. Knott.

**Most dismissals in an innings:** 6 (5 ct, 1 st), R. W. Taylor, Derbyshire v Essex, Derby, 1981; 6 (4 ct, 2 st), T. Davies, Glamorgan v Staffordshire, Stone, 1986.

**Most catches by a fielder:** 26, J. Simmons; 24, G. Cook and P. J. Sharpe.

**Most catches by a fielder in an innings:** 4 – A. S. Brown, Gloucestershire v Middlesex, Bristol, 1963; G. Cook, Northamptonshire v Glamorgan, Northampton, 1972; C. G. Greenidge, Hampshire v Cheshire, Southampton, 1981; D. C. Jackson, Durham v Northamptonshire, Darlington, 1984; T. S. Smith, Hertfordshire v Somerset, St Albans, 1984; H. Morris, Glamorgan v Scotland, Edinburgh, 1988.

## Results

**Largest victories in runs:** Somerset by 346 runs v Devon, Torquay, 1990; Worcestershire by 299 runs v Devon, Worcester, 1987; Essex by 291 runs v Wiltshire, Chelmsford, 1988; Sussex by 244 runs v Ireland, Hove, 1985; Lancashire by 241 runs v Gloucestershire, Manchester, 1990; Warwickshire by 227 runs v Oxfordshire, Birmingham, 1984; Essex by 226 runs v Oxfordshire, Chelmsford, 1985; Northamptonshire by 216 runs v Staffordshire, Northampton, 1990; Leicestershire by 214 runs v Staffordshire, Longton, 1975; Hampshire by 209 runs v Dorset, Southampton, 1987; Derbyshire by 204 runs v Cornwall, Derby, 1986; Warwickshire by 201 runs v Buckinghamshire, Birmingham, 1987; Sussex by 200 runs v Durham, Hove, 1964. *In the final:* 175 runs, Yorkshire v Surrey, Lord's, 1965.

**Victories by ten wickets (11):** Northamptonshire v Leicestershire, Leicester, 1964; Warwickshire v Cambridgeshire, Birmingham, 1965; Sussex v Derbyshire, Hove, 1968; Hampshire v Nottinghamshire, Southampton, 1977; Middlesex v Worcestershire, Worcester, 1980; Yorkshire v Cheshire, Birkenhead, 1985; Yorkshire v Berkshire, Finchampstead, 1988; Yorkshire v Norfolk, Leeds, 1990; Yorkshire v Warwickshire, Leeds, 1990; Hampshire v Berkshire, Reading, 1991; Warwickshire v Hertfordshire, Birmingham, 1991.

**Earliest finishes:** both at 2.20 p.m. Worcestershire beat Lancashire by nine wickets at Worcester, 1963; Essex beat Middlesex by eight wickets at Westcliff, 1972.

**Scores level (9):** Nottinghamshire 215, Somerset 215 for nine at Taunton, 1964; Surrey 196, Sussex 196 for eight at The Oval, 1970; Somerset 287 for six, Essex 287 at Taunton, 1978; Surrey 195 for seven, Essex 195 at Chelmsford, 1980; Essex 149, Derbyshire 149 for eight at Derby, 1981; Northamptonshire 235 for nine, Derbyshire 235 for six in the final at Lord's, 1981; Middlesex 222 for nine, Somerset 222 for eight at Lord's, 1983; Hampshire 224 for eight, Essex 224 for seven at Southampton, 1985; Essex 307 for six, Hampshire 307 for five at Chelmsford, 1990. Under the rules the side which lost fewer wickets won.

**Wins by a minor county over a first-class county (8):** Durham v Yorkshire (by five wickets), Harrogate, 1973; Lincolnshire v Glamorgan (by six wickets), Swansea, 1974; Hertfordshire v Essex (by 33 runs), 2nd round, Hitchin, 1976; Shropshire v Yorkshire (by 37 runs), Telford, 1984; Durham v Derbyshire (by seven wickets), Derby, 1985; Buckinghamshire v Somerset (by 7 runs), High Wycombe, 1987; Cheshire v Northamptonshire (by one wicket), Chester, 1988; Hertfordshire v Derbyshire (2–1 in a bowling contest after the match was abandoned), Bishop's Stortford, 1991.

# WINNERS

## Gillette Cup

1963 SUSSEX beat Worcestershire by 14 runs.
1964 SUSSEX beat Warwickshire by eight wickets.
1965 YORKSHIRE beat Surrey by 175 runs.
1966 WARWICKSHIRE beat Worcestershire by five wickets.
1967 KENT beat Somerset by 32 runs.
1968 WARWICKSHIRE beat Sussex by four wickets.
1969 YORKSHIRE beat Derbyshire by 69 runs.
1970 LANCASHIRE beat Sussex by six wickets.
1971 LANCASHIRE beat Kent by 24 runs.
1972 LANCASHIRE beat Warwickshire by four wickets.
1973 GLOUCESTERSHIRE beat Sussex by 40 runs.
1974 KENT beat Lancashire by four wickets.
1975 LANCASHIRE beat Middlesex by seven wickets.
1976 NORTHAMPTONSHIRE beat Lancashire by four wickets.
1977 MIDDLESEX beat Glamorgan by five wickets.
1978 SUSSEX beat Somerset by five wickets.
1979 SOMERSET beat Northamptonshire by 45 runs.
1980 MIDDLESEX beat Surrey by seven wickets.

## NatWest Bank Trophy

1981 DERBYSHIRE beat Northamptonshire by losing fewer wickets with the scores level.
1982 SURREY beat Warwickshire by nine wickets.
1983 SOMERSET beat Kent by 24 runs.
1984 MIDDLESEX beat Kent by four wickets.
1985 ESSEX beat Nottinghamshire by 1 run.
1986 SUSSEX beat Lancashire by seven wickets.
1987 NOTTINGHAMSHIRE beat Northamptonshire by three wickets.
1988 MIDDLESEX beat Worcestershire by three wickets.
1989 WARWICKSHIRE beat Middlesex by four wickets.
1990 LANCASHIRE beat Northamptonshire by seven wickets.
1991 HAMPSHIRE beat Surrey by four wickets.

# BENSON AND HEDGES CUP, 1991

Worcestershire, losing finalists in their six previous visits to Lord's, put the record right by winning the Benson and Hedges Cup at their fourth attempt. The 1991 final brought together the 1990 finalists, but whereas Lancashire had won the previous year by 69 runs, in 1991 Worcestershire triumphed over the holders by 65 runs. For only the second time in the twenty years of the competition, the final went into a second day, providing the first instance of Sunday play in a final at Lord's. Both finalists had played their Sunday League fixtures earlier in anticipation of this contingency.

The total prizemoney in 1991 was £105,650, an increase of £8,750 from 1990. Worcestershire won £26,500 in prizemoney, in addition to the Benson and Hedges Cup, while the runners-up, Lancashire, received £13,000. Essex and Yorkshire, the losing semi-finalists, each received £6,500, while the losing quarter-finalists, Hampshire, Kent, Northamptonshire and Warwickshire, received £3,250 each. The winners of each group match won £800. Gold Award winners, in addition to a gold medallion, received £150 in the group matches, £250 in the quarter-finals, £300 in the semi-finals and £550 in the final.

Benson and Hedges increased their total sponsorship to the TCCB in 1991 by £50,540 to £571,571.

## FINAL GROUP TABLE

| | Played | Won | Lost | Pts | Run-rate |
|---|---|---|---|---|---|
| *Group A* | | | | | |
| WORCESTERSHIRE | 4 | 3 | 1 | 6 | 64.67 |
| NORTHAMPTONSHIRE | 4 | 3 | 1 | 6 | 63.57 |
| Derbyshire | 4 | 2 | 2 | 4 | 71.06 |
| Gloucestershire | 4 | 2 | 2 | 4 | 56.60 |
| Combined Universities | 4 | 0 | 4 | 0 | 43.71 |
| *Group B* | | | | | |
| ESSEX | 4 | 4 | 0 | 8 | 79.74 |
| WARWICKSHIRE | 4 | 3 | 1 | 6 | 77.19 |
| Somerset | 4 | 1 | 3 | 2 | 68.54 |
| Surrey | 4 | 1 | 3 | 2 | 65.90 |
| Middlesex | 4 | 1 | 3 | 2 | 59.79 |
| *Group C* | | | | | |
| LANCASHIRE | 4 | 4 | 0 | 8 | 74.13 |
| KENT | 4 | 3 | 1 | 6 | 76.25 |
| Sussex | 4 | 2 | 2 | 4 | 69.24 |
| Leicestershire | 4 | 1 | 3 | 2 | 64.31 |
| Scotland | 4 | 0 | 4 | 0 | 58.48 |
| *Group D* | | | | | |
| YORKSHIRE | 4 | 3 | 1 | 6 | 70.17 |
| HAMPSHIRE | 4 | 3 | 1 | 6 | 64.23 |
| Nottinghamshire | 4 | 2 | 2 | 4 | 76.13 |
| Glamorgan | 4 | 2 | 2 | 4 | 70.98 |
| Minor Counties | 4 | 0 | 4 | 0 | 63.63 |

*The top two teams in each group qualified for the quarter-finals.*
*Where two or more teams finished with the same number of points, the position in the group was based on run-rate.*

## GROUP A

The Combined Universities' squad of thirteen named for the competition was: N. V. Knight (Loughborough) *(captain)*, J. P. Crawley (Cambridge), I. Fletcher (Loughborough), J. C. Hallett (Durham), A. R. Hansford (Surrey), P. C. L. Holloway (Loughborough), R. H. J. Jenkins (Cambridge), J. I. Longley (Durham), R. H. Macdonald (Oxford), R. E. Morris (Oxford), T. Parker (Swansea), P. J. Rendall (Loughborough) and G. J. Turner (Oxford). R. M. Pearson (Cambridge) was added to the squad subsequently.

## DERBYSHIRE v NORTHAMPTONSHIRE

At Derby, April 23. Northamptonshire won by 66 runs. Toss: Derbyshire. Northamptonshire scored only 14 in the first hour. Thomas took five wickets for the first time in the competition, including three wickets for no runs in eight balls, while Capel took his four wickets for 9 runs in 23 balls.

*Gold Award:* J. G. Thomas.

### Northamptonshire

| | | | | |
|---|---|---|---|---|
| A. Fordham c Bowler b Mortensen | .... 1 | E. A. E. Baptiste not out | ............... | 15 |
| N. A. Felton c Barnett b Base | ........ 23 | J. G. Thomas not out | ............... | 4 |
| R. J. Bailey c Morris b Mortensen | .... 38 | B 1, l-b 6, w 7 | ............. | 14 |
| *A. J. Lamb c Azharuddin b Malcolm | .. 45 | | | |
| D. J. Capel c Roberts b Base | ........ 3 | 1/4 2/43 3/93 | (7 wkts, 55 overs) | 191 |
| K. M. Curran b Warner | ............ 26 | 4/108 5/134 | | |
| R. G. Williams c Azharuddin b Barnett | 22 | 6/156 7/181 | | |

†D. Ripley and J. P. Taylor did not bat.

Bowling: Mortensen 11–5–16–2; Warner 11–4–25–1; Base 11–0–40–2; Malcolm 11–1–42–1; Roberts 4–0–26–0; Barnett 7–1–35–1.

### Derbyshire

| | | | | |
|---|---|---|---|---|
| *K. J. Barnett c Ripley b Thomas | ..... 6 | D. E. Malcolm c Williams b Thomas | .. | 14 |
| †P. D. Bowler c Ripley b Thomas | ..... 5 | S. J. Base b Capel | ................. | 7 |
| J. E. Morris c Felton b Thomas | ....... 0 | O. H. Mortensen not out | ............ | 4 |
| M. Azharuddin b Capel | ............. 29 | L-b 4, w 5 | | 9 |
| B. Roberts c Ripley b Thomas | ........ 2 | | | |
| T. J. G. O'Gorman c Capel | ......... 49 | 1/12 2/12 3/13 | (38.3 overs) | 125 |
| C. J. Adams b Taylor | .............. 0 | 4/20 5/96 6/97 | | |
| A. E. Warner c Bailey b Capel | ....... 0 | 7/98 8/98 9/110 | | |

Bowling: Thomas 9.3–1–29–5; Taylor 11–3–14–1; Curran 3–0–15–0; Capel 11–1–37–4; Baptiste 4–0–26–0.

Umpires: H. D. Bird and B. Hassan.

## GLOUCESTERSHIRE v COMBINED UNIVERSITIES

At Bristol, April 23. Gloucestershire won by 66 runs. Toss: Gloucestershire. Macdonald's six for 36 on his Benson and Hedges début, the best bowling analysis from a university player in the competition, gave his team a realistic target of 150. They reached 50 without loss before Lawrence took six wickets for 8 runs in a six-over spell; all ten wickets were lost for 33 runs.

*Gold Award:* D. V. Lawrence.

## Gloucestershire

| | | | | |
|---|---|---|---|---|
| G. D. Hodgson c Knight b Hallett | 7 | D. R. Gilbert c Holloway b Macdonald | 1 |
| R. J. Scott c Holloway b Macdonald | 29 | A. M. Smith run out | 8 |
| *A. J. Wright c Crawley b Macdonald | 13 | A. M. Babington not out | 1 |
| C. W. J. Athey c Holloway b Macdonald | 0 | B 3, l-b 4, w 9, n-b 1 | 17 |
| M. W. Alleyne b Macdonald | 6 | | |
| J. W. Lloyds c Knight b Turner | 19 | 1/13 2/49 3/50 | (50.5 overs) 149 |
| †R. C. Russell c Jenkins b Turner | 25 | 4/59 5/66 6/96 | |
| D. V. Lawrence c Knight b Macdonald | 23 | 7/132 8/133 9/141 | |

Bowling: Hansford 8.5–1–21–0; Hallett 11–0–32–1; Macdonald 10–1–36–6; Jenkins 11–1–35–0; Turner 10–2–18–2.

## Combined Universities

| | | | | |
|---|---|---|---|---|
| R. E. Morris c Lloyds b Lawrence | 19 | J. C. Hallett b Lloyds | 0 |
| *N. V. Knight c Alleyne b Lawrence | 36 | A. R. Hansford b Lloyds | 0 |
| J. P. Crawley b Lawrence | 0 | R. H. J. Jenkins not out | 0 |
| J. I. Longley lbw b Lawrence | 1 | L-b 4, w 6, n-b 4 | 14 |
| G. J. Turner c Russell b Gilbert | 8 | | |
| †P. C. L. Holloway b Lawrence | 0 | 1/50 2/53 3/60 | (38 overs) 83 |
| P. J. Rendall b Lawrence | 0 | 4/67 5/69 6/69 | |
| R. H. Macdonald c Smith b Lloyds | 5 | 7/76 8/80 9/80 | |

Bowling: Gilbert 11–2–34–1; Lawrence 11–3–20–6; Babington 7–3–11–0; Lloyds 9–2–14–3.

Umpires: G. I. Burgess and K. J. Lyons.

## COMBINED UNIVERSITIES v DERBYSHIRE

At Oxford, April 25. Derbyshire won by 206 runs. Toss: Derbyshire. The county's total was a record for the Benson and Hedges Cup, passing Essex's 350 for three against Oxford & Cambridge Universities at Chelmsford in 1979. Morris scored 71 from 47 balls, hitting ten fours and a six. In Combined Universities' innings all the Derbyshire players bowled, apart from Bowler.

*Gold Award:* P. D. Bowler.

## Derbyshire

| | | | | |
|---|---|---|---|---|
| *K. J. Barnett c Hallett b Turner | 82 | A. E. Warner not out | 35 |
| †P. D. Bowler c Rendall b Jenkins | 100 | L-b 4, w 4, n-b 11 | 19 |
| J. E. Morris c Knight b Rendall | 71 | | |
| M. Azharuddin not out | 44 | 1/177 2/231 | (4 wkts, 55 overs) 366 |
| D. E. Malcolm b Hansford | 15 | 3/278 4/302 | |

B. Roberts, T. J. G. O'Gorman, C. J. Adams, S. J. Base and O. H. Mortensen did not bat.

Bowling: Hansford 11–2–55–1; Hallett 11–0–43–0; Turner 11–0–61–1; Jenkins 7–0–58–1; Rendall 6–0–55–1; Macdonald 9–0–90–0.

## Combined Universities

| | | | | |
|---|---|---|---|---|
| *N. V. Knight b Mortensen | 5 | P. J. Rendall c Bowler b Roberts | 8 |
| R. E. Morris c Roberts b Mortensen | 12 | R. H. Macdonald not out | 1 |
| J. P. Crawley c Adams b Malcolm | 18 | | |
| J. I. Longley c Bowler b Malcolm | 6 | B 3, l-b 3, w 6, n-b 1 | 13 |
| G. J. Turner not out | 70 | | |
| †P. C. L. Holloway c Azharuddin b Barnett | 27 | 1/19 2/20 3/37 | (6 wkts, 55 overs) 160 |
| | | 4/66 5/121 6/147 | |

J. C. Hallett, A. R. Hansford and R. H. J. Jenkins did not bat.

Bowling: Mortensen 7–2–16–2; Warner 6–2–14–0; Base 5–0–24–0; Malcolm 6–1–14–2; Azharuddin 11–0–29–0; Barnett 11–2–28–1; Morris 4–0–14–0; Roberts 3–1–11–1; Adams 1–0–3–0; O'Gorman 1–0–1–0.

Umpires: J. H. Harris and P. B. Wight.

## WORCESTERSHIRE v GLOUCESTERSHIRE

At Worcester, April 25, 26. Worcestershire won by six wickets. Toss: Worcestershire. Close of play: Worcestershire 60-1 (19 overs) (T. S. Curtis 21*, G. A. Hick 12*).
*Gold Award:* S. R. Lampitt.

### Gloucestershire

| | | | | |
|---|---|---|---|---|
| G. D. Hodgson c D'Oliveira b Newport | 9 | D. R. Gilbert c Curtis b Lampitt | 16 |
| R. J. Scott c Curtis b Radford | 10 | A. M. Smith not out | 3 |
| *A. J. Wright c Rhodes b Moody | 36 | A. M. Babington c Moody b Lampitt | 8 |
| C. W. J. Athey c Hick b Lampitt | 5 | B 1, l-b 9, w 8, n-b 7 | 25 |
| M. W. Alleyne c Hick b Lampitt | 0 | | |
| J. W. Lloyds c Lampitt b Moody | 24 | 1/17 2/32 3/52 (54.1 overs) | 197 |
| †R. C. Russell c Newport b Radford | 51 | 4/52 5/98 6/120 | |
| D. V. Lawrence c Hick b Radford | 10 | 7/145 8/181 9/186 | |

Bowling: Radford 11–2–40–3; Newport 11–1–30–1; Lampitt 10.1–2–46–4; Botham 11–1–28–0; Moody 6–0–22–2; Illingworth 5–0–21–0.

### Worcestershire

| | | | | |
|---|---|---|---|---|
| T. S. Curtis c Russell b Smith | 36 | I. T. Botham not out | 18 |
| T. M. Moody c Lloyds b Lawrence | 21 | L-b 9, w 1, n-b 3 | 13 |
| G. A. Hick b Lawrence | 56 | | |
| D. B. D'Oliveira c Hodgson b Scott | 24 | 1/39 2/105 (4 wkts, 53.5 overs) | 198 |
| *P. A. Neale not out | 48 | 3/114 4/140 | |

†S. J. Rhodes, P. J. Newport, R. K. Illingworth, S. R. Lampitt and N. V. Radford did not bat.

Bowling: Gilbert 11–0–36–0; Lawrence 11–3–35–2; Babington 11–3–27–0; Smith 11–2–30–1; Scott 7.5–0–42–1; Alleyne 2–0–19–0.

Umpires: A. A. Jones and N. T. Plews.

## COMBINED UNIVERSITIES v WORCESTERSHIRE

At Cambridge, May 2. Worcestershire won by six wickets. Toss: Worcestershire. Combined Universities lost three wickets in eight balls after reaching 16 without loss by their fifth over. Moody's maiden fifty in the competition came from 58 balls.
*Gold Award:* T. M. Moody.

### Combined Universities

| | | | | |
|---|---|---|---|---|
| R. E. Morris c Rhodes b Radford | 6 | J. C. Hallett c Botham b Newport | 5 |
| *N. V. Knight lbw b Radford | 9 | R. H. J. Jenkins c Rhodes b Radford | 9 |
| J. P. Crawley lbw b Botham | 0 | A. R. Hansford not out | 13 |
| J. I. Longley run out | 47 | L-b 7, w 3, n-b 3 | 13 |
| G. J. Turner c D'Oliveira b Newport | 12 | | |
| †P. C. L. Holloway c D'Oliveira b Lampitt | 22 | 1/16 2/17 3/17 (8 wkts, 55 overs) | 148 |
| | | 4/33 5/92 6/113 | |
| R. H. Macdonald not out | 12 | 7/118 8/131 | |

R. M. Pearson did not bat.

Bowling: Radford 11–5–22–3; Botham 11–5–26–1; Illingworth 11–1–28–0; Lampitt 11–1–29–1; Newport 11–2–36–2.

### Worcestershire

| | | | | |
|---|---|---|---|---|
| T. S. Curtis c Jenkins b Macdonald | 2 | I. T. Botham not out | 16 |
| T. M. Moody c Longley b Hallett | 50 | L-b 4, w 6 | 10 |
| G. A. Hick lbw b Hallett | 55 | | |
| D. B. D'Oliveira b Hallett | 8 | 1/9 2/104 (4 wkts, 32.1 overs) | 149 |
| *P. A. Neale not out | 8 | 3/116 4/128 | |

P. J. Newport, †S. J. Rhodes, R. K. Illingworth, S. R. Lampitt and N. V. Radford did not bat.

Bowling: Hansford 6–0–31–0; Macdonald 6–0–31–1; Pearson 6–0–24–0; Hallett 10.1–0–36–3; Jenkins 4–0–23–0.

Umpires: J. D. Bond and B. Hassan.

## GLOUCESTERSHIRE v NORTHAMPTONSHIRE

At Bristol, May 2. Gloucestershire won by seven wickets. Toss: Gloucestershire. Lawrence took three wickets for 2 runs in seventeen balls to reduce Northamptonshire to 44 for four.
*Gold Award:* A. J. Wright.

### Northamptonshire

| | | |
|---|---|---|
| A. Fordham lbw b Gilbert | 0 | J. G. Thomas c Athey b Lawrence .... 3 |
| N. A. Felton c Russell b Lawrence | 22 | N. G. B. Cook run out .............. 1 |
| R. J. Bailey c Athey b Lawrence | 15 | J. P. Taylor not out ............... 1 |
| *A. J. Lamb b Lawrence | 0 | B 1, l-b 5, w 3, n-b 1 ........ 10 |
| D. J. Capel run out | 42 | |
| R. G. Williams c and b Alleyne | 29 | 1/0 2/36 3/40    (9 wkts, 55 overs) 170 |
| E. A. E. Baptiste c and b Babington | 11 | 4/44 5/92 6/110 |
| †D. Ripley not out | 36 | 7/138 8/147 9/158 |

Bowling: Gilbert 11–1–31–1; Babington 11–3–24–1; Lawrence 11–1–44–4; Smith 11–0–26–0; Scott 3–0–15–0; Alleyne 8–0–24–1.

### Gloucestershire

| | | |
|---|---|---|
| G. D. Hodgson c Taylor b Thomas | 3 | †R. C. Russell not out .............. 0 |
| R. J. Scott st Ripley b Williams | 46 | L-b 10, w 9 ................. 19 |
| *A. J. Wright c Lamb b Taylor | 81 | |
| C. W. J. Athey not out | 22 | 1/10 2/86 3/165    (3 wkts, 53.1 overs) 171 |

M. W. Alleyne, J. W. Lloyds, D. V. Lawrence, D. R. Gilbert, A. M. Smith and A. M. Babington did not bat.

Bowling: Thomas 10–3–22–1; Taylor 11–3–25–1; Baptiste 6.1–0–38–0; Capel 11–1–29–0; Cook 4–1–16–0; Williams 11–2–31–1.

Umpires: R. Julian and A. G. T. Whitehead.

## NORTHAMPTONSHIRE v COMBINED UNIVERSITIES

At Northampton, May 4. Northamptonshire won by six wickets. Toss: Combined Universities. The first 25 overs of Combined Universities' innings included ten maidens, but the final ten yielded 71 runs. Turner faced 76 balls and struck three fours and a six; he registered his highest score in the competition, as did Crawley and Fordham.
*Gold Award:* A. Fordham.

### Combined Universities

| | | |
|---|---|---|
| R. E. Morris b Penberthy | 7 | †P. C. L. Holloway run out ......... 10 |
| *N. V. Knight c Ripley b Penberthy | 12 | |
| J. P. Crawley c Ripley b Thomas | 40 | B 1, l-b 8, w 8, n-b 2 ........ 19 |
| J. I. Longley run out | 9 | |
| G. J. Turner not out | 80 | 1/22 2/23 3/49    (6 wkts, 55 overs) 186 |
| I. Fletcher c Ripley b Williams | 9 | 4/106 5/142 6/186 |

R. H. Macdonald, J. C. Hallett, A. R. Hansford and R. H. J. Jenkins did not bat.

Bowling: Thomas 11–1–30–1; Baptiste 10–3–24–0; Taylor 10–3–37–0; Penberthy 9–3–22–2; Capel 4–0–20–0; Williams 11–0–44–1.

## Northamptonshire

| | | | | |
|---|---|---|---|---|
| A. Fordham not out | 93 | R. G. Williams not out | | 17 |
| N. A. Felton c Fletcher b Hallett | 20 | L-b 2, w 7, n-b 2 | | 11 |
| R. J. Bailey c Holloway b Hallett | 1 | | | — |
| *A. J. Lamb c Knight b Macdonald | 34 | 1/54  2/56 | (4 wkts, 43.4 overs) | 187 |
| D. J. Capel run out | 11 | 3/122  4/135 | | |

E. A. E. Baptiste, †D. Ripley, J. G. Thomas, A. L. Penberthy and J. P. Taylor did not bat.

Bowling: Hansford 7–0–18–0; Hallett 11–0–38–2; Macdonald 11–0–59–1; Turner 9.4–2–41–0; Jenkins 4–0–25–0; Knight 1–0–4–0.

Umpires: A. A. Jones and K. E. Palmer.

## WORCESTERSHIRE v DERBYSHIRE

At Worcester, May 4. Worcestershire won by seven wickets. Toss: Worcestershire. Moody reached his maiden hundred in the Benson and Hedges Cup from 128 balls, hitting nine fours, and in all he received 139 balls. He added 101 in eighteen overs with Botham.

*Gold Award:* T. M. Moody.

## Derbyshire

| | | | | |
|---|---|---|---|---|
| *K. J. Barnett c Radford b Lampitt | 66 | D. E. Malcolm b Lampitt | | 8 |
| †P. D. Bowler c Hick b Radford | 29 | S. J. Base run out | | 1 |
| J. E. Morris b Lampitt | 18 | O. H. Mortensen lbw b Radford | | 2 |
| M. Azharuddin run out | 30 | L-b 8, w 1, n-b 10 | | 19 |
| B. Roberts c Newport b Dilley | 24 | | | — |
| T. J. G. O'Gorman lbw b Newport | 4 | 1/73  2/104  3/133 | (53 overs) | 223 |
| C. J. Adams not out | 16 | 4/176  5/188  6/192 | | |
| A. E. Warner c Rhodes b Dilley | 4 | 7/201  8/218  9/219 | | |

Bowling: Dilley 11–0–57–2; Radford 10–2–36–2; Botham 11–0–40–0; Lampitt 10–0–46–3; Newport 11–0–36–1.

## Worcestershire

| | | | | |
|---|---|---|---|---|
| T. S. Curtis b Warner | 30 | I. T. Botham not out | | 35 |
| T. M. Moody not out | 110 | B 1, l-b 11, w 14, n-b 3 | | 29 |
| G. A. Hick b Roberts | 6 | | | — |
| D. B. D'Oliveira c Bowler b Mortensen | 17 | 1/75  2/87  3/126 | (3 wkts, 51.3 overs) | 227 |

*P. A. Neale, †S. J. Rhodes, P. J. Newport, S. R. Lampitt, N. V. Radford and G. R. Dilley did not bat.

Bowling: Malcolm 11–1–46–0; Mortensen 11–0–47–1; Base 11–1–44–0; Warner 9.3–0–34–1; Roberts 6–0–32–1; Azharuddin 3–0–12–0.

Umpires: J. H. Harris and B. Hassan.

## DERBYSHIRE v GLOUCESTERSHIRE

At Derby, May 7, 8. Derbyshire won by virtue of losing fewer wickets with the scores tied. Toss: Derbyshire. Barnett's eleventh one-day hundred came in 149 balls, with seven fours, and he put on 119 in 30 overs for the fourth wicket with Roberts. The first day's play, delayed by rain and curtailed by bad light, ended with Derbyshire 139 for three from 39 overs (K. J. Barnett 68*, B. Roberts 30*).

*Gold Award:* K. J. Barnett.

## Gloucestershire

| | | | | |
|---|---|---|---|---|
| R. J. Scott c Bowler b Warner | 14 | D. R. Gilbert run out | | 8 |
| C. W. J. Athey b Mortensen | 81 | A. M. Babington c Barnett b Base | | 4 |
| *A. J. Wright c and b Azharuddin | 45 | A. M. Smith not out | | 1 |
| J. J. E. Hardy b Barnett | 6 | L-b 5, w 8, n-b 2 | | 15 |
| M. W. Alleyne c Barnett b Malcolm | 1 | | | |
| P. W. Romaines c Bowler b Malcolm | 22 | 1/37 2/133 3/151 | (9 wkts, 55 overs) | 224 |
| †R. C. Russell c O'Gorman b Warner | 9 | 4/153 5/165 6/189 | | |
| D. V. Lawrence not out | 18 | 7/193 8/217 9/222 | | |

Bowling: Mortensen 11–3–36–1; Base 9–3–26–1; Warner 11–0–57–2; Barnett 11–1–34–1; Malcolm 11–0–49–2; Azharuddin 2–0–17–1.

## Derbyshire

| | | | | |
|---|---|---|---|---|
| *K. J. Barnett b Smith | 102 | C. J. Adams run out | | 2 |
| †P. D. Bowler lbw b Gilbert | 7 | A. E. Warner not out | | 0 |
| J. E. Morris b Babington | 0 | B 2, l-b 11, w 6 | | 19 |
| M. Azharuddin c Russell b Lawrence | 2 | | | |
| B. Roberts c Romaines b Babington | 49 | 1/20 2/21 3/67 | (6 wkts, 55 overs) | 224 |
| T. J. G. O'Gorman not out | 23 | 4/186 5/216 6/219 | | |

S. J. Base, D. E. Malcolm and O. H. Mortensen did not bat.

Bowling: Gilbert 11–2–37–1; Babington 11–0–49–2; Lawrence 11–0–38–1; Smith 11–0–39–1; Alleyne 5–0–24–0; Scott 6–0–24–0.

Umpires: B. Dudleston and D. O. Oslear.

# NORTHAMPTONSHIRE v WORCESTERSHIRE

At Northampton, May 7. Northamptonshire won by 75 runs. Toss: Worcestershire. Worcestershire lost the match but succeeded in their primary object of scoring 161 to head Group A on run-rate.

*Gold Award:* A. Fordham.

## Northamptonshire

| | | | | |
|---|---|---|---|---|
| A. Fordham run out | 70 | J. G. Thomas c Newport b Dilley | | 3 |
| N. A. Felton lbw b Dilley | 10 | N. G. B. Cook b Dilley | | 0 |
| R. J. Bailey c Rhodes b Dilley | 55 | J. P. Taylor not out | | 1 |
| *A. J. Lamb c Moody b Weston | 23 | B 1, l-b 9, w 12, n-b 2 | | 24 |
| D. J. Capel c Newport b Botham | 27 | | | |
| R. G. Williams not out | 28 | 1/29 2/132 3/157 | (9 wkts, 55 overs) | 248 |
| E. A. E. Baptiste c Illingworth b Botham | 2 | 4/180 5/211 6/222 | | |
| †D. Ripley b Botham | 5 | 7/237 8/246 9/247 | | |

Bowling: Dilley 11–1–35–4; Botham 11–1–46–3; Newport 11–0–64–0; Illingworth 11–0–52–0; Weston 11–0–41–1.

## Worcestershire

| | | | | |
|---|---|---|---|---|
| T. S. Curtis b Taylor | 11 | M. J. Weston run out | | 30 |
| T. M. Moody b Baptiste | 17 | †S. J. Rhodes not out | | 13 |
| G. A. Hick c Felton b Taylor | 4 | B 1, l-b 10, w 14 | | 25 |
| D. B. D'Oliveira b Cook | 21 | | | |
| I. T. Botham c Fordham b Capel | 0 | 1/32 2/32 3/50 | (6 wkts, 55 overs) | 173 |
| *P. A. Neale not out | 52 | 4/58 5/65 6/146 | | |

R. K. Illingworth, P. J. Newport and G. R. Dilley did not bat.

Bowling: Thomas 8–0–38–0; Baptiste 11–2–30–1; Taylor 10–0–30–2; Capel 4–0–9–1; Cook 11–1–21–1; Williams 11–0–34–0.

Umpires: D. J. Constant and J. W. Holder.

# GROUP B

## SOMERSET v MIDDLESEX

At Taunton, April 23. Middlesex won by eight wickets. Toss: Middlesex. Gatting hit seventeen fours and faced 129 balls. He and Ramprakash, whose unbeaten 78 was his best in this competition, added 198 in 40 overs for the second wicket, two days after their Sunday League stand of 194.

*Gold Award:* M. W. Gatting.

### Somerset

| | | | | |
|---|---|---|---|---|
| S. J. Cook b Emburey | 41 | N. A. Mallender c Cowans b Emburey | 1 |
| P. M. Roebuck run out | 61 | D. A. Graveney not out | 3 |
| R. J. Harden c Ramprakash b Emburey | 3 | D. Beal b Emburey | 1 |
| G. D. Rose c Downton b Williams | 11 | B 1, l-b 6, w 4, n-b 1 | 12 |
| *C. J. Tavaré c Downton b Tufnell | 1 | | |
| A. N. Hayhurst c Downton b Cowans | 32 | 1/101 2/107 3/116 | (55 overs) 208 |
| †N. D. Burns c Tufnell b Cowans | 37 | 4/123 5/127 6/187 | |
| R. P. Lefebvre st Downton b Emburey | 5 | 7/200 8/204 9/206 | |

Bowling: Williams 11–0–26–1; Cowans 11–1–49–2; Headley 11–2–48–0; Tufnell 11–0–41–1; Emburey 11–0–37–5.

### Middlesex

| | | | |
|---|---|---|---|
| *M. W. Gatting b Beal | 112 | | |
| J. C. Pooley b Mallender | 2 | | |
| M. R. Ramprakash not out | 78 | | |
| K. R. Brown not out | 0 | | |
| L-b 10, w 3, n-b 5 | 18 | | |
| | | | |
| 1/8 2/206 | (2 wkts, 45.1 overs) 210 | | |

M. A. Roseberry, †P. R. Downton, J. E. Emburey, P. C. R. Tufnell, D. W. Headley, N. F. Williams and N. G. Cowans did not bat.

Bowling: Mallender 10–2–45–1; Lefebvre 8–2–22–0; Beal 8–1–51–1; Rose 7–0–31–0; Graveney 7–0–33–0; Hayhurst 5.1–0–18–0.

Umpires: K. E. Palmer and D. R. Shepherd.

## SURREY v ESSEX

At The Oval, April 23, 24. Essex won by 53 runs. Toss: Surrey. Salim Malik struck an unbeaten 90 from 99 balls, including five fours, all off the bowling of his Pakistan team-mate, Waqar Younis. Bad light ended play on the first day when Surrey were 148 for four from 40 overs (D. M. Ward 33*, I. A. Greig 32*).

*Gold Award:* Salim Malik.

### Essex

| | | | | |
|---|---|---|---|---|
| *G. A. Gooch c Greig b Feltham | 34 | N. Shahid run out | 8 |
| J. P. Stephenson c and b Bullen | 73 | †M. A. Garnham not out | 6 |
| P. J. Prichard c and b Feltham | 10 | L-b 7, w 7 | 14 |
| Salim Malik not out | 90 | | |
| N. Hussain c Stewart b M. P. Bicknell | 1 | 1/82 2/96 3/160 | (6 wkts, 55 overs) 261 |
| D. R. Pringle run out | 25 | 4/161 5/212 6/237 | |

N. A. Foster, M. C. Ilott and P. M. Such did not bat.

Bowling: Waqar Younis 11–0–63–0; M. P. Bicknell 11–0–55–1; Murphy 11–1–46–0; Feltham 11–1–45–2; Thorpe 4–0–16–0; Bullen 7–0–29–1.

## Surrey

| | | | | |
|---|---|---|---|---|
| D. J. Bicknell lbw b Such | 43 | M. P. Bicknell c Stephenson b Ilott | 6 |
| G. P. Thorpe c Pringle b Ilott | 3 | Waqar Younis not out | 5 |
| †A. J. Stewart c Prichard b Such | 30 | A. J. Murphy not out | 0 |
| D. M. Ward b Ilott | 41 | L-b 6, w 7 | 13 |
| M. A. Lynch lbw b Pringle | 0 | | |
| *I. A. Greig c Stephenson b Gooch | 47 | 1/13 2/67 3/91 (9 wkts, 55 overs) 208 | |
| M. A. Feltham c Gooch b Foster | 4 | 4/92 5/172 6/177 | |
| C. K. Bullen c Stephenson b Salim Malik | 16 | 7/177 8/193 9/208 | |

Bowling: Foster 11–3–26–1; Ilott 11–3–34–3; Gooch 9–0–52–1; Such 11–1–52–2; Pringle 9–0–25–1; Stephenson 2–0–6–0; Salim Malik 2–0–7–1.

Umpires: J. C. Balderstone and J. H. Harris.

## MIDDLESEX v SURREY

At Lord's, April 25. Surrey won by 75 runs. Toss: Middlesex. Surrey's victory was their second in ten meetings with Middlesex in this competition.
*Gold Award:* A. J. Stewart.

## Surrey

| | | | | |
|---|---|---|---|---|
| D. J. Bicknell b Williams | 1 | J. Boiling not out | 3 |
| M. A. Lynch c Downton b Headley | 20 | Waqar Younis c Brown b Tufnell | 3 |
| †A. J. Stewart c Emburey b Tufnell | 55 | | |
| D. M. Ward run out | 46 | L-b 9, w 6, n-b 3 | 18 |
| G. P. Thorpe c Weekes b Tufnell | 40 | | |
| *I. A. Greig c Cowans | 38 | 1/10 2/41 3/113 (9 wkts, 55 overs) 235 | |
| J. D. Robinson c Ramprakash b Cowans | 4 | 4/151 5/206 6/215 | |
| M. P. Bicknell c Cowans | 7 | 7/227 8/228 9/235 | |

A. J. Murphy did not bat.

Bowling: Cowans 11–1–42–3; Williams 11–2–37–1; Headley 11–0–54–1; Emburey 11–1–43–0; Tufnell 11–0–50–3.

## Middlesex

| | | | | |
|---|---|---|---|---|
| *M. W. Gatting b Murphy | 34 | D. W. Headley b Robinson | 26 |
| J. C. Pooley b Waqar Younis | 8 | P. C. R. Tufnell run out | 1 |
| M. R. Ramprakash c Robinson b M. P. Bicknell | 2 | N. G. Cowans c Thorpe b Robinson | 5 |
| K. R. Brown c D. J. Bicknell b Boiling | 25 | | |
| P. N. Weekes lbw b Murphy | 0 | L-b 3, w 6 | 9 |
| †P. R. Downton not out | 35 | | |
| J. E. Emburey c Stewart b M. P. Bicknell | 9 | 1/26 2/29 3/55 (45.2 overs) 160 | |
| N. F. Williams c Stewart b M. P. Bicknell | 6 | 4/55 5/87 6/102 | |
| | | 7/111 8/153 9/154 | |

Bowling: M. P. Bicknell 11–1–28–3; Waqar Younis 8–0–32–1; Robinson 8.2–1–31–2; Murphy 9–2–23–2; Boiling 9–0–43–1.

Umpires: B. Dudleston and M. J. Kitchen.

## WARWICKSHIRE v ESSEX

At Birmingham, April 25. Essex won by 12 runs. Toss: Essex. Stephenson's first 50 came in 93 balls, with four fours; his next 92 runs took 62 balls, and featured eight fours and three sixes. It was his maiden hundred in the Benson and Hedges Cup, and with Salim Malik (46 balls) he added 180 in twenty overs for the third wicket. Warwickshire were ahead of the required run-rate into the final ten overs, thanks to Reeve and Ostler, who put on 78 in eleven overs for the fifth wicket.
*Gold Award:* J. P. Stephenson.

## Essex

| | |
|---|---|
| *G. A. Gooch c Moles b Munton ...... 26 | N. Hussain not out ................. 2 |
| J. P. Stephenson c Lloyd b Donald ....142 | B 6, l-b 4, w 7, n-b 1 ........ 18 |
| P. J. Prichard c Small b Moles........ 38 | |
| Salim Malik b Donald ................ 72 | 1/44 2/114    (4 wkts, 55 overs) 307 |
| D. R. Pringle not out ................ 9 | 3/294 4/295 |

N. Shahid, †M. A. Garnham, N. A. Foster, T. D. Topley and P. M. Such did not bat.

Bowling: Donald 11–0–78–2; Small 11–0–43–0; Reeve 11–0–64–0; Munton 11–0–40–1; N. M. K. Smith 4–0–32–0; Moles 4–1–19–1; P. A. Smith 3–0–21–0.

## Warwickshire

| | |
|---|---|
| A. J. Moles c Hussain b Foster ....... 19 | G. C. Small c Such b Pringle ......... 2 |
| Asif Din lbw b Gooch ............... 34 | T. A. Munton b Pringle .............. 6 |
| *T. A. Lloyd c Salim Malik b Pringle .. 58 | A. A. Donald not out ............... 6 |
| P. A. Smith c Garnham b Gooch ..... 3 | L-b 9, w 6, n-b 1 ........... 16 |
| D. A. Reeve run out ................ 80 | |
| D. P. Ostler b Pringle .............. 45 | 1/24 2/87 3/99       (54.2 overs) 295 |
| N. M. K. Smith c Prichard b Pringle .. 23 | 4/159 5/237 6/268 |
| †M. Burns c Hussain b Foster ........ 3 | 7/278 8/283 9/283 |

Bowling: Pringle 10.2–1–51–5; Foster 11–0–52–2; Topley 9–0–57–0; Such 10–0–47–0; Gooch 11–0–54–2; Stephenson 3–0–25–0.

Umpires: K. J. Lyons and B. J. Meyer.

## ESSEX v MIDDLESEX

At Chelmsford, May 2. Essex won by three wickets. Toss: Essex. Foster took Pooley's wicket with his first ball, and later Middlesex lost their last five wickets for 14 runs in four overs. Essex in turn collapsed from 93 for one to 105 for six, but Pringle and Foster, the latter making his highest score in the Benson and Hedges Cup with four fours and two sixes in 41 balls, put on 69 in eleven overs. They took 22 off the last two in heavy rain. It was Essex's fifth successive win over Middlesex in the competition.

*Gold Award:* N. A. Foster.

## Middlesex

| | |
|---|---|
| *M. W. Gatting lbw b Ilott .......... 6 | R. M. Ellcock run out ................ 0 |
| J. C. Pooley lbw b Foster ........... 1 | D. W. Headley run out .............. 2 |
| M. R. Ramprakash run out .......... 33 | P. C. R. Tufnell not out ............. 0 |
| K. R. Brown lbw b Stephenson ....... 20 | L-b 2, w 15, n-b 5 ......... 22 |
| M. Keech run out ................. 37 | |
| †P. R. Downton c Shahid b Foster .... 58 | 1/4 2/13 3/68       (54 overs) 186 |
| J. E. Emburey st Garnham b Such .... 6 | 4/76 5/137 6/172 |
| N. F. Williams c Prichard b Pringle ... 1 | 7/178 8/182 9/184 |

Bowling: Ilott 10–1–32–1; Foster 10–1–28–2; Pringle 9–1–32–1; Gooch 9–0–41–0; Stephenson 5–0–17–1; Such 11–1–34–1.

## Essex

| | |
|---|---|
| *G. A. Gooch c Downton b Ellcock ... 29 | †M. A. Garnham c Keech b Headley .. 8 |
| J. P. Stephenson c Downton b Emburey 23 | N. A. Foster not out ............... 39 |
| P. J. Prichard lbw b Emburey ........ 31 | B 1, l-b 4, w 10, n-b 6 ....... 21 |
| Salim Malik b Emburey ............. 3 | |
| N. Hussain b Williams .............. 0 | 1/59 2/93 3/100   (7 wkts, 47.1 overs) 190 |
| N. Shahid c Gatting b Williams ...... 0 | 4/101 5/101 |
| D. R. Pringle not out .............. 36 | 6/105 7/121 |

M. C. Ilott and P. M. Such did not bat.

Bowling: Ellcock 10–0–55–1; Williams 11–4–19–2; Headley 9.1–1–34–1; Tufnell 6–0–37–0; Emburey 11–2–40–3.

Umpires: G. I. Burgess and R. A. White.

## WARWICKSHIRE v SOMERSET

At Birmingham, May 2. Warwickshire won by 33 runs. Toss: Somerset. Asif Din's highest score in the Benson and Hedges Cup came from 142 balls, and included twelve fours and two sixes. His partnership of 146 with Moles was Warwickshire's best for the first wicket in this competition, and he added another 92 in fourteen overs with Lloyd (42 balls). In Somerset's reply, Hayhurst put on 100 in sixteen overs with Tavaré before retiring hurt.

*Gold Award:* Asif Din.

### Warwickshire

| | | | |
|---|---|---|---|
| A. J. Moles st Burns b Swallow | 65 | †K. J. Piper not out | 6 |
| Asif Din c Cook b Mallender | 137 | | |
| *T. A. Lloyd c Hayhurst b Beal | 40 | B 4, l-b 12, w 2, n-b 1 | 19 |
| P. A. Smith lbw b Lefebvre | 5 | | — |
| D. A. Reeve b Beal | 19 | 1/146 2/238 3/256 (6 wkts, 55 overs) | 303 |
| D. P. Ostler run out | 12 | 4/277 5/286 6/303 | |

P. A. Booth, G. C. Small, A. A. Donald and T. A. Munton did not bat.

Bowling: Mallender 11-1-47-1; Rose 10-1-38-0; Lefebvre 11-1-59-1; Beal 8-0-63-2; Swallow 10-0-58-1; Roebuck 5-0-22-0.

### Somerset

| | | | |
|---|---|---|---|
| S. J. Cook b Booth | 58 | I. G. Swallow b Reeve | 3 |
| P. M. Roebuck b Munton | 11 | N. A. Mallender run out | 1 |
| A. N. Hayhurst c Lloyd b Donald | 70 | D. Beal not out | 0 |
| *C. J. Tavaré c Lloyd b Donald | 53 | B 9, l-b 10, w 5, n-b 4 | 28 |
| G. D. Rose c Munton b Donald | 2 | | — |
| R. J. Harden c Smith b Reeve | 21 | 1/36 2/100 3/207 (54.2 overs) | 270 |
| †N. D. Burns b Donald | 21 | 4/213 5/255 6/257 | |
| R. P. Lefebvre c and b Reeve | 2 | 7/262 8/264 9/267 | |

*A. N. Hayhurst, when 69, retired hurt at 200 and resumed at 255.*

Bowling: Munton 11-0-48-1; Donald 11-0-55-4; Small 11-1-52-0; Reeve 9.2-0-43-3; Booth 7-0-35-1; Smith 5-0-18-0.

Umpires: D. O. Oslear and R. Palmer.

### MIDDLESEX v WARWICKSHIRE

At Lord's, May 4, 6. Warwickshire won by 39 runs. Toss: Middlesex. Close of play: Middlesex 29-0 (13 overs) (I. J. F. Hutchinson 6*, M. W. Gatting 15*).

*Gold Award:* P. A. Smith.

### Warwickshire

| | | | |
|---|---|---|---|
| A. J. Moles c Williams b Headley | 51 | P. A. Booth run out | 11 |
| Asif Din run out | 97 | T. A. Munton not out | 2 |
| P. A. Smith c Downton b Williams | 34 | A. A. Donald not out | 2 |
| *T. A. Lloyd c and b Emburey | 0 | L-b 7, w 5, n-b 1 | 13 |
| D. A. Reeve c Headley b Cowans | 12 | | — |
| D. P. Ostler c Emburey b Cowans | 7 | 1/120 2/186 3/187 (9 wkts, 55 overs) | 237 |
| †K. J. Piper run out | 7 | 4/202 5/206 6/213 | |
| G. C. Small c Ramprakash b Cowans | 1 | 7/219 8/232 9/232 | |

Bowling: Cowans 11-0-39-3; Williams 11-2-41-1; Headley 11-1-44-1; Emburey 11-0-47-1; Tufnell 11-0-59-0.

## Middlesex

| | | | | |
|---|---|---|---|---|
| I. J. F. Hutchinson c Piper b Smith | ... | 8 | D. W. Headley c Ostler b Munton | 2 |
| *M. W. Gatting c Piper b Reeve | | 17 | P. C. R. Tufnell run out | 18 |
| M. R. Ramprakash b Smith | | 7 | N. G. Cowans not out | 0 |
| K. R. Brown c Reeve b Smith | | 12 | B 2, l-b 6, w 11, n-b 1 | 20 |
| M. Keech run out | | 47 | | |
| †P. R. Downton c Piper b Reeve | | 41 | 1/34 2/36 3/55 | (51.3 overs) 198 |
| J. E. Emburey b Reeve | | 23 | 4/57 5/132 6/153 | |
| N. F. Williams c Donald b Small | ... | 3 | 7/161 8/166 9/198 | |

Bowling: Donald 9–1–32–0; Munton 11–2–27–1; Smith 11–1–28–3; Reeve 9.3–0–48–3; Small 11–0–55–1.

Umpires: J. D. Bond and P. B. Wight.

## SOMERSET v SURREY

At Taunton, May 4. Somerset won by four wickets. Toss: Somerset. Stewart's maiden Benson and Hedges Cup hundred came from 121 balls. In all he faced 125 balls and struck ten fours. Tavaré became the third player to take 50 catches in the competition.

*Gold Award:* S. J. Cook.

## Surrey

| | | | | |
|---|---|---|---|---|
| D. J. Bicknell run out | | 11 | C. K. Bullen c Mallender b Lefebvre | 0 |
| J. D. Robinson c Tavaré b Swallow | | 35 | | |
| †A. J. Stewart not out | | 110 | L-b 5, w 6, n-b 2 | 13 |
| D. M. Ward b Rose | | 28 | | |
| G. P. Thorpe c Swallow b Lefebvre | ... | 41 | 1/31 2/68 3/133 | (7 wkts, 55 overs) 244 |
| *I. A. Greig c Lefebvre b Rose | | 4 | 4/226 5/231 | |
| M. A. Feltham c Tavaré b Lefebvre | ... | 2 | 6/243 7/244 | |

M. P. Bicknell, Waqar Younis and A. J. Murphy did not bat.

Bowling: Mallender 10–0–54–0; Rose 11–1–48–2; Swallow 11–1–31–1; Lefebvre 11–1–44–3; Cleal 4–0–21–0; Roebuck 8–0–41–0.

## Somerset

| | | | | |
|---|---|---|---|---|
| S. J. Cook c Bullen b Feltham | | 76 | G. D. Rose b M. P. Bicknell | 23 |
| P. M. Roebuck b Waqar Younis | | 0 | R. P. Lefebvre not out | 21 |
| R. J. Harden c and b Waqar Younis | | 1 | B 4, l-b 10, w 15 | 29 |
| *C. J. Tavaré b Murphy | | 39 | | |
| R. J. Bartlett b Waqar Younis | | 14 | 1/1 2/11 3/110 | (6 wkts, 53.2 overs) 246 |
| †N. D. Burns not out | | 43 | 4/134 5/157 6/212 | |

I. G. Swallow, M. W. Cleal and N. A. Mallender did not bat.

Bowling: Waqar Younis 11–2–29–3; M. P. Bicknell 11–0–49–1; Feltham 10.2–0–58–1; Murphy 11–0–48–1; Bullen 6–0–29–0; Thorpe 4–0–19–0.

Umpires: K. J. Lyons and D. R. Shepherd.

## ESSEX v SOMERSET

At Chelmsford, May 7, 8. Essex won by eight wickets. Toss: Essex. Gooch, who hit ten fours, shared a first-wicket partnership of 151 with Stephenson (six fours, two sixes). Overnight Essex were 6 for no wicket from two overs (G. A. Gooch 5*, J. P. Stephenson 0*).

*Gold Award:* G. A. Gooch.

## Somerset

| | | | | | |
|---|---|---|---|---|---|
| S. J. Cook c and b Gooch | 38 | | I. G. Swallow c Garnham b Pringle | 2 |
| P. M. Roebuck run out | 2 | | M. W. Cleal lbw b Foster | 18 |
| R. J. Harden c Garnham b Ilott | 1 | | N. A. Mallender not out | 2 |
| *C. J. Tavaré lbw b Such | 46 | | B 1, l-b 4, w 10, n-b 3 | 18 |
| R. J. Bartlett lbw b Gooch | 14 | | | |
| †N. D. Burns c Garnham b Pringle | 9 | | 1/8 2/11 3/69 | (9 wkts, 55 overs) 174 |
| G. D. Rose c Garnham b Pringle | 1 | | 4/96 5/122 6/123 | |
| R. P. Lefebvre not out | 23 | | 7/124 8/131 9/166 | |

Bowling: Foster 11–1–41–1; Ilott 10–2–35–1; Pringle 11–1–31–3; Gooch 11–1–19–2; Such 11–1–34–1; Stephenson 1–0–9–0.

## Essex

| | |
|---|---|
| *G. A. Gooch c Burns b Mallender | 72 |
| J. P. Stephenson c Bartlett b Rose | 60 |
| P. J. Prichard not out | 12 |
| Salim Malik not out | 12 |
| L-b 4, w 4, n-b 11 | 19 |

1/151 2/152     (2 wkts, 37.5 overs) 175

N. Hussain, N. Shahid, D. R. Pringle, †M. A. Garnham, N. A. Foster, M. C. Ilott and P. M. Such did not bat.

Bowling: Mallender 10–0–35–1; Rose 10.5–0–55–1; Lefebvre 8–2–25–0; Cleal 6–0–34–0; Swallow 3–0–22–0.

Umpires: J. D. Bond and N. T. Plews.

## SURREY v WARWICKSHIRE

At The Oval, May 7. Warwickshire won by 1 run. Toss: Surrey. Surrey, needing to win in 23.2 overs to reach the quarter-finals on run-rate, fell 13 runs short of this target. Darren Bicknell, batting at an unaccustomed No. 7, needed only 34 balls for his 50, hitting six fours and a six and taking 12 and 14 off consecutive overs from Donald. He added 90 in ten overs with Robinson for the sixth wicket. Waqar Younis sprained his left ankle while bowling, and batted with a runner. Munton's figures were his best in the competition.

*Gold Award:* D. A. Reeve.

## Warwickshire

| | | | | | |
|---|---|---|---|---|---|
| A. J. Moles run out | 21 | | †K. J. Piper not out | 11 |
| J. D. Ratcliffe c Greig b Murphy | 29 | | P. A. Booth not out | 4 |
| *T. A. Lloyd c Robinson b Greig | 32 | | B 4, l-b 11, w 8, n-b 1 | 24 |
| P. A. Smith b Boiling | 17 | | | |
| D. A. Reeve b Greig | 13 | | 1/57 2/58 3/85 | (7 wkts, 55 overs) 184 |
| D. P. Ostler b Robinson | 28 | | 4/127 5/140 | |
| R. G. Twose run out | 5 | | 6/151 7/177 | |

T. A. Munton and A. A. Donald did not bat.

Bowling: Waqar Younis 5.4–0–16–0; M. P. Bicknell 8–1–26–0; Murphy 10–1–34–1; Robinson 11–2–29–1; Boiling 11–0–38–1; Greig 9.2–0–26–2.

## Surrey

| | | | | | |
|---|---|---|---|---|---|
| A. D. Brown c Booth b Reeve | 37 | | J. Boiling c Moles b Munton | 7 |
| *I. A. Greig c Moles b Donald | 4 | | A. J. Murphy b Munton | 1 |
| †A. J. Stewart b Munton | 0 | | Waqar Younis not out | 0 |
| D. M. Ward c Booth b Donald | 5 | | B 1, l-b 3, w 2 | 6 |
| G. P. Thorpe c Piper b Reeve | 28 | | | |
| J. D. Robinson c Moles b Reeve | 38 | | 1/5 2/7 3/30 | (31.4 overs) 183 |
| D. J. Bicknell c Booth b Reeve | 53 | | 4/66 5/80 6/170 | |
| M. P. Bicknell c Ostler b Munton | 24 | | 7/170 8/179 9/182 | |

Bowling: Donald 7–0–55–2; Munton 7.4–0–35–4; Booth 6–0–46–0; Reeve 11–0–43–4.

Umpires: K. E. Palmer and A. G. T. Whitehead.

## GROUP C

## KENT v LEICESTERSHIRE

At Canterbury, April 23. Kent won by 74 runs. Toss: Leicestershire. After a slow start, with only 25 runs coming in their first ten overs, Kent reached their highest total in the Benson and Hedges Cup, previously 293 for six against Somerset at Taunton in 1985. Benson and Ward put on 170 together, a county record for the second wicket in the competition, and at the end Graham Cowdrey (48 balls, eight fours) added 76 in six overs with Marsh. For Leicestershire, Whitaker hit his first Benson and Hedges hundred.

*Gold Award:* M. R. Benson.

### Kent

| | | | | |
|---|---|---|---|---|
| *M. R. Benson c Briers b Maguire | .... 76 | †S. A. Marsh not out | ............... | 23 |
| N. R. Taylor c Wilkinson b Lewis | ..... 1 | | | |
| T. R. Ward b Mullally | ............. 87 | B 1, l-b 10, w 15, n-b 2 | ...... | 28 |
| G. R. Cowdrey not out | ............. 70 | | | — |
| C. S. Cowdrey b Lewis | ............. 4 | 1/4 2/174 3/188 | (5 wkts, 55 overs) | 297 |
| M. V. Fleming b Lewis | ............. 8 | 4/201 5/221 | | |

R. M. Ellison, M. J. McCague, T. A. Merrick and A. P. Igglesden did not bat.

Bowling: Lewis 11–0–62–3; Mullally 11–0–45–1; Maguire 11–3–59–1; Wilkinson 11–0–58–0; Willey 6–0–33–0; Benson 5–0–29–0.

### Leicestershire

| | | | | |
|---|---|---|---|---|
| L. Potter c C. S. Cowdrey b Igglesden | . 6 | J. N. Maguire c Taylor b Igglesden | .... | 2 |
| *N. E. Briers c Marsh b McCague | .... 12 | A. D. Mullally c and b Igglesden | ...... | 5 |
| J. J. Whitaker b Merrick | ........... 100 | T. J. Boon absent injured | | |
| P. Willey c G. R. Cowdrey b Fleming | . 36 | L-b 8, w 10, n-b 1 | ........... | 19 |
| C. C. Lewis c Taylor b Fleming | ....... 5 | | | — |
| J. D. R. Benson b McCague | .......... 27 | 1/20 2/25 3/112 | (54.5 overs) | 223 |
| †P. Whitticase c Marsh b Merrick | ..... 2 | 4/126 5/199 6/205 | | |
| C. W. Wilkinson not out | ............. 9 | 7/207 8/210 9/223 | | |

Bowling: McCague 11–1–53–2; Igglesden 10.5–1–32–3; Merrick 11–2–34–2; Ellison 11–0–44–0; Fleming 11–0–52–2.

Umpires: M. J. Kitchen and D. O. Oslear.

## SCOTLAND v LANCASHIRE

At Forfar, April 23. Lancashire won by seven wickets. Toss: Lancashire. Scotland's first Benson and Hedges match at Forfar began disastrously when Philip was out first ball; DeFreitas reduced them to 9 for three in the first nine overs of the innings.

*Gold Award:* P. A. J. DeFreitas.

### Scotland

| | | | | |
|---|---|---|---|---|
| I. L. Philip lbw b DeFreitas | ......... 0 | †D. J. Haggo not out | ............... | 22 |
| B. M. W. Patterson c Atherton | | A. Bee b Austin | ......... | 13 |
| | b DeFreitas . 2 | D. Cowan not out | ................. | 3 |
| G. Salmond c Fairbrother b DeFreitas | . 6 | L-b 9, w 21, n-b 5 | ........... | 35 |
| G. N. Reifer lbw b Watkinson | ....... 25 | | | — |
| *O. Henry c Hegg b Watkinson | ....... 8 | 1/0 2/6 3/9 | (8 wkts, 55 overs) | 163 |
| A. B. Russell c Hegg b DeFreitas | ..... 31 | 4/43 5/68 6/116 | | |
| J. W. Govan b Austin | ............. 18 | 7/123 8/154 | | |

J. D. Moir did not bat.

Bowling: DeFreitas 11–5–21–4; Allott 11–3–21–0; Wasim Akram 11–0–32–0; Watkinson 11–2–30–2; Austin 11–0–50–2.

## Lancashire

| | | | |
|---|---|---|---|
| G. D. Mendis c Philip b Cowan | 63 | M. Watkinson not out | 15 |
| G. Fowler c Reifer b Govan | 45 | L-b 1, w 8 | 9 |
| M. A. Atherton c Haggo b Cowan | 10 | | |
| *N. H. Fairbrother not out | 22 | 1/97 2/115 3/132 (3 wkts, 46.2 overs) | 164 |

N. J. Speak, Wasim Akram, †W. K. Hegg, I. D. Austin, P. A. J. DeFreitas and P. J. W. Allott did not bat.

Bowling: Bee 4–0–18–0; Moir 8–1–26–0; Reifer 8.2–2–27–0; Cowan 9–0–47–2; Govan 11–4–26–1; Henry 6–1–19–0.

Umpires: J. H. Hampshire and R. Julian.

## LANCASHIRE v KENT

At Manchester, April 25. Lancashire won by six wickets. Toss: Kent. Marsh hit five fours and two sixes while making his highest score in this competition, and added 80 for the ninth wicket with Merrick.
*Gold Award*: P. A. J. DeFreitas.

## Kent

| | | | |
|---|---|---|---|
| *M. R. Benson c Allott b DeFreitas | 4 | M. J. McCague c Mendis b Watkinson | 12 |
| N. R. Taylor b DeFreitas | 9 | T. A. Merrick not out | 22 |
| T. R. Ward c Hegg b Allott | 1 | A. P. Igglesden c Yates b DeFreitas | 3 |
| G. R. Cowdrey c Mendis b Watkinson | 10 | L-b 6, w 11, n-b 4 | 21 |
| C. S. Cowdrey c Fairbrother b Allott | 0 | | |
| M. V. Fleming c Fairbrother b Allott | 8 | 1/7 2/14 3/14 (53.4 overs) | 167 |
| †S. A. Marsh c Mendis b DeFreitas | 71 | 4/14 5/26 6/40 | |
| R. M. Ellison c DeFreitas b Watkinson | 6 | 7/57 8/83 9/163 | |

Bowling: DeFreitas 10.4–3–15–4; Allott 11–4–17–3; Watkinson 11–1–42–3; Wasim Akram 11–1–49–0; Austin 10–1–38–0.

## Lancashire

| | | | |
|---|---|---|---|
| G. D. Mendis b Merrick | 22 | Wasim Akram not out | 45 |
| G. Fowler c Ward b McCague | 1 | L-b 6, w 6 | 12 |
| M. A. Atherton c Marsh b McCague | 22 | | |
| *N. H. Fairbrother c Marsh b Ellison | 46 | 1/3 2/31 (4 wkts, 37.3 overs) | 170 |
| M. Watkinson not out | 22 | 3/98 4/98 | |

P. A. J. DeFreitas, †W. K. Hegg, G. Yates, I. D. Austin and P. J. W. Allott did not bat.

Bowling: McCague 7–1–32–2; Igglesden 10–0–48–0; Merrick 10–0–30–1; Ellison 8–1–45–1; Fleming 2.3–0–9–0.

Umpires: J. H. Hampshire and R. Julian.

## SUSSEX v LEICESTERSHIRE

At Hove, April 25. Sussex won by 72 runs. Toss: Leicestershire. Parker, who had recently recovered from a hamstring strain, made his highest score in the Benson and Hedges Cup, in 79 balls with seven fours and a six. Jones took three wickets on his first appearance at Hove since rejoining Sussex after four seasons with Somerset.
*Gold Award*: P. W. G. Parker.

## Sussex

| | | | | |
|---|---|---|---|---|
| D. M. Smith c Briers b Willey | 76 | K. Greenfield not out | 0 |
| J. W. Hall c Potter b Benson | 43 | | |
| *P. W. G. Parker run out | 87 | B 2, l-b 19, w 10, n-b 3 | 34 |
| A. P. Wells not out | 23 | 1/94 2/202 3/260 (3 wkts, 55 overs) 263 | |

A. I. C. Dodemaide, J. A. North, †P. Moores, A. C. S. Pigott, I. D. K. Salisbury and
A. N. Jones did not bat.

Bowling: Lewis 11–0–53–0; Millns 9–3–39–0; Maguire 11–2–43–0; Mullally 11–0–63–0;
Willey 11–1–34–1; Benson 2–0–10–1.

## Leicestershire

| | | | | |
|---|---|---|---|---|
| L. Potter c Parker b Jones | 2 | J. N. Maguire b Pigott | 35 |
| *N. E. Briers b Salisbury | 46 | D. J. Millns not out | 11 |
| J. J. Whitaker c Moores b Jones | 2 | A. D. Mullally c Greenfield b Pigott | 1 |
| P. Willey c Greenfield b Dodemaide | 4 | L-b 4, w 11 | 15 |
| J. D. R. Benson c and b Pigott | 3 | | |
| C. C. Lewis c Moores b Jones | 8 | 1/4 2/19 3/37 (50.4 overs) 191 | |
| P. N. Hepworth b Greenfield | 33 | 4/40 5/51 6/111 | |
| †P. Whitticase c Greenfield b North | 31 | 7/111 8/157 9/189 | |

Bowling: Jones 9–0–33–3; Dodemaide 7–3–17–1; Pigott 8.4–2–29–3; Salisbury 8–0–32–1;
North 10–0–41–1; Greenfield 8–0–35–1.

Umpires: R. Palmer and R. C. Tolchard.

# KENT v SUSSEX

At Canterbury, May 2, 3. Kent won by four wickets. Toss: Sussex. Chris Cowdrey struck
50 in 54 balls, with four fours. Close of play: Sussex 120-4 (34 overs) (A. P. Wells 43*,
J. A. North 13*).

*Gold Award:* C. S. Cowdrey.

## Sussex

| | | | | |
|---|---|---|---|---|
| D. M. Smith lbw b Igglesden | 4 | I. D. K. Salisbury not out | 17 |
| J. W. Hall lbw b Ellison | 8 | B. T. P. Donelan not out | 8 |
| *P. W. G. Parker lbw b Ellison | 1 | | |
| A. P. Wells c and b Ealham | 66 | B 1, l-b 23, w 5, n-b 1 | 30 |
| M. P. Speight run out | 35 | | |
| J. A. North run out | 13 | 1/12 2/17 3/18 (8 wkts, 55 overs) 218 | |
| †P. Moores c Ellison b Fleming | 20 | 4/101 5/122 6/153 | |
| A. C. S. Pigott b Igglesden | 16 | 7/183 8/191 | |

A. N. Jones did not bat.

Bowling: Ellison 11–5–19–2; Igglesden 11–2–35–2; Ealham 11–0–46–1; Merrick
11–0–53–0; Fleming 11–0–41–1.

## Kent

| | | | | |
|---|---|---|---|---|
| *M. R. Benson b Salisbury | 28 | †V. J. Wells st Moores b Salisbury | 25 |
| N. R. Taylor b North | 21 | R. M. Ellison not out | 7 |
| T. R. Ward c Wells b Salisbury | 38 | L-b 16, w 11, n-b 1 | 28 |
| G. R. Cowdrey c Moores b Pigott | 18 | | |
| C. S. Cowdrey not out | 57 | 1/58 2/62 3/111 (6 wkts, 54.4 overs) 222 | |
| M. V. Fleming c Smith b Jones | 0 | 4/153 5/154 6/201 | |

T. A. Merrick, A. P. Igglesden and M. A. Ealham did not bat.

Bowling: Jones 10.4–1–41–1; Pigott 11–0–41–1; Donelan 11–0–54–0; North 11–1–30–1;
Salisbury 11–0–40–3.

Umpires: A. A. Jones and M. J. Kitchen.

## LEICESTERSHIRE v SCOTLAND

At Leicester, May 2. Leicestershire won by 45 runs. Toss: Leicestershire. Boon, whose hundred was his first in limited-overs cricket, added 160 in 30 overs with Whitaker (88 balls) for Leicestershire's second wicket. In Scotland's innings, Hepworth took his first wickets for Leicestershire in any first-team competition.

*Gold Award*: T. J. Boon.

### Leicestershire

| | | | |
|---|---|---|---|
| T. J. Boon lbw b Cowan | 103 | J. D. R. Benson not out | 6 |
| *N. E. Briers c Haggo b Reifer | 36 | L-b 6, w 4, n-b 1 | 11 |
| J. J. Whitaker c Reifer b Bee | 84 | | |
| P. Willey b Cowan | 0 | 1/71 2/231 (4 wkts, 55 overs) | 243 |
| L. Potter not out | 3 | 3/231 4/232 | |

P. N. Hepworth, †P. Whitticase, C. W. Wilkinson, J. N. Maguire and D. J. Millns did not bat.

Bowling: Moir 11–6–16–0; Bee 6–0–38–1; Cowan 8–0–54–2; Reifer 9–0–36–1; Henry 11–0–43–0; Govan 10–0–50–0.

### Scotland

| | | | |
|---|---|---|---|
| I. L. Philip c Whitticase b Wilkinson | 35 | †D. J. Haggo not out | 10 |
| B. M. W. Patterson run out | 12 | D. Cowan c Maguire b Hepworth | 0 |
| G. N. Reifer c Millns b Wilkinson | 31 | J. D. Moir not out | 6 |
| R. G. Swan lbw b Wilkinson | 55 | L-b 6, w 6 | 12 |
| A. B. Russell lbw b Hepworth | 2 | | |
| *O. Henry c Wilkinson b Hepworth | 22 | 1/47 2/51 3/138 (9 wkts, 55 overs) | 198 |
| J. W. Govan st Whitticase b Hepworth | 10 | 4/144 5/144 6/176 | |
| A. Bee c Briers b Millns | 3 | 7/179 8/182 9/182 | |

Bowling: Maguire 6–0–25–0; Millns 7–0–25–1; Wilkinson 11–1–46–3; Willey 11–3–15–0; Potter 9–0–42–0; Hepworth 11–1–39–4.

Umpires: B. Leadbeater and P. B. Wight.

## LEICESTERSHIRE v LANCASHIRE

At Leicester, May 4. Lancashire won by seven wickets. Toss: Lancashire. Allott's bowling figures were his best in the Benson and Hedges Cup, and Atherton equalled his highest score in the competition.

*Gold Award*: P. J. W. Allott.

### Leicestershire

| | | | |
|---|---|---|---|
| T. J. Boon run out | 16 | J. N. Maguire b Allott | 0 |
| *N. E. Briers c Austin b Allott | 9 | C. W. Wilkinson not out | 19 |
| J. J. Whitaker lbw b Allott | 1 | B 4, l-b 5, w 11, n-b 1 | 21 |
| P. Willey c Hegg b Austin | 29 | | |
| L. Potter b Allott | 54 | 1/12 2/16 3/41 (7 wkts, 55 overs) | 192 |
| P. N. Hepworth b Fitton | 9 | 4/88 5/111 | |
| †P. Whitticase not out | 34 | 6/148 7/148 | |

D. J. Millns and A. D. Mullally did not bat.

Bowling: DeFreitas 11–3–37–0; Allott 11–4–23–4; Yates 11–3–35–0; Austin 11–1–41–1; Fitton 11–0–47–1.

## Lancashire

| | |
|---|---|
| G. D. Mendis c Boon b Hepworth..... 36 | G. D. Lloyd not out.................... 1 |
| G. Fowler c Briers b Maguire ....... 17 | L-b 4, w 7, n-b 1 ............ 12 |
| M. A. Atherton c Hepworth b Willey .. 74 | |
| *N. H. Fairbrother not out.......... 53 | 1/42 2/69 3/189    (3 wkts, 53.5 overs) 193 |

P. A. J. DeFreitas, †W. K. Hegg, G. Yates, J. D. Fitton, I. D. Austin and P. J. W. Allott did not bat.

Bowling: Mullally 11-2-26-0; Millns 7-0-37-0; Wilkinson 9-2-26-0; Maguire 9-2-27-1; Willey 8.5-0-29-1; Hepworth 9-1-44-1.

Umpires: J. W. Holder and R. A. White.

## SUSSEX v SCOTLAND

At Hove, May 4, 5. Sussex won by 4 runs. Toss: Scotland. Close of play: Scotland 100-3 (28.3 overs) (G. N. Reifer 42*, A. B. Russell 15*).
*Gold Award:* D. M. Smith.

### Sussex

| | |
|---|---|
| D. M. Smith b Bee ................102 | I. D. K. Salisbury c Russell b Bee ..... 5 |
| J. W. Hall run out .................. 28 | A. N. Jones not out ............... 0 |
| *P. W. G. Parker c Cowan b Bee ..... 35 | R. A. Bunting not out .............. 1 |
| A. P. Wells c Govan b Henry ........ 0 | B 3, l-b 9, w 4............ 16 |
| M. P. Speight run out ............. 6 | |
| J. A. North st Haggo b Moir ....... 22 | 1/74 2/134 3/140    (9 wkts, 55 overs) 226 |
| A. C. S. Pigott c Russell b Moir .... 2 | 4/150 5/202 6/204 |
| †P. Moores st Haggo b Bee ......... 9 | 7/211 8/223 9/225 |

Bowling: Reifer 9-2-30-0; Moir 11-1-47-2; Govan 10-0-52-0; Henry 11-1-31-1; Cowan 5-1-23-0; Bee 9-0-31-4.

### Scotland

| | |
|---|---|
| I. L. Philip c Moores b Jones ........ 2 | †D. J. Haggo b Pigott ............... 1 |
| B. M. W. Patterson c Pigott b Jones ... 0 | A. Bee not out .................... 1 |
| G. N. Reifer c Salisbury b Bunting .... 76 | B 1, l-b 9, w 22.............. 32 |
| G. Salmond run out ................ 24 | |
| A. B. Russell c Pigott b Jones ........ 45 | 1/1 2/3 3/73    (8 wkts, 55 overs) 222 |
| *O. Henry c Smith b Salisbury........ 32 | 4/160 5/187 6/218 |
| J. W. Govan run out ............... 9 | 7/221 8/222 |

J. D. Moir and D. Cowan did not bat.

Bowling: Jones 11-3-43-3; Bunting 11-1-34-1; Pigott 11-1-34-1; North 11-0-57-0; Salisbury 11-1-44-1.

Umpires: D. J. Constant and R. C. Tolchard.

## LANCASHIRE v SUSSEX

At Manchester, May 7. Lancashire won by 123 runs. Toss: Sussex. Lancashire completed a clean sweep of their group matches, recording their highest total in the Benson and Hedges Cup (apart from 352 for six against Hampshire in the abandoned game declared void in 1990). Fowler's 136, his maiden hundred in the competition, came from 153 balls and included eleven fours and three sixes. It was the highest innings by a Lancashire batsman in the Benson and Hedges Cup, or in any limited-overs contest, both records previously held by C. H. Lloyd. Fairbrother hit his 50 in 21 balls, with six fours and a six; Atherton and Hall also registered their highest scores in the competition.
*Gold Award:* G. Fowler.

## Lancashire

| | | | |
|---|---|---|---|
| G. D. Mendis lbw b Salisbury | 31 | Wasim Akram not out | 6 |
| G. Fowler c Moores b North | 136 | L-b 5, w 5 | 10 |
| M. A. Atherton c Bunting b Giddins | 91 | | |
| *N. H. Fairbrother c Salisbury b North | 50 | 1/84 2/252 (4 wkts, 55 overs) | 330 |
| G. D. Lloyd not out | 6 | 3/317 4/321 | |

G. Yates, P. A. J. DeFreitas, †W. K. Hegg, I. D. Austin and P. J. W. Allott did not bat.

Bowling: Pigott 11–0–71–0; Giddins 8–2–46–1; North 9–0–80–2; Salisbury 11–2–33–1; Bunting 6–0–41–0; Greenfield 10–0–54–0.

## Sussex

| | | | |
|---|---|---|---|
| D. M. Smith lbw b Wasim Akram | 27 | A. C. S. Pigott c and b DeFreitas | 29 |
| J. W. Hall c Atherton b Yates | 71 | I. D. K. Salisbury b Austin | 10 |
| M. P. Speight c Atherton b Wasim Akram | 1 | R. A. Bunting not out | 2 |
| *A. P. Wells c Mendis b Yates | 7 | E. S. H. Giddins b DeFreitas | 0 |
| K. Greenfield c Hegg b Wasim Akram | 33 | B 3, l-b 9, w 4 | 16 |
| J. A. North run out | 9 | 1/64 2/68 3/91 (44.3 overs) | 207 |
| †P. Moores c Fairbrother b Wasim Akram | 2 | 4/138 5/153 6/156 | |
| | | 7/170 8/205 9/207 | |

Bowling: Allott 8–2–29–0; DeFreitas 7.3–1–36–2; Austin 9–0–62–1; Wasim Akram 9–3–18–4; Yates 11–0–50–2.

Umpires: B. Leadbeater and R. A. White.

## SCOTLAND v KENT

At Glasgow, May 7. Kent won by 130 runs. Toss: Scotland. Kent passed their record total of 297 for five, set on April 23 against Leicestershire. Fleming's 50 came from sixteen balls (he faced nineteen in all) and included four consecutive sixes off Moir, in an over costing 27 runs. Earlier the Kent openers, Taylor and Benson, had taken 140 balls and 65 balls respectively, with Taylor hitting a six and nine fours in his 110.

*Gold Award:* N. R. Taylor.

## Kent

| | | | |
|---|---|---|---|
| N. R. Taylor c Govan b Russell | 110 | M. A. Ealham not out | 0 |
| *M. R. Benson b Govan | 64 | T. A. Merrick not out | 4 |
| T. R. Ward c Philip b Russell | 29 | | |
| G. R. Cowdrey st Haggo b Russell | 5 | B 1, l-b 10, w 11 | 22 |
| C. S. Cowdrey c Reifer b Russell | 11 | | |
| M. V. Fleming b Henry b Cowan | 52 | 1/127 2/210 3/217 (8 wkts, 55 overs) | 319 |
| R. M. Ellison run out | 15 | 4/236 5/247 6/296 | |
| †V. J. Wells c Henry b Bee | 7 | 7/307 8/315 | |

A. P. Igglesden did not bat.

Bowling: Moir 10–3–57–0; Reifer 3–0–16–0; Bee 7–0–47–1; Govan 11–0–63–1; Cowan 6–0–33–1; Henry 11–0–50–0; Russell 7–0–42–4.

## Scotland

| | | | |
|---|---|---|---|
| I. L. Philip c C. S. Cowdrey b Igglesden | 2 | A. Bee b C. S. Cowdrey | 35 |
| B. M. W. Patterson c Wells b Igglesden | 23 | D. Cowan b Fleming | 6 |
| G. N. Reifer lbw b Merrick | 9 | J. D. Moir not out | 2 |
| G. Salmond c Merrick b Igglesden | 4 | B 4, l-b 16, w 21, n-b 1 | 42 |
| A. B. Russell c C. S. Cowdrey b Merrick | 0 | | |
| *O. Henry c Wells b Ellison | 18 | 1/13 2/45 3/51 (47.3 overs) | 189 |
| J. W. Govan c Ward b Ellison | 23 | 4/58 5/58 6/104 | |
| †D. J. Haggo c Ealham b C. S. Cowdrey | 25 | 7/124 8/162 9/187 | |

Bowling: Igglesden 8–3–24–3; Ealham 8–1–32–0; Merrick 7–0–31–2; Ellison 11–1–42–2; Fleming 8.3–0–23–1; C. S. Cowdrey 5–1–17–2.

Umpires: H. D. Bird and R. Palmer.

## GROUP D

### HAMPSHIRE v NOTTINGHAMSHIRE

At Southampton, April 23. Hampshire won by 4 runs. Toss: Nottinghamshire. Smith's unbeaten 121, off 159 balls, included a six and thirteen fours. With his captain, Nicholas, who faced 43 balls, he added 89 in thirteen overs after Hampshire had lost three wickets for 5 runs in nine balls.

*Gold Award:* C. L. Smith.

#### Hampshire

| | | | |
|---|---|---|---|
| T. C. Middleton b Cooper | 60 | J. R. Ayling not out | 3 |
| C. L. Smith not out | 121 | B 17, w 4, n-b 4 | 25 |
| D. I. Gower c French b Hemmings | 5 | | — |
| J. R. Wood c Randall b Hemmings | 0 | 1/163 2/168　(4 wkts, 55 overs) | 264 |
| *M. C. J. Nicholas b Pick | 50 | 3/168 4/257 | |

K. D. James, †A. N. Aymes, S. D. Udal, C. A. Connor and Aqib Javed did not bat.

Bowling: Stephenson 11-0-56-0; Pick 11-0-61-1; Cooper 11-2-42-1; Saxelby 11-1-39-0; Hemmings 11-0-49-2.

#### Nottinghamshire

| | | | |
|---|---|---|---|
| B. C. Broad b Connor | 8 | E. E. Hemmings c Connor b Udal | 9 |
| M. Newell c Wood b Udal | 18 | K. E. Cooper run out | 0 |
| *R. T. Robinson st Aymes b Ayling | 54 | R. A. Pick not out | 25 |
| P. Johnson c Middleton b Ayling | 24 | B 2, l-b 14, w 17, n-b 1 | 34 |
| D. W. Randall c and b Connor | 5 | | — |
| M. Saxelby lbw b Udal | 32 | 1/11 2/52 3/116　(9 wkts, 55 overs) | 260 |
| F. D. Stephenson c Connor b Aqib Javed | 14 | 4/126 5/135 6/160 | |
| †B. N. French not out | 37 | 7/194 8/212 9/216 | |

Bowling: Aqib Javed 11-2-35-1; Connor 11-1-50-2; James 11-0-55-0; Udal 11-1-48-3; Ayling 11-0-56-2.

Umpires: R. Palmer and R. C. Tolchard.

### MINOR COUNTIES v GLAMORGAN

At Trowbridge, April 23. Glamorgan won by 17 runs. Toss: Minor Counties. Shastri's first hundred in an English domestic limited-overs competition included thirteen fours and two sixes. For Minor Counties, Love hit 81 from 78 balls.

*Gold Award:* R. J. Shastri.

#### Glamorgan

| | | | |
|---|---|---|---|
| *A. R. Butcher c Roberts b Greensword | 25 | †C. P. Metson b Taylor | 0 |
| H. Morris c Fothergill b Taylor | 1 | S. L. Watkin not out | 5 |
| R. J. Shastri not out | 138 | B 4, l-b 11, w 5, n-b 1 | 21 |
| M. P. Maynard c Brown b Greensword | 7 | | — |
| I. Smith run out | 2 | 1/7 2/68 3/84　(7 wkts, 55 overs) | 233 |
| G. C. Holmes c Mack b Green | 34 | 4/109 5/190 | |
| R. D. B. Croft c Fothergill b Green | 0 | 6/191 7/202 | |

S. R. Barwick and M. Frost did not bat.

Bowling: Taylor 11-4-33-2; Mack 11-3-49-0; Green 10-0-55-2; Greensword 11-3-31-2; Evans 10-0-35-0; Plumb 2-0-15-0.

## Minor Counties

| | | | |
|---|---|---|---|
| G. K. Brown b Barwick | 2 | R. C. Green not out | 0 |
| M. J. Roberts c Shastri b Croft | 40 | N. R. Taylor not out | 1 |
| N. A. Folland c Barwick b Croft | 45 | | |
| J. D. Love c Butcher b Watkin | 81 | L-b 9, w 7 | 16 |
| S. G. Plumb b Watkin | 23 | | |
| *S. Greensword run out | 3 | 1/6 2/76 3/108 (8 wkts, 55 overs) 216 | |
| †A. R. Fothergill lbw b Frost | 0 | 4/174 5/180 6/186 | |
| R. A. Evans b Watkin | 5 | 7/215 8/215 | |

A. J. Mack did not bat.

Bowling: Watkin 11–4–28–3; Frost 11–1–45–1; Barwick 10–3–31–1; Shastri 11–1–36–0; Croft 9–0–49–2; Smith 3–0–18–0.

Umpires: B. Dudleston and B. J. Meyer.

## MINOR COUNTIES v HAMPSHIRE

At Trowbridge, April 25, 26. Hampshire won by eight wickets. Toss: Minor Counties. Brown, who hit six fours, and Love, with nine fours and a six, put on 154 for the third wicket after Minor Counties were 9 for two. Ninety minutes were lost on the first day, and overnight Hampshire were 141 for two from 39 overs (C. L. Smith 62*, J. R. Wood 16*).

*Gold Award:* J. R. Wood.

## Minor Counties

| | | | |
|---|---|---|---|
| G. K. Brown st Aymes b Connor | 82 | R. A. Evans not out | 5 |
| M. J. Roberts lbw b Aqib Javed | 4 | | |
| N. A. Folland b Aqib Javed | 0 | B 4, l-b 4, w 9, n-b 3 | 20 |
| J. D. Love st Aymes b Bakker | 75 | | |
| S. G. Plumb not out | 23 | 1/7 2/9 3/163 (5 wkts, 55 overs) 214 | |
| †A. R. Fothergill b Aqib Javed | 5 | 4/199 5/204 | |

*S. Greensword, R. C. Green, N. R. Taylor and A. J. Mack did not bat.

Bowling: Bakker 11–3–21–1; Aqib Javed 11–0–43–3; Ayling 11–0–28–0; Connor 11–0–64–1; Udal 11–2–50–0.

## Hampshire

| | |
|---|---|
| T. C. Middleton run out | 40 |
| C. L. Smith not out | 78 |
| D. I. Gower c Roberts b Greensword | 6 |
| J. R. Wood not out | 70 |
| L-b 9, w 11, n-b 1 | 21 |

1/76 2/99 (2 wkts, 49.5 overs) 215

*M. C. J. Nicholas, J. R. Ayling, †A. N. Aymes, S. D. Udal, C. A. Connor, Aqib Javed and P. J. Bakker did not bat.

Bowling: Taylor 9–2–41–0; Green 10.5–0–35–0; Mack 10–1–48–0; Greensword 11–2–35–1; Evans 9–1–47–0.

Umpires: G. I. Burgess and J. W. Holder.

## NOTTINGHAMSHIRE v YORKSHIRE

At Nottingham, April 25. Nottinghamshire won by seven wickets. Toss: Yorkshire. Stephenson, who returned his best figures in the competition, took three wickets in nine balls as five Yorkshire wickets fell for 13 runs in seven overs.

*Gold Award:* F. D. Stephenson.

## Yorkshire

| | | | | |
|---|---|---|---|---|
| *M. D. Moxon b Stephenson | 95 | P. W. Jarvis not out | | 3 |
| A. A. Metcalfe b Evans | 20 | S. D. Fletcher not out | | 2 |
| D. Byas lbw b Stephenson | 47 | | | |
| †R. J. Blakey c Randall b Stephenson | 39 | L-b 10, w 2, n-b 1 | | 13 |
| P. E. Robinson b Stephenson | 0 | | | |
| K. Sharp b Evans | 0 | 1/60 2/169 3/176 | (8 wkts, 55 overs) | 234 |
| P. Carrick c French b Cooper | 2 | 4/178 5/179 6/182 | | |
| P. J. Hartley c Johnson b Stephenson | 13 | 7/216 8/232 | | |

M. A. Robinson did not bat.

Bowling: Stephenson 11–5–30–5; Cooper 10–2–27–1; Evans 11–0–50–2; Saxelby 6–0–43–0; Hemmings 11–0–52–0; Crawley 6–0–22–0.

## Nottinghamshire

| | | | | |
|---|---|---|---|---|
| B. C. Broad not out | 108 | M. A. Crawley not out | | 0 |
| D. W. Randall c Blakey b Hartley | 86 | L-b 5, w 5 | | 10 |
| *R. T. Robinson b Jarvis | 27 | | | |
| P. Johnson c Metcalfe b M. A. Robinson | 4 | 1/177 2/227 3/232 | (3 wkts, 54.2 overs) | 235 |

M. Saxelby, K. P. Evans, F. D. Stephenson, †B. N. French, E. E. Hemmings and K. E. Cooper did not bat.

Bowling: Jarvis 10.2–2–34–1; M. A. Robinson 11–0–52–1; Fletcher 11–2–40–0; Hartley 11–0–56–1; Carrick 11–0–48–0.

Umpires: D. J. Constant and B. Leadbeater.

# HAMPSHIRE v GLAMORGAN

At Southampton, May 2. Hampshire won by 59 runs. Toss: Glamorgan. Chris Smith, whose 142 came from 154 balls, put on 140 in 33 overs with Middleton and added 124 in eighteen with Gower, who scored his first fifty of the season. Ian Smith and Dennis, who shared a 76-run stand for Glamorgan's seventh wicket, both hit maiden fifties in the competition.
*Gold Award:* C. L. Smith.

## Hampshire

| | | | | |
|---|---|---|---|---|
| T. C. Middleton c Roberts b Smith | 54 | J. R. Ayling not out | | 5 |
| C. L. Smith b Barwick | 142 | B 4, l-b 5, w 5 | | 14 |
| D. I. Gower b Frost | 63 | | | |
| *M. C. J. Nicholas not out | 15 | 1/140 2/264 | (4 wkts, 55 overs) | 299 |
| J. R. Wood lbw b Barwick | 6 | 3/274 4/289 | | |

†A. N. Aymes, S. D. Udal, C. A. Connor, P. J. Bakker and Aqib Javed did not bat.

Bowling: Watkin 11–0–69–0; Frost 11–2–50–1; Barwick 11–0–61–2; Dennis 11–1–29–0; Dale 4–0–30–0; Smith 7–0–51–1.

## Glamorgan

| | | | | |
|---|---|---|---|---|
| *A. R. Butcher c Gower b Udal | 70 | S. L. Watkin c Middleton b Nicholas | | 15 |
| H. Morris c Aymes b Bakker | 3 | S. R. Barwick not out | | 1 |
| A. Dale c Middleton b Ayling | 19 | M. Frost c Wood b Nicholas | | 0 |
| M. P. Maynard b Connor | 6 | B 1, l-b 7, w 9, n-b 6 | | 23 |
| G. C. Holmes c Aymes b Connor | 1 | | | |
| I. Smith b Bakker | 51 | 1/18 2/86 3/107 | (55 overs) | 240 |
| †M. L. Roberts c and b Udal | 1 | 4/111 5/111 6/117 | | |
| S. J. Dennis c Bakker b Connor | 50 | 7/193 8/230 9/239 | | |

Bowling: Aqib Javed 9–1–30–0; Bakker 11–2–37–2; Connor 11–0–54–3; Ayling 9–0–51–1; Udal 11–2–33–2; Nicholas 4–0–27–2.

Umpires: J. C. Balderstone and D. R. Shepherd.

## YORKSHIRE v MINOR COUNTIES

At Leeds, May 2. Yorkshire won by seven wickets. Toss: Yorkshire. After sixteen overs Minor Counties were 20 for two, but Yorkshire exile Love added 118 for the third wicket with Folland and, unbeaten with 80, took his aggregate in three Benson and Hedges Cup innings in 1991 to 236.

*Gold Award:* M. D. Moxon.

### Minor Counties

| | | | |
|---|---|---|---|
| G. K. Brown c Fletcher b Pickles | 6 | †A. R. Fothergill not out | 15 |
| M. J. Roberts c Blakey b Jarvis | 6 | | |
| N. A. Folland c Fletcher b Pickles | 54 | L-b 6, w 9 | 15 |
| J. D. Love not out | 80 | | |
| S. G. Plumb c Blakey b M. A. Robinson | 0 | 1/11 2/20 3/138 (5 wkts, 55 overs) 182 | |
| D. R. Thomas b Jarvis | 6 | 4/138 5/160 | |

*S. Greensword, R. A. Evans, N. R. Taylor and A. J. Mack did not bat.

Bowling: Jarvis 11–5–27–2; Fletcher 11–3–26–0; M. A. Robinson 11–2–33–1; Pickles 11–0–49–2; Batty 11–2–41–0.

### Yorkshire

| | | | |
|---|---|---|---|
| *M. D. Moxon b Greensword | 65 | P. E. Robinson not out | 11 |
| A. A. Metcalfe not out | 92 | L-b 6, w 6, n-b 1 | 13 |
| D. Byas run out | 3 | | |
| †R. J. Blakey c Folland b Greensword | 0 | 1/135 2/148 3/160 (3 wkts, 53.2 overs) 184 | |

S. A. Kellett, P. W. Jarvis, C. S. Pickles, J. D. Batty, S. D. Fletcher and M. A. Robinson did not bat.

Bowling: Taylor 10.2–3–36–0; Mack 9–2–32–0; Thomas 11–0–49–0; Evans 11–0–37–0; Greensword 11–3–21–2; Plumb 1–0–3–0.

Umpires: H. D. Bird and K. E. Palmer.

## GLAMORGAN v NOTTINGHAMSHIRE

At Cardiff, May 4. Glamorgan won by 1 run. Toss: Nottinghamshire. Robinson, taking 140 balls for his 100, added 147 for Nottinghamshire's fourth wicket with Crawley, whose 58 was his highest score in the competition. Evans's return was his best in the Benson and Hedges Cup.

*Gold Award:* R. T. Robinson.

### Glamorgan

| | | | |
|---|---|---|---|
| *A. R. Butcher run out | 57 | S. L. Watkin c and b Stephenson | 5 |
| H. Morris c French b Stephenson | 3 | S. R. Barwick not out | 4 |
| R. J. Shastri lbw b Evans | 16 | M. Frost not out | 0 |
| M. P. Maynard c Randall b Saxelby | 62 | L-b 8, w 6, n-b 5 | 19 |
| G. C. Holmes b Hemmings | 22 | | |
| I. Smith lbw b Evans | 36 | 1/15 2/56 3/97 (9 wkts, 55 overs) 229 | |
| †M. L. Roberts lbw b Evans | 0 | 4/153 5/207 6/207 | |
| S. J. Dennis c Randall b Evans | 5 | 7/219 8/221 9/225 | |

Bowling: Stephenson 11–1–46–2; Cooper 10–1–34–0; Evans 11–0–43–4; Saxelby 9–0–36–1; Hemmings 11–1–46–1; Crawley 3–0–16–0.

## Nottinghamshire

| | | | |
|---|---|---|---|
| B. C. Broad c Smith b Frost | 0 | F. D. Stephenson not out | 4 |
| D. W. Randall c Roberts b Watkin | 14 | K. P. Evans not out | 5 |
| *R. T. Robinson b Frost | 116 | L-b 9, w 3 | 12 |
| P. Johnson c Maynard b Shastri | 14 | | — |
| M. A. Crawley c and b Barwick | 58 | 1/0 2/29 3/53 (6 wkts, 55 overs) 228 |
| M. Saxelby c Maynard b Frost | 5 | 4/200 5/214 6/214 |

†B. N. French, E. E. Hemmings and K. E. Cooper did not bat.

Bowling: Frost 9–1–38–3; Dennis 11–1–41–0; Watkin 11–3–42–1; Barwick 10–1–42–1; Shastri 11–0–40–1; Butcher 3–0–16–0.

Umpires: J. C. Balderstone and D. O. Oslear.

## YORKSHIRE v HAMPSHIRE

At Leeds, May 4. Yorkshire won by 189 runs. Toss: Hampshire. Hampshire's total was the lowest in the Benson and Hedges Cup, undercutting Leicestershire's 56 against Minor Counties at Wellington in 1982. Smith followed his scores of 121 not out, 78 not out and 142 in the previous rounds with 1. Two of Robinson's catches were taken behind the wicket while he was deputising for Blakey, off the field with a migraine. Earlier Robinson had scored 43 runs from 28 balls, and Byas had compiled a determined 92, his highest score in the competition, from 133 balls.

*Gold Award:* A. Sidebottom.

## Yorkshire

| | | | |
|---|---|---|---|
| *M. D. Moxon b Connor | 24 | S. A. Kellett not out | 0 |
| A. A. Metcalfe c and b Udal | 37 | | |
| D. Byas c Ayling b Aqib Javed | 92 | L-b 7, w 13, n-b 2 | 22 |
| †R. J. Blakey c Smith b Ayling | 20 | | — |
| P. E. Robinson c Connor | 43 | 1/42 2/106 3/165 (7 wkts, 55 overs) 239 |
| P. W. Jarvis c Ayling b Aqib Javed | 0 | 4/228 5/231 |
| P. J. Hartley c Wood b Aqib Javed | 1 | 6/237 7/239 |

A. Sidebottom, J. D. Batty and S. D. Fletcher did not bat.

Bowling: Aqib Javed 11–2–51–3; Bakker 11–1–54–0; Connor 11–2–59–2; Ayling 11–0–51–1; Udal 11–3–17–1.

## Hampshire

| | | | |
|---|---|---|---|
| T. C. Middleton b Jarvis | 2 | C. A. Connor c Blakey b Hartley | 3 |
| C. L. Smith c Robinson b Sidebottom | 1 | P. J. Bakker b Fletcher | 7 |
| D. I. Gower lbw b Jarvis | 5 | Aqib Javed not out | 0 |
| J. R. Wood c Robinson b Sidebottom | 14 | W 1, n-b 4 | 5 |
| *M. C. J. Nicholas run out | 0 | | — |
| J. R. Ayling lbw b Sidebottom | 2 | 1/2 2/11 3/11 (27.2 overs) 50 |
| †A. N. Aymes c Robinson b Hartley | 10 | 4/14 5/24 6/29 |
| S. D. Udal c Moxon b Sidebottom | 1 | 7/33 8/43 9/50 |

Bowling: Jarvis 7–2–13–2; Sidebottom 11–5–19–4; Hartley 7–3–7–2; Fletcher 2.2–0–11–1.

Umpires: B. Dudleston and J. H. Hampshire.

## GLAMORGAN v YORKSHIRE

At Cardiff, May 7. Yorkshire won by eight wickets. Toss: Glamorgan. Butcher scored his maiden hundred in the competition, striking twelve fours and facing 147 balls in all. He shared stands of 105 with Morris and 89 in thirteen overs with Holmes. Moxon, whose hundred came from 122 balls during his third double-century partnership with Metcalfe in one-day cricket, also reached his highest score in the competition, 1 short of the Yorkshire record of 142 held by G. Boycott.

*Gold Award:* M. D. Moxon.

## Glamorgan

| | | | |
|---|---|---|---|
| A. R. Butcher c Sidebottom b Hartley . . | 127 | †M. L. Roberts not out . . . . . . . . . . . . | 1 |
| *H. Morris b Fletcher . . . . . . . . . . . . . | 36 | | |
| R. J. Shastri c Blakey b Fletcher . . . . . . | 7 | L-b 6, w 3 . . . . . . . . . . . . | 9 |
| M. P. Maynard c Fletcher b Batty . . . . . | 19 | | |
| G. C. Holmes not out . . . . . . . . . . . . . | 35 | 1/105 2/117 3/140    (5 wkts, 55 overs) 235 | |
| I. Smith b Jarvis . . . . . . . . . . . . . . . . | 1 | 4/229 5/232 | |

M. Frost, S. J. Dennis, S. L. Watkin and S. R. Barwick did not bat.

Bowling: Jarvis 11–0–57–1; Sidebottom 11–2–22–0; Hartley 11–0–47–1; Batty 11–1–34–1; Fletcher 11–0–69–2.

## Yorkshire

| | |
|---|---|
| *M. D. Moxon not out . . . . . . . . . . . . | 141 |
| A. A. Metcalfe c Barwick b Shastri . . . . | 84 |
| D. Byas lbw b Watkin . . . . . . . . . . . . | 7 |
| †R. J. Blakey not out . . . . . . . . . . . . | 1 |
| L-b 4 . . . . . . . . . . . . . . . . . . | 4 |

1/213 2/225        (2 wkts, 49 overs) 237

P. E. Robinson, S. A. Kellett, P. J. Hartley, A. Sidebottom, S. D. Fletcher, P. W. Jarvis and J. D. Batty did not bat.

Bowling: Frost 9–2–44–0; Dennis 11–1–49–0; Watkin 11–0–51–1; Barwick 8–0–41–0; Shastri 10–0–48–1.

Umpires: B. Hassan and R. Julian.

## NOTTINGHAMSHIRE v MINOR COUNTIES

At Nottingham, May 7. Nottinghamshire won by 51 runs. Toss: Minor Counties. Johnson's unbeaten 102 came from 75 balls. Folland reached his hundred from the last ball of the match, the 132nd he received; he struck six fours, and added 94 in sixteen overs with Plumb for the fourth wicket.

*Gold Award:* N. A. Folland.

## Nottinghamshire

| | | | |
|---|---|---|---|
| B. C. Broad c Brown b Arnold . . . . . . . | 24 | K. P. Evans not out . . . . . . . . . . . . . . | 1 |
| D. W. Randall b Thomas . . . . . . . . . . . | 84 | | |
| *R. T. Robinson c Folland b Taylor . . . . | 42 | L-b 2, w 7 . . . . . . . . . . . . | 9 |
| P. Johnson not out . . . . . . . . . . . . . . . | 102 | | |
| M. A. Crawley run out . . . . . . . . . . . . | 5 | 1/39 2/133 3/201    (5 wkts, 55 overs) 279 | |
| F. D. Stephenson c Plumb b Arnold . . . | 1 | 4/249 5/274 | |

†B. N. French, E. E. Hemmings, R. A. Pick and J. A. Afford did not bat.

Bowling: Taylor 11–1–63–1; Arnold 11–0–52–2; Conn 11–1–40–0; Thomas 11–1–61–1; Greensword 5–0–28–0; Plumb 6–0–33–0.

## Minor Counties

| | | | |
|---|---|---|---|
| G. K. Brown c Randall b Hemmings . . | 17 | †A. R. Fothergill run out . . . . . . . . . . . | 4 |
| M. J. Roberts c Evans b Pick . . . . . . . . | 1 | I. E. Conn not out . . . . . . . . . . . . . . . | 23 |
| N. A. Folland not out . . . . . . . . . . . . . | 100 | L-b 9, w 5, n-b 2 . . . . . . . . . . . | 16 |
| D. R. Turner b Afford . . . . . . . . . . . . . | 15 | | |
| S. G. Plumb c Robinson b Crawley . . . . | 52 | 1/21 2/25 3/63    (6 wkts, 55 overs) 228 | |
| D. R. Thomas run out . . . . . . . . . . . . . | 0 | 4/157 5/158 6/169 | |

*S. Greensword, N. R. Taylor and K. A. Arnold did not bat.

Bowling: Pick 11–1–36–1; Stephenson 4–3–3–0; Evans 10–2–39–0; Hemmings 11–3–54–1; Afford 11–0–43–1; Crawley 8–0–44–1.

Umpires: J. H. Hampshire and P. B. Wight.

## QUARTER-FINALS

### ESSEX v HAMPSHIRE

At Chelmsford, May 29. Essex won by 32 runs. Toss: Hampshire. After reaching the final twenty overs requiring 109 with eight wickets in hand, Hampshire capitulated on a pitch which gave some encouragement to seam throughout. Topley claimed three wickets for 6 runs during a 23-ball spell, in between which Foster, who combined accuracy with hostility, broke through the defences of Chris Smith. The Hampshire opener had resisted for 43 overs. Earlier in the day, several of the Essex batsmen had been dismissed when seemingly well set, and it was left to Shahid, with 42 off 60 balls, to see the total past 200. Off-spinner Udal presented the major problem, and his three wickets were just reward.

*Gold Award:* T. D. Topley.

### Essex

| | | | | |
|---|---|---|---|---|
| *G. A. Gooch lbw b James | 29 | N. A. Foster b Aqib Javed | | 5 |
| J. P. Stephenson run out | 38 | T. D. Topley not out | | 6 |
| P. J. Prichard b Connor | 2 | P. M. Such b Connor | | 4 |
| Salim Malik c R. A. Smith b Aqib Javed | 38 | L-b 9, w 16, n-b 3 | | 28 |
| N. Hussain c Aymes b Bakker | 17 | | | — |
| D. R. Pringle c Aymes b Udal | 3 | 1/56 2/60 3/110 | (55 overs) | 223 |
| N. Shahid st Aymes b Udal | 42 | 4/132 5/135 6/175 | | |
| †M. A. Garnham b Udal | 11 | 7/204 8/205 9/214 | | |

Bowling: Bakker 11-0-34-1; Aqib Javed 11-1-49-2; Connor 11-1-45-2; James 11-0-45-1; Udal 11-1-41-3.

### Hampshire

| | | | | |
|---|---|---|---|---|
| V. P. Terry c and b Topley | 10 | C. A. Connor run out | | 0 |
| C. L. Smith b Foster | 71 | P. J. Bakker c Stephenson b Pringle | | 4 |
| D. I. Gower lbw b Gooch | 18 | Aqib Javed b Gooch | | 3 |
| R. A. Smith c Garnham b Topley | 35 | L-b 8, w 2, n-b 5 | | 15 |
| *M. C. J. Nicholas not out | 22 | | | — |
| K. D. James c Gooch b Topley | 2 | 1/27 2/72 3/142 | (53.5 overs) | 191 |
| †A. N. Aymes c Garnham b Topley | 2 | 4/146 5/153 6/156 | | |
| S. D. Udal b Pringle | 9 | 7/176 8/176 9/183 | | |

Bowling: Foster 11-3-24-1; Pringle 10-2-36-2; Topley 11-3-41-4; Gooch 10.5-1-42-2; Such 11-1-40-0.

Umpires: M. J. Kitchen and R. A. White.

### LANCASHIRE v NORTHAMPTONSHIRE

At Manchester, May 29. Lancashire won by seven wickets. Toss: Lancashire. Lamb, with 48 in 52 balls, and Bailey shared in a third-wicket stand of 81 in thirteen overs, but Northamptonshire's total on a true pitch did not look enough to stretch Lancashire's strong batting line-up. Mendis led the chase to a comfortable win, his second-wicket partnership of 142 in 32 overs with Atherton virtually settling the result. He reached his century in 111 balls and went on to his highest score in the competition.

*Gold Award:* G. D. Mendis.

### Northamptonshire

| | | | | |
|---|---|---|---|---|
| A. Fordham c Fairbrother b Allott | 19 | †D. Ripley not out | | 6 |
| N. A. Felton run out | 44 | A. Walker not out | | 0 |
| R. J. Bailey b Austin | 75 | | | |
| *A. J. Lamb c Fowler b Allott | 48 | | | |
| D. J. Capel c Hughes b Watkinson | 19 | B 3, l-b 8, w 7, n-b 5 | | 23 |
| K. M. Curran b Wasim Akram | 0 | | | — |
| A. L. Penberthy b Wasim Akram | 3 | 1/40 2/101 3/182 | (8 wkts, 55 overs) | 246 |
| J. G. Thomas c DeFreitas b Wasim Akram | 9 | 4/219 5/219 6/227 | | |
| | | 7/229 8/244 | | |

N. G. B. Cook did not bat.

Bowling: DeFreitas 11–0–54–0; Allott 11–0–38–2; Wasim Akram 11–0–57–3; Watkinson 11–1–46–1; Austin 11–0–40–1.

## Lancashire

| | |
|---|---|
| G. D. Mendis not out . . . . . . . . . . . . . .125 | M. Watkinson not out . . . . . . . . . . . . . . 32 |
| G. Fowler c Ripley b Thomas . . . . . . . . 9 | L-b 4, w 7, n-b 1 . . . . . . . . . . . 12 |
| M. A. Atherton c Cook b Walker . . . . . 56 | |
| N. H. Fairbrother c Lamb b Thomas . . 13 | 1/28 2/170 3/192 (3 wkts, 52.4 overs) 247 |

Wasim Akram, P. A. J. DeFreitas, †W. K. Hegg, *D. P. Hughes, I. D. Austin and P. J. W. Allott did not bat.

Bowling: Thomas 11–0–54–2; Walker 9–1–33–1; Capel 10.4–1–52–0; Cook 11–0–40–0; Curran 3–0–21–0; Penberthy 8–0–43–0.

Umpires: H. D. Bird and N. T. Plews.

## WORCESTERSHIRE v KENT

At Worcester, May 29. Worcestershire won by 27 runs. Toss: Worcestershire. Curtis and Moody set the home side on course for a semi-final place with an opening stand of 138 in 27 overs, and with Hick hitting his last 35 runs from eleven deliveries (two sixes, five fours), the other end of the innings was even more productive. The last ten overs brought 88 runs, with 55 of those coming from the final five overs. Moody's hundred before lunch, off 104 balls, contained two sixes and ten fours, and won him his third Gold Award in five games for Worcestershire. No side batting second had scored 300 runs in the competition and won. Kent, moreover, had never totalled 300 runs in 55 overs against another county. But they made a good try. Benson gave them a solid start, hitting 56 of the first 113 runs, and Taylor's unbeaten 89 from 82 balls saw to it that they were not eclipsed without honour.

*Gold Award:* T. M. Moody.

## Worcestershire

| | |
|---|---|
| T. S. Curtis c Marsh b Igglesden . . . . . . 53 | R. K. Illingworth not out . . . . . . . . . . . 1 |
| T. M. Moody lbw b Fleming . . . . . . . . .100 | |
| G. A. Hick not out . . . . . . . . . . . . . . . . 84 | B 1, l-b 7, w 5 . . . . . . . . . . . . . 13 |
| D. B. D'Oliveira run out . . . . . . . . . . . . 2 | |
| *P. A. Neale c C. S. Cowdrey b Igglesden 47 | 1/138 2/168 3/178 (5 wkts, 55 overs) 308 |
| †S. J. Rhodes b Merrick . . . . . . . . . . . . 8 | 4/263 5/307 |

P. J. Newport, S. R. Lampitt, N. V. Radford and G. R. Dilley did not bat.

Bowling: Merrick 11–0–59–1; Igglesden 11–1–85–2; Ellison 11–0–49–0; Davis 11–1–62–0; Fleming 11–0–45–1.

## Kent

| | |
|---|---|
| *M. R. Benson st Rhodes b Illingworth . 56 | R. P. Davis c Neale b Lampitt . . . . . . . 1 |
| M. V. Fleming c Hick b Radford . . . . . 22 | T. A. Merrick c Neale b Lampitt . . . . . 0 |
| C. S. Cowdrey b Illingworth . . . . . . . . . 25 | A. P. Igglesden not out . . . . . . . . . . . . 26 |
| N. R. Taylor not out . . . . . . . . . . . . . . . 89 | L-b 5, w 8, n-b 1 . . . . . . . . . . . 14 |
| T. R. Ward c Neale b Newport . . . . . . . 10 | |
| G. R. Cowdrey b Dilley . . . . . . . . . . . . 8 | 1/47 2/110 3/113 (9 wkts, 55 overs) 281 |
| †S. A. Marsh c Curtis b Radford . . . . . . 24 | 4/137 5/159 6/215 |
| R. M. Ellison run out . . . . . . . . . . . . . . 6 | 7/229 8/231 9/231 |

Bowling: Dilley 11–0–72–1; Radford 11–1–57–2; Illingworth 11–1–50–2; Lampitt 11–0–59–2; Newport 11–1–38–1.

Umpires: J. D. Bond and J. H. Harris.

## YORKSHIRE v WARWICKSHIRE

At Leeds, May 29. Yorkshire won by 122 runs. Toss: Warwickshire. Moxon led Yorkshire in fine style, making a solid 30 when the conditions favoured the bowlers and later taking a career-best five for 31, including three wickets in fourteen balls. Kellett and Byas also batted well, but Donald was wayward and Warwickshire conceded 41 extras. Jarvis, with hamstring trouble, and Sidebottom, with a groin strain, broke down and could not complete their allocation of overs, but the pitch suited Moxon's tidy medium-pace deliveries, and Warwickshire paid the penalty for some hesitant batting.

*Gold Award:* M. D. Moxon.

### Yorkshire

| | | | |
|---|---:|---|---:|
| *M. D. Moxon b Smith | 30 | P. W. Jarvis not out | 12 |
| A. A. Metcalfe c Piper b Donald | 3 | P. J. Hartley not out | 1 |
| S. A. Kellett b Donald | 44 | B 4, l-b 20, w 15, n-b 2 | 41 |
| D. Byas c Reeve b Munton | 58 | | |
| †R. J. Blakey b Donald | 15 | 1/7 2/63 3/104 (6 wkts, 55 overs) 233 | |
| P. E. Robinson b Munton | 29 | 4/157 5/194 6/224 | |

P. Carrick, A. Sidebottom and S. D. Fletcher did not bat.

Bowling: Munton 11–3–37–2; Donald 11–1–46–3; Small 11–1–43–0; Reeve 11–0–35–0; Smith 9–2–41–1; Pierson 2–0–7–0.

### Warwickshire

| | | | |
|---|---:|---|---:|
| A. J. Moles c Blakey b Hartley | 10 | T. A. Munton c Hartley b Carrick | 10 |
| Asif Din c Blakey b Fletcher | 23 | A. A. Donald c Carrick b Moxon | 0 |
| *T. A. Lloyd c Moxon b Carrick | 24 | A. R. K. Pierson not out | 3 |
| P. A. Smith c and b Moxon | 3 | L-b 6, w 9, n-b 2 | 17 |
| D. A. Reeve c Blakey b Moxon | 0 | | |
| D. P. Ostler lbw b Moxon | 8 | 1/24 2/44 3/59 (42 overs) 111 | |
| †K. J. Piper c and b Moxon | 11 | 4/59 5/75 6/96 | |
| G. C. Small lbw b Carrick | 2 | 7/96 8/101 9/106 | |

Bowling: Sidebottom 9–4–11–0; Jarvis 5–0–11–0; Hartley 6–2–19–1; Fletcher 4–1–11–1; Carrick 10–1–22–3; Moxon 8–0–31–5.

Umpires: J. C. Balderstone and B. J. Meyer.

## SEMI-FINALS

### ESSEX v WORCESTERSHIRE

At Chelmsford, June 12. Worcestershire won by nine wickets. Toss: Worcestershire. Not even the amount of cloud cover, combining with some moisture in the pitch, could explain the way in which Essex were dismissed in two and a quarter hours. Dilley set them on the slide when he found enough movement to have Gooch caught behind, and he removed Salim Malik soon afterwards before returning to the deep to watch the nagging accuracy of Botham inflict further damage. Botham conceded just 11 runs in as many overs – he conceded a wide and a boundary with his first two deliveries – and only Foster's defiant six and four off Radford in one over saved Essex from their lowest total in the competition: 100 against Hampshire at Chelmsford in 1987. Worcestershire, with no need to hurry, did not raise 50 until the 24th over. Thereafter Moody struck four sixes, the last of them against Gooch to put his side ahead with nearly 24 overs to spare. His 72 not out came from 99 balls and also included half a dozen boundaries.

*Gold Award:* I. T. Botham.

## Essex

| | | | |
|---|---|---|---|
| *G. A. Gooch c Rhodes b Dilley | 12 | N. A. Foster b Radford | 16 |
| J. P. Stephenson c Rhodes b Lampitt | 13 | T. D. Topley b Botham | 1 |
| P. J. Prichard c Rhodes b Botham | 18 | P. M. Such not out | 1 |
| Salim Malik c Neale b Dilley | 2 | L-b 4, w 2, n-b 2 | 8 |
| N. Hussain c Rhodes b Radford | 26 | | |
| D. R. Pringle run out | 4 | 1/26 2/27 3/43 | (34.5 overs) 104 |
| N. Shahid c and b Radford | 1 | 4/56 5/71 6/74 | |
| †M. A. Garnham lbw b Botham | 2 | 7/85 8/85 9/89 | |

Bowling: Dilley 8–1–17–2; Lampitt 6–1–31–1; Botham 11–6–11–3; Radford 9.5–2–41–3.

## Worcestershire

| | |
|---|---|
| T. S. Curtis run out | 27 |
| T. M. Moody not out | 72 |
| G. A. Hick not out | 4 |
| L-b 2, w 3, n-b 2 | 7 |
| | — |
| 1/100      (1 wkt, 31.1 overs) | 110 |

D. B. D'Oliveira, *P. A. Neale, I. T. Botham, †S. J. Rhodes, R. K. Illingworth, S. R. Lampitt, N. V. Radford and G. R. Dilley did not bat.

Bowling: Foster 7–0–14–0; Pringle 7–1–16–0; Topley 8–1–26–0; Gooch 5.1–0–27–0; Such 4–0–25–0.

Umpires: D. J. Constant and B. Leadbeater.

# LANCASHIRE v YORKSHIRE

At Manchester, June 12. Lancashire won by 68 runs. Toss: Yorkshire. The Gold Award went to Yorkshire's opening batsman, Metcalfe, but it was team effort which saw Lancashire through to their third successive Lord's final. Mendis and Fowler gave Lancashire a flying start with 125 runs in 27 overs, and although the last seven wickets fell in ten overs for 58 runs, a total of 268 always looked too high for Yorkshire. Metcalfe's sterling effort kept him at the crease through 48 overs; he reached his first hundred in the competition from 121 balls, and faced 132 in all, hitting seven fours. His partnership of 109 in 21 overs with Blakey raised the hopes of Yorkshire supporters among the 18,200 spectators, but once Watkinson had broken through the end came quickly. Yorkshire lost their last seven wickets for 38 runs, five of them to Watkinson.

*Gold Award:* A. A. Metcalfe.

## Lancashire

| | | | |
|---|---|---|---|
| G. D. Mendis b Carrick | 75 | †W. K. Hegg b Gough | 0 |
| G. Fowler c Blakey b Carrick | 58 | I. D. Austin b Fletcher | 22 |
| M. A. Atherton c Moxon b Fletcher | 24 | *D. P. Hughes not out | 1 |
| N. H. Fairbrother c Blakey b Gough | 40 | P. J. W. Allott b Fletcher | 0 |
| M. Watkinson c Blakey | | L-b 11, w 4, n-b 3 | 18 |
|      b M. A. Robinson | 12 | | — |
| Wasim Akram c Fletcher | | 1/125 2/163 3/179 | (54 overs) 268 |
|      b M. A. Robinson | 6 | 4/210 5/224 6/234 | |
| P. A. J. DeFreitas c Carrick b Fletcher | 12 | 7/234 8/266 9/268 | |

Bowling: Hartley 11–0–56–0; M. A. Robinson 9–1–43–2; Gough 8–0–41–2; Fletcher 10–0–51–4; Carrick 11–0–36–2; Moxon 5–0–30–0.

## Yorkshire

| | | | | |
|---|---|---|---|---|
| *M. D. Moxon c Hegg b DeFreitas | 15 | P. J. Hartley b Watkinson | | 0 |
| A. A. Metcalfe b Watkinson | 114 | S. D. Fletcher b Watkinson | | 1 |
| S. A. Kellett run out | 2 | M. A. Robinson not out | | 1 |
| D. Byas c Allott b Wasim Akram | 0 | B 1, l-b 2, w 7, n-b 2 | | 12 |
| †R. J. Blakey b Watkinson | 38 | | | |
| P. E. Robinson b Watkinson | 9 | 1/22 2/49 3/53 | (49.4 overs) | 200 |
| P. Carrick b DeFreitas | 7 | 4/162 5/182 6/193 | | |
| D. Gough c Allott b DeFreitas | 1 | 7/198 8/198 9/199 | | |

Bowling: DeFreitas 11–0–34–3; Allott 11–1–46–0; Austin 9–0–36–0; Wasim Akram 8–0–32–1; Watkinson 10.4–0–49–5.

Umpires: K. J. Lyons and A. G. T. Whitehead.

# FINAL

## LANCASHIRE v WORCESTERSHIRE

At Lord's, July 13, 14. Worcestershire won by 65 runs. Toss: Lancashire. Hughes, who had captained Lancashire to victory in both Lord's finals in 1990, omitted himself a year later in order to strengthen their batting. However, Fairbrother's inexperience told against him, not least in his decision to bowl his steady openers, DeFreitas and Allott, until the fourteenth over, by which time Hick had settled in to play the match-winning innings. Well though Wasim Akram bowled to him in his opening spell, it was too late by then.

When play began 30 minutes late, after light rain, Worcestershire quickly lost Curtis, playing on to the last ball of the first over. Hick, however, struck his first ball, off Allott, for four, and he had hit another nine fours before, checking his drive against Allott's slower ball, he was marvellously caught by the bowler, diving to his left. Hick's 88 came from 126 balls, but Worcestershire, 166 for four, still had a lot to do. At 203 for eight, when Newport was out in the 52nd over, it seemed they had been contained. But Radford and Illingworth added 33 in 22 balls to snatch back the advantage. Wasim and Austin conceded 18 and 10 runs respectively from the last two overs.

An unfortunate feature was Lancashire's slow over-rate: they bowled only 49 overs within the 3 hours 25 minutes stipulated, and subsequently they were fined £500. The consequence of this tactic was a reduction in the time available for their own innings that afternoon, for it had always been likely that bad light would take play into a second day. The first stoppage came when Lancashire were 32 for three, having just lost Fairbrother second ball, spectacularly run out by D'Oliveira with a direct hit from mid-wicket on the non-striker's wicket. When play was finally called off for the day, they were 55 for three from eighteen overs (G. Fowler 21*, G. D. Lloyd 10*).

The next day, in pleasant contrast, provided beautiful weather, and a good crowd turned up for the first Sunday play in a Lord's final. They saw Worcestershire win confidently. Fowler went on to reach his half-century, out of 105, in the 35th over, after which he managed just one more four, his seventh, before Hick took his third successive catch – all at second slip. Good work by Rhodes ran out the dangerous Wasim Akram, and Neale, the Worcestershire captain, sealed his triumph with two late catches at cover.

*Gold Award:* G. A. Hick.　　*Attendance:* 22,000 (excl. members); *receipts* £595,000.

## Worcestershire

| | | | | |
|---|---|---|---|---|
| T. S. Curtis b DeFreitas | 4 | P. J. Newport c DeFreitas | | |
| T. M. Moody b Allott | 12 | b Wasim Akram | | 2 |
| G. A. Hick c and b Allott | 88 | N. V. Radford not out | | 25 |
| D. B. D'Oliveira c DeFreitas | | L-b 8, w 15, n-b 4 | | 27 |
| b Wasim Akram | 25 | | | |
| I. T. Botham c Fowler b Watkinson | 19 | 1/4 (1) 2/38 (2) | (8 wkts, 55 overs) | 236 |
| *P. A. Neale c Watkinson b Austin | 4 | 3/97 (4) 4/166 (3) | | |
| †S. J. Rhodes c Allott b Wasim Akram | 13 | 5/172 (5) 6/175 (6) | | |
| R. K. Illingworth not out | 17 | 7/195 (7) 8/203 (9) | | |

G. R. Dilley did not bat.

Bowling: DeFreitas 11–1–38–1; Allott 11–3–26–2; Watkinson 11–0–54–1; Wasim Akram 11–1–58–3; Austin 11–0–52–1.

## Lancashire

| | | | | |
|---|---|---|---|---|
| G. D. Mendis b Radford | 14 | I. D. Austin c Illingworth b Newport | 7 |
| G. Fowler c Hick b Radford | 54 | P. J. W. Allott c Neale b Dilley | 10 |
| M. A. Atherton c Rhodes b Radford | 5 | | |
| *N. H. Fairbrother run out | 1 | L-b 5, w 4, n-b 2 | 11 |
| G. D. Lloyd c Hick b Botham | 10 | | |
| M. Watkinson c Hick b Dilley | 13 | 1/24 (1) 2/31 (3) 3/32 (4)    (47.2 overs) 171 | |
| Wasim Akram run out | 14 | 4/64 (5) 5/92 (6) 6/111 (2) | |
| P. A. J. DeFreitas c Neale b Newport | 19 | 7/134 (7) 8/140 (8) | |
| †W. K. Hegg not out | 13 | 9/158 (10) 10/171 (11) | |

Bowling: Dilley 8.2–2–19–2; Radford 9–1–48–3; Botham 8–1–23–1; Newport 11–1–38–2; Illingworth 11–0–38–0.

Umpires: J. W. Holder and D. R. Shepherd.

# BENSON AND HEDGES CUP RECORDS

## Batting

**Highest individual scores:** 198*, G. A. Gooch, Essex v Sussex, Hove, 1982; 177, S. J. Cook, Somerset v Sussex, Hove, 1990; 173*, C. G. Greenidge, Hampshire v Minor Counties (South), Amersham, 1973; 158*, B. F. Davison, Leicestershire v Warwickshire, Coventry, 1972; 155*, M. D. Crowe, Somerset v Hampshire, Southampton, 1987; 155*, R. A. Smith, Hampshire v Glamorgan, Southampton, 1989; 154*, M. J. Procter, Gloucestershire v Somerset, Taunton, 1972; 154*, C. L. Smith, Hampshire v Combined Universities, Southampton, 1990. *In the final:* 132*, I. V. A. Richards, Somerset v Surrey, 1981. (212 hundreds have been scored in the competition. The most hundreds in one season is 24 in 1991.)

**Most runs:** 4,156, G. A. Gooch; 2,647, D. W. Randall.

**Fastest hundred:** M. A. Nash in 62 minutes, Glamorgan v Hampshire at Swansea, 1976.

**Most hundreds:** 9, G. A. Gooch; 5, C. G. Greenidge, W. Larkins and N. R. Taylor.

**Highest totals in 55 overs:** 366 for four, Derbyshire v Combined Universities, Oxford, 1991; 350 for three, Essex v Oxford & Cambridge Univs, Chelmsford, 1979; 333 for four, Essex v Oxford & Cambridge Univs, Chelmsford, 1985; 331 for five, Surrey v Hampshire, The Oval, 1990; 330 for four, Lancashire v Sussex, Manchester, 1991; 327 for four, Leicestershire v Warwickshire, Coventry, 1972; 327 for two, Essex v Sussex, Hove, 1982; 321 for one, Hampshire v Minor Counties (South), Amersham, 1973; 321 for five, Somerset v Sussex, Hove, 1990. *In the final:* 290 for six, Essex v Surrey, 1979.

**Highest total by a side batting second and winning:** 291 for five (53.5 overs), Warwickshire v Lancashire (288 for nine), Manchester, 1981. *In the final:* 244 for six (55 overs), Yorkshire v Northamptonshire (244 for seven), 1987; 244 for seven (55 overs), Nottinghamshire v Essex (243 for seven), 1989.

**Highest total by a side batting second and losing:** 303 for seven (55 overs), Derbyshire v Somerset (310 for three), Taunton, 1990. *In the final:* 255 (51.4 overs), Surrey v Essex (290 for six), 1979.

**Highest match aggregates:** 613 for ten wickets, Somerset (310-3) v Derbyshire (303-7), Taunton, 1990; 602 runs for fourteen wickets, Essex (307-4) v Warwickshire (295), Birmingham, 1991; 601 runs for thirteen wickets, Somerset (307-6) v Gloucestershire (294-7), Taunton, 1982; 600 runs for sixteen wickets, Derbyshire (300-6) v Northamptonshire (300), Derby, 1987.

**Lowest totals:** 50 in 27.2 overs, Hampshire v Yorkshire, Leeds, 1991; 56 in 26.2 overs, Leicestershire v Minor Counties, Wellington, 1982; 59 in 34 overs, Oxford & Cambridge Univs v Glamorgan, Cambridge, 1983; 61 in 26 overs, Sussex v Middlesex, Hove, 1978; 62 in 26.5 overs, Gloucestershire v Hampshire, Bristol, 1975. *In the final:* 117 in 46.3 overs, Derbyshire v Hampshire, 1988.

**Shortest completed innings:** 21.4 overs (156), Surrey v Sussex, Hove, 1988.

**Record partnership for each wicket**

| | | | |
|---|---|---|---|
| 252 | for 1st | V. P. Terry and C. L. Smith, Hampshire v Combined Universities at Southampton | 1990 |
| 285* | for 2nd | C. G. Greenidge and D. R. Turner, Hampshire v Minor Counties (South) at Amersham | 1973 |
| 269* | for 3rd | P. M. Roebuck and M. D. Crowe, Somerset v Hampshire at Southampton | 1987 |
| 184* | for 4th | D. Lloyd and B. W. Reidy, Lancashire v Derbyshire at Chesterfield. | 1980 |
| 160 | for 5th | A. J. Lamb and D. J. Capel, Northamptonshire v Leicestershire at Northampton | 1986 |
| 121 | for 6th | P. A. Neale and S. J. Rhodes, Worcestershire v Yorkshire at Worcester | 1988 |
| 149* | for 7th | J. D. Love and C. M. Old, Yorkshire v Scotland at Bradford | 1981 |
| 109 | for 8th | R. E. East and N. Smith, Essex v Northamptonshire at Chelmsford. | 1977 |
| 83 | for 9th | P. G. Newman and M. A. Holding, Derbyshire v Nottinghamshire at Nottingham | 1985 |
| 80* | for 10th | D. L. Bairstow and M. Johnson, Yorkshire v Derbyshire at Derby .. | 1981 |

## Bowling

**Most wickets:** 147, J. K. Lever; 127, I. T. Botham.

**Best bowling:** Seven for 12, W. W. Daniel, Middlesex v Minor Counties (East), Ipswich, 1978; seven for 22, J. R. Thomson, Middlesex v Hampshire, Lord's, 1981; seven for 32, R. G. D. Willis, Warwickshire v Yorkshire, Birmingham, 1981. *In the final:* Five for 13, S. T. Jefferies, Hampshire v Derbyshire, 1988.

**Hat-tricks (10):** G. D. McKenzie, Leicestershire v Worcestershire, Worcester, 1972; K. Higgs, Leicestershire v Surrey in the final, Lord's, 1974; A. A. Jones, Middlesex v Essex, Lord's, 1977; M. J. Procter, Gloucestershire v Hampshire, Southampton, 1977; W. Larkins, Northamptonshire v Oxford & Cambridge Univs, Northampton, 1980; E. A. Moseley, Glamorgan v Kent, Cardiff, 1981; G. C. Small, Warwickshire v Leicestershire, Leicester, 1984; N. A. Mallender, Somerset v Combined Universities, Taunton, 1987; W. K. M. Benjamin, Leicestershire v Nottinghamshire, Leicester, 1987; A. R. C. Fraser, Middlesex v Sussex, Lord's, 1988.

## Wicket-keeping and Fielding

**Most dismissals:** 122 (117 ct, 5 st), D. L. Bairstow.

**Most dismissals in an innings:** 8 (all ct), D. J. S. Taylor, Somerset v Oxford & Cambridge Univs, Taunton, 1982.

**Most catches by a fielder:** 60, G. A. Gooch; 50, I. T. Botham, C. J. Tavaré.

**Most catches by a fielder in an innings:** 5, V. J. Marks, Oxford & Cambridge Univs v Kent, Oxford, 1976.

## Results

**Largest victories in runs:** Essex by 214 runs v Combined Universities, Chelmsford, 1979; Derbyshire by 206 runs v Combined Universities, Oxford, 1991; Yorkshire by 189 runs v Hampshire, Leeds, 1991; Sussex by 186 runs v Cambridge University, Hove, 1974.

**Victories by ten wickets (14):** By Derbyshire, Essex (twice), Glamorgan, Hampshire, Kent, Lancashire, Leicestershire, Northamptonshire, Somerset, Warwickshire, Worcestershire, Yorkshire (twice).

## WINNERS 1972-91

1972 LEICESTERSHIRE beat Yorkshire by five wickets.
1973 KENT beat Worcestershire by 39 runs.
1974 SURREY beat Leicestershire by 27 runs.
1975 LEICESTERSHIRE beat Middlesex by five wickets.
1976 KENT beat Worcestershire by 43 runs.
1977 GLOUCESTERSHIRE beat Kent by 64 runs.
1978 KENT beat Derbyshire by six wickets.
1979 ESSEX beat Surrey by 35 runs.
1980 NORTHAMPTONSHIRE beat Essex by 6 runs.
1981 SOMERSET beat Surrey by seven wickets.
1982 SOMERSET beat Nottinghamshire by nine wickets.
1983 MIDDLESEX beat Essex by 4 runs.
1984 LANCASHIRE beat Warwickshire by six wickets.
1985 LEICESTERSHIRE beat Essex by five wickets.
1986 MIDDLESEX beat Kent by 2 runs.
1987 YORKSHIRE beat Northamptonshire, having taken more wickets with the scores tied.
1988 HAMPSHIRE beat Derbyshire by seven wickets.
1989 NOTTINGHAMSHIRE beat Essex by three wickets.
1990 LANCASHIRE beat Worcestershire by 69 runs.
1991 WORCESTERSHIRE beat Lancashire by 65 runs.

## WINS BY UNIVERSITIES

1973   OXFORD beat Northamptonshire at Northampton by two wickets.
1975 { OXFORD & CAMBRIDGE beat Worcestershire at Cambridge by 66 runs.
     OXFORD & CAMBRIDGE beat Northamptonshire at Oxford by three wickets.
1976   OXFORD & CAMBRIDGE beat Yorkshire at Barnsley by seven wickets.
1984   OXFORD & CAMBRIDGE beat Gloucestershire at Bristol by 27 runs.
1989 { COMBINED UNIVERSITIES beat Surrey at Cambridge by 9 runs.
     COMBINED UNIVERSITIES beat Worcestershire at Worcester by five wickets.
1990   COMBINED UNIVERSITIES beat Yorkshire at Leeds by two wickets.

## WINS BY MINOR COUNTIES AND SCOTLAND

1980 MINOR COUNTIES beat Gloucestershire at Chippenham by 3 runs.
1981 MINOR COUNTIES beat Hampshire at Southampton by 3 runs.
1982 MINOR COUNTIES beat Leicestershire at Wellington by 131 runs.
1986 SCOTLAND beat Lancashire at Perth by 3 runs.
1987 MINOR COUNTIES beat Glamorgan at Oxford (Christ Church) by seven wickets.
1990 SCOTLAND beat Northamptonshire at Northampton by 2 runs.

# REFUGE ASSURANCE LEAGUE, 1991

Nottinghamshire, unbeaten until June 23, by which time they had won their first seven games, fought off the strong challenge of Lancashire to win the Sunday League for the first time. They had been runners-up in 1984 and 1987. For Lancashire, the champions in 1989, it was their second year in succession as runners-up, and their fourth year in the top three. In the end, what separated the two sides was the weather, which prevented a result in Lancashire's home game against lowly-placed Glamorgan. Both counties were beaten three times, and Nottinghamshire's nine-wicket victory over Lancashire on the opening Sunday of the season, their first win at Old Trafford in the competition, ultimately proved to be the decisive result.

A feature of the season, the last for Refuge Assurance after five years as sponsor of the Sunday League, was the transfer of two matches from Sunday to a weekday, in order to make Sunday, July 14 available as the reserve day for the Benson and Hedges Cup final. Lancashire broke new ground by playing their Sunday League game against Somerset on a Friday – Worcestershire played their rearranged fixture against Derbyshire the following Tuesday – and as a result of winning two Sunday League games in three days, Lancashire temporarily dislodged Nottinghamshire from the top of the table on July 7. When Lancashire lost to Yorkshire four weeks later, they had gone

*Continued over*

## REFUGE ASSURANCE LEAGUE

| | P | W | L | T | NR | Pts | Away Wins | Run-Rate |
|---|---|---|---|---|---|---|---|---|
| 1 – Nottinghamshire (4) .... | 16 | 13 | 3 | 0 | 0 | 52 | 7 | 83.47 |
| 2 – Lancashire (2) ......... | 16 | 12 | 3 | 0 | 1 | 50 | 8 | 89.78 |
| 3 – Northamptonshire (17).. | 15 | 10 | 4 | 0 | 2 | 44 | 3 | 86.26 |
| 4 – Worcestershire (10)..... | 16 | 9 | 4 | 1 | 2 | 42 | 4 | 95.16 |
| 5 – Warwickshire (14) ..... | 14 | 8 | 4 | 1 | 3 | 40 | 4 | 82.53 |
| 6 – Essex (12) ............. | 14 | 7 | 4 | 1 | 4 | 38 | 1 | 84.41 |
| 7 – Yorkshire (6) .......... | 16 | 9 | 7 | 0 | 0 | 36 | 4 | 86.38 |
| 8 ⎰ Surrey (6) ............. | 15 | 7 | 7 | 0 | 2 | 32 | 5 | 81.94 |
| 8 ⎱ Somerset (8) ........... | 15 | 7 | 7 | 0 | 2 | 32 | 4 | 80.85 |
| 10 – Kent (10) ............. | 15 | 6 | 8 | 1 | 1 | 28 | 2 | 87.46 |
| 11 – Middlesex (3) ......... | 15 | 6 | 9 | 0 | 1 | 26 | 4 | 79.14 |
| 12 ⎰ Gloucestershire (8) .... | 15 | 5 | 9 | 0 | 2 | 24 | 4 | 77.68 |
| 12 ⎱ Sussex (13) ........... | 15 | 5 | 9 | 0 | 2 | 24 | 3 | 81.42 |
| 14 – Leicestershire (15).... | 15 | 5 | 10 | 0 | 1 | 22 | 3 | 78.29 |
| 15 ⎰ Derbyshire (1) ........ | 16 | 5 | 11 | 0 | 0 | 20 | 2 | 84.38 |
| 15 ⎱ Glamorgan (15)........ | 16 | 4 | 10 | 0 | 2 | 20 | 1 | 82.60 |
| 17 – Hampshire (5)......... | 16 | 3 | 12 | 0 | 1 | 14 | 1 | 79.24 |

*1990 positions are shown in brackets.*

*When two or more counties finish with an equal number of points for any of the first four places, the positions are decided by a) most wins, b) most away wins, c) runs per 100 balls.*

No play was possible in the following six matches: May 5 – Essex v Leicestershire at Chelmsford, Kent v Warwickshire at Canterbury, Middlesex v Northamptonshire at Lord's; June 23 – Somerset v Gloucestershire at Bath, Sussex v Essex at Horsham, Warwickshire v Surrey at Birmingham.

eleven games without defeat; by now they were back in first place, and with Nottinghamshire suffering their third loss of the season, to Worcestershire, there was no change at the top. What allowed Nottinghamshire to forge ahead was Lancashire's defeat by Surrey, at Old Trafford, on the second-last Sunday of the season.

In May, Somerset had shared the top of the table with Nottinghamshire after winning their first four games. But defeat by Middlesex, coming into the leading four, ended Somerset's run, and five consecutive defeats from the end of June took them from third to tenth before they won their last two games. Yorkshire, in contrast, lost their first four games but won nine of their next ten, including six in succession, a county record. Defeat in their last two games pushed them out of the running for a share of the prizemoney. Derbyshire, the defending champions, went eight games without victory after winning their first two games, and defeat by the new champions, Nottinghamshire, on the last Sunday of the season condemned them to fifteenth place, a dramatic fall comparable to Yorkshire's drop from champions in 1983 to second last in 1984. Glamorgan, who shared fifteenth place with Derbyshire, also went eight games without a win, not tasting victory until June 16.

Essex, despite four "no results" in their first nine games, held a top-four place throughout July and into August. But defeat at Northampton three rounds from the end let Northamptonshire leapfrog over them; and by beating Warwickshire on the last Sunday of the season, Allan Lamb's team claimed third place. That defeat not only cost Warwickshire third place; Worcestershire's victory over Middlesex the same day pushed them out of the Refuge Assurance Cup.

Worcestershire, Refuge League champions in 1987 and 1988, had in Tom Moody and Tim Curtis the season's leading run-makers. Moody's aggregate of 917 runs, containing four hundreds and five fifties, was the highest in a Sunday League season, beating Jimmy Cook's record of 902 for Somerset in 1990. Curtis's 769 runs included nine fifties, and together these two put on 1,158 runs for Worcestershire's first wicket, passing the 949 by G. Boycott and J. H. Hampshire for Yorkshire in 1975. Their six century partnerships were another League record, and Curtis also shared in two with Graeme Hick, giving him a record eight century stands. At the other end of the record scale, Nottinghamshire's Kevin Evans conceded the most runs by a bowler in a season, 679, and Glamorgan became the first county to record 200 defeats in the competition.

Nottinghamshire's Derek Randall showed at 40 that 40-overs cricket is not necessarily a young man's game, scoring 673 runs to follow Moody and Curtis, and after him came his opening partner, Chris Broad (635 runs), and the Yorkshire captain, Martyn Moxon (561 runs). Nottinghamshire's Franklyn Stephenson was the leading wicket-taker, with 30, while Ian Austin of Lancashire and Middlesex's John Emburey each took four wickets in an innings three times in capturing 28 wickets apiece. Tony Pigott of Sussex took 27 wickets, and Kent's Alan Igglesden was next with 23. The season's leading wicket-keepers were Lancashire's Warren Hegg, who took 21 catches, Richard Blakey of Yorkshire (18 ct, 1 st) and Neil Burns of Somerset (12 ct, 6 st).

## DISTRIBUTION OF PRIZEMONEY

**Team awards**

£26,500 and Refuge Assurance Trophy: NOTTINGHAMSHIRE.
£13,000 to runners-up: LANCASHIRE.
£6,500 for third place: NORTHAMPTONSHIRE.
£3,250 for fourth place: WORCESTERSHIRE.
£275 each match to the winner – shared if tied or no result.

**Individual awards**

£300 for highest innings: T. M. Moody (Worcestershire), 160 v Kent at Worcester.
£300 for best bowling: N. G. Cowans (Middlesex), six for 9 v Lancashire at Lord's.

**Fastest televised fifty**

£250 to P. E. Robinson (Yorkshire) – 20 balls v Derbyshire at Chesterfield.

# DERBYSHIRE

At Leicester, April 21. DERBYSHIRE beat LEICESTERSHIRE on scoring-rate.

## DERBYSHIRE v HAMPSHIRE

At Derby, May 5. Derbyshire won by four wickets. Toss: Derbyshire. Adams and Warner added 39 in 28 balls for the seventh wicket.

### Hampshire

| | | | |
|---|---|---|---|
| V. P. Terry c Bowler b Mortensen | 5 | S. D. Udal c Azharuddin b Warner | 6 |
| C. L. Smith run out | 29 | C. A. Connor not out | 0 |
| D. I. Gower b Warner | 37 | | |
| J. R. Wood c Warner b Roberts | 19 | B 3, l-b 6, w 9 | 18 |
| *M. C. J. Nicholas c Azharuddin b Malcolm | 23 | 1/12 2/76 3/81 (7 wkts, 40 overs) 166 | |
| K. D. James c Warner b Base | 12 | 4/106 5/125 | |
| †A. N. Aymes not out | 17 | 6/155 7/165 | |

Aqib Javed and P. J. Bakker did not bat.

Bowling: Base 8-1-27-1; Mortensen 8-2-27-1; Malcolm 8-0-35-1; Warner 8-2-34-2; Roberts 8-1-34-1.

### Derbyshire

| | | | |
|---|---|---|---|
| *K. J. Barnett run out | 11 | C. J. Adams not out | 34 |
| †P. D. Bowler b James | 8 | A. E. Warner not out | 22 |
| J. E. Morris st Aymes b Udal | 32 | L-b 7, w 9, n-b 1 | 17 |
| M. Azharuddin lbw b Connor | 9 | | |
| B. Roberts run out | 12 | 1/22 2/27 3/57 (6 wkts, 39.1 overs) 167 | |
| T. J. G. O'Gorman c Smith b James | 22 | 4/71 5/91 6/128 | |

S. J. Base, D. E. Malcolm and O. H. Mortensen did not bat.

Bowling: James 8-1-29-2; Aqib Javed 7.1-1-26-0; Bakker 8-1-31-0; Connor 8-0-48-1; Udal 8-2-26-1.

Umpires: H. D. Bird and B. Leadbeater.

## DERBYSHIRE v LANCASHIRE

At Derby, May 19. Lancashire won by 63 runs. Toss: Derbyshire. Hughes's team celebrated his first appearance of the season with their highest score in the Refuge Assurance League, beating their 268 for three against Surrey at The Oval in 1990. Watkinson, who faced 57 balls and struck nine fours and two sixes, also reached a Sunday best, adding 90 in eleven overs with Lloyd and 37 in four with Wasim Akram. When Derbyshire replied, Barnett reached 5,000 runs in the competition. Austin's bowling figures were his best in the League, and Adams completed a day of records with his highest Sunday score for Derbyshire.

### Lancashire

| | | | |
|---|---|---|---|
| G. D. Mendis c Bowler b Mortensen... | 0 | P. A. J. DeFreitas not out .......... | 14 |
| G. Fowler b Malcolm .............. | 59 | †W. K. Hegg not out............... | 11 |
| M. A. Atherton c Adams b Base ..... | 48 | L-b 7, w 5, n-b 6........... | 18 |
| G. D. Lloyd b Base b Malcolm ....... | 26 | | — |
| M. Watkinson c Base b Jean-Jacques .. | 82 | 1/0 2/95 3/118        (6 wkts, 40 overs) 276 | |
| Wasim Akram c Barnett b Jean-Jacques | 18 | 4/208 5/245 6/251 | |

*D. P. Hughes, I. D. Austin and P. J. W. Allott did not bat.

Bowling: Mortensen 8–1–41–1; Base 8–0–51–1; Jean-Jacques 8–1–56–2; Warner 8–0–70–0; Malcolm 8–0–51–2.

### Derbyshire

| | | | |
|---|---|---|---|
| *K. J. Barnett c Mendis b DeFreitas... | 15 | S. J. Base b Austin ............... | 1 |
| †P. D. Bowler c Hughes b Austin ..... | 51 | D. E. Malcolm b Austin ........... | 11 |
| T. J. G. O'Gorman c Atherton b Allott. | 5 | O. H. Mortensen not out........... | 1 |
| M. Azharuddin c Hughes b Allott ..... | 2 | L-b 5, w 3, n-b 1........... | 9 |
| B. Roberts b Watkinson ........... | 8 | | — |
| C. J. Adams b Wasim Akram ....... | 71 | 1/26 2/44 3/49        (39.3 overs) 213 | |
| A. E. Warner b Austin ........... | 16 | 4/66 5/109 6/135 | |
| M. Jean-Jacques b Austin............ | 23 | 7/199 8/201 9/202 | |

Bowling: DeFreitas 8–1–29–1; Allott 8–1–45–2; Wasim Akram 8–0–42–1; Watkinson 8–1–36–1; Austin 7.3–0–56–5.

Umpires: K. J. Lyons and D. O. Oslear.

At Canterbury, May 26. DERBYSHIRE lost to KENT by 6 runs.

## DERBYSHIRE v YORKSHIRE

At Chesterfield, June 2. Yorkshire won by three wickets. Toss: Yorkshire. The game was reduced to ten overs a side after an earlier, nineteen-over attempt was ended by rain, with Yorkshire 57 for one after 10.1 overs. Phil Robinson, who hit six fours and six sixes in 21 balls, took 19 (41644) from the last over, bowled by Warner, to win the match. (Hartley was run out as they tried for a second run from the second ball.)

### Derbyshire

| | | | |
|---|---|---|---|
| *K. J. Barnett c Blakey b Hartley ..... | 9 | A. E. Warner run out .............. | 23 |
| †P. D. Bowler c P. E. Robinson b Hartley | 30 | L-b 4, w 1 .............. | 5 |
| J. E. Morris c Pickles b Hartley....... | 0 | | — |
| M. Azharuddin not out .............. | 29 | 1/28 2/28 3/50        (5 wkts, 10 overs) 105 | |
| B. Roberts c Pickles b Fletcher ....... | 9 | 4/80 5/105 | |

T. J. G. O'Gorman, C. J. Adams, S. J. Base, D. E. Malcolm and D. G. Cork did not bat.

Bowling: M. A. Robinson 2–0–33–0; Pickles 2–0–25–0; Hartley 2–0–6–3; Gough 2–0–20–0; Fletcher 2–0–17–1.

## Yorkshire

| | | | |
|---|---|---|---|
| *M. D. Moxon c and b Warner | 20 | P. J. Hartley run out | 0 |
| A. A. Metcalfe c O'Gorman b Roberts | 0 | S. A. Kellett not out | 0 |
| †R. J. Blakey c Malcolm b Cork | 7 | B 1, l-b 2, w 5 | 8 |
| D. Byas c and b Malcolm | 14 | | |
| P. E. Robinson not out | 57 | 1/2 2/16 3/34 (7 wkts, 9.5 overs) | 106 |
| C. S. Pickles run out | 0 | 4/72 5/72 | |
| D. Gough run out | 0 | 6/82 7/92 | |

S. D. Fletcher and M. A. Robinson did not bat.

Bowling: Roberts 2–0–27–1; Cork 2–0–15–1; Base 2–0–15–0; Warner 1.5–0–27–1; Malcolm 2–0–19–1.

Umpires: M. J. Kitchen and N. T. Plews.

## DERBYSHIRE v SURREY

At Chesterfield, June 9. Surrey won on scoring-rate. Toss: Derbyshire. Rain interrupted Derbyshire's innings when they were 100 for one from 20.3 overs. Their target was adjusted to 151 from 27 overs, and then, after a further break, 129 from 23, but they fell 9 runs short as Waqar Younis and Murphy restricted them to 11 from eleven balls at the end.

## Surrey

| | | | |
|---|---|---|---|
| M. A. Lynch c Bowler b Base | 10 | C. K. Bullen not out | 0 |
| D. J. Bicknell b Cork | 68 | Waqar Younis b Goldsmith | 0 |
| †A. J. Stewart b Base | 60 | A. J. Murphy not out | 0 |
| D. M. Ward b Warner | 15 | L-b 5, w 4 | 9 |
| G. P. Thorpe c Bowler b Cork | 1 | | |
| *I. A. Greig c Cork | 24 | 1/25 2/144 3/144 (9 wkts, 40 overs) | 223 |
| J. D. Robinson c Cork b Goldsmith | 17 | 4/146 5/182 6/188 | |
| M. A. Feltham c Cork b Goldsmith | 19 | 7/220 8/222 9/222 | |

Bowling: Warner 8–0–52–1; Base 8–0–21–2; Cork 8–0–45–3; Goldsmith 8–0–48–3; Folley 4–0–28–0; Griffith 4–0–24–0.

## Derbyshire

| | | | |
|---|---|---|---|
| *K. J. Barnett c Stewart b Murphy | 11 | | |
| †P. D. Bowler not out | 47 | | |
| T. J. G. O'Gorman not out | 49 | | |
| L-b 4, w 9 | 13 | | |
| 1/25 | | (1 wkt, 23 overs) | 120 |

S. C. Goldsmith, M. Azharuddin, C. J. Adams, F. A. Griffith, D. G. Cork, A. E. Warner, S. J. Base and I. Folley did not bat.

Bowling: Feltham 7–0–33–0; Murphy 6–0–35–1; Robinson 2–0–9–0; Greig 4–0–16–0; Waqar Younis 4–0–33–0.

Umpires: J. H. Hampshire and B. J. Meyer.

## DERBYSHIRE v SOMERSET

At Derby, June 16. Somerset won by 46 runs. Toss: Derbyshire. The match, which ended in Derbyshire's fifth consecutive Sunday defeat, was to have taken place at Checkley, but the ground was waterlogged. Somerset's innings contained only two boundaries, both from Cook.

## Somerset

| | | | | |
|---|---|---|---|---|
| S. J. Cook c Bowler b Griffith | 32 | A. N. Hayhurst not out | | 18 |
| P. M. Roebuck run out | 45 | N. A. Mallender b Base | | 0 |
| *C. J. Tavaré c Barnett b Griffith | 3 | D. A. Graveney not out | | 2 |
| R. J. Harden b Malcolm | 4 | L-b 10, w 12, n-b 1 | | 23 |
| †N. D. Burns c Azharuddin b Warner | 32 | | | |
| G. D. Rose c Warner b Griffith | 17 | 1/61 2/69 3/94 | (9 wkts, 40 overs) | 198 |
| K. H. MacLeay b Malcolm | 9 | 4/103 5/140 6/161 | | |
| R. P. Lefebvre run out | 13 | 7/165 8/191 9/193 | | |

Bowling: Warner 8–0–34–1; Cork 8–1–30–0; Base 8–0–46–1; Griffith 8–0–37–3; Malcolm 8–0–41–2.

## Derbyshire

| | | | | |
|---|---|---|---|---|
| *K. J. Barnett c Lefebvre b Hayhurst | 17 | A. E. Warner b Roebuck | | 12 |
| †P. D. Bowler b Lefebvre | 9 | D. E. Malcolm not out | | 3 |
| J. E. Morris c Roebuck b MacLeay | 27 | S. J. Base c Tavaré b Roebuck | | 0 |
| M. Azharuddin c Burns b Graveney | 20 | L-b 9, w 2 | | 11 |
| T. J. G. O'Gorman b Roebuck | 31 | | | |
| C. J. Adams st Burns b Graveney | 9 | 1/21 2/31 3/66 | (35.4 overs) | 152 |
| F. A. Griffith c Cook b Roebuck | 6 | 4/82 5/113 6/129 | | |
| D. G. Cork run out | 7 | 7/130 8/139 9/152 | | |

Bowling: Mallender 4–0–13–0; Lefebvre 6–0–28–1; Hayhurst 5–0–23–1; MacLeay 8–0–31–1; Graveney 8–0–37–2; Roebuck 4.4–0–11–4.

Umpires: A. A. Jones and R. A. White.

At Chelmsford, June 30. DERBYSHIRE lost to ESSEX by 11 runs.

# DERBYSHIRE v SUSSEX

At Derby, July 7. Sussex won by 5 runs. Toss: Sussex. Smith, who faced 86 balls, and Greenfield, scoring 50 from 46, added 107 for the fourth wicket in sixteen overs to help set up a seventh consecutive defeat for the League champions.

## Sussex

| | | | | |
|---|---|---|---|---|
| N. J. Lenham run out | 11 | A. C. S. Pigott not out | | 4 |
| *P. W. G. Parker b Goldsmith | 27 | | | |
| D. M. Smith c Adams b Base | 78 | L-b 13, w 8 | | 21 |
| M. P. Speight c and b Goldsmith | 3 | | | |
| K. Greenfield c Goldsmith b Barnett | 53 | 1/28 2/66 3/75 | (5 wkts, 40 overs) | 231 |
| C. M. Wells not out | 34 | 4/182 5/220 | | |

A. I. C. Dodemaide, †P. Moores, I. D. K. Salisbury and A. N. Jones did not bat.

Bowling: Base 8–0–42–1; Warner 8–0–56–0; Goldsmith 8–1–33–2; Griffith 8–0–49–0; Barnett 8–0–38–1.

## Derbyshire

| | | | | |
|---|---|---|---|---|
| P. D. Bowler lbw b Pigott | 26 | A. E. Warner b Pigott | | 8 |
| C. J. Adams run out | 44 | F. A. Griffith not out | | 12 |
| J. E. Morris c and b Pigott | 6 | B 2, l-b 12, w 7, n-b 1 | | 22 |
| M. Azharuddin b Jones | 3 | | | |
| T. J. G. O'Gorman b Jones | 3 | 1/40 2/52 3/64 | (7 wkts, 40 overs) | 226 |
| S. C. Goldsmith b Lenham | 42 | 4/70 5/104 | | |
| *K. J. Barnett not out | 60 | 6/185 7/205 | | |

†K. M. Krikken and S. J. Base did not bat.

Bowling: Dodemaide 8–0–25–0; Wells 8–0–35–0; Jones 8–0–55–2; Pigott 8–0–44–3; Salisbury 6–0–34–0; Lenham 2–0–19–1.

Umpires: J. W. Holder and B. Leadbeater.

At Worcester, July 9. DERBYSHIRE lost to WORCESTERSHIRE by eight wickets.

At Cheltenham, July 21. DERBYSHIRE beat GLOUCESTERSHIRE by 94 runs.

## DERBYSHIRE v NORTHAMPTONSHIRE

At Derby, July 28. Derbyshire won by 46 runs. Toss: Derbyshire. Base's figures were his best in the competition.

### Derbyshire

| | | |
|---|---|---|
| *J. E. Morris c Walker b Curran . . . . . | 40 | A. E. Warner not out . . . . . . . . . . . . . . 16 |
| D. G. Cork run out . . . . . . . . . . . . . . | 7 | †B. J. M. Maher not out . . . . . . . . . . . 0 |
| T. J. G. O'Gorman b Williams . . . . . . | 38 | B 1, l-b 10, w 4 . . . . . . . . . . . . 15 |
| M. Azharuddin c Walker b Capel . . . . | 25 | |
| S. C. Goldsmith lbw b Williams . . . . . | 5 | 1/28 2/59 3/109    (7 wkts, 40 overs) 184 |
| F. A. Griffith b Taylor . . . . . . . . . . . . | 20 | 4/124 5/126 |
| E. McCray c Curran b Taylor . . . . . . . | 18 | 6/155 7/178 |

S. J. Base and O. H. Mortensen did not bat.

Bowling: Walker 8–0–36–0; Taylor 7–1–24–2; Baptiste 5–0–26–0; Curran 7–1–32–1; Capel 5–0–33–1; Williams 8–0–22–2.

### Northamptonshire

| | | |
|---|---|---|
| A. Fordham run out . . . . . . . . . . . . . . | 7 | †D. Ripley c Morris b Base . . . . . . . . . . 14 |
| N. A. Felton c O'Gorman b Base . . . . . | 4 | A. Walker c Azharuddin b Base . . . . . 5 |
| W. Larkins lbw b Mortensen . . . . . . . . | 2 | J. P. Taylor c O'Gorman b Base . . . . . . 0 |
| D. J. Capel c Base b McCray . . . . . . . . | 10 | L-b 9, w 6, n-b 1 . . . . . . . . . . . 16 |
| *R. J. Bailey c Maher b McCray . . . . . . | 22 | |
| K. M. Curran c Cork b Warner . . . . . . . | 21 | 1/10 2/15 3/16        (36.5 overs) 138 |
| E. A. E. Baptiste st Maher b McCray . . . | 9 | 4/48 5/72 6/86 |
| R. G. Williams not out . . . . . . . . . . . . . | 28 | 7/90 8/124 9/137 |

Bowling: Base 6.5–1–14–4; Mortensen 8–1–19–1; Cork 6–0–25–0; McCray 8–0–38–3; Warner 6–0–21–1; Goldsmith 2–0–12–0.

Umpires: J. C. Balderstone and B. Hassan.

At Birmingham, August 4. DERBYSHIRE lost to WARWICKSHIRE by 32 runs.

At Lord's, August 11. DERBYSHIRE lost to MIDDLESEX on scoring-rate.

## DERBYSHIRE v GLAMORGAN

At Checkley, August 18. Derbyshire won by 29 runs. Toss: Glamorgan. Warner made his runs from 26 balls, with five sixes and three fours, and shared a fourth-wicket partnership of 70 in 6.2 overs with Azharuddin. When Glamorgan replied, Maynard made his highest score in the competition, his 101 coming from 88 balls with fifteen fours and two sixes, and McCray took three wickets in one over. Checkley, which was due to stage the match of June 16, became Derbyshire's thirteenth Sunday League venue.

## Derbyshire

| | | | | |
|---|---|---|---|---|
| P. D. Bowler st Metson b Shastri | 39 | D. G. Cork lbw b Frost | 28 |
| C. J. Adams run out | 0 | E. McCray c Metson b Foster | 1 |
| T. J. G. O'Gorman lbw b Frost | 11 | O. H. Mortensen not out | 7 |
| M. Azharuddin c Frost b Watkin | 36 | L-b 15, w 9, n-b 1 | 25 |
| A. E. Warner c Dale b Watkin | 51 | | |
| S. C. Goldsmith b Foster | 31 | 1/1 2/29 3/79 (39 overs) 251 |
| *K. J. Barnett c Metson b Dale | 14 | 4/149 5/167 6/195 |
| †K. M. Krikken lbw b Foster | 8 | 7/212 8/230 9/239 |

Bowling: Frost 7–1–39–2; Foster 7–0–30–3; Croft 8–0–33–0; Watkin 8–0–50–2; Shastri 4–0–33–1; Dale 5–0–51–1.

## Glamorgan

| | | | | |
|---|---|---|---|---|
| M. P. Maynard st Krikken b McCray | 101 | S. L. Watkin not out | 31 |
| H. Morris b Mortensen | 21 | M. Frost run out | 2 |
| A. Dale c Krikken b Cork | 4 | D. J. Foster not out | 2 |
| R. J. Shastri b Cork | 16 | L-b 4, n-b 1 | 5 |
| P. A. Cottey c O'Gorman b McCray | 14 | | |
| *A. R. Butcher st Krikken b McCray | 7 | 1/47 2/81 3/123 (9 wkts, 40 overs) 222 |
| R. D. B. Croft lbw b McCray | 0 | 4/157 5/161 6/161 |
| †C. P. Metson c Goldsmith b Mortensen | 20 | 7/176 8/197 9/209 |

Bowling: McCray 8–0–49–4; Mortensen 8–1–36–2; Goldsmith 8–0–62–0; Warner 8–0–51–0; Cork 8–2–20–2.

Umpires: D. J. Constant and J. H. Harris.

At Nottingham, August 25. DERBYSHIRE lost to NOTTINGHAMSHIRE by nine wickets.

# ESSEX

## ESSEX v YORKSHIRE

At Chelmsford, April 28. Essex won by nine wickets. Toss: Yorkshire.

## Yorkshire

| | | | | |
|---|---|---|---|---|
| *M. D. Moxon c Garnham b Ilott | 6 | A. Sidebottom c Garnham b Pringle | 6 |
| A. A. Metcalfe c Garnham b Ilott | 4 | S. D. Fletcher not out | 11 |
| †R. J. Blakey lbw b Gooch | 18 | | |
| D. Byas c Ilott b Gooch | 5 | L-b 4, w 14 | 18 |
| P. E. Robinson run out | 20 | | |
| K. Sharp c Such b Gooch | 37 | 1/11 2/17 3/28 (8 wkts, 40 overs) 149 |
| P. W. Jarvis c Garnham b Pringle | 5 | 4/48 5/74 6/99 |
| P. Carrick not out | 20 | 7/116 8/128 |

M. A. Robinson did not bat.

Bowling: Pringle 8–1–28–2; Ilott 6–0–26–2; Gooch 8–1–25–3; Topley 6–0–18–0; Stephenson 4–0–19–0; Such 8–0–29–0.

## Essex

| | | |
|---|---|---|
| *G. A. Gooch not out | 59 |
| J. P. Stephenson c Blakey b Fletcher | 32 |
| Salim Malik not out | 48 |
| B 1, l-b 8, w 2, n-b 3 | 14 |

1/56 (1 wkt, 33.3 overs) 153

P. J. Prichard, N. Hussain, N. Shahid, D. R. Pringle, †M. A. Garnham, M. C. Ilott, T. D. Topley and P. M. Such did not bat.

Bowling: Jarvis 8–1–39–0; Sidebottom 8–0–26–0; Fletcher 8–1–37–1; M. A. Robinson 6–1–25–0; Carrick 2–0–10–0; Moxon 1.3–0–7–0.

Umpires: K. J. Lyons and P. B. Wight.

## ESSEX v LEICESTERSHIRE

At Chelmsford, May 5. No result.

At Nottingham, May 12. ESSEX lost to NOTTINGHAMSHIRE by 10 runs.

At Folkestone, May 19. ESSEX tied with KENT.

At The Oval, May 26. ESSEX lost to SURREY by seven wickets.

At Pontypridd, June 2. GLAMORGAN v ESSEX. No result.

## ESSEX v WORCESTERSHIRE

At Ilford, June 9. Essex won by 34 runs. Toss: Worcestershire. Botham celebrated his return after suffering a hamstring strain in the first Texaco Trophy international by taking Stephenson's wicket with his third delivery and hitting 33 from 55 balls. His team-mate, Moody, faced a comedown: after averaging 109 in the first six Sunday games of the season, he was out to the first delivery he received. Earlier, Salim Malik had made 89 from 81 balls for Essex.

### Essex

| | | | | |
|---|---|---|---|---|
| J. P. Stephenson c Weston b Botham | 67 | *N. A. Foster run out | | 5 |
| A. C. H. Seymour lbw b Weston | 20 | | | |
| Salim Malik c Newport b Radford | 89 | L-b 5, w 4, n-b 1 | | 10 |
| P. J. Prichard c Botham b Radford | 36 | | | |
| N. Hussain not out | 22 | 1/47 2/151 3/193 | (6 wkts, 40 overs) | 250 |
| †M. A. Garnham b Botham | 1 | 4/232 5/233 6/250 | | |

N. Shahid, T. D. Topley, S. J. W. Andrew and P. M. Such did not bat.

Bowling: Weston 8–0–37–1; Newport 4–0–28–0; Lampitt 5–0–29–0; Radford 8–0–67–2; Illingworth 8–0–45–0; Botham 7–1–39–2.

### Worcestershire

| | | | | |
|---|---|---|---|---|
| T. S. Curtis c Topley b Stephenson | 46 | S. R. Lampitt c Stephenson b Foster | | 4 |
| T. M. Moody b Foster | 0 | R. K. Illingworth not out | | 25 |
| M. J. Weston c Hussain b Andrew | 4 | P. J. Newport not out | | 3 |
| D. B. D'Oliveira c Salim Malik b Topley | 25 | | | |
| I. T. Botham c Shahid b Andrew | 33 | B 5, l-b 18, w 4, n-b 5 | | 32 |
| *P. A. Neale c Salim Malik b Foster | 39 | | | |
| †S. J. Rhodes c Salim Malik b Stephenson | 0 | 1/1 2/11 3/58 | (9 wkts, 40 overs) | 216 |
| | | 4/117 5/149 6/150 | | |
| N. V. Radford b Stephenson | 5 | 7/158 8/175 9/205 | | |

Bowling: Foster 8–0–28–3; Andrew 8–0–45–2; Such 8–1–38–0; Topley 8–0–65–1; Stephenson 8–1–17–3.

Umpires: D. O. Oslear and A. G. T. Whitehead.

## ESSEX v HAMPSHIRE

At Chelmsford, June 16. No result. Toss: Hampshire. Rain ended the match.

### Essex

| | | | |
|---|---|---|---|
| *G. A. Gooch run out | 50 | †M. A. Garnham not out | 0 |
| J. P. Stephenson c Connor b Ayling | 38 | | |
| P. J. Prichard c Aqib Javed b Tremlett | 34 | B 3, l-b 5, w 5, n-b 1 | 14 |
| N. Hussain c Ayling b Udal | 10 | | |
| D. R. Pringle b Connor | 17 | 1/69 2/116 3/142 (5 wkts, 33.3 overs) | 180 |
| N. Shahid not out | 17 | 4/145 5/180 | |

A. C. H. Seymour, T. D. Topley, S. J. W. Andrew and P. M. Such did not bat.

Bowling: Connor 6.3–0–31–1; Aqib Javed 7–0–41–0; Tremlett 8–0–30–1; Ayling 4–0–29–1; Udal 8–1–41–1.

### Hampshire

V. P. Terry, J. R. Wood, R. A. Smith, D. I. Gower, *M. C. J. Nicholas, T. M. Tremlett, J. R. Ayling, †A. N. Aymes, S. D. Udal, C. A. Connor and Aqib Javed.

Umpires: B. Hassan and M. J. Kitchen.

At Horsham, June 23. SUSSEX v ESSEX. No result.

## ESSEX v DERBYSHIRE

At Chelmsford, June 30. Essex won by 11 runs. Toss: Derbyshire. Prichard's 40 runs came from 25 balls and included five fours and a six. With his 26th run, Gooch became the fourth batsman to score 6,500 Sunday League runs.

### Essex

| | | | |
|---|---|---|---|
| *G. A. Gooch lbw b Base | 56 | T. D. Topley run out | 1 |
| J. P. Stephenson c Krikken b Malcolm | 27 | S. J. W. Andrew run out | 0 |
| Salim Malik c Krikken b Malcolm | 36 | | |
| P. J. Prichard c Mortensen b Malcolm | 40 | B 1, l-b 6, w 7, n-b 2 | 16 |
| N. Hussain b Warner | 15 | | |
| D. R. Pringle c Goldsmith b Warner | 4 | 1/81 2/97 3/171 (9 wkts, 40 overs) | 202 |
| N. Shahid b Warner | 6 | 4/171 5/185 6/199 | |
| †M. A. Garnham not out | 1 | 7/201 8/202 9/202 | |

P. M. Such did not bat.

Bowling: Mortensen 8–1–22–0; Warner 8–0–38–3; Base 8–0–46–1; Goldsmith 8–0–46–0; Malcolm 8–1–43–3.

### Derbyshire

| | | | |
|---|---|---|---|
| P. D. Bowler run out | 30 | S. J. Base lbw b Topley | 1 |
| C. J. Adams c Garnham b Andrew | 0 | D. E. Malcolm c Stephenson b Pringle | 18 |
| *J. E. Morris c Prichard b Such | 46 | O. H. Mortensen not out | 3 |
| M. Azharuddin c Salim Malik b Such | 23 | L-b 4, w 3 | 7 |
| T. J. G. O'Gorman b Such | 3 | | |
| S. C. Goldsmith c Hussain b Such | 4 | 1/2 2/61 3/87 (9 wkts, 40 overs) | 191 |
| †K. M. Krikken not out | 44 | 4/98 5/106 6/111 | |
| A. E. Warner run out | 12 | 7/136 8/141 9/186 | |

Bowling: Andrew 8–0–43–1; Pringle 8–0–49–1; Topley 8–1–29–1; Gooch 8–0–36–0; Such 8–0–30–4.

Umpires: G. I. Burgess and D. J. Constant.

## ESSEX v WARWICKSHIRE

At Chelmsford, July 7. Essex won by six wickets. Toss: Essex. Warwickshire were 101 without loss when Stephenson came on to bowl; he returned his best figures for Essex in any competition, and also ran out Ostler with a direct hit from long leg. In the Essex innings he made 60 from 68 balls, adding 115 for the second wicket with Salim Malik.

### Warwickshire

| | | | | |
|---|---|---|---|---|
| A. J. Moles run out | 53 | †P. C. L. Holloway lbw b Stephenson | 8 |
| Asif Din c Garnham b Stephenson | 45 | J. E. Benjamin not out | 12 |
| *T. A. Lloyd lbw b Stephenson | 1 | B 6, l-b 7, w 3, n-b 2 | 18 |
| D. A. Reeve st Garnham b Stephenson | 2 | | |
| D. P. Ostler run out | 4 | 1/106 2/107 3/111 (7 wkts, 40 overs) 184 |
| P. A. Smith c and b Salim Malik | 3 | 4/112 5/117 |
| N. M. K. Smith not out | 38 | 6/123 7/138 |

T. A. Munton and A. A. Donald did not bat.

Bowling: Foster 6–1–19–0; Topley 6–0–44–0; Fraser 6–0–33–0; Such 6–0–33–0; Stephenson 8–0–17–4; Salim Malik 8–0–25–1.

### Essex

| | | | | |
|---|---|---|---|---|
| †M. A. Garnham b Donald | 8 | *N. A. Foster not out | 16 |
| J. P. Stephenson c Moles b Donald | 60 | B 1, l-b 6, w 6, n-b 4 | 17 |
| Salim Malik b Benjamin | 64 | | |
| P. J. Prichard lbw b P. A. Smith | 5 | 1/18 2/133 (4 wkts, 37 overs) 187 |
| N. Hussain not out | 17 | 3/142 4/154 |

K. A. Butler, N. Shahid, A. G. J. Fraser, T. D. Topley and P. M. Such did not bat.

Bowling: Donald 8–0–30–2; Munton 8–0–34–0; Benjamin 7–0–41–1; Reeve 3–0–24–0; N. M. K. Smith 7–0–27–0; P. A. Smith 4–0–24–1.

Umpires: J. C. Balderstone and R. A. White.

## ESSEX v SOMERSET

At Southend, July 21. Essex won by 30 runs. Toss: Somerset. Gooch equalled C. G. Greenidge's record of eleven Sunday League hundreds with a century which included six fours; he faced 102 balls. It was his third hundred in the competition at Southend in three years.

### Essex

| | | | | |
|---|---|---|---|---|
| *G. A. Gooch c Burns b Lefebvre | 107 | D. R. Pringle not out | 27 |
| J. P. Stephenson c Lefebvre b Hallett | 10 | L-b 6, w 1 | 7 |
| Salim Malik c and b Trump | 41 | | |
| P. J. Prichard lbw b Lefebvre | 22 | 1/30 2/126 (4 wkts, 40 overs) 247 |
| N. Hussain not out | 33 | 3/182 4/187 |

N. Shahid, †M. A. Garnham, T. D. Topley, S. J. W. Andrew and P. M. Such did not bat.

Bowling: Lefebvre 8–0–40–2; Hallett 5–0–22–1; MacLeay 8–0–67–0; Trump 8–0–39–1; Roebuck 7–0–38–0; Hayhurst 4–0–35–0.

### Somerset

| | | | | |
|---|---|---|---|---|
| S. J. Cook c Shahid b Topley | 93 | K. H. MacLeay not out | 10 |
| P. M. Roebuck c Hussain b Such | 41 | †N. D. Burns not out | 10 |
| *C. J. Tavaré b Stephenson | 34 | L-b 9, w 5, n-b 1 | 15 |
| R. J. Harden b Topley | 13 | | |
| R. P. Lefebvre lbw b Topley | 0 | 1/92 2/152 3/180 (6 wkts, 40 overs) 217 |
| N. J. Pringle c Prichard b Stephenson | 1 | 4/180 5/183 6/202 |

A. N. Hayhurst, H. R. J. Trump and J. C. Hallett did not bat.

Bowling: Andrew 4–0–38–0; Pringle 6–0–29–0; Topley 8–0–36–3; Such 8–0–32–1; Gooch 6–0–24–0; Stephenson 8–0–49–2.

Umpires: J. D. Bond and K. E. Palmer.

At Cheltenham, July 28. ESSEX beat GLOUCESTERSHIRE by four wickets.

At Northampton, August 11. ESSEX lost to NORTHAMPTONSHIRE by 62 runs.

## ESSEX v MIDDLESEX

At Colchester, August 18. Essex won by 95 runs. Toss: Essex. When 14, Gooch became the second-highest run-scorer in Sunday League cricket.

### Essex

| | | | | |
|---|---|---|---|---|
| *G. A. Gooch b Weekes | 45 | D. R. Pringle c sub b Cowans | | 34 |
| J. P. Stephenson c Ramprakash | | N. A. Foster not out | | 14 |
| b Emburey | 44 | L-b 11, w 4 | | 15 |
| Salim Malik c Taylor b Cowans | 33 | | | |
| P. J. Prichard not out | 54 | 1/96 2/103 3/150 | (5 wkts, 40 overs) | 239 |
| N. Hussain c Farbrace b Cowans | 0 | 4/150 5/223 | | |

†M. A. Garnham, T. D. Topley, J. H. Childs and P. M. Such did not bat.

Bowling: Taylor 4–0–32–0; Cowans 8–2–35–3; Headley 8–0–56–0; Emburey 8–1–37–1; Weekes 8–0–42–1; Gatting 4–0–26–0.

### Middlesex

| | | | | |
|---|---|---|---|---|
| M. A. Roseberry c Garnham b Pringle | 2 | D. W. Headley not out | | 6 |
| J. C. Pooley c Pringle b Foster | 12 | C. W. Taylor lbw b Childs | | 3 |
| *M. W. Gatting lbw b Topley | 8 | N. G. Cowans b Topley | | 4 |
| M. R. Ramprakash b Topley | 59 | L-b 4 | | 4 |
| K. R. Brown c Topley b Such | 33 | | | |
| P. N. Weekes run out | 0 | 1/2 2/18 3/31 | (33.4 overs) | 144 |
| J. E. Emburey c Hussain b Childs | 8 | 4/100 5/101 6/116 | | |
| †P. Farbrace run out | 5 | 7/130 8/132 9/135 | | |

Bowling: Pringle 4–0–6–1; Foster 6–0–23–1; Topley 7.4–0–36–3; Such 8–0–40–1; Childs 8–0–35–2.

Umpires: R. Julian and R. C. Tolchard.

At Manchester, August 25. ESSEX lost to LANCASHIRE by five wickets.

# GLAMORGAN

## GLAMORGAN v NORTHAMPTONSHIRE

At Cardiff, April 21. Northamptonshire won by one wicket. Toss: Northamptonshire. The visitors' target was adjusted to 168 off 36 overs after rain interrupted their innings.

## Glamorgan

| | | | |
|---|---|---|---|
| *A. R. Butcher b Taylor | 77 | G. C. Holmes not out | 13 |
| H. Morris c Lamb b Taylor | 2 | B 1, l-b 9, w 1 | 11 |
| M. P. Maynard c Baptiste b Curran | 13 | | |
| R. J. Shastri not out | 64 | 1/32 2/54 | (4 wkts, 40 overs) 186 |
| I. Smith c Thomas b Williams | 6 | 3/131 4/150 | |

R. D. B. Croft, †C. P. Metson, S. L. Watkin, S. R. Barwick and M. Frost did not bat.

Bowling: Baptiste 8–0–39–0; Thomas 4–0–27–0; Curran 8–0–37–1; Taylor 8–0–27–2; Cook 5–0–19–0; Williams 7–0–27–1.

## Northamptonshire

| | | | |
|---|---|---|---|
| A. Fordham c Barwick b Watkin | 3 | J. G. Thomas c Butcher b Barwick | 5 |
| R. J. Bailey run out | 8 | N. G. B. Cook c Morris b Barwick | 6 |
| *A. J. Lamb lbw b Watkin | 2 | J. P. Taylor not out | 2 |
| D. J. Capel b Watkin | 20 | B 1, l-b 15, w 4, n-b 1 | 21 |
| K. M. Curran c Metson b Barwick | 13 | | |
| R. G. Williams not out | 66 | 1/7 2/20 3/20 | (9 wkts, 35.5 overs) 171 |
| E. A. E. Baptiste run out | 11 | 4/51 5/64 6/80 | |
| †D. Ripley b Frost | 14 | 7/126 8/141 9/155 | |

Bowling: Frost 8–1–24–1; Watkin 8–0–30–3; Barwick 8–0–30–3; Shastri 8–0–31–0; Croft 2–0–16–0; Holmes 1.5–0–24–0.

Umpires: D. R. Shepherd and A. G. T. Whitehead.

At Leicester, April 28. GLAMORGAN lost to LEICESTERSHIRE by 13 runs.

## GLAMORGAN v NOTTINGHAMSHIRE

At Cardiff, May 5. Nottinghamshire won by four wickets. Toss: Glamorgan. Nottinghamshire's third successive win kept them at the head of the Sunday League. Broad's 108, a Sunday best, came from 106 balls and included eight fours and a six.

## Glamorgan

| | | | |
|---|---|---|---|
| *A. R. Butcher b Saxelby | 77 | | |
| H. Morris c Hemmings b Evans | 46 | | |
| M. P. Maynard not out | 57 | | |
| I. Smith not out | 28 | | |
| L-b 8, w 4, n-b 3 | 15 | | |
| | | 1/104 2/146 | (2 wkts, 40 overs) 223 |

R. D. B. Croft, G. C. Holmes, A. Dale, †M. L. Roberts, S. L. Watkin, S. R. Barwick and M. Frost did not bat.

Bowling: Cooper 8–1–40–0; Stephenson 8–1–42–0; Saxelby 8–1–36–1; Hemmings 6–1–27–0; Evans 8–0–54–1; Crawley 2–0–16–0.

## Nottinghamshire

| | | | |
|---|---|---|---|
| B. C. Broad c Morris b Smith | 108 | †B. N. French not out | 8 |
| D. W. Randall lbw b Croft | 24 | M. A. Crawley not out | 5 |
| *R. T. Robinson c Watkin b Smith | 10 | B 1, l-b 6, w 6, n-b 1 | 14 |
| P. Johnson c Roberts b Frost | 22 | | |
| M. Saxelby run out | 19 | 1/59 2/87 3/144 | (6 wkts, 39 overs) 225 |
| F. D. Stephenson run out | 15 | 4/188 5/204 6/218 | |

K. P. Evans, E. E. Hemmings and K. E. Cooper did not bat.

Bowling: Frost 8–0–41–1; Watkin 7–0–33–0; Dale 2–0–16–0; Barwick 1–0–8–0; Croft 8–0–39–1; Smith 8–0–49–2; Butcher 5–0–32–0.

Umpires: J. C. Balderstone and D. O. Oslear.

At Taunton, May 12. GLAMORGAN lost to SOMERSET by 35 runs.

## GLAMORGAN v WARWICKSHIRE

At Swansea, May 19. Warwickshire won by 13 runs. Toss: Glamorgan. Frost took three wickets for 4 runs in twelve balls to reduce Warwickshire to 104 for four, but Moles remained to add 105 in fifteen overs with Ostler and reach his highest score in the competition. Holmes and Smith also scored at 7 runs an over in their fourth-wicket partnership for Glamorgan, but they were unable to prevent Glamorgan's fifth successive Sunday defeat of the season.

### Warwickshire

| | | | |
|---|---|---|---|
| A. J. Moles not out | 93 | †K. J. Piper not out | 0 |
| Asif Din c Shastri b Frost | 46 | | |
| S. J. Green c Morris b Frost | 2 | L-b 10, w 3 | 13 |
| P. A. Smith c Metson b Barwick | 0 | | |
| *D. A. Reeve c Metson b Frost | 2 | 1/92 2/100 3/100 (5 wkts, 40 overs) 211 |
| D. P. Ostler c Dennis b Barwick | 55 | 4/104 5/209 |

A. R. K. Pierson, G. C. Small, A. A. Donald and T. A. Munton did not bat.

Bowling: Watkin 8–0–27–0; Frost 8–0–42–3; Dale 4–0–12–0; Dennis 8–0–46–0; Shastri 4–0–21–0; Barwick 8–0–53–2.

### Glamorgan

| | | | |
|---|---|---|---|
| *A. R. Butcher c Ostler b Munton | 0 | S. L. Watkin b Smith | 0 |
| H. Morris lbw b Small | 39 | S. R. Barwick b Smith | 0 |
| R. J. Shastri c Asif Din b Small | 32 | M. Frost not out | 0 |
| G. C. Holmes c Piper b Reeve | 46 | B 1, l-b 8, w 8, n-b 2 | 19 |
| I. Smith b Reeve | 41 | |
| A. Dale b Smith | 3 | 1/0 2/64 3/79 (9 wkts, 40 overs) 198 |
| †C. P. Metson not out | 12 | 4/170 5/175 6/177 |
| S. J. Dennis run out | 6 | 7/196 8/198 9/198 |

Bowling: Munton 8–1–15–1; Donald 8–0–43–0; Reeve 8–0–45–2; Small 8–1–33–2; Pierson 1–0–11–0; Smith 7–1–42–3.

Umpires: A. G. T. Whitehead and P. B. Wight.

## GLAMORGAN v SUSSEX

At Swansea, May 26. Sussex won by 113 runs. Toss: Glamorgan.

### Sussex

| | | | |
|---|---|---|---|
| N. J. Lenham c Holmes b Watkin | 13 | I. D. K. Salisbury b Frost | 4 |
| K. Greenfield c Holmes b Dale | 38 | R. A. Bunting not out | 2 |
| *P. W. G. Parker lbw b Dale | 32 | A. N. Jones c Dale b Barwick | 2 |
| A. P. Wells c Barwick b Smith | 5 | B 1, l-b 7, w 8, n-b 1 | 17 |
| M. P. Speight c Maynard b Frost | 47 | |
| A. I. C. Dodemaide c Shastri b Smith | 9 | 1/30 2/77 3/96 (37.5 overs) 205 |
| †P. Moores run out | 34 | 4/97 5/117 6/187 |
| A. C. S. Pigott lbw b Watkin | 2 | 7/193 8/200 9/200 |

Bowling: Watkin 8–0–44–2; Frost 7–0–46–2; Barwick 6.5–0–35–1; Dale 8–0–37–2; Smith 8–0–35–2.

## Glamorgan

| | | | |
|---|---|---|---|
| *A. R. Butcher c Moores b Pigott | 9 | S. L. Watkin b Salisbury | 0 |
| H. Morris c and b Pigott | 24 | S. R. Barwick b Salisbury | 2 |
| M. P. Maynard run out | 0 | M. Frost not out | 0 |
| R. J. Shastri c Parker b Pigott | 14 | L-b 3, w 8 | 11 |
| G. C. Holmes c Moores b Bunting | 5 | | |
| I. Smith c Parker b Bunting | 8 | 1/5 2/24 3/29 (30.1 overs) 92 | |
| A. Dale c Jones b Salisbury | 17 | 4/33 5/47 6/54 | |
| †C. P. Metson run out | 2 | 7/73 8/80 9/92 | |

*H. Morris, when 1, retired hurt at 4 and resumed at 54.*

Bowling: Jones 5–2–11–0; Dodemaide 5–0–10–0; Pigott 8–0–26–3; Bunting 8–0–32–2; Salisbury 4.1–0–10–3.

Umpires: J. D. Bond and A. A. Jones.

## GLAMORGAN v ESSEX

At Pontypridd, June 2. No result. Toss: Essex. Glamorgan gained their first two League points of the season when this match, their seventh, was abandoned.

## Glamorgan

| | | | |
|---|---|---|---|
| *A. R. Butcher c Prichard b Andrew | 14 | †C. P. Metson not out | 6 |
| H. Morris c Garnham b Andrew | 3 | | |
| M. P. Maynard b Andrew | 6 | L-b 5, w 7, n-b 1 | 13 |
| R. J. Shastri c Gooch b Stephenson | 22 | | |
| I. Smith c Garnham b Topley | 8 | 1/16 2/27 3/29 (7 wkts, 27.3 overs) 99 | |
| A. Dale run out | 2 | 4/52 5/66 | |
| J. Derrick b Pringle | 25 | 6/66 7/99 | |

S. Bastien, S. L. Watkin and S. R. Barwick did not bat.

Bowling: Andrew 8–1–33–3; Pringle 5.3–0–26–1; Gooch 5–1–11–0; Topley 6–1–16–1; Stephenson 3–1–8–1.

## Essex

*G. A. Gooch, J. P. Stephenson, P. J. Prichard, N. Shahid, N. Hussain, D. R. Pringle, N. A. Foster, †M. A. Garnham, T. D. Topley, S. J. W. Andrew and P. M. Such.

Umpires: J. W. Holder and R. Palmer.

At Manchester, June 9. LANCASHIRE v GLAMORGAN. No result.

## GLAMORGAN v MIDDLESEX

At Cardiff, June 16. Glamorgan won by 54 runs. Toss: Middlesex. Morris, who hit two sixes in his 75, led Glamorgan to their first victory in the League since July 15, 1990.

## Glamorgan

| | | | |
|---|---|---|---|
| M. P. Maynard b Williams | 25 | S. L. Watkin c Weekes b Emburey | 2 |
| *H. Morris c Gatting b Cowans | 75 | S. R. Barwick not out | 3 |
| G. C. Holmes st Farbrace b Weekes | 15 | | |
| R. J. Shastri run out | 4 | L-b 14, w 1 | 15 |
| I. Smith b Cowans | 22 | | |
| A. Dale not out | 25 | 1/52 2/75 3/86 (8 wkts, 40 overs) 198 | |
| J. Derrick run out | 5 | 4/133 5/158 6/169 | |
| †C. P. Metson b Hughes | 7 | 7/179 8/182 | |

M. Frost did not bat.

Bowling: Cowans 8–0–44–2; Williams 7–0–32–1; Weekes 8–0–40–1; Hughes 8–2–23–1; Emburey 8–1–33–1; Ramprakash 1–0–12–0.

## Middlesex

| | | | | |
|---|---|---|---|---|
| J. F. Hutchinson c Maynard b Derrick | 42 | N. F. Williams c Smith b Dale | | 11 |
| M. A. Roseberry lbw b Watkin | 6 | †P. Farbrace b Watkin | | 3 |
| M. W. Gatting b Watkin | 8 | S. P. Hughes lbw b Barwick | | 4 |
| M. R. Ramprakash c Maynard b Derrick | 18 | B 1, l-b 10 | | 11 |
| K. R. Brown c Holmes b Derrick | 16 | | | |
| P. N. Weekes lbw b Derrick | 1 | 1/23 2/53 3/68 | (35.2 overs) | 144 |
| J. E. Emburey not out | 20 | 4/85 5/91 6/108 | | |
| N. G. Cowans c Smith b Dale | 4 | 7/112 8/129 9/135 | | |

Bowling: Watkin 8–0–34–3; Frost 6–0–20–0; Barwick 5.2–0–18–1; Derrick 8–0–25–4; Dale 7–0–36–2.

Umpires: D. J. Constant and K. J. Lyons.

At Leeds, June 30. GLAMORGAN lost to YORKSHIRE by 95 runs.

At Maidstone, July 7. GLAMORGAN lost to KENT by eight wickets.

At Worcester, July 21. GLAMORGAN lost to WORCESTERSHIRE by seven wickets.

At The Oval, July 28. GLAMORGAN beat SURREY by 3 runs.

## GLAMORGAN v GLOUCESTERSHIRE

At Swansea, August 4. Glamorgan won by 100 runs. Toss: Glamorgan. Maynard hit the first ball of the match for six and went on to make 81 from 79 balls. Glamorgan's winning margin was its largest in a Sunday match since they beat Middlesex by 124 runs in 1984.

### Glamorgan

| | | | | |
|---|---|---|---|---|
| M. P. Maynard c Russell b Alleyne | 81 | S. L. Watkin c Athey b Babington | | 6 |
| S. P. James c Russell b Gerrard | 23 | S. R. Barwick not out | | 1 |
| R. J. Shastri run out | 6 | D. J. Foster b Babington | | 0 |
| A. Dale b Lawrence | 32 | B 1, l-b 16, w 5, n-b 4 | | 26 |
| M. A. Cottey b Babington | 33 | | | |
| A. R. Butcher b Lawrence | 20 | 1/71 2/100 3/128 | (40 overs) | 236 |
| R. D. B. Croft run out | 1 | 4/180 5/219 6/220 | | |
| C. P. Metson c Milburn b Babington | 7 | 7/222 8/233 9/235 | | |

Bowling: Lawrence 8–0–48–2; Babington 8–0–53–4; Gerrard 8–2–35–1; Scott 8–0–29–0; Alleyne 7–0–44–1; Ball 1–0–10–0.

### Gloucestershire

| | | | | |
|---|---|---|---|---|
| R. J. Scott c Cottey b Foster | 2 | A. M. Babington c Maynard b Shastri | | 4 |
| C. W. J. Athey c Metson b Watkin | 3 | M. C. J. Ball not out | | 2 |
| R. C. Russell b Dale | 40 | M. J. Gerrard b Foster | | 4 |
| A. J. Wright c Dale b Croft | 23 | L-b 2, w 2 | | 4 |
| M. W. Alleyne b Croft | 8 | | | |
| D. W. Lloyds c James b Dale | 20 | 1/3 2/6 3/63 | (35 overs) | 136 |
| J. T. Milburn run out | 13 | 4/79 5/83 6/113 | | |
| D. V. Lawrence c Maynard b Dale | 13 | 7/114 8/127 9/132 | | |

Bowling: Watkin 5–2–11–1; Foster 6–0–16–2; Barwick 4–0–18–0; Croft 8–0–30–2; Dale 8–0–44–3; Shastri 4–1–15–1.

Umpires: J. C. Balderstone and J. H. Harris.

## GLAMORGAN v HAMPSHIRE

At Ebbw Vale, August 11. Glamorgan won by 6 runs. Toss: Glamorgan. Cottey's 92 not out, his highest score in the League, came from 70 balls, and he added 84 in nine overs for the seventh wicket with Metson. The match was reduced to 36 overs a side by the weather.

### Glamorgan

| | | | |
|---|---:|---|---:|
| M. P. Maynard b Connor | 2 | S. L. Watkin lbw b Udal | 2 |
| S. P. James b Shine | 11 | S. R. Barwick not out | 5 |
| A. Dale b Connor | 7 | | |
| R. J. Shastri c Aymes b Ayling | 36 | B 1, l-b 8, w 7 | 16 |
| P. A. Cottey not out | 92 | | — |
| *A. R. Butcher b Udal | 6 | 1/4 2/19 3/39 | (8 wkts, 36 overs) 197 |
| R. D. B. Croft lbw b Udal | 0 | 4/80 5/103 6/103 | |
| †C. P. Metson c Maru b Connor | 20 | 7/187 8/191 | |

D. J. Foster did not bat.

Bowling: Connor 7-0-36-3; Shine 8-0-17-1; Ayling 7-0-53-1; James 6-1-30-0; Udal 6-0-40-3; Maru 2-0-12-0.

### Hampshire

| | | | |
|---|---:|---|---:|
| T. C. Middleton c Croft b Shastri | 32 | S. D. Udal c Butcher b Dale | 23 |
| V. P. Terry lbw b Croft | 24 | C. A. Connor c Maynard b Foster | 8 |
| R. M. F. Cox b Shastri | 2 | K. J. Shine not out | 2 |
| *M. C. J. Nicholas c Maynard b Dale | 29 | L-b 4, w 5 | 9 |
| K. D. James st Metson b Shastri | 8 | | — |
| J. R. Ayling c Metson b Watkin | 13 | 1/58 2/61 3/61 | (9 wkts, 36 overs) 191 |
| †A. N. Aymes c Dale b Watkin | 8 | 4/77 5/114 6/119 | |
| R. J. Maru not out | 33 | 7/141 8/176 9/188 | |

Bowling: Watkin 7-0-37-2; Foster 5-0-27-1; Shastri 8-0-26-3; Barwick 3-0-29-0; Croft 7-0-30-1; Dale 6-0-38-2.

Umpires: D. J. Constant and R. C. Tolchard.

At Checkley, August 18. GLAMORGAN lost to DERBYSHIRE by 29 runs.

# GLOUCESTERSHIRE

## GLOUCESTERSHIRE v MIDDLESEX

At Bristol, April 21. Middlesex won on scoring-rate. Toss: Middlesex. Gloucestershire's target was adjusted to 204 from 34 overs after rain. Gatting (117 balls) and Ramprakash (107 balls) added 194 in 34 overs for the second wicket, a Middlesex record for any wicket in the Sunday League.

### Middlesex

| | |
|---|---:|
| *M. W. Gatting run out | 111 |
| M. A. Roseberry c Wright b Babington | 2 |
| M. R. Ramprakash not out | 111 |
| K. R. Brown not out | 8 |
| L-b 6, n-b 1 | 7 |

1/10 2/204          (2 wkts, 40 overs) 239

P. N. Weekes, †P. R. Downton, J. E. Emburey, N. F. Williams, D. W. Headley, C. W. Taylor and N. G. Cowans did not bat.

Bowling: Gilbert 8-0-47-0; Babington 8-0-33-1; Lawrence 8-0-52-0; Smith 6-0-36-0; Scott 4-0-23-0; Alleyne 6-0-42-0.

## Gloucestershire

| | | | | |
|---|---|---|---|---|
| R. J. Scott c Downton b Taylor | 44 | D. R. Gilbert c Weekes b Emburey | | 0 |
| C. W. J. Athey run out | 1 | A. M. Smith not out | | 0 |
| *A. J. Wright c Roseberry b Williams | 1 | A. M. Babington c Ramprakash | | |
| M. W. Alleyne st Downton b Emburey | 48 | | b Cowans | 6 |
| J. W. Lloyds c Taylor b Emburey | 11 | L-b 3, w 10, n-b 1 | | 14 |
| P. W. Romaines st Downton | | | | |
| b Emburey | 13 | 1/15 2/26 3/82 | (32.5 overs) | 159 |
| †R. C. Russell b Cowans | 12 | 4/116 5/116 6/141 | | |
| D. V. Lawrence c Williams b Cowans | 9 | 7/148 8/148 9/152 | | |

Bowling: Williams 7–1–26–1; Cowans 6.5–0–33–3; Emburey 7–0–39–4; Headley 8–0–38–0; Taylor 4–0–20–1.

Umpires: J. H. Harris and K. J. Lyons.

## GLOUCESTERSHIRE v WORCESTERSHIRE

At Bristol, May 5. Worcestershire won by ten wickets. Toss: Gloucestershire. It took Worcestershire only 95 minutes to make the highest score achieved for a ten-wicket win in the Sunday League. Moody followed his 160 in his first Sunday game of the season with an unbeaten 128 in 97 balls (fifteen fours and three sixes). His first 50 took 49 balls, the next 29, and he hit 24 off one over from Alleyne. This innings took his aggregate in his first six games for Worcestershire in all competitions to 551 runs from 552 balls.

## Gloucestershire

| | | | | |
|---|---|---|---|---|
| R. J. Scott c Rhodes b Weston | 32 | D. V. Lawrence c D'Oliveira b Radford | | 0 |
| C. W. J. Athey c and b Illingworth | 26 | D. R. Gilbert not out | | 10 |
| *A. J. Wright c Curtis b Illingworth | 23 | B 1, w 5, n-b 1 | | 7 |
| M. W. Alleyne c Weston b Newport | 44 | | | |
| J. J. E. Hardy run out | 20 | 1/52 2/67 3/98 | (7 wkts, 39 overs) | 193 |
| P. W. Romaines not out | 27 | 4/148 5/149 | | |
| †R. C. Russell c Weston b Radford | 4 | 6/161 7/161 | | |

M. C. J. Ball and A. M. Babington did not bat.

Bowling: Newport 8–0–47–1; Weston 8–1–24–1; Radford 8–0–37–2; Illingworth 8–1–37–2; Botham 7–0–47–0.

## Worcestershire

| | |
|---|---|
| T. S. Curtis not out | 61 |
| T. M. Moody not out | 128 |
| L-b 6, w 1, n-b 1 | 8 |

(no wkt, 29.4 overs) 197

G. A. Hick, I. T. Botham, D. B. D'Oliveira, *P. A. Neale, †S. J. Rhodes, P. J. Newport, R. K. Illingworth, M. J. Weston and N. V. Radford did not bat.

Bowling: Gilbert 8–0–38–0; Babington 6.4–0–48–0; Lawrence 8–0–42–0; Ball 2–0–19–0; Alleyne 3–0–33–0; Scott 2–0–11–0.

Umpires: M. J. Kitchen and R. Palmer.

At The Oval, May 12. GLOUCESTERSHIRE beat SURREY by 25 runs.

At Hove, May 19. GLOUCESTERSHIRE beat SUSSEX by 62 runs.

## GLOUCESTERSHIRE v HAMPSHIRE

At Swindon, May 26. Gloucestershire won by 26 runs. Toss: Hampshire. Gloucestershire reached their highest total in the Sunday League, passing their previous best of 272 (for four against Middlesex at Lord's in 1983, and for seven against Northamptonshire at Northampton in 1990). Scott (78 balls, nine fours, one six) and Athey (99 balls, eight fours, one six) gave them a sound start, and Wright, who reached 50 from 37 balls, and Alleyne (17 balls) added 73 in the last six overs. Terry's 123 for Hampshire, from 103 balls, contained eight fours and three sixes.

### Gloucestershire

R. J. Scott lbw b Udal .............. 77
C. W. J. Athey c Smith b Bakker ..... 85
*A. J. Wright not out .............. 60
M. W. Alleyne not out ............. 37
    B 4, l-b 8, w 10 ............. 22

1/130 2/208     (2 wkts, 40 overs) 281

P. W. Romaines, J. W. Lloyds, J. J. E. Hardy, †R. C. J. Williams, D. R. Gilbert, A. M. Smith and A. M. Babington did not bat.

Bowling: James 4–0–25–0; Aqib Javed 8–0–51–0; Bakker 8–0–45–1; Ayling 7–0–49–0; Nicholas 5–0–42–0; Udal 8–0–57–1.

### Hampshire

V. P. Terry b Smith ................ 123
T. C. Middleton b Smith ........... 36
R. A. Smith c and b Lloyds ......... 16
D. I. Gower c Alleyne b Lloyds ...... 2
*M. C. J. Nicholas b Gilbert ........ 45
K. D. James c Athey b Smith ....... 8
J. R. Ayling not out ................ 9
†A. N. Aymes not out .............. 4
    L-b 7, w 5 ............. 12

1/62 2/88 3/99     (6 wkts, 40 overs) 255
4/219 5/238 6/240

S. D. Udal, P. J. Bakker and Aqib Javed did not bat.

Bowling: Gilbert 8–0–51–1; Babington 8–0–50–0; Athey 5–0–28–0; Smith 8–0–47–3; Lloyds 7–0–47–2; Alleyne 4–0–25–0.

Umpires: D. O. Oslear and R. Palmer.

## GLOUCESTERSHIRE v NORTHAMPTONSHIRE

At Moreton-in-Marsh, June 9. No result. Toss: Northamptonshire. Only one ball was bowled before rain drove the players from the field.

### Gloucestershire

R. J. Scott not out ................. 0
†C. W. J. Athey not out ............ 0

    (no wkt, 0.1 over) 0

*A. J. Wright, M. W. Alleyne, J. W. Lloyds, P. W. Romaines, D. R. Gilbert, D. V. Lawrence, A. M. Babington, A. M. Smith and T. H. C. Hancock did not bat.

Bowling: Walker 0.1–0–0–0.

### Northamptonshire

A. Fordham, N. A. Felton, D. J. Capel, *R. J. Bailey, K. M. Curran, R. G. Williams, J. G. Thomas, †D. Ripley, A. L. Penberthy, A. Walker and N. G. B. Cook.

Umpires: A. A. Jones and K. E. Palmer.

## GLOUCESTERSHIRE v NOTTINGHAMSHIRE

At Gloucester, June 16. Nottinghamshire won by eight wickets. Toss: Nottinghamshire. Nottinghamshire's seventh straight win in the League came after their target had been adjusted to 149 in 33 overs. Rain had already restricted Gloucestershire's innings, in which Hardy's 42 runs were made from 29 balls, to 37 overs. Nottinghamshire had almost three overs to spare after Johnson raced to 52 from 51 balls while adding 78 with Robinson.

### Gloucestershire

| | | | |
|---|---|---|---|
| R. J. Scott lbw b Cooper | 1 | †R. C. Russell not out | 7 |
| C. W. J. Athey b Crawley | 44 | D. V. Lawrence not out | 9 |
| J. W. Lloyds c Evans b Saxelby | 15 | L-b 4, w 2, n-b 1 | 7 |
| *A. J. Wright b Evans | 4 | | |
| M. W. Alleyne c Saxelby b Stephenson | 37 | 1/4 2/31 3/52 (6 wkts, 37 overs) 166 | |
| J. J. E. Hardy b Stephenson | 42 | 4/83 5/135 6/151 | |

D. R. Gilbert, A. M. Babington and A. M. Smith did not bat.

Bowling: Cooper 8–1–30–1; Stephenson 6–0–25–2; Saxelby 4–0–18–1; Evans 6–1–34–1; Hemmings 8–0–39–0; Crawley 5–0–16–1.

### Nottinghamshire

| | |
|---|---|
| B. C. Broad run out | 36 |
| D. W. Randall c and b Lawrence | 27 |
| *R. T. Robinson not out | 24 |
| P. Johnson not out | 52 |
| L-b 3, w 7 | 10 |

1/64 2/71 (2 wkts, 30.1 overs) 149

M. A. Crawley, M. Saxelby, F. D. Stephenson, †B. N. French, K. P. Evans, E. E. Hemmings and K. E. Cooper did not bat.

Bowling: Gilbert 8–0–39–0; Babington 7–0–38–0; Smith 6.1–1–29–0; Lawrence 8–0–35–1; Lloyds 1–0–5–0.

Umpires: B. Leadbeater and N. T. Plews.

At Bath, June 23. SOMERSET v GLOUCESTERSHIRE. No result.

At Canterbury, June 30. GLOUCESTERSHIRE lost to KENT by 67 runs.

At Scarborough, July 14. GLOUCESTERSHIRE beat YORKSHIRE by 10 runs.

## GLOUCESTERSHIRE v DERBYSHIRE

At Cheltenham, July 21. Derbyshire won by 94 runs. Toss: Derbyshire. After a string of eight defeats, the title holders won their first League match since May 5. The unbroken stand of 94 between Goldsmith, whose 67 not out was a competition best, and Barnett was a record for Derbyshire's seventh wicket in limited-overs matches.

### Derbyshire

| | | | |
|---|---|---|---|
| P. D. Bowler b Lawrence | 8 | A. E. Warner c Ball b Lawrence | 8 |
| C. J. Adams c Russell b Gilbert | 67 | *K. J. Barnett not out | 36 |
| J. E. Morris c Russell b Scott | 21 | L-b 3, w 3 | 6 |
| M. Azharuddin c Russell b Alleyne | 26 | | |
| T. J. G. O'Gorman c Ball b Lawrence | 16 | 1/26 2/63 3/120 (6 wkts, 40 overs) 255 | |
| S. C. Goldsmith not out | 67 | 4/127 5/150 6/161 | |

†K. M. Krikken, D. G. Cork and S. J. Base did not bat.

Bowling: Lawrence 7–0–51–3; Gilbert 8–0–49–1; Smith 6–0–47–0; Scott 7–0–48–1; Ball 8–0–35–0; Alleyne 4–0–22–1.

## Gloucestershire

| | | | |
|---|---|---|---|
| R. J. Scott c Krikken b Base | 17 | M. C. J. Ball c Barnett b Bowler | 5 |
| C. W. J. Athey c O'Gorman b Cork | 9 | D. R. Gilbert c Azharuddin b Bowler | 7 |
| †R. C. Russell c Krikken b Cork | 7 | A. M. Smith not out | 2 |
| *A. J. Wright c Krikken b Warner | 19 | L-b 3, w 8 | 11 |
| M. W. Alleyne c O'Gorman b Warner | 17 | | |
| J. J. E. Hardy c sub b Bowler | 54 | 1/27 2/33 3/35 | (35.2 overs) 161 |
| J. W. Lloyds c Adams b Barnett | 0 | 4/56 5/85 6/88 | |
| D. V. Lawrence c Morris b Base | 13 | 7/110 8/142 9/155 | |

Bowling: Cork 6–0–27–2; Base 8–0–37–2; Warner 8–0–36–2; Barnett 8–0–27–1; Bowler 5.2–0–31–3.

Umpires: G. I. Burgess and P. B. Wight.

## GLOUCESTERSHIRE v ESSEX

At Cheltenham, July 28. Essex won by four wickets. Toss: Essex.

### Gloucestershire

| | | | |
|---|---|---|---|
| R. J. Scott b Topley | 11 | A. M. Babington c Foster b Such | 11 |
| †C. W. J. Athey lbw b Stephenson | 49 | A. M. Smith not out | 15 |
| *A. J. Wright c Garnham b Fraser | 10 | M. J. Gerrard c Shahid b Topley | 3 |
| M. W. Alleyne c Seymour b Stephenson | 13 | L-b 6, w 3, n-b 3 | 12 |
| T. H. C. Hancock b Stephenson | 0 | | |
| J. W. Lloyds c Fraser b Such | 12 | 1/21 2/39 3/79 | (38.1 overs) 158 |
| E. T. Milburn c Prichard b Topley | 21 | 4/79 5/100 6/111 | |
| M. C. J. Ball run out | 1 | 7/112 8/127 9/152 | |

Bowling: Foster 7–0–24–0; Fraser 8–0–21–1; Topley 7.1–1–35–3; Stephenson 8–1–31–3; Such 8–0–41–2.

### Essex

| | | | |
|---|---|---|---|
| A. C. H. Seymour b Gerrard | 1 | *N. A. Foster not out | 29 |
| J. P. Stephenson c Athey b Babington | 0 | †M. A. Garnham not out | 18 |
| Salim Malik lbw b Scott | 27 | L-b 1, w 1, n-b 2 | 4 |
| P. J. Prichard b Babington | 0 | | |
| N. Hussain lbw b Alleyne | 44 | 1/1 2/1 3/2 | (6 wkts, 37.4 overs) 159 |
| N. Shahid c Athey b Alleyne | 36 | 4/58 5/109 6/112 | |

A. G. J. Fraser, T. D. Topley and P. M. Such did not bat.

Bowling: Babington 8–0–24–2; Gerrard 8–1–42–1; Scott 8–0–23–1; Smith 3–0–23–0; Ball 5–0–27–0; Alleyne 5.4–0–19–2.

Umpires: J. D. Bond and D. J. Constant.

At Swansea, August 4. GLOUCESTERSHIRE lost to GLAMORGAN by 100 runs.

## GLOUCESTERSHIRE v LANCASHIRE

At Bristol, August 11. Lancashire won by eight wickets. Toss: Lancashire. Rain interrupted Gloucestershire's innings when they were 93 for four from 24 overs, and the match was subsequently restricted to 29 overs a side. On the resumption, Gloucestershire lost six wickets for 15 runs as Austin set a Lancashire record of 28 wickets in a Sunday League season.

## Gloucestershire

| | | | | |
|---|---|---|---|---|
| C. W. J. Athey lbw b Allott | 5 | A. M. Babington b Austin | 0 |
| †R. C. Russell run out | 12 | A. M. Smith run out | 4 |
| *A. J. Wright c and b Watkinson | 33 | M. J. Gerrard not out | 3 |
| M. W. Alleyne c Wasim Akram | | | |
| b Watkinson | 11 | L-b 8, w 5 | 13 |
| J. J. E. Hardy b Austin | 20 | | |
| J. W. Lloyds c Lloyd b Wasim Akram | 5 | 1/13 2/22 3/65 | (29 overs) 108 |
| E. T. Milburn b Austin | 0 | 4/72 5/93 6/98 | |
| M. C. J. Ball c Hegg b Austin | 2 | 7/98 8/100 9/101 | |

Bowling: Allott 6–0–17–1; Wasim Akram 8–0–25–1; Martin 7–0–28–0; Watkinson 4–0–20–2; Austin 4–0–10–4.

## Lancashire

| | |
|---|---|
| G. D. Mendis c Hardy b Smith | 23 |
| G. Fowler b Alleyne | 15 |
| G. D. Lloyd not out | 25 |
| *N. H. Fairbrother not out | 43 |
| L-b 3, w 2, n-b 1 | 6 |

1/35 2/43    (2 wkts, 22.5 overs) 112

M. Watkinson, N. J. Speak, Wasim Akram, †W. K. Hegg, I. D. Austin, P. J. W. Allott and P. J. Martin did not bat.

Bowling: Babington 7–0–41–0; Gerrard 5–0–35–0; Smith 4–0–10–1; Alleyne 4–1–7–1; Ball 2.5–0–16–0.

Umpires: B. Hassan and D. R. Shepherd.

At Birmingham, August 18. GLOUCESTERSHIRE lost to WARWICKSHIRE by nine wickets.

At Leicester, August 25. GLOUCESTERSHIRE beat LEICESTERSHIRE by 12 runs.

# HAMPSHIRE

## HAMPSHIRE v YORKSHIRE

At Southampton, April 21. Hampshire won by 49 runs. Toss: Yorkshire. Smith, who hit eight fours and a six in 107 balls, and Gower added 102 in eighteen overs for Hampshire's second wicket.

## Hampshire

| | | | | |
|---|---|---|---|---|
| T. C. Middleton c Fletcher b Hartley | 22 | J. R. Ayling not out | 2 |
| C. L. Smith c Moxon b Hartley | 86 | L-b 3, w 2, n-b 1 | 6 |
| D. I. Gower c Sharp b Sidebottom | 45 | | |
| J. R. Wood c and b Fletcher | 14 | 1/40 2/142 | (4 wkts, 39 overs) 197 |
| *M. C. J. Nicholas not out | 22 | 3/160 4/190 | |

K. D. James, †A. N. Aymes, C. A. Connor, Aqib Javed and S. D. Udal did not bat.

Bowling: Jarvis 7–2–27–0; Sidebottom 8–0–42–1; M. A. Robinson 8–0–45–0; Hartley 8–0–36–2; Fletcher 8–0–44–1.

## Yorkshire

| | | |
|---|---|---|
| *M. D. Moxon c Aymes b James | 15 | A. Sidebottom not out | 7 |
| A. A. Metcalfe c Aymes b Connor | 7 | S. D. Fletcher b Aqib Javed | 1 |
| †R. J. Blakey b Udal | 24 | M. A. Robinson not out | 2 |
| K. Sharp c Wood b James | 41 | L-b 18, w 4 | 22 |
| P. E. Robinson run out | 15 | | |
| D. Byas lbw b James | 2 | 1/27 2/31 3/78 (9 wkts, 39 overs) 148 |
| P. J. Hartley b Aqib Javed | 8 | 4/102 5/120 6/123 |
| P. W. Jarvis st Aymes b Ayling | 4 | 7/129 8/137 9/139 |

Bowling: James 8–0–24–3; Aqib Javed 8–0–21–2; Connor 7–0–25–1; Ayling 8–0–33–1; Udal 8–0–27–1.

Umpires: A. A. Jones and P. B. Wight.

At Derby, May 5. HAMPSHIRE lost to DERBYSHIRE by four wickets.

## HAMPSHIRE v KENT

At Southampton, May 12. Hampshire won by five wickets. Toss: Kent. The fastest scoring of the match came from James, who faced 44 balls for his unbeaten 58, hitting four fours. Kent's captain, Benson, hit three fours and a six in his 78-ball 65.

### Kent

| | | |
|---|---|---|
| *M. R. Benson run out | 65 | R. P. Davis run out | 0 |
| N. R. Taylor lbw b James | 2 | T. A. Merrick c Wood b Connor | 4 |
| T. R. Ward c Udal b Aqib Javed | 2 | A. P. Igglesden not out | 1 |
| G. R. Cowdrey c Udal b Bakker | 35 | L-b 7, w 6 | 13 |
| C. S. Cowdrey run out | 14 | | |
| M. V. Fleming c Smith b Bakker | 19 | 1/12 2/27 3/105 (9 wkts, 39 overs) 187 |
| †V. J. Wells c Terry b James | 8 | 4/121 5/133 6/145 |
| R. M. Ellison not out | 24 | 7/171 8/171 9/185 |

Bowling: James 8–1–31–2; Aqib Javed 7–0–33–1; Bakker 8–0–36–2; Connor 8–0–33–1; Udal 8–0–47–0.

### Hampshire

| | | |
|---|---|---|
| V. P. Terry c and b Igglesden | 1 | †A. N. Aymes not out | 15 |
| C. L. Smith c and b Davis | 40 | | |
| D. I. Gower c C. S. Cowdrey b Igglesden | 3 | B 1, l-b 9, w 3 | 13 |
| J. R. Wood c C. S. Cowdrey b Merrick | 18 | | |
| *M. C. J. Nicholas b Igglesden | 43 | 1/10 2/16 3/48 (5 wkts, 38.4 overs) 191 |
| K. D. James not out | 58 | 4/76 5/146 |

S. D. Udal, C. A. Connor, P. J. Bakker and Aqib Javed did not bat.

Bowling: Igglesden 7.4–0–33–3; Ellison 8–0–25–0; Merrick 8–0–56–1; Davis 7–0–34–1; Fleming 8–0–33–0.

Umpires: D. J. Constant and B. J. Meyer.

## HAMPSHIRE v SOMERSET

At Bournemouth, May 19. Somerset won by seven wickets. Toss: Somerset. Tavaré hit eleven fours, and faced 82 balls for his unbeaten 75, in helping maintain Somerset's unbeaten start to the season with their fourth win.

## Hampshire

| | | | |
|---|---|---|---|
| V. P. Terry lbw b Mallender | 6 | †A. N. Aymes not out | 18 |
| C. L. Smith c Burns b Hayhurst | 47 | S. D. Udal not out | 4 |
| R. A. Smith b Lefebvre | 1 | L-b 2, w 4 | 6 |
| O. I. Gower c Tavaré b MacLeay | 8 | | |
| *M. C. J. Nicholas c Burns b Rose | 43 | 1/12 2/15 3/45 (6 wkts, 40 overs) 149 | |
| K. D. James c Cook b Mallender | 16 | 4/81 5/114 6/137 | |

C. A. Connor, P. J. Bakker and Aqib Javed did not bat.

Bowling: Mallender 8-0-21-2; Lefebvre 8-1-35-1; MacLeay 8-1-16-1; Rose 8-0-31-1; Hayhurst 8-0-44-1.

## Somerset

| | | | |
|---|---|---|---|
| S. J. Cook c Aymes b Udal | 43 | G. D. Rose not out | 11 |
| R. J. Bartlett c Aymes b James | 6 | L-b 5, w 7, n-b 1 | 13 |
| *C. J. Tavaré not out | 75 | | |
| R. J. Harden c Aymes b Aqib Javed | 5 | 1/23 2/92 3/102 (3 wkts, 39 overs) 153 | |

A. N. Hayhurst, P. M. Roebuck, †N. D. Burns, K. H. MacLeay, R. P. Lefebvre and N. A. Mallender did not bat.

Bowling: Aqib Javed 8-1-20-1; Bakker 8-1-21-0; Connor 8-0-31-0; James 7-0-43-1; Udal 8-0-33-1.

Umpires: D. J. Constant and K. E. Palmer.

At Swindon, May 26. HAMPSHIRE lost to GLOUCESTERSHIRE by 26 runs.

At Northampton, June 2. HAMPSHIRE lost to NORTHAMPTONSHIRE by 99 runs.

## HAMPSHIRE v SUSSEX

At Basingstoke, June 9. Sussex won by 14 runs. Toss: Hampshire. Greenfield's unbeaten 78 for Sussex, his maiden fifty in the competition, came from 88 balls and contained eight fours.

## Sussex

| | | | |
|---|---|---|---|
| N. J. Lenham b Connor | 9 | A. C. S. Pigott c Gower b Connor | 4 |
| *P. W. G. Parker c Terry b Connor | 1 | I. D. K. Salisbury c Gower b Connor | 2 |
| A. P. Wells c Gower b Aqib Javed | 1 | A. N. Jones not out | 3 |
| M. P. Speight c Udal b Aqib Javed | 7 | B 3, l-b 10, w 4, n-b 1 | 18 |
| K. Greenfield not out | 78 | | |
| C. M. Wells c and b Ayling | 16 | 1/7 2/8 3/18 (9 wkts, 40 overs) 172 | |
| A. I. C. Dodemaide lbw b Ayling | 0 | 4/18 5/59 6/59 | |
| †P. Moores b Udal | 33 | 7/138 8/150 9/159 | |

Bowling: Connor 8-0-29-4; Aqib Javed 8-2-16-2; Tremlett 8-0-33-0; Ayling 8-1-41-2; Udal 8-0-40-1.

## Hampshire

| | | | |
|---|---|---|---|
| V. P. Terry lbw b Pigott | 42 | S. D. Udal c Moores b Pigott | 3 |
| T. C. Middleton c Speight b Jones | 8 | C. A. Connor b Pigott | 2 |
| J. R. Wood c Jones b Pigott | 39 | Aqib Javed not out | 4 |
| D. I. Gower c C. M. Wells b Pigott | 0 | L-b 10, w 6, n-b 1 | 17 |
| *M. C. J. Nicholas b Jones | 23 | | |
| J. R. Ayling c and b Salisbury | 7 | 1/31 2/94 3/97 (39.1 overs) 158 | |
| †A. N. Aymes lbw b Jones | 5 | 4/108 5/132 6/138 | |
| T. M. Tremlett c Pigott b Salisbury | 8 | 7/143 8/151 9/151 | |

Bowling: Dodemaide 8-0-20-0; Jones 8-0-33-3; C. M. Wells 8-0-32-0; Pigott 7.1-1-30-5; Salisbury 8-1-33-2.

Umpires: B. Dudleston and R. Julian.

At Chelmsford, June 16. ESSEX v HAMPSHIRE. No result.

## HAMPSHIRE v WORCESTERSHIRE

At Southampton, July 7. Worcestershire won by six wickets. Toss: Worcestershire. The visitors' target was adjusted to 205 from 32 overs after rain halted their innings at 47 for no wicket from seven overs. Curtis and Moody went on to 126 before being parted, Moody reaching 1,000 runs in the League in only 24 innings, beating B. A. Richards's record of 25 in 1971. In Hampshire's innings, Smith made his first hundred in the competition, in his thirteenth year; he faced 113 balls and hit sixteen boundaries. With Wood, whose half-century contained three fours and three sixes, Smith added 114 for the third wicket.

### Hampshire

| | | |
|---|---|---|
| *M. C. J. Nicholas c Rhodes b Weston. | 2 | J. R. Ayling not out............... 14 |
| C. L. Smith c and b Newport........ | 114 | |
| D. I. Gower c Radford b Newport.... | 16 | L-b 8, w 1, n-b 1............ 10 |
| J. R. Wood c Lampitt b Radford..... | 54 | — |
| V. P. Terry not out ............... | 42 | 1/4 2/64 3/178 (5 wkts, 40 overs) 255 |
| K. D. James c D'Oliveira b Lampitt ... | 3 | 4/204 5/213 |

†R. J. Parks, S. D. Udal, C. A. Connor and Aqib Javed did not bat.

Bowling: Radford 8-1-37-1; Weston 4-0-21-1; Newport 7-0-53-2; Lampitt 8-0-52-1; Stemp 5-0-33-0; Botham 8-0-51-0.

### Worcestershire

| | | |
|---|---|---|
| T. S. Curtis c Nicholas b Aqib Javed .. | 76 | M. J. Weston not out ............ 0 |
| T. M. Moody c James b Udal ........ | 66 | L-b 4, w 8 ............ 12 |
| D. B. D'Oliveira b Aqib Javed........ | 32 | — |
| I. T. Botham c Gower b Aqib Javed... | 7 | 1/126 2/177 (4 wkts, 31.4 overs) 205 |
| *P. A. Neale not out ............... | 12 | 3/189 4/196 |

†S. J. Rhodes, S. R. Lampitt, P. J. Newport, N. V. Radford and R. D. Stemp did not bat.

Bowling: Aqib Javed 8-0-50-3; James 2-0-14-0; Connor 8-0-46-0; Udal 8-0-47-1; Ayling 5.4-0-44-0.

Umpires: K. J. Lyons and D. R. Shepherd.

At Nottingham, July 14. HAMPSHIRE lost to NOTTINGHAMSHIRE by three wickets.

## HAMPSHIRE v WARWICKSHIRE

At Portsmouth, July 21. Warwickshire won by five wickets. Toss: Warwickshire.

### Hampshire

| | | |
|---|---|---|
| V. P. Terry c N. M. K. Smith b Small .. | 27 | R. J. Maru c Moles b N. M. K. Smith . 1 |
| C. L. Smith b Munton............ | 2 | T. M. Tremlett not out ............ 5 |
| J. R. Wood c Piper b Reeve........ | 19 | L-b 2, w 5 ............... 7 |
| *M. C. J. Nicholas lbw b Reeve ..... | 4 | — |
| K. D. James c Munton b P. A. Smith.. | 21 | 1/7 2/47 3/53 (7 wkts, 40 overs) 153 |
| J. R. Ayling st Piper b N. M. K. Smith | 37 | 4/65 5/107 |
| †A. N. Aymes not out............... | 14 | 6/119 7/141 |

S. D. Udal and C. A. Connor did not bat.

Bowling: Munton 7-0-21-1; Benjamin 4-0-17-0; Reeve 6-0-27-2; Small 7-1-33-1; P. A. Smith 8-0-29-1; N. M. K. Smith 8-0-24-2.

## Warwickshire

| | | | |
|---|---|---|---|
| A. J. Moles c Aymes b James | 13 | N. M. K. Smith not out | 8 |
| Asif Din c Maru b Ayling | 30 | | |
| P. A. Smith c Aymes b Ayling | 10 | L-b 6, w 10, n-b 5 | 21 |
| D. P. Ostler c Aymes b Ayling | 4 | | |
| D. A. Reeve not out | 44 | 1/51 2/61 3/66 (5 wkts, 37.1 overs) 154 | |
| *T. A. Lloyd c Maru b Tremlett | 24 | 4/71 5/137 | |

†K. J. Piper, J. E. Benjamin, G. C. Small and T. A. Munton did not bat.

Bowling: Connor 6–0–20–0; Tremlett 6.1–0–27–1; Udal 7–0–23–0; Ayling 8–0–25–3; James 8–0–38–1; Maru 2–0–15–0.

Umpires: J. H. Harris and A. G. T. Whitehead.

## HAMPSHIRE v LANCASHIRE

At Southampton, July 28. Lancashire won by two wickets. Toss: Lancashire. For the second week running, Hegg rescued Lancashire to keep them at the top of the League. Coming in when Lancashire were 127 for six, he struck seven fours and a six in making 42 not out from 25 balls; 24 of the 45 runs he shared with Allott came in two overs.

### Hampshire

| | | | |
|---|---|---|---|
| V. P. Terry lbw b Watkinson | 1 | †A. N. Aymes not out | 18 |
| K. D. James c Hegg b Watkinson | 10 | | |
| J. R. Wood c Hegg b Allott | 10 | L-b 5, w 2, n-b 2 | 9 |
| C. L. Smith c Hegg b Austin | 60 | | |
| *M. C. J. Nicholas not out | 65 | 1/2 2/19 3/28 (5 wkts, 40 overs) 182 | |
| J. R. Ayling c Mendis b Watkinson | 9 | 4/113 5/137 | |

S. D. Udal, R. J. Maru, C. A. Connor and K. J. Shine did not bat.

Bowling: Watkinson 8–0–34–3; Allott 8–2–28–1; Yates 8–0–42–0; Wasim Akram 8–0–35–0; Austin 8–0–38–1.

### Lancashire

| | | | |
|---|---|---|---|
| G. D. Mendis c Aymes b Shine | 5 | I. D. Austin b Connor | 1 |
| G. Fowler c Smith b Maru | 38 | P. J. W. Allott not out | 10 |
| G. D. Lloyd c Terry b Shine | 9 | | |
| *N. H. Fairbrother c Aymes b Ayling | 37 | L-b 4, w 5, n-b 1 | 10 |
| N. J. Speak b Udal | 8 | | |
| M. Watkinson b Connor | 25 | 1/9 2/27 3/82 (8 wkts, 38.2 overs) 185 | |
| Wasim Akram c Nicholas b Connor | 0 | 4/96 5/125 6/127 | |
| †W. K. Hegg not out | 42 | 7/133 8/140 | |

G. Yates did not bat.

Bowling: Connor 8–0–33–3; Shine 7–0–35–2; Maru 8–0–31–1; Ayling 7.2–0–52–1; Udal 8–1–30–1.

Umpires: G. I. Burgess and K. E. Palmer.

At Lord's, August 4. HAMPSHIRE lost to MIDDLESEX by seven wickets.

At Ebbw Vale, August 11. HAMPSHIRE lost to GLAMORGAN by 6 runs.

## HAMPSHIRE v LEICESTERSHIRE

At Bournemouth, August 18. Leicestershire won by four wickets. Toss: Leicestershire. Hampshire's twelfth consecutive match without victory consigned them to last place in the League for the first time. Their innings had started well, with Smith scoring 75 in 73 balls as he and Nicholas added 98 for the third wicket, but only 40 runs came from the last ten overs.

### Hampshire

| | | | |
|---|---|---|---|
| V. P. Terry lbw b Maguire | 20 | R. J. Maru not out | 3 |
| T. C. Middleton run out | 8 | S. D. Udal not out | 1 |
| R. A. Smith b Maguire | 75 | L-b 4, w 1 | 5 |
| *M. C. J. Nicholas c Whitaker b Millns | 56 | | |
| K. D. James b Maguire | 2 | 1/14 2/56 3/154 (7 wkts, 40 overs) 195 | |
| J. R. Ayling b Lewis | 17 | 4/156 5/180 | |
| †R. J. Parks b Millns | 8 | 6/191 7/193 | |

Aqib Javed and K. J. Shine did not bat.

Bowling: Millns 8–0–33–2; Lewis 8–0–28–1; Wilkinson 8–0–32–0; Maguire 8–1–44–3; Benson 4–0–21–0; Gidley 4–0–33–0.

### Leicestershire

| | | | |
|---|---|---|---|
| J. J. Whitaker c Udal b Shine | 1 | †P. Whitticase c Terry b Udal | 17 |
| *N. E. Briers c Ayling b James | 42 | M. I. Gidley not out | 12 |
| T. J. Boon c Nicholas b Ayling | 68 | L-b 4, w 12, n-b 1 | 17 |
| C. C. Lewis c James b Ayling | 16 | | |
| L. Potter run out | 2 | 1/8 2/110 3/138 (6 wkts, 39.3 overs) 198 | |
| J. D. R. Benson not out | 23 | 4/144 5/146 6/178 | |

C. W. Wilkinson, D. J. Millns and J. N. Maguire did not bat.

Bowling: Aqib Javed 8–0–36–0; Shine 5–0–28–1; Ayling 7–0–29–2; Udal 7.3–0–46–1; Maru 8–0–32–0; James 4–0–23–1.

Umpires: N. T. Plews and R. A. White.

At The Oval, August 25. HAMPSHIRE beat SURREY by three wickets.

# KENT

At Worcester, April 21. KENT lost to WORCESTERSHIRE on scoring-rate.

## KENT v WARWICKSHIRE

At Canterbury, May 5. No result.

At Southampton, May 12. KENT lost to HAMPSHIRE by five wickets.

## KENT v ESSEX

At Folkestone, May 19. Tied. Toss: Essex. Essex needed 7 runs from their last over, bowled by Merrick, and 3 from the last ball. Andrew, whose previous highest score in the competition was 5, managed only 2. Earlier, Fleming's maiden fifty in the League included six fours; he faced 50 balls.

## Kent

| | | | | |
|---|---|---|---|---|
| N. R. Taylor lbw b Pringle | 4 | R. M. Ellison not out | | 15 |
| *M. R. Benson c Stephenson b Topley | 43 | R. P. Davis not out | | 8 |
| S. G. Hinks c Pringle b Such | 25 | L-b 6, w 5 | | 11 |
| G. R. Cowdrey c Gooch b Topley | 14 | | | |
| N. J. Llong st Garnham b Such | 5 | 1/11 2/54 3/76 | (7 wkts, 40 overs) | 183 |
| M. V. Fleming b Gooch | 51 | 4/86 5/100 | | |
| †S. A. Marsh b Andrew | 7 | 6/142 7/166 | | |

A. P. Igglesden and T. A. Merrick did not bat.

Bowling: Andrew 8–1–30–1; Pringle 8–1–41–1; Gooch 8–0–43–1; Such 8–0–22–2; Topley 8–0–41–2.

## Essex

| | | | | |
|---|---|---|---|---|
| *G. A. Gooch b Igglesden | 0 | T. D. Topley not out | | 3 |
| J. P. Stephenson b Ellison | 4 | S. J. W. Andrew not out | | 6 |
| Salim Malik c Marsh b Merrick | 37 | | | |
| P. J. Prichard c Cowdrey b Fleming | 25 | B 1, l-b 8, w 1 | | 10 |
| N. Hussain c Marsh b Igglesden | 48 | | | |
| D. R. Pringle run out | 9 | 1/0 2/22 3/62 | (8 wkts, 40 overs) | 183 |
| N. Shahid c Marsh b Ellison | 27 | 4/80 5/93 6/147 | | |
| †M. A. Garnham b Igglesden | 14 | 7/163 8/174 | | |

P. M. Such did not bat.

Bowling: Igglesden 8–1–34–3; Ellison 8–0–37–2; Merrick 8–0–39–1; Fleming 8–0–40–1; Davis 8–0–24–0.

Umpires: B. Dudleston and A. A. Jones.

# KENT v DERBYSHIRE

At Canterbury, May 26. Kent won by 6 runs. Toss: Derbyshire. In the unfamiliar role of opener, Fleming scored his 35 at a run a ball, while Chris Cowdrey's 45 came from 40 balls, with four fours and a six. Azharuddin reached 73, his highest score in the competition to date, from 72 balls, but McCague's bowling secured Kent their first Sunday win of the season.

## Kent

| | | | | |
|---|---|---|---|---|
| M. V. Fleming c Jean-Jacques b Malcolm | 35 | R. M. Ellison not out | | 8 |
| *M. R. Benson c Roberts b Base | 24 | M. J. McCague not out | | 5 |
| N. R. Taylor b Base | 56 | B 1, l-b 7, w 2 | | 10 |
| G. R. Cowdrey c Bowler b Mortensen | 17 | | | |
| T. R. Ward c Bowler b Malcolm | 14 | 1/47 2/69 3/109 | (7 wkts, 40 overs) | 214 |
| C. S. Cowdrey c Adams b Barnett | 45 | 4/131 5/195 | | |
| †S. A. Marsh c Base b Barnett | 0 | 6/198 7/202 | | |

A. P. Igglesden and R. P. Davis did not bat.

Bowling: Jean-Jacques 8–0–55–0; Mortensen 8–0–42–1; Malcolm 8–1–34–2; Base 8–1–35–2; Barnett 8–0–40–2.

## Derbyshire

| | | | | |
|---|---|---|---|---|
| *K. J. Barnett c and b Davis | 16 | D. E. Malcolm not out | | 4 |
| †P. D. Bowler lbw b Fleming | 25 | S. J. Base c Benson b McCague | | 3 |
| J. E. Morris c Ward b Davis | 11 | | | |
| M. Azharuddin c sub b McCague | 73 | L-b 6, w 5, n-b 1 | | 12 |
| B. Roberts c C. S. Cowdrey b Ellison | 15 | | | |
| T. J. G. O'Gorman c Benson b Ellison | 41 | 1/38 2/50 3/68 | (9 wkts, 40 overs) | 208 |
| C. J. Adams c Marsh b McCague | 8 | 4/95 5/174 6/199 | | |
| M. Jean-Jacques b McCague | 0 | 7/199 8/202 9/208 | | |

O. H. Mortensen did not bat.

Bowling: Igglesden 8–0–32–0; Ellison 8–0–46–2; McCague 8–0–51–4; Davis 8–1–29–2; Fleming 8–1–44–1.

Umpires: J. W. Holder and N. T. Plews.

At Southgate, June 2. KENT beat MIDDLESEX by 21 runs.

At Scarborough, June 16. KENT lost to YORKSHIRE by 67 runs.

At Manchester, June 23. KENT lost to LANCASHIRE by six wickets.

## KENT v GLOUCESTERSHIRE

At Canterbury, June 30. Kent won by 67 runs. Toss: Gloucestershire. Graham Cowdrey's 91-ball innings, with four fours and four sixes, regained the initiative for Kent after they lost three wickets for 26. In contrast, Gloucestershire began well but collapsed after Scott was run out when the score was 102.

### Kent

| | | | | |
|---|---|---|---|---|
| M. V. Fleming c Babington b Gerrard | 13 | †S. A. Marsh not out | | 24 |
| *M. R. Benson run out | 7 | R. P. Davis not out | | 2 |
| N. R. Taylor c Russell b Alleyne | 39 | B 1, l-b 13, w 9 | | 23 |
| T. R. Ward c Russell b Babington | 0 | | | |
| G. R. Cowdrey b Smith | 80 | 1/22 2/24 3/26 | (6 wkts, 40 overs) | 210 |
| C. S. Cowdrey b Smith | 22 | 4/105 5/147 6/186 | | |

T. A. Merrick, A. P. Igglesden and M. J. McCague did not bat.

Bowling: Gerrard 8–0–52–1; Babington 4–0–15–1; Smith 8–1–35–2; Scott 8–1–24–0; Alleyne 8–0–46–1; Athey 4–0–24–0.

### Gloucestershire

| | | | | |
|---|---|---|---|---|
| R. J. Scott run out | 58 | M. J. Gerrard run out | | 7 |
| C. W. J. Athey c Ward b Davis | 18 | A. M. Smith not out | | 0 |
| *A. J. Wright c Benson b McCague | 24 | A. M. Babington absent injured | | |
| J. J. E. Hardy b McCague | 1 | | | |
| M. W. Alleyne c G. R. Cowdrey | | B 8 | | 8 |
| b Igglesden | 1 | | | |
| †R. C. Russell c C. S. Cowdrey b Merrick | 22 | 1/41 2/102 3/104 | (35.2 overs) | 143 |
| J. W. Lloyds b Igglesden | 4 | 4/105 5/105 6/115 | | |
| T. H. C. Hancock b McCague | 0 | 7/118 8/142 9/143 | | |

Bowling: McCague 8–0–39–3; Igglesden 8–1–18–2; Davis 8–0–37–1; Merrick 5.2–1–16–1; Fleming 6–0–25–0.

Umpires: J. C. Balderstone and D. R. Shepherd.

## KENT v GLAMORGAN

At Maidstone, July 7. Kent won by eight wickets. Toss: Kent. Benson, who reached 3,000 Sunday League runs when he was 24, and Taylor added 147 in 28 overs.

## Glamorgan

| | | | | |
|---|---|---|---|---|
| M. P. Maynard c Fleming b Igglesden | . | 23 | P. A. Cottey not out | 18 |
| H. Morris b Fleming | | 32 | L-b 4, w 7 | 11 |
| R. J. Shastri not out | | 90 | | — |
| *A. R. Butcher c and b Fleming | | 30 | 1/34 2/102 3/170     (3 wkts, 40 overs) | 204 |

A. Dale, R. D. B. Croft, S. L. Watkin, S. R. Barwick, †C. P. Metson and S. Bastien did not bat.

Bowling: McCague 8-0-42-0; Igglesden 8-0-38-1; Davis 8-1-46-0; Merrick 8-1-29-0; Fleming 8-0-45-2.

## Kent

| | | | |
|---|---|---|---|
| M. V. Fleming c Morris b Bastien | | | 2 |
| *M. R. Benson c Morris b Bastien | | | 84 |
| N. R. Taylor not out | | | 82 |
| T. R. Ward not out | | | 33 |
| L-b 5, w 2 | | | 7 |
| | | | — |
| 1/3 2/150     (2 wkts, 37 overs) | | | 208 |

G. R. Cowdrey, C. S. Cowdrey, †S. A. Marsh, R. P. Davis, T. A. Merrick, A. P. Igglesden and M. J. McCague did not bat.

Bowling: Watkin 8-0-48-0; Bastien 8-0-42-2; Croft 8-1-34-0; Shastri 6-0-35-0; Barwick 5-0-26-0; Dale 2-0-18-0.

Umpires: G. I. Burgess and R. Palmer.

## KENT v LEICESTERSHIRE

At Canterbury, July 14. Kent won by three wickets. Toss: Kent. Struggling at 76 for five, Kent were rescued by Hinks and Marsh, the wicket-keeper making his highest League score, 59, from 46 balls. When 25, Willey became the fifth batsman to score 6,500 runs in the Sunday League.

## Leicestershire

| | | | |
|---|---|---|---|
| J. J. Whitaker c Cowdrey b Davis | 48 | †P. Whitticase c Davis b Fleming | 9 |
| *N. E. Briers run out | 16 | D. J. Millns b Fleming | 13 |
| B. F. Smith c and b Davis | 21 | J. N. Maguire not out | 0 |
| C. C. Lewis b Davis | 8 | L-b 8, w 5, n-b 2 | 15 |
| L. Potter c Ward b Merrick | 19 | | — |
| J. D. R. Benson c Marsh b Fleming | 2 | 1/36 2/75 3/91     (39.4 overs) | 184 |
| P. Willey b McCague | 31 | 4/104 5/107 6/153 | |
| M. I. Gidley c and b McCague | 2 | 7/159 8/159 9/180 | |

Bowling: Igglesden 8-1-27-0; Merrick 8-0-38-1; McCague 8-0-37-2; Fleming 7.4-0-41-3; Davis 8-0-33-3.

## Kent

| | | | |
|---|---|---|---|
| M. V. Fleming c Potter b Lewis | 5 | R. P. Davis not out | 11 |
| *M. R. Benson c Smith b Benson | 12 | M. J. McCague not out | 17 |
| N. R. Taylor lbw b Lewis | 0 | L-b 5, w 8, n-b 1 | 14 |
| T. R. Ward c Potter b Benson | 15 | | — |
| G. R. Cowdrey lbw b Willey | 17 | 1/12 2/12 3/40     (7 wkts, 39.3 overs) | 185 |
| S. G. Hinks c and b Benson | 35 | 4/46 5/76 | |
| †S. A. Marsh c Whitticase b Lewis | 59 | 6/131 7/163 | |

T. A. Merrick and A. P. Igglesden did not bat.

Bowling: Lewis 8-2-25-3; Maguire 7.3-0-30-0; Millns 8-0-41-0; Benson 7-0-39-3; Willey 5-0-25-1; Potter 4-0-20-0.

Umpires: B. Dudleston and M. J. Kitchen.

At Taunton, July 28. KENT beat SOMERSET by 35 runs.

## KENT v SURREY

At Canterbury, August 4. Surrey won by six wickets. Toss: Surrey.

### Kent

| | | | |
|---|---|---|---|
| T. R. Ward c D. J. Bicknell b Robinson | 27 | R. P. Davis b M. P. Bicknell | 0 |
| *M. R. Benson b Robson | 14 | T. A. Merrick not out | 2 |
| N. R. Taylor c Stewart b Waqar Younis | 29 | | |
| S. G. Hinks b Waqar Younis | 18 | L-b 8, w 4 | 12 |
| G. R. Cowdrey lbw b Waqar Younis | 36 | | |
| M. V. Fleming c Robinson b Robson | 15 | 1/36 2/48 3/86 (8 wkts, 39 overs) | 183 |
| †S. A. Marsh not out | 28 | 4/106 5/144 6/158 | |
| M. A. Ealham lbw b Waqar Younis | 2 | 7/176 8/179 | |

A. P. Igglesden did not bat.

Bowling: M. P. Bicknell 8–0–34–1; Robson 8–0–40–2; Robinson 8–1–26–1; Boiling 6–0–33–0; Waqar Younis 7–1–21–4; Greig 2–0–21–0.

### Surrey

| | | | |
|---|---|---|---|
| D. J. Bicknell b Ealham | 13 | J. D. Robinson not out | 7 |
| G. P. Thorpe c Marsh b Fleming | 54 | L-b 4, w 5 | 9 |
| †A. J. Stewart c Taylor b Ealham | 64 | | |
| D. M. Ward c Igglesden b Fleming | 22 | 1/29 2/125 (4 wkts, 38.4 overs) | 186 |
| M. A. Lynch not out | 17 | 3/144 4/169 | |

*I. A. Greig, M. P. Bicknell, J. Boiling, Waqar Younis and A. G. Robson did not bat.

Bowling: Igglesden 8–0–32–0; Merrick 7–0–47–0; Ealham 8–0–25–2; Davis 8–2–41–0; Fleming 7.4–0–37–2.

Umpires: R. Julian and K. J. Lyons.

At Nottingham, August 11. KENT lost to NOTTINGHAMSHIRE by four wickets.

## KENT v NORTHAMPTONSHIRE

At Canterbury, August 18. Northamptonshire won by 2 runs. Toss: Kent. Marsh, hitting his third fifty in five Sunday innings, from 35 balls, added 67 in seven overs with Davis, who made his highest score in the competition. Needing 7 runs from the final over, Kent could manage only 4.

### Northamptonshire

| | | | |
|---|---|---|---|
| A. Fordham run out | 30 | E. A. E. Baptiste not out | 15 |
| W. Larkins c and b Davis | 56 | | |
| *A. J. Lamb c Cowdrey b Igglesden | 30 | L-b 5, w 5 | 10 |
| R. J. Bailey c Cowdrey b Igglesden | 23 | | |
| K. M. Curran not out | 35 | 1/88 2/95 3/143 (5 wkts, 40 overs) | 202 |
| D. J. Capel c Ellison b Fleming | 3 | 4/152 5/161 | |

R. G. Williams, †D. Ripley, A. Walker and A. L. Penberthy did not bat.

Bowling: Igglesden 8–0–27–2; Ellison 4–0–28–0; Merrick 6–0–42–0; Davis 8–0–28–1; Ealham 6–0–26–0; Fleming 8–0–46–1.

## Kent

| | |
|---|---|
| T. R. Ward run out | 9 |
| *M. R. Benson b Curran | 45 |
| N. R. Taylor b Walker | 2 |
| M. A. Ealham lbw b Capel | 3 |
| G. R. Cowdrey lbw b Capel | 13 |
| M. V. Fleming lbw b Williams | 18 |
| †S. A. Marsh b Baptiste | 52 |
| R. M. Ellison run out | 0 |

A. P. Igglesden did not bat.

R. P. Davis not out ............ 40
T. A. Merrick not out .......... 3

B 2, l-b 11, w 2 ........... 15

1/29 2/33 3/51     (8 wkts, 40 overs) 200
4/69 5/81 6/111
7/116 8/183

Bowling: Walker 8-0-27-1; Baptiste 8-1-20-1; Capel 6-0-24-2; Curran 8-0-49-1; Williams 6-0-46-1; Penberthy 4-0-21-0.

Umpires: J. C. Balderstone and B. Hassan.

At Hove, August 25. KENT lost to SUSSEX by four wickets.

# LANCASHIRE

## LANCASHIRE v NOTTINGHAMSHIRE

At Manchester, April 21. Nottinghamshire won by nine wickets. Toss: Nottinghamshire. Nottinghamshire's victory was their first at Old Trafford in the Sunday League in thirteen visits since the competition began in 1969. Broad, who had twelve fours in his unbeaten hundred (107 balls), and Randall put them on course with a first-wicket partnership of 106.

## Lancashire

| | |
|---|---|
| G. Fowler c French b Evans | 36 |
| G. D. Mendis c Robinson b Crawley | 34 |
| M. A. Atherton c Johnson b Hemmings | 45 |
| *N. H. Fairbrother run out | 4 |
| G. D. Lloyd lbw b Hemmings | 2 |
| M. Watkinson c Broad b Stephenson | 25 |
| Wasim Akram c Hemmings b Stephenson | 12 |
| P. A. J. DeFreitas b Evans | 7 |

†W. K. Hegg c Johnson b Evans ...... 7
I. D. Austin not out .......... 4
P. J. W. Allott not out ........... 1

L-b 2, w 6, n-b 1 ........... 9

1/60 2/90 3/105    (9 wkts, 40 overs) 186
4/116 5/137 6/158
7/173 8/176 9/183

Bowling: Stephenson 8-0-41-2; Cooper 5-0-19-0; Saxelby 8-0-37-0; Evans 7-0-46-3; Crawley 4-0-20-1; Hemmings 8-1-21-2.

## Nottinghamshire

| | |
|---|---|
| B. C. Broad not out | 100 |
| D. W. Randall c Atherton b Allott | 49 |
| *R. T. Robinson not out | 29 |
| L-b 6, w 1, n-b 5 | 12 |

1/106    (1 wkt, 37.5 overs) 190

P. Johnson, M. A. Crawley, M. Saxelby, K. P. Evans, F. D. Stephenson, †B. N. French, E. E. Hemmings and K. E. Cooper did not bat.

Bowling: Allott 8-0-30-1; DeFreitas 8-1-30-0; Watkinson 8-0-40-0; Wasim Akram 6.5-0-54-0; Austin 7-0-30-0.

Umpires: J. C. Balderstone and J. D. Bond.

## LANCASHIRE v NORTHAMPTONSHIRE

At Manchester, April 28. Lancashire won by five wickets. Toss: Lancashire. Lloyd, whose 71 came from 63 balls and included eight fours, put on 71 in thirteen overs for the second wicket with Fowler.

### Northamptonshire

| | | | | |
|---|---|---|---|---|
| A. Fordham c Hegg b Allott | 12 | E. A. E. Baptiste not out | 5 |
| R. J. Bailey b Austin | 99 | B 2, l-b 13, w 5, n-b 1 | 21 |
| *A. J. Lamb b DeFreitas | 13 | | |
| D. J. Capel c Fowler b DeFreitas | 53 | 1/19 2/40 (4 wkts, 40 overs) 219 | |
| R. G. Williams not out | 16 | 3/163 4/211 | |

A. L. Penberthy, †D. Ripley, J. G. Thomas, N. G. B. Cook and J. P. Taylor did not bat.

Bowling: DeFreitas 8–0–39–2; Allott 8–0–27–1; Watkinson 8–0–53–0; Wasim Akram 8–1–33–0; Austin 6–0–32–1; Yates 2–0–20–0.

### Lancashire

| | | | | |
|---|---|---|---|---|
| G. Fowler c Ripley b Taylor | 52 | P. A. J. DeFreitas not out | 6 |
| M. A. Atherton b Thomas | 25 | | |
| G. D. Lloyd c Cook b Capel | 71 | B 1, l-b 12, w 5, n-b 1 | 19 |
| *N. H. Fairbrother not out | 39 | | |
| M. Watkinson c Penberthy b Taylor | 4 | 1/50 2/121 3/180 (5 wkts, 39.1 overs) 222 | |
| Wasim Akram c Bailey b Capel | 6 | 4/189 5/195 | |

†W. K. Hegg, G. Yates, I. D. Austin and P. J. W. Allott did not bat.

Bowling: Taylor 8–1–27–2; Baptiste 7.1–0–34–0; Cook 8–0–36–0; Thomas 8–0–47–1; Capel 6–0–43–2; Williams 2–0–22–0.

Umpires: M. J. Kitchen and B. J. Meyer.

At Worcester, May 12. LANCASHIRE beat WORCESTERSHIRE by six wickets.

At Derby, May 19. LANCASHIRE beat DERBYSHIRE by 63 runs.

## LANCASHIRE v SUSSEX

At Manchester, June 2. Lancashire won by 53 runs. Toss: Sussex. Reduced by rain to eighteen overs a side, the game was dominated by Watkinson, who hit three fours and four sixes in his 45-ball 83 (50 from 27 balls), took three wickets, held two catches and was involved in a run-out.

### Lancashire

| | | | | |
|---|---|---|---|---|
| G. Fowler b Jones | 22 | P. A. J. DeFreitas c Speight b Jones | 19 |
| G. D. Lloyd c Moores b Pigott | 22 | M. A. Atherton not out | 1 |
| N. H. Fairbrother c C. M. Wells b Bunting | 12 | B 1, l-b 1, w 1 | 3 |
| M. Watkinson c Salisbury b Jones | 83 | 1/33 2/49 3/75 (6 wkts, 18 overs) 176 | |
| Wasim Akram c Jones b C. M. Wells | 14 | 4/139 5/174 6/176 | |

†W. K. Hegg, *D. P. Hughes, I. D. Austin and P. J. W. Allott did not bat.

Bowling: C. M. Wells 3–0–31–1; Jones 4–0–39–3; Bunting 4–0–43–1; Pigott 4–0–21–1; Salisbury 2–0–24–0; Greenfield 1–0–16–0.

## Sussex

| | | |
|---|---|---|
| K. Greenfield run out .............. | 6 | |
| *P. W. G. Parker c Fairbrother | | |
| b Watkinson . | 28 | |
| A. P. Wells c Hughes b DeFreitas..... | 1 | |
| M. P. Speight c Watkinson b DeFreitas | 39 | |
| N. J. Lenham not out .............. | 24 | |
| C. M. Wells b Austin .............. | 3 | |
| †P. Moores c Watkinson b DeFreitas .. | 4 | |
| A. C. S. Pigott c Austin b Watkinson .. | 5 | |

| | |
|---|---|
| I. D. K. Salisbury c Wasim Akram | |
| b Watkinson . | 0 |
| R. A. Bunting run out .............. | 0 |
| A. N. Jones not out.............. | 6 |
| L-b 3, w 4 .............. | 7 |

1/17 2/20 3/68     (9 wkts, 18 overs) 123
4/81 5/86 6/91
7/105 8/106 9/107

Bowling: Allott 3–0–23–0; DeFreitas 4–0–28–3; Wasim Akram 4–0–22–0; Watkinson 3–0–27–3; Austin 4–0–20–1.

Umpires: J. C. Balderstone and J. D. Bond.

## LANCASHIRE v GLAMORGAN

At Manchester, June 9. No result. Toss: Lancashire. Rain reduced the match first to 31 overs a side, then to 27; another shower led to Lancashire's target being revised to 129 from twenty overs, but they were unable to complete their innings. For Glamorgan, Morris hit three sixes, all off the bowling of Watkinson, and six fours in his 66.

## Glamorgan

| | | |
|---|---|---|
| *H. Morris b Austin .............. | 66 | |
| M. P. Maynard lbw b Wasim Akram .. | 19 | |
| G. C. Holmes not out .............. | 50 | |
| I. Smith b Austin.............. | 23 | |
| M. J. Cann b Wasim Akram ........ | 2 | |

| | |
|---|---|
| J. Derrick not out .............. | 4 |
| L-b 7, w 2, n-b 1............ | 10 |

1/40 2/124     (4 wkts, 27 overs) 174
3/163 4/167

A. Dale, †C. P. Metson, S. J. Dennis, M. Frost and S. R. Barwick did not bat.

Bowling: Martin 4–0–19–0; Allott 6–1–26–0; Wasim Akram 7–0–46–2; Watkinson 5–0–43–0; Austin 5–0–33–2.

## Lancashire

| | |
|---|---|
| G. D. Mendis c sub b Derrick ....... | 11 |
| G. Fowler not out .............. | 38 |
| G. D. Lloyd not out.............. | 4 |

1/40     (1 wkt, 8.2 overs) 53

N. H. Fairbrother, M. Watkinson, Wasim Akram, †W. K. Hegg, P. J. Martin, *D. P. Hughes, I. D. Austin and P. J. W. Allott did not bat.

Bowling: Dennis 2–0–13–0; Frost 2–0–9–0; Derrick 2.2–0–17–1; Barwick 2–0–14–0.

Umpires: N. T. Plews and R. A. White.

At Birmingham, June 16. LANCASHIRE beat WARWICKSHIRE by four wickets.

## LANCASHIRE v KENT

At Manchester, June 23. Lancashire won by six wickets. Toss: Lancashire. Mendis and Fowler set up Lancashire's victory with an opening stand of 91 in under twelve overs. In Kent's innings, restricted by rain initially to 30 overs and then further reduced to 23, Ward made his unbeaten 62 from 50 balls.

## Kent

| | | | | |
|---|---|---|---|---|
| M. V. Fleming c Watkinson b Wasim Akram . | 44 | C. S. Cowdrey c Hegg b Austin | 11 |
| *M. R. Benson b Martin | 1 | †S. A. Marsh not out | 4 |
| N. R. Taylor c Hegg b Watkinson | 10 | B 1, l-b 11, w 6, n-b 2 | 20 |
| T. R. Ward not out | 62 | | |
| G. R. Cowdrey b Wasim Akram | 10 | 1/7 2/36 3/105    (5 wkts, 23 overs) 162 |
| | | 4/127 5/153 | |

M. J. McCague, R. M. Ellison, C. Penn and A. P. Igglesden did not bat.

Bowling: Watkinson 6–0–34–1; Martin 4–0–20–1; Wasim Akram 6–0–40–2; Yates 2–0–18–0; Austin 5–0–38–1.

## Lancashire

| | | | | |
|---|---|---|---|---|
| G. D. Mendis c and b Fleming | 44 | Wasim Akram not out | 16 |
| G. Fowler c Penn b Igglesden | 46 | L-b 1, w 2, n-b 1 | 4 |
| G. D. Lloyd run out | 18 | | |
| N. H. Fairbrother not out | 31 | 1/91 2/95    (4 wkts, 22.2 overs) 165 |
| M. Watkinson c Fleming b Penn | 6 | 3/118 4/129 | |

†W. K. Hegg, I. D. Austin, G. Yates, *D. P. Hughes and P. J. Martin did not bat.

Bowling: Igglesden 5.2–0–34–1; McCague 6–0–43–0; Penn 6–0–56–1; Fleming 5–0–31–1.

Umpires: D. O. Oslear and P. B. Wight.

At Taunton, July 5. LANCASHIRE beat SOMERSET by eight wickets.

At Leicester, July 7. LANCASHIRE beat LEICESTERSHIRE by five wickets.

At Lord's, July 21. LANCASHIRE beat MIDDLESEX by two wickets.

At Southampton, July 28. LANCASHIRE beat HAMPSHIRE by two wickets.

## LANCASHIRE v YORKSHIRE

At Manchester, August 4. Yorkshire won by five wickets. Toss: Yorkshire. A crowd of 16,000, bringing in receipts of £46,700, a record for a Sunday League game, saw Yorkshire end Lancashire's unbeaten run of eleven League games since their defeat by Nottinghamshire on the first Sunday of the season. Hegg gave Lancashire's total a degree of substance with his unbeaten 27 from ten balls, including three sixes, while for Yorkshire, Carrick took his 150th wicket in the competition. Later, Austin delayed Yorkshire's victory by taking two wickets with successive balls when the scores were level.

## Lancashire

| | | | | |
|---|---|---|---|---|
| G. D. Mendis c Moxon b Carrick | 39 | †W. K. Hegg not out | 27 |
| G. Fowler c Metcalfe b Carrick | 39 | I. D. Austin lbw b M. A. Robinson | 3 |
| G. D. Lloyd c and b Carrick | 21 | P. J. W. Allott not out | 1 |
| *N. H. Fairbrother c Blakey b Pickles | 39 | B 1, l-b 5 | 6 |
| M. Watkinson c Hartley b Carrick | 4 | | |
| Wasim Akram c Blakey b Pickles | 1 | 1/76 2/89 3/116    (9 wkts, 40 overs) 196 |
| M. A. Atherton c and b Pickles | 11 | 4/122 5/126 6/146 | |
| P. A. J. DeFreitas c Pickles b Hartley | 5 | 7/153 8/176 9/185 | |

Bowling: Hartley 8–0–29–1; M. A. Robinson 8–1–48–1; Pickles 8–0–49–3; Batty 8–0–36–0; Carrick 8–0–28–4.

## Yorkshire

| | | | |
|---|---|---|---|
| *M. D. Moxon c DeFreitas b Austin | 76 | C. S. Pickles not out | 1 |
| A. A. Metcalfe b Austin | 41 | | |
| †R. J. Blakey c Fairbrother b Watkinson | 32 | B 1, l-b 3, w 1, n-b 2 | 7 |
| D. Byas not out | 31 | | — |
| P. E. Robinson b Austin | 9 | 1/78 2/138 3/166   (5 wkts, 38 overs) 197 | |
| S. A. Kellett c Hegg b Austin | 0 | 4/196 5/196 | |

P. Carrick, P. J. Hartley, J. D. Batty and M. A. Robinson did not bat.

Bowling: DeFreitas 8–0–33–0; Allott 8–0–37–0; Wasim Akram 7–0–32–0; Watkinson 8–0–51–1; Austin 7–0–40–4.

Umpires: A. A. Jones and A. G. T. Whitehead.

At Bristol, August 11. LANCASHIRE beat GLOUCESTERSHIRE by eight wickets.

## LANCASHIRE v SURREY

At Manchester, August 18. Surrey won by 21 runs. Toss: Lancashire. Thorpe, making his maiden hundred in the competition, began by putting on 61 in the first ten overs with Brown, and later added 93 in fourteen overs with Lynch for the fourth wicket. Lancashire's captain, Fairbrother, took 58 balls for his 62 and hit five fours.

## Surrey

| | | | |
|---|---|---|---|
| A. D. Brown c Mendis b Watkinson | 44 | *I. A. Greig not out | 0 |
| G. P. Thorpe not out | 115 | | |
| †A. J. Stewart b Allott | 16 | B 3, l-b 3, w 6, n-b 1 | 13 |
| D. M. Ward c Hegg b Wasim Akram | 3 | | — |
| M. A. Lynch c Hegg b Wasim Akram | 37 | 1/76 2/119 3/130   (5 wkts, 40 overs) 228 | |
| J. D. Robinson run out | 0 | 4/223 5/223 | |

M. P. Bicknell, J. Boiling, A. J. Murphy and A. G. Robson did not bat.

Bowling: Allott 8–0–37–1; DeFreitas 8–0–51–0; Watkinson 8–0–48–1; Wasim Akram 8–0–49–2; Austin 8–0–37–0.

## Lancashire

| | | | |
|---|---|---|---|
| G. D. Mendis b Bicknell | 0 | †W. K. Hegg c Lynch b Bicknell | 7 |
| G. Fowler c Greig b Robson | 12 | I. D. Austin not out | 10 |
| M. A. Atherton b Murphy | 34 | P. J. W. Allott not out | 3 |
| G. D. Lloyd run out | 11 | B 1, l-b 4, w 4, n-b 1 | 10 |
| *N. H. Fairbrother run out | 62 | | — |
| M. Watkinson c Greig b Boiling | 9 | 1/1 2/29 3/55   (9 wkts, 40 overs) 207 | |
| Wasim Akram b Robson | 38 | 4/85 5/98 6/173 | |
| P. A. J. DeFreitas b Bicknell | 11 | 7/179 8/193 9/194 | |

Bowling: Bicknell 8–0–36–3; Robson 8–0–46–2; Robinson 8–0–41–0; Boiling 8–0–34–1; Murphy 8–0–45–1.

Umpires: A. A. Jones and B. J. Meyer.

## LANCASHIRE v ESSEX

At Manchester, August 25. Lancashire won by five wickets. Toss: Lancashire. Victory was not enough for Lancashire to overtake Nottinghamshire, and they finished runners-up for the second year. They remained the only team to have qualified for the Refuge Assurance Cup every year since its inauguration in 1988. Fairbrother saw his side home with an unbeaten 52 from 59 balls, after Pringle and Topley's unbroken stand of 78 in thirteen overs had given the Essex total respectability.

## Essex

| | | | |
|---|---|---|---|
| A. C. H. Seymour run out | 25 | †M. A. Garnham c and b Watkinson | 12 |
| J. P. Stephenson c Speak b Allott | 12 | T. D. Topley not out | 38 |
| N. Hussain c Hegg b Allott | 0 | L-b 5, w 3, n-b 4 | 12 |
| J. J. B. Lewis c Hegg b Watkinson | 19 | | |
| N. V. Knight lbw b Wasim Akram | 0 | 1/32 2/32 3/50    (6 wkts, 40 overs) 169 | |
| *D. R. Pringle not out | 51 | 4/57 5/63 6/91 | |

S. J. W. Andrew, J. H. Childs and W. G. Lovell did not bat.

Bowling: Allott 8–0–30–2; Martin 8–0–37–0; Wasim Akram 8–0–35–1; Watkinson 8–0–34–2; Austin 8–1–28–0.

## Lancashire

| | | | |
|---|---|---|---|
| G. D. Mendis c Stephenson b Topley | 24 | Wasim Akram not out | 11 |
| G. Fowler lbw b Childs | 41 | | |
| G. D. Lloyd b Pringle | 23 | L-b 10, w 6, n-b 1 | 17 |
| *N. H. Fairbrother not out | 52 | | |
| N. J. Speak lbw b Topley | 0 | 1/73 2/83 3/139    (5 wkts, 39.1 overs) 171 | |
| M. Watkinson c Knight b Topley | 3 | 4/140 5/146 | |

†W. K. Hegg, I. D. Austin, P. J. W. Allott and P. J. Martin did not bat.

Bowling: Andrew 5–0–20–0; Pringle 7.1–0–34–1; Stephenson 6–0–17–0; Topley 7–1–29–3; Childs 8–1–27–1; Lovell 6–0–34–0.

Umpires: B. Dudleston and J. W. Holder.

# LEICESTERSHIRE

## LEICESTERSHIRE v DERBYSHIRE

At Leicester, April 21. Derbyshire won on scoring-rate. Toss: Leicestershire. Rain brought Derbyshire's innings to an early close, and when play could resume, the revised target for Leicestershire was 101 in twenty overs. Barnett and Bowler put on 102 in 21 overs for Derbyshire's first wicket.

## Derbyshire

| | | | |
|---|---|---|---|
| *K. J. Barnett c Mullally b Potter | 46 | C. J. Adams not out | 4 |
| †P. D. Bowler c Willey b Mullally | 77 | | |
| J. E. Morris c Whitaker b Wilkinson | 26 | L-b 8, w 1 | 9 |
| M. Azharuddin run out | 11 | | |
| B. Roberts c Maguire b Mullally | 0 | 1/102 2/147 3/166    (5 wkts, 36.3 overs) 183 | |
| T. J. G. O'Gorman not out | 10 | 4/167 5/172 | |

S. J. Base, M. Jean-Jacques, O. H. Mortensen and D. E. Malcolm did not bat.

Bowling: Lewis 6.3–0–21–0; Mullally 8–0–31–2; Maguire 6–0–25–0; Wilkinson 6–0–28–1; Willey 6–0–33–0; Potter 4–0–37–1.

## Leicestershire

| | | | |
|---|---|---|---|
| T. J. Boon lbw b Mortensen | 22 | †P. Whitticase not out | 0 |
| *N. E. Briers c Azharuddin b Mortensen | 21 | C. W. Wilkinson not out | 3 |
| C. C. Lewis c Bowler b Malcolm | 1 | B 1, l-b 6, w 11 | 18 |
| J. J. Whitaker c Barnett b Malcolm | 22 | | |
| L. Potter run out | 12 | 1/51 2/51 3/55    (7 wkts, 20 overs) 100 | |
| P. Willey c Barnett b Base | 1 | 4/86 5/87 | |
| J. D. R. Benson c Barnett b Base | 4 | 6/90 7/95 | |

J. N. Maguire and A. D. Mullally did not bat.

Bowling: Mortensen 8–0–36–2; Jean-Jacques 2–0–13–0; Malcolm 8–0–39–2; Base 2–0–5–2.

Umpires: B. Leadbeater and R. Palmer.

## LEICESTERSHIRE v GLAMORGAN

At Leicester, April 28. Leicestershire won by 13 runs. Toss: Glamorgan.

### Leicestershire

| | | | |
|---|---|---|---|
| †P. Whitticase run out | 8 | P. N. Hepworth run out | 5 |
| *N. E. Briers lbw b Watkin | 11 | J. N. Maguire not out | 2 |
| J. J. Whitaker c Frost b Watkin | 73 | L-b 8, w 6 | 14 |
| P. Willey c Metson b Shastri | 27 | | |
| C. C. Lewis c Barwick b Croft | 8 | 1/21 2/21 3/75  (7 wkts, 40 overs) 207 | |
| L. Potter lbw b Barwick | 45 | 4/91 5/176 | |
| J. D. R. Benson not out | 14 | 6/188 7/204 | |

C. W. Wilkinson and L. Tennant did not bat.

Bowling: Watkin 8-2-28-2; Frost 8-0-48-0; Barwick 8-0-29-1; Shastri 8-0-38-1; Croft 7-0-49-1; Smith 1-0-7-0.

### Glamorgan

| | | | |
|---|---|---|---|
| P. A. Cottey lbw b Lewis | 3 | R. D. B. Croft c Benson b Maguire | 6 |
| M. P. Maynard lbw b Maguire | 2 | †C. P. Metson not out | 1 |
| *H. Morris c Lewis b Benson | 62 | L-b 4, w 11, n-b 1 | 16 |
| R. J. Shastri c Benson b Maguire | 5 | | |
| G. C. Holmes b Lewis | 72 | 1/8 2/15 3/22  (6 wkts, 40 overs) 194 | |
| I. Smith not out | 27 | 4/131 5/185 6/192 | |

S. L. Watkin, S. R. Barwick and M. Frost did not bat.

Bowling: Lewis 8-2-33-2; Maguire 8-0-31-3; Wilkinson 8-0-39-0; Tennant 6-0-30-0; Willey 5-0-25-0; Benson 5-0-32-1.

Umpires: H. D. Bird and J. D. Bond.

At Chelmsford, May 5. ESSEX v LEICESTERSHIRE. No result.

At Northampton, May 12. LEICESTERSHIRE lost to NORTHAMPTONSHIRE by five wickets.

## LEICESTERSHIRE v YORKSHIRE

At Leicester, May 19. Leicestershire won by 7 runs. Toss: Yorkshire. Byas and Gough (73 balls, two sixes), both of whom made their highest scores in the competition, added 129 without being parted after Yorkshire had been 67 for six.

### Leicestershire

| | | | |
|---|---|---|---|
| *N. E. Briers c Sidebottom b Fletcher | 25 | B. F. Smith not out | 20 |
| †P. Whitticase lbw b Sidebottom | 24 | | |
| J. J. Whitaker b Gough | 31 | B 1, l-b 14, w 5 | 20 |
| P. Willey c Byas b Batty | 16 | | |
| C. C. Lewis lbw b Hartley | 27 | 1/46 2/60 3/101  (5 wkts, 40 overs) 203 | |
| L. Potter not out | 40 | 4/120 5/156 | |

P. N. Hepworth, D. J. Millns, C. W. Wilkinson and J. N. Maguire did not bat.

Bowling: Sidebottom 8-0-25-1; Hartley 8-1-43-1; Fletcher 7-0-34-1; M. A. Robinson 5-0-20-0; Batty 8-0-40-1; Gough 4-0-26-1.

## Yorkshire

| | | | |
|---|---|---|---|
| *M. D. Moxon b Maguire | 8 | P. J. Hartley c Whitticase b Maguire | 2 |
| A. A. Metcalfe c Briers b Lewis | 5 | D. Gough not out | 72 |
| D. Byas not out | 74 | L-b 9, w 11, n-b 1 | 21 |
| P. E. Robinson lbw b Millns | 2 | | |
| †C. A. Chapman lbw b Wilkinson | 2 | 1/14 2/22 3/28     (6 wkts, 40 overs) 196 | |
| A. Sidebottom b Wilkinson | 10 | 4/39 5/65 6/67 | |

J. D. Batty, S. D. Fletcher and M. A. Robinson did not bat.

Bowling: Lewis 8–0–46–1; Maguire 8–0–46–2; Millns 8–1–38–1; Wilkinson 8–0–31–2; Willey 8–1–26–0.

Umpires: R. Julian and D. R. Shepherd.

## LEICESTERSHIRE v NOTTINGHAMSHIRE

At Leicester, May 26. Nottinghamshire won by five wickets. Toss: Nottinghamshire. Hemmings's two wickets, his 267th and 268th in the Sunday League, moved him into seventh place on the list of leading wicket-takers in the competition. Nottinghamshire's win was their fifth in five Sunday games since the start of the season.

### Leicestershire

| | | | |
|---|---|---|---|
| T. J. Boon c French b Saxelby | 50 | C. W. Wilkinson c Robinson b Crawley | 2 |
| *N. E. Briers lbw b Saxelby | 19 | D. J. Millns not out | 20 |
| J. J. Whitaker b Saxelby | 10 | | |
| P. Willey c French b Saxelby | 12 | L-b 6, w 6, n-b 1 | 13 |
| L. Potter not out | 42 | | |
| B. F. Smith lbw b Hemmings | 2 | 1/57 2/74 3/98     (8 wkts, 40 overs) 170 | |
| †P. Whitticase c French b Crawley | 0 | 4/105 5/108 6/109 | |
| P. N. Hepworth b Hemmings | 0 | 7/110 8/117 | |

J. N. Maguire did not bat.

Bowling: Pick 5–0–20–0; Stephenson 7–1–30–0; Saxelby 8–0–29–4; Evans 7–0–51–0; Hemmings 8–0–21–2; Crawley 5–0–13–2.

### Nottinghamshire

| | | | |
|---|---|---|---|
| B. C. Broad lbw b Maguire | 3 | †B. N. French not out | 16 |
| D. W. Randall not out | 83 | | |
| *R. T. Robinson c Whitticase b Millns | 8 | B 2, l-b 3, w 3, n-b 2 | 10 |
| P. Johnson b Hepworth | 46 | | |
| M. A. Crawley c Whitticase b Wilkinson | 6 | 1/12 2/34 3/126    (5 wkts, 36.3 overs) 174 | |
| M. Saxelby c Millns b Hepworth | 2 | 4/136 5/143 | |

F. D. Stephenson, K. P. Evans, E. E. Hemmings and R. A. Pick did not bat.

Bowling: Maguire 6–0–30–1; Millns 8–1–30–1; Wilkinson 6.3–1–27–1; Willey 4–0–17–0; Smith 3–0–15–0; Potter 3–0–17–0; Hepworth 6–1–33–2.

Umpires: G. I. Burgess and R. Julian.

At Uxbridge, June 9. LEICESTERSHIRE beat MIDDLESEX by 73 runs.

## LEICESTERSHIRE v SURREY

At Leicester, June 16. Surrey won by 51 runs. Toss: Leicestershire. The visitors seemed unlikely winners when Willey's best bowling return in the competition reduced them to 99 for seven. However, they recovered to reach 134, and then bowled out Leicestershire with 8.1 overs to spare, the last five wickets falling for 16 runs in six overs.

## Surrey

| | | | | |
|---|---|---|---|---|
| M. A. Lynch b Maguire | 1 | C. K. Bullen not out | 16 |
| D. J. Bicknell b Maguire | 1 | Waqar Younis c Briers b Lewis | 1 |
| †A. J. Stewart c Lewis b Wilkinson | 13 | A. J. Murphy not out | 5 |
| D. M. Ward c Smith b Willey | 19 | B 2, l-b 4, w 8, n-b 1 | 15 |
| G. P. Thorpe b Willey | 28 | | |
| *I. A. Greig lbw b Willey | 2 | 1/1 2/3 3/23 | (9 wkts, 40 overs) 134 |
| J. D. Robinson lbw b Lewis | 22 | 4/65 5/68 6/78 | |
| M. A. Feltham c and b Willey | 11 | 7/99 8/116 9/120 | |

Bowling: Lewis 8-1-14-2; Maguire 8-3-20-2; Millns 4-0-18-0; Wilkinson 5-0-25-1; Willey 8-1-17-4; Benson 7-0-34-0.

## Leicestershire

| | | | | |
|---|---|---|---|---|
| *N. E. Briers lbw b Murphy | 3 | D. J. Millns c Ward b Feltham | 7 |
| J. J. Whitaker c Bicknell b Murphy | 19 | C. W. Wilkinson not out | 0 |
| B. F. Smith c Bullen b Murphy | 12 | J. N. Maguire c Waqar Younis b Greig | 0 |
| C. C. Lewis run out | 7 | L-b 5, w 2 | 7 |
| L. Potter c Bicknell b Robinson | 9 | | |
| J. D. R. Benson b Waqar Younis | 0 | 1/12 2/29 3/38 | (31.5 overs) 83 |
| P. Willey c Stewart b Greig | 17 | 4/46 5/47 6/67 | |
| †P. Whitticase lbw b Greig | 2 | 7/70 8/83 9/83 | |

Bowling: Feltham 7-1-23-1; Murphy 6-2-15-3; Waqar Younis 6-2-10-1; Robinson 8-1-20-1; Greig 4.5-0-10-3.

Umpires: J. W. Holder and R. Julian.

At Worcester, June 30. LEICESTERSHIRE lost to WORCESTERSHIRE by seven wickets.

## LEICESTERSHIRE v LANCASHIRE

At Leicester, July 7. Lancashire won by five wickets. Toss: Lancashire. Lancashire, winning their second "Sunday" game in three days, after their match against Somerset had been moved to Friday, July 5 to accommodate the Benson and Hedges Cup final, pushed Nottinghamshire off the top of the League table for the first time in 1991. Since Nottinghamshire, who had no fixture, won at Old Trafford on April 21, Lancashire had not been beaten in any of their seventeen one-day games. For Leicestershire, the last team to beat them away from home on a Sunday, in June 1989, only Whitaker, with seven fours in his 88, put up much resistance.

## Leicestershire

| | | | | |
|---|---|---|---|---|
| *N. E. Briers c Speak b Martin | 8 | †P. Whitticase not out | 14 |
| J. J. Whitaker run out | 88 | P. Willey not out | 12 |
| C. C. Lewis b Martin | 9 | L-b 7, w 1, n-b 1 | 9 |
| B. F. Smith lbw b Watkinson | 26 | | |
| L. Potter c Hegg b Watkinson | 1 | 1/12 2/38 3/98 | (6 wkts, 40 overs) 196 |
| J. D. R. Benson c Speak b Allott | 29 | 4/100 5/161 6/179 | |

C. W. Wilkinson, J. N. Maguire and D. J. Millns did not bat.

Bowling: Allott 8-0-31-1; Martin 8-0-38-2; Wasim Akram 8-0-40-0; Watkinson 8-0-33-2; Austin 8-0-47-0.

## Lancashire

| | | | | |
|---|---|---|---|---|
| G. D. Mendis c Whitaker b Maguire | . 13 | Wasim Akram not out | | 8 |
| G. Fowler c Potter b Benson | 49 | | | |
| G. D. Lloyd b Willey | 33 | L-b 11, w 7 | | 18 |
| *N. H. Fairbrother c Wilkinson b Benson | 18 | | | |
| N. J. Speak not out | 27 | 1/30 2/88 3/118 | (5 wkts, 39 overs) | 197 |
| M. Watkinson c Millns b Maguire | 31 | 4/136 5/186 | | |

†W. K. Hegg, I. D. Austin, P. J. W. Allott and P. J. Martin did not bat.

Bowling: Lewis 8–0–33–0; Maguire 8–0–33–2; Millns 4–0–21–0; Wilkinson 4–0–19–0; Willey 8–0–30–1; Benson 7–0–50–2.

Umpires: A. A. Jones and N. T. Plews.

At Canterbury, July 14. LEICESTERSHIRE lost to KENT by three wickets.

At Hove, July 21. LEICESTERSHIRE lost to SUSSEX by 14 runs.

At Weston-super-Mare, August 4. LEICESTERSHIRE beat SOMERSET by seven wickets.

## LEICESTERSHIRE v WARWICKSHIRE

At Leicester, August 11. Warwickshire won by 2 runs. Toss: Warwickshire. Bad light interrupted Warwickshire's innings after eight balls, causing the match to be reduced to 36 overs a side. When the umpires called the players off at 4.20 p.m. for tea, the statutory time in a 40-overs match, only 31 overs had been bowled, and both teams objected, claiming that tea should be delayed until 4.34 p.m. to allow equal time for each innings. The umpires maintained their point, but later the TCCB agreed that tea could have been delayed, and waived a £500 fine on Leicestershire for failing to bowl 36 overs in the time given.

## Warwickshire

| | | | | |
|---|---|---|---|---|
| A. J. Moles c Maguire b Parsons | 1 | G. C. Small b Maguire | | 0 |
| Asif Din lbw b Parsons | 0 | J. E. Benjamin c Potter b Benson | | 0 |
| *T. A. Lloyd c Whitaker b Benson | 39 | T. A. Munton not out | | 0 |
| D. P. Ostler b Millns | 2 | L-b 14, w 14, n-b 1 | | 29 |
| D. A. Reeve b Millns | 2 | | | |
| P. A. Smith c Wilkinson b Benson | 38 | 1/1 2/2 3/9 | (9 wkts, 31 overs) | 151 |
| N. M. K. Smith b Wilkinson | 25 | 4/19 5/79 6/104 | | |
| †P. C. L. Holloway not out | 25 | 7/128 8/140 9/145 | | |

Bowling: Millns 6–0–20–2; Parsons 5–0–28–2; Maguire 6–0–20–1; Wilkinson 8–0–32–1; Benson 6–0–37–3.

## Leicestershire

| | | | | |
|---|---|---|---|---|
| J. J. Whitaker b N. M. K. Smith | 29 | †P. Whitticase not out | | 16 |
| *N. E. Briers c Holloway b Small | 40 | | | |
| T. J. Boon c Moles b Reeve | 11 | L-b 7, w 6, n-b 1 | | 14 |
| B. F. Smith not out | 21 | | | |
| L. Potter b Small | 15 | 1/49 2/76 3/100 | (5 wkts, 31 overs) | 149 |
| J. D. R. Benson run out | 3 | 4/121 5/126 | | |

G. J. Parsons, C. W. Wilkinson, D. J. Millns and J. N. Maguire did not bat.

Bowling: Munton 6–0–27–0; Benjamin 4–0–25–0; Reeve 7–0–24–1; N. M. K. Smith 6–0–27–1; Small 5–0–25–2; P. A. Smith 3–0–14–0.

Umpires: J. D. Bond and D. O. Oslear.

At Bournemouth, August 18. LEICESTERSHIRE beat HAMPSHIRE by four wickets.

## LEICESTERSHIRE v GLOUCESTERSHIRE

At Leicester, August 25. Gloucestershire won by 12 runs. Toss: Leicestershire. Alleyne went on to his highest score in the competition after he and Scott had put on 108 for the first wicket.

### Gloucestershire

| | | | |
|---|---|---|---|
| R. J. Scott c Whitaker b Hepworth .... | 56 | J. J. E. Hardy not out ............... | 11 |
| M. W. Alleyne not out ............. | 76 | B 1, l-b 7, w 10, n-b 3 ....... | 21 |
| *A. J. Wright c Whitticase b Wilkinson | 29 | | |
| C. W. J. Athey c Parsons b Maguire ... | 25 | 1/108 2/148 3/198 (3 wkts, 40 overs) | 218 |

†R. C. J. Williams, T. H. C. Hancock, M. C. J. Ball, D. R. Gilbert, A. M. Babington and A. M. Smith did not bat.

Bowling: Millns 8-0-36-0; Parsons 8-0-23-0; Wilkinson 8-0-55-1; Maguire 8-0-58-1; Hepworth 8-0-38-1.

### Leicestershire

| | | | |
|---|---|---|---|
| J. J. Whitaker c Athey b Scott ........ | 30 | G. J. Parsons c Babington b Smith .... | 9 |
| *N. E. Briers b Smith .............. | 0 | C. W. Wilkinson not out............. | 12 |
| T. J. Boon c Smith b Babington....... | 18 | J. N. Maguire not out ............. | 0 |
| B. F. Smith lbw b Gilbert........... | 23 | L-b 5, w 3, n-b 1............ | 9 |
| L. Potter c Smith b Gilbert .......... | 53 | | |
| †P. Whitticase c Hancock b Scott ...... | 17 | 1/6 2/38 3/71 (9 wkts, 40 overs) | 206 |
| P. N. Hepworth run out ............. | 31 | 4/80 5/111 6/178 | |
| D. J. Millns c Athey b Smith ........ | 4 | 7/181 8/185 9/206 | |

Bowling: Smith 8-0-52-3; Babington 8-2-34-1; Gilbert 8-0-37-2; Ball 8-0-40-0; Scott 8-1-38-2.

Umpires: D. J. Constant and K. E. Palmer.

## MIDDLESEX

At Bristol, April 21. MIDDLESEX beat GLOUCESTERSHIRE on scoring-rate.

### MIDDLESEX v SURREY

At Lord's, April 28. Surrey won by four wickets. Toss: Middlesex. Brown's undefeated 81 for Middlesex came from 78 balls; he added 80 in fifteen overs for the third wicket with Keech, who was making his début for the county. In Surrey's reply, Greig, who hit a six over Father Time, faced 70 balls for his 68 not out, and Stewart 69 balls, two of which he hit for six, for his 71.

### Middlesex

| | | | |
|---|---|---|---|
| *M. W. Gatting b Boiling............ | 22 | P. N. Weekes c Ward b Greig ........ | 3 |
| J. C. Pooley c Robinson b Waqar Younis | 42 | J. E. Emburey not out ............... | 16 |
| K. R. Brown not out ............... | 81 | B 4, l-b 7, w 5............ | 16 |
| M. Keech c Bicknell b Greig ......... | 36 | | |
| †P. R. Downton c Waqar Younis | | 1/67 2/71 3/151 (5 wkts, 40 overs) | 221 |
| b Bicknell . | 5 | 4/159 5/166 | |

D. W. Headley, S. P. Hughes, P. C. R. Tufnell and C. W. Taylor did not bat.

Bowling: Bicknell 7-0-37-1; Murphy 8-1-31-0; Robinson 5-0-34-0; Waqar Younis 8-1-41-1; Boiling 3-0-21-1; Thorpe 2-0-16-0; Greig 7-0-30-2.

## Surrey

| | | | |
|---|---|---|---|
| M. A. Lynch c Keech b Taylor | 5 | J. D. Robinson b Hughes | 26 |
| A. D. Brown b Tufnell | 15 | M. P. Bicknell not out | 7 |
| †A. J. Stewart c Brown b Tufnell | 71 | L-b 15, w 5, n-b 3 | 23 |
| D. M. Ward c Brown b Tufnell | 7 | | |
| G. P. Thorpe b Hughes | 2 | 1/6 2/49 3/59 (6 wkts, 38.2 overs) | 224 |
| *I. A. Greig not out | 68 | 4/67 5/128 6/198 | |

J. Boiling, A. J. Murphy and Waqar Younis did not bat.

Bowling: Headley 8-0-41-0; Taylor 7.2-0-50-1; Tufnell 8-0-28-3; Hughes 8-0-46-2; Emburey 7-0-44-0.

Umpires: B. Hassan and A. A. Jones.


## MIDDLESEX v NORTHAMPTONSHIRE

At Lord's, May 5. No result.


At Hove, May 12. MIDDLESEX beat SUSSEX by five wickets.


At Taunton, May 26. MIDDLESEX beat SOMERSET by seven wickets.


## MIDDLESEX v KENT

At Southgate, June 2. Kent won by 21 runs. Toss: Kent. Middlesex's first senior game at Southgate since 1859, and their first Sunday League home tie away from Lord's, was enjoyed by Kent's batsmen. Taylor hit eight fours and two sixes in his 66, Ward six fours and two sixes in making 55 from 34 balls, and Chris Cowdrey two fours and two sixes in his 29-ball 38 not out.

### Kent

| | | | |
|---|---|---|---|
| M. V. Fleming c Roseberry b Ellcock | 2 | †S. A. Marsh c Farbrace b Williams | 2 |
| *M. R. Benson c Farbrace b Fraser | 78 | M. A. Ealham not out | 6 |
| N. R. Taylor c Ramprakash b Emburey | 66 | B 8, l-b 12 | 20 |
| T. R. Ward c Williams b Emburey | 55 | | |
| G. R. Cowdrey c Farbrace b Cowans | 9 | 1/2 2/137 3/178 (6 wkts, 40 overs) | 276 |
| C. S. Cowdrey not out | 38 | 4/214 5/235 6/256 | |

R. P. Davis, A. P. Igglesden and T. A. Merrick did not bat.

Bowling: Ellcock 6-0-33-1; Cowans 8-1-49-1; Williams 6-0-55-1; Fraser 8-0-44-1; Emburey 8-0-48-2; Ramprakash 4-0-27-0.


### Middlesex

| | | | |
|---|---|---|---|
| *M. W. Gatting run out | 15 | N. G. Cowans b Fleming | 1 |
| M. A. Roseberry c Marsh b Fleming | 79 | R. M. Ellcock not out | 8 |
| M. R. Ramprakash lbw b Igglesden | 47 | A. R. C. Fraser not out | 8 |
| K. R. Brown c Fleming b Merrick | 34 | | |
| M. Keech lbw b Igglesden | 4 | L-b 15, w 5, n-b 1 | 21 |
| J. E. Emburey c G. R. Cowdrey b Ealham | 5 | 1/43 2/126 3/188 (9 wkts, 40 overs) | 255 |
| N. F. Williams run out | 27 | 4/196 5/199 6/203 | |
| †P. Farbrace b Ealham | 6 | 7/230 8/235 9/242 | |

Bowling: Igglesden 8-1-37-2; Merrick 8-0-41-1; Davis 8-0-48-0; Ealham 8-0-56-2; Fleming 8-0-58-2.

Umpires: B. Dudleston and P. B. Wight.

## MIDDLESEX v LEICESTERSHIRE

At Uxbridge, June 9. Leicestershire won by 73 runs. Toss: Middlesex. Wilkinson made his unbeaten 35 from 24 balls as Leicestershire added 45 in the last six overs. Emburey's two wickets made him the fifth-highest wicket-taker in the Sunday League, with 285.

### Leicestershire

| | | | |
|---|---|---|---|
| T. J. Boon lbw b Cowans | 4 | D. J. Millns c Farbrace b Hughes | 5 |
| *N. E. Briers run out | 44 | C. W. Wilkinson not out | 35 |
| P. N. Hepworth b Hughes | 1 | J. N. Maguire not out | 0 |
| C. C. Lewis st Farbrace b Weekes | 10 | L-b 9, w 6, n-b 2 | 17 |
| B. F. Smith c Gatting b Emburey | 33 | | |
| J. D. R. Benson run out | 42 | 1/10 2/17 3/41 (9 wkts, 40 overs) 202 | |
| P. Willey c Emburey b Hutchinson | 10 | 4/98 5/118 6/153 | |
| †P. Whitticase b Emburey | 1 | 7/156 8/157 9/191 | |

Bowling: Cowans 8–0–30–1; Hughes 8–0–29–2; Williams 6–0–40–0; Weekes 8–0–45–1; Emburey 8–0–39–2; Hutchinson 2–0–10–1.

### Middlesex

| | | | |
|---|---|---|---|
| I. J. F. Hutchinson lbw b Lewis | 0 | †P. Farbrace not out | 14 |
| M. A. Roseberry b Maguire | 1 | S. P. Hughes c Wilkinson b Lewis | 4 |
| *M. W. Gatting lbw b Millns | 16 | N. G. Cowans not out | 0 |
| K. R. Brown c Hepworth b Benson | 40 | L-b 6, w 3, n-b 2 | 11 |
| M. Keech run out | 20 | | |
| P. N. Weekes lbw b Maguire | 20 | 1/0 2/2 3/39 (9 wkts, 40 overs) 129 | |
| J. E. Emburey b Willey | 2 | 4/82 5/87 6/91 | |
| N. F. Williams c Millns b Benson | 1 | 7/100 8/119 9/128 | |

Bowling: Lewis 6–1–14–2; Maguire 8–2–16–2; Millns 6–0–27–1; Wilkinson 4–0–18–0; Willey 8–0–22–1; Benson 8–0–26–2.

Umpires: M. J. Kitchen and R. C. Tolchard.

At Cardiff, June 16. MIDDLESEX lost to GLAMORGAN by 54 runs.

At Nottingham, June 23. MIDDLESEX beat NOTTINGHAMSHIRE by seven wickets.

## MIDDLESEX v YORKSHIRE

At Lord's, July 7. Yorkshire won by seven wickets. Toss: Middlesex. Yorkshire won their sixth successive Sunday game, a county record, after Moxon and Metcalfe put on 167 for the first wicket. Metcalfe's 116, from 114 balls, was a personal best in the competition. Roseberry's maiden hundred in the Sunday League came from 114 balls; his second fifty took only 33 balls, and he hit three sixes.

### Middlesex

| | | | |
|---|---|---|---|
| *M. W. Gatting c Blakey b Fletcher | 14 | P. N. Weekes not out | 32 |
| M. A. Roseberry not out | 106 | | |
| K. R. Brown c Robinson b Pickles | 6 | L-b 8, w 7 | 15 |
| M. Keech c Moxon b Gough | 5 | | |
| I. J. F. Hutchinson run out | 17 | 1/23 2/50 3/65 (5 wkts, 40 overs) 210 | |
| J. E. Emburey c Metcalfe b Fletcher | 15 | 4/91 5/126 | |

†P. Farbrace, N. F. Williams, C. W. Taylor and N. G. Cowans did not bat.

Bowling: Hartley 8–0–46–0; Fletcher 8–0–43–2; Gough 8–0–35–1; Pickles 4–0–13–1; Carrick 8–0–38–0; Batty 4–0–27–0.

## Yorkshire

| | | | |
|---|---|---|---|
| *M. D. Moxon b Emburey | 64 | P. E. Robinson not out | 3 |
| A. A. Metcalfe c Taylor b Emburey | 116 | B 2, l-b 13, w 2, n-b 3 | 20 |
| †R. J. Blakey c Hutchinson b Emburey | 2 | | |
| D. Byas not out | 6 | 1/167 2/172 3/204 (3 wkts, 39.2 overs) 211 | |

C. S. Pickles, P. Carrick, P. J. Hartley, D. Gough, J. D. Batty and S. D. Fletcher did not bat.

Bowling: Williams 8–0–47–0; Taylor 8–0–37–0; Emburey 8–0–34–3; Cowans 8–0–42–0; Weekes 7.2–0–36–0.

Umpires: R. Julian and B. J. Meyer.

At Birmingham, July 14. MIDDLESEX lost to WARWICKSHIRE by nine wickets.

## MIDDLESEX v LANCASHIRE

At Lord's, July 21. Lancashire won by two wickets. Toss: Lancashire. Cowans reduced Lancashire to 4 for four by the end of his third over, and they were 36 for seven when he completed his eighth, having returned his best figures in the competition – and the best by any bowler in 1991. However, Austin and Hegg, both of whom made their highest scores in the League, added 105 in 23 overs, an eighth-wicket record for the Sunday League, and Lancashire's victory kept them on top of the Refuge Assurance League table after a disastrous fortnight in the other three competitions.

## Middlesex

| | | | |
|---|---|---|---|
| M. A. Roseberry c Hegg b Austin | 42 | J. E. Emburey lbw b Austin | 2 |
| *M. W. Gatting c Lloyd b DeFreitas | 7 | †P. Farbrace not out | 26 |
| M. R. Ramprakash c Hegg b Wasim Akram | 6 | L-b 4, w 10, n-b 3 | 17 |
| K. R. Brown c Atherton b Watkinson | 1 | | |
| M. Keech c Fairbrother b Austin | 16 | 1/21 2/45 3/49 (6 wkts, 38 overs) 143 | |
| P. N. Weekes not out | 26 | 4/82 5/92 6/95 | |

D. W. Headley, N. F. Williams and N. G. Cowans did not bat.

Bowling: DeFreitas 8–0–25–1; Allott 8–2–21–0; Wasim Akram 7–0–30–1; Watkinson 8–0–21–1; Austin 7–0–42–3.

## Lancashire

| | | | |
|---|---|---|---|
| G. Fowler run out | 1 | I. D. Austin run out | 48 |
| M. A. Atherton lbw b Cowans | 1 | *D. P. Hughes not out | 4 |
| G. D. Lloyd lbw b Cowans | 5 | | |
| N. H. Fairbrother b Cowans | 0 | B 8, l-b 10, w 10, n-b 1 | 29 |
| M. Watkinson c Farbrace b Cowans | 2 | | |
| Wasim Akram c Roseberry b Cowans | 10 | 1/1 2/2 3/2 (8 wkts, 37.5 overs) 147 | |
| P. A. J. DeFreitas lbw b Cowans | 0 | 4/4 5/22 6/22 | |
| †W. K. Hegg not out | 47 | 7/36 8/141 | |

P. J. W. Allott did not bat.

Bowling: Cowans 8–2–9–6; Williams 8–0–23–0; Headley 6–0–29–0; Emburey 8–0–28–0; Gatting 5.5–0–32–0; Weekes 2–0–8–0.

Umpires: J. C. Balderstone and R. C. Tolchard.

## MIDDLESEX v HAMPSHIRE

At Lord's, August 4. Middlesex won by seven wickets. Toss: Middlesex. Middlesex registered their first home win in any competition in 1991, thanks to Weekes's best bowling in any match for the first team, and the second-wicket partnership of 116 between Gatting and Ramprakash.

### Hampshire

| | | | |
|---|---|---|---|
| V. P. Terry c Roseberry b Emburey | ... 34 | †R. J. Parks c Taylor b Weekes | ...... 6 |
| R. A. Smith c Farbrace b Taylor | ...... 14 | | |
| J. R. Wood b Emburey | ............ 17 | B 2, l-b 6, w 10 | ............ 18 |
| *M. C. J. Nicholas not out | .......... 50 | | — |
| K. D. James st Farbrace b Weekes | .... 9 | 1/37 2/67 3/76 (6 wkts, 40 overs) 152 | |
| J. R. Ayling b Weekes | ............. 4 | 4/116 5/132 6/152 | |

R. J. Maru, S. D. Udal, C. A. Connor and K. J. Shine did not bat.

Bowling: Cowans 8-0-39-0; Headley 6-0-16-0; Taylor 4-0-14-1; Gatting 8-0-27-0; Emburey 8-1-21-2; Weekes 6-0-27-3.

### Middlesex

| | | | |
|---|---|---|---|
| M. A. Roseberry b Connor | .......... 5 | M. Keech not out | ............ 0 |
| *M. W. Gatting c James b Connor | .... 58 | L-b 1, w 4, n-b 4 | ............ 9 |
| M. R. Ramprakash c Parks b Shine | ... 68 | | — |
| K. R. Brown not out | ............ 14 | 1/12 2/128 3/145 (3 wkts, 33.5 overs) 154 | |

J. E. Emburey, †P. Farbrace, D. W. Headley, C. W. Taylor, P. N. Weekes and N. G. Cowans did not bat.

Bowling: Connor 8-0-30-2; Shine 7-0-22-1; Ayling 7-0-37-0; Udal 4.5-0-29-0; Maru 3-0-19-0; James 4-0-16-0.

Umpires: B. Leadbeater and K. E. Palmer.

## MIDDLESEX v DERBYSHIRE

At Lord's, August 11. Middlesex won on faster scoring-rate. Toss: Derbyshire. Middlesex started briskly, with Roseberry and Pooley putting on 167 from 140 balls; but their last five wickets fell for 19 runs in 22 balls. Pooley, making his third appearance in the competition, hit four sixes and nine fours in racing to a maiden Sunday League hundred off 78 balls. Rain revised Derbyshire's target to 211 from 34 overs, and then ended play four overs early. The Middlesex captain, Gatting, had planned to wear a microphone in order to join in television commentary while in the field, but he was forbidden to do so by the TCCB.

### Middlesex

| | | | |
|---|---|---|---|
| M. A. Roseberry st Krikken b Goldsmith | 63 | N. F. Williams not out | ......... 2 |
| J. C. Pooley c Mortensen b Goldsmith | .109 | D. W. Headley c Krikken b Base | ..... 4 |
| *M. W. Gatting run out | ............. 22 | N. G. Cowans not out | ............ 5 |
| K. R. Brown lbw b Mortensen | ...... 2 | L-b 8, w 5 | ............ 13 |
| M. Keech c Krikken b Malcolm | ...... 2 | | — |
| P. N. Weekes c Cork b Mortensen | ... 13 | 1/167 2/184 3/187 (9 wkts, 39 overs) 242 | |
| J. E. Emburey run out | ............. 7 | 4/192 5/222 6/223 | |
| †P. Farbrace lbw b Mortensen | ....... 0 | 7/225 8/231 9/236 | |

Bowling: Base 8-0-39-1; Mortensen 8-0-29-3; Cork 8-0-56-0; Malcolm 8-0-65-1; Goldsmith 7-0-45-2.

### Derbyshire

| | | | |
|---|---|---|---|
| P. D. Bowler b Gatting | ............. 37 | *K. J. Barnett not out | ............ 22 |
| C. J. Adams c Roseberry b Williams | ... 20 | L-b 4, w 5 | ............ 9 |
| T. J. G. O'Gorman c Weekes b Gatting | 12 | | — |
| D. E. Malcolm b Emburey | .......... 0 | 1/50 2/70 (4 wkts, 30 overs) 137 | |
| M. Azharuddin not out | ............. 37 | 3/74 4/76 | |

S. C. Goldsmith, †K. M. Krikken, D. G. Cork, S. J. Base and O. H. Mortensen did not bat.

Bowling: Cowans 5-0-18-0; Williams 8-0-24-1; Emburey 6-0-39-1; Gatting 7-0-34-2; Headley 4-0-18-0.

Umpires: R. Palmer and R. A. White.

At Colchester, August 18. MIDDLESEX lost to ESSEX by 95 runs.


At Worcester, August 25. MIDDLESEX lost to WORCESTERSHIRE by 103 runs.


# NORTHAMPTONSHIRE

At Cardiff, April 21. NORTHAMPTONSHIRE beat GLAMORGAN by one wicket.


At Manchester, April 28. NORTHAMPTONSHIRE lost to LANCASHIRE by five wickets.


At Lord's, May 5. MIDDLESEX v NORTHAMPTONSHIRE. No result.


## NORTHAMPTONSHIRE v LEICESTERSHIRE

At Northampton, May 12. Northamptonshire won by five wickets. Toss: Northamptonshire. Capel's undefeated 77 came from 71 balls.

### Leicestershire

| | | | |
|---|---:|---|---:|
| †P. Whitticase c Ripley b Taylor | 0 | P. N. Hepworth not out | 17 |
| *N. E. Briers b Penberthy | 48 | C. W. Wilkinson not out | 0 |
| J. J. Whitaker c Walker b Capel | 34 | L-b 22, w 7 | 29 |
| P. Willey run out | 27 | | |
| C. C. Lewis c Ripley b Penberthy | 6 | 1/2 2/77 3/119 (7 wkts, 40 overs) 210 | |
| L. Potter c and b Thomas | 33 | 4/129 5/133 | |
| B. F. Smith run out | 16 | 6/159 7/210 | |

J. N. Maguire and D. J. Millns did not bat.

Bowling: Taylor 8–1–32–1; Walker 8–2–31–0; Thomas 6–0–42–1; Capel 7–0–31–1; Williams 6–0–32–0; Penberthy 5–0–20–2.

### Northamptonshire

| | | | |
|---|---:|---|---:|
| A. Fordham lbw b Wilkinson | 40 | A. L. Penberthy not out | 22 |
| W. Larkins c Briers b Millns | 5 | | |
| R. J. Bailey c Lewis b Willey | 22 | L-b 9, w 6, n-b 2 | 17 |
| D. J. Capel not out | 77 | | |
| *A. J. Lamb c Briers b Hepworth | 23 | 1/6 2/61 3/90 (5 wkts, 39.3 overs) 214 | |
| R. G. Williams c Millns b Hepworth | 8 | 4/129 5/144 | |

†D. Ripley, J. G. Thomas, A. Walker and J. P. Taylor did not bat.

Bowling: Lewis 7.3–1–26–0; Millns 7–0–36–1; Maguire 8–0–48–0; Wilkinson 8–0–50–2; Willey 4–0–19–1; Hepworth 5–0–26–1.

Umpires: J. D. Bond and J. H. Hampshire.


## NORTHAMPTONSHIRE v WORCESTERSHIRE

At Northampton, May 19. Worcestershire won by 27 runs. Toss: Northamptonshire. Moody's 80-ball 100, including twelve fours and two sixes, was his third in four Refuge Assurance matches for Worcestershire, taking him to a total of 438 runs, well past his 382 from fourteen Sunday games for Warwickshire in 1990. With Curtis, he put on 152 in 21.3 overs for the first wicket. When Northamptonshire replied, Penberthy made his highest score in the competition and Thomas ran up 34 in 23 balls.

## Worcestershire

| | | | |
|---|---|---|---|
| T. S. Curtis run out | 49 | M. J. Weston not out | 1 |
| T. M. Moody c Walker b Roberts | 100 | | |
| G. A. Hick c Lamb b Walker | 47 | L-b 12, w 10 | 22 |
| I. T. Botham b Thomas | 10 | | |
| D. B. D'Oliveira run out | 3 | 1/152 2/176 3/195    (5 wkts, 40 overs) 251 | |
| *P. A. Neale not out | 19 | 4/200 5/247 | |

†S. R. Bevins, R. K. Illingworth, N. V. Radford and S. R. Lampitt did not bat.

Bowling: Taylor 7–0–48–0; Walker 7–0–38–1; Penberthy 6–0–35–0; Capel 5–0–46–0; Thomas 8–0–36–1; Roberts 7–0–36–1.

## Northamptonshire

| | | | |
|---|---|---|---|
| A. Fordham c Moody b Radford | 13 | A. R. Roberts c Curtis b Illingworth | 14 |
| N. A. Felton c Neale b Lampitt | 65 | A. Walker b Illingworth | 6 |
| *A. J. Lamb b Radford | 1 | J. P. Taylor b Botham | 5 |
| D. J. Capel c D'Oliveira b Radford | 12 | L-b 1, w 7 | 8 |
| R. J. Bailey c Curtis b Illingworth | 25 | | |
| A. L. Penberthy not out | 41 | 1/21 2/36 3/50        (38.3 overs) 224 | |
| †D. Ripley b Illingworth | 0 | 4/113 5/125 6/125 | |
| J. G. Thomas c Curtis b Illingworth | 34 | 7/170 8/203 9/210 | |

Bowling: Weston 7–0–36–0; Radford 7–0–31–3; Botham 6.3–0–46–1; Lampitt 8–0–44–1; Illingworth 8–0–49–5; Hick 2–0–17–0.

Umpires: J. C. Balderstone and J. H. Harris.

At Leeds, May 26. NORTHAMPTONSHIRE lost to YORKSHIRE by three wickets.

## NORTHAMPTONSHIRE v HAMPSHIRE

At Northampton, June 2. Northamptonshire won by 99 runs. Toss: Hampshire. Although their innings was restricted by rain to 36 overs, Northamptonshire put together their fifth-highest score in the competition. Lamb faced 44 balls for his 61, and struck six fours, while Capel and Bailey (nineteen balls, two sixes, six fours) added 75 in five overs for the fourth wicket.

## Northamptonshire

| | | | |
|---|---|---|---|
| A. Fordham c Connor b Udal | 41 | K. M. Curran not out | 2 |
| N. A. Felton b Bakker | 69 | B 4, l-b 14, w 11, n-b 1 | 30 |
| *A. J. Lamb c Nicholas b Ayling | 61 | | |
| D. J. Capel not out | 30 | 1/101 2/166      (4 wkts, 36 overs) 280 | |
| R. J. Bailey b Udal | 47 | 3/203 4/278 | |

A. L. Penberthy, †D. Ripley, J. G. Thomas, A. R. Roberts and A. Walker did not bat.

Bowling: Bakker 8–0–53–1; Aqib Javed 7–0–50–0; Connor 8–0–60–0; Ayling 7–0–52–1; Udal 6–0–47–2.

## Hampshire

| | | | |
|---|---|---|---|
| V. P. Terry c Lamb b Thomas | 14 | C. A. Connor c Capel b Roberts | 18 |
| T. C. Middleton c Fordham b Curran | 56 | P. J. Bakker b Roberts | 4 |
| R. A. Smith c Roberts b Thomas | 2 | Aqib Javed not out | 1 |
| *M. C. J. Nicholas b Walker | 1 | B 4, l-b 6, w 6 | 16 |
| C. L. Smith b Penberthy | 19 | | |
| J. R. Ayling c Fordham b Curran | 4 | 1/22 2/28 3/32       (9 wkts, 36 overs) 181 | |
| †A. N. Aymes not out | 33 | 4/70 5/87 6/108 | |
| S. D. Udal c Fordham b Roberts | 13 | 7/140 8/170 9/180 | |

Bowling: Walker 7–0–24–1; Thomas 5–0–20–2; Curran 7–0–30–2; Penberthy 8–0–45–1; Roberts 6–0–26–3; Bailey 3–0–26–0.

Umpires: K. J. Lyons and R. A. White.

At Moreton-in-Marsh, June 9. GLOUCESTERSHIRE v NORTHAMPTONSHIRE. No result.

## NORTHAMPTONSHIRE v SOMERSET

At Luton, June 30. Northamptonshire won by four wickets. Toss: Northamptonshire. Northamptonshire's progress to victory was interrupted when Roebuck took three wickets in fifteen balls, reducing them to 118 for six.

### Somerset

| | | |
|---|---|---|
| S. J. Cook c Bailey b Walker | 5 | K. H. MacLeay not out .............. 12 |
| P. M. Roebuck b Walker | 0 | N. A. Mallender not out ............. 13 |
| *C. J. Tavaré c Ripley b Curran | 23 | |
| R. J. Harden run out | 1 | L-b 4, w 16 .......... 20 |
| A. N. Hayhurst run out | 2 | |
| †N. D. Burns c Bailey b Curran | 24 | 1/5 2/6 3/11 (8 wkts, 40 overs) 126 |
| G. D. Rose b Curran | 2 | 4/22 5/68 6/70 |
| R. P. Lefebvre c Taylor b Capel | 24 | 7/81 8/103 |

D. A. Graveney did not bat.

Bowling: Taylor 8–1–22–0; Walker 8–2–7–2; Baptiste 8–0–43–0; Curran 8–1–24–3; Capel 8–0–26–1.

### Northamptonshire

| | | |
|---|---|---|
| A. Fordham lbw b Roebuck | 67 | E. A. E. Baptiste not out ........... 10 |
| N. A. Felton b Mallender | 10 | †D. Ripley not out ................. 6 |
| D. J. Capel lbw b MacLeay | 1 | B 1, l-b 6, w 2, n-b 1 ........ 10 |
| R. J. Bailey c Hayhurst b Graveney | 19 | |
| *A. J. Lamb b Roebuck | 3 | 1/36 2/45 3/100 (6 wkts, 37.2 overs) 129 |
| K. M. Curran b Roebuck | 3 | 4/103 5/109 6/118 |

N. G. B. Cook, A. Walker and J. P. Taylor did not bat.

Bowling: Mallender 8–0–31–1; Lefebvre 5–0–25–0; MacLeay 8–0–24–1; Graveney 8–1–23–1; Roebuck 8–2–15–3; Hayhurst 0.2–0–4–0.

Umpires: J. H. Harris and R. A. White.

## NORTHAMPTONSHIRE v SURREY

At Tring, July 7. Northamptonshire won by 15 runs. Toss: Northamptonshire. Fordham made his 49 from 52 balls, but his side slipped from 113 for three, losing six wickets for 32. Surrey, in contrast, began badly, and were three down for 17, but Lynch and Thorpe revived them with an 86-run stand in twenty overs.

### Northamptonshire

| | | |
|---|---|---|
| A. Fordham c Stewart b Waqar Younis | 49 | A. Walker c and b M. P. Bicknell .... 4 |
| N. A. Felton c Stewart b Murphy | 4 | N. G. B. Cook not out ............. 17 |
| D. J. Capel c Medlycott b Robinson | 16 | J. P. Taylor run out .............. 16 |
| *R. J. Bailey c Ward b Boiling | 33 | |
| K. M. Curran c Lynch b Murphy | 13 | L-b 9, w 4, n-b 2 ........ 15 |
| E. A. E. Baptiste lbw b Waqar Younis | 1 | |
| R. G. Williams c Stewart | | 1/22 2/46 3/98 (39.1 overs) 181 |
| b Waqar Younis | 0 | 4/113 5/115 6/115 |
| †D. Ripley b Boiling | 13 | 7/134 8/145 9/145 |

Bowling: M. P. Bicknell 8–0–28–1; Murphy 8–2–26–2; Robinson 5.1–0–26–1; Thorpe 2–0–14–0; Boiling 8–0–41–2; Waqar Younis 8–1–37–3.

## Surrey

| | | | | |
|---|---|---|---|---|
| D. J. Bicknell b Taylor | 0 | Waqar Younis b Baptiste | | 1 |
| M. A. Lynch c Baptiste b Williams | 55 | J. Boiling not out | | 3 |
| *†A. J. Stewart lbw b Taylor | 1 | | | |
| D. M. Ward b Walker | 3 | B 1, l-b 5, w 7 | | 13 |
| G. P. Thorpe c and b Capel | 50 | | | |
| J. D. Robinson c Walker b Capel | 11 | 1/3 2/12 3/17 | (8 wkts, 40 overs) | 166 |
| K. T. Medlycott run out | 9 | 4/103 5/125 6/136 | | |
| M. P. Bicknell not out | 20 | 7/152 8/156 | | |

A. J. Murphy did not bat.

Bowling: Walker 8-1-14-1; Taylor 7-2-18-2; Curran 4-0-21-0; Baptiste 7-1-25-1; Cook 4-0-25-0; Williams 5-0-28-1; Capel 5-0-29-2.

Umpires: K. E. Palmer and P. B. Wight.

## NORTHAMPTONSHIRE v NOTTINGHAMSHIRE

At Wellingborough School, July 21. Northamptonshire won by 5 runs. Toss: Nottinghamshire. Nottinghamshire lost their second Refuge Assurance match of the season, and with it the League leadership, one day after beating the same opponents in a County Championship game in two days. Stephenson took five Northamptonshire wickets for the third day running, but there was too little support from the batsmen. The Northamptonshire innings was dominated by Larkins, who, returning after two months out of the side with a broken thumb, hit five fours and two sixes in 63 from 71 balls.

## Northamptonshire

| | | | | |
|---|---|---|---|---|
| A. Fordham c French b Stephenson | 8 | †W. M. Noon b Evans | | 4 |
| N. A. Felton run out | 37 | A. Walker b Evans | | 2 |
| W. Larkins c Pollard b Evans | 63 | J. P. Taylor not out | | 1 |
| *A. J. Lamb c French b Stephenson | 2 | L-b 9, w 6, n-b 1 | | 16 |
| D. J. Capel b Stephenson | 28 | | | |
| M. K. Curran c Johnson b Pick | 26 | 1/12 2/104 3/109 | (40 overs) | 202 |
| E. A. E. Baptiste lbw b Stephenson | 5 | 4/120 5/166 6/184 | | |
| R. G. Williams b Stephenson | 10 | 7/185 8/199 9/199 | | |

Bowling: Stephenson 8-0-31-5; Pick 8-0-37-1; Saxelby 8-1-46-0; Hemmings 8-0-38-0; Evans 8-1-41-3.

## Nottinghamshire

| | | | | |
|---|---|---|---|---|
| P. R. Pollard c Noon b Taylor | 6 | †B. N. French c Lamb b Walker | | 26 |
| D. W. Randall b Williams | 48 | E. E. Hemmings b Taylor | | 17 |
| P. Johnson c Felton b Walker | 0 | R. A. Pick not out | | 2 |
| *R. T. Robinson b Capel | 35 | L-b 18, w 4 | | 22 |
| M. Saxelby b Williams | 2 | | | |
| F. D. Stephenson b Baptiste | 19 | 1/19 2/21 3/84 | (40 overs) | 197 |
| M. Newell c Felton b Curran | 12 | 4/93 5/106 6/136 | | |
| K. P. Evans b Curran | 8 | 7/141 8/155 9/191 | | |

Bowling: Walker 8-0-24-2; Taylor 7-0-45-2; Curran 7-0-28-2; Baptiste 8-0-37-1; Capel 5-0-23-1; Williams 5-0-22-2.

Umpires: H. D. Bird and B. J. Meyer.

At Derby, July 28. NORTHAMPTONSHIRE lost to DERBYSHIRE by 46 runs.

At Eastbourne, August 4. NORTHAMPTONSHIRE beat SUSSEX by five wickets.

## NORTHAMPTONSHIRE v ESSEX

At Northampton, August 11. Northamptonshire won by 62 runs. Toss: Northamptonshire. Larkins's tenth hundred in the competition came off 94 balls, with eleven fours and a six. He and Fordham put on 155 in 24 overs, and then Lamb hit five fours in his 22-ball 36. For Essex, Foster scored a maiden Sunday fifty, and Pringle claimed his 150th League wicket. The fixture was originally scheduled for Peterborough but was transferred to the county ground for financial reasons.

### Northamptonshire

| | | | |
|---|---|---|---|
| A. Fordham c Such b Topley | 73 | †D. Ripley not out | 0 |
| W. Larkins c Stephenson b Pringle | 108 | | |
| *A. J. Lamb b Such | 36 | L-b 11, w 1, n-b 1 | 13 |
| D. J. Capel c Knight b Pringle | 23 | | |
| R. J. Bailey b Topley | 2 | 1/155 2/228 3/228 (7 wkts, 40 overs) | 277 |
| K. M. Curran c Prichard b Foster | 19 | 4/231 5/270 | |
| E. A. E. Baptiste c Stephenson b Pringle | 3 | 6/277 7/277 | |

R. G. Williams, A. Walker and J. P. Taylor did not bat.

Bowling: Foster 8–0–45–1; Pringle 8–0–43–3; Stephenson 2–0–20–0; Topley 8–0–57–2; Such 8–1–67–1; Salim Malik 6–0–34–0.

### Essex

| | | | |
|---|---|---|---|
| J. P. Stephenson b Taylor | 12 | N. V. Knight not out | 31 |
| A. C. H. Seymour b Taylor | 0 | T. D. Topley b Walker | 4 |
| Salim Malik c sub b Capel | 58 | P. M. Such not out | 1 |
| P. J. Prichard c Williams b Curran | 13 | B 4, l-b 16, w 3, n-b 1 | 24 |
| N. Hussain c Ripley b Capel | 0 | | |
| *D. R. Pringle c Ripley b Capel | 6 | 1/1 2/22 3/60 (9 wkts, 40 overs) | 215 |
| N. A. Foster run out | 57 | 4/68 5/82 6/111 | |
| †M. A. Garnham lbw b Williams | 9 | 7/145 8/190 9/214 | |

Bowling: Taylor 8–0–33–2; Walker 8–0–30–1; Baptiste 8–2–30–0; Curran 3–0–7–1; Capel 6–0–30–3; Williams 7–0–65–1.

Umpires: G. I. Burgess and B. Leadbeater.

At Canterbury, August 18. NORTHAMPTONSHIRE beat KENT by 2 runs.

## NORTHAMPTONSHIRE v WARWICKSHIRE

At Northampton, August 25. Northamptonshire won by 8 runs. Toss: Northamptonshire. Bailey's unbeaten 78 came from 85 balls, and helped keep his county in third place in the League, their highest position yet. Had Warwickshire won they would have moved up into third, and Northamptonshire would have slipped to fifth, behind Worcestershire.

### Northamptonshire

| | | | |
|---|---|---|---|
| A. Fordham c and b Benjamin | 16 | K. M. Curran c Small b N. M. K. Smith | 10 |
| W. Larkins b N. M. K. Smith | 66 | D. J. Capel not out | 14 |
| *A. J. Lamb c Moles b Benjamin | 4 | B 5, l-b 6, w 9 | 20 |
| R. J. Bailey not out | 78 | | |
| E. A. E. Baptiste c Moles b N. M. K. Smith | 10 | 1/36 2/50 3/122 (5 wkts, 40 overs) | 218 |
| | | 4/138 5/169 | |

R. G. Williams, A. L. Penberthy, †W. M. Noon and A. Walker did not bat.

Bowling: Munton 8–1–38–0; Benjamin 8–0–26–2; Small 6–1–26–0; Reeve 5.3–0–26–0; P. A. Smith 6–0–39–0; N. M. K. Smith 6.3–0–52–3.

## Warwickshire

| | | | | |
|---|---|---|---|---|
| A. J. Moles b Walker | 4 | G. C. Small b Curran | | 3 |
| Asif Din c Noon b Baptiste | 7 | J. E. Benjamin run out | | 2 |
| *T. A. Lloyd c Curran b Williams | 24 | T. A. Munton not out | | 10 |
| D. P. Ostler st Noon b Williams | 26 | L-b 11, w 5 | | 16 |
| D. A. Reeve c Curran | 43 | | | |
| P. A. Smith c Noon b Capel | 2 | 1/10 2/20 3/41 | (9 wkts, 40 overs) | 210 |
| N. M. K. Smith c Capel b Penberthy | 39 | 4/74 5/80 6/152 | | |
| †P. C. L. Holloway not out | 34 | 7/158 8/176 9/190 | | |

Bowling: Walker 7–0–24–1; Baptiste 8–0–36–1; Williams 8–0–42–2; Capel 8–1–40–1; Curran 8–0–56–2; Penberthy 1–0–1–1.

Umpires: B. Leadbeater and K. J. Lyons.

# NOTTINGHAMSHIRE

At Manchester, April 21. NOTTINGHAMSHIRE beat LANCASHIRE by nine wickets.

## NOTTINGHAMSHIRE v WARWICKSHIRE

At Nottingham, April 28. Nottinghamshire won by 82 runs. Toss: Warwickshire. Johnson, whose 80 included three sixes, shared a fourth-wicket partnership of 74 in ten overs with Crawley. After Nottinghamshire then lost three wickets for 7 runs, Stephenson, who faced 25 balls for his unbeaten 36 and struck four fours and two sixes, added 56 with Evans before the innings closed.

## Nottinghamshire

| | | | | |
|---|---|---|---|---|
| B. C. Broad c Piper b Munton | 2 | F. D. Stephenson not out | | 36 |
| D. W. Randall c and b N. M. K. Smith | 32 | K. P. Evans not out | | 14 |
| *R. T. Robinson c and b Munton | 3 | B 1, l-b 8, w 5, n-b 2 | | 16 |
| P. Johnson c P. A. Smith b Small | 80 | | | |
| M. A. Crawley b P. A. Smith | 29 | 1/12 2/20 3/75 | (6 wkts, 40 overs) | 212 |
| M. Saxelby c Piper b P. A. Smith | 0 | 4/149 5/155 6/156 | | |

†B. N. French, E. E. Hemmings and K. E. Cooper did not bat.

Bowling: Munton 8–1–35–2; Donald 8–0–41–0; P. A. Smith 8–0–36–2; Small 8–0–37–1; Moles 4–0–24–0; N. M. K. Smith 4–0–30–1.

## Warwickshire

| | | | | |
|---|---|---|---|---|
| A. J. Moles b Cooper | 0 | G. C. Small b Stephenson | | 1 |
| Asif Din b Stephenson | 6 | A. A. Donald c Broad b Stephenson | | 7 |
| *T. A. Lloyd lbw b Hemmings | 45 | T. A. Munton not out | | 3 |
| P. A. Smith c Robinson b Hemmings | 15 | L-b 6, w 1, n-b 4 | | 11 |
| D. A. Reeve b Crawley | 17 | | | |
| D. P. Ostler b Crawley | 16 | 1/0 2/17 3/76 | (35.2 overs) | 130 |
| N. M. K. Smith c Broad b Hemmings | 8 | 4/77 5/108 6/111 | | |
| †K. J. Piper st French b Hemmings | 1 | 7/119 8/119 9/127 | | |

Bowling: Cooper 8–1–20–1; Stephenson 5.2–0–17–3; Saxelby 4–0–20–0; Evans 4–0–16–0; Hemmings 8–0–26–4; Crawley 6–0–25–2.

Umpires: D. O. Oslear and K. E. Palmer.

At Cardiff, May 5. NOTTINGHAMSHIRE beat GLAMORGAN by four wickets.

## NOTTINGHAMSHIRE v ESSEX

At Nottingham, May 12. Nottinghamshire won by 10 runs. Toss: Essex. Nottinghamshire looked unlikely to register their fourth win in four Sunday games when Essex, chasing 195 were 180 for six. But the last four wickets fell for 4 runs, with Stephenson claiming three of them in six balls. Earlier, Randall, when 12, reached 6,000 runs in the competition, and Johnson hit three sixes and two fours in his half-century.

### Nottinghamshire

| | | | | |
|---|---|---|---|---|
| B. C. Broad run out | 14 | K. P. Evans c Prichard b Gooch | 3 | |
| D. W. Randall c Stephenson b Such | 19 | K. E. Cooper not out | 4 | |
| *R. T. Robinson b Pringle | 25 | E. E. Hemmings not out | 2 | |
| P. Johnson b Gooch | 55 | L-b 5, w 4, n-b 2 | 11 | |
| M. A. Crawley st Garnham b Such | 19 | | — | |
| M. Saxelby c Pringle b Ilott | 20 | 1/24 2/47 3/95 | (9 wkts, 40 overs) 194 | |
| F. D. Stephenson c Gooch b Pringle | 13 | 4/132 5/153 6/167 | | |
| †B. N. French run out | 9 | 7/179 8/187 9/187 | | |

Bowling: Ilott 8-1-28-1; Pringle 8-0-45-2; Gooch 8-0-36-2; Topley 8-0-35-0; Such 8-0-45-2.

### Essex

| | | | | |
|---|---|---|---|---|
| *G. A. Gooch c French b Saxelby | 41 | T. D. Topley lbw b Stephenson | 0 | |
| J. P. Stephenson c and b Hemmings | 29 | M. C. Ilott b Stephenson | 0 | |
| Salim Malik c French b Hemmings | 6 | P. M. Such not out | 2 | |
| P. J. Prichard c French b Saxelby | 15 | L-b 7, w 4, n-b 1 | 12 | |
| N. Hussain c Johnson b Evans | 45 | | — | |
| D. R. Pringle b Evans | 28 | 1/73 2/75 3/95 | (38 overs) 184 | |
| N. Shahid run out | 1 | 4/103 5/167 6/170 | | |
| †M. A. Garnham b Stephenson | 4 | 7/180 8/181 9/184 | | |

Bowling: Cooper 8-0-33-0; Stephenson 7-0-33-3; Saxelby 8-0-28-2; Evans 7-0-54-2; Hemmings 8-0-29-2.

Umpires: B. Dudleston and N. T. Plews.

At Leicester, May 26. NOTTINGHAMSHIRE beat LEICESTERSHIRE by five wickets.

## NOTTINGHAMSHIRE v SOMERSET

At Nottingham, June 9. Nottinghamshire won by 4 runs. Toss: Somerset. Nottinghamshire's sixth consecutive win in the League in 1991 was also their first victory over Somerset at Nottingham in any one-day competition. It was gained despite Harden's Sunday best score of 79 not out, made from 69 balls with six fours and two sixes; he and Hayhurst added 68 in eleven overs for the sixth wicket. MacLeay's spell of three wickets for 5 runs in eleven balls had earlier helped to restrict the League leaders to an unpromising 180.

### Nottinghamshire

| | | | | |
|---|---|---|---|---|
| B. C. Broad c Harden b Trump | 41 | †B. N. French not out | 5 | |
| D. W. Randall lbw b Hayhurst | 39 | | | |
| *R. T. Robinson run out | 15 | L-b 8, w 5 | 13 | |
| P. Johnson c Burns b MacLeay | 31 | | — | |
| M. A. Crawley c and b MacLeay | 9 | 1/80 2/99 3/129 | (7 wkts, 40 overs) 180 | |
| M. Saxelby lbw b Lefebvre | 27 | 4/139 5/153 | | |
| F. D. Stephenson c Tavaré b MacLeay | 0 | 6/153 7/180 | | |

K. P. Evans, E. E. Hemmings and K. E. Cooper did not bat.

Bowling: Mallender 8-0-41-0; Lefebvre 7-0-25-1; Hayhurst 6-0-33-1; MacLeay 8-0-31-3; Graveney 5-0-20-0; Trump 6-0-22-1.

## Somerset

| | | | | |
|---|---|---|---|---|
| S. J. Cook lbw b Stephenson | 2 | R. P. Lefebvre run out | | 4 |
| R. J. Bartlett c Broad b Cooper | 19 | N. A. Mallender not out | | 5 |
| *C. J. Tavaré c Randall b Evans | 16 | L-b 10, w 3 | | 13 |
| R. J. Harden not out | 79 | | | |
| †N. D. Burns c Broad b Saxelby | 9 | 1/8 2/36 3/49 | (7 wkts, 40 overs) | 176 |
| K. H. MacLeay c and b Hemmings | 2 | 4/76 5/88 | | |
| A. N. Hayhurst c French b Saxelby | 27 | 6/156 7/167 | | |

H. R. J. Trump and D. A. Graveney did not bat.

Bowling: Cooper 8–0–20–1; Stephenson 8–1–26–1; Evans 8–0–40–1; Hemmings 8–1–33–1; Saxelby 6–0–31–2; Crawley 2–0–16–0.

Umpires: K. J. Lyons and R. Palmer.

At Gloucester, June 16. NOTTINGHAMSHIRE beat GLOUCESTERSHIRE by eight wickets.

## NOTTINGHAMSHIRE v MIDDLESEX

At Nottingham, June 23. Middlesex won by seven wickets. Toss: Middlesex. Nottinghamshire dropped their first League points of the season in their eighth match. Gatting's 60-ball 61, which included eight fours and a six, ensured that Middlesex would win comfortably a game reduced to 36 overs a side because of rain.

## Nottinghamshire

| | | | | |
|---|---|---|---|---|
| B. C. Broad c Roseberry b Cowans | 0 | †B. N. French not out | | 17 |
| D. W. Randall c Williams b Emburey | 37 | E. E. Hemmings c Keech b Emburey | | 0 |
| *R. T. Robinson c Gatting b Weekes | 23 | K. E. Cooper not out | | 0 |
| P. Johnson c Hutchinson b Williams | 0 | B 1, l-b 11, w 6, n-b 1 | | 19 |
| M. A. Crawley b Weekes | 0 | | | |
| M. Saxelby st Farbrace b Emburey | 22 | 1/0 2/51 3/69 | (9 wkts, 36 overs) | 160 |
| F. D. Stephenson c Weekes b Cowans | 27 | 4/69 5/83 6/128 | | |
| K. P. Evans b Emburey | 6 | 7/134 8/151 9/153 | | |

Bowling: Cowans 7–1–30–2; Hughes 7–0–35–0; Weekes 7–1–20–2; Williams 7–1–25–1; Emburey 8–0–38–4.

## Middlesex

| | | | | |
|---|---|---|---|---|
| I. J. F. Hutchinson lbw b Stephenson | 25 | M. Keech not out | | 14 |
| M. A. Roseberry lbw b Stephenson | 3 | L-b 5, w 5, n-b 1 | | 11 |
| *M. W. Gatting c Robinson | | | | |
|     b Stephenson | 61 | | | |
| K. R. Brown not out | 47 | 1/19 2/31 3/126 | (3 wkts, 33 overs) | 161 |

P. N. Weekes, J. E. Emburey, N. F. Williams, †P. Farbrace, S. P. Hughes and N. G. Cowans did not bat.

Bowling: Cooper 5–0–38–0; Stephenson 8–0–20–3; Evans 7–0–26–0; Hemmings 7–0–30–0; Saxelby 2–0–21–0; Crawley 4–0–21–0.

Umpires: J. D. Bond and M. J. Kitchen.

At The Oval, June 30. NOTTINGHAMSHIRE beat SURREY by eight wickets.

## NOTTINGHAMSHIRE v HAMPSHIRE

At Nottingham, July 14. Nottinghamshire won by three wickets. Toss: Nottinghamshire. Evans hit the last ball for four to put Nottinghamshire back on top of the Sunday League. They had slipped to second the previous week, when they were without a fixture and their closest rivals, Lancashire, had two.

### Hampshire

| | | | |
|---|---|---|---|
| V. P. Terry c Saxelby b Hemmings | 61 | †A. N. Aymes run out | 8 |
| R. A. Smith b Pick | 9 | | |
| J. R. Wood b Pick | 11 | B 1, l-b 10, w 7, n-b 5 | 23 |
| *M. C. J. Nicholas c Hemmings b Evans | 32 | | — |
| K. D. James not out | 28 | 1/23 2/45 3/131 (6 wkts, 40 overs) | 206 |
| J. R. Ayling run out | 34 | 4/132 5/194 6/206 | |

S. D. Udal, R. J. Maru, C. A. Connor and Aqib Javed did not bat.

Bowling: Stephenson 8–1–32–0; Pick 8–1–27–2; Evans 8–0–52–1; Crawley 8–0–49–0; Hemmings 8–0–35–1.

### Nottinghamshire

| | | | |
|---|---|---|---|
| B. C. Broad c Aymes b Connor | 12 | †B. N. French not out | 1 |
| D. W. Randall c Smith b Udal | 83 | K. P. Evans not out | 4 |
| *R. T. Robinson b Maru | 7 | B 4, l-b 9, w 7, n-b 1 | 21 |
| P. Johnson b Udal | 31 | | — |
| M. A. Crawley c Terry b Ayling | 6 | 1/22 2/35 3/122 (7 wkts, 40 overs) | 210 |
| M. Saxelby run out | 24 | 4/146 5/160 | |
| F. D. Stephenson run out | 21 | 6/204 7/206 | |

E. E. Hemmings and R. A. Pick did not bat.

Bowling: Connor 7–0–40–1; Aqib Javed 8–0–43–0; Ayling 7–1–34–1; Maru 8–1–27–1; Udal 8–1–42–2; James 2–0–11–0.

Umpires: J. H. Hampshire and D. O. Oslear.

At Wellingborough School, July 21. NOTTINGHAMSHIRE lost to NORTHAMPTON-SHIRE by 5 runs.

At Hove, July 28. NOTTINGHAMSHIRE beat SUSSEX by six wickets.

## NOTTINGHAMSHIRE v WORCESTERSHIRE

At Nottingham, August 4. Worcestershire won by eight wickets. Toss: Worcestershire. Curtis and Hick, who struck six fours and four sixes in 109 from 98 balls, added 187 in 35 overs after Moody was out to the fifth ball of the innings. It was the second partnership of more than 150 that Curtis had shared with Hick in the Sunday League season, as well as his three with Moody.

### Nottinghamshire

| | | | |
|---|---|---|---|
| B. C. Broad lbw b Newport | 11 | F. D. Stephenson not out | 18 |
| D. W. Randall c and b Illingworth | 50 | †B. N. French not out | 4 |
| *R. T. Robinson c and b Radford | 8 | L-b 10, w 4, n-b 1 | 15 |
| P. Johnson c Hick b Illingworth | 15 | | — |
| P. R. Pollard lbw b Lampitt | 73 | 1/22 2/32 3/70 (6 wkts, 40 overs) | 209 |
| M. Saxelby run out | 12 | 4/125 5/146 6/204 | |

K. P. Evans, E. E. Hemmings and R. A. Pick did not bat.

Bowling: Weston 8–0–22–0; Newport 8–0–38–1; Radford 4–0–25–1; Illingworth 8–1–30–2; Botham 6–0–38–0; Lampitt 6–0–46–1.

## Worcestershire

| | |
|---|---|
| *T. S. Curtis not out . . . . . . . . . . . . . . . | 66 |
| T. M. Moody c French b Pick . . . . . . . . | 0 |
| G. A. Hick b Stephenson . . . . . . . . . . . .| 109 |
| D. B. D'Oliveira not out . . . . . . . . . . . . | 16 |
| L-b 9, w 10, n-b 1 . . . . . . . . . . | 20 |

1/1 2/188          (2 wkts, 39.1 overs) 211

I. T. Botham, M. J. Weston, †S. J. Rhodes, P. J. Newport, R. K. Illingworth, N. V. Radford and S. R. Lampitt did not bat.

Bowling: Pick 8-0-34-1; Stephenson 8-2-26-1; Saxelby 8-1-47-0; Evans 8-0-35-0; Hemmings 7.1-0-60-0.

Umpires: B. Dudleston and R. A. White.

## NOTTINGHAMSHIRE v KENT

At Nottingham, August 11. Nottinghamshire won by four wickets. Toss: Kent. Marsh faced 47 balls for his 56, hitting seven fours and a six, and he added 59 in seven overs with Ellison for the seventh wicket. Pollard's 56 came from 52 deliveries.

### Kent

| | | | | |
|---|---|---|---|---|
| T. R. Ward c Hemmings b Saxelby | 15 | M. J. McCague b Stephenson | | 0 |
| S. G. Hinks b Stephenson | 10 | R. P. Davis not out | | 7 |
| N. R. Taylor c Stephenson b Saxelby | 38 | | | |
| G. R. Cowdrey c Randall b Evans | 26 | L-b 2, w 5, n-b 2 | | 9 |
| M. V. Fleming c Pollard b Saxelby | 9 | | | |
| M. A. Ealham b Pick | 18 | 1/18 2/40 3/78 | (8 wkts, 40 overs) | 217 |
| *†S. A. Marsh b Stephenson | 56 | 4/94 5/104 6/137 | | |
| R. M. Ellison not out | 29 | 7/196 8/196 | | |

T. A. Merrick did not bat.

Bowling: Pick 8-0-32-1; Stephenson 8-0-48-3; Hemmings 8-0-46-0; Saxelby 8-0-40-3; Evans 8-0-49-1.

### Nottinghamshire

| | | | | |
|---|---|---|---|---|
| B. C. Broad b Ealham | 76 | †B. N. French c Ellison b McCague | | 12 |
| D. W. Randall lbw b Ellison | 16 | F. D. Stephenson not out | | 15 |
| *R. T. Robinson c Hinks b Ellison | 30 | L-b 6, w 1, n-b 2 | | 9 |
| P. Johnson b Ealham | 3 | | | |
| P. R. Pollard not out | 56 | 1/51 2/108 3/114 | (6 wkts, 39 overs) | 218 |
| M. Saxelby lbw b Ealham | 1 | 4/156 5/160 6/194 | | |

K. P. Evans, E. E. Hemmings and R. A. Pick did not bat.

Bowling: McCague 6-0-42-1; Merrick 7-0-36-0; Davis 5-0-33-0; Ellison 8-0-29-2; Fleming 5-0-36-0; Ealham 8-0-36-3.

Umpires: J. H. Harris and K. E. Palmer.

At Scarborough, August 18. NOTTINGHAMSHIRE beat YORKSHIRE by two wickets.

## NOTTINGHAMSHIRE v DERBYSHIRE

At Nottingham, August 25. Nottinghamshire won by nine wickets. Toss: Nottinghamshire. The home team defeated the Refuge Assurance champions of 1990 to win the Sunday League for the first time, and so complete the set of the four county competitions in five years. Stephenson's two wickets gave him a final total of 30, the highest in the competition in 1991. Derbyshire's innings had depended heavily on the third-wicket stand between Adams and Azharuddin (56 balls), who added 51 in eight overs; each of them took two sixes off the bowling of Field-Buss. In Nottinghamshire's reply, Broad and Randall hit six fours each.

## Derbyshire

| | | | |
|---|---|---|---|
| *K. J. Barnett c Robinson b Stephenson | 6 | I. Folley not out | 6 |
| C. J. Adams c Johnson b Field-Buss | 47 | S. J. Base c Randall b Stephenson | 4 |
| T. J. G. O'Gorman b Field-Buss | 16 | O. H. Mortensen not out | 1 |
| M. Azharuddin b Saxelby | 53 | L-b 7, w 5, n-b 1 | 13 |
| S. C. Goldsmith run out | 2 | | |
| †K. M. Krikken run out | 15 | 1/12 2/55 3/106　　(9 wkts, 40 overs) 176 | |
| D. G. Cork run out | 11 | 4/110 5/146 6/149 | |
| E. McCray c French b Pick | 2 | 7/160 8/164 9/171 | |

Bowling: Stephenson 8–4–13–2; Pick 8–0–34–1; Saxelby 8–0–38–1; Evans 8–0–41–0; Field-Buss 8–0–43–2.

## Nottinghamshire

| | | |
|---|---|---|
| B. C. Broad not out | 73 | |
| D. W. Randall c Mortensen b Cork | 67 | |
| *R. T. Robinson not out | 25 | |
| L-b 7, w 8 | 15 | |

1/134　　　　　(1 wkt, 37.5 overs) 180

P. Johnson, P. R. Pollard, M. Saxelby, K. P. Evans, †B. N. French, F. D. Stephenson, R. A. Pick and M. G. Field-Buss did not bat.

Bowling: Mortensen 8–0–24–0; Base 6–0–30–0; Cork 8–0–35–1; McCray 8–0–42–0; Folley 4–0–26–0; Goldsmith 3–0–11–0; Azharuddin 0.5–0–5–0.

Umpires: M. J. Kitchen and P. B. Wight.

# SOMERSET

At The Oval, April 21. SOMERSET beat SURREY by two wickets.

## SOMERSET v SUSSEX

At Taunton, April 28. Somerset won by three wickets. Toss: Somerset. Rose reached his half-century from 43 balls, having hit five fours and a six, and was out two balls later.

## Sussex

| | | | |
|---|---|---|---|
| J. W. Hall b Graveney | 50 | I. D. K. Salisbury run out | 2 |
| D. M. Smith c Rose b Lefebvre | 48 | R. A. Bunting not out | 1 |
| *P. W. G. Parker run out | 3 | A. N. Jones not out | 0 |
| A. P. Wells c and b Rose | 38 | B 1, l-b 7, w 1, n-b 1 | 10 |
| K. Greenfield b Lefebvre | 5 | | |
| J. A. North c Cook b Rose | 5 | 1/83 2/87 3/132　　(9 wkts, 39 overs) 188 | |
| †P. Moores b Lefebvre | 12 | 4/142 5/158 6/158 | |
| A. C. S. Pigott run out | 14 | 7/183 8/185 9/187 | |

Bowling: Mallender 8–0–37–0; Lefebvre 8–1–29–3; Rose 5–0–40–2; Swallow 3–0–16–0; Hayhurst 8–0–25–0; Graveney 7–0–33–1.

## Somerset

| | | | |
|---|---|---|---|
| S. J. Cook c Parker b Jones | 33 | R. P. Lefebvre c Wells b North | 4 |
| R. J. Bartlett c Moores b Pigott | 26 | I. G. Swallow not out | 4 |
| *C. J. Tavaré b Salisbury | 15 | L-b 1, w 11 | 12 |
| R. J. Harden c Moores b Jones | 15 | | |
| †N. D. Burns c Moores b North | 6 | 1/42 2/78 3/90　　(7 wkts, 38.3 overs) 191 | |
| G. D. Rose b Bunting | 50 | 4/102 5/111 | |
| A. N. Hayhurst not out | 26 | 6/179 7/186 | |

N. A. Mallender and D. A. Graveney did not bat.

Bowling: Jones 8–0–49–2; Bunting 5–0–27–1; Pigott 8–0–30–1; Salisbury 8–1–16–1; North 5–0–39–2; Greenfield 4.3–0–29–0.

Umpires: J. C. Balderstone and A. G. T. Whitehead.

## SOMERSET v GLAMORGAN

At Taunton, May 12. Somerset won by 35 runs. Toss: Glamorgan. Given impetus by Rose, who scored his 59 in 42 balls, Somerset took 108 off the last ten overs of their innings.

### Somerset

| | | | |
|---|---|---|---|
| R. J. Bartlett c Metson b Frost | 0 | R. P. Lefebvre c Dennis b Barwick | 3 |
| S. J. Cook lbw b Dennis | 10 | | |
| *C. J. Tavaré c Metson b Frost | 46 | B 1, l-b 6, w 6 | 13 |
| R. J. Harden lbw b Croft | 40 | | — |
| G. D. Rose c Morris b Barwick | 59 | 1/1 2/22 3/100 (7 wkts, 40 overs) 225 | |
| †N. D. Burns not out | 52 | 4/108 5/200 | |
| K. H. MacLeay lbw b Frost | 2 | 6/214 7/225 | |

P. M. Roebuck, D. A. Graveney and N. A. Mallender did not bat.

Bowling: Frost 8–0–35–3; Dennis 8–0–36–1; Barwick 8–0–46–2; Dale 8–0–60–0; Shastri 3–0–13–0; Croft 5–1–28–1.

### Glamorgan

| | | | |
|---|---|---|---|
| A. Dale c and b MacLeay | 24 | S. J. Dennis b Lefebvre | 3 |
| *H. Morris b Graveney | 27 | S. R. Barwick not out | 1 |
| M. P. Maynard c Cook b Graveney | 19 | | |
| R. J. Shastri c Tavaré b Roebuck | 27 | B 2, l-b 6, w 1 | 9 |
| G. C. Holmes c Burns b Rose | 33 | | — |
| I. Smith not out | 34 | 1/49 2/69 3/82 (8 wkts, 40 overs) 190 | |
| R. D. B. Croft c Bartlett b Lefebvre | 9 | 4/130 5/142 6/164 | |
| †C. P. Metson c and b Lefebvre | 4 | 7/176 8/189 | |

M. Frost did not bat.

Bowling: Mallender 7–1–29–0; Lefebvre 8–1–30–3; Rose 6–0–43–1; MacLeay 8–0–30–1; Graveney 8–0–39–2; Roebuck 3–0–11–1.

Umpires: R. Julian and M. J. Kitchen.

At Bournemouth, May 19. SOMERSET beat HAMPSHIRE by seven wickets.

## SOMERSET v MIDDLESEX

At Taunton, May 26. Middlesex won by seven wickets. Toss: Middlesex. With Emburey returning his best figures in the competition, and Keech reaching his highest Sunday score as he and Gatting added 87 in under twelve overs, Middlesex brought to an end Somerset's unbeaten start to the season.

### Somerset

| | | | |
|---|---|---|---|
| S. J. Cook b Hughes | 1 | R. P. Lefebvre c Weekes b Emburey | 11 |
| A. N. Hayhurst c Williams b Emburey | 19 | P. M. Roebuck run out | 2 |
| *C. J. Tavaré c Gatting b Hughes | 65 | N. A. Mallender not out | 6 |
| R. J. Harden run out | 35 | L-b 14, w 3, n-b 3 | 20 |
| G. D. Rose c Farbrace b Williams | 0 | | — |
| R. J. Bartlett c Farbrace b Emburey | 6 | 1/3 2/62 3/122 (40 overs) 192 | |
| †N. D. Burns st Farbrace b Emburey | 8 | 4/124 5/137 6/142 | |
| K. H. MacLeay st Farbrace b Emburey | 19 | 7/154 8/182 9/182 | |

Bowling: Hughes 8–0–42–2; Cowans 8–0–31–0; Williams 8–0–40–1; Weekes 8–0–42–0; Emburey 8–0–23–5.

## Middlesex

| | |
|---|---|
| I. J. F. Hutchinson c Lefebvre | M. Keech not out . . . . . . . . . . . . . . . . . 49 |
|           b MacLeay . 20 | |
| M. A. Roseberry c MacLeay b Roebuck 30 | B 1, l-b 9, w 3 . . . . . . . . . . . . . 13 |
| *M. W. Gatting not out . . . . . . . . . . . . 65 | ——— |
| K. R. Brown c Burns b Hayhurst . . . . . . 18 | 1/31 2/70 3/108    (3 wkts, 38 overs) 195 |

†P. Farbrace, J. E. Emburey, P. N. Weekes, N. F. Williams, S. P. Hughes and N. G. Cowans did not bat.

Bowling: Mallender 8–0–36–0; Lefebvre 7–1–39–0; Rose 4–0–18–0; MacLeay 8–0–28–1; Roebuck 7–0–47–1; Hayhurst 4–0–17–1.

Umpires: J. H. Harris and B. J. Meyer.

At Birmingham, June 2. WARWICKSHIRE v SOMERSET. No result.

At Nottingham, June 9. SOMERSET lost to NOTTINGHAMSHIRE by 4 runs.

At Derby, June 16. SOMERSET beat DERBYSHIRE by 46 runs.

## SOMERSET v GLOUCESTERSHIRE

At Bath, June 23. No result.

At Luton, June 30. SOMERSET lost to NORTHAMPTONSHIRE by four wickets.

## SOMERSET v LANCASHIRE

At Taunton, July 5. Lancashire won by eight wickets. Toss: Lancashire. Originally scheduled for July 14, this match, played on a Friday because of Lancashire's Benson and Hedges Cup Final commitments, was the first in the Sunday League not to be staged on a Sunday. Somerset, 170 for two in the 34th over, collapsed badly, and with Mendis (five fours and a six in 83 balls) and Lloyd (seven fours in 94 balls) adding 117 for the second wicket, Lancashire ran out comfortable winners.

## Somerset

| | |
|---|---|
| S. J. Cook b Austin . . . . . . . . . . . . . . . . 53 | A. N. Hayhurst not out . . . . . . . . . . . . . 2 |
| P. M. Roebuck c Hegg b Wasim Akram 20 | H. R. J. Trump not out . . . . . . . . . . . . . 2 |
| *C. J. Tavaré run out . . . . . . . . . . . . . . 57 | |
| R. J. Harden c Hegg b Watkinson . . 25 | B 2, l-b 4, w 4, n-b 6 . . . . . . . . 21 |
| N. J. Pringle c Allott b Wasim Akram . 7 | ——— |
| †N. D. Burns c and b Austin . . . . . . . . . 6 | 1/53 2/104 3/170    (8 wkts, 40 overs) 196 |
| R. P. Lefebvre run out . . . . . . . . . . . . 2 | 4/173 5/185 6/187 |
| K. H. MacLeay b Austin . . . . . . . . . . . . 1 | 7/192 8/192 |

J. C. Hallett did not bat.

Bowling: Allott 8–0–41–0; Martin 8–1–32–0; Wasim Akram 8–0–30–2; Watkinson 8–0–42–1; Austin 8–0–40–3.

## Lancashire

| | |
|---|---|
| G. D. Mendis c Tavaré b Hallett | 79 |
| G. Fowler c Hallett b MacLeay | 20 |
| G. D. Lloyd not out | 78 |
| *N. H. Fairbrother not out | 12 |
| L-b 4, w 2, n-b 2 | 8 |

1/38 2/155          (2 wkts, 37 overs) 197

M. Watkinson, Wasim Akram, †W. K. Hegg, I. D. Austin, N. J. Speak, P. J. W. Allott and P. J. Martin did not bat.

Bowling: Lefebvre 7-0-35-0; Hallett 7-0-33-1; MacLeay 7-0-25-1; Roebuck 4-0-26-0; Trump 8-0-59-0; Hayhurst 4-0-15-0.

Umpires: D. O. Oslear and R. C. Tolchard.

At Southend, July 21. SOMERSET lost to ESSEX by 30 runs.

## SOMERSET v KENT

At Taunton, July 28. Kent won by 35 runs. Toss: Kent. Cowdrey's 50 for Kent came from 44 balls, and later his team-mate, Fleming, returned his best bowling figures in the competition.

### Kent

| | | | |
|---|---|---|---|
| *M. R. Benson c Tavaré b Hallett | 8 | M. J. McCague b Lefebvre | 4 |
| T. R. Ward st Burns b Graveney | 56 | T. A. Merrick not out | 13 |
| N. R. Taylor st Burns b Graveney | 36 | A. P. Igglesden not out | 3 |
| S. G. Hinks st Burns b Graveney | 11 | L-b 5, w 8, n-b 1 | 14 |
| G. R. Cowdrey b Lefebvre | 50 | | |
| M. V. Fleming st Burns b Trump | 20 | 1/17 2/107 3/114 (9 wkts, 40 overs) 220 |
| †S. A. Marsh lbw b Trump | 3 | 4/121 5/163 6/181 |
| R. P. Davis c Roebuck b Lefebvre | 2 | 7/186 8/203 9/208 |

Bowling: Hallett 6-0-25-1; Lefebvre 7-1-30-3; Rose 3-0-25-0; Graveney 8-1-21-3; Trump 8-0-58-2; Roebuck 8-0-56-0.

### Somerset

| | | | |
|---|---|---|---|
| S. J. Cook c Marsh b Merrick | 1 | H. R. J. Trump b Igglesden | 19 |
| P. M. Roebuck c and b Fleming | 34 | J. C. Hallett c Cowdrey b Igglesden | 1 |
| *C. J. Tavaré b Fleming | 19 | D. A. Graveney not out | 14 |
| R. J. Harden b Fleming | 46 | W 4 | 4 |
| M. N. Lathwell st Marsh b Davis | 15 | | |
| †N. D. Burns c Marsh b Davis | 5 | 1/9 2/48 3/82 (38.1 overs) 185 |
| G. D. Rose lbw b Igglesden | 0 | 4/107 5/115 6/117 |
| R. P. Lefebvre c Ward b Fleming | 27 | 7/130 8/163 9/165 |

Bowling: Merrick 8-0-33-1; Igglesden 8-0-38-3; McCague 7-0-42-0; Fleming 7.1-0-45-4; Davis 8-0-27-2.

Umpires: J. H. Harris and R. Julian.

## SOMERSET v LEICESTERSHIRE

At Weston-super-Mare, August 4. Leicestershire won by seven wickets. Toss: Leicestershire. Whitaker hit ten fours and two sixes in making 85 from 104 balls.

## Somerset

| | | | |
|---|---|---|---|
| S. J. Cook lbw b Mullally | 2 | †N. D. Burns not out | 51 |
| P. M. Roebuck c Whitticase b Lewis | 10 | G. D. Rose not out | 0 |
| *C. J. Tavaré c Benson b Wilkinson | 41 | L-b 9, n-b 1 | 10 |
| R. J. Harden c Whitticase b Mullally | 4 | | — |
| M. N. Lathwell c Briers b Benson | 20 | 1/9 2/23 3/38 (6 wkts, 40 overs) 173 |
| A. N. Hayhurst c Mullally b Maguire | 35 | 4/84 5/84 6/170 | |

R. P. Lefebvre, J. C. Hallett and H. R. J. Trump did not bat.

Bowling: Lewis 8-1-31-1; Mullally 8-1-19-2; Maguire 8-1-42-1; Benson 8-0-37-1; Wilkinson 8-0-35-1.

## Leicestershire

| | | | |
|---|---|---|---|
| J. J. Whitaker c Lathwell b Roebuck | 85 | L. Potter not out | 13 |
| *N. E. Briers st Burns b Roebuck | 26 | B 1, l-b 8, w 3 | 12 |
| B. F. Smith b Rose | 22 | | — |
| C. C. Lewis not out | 18 | 1/93 2/141 3/150 (3 wkts, 39.1 overs) 176 |

J. D. R. Benson, P. N. Hepworth, †P. Whitticase, C. W. Wilkinson, A. D. Mullally and J. N. Maguire did not bat.

Bowling: Lefebvre 8-0-24-0; Hallett 6-0-29-0; Rose 5.1-0-33-1; Lathwell 4-0-19-0; Trump 8-1-30-0; Roebuck 8-1-32-2.

Umpires: B. Hassan and B. J. Meyer.

At Worcester, August 18. SOMERSET beat WORCESTERSHIRE by 18 runs.

## SOMERSET v YORKSHIRE

At Taunton, August 25. Somerset won by 46 runs. Toss: Somerset. Tavaré's 65 not out came from 66 balls.

## Somerset

| | | | |
|---|---|---|---|
| S. J. Cook c and b Carrick | 44 | †N. D. Burns not out | 25 |
| G. T. J. Townsend c Moxon b Carrick | 27 | | |
| R. J. Harden c P. E. Robinson b Carrick | 29 | | |
| *C. J. Tavaré not out | 65 | B 6, l-b 3, w 7, n-b 1 | 17 |
| G. D. Rose c and b Batty | 3 | | — |
| A. N. Hayhurst c Gough | | 1/77 2/88 3/136 (5 wkts, 40 overs) 224 |
| b M. A. Robinson | 14 | 4/148 5/178 | |

D. Beal, H. R. J. Trump, D. A. Graveney and J. C. Hallett did not bat.

Bowling: M. A. Robinson 7-0-48-1; Gough 8-0-45-0; Pickles 6-0-30-0; Kellett 3-0-16-0; Carrick 8-0-38-3; Batty 8-0-38-1.

## Yorkshire

| | | | |
|---|---|---|---|
| *M. D. Moxon b Rose | 0 | D. Gough c Trump b Hallett | 6 |
| A. A. Metcalfe c Townsend b Trump | 49 | J. D. Batty b Hayhurst | 12 |
| †R. J. Blakey c Burns b Rose | 1 | M. A. Robinson b Hayhurst | 2 |
| D. Byas run out | 2 | B 3, l-b 13, w 7 | 23 |
| P. E. Robinson run out | 39 | | — |
| S. A. Kellett b Hallett | 10 | 1/0 2/12 3/17 (37.1 overs) 178 |
| C. S. Pickles b Graveney | 16 | 4/102 5/107 6/132 | |
| P. Carrick not out | 18 | 7/137 8/149 9/172 | |

Bowling: Rose 7-0-21-2; Hallett 8-0-32-2; Hayhurst 6.1-0-27-2; Graveney 8-0-44-1; Trump 8-0-38-1.

Umpires: J. C. Balderstone and N. T. Plews.

# SURREY

## SURREY v SOMERSET

At The Oval, April 21. Somerset won by two wickets. Toss: Somerset. Rain interrupted Somerset's innings, so that their target was adjusted to 104 off 22 overs.

### Surrey

| | | | | |
|---|---|---|---|---|
| †A. J. Stewart c Tavaré b Rose | 14 | *I. A. Greig c Burns b Beal | 30 |
| A. D. Brown run out | 3 | C. K. Bullen not out | 2 |
| G. P. Thorpe c Hayhurst b Beal | 8 | L-b 7, w 6, n-b 4 | 17 |
| D. M. Ward b Lefebvre | 51 | | |
| M. A. Lynch c Burns b Rose | 9 | 1/6 2/28 3/30 | (6 wkts, 40 overs) 189 |
| J. D. Robinson not out | 55 | 4/69 5/129 6/180 | |

M. P. Bicknell, Waqar Younis and A. J. Murphy did not bat.

Bowling: Mallender 8-0-38-0; Lefebvre 8-0-27-1; Rose 8-0-30-2; Beal 8-0-40-2; Hayhurst 8-0-47-0.

### Somerset

| | | | | |
|---|---|---|---|---|
| S. J. Cook b Waqar Younis | 31 | R. P. Lefebvre not out | 15 |
| R. J. Bartlett c Stewart b Waqar Younis | 34 | N. A. Mallender run out | 0 |
| *C. J. Tavaré c Stewart b Thorpe | 0 | D. A. Graveney not out | 4 |
| R. J. Harden c Robinson b Thorpe | 2 | B 1, l-b 7, w 2 | 10 |
| G. D. Rose b Thorpe | 2 | | |
| †N. D. Burns b Waqar Younis | 5 | 1/73 2/74 3/76 | (8 wkts, 21.4 overs) 104 |
| A. N. Hayhurst c Stewart | | 4/79 5/80 6/84 | |
| b Waqar Younis | 1 | 7/85 8/85 | |

D. Beal did not bat.

Bowling: Bicknell 4-0-24-0; Murphy 6-0-21-0; Waqar Younis 7.4-0-30-4; Thorpe 4-0-21-3.

Umpires: D. J. Constant and M. J. Kitchen.


At Lord's, April 28. SURREY beat MIDDLESEX by four wickets.


## SURREY v GLOUCESTERSHIRE

At The Oval, May 12. Gloucestershire won by 25 runs. Toss: Surrey. Wright's 71, from 84 balls, contained nine fours and a six, but it was Alleyne, needing only 24 balls for his 37, who caught the eye as Gloucestershire added 86 in the last ten overs. After Surrey had limped to 91 for five, Thorpe and Robinson put on 66 in as many balls for the sixth wicket.

### Gloucestershire

| | | | | |
|---|---|---|---|---|
| C. W. J. Athey c Greig b Murphy | 79 | P. W. Romaines not out | 5 |
| R. J. Scott b M. P. Bicknell | 2 | B 1, l-b 10, w 9 | 20 |
| *A. J. Wright b Murphy | 71 | | |
| M. W. Alleyne b Waqar Younis | 37 | 1/6 2/145 3/194 | (5 wkts, 40 overs) 225 |
| †R. C. Russell b Murphy | 11 | 4/213 5/225 | |

S. N. Barnes, J. W. Lloyds, D. R. Gilbert, A. M. Smith and A. M. Babington did not bat.

Bowling: M. P. Bicknell 8-1-41-1; Murphy 8-1-45-3; Robinson 8-0-40-0; Boiling 3-0-19-0; Waqar Younis 8-1-43-1; Greig 3-0-16-0; Thorpe 2-0-10-0.

## Surrey

| | | |
|---|---|---|
| D. J. Bicknell run out | 36 | J. Boiling c Lloyds b Babington | 4 |
| A. D. Brown c Russell b Gilbert | 10 | Waqar Younis c Wright b Gilbert | 8 |
| †A. J. Stewart c Russell b Alleyne | 9 | A. J. Murphy not out | 1 |
| D. M. Ward c Russell b Babington | 3 | L-b 5, w 10 | 15 |
| G. P. Thorpe c Russell b Barnes | 47 | | |
| *I. A. Greig c Athey b Scott | 5 | 1/24 2/43 3/50 (39.4 overs) 200 |
| J. D. Robinson c Romaines b Babington | 50 | 4/76 5/91 6/157 |
| M. P. Bicknell run out | 12 | 7/179 8/191 9/191 |

Bowling: Gilbert 7.4–0–27–2; Barnes 8–0–33–1; Smith 0.3–0–3–0; Alleyne 7.3–0–32–1; Babington 8–0–39–3; Scott 7–0–52–1; Athey 1–0–9–0.

Umpires: H. D. Bird and R. Palmer.

## SURREY v ESSEX

At The Oval, May 26. Surrey won by seven wickets. Toss: Surrey. Lynch, who struck eight fours and a six from 117 balls, put on 97 in fifteen overs with Brown at the start of Surrey's reply. Medlycott captained Surrey in the absence of the injured Greig.

### Essex

| | | |
|---|---|---|
| J. P. Stephenson b Waqar Younis | 64 | T. D. Topley b Waqar Younis | 3 |
| P. J. Prichard b Murphy | 4 | S. J. W. Andrew c Ward b Murphy | 8 |
| Salim Malik c Sargeant b Feltham | 3 | P. M. Such not out | 1 |
| N. Hussain c Medlycott b Robinson | 22 | L-b 6, w 6, n-b 1 | 13 |
| N. Shahid c Lynch b Murphy | 16 | | |
| K. A. Butler lbw b Waqar Younis | 1 | 1/10 2/31 3/77 (9 wkts, 40 overs) 173 |
| *N. A. Foster not out | 27 | 4/121 5/126 6/139 |
| †D. E. East run out | 2 | 7/144 8/148 9/162 |

Bowling: Feltham 8–0–22–1; Murphy 8–0–28–3; Robinson 8–1–28–1; Bullen 6–0–45–0; Thorpe 2–0–17–0; Waqar Younis 8–1–27–3.

### Surrey

| | | |
|---|---|---|
| M. A. Lynch c Salim Malik b Andrew | 85 | J. D. Robinson not out | 2 |
| A. D. Brown c Prichard b Foster | 45 | L-b 6, w 2 | 8 |
| D. M. Ward c Butler b Topley | 5 | | |
| G. P. Thorpe not out | 29 | 1/97 2/103 3/167 (3 wkts, 38.2 overs) 174 |

†N. F. Sargeant, *K. T. Medlycott, C. K. Bullen, M. A. Feltham, A. J. Murphy and Waqar Younis did not bat.

Bowling: Andrew 8–1–44–1; Foster 6–0–22–1; Topley 8–1–28–1; Such 8–1–46–0; Stephenson 4–0–16–0; Salim Malik 4.2–1–12–0.

Umpires: B. Hassan and A. G. T. Whitehead.

At Worcester, June 2. WORCESTERSHIRE v SURREY. No result.

At Chesterfield, June 9. SURREY beat DERBYSHIRE on scoring-rate.

At Leicester, June 16. SURREY beat LEICESTERSHIRE by 51 runs.

At Birmingham, June 23. WARWICKSHIRE v SURREY. No result.

## SURREY v NOTTINGHAMSHIRE

At The Oval, June 30. Nottinghamshire won by eight wickets. Toss: Nottinghamshire. Nottinghamshire's target was adjusted to 162 from 35 overs after rain interrupted their innings in the ninth over. Broad (88 balls) and Randall had seen them to victory by the time Waqar Younis, in his last over, dismissed Randall and Johnson with consecutive balls.

### Surrey

| | | | |
|---|---|---|---|
| D. J. Bicknell run out | 64 | M. P. Bicknell c Robinson b Stephenson | 11 |
| M. A. Lynch c Johnson b Hemmings | 33 | Waqar Younis run out | 0 |
| †A. J. Stewart lbw b Stephenson | 1 | | |
| D. M. Ward c and b Crawley | 4 | L-b 7, w 6, n-b 2 | 15 |
| G. P. Thorpe c Crawley b Evans | 34 | | |
| J. D. Robinson b Evans | 6 | 1/98 2/100 3/111 (9 wkts, 40 overs) | 185 |
| *I. A. Greig c and b Crawley | 3 | 4/116 5/139 6/150 | |
| M. A. Feltham not out | 14 | 7/161 8/185 9/185 | |

A. J. Murphy did not bat.

Bowling: Pick 6–0–24–0; Stephenson 8–1–27–2; Evans 8–0–43–2; Saxelby 4–0–28–0; Hemmings 8–0–36–1; Crawley 6–1–20–2.

### Nottinghamshire

| | | |
|---|---|---|
| B. C. Broad not out | 79 | |
| D. W. Randall b Waqar Younis | 67 | |
| P. Johnson lbw b Waqar Younis | 0 | |
| *R. T. Robinson not out | 3 | |
| L-b 7, w 6 | 13 | |

1/154 2/154      (2 wkts, 32 overs) 162

M. A. Crawley, M. Saxelby, F. D. Stephenson, †B. N. French, K. P. Evans, E. E. Hemmings and R. A. Pick did not bat.

Bowling: Murphy 8–0–26–0; M. P. Bicknell 8–0–39–0; Feltham 6–0–43–0; Waqar Younis 8–0–33–2; Robinson 2–0–14–0.

Umpires: H. D. Bird and B. Leadbeater.

At Tring, July 7. SURREY lost to NORTHAMPTONSHIRE by 15 runs.

## SURREY v SUSSEX

At The Oval, July 14. Surrey won by eight wickets. Toss: Sussex. An unbroken third-wicket partnership of 120, from 128 balls, between Stewart (four fours) and Ward (57 balls, five fours) carried the home side to victory.

### Sussex

| | | | |
|---|---|---|---|
| N. J. Lenham c Stewart b Feltham | 11 | A. C. S. Pigott c Stewart b Feltham | 14 |
| *P. W. G. Parker c Thorpe b Robinson | 60 | I. D. K. Salisbury b Feltham | 8 |
| D. M. Smith st Stewart b Boiling | 19 | A. N. Jones not out | 0 |
| M. P. Speight c Ward b Boiling | 9 | B 1, l-b 10, w 4, n-b 3 | 18 |
| K. Greenfield run out | 22 | | |
| C. M. Wells c Feltham b Murphy | 10 | 1/27 2/66 3/95 (9 wkts, 40 overs) | 190 |
| A. I. C. Dodemaide not out | 17 | 4/134 5/137 6/151 | |
| †P. Moores c Stewart b Murphy | 2 | 7/154 8/174 9/189 | |

Bowling: Feltham 8–0–44–3; Murphy 8–1–36–2; Robinson 8–0–39–1; Boiling 8–0–24–2; Waqar Younis 8–1–36–0.

## Surrey

| | |
|---|---|
| D. J. Bicknell c Smith b Lenham | 40 |
| M. A. Lynch c Smith b Dodemaide | 6 |
| †A. J. Stewart not out | 84 |
| D. M. Ward not out | 51 |
| L-b 4, w 9 | 13 |

1/7 2/74    (2 wkts, 38.5 overs) 194

G. P. Thorpe, *I. A. Greig, J. D. Robinson, M. A. Feltham, J. Boiling, Waqar Younis and A. J. Murphy did not bat.

Bowling: Dodemaide 7–1–32–1; Wells 7–0–26–0; Pigott 7.5–0–43–0; Salisbury 8–0–52–0; Lenham 2–0–12–1; Jones 7–1–25–0.

Umpires: J. H. Harris and P. B. Wight.

---

### SURREY v YORKSHIRE

At The Oval, July 21. Yorkshire won by eight wickets. Toss: Yorkshire. For Yorkshire, Moxon scored his highest innings, with fourteen fours and a six, and Mark Robinson returned his best figures in the competition. Surrey's Lynch reached 4,000 runs in the League.

## Surrey

| | | | |
|---|---|---|---|
| D. J. Bicknell lbw b M. A. Robinson | 7 | J. Boiling run out | 1 |
| M. A. Lynch b Grayson | 97 | Waqar Younis not out | 0 |
| †A. J. Stewart c Blakey b Hartley | 5 | | |
| D. M. Ward c Blakey b M. A. Robinson | 56 | L-b 4, w 7, n-b 3 | 14 |
| G. P. Thorpe c Moxon b Fletcher | 4 | | |
| *I. A. Greig b M. A. Robinson | 15 | 1/9 2/23 3/179  (8 wkts, 40 overs) 227 |
| J. D. Robinson b M. A. Robinson | 16 | 4/179 5/185 6/205 |
| M. A. Feltham not out | 12 | 7/224 8/226 |

A. J. Murphy did not bat.

Bowling: Hartley 8–0–25–1; M. A. Robinson 8–1–33–4; Pickles 8–0–48–0; Fletcher 8–0–51–1; Batty 3–0–34–0; Grayson 5–0–32–1.

## Yorkshire

| | |
|---|---|
| *M. D. Moxon not out | 129 |
| A. A. Metcalfe c Feltham b Boiling | 31 |
| †R. J. Blakey c Stewart b Waqar Younis | 24 |
| D. Byas not out | 28 |
| L-b 11, w 5 | 16 |

1/89 2/161    (2 wkts, 36.1 overs) 228

P. E. Robinson, C. S. Pickles, A. P. Grayson, P. J. Hartley, M. A. Robinson, J. D. Batty and S. D. Fletcher did not bat.

Bowling: Murphy 7–0–46–0; Feltham 6.1–0–41–0; Robinson 5–0–26–0; Waqar Younis 8–0–34–1; Boiling 8–0–54–1; Greig 2–0–16–0.

Umpires: D. O. Oslear and R. A. White.

---

### SURREY v GLAMORGAN

At The Oval, July 28. Glamorgan won by 3 runs. Toss: Surrey. Mark Butcher made a spectacular début for Surrey, almost robbing his father Alan's team of victory. Coming in at 121 for seven, he scored his unbeaten 48 in 36 balls, and added an undefeated 58 in 6.2 overs for the ninth wicket with Bullen. The match provided the first instance in the Sunday League of a father and son playing against each other.

## Glamorgan

| | | | |
|---|--:|---|--:|
| M. P. Maynard b Robinson | 51 | †C. P. Metson not out | 18 |
| M. J. Cann lbw b Feltham | 2 | S. R. Barwick c Lynch b Bullen | 3 |
| A. Dale c Feltham b Robinson | 23 | D. J. Foster not out | 0 |
| *A. R. Butcher c Ward b Greig | 39 | L-b 7, w 8, n-b 1 | 16 |
| P. A. Cottey c Thorpe b Feltham | 47 | | |
| D. L. Hemp lbw b Bullen | 7 | 1/14 2/74 3/93 | (9 wkts, 40 overs) 225 |
| S. Kirnon lbw b Bullen | 0 | 4/150 5/182 6/182 | |
| R. D. B. Croft b Bullen b Feltham | 19 | 7/189 8/206 9/221 | |

Bowling: Feltham 8–0–60–3; Butcher 3–0–16–0; Robinson 8–0–32–2; Boiling 8–0–51–0; Bullen 8–0–38–3; Greig 5–0–21–1.

## Surrey

| | | | |
|---|--:|---|--:|
| D. J. Bicknell c Metson b Kirnon | 31 | M. A. Butcher not out | 48 |
| M. A. Lynch c Butcher b Barwick | 28 | C. K. Bullen not out | 22 |
| †A. J. Stewart c Foster b Dale | 3 | | |
| D. M. Ward c Metson b Dale | 0 | L-b 5, w 7 | 12 |
| G. P. Thorpe c Croft b Kirnon | 58 | | |
| J. D. Robinson c and b Croft | 8 | 1/53 2/58 3/58 | (8 wkts, 40 overs) 222 |
| *I. A. Greig b Barwick | 5 | 4/79 5/97 6/102 | |
| M. A. Feltham c Maynard b Croft | 7 | 7/121 8/164 | |

J. Boiling did not bat.

Bowling: Foster 8–0–39–0; Kirnon 8–0–48–2; Dale 8–1–48–2; Barwick 8–0–44–2; Croft 8–0–38–2.

Umpires: J. H. Hampshire and M. J. Kitchen.

At Canterbury, August 4. SURREY beat KENT by six wickets.

At Manchester, August 18. SURREY beat LANCASHIRE by 21 runs.

## SURREY v HAMPSHIRE

At The Oval, August 25. Hampshire won by three wickets. Toss: Hampshire. Ayling's highest score in the League helped Hampshire to their first win since May 12. This saved them from becoming the third team, after Glamorgan in 1972 and Warwickshire in 1979, to finish a season with only ten points.

## Surrey

| | | | |
|---|--:|---|--:|
| G. P. Thorpe c Cox b Aqib Javed | 1 | †N. F. Sargeant not out | 13 |
| A. D. Brown b Connor | 16 | J. Boiling not out | 12 |
| D. M. Ward st Aymes b Udal | 29 | L-b 5, w 8, n-b 1 | 14 |
| M. A. Lynch c Ayling b Maru | 32 | | |
| J. D. Robinson c Maru b James | 33 | 1/9 2/21 3/75 | (7 wkts, 40 overs) 167 |
| *I. A. Greig c Aymes b Ayling | 10 | 4/98 5/118 | |
| M. A. Feltham run out | 7 | 6/136 7/142 | |

A. G. Robson and A. J. Murphy did not bat.

Bowling: Connor 6–1–19–1; Aqib Javed 8–0–36–1; Ayling 8–0–34–1; James 5–0–20–1; Udal 8–1–19–1; Maru 5–0–34–1.

## Hampshire

| | | | |
|---|---|---|---|
| R. M. F. Cox b Robinson | 13 | R. J. Maru b Robson | 10 |
| V. P. Terry b Robson | 8 | S. D. Udal not out | 16 |
| J. R. Wood b Murphy | 3 | L-b 2, w 8, n-b 1 | 11 |
| J. R. Ayling c Murphy b Robinson | 56 | | — |
| †A. N. Aymes b Robson | 29 | 1/16 2/19 3/57 (7 wkts, 39.4 overs) 171 | |
| K. D. James c Robinson b Boiling | 1 | 4/116 5/118 | |
| *M. C. J. Nicholas not out | 24 | 6/118 7/140 | |

C. A. Connor and Aqib Javed did not bat.

Bowling: Murphy 8–0–32–1; Robson 8–0–42–3; Feltham 7–0–20–0; Robinson 8–0–34–2; Boiling 8–0–35–1; Lynch 0.4–0–6–0.

Umpires: G. I. Burgess and R. A. White.

# SUSSEX

At Birmingham, April 21. SUSSEX lost to WARWICKSHIRE by 21 runs.

At Taunton, April 28. SUSSEX lost to SOMERSET by three wickets.

## SUSSEX v MIDDLESEX

At Hove, May 12. Middlesex won by five wickets. Toss: Sussex. Ramprakash faced 68 balls for his unbeaten 62, and added 84 in seventeen overs with Keech for the fourth wicket. Bunting's figures were his best in the competition.

### Sussex

| | | | |
|---|---|---|---|
| †P. Moores b Emburey | 25 | A. C. S. Pigott c Gatting b Ramprakash | 10 |
| J. W. Hall c Fraser b Hughes | 34 | I. D. K. Salisbury not out | 2 |
| *P. W. G. Parker lbw b Fraser | 33 | L-b 5, w 1, n-b 4 | 10 |
| A. P. Wells c Williams b Emburey | 10 | | — |
| M. P. Speight c Brown b Ramprakash | 15 | 1/65 2/65 3/81 (6 wkts, 40 overs) 171 | |
| K. Greenfield not out | 32 | 4/104 5/148 6/161 | |

A. N. Jones, E. S. H. Giddins and R. A. Bunting did not bat.

Bowling: Williams 4–0–18–0; Ellcock 5–0–25–0; Hughes 8–1–39–1; Emburey 8–2–18–2; Fraser 8–0–34–1; Ramprakash 7–0–32–2.

### Middlesex

| | | | |
|---|---|---|---|
| *M. W. Gatting c Wells b Bunting | 25 | J. E. Emburey not out | 2 |
| M. A. Roseberry c Speight b Bunting | 21 | | |
| M. R. Ramprakash not out | 62 | B 1, l-b 6, w 10 | 17 |
| K. R. Brown run out | 4 | | — |
| M. Keech b Bunting | 38 | 1/56 2/59 3/68 (5 wkts, 38.3 overs) 172 | |
| †P. R. Downton c Wells b Bunting | 3 | 4/152 5/158 | |

N. F. Williams, A. R. C. Fraser, S. P. Hughes and R. M. Ellcock did not bat.

Bowling: Jones 4–0–23–0; Pigott 7–0–28–0; Bunting 7.3–0–35–4; Giddins 5–0–19–0; Salisbury 8–0–23–0; Greenfield 7–0–37–0.

Umpires: D. O. Oslear and K. E. Palmer.

## SUSSEX v GLOUCESTERSHIRE

At Hove, May 19. Gloucestershire won by 62 runs. Toss: Gloucestershire. Alleyne, with his highest score of the competition, from 55 balls, and Russell (42 balls) revived Gloucestershire from a position of 79 for three.

### Gloucestershire

| | | |
|---|---|---|
| C. W. J. Athey b Jones | 3 | D. R. Gilbert not out .......... 0 |
| R. J. Scott b Donelan | 44 | A. M. Smith not out ........... 1 |
| *A. J. Wright b Salisbury | 20 | |
| M. W. Alleyne c Lenham b Jones | 59 | L-b 14, w 14, n-b 1 ......... 29 |
| †R. C. Russell c and b Jones | 42 | |
| P. W. Romaines c North b Pigott | 2 | 1/22 2/75 3/79  (8 wkts, 40 overs) 207 |
| J. W. Lloyds c Donelan b Pigott | 7 | 4/189 5/193 6/198 |
| D. V. Lawrence b Pigott | 0 | 7/206 8/206 |

A. M. Babington did not bat.

Bowling: Jones 8–2–25–3; Pigott 8–0–40–3; Donelan 8–1–35–1; North 7–0–44–0; Salisbury 7–1–36–1; Greenfield 2–0–13–0.

### Sussex

| | | |
|---|---|---|
| D. M. Smith c Athey b Alleyne | 40 | I. D. K. Salisbury c Smith b Babington. 14 |
| J. W. Hall c Babington b Lawrence | 12 | B. T. P. Donelan b Smith ......... 19 |
| N. J. Lenham b Babington | 12 | A. N. Jones not out ............. 0 |
| *A. P. Wells c Lloyds b Smith | 3 | L-b 9, w 3, n-b 1 ......... 13 |
| K. Greenfield c Wright b Smith | 5 | |
| J. A. North c Russell b Alleyne | 14 | 1/32 2/45 3/53  (35.1 overs) 145 |
| †P. Moores c Russell b Athey | 6 | 4/59 5/79 6/95 |
| A. C. S. Pigott st Russell b Athey | 7 | 7/106 8/112 9/136 |

Bowling: Gilbert 6–0–27–0; Babington 8–0–26–2; Lawrence 8–0–30–1; Smith 4.1–0–16–3; Alleyne 5–0–19–2; Athey 4–0–18–2.

Umpires: H. D. Bird and R. C. Tolchard.

At Swansea, May 26. SUSSEX beat GLAMORGAN by 113 runs.

At Manchester, June 2. SUSSEX lost to LANCASHIRE by 53 runs.

At Basingstoke, June 9. SUSSEX beat HAMPSHIRE by 14 runs.

## SUSSEX v WORCESTERSHIRE

At Hove, June 16. No result. Toss: Worcestershire. Speight's maiden hundred in the League – he was still undefeated when rain stopped play – came in 68 balls, with the second fifty coming in only 23. He hit four sixes off the bowling of Newport, whose last three overs cost 44 runs, as well as eleven fours, and together with Alan Wells he added 152 in 21 overs for the third wicket.

### Sussex

| | | |
|---|---|---|
| N. J. Lenham b Radford | 8 | K. Greenfield not out ........ 4 |
| *P. W. G. Parker b Weston | 14 | L-b 8, w 2, n-b 2 ......... 12 |
| A. P. Wells c Neale b Hick | 58 | |
| M. P. Speight not out | 106 | 1/18 2/24 3/176  (3 wkts, 30.2 overs) 202 |

C. M. Wells, A. I. C. Dodemaide, A. C. S. Pigott, †P. Moores, I. D. K. Salisbury and A. N. Jones did not bat.

Bowling: Radford 5–0–11–1; Weston 8–0–33–1; Newport 8–0–70–0; Illingworth 4–0–40–0; Lampitt 4–0–35–0; Hick 1.2–0–5–1.

## Worcestershire

T. S. Curtis, T. M. Moody, G. A. Hick, M. J. Weston, D. B. D'Oliveira, *P. A. Neale, †S. J. Rhodes, P. J. Newport, R. K. Illingworth, N. V. Radford and S. R. Lampitt.

Umpires: H. D. Bird and J. H. Harris.

## SUSSEX v ESSEX

At Horsham, June 23. No result.

At Derby, July 7. SUSSEX beat DERBYSHIRE by 5 runs.

At The Oval, July 14. SUSSEX lost to SURREY by eight wickets.

## SUSSEX v LEICESTERSHIRE

At Hove, July 21. Sussex won by 14 runs. Toss: Sussex.

### Sussex

| | | | | |
|---|--:|---|---|--:|
| N. J. Lenham c Nixon b Lewis | 10 | †P. Moores not out | | 4 |
| *P. W. G. Parker b Lewis | 104 | A. C. S. Pigott not out | | 1 |
| A. P. Wells c Maguire b Hepworth | 36 | B 1, l-b 2, w 3 | | 6 |
| M. P. Speight lbw b Maguire | 4 | | | — |
| K. Greenfield c Nixon b Maguire | 13 | 1/19 2/80 3/96 | (7 wkts, 40 overs) | 203 |
| C. M. Wells c Nixon b Hepworth | 7 | 4/139 5/151 | | |
| A. I. C. Dodemaide c Lewis b Benson | 18 | 6/192 7/199 | | |

I. D. K. Salisbury and A. N. Jones did not bat.

Bowling: Millns 6–0–24–0; Lewis 8–1–33–2; Benson 7–0–40–1; Tennant 3–0–26–0; Maguire 8–0–34–2; Hepworth 8–0–43–2.

### Leicestershire

| | | | | |
|---|--:|---|---|--:|
| J. J. Whitaker c Moores b Jones | 17 | D. J. Millns not out | | 10 |
| *N. E. Briers c Moores b Jones | 20 | L. Tennant c Speight b Jones | | 0 |
| B. F. Smith c Moores b Jones | 0 | J. N. Maguire not out | | 0 |
| L. Potter c Parker b Pigott | 59 | L-b 9, w 7, n-b 1 | | 17 |
| C. C. Lewis run out | 36 | | | |
| J. D. R. Benson run out | 23 | 1/40 2/40 3/46 | (9 wkts, 40 overs) | 189 |
| P. N. Hepworth b Pigott | 2 | 4/113 5/169 6/170 | | |
| †P. A. Nixon lbw b Jones | 5 | 7/173 8/188 9/188 | | |

Bowling: C. M. Wells 8–0–36–0; Dodemaide 8–2–19–0; Pigott 8–1–35–2; Jones 8–0–32–5; Salisbury 5–0–34–0; Lenham 3–0–24–0.

Umpires: B. Hassan and K. J. Lyons.

## SUSSEX v NOTTINGHAMSHIRE

At Hove, July 28. Nottinghamshire won by six wickets. Toss: Nottinghamshire. Pollard's unbeaten 30 included four successive fours in one over from Jones.

## Sussex

| | | | | |
|---|---|---|---|---|
| N. J. Lenham c Randall b Saxelby | ... 21 | A. C. S. Pigott b Evans | ............. | 2 |
| *P. W. G. Parker c French b Stephenson | 4 | †P. Moores not out | ................. | 7 |
| A. P. Wells c and b Hemmings | ....... 33 | L-b 12, w 4, n-b 2 | ........... | 18 |
| M. P. Speight c French b Evans | ...... 44 | | | |
| K. Greenfield c French b Saxelby | ..... 0 | 1/14 2/42 3/79 | (7 wkts, 40 overs) | 188 |
| C. M. Wells c and b Stephenson | ...... 28 | 4/82 5/137 | | |
| A. I. C. Dodemaide not out | .......... 31 | 6/160 7/168 | | |

I. D. K. Salisbury and A. N. Jones did not bat.

Bowling: Stephenson 8–0–36–2; Pick 8–1–30–0; Saxelby 8–0–26–2; Evans 8–0–50–2; Hemmings 8–0–34–1.

## Nottinghamshire

| | | | | |
|---|---|---|---|---|
| B. C. Broad c Moores b Salisbury | ..... 65 | M. Saxelby not out | ................. | 23 |
| D. W. Randall b Jones | ............. 22 | L-b 12, w 8, n-b 2 | ........... | 22 |
| *R. T. Robinson b Dodemaide | ........ 10 | | | |
| P. Johnson lbw b Lenham | ............ 20 | 1/53 2/114 | (4 wkts, 38.5 overs) | 192 |
| P. R. Pollard not out | ............... 30 | 3/136 4/141 | | |

F. D. Stephenson, K. P. Evans, †B. N. French, E. E. Hemmings and R. A. Pick did not bat.

Bowling: C. M. Wells 7–0–23–0; Dodemaide 8–0–35–1; Pigott 7.5–0–47–0; Jones 7–0–45–1; Salisbury 8–1–22–1; Lenham 1–0–8–1.

Umpires: A. G. T. Whitehead and P. B. Wight.

# SUSSEX v NORTHAMPTONSHIRE

At Eastbourne, August 4. Northamptonshire won by five wickets. Toss: Sussex.

## Sussex

| | | | | |
|---|---|---|---|---|
| K. Greenfield c Larkins b Williams | .... 57 | †P. Moores b Baptiste | ................. | 0 |
| *P. W. G. Parker c Felton b Taylor | ... 1 | I. D. K. Salisbury not out | ........... | 6 |
| A. P. Wells c Williams b Curran | ...... 38 | L-b 10, w 6 | ........... | 16 |
| M. P. Speight c Walker b Williams | .... 2 | | | |
| C. M. Wells not out | ............... 24 | 1/17 2/103 3/108 | (8 wkts, 40 overs) | 170 |
| J. A. North b Taylor | ............... 18 | 4/111 5/142 6/154 | | |
| A. I. C. Dodemaide c Felton b Walker | . 8 | 7/154 8/158 | | |
| A. C. S. Pigott b Baptiste | ........... 0 | | | |

A. N. Jones did not bat.

Bowling: Taylor 6–1–25–2; Walker 8–1–26–1; Capel 5–0–23–0; Baptiste 8–1–25–2; Williams 8–0–32–2; Curran 5–0–29–1.

## Northamptonshire

| | | | | |
|---|---|---|---|---|
| A. Fordham st Moores b Salisbury | .... 20 | E. A. E. Baptiste not out | ........... | 14 |
| N. A. Felton c Parker b Dodemaide | ... 5 | L-b 7, w 3 | ............. | 10 |
| W. Larkins c Moores b Jones | ........ 43 | | | |
| *A. J. Lamb c Moores b Dodemaide | ... 35 | | | |
| D. J. Capel b Salisbury | ............. 22 | 1/8 2/60 3/94 | (5 wkts, 37.2 overs) | 174 |
| K. M. Curran not out | ............ 25 | 4/130 5/148 | | |

R. G. Williams, †D. Ripley, A. Walker and J. P. Taylor did not bat.

Bowling: C. M. Wells 7–0–22–0; Dodemaide 8–1–22–2; Greenfield 7–0–29–0; Salisbury 8–0–43–2; Jones 3.2–0–28–1; Pigott 4–0–23–0.

Umpires: R. Palmer and D. R. Shepherd.

At Middlesbrough, August 11. SUSSEX lost to YORKSHIRE by 77 runs.

## SUSSEX v KENT

At Hove, August 25. Sussex won by four wickets. Toss: Sussex. Fleming and Lenham both made their highest scores in the competition.

### Kent

| | | | |
|---|---|---|---|
| T. R. Ward c and b Pigott | 3 | R. P. Davis run out | 6 |
| *M. R. Benson c Moores b Dodemaide | 6 | A. P. Igglesden not out | 13 |
| J. I. Longley c Greenfield b Pigott | 1 | T. N. Wren not out | 0 |
| G. R. Cowdrey lbw b North | 18 | L-b 4, w 7, n-b 7 | 18 |
| M. A. Ealham c Hanley b North | 17 | | |
| M. V. Fleming c Dodemaide b Pigott | 77 | 1/9 2/11 3/13    (9 wkts, 40 overs) 171 | |
| †S. A. Marsh c and b North | 4 | 4/40 5/56 6/77 | |
| N. J. Llong run out | 8 | 7/96 8/115 9/168 | |

Bowling: Pigott 8–0–26–3; Dodemaide 8–1–29–1; North 8–1–29–3; Jones 7–0–49–0; Salisbury 2–0–11–0; Donelan 7–0–23–0.

### Sussex

| | | | |
|---|---|---|---|
| N. J. Lenham b Igglesden | 86 | †P. Moores run out | 11 |
| K. Greenfield b Davis | 26 | A. C. S. Pigott not out | 1 |
| *A. P. Wells c Longley b Davis | 28 | L-b 4, w 2 | 6 |
| R. Hanley c and b Igglesden | 2 | | |
| J. A. North c Cowdrey b Wren | 6 | 1/56 2/139 3/144   (6 wkts, 40 overs) 172 | |
| A. I. C. Dodemaide not out | 6 | 4/153 5/155 6/169 | |

I. D. K. Salisbury, B. T. P. Donelan and A. N. Jones did not bat.

Bowling: Igglesden 8–2–21–2; Wren 5–0–33–1; Ealham 8–0–35–0; Davis 8–0–23–2; Fleming 8–0–39–0; Llong 3–0–17–0.

Umpires: J. H. Harris and D. R. Shepherd.

# WARWICKSHIRE

## WARWICKSHIRE v SUSSEX

At Birmingham, April 21. Warwickshire won by 21 runs. Toss: Sussex. A match of ten overs a side was played after rain had caused an earlier game to be abandoned when Sussex were 8 for no wicket off one over.

### Warwickshire

| | | | |
|---|---|---|---|
| D. A. Reeve c Dodemaide b Jones | 10 | R. G. Twose not out | 0 |
| Asif Din c North b Pigott | 3 | | |
| P. A. Smith c Smith b Pigott | 44 | L-b 3, w 6 | 9 |
| D. P. Ostler b Pigott | 15 | | |
| N. M. K. Smith c and b Jones | 1 | 1/14 2/18 3/76   (5 wkts, 10 overs) 89 | |
| *T. A. Lloyd not out | 7 | 4/82 5/82 | |

†P. C. L. Holloway, G. C. Small, A. A. Donald and T. A. Munton did not bat.

Bowling: North 1–0–12–0; Jones 2–0–13–2; Pigott 2–0–11–3; Giddins 2–0–19–0; Dodemaide 2–0–20–0; Salisbury 1–0–11–0.

### Sussex

| | | | |
|---|---|---|---|
| N. J. Lenham c and b Donald | 3 | J. A. North not out | 1 |
| D. M. Smith c Ostler b N. M. K. Smith | 23 | L-b 5, w 2 | 7 |
| †I. J. Gould run out | 21 | | |
| *A. P. Wells run out | 8 | 1/4 2/49 3/54   (5 wkts, 10 overs) 68 | |
| A. C. S. Pigott c Twose b Donald | 5 | 4/67 5/68 | |

K. Greenfield, A. I. C. Dodemaide, E. S. H. Giddins, I. D. K. Salisbury and A. N. Jones did not bat.

Bowling: Donald 2–0–7–2; Munton 2–0–16–0; Small 2–0–8–0; N. M. K. Smith 2–0–14–1; Reeve 2–0–18–0.

Umpires: J. H. Hampshire and B. Hassan.

At Nottingham, April 28. WARWICKSHIRE lost to NOTTINGHAMSHIRE by 82 runs.

At Canterbury, May 5. KENT v WARWICKSHIRE. No result.

At Leeds, May 12. WARWICKSHIRE beat YORKSHIRE by 2 runs.

At Swansea, May 19. WARWICKSHIRE beat GLAMORGAN by 13 runs.

## WARWICKSHIRE v WORCESTERSHIRE

At Birmingham, May 26. Tied. Toss: Warwickshire. The drama of Moody's return to face his colleagues of the previous season was overshadowed by a comedy of error which produced the tie. Worcestershire entered the final over needing 4 to win, but lost three wickets in consecutive balls. Lampitt wanted 2 from the last ball, failed to connect, and ran a bye while Piper, mistakenly believing Warwickshire would win if the scores were level, because they had lost fewer wickets, began to celebrate as his team-mates were urging him to throw down the wicket.

### Warwickshire

| | | | |
|---|---|---|---|
| Asif Din b Dilley | 11 | †K. J. Piper not out | 15 |
| A. J. Moles b Radford | 39 | | |
| *T. A. Lloyd lbw b Stemp | 34 | L-b 6, w 8 | 14 |
| P. A. Smith c Stemp b Newport | 16 | | |
| D. P. Ostler c Newport b Dilley | 48 | 1/16 2/89 3/89 (5 wkts, 40 overs) 203 |
| R. G. Twose not out | 26 | 4/135 5/174 | |

A. R. K. Pierson, G. C. Small, A. A. Donald and T. A. Munton did not bat.

Bowling: Dilley 8–0–48–2; Weston 6–0–28–0; Radford 8–1–42–1; Stemp 7–0–22–1; Newport 5–0–25–1; Lampitt 6–0–32–0.

### Worcestershire

| | | | |
|---|---|---|---|
| *T. S. Curtis c Lloyd b Donald | 67 | S. R. Lampitt not out | 0 |
| T. M. Moody b Smith | 45 | N. V. Radford not out | 1 |
| M. J. Weston c Twose b Smith | 51 | B 2, l-b 7, w 12, n-b 1 | 22 |
| D. B. D'Oliveira c Donald b Pierson | 4 | | |
| D. A. Leatherdale c Piper b Munton | 12 | 1/92 2/158 3/162 (7 wkts, 40 overs) 203 |
| †S. J. Rhodes run out | 1 | 4/200 5/201 | |
| P. J. Newport c Asif Din b Munton | 0 | 6/201 7/201 | |

R. D. Stemp and G. R. Dilley did not bat.

Bowling: Munton 8–2–20–2; Donald 8–0–43–1; Twose 1–0–9–0; Pierson 7–0–45–1; Small 8–0–32–0; Smith 8–0–45–2.

Umpires: J. C. Balderstone and B. Dudleston.

## WARWICKSHIRE v SOMERSET

At Birmingham, June 2. No result. Toss: Warwickshire. Rain reduced the game to 32 overs a side, and then prevented Warwickshire from starting their innings. Paul Smith's bowling return was his best in the competition.

## Somerset

| | | | | |
|---|---|---|---|---|
| S. J. Cook b Reeve | 67 | R. P. Lefebvre b Small | | 4 |
| R. J. Bartlett run out | 7 | K. H. MacLeay not out | | 1 |
| *C. J. Tavaré c Benjamin b P. A. Smith | 59 | L-b 6, w 3 | | 9 |
| G. D. Rose c Benjamin b P. A. Smith | 2 | | | |
| R. J. Harden c Benjamin b P. A. Smith | 13 | 1/28 2/124 3/127 | (7 wkts, 32 overs) | 176 |
| †N. D. Burns c and b P. A. Smith | 2 | 4/149 5/153 | | |
| A. N. Hayhurst not out | 12 | 6/167 7/173 | | |

D. A. Graveney and N. A. Mallender did not bat.

Bowling: Donald 8–1–21–0; Benjamin 7–0–29–0; Reeve 8–0–60–1; Small 6–0–39–1; P. A. Smith 3–0–21–4.

## Warwickshire

A. J. Moles, R. G. Twose, *T. A. Lloyd, P. A. Smith, D. A. Reeve, D. P. Ostler, †K. J. Piper, N. M. K. Smith, G. C. Small, A. A. Donald and J. E. Benjamin.

Umpires: J. H. Hampshire and A. A. Jones.

# WARWICKSHIRE v LANCASHIRE

At Birmingham, June 16. Lancashire won by four wickets. Toss: Lancashire. A sixth-wicket partnership of 80 in nine overs from Wasim Akram and DeFreitas, who faced 28 balls and registered his highest Sunday score, 41 not out, earned Lancashire their first Sunday League victory at Edgbaston in thirteen years. Earlier Reeve's maiden hundred in the competition, from 96 balls and featuring eight fours and a six, had rescued Warwickshire after DeFreitas reduced them to 45 for four in eleven overs. Reeve added 143 in 27 overs with Paul Smith.

## Warwickshire

| | | | | |
|---|---|---|---|---|
| A. J. Moles c Atherton b DeFreitas | 7 | N. M. K. Smith not out | | 4 |
| *T. A. Lloyd c Fowler b DeFreitas | 16 | | | |
| S. J. Green c Hegg b Watkinson | 5 | B 2, l-b 7, w 8, n-b 1 | | 18 |
| D. P. Ostler c Lloyd b DeFreitas | 7 | | | |
| D. A. Reeve c Fairbrother b Austin | 100 | 1/24 2/30 3/30 | (6 wkts, 40 overs) | 206 |
| P. A. Smith c Atherton b Austin | 49 | 4/45 5/188 6/206 | | |

†K. J. Piper, G. C. Small, J. E. Benjamin and T. A. Munton did not bat.

Bowling: DeFreitas 8–1–27–3; Allott 2–0–13–0; Watkinson 8–0–37–1; Wasim Akram 8–0–51–0; Hughes 6–0–33–0; Austin 8–1–36–2.

## Lancashire

| | | | | |
|---|---|---|---|---|
| G. Fowler b P. A. Smith | 26 | P. A. J. DeFreitas not out | | 41 |
| M. A. Atherton c Piper b Benjamin | 0 | †W. K. Hegg not out | | 2 |
| G. D. Lloyd b Small | 50 | | | |
| N. H. Fairbrother c N. M. K. Smith b Small | 20 | L-b 12, w 7, n-b 4 | | 23 |
| M. Watkinson c Small b Reeve | 7 | 1/1 2/64 3/107 | (6 wkts, 38.3 overs) | 207 |
| Wasim Akram run out | 38 | 4/119 5/121 6/201 | | |

*D. P. Hughes, I. D. Austin and P. J. W. Allott did not bat.

Bowling: Benjamin 8–0–26–1; Munton 7–0–20–0; Reeve 8–1–38–1; P. A. Smith 7.3–0–51–1; Small 8–0–60–2.

Umpires: D. R. Shepherd and R. C. Tolchard.

# WARWICKSHIRE v SURREY

At Birmingham, June 23. No result.

At Chelmsford, July 7. WARWICKSHIRE lost to ESSEX by six wickets.

## WARWICKSHIRE v MIDDLESEX

At Birmingham, July 14. Warwickshire won by nine wickets. Toss: Middlesex. Asif Din virtually doubled his aggregate for the Sunday season with his first score of fifty or more; he hit ten fours and a six, and added 107 in fifteen overs with his captain, Lloyd.

## Middlesex

| | |
|---|---|
| *M. W. Gatting lbw b P. A. Smith . . . . 33 | J. E. Emburey not out . . . . . . . . . . . . . . 33 |
| M. A. Roseberry c Lloyd b P. A. Smith 17 | †P. Farbrace c Benjamin b Donald . . . . 4 |
| M. R. Ramprakash st Piper | N. F. Williams not out . . . . . . . . . . . . 7 |
|      b N. M. K. Smith . 11 |      B 1, l-b 10, w 3, n-b 2 . . . . . . . 16 |
| K. R. Brown c N. M. K. Smith | |
|      b P. A. Smith . 52 | 1/51 2/56 3/91      (7 wkts, 40 overs) 193 |
| M. Keech b Donald . . . . . . . . . . . . . . . . 4 | 4/98 5/135 |
| P. N. Weekes run out . . . . . . . . . . . . 16 | 6/165 7/177 |

D. W. Headley and N. G. Cowans did not bat.

Bowling: Benjamin 4–0–29–0; Munton 8–1–33–0; P. A. Smith 8–0–33–3; Reeve 8–1–32–0; Donald 8–0–44–2; N. M. K. Smith 4–0–11–1.

## Warwickshire

| | |
|---|---|
| A. J. Moles c Roseberry b Williams . . . 38 | |
| Asif Din not out . . . . . . . . . . . . . . . . 101 | |
| *T. A. Lloyd not out . . . . . . . . . . . . . . 44 | |
|      L-b 5, w 2, n-b 4 . . . . . . . . . . . 11 | |

1/87      (1 wkt, 36.2 overs) 194

D. P. Ostler, D. A. Reeve, P. A. Smith, N. M. K. Smith, †K. J. Piper, J. E. Benjamin, A. A. Donald and T. A. Munton did not bat.

Bowling: Headley 8–0–28–0; Cowans 8–0–31–0; Weekes 8–0–50–0; Williams 6–0–34–1; Emburey 6–0–44–0; Brown 0.2–0–2–0.

Umpires: G. I. Burgess and N. T. Plews.

At Portsmouth, July 21. WARWICKSHIRE beat HAMPSHIRE by five wickets.

## WARWICKSHIRE v DERBYSHIRE

At Birmingham, August 4. Warwickshire won by 32 runs. Toss: Warwickshire. Lloyd reached 4,000 runs in the competition, and Ostler his highest score; Reeve made his 38 at a run a ball.

## Warwickshire

| | |
|---|---|
| A. J. Moles lbw b Cork . . . . . . . . . . . . 44 | N. M. K. Smith not out . . . . . . . . . . . 14 |
| J. D. Ratcliffe lbw b Mortensen . . . . . . . 1 | L-b 16, w 4, n-b 1 . . . . . . . . 21 |
| *T. A. Lloyd c Base b McCray . . . . . . 45 | |
| D. P. Ostler not out . . . . . . . . . . . . . . . . 62 | 1/2 2/76      (4 wkts, 40 overs) 225 |
| D. A. Reeve c Bork . . . . . . . . . . . . . . . 38 | 3/121 4/210 |

R. G. Twose, †P. C. L. Holloway, J. E. Benjamin, T. A. Munton and D. R. Brown did not bat.

Bowling: Base 8–0–38–0; Mortensen 8–1–41–1; McCray 8–0–37–1; Cork 8–0–38–2; Goldsmith 8–1–55–0.

## Derbyshire

| | | | | |
|---|---|---|---|---|
| *K. J. Barnett b Benjamin | 10 | E. McCray b Munton | 1 |
| C. J. Adams c Holloway b Reeve | 35 | †B. J. M. Maher c Benjamin b Reeve | 4 |
| J. E. Morris c Lloyd b Benjamin | 17 | O. H. Mortensen not out | 1 |
| T. J. G. O'Gorman c and b Reeve | 32 | L-b 11, w 6 | 17 |
| M. Azharuddin lbw b Brown | 24 | | |
| S. C. Goldsmith lbw b Benjamin | 10 | 1/13 2/38 3/93 | (37.4 overs) 193 |
| S. J. Base b Smith | 12 | 4/122 5/140 6/142 | |
| D. G. Cork c Moles b Reeve | 30 | 7/182 8/183 9/191 | |

Bowling: Brown 6–0–35–1; Benjamin 8–0–33–3; Munton 7–0–29–1; Smith 8–0–50–1; Reeve 6.4–0–18–4; Twose 2–0–17–0.

Umpires: J. W. Holder and R. C. Tolchard.

At Leicester, August 11. WARWICKSHIRE beat LEICESTERSHIRE by 2 runs.

## WARWICKSHIRE v GLOUCESTERSHIRE

At Birmingham, August 18. Warwickshire won by nine wickets. Toss: Gloucestershire. Warwickshire recorded their fifth consecutive win, to enter the reckoning for a place in the Refuge Assurance Cup, but for Gloucestershire it was their fifth successive defeat. Munton's return included three wickets in four balls.

## Gloucestershire

| | | | | |
|---|---|---|---|---|
| R. J. Scott lbw b Munton | 1 | D. R. Gilbert b Munton | 0 |
| M. W. Alleyne b Munton | 17 | A. M. Babington not out | 6 |
| *A. J. Wright c Donald b Benjamin | 56 | A. M. Smith not out | 5 |
| C. W. J. Athey c Reeve b Benjamin | 2 | L-b 18, w 7 | 25 |
| †R. C. Russell c Piper b Donald | 28 | | |
| J. J. E. Hardy lbw b P. A. Smith | 13 | 1/5 2/39 3/42 | (9 wkts, 40 overs) 177 |
| T. H. C. Hancock b Munton | 20 | 4/112 5/131 6/144 | |
| M. C. J. Ball b Munton | 4 | 7/165 8/165 9/166 | |

Bowling: Donald 8–0–35–1; Munton 8–0–28–5; Benjamin 8–0–36–2; P. A. Smith 8–0–27–1; N. M. K. Smith 8–0–33–0.

## Warwickshire

| | |
|---|---|
| A. J. Moles b Scott | 26 |
| Asif Din not out | 81 |
| *T. A. Lloyd not out | 56 |
| L-b 6, w 7, n-b 2 | 15 |

1/76      (1 wkt, 37.5 overs) 178

D. P. Ostler, D. A. Reeve, P. A. Smith, N. M. K. Smith, †K. J. Piper, J. E. Benjamin, T. A. Munton and A. A. Donald did not bat.

Bowling: Gilbert 8–1–35–0; Babington 8–1–25–0; Ball 8–0–27–0; Smith 5–0–39–0; Scott 6–0–29–1; Alleyne 2.5–0–17–0.

Umpires: J. H. Hampshire and P. B. Wight.

At Northampton, August 25. WARWICKSHIRE lost to NORTHAMPTONSHIRE by 8 runs.

# WORCESTERSHIRE

## WORCESTERSHIRE v KENT

At Worcester, April 21. Worcestershire won on scoring-rate. Toss: Kent. Kent's innings was interrupted by rain, which reduced their target to 269 from 38 overs. Moody, who played for Warwickshire in 1990, struck sixteen fours and six sixes, and scored his 160 from 111 balls; his first 50 came in 51 deliveries, his second in 35 and his third in nineteen. His maiden hundred in English limited-overs cricket, on his début for the county, was the highest score by a Worcestershire batsman in the Sunday League, and with Curtis he put on 198 for the first wicket in 30 overs, the first of their six century opening partnerships in 1991.

### Worcestershire

| | | | | |
|---|---|---|---|---|
| T. S. Curtis c Davis b Igglesden | 70 | *P. A. Neale not out | | 5 |
| T. M. Moody b Igglesden | 160 | B 1, l-b 5, w 5 | | 11 |
| G. A. Hick c Davis b Igglesden | 8 | | | — |
| I. T. Botham b Igglesden | 20 | 1/198 2/242 | (4 wkts, 40 overs) | 283 |
| D. B. D'Oliveira not out | 9 | 3/256 4/273 | | |

M. J. Weston, †S. J. Rhodes, R. K. Illingworth, S. R. Lampitt and N. V. Radford did not bat.

Bowling: Igglesden 8-0-59-4; Ellison 8-0-47-0; Merrick 8-1-38-0; Fleming 8-0-56-0; Davis 5-0-40-0; C. S. Cowdrey 3-0-37-0.

### Kent

| | | | | |
|---|---|---|---|---|
| *M. R. Benson lbw b Radford | 12 | R. P. Davis lbw b Radford | | 7 |
| N. R. Taylor c Weston b Botham | 62 | T. A. Merrick run out | | 1 |
| T. R. Ward c Curtis b Botham | 40 | A. P. Igglesden c D'Oliveira b Moody | | 1 |
| G. R. Cowdrey c Radford b Lampitt | 0 | B 2, l-b 10, w 6 | | 18 |
| C. S. Cowdrey c Neale b Botham | 24 | | | — |
| M. V. Fleming b Lampitt | 26 | 1/25 2/99 3/103 | (38 overs) | 230 |
| †S. A. Marsh c Hick b Radford | 27 | 4/137 5/164 6/208 | | |
| R. M. Ellison not out | 12 | 7/210 8/225 9/227 | | |

Bowling: Radford 8-0-46-3; Weston 6-0-26-0; Illingworth 3-0-32-0; Lampitt 8-0-42-2; Botham 8-0-34-3; Moody 5-0-38-1.

Umpires: B. J. Meyer and R. C. Tolchard.

At Bristol, May 5. WORCESTERSHIRE beat GLOUCESTERSHIRE by ten wickets.

## WORCESTERSHIRE v LANCASHIRE

At Worcester, May 12. Lancashire won by six wickets. Toss: Lancashire. Fairbrother and Lloyd added 118 in twenty overs for the fourth wicket; Lloyd's 79 not out came in 70 balls.

### Worcestershire

| | | | | |
|---|---|---|---|---|
| T. S. Curtis lbw b DeFreitas | 2 | R. K. Illingworth not out | | 24 |
| T. M. Moody run out | 50 | P. J. Newport not out | | 11 |
| G. A. Hick c Hegg b DeFreitas | 5 | | | |
| I. T. Botham b Austin | 58 | L-b 2, w 2 | | 4 |
| D. B. D'Oliveira c Hegg b Yates | 12 | | | — |
| *P. A. Neale c Fairbrother | | 1/8 2/20 3/99 | (7 wkts, 40 overs) | 209 |
|     b Wasim Akram | 39 | 4/121 5/136 | | |
| M. J. Weston c Hegg b Yates | 4 | 6/144 7/188 | | |

S. R. Lampitt and †S. R. Bevins did not bat.

Bowling: DeFreitas 8-0-35-2; Allott 8-0-31-0; Yates 8-1-45-2; Wasim Akram 8-0-56-1; Austin 8-1-40-1.

## Lancashire

| | | | | |
|---|---|---|---|---|
| G. Fowler b Illingworth | 27 | Wasim Akram not out | 7 | |
| G. D. Mendis c and b Illingworth | 31 | L-b 14, w 1 | 15 | |
| M. A. Atherton b Hick | 6 | | — | |
| *N. H. Fairbrother lbw b Hick | 46 | 1/54 2/67 | (4 wkts, 39.2 overs) 211 | |
| G. D. Lloyd not out | 79 | 3/71 4/189 | | |

P. A. J. DeFreitas, †W. K. Hegg, I. D. Austin, G. Yates and P. J. W. Allott did not bat.

Bowling: Weston 8–0–30–0; Newport 5.2–0–32–0; Illingworth 8–1–26–2; Hick 8–0–42–2; Botham 6–0–41–0; Lampitt 4–0–26–0.

*Umpires: B. Hassan and P. B. Wight.*

At Northampton, May 19. WORCESTERSHIRE beat NORTHAMPTONSHIRE by 27 runs.

At Birmingham, May 26. WORCESTERSHIRE tied with WARWICKSHIRE.

## WORCESTERSHIRE v SURREY

At Worcester, June 2. No result. Toss: Surrey. Before the match the Worcestershire groundsman, Roy McLaren, was taken to hospital after Waqar Younis crashed into him during fielding practice, knocking him unconscious. Despite interruptions from rain, Curtis and Moody compiled their fourth century opening partnership in six Sunday innings, with Moody, when 17, reaching 500 runs. This equalled D. I. Gower's record of 1982, though Gower did not play his sixth innings until July 4. Moody faced 60 balls for his 62 and was capped during the game, only nine months after receiving a county cap from Warwickshire.

## Worcestershire

| | | | | |
|---|---|---|---|---|
| T. S. Curtis c Lynch b Murphy | 65 | D. A. Leatherdale not out | 0 | |
| T. M. Moody c Lynch b Murphy | 62 | L-b 5, w 5, n-b 2 | 12 | |
| M. J. Weston c Greig b Waqar Younis | 27 | | — | |
| D. B. D'Oliveira not out | 28 | 1/116 2/156 | (4 wkts, 31 overs) 199 | |
| *P. A. Neale c sub b Feltham | 5 | 3/173 4/187 | | |

†S. J. Rhodes, P. J. Newport, R. K. Illingworth, S. R. Lampitt and N. V. Radford did not bat.

Bowling: Feltham 8–1–51–1; Murphy 8–0–58–2; Waqar Younis 8–0–36–1; Robinson 5–0–33–0; Greig 2–0–16–0.

## Surrey

| | | | | |
|---|---|---|---|---|
| M. A. Lynch not out | 18 | | | |
| M. A. Feltham not out | 23 | | | |
| L-b 2, w 1, n-b 1 | 4 | | | |
| | | (no wkt, 8 overs) 45 | | |

A. D. Brown, D. M. Ward, †A. J. Stewart, G. P. Thorpe, J. D. Robinson, *I. A. Greig, C. K. Bullen, A. J. Murphy and Waqar Younis did not bat.

Bowling: Weston 4–0–16–0; Newport 4–0–27–0.

*Umpires: G. I. Burgess and B. Leadbeater.*

At Ilford, June 9. WORCESTERSHIRE lost to ESSEX by 34 runs.

At Hove, June 16. SUSSEX v WORCESTERSHIRE. No result.

At Sheffield, June 23. WORCESTERSHIRE lost to YORKSHIRE by four wickets.

## WORCESTERSHIRE v LEICESTERSHIRE

At Worcester, June 30. Worcestershire won by seven wickets. Toss: Leicestershire. Hick, whose previous three innings – in the Test match at Lord's, the NatWest Trophy and the County Championship – had brought him no runs, returned to form with 84 in 82 balls. One of his two sixes smashed a car window, and he also hit four fours.

### Leicestershire

| | | | |
|---|---|---|---|
| *N. E. Briers st Rhodes b Illingworth . . | 29 | L. Potter not out . . . . . . . . . . . . . . . . . . | 31 |
| J. J. Whitaker c Lampitt b Radford . . . | 63 | L-b 4, w 1 . . . . . . . . . . . . . . | 5 |
| †P. A. Nixon b Illingworth . . . . . . . . . . | 17 | | |
| C. C. Lewis c D'Oliveira b Newport . . | 28 | 1/65 2/91 | (4 wkts, 40 overs) 203 |
| B. F. Smith not out . . . . . . . . . . . . . . . | 30 | 3/137 4/148 | |

J. D. R. Benson, P. Willey, D. J. Millns, C. W. Wilkinson and J. N. Maguire did not bat.

Bowling: Radford 8-0-48-1; Tolley 5-0-41-0; Lampitt 8-0-35-0; Illingworth 8-1-19-2; Newport 8-0-37-1; Hick 3-0-19-0.

### Worcestershire

| | | | |
|---|---|---|---|
| T. S. Curtis not out . . . . . . . . . . . . . . . | 88 | *P. A. Neale not out . . . . . . . . . . . . . . | 18 |
| T. M. Moody b Lewis . . . . . . . . . . . | 9 | L-b 6, w 1 . . . . . . . . . . . . . | 7 |
| G. A. Hick c Whitaker b Maguire . . . . . | 84 | | |
| D. B. D'Oliveira c and b Benson . . . . . . | 1 | 1/13 2/170 3/173 | (3 wkts, 38.2 overs) 207 |

C. M. Tolley, †S. J. Rhodes, R. K. Illingworth, S. R. Lampitt, P. J. Newport and N. V. Radford did not bat.

Bowling: Lewis 7.2-1-37-1; Maguire 8-0-28-1; Millns 4-0-28-0; Benson 8-0-38-1; Wilkinson 7-0-46-0; Willey 4-0-24-0.

Umpires: J. H. Hampshire and K. J. Lyons.

At Southampton, July 7. WORCESTERSHIRE beat HAMPSHIRE by six wickets.

## WORCESTERSHIRE v DERBYSHIRE

At Worcester, July 9. Worcestershire won by eight wickets. Toss: Worcestershire. Worcestershire had to rearrange their fixture of July 14 because of the Benson and Hedges Cup final, and played it on a Tuesday. They won comfortably as, in support of Curtis, D'Oliveira made his fifty from 62 balls and Botham hit 36 off 28 deliveries including four fours and a six. Morris had a similar tally of boundaries in his 62-minute innings for Derbyshire, who, from 117 for two, lost five wickets for 12 runs.

### Derbyshire

| | | | |
|---|---|---|---|
| P. D. Bowler b Radford . . . . . . . . . . . . | 9 | A. E. Warner c Newport b Radford . . . | 21 |
| C. J. Adams c Newport b Botham . . . . . | 36 | S. J. Base b Radford . . . . . . . . . . . . . . . | 0 |
| J. E. Morris c and b Stemp . . . . . . . . . . | 51 | D. E. Malcolm not out . . . . . . . . . . . . . | 2 |
| F. A. Griffith lbw b Botham . . . . . . . . . | 9 | B 2, l-b 8, w 3, n-b 4 . . . . . . . . | 17 |
| T. J. G. O'Gorman c Rhodes b Stemp . . | 4 | | |
| S. C. Goldsmith b Stemp . . . . . . . . . . . | 4 | 1/16 2/91 3/117 | (9 wkts, 40 overs) 169 |
| *K. J. Barnett not out . . . . . . . . . . . . . . | 16 | 4/119 5/125 6/128 | |
| †K. M. Krikken b Botham . . . . . . . . . . . | 0 | 7/129 8/162 9/163 | |

Bowling: Radford 7-0-16-3; Weston 5-0-24-0; Newport 5-0-23-0; Lampitt 7-0-57-0; Botham 8-1-21-3; Stemp 8-1-18-3.

## Worcestershire

| | |
|---|---|
| T. S. Curtis not out | 63 |
| T. M. Moody c Krikken b Warner | 1 |
| D. B. D'Oliveira c O'Gorman b Malcolm | 54 |
| I. T. Botham not out | 36 |
| B 4, l-b 10, w 2, n-b 1 | 17 |

1/2 2/100          (2 wkts, 32.3 overs) 171

*P. A. Neale, M. J. Weston, †S. J. Rhodes, S. R. Lampitt, P. J. Newport, N. V. Radford and R. D. Stemp did not bat.

Bowling: Base 8–1–28–0; Warner 5–1–10–1; Malcolm 8–0–57–1; Goldsmith 8–1–33–0; Griffith 3–0–22–0; Morris 0.3–0–7–0.

Umpires: R. Julian and R. Palmer.

## WORCESTERSHIRE v GLAMORGAN

At Worcester, July 21. Worcestershire won by seven wickets. Toss: Worcestershire. The 111-run opening partnership of Curtis and Moody was their sixth stand of 100 or more since Moody joined Worcestershire three months earlier. Their aggregate of partnerships stood at 1,038, beating the League record of 949 set in fifteen innings by G. Boycott and J. H. Hampshire of Yorkshire in 1975. Later, D'Oliveira hit 45 from 30 balls, with three fours and three sixes.

## Glamorgan

| | | | |
|---|---|---|---|
| M. P. Maynard c D'Oliveira b Newport | 15 | P. A. Cottey not out | 26 |
| H. Morris c Curtis b Radford | 16 | | |
| R. J. Shastri c D'Oliveira b Illingworth | 22 | L-b 14, w 6 | 20 |
| A. Dale c Radford b Stemp | 56 | | |
| I. Smith c Radford b Newport | 24 | 1/20 2/54 3/74     (5 wkts, 40 overs) 230 |
| *A. R. Butcher not out | 51 | 4/117 5/168 | |

R. D. B. Croft, †C. P. Metson, S. Bastien and S. R. Barwick did not bat.

Bowling: Weston 8–2–17–0; Newport 8–0–43–2; Radford 6–0–37–1; Illingworth 8–0–38–1; Botham 8–0–65–0; Stemp 2–0–16–1.

## Worcestershire

| | | | |
|---|---|---|---|
| *T. S. Curtis c Maynard b Croft | 55 | I. T. Botham not out | 24 |
| T. M. Moody c Shastri b Croft | 58 | L-b 13, w 5 | 18 |
| G. A. Hick not out | 34 | | |
| D. B. D'Oliveira c Smith b Shastri | 45 | 1/111 2/130 3/186   (3 wkts, 39.1 overs) 234 |

M. J. Weston, †S. J. Rhodes, R. K. Illingworth, P. J. Newport, N. V. Radford and R. D. Stemp did not bat.

Bowling: Barwick 7–0–44–0; Bastien 6–0–37–0; Dale 5–0–27–0; Croft 8–0–36–2; Smith 6–0–42–0; Shastri 6–0–29–1; Maynard 1–0–2–0; Butcher 0.1–0–4–0.

Umpires: M. J. Kitchen and B. Leadbeater.

At Nottingham, August 4. WORCESTERSHIRE beat NOTTINGHAMSHIRE by eight wickets.

## WORCESTERSHIRE v SOMERSET

At Worcester, August 18. Somerset won by 18 runs. Toss: Somerset. Cook scored his runs from 112 balls, with the last 66 coming from 36 deliveries as Somerset took 98 from their last ten overs.

## Somerset

| | | | |
|---|---|---|---|
| S. J. Cook not out | 129 | A. N. Hayhurst not out | 7 |
| G. T. J. Townsend c Curtis b Newport | 27 | W 1, n-b 2 | 3 |
| R. J. Harden c and b Botham | 31 | | |
| *C. J. Tavaré b Botham | 24 | 1/73 2/133 | (4 wkts, 40 overs) 235 |
| G. D. Rose run out | 14 | 3/196 4/215 | |

†N. D. Burns, D. A. Graveney, D. Beal, J. C. Hallett and H. R. J. Trump did not bat.

Bowling: Weston 4–0–22–0; Radford 8–0–63–0; Newport 8–1–18–1; Illingworth 8–0–45–0; Lampitt 4–0–29–0; Botham 8–0–58–2.

## Worcestershire

| | | | |
|---|---|---|---|
| *T. S. Curtis b Trump | 16 | M. J. Weston not out | 30 |
| T. M. Moody c Burns b Hayhurst | 91 | N. V. Radford not out | 20 |
| G. A. Hick c Beal b Trump | 11 | L-b 6, w 3 | 9 |
| D. B. D'Oliveira c and b Graveney | 23 | | |
| I. T. Botham c Trump b Hayhurst | 17 | 1/40 2/58 3/104 | (6 wkts, 40 overs) 217 |
| †S. J. Rhodes c Burns b Hayhurst | 0 | 4/147 5/147 6/185 | |

R. K. Illingworth, S. R. Lampitt and P. J. Newport did not bat.

Bowling: Rose 8–0–49–0; Hallett 8–0–57–0; Trump 8–0–31–2; Hayhurst 8–0–38–3; Graveney 8–0–36–1.

Umpires: B. Dudleston and D. O. Oslear.

## WORCESTERSHIRE v MIDDLESEX

At Worcester, August 25. Worcestershire won by 103 runs. Toss: Middlesex. Moody ended the Sunday League season as he had begun it, with a century. He became the first player to score four hundreds in the competition in one year, and also reached an aggregate of 917 runs, beating the record of 902 set by S. J. Cook of Somerset in 1990. Moody's 128 not out included eleven fours and two sixes, and ensured that Worcestershire qualified for the Refuge Assurance Cup.

## Worcestershire

| | | | |
|---|---|---|---|
| *T. S. Curtis b Weekes | 37 | †S. J. Rhodes not out | 11 |
| T. M. Moody not out | 128 | B 1, l-b 2, w 1, n-b 1 | 5 |
| G. A. Hick c Weekes b Emburey | 65 | | |
| D. B. D'Oliveira c and b Williams | 11 | 1/79 2/207 | (4 wkts, 40 overs) 257 |
| M. J. Weston c Brown b Headley | 0 | 3/228 4/239 | |

S. R. Lampitt, R. K. Illingworth, C. M. Tolley, P. J. Newport and G. R. Dilley did not bat.

Bowling: Cowans 8–1–34–0; Williams 8–0–44–1; Emburey 8–0–43–1; Weekes 8–1–63–1; Headley 8–0–70–1.

## Middlesex

| | | | |
|---|---|---|---|
| M. A. Roseberry b Weston | 6 | J. E. Emburey st Rhodes b Hick | 32 |
| J. C. Pooley c Moody b Weston | 22 | †P. Farbrace not out | 9 |
| *M. W. Gatting not out | 60 | L-b 7, w 3, n-b 1 | 11 |
| P. N. Weekes b Lampitt | 4 | | |
| K. R. Brown c Tolley b Lampitt | 3 | 1/15 2/40 3/59 | (6 wkts, 40 overs) 154 |
| M. Keech c Rhodes b Lampitt | 7 | 4/67 5/81 6/135 | |

N. F. Williams, D. W. Headley and N. G. Cowans did not bat.

Bowling: Weston 8–0–27–2; Dilley 4–0–24–0; Lampitt 8–0–23–3; Newport 6–0–24–0; Tolley 3–0–11–0; Illingworth 6–0–18–0; Hick 5–0–20–1.

Umpires: A. A. Jones and D. O. Oslear.

# YORKSHIRE

At Southampton, April 21. YORKSHIRE lost to HAMPSHIRE by 49 runs.

At Chelmsford, April 28. YORKSHIRE lost to ESSEX by nine wickets.

## YORKSHIRE v WARWICKSHIRE

At Leeds, May 12. Warwickshire won by 2 runs. Toss: Yorkshire. Moles and Smith, whose 75 from 69 balls contained five fours and a six, added 91 in sixteen overs for the third wicket, and Smith went on to take three for 43 in Yorkshire's reply.

### Warwickshire

| | | | | |
|---|---|---|---|---|
| A. J. Moles c Kellett b Jarvis | 67 | R. G. Twose b Fletcher | 1 |
| Asif Din b Jarvis | 0 | †K. J. Piper not out | 1 |
| *T. A. Lloyd lbw b Carrick | 38 | B 2, l-b 3, w 1 | 6 |
| P. A. Smith c and b Fletcher | 75 | | |
| D. A. Reeve c Kellett b Fletcher | 2 | 1/1 2/67 3/158 (6 wkts, 40 overs) 204 |
| D. P. Ostler not out | 14 | 4/163 5/201 6/203 |

G. C. Small, A. R. K. Pierson and T. A. Munton did not bat.

Bowling: Jarvis 8–0–37–2; Sidebottom 8–0–22–0; Hartley 6–0–41–0; Carrick 8–0–38–1; Fletcher 8–0–47–3; Moxon 2–0–14–0.

### Yorkshire

| | | | | |
|---|---|---|---|---|
| *M. D. Moxon st Piper b Pierson | 39 | P. J. Hartley not out | 0 |
| A. A. Metcalfe c Lloyd b Small | 27 | A. Sidebottom not out | 1 |
| †R. J. Blakey c Asif Din b Smith | 51 | B 1, l-b 14, w 11 | 26 |
| D. Byas lbw b Smith | 23 | | |
| P. E. Robinson c Small b Smith | 3 | 1/59 2/74 3/137 (8 wkts, 40 overs) 202 |
| S. A. Kellett run out | 17 | 4/148 5/180 6/182 |
| P. Carrick b Munton | 6 | 7/189 8/201 |
| P. W. Jarvis run out | 9 | |

S. D. Fletcher did not bat.

Bowling: Munton 5–0–17–1; Twose 5–0–23–0; Reeve 8–0–40–0; Pierson 8–1–35–1; Small 7–0–29–1; Smith 7–0–43–3.

Umpires: J. C. Balderstone and R. A. White.

At Leicester, May 19. YORKSHIRE lost to LEICESTERSHIRE by 7 runs.

## YORKSHIRE v NORTHAMPTONSHIRE

At Leeds, May 26. Yorkshire won by three wickets. Toss: Yorkshire. For Northamptonshire, Fordham made his highest score in the League, hitting six fours and a six in his 76. Blakey's unbeaten 71, from 77 balls with three fours and three sixes, saw Yorkshire to their first Refuge Assurance win of the season after four defeats.

## Northamptonshire

| | | | |
|---|---|---|---|
| A. Fordham c and b Batty | 76 | †D. Ripley c Blakey b M. A. Robinson | 10 |
| N. A. Felton c Batty b M. A. Robinson | 9 | W. M. Noon not out | 8 |
| *R. J. Bailey lbw b Fletcher | 1 | B 1, l-b 7, w 9, n-b 2 | 19 |
| D. J. Capel run out | 30 | | |
| K. M. Curran c Moxon b Batty | 8 | 1/33 2/36 3/131 (7 wkts, 40 overs) | 197 |
| A. L. Penberthy c Hartley b Moxon | 6 | 4/134 5/141 | |
| J. G. Thomas not out | 30 | 6/159 7/186 | |

A. Walker and A. R. Roberts did not bat.

Bowling: M. A. Robinson 7-0-24-2; Gough 3-0-21-0; Fletcher 6-0-31-1; Hartley 8-0-47-0; Batty 8-2-32-2; Moxon 8-0-34-1.

## Yorkshire

| | | | |
|---|---|---|---|
| *M. D. Moxon c Ripley b Penberthy | 31 | P. J. Hartley run out | 5 |
| A. A. Metcalfe c Ripley b Curran | 33 | J. D. Batty not out | 2 |
| †R. J. Blakey not out | 71 | B 2, l-b 4, w 7 | 13 |
| D. Byas b Capel | 27 | | |
| P. E. Robinson lbw b Capel | 2 | 1/47 2/81 3/146 (7 wkts, 39.4 overs) | 198 |
| D. Gough c Penberthy b Walker | 13 | 4/158 5/177 | |
| C. A. Chapman b Thomas | 1 | 6/181 7/195 | |

S. D. Fletcher and M. A. Robinson did not bat.

Bowling: Thomas 8-0-37-1; Walker 7.4-2-27-1; Capel 8-0-29-2; Penberthy 8-2-43-1; Roberts 2-0-15-0; Curran 6-0-41-1.

Umpires: R. C. Tolchard and P. B. Wight.

At Chesterfield, June 2. YORKSHIRE beat DERBYSHIRE by three wickets.

## YORKSHIRE v KENT

At Scarborough, June 16. Yorkshire won by 67 runs. Toss: Kent. Blakey's 130 not out was the highest for Yorkshire in the Sunday League; it came from 123 balls with fourteen fours, and he added 116 in eighteen overs with Byas (48 balls). Yorkshire's victory was secured when Batty removed four of Kent's top six batsmen for his best bowling figures in the competition.

## Yorkshire

| | | | |
|---|---|---|---|
| *M. D. Moxon retired hurt | 3 | D. Gough c Benson b Davis | 0 |
| A. A. Metcalfe run out | 20 | J. D. Batty not out | 13 |
| †R. J. Blakey not out | 130 | | |
| D. Byas c Cowdrey b Ellison | 45 | L-b 7, w 9 | 16 |
| P. E. Robinson c Benson b Davis | 11 | | |
| C. White lbw b McCague | 3 | 1/52 2/168 3/187 (6 wkts, 40 overs) | 241 |
| C. S. Pickles c Ward b Davis | 0 | 4/192 5/197 6/198 | |

M. Broadhurst and S. D. Fletcher did not bat.

*M. D. Moxon retired hurt at 12.*

Bowling: Igglesden 8-0-31-0; Ellison 8-1-60-1; Merrick 8-0-48-0; Davis 8-1-42-3; McCague 8-0-53-1.

## Kent

†S. A. Marsh c Blakey b Fletcher ..... 3
*M. R. Benson c Robinson b Batty .... 23
N. R. Taylor c sub b Batty .......... 41
T. R. Ward c Gough b Batty ......... 16
G. R. Cowdrey c Blakey b Pickles..... 2
N. J. Llong c Blakey b Batty ........ 23
M. J. McCague b Fletcher ........... 13
R. M. Ellison b Pickles ............. 14

R. P. Davis lbw b Gough ........... 25
T. A. Merrick not out .............. 0
A. P. Igglesden b Gough............. 0
    B 1, l-b 7, w 6 ........... 14
                     —
1/4 2/62 3/82      (35.2 overs) 174
4/88 5/110 6/130
7/130 8/174 9/174

Bowling: Broadhurst 8–0–27–0; Fletcher 6–0–23–2; Gough 7.2–0–32–2; Batty 8–0–33–4; Pickles 6–0–51–2.

Umpires: J. D. Bond and G. I. Burgess.


## YORKSHIRE v WORCESTERSHIRE

At Sheffield, June 23. Yorkshire won by four wickets. Toss: Yorkshire. This was the only game of the day unaffected by rain. Worcestershire's innings included only two fours, but four sixes.

### Worcestershire

T. S. Curtis lbw b Hartley ........... 8
T. M. Moody c Gough b Carrick ...... 19
M. J. Weston c Robinson b Batty .... 13
D. B. D'Oliveira b Pickles .......... 27
N. V. Radford c Batty b Fletcher ..... 12
*P. A. Neale lbw b Pickles .......... 2
D. A. Leatherdale c Robinson b Fletcher 15
†S. J. Rhodes lbw b Pickles .......... 0

S. R. Lampitt c Blakey b Pickles ...... 1
R. K. Illingworth not out ........... 17
P. J. Newport not out .............. 17
    L-b 3, w 11, n-b 1 .......... 15
                     —
1/22 2/38 3/46    (9 wkts, 40 overs) 146
4/76 5/81 6/99
7/100 8/102 9/123

Bowling: Hartley 7–1–28–1; Gough 8–0–29–0; Carrick 8–0–15–1; Batty 8–2–33–1; Fletcher 6–1–26–3; Pickles 3–0–12–3.

### Yorkshire

*A. A. Metcalfe c Leatherdale b Radford 0
D. Byas c Illingworth b Newport ...... 54
†R. J. Blakey lbw b Weston ......... 3
P. E. Robinson c Radford b Illingworth 10
P. J. Hartley b Lampitt ............. 11
C. White c Illingworth b Lampitt ..... 9

C. S. Pickles not out ............... 30
P. Carrick not out ................. 17
    L-b 9, w 6 ................ 15
                     —
1/0 2/15 3/53    (6 wkts, 39.1 overs) 149
4/76 5/90 6/100

D. Gough, J. D. Batty and S. D. Fletcher did not bat.

Bowling: Radford 8–0–33–1; Weston 7.1–1–21–1; Newport 8–0–29–1; Illingworth 8–0–30–1; Lampitt 8–1–27–2.

Umpires: J. H. Hampshire and J. W. Holder.


## YORKSHIRE v GLAMORGAN

At Leeds, June 30. Yorkshire won by 95 runs. Toss: Glamorgan. Yorkshire, gaining their fifth successive win, equalled their best run in the Sunday League. Metcalfe's 96 came from 98 balls, and when Glamorgan batted, Carrick took five wickets in a Sunday League game for the first time. Maynard took over as wicket-keeper for Glamorgan when Metson was taken to hospital, having been struck in the face by a delivery from Barwick which was deflected by the batsman's pad.

## Yorkshire

| | | | | |
|---|---|---|---|---|
| *M. D. Moxon c Frost b Dale | 52 | C. S. Pickles not out | 8 |
| A. A. Metcalfe lbw b Watkin | 96 | L-b 8, w 6, n-b 1 | 15 |
| †R. J. Blakey c Dale b Frost | 47 | | |
| D. Byas c Dale b Frost | 14 | 1/116 2/207 | (4 wkts, 40 overs) 253 |
| P. E. Robinson not out | 21 | 3/214 4/224 | |

P. Carrick, D. Gough, P. J. Hartley, J. D. Batty and S. D. Fletcher did not bat.

Bowling: Frost 8–0–53–2; Watkin 8–0–40–1; Derrick 4–0–37–0; Barwick 7–0–47–0; Dale 8–0–43–1; Smith 5–0–25–0.

## Glamorgan

| | | | | |
|---|---|---|---|---|
| M. P. Maynard c Blakey b Carrick | 44 | S. L. Watkin b Fletcher | 14 |
| *H. Morris c Blakey b Gough | 20 | S. R. Barwick b Hartley | 8 |
| G. C. Holmes c Batty b Carrick | 6 | B 3, l-b 7, w 4 | 14 |
| R. J. Shastri c Fletcher b Carrick | 4 | | |
| I. Smith c Robinson b Carrick | 23 | 1/49 2/77 3/78 | (8 wkts, 40 overs) 158 |
| A. Dale not out | 20 | 4/89 5/112 6/123 | |
| J. Derrick c Fletcher b Carrick | 5 | 7/147 8/158 | |

†C. P. Metson and M. Frost did not bat.

Bowling: Fletcher 7–0–31–1; Hartley 8–0–24–1; Gough 5–0–26–1; Pickles 4–0–11–0; Carrick 8–1–22–5; Batty 8–0–34–0.

Umpires: B. Hassan and J. W. Holder.

At Lord's, July 7. YORKSHIRE beat MIDDLESEX by seven wickets.

## YORKSHIRE v GLOUCESTERSHIRE

At Scarborough, July 14. Gloucestershire won by 10 runs. Toss: Gloucestershire. Spectacular hitting from Lloyds (30 balls, six fours) and Lawrence, whose highest Sunday League score, 38 not out, came in 26 balls, with three fours and a six, produced 60 runs in the last six overs of Gloucestershire's innings. Yorkshire's six-match winning sequence was halted when they lost their last five wickets for 15 runs.

## Gloucestershire

| | | | | |
|---|---|---|---|---|
| R. J. Scott c Byas b Gough | 31 | J. W. Lloyds not out | 42 |
| C. W. J. Athey b Fletcher | 3 | D. V. Lawrence not out | 38 |
| *A. J. Wright c Robinson b Batty | 41 | L-b 2, w 2, n-b 1 | 11 |
| †R. C. Russell c Fletcher b Pickles | 29 | | |
| M. W. Alleyne b Pickles | 4 | 1/14 2/60 3/104 | (6 wkts, 40 overs) 209 |
| J. J. E. Hardy b Pickles | 10 | 4/112 5/121 6/149 | |

M. C. J. Ball, A. M. Smith and D. R. Gilbert did not bat.

Bowling: Hartley 7–1–33–0; Fletcher 6–0–42–1; Carrick 8–0–23–0; Gough 7–1–35–1; Batty 6–0–38–1; Pickles 6–0–30–3.

## Yorkshire

| | | | | |
|---|---|---|---|---|
| *M. D. Moxon c Ball b Lawrence | 6 | P. J. Hartley c Hardy b Scott | 1 |
| A. A. Metcalfe c Russell b Lawrence | 11 | J. D. Batty b Scott | 0 |
| †R. J. Blakey lbw b Lawrence | 43 | S. D. Fletcher not out | 3 |
| D. Byas c Russell b Smith | 19 | L-b 5, w 6, n-b 4 | 13 |
| P. E. Robinson b Alleyne | 64 | | |
| C. S. Pickles c Gilbert b Lawrence | 7 | 1/21 2/22 3/56 | (39.5 overs) 199 |
| P. Carrick c Lloyds b Smith | 25 | 4/119 5/130 6/184 | |
| D. Gough b Smith | 7 | 7/192 8/194 9/195 | |

Bowling: Lawrence 8–1–27–4; Gilbert 8–0–41–0; Smith 7.5–0–41–3; Lloyds 4–0–23–0; Scott 4–0–26–2; Alleyne 8–0–38–1.

Umpires: J. D. Bond and R. A. White.

At The Oval, July 21. YORKSHIRE beat SURREY by eight wickets.

At Manchester, August 4. YORKSHIRE beat LANCASHIRE by five wickets.

## YORKSHIRE v SUSSEX

At Middlesbrough, August 11. Yorkshire won by 77 runs. Toss: Sussex. Yorkshire's highest total in the competition was more than enough to achieve the victory which took them into the top four. Moxon, who struck nine fours and two sixes in 109 balls, and Metcalfe shared an opening partnership of 171 in 27 overs.

### Yorkshire

| | |
|---|---|
| *M. D. Moxon c Dodemaide b North ..112 | P. J. Hartley not out .............. 5 |
| A. A. Metcalfe c North b Pigott ...... 68 | P. Carrick not out .............. 1 |
| †R. J. Blakey c Speight b North ...... 26 | |
| D. Byas c Lenham b Dodemaide ..... 16 | L-b 7, w 4, n-b 1 ........... 12 |
| P. E. Robinson c Moores b Dodemaide 13 | |
| S. A. Kellett c North b Pigott ..... 13 | 1/171 2/216 3/216 (8 wkts, 40 overs) 274 |
| C. S. Pickles c and b Pigott ......... 1 | 4/243 5/258 6/260 |
| D. Gough b North ................ 7 | 7/261 8/270 |

M. A. Robinson did not bat.

Bowling: C. M. Wells 5–0–23–0; Dodemaide 8–0–48–2; Jones 2–0–21–0; North 6–0–38–3; Salisbury 7–0–50–0; Pigott 8–0–57–3; Greenfield 4–0–30–0.

### Sussex

| | |
|---|---|
| N. J. Lenham c M. A. Robinson | †P. Moores b Gough .............. 15 |
|     b Carrick . 64 | A. C. S. Pigott st Blakey b Carrick .... 4 |
| K. Greenfield c Metcalfe | I. D. K. Salisbury c Pickles b Hartley .. 23 |
|     b M. A. Robinson . 2 | A. N. Jones not out ............... 7 |
| *A. P. Wells run out ............... 30 | B 2, l-b 8, w 3, n-b 1 ........ 14 |
| M. P. Speight c Blakey b Carrick ..... 19 | |
| C. M. Wells c Gough b Carrick ...... 6 | 1/9 2/67 3/99 (36.2 overs) 197 |
| J. A. North c Pickles b Carrick ...... 6 | 4/107 5/129 6/131 |
| A. I. C. Dodemaide lbw b Hartley .... 7 | 7/141 8/156 9/178 |

Bowling: Hartley 6.2–0–16–2; M. A. Robinson 6–0–27–1; Gough 8–0–47–1; Pickles 8–0–57–0; Carrick 8–0–40–5.

Umpires: B. Dudleston and A. G. T. Whitehead.

## YORKSHIRE v NOTTINGHAMSHIRE

At Scarborough, August 18. Nottinghamshire won by two wickets. Toss: Nottinghamshire. Nottinghamshire's fortunes were revived by Pollard and Saxelby, the latter making his highest score in the competition, as they added 97 in fifteen overs for the fifth wicket. The 9 runs needed for victory from Mark Robinson's final over were scored by Evans, who had earlier set a record for the highest number of runs conceded by a bowler in a Sunday League season. His 638, with a game still to play, passed the 610 conceded by E. E. Hemmings, for Warwickshire in 1975, and G. D. Rose, for Somerset in 1990. Nottinghamshire's win, with Lancashire losing at home to Surrey, put them back at the top of the table.

## Yorkshire

| | | | |
|---|---|---|---|
| S. A. Kellett run out | 26 | P. Carrick c and b Pick | 2 |
| *A. A. Metcalfe b Evans | 33 | | |
| †R. J. Blakey c French b Field-Buss | 11 | L-b 14, w 8 | 22 |
| D. Byas c Broad b Field-Buss | 9 | | |
| P. E. Robinson run out | 32 | 1/60 2/65 3/83 (7 wkts, 40 overs) 187 | |
| C. White b Stephenson | 37 | 4/84 5/160 | |
| C. S. Pickles not out | 15 | 6/178 7/187 | |

P. J. Hartley, J. D. Batty and M. A. Robinson did not bat.

Bowling: Pick 8–0–35–1; Stephenson 8–0–39–1; Saxelby 8–0–30–0; Evans 8–0–47–1; Field-Buss 8–1–22–2.

## Nottinghamshire

| | | | |
|---|---|---|---|
| B. C. Broad c Batty b Hartley | 15 | †B. N. French c Blakey b Pickles | 8 |
| D. W. Randall c P. E. Robinson b Batty | 10 | K. P. Evans not out | 12 |
| *R. T. Robinson c Blakey b Batty | 23 | M. G. Field-Buss not out | 0 |
| P. Johnson run out | 0 | L-b 10, w 2 | 12 |
| P. R. Pollard c White b M. A. Robinson | 53 | | |
| M. Saxelby c Byas b Pickles | 55 | 1/23 2/32 3/32 (8 wkts, 39.5 overs) 188 | |
| F. D. Stephenson c Blakey | | 4/70 5/167 6/168 | |
| b M. A. Robinson | 0 | 7/171 8/179 | |

R. A. Pick did not bat.

Bowling: M. A. Robinson 7.5–0–46–2; Hartley 8–0–42–1; Carrick 8–1–24–0; Batty 8–0–31–2; Pickles 8–0–35–2.

Umpires: K. E. Palmer and R. Palmer.

At Taunton, August 25. YORKSHIRE lost to SOMERSET by 46 runs.

# SUNDAY LEAGUE RECORDS

## Batting

**Highest score:** 176 – G. A. Gooch, Essex v Glamorgan (Southend), 1983.

**Most hundreds:** 11 – C. G. Greenidge and G. A. Gooch; 10 – W. Larkins; 9 – K. S. McEwan and B. A. Richards. 394 hundreds have been scored in the League. The most in one season is 40 in 1990.

**Most runs:** D. L. Amiss 7,040; G. A. Gooch 6,682; C. T. Radley 6,650; D. R. Turner 6,639; D. W. Randall 6,556; P. Willey 6,506; C. G. Greenidge 6,344; C. E. B. Rice 6,265; G. M. Turner 6,144.

**Most runs in a season:** 917 – T. M. Moody (Worcestershire), 1991.

**Most sixes in an innings:** 13 – I. T. Botham, Somerset v Northamptonshire (Wellingborough School), 1986.

**Most sixes by a team in an innings:** 18 – Derbyshire v Worcestershire (Knypersley), 1985.

**Most sixes in a season:** 26 – I. V. A. Richards (Somerset), 1977.

**Highest total:** 360 for three – Somerset v Glamorgan (Neath), 1990.

**Highest total – batting second:** 301 for six – Warwickshire v Essex (Colchester), 1982.

**Highest match aggregate:** 604 – Surrey (304) v Warwickshire (300 for nine) (The Oval), 1985.

**Lowest total:** 23 (19.4 overs) – Middlesex v Yorkshire (Leeds), 1974.

**Shortest completed innings:** 16 overs – Northamptonshire 59 v Middlesex (Tring), 1974.

**Shortest match:** 2 hr 13 min (40.3 overs) – Essex v Northamptonshire (Ilford), 1971.

**Biggest victories:** 220 runs, Somerset beat Glamorgan (Neath), 1990.
  There have been 22 instances of victory by ten wickets – by Derbyshire, Essex (twice), Glamorgan, Hampshire, Leicestershire (twice), Middlesex (twice), Northamptonshire, Nottinghamshire, Somerset (twice), Surrey (twice), Warwickshire, Worcestershire (three times) and Yorkshire (three times). This does not include those matches in which the side batting second was set a reduced target.

**Ties (32):** Nottinghamshire v Kent (Nottingham), 1969, in a match reduced to twenty overs.
  Gloucestershire v Hampshire (Bristol), 1972; Gloucestershire v Northamptonshire (Bristol), 1972.
  Surrey v Worcestershire (Byfleet), 1973.
  Middlesex v Lancashire (Lord's), 1974; Sussex v Leicestershire (Hove), 1974.
  Lancashire v Worcestershire (Manchester), 1975; Somerset v Glamorgan (Taunton), 1975.
  Warwickshire v Kent (Birmingham), 1980.
  Kent v Lancashire (Maidstone), 1981.
  Yorkshire v Nottinghamshire (Hull), 1982; Hampshire v Lancashire (Southampton), 1982; Surrey v Hampshire (The Oval), 1982.
  Worcestershire v Nottinghamshire (Hereford), 1983; Lancashire v Worcestershire (Manchester), 1983, in a match reduced to nineteen overs; Warwickshire v Worcestershire (Birmingham), 1983, Warwickshire's innings having been reduced to ten overs.
  Middlesex v Essex (Lord's), 1984.
  Essex v Leicestershire (Chelmsford), 1985; Northamptonshire v Lancashire (Northampton), 1985; Lancashire v Glamorgan (Manchester), 1985.
  Kent v Surrey (Canterbury), 1986; Middlesex v Warwickshire (Lord's), 1986; Yorkshire v Warwickshire (Leeds), 1986.
  Hampshire v Gloucestershire (Southampton), 1987; Hampshire v Derbyshire (Southampton), 1987.
  Essex v Sussex (Ilford), 1988; Surrey v Derbyshire (The Oval), 1988; Sussex v Glamorgan (Eastbourne), 1988.
  Middlesex v Hampshire (Lord's), 1989; Somerset v Sussex (Taunton), 1989.
  Kent v Essex (Folkestone), 1991; Warwickshire v Worcestershire (Birmingham), 1991.

**Record partnerships for each wicket**

| | | | |
|---|---|---|---:|
| 239 | for 1st | G. A. Gooch and B. R. Hardie, Essex v Nottinghamshire at Nottingham | 1985 |
| 273 | for 2nd | G. A. Gooch and K. S. McEwan, Essex v Nottinghamshire at Nottingham | 1983 |
| 223 | for 3rd | S. J. Cook and G. D. Rose, Somerset v Glamorgan at Neath | 1990 |
| 219 | for 4th | C. G. Greenidge and C. L. Smith, Hampshire v Surrey at Southampton | 1987 |
| 185* | for 5th | B. M. McMillan and Asif Din, Warwickshire v Essex at Chelmsford | 1986 |
| 121 | for 6th | C. P. Wilkins and A. J. Borrington, Derbyshire v Warwickshire at Chesterfield | 1972 |
| 132 | for 7th | K. R. Brown and N. F. Williams, Middlesex v Somerset at Lord's | 1988 |
| 105 | for 8th | W. K. Hegg and I. D. Austin, Lancashire v Middlesex at Lord's | 1991 |
| 105 | for 9th | D. G. Moir and R. W. Taylor, Derbyshire v Kent at Derby | 1984 |
| 57 | for 10th | D. A. Graveney and J. B. Mortimore, Gloucestershire v Lancashire at Tewkesbury | 1973 |

# Bowling

**Best analyses:** eight for 26, K. D. Boyce, Essex v Lancashire (Manchester), 1971; seven for 15, R. A. Hutton, Yorkshire v Worcestershire (Leeds), 1969; seven for 39, A. Hodgson, Northamptonshire v Somerset (Northampton), 1976; seven for 41, A. N. Jones, Sussex v Nottinghamshire (Nottingham), 1986; six for 6, R. W. Hooker, Middlesex v Surrey (Lord's), 1969; six for 7, M. Hendrick, Derbyshire v Nottinghamshire (Nottingham), 1972; six for 9, N. G. Cowans, Middlesex v Lancashire (Lord's), 1991.

**Four wickets in four balls:** A. Ward, Derbyshire v Sussex (Derby), 1970.

**Hat-tricks** (19): A. Ward, Derbyshire v Sussex (Derby), 1970; R. Palmer, Somerset v Gloucestershire (Bristol), 1970; K. D. Boyce, Essex v Somerset (Westcliff), 1971; G. D. McKenzie, Leicestershire v Essex (Leicester), 1972; R. G. D. Willis, Warwickshire v Yorkshire (Birmingham), 1973; W. Blenkiron, Warwickshire v Derbyshire (Buxton), 1974; A. Buss, Sussex v Worcestershire (Hastings), 1974; J. M. Rice, Hampshire v Northamptonshire (Southampton), 1975; M. A. Nash, Glamorgan v Worcestershire (Worcester), 1975; A. Hodgson, Northamptonshire v Somerset (Northampton), 1976; A. E. Cordle, Glamorgan v Hampshire (Portsmouth), 1979; C. J. Tunnicliffe, Derbyshire v Worcestershire (Derby), 1979; M. D. Marshall, Hampshire v Surrey (Southampton), 1981; I. V. A. Richards, Somerset v Essex (Chelmsford), 1982; P. W. Jarvis, Yorkshire v Derbyshire (Derby), 1982; R. M. Ellison, Kent v Hampshire (Canterbury), 1983; G. C. Holmes, Glamorgan v Nottinghamshire (Ebbw Vale), 1987; K. Saxelby, Nottinghamshire v Worcestershire (Nottingham), 1987; K. M. Curran, Gloucestershire v Warwickshire (Birmingham), 1989.

**Most economical analysis:** 8–8–0–0, B. A. Langford, Somerset v Essex (Yeovil), 1969.

**Most expensive analyses:** 7.5–0–89–3, G. Miller, Derbyshire v Gloucestershire (Gloucester), 1984; 8–0–88–1, E. E. Hemmings, Nottinghamshire v Somerset (Nottingham), 1983.

**Most wickets in a season:** 34 – R. J. Clapp (Somerset), 1974, and C. E. B. Rice (Nottinghamshire), 1986.

**Most wickets:** J. K. Lever 386; D. L. Underwood 346; J. Simmons 307; S. Turner 303; J. E. Emburey 298; N. Gifford 284; E. E. Hemmings 272; J. N. Shepherd 267; T. E. Jesty 249; R. D. Jackman 234; P. Willey 234.

## Wicket-keeping and Fielding

**Most dismissals:** D. L. Bairstow 255 (231 ct, 24 st); R. W. Taylor 236 (187 ct, 49 st); E. W. Jones 223 (184 ct, 39 st).

**Most dismissals in a season:** 29 (26 ct, 3 st) – S. J. Rhodes (Worcestershire), 1988.

**Most dismissals in an innings:** 7 (6 ct, 1 st) – R. W. Taylor, Derbyshire v Lancashire (Manchester), 1975.

**Most catches in an innings:** 6 – K. Goodwin, Lancashire v Worcestershire (Worcester), 1969; R. W. Taylor, Derbyshire v Lancashire (Manchester), 1975.

**Most stumpings in an innings:** 4 – S. J. Rhodes, Worcestershire v Warwickshire (Birmingham), 1986; N. D. Burns, Somerset v Kent (Taunton), 1991.

**Most catches by a fielder** (not a wicket-keeper): J. F. Steele 101; D. P. Hughes 97; G. Cook 94; C. T. Radley 91.

**Most catches in a season:** 16 – J. M. Rice (Hampshire), 1978.

**Most catches in an innings:** 5 – J. M. Rice, Hampshire v Warwickshire (Southampton), 1978.

## CHAMPIONS 1969-91

| *John Player League* | | | |
|---|---|---|---|
| 1969 | Lancashire | 1981 | Essex |
| 1970 | Lancashire | 1982 | Sussex |
| 1971 | Worcestershire | 1983 | Yorkshire |
| 1972 | Kent | 1984 | Essex |
| 1973 | Kent | 1985 | Essex |
| 1974 | Leicestershire | 1986 | Hampshire |
| 1975 | Hampshire | *Refuge Assurance League* | |
| 1976 | Kent | 1987 | Worcestershire |
| 1977 | Leicestershire | 1988 | Worcestershire |
| 1978 | Hampshire | 1989 | Lancashire |
| 1979 | Somerset | 1990 | Derbyshire |
| 1980 | Warwickshire | 1991 | Nottinghamshire |

# REFUGE ASSURANCE CUP, 1991

Worcestershire reversed the result of the first Refuge Assurance Cup final when they beat Lancashire by 7 runs at Old Trafford, the final being played in Manchester for the first time after being staged at Edgbaston, Birmingham, for three years. In 1988, Lancashire had beaten Worcestershire by 52 runs. In addition to becoming the last holders of the trophy, Worcestershire won £6,000 in prizemoney, while the runners-up received £3,000. Northamptonshire and Nottinghamshire, the losing semi-finalists, each received £1,500. The Man of the Match award in the final was worth £350, and £175 in the semi-finals.

## LANCASHIRE v NORTHAMPTONSHIRE

At Manchester, September 1. Lancashire won by four wickets. Toss: Lancashire. Calm batting by Speak, amid flurries from his senior colleagues, saw Lancashire to another final. Included because Fowler was troubled by a neck injury, he hit nine fours in 115 balls, remaining unbeaten on 94. Lancashire had faltered when the leg-spinner, Roberts, came on; Fairbrother began with a six over mid-wicket, but was caught attempting a second two balls later. However, Austin, promoted to No. 6, regained the initiative with two successive sixes as he and Speak took 17 off Roberts in one over. Earlier, Northamptonshire's openers had put on 50 before Larkins was run out by DeFreitas. Thereafter only Curran, with 61 not out from 60 balls, successfully took the fight to the home bowling.

*Man of the Match:* N. J. Speak.

### Northamptonshire

| | | | | | |
|---|---|---|---|---|---|
| A. Fordham c and b Austin | 54 | | E. A. E. Baptiste lbw b Allott | 0 |
| W. Larkins run out | 20 | | R. G. Williams not out | 13 |
| *A. J. Lamb c Hegg b Watkinson | 2 | | L-b 4, w 1 | 5 |
| R. J. Bailey st Hegg b Watkinson | 9 | | | |
| D. J. Capel c Fairbrother b Watkinson | 21 | | 1/50 2/58 3/87 (6 wkts, 40 overs) | 185 |
| K. M. Curran not out | 61 | | 4/89 5/150 6/151 | |

A. R. Roberts, †W. M. Noon and A. Walker did not bat.

Bowling: DeFreitas 8-0-30-0; Allott 8-0-27-1; Watkinson 8-0-47-2; Fitton 8-0-31-1; Austin 8-0-46-1.

### Lancashire

| | | | | | |
|---|---|---|---|---|---|
| G. D. Mendis run out | 23 | | M. Watkinson c Lamb b Roberts | 0 |
| N. J. Speak not out | 94 | | J. D. Fitton not out | 14 |
| G. D. Lloyd lbw b Capel | 10 | | L-b 7, w 2 | 9 |
| *N. H. Fairbrother c Larkins b Roberts | 6 | | | |
| S. P. Titchard run out | 13 | | 1/59 2/84 3/94 (6 wkts, 39.1 overs) | 186 |
| I. D. Austin c Williams b Curran | 17 | | 4/126 5/149 6/155 | |

P. A. J. DeFreitas, †W. K. Hegg and P. J. W. Allott did not bat.

Bowling: Walker 6-0-27-0; Baptiste 6-0-25-0; Curran 6.1-0-30-1; Williams 8-0-22-0; Capel 6-0-23-1; Roberts 6-0-41-2; Bailey 1-0-11-0.

Umpires: D. J. Constant and B. J. Meyer.

## NOTTINGHAMSHIRE v WORCESTERSHIRE

At Nottingham, September 1. Worcestershire won by 14 runs. Toss: Nottinghamshire. The Refuge Assurance League champions were overthrown by Hick's best bowling for his county in any competition. Nottinghamshire had reached 112 for one when he took five wickets for 6 runs in seventeen balls: Randall was stumped attempting a reverse sweep and Johnson caught low by Curtis at mid-wicket; Pollard top-edged a ball to fine short leg, Saxelby was bowled off the pad, and Stephenson fell to another good catch by Curtis. Despite the efforts of Crawley, returning six weeks after breaking his thumb, Nottinghamshire could not score 30 from the last two overs. In the Worcestershire innings, Hick hit four successive fours in Saxelby's first over, but when he gave the bowler a low return catch, Worcestershire were 82 for three, with Curtis and Moody, the highest scorers of the Refuge League season, already out. Their eventual total owed much to a 77-run stand in 53 balls from Rhodes and Illingworth.

*Man of the Match:* G. A. Hick.

### Worcestershire

| | | | | |
|---|---|---|---|---|
| *T. S. Curtis c Saxelby | 16 | R. K. Illingworth lbw b Stephenson | ... | 24 |
| T. M. Moody lbw b Stephenson | 9 | | | |
| G. A. Hick c and b Saxelby | 33 | B 1, l-b 18, w 8 | | 27 |
| D. B. D'Oliveira c Saxelby b Pick | 28 | | | |
| I. T. Botham c Stephenson b Field-Buss | 23 | 1/24 2/60 3/82 (7 wkts, 40 overs) | | 225 |
| M. J. Weston c French b Pick | 18 | 4/116 5/143 | | |
| †S. J. Rhodes not out | 47 | 6/148 7/225 | | |

C. M. Tolley, P. J. Newport and N. V. Radford did not bat.

Bowling: Stephenson 8–0–39–2; Pick 8–0–35–2; Saxelby 8–0–41–2; Hemmings 4–1–13–0; Field-Buss 8–0–42–1; Crawley 4–0–36–0.

### Nottinghamshire

| | | | | |
|---|---|---|---|---|
| B. C. Broad c Moody b Weston | 12 | E. E. Hemmings run out | | 9 |
| D. W. Randall st Rhodes b Hick | 45 | M. G. Field-Buss not out | | 0 |
| P. R. Pollard c Botham b Hick | 50 | | | |
| *P. Johnson c Curtis b Hick | 3 | B 2, l-b 9, w 2 | | 13 |
| M. A. Crawley not out | 47 | | | |
| M. Saxelby b Hick | 1 | 1/28 2/112 3/118 (8 wkts, 40 overs) | | 211 |
| F. D. Stephenson c Curtis b Hick | 0 | 4/123 5/133 6/133 | | |
| †B. N. French c and b Tolley | 31 | 7/195 8/208 | | |

R. A. Pick did not bat.

Bowling: Weston 6–0–28–1; Radford 7–0–36–0; Illingworth 8–0–26–0; Newport 8–0–52–0; Hick 8–1–35–5; Tolley 3–0–23–1.

Umpires: R. Palmer and N. T. Plews.

## FINAL

## LANCASHIRE v WORCESTERSHIRE

At Manchester, September 15. Worcestershire won by 7 runs. Toss: Lancashire. Ground advantage did not help Lancashire as Worcestershire completed a Cup double over them following their Benson and Hedges Cup win at Lord's in July. Worcestershire were handsomely served by Rhodes, who, opening the batting, scored his first one-day century, and Radford, who ended Lancashire's challenge with four wickets for 6 runs in nine balls. Rhodes's 105, from 127 balls, contained nine fours and two sixes, but Fairbrother's gamble in promoting DeFreitas proved less successful for Lancashire. They were better served by Watkinson, who hit 34 from twenty balls before he was ninth out. This was the last of the Refuge Assurance Cup competitions, following the withdrawal of the sponsors, and it was also Botham's last match for Worcestershire after five seasons with them.

*Man of the Match:* S. J. Rhodes. *Attendance:* 9,025; *receipts* £70,913.

## Worcestershire

| | |
|---|---|
| *T. S. Curtis run out .............. 31 | M. J. Weston not out ............. 14 |
| †S. J. Rhodes c Allott b Watkinson ....105 | B 2, l-b 16, w 6, n-b 2 ....... 26 |
| G. A. Hick c Lloyd b Fitton ......... 37 | — |
| D. A. Leatherdale run out........... 0 | 1/114 (1) 2/190 (3)  (5 wkts, 40 overs) 235 |
| I. T. Botham not out ............... 21 | 3/191 (4) 4/194 (2) |
| D. B. D'Oliveira b Fitton ............ 1 | 5/197 (6) |

R. K. Illingworth, C. M. Tolley, P. J. Newport and N. V. Radford did not bat.

Bowling: DeFreitas 8–0–42–0; Allott 8–2–17–0; Watkinson 8–0–44–1; Fitton 8–0–67–2; Austin 8–0–47–0.

## Lancashire

| | |
|---|---|
| G. D. Mendis c Curtis b Weston ...... 18 | J. D. Fitton c Illingworth b Radford ... 8 |
| G. Fowler c Radford b Illingworth .... 51 | P. J. W. Allott not out ............. 5 |
| P. A. J. DeFreitas c Hick b Weston ... 2 | |
| G. D. Lloyd lbw b Botham........... 32 | L-b 8, w 5 ................ 13 |
| *N. H. Fairbrother c Newport b Tolley 30 | — |
| N. J. Speak b Radford ............. 26 | 1/30 (1) 2/38 (3) 3/104 (2)   (40 overs) 228 |
| M. Watkinson c Newport b Radford... 34 | 4/111 (4) 5/165 (5) 6/188 (6) |
| I. D. Austin b Radford ............. 0 | 7/188 (8) 8/212 (9) |
| †W. K. Hegg lbw b Radford ......... 9 | 9/213 (7) 10/228 (10) |

Bowling: Weston 8–0–25–2; Radford 8–1–42–5; Newport 6–0–30–0; Botham 8–0–53–1; Illingworth 7–0–38–1; Tolley 3–0–32–1.

Umpires: H. D. Bird and J. H. Hampshire.

## WINNERS 1988-91

| | |
|---|---|
| 1988 | LANCASHIRE beat Worcestershire by 52 runs. |
| 1989 | ESSEX beat Nottinghamshire by 5 runs. |
| 1990 | MIDDLESEX beat Derbyshire by five wickets. |
| 1991 | WORCESTERSHIRE beat Lancashire by 7 runs. |

# THE MINOR COUNTIES IN 1991

By MICHAEL BERRY and ROBERT BROOKE

Staffordshire's achievement in becoming the first side to win both the Minor Counties Championship and the Holt Cup limited-overs competition in the same season earned them a historic place in the Minor Counties record books. Captained by Nick Archer, they at last fulfilled their potential, and their stunning, if contrasting, victories in the respective finals wrapped up a spectacular summer for a county which had last won the championship in 1927, during the days of the legendary S. F. Barnes.

A revamped points system was introduced into the Minor Counties Championship in 1991, with the points for a win being increased from ten to sixteen, and both batting and bowling bonus points being available in the first innings. Batting points were awarded for 150 runs (1 pt), 175 (2 pts), 200 (3 pts) and 225 runs (4 pts) scored in the first 50 overs, and bowling points were awarded for three wickets (1 pt), five (2 pts), seven (3 pts) and nine wickets (4 pts) taken, but with no restriction of overs.

After almost a decade of near misses in the Eastern Division – they were runners-up in four successive seasons from 1984 to 1987 – **Staffordshire** finally found the right formula to take the title. Their success was built around the contributions of Steve Dean and David Cartledge, their swashbuckling opening batsmen, who enjoyed a summer rich in runs. By far their most spectacular offering came in the six-wicket triumph over Lincolnshire at Stone, where they powered their way to a partnership of 122 in just fourteen overs. At the end of the tenth over, Staffordshire's score stood at 100 without loss. As Staffordshire won five of their nine championship fixtures, Tony Dutton established himself as a genuine all-rounder, Nigel

*Continued over*

## MINOR COUNTIES CHAMPIONSHIP, 1991

| Eastern Division | M | W | L | T | D | NR | Bonus Points Batting | Bowling | Total Pts |
|---|---|---|---|---|---|---|---|---|---|
| Staffordshire<sup>NW</sup> | 9 | 5 | 0 | 0 | 4 | 0 | 17 | 17 | 114 |
| Cumberland<sup>NW</sup> | 9 | 3 | 1 | 1 | 3 | 1 | 20 | 24 | 105 |
| Durham | 9 | 4 | 3 | 0 | 2 | 0 | 18 | 21 | 103 |
| Cambridgeshire<sup>NW</sup> | 9 | 4 | 0 | 0 | 5 | 0 | 14 | 20 | 98 |
| Norfolk<sup>NW</sup> | 9 | 3 | 3 | 0 | 2 | 1 | 22 | 21 | 96 |
| Northumberland<sup>NW</sup> | 9 | 2 | 3 | 0 | 3 | 1 | 8 | 25 | 70 |
| Lincolnshire | 9 | 1 | 2 | 1 | 5 | 0 | 19 | 18 | 61 |
| Hertfordshire | 9 | 1 | 2 | 0 | 4 | 2 | 20 | 12 | 58 |
| Suffolk | 9 | 1 | 4 | 0 | 4 | 0 | 14 | 21 | 51 |
| Bedfordshire | 9 | 0 | 6 | 0 | 2 | 1 | 7 | 12 | 24 |

| Western Division | M | W | L | T | D | NR | Bonus Points Batting | Bowling | Total Pts |
|---|---|---|---|---|---|---|---|---|---|
| Oxfordshire<sup>NW</sup> | 9 | 3 | 0 | 1 | 3 | 2 | 15 | 19 | 100 |
| Buckinghamshire<sup>NW</sup> | 9 | 3 | 1 | 1 | 3 | 1 | 15 | 22 | 98 |
| Cheshire<sup>NW</sup> | 9 | 3 | 1 | 0 | 5 | 0 | 20 | 27 | 95 |
| Devon<sup>NW</sup> | 9 | 3 | 2 | 0 | 2 | 2 | 20 | 15 | 93 |
| Berkshire<sup>NW</sup> | 9 | 2 | 1 | 0 | 6 | 0 | 21 | 21 | 74 |
| Dorset<sup>NW</sup> | 9 | 2 | 3 | 0 | 3 | 1 | 9 | 21 | 67 |
| Shropshire<sup>NW</sup> | 9 | 2 | 1 | 0 | 6 | 0 | 11 | 22 | 65 |
| Cornwall | 9 | 1 | 4 | 2 | 1 | 1 | 5 | 18 | 60 |
| Wiltshire | 9 | 1 | 3 | 0 | 3 | 2 | 11 | 16 | 53 |
| Wales | 9 | 0 | 4 | 0 | 4 | 1 | 17 | 23 | 45 |

*Win = 16 pts, Tie = 8 pts, No result (including abandoned games) = 5 pts.*
<sup>NW</sup> *Denotes qualified for NatWest Bank Trophy in 1992. Durham qualified by virtue of becoming a first-class county in 1992.*

Hackett, a new left-arm swing bowler, finished with 25 wickets, including a return of eight for 62 against Hertfordshire, and Jonathan Addison re-emerged as a slow left-arm bowler to capture 25.

**Cumberland** were runners-up in the Eastern Division, a welcome return to the right end of the table after twice finishing in ninth place. The first of three championship wins – against Bedfordshire – broke a barren sequence that stretched back to August 1988, and they were also involved in a remarkable last-ball tie with Lincolnshire. Needing 1 run to win with two wickets in hand and ten balls left, they contrived to lose all three wickets without managing the run required. Simon Dutton (625 runs) graduated into a top-quality county batsman, and Steve Sharp made 592 runs. Bernard Reidy, the former Lancashire all-rounder, claimed 23 wickets at just 19.00 runs each, and worthy support came from David Makinson and Malcolm Woods.

In third place, after three wins in their last four games, came **Durham**, playing their final season of Minor Counties cricket before becoming the eighteenth first-class county. They had only 31 points from their first five matches, but they then defeated Northumberland and Lincolnshire, lost narrowly to Norfolk, and bowed out with a victory over Suffolk. The game against Norfolk at Durham University boiled up into a dramatic climax, with the East Anglian county clinching a one-wicket win with one ball to spare, Roger Finney's match-winning boundary also bringing him his century. Durham tried out many players during the course of the season, and sixteen of the 22 players used in the championship were newcomers. Gary Brown, with 633 runs, was the leading run-scorer, while Mark Briers, recruited from Bedfordshire, was close behind him with 582 runs, as well as taking twenty wickets. Stewart Hutton, John Glendenen and John Wood also impressed, but it was the younger players who offered encouragement for the future. Teenagers Paul Henderson, Darren Blenkiron, son of Bill, the former Warwickshire player, Quentin Hughes and Robin Weston all showed great promise, and Weston became the youngest player in Durham's history when he made his début at the age of fifteen.

**Cambridgeshire's** season was again noteworthy for the individual performance of Stuart Turner, whose 31 wickets took his tally of championship victims to 206 in the five seasons since he retired from Essex. Ajaz Akhtar equalled Turner's 1991 haul, while Nigel Gadsby, the Cambridgeshire captain, and Nick Adams dominated the batting. Gadsby, who had missed much of the previous two seasons with injury, piled up 831 runs, the best for the county since 1982, and the promising Adams contributed 565.

Even so, Gadsby failed to finish as the leading run-scorer in the championship. That honour went to Steve Plumb of **Norfolk**, who was only 8 runs short of becoming the first batsman since 1979 to reach 1,000 championship runs in a season. Plumb, stripped of the Minor Counties representative captaincy, and almost discarded as Norfolk's professional the previous winter, proved a point in the best way possible. He made his 992 runs at an average of 90.18 to claim the Wilfred Rhodes Trophy, and he went into the record books as the first Minor Counties player to score two centuries in a match twice. Making 111 not out and 120 not out against Hertfordshire, Plumb repeated the feat he had previously performed against Bedfordshire in 1986. Ray Kingshott was Norfolk's leading bowler with 30 wickets, and Plumb, in addition to making runs, took 21 wickets.

**Northumberland**, bottom in 1989 and 1990, enjoyed one of their most profitable summers for years, and qualified for the 1992 NatWest Bank Trophy. They won two of their first three championship matches, and also reached the semi-finals of the Holt Cup. Peter Graham returned figures of nine for 37 in the victory over Suffolk, claiming the first nine wickets to fall in the second innings, and he finished the championship with 28 wickets, while Steve Greensword, having switched from Durham, picked up 24. But Northumberland's normally solid batting was below par, despite Jonathan Benn making 604 runs and Graeme Morris hitting 474.

**Lincolnshire**, captained for the first time by Jim Love, had enough batting but struggled on the bowling front. Although David Storer (747 runs), Steve Warman (546 runs) and Love (620 runs) ensured that they never went short of runs, only Paul McKeown, with 26 wickets, provided any consistency among the bowlers. Ian Pont, having started the summer as one of Lincolnshire's strike bowlers, retired from the game at the start of June to concentrate on playing amateur baseball.

A final placing of eighth represented **Hertfordshire's** worst season since the championship was split into two divisions in 1983; but being able to play only one session in four days of cricket on home territory in June left them in a forlorn position. Pete Waterman performed the hat-trick in the weather-ruined home game with Northumberland, and Martin James (594 runs) and Neil MacLaurin (508 runs) each had an excellent season with the bat. John Carr would surely have done so, too, had he played more than just the one championship game, in which he scored 148 not out and 62 against Lincolnshire in the same day.

**Suffolk's** recruitment of Roland Butcher failed to improve their fortunes, particularly as the former Middlesex batsman found runs hard to come by in the early weeks of the season on some far from helpful wickets. His first six innings realised just 62 runs, and although things then improved, he was not retained for a second season. Mark Bailey, the Suffolk captain, called it a day at the end of the year, and in 1992 the county will be captained by Ray East, the former Essex left-arm spinner. Simon Clements, with 793 runs, was the only batsman to score consistently, while the slow left-arm bowling of Andy Golding provided the bulk of the wickets (34).

Six defeats in nine games, and no wins, left **Bedfordshire** stranded at the foot of the Eastern Division table. Mark Gouldstone (613 runs) and Ray Swann (564 runs) weighed in with consistent performances and Mark Vincent, a teenage newcomer, impressed as a future prospect with several useful innings. However, the Bedfordshire bowling was cause for serious concern.

**Oxfordshire**, seemingly out of the running after rain had interfered with some early fixtures, pipped Buckinghamshire for the Western Division title by just two points, having accrued 58 points from their final three matches. They tied with Cornwall, defeated Devon with one ball and one wicket to spare, and then beat Dorset by eight wickets in their last game. Phil Garner, their captain, led astutely and wicket-keeper Stuart Waterton once more topped 500 runs. Rupert Evans, the off-spinner, collected 27 wickets.

**Buckinghamshire**, captained for the last time by Neil Hames, also finished strongly, winning two of their last three fixtures. But defeat by Shropshire in their penultimate game proved to be decisive. Malcolm Roberts (565 runs) and Andrew Harwood (554 runs) were the chief run-scorers, with Tim Scriven and Steve Burrow leading the wicket-takers with 33 and 22 respectively in what was Buckinghamshire's last season, for the time being, in the Western Division. They switch to the Eastern Division for 1992 to accommodate the entry of Hereford-shire, who have joined the Western Division to balance the numbers, following Durham's departure.

One of four Western Division sides to collect three wins, **Cheshire** return to the NatWest Bank Trophy in 1992 after an absence of two seasons. Geoff Miller, in his début season for them, began inauspiciously when his first delivery in Minor Counties cricket – against Cumberland in the Holt Cup – was despatched for six by Steve Sharp. Thereafter he became a major asset, scoring 355 championship runs at an average of 71.00 and taking 37 wickets to finish as the leading wicket-taker in the competition. Steve Crawley compiled 761 runs and Ian Cockbain, their captain, made 696. Nigel Peel went some way to solving their problem of new-ball bowling by capturing 32 wickets.

For **Devon**, who began their summer watching the rain wash out two games without a ball being bowled, 1992 will be remembered as the season of what so easily might have been. Up until their final game they were in contention for the Western Division title, only for their hopes to be dashed when they lost to Cheshire off the last ball of their final championship match. And 24 hours later they allowed victory to slip through their fingers in the Holt Cup final against Staffordshire at Lord's. Andy Pugh, Nick Folland and Bobby Dawson were in fine fettle with the bat, while Keith Donohue and Giles White, the latter a leg-spinner who came of age in the county game, shared the wicket-taking honours.

Peter Lewington's feat in passing 500 championship wickets was the highlight for **Berkshire**, the previous season's Western Division champions. Lewington, formerly of Warwickshire, first played for Berkshire in 1967, and his 35 wickets in 1991 were bettered only by Geoff Miller's return. Gary Loveday was in prolific form with the bat, scoring 820 runs, and Martin Lickley, David Mercer and Mark Simmons, the captain, all broke the 500-run mark. Neil Fusedale, a left-arm slow bowler, performed the hat-trick in the game against Shropshire.

Graeme Calway furthered his reputation as an authentic all-rounder to boost an otherwise ordinary season for **Dorset**. Calway made 486 runs and took 21 wickets, and although support was generally thin on the ground, Giles Reynolds had a good season with the bat, contributing 446 runs. The retirement of both Andrew Wingfield Digby, the former captain, and Chris Stone, their long-serving all-rounder, hit Dorset hard.

The unavailability of John Abrahams for all but three games, and the loss through injury of John Foster, their captain, hampered **Shropshire's** championship campaign. They just managed to scrape into the frame as NatWest Bank Trophy qualifiers, but a final Western Division position of seventh was a big disappointment. Bryan Jones was the only batsman to score 500 runs, but the bowlers enjoyed a measure of success. Geoff Edmunds finished with 33 wickets and Paul Pridgeon, the former Worcestershire bowler, snapped up 29 in his début season.

**Cornwall**, long-time holders of the wooden spoon in the Western Division, lifted themselves off the bottom for the first time since 1985. As well as beating Wales – only their third championship victory in six years – they were also involved in last-ball ties against Buckinghamshire and Oxfordshire. In both games they threw away match-winning positions, collapsing from 153 for no wicket to 209 all out against Buckinghamshire, and losing their last six wickets for 22 runs against Oxfordshire. Ed Nicolson hit 677 runs, and David Toseland inched closer to the milestone of 400 wickets, claiming a further 33 victims to take his tally to 390. Graham Watts marked his first season as captain with 27 wickets.

Lawrence Smith of **Wiltshire** amassed the highest individual score of the summer, a memorable 200 not out against Cheshire at Trowbridge in only his third innings for the county. The former Worcestershire batsman shared in a third-wicket stand of 238 with David Turner, who made 103 not out. Smith netted 730 runs in the championship, but Wiltshire managed only one win, Grant Sheppard taking three wickets in the same over towards final figures of six for 67 in the victory over Wales.

**Wales**, who used 31 players, finished at the foot of the table for the first time since joining the championship in 1988. Ironically they showed positive signs of improvement, but they still lacked consistency over two days. Their total of bonus points, 40, was bettered by only four other counties in either division, but they were one of only two counties not to win a championship game. They did, however, pick up an individual honour, with Tony Smith, their slow left-arm bowler, winning the Frank Edwards Trophy for heading the championship bowling averages; his 23 wickets came at 18.39 runs each. The potential of Andy Harris shone brightly in his aggregate of 485 runs, and Andy Puddle, the captain, made 442.

# CHAMPIONSHIP FINAL

## OXFORDSHIRE v STAFFORDSHIRE

At Luton, September 8. Staffordshire won by ten wickets. Toss: Staffordshire. Dean and Cartledge led Staffordshire home to the most comprehensive of victories, their unbroken opening stand of 216 in 141 minutes overwhelming Oxfordshire. Put in, Oxfordshire had reached a useful 131 for two off 37 overs by lunch, but they subsided afterwards. Garner, their captain, made 75 from 126 deliveries before top-edging a pull to long leg, and Humphries, the Staffordshire wicket-keeper, took two catches in one over standing up to the medium-pace swing of Dutton. A hostile opening spell from Arnold briefly contained Dean and Cartledge, but Oxfordshire allowed both batsmen crucial lives, and they needed no second invitation to unleash their talents. Dean reached three figures off 107 balls when he hoisted Arnold over square leg for six in the 31st over, and in all he faced 133 balls, hitting two sixes and thirteen fours in his 117 not out. Cartledge had eleven fours in his unbeaten 83 off 99 balls.

## Oxfordshire

| | |
|---|---|
| J. S. Hartley b Hackett | 4 |
| †S. N. V. Waterton c Humphries b Spiers | 32 |
| *P. J. Garner c Hackett b Blank | 75 |
| T. A. Lester c Humphries b Blank | 23 |
| P. M. Jobson c Dean b Newman | 14 |
| G. P. Savin c Humphries b Dutton | 13 |
| R. J. Cunliffe c Humphries b Dutton | 0 |

| | |
|---|---|
| D. A. Hale not out | 13 |
| K. A. Arnold c and b Newman | 15 |
| L-b 13, w 12, n-b 1 | 26 |

1/5 2/96 3/138     (8 wkts, 55 overs) 215
4/151 5/176 6/176
7/185 8/215

R. A. Evans and I. J. Curtis did not bat.

Bowling: Newman 11–1–33–2; Hackett 11–0–43–1; Blank 11–0–40–2; Spiers 11–0–35–1; Dutton 9–0–41–2; Cartledge 2–0–10–0.

## Staffordshire

| | |
|---|---|
| S. J. Dean not out | 117 |
| D. Cartledge not out | 83 |
| B 4, l-b 7, w 4, n-b 1 | 16 |

(no wkt, 37.5 overs) 216

A. D. Hobson, D. A. Banks, *N. J. Archer, A. J. Dutton, P. G. Newman, †M. I. Humphries, R. A. Spiers, D. C. Blank and N. P. Hackett did not bat.

Bowling: Arnold 9–1–55–0; Hale 5–0–20–0; Curtis 9–0–72–0; Savin 2–0–19–0; Evans 10.5–3–28–0; Hartley 2–0–11–0.

Umpires: P. Adams and K. Bray.

## HOLT CUP FINAL

### DEVON v STAFFORDSHIRE

At Lord's, August 29. Staffordshire won by four wickets. Toss: Staffordshire. A remarkable last-over finish saw Humphries, the Staffordshire wicket-keeper, claw a dramatic victory from what had seemed a certain defeat. Staffordshire needed 17 to win off the final over from Tierney, but Humphries, a left-hander, made the most of the short Tavern boundary, and by hitting 2, 2, 4, 4, 6 he became the toast of the large following from the Potteries. Half-centuries from Folland and Pugh had fortified the Devon innings, with White helping Pugh add 74 in nine overs after lunch. Staffordshire then struggled to build on an opening partnership of 43 between Dean and Cartledge, but Banks held the innings together with an unbeaten 68.

## Devon

| | |
|---|---|
| *J. H. Edwards b Spiers | 26 |
| S. M. Willis lbw b Hackett | 8 |
| N. A. Folland c and b Spiers | 57 |
| A. J. Pugh c Humphries b Newman | 59 |
| R. I. Dawson b Blank | 12 |
| G. W. White c Humphries b Hackett | 31 |
| J. K. Tierney c Dean b Hackett | 14 |
| T. W. Ward not out | 7 |

| | |
|---|---|
| K. Donohue run out | 0 |
| M. C. Woodman not out | 1 |
| L-b 12, w 9, n-b 3 | 24 |

1/11 2/81 3/118     (8 wkts, 55 overs) 239
4/140 5/214 6/215
7/232 8/236

†C. S. Pritchard did not bat.

Bowling: Newman 11–3–32–1; Hackett 11–0–62–3; Blank 11–0–56–1; Spiers 11–4–33–2; Dutton 8–3–26–0; Cartledge 3–0–18–0.

## Staffordshire

| | | | |
|---|---|---|---|
| S. J. Dean c Dawson b Ward | 24 | P. G. Newman c Pritchard b Tierney | 18 |
| D. Cartledge b Woodman | 26 | †M. I. Humphries not out | 20 |
| J. P. Addison run out | 9 | L-b 4, w 10, n-b 1 | 15 |
| D. A. Banks not out | 68 | | |
| A. J. Dutton lbw b Dawson | 31 | 1/43 2/54 3/70 (6 wkts, 54.5 overs) 241 | |
| *N. J. Archer b Donohue | 30 | 4/117 5/187 6/219 | |

D. C. Blank, R. A. Spiers and N. P. Hackett did not bat.

Bowling: Donohue 11-0-50-1; Woodman 11-1-51-1; Ward 6-1-28-1; Tierney 8.5-1-49-1; Folland 6-0-22-0; Dawson 9-1-26-1; White 3-0-11-0.

Umpires: P. Adams and D. J. Halfyard.

*In the averages that follow, * against a score signifies not out, * against a name signifies the captain and † signifies a wicket-keeper.*

# BEDFORDSHIRE

Secretary – D. J. F. HOARE, 5 Brecon Way, Bedford MK41 8DF

*Matches 9: Lost – Cambridgeshire, Cumberland, Durham, Northumberland, Staffordshire, Suffolk. Drawn – Hertfordshire, Lincolnshire. No result – Norfolk.*

## Batting Averages

| | M | I | NO | R | HI | 100s | 50s | Avge |
|---|---|---|---|---|---|---|---|---|
| N. G. Folland | 7 | 12 | 3 | 376 | 71 | 0 | 4 | 41.77 |
| R. Swann | 8 | 15 | 1 | 564 | 130* | 1 | 5 | 40.28 |
| M. R. Gouldstone | 9 | 17 | 1 | 613 | 100* | 1 | 4 | 38.31 |
| R. Dalton | 5 | 8 | 3 | 129 | 65* | 0 | 1 | 25.80 |
| *J. R. Wake | 9 | 13 | 3 | 170 | 31* | 0 | 0 | 17.00 |
| S. D. L. Davis | 4 | 7 | 1 | 89 | 23* | 0 | 0 | 14.83 |
| P. D. B. Hoare | 7 | 13 | 0 | 189 | 39 | 0 | 0 | 14.53 |
| R. Ashton | 3 | 6 | 0 | 74 | 24 | 0 | 0 | 12.33 |
| M. R. White | 8 | 8 | 6 | 24 | 14* | 0 | 0 | 12.00 |
| A. Dean | 7 | 10 | 1 | 74 | 26 | 0 | 0 | 8.22 |
| P. A. Owen | 8 | 8 | 1 | 18 | 10* | 0 | 0 | 2.57 |

Played in five matches: †E. R. Osborn 3, 13, 12, 0. Played in four matches: K. Gentle 27*, 8, 4, 16, 67; †G. D. Sandford 1, 15, 17, 7, 0. Played in three matches: M. Vincent 47, 38, 21, 25. Played in two matches: K. Standring 26, 5, 19*, 18; P. D. Thomas 0, 3. Played in one match: B. C. Banks 14; R. G. Blair 28, 31; I. M. Henderson 17*; R. W. Morris 25, 3.

## Bowling Averages

| | O | M | R | W | BB | 5W/i | Avge |
|---|---|---|---|---|---|---|---|
| J. R. Wake | 244.5 | 43 | 771 | 25 | 5-8 | 1 | 30.84 |
| R. Swann | 120.2 | 23 | 404 | 13 | 3-40 | 0 | 31.07 |
| P. A. Owen | 195.5 | 41 | 650 | 17 | 3-20 | 0 | 38.23 |

Also bowled: R. Ashton 15-4-52-0; B. C. Banks 8-0-48-1; R. Dalton 90-17-271-9; A. Dean 62-11-231-4; I. M. Henderson 8-1-39-2; K. Standring 28-0-134-3; P. D. Thomas 8-0-59-0; M. R. White 127.5-19-460-8.

# BERKSHIRE

Secretary – C. M. S. CROMBIE, Orchard Cottage, Waltham St Lawrence

*Matches 9: Won – Cornwall, Wiltshire. Lost – Devon. Drawn – Buckinghamshire, Cheshire, Dorset, Oxfordshire, Shropshire, Wales.*

## Batting Averages

| | M | I | NO | R | HI | 100s | 50s | Avge |
|---|---|---|---|---|---|---|---|---|
| G. E. Loveday | 9 | 18 | 2 | 820 | 113* | 2 | 5 | 51.25 |
| *M. L. Simmons | 9 | 16 | 3 | 520 | 93* | 0 | 4 | 40.00 |
| D. J. M. Mercer | 8 | 16 | 3 | 512 | 93 | 0 | 3 | 39.38 |
| M. G. Lickley | 7 | 14 | 0 | 515 | 119 | 1 | 3 | 36.78 |
| D. A. Shaw | 8 | 14 | 4 | 263 | 61 | 0 | 1 | 26.30 |
| G. T. Headley | 5 | 10 | 1 | 196 | 37 | 0 | 0 | 21.77 |
| P. J. Oxley | 9 | 12 | 1 | 192 | 53 | 0 | 1 | 17.45 |
| †M. E. Stevens | 9 | 8 | 2 | 58 | 23 | 0 | 0 | 9.66 |
| D. J. B. Hartley | 5 | 6 | 2 | 27 | 19* | 0 | 0 | 6.75 |

Played in nine matches: P. J. Lewington 9*, 11, 9, 0, 0*. Played in seven matches: J. H. Jones 2*, 4*, 7, 5, 9. Played in four matches: M. G. Stear 27, 18*, 0. Played in three matches: J. K. Barrow 13*, 17; N. A. Fusedale 10*, 19, 2. Played in two matches: T. P. J. Dodd 18, 31, 10*, 0. Played in one match: N. Cartmell 11*, 3*; N. Pitcher 3*.

## Bowling Averages

| | O | M | R | W | BB | 5W/i | Avge |
|---|---|---|---|---|---|---|---|
| N. A. Fusedale | 57.4 | 19 | 151 | 10 | 4-35 | 0 | 15.10 |
| P. J. Lewington | 304 | 107 | 656 | 35 | 5-42 | 1 | 18.74 |
| D. J. B. Hartley | 125.5 | 16 | 511 | 21 | 5-36 | 2 | 24.33 |
| J. H. Jones | 159 | 29 | 464 | 18 | 4-53 | 0 | 25.77 |

Also bowled: J. K. Barrow 65-18-182-9; T. P. J. Dodd 21-4-90-1; G. T. Headley 42-10-191-3; M. G. Lickley 35.2-10-98-8; D. J. M. Mercer 5-0-51-0; P. J. Oxley 28-4-102-5; D. A. Shaw 38-6-146-3; M. L. Simmons 3-1-17-0; M. G. Stear 86-12-286-8.

# BUCKINGHAMSHIRE

Secretary – S. J. TOMLIN, Orchardleigh Cottage, Bigfrith Lane, Cookham Dean SL6 9PH

*Matches 9: Won – Cheshire, Dorset, Wiltshire. Lost – Shropshire. Tied – Cornwall. Drawn – Berkshire, Devon, Wales. Abandoned – Oxfordshire.*

## Batting Averages

| | M | I | NO | R | HI | 100s | 50s | Avge |
|---|---|---|---|---|---|---|---|---|
| B. S. Percy | 3 | 6 | 1 | 277 | 123 | 1 | 1 | 55.40 |
| M. J. Roberts | 8 | 16 | 2 | 565 | 131 | 2 | 1 | 40.35 |
| S. M. Shearman | 4 | 8 | 2 | 233 | 72 | 0 | 1 | 38.83 |
| A. R. Harwood | 8 | 16 | 0 | 554 | 76 | 0 | 6 | 34.62 |
| S. Burrow | 7 | 12 | 2 | 292 | 47 | 0 | 0 | 29.20 |
| C. D. Booden | 6 | 6 | 3 | 84 | 25* | 0 | 0 | 28.00 |
| T. J. A. Scriven | 7 | 12 | 1 | 291 | 72 | 0 | 2 | 26.45 |
| J. N. B. Bovill | 4 | 7 | 5 | 48 | 16* | 0 | 0 | 24.00 |
| P. G. Roshier | 5 | 8 | 2 | 106 | 29 | 0 | 0 | 17.66 |
| *N. G. Hames | 8 | 13 | 2 | 169 | 47 | 0 | 0 | 15.36 |
| J. C. Harrison | 4 | 6 | 0 | 88 | 47 | 0 | 0 | 14.66 |
| G. R. Black | 7 | 12 | 0 | 92 | 25 | 0 | 0 | 8.36 |

Played in six matches: †D. J. Goldsmith 0*, 0, 2*, 0*, 0. Played in two matches: J. W. D. Lishmann 0, 6; D. Porter 2, 0, 4*. Played in one match: P. D. Atkins 2*; T. J. Barry 29*; S. J. Edwards 9, 17; †G. R. Fryer 6; †T. P. Russell 4, 2; S. F. Stanway 0*, 5; S. A. Sylvester 4.

## Bowling Averages

|  | O | M | R | W | BB | 5W/i | Avge |
|---|---|---|---|---|---|---|---|
| J. C. Harrison . . . . . . . | 66 | 9 | 197 | 11 | 5-35 | 1 | 17.90 |
| S. Burrow. . . . . . . . . . | 159 | 42 | 421 | 22 | 5-46 | 1 | 19.13 |
| T. J. A. Scriven . . . . | 230.2 | 57 | 664 | 33 | 6-57 | 3 | 20.12 |
| G. R. Black . . . . . . . | 86.4 | 13 | 311 | 10 | 3-49 | 0 | 31.10 |
| P. G. Roshier . . . . . . . | 146.3 | 37 | 397 | 12 | 2-29 | 0 | 33.08 |

Also bowled: T. J. Barry 23.5–6–65–3; C. D. Booden 98.4–25–269–6; J. N. B. Bovill 37.2–5–137–3; S. J. Edwards 9–1–44–0; D. J. Goldsmith 0.2–0–0–0; J. W. D. Lishmann 22–3–87–1; B. S. Percy 12–1–35–1; D. Porter 54–20–156–8; S. F. Stanway 4–0–20–0; S. A. Sylvester 22–2–109–1.

# CAMBRIDGESHIRE

Secretary – P. W. GOODEN, The Redlands, Oakington Road, Cottenham, Cambridge CB4 4TW

*Matches 9: Won – Bedfordshire, Cumberland, Norfolk, Suffolk. Drawn – Durham, Hertfordshire, Lincolnshire, Northumberland, Staffordshire.*

## Batting Averages

|  | M | I | NO | R | HI | 100s | 50s | Avge |
|---|---|---|---|---|---|---|---|---|
| S. C. Ecclestone . . . . . | 6 | 9 | 4 | 286 | 72 | 0 | 2 | 57.20 |
| *N. T. Gadsby . . . . . . | 9 | 18 | 3 | 831 | 131 | 3 | 3 | 55.40 |
| N. J. Adams . . . . . . . | 8 | 16 | 4 | 565 | 91* | 0 | 5 | 47.08 |
| A. M. Cade . . . . . . . . | 8 | 11 | 5 | 145 | 38 | 0 | 0 | 24.16 |
| D. P. Norman . . . . . . | 9 | 17 | 2 | 354 | 88 | 0 | 2 | 23.60 |
| S. Turner . . . . . . . . . . | 7 | 8 | 2 | 101 | 33* | 0 | 0 | 16.83 |
| R. A. Milne . . . . . . . . | 5 | 9 | 0 | 125 | 40 | 0 | 0 | 13.88 |
| R. P. Merriman . . . . . | 6 | 11 | 1 | 128 | 54 | 0 | 1 | 12.80 |
| †M. W. C. Olley . . . . . | 9 | 8 | 2 | 37 | 12 | 0 | 0 | 6.16 |
| Ajaz Akhtar. . . . . . . . | 9 | 12 | 3 | 55 | 19* | 0 | 0 | 6.11 |

Played in five matches: M. G. Stephenson 14, 6*. Played in four matches: J. K. Lever 1*, 3*. Played in three matches: C. R. F. Green 0, 0*. Played in two matches: I. S. Lawrence 16, 20, 62, 16; D. W. S. Pimlett 8, 5*, 5, 8*; K. O. Thomas 7, 8*; D. M. Cousins did not bat. Played in one match: G. W. Ecclestone 0, 53*; D. C. Collard and D. Ralf did not bat.

## Bowling Averages

|  | O | M | R | W | BB | 5W/i | Avge |
|---|---|---|---|---|---|---|---|
| S. Turner . . . . . . . . | 253 | 69 | 647 | 31 | 6-46 | 1 | 20.87 |
| Ajaz Akhtar . . . . . | 244.4 | 58 | 735 | 31 | 6-49 | 2 | 23.70 |
| J. K. Lever . . . . . . | 144.5 | 29 | 428 | 13 | 5-41 | 1 | 32.92 |

Also bowled: N. J. Adams 32.5–7–107–4; D. C. Collard 28–3–87–6; D. M. Cousins 37–6–129–4; N. T. Gadsby 7–0–24–0; C. R. F. Green 96.2–17–359–7; R. P. Merriman 27–1–114–4; D. Ralf 10–4–25–0; M. G. Stephenson 83–23–237–5; K. O. Thomas 58–12–180–4.

# CHESHIRE

Secretary – J. B. PICKUP, 2 Castle Street, Northwich CW8 1AB

*Matches 9: Won – Devon, Dorset, Wales. Lost – Buckinghamshire. Drawn – Berkshire, Cornwall, Oxfordshire, Shropshire, Wiltshire.*

## Batting Averages

|  | M | I | NO | R | HI | 100s | 50s | Avge |
|---|---|---|---|---|---|---|---|---|
| G. Miller ............ | 9 | 13 | 8 | 355 | 79* | 0 | 3 | 71.00 |
| D. W. Varey ........ | 5 | 10 | 2 | 446 | 91 | 0 | 5 | 55.75 |
| *I. Cockbain ........ | 9 | 18 | 3 | 696 | 120 | 1 | 5 | 46.40 |
| S. T. Crawley ....... | 9 | 18 | 0 | 761 | 104 | 1 | 6 | 42.27 |
| J. Gray ............. | 7 | 11 | 3 | 295 | 66* | 0 | 2 | 36.87 |
| J. J. Hitchmough ..... | 9 | 17 | 3 | 335 | 74 | 0 | 1 | 23.92 |
| J. Bean ............. | 9 | 14 | 3 | 233 | 54 | 0 | 1 | 21.18 |
| †S. Bramhall ........ | 9 | 9 | 2 | 90 | 32* | 0 | 0 | 12.85 |
| J. F. M. O'Brien ..... | 8 | 6 | 4 | 19 | 10 | 0 | 0 | 9.50 |

Played in eight matches: N. D. Peel 4*, 0, 0. Played in seven matches: A. Fox 2, 2, 1*, 2. Played in four matches: A. D. Greasley 30, 0. Played in two matches: M. G. Boocock 13; P. A. Davis 0, 1, 34, 11. Played in one match: N. T. O'Brien 16, 58; J. Potts 3*.

## Bowling Averages

|  | O | M | R | W | BB | 5W/i | Avge |
|---|---|---|---|---|---|---|---|
| N. D. Peel .......... | 254.4 | 48 | 861 | 32 | 7-86 | 2 | 26.90 |
| G. Miller ........... | 337.2 | 82 | 996 | 37 | 5-87 | 1 | 26.91 |
| J. F. M. O'Brien ..... | 210.2 | 31 | 775 | 22 | 5-98 | 1 | 35.22 |
| A. Fox ............. | 96 | 23 | 359 | 10 | 4-46 | 0 | 35.90 |

Also bowled: M. G. Boocock 14-0-56-3; S. T. Crawley 43-9-147-3; A. D. Greasley 59-5-232-4; J. Potts 36-3-157-5.

## CORNWALL

Secretary – T. D. MENEER, Falbridge, Penvale Cross, Penryn

*Matches 9: Won – Wales. Lost – Berkshire, Devon, Dorset, Shropshire. Tied – Buckinghamshire, Oxfordshire. Drawn – Cheshire. Abandoned – Wiltshire.*

## Batting Averages

|  | M | I | NO | R | HI | 100s | 50s | Avge |
|---|---|---|---|---|---|---|---|---|
| E. Nicolson ........ | 8 | 16 | 0 | 677 | 93 | 0 | 5 | 42.31 |
| R. T. Walton ....... | 6 | 12 | 0 | 378 | 105 | 1 | 2 | 31.50 |
| S. M. Williams ..... | 8 | 16 | 1 | 407 | 114* | 1 | 1 | 27.13 |
| R. G. Furse ........ | 8 | 16 | 7 | 236 | 58 | 0 | 1 | 26.22 |
| S. Hooper .......... | 7 | 14 | 0 | 240 | 52 | 0 | 1 | 17.14 |
| C. C. Lovell ........ | 5 | 10 | 2 | 119 | 35 | 0 | 0 | 14.87 |
| J. Kent ............ | 3 | 6 | 0 | 81 | 38 | 0 | 0 | 13.50 |
| †D. Rowe ........... | 8 | 13 | 2 | 113 | 21 | 0 | 0 | 10.27 |
| *G. G. Watts ....... | 8 | 12 | 1 | 111 | 50* | 0 | 1 | 10.09 |
| B. F. Purchase ...... | 4 | 8 | 0 | 62 | 30 | 0 | 0 | 7.75 |
| D. A. Toseland ..... | 6 | 9 | 5 | 29 | 12* | 0 | 0 | 7.25 |
| G. Trenwith ........ | 5 | 8 | 3 | 22 | 6* | 0 | 0 | 4.40 |

Played in three matches: S. Moyle 6, 43, 28, 2, 15; S. Turner 2, 20, 0, 11, 22. Played in two matches: K. Blackburn 2, 5, 7, 31; S. Pedlar 18, 24, 0, 12. Played in one match: C. Libby 5*; P. Thomas 19, 0*.

## Bowling Averages

|  | O | M | R | W | BB | 5W/i | Avge |
|---|---|---|---|---|---|---|---|
| D. A. Toseland ..... | 230 | 49 | 647 | 33 | 6-44 | 3 | 19.60 |
| G. G. Watts ........ | 204.2 | 49 | 658 | 27 | 5-65 | 1 | 24.37 |

Also bowled: R. G. Furse 55.5-14-231-4; S. Hooper 3-0-27-0; J. Kent 23-4-85-3; C. C. Lovell 88.2-15-355-6; S. Moyle 43.1-3-215-5; S. Pedlar 32-4-132-4; P. Thomas 11-1-39-0; G. Trenwith 80-24-215-4; S. Turner 63-11-237-6.

# CUMBERLAND

Secretary – M. BEATY, 9 Abbey Drive, Natland, Kendal,
Cumbria LA9 7QN

*Matches 9: Won – Bedfordshire, Norfolk, Northumberland. Lost – Cambridgeshire. Tied –*
*Lincolnshire. Drawn – Durham, Staffordshire, Suffolk. Abandoned – Hertfordshire.*

## Batting Averages

|                   | M  | I  | NO | R   | HI   | 100s | 50s | Avge  |
|-------------------|----|----|----|-----|------|------|-----|-------|
| †S. M. Dutton ....| 8  | 16 | 4  | 625 | 101* | 1    | 4   | 52.08 |
| S. Sharp .........| 8  | 16 | 1  | 592 | 136  | 2    | 3   | 39.46 |
| K. A. Hayes.......| 4  | 8  | 0  | 266 | 73   | 0    | 3   | 33.25 |
| C. J. Stockdale ..| 8  | 16 | 1  | 460 | 126* | 1    | 2   | 30.66 |
| B. W. Reidy.......| 8  | 14 | 1  | 376 | 84   | 0    | 2   | 28.92 |
| D. J. Makinson ...| 8  | 13 | 3  | 158 | 49*  | 0    | 0   | 15.80 |
| D. Patel .........| 8  | 14 | 0  | 209 | 42   | 0    | 0   | 14.92 |
| M. D. Woods.......| 7  | 6  | 4  | 28  | 18*  | 0    | 0   | 14.00 |
| *J. R. Moyes .....| 7  | 10 | 3  | 91  | 39   | 0    | 0   | 13.00 |
| M. G. Scothern ...| 7  | 8  | 3  | 53  | 14*  | 0    | 0   | 10.60 |
| R. Ellwood .......| 6  | 6  | 3  | 11  | 5*   | 0    | 0   | 3.66  |

Played in three matches: G. Bolton 0, 6, 18, 0, 1; S. Wall 15, 4, 3*, 6*. Played in
two matches: S. James 35, 5*. Played in one match: S. Adam 2, 0*.

## Bowling Averages

|                   | O     | M  | R   | W  | BB   | 5W/i | Avge  |
|-------------------|-------|----|-----|----|------|------|-------|
| B. W. Reidy ......| 153   | 48 | 437 | 23 | 4-58 | 0    | 19.00 |
| M. G. Scothern ...| 145   | 35 | 423 | 18 | 5-53 | 1    | 23.50 |
| M. D. Woods ......| 182.2 | 40 | 598 | 22 | 4-59 | 0    | 27.18 |
| D. J. Makinson ...| 243.1 | 58 | 698 | 25 | 7-32 | 1    | 27.92 |

Also bowled: S. Adam 16–7–37–2; G. Bolton 45–10–137–5; R. Ellwood 77–25–200–0;
S. Wall 26–4–93–0.

# DEVON

Secretary – G. R. EVANS, Blueberry Haven, 20 Boucher Road,
Budleigh Salterton EX9 6JF

*Matches 9: Won – Berkshire, Cornwall, Shropshire. Lost – Cheshire, Oxfordshire. Drawn –*
*Buckinghamshire, Wiltshire. Abandoned – Dorset, Wales.*

## Batting Averages

|                   | M  | I  | NO | R   | HI   | 100s | 50s | Avge  |
|-------------------|----|----|----|-----|------|------|-----|-------|
| A. J. Pugh .......| 7  | 14 | 4  | 638 | 97*  | 0    | 5   | 63.80 |
| R. I. Dawson .....| 6  | 12 | 3  | 421 | 118  | 1    | 2   | 46.77 |
| N. A. Folland.....| 7  | 14 | 1  | 565 | 95   | 0    | 5   | 43.46 |
| *J. H. Edwards ...| 7  | 11 | 2  | 385 | 92*  | 0    | 4   | 42.77 |
| S. M. Willis .....| 4  | 8  | 0  | 331 | 100  | 1    | 2   | 41.37 |
| K. Donohue .......| 7  | 11 | 7  | 148 | 55   | 0    | 1   | 37.00 |
| J. K. Tierney ....| 5  | 7  | 1  | 98  | 24   | 0    | 0   | 16.33 |
| G. W. White ......| 5  | 8  | 0  | 64  | 16   | 0    | 0   | 8.00  |

Played in six matches: †C. S. Pritchard 0; M. C. Woodman 19*, 2, 10. Played in five
matches: T. W. Ward 4, 23*, 62*, 20, 91. Played in three matches: N. R. Gaywood 0,
4, 19, 23, 46; R. Horrell 0*. Played in two matches: M. J. Record 1*, 4*, 9*. Played in
one match: †A. Maddock 2*, 0; S. M. Moore 3; K. G. Rice 39, 6; J. Rhodes did not bat.

## Bowling Averages

|  | O | M | R | W | BB | 5W/i | Avge |
|---|---|---|---|---|---|---|---|
| T. W. Ward ......... | 86 | 9 | 374 | 19 | 5-26 | 2 | 19.68 |
| K. Donohue ......... | 176.4 | 44 | 495 | 20 | 3-14 | 0 | 24.75 |
| R. Horrell .......... | 83.3 | 15 | 323 | 13 | 6-43 | 1 | 24.84 |
| G. W. White......... | 122.1 | 14 | 528 | 20 | 5-48 | 2 | 26.40 |
| M. C. Woodman ..... | 135 | 24 | 399 | 13 | 3-47 | 0 | 30.69 |

Also bowled: R. I. Dawson 4–1–9–0; J. H. Edwards 1–0–23–0; N. A. Folland 15–1–61–0; N. R. Gaywood 4–0–35–0; S. M. Moore 11–0–63–1; A. J. Pugh 5–0–39–0; M. J. Record 45.4–5–187–3; J. Rhodes 23–3–84–1; K. G. Rice 13–4–31–0; J. K. Tierney 60–12–224–4.

## DORSET

Secretary – D. J. W. BRIDGE, Long Acre, Tinney's Lane, Sherborne DT9 3DY

*Matches 9: Won – Cornwall, Wiltshire. Lost – Buckinghamshire, Cheshire, Oxfordshire. Drawn – Berkshire, Shropshire, Wales. Abandoned – Devon.*

## Batting Averages

|  | M | I | NO | R | HI | 100s | 50s | Avge |
|---|---|---|---|---|---|---|---|---|
| R. J. Morgan........ | 4 | 8 | 3 | 178 | 44 | 0 | 0 | 35.60 |
| G. S. Calway ........ | 8 | 16 | 1 | 486 | 101 | 1 | 3 | 32.40 |
| †G. D. Reynolds..... | 8 | 15 | 1 | 446 | 76 | 0 | 5 | 31.85 |
| J. R. Hall .......... | 5 | 10 | 1 | 253 | 53 | 0 | 2 | 28.11 |
| J. A. Claughton ..... | 5 | 10 | 0 | 263 | 43 | 0 | 0 | 26.30 |
| S. W. D. Rintoul .... | 4 | 8 | 2 | 151 | 55 | 0 | 2 | 25.16 |
| *V. B. Lewis ........ | 8 | 14 | 2 | 275 | 53* | 0 | 1 | 22.91 |
| R. A. Pyman ........ | 6 | 11 | 2 | 107 | 28 | 0 | 0 | 11.88 |
| A. Willows .......... | 5 | 7 | 2 | 54 | 16 | 0 | 0 | 10.80 |
| S. Sawney .......... | 7 | 12 | 3 | 88 | 22* | 0 | 0 | 8.80 |
| N. R. Taylor ........ | 6 | 8 | 1 | 60 | 24 | 0 | 0 | 8.57 |

Played in five matches: †S. M. Fitzgerald 0*, 0*, 5*, 4*, 14*. Played in three matches: S. R. Knight 4, 27, 0*, 23*; S. R. Walbridge 1. Played in two matches: J. W. Dike 2; J. M. H. Graham-Brown 22, 51, 10*, 8; D. J. Pepperell 17, 47, 0, 6; J. H. Shackleton 5*, 7*. Played in one match: S. J. Legg 9, 1; D. J. McBride 20; P. L. Garlick did not bat.

## Bowling Averages

|  | O | M | R | W | BB | 5W/i | Avge |
|---|---|---|---|---|---|---|---|
| S. R. Walbridge ..... | 75 | 13 | 282 | 13 | 5-46 | 1 | 21.69 |
| A. Willows .......... | 76.5 | 20 | 235 | 10 | 3-63 | 0 | 23.50 |
| G. S. Calway ........ | 176 | 29 | 586 | 21 | 5-65 | 1 | 27.90 |
| N. R. Taylor ........ | 159.5 | 27 | 558 | 18 | 4-44 | 0 | 31.00 |
| R. A. Pyman ........ | 131 | 23 | 523 | 10 | 4-69 | 0 | 52.30 |

Also bowled: J. A. Claughton 1–0–4–0; J. W. Dike 38–12–75–5; P. L. Garlick 23–2–99–4; J. M. H. Graham-Brown 22–7–80–2; J. R. Hall 3–0–14–0; V. B. Lewis 0.4–0–7–0; G. D. Reynolds 2.5–0–17–0; S. Sawney 68.4–13–252–9; J. H. Shackleton 64–16–145–5.

## DURHAM

*Matches 9: Won – Bedfordshire, Lincolnshire, Northumberland, Suffolk. Lost – Hertfordshire, Norfolk, Staffordshire. Drawn – Cambridgeshire, Cumberland.*

## Batting Averages

|  | M | I | NO | R | HI | 100s | 50s | Avge |
|---|---|---|---|---|---|---|---|---|
| S. Hutton . . . . . . . . . . . | 3 | 6 | 2 | 315 | 112* | 1 | 2 | 78.75 |
| P. Burn . . . . . . . . . . . . | 4 | 8 | 2 | 357 | 71 | 0 | 5 | 59.50 |
| M. P. Briers . . . . . . . . | 8 | 14 | 3 | 582 | 90 | 0 | 6 | 52.90 |
| *G. Cook . . . . . . . . . . | 9 | 13 | 6 | 366 | 67* | 0 | 2 | 52.28 |
| G. K. Brown . . . . . . . . | 8 | 16 | 2 | 633 | 114* | 1 | 4 | 45.21 |
| †A. R. Fothergill . . . . . | 7 | 9 | 5 | 140 | 61 | 0 | 1 | 35.00 |
| D. A. Blenkiron . . . . . | 5 | 8 | 1 | 209 | 71 | 0 | 1 | 29.85 |
| J. D. Glendenen . . . . . | 8 | 16 | 1 | 441 | 85 | 0 | 3 | 29.40 |
| P. Bainbridge . . . . . . . | 7 | 13 | 2 | 297 | 68* | 0 | 2 | 27.00 |
| P. W. Henderson . . . . | 5 | 7 | 2 | 113 | 61* | 0 | 1 | 22.60 |

Played in eight matches: S. J. E. Brown 0, 7*, 0*. Played in seven matches: J. Wood 8, 40*, 6, 4*. Played in six matches: L. Beaumont 0. Played in four matches: I. E. Conn 12*, 7*, 0. Played in two matches: †J. D. Harvey 7, 10*; Q. J. Hughes did not bat. Played in one match: G. J. Weeks 5, 8; R. M. S. Weston 6, 2; P. Christie, A. C. Day, P. A. W. Heseltine and G. Wigham did not bat.

## Bowling Averages

|  | O | M | R | W | BB | 5W/i | Avge |
|---|---|---|---|---|---|---|---|
| P. W. Henderson . . . . | 49 | 11 | 174 | 10 | 4-34 | 0 | 17.40 |
| J. Wood . . . . . . . . . . . . | 123.5 | 25 | 353 | 19 | 5-22 | 1 | 18.57 |
| I. E. Conn . . . . . . . . . | 109.4 | 20 | 295 | 14 | 4-42 | 0 | 21.07 |
| P. Bainbridge . . . . . . . | 120 | 35 | 322 | 15 | 3-22 | 0 | 21.46 |
| M. P. Briers . . . . . . . . . | 136 | 19 | 510 | 20 | 5-71 | 1 | 25.50 |
| L. Beaumont . . . . . . . . | 142.1 | 28 | 449 | 17 | 4-55 | 0 | 26.41 |
| S. J. E. Brown . . . . . . | 185.2 | 38 | 574 | 20 | 5-60 | 1 | 28.70 |

Also bowled: D. A. Blenkiron 13–1–73–0; G. K. Brown 1.1–1–0–0; P. Christie 18–2–81–1; A. C. Day 17–1–81–1; P. A. W. Heseltine 23–4–92–1; Q. J. Hughes 50.5–9–175–8; G. Wigham 32–3–128–3.

# HEREFORDSHIRE

Secretary – P. SYKES, The Mews House, Mordiford, Herefordshire HR1 4LN

Herefordshire enter the Minor Counties Championship and Holt Cup in 1992 in place of Durham.

# HERTFORDSHIRE

Secretary – D. DREDGE, 38 Santers Lane, Potters Bar EN6 2BX

*Matches 9: Won – Durham. Lost – Norfolk, Staffordshire. Drawn – Bedfordshire, Cambridge-shire, Lincolnshire, Suffolk. No result – Northumberland. Abandoned – Cumberland.*

## Batting Averages

|  | M | I | NO | R | HI | 100s | 50s | Avge |
|---|---|---|---|---|---|---|---|---|
| A. Needham . . . . . . . . . . | 8 | 10 | 3 | 451 | 84* | 0 | 3 | 64.42 |
| N. R. C. MacLaurin . . . . | 7 | 12 | 2 | 508 | 89* | 0 | 4 | 50.80 |
| †M. James . . . . . . . . . . | 7 | 12 | 0 | 594 | 102 | 1 | 7 | 49.50 |
| M. D. Dale . . . . . . . . . . . | 6 | 10 | 6 | 176 | 40* | 0 | 0 | 44.00 |
| B. G. Evans . . . . . . . . . . | 8 | 13 | 3 | 407 | 106* | 1 | 1 | 40.70 |
| D. M. Smith . . . . . . . . . | 5 | 6 | 3 | 59 | 30* | 0 | 0 | 19.66 |
| N. J. Ilott . . . . . . . . . . . | 4 | 8 | 0 | 124 | 60 | 0 | 1 | 15.50 |

Played in eight matches: W. G. Merry 0, 0, 0. Played in seven matches: P. A. Waterman 0*, 0, 4, 0. Played in six matches: *D. Surridge 6*, 1*. Played in five matches: G. A. R. Harris 30; †D. G. C. Ligertwood 55, 10*, 35, 27*, 18. Played in three matches: M. M. Blackburn 2; R. S. Shakespeare 26, 7, 34, 9*, 3; N. P. G. Wright 4, 0, 68, 19. Played in one match: J. D. Carr 148*, 62; C. N. Cavenor 5; †S. March 0.

## Bowling Averages

|  | O | M | R | W | BB | 5W/i | Avge |
|---|---|---|---|---|---|---|---|
| D. Surridge . . . . . . . . . . | 95 | 23 | 285 | 14 | 7-48 | 1 | 20.35 |
| P. A. Waterman . . . . . | 105.2 | 17 | 435 | 20 | 5-25 | 1 | 21.75 |
| A. Needham . . . . . . . . . | 164.3 | 32 | 543 | 15 | 3-32 | 0 | 36.20 |
| W. G. Merry . . . . . . . . | 153.1 | 30 | 449 | 10 | 3-25 | 0 | 44.90 |

Also bowled: M. M. Blackburn 46-3-238-3; J. D. Carr 7-1-14-0; C. N. Cavenor 5-1-35-0; M. D. Dale 7.1-0-60-0; G. A. R. Harris 98.2-14-362-9; M. James 1.1-0-9-0; N. R. C. MacLaurin 3-0-23-0; R. S. Shakespeare 9-2-40-2; D. M. Smith 74-12-289-1; N. P. G. Wright 9-0-27-0.

# LINCOLNSHIRE

Secretary – D. H. WRIGHT, 18 Spencers Road, Ketton, Stamford

*Matches 9 : Won – Norfolk. Lost – Durham, Staffordshire. Tied – Cumberland. Drawn – Bedford-shire, Cambridgeshire, Hertfordshire, Northumberland, Suffolk.*

## Batting Averages

|  | M | I | NO | R | HI | 100s | 50s | Avge |
|---|---|---|---|---|---|---|---|---|
| D. B. Storer . . . . . . . . | 8 | 16 | 3 | 747 | 112* | 1 | 6 | 57.46 |
| *J. D. Love . . . . . . . . | 7 | 14 | 1 | 620 | 90 | 0 | 6 | 47.69 |
| P. J. Heseltine . . . . . | 8 | 15 | 4 | 435 | 106* | 1 | 1 | 39.54 |
| S. N. Warman . . . . . | 9 | 17 | 2 | 546 | 112* | 2 | 1 | 36.40 |
| N. J. C. Gandon . . . . | 8 | 16 | 3 | 270 | 48 | 0 | 0 | 20.76 |
| D. A. Christmas . . . . | 9 | 13 | 2 | 221 | 74 | 0 | 1 | 20.09 |
| M. A. Fell . . . . . . . . | 7 | 14 | 2 | 218 | 65 | 0 | 1 | 18.16 |
| A. C. Jelfs . . . . . . . . . | 5 | 8 | 2 | 80 | 23* | 0 | 0 | 13.33 |
| R. C. Hibbitt . . . . . . | 5 | 7 | 0 | 77 | 38 | 0 | 0 | 11.00 |
| †N. P. Dobbs . . . . . . | 9 | 8 | 3 | 32 | 18 | 0 | 0 | 6.40 |
| P. D. McKeown . . . . | 7 | 8 | 3 | 24 | 6* | 0 | 0 | 4.80 |

Played in four matches: D. A. Marshall 4*, 0. Played in two matches: A. Afford 33, 2; S. A. Bradford 0, 0, 8; J. H. T. Bramhill 1, 1, 19, 15; R. L. Burton 0. Played in one match: R. T. Bates 1, 1; D. R. Brewis 10*, 2*; N. French 6*; I. L. Pont 13, 3; K. Tillison 9*.

## Bowling Averages

|  | O | M | R | W | BB | 5W/i | Avge |
|---|---|---|---|---|---|---|---|
| A. C. Jelfs . . . . . . . . | 124.3 | 37 | 348 | 15 | 5-39 | 1 | 23.20 |
| S. A. Bradford . . . . . . | 73.5 | 15 | 257 | 11 | 5-53 | 1 | 23.36 |
| P. D. McKeown . . . . | 202 | 40 | 694 | 26 | 5-59 | 2 | 26.69 |
| D. A. Marshall . . . . . . | 119 | 21 | 405 | 14 | 6-47 | 1 | 28.92 |
| D. A. Christmas . . . . . | 205.1 | 41 | 777 | 19 | 4-37 | 0 | 40.89 |

Also bowled: A. Afford 54-14-161-8; D. R. Brewis 18-5-44-0; R. L. Burton 27-5-120-1; M. A. Fell 34.2-3-144-0; N. French 20-2-84-2; N. J. C. Gandon 1-0-8-0; J. D. Love 59.4-7-264-3; I. L. Pont 27-2-124-2; D. B. Storer 7-0-39-1; K. Tillison 24-7-49-1.

# NORFOLK

Secretary – S. J. SKINNER, 27 Colkett Drive, Old Catton,
Norwich NR6 7ND

*Matches 9: Won – Durham, Hertfordshire, Northumberland. Lost – Cambridgeshire, Cumberland,
Lincolnshire. Drawn – Staffordshire, Suffolk. No result – Bedfordshire.*

## Batting Averages

|  | M | I | NO | R | HI | 100s | 50s | Avge |
|---|---|---|---|---|---|---|---|---|
| *S. G. Plumb ........ | 9 | 16 | 5 | 992 | 150* | 3 | 7 | 90.18 |
| R. J. Finney ......... | 9 | 15 | 4 | 476 | 101* | 1 | 3 | 43.27 |
| S. B. Dixon .......... | 9 | 15 | 3 | 469 | 76 | 0 | 4 | 39.08 |
| C. J. Rogers ........ | 6 | 11 | 0 | 381 | 107 | 1 | 2 | 34.63 |
| S. K. Taylor ......... | 4 | 7 | 3 | 126 | 77 | 0 | 1 | 31.50 |
| D. M. Stamp ........ | 7 | 14 | 3 | 346 | 74 | 0 | 2 | 31.45 |
| R. D. E. Farrow ..... | 5 | 7 | 1 | 123 | 42 | 0 | 0 | 20.50 |
| J. C. M. Lewis ...... | 8 | 7 | 2 | 87 | 33 | 0 | 0 | 17.40 |
| D. R. Thomas ...... | 9 | 9 | 2 | 99 | 46 | 0 | 0 | 14.14 |
| R. Kingshott ........ | 8 | 6 | 1 | 13 | 6 | 0 | 0 | 2.60 |

Played in four matches: S. J. Bunting 0*, 1*; M. T. Ellis 5; †D. M. Morrell 6. Played in
three matches: †D. E. Mattocks 23, 4; P. A. Roff 20, 10*, 3, 15*. Played in two matches:
†J. P. Garner 0. Played in one match: R. J. Belmont 0*; B. C. A. Ellison 24*; S. J. B.
Livermore 18; N. Fox and A. J. Mack did not bat.

## Bowling Averages

|  | O | M | R | W | BB | 5W/i | Avge |
|---|---|---|---|---|---|---|---|
| R. Kingshott ..... | 280.3 | 79 | 827 | 30 | 5-78 | 2 | 27.56 |
| S. G. Plumb ...... | 204 | 57 | 668 | 21 | 4-33 | 0 | 31.80 |
| J. C. M. Lewis .... | 197 | 46 | 636 | 19 | 5-81 | 1 | 33.47 |
| D. R. Thomas .... | 104.3 | 15 | 359 | 10 | 2-20 | 0 | 35.90 |

Also bowled: R. J. Belmont 16–3–57–2; S. J. Bunting 60–14–178–4; S. B. Dixon 13–2–33–0;
M. T. Ellis 87.1–24–270–6; B. C. A. Ellison 24–6–82–1; N. Fox 5–0–29–0; A. J. Mack
34–12–66–5; P. A. Roff 43.4–7–190–6; C. J. Rogers 8.1–1–23–4; D. M. Stamp 8–1–24–0.

# NORTHUMBERLAND

Secretary – A. B. STEPHENSON, Northumberland County Cricket
Ground, Osborne Avenue, Jesmond, Newcastle upon Tyne NE2 1JS

*Matches 9: Won – Bedfordshire, Suffolk. Lost – Cumberland, Durham, Norfolk. Drawn –
Cambridgeshire, Lincolnshire, Staffordshire. No result – Hertfordshire.*

## Batting Averages

|  | M | I | NO | R | HI | 100s | 50s | Avge |
|---|---|---|---|---|---|---|---|---|
| J. A. Benn............ | 9 | 17 | 1 | 604 | 143 | 1 | 2 | 37.75 |
| G. R. Morris............ | 7 | 13 | 0 | 474 | 105 | 2 | 1 | 36.46 |
| P. N. S. Dutton ...... | 6 | 10 | 0 | 288 | 61 | 0 | 3 | 28.80 |
| S. C. Dunsford ...... | 5 | 10 | 2 | 221 | 57 | 0 | 1 | 27.62 |
| J. R. Purvis.......... | 9 | 13 | 4 | 185 | 46 | 0 | 0 | 20.55 |
| *M. E. Younger ...... | 9 | 15 | 3 | 231 | 45* | 0 | 0 | 19.25 |
| S. Greensword ...... | 9 | 14 | 3 | 184 | 53* | 0 | 1 | 16.72 |
| †M. S. Tiffin.......... | 6 | 10 | 2 | 119 | 36 | 0 | 0 | 14.87 |
| H. M. Sidney-Wilmot ..... | 4 | 8 | 2 | 88 | 55* | 0 | 1 | 14.66 |
| P. C. Graham ........ | 8 | 9 | 2 | 37 | 16 | 0 | 0 | 5.28 |

Played in seven matches: C. Stanley 1, 4, 12, 3, 13*. Played in five matches: C. J. Harker 1*, 12, 0, 12, 1. Played in four matches: P. G. Cormack 31, 18, 1, 27, 63. Played in two matches: †N. H. G. Bates 2, 3; †K. Corby 6*; R. Darling 2*; P. J. Dicks 28, 20; W. Falla 0*; †P. J. Nicholson 4*, 0*; C. Pleasants 3*; B. S. Brar and N. B. Campbell did not bat.

## Bowling Averages

|                | O     | M  | R   | W  | BB   | 5W/i | Avge  |
|----------------|-------|----|-----|----|------|------|-------|
| P. C. Graham . . . . . . | 189.1 | 47 | 561 | 28 | 9-37 | 2    | 20.03 |
| S. Greensword . . . . . | 176.3 | 50 | 487 | 24 | 5-33 | 1    | 20.29 |
| C. Stanley . . . . . . . | 112.5 | 14 | 500 | 16 | 3-36 | 0    | 31.25 |

Also bowled: J. A. Benn 1.1–1–4–0; B. S. Brar 18-6–33–0; T. A. S. Brown 5.4–0–36–0; R. Darling 18.5–1–110–3; P. J. Dicks 6.5–0–48–1; P. N. S. Dutton 48.2–12–122–8; C. J. Harker 93.3–24–384–9; C. Pleasants 17–5–35–2; J. R. Purvis 82–11–282–6; M. E. Younger 53.3–8–238–5.

# OXFORDSHIRE

Secretary – J. E. O. SMITH, 2 The Green, Horton-cum-Studley OX9 1AE

*Matches 9: Won – Devon, Dorset, Wales. Tied – Cornwall. Drawn – Berkshire, Cheshire, Shropshire. No result – Wiltshire. Abandoned – Buckinghamshire.*

## Batting Averages

|                    | M | I  | NO | R   | HI   | 100s | 50s | Avge  |
|--------------------|---|----|----|-----|------|------|-----|-------|
| G. P. Savin . . . . . . . . . . . | 8 | 10 | 7  | 263 | 62*  | 0    | 1   | 87.66 |
| †S. N. V. Waterton . . . . . | 8 | 14 | 2  | 502 | 100* | 1    | 3   | 41.83 |
| T. A. Lester . . . . . . . . . . . | 7 | 12 | 3  | 290 | 65*  | 0    | 2   | 32.22 |
| P. M. Jobson . . . . . . . . . . | 5 | 8  | 1  | 209 | 67   | 0    | 2   | 29.85 |
| *P. J. Garner . . . . . . . . . . | 8 | 14 | 1  | 353 | 80   | 0    | 3   | 27.15 |
| D. A. J. Wise . . . . . . . . . . | 8 | 13 | 2  | 293 | 53   | 0    | 1   | 26.63 |
| J. S. Hartley . . . . . . . . . . | 8 | 12 | 0  | 254 | 47   | 0    | 0   | 21.16 |
| R. A. Evans . . . . . . . . . . . | 8 | 6  | 3  | 42  | 33   | 0    | 0   | 14.00 |

Played in eight matches: I. J. Curtis 17, 10*. Played in seven matches: K. A. Arnold 0, 25, 0*, 0. Played in four matches: R. J. Cunliffe 16, 0, 32, 14*; D. A. Hale 0, 5, 12*, 10. Played in three matches: D. C. Woods 5, 50, 13, 1, 2. Played in one match: A. G. Sabin 10; M. C. Cox did not bat.

## Bowling Averages

|                | O     | M  | R   | W  | BB   | 5W/i | Avge  |
|----------------|-------|----|-----|----|------|------|-------|
| J. S. Hartley . . . . . | 89.4  | 11 | 278 | 14 | 5-67 | 1    | 19.85 |
| R. A. Evans . . . . . . | 217.2 | 61 | 565 | 27 | 5-23 | 1    | 20.92 |
| K. A. Arnold . . . . . | 179.5 | 37 | 505 | 20 | 6-50 | 1    | 25.25 |
| G. P. Savin . . . . . . | 134   | 30 | 398 | 12 | 4-48 | 0    | 33.16 |
| I. J. Curtis . . . . . . | 188.3 | 39 | 584 | 16 | 3-31 | 0    | 36.50 |

Also bowled: M. C. Cox 6-4–3–0; P. J. Garner 7–2–14–0; D. A. Hale 47–5–178–3; P. M. Jobson 9–0–100–1; D. A. J. Wise 10–0–108–1.

# SHROPSHIRE

Secretary – N. H. BIRCH, 8 Port Hill Close, Copthorne,
Shrewsbury SY3 8RR

*Matches 9: Won – Buckinghamshire, Cornwall. Lost – Devon. Drawn – Berkshire, Cheshire, Dorset, Oxfordshire, Wales, Wiltshire.*

## Batting Averages

|  | M | I | NO | R | HI | 100s | 50s | Avge |
|---|---|---|---|---|---|---|---|---|
| J. B. R. Jones | 8 | 16 | 5 | 540 | 100* | 1 | 4 | 49.09 |
| T. Parton | 9 | 15 | 4 | 483 | 78 | 0 | 5 | 43.90 |
| *J. Foster | 6 | 9 | 1 | 301 | 69 | 0 | 3 | 37.62 |
| J. S. Johnson | 4 | 8 | 1 | 222 | 79 | 0 | 2 | 31.71 |
| M. R. Davies | 6 | 10 | 1 | 269 | 90 | 0 | 2 | 29.88 |
| A. B. Byram | 7 | 11 | 4 | 196 | 47 | 0 | 0 | 28.00 |
| J. P. Wright | 3 | 6 | 0 | 161 | 70 | 0 | 2 | 26.83 |
| G. L. Home | 4 | 7 | 0 | 148 | 39 | 0 | 0 | 21.14 |
| J. Abrahams | 3 | 6 | 1 | 105 | 38 | 0 | 1 | 21.00 |
| †M. J. Davidson | 7 | 11 | 1 | 142 | 30 | 0 | 0 | 14.20 |
| A. P. Pridgeon | 9 | 8 | 1 | 80 | 17 | 0 | 0 | 11.42 |
| G. Edmunds | 9 | 6 | 5 | 9 | 4* | 0 | 0 | 9.00 |
| A. S. Barnard | 7 | 8 | 3 | 32 | 12* | 0 | 0 | 6.40 |

Played in five matches: P. B. Wormald 3, 3, 9. Played in two matches: P. T. Massey 2, 0, 22; J. S. Roberts 0*; B. K. Shantry 0. Played in one match: A. N. Johnson 17; J. G. Slater 2; G. J. Toogood 2*; †J. R. Weaver 35*, 0; J. V. Anders and †G. D. Hughes did not bat.

## Bowling Averages

|  | O | M | R | W | BB | 5W/i | Avge |
|---|---|---|---|---|---|---|---|
| G. Edmunds | 279.2 | 90 | 667 | 33 | 5-61 | 1 | 20.21 |
| A. S. Barnard | 157.1 | 43 | 387 | 17 | 4-24 | 0 | 22.76 |
| A. P. Pridgeon | 260.4 | 62 | 670 | 29 | 5-38 | 1 | 23.10 |
| A. B. Byram | 112.3 | 18 | 395 | 17 | 7-20 | 2 | 23.23 |
| P. B. Wormald | 81 | 16 | 288 | 11 | 4-28 | 0 | 26.18 |

Also bowled: J. Abrahams 44-9-124-3; P. T. Massey 15-2-33-1; T. Parton 4-0-16-0; J. S. Roberts 43.3-8-145-7; B. K. Shantry 30-2-135-1; J. G. Slater 9-2-22-1.

# STAFFORDSHIRE

Secretary – W. S. BOURNE, 10 The Pavement, Brewood ST19 9BZ

*Matches 9: Won – Bedfordshire, Durham, Hertfordshire, Lincolnshire, Suffolk. Drawn – Cambridgeshire, Cumberland, Norfolk, Northumberland.*

## Batting Averages

|  | M | I | NO | R | HI | 100s | 50s | Avge |
|---|---|---|---|---|---|---|---|---|
| A. J. Dutton | 8 | 10 | 4 | 336 | 63 | 0 | 3 | 56.00 |
| S. J. Dean | 9 | 16 | 1 | 678 | 134* | 2 | 3 | 45.20 |
| A. D. Hobson | 9 | 15 | 4 | 481 | 120* | 1 | 4 | 43.72 |
| D. Cartledge | 8 | 14 | 0 | 562 | 109 | 1 | 4 | 40.14 |
| J. P. Addison | 7 | 11 | 3 | 245 | 84* | 0 | 2 | 30.62 |
| †M. I. Humphries | 9 | 7 | 4 | 82 | 67* | 0 | 1 | 27.33 |
| *N. J. Archer | 9 | 11 | 4 | 186 | 62 | 0 | 1 | 26.57 |
| J. A. Waterhouse | 4 | 7 | 2 | 121 | 104* | 1 | 0 | 24.20 |

Played in eight matches: N. P. Hackett 2*, 7. Played in five matches: D. C. Blank 0; P. G. Newman 14*, 12*, 8*, 32, 1. Played in four matches: A. P. Bryan 5*, 2*, 1; R. A. Spiers 10, 0. Played in three matches: D. A. Banks 14, 28, 19, 39*, 75; P. F. Ridgway 1, 0. Played in two matches: P. R. Oliver 10, 19, 0, 40; G. D. Williams 2*, 1*.

## Bowling Averages

|  | O | M | R | W | BB | 5W/i | Avge |
|---|---|---|---|---|---|---|---|
| A. J. Dutton . . . . . . . | 87.1 | 23 | 293 | 14 | 3-29 | 0 | 20.92 |
| J. P. Addison . . . . . . | 162 | 22 | 616 | 25 | 6-83 | 1 | 24.64 |
| D. C. Blank . . . . . . . | 103.3 | 22 | 340 | 13 | 4-56 | 0 | 26.15 |
| N. P. Hackett . . . . . | 205.4 | 52 | 658 | 25 | 8-62 | 1 | 26.32 |

Also bowled: A. P. Bryan 73–9–305–8; D. Cartledge 55–8–207–4; S. J. Dean 1–0–1–0;
P. G. Newman 129.5–24–386–9; P. F. Ridgway 59.4–8–221–5; R. A. Spiers 117–32–339–8;
G. D. Williams 39–7–104–3.

## SUFFOLK

Secretary – T. POUND, 94 Henley Road, Ipswich IP1 4NJ

*Matches 9: Won – Bedfordshire. Lost – Cambridgeshire, Durham, Northumberland, Staffordshire.
Drawn – Cumberland, Hertfordshire, Lincolnshire, Norfolk.*

## Batting Averages

|  | M | I | NO | R | HI | 100s | 50s | Avge |
|---|---|---|---|---|---|---|---|---|
| S. M. Clements . . . . | 9 | 18 | 1 | 793 | 112 | 2 | 6 | 46.64 |
| S. J. Halliday . . . . . | 3 | 6 | 0 | 204 | 81 | 0 | 2 | 34.00 |
| R. O. Butcher . . . . . | 7 | 14 | 0 | 391 | 74 | 0 | 3 | 27.92 |
| R. R. Gregg . . . . . . | 6 | 11 | 3 | 196 | 35* | 0 | 0 | 24.50 |
| †A. D. Brown . . . . . | 9 | 12 | 6 | 128 | 33* | 0 | 0 | 21.33 |
| J. W. Edrich . . . . . | 3 | 6 | 0 | 125 | 58 | 0 | 1 | 20.83 |
| A. J. Squire . . . . . . . | 7 | 14 | 1 | 261 | 79 | 0 | 1 | 20.07 |
| M. J. Peck . . . . . . . | 8 | 15 | 1 | 256 | 70 | 0 | 2 | 18.28 |
| I. D. Graham . . . . . | 5 | 8 | 1 | 110 | 33 | 0 | 0 | 15.71 |
| P. J. Caley . . . . . . . . | 9 | 17 | 2 | 231 | 40 | 0 | 0 | 15.40 |
| A. K. Golding . . . . . | 9 | 12 | 2 | 153 | 79 | 0 | 1 | 15.30 |
| *M. D. Bailey . . . . . | 9 | 10 | 3 | 40 | 11 | 0 | 0 | 5.71 |
| R. C. Green . . . . . . | 5 | 6 | 0 | 5 | 3 | 0 | 0 | 0.83 |

Played in three matches: P. Toogood 1, 8*, 9*, 22*, 16*. Played in two matches:
C. C. Graham 4*, 2*, 1*. Played in one match: R. Barber 2, 9; R. E. East 18, 29;
N. F. Gregory 19, 3; M. S. A. McEvoy 7, 9; R. A. Pybus 24.

## Bowling Averages

|  | O | M | R | W | BB | 5W/i | Avge |
|---|---|---|---|---|---|---|---|
| R. C. Green . . . . . . . | 88.3 | 12 | 275 | 13 | 6-49 | 1 | 21.15 |
| A. K. Golding . . . . . | 265.1 | 50 | 858 | 34 | 6-65 | 1 | 25.23 |
| M. D. Bailey . . . . . . | 114 | 21 | 393 | 12 | 5-47 | 2 | 32.75 |
| R. R. Gregg . . . . . . | 105.4 | 10 | 425 | 11 | 6-52 | 1 | 38.63 |

Also bowled: P. J. Caley 62.5–15–248–6; S. M. Clements 4.1–0–33–0; R. E. East
14.3–3–48–1; J. W. Edrich 12–0–94–2; C. C. Graham 11–0–56–1; I. D. Graham
84.3–9–378–8; R. A. Pybus 34–4–118–4; A. J. Squire 1–0–2–0; P. Toogood 45.3–8–178–7.

## WALES MINOR COUNTIES

Secretary – BILL EDWARDS, 59a King Edward Road,
Swansea SA1 4LN

*Matches 9: Lost – Cheshire, Cornwall, Oxfordshire, Wiltshire. Drawn – Berkshire, Buckingham-
shire, Dorset, Shropshire. Abandoned – Devon.*

## Batting Averages

|  | M | I | NO | R | HI | 100s | 50s | Avge |
|---|---|---|---|---|---|---|---|---|
| A. W. Harris ...... | 6 | 12 | 1 | 485 | 82 | 0 | 5 | 44.09 |
| S. G. Watkins ..... | 5 | 10 | 0 | 380 | 71 | 0 | 3 | 38.00 |
| *A. C. Puddle ..... | 8 | 16 | 2 | 442 | 100 | 1 | 1 | 31.57 |
| M. A. G. Jones .... | 3 | 6 | 0 | 178 | 97 | 0 | 2 | 29.66 |
| J. Griffiths ........ | 3 | 6 | 0 | 155 | 42 | 0 | 0 | 25.83 |
| M. Davies.......... | 3 | 6 | 3 | 73 | 26 | 0 | 0 | 24.33 |
| N. G. Roberts ..... | 6 | 12 | 0 | 247 | 60 | 0 | 1 | 20.58 |
| G. Edwards ....... | 4 | 6 | 3 | 54 | 26 | 0 | 0 | 18.00 |
| †J. B. Bishop ..... | 4 | 8 | 0 | 133 | 56 | 0 | 1 | 16.62 |
| A. D. Griffith ..... | 4 | 6 | 0 | 87 | 33 | 0 | 0 | 14.50 |
| B. J. Lloyd ........ | 6 | 10 | 3 | 84 | 26* | 0 | 0 | 12.00 |
| T. C. Hughes ..... | 5 | 10 | 1 | 83 | 22 | 0 | 0 | 9.22 |

Played in four matches: A. Smith 4, 3, 0, 1. Played in three matches: G. Hughes 0, 4*, 0; †A. D. Shaw 9, 17, 0*, 0. Played in two matches: C. Elward 46, 0, 14, 23; R. Hicks 21*, 26, 13; B. Metcalf 25, 14, 36*, 14; R. E. Morris 6, 8, 30, 1; S. Pearce 13*, 1, 8. Played in one match: M. H. Davies 0; S. W. Evans 11, 31; P. Makinson 9*; R. Moore 54, 29; †I. Poole 9; R. Thomas 2*; C. G. Williams 1*; S. A. Williams 10, 23; R. Wiseman 2, 25*; G. Wood 1, 2; H. G. Rogers did not bat.

## Bowling Averages

|  | O | M | R | W | BB | 5W/i | Avge |
|---|---|---|---|---|---|---|---|
| A. Smith .......... | 170.5 | 53 | 423 | 23 | 7-51 | 3 | 18.39 |
| A. D. Griffith ...... | 82 | 12 | 348 | 17 | 5-62 | 1 | 20.47 |
| M. Davies.......... | 99.4 | 20 | 391 | 10 | 6-52 | 1 | 39.10 |
| B. J. Lloyd ........ | 181 | 31 | 529 | 10 | 3-69 | 0 | 52.90 |

Also bowled: G. Edwards 83.2-17-260-9; G. Hughes 60-8-277-5; P. Makinson 14-3-73-0; S. Pearce 36-6-116-3; N. G. Roberts 52-10-165-4; H. G. Rogers 18-3-60-0; R. Thomas 8-0-39-1; S. G. Watkins 48-6-187-6; C. G. Williams 17-4-47-0; R. Wiseman 15-4-35-2.

# WILTSHIRE

Secretary – C. R. SHEPPARD, 45 Ipswich Street, Swindon SN2 1DB

*Matches 9: Won – Wales. Lost – Berkshire, Buckinghamshire, Dorset. Drawn – Cheshire, Devon, Shropshire. No result – Oxfordshire. Abandoned – Cornwall.*

## Batting Averages

|  | M | I | NO | R | HI | 100s | 50s | Avge |
|---|---|---|---|---|---|---|---|---|
| L. K. Smith ........ | 8 | 14 | 2 | 730 | 200* | 3 | 3 | 60.83 |
| D. R. Turner ...... | 7 | 12 | 2 | 406 | 103* | 1 | 4 | 40.60 |
| J. J. Newman ...... | 7 | 12 | 1 | 358 | 70* | 0 | 3 | 32.54 |
| †S. M. Perrin ...... | 8 | 12 | 2 | 308 | 67 | 0 | 2 | 30.80 |
| P. A. C. Bail ...... | 5 | 9 | 0 | 149 | 77 | 0 | 1 | 16.55 |
| *B. H. White ...... | 7 | 11 | 0 | 147 | 45 | 0 | 0 | 13.36 |
| S. J. Malone........ | 8 | 10 | 3 | 85 | 20* | 0 | 0 | 12.14 |
| D. P. Simpkins ..... | 8 | 12 | 1 | 130 | 41 | 0 | 0 | 11.81 |
| I. G. Osborne ..... | 8 | 10 | 1 | 98 | 41 | 0 | 0 | 10.88 |
| G. Sheppard........ | 5 | 7 | 3 | 37 | 15* | 0 | 0 | 9.25 |
| A. Webb........... | 8 | 8 | 3 | 15 | 11* | 0 | 0 | 3.00 |

Played in four matches: R. R. Savage 0, 14, 0, 37*, 33. Played in two matches: N. Prigent 5*, 9, 4*. Played in one match: K. N. Foyle 0, 37; D. R. Parry 26, 49; C. R. Trembath 13.

**Bowling Averages**

|  | O | M | R | W | BB | 5W/i | Avge |
|---|---|---|---|---|---|---|---|
| D. P. Simpkins ..... | 89 | 19 | 282 | 12 | 4-54 | 0 | 23.50 |
| G. Sheppard ........ | 110.4 | 15 | 444 | 17 | 6-67 | 1 | 26.11 |
| A. Webb............ | 177.1 | 19 | 740 | 18 | 4-72 | 0 | 41.11 |
| S. J. Malone........ | 153.2 | 16 | 611 | 10 | 3-39 | 0 | 61.10 |

Also bowled: P. A. C. Bail 12–1–46–2; I. G. Osborne 142.4–24–467–9; N. Prigent 48–2–224–7; C. R. Trembath 16–7–29–2.

## TOP TEN MINOR COUNTIES CHAMPIONSHIP AVERAGES, 1991

### BATTING

(Qualification: 8 innings)

|  | M | I | NO | R | HI | 100s | Avge |
|---|---|---|---|---|---|---|---|
| S. G. Plumb (*Norfolk*)............... | 9 | 16 | 5 | 992 | 150* | 3 | 90.18 |
| G. P. Savin (*Oxfordshire*) ........... | 8 | 10 | 7 | 263 | 62* | 0 | 87.66 |
| G. Miller (*Cheshire*)............... | 9 | 13 | 8 | 355 | 79* | 0 | 71.00 |
| A. Needham (*Hertfordshire*) ......... | 8 | 10 | 3 | 451 | 84* | 0 | 64.42 |
| A. J. Pugh (*Devon*) .............. | 7 | 14 | 4 | 638 | 97* | 0 | 63.80 |
| L. K. Smith (*Wiltshire*) ........... | 8 | 14 | 2 | 730 | 200* | 3 | 60.83 |
| P. Burn (*Durham*) ............... | 4 | 8 | 2 | 357 | 71 | 0 | 59.50 |
| D. B. Storer (*Lincolnshire*) ......... | 8 | 16 | 3 | 747 | 112* | 1 | 57.46 |
| S. C. Ecclestone (*Cambridgeshire*) ..... | 6 | 9 | 4 | 286 | 72 | 0 | 57.20 |
| A. J. Dutton (*Staffordshire*)........... | 8 | 10 | 4 | 336 | 63 | 0 | 56.00 |

### BOWLING

(Qualification: 20 wickets)

|  | O | M | R | W | BB | Avge |
|---|---|---|---|---|---|---|
| A. Smith (*Wales MC*)............... | 170.5 | 53 | 423 | 23 | 7-51 | 18.39 |
| P. J. Lewington (*Berkshire*) ........... | 304 | 107 | 656 | 35 | 5-42 | 18.74 |
| B. W. Reidy (*Cumberland*) ........... | 153 | 48 | 437 | 23 | 4-58 | 19.00 |
| S. Burrow (*Buckinghamshire*)........... | 159 | 42 | 421 | 22 | 5-46 | 19.13 |
| D. A. Toseland (*Cornwall*) ........... | 230 | 49 | 647 | 33 | 6-44 | 19.60 |
| P. C. Graham (*Northumberland*) ....... | 189.1 | 47 | 561 | 28 | 9-37 | 20.03 |
| T. J. A. Scriven (*Buckinghamshire*) ..... | 230.2 | 57 | 664 | 33 | 6-57 | 20.12 |
| G. Edmunds (*Shropshire*) ........... | 279.2 | 90 | 667 | 33 | 5-61 | 20.21 |
| S. Greensword (*Northumberland*) ....... | 176.3 | 50 | 487 | 24 | 5-33 | 20.29 |
| S. Turner (*Cambridgeshire*) ........... | 253 | 69 | 647 | 31 | 6-46 | 20.87 |

## THE MINOR COUNTIES CHAMPIONS

| | | | |
|---|---|---|---|
| 1895 { Norfolk / Durham / Worcestershire | 1901 | Durham | 1912 | In abeyance |
| 1896 Worcestershire | 1902 | Wiltshire | 1913 | Norfolk |
| 1897 Worcestershire | 1903 | Northamptonshire | 1914 | Staffordshire |
| 1898 Worcestershire | 1904 | Northamptonshire | 1920 | Staffordshire |
| 1899 { Northamptonshire / Buckinghamshire | 1905 | Norfolk | 1921 | Staffordshire |
| | 1906 | Staffordshire | 1922 | Buckinghamshire |
| Glamorgan | 1907 | Lancashire II | 1923 | Buckinghamshire |
| 1900 { Durham / Northamptonshire | 1908 | Staffordshire | 1924 | Berkshire |
| | 1909 | Wiltshire | 1925 | Buckinghamshire |
| | 1910 | Norfolk | 1926 | Durham |
| | 1911 | Staffordshire | 1927 | Staffordshire |

| | | | | | | |
|---|---|---|---|---|---|---|
| 1928 | Berkshire | 1954 | Surrey II | 1974 | Oxfordshire |
| 1929 | Oxfordshire | 1955 | Surrey II | 1975 | Hertfordshire |
| 1930 | Durham | 1956 | Kent II | 1976 | Durham |
| 1931 | Leicestershire II | 1957 | Yorkshire II | 1977 | Suffolk |
| 1932 | Buckinghamshire | 1958 | Yorkshire II | 1978 | Devon |
| 1933 | Undecided | 1959 | Warwickshire II | 1979 | Suffolk |
| 1934 | Lancashire II | 1960 | Lancashire II | 1980 | Durham |
| 1935 | Middlesex II | 1961 | Somerset II | 1981 | Durham |
| 1936 | Hertfordshire | 1962 | Warwickshire II | 1982 | Oxfordshire |
| 1937 | Lancashire II | 1963 | Cambridgeshire | 1983 | Hertfordshire |
| 1938 | Buckinghamshire | 1964 | Lancashire II | 1984 | Durham |
| 1939 | Surrey II | 1965 | Somerset II | 1985 | Cheshire |
| 1946 | Suffolk | 1966 | Lincolnshire | 1986 | Cumberland |
| 1947 | Yorkshire | 1967 | Cheshire | 1987 | Buckinghamshire |
| 1948 | Lancashire II | 1968 | Yorkshire II | 1988 | Cheshire |
| 1949 | Lancashire II | 1969 | Buckinghamshire | 1989 | Oxfordshire |
| 1950 | Surrey II | 1970 | Bedfordshire | 1990 | Hertfordshire |
| 1951 | Kent II | 1971 | Yorkshire II | 1991 | Staffordshire |
| 1952 | Buckinghamshire | 1972 | Bedfordshire | | |
| 1953 | Berkshire | 1973 | Shropshire | | |

---

## I ZINGARI RESULTS, 1991

*Matches 25: Won 13, Lost 4, Drawn 8.*

| | | |
|---|---|---|
| April 23 | Eton College | Lost by nine wickets |
| May 2 | Winchester College | Won by 78 runs |
| May 12 | Honourable Artillery Company | Drawn |
| May 18 | Royal Artillery | Won by two wickets |
| May 19 | Staff College | Lost by seven wickets |
| May 25 | Eton Ramblers | Won by three wickets |
| May 30 | Harrow School | Lost by 59 runs |
| June 8 | Hurlingham CC | Won by five wickets |
| June 9 | Earl of Carnarvon's XI | Drawn |
| June 15 | Charterhouse School | Drawn |
| June 16 | Sandhurst Wanderers | Drawn |
| June 22 | Guards CC | Drawn |
| July 6 | Bradfield Waifs | Won by seven wickets |
| July 7 | Hagley CC | Won by five wickets |
| July 13 | Green Jackets Club | Drawn |
| July 20 | Leicester Gentlemen | Drawn |
| July 21 | Sir John Starkey's XI | Won by 92 runs |
| July 28 | Lavinia, Duchess of Norfolk's XI | Won by 53 runs |
| August 3 | R. Leigh Pemberton's XI | Won by six wickets |
| August 4 | Band of Brothers | Won by five wickets |
| August 10, 11 | South Wales Hunts XI | Lost by two wickets |
| August 18 | Royal Navy CC | Won by 119 runs |
| August 31 | Hampshire Hogs | Drawn |
| September 1 | Captain R. H. Hawkins' XI | Won by five wickets |
| September 8 | J. H. Pawle's XI | Won by three wickets |

I Zingari's number of wins in 1991, thirteen, was the most since 1912, when fifteen wins were recorded in 30 matches.

# RAPID CRICKETLINE SECOND ELEVEN CHAMPIONSHIP, 1991

With a late-season surge, Yorkshire, bottom of the table in 1990, came through to win the Second Eleven Championship in 1991, finishing six points ahead of their nearest rivals. It was the third time they had won the title outright, having been champions in 1977 and 1984 and shared the title with Kent in 1987. Runners-up Warwickshire, seventh the previous season, finished a comfortable seventeen points ahead of third-placed Somerset. At one stage in mid-August, both Warwickshire's first and second teams looked to be in contention for their respective Championships, a double previously achieved only by Kent in 1970. As it was, they finished with neither. Nor did they find any consolation in the Bain Clarkson Trophy, which was won by Nottinghamshire, fifth in the Championship table, who comfortably beat Surrey (sixth) by eight wickets at The Oval. The two sides had respectively beaten Kent and Hampshire in the semi-finals.

Seven batsmen passed 1,000 runs in the Championship, the highest aggregate being 1,222 at 47.00 by Rupert Cox of Hampshire, one of sixteen players who appeared in all their county's matches in the Championship. Close behind him was Lancashire's Stephen Titchard, whose 1,212 came in twenty innings at the impressive average of 93.23. His five hundreds were the most by anyone, although three scored four each. Roger Twose of Warwickshire needed only sixteen innings for his 1,042 at 74.42. There were six scores in excess of 200, the highest being 213 by Kent's Mark Ealham.

Although only four bowlers took 50 wickets in 1990, Somerset's New Zealand-born seam bowler, Andrew Caddick, did it in some style with 96 at 12.84. He bettered by one the record set in 1961 by the Leicestershire fast bowler, P. N. Broughton, who sent down two fewer overs for his 95 at 15.24. Caddick, whose tally was 33 more than the next highest, achieved by the Middlesex slow left-armer, Alex Barnett, was named Rapid Cricketline Player of the Season, an award worth £550. Two young all-rounders also stood out. In twelve matches for Middlesex, Paul Weekes compiled 739 runs at 49.26 and took 43 wickets at 26.02, while in fifteen appearances Yorkshire's Paul Grayson scored 705 runs at 29.37 to set alongside his 40 wickets at 21.97.

*Continued over*

## SECOND ELEVEN CHAMPIONSHIP, 1991

| Win = 16 points | P | W | L | D | Bonus points Batting | Bowling | Points |
|---|---|---|---|---|---|---|---|
| 1 – Yorkshire (17) . . . . . . . | 16 | 8 | 1 | 7 | 38 | 36 | 202 |
| 2 – Warwickshire (7) . . . . | 16 | 7 | 1 | 8 | 45 | 43 | 196 |
| 3 – Somerset (15) . . . . . . . . | 16 | 6 | 4 | 6 | 36 | 47 | 179 |
| 4 – Hampshire (11) . . . . . . | 16 | 5 | 0 | 11 | 44 | 40 | 164 |
| 5 – Nottinghamshire (4) . . | 16 | 5 | 2 | 9 | 38 | 33 | 151 |
| 6 – Surrey (3) . . . . . . . . . . | 16 | 4 | 4 | 8 | 33 | 46 | 143 |
| 7 – Sussex (1) . . . . . . . . . . . | 16 | 4 | 3 | 9 | 37 | 41 | 142 |
| 8 – Derbyshire (13) . . . . . . | 16 | 3 | 5 | 8 | 34 | 50 | 132 |
| 9 – Worcestershire (10) . . | 16 | 3 | 5 | 8 | 36 | 45 | 129 |
| 10 – Leicestershire (16) . . . . | 16 | 3 | 6 | 7 | 34 | 41 | 123 |
| 11 { Lancashire (8) . . . . . . . | 16 | 2 | 3 | 11 | 39 | 40 | 111 |
| Middlesex (6) . . . . . . . | 16 | 2 | 4 | 10 | 36 | 43 | 111 |
| 13 – Glamorgan (2) . . . . . . . | 15 | 2 | 2 | 11 | 36 | 40 | 108 |
| 14 – Kent (5) . . . . . . . . . . . | 16 | 1 | 3 | 12 | 48 | 37 | 101 |
| 15 – Essex (9) . . . . . . . . . . | 16 | 1 | 6 | 9 | 34 | 37 | 87 |
| 16 – Gloucestershire (14) . . | 15 | 1 | 4 | 10 | 25 | 37 | 78 |
| 17 – Northamptonshire (12) | 16 | 0 | 4 | 12 | 33 | 39 | 72 |

*1990 positions are shown in brackets.*

*The total for Warwickshire includes 12 points for a win in a one-innings match.*

*The match between Glamorgan and Gloucestershire at BP Llandarcy on June 25, 26, 27 was abandoned without a ball bowled and is not included in the above table.*

With their players showing a greater maturity, **Derbyshire** enjoyed a more successful season and, after heading the table for a time in July and early August, finished eighth, an improvement of five places. Although first-team calls enabled more colts and trialists to gain valuable experience, helping to produce a good pool of players for the future, this benefit was offset by some loss of the team's competitive edge. Had they been able to make more out of winning positions against Glamorgan and Yorkshire, for example, they would have finished higher. Imtiaz Ahmed produced a string of entertaining innings in his 648 runs, including 165 against Worcestershire at Halesowen and 102 against Northamptonshire at Oundle, while Frank Griffith, another to reach 600 runs, made an unbeaten 128 against Glamorgan at Belper Meadow. Runs also came from Chris Adams and Steve Goldsmith – with hundreds at Nottingham and Sittingbourne respectively – while Dominic Cork, the young all-rounder, was soon performing with distinction in the first team. In an attack which earned more bowling bonus points (50) than any other county, Ian Folley, the former Lancashire slow left-armer, took 42 wickets and Ewen McCray, in 500 overs of off-breaks, picked up 44, including Derbyshire's best innings return of six for 51 in the rain-restricted match at Gloucester. For financial reasons, however, neither was retained. At the end of the season, Stuart Stoneman produced several useful spells.

**Essex** finished a disappointing fifteenth, managing only one win. With two of the first team frequently on England duty, and Mark Ilott injured for most of the season, their resources were often strained, and generally they found difficulty in bowling sides out. The principal wicket-takers were David Boden and Craig Miller, both around medium pace, and the slow left-armer, Guy Lovell, but none of them managed an average below 35. Lovell was particularly expensive. However, seven batsmen averaged more than 34 and produced eleven centuries between them. Adam Seymour, the leading scorer, made two – 140 not out against Middlesex at Chelmsford and 115 against Sussex at Southend – while Nadeem Shahid hit 108 not out against both Middlesex and Leicestershire at Chelmsford, and David East 146 at Northampton and 123 at Elland. East also kept wicket to his usual high standard and was an inspiration as captain when Keith Fletcher was absent. Nick Knight made the side's highest innings, 155 against Sussex at Southend, in his two hundreds, and Darren Robinson followed his maiden century (119 against Yorkshire at Elland) with 109 not out against Hampshire at Bournemouth a week later. He had earlier won the batting award at the International Youth Tournament in Canada, playing for England Under-18, for whom Robert Rollins kept wicket. Both were later selected for the winter tour to Pakistan with the England Under-19 side. Others among the runs were Jonathan Lewis and Keith Butler.

After their success of the previous season, 1991 was one of relative disappointment for **Glamorgan**, who salvaged just two wins from a heavily rain-affected programme, which saw them slide from the runners-up spot to thirteenth. Tony Cottey headed the batting averages, his 637 at nearly 80 including 101 against Derbyshire at Belper Meadow and 106 not out against Leicestershire at Hinckley. Mike Cann was the leading run-maker, with 735, Steve James and David Hemp were also productive, and there was promise for the future in the performances of Alistair Dalton, James Williams and Andrew Jones, captain of the Welsh Under-19 side and son of Alan Jones. Hemp and Williams each recorded a maiden century – Hemp against Northamptonshire at Ammanford and Williams against Yorkshire at Usk. The bowling honours went to Mark Davies, slow left-arm, supported by Sam Kirnon, at medium-fast, and Simon Dennis, who took seven for 30 against Surrey at Swansea. Ewan Holland looked an interesting prospect.

**Gloucestershire** generally lacked the consistency to force victory, failing on four occasions to capitalise on a strong position, and had to wait until their last match for their first win. It came at the expense of Middlesex at Enfield and was set up by an innings of 104 from the left-handed Richard Scott. Alan Hunt followed his maiden century – 100 not out at Bournemouth – with 137 against Surrey at Bristol, but was beaten to the highest aggregate by nineteen-year-old Tim Hancock, also a fine fielder, whose maiden hundred, against Nottinghamshire at Bristol, was preceded by a score of 91 in the first innings. Nick Pringle's unbeaten 198 against Sussex at Horsham, in his only match, was the highest for Gloucestershire since Alastair Hignell's 217 in 1983. Ricardo Williams was an outstanding all-rounder with 39 wickets and 535 runs, including a maiden century against Warwickshire at Walmley, but overall the bowlers tended to be expensive. Only Martyn Ball and Martin Gerrard, a left-arm seamer, averaged less than 30, and with off-spinner Ball the only regular slow bowler, the attacking options tended to be limited. Richard Williams broke the club record of wicket-keeping dismissals with 33 catches and three stumpings.

Batting was again the strong suit at **Hampshire**, where tremendous team spirit, enthusiastic fielding and fewer injuries saw a move up to fourth place. Rupert Cox, with the highest aggregate of any batsman in the Championship, 1,222, passed 1,000 runs for the second successive season, and Julian Wood also reached that landmark. Sean Morris fell just 3 runs short in his nine matches after returning from Durham University, averaging 90.63, and his aggregate included six fifties and four hundreds – 135 (and 94 not out) against Worcestershire and 134 not out against Northamptonshire, both at Southampton, 136 not out at Manchester, and 116 not out at Hove. Cox hit three hundreds, with 147 not out and 108 at Southampton against Northamptonshire and Yorkshire respectively, and 146 against Nottinghamshire at Bournemouth. The Worcestershire match, the last of the season, brought victory by nine wickets, and in addition to Morris's hundred there was one also from Bob Parks, as well as returns of six for 29 from Ian Turner and six for 94 from Darren Flint. Flint, a left-arm spinner, also took six for 47 against Essex at Bournemouth and had valuable support from Turner, another slow left-armer, and off-spinner Shaun Udal. The experienced Parks led the side well and encouraged the younger players, one of whom was the promising medium-paced bowler, Martin Thursfield, making a comeback after breaking a leg on the England Under-19 tour to New Zealand during the winter.

It was a disappointing season for **Kent** who dropped nine places to fourteenth. Although their strong line-up brought them more batting points than any other county, they did not have the bowling strength to translate that advantage into more than one victory. Their bowlers were also unhappy with the machine-stitched balls used in the Championship as part of an experiment by the TCCB. Vince Wells headed the batting with 930 runs, including 205 against Leicestershire at Market Harborough in May, and in July at Bristol Mark Ealham bettered that score with 213, the season's highest in the Championship. Ealham and Nigel Llong both passed 800 runs, and five batsmen averaged 50, including Jon Longley, who returned to the side after completing his studies at Durham University. Another, Mark Dobson, was not retained by the county. The wicket-keeper, Graham Kersey, made great strides with 428 runs, 31 catches and five stumpings, as well as making his first-team début, while of the younger players David Fulton, from Kent University, hit a maiden hundred at Cardiff. Only Tim Wren, Min Patel and Ealham took twenty wickets, and the season's best return was recorded by the young New South Wales batsman, Michael Bevan, who marked his one appearance by taking six Sussex wickets for 68 and hitting two fifties. Patel also took six in an innings – in the final match of the season against Somerset at Canterbury.

**Lancashire** finished in the bottom half of the table and, for the first time in many seasons, were never in contention for the title at any stage. First-team calls weakened them, though against this was set a satisfaction in the contribution their promoted players made at the higher level. Outstanding with the bat were Stephen Titchard and the young Australian, Jason Gallian, both of whom reached 1,000 runs with five and four centuries respectively. Titchard hit hundreds against Leicestershire (182 not out), Middlesex (161 not out), Northamptonshire (138 not out) and Gloucestershire (121 not out) and Kent (117). Gallian's 143 against Sussex at Hove, his maiden century, was followed by 125 not out against Northamptonshire, 102 against Hampshire and 107 against Nottinghamshire. Gallian was also the leading wicket-taker, but at 47 apiece his twenty wickets were expensive. In contrast, Peter Martin's nineteen came from half the number of overs and at less than half the cost. Martin's return of six for 33 against Yorkshire at Todmorden was the season's best by a Lancashire bowler.

**Leicestershire** improved on their performance of the previous season, recording three wins as they moved up to tenth place. They might have had a fourth win had they not been obliged to forfeit the match against Sussex at Hove, for they were in a strong position when most of the team were stricken on the third day with food poisoning. The batting averages were headed by Damien Martyn, the Australian Under-19 captain, on a cricket scholarship from Western Australia and scorer of a superb unbeaten 201 against Essex at Chelmsford. Paul Nixon scored the most runs, though, his aggregate of 785 including a maiden century at the expense of Kent at Leicester. Others to play three-figure innings were the England Under-19 representative, Ben Smith, with 119 at Manchester; Russell Cobb, whose career-best 160 came in a total of 479 for four at Hove; Tim Boon and Martyn Gidley, who scored 113 not out and 100 respectively against Yorkshire at Leicester; and Peter Hepworth, whose only appearance featured an innings of 122 against Gloucestershire at Oakham. The experienced Gordon Parsons took the most wickets, 24, and there were 21 apiece from Lloyd Tennant and the economical slow left-armer, Chris Hawkes, who achieved the county's best return with seven for 65 at Derby.

Slipping to eleventh place, **Middlesex** could reflect on a season in which the side was unsettled by first-team calls on eight leading players. Paul Weekes, one of them, confirmed his promise as a valuable all-rounder in his twelve matches, making major contributions as a left-handed batsman and off-spinner to the tune of 739 runs and 43 wickets; there was a match return of eleven for 119 (seven for 80 in the first innings) against Sussex at Teddington and a maiden century against Worcestershire at Flagge Meadow. Other promoted players, available for only half the programme, were Matthew Keech, who headed the batting averages with 605 runs, and the left-handed Jason Pooley, whose 556 runs included 162 at Weston-super-Mare and 135 against Lancashire at Uxbridge. Alex Barnett again took the bowling honours with 63 wickets, including match figures of ten for 162 at Derby and an innings return of six for 29 in the Sussex match, and he subsequently moved to Old Trafford in search of regular first-team cricket. Of the younger players Toby Radford made 603 runs and Jonathan Whittington, the Eton and English Schools slow left-armer, returned seven for 114 at Leeds.

Any disappointment **Northamptonshire** may have felt at finishing bottom of the table, without a win, was tempered by the development of many of the younger players. In the first half of the season the side were frequently frustrated by the weather, several times when victory had looked likely, and injury problems throughout the playing staff required the Second Eleven to call on as many as 39 players. Neil Stanley made a successful return after missing the whole of 1990 with a serious back injury; he finished just 8 short of 1,000 runs, a highlight being his unbeaten double-hundred at Southampton. Other significant batting contributions came from Malachy Loye and Russell Warren, both of whom represented England Under-19 during 1991, and the county have a promising recruit in Tim Walton, whose maiden century came against Warwickshire at Moseley in the last match of the season. Loye, Walton and Jeremy Snape were all selected to tour Pakistan with England Under-19. The leading bowler, Tony Penberthy, took 22 economical wickets, including seven for 57 at Cheltenham, and while Derrick Page, a Jamaican-born medium-pacer, took one more, his 23 were expensive at 37.78. Andy Roberts, a leg-spinner, took the chance to show his potential when called up by the first team, and Richard Pearson, the Cambridge University off-spinner, looked a promising recruit.

Under the new management team of John Birch and Kevin Saxelby, **Nottinghamshire** enjoyed a successful season, winning the Bain Clarkson Trophy for the first time and being the only side to beat the eventual champions, Yorkshire. Mike Newell had an excellent season as captain. His 1,052 runs included scores of 139 against Essex at Worthington Simpson, 145 not out at Liverpool and 106 at Bournemouth, as well as four fifties – and for good measure he held twenty catches. Graeme Archer, who topped the averages, put together 839 runs in his first full season, with a top score of 149 against Derbyshire, and there was an unbeaten 208 by Wayne Dessaur when he was promoted from No. 7 to open against Gloucestershire at Bristol. Michael Field-Buss sent down nearly 600 overs of off-spin for his 49 wickets, while Andy Afford, whose 21 wickets cost just 11.42 apiece, recorded the season's most economical average by a bowler taking ten or more wickets in the Championship. He returned ten for 116 against Essex at Worthington Simpson. Excellent progress was made by Pascal Broadley, a local all-rounder who began the season in the county Colts XI and finished with a first-team début against Derbyshire in the Britannic Assurance Championship.

For their improvement from fifteenth in 1990 to a best-ever position of third, **Somerset** owed much to Andrew Caddick, the New Zealand-born fast bowler who was named Rapid Cricketline Player of the Year. His record 96 wickets at 12.84 included match returns of eleven for 128 against Surrey at Guildford and ten for 107 against Lancashire at Taunton, as well as his best innings figures of eight for 39 against Essex at Chelmsford. Somerset will be expecting much from him now that he has qualified for county cricket in 1992. Gareth Townsend scored the most runs, his 723 featuring an unbeaten 129 at Chelmsford, while in only eleven matches Ricky Bartlett totalled 602, including 106 against Glamorgan at North Perrott. Mark Lathwell, an England Under-19 representative, batted well in his first season on the staff; wicket-keeper Robert Turner made a solid contribution with 421 runs and 31 dismissals; and Ian Fletcher, who began slowly after joining the side mid-season from Loughborough University, found form to play a match-winning innings of 119 against Kent in the final match of the season. The departure of Jimmy Cook and Peter Roebuck should offer more opportunities for the young batsmen in 1992. In the slow bowling department the presence in the second team of both off-spinners, Harvey Trump and Ian Swallow, meant there was less early in the season than had been expected for Andrew Cottam, who went with England Under-18 to Canada.

**Surrey**, runners-up in the Bain Clarkson Trophy, could not maintain their significant progress of the previous season and slipped down to sixth in the Championship. Alistair Brown again impressed, his 1,199 runs including 207 not out at Colchester, 182 not out against Yorkshire at The Oval and 171 at Crosby. Others with more than 700 runs were Jonathan Robinson, who hit hundreds against Lancashire (134) and Gloucestershire (135), and Chris Bullen, with 111 not out at Leicester. In the second innings of that match Mark Butcher scored 102, and a fortnight later he hit 101 in a total of 414 for five as Surrey beat Essex at Colchester. The bowling honours went to Neil Kendrick, one of the season's leading all-rounders, whose slow left-arm spin captured 61 wickets, including returns of six for 42 at Swansea, six for 45 at Leicester and six for 83 against Derbyshire at Banstead. He was ably supported by Bullen's off-spin bowling.

Failure to complete victories in two or three matches prevented **Sussex** from retaining the title and, although they were at one stage in contention for honours, they had to be content with a middle-of-the-table position. Rupert Hanley scored consistently, with six fifties but no three-figure innings, and close behind him in aggregate was Keith Greenfield, whose 702 runs included 138 not out against Surrey at Eastbourne, 117 at Worcester and 101 against Nottinghamshire at Collingham. In the defeat of Derbyshire at Heanor, Hanley hit eight sixes in his unbeaten 51, and John North took nine for 35, the season's best innings figures by any player in the Championship. Rodney Bunting, at medium pace, and Jacob Dean, bowling slow left-arm, captured the most wickets, with Dean's 29 including a six-wicket return against Glamorgan at Hastings. Against Warwickshire at Hove, Bradleigh Donelan hit a maiden century and had innings figures of six for 62.

**Warwickshire** capped a good season by finishing as runners-up, just six points behind Yorkshire, who inflicted on them their only defeat, at Bradford in a game that could have gone either way. They won seven matches and accumulated more bonus points (88) than any other county. Roger Twose had an outstanding season with 1,042 runs in ten matches, including centuries against Middlesex (171 not out), Derbyshire (125), Gloucestershire (108) and Leicestershire (101 not out). He also chipped in with sixteen wickets. Sound support with the bat came from Simon Green, Graham Charlesworth, Trevor Penney and Gary Steer, all of whom passed 500 runs. Charlesworth compiled a maiden century (143 not out) at Chelmsford, while Green reached three figures at Chesterfield. Asif Din scored hundreds in each of his two matches, 100 against Sussex and 107 not out against Leicestershire, and Paul Smith marked his single appearance with an unbeaten hundred at Worcester. All the bowlers contributed at times, with the medium-paced Doug Brown capturing the most wickets (43); in addition he hit a maiden hundred against Surrey at Guildford. Others to take twenty wickets were the off-spinner, Adrian Pierson, and the England Under-19 medium-pacer, Graeme Welch.

**Worcestershire**, a strong all-round combination, continued their movement up the table to ninth place, with one win more than in 1990. There were no four-figure aggregates in 1991, although five batsmen passed 500 and eight played three-figure innings. The highest was 181 at Southampton by Mark Scott, the captain, while there were two from Chris Tolley – 135 against Somerset and 101 against Leicestershire, both at Worcester – in the leading aggregate of 668 runs. Gavin Haynes was an outstanding all-rounder, and it came as little surprise when he was called into the first team. He compiled the second-highest aggregate of 653, including 101 not out against Middlesex at Flagge Meadow, and his 25 wickets at medium pace were bettered only by Richard Stemp. The left-arm spinner's tally of 31 was boosted by match figures of ten for 125 against Nottinghamshire at Shireoaks and an innings return of six for 121 at Dartford. The Kent match was also noteworthy for an innings of 135 not out by Philip Weston, who played for England Under-19 against the touring Australian Under-19s and was selected to captain them in Pakistan in the winter.

When **Yorkshire** beat Middlesex by an innings at the end of August, they had gained an unassailable position at the top of the table with a game in hand. Overcoming a stuttering start, they had swept from the bottom of the table the previous season to take the title outright for the third time. Only Nottinghamshire and the three last-placed counties – Essex, Gloucestershire and Northamptonshire – collected fewer bonus points than their 74, but eight wins, offset by only one defeat, saw them to the Championship. Craig White, ever present, was the leading batsman, his 963 runs including 153 against Worcestershire at Marske-by-Sea and 104 against Essex at Elland. Also among the runs were Colin Chapman, the wicket-keeper, whose 840 contained an unbeaten hundred against Worcestershire, and twenty-year-old Paul Grayson, who, in addition to his 705 runs, headed the bowling with 40 economical wickets. His all-round ability was highlighted at Folkestone in the last match of the season, where he scored a century in the first innings and returned match figures of ten for 156, with innings figures of seven for 90. Chris Pickles had enjoyed a similar success at Bristol, where, having compiled the side's highest innings of 189 not out, he took six for 33 in Gloucestershire's first innings. The Essex match at Elland was particularly memorable for the batting of Kevin Sharp, who followed his unbeaten 150 in the first innings with 127 in the second. With the ball, Grayson, who bowled slow left-arm, was strongly supported by Ian Houseman, at fast-medium, and the off-spinner, Philip Berry. Houseman took six for 39 against Warwickshire and six for 58 against Sussex, while Berry had the side's best innings return of eight for 79 against Derbyshire at Harrogate.

*In the averages that follow,* * *against a score signifies not out,* * *against a name signifies the captain and* † *signifies a wicket-keeper.*

## DERBYSHIRE SECOND ELEVEN

*Matches 16: Won – Essex, Kent, Somerset. Lost – Hampshire, Nottinghamshire, Sussex, Warwickshire, Worcestershire. Drawn – Glamorgan, Gloucestershire, Lancashire, Leicestershire, Middlesex, Northamptonshire, Surrey, Yorkshire.*

## Batting Averages

|  | M | I | NO | R | HI | 100s | Avge |
|---|---|---|---|---|---|---|---|
| Imtiaz Ahmed | 5 | 10 | 0 | 648 | 165 | 2 | 64.80 |
| C. J. Adams | 6 | 10 | 1 | 400 | 139* | 1 | 44.44 |
| S. C. Goldsmith | 5 | 10 | 0 | 420 | 124 | 1 | 42.00 |
| D. G. Cork | 7 | 12 | 1 | 404 | 80 | 0 | 36.72 |
| M. Jean-Jacques | 3 | 4 | 2 | 71 | 61* | 0 | 35.50 |
| B. Roberts | 8 | 14 | 2 | 366 | 60 | 0 | 30.50 |
| A. M. Brown | 11 | 20 | 2 | 519 | 126 | 1 | 28.83 |
| F. A. Griffith | 13 | 25 | 2 | 640 | 128* | 1 | 27.82 |
| *†B. J. M. Maher | 15 | 20 | 11 | 229 | 41 | 0 | 25.44 |
| M. R. Spencer | 7 | 8 | 0 | 193 | 59 | 0 | 24.12 |
| G. A. Bethell | 6 | 11 | 1 | 228 | 56 | 0 | 22.80 |
| G. V. Palmer | 16 | 24 | 4 | 401 | 57 | 0 | 20.05 |
| T. A. Tweats | 2 | 4 | 1 | 53 | 30 | 0 | 17.66 |
| E. McCray | 15 | 26 | 3 | 378 | 72 | 0 | 16.43 |
| I. Folley | 11 | 17 | 2 | 224 | 36 | 0 | 14.93 |
| S. A. Stoneman | 4 | 6 | 0 | 87 | 31 | 0 | 14.50 |
| R. I. Biggin | 2 | 4 | 0 | 53 | 24 | 0 | 13.25 |
| J. R. Goldthorp | 9 | 15 | 0 | 192 | 75 | 0 | 12.80 |
| A. M. A. Aduhene | 2 | 3 | 0 | 38 | 15 | 0 | 12.66 |
| P. R. Whitaker | 5 | 5 | 2 | 38 | 24 | 0 | 12.66 |
| M. C. Russell | 4 | 7 | 1 | 64 | 27 | 0 | 10.66 |
| R. W. Sladdin | 9 | 12 | 1 | 68 | 15* | 0 | 6.18 |

Played in two matches: S. A. Aslam 12; R. Bhanabhai 8*, 0. Played in one match: M. Crookson 1, 5*; K. Hunter 0, 8; K. Jahangir 2, 0; K. M. Krikken 35, 31; A. W. Richardson 1, 1; M. J. Saggers 4; R. M. Wight 44*; †M. Godber did not bat.

*Note:* During the second innings of the match v Worcestershire at Halesowen, and after he had been dismissed for 36, C. J. Adams was replaced by P. R. Whitaker.

## Bowling Averages

|  | O | M | R | W | BB | Avge |
|---|---|---|---|---|---|---|
| M. Crookson . . . . . . . | 25 | 10 | 54 | 6 | 3-15 | 9.00 |
| M. R. Spencer . . . . . . | 30 | 5 | 87 | 6 | 4-31 | 14.50 |
| S. A. Stoneman . . . . . | 82 | 20 | 236 | 13 | 4-35 | 18.15 |
| I. Folley . . . . . . . | 359.1 | 113 | 800 | 42 | 5-41 | 19.04 |
| C. J. Adams . . . . . . . | 47 | 13 | 122 | 6 | 4-60 | 20.33 |
| D. G. Cork . . . . . . . | 132.2 | 34 | 348 | 16 | 5-26 | 21.75 |
| R. W. Sladdin . . . . . . | 248 | 80 | 588 | 23 | 3-30 | 25.56 |
| F. A. Griffith . . . . . . | 125.4 | 33 | 312 | 12 | 3-57 | 26.00 |
| P. R. Whitaker . . . . . . | 108.3 | 28 | 295 | 11 | 3-72 | 26.81 |
| E. McCray . . . . . . . | 502.1 | 128 | 1,372 | 44 | 6-51 | 31.18 |
| M. Jean-Jacques . . . . . | 68 | 19 | 177 | 5 | 2-8 | 35.40 |
| G. V. Palmer . . . . . . | 327.3 | 74 | 1,103 | 31 | 4-30 | 35.58 |
| S. C. Goldsmith . . . . . . | 93.2 | 27 | 271 | 7 | 4-59 | 38.71 |
| S. A. Aslam . . . . . . . . | 63 | 6 | 177 | 4 | 2-60 | 44.25 |

Also bowled: A. M. A. Aduhene 20–3–89–0; R. Bhanabhai 22–4–61–1; K. Hunter 14–5–32–1; Imtiaz Ahmed 1–0–5–0; K. Jahangir 6–3–12–0; A. W. Richardson 16–7–26–2; B. Roberts 55–21–125–1; M. J. Saggers 23–8–74–1; T. A. Tweats 4–1–16–1; R. M. Wight 19–3–70–1.

## ESSEX SECOND ELEVEN

*Matches 16 : Won – Lancashire. Lost – Derbyshire, Glamorgan, Hampshire, Nottinghamshire, Surrey, Yorkshire. Drawn – Gloucestershire, Kent, Leicestershire, Middlesex, Northamptonshire, Somerset, Sussex, Warwickshire, Worcestershire.*

## Batting Averages

|  | M | I | NO | R | HI | 100s | Avge |
|---|---|---|---|---|---|---|---|
| N. Shahid . . . . . . . . . . | 5 | 8 | 3 | 258 | 108* | 2 | 51.60 |
| N. V. Knight . . . . . . . . . | 9 | 16 | 2 | 665 | 155 | 2 | 47.50 |
| A. C. H. Seymour . . . . . | 11 | 19 | 1 | 757 | 140* | 2 | 42.05 |
| D. J. Robinson . . . . . . . | 6 | 11 | 2 | 371 | 119 | 2 | 41.22 |
| †D. E. East . . . . . . . . . | 11 | 16 | 0 | 623 | 146 | 2 | 38.93 |
| K. A. Butler . . . . . . . . | 13 | 20 | 4 | 573 | 87 | 0 | 35.81 |
| J. J. B. Lewis . . . . . . . . | 11 | 20 | 4 | 545 | 110 | 1 | 34.06 |
| †R. J. Rollins . . . . . . . . | 7 | 10 | 4 | 174 | 45 | 0 | 29.00 |
| A. G. J. Fraser . . . . . . . | 10 | 14 | 1 | 363 | 73 | 0 | 27.92 |
| A. C. Richards . . . . . . . | 14 | 21 | 4 | 436 | 79 | 0 | 25.64 |
| G. W. Ecclestone . . . . . | 10 | 16 | 2 | 346 | 31* | 0 | 24.71 |
| *K. W. R. Fletcher . . . . . | 13 | 8 | 4 | 86 | 33 | 0 | 21.50 |
| C. A. Miller . . . . . . . . . | 15 | 19 | 7 | 195 | 52 | 0 | 16.25 |
| D. J. P. Boden . . . . . . . | 12 | 13 | 1 | 182 | 49* | 0 | 15.16 |
| W. G. Lovell . . . . . . . . . | 14 | 9 | 4 | 21 | 12 | 0 | 4.20 |
| P. Bashford . . . . . . . . | 4 | 4 | 0 | 11 | 8 | 0 | 2.75 |

Played in two matches: M. R. Bate 20, 16*, 17; G. A. Khan 39, 3, 4. Played in one match: S. J. W. Andrew 0, 0; J. Chambers 16, 41; A. C. Churchill 1, 25*; S. Hale 5*; K. D. Hockley 0*; T. Kemp 0*, 1; A. W. Lilley 8, 0; P. M. Such 4; D. M. Cousins did not bat.

*Note:* Owing to first-team calls, N. Shahid was replaced by R. J. Rollins in the match v Somerset and A. C. H. Seymour was replaced by D. J. Robinson in the match v Sussex.

## Bowling Averages

|                     | O     | M   | R     | W   | BB    | Avge  |
| ------------------- | ----- | --- | ----- | --- | ----- | ----- |
| S. J. W. Andrew ... | 37    | 9   | 92    | 5   | 3-55  | 18.40 |
| C. A. Miller ...... | 355.5 | 47  | 1,272 | 35  | 5-85  | 36.34 |
| D. J. P. Boden ..... | 367.5 | 62  | 1,242 | 34  | 5-73  | 36.52 |
| N. Shahid ......... | 54    | 13  | 189   | 5   | 4-16  | 37.80 |
| W. G. Lovell ...... | 539.1 | 117 | 1,590 | 31  | 5-80  | 51.29 |
| A. G. J. Fraser .... | 203.1 | 37  | 637   | 11  | 4-80  | 57.90 |
| A. C. Richards ..... | 259.5 | 32  | 988   | 16  | 3-72  | 61.75 |

Also bowled: A. C. Churchill 5-0-24-0; D. M. Cousins 13-3-24-0; G. W. Eccleston 20.5-1-134-0; S. Hale 15-4-72-0; K. D. Hockley 15-2-64-1; T. Kemp 44.1-3-217-3; N. V. Knight 43-10-132-4; J. J. B. Lewis 10-1-28-1; D. J. Robinson 10-0-66-0; A. C. H. Seymour 29-7-84-2; P. M. Such 65-21-162-3.

## GLAMORGAN SECOND ELEVEN

*Matches 15: Won – Essex, Surrey. Lost – Sussex, Yorkshire. Drawn – Derbyshire, Hampshire, Kent, Lancashire, Leicestershire, Middlesex, Northamptonshire, Nottinghamshire, Somerset, Warwickshire, Worcestershire. Abandoned – Gloucestershire.*

### Batting Averages

|                      | M   | I   | NO  | R   | HI   | 100s | Avge  |
| -------------------- | --- | --- | --- | --- | ---- | ---- | ----- |
| P. A. Cottey ......  | 6   | 11  | 3   | 637 | 106* | 2    | 79.62 |
| *J. F. Steele ...... | 11  | 6   | 5   | 48  | 17*  | 0    | 48.00 |
| S. P. James ......   | 7   | 12  | 2   | 475 | 150  | 1    | 47.50 |
| J. R. A. Williams .. | 4   | 6   | 1   | 213 | 112  | 1    | 42.60 |
| †M. L. Roberts ....  | 12  | 16  | 5   | 463 | 60   | 0    | 42.09 |
| M. J. Cann ......    | 11  | 20  | 2   | 735 | 162  | 1    | 40.83 |
| S. J. Dennis ......  | 8   | 8   | 5   | 113 | 33*  | 0    | 37.66 |
| D. L. Hemp ......    | 14  | 24  | 5   | 599 | 108* | 1    | 31.52 |
| I. Smith ......      | 5   | 8   | 0   | 211 | 51   | 0    | 26.37 |
| S. Kirnon ......     | 14  | 15  | 1   | 309 | 89   | 0    | 22.07 |
| A. Dale ......       | 5   | 10  | 0   | 214 | 55   | 0    | 21.40 |
| *J. Derrick ......   | 13  | 16  | 2   | 262 | 62*  | 0    | 18.71 |
| J. Bishop ......     | 9   | 13  | 0   | 177 | 36   | 0    | 13.61 |
| S. Bastien ......    | 5   | 4   | 0   | 47  | 19   | 0    | 11.75 |
| M. Davies ......     | 15  | 16  | 2   | 135 | 41   | 0    | 9.64  |
| S. R. Barwick .....  | 4   | 4   | 3   | 9   | 4    | 0    | 9.00  |
| D. J. Foster ......  | 7   | 4   | 1   | 21  | 15*  | 0    | 7.00  |

Played in three matches: E. P. M. Holland 0*, 6, 8; †A. D. Shaw 6*, 77. Played in two matches: A. J. Dalton 3*, 39; A. J. Jones 11, 78, 27. Played in one match: N. B. Driscoll 14; M. Frost 26*; G. C. Holmes 41, 67*; †G. Norris 5; P. C. E. Simmonite 36, 15*.

### Bowling Averages

|                      | O     | M   | R   | W   | BB    | Avge  |
| -------------------- | ----- | --- | --- | --- | ----- | ----- |
| M. Davies ......     | 415.1 | 136 | 951 | 43  | 5-54  | 22.11 |
| S. J. Dennis ......  | 170.5 | 49  | 475 | 19  | 7-30  | 25.00 |
| S. Kirnon ......     | 258.5 | 58  | 817 | 30  | 5-87  | 27.23 |
| S. R. Barwick .....  | 194.5 | 63  | 455 | 15  | 5-66  | 30.33 |
| D. J. Foster ......  | 138.1 | 25  | 423 | 13  | 2-72  | 32.53 |
| S. Bastien ......    | 104   | 20  | 277 | 8   | 2-39  | 34.62 |
| E. P. M. Holland ... | 73    | 18  | 222 | 6   | 3-55  | 37.00 |
| M. J. Cann ......    | 197.5 | 49  | 541 | 14  | 3-20  | 38.64 |
| J. Derrick ......    | 104.4 | 24  | 323 | 8   | 2-22  | 40.37 |

Also bowled: J. Bishop 1-0-4-0; P. A. Cottey 45-14-127-3; A. Dale 38-7-109-1; A. J. Dalton 6-0-18-1; M. Frost 22-5-57-1; D. L. Hemp 20-1-109-0; S. P. James 1-1-0-0; M. L. Roberts 10.1-1-49-0; I. Smith 17-9-21-3; J. F. Steele 9-1-46-1; J. R. A. Williams 1-0-9-0.

## GLOUCESTERSHIRE SECOND ELEVEN

*Matches 15: Won – Middlesex. Lost – Lancashire, Somerset, Surrey, Yorkshire. Drawn – Derbyshire, Essex, Hampshire, Kent, Leicestershire, Northamptonshire, Nottinghamshire, Sussex, Warwickshire, Worcestershire. Abandoned – Glamorgan.*

### Batting Averages

|  | M | I | NO | R | HI | 100s | Avge |
|---|---|---|---|---|---|---|---|
| T. H. C. Hancock ...... | 12 | 20 | 4 | 715 | 107* | 1 | 44.68 |
| J. L. P. Meadows ...... | 3 | 5 | 0 | 212 | 93 | 0 | 42.40 |
| R. I. Dawson ...... | 8 | 15 | 1 | 569 | 101 | 1 | 40.64 |
| J. J. E. Hardy ......... | 5 | 9 | 2 | 260 | 81 | 0 | 37.14 |
| R. C. Williams......... | 13 | 20 | 5 | 535 | 104 | 1 | 35.66 |
| P. W. Romaines ...... | 7 | 10 | 1 | 272 | 81 | 0 | 30.22 |
| R. J. Scott ............ | 3 | 6 | 0 | 178 | 104 | 1 | 29.66 |
| †J. R. Tegg ......... | 5 | 5 | 2 | 88 | 35* | 0 | 29.33 |
| A. J. Hunt ......... | 14 | 25 | 2 | 652 | 137 | 2 | 28.34 |
| R. J. Cunliffe ......... | 3 | 5 | 2 | 83 | 39* | 0 | 27.66 |
| *A. W. Stovold ........ | 11 | 11 | 4 | 181 | 49 | 0 | 25.85 |
| M. G. N. Windows..... | 3 | 5 | 0 | 114 | 77 | 0 | 22.80 |
| E. T. Milburn ........ | 10 | 17 | 1 | 301 | 75 | 0 | 18.81 |
| M. C. J. Ball ......... | 9 | 10 | 2 | 126 | 43 | 0 | 15.75 |
| †R. C. J. Williams ..... | 9 | 13 | 0 | 174 | 68 | 0 | 13.38 |
| S. N. Barnes ......... | 9 | 9 | 2 | 62 | 26 | 0 | 8.85 |
| M. J. Gerrard ....... | 6 | 9 | 2 | 52 | 18 | 0 | 7.42 |
| A. M. Smith ........ | 5 | 8 | 1 | 48 | 18 | 0 | 6.85 |
| R. M. Bell ......... | 9 | 10 | 5 | 17 | 8* | 0 | 3.40 |
| J. M. de la Pena ....... | 6 | 7 | 2 | 10 | 4 | 0 | 2.00 |

Played in two matches: G. B. Agg 0, 0; S. G. Joyner 0, 1; K. Patel 7, 0. Played in one match: A. M. Babington 22; P. J. Bird 8, 29; K. Britton 14; A. J. Freeman 0; R. Horrell 0; †J. Huxtable 2, 2; N. J. Pringle 198*, 33; S. R. Walbridge 8, 6; L. James did not bat.

### Bowling Averages

|  | O | M | R | W | BB | Avge |
|---|---|---|---|---|---|---|
| M. C. J. Ball ........ | 261.4 | 61 | 752 | 29 | 5-66 | 25.93 |
| M. J. Gerrard ....... | 179.2 | 35 | 573 | 22 | 4-33 | 26.04 |
| R. C. Williams....... | 418.4 | 88 | 1,230 | 39 | 5-107 | 31.53 |
| A. M. Smith......... | 157.5 | 34 | 480 | 12 | 3-51 | 40.00 |
| R. M. Bell ......... | 168.1 | 41 | 551 | 13 | 5-42 | 42.38 |
| S. N. Barnes........ | 188.3 | 40 | 571 | 9 | 2-42 | 63.44 |
| J. M. de la Pena ..... | 121.4 | 16 | 483 | 7 | 3-55 | 69.00 |
| E. T. Milburn ....... | 146 | 20 | 535 | 7 | 2-47 | 76.42 |

Also bowled: G. B. Agg 27–3–126–1; A. M. Babington 20–10–33–1; P. J. Bird 17–0–114–0; R. I. Dawson 4–0–11–0; A. J. Freeman 10–1–39–0; T. H. C. Hancock 39–10–141–1; R. Horrell 26–6–59–4; S. G. Joyner 31–10–84–3; K. Patel 56.2–9–213–4; P. W. Romaines 10–3–25–1; R. J. Scott 32–9–113–2; A. W. Stovold 2–1–1–0; S. R. Walbridge 52–12–146–1.

## HAMPSHIRE SECOND ELEVEN

*Matches 16: Won – Derbyshire, Essex, Northamptonshire, Somerset, Worcestershire. Drawn – Glamorgan, Gloucestershire, Kent, Lancashire, Leicestershire, Middlesex, Nottinghamshire, Surrey, Sussex, Warwickshire, Yorkshire.*

## Batting Averages

|  | M | I | NO | R | HI | 100s | Avge |
|---|---|---|---|---|---|---|---|
| R. S. M. Morris . . . . . | 9 | 18 | 7 | 997 | 136* | 4 | 90.63 |
| R. M. F. Cox . . . . . . . | 16 | 28 | 2 | 1,222 | 147* | 3 | 47.00 |
| I. J. Turner . . . . . . . . | 11 | 10 | 4 | 278 | 85* | 0 | 46.33 |
| J. R. Wood . . . . . . . . | 15 | 27 | 3 | 1,015 | 148 | 1 | 42.29 |
| J. R. Ayling . . . . . . . . | 7 | 13 | 4 | 365 | 86 | 0 | 40.55 |
| *†R. J. Parks . . . . . . . . | 15 | 23 | 3 | 726 | 102 | 1 | 36.30 |
| K. D. James . . . . . . . | 3 | 5 | 0 | 159 | 58 | 0 | 31.80 |
| J. S. Laney . . . . . . . . . | 6 | 8 | 3 | 158 | 48* | 0 | 31.60 |
| T. C. Middleton . . . . . | 3 | 6 | 0 | 166 | 79 | 0 | 27.66 |
| I. K. Maynard . . . . . . | 3 | 6 | 0 | 153 | 47 | 0 | 25.50 |
| S. D. Udal . . . . . . . . | 10 | 12 | 2 | 197 | 84* | 0 | 19.70 |
| M. J. Thursfield . . . . . | 13 | 11 | 1 | 180 | 33 | 0 | 18.00 |
| T. M. Tremlett . . . . . | 7 | 6 | 1 | 71 | 39 | 0 | 14.20 |
| J. N. B. Bovill . . . . . . | 4 | 6 | 2 | 50 | 37 | 0 | 12.50 |
| D. P. J. Flint . . . . . . . | 15 | 9 | 4 | 11 | 5* | 0 | 2.20 |

Also batted: P. J. Bakker 5, 0; D. G. J. Carson 2, 6*, 49, 9; P. Chrispin 42, 36*; C. A. Connor 7, 1, 4, 2; M. Garaway 3; B. A. Hames 16*; J. C. Harrison 1*, 14; J. E. Hayward 0, 29*; J. P. Kent 56*, 38; A. Lang 1*; R. J. Maru 11; G. I. Macmillan 9, 28; O. T. Parkin 9; M. J. Russell 1, 29; Sagheer Mohammed 0; K. J. Shine 3, 1, 0*, 10, 1; V. P. Terry 129; C. J. Thomason 12, 4, 27*, 10. J. Boyce, P. Mirza and N. R. Taylor each played in one match but did not bat.

## Bowling Averages

|  | O | M | R | W | BB | Avge |
|---|---|---|---|---|---|---|
| P. J. Bakker . . . . . . . . | 45 | 20 | 111 | 7 | 3-42 | 15.85 |
| T. M. Tremlett . . . . . . | 47 | 9 | 125 | 7 | 5-48 | 17.85 |
| K. D. James . . . . . . . . | 45.1 | 14 | 146 | 8 | 4-42 | 18.25 |
| C. A. Connor . . . . . . . | 62.1 | 15 | 159 | 7 | 3-23 | 22.71 |
| D. P. J. Flint . . . . . . . | 420 | 120 | 1,263 | 53 | 6-47 | 23.83 |
| I. J. Turner . . . . . . . . | 290 | 77 | 741 | 30 | 6-29 | 24.70 |
| J. N. B. Bovill . . . . . . | 94 | 15 | 305 | 12 | 4-41 | 25.41 |
| S. D. Udal . . . . . . . . | 286.4 | 72 | 819 | 27 | 4-30 | 30.33 |
| J. R. Ayling . . . . . . . . | 142.3 | 33 | 354 | 11 | 3-43 | 32.18 |
| M. J. Thursfield . . . . . | 198 | 55 | 550 | 16 | 2-18 | 34.37 |
| K. J. Shine . . . . . . . . . | 159.2 | 35 | 477 | 13 | 3-58 | 36.69 |

Also bowled: J. Boyce 19-3-57-1; P. Chrispin 16-4-53-2; R. M. F. Cox 9-2-45-1; J. C. Harrison 10-2-44-1; J. P. Kent 6-1-33-1; J. S. Laney 4-1-10-0; A. Lang 7-0-23-0; R. J. Maru 24-10-35-1; P. Mirza 12-1-63-0; R. S. M. Morris 2-1-5-0; O. T. Parkin 26-6-66-1; Sagheer Mohammed 7.5-2-41-2; N. R. Taylor 24-8-57-1.

# KENT SECOND ELEVEN

*Matches 16: Won – Nottinghamshire. Lost – Derbyshire, Leicestershire, Somerset. Drawn – Essex, Glamorgan, Gloucestershire, Hampshire, Lancashire, Middlesex, Northamptonshire, Surrey, Sussex, Warwickshire, Worcestershire, Yorkshire.*

## Batting Averages

|  | M | I | NO | R | HI | Avge |
|---|---|---|---|---|---|---|
| †V. J. Wells . . . . . . . . . | 12 | 21 | 4 | 930 | 205 | 54.70 |
| J. I. Longley . . . . . . . . . | 8 | 12 | 2 | 546 | 119* | 54.60 |
| S. G. Hinks . . . . . . . . . | 4 | 6 | 1 | 271 | 91 | 54.20 |
| M. A. Ealham . . . . . . . | 13 | 19 | 3 | 827 | 213 | 51.68 |
| M. C. Dobson . . . . . . . | 10 | 19 | 4 | 750 | 123* | 50.00 |
| N. J. Llong . . . . . . . . . . | 13 | 21 | 2 | 898 | 96 | 47.26 |
| D. J. M. Kelleher . . . . | 10 | 14 | 3 | 494 | 108 | 44.90 |

| | M | I | NO | R | HI | | Avge |
|---|---|---|---|---|---|---|---|
| R. M. Ellison | 4 | 4 | 2 | 85 | 38 | | 42.50 |
| D. P. Fulton | 8 | 12 | 2 | 349 | 116 | | 34.90 |
| M. M. Patel | 8 | 5 | 2 | 103 | 51 | | 34.33 |
| C. S. Cowdrey | 3 | 4 | 0 | 120 | 70 | | 30.00 |
| †G. J. Kersey | 15 | 19 | 4 | 428 | 70* | | 28.53 |
| J. F. Barr | 3 | 3 | 1 | 53 | 52* | | 26.50 |
| D. J. T. Moon | 2 | 4 | 0 | 99 | 63 | | 24.75 |
| G. D. Myers | 6 | 9 | 2 | 158 | 55 | | 22.57 |
| A. J. Planck | 2 | 3 | 0 | 52 | 34 | | 17.33 |
| *A. G. E. Ealham | 6 | 3 | 2 | 17 | 17 | | 17.00 |
| T. N. Wren | 14 | 12 | 6 | 98 | 26* | | 16.33 |
| M. T. Brimson | 4 | 5 | 2 | 42 | 16* | | 14.00 |
| S. C. Willis | 8 | 10 | 2 | 88 | 26* | | 11.00 |
| P. A. Westrop | 4 | 3 | 0 | 19 | 14 | | 6.33 |
| S. G. Milroy | 3 | 3 | 0 | 11 | 9 | | 3.66 |
| N. W. Preston | 4 | 3 | 2 | 2 | 2* | | 2.00 |

Played in three matches: L. A. C. Clarke 8, 2; M. J. McCague 24, 6. Played in one match: M. G. Bevan 61, 73; R. Bhanabhai 13; J. Creed 2; M. V. Fleming 38, 35; C. J. Hollins 4, 34*; M. Luckhurst 5.

## Bowling Averages

| | O | M | R | W | BB | Avge |
|---|---|---|---|---|---|---|
| M. G. Bevan | 41.4 | 15 | 105 | 6 | 6-68 | 17.50 |
| M. M. Patel | 219 | 89 | 513 | 23 | 6-99 | 22.30 |
| L. A. C. Clarke | 29 | 6 | 85 | 3 | 2-13 | 28.33 |
| M. A. Ealham | 210.5 | 38 | 673 | 22 | 4-49 | 30.59 |
| V. J. Wells | 174.2 | 37 | 534 | 17 | 4-34 | 31.41 |
| R. M. Ellison | 58 | 21 | 131 | 4 | 3-42 | 32.75 |
| M. J. McCague | 62 | 12 | 164 | 5 | 2-55 | 32.80 |
| M. C. Dobson | 160.1 | 28 | 530 | 16 | 3-49 | 33.12 |
| T. N. Wren | 337.5 | 79 | 1,016 | 29 | 4-45 | 35.03 |
| D. J. M. Kelleher | 119.4 | 24 | 358 | 10 | 2-12 | 35.80 |
| P. A. Westrop | 33 | 5 | 130 | 3 | 3-30 | 43.33 |
| N. W. Preston | 79 | 17 | 196 | 4 | 2-61 | 49.00 |
| N. J. Llong | 230.2 | 41 | 751 | 12 | 5-87 | 62.58 |

Also bowled: R. Bhanabhai 3-1-8-1; M. T. Brimson 114-27-298-2; C. S. Cowdrey 7-3-17-1; M. V. Fleming 10-4-24-1; D. P. Fulton 1-0-2-0; S. G. Hinks 1-0-11-1; J. I. Longley 1-0-1-0; M. Luckhurst 6-1-23-0; S. C. Willis 8.1-4-17-1.

## LANCASHIRE SECOND ELEVEN

*Matches 16: Won – Gloucestershire, Surrey. Lost – Essex, Leicestershire, Somerset. Drawn – Derbyshire, Glamorgan, Hampshire, Kent, Middlesex, Northamptonshire, Nottinghamshire, Sussex, Warwickshire, Worcestershire, Yorkshire.*

## Batting Averages

| | M | I | NO | R | HI | 100s | Avge |
|---|---|---|---|---|---|---|---|
| J. P. Crawley | 4 | 6 | 3 | 286 | 80 | 0 | 95.33 |
| S. P. Titchard | 12 | 20 | 7 | 1,212 | 182* | 5 | 93.23 |
| N. J. Speak | 6 | 8 | 2 | 376 | 108* | 1 | 62.66 |
| J. E. R. Gallian | 16 | 25 | 8 | 1,009 | 143 | 4 | 59.35 |
| G. D. Lloyd | 5 | 10 | 0 | 578 | 152 | 2 | 57.80 |
| T. E. Jesty | 14 | 20 | 4 | 594 | 105 | 1 | 37.12 |
| T. M. Orrell | 16 | 24 | 2 | 741 | 84 | 0 | 33.68 |
| J. D. Fitton | 12 | 13 | 3 | 333 | 108* | 1 | 33.30 |
| R. C. Irani | 9 | 8 | 2 | 197 | 73 | 0 | 32.83 |

|  | M | I | NO | R | HI | 100s | Avge |
|---|---|---|---|---|---|---|---|
| M. A. Sharp.......... | 9 | 5 | 4 | 32 | 13* | 0 | 32.00 |
| N. A. Derbyshire ..... | 8 | 5 | 2 | 83 | 59 | 0 | 27.66 |
| *†J. Stanworth........ | 13 | 5 | 3 | 55 | 20* | 0 | 27.50 |
| M. J. P. Ward ........ | 9 | 9 | 3 | 163 | 47 | 0 | 27.16 |
| D. T. Foy............ | 3 | 4 | 1 | 57 | 21 | 0 | 19.00 |
| J. I. D. Kerr ........ | 4 | 4 | 0 | 66 | 55 | 0 | 16.50 |
| G. Yates ............ | 4 | 3 | 1 | 29 | 17 | 0 | 14.50 |
| P. J. Martin ......... | 5 | 4 | 1 | 27 | 19* | 0 | 9.00 |
| R. O. Jones ......... | 3 | 3 | 0 | 21 | 20 | 0 | 7.00 |
| S. J. Speak .......... | 6 | 4 | 0 | 15 | 10 | 0 | 3.75 |

Played in four matches: A. Payne 1*. Played in three matches: I. D. Austin did not bat. Played in two matches: P. J. Heaton 17*, 1*. Played in one match: P. J. W. Allott 18; J. Fielding 26*; M. E. Harvey 9*; D. P. Hughes 27; G. A. Knowles 7; J. D. Simpson 7, 6; †T. Wallwork 29*, 1; P. J. Wilcock 10; A. B. Byram, J. A. L. Henderson, M. Taylor and R. Vigars did not bat.

*Note:* Owing to first-team calls, N. J. Speak and I. D. Austin were replaced by M. J. P. Ward and S. J. Speak in the match v Derbyshire and G. Yates was replaced by M. J. P. Ward in the match v Middlesex.

## Bowling Averages

|  | O | M | R | W | BB | Avge |
|---|---|---|---|---|---|---|
| J. Fielding ........... | 29 | 8 | 74 | 5 | 4-36 | 14.80 |
| P. J. Martin ......... | 127.3 | 38 | 363 | 19 | 6-33 | 19.10 |
| D. T. Foy ........... | 45 | 7 | 130 | 6 | 2-40 | 21.66 |
| T. E. Jesty .......... | 54.4 | 13 | 168 | 7 | 3-92 | 24.00 |
| A. Payne ........... | 94.5 | 18 | 278 | 8 | 4-59 | 34.75 |
| N. A. Derbyshire ..... | 152.3 | 13 | 614 | 16 | 5-67 | 38.37 |
| R. C. Irani .......... | 208.5 | 57 | 673 | 15 | 3-33 | 44.86 |
| J. E. R. Gallian....... | 245.5 | 33 | 940 | 20 | 3-62 | 47.00 |
| M. A. Sharp.......... | 266.1 | 66 | 791 | 16 | 3-33 | 49.43 |
| G. Yates............. | 82.5 | 18 | 273 | 5 | 4-116 | 54.60 |
| J. D. Fitton ......... | 331 | 78 | 893 | 13 | 2-44 | 68.69 |
| R. O. Jones ......... | 77.2 | 15 | 297 | 4 | 3-98 | 74.25 |

Also bowled: P. J. W. Allott 14–6–30–2; I. D. Austin 61–15–160–3; A. B. Byram 23–6–54–0; P. J. Heaton 35.4–6–133–3; J. A. L. Henderson 23–7–57–0; D. P. Hughes 11–8–7–0; J. I. D. Kerr 3–1–18–2; G. D. Lloyd 4–1–43–1; T. M. Orrell 3–0–29–0; N. J. Speak 18–5–59–2; S. J. Speak 42.5–8–174–2; M. Taylor 31–11–114–2; R. Vigars 28.3–3–106–2; M. J. P. Ward 64–12–262–2.

## LEICESTERSHIRE SECOND ELEVEN

*Matches 16:* Won – Kent, Lancashire, Middlesex. Lost – Nottinghamshire, Somerset, Surrey, Sussex, Warwickshire, Worcestershire. Drawn – Derbyshire, Essex, Glamorgan, Gloucestershire, Hampshire, Northamptonshire, Yorkshire.

## Batting Averages

|  | M | I | NO | R | HI | 100s | Avge |
|---|---|---|---|---|---|---|---|
| D. R. Martyn .......... | 9 | 16 | 6 | 656 | 201* | 1 | 65.60 |
| B. F. Smith .......... | 3 | 5 | 1 | 248 | 119 | 1 | 62.00 |
| G. E. Charles ......... | 2 | 3 | 0 | 178 | 93 | 0 | 59.33 |
| P. Willey............. | 5 | 9 | 3 | 274 | 76* | 0 | 45.66 |
| J. D. R. Benson ...... | 4 | 6 | 0 | 243 | 98 | 0 | 40.50 |
| *R. A. Cobb.......... | 15 | 22 | 6 | 627 | 160 | 1 | 39.18 |
| D. Maddy ........... | 9 | 10 | 3 | 229 | 87 | 0 | 32.71 |
| M. I. Gidley ......... | 9 | 13 | 2 | 359 | 100 | 1 | 32.63 |
| †P. A. Nixon .......... | 15 | 26 | 1 | 785 | 125 | 1 | 31.40 |

| | M | I | NO | R | HI | 100s | Avge |
|---|---|---|---|---|---|---|---|
| G. J. Parsons .......... | 13 | 19 | 4 | 390 | 75 | 0 | 26.00 |
| N. G. Gamble ........ | 4 | 6 | 4 | 48 | 16 | 0 | 24.00 |
| I. F. Plender .......... | 14 | 25 | 1 | 512 | 66 | 0 | 21.33 |
| A. O. Rooke .......... | 13 | 8 | 7 | 20 | 10* | 0 | 20.00 |
| C. J. Hawkes ......... | 8 | 12 | 2 | 192 | 40 | 0 | 19.20 |
| A. Roseberry ......... | 16 | 28 | 1 | 412 | 63 | 0 | 15.25 |
| A. F. Haye .......... | 6 | 7 | 0 | 77 | 31 | 0 | 11.00 |
| L. Tennant .......... | 9 | 8 | 2 | 56 | 16 | 0 | 9.33 |
| N. Adams .......... | 2 | 4 | 0 | 34 | 21 | 0 | 8.50 |
| I. J. Sutcliffe ........ | 2 | 4 | 1 | 19 | 12 | 0 | 6.33 |
| C. W. Wilkinson ....... | 4 | 3 | 0 | 17 | 17 | 0 | 5.66 |
| Sagheer Mohammed ..... | 2 | 3 | 0 | 12 | 12 | 0 | 4.00 |

Played in two matches: D. J. Miller 13*, 2*; A. D. Mullally 0*, 6. Played in one match:
J. Addison 40, 44; T. J. Boon 113*, 10; M. A. Challenger 2*, 4*; S. J. Cooper 36; P. E. Ellis
12, 22; A. K. Golding 15, 4; J. R. Goldthorp 4, 59; P. N. Hepworth 4, 122; I. Mason 3;
S. Schofield 36*; V. Walsh 8, 33; N. Whitmore 10; M. Rutterford did not bat.

*Note:* Owing to first-team calls, M. I. Gidley was replaced by A. F. Haye in the match v
Middlesex, L. Tennant was replaced by D. J. Miller in the match v Northamptonshire,
G. J. Parsons was replaced by D. Maddy in the match v Derbyshire and J. D. R. Benson was
replaced by I. Mason in the match v Surrey.

## Bowling Averages

| | O | M | R | W | BB | Avge |
|---|---|---|---|---|---|---|
| T. J. Boon .......... | 10 | 2 | 24 | 4 | 4-24 | 6.00 |
| C. W. Wilkinson ..... | 112 | 35 | 250 | 16 | 4-45 | 15.62 |
| V. Walsh .......... | 33.4 | 6 | 103 | 5 | 4-81 | 20.60 |
| C. J. Hawkes ........ | 225 | 75 | 549 | 21 | 7-65 | 26.14 |
| A. F. Haye ......... | 58 | 9 | 222 | 8 | 5-48 | 27.75 |
| D. R. Martyn ....... | 85.2 | 20 | 239 | 8 | 3-46 | 29.87 |
| G. J. Parsons ....... | 241.2 | 48 | 732 | 24 | 4-60 | 30.50 |
| M. I. Gidley ........ | 235.2 | 78 | 521 | 15 | 4-74 | 34.73 |
| L. Tennant ......... | 214.2 | 32 | 753 | 21 | 5-66 | 35.85 |
| N. G. Gamble ....... | 88.3 | 22 | 280 | 7 | 3-42 | 40.00 |
| A. O. Rooke ........ | 271.4 | 63 | 818 | 20 | 4-25 | 40.90 |
| P. Willey .......... | 132.4 | 46 | 286 | 6 | 2-54 | 47.66 |
| I. F. Plender ........ | 113.5 | 24 | 405 | 5 | 1-20 | 81.00 |

Also bowled: J. Addison 19–3–73–1; J. D. R. Benson 34–10–91–1; M. A. Challenger
18–1–74–0; G. E. Charles 53–11–154–3; S. J. Cooper 2–0–24–0; P. E. Ellis 7–0–33–0;
A. K. Golding 30–9–81–2; P. N. Hepworth 3–1–9–0; D. Maddy 30–4–100–1; I. Mason
11–3–35–0; D. J. Miller 20–4–72–1; A. D. Mullally 34–10–79–3; P. A. Nixon 4–0–20–0;
M. Rutterford 8.1–0–48–0; Sagheer Mohammed 18–1–73–1; B. F. Smith 36.1–3–163–0;
N. Whitmore 21.4–3–80–1.

# MIDDLESEX SECOND ELEVEN

*Matches 16: Won – Nottinghamshire, Sussex. Lost – Gloucestershire, Leicestershire, Warwick-
shire, Yorkshire. Drawn – Derbyshire, Essex, Glamorgan, Hampshire, Kent, Lancashire,
Northamptonshire, Somerset, Surrey, Worcestershire.*

## Batting Averages

| | M | I | NO | R | HI | Avge |
|---|---|---|---|---|---|---|
| M. Keech .............. | 8 | 14 | 3 | 605 | 121 | 55.00 |
| M. A. Roseberry ......... | 2 | 4 | 0 | 204 | 74 | 51.00 |
| *I. J. Gould ............. | 11 | 10 | 6 | 203 | 41* | 50.75 |
| J. C. Pooley ............. | 8 | 14 | 3 | 556 | 162 | 50.54 |
| P. N. Weekes ........... | 12 | 19 | 4 | 739 | 101* | 49.26 |

| | M | I | NO | R | HI | Avge |
|---|---|---|---|---|---|---|
| †R. J. Sims . . . . . . . . . . . . | 12 | 16 | 5 | 443 | 113 | 40.27 |
| M. J. Lowrey . . . . . . . . . . . | 8 | 15 | 3 | 440 | 113* | 36.66 |
| †G. M. Pooley . . . . . . . . . . . | 7 | 11 | 1 | 354 | 61 | 35.40 |
| A. Habib . . . . . . . . . . . . . | 5 | 8 | 1 | 244 | 77 | 34.85 |
| T. A. Radford . . . . . . . . . . | 13 | 24 | 6 | 603 | 93 | 33.50 |
| I. J. F. Hutchinson . . . . . . | 7 | 13 | 0 | 392 | 75 | 30.15 |
| †P. Farbrace . . . . . . . . . . . | 4 | 5 | 0 | 137 | 51 | 27.40 |
| S. P. Hughes . . . . . . . . . . . | 4 | 5 | 2 | 74 | 43 | 24.66 |
| P. J. Atherley . . . . . . . . . . | 3 | 3 | 1 | 41 | 35 | 20.50 |
| D. J. Bowen . . . . . . . . . . . | 3 | 6 | 0 | 108 | 36 | 18.00 |
| A. A. Barnett . . . . . . . . . . | 16 | 20 | 4 | 257 | 61 | 16.06 |
| J. W. A. Gilson . . . . . . . . . | 3 | 5 | 0 | 70 | 48 | 14.00 |
| C. W. Taylor . . . . . . . . . . . | 9 | 10 | 2 | 110 | 35 | 13.75 |
| R. Johnson . . . . . . . . . . . . | 5 | 6 | 0 | 61 | 23 | 10.16 |
| J. M. S. Whittington . . . . . . | 3 | 4 | 1 | 18 | 17 | 6.00 |
| C. Patel . . . . . . . . . . . . . | 4 | 4 | 1 | 14 | 8* | 4.66 |
| R. S. Yeabsley . . . . . . . . . . | 3 | 3 | 0 | 10 | 7 | 3.33 |
| S. A. Sylvester . . . . . . . . . . | 11 | 7 | 1 | 15 | 4 | 2.50 |

Played in two matches: N. P. Harvey 0, 11*, 0*; N. F. Williams 9, 6. Played in one match: M. R. Bate 14*, 64; D. J. Bowett 6; K. R. Brown 43, 23; C. L. Cairns 25, 15; N. G. Cowans 0; A. R. C. Fraser 7; D. W. Headley 11; G. I. Macmillan 56, 59; C. J. Rogers 15, 0; E. W. Thacker 7; M. J. Thewlis 0; P. C. R. Tufnell 2; J. P. Dickson did not bat.

*Note:* Owing to first-team calls, S. P. Hughes and C. W. Taylor were replaced by P. C. R. Tufnell and P. J. Atherley in the match v Lancashire.

## Bowling Averages

| | O | M | R | W | BB | Avge |
|---|---|---|---|---|---|---|
| S. P. Hughes . . . . . . . . . . . | 93.3 | 19 | 265 | 12 | 5-46 | 22.08 |
| A. A. Barnett . . . . . . . . . . | 592.4 | 161 | 1,540 | 63 | 7-130 | 24.44 |
| P. N. Weekes . . . . . . . . . . | 418.5 | 102 | 1,119 | 43 | 7-80 | 26.02 |
| C. W. Taylor . . . . . . . . . . . | 186.4 | 46 | 563 | 21 | 5-51 | 26.80 |
| J. M. S. Whittington . . . . . | 84 | 24 | 239 | 8 | 7-114 | 29.87 |
| S. A. Sylvester . . . . . . . . . . | 142.2 | 23 | 518 | 15 | 3-38 | 34.53 |

Also bowled: C. L. Cairns 26.5-9-72-3; N. G. Cowans 11-4-25-0; J. P. Dickson 16-1-45-1; A. R. C. Fraser 10-4-13-1; I. J. Gould 19.5-4-82-0; A. Habib 12-1-52-0; D. W. Headley 18.5-2-86-1; I. J. F. Hutchinson 13-1-66-1; R. Johnson 87-17-295-5; M. Keech 22.1-3-60-0; M. J. Lowrey 9.2-3-35-2; C. Patel 34-7-87-3; T. A. Radford 6-1-9-0; M. A. Roseberry 11-0-57-0; M. J. Thewlis 13-1-56-0; P. C. R. Tufnell 10-7-10-0; N. F. Williams 49-13-129-4; R. S. Yeabsley 42-2-176-3.

# NORTHAMPTONSHIRE SECOND ELEVEN

*Matches 16: Lost – Hampshire, Somerset, Sussex, Warwickshire. Drawn – Derbyshire, Essex, Glamorgan, Gloucestershire, Kent, Lancashire, Leicestershire, Middlesex, Nottinghamshire, Surrey, Worcestershire, Yorkshire.*

## Batting Averages

| | M | I | NO | R | HI | Avge |
|---|---|---|---|---|---|---|
| *R. M. Carter . . . . . . . . . . | 11 | 9 | 5 | 241 | 60 | 60.25 |
| N. A. Stanley . . . . . . . . . . | 14 | 23 | 4 | 992 | 203* | 52.21 |
| N. A. Felton . . . . . . . . . . | 4 | 7 | 1 | 299 | 131 | 49.83 |
| A. R. Roberts . . . . . . . . . . | 9 | 13 | 4 | 392 | 94 | 43.55 |
| †W. M. Noon . . . . . . . . . . | 13 | 18 | 5 | 523 | 91 | 40.23 |
| M. B. Loye . . . . . . . . . . . | 12 | 21 | 2 | 694 | 156* | 36.52 |
| R. J. Warren . . . . . . . . . . | 12 | 21 | 4 | 609 | 170* | 35.82 |
| D. B. K. Page . . . . . . . . . . | 11 | 16 | 5 | 376 | 54 | 34.18 |
| T. C. Walton . . . . . . . . . . | 5 | 6 | 0 | 187 | 118 | 31.16 |

| | M | I | NO | R | HI | Avge |
|---|---|---|---|---|---|---|
| A. L. Penberthy . . . . . . . | 7 | 10 | 1 | 272 | 84 | 30.22 |
| P. E. Ellis . . . . . . . . . . . | 4 | 7 | 0 | 189 | 74 | 27.00 |
| R. R. Montgomerie . . . . | 5 | 10 | 1 | 223 | 92 | 24.77 |
| M. A. Sharpe . . . . . . . . . | 8 | 7 | 2 | 76 | 34 | 15.20 |
| A. Walker . . . . . . . . . . . | 4 | 6 | 1 | 72 | 33 | 14.40 |
| R. M. Pearson . . . . . . . | 7 | 8 | 1 | 79 | 39 | 11.28 |
| J. G. Hughes . . . . . . . . . | 8 | 8 | 3 | 54 | 16* | 10.80 |
| J. N. Snape . . . . . . . . . . | 4 | 7 | 1 | 31 | 18 | 5.16 |
| K. Bird . . . . . . . . . . . . | 8 | 7 | 3 | 14 | 5* | 3.50 |

Also batted: Ajaz Akhtar 18; J. M. Attfield 25; L. M. Banfield 0; R. E. Bryson 12; M. T. Burt 0; D. J. Capel 86, 4; J. R. Carruthers 0; D. R. Clarke 13, 94; D. M. Cousins 0, 7*; J. R. Goode 10, 29*, 2*; A. Howorth 9, 10; W. Larkins 72, 185; P. Mirza 6; R. J. Pack 14*; D. Ripley 4, 97; J. G. Thomas 18, 21; R. J. Williams 6. M. H. Colclough, D. M. Jones, S. G. Joyner and J. P. Taylor did not bat.

## Bowling Averages

| | O | M | R | W | BB | Avge |
|---|---|---|---|---|---|---|
| A. L. Penberthy . . . . . | 157.4 | 39 | 360 | 22 | 7-57 | 16.36 |
| M. A. Sharpe . . . . . . . . | 168.5 | 28 | 498 | 17 | 4-54 | 29.29 |
| R. M. Pearson . . . . . . . | 251.3 | 76 | 634 | 21 | 4-42 | 30.19 |
| A. R. Roberts . . . . . . . | 219.3 | 53 | 640 | 17 | 3-18 | 37.64 |
| D. B. K. Page . . . . . . . | 235.3 | 41 | 869 | 23 | 4-25 | 37.78 |
| T. C. Walton . . . . . . . . | 56 | 10 | 219 | 5 | 3-54 | 43.80 |
| J. G. Hughes . . . . . . . . | 171.1 | 29 | 505 | 10 | 5-36 | 50.50 |
| A. Walker . . . . . . . . . . | 119.3 | 21 | 356 | 6 | 3-12 | 59.33 |
| K. Bird . . . . . . . . . . . . | 112 | 16 | 493 | 7 | 2-62 | 70.42 |

Also bowled: Ajaz Akhtar 20-4-56-0; L. M. Banfield 30-4-95-0; R. E. Bryson 30-1-109-1; D. J. Capel 23.1-8-50-4; J. R. Carruthers 12-2-36-1; D. M. Cousins 22-1-88-1; P. E. Ellis 7-1-53-0; N. A. Felton 10-7-6-0; A. Howorth 43-14-103-3; D. M. Jones 20-4-77-0; S. G. Joyner 7-1-44-0; P. Mirza 18-5-74-0; R. R. Montgomerie 4-1-13-0; W. M. Noon 8-0-60-0; R. J. Pack 16-6-51-1; J. N. Snape 5-0-13-1; N. A. Stanley 35-4-132-4; J. P. Taylor 24.5-6-83-3; J. G. Thomas 38-5-132-6.

# NOTTINGHAMSHIRE SECOND ELEVEN

*Matches 16: Won – Derbyshire, Essex, Leicestershire, Worcestershire, Yorkshire. Lost – Kent, Middlesex. Drawn – Glamorgan, Gloucestershire, Hampshire, Lancashire, Northamptonshire, Somerset, Surrey, Sussex, Warwickshire.*

## Batting Averages

| | M | I | NO | R | HI | 100s | Avge |
|---|---|---|---|---|---|---|---|
| P. R. Pollard . . . . . . . . | 2 | 3 | 0 | 217 | 154 | 1 | 72.33 |
| M. P. Dowman . . . . . . . . | 2 | 4 | 1 | 207 | 124 | 1 | 69.00 |
| G. F. Archer . . . . . . . . . | 13 | 20 | 4 | 839 | 149 | 2 | 52.43 |
| *M. Newell . . . . . . . . . | 16 | 26 | 5 | 1,052 | 145* | 3 | 50.09 |
| D. J. R. Martindale . . . . | 14 | 23 | 5 | 749 | 139* | 2 | 41.61 |
| M. Saxelby . . . . . . . . . | 9 | 14 | 4 | 413 | 85 | 0 | 41.30 |
| S. M. Brogan . . . . . . . . | 13 | 24 | 4 | 750 | 118* | 2 | 37.50 |
| W. A. Dessaur . . . . . . . | 14 | 20 | 2 | 675 | 208* | 2 | 37.50 |
| M. A. Crawley . . . . . . . . | 4 | 7 | 2 | 184 | 51 | 0 | 36.80 |
| †C. W. Scott . . . . . . . . | 14 | 13 | 4 | 277 | 85 | 0 | 30.77 |
| R. T. Bates . . . . . . . . . | 13 | 17 | 5 | 353 | 72* | 0 | 29.41 |
| M. G. Field-Buss . . . . . | 15 | 12 | 2 | 188 | 60 | 0 | 18.80 |
| V. J. P. Broadley . . . . . | 8 | 5 | 3 | 36 | 20* | 0 | 18.00 |
| J. Hodgson . . . . . . . . . | 10 | 9 | 3 | 66 | 42 | 0 | 11.00 |
| G. W. Mike . . . . . . . . . | 2 | 4 | 0 | 8 | 7 | 0 | 2.00 |

Played in six matches: R. J. Chapman 0. Played in five matches: D. R. Brewis 8, 8. Played in four matches: K. Saxelby 8, 1*. Played in three matches: J. A. Afford 1*. Played in two matches: P. Aldred 4, 16; K. E. Cooper 0*, 18. Played in one match: †S. Bramhall 1, 10*; †P. W. Hampshire 21, 14*; G. James 18, 0; S. J. Musgrove 0; B. Helps did not bat.

## Bowling Averages

|  | O | M | R | W | BB | Avge |
|---|---|---|---|---|---|---|
| K. E. Cooper . . . . . . . . . . | 54.4 | 19 | 72 | 8 | 4-15 | 9.00 |
| J. A. Afford . . . . . . . . . . | 125 | 41 | 240 | 21 | 6-68 | 11.42 |
| M. G. Field-Buss . . . . . | 582.1 | 174 | 1,356 | 49 | 5-81 | 27.67 |
| M. Saxelby . . . . . . . . . . | 158.3 | 32 | 390 | 14 | 4-55 | 27.85 |
| R. T. Bates . . . . . . . . . . | 349.4 | 58 | 1,215 | 28 | 4-86 | 43.39 |
| V. J. P. Broadley . . . . . | 222.5 | 42 | 727 | 16 | 3-37 | 45.43 |
| J. Hodgson . . . . . . . . . . | 151.1 | 22 | 518 | 11 | 3-68 | 47.09 |
| D. R. Brewis . . . . . . . . | 95 | 12 | 381 | 7 | 2-59 | 54.42 |
| R. J. Chapman . . . . . . . | 95.3 | 11 | 369 | 6 | 2-31 | 61.50 |

Also bowled: P. Aldred 40–6–158–0; S. M. Brogan 3–0–32–0; M. A. Crawley 63–13–187–1; W. A. Dessaur 13–4–43–0; M. P. Dowman 48–11–133–3; B. Helps 33–8–80–3; G. W. Mike 39.4–4–137–2; S. J. Musgrove 5–0–24–0; M. Newell 41.2–5–162–2; K. Saxelby 43–9–146–2.

## SOMERSET SECOND ELEVEN

*Matches 16: Won – Gloucestershire, Kent, Lancashire, Leicestershire, Northamptonshire, Surrey. Lost – Derbyshire, Hampshire, Worcestershire, Yorkshire. Drawn – Essex, Glamorgan, Middlesex, Nottinghamshire, Sussex, Warwickshire.*

## Batting Averages

|  | M | I | NO | R | HI | Avge |
|---|---|---|---|---|---|---|
| K. G. Sedgbeer . . . . . . . | 2 | 3 | 2 | 142 | 80* | 142.00 |
| R. J. Bartlett . . . . . . . . . | 11 | 15 | 2 | 602 | 106 | 46.30 |
| M. N. Lathwell . . . . . . . | 9 | 13 | 1 | 522 | 87 | 43.50 |
| G. Brown . . . . . . . . . . . | 2 | 3 | 2 | 42 | 38* | 42.00 |
| Kevin J. Parsons . . . . . . | 2 | 4 | 1 | 122 | 57 | 40.66 |
| †R. J. Turner . . . . . . . . . | 8 | 12 | 1 | 421 | 72* | 38.27 |
| G. T. J. Townsend . . . . . | 14 | 24 | 5 | 723 | 129* | 38.05 |
| I. G. Swallow . . . . . . . . | 10 | 10 | 3 | 259 | 85* | 37.00 |
| Keith A. Parsons . . . . . . | 3 | 6 | 1 | 177 | 55 | 35.40 |
| G. D. Rose . . . . . . . . . . | 2 | 3 | 0 | 102 | 71 | 34.00 |
| I. Fletcher . . . . . . . . . . | 9 | 16 | 1 | 479 | 119 | 31.93 |
| *N. J. Pringle . . . . . . . . . | 13 | 19 | 1 | 550 | 87 | 30.55 |
| G. W. White . . . . . . . . . | 13 | 20 | 2 | 469 | 91 | 26.05 |
| H. R. J. Trump . . . . . . . | 4 | 6 | 1 | 120 | 71 | 24.00 |
| M. W. Cleal . . . . . . . . . | 3 | 4 | 1 | 69 | 32 | 23.00 |
| K. H. MacLeay . . . . . . . | 2 | 3 | 0 | 65 | 50 | 21.66 |
| A. R. Caddick . . . . . . . . | 15 | 15 | 5 | 152 | 28* | 15.20 |
| †T. Edwards . . . . . . . . . . | 8 | 9 | 2 | 83 | 56* | 11.85 |
| D. Beal . . . . . . . . . . . . | 8 | 10 | 2 | 93 | 34 | 11.62 |
| A. C. Cottam . . . . . . . . | 12 | 11 | 4 | 63 | 26 | 9.00 |
| V. Walsh . . . . . . . . . . . | 2 | 3 | 1 | 11 | 11 | 5.50 |

Played in four matches: A. P. van Troost did not bat. Played in two matches: P. C. Turner did not bat. Played in one match: K. C. G. Benjamin 1; J. Gosling 0*, 8; J. C. Hallett 41*; M. A. Harris 10, 0; M. James 23; N. A. Mallender 0*; R. J. Pannel 0; D. Perryman 1*; D. W. Pippett 0*; S. P. Pollard 0; J. Prosser 0, 1; T. Ramshaw 43, 13; P. J. Rendell 12*; J. B. Robertson 1*; M. F. Robinson 0; M. P. Sage 0, 8; B. M. Wellington 1; N. R. Williams 2. K. J. Moyse and P. J. Robinson did not bat.

*Note:* Owing to first-team calls, D. Beal was replaced by P. J. Rendell in the match v Middlesex and H. R. J. Trump was replaced by P. J. Robinson in the match v Derbyshire.

## Bowling Averages

|                    | O      | M   | R     | W  | BB       | Avge  |
|--------------------|--------|-----|-------|----|----------|-------|
| A. R. Caddick .........  | 515.2  | 120 | 1,233 | 96 | 8-39     | 12.84 |
| K. C. G. Benjamin .....  | 33     | 10  | 78    | 5  | 3-17     | 15.60 |
| A. P. van Troost .......  | 54     | 8   | 156   | 8  | 4-15     | 19.50 |
| R. J. Bartlett...........  | 24.2   | 5   | 105   | 5  | 3-26     | 21.00 |
| I. G. Swallow .........  | 159.3  | 57  | 379   | 17 | 4-24     | 22.29 |
| D. Beal ..............  | 176    | 30  | 588   | 24 | 6-41     | 24.50 |
| H. R. J. Trump ........  | 143    | 45  | 298   | 10 | 4-44     | 29.80 |
| G. D. Rose ............  | 32     | 8   | 128   | 4  | 2-25     | 32.00 |
| A. C. Cottam ..........  | 219.3  | 60  | 618   | 19 | 4-38     | 32.52 |
| M. N. Lathwell .......  | 79     | 21  | 230   | 6  | 2-32     | 38.33 |
| V. Walsh ..............  | 64     | 12  | 154   | 4  | 2-37     | 38.50 |
| G. W. White...........  | 164.3  | 38  | 557   | 9  | 2-48     | 61.88 |

Also bowled: G. Brown 2–0–4–0; M. W. Cleal 5–1–17–0; J. C. Hallett 38–10–148–3; M. James 8–0–32–0; K. H. MacLeay 24–5–60–1; N. A. Mallender 15–2–38–1; K. J. Moyse 5–0–31–1; R. J. Pannel 5–0–21–0; Keith A. Parsons 26–7–99–2; D. Perryman 6–2–21–1; D. W. Pippett 11–1–57–0; N. J. Pringle 25–2–113–2; T. Ramshaw 6–0–25–0; P. J. Rendell 6–1–16–0; J. B. Robertson 30–4–104–2; K. G. Sedgbeer 3–0–14–0; G. T. J. Townsend 1–0–4–0; P. C. Turner 12–4–34–1; B. M. Wellington 11–0–51–0.

## SURREY SECOND ELEVEN

*Matches 16: Won – Essex, Gloucestershire, Leicestershire, Worcestershire. Lost – Glamorgan, Lancashire, Somerset, Warwickshire. Drawn – Derbyshire, Hampshire, Kent, Middlesex, Northamptonshire, Nottinghamshire, Sussex, Yorkshire.*

## Batting Averages

|                        | M  | I  | NO | R     | HI    | 100s | Avge  |
|------------------------|----|----|----|-------|-------|------|-------|
| A. D. Brown .........  | 15 | 26 | 5  | 1,199 | 207*  | 3    | 57.09 |
| C. K. Bullen .........  | 16 | 23 | 7  | 727   | 111*  | 1    | 45.43 |
| M. A. Lynch .........  | 2  | 4  | 0  | 167   | 104   | 1    | 41.75 |
| J. D. Robinson .........  | 11 | 22 | 4  | 748   | 135   | 2    | 41.55 |
| R. I. Alikhan.............  | 2  | 4  | 0  | 155   | 121   | 1    | 38.75 |
| N. M. Kendrick .......  | 15 | 20 | 6  | 469   | 78    | 0    | 33.50 |
| K. T. Medlycott .......  | 2  | 4  | 2  | 67    | 22    | 0    | 33.50 |
| P. D. Atkins .........  | 11 | 19 | 2  | 474   | 81*   | 0    | 27.88 |
| A. J. Hollioake .......  | 10 | 14 | 1  | 344   | 80    | 0    | 26.46 |
| M. A. Feltham .......  | 5  | 9  | 1  | 204   | 57    | 0    | 25.50 |
| M. A. Butcher .......  | 14 | 25 | 1  | 569   | 102   | 2    | 23.70 |
| N. H. Peters .........  | 15 | 19 | 5  | 304   | 46    | 0    | 21.71 |
| A. W. Smith .........  | 16 | 28 | 3  | 501   | 77    | 0    | 20.04 |
| L. Tennant.............  | 3  | 5  | 2  | 49    | 32    | 0    | 16.33 |
| †D. G. C. Ligertwood .....  | 11 | 13 | 2  | 142   | 38*   | 0    | 12.90 |
| †P. M. James .........  | 4  | 4  | 2  | 16    | 8     | 0    | 8.00  |
| A. G. Robson .........  | 5  | 4  | 2  | 11    | 9*    | 0    | 5.50  |

Played in six matches: J. Boiling 24*, 2*; M. R. Lee 0, 1. Played in one match: D. Blackwood 2; A. Giles 0, 0*; G. C. Luxon 0; T. P. Marsden 3, 16; A. J. Murphy 0*; A. J. Stewart 56*, 12; C. E. Waller did not bat.

## Bowling Averages

|                     | O     | M   | R     | W  | BB     | Avge  |
|---------------------|-------|-----|-------|----|--------|-------|
| N. M. Kendrick .....  | 539.1 | 164 | 1,326 | 61 | 6-42   | 21.73 |
| C. K. Bullen .......  | 239   | 75  | 656   | 27 | 4-82   | 24.29 |
| A. G. Robson .......  | 134   | 29  | 406   | 16 | 4-50   | 25.37 |
| L. Tennant..........  | 85.2  | 11  | 389   | 14 | 5-141  | 27.78 |
| A. J. Hollioake ......  | 27    | 2   | 113   | 4  | 4-79   | 28.25 |
| M. R. Lee ..........  | 121.2 | 20  | 376   | 13 | 4-91   | 28.92 |
| M. A. Butcher .......  | 112.5 | 30  | 319   | 11 | 2-12   | 29.00 |

| | O | M | R | W | BB | Avge |
|---|---|---|---|---|---|---|
| J. Boiling . . . . . . . . . . . | 206.1 | 61 | 509 | 17 | 4-66 | 29.94 |
| M. A. Feltham . . . . . . | 125 | 31 | 368 | 11 | 3-79 | 33.45 |
| K. T. Medlycott . . . . . | 67.2 | 10 | 237 | 4 | 2-99 | 59.25 |
| N. H. Peters . . . . . . . | 210.5 | 23 | 791 | 13 | 2-19 | 60.84 |
| J. D. Robinson . . . . . . | 129.5 | 31 | 441 | 6 | 2-41 | 73.50 |

Also bowled: R. I. Alikhan 10–1–39–0; D. Blackwood 21–2–83–1; A. D. Brown 16.2–0–83–0; A. Giles 12–1–33–0; M. A. Lynch 1–1–0–0; A. J. Murphy 25–0–98–2.

## SUSSEX SECOND ELEVEN

*Matches 16: Won – Derbyshire, Glamorgan, Leicestershire, Northamptonshire. Lost – Middlesex, Warwickshire, Yorkshire. Drawn – Essex, Gloucestershire, Hampshire, Kent, Lancashire, Nottinghamshire, Somerset, Surrey, Worcestershire.*

### Batting Averages

| | M | I | NO | R | HI | 100s | Avge |
|---|---|---|---|---|---|---|---|
| T. B. M. de Leede . . . | 3 | 5 | 3 | 195 | 63* | 0 | 97.50 |
| N. J. Lenham . . . . . . | 2 | 3 | 0 | 224 | 94 | 0 | 74.66 |
| C. M. Wells . . . . . . . | 2 | 3 | 1 | 113 | 109 | 1 | 56.50 |
| M. T. E. Peirce . . . . . | 2 | 3 | 0 | 169 | 134 | 1 | 56.33 |
| *K. Greenfield . . . . . . | 10 | 15 | 2 | 702 | 138* | 3 | 54.00 |
| †M. P. Speight . . . . . . | 5 | 9 | 1 | 392 | 103 | 2 | 49.00 |
| J. W. Hall . . . . . . . . | 5 | 9 | 2 | 307 | 88* | 0 | 43.85 |
| K. Newell . . . . . . . . | 9 | 16 | 4 | 409 | 113* | 1 | 34.08 |
| J. M. Finch . . . . . . . | 3 | 5 | 0 | 165 | 56 | 0 | 33.00 |
| R. Hanley . . . . . . . . . | 16 | 26 | 2 | 756 | 91 | 0 | 31.50 |
| B. R. Williams . . . . . . | 10 | 13 | 5 | 245 | 72* | 0 | 30.62 |
| A. R. Hansford . . . . . | 7 | 5 | 2 | 83 | 42* | 0 | 27.66 |
| †J. N. Smith . . . . . . . | 13 | 16 | 4 | 322 | 80 | 0 | 26.83 |
| B. T. P. Donelan . . . . | 6 | 10 | 0 | 226 | 103 | 1 | 22.60 |
| C. C. Remy . . . . . . . . | 8 | 13 | 0 | 249 | 97 | 0 | 19.15 |
| A. R. Cornford . . . . . | 12 | 18 | 1 | 320 | 44 | 0 | 18.82 |
| R. A. Bunting . . . . . . | 12 | 17 | 5 | 199 | 49* | 0 | 16.58 |
| J. W. Dean . . . . . . . . | 13 | 12 | 5 | 114 | 54 | 0 | 16.28 |
| P. W. Threlfall . . . . . | 9 | 3 | 1 | 31 | 15 | 0 | 15.50 |
| J. A. North . . . . . . . . | 12 | 17 | 2 | 187 | 39 | 0 | 12.46 |
| E. S. H. Giddins . . . . | 3 | 3 | 0 | 12 | 7 | 0 | 4.00 |

Played in five matches: A. M. A. Aduhene 10*. Played in one match: R. G. Bickell 0, 27; O. Fattani 0; D. Law 4*; H. Nankivell 0*, 4*; N. Phillips 4; C. J. Rogers 31; I. D. K. Salisbury 30, 0; R. F. van Oosterom 0, 46; P. Wicker 4, 13.

### Bowling Averages

| | O | M | R | W | BB | Avge |
|---|---|---|---|---|---|---|
| C. M. Wells . . . . . . . . | 50 | 10 | 117 | 7 | 3-24 | 16.71 |
| E. S. H. Giddins . . . . | 45.3 | 10 | 138 | 6 | 4-74 | 23.00 |
| N. Phillips . . . . . . . . . | 41 | 9 | 141 | 6 | 5-102 | 23.50 |
| J. A. North . . . . . . . . | 194.5 | 38 | 529 | 22 | 9-35 | 24.04 |
| T. B. M. de Leede . . . | 38.1 | 3 | 145 | 6 | 3-72 | 24.16 |
| B. T. P. Donelan . . . . | 229 | 75 | 828 | 24 | 6-62 | 34.50 |
| R. A. Bunting . . . . . . | 328.4 | 43 | 1,085 | 31 | 5-70 | 35.00 |
| J. W. Dean . . . . . . . . | 386.2 | 98 | 1,079 | 29 | 6-66 | 37.20 |
| A. R. Cornford . . . . . | 111.3 | 30 | 298 | 8 | 3-70 | 37.25 |
| P. W. Threlfall . . . . . | 171 | 25 | 553 | 13 | 3-45 | 42.53 |
| A. M. A. Aduhene . . | 135.4 | 17 | 494 | 10 | 3-66 | 49.40 |
| A. R. Hansford . . . . . | 163 | 39 | 399 | 8 | 3-48 | 49.87 |
| B. R. Williams . . . . . . | 144.3 | 34 | 424 | 8 | 2-13 | 53.00 |

Also bowled: O. Fattani 6–2–19–0; K. Greenfield 68.5–9–251–2; D. Law 16–2–57–0; H. Nankivell 9–0–32–0; M. T. E. Peirce 13–1–49–0; C. C. Remy 4–0–10–1; I. D. K. Salisbury 12–2–44–1; P. Wicker 11.1–2–25–2.

# WARWICKSHIRE SECOND ELEVEN

*Matches 16: Won – Derbyshire, Leicestershire, Middlesex, Northamptonshire, Surrey, Sussex, Worcestershire. Lost – Yorkshire. Drawn – Essex, Glamorgan, Gloucestershire, Hampshire, Kent, Lancashire, Nottinghamshire, Somerset.*

## Batting Averages

|  | M | I | NO | R | HI | 100s | Avge |
|---|---|---|---|---|---|---|---|
| Asif Din | 2 | 3 | 1 | 209 | 107* | 2 | 104.50 |
| R. G. Twose | 10 | 16 | 2 | 1,042 | 171* | 4 | 74.42 |
| I. G. S. Steer | 14 | 18 | 7 | 566 | 75* | 0 | 51.45 |
| *T. L. Penney | 10 | 16 | 3 | 596 | 87* | 0 | 45.84 |
| †P. C. L. Holloway | 4 | 5 | 2 | 134 | 45 | 0 | 44.66 |
| N. M. K. Smith | 10 | 12 | 3 | 389 | 121* | 1 | 43.22 |
| J. D. Ratcliffe | 6 | 10 | 0 | 390 | 104 | 1 | 39.00 |
| G. M. Charlesworth | 12 | 20 | 4 | 598 | 143* | 1 | 37.37 |
| †K. J. Piper | 4 | 7 | 2 | 178 | 88 | 0 | 35.60 |
| S. J. Green | 13 | 20 | 0 | 646 | 108 | 1 | 32.30 |
| D. R. Brown | 11 | 12 | 2 | 320 | 111* | 1 | 32.00 |
| P. A. Booth | 8 | 7 | 3 | 117 | 42* | 0 | 29.25 |
| A. R. K. Pierson | 11 | 9 | 4 | 140 | 68* | 0 | 28.00 |
| Wasim Khan | 10 | 17 | 0 | 435 | 69 | 0 | 25.58 |
| †M. Burns | 12 | 16 | 3 | 331 | 62 | 0 | 25.46 |
| G. Welch | 10 | 9 | 4 | 78 | 34* | 0 | 15.60 |
| O. S. Chagar | 9 | 7 | 2 | 56 | 27 | 0 | 11.20 |
| G. Smith | 8 | 3 | 2 | 5 | 4* | 0 | 5.00 |

Played in six matches: J. E. Benjamin 1*, 0, 0. Played in four matches: B. C. Usher 0. Played in one match: P. A. Smith 110*; J. R. Carruthers did not bat.

*Note:* In the match v Middlesex, Wasim Khan replaced P. C. L. Holloway, who was called to the first team.

## Bowling Averages

|  | O | M | R | W | BB | Avge |
|---|---|---|---|---|---|---|
| R. G. Twose | 134.2 | 25 | 385 | 16 | 4-42 | 24.06 |
| G. Welch | 239 | 69 | 604 | 24 | 5-40 | 25.16 |
| D. R. Brown | 355.3 | 75 | 1,109 | 43 | 4-37 | 25.79 |
| J. E. Benjamin | 151.5 | 26 | 466 | 18 | 5-79 | 25.88 |
| N. M. K. Smith | 171.2 | 36 | 530 | 19 | 4-17 | 27.89 |
| I. G. S. Steer | 76.1 | 16 | 229 | 8 | 3-32 | 28.62 |
| P. A. Booth | 181.4 | 50 | 508 | 17 | 3-40 | 29.88 |
| A. R. K. Pierson | 334 | 82 | 838 | 27 | 4-32 | 31.03 |
| O. S. Chagar | 179 | 36 | 544 | 16 | 2-23 | 34.00 |
| G. Smith | 133 | 23 | 463 | 8 | 2-22 | 57.87 |

Also bowled: Asif Din 5–0–37–0; J. R. Carruthers 8–0–31–0; G. M. Charlesworth 18–5–53–0; S. J. Green 15.5–0–120–1; Wasim Khan 8–0–38–0; T. L. Penney 4–0–39–0; J. D. Ratcliffe 4–0–41–0; P. A. Smith 9–3–23–1; B. C. Usher 34–6–126–1.

# WORCESTERSHIRE SECOND ELEVEN

*Matches 16: Won – Derbyshire, Leicestershire, Somerset. Lost – Hampshire, Nottinghamshire, Surrey, Warwickshire, Yorkshire. Drawn – Essex, Glamorgan, Gloucestershire, Kent, Lancashire, Middlesex, Northamptonshire, Sussex.*

## Batting Averages

|  | M | I | NO | R | HI | 100s | Avge |
|---|---|---|---|---|---|---|---|
| D. B. D'Oliveira . . . . . . . . . . | 4 | 8 | 3 | 321 | 86* | 0 | 64.20 |
| G. R. Haynes . . . . . . . . . . . | 10 | 17 | 6 | 653 | 101* | 1 | 59.36 |
| *M. S. Scott . . . . . . . . . . . . | 15 | 12 | 6 | 320 | 181 | 1 | 53.33 |
| †J. D. Harvey . . . . . . . . . . | 2 | 4 | 1 | 142 | 66 | 0 | 47.33 |
| W. P. C. Weston . . . . . . . . . | 3 | 6 | 1 | 206 | 135* | 1 | 41.20 |
| S. M. McEwan . . . . . . . . . . | 10 | 10 | 4 | 245 | 74* | 0 | 40.83 |
| C. M. Tolley . . . . . . . . . . . | 10 | 18 | 0 | 668 | 135 | 2 | 37.11 |
| S. R. Froggatt . . . . . . . . . . | 4 | 4 | 2 | 71 | 47 | 0 | 35.50 |
| G. J. Lord . . . . . . . . . . . . | 7 | 14 | 0 | 492 | 110 | 1 | 35.14 |
| R. P. Gofton . . . . . . . . . . . | 7 | 10 | 3 | 227 | 85* | 0 | 32.42 |
| P. Bent . . . . . . . . . . . . . . | 9 | 16 | 0 | 502 | 133 | 1 | 31.37 |
| M. J. Weston . . . . . . . . . . | 10 | 20 | 1 | 566 | 105 | 1 | 29.78 |
| S. Herzberg . . . . . . . . . . . | 11 | 20 | 6 | 402 | 50* | 0 | 28.71 |
| D. A. Leatherdale . . . . . . . . | 14 | 26 | 2 | 634 | 117 | 1 | 26.41 |
| M. J. Dallaway . . . . . . . . . | 2 | 4 | 0 | 95 | 34 | 0 | 23.75 |
| †S. R. Bevins . . . . . . . . . . | 13 | 18 | 5 | 286 | 60* | 0 | 22.00 |
| N. Davey . . . . . . . . . . . . | 4 | 5 | 1 | 74 | 33* | 0 | 18.50 |
| J. Grant . . . . . . . . . . . . . | 2 | 4 | 0 | 70 | 47 | 0 | 17.50 |
| R. D. Stemp . . . . . . . . . . . | 10 | 11 | 3 | 131 | 31 | 0 | 16.37 |
| C. J. Eyers . . . . . . . . . . . | 6 | 5 | 1 | 60 | 28 | 0 | 15.00 |
| A. Wylie . . . . . . . . . . . . . | 5 | 7 | 2 | 47 | 22 | 0 | 9.40 |
| G. J. P. B. Williamson . . . . | 3 | 4 | 1 | 13 | 12* | 0 | 4.33 |

Played in one match: S. Aldis 0; D. M. Cousins 7*; †R. J. Coyle 0, 12; I. Cutler 0, 12; N. M. Davies 13*, 13*; P. J. Deakin 6; M. G. Fowles 4; M. E. Harvey 26, 0; P. J. Heaton 0, 7; D. R. McDonnell 11, 28; P. Mirza 9; R. E. Morris 71, 11; S. Silva 2, 21; V. S. Solanki 0, 9; I. J. Sutcliffe 0, 14.

## Bowling Averages

|  | O | M | R | W | BB | Avge |
|---|---|---|---|---|---|---|
| J. Grant . . . . . . . . . . | 82 | 21 | 233 | 10 | 4-47 | 23.30 |
| G. R. Haynes . . . . . . . . | 193.1 | 44 | 595 | 25 | 5-28 | 23.80 |
| D. A. Leatherdale . . . . . | 62 | 15 | 210 | 8 | 3-20 | 26.25 |
| P. Bent . . . . . . . . . . . | 44.4 | 14 | 166 | 6 | 3-22 | 27.66 |
| R. P. Gofton . . . . . . . . . | 122 | 22 | 340 | 12 | 4-56 | 28.33 |
| S. Herzberg . . . . . . . . . . | 192.3 | 40 | 737 | 23 | 4-94 | 32.04 |
| R. D. Stemp . . . . . . . . . | 375 | 94 | 1,107 | 31 | 6-27 | 35.70 |
| S. M. McEwan . . . . . . . . | 221.4 | 56 | 667 | 17 | 4-26 | 39.23 |
| C. M. Tolley . . . . . . . . . | 240.2 | 59 | 708 | 18 | 4-56 | 39.33 |
| M. J. Weston . . . . . . . . . | 127 | 24 | 423 | 10 | 4-71 | 42.30 |
| C. J. Eyers . . . . . . . . . . | 89.4 | 12 | 332 | 4 | 1-16 | 83.00 |

Also bowled: S. Aldis 11.5-2-40-2; D. M. Cousins 8-0-42-0; I. Cutler 15-0-102-0; N. M. Davies 24-1-103-1; P. J. Deakin 4-1-15-0; D. B. D'Oliveira 9-0-29-0; M. G. Fowles 9.5-2-33-0; P. J. Heaton 13-0-63-0; G. J. Lord 6.1-1-35-0; P. Mirza 15-4-42-2; S. Silva 18-4-73-1; A. Wylie 52-5-200-3.

# YORKSHIRE SECOND ELEVEN

*Matches 16: Won – Essex, Glamorgan, Gloucestershire, Middlesex, Somerset, Sussex, Warwickshire, Worcestershire. Lost – Nottinghamshire. Drawn – Derbyshire, Hampshire, Kent, Lancashire, Leicestershire, Northamptonshire, Surrey.*

## Batting Averages

|  | M | I | NO | R | HI | 100s | Avge |
|---|---|---|---|---|---|---|---|
| S. Bartle............. | 6 | 9 | 6 | 201 | 50* | 0 | 67.00 |
| K. Sharp ............. | 7 | 12 | 1 | 590 | 150* | 2 | 53.63 |
| C. S. Pickles ......... | 10 | 13 | 2 | 556 | 189* | 2 | 50.54 |
| *S. N. Hartley........ | 15 | 19 | 7 | 494 | 84* | 0 | 41.16 |
| C. White ............. | 16 | 26 | 1 | 963 | 153 | 2 | 38.52 |
| S. Bethel ............ | 5 | 7 | 2 | 178 | 63 | 0 | 35.60 |
| †C. A. Chapman....... | 16 | 27 | 3 | 840 | 100* | 1 | 35.00 |
| A. P. Grayson........ | 15 | 26 | 2 | 705 | 100 | 1 | 29.37 |
| B. Parker ........... | 16 | 26 | 2 | 629 | 110 | 1 | 26.20 |
| D. Gough ........... | 2 | 3 | 0 | 66 | 62 | 0 | 22.00 |
| P. J. Berry .......... | 16 | 16 | 4 | 237 | 40* | 0 | 19.75 |
| M. Broadhurst........ | 8 | 7 | 3 | 71 | 20* | 0 | 17.75 |
| M. J. Doidge......... | 5 | 7 | 2 | 85 | 65 | 0 | 17.00 |
| C. S. Gott ........... | 6 | 10 | 1 | 151 | 41 | 0 | 16.77 |
| I. J. Houseman ...... | 16 | 13 | 6 | 34 | 6 | 0 | 4.85 |

Played in five matches: M. A. Robinson 0*, 0*, 0, 5*. Played in three matches: S. D. Fletcher 4. Played in two matches: P. W. Jarvis 27, 1, 0. Played in one match: D. Bates 9; M. Bowen 1*; M. J. Foster 6, 11; S. A. Kellett 8, 21; R. Kettleborough 0; †A. Mynett 11; M. Vaughan 6, 11. D. B. Pennett did not bat.

*Note:* On the third day of the match v Warwickshire at Bradford, D. Gough, called up for a first-team match, was replaced by C. A. Chapman, who batted in the second innings.

## Bowling Averages

|  | O | M | R | W | BB | Avge |
|---|---|---|---|---|---|---|
| A. P. Grayson ..... | 320.4 | 91 | 879 | 40 | 7-90 | 21.97 |
| D. Gough ......... | 47.3 | 5 | 173 | 7 | 3-59 | 24.71 |
| P. W. Jarvis ....... | 53 | 19 | 102 | 4 | 2-48 | 25.50 |
| C. S. Pickles ...... | 207.2 | 57 | 566 | 20 | 6-33 | 28.30 |
| I. J. Houseman..... | 356.5 | 82 | 1,099 | 38 | 6-39 | 28.92 |
| P. J. Berry ........ | 438.5 | 123 | 1,205 | 38 | 8-79 | 31.71 |
| C. White .......... | 140.1 | 23 | 527 | 14 | 3-43 | 37.64 |
| S. D. Fletcher ...... | 101 | 26 | 247 | 6 | 4-34 | 41.16 |
| M. A. Robinson .... | 116.3 | 23 | 371 | 8 | 2-72 | 46.37 |
| S. Bartle .......... | 88 | 20 | 260 | 4 | 2-44 | 65.00 |
| M. Broadhurst ..... | 161.4 | 23 | 561 | 7 | 2-61 | 80.14 |

Also bowled: S. Bethel 1-0-8-0; M. Bowen 21-6-55-1; M. J. Doidge 31-14-78-1; B. Parker 2-0-17-0; D. B. Pennett 16-2-76-0; K. Sharp 8.2-1-70-2; M. Vaughan 13-3-36-0.

## SECOND ELEVEN CHAMPIONS

| | | | | | |
|---|---|---|---|---|---|
| 1959 | Gloucestershire | 1971 | Hampshire | 1983 | Leicestershire |
| 1960 | Northamptonshire | 1972 | Nottinghamshire | 1984 | Yorkshire |
| 1961 | Kent | 1973 | Essex | 1985 | Nottinghamshire |
| 1962 | Worcestershire | 1974 | Middlesex | 1986 | Lancashire |
| 1963 | Worcestershire | 1975 | Surrey | 1987 | { Kent |
| 1964 | Lancashire | 1976 | Kent | | Yorkshire |
| 1965 | Glamorgan | 1977 | Yorkshire | 1988 | Surrey |
| 1966 | Surrey | 1978 | Sussex | 1989 | Middlesex |
| 1967 | Hampshire | 1979 | Warwickshire | 1990 | Sussex |
| 1968 | Surrey | 1980 | Glamorgan | 1991 | Yorkshire |
| 1969 | Kent | 1981 | Hampshire | | |
| 1970 | Kent | 1982 | Worcestershire | | |

# BAIN CLARKSON TROPHY, 1991

| North Zone | P | W | L | NR | Pts | Runs/100b |
|---|---|---|---|---|---|---|
| Nottinghamshire . . . . . . | 10 | 6 | 3 | 1 | 13 | 74.85 |
| Yorkshire . . . . . . . . . . . . | 10 | 5 | 4 | 1 | 11 | 68.68 |
| Northamptonshire . . . . | 10 | 5 | 5 | 0 | 10 | 70.44 |
| Leicestershire . . . . . . . . | 10 | 5 | 5 | 0 | 10 | 69.67 |
| Lancashire . . . . . . . . . . . | 10 | 4 | 5 | 1 | 9 | 69.51 |
| Derbyshire . . . . . . . . . . . | 10 | 3 | 6 | 1 | 7 | 68.60 |

| South-West Zone | P | W | L | NR | Pts | Runs/100b |
|---|---|---|---|---|---|---|
| Hampshire . . . . . . . . . . . | 10 | 8 | 1 | 1 | 17 | 76.61 |
| Glamorgan . . . . . . . . . . | 10 | 5 | 3 | 2 | 12 | 75.84 |
| Warwickshire . . . . . . . . | 10 | 6 | 4 | 0 | 12 | 63.04 |
| Worcestershire . . . . . . . | 10 | 3 | 6 | 1 | 7 | 76.91 |
| Somerset . . . . . . . . . . . . | 10 | 3 | 6 | 1 | 7 | 65.09 |
| Gloucestershire . . . . . . . | 10 | 2 | 7 | 1 | 5 | 61.79 |

| South-East Zone | P | W | L | NR | Pts | Runs/100b |
|---|---|---|---|---|---|---|
| Kent . . . . . . . . . . . . . . . | 10 | 7 | 1 | 2 | 16 | 69.51 |
| Surrey . . . . . . . . . . . . . | 10 | 7 | 3 | 0 | 14 | 65.53 |
| Essex . . . . . . . . . . . . . . | 10 | 4 | 3 | 3 | 11 | 63.60 |
| Middlesex . . . . . . . . . . . | 10 | 3 | 4 | 3 | 9 | 66.62 |
| Sussex . . . . . . . . . . . . . | 10 | 3 | 6 | 1 | 7 | 53.57 |
| MCC Young Cricketers . | 10 | 1 | 8 | 1 | 3 | 64.89 |

*Notes:* Surrey qualified for the semi-finals as the best runners-up after the zone matches.
    Counties are restricted to players qualified for England and for competitive county cricket, only two of whom may be capped players. The matches are of 55 overs per side.

## SEMI-FINALS

At Southampton, August 13. Surrey won by 22 runs. Toss: Surrey. Surrey 279 for eight (55 overs) (M. A. Butcher 65, J. D. Robinson 31, A. D. Brown 78; M. J. Thursfield three for 35); Hampshire 257 (54.1 overs) (T. C. Middleton 32, J. R. Wood 32, J. R. Ayling 38, S. D. Udal 36; A. G. Robson three for 55).

At Canterbury, August 13. Nottinghamshire won by four wickets. Toss: Kent. Kent 248 (54.4 overs) (M. A. Ealham 100, N. J. Llong 47; R. T. Bates three for 27); Nottinghamshire 249 for six (54 overs) (M. Newell 57, M. Saxelby 46, D. J. R. Martindale 45, P. R. Pollard 36).

## FINAL

## SURREY v NOTTINGHAMSHIRE

At The Oval, September 9. Nottinghamshire won by eight wickets. Toss: Nottinghamshire.

## Surrey

| | | | | |
|---|---|---|---|---|
| A. W. Smith c Newell b Saxelby . . . . . | 5 | N. M. Kendrick b Crawley . . . . . . . . . . . | 1 |
| M. A. Butcher c Saxelby b Field-Buss . . | 42 | J. Boiling run out . . . . . . . . . . . . . . . . . . | 9 |
| J. D. Robinson c Broadley b Crawley . . | 29 | B 6, l-b 16, w 4 . . . . . . . . . . . . . | 26 |
| G. P. Thorpe c Pollard b Crawley . . . . . | 18 | | |
| A. D. Brown c Broadley b Afford . . . . . | 11 | 1/22 2/66 3/99 (8 wkts, 55 overs) 196 |
| *C. K. Bullen not out . . . . . . . . . . . . . . | 45 | 4/115 5/121 6/156 |
| †N. F. Sargeant b Crawley . . . . . . . . . . | 10 | 7/162 8/196 |

A. J. Murphy and A. G. Robson did not bat.

Bowling: Saxelby 8–1–35–1; Broadley 8–1–10–0; Field-Buss 11–0–31–1; Afford 11–1–33–1; Bates 6–0–25–0; Crawley 11–1–40–4.

## Nottinghamshire

P. R. Pollard lbw b Boiling .......... 75
S. M. Brogan lbw b Robinson ........ 12
D. J. R. Martindale not out .......... 76
*†M. Newell not out ................. 21
    L-b 8, w 1, n-b 4............ 13

1/31 2/150      (2 wkts, 48.1 overs) 197

G. F. Archer, M. A. Crawley, M. Saxelby, R. T. Bates, M. G. Field-Buss, J. A. Afford and
V. J. P. Broadley did not bat.

Bowling: Murphy 10.1–0–44–0; Robson 8–0–36–0; Robinson 4–1–18–1; Boiling 11–2–33–1;
Kendrick 11–0–37–0; Bullen 3–0–15–0; Brown 1–0–6–0.

Umpires: J. D. Bond and P. B. Wight.

## WINNERS 1986-91

1986    NORTHAMPTONSHIRE beat Essex by 14 runs at Chelmsford.
1987    DERBYSHIRE beat Hampshire by seven wickets at Southampton.
1988    YORKSHIRE beat Kent by seven wickets at Leeds.
1989    MIDDLESEX beat Kent by six wickets at Canterbury.
1990    LANCASHIRE beat Somerset by eight wickets at Manchester.
1991    NOTTINGHAMSHIRE beat Surrey by eight wickets at The Oval.

# CAREER FIGURES OF PLAYERS RETIRING OR NOT RETAINED

## BATTING

| | M | I | NO | R | HI | 100s | Avge | 1,000r/ season |
|---|---|---|---|---|---|---|---|---|
| P. Bent ........... | 32 | 54 | 2 | 1,289 | 144 | 2 | 24.78 | 0 |
| M. J. Cann........ | 46 | 71 | 6 | 1,916 | 141 | 4 | 29.47 | 0 |
| C. S. Cowdrey ..... | 297 | 451 | 68 | 12,202 | 159 | 21 | 31.85 | 4 |
| S. J. Dennis ....... | 102 | 98 | 29 | 666 | 53* | 0 | 9.65 | 0 |
| J. Derrick ........ | 95 | 125 | 38 | 1,995 | 78* | 0 | 22.93 | 0 |
| M. C. Dobson ..... | 9 | 14 | 2 | 206 | 52 | 0 | 17.16 | 0 |
| P. R. Downton ..... | 313 | 405 | 76 | 8,270 | 126* | 6 | 25.13 | 1 |
| D. E. East........ | 190 | 254 | 32 | 4,553 | 134 | 4 | 20.50 | 0 |
| S. J. Green ....... | 5 | 8 | 1 | 168 | 77* | 0 | 24.00 | 0 |
| S. N. Hartley ..... | 142 | 215 | 28 | 4,667 | 114 | 4 | 24.95 | 0 |
| S. G. Hinks ...... | 154 | 267 | 15 | 7,569 | 234 | 11 | 30.03 | 3 |
| G. C. Holmes ...... | 209 | 335 | 51 | 8,092 | 182 | 11 | 28.49 | 3 |
| T. E. Jesty ........ | 490 | 777 | 107 | 21,916 | 248 | 35 | 32.71 | 10 |
| D. J. M. Kelleher .. | 34 | 43 | 6 | 565 | 53* | 0 | 15.27 | 0 |
| J. W. Lloyds ...... | 267 | 408 | 64 | 10,679 | 132* | 10 | 31.04 | 3 |
| G. J. Lord........ | 85 | 137 | 10 | 3,406 | 199 | 5 | 26.81 | 1 |
| D. J. R. Martindale . | 55 | 85 | 10 | 1,861 | 138 | 4 | 24.81 | 0 |
| A. R. K. Pierson ... | 57 | 64 | 29 | 427 | 42* | 0 | 12.20 | 0 |
| B. Roberts........ | 205 | 333 | 34 | 9,182 | 184 | 13 | 30.70 | 3 |
| M. L. Roberts ..... | 10 | 10 | 2 | 100 | 25 | 0 | 12.50 | 0 |
| P. M. Roebuck .... | 335 | 552 | 81 | 17,552 | 221* | 33 | 37.26 | 9 |
| P. W. Romaines.... | 173 | 309 | 23 | 8,120 | 186 | 13 | 28.39 | 3 |
| C. Shaw .......... | 61 | 58 | 27 | 340 | 31 | 0 | 10.96 | 0 |
| A. Sidebottom ..... | 228 | 263 | 62 | 4,508 | 124 | 1 | 22.42 | 0 |
| C. L. Smith........ | 269 | 466 | 60 | 18,028 | 217 | 47 | 44.40 | 10 |
| J. G. Thomas ..... | 192 | 253 | 45 | 2,419 | 110 | 2 | 16.43 | 0 |
| P. Willey......... | 559 | 918 | 121 | 24,361 | 227 | 44 | 30.56 | 10 |

   *Signifies not out.*

## BOWLING AND FIELDING

| | R | W | BB | Avge | 5W/i | 10W/m | Ct/St |
|---|---|---|---|---|---|---|---|
| P. Bent .......... | 5 | 0 | — | — | — | — | 4 |
| M. J. Cann ....... | 1,226 | 19 | 3-30 | 64.52 | — | — | 17 |
| C. S. Cowdrey ..... | 7,962 | 200 | 5-46 | 39.81 | 2 | 0 | 290 |
| S. J. Dennis ...... | 8,359 | 254 | 5-35 | 32.90 | 7 | 0 | 26 |
| J. Derrick ........ | 5,213 | 137 | 6-54 | 38.05 | 2 | 0 | 40 |
| M. C. Dobson ..... | 424 | 8 | 2-20 | 53.00 | — | — | 1 |
| P. R. Downton ..... | 9 | 1 | 1-4 | 9.00 | — | — | 690/89 |
| D. E. East......... | 17 | 0 | — | — | — | — | 480/53 |
| S. J. Green ........ | — | — | — | — | — | — | 2 |
| S. N. Hartley ...... | 2,182 | 48 | 4-51 | 45.45 | — | — | 54 |
| S. G. Hinks ....... | 367 | 8 | 2-18 | 45.87 | — | — | 96 |
| G. C. Holmes ...... | 3,963 | 88 | 5-38 | 45.03 | 2 | 0 | 85 |
| T. E. Jesty ........ | 16,075 | 585 | 7-75 | 27.47 | 19 | 0 | 265/1 |
| D. J. M. Kelleher .. | 2,533 | 77 | 6-109 | 32.89 | 2 | 0 | 8 |
| J. W. Lloyds ....... | 12,943 | 333 | 7-88 | 38.86 | 13 | 1 | 229 |
| G. J. Lord......... | 61 | 0 | — | — | — | — | 22 |
| D. J. R. Martindale . | 8 | 0 | — | — | — | — | 23 |
| A. R. K. Pierson ... | 3,753 | 85 | 6-82 | 44.15 | 3 | 0 | 17 |
| B. Roberts......... | 2,948 | 89 | 5-68 | 33.12 | 1 | — | 166/1 |
| M. L. Roberts ..... | — | — | — | — | — | — | 16/4 |
| P. M. Roebuck .... | 3,540 | 72 | 6-50 | 49.16 | 1 | 0 | 162 |
| P. W. Romaines.... | 247 | 4 | 3-42 | 61.75 | — | — | 68 |
| C. Shaw .......... | 4,101 | 123 | 6-64 | 33.34 | 3 | 0 | 9 |
| A. Sidebottom ..... | 14,558 | 596 | 8-72 | 24.42 | 23 | 3 | 63 |
| C. L. Smith........ | 2,685 | 50 | 5-69 | 53.70 | 1 | — | 176 |
| J. G. Thomas ...... | 16,303 | 525 | 7-75 | 31.05 | 18 | 1 | 74 |
| P. Willey.......... | 23,300 | 756 | 7-37 | 30.82 | 26 | 3 | 235 |

# UAU CHAMPIONSHIP, 1991

## By GRENVILLE HOLLAND

The short UAU season again encountered difficulties at its culmination. In a repetition of 1990 the final rounds were staged at Liverpool, and once again they fell victim to the weather. Furthermore, the lessons that should have been learned in 1990 were not put into practice, and the eventual resolution of the championship owed much to the determination, good sense and unfailing good manners of the students.

The quartet that reached Liverpool in mid-June included fresh faces in the form of Bangor, Kent and Southampton, who were joined by the durable Durham. Bangor began their campaign in uncertain fashion, for they qualified only as runners-up in their regional league. Yet in the challenge round a match-winning six for 43 by Neil Pratt at Warwick gave them a home draw against Aberystwyth, whom they defeated by five wickets. In the quarter-finals, Bangor crossed the Mersey to Liverpool and invited the home side to bat first on a rain-affected pitch. Liverpool struggled to 112 in 53 overs and, as conditions eased, Bangor passed this for the loss of two wickets in the 42nd over.

Kent's progress was equally assured. In their south-eastern league they entertained LSE at Canterbury, and after a sustaining 60 from Julian Mountford had helped them reach 157, Angus McGoogan (five for 26) and Aman Zafar (four for 22) bowled out the visitors for 58. The second league game, at Brighton, was much closer. Sussex elected to bat first, and in hazy sunshine Mike Murray (55) and Andy Griffin (61) provided an invaluable partnership which helped them score 177 for nine in their 60 overs. Kent's early reply was hesitant, and by the 36th over they were only 91 for six; but 40 from David Jowett and 35 from Andy Rogers earned them victory by one wicket with one over to spare. They had a bye in the challenge round and then travelled to King's College, London, for a brief encounter. King's managed just 60 in 30 overs, Jowett's five for 24 causing the most damage, and Kent needed only twelve overs to gain a nine-wicket victory. In the quarter-finals they were back in London, this time to meet University College, and while victory took rather longer, it was still achieved comfortably. Early wickets by Jowett (four for 18) confined University College to 140 off 56 overs, whereupon opener David Fulton (59) led the way as Kent moved on to the semi-finals in the 47th over by a margin of three wickets.

Southampton have long been a competent side, and still hold the record of three consecutive UAU championships, from 1968 to 1970. Their students have the advantage of a well-maintained ground, and in 1991 they also had the benefit of skilful leadership from their opening batsman, Greg Macmillan. In their Wessex league they began with a comfortable six-wicket home win over Surrey, but their visit to Reading posed greater difficulties. The pitch there offered the bowlers encouragement, and only half-centuries from Macmillan and Nigel Reynolds carried Southampton to 160 in 50 overs. Reading's initial response was positive and by tea they had reached 90 for one. After the break, however, tight fielding and an invigorating six-wicket burst from Stuart Godden brought about Reading's collapse and a 40-run victory for the visitors. A bye in round four was followed by an away tie at Bristol, who were dismissed for 142 in the 42nd over. Anthony Powell (65), on his first-team début, helped Southampton put on 81 for the first wicket, which paved the way for a convincing six-wicket win. Their quarter-final at Exeter, described as the "southern showdown", provided an exciting and entertaining game. Conditions were far from ideal when Southampton, on losing the toss, were asked to bat, and after repeated disruptions from the rain they were 71 for eight off 39 overs at lunch. However, Jeremy Carr-Smith (65), ably supported by John Lishman (27), then launched a vigorous assault on Exeter's bowling and, in a stand of 91 in just twelve overs, they swept Southampton to 162. Exeter steadily retrieved the lost ground, and Philip Relf (52) held their middle order together as Macmillan's off-spin (18–7–35–5) steadily took its toll. With ten overs left, Exeter required 30 runs with four wickets in hand, but Southampton's fielding kept them in check. When the last over began Exeter needed 9 more runs with their last pair together. It proved 2 runs too many, and Southampton had cleared another hurdle on their path to the final.

For more than a decade Durham had been in contention and had already reached seven consecutive finals. As an added attraction, their Racecourse ground had been selected as a first-class venue, and a unique partnership was being forged so that from 1992 the students and the county would share their facilities, to the benefit of both. They began their 1991 campaign with a match against Hull, and an opening stand of 94 between Sean Morris (83) and Chris Keey (37) gave early notice that Durham again meant business. A total of 236, despite a late burst of five for 35 from Christopher Clay, was well beyond Hull, who were dismissed for 86. At Newcastle, Durham reached 278, Keey (124) and Jon Longley (58) contributing a stand of 130, while Marcus Marvel, with six for 78, did his best to stem the flow. Despite an eye-catching 42 from Jeremy Casey, Newcastle found the left-arm spin of Matt Brimson (five for 34) too much for them, and they were dismissed for 115 in the 41st over. In the challenge round Bradford visited the Racecourse, where a polished 66 from Morris and a thundering 87 not out from Simon Ecclestone took Durham to 252 for five in their 60 overs. Once again Brimson's spin (six for 28) proved beyond Durham's opponents and Bradford trailed in for 106 in the 40th over. Round five took Newcastle to the Racecourse but, rain interfered, and reversing venues still produced no result after three attempts and two weekends. Both sides then agreed to play to a finish over several days, but with examinations looming Newcastle scratched from the competition. The weather was just as grim when, a few days later, Durham took the field at Loughborough. A wet and uncovered wicket offered the home side little comfort as they struggled to 135 for seven off 60 overs, which Durham passed with ten overs and five wickets to spare.

The semi-finals were scheduled for June 19, but heavy overnight rain and early morning drizzle left the uncovered wicket at Sefton, where Bangor and Durham were due to meet, in an unplayable state. In contrast, at Liverpool CC the covers were rolled back and the second semi-final, reduced to 40 overs, began at 3.00 p.m. in bright sunshine. Macmillan invited Kent to bat first on a benign wicket and used his opener, Lishmann (20–4–45–7), to great effect as Kent were restricted to 100 for nine. Macmillan then led the way with 54 not out as Southampton cruised into the final in the 24th over. The following day Bangor and Durham met on the same strip, and Durham, batting first, took full advantage of the conditions. Morris (123) and Keey (115) put on 241 for the first wicket and the final total of 314 for seven was well beyond Bangor, who succumbed for 140 in the 46th over. In the meantime, UAU officials had been trying to secure a venue for the final the following day. Sefton generously offered their facilities, but more overnight rain left the pitch in an unsatisfactory state, and both captains declined to play a UAU final under such conditions. A new venue, Clifton College, was agreed upon and the two sides met a week later.

# COMMERCIAL UNION UAU FINAL

## DURHAM v SOUTHAMPTON

At Clifton College, Bristol, June 30. Durham won by eight wickets. Toss: Durham. It was still raining as the players gathered at the picturesque Close, but despite the gloomy forecast of persisting rain, the clouds lifted and gave way to a sunlit day. Durham's captain, Sam Watkinson, invited Southampton to bat first on a damp pitch with a wet, slow outfield. By the 25th over they had progressed steadily to 77 for one, but three wickets in quick succession by Andy Webster, and six maiden overs on the trot, left them 82 for four after 32 overs. Worse followed after lunch. Off the very first ball Macmillan ran a comfortable single to fine leg, but Chakrabarti thought it was worth a second. Rightly sent back by his captain, he failed by inches to beat Longley's long, low throw from the boundary. Just 4 runs later Chris Hawkes bowled David Blomfield, and then Macmillan, whose beautifully crafted innings of 63 had sustained his side, was smartly run out by Webster's underarm throw from mid-wicket. All resistance evaporated and Southampton's innings closed peacefully in the 49th over. By now the warm sunshine had settled the pitch and quickened the outfield, and Durham's experienced openers set about their task in a calm, unhurried manner. Eventually Macmillan tempted Keey into a mistimed drive, but by then the game was won and lost. Morris, surely destined for higher things, was steadiness itself, and his fierce square drive for four brought Durham their eleventh UAU championship. The game was enhanced by high-quality umpiring, Clifton College provided an excellent venue, and that the season ended on such a high note was as welcome as it was unexpected.

*Man of the Match:* A. G. Webster.

## Southampton

| | | | | |
|---|---|---|---|---|
| *G. I. Macmillan run out | 63 | J. D. C. Carr-Smith c Morris b Hawkes | 4 |
| A. J. Powell lbw b Webster | 8 | J. W. D. Lishmann c Webster b Brimson | 5 |
| T. W. Butterworth b Webster | 12 | S. D. Godden not out | 0 |
| N. H. Reynolds b Webster | 0 | B 2, l-b 2, w 10, n-b 2 | 16 |
| J. P. B. Barnes b Webster | 1 | | |
| I. Chakrabarti run out | 5 | 1/33 2/79 3/80 | (48.2 overs) 120 |
| D. R. Blomfield b Hawkes | 4 | 4/82 5/103 6/108 | |
| †O. C. J. Saxelby c Watkinson b Brimson | 2 | 7/109 8/111 9/120 | |

Bowling: Hallett 12–4–23–0; Watkinson 3–0–15–0; Webster 14–4–44–4; Brimson 12.2–5–19–2; Hawkes 7–3–15–2.

## Durham

| | |
|---|---|
| R. S. M. Morris not out | 50 |
| C. L. Keey c and b Macmillan | 42 |
| J. I. Longley lbw b Lishmann | 3 |
| C. J. Hawkes not out | 9 |
| L-b 8, w 7, n-b 2 | 17 |

1/71 2/92                    (2 wkts, 44.4 overs) 121

C. J. Hollins, S. C. Ecclestone, †W. M. I. Bailey, *S. J. Watkinson, J. C. Hallett, M. T. Brimson and A. G. Webster did not bat.

Bowling: Lishmann 22.4–5–55–1; Godden 6–0–26–0; Macmillan 16–3–32–1.

Umpires: M. J. Kitchen and T. Stevens.

---

## THE CRICKETER CUP WINNERS, 1967-1991

| | | |
|---|---|---|
| 1967 | REPTON PILGRIMS | beat Radley Rangers by 96 runs. |
| 1968 | OLD MALVERNIANS | beat Harrow Wanderers by five wickets. |
| 1969 | OLD BRIGHTONIANS | beat Stowe Templars by 156 runs. |
| 1970 | OLD WYKEHAMISTS | beat Old Tonbridgians by 94 runs. |
| 1971 | OLD TONBRIDGIANS | beat Charterhouse Friars on faster scoring-rate. |
| 1972 | OLD TONBRIDGIANS | beat Old Malvernians by 114 runs. |
| 1973 | RUGBY METEORS | beat Old Tonbridgians by five wickets. |
| 1974 | OLD WYKEHAMISTS | beat Old Alleynians on faster scoring-rate. |
| 1975 | OLD MALVERNIANS | beat Harrow Wanderers by 97 runs. |
| 1976 | OLD TONBRIDGIANS | beat Old Blundellians by 170 runs. |
| 1977 | SHREWSBURY SARACENS | beat Oundle Rovers by nine wickets. |
| 1978 | CHARTERHOUSE FRIARS | beat Oundle Rovers by nine wickets. |
| 1979 | OLD TONBRIDGIANS | beat Uppingham Rovers by 5 runs. |
| 1980 | MARLBOROUGH BLUES | beat Old Wellingtonians by 31 runs. |
| 1981 | CHARTERHOUSE FRIARS | beat Old Wykehamists by nine wickets. |
| 1982 | OLD WYKEHAMISTS | beat Old Malvernians on faster scoring-rate. |
| 1983 | REPTON PILGRIMS | beat Haileybury Hermits by seven wickets. |
| 1984 | OLD TONBRIDGIANS | beat Old Malvernians by seven wickets. |
| 1985 | OUNDLE ROVERS | beat Repton Pilgrims by three wickets. |
| 1986 | OLD MALVERNIANS | beat Downside Wanderers by six wickets. |
| 1987 | SHREWSBURY SARACENS | beat Old Cliftonians by 58 runs. |
| 1988 | OUNDLE ROVERS | beat Shrewsbury Saracens by 19 runs. |
| 1989 | OUNDLE ROVERS | beat Shrewsbury Saracens by 9 runs. |
| 1990 | OLD MALVERNIANS | beat Harrow Wanderers by four wickets. |
| 1991 | OLD TONBRIDGIANS | beat Charterhouse Friars by 27 runs. |

*From 1967 to 1983 the final was played at Burton Court, Chelsea. Since then, it has been played at Vincent Square, Westminster.*

# THE LANCASHIRE LEAGUES, 1991

## By CHRIS ASPIN

Fielding sides had an exhausting season as batsmen scored freely and broke several long-standing records; only two bowlers, one in each of the two major leagues, took 100 wickets. By rescheduling all games spoiled by bad weather, the Lancashire League enabled the Australian, Peter Sleep, to become the highest-scoring professional, and the Rawtenstall opener, Peter Wood, the highest-scoring amateur in the 99-year history of the competition. Both men achieved their ambition on the penultimate weekend of the season, but were upstaged by Phil Simmons, the West Indian opener, who made the most dramatic début seen in east Lancashire. Haslingden, who recruited Simmons when their professional, Rod Tucker, was called up for the Australia B tour of Zimbabwe, began the weekend needing five points to clinch their fourth championship in five years. The first of their two games was at Nelson, where Simmons, going in first wicket down, scored 178 not out – 1 short of the League record for limited-overs cricket – as the total soared to 298 for four, a record for a 46-over innings. Haslingden gained four points and moved on to Rawtenstall, where Simmons raced from 50 to 100 in thirteen balls and finished with 135 in Haslingden's 302 for four, the highest total in a League game for more than half a century. In the two games he hit sixteen sixes and 31 fours.

Until its closing stages, the struggle for the championship was closer than for many years, with East Lancashire, who finished runners-up, Bacup, Rishton and Todmorden all having spells at the top. In the Worsley Cup final, Enfield, the underdogs, had an easy win against East Lancashire. Sleep hit seven centuries and finished with 1,621 runs, beating by 103 the record set by Everton Weekes when he was with Bacup in 1951. Wood, only the fifth amateur to score 1,000 runs in a season, made 1,228 (53.35), the previous best being 1,130 by James Midgley jun., of Bacup, in 1929. Two other professionals, the Australian Joe Scuderi and the West Indian Roger Harper, also topped 1,000. The leading amateurs were Michael Ingham of Haslingden with 972 (44.18), Gary Barker of Enfield, a club-record 888 (40.36), Ian Clarkson of Nelson, 795 (33.13), and Chris Bleazard of Lowerhouse with 788 (41.47). The long-serving Steve Metcalf completed 10,000 runs for Church.

The most successful bowler was the Rawtenstall professional, Colin Miller of South Australia; his 108 wickets cost 13.95 apiece. The young Ramsbottom spinner, Jonathon Fielding, had the best amateur return for twelve years, with 72 wickets at 15.24, while Alan Barnes (Haslingden) and Neil Westwell (Church) each took 52 wickets at 18.00 and 24.06 respectively.

Rochdale did the double in the Central Lancashire League, comfortably winning the championship and, when all seemed lost, gaining the Lees Wood Cup for the first time since 1958. In the 50-over final against Littleborough, Rochdale began the 48th over needing 33 to win, but their professional and captain, David Callaghan, transformed the game by hitting four sixes and a single off Phil Deakin's over. He completed an unbeaten century and made the winning hit, another six, in the final over. In 31 League and Cup games, the South African made 1,823 runs (76.96), the second-largest aggregate in the CLL's history, and good support came from his colleagues, notably seventeen-year-old Peter Wilcock, who scored 942 runs (34.22) in 28 innings, and Neil Avery, who set a club amateur record with 60 wickets at 12.06.

Another South African, the Middleton professional, Brad Osborne, hit a record 223 not out against Hyde, only the third double-century in the 99 years since the League was formed. The leading amateurs were Chris Dearden of Littleborough with 1,060 runs (36.66) and Alan Howard of Norden with 1,039 (35.82). Norden made the season's highest score: 327 for five against Unsworth.

The Royton professional, Aaron Daley, headed the bowling averages with 121 wickets at 11.38, while Stockport's Australian professional, Steve Wundke, was just one wicket away from a season's double. Osborne took eight for 8 in Middleton's home game with Ashton. Mel Whittle of Oldham was the most successful amateur, taking 78 wickets at 16.06, and Heywood's Scott Bannermann captured 67 at 20.20. However, they were all out-bowled by Cec Wright, at 58 the oldest player in the League. After many years in the amateur ranks, he became a professional again for none-too-wealthy Crompton, bowled 564 overs – 44 more than Daley – and finished with 94 wickets at 17.35. His best figures were eight for 44 against Ashton.

## MARSDEN BS LANCASHIRE LEAGUE

|  | P | W | L | NR | Pts | Professional | Runs | Avge | Wkts | Avge |
|---|---|---|---|---|---|---|---|---|---|---|
| Haslingden . . . . . | 26 | 21 | 4 | 1 | 92 | R. J. Tucker . . | 715 | 42.06 | 65 | 15.29 |
| East Lancashire . | 26 | 17 | 9 | 0 | 74 | P. R. Reiffel . . | 617 | 38.56 | 64 | 13.72 |
| Bacup . . . . . . . . | 26 | 16 | 10 | 0 | 73 | R. A. Harper . . | 1,032 | 57.28 | 80 | 14.65 |
| Rishton . . . . . . . | 26 | 15 | 10 | 0 | 73* | P. R. Sleep . . . | 1,621 | 81.05 | 57 | 20.49 |
| Nelson . . . . . . . | 26 | 15 | 10 | 0 | 72* | J. C. Scuderi . . | 1,501 | 71.48 | 78 | 16.79 |
| Church . . . . . . . | 26 | 15 | 11 | 0 | 69 | M. W. Priest . . | 918 | 36.72 | 85 | 17.23 |
| Rawtenstall . . . . | 26 | 15 | 11 | 0 | 68 | C. R. Miller . . | 780 | 33.90 | 108 | 13.95 |
| Todmorden . . . . | 26 | 15 | 11 | 0 | 68 | C. Yorke . . . | 981 | 42.64 | 43 | 24.90 |
| Ramsbottom . . . . | 26 | 11 | 14 | 1 | 55 | R. E. Bryson . | 428 | 18.60 | 44 | 26.29 |
| Enfield . . . . . . . . | 26 | 12 | 13 | 0 | 53 | L. A. Joseph . | 700 | 35.00 | 64 | 20.07 |
| Lowerhouse . . . . | 26 | 11 | 14 | 1 | 50 | M. Prabhakar . | 716 | 39.78 | 45 | 19.20 |
| Burnley . . . . . . | 26 | 9 | 16 | 1 | 43 | C. D. Mack . . | 313 | 13.60 | 77 | 20.20 |
| Accrington . . . . . | 26 | 5 | 21 | 0 | 26 | S. K. Warne . . | 329 | 14.95 | 73 | 15.42 |
| Colne . . . . . . . . . | 26 | 2 | 24 | 0 | 12 | H. L. Alleyne . | 319 | 15.95 | 44 | 27.81 |

*\* Includes two points awarded for a tie.*

*Note: Four points awarded for a win; one point awarded for dismissing the opposition.*

## BROTHER CENTRAL LANCASHIRE LEAGUE

|  | P | W | L | NR | Pts | Professional | Runs | Avge | Wkts | Avge |
|---|---|---|---|---|---|---|---|---|---|---|
| Rochdale . . . . . . | 30 | 23 | 3 | 4 | 110 | D. J. Callaghan . | 1,823 | 75.95 | 64 | 16.65 |
| Royton . . . . . . . | 30 | 19 | 8 | 3 | 91 | A. G. Daley . . . . | 970 | 38.80 | 121 | 11.38 |
| Stockport . . . . . . | 30 | 19 | 8 | 3 | 90 | S. C. Wundke . . . . . | 1,217 | 48.68 | 99 | 14.79 |
| Oldham . . . . . . . | 30 | 18 | 7 | 5 | 86 | B. E. McNamara . . | 998 | 49.90 | 55 | 19.16 |
| Walsden . . . . . . | 30 | 15 | 10 | 5 | 75 | C. Jesberg . . . . . | 768 | 30.72 | 70 | 22.18 |
| Middleton . . . . . . | 30 | 15 | 12 | 3 | 71 | B. M. Osborne . . | 918 | 36.72 | 81 | 16.45 |
| Littleborough . . . | 30 | 13 | 11 | 6 | 69 | V. deC. Walcott . . | 233 | 11.09 | 75 | 18.12 |
| Heywood . . . . . . | 30 | 12 | 11 | 7 | 62 | P. J. S. Alley . . . . . | 540 | 22.50 | 73 | 19.13 |
| Milnrow . . . . . . . | 30 | 12 | 11 | 7 | 61 | G. I. Foley . . . . . | 1,179 | 51.26 | 53 | 22.75 |
| Radcliffe . . . . . . . | 30 | 10 | 14 | 6 | 53 | Saleem Sajjad . . . | 608 | 24.32 | 61 | 22.67 |
| Norden . . . . . . . | 30 | 10 | 15 | 5 | 50 | P. W. Gladigau . . | 827 | 34.45 | 79 | 17.83 |
| Unsworth . . . . . . | 30 | 10 | 16 | 4 | 49 | Imtiaz Ahmed . . . . | 858 | 31.77 | 15 | 29.86 |
| Ashton . . . . . . . . | 30 | 7 | 16 | 7 | 41 | Ajay Sharma . . . . | 1,030 | 44.78 | 67 | 17.46 |
| Hyde . . . . . . . . . | 30 | 7 | 18 | 5 | 39 | P. Smith . . . . . . . | 393 | 17.86 | 86 | 15.84 |
| Werneth . . . . . . . | 30 | 7 | 18 | 5 | 39 | J. E. R. Gallian . . . | 1,161 | 41.46 | 45 | 28.22 |
| Crompton . . . . . . | 30 | 4 | 23 | 3 | 22 | C. Wright . . . . . . . | 109 | 6.05 | 94 | 17.35 |

*Notes: Five points awarded for an outright win; four for a limited win.*
*Averages include Cup games.*

# IRISH CRICKET IN 1991

## By DEREK SCOTT

Ireland's cricketing year opened in March when, through the good offices of the Zimbabwe Cricket Union and the Mashonaland Districts, the second three-week tour to Zimbabwe in five years was undertaken. A tour of that country is always a success, because of the warm hospitality, the exotic sights and the good standard of cricket, and nine matches of various durations were undertaken. Six ranked as "cap" matches for the Irish, and while some experienced players were unavailable, the younger players benefited greatly from the visit.

A limited-overs game, played 48 hours after arrival, was lost, and the second match, over three days against the President's XI at the beautiful Harare Sports Club, was drawn when a dramatic thunderstorm brought it to a sudden end with the home team requiring 88 to win in 16.3 overs, with four wickets in hand. In a match of declarations, eighteen-year-old Alistair Campbell made 51 and 75 not out for the President's XI and Alan Lewis scored 96 for Ireland. The two-day match at Wedza, against Mashonaland Country Districts, also reached an exciting climax, though this time for cricketing reasons. Kevin Arnott made 100 not out for the Districts, having hit 99 in the first match, but after Ireland had declared 80 behind, Conor Hoey, their young leg-spinner, took six for 19 as the Districts crashed from 80 without loss to 124 all out. Rain interfered with Ireland's chase, and with twelve overs to go 111 were needed. Thanks to Lewis's unbeaten 67, they finished only 7 runs short, leaving the game drawn. Next a Zimbabwe XI were played over three days at the Old Hararians ground. They were strong in batting – Gavin Briant scored 102 – but no real challenge was issued to Ireland in the fourth innings and the match petered out. Finally, a win and a draw were recorded in the Bulawayo area. For Ireland, bowled out only once on the tour, the batting stars were Lewis (44.37), T. J. T. Patterson (41.12) and G. D. Harrison (32.66). Hoey and P. McCrum each took twelve wickets, with good support coming from A. N. Nelson and P. M. O'Reilly, while P. B. Jackson's wicket-keeping was again superb.

The domestic international season opened at Malahide near Dublin, a new venue for a first-class match, with an extraordinary victory over Scotland, the first for eight years. The fixture was sponsored by JMA. A fifth-wicket stand of 141 between Patterson and Harrison helped the Irish to a declaration at 284 for six. But Scotland's openers, Philip and Patterson, then broke all records for any wicket against Ireland by putting on 236, and when Patterson was run out, Scotland declared 48 behind. Warke's 78 for Ireland saw Scotland set 282 in 130 minutes plus twenty overs, and while it did not look as if either team could win from that position, Scotland lost their way and were all out in the second-last over for 186. Two days later Ireland bowled and fielded splendidly against Middlesex in the NatWest Bank Trophy match at Castle Avenue, Dublin, but they could never match the run-rate and lost by 45 runs. Reg Simpson adjudged Lewis of Ireland to be Man of the Match.

In July the West Indies visited Downpatrick for a one-day match, sponsored by Gilbey's Ulster Games and Allied Irish Banks, which attracted the biggest crowd ever for cricket in Ireland. Lambert and Logie scored centuries in the tourists' 321 for four declared, and Ireland held out at 165 for five for a draw.

The usual biennial tour of England and Wales was undertaken later in July, helped by the sponsorship of Allied Irish Banks. After a 34-year gap there was a fixture against Free Foresters, at Lancing College. Rain delayed the start for two hours, after which Lawry hit 113 not out as the Foresters reached 212 for three in 61 overs. When time was called, Ireland had received 41 overs and were 17 runs away from winning. At Arundel, however, the situation was reversed, with Ireland, sent in, declaring at 191 for seven and the Duchess of Norfolk's XI, inspired by Robin Dyer's 111 not out, finishing 9 runs short with two wickets in hand. Another drawn match! And the same again at Lord's, where the game against MCC had arrived at an exciting stage when rain prevented play after tea on the second day. At that stage Ireland required 152 to win with seven wickets in hand. An opening stand of 119 by Warke and Cohen had allowed Ireland to declare their first innings 47 behind, whereupon Hoey, taking five for 48, helped bowl MCC out for 171. At Usk, the venue for the three-day match against Wales, the home team made a slow 251 as Hoey returned figures of six for 82. However, Ireland compiled an even slower 243, the feature of which was a last-wicket stand of 58, Ireland's best since 1932; and when S. W. Evans occupied a further four and a half hours for his 106, the Irish had to content themselves with all four tour matches being drawn.

In the season's seven international matches, Warke scored 426 runs, for an average of 42.60, and he hit four of the side's eight half-centuries. The principal batting support came from Cohen, Harrison, Lewis and Patterson. Hoey captured 21 wickets at 27.19, but no other bowler reached double figures. Dunlop's nine wickets cost 19.77 each.

Ireland did less well than usual at the International Under-19 tournament, held in 1991 in Winnipeg, Canada. Denmark and Canada were beaten, but England, The Netherlands and Bermuda beat them, the Irish cause not being helped by poor bowling and catching. The three-day schools international against Wales at Cardiff was a high-scoring draw, with 958 runs scored for the loss of 22 wickets. The most promising Graham Russell hit a century for Ireland.

At interprovincial level, South Leinster brought off a double by winning the Senior and Under-19 titles, while Northern Union prevented a clean sweep by taking the Under-15 title. All these competitions were sponsored by Allied Irish Banks, with the Lord's Taverners assisting at the Under-15 level. The Schweppes Cup, in its tenth year, was won by Downpatrick, who beat North of Ireland CC by 3 runs in an exciting final.

In the North-West (Derry), Donemana won their seventh successive League title, needing just one more to equal the record of Dublin's Leinster CC, who won eight League championships in a row from 1928 to 1935. However, Eglinton failed to retain the knockout cup. Set 197 to win in a two-innings match, Brigade won in the last over when their No. 7 hit the Eglinton professional for two fours. In the Northern Union (Belfast), Waringstown, after a barren year in 1990, won their sixteenth league title in the last 25 seasons, while in an unexpectedly close cup final Woodvale, heavy under-dogs, lost to North Down by only 7 runs, having been set 245 to win. This match was dominated by the professionals on each side, but in the 1992 knockout cup professionals will not be allowed.

YMCA, who won their sixth cup final in eight seasons, and Clontarf, who took the league, were the leading teams in the Leinster Union (Dublin). A third competition, of 50 overs per side, was shared by these two clubs after the first final was tied and rain ruined the replay. A. Brophy of Malahide took all ten wickets in a Leinster Union league match, a feat last done in 1943, and Alan Lewis scored his third cup final century for YMCA.

# SCOTTISH CRICKET IN 1991

## By J. WATSON BLAIR

Although 1991 was a memorable year in many ways for cricket in Scotland, in neither the Benson and Hedges Cup nor the NatWest Bank Trophy did the national team taste success. Moreover, the first-class match against Ireland was also lost, despite a record opening stand of 236, in Scotland's first innings, between Ian Philip and Bruce Patterson.

The Benson and Hedges programme began on April 23, in advance of the start of the Scottish season. Lancashire were the first opponents, and at Lochside Park, Forfar, the home team's lack of match practice was apparent as the trophy holders won comfortably. Set a modest target of 164, Lancashire achieved it in 46.2 overs for the loss of three wickets. Scotland then travelled south, first to Grace Road, where a hard-hitting partnership of 160 for the second wicket between Boon and Whitaker set Leicestershire up for a 45-run victory. Richard Swan hit a brave 55, but Scotland were unable to match the required run-rate and at the end of 55 overs were 198 for nine.

Two days later the Scots were at Hove, for their first-ever match against Sussex. Rain delayed the start for more than an hour, and with stoppages throughout the afternoon the match went over into a second day. Scotland, chasing 227, resumed at 100 for three and made steady progress to reach 218 in the 54th over for the loss of five wickets. With Omar Henry, their captain, still at the wicket, a third Benson and Hedges victory looked a possibility for the Scots, but his dismissal and the return of Pigott for the final over saved the county from embarrassment. Only 4 runs separated the sides at the end, with Scotland having lost one fewer wicket. Returning to Glasgow, the disappointed squad had a day's training before meeting Kent at Hamilton Crescent, where a century opening partnership between Taylor and Benson put the game out of Scotland's reach. As fate would have it, Scotland clashed with Sussex for a second time in the season when the county travelled to Myreside, Edinburgh, in the first round of the NatWest. Remembering their earlier close encounter, Sussex made no mistakes this time and won by 72 runs.

A new feature in 1991 was an attractive, eight-match fixture list arranged by the recently formed Scottish Touring Cricket Board for a Pakistan All-Stars side, captained by Majid Khan and managed by Javed Burki. Included in the touring party were other former Test cricketers, such as Zaheer Abbas, Asif Masood, Salah-ud-Din and Sadiq Mohammad. All the games were of the limited-overs variety, but while those against club representative sides at Prestwick, Glasgow, Greenock and Paisley produced entertaining cricket, the three challenge matches against a Scotland XI, scheduled for Titwood, Glasgow, were completely ruined by the weather. It is to be hoped that further visits from Test-playing countries can be arranged by the STCB, which has also contemplated making overseas tours in the spring. Such trips would give Scotland's leading players invaluable practice prior to the Benson and Hedges Cup group matches and the start of the Scottish season.

The Scots finally had a taste of victory when, for the second year in succession, they played two games against the NCA England Amateur XI. The first, at Gateshead Fell on July 17, provided the England side with a good win, but the following day, at Jesmond, Scotland turned the tables thanks to Philip's unbeaten 153. The win gave Scotland a 3-1 lead in this new series of limited-overs games, but it was overshadowed a month later at Titwood, where the Scots demolished MCC in their traditional three-day fixture. The new opening partnership of Philip and Alastair Storie set a new record of 301, and after Storie was out for 106, Philip went on to score 234, the highest individual score in Scottish international cricket. With Henry hitting an unbeaten 102 from just 66 balls, Scotland totalled 537 for five declared and went on to win by an innings and 37 runs. Several weeks earlier Storie had made 126 for Scotland B against Lancashire Second Eleven, and also in that match, at Hamilton Crescent, George Salmond, one of Scotland's most promising batsmen, compiled an excellent 165.

New batting records were established on the domestic scene as well. In the Ryden's East League, Storie, playing as the professional for Watsonians, accumulated 977 runs, while at West of Scotland, in the D. M. Hall Western Union, Mark Harper from Guyana, brother of Roger, put together 1,158 runs in majestic style. Coming from seventeen innings in the championship, with a highest score of 134 not out and an average of 128.67, Harper's aggregate passed the previous best of 1,012 scored in 1983 by Omar Henry, when he was with Poloc.

Without question the club to achieve the outstanding success in 1991 were Grange, winners of the prestigious "Famous Grouse" award for the best team of the season. They not only retained the Ryden's East League title but also repeated their 1990 triumphs in the Whyte and Mackay Scottish Cup and the Masterton Trophy. West Lothian were beaten in the final of the Masterton while in the Scottish Cup final Clydesdale, six times winners, met their match in the all-conquering Edinburgh club.

While in the space available it is not possible to list all the winners of the many league and cup competitions from the Shetland Isles to the Borders most of them were as follows: *Ryden East League:* Grange; *Division 2:* St Modan's HSFP; *Division 3:* Marchmont. *Masterton Trophy:* Grange. *D. M Hall Western Union:* West of Scotland. *West League Cup:* Drumpellier *Rowan Charity Cup:* Ayr. *Small Clubs Cup:* Stoneywood. *Scottish Counties Championship:* Ayrshire; *Scottish Counties Cup:* Aberdeenshire. *National Club Championship* (Scottish section): West of Scotland. *National Village Championship* (Scottish section): Meigle. *Border League:* Kelso; *Border Cup* Gala. *Perthshire League* and *Perthshire Cup:* Crieff. *Strathmore Union* Strathmore; *Division 2:* Montrose. *Three Counties Cup:* Aberdeen Grades Select XI. *Two Counties Cup:* Montrose. *Western Cup:* Weirs. *Glasgow Evening League:* Queen's Park; *Glasgow Evening League Cup:* Hyndland FP *Strathclyde League* and *Strathclyde Shield:* West of Scotland (Hamilton Crescent XI. *North of Scotland League:* Elgin; *Reserve League:* Dornoch *North of Scotland Cup:* Nairn; *Reserve League Cup:* Northern Counties. *Forth Cricket Union:* Clackmannanshire. *Ryden Aberdeenshire Grade 1* (Bain Cup) Cults; *Grade 2:* Bon Accord; *Grade 3:* Dunecht. *Glasgow and District League*

*Division 1:* East Kilbride; *Division 2:* Prestwick; *Division 3:* Bishopbriggs; *Glasgow and District League Cup:* GHS/KA.

The *Scotland on Sunday* Player of the Year award was won by John Everett of Grange, while Arbroath's George Salmond received the Jean and Henry Thow Rosebowl as the outstanding young player of 1991. Other awards went to Ian Philip of Selkirk (Batsman of the Season), David Cowan of Freuchie (Bowler of the Season), Ayrshire's David Haggo (All-rounder of the Season), and Donald Orr of Clydesdale (Wicket-keeper of the Season).

At the Scottish Cricket Union headquarters there was a change of management, with Peter Wilkinson resigning as general manager after a sojourn of just over a year and Alec Ritchie assuming the post. With so many developments taking place, and more to follow, the new manager faced a daunting programme. Andy Little relinquished the presidency in December, to be succeeded for 1992 by Ralph Laing, the former Perthshire and Scotland batsman, who still plays for the village club, Meigle. The possible formation of a national league for Scottish clubs received a setback when 22 of the 66 clubs contacted voted against such a move: 40 were in favour and the remaining four made no return. The entire Western Union, comprising ten clubs, was against a national league, and opinion in the East League was divided 5-5. As these two competitions are considered to be among the best in Scotland – along with the Scottish Counties Championship, whose ten clubs all voted in favour – a national league involving so few of their clubs would be meaningless. The committee set up by the SCU have, however, decided to continue their consultations with the interested clubs, and further information was expected in 1992.

There was a body of opinion which considered that a reorganised Area Championship would be a better basis on which to operate a national competition that would provide a higher standard of competitive cricket for players throughout the country. The 1991 Area Championship was won for the first time by Central, and the knockout competition, which features the league section winners and runners-up, was won convincingly by Strathclyde East.

In the youth competitions Aberdeenshire excelled, winning the Bank of Scotland leagues at Under-15 and Under-18, while their Under-13s carried all before them in the NCA national eight-a-side tournament. The Under-19 and Under-16 district championship titles were won by the West District. The introduction of Kwik Cricket at primary school level, the establishment of a Cricket 2000 foundation in Edinburgh, and an increase in the number of teams being provided by clubs for minors and juniors have all helped to fill the void brought about by the demise of cricket at many schools. The SCU, assisted by a number of generous sponsors, has been making every effort to continue and improve the opportunities for young cricketers, and such a policy augurs well for the future of the game in Scotland.

# AUSTRALIAN YOUNG CRICKETERS IN ENGLAND, 1991

### By JOHN MINSHULL-FOGG

The Bull Development of Excellence programme for youth cricket was the principal sponsor of the visit by the Australian Young Cricketers, who enjoyed a successful tour, playing sixteen matches and losing only one, the second "Test" at Chelmsford. The tour actually started with three matches in The Netherlands and an intensive training spell under the watchful eyes of the Australian manager, Bobby Simpson, at Leicester. Three four-day "Tests" were played, with one victory to each country and the final match drawn. The Young Australians, though, won both the one-day "international" matches.

The tourists, as is often the case at this Under-19 level, seemed the more mature of the two teams, and certainly some of them showed the benefit of playing in the senior echelons of the game on equal status, rather than as raw newcomers. Damien Martyn, the captain, and Michael Kasprowicz, the main strike bowler, had Sheffield Shield experience, while the wicket-keeper-batsman, Adam Gilchrist, Greg Blewett and the promising Michael Foster seemed ready for higher things. Of the England team, John Crawley and Ben Smith had played regularly at county level. Both sides, however, felt the lack of penetrative, accurate attacks on good pitches, and when Kasprowicz was injured before the final "Test", the Australians lacked a true substitute. Crawley, England's captain, was their one batsman of real class, although Philip Weston, a tall, determined left-hander, was fast-improving. Richard Pearson, a Cambridge Blue and contracted to Northamptonshire, showed excellent qualities as an off-spinner when he was brought into the side after the disastrous defeat at Leicester in the first "Test".

Players' conduct on the field received careful scrutiny from the umpires. "Sledging", according to the team managers, Graham Saville and Brian Taber, was minimal, and they described this series as being "as worthy" as any in which they had been involved. Whooping and dancing on the pitch at the fall of a wicket were, however, still part of the Australian scene. All in all, from the defeats at Lord's, Trent Bridge and Leicester, England's Young Cricketers stuck manfully to their task, almost to the point of winning the series at Old Trafford. The Australian batting, on the other hand, seemed to lose some of its purpose during and after their second innings at Chelmsford. A drawn "Test" series was a fair result.

The tour party was: H. B. Taber (*manager*), S. R. Bernard (*coach*), D. R. Martyn (Western Australia, *captain*), A. C. Gilchrist (New South Wales, *vice-captain*), G. D. Barr (Western Australia), G. S. Blewett (South Australia), D. J. Castle (Tasmania), S. H. Cook (Victoria), M. J. Fraser (Queensland), M. R. Foster (Victoria), S. D. Godwin (ACT), G. J. Hayne (New South Wales), M. S. Kasprowicz (Queensland), C. B. Linhart (South Australia), A. R. Littlejohn (Western Australia) and K. J. Roberts (New South Wales).

## RESULTS

*Matches 17: Won 10, Lost 1, Drawn 5, Abandoned 1.*

*Note:* None of the matches played was first-class.

**v KNCB President's XI:** at The Hague, July 21. Australian Young Cricketers won by 129 runs. Australian Young Cricketers 216 for six (55 overs) (C. B. Linhart 77); KNCB President's XI 87 (D. J. Castle four for 19).

**v Netherlands Under-23:** at Rotterdam, July 23. Australian Young Cricketers won by 19 runs. Australian Young Cricketers 235 for six (55 overs) (G. J. Hayne 63, A. C. Gilchrist 80 not out); Netherlands Under-23 216 for nine (55 overs) (A. Zulfiqar 70 not out).

**v Quick:** at The Hague, July 25. Australian Young Cricketers won by 84 runs. Australian Young Cricketers 264 for nine (55 overs) (M. J. Fraser 76, A. C. Gilchrist 53 not out); Quick 180 (55 overs) (L. Troost 53 not out).

**v England Under-17:** at RAF Uxbridge, July 31. Australian Young Cricketers won by 122 runs. Australian Young Cricketers 210 for five dec. (K. J. Roberts 68 not out); England Under-17 88 (D. J. Castle four for 5).

**v England Amateur XI:** at Maidenhead and Bray CC, August 1. Abandoned.

**v Bull Development Squad:** at Winchester College, August 2, 3, 4. Australian Young Cricketers won by nine wickets. Toss: Australian Young Cricketers. Australian Young Cricketers 317 for four dec. (G. S. Blewett 109, G. J. Hayne 53, D. R. Martyn 90 not out) and 46 for one; Bull Development Squad 120 (M. J. Lowrey 63; S. H. Cook four for 27) and 242 (M. J. Lowrey 81, G. Welch 65; M. S. Kasprowicz four for 42).

**v England Young Cricketers** (First one-day "international"): at Lord's, August 6. Australian Young Cricketers won by 9 runs. Toss: England Young Cricketers. Australian Young Cricketers 283 for five (55 overs) (G. J. Hayne 112 not out, D. R. Martyn 37, A. C. Gilchrist 65); England Young Cricketers 274 for nine (55 overs) (J. P. Crawley 89, W. P. C. Weston 44, R. C. Irani 34).

**v England Young Cricketers** (Second one-day "international"): at Nottingham, August 8. Australian Young Cricketers won by five wickets. Toss: England Young Cricketers. England Young Cricketers 183 (52.1 overs) (M. N. Lathwell 31, R. C. Irani 31, G. Welch 55; M. S. Kasprowicz three for 11); Australian Young Cricketers 185 for five (46 overs) (D. R. Martyn 43, A. C. Gilchrist 48 not out).

**v English Schools CA Under-19:** at Worksop College, August 9, 10. Drawn. Toss: Australian Young Cricketers. Australian Young Cricketers 367 (M. J. Fraser 86, M. R. Foster 102, A. C. Gilchrist 61) and 52 for three; English Schools CA Under-19 198 (A. Payne 82 not out; S. H. Cook four for 48).

**v Leicestershire Second Eleven:** at Hinckley, August 12, 13, 14. Australian Young Cricketers won by 78 runs. Toss: Australian Young Cricketers. Australian Young Cricketers 313 for seven dec. (G. S. Blewett 72, M. R. Foster 62 not out, A. C. Gilchrist 59) and 251 for four dec. (D. R. Martyn 85 not out); Leicestershire Second Eleven 236 (P. A. Nixon 64; M. S. Kasprowicz five for 68) and 250 (P. Willey 71 not out; D. J. Castle five for 81).

# ENGLAND YOUNG CRICKETERS v
# AUSTRALIAN YOUNG CRICKETERS

## First "Test" Match

At Leicester, August 16, 17, 18. Australian Young Cricketers won by ten wickets. Toss: Australian Young Cricketers. Buoyed by satisfactory wins in the one-day "internationals", and ample batting practice against insufficiently strong sides, the Young Australians came to

Grace Road confident of victory. If their ebullience was in over-supply at times, their confidence was fully justified in all playing sections of the game, which they won with more than a day to spare. Martyn led his team from the front: his 179 came in just under four and a half hours, with 34 fours, and there was excellent, entertaining support from Foster's 132 and the crisp half-centuries of Gilchrist and Kasprowicz. The innings was declared shortly before noon on the second day at 525 for seven, the runs having come at more than 70 an hour. England needed 376 to avoid the follow-on and were dismissed for 117, mainly by the speed and accuracy of Kasprowicz and Cook, backed up by some stunning catching and Castle's looping off-breaks. The low total quite overshadowed the first-wicket partnership of 61 between Radford and Weston. England's second innings started well and they ended the day on 61 for the loss of Lathwell. The third day saw Weston in defiant mood, and with good support coming from the middle order, England achieved respectability and avoided an innings defeat. Kasprowicz was the main destroyer with five for 62, but their fight back had given Young England something to aim for in the remaining "Tests", even if their bowling and fielding looked far from adequate.

## Australian Young Cricketers

| | | |
|---|---|---|
| G. S. Blewett lbw b Welch | 34 – not out | 5 |
| G. J. Hayne c Crawley b Irani | 21 – not out | 4 |
| *D. R. Martyn c Lathwell b Chapple | 179 | |
| K. J. Roberts c Lathwell b Irani | 8 | |
| †A. C. Gilchrist b Welch | 54 | |
| M. R. Foster c Irani b Chapple | 132 | |
| M. J. Fraser run out | 7 | |
| M. S. Kasprowicz not out | 63 | |
| B 13, l-b 5, w 8, n-b 1 | 27 | |

1/66 2/79 3/113 4/228 5/370          (7 wkts dec.) 525          (no wkt) 9
6/388 7/525

D. J. Castle, S. H. Cook and A. R. Littlejohn did not bat.

Bowling: *First Innings*—Broadhurst 27-3-123-0; Chapple 18.5-1-81-2; Welch 18-2-87-2; Irani 21-4-89-2; Bainbridge 28-6-74-0; Smith 3-0-15-0; Lathwell 9-2-38-0. *Second Innings*—Broadhurst 0.5-0-9-0.

## England Young Cricketers

| | | |
|---|---|---|
| T. A. Radford b Castle | 26 – (8) c sub b Kasprowicz | 0 |
| W. P. C. Weston c Gilchrist b Kasprowicz | 30 – lbw b Castle | 93 |
| *J. P. Crawley b Kasprowicz | 9 – (4) c Hayne b Castle | 57 |
| B. F. Smith c Foster b Castle | 4 – (5) lbw b Kasprowicz | 54 |
| M. N. Lathwell lbw b Kasprowicz | 0 – (1) c Martyn b Castle | 29 |
| R. C. Irani b Kasprowicz | 0 – 1 c sub b Kasprowicz | 61 |
| G. Welch c Roberts b Cook | 10 – c Fraser b Kasprowicz | 48 |
| G. Chapple not out | 9 – (9) st Gilchrist b Blewett | 13 |
| M. Bainbridge c Gilchrist b Cook | 13 – (10) not out | 14 |
| †A. D. Shaw c Fraser b Cook | 0 – (3) c Castle b Cook | 22 |
| M. Broadhurst c Martyn b Cook | 4 – b Kasprowicz | 4 |
| L-b 3, w 1, n-b 7 | 11 | B 2, l-b 11, w 7 | 20 |

1/61 2/71 3/76 4/76 5/76          117          1/46 2/110 3/197 4/238 5/304          415
6/82 7/98 8/112 9/113                          6/344 7/346 8/375 9/399

Bowling: *First Innings*—Kasprowicz 17-4-33-4; Cook 14.3-6-16-4; Littlejohn 10-2-24-0; Blewett 5-0-18-0; Castle 16-10-23-2. *Second Innings*—Cook 16.4-4-58-1; Littlejohn 17-3-64-0; Kasprowicz 20.2-8-62-5; Blewett 17-3-60-1; Castle 29-12-87-3; Fraser 17-3-71-0.

Umpires: J. W. Holder and M. J. Kitchen.

**v National Association of Young Cricketers:** at Market Harborough, August 21, 22. Drawn. Toss: Australian Young Cricketers. Australian Young Cricketers 355 for four dec. (M. J. Fraser 127, C. B. Linhart 124 not out) and 130 for four; National Association of Young Cricketers 210 (A. R. Littlejohn five for 60).

**v Bull Development Squad:** at Oundle School, August 23, 24, 25. Drawn. Toss: Bull Development Squad. Bull Development Squad 248 (M. A. Butcher 75, J. N. Snape 65; D. J. Castle four for 50) and 289 (M. A. Butcher 64, M. J. Foster 68, J. N. Snape 54 not out; D. J. Castle four for 126, G. D. Barr five for 64); Australian Young Cricketers 334 for nine dec. (G. S. Blewett 119, K. J. Roberts 65, A. C. Gilchrist 58; D. Cousens four for 117) and 124 for five (D. Cousens four for 43).

## ENGLAND YOUNG CRICKETERS v
## AUSTRALIAN YOUNG CRICKETERS

### Second "Test" Match

At Chelmsford, August 27, 28, 29, 30. England Young Cricketers won by four wickets. Toss: Australian Young Cricketers. England were indebted mainly to Crawley, their captain, for an excellent, if unexpected, victory with three balls to spare. His considerable experience at this level was a major factor as England set about reaching a target of 401 on the final day, and full credit is also due to splendid stints of controlled off-spin from Pearson, who bowled 83.4 overs in the match and may well have induced the inexplicably pointless Australian batting on the third afternoon. The Australians had played much more positive cricket on the first day, declaring at 375 for seven and getting rid of Weston just before the close. Crawley went early on the second day, but the experienced Smith, Lathwell, Irani and Welch put matters right and England finished just 62 behind. In the last eighteen overs of the day, Australia made 78 for the loss of Blewett, extending their lead to 140 runs. Next day they added 100 runs in the pre-lunch session for the loss of Hayne. Thereafter, Martyn and Roberts batted slowly, adding only 86 runs before tea and continuing at that sort of pace until the close. Pearson and Bainbridge, slow left-arm, bowled 109 overs between them. At lunch on the final day, with England 91 for three, the odds favoured Australia or a draw. But Crawley was soon in the driving seat. With Lathwell he added 98 for the fourth wicket, and with Irani 134 for the fifth. When he was out, Irani and Welch and then Welch and Rollins carried England to victory. In the previous Young Australians tour, in 1983, England beat the tourists by 67 runs at Chelmsford – but the series had been lost by then.

## Australian Young Cricketers

| | | | | |
|---|---|---|---|---|
| G. S. Blewett c Welch b Broadhurst | 164 | – b Welch | 0 |
| G. J. Hayne c Loye b Broadhurst | 22 | – lbw b Pearson | 47 |
| *D. R. Martyn c Rollins b Broadhurst | 13 | – not out | 181 |
| K. J. Roberts lbw b Pearson | 18 | – lbw b Pearson | 65 |
| †A. C. Gilchrist c Bainbridge b Irani | 106 | – not out | 23 |
| G. D. Barr b Broadhurst | 0 | | |
| M. R. Foster not out | 26 | | |
| M. S. Kasprowicz c Smith b Pearson | 10 | | |
| B 2, l-b 4, w 1, n-b 9 | 16 | B 12, l-b 4, n-b 6 | 22 |

1/47 2/65 3/107 4/319 5/326      (7 wkts dec.) 375      1/13 2/199 3/265      (3 wkts dec.) 338
6/356 7/375

D. J. Castle, S. D. Godwin and S. H. Cook did not bat.

Bowling: *First Innings*—Broadhurst 20–2–85–4; Welch 14–1–68–0; Bainbridge 28–7–91–0; Pearson 22.4–2–69–2; Irani 12–4–44–1; Smith 4–1–12–0. *Second Innings*—Broadhurst 14–2–74–0; Welch 15–3–48–1; Bainbridge 48–17–97–0; Pearson 61–19–103–2.

## England Young Cricketers

| | | | |
|---|---|---|---|
| W. P. C. Weston c Hayne b Cook | 16 | – c Gilchrist b Godwin | 45 |
| M. B. Loye c Gilchrist b Kasprowicz | 19 | – c and b Cook | 5 |
| M. Bainbridge c Hayne b Cook | 26 | | |
| *J. P. Crawley c Gilchrist b Barr | 9 | – lbw b Kasprowicz | 130 |
| B. F. Smith c Foster b Cook | 77 | – (3) b Barr | 16 |
| M. N. Lathwell c Foster b Castle | 38 | – (5) c Gilchrist b Castle | 45 |
| R. C. Irani b Kasprowicz | 56 | – (6) run out | 73 |
| G. Welch c Blewett b Cook | 53 | – (7) not out | 46 |
| †R. J. Rollins b Kasprowicz | 2 | – (8) not out | 12 |
| R. M. Pearson b Kasprowicz | 0 | | |
| M. Broadhurst not out | 2 | | |
| L-b 3, n-b 12 | 15 | B 1, l-b 13, w 4, n-b 14 | 32 |

1/21 2/46 3/67 4/113 5/187　　　313　　1/29 2/55 3/89　　　(6 wkts) 404
6/203 7/297 8/304 9/304　　　　　　　4/187 5/321 6/373

Bowling: *First Innings*—Kasprowicz 28.5-4-77-4; Cook 19-3-75-4; Godwin 15-2-51-0; Barr 12-2-55-1; Castle 24-7-52-1. *Second Innings*—Kasprowicz 25-3-94-1; Cook 13-2-55-1; Barr 20.3-5-71-1; Godwin 16-3-68-1; Castle 24-4-88-1; Blewett 3-0-14-0.

Umpires: D. J. Constant and B. J. Meyer.

**v Bull Development Squad:** at Old Hill CC, September 1, 2, 3. Drawn. Toss: Australian Young Cricketers. Australian Young Cricketers 564 for six dec. (G. J. Hayne 183, A. C. Gilchrist 200 not out, D. R. Martyn 65) and 201 for three dec. (M. J. Fraser 51); Bull Development Squad 164 (M. J. Walker 54) and 350 for nine (M. J. Walker 54, R. Cunliffe 54).

**v MCC Young Cricketers:** at Neston CC, September 4, 5, 6. Australian Young Cricketers won by seven wickets. Toss: MCC Young Cricketers. MCC Young Cricketers 340 (N. Pratt 68, J. Daley 67, T. Chadwick 61) and 259 (S. J. Cooper 63 not out; M. J. Fraser five for 107); Australian Young Cricketers 365 (G. J. Hayne 77, M. J. Fraser 61, A. C. Gilchrist 65) and 235 for three (G. J. Hayne 105).

## ENGLAND YOUNG CRICKETERS v
## AUSTRALIAN YOUNG CRICKETERS

### Third "Test" Match

At Manchester, September 9, 10, 11, 12. Drawn. Toss: Australian Young Cricketers. Their first day's score of 367 for six provided the Australians with an ideal launching-pad for victory in the deciding match of the series; and on the final day, with 49 runs needed from ten overs, victory was still a possibility for the tourists. But with the pitch taking quite some spin, so, too, was defeat. Martyn played it safe, and Australia finished 31 runs short with three wickets in hand. Between times there had been some excellent cricket, with Crawley ending his England Under-19 career with a classic 121, Worcestershire's Weston scoring a dogged 146, and Irani on his home ground, making a typically breezy undefeated 106 to save England's first innings. Despite Irani's effort, England still finished well short of the follow-on, but Weston and Crawley together added 178 in the second innings, and eventually Australia were left with 59 overs to make 254 for victory. Blewett, Martyn and Hayne each played confidently, but Pearson, flighting the ball well, took four wickets to equal Castle's match tally of eleven wickets and, significantly, put Martyn on the defensive. The three Australian run-outs, all suggesting poor judgment, must also have made the captain doubt his side's ability to finish the job under pressure.

## Australian Young Cricketers

| | | |
|---|---|---|
| G. S. Blewett b Pearson | 78 – c Weston b Pearson | 42 |
| G. J. Hayne c Rollins b Broadhurst | 3 – st Rollins b Pearson | 51 |
| *D. R. Martyn c Crawley b Bainbridge | 31 – not out | 62 |
| M. R. Foster b Pearson | 45 – run out | 9 |
| †A. C. Gilchrist b Pearson | 45 – run out | 28 |
| M. J. Fraser lbw b Welch | 23 – c Crawley b Pearson | 2 |
| C. B. Linhart c Weston b Pearson | 88 – lbw b Pearson | 13 |
| G. D. Barr not out | 113 – run out | 2 |
| D. J. Castle st Rollins b Pearson | 6 – not out | 0 |
| S. H. Cook c Welch b Pearson | 6 | |
| A. R. Littlejohn c Welch b Pearson | 3 | |
| B 7, l-b 9, w 2, n-b 17 | 35 | B 6, l-b 5, w 1, n-b 2 .... 14 |

1/37 2/111 3/141 4/217 5/238    476    1/94 2/101 3/118 4/171  (7 wkts) 223
6/261 7/447 8/462 9/472                5/180 6/206 7/209

Bowling: *First Innings*—Broadhurst 21–1–87–1; Welch 17–2–52–1; Lathwell 6–1–37–0; Irani 9–2–42–0; Bainbridge 43–12–96–1; Pearson 54–14–146–7. *Second Innings*—Broadhurst 4–0–38–0; Welch 3–0–15–0; Pearson 26–5–66–4; Irani 2–0–19–0; Bainbridge 24–3–74–0.

## England Young Cricketers

| | | |
|---|---|---|
| W. P. C. Weston c Hayne b Castle | 36 – c Littlejohn b Fraser | 146 |
| M. B. Loye c Gilchrist b Castle | 8 – c and b Blewett | 11 |
| *J. P. Crawley c and b Fraser | 35 – c Martyn b Fraser | 121 |
| B. F. Smith c Castle b Fraser | 6 – c Hayne b Castle | 29 |
| M. N. Lathwell b Castle | 27 – c Martyn b Fraser | 66 |
| R. C. Irani not out | 106 – c Barr b Littlejohn | 1 |
| G. Welch c Fraser b Castle | 14 – c Foster b Castle | 6 |
| †R. J. Rollins c Gilchrist b Fraser | 5 – b Castle | 0 |
| M. Bainbridge lbw b Castle | 9 – b Castle | 14 |
| R. M. Pearson run out | 5 – c and b Castle | 0 |
| M. Broadhurst b Castle | 20 – not out | 2 |
| B 12, l-b 7, w 2, n-b 4 | 25 | B 18, l-b 12, w 5, n-b 2 .. 37 |

1/37 2/92 3/98 4/98 5/140    296    1/24 2/202 3/261 4/382 5/385    433
6/168 7/201 8/239 9/255            6/405 7/406 8/423 9/427

Bowling: *First Innings*—Cook 6–1–16–0; Littlejohn 3–0–12–0; Barr 15–2–42–0; Castle 37.2–15–87–6; Fraser 29–7–103–3; Blewett 4–1–17–0. *Second Innings*—Barr 18–3–67–0; Blewett 14–4–35–1; Castle 60–26–103–5; Fraser 53.4–22–140–3; Littlejohn 15–2–58–1.

Umpires: J. H. Hampshire and B. Leadbeater.

# ESSO/NAYC UNDER-19 COUNTY FESTIVALS, 1991

By JOHN MINSHULL-FOGG

Middlesex won the sixth Under-19 County Festival championship, sponsored by Esso Youth Sport, beating Kent by eight wickets and with 30 overs in hand at the Christ Church ground, Oxford. It was Middlesex's first victory in this premier youth tournament, in which 34 counties – first-class and minor, including Cornwall and Wiltshire for the first time – took part at venues in Oxford and Cambridge, utilising mainly college grounds and accommodation. The competition, it seems, grows annually in popularity. Play commenced each day at 10.45 a.m., and the matches, 60 overs a side, were governed by the National Association of Young Cricketers.

Throughout the week there were interesting performances in the various section results. Kent's bowling strength was exemplified by J. F. Barr's five for 13 against Worcestershire and five for 31 against Gloucestershire, J. Boreham's six for 103 against Oxfordshire, and L. A. C. Clarke's five for 100 against Hertfordshire. For Buckinghamshire, J. W. D. Lishmann took eight for 73 against Derbyshire and seven for 53 against Hertfordshire, and L. Banfield of Cornwall had six for 66 against Hampshire. Staffordshire's J. N. Snape headed the Oxford century-makers with 171 against Somerset, while S. Moffat, of Hertfordshire, took 145 off Kent and Barr, Kent's all-rounder, 143 off Worcestershire and 130 off Hertfordshire. At Cambridge, A. Payne of Lancashire took seven for 37 against Norfolk, and J. E. Hindson of Nottinghamshire captured seven for 20 against Huntingdon & Peterborough. Their batsmen also suffered against T. Singh of Bedfordshire (five for 27) and L. Hunt of Leicestershire (seven for 70). Nottinghamshire's S. N. Neal made 191 against Suffolk, and the Lincolnshire batsmen, M. Dowman and P. Rawden, plundered 157 and 141 respectively off Huntingdon & Peterborough. D. J. Bowen of Middlesex scored 131 against Northampton-shire, and B. Moore, also Middlesex, was undefeated with 112 against Bedfordshire.

The counties playing in the four Oxford groups were: Warwickshire, Somerset, Durham, Staffordshire, Berkshire and Shropshire; Glamorgan, Hampshire, Cornwall and Leinster; Derbyshire, Gloucestershire, Wiltshire and Buckinghamshire; Kent, Worcestershire, Oxfordshire and Hertfordshire. Those at Cambridge were: Essex, Lancashire, Surrey and Lincolnshire; Sussex, Yorkshire, Cheshire and Norfolk; Middlesex, Northamptonshire, Suffolk and Bedfordshire; Leicestershire, Nottinghamshire, Huntingdon & Peterborough and Cambridgeshire.

In the Oxford area semi-finals Kent, 274 for five (S. N. Warley 130 not out), beat Gloucestershire, 140 (J. F. Barr five for 31), by 134 runs; and Staffordshire, 236 for nine (J. N. Snape 80; R. Weisman six for 59), beat Glamorgan, 184, by 52 runs. At Cambridge, Middlesex, 209 for six (R. Thacker 79), beat Yorkshire, 184 (M. J. Foster 61; R. Johnson five for 49), by 25 runs; and Surrey, 288 for five (M. Church 112 not out; L. Hunt four for 89), beat Leicestershire, 201 (H. C. Watkinson five for 49), by 87 runs.

## AREA FINALS

At Clare College, Cambridge, August 16. Middlesex won by eight wickets. Surrey 158 (J. M. S. Whittington four for 31); Middlesex 161 for two (B. Moore 63, G. M. Pooley 62).

At Jesus College, Oxford, August 16. Kent won by 44 runs. Kent 291 for five (A. J. Planck 83, D. J. T. Moon 76); Staffordshire 247 (N. Hunt 56, T. A. Tweats 58, D. Long 62).

## FINAL

### KENT v MIDDLESEX

At Christ Church, Oxford, August 17. Middlesex won by eight wickets. Toss: Kent. Kent, electing to bat first, were soon struggling on a pitch with little bounce, and they were in trouble at 36 for seven. Fay, a sixteen-year-old seam bowler, used the conditions especially well, and all the Middlesex bowlers were backed up by excellent work in the field. Senneck provided some resistance at the end and, with Boreham, took the total into three figures. Fifteen of Kent's 60 overs remained unused. Middlesex lost Bowen, their captain, early on, but Moore's unbeaten and unhurried 50 brought them victory before tea. For many of the spectators who had come expecting a full and entertaining day's cricket, among them the chairman of the England selectors, E. R. Dexter, the match proved to be disappointing. But it was more so for the Kent batsmen, who had scored some 1,400 runs in their five games *en route* to the final.

### Kent

| | | | | |
|---|---|---|---|---|
| J. F. Barr lbw b Fay | 3 | O. Senneck not out | | 23 |
| S. N. Warley b Johnson | 6 | L. A. C. Clarke c Pooley b Fay | | 6 |
| *N. Mobey c Pooley b Fay | 0 | J. Boreham c Whittington b Dutch | | 10 |
| D. J. T. Moon c Bowen b Johnson | 3 | B 4, l-b 7, w 1, n-b 1 | | 13 |
| A. J. Planck lbw b Walker | 14 | | | |
| S. C. Willis c Pooley b Whittington | 4 | 1/5 2/7 3/9 | (44.1 overs) | 100 |
| †M. Roberts c Whittington b Walker | 0 | 4/15 5/34 6/34 | | |
| J. Ramsey b Fay | 18 | 7/36 8/64 9/74 | | |

Bowling: Johnson 9–2–13–2; Fay 14–2–31–4; Whittington 5–0–11–1; Walker 5–1–13–2; Dutch 11.1–4–21–1.

### Middlesex

| | | |
|---|---|---|
| B. Moore not out | | 50 |
| *D. J. Bowen b Clarke | | 5 |
| †G. M. Pooley c and b Barr | | 18 |
| R. Nadim not out | | 15 |
| B 11, l-b 1, w 1 | | 13 |

1/11 2/48     (2 wkts, 30 overs) 101

R. Thacker, C. Gupta, D. Walker, K. Dutch, J. M. S. Whittington, R. Fay and R. Johnson did not bat.

Bowling: Clarke 7–3–5–1; Boreham 8–2–19–0; Senneck 4–0–24–0; Barr 7–2–20–1; Willis 4–0–21–0.

Umpires: B. Hassan and B. J. Meyer.

# SCHOOLS CRICKET IN 1991

With J. S. Laney, J. N. Snape and W. P. C. Weston representing England Under-18 at the International Youth Tournament in Winnipeg, Canada, in mid-July, and T. C. Walton, like Snape and Weston, having county commitments, not one of the players capped by the English Schools in 1990 was available for selection in 1991. Although the three at the Winnipeg tournament could in theory have been picked for the English Schools international programme, which commenced at the end of July, the Schools selectors stuck to their policy of choosing their side from those who played in the trial matches at the Oxford Festival. Including the two matches at Lord's, played under the appellation of MCC Schools, fifteen players appeared for the senior Schools side. They were: R. J. Ballinger, A. J. Hall (captain), M. E. Harvey, J. E. Hindson, Keith A. Parsons, Kevin J. Parsons, A. Payne, M. F. D. Robinson, K. G. Sedgeber, M. J. Semmence, M. J. Walker, R. M. S. Weston, J. M. S. Whittington, N. J. Workman and R. S. Yeabsley. Their schools may be found in the scorecards of matches played at the MCC Festival, Oxford.

The regional matches prior to the Oxford Festival revealed a lack of real quality and variety. This was particularly so in the bowling, although the batsmen did not dominate as much as they had in 1990, and was a contributive factor in the international matches being drawn, after the two matches at Lord's had produced positive results. The Schools beat MCC but lost to the National Association of Young Cricketers.

The batting was led by Weston, who at sixteen showed the concentration to play long innings. He was well supported by his opening partner, Keith Parsons, but apart from Hall, the rest of the batting was disappointing. Several good players were unable to perform to their known ability. This may have been the result of a surfeit of cricket and travel, a problem which was viewed with concern by the appropriate authorities. A rationalisation of the youth cricket programme appears to be necessary, for some of the injuries to young bowlers could perhaps be attributed to the demands placed on them. Both Ballinger and Payne, for example, suffered in this respect. The principal wicket-takers were Hindson, slow left-arm, and Robinson, medium fast, with support coming chiefly from Whittington, another slow left-armer, and Payne, who in two matches took five wickets against Scotland at medium pace and scored 82 against the Young Australians to confirm his all-round potential. The fielding was reliable – the wicket-keeping was shared between Sedgeber and Workman – and the side was ably led by Hall, who engendered a fine team spirit in a quiet but effective way.

In the first international, against Wales at Clifton College on July 29, 30, English Schools were restricted to 134, one of their lowest totals for some years. Wales, in reply, fared little better, reaching 170 in 59 overs (Robinson six for 31, Hindson two for 37 in twenty overs). An unbeaten 114 from Weston enabled English Schools to declare their second innings at 245 for eight, but rain prevented any further play after tea, with Wales 37 for one.

Against Scottish Young Cricketers at Broughty Ferry on August 6, 7, Weston was again to the fore, scoring 73 of England's 198. The Scots, 77 for three overnight, lost their seven remaining wickets for 48 (Hindson five for 27), to give English Schools a lead of 73. The loss of Weston for 12 was brushed aside by Keith Parsons and Hall, who put on 141 unbroken for the second wicket before Hall's declaration at 174 invited the home side to score 248 in two hours plus twenty overs. With 140 required from the last twenty, the Scots looked to be out of the hunt, but there followed a whirlwind century partnership between I. M. Stanger (50) and N. Bell (63), before Stanger was brilliantly caught and bowled by Hindson. The last over began with 11 runs needed and two wickets in hand; 3 came from the first three balls, Payne bowled Stewart with the fourth, and Scotland played out the last two balls for a draw.

An injury in that match to Ballinger, the quickest of the new-ball bowlers, further weakened the Schools team, who travelled directly to Worksop College to face the formidable Australian Under-19 side on August 9, 10. Fresh from their one-day success against England Under-19 at Trent Bridge, the Australians put paid to any meaningful contest by batting through most of the first day for 367 in 104 overs – the first time on the tour they had lost all ten wickets. At 55 for five at lunch on the second day, English Schools looked in danger of an innings defeat, but some aggressive batting by Kevin Parsons and Payne in a stand of 86 restricted Australia's lead to 169, Payne showing great composure in his fine innings of 82. There being insufficient time to press for victory, the tourists settled for batting practice, though Robinson responsed with a lively spell of bowling and took all three wickets to fall as the Australians progressed to 52.

The Welsh Schools enjoyed an encouraging season, overcoming a shaky start against Scottish Young Cricketers, who reduced them to 13 to five at Ebbw Vale. H. Evans (67) and R. Cogbill (28) pulled the innings round to a more respectable 150, in reply to which Scotland had reached 26 for no wicket when the rain came. That match was then abandoned and replaced by the first limited-overs international between the two sides; the Scots made 199 for four in 50 overs (Stanger 59 not out) and dismissed their hosts for 179 (A. J. Dalton 58).

After their encouraging performance against English Schools, the Welsh Schools met the Irish Schools at Sophia Gardens, Cardiff. Irish Schools, batting first, declared at 264 for five (G. Russell 102 not out), to which the Welsh responded by declaring behind at 235 for five (A. D. Shaw 65 not out). The visitors then batted on into the last afternoon, eventually declaring a second time at 264 for seven (N. Curzon 58, J. Molins 56, E. Armstrong 53 not out), and with the Welsh needing 294 in 100 minutes and twenty overs, the match seemed dead. However, Dalton (83) and A. J. Jones (69) rose to the challenge and set them well on course with a century opening stand. When wickets began to fall in the last hour, though, the Welsh closed ranks and settled for a draw, finishing at 195 for five (K. Banks four for 36).

The Welsh Schools side was captained by A. J. Jones, son of the former Glamorgan batsman, Alan Jones, while Shaw, the England Under-19 wicket-keeper, was chosen as the first Welsh Schools player of the year. The Welsh Under-16 side, coached by T. W. Cartwright, formerly of England, Warwickshire, Somerset and Glamorgan, won the Texaco Under-16 County Championship. In the three-day round-robin final, held at Uppingham School, they took the title by virtue of having lost fewer wickets than Lancashire and Hampshire, with whom they finished level on points.

## HMC SOUTHERN SCHOOLS v THE REST

At Wadham College, July 12, 13. Drawn. There was little in the slow pitch for the bowlers on the first day, when Jones compiled a neat, assured century, and Robinson's fierce hitting hastened the way to a declaration at 251. The Rest's reply was built around a well-organised, unbeaten century by Weston, supported by a fluent fifty from Parsons. Overnight rain tilted the balance more in favour of the bowlers, and Southern Schools struggled somewhat against tight seam bowling from White and the teasing left-arm spin of Whittington. Although Semmence, promoted to open, scored a good fifty and Walker injected some momentum at the end, they needed 71 overs to reach 186 for eight. The Rest's target of 233 was always beyond them, and for a time they looked likely losers as Carpenter and Richardson bowled well at the start, and Peirce contributed an accurate spell of left-arm spin.

## Southern Schools

| | | | |
|---|---|---|---|
| M. J. Walker (*King's, Rochester*) c Langworth b Yeabsley . 37 | – (7) c Slater b Whittington | 49 |
| *A. J. Jones (*Monmouth*) b Whittington . 102 | | |
| G. A. Khan (*Ipswich*) c Parsons b Whittington . 29 | – (1) c Slater b White | 12 |
| M. T. E. Peirce (*Ardingly*) c Colclough b Whittington . 0 | – (3) b White | 5 |
| M. F. D. Robinson (*King's, Taunton*) not out . 57 | – (9) not out | 10 |
| M. J. Semmence (*Hurstpierpoint*) not out . 15 | – (2) st Langworth b Yeabsley | 55 |
| A. W. Richardson (*Oundle*) (did not bat) | – (8) b White | 0 |
| A. J. Scott-Gall (*Stowe*) (did not bat) | – (4) c Yeabsley b Whittington | 14 |
| †K. G. Sedgbeer (*Taunton*) (did not bat) | – (5) b White | 18 |
| S. P. Moffat (*Aldenham*) (did not bat) | – (6) c and b White | 13 |
| Extras | 11 | Extras | 10 |

1/71 2/123 3/125 4/189          (4 wkts dec.) 251     1/28 2/39 3/63      (8 wkts dec.) 186
                                                       4/89 5/127 6/151
                                                       7/153 8/186

J. F. Carpenter (*Chigwell*) did not bat.

*Bowling: First Innings*—White 10–0–47–0; Slater 8–1–17–0; Whittington 20–2–71–3; Yeabsley 6–0–32–1; Atkinson 16–3–76–0. *Second Innings*—White 18–3–57–5; Slater 16–3–50–0; Atkinson 12–7–24–0; Yeabsley 10–5–15–1; Whittington 15–6–36–2.

## The Rest

| | | | |
|---|---|---|---|
| K. A. Graham (*King's, Macclesfield*) c Khan b Carpenter . 18 | – b Carpenter | 20 |
| R. M. S. Weston (*Durham*) not out . 101 | – (6) c Walker b Carpenter | 10 |
| *K. A. Parsons (*Richard Huish*) c Sedgbeer b Semmence . 54 | – (5) st Sedgbeer b Scott-Gall | 23 |
| M. H. Colclough (*Newcastle-under-Lyme*) not out 18 | – (3) c Semmence b Peirce | 24 |
| †J. H. Langworth (*Monmouth*) (did not bat) | – (2) c Peirce b Carpenter | 8 |
| C. Mulraine (*Warwick*) (did not bat) | – (4) c and b Peirce | 10 |
| R. M. Atkinson (*Leeds GS*) (did not bat) | – not out | 23 |
| J. G. Slater (*Ellesmere*) (did not bat) | – lbw b Richardson | 4 |
| M. T. White (*Trent*) (did not bat) | – not out | 2 |
| Extras | 14 | Extras | 5 |

1/59 2/162                    (2 wkts dec.) 205     1/24 2/29 3/58 4/64      (7 wkts) 129
                                                    5/95 6/122 7/125

R. S. Yeabsley (*Haberdashers' Aske's*) and J. M. S. Whittington (*Eton*) did not bat.

*Bowling: First Innings*—Carpenter 13–2–36–1; Richardson 9–0–34–0; Robinson 16–4–29–0; Peirce 7–2–34–0; Semmence 6–0–34–1; Scott-Gall 6–0–26–0. *Second Innings*—Carpenter 9–2–25–3; Richardson 9–2–21–1; Peirce 14–8–20–2; Semmence 6–1–13–0; Robinson 4–0–9–0; Scott-Gall 8–1–26–1; Khan 4–0–13–0.

## ESCA NORTH v ESCA SOUTH

At St Edward's School, July 12, 13. ESCA North won by five wickets in a match generally dominated by batsmen on a pitch with some pace and a large outfield. ESCA South's innings was founded on a fourth-wicket century partnership between Parsons and Thomas, but with Harvey and Hall impressing with the quality of their strokeplay, ESCA North comfortably established a first-innings lead in fewer overs. Although the South fared better in their second innings, thanks mainly to a swashbuckling half-century from Thomas, they still scored too slowly to set a sufficiently challenging target. North, in pursuit of 230, slumped to 92 for five, but were rescued by a hard-hitting stand of 138 from Payne and Whitaker, which swept them to victory in only 53 overs.

## ESCA South

| | | | |
|---|---|---|---|
| *H. Morgan (Westlands; Devon)* c Luntley b Hindson . 19 | – run out | 41 |
| I. Johns (*QEGS, Barnet; Middx*) c Luntley b Whitaker . 39 | – c Luntley b Hindson | 31 |
| C. M. Pitcher (*St Edward's, Oxford; Oxon.*) c Whitaker b Payne . 4 | – b Whitaker | 16 |
| K. J. Parsons (*Richard Huish; Somerset*) b Sheriya . 73 | – c Hall b Whitaker | 5 |
| K. Thomas (*Bilborough SFC; Notts.*) c Payne b Sheriya . 28 | – st Luntley b Hindson | 65 |
| A. Collins (*Cricklade; Hants*) not out . 12 | – st Luntley b Hindson | 26 |
| A. Thornley (*Warwicks.*) not out . 0 | – b Sheriya | 26 |
| †N. J. Workman (*King Edward VI, Stourbridge; Worcs.*) (did not bat) . | – c Heseltine b Whitaker | 15 |
| R. J. Ballinger (*Millfield; Middx*) (did not bat) . . | – not out | 7 |
| C. Sketchley (*Medina; Isle of Wight*) (did not bat) . | – not out | 1 |
| Extras . 12 | Extras | 13 |

1/53 2/64 3/74 4/174 5/178     (5 wkts dec.) 187      1/65 2/79 3/131   (8 wkts dec.) 246
                                                           4/145 5/167 6/179
                                                            7/213 8/232

P. T. Jacques (*Millfield; Somerset*) did not bat.

Bowling: *First Innings*—Sheriya 12–3–36–2; Heseltine 14–3–56–0; Payne 9–2–25–1; Hindson 15–5–41–1; Whitaker 10–2–25–1. *Second Innings*—Sheriya 10–1–39–1; Heseltine 15–3–42–0; Hindson 28–7–80–3; Whitaker 23–4–77–3.

## ESCA North

| | | | |
|---|---|---|---|
| P. Wilcock (*Hopwood Hall; Lancs.*) lbw b Thornley . 27 | – b Jacques | 43 |
| M. E. Harvey (*Habergham HS; Lancs.*) lbw b Jacques . 80 | – b Ballinger | 9 |
| R. Hughes (*Lawrence Sheriff; Warwicks.*) run out . 23 | – c Workman b Jacques | 8 |
| *A. J. Hall (*Marple Hall; Cheshire*) not out . 54 | – (5) lbw b Pitcher | 12 |
| M. Brooke (*Batley GS; Yorks.*) not out . 13 | – (4) c Parsons b Sketchley | 7 |
| A. Payne (*Accrington; Lancs.*) (did not bat) . | – not out | 86 |
| P. Whitaker (*Whitcliffe Mount; Yorks.*) (did not bat) . | – not out | 57 |
| Extras . 7 | Extras | 8 |

1/51 2/92 3/180     (3 wkts dec.) 204      1/26 2/62 3/69   (5 wkts) 230
                                                               4/77 5/92

J. E. Hindson (*Toothill; Notts.*), A. Sheriya (*Joseph Chamberlain; Warwicks.*), †W. Luntley (*Ribbington; Lancs.*) and S. Heseltine (*Guiseley; Yorks.*) did not bat.

Bowling: *First Innings*—Ballinger 5–0–28–0; Collins 8–2–40–0; Pitcher 8–1–38–0; Thornley 6–1–26–1; Jacques 13–2–41–1; Sketchley 8–1–24–0. *Second Innings*—Ballinger 9–0–40–1; Collins 6–1–22–0; Pitcher 4–0–26–1; Thornley 6–0–34–0; Jacques 14–1–54–2; Sketchley 14–5–49–1.

At Keble College, July 14. Drawn. H. Morgan's XI 206 (M. F. D. Robinson 82; R. J. Ballinger three for 59); A. J. Jones's XI 163 for six (K. A. Graham 56, K. Thomas 40).

At Wadham College, July 14. K. A. Parsons's XI won by three wickets. A. J. Hall's XI 209 for four dec. (S. P. Moffat 40, A. J. Hall 91 not out, M. J. Semmence 64 not out); K. A. Parsons's XI 213 for seven (M. T. E. Peirce 92, K. A. Parsons 35; A. W. Richardson four for 50).

At Christ Church, July 15. MCC Schools West won by six wickets. MCC Schools East 208 for five dec. (M. J. Walker 38, M. E. Harvey 50, K. Thomas 32 not out); MCC Schools West 212 for four (A. J. Jones 62, A. J. Hall 75).

More details of the Oxford Festival may be found in the article by Gerald Howat, which appears elsewhere in the Almanack. The match at Lord's between MCC and MCC Schools may be found in the MCC section, and that at Lord's between MCC Schools and the National Association of Young Cricketers may be found in Other Matches at Lord's, 1991.

*Highlights from the Schools*

The dismal weather of 1991 curtailed so many schools matches that batsmen and bowlers alike were restricted. Only three batsmen from the schools reviewed here passed 1,000 runs – the fewest since the wet summer of 1985 – with just five more topping 900. The leading scorers were: K. A. Graham of King's, Macclesfield (1,128 runs at 75.20), J. Hargrove of Victoria College, Jersey (1,046 at 52.30), G. A. Khan of Ipswich (1,006 at 83.83), R. Q. Cake of King's College School, Wimbledon (979 at 57.58), G. J. Kennis of Tiffin (946 at 55.64), R. J. Ayre of University College School (920 at 83.63), R. W. Nowell of Trinity (911 at 47.94) and A. V. Powell of Royal GS, Worcester (903 at 53.11). Of these Ayre and Khan went to the wicket just fifteen times each, while Hargrove, with 23 innings, played the most. Two batsmen recorded three-figure averages, M. G. N. Windows of Clifton compiling 615 runs at 123.00 and E. J. Meredith of Ratcliffe averaging 105.16 for his 631. There were no double-centuries, although ten batsmen reached 150, the two highest scores being 181 not out by R. C. Weston of The Leys and 176 not out by Khan, who reached 150 three times. He alone made five centuries, while four each were scored by Ayre, Cake, Graham, Nowell, M. J. Walker of King's, Rochester and Kennis; the last-mentioned followed his thousand runs and three centuries in 1990 with four hundreds in his first five innings in 1991. In representative schoolboy cricket R. M. S. Weston, who made 700 runs at 63.63 for Durham, scored centuries at the Oxford Festival and for English Schools against Welsh Schools.

Again no bowler took 60 wickets, and 50 or more were taken by only five, the lowest number for many years: A. R. C. Gilmour of Merchiston Castle (53 at 10.50), J. G. Slater of Ellesmere (52 at 8.78), R. S. Jayatileke of Bishop's Stortford (52 at 11.28), B. J. Walters of Tiffin (51 at 12.72) and I. Ritchie of Victoria College, Jersey (50 at 19.08). Of these, Slater bowled the fewest overs (209), while Ritchie's 329 were by far the most. Slater was also the season's most frugal bowler, others with economical averages being J. R. Carpenter of Birkenhead (43 wickets at 8.83), J. M. S. Whittington of Eton (42 at 8.88) and J. L. Cunningham of Bangor GS (47 at 9.82). The best innings returns came from D. G. Gourlay of Glasgow Academy (nine for 9), I. R. Harris of Epsom (nine for 23), N. A. Doggett of Merchant Taylors', Crosby (eight for 4), Whittington (eight for 13) and Gilmour (eight for 18), while ten other bowlers recorded eight-wicket returns and 49 more had seven-wicket hauls.

The most impressive of these was the seven for 7 taken by S. T. Fearon of Wyggeston & Queen Elizabeth I Sixth Form College. Nine hat-tricks were reported, taken by: M. H. Colclough of Newcastle-under-Lyme, A. M. Denslow and D. P. Frost, both of King's College School, Wimbledon, T. J. Gladwin of Highgate, Khan of Ipswich, A. T. Lark of Whitgift, P. A. B. Page of Abingdon, S. J. Perkins of Truro and A. W. Richardson of Oundle.

Without doubt the leading all-rounder was the England Under-15 Schools representative, Nowell, with 911 runs and 49 wickets, followed by J. M. Ramsey of Eltham (829 runs, 47 wickets). Other notable all-round contributions came from R. A. Hawkey of Merchant Taylors', Northwood (676 runs, 46 wickets), B. C. Ray of Royal GS, Guildford (637 runs, 41 wickets), Carpenter, another Under-15 player (548 runs, 43 wickets) and L. J. Crozier of Royal GS, Newcastle (527 runs, 41 wickets).

Thirteen of the Schools who appear in this *Wisden* were unbeaten. Of these, King's, Macclesfield recorded eleven wins and Ellesmere beat ten sides, while at the other end of the scale Nottingham HS won just once, their other twelve games being drawn. The remaining undefeated sides were Chigwell, Clifton, Haileybury, St John's Leatherhead, Sevenoaks, Simon Langton GS, Tiffin, Warwick, Wellingborough and Woodhouse Grove. Among those unbeaten by schools were Bishop's Stortford and Highgate, both of whom lost only to MCC; King's College School, Wimbledon, whose single defeat was at the hands of Guernsey Island Under-23; Dover College, who drew all their schools matches, and Glenalmond.

It was good to read, in reports from the schools, of the popularity of the game, despite the pressure of examinations and the plethora of interests available to today's schoolboys and schoolgirls. Less encouraging, perhaps, was the comment from some masters that opposing sides would have preferred a limited-overs match. This seems to have been the case in instances when one side has played for a draw from the start, and as Gerald Howat says in his report of the Oxford Festival, "at the heart of such a situation is the fear of losing". If interest in cricket is to continue, both for boys at school and after they leave, it is important that a more positive attitude is fostered.

Such an attitude was exemplified by **Haileybury's** competitive and good-humoured XI, who were determined always to play positively and were rewarded with an unbeaten record, although that was never a primary aim. Against Tonbridge, for example, they rose to the challenge of scoring 40 off the last four overs, 20 off the last two and 13 off the final over, to snatch an exciting victory. Another school similarly unwilling to settle for a draw were **Durham**, who recorded eleven wins in their sixteen matches. Against **St Bees**, they made a valiant effort to score 11 from the last over in pursuit of 175, but the last batsman fell 1 short to tie the match with two balls remaining. Even closer was the tie between **The Leys** and **Monkton Combe**: in their reply to the former's 271 for four, Monkton Combe's last batsman was dismissed off the last ball with the score 271 from the same number of overs.

More schools found it easier to win chasing runs than to score quickly batting first and then bowl sides out. Thus the toss often played an undue part in success or failure, and at least one school felt that their record of wins and losses simply reflected their success with the toss. An exception was **Christ's Hospital**, who succeeded in bowling out the opposition nine times in their twelve matches. Similarly successful in that respect were **Hampton**, a feature of whose season was the number of games won when defending low scores, such as 112 and 132 against Enfield GS and Watford GS respectively. That they could also chase runs was demonstrated in their one-wicket victory off the last ball over Latymer, when chasing 241. Durham, too, while agreeing that a run-chase tended to be easier, achieved more than half their victories when batting first.

Masters reported a number of other outstanding performances and records broken, and these may be found in the returns from schools which follow.

# THE SCHOOLS

(Qualification: Batting 100 runs; Bowling 10 wickets)

* *On name indicates captain.*   * *On figures indicates not out.*

*Note:* The line for batting reads Innings–Not Outs–Runs–Highest Innings–100s–Average; that for bowling reads Overs–Maidens–Runs–Wickets–Best Bowling–Average.

## ABINGDON SCHOOL

*Played 18: Won 6, Lost 6, Drawn 6, Abandoned 1*

Master i/c: A. M. Broadbent

*Wins v:* Oratory; Douai; Berkhamsted; Lord Williams's, Thame; UCS; South Oxfordshire Amateurs.

P. A. B. Page took a hat-trick against Douai, while against Pangbourne J. M. Allen (101 not out) featured with J. S. Tilley (112 not out) in an unbroken second-wicket partnership of 210. The two-wicket victory over Berkhamsted, when chasing a target of 190 in 34 overs, came off the final delivery, and against South Oxfordshire Amateurs, Abingdon recovered from 4 for four, needing 193, to win by three wickets.

*Batting*—P. A. B. Page 16-3-462-92-0-35.53; J. S. Tilley 16-1-447-112*-1-29.80; *J. M. Allen 18-2-432-101*-1-27.00; A. N. Janisch 11-3-323-59-0-26.91; A. J. C. Smith 7-2-124-77*-0-24.80; J. M. Wilkinson 13-1-207-55-0-17.25; A. P. Harding 16-0-237-48-0-14.81; E. J. Paleit 12-1-157-30*-0-14.27.

*Bowling*—P. A. B. Page 212.3-72-447-38-6/11-11.76; J. M. Wilkinson 121-31-358-21-4/12-17.04; J. M. Allen 61.3-8-227-12-5/11-18.91; N. F. Pree 106-22-353-17-4/56-20.76; B. W. Gannon 109-27-347-14-3/5-24.78; J. S. Tilley 139-27-487-16-3/25-30.43.

## ALDENHAM SCHOOL

*Played 12: Won 6, Lost 4, Drawn 2, Abandoned 1*

Master i/c: P. K. Smith

*Wins v:* Westminster; Berkhamsted; St George's, Weybridge; Cricket Master's XI; UCS; Liverpool.

*Batting*—*S. P. Moffat 11-4-573-118*-2-81.85; C. S. Molyneux 12-4-406-81*-0-50.75; D. P. Marsh 7-1-214-103*-1-35.66; R. J. Robertson 9-2-216-58*-0-30.85; R. L. Ullman 9-0-162-50-0-18.00.

*Bowling*—D. M. Rawlinson 44-4-155-12-6/35-12.91; R. G. May 75-10-275-15-4/51-18.33; R. J. Robertson 144-28-474-24-5/26-19.75; T. J. McAllister 144-24-441-20-4/31-22.05.

## ALLEYN'S SCHOOL

*Played 16: Won 1, Lost 6, Drawn 9*

Master i/c: S. E. Smith

*Win v:* Westminster.

*Batting*—G. W. Francis 16-3-461-82-0-35.46; N. P. Wharton 9-3-124-50-0-20.66; C. P. Hankey 12-1-213-57-0-19.36; D. J. Dare 11-1-152-32-0-15.20; B. McGill 11-1-124-28-0-12.40; M. T. Roberts 12-1-116-37-0-10.54.

*Bowling*—*P. J. B. Haslam 167.5-32-445-24-6/33-18.54; B. McGill 151-27-449-23-5/38-19.52; R. M. Whittall 168.2-36-424-20-4/45-21.20.

## ALLHALLOWS SCHOOL

*Played 10: Won 2, Lost 7, Drawn 1, Abandoned 2*

Masters i/c: C. G. McNee and M. Hill

*Wins v:* Devon Dumplings; Free Foresters.

*Batting*—A. W. E. Crawford 7-0-156-77-0-22.28; G. D. Moxon 10-0-189-62-0-18.90; A. C. Boddy 10-1-162-87*-0-18.00; A. M. Frampton 10-1-131-64*-0-14.55.

*Bowling*—A. C. Boddy 80-13-324-12-3/32-27.00; K. W. W. Clarke 87-12-277-10-3/29-27.70; G. D. Moxon 83-13-309-11-4/33-28.09.

## AMPLEFORTH COLLEGE

*Played 17: Won 3, Lost 3, Drawn 11*

Master i/c: G. D. Thurman             Cricket professional: D. Wilson

*Wins v:* Worksop; Free Foresters; Pocklington.

*Batting*—A. J. Zino 10–1–308–130*–1–34.22; N. R. Lamb 17–2–497–100*–1–33.13; O. R. Mathias 10–3–221–53*–0–31.57; R. M. Wilson 15–1–400–108*–1–28.57; G. Finch 15–2–227–52–0–17.46; *T. S. Codrington 16–1–221–50–0–14.73; R. J. Gilmore 13–2–137–32–0–12.45; S. B. Pilkington 14–2–132–29–0–11.00.

*Bowling*—J. W. Acton 63.2–15–221–14–4/24–15.78; D. A. Thompson 123–30–271–14–3/17–19.35; A. R. Freeland 194.2–24–713–29–5/40–24.58; R. J. Gilmore 240.1–37–769–29–6/72–26.51; S. B. Pilkington 127.4–13–456–17–3/25–26.82; C. P. Williams 96–22–274–10–3/11–27.40.

## ARDINGLY COLLEGE

*Played 12: Won 3, Lost 6, Drawn 3. Abandoned 5*

Master i/c: T. J. Brooker             Cricket professional: S. S. Sawant

*Wins v:* Eastbourne; St George's, Weybridge; Headmaster's XI.

*Batting*—M. T. E. Peirce 11–2–564–153*–3–62.66; A. C. C. Slight 11–1–360–104–1–36.00; C. S. Spencer 10–0–251–64–0–25.10; M. Newcomb 10–0–222–41–0–22.20; N. Bradley Hole 10–0–103–19–0–10.30.

*Bowling*—M. T. E. Peirce 186.1–51–486–34–4/32–14.29; C. S. Spencer 115.3–23–372–14–3/27–26.57; S. Skeel 121–23–359–12–3/20–29.91.

## ARNOLD SCHOOL

*Played 21: Won 4, Lost 7, Drawn 10*

Master i/c: S. Burnage             Cricket professional: J. Simmons

*Wins v:* RGS, Clitheroe; Kirkham GS; Stockport GS; Edinburgh Acad.

*Batting*—C. J. Outram 18–1–635–122–1–37.35; I. Best 16–5–323–63*–0–29.36; R. Day 15–5–257–58*–0–25.70; S. Knapman 19–1–396–78–0–22.00; R. Chew 19–0–409–64–0–21.52; D. Chant 12–2–204–65*–0–20.40; P. Bentley 17–2–297–60–0–19.80; A. Stewart 16–1–168–39–0–11.20.

*Bowling*—I. Best 175.4–36–563–26–5/18–21.65; S. Whittle 148.2–35–571–21–4/21–27.19; R. Chew 198–53–741–21–4/17–35.28; D. Miller 182.1–31–752–20–3/62–37.60.

## ASHVILLE COLLEGE, HARROGATE

*Played 17: Won 4, Lost 7, Drawn 6. Abandoned 1*

Master i/c: J. M. Bromley             Cricket professional: P. J. Kippax

*Wins v:* QEGS, Wakefield; Silcoates S.; Read S.; Old Ashvillians.

*Batting*—S. R. Alexander 17–4–428–92–0–32.92; *K. D. Crack 16–0–423–76–0–26.43; A. J. Hyslop 8–1–146–53–0–20.85; D. J. Lupton 17–1–253–65*–0–15.81; A. R. White 16–2–186–36–0–13.28; S. Creber 15–1–177–40–0–12.64.

*Bowling*—K. D. Crack 186–55–459–37–8/34–12.40; N. L. Ahmad 149–39–447–28–7/15–15.96; S. R. Alexander 80–16–225–13–4/23–17.30; D. J. Lupton 65–7–257–11–4/16–23.36.

## BANCROFT'S SCHOOL

*Played 21: Won 4, Lost 7, Drawn 10. Abandoned 2*

Master i/c: J. G. Bromfield                    Cricket professional: J. K. Lever

*Wins v:* St Albans; Chelmsford Clergy; Fredericia CC, Denmark; Kolding CC, Denmark.

Against St Dunstan's, a second-wicket record of 212 was set by T. W. Clark (121) and C. S. Greenhill (93), the latter a sixteen-year-old who passed 600 runs for the second successive season.

*Batting*—C. S. Greenhill 18–3–635–93–0–42.33; T. W. Clark 18–1–412–121–1–24.23; A. A. Khan 18–2–356–59–0–22.25; R. Patel 14–1–170–46*–0–13.07; D. W. Strong 10–2–102–31–0–12.75; *T. M. Dowling 20–4–199–42*–0–12.43; P. T. Vohmann 12–2–106–20*–0–10.60.

*Bowling*—C. C. Barlow 25–4–88–10–5/18–8.80; A. A. Khan 180.5–25–652–36–4/12–18.11; T. W. Clark 150.1–33–482–24–4/10–20.08; R. Patel 182.3–35–620–30–6/34–20.66; C. S. Greenhill 106–19–322–15–5/23–21.46.

## BANGOR GRAMMAR SCHOOL

*Played 23: Won 16, Lost 2, Drawn 5. Abandoned 3*

Master i/c: C. C. J. Harte

*Wins v:* Bangor CC; Limavady GS; Dacriada; Foyle and Londonderry C. (twice); Down HS; Ballymena Acad. (three times); The Leprechauns; RBAI; RS Dungannon; Sullivan US; Ballyclare HS; Coleraine AI; Arnold.

In a season when Bangor won both the Schools and McCullough Cups, sixteen-year-old J. L. Cunningham's 47 wickets at 9.82 were just one short of the record set in 1980 by C. D. Capper.

*Batting*—P. J. English 20–6–461–73*–0–32.92; M. S. J. Law 18–1–409–61–0–24.05; J. L. Cunningham 18–5–221–48–0–17.00; M. L. Edwards 23–2–290–54*–0–13.80; M. N. Wade 19–3–187–27*–0–11.68; W. P. McMillan 18–0–136–34–0–7.55.

*Bowling*—R. M. McCord 91.5–14–272–31–5/6–8.77; P. J. English 87–18–219–23–5/53–9.52; J. L. Cunningham 188–54–462–47–5/33–9.82; *C. P. Escott 156.2–44–375–36–6/15–10.41; A. R. P. McVicar 141–34–311–26–6/24–11.96.

## BARNARD CASTLE SCHOOL

*Played 20: Won 9, Lost 2, Drawn 9. Abandoned 1*

Master i/c: C. P. Johnson

*Wins v:* Scotton Banks CC; RGS, Newcastle; Edinburgh Acad.; Pocklington; Dame Allan's; UCS (twice); Woodbridge; King Edward VII, Lytham.

*Batting*—S. G. Riddell 19–0–625–88–0–32.89; *R. Brewis 15–4–319–73–0–29.00; J. W. Foster 18–2–457–74–0–28.56; T. Mardon 16–3–307–81–0–23.61; A. W. Hutchinson 20–1–398–59–0–20.94; K. Lowe 9–2–134–52*–0–19.14; N. R. Walker 15–1–256–59–0–18.28.

*Bowling*—T. Mardon 108.4–24–332–22–8/49–15.09; R. Brewis 224.2–57–627–33–7/32–19.00; N. R. Walker 93–16–292–14–4/33–20.85; A. D. Ballantyne 257.1–82–647–29–6/15–22.31; J. M. Watson 179.3–46–498–19–3/27–26.21.

## BEDFORD SCHOOL

*Played 15: Won 7, Lost 2, Drawn 6. Abandoned 4*

Master i/c: D. W. Jarrett                    Cricket professional: R. G. Caple

*Wins v:* Buccaneers CC; XL Club; Old Bedfordians; The Leys; Bedford Modern; St Edward's, Oxford; Stowe.

An excellent début season was enjoyed by M. R. Evans, a young all-rounder who should have another two years at the School. B. J. A. Miller, the captain and wicket-keeper, hit an exciting 123 off 24 overs in the victory over Bedford Modern.

*Batting*—G. D. Cruse 16–5–769–144*–1–69.90; M. R. Evans 16–2–543–96–0–38.78; *B. J. A. Miller 14–0–397–123–1–28.35; G. I. Green 13–6–196–43–0–28.00; R. G. Simmonds 10–1–228–63–0–25.33; L. J. Wood 11–1–124–29–0–12.40.

*Bowling*—G. D. Cruse 173–29–587–26–4/38–22.57; M. R. Evans 183–33–571–24–5/41–23.79; G. I. Green 161–30–484–20–6/35–24.20; A. J. Penn 82–8–286–11–4/11–26.00; R. J. Stone 88–15–314–10–2/14–31.40.


## BEDFORD MODERN SCHOOL

*Played 18: Won 1, Lost 3, Drawn 14. Abandoned 3*

Master i/c: N. J. Chinneck

*Win v:* Gentlemen of Bedfordshire.

*Batting*—A. R. Woodcock 16–3–727–137*–2–55.92; P. D. Brownridge 10–6–140–39*–0–35.00; G. S. Pilgrim 18–4–435–81*–0–31.07; *D. B. Reavill 18–1–425–87–0–25.00; B. J. Young 7–1–129–64–0–21.50; R. C. Shah 9–1–139–29–0–17.37.

*Bowling*—A. R. Woodcock 227.2–32–941–36–6/32–26.13; P. D. Brownridge 226.2–47–771–26–6/55–29.65; M. J. Brownridge 123.1–25–479–16–3/24–29.93; J. P. Gray 136–20–427–12–3/81–35.58.


## BEECHEN CLIFF SCHOOL, BATH

*Played 11: Won 3, Lost 1, Drawn 7. Abandoned 2*

Master i/c: K. J. L. Mabe        Cricket professional: P. J. Colbourne

*Wins v:* Queen Elizabeth's Hospital; Norton Hill S.; Prior Park.

P. R. Tisdale's total of 1,244 runs for the XI since 1987, at an average of 62.20, was a school record, as were his four centuries. He scored two in 1991, including 126 in a record first-wicket partnership of 213 with L. Davis (100 not out) against Monkton Combe.

*Batting*—*P. R. Tisdale 9–1–381–126–2–47.62; L. Davis 8–2–184–100*–1–30.66; N. J. Welch 7–1–106–44–0–17.66; N. P. Bursell 10–1–116–40–0–12.88.

*Bowling*—P. R. Tisdale 62–29–80–14–3/6–5.71; D. Jones 74–27–146–14–4/20–10.42; D. M. Barnes 56.4–15–177–12–3/45–14.75.


## BERKHAMSTED SCHOOL

*Played 14: Won 1, Lost 9, Drawn 4. Abandoned 3*

Master i/c: J. G. Tolchard        Cricket professional: M. Herring

*Win v:* Gentlemen of Hertfordshire.

At the Kimbolton Festival, B. A. King carried his bat for 37 against Hyderabad Blues.

*Batting*—N. A. Wolstenholme 14–2–448–100*–1–37.33; N. E. Mawdsley 13–1–264–66–0–22.00; *R. D. Collett 14–1–281–74–0–21.61; R. L. Cunliffe 10–3–145–47*–0–20.71; B. A. King 8–1–119–37*–0–17.00; M. H. Robinson 9–0–138–36–0–15.33; A. C. Lovegrove 12–2–101–24–0–10.10.

*Bowling*—B. P. Howard 135–25–476–22–5/30–21.63; R. D. Collett 108–29–326–12–3/21–27.16; A. C. Lovegrove 124–31–387–10–3/32–38.70; M. H. Robinson 142–28–472–10–3/57–47.20.

# BIRKENHEAD SCHOOL

*Played 17: Won 12, Lost 2, Drawn 3. Abandoned 1*

Master i/c: G. Prescott

*Wins v:* Wallasey S.; Merchant Taylors', Crosby; Rydal; Wirral GS; Stonyhurst; XL School; Manchester GS; St David's, Llandudno; Liverpool; Foyle and Londonderry C.; King's, Chester; Old Birkonians.

J. R. Carpenter made an outstanding all-round contribution, his 43 wickets representing a particularly impressive performance in his first season bowling slow left-arm after switching from left-arm medium pace. The School won the Barclays Under-17 Cup, beating the strong Ipswich side in the final.

*Batting*—J. R. Carpenter 13–5–548–100*–1–68.50; N. D. Cross 10–1–507–129–2–56.33; S. J. Renshaw 10–2–393–103–2–49.12; M. W. Southworth 10–3–263–58–0–37.57; *I. G. Berry 13–3–373–92–0–37.30.

*Bowling*—J. R. Carpenter 183.2–81–380–43–7/38–8.83; N. D. Cross 92.1–29–246–21–5/50–11.71; J. L. Cooper 88.4–30–243–20–6/37–12.15; S. J. Renshaw 141.4–48–316–24–6/24–13.16; A. G. Cook 76.1–12–229–13–3/17–17.61.

# BISHOP'S STORTFORD COLLEGE

*Played 15: Won 9, Lost 1, Drawn 5. Abandoned 4*

Master i/c: D. A. Hopper          Cricket professional: C. S. Bannister

*Wins v:* St Edmund's, Ware; Aldenham; The Perse; Berkhamsted; Framlingham; Wrekin; Gresham's; Oakham; Stamford.

For the nine wins, which equalled the college record, the XI owed a considerable amount to their Sri Lankan off-spinner, R. S. Jayatileke, as well as to their opening attack of two left-armers, M. G. Burle and R. J. Walters.

*Batting*—L. E. M. Riddell 15–4–595–124–2–54.09; *D. N. Child 14–1–370–78–0–28.46; I. M. Bateman 15–2–335–97–0–25.76; E. M. Peachey 13–3–249–90–0–24.90; R. F. Hudson 9–3–134–29*–0–22.33; M. G. Burle 10–3–133–35–0–19.00.

*Bowling*—R. S. Jayatileke 250–79–587–52–7/30–11.28; M. G. Burle 213.1–70–473–31–5/22–15.25; R. J. Walters 130.5–34–337–22–5/23–15.31.

# BLOXHAM SCHOOL

*Played 17: Won 5, Lost 3, Drawn 9. Abandoned 2*

Master i/c: J. P. Horton

*Wins v:* Bromsgrove; Rendcomb; Oratory; Old Bloxhamists; Abingdon.

*Batting*—R. A. F. Whitton 11–4–336–86*–0–48.00; C. T. G. Carr 8–1–217–106*–1–31.00; *S. P. Johnson 14–3–299–102*–1–27.18; M. G. Wood 15–2–341–99–0–26.23; S. Hehir 15–1–307–51–0–21.92; A. M. Kenward 12–3–195–41*–0–21.66; A. W. A. Adejumo 7–0–118–49–0–16.85.

*Bowling*—R. A. F. Whitton 202.5–82–439–32–5/46–13.71; P. R. Arber 139–18–501–22–5/37–22.77; J. F. F. Diamond 91–20–305–13–3/12–23.46; C. D. Muldoon 148.5–31–451–17–4/9–26.52.

## BLUNDELL'S SCHOOL

*Played 15: Won 4, Lost 4, Drawn 7. Abandoned 2*

Master i/c: G. P. Randall Johnson

*Wins v:* MCC; Old Blundellians; Wellington S.; Uppingham.

A mature innings of 130 by fifteen-year-old I. Gompertz was the basis of the last-ball victory against MCC, while at the Ampleforth Festival, the last wicket put on 97 to defeat a strong Uppingham XI. The side was captained in the first half of the term by M. R. N. Hunt and in the second by P. Steward.

*Batting*—I. Gompertz 15-1-642-130-1-45.85; *P. Steward 12-2-298-62-0-29.80; J. R. Stormonth 8-2-170-42-0-28.33; S. M. P. Patidar 15-2-317-88-0-24.38; *M. R. N. Hunt 15-1-318-92-0-22.71; E. T. C. Whitefield 13-1-271-80-0-22.58; J. E. McGough 10-2-112-29-0-14.00.

*Bowling*—I. Gompertz 99-34-259-15-?-17.26; J. E. McGough 160.1-25-517-25-4/42-20.68; P. Steward 157-39-469-17-2/9-27.58.

## BRADFIELD COLLEGE

*Played 13: Won 1, Lost 3, Drawn 9. Abandoned 1*

Master i/c: F. R. Dethridge                    Cricket professional: J. F. Harvey

*Win v:* Wellington C.

*Batting*—*W. S. Kendall 12-1-646-125-3-58.72; R. J. Cane 11-0-228-62-0-20.72; C. D. Gent 11-2-179-44-0-19.88; R. A. W. Oscroft 12-1-217-62-0-19.72; S. A. Seymour 12-2-175-87-0-17.50; A. J. Williams 12-2-158-38-0-15.80; S. J. S. Dennis 11-2-127-32-0-14.11.

*Bowling*—R. J. Cane 109-33-301-16-3/20-18.81; A. J. Williams 154-52-444-20-3/12-22.20; B. H. Maxwell 155-49-436-19-6/41-22.94.

## BRADFORD GRAMMAR SCHOOL

*Played 23: Won 12, Lost 3, Drawn 8. Abandoned 2*

Master i/c: A. G. Smith

*Wins v:* King Edward's, Birmingham; Ashville; Pocklington; Hymers; Hipperholme GS; Wells Cathedral S.; plus six club sides and invitation XIs.

*Batting*—J. S. Pearson 15-7-314-48-0-39.25; N. J. Gomersall 20-3-642-97-0-37.76; S. A. W. Davies 20-2-668-150-1-37.11; A. B. Wharton 23-5-550-112*-1-30.55; A. M. Bretherton 8-2-155-35-0-25.83; A. J. Brosnan 19-4-371-64-0-24.73; C. W. A. McIntosh 18-4-258-49-0-18.42; J. R. I. McIntosh 8-0-118-32-0-14.75.

*Bowling*—S. W. Elson 59-10-206-13-3/19-15.84; C. W. A. McIntosh 187.1-53-570-33-4/15-17.27; N. A. Joy 196.2-53-654-35-4/27-18.68; D. J. Collinge 135.2-36-393-21-4/28-18.71; A. K. Barker 91.4-16-308-15-4/4-20.53; P. S. Bachra 111.5-20-397-19-3/5-20.89; *M. J. Hannan 146.4-33-525-19-3/6-27.63.

## BRENTWOOD SCHOOL

*Played 11: Won 1, Lost 2, Drawn 8. Abandoned 5*

Master i/c: B. R. Hardie

*Win v:* Berkhamsted.

*Batting*—D. A. R. Gilbert 10-4-213-117*-1-35.50; G. K. Fletcher 11-0-302-62-0-27.45; *P. J. Collier 10-1-236-73-0-26.22; J. L. G. Cameron 10-2-200-38*-0-25.00; D. P. McAllister 6-2-100-35-0-25.00; S. I. Reeve 10-1-178-54-0-19.77; A. R. J. Sansom 9-0-160-33-0-17.77.

*Bowling*—J. E. B. Vereker 79.3–16–269–17–5/35–15.82; A. R. J. Sansom 60–14–183–10–4/48–18.30; R. E. D. Crapnell 85–19–245–12–2/22–20.41; D. P. McAllister 164–41–456–18–4/61–25.33.

## BRIGHTON COLLEGE

*Played 18: Won 6, Lost 5, Drawn 7. Abandoned 1*

Master i/c: J. Spencer                                   Cricket professional: J. D. Morley

*Wins v:* King Edward VI, Southampton; Ardingly; Eastbourne; Christ's Hospital; Arnold; Common Room XI.

The College retained the 40-overs Langdale Trophy, beating Christ's Hospital in the final.

*Batting*—R. J. Gibson 19–5–522–89–0–37.28; A. J. Sweet 19–1–595–106–2–33.05; P. D. L. Rennie 18–0–484–99–0–26.88; M. R. Strong 14–8–150–22*–0–25.00; A. R. Bidwell 18–3–311–73–0–20.73; T. W. Earl 18–2–325–63–0–20.31; A. D. King 14–3–179–58*–0–16.27; M. N. Dovey 13–1–130–30–0–10.83.

*Bowling*—T. W. Earl 79–8–279–15–3/26–18.60; R. J. Gibson 174.1–45–511–25–5/9–20.44; M. R. Strong 250.4–46–904–34–6/76–26.58; P. E. Fokes 117.3–7–518–15–3/22–34.53; A. J. Sweet 219–40–778–19–4/40–40.94.

## BRISTOL GRAMMAR SCHOOL

*Played 12: Won 4, Lost 1, Drawn 7. Abandoned 1*

Master i/c: R. Sellers

*Wins v:* Old Bristolians; Queen Elizabeth's Hospital; Wells Cathedral S.; Wellington S.

*Batting*—*M. Meredith 11–5–487–100*–1–81.16; S. Tyler 11–5–276–76*–0–46.00; A. Richardson 6–1–107–88–0–21.40; S. Beckett 11–1–179–52*–0–17.90; S. Hawkins 8–0–104–26–0–13.00.

*Bowling*—S. Beckett 62–10–205–13–5/25–15.76; F. Inglis 85.2–14–286–16–3/15–17.87; A. Richardson 140.3–41–387–21–4/18–18.42; M. Dobson 86.1–12–303–14–4/41–21.64; M. Meredith 164–44–431–15–4/47–28.73.

## BROMSGROVE SCHOOL

*Played 15: Won 3, Lost 5, Drawn 7. Abandoned 3*

Master i/c: D. Langlands                                 Cricket professional: P. G. Newman

*Wins v:* Oakham; Martlets; West Mercia Police.

*Batting*—S. C. Davis 9–4–182–46*–0–36.40; S. D. Coates 14–2–392–89–0–32.66; D. D. Griffiths 14–0–328–70–0–23.42; G. A. Hughes 14–3–235–56–0–21.36; *J. J. Court 15–2–265–51–0–20.38; M. J. Eckersley 12–2–192–34–0–19.20; P. D. Howard 11–0–147–29–0–13.36.

*Bowling*—C. G. R. Battelley 145.2–28–449–27–8/34–16.62; D. D. Griffiths 59.5–6–227–13–5/41–17.46; K. K. Haji 87.4–16–286–14–4/19–20.42; G. A. Harrhy 110–15–418–13–5/63–32.15.

## BRYANSTON SCHOOL

*Played 18: Won 2, Lost 8, Drawn 8. Abandoned 2*

Master i/c: T. J. Hill

*Wins v:* Ventnor CC; Blundell's.

*Batting*—N. P. Lind 11–3–357–79–0–44.62; G. A. Bucknell 18–1–683–117–1–40.17; W. J. Freisenbruch 17–1–473–51–0–29.56; J. E. Markham 16–2–413–73*–0–29.50; R. S. Wagstaffe 16–1–410–81*–0–27.33; I. E. Ronald 9–0–123–41–0–13.66; C. F. Austin 15–4–126–45*–0–11.45.

*Bowling*—J. E. Markham 169–31–557–29–6/39–19.20; C. F. Austin 174–21–556–21–4/43–26.47; R. T. Cuthill 95–10–406–12–3/34–33.83.

## CAMPBELL COLLEGE

*Played 17: Won 6, Lost 3, Drawn 8*

Master i/c: E. T. Cooke

*Wins v:* Regent House; Sullivan HS; Antrim GS; Royal S., Armagh; Limavady GS; Coleraine AI.

*Batting*—S. A. I. Dyer 15–2–542–108–1–41.69; A. E. Logan 17–2–310–61–0–20.66; C. R. T. Mounstephen 17–3–254–52–0–18.14; C. R. M. Caves 9–1–115–35–0–14.37; R. H. Lucas 13–1–164–30–0–13.66; G. M. Egan 15–3–136–46–0–11.33.

*Bowling*—N. J. Brown 47–9–144–13–4/24–11.07; J. G. N. Lucas 100–26–282–21–4/30–13.42; R. H. Lucas 165–40–491–33–5/22–14.87; J. L. Waterworth 111–14–314–21–3/12–14.95; B. J. Mockford 84–22–221–10–4/34–22.10.

## CANFORD SCHOOL

*Played 14: Won 9, Lost 3, Drawn 2. Abandoned 2*

Master i/c: S. J. Turrill                    Cricket professional: A. Kritzinger

*Wins v:* Wimborne CC; Milton Abbey; XL Club; Blundell's; King Edward VI, Southampton; Bryanston; King's, Bruton; Taunton; Ampleforth.

A fine team effort led to the XI winning nine games, which equalled the school record and took to seventeen their tally of wins in the last two seasons.

*Batting*—M. Kind 12–4–374–114*–1–46.75; *D. A. W. Young 14–1–413–96–0–31.76; T. Allen 13–3–304–100*–1–30.40; A. M. Scott 13–7–148–30*–0–24.66; M. Allom 14–0–343–75–0–24.50; J. Blacker 12–1–116–33–0–10.54.

*Bowling*—M. Allom 261.4–56–649–37–6/37–17.54; G. Rees 184–46–537–30–7/32–17.90; M. Noble 83.3–21–234–13–2/17–18.00; S. White-Cooper 77–13–216–10–3/25–21.60; G. Herring 132.3–24–471–16–4/56–29.43.

## CATERHAM SCHOOL

*Played 11: Won 1, Lost 4, Drawn 6. Abandoned 2*

Master i/c: A. G. Tapp                    Cricket professional: Wasim Raja

*Win v:* Alleyn's.

*Batting*—G. E. Owen 7–3–154–69*–0–38.50; *S. M. Lillicrap 9–1–190–61–0–23.75; T. G. W. Bailey 9–1–187–48–0–23.37; A. P. McKeran 10–0–211–71–0–21.10; R. G. H. Turner 8–1–120–28–0–17.14.

*Bowling*—S. M. Lillicrap 69.3–5–258–15–4/40–17.20; S. C. Turner 136.2–31–541–14–4/35–38.64.

## CHARTERHOUSE

*Played 18: Won 2, Lost 3, Drawn 13. Abandoned 1*

Master i/c: J. M. Knight        Cricket professional: R. V. Lewis

*Wins v:* Westminster; Free Foresters.

The highlight was the resounding victory over Westminster, in which J. F. Wilson returned the impressive figures of 8-4-6-6 on a good pitch.

*Batting*—*T. A. Bristowe 17-1-474-112-1-29.62; D. M. H. Shah 15-4-310-76-0-28.18; M. S. P. Benka 7-1-159-58-0-26.50; C. A. M. Ayres 15-1-349-61-0-24.92; A. Gompertz 8-2-145-32-0-24.16; E. L. Green 17-2-291-65-0-19.40; R. Ashby 8-1-130-57-0-18.57; J. F. Wilson 16-3-205-50-0-15.76; T. D. Courtenay-Evans 3-1-181-28-0-15.08; J. D. Wallace 16-2-210-43-0-15.00; M. J. Mitten 16-1-187-56-0-12.46.

*Bowling*—M. G. Bristowe 83-21-242-14-3/34-17.28; C. A. M. Ayres 159.5-24-460-26-4/31-17.69; T. D. Courtenay-Evans 60-12-202-10-3/17-20.20; J. F. Wilson 196-35-628-27-6/6-23.25; E. J. Rees 187-36-557-17-3/21-32.76.

## CHELTENHAM COLLEGE

*Played 20: Won 8, Lost 1, Drawn 11*

Master i/c: W. J. Wesson        Cricket professional: M. W. Stovold

*Wins v:* Malvern; Marlborough; Rugby; Monmouth; King's, Worcester; Rendcomb; Dean Close; Gloucestershire Gipsies.

The College celebrated its 150th anniversary by winning the first-ever Chesterton Cup, a 40-overs knockout competition instigated by G. H. Chesterton, President of Worcestershire CCC, and contested between eight schools in the Gloucestershire/Worcestershire/Monmouth area. In the final at New Road, Cheltenham won with a four off the last ball in reply to Monmouth's 186 for seven.

*Batting*—D. R. Hewson 19-5-679-99*-0-48.50; M. J. Cawdron 19-3-671-90-0-41.93; B. J. C. Lawrence 20-2-712-117*-1-39.55; A. C. J. Bridgwood 18-8-341-58*-0-34.10; M. E. Dalton-Morris 6-1-101-94*-0-20.20; C. L. Foster 13-4-177-31*-0-19.66; J. T. G. Westbrook 15-3-180-38*-0-15.00; *P. M. Evans 17-5-163-44-0-13.58.

*Bowling*—A. C. J. Bridgwood 56.2-12-224-10-2/29-22.40; B. J. C. Lawrence 220-49-652-28-5/50-23.28; M. J. Cawdron 282.4-71-773-32-6/23-24.15; C. L. T. Speed 167.2-24-585-23-5/18-25.43; P. W. Foster 229-52-623-24-6/42-25.95; D. R. Hewson 128-24-526-16-3/48-32.87.

## CHIGWELL SCHOOL

*Played 13: Won 5, Lost 0, Drawn 8*

Master i/c: D. N. Morrison        Cricket professional: F. Griffiths

*Wins v:* Romford Police XI; XL Club; Old Chigwellians; Pocklington; William Hulme's GS.

Having achieved a school record total of 292 for seven against Forest in 1990, the XI bettered it at the expense of Latymer in 1991, with 320 for five, to which J. F. Carpenter (97) and the left-handed D. J. Timpson contributed a second-wicket stand of 142. Carpenter and P. C. Harvey represented Essex Under-19, and I. Harvey played for Essex Under-17 and England Under-17.

*Batting*—P. C. Harvey 13-5-679-100*-1-84.87; I. Harvey 6-2-240-101-1-60.00; *J. F. Carpenter 12-1-367-97-0-33.36; G. Offen 12-0-335-61-0-27.91; D. J. Timpson 12-0-239-89-0-19.91; D. J. Goddard 10-1-102-30*-0-11.33.

*Bowling*—I. R. Mafti 69-14-186-12-4/37-15.50; J. F. Carpenter 222-52-584-33-5/56-17.69; I. Harvey 104.2-23-274-15-5/31-18.26; P. C. Harvey 173-58-394-18-5/13-21.88.

## CHRIST COLLEGE, BRECON

*Played 12: Won 2, Lost 3, Drawn 7. Abandoned 5*

Master i/c: C. W. Kleiser

*Wins v:* Belmont Abbey; King's, Worcester.

*Batting*—*M. E. Morris 10–1–308–76–0–34.22; L. A. Dovey 11–2–210–72–0–23.33; J. N. Davies 10–4–139–60*–0–23.16; A. L. P. Lewis 8–0–174–42–0–21.75; J. Digby 12–0–193–43–0–16.08.

*Bowling*—P. J. B. Davies 126.2–13–474–24–6/29–19.75; R. J. Strawbridge 107.5–26–340–12–4/21–28.33.

## CHRIST'S HOSPITAL

*Played 12: Won 8, Lost 1, Drawn 3*

Master i/c: R. C. Bond          Cricket professionals: G. R. J. Roope and P. J. Graves

*Wins v:* Worth; Caterham; Ardingly; Hurstpierpoint; Brighton; Whitgift; Sussex Martlets; Epsom.

Penetrative bowling resulted in opposing sides being dismissed nine times, a major factor in the XI's most successful season for decades. The one defeat was by Brighton, in the final of the Langdale Trophy.

*Batting*—*C. E. Igolen-Robinson 12–3–474–134–1–52.66; M. A. S. Lemon 6–3–103–50*–0–34.33; I. B. G. Bond 10–2–246–79–0–30.75; N. J. Atkinson 6–2–102–29*–0–25.50.

*Bowling*—R. A. S. Learmonth 133.3–43–271–33–7/26–8.21; R. Howard 63–16–185–15–6/25–12.33; A. J. Walker 115.4–29–300–21–5/31–14.28; M. A. S. Lemon 69.5–13–232–12–2/19–19.33.

## CLIFTON COLLEGE

*Played 17: Won 4, Lost 0, Drawn 12, Tied 1. Abandoned 2*

Master i/c: C. M. E. Colquhoun          Cricket professional: F. J. Andrew

*Wins v:* Cheltenham; Marlborough; Eastbourne; Old Cliftonians.

M. G. N. Windows, son of the Cambridge Blue, A. R. Windows, overcame the loss of five weeks owing to injury to score 615 runs at the impressive average of 123.00. He played for Gloucestershire Second XI, was a reserve for the England Under-18 team to Canada, and was selected for the England Under-19 tour of Pakistan. R. J. Kirtley, a sixteen-year-old fast bowler, looked an exciting prospect.

*Batting*—M. G. N. Windows 8–3–615–134*–2–123.00; G. H. J. Rees 10–2–460–147*–2–57.50; C. D. Bevan 10–2–268–95–0–33.50; J. R. A. Williams 14–1–388–81–0–29.84; R. G. B. Moffat 11–1–253–90–0–25.30; B. M. O. Gibbs 10–2–161–45*–0–20.12.

*Bowling*—R. J. Kirtley 201–59–475–45–7/33–10.55; J. Whitby-Coles 95–28–209–13–3/8–16.07; N. E. L. Howe 171–40–444–14–3/47–31.71.

## COLSTON'S SCHOOL

*Played 16: Won 3, Lost 4, Drawn 9. Abandoned 4*

Master i/c: M. P. B. Tayler

*Wins v:* King Edward's, Bath; Bristol Cathedral S.; Monkton Combe.

*Batting*—A. R. Nicholls 8–5–103–27*–0–34.33; I. J. Webb 15–2–405–83–0–31.15; R. J. Pandya 16–1–405–108–1–27.00; *L. A. Collins 15–0–350–54–0–23.33; P. A. Curtis 15–4–187–58*–0–17.00; M. J. Baldwin 14–4–147–32*–0–14.70; M. J. Sheedy 15–0–176–40–0–11.73.

*Bowling*—S. M. Shepherd 78.5–21–219–15–7/39–14.60; R. J. Pandya 150.2–21–489–27–4/23–18.11; R. I. Phillipson-Masters 56.1–6–207–11–5/43–18.81; S. W. Brown 244.2–47–776–37–6/42–20.97.

## COVENTRY SCHOOL, BABLAKE

*Played 13: Won 5, Lost 4, Drawn 4. Abandoned 2*

Master i/c: B. J. Sutton

*Wins v:* Wolverhampton GS; King Edward's, Five Ways; Handsworth GS; Lawrence Sheriff; King Henry VIII, Coventry.

*Batting*—M. A. Ward 10–4–378–103*–1–63.00; G. Dowall 13–4–482–131–1–53.55; A. Cronin 12–3–223–53–0–24.77; D. A. Hart 8–2–140–64*–0–23.33; *M. G. H. Sutton 9–0–209–50–0–23.22; R. Bull 7–0–110–57–0–15.71.

*Bowling*—J. Hart 93.5–35–184–22–6/24–8.36; J. Myton 93–24–238–17–5/15–14.00; M. G. H. Sutton 81.5–24–223–13–3/15–17.15.

## CRANBROOK SCHOOL

*Played 8: Won 3, Lost 2, Drawn 3. Abandoned 6*

Master i/c: A. J. Presnell

*Wins v:* Maidstone GS; Bethany; Ewell Castle.

*Batting*—C. Botsman 8–0–225–43–0–28.12; J. Barron 8–0–178–41–0–22.25; M. Taylor 7–0–138–37–0–19.71.

*Bowling*—C. Peskett 63–21–150–16–5/20–9.37; C. Botsman 78–24–210–19–5/16–11.05; J. Thompson 79–30–178–15–4/24–11.86.

## CRANLEIGH SCHOOL

*Played 16: Won 6, Lost 1, Drawn 9. Abandoned 2*

Master i/c: D. C. Williams

*Wins v:* Cryptics; Hurstpierpoint; Epsom; Brighton; Loretto; Bryanston.

H. C. Watkinson had an excellent season with both bat and ball; he bowled with genuine pace, despite some slow, wet wickets in May and June, and went on to represent Surrey in the Esso Under-19 Festival.

*Batting*—N. J. G. Read 14–6–258–51*–0–32.25; R. L. Johnson 10–1–278–61–0–30.88; B. R. Seal 13–7–165–38*–0–27.50; H. C. Watkinson 15–1–364–73–0–26.00; S. C. G. Copleston 16–2–343–56–0–24.50; G. R. Atkinson 11–1–159–41–0–15.90; I. Tabor 15–1–209–45–0–14.92.

*Bowling*—H. C. Watkinson 278–67–768–41–7/27–18.73; B. R. Seal 124.3–28–334–17–3/55–19.64; A. Kyle 188.1–53–493–18–4/10–27.38; G. R. Atkinson 134.4–32–382–11–2/4–34.72.

## DAME ALLAN'S SCHOOL

*Played 11: Won 6, Lost 3, Drawn 2. Abandoned 1*

Master i/c: J. A. Benn

*Wins v:* Northumberland CCC Club and Ground; King's School, Tynemouth; Morpeth HS; St Cuthbert's HS; Haydon Bridge HS; Old Boys' XI.

*Batting*—*P. J. Nicholson 10–3–361–72–0–51.57; M. J. Thompson 5–2–122–108*–1–40.66; T. P. Ditchburn 9–2–165–42*–0–23.57.

*Bowling*—M. J. Thompson 31.1–11–60–14–7/12–4.28; R. Black 59–19–182–12–4/19–15.16.

## DAUNTSEY'S SCHOOL

*Played 12: Won 6, Lost 2, Drawn 4. Abandoned 1*

Master i/c: D. C. R. Baker                    Cricket professional: P. Knowles

*Wins v:* Monkton Combe; Prior Park; Kingswood; King Edward's, Bath; XL Club; Staff XI.

*Batting*—*M. Whistler 9–5–197–65–0–49.25; I. Hardman 10–2–233–63–0–29.12; A. Field 8–2–136–34–0–22.66; S. Gilmour 11–1–195–64–0–19.50; M. Duncan 11–0–190–62–0–17.27.

*Bowling*—I. Hardman 28.4–5–83–11–5/39–7.54; D. Atkins 44.5–6–161–13–6/16–12.38; A. Darbyshire 85.4–17–251–17–4/9–14.76; A. Field 106.2–20–309–19–7/28–16.26.

## DEAN CLOSE SCHOOL

*Played 15: Won 3, Lost 2, Drawn 10*

Master i/c: C. M. Kenyon                    Cricket professional: S. Hansford

*Wins v:* Rendcomb; Magdalen College S.; Old Decanians.

*Batting*—M. Butler 13–2–323–63–0–29.36; A. H. Odell 14–2–348–74–0–29.00; *S. H. Odell 15–3–346–71–0–28.83; A. J. Negus 11–2–219–60*–0–24.33; B. M. Hyde 12–3–216–44–0–24.00; R. S. Gill 11–1–106–26–0–10.60.

*Bowling*—M. Butler 159–37–437–27–4/11–16.18; J. L. Watts 75.4–15–221–13–4/32–17.00; M. R. James 106.2–16–394–17–4/42–23.17; J. A. Simmonds 144.1–30–444–19–5/47–23.36.

## DENSTONE COLLEGE (BOYS)

*Played 19: Won 6, Lost 2, Drawn 11. Abandoned 3*

Master i/c: A. N. James

*Wins v:* Queen Mary's, Walsall; Worksop; Old Denstonians; Borden GS; MCC; Christchurch GS, Australia.

J. N. Snape was again outstanding, his 682 runs including three centuries, of which his 167 not out was the third-highest score for the College. He finished his career in the First XI, before going on to Durham University, with 2,485 runs at 65.39, an average 13 higher than the previous best, while his aggregate was just 52 runs short of A. J. Hignell's record – but was achieved in seventeen fewer innings. Snape also captained the England Under-18 side at the International Youth Tournament in Canada, played for Northamptonshire Second Eleven and was selected for the England Under-19 tour to Pakistan. The side's defeat by South African College High School was their first in 28 games.

*Batting*—*J. N. Snape 16–3–682–167*–3–52.46; T. J. Mason 16–3–381–78*–0–29.30; C. C. Tissainayagam 14–3–286–80*–0–26.00; T. O. Kemp 11–7–104–29*–0–26.00; P. J. Barnes 17–3–357–82–0–25.50; J. J. Mason 11–2–176–53*–0–19.55; A. N. Johnson 17–2–246–51–0–16.40; P. A. Handford 11–0–139–39–0–12.63.

*Bowling*—P. J. Barnes 187–51–460–30–6/26–15.33; J. N. Snape 183.2–52–551–34–4/41–16.20; N. A. Warr 166–36–421–20–8/28–21.05; C. C. Tissainayagam 145.2–21–465–22–7/44–21.13; T. J. Mason 143.1–40–315–14–3/34–22.50.

## DENSTONE COLLEGE (GIRLS)

*Played 10: Won 6, Lost 2, Drawn 2*

Mistress i/c: Miss J. R. Morris

*Wins v:* Ellesmere; Wrekin; Bromsgrove; Chase HS; Newcastle; Queen Elizabeth, Ashbourne.

*Batting*—E. L. Hoten 10–4–148–34*–0–24.66; *C. P. Sawyer 10–2–130–50*–0–16.25; A. L. Bennett 10–1–101–25*–0–11.22.

*Bowling*—E. C. Hawksley 59–11–147–27–5/14–5.44; C. P. Sawyer 78–10–161–26–5/14–6.19.

# DOUAI SCHOOL

*Played 10: Won 0, Lost 3, Drawn 7*

Master i/c: J. Shaw

*Batting*—E. J. A. Opia 10–1–210–69*–0–23.33; *N. J. A. Saw 10–0–221–59–0–22.10; R. J. Leach 10–0–211–70–0–21.10; M. E. Roddis 10–1–114–42–0–12.66.

*Bowling*—N. J. A. Saw 110–12–343–12–5/20–28.58; R. J. Leach 126–7–448–10–4/26–44.80.

# DOVER COLLEGE

*Played 11: Won 0, Lost 2, Drawn 9. Abandoned 4*

Master i/c: D. C. Butler

S. J. Schilder, one of a small band of Dovorians to score 1,000 runs for the XI, took his career aggregate to 1,338 in his final year.

*Batting*—*S. J. Schilder 9–2–295–72–0–42.14; A. B. Dandeh-N'Jie 9–1–165–43–0–20.62; A. S. Burrell 9–1–141–51*–0–17.62; M. D. Schilder 9–1–112–39–0–14.00.

*Bowling*—R. V. Price 123.3–29–377–21–4/32–17.95; A. B. Dandeh-N'Jie 54–9–208–11–5/37–18.90; D. A. Cruickshank 99.4–20–356–10–4/40–35.60.

# DOWNSIDE SCHOOL

*Played 11: Won 4, Lost 5, Drawn 2. Abandoned 3*

Master i/c: K. J. Burke                    Cricket professional: B. Bing

*Wins v*: XL Club; Prior Park; Downside Wanderers; Strathallan.

*Batting*—O. B. Ratcliffe 14–4–294–62–0–29.40; *B. P. N. Ramsay 10–2–221–76–0–27.62; M. F. Fitzgerald 12–2–271–81–0–27.10; M. R. Kennedy 14–0–285–41–0–20.35; M. J. Tory 12–0–225–76–0–18.75; T. V. E. Hansom 14–2–185–59–0–15.41; J. A. Wilson 9–2–106–40–0–15.14; B. M. Kennard 13–1–129–40–0–10.75.

*Bowling*—B. M. Kennard 73.1–9–288–15–5/21–19.20; G. J. Bell 125–25–425–19–5/49–22.36; M. F. Fitzgerald 157.3–35–500–22–4/62–22.72; O. B. Ratcliffe 117–23–366–14–3/58–26.14.

# DUKE OF YORK'S ROYAL MILITARY SCHOOL

*Played 9: Won 1, Lost 4, Drawn 4. Abandoned 7*

Master i/c: S. Salisbury                    Cricket professional: I. J. Hansen

*Win v*: St Augustine's.

*Batting*—*G. Kennett 8–1–155–76–0–22.14; M. Goodinson 9–0–179–52–0–19.88; M. Muir 9–0–134–35–0–14.88.

*Bowling*—G. Kennett 50.1–6–205–14–6/22–14.64; G. Stanley 105.3–24–311–15–4/19–20.73; J. Wilkinson 75.3–16–244–11–3/29–22.18.

# DULWICH COLLEGE

*Played 16: Won 7, Lost 2, Drawn 7. Abandoned 1*

Master i/c: F. R. F. Wilson          Cricket professionals: W. A. Smith and A. Ranson.

*Wins v*: Old Alleynians; Whitgift; MCC; Mill Hill; Strathallan; Downside; Dusters.

*Batting*—T. R. Sandars 6–2–152–77–0–38.00; *R. W. Scholar 11–2–223–61*–0–24.77; S. C. Davey 14–3–262–115*–1–23.81; W. R. Morley 12–1–258–64–0–23.45; P. D. S. Battley 12–4–174–72–0–21.75; W. E. S. Warrell 13–1–259–60–0–21.58; S. C. Teesdale 8–1–140–55*–0–20.00.

*Bowling*—P. J. Smith 205.2–68–442–30–6/25–14.73; K. K. Duodu 118.4–15–381–15–4/32–25.40; R. W. Scholar 92–14–334–10–3/55–33.40.

## DURHAM SCHOOL

*Played 16: Won 11, Lost 1, Drawn 3, Tied 1*

Master i/c: N. J. Willings                    Cricket professional: M. Hirsch

*Wins v:* Barnard Castle; Hatfield C.; Dame Allan's; Ampleforth; Sedbergh; Pocklington; Giggleswick; Durham Pilgrims; Yarm S.; Old Dunelmians; Manchester GS.

Durham's eleven wins were a season's best, and the winning trend was maintained by the Under-15 side, who shared the Lord's Taverners Trophy with Millfield after poor weather had prevented the final being played. The XI owed much to the Weston brothers, whose many achievements included an opening partnership of 190 against Pocklington. The elder, W. P. C. Weston, hit two hundreds and six fifties in nine innings for the school and went on to make his first-class début for Worcestershire at the end of the season. In between, he opened the batting for England Under-19 against Australia Under-19, having originally been selected as a fast bowler, and scored 93 in the First "Test" and 146 in the third; he was subsequently chosen to captain the England Under-19 side to Pakistan. R. M. S. Weston hit three hundreds for the XI, before captaining England Under-16 against the touring Zimbabwe Under-17 side, against whom he also played for England Under-17. Having made 101 not out at the Oxford Festival and played for MCC Schools v NAYC, he represented English Schools Under-19 v Scotland and Wales, scoring 114 not out against Wales. In addition, at fifteen he was the youngest to play for Durham in the Minor Counties Championship when he made his début for the county against Hertfordshire in May.

*Batting*—*W. P. C. Weston 13–3–794–136–2–72.18; R. M. S. Weston 14–3–700–111*–3–63.63; J. B. Windows 5–2–137–75–0–45.66; P. McCutcheon 10–2–249–61–0–31.12; D. Parkin 9–4–130–32*–0–26.00; J. M. W. Taylor 13–1–293–109–1–24.41.

*Bowling*—W. P. C. Weston 128.5–24–300–30–5/39–10.00; P. McCutcheon 74–26–170–14–6/16–12.14; N. C. F. Taylor 152.3–54–322–26–4/6–12.38; N. W. Darling 140.5–38–349–22–4/51–15.86.

## EASTBOURNE COLLEGE

*Played 17: Won 5, Lost 5, Drawn 7*

Master i/c: N. L. Wheeler                    Cricket professional: A. E. James

*Wins v:* Lancing; King's, Canterbury; MCC; Old Eastbournians; Bradfield.

*Batting*—W. R. Green 16–3–498–58*–0–38.30; T. J. W. Parker 13–1–335–91–0–27.91; C. D. Grove 10–5–139–40–0–27.80; P. J. Hillman 14–1–278–110–1–21.38; P. F. Divito 14–0–280–70–0–20.00; *B. H. Miller 15–1–252–49–0–18.00; D. C. Richards 13–3–169–38–0–16.90.

*Bowling*—M. C. G. Dennis 74–21–169–10–4/40–16.90; D. A. Brown 215–52–656–35–6/34–18.74; T. C. Russell 203.2–70–571–27–3/31–21.14; C. D. Grove 77–16–327–14–5/39–23.35; P. J. Hillman 97–17–373–14–6/12–26.64.

# THE EDINBURGH ACADEMY

*Played 21: Won 1, Lost 18, Drawn 2*

Master i/c: G. R. Bowe                      Cricket professional: N. O. Perry

*Win v:* Holy Cross.

*Batting*—*J. M. Anderson 21–1–320–55–0–16.00; M. G. Ridge 11–1–128–42–0–12.80; D. I. S. Cowper 20–2–217–42–0–12.05; R. E. Boyd 21–1–238–67–0–11.90; S. E. McGlynn 16–2–128–21–0–9.14; P. D. Anderson 21–1–170–43*–0–8.50; J. A. K. Macleod 20–1–151–24–0–7.94.

*Bowling*—D. I. S. Cowper 47.4–3–235–14–5/35–16.78; J. M. Anderson 271–52–855–42–6/61–20.35; J. A. K. Macleod 189–49–586–25–4/10–23.44; N. C. A. Moule 240.5–55–734–30–5/44–24.46.

# ELIZABETH COLLEGE, GUERNSEY

*Played 22: Won 4, Lost 3, Drawn 15*

Master i/c: M. E. Kinder

*Wins v:* Occasionals CC (London); Reed's; Guernsey Island CC; Police CC.

T. Hollyer-Hill's 73 against Victoria College was a particular highlight for the XI, of which he was captain, for he played several games knowing of a serious illness.

*Batting*—*T. Hollyer-Hill 10–4–288–73–0–48.00; A. Biggins 9–1–201–66–0–25.12; P. le Ray 8–1–147–42–0–21.00; D. B. L. Mackay 17–1–325–69–0–20.31; T. Carey 11–4–121–25*–0–17.28; J. Sherbourne 15–3–187–41–0–15.58; S. P. Noyon 16–2–192–56*–0–13.71; M. Veillaro 12–0–160–30–0–13.33.

*Bowling*—M. Smith 228.1–47–631–33–6/31–19.12; G. Bent 141–32–479–25–5/34–19.16; A. Mitchell 197.3–35–709–30–5/43–23.63.

# ELLESMERE COLLEGE

*Played 17: Won 10, Lost 0, Drawn 7. Abandoned 1*

Master i/c: E. Marsh                      Cricket professional: R. G. Mapp

*Wins v:* Oswestry S.; Birkenhead; Rydal; Foyle and Londonderry C.; Old Ellesmerians; Hurstpierpoint; Bloxham; Frankton CC; Mold CC; Gentlemen of Shropshire.

J. G. Slater, winner of the *Daily Telegraph* Under-19 bowling award, took a school record of 52 wickets at 8.78 and went on to play for Shropshire. An unbroken opening stand of 216 against Oswestry was compiled by R. C. Carew and the sixteen-year-old M. E. Gillison who passed 600 runs in his first season.

*Batting*—M. E. Gillison 16–4–619–102*–1–51.58; R. C. Carew 17–3–379–101*–1–27.07; *J. G. Slater 13–6–186–65*–0–26.57; G. N. Phillips 14–2–309–62–0–25.75; S. R. Montgomery 14–0–352–70–0–25.14; R. M. Bruce-Payne 15–2–296–41–0–22.76; R. J. Slater 10–1–131–37–0–14.55.

*Bowling*—J. G. Slater 209–57–457–52–6/33–8.78; G. N. Phillips 130–45–279–29–4/20–9.62; M. J. Noakes 143–43–322–22–4/47–14.63; D. C. Gervis 197–48–508–30–4/38–16.93.

# ELTHAM COLLEGE

*Played 22: Won 9, Lost 2, Drawn 11*

Masters i/c: B. M. Withecombe and P. McCartney                      Cricket professional: R. Winup

*Wins v:* Emanuel; St Dunstan's; Gravesend GS; Judd GS; Harvey GS; Old Elthamians (twice); Alexandra Exiles; Mottingham CC.

The College won the Under-19 Kent Cup, with a 66-run victory over Harvey GS in the final.

*Batting*—J. M. Ramsey 20–1–829–99–0–43.63; K. M. Morrell 19–2–560–100*–1–32.94; S. B. Dissanayake 14–4–316–50–0–31.60; S. Baksh 16–5–294–48–0–26.72; F. Kavina 19–0–453–93–0–23.84; K. Shanmuganathan 16–4–223–90–0–18.58; N. R. Wellard 12–3–143–54–0–15.88; G. B. Tibbs 19–3–208–35–0–13.00.

*Bowling*—J. M. Ramsey 248–68–646–47–5/12–13.74; J. M. Arber 52–12–182–10–5/18–18.20; S. B. Dissanayake 87.2–17–278–15–6/56–18.53; N. R. Wellard 144.5–27–412–20–4/10–20.60; K. M. Morrell 182.5–41–544–26–4/51–20.92; F. Kavina 72–1–360–15–4/11–24.00; G. B. Tibbs 70–6–343–10–3/29–34.30.

## ENFIELD GRAMMAR SCHOOL

*Played 18: Won 1, Lost 6, Drawn 11. Abandoned 4*

Master i/c: J. J. Conroy.

*Win v:* Dr Challoner's.

*Batting*—M. Stevens 17–4–384–63*–0–29.53; E. Morris 17–4–270–51–0–20.76; D. Alleyne 17–0–343–95–0–20.17; C. Browne 11–1–200–74*–0–20.00; N. Martin 9–2–102–33*–0–14.57; L. Beskeen 12–0–155–30–0–12.91; *I. Cully 15–2–129–28–0–9.92.

*Bowling*—M. Stevens 195.3–44–517–37–5/14–13.97; J. Downing 51–8–162–10–4/24–16.20; L. Beskeen 58–9–254–12–4/65–21.16; R. Hore 117–18–404–12–3/33–33.66.

## EPSOM COLLEGE

*Played 13: Won 5, Lost 5, Drawn 3*

Master i/c: M. D. Hobbs

*Wins v:* King's School, Canterbury; MCC; Dulwich; Lancing; Common Room XI.

I. R. Harris returned nine for 23 against Free Foresters, and M. D. G. Day provided another highlight when he carried his bat for 103 against Dulwich.

*Batting*—N. J. Saunders-Griffiths 13–1–454–83–0–37.83; M. D. G. Day 14–1–401–103*–1–30.84; P. E. Roche 6–1–152–71*–0–30.40; *J. C. Harris 13–0–322–79–0–24.76; C. E. Bowden 9–1–158–56–0–19.75; S. J. Head 13–3–175–47*–0–17.50; J. A. Shattock 13–0–191–51–0–14.69.

*Bowling*—P. E. Roche 61.5–12–197–19–6/20–10.36; D. D. J. Edwards 115–42–289–20–4/32–14.45; J. D. Bushell 68–13–219–12–6/35–18.25; I. R. Harris 167.4–34–491–26–9/23–18.88; N. J. Caffarate 89.5–10–398–10–3/59–39.80.

## ETON COLLEGE

*Played 15: Won 9, Lost 1, Drawn 5*

Master i/c: J. A. Claughton        Cricket professional: J. M. Rice

*Wins v:* I Zingari; St Edward's, Oxford; Bradfield; Wellington C.; Northamptonshire CA U-19; Harrow; Winchester; Shrewsbury; Radley.

The XI's only defeat was at the hands of the Antipodeans – an Australian touring side selected from eight New South Wales schools – who won the 55-overs Silk Trophy, hosted in 1991 by Eton. The College were thus unbeaten by English sides, and were particularly satisfied to number among their nine victories that over Harrow at Lord's, winning there in consecutive seasons for the first time in 60 years. The side owed much to the captain and slow left-arm bowler, J. M. S. Whittington, who went on to play for MCC Schools, English Schools and Middlesex Second XI. With 42 wickets, including eight for 13 against Wellington College, he took to 91 his total during two years in the XI.

*Batting*—G. L. Dunning 14–3–358–78*–0–32.54; J. J. S. Larken 10–1–278–71–0–30.88; R. M. Wagg 6–0–162–78–0–27.00; R. J. M. Thomas 12–3–227–63*–0–25.22; W. R. G. Sellar 11–2–221–61–0–24.55; S. C. E. Strickland 12–2–169–36–0–16.90; P. G. Morgan 10–1–129–45–0–14.33.

*Bowling*—*J. M. S. Whittington 232.3–91–373–42–8/13–8.88; B. K. Ssennyamantono 162.3–56–311–24–5/37–12.95; G. H. B. Lewis 206.2–63–459–34–5/16–13.50; E. J. M. Amies 111–33–223–15–4/33–14.86.

## EXETER SCHOOL

*Played 18: Won 6, Lost 2, Drawn 10*

Master i/c: M. C. Wilcock

*Wins v:* Exeter St James CC; Allhallows; Exeter C.; Wellington S.; Herefordshire CA U-16; Hereford Cathedral S.

The Under-16 player, P. B. Hughes, was outstanding with the bat in one of the best Exeter XIs in recent years.

*Batting*—P. B. Hughes 17–4–857–149*–3–65.92; O. F. A. le Fleming 13–2–318–63–0–28.90; *M. W. Evans 15–2–340–60*–0–26.15; M. J. Perring 16–3–338–59–0–26.00; M. D. Keylock 10–3–159–45–0–22.71; J. J. B. Lawford 7–2–102–56–0–20.40; J. D. Evennett 10–1–175–40–0–19.44; H. S. V. Thomas 15–1–215–45–0–15.35.

*Bowling*—O. F. A. le Fleming 128–32–310–22–5/18–14.09; M. D. Keylock 122–30–335–22–4/25–15.22; T. P. Quartley 198.2–47–481–30–5/44–16.03; M. J. Perring 56–10–192–10–5/14–19.20; N. A. Padget 110–22–392–17–4/6–23.05; J. R. Price 117–16–422–15–4/39–28.13.

## FELSTED SCHOOL

*Played 16: Won 2, Lost 1, Drawn 13. Abandoned 5*

Master i/c: A. N. Grierson Rickford　　　　　　　Cricket professional: G. Barker

*Wins v:* Christchurch GS, Australia; Gentlemen of Essex.

*Batting*—A. C. M. Woods 15–1–649–109–2–46.35; M. J. S. Martin 14–3–425–100*–1–38.63; *M. J. Crisp 15–2–373–92–0–28.69; W. C. C. Cooper 13–0–348–95–0–26.76; R. D. Harvard-Davies 7–0–182–60–0–26.00; M. J. Slater 11–3–189–41*–0–23.62; J. D. G. Goodwin 8–0–115–32–0–14.37.

*Bowling*—M. J. S. Martin 111–25–346–18–4/18–19.22; A. C. M. Woods 116–19–401–20–5/30–20.05; G. J. A. Goodwin 124–41–325–15–4/18–21.66; M. G. Mixer 166–33–536–16–3/15–33.50; A. J. Butler 105–18–347–10–3/36–34.70.

## FETTES COLLEGE

*Played 15: Won 4, Lost 7, Drawn 4*

Master i/c: C. H. Carruthers　　　　　　　Cricket professional: J. van Geloven

*Wins v:* George Watson's; Edinburgh Acad.; Headmaster's XI; The Leys.

For their first victory over The Edinburgh Academy since 1971, the College were indebted to their opening batsman, R. A. N. R. Llewellyn, who made an unbeaten 139 in their total of 189 for nine.

*Batting*—R. A. N. R. Llewellyn 15–1–375–139*–1–26.78; So. Zindani 16–0–379–74–0–23.68; A. F. Zulfiqar 16–1–313–64*–0–20.86; Sh. Zindani 15–3–244–44–0–20.33; D. C. A. Thain 14–6–109–24*–0–13.62; C. D. Mayo 11–0–147–58–0–13.36; A. J. S. Kennedy 14–1–155–76*–0–11.92; M. J. Neville 16–1–146–23–0–9.73.

*Bowling*—J. G. M. Burns 182.3–63–389–26–4/31–14.96; So. Zindani 92.4–25–203–11–3/26–18.45; D. C. A. Thain 194.1–38–723–35–6/46–20.65; J. D. Lamb 98.3–17–338–11–4/53–30.72.

## FOREST SCHOOL

*Played 14: Won 3, Lost 3, Drawn 8. Abandoned 3*

Master i/c: S. Turner

*Wins v:* Bancroft's; Essex U-16; Ilford CHS.

*Batting*—D. Pratt 11-3-317-75*-0-39.62; J. Moore 11-0-233-48-0-21.18; P. Alexander 10-0-209-58-0-20.90; K. Oram 9-1-149-39-0-18.62; Py. Sharma 9-0-103-25-0-11.44.

*Bowling*—J. Dwyer 126-32-357-23-6/49-15.52; A. Hashmi 78-19-198-10-3/25-19.80; D. Pratt 128.4-29-385-17-3/45-22.64.

## FOYLE AND LONDONDERRY COLLEGE

*Played 16: Won 6, Lost 7, Drawn 3*

Masters i/c: G. R. McCarter and I. McCracken

*Wins v:* Royal S., Dungannon; Armagh CFE; Limavady GS; Royal S., Armagh; Ballymena Acad.; Coleraine AI.

*Batting*—*A. Brown 13-2-381-77-0-34.63; C. Donaghy 11-1-298-89-0-29.80; J. Torrens 14-1-185-56*-0-14.23; S. Craig 12-1-120-25-0-10.90; A. Cooke 14-0-146-41-0-10.42; M. McAuley 13-2-104-46*-0-9.45; A. Henderson 14-2-112-38-0-9.33.

*Bowling*—S. Craig 130.1-29-335-36-7/37-9.30; B. Galbraith 60-19-131-13-3/13-10.07; S. Lapsley 68.3-12-223-20-6/20-11.15; A. Cooke 103.6-16-341-26-3/6-13.11; J. Torrens 144.2-42-383-26-4/14-14.73.

## FRAMLINGHAM COLLEGE

*Played 14: Won 6, Lost 3, Drawn 5. Abandoned 2*

Master i/c: P. J. Hayes                    Cricket professional: C. Rutterford

*Wins v:* St Joseph's, Ipswich; Brentwood; Old Framlinghamians; Royal Anglian Regiment; Berkhamsted; Kimbolton.

*Batting*—*W. J. Earl 13-1-562-100-1-46.83; J. R. Menzies 12-2-307-109-1-30.70; J. A. Newton 12-2-292-72*-0-29.20; R. I. Roberts 12-1-307-75*-0-27.90; A. P. Cowan 11-4-189-42-0-27.00; D. R. Wilson 9-3-126-38-0-21.00; D. M. Vipond 8-2-107-52*-0-17.83; B. N. Chamberlain 8-0-106-53-0-13.25.

*Bowling*—A. P. Cowan 190.3-42-499-30-5/40-16.63; W. J. Earl 82-10-322-13-5/90-24.76; B. N. Chamberlain 90.4-14-307-12-5/26-25.58; D. R. Wilson 84-10-362-12-2/21-30.16; S. H. Cartwright 122.5-18-413-13-3/20-31.76.

## THE GLASGOW ACADEMY

*Played 10: Won 3, Lost 1, Drawn 6*

Master i/c: D. N. Barrett                    Cricket professional: B. M. W. Patterson

*Wins v:* Edinburgh Acad.; XL Club; Keil S.

J. M. Gayfer's unbeaten 103 was the first hundred for the XI in 35 years and the highest score for 40; it was matched as a highlight of the season by D. G. Gourlay's nine for 9 in his side's victory over The Edinburgh Academy. D. R. Lockhart was selected to keep wicket for the Glasgow District League senior side against the touring Pakistani All Stars.

*Batting*—J. M. Gayfer 9-1-276-103*-1-34.50; S. C. Matthews 10-2-244-59-0-30.50; D. R. Lockhart 9-3-159-45-0-26.50; J. M. Graham 8-0-106-37-0-13.25.

*Bowling*—*D. G. Gourlay 130.5-31-337-34-9/9-9.91; J. M. Gayfer 121.2-32-253-20-5/11-12.65; M. J. A. Cassidy 65-12-196-10-2/11-19.60.

## GLENALMOND

*Played 11: Won 5, Lost 1, Drawn 5. Abandoned 2*

Master i/c: A. J. N. James

*Wins v:* Wayfarers; Fettes; Edinburgh Acad.; Loretto; Merchiston Castle.

Unbeaten by schools, and never bowled out by any of its opponents, the XI was considered one of Glenalmond's strongest on record. C. J. C. Breese, wicket-keeper and the side's leading batsman, proved an inspirational captain of a side which fielded to a high standard in support of a varied attack.

*Batting*—*C. J. C. Breese 12–1–429–93–0–39.00; C. J. Jack 12–3–346–62*–0–38.44; G. J. N. Nardini 12–4–291–50*–0–36.37; S. C. Scott-Elliot 12–0–421–104–1–35.08; J. D. Thomson 12–1–238–60*–0–21.63; J. I. M. Gully 8–1–140–60–0–20.00; E. R. Lindsay 7–0–139–67–0–19.85.

*Bowling*—S. C. Scott-Elliot 101.2–21–302–21–5/28–14.38; A. R. L. Wager 141.4–31–419–26–7/37–16.11; J. I. M. Gully 171–54–438–22–6/26–19.90; J. A. Buchanan 120–29–366–13–2/15–28.15.

## GORDONSTOUN SCHOOL

*Played 9: Won 5, Lost 4, Drawn 0*

Master i/c: C. J. Barton

*Wins v:* R. S. Mellis's XI; Old Gordonstounians; Headmaster's XI; Robert Gordon's C.; Dundee HS.

*Batting*—G. N. E. Brown 9–1–258–96–0–32.25; J. D. Cave 6–1–117–38*–0–23.40; A. J. E. Clark 9–0–183–58–0–20.33; S. A. B. MacDonald 8–0–138–57–0–17.25; S. A. Walton 9–1–135–41–0–16.87.

*Bowling*—S. A. Shraeo 51.2–9–170–15–4/11–11.33; B. Clarke 94–20–219–18–5/28–12.16; R. S. Larkman 51–12–264–20–7/43–13.20.

## GRENVILLE COLLEGE

*Played 10: Won 3, Lost 2, Drawn 5*

Master i/c: C. R. Beechey

*Wins v:* Gremlins; Kelly C.; West Buckland.

*Batting*—J. Billington 10–1–165–57–0–18.33; T. Greer 9–2–117–30–0–16.71; J. P. Eyer 10–0–145–43–0–14.50; C. J. Walker 7–0–101–34–0–14.42.

*Bowling*—R. Hann 45–5–221–14–4/33–15.78; J. P. Eyer 87–8–349–21–5/44–16.61; J. Billington 49–6–206–11–4/36–18.72.

## GRESHAM'S SCHOOL

*Played 16: Won 4, Lost 3, Drawn 9. Abandoned 2*

Master i/c: A. M. Ponder

*Wins v:* Bromsgrove; Oakham; Wymondham; Royal Anglian Regiment.

D. A. Jackson, a fifth-former, set a school record of 40 wickets with his accurate left-arm spin bowling.

*Batting*—K. S. C. Tuck 16–4–511–100–1–42.58; N. M. Park 14–6–269–42*–0–33.62; *P. D. Holliday 17–1–472–87–0–29.50; A. J. Ward 12–4–220–61–0–27.50; M. V. A. Robins 6–1–136–72–0–27.20; H. T. Semple 15–3–252–46*–0–21.00; K. H. I. Crampsie 7–0–110–39–0–15.71.

Bowling—D. A. Jackson 199–44–690–40–6/55–17.25; B. J. Threlfall 90.5–19–298–13–3/28–22.92; A. Iacovides 98.3–21–302–13–3/12–23.23; N. Coman 179.3–43–540–23–4/14–23.47; A. J. Ward 107.4–10–396–16–3/12–24.75.

## HABERDASHERS' ASKE'S SCHOOL, ELSTREE

*Played 14: Won 8, Lost 1, Drawn 5. Abandoned 3*

Master i/c: N. G. Folland

*Wins v:* Watford GS; XL Club; UCS; Gentlemen of Hertfordshire; Merchant Taylors', Northwood; Staff XI; Colonel Fraser Bird's XI; Exmouth CC.

The brothers M. I. and R. S. Yeabsley dominated with both bat and ball, the younger, R. S. Yeabsley, going on to play for English Schools and Middlesex Second XI. Sleet and hail in the first game of the season, against Forest School, interrupted play for half an hour, during which time the square became completely white.

*Batting*—*R. S. Yeabsley 13–5–394–81*–0–49.25; G. I. Smart 8–4–172–50–0–43.00; S. V. Arumugam 13–4–339–84*–0–37.66; M. I. Yeabsley 14–0–407–98–0–29.07; C. V. Harris 13–1–348–92–0–29.00.

*Bowling*—C. V. Harris 116.2–34–348–23–8/90–15.13; R. S. Yeabsley 187.1–53–480–29–5/37–16.55; M. I. Yeabsley 173–54–440–24–4/29–18.33; J. A. Cameron 135.2–26–350–18–4/26–19.44.

## HAILEYBURY

*Played 16: Won 4, Lost 0, Drawn 12*

Master i/c: M. S. Seymour                    Cricket professional: P. M. Ellis

*Wins v:* Tonbridge; Uppingham; Oundle; Gentlemen of Hertfordshire.

N. P. Broughton, the 1991 Nomad Scholar, and P. Bhatia, an exchange student from the Doon School, India, frequently caught the eye in a mature XI whose season is highlighted in the introduction to this section. The match against Tonbridge coincided with the opening of Haileybury's refurbished pavilion.

*Batting*—P. Bhatia 16–5–543–80*–0–49.36; B. M. Todd 9–5–155–48*–0–38.75; N. W. Oakden 15–0–452–83–0–30.13; N. P. Broughton 15–3–346–60*–0–28.83; T. C. Roundell 16–1–424–97–0–28.26; S. J. Ansell 14–1–285–66–0–21.92.

*Bowling*—N. P. Broughton 234–66–488–34–6/18–14.35; J. W. Holding 120–22–364–16–4/14–22.75; *R. G. A. Gunn 203–69–578–22–4/15–26.27; P. Bhatia 156–30–358–10–2/15–35.80.

## HAMPTON SCHOOL

*Played 19: Won 9, Lost 5, Drawn 5. Abandoned 4*

Master i/c: A. J. Cook                    Cricket professional: P. Farbrace

*Wins v:* RGS, High Wycombe; Enfield; Reigate; Latymer; RGS, Guildford; Reed's; Watford GS; Kongonis CC, Kenya; Mombasa Sports Club, Kenya.

A five-match tour of Kenya provided a worthy finale to an enjoyable season which is mentioned in more detail in the introduction to this section.

*Batting*—S. C. Janes 16–2–522–117–1–37.28; M. E. Hurles 15–0–529–102–1–35.26; N. J. Wright 4–0–120–84–0–30.00; S. E. J. Weller 14–6–220–42–0–27.50; J. Dave 15–0–369–59–0–24.60; J. W. J. Reid 18–0–357–50–0–19.83; E. D. Parker 17–1–312–73–0–19.50; M. H. Chalavatzis 8–1–111–41–0–15.85; N. A. Taylor 13–3–154–27–0–15.40.

*Bowling*—*S. R. Caruana 191.1–58–529–33–7/54–16.03; J. A. Scowen 137.5–25–451–23–4/21–19.60; J. E. Saunders 171–45–597–30–6/12–19.90; A. C. King 100–25–319–12–3/14–26.58.

# HARROW SCHOOL

*Played 13: Won 5, Lost 1, Drawn 7. Abandoned 3*

Master i/c: W. Snowden

Cricket professional: R. K. Sethi

*Wins v:* Bradfield; Malvern; Tonbridge; Harrow Wanderers; I Zingari.

*Batting*—C. E. Williams 13–2–376–94\*–0–34.18; \*S. M. Guillebaud 13–3–340–53–0–34.00; C. G. Hill 13–1–393–84–0–32.75; J. G. Fleming 5–1–104–45\*–0–26.00; R. J. Preece 11–2–196–76\*–0–21.77; M. A. Holyoake 10–1–179–55–0–19.88; C. B. J. Danby 11–1–173–32\*–0–17.30.

*Bowling*—J. G. Fleming 92.2–21–221–18–4/17–12.27; M. M. J. Hawkins 207.1–52–460–32–5/50–14.37; R. A. H. Peasgood 103.1–16–308–20–6/54–15.40; R. E. Sexton 197.5–54–474–17–5/62–27.88.

# THE HARVEY GRAMMAR SCHOOL

*Played 21: Won 11, Lost 3, Drawn 7*

Master i/c: P. J. Harding

*Wins v:* Kent C.; Oakwood Park GS; Howard GS; Norton Knatchbull S.; Chatham GS (twice); Sir Roger Manwood's GS; Folkestone CC; Old Harveians; Wootton Courtenay CC; Roadwater CC.

For the XI, runners-up in the Kent Under-19 Cup, S. F. Hobbs scored a post-war best of 141 not out, against Folkestone CC.

*Batting*—M. R. Fletcher 14–2–644–105\*–2–53.66; \*S. F. Hobbs 20–6–549–141\*–1–39.21; G. N. Thompson 17–2–393–78\*–0–26.20; S. Norman 17–0–337–53–0–19.82; R. J. N. Davis 12–3–161–59\*–0–17.88; D. Carney 16–1–241–46\*–0–16.06.

*Bowling*—M. R. Fletcher 43–6–114–14–3/6–8.14; R. J. N. Davis 239.1–56–680–49–6/28–13.87; S. G. Rees 64.3–19–162–11–4/20–14.72; S. Norman 166–45–454–29–4/20–15.65; J. Griggs 50–6–190–10–4/26–19.00.

# HEREFORD CATHEDRAL SCHOOL

*Played 12: Won 1, Lost 5, Drawn 6. Abandoned 2*

Master i/c: A. H. Connop

*Win v:* Chairman's XI.

*Batting*—\*E. Symonds 11–0–321–70–0–29.18; N. Priday 12–0–344–86–0–28.66; L. James 7–0–185–61–0–26.42; B. Plane 11–5–111–38\*–0–18.50; C. Banks 8–0–139–39–0–17.37; S. Albright 9–0–146–40–0–16.22.

*Bowling*—B. Plane 161–38–547–26–4/40–21.03; N. Foster 68.1–6–299–11–5/60–27.18; D. Kings 105.5–10–409–14–3/60–29.21.

# HIGHGATE SCHOOL

*Played 11: Won 4, Lost 1, Drawn 6*

Master i/c: C. J. Davies

Cricket professional: R. E. O. Jones

*Wins v:* Merchant Taylors', Northwood; Abingdon; Westminster; Mill Hill.

Undefeated by schools for the first time since 1971, Highgate beat Mill Hill by 218 runs – the highest margin for many years. In that match E. N. Gladwin, a fourth-former, scored 139, whereupon his elder brother, T. J. Gladwin, returned five for 14, including a hat-trick.

*Batting*—M. Robinson 9–3–266–55–0–44.33; E. N. Gladwin 8–0–322–139–1–40.25; D. Davis 9–4–158–44–0–31.60; T. J. Gladwin 11–0–284–58–0–25.81; M. A. Shams 11–0–251–77–0–22.81; R. Tillett 9–3–133–52\*–0–22.16.

*Bowling*—T. J. Gladwin 188.2–56–616–39–5/13–15.79; *M. W. Tudor 44.1–10–170–10–3/9–17.00; D. Davis 68–11–205–11–5/41–18.63; R. Parbhoo 112.1–29–336–14–4/14–24.00.

## HURSTPIERPOINT COLLEGE

*Played 16: Won 6, Lost 3, Drawn 7. Abandoned 3*

Master i/c: M. E. Allbrook          Cricket professional: D. J. Semmence

*Wins v:* Seaford (twice); Reigate; Lancing; OJS; Bloxham.

The leading all-rounder, M. J. Semmence, represented English Schools.

*Batting*—*M. J. Semmence 15–5–458–73*–0–45.80; P. T. Wicker 15–2–527–131–1–40.53; G. W. Budibent 15–1–308–62*–0–22.00; C. K. Bates 13–1–263–38–0–21.91; S. L. Lilly 13–4–170–27–0–18.88; J. Bates 10–2–144–41*–0–18.00.

*Bowling*—P. T. Wicker 155.4–58–297–23–5/30–12.91; S. R. J. Hall 170.3–43–407–27–5/24–15.07; M. J. Semmence 155.1–43–363–24–4/22–15.12; J. Bates 78–14–304–13–5/21–23.38.

## IPSWICH SCHOOL

*Played 16: Won 6, Lost 2, Drawn 8*

Master i/c: P. M. Rees          Cricket professional: R. E. East

*Wins v:* Suffolk Club and Ground; Woodbridge; Framlingham; Gentlemen of Suffolk; Edinburgh Acad.; Arnold.

G. A. Khan, a wristy batsman with shots all round the wicket, was outstanding with 1,300 in schools and representative cricket, the second-highest aggregate by a schoolboy in 1991. His aggregate of 1,006 for the school was certainly a post-war best, and was considered likely to be the highest ever. He broke another school record with five centuries: 176 not out in the first game of the season against a strong Suffolk Club and Ground side, 152 against Gresham's, 150 against Framlingham, 133 against Christchurch College, Perth, Australia and 100 against St Joseph's, Ipswich. His three innings of 150 or more were also a first for the XI. In addition to his achievements with the bat, his leg-breaks and googlies earned him a hat-trick against Royal GS, Colchester. He played for Suffolk Under-19 and Essex Second XI, and is expected to be available for the XI again in 1992. The Under-17 side reached the final of the Barclays Cup, losing to Birkenhead, and in a younger age-group J. Collins took all ten wickets for 15 as Orwell Park were bowled out for 35.

*Batting*—G. A. Khan 15–3–1,006–176*–5–83.83; O. Magnus 13–3–432–119–1–43.20; J. Douglas 4–1–117–55–0–39.00; M. Holland 12–4–215–55–0–26.87; G. Warrington 14–1–288–101*–1–22.15; R. Catley 7–1–126–62–0–21.00; J. Bacon 13–2–142–46–0–12.90.

*Bowling*—G. A. Khan 93–20–166–17–5/55–9.76; E. Hughes 134.4–34–287–21–5/7–13.66; C. Earley 131–33–333–21–4/6–15.85; S. Gladwell 137–29–405–19–4/71–21.31.

## KELLY COLLEGE

*Played 12: Won 2, Lost 4, Drawn 6. Abandoned 2*

Master i/c: G. C. L. Cooper

*Wins v:* XL Club; Allhallows.

*Batting*—D. S. Edwards 12–2–262–72*–0–26.20; A. M. Dakin 11–4–159–67*–0–22.71; G. E. M. Baber 11–1–198–52–0–19.80; J. R. Hurst 10–1–138–45*–0–15.33; *J. J. Wood 8–0–102–44–0–12.75; A. Chung 11–1–121–42–0–12.10; P. W. H. Spry 11–1–114–36*–0–11.40.

*Bowling*—J. M. Rowan 86–13–267–11–3/30–24.27; J. J. Wood 135.4–22–489–19–3/52–25.73.

## KIMBOLTON SCHOOL

*Played 19: Won 1, Lost 4, Drawn 14*

Master i/c: R. P. Merriman                    Cricket professional: M. E. Latham

*Win v:* Berkhamsted.

*Batting*—C. Mear 19–1–458–63–0–25.44; G. Sowter 16–2–243–58*–0–17.35; R. Butler 14–2–192–40*–0–16.00; D. Dattagupta 14–3–170–40–0–15.45; D. Harris 12–1–151–39–0–13.72; *S. G. Wood 18–0–233–48–0–12.94; T. Littlewood 12–3–106–40–0–11.77.

*Bowling*—T. Littlewood 189.4–35–536–26–5/27–20.61; G. R. Wardle 116.2–16–507–22–5/56–23.04; A. Crowe 72–9–303–12–7/31–25.25; R. Butler 122–23–420–16–4/50–26.25; T. J. McCreadie 83.3–11–335–10–2/16–33.50.

## KING EDWARD VI COLLEGE, STOURBRIDGE

*Played 12: Won 2, Lost 2, Drawn 8. Abandoned 5*

Masters i/c: D. E. D. Campbell and M. L. Ryan

*Wins v:* King Edward's, Birmingham; Hagley S.

The wicket-keeper, N. J. Workman, played in that capacity for English Schools – against Scotland and the Australian Under-19 side – MCC Schools v NAYC and NCA Young Cricketers v Combined Services.

*Batting*—J. R. T. Burn 9–5–100–47*–0–25.00; S. R. Lawson 12–0–293–70–0–24.41; N. J. Workman 11–0–188–46–0–17.09; I. A. Sommerville 12–0–192–50–0–16.00; G. M. Williams 10–2–109–22–0–13.62; C. G. Willetts 12–1–133–37–0–12.09.

*Bowling*—R. J. Trethewey 65–13–204–17–5/26–12.00; J. R. T. Burn 92–24–216–17–5/21–12.70; *N. Bell 64.5–8–257–17–5/33–15.11; M. N. Khan 96.1–32–238–15–3/10–15.86.

## KING EDWARD VI SCHOOL, SOUTHAMPTON

*Played 19: Won 5, Lost 7, Drawn 7. Abandoned 4*

Master i/c: R. J. Putt

*Wins v:* Totton C.; St George's, Weybridge; Retiring Captain's XI; Taunton's C.; Hampshire U-19 B.

G. R. Treagus, a fifth-former, made 545 runs and for the second successive season was the only member of the XI to play a three-figure innings.

*Batting*—G. R. Treagus 14–3–545–103*–1–49.54; E. D. M. Taylor 16–4–305–64–0–25.41; N. D. Osman 8–1–163–75–0–23.28; D. O. Arnold 13–4–176–46*–0–19.55; J. D. Chrispin 17–4–242–53*–0–18.61; M. E. Munro 15–2–233–55–0–17.92; *A. J. Tidby 16–1–266–85–0–17.73.

*Bowling*—A. J. Tidby 48–7–172–14–5/14–12.28; N. C. Jackman 122.4–41–321–18–3/23–17.83; D. N. Ayton 84.3–16–301–16–4/32–18.81; M. P. Perry-Lewis 134–41–349–18–5/33–19.38; G. R. Treagus 118.2–40–319–15–4/8–21.26; J. D. Chrispin 147.3–35–420–13–2/21–32.30.

## KING EDWARD VII SCHOOL, LYTHAM

*Played 20: Won 4, Lost 5, Drawn 11*

Master i/c: A. Crowther

*Wins v:* Invitation XI; Old Boys; UCS; Woodbridge.

G. Maitland and P. Macauley put on 176 runs in nineteen overs at the end-of-season festival at UCS Hampstead, with Maitland making 111 not out off 46 scoring shots and Macauley finishing with 80 not out.

*Batting*—\*P. Macauley 19–7–570–102\*–1–47.50; G. Maitland 19–5–604–111\*–2–43.14; D. Tomlinson 14–3–310–53\*–0–28.18; M. Dawson 15–0–301–67–0–20.06; T. Shaw 12–2–178–46–0–17.80; G. Kempston 10–3–100–23\*–0–14.28; M. Clague 12–3–127–40–0–14.11.

*Bowling*—D. Tomlinson 136.5–29–392–21–3/8–18.66; P. Young 212–48–623–32–5/30–19.46; R. Tufft 134.3–32–433–17–6/57–25.47; G. Maitland 145.3–21–549–21–4/25–26.14.


## KING EDWARD'S SCHOOL, BIRMINGHAM

*Played 21: Won 6, Lost 3, Drawn 12. Abandoned 2*

Master i/c: M. D. Stead        Cricket professional: R. J. Newman

*Wins v:* RGS, Worcester; Wolverhampton GS; Old Edwardians; Common Room XI; Gentlemen of Worcestershire; Hereford Cathedral S.

*Batting*—C. E. Hitchins 13–5–448–65–0–56.00; D. A. Bhadri 8–4–218–64–0–54.60; \*C. E. R. Meyer 16–5–545–87\*–0–49.54; N. M. Linehan 15–5–452–92–0–45.20; C. N. Ashton 19–3–515–115–1–32.18; J. D. T. West 19–4–457–83–0–30.46.

*Bowling*—O. J. Sharp 87.5–17–273–19–4/21–14.36; D. A. Bhadri 96–13–354–17–3/32–20.82; N. M. Linehan 250–58–717–33–6/31–21.72; F. A. Izfan 258.3–85–704–29–5/18–24.27; P. N. W. Button 165–37–531–12–2/26–44.25.


## KING HENRY VIII SCHOOL, COVENTRY

*Played 15: Won 6, Lost 3, Drawn 6. Abandoned 2*

Master i/c: G. P. C. Courtois

*Wins v:* Abbot Beyne; King Edward's, Stratford; King Edward's, Birmingham; Bishop Vesey's GS; King Edward's, Five Ways; Old Coventrians' XI.

*Batting*—C. H. Field 14–3–507–102\*–1–46.09; \*G. O. Thomas 15–0–645–109–2–43.00; A. M. H. Crowter 6–2–139–50\*–0–34.75; A. Saeed 14–2–200–73\*–0–16.66; N. C. Ward 10–1–123–40–0–13.66; M. G. Dow 12–0–138–28–0–11.50.

*Bowling*—A. Saeed 51.5–16–198–15–6/21–13.20; R. G. Whitehall 150.4–35–420–30–5/20–14.00; M. J. Gough 65.2–12–236–15–6/31–15.73; A. J. Stanley 53.4–9–203–10–6/40–20.30; P. R. Norris 80–11–289–13–4/44–22.23.


## KING WILLIAM'S COLLEGE, ISLE OF MAN

*Played 16: Won 6, Lost 4, Drawn 6*

Master i/c: T. M. Manning        Cricket professional: D. Mark

*Wins v:* Fencibles CC; OKW XI; Oswestry S.; QEGS, Wakefield; Aldenham; Liverpool.

*Batting*—G. M. Kermode 10–0–239–118–1–23.90; L. W. H. Moreton 13–4–196–57\*–0–21.77; E. J. S. Corlett 10–2–151–62\*–0–18.87; \*J. C. D. Hinds 13–2–181–74\*–0–16.45; G. M. Atchison 16–1–233–77\*–0–15.53; J. F. K. Bregazzi 12–4–106–30–0–13.25; L. R. Clarke 14–1–150–33–0–11.53; R. C. Turner 16–1–132–42–0–8.80.

*Bowling*—L. R. Clarke 284.3–71–737–48–7/52–15.35; J. F. K. Bregazzi 191.1–48–499–29–6/47–17.20; R. C. Turner 64.3–14–240–12–4/6–20.00; T. C. Walters 99–17–331–14–2/5–23.64.

## KING'S COLLEGE, TAUNTON

*Played 12: Won 4, Lost 2, Drawn 6. Abandoned 4*

Master i/c: R. J. R. Yeates        Cricket professional: D. Breakwell

*Wins v:* Wellington S.; Queen's, Taunton; Canford; Allhallows.

M. F. D. Robinson, the side's most prolific batsman, played for English Schools.

*Batting*—\*M. K. Coley 10–6–208–78\*–0–52.00; M. F. D. Robinson 11–1–459–164\*–1–45.90; R. E. Berry 12–1–346–67–0–31.45; C. P. W. Cashell 12–1–338–100–1–30.72; T. J. V. Rainey 10–2–191–40\*–0–23.87; M. Hiles 10–2–141–51\*–0–17.62; J. G. M. Ross 10–2–112–29\*–0–14.00.

*Bowling*—M. J. Scott 120–36–314–23–5/36–13.65; A. F. Lacy-Smith 132–20–332–19–4/64–17.47; M. K. Coley 115–26–336–17–4/63–19.76; M. F. D. Robinson 89–17–243–10–2/13–24.30.

## KING'S COLLEGE SCHOOL, WIMBLEDON

*Played 21: Won 11, Lost 1, Drawn 9. Abandoned 1*

Master i/c: G. C. McGinn        Cricket professional: L. J. Moody

*Wins v:* Wimbledon CC; Strodes; Kingston GS; Caterham; Emanuel; Whitgift; Rutlish; KCS Old Boys; Guernsey Island CC (twice); Alleyn's.

Opening the batting for what may have been the best KCS XI for some time, R. Q. Cake and J. Parrish compiled a record unbroken partnership of 216 against Emanuel, only to overtake it in their next match three days later, when they put on 230 against Epsom. Cake made three consecutive centuries when he followed his 140 not out and 122 respectively in these two matches with 117 against Tiffin. The Epsom match was memorable, too, for a hat-trick by D. P. Frost, while the feat was also performed against St John's by A. M. Denslow. The one defeat was by Guernsey Island Under-23 in a 40-overs match.

*Batting*—\*R. Q. Cake 18–1–979–140\*–4–57.58; J. Parrish 16–3–617–101–1–47.46; S. J. Bayly 14–8–231–58\*–0–38.50; T. P. Howland 19–2–473–111–1–27.82; H. S. Malik 19–2–428–71–0–25.17; B. J. Howland 8–1–175–55–0–25.00; B. C. M. Gardner 13–4–161–50–0–17.88; R. T. H. Carter 10–3–109–41–0–15.57.

*Bowling*—H. S. Malik 160.5–33–484–34–6/53–14.23; S. J. Bayly 87.2–11–295–20–5/14–14.75; A. M. Denslow 101–30–269–18–5/21–14.94; I. M. Hepburn 176.2–38–496–31–5/18–16.00; T. P. Howland 116–21–349–19–4/22–18.36; D. P. Frost 55–6–223–12–5/20–18.58; N. H. C. Kidd 165–49–366–19–3/9–19.26.

## KING'S SCHOOL, BRUTON

*Played 13: Won 4, Lost 2, Drawn 7. Abandoned 3*

Master i/c: P. Platts-Martin        Cricket professional: N. J. Lockhart

*Wins v:* Bryanston; Compton House CC; Allhallows; Wellington S.

*Batting*—F. L. Stewart 12–3–522–107–1–58.00; \*N. J. Gammon 10–3–284–56–0–40.57; A. R. MacEwen 11–3–184–35\*–0–23.00; P. K. Harding 9–1–166–50–0–20.75; C. J. S. Upton 7–0–131–70–0–18.71; J. L. Hayes 10–0–166–77–0–16.60.

*Bowling*—T. R. Fowlston 53.1–12–129–12–4/15–10.75; M. D. Cooper 66.2–16–187–16–5/12–11.68; N. J. Gammon 152.1–33–400–27–7/60–14.81; P. K. Harding 89.3–23–286–15–4/35–19.06; N. I. Paul 101–14–333–14–4/62–23.78.

## THE KING'S SCHOOL, CANTERBURY

*Played 9: Won 1, Lost 2, Drawn 6. Abandoned 5*

Master i/c: A. W. Dyer

*Win v:* Band of Brothers.

*Batting*—K. O. O. Sonaike 10–1–279–102*–1–31.00; J. J. Rhodes 10–1–193–75–0–21.44; R. J. Weston 10–2–155–46*–0–19.37; J. R. E. Parker 9–1–152–57–0–19.00; A. S. Davies 10–3–133–46*–0–19.00.

*Bowling*—M. I. Odgers 81–18–228–18–4/36–12.66; *S. R. Maggs 146.4–26–447–20–5/38–22.35.

## THE KING'S SCHOOL, CHESTER

*Played 16: Won 6, Lost 3, Drawn 7*

Master i/c: K. H. Mellor

*Wins v:* Cheadle Hulme; Rydal; King William's, IOM; Aldenham; Liverpool; OKS.

*Batting*—N. J. Phillingham 13–7–287–53–0–47.83; J. M. Thomas 13–4–294–55–0–32.66; *J. R. H. Spencer 14–2–376–91–0–31.33; G. P. Barrett 14–2–340–65–0–28.33; A. C. Richardson 9–0–199–61–0–22.11; B. J. Mitchell 16–1–299–58–0–19.93; E. A. Spencer 13–1–230–54–0–19.16; A. M. Miln 13–0–183–32–0–14.07.

*Bowling*—C. B. Place 142.4–29–428–27–7/44–15.85; G. Benton 129.2–25–419–22–4/8–19.04; M. J. Cox 121.4–21–326–15–4/27–21.73; J. M. Thomas 157.4–26–515–20–4/49–25.75.

## THE KING'S SCHOOL, ELY

*Played 13: Won 4, Lost 3, Drawn 6. Abandoned 2*

Master i/c: C. J. Limb                    Cricket professional: T. G. A. Morley

*Wins v:* Wisbech GS; Cambridge CSFS; Saffron Walden CHS; Culford.

*Batting*—M. C. Savage 14–3–452–102*–1–41.09; R. M. James 11–3–324–78–0–40.50; E. L. Steyn 11–4–280–72*–0–40.00; *P. D. Griffiths 14–2–383–100*–1–31.91; C. J. Kisby 10–4–109–43–0–18.16.

*Bowling*—R. M. James 62–10–217–17–4/23–12.76; C. D. Marshall 54.3–5–295–18–5/12–16.38; D. J. Parker 89.2–15–253–14–7/18–18.07; J. F. Manchett 57–10–244–13–3/36–18.76; C. J. Kisby 106–17–390–14–3/23–27.85.

## THE KING'S SCHOOL, MACCLESFIELD

*Played 21: Won 11, Lost 0, Drawn 10. Abandoned 2*

Master i/c: D. M. Harbord                    Cricket professional: S. Moores

*Wins v:* William Hulme's GS; Arnold (twice); Bolton; Hulme GS; Newcastle HS; MCC; Bangor GS; QEGS, Blackburn; Edinburgh Acad.; Ipswich.

The XI enjoyed their first unbeaten season since 1965, and remained undefeated by schools for two years, having lost in 1990 only to MCC. K. A. Graham, their Australian opening batsman, broke his own record with 1,128 runs as he passed 1,000 for the second successive season, and won the *Daily Telegraph* batting award.

*Batting*—K. A. Graham 21–6–1,128–157–4–75.20; A. N. Owens 20–5–607–111*–1–40.46; G. A. J. Mason 16–6–380–85–0–38.00; M. J. Hammond 12–2–248–61*–0–24.80; *S. C. James 9–1–172–60*–0–21.50; E. K. Dalboth 9–0–189–65–0–21.00; M. J. Simpson 17–3–277–52–0–19.78.

*Bowling*—S. C. James 242–70–573–47–6/27–12.19; A. M. James 242–76–575–45–5/8–12.77; B. J. Cutbill 214.3–36–692–40–5/20–17.30; C. M. Watson 176–56–483–25–3/21–19.32.

## KING'S SCHOOL, ROCHESTER

*Played 15: Won 4, Lost 2, Drawn 9. Abandoned 1*

Master i/c: J. S. Irvine

*Wins v:* Cranbrook; Band of Brothers; Sutton Valence; Chatham House.

The outstanding batsman was the English Schools representative, M. J. Walker, who in four seasons in the XI – three as captain – scored 3,270 runs; he is expected to return in 1992.

*Batting*—*M. J. Walker 12–3–746–135*–4–82.88; D. P. Johnson 9–1–247–72–0–30.87; J. Mitchell 11–3–243–57–0–30.37; M. Vowls 7–1–144–47–0–24.00; R. Greer 13–1–285–40–0–23.75.

*Bowling*—M. J. Walker 175–49–489–31–5/67–15.77; J. Mitchell 136–31–409–19–3/72–21.52; R. E. C. Jones 117–27–388–15–5/23–25.86; D. P. Johnson 130–20–408–15–4/51–27.20.

## THE KING'S SCHOOL, WORCESTER

*Played 21: Won 7, Lost 5, Drawn 9*

Master i/c: D. P. Iddon

*Wins v:* Belmont Abbey; Malvern Chase; King Edward VI, Stourbridge; Kelvinside Acad.; Common Room XI; Old Vigornians CC; Victoria C., Jersey.

*Batting*—*D. A. W. Hughes 20–5–832–104*–1–55.46; J. H. Richardson 19–3–662–67–0–41.37; D. J. L. Wheeler 11–2–178–31–0–19.77; J. S. E. Rogers 19–2–296–58–0–17.41; R. B. Cook 12–2–142–44–0–14.20; P. J. W. O'Neill 20–3–236–71*–0–13.88; C. M. Way 17–2–206–31–0–13.73; T. P. Booton 13–2–100–30–0–9.09.

*Bowling*—P. J. W. O'Neill 51–4–217–12–3/20–18.08; T. P. Bawden 164–27–582–30–5/25–19.40; J. H. Richardson 216–45–662–33–6/43–20.06; D. A. W. Hughes 169–25–585–21–4/28–27.85; B. T. T. Crabbe 112–23–450–16–3/26–28.12.

## KINGSTON GRAMMAR SCHOOL

*Played 16: Won 3, Lost 5, Drawn 8*

Master i/c: J. A. Royce

*Wins v:* Glyn; Reed's; Teddington.

*Batting*—J. M. Wallis 15–1–559–80–0–39.92; D. Spencer 15–1–370–91–0–26.42; N. Gardiner 13–3–200–59–0–20.00; I. M. Dowle 11–0–169–52–0–15.36; D. J. Lipscomb 15–0–222–54–0–14.80; A. O. Malpas-Sands 14–0–112–21–0–8.00.

*Bowling*—D. J. Lipscomb 69–12–274–15–4/53–18.26; D. Spencer 227–32–735–33–6/24–22.27; *S. P. Temlett 182–29–631–21–5/33–30.04; A. O. Malpas-Sands 98–9–407–13–4/108–31.30.

## KINGSWOOD SCHOOL

*Played 10: Won 1, Lost 3, Drawn 6*

Master i/c: R. J. Lewis

*Win v:* Prior Park.

*Batting*—*D. R. Bowden 9–1–281–97–0–35.12; N. P. Dowling 10–3–219–76*–0–31.28; J. D. Pillinger 10–2–220–43–0–27.50; J. Dyson 9–0–154–67–0–17.11; S. Redman 9–1–126–41–0–15.75.

*Bowling*—J. Dyson 114.4–21–362–25–5/57–14.48; N. J. Page 62–16–236–16–7/60–14.75; N. P. Dowling 43.5–7–149–8–4/22–18.62; J. D. Pillinger 54.2–8–261–11–5/29–23.72.

## LANCING COLLEGE

*Played 13: Won 2, Lost 6, Drawn 5. Abandoned 1*

Master i/c: I. D. Perrins       Cricket professional: R. H. C. Davis

*Wins v:* Tonbridge; Sussex Martlets.

A highlight was the first defeat of Tonbridge since 1959.

*Batting*—A. Lutwyche 13–0–329–67–0–25.30; J. Southorn 10–1–177–41*–0–19.66; J. Annetts 11–0–201–51–0–18.27; D. Gurney 11–0–169–48–0–16.90; J. Rees 12–1–185–56–0–16.81; *I. Meadows 13–0–217–61–0–16.69; M. Couling 11–1–147–33–0–14.70; A. Pierce 13–2–132–42*–0–12.00.

*Bowling*—B. Clark 101–23–301–12–4/20–25.08; A. Lutwyche 149–33–457–16–4/22–28.56; I. Meadows 98–13–378–10–4/52–37.80.


## LATYMER UPPER SCHOOL

*Played 14: Won 2, Lost 4, Drawn 8*

Master i/c: A. M. Weston       Cricket professional: K. Mayers

*Wins v:* Mill Hill; Enfield.

*Batting*—S. Phillips 13–0–328–44–0–25.23; O. Ghaffar 10–0–233–75–0–23.30; S. Kakar 12–1–226–44–0–20.54; S. Thavam 10–2–147–36–0–18.37; J. Brooke-Partridge 13–1–219–50–0–18.25; M. Smith 13–0–117–40*–0–16.71; *C. Craddock 10–1–147–29–0–16.33; M. Pryor 10–1–103–38–0–11.44.

*Bowling*—C. Craddock 107–18–389–23–6/51–16.91; M. Pryor 84–18–214–10–3/7–21.40; S. Phillips 116.3–24–323–13–3/20–24.84.


## LEEDS GRAMMAR SCHOOL

*Played 14: Won 4, Lost 1, Drawn 9. Abandoned 3*

Master i/c: R. Hill

*Wins v:* Pocklington; Ashville; Leodiensian CC; Past XI.

*Batting*—I. C. Sutcliffe 13–5–550–99*–0–68.75; *T. C. Walton 11–3–420–116–1–52.50; R. M. Atkinson 13–3–447–116*–1–44.70; D. P. Gait 8–2–184–104*–1–30.66; G. D. Simmonds 10–2–189–54*–0–23.62.

*Bowling*—R. M. Atkinson 155–45–433–28–6/39–15.46; T. C. Walton 134.3–22–427–22–4/16–19.40.


## THE LEYS SCHOOL

*Played 16: Won 3, Lost 2, Drawn 10, Tied 1. Abandoned 2*

Master i/c: P. S. D. Carpenter       Cricket professional: D. Gibson

*Wins v:* Stamford; Oakham; Old Leysians.

R. C. Weston's 181 not out against Mill Hill, in a total of 276 for two declared, won him the Slazenger Young Cricketer of the Month award for May, but M. C. Donnor's unbeaten 112 against Highgate was considered the better of the XI's two centuries. The tie, against Monkton Combe, was achieved off the last ball after The Leys had earlier declared at 271 for four.

*Batting*—M. C. Donnor 14–3–510–112*–1–46.36; R. C. Weston 14–1–548–181*–1–42.15; *D. J. Woods 13–2–459–90–0–41.72; A. J. C. Kinnear 6–2–109–26–0–27.25; J. R. Tilbrook 7–1–143–70–0–23.83; A. S. Bruce-Ball 14–4–237–37*–0–23.70; J. Crilley 10–3–165–56–0–23.57.

*Bowling*—D. M. Wingfield 171.1–40–439–27–5/36–16.25; D. M. A. Bullen 185–38–540–21–4/18–25.71; M. C. Donnor 133–20–477–11–2/33–43.36.

## LIVERPOOL COLLEGE

*Played 14: Won 1, Lost 8, Drawn 5*

Master i/c: The Revd J. R. Macaulay

*Win v:* Rydal.

*Batting*—*B. H. Latto 12–2–239–73*–0–23.90; D. J. Talisman 11–3–188–54*–0–23.50; J. L. Perry 9–0–174–59–0–19.33; T. F. Henderson 13–3–162–47*–0–16.20; D. P. Hines 11–1–145–25*–0–14.50.

*Bowling*—J. M. Rylance 160–37–499–27–6/39–18.48; B. H. Latto 79–7–359–15–4/35–23.93.

## LLANDOVERY COLLEGE

*Played 14: Won 3, Lost 3, Drawn 8. Abandoned 4*

Master i/c: T. G. Marks

*Wins v:* Hereford Cathedral S.; Bishop Gore S.; Gowerton CC President's XI.

*Batting*—*S. A. Richards 13–1–412–79–0–34.33; S. Howells 12–3–295–59–0–32.77; H. G. Davies 9–1–165–38–0–20.62; R. G. Jones 8–2–100–35*–0–16.66.

*Bowling*—G. D. A. Lyddon-Jones 90–16–241–25–7/21–9.64; S. A. Richards 66–14–189–18–6/25–10.50; H. G. Davies 114–21–276–23–5/11–12.00; S. Howells 76–7–260–18–4/29–14.44; R. Mably 73–9–239–13–4/33–18.38.

## LORD WANDSWORTH COLLEGE

*Played 14: Won 4, Lost 2, Drawn 8*

Master i/c: G. R. Smith

*Wins v:* Leighton Park; St John's, Southsea; Salesian C.; Acorns CC.

The XI's sixteen-year-old captain, B. A. Hames, set a new school record with his unbeaten innings of 151 against Ryde School, Isle of Wight.

*Batting*—*B. A. Hames 14–2–831–151*–3–69.25; G. Rodwell 12–4–200–54–0–25.00; T. A. Dyson 12–1–188–52–0–17.09; S. J. English 12–2–166–43*–0–16.60; C. J. Fairley 13–2–137–35*–0–12.45.

*Bowling*—N. A. Bellamy 141.2–41–346–28–5/38–12.35; D. A. Higgins 72–14–217–15–3/9–14.46; G. Rodwell 133.5–30–382–23–5/38–16.60; B. A. Hames 62–9–237–11–3/52–21.54; E. T. Bryce 47–3–219–10–2/20–21.90.

## LORD WILLIAMS'S SCHOOL, THAME

*Played 14: Won 4, Lost 8, Drawn 2*

Master i/c: A. M. Brannan

*Wins v:* Burford; Desborough; Oxford S.; Henley.

*Batting*—P. Kelloway 8–1–248–102*–1–35.42; G. B. G. Yates 13–1–217–60–0–18.08; S. R. Almutair 12–1–161–40–0–14.63; S. Lazurak 12–4–107–28*–0–13.37; J. R. Gibbs 12–0–114–29–0–9.50.

*Bowling*—C. D. Pigden 37.1–6–155–12–7/43–12.91; G. B. G. Yates 157.1–30–487–28–7/74–17.39; S. R. Almutair 126–18–406–19–4/35–21.36; R. D. Halliwell 105.5–19–381–12–3/15–31.75.

## LORETTO SCHOOL

*Played 16: Won 6, Lost 4, Drawn 6. Abandoned 2*

Master i/c: R. G. Selley

*Wins v:* Fettes; George Watson's; Edinburgh Acad.; MCC; Merchant Taylors', Northwood; Scottish Wayfarers.

A. C. F. Mason, a fast left-arm bowler, and J. S. Bedi, an off-spinner, each passed 100 wickets for the XI in three seasons.

*Batting*—J. N. Garbutt 13–2–310–54*–0–28.18; E. Barbour 12–4–204–70*–0–25.50; *A. C. F. Mason 10–2–179–42–0–22.37; S. C. Fraser 16–5–240–45–0–21.81.

*Bowling*—J. S. Bedi 209–58–549–48–7/32–11.43; A. C. F. Mason 305–107–612–48–7/39–12.75; G. C. Harden 101–26–328–14–3/33–23.42; L. Montgomery 217–63–610–22–5/40–27.72.

## LOUGHBOROUGH GRAMMAR SCHOOL

*Played 13: Won 3, Lost 2, Drawn 8. Abandoned 3*

Master i/c: E. Thorpe

*Wins v:* Coventry S., Bablake; Abbot Beyne; Gentlemen of Lincolnshire.

*Batting*—A. E. D. Duncombe 8–2–218–52*–0–36.33; P. J. Noon 11–2–293–139–1–32.55; *I. R. Partridge 12–2–303–84–0–30.30; P. J. Gidley 10–2–229–63*–0–28.62; J. C. Malpas 9–0–133–38–0–14.77; C. A. Hill 8–0–113–68–0–14.12.

*Bowling*—P. J. Noon 105–18–383–20–5/40–19.15; I. R. Partridge 67.3–11–279–10–2/6–27.90; P. P. Kelly 120–28–484–16–3/49–30.25; P. J. Gidley 116–17–421–12–2/18–35.08.

## MAGDALEN COLLEGE SCHOOL

*Played 19: Won 4, Lost 3, Drawn 12. Abandoned 1*

Master i/c: P. Askew

*Wins v:* Lord Williams's, Thame; Douai; Shiplake; King Edward VI, Southampton.

In the win over Douai, two sixteen-year-olds, D. A. Bixby and N. S. Hawken, established a school record for the first wicket, putting on 195; both scored hundreds in the match.

*Batting*—D. A. Ross 20–5–634–92–0–42.26; *S. D. Stinchcombe 19–4–580–81–0–38.66; N. S. Hawken 18–1–520–100–1–30.58; D. A. Bixby 20–1–422–101*–1–22.21; S. D. Hayes 16–4–224–44*–0–18.66; C. S. Winson 11–3–121–58–0–15.12; J. H. Rea 13–3–111–22–0–11.10.

*Bowling*—S. D. Stinchcombe 231–43–594–39–5/48–15.23; J. H. Rea 371–59–591–36–4/32–16.41; P. M. Woodard 194–43–574–31–6/21–18.51.

## MALVERN COLLEGE

*Played 12: Won 4, Lost 4, Drawn 4. Abandoned 5*

Master i/c: R. W. Tolchard

*Wins v:* Gentlemen of Worcestershire; Masters' XI; Lancing; Rugby.

A highlight was A. J. P. Lenard's return of eight for 56 in the defeat by Radley. Generally, a good bowling attack suffered from the number of slow pitches encountered, while the uneven bounce of their home square did not help the batsmen acquire confidence.

*Batting*—*J. H. Verity 12–3–259–79*–0–28.77; J. T. Tolchard 14–6–227–104*–1–28.37; O. W. C. Brough 7–2–134–54–0–26.80; P. V. Sykes 11–1–246–85–0–24.60; J. R. A. Poulton 10–2–193–46–0–24.12; J. T. B. Crawley 10–2–190–48–0–23.75.

*Bowling*—J. T. B. Crawley 91–21–184–19–6/36–9.68; A. J. P. Lenard 115–36–251–21–8/56–11.95; F. S. O. Nyaseme 96–19–290–15–4/48–19.33; A. C. M. Scammell 113–21–311–15–5/56–20.73.

## MANCHESTER GRAMMAR SCHOOL

*Played 19: Won 2, Lost 4, Drawn 13. Abandoned 2*

Master i/c: D. Moss

*Wins v:* Bolton; Bangor GS.

The young opening batsman, L. J. Marland, scored 618 runs for the XI, captained English Schools Under-15, and won the *Daily Telegraph* Under-15 batting award.

*Batting*—L. J. Marland 17–3–618–100*–1–44.14; S. M. Hogg 14–4–342–56*–0–34.20; *C. M. Gresty 18–2–430–91*–0–26.87; C. F. Sinton 17–3–271–46–0–19.35; S. J. O'Hare 11–4–125–25*–0–17.85; P. D. Knott 16–5–193–58–0–17.54; G. J. Wilkinson 17–1–246–47–0–15.37.

*Bowling*—J. R. Wickins 204.1–59–559–27–5/42–20.70; P. N. Stanyard 231.3–72–592–28–5/64–21.14; P. J. Galvin 168.4–47–459–15–6/32–30.60; C. F. Sinton 226–49–765–22–4/66–34.77.

## MARLBOROUGH COLLEGE

*Played 13: Won 0, Lost 8, Drawn 5. Abandoned 3*

Master i/c: R. B. Pick        Cricket professional: R. M. Ratcliffe

*Batting*—T. C. Stewart-Liberty 13–0–381–88–0–29.30; R. A. I. Chisholm Batten 12–2–209–48*–0–20.90; J. H. M. Gordon 12–0–222–42–0–18.50; M. E. C. Harris 12–1–188–43–0–17.09; *J. Simkins 13–1–177–39*–0–14.75; C. M. M. Youens 12–3–110–36–0–12.22; D. J. Snelling 12–1–120–59–0–10.90.

*Bowling*—C. M. M. Youens 111–12–441–15–4/56–29.40; N. F. Outram 96–14–337–10–3/28–33.70; D. F. Anderson 154–18–563–10–3/26–56.30.

## MERCHANT TAYLORS' SCHOOL, CROSBY

*Played 17: Won 3, Lost 4, Drawn 10. Abandoned 1*

Master i/c: The Revd D. A. Smith        Cricket professional: M. Chee Quee

*Wins v:* Rossall; St Mary's, Crosby; King William's, IOM.

N. A. Doggett (fast-medium) returned the remarkable figures of 16.5–13–4–8 against St Mary's, Crosby, who were bundled out for 27 following a declaration at 178 for three. Another side to feel the force of the XI's attack were King William's College, Isle of Man, who were dismissed for 79 in reply to 185.

*Batting*—G. M. M. Cannock 10–3–214–63–0–30.57; *M. G. Doggett 17–3–382–83–0–27.28; D. G. Garland 11–5–146–41–0–24.33; M. P. Edwards 16–0–383–74–0–23.93; P. C. McKeown 13–1–268–83–0–22.33; A. Sharma 15–3–197–32–0–16.41; N. D. Wells 17–2–245–50–0–16.33.

*Bowling*—N. A. Doggett 188–60–481–40–8/4–12.02; M. G. Doggett 91.2–29–285–23–5/20–12.39; G. N. Hedger 171–33–566–24–5/27–23.58; M. D. Thomas 161.5–45–530–17–4/47–31.17.

## MERCHANT TAYLORS' SCHOOL, NORTHWOOD

*Played 23: Won 8, Lost 4, Drawn 11. Abandoned 3*

Master i/c: W. M. B. Ritchie        Cricket professional: H. C. Latchman

*Wins v:* St John's Coll., Oxford; St Albans; Watford GS; Isleworth and Syon S.; Enfield GS; Mill Hill; St Peter's, York; Cranleigh.

The all-rounder, R. A. Hawkey, bowling slow left-arm, became only the second cricketer in recent history to take 200 wickets for the XI, his 204 falling just twelve short of the record set in the 1960s by J. M. H. Grimsdyke, also a left-arm spinner.

*Batting*—A. J. Powell-Williams 17–4–546–84*–0–42.00; *R. A. Hawkey 23–3–676–113*–1–33.80; C. M. Jaggard 15–1–386–100*–1–27.57; N. J. Hutchinson 16–6–240–49*–0–24.00; A. J. M. Smee 13–1–215–70–0–17.91; S. Roy 16–1–250–59–0–16.66; J. A. Roberts 16–3–188–82–0–14.46; T. N. S. Hewage 19–5–177–35*–0–12.64; P. Knowles 15–2–141–35–0–10.84.

*Bowling*—J. A. Roberts 163.3–35–494–36–6/13–13.72; R. A. Hawkey 296.5–81–761–46–5/9–16.54; P. Knowles 175–33–529–20–4/16–26.45; P. Parekh 174.5–19–663–22–5/61–30.13.

## MERCHISTON CASTLE SCHOOL

*Played 17: Won 12, Lost 3, Drawn 2. Abandoned 3*

Master i/c: C. W. Swan

Cricket professional: I. Philip

*Wins v:* Scottish Wayfarers CC; George Watson's; George Heriot's; S. D. Stranock's XI; Merchistonians; Stewart's Melville; Strathallan; Dundee HS; RGS, Newcastle; Royal Belfast AI; Fettes; Llandovery.

A. R. C. Gilmour, a medium-pace bowler, followed his 59 wickets in 1990 with 53 in 1991 to take his tally from three seasons in the XI to 131.

*Batting*—D. W. Hodge 18–1–449–92–0–26.41; J. D. Taylor 17–2–380–84*–0–25.33; J. M. Prescott 18–3–358–68–0–23.86; A. W. Ritchie 13–5–141–47–0–17.62; J. A. A. M. Kerr 12–6–103–51*–0–17.16; A. C. Wearmouth 17–0–288–52–0–16.94.

*Bowling*—R. A. F. Dobson 63–17–244–26–7/11–9.38; J. D. Taylor 138–34–350–35–8/23–10.00; *A. R. C. Gilmour 252–77–557–53–8/18–10.50; A. W. Ritchie 159–29–469–25–5/39–18.76.

## MILL HILL SCHOOL

*Played 13: Won 2, Lost 6, Drawn 5. Abandoned 2*

Master i/c: S. T. Plummer

Cricket professional: G. A. R. Lock

*Wins v:* Christ's College; Queen Elizabeth, Barnet.

The captain and slow left-arm bowler, G. E. S. Brock, completed five seasons in the XI with a total of 110 wickets.

*Batting*—N. Kamath 12–1–224–50–0–20.36; M. R. Davis 8–0–120–68–0–15.00; D. M. J. Kraft 13–0–182–38–0–14.00; D. L. Goodwin 10–1–124–31–0–13.77; T. M. F. Harris 10–0–121–52–0–12.10; C. L. L. Mortali 11–0–132–43–0–12.00.

*Bowling*—C. L. L. Mortali 72–13–250–11–3/22–22.72; *G. E. S. Brock 147–31–533–16–4/80–33.31; K. B. Patel 163–24–649–19–4/103–34.15.

## MILLFIELD SCHOOL

*Played 14: Won 5, Lost 1, Drawn 8. Abandoned 1*

Master i/c: A. D. Curtis

Cricket professional: G. C. Wilson

*Wins v:* Downside; Taunton; King's, Taunton; Exeter Univ.; Monmouth.

R. J. Ballinger, the leading fast bowler, represented English Schools.

*Batting*—A. J. Dalton 15–2–723–101–1–55.61; R. O. Jones 14–3–459–90–0–41.72; I. J. Ward 13–1–425–96–0–35.41; A. S. Golder 13–2–291–65–0–26.45; C. T. Thomas 8–1–155–61–0–22.14; P. T. Jacques 9–3–108–45–0–18.00.

*Bowling*—*R. J. Ballinger 156–49–341–37–7/15–9.21; P. T. Jacques 191.3–72–431–34–7/31–12.67; M. C. Jeffries 148–42–353–18–5/32–19.61; R. O. Jones 88–22–282–10–4/24–28.20.

## MILTON ABBEY SCHOOL

*Played 14: Won 2, Lost 5, Drawn 7. Abandoned 3.*

Master i/c: P. W. Wood

*Wins v:* Allhallows; XL Club.

*Batting*—*N. J. Smallman 14-2-350-56-0-29.16; A. W. Harvey 14-2-219-78-0-18.25; M. C. W. Williams 14-0-248-60-0-17.71; P. Le Q. Herbert 14-1-223-58-0-17.15; G. E. Bundock 9-0-132-41-0-14.66; N. J. D. Foster 14-1-168-35-0-12.92.

*Bowling*—A. W. Harvey 110.4-23-435-23-6/40-18.91; M. C. W. Williams 72-15-264-12-5/36-22.00; N. J. Smallman 98.5-22-339-14-3/13-24.21; P. Le Q. Herbert 94.4-11-365-14-5/21-26.07.

## MONKTON COMBE SCHOOL

*Played 15: Won 2, Lost 6, Drawn 6, Tied 1.*

Masters i/c: P. C. Sibley and N. D. Botton

*Wins v:* Wycliffe; Monkton Combe Cavaliers.

*Batting*—J. B. A. Smith 13-1-291-41*-0-24.25; *N. C. L. Sinfield 15-0-361-56-0-24.06; E. Weale 10-0-226-64-0-22.60; S. Lockyer 14-0-231-36-0-16.50; J. Ward 15-1-231-50*-0-16.50; J. Dollery 12-2-121-36-0-12.10; J. Cary 13-0-119-22-0-9.15.

*Bowling*—E. Weale 57-10-232-10-5/63-23.20; N. C. L. Sinfield 221.2-57-646-22-4/28-29.36; J. B. A. Smith 78-10-351-11-4/54-31.90; C. Owen 128.3-29-451-12-2/18-37.58.

## MONMOUTH SCHOOL

*Played 19: Won 4, Lost 3, Drawn 11, Tied 1. Abandoned 1.*

Master i/c: D. H. Messenger

*Wins v:* RGS, Worcester; Malvern; Colston's; Old Monmouthians.

Runners-up in the Chesterton Cup, the XI owed much to their batsmen. In the ten-wicket win over Colston's, A. J. Jones (123 not out) and M. J. Tamplin (64 not out) put on a school-record 195. There were two other century opening partnerships – an undefeated 175 against Wycliffe (Jones 102 not out, Tamplin 63 not out) and 120 against MCC (Tamplin 67, J. Williams 53). In the tied match against Clifton, a record stand of 106 unbroken for the fifth wicket was compiled by two fifth-formers, A. Mohindru (59 not out) and K. R. Spiring (55 not out). Jones, son of the former Glamorgan batsman, Alan Jones, went on to captain HMC Southern Schools at the Oxford Festival, where he scored a century, following with another at Lord's for MCC Schools v MCC. He also captained Wales Under-19, Glamorgan Under-19 and the Bull Development of Excellence side v Australia Under-19; he was offered a summer contract with Glamorgan for 1992. J. H. Langworth played for The Rest at Oxford and was subsequently awarded a Glamorgan CCC scholarship while at Swansea University.

*Batting*—A. Mohindru 6-3-181-59*-0-60.33; P. A. Clitheroe 13-5-416-103*-1-52.00; K. R. Spiring 12-6-312-55*-0-52.00; *A. J. Jones 16-3-595-123*-2-45.76; M. J. Tamplin 18-3-640-80-0-42.66; J. H. Langworth 13-1-280-65-0-23.33.

*Bowling*—P. A. Clitheroe 189.1-41-585-29-5/63-20.17; D. J. R. Price 157.4-33-526-23-6/24-22.86; M. J. Tamplin 80-13-303-12-4/41-25.25.

## NEWCASTLE-UNDER-LYME SCHOOL

*Played 15: Won 4, Lost 1, Drawn 10. Abandoned 3.*

Master i/c: S. A. Robson                     Cricket professional: A. H. Manack

*Wins v:* Tettenhall C.; MCC; Birkenhead; Old Newcastilians.

M. H. Colclough featured in two of the season's most memorable moments: he took a hat-trick against Stockport GS, and clinched a thrilling six-wicket win over MCC when he hit two sixes in the last over. He went on to play for Northamptonshire Second XI.

*Batting*—*M. H. Colclough 14–6–466–79*–0–58.25; R. J. Howell 15–2–374–73*–0–28.76; M. A. Smith 13–5–223–51–0–27.87; P. R. Leverett 8–1–137–49–0–19.57; N. S. J. Clarke 9–0–160–38–0–17.77; M. H. Foster 8–2–101–21–0–16.83; R. A. Spence 12–1–153–36–0–13.90; S. J. Currie 8–0–101–27–0–12.62.

*Bowling*—I. Bradbury 140–35–368–28–6/30–13.14; M. H. Colclough 122.5–36–349–22–5/32–15.86; R. M. Taylor 69–19–225–12–4/19–18.75; R. J. Howell 121.2–25–363–17–4/30–21.35.

## NOTTINGHAM HIGH SCHOOL

*Played 13: Won 1, Lost 0, Drawn 12. Abandoned 1*

Master i/c: Dr D. A. Slack                    Cricket professional: K. Poole

*Win v:* Bedford Modern.

*Batting*—S. W. Holliday 11–2–422–106*–1–46.88; *M. J. Bonsall 13–0–352–109–1–27.07; A. H. Rose 7–2–116–51*–0–23.20; M. Kennedy 6–1–104–53*–0–20.80; D. D. Williams 8–0–147–50–0–18.37; J. W. Phillips 9–2–128–27–0–18.28; S. H. Ferguson 9–3–103–30–0–17.16; D. T. Wootton 10–0–104–26–0–10.40.

*Bowling*—S. W. Holliday 97–24–344–14–4/76–24.57; A. H. Rose 124–15–446–17–4/46–26.23.

## OAKHAM SCHOOL

*Played 19: Won 0, Lost 7, Drawn 12*

Master i/c: J. Wills

*Batting*—J. Singh 16–1–437–67–0–29.13; P. M. J. Webb 17–1–454–100*–1–28.37; C. D. Durant 11–3–207–56–0–25.87; D. J. Ball 8–3–122–80*–0–24.40; S. I. Gilliver 13–1–247–54–0–20.58; *A. T. Craig 15–5–185–36–0–18.50; A. J. Aldridge 9–0–121–31–0–13.44; M. J. Astill 13–1–159–34*–0–13.25; M. J. Lavey 15–1–174–56*–0–12.42.

*Bowling*—J. M. Astill 172–46–525–24–6/89–21.87; S. I. Gilliver 96–12–368–13–2/32–28.30; J. J. Bull 66–5–332–11–3/36–30.18; D. Carrier 100–13–395–11–4/49–35.90.

## THE ORATORY SCHOOL

*Played 14: Won 3, Lost 3, Drawn 8. Abandoned 8*

Master i/c: P. L. Tomlinson                    Cricket professional: J. B. K. Howell

*Wins v:* Douai; Berkshire Gentlemen; P. L. Tomlinson's Invitation XI.

In his first full season in the XI, the fifteen-year-old left-hander, J. P. S. Tomlinson, scored 507 runs.

*Batting*—J. P. S. Tomlinson 14–2–507–92*–0–42.25; *J. D. Clarke 10–1–346–80–0–38.44; S. F. Hasslacher 8–0–146–40–0–18.25; A. J. E. Flower 8–1–120–34–0–17.14; R. W. Atkins 12–1–168–51–0–15.27; R. D. Louisson 9–0–116–50–0–12.88; P. D. Hemming-Tayler 10–0–118–31–0–11.80; A. S. O. Fraser 12–0–124–35–0–10.33.

*Bowling*—W. P. C. Outram 77–16–270–16–3/31–16.87; P. D. Hemming-Tayler 65–14–182–10–5/30–18.20; J. P. S. Tomlinson 92–16–339–15–3/22–22.60; D. J. Cole 106–20–271–10–5/20–27.10.

# OUNDLE SCHOOL

*Played 14: Won 3, Lost 1, Drawn 10. Abandoned 4*

Master i/c: V. G. B. Cushing        Cricket professional: A. Howorth

*Wins v:* Repton; MCC; Rugby.

A. W. Richardson took a hat-trick against Repton, bowling their last three batsmen. The win over MCC was Oundle's first for many years.

*Batting*—*A. W. Richardson 11–4–387–83*–0–55.28; H. Simpson 8–3–253–61–0–50.60; M. Milton 8–1–212–47*–0–30.28; J. J. Harris 10–2–209–90–0–26.12; S. Morgan 12–2–249–76–0–24.90; M. Epton 11–2–183–55*–0–20.33; C. Herbert 10–1–167–47–0–18.55.

*Bowling*—M. Epton 119.5–26–408–23–7/43–17.73; A. W. Richardson 179.1–35–516–21–7/40–24.57; C. Turpin 126.2–26–369–14–5/28–26.35.


# THE PERSE SCHOOL

*Played 15: Won 2, Lost 1, Drawn 12*

Master i/c: A. C. Porter        Cricket professional: D. C. Collard

*Wins v:* Kimbolton; Norwich.

*Batting*—P. C. Armstrong 12–3–351–77*–0–39.00; *D. M. Johnson 15–1–335–49–0–23.92; D. R. Sutton 10–0–203–38–0–20.30; R. T. Ragnauth 12–0–200–37–0–16.66; J. E. B. Stobbs 11–2–108–50*–0–12.00.

*Bowling*—D. J. Bentley 173–50–418–26–5/46–16.07; J. R. N. Jack 186–41–474–26–5/35–18.23; B. J. Bridgen 98–28–301–16–3/37–18.81; R. T. Ragnauth 76–8–265–14–3/42–18.92.


# PLYMOUTH COLLEGE

*Played 20: Won 6, Lost 4, Drawn 10. Abandoned 5*

Master i/c: T. J. Stevens

*Wins v:* Plymouth Hospitals CC; Philanthropists CC; Plymouth CC; Coleridge and Parry C., Barbados; Alexandra C., Barbados; Christchurch S., Barbados.

A. R. Maddock hit three fine hundreds – 124 not out v Plymouth CC, 131 v Plymouth Polytechnic and 100 not out v Alexandra College, Barbados – and took his aggregate for the XI in three seasons to more than 2,800 runs.

*Batting*—*A. R. Maddock 18–3–806–131–3–53.73; D. Roke 18–1–642–93–0–37.76; J. Whittall 6–0–181–108–1–30.16; K. Willcock 12–2–286–73*–0–28.60; G. Roberts 15–3–252–78*–0–21.00; S. Hunt 12–5–131–24*–0–18.71; S. Nicholson 12–3–144–21–0–16.00; K. Throgmorton 10–2–106–28–0–13.25; J. Dadge 16–3–154–47–0–11.84.

*Bowling*—A. Battersby 113.2–16–369–28–5/45–13.17; S. Nicholson 163–48–470–29–4/17–16.20; S. Hunt 160.3–38–503–29–4/27–17.34; K. Willcock 101.1–24–385–21–6/50–18.33; A. Barry 80.5–17–294–14–3/10–21.00.


# POCKLINGTON SCHOOL

*Played 23: Won 6, Lost 11, Drawn 6*

Master i/c: D. Nuttall

*Wins v:* Magdalen College S., Oxford; Hymers; Saints CC; Craven Gentlemen; Old Pocklingtonians; Londesborough Park CC.

*Batting*—*D. Edwards 23–0–821–94–0–35.69; C. E. Wilks 23–4–608–85*–0–32.00; A. H. Wood 23–1–491–92*–0–22.31; S. A. Boswell 20–3–294–62*–0–17.29; M. T. Atkinson 18–3–195–34–0–13.00.

*Bowling*—K. P. Robinson 199.5–53–525–29–4/27–18.10; S. A. Boswell 228.3–41–713–26–4/22–27.42; A. H. Wood 278–56–941–32–4/52–29.40; J. E. Dowling 135.1–19–572–19–4/55–30.10.

## PORTSMOUTH GRAMMAR SCHOOL

*Played 17: Won 4, Lost 3, Drawn 10*

Master i/c: G. D. Payne                     Cricket professional: L. Botha

*Wins v:* Milton Abbey; Victoria C. XI; United Services, Portsmouth; Portsmouth CC.

*Batting*—D. K. Pickup 8–3–179–49*–0–35.80; R. A. Compton 16–1–377–62–0–25.13; *A. M. Small 16–1–314–77–0–20.93; N. J. Macmillan 16–0–303–65–0–18.93; J. R. N. Brooke 11–0–181–73–0–16.45; H. Rushin 10–0–161–57–0–16.10; E. J. Anderson 15–1–224–36–0–16.00; J. Herman 12–4–101–57*–0–12.62.

*Bowling*—R. D. Saulet 52.2–10–163–10–4/21–16.30; R. J. Bridger 82.3–18–286–14–3/11–20.42; J. Herman 119.3–18–427–18–3/22–23.72; A. M. Small 84–17–371–14–6/39–26.50; W. A. Humphries 100–26–322–12–3/44–26.83; H. Rushin 99–11–318–10–6/45–31.80.

## QUEEN ELIZABETH GRAMMAR SCHOOL, WAKEFIELD

*Played 12: Won 1, Lost 2, Drawn 9. Abandoned 1*

Master i/c: T. Barker

*Win v:* 1990 Captain's XI.

*Batting*—S. Mandal 10–4–215–55*–0–35.83; D. Woffinden 11–0–255–67–0–23.18; R. Hames 9–1–173–58–0–21.62; D. Downham 10–0–200–57–0–20.00; K. Jayarajasingam 9–2–137–36*–0–19.57; J. Dunk 11–0–206–64–0–18.72.

*Bowling*—K. Jayarajasingam 39–9–151–10–3/11–15.10; T. Clegg 134–25–391–23–7/31–17.00; R. Fewster 100–15–349–11–5/23–31.72.

## QUEEN'S COLLEGE, TAUNTON

*Played 17: Won 5, Lost 3, Drawn 9. Abandoned 1*

Master i/c: J. W. Davies

*Wins v:* Clifton; Monmouth; Exeter; Richard Huish; Dwr-y-Felin Old Boys.

*Batting*—W. R. Thresher 13–2–495–88–0–45.00; N. J. Burke 17–1–611–128*–1–38.18; R. G. Jones 15–0–388–71–0–25.86; T. Aish 11–3–171–47–0–21.37; N. Rowcliffe 16–3–273–64–0–21.00; D. Wilson 7–2–101–54–0–20.20; S. Holland 11–3–156–64–0–19.50; C. Ameer 10–2–149–58*–0–18.62; *D. A. Williams 15–1–229–65*–0–16.35; W. Pilcher 10–1–113–42*–0–12.55.

*Bowling*—D. Wilson 54.3–4–142–12–5/47–11/83; N. J. Burke 110.4–23–341–21–5/23–16.23; D. A. Williams 174.4–37–470–28–6/31–16.78; P. Spencer-Ward 88.1–23–208–11–3/20–18.90; S. Holland 92–10–252–10–3/26–25.20.

# RADLEY COLLEGE

*Played 18: Won 7, Lost 3, Drawn 8*

Master i/c: G. de W. Waller     Cricket professionals: A. G. Robinson and A. R. Wagner

*Wins v:* MCC; Free Foresters; Abingdon; MCC School of Merit; Stowe; Malvern; Radley Rangers.

Until the Silk Trophy matches at Eton, the XI was one of Radley's best in terms of results. In addition to their seven wins, they levelled the scores against Cheltenham, chasing 171 in 36 overs. To beat Free Foresters, P. L. Hollis (118 not out) and T. P. Robinson (84 not out) put on a record unbroken third-wicket partnership of 193, at just under 9 an over, as Radley met a target of 226 in 44 overs. In the 55-overs matches at Eton, however, they were bowled out for low scores three days running.

*Batting*—T. P. Robinson 18–4–469–87*–0–33.50; *R. A. MacDowel 18–1–555–74–0–32.64; P. L. Hollis 17–1–451–118*–1–28.18; R. C. D. Hunter 15–4–288–51–0–26.18; J. T. A. Martin-Jenkins 15–0–355–52–0–23.66; E. R. Cropley 9–2–142–55*–0–20.28; R. J. Dearden 13–3–155–33–0–15.50; J. C. Barker 12–3–120–35–0–13.33.

*Bowling*—J. T. A. Martin-Jenkins 92–25–205–14–3/20–14.64; R. A. G. Sinclair 278–73–650–42–6/49–15.47; P. L. Hollis 100–18–330–19–5/43–17.36; E. R. Cropley 104–25–327–18–4/25–18.16; N. J. Walker 241–46–674–26–4/31–25.92.

# RATCLIFFE COLLEGE

*Played 11: Won 5, Lost 1, Drawn 5. Abandoned 4*

Master i/c: R. M. Hughes                    Cricket professional: S. G. Peall

*Wins v:* Welbeck C.; Guthlaxton S.; Laxton S.; Gentlemen of Leicestershire; Ratcliffe Old Boys.

Between May 8 and June 12, sixteen-year-old E. J. Meredith scored 432 runs in six innings before being dismissed.

*Batting*—E. J. Meredith 11–5–631–121*–2–105.16; *P. G. Meredith 8–5–144–58–0–48.00; P. Ferguson 9–2–217–56*–0–31.00.

*Bowling*—P. G. Meredith 112.5–22–276–31–7/44–8.90; E. J. Meredith 136.1–22–385–24–6/36–16.04; A. Roga 83–13–272–13–4/21–20.92.

# READING SCHOOL

*Played 13: Won 1, Lost 5, Drawn 7. Abandoned 2*

Master i/c: R. G. Owen

*Win v:* Lord Williams's, Thame.

*Batting*—M. L. Dykes 6–3–137–60*–0–45.66; A. C. Clouting 12–1–436–108–2–39.63; B. Mayhew 10–0–200–71–0–20.00; B. T. Clacy 12–0–239–51–0–19.91; M. P. Bold 12–0–202–51–0–16.83; *A. J. Cole 12–2–165–53–0–16.50; S. Gibson 13–0–191–69–0–14.69; J. R. Parkhouse 9–1–113–32–0–14.12.

*Bowling*—G. J. Tollervey 99–19–350–17–4/25–20.58; M. P. Bold 104–17–446–15–3/10–29.73; R. F. Mascarenhas 72–5–355–11–3/46–32.27.

# REED'S SCHOOL

*Played 12: Won 1, Lost 8, Drawn 3. Abandoned 3*

Master i/c: G. R. Martin

*Win v:* Glyn S.

*Batting*—*M. R. Neal-Smith 12–0–296–51–0–24.66; C. R. Hagan 11–3–190–64*–0–23.75; T. Makhzangi 11–2–194–61–0–21.55; D. Keep 12–1–186–59–0–16.90; R. B. Thompson 12–0–179–51–0–14.91; B. B. Woolnough 10–0–127–43–0–12.70; D. R. Bayat 12–0–122–25–0–10.16.

*Bowling*—D. S. Faulkner 136–32–469–19–5/11–24.68; R. Coleman 104.5–26–357–13–3/8–27.46; C. R. Hagan 95–21–400–13–5/64–30.76.

## REIGATE GRAMMAR SCHOOL

*Played 19: Won 4, Lost 3, Drawn 12. Abandoned 3*

Master i/c: D. C. R. Jones                    Cricket professional: H. Newton

*Wins v:* XL Club; Ardingly; Trinity; Victoria C., Jersey.

*Batting*—N. R. Cook 12–3–270–40–0–30.00; J. B. Drewett 12–3–254–53–0–28.22; *S. J. Hygate 17–0–378–88–0–22.23; M. C. Pritchard 15–0–310–53–0–20.66; N. J. Chapman 13–3–203–42–0–20.30; M. H. Hetherington 7–1–118–48–0–19.66; S. R. G. Roberts 17–3–246–34–0–17.57.

*Bowling*—D. R. C. Holder 217.2–55–533–41–6/48–13.00; J. O. M. Whyte 161.5–39–476–23–6/43–20.69; N. J. Chapman 200.3–45–600–24–4/42–25.00; T. J. H. Martin 98.1–17–335–13–3/8–25.76.

## RENDCOMB COLLEGE

*Played 19: Won 2, Lost 8, Drawn 9. Abandoned 1*

Master i/c: C. Burden                    Cricket professional: D. Essenhigh

*Wins v:* Marling S.; Cokethorpe S.

*Batting*—*M. Head 18–2–565–97–0–35.31; M. Valentine 14–1–234–51–0–18.00; N. J. Smith 17–1–247–73–0–15.43; P. Irving 12–2–105–34–0–10.50; J. Wheeler 20–1–191–37–0–10.05; D. Chapman 15–3–117–33–0–9.75; W. King 17–0–135–33–0–7.94; J. Grafton 17–0–122–30–0–7.17.

*Bowling*—W. King 195.2–33–716–35–7/54–20.45; J. Tate 134–34–394–18–5/24–21.88; A. Sylvester 105–9–401–14–5/15–28.64; D. Chapman 133–21–533–15–4/54–35.53.

## REPTON SCHOOL

*Played 16: Won 9, Lost 3, Drawn 4. Abandoned 3*

Masters i/c: M. Stones and J. M. G. Willatt                    Cricket professional: M. K. Kettle

*Wins v:* Pocklington; Ashby Hastings CC; Malvern; Wrekin; Repton Pilgrims; Worksop; King Edward's, Birmingham; Stowe; Bedford.

*Batting*—A. R. Paulett 18–2–831–103–2–51.93; R. I. Biggin 18–3–734–125–2–48.93; L. J. Allen 13–4–320–100*–1–35.55; G. E. Shipley 11–0–330–87–0–30.00; J. N. Batty 16–4–327–97*–0–27.25; *N. J. W. Campion 11–3–206–44–0–25.75.

*Bowling*—J. N. Batty 72–9–212–11–4/28–19.27; J. W. S. Piper 137.5–23–523–24–5/34–21.79; A. R. Paulett 85.4–17–260–11–5/45–23.63; N. F. Murray 78.3–10–268–11–3/17–24.36; R. I. Biggin 92.4–17–315–11–4/54–28.28; E. G. Prince 199–61–578–18–3/9–32.11.

## RICHARD HUISH COLLEGE, TAUNTON

*Played 16: Won 5, Lost 4, Drawn 7. Abandoned 2*

Master i/c: W. J. Maidlow

*Wins v:* Sexey's; Exeter Univ.; Britannia Royal Naval C., Dartmouth; Huish Staff; Purbeck S.

M. J. Saunders established two new records in the Barclays Cup match v Purbeck School, Wareham: he scored 137 not out and shared in a second-wicket partnership of 223 with J. M. Paul (107). Kevin J. Parsons completed his school career with a record aggregate of 1,533 runs and five centuries in 26 innings, and was selected, along with his identical twin, Keith A. Parsons, for English Schools.

*Batting*—Keith A. Parsons 7–1–362–116–1–60.33; B. T. Collins 6–1–296–74–0–59.20; J. M. Paul 7–2–290–107–1–58.00; *Kevin J. Parsons 9–1–460–115*–1–57.50; M. J. Saunders 7–3–179–137*–1–44.75; B. A. Law 11–2–181–54–0–20.11; A. J. Coupé 6–0–105–43–0–17.50.

*Bowling*—B. T. Collins 44–8–126–13–5/20–9.69; P. Dimond 88.1–17–345–23–4/31–15.00; S. J. Nelson 66–13–216–12–3/7–18.00; B. A. Law 60.2–8–224–11–3/29–20.36.

## ROEDEAN SCHOOL

*Played 8: Won 6, Lost 1, Drawn 0, Tied 1. Abandoned 4*

Staff i/c: A. S. England and Mrs A. F. Romanov

*Wins v:* Newland's Manor; Sevenoaks; Cottesmore; Charterhouse; Cranleigh; Staff XI.

With an innings of 109 against Cranleigh, K. Mills, an Australian, became the first to score a century for the XI; she also achieved a post-war record aggregate of 266 runs.

*Batting*—K. Mills 7–1–266–109–1–44.33; V. L. Tassell 8–2–228–74–0–38.00.

*Bowling*—G. M. Baker 32.1–5–82–15–4/16–5.46; K. Mills 42–11–131–12–4/51–10.91.

## ROSSALL SCHOOL

*Played 16: Won 1, Lost 8, Drawn 7*

Master i/c: A. T. Crouch

*Win v:* Stonyhurst.

At thirteen, L. Botham became the youngest player to appear in the Rossall XI, but he played in the first three matches only (highest score, 57 against Manchester GS) before a back injury kept him out for the rest of the season.

*Batting*—J. Elliott 16–1–579–76–0–38.60; A. Greenwood 9–1–176–48–0–22.00; C. Mawdsley 7–1–120–51*–0–20.00; J. Newbold 16–0–314–56–0–19.62; A. Holmes 11–3–108–30*–0–13.50; H. Parr 11–0–139–41–0–12.63.

*Bowling*—A. Holmes 106–26–289–17–4/46–17.00; C. Mawdsley 62.4–9–245–10–4/26–24.50; J. Mathers 221–35–747–29–5/39–25.75; H. Parr 118–22–373–13–2/19–28.69.

## ROYAL GRAMMAR SCHOOL, GUILDFORD

*Played 19: Won 7, Lost 5, Drawn 7. Abandoned 2*

Master i/c: S. B. R. Shore

*Wins v:* Judd GS; Charterhouse; RGS, High Wycombe; Emanuel; Reed's; Wallington; Trinity.

The captain and leading all-rounder, B. C. Ray, came within 36 runs of his own batting record, set the previous year. Four of the XI's defeats were inflicted at the RGS festival at Worcester, spoiling what prior to then had been a good record.

*Batting*—\*B. C. Ray 18–2–637–111–2–39.81; W. R. Skottowe 13–3–306–81–0–30.60; S. J. Derrick 18–2–419–74–0–26.18; A. J. Moss 16–2–360–55\*–0–25.71; J. D. C. Wydenbach 11–1–223–41\*–0–22.30; R. M. Gilbert 17–2–300–61–0–20.00; M. P. Arnull 13–3–173–31\*–0–17.30.

*Bowling*—B. C. Ray 229.1–80–512–41–6/28–12.48; A. J. Moss 158–29–444–24–5/46–18.50; P. Z. Brown 183–54–457–23–4/18–19.86; T. C. Fraser 80–14–287–14–4/50–20.50; G. B. Morley 126.1–32–381–11–2/5–34.63.

## ROYAL GRAMMAR SCHOOL, NEWCASTLE

*Played 17: Won 11, Lost 5, Drawn 1*

Master i/c: D. W. Smith

*Wins v*: Queen Elizabeth GS, Penrith; St Bees; Austin Friars; King's, Tynemouth; Durham; Whitley Bay HS; Alnwick HS; Berwick HS; Dame Allan's; RGS, High Wycombe; RGS, Guildford.

*Batting*—\*R. S. Papps 17–3–546–85–0–39.00; L. J. Crozier 17–2–527–126\*–1–35.13; J. C. Hammill 17–2–392–63–0–26.13; A. J. Proctor 15–3–313–88\*–0–26.08; J. D. V. Ryan 15–4–223–50\*–0–20.27; N. R. Gandy 14–3–201–47–0–18.27.

*Bowling*—R. S. Papps 111.3–30–331–32–5/25–10.34; L. J. Crozier 166.4–38–469–41–6/28–11.43; J. D. V. Ryan 138–27–395–21–3/36–18.80; K. Walton 154–30–453–23–4/8–19.69.

## ROYAL GRAMMAR SCHOOL, WORCESTER

*Played 25: Won 12, Lost 3, Drawn 10. Abandoned 3*

Master i/c: B. M. Rees                    Cricket professional: M. J. Horton

*Wins v*: Coventry GS, Bablake; Old Elizabethans; Wolverhampton GS; Christ C., Brecon; King's, Worcester; Loughborough GS; Brighton; RGS, Colchester; RGS, Guildford; RGS, High Wycombe; RGS, Newcastle; RGS Masters.

The highlight of the season was the Royal GS festival, which the School hosted in its septcentenary and where they won four of five matches, as did Royal GS, Colchester. A. V. Powell, who passed 900 runs for the second successive season, won the *Daily Telegraph* award for Midlands schools.

*Batting*—A. V. Powell 21–4–903–127–1–53.11; J. E. Phillips 22–5–846–113\*–1–49.76; J. A. Davies 6–2–198–82\*–0–49.50; G. Pilgrim 22–3–676–78\*–0–35.57; M. W. Williams 13–3–285–94–0–28.50; J. M. Connor 17–5–259–41–0–21.58; \*N. P. Haddock 12–3–160–43–0–17.77; N. M. Davies 9–2–100–21–0–14.28.

*Bowling*—S. D. C. Haynes 113.3–33–283–17–6/23–16.64; C. M. B. Tetley 180.3–51–528–31–5/45–17.03; M. W. Williams 155.5–35–397–20–6/50–19.85; N. P. Haddock 281.1–64–872–38–5/58–22.94; N. M. Davies 99–22–305–12–3/22–25.41; J. A. Osborn 188.2–54–433–16–3/21–27.06.

## RUGBY SCHOOL

*Played 18: Won 1, Lost 5, Drawn 12. Abandoned 1*

Master i/c: K. Siviter                    Cricket professional: W. J. Stewart

*Win v*: Charterhouse.

*Batting*—\*A. M. Alexander 12–2–477–109–1–47.70; M. A. Goodhart 17–3–540–82\*–0–38.57; N. J. Wood 17–1–435–73–0–27.18; R. W. S. Seabrook 10–1–201–59–0–22.33; C. J. C. Robards 14–3–242–51\*–0–22.00; C. H. D. Boddington 11–3–114–62–0–14.25.

*Bowling*—K. J. Edwards 49–11–162–10–4/31–16.20; N. J. Wood 243.2–62–747–35–5/48–21.34; D. Jain 121–29–396–14–3/13–28.28; R. W. S. Seabrook 123–22–389–13–3/35–29.92; A. W. Whittle 154.5–16–544–17–3/22–32.00.

# RYDAL SCHOOL

*Played 12: Won 2, Lost 5, Drawn 5*

Master i/c: M. T. Leach                           Cricket professional: R. W. Pitman

*Wins v:* St David's, Llandudno; MCC.

*Batting*—M. H. Bennett 12–1–306–101*–1–27.81; S. M. Ashley 11–0–169–89–0–15.36; R. A. Finney 9–0–107–43–0–11.88; J. C. Davies 12–1–106–30–0–9.63.

*Bowling*—R. J. Brook 47–9–154–13–4/21–11.84; M. G. Macdonald 109–32–292–23–4/17–12.69; G. W. Williams 60.1–17–147–10–3/11–14.70; S. M. Ashley 118.1–22–347–20–4/16–17.35; J. C. Davies 68–19–255–10–2/3–25.50.

# ST ALBANS SCHOOL

*Played 21: Won 5, Lost 8, Drawn 8*

Master i/c: I. P. Jordan

*Wins v:* C. C. Hudson's XI; Cavendish; Luton; John Lyon; Roundwood.

*Batting*—*I. Mote 17–4–263–51–0–20.23; J. Baines 20–1–364–48–0–19.15; M. Seller 17–2–260–38–0–17.33; A. Harwood 17–3–219–47–0–15.64; J. Newbery 20–1–280–60–0–14.73; R. Walker 16–0–219–49–0–13.68.

*Bowling*—T. Hunt 95–9–362–23–7/33–15.73; M. Seller 48–7–217–10–4/10–21.70; R. Walker 143–14–662–28–4/47–23.64; J. Newbery 47–5–245–10–2/1–24.50; G. Kan 70–11–264–10–4/54–26.40; R. White 95–16–314–11–3/33–28.54.

# ST DUNSTAN'S COLLEGE

*Played 14: Won 0, Lost 6, Drawn 8. Abandoned 2*

Master i/c: C. Matten

*Batting*—J. M. Bennett 13–4–379–115*–1–42.11; N. J. Andrews 11–1–377–60–0–37.70; M. C. Allen 9–2–242–96–0–34.57; P. A. R. Hobson 11–1–170–46*–0–17.00; P. J. Gaskell 11–1–163–31–0–16.30; C. J. Cowley 14–1–203–64–0–15.61.

*Bowling*—J. M. Bennett 122.3–27–367–19–6/40–19.31; D. L. Kirby 163.2–35–483–23–5/17–21.00.

# ST EDWARD'S SCHOOL, OXFORD

*Played 14: Won 5, Lost 2, Drawn 7. Abandoned 1*

Master i/c: M. D. Peregrine

*Wins v:* Abingdon; MCC; Worcester Coll., Oxford; St Edward's Martyrs; Berkhamsted.

C. M. Pitcher's aggregate of 507, the highest for the XI for some years, featured two innings of 100 not out in three days – against Bradfield on June 20, and Marlborough on June 22. For the second successive season, Pitcher was also the leading wicket-taker.

*Batting*—*C. M. Pitcher 14–4–507–100*–2–50.70; E. J. Montague 14–1–216–80–0–16.61; A. J. Stewart 13–0–208–44–0–16.00; J. G. Drake-Brockman 11–0–161–80–0–14.63; T. W. T. Stanley 11–2–125–35–0–13.88; A. M. B. Goodwin 14–2–152–35–0–12.66.

*Bowling*—E. C. Lonsdale 120.3–29–284–21–5/26–13.52; C. M. Pitcher 172.1–43–442–27–5/16–16.37; L. Siriwardene 101.1–17–337–14–4/35–24.07; M. C. Brodie 141–29–460–14–3/42–32.85.

## ST GEORGE'S COLLEGE, WEYBRIDGE

*Played 15: Won 0, Lost 9, Drawn 6. Abandoned 4*

Master i/c: B. V. O'Gorman

*Batting*—M. Miller 13–1–672–113–1–56.00; J. Barwell 10–0–214–60–0–21.40; J. Stephens 10–1–176–58–0–19.55; R. Hirst 15–2–225–56–0–17.30; C. Segal 15–0–251–73–0–16.73; T. Carroll 12–1–143–42*–0–13.00.

*Bowling*—R. Hirst 194–18–852–26–5/48–32.76.

## ST JOHN'S SCHOOL, LEATHERHEAD

*Played 14: Won 4, Lost 0, Drawn 10. Abandoned 1*

Master i/c: A. B. Gale                                   Cricket professional: E. Shepperd

*Wins v:* Alleyn's; Grasshoppers CC; St George's, Weybridge; St Benedict's, Ealing.

*Batting*—M. N. Cooper 14–4–419–81*–0–41.90; *T. S. S. Walton 14–3–434–102*–1–39.45; C. A. Musson 12–5–219–55*–0–31.28; J. K. Patel 13–0–287–118–1–22.07; R. J. Vickery 14–0–297–74–0–21.21; R. I. Elliott 10–0–190–47–0–19.00; I. A. D. Grove 10–4–105–35*–0–17.50; R. A. Brookes 13–3–150–35*–0–15.00.

*Bowling*—R. J. Vickery 114–23–316–21–4/15–15.04; C. A. Musson 151–41–355–18–5/42–19.72; G. J. Thompson 128–21–429–10–3/65–42.90.

## ST JOSEPH'S COLLEGE, IPSWICH

*Played 17: Won 6, Lost 4, Drawn 7*

Master i/c: A. C. Rutherford                             Cricket professional: J. Pugh

*Wins v:* Culford; Wymondham C.; Royal Hospital S.; Pimpernells CC; J. Bidwell's XI; Old Oakhillians.

*Batting*—D. White 12–4–362–95*–0–45.25; J. McLoughlin 14–6–352–72*–0–44.00; J. King 15–0–335–101–1–22.33; A. Heyland 12–0–235–37–0–19.58; R. Farrow 11–4–133–73*–0–19.00; M. Noah 9–3–100–27–0–16.66; S. Prestney 8–0–110–38–0–13.75.

*Bowling*—R. Farrow 98.2–21–260–20–8/54–13.00; D. Dellamaestra 150.1–27–483–35–8/39–13.80; J. McLoughlin 84.2–21–280–14–3/39–20.00; A. George 107.2–18–384–17–3/19–22.58; *S. McGrath 95–16–335–13–4/36–25.76; J. King 74.2–11–284–11–3/39–25.81.

## ST LAWRENCE COLLEGE, RAMSGATE

*Played 11: Won 3, Lost 1, Drawn 7. Abandoned 2*

Master i/c: N. O. S. Jones        Cricket professionals: L. A. C. D'Arcy and A. P. E. Knott

*Wins v:* Sir Roger Manwood's GS; Duke of York's RMS; Old Lawrentians.

*Batting*—D. J. Gear 11–1–358–87*–0–35.80; J. M. Huddy 11–3–277–97–0–34.62; T. R. Burles 11–2–298–56–0–33.11; *B. T. Everett 11–1–322–104*–1–32.20; C. M. Relfe 9–4–108–32–0–21.60; W. A. Taylaur 11–1–100–35–0–10.00.

*Bowling*—J. M. Huddy 117.4–26–318–20–5/39–15.90; W. A. Taylaur 137–34–399–14–5/50–28.50.

# ST PAUL'S SCHOOL

*Played 15: Won 2, Lost 1, Drawn 11, Tied 1. Abandoned 1*

Master i/c: G. Hughes                    Cricket professional: E. W. Whitfield

*Wins v:* Fettes; Monkton Combe.

The cricket professional, E. W. Whitfield, retired after twenty years with the School and having celebrated his 80th birthday. The tied match was against the Incogniti.

*Batting*—J. O. Morris 14-1-465-78-0-35.76; S. Patel 14-0-447-93-0-31.92; P. A. Shapiro 14-1-391-66*-0-30.07; T. J. Taberner 11-1-235-57*-0-23.50; *S. D. S. Kaikini 13-1-268-59-0-22.33; C. M. Rampling 13-1-185-55*-0-15.41.

*Bowling*—D. C. Hitchins 156.3-35-405-27-6/20-15.00; S. H. Clark 86.1-20-245-15-4/30-16.33; F. S. Walden 81-25-205-11-2/26-18.63; S. B. Clarke 195.2-44-523-28-5/34-18.67.

# ST PETER'S SCHOOL, YORK

*Played 20: Won 2, Lost 3, Drawn 15*

Master i/c: D. Kirby                    Cricket professional: K. F. Mohan

*Wins v:* Loretto; Old Peterites.

*Batting*—M. P. Forrester 20-1-744-116-2-39.15; M. J. Davies 20-5-582-101*-1-38.80; P. F. Carvosso 19-2-342-59*-0-20.11; O. Gardner 17-8-167-45-0-18.55; *J. D. Rigby 19-0-349-83-0-18.36; G. J. Harding 19-0-305-66-0-16.05; B. R. Neary 13-4-139-57-0-15.44.

*Bowling*—R. F. T. Musgrave 147-34-453-21-4/26-21.57; B. R. Neary 128-22-561-19-5/15-29.52; D. Bundy 106-21-427-12-3/28-35.58; M. P. Forrester 161-22-572-13-2/15-44.00.

# SEDBERGH SCHOOL

*Played 12: Won 6, Lost 2, Drawn 4. Abandoned 5*

Master i/c: N. A. Rollings                  Cricket professional: K. Benjamin

*Wins v:* Pocklington; Ampleforth; MCC; Incomparables; Stonyhurst; St Paul's, Brisbane.

*Batting*—D. J. Player 7-0-280-68-0-40.00; *W. J. H. Greenwood 12-3-285-55*-0-31.66; S. G. Lewis 11-4-187-57*-0-26.71; P. M. Birkbeck 11-0-263-66-0-23.90; R. C. F. Smailes 12-1-261-57-0-23.72; M. L. Parrish 11-0-234-40-0-21.27; M. Manson 11-2-167-53*-0-18.55.

*Bowling*—R. C. F. Smailes 78-17-227-15-3/51-15.13; S. C. V. Light 154-42-431-21-4/24-20.52; D. J. Player 74-15-222-10-3/44-22.20; W. J. H. Greenwood 131-35-341-11-3/25-31.00.

# SEVENOAKS SCHOOL

*Played 14: Won 3, Lost 0, Drawn 11. Abandoned 5*

Master i/c: I. J. B. Walker

*Wins v:* Ardingly; Worth; Old Sennockians.

H. Iqbal, son of the Pakistani Test cricketer, Asif Iqbal, headed the batting in a young XI, which was Sevenoaks' first unbeaten side since 1980. J. S. Smeeton, a fifteen-year-old off-spinner, was the leading wicket-taker.

*Batting*—H. Iqbal 14–2–578–97–0–48.16; W. J. House 6–2–179–44*–0–44.75; *J. D. M. Brearley 13–0–324–104–1–24.92; C. J. Peters 13–2–183–31*–0–16.63; N. R. Payton 9–0–107–36–0–11.88; A. M. H. Hook 13–3–100–28*–0–10.00.

*Bowling*—J. S. Smeeton 166.2–35–489–29–5/12–16.86; C. J. Peters 170.4–44–427–25–5/35–17.08.

## SHEBBEAR COLLEGE

*Played 11: Won 3, Lost 3, Drawn 5*

Master i/c: A. Bryan                    Cricket professional: G. V. Palmer

*Wins v:* Grenville; Chatham GS; Old Shebbearians.

*Batting*—A. Skinner 11–3–272–59–0–34.00; J. Spires 10–1–134–46–0–14.88; S. Jackson 11–1–143–30*–0–14.30.

*Bowling*—P. Muirhead 132–35–295–33–5/22–8.93; M. Dale 131.1–34–367–34–6/41–10.79; *A. Armstrong 71.4–8–201–16–4/59–12.56.

## SHERBORNE SCHOOL

*Played 15: Won 6, Lost 2, Drawn 7. Abandoned 1*

Master i/c: G. C. Allen                    Cricket professional: A. Willows

*Wins v:* Free Foresters; King's, Taunton; Blundell's; Westminster S., Adelaide; Sherborne Pilgrims; Marlborough.

R. H. F. Pugsley, the captain, took five or more wickets on five occasions with his off-spin bowling, while J. D. Ricketts hit hundreds against Dorset Rangers and Downside.

*Batting*—J. D. Ricketts 16–2–641–111*–2–45.78; A. R. Baines 16–0–510–95–0–31.87; E. J. Sangster 16–5–330–69*–0–30.00; C. J. Colby 10–0–216–81–0–21.60; J. L. Pexton 13–1–255–65–0–21.25; S. C. G. Watling 12–1–157–42–0–14.27.

*Bowling*—*R. H. F. Pugsley 214.1–68–538–43–7/44–12.51; J. L. Pexton 138–54–322–25–5/32–12.88; P. A. Evans 150.3–47–344–24–4/46–14.33; A. J. Rutherford 78–11–258–10–2/28–25.80; J. D. Ricketts 167.3–53–467–17–3/41–27.47.

## SHIPLAKE COLLEGE

*Played 12: Won 5, Lost 1, Drawn 6. Abandoned 1*

Master i/c: P. M. Davey                    Cricket professional: M. Hobbs

*Wins v:* Reading; Pangbourne C.; St Bartholomews, Newbury; Free Foresters; Cokethorpe S.

*Batting*—T. P. Caston 10–4–409–98–0–68.16; *A. J. Hall 10–3–390–77–0–55.71; A. E. Rouse 11–1–315–78–0–31.50; M. J. Baker 11–1–140–32–0–14.00.

*Bowling*—A. J. Hall 161.2–33–479–38–6/44–12.60; G. Philp 140.3–33–362–26–7/50–13.92; T. Ratcliff 73–9–268–11–5/29–24.36.

## SHREWSBURY SCHOOL

*Played 13: Won 2, Lost 4, Drawn 7. Abandoned 2*

Master i/c: S. M. Holroyd                    Cricket professional: A. P. Pridgeon

*Wins v:* Free Foresters; Radley.

*Batting*—J. W. Laycock 6–2–119–29*–0–29.75; S. W. K. Ellis 5–1–116–63*–0–29.00; D. P. Watson 13–3–272–76–0–27.20; A. F. Cutler 13–1–304–60–0–25.33; C. G. B. Sankey 11–1–214–51*–0–21.40; B. R. Parfitt 15–3–223–50–0–18.58.

*Bowling*—R. J. Hanson 104–31–249–21–6/59–11.85; I. K. Mainwaring 214–53–499–34–7/46–14.67; D. P. Watson 182–37–484–26–6/31–18.61; R. A. D. Holden 60–14–191–10–5/19–19.10; *M. D. Tattersall 91–20–320–14–3/43–22.85.

## SIMON LANGTON GRAMMAR SCHOOL

*Played 12: Won 8, Lost 0, Drawn 4*

Master i/c: R. H. Green

*Wins v:* Bexley-Erith THS; Borden GS; Sir Joseph Williamson's Math School, Rochester (twice); Norton Knatchbull; Gravesend GS; Chislehurst and Sidcup GS; Simon Langton Staff XI.

Simon Langton won the Kent Schools' CA Under-19 League.

*Batting*—J. Chadwick 5–2–107–45*–0–35.66; *N. Jones 11–1–344–107*–1–34.40; D. Isard 9–3–159–49*–0–26.50; S. Hart 8–3–123–50*–0–24.60; P. Livesey 11–1–243–70–0–24.30; J. Kember 10–1–191–44–0–21.22.

*Bowling*—P. Livesey 25.1–6–67–11–5/3–6.09; D. Clark 56–21–85–12–4/18–7.08; M. Relf 79.3–19–146–15–5/25–9.73; N. Jones 51.4–6–187–17–5/21–11.00; N. Bielby 107.1–21–307–24–5/32–12.79.

## SOLIHULL SCHOOL

*Played 16: Won 4, Lost 2, Drawn 10. Abandoned 2*

Master i/c: D. J. Dunn                    Cricket professional: S. P. Perryman

*Wins v:* King William's, IOM; Campbell C., Belfast; Bishop Vesey GS; Recent Old Silhillians.

*Batting*—J. R. Vaughan 12–5–275–54*–0–39.28; *K. A. Mortimer 16–0–498–77–0–31.12; M. A. Jones 10–1–248–109*–1–27.55; R. A. Chapman 16–2–307–71–0–21.92; M. J. Ketland-Jones 11–2–182–68*–0–20.22; R. A. Kallicharran 15–1–277–101*–1–19.78; P. S. Amiss 12–0–153–35–0–12.75.

*Bowling*—J. R. Vaughan 103.2–20–384–23–5/55–16.69; K. A. Mortimer 147.3–33–499–24–5/36–20.79; R. A. Kallicharran 119.2–20–427–14–3/17–30.50; J. E. Vertigen 85–10–376–11–3/33–34.18.

## STAMFORD SCHOOL

*Played 16: Won 3, Lost 5, Drawn 8*

Master i/c: P. D. McKeown

*Wins v:* King's, Peterborough; Gresham's; Bromsgrove.

*Batting*—D. G. Bartle 6–1–117–56–0–23.40; R. E. Grundy 14–2–267–48*–0–22.25; J. P. Moore 12–2–193–39–0–19.30; *P. Banbury 15–0–284–55–0–18.93; B. T. Bonney-James 9–0–164–35–0–18.22; D. P. M. Herrick 10–2–131–58*–0–16.37; M. D. Anstey 14–2–185–51–0–15.41; D. M. Palmer 11–2–132–31–0–14.66; T. D. Bonney-James 13–2–150–25*–0–13.63.

*Bowling*—P. Holland 118–24–363–18–6/7–20.16; G. S. Paulson 95–11–381–18–4/27–21.16; M. D. Anstey 117–16–375–14–5/30–26.78; T. D. Bonney-James 162–36–517–18–3/26–28.72.

## STOCKPORT GRAMMAR SCHOOL

*Played 12: Won 4, Lost 1, Drawn 7*

Master i/c: C. Dunkerley        Cricket professional: D. J. Makinson

*Wins v:* Cheadle Hulme; Manchester GS; King's, Tynemouth; St Ambrose.

In addition to their ten-wicket victory over Cheadle Hulme, the XI enjoyed a nine-wicket win over Manchester GS, at Manchester.

*Batting*—*J. S. Mellor 11–3–549–66–0–68.62; S. Lapsia 10–2–335–77–0–41.87; J. M. A. Reeman 7–4–108–44\*–0–36.00; F. I. Macdonald 8–1–155–64–0–22.14; D. A. Whitehead 9–3–120–39\*–0–20.00; R. Bowden 7–1–103–65\*–0–17.16.

*Bowling*—S. Lapsia 149.2–33–413–36–6/17–11.47; F. I. Macdonald 119–31–359–11–3/14–32.63.

## STOWE SCHOOL

*Played 16: Won 5, Lost 5, Drawn 6. Abandoned 2*

Master i/c: G. A. Cottrell        Cricket professional: M. J. Harris

*Wins v:* Winchester; Bradfield; Berkhamsted; Bloxham; Northamptonshire YCA.

*Batting*—D. J. Amdor 11–3–353–74\*–0–44.12; A. J. Scott-Gall 15–2–475–74\*–0–36.53; A. R. B. Bellew 7–3–108–34\*–0–27.00; R. D. S. Burrough 5–0–123–83–0–24.60; M. P. Bazeley 12–1–267–48–0–24.27; W. L. C. Morris 10–2–169–94\*–0–21.12; R. J. Q. Green 14–1–233–48–0–17.92; D. H. Westinghouse 9–2–115–23–0–16.42; \*D. J. Raynor 12–0–119–46–0–9.91.

*Bowling*—D. J. Raynor 231–63–578–36–7/48–16.05; D. J. Amdor 60.2–16–170–10–3/12–17.00; A. J. Scott-Gall 267–77–671–36–5/37–18.63; W. D. H. Jones 97–20–320–11–3/35–29.09.

## STRATHALLAN SCHOOL

*Played 14: Won 7, Lost 4, Drawn 3. Abandoned 4*

Master i/c: R. J. W. Proctor        Cricket professional: C. L. Parfitt

*Wins v:* Loretto; Fettes; Edinburgh Acad.; RGS, Lancaster; XL Club; Scottish Wayfarers; Perth Northern CC.

Despite being unable to bowl before half-term, owing to injury, H. A. D. McKenzie-Wilson was again the most successful bowler. In his second match back, he returned figures of 19–13–22–8 and eventually took his total for the XI to 112 at 12.96.

*Batting*—R. G. J. Johnston 13–3–343–77–0–34.30; \*K. L. Salters 11–2–259–78–0–28.77; H. A. D. McKenzie-Wilson 13–2–311–74–0–28.27; N. A. Gray 11–0–290–74–0–26.36; M. A. Smith 12–1–150–34–0–13.63; E. D. Anderson 10–1–104–38–0–11.55.

*Bowling*—H. A. D. McKenzie-Wilson 132.4–43–310–27–8/22–11.48; M. R. Tench 166–34–461–24–6/42–19.20; K. L. Salters 134.5–28–375–19–4/41–19.73; E. D. Anderson 96.3–20–282–14–3/30–20.14.

## SUTTON VALENCE SCHOOL

*Played 13: Won 2, Lost 6, Drawn 5. Abandoned 5*

Master i/c: D. Pickard

*Wins v:* XL Club; Duke of York's RMS.

*Batting*—\*J. M. Cowell 10–2–598–117\*–2–74.75; A. P. Hudd 9–0–272–73–0–30.22; D. Poole-Connor 12–0–249–65–0–20.75; A. Barr 10–1–166–47–0–18.44; S. Young 7–0–109–43–0–15.57.

*Bowling*—J. H. Waters 78.5–5–327–12–4/40–27.25; D. Poole-Connor 93.5–13–342–10–5/51–34.20.

# TAUNTON SCHOOL

*Played 15: Won 7, Lost 2, Drawn 6. Abandoned 2*

Master i/c: D. Baty                              Cricket professional: A. Kennedy

*Wins v:* King's, Bruton; XL Club; Sherborne; Downside; Blundell's; Bradford GS; MCC.

K. G. Sedgbeer kept wicket for MCC Schools and English Schools, as well as playing for Somerset Second XI.

*Batting*—G. Crompton 15–2–392–56–0–30.15; P. E. S. Tarr 15–1–411–69–0–29.35; J. P. Hunt 5–0–132–71–0–26.40; K. G. Sedgbeer 14–1–329–94–0–25.30; B. M. Wellington 13–3–214–61–0–21.40; N. L. Smith 13–2–211–48–0–19.18.

*Bowling*—J. S. Hales 196.2–61–390–26–6/25–15.00; B. M. Wellington 221.2–64–597–33–7/27–18.09; J. Skittrall 84.4–20–272–13–3/47–20.92; E. S. Little 153.2–35–424–17–3/28–24.94.

# TIFFIN SCHOOL

*Played 20: Won 4, Lost 0, Drawn 16. Abandoned 2*

Master i/c: M. J. Williams

*Wins v:* Emanuel; Kingston GS; Caterham; John Fisher.

Outstanding again was the opening batsman, G. J. Kennis, who followed his 1,008 runs and three centuries in 1990 with 946 runs and four centuries in 1991, thus passing D. G. Ottley's record of six hundreds for the XI. B. J. Walters was once more the leading wicket-taker, his left-arm spin bringing him 51 wickets to set alongside his 41 of the previous season and taking his tally for the XI to 125 in three full seasons. Kennis was expected to return for another season, while Walters was offered a place at Durham University for 1992.

*Batting*—G. J. Kennis 19–2–946–145*–4–55.64; N. G. Hodgson 17–1–558–130–2–34.87; S. R. A. Leeds 15–0–443–101–1–29.53; *B. J. Walters 12–1–300–58*–0–27.27; N. Evans 15–5–249–44*–0–24.90; H. D. Steel 19–4–203–44–0–13.53; M. A. Rafique 14–4–129–41*–0–12.90; M. D. McPherson 13–0–153–31–0–11.76.

*Bowling*—B. J. Walters 242.2–98–649–51–6/40–12.72; A. M. Hickman 218–59–580–33–5/12–17.57; N. Evans 138.5–30–420–16–5/64–26.25; G. J. Kennis 93–25–267–10–4/20–26.70; S. R. Vinnicombe 202.5–42–649–19–3/32–34.15.

# TONBRIDGE SCHOOL

*Played 11: Won 3, Lost 4, Drawn 4. Abandoned 5*

Master i/c: I. S. MacEwen                        Cricket professional: C. Stone

*Wins v:* Tonbridge CC; Free Foresters; Felsted.

*Batting*—C. S. Madderson 10–1–292–72–0–32.44; *S. J. Jobber 13–3–261–102*–1–26.10; S. D. Gilbert 10–2–187–36–0–23.37; M. O. Church 12–0–272–47–0–22.66; W. R. Tomkins 12–2–193–67–0–19.30; P. E. M. Le Marchand 7–0–128–35–0–18.28; P. J. Kemp 13–0–225–54–0–17.30.

*Bowling*—W. R. Tomkins 88–21–275–19–6/35–14.47; M. J. H. Bryant 183.1–46–508–29–6/12–17.51; J. E. Baird 105–18–349–17–5/38–20.52; P. S. Shea 82.4–14–306–11–3/34–27.81.

## TRENT COLLEGE

*Played 15: Won 3, Lost 4, Drawn 8*

Master i/c: Dr T. P. Woods          Cricket professional: L. Spendlove

*Wins v:* Oakham; Bradford GS; Headmaster's XI.

M. T. White would almost certainly have taken more than his 39 wickets but for the handicap of a leg injury after half-term; until then, he had taken 27 in seven matches at an average of just over 10.

*Batting—*R. S. Brooks 12–1–379–90–0–34.45; *J. Pavis 13–1–394–100\*–1–32.83; N. D. Johnson 15–0–447–82–0–29.80; J. D. Pratt 13–1–254–52–0–21.16; A. J. Vaughan 13–2–223–69–0–20.27; M. T. White 13–2–145–38–0–13.18; M. J. Goodley 13–2–101–49–0–9.18.

*Bowling—*M. T. White 200.4–31–611–39–6/57–15.66; A. J. Vaughan 104–16–371–16–4/25–23.18; B. L. Tyack 88.2–12–331–11–4/26–30.09; M. B. Wilson 132–29–369–12–3/13–30.75.

## TRINITY SCHOOL

*Played 22: Won 10, Lost 3, Drawn 9. Abandoned 3*

Masters i/c: D. Coleman and B. Widger

*Wins v:* Hampton; Alleyn's; St Dunstan's; Eltham; Whitgift; Parents' XI; Past Captain's XI; East Holland District U-19 XI; Rotterdam and District U-19 XI; The Hague District U-19 XI.

R. W. Nowell, who went on to play for England Schools Under-15, was an outstanding all-rounder. Bowling left-arm spin, he took 49 wickets, while his 911 runs included four centuries, equalling the school record.

*Batting—*R. W. Nowell 21–2–911–119\*–4–47.94; A. J. Derosa 14–9–216–72\*–0–43.20; A. J. Codling 21–3–687–100\*–1–38.16; D. O. Dyer 8–4–120–27\*–0–30.00; *C. H. Maiden 21–2–532–107\*–1–28.00; C. M. Brown 19–4–348–59–0–23.20; D. L. Fifield 19–0–363–55–0–19.10; P. S. Kember 13–4–170–33\*–0–18.88; R. J. Anderson 10–2–122–34\*–0–15.25.

*Bowling—*R. W. Nowell 242–68–653–49–6/25–13.32; P. S. Kember 219.1–44–616–32–5/31–19.25; J. R. Mills 130.5–22–410–20–5/24–20.50; A. J. Derosa 125–25–379–18–5/21–21.05; M. D. C. Butterworth 185–38–511–23–4/44–22.21.

## TRURO SCHOOL

*Played 10: Won 1, Lost 3, Drawn 6. Abandoned 3*

Master i/c: D. M. Phillips

*Win v:* Kelly C.

*Batting—*D. F. Simcock 10–2–242–66\*–0–30.25; *T. R. Perkins 10–1–159–82\*–0–17.66; M. R. Thomas 10–0–173–45–0–17.30; D. P. Griffiths 7–1–100–30–0–16.66; E. L. Smith 8–0–105–44–0–13.12.

*Bowling—*S. J. Perkins 61.5–10–181–18–5/23–10.05; M. R. Thomas 124–29–376–23–7/53–16.34; T. R. Perkins 105.3–14–319–15–3/27–21.26.

## UNIVERSITY COLLEGE SCHOOL

*Played 14: Won 2, Lost 5, Drawn 7. Abandoned 3*

Master i/c: S. M. Bloomfield      Cricket professional: W. G. Jones

*Wins v:* Enfield GS; Woodbridge.

Despite the pressures of captaining a young, inexperienced side, R. J. Ayre made an outstanding contribution with the bat. He overcame the handicap of slow pitches to average 100 for much of the season and finished his four years in the XI with eight centuries, the four scored in 1991 thought to be a school record.

*Batting*—*R. J. Ayre 15-4-920-156*-4-83.63; A. R. Gishen 14-2-298-68-0-24.83; D. S. Quint 11-1-184-70*-0-18.40; G. M. Burnham 11-2-108-30*-0-12.00.

*Bowling*—A. Slatter 66-21-222-17-5/43-13.05; D. S. Quint 147-20-563-15-6/36-37.53; A. M. Quint 149-26-435-10-3/31-43.50.

## UPPINGHAM SCHOOL

*Played 17: Won 5, Lost 4, Drawn 8. Abandoned 2*

Master i/c: I. E. W. Sanders      Cricket professional: M. R. Hallam

*Wins v:* Trent; Oakham; Gentlemen of Leicestershire; Old Uppinghamians; Canford.

*Batting*—A. B. Greig 16-3-440-86*-0-33.84; S. D. Smith 17-1-524-73-0-32.75; C. E. Ferry 17-2-483-63-0-32.20; J. N. Beaumont 11-0-234-50-0-21.27; T. O. Hamilton 17-0-293-57-0-17.23; A. M. W. Green 14-6-124-47-0-15.50; C. J. Maitland 16-0-229-47-0-14.31; B. G. Helps 16-0-179-43-0-11.18.

*Bowling*—C. E. Ferry 59.3-11-181-13-5/10-13.92; M. R. W. Worrall 216.3-50-508-31-7/35-16.38; B. G. Helps 190.1-40-483-29-4/54-16.65; *R. L. Perkins 215.3-74-549-32-5/54-17.15; A. D. Bain 157-60-417-19-4/50-21.94.

## VICTORIA COLLEGE, JERSEY

*Played 25: Won 8, Lost 5, Drawn 12*

Master i/c: D. Ferguson      Cricket professional: R. Pearce

*Wins v:* Jersey Academicals; Rendcomb; Claysmore; Irish Taverners; Hereford Cathedral S.; OV President's XI; Bearwood; Reigate Cats.

J. Hargrove became the first player since 1983 to score 1,000 runs in a season for the College.

*Batting*—C. Jones 16-9-571-111*-1-81.57; J. Hargrove 23-3-1,046-116*-2-52.30; *R. le Quesne 23-5-655-100-1-36.38; T. Colclough 17-3-462-78*-0-33.00; I. Rogers 17-2-296-63-0-19.73; A. Barr 17-0-326-46-0-19.17; S. Billingham 13-4-107-29*-0-11.88; A. Ray 14-3-122-44-0-11.09; D. McKeon 18-1-166-34-0-9.76.

*Bowling*—I. Ritchie 329-91-954-50-6/36-19.08; A. Ray 275-56-778-40-6/56-19.45; S. Ramskill 161-31-585-29-5/22-20.17; R. le Quesne 130-22-487-14-2/7-34.78.

## WARWICK SCHOOL

*Played 10: Won 2, Lost 0, Drawn 8. Abandoned 2*

Master i/c: D. C. Elstone

*Wins v:* King's, Worcester; Trent.

*Batting*—S. Ensall 9-3-245-63*-0-40.83; C. Mulraine 7-0-243-89-0-34.71; D. Dalton 9-1-258-79-0-32.25; S. Kelley 6-0-189-71-0-31.50; J. Wilsden 8-1-167-48-0-23.85; T. McCann 9-0-119-31-0-13.22.

*Bowling*—D. Dalton 112.2-25-369-16-7/39-23.06; S. Webb 114.2-18-392-14-5/55-28.00; M. Covington 134-32-398-14-3/40-28.42.

## WATFORD GRAMMAR SCHOOL

*Played 15: Won 5, Lost 7, Drawn 3. Abandoned 3*

Master i/c: W. E. Miller

*Wins v:* Aldenham; John Lyon; Latymer Upper; Gentlemen of Hertfordshire; Old Fullerians.

*Batting*—D. H. T. Warren 13–0–485–109–1–37.30; D. W. K. Spray 9–2–232–63*–0–33.14; M. C. Dunstone 10–3–225–99*–0–32.14; A. J. Moore 8–0–171–59–0–21.37; G. McDonald 11–2–162–49–0–18.00; R. S. Ambrose 12–2–174–55–0–17.40; R. J. Emson 9–1–116–26–0–14.50.

*Bowling*—R. S. Ambrose 134–34–375–25–6/45–15.00; D. H. T. Warren 185.5–36–543–34–7/21–15.97.

## WELLINGBOROUGH SCHOOL

*Played 18: Won 2, Lost 0, Drawn 16. Abandoned 4*

Master i/c: M. H. Askham          Cricket professional: J. C. J. Dye

*Wins v:* Kimbolton; Ivanhoe GS, Melbourne.

*Batting*—R. D. Mann 18–2–841–102*–2–52.56; *N. J. Haste 17–2–484–66–0–32.26; M. V. Steele 13–5–161–49–0–20.12; M. J. Haste 17–6–210–44*–0–19.09; P. S. Smith 11–1–135–51*–0–13.50; P. J. Dolman 15–0–197–46–0–13.13; S. Swaroop 17–0–213–46–0–12.52.

*Bowling*—N. J. Haste 180.4–33–460–36–6/32–12.77; D. W. Hallworth 177–38–484–27–4/25–17.92; R. I. J. Matheson 135–24–408–16–5/44–25.50; M. V. Steele 71–6–356–13–3/49–27.38; S. Swaroop 88.2–23–298–10–2/7–29.80.

## WELLINGTON COLLEGE

*Played 15: Won 5, Lost 4, Drawn 6*

Masters i/c: C. M. St G. Potter and R. I. H. B. Dyer     Cricket professional: P. J. Lewington

*Wins v:* Marlborough; Charterhouse; Bedford; Repton; Stowe.

T. N. Sawrey-Cookson completed his career in the XI as the College's second most prolific batsman, his total of 2,216 falling just 71 short of the record.

*Batting*—T. P. Newman 11–5–434–79*–0–72.33; *T. N. Sawrey-Cookson 16–1–731–157*–2–48.73; W. P. G. Waugh 15–3–504–76–0–42.00; A. J. Parker 8–3–196–88–0–39.20; J. A. D. Wyke 15–1–521–98–0–37.21; J. M. Gowar 11–6–122–41*–0–24.40; S. C. Thompson 6–1–111–39–0–22.20.

*Bowling*—A. P. M. Samuel 156–42–402–21–4/23–19.14; J. G. Roberts 137.4–32–398–20–4/9–19.90; T. P. Newman 126–28–377–15–2/5–25.13; A. J. Parker 227.2–48–834–26–5/78–32.07; R. W. D. Waters 107.1–16–378–10–3/29–37.80.

## WELLINGTON SCHOOL

*Played 16: Won 4, Lost 8, Drawn 4. Abandoned 2*

Master i/c: P. M. Pearce

*Wins v:* Mallards CC; Kelly C.; Wellington CC; Christ C., Brecon.

*Batting*—D. R. Davidson 15–3–401–67–0–33.41; D. W. Hine 16–2–435–100*–1–31.07; L. J. Wardell 11–0–187–40–0–17.00; M. A. Hall 12–1–184–39–0–16.72; J. C. Clarke 10–1–141–46–0–15.66; *R. G. Wolfenden 15–1–216–68–0–15.42; N. J. Hutchings 12–1–138–45–0–12.54; T. J. Salter 16–1–181–56*–0–12.06; M. J. Fulker 11–1–116–47–0–11.60.

*Bowling*—D. R. Davidson 39.4–8–167–11–4/31–15.18; N. J. Hutchings 222–52–622–39–7/33–15.94; J. C. Clarke 117.1–20–384–21–7/35–18.28; D. W. Hine 97.1–16–370–16–5/31–23.12; S. Weetch 104.3–14–471–14–3/21–33.64.

## WESTMINSTER SCHOOL

*Played 10: Won 2, Lost 4, Drawn 4. Abandoned 4*

Master i/c: D. Cook                                    Cricket professional: R. Gilson

*Wins v:* MCC; Westminster City.

*Batting*—N. Mehra 6–0–155–63–0–25.83; C. Luke 9–0–150–37–0–16.66; S. Goulden 7–0–104–22–0–14.85; T. Hyam 10–0–147–52–0–14.70; M. Cornes 8–0–113–22–0–14.12.

*Bowling*—M. Cornes 35–2–159–10–2/21–15.90; V. Eatwell 35–5–160–10–3/34–16.00; L. Gillam 51–0–193–11–2/40–17.54; T. Hyam 61–8–234–13–2/36–18.00.

## WHITGIFT SCHOOL

*Played 16: Won 3, Lost 4, Drawn 9*

Master i/c: P. C. Fladgate                              Cricket professional: M. Phelps

*Wins v:* Honesti; P. C. Fladgate's XI; OWs.

On successive days, J. D. G. Ufton scored 101 not out against Kingston GS and 100 not out against The Hague Colts. The second match was also memorable for a hat-trick by the off-spinner, A. T. Lark.

*Batting*—J. D. G. Ufton 15–6–485–101*–2–53.88; C. E. Catling 5–0–200–69–0–40.00; *R. Shah 16–2–468–74–0–33.42; R. S. Gibson 14–2–363–91–0–30.25; T. J. Colbourn 10–2–234–61–0–29.25; P. M. Horne 16–2–345–71*–0–24.64; J. P. Blasco 12–0–153–49–0–12.75.

*Bowling*—J. D. G. Ufton 243.3–45–647–33–5/43–19.60; A. T. Lark 192–39–618–31–6/12–19.93; P. S. V. Middleton 79–14–299–15–4/50–19.93; T. J. Colbourn 73–10–236–11–4/59–21.45; S. N. Jackson 140–28–396–16–6/22–24.75.

## WILLIAM HULME'S GRAMMAR SCHOOL

*Played 16: Won 3, Lost 2, Drawn 11. Abandoned 1*

Master i/c: H. W. Timm                                 Cricket professional: R. Collins

*Wins v:* King Edward VII, Lytham; Merchant Taylors', Crosby; XL Club.

*Batting*—N. T. Wood 12–3–672–112*–2–74.66; *A. K. Hollingworth 13–2–440–96–0–40.00; I. A. Brassell 11–2–359–103*–1–39.88; M. Ekstein 9–3–160–56–0–26.66; L. E. Tilston 11–1–204–54–0–20.40; F. J. Baama 8–1–137–27–0–19.57; A. K. Doney 10–3–128–37*–0–18.28.

*Bowling*—I. A. Brassell 52–11–199–14–5/65–14.21; A. K. Hollingworth 109.2–16–429–18–3/30–23.83; A. R. Ladd 125.1–30–398–15–4/33–26.53.

## WINCHESTER COLLEGE

*Played 17: Won 3, Lost 4, Drawn 10. Abandoned 1*

Master i/c: P. J. Metcalfe                              Cricket professional: K. N. Foyle

*Wins v:* Portsmouth GS; Bryanston; Marlborough.

*Batting*—S. H. R. Brooke 3–1–111–74*–0–55.50; W. F. Poole-Wilson 17–2–530–94–0–35.33; *A. W. Maclay 13–3–262–52*–0–26.20; E. J. Daniels 17–1–374–69–0–23.37; N. R. Hall 17–3–293–76*–0–20.92; J. C. Guise 11–2–181–50–0–20.11; J. M. Healey 12–1–211–61–0–19.18.

*Bowling*—A. W. Maclay 242.5–46–622–38–6/32–16.36; J. W. W. Smith 262–61–764–27–6/85–28.29; H. W. Foster 117.1–23–360–10–3/37–36.00.

## WOODHOUSE GROVE SCHOOL

*Played 14: Won 5, Lost 0, Drawn 8, Tied 1. Abandoned 2*

Master i/c: E. R. Howard                    Cricket professional: R. Burgess

*Wins v:* Bootham; Old Boys; Ashville; Cowley S.; Hawks CC.

R. D. Webster, opening bat and fast-medium opening bowler, finished the season with a significant contribution in the defeat of Cowley School. He first made a powerful, unbeaten 121 in two hours and then took five for 3 to secure the victory. S. N. Lee, the captain, opening batsman and leg-spin bowler, made a useful all-round contribution and captured his 100th wicket for the XI.

*Batting*—R. D. Webster 11–3–541–121*–1–67.62; C. J. Rika 11–1–396–81–0–39.60; *S. N. Lee 12–0–450–86–0–37.50.

*Bowling*—R. D. Webster 122.3–39–260–27–6/16–9.62; C. J. Rika 130.2–26–362–26–4/18–13.92; R. C. Ham 80–18–207–14–6/39–14.78; S. N. Lee 82–12–285–16–5/38–17.81.

## WORKSOP COLLEGE

*Played 14: Won 1, Lost 4, Drawn 9. Abandoned 1*

Master i/c: B. Wilks                    Cricket professional: A. Kettleborough

*Win v:* XL Club.

*Batting*—J. C. Butt 11–1–344–62–0–34.40; M. A. Czernek 11–3–192–51–0–24.00; *J. S. T. Rowe 14–0–316–73–0–22.57; R. J. Fox-Andrews 8–3–108–27*–0–21.60; A. S. Hunter 9–2–132–31–0–18.85; J. M. Meir 13–4–155–35–0–17.22; J. S. Berry 9–1–110–26–0–13.75; I. P. Jenkinson 12–0–163–55–0–13.58; A. Stoddard 12–1–142–56–0–12.90.

*Bowling*—A. S. Hunter 171–25–560–25–5/36–22.40.

## WREKIN COLLEGE

*Played 15: Won 6, Lost 2, Drawn 7. Abandoned 4*

Master i/c: M. de Weymarn                    Cricket professional: D. A. Banks

*Wins v:* Gentlemen of Staffordshire; Liverpool; Sundowners CC; Gentlemen of Shropshire; Oswestry; Newport GS.

*Batting*—C. Ingram 17–4–570–103*–1–43.84; M. Savage 18–2–434–81–0–27.12; *C. Davies 17–2–378–65–0–25.20; G. Howell 17–1–320–85–0–20.00; B. Cox 12–2–195–45–0–19.50; N. Harrison 14–4–109–36–0–10.90.

*Bowling*—S. Phillips-Broadhurst 234.1–48–684–42–6/59–16.28; G. Howell 194.1–47–526–30–5/18–17.53; C. Davies 109–25–299–15–4/39–19.93; N. Edwards 70–8–260–13–5/50–20.00.

## WYCLIFFE COLLEGE

*Played 10: Won 4, Lost 1, Drawn 5. Abandoned 3*

Master i/c: P. Woolley                              Cricket professional: K. Biddulph

*Wins v:* Bristol GS; Queen's, Taunton; Colston's; Dean Close.

I. M. Collins, a left-handed opening batsman, represented Gloucestershire Under-16, while B. Harding, M. A. House and A. Baker, the wicket-keeper, all appeared for Gloucestershire Under-19.

*Batting*—I. M. Collins 13–2–362–77–0–32.90; S. P. Collins 11–3–254–64\*–0–31.75; G. A. McDade 10–2–213–54–0–26.62; M. A. House 8–1–136–53–0–19.42; B. Harding 10–2–149–40–0–18.62; M. J. Singer 7–1–106–38\*–0–17.66; P. W. Lewis 8–2–105–48\*–0–17.50.

*Bowling*—W. R. Tovey 137.4–23–472–31–7/36–15.22; B. Harding 92.5–18–229–12–3/28–19.08; M. A. House 99–27–298–15–4/37–19.86; S. B. Thomas 118–34–265–11–3/36–24.09.

## WYGGESTON & QUEEN ELIZABETH I SIXTH FORM COLLEGE

*Played 10: Won 4, Lost 1, Drawn 5. Abandoned 2*

Master i/c: G. G. Wells

*Wins v:* High Pavement; Abbot Beyne; Wreake Valley; Guthlaxton.

*Batting*—J. Kataria 6–3–141–72\*–0–47.00; \*S. J. Patel 8–2–175–80\*–0–29.16; J. S. Sangha 9–4–136–62\*–0–27.20; P. Wright 10–1–205–55–0–22.77; J. E. Kent 6–0–105–39–0–17.50; G. J. P. Thornton 10–1–135–28–0–15.00.

*Bowling*—S. T. Fearon 91.2–29–203–23–7/7–8.82; J. Kataria 45.4–9–151–14–6/6–10.78; S. J. Patel 111–32–273–22–6/37–12.40.

# OVERSEAS CRICKET, 1990-91

*Note:* Throughout this section, matches not first-class are denoted by the use of a dagger.

# ENGLAND IN AUSTRALIA AND
# NEW ZEALAND, 1990-91

### By JOHN THICKNESSE

England were badly beaten in Australia, and against a strong and well-knit team they might well have suffered the same fate even had luck been on their side. In the event, deprived of Graham Gooch, the captain, for a month spanning the First Test, Allan Lamb, another mainstay of the batting, for the Second and Third Tests, and Angus Fraser, the best bowler, for the Third and Fifth, they were never in contention.

It had been apparent from the outset that to recover the Ashes, won so convincingly by Australia in England in 1989, a minimum of six players – the three already named plus Mike Atherton, Robin Smith and Devon Malcolm – had to strike their best form and maintain it. When that condition was not met, it was predictable that the upshot should be a series dominated by Australia. Admirably led by Allan Border, they won 3-0 on merit, England's one minor consolation being that, unlike in 1989, there were moments in each Test when the initiative was theirs. Contrary to expectation, batting was the touring team's chief weakness. Collapses developed from the unlikeliest positions in November and December and became habitual long before the tour ended in New Zealand in mid-February. Overall, England lost sixteen and won only nine of 31 fixtures, and the record was a true reflection of their cricket.

Using fourteen players in the series, compared with England's sixteen, and reinforced by the return of Bruce Reid, the 6ft 8in fast left-armer, Australia were even more impressive than in the previous Ashes series, despite the fact that Mark Taylor, Dean Jones and Steve Waugh, the batting successes on the tour of England, scored only 458 runs between them in 21 innings. Waugh was dropped midway through the rubber after an unbroken run of 42 Tests since his first appearance. Under Border and their coach, former captain Bob Simpson, they had developed into a formidable combination, with plenty in reserve: Tom Moody and Carl Rackemann, both of whom missed selection for the tour of the West Indies that followed the Fifth Test, would have been in or close to England's team, and so might Geoff Lawson.

Reid, with 27 wickets in four Tests, after two years out of cricket with a back condition which had threatened his career, took as many wickets as were shared by Malcolm and Fraser, England's leading wicket-takers, while the boisterous Craig McDermott grabbed eighteen, even though he was not picked until the Fourth Test. David Boon, solid as an oak, was the leading run-scorer with 530, while Mark Waugh, replacing his elder twin, gave 17,000 Adelaide spectators memories for life with a maiden hundred that, for balance, footwork, timing and variety of stroke, stood comparison with any hundred in a Test between the countries since the end of the Second World War. It was an ironic reflection on the gulf between the teams that Jack

Russell, the one Englishman other than Gooch who could have been certain of selection for a Combined XI, was unable to hold his place as England's wicket-keeper because of the length and helplessness of the tail.

More culpable than losing the Test series, however, was England's failure to reach the finals of the 50-overs World Series Cup competition, in which the third team was New Zealand. Despite being without Gooch for the first three of eight qualifying games, and embarking on the programme within a week of losing the First Test by ten wickets in three days, the tourists should have been able to out-point a New Zealand side in the early stages of rebuilding. Had Gooch been one to seek excuses, he could have pointed out that England, though winning only twice, would still have reached the finals but for Australia's batsmen collectively hallucinating in pursuit of a sitting target in Hobart, in New Zealand's last qualifying game. But playing as they did, England undoubtedly got what they deserved.

It was during the sixteen-day period of exclusively one-day cricket at the beginning of December that the team's technical and mental shortcomings were exposed. As they lost six games out of eight – twice to each opponent in World Series matches, the others to scratch teams at Canberra and Bowral – no fewer than ten wickets fell to run-outs, the silliest of them in ways that would have been scoffed at in club cricket. It was one of the most depressing aspects of the tour that the same sort of amateurish errors were still being perpetrated two months later, when England signed off with three one-day internationals in New Zealand and lost that series too. The team had been beaten too heavily in Australia to save face by winning in New Zealand, but victory there would have saved them additional embarrassment when they flew home to Heathrow.

Gooch's absence from November 10, when he had an operation on a poisoned hand, to December 11, when in the hope of refloating a sinking ship he returned a week ahead of schedule for the match at Bowral, was far and away the most damaging of England's many injuries: indeed, a blow from which they never recovered. It stemmed from what seemed an insignificant injury. Attempting a caught and bowled off a hard drive by Smith in the opening practice game in Perth, Gooch gashed the fourth finger of his right hand below the lower knuckle. Though the cut was deep enough to expose the bone, the doctor who inspected it decided that stitches were unnecessary, and used "butterfly tape" to hold the skin together. All seemed well when, having tested the finger later that week at Geraldton, where a Western Australian Country XI willingly agreed that he could play as a batsman only, Gooch suffered no reaction for more than a fortnight. In this time he played nine days of cricket, only to feel "acute pain" in the finger while batting in the nets before the second day of the South Australia match at Adelaide. The initial diagnosis then was that the finger had turned septic; but a second examination, carried out in hospital, revealed that the poison had spread dangerously to the palm of Gooch's hand, which was operated on that evening.

The loss of the captain and main run-scorer, midway through the build-up to the Brisbane Test, was shattering, and had immediate and dire effects. The first was an astonishing decision not to send for a replacement, despite the fact that Atherton and Wayne Larkins were the only other opening batsmen in the party, and that in the last match before the Test, England were meeting an Australian XI containing, in McDermott, a fast bowler who would be flat out to leave his mark. The policy was arrived at jointly by Peter Lush, the manager, Micky Stewart, the team manager, Gooch as captain, and the vice-captain, Lamb, on the grounds that, even if the replacement boarded a plane within 24 hours, there would be no possibility of playing him in the Test, but it ranked among the least far-sighted decisions taken by an England touring team in two decades.

By luck rather than management they got away with it. The Hobart pitch lacked pace, and Atherton and Larkins, scoring only 12 runs in the match between them, scarcely batted long enough to risk injury. Within days, though, Lush and Stewart acknowledged their misjudgment by sending for the Glamorgan left-hander, Hugh Morris, who but for Gooch's faith in Larkins must have been among the original sixteen. Insisting on labelling him a "reinforcement", rather than a replacement, England granted Morris only two minor games in just over a month, in which he scored 33 and 50, before he flew home in time to lead the A team to Pakistan in early January. Certainly he was used less than two other makeweights who subsequently joined the team. Phillip DeFreitas, initially a "reinforcement" for Gladstone Small, blossomed into a fully fledged replacement when, on December 27, it was decided that Chris Lewis should return to England for treatment on a stress fracture in his back; while Phil Newport, on a brief absence from the A team, which was by that time in Sri Lanka, played in the final Test at Perth when Fraser and Martin Bicknell were unfit. Fraser was suffering from a recurrence of the hip injury which first troubled him during his lion-hearted six for 82 at Melbourne in the Second Test.

Taking into account that Micky Stewart spent a night in hospital during the Victoria match at Ballarat, as a precaution after he complained of prolonged numbness in a leg, it can be judged that the party's health was a source of continuous anxiety. Only a handful of players avoided injury, among them Atherton and Alec Stewart, both of whom played in every Test. As the side mostly trained diligently under Lawrie Brown, the hard-working physiotherapist, the appalling fitness record added to the problems facing the England Committee, whom the Test and County Cricket Board listlessly reappointed *en bloc* for another year within a month of the end of the tour.

Lamb's injury, the most serious after Gooch's, was effectively self-inflicted. He tore a calf muscle jogging back to his Ballarat hotel a short time after completing a three-hour 143 against Victoria. Considering he had torn the same muscle in the same way eight months earlier in Barbados, it was a foolish thing to do. It compounded his shocking error of judgment at Brisbane when, as captain, and 10 not out in a parlous score of 56 for three on the night before what turned out to be the final day of the First Test, he went to a casino 50 miles from base in a party that included David Gower, Tony Greig, the former England captain, and Kerry Packer, one of the highest rollers in Australia, on whom Lamb was relying for transport back to Brisbane. When he was out in the first over next morning, he was lucky to get no worse than a rap over the knuckles; the tour manager accepted his word that he was back in the hotel by midnight.

On and off the field, bad thinking was an ever-present feature of the tour. If the team weren't running between wickets like headless chickens, they were behaving like lemmings searching for a cliff. That there was a shortage of strong leadership in Gooch's absence can be gauged from the fact that Gower and Lamb were the only past or present county captains in the side. Yet it could equally be argued that a by-product of the squad system dear to

Gooch and Stewart was that it discouraged players from thinking for themselves.

By crowning a Second and Third Test sequence of 20, 58, 59 and 54 with a magnificent double of 87 and 117 at Adelaide, Gooch scored 426 runs at 53.25, a tribute to his mental strength (his previous average against Australia, in 27 Tests, was 26.28). But his innings were inadequately supported; and put together only after Australia had gone one up at Brisbane, they could not alter the series result. From Ashes history, and Australia's home record through the 1980s, it was clear that for England to win they had to be in the lead after the Second Test at Melbourne. Only two England teams had won in Australia coming from behind, in 1911-12 and 1954-55, and both had had better attacks than Gooch possessed.

Australia, on their record over a decade, had shown themselves to be most vulnerable at Brisbane (won four, lost four, drawn two) and Melbourne, their bogey ground, where they had won only two of twelve Tests in the 1980s and lost five, two of them at England's hands. Yet England lost on both grounds, at Melbourne after the most dramatic of their many collapses: six wickets fell for 3 runs in 53 minutes, from a point when they held the upper hand – 193 runs ahead with six wickets standing and four sessions left for play. When Australia went on to win by eight wickets, through an unbroken stand of 187 between Geoff Marsh and Boon, England, two down with three to go against a buoyant side, had only pride to play for.

Some was regained at Sydney, where Gower made his second hundred in successive Tests and Atherton his first against Australia, and more at Adelaide. There, inspired by Gooch, the tourists briefly looked capable of conjuring an epic out of a match doomed to be a draw. But at Perth Australia reasserted their superiority. When they won by nine wickets on the fourth morning, after England had been 212 for three at tea on the first day, it was their eighth victory over England in thirteen Tests, with the other five all drawn.

Of the established players, other than Russell, whose reaction to being dropped was to work ever harder on his mislaid batting touch, surprisingly it was Malcolm who made the biggest advance, despite his costly wickets. Even by Australian standards it was a scorching summer, and in the last four Tests, under Gooch, Derbyshire's big Jamaican averaged 25 overs an innings. But he came back full of running for every spell, bowling with pace and heart, and he might well have won the Sydney Test if Gooch had given him an early chance to attack Rackemann. Instead, Australia's No. 9 held off the spin of Phil Tufnell and Eddie Hemmings for 32 overs when Australia were in trouble in their second innings. Among the new caps, Tufnell provided the brightest hope for the future with his left-arm spin. Overtaking Hemmings, he looked in four Tests to be England's slowest spinner since Fred Titmus, at his best when tossing the ball up with a man out straight. A bad match in the Sydney outfield earned his fielding a reputation he could not shake off, and this affected his self-confidence; but in the same match he showed he could make use of favourable conditions, dismissing Boon, Border and Jones in a return of five for 61. He seemed young for his age at 24, but as a bowler he looked worthy of encouragement.

John Morris had the misfortune to make his only hundred against Queensland in the final state game, when, because Smith also made a hundred to protect his threatened place, and Stewart was pencilled in to keep wicket at Adelaide and Perth, it was too late to challenge for a Test role. It added to Morris's chagrin that Carrara was the scene of his escapade with Gower in a pair of 1938 Tiger Moths. To greet Smith's century they prevailed upon the pilots of their hired planes to "buzz" the ground at low altitude, for which each was fined £1,000. For all their dereliction of duty in leaving without permission a game in which they were playing, it was a harsh penalty for an essentially light-hearted prank, reflecting all too accurately the joyless nature of the tour. Impressive as Gooch's captaincy was, a hair shirt was usually to be found hanging in his wardrobe.

That teams tend to play all the better for enjoying themselves was borne out at Carrara, where Queensland's defeat spared Gooch the ignominy of becoming the first England captain to go through a tour of Australia without a win in first-class cricket. No summary would be fair that failed to draw attention to the fact that Gooch, Lamb and Fraser played only one Test together, in Adelaide, and even there the Middlesex bowler was less than fully fit. Nevertheless, for all their efforts and commitment, it was clear that Gooch and Stewart had failed to get the balance right. For England in Australia, the diet was cricket morning, noon and night, and for too many of the players it was indigestible.

## ENGLAND TOUR PARTY

G. A. Gooch (Essex) (*captain*), A. J. Lamb (Northants) (*vice-captain*), M. A. Atherton (Lancs.), M. P. Bicknell (Surrey), A. R. C. Fraser (Middx), D. I. Gower (Hants), E. E. Hemmings (Notts.), W. Larkins (Northants), C. C. Lewis (Leics.), D. E. Malcolm (Derbys.), J. E. Morris (Derbys.), R. C. Russell (Glos.), G. C. Small (Warwicks.), R. A. Smith (Hants), A. J. Stewart (Surrey) and P. C. R. Tufnell (Middx).

P. A. J. DeFreitas (Lancs.), H. Morris (Glam.) and P. J. Newport (Worcs.) joined the party subsequently as cover or replacements for injured players.

*Tour manager:* P. M. Lush.   *Team manager:* M. J. Stewart.

## ENGLAND TOUR RESULTS

*Test matches* – Played 5: Lost 3, Drawn 2.
*First-class matches* – Played 11: Won 1, Lost 5, Drawn 5.
*Win* – Queensland.
*Losses* – Australia (3), South Australia, New South Wales.
*Draws* – Australia (2), Western Australia, Australian XI, Victoria.
*One-day internationals* – Played 11: Won 3, Lost 8. *Wins* – New Zealand (3). *Losses* – Australia (4), New Zealand (4).
*Other non first-class matches* – Played 9: Won 5, Lost 3, Drawn 1. *Wins* – WACA President's XI, South Australian Country XI, Tasmania, Australian Cricket Academy (2). *Losses* – Western Australian Invitation XI, Prime Minister's XI, Sir Donald Bradman Invitation XI.
*Draw* – Western Australian Country XI.

## TEST MATCH AVERAGES

## AUSTRALIA – BATTING

|  | T | I | NO | R | HI | 100s | Avge |
|---|---|---|---|---|---|---|---|
| D. C. Boon . . . . . . . . . . | 5 | 9 | 2 | 530 | 121 | 1 | 75.71 |
| G. R. J. Matthews . . . . | 5 | 7 | 2 | 353 | 128 | 1 | 70.60 |
| M. E. Waugh . . . . . . . . | 2 | 3 | 0 | 187 | 138 | 1 | 62.33 |
| A. R. Border . . . . . . . . | 5 | 7 | 1 | 281 | 83* | 0 | 46.83 |
| G. R. Marsh . . . . . . . . | 5 | 10 | 3 | 314 | 79* | 0 | 44.85 |

| | T | I | NO | R | HI | 100s | Avge |
|---|---|---|---|---|---|---|---|
| I. A. Healy . . . . . . . . . | 5 | 7 | 0 | 175 | 69 | 0 | 25.00 |
| M. A. Taylor . . . . . . . | 5 | 10 | 1 | 213 | 67* | 0 | 23.66 |
| D. M. Jones . . . . . . . . | 5 | 7 | 0 | 163 | 60 | 0 | 23.28 |
| S. R. Waugh . . . . . . . . | 3 | 4 | 0 | 82 | 48 | 0 | 20.50 |
| T. M. Alderman . . . . . | 4 | 5 | 2 | 34 | 26* | 0 | 11.33 |
| M. G. Hughes . . . . . . | 4 | 5 | 0 | 44 | 30 | 0 | 8.80 |
| B. A. Reid . . . . . . . . . | 4 | 5 | 2 | 13 | 5* | 0 | 4.33 |

Played in two Tests: C. J. McDermott 42*, 25. Played in one Test: C. G. Rackemann 1, 9.

* *Signifies not out.*

## BOWLING

| | O | M | R | W | BB | 5W/i | Avge |
|---|---|---|---|---|---|---|---|
| B. A. Reid . . . . . . . . | 180.1 | 49 | 432 | 27 | 7-51 | 2 | 16.00 |
| C. J. McDermott . . . . | 97.4 | 12 | 360 | 18 | 8-97 | 2 | 20.00 |
| M. G. Hughes . . . . . . | 142.1 | 38 | 365 | 15 | 4-37 | 0 | 24.33 |
| T. M. Alderman . . . . . | 148.5 | 33 | 428 | 16 | 6-47 | 1 | 26.75 |
| G. R. J. Matthews . . . . | 169 | 51 | 422 | 7 | 3-40 | 0 | 60.28 |

Also bowled: A. R. Border 28-6-82-1; C. G. Rackemann 28.5-5-109-0; M. E. Waugh 6-1-26-0; S. R. Waugh 38-15-90-1.

## ENGLAND – BATTING

| | T | I | NO | R | HI | 100s | Avge |
|---|---|---|---|---|---|---|---|
| G. A. Gooch . . . . . . . | 4 | 8 | 0 | 426 | 117 | 1 | 53.25 |
| D. I. Gower . . . . . . . . | 5 | 10 | 1 | 407 | 123 | 2 | 45.22 |
| A. J. Lamb . . . . . . . . | 3 | 6 | 0 | 195 | 91 | 0 | 32.50 |
| M. A. Atherton . . . . . | 5 | 10 | 1 | 279 | 105 | 1 | 31.00 |
| R. A. Smith . . . . . . . | 5 | 10 | 2 | 238 | 58 | 0 | 29.75 |
| W. Larkins . . . . . . . . | 3 | 6 | 0 | 141 | 64 | 0 | 23.50 |
| A. J. Stewart . . . . . . | 5 | 10 | 0 | 224 | 91 | 0 | 22.40 |
| R. C. Russell . . . . . . | 3 | 5 | 1 | 77 | 30* | 0 | 19.25 |
| P. A. J. DeFreitas . . . . | 3 | 6 | 1 | 77 | 45 | 0 | 15.40 |
| G. C. Small . . . . . . . | 4 | 6 | 1 | 42 | 15 | 0 | 8.40 |
| P. C. R. Tufnell . . . . | 4 | 6 | 4 | 13 | 8 | 0 | 6.50 |
| A. R. C. Fraser . . . . . | 3 | 5 | 0 | 27 | 24 | 0 | 5.40 |
| D. E. Malcolm . . . . . | 5 | 7 | 1 | 27 | 7 | 0 | 4.50 |

Played in one Test: E. E. Hemmings 0; C. C. Lewis 20, 14; P. J. Newport 0, 40*.

* *Signifies not out.*

## BOWLING

| | O | M | R | W | BB | 5W/i | Avge |
|---|---|---|---|---|---|---|---|
| A. R. C. Fraser . . . . . . | 143 | 31 | 311 | 11 | 6-82 | 1 | 28.27 |
| P. A. J. DeFreitas . . . . | 113.3 | 22 | 318 | 10 | 4-56 | 0 | 31.80 |
| E. E. Hemmings . . . . . | 73 | 16 | 199 | 6 | 3-94 | 0 | 33.16 |
| P. C. R. Tufnell . . . . | 140 | 45 | 345 | 9 | 5-61 | 1 | 38.33 |
| D. E. Malcolm . . . . . | 223.5 | 42 | 665 | 16 | 4-128 | 0 | 41.56 |
| G. C. Small . . . . . . . . | 149 | 33 | 424 | 9 | 3-34 | 0 | 47.11 |

Also bowled: M. A. Atherton 15-2-70-0; G. A. Gooch 23-5-69-2; C. C. Lewis 15-0-58-3; P. J. Newport 20-0-78-1.

## ENGLAND AVERAGES – FIRST-CLASS MATCHES

### BATTING

|  | M | I | NO | R | HI | 100s | Avge |
|---|---|---|---|---|---|---|---|
| A. J. Lamb ......... | 8 | 14 | 1 | 757 | 154 | 3 | 58.23 |
| R. A. Smith ......... | 10 | 19 | 6 | 755 | 108 | 1 | 58.07 |
| G. A. Gooch ........ | 8 | 14 | 1 | 623 | 117 | 1 | 47.92 |
| J. E. Morris ......... | 4 | 7 | 0 | 252 | 132 | 1 | 36.00 |
| D. I. Gower ......... | 10 | 19 | 1 | 578 | 123 | 2 | 32.11 |
| C. C. Lewis ......... | 3 | 6 | 0 | 181 | 73 | 0 | 30.16 |
| A. J. Stewart ....... | 9 | 17 | 0 | 497 | 95 | 0 | 29.23 |
| M. A. Atherton ...... | 11 | 22 | 2 | 577 | 114 | 2 | 28.85 |
| P. A. J. DeFreitas .... | 4 | 8 | 1 | 139 | 54 | 0 | 19.85 |
| W. Larkins .......... | 6 | 12 | 0 | 205 | 64 | 0 | 17.08 |
| R. C. Russell ........ | 8 | 13 | 1 | 168 | 36 | 0 | 14.00 |
| G. C. Small ......... | 9 | 14 | 3 | 147 | 37* | 0 | 13.36 |
| M. P. Bicknell ...... | 4 | 6 | 2 | 28 | 17 | 0 | 7.00 |
| A. R. C. Fraser ..... | 5 | 7 | 0 | 48 | 24 | 0 | 6.85 |
| D. E. Malcolm ...... | 10 | 14 | 2 | 52 | 18 | 0 | 4.33 |
| P. C. R. Tufnell ..... | 8 | 10 | 7 | 13 | 13 | 0 | 4.33 |
| E. E. Hemmings ..... | 3 | 5 | 0 | 19 | 13 | 0 | 3.80 |

Played in one match: P. J. Newport 0, 40*.

* *Signifies not out.*

### BOWLING

|  | O | M | R | W | BB | 5W/i | Avge |
|---|---|---|---|---|---|---|---|
| E. E. Hemmings ..... | 164 | 46 | 391 | 15 | 4-29 | 0 | 26.06 |
| P. A. J. DeFreitas ... | 126 | 25 | 353 | 11 | 4-56 | 0 | 32.09 |
| D. E. Malcolm ...... | 422.4 | 78 | 1,269 | 39 | 7-74 | 1 | 32.53 |
| P. C. R. Tufnell ..... | 318 | 73 | 887 | 26 | 5-61 | 2 | 34.11 |
| A. R. C. Fraser ..... | 237 | 51 | 596 | 17 | 6-82 | 1 | 35.05 |
| G. C. Small ......... | 277 | 63 | 774 | 19 | 4-38 | 0 | 40.73 |
| M. P. Bicknell ...... | 120.4 | 22 | 409 | 9 | 3-124 | 0 | 45.44 |
| M. A. Atherton ...... | 79.1 | 10 | 330 | 6 | 3-27 | 0 | 55.00 |
| C. C. Lewis .......... | 93 | 8 | 342 | 6 | 3-29 | 0 | 57.00 |

Also bowled: G. A. Gooch 33-8-90-2; P. J. Newport 20-0-78-1.

### FIELDING

31 – R. C. Russell (27 ct, 4 st); 10 – M. A. Atherton, A. J. Lamb, A. J. Stewart; 7 – G. A. Gooch, G. C. Small; 6 – P. C. R. Tufnell; 5 – R. A. Smith; 4 – W. Larkins; 3 – D. I. Gower, C. C. Lewis, D. E. Malcolm; 2 – M. P. Bicknell, A. R. C. Fraser, E. E. Hemmings, J. E. Morris; 1 – Substitute (A. J. Lamb).

†At Lilac Hill, October 25. England XI won by six wickets. Toss: WACA President's XI. WACA President's XI 205 for seven (47 overs) (M. R. J. Veletta 30, T. M. Moody 100 not out; C. C. Lewis three for 37); England XI 206 for four (40 overs) (D. I. Gower 33, J. E. Morris 68 not out, A. J. Stewart 70 not out).

†At Geraldton, October 27, 28. Drawn. Toss: England XI. England XI 197 for eight dec. (W. Larkins 55, M. A. Atherton 40, A. J. Lamb 37; M. Obst four for 36) and 121 for four (G. A. Gooch 47); Western Australian Country XI 181 (P. Shine 43, B. Woods 40, T. Waldron 35; M. A. Atherton three for 46).

†At Perth, October 30 (day/night). Western Australian Invitation XI won by three wickets. Toss: Western Australian Invitation XI. England XI 180 (49.2 overs) (A. J. Lamb 50, R. C. Russell 31; C. D. Mack three for 51); Western Australian Invitation XI 181 for seven (48.3 overs) (M. E. Waugh 36, D. S. Lehmann 50; M. P. Bicknell three for 43).

## WESTERN AUSTRALIA v ENGLAND XI

At Perth, November 2, 3, 4, 5. Drawn. Toss: England XI. Decisively outplayed after winning a valuable toss, England would have lost their opening state match for the third successive tour of Australia but for a determined rearguard action inspired by Smith. When Western Australia were 14 for three in the first hour of an overcast opening day, few could suppose that on the final afternoon England would be 90 for six, nominally pursuing 373 to win. It was Wood, in his second game for Western Australia since his dismissal as captain the previous season, who turned the match with a determined five-hour hundred. As the skies cleared on the second day, every England batsman made a start, but Lamb and Smith, adding 101 in 91 minutes, shared the only worthwhile stand. Matthews's left-arm fast-medium in-swing attracted some livelier strokes and earned him five for 66. Marsh and Veletta then pressed home the advantage next day; the captain's 151, in 333 minutes with 21 fours, beat his own 124 in 1986-87 as a Western Australian record against England. He might have declared at stumps, but reluctant to risk giving England a winning start to the tour, he batted on for half an hour on the last day. It was not Marsh's caution that cost his side the match, however, but faulty catching. Smith was badly missed by Zoehrer at 35, and Malcolm survived two chances in the slips as Smith coaxed three hours' resistance from the tail. When Malcolm succumbed, 39 balls remained. But Lamb, returning to the wicket after being rapped on the elbow earlier by Reid, made sure that Smith's dedication was not wasted. Putting safety before his hundred, Smith batted 282 minutes and hit fourteen fours off 231 balls. Reid, returning after 21 months out of the game, bowled brilliantly but unluckily.

*Close of play:* First day, Western Australia 289; Second day, Western Australia 28-0 (M. R. J. Veletta 9*, G. R. Marsh 14*); Third day, Western Australia 308-4 (G. M. Wood 17*, T. J. Zoehrer 7*).

## Western Australia

| | | | |
|---|---|---|---|
| *G. R. Marsh c Russell b Malcolm | 1 | - (2) b Lewis | 151 |
| M. R. J. Veletta c Russell b Malcolm | 7 | - (1) c Russell b Fraser | 77 |
| T. M. Moody c Russell b Fraser | 0 | - c Gower b Malcolm | 25 |
| G. M. Wood lbw b Atherton | 108 | - not out | 23 |
| W. S. Andrews lbw b Small | 31 | - lbw b Small | 10 |
| †T. J. Zoehrer run out | 16 | - not out | 21 |
| K. H. MacLeay c Lamb b Small | 63 | | |
| T. G. Hogan c Lamb b Small | 5 | | |
| C. D. Matthews c Fraser b Atherton | 28 | | |
| B. A. Reid not out | 0 | | |
| T. M. Alderman st Russell b Atherton | 12 | | |
| B 1, l-b 8, w 4, n-b 5 | 18 | L-b 17, n-b 5 | 22 |

1/11 2/12 3/14 4/71 5/91    289    1/195 2/272 3/272  (4 wkts dec.) 329
6/186 7/195 8/276 9/277            4/297

Bowling: *First Innings*—Malcolm 24-4-60-2; Fraser 22-5-70-1; Lewis 16-2-64-0; Small 19-2-59-3; Atherton 4.1-0-27-3. *Second Innings*—Malcolm 22-6-54-1; Fraser 31-9-88-1; Small 27-6-71-1; Lewis 18-1-70-1; Atherton 6-1-29-0.

## England XI

| | | | | | |
|---|---|---|---|---|---|
| *G. A. Gooch b Matthews | 26 | – c Zoehrer b Alderman | 12 |
| M. A. Atherton c Veletta b Matthews | 15 | – lbw b Reid | 3 |
| D. I. Gower c Andrews b MacLeay | 14 | – lbw b Reid | 10 |
| A. J. Lamb c Andrews b Matthews | 84 | – not out | 4 |
| R. A. Smith c and b Matthews | 41 | – not out | 98 |
| J. E. Morris c Zoehrer b Matthews | 10 | – c Hogan b Matthews | 18 |
| C. C. Lewis lbw b Alderman | 26 | – b Matthews | 4 |
| †R. C. Russell run out | 18 | – c Zoehrer b MacLeay | 6 |
| G. C. Small c Andrews b Alderman | 4 | – c Zoehrer b Moody | 15 |
| A. R. C. Fraser not out | 1 | – c sub b Alderman | 18 |
| D. E. Malcolm c Matthews b Alderman | 0 | – c Zoehrer b Alderman | 18 |
| B 2, l-b 4, n-b 1 | 7 | B 12, l-b 1, w 1, n-b 2 | 16 |

1/37 2/50 3/62 4/163 5/193     246     1/14 2/22 3/30     (9 wkts) 222
6/200 7/234 8/241 9/246                       4/69 5/73 6/90
                                          7/123 8/178 9/210

*In the second innings A. J. Lamb, when 4, retired hurt at 29 and resumed at 210.*

Bowling: *First Innings*—Alderman 19.4–7–60–3; Reid 19–5–57–0; Matthews 16–3–66–5; MacLeay 14–7–22–1; Hogan 10–4–35–0. *Second Innings*—Alderman 17–6–49–3; Reid 16–5–44–2; Matthews 17–4–44–2; Hogan 11–5–17–0; MacLeay 8–1–21–1; Moody 8–2–18–1; Andrews 6–2–16–0.

Umpires: R. J. Evans and P. J. McConnell.

†At Port Pirie, November 7. England XI won by 111 runs. Toss: South Australian Country XI. England XI 239 for seven dec. (52 overs) (M. A. Atherton 36, W. Larkins 110, J. E. Morris 30; S. Fuchs three for 84); South Australian Country XI 128 (40.1 overs) (C. Richards 57; M. P. Bicknell three for 24, P. C. R. Tufnell three for 41).

## SOUTH AUSTRALIA v ENGLAND XI

At Adelaide, November 9, 10, 11, 12. South Australia won by six wickets. Toss: England XI. Gooch's sudden withdrawal for the operation on his finger, on the second day, was the worst blow in a match which exposed England's lack of depth. Without his batting in either innings, and with Lamb, Smith, Fraser and Small resting, they were flattered to lose with only four overs left; Stewart, who stayed 188 minutes for his 92, had had two lives before scoring. South Australia's dominance was built on a second-wicket stand of 275 – a state record against MCC/England – between Bishop (eighteen fours), a powerful driver, and the stocky Nobes (sixteen fours), whose strength lay in the pull stroke. Having survived without difficulty what might have been a testing first hour on a green pitch in overcast conditions, they remained together for 289 minutes before Nobes fell to the second new ball. In reply none of the tourists could reach 50, but after following on, 214 behind, they stood a good chance of saving the game on the last day. Lewis (203 minutes) and Russell (107 minutes) put their side in sight of the tea interval with only five wickets down. However, England's resistance ended dramatically when Hickey, maintaining his pace well, claimed four victims in five balls, with Hemmings denying him a hat-trick. Although losing two early wickets to Bicknell, South Australia reached their target in 137 minutes.

*Close of play:* First day, South Australia 316-3 (G. A. Bishop 146*); Second day, England XI 149-5 (C. C. Lewis 18*, R. C. Russell 14*); Third day, England XI 186-4 (A. J. Stewart 43*).

## South Australia

| | | | |
|---|---|---|---|
| *A. M. J. Hilditch c Lewis b Malcolm | 14 | – c Atherton b Bicknell | 3 |
| G. A. Bishop run out | 154 | | |
| P. C. Nobes c Russell b Bicknell | 131 | – lbw b Lewis | 32 |
| D. W. Hookes c Gower b Lewis | 6 | – st Russell b Hemmings | 26 |
| P. R. Sleep not out | 71 | – not out | 20 |
| W. B. Phillips lbw b Bicknell | 5 | – (2) c Lewis b Bicknell | 8 |
| J. C. Scuderi c sub b Bicknell | 24 | – (6) not out | 21 |
| †T. J. Nielsen not out | 4 | | |
| L-b 14, n-b 8 | 22 | L-b 1, n-b 1 | 2 |

1/23 2/298 3/316 4/338        (6 wkts. dec.) 431    1/12 2/13 3/50 4/84        (4 wkts) 112
5/354 6/414

T. B. A. May, C. R. Miller and D. J. Hickey did not bat.

Bowling: *First Innings*—Malcolm 31-4-105-1; Lewis 33-2-102-1; Bicknell 32.4-5-124-3; Hemmings 23-6-53-0; Gooch 9-3-20-0; Atherton 4-0-13-0. *Second Innings*—Malcolm 1-0-4-0; Lewis 11-3-48-1; Bicknell 11-2-34-2; Hemmings 10-1-25-1.

## England XI

| | | | |
|---|---|---|---|
| M. A. Atherton b Miller | 8 | – b May | 40 |
| W. Larkins b Hickey | 31 | – b Hickey | 14 |
| D. I. Gower lbw b Hickey | 12 | – c Miller b Sleep | 56 |
| A. J. Stewart st Nielsen b Sleep | 41 | – (5) c Hilditch b Scuderi | 92 |
| J. E. Morris c Sleep b Miller | 19 | – (4) b Scuderi | 18 |
| C. C. Lewis run out | 44 | – c Scuderi b Hickey | 73 |
| †R. C. Russell c Nielsen b Sleep | 36 | – c Nielsen b Hickey | 13 |
| E. E. Hemmings c Nielsen b Scuderi | 13 | – c Hilditch b Hickey | 0 |
| M. P. Bicknell not out | 1 | – not out | 0 |
| D. E. Malcolm c May b Scuderi | 3 | – b Hickey | 0 |
| *G. A. Gooch absent injured | | – absent injured | |
| B 4, l-b 4, n-b 1 | 9 | B 6, l-b 10, n-b 3 | 19 |

1/30 2/53 3/54 4/93 5/124                        217    1/24 2/116 3/116 4/186 5/274                        325
6/186 7/203 8/214 9/217                                6/325 7/325 8/325 9/325

Bowling: *First Innings*—Miller 13-2-57-2; Hickey 16-4-42-2; Scuderi 11.1-4-30-2; May 20-5-50-0; Sleep 14-2-30-2. *Second Innings*—Miller 18-7-58-0; Hickey 25-6-83-5; May 26-5-60-1; Scuderi 25-10-41-2; Sleep 24-8-67-1.

Umpires: A. R. Crafter and D. J. Harper.

†At Hobart, November 14. England XI won by eight wickets. Toss: Tasmania. Tasmania 173 for six (50 overs) (M. G. Farrell 36, D. M. Wellham 63; C. C. Lewis three for 36); England XI 175 for two (46 overs) (M. A. Atherton 88 not out, D. I. Gower 30).

# AUSTRALIAN XI v ENGLAND XI

At Hobart, November 16, 17, 18, 19. Drawn. Toss: England XI. Two dazzling hundreds from Lamb, supported by the excellent Smith and Stewart, spared England's blushes at the chilly Bellerive Oval after inept batting in both innings by their top three. With 154 (twenty fours, two sixes) and 105, Lamb became the first player to score two centuries in a match for MCC/England in Australia since P. B. H. May in 1958-59, also against an Australian XI, in Sydney. Recovering from 9 for three, England reached 333 for four before Chris Matthews and McDermott shared six wickets for 7 runs with the second new ball. Four of those fell for 2 during the 52 minutes of play possible on the second day. Another thirteen wickets went on the third day, including seven to Malcolm in a career-best performance of sustained accuracy and pace which only Boon withstood. England, leading by 148, were 19 for three after eight overs, with Cantrell in the gully and Campbell at backward short leg taking superb catches.

However, Smith and Lamb then added 173 in 130 minutes, and when the latter declared at lunch, after completing his second 50 off 40 balls, the Australian XI's target was 341. Thanks to the solidity and power of their captain, Boon, they were just in the hunt at tea, but Lamb pushed his fields back afterwards, and the match petered to a draw. Boon, batting 221 minutes in the first innings and 201 in the second, attuned himself impressively for the Brisbane Test which followed.

*Close of play:* First day, England XI 338-6 (A. R. C. Fraser 2\*, R. C. Russell 1\*); Second day, Australian XI 15-0 (P. E. Cantrell 5\*, D. C. Boon 5\*); Third day, England XI 29-3 (R. A. Smith 6\*, A. J. Lamb 2\*).

## England XI

| | | | |
|---|---|---|---|
| M. A. Atherton c Healy b C. D. Matthews | 3 | – c Waugh b C. D. Matthews | 0 |
| W. Larkins c G. R. J. Matthews b McDermott | 1 | – c Campbell b C. D. Matthews | 8 |
| D. I. Gower lbw b C. D. Matthews | 4 | – c Cantrell b McDermott | 8 |
| \*A. J. Lamb b McDermott | 154 | – (5) c Waugh b Campbell | 105 |
| R. A. Smith c Cantrell b C. D. Matthews | 71 | – (4) not out | 58 |
| A. J. Stewart c and b McDermott | 95 | | |
| A. R. C. Fraser c Cantrell b C. D. Matthews | 2 | | |
| †R. C. Russell c Healy b McDermott | 1 | | |
| G. C. Small c Healy b C. D. Matthews | 2 | | |
| P. C. R. Tufnell not out | 0 | | |
| D. E. Malcolm c and b C. D. Matthews | 0 | | |
| L-b 3, n-b 4 | 7 | B 6, l-b 2, w 1, n-b 4 | 13 |

1/5 2/9 3/9 4/145 5/333     340     1/1 2/13 3/19    (4 wkts dec.) 192
6/336 7/338 8/340 9/340       4/192

*Bowling: First Innings*—McDermott 20-7-70-4; C. D. Matthews 25-7-71-6; Campbell 15-5-37-0; McIntyre 14-1-71-0; G. R. J. Matthews 15-3-50-0; Moody 5-0-30-0; Waugh 2-0-8-0. *Second Innings*—McDermott 13-3-71-0; C. D. Matthews 12-0-44-2; McIntyre 12-3-71-0; Campbell 3.2-0-15-1.

## Australian XI

| | | | |
|---|---|---|---|
| P. E. Cantrell b Malcolm | 14 | – hit wkt b Fraser | 17 |
| \*D. C. Boon c Stewart b Malcolm | 67 | – c Larkins b Malcolm | 108 |
| T. M. Moody b Malcolm | 14 | – c Lamb b Fraser | 10 |
| M. E. Waugh b Malcolm | 4 | – c Atherton b Tufnell | 12 |
| D. S. Lehmann c Larkins b Malcolm | 2 | – run out | 29 |
| †I. A. Healy c Russell b Small | 5 | – c Russell b Fraser | 0 |
| G. R. J. Matthews c Tufnell b Malcolm | 14 | – not out | 21 |
| C. D. Matthews c Small b Tufnell | 16 | – not out | 2 |
| C. J. McDermott c Lamb b Malcolm | 21 | | |
| G. D. Campbell c Russell b Fraser | 7 | | |
| P. E. McIntyre not out | 0 | | |
| B 4, l-b 3, n-b 10 | 17 | B 4, l-b 3, n-b 8 | 15 |

1/25 2/61 3/89 4/93 5/101     192     1/42 2/75 3/113 4/179    (6 wkts) 214
6/140 7/145 8/174 9/191       5/185 6/201

*Bowling: First Innings*—Malcolm 22-3-74-7; Fraser 22-3-52-1; Small 13-3-39-1; Tufnell 11.1-2-20-1. *Second Innings*—Malcolm 10-5-34-1; Fraser 19-3-75-3; Small 9-3-31-0; Tufnell 15-0-60-1; Atherton 4-2-7-0.

Umpires: S. G. Randell and I. S. Thomas.

## AUSTRALIA v ENGLAND

### First Test Match

At Brisbane, November 23, 24, 25. Australia won by ten wickets. Toss: Australia. A Test which looked evenly balanced after two days ended in an astonishingly easy win for Australia on the evening of the third, following a familiar England collapse in the face of Alderman. Outshone by Reid in the first innings, the 34-year-old Western Australian bowled his out-swing with excellent control to take six for 47, his best figures in Test cricket. Yet future generations will surely wonder how Marsh and Taylor scored 157 without being parted, a ground record against England, to complete Australia's win, after the first three innings had yielded 194, 152 and 114. The short answer is that England had no bowler to match Alderman or Reid, and that by the third day the pitch had belatedly turned in favour of the bat. Australia reached their target at 3.41 runs per over, the fastest scoring of the match by nearly 1 run an over. In effect the game had begun a day too early.

In humid weather after a rainy night, which had turned the pitch green under its tarpaulin covers, there was enough moisture in the pitch to make Border's decision to field a formality. Enough remained on the second day for England, bowling well and catching brilliantly, to find themselves with an unexpected lead, but the position was deceptive in that nearly every uppish stroke had gone to hand. Moreover, England's good fortune was to rebound on them. Batting again before the pitch was fully dry, they lost three wickets before the close.

Gooch's absence was a huge blow to England, both in psychological terms and the loss of the runs he might have scored. But with the ball swinging and seaming as it did, there was nothing to be ashamed of in their first-day batting, disappointing as it was to make only 194 after reaching 117 before the third wicket, that of Lamb, fell. The acting-captain's 32 took him past 4,000 Test runs and 25,000 in first-class cricket. Had Gower not used up three innings' worth of luck in making 61, however, England's limit might well have been 150. Smith, yorked by a fast in-ducker from Reid, was the victim of the day's most fiendish ball, while Border took a lovely catch, right-handed at second slip, to see the back of Lewis.

Australia's troubles on the Saturday began in the second over when Fraser had Marsh lbw with a ball that straightened. Then, 39 minutes later, Lewis in the gully took a firmly hit square-cut by Taylor with sublime ease, and the pattern of the match was set. Of seven later chances, six were taken, among them outstanding efforts at mid-off by Small and at cover by Smith, and two very droppable ones by Atherton at second slip. Australia had every right to be dissatisfied with their batting. Only Matthews, back in favour after four years, and Healy played as the situation demanded, in a stand of 46. Nevertheless the ball did run badly for them.

Reid struck an immediate blow in the second innings when Larkins, who had fielded only in the later stages because of an infected tooth, went back to a full-length in-swinger first ball and was lbw. Even so, England were in sight of finishing the day strongly placed until, in the last half-hour, Atherton lost his off stump to an unplayable late out-swinger from Alderman, and Gower, in the next over, dragged a wide ball from Hughes into his stumps. It was the second time in the match that Gower had been out in the over after the loss of an important wicket, and both times to strokes of poor conception. When next morning Lamb was lbw to the sixth ball of the first over, mistakenly on the back foot, England had lost three wickets for 18 runs. With the exception of the night-watchman, Russell, who stayed for 116 minutes, they subsided without fight.

*Man of the Match:* T. M. Alderman.      *Attendance:* 32,244.

*Close of play:* First day, Australia 16-0 (G. R. Marsh 6*, M. A. Taylor 4*); Second day, England 56-3 (A. J. Lamb 10*, R. C. Russell 1*).

## England

| | | | | |
|---|---|---|---|---|
| M. A. Atherton lbw b Reid | 13 | – b Alderman | 15 |
| W. Larkins c Healy b Hughes | 12 | – lbw b Reid | 0 |
| D. I. Gower c Healy b Reid | 61 | – b Hughes | 27 |
| *A. J. Lamb c Hughes b Matthews | 32 | – lbw b Alderman | 14 |
| R. A. Smith b Reid | 7 | – (6) c Taylor b Alderman | 1 |
| A. J. Stewart lbw b Reid | 4 | – (7) c sub (P. E. Cantrell) b Alderman | 6 |
| †R. C. Russell c and b Alderman | 16 | – (5) lbw b Waugh | 15 |
| C. C. Lewis c Border b Hughes | 20 | – lbw b Alderman | 14 |
| G. C. Small not out | 12 | – c Alderman b Hughes | 15 |
| A. R. C. Fraser c Healy b Alderman | 1 | – c sub (P. E. Cantrell) b Alderman | 0 |
| D. E. Malcolm c Waugh b Hughes | 5 | – not out | 0 |
| B 1, l-b 7, n-b 3 | 11 | L-b 3, n-b 4 | 7 |

1/23 (2) 2/43 (1) 3/117 (4) 4/123 (3)         194     1/0 (2) 2/42 (1) 3/46 (3)        114
5/134 (5) 6/135 (6) 7/167 (8)                      4/60 (4) 5/78 (6) 6/84 (7)
8/181 (7) 9/187 (10) 10/194 (11)                 7/93 (5) 8/112 (8)
                                        9/114 (10) 10/114 (9)

Bowling: *First Innings*—Alderman 18–5–44–2; Reid 18–3–53–4; Hughes 19–5–39–3; Waugh 7–2–20–0; Matthews 16–8–30–1. *Second Innings*—Alderman 22–7–47–6; Reid 14–3–40–1; Hughes 12.1–5–17–2; Matthews 1–1–0–0; Waugh 4–2–7–1.

## Australia

| | | |
|---|---|---|
| G. R. Marsh lbw b Fraser | 9 – (2) | not out ................... 72 |
| M. A. Taylor c Lewis b Fraser | 10 – (1) | not out ................... 67 |
| D. C. Boon lbw b Small | 18 | |
| *A. R. Border c Atherton b Small | 9 | |
| D. M. Jones c Small b Lewis | 17 | |
| S. R. Waugh b Smith b Small | 1 | |
| G. R. J. Matthews c Small b Malcolm | 35 | |
| †I. A. Healy c Atherton b Lewis | 22 | |
| M. G. Hughes c Russell b Fraser | 9 | |
| B. A. Reid b Lewis | 0 | |
| T. M. Alderman not out | 0 | |
| B 1, l-b 10, n-b 11 | 22 | B 3, l-b 2, w 3, n-b 10 ... 18 |

1/22 (1) 2/35 (2) 3/49 (4) 4/60 (3)   152   (no wkt) 157
5/64 (6) 6/89 (5) 7/135 (7) 8/150 (9)
9/150 (8) 10/152 (10)

Bowling: *First Innings*—Malcolm 17–2–45–1; Fraser 21–6–33–3; Small 16–4–34–3; Lewis 9–0–29–3. *Second Innings*—Fraser 14–2–49–0; Small 15–2–36–0; Malcolm 9–5–22–0; Lewis 6–0–29–0; Atherton 2–0–16–0.

Umpires: A. R. Crafter and P. J. McConnell.

†At Adelaide, November 29. England XI won by five wickets. Toss: England XI. Australian Cricket Academy 95 (42 overs) (D. E. Malcolm three for 13, G. C. Small three for 7); England XI 96 for five (32.2 overs).

†At Adelaide, November 30. England XI won by 150 runs. It was agreed without a toss that England should bat. England XI 237 for six (45 overs) (H. Morris 33, J. E. Morris 63, R. A. Smith 37); Australian Cricket Academy 87 (32.2 overs) (D. R. Martyn 32; M. P. Bicknell four for 30, P. C. R. Tufnell three for 11).

*England's matches v Australia and New Zealand in the Benson and Hedges World Series Cup (December 1 – January 10) may be found in that section.*

†At Canberra, December 4. Prime Minister's XI won by 31 runs. Toss: England XI. Prime Minister's XI 226 for eight (48 overs) (D. S. Lehmann 37, A. R. Border 55 not out, C. J. McDermott 39; P. C. R. Tufnell three for 40); England XI 195 for nine (48 overs) (J. E. Morris 30, W. Larkins 34; C. J. McDermott three for 41).

†At Bowral, December 11. Sir Donald Bradman Invitation XI won by seven wickets. Toss: England XI. England XI 229 for seven (50 overs) (H. Morris 50, A. J. Lamb 55, R. A. Smith 39, A. J. Stewart 53 not out); Sir Donald Bradman Invitation XI 231 for three (42.1 overs) (J. C. Young 55, D. S. Lehmann 112 not out, M. G. Bevan 51 not out).

## VICTORIA v ENGLAND XI

At Ballarat, December 20, 21, 22, 23. Drawn. Toss: Victoria. Played away from the MCG so as not to hinder preparations for the Second Test, the Menzies Memorial match drew good crowds to the Eastern Oval. Hundreds by Ayres and Jones, the one stylishly unhurried in 432 minutes, the other savagely athletic in two and a quarter hours, with 62 runs coming from boundaries, won Victoria the initiative. And despite an attacking 143 by Lamb, scored during a third-wicket stand of 198 with Atherton, England might have lost but for Smith's dogged 56 not out, in 187 minutes, on the final afternoon. Both Jones and Lamb, who scored his runs off 129 balls, found a bowling green by the short boundary at wide mid-on magnetic; seven of their eleven sixes landed on or near it at the expense of Tufnell and Jackson, the rival left-arm spinners. Challenged to score 304 in 71 overs, England should have had no trouble holding out when the chase was abandoned following Gower's dismissal. But with Lamb out of the game – he had torn a calf muscle jogging back to the hotel after his hundred – only 23 minutes' resistance by Malcolm spared Tufnell from coming to the wicket as Smith's last partner. Jackson and Hughes, who had an impressive match with bat and ball, had been principally responsible for England's slide to 188 for seven.

*Close of play:* First day, Victoria 336-4 (W. G. Ayres 123*, S. P. O'Donnell 11*); Second day, England XI 220-3 (M. A. Atherton 59*, R. C. Russell 1*); Third day, Victoria 155-7 (M. G. Hughes 17*, P. R. Reiffel 4*).

### Victoria

| | | | |
|---|---|---|---|
| G. M. Watts lbw b Atherton | 65 | – (2) b Malcolm | 4 |
| W. G. Ayres c Tufnell b Malcolm | 139 | – (1) c and b Tufnell | 53 |
| D. M. Jones c Malcolm b Atherton | 110 | – c Russell b Malcolm | 0 |
| D. S. Lehmann run out | 3 | – c Russell b Malcolm | 17 |
| J. D. Siddons c Russell b Tufnell | 11 | – st Russell b Atherton | 50 |
| *S. P. O'Donnell c Russell b Malcolm | 12 | – b Tufnell | 3 |
| †D. S. Berry c Lamb b Tufnell | 45 | – c Atherton b Malcolm | 0 |
| M. G. Hughes not out | 36 | – not out | 64 |
| P. R. Reiffel (did not bat) | | – not out | 15 |
| B 6, l-b 8, w 1, n-b 5 | 20 | L-b 5, n-b 4 | 9 |

1/124 2/301 3/306 4/319 5/342    (7 wkts dec.) 441    1/9 2/9 3/29    (7 wkts dec.) 215
6/367 7/441    4/126 5/129
   6/134 7/134

D. W. Fleming and P. W. Jackson did not bat.

Bowling: *First Innings*—Malcolm 31-6-95-2; Small 13-2-35-0; Bicknell 22-3-94-0; Tufnell 38-8-125-2; Atherton 19-2-78-2. *Second Innings*—Malcolm 23-4-62-4; Bicknell 9-1-37-0; Tufnell 24-6-60-2; Atherton 8-0-51-1.

### England XI

| | | | |
|---|---|---|---|
| *G. A. Gooch run out | 7 | – c O'Donnell b Jackson | 38 |
| M. A. Atherton c Lehmann b O'Donnell | 73 | – c Fleming b Hughes | 9 |
| A. J. Stewart c and b Fleming | 1 | – b Jackson | 8 |
| A. J. Lamb c Reiffel b Jones | 143 | | |
| †R. C. Russell c Berry b Hughes | 4 | – (6) b Jackson | 11 |
| D. I. Gower b Hughes | 0 | – (4) c Berry b Fleming | 54 |
| R. A. Smith not out | 71 | – (5) not out | 56 |
| G. C. Small not out | 37 | – (7) c Lehmann b Jackson | 0 |
| M. P. Bicknell (did not bat) | | – (8) c and b Hughes | 17 |
| D. E. Malcolm (did not bat) | | – (9) not out | 4 |
| B 5, l-b 3, w 1, n-b 8 | 17 | B 4, l-b 1, n-b 2 | 7 |

1/20 2/21 3/219 4/225    (6 wkts dec.) 353    1/20 2/39 3/71 4/139    (7 wkts) 204
5/227 6/259    5/163 6/163 7/188

P. C. R. Tufnell did not bat.

Bowling: *First Innings*—Hughes 23.5–6–62–2; Fleming 19–4–53–1; O'Donnell 16–1–65–1; Reiffel 22–6–82–0; Jackson 13–2–76–0; Jones 1–0–7–1. *Second Innings*—Hughes 20–4–42–2; Fleming 15–4–50–1; Jackson 21–7–62–4; Reiffel 11–4–29–0; O'Donnell 4–0–16–0.

Umpires: D. W. Holt and L. J. King.

## AUSTRALIA v ENGLAND

### Second Test Match

At Melbourne, December 26, 27, 28, 29, 30. Australia won by eight wickets. Toss: England. A hard-fought Test match of many fluctuations was won by Australia with surprising ease. They were apparently in difficulties at 28 for two at the start of the last day, but Marsh and Boon scored the remaining 169 in five hours without being parted. It was an excellent, single-minded piece of batting on a slow, low-bouncing pitch, and showed what could be done by concentrating on strokes which could be played with a straight bat. Had England's batsmen followed the same principles, the best Australia could have hoped for would have been a draw; instead they indulged in what the team manager, in understandable irritation, described as "fifty minutes of madness" after tea on the fourth day, when Reid and Matthews shared six wickets in twelve overs while 3 runs were scored.

Reid, who had never taken more than four wickets in an innings in nineteen Tests, came out of his twentieth with six for 97 and seven for 51, without seeming to bowl any better than when he took two for 101 for Western Australia at the beginning of the tour. His height, deceptive changes of pace, left-arm-over angle and control made him a bowler any team would welcome. Yet there was little sign of the in-swing that gave England such problems against Western Australia and in the First Test at Brisbane. At Melbourne he slanted the ball across the batsmen and waited for mistakes: nine of his wickets came from catches off the outside edge from balls missing the off stump. For England, Gower made his eighth hundred against Australia and seventeenth in all Tests, despite a badly bruised right wrist, and Fraser returned his best figures in Test cricket, six for 82, at the expense of a hip injury in a marathon of 39 overs.

This was the first match played at the MCG since the demolition of the Southern Stand, which reduced capacity to 60,000 and opened up a view of leafy Yarra Park. The removal of this 200-yard wind-break may have added to the ball's reluctance to swing. While Australia fielded their Brisbane side, Gooch's return for Lamb, still hobbling from his calf injury, was one of the three England changes. Tufnell, winning his first cap, and DeFreitas replaced the injured Small and Lewis.

When Atherton and Gooch were dismissed in the first 40 minutes, the captain shouldering arms to an in-coming ball from Alderman, England were in danger of wasting a good toss. But Larkins, who would have lost his place had Lamb been fit, spent three and threequarter hours patiently building a platform for recovery before giving Healy the second of five first-innings catches, nibbling at Reid. Gower, taking pain-killers, was smoothly in command, and added 122 with the impetuous but lucky Stewart before being caught off the splice, mistiming a leg-side turn two balls after completing his hundred. He had batted for 254 minutes and 170 balls. Though Stewart lasted another 100 minutes, surviving a fast and short-pitched spell from Hughes, the last five wickets added only 78.

Solid batting by Taylor (256 minutes) and Border (239 minutes), plus a cameo by Jones, whose pattering 44 from 57 balls was by far the fastest scoring of the game, looked to have given Australia control when they were 259 for four at tea on the third day. However, Fraser, armed with a new ball, straightened one to hit Waugh's off stump two overs afterwards. And spurred by a piece of luck 37 minutes later, when Border was caught off a leg-glance, he bowled unchanged until the close to hem England a lead of 46. Wicket to wicket his spell was six for 23 in 13.4 overs, and on the day he took six for 34 off 26, a workload that stirred memories for the watching Alec Bedser.

Soon after lunch on the fourth day, with Gooch playing freely and Larkins (232 minutes) on the way to his second patient fifty of the match, England's one problem on the slow, low pitch looked to be dismissing Australia a second time. They remained comfortably placed at tea – 147 for four, 193 ahead. But in the first over of the final session, an ambitious drive by

Stewart against Reid's angle was brilliantly taken low to his right by Marsh at gully, and the innings fell to pieces. Two catches by Atherton at gully revived English hopes before the close, and they might still have had an outside chance if, in the fourth over next morning, Malcolm had won an lbw appeal against Boon, who had moved across the stumps to play a ball to leg. Otherwise neither batsman gave England another chance until Australia were within 31 runs of victory. Tufnell was unlucky to miss a first Test wicket when Boon, cutting, edged to Russell. Marsh, steady as a rock, batted 363 minutes (257 balls) and Boon 321 minutes (234 balls) for the second highest of their six three-figure stands in Tests.

*Man of the Match*: B. A. Reid.

*Close of play*: First day, England 239-4 (D. I. Gower 73*, A. J. Stewart 42*); Second day, Australia 109-1 (M. A. Taylor 42*, D. C. Boon 18*); Third day, Australia 306; Fourth day, Australia 28-2 (G. R. Marsh 11*, D. C. Boon 8*).

## England

| | | | |
|---|---|---|---|
| *G. A. Gooch lbw b Alderman | 20 | – c Alderman b Reid | 58 |
| M. A. Atherton c Boon b Reid | 0 | – c Healy b Reid | 4 |
| W. Larkins c Healy b Reid | 64 | – c Healy b Reid | 54 |
| R. A. Smith c Healy b Hughes | 30 | – c Taylor b Reid | 8 |
| D. I. Gower c and b Reid | 100 | – c Border b Matthews | 0 |
| A. J. Stewart c Healy b Reid | 79 | – c Marsh b Reid | 8 |
| †R. C. Russell c Healy b Hughes | 15 | – c Jones b Matthews | 1 |
| P. A. J. DeFreitas c Healy b Reid | 3 | – lbw b Reid | 0 |
| A. R. C. Fraser c Jones b Alderman | 24 | – c Taylor b Reid | 0 |
| D. E. Malcolm c Taylor b Reid | 6 | – lbw b Matthews | 1 |
| P. C. R. Tufnell not out | 0 | – not out | 0 |
| L-b 2, n-b 9 | 11 | B 7, l-b 3, n-b 6 | 16 |

1/12 (2) 2/30 (1) 3/109 (4) 4/152 (3)      352      1/17 (2) 2/103 (1) 3/115 (4)      150
5/274 (5) 6/303 (7) 7/307 (8)                       4/122 (5) 5/147 (6) 6/148 (3)
8/324 (6) 9/344 (10) 10/352 (9)                    7/148 (8) 8/148 (9)
                                             9/150 (7) 10/150 (10)

Bowling: *First Innings*—Alderman 30.4-7-86-2; Reid 39-8-97-6; Hughes 29-7-83-2; Matthews 27-8-65-0; Waugh 6-2-19-0. *Second Innings*—Alderman 10-2-19-0; Reid 22-12-51-7; Hughes 9-4-26-0; Matthews 25-9-40-3; Waugh 7-6-4-0.

## Australia

| | | | |
|---|---|---|---|
| G. R. Marsh c Russell b DeFreitas | 36 | – (2) not out | 79 |
| M. A. Taylor c Russell b DeFreitas | 61 | – (1) c Atherton b Malcolm | 5 |
| D. C. Boon c Russell b Malcolm | 28 | – (4) not out | 94 |
| *A. R. Border c Russell b Fraser | 62 | | |
| D. M. Jones c Russell b Fraser | 44 | | |
| S. R. Waugh b Fraser | 19 | | |
| G. R. J. Matthews lbw b Fraser | 12 | | |
| †I. A. Healy c Russell b Fraser | 5 | – (3) c Atherton b Fraser | 1 |
| M. G. Hughes lbw b Malcolm | 4 | | |
| T. M. Alderman b Fraser | 0 | | |
| B. A. Reid not out | 3 | | |
| B 4, l-b 12, n-b 16 | 32 | B 4, l-b 12, n-b 2 | 18 |

1/63 (1) 2/133 (3) 3/149 (2) 4/224 (5)      306      1/9 (1) 2/10 (3)      (2 wkts) 197
5/264 (6) 6/281 (4) 7/289 (8)
8/298 (7) 9/302 (10) 10/306 (9)

Bowling: *First Innings*—Malcolm 25.5-4-74-2; Fraser 39-10-82-6; Tufnell 21-5-62-0; DeFreitas 25-5-69-2; Atherton 2-1-3-0. *Second Innings*—Malcolm 23-7-52-1; Fraser 20-4-33-1; Tufnell 24-12-36-0; DeFreitas 16-3-46-0; Atherton 3-0-14-0.

Umpires: A. R. Crafter and P. J. McConnell.

## AUSTRALIA v ENGLAND

### Third Test Match

At Sydney, January 4, 5, 6, 7, 8. Drawn. Toss: Australia. The enterprise of Gooch and the competitive response of his players kept alive until the final hour a game which had seemed Australia's after they had scored 518 in 652 minutes in the first innings. It was not until the fourth morning that England, anchored by Atherton's 105 in 451 minutes and embellished by Gower's cultured 123, saved the follow-on, but Gooch's declaration at 469 for eight, 49 behind, brought the game to life in a quite unexpected way. The ball was turning – Matthews had often worried Gower, bowling what were leg-breaks to the left-hander – and Gooch wasted no time in bringing on his spin bowlers.

There was no mistaking the psychological effect of England's declaration. That evening Marsh and Taylor fell cheaply for the second time – in nine Tests against England, Taylor had never before failed to pass 50 – and Australia entered the final day without their usual buoyancy. In the event they survived until two and a quarter hours from the scheduled close, leaving England the almost impossible task of scoring 255 in 28 overs, a rate of 9.1 an over. They made a valiant stab at it, and Gooch's aggression could well have set up a brilliant win had the game followed only a slightly different pattern. The night-watchman, Healy, for example, who made 69 and lasted until seventeen minutes after lunch, gave an awkward chance low to the left of Gower at square leg in Hemmings's first over of the day; while Rackemann, abetted by Gooch's pessimistic view that Malcolm's back strain prevented him bowling, held out for 32 overs against the spinners, a well-advanced left pad thwarting them as often as his bat.

Well as Tufnell bowled, turning the ball perceptibly more than Hemmings and giving full value for his figures of five for 61, Gooch was over-committed to his spinners. When, after four hours in the field, Malcolm was finally handed an overdue new ball – the last pair had been together 25 minutes – he bowled Rackemann with his sixth delivery. Theoretically, England retained a chance while Gooch and Gower were scoring 84 at 7 runs an over, before the latter, having passed 8,000 Test runs, was caught a few yards inside the long-off boundary. Realistically, hopes had ended during Rackemann's 112-minute occupation.

Consistency underlay Australia's batting on the first two days. Malcolm had made good use of the pitch's early pace, having Marsh caught at first slip and Taylor down the leg side, off his gloves, but from the start England tended to bowl too short. Boon, adding 147 with Border, scarcely missed a chance to cut, and his fourth successive Sydney Test hundred looked there for the taking when, having cut and driven Gooch for three fours in four balls to leap from 85 to 97, he sliced an off-side long hop to deep gully. The selectiveness of Boon's attacking play is illustrated by his tally of seventeen boundaries in an innings of 174 balls and 201 minutes. Border, Jones and Waugh consolidated, and Matthews, unsettling Hemmings by his darting footwork, made 128 in 242 minutes (175 balls, seventeen fours), his fourth hundred in 24 Tests. Only Malcolm's stamina and strength saved England from submersion.

The only rain in a sweltering match restricted England's reply that evening to one over, sparing them a testing hour. Gooch and Atherton turned their good fortune to good account with a stand of 95 that lasted until twenty minutes after lunch on the third day, when Reid had Gooch caught down the leg side. And after Larkins and Smith had gone cheaply, the former run out by Border's direct hit from mid-wicket, Gower and Atherton swept away the danger of the follow-on in a stand of 139. The Lancastrian completed a dogged hundred, at 451 minutes the slowest in Ashes Tests, with a lovely cover-drive off Rackemann, one of only eight fours in his innings, before succumbing to his 349th ball, caught off Matthews at short leg. For the past hour he had been little more than a spectator of his partner's spectacular hitting, but he had already done enough to earn unexpected selection for the Man of the Match award. Gower went on to adorn the SCG with his first hundred there in any form of cricket (312 minutes, 236 balls, fifteen fours). When he had added 99 with Stewart, who scored a crisp 91 from 146 balls, Gooch had the material for his declaration.

*Man of the Match:* M. A. Atherton.        *Attendance:* 106,304.

*Close of play:* First day, Australia 259-4 (D. M. Jones 27*, S. R. Waugh 22*); Second day, England 1-0 (G. A. Gooch 1*, M. A. Atherton 0*); Third day, England 227-3 (M. A. Atherton 94*, D. I. Gower 33*); Fourth day, Australia 38-2 (I. A. Healy 9*, D. C. Boon 3*).

## Australia

| | | | |
|---|---:|---|---:|
| G. R. Marsh c Larkins b Malcolm | 13 | – (2) c Stewart b Malcolm | 4 |
| M. A. Taylor c Russell b Malcolm | 11 | – (1) lbw b Hemmings | 19 |
| D. C. Boon c Atherton b Gooch | 97 | – (4) c Gooch b Tufnell | 29 |
| *A. R. Border b Hemmings | 78 | – (5) c Gooch b Tufnell | 20 |
| D. M. Jones st Russell b Small | 60 | – (6) c and b Tufnell | 0 |
| S. R. Waugh c Stewart b Malcolm | 48 | – (7) c Russell b Hemmings | 14 |
| G. R. J. Matthews c Hemmings b Tufnell | 128 | – (8) b Hemmings | 19 |
| †I. A. Healy c Small b Hemmings | 35 | – (3) c Smith b Tufnell | 69 |
| C. G. Rackemann b Hemmings | 1 | – b Malcolm | 9 |
| T. M. Alderman not out | 26 | – c Gower b Tufnell | 1 |
| B. A. Reid c Smith b Malcolm | 0 | – not out | 5 |
| B 5, l-b 8, n-b 8 | 21 | L-b 16 | 16 |

1/21 (1) 2/38 (2) 3/185 (3) 4/226 (4)     518     1/21 (2) 2/29 (1) 3/81 (4)     205
5/292 (6) 6/347 (5) 7/442 (8)     4/129 (5) 5/129 (6) 6/166 (7)
8/457 (9) 9/512 (7) 10/518 (11)     7/166 (3) 8/189 (8) 9/192 (10)
    10/205 (9)

Bowling: *First Innings*—Malcolm 45-12-128-4; Small 31-5-103-1; Hemmings 32-7-105-3; Tufnell 30-6-95-1; Gooch 14-3-46-1; Atherton 5-0-28-0. *Second Innings*—Malcolm 6-1-19-2; Small 2-1-6-0; Hemmings 41-9-94-3; Tufnell 37-18-61-5; Atherton 3-1-9-0.

## England

| | | | |
|---|---:|---|---:|
| *G. A. Gooch c Healy b Reid | 59 | – c Border b Matthews | 54 |
| M. A. Atherton c Boon b Matthews | 105 | – (6) not out | 3 |
| W. Larkins run out | 11 | – lbw b Border | 0 |
| R. A. Smith c Healy b Reid | 18 | – (5) not out | 10 |
| D. I. Gower c Marsh b Reid | 123 | – (2) c Taylor b Matthews | 36 |
| A. J. Stewart lbw b Alderman | 91 | – (4) run out | 7 |
| †R. C. Russell not out | 30 | | |
| G. C. Small lbw b Alderman | 10 | | |
| E. E. Hemmings b Alderman | 0 | | |
| P. C. R. Tufnell not out | 5 | | |
| B 1, l-b 8, n-b 8 | 17 | L-b 1, n-b 2 | 3 |

1/95 (1) 2/116 (3) 3/156 (4)     (8 wkts dec.) 469     1/84 (2) 2/84 (3)     (4 wkts) 113
4/295 (2) 5/394 (5) 6/426 (6)     3/100 (1) 3/100 (4)
7/444 (8) 8/444 (9)

D. E. Malcolm did not bat.

Bowling: *First Innings*—Alderman 20.1-4-62-3; Reid 35.1-9-79-3; Rackemann 25.5-5-89-0; Matthews 58-16-145-1; Border 19-5-45-0; Waugh 14-3-40-0. *Second Innings*—Alderman 4-0-29-0; Rackemann 3-0-20-0; Matthews 9-2-26-2; Border 9-1-37-1.

Umpires: A. R. Crafter and P. J. McConnell.

## NEW SOUTH WALES v ENGLAND XI

At Albury, January 13, 14, 15, 16. New South Wales won by six wickets. Toss: England XI. Lack of spirit on the first day, when they were dismissed in four and a quarter hours on a good pitch, saw to it that England wasted the game worked into the itinerary after their failure to reach the World Series finals. Their punishment was prolonged: an innings by the Sheffield Shield champions which began 95 minutes before stumps on the first day and ended 21 minutes into the morning of the third, in heat that justified two drinks intervals a session. For 342 minutes it was anchored by Milliken, a dour 26-year-old left-hander standing in for M. A. Taylor, on duty like the Waugh twins against New Zealand. Three flowing fours through extra cover in a Tufnell over, played with perfect footwork from well down the pitch, proved he had strokes, but caution often prevailed. He passed 27 minutes on 99, during which Stewart missed a stumping. Batting again 157 behind, England were spared an innings defeat by a five-hour hundred from Atherton, the last man out. Otherwise most of the batting was again half-hearted. Lamb, acting-captain while Gooch rested in Melbourne, set an unfortunate example when he drove his fifth ball to mid-on after hitting its predecessor over the bowler's head for four. Even 50 more runs might have made a difference, as Hemmings showed when he reduced New South Wales to 44 for four on their way to victory.

*Close of play:* First day, New South Wales 73-1 (G. S. Milliken 20*, B. E. McNamara 13*); Second day, New South Wales 311-9 (P. A. Emery 49*, W. J. Holdsworth 0*); Third day, New South Wales 3-0 (S. M. Small 3*, G. S. Milliken 0*).

## England XI

| | | | |
|---|---|---|---|
| M. A. Atherton c Emery b Whitney | 15 | – (2) b Tucker | 114 |
| W. Larkins c Bevan b Whitney | 8 | – (8) b Matthews | 2 |
| J. E. Morris c Milliken b Holdsworth | 14 | – (1) c Milliken b Tucker | 41 |
| *A. J. Lamb c Emery b Lawson | 13 | – c Tucker b Matthews | 4 |
| R. A. Smith b Holdsworth | 5 | – (3) c Whitney b Tucker | 9 |
| †A. J. Stewart c Holdsworth b Lawson | 25 | – (5) st Emery b Tucker | 11 |
| P. A. J. DeFreitas c and b Tucker | 54 | – (6) c Whitney b Matthews | 8 |
| M. P. Bicknell c Bevan b Matthews | 10 | – (7) c Small b Matthews | 0 |
| G. C. Small not out | 9 | – b Whitney | 34 |
| E. E. Hemmings b Matthews | 2 | – c and b Whitney | 4 |
| P. C. R. Tufnell c Emery b Tucker | 0 | – not out | 0 |
| B 2, l-b 3, n-b 4 | 9 | B 6, l-b 2 | 8 |
| | **164** | | **235** |

1/10 2/39 3/39 4/56 5/58      164    1/69 2/81 3/86 4/111 5/128
6/129 7/152 8/152 9/163                         6/143 7/159 8/211 9/221      235

*Bowling: First Innings*—Lawson 13-3-29-2; Whitney 11-2-35-2; Holdsworth 13-2-50-2; McNamara 1-1-0-0; Matthews 15-5-34-2; Tucker 9.1-5-11-2. *Second Innings*—Lawson 6-1-17-0; Whitney 10-1-28-2; Matthews 32-10-77-4; Holdsworth 5-1-12-0; Bevan 2-1-4-0; Tucker 29.4-4-89-4.

## New South Wales

| | | | |
|---|---|---|---|
| S. M. Small c Stewart b Hemmings | 35 | – c Bicknell b Hemmings | 8 |
| G. S. Milliken lbw b Hemmings | 107 | – lbw b Hemmings | 3 |
| B. E. McNamara c Smith b Hemmings | 28 | – (4) c Morris b Hemmings | 3 |
| T. H. Bayliss c Lamb b Hemmings | 0 | – (3) c Smith b Hemmings | 22 |
| M. G. Bevan c Larkins b Tufnell | 42 | – not out | 14 |
| †P. A. Emery not out | 53 | – not out | 17 |
| G. R. J. Matthews c Hemmings b Tufnell | 5 | | |
| A. E. Tucker b Tufnell | 0 | | |
| *G. F. Lawson b Bicknell | 10 | | |
| M. R. Whitney c Small b Tufnell | 19 | | |
| W. J. Holdsworth c Lamb b DeFreitas | 6 | | |
| B 7, l-b 3, w 1, n-b 6 | 17 | B 8, l-b 5 | 13 |
| | **321** | | **(4 wkts) 79** |

1/48 2/123 3/123 4/219 5/229     321    1/11 2/24 3/39 4/44     (4 wkts) 79
6/234 7/238 8/254 9/302

*Bowling: First Innings*—Bicknell 18-5-47-1; DeFreitas 11.3-2-35-1; Hemmings 40-16-85-4; Small 16-6-30-0; Tufnell 32-6-97-4; Atherton 7-2-17-0. *Second Innings*—Bicknell 8-3-16-0; DeFreitas 1-1-0-0; Tufnell 12.5-2-21-0; Hemmings 18-7-29-4.

Umpires: D. B. Hair and I. S. Thomas.

## QUEENSLAND v ENGLAND XI

At Carrara, January 19, 20, 21, 22. England XI won by ten wickets. Toss: Queensland. For the first time since the Australian XI match in Hobart two months before, England won control early in the piece, and on this occasion they pressed home their advantage, sparing Gooch the stigma of becoming the first England captain to tour Australia without a first-class win.

Missing Border, nursing the groin strain which kept him out of the World Series finals, Queensland performed below their capabilities. The top-order batting twice failed in steamy conditions demanding stamina and patience, though Law was a stylish exception. Gooch, given three lives, and Morris and Smith, with their first hundreds of the tour, consolidated an England innings spanning 518 minutes on an outfield so big and slow that 38 threes were run and only 31 fours hit. (The playing area, normally used for Australian Rules football, matched Melbourne Cricket Ground's dimensions, and at 65 metres its floodlights were comfortably high enough for Gower and Morris to be flown between them on their expensive trip in Tiger Moths.) In arrears by 144, Queensland collapsed to 42 for five in 99 minutes, Hick following his first-innings dismissal to a full toss by slicing a cover-drive to gully. Healy and McDermott again resisted strongly, but Atherton made the winning hit with 90 minutes in hand.

*Close of play:* First day, England XI 27-1 (G. A. Gooch 18*, R. C. Russell 1*); Second day, England XI 253-3 (J. E. Morris 118*, R. A. Smith 25*); Third day, Queensland 94-5 (S. G. Law 36*, I. A. Healy 26*).

## Queensland

| | | | |
|---|---:|---|---:|
| P. E. Cantrell lbw b Small | 10 | – (2) b Small | 8 |
| S. Monty b Malcolm | 5 | – (1) c Russell b Bicknell | 2 |
| G. A. Hick c Malcolm b Tufnell | 45 | – c Atherton b Bicknell | 14 |
| P. S. Clifford c Atherton b Bicknell | 17 | – c Russell b Malcolm | 0 |
| S. G. Law c Gooch b Tufnell | 73 | – c Tufnell b Small | 44 |
| P. L. Taylor c and b Tufnell | 2 | – c Malcolm b Tufnell | 2 |
| †I. A. Healy c Bicknell b Tufnell | 56 | – c Russell b Small | 37 |
| C. J. McDermott not out | 50 | – c Russell b Small | 29 |
| *T. V. Hohns c Lamb b Tufnell | 10 | – not out | 16 |
| M. S. Kasprowicz c Russell b Malcolm | 12 | – c Morris b Tufnell | 3 |
| C. G. Rackemann c Small b Malcolm | 0 | – c Russell b Malcolm | 14 |
| B 1, l-b 3, n-b 2 | 6 | L-b 1, n-b 5 | 6 |
| | **286** | | **175** |

1/15 2/15 3/45 4/113 5/123 **286**  1/10 2/23 3/24 4/28 5/42 **175**
6/185 7/228 8/257 9/286  6/105 7/134 8/143 9/150

*Bowling: First Innings*—Malcolm 17.3–0–65–3; Small 14–2–47–1; Bicknell 12–1–39–1; Tufnell 30–2–108–5; Gooch 1–0–1–0; Atherton 9–1–22–0. *Second Innings*—Malcolm 17.2–4–51–2; Small 17–6–38–4; Bicknell 8–2–18–2; Tufnell 15–2–51–2; Atherton 3–0–16–0.

## England XI

| | | | |
|---|---:|---|---:|
| *G. A. Gooch c Healy b Rackemann | 93 | – not out | 21 |
| M. A. Atherton lbw b McDermott | 7 | – not out | 11 |
| †R. C. Russell c Healy b Rackemann | 2 | | |
| J. E. Morris c Hohns b Kasprowicz | 132 | | |
| R. A. Smith c Cantrell b Rackemann | 108 | | |
| D. I. Gower c McDermott b Taylor | 13 | | |
| A. J. Lamb c Healy b McDermott | 55 | | |
| G. C. Small c Healy b Hohns | 4 | | |
| M. P. Bicknell c Monty b Hohns | 0 | | |
| P. C. R. Tufnell not out | 0 | | |
| D. E. Malcolm b McDermott | 0 | | |
| B 2, l-b 5, w 2, n-b 7 | 16 | | |
| | **430** | | **(no wkt) 32** |

1/13 2/41 3/210 4/276 5/303 **430**  (no wkt) 32
6/411 7/420 8/420 9/430

*Bowling: First Innings*—McDermott 26.1–4–74–3; Kasprowicz 25–4–87–1; Rackemann 21–4–87–3; Taylor 24–4–77–1; Hohns 31–8–71–2; Monty 5–1–22–0; Cantrell 2–0–5–0. *Second Innings*—Kasprowicz 6.3–2–18–0; Cantrell 4–1–7–0; Monty 2–0–7–0.

Umpires: P. D. Parker and C. D. Timmins.

## AUSTRALIA v ENGLAND

### Fourth Test Match

At Adelaide, January 25, 26, 27, 28, 29. Drawn. Toss: Australia. For the second Test in succession, an engagingly irrational batting display by England on the final day transformed a routine draw into something that briefly promised more. History, as much as England's lack of depth, proclaimed that they had no chance of scoring 472 when Border declared three-quarters of an hour before the close of the fourth day. The scoreboard proved history and the form-book correct, but only after England had gone to tea on the fifth afternoon at 267 for two, thanks to an opening stand of 203 between Gooch and Atherton, and a cameo by Lamb. England had scored 152 in 30 overs since lunch, and Border was disconcerted enough to let the game drift to stalemate, rather than move on to the attack when England lost Lamb, Gower and Stewart within 10 runs.

Australia made their one batting change of the series, bringing in Mark Waugh at the expense of his twin brother, Steve, whose sequence of 42 Tests since his début against India at Melbourne in 1985-86 was thus broken. McDermott and Hughes replaced Alderman and Rackemann. Missing on the England side was Russell, whose run of twenty Tests as wicket-keeper ended when misgivings about Fraser's hip prompted the inclusion of a fifth bowler, with Stewart keeping wicket. It turned out to be a worthwhile precaution; Fraser twisted an ankle in the first innings, though he came back to bowl at less than full pace in the second, while Tufnell missed most of the second and third days with tonsillitis. Lamb and DeFreitas returned to displace Larkins and Hemmings.

For Waugh, by four minutes the younger of the 25-year-old twins, it proved a glorious début. He produced an innings which a batsman of any generation would have been overjoyed to play any time in his career, let alone on a first Test appearance and in a situation which verged on crisis. When he came in 52 minutes after lunch, DeFreitas had dismissed Border and Jones in four balls, the former cramped by a quick break-back making extra height, which he played into his stumps. Boon followed 38 minutes later, caught at deep third man, to leave Australia 124 for five.

Waugh's shot off the mark, a flowing straight three off his second ball, was a portent of what was in store. In the evening his timing, range of strokes, and quick and confident footwork dazzled. He passed 50 in 74 balls, and needed only another 52 to reach his hundred, which came out of 148 runs in 176 minutes with his fifteenth four. Tufnell, unable to find either a trajectory or a length to hold him, was picked up over the on-side from down the pitch or hit off the back foot through the covers with equal certainty and style. On the second day Waugh lost his touch, but Matthews, almost unnoticed in their stand of 171, stretched a valuable but tedious innings to five and a quarter hours, and with McDermott steered Australia to 386 in 584 minutes.

England made a bad start when, in McDermott's third over, Atherton was judged lbw, padding up well outside off stump, and Lamb was caught at the wicket, the first of five catches for Healy. However, Gooch (284 minutes) and Smith added 126 in 200 minutes, but Gower, obligingly chipping the last ball of the morning to long leg, one of three men positioned for the stroke, ushered in a collapse that saw seven wickets fall for 69 runs. McDermott could have no complaint with figures of five for 97 in his first Test since 1988-89. Australia, leading by 157 with seven sessions to go, lost momentum when Marsh, Taylor and Jones were out by the tenth over. But the immovable Boon more than atoned for running out Taylor, adding 66 with Hughes, the night-watchman, and 110 with Border. Nothing he played at passed the bat in 368 minutes until he swept clumsily at Tufnell and was bowled for 121, his second Adelaide hundred against England. Border batted another 71 minutes, adding 74 with Matthews before his declaration.

When, in the first over of the final day, Atherton and Gooch sprinted four runs from a stroke to third man, rather than jogging three, it was obvious that Gooch had more than survival on his mind. Atherton confirmed it with three hooked fours, hitting each so well it was a mystery he played the stroke so rarely. It was only at lunch, though, with England 115 for no wicket, that Gooch decided the distant goal was worth a try. His explosive driving, mainly through mid-off and extra cover off Matthews and McDermott, brought him another 58 in 57 minutes before Marsh, at gully, caught a full-blooded slash off Reid. His first Test hundred in Australia contained twelve fours and lasted 214 minutes and 188 balls. Atherton followed 36 minutes later, hitting Reid to cover, but Lamb, 46 at tea off 38 balls, kept the goal in sight until McDermott and Hughes forced England on to the defensive.

*Man of the Match*: G. A. Gooch.     *Attendance*: 78,676.

*Close of play:* First day, Australia 269-5 (M. E. Waugh 116\*, G. R. J. Matthews 29\*); Second day, England 95-2 (G. A. Gooch 50\*, R. A. Smith 36\*); Third day, Australia 68-4 (D. C. Boon 24\*, M. G. Hughes 3\*); Fourth day, England 19-0 (G. A. Gooch 14\*, M. A. Atherton 1\*).

## Australia

| | | | |
|---|---:|---|---:|
| G. R. Marsh c Gooch b Small | 37 | – (2) c Gooch b Small | 0 |
| M. A. Taylor run out | 5 | – (1) run out | 4 |
| D. C. Boon c Fraser b Malcolm | 49 | – b Tufnell | 121 |
| \*A. R. Border b DeFreitas | 12 | – (7) not out | 83 |
| D. M. Jones lbw b DeFreitas | 0 | – (4) lbw b DeFreitas | 8 |
| M. E. Waugh b Malcolm | 138 | – (5) b Malcolm | 23 |
| G. R. J. Matthews c Stewart b Gooch | 65 | – (8) not out | 34 |
| †I. A. Healy c Stewart b DeFreitas | 1 | | |
| C. J. McDermott not out | 42 | | |
| M. G. Hughes lbw b Small | 1 | – (6) c Gooch b Fraser | 30 |
| B. A. Reid c Lamb b DeFreitas | 5 | | |
| B 2, l-b 23, w 2, n-b 4 | 31 | B 1, l-b 7, w 1, n-b 2 | 11 |
| | 386 | (6 wkts dec.) | 314 |

1/11 (2) 2/62 (1) 3/104 (4) 4/104 (5)     1/1 (2) 2/8 (1)    (6 wkts dec.) 314
5/124 (3) 6/295 (6) 7/298 (8)              3/25 (4) 4/64 (5)
8/358 (9) 9/373 (10) 10/386 (11)        5/130 (6) 6/240 (3)

Bowling: *First Innings*—Malcolm 38-7-104-2; Fraser 23-6-48-0; Small 34-10-92-2; DeFreitas 26.2-6-56-4; Tufnell 5-0-38-0; Gooch 9-2-23-1. *Second Innings*—Malcolm 21-0-87-1; Small 18-3-64-1; DeFreitas 23-6-61-1; Fraser 26-3-66-1; Tufnell 16-3-28-1.

## England

| | | | |
|---|---:|---|---:|
| \*G. A. Gooch c Healy b Reid | 87 | – c Marsh b Reid | 117 |
| M. A. Atherton lbw b McDermott | 0 | – c Waugh b Reid | 87 |
| A. J. Lamb c Healy b McDermott | 0 | – b McDermott | 53 |
| R. A. Smith c and b Hughes | 53 | – (5) not out | 10 |
| D. I. Gower c Hughes b McDermott | 11 | – (4) lbw b Hughes | 16 |
| †A. J. Stewart c Healy b Reid | 11 | – c Jones b McDermott | 9 |
| P. A. J. DeFreitas c Matthews b McDermott | 45 | – not out | 19 |
| G. C. Small b McDermott | 1 | | |
| A. R. C. Fraser c Healy b Reid | 2 | | |
| D. E. Malcolm c Healy b Reid | 2 | | |
| P. C. R. Tufnell not out | 0 | | |
| B 1, l-b 3, n-b 13 | 17 | B 5, l-b 9, w 1, n-b 9 | 24 |
| | 229 | (5 wkts) | 335 |

1/10 (2) 2/11 (3) 3/137 (4) 4/160 (5)     1/203 (1) 2/246 (2)    (5 wkts) 335
5/176 (1) 6/179 (6) 7/198 (8)             3/287 (3) 4/287 (4)
8/215 (9) 9/219 (10) 10/229 (7)          5/297 (6)

Bowling: *First Innings*—Reid 29-9-53-4; McDermott 26.3-3-97-5; Hughes 22-4-62-1; Waugh 4-1-13-0. *Second Innings*—Reid 23-5-59-2; McDermott 27-5-106-2; Matthews 31-7-100-0; Hughes 14-3-52-1; Waugh 1-0-4-0.

Umpires: L. J. King and T. A. Prue.

## AUSTRALIA v ENGLAND

### Fifth Test Match

At Perth, February 1, 2, 3, 5. Australia won by nine wickets. Toss: England. Australia took only ten sessions to improve their unbeaten run against England to eight victories and four draws since the Sydney Test of 1986-87, despite Reid's absence with a callus on his foot and the fact that at tea on the first day they were looking at an England scoreboard reading 212 for three. Dashing, attacking play from Lamb and Smith, combined with Australia's loosest bowling of the series on the fastest outfield, lifted England's hopes; a moment's overconfidence, a dubious lbw decision, the well-established temperamental and technical flaws of the lower-order batting, and fiery bowling by McDermott reversed the position in the twinkling of an eye.

Although McDermott disposed of Gooch, Atherton and later Smith in the first two sessions, his eighteen overs had cost 80 runs. After tea he had five for 17 in 6.4 overs, giving him eight England wickets for the second time in ten Tests. He had taken eight for 141 at Old Trafford in 1985. The critical dismissal came in the first over after the resumption when Lamb tried to pull a ball from clear of his off stump and was caught behind the bowler by Border, running from mid-on. If it was a dangerous stroke immediately after an interval, the under-pitched ball had proved highly profitable for both Lamb and Smith in a third-wicket stand of 141 at three an over. Lamb's highest Test score in Australia, beating his 83 at Melbourne in 1982-83, was crisply struck off 122 balls in 206 minutes, and contained a straight six off Matthews and thirteen fours. Smith, who was caught head high at second slip off a fast-flying edged drive 25 minutes before tea, hit a six and nine fours off 120 balls in 153 minutes.

On an ideal batting pitch, in perfect weather and with an outfield so quick that Atherton found the 95-yard boundary only just behind square leg when he jammed down on a yorker in the second over, a score of 400 was still possible. But in McDermott's next over after Lamb's dismissal, Stewart was given out lbw off a ball that seemed likely to miss the leg stump, and the innings folded. From 212 for three, England were all out for 244 in 70 minutes and 12.4 overs. Newport, borrowed from the England A team in Sri Lanka three days before the match, was out first ball, McDermott's seventh victim.

Australia's innings illustrated one of the essential differences between the teams – lower-order batting strength. Midway through the second day they were 168 for six, but for the third time Matthews became England's stumbling block, supervising the addition of 139 runs for the last four wickets in a typically adhesive, three-and-a-quarter-hour innings. He also displayed tactical flair, for the first time in the series exercising the right to continue batting after 6.00 p.m. if fewer than 90 overs had been bowled. With nine overs due, and Alderman looking untroubled, it was the right decision against a team flagging after six hours in a temperature of 82 degrees. Ironically the No. 11 fell five balls later to DeFreitas.

Only 63 behind, England still had hopes of fighting back to win. In the event there was more movement for the fast bowlers than Western Australians could recall on a third day at Perth. But for luck running against Hughes, and Newport's robust 38-run stand with Malcolm at the end, Australia could have finished the series as they started, with a three-day win. Hughes's line hardly wavered from off stump or just outside, and figures of four for 37 did not do him justice. They did, however, take him past 100 Test wickets; and when DeFreitas was caught behind, Alderman had his 100th wicket in Ashes Tests.

Australia, needing 120, lost Taylor in the final over of the day, but Marsh and Boon scored the remaining 81 in 87 minutes after the only rest day of the series. Fittingly, the winning runs, a sprinted two, came from a defensive stroke by Boon that rolled no further than the square-leg umpire, a range that, because of the speed of Australia's fielding, would have restricted England to a single.

*Man of the Match*: C. J. McDermott.　　　*Attendance*: 47,500.

*Man of the Series*: B. A. Reid.

*Close of play*: First day, Australia 19-1 (M. A. Taylor 9*, D. C. Boon 9*); Second day, Australia 307; Third day, Australia 39-1 (G. R. Marsh 19*).

# England

| | | | |
|---|---|---|---|
| *G. A. Gooch c Healy b McDermott | 13 | – c Alderman b Hughes | 18 |
| M. A. Atherton c Healy b McDermott | 27 | – c Boon b Hughes | 25 |
| A. J. Lamb c Border b McDermott | 91 | – lbw b McDermott | 5 |
| R. A. Smith c Taylor b McDermott | 58 | – lbw b Alderman | 43 |
| D. I. Gower not out | 28 | – c Taylor b Alderman | 5 |
| †A. J. Stewart lbw b McDermott | 2 | – c Healy b McDermott | 7 |
| P. A. J. DeFreitas c Marsh b McDermott | 5 | – c Healy b Alderman | 5 |
| P. J. Newport c Healy b McDermott | 0 | – not out | 40 |
| G. C. Small c Boon b Hughes | 0 | – c Taylor b Hughes | 4 |
| P. C. R. Tufnell c Healy b Hughes | 0 | – c Healy b Hughes | 8 |
| D. E. Malcolm c Marsh b McDermott | 7 | – c Jones b McDermott | 6 |
| B 1, l-b 6, w 1, n-b 5 | 13 | B 5, l-b 5, n-b 6 | 16 |

1/27 (1) 2/50 (2) 3/191 (4) 4/212 (3) 　　　　244　　1/41 (1) 2/49 (3) 3/75 (2) 　　　182
5/220 (6) 6/226 (7) 7/226 (8) 　　　　　　　　　　　4/80 (5) 5/114 (6) 6/118 (4)
8/227 (9) 9/227 (10) 10/244 (11) 　　　　　　　　　7/125 (7) 8/134 (9)
　　　　　　　　　　　　　　　　　　　　　　　　　9/144 (10) 10/182 (11)

Bowling: *First Innings*—Alderman 22–5–66–0; McDermott 24.4–2–97–8; Hughes 17–3–49–2; Waugh 1–0–9–0; Matthews 2–0–16–0. *Second Innings*—McDermott 19.3–2–60–3; Alderman 22–3–75–3; Hughes 20–7–37–4.

## Australia

| | | | |
|---|---|---|---|
| G. R. Marsh c Stewart b Small | 1 | – (2) not out | 63 |
| M. A. Taylor c Stewart b Malcolm | 12 | – (1) c Stewart b DeFreitas | 19 |
| D. C. Boon c Stewart b Malcolm | 64 | – not out | 30 |
| *A. R. Border lbw b DeFreitas | 17 | | |
| D. M. Jones b Newport | 34 | | |
| M. E. Waugh c Small b Malcolm | 26 | | |
| G. R. J. Matthews not out | 60 | | |
| †I. A. Healy c Lamb b Small | 42 | | |
| C. J. McDermott b Tufnell | 25 | | |
| M. G. Hughes c Gooch b Tufnell | 0 | | |
| T. M. Alderman lbw b DeFreitas | 7 | | |
| B 2, l-b 8, w 1, n-b 8 | 19 | L-b 5, w 2, n-b 1 | 8 |

1/1 (1) 2/44 (2) 3/90 (4) 4/113 (3)      307    1/39 (1)    (1 wkt) 120
5/161 (5) 6/168 (6) 7/230 (8) 8/281 (9)
9/283 (10) 10/307 (11)

Bowling: *First Innings*—Malcolm 30–4–94–3; Small 23–3–65–2; DeFreitas 16.5–2–57–2; Newport 14–0–56–1; Tufnell 7–1–25–2. *Second Innings*—Malcolm 9–0–40–0; Small 10–5–24–0; DeFreitas 6.2–0–29–1; Newport 6–0–22–0.

Umpires: S. G. Randell and C. D. Timmins.

## †NEW ZEALAND v ENGLAND

### First One-day International

At Christchurch, February 9. England won by 14 runs. Toss: England. Successive stands of 83 and 63 involving Smith saw England to a competitive total after a start of 46 for three. Before the sun broke through there was encouragement for the bowlers on a slow, uneven pitch, and Watson combined accuracy with variable movement off the seam in ten unbroken overs for 15 runs. In the best innings of the day Lamb scored 61 off 62 balls – he was run out off a no-ball – and Stewart's 40-ball 40 made sure the momentum was not lost. With Wright taking to Bicknell, New Zealand put on 38 off eight overs. But Crowe then mistimed a straight drive, and two run-outs helped drag the home side down to 94 for five at the halfway stage. However, to the delight of a crowd of 16,800, Rutherford and the left-handed Harris coolly added 122 to cut the target to 19 from three overs. When Rutherford drove Bicknell to mid-off, and Harris desperately slashed at the last ball of the over, a fine effort came to nothing. *Man of the Match:* K. R. Rutherford.

## England

| | | |
|---|---|---|
| *G. A. Gooch b Pringle | 17 | P. A. J. DeFreitas not out .......... 10 |
| D. I. Gower b Petrie | 4 | M. P. Bicknell not out ............. 0 |
| M. A. Atherton b Watson | 0 | L-b 8, w 12, n-b 3 ......... 23 |
| A. J. Lamb run out | 61 | |
| R. A. Smith c Jones b Pringle | 65 | 1/6 (2) 2/9 (3)    (7 wkts, 50 overs) 230 |
| A. J. Stewart c Wright b Pringle | 40 | 3/46 (1) 4/129 (4) |
| †R. C. Russell c sub (R. T. Latham) | | 5/192 (5) 6/217 (7) |
| b Petrie . | 10 | 7/220 (6) |

A. R. C. Fraser and E. E. Hemmings did not bat.

Bowling: Petrie 10–0–51–2; Watson 10–2–15–1; Pringle 10–0–54–3; Larsen 10–0–47–0; Harris 8–0–46–0; Rutherford 2–0–9–0.

## New Zealand

| | | | |
|---|---|---|---|
| *M. D. Crowe c and b Bicknell | 13 | R. G. Petrie c Gower b Fraser | 0 |
| J. G. Wright c Smith b DeFreitas | 27 | C. Pringle not out | 0 |
| A. H. Jones run out | 17 | B 2, l-b 14, w 5 | 21 |
| K. R. Rutherford c Gooch b Bicknell | 77 | | |
| M. J. Greatbatch c Russell b Hemmings | 0 | 1/38 (1) 2/50 (2) | (8 wkts, 50 overs) 216 |
| †I. D. S. Smith run out | 4 | 3/82 (3) 4/86 (5) | |
| C. Z. Harris c Russell b Bicknell | 56 | 5/90 (6) 6/212 (4) | |
| G. R. Larsen not out | 1 | 7/213 (7) 8/215 (9) | |

W. Watson did not bat.

Bowling: Fraser 10-0-28-1; Bicknell 10-2-55-3; DeFreitas 10-3-36-1; Gooch 10-0-31-0; Hemmings 10-0-50-1.

Umpires: B. L. Aldridge and R. S. Dunne.

## †NEW ZEALAND v ENGLAND

### Second One-day International

At Wellington, February 13. New Zealand won by 9 runs. Toss: England. Generous to a fault, England reserved for their hosts a collapse that was a collector's item, even by their standards in Australia. After good bowling and brilliant fielding had pegged New Zealand to 196 for eight, England progressed from 73 for no wicket to 147 for three and 160 for four, needing 37 off nine overs. And still they lost the match with ease, through a mixture of arrogance, stupidity and panic. A full house of 11,000 watched in mounting disbelief until Bicknell and Fraser were caught within three balls from Pringle. England had controlled the game from the moment Gooch won the toss. With Fraser making the ball bounce and seam on a pitch that had sweated under tarpaulins on a rainy night, and Bicknell disposing of Crowe with a devastating leg-cutter, New Zealand were 43 for three in an hour. When Gooch and Atherton launched England's reply in bright sunshine at almost 4 an over, it seemed that Jones's 64 from 91 balls had merely postponed the inevitable. But four wickets fell to catches at mid-off and mid-on, and two to run-outs. Once more England had tackled the impossible and made it look commonplace.

*Man of the Match*: A. H. Jones.

## New Zealand

| | | | |
|---|---|---|---|
| R. B. Reid c Russell b Fraser | 9 | G. R. Larsen not out | 10 |
| J. G. Wright b Fraser | 9 | C. Pringle not out | 18 |
| *M. D. Crowe c Russell b Bicknell | 5 | L-b 9, w 11 | 20 |
| A. H. Jones b Fraser | 64 | | |
| K. R. Rutherford c and b Tufnell | 19 | 1/20 (2) 2/25 (1) | (8 wkts, 49 overs) 196 |
| C. Z. Harris st Russell b Tufnell | 9 | 3/43 (3) 4/91 (5) | |
| †I. D. S. Smith b Bicknell | 28 | 5/109 (6) 6/150 (4) | |
| C. L. Cairns c Smith b DeFreitas | 5 | 7/158 (8) 8/171 (7) | |

W. Watson did not bat.

Bowling: Fraser 9-1-22-3; Bicknell 10-0-65-2; DeFreitas 10-2-22-1; Gooch 10-2-33-0; Tufnell 10-0-45-2.

## England

| | | | |
|---|---|---|---|
| *G. A. Gooch c Wright b Cairns | 41 | A. R. C. Fraser c Crowe b Pringle | 5 |
| M. A. Atherton c Cairns b Harris | 26 | P. C. R. Tufnell not out | 0 |
| D. I. Gower run out | 11 | | |
| A. J. Lamb c Cairns | 33 | L-b 8, w 7 | 15 |
| R. A. Smith b Pringle | 38 | | |
| A. J. Stewart c Watson b Harris | 5 | 1/73 (1) 2/81 (2) 3/93 (3) | (48 overs) 187 |
| †R. C. Russell c Cairns b Harris | 2 | 4/147 (4) 5/160 (6) 6/170 (7) | |
| P. A. J. DeFreitas run out | 2 | 7/173 (8) 8/174 (5) 9/187 (9) | |
| M. P. Bicknell c Jones b Pringle | 9 | 10/187 (10) | |

Bowling: Pringle 10-1-43-3; Watson 10-1-34-0; Cairns 9-1-41-2; Larsen 9-1-28-0; Harris 10-0-33-3.

Umpires: G. I. J. Cowan and S. J. Woodward.

## †NEW ZEALAND v ENGLAND

### Third One-day International

At Auckland, February 16. New Zealand won by 7 runs. Toss: England. As in the previous game, England looked sure winners at 170 for three with ten overs to go, needing 30 fewer than the home team scored in the same period when Harris and Smith hit 74 in 55 balls. (The New Zealanders, despite Jones's energy, had taken 30.2 overs to reach 100.) This time, however, the match was won by New Zealand rather than lost by England. In the 41st over, Cairns accounted for Lamb with a quick leg-cutter, after which England cracked under pressure. Stewart was well caught above his head by wicket-keeper Smith, mistiming a short-arm pull, and England's Smith lost his off stump as he made room to force Cairns through the covers. When Crowe, backing out of the circle at mid-off, caught DeFreitas off Pringle in the 48th over, England's chance was gone. Hindsight pointed to mistakes by Gooch, who was out here and at Wellington to misplayed attacking strokes; and in view of England's diffident batting, his decision to field first was also debatable.

*Man of the Match:* C. Z. Harris.

### New Zealand

| | | | |
|---|---|---|---|
| *M. D. Crowe b DeFreitas | 6 | C. Pringle not out | 0 |
| R. B. Reid c Lamb b Tufnell | 26 | | |
| A. H. Jones run out | 64 | L-b 5, w 3 | 8 |
| K. R. Rutherford lbw b Gooch | 12 | | |
| M. J. Greatbatch c Lamb b DeFreitas | 12 | 1/7 (1) 2/66 (2)　　(7 wkts, 50 overs) 224 | |
| C. Z. Harris b Fraser | 39 | 3/98 (4) 4/120 (5) | |
| †I. D. S. Smith not out | 51 | 5/135 (3) 6/209 (6) | |
| C. L. Cairns run out | 6 | 7/220 (8) | |

G. R. Larsen and W. Watson did not bat.

Bowling: Fraser 10-3-31-1; DeFreitas 10-0-51-2; Small 10-2-51-0; Gooch 10-0-40-1; Tufnell 10-1-46-1.

### England

| | | | |
|---|---|---|---|
| *G. A. Gooch b Larsen | 47 | A. R. C. Fraser b Pringle | 6 |
| M. A. Atherton c Crowe b Harris | 34 | P. C. R. Tufnell not out | 3 |
| D. I. Gower c Jones b Harris | 13 | | |
| A. J. Lamb b Smith b Cairns | 42 | L-b 10, w 4 | 14 |
| R. A. Smith b Cairns | 35 | | |
| A. J. Stewart c Smith b Cairns | 3 | 1/83 (1) 2/91 (2) 3/118 (3)　(49.5 overs) 217 | |
| P. A. J. DeFreitas c Crowe b Pringle | 7 | 4/171 (4) 5/185 (6) 6/194 (5) | |
| †R. C. Russell b Cairns | 13 | 7/200 (7) 8/203 (9) | |
| G. C. Small b Pringle | 0 | 9/209 (8) 10/217 (10) | |

Bowling: Pringle 9.5-0-43-3; Watson 10-1-38-0; Cairns 10-0-55-4; Larsen 10-0-35-1; Harris 10-1-36-2.

Umpires: R. L. McHarg and S. J. Woodward.

# ENGLAND A IN PAKISTAN AND SRI LANKA, 1990-91

## By MARK BALDWIN

"This tour is not about results," said Ted Dexter, chairman of the England selectors. "It's about producing future Test cricketers for England." Yet if Dexter, spending a week in Sri Lanka, watching the second unofficial "Test" unfold at Colombo's attractive SSC ground, had uttered those sentiments in the England A team's dressing-room at the end of that taut, draining match, he might well have become a late chairman of selectors – if England's weary young cricketers had been able to summon the strength.

As in the first "Test" at Kandy, they had only drawn a match they should have won. But this time it had been heat, exhaustion and a superlative Sri Lankan rearguard action – rather than a clutch of unfortunate umpiring decisions – which had conspired to frustrate them. However, it was the very way they took bitter disappointment to heart – their will to win – coupled with their often considerable restraint in the face of debatable decisions, that marked out Hugh Morris's side as one full of future Test players.

This was a tough team, resilient and ambitious. A pleasure to be with off the field, but single-minded and ruthless on it. It rankled to young men like Morris, Andy Pick, Mark Ramprakash, Nasser Hussain, Richard Illingworth and Graham Thorpe that on paper their tour record looked poor: the three-match "Test" series drawn, and a 4-1 defeat in the one-day "internationals". Only in the final match of the nine-week tour, Sri Lanka's spectacular inaugural day/night international in Colombo, did England translate their potential into success. Even without an unwell Pick, their leading strike bowler and one of the tour's successes, they capped forceful batting and disciplined bowling with, in the words of Bruce Yardley, the former Australian off-spinner, "the most stunning fielding display I have seen from an England team". The athleticism and commitment of England's fielding, with Thorpe, Hussain, Fairbrother, Ramprakash and Blakey outstanding, was particularly welcome following the shortcomings in that department of the senior side in Australia.

In retrospect, England's selectors might well have wished they had chosen the likes of Morris (for Larkins), Ramprakash (for John Morris) and Illingworth (for Hemmings) on the Ashes tour. As it was, Phil Newport was summoned to Perth to play in the final Ashes Test, after which he returned to Sri Lanka for the three five-day matches there. And, while his side attended pre-tour training sessions at Lilleshall, the captain, Morris, was detained for six weeks in Australia as stand-by for the injured Gooch. In that time he had only two innings, both in low-key one-day games, and his subsequent efforts in Pakistan and Sri Lanka were a triumph for his stamina. Morris returned home from Australia just four days before boarding an international flight for Pakistan. A succession of gruelling air journeys was hardly ideal preparation for a personally vital tour, and it undoubtedly cost him some of his batting form.

Phillip DeFreitas, an original A team selection, was another called to Australia, but unlike Morris he stayed with Gooch's team until the end of their tour. DeFreitas was replaced in the sixteen-man party by Steve Watkin, and when the Glamorgan fast bowler's tour was cut short by injury, twenty-year-old Mark Ilott of Essex joined the team to great effect in the last month.

He quickly showed that he had the action, pace and attitude to become a top-class left-arm fast bowler. In the "Test" at the SSC ground in Colombo, Ilott and Pick ran through the Sri Lankan second innings with sharp, penetrative bowling, in largely unhelpful conditions, before they tired, and Dileepa Wickremasinghe and Chintaka Edirimanne were able to save the match.

For Pick, 27 and with a history of injury troubles, international recognition had come late. And in spite of the slow pitches and the intense heat and humidity – not ideal conditions for fast bowling – he took his chance. "I don't think he can recognise himself from the county cricketer he was before this tour", said Keith Fletcher, the team's coach.

Among the batsmen, Ramprakash and Hussain made the major headlines with their innings of 158 and 161 respectively in the "Tests" at Kandy and at the SSC in Colombo. Ramprakash revealed immense concentration, sound temperament and steely resolve to go with his already known gifts of style, ability and technique. Hussain, fully recovered from the broken wrist he had suffered the previous spring in the West Indies, reasserted his claim for a place in the full England side.

Yet it was Thorpe who most caught the eye, simply because he started the tour with the biggest question mark against his name. After impressing the previous winter on the A tour of Zimbabwe, the Surrey left-hander had had a poor summer in county cricket. His selection ahead of other middle-order candidates could not be justified by figures; it was, rather, a case of backing a class player, and the England selectors should be applauded for it. Thorpe's morale was clearly boosted by this expression of confidence in him, and he spoke glowingly of the help Fletcher gave him at Lilleshall. In Pakistan and Sri Lanka he became the team's most consistent scorer, and he was rated by the Sri Lankan spinners as their most accomplished opponent.

Darren Bicknell and Richard Blakey just about kept their batting reputations alive, but the vice-captain, Neil Fairbrother, had a largely disappointing time. He began the tour as the senior batsman, in terms of Test caps; he ended it by being omitted from the side for the final "Test". A rash stroke in the first innings of the Kandy "Test", and a poor decision in the second, set him back early on, and his promising 71 at the SSC was cut short by another ill-advised choice of stroke – a top-edged sweep going to a fielder specifically positioned for such a mistake. Fletcher's opinion was that Fairbrother still needed to realise fully the importance of organising an innings in relation to the conditions encountered.

Like Fairbrother's, Illingworth's performances marked him out for limited-overs internationals rather than the five-day game. Illingworth, a fine all-round cricketer, let no-one down, but slow left-arm spinning is his stock-in-trade, and direct comparison with Sri Lanka's second string, on mainly helpful pitches, showed up his lack of penetration. His best asset was his control.

Of the two other spinners, Ian Salisbury had a tour to remember with affection, and Keith Medlycott one to put behind him. Salisbury, the 21-year-old leg-spinner from Sussex, was an imaginative choice and he learned more than simple figures can show. But Medlycott, the second slow left-armer, who the previous year had toured the Caribbean with the senior England side, suffered such a chronic plunge in confidence that it could be argued he should not have stayed on in Sri Lanka. In seven weeks on the island, he played in just a couple of two-day matches and sent down only 32 overs, few of them without either a full toss or a long hop.

Despite this setback, Medlycott conducted himself with great cheerfulness and was never less than helpful to his tour colleagues. Also to his credit was a willingness, unfortunately not always shared by many of the other tourists, to mix with the Sri Lankan opposition. Socialising between rival international teams may seldom be easy these days, but in the low-key atmosphere of an A tour it should be encouraged. Both sides could have benefited from more communication with each other; it would have prevented much of the niggly ill-feeling which became an unhappy side-issue between the two sets of players.

The England management, Bob Bennett and Fletcher, who were such a success in Zimbabwe, found this a more difficult tour. Bennett acquitted himself well when diplomacy and important decisions were required in Pakistan, the original seven-week tour there being aborted after a fortnight following the outbreak of war in the Gulf and growing civil disturbances throughout the country. Sri Lanka, originally due to host England A for just two weeks, stepped in quickly to offer not only a safe haven but also a full itinerary. The Test and County Cricket Board was delighted with the Sri Lankan initiative, which is perhaps why it was less than pleased either with Fletcher's comments on the standard of umpiring, and the general facilities offered to England, or with Bennett's request that umpire Basil Anthony be stood down from the final "Test", following a controversial performance in the fourth one-day "international".

The popularity of the two men with the players, and the respect they commanded, cannot be overstated. Both in Zimbabwe in 1989-90 and in Sri Lanka, the young England players without exception spoke of the amount they had learned from Fletcher. The TCCB, when the time comes to appoint a successor to Micky Stewart as England team manager, might even be wise to overlook Fletcher, simply because of the invaluable work he is doing with players at the formative stage of their international careers. One area which Fletcher wants developed, for all England players, is the autumn "talk-in" and "practical" sessions at Lilleshall. He is seen at his best there, and the England committee would do well to use his sage teaching to the full.

## ENGLAND A TOUR PARTY

H. Morris (Glam.) (*captain*), N. H. Fairbrother (Lancs.) (*vice-captain*), D. J. Bicknell (Surrey), R. J. Blakey (Yorks.), W. K. Hegg (Lancs.), N. Hussain (Essex), R. K. Illingworth (Worcs.), K. T. Medlycott (Surrey), T. A. Munton (Warwicks.), P. J. Newport (Worcs.), R. A. Pick (Notts.), M. R. Ramprakash (Middx), S. J. Rhodes (Worcs.), I. D. K. Salisbury (Sussex), G. P. Thorpe (Surrey) and S. L. Watkin (Glam.).

Watkin joined the tour party after P. A. J. DeFreitas (Lancs.), an original selection, had been called up by the England team in Australia before the England A tour began. M. C. Ilott (Essex) joined the team in Sri Lanka as a replacement when Watkin was injured.

*Tour manager:* R. M. Bennett (Lancs.). *Team manager:* K. W. R. Fletcher (Essex).

## ENGLAND A TOUR RESULTS

*First-class matches* – Played 5: Won 1, Drawn 4.
*Win* – Southern Districts XI.
*Draws* – Combined Universities, Sri Lanka A (3).
*Non first-class matches* – Played 9: Won 2, Lost 5, Drawn 2. *Wins* – Hyderabad Divisional CA, Sri Lanka A. *Losses* – Karachi City CA, Sri Lanka A (4). *Drawn* – Mercantile CA, Gampaha District XI.

## ENGLAND A AVERAGES – FIRST-CLASS MATCHES

### BATTING

|                      | M | I | NO | R   | HI  | 100s | Avge  |
|----------------------|---|---|----|-----|-----|------|-------|
| G. P. Thorpe ........ | 4 | 5 | 0  | 286 | 98  | 0    | 57.20 |
| N. Hussain .......... | 5 | 8 | 1  | 391 | 161 | 1    | 55.85 |
| R. J. Blakey ........ | 2 | 3 | 1  | 77  | 35* | 0    | 38.50 |
| M. R. Ramprakash .. | 5 | 7 | 0  | 250 | 158 | 1    | 35.71 |
| S. J. Rhodes ........ | 3 | 5 | 1  | 133 | 60* | 0    | 33.25 |
| P. J. Newport ....... | 4 | 5 | 1  | 125 | 49  | 0    | 31.25 |
| N. H. Fairbrother ... | 4 | 6 | 0  | 175 | 71  | 0    | 29.16 |
| D. J. Bicknell ....... | 5 | 8 | 0  | 228 | 75  | 0    | 28.50 |
| R. K. Illingworth .... | 4 | 7 | 3  | 90  | 41  | 0    | 22.50 |
| H. Morris ........... | 4 | 6 | 0  | 72  | 23  | 0    | 12.00 |
| R. A. Pick .......... | 4 | 4 | 1  | 36  | 18* | 0    | 12.00 |

Played in three matches: T. A. Munton 1*, 0*, 0*; I. D. K. Salisbury 1*, 0, 0, 1. Played in two matches: M. C. Ilott 4*, 12; S. L. Watkin 5, 8. Played in one match: W. K. Hegg 24.

*\* Signifies not out.*

### BOWLING

|                      | O     | M  | R   | W  | BB    | 5W/i | Avge  |
|----------------------|-------|----|-----|----|-------|------|-------|
| R. A. Pick ......... | 121.1 | 23 | 357 | 21 | 5-41  | 2    | 17.00 |
| T. A. Munton ...... | 81    | 21 | 176 | 10 | 4-61  | 0    | 17.60 |
| R. K. Illingworth .... | 110.4 | 50 | 182 | 10 | 3-19  | 0    | 18.20 |
| S. L. Watkin ....... | 46    | 11 | 110 | 6  | 3-36  | 0    | 18.33 |
| M. C. Ilott ......... | 64    | 19 | 142 | 6  | 4-42  | 0    | 23.66 |
| P. J. Newport ...... | 121   | 33 | 330 | 10 | 4-39  | 0    | 33.00 |
| I. D. K. Salisbury ... | 112   | 38 | 256 | 4  | 2-110 | 0    | 64.00 |

Also bowled: M. R. Ramprakash 48–16–100–2; G. P. Thorpe 15–5–36–0.

### FIELDING

14 – S. J. Rhodes (13 ct, 1 st); 9 – N. Hussain; 5 – I. D. K. Salisbury, G. P. Thorpe; 3 – D. J. Bicknell, R. J. Blakey; 2 – N. H. Fairbrother, R. K. Illingworth, H. Morris, T. A. Munton; 1 – M. C. Ilott, P. J. Newport, R. A. Pick, Substitute (K. T. Medlycott).

†At Karachi, January 11. Karachi City CA won by 29 runs. Toss: England A. Karachi City CA 176 (40 overs) (Ghulam Ali 32; R. A. Pick three for 34, T. A. Munton three for 28); England A 147 for seven (40 overs) (H. Morris 54).

†At Hyderabad, January 12. England A won by 3 runs. Toss: Hyderabad Divisional CA. England A 223 for five (40 overs) (R. J. Blakey 69, H. Morris 39, M. R. Ramprakash 39); Hyderabad Divisional CA 220 for eight (40 overs) (Mehfooz Ali 55, Sajid Ali 47, Abdul Waheed Rashid 38; M. R. Ramprakash four for 33).

## COMBINED UNIVERSITIES v ENGLAND A

At Lahore, January 14, 15, 16. Drawn. Toss: England A. A good, competitive game petered out on the final afternoon, by which stage the England players were more concerned with their imminent withdrawal from Pakistan, because of the Gulf War. The early pace and bounce in the pitch was well exploited by the young Universities attack, in which Nadeem Afzal looked a quick bowler of promise. England were 39 for three after 40 minutes, but some scintillating strokeplay from Fairbrother and Ramprakash redressed the balance, and there followed a fine stand of 131 in 36 overs between Thorpe and Newport. Thorpe hit eight fours in his first 44 runs, and in all he struck two sixes and fifteen fours in an innings which set him up for the tour. When the Universities replied, Munton and Watkin found the ball, thought to be lightweight, virtually impossible to control. Only five deliveries hit the bat in the first 35 minutes. When the shine went off it, however, England's bowlers soon had the Universities batsmen struggling. With Bicknell and Hussain making up for their first-innings failures, Fairbrother was able to set a target of 339, and when the Universities were 113 for four, England had a chance of victory. A couple of dropped catches ended that ambition, in front of a crowd by now containing a sprinkling of plain-clothes policemen. Two nights later, under armed guard, England left their Lahore hotel for a flight to Colombo.

*Close of play:* First day, England A 298-7 (R. K. Illingworth 4*, I. D. K. Salisbury 1*); Second day, England A 81-0 (R. J. Blakey 35*, D. J. Bicknell 35*).

## England A

| | | | |
|---|---|---|---|
| D. J. Bicknell lbw b Nadeem Afzal | 0 | – c Ahmad Munir b Shahid Ali Khan | 75 |
| †R. J. Blakey b Sajjad Ali | 12 | – retired hurt | 35 |
| N. Hussain c Mohammad Riaz b Nadeem Afzal | 0 | – not out | 69 |
| *N. H. Fairbrother lbw b Sajjad Ali | 62 | | |
| M. R. Ramprakash c Sajjad Ali b Nadeem Afzal | 44 | | |
| G. P. Thorpe c Babar Zaman b Nadeem Afzal | 98 | | |
| P. J. Newport b Nadeem Afzal | 49 | | |
| R. K. Illingworth not out | 4 | – (4) not out | 19 |
| I. D. K. Salisbury not out | 1 | | |
| B 4, l-b 9, n-b 15 | 28 | B 12, l-b 3, n-b 2 | 17 |

1/0 2/8 3/39 4/134 5/146     (7 wkts dec.) 298    1/147      (1 wkt dec.) 215
6/277 7/294

T. A. Munton and S. L. Watkin did not bat.

*In the second innings R. J. Blakey did not resume on the last day.*

Bowling: *First Innings*—Nadeem Afzal 16–3–56–5; Sajjad Ali 15–1–81–2; Shahid Ali Khan 19–6–57–0; Rizwan Qazi 7–0–20–0; Aziz-ur-Rehman 10–2–26–0; Babar Zaman 2–0–6–0; Ahmad Munir 8–1–39–0. *Second Innings*—Nadeem Afzal 12–1–55–0; Sajjad Ali 5–1–27–0; Shahid Ali Khan 15–1–56–1; Aziz-ur-Rehman 7–0–28–0; Ahmad Munir 1–0–17–0; Rizwan Qazi 7–2–17–0.

## Combined Universities

| | | | |
|---|---|---|---|
| Riffat Ijaz b Salisbury | 42 | | |
| Ghulam Ali c Illingworth b Munton | 4 | – c sub b Newport | 8 |
| Babar Zaman c Fairbrother b Munton | 0 | – (1) c Blakey b Watkin | 45 |
| Kamran Khan c Munton b Watkin | 47 | – c Blakey b Newport | 8 |
| Ahmad Munir c Munton b Watkin | 9 | – (3) c Salisbury b Munton | 27 |
| Rizwan Qazi c Thorpe b Watkin | 5 | | |
| Aziz-ur-Rehman c Blakey b Newport | 23 | – (5) not out | 50 |
| Sajjad Ali c Salisbury b Illingworth | 13 | – (6) not out | 21 |
| †Mohammad Riaz b Hussain b Illingworth | 12 | | |
| Nadeem Afzal not out | 0 | | |
| B 8, l-b 10, w 3, n-b 9 | 30 | B 5, l-b 3, n-b 8 | 16 |

1/23 2/23 3/118 4/118 5/128    (9 wkts dec.) 185    1/12 2/53 3/66 4/113    (4 wkts) 175
6/137 7/172 8/172 9/185

*Shahid Ali Khan did not bat.

Bowling: *First Innings*—Munton 11–4–11–2; Watkin 16–4–36–3; Newport 14–3–47–1; Salisbury 15–4–60–1; Illingworth 4.2–2–13–2. *Second Innings*—Munton 7–0–35–1; Newport 8–2–43–2; Watkin 8–3–18–1; Illingworth 11–4–21–0; Salisbury 8–3–23–0; Ramprakash 5–1–20–0; Thorpe 2–0–7–0.

Umpires: Khizar Hayat and Mahboob Shah.

†At Colombo, January 26, 27. Drawn. Toss: England A. England A 233 for six dec. (N. H. Fairbrother 45, G. P. Thorpe 103 not out) and 128 for two dec. (R. J. Blakey 63 not out, H. Morris 53); Mercantile CA 189 for five dec. (T. M. Wijesinghe 33, A. M. de Silva 65 not out, S. H. U. Karnain 31; P. J. Newport three for 21) and 38 for three.

## SOUTHERN DISTRICTS XI v ENGLAND A

At Matara, January 29, 30, 31. England A won by 171 runs. Toss: Southern Districts XI. An innings of great skill by Hussain, and a determined one from Illingworth, enabled England to recover from 81 for five after being put in on a damp, under-prepared pitch that was unworthy of the first-class status awarded this match. A total of 193 proved too much for the local side to match, particularly against the pace of Pick and Munton's steadiness. Professional application enabled England to do better second time around, with Rhodes producing a typically combative 60 not out from 93 balls. On the last day Pick took five for 43, to add to his first-innings five for 41, but Liyanage made the tourists work hard for victory with an eighth-wicket stand of 47 with Munasinghe. It took an outstanding catch by Morris at fourth slip to remove him. Hordes of schoolchildren helped give the match a festive atmosphere, and the passion for cricket was clear to see in this southerly outpost.

*Close of play:* First day, Southern Districts XI 34-5 (K. P. J. A. de Silva 0*, H. Munasinghe 0*); Second day, England A 231-9 dec.

### England A

| | | |
|---|---|---|
| D. J. Bicknell c Liyanage b Ekanayake | 0 | – c sub b Faumi ..... 39 |
| *H. Morris lbw b Palliyaguru | 23 | – lbw b Palliyaguru ..... 22 |
| M. R. Ramprakash c Bandara b Milton | 3 | – c Bandara b Faumi ..... 32 |
| N. Hussain st Liyanage b Palliyaguru | 56 | – c Liyanage b Palliyaguru ..... 27 |
| N. H. Fairbrother c Munasinghe b Milton | 21 | – c de Silva b Faumi ..... 0 |
| †S. J. Rhodes c de Silva b Faumi | 4 | – not out ..... 60 |
| R. K. Illingworth c sub b Faumi | 41 | – c Liyanage b Munasinghe ..... 8 |
| I. D. K. Salisbury lbw b Palliyaguru | 0 | – c Premasiri b Munasinghe ..... 0 |
| R. A. Pick b Munasinghe | 16 | – b Palliyaguru ..... 2 |
| S. L. Watkin c and b Faumi | 5 | – run out ..... 8 |
| T. A. Munton not out | 1 | – not out ..... 0 |
| L-b 3, w 2, n-b 18 | 23 | B 3, l-b 7, w 2, n-b 21 ..... 33 |

1/0 2/26 3/28 4/66 5/81          193    1/53 2/112 3/120    (9 wkts dec.) 231
6/135 7/135 8/171 9/192              4/134 5/147 6/165
                                     7/173 8/191 9/225

Bowling: *First Innings*—Ekanayake 11–4–17–1; Milton 20–2–60–2; Palliyaguru 17.2–3–48–3; Faumi 5.4-0-18-3; Munasinghe 11-0-40-1; Wimalasiri 3-0-7-0. *Second Innings*—Milton 18-2-63-0; Faumi 21-2-65-3; Palliyaguru 15-2-55-3; Munasinghe 20-4-38-2.

### Southern Districts XI

| | | |
|---|---|---|
| T. M. Wijesinghe c Salisbury b Pick | 0 | – (2) c Hussain b Illingworth ..... 33 |
| H. Premasiri lbw b Pick | 13 | – (1) lbw b Bicknell b Pick ..... 0 |
| R. Wimalasiri b Munton | 11 | – c Rhodes b Pick ..... 1 |
| R. Palliyaguru c Rhodes b Munton | 0 | – b Watkin ..... 12 |
| S. M. Faumi lbw b Pick | 3 | – lbw b Watkin ..... 43 |
| K. P. J. A. de Silva lbw b Pick | 35 | – c Salisbury b Illingworth ..... 5 |
| H. Munasinghe run out | 8 | – (9) lbw b Pick ..... 8 |
| †G. Liyanage b Munton | 5 | – c Morris b Pick ..... 32 |
| P. Bandara not out | 13 | – (7) st Rhodes b Illingworth ..... 4 |
| P. Milton c Illingworth b Pick | 0 | – not out ..... 2 |
| *M. Ekanayake absent ill | | – b Pick ..... 0 |
| B 4, l-b 1, w 1, n-b 4 | 10 | B 4, l-b 6, n-b 5 ..... 15 |

1/0 2/30 3/30 4/34 5/34        98    1/0 2/2 3/32 4/91 5/95    155
6/72 7/81 8/83 9/98             6/101 7/104 8/151 9/155

Bowling: *First Innings*—Pick 12.3–2–41–5; Watkin 6–2–25–0; Munton 9–2–27–3. *Second Innings*—Pick 14.5-2-43-5; Watkin 16-2-31-2; Munton 12-2-26-0; Salisbury 14-4-19-0; Illingworth 14-7-19-3; Ramprakash 8-4-7-0.

Umpires: B. C. Cooray and T. M. Samarasinghe.

## †SRI LANKA A v ENGLAND A

### First One-day "International"

At Galle, February 2. Sri Lanka A won by four wickets. Toss: Sri Lanka A. England, put in on a damp, drying pitch, were 59 for four from 24 overs and needed a stand of 85 in eighteen overs between Ramprakash and Thorpe to reach a defendable total. Ramprakash played a superb, mature innings of 91 from 119 balls, while Thorpe's 42 came from 52 balls. As the conditions eased in the fierce heat, the experienced Kuruppu launched Sri Lanka's reply with a fine 71 out of 121. Tight spin bowling by Illingworth and Ramprakash, who continued a top-class display, kept England in contention, but Wickremasinghe, chancing his arm, hit 32 off 33 balls and the home side went on to win off the penultimate delivery.

*Man of the Match:* M. R. Ramprakash.

### England A

| | | |
|---|---|---|
| R. J. Blakey c de Silva | | |
|   b G. P. Wickremasinghe . | 0 | |
| *H. Morris c de Silva | | |
|   b G. P. Wickremasinghe . | 0 | |
| M. R. Ramprakash c Kalpage b Karnain | 91 | |
| N. H. Fairbrother b Hathurusinghe | 10 | |
| N. Hussain lbw b Rajadurai | 7 | |

| | | |
|---|---|---|
| G. P. Thorpe c Rajadurai | | |
|   b G. P. Wickremasinghe . | 42 | |
| †S. J. Rhodes not out | 7 | |
| L-b 3, w 4, n-b 1 | 8 | |
| | | |
| 1/4 2/9 3/46        (6 wkts, 45 overs) | 171 | |
| 4/59 5/144 6/171 | | |

R. K. Illingworth, R. A. Pick, S. L. Watkin and T. A. Munton did not bat.

Bowling: G. P. Wickremasinghe 8-2-28-3; Halangoda 5-1-14-0; Karnain 8-0-30-1; Hathurusinghe 7-0-19-1; Rajadurai 9-0-37-1; Anurasiri 8-1-40-0.

### Sri Lanka A

| | | |
|---|---|---|
| D. S. B. P. Kuruppu lbw b Thorpe | 71 | |
| U. C. Hathurusinghe b Illingworth | 24 | |
| D. S. G. Bulankulame | | |
|   c and b Illingworth | 7 | |
| R. S. Kalpage st Rhodes b Ramprakash | 10 | |
| D. C. Wickremasinghe lbw b Pick | 32 | |
| S. H. U. Karnain lbw b Munton | 2 | |

| | | |
|---|---|---|
| †A. M. de Silva not out | 16 | |
| *M. B. Halangoda not out | 4 | |
| | | |
| L-b 7, w 1, n-b 1 | 9 | |
| | | |
| 1/56 2/78 3/105     (6 wkts, 44.5 overs) | 175 | |
| 4/121 5/131 6/171 | | |

B. E. A. Rajadurai, S. D. Anurasiri and G. P. Wickremasinghe did not bat.

Bowling: Pick 8.5-0-45-1; Watkin 6-2-18-0; Munton 9-0-39-1; Illingworth 9-1-19-2; Ramprakash 9-1-25-1; Thorpe 3-0-22-1.

Umpires: K. T. Francis and T. M. Samarasinghe.

## †SRI LANKA A v ENGLAND A

### Second One-day "International"

At Kurunegala, February 4. Sri Lanka A won by 40 runs. Toss: England A. Injury to Watkin, who tore a muscle in his side during the previous match, left England short of seam bowling, as became plain when Morris won the toss and rightly inserted the Sri Lankans on a wet pitch. With Newport "on loan" in Australia, England had just Pick and Munton to exploit the conditions. Both bowled well, but the Sri Lankan score was given a late boost by de Silva's unbeaten 37 from 45 balls. A day which began as a seamers' paradise ended with Sri Lanka's four good-class spinners bamboozling the England batting on a drying strip. Despite a solid opening stand of 59 between Morris and Blakey, the target of 174 was enough to embarrass the highly rated English middle order in unfamiliar, turning conditions. The dismissal of Fairbrother, bowled by off-spinner Jurangpathy for 20 when the score was 112, left England with little hope of victory.

*Man of the Match:* B. R. Jurangpathy.

## Sri Lanka A

| | | | |
|---|---|---|---|
| †D. S. B. P. Kuruppu c Blakey b Salisbury | 31 | S. H. U. Karnain run out | 14 |
| D. S. G. Bulankulame b Illingworth | 4 | *M. B. Halangoda b Pick | 18 |
| D. C. Wickremasinghe c Pick b Munton | 26 | B. E. A. Rajadurai not out | 3 |
| R. S. Kalpage c Rhodes b Munton | 19 | B 3, l-b 8, w 1, n-b 4 | 16 |
| B. R. Jurangpathy c Fairbrother b Munton | 5 | | |
| A. M. de Silva not out | 37 | | |

1/14 2/52 3/89     (7 wkts, 44 overs) 173
4/90 5/99
6/130 7/162

S. D. Anurasiri and G. P. Wickremasinghe did not bat.

Bowling: Pick 8–3–20–1; Munton 9–1–31–3; Illingworth 9–2–36–1; Salisbury 9–1–35–1; Ramprakash 9–0–40–0.

## England A

| | | | |
|---|---|---|---|
| R. J. Blakey b Kalpage | 31 | I. D. K. Salisbury not out | 13 |
| *H. Morris lbw b Kalpage | 31 | R. A. Pick st Kuruppu b Jurangpathy | 5 |
| M. R. Ramprakash b Rajadurai | 15 | T. A. Munton lbw b Jurangpathy | 0 |
| N. H. Fairbrother b Jurangpathy | 20 | | |
| G. P. Thorpe c Karnain b Rajadurai | 2 | L-b 3, w 4 | 7 |
| D. J. Bicknell c and b Jurangpathy | 4 | | |
| †S. J. Rhodes hit wkt b Jurangpathy | 5 | 1/59 2/72 3/88     (42.2 overs) 133 |
| R. K. Illingworth st Kuruppu b Rajadurai | 0 | 4/94 5/107 6/112 |
| | | 7/115 8/117 9/127 |

Bowling: G. P. Wickremasinghe 6–1–9–0; Halangoda 5–1–13–0; Anurasiri 8–0–29–0; Kalpage 9–0–30–2; Rajadurai 8–0–29–3; Jurangpathy 6.2–0–20–5.

Umpires: W. A. U. Wickramasinghe and K. J. P. Wijedasa.

## SRI LANKA A v ENGLAND A

### First Unofficial "Test"

At Kandy, February 8, 9, 10, 11, 12. Drawn. Toss: England A. A fine, attritional match unfortunately ended in acrimony on the final afternoon, when England felt that their chase towards a target of 145 from 48 overs was set back by several incorrect umpiring decisions. Bicknell, after an authoritative 36, Fairbrother and Rhodes all returned to the pavilion with the air of men told that their winning lottery ticket was, in fact, invalid. The barely concealed sense of outrage was not improved when the umpires signalled a four after a superb pull-sweep by Thorpe, who was leading a last surge, had clearly landed yards over the boundary rope. England, with Newport and Illingworth playing out the last five overs to ultra-defensive fields, finished 33 runs adrift.

The bitter last act was unworthy of a drama which, over the five days, contained a host of eye-catching performances. England's star was Ramprakash, whose first-innings 158 could not be praised too highly. England, having resumed on the third morning at 92 for two, were soon 109 for five after Ahangama had produced the ball of the match to account for Hussain. The batsman avoided being hit between the eyes by a wicked lifter, only for his helmet to fall on to his stumps. But Ramprakash, his concentration unwavering and his technique against the turning ball secure, masterminded a recovery with Thorpe and Rhodes. He batted in all for sixteen minutes under ten hours, faced 424 balls and hit 21 fours; his first mistake was also his last.

England's 354 gave them a lead of 11 runs, and by the close of the fourth day they had Sri Lanka 78 for five, Newport having taken three for 14 in nine overs of skilful swing bowling. On the final day, however, the Sri Lankan lower order hung on grimly and bravely until Pick launched himself into one last, energy-draining effort.

The consequent controversial finish obscured a high-class spell of five for 35 from 21 overs by the left-arm spinner, Anurasiri, who fully exploited the helpful conditions. In England's first innings he had taken six for 84 in 61 overs, and his accuracy pinned down batsmen unwilling to use their feet for fear of becoming stranded down the pitch. Illingworth's match figures of five for 129 from 81.2 overs paled in comparison, but nevertheless represented a worthy effort.

*Men of the Match:* S. D. Anurasiri and M. R. Ramprakash.

*Close of play:* First day, Sri Lanka A 226-7 (A. M. de Silva 10*); Second day, England A 92-2 (M. R. Ramprakash 44*, R. K. Illingworth 6*); Third day, England A 257-6 (M. R. Ramprakash 116*, S. J. Rhodes 17*); Fourth day, Sri Lanka A 78-5 (A. M. de Silva 8*, A. G. D. Wickremasinghe 0*).

## Sri Lanka A

| | | | |
|---|---|---|---|
| *D. S. B. P. Kuruppu c Rhodes b Newport | 11 | – c Rhodes b Newport | 39 |
| D. S. G. Bulankulame c Thorpe b Newport | 28 | – c Hussain b Illingworth | 1 |
| D. C. Wickremasinghe b Munton | 71 | – c Morris b Pick | 7 |
| H. Premasiri run out | 56 | – c Bicknell b Newport | 10 |
| B. R. Jurangpathy c Hussain b Munton | 25 | – b Newport | 5 |
| A. M. de Silva hit wkt b Illingworth | 31 | – c Newport b Ramprakash | 28 |
| †A. G. D. Wickremasinghe c Rhodes b Munton | 4 | – c Rhodes b Newport | 4 |
| B. E. A. Rajadurai c Hussain b Munton | 1 | – c Fairbrother b Pick | 19 |
| S. D. Anurasiri c Hussain b Illingworth | 41 | – c Hussain b Illingworth | 0 |
| G. P. Wickremasinghe c Hussain b Illingworth | 36 | – c Thorpe b Pick | 23 |
| F. S. Ahangama not out | 4 | – not out | 6 |
| B 7, l-b 5, w 7, n-b 20 | 39 | B 2, n-b 11 | 13 |

1/31 2/64 3/164 4/188 5/218          343     1/23 2/35 3/57 4/70 5/71          155
6/218 7/226 8/267 9/328                      6/84 7/118 8/118 9/128

Bowling: *First Innings*—Pick 26-4-87-0; Munton 35-9-61-4; Newport 30-6-88-2; Illingworth 47.2-21-78-3; Ramprakash 9-2-17-0. *Second Innings*—Pick 14.5-4-37-3; Munton 7-4-16-0; Illingworth 34-16-51-2; Newport 19-8-39-4; Ramprakash 5-1-10-1.

## England A

| | | | |
|---|---|---|---|
| D. J. Bicknell lbw b Jurangpathy | 32 | – st A. G. D. Wickremasinghe b Anurasiri | 36 |
| *H. Morris lbw b Ahangama | 1 | – c Anurasiri b Jurangpathy | 15 |
| M. R. Ramprakash b Anurasiri | 158 | – c A. G. D. Wickremasinghe b Anurasiri | 6 |
| R. K. Illingworth c Bulankulame b Anurasiri | 17 | – (9) not out | 0 |
| N. H. Fairbrother c A. G. D. Wickremasinghe b Ahangama | 0 | – (4) c A. G. D. Wickremasinghe b Anurasiri | 21 |
| N. Hussain hit wkt b Ahangama | 0 | – (5) b Anurasiri | 1 |
| G. P. Thorpe lbw b Anurasiri | 51 | – (6) b Anurasiri | 16 |
| †S. J. Rhodes c Jurangpathy b Anurasiri | 57 | – (7) run out | 8 |
| P. J. Newport c A. G. D. Wickremasinghe b Anurasiri | 8 | – (8) not out | 5 |
| R. A. Pick c A. G. D. Wickremasinghe b Anurasiri | 0 | | |
| T. A. Munton not out | 0 | | |
| B 6, l-b 7, w 1, n-b 16 | 30 | L-b 4 | 4 |

1/10 2/78 3/106 4/109 5/109          354     1/29 2/44 3/73 4/81          (7 wkts) 112
6/193 7/322 8/343 9/347                      5/84 6/100 7/110

Bowling: *First Innings*—G. P. Wickremasinghe 12-1-56-0; Ahangama 24-7-66-3; Jurangpathy 49-22-79-1; Anurasiri 61-25-84-6; Rajadurai 24-8-41-0; Bulankulame 10-2-15-0. *Second Innings*—G. P. Wickremasinghe 2-1-6-0; Ahangama 2-0-4-0; Jurangpathy 22-4-63-1; Anurasiri 21-5-35-5.

Umpires: K. T. Francis and T. M. Samarasinghe.

## SRI LANKA A v ENGLAND A

### Second Unofficial "Test"

At Sinhalese Sports Club, Colombo, February 15, 16, 17, 19, 20. Drawn. Toss: Sri Lanka A. A match which for four days mirrored the Kandy "Test" ended in great tension as England went desperately close to victory. This time, however, there was no controversy. Sri Lanka's survival was due entirely to a brilliant 105 not out from 194 balls by Dileepa Wickremasinghe, who brought off one of cricket's great escapes in a ninth-wicket partnership of 120 in 43 overs with Edirimanne. The pair had come together ten minutes before lunch on the final day with Sri Lanka, 61 for eight, only 59 runs ahead.

England brought in the newly arrived replacement, Ilott, for Munton and promoted the equally inexperienced Salisbury ahead of Illingworth. But the reshaped attack suffered initially at the hands of Sri Lanka's captain, Kuruppu, who completed a very good hundred before the close and extended it to 168 on the second day. England were also impressed by Atapattu, who had toured England the previous summer, though Newport was less than impressed when his appeal for a catch at the wicket against the young batsman was turned down. He let himself down badly with a prolonged show of dissent. Publicly this went unpunished by the England management, although some action may have been taken in private.

Sri Lanka declared at their overnight score of 409 for nine, Pick's four for 75 representing a fine effort, and England's reply began badly on the third day with the cheap dismissals of Morris and Ramprakash. However, Bicknell made a painstaking 40, Fairbrother a comparatively rapid 71, including twelve fours, and a slow day ended promisingly with purposeful batting from Hussain and Thorpe. After the rest day they took their fifth-wicket stand to 114 before Thorpe fell for 53, and Hussain opened up with some magnificent strokes to reach his century. He then turned it into a score of major significance by continuing to take the attack to the Sri Lankan bowling, and he batted in all for just over seven and a half hours, facing 355 balls and hitting twenty fours.

Morris might have declared when Hussain and Newport, who added 138 for the seventh wicket, were both out at 403, for England could have used the extra time when Pick and Ilott, in seven hostile overs before the close, reduced Sri Lanka to 23 for three. Both opening bowlers captured two more wickets apiece on the final morning, and at lunch an England victory looked a formality. By now, though, Pick and Ilott were spent forces under the merciless sun, and tailender Edirimanne survived for three hours (145 balls) while Wickremasinghe sensibly went for his shots to stretch England's target. He hit fifteen boundaries in what proved to be his maiden first-class century. The last chance of victory probably came just before tea, when Edirimanne, then 20, edged Salisbury just short of Fairbrother at slip. Pick's match figures of eight for 136 were outstanding, while Ilott's four for 42 in the second innings was a courageous effort after he had suffered from dehydration following his 36 overs in the first innings.

*Man of the Match:* D. C. Wickremasinghe.

*Close of play:* First day, Sri Lanka A 205-3 (D. S. B. P. Kuruppu 116*, M. S. Atapattu 1*); Second day, Sri Lanka A 409-9 (P. K. Wijetunge 17*, C. D. C. Edirimanne 2*); Third day, England A 217-4 (N. Hussain 35*, G. P. Thorpe 42*); Fourth day, Sri Lanka A 23-3 (D. S. B. P. Kuruppu 15*, R. S. Kalpage 1*).

## Sri Lanka A

| | | |
|---|---|---|
| *D. S. B. P. Kuruppu c Ilott b Ramprakash | .168 | – c Salisbury b Pick .... 27 |
| D. C. Wickremasinghe c Hussain b Salisbury | . 17 | – (6) not out .... 105 |
| †A. G. D. Wickremasinghe lbw b Salisbury | . 51 | – lbw b Pick .... 0 |
| H. Premasiri c Rhodes b Pick | . 0 | – (2) c Rhodes b Ilott .... 4 |
| M. S. Atapattu c Rhodes b Pick | . 67 | – (7) c Rhodes b Ilott .... 3 |
| R. S. Kalpage c Rhodes b Ilott | . 0 | – (5) c Thorpe b Pick .... 7 |
| B. R. Jurangpathy c Rhodes b Pick | . 41 | – (8) b Ilott .... 0 |
| S. H. U. Karnain b Newport | . 9 | – (4) c Rhodes b Pick .... 0 |
| P. K. Wijetunge not out | . 17 | – c Pick b Salisbury .... 0 |
| F. S. Ahangama c Thorpe b Pick | . 1 | – (11) not out .... 10 |
| C. D. C. Edirimanne not out | . 2 | – (10) lbw b Ilott .... 28 |
| B 4, l-b 10, n-b 22 | . 36 | L-b 7, w 1, n-b 6 .... 14 |

1/45 2/197 3/198 4/315 5/318      (9 wkts dec.) 409      1/8 2/14 3/22      (9 wkts dec.) 198
6/344 7/372 8/402 9/407                                  4/38 5/43 6/56
                                                         7/60 8/61 9/181

Bowling: *First Innings*—Pick 28–8–75–4; Ilott 36–11–80–1; Newport 32–11–55–1; Salisbury 50–17–110–2; Ramprakash 21–8–46–1; Thorpe 13–5–29–0. *Second Innings*—Pick 17–1–61–4; Ilott 20–8–42–4; Newport 17–5–44–0; Salisbury 25–10–44–1.

## England A

| | |
|---|---|
| D. J. Bicknell c D. C. Wickremasinghe | †S. J. Rhodes lbw b Ahangama . . . . . . . 4 |
|     b Wijetunge . 40 | P. J. Newport run out . . . . . . . . . . . . . . 35 |
| *H. Morris c A. G. D. Wickremasinghe | I. D. K. Salisbury c A. G. D. |
|     b Ahangama . 2 |     Wickremasinghe b Ahangama . 1 |
| M. R. Ramprakash c D. C. | M. C. Ilott not out . . . . . . . . . . . . . . . . 4 |
|     Wickremasinghe b Ahangama . 0 | |
| N. H. Fairbrother c Jurangpathy | B 9, l-b 14, w 5, n-b 12 . . . . . . 40 |
|     b Wijetunge . 71 | |
| N. Hussain c Kalpage b Ahangama . . .161 | 1/12 2/12 3/120      (9 wkts dec.) 411 |
| G. P. Thorpe c sub | 4/138 5/252 6/265 |
|     (D. S. G. Bulankulame) b Kalpage . 53 | 7/403 8/403 9/411 |

R. A. Pick did not bat.

Bowling: Edirimanne 31–9–84–0; Ahangama 29.5–9–81–5; Karnain 9–3–26–0; Kalpage 54–21–85–1; Jurangpathy 12–4–27–0; Wijetunge 32–6–82–2; Atapattu 5–4–3–0.

Umpires: B. C. Cooray and W. A. U. Wickramasinghe.

## †SRI LANKA A v ENGLAND A

### Third One-day "International"

At Moratuwa, February 23. Sri Lanka A won by eight wickets. Toss: England A. Exhilarating batting by the 21-year-old Fernando and 20-year-old Atapattu, as they added 74 in fewer than nine overs, clinched an eight-wicket victory – and the one-day series – for Sri Lanka in front of 2,000 jubilant supporters at this compact ground in Colombo's southern suburbs. Fernando's unbeaten 88 required just 90 balls; earlier Wickremasinghe had followed up his match-saving hundred in the "Test" with 75 from 117 balls. England's innings was built around Morris, who returned to form with 118 from 115 balls, which included five sixes and eight fours. The England A captain scored more than half his team's total, yet received considerably less than 50 per cent of the strike. England's slow start, in which only 18 runs came from the first ten overs, was the decisive factor between the two innings.

*Man of the Match:* N. Fernando.

## England A

| | |
|---|---|
| †R. J. Blakey c Fernando b Anurasiri . . 52 | N. H. Fairbrother not out . . . . . . . . . . . 9 |
| *H. Morris c Halangoda b Edirimanne .118 | L-b 7, w 1, n-b 1 . . . . . . . . . . . 9 |
| M. R. Ramprakash c Kalpage | |
|     b Halangoda . 38 | 1/103 2/193 3/226    (3 wkts, 45 overs) 226 |

N. Hussain, G. P. Thorpe, P. J. Newport, R. K. Illingworth, M. C. Ilott, R. A. Pick and T. A. Munton did not bat.

Bowling: Edirimanne 9–1–36–1; Halangoda 9–1–40–1; Rajadurai 5–0–24–0; Karnain 4–0–24–0; Kalpage 9–0–41–0; Anurasiri 9–0–54–1.

## Sri Lanka A

| | |
|---|---|
| D. C. Wickremasinghe c Ilott b Pick . . 75 | |
| H. Premasiri c Morris b Munton . . . . . . 21 | |
| †N. Fernando not out . . . . . . . . . . . . . . 88 | |
| M. S. Atapattu not out . . . . . . . . . . . . . 33 | |
| L-b 6, w 3, n-b 1 . . . . . . . . . . . . 10 | |

1/42 2/153     (2 wkts, 43.5 overs) 227

D. S. B. P. Kuruppu, R. S. Kalpage, *M. B. Halangoda, S. H. U. Karnain, S. D. Anurasiri, B. E. A. Rajadurai and C. D. C. Edirimanne did not bat.

Bowling: Pick 8.5–1–42–1; Ilott 9–0–41–0; Newport 7–0–40–0; Munton 8–1–42–1; Illingworth 9–1–36–0; Ramprakash 2–0–20–0.

Umpires: I. Anandappa and D. Buultjens.

## †SRI LANKA A v ENGLAND A

### Fourth One-day "International"

At Sinhalese Sports Club, Colombo, February 24. Sri Lanka A won by 1 run. Toss: Sri Lanka A. Controversy over an umpiring decision again clouded a closely fought match. Ramprakash, attempting to sweep, was clearly astonished at being adjudged lbw to off-spinner Jurangpathy, who was bowling from round the wicket. Tenacious late-order batting took England nearer their target, but after Pick and Munton had taken 9 runs from the first four balls of the final over, Munton failed to score from Ahangama's last two deliveries. Atapattu's mature 51 was the highlight of Sri Lanka's innings on a day when the blistering heat added to the difficult conditions for strokemaking. The need for several drinks breaks contributed to England's bowling only 40 overs in the prescribed time.

*Man of the Match:* C. D. C. Edirimanne.

### Sri Lanka A

| | | | |
|---|---|---|---|
| H. Premasiri c Fairbrother b Ilott | 6 | S. Weerasinghe not out | 3 |
| D. C. Wickremasinghe c Illingworth | | *M. B. Halangoda c Blakey b Ilott | 0 |
| b Munton | 20 | C. D. C. Edirimanne not out | 1 |
| †N. Fernando c Hussain b Illingworth | 21 | B 1, l-b 4, w 10, n-b 4 | 19 |
| M. S. Atapattu c Morris b Pick | 51 | | |
| H. Wickremaratne b Munton | 28 | 1/13 2/59 3/59 (8 wkts, 40 overs) 164 |
| R. S. Kalpage run out | 3 | 4/129 5/134 6/152 |
| B. R. Jurangpathy b Ilott | 12 | 7/162 8/162 |

F. S. Ahangama did not bat.

Bowling: Pick 8–1–24–1; Ilott 8–1–24–3; Illingworth 9–0–36–1; Munton 9–0–43–2; Salisbury 6–0–32–0.

### England A

| | | | |
|---|---|---|---|
| †R. J. Blakey lbw b Kalpage | 20 | M. C. Ilott b Edirimanne | 1 |
| *H. Morris c sub b Ahangama | 30 | R. A. Pick not out | 8 |
| M. R. Ramprakash lbw b Jurangpathy | 35 | T. A. Munton not out | 2 |
| N. H. Fairbrother c Atapattu b Kalpage | 1 | | |
| N. Hussain b Jurangpathy | 15 | B 1, l-b 3, w 1, n-b 1 | 6 |
| G. P. Thorpe c Wickremaratne | | | |
| b Edirimanne | 14 | 1/46 2/60 3/66 (9 wkts, 40 overs) 163 |
| R. K. Illingworth lbw b Edirimanne | 12 | 4/92 5/115 6/119 |
| I. D. K. Salisbury b Edirimanne | 19 | 7/152 8/153 9/154 |

Bowling: Edirimanne 9–2–29–4; Halangoda 6–1–23–0; Ahangama 8–0–39–1; Kalpage 9–0–30–2; Jurangpathy 8–0–38–2.

Umpires: C. E. B. Anthony and D. Buultjens.

†At Katunayake, February 26, 27. Drawn. Toss: England A. England A 283 for nine dec. (D. J. Bicknell 121, R. K. Illingworth 43 not out; M. Muralitharan six for 68, N. Devarajan three for 49); Gampaha District XI 200 for five (S. Guneratne 64, H. Perera 30, U. Koddituwakku 44 not out).

## SRI LANKA A v ENGLAND A

### Third Unofficial "Test"

At P. Saravanamuttu Stadium, Colombo, March 1, 2, 3, 4, 5. Drawn. Toss: Sri Lanka A. Inadequate covering failed to protect the square from three successive nights of thunderstorms and resulted in the final "Test" being abandoned as a draw. Only ten overs were possible on the third day, after five inspections of a sodden square which was drying rapidly in hot sunshine. England felt that play should have started at noon, but umpires Buultjens and Anthony ruled that one damp spot – in a bowlers' foot-hole, just outside a left-hander's off stump – should be allowed to dry fully, and it was 3.30 p.m. before play finally got under way. England had also been frustrated the previous evening, when bad light and then rain had denied them ten overs at the Sri Lankans as the home side were struggling at 9 for one. However, all the wrangling on day three became immaterial when further thunderstorms prevented any play on the last two days. The tarpaulins which were hauled over the pitch every evening were useless against these overnight downpours. The square became a mud-heap, and England's cricketers were left to lounge around their hotel pool, ironically under sunny skies.

The opening day had brought the best cricket of an otherwise forgettable match, Hussain and Thorpe rescuing England from 59 for four with a partnership that was worth 144 when they were eventually parted on the second morning. Hussain's 77 took four and a half hours, while Thorpe batted an hour longer for his 68, which included eleven boundaries. Ahangama once again bowled with skill and spirit, claiming five for 81 on a pitch helping seam.

Play had originally been scheduled for March 6, with March 4 set aside as the rest day, but this was rearranged when March 6 was declared a national day of mourning following the assassination of Sri Lanka's State Minister for Defence on March 2.

*Close of play:* First day, England A 192-4 (N. Hussain 68*, G. P. Thorpe 59*); Second day, Sri Lanka A 9-1 (D. C. Wickremasinghe 2*, N. Fernando 1*); Third day, Sri Lanka A 48-1 (D. C. Wickremasinghe 11*, N. Fernando 30*); Fourth day, No play.

## England A

| | | | |
|---|---|---|---|
| D. J. Bicknell c Kuruppu b Ahangama . | 6 | R. K. Illingworth c Fernando b Kalpage | 1 |
| *H. Morris c Wijesinghe b Edirimanne . | 9 | M. C. Ilott lbw b Edirimanne ........ | 12 |
| R. J. Blakey c Kuruppu b Deshapriya . | 30 | R. A. Pick not out................. | 18 |
| M. R. Ramprakash b Anurasiri ....... | 7 | | |
| N. Hussain b Ahangama............. | 77 | B 5, l-b 13, w 1, n-b 7 ....... | 26 |
| G. P. Thorpe lbw b Ahangama ....... | 68 | | |
| †W. K. Hegg c Deshapriya b Ahangama | 24 | 1/8 2/24 3/59 4/59 5/203 | 306 |
| P. J. Newport lbw b Ahangama....... | 28 | 6/216 7/267 8/270 9/270 | |

Bowling: Edirimanne 30.5–6–66–2; Ahangama 38–15–81–5; Anurasiri 21–3–45–1; Kalpage 36–10–45–1; Deshapriya 16–5–22–1; Jurangpathy 17–6–29–0.

## Sri Lanka A

| | |
|---|---|
| T. M. Wijesinghe c Bicknell b Ilott .... | 4 |
| D. C. Wickremasinghe not out........ | 11 |
| †N. Fernando not out ............... | 30 |
| L-b 1, n-b 2................ | 3 |
| | |
| 1/5                    (1 wkt) | 48 |

*D. S. B. P. Kuruppu, M. S. Atapattu, R. S. Kalpage, B. R. Jurangpathy, C. D. C. Edirimanne, P. M. V. Deshapriya, S. D. Anurasiri and F. S. Ahangama did not bat.

Bowling: Pick 8–2–13–0; Ilott 8–0–20–1; Newport 1–0–14–0.

Umpires: C. E. B. Anthony and D. Buultjens.

## †SRI LANKA A v ENGLAND A

### Fifth One-day "International"

At Khetterama Stadium, Colombo, March 8 (day/night). England A won by 51 runs. Toss: England A. Sri Lanka's first international under lights brought out the best in Morris's side, who dampened the enthusiasm of a near-30,000 crowd in this magnificent, modern stadium with a faultless performance. England were determined to prevent a one-day "whitewash", and not even the late withdrawal of Pick, who was ill, could shake their resolve. Morris hit a fine 54 to launch his side towards a challenging total, and Blakey, Thorpe and Hussain all made useful scores. These three, Ramprakash and Fairbrother were then quite outstanding in the field as England, inspired by Newport's opening spell, kept Sri Lanka's reply in check.

*Man of the Match:* H. Morris.

### England A

| | | |
|---|---|---|
| N. H. Fairbrother c Kalpage b Halangoda . | 14 | †S. J. Rhodes c sub b Kalpage . . . . . . . . 17 |
| *H. Morris run out . . . . . . . . . . . . . . . | 54 | P. J. Newport not out . . . . . . . . . . . . . . 15 |
| R. J. Blakey c and b Jurangpathy . . . . . | 39 | R. K. Illingworth not out . . . . . . . . . . 6 |
| M. R. Ramprakash c Wickremaratne b Jurangpathy . | 9 | B 3, l-b 9, w 10 . . . . . . . . . . . . 22 |
| G. P. Thorpe c Edirimanne b Kalpage . | 35 | 1/35 2/122 3/125    (7 wkts, 45 overs) 246 |
| N. Hussain b Ahangama . . . . . . . . . . . . | 35 | 4/135 5/191 |
| | | 6/210 7/222 |

M. C. Ilott and T. A. Munton did not bat.

Bowling: Edirimanne 6-0-43-0; Halangoda 6-0-32-1; Ahangama 7-0-33-1; Kalpage 8-0-53-2; Anurasiri 9-0-31-0; Jurangpathy 9-0-42-2.

### Sri Lanka A

| | | |
|---|---|---|
| D. S. B. P. Kuruppu c Hussain b Newport . | 6 | S. D. Anurasiri not out . . . . . . . . . . . . . 28 |
| D. C. Wickremasinghe c Thorpe b Newport . | 13 | C. D. C. Edirimanne st Rhodes b Illingworth . 15 |
| †N. Fernando c Rhodes b Newport . . . . | 6 | F. S. Ahangama not out . . . . . . . . . . . . 13 |
| M. S. Atapattu b Ramprakash . . . . . . . . | 24 | B 2, l-b 2, w 16, n-b 5 . . . . . . . 25 |
| H. Wickremaratne c Thorpe b Munton . | 38 | |
| B. R. Jurangpathy c Morris b Illingworth | 2 | 1/9 2/34 3/39    (9 wkts, 45 overs) 195 |
| R. S. Kalpage c Hussain b Munton . . . . | 25 | 4/82 5/87 6/134 |
| *M. B. Halangoda c Rhodes b Ilott . . . . | 0 | 7/134 8/143 9/176 |

Bowling: Newport 8-0-39-3; Ilott 8-0-36-1; Munton 9-0-40-2; Ramprakash 9-1-25-1; Illingworth 9-0-35-2; Fairbrother 1-0-8-0; Thorpe 1-0-8-0.

Umpires: K. T. Francis and W. A. U. Wickremasinghe.

# THE NEW ZEALANDERS IN PAKISTAN, 1990-91

## By QAMAR AHMED

Without Sir Richard Hadlee and Martin Snedden, both of whom had retired following the recent tour of England, and with John Wright, Andrew Jones and John Bracewell all unavailable, it was a much weakened New Zealand team which arrived in Pakistan at the end of September. Consequently it came as little surprise when they lost all three Test matches, the first two by convincing margins, and the three one-day internationals, giving Pakistan their second clean sweep in a three-Test series after that of October 1982, when they comprehensively defeated K. J. Hughes's Australian side. The tourists' three-day games against Karachi and PIA were both drawn.

The tour was not without controversy. Even before it began, Imran Khan declined the Pakistan Board's invitation to play in the series, branding the New Zealanders a "B" team and appealing to the Board to cancel the tour altogether. Then, just days before it started, Pakistan withdrew their offer of third-country umpires for the Tests, following remarks allegedly made by the New Zealand captain, Martin Crowe. He was reported as saying that any umpire standing in the series "will be better than having two Pakistani umpires", a statement he strongly denied having made. But the damage was done.

Finally, the New Zealand manager, Mr Ian Taylor, on the team's return home, accused the Pakistan bowlers of doctoring the ball, by lifting the seam or damaging the surface, in order to obtain extra swing. The New Zealand manager even admitted that Chris Pringle, their medium-pace bowler, had experimented with such tactics during the Third Test at Faisalabad, in which he took seven for 52 in the first innings as Pakistan were bowled out for 102, their lowest total against New Zealand. The claim was strongly denied by the Pakistan players and their Board, while Intikhab Alam, the manager of the Pakistan team, described it as "rubbish".

Imran's allegation that New Zealand were sending a second-rate side was in the end justified by the results. The tourists' inexperience was manifested by their inability to handle the fire, pace and swing of Wasim Akram and Waqar Younis, who between them claimed 39 wickets in the Test matches. Younis's share, 29, was a record for a three-match series in Pakistan, and twice he captured ten or more wickets in a match. Not even the absence through injury of his strike partner, Akram, at Faisalabad could make a difference: he continued to frustrate the New Zealanders with his swing and devastating yorkers.

However, it was not just the New Zealand batsmen who had trouble coming to terms with the seaming pitches produced for the Test matches. Despite the weakness of the New Zealand bowling generally, most of the leading Pakistan batsmen had disappointing aggregates. The exception was Shoaib Mohammad, who scored 507 runs at an average of 169 and became the highest run-maker for Pakistan in a series against New Zealand. The previous record had been held by Javed Miandad, who made 504 runs in his début series in 1976-77. Shoaib also had the distinction of scoring five hundreds in five consecutive Tests against the New Zealanders, having begun the sequence in New Zealand in 1988-89. Although Miandad's lack of form surprised many observers, he did have the consolation in his final innings, at Faisalabad, of becoming the fifth batsman to score 8,000 runs in Tests.

For New Zealand, Crowe was the pick of their batting, being the only one to reach three figures in the Tests and finishing with an average of 61. At Faisalabad, Mark Greatbatch completed 1,000 runs in his seventeenth Test, but with the tourists looking to him and to Ken Rutherford for experience and depth in batting, neither really resolved the struggle against the pace and swing of the Pakistan attack. Wicket-keeper Ian Smith again displayed his fighting spirit lower down the order, but Wright, the former captain, was sorely missed at the top: only once in the Tests did New Zealand manage more than 30 for the first wicket.

## NEW ZEALAND TOUR RESULTS

*Test matches* – Played 3: Lost 3.
*First-class matches* – Played 5: Lost 3, Drawn 2.
*Losses* – Pakistan (3).
*Draws* – Karachi, PIA.
*One-day internationals* – Played 3: Lost 3.

## TEST MATCH AVERAGES

### PAKISTAN – BATTING

| | T | I | NO | R | HI | 100s | Avge |
|---|---|---|---|---|---|---|---|
| Shoaib Mohammad.... | 3 | 5 | 2 | 507 | 203* | 3 | 169.00 |
| Javed Miandad ....... | 3 | 4 | 0 | 150 | 55 | 0 | 37.50 |
| Salim Malik.......... | 3 | 5 | 1 | 143 | 71 | 0 | 35.75 |
| Ramiz Raja ......... | 3 | 5 | 0 | 173 | 78 | 0 | 34.60 |
| Ijaz Ahmed ......... | 3 | 4 | 0 | 106 | 86 | 0 | 26.50 |
| Salim Yousuf........ | 3 | 4 | 0 | 73 | 33 | 0 | 18.25 |
| Saleem Jaffer........ | 2 | 3 | 1 | 12 | 10* | 0 | 6.00 |
| Waqar Younis........ | 3 | 3 | 0 | 17 | 17 | 0 | 5.66 |
| Aqib Javed ......... | 3 | 3 | 1 | 11 | 7 | 0 | 5.50 |

Played in two Tests: Abdul Qadir 6*; Tauseef Ahmed 1, 12*; Wasim Akram 28, 1. Played in one Test: Naved Anjum 10, 22.

* *Signifies not out.*

### BOWLING

| | O | M | R | W | BB | 5W/i | Avge |
|---|---|---|---|---|---|---|---|
| Waqar Younis ... | 144.4 | 51 | 315 | 29 | 7-76 | 3 | 10.86 |
| Wasim Akram ... | 78.5 | 24 | 162 | 10 | 4-44 | 0 | 16.20 |
| Saleem Jaffer .... | 75 | 19 | 197 | 8 | 2-37 | 0 | 24.62 |
| Abdul Qadir .... | 39 | 8 | 112 | 4 | 2-5 | 0 | 28.00 |
| Aqib Javed ..... | 89 | 22 | 240 | 7 | 3-57 | 0 | 34.28 |

Also bowled: Ijaz Ahmed 7-0-15-1; Naved Anjum 6-4-13-0; Shoaib Mohammad 2-0-8-0; Tauseef Ahmed 16-2-57-1.

## NEW ZEALAND – BATTING

|  | T | I | NO | R | HI | 100s | Avge |
|---|---|---|---|---|---|---|---|
| M. D. Crowe . . . . . . | 3 | 6 | 2 | 244 | 108* | 1 | 61.00 |
| K. R. Rutherford . . . | 3 | 6 | 0 | 187 | 79 | 0 | 31.16 |
| I. D. S. Smith . . . . . . | 3 | 6 | 0 | 141 | 61 | 0 | 23.50 |
| G. E. Bradburn . . . . . | 3 | 6 | 2 | 83 | 30* | 0 | 20.75 |
| M. J. Greatbatch . . . . | 3 | 6 | 0 | 89 | 43 | 0 | 14.83 |
| T. J. Franklin . . . . . . | 3 | 6 | 0 | 89 | 25 | 0 | 14.83 |
| D. N. Patel . . . . . . . | 3 | 6 | 0 | 77 | 45 | 0 | 12.83 |
| C. Pringle . . . . . . . . | 3 | 6 | 1 | 60 | 24* | 0 | 12.00 |
| D. J. White . . . . . . . | 2 | 4 | 0 | 31 | 18 | 0 | 7.75 |
| D. K. Morrison . . . . . | 3 | 6 | 0 | 36 | 25 | 0 | 6.00 |
| W. Watson . . . . . . . | 3 | 6 | 1 | 15 | 11 | 0 | 3.00 |

Played in one Test: P. A. Horne 0, 12.

*\* Signifies not out.*

## BOWLING

|  | O | M | R | W | BB | 5W/i | Avge |
|---|---|---|---|---|---|---|---|
| C. Pringle . . . . . . . | 122 | 30 | 342 | 13 | 7-52 | 1 | 26.30 |
| W. Watson . . . . . . . | 137.3 | 46 | 321 | 11 | 6-78 | 1 | 29.18 |
| D. K. Morrison . . . . | 104.2 | 22 | 348 | 8 | 4-105 | 0 | 43.50 |

Also bowled: G. E. Bradburn 36-8-111-2; M. D. Crowe 17-6-44-1; D. N. Patel 49-11-139-0; D. J. White 0.3-0-5-0.

# NEW ZEALAND AVERAGES – FIRST-CLASS MATCHES

## BATTING

|  | M | I | NO | R | HI | 100s | Avge |
|---|---|---|---|---|---|---|---|
| M. D. Crowe . . . . . . | 5 | 9 | 3 | 356 | 108* | 2 | 59.33 |
| K. R. Rutherford . . . | 5 | 10 | 1 | 325 | 92 | 0 | 36.11 |
| M. J. Greatbatch . . . . | 5 | 9 | 1 | 251 | 102* | 1 | 31.37 |
| I. D. S. Smith . . . . . . | 4 | 7 | 1 | 186 | 61 | 0 | 31.00 |
| T. J. Franklin . . . . . . | 4 | 8 | 1 | 163 | 66* | 0 | 23.28 |
| D. J. White . . . . . . . | 3 | 6 | 0 | 120 | 50 | 0 | 20.00 |
| G. E. Bradburn . . . . . | 4 | 8 | 3 | 98 | 30* | 0 | 19.60 |
| D. N. Patel . . . . . . . | 5 | 9 | 2 | 98 | 45 | 0 | 14.00 |
| C. Pringle . . . . . . . . | 4 | 6 | 1 | 60 | 24* | 0 | 12.00 |
| P. A. Horne . . . . . . . | 3 | 6 | 0 | 38 | 12 | 0 | 6.33 |
| D. K. Morrison . . . . | 4 | 6 | 0 | 36 | 25 | 0 | 6.00 |
| W. Watson . . . . . . . | 5 | 6 | 1 | 15 | 11 | 0 | 3.00 |

Played in two matches: M. W. Priest 0. Played in one match: A. C. Parore and S. J. Roberts did not bat.

*\* Signifies not out.*

## BOWLING

|  | O | M | R | W | BB | 5W/i | Avge |
|---|---|---|---|---|---|---|---|
| C. Pringle . . . . . . . | 148 | 36 | 420 | 18 | 7-52 | 1 | 23.33 |
| G. E. Bradburn . . . . | 63.3 | 16 | 196 | 7 | 5-44 | 1 | 28.00 |
| W. Watson . . . . . . . | 182.5 | 54 | 442 | 14 | 6-78 | 1 | 31.57 |
| D. K. Morrison . . . . | 117 | 23 | 384 | 10 | 4-105 | 0 | 38.40 |
| D. N. Patel . . . . . . . | 106.1 | 22 | 324 | 6 | 4-62 | 0 | 54.00 |

Also bowled: M. D. Crowe 23-7-68-1; M. W. Priest 71-13-257-3; S. J. Roberts 20-4-100-2; K. R. Rutherford 2-0-8-0; D. J. White 1.3-1-5-0.

## FIELDING

11 – I. D. S. Smith (10 ct, 1 st); 10 – M. D. Crowe; 5 – K. R. Rutherford; 2 – G. E. Bradburn,
M. J. Greatbatch, P. A. Horne, W. Watson, Substitute (A. C. Parore); 1 – T. J. Franklin,
D. K. Morrison, A. C. Parore (1 st), D. N. Patel, M. W. Priest.


## KARACHI v NEW ZEALANDERS

At Karachi, October 1, 2, 3. Drawn. Toss: Karachi. Set to score 268 in 110 minutes and
twenty overs, the New Zealanders emerged with an honourable draw thanks to an unbeaten
105 by Crowe, their captain. Karachi had followed their declaration, half an hour after lunch,
by removing both openers for 16, but Crowe, adding 47 with Greatbatch and 115 with
Rutherford, made sure the tour would not begin with a defeat. He batted for 142 minutes and
hit three sixes and thirteen fours in his century from 110 balls. On the opening day Mansoor
Akhtar batted for almost four hours and hit seventeen boundaries in his chanceless 103, while
on the final morning Ghulam Ali progressed to a maiden century which included three sixes
and thirteen fours in 190 minutes. The New Zealanders' first innings was sustained by
Franklin's dour 66 not out and given some guidance by Smith's seventh-wicket stand of 69
with the tall opener before Crowe declared 40 runs in arrears at tea on the second day.

*Close of play:* First day, New Zealanders 9-0 (T. J. Franklin 3\*, P. A. Horne 6\*); Second
day, Karachi 74-1 (Ghulam Ali 30\*, Anwar Miandad 12\*).

## Karachi

| | | | |
|---|---:|---|---:|
| Mansoor Akhtar c Watson b Patel | 103 | – b Watson | 29 |
| Ghulam Ali c Smith b Priest | 14 | – c Franklin b Patel | 101 |
| Anwar Miandad c Smith b Morrison | 14 | – c Smith b Roberts | 20 |
| Shaukat Mirza c Smith b Roberts | 8 | – not out | 38 |
| *Ijaz Faqih c Smith b Morrison | 22 | – c Crowe b Priest | 12 |
| †Rashid Latif c Crowe b Patel | 30 | | |
| Shakil Sajjad st Smith b Patel | 10 | – not out | 9 |
| Shahid Mahboob b Priest | 25 | – (6) b Watson | 13 |
| Sohail Mehdi lbw b Patel | 0 | | |
| Baqar Rizvi not out | 13 | | |
| B 2, n-b 1 | 3 | B 2, l-b 1, n-b 2 | 5 |

1/26 2/55 3/82 4/125 5/173          (9 wkts dec.) 242     1/52 2/83 3/177     (5 wkts dec.) 227
6/187 7/214 8/219 9/242                                   4/192 5/209

Haaris Khan did not bat.

Bowling: *First Innings*—Morrison 12-1-35-2; Roberts 11-4-39-1; Watson 10-1-40-0;
Priest 20-6-64-2; Patel 19.1-4-62-4. *Second Innings*—Morrison 0.4-0-1-0; Watson
16.2-3-37-2; Roberts 9-0-61-1; Priest 17-1-81-1; Patel 14-4-27-1; Crowe 4-0-17-0.

## New Zealanders

| | | | |
|---|---:|---|---:|
| T. J. Franklin not out | 66 | – (2) c Shahid Mahboob | |
| | | b Baqar Rizvi . | 8 |
| P. A. Horne c Rashid Latif b Baqar Rizvi | 11 | – (1) lbw b Shahid Mahboob | 2 |
| M. J. Greatbatch lbw b Shahid Mahboob | 37 | – b Haaris Khan | 23 |
| *M. D. Crowe b Shahid Mahboob | 0 | – not out | 105 |
| K. R. Rutherford b Baqar Rizvi | 14 | – not out | 29 |
| D. N. Patel c sub b Haaris Khan | 12 | | |
| M. W. Priest b Haaris Khan | 0 | | |
| †I. D. S. Smith not out | 45 | | |
| B 4, l-b 11, n-b 2 | 17 | B 6, l-b 3, w 2 | 11 |

1/19 2/90 3/90 4/117 5/133          (6 wkts dec.) 202     1/2 2/16 3/63          (3 wkts) 178
6/133

D. K. Morrison, W. Watson and S. J. Roberts did not bat.

Bowling: *First Innings*—Shahid Mahboob 17–3–54–2; Baqar Rizvi 14–3–41–2; Ijaz Faqih 13–3–39–0; Sohail Mehdi 10–6–10–0; Haaris Khan 14–5–43–2. *Second Innings*—Shahid Mahboob 16–1–69–1; Baqar Rizvi 4–1–7–1; Shakil Sajjad 3–0–12–0; Sohail Mehdi 12–3–34–0; Haaris Khan 8–0–47–1.

Umpires: Athar Zaidi and Feroze Butt.

## PIA v NEW ZEALANDERS

At Rawalpindi, October 5, 6, 7. Drawn. Toss: PIA. With Test opener Shoaib Mohammad reminding the New Zealanders of his appetite for their bowling by accumulating an unbeaten 123 in a 260-minute stay, PIA were able to declare twenty minutes after tea on the first day for the loss of just two wickets. Only Aamer Malik missed out, adjudged lbw first ball either side of century partnerships. Shoaib hit thirteen fours and a six. The New Zealanders declared at tea on the second day, Greatbatch having made 102, with seven fours and three sixes, before retiring with cramp in the leg. He put on 111 for the second wicket with White and batted in all for 222 minutes, facing 209 balls. Although the New Zealanders then bowled out PIA, a target of 249 to win in 165 minutes was never on. Rutherford availed himself of the opportunity to prepare for the forthcoming Test matches, and when he was out, just short of a century, play was called off.

*Close of play:* First day, New Zealanders 38-1 (D. J. White 24\*, M. J. Greatbatch 7\*); Second day, PIA 62-1 (Shoaib Mohammad 23\*, Rizwan-uz-Zaman 9\*).

## PIA

| | | | | |
|---|---|---|---|---|
| Rizwan-uz-Zaman lbw b Pringle | 52 | – (3) hit wkt b Pringle | | 65 |
| Shoaib Mohammad not out | 123 | – c Rutherford b Patel | | 45 |
| Aamer Malik lbw b Pringle | 0 | – (1) c Crowe b Bradburn | | 26 |
| Sagheer Abbas not out | 51 | – c and b Watson | | 16 |
| Zahid Ahmed (did not bat) | | – b Pringle | | 2 |
| Asif Mohammad (did not bat) | | – c Priest b Bradburn | | 8 |
| Wasim Hyder (did not bat) | | – b Pringle | | 11 |
| Iqbal Sikandar (did not bat) | | – c Patel b Bradburn | | 6 |
| *Rashid Khan (did not bat) | | – st Parore b Bradburn | | 12 |
| Tanvir Ali (did not bat) | | – b Bradburn | | 0 |
| †Haider Nisar (did not bat) | | – not out | | 6 |
| B 4, n-b 4 | 8 | L-b 5, n-b 3 | | 8 |

1/134 2/134  (2 wkts dec.) 234    1/45 2/119 3/141 4/152 5/165    205
6/177 7/181 8/194 9/194

Bowling: *First Innings*—Pringle 10–2–27–2; Watson 11–4–21–0; Rutherford 2–0–8–0; Priest 20–3–68–0; Crowe 2–1–7–0; Patel 13–2–58–0; Bradburn 16–6–41–0. *Second Innings*—Pringle 16–4–51–3; Watson 8–0–23–1; Bradburn 11.3–2–44–5; Priest 14–3–44–0; White 1–1–0–0; Patel 11–1–38–1.

## New Zealanders

| | | | | |
|---|---|---|---|---|
| P. A. Horne lbw b Iqbal Sikandar | 5 | – c Aamer Malik b Wasim Hyder | | 8 |
| D. J. White run out | 50 | – c and b Zahid Ahmed | | 39 |
| M. J. Greatbatch retired hurt | 102 | | | |
| *M. D. Crowe st Haider Nisar b Iqbal Sikandar | 7 | | | |
| K. R. Rutherford c Haider Nisar | | – (3) c Sagheer Abbas | | |
| b Iqbal Sikandar | 3 | b Zahid Ahmed | | 92 |
| G. E. Bradburn not out | 13 | – (4) c Haider Nisar | | |
| | | b Zahid Ahmed | | 2 |
| D. N. Patel not out | 0 | – (5) not out | | 9 |
| B 2, l-b 7, n-b 2 | 11 | L-b 3, n-b 1 | | 4 |

1/28 2/139 3/159 4/185  (4 wkts dec.) 191    1/22 2/85 3/111 4/154    (4 wkts) 154

M. W. Priest, †A. C. Parore, W. Watson and C. Pringle did not bat.

*In the first innings, M. J. Greatbatch retired hurt at 178.*

Bowling: *First Innings*—Rashid Khan 5–3–5–0; Wasim Hyder 9–1–24–0; Tanvir Ali 22–9–52–0; Iqbal Sikandar 33–8–63–3; Shoaib Mohammad 3–0–5–0; Zahid Ahmed 17–2–33–0. *Second Innings*—Rashid Khan 5–2–13–0; Wasim Hyder 10–3–17–1; Tanvir Ali 4–0–29–0; Iqbal Sikandar 11–2–39–0; Zahid Ahmed 13.5–3–53–3.

Umpires: Javed Akhtar and Mahboob Shah.

## PAKISTAN v NEW ZEALAND

### First Test Match

At Karachi, October 10, 11, 12, 14, 15. Pakistan won by an innings and 43 runs. Toss: Pakistan. Always in difficulty against Wasim Akram and Waqar Younis on a seaming pitch, New Zealand were twice dismissed for less than 200 and lacked the bowling to prevent Pakistan amassing a winning total. Put in, they managed just 45 runs in the 26 overs before lunch on the opening day, and the loss of their captain, Crowe, minutes into the afternoon session was a vital blow. Greatbatch (250 minutes) and Rutherford added 116 for the fourth wicket, with Rutherford, the dominant partner, hitting fourteen fours in a fine 79 made in three hours six minutes; but next morning Waqar and Wasim swept aside the last five wickets while 21 runs were added to the overnight score.

No further wickets fell that day as Shoaib Mohammad and Ramiz Raja took Pakistan to within 37 of New Zealand's total with a record-equalling first-wicket stand for Tests between the two countries. On the third day they increased this to 172 before Ramiz, after 287 minutes' batting and eight fours, became the first Test wicket of off-spinner Bradburn on his début. Shoaib, however, batted on and on; when Miandad declared on the fourth day, he had batted for 10 hours 55 minutes, faced 414 balls and hit 23 fours in his unbeaten 203, equalling his highest score in Tests and coincidentally equalling his father, Hanif Mohammad's personal best against New Zealand. Facing a deficit of 237, New Zealand made a poor start and never recovered. Crowe batted skilfully to take the match into the fifth day, but ten balls were all that Pakistan needed on the final morning to go one up in the series.

*Man of the Match:* Shoaib Mohammad.

*Close of play:* First day, New Zealand 175-5 (D. N. Patel 2*, D. K. Morrison 0*); Second day, Pakistan 159-0 (Ramiz Raja 68*, Shoaib Mohammad 82*); Third day, Pakistan 386-5 (Shoaib Mohammad 175*, Salim Yousuf 1*); Fourth day, New Zealand 192-9 (M. D. Crowe 67*, W. Watson 11*).

## New Zealand

| | | | |
|---|---|---|---|
| T. J. Franklin c Salim Yousuf b Waqar Younis . | 16 | – b Wasim Akram | 0 |
| D. J. White c Salim Yousuf b Wasim Akram | 9 | – b Wasim Akram | 18 |
| M. J. Greatbatch c and b Ijaz Ahmed | 43 | – lbw b Aqib Javed | 21 |
| *M. D. Crowe c Ramiz Raja b Waqar Younis . . | 7 | – not out | 68 |
| K. R. Rutherford b Aqib Javed | 79 | – lbw b Aqib Javed | 0 |
| D. N. Patel lbw b Waqar Younis | 2 | – lbw b Wasim Akram | 19 |
| D. K. Morrison lbw b Wasim Akram | 4 | – (9) b Wasim Akram | 0 |
| G. E. Bradburn not out | 11 | – (7) c Salim Yousuf b Waqar Younis . | 2 |
| †I. D. S. Smith lbw b Wasim Akram | 4 | – (8) b Waqar Younis | 14 |
| C. Pringle b Waqar Younis | 0 | – lbw b Abdul Qadir | 20 |
| W. Watson lbw b Wasim Akram | 0 | – lbw b Waqar Younis | 11 |
| B 5, l-b 11, w 2, n-b 3 | 21 | B 7, l-b 9, n-b 5 | 21 |
| | **196** | | **194** |

1/28 2/37 3/51 4/167 5/174      196     1/4 2/23 3/56 4/57 5/96     194
6/181 7/181 8/194 9/195                  6/103 7/119 8/120 9/173

Bowling: *First Innings*—Wasim Akram 29.5–12–44–4; Waqar Younis 22–7–40–4; Aqib Javed 16–4–37–1; Abdul Qadir 7–1–32–0; Tauseef Ahmed 5–0–18–0; Ijaz Ahmed 5–0–9–1. *Second Innings*—Wasim 24.5–6–60–4; Aqib Javed 12–1–45–2; Waqar Younis 15.4–4–39–3; Abdul Qadir 10–2–32–1, Tauseef Ahmed 1–0–2–0.

## Pakistan

| | | | | |
|---|---|---|---|---|
| Ramiz Raja c Crowe b Bradburn | 78 | †Salim Yousuf c Crowe b Morrison | 13 |
| Shoaib Mohammad not out | 203 | Abdul Qadir not out | 6 |
| Salim Malik c Rutherford b Pringle | 43 | B 3, l-b 11, w 1, n-b 11 | 26 |
| *Javed Miandad lbw b Morrison | 27 | | |
| Wasim Akram run out | 28 | 1/172 2/239 3/288 (6 wkts dec.) 433 |
| Ijaz Ahmed b Watson | 9 | 4/360 5/384 6/413 |

Tauseef Ahmed, Waqar Younis and Aqib Javed did not bat.

Bowling: Morrison 28.3–5–86–2; Pringle 25–3–68–1; Watson 40–8–125–1; Bradburn 17–3–56–1; Patel 24–6–62–0; Crowe 6–1–22–0.

Umpires: Feroze Butt and Mahboob Shah.

## PAKISTAN v NEW ZEALAND

### Second Test Match

At Lahore, October 18, 19, 20, 22, 23. Pakistan won by nine wickets. Toss: New Zealand. A cover drive by Shoaib Mohammad took Pakistan to a comfortable victory an hour and a quarter after lunch on the final day. While it was fitting that Shoaib hit the winning runs, having given the Pakistan first innings its foundation with his fourth hundred against New Zealand in consecutive innings, it was Waqar Younis who set up victory when he took seven wickets for 86 in New Zealand's second innings. These figures gave him his first ten-wicket return in Tests, and afterwards Crowe, who had remained unbeaten with 108, said that he had never faced such quality pace and swing bowling in his Test career as he had from Younis.

Batting first on a slightly green pitch was a mistake New Zealand quickly rued. Only Smith, hitting six fours in his 33, played the fast bowlers with confidence, and extras, 38, provided the highest score of the innings. By the close on the second day Pakistan were 92 runs ahead, with six wickets in hand, Shoaib having reached his sixth Test innings in five hours thirteen minutes, including fourteen fours and a six. An entertaining stand of 71 in 116 minutes for the fifth wicket between Ijaz Ahmed and Salim Yousuf extended the lead on the third day, Ijaz batting in all for 234 minutes and hitting seven fours and two sixes in his 86, and when the declaration came Pakistan were 213 ahead.

New Zealand went into the rest day already three wickets down and needing another 144 runs to avoid a second consecutive innings defeat. A twelfth Test century by Crowe and a polished half-century from Rutherford, who together added 132 for the fifth wicket, prevented that embarrassment, and New Zealand were 40 runs on with four wickets in hand when bad light stopped play. However, those four wickets could manage only 34 more runs next morning and, as at Karachi, Crowe was left stranded, having batted for almost nine and a quarter hours, in which time he hit ten fours.

*Man of the Match*: Waqar Younis.

*Close of play*: First day, Pakistan 43-0 (Ramiz Raja 23*, Shoaib Mohammad 17*); Second day, Pakistan 252-4 (Ijaz Ahmed 33*, Salim Yousuf 4*); Third day, New Zealand 69-3 (M. D. Crowe 17*, D. K. Morrison 7*); Fourth day, New Zealand 253-6 (M. D. Crowe 100*, G. E. Bradburn 5*).

## New Zealand

| | | | |
|---|---|---|---|
| T. J. Franklin c Wasim Akram b Saleem Jaffer | 11 | – c Salim Yousuf b Saleem Jaffer | 25 |
| D. J. White c Salim Yousuf b Wasim Akram | 3 | – b Waqar Younis | 1 |
| M. J. Greatbatch b Waqar Younis | 11 | – b Waqar Younis | 6 |
| *M. D. Crowe c Salim Malik b Aqib Javed | 20 | – not out | 108 |
| K. R. Rutherford lbw b Wasim Akram | 23 | – (6) lbw b Waqar Younis | 60 |
| D. N. Patel b Waqar Younis | 4 | – (7) c Salim Yousuf b Saleem Jaffer | 7 |
| G. E. Bradburn lbw b Saleem Jaffer | 8 | – (8) c sub (Aamer Sohail) b Waqar Younis | 14 |
| †I. D. S. Smith c Salim Yousuf b Abdul Qadir | 33 | – (9) c Saleem Jaffer b Abdul Qadir | 8 |
| C. Pringle c Ramiz Raja b Waqar Younis | 9 | – (10) b Waqar Younis | 7 |
| D. K. Morrison c Salim Yousuf b Abdul Qadir | 0 | – (5) b Waqar Younis | 7 |
| W. Watson not out | 0 | – lbw b Waqar Younis | 0 |
| B 5, l-b 13, w 5, n-b 15 | 38 | B 17, l-b 10, n-b 17 | 44 |

1/7 2/30 3/39 4/79 5/99                   160          1/10 2/18 3/57 4/74 5/206          287
6/103 7/143 8/147 9/154                                6/228 7/264 8/277 9/287

Bowling: *First Innings*—Wasim Akram 16-3-43-2; Waqar Younis 15-7-20-3; Saleem Jaffer 12-2-37-2; Aqib Javed 13-2-37-1; Abdul Qadir 3-1-5-2. *Second Innings*—Wasim Akram 9-4-15-0; Waqar Younis 37.5-11-86-7; Aqib Javed 21-9-40-0; Saleem Jaffer 25-8-62-2; Abdul Qadir 19-4-43-1; Shoaib Mohammad 2-0-8-0; Ijaz Ahmed 2-0-6-0.

## Pakistan

| | | |
|---|---|---|
| Ramiz Raja c Greatbatch b Watson | 48 | – c Crowe b Morrison........... 11 |
| Shoaib Mohammad b Morrison | 105 | – not out .................... 42 |
| Salim Malik lbw b Watson | 6 | – not out .................... 19 |
| *Javed Miandad c Smith b Bradburn | 43 | |
| Ijaz Ahmed c Greatbatch b Watson | 86 | |
| †Salim Yousuf c Rutherford b Pringle | 33 | |
| Wasim Akram c Bradburn b Watson | 1 | |
| Waqar Younis b Watson | 17 | |
| Saleem Jaffer not out | 10 | |
| Aqib Javed c Crowe b Watson | 7 | |
| B 4, l-b 1, n-b 12 | 17 | L-b 1, w 1, n-b 3 ....... 5 |

1/98 2/117 3/192 4/246 5/317     (9 wkts dec.) 373   1/27                  (1 wkt) 77
6/337 7/342 8/363 9/373

Abdul Qadir did not bat.

Bowling: *First Innings*—Morrison 29-9-103-1; Pringle 31-6-112-1; Watson 36-10-78-6; Patel 16-5-43-0; Bradburn 13-4-32-1. *Second Innings*—Morrison 8-2-36-1; Pringle 7-4-10-0; Patel 3-0-13-0; Watson 2-0-12-0; White 0.3-0-5-0.

Umpires: Athar Zaidi and Salim Badar.

## PAKISTAN v NEW ZEALAND

### Third Test Match

At Faisalabad, October 26, 28, 29, 30, 31. Pakistan won by 65 runs. Toss: New Zealand. Put in, Pakistan were dismissed for 102, their lowest total against New Zealand, as Pringle, bowling with sustained accuracy, and Watson availed themselves of the favourable conditions. By the close New Zealand themselves were in trouble at 40 for four, with Horne having retired hurt after ducking into a delivery from Waqar Younis early on. Younis, in his last three overs of the day, had Greatbatch caught behind, yorked Rutherford first ball, and sent back Patel, who had averted the hat-trick. After the rest day (brought forward to coincide with provincial elections) Crowe, Morrison and Smith began the recovery which saw New Zealand lead by 115 runs. Morrison, who batted for more than four hours as night-watchman, helped add 77 for the sixth wicket with Smith, whose 61 came from 44 balls and contained eleven fours.

Before the second day was over, Shoaib Mohammad had passed 2,000 runs in Tests, and on the third day Javed Miandad, when 14, reached 8,000 runs in his 107th Test, the fifth to do so after Sir Garfield Sobers, G. Boycott, S. M. Gavaskar and A. R. Border. Shoaib, meanwhile, had moved on to his seventh Test hundred, after 5 hours 39 minutes, and with Salim Malik (126 balls, twelve fours) had added 131 for the third wicket to wipe out the arrears. Another century partnership with Miandad put Pakistan in a good position, but Morrison, taking four wickets in seventeen balls, prevented it from becoming a commanding one. Pringle, with another four wickets, became the first New Zealander to take ten or more wickets in a Test against Pakistan.

Needing 243 to win, New Zealand were 31 for four at stumps, Aqib Javed having removed three batsmen in seventeen balls. Hopes that Crowe and Rutherford would redeem the situation were dashed next morning when the captain was caught at the wicket in Younis's fourth over and Rutherford followed in a similar fashion to Saleem Jaffer 19 runs later. Patel and Bradburn batted defiantly, adding 84 for the seventh wicket and getting New Zealand closer to their target, but in the end there was no denying Waqar Younis.

*Man of the Match:* Waqar Younis.

*Close of play:* First day, New Zealand 40-4 (M. D. Crowe 1*, D. K. Morrison 2*); Second day, Pakistan 43-1 (Shoaib Mohammad 24*, Salim Yousuf 0*); Third day, Pakistan 252-3 (Shoaib Mohammad 122*, Javed Miandad 22*); Fourth day, New Zealand 31-4 (M. D. Crowe 3*, K. R. Rutherford 0*).

## Pakistan

| | | | | |
|---|---|---|---|---|
| Ramiz Raja c Smith b Pringle | 20 | – lbw b Watson | 16 |
| Shoaib Mohammad c Crowe b Pringle | 15 | – c sub (A. C. Parore) b Pringle | 142 |
| Salim Malik c Smith b Pringle | 4 | – (4) c and b Crowe | 71 |
| *Javed Miandad c Smith b Pringle | 25 | – (5) c Bradburn b Pringle | 55 |
| Ijaz Ahmed c Horne b Watson | 5 | – (6) c Horne b Pringle | 6 |
| †Salim Yousuf c Morrison b Watson | 14 | – (3) c Crowe b Pringle | 13 |
| Naved Anjum b Smith b Pringle | 10 | – b Morrison | 22 |
| Tauseef Ahmed c Rutherford b Pringle | 1 | – not out | 12 |
| Waqar Younis b Pringle | 0 | – c Rutherford b Morrison | 0 |
| Saleem Jaffer lbw b Watson | 0 | – b Morrison | 2 |
| Aqib Javed not out | 0 | – c sub (A. C. Parore) b Morrison | 4 |
| B 3, n-b 5 | 8 | B 1, l-b 8, n-b 5 | 14 |

1/35 2/37 3/42 4/65 5/82    102    1/33 2/61 3/192 4/309 5/314    357
6/92 7/98 8/102 9/102               6/321 7/349 8/349 9/353

*Bowling: First Innings*—Morrison 9-3-18-0; Pringle 16-4-52-7; Watson 15.3-5-29-3. *Second Innings*—Morrison 29.5-3-105-4; Pringle 43-13-100-4; Watson 44-23-77-1; Patel 6-0-21-0; Crowe 11-5-22-1; Bradburn 6-1-23-0.

## New Zealand

| | | | | |
|---|---|---|---|---|
| T. J. Franklin b Waqar Younis | 25 | – c Ijaz Ahmed b Aqib Javed | 12 |
| P. A. Horne c Ramiz Raja b Saleem Jaffer | 0 | – lbw b Waqar Younis | 12 |
| M. J. Greatbatch c Salim Yousuf b Waqar Younis | 8 | – (4) c Aqib Javed | 0 |
| *M. D. Crowe c Tauseef Ahmed b Saleem Jaffer | 31 | – (5) c Salim Yousuf b Waqar Younis | 10 |
| K. R. Rutherford b Waqar Younis | 0 | – (6) c Salim Yousuf b Saleem Jaffer | 25 |
| D. N. Patel lbw b Waqar Younis | 0 | – (7) c Salim Yousuf b Saleem Jaffer | 45 |
| D. K. Morrison c Shoaib Mohammad b Waqar Younis | 25 | – (3) c Salim Yousuf b Aqib Javed | 0 |
| †I. D. S. Smith c Salim Malik b Tauseef Ahmed | 61 | – (9) c and b Waqar Younis | 21 |
| G. E. Bradburn c Salim Yousuf b Waqar Younis | 18 | – (8) not out | 30 |
| C. Pringle not out | 24 | – c Salim Yousuf b Waqar Younis | 0 |
| W. Watson lbw b Waqar Younis | 2 | – lbw b Waqar Younis | 2 |
| B 12, l-b 8, n-b 3 | 23 | B 10, l-b 5, w 1, n-b 4 | 20 |

1/36 2/37 3/37 4/37 5/89    217    1/23 2/25 3/28 4/31 5/45    177
6/166 7/171 8/178 9/207            6/64 7/148 8/171 9/171

*In the first innings P. A. Horne, when 0, retired hurt at 7 and resumed at 166.*

*Bowling: First Innings*—Waqar Younis 30.2-13-76-7; Aqib Javed 10-5-24-0; Naved Anjum 6-4-13-0; Saleem Jaffer 20-5-47-2; Tauseef Ahmed 10-2-37-1. *Second Innings*—Waqar Younis 23.5-9-54-5; Saleem Jaffer 18-4-51-2; Aqib Javed 17-1-57-3.

Umpires: Athar Zaidi and Salim Badar.

## †PAKISTAN v NEW ZEALAND

### First One-day International

At Lahore, November 2. Pakistan won by 19 runs. Toss: New Zealand. Put in, Pakistan made a good start with Saeed Anwar and Shoaib Mohammad putting on 59 before Shoaib went in the fourteenth over. Saeed was soon to his fifty, from just 59 balls, and he continued on his authoritative way to reach his century in 114 balls, including eleven fours. New Zealand, chasing nearly 5 runs an over, were 100 for three in the 25th over, with Greatbatch and Patel keeping them in touch with the run-rate. But the introduction of Salim Malik changed the course of the match. He broke the stand by bowling Patel, and when Greatbatch was splendidly caught by Saeed off Akram Raza, the off-spinner, only Smith, cutting and driving with purpose, could keep the runs coming.

*Man of the Match:* Saeed Anwar.

## Pakistan

| | |
|---|---|
| Saeed Anwar c Smith b Morrison . . . . .101 | Akram Raza not out . . . . . . . . . . . . . . . 13 |
| Shoaib Mohammad c Smith b Morrison 12 | Mushtaq Ahmed run out . . . . . . . . . . . . 7 |
| Salim Malik c Morrison b Crowe . . . . . . 17 | L-b 7, w 5 . . . . . . . . . . . . . . . . 12 |
| Manzoor Elahi c and b Watson . . . . . . . 17 | — |
| Ijaz Ahmed run out . . . . . . . . . . . . . . . . 5 | 1/59 2/114 3/152      (8 wkts, 40 overs) 196 |
| *Javed Miandad run out . . . . . . . . . . . . . 11 | 4/161 5/164 6/168 |
| †Salim Yousuf c Smith b Morrison . . . . 1 | 7/189 8/196 |

Saleem Jaffer and Waqar Younis did not bat.

Bowling: Pringle 6-0-22-0; Roberts 3-0-21-0; Watson 7-0-34-1; Morrison 8-0-28-3; Patel 8-0-36-0; Priest 4-0-24-0; Crowe 4-1-24-1.

## New Zealand

| | |
|---|---|
| D. J. White c Saeed Anwar | C. Pringle st Salim Yousuf |
|     b Manzoor Elahi . 13 |     b Salim Malik . 2 |
| *M. D. Crowe b Manzoor Elahi . . . . . . 20 | D. K. Morrison lbw b Salim Malik . . . . 0 |
| K. R. Rutherford run out . . . . . . . . . . . 12 | W. Watson b Waqar Younis . . . . . . . . . 5 |
| M. J. Greatbatch c Saeed Anwar | S. J. Roberts not out . . . . . . . . . . . . . . . 1 |
|     b Akram Raza . 36 | |
| D. N. Patel b Salim Malik . . . . . . . . . . 16 | |
| †I. D. S. Smith st Salim Yousuf | B 1, l-b 8, w 4, n-b 3 . . . . . . . 16 |
|     b Salim Malik . 47 | |
| M. W. Priest st Salim Yousuf | 1/27 2/40 3/79 4/104 5/117   (39.2 overs) 177 |
|     b Salim Malik . 9 | 6/149 7/164 8/164 9/175 |

Bowling: Saleem Jaffer 5-0-16-0; Manzoor Elahi 8-1-32-2; Waqar Younis 7.2-0-26-1; Akram Raza 8-0-40-1; Mushtaq Ahmed 4-0-19-0; Salim Malik 7-2-35-5.

Umpires: Khizar Hayat and Mian Aslam.

## †PAKISTAN v NEW ZEALAND

### Second One-day International

At Peshawar, November 4. Pakistan won by eight wickets. Toss: Pakistan. After White and Crowe had put on 50 for the first wicket, Waqar Younis shattered the New Zealand innings by taking five wickets for just 11 runs. First he removed White and Rutherford with consecutive deliveries, and although Greatbatch prevented the hat-trick, he did not last long. Nor did Patel, and it was left to Bradburn and the tail, wagging against the spinners, to set some kind of target. By the time Saeed Anwar was out in the nineteenth over of Pakistan's innings, the match was as good as won. He had hit Watson for three successive fours in his opening over, and in all he hit seven fours and two sixes. Ramiz Raja had five fours in his unbeaten 50 from 75 balls.

*Man of the Match:* Saeed Anwar.

## New Zealand

| | |
|---|---|
| D. J. White c Salim Malik b Waqar Younis . | 15 |
| *M. D. Crowe lbw b Waqar Younis ... | 46 |
| K. R. Rutherford lbw b Waqar Younis . | 0 |
| M. J. Greatbatch run out ............ | 5 |
| D. N. Patel b Waqar Younis .......... | 2 |
| G. E. Bradburn c Saeed Anwar b Akram Raza | 30 |
| †I. D. S. Smith b Mushtaq Ahmed .... | 6 |
| M. W. Priest c Ramiz Raja b Salim Malik . | 10 |
| C. Pringle c Javed Miandad b Salim Malik . | 3 |
| D. K. Morrison lbw b Waqar Younis .. | 0 |
| W. Watson not out ................. | 0 |
| L-b 7, w 2, n-b 1 ............ | 10 |

1/50 2/50 3/58 4/65 5/82 (37.4 overs) 127
6/95 7/117 8/127 9/127

Bowling: Manzoor Elahi 8–0–35–0; Zakir Khan 5–0–19–0; Waqar Younis 6.4–2–11–5; Mushtaq Ahmed 8–1–26–1; Akram Raza 7–0–22–1; Salim Malik 3–0–7–2.

## Pakistan

| | |
|---|---|
| Saeed Anwar c Smith b Bradburn ..... | 67 |
| Ramiz Raja not out ................ | 50 |
| Salim Malik c Smith b Bradburn ...... | 1 |
| Ijaz Ahmed not out ................ | 7 |
| L-b 1, w 2 ................ | 3 |

1/96 2/98 (2 wkts, 29.1 overs) 128

*Javed Miandad, Manzoor Elahi, †Salim Yousuf, Akram Raza, Mushtaq Ahmed, Zakir Khan and Waqar Younis did not bat.

Bowling: Pringle 4–0–15–0; Watson 3–0–16–0; Patel 8–0–35–0; Morrison 2–0–11–0; Priest 3–0–23–0; Bradburn 6–2–18–2; Crowe 3.1–0–9–0.

Umpires: Javed Akhtar and Said Shah.

## †PAKISTAN v NEW ZEALAND

### Third One-day International

At Sialkot, November 6. Pakistan won by 105 runs. Toss: New Zealand. Crowe's decision to put Pakistan in backfired when Saeed Anwar and Ramiz Raja again tucked into the New Zealand bowlers, putting on 78 before Saeed was out in the eighteenth over. In the next 22 overs Ramiz and Salim Malik added 139, Ramiz's 114, his fifth one-day century, being lit with fourteen fours in 123 balls. Malik's unbeaten 65 came from 68 balls. New Zealand's openers raced to 36 in seven overs, but both went in quick succession and Greatbatch was unlucky to be caught at the wicket off his pads. Waqar Younis proved too much for the later batsmen, and his five wickets in six overs gave him a haul of 40 wickets against the tourists in the Tests and one-day games.

*Man of the Match:* Ramiz Raja.

## Pakistan

| | |
|---|---|
| Saeed Anwar c White b Patel ......... | 35 |
| Ramiz Raja run out ................ | 114 |
| Salim Malik not out ................ | 65 |
| Zahid Fazal not out ................ | 5 |
| B 2, w 1, n-b 1 ............ | 4 |

1/78 2/217 (2 wkts, 40 overs) 223

Ijaz Ahmed, *Javed Miandad, †Salim Yousuf, Manzoor Elahi, Zakir Khan, Akram Raza and Waqar Younis did not bat.

Bowling: Pringle 8–0–46–0; Watson 8–1–32–0; Morrison 3–0–17–0; Patel 7–0–44–1; Bradburn 4–0–24–0; Priest 5–0–27–0; Crowe 5–0–31–0.

## New Zealand

| | | | |
|---|---|---|---|
| D. J. White b Manzoor Elahi | 9 | G. E. Bradburn c Salim Yousuf | |
| *M. D. Crowe lbw b Manzoor Elahi | 22 | b Waqar Younis | 0 |
| K. R. Rutherford | | M. W. Priest lbw b Waqar Younis | 0 |
| c and b Ijaz Ahmed | 24 | C. Pringle lbw b Waqar Younis | 0 |
| M. J. Greatbatch c Salim Yousuf | | D. K. Morrison not out | 4 |
| b Manzoor Elahi | 3 | W. Watson lbw b Waqar Younis | 0 |
| D. N. Patel c Salim Yousuf | | B 4, l-b 5, w 10, n-b 3 | 22 |
| b Waqar Younis | 23 | | — |
| †I. D. S. Smith c sub (Mushtaq Ahmed) | | 1/36 2/47 3/60 4/74 5/94 (25 overs) 118 |
| b Ijaz Ahmed | 11 | 6/97 7/97 8/107 9/118 |

Bowling: Manzoor Elahi 7-0-36-3; Zakir Khan 5-0-26-0; Ijaz Ahmed 7-0-31-2; Waqar Younis 6-1-16-5.

Umpires: Khalid Aziz and Shakeel Khan.

# THE NEW ZEALANDERS IN AUSTRALIA, 1990-91

## NEW ZEALAND TOUR RESULTS

*One-day internationals* – Played 10: Won 3, Lost 7. *Wins* – England (2), Australia (1). *Losses* – Australia (5), England (2).
*Other non first-class match* – Won v New South Wales.

†At Wollongong, November 27. New Zealanders won by seven wickets. Toss: New Zealanders. New South Wales 130 (45.3 overs) (W. Watson four for 21); New Zealanders 131 for three (33.4 overs) (J. G. Wright 59, M. J. Greatbatch 43 not out).

*New Zealand's matches v Australia and England in the Benson and Hedges World Series Cup (November 29–January 15) may be found in that section.*

# THE WEST INDIANS IN PAKISTAN, 1990-91

## By QAMAR AHMED

With the third series in succession between Pakistan and West Indies being drawn, each side winning one Test, the unofficial world championship of cricket – as this three-match series was labelled – remained undecided. It was a low-scoring series, for the pitches were not conducive to strokemaking, and yet it was an absorbing one. If ultimately West Indies appeared to be the better Test side, there was the consolation for Pakistan of their first series victory over West Indies in one-day internationals.

Although accusations were levelled at the authorities for preparing slow pitches to suit the Pakistani spinners, it was the fast bowlers who dominated the Test matches. Of the 97 wickets which fell to bowlers, 85 were taken by the fast men, with the pace and swing of the Pakistani pair, Wasim Akram and Waqar Younis, catching the West Indians unawares in the First Test. This made it all the more surprising that, after they had shared fifteen wickets in Pakistan's victory, a slow pitch was provided at Faisalabad for the Second Test. The spinners, on whom Imran Khan had been banking, let him down, though had Imran played in the series against New Zealand, which preceded this one, he would have known that his spin bowlers had lost their edge and were no longer so reliable. On a pitch of uneven bounce, it was the West Indian pacemen who did the damage and the match was over in three days.

Malcolm Marshall made the decisive breakthrough there, taking four wickets in thirteen balls after lunch on the third day. That, however, was his only significant contribution on the tour with the ball. Gordon Greenidge was an even bigger disappointment, unable to average 10 from his six Test innings, and Jeffrey Dujon was another established player to have an unsatisfactory series. Desmond Haynes, captaining the West Indians while Vivian Richards recuperated from a recent operation, and Carl Hooper hit the only Test hundreds for the tourists, and while Richie Richardson and Gus Logie also batted well, they did so in patches. The left-handed Brian Lara, coming into the side for the final Test after Carlisle Best had split the webbing of his right hand, quickly proved his worth with a gritty disciplined first innings to follow his 139 against the Combined XI at Sargodha. This was the only fixture of the tour which was not an international of one kind or another.

Ian Bishop, the Wills Man of the Series for West Indies, was the pick of their bowlers, his sixteen wickets costing 18.87 apiece, and with Curtly Ambrose he provided a potent spearhead. Courtney Walsh, like Marshall, was more expensive and less penetrative, but he gave tireless support throughout. He was also the target in one of the less savoury moments on the tour, being hit by an object thrown from one of the stands during the tense final day of the last Test. While the matter was soon sorted out, with the culprit being taken to task by ground security officials, play was halted for five minutes when Walsh ran to the middle from the third-man boundary and pulled out a stump to vent his disgust at the crowd's behaviour. He subsequently left the field for treatment.

Time was lost throughout the series for reasons of a less controversial nature. Heavy morning dew and fading light in the late afternoon several times cut into the hours of play, with the result that even a requirement of 72 overs a day became an unattainable target.

For Pakistan, Salim Malik batted splendidly for an aggregate of 285 runs at 57.00 in the Tests, including the home team's only century, and of 179 in the three one-day internationals. It came as no surprise that Shoaib could not repeat his heavy scoring of the New Zealand series, but he made a key contribution to the First Test victory. And Imran Khan compensated with his batting for what he was beginning to lose as a bowler. Without his defiant half-century in the last Test, the series would probably have been lost. Wasim Akram, with 21 wickets at 14.19 and two important innings at Lahore, was Pakistan's Wills Man of the Series.

The umpiring of Khizar Hayat and Riazuddin throughout the series made a good impression, with the newcomer, Riazuddin, winning admiration for his coolness under pressure. There were mistakes, but because these favoured neither side in particular, there were no grounds for recriminations. However, as after the New Zealand series, there were complaints from the visiting team's management that the Pakistanis were tampering with the ball to help it swing. The charge was promptly denied by Imran Khan and the Pakistan Board.

"It's a ridiculous charge", Imran said. "The Pakistan bowlers play in county games and have never been accused by any player or umpire. They played under the close scrutiny of John Hampshire and John Holder in the series against India and not a finger was raised. I am surprised at the allegations."

Arif Ali Abbasi, then secretary of the Pakistan Board, stated that after the First Test he had shown the ball used by the Pakistan bowlers to Lance Gibbs, the West Indies manager, and also the ball used by the West Indians. "The manager agreed that the ball used by the West Indians was in a much worse condition than the one used by Pakistan", he said.

## WEST INDIAN TOUR RESULTS

*Test matches* – Played 3: Won 1, Lost 1, Drawn 1.
*First-class matches* – Played 4: Won 1, Lost 1, Drawn 2.
*Win* – Pakistan.
*Loss* – Pakistan.
*Draws* – Pakistan, Pakistan Combined XI.
*One-day internationals* – Played 3: Lost 3.

## TEST MATCH AVERAGES

### PAKISTAN – BATTING

|  | T | I | NO | R | HI | 100s | Avge |
|---|---|---|---|---|---|---|---|
| Salim Malik......... | 3 | 6 | 1 | 285 | 102 | 1 | 57.00 |
| Imran Khan ......... | 3 | 5 | 2 | 151 | 73* | 0 | 50.33 |
| Shoaib Mohammad.... | 3 | 6 | 1 | 189 | 86 | 0 | 37.80 |
| Moin Khan .......... | 2 | 3 | 0 | 63 | 32 | 0 | 21.00 |
| Wasim Akram........ | 3 | 5 | 1 | 72 | 38 | 0 | 18.00 |
| Ramiz Raja .......... | 2 | 4 | 0 | 54 | 41 | 0 | 13.50 |

| | T | I | NO | R | HI | 100s | Avge |
|---|---|---|---|---|---|---|---|
| Zahid Fazal.......... | 3 | 6 | 0 | 75 | 32 | 0 | 12.50 |
| Mushtaq Ahmed ...... | 2 | 3 | 2 | 10 | 5* | 0 | 10.00 |
| Javed Miandad ....... | 2 | 3 | 0 | 23 | 9 | 0 | 7.66 |
| Waqar Younis........ | 3 | 4 | 1 | 9 | 5 | 0 | 3.00 |

Played in two Tests: Abdul Qadir 0, 1. Played in one Test: Aamer Malik 3, 0; Akram Raza 5, 0; Masood Anwar 2, 37; Saeed Anwar 0, 0; Salim Yousuf 5.

*\* Signifies not out.*

## BOWLING

| | O | M | R | W | BB | 5W/i | Avge |
|---|---|---|---|---|---|---|---|
| Imran Khan ..... | 19 | 5 | 54 | 4 | 2-22 | 0 | 13.50 |
| Wasim Akram ... | 106 | 12 | 298 | 21 | 5-28 | 1 | 14.19 |
| Waqar Younis.... | 89 | 8 | 296 | 16 | 5-46 | 2 | 18.50 |

Also bowled: Abdul Qadir 50-4-172-2; Akram Raza 26.2-5-89-2; Masood Anwar 26.5-4-102-3; Mushtaq Ahmed 38-10-100-3; Salim Malik 1-0-5-0; Shoaib Mohammad 7-1-16-1.

## WEST INDIES – BATTING

| | T | I | NO | R | HI | 100s | Avge |
|---|---|---|---|---|---|---|---|
| C. L. Hooper ....... | 3 | 6 | 1 | 229 | 134 | 1 | 45.80 |
| A. L. Logie ........ | 3 | 5 | 1 | 170 | 59 | 0 | 42.50 |
| D. L. Haynes ....... | 3 | 6 | 0 | 198 | 117 | 1 | 33.00 |
| R. B. Richardson.... | 3 | 6 | 1 | 162 | 70* | 0 | 32.40 |
| M. D. Marshall .... | 3 | 5 | 0 | 92 | 27 | 0 | 18.40 |
| C. A. Walsh........ | 3 | 5 | 3 | 25 | 14* | 0 | 12.50 |
| C. G. Greenidge .... | 3 | 6 | 0 | 58 | 21 | 0 | 9.66 |
| I. R. Bishop ....... | 3 | 5 | 1 | 32 | 22 | 0 | 8.00 |
| P. J. L. Dujon ...... | 3 | 5 | 0 | 30 | 17 | 0 | 6.00 |
| C. A. Best ........ | 2 | 4 | 0 | 22 | 8 | 0 | 5.50 |
| C. E. L. Ambrose ... | 3 | 5 | 0 | 17 | 15 | 0 | 3.40 |

Played in one Test: B. C. Lara 44, 5.

*\* Signifies not out.*

## BOWLING

| | O | M | R | W | BB | 5W/i | Avge |
|---|---|---|---|---|---|---|---|
| C. E. L. Ambrose.... | 106.4 | 25 | 239 | 14 | 5-35 | 1 | 17.07 |
| I. R. Bishop ........ | 105 | 23 | 302 | 16 | 5-41 | 1 | 18.87 |
| M. D. Marshall .... | 65.2 | 14 | 166 | 6 | 4-24 | 0 | 27.66 |
| C. A. Walsh ....... | 74 | 7 | 222 | 8 | 2-27 | 0 | 27.75 |

Also bowled: C. A. Best 1-0-2-0; C. L. Hooper 59-14-144-1.

## WEST INDIAN AVERAGES – FIRST-CLASS MATCHES

### BATTING

| | M | I | NO | R | HI | 100s | Avge |
|---|---|---|---|---|---|---|---|
| B. C. Lara ......... | 2 | 4 | 1 | 212 | 139 | 1 | 70.66 |
| D. L. Haynes ....... | 4 | 7 | 1 | 234 | 117 | 1 | 39.00 |
| C. L. Hooper ....... | 4 | 8 | 1 | 269 | 134 | 1 | 38.42 |
| A. L. Logie ........ | 4 | 7 | 1 | 208 | 59 | 0 | 34.66 |
| R. B. Richardson.... | 4 | 8 | 2 | 201 | 70* | 0 | 33.50 |
| M. D. Marshall ..... | 3 | 5 | 0 | 92 | 27 | 0 | 18.40 |
| C. G. Greenidge .... | 4 | 8 | 0 | 139 | 76 | 0 | 17.37 |
| P. J. L. Dujon ..... | 4 | 7 | 0 | 110 | 63 | 0 | 15.71 |
| C. A. Walsh ........ | 3 | 5 | 3 | 25 | 14* | 0 | 12.50 |
| I. R. Bishop ....... | 4 | 6 | 1 | 32 | 22 | 0 | 6.40 |
| C. A. Best ........ | 2 | 4 | 0 | 22 | 8 | 0 | 5.50 |
| C. E. L. Ambrose ... | 3 | 5 | 0 | 17 | 15 | 0 | 3.40 |

Played in one match: R. C. Haynes 20; E. A. Moseley 13; D. Williams 4.

*\* Signifies not out.*

### BOWLING

| | O | M | R | W | BB | 5W/i | Avge |
|---|---|---|---|---|---|---|---|
| C. E. L. Ambrose.... | 106.4 | 25 | 239 | 14 | 5-35 | 1 | 17.07 |
| I. R. Bishop ....... | 121 | 25 | 361 | 20 | 5-41 | 1 | 18.05 |
| M. D. Marshall ..... | 65.2 | 14 | 166 | 6 | 4-24 | 0 | 27.66 |
| C. A. Walsh ........ | 74 | 7 | 222 | 8 | 2-27 | 0 | 27.75 |

Also bowled: C. A. Best 1–0–2–0; R. C. Haynes 20–4–56–3; C. L. Hooper 64–14–172–1; E. A. Moseley 20.1–3–57–3.

### FIELDING

9 – P. J. L. Dujon; 7 – A. L. Logie; 5 – R. B. Richardson; 2 – C. G. Greenidge; 1 – C. A. Best, D. L. Haynes, C. L. Hooper, B. C. Lara, D. Williams.

## †PAKISTAN v WEST INDIES

### First One-day International

At Karachi, November 9. Pakistan won by 6 runs. Toss: Pakistan. A capacity crowd of 25,000 saw Pakistan lose three wickets to Ambrose and Bishop after choosing to bat first. However, Salim Malik and Zahid Fazal added 42 runs in seven overs, and then Imran Khan and Malik, seeing Pakistan past 100 in the 22nd over, put on 75 in 78 balls before Malik was caught at mid-wicket. Imran continued to flourish, and his unbeaten 53 contained five fours and a six in 50 balls. West Indies lost Best to the fifth ball of the innings, but Richardson, dropped at long leg by Saleem Jaffer off Imran soon after, went on a run-spree, adding 138 for the second wicket with Haynes. His fifty, coming in 64 balls, contained two sixes and four fours. Logie was then bowled first ball by Waqar Younis, and while Lara avoided the hat-trick, Haynes soon fell victim to the same bowler, having hit nine fours in his 67. In seven balls Younis had taken three for 6 and in finishing with five wickets he did much to ensure that West Indies did not mark their 200th one-day international with a victory.

*Man of the Match:* Waqar Younis.

## Pakistan

| | | | | |
|---|---|---|---|---|
| Saeed Anwar c and b Ambrose | 20 | †Salim Yousuf not out | 27 |
| Ramiz Raja b Ambrose | 10 | | |
| Zahid Fazal c Dujon b Hooper | 22 | L-b 8, w 4, n-b 4 | 16 |
| Javed Miandad hit wkt b Bishop | 5 | | |
| Salim Malik c Haynes b Bishop | 58 | 1/32 2/35 3/49 (5 wkts, 40 overs) 211 | |
| *Imran Khan not out | 53 | 4/91 5/166 | |

Akram Raza, Waqar Younis, Mushtaq Ahmed and Saleem Jaffer did not bat.

Bowling: Bishop 8-1-45-2; Ambrose 8-0-40-2; Marshall 8-0-30-0; Walsh 8-0-51-0; Hooper 8-0-37-1.

## West Indies

| | | | | |
|---|---|---|---|---|
| *D. L. Haynes b Waqar Younis | 67 | †P. J. L. Dujon c Salim Yousuf | |
| C. A. Best c Akram Raza | | b Mushtaq Ahmed | 3 |
| b Imran Khan | 0 | M. D. Marshall not out | 26 |
| R. B. Richardson c sub (Ijaz Ahmed) | | C. E. L. Ambrose not out | 1 |
| b Waqar Younis | 69 | B 1, l-b 5, w 3, n-b 4 | 13 |
| A. L. Logie b Waqar Younis | 0 | | |
| B. C. Lara lbw b Waqar Younis | 11 | 1/1 2/139 3/139 (7 wkts, 40 overs) 205 | |
| C. L. Hooper lbw b Waqar Younis | 15 | 4/149 5/158 6/171 7/181 | |

I. R. Bishop and C. A. Walsh did not bat.

Bowling: Imran Khan 7-0-53-1; Saleem Jaffer 8-0-19-0; Akram Raza 8-0-37-0; Waqar Younis 8-0-52-5; Mushtaq Ahmed 8-0-32-1; Salim Malik 1-0-6-0.

Umpires: Khizar Hayat and Mahboob Shah.

## †PAKISTAN v WEST INDIES

### Second One-day International

At Lahore, November 11. Pakistan won by five wickets. Toss: West Indies. This was Pakistan's 200th one-day international, and after being 23 for three in the tenth over they came back well to win it. As in Karachi, Salim Malik first steadied the innings and then dominated it, taking Pakistan to victory with a superbly struck 91 not out from 98 balls. Imran batted defiantly at the other end. West Indies, electing to bat first, had lost Greenidge and Richardson at 29 within the space of three balls to Saleem Jaffer, but Haynes and Best put on 50 in fifteen overs. Haynes was twice dropped by Jaffer off Akram Raza and Saeed Anwar. When leg-spinner Mushtaq Ahmed bowled Marshall and Logie, the West Indians were struggling, but Hooper and Dujon thrashed 36 in five overs to give their bowlers something to defend.

*Man of the Match:* Salim Malik.

## West Indies

| | | | | |
|---|---|---|---|---|
| C. G. Greenidge c Salim Yousuf | | C. L. Hooper not out | 27 |
| b Saleem Jaffer | 9 | †P. J. L. Dujon run out | 14 |
| *D. L. Haynes c Waqar Younis | | E. A. Moseley not out | 2 |
| b Saeed Anwar | 66 | | |
| R. B. Richardson c Salim Yousuf | | B 1, l-b 10, w 4, n-b 2 | 17 |
| b Saleem Jaffer | 0 | | |
| C. A. Best c and b Akram Raza | 19 | 1/29 2/29 3/79 (7 wkts, 39 overs) 176 | |
| A. L. Logie b Mushtaq Ahmed | 18 | 4/123 5/124 | |
| M. D. Marshall b Mushtaq Ahmed | 4 | 6/134 7/170 | |

C. E. L. Ambrose and I. R. Bishop did not bat.

Bowling: Imran Khan 5-2-13-0; Saleem Jaffer 8-0-20-2; Akram Raza 8-0-32-1; Waqar Younis 8-1-33-0; Mushtaq Ahmed 7-0-48-2; Saeed Anwar 3-0-19-1.

## Pakistan

| | | | |
|---|---|---|---|
| Saeed Anwar c Dujon b Bishop | 5 | †Salim Yousuf not out | 0 |
| Ramiz Raja b Ambrose | 1 | | |
| Zahid Fazal c Richardson b Marshall | 5 | L-b 5, w 8, n-b 7 | 20 |
| Javed Miandad c Dujon b Marshall | 23 | | |
| Salim Malik not out | 91 | 1/4 2/6 3/23    (5 wkts, 37.1 overs) 177 | |
| *Imran Khan c Richardson b Moseley | 32 | 4/52 5/175 | |

Akram Raza, Mushtaq Ahmed, Waqar Younis and Saleem Jaffer did not bat.

Bowling: Bishop 7–0–36–2; Ambrose 8–2–20–1; Marshall 8–1–36–1; Moseley 8–0–47–1; Hooper 6.1–0–33–0.

Umpires: Javed Akhtar and Ikram Rabbani.

## †PAKISTAN v WEST INDIES

### Third One-day International

At Multan, November 13. Pakistan won by 31 runs. Toss: Pakistan. West Indies were beaten 3-0 in a three-match one-day series for only the second time, and the defeat provided Pakistan with their first series win against them. Pakistan, batting first, lost Shoaib Mohammad and Zahid Fazal within seven balls, but Saeed Anwar and Salim Malik added 51 runs before Malik was caught at the wicket in the twelfth over. Newcomer Moin Khan batted bravely to add 58 runs for the sixth wicket with Imran Khan, who when 12 reached 1,000 runs against West Indies. The West Indians were 35 without loss in the tenth over, with Greenidge having passed 5,000 runs in one-day internationals, but the dismissals of Haynes and Richardson arrested the run-rate: only 23 runs came in the next ten overs. Then in successive overs Mushtaq Ahmed bowled Best and Logie and the tourists were out of contention. Hooper, however, stayed until the end and gained useful practice against the spinners.

*Man of the Match:* Imran Khan.

## Pakistan

| | | | |
|---|---|---|---|
| Saeed Anwar b Hooper | 31 | Akram Raza b Walsh | 0 |
| Shoaib Mohammad c Richardson | | Mushtaq Ahmed b Walsh | 0 |
|     b Bishop | 0 | Abdul Qadir run out | 1 |
| Zahid Fazal c Williams b Moseley | 1 | L-b 5, w 9 | 14 |
| Salim Malik c Williams b Walsh | 30 | | |
| Ijaz Ahmed b R. C. Haynes | 22 | 1/2 2/3 3/54    (9 wkts, 40 overs) 168 | |
| *Imran Khan not out | 46 | 4/88 5/99 6/157 | |
| †Moin Khan b Bishop | 23 | 7/161 8/161 9/168 | |

Waqar Younis did not bat.

Bowling: Bishop 8–0–35–2; Moseley 8–0–45–1; Walsh 8–0–28–3; Hooper 8–0–26–1; R. C. Haynes 8–0–29–1.

## West Indies

| | | | |
|---|---|---|---|
| C. G. Greenidge b Waqar Younis | 35 | E. A. Moseley c Saeed Anwar | |
| *D. L. Haynes b Akram Raza | 18 |     b Mushtaq Ahmed | 0 |
| R. B. Richardson c Akram Raza | | †D. Williams not out | 10 |
|     b Imran Khan | 7 | B 2, l-b 11, w 5 | 18 |
| C. A. Best b Mushtaq Ahmed | 10 | | |
| A. L. Logie b Mushtaq Ahmed | 7 | 1/35 2/44 3/67    (7 wkts, 40 overs) 137 | |
| C. L. Hooper not out | 32 | 4/79 5/107 | |
| R. C. Haynes b Waqar Younis | 0 | 6/107 7/110 | |

I. R. Bishop and C. A. Walsh did not bat.

Bowling: Imran Khan 8–1–26–1; Waqar Younis 7–0–19–2; Akram Raza 8–0–20–1; Mushtaq Ahmed 8–0–31–3; Abdul Qadir 8–0–24–0; Saeed Anwar 1–0–4–0.

Umpires: Riazuddin and Siddiq Khan.

## PAKISTAN v WEST INDIES

### First Test Match

At Karachi, November 15, 16, 17, 19, 20. Pakistan won by eight wickets. Toss: West Indies. Haynes, hitting his fifteenth hundred in 90 Tests, was the only West Indian batsman to prosper after his decision to bat first on a pitch devoid of grass and subsequently revealing uneven bounce. He lost Greenidge in Waqar Younis's first over, and just when a second-wicket partnership of 73 had put the innings on course, Richardson was made to pay for his impetuosity against the leg-spinner, Mushtaq Ahmed. Logie, too, suffered from a lapse in concentration when seemingly set, and West Indies owed everything to their captain's first Test hundred against Pakistan. Younis bowled well to take five wickets for the fourth successive Test innings and was unlucky not to have Haynes caught behind when he was 92.

Initially the second day looked less likely to go Pakistan's way. The West Indians batted for almost an hour while adding 24 runs, and then they had Pakistan 27 for three. However, that was the turning-point. Shoaib Mohammad and Salim Malik remained unbeaten until the close, and early next day they passed Pakistan's fourth-wicket record against West Indies, 154 set in 1957-58 by Shoaib's father, Hanif, and uncle, Wazir. When Malik was caught behind off Marshall, having batted 268 minutes (208 balls) for his eighth Test hundred, Shoaib added 80 for the fifth wicket with Imran Khan before Marshall dismissed him too, after almost eight hours' batting (314 balls). Imran, reprieved behind the wicket when 35, batted for more than five hours for his unbeaten 73, but a blow on the leg was to prevent him fielding.

A sound start saw West Indies clear their first-innings deficit for the loss of Greenidge. No sooner was that achieved, though, than they lost five wickets for 42 runs in fifteen overs, and at the close they were only 88 runs ahead with just three wickets in hand. Logie batted valiantly for an unbeaten 58 (163 minutes, eight fours), but the Pakistan fast bowlers needed no more than 21 balls on the final morning to finish the innings and leave Pakistan a comfortable target of 98. This they achieved cautiously, and with a session to spare.

*Man of the Match*: Salim Malik.

*Close of play*: First day, West Indies 237-8 (D. L. Haynes 113*, I. R. Bishop 12*); Second day, Pakistan 171-3 (Shoaib Mohammad 48*, Salim Malik 88*); Third day, Pakistan 332-9 (Imran Khan 60*, Waqar Younis 5*); Fourth day, West Indies 172-7 (A. L. Logie 51*, C. E. L. Ambrose 0*).

## West Indies

| | | | |
|---|---|---|---|
| C. G. Greenidge lbw b Waqar Younis | 3 | – st Salim Yousuf b Abdul Qadir | 11 |
| *D. L. Haynes lbw b Wasim Akram | 117 | – c Salim Yousuf b Waqar Younis | 47 |
| R. B. Richardson st Salim Yousuf b Mushtaq Ahmed | 26 | – lbw b Waqar Younis | 11 |
| C. A. Best c Ramiz Raja b Mushtaq Ahmed | 1 | – lbw b Mushtaq Ahmed | 8 |
| C. L. Hooper lbw b Waqar Younis | 0 | – b Wasim Akram | 0 |
| A. L. Logie c Salim Yousuf b Wasim Akram | 25 | – not out | 58 |
| †P. J. L. Dujon c Javed Miandad b Waqar Younis | 17 | – b Shoaib Mohammad | 1 |
| M. D. Marshall b Waqar Younis | 13 | – b Wasim Akram | 21 |
| C. E. L. Ambrose lbw b Waqar Younis | 2 | – lbw b Waqar Younis | 0 |
| I. R. Bishop c Salim Yousuf b Wasim Akram | 22 | – b Waqar Younis | 0 |
| C. A. Walsh not out | 6 | – b Wasim Akram | 0 |
| B 6, l-b 6, n-b 9 | 21 | B 10, l-b 8, n-b 6 | 24 |
| | **261** | | **181** |

1/4 2/77 3/81 4/96 5/151 6/178 7/200 8/204 9/243    **261**

1/47 2/85 3/86 4/90 5/111 6/127 7/166 8/174 9/174    **181**

*Bowling: First Innings*—Wasim Akram 23.3–1–61–3; Waqar Younis 22–0–76–5; Abdul Qadir 20–2–56–0; Mushtaq Ahmed 18–3–56–2. *Second Innings*—Wasim Akram 20.3–6–39–3; Waqar Younis 17–3–44–4; Abdul Qadir 8–1–22–1; Mushtaq Ahmed 15–5–38–1; Shoaib Mohammad 6–1–15–1; Salim Malik 1–0–5–0.

## Pakistan

| | | | |
|---|---|---|---|
| Shoaib Mohammad c Richardson b Marshall ... | 86 | – not out .......................... | 32 |
| Ramiz Raja b Bishop ...................... | 0 | – lbw b Walsh ..................... | 7 |
| Zahid Fazal c Logie b Ambrose............. | 7 | – c Richardson b Walsh ......... | 12 |
| Javed Miandad c Dujon b Bishop ........... | 7 | | |
| Salim Malik c Dujon b Marshall ........... | 102 | – (4) not out .................... | 30 |
| *Imran Khan not out ..................... | 73 | | |
| †Salim Yousuf b Ambrose.................. | 5 | | |
| Wasim Akram c Richardson b Walsh ......... | 9 | | |
| Mushtaq Ahmed c Richardson b Ambrose ..... | 3 | | |
| Abdul Qadir c Dujon b Ambrose............ | 0 | | |
| Waqar Younis c Hooper b Bishop .......... | 5 | | |
| B 7, l-b 14, w 1, n-b 26 ........ | 48 | L-b 8, n-b 9 ........... | 17 |

1/2 2/16 3/27 4/201 5/281　　　　　345　　1/15 2/56　　　　(2 wkts) 98
6/298 7/313 8/318 9/318

Bowling: *First Innings*—Ambrose 34-7-78-4; Bishop 27.2-3-81-3; Marshall 24-5-48-2; Walsh 19-0-50-1; Hooper 28-6-65-0; Best 1-0-2-0. *Second Innings*—Bishop 7-0-21-0; Ambrose 2-0-4-0; Marshall 5-1-8-0; Walsh 12-2-27-2; Hooper 11-2-30-0.

Umpires: Khizar Hayat and Riazuddin.

## PAKISTAN v WEST INDIES

### Second Test Match

At Faisalabad, November 23, 24, 25. West Indies won by seven wickets. Toss: Pakistan. It took just three days for West Indies to square the series in conditions which provided movement through the air and off the seam for the fast bowlers. Only 25 runs separated the sides after the first innings, but a devastating spell of fast bowling by Marshall, who took four wickets in thirteen balls, precipitated a batting collapse which saw Pakistan crash from 145 for four to 146 for nine in their second innings. Needing 130 to win, West Indies lost their captain first ball, driving to cover, and in the seventeenth over they were 34 for three. From that point, however, Richardson and Hooper steered them to victory, 50 minutes after tea, with an unbroken partnership of 98.

Imran Khan's decision to bat first was never supported by his batsmen. Only Salim Malik's fighting 74 from 113 balls, with 40 runs in boundaries, lit a day shortened at one end by heavy dew and at the other by bad light. Malik shared stands of 47 with both Zahid Fazal, playing in his second Test, and the wicket-keeper, Moin Khan, who was making his Test début. Another newcomer, the left-handed opener, Saeed Anwar, had faced just five balls and was to collect a pair before the match was two days old.

West Indies made a sound start on the second day, going to lunch at 90 for two. But in the afternoon, unable to settle against the pace and swing of Waqar Younis and Wasim Akram, or the off-spin of Akram Raza, they could manage just 105 more runs as eight wickets fell. Only the last-wicket stand of 33 between Ambrose and Walsh gave West Indies, rather than Pakistan, the first-innings lead. Younis once again finished with five wickets, and in taking his 50th wicket in his tenth Test he reached this landmark faster than any Pakistan bowler before him. Stunned by the West Indian fast men before the close, Pakistan fought back next morning as Malik and Moin, the overnight pair, put on 89. Moin's was the one wicket to fall before lunch, but it was a different story afterwards.

*Man of the Match:* R. B. Richardson.

*Close of play:* First day, Pakistan 170; Second day, Pakistan 38-3 (Salim Malik 16*, Moin Khan 0*).

## Pakistan

| | | | |
|---|---|---|---|
| Saeed Anwar c Best b Ambrose | 0 | – lbw b Bishop | 0 |
| Shoaib Mohammad c Dujon b Bishop | 7 | – b Ambrose | 15 |
| Zahid Fazal run out | 32 | – b Bishop | 5 |
| Javed Miandad c Dujon b Walsh | 7 | – (6) c Dujon b Ambrose | 9 |
| Salim Malik c Richardson b Bishop | 74 | – (4) b Marshall | 71 |
| *Imran Khan lbw b Walsh | 3 | – (7) c Dujon b Marshall | 0 |
| Wasim Akram run out | 4 | – (8) run out | 0 |
| †Moin Khan c Greenidge b Ambrose | 24 | – (5) c Logie b Walsh | 32 |
| Akram Raza b Bishop | 5 | – b Marshall | 0 |
| Mushtaq Ahmed not out | 2 | – not out | 5 |
| Waqar Younis c Dujon b Bishop | 1 | – c Dujon b Marshall | 3 |
| L-b 3, n-b 8 | 11 | L-b 4, n-b 10 | 14 |
| | **170** | | **154** |

1/1 2/15 3/29 4/76 5/91                    1/0 2/10 3/38 4/127 5/145
6/99 7/146 8/157 9/169                    6/146 7/146 8/146 9/146

*Bowling: First Innings*—Bishop 17.2–6–47–4; Ambrose 17–3–47–2; Walsh 10–1–38–2; Marshall 8–1–30–0; Hooper 2–1–5–0. *Second Innings*—Bishop 11–1–53–2; Ambrose 13–5–32–2; Walsh 9–0–32–1; Marshall 4.2–0–24–4; Hooper 3–1–9–0.

## West Indies

| | | | |
|---|---|---|---|
| C. G. Greenidge lbw b Waqar Younis | 12 | – (4) lbw b Wasim Akram | 10 |
| *D. L. Haynes lbw b Akram Raza | 19 | – (1) c Akram Raza b Wasim Akram | 0 |
| R. B. Richardson c Saeed Anwar b Akram Raza | 44 | – not out | 70 |
| C. A. Best c Moin Khan b Waqar Younis | 6 | – (2) b Wasim Akram | 7 |
| C. L. Hooper lbw b Waqar Younis | 5 | – not out | 33 |
| A. L. Logie c Moin Khan b Waqar Younis | 12 | | |
| †P. J. L. Dujon lbw b Wasim Akram | 9 | | |
| M. D. Marshall b Wasim Akram | 20 | | |
| C. E. L. Ambrose b Waqar Younis | 15 | | |
| I. R. Bishop lbw b Wasim Akram | 0 | | |
| C. A. Walsh not out | 14 | | |
| B 9, l-b 19, n-b 11 | 39 | B 4, l-b 2, n-b 4 | 10 |
| | **195** | (3 wkts) | **130** |

1/26 2/78 3/101 4/101 5/108                    1/0 2/11 3/34
6/121 7/143 8/162 9/162

*Bowling: First Innings*—Wasim Akram 17–1–63–3; Waqar Younis 16–3–46–5; Akram Raza 19–4–52–2; Mushtaq Ahmed 4–1–6–0. *Second Innings*—Wasim Akram 12–0–46–3; Waqar Younis 9–2–41–0; Akram Raza 7.2–1–37–0; Mushtaq Ahmed 1–1–0–0.

Umpires: Khizar Hayat and Riazuddin.

## PAKISTAN COMBINED XI v WEST INDIANS

At Sargodha, December 1, 2, 3. Drawn. Toss: Pakistan Combined XI. Greenidge, struggling to make runs on the tour, batted for 4 hours 39 minutes and put on 170 for the third wicket with Lara after Dujon and Richardson had departed within the space of 9 runs. Lara remained unbeaten at the close with 118, scored in 283 minutes with eleven fours, and he hit another five boundaries next morning before being bowled for 139. All out twenty minutes after lunch, the touring team were in a strong position to force a win when they had the Combined XI 57 for five, but a solid sixth-wicket stand of 107 between Aamer Hanif and

Iqbal Sikandar held them up for the rest of the afternoon. The final morning saw the home side struggle to avoid the follow-on, but although they failed in this by 1 run, Richardson preferred to give his team-mates batting practice rather than make the opposition bat again. Greenidge missed out this time, but there was a half-century, including a six and seven fours, for the out-of-touch Dujon.

*Close of play:* First day, West Indians 252-3 (B. C. Lara 118*, C. L. Hooper 18*); Second day, Pakistan Combined XI 164-5 (Aamer Hanif 54*, Iqbal Sikandar 59*).

## West Indians

| | | | |
|---|---|---|---|
| C. G. Greenidge lbw b Amin Lakhani | 76 | – b Naeem Khan | 5 |
| P. J. L. Dujon c Shakeel Ahmed b Naeem Khan | 17 | – c Aamer Hanif b Aamer Sohail | 63 |
| *R. B. Richardson lbw b Athar Laeeq | 8 | – (5) not out | 31 |
| B. C. Lara b Naeem Khan | 139 | – (6) not out | 24 |
| C. L. Hooper lbw b Naeem Khan | 25 | – (4) st Shakeel Ahmed b Iqbal Sikandar | 15 |
| A. L. Logie lbw b Naeem Khan | 6 | – (3) b Amin Lakhani | 32 |
| D. L. Haynes not out | 36 | | |
| †D. Williams c Aamer Hanif b Shahid Saeed | 4 | | |
| R. C. Haynes b Iqbal Sikandar | 20 | | |
| E. A. Moseley b Amin Lakhani | 13 | | |
| I. R. Bishop run out | 0 | | |
| B 8, l-b 12, n-b 3 | 23 | B 2, l-b 11, n-b 2 | 15 |

1/32 2/41 3/211 4/260 5/276      367      1/8 2/49 3/97 4/145      (4 wkts) 185
6/291 7/310 8/342 9/365

*Bowling: First Innings*—Athar Laeeq 11-3-43-1; Naeem Khan 20-5-65-4; Amin Lakhani 35.4-5-77-2; Iqbal Sikandar 40-4-127-1; Shahid Saeed 9-2-22-1; Aamer Sohail 5-0-11-0; Mansoor Rana 3-1-2-0. *Second Innings*—Naeem Khan 6-2-23-1; Athar Laeeq 5-1-19-0; Amin Lakhani 7-0-18-1; Iqbal Sikandar 23-7-60-1; Aamer Sohail 17-2-52-1.

## Pakistan Combined XI

| | | | |
|---|---|---|---|
| Aamer Sohail b Bishop | 7 | Naeem Khan lbw b R. C. Haynes | 23 |
| Shahid Saeed lbw b Moseley | 5 | Amin Lakhani not out | 22 |
| Ghulam Ali b R. C. Haynes | 14 | Athar Laeeq lbw b Moseley | 2 |
| *Mansoor Rana b Moseley | 1 | | |
| Aamer Hanif lbw b Bishop | 56 | B 8, l-b 9, n-b 6 | 23 |
| Shahid Nawaz lbw b R. C. Haynes | 3 | | |
| Iqbal Sikandar c Williams b Bishop | 59 | 1/15 2/39 3/40 4/41 5/57 | 217 |
| †Shakeel Ahmed b Bishop | 2 | 6/164 7/166 8/172 9/204 | |

*Bowling:* Bishop 16-2-59-4; Moseley 20.1-3-57-3; R. C. Haynes 20-4-56-3; Hooper 5-0-28-0.

Umpires: Mohammad Iqbal and Taufiq Khan.

# PAKISTAN v WEST INDIES

## Third Test Match

At Lahore, December 6, 7, 8, 10, 11. Drawn. Toss: West Indies. Imran Khan's fighting, unbeaten 58, and his defiant stand of 67 for the fifth wicket with Masood Anwar, making his Test début, saved Pakistan not only the match but the series. Needing 346 for victory, they were 110 for four on the final morning when Imran joined night-watchman Anwar, and he kept the West Indian bowlers at bay for just over four hours. Anwar, a left-arm spinner, was one of four changes made by Pakistan after their defeat at Faisalabad; Javed Miandad was unable to play because of illness. In the West Indies side, Lara came in for Best, who had a hand injury.

Again the pitch played an unduly significant role, with the cracks widening and the surface breaking up as the match progressed. Thus the toss was a good one for West Indies to win, but they needed a special innings from Hooper to gain from their advantage after Imran Khan, bowling for the first time in the series, had removed the openers, and Wasim Akram had sent back Richardson. Hooper, dropped by Salim Malik at slip off Waqar Younis when 31, finished the day 107 not out, having reached his second Test hundred in 242 minutes, with eight fours and a six. He had added 95 for the fourth wicket with Lara, who batted solidly for 44 in his first Test, and 61 in 56 minutes with Marshall for the seventh wicket.

After a delay of 45 minutes because of heavy dew, West Indies added a further 44 runs on the second morning, and when poor light forced an early finish they had Pakistan 93 for six. That represented a recovery from 48 for five, after Imran, who batted for an hour and a quarter for 17, and Akram had added 45 for the sixth wicket. On the third morning Akram's overnight partner, Moin Khan, was hit on the face by a Bishop bouncer, and he did not keep wicket in West Indies' second innings, the gloves being taken by Aamer Malik. Bishop and Ambrose finished with five wickets each, with Bishop, in his eleventh Test, taking his 50th Test wicket.

A poor start again left West Indies looking to Hooper, and with Logie helping him add 107 for the fifth wicket he secured his side's position. However, Akram swung the course of the game on the final morning by taking the last four wickets in five balls, emulating a feat previously achieved in Test cricket only by M. J. C. Allom and C. M. Old. Dujon and Ambrose went to successive balls, Bishop edged the hat-trick ball just wide of Imran, and the next two deliveries claimed Marshall and Walsh.

Even on a better pitch Pakistan's target would have been a difficult one. They lost Aamer Malik in the first over, but Ramiz Raja and Shoaib Mohammad countered bravely with a stand that was worth 90 when Walsh bowled Ramiz just as the fading light heralded another early finish. Bishop's dismissing Shoaib and Salim Malik on the final morning seemingly opened the way for West Indies to win the series. Instead, Anwar defied them for three hours ten minutes (130 balls), and when Imran and Akram had added 55 in 86 minutes Haynes recognised the inevitability of the draw. Imran's resolve was such that he hit just three boundaries from the 196 deliveries he received.

*Man of the Match:* C. L. Hooper.

*Close of play:* First day, West Indies 250-8 (C. L. Hooper 107*, I. R. Bishop 0*); Second day, Pakistan 93-6 (Wasim Akram 21*, Moin Khan 0*); Third day, West Indies 128-4 (C. L. Hooper 39*, A. L. Logie 43*); Fourth day, Pakistan 90-2 (Shoaib Mohammad 36*, Masood Anwar 0*).

## West Indies

| | | | |
|---|---|---|---|
| C. G. Greenidge lbw b Imran Khan | 21 | – c Zahid Fazal b Waqar Younis | 1 |
| *D. L. Haynes c Moin Khan b Imran Khan | 3 | – c Shoaib Mohammad b Masood Anwar | 12 |
| R. B. Richardson lbw b Wasim Akram | 5 | – c Aamer Malik b Imran Khan | 6 |
| B. C. Lara c Aamer Malik b Abdul Qadir | 44 | – c Salim Malik b Imran Khan | 5 |
| C. L. Hooper c Zahid Fazal b Masood Anwar | 134 | – run out | 49 |
| A. L. Logie lbw b Waqar Younis | 16 | – lbw b Wasim Akram | 59 |
| †P. J. L. Dujon st Moin Khan b Masood Anwar | 0 | – c Moin Khan b Wasim Akram | 3 |
| M. D. Marshall b Wasim Akram | 27 | – b Wasim Akram | 11 |
| C. E. L. Ambrose lbw b Wasim Akram | 0 | – lbw b Wasim Akram | 0 |
| I. R. Bishop c Moin Khan b Wasim Akram | 9 | – not out | 1 |
| C. A. Walsh not out | 5 | – b Wasim Akram | 0 |
| B 8, l-b 12, n-b 10 | 30 | B 14, l-b 4, n-b 8 | 26 |
| | **294** | | **173** |

1/13 2/24 3/37 4/132 5/185       294       1/1 2/13 3/27 4/47 5/154       173
6/186 7/247 8/249 9/278                         6/155 7/172 8/172 9/173

*Bowling: First Innings*—Imran Khan 6-0-22-2; Wasim Akram 24-4-61-4; Waqar Younis 17-0-57-1; Abdul Qadir 18-1-75-1; Masood Anwar 13.5-3-59-2. *Second Innings*—Imran Khan 13-5-32-2; Waqar Younis 8-0-32-1; Masood Anwar 13-1-43-1; Wasim Akram 9-0-28-5; Abdul Qadir 4-0-19-0; Shoaib Mohammad 1-0-1-0.

## Pakistan

| | | |
|---|---|---|
| Aamer Malik b Bishop | 3 | – c Logie b Ambrose 0 |
| Shoaib Mohammad b Bishop | 0 | – (3) b Bishop 49 |
| Zahid Fazal c Haynes b Ambrose | 13 | – (7) b Walsh 6 |
| Ramiz Raja c Logie b Ambrose | 6 | – (2) b Walsh 41 |
| Salim Malik c Greenidge b Bishop | 8 | – b Bishop 0 |
| *Imran Khan c Logie b Ambrose | 17 | – not out 58 |
| Wasim Akram b Ambrose | 38 | – (8) not out 21 |
| †Moin Khan c Logie b Ambrose | 7 | |
| Masood Anwar c Logie b Bishop | 2 | – (4) c Lara b Hooper 37 |
| Abdul Qadir lbw b Bishop | 1 | |
| Waqar Younis not out | 0 | |
| B 4, l-b 12, w 1, n-b 10 | 27 | L-b 4, n-b 26 30 |

1/2 2/11 3/33 4/34 5/48      122      1/0 2/90 3/107 4/110    (6 wkts) 242
6/93 7/108 8/120 9/121                  5/177 6/187

Bowling: *First Innings*—Ambrose 20-5-35-5; Bishop 19.2-7-41-5; Marshall 5-2-8-0; Walsh 5-1-22-0. *Second Innings*—Ambrose 20.4-5-43-1; Bishop 23-6-59-2; Walsh 19-3-53-2; Marshall 19-5-48-0; Hooper 15-4-35-1.

Umpires: Khizar Hayat and Riazuddin.

---

# FUTURE TOURS

At the time of going to press, future tours involving South Africa had not been arranged, other than those shown below, and some of the tours listed here may be subject to change.

| | | | |
|---|---|---|---|
| 1992 | Pakistanis to England | 1993-94 | New Zealanders to Australia |
| | Australians to Sri Lanka | | Indians to Pakistan |
| | | | Sri Lankans to Australia |
| | | | England to West Indies |
| 1992-93 | West Indians to Australia | | Indians to Sri Lanka |
| | New Zealanders to Sri Lanka | | Pakistanis to New Zealand |
| | Pakistanis to Australia | | Australians to Pakistan* |
| | Indians to South Africa* | | |
| | England to India and *Sri Lanka | 1994 | Indians to England* |
| | Australians to New Zealand | | New Zealanders to England* |
| | Pakistanis to West Indies | | |
| | West Indians to Sri Lanka* | 1994-95 | England to Australia |
| | | | West Indians to India* |
| 1993 | Australians to England | | Pakistanis to India |
| | South Africans to Sri Lanka* | | West Indians to New Zealand |
| | | | Australians to West Indies* |

* *Signifies unconfirmed.*

*Note:* The following tours were scheduled for 1991-92: Indians and West Indians to Australia, Sri Lankans to Pakistan, England to New Zealand, and Sri Lankans to India. In addition, South Africa made a short visit to India and the World Cup was staged in Australia and New Zealand.

# THE SRI LANKANS IN INDIA, 1990-91

## By R. MOHAN

After a largely successful tour of the English counties in 1990, the Sri Lankans were keen for international cricket. But they were ill prepared for their single Test on a visit to India which was hastily arranged amid uncertainty about the series proposed for later in the season. For the Indians, it was their first home Test for two years, during which time they had played fourteen Test matches on four overseas trips without a win. Eagerness to register the long-awaited victory was one factor blamed for the under-preparation of the pitch at Chandigarh, the fourteenth Indian city to host a Test, as was the late transfer from the proposed venue of Jullundur. Certainly the pitch was nowhere near standard at the start of the match.

The chief architect of India's win was the 21-year-old orthodox left-arm spinner from Hyderabad, Venkatapathy Raju. His nagging accuracy, genuine spin and even some bounce, on a pitch where the ball kept disturbingly low, brought him figures of six for 12 as Sri Lanka were dismissed for 82, their lowest Test score, and eight for 37 in the match. It was a welcome return for Raju, who had missed most of India's 1990 tour of England after a knuckle on his bowling hand was broken by a ball from Courtney Walsh. Another Indian bowler with cause for celebration was Kapil Dev, who equalled I. T. Botham's return of 376 Test wickets, second only to Sir Richard Hadlee's record 431. Kapil bowled with fire, his spirits rejuvenated by the helpful conditions in his native city. The older version of the Duke ball, with its more pronounced seam, may also have offered him more movement than he could obtain from the nine-strand ball in a whole English summer. On the batting side, India could be grateful to the patience of opener Ravi Shastri, who followed his successes in England with the Test's longest innings, 88 in more than five hours. Ironically, it was the omission of Arun Lal, the opening batsman seeking to make a comeback after a year and a half out of the team, which let in Raju. Originally the selectors had planned to play only two spinners, Narendra Hirwani and Gopal Sharma.

The Sri Lankan batsmen looked woefully out of touch, apart from Asanka Gurusinha, who made a delightful unbeaten 52 in the first innings, though Roshan Mahanama, Arjuna Ranatunga, the captain, and Hashan Tillekeratne suggested what might have been on an improving pitch in the second innings. Five batsmen went without scoring in the first innings, and four in the second, while another was 0 not out. Jayananda Warnaweera and Ranjith Madurasinghe, both off-spinners, enjoyed a fine spell on the first day as three Indian wickets fell for 12 runs, and Rumesh Ratnayake became the third Sri Lankan to take 50 Test wickets when he dismissed Vengsarkar. The players' morale was not lifted by some of the decisions made by the two novice Test umpires – one over-eager to give the batsman out, the other quite the opposite – but in fact none had any material effect on the game.

The one-day series was far more entertaining and better patronised, with the Sri Lankans proving a better match for the Indians in limited-overs cricket. After losing the first two games, they finished an otherwise unsuccessful tour on a winning note, doing well to pull off victory in Margao on a heavily watered pitch that baffled the home batsmen, who unwisely chose to go in first. Conditions were not very different when Sri Lanka batted, but the boldness of de Silva saw them home with more than seventeen overs to spare. Thus honour was restored to a team so anxious to play that they offered to take part in any additional Test or one-day internationals that could be arranged. The Indian Board, however, was unwilling to extend the eleventh-hour exercise.

## SRI LANKAN TOUR RESULTS

*Test match* – Played 1: Lost 1.
*One-day internationals* – Played 3: Won 1, Lost 2.

## INDIA v SRI LANKA

### Test Match

At Chandigarh, November 23, 24, 25, 27. India won by an innings and 8 runs. Toss: India. This was Azharuddin's first win in seven Tests as captain, and he began by winning the toss on a pitch viewed with justified suspicion. With Shastri playing circumspectly early on, when the ball kept low, the first-wicket stand was dominated by Prabhakar, and Manjrekar helped to build on the solid start, batting with assurance and elegance despite the conditions. In the last session, however, India slid from 208 for three to 220 for six. There were poor shots from Azharuddin, Shastri and Kapil Dev, but it was also the well-directed off-spin of Warnaweera and Madurasinghe which wrested the initiative for Sri Lanka. Shastri batted for more than five and a quarter hours and faced 224 balls for his 88, which included five fours and two sixes. Another vital innings, in worsening conditions the next day, came from More, who added 36 with Raju in a brave stand which saw Raju, on his return to Test cricket, the recipient of over-frequent bouncers from Labrooy.

Sri Lanka's joy at keeping India's total under 300 was short-lived, for the appearance of Raju, after sixteen overs, changed the complexion of the match. He spun out the middle order with five wickets for just 2 runs in 39 balls, and the visitors began the third morning needing 14 to avoid the follow-on with two wickets in hand. Their difficulties increased when a deceptively lazy Kapil Dev, at long-off, sent his throw humming over the non-striker's wicket into the hands of Azharuddin to run out Madurasinghe. Five runs later Raju bowled Warnaweera off the inside edge, to return figures of six for 12 from 17.5 overs and dismiss Sri Lanka for 82. Gurusinha was left high and dry after batting for 181 minutes and facing 159 balls.

He was soon in again, but this time he hooked his second ball in the air. Only Mahanama's patience, which brought him 48 runs from 213 deliveries, held Sri Lanka's second innings together. As the pitch improved, Ranatunga looked to repair the reputation of his team's batting, but hopes of making India bat again were effectively dashed when Raju beat him in the air to set up a catch at mid-wicket. The only balm for the visitors was the 60-run partnership between Tillekeratne and Madurasinghe, a ninth-wicket record for Sri Lanka, which denied India for two hours. Tillekeratne completed his first Test fifty, with eight fours, before he was last out, driving a head-high catch to mid-on to give Kapil Dev his 376th Test wicket.

*Man of the Match:* S. L. V. Raju.

*Close of play:* First day, India 220-6 (S. R. Tendulkar 7*, K. S. More 0*); Second day, Sri Lanka 75-8 (A. P. Gurusinha 47*, A. W. R. Madurasinghe 0*); Third day, Sri Lanka 125-5 (A. Ranatunga 36*, H. P. Tillekeratne 11*).

## India

| | | | |
|---|---|---|---|
| R. J. Shastri c de Silva b Warnaweera . | 88 | †K. S. More not out | 37 |
| M. Prabhakar lbw b Warnaweera | 31 | S. L. V. Raju lbw b Ratnayake | 14 |
| S. V. Manjrekar lbw b Madurasinghe . | 39 | Gopal Sharma lbw b Ratnayake | 0 |
| D. B. Vengsarkar lbw b Ratnayake | 7 | N. D. Hirwani run out | 0 |
| *M. Azharuddin c Labrooy | | B 5, l-b 10, n-b 19 | 34 |
| b Madurasinghe . | 23 | | |
| S. R. Tendulkar lbw b Madurasinghe . | 11 | 1/58 2/134 3/158 4/208 5/210 | 288 |
| Kapil Dev c de Silva b Warnaweera | 4 | 6/220 7/240 8/276 9/276 | |

Bowling: Ratnayake 21.5–3–60–3; Labrooy 12–1–59–0; Warnaweera 46–17–90–3; Ranatunga 5–2–4–0; Madurasinghe 26–6–60–3.

## Sri Lanka

| | | | |
|---|---|---|---|
| R. S. Mahanama c More b Kapil Dev | 1 | – c More b Kapil Dev | 48 |
| M. A. R. Samarasekera lbw b Prabhakar | 13 | – c More b Prabhakar | 5 |
| A. P. Gurusinha not out | 52 | – c G. Sharma b Prabhakar | 0 |
| P. A. de Silva b Raju | 5 | – lbw b Hirwani | 7 |
| *A. Ranatunga b Raju | 1 | – c Azharuddin b Raju | 42 |
| †H. P. Tillekeratne b Raju | 0 | – (7) c Shastri b Kapil Dev | 55 |
| M. S. Atapattu c More b Raju | 0 | – (6) lbw b Kapil Dev | 0 |
| R. J. Ratnayake b Raju | 0 | – lbw b Raju | 0 |
| G. F. Labrooy b G. Sharma | 0 | – b Kapil Dev | 0 |
| A. W. R. Madurasinghe run out | 2 | – b Prabhakar | 11 |
| K. P. J. Warnaweera b Raju | 0 | – not out | 0 |
| B 1, l-b 2, n-b 5 | 8 | B 5, l-b 15, n-b 10 | 30 |
| | | | |
| 1/4 2/34 3/50 4/54 5/54 | 82 | 1/14 2/14 3/47 4/110 5/110 | 198 |
| 6/54 7/60 8/65 9/77 | | 6/135 7/135 8/136 9/196 | |

Bowling: *First Innings*—Kapil Dev 8–3–14–1; Prabhakar 9–0–27–1; Raju 17.5–13–12–6; G. Sharma 17–5–26–1. *Second Innings*—Kapil Dev 29.4–15–36–4; Prabhakar 15–4–44–3; G. Sharma 20–7–39–0; Raju 36–25–25–2; Hirwani 20–9–34–1.

Umpires: S. B. Kulkarni and R. S. Rathore.

## †INDIA v SRI LANKA

### First One-day International

At Nagpur, December 1. India won by 19 runs. Toss: Sri Lanka. India's victory was built on a solid opening partnership of 133, after impressive seam bowling from the Sri Lankans had restricted Shastri and Sidhu to 67 from the first 25 overs. They almost doubled that score in the next five overs of spin, and Tendulkar enlivened proceedings with a 22-ball 36 (three fours and two sixes, both off Labrooy). As the innings closed Shastri reached his hundred, which had taken 147 balls and included twelve fours and a six. Sri Lanka's run-chase centred around the brilliance of de Silva. After early setbacks, when three batsmen fell for 21 runs, his stand of 94 with Tillekeratne looked like putting the match in the balance. However, the rising run-rate proved too much for him, and he was out soon after completing his maiden century in one-day internationals, from 118 balls.

*Man of the Match*: R. J. Shastri.

## India

| | | | |
|---|---|---|---|
| R. J. Shastri not out | 101 | Kapil Dev c Mahanama b Labrooy | 7 |
| N. S. Sidhu lbw b Ratnayake | 52 | V. Razdan not out | 4 |
| S. V. Manjrekar c Tillekeratne | | L-b 9, w 5, n-b 15 | 29 |
| b Wijegunawardene . | 14 | | |
| *M. Azharuddin b Gurusinha | 2 | 1/133 2/164 3/177 (5 wkts, 45 overs) 245 | |
| S. R. Tendulkar b Ratnayake | 36 | 4/224 5/235 | |

M. Prabhakar, †K. S. More, Arshad Ayub and A. Kumble did not bat.

Bowling: Ratnayake 10–0–36–2; Labrooy 10–1–58–1; Wijegunawardene 8–0–49–1; Ranatunga 8–0–36–0; Madurasinghe 3–0–29–0; Gurusinha 6–0–28–1.

## Sri Lanka

| | | | | |
|---|---|---|---|---|
| R. S. Mahanama c More b Prabhakar . | 4 | G. F. Labrooy c More b Prabhakar.... | 0 |
| M. A. R. Samarasekera | | M. S. Atapattu not out ............. | 8 |
| lbw b Kapil Dev . | 0 | | |
| A. P. Gurusinha b Prabhakar........ | 6 | L-b 11, w 4, n-b 3......... | 18 |
| P. A. de Silva c Razdan b Kapil Dev ..104 | | | |
| *A. Ranatunga run out ............. | 14 | 1/1 2/11 3/21 | (7 wkts, 45 overs) 226 |
| †H. P. Tillekeratne c Razdan b Shastri . | 39 | 4/61 5/155 | |
| R. J. Ratnayake not out ........... | 33 | 6/204 7/208 | |

K. I. W. Wijegunawardene and A. W. R. Madurasinghe did not bat.

Bowling: Kapil Dev 10–1–46–2; Prabhakar 10–1–47–3; Kumble 10–0–35–0; Razdan 4–0–31–0; Arshad Ayub 8–0–43–0; Shastri 3–0–13–1.

Umpires: S. Banerjee and S. K. Bansal.

## †INDIA v SRI LANKA

### Second One-day International

At Pune, December 5. India won by six wickets. Toss: India. The Indians changed their strategy, putting their visitors in to exploit the early damp conditions, and Sri Lanka's slow progress seemed to vindicate the decision, until the left-handers, Gurusinha and Arjuna Ranatunga, pushed the score along in a stand of 97. The turning-point was Tendulkar's misfield and subsequent throw from long-on to run out Ranatunga. He had already dismissed the two openers with his gentle medium pace, and he added two catches as Sri Lanka had to settle for a total of 227. India's reply began with a well-paced stand of 76, but when the openers went, Manjrekar and Azharuddin were pegged down by spin. Again it was Tendulkar who tilted the scales: he hit 53 from 40 balls, with seven fours and a six. Azharuddin had the satisfaction of striking the winning runs as India registered their second one-day series triumph under his captaincy.

*Man of the Match:* S. R. Tendulkar.

## Sri Lanka

| | | | | |
|---|---|---|---|---|
| R. S. Mahanama c More b Tendulkar .. | 24 | †H. P. Tillekeratne not out........... | 13 |
| D. Ranatunga b Tendulkar........... | 25 | G. F. Labrooy c Kumble | |
| A. P. Gurusinha c Tendulkar | | b Arshad Ayub . | 21 |
| b Prabhakar . | 44 | S. D. Anurasiri not out ........... | 6 |
| P. A. de Silva c Shastri b Wassan .... | 1 | L-b 10, w 16, n-b 8.......... | 34 |
| *A. Ranatunga run out ............. | 58 | | |
| R. J. Ratnayake c Tendulkar | | 1/52 2/77 3/80 | (8 wkts, 49 overs) 227 |
| b Arshad Ayub . | 1 | 4/177 5/178 6/179 | |
| M. S. Atapattu run out ............. | 0 | 7/180 8/214 | |

K. I. W. Wijegunawardene did not bat.

Bowling: Kapil Dev 7–1–15–0; Prabhakar 9–0–45–1; Tendulkar 9–0–39–2; Wassan 10–0–29–1; Kumble 6–0–51–0; Arshad Ayub 8–1–38–2.

## India

| | | | | |
|---|---|---|---|---|
| R. J. Shastri c Labrooy b Anurasiri ... | 53 | Kapil Dev not out ................ | 0 |
| N. S. Sidhu b Anurasiri ........... | 38 | | |
| S. V. Manjrekar c Wijegunawardene | | L-b 1, w 6, n-b 4........... | 11 |
| b Labrooy . | 23 | | |
| *M. Azharuddin not out ........... | 52 | 1/76 2/108 3/146 | (4 wkts, 45.3 overs) 230 |
| S. R. Tendulkar b Labrooy ........... | 53 | 4/226 | |

M. Prabhakar, †K. S. More, Arshad Ayub, A. Kumble and A. S. Wassan did not bat.

Bowling: Ratnayake 9–1–43–0; Labrooy 9–0–50–2; Wijegunawardene 10–1–56–0; Anurasiri 10–0–44–2; A. Ranatunga 7–0–32–0; Atapattu 0.3–0–4–0.

Umpires: N. Dutta and S. T. Sambandam.

## †INDIA v SRI LANKA

### Third One-day International

At Margao, December 8. Sri Lanka won by seven wickets. Toss: India. The home team paid the penalty for their decision, based on the premise that the pitch would deteriorate, to bat first. The ball tended to leap, especially from the spinners, but there were not as many devils in the pitch as the Indian batsmen suggested in their higgledy-piggledy innings. Ramanayake bowled a tight line at medium pace to pick up the first three wickets, and Anurasiri and Warnaweera, with contrasting spin, sent the others sliding to a poor total of 136, with nearly ten overs unused. India's hopes of making a fight of it, when Sri Lanka's openers went cheaply, were dispelled by de Silva, who waited for the loose ball to drive, cut or pull. His captain, Arjuna Ranatunga, was the ideal foil, and their unbroken stand of 82 made a telling contrast with the Indians' surrender to their apprehensions about the pitch. De Silva struck eleven fours and scored 63 in 76 balls, steering his team to Sri Lanka's second one-day international victory in India.

*Man of the Match*: P. A. de Silva.

### India

| | | | |
|---|---|---|---|
| R. J. Shastri c Gurusinha b Ramanayake | 12 | †K. S. More c Kaluwitharana | |
| N. S. Sidhu b Ramanayake | 0 | b Warnaweera | 6 |
| S. V. Manjrekar c Mahanama | | Arshad Ayub c D. Ranatunga b de Silva | 6 |
| b Ramanayake | 14 | A. Kumble lbw b Ratnayake | 0 |
| *M. Azharuddin c Mahanama | | A. S. Wassan b Ratnayake | 0 |
| b Anurasiri | 20 | B 5, l-b 5, w 6, n-b 3 | 19 |
| S. R. Tendulkar c and b Anurasiri | 30 | | |
| Kapil Dev c Tillekeratne b Warnaweera | 9 | 1/0 2/27 3/40 4/69 5/94 (40.3 overs) | 136 |
| M. Prabhakar not out | 23 | 6/106 7/119 8/132 9/134 | |

Bowling: Ratnayake 6.3-3-17-2; Ramanayake 7-3-15-3; A. Ranatunga 4-0-22-0; Anurasiri 10-1-39-2; Warnaweera 10-1-24-2; de Silva 3-0-9-1.

### Sri Lanka

| | | | |
|---|---|---|---|
| R. S. Mahanama lbw b Kumble | 8 | *A. Ranatunga not out | 30 |
| D. Ranatunga c and b Kapil Dev | 5 | | |
| A. P. Gurusinha c Azharuddin | | L-b 5, w 4, n-b 3 | 12 |
| b Arshad Ayub | 19 | | |
| P. A. de Silva not out | 63 | 1/10 2/24 3/55 (3 wkts, 32.5 overs) | 137 |

†R. S. Kaluwitharana, H. P. Tillekeratne, R. J. Ratnayake, S. D. Anurasiri, C. P. H. Ramanayake and K. P. J. Warnaweera did not bat.

Bowling: Kapil Dev 4-0-15-1; Prabhakar 5-1-15-0; Kumble 10-1-41-1; Arshad Ayub 8.5-3-34-1; Shastri 3-0-16-0; Wassan 2-0-11-0.

Umpires: R. A. Jamula and C. R. Vijayaraghavan.

# THE SRI LANKANS IN NEW ZEALAND, 1990-91

By DICK BRITTENDEN

The Sri Lankans arrived in New Zealand for their second tour – the first was in 1982-83 – with no great reputation, and Martin Crowe, the New Zealand captain, predicted a 3-0 win for his team. In the event, all three Tests were drawn, and Sri Lanka had the upper hand in at least two of them. New Zealand had to be satisfied by their twelfth consecutive season without losing a Test rubber at home, though they won all three one-day internationals easily.

The cricket was never dull. The retirement of Sir Richard Hadlee, Ewen Chatfield and John Bracewell had undeniably weakened the New Zealand attack, but the Sri Lankans won many admirers for their attacking batting and their friendliness towards crowds and opponents. Aravinda de Silva, dubbed "Quicksilver" by the crowds, had remarkable success. His 267 in the First Test at Wellington was a record for Sri Lanka, and the power of his hooking brought him runs at a very brisk rate. He was dismissed twice in the Hamilton Test attempting to hook within minutes of his arrival, but when New Zealand tried to bounce him out in Auckland, he scored 96 and 123. While the hook was his most powerful weapon, his square cut and cover drive were also perfectly timed. The most consistent batsman was Asanka Gurusinha, who played in every match and was the leading run-scorer on the tour. With every stroke at his command, he steadied the side regularly. However, all the batsmen had more than a measure of success – Chandika Hathurusinghe scored 191 runs in his first two Tests – even if they were left in the shadows by the explosive power of Graeme Labrooy at Auckland, where he reached 50 in thirteen scoring strokes, a Test record, without the aid of a single.

The Sri Lankan bowling was average, though Labrooy and Rumesh Ratnayake, the only survivor of the previous tour, had their moments. Labrooy was a man of moods. He took only seventeen first-class wickets, but thirteen of those were in the Tests; he bowled with accuracy and persistence into a howling wind at Wellington, and he had match figures of seven for 90 at Auckland. Arjuna Ranatunga, the captain, was a useful all-rounder, although his Test performances suffered from his being handicapped by injury. The team lacked a penetrative spinner: Asoka de Silva bowled his minimal leg-breaks tidily, but his four Test wickets cost nearly 100 runs apiece. The fielding, lack-lustre at first, improved steadily, with Sanath Jayasuriya an athletic outfielder.

New Zealand's bowling was far from impressive, until Chris Cairns returned for the final Test, after sixteen months' absence with a back injury. If, like the other fast-medium bowlers, he was guilty of too many loose deliveries, and tended to invite the hook, his splendid action suggested a Test bowler in the making. Willie Watson was steady, but Danny Morrison showed the effects of a strenuous summer. After his successes in Pakistan and Australia, Chris Pringle was dropped for the Third Test, suffering from fatigue, which was hardly surprising when the team had to play international cricket from October to March. With the departure of Bracewell and Stephen Boock, New Zealand also lacked quality spin bowling.

Their batting prospered, however, with Andrew Jones, a master of the unorthodox, scoring three successive hundreds, including two in the Hamilton Test, and an aggregate of 513 runs, a record for a New Zealander in a home series. Martin Crowe's 299 at Wellington was another New Zealand Test record, and in that match he and Jones shared a third-wicket partnership of 467, the highest for any wicket in a Test match. Crowe is very much a stylist; Jones is not. But their combined talents shredded Sri Lanka's first-innings lead of 323 into the wastepaper-basket. Crowe made his thirteenth Test hundred in commanding style, and Jones unleashed some fluent cover drives off either foot. They provided the bulk of a total of 671 for four, a record for their country, and also beat New Zealand's first-class record stand of 445 between W. N. Carson and P. E. Whitelaw for Auckland against Otago in 1936-37. John Wright contributed generously throughout the series, and Shane Thomson delighted spectators with his polished batting in the last two Tests.

It was a pity that so enjoyable a visit ended in controversy, not in New Zealand but in Colombo. A Sri Lankan newspaper report said that the manager, Stanley Jayasinghe, had alleged that Ranatunga and the assistant-manager, Jayantha Paranathala, had displayed "haughty" attitudes and "double standards". The trouble appeared to stem from the manager's decision to send home the injured opener, Dammika Ranatunga, the captain's elder brother, and it was to result in Ranatunga's losing the captaincy and missing the tour of England later in the year.

## SRI LANKAN TOUR RESULTS

*Test matches* – Played 3: Drawn 3.
*First-class matches* – Played 7: Won 1, Drawn 6.
*Win* – Central Districts.
*Draws* – New Zealand (3), Emerging Players, Wellington, Canterbury.
*One-day internationals* – Played 3: Lost 3.

## TEST MATCH AVERAGES

## NEW ZEALAND – BATTING

|  | T | I | NO | R | HI | 100s | Avge |
|---|---|---|---|---|---|---|---|
| M. D. Crowe .......... | 2 | 3 | 0 | 365 | 299 | 1 | 121.66 |
| A. H. Jones............ | 3 | 6 | 1 | 513 | 186 | 3 | 102.60 |
| S. A. Thomson ........ | 2 | 4 | 1 | 172 | 80* | 0 | 57.33 |
| J. G. Wright .......... | 3 | 6 | 0 | 329 | 101 | 1 | 54.83 |
| D. N. Patel ........... | 2 | 4 | 2 | 92 | 41 | 0 | 46.00 |
| M. J. Greatbatch ...... | 2 | 4 | 1 | 99 | 65 | 0 | 33.00 |
| T. J. Franklin ........ | 3 | 6 | 0 | 170 | 69 | 0 | 28.33 |
| W. Watson ........... | 3 | 3 | 2 | 19 | 10* | 0 | 19.00 |
| I. D. S. Smith ........ | 3 | 4 | 1 | 44 | 28 | 0 | 14.66 |
| K. R. Rutherford ...... | 3 | 5 | 0 | 52 | 25 | 0 | 10.40 |
| D. K. Morrison ....... | 3 | 4 | 0 | 20 | 13 | 0 | 5.00 |

Played in two Tests: C. Pringle 0, 9. Played in one Test: G. E. Bradburn 14; C. L. Cairns 17.

\* *Signifies not out.*

## BOWLING

| | O | M | R | W | BB | 5W/i | Avge |
|---|---|---|---|---|---|---|---|
| C. L. Cairns ...... | 59 | 11 | 211 | 9 | 5-75 | 1 | 23.44 |
| S. A. Thomson .... | 45.1 | 15 | 113 | 4 | 3-63 | 0 | 28.25 |
| W. Watson ....... | 150.4 | 38 | 365 | 12 | 4-121 | 0 | 30.41 |
| D. K. Morrison ... | 136 | 23 | 476 | 13 | 5-153 | 1 | 36.61 |
| D. N. Patel ....... | 85 | 25 | 238 | 4 | 2-90 | 0 | 59.50 |

Also bowled: G. E. Bradburn 26-5-83-0; A. H. Jones 6-1-21-0; C. Pringle 63-11-226-2; K. R. Rutherford 2-0-11-0.

## SRI LANKA – BATTING

| | T | I | NO | R | HI | 100s | Avge |
|---|---|---|---|---|---|---|---|
| P. A. de Silva .......... | 3 | 5 | 0 | 493 | 267 | 2 | 98.60 |
| A. P. Gurusinha ........ | 3 | 5 | 0 | 370 | 119 | 2 | 74.00 |
| U. C. Hathurusinghe .... | 2 | 4 | 0 | 191 | 81 | 0 | 47.75 |
| A. Ranatunga ......... | 3 | 5 | 1 | 160 | 55 | 0 | 40.00 |
| S. T. Jayasuriya ........ | 3 | 3 | 1 | 65 | 35 | 0 | 32.50 |
| G. F. Labrooy ......... | 3 | 4 | 1 | 77 | 70* | 0 | 25.66 |
| R. J. Ratnayake ........ | 3 | 4 | 1 | 65 | 26 | 0 | 21.66 |
| C. P. Senanayake ....... | 3 | 5 | 0 | 97 | 64 | 0 | 19.40 |
| H. P. Tillekeratne ...... | 3 | 5 | 0 | 93 | 31 | 0 | 18.60 |
| E. A. R. de Silva ....... | 3 | 5 | 1 | 39 | 26 | 0 | 9.75 |
| C. P. H. Ramanayake ... | 3 | 5 | 1 | 39 | 14* | 0 | 9.75 |

Played in one Test: K. P. J. Warnaweera 3; R. S. Mahanama did not bat.

*\* Signifies not out.*

## BOWLING

| | O | M | R | W | BB | 5W/i | Avge |
|---|---|---|---|---|---|---|---|
| G. F. Labrooy ......... | 131.3 | 26 | 357 | 13 | 4-42 | 0 | 27.46 |
| R. J. Ratnayake ........ | 160 | 27 | 420 | 13 | 5-77 | 1 | 32.30 |
| C. P. H. Ramanayake ... | 149 | 33 | 468 | 11 | 2-39 | 0 | 42.54 |
| E. A. R. de Silva ....... | 148 | 34 | 393 | 4 | 2-67 | 0 | 98.25 |

Also bowled: P. A. de Silva 10-0-73-0; A. P. Gurusinha 33.2-7-80-1; U. C. Hathurusinghe 2-0-15-0; S. T. Jayasuriya 6-1-18-0; A. Ranatunga 40.1-6-117-3; K. P. J. Warnaweera 40-9-89-0.

## SRI LANKAN TOUR AVERAGES – FIRST-CLASS MATCHES

### BATTING

| | M | I | NO | R | HI | 100s | Avge |
|---|---|---|---|---|---|---|---|
| P. A. de Silva ......... | 6 | 9 | 0 | 709 | 267 | 3 | 78.77 |
| A. P. Gurusinha ....... | 7 | 10 | 0 | 713 | 121 | 3 | 71.30 |
| U. C. Hathurusinghe ... | 4 | 6 | 0 | 257 | 81 | 0 | 42.83 |
| A. Ranatunga ......... | 6 | 8 | 1 | 229 | 55 | 0 | 32.71 |
| G. F. Labrooy ......... | 6 | 6 | 1 | 146 | 70* | 0 | 29.20 |
| S. T. Jayasuriya ....... | 6 | 8 | 2 | 173 | 42* | 0 | 28.83 |
| C. P. H. Ramanayake .. | 6 | 8 | 3 | 130 | 67 | 0 | 26.00 |
| H. P. Tillekeratne ...... | 7 | 8 | 0 | 182 | 48 | 0 | 22.75 |
| C. P. Senanayake ...... | 6 | 9 | 0 | 198 | 64 | 0 | 22.00 |
| R. J. Ratnayake ....... | 3 | 4 | 1 | 65 | 26 | 0 | 21.66 |
| E. A. R. de Silva ...... | 6 | 8 | 1 | 73 | 26 | 0 | 10.42 |

Played in three matches: R. S. Mahanama 35, 22; K. P. J. Warnaweera 3, 4*, 1; K. I. W. Wijegunawardene 0*, 7, 5*. Played in two matches: R. S. Kaluwitharana 9, 61*, 62; A. W. R. Madurasinghe 0*, 29. Played in one match: D. Ranatunga 0*.

*\* Signifies not out.*

## BOWLING

|  | O | M | R | W | BB | 5W/i | Avge |
|---|---|---|---|---|---|---|---|
| A. W. R. Madurasinghe ...... | 77 | 17 | 190 | 7 | 3-68 | 0 | 27.14 |
| A. Ranatunga ............ | 63.1 | 14 | 167 | 6 | 2-33 | 0 | 27.83 |
| K. I. W. Wijegunawardene ... | 98.1 | 8 | 285 | 9 | 5-65 | 1 | 31.66 |
| R. J. Ratnayake ........... | 160 | 27 | 420 | 13 | 5-77 | 1 | 32.30 |
| G. F. Labrooy ............ | 213.3 | 52 | 566 | 17 | 4-42 | 0 | 33.29 |
| A. P. Gurusinha .......... | 79.2 | 16 | 211 | 6 | 2-25 | 0 | 35.16 |
| C. P. H. Ramanayake ...... | 229.5 | 44 | 730 | 20 | 6-79 | 1 | 36.50 |
| E. A. R. de Silva .......... | 245 | 62 | 600 | 10 | 2-46 | 0 | 60.00 |
| K. P. J. Warnaweera ....... | 110 | 31 | 254 | 4 | 3-68 | 0 | 63.50 |

Also bowled: P. A. de Silva 17.2–1–94–0; U. C. Hathurusinghe 24–5–71–0; S. T. Jayasuriya 27–7–82–1; H. P. Tillekeratne 2–0–7–0.

## FIELDING

20 – H. P. Tillekeratne (19 ct, 1 st); 5 – A. P. Gurusinha, U. C. Hathurusinghe; 4 – P. A. de Silva, A. W. R. Madurasinghe; 3 – R. S. Kaluwitharana (2 ct, 1 st), R. S. Mahanama, C. P. Senanayake, Substitutes (S. T. Jayasuriya, G. F. Labrooy, A. W. R. Madurasinghe); 2 – S. T. Jayasuriya, G. F. Labrooy, K. I. W. Wijegunawardene, A. Ranatunga; 1 – E. A. R. de Silva, C. P. H. Ramanayake, R. J. Ratnayake.

## EMERGING PLAYERS v SRI LANKANS

At Palmerston North, January 17, 18, 19. Drawn. Toss: Emerging Players. The Sri Lankans came close to winning their first match, but the Emerging Players, mostly drawn from the provincial second elevens, performed creditably. Hunt declared on the second morning, after the first day was shortened by rain, and the tourists met his challenge emphatically. In their first over, however, Dammika Ranatunga was struck on his right thumb by probably the fastest bowler in New Zealand, the raw but promising Furlong. A hairline fracture ended the opener's tour. The Sri Lankan batsmen counter-attacked with a fine fury, and Aravinda de Silva and Gurusinha took 54 off four Furlong overs after lunch. In a partnership of 173, there was a clear warning to New Zealand bowlers that anything off line or length would be punished.

De Silva reached 100 in 71 balls and 94 minutes, and hit 24 fours and three sixes in all, while Gurusinha's 79 included thirteen boundaries. Declaring 152 ahead, the Sri Lankans had their opponents 163 for eight, but Furlong and Gale held out until the end. Parore, who toured England and Pakistan in 1990, batted well, and the medium-pace bowling of Gale and slow left-arm spin of Kember made a good impression.

*Close of play:* First day, Emerging Players 169-6 (A. C. Parore 9*, J. B. M. Furlong 1*); Second day, Sri Lankans 354-7 (E. A. R. de Silva 15*).

## Emerging Players

| | | | |
|---|---|---|---|
| M. J. Clark c Mahanama b A. Ranatunga ..... | 21 | – c Gurusinha b Ramanayake .... | 4 |
| C. D. Ingham lbw b Labrooy ................ | 0 | – lbw b E. A. R. de Silva ........ | 51 |
| R. J. McLeod c Gurusinha b E. A. R. de Silva | 73 | – c Jayasuriya b Madurasinghe ... | 21 |
| M. R. Pringle c Tillekeratne b A. Ranatunga .. | 2 | – c and b Madurasinghe ........ | 29 |
| S. W. J. Wilson b E. A. R. de Silva ......... | 30 | – c E. A. R. de Silva b Madurasinghe . | 3 |
| *A. J. Hunt c Mahanama b Ramanayake ..... | 25 | – run out ..................... | 5 |
| †A. C. Parore not out ...................... | 39 | – c Labrooy b Jayasuriya ........ | 36 |
| J. B. M. Furlong not out ................... | 8 | – not out ..................... | 50 |
| E. J. Marshall (did not bat) ............... | | – c Tillekeratne b Labrooy ...... | 0 |
| A. J. Gale (did not bat) ................... | | – not out ..................... | 14 |
| B 4, l-b 5, n-b 6 ................... | 15 | L-b 4, n-b 3 ........... | 7 |

1/6 2/26 3/30 4/113     (6 wkts dec.) 213    1/5 2/56 3/99 4/113    (8 wkts) 220
5/154 6/158                         5/113 6/130
                                      7/163 8/163

H. J. Kember did not bat.

Bowling: *First Innings*—Labrooy 20–8–33–1; Ramanayake 22–4–61–1; A. Ranatunga 16–6–33–2; E. A. R. de Silva 21–4–46–2; Madurasinghe 13–3–31–0. *Second Innings*—Labrooy 16–4–33–1; Ramanayake 7–0–33–1; E. A. R. de Silva 27–7–50–1; Madurasinghe 29–6–68–3; Jayasuriya 9–3–26–1; P. A. de Silva 0.2–0–6–0.

## Sri Lankans

| | | | | |
|---|---|---|---|---|
| D. Ranatunga retired hurt | 0 | G. F. Labrooy st Parore b Kember | 17 |
| †H. P. Tillekeratne b Gale | 4 | C. P. H. Ramanayake not out | 5 |
| A. P. Gurusinha c Clark b Kember | 79 | A. W. R. Madurasinghe not out | 0 |
| P. A. de Silva c Clark b Marshall | 174 | L-b 7, w 1, n-b 8 | 16 |
| *A. Ranatunga c Marshall b Hunt | 14 | | |
| R. S. Mahanama c Kember b Gale | 35 | 1/23 2/196 3/239 | (8 wkts dec.) 365 |
| S. T. Jayasuriya run out | 1 | 4/312 5/316 6/325 | |
| E. A. R. de Silva b Kember | 20 | 7/354 8/365 | |

*D. Ranatunga retired hurt at 0.*

Bowling: Furlong 16–1–90–0; Marshall 14–5–48–1; Gale 21–3–88–2; Kember 18–6–60–3; Hunt 14–1–71–1; Pringle 1–0–1–0.

Umpires: B. L. Aldridge and R. W. Hutchison.

## WELLINGTON v SRI LANKANS

At Wellington, January 21, 22, 23, 24. Drawn. Toss: Sri Lankans. Only 100 minutes were possible on the first day, and the fourth was washed out, but the midsummer weather of the second was graced by Crowe's 57th first-class hundred. In an innings of four and a quarter hours, he hit fourteen fours and faced 174 balls. The rest of the Wellington batting was less pleasing, however, with Larsen lucky to reach 50. Ramanayake took six wickets in nearly 25 overs of persistent fast-medium bowling in uncomfortable heat. The Sri Lankans declared on the third evening, still 55 behind, after a day of spendthrift batting. Their extravagance reduced them to 116 for seven – Aravinda de Silva may have batted for half an hour (21 balls), but his 14 consisted of two fours and a six – and it was left to Labrooy and Tillekeratne to restore some order with a determined eighth-wicket stand of 81. Wellington began their second innings safely in what became the final session.

*Close of play:* First day, Wellington 59-1 (E. B. McSweeney 29*, M. D. Crowe 19*); Second day, Sri Lankans 30-1 (R. S. Mahanama 9*, E. A. R. de Silva 0*); Third day, Wellington 46-0 (G. P. Burnett 22*, J. D. Wells 16*).

## Wellington

| | | | | |
|---|---|---|---|---|
| *†E. B. McSweeney c Mahanama b Ramanayake | 36 | | |
| G. P. Burnett lbw b Ramanayake | 2 | – (1) not out | 22 |
| M. D. Crowe c Wijegunawardene b E. A. R. de Silva | 101 | | |
| A. H. Jones c Tillekeratne b Gurusinha | 17 | | |
| R. H. Vance b Ramanayake | 14 | | |
| G. R. Larsen c P. A. de Silva b Ramanayake | 57 | | |
| J. D. Wells b Labrooy | 5 | – (2) not out | 16 |
| B. R. Williams c Ramanayake b Wijegunawardene | 29 | | |
| L. J. Doull c Senanayake b Ramanayake | 2 | | |
| G. J. Mackenzie lbw b Ramanayake | 2 | | |
| P. W. O'Rourke not out | 1 | | |
| B 3, l-b 13, w 1, n-b 12 | 29 | L-b 5, n-b 3 | 8 |

| | | |
|---|---|---|
| 1/10 2/86 3/126 4/176 5/196 | 295 | (no wkt) 46 |
| 6/207 7/277 8/289 9/294 | | |

Bowling: *First Innings*—Labrooy 20–10–51–1; Ramanayake 24.5–5–79–6; Wijegunawardene 17–1–52–1; Ranatunga 3–1–5–0; Gurusinha 6–0–29–1; E. A. R. de Silva 21–8–44–1; Jayasuriya 5–1–19–0. *Second Innings*—Labrooy 3–1–9–0; Ramanayake 7–0–22–0; Wijegunawardene 4–1–10–0.

## Sri Lankans

| | | | | |
|---|---|---|---|---|
| R. S. Mahanama b O'Rourke | ....... 22 | | G. F. Labrooy c and b Doull | ......... 52 |
| C. P. Senanayake b O'Rourke | ........ 20 | | C. P. H. Ramanayake not out | ........ 19 |
| E. A. R. de Silva c McSweeney | | | K. I. W. Wijegunawardene not out | .... 0 |
| | b O'Rourke . 10 | | | |
| A. P. Gurusinha run out | ............. 20 | | L-b 9, n-b 5 | .............. 14 |
| P. A. de Silva c Vance b Mackenzie | ... 14 | | | |
| *A. Ranatunga c Jones b Mackenzie | .. 12 | | 1/29 2/48 3/61 | (9 wkts dec.) 240 |
| †H. P. Tillekeratne c Jones b Larsen | .. 48 | | 4/84 5/100 6/104 | |
| S. T. Jayasuriya b Mackenzie | ..... 9 | | 7/116 8/197 9/240 | |

Bowling: O'Rourke 21–6–59–3; Mackenzie 25–6–80–3; Doull 10–2–33–1; Larsen 9–3–24–1; Williams 13–3–35–0; Jones 1–1–0–0.

Umpires: G. I. J. Cowan and S. J. Woodward.

## †NEW ZEALAND v SRI LANKA

### First One-day International

At Napier, January 26. New Zealand won by five wickets. Toss: New Zealand. The Sri Lankans lost their way after being sent in on a pitch mildly helpful to the bowlers, and with recent rain having made the outfield slow. Five batsmen attained 20, but none could go on to a significant score: Senanayake was briefly competitive and later Labrooy hit 22 off 29 balls, with a six his only boundary. New Zealand's fielding was first-rate, almost unrecognisable from some of their performances in Australia at the start of the season. The home team had a simple task, and Wright made it simpler by scoring 64 from 113 balls. The tourists did themselves no service by bowling sixteen wides in 42.3 overs.

*Man of the Match*: J. G. Wright.

### Sri Lanka

| | | | | |
|---|---|---|---|---|
| C. P. Senanayake c Smith b Watson | ... 26 | | G. F. Labrooy not out | .............. 22 |
| †H. P. Tillekeratne b Larsen | ......... 26 | | R. J. Ratnayake not out | ......... 3 |
| A. P. Gurusinha run out | .............. 28 | | | |
| P. A. de Silva b Larsen | ............. 6 | | B 1, l-b 10, w 7 | ............ 18 |
| *A. Ranatunga b Pringle | ............. 29 | | | |
| R. S. Mahanama b Harris | ............ 8 | | 1/41 2/87 3/96 | (8 wkts, 50 overs) 177 |
| S. T. Jayasuriya run out | ............. 29 | | 4/99 5/114 6/114 | |
| E. A. R. de Silva c Reid b Pringle | .... 11 | | 7/131 8/171 | |

C. P. H. Ramanayake did not bat.

Bowling: Pringle 10–0–44–2; Watson 10–0–31–1; Morrison 10–0–30–0; Larsen 10–3–25–2; Harris 10–0–36–1.

### New Zealand

| | | | | |
|---|---|---|---|---|
| R. B. Reid c Gurusinha b Ratnayake | .. 19 | | M. J. Greatbatch not out | ......... 29 |
| J. G. Wright c Ratnayake | | | C. Z. Harris not out | ............... 11 |
| | b E. A. R. de Silva . 64 | | | |
| *M. D. Crowe c Tillekeratne | | | | |
| | b Ramanayake . 3 | | L-b 4, w 16, n-b 3 | .......... 23 |
| A. H. Jones c Tillekeratne | | | | |
| | b E. A. R. de Silva . 29 | | 1/46 2/63 | (5 wkts, 42.3 overs) 178 |
| †I. D. S. Smith c Tillekeratne | | | 3/126 4/127 | |
| | b Ratnayake . 0 | | 5/153 | |

G. R. Larsen, C. Pringle, D. K. Morrison and W. Watson did not bat.

Bowling: Labrooy 9–0–38–0; Ramanayake 10–1–38–1; Ratnayake 8.3–1–27–2; Ranatunga 4–0–21–0; E. A. R. de Silva 10–1–36–2; Gurusinha 1–0–14–0.

Umpires: G. I. J. Cowan and S. J. Woodward.

## †NEW ZEALAND v SRI LANKA

### Second One-day International

At Auckland, January 28. New Zealand won by 41 runs. Toss: Sri Lanka. Again Sri Lanka started nervously, with Labrooy bowling three wides in his first over before dismissing Wright early on. Reid, who was strong on the hook and the drive, and Crowe, sweeping with particular effect, added 83 for the second wicket from 113 balls, and Jones embellished his outstanding one-day record with an unbeaten 64 from 76 deliveries. The Sri Lankans batted positively, though taking till the 29th over to reach three figures. The acquisitive Gurusinha scored a busy 81 from 90 balls, with six fours and two sixes, and Ratnayake caused a flutter with 22 in nineteen balls. At 185 for seven Sri Lanka still had a chance, but the tail went quickly.

*Man of the Match:* C. Pringle.

### New Zealand

| | | | | |
|---|---|---|---|---|
| R. B. Reid run out | 44 | M. J. Greatbatch c P. A. de Silva | | |
| J. G. Wright c E. A. R. de Silva | | | b Ramanayake | 14 |
| b Labrooy | 4 | C. Z. Harris not out | | 18 |
| *M. D. Crowe c Gurusinha | | | | |
| b E. A. R. de Silva | 64 | B 2, l-b 4, w 4, n-b 3 | | 13 |
| A. H. Jones not out | 64 | | | |
| †I. D. S. Smith c E. A. R. de Silva | | 1/16 2/99 3/134 | (5 wkts, 50 overs) | 242 |
| b Ratnayake | 21 | 4/164 5/200 | | |

G. R. Larsen, R. G. Petrie, C. Pringle and W. Watson did not bat.

Bowling: Labrooy 10–0–57–1; Ramanayake 10–0–49–1; Ratnayake 10–1–45–1; E. A. R. de Silva 10–0–41–1; Ranatunga 10–0–44–0.

### Sri Lanka

| | | | | |
|---|---|---|---|---|
| C. P. Senanayake c Wright b Watson | 12 | E. A. R. de Silva not out | | 10 |
| †H. P. Tillekeratne run out | 25 | G. F. Labrooy b Watson | | 3 |
| A. P. Gurusinha c Larsen b Harris | 81 | C. P. H. Ramanayake run out | | 0 |
| P. A. de Silva c Smith b Larsen | 0 | L-b 6, w 4 | | 10 |
| *A. Ranatunga b Harris | 24 | | | |
| R. S. Mahanama c Reid b Jones | 10 | 1/25 2/63 3/64 | (44.4 overs) | 201 |
| R. J. Ratnayake c Petrie b Pringle | 22 | 4/110 5/123 6/169 | | |
| S. T. Jayasuriya b Pringle | 4 | 7/185 8/191 9/201 | | |

Bowling: Watson 7.4–0–25–2; Petrie 8–1–41–0; Pringle 9–1–27–2; Larsen 10–1–37–1; Harris 6–0–38–2; Jones 4–0–27–1.

Umpires: B. L. Aldridge and R. S. Dunne.

## NEW ZEALAND v SRI LANKA

### First Test Match

At Wellington, January 31, February 1, 2, 3, 4. Drawn. Toss: Sri Lanka. New Zealand had not lost a Test at the Basin Reserve since 1967-68, but this run seemed to be over when they were dismissed for 174 on the opening day. After that dismal performance, however, batsmen prospered; whereas twelve wickets fell on the first day, only eleven went during the next four, while a host of records were rewritten. Most notably, Jones and Crowe shared a world-record Test partnership of 467, also the highest first-class stand by a New Zealand side, and a record for the third wicket anywhere. Aravinda de Silva's 267 was the best Test score by a Sri Lankan, and a Test record for the Basin Reserve until, two days later, it was surpassed by Crowe's 299, also the highest Test innings for his country, and the highest first-class score on the ground. Sri Lanka and New Zealand both made their biggest totals, with the latter's 671 for four being the highest in the second innings of a Test, and the first over 600 in a Test at the Basin Reserve.

There had been much rain before the match, and Wellington lived up to its "windy city" reputation. On the first day, a gale often reached 85 miles per hour: the umpires dispensed with bails, until they found some lined with steel rods; batsmen struggled against the wind on their all-too-regular return to the haven of the pavilion; and some television cameramen had to abandon scaffolding which looked dangerously askance. Even if the pitch, initially, favoured the seamers, Sri Lanka deserved their success in bundling out New Zealand for the lowest score of the series. Labrooy had a stiff task, bowling all but six overs into the fierce wind, but he was remarkably accurate and did so much with the ball that he won wide admiration for his stamina and skill. He had figures of two for 9 in his first nine overs. His partner, Ratnayake, bowled a demanding 105-minute spell downwind, the Sri Lankan fielding was sound, and Tillekeratne held four catches behind the stumps, including a blinder off Crowe. At the start Mahanama injured a finger in the slips, which ended his tour, while the only flaw occurred when Morrison was dropped in the slips; he and Watson added 24 for the last wicket. Of the batsmen, only Smith, with 28 at a run a ball, looked at home.

Sri Lanka lost two wickets before the close, but the next day they advanced by 318 for the loss of only one wicket, that of Gurusinha, who played a competent innings to add 143 with Aravinda de Silva. The bowlers were wildly erratic, evidently expecting the ball to move awkwardly and to steeple occasionally, and they were taught a stern lesson by the magnificent de Silva. He hooked anything short with immense profit during his first 100 runs, made from 124 balls, and then added almost arrogant cover drives and square cuts. He reached 203 in six hours, and remained dominant on the third morning, adding 64 in 83 balls. His partnership of 178 with Ranatunga was a record for Sri Lanka against New Zealand, and when, after lunch, de Silva was one of three victims for Morrison in seven balls, he had batted for 509 minutes, faced 380 balls and, in an unforgettable display, hit 40 fours. Sri Lanka went from 427 for four at lunch to 497 all out.

New Zealand faced a deficit of 323, but the weather was fine, there was little wind and the pitch was ideal. Wright and Franklin put on a studious 91 in 41 overs before stumps, and on the fourth day New Zealand added 278 for the loss of two wickets, notwithstanding stout-hearted Sri Lankan bowling and 45 minutes lost to rain. The openers' 134 was a new mark for New Zealand's first wicket against Sri Lanka, and although Franklin was ill at ease, Wright played confidently. Similarly in the record third-wicket partnership, Jones was, in the main, defensive, whereas Crowe was at the top of his bent. They made the draw almost inevitable. On the final day, Jones was in more assertive mood on his way to a career-best 186. He stayed 562 minutes and 454 balls, striking fifteen fours, while his captain, Crowe, batted for 610 minutes and 523 balls, hitting 29 fours and three sixes. Everybody, including the Sri Lankans, was disappointed that he did not reach 300. He was caught behind 1 run short, with three more balls possible, and after the match commented: "It's a bit like climbing Everest and pulling a hamstring in the last stride."

Sri Lanka had competed all the way, but the pitch was easy, and they compounded their difficulties by bowling 35 no-balls. Tillekeratne did not concede a bye in 220.3 overs and 671 runs, yet another record in Test cricket, and there was only one bye in the 1,342 runs scored in the match.

*Man of the Match:* M. D. Crowe.

*Close of play:* First day, Sri Lanka 41-2 (A. P. Gurusinha 17*, P. A. de Silva 0*); Second day, Sri Lanka 359-3 (P. A. de Silva 203*, A. Ranatunga 52*); Third day, New Zealand 91-0 (T. J. Franklin 24*, J. G. Wright 55*); Fourth day, New Zealand 369-2 (A. H. Jones 82*, M. D. Crowe 126*).

## New Zealand

| | | | |
|---|---|---|---|
| T. J. Franklin c sub (S. T. Jayasuriya) b Labrooy | 3 | – lbw b Ramanayake | 39 |
| J. G. Wright c Gurusinha b Labrooy | 15 | – c Tillekeratne b Ramanayake | 88 |
| A. H. Jones c Tillekeratne b Ratnayake | 5 | – c sub (A. W. R. Madurasinghe) b Ranatunga | 186 |
| *M. D. Crowe c Tillekeratne b Ramanayake | 30 | – c Tillekeratne b Ranatunga | 299 |
| M. J. Greatbatch c Gurusinha b Labrooy | 13 | – not out | 14 |
| K. R. Rutherford c Tillekeratne b Ratnayake | 25 | | |
| G. E. Bradburn c Tillekeratne b Ramanayake | 14 | | |
| †D. S. Smith c Senanayake b Ratnayake | 28 | | |
| C. Pringle lbw b Labrooy | 0 | | |
| D. K. Morrison b Ratnayake | 13 | | |
| W. Watson not out | 10 | | |
| B 1, l-b 7, w 1, n-b 9 | 18 | L-b 9, w 1, n-b 35 | 45 |
| | **174** | | **(4 wkts) 671** |

1/5 2/18 3/33 4/75 5/78
6/108 7/124 8/131 9/150

1/134 2/148
3/615 4/671

Bowling: *First Innings*—Ratnayake 18.2-6-45-4; Labrooy 23-5-68-4; Ramanayake 11-3-39-2; Warnaweera 6-1-14-0. *Second Innings*—Ratnayake 30-1-101-0; Labrooy 26-1-88-0; Ramanayake 40-5-122-2; Ranatunga 19.3-4-60-2; E. A. R. de Silva 56-14-141-0; Warnaweera 34-8-75-0; P. A. de Silva 8-0-59-0; Gurusinha 7-0-16-0.

## Sri Lanka

| | | | |
|---|---|---|---|
| C. P. Senanayake c Smith b Watson ... | 0 | R. J. Ratnayake b Watson ........... | 26 |
| †H. P. Tillekeratne c Greatbatch | | C. P. H. Ramanayake not out ........ | 14 |
| b Morrison . | 21 | K. P. J. Warnaweera b Watson ....... | 3 |
| A. P. Gurusinha c Crowe b Watson ... | 70 | R. S. Mahanama absent injured | |
| P. A. de Silva c Bradburn b Morrison .267 | | L-b 7, n-b 8 .............. | 15 |
| *A. Ranatunga hit wkt b Morrison .... | 55 | | |
| E. A. R. de Silva c Smith b Morrison . | 26 | 1/8 2/41 3/184 4/362 5/449 | 497 |
| G. F. Labrooy c Wright b Morrison ... | 0 | 6/449 7/454 8/487 9/497 | |

Bowling: Morrison 44-6-153-5; Watson 46.1-10-121-4; Pringle 31-4-116-0; Bradburn 26-5-83-0; Rutherford 2-0-11-0; Jones 2-0-6-0.

Umpires: B. L. Aldridge and S. J. Woodward.

## †NEW ZEALAND v SRI LANKA

### Third One-day International

At Dunedin, February 6. New Zealand won by 107 runs. Toss: Sri Lanka. Both New Zealand openers were missed early in the innings, and from then on it was a cakewalk for the home team. All the top-order batsmen scored at a good rate, and Smith plundered his undefeated 42 from 21 balls. Ranatunga was the best of the bowlers, and the best of Sri Lanka's batsmen, too, with a well-compiled 50 in 59 balls. But his colleagues squandered their chances, preferring to score runs quickly instead of building their innings. The only blow for New Zealand was the injury to Morrison, who twisted an ankle badly when Sri Lanka began their reply, and was unable to play in the one-day series against England which followed.

*Man of the Match*: K. R. Rutherford.

## New Zealand

| | | | |
|---|---|---|---|
| *M. D. Crowe lbw b Wijegunawardene. | 31 | †I. D. S. Smith not out ............. | 42 |
| R. B. Reid c Wijegunawardene | | C. Z. Harris c Gurusinha b Ramanayake | 5 |
| b Ranatunga . | 53 | C. Pringle not out ................. | 1 |
| A. H. Jones c Ratnayake b Ranatunga . | 35 | L-b 10, w 4 ............... | 14 |
| K. R. Rutherford b Ramanayake ..... | 65 | | |
| M. J. Greatbatch c Senanayake | | 1/79 2/110 3/133    (6 wkts, 50 overs) 272 | |
| b Gurusinha . | 26 | 4/203 5/243 6/260 | |

G. R. Larsen, D. K. Morrison and W. Watson did not bat.

Bowling: Ratnayake 10-0-52-0; Ramanayake 9-0-60-2; Wijegunawardene 5-0-33-1; E. A. R. de Silva 10-0-44-0; Ranatunga 10-0-39-2; Gurusinha 6-0-34-1.

## Sri Lanka

| | | | |
|---|---|---|---|
| C. P. Senanayake c Crowe b Watson .. | 12 | R. J. Ratnayake c sub (J. G. Wright) | |
| †R. S. Kaluwitharana c Reid b Pringle . | 14 | b Reid . | 19 |
| A. P. Gurusinha b Watson .......... | 15 | C. P. H. Ramanayake b Rutherford ... | 0 |
| P. A. de Silva c Rutherford b Watson.. | 21 | K. I. W. Wijegunawardene not out .... | 0 |
| *A. Ranatunga run out .............. | 50 | L-b 1, w 7, n-b 1 .......... | 9 |
| H. P. Tillekeratne c Crowe b Harris ... | 8 | | |
| S. T. Jayasuriya c Smith b Larsen .... | 1 | 1/15 2/41 3/43        (33.1 overs) 165 | |
| E. A. R. de Silva c sub (J. G. Wright) | | 4/74 5/102 6/105 | |
| b Crowe . | 16 | 7/139 8/151 9/151 | |

Bowling: Pringle 5-0-29-1; Watson 7-0-39-3; Larsen 10-0-36-1; Harris 5-0-30-1; Crowe 3-0-12-1; Rutherford 2-0-5-1; Reid 1.1-0-13-1.

Umpires: R. S. Dunne and R. L. McHarg.

## CENTRAL DISTRICTS v SRI LANKANS

At Nelson, February 9, 10, 11, 12. Sri Lankans won by seven wickets. Toss: Central Districts. The tourists' enterprising batting made them thoroughly deserving victors in this entertaining match. Central Districts lost three wickets in quick succession early on, but solid, defensive batting saw them through to a respectable score at close of play, and their eventual total of 353 looked substantial. The captain, Briasco, led the way for two and a half hours, Blain hit eight fours in his two-and-threequarter-hour fifty, and Duff's 80 in 217 minutes (185 balls) underlined his growing value as an all-rounder. In Sri Lanka's reply, Gurusinha mastered the situation expertly. He reached his first century of the tour in four hours, from 203 balls, and hit thirteen fours and two sixes in his 121 from 242 balls. Central Districts' top order failed again, with the fast-medium bowler, Wijegunawardene, returning his most successful figures in New Zealand; but the match seemed safe when the Sri Lankans were left needing 179 from 26 overs to win. However, their first 27 runs came inside three overs, 50 arrived off 6.1 overs and 100 off 12.2. The unbroken 83-run stand between Kaluwitharana and Jayasuriya took just 43 minutes, and the win was accomplished with 3.5 overs to spare.

*Close of play:* First day, Central Districts 249-6 (S. W. Duff 62*, D. J. Leonard 11*); Second day, Sri Lankans 199-3 (A. P. Gurusinha 106*, A. W. R. Madurasinghe 0*); Third day, Central Districts 42-3 (P. S. Briasco 22*, T. E. Blain 12*).

## Central Districts

| | | | | |
|---|---|---|---|---|
| R. T. Hart c Kaluwitharana b Ramanayake | 9 | – (2) b Wijegunawardene | 1 | |
| C. J. Smith c Hathurusinghe b Gurusinha | 12 | – (1) c Hathurusinghe b Gurusinha | 4 | |
| M. W. Douglas c Kaluwitharana b Gurusinha | 5 | – lbw b Wijegunawardene | 0 | |
| *P. S. Briasco lbw b Warnaweera | 41 | – c and b Madurasinghe | 92 | |
| †T. E. Blain c Madurasinghe b Wijegunawardene | 57 | – b Wijegunawardene | 15 | |
| S. W. Duff run out | 80 | – c Hathurusinghe b Warnaweera | 42 | |
| R. K. Brown c and b Madurasinghe | 24 | – b Wijegunawardene | 1 | |
| D. J. Leonard c sub b Madurasinghe | 48 | – lbw b Gurusinha | 1 | |
| M. J. Pawson st Kaluwitharana b Warnaweera | 17 | – not out | 54 | |
| P. R. Lowes lbw b Warnaweera | 24 | – c de Silva b Madurasinghe | 0 | |
| P. B. Gibbs not out | 3 | – c Tillekeratne | | |
| | | b Wijegunawardene | 9 | |
| B 4, l-b 6, n-b 23 | 33 | L-b 8, n-b 17 | 25 | |

1/26 2/26 3/37 4/131 5/143     353     1/4 2/4 3/10 4/49 5/125     244
6/199 7/270 8/315 9/336     6/131 7/151 8/209 9/209

*Bowling: First Innings*—Ramanayake 20–2–67–1; Wijegunawardene 25–1–74–1; Gurusinha 15–4–25–2; Madurasinghe 23–3–77–2; Warnaweera 30.2–10–68–3; de Silva 5–1–8–0; Jayasuriya 2–0–7–0; Hathurusinghe 8–2–17–0. *Second Innings*—Wijegunawardene 22.1–3–65–5; Gurusinha 19–3–64–2; Hathurusinghe 9–1–30–0; Warnaweera 18–5–40–1; Madurasinghe 12–5–14–2; Jayasuriya 2–0–9–0; de Silva 2–0–7–0; Tillekeratne 2–0–7–0.

## Sri Lankans

| | | | | |
|---|---|---|---|---|
| C. P. Senanayake c Douglas b Duff | 39 | – (2) c Brown b Leonard | 21 | |
| U. C. Hathurusinghe c Blain b Pawson | 21 | | | |
| A. P. Gurusinha c Douglas b Duff | 121 | – (4) c Brown b Duff | 36 | |
| *P. A. de Silva c and b Duff | 14 | – (1) c Douglas b Leonard | 14 | |
| A. W. R. Madurasinghe c Blain b Lowes | 29 | | | |
| H. P. Tillekeratne run out | 37 | | | |
| S. T. Jayasuriya lbw b Pawson | 39 | – (5) not out | 42 | |
| †R. S. Kaluwitharana c Blain b Pawson | 9 | – (3) not out | 61 | |
| C. P. H. Ramanayake c Hart b Pawson | 67 | | | |
| K. I. W. Wijegunawardene c Douglas b Lowes | 7 | | | |
| K. P. J. Warnaweera not out | 4 | | | |
| B 7, l-b 7, w 2, n-b 16 | 32 | L-b 4, n-b 1 | 5 | |

1/76 2/157 3/185 4/225 5/262     419     1/27 2/45 3/96     (3 wkts) 179
6/300 7/306 8/388 9/415

*In the first innings C. P. Senanayake, when 0, retired hurt at 3 and resumed at 76. On the third morning A. W. R. Madurasinghe did not resume until 306.*

Bowling: *First Innings*—Leonard 21–4–78–0; Pawson 25.2–5–87–4; Gibbs 21–4–63–0; Duff 44–8–92–3; Lowes 31–10–82–2; Brown 2–1–3–0. *Second Innings*—Leonard 5–0–49–2; Pawson 6–0–40–0; Gibbs 1–0–12–0; Duff 9–0–65–1; Smith 1.1–0–9–0.

Umpires: L. F. Jones and R. L. McHarg.

## CANTERBURY v SRI LANKANS

At Christchurch, February 15, 16, 17, 18. Drawn. Toss: Sri Lankans. Only fourteen wickets fell in a game spoiled by rain. All four days were disrupted by the weather, and the third was abandoned. After a delayed start the Canterbury openers, Hartland and David Boyle, added to their Shell Trophy successes with a stand of 105 in 138 minutes, which they followed in the second innings with an unbroken 51. Boyle's older brother, Justin, almost completed a competent half-century, while, in his first match for the province, Murray achieved that landmark from 136 balls after 226 minutes' batting. The Sri Lankan innings again was built around Gurusinha; on a placid pitch, he was unhurried in making the match's top score. Kaluwitharana, who also deputised as wicket-keeper after the first day, added to such entertainment as there was with some firm hits on the leg side.

*Close of play:* First day, Canterbury 237-5 (D. J. Murray 29*, M. W. Priest 28*); Second day, Sri Lankans 153-2 (A. P. Gurusinha 69*, S. T. Jayasuriya 16*); Third day, No play.

## Canterbury

| | | | | |
|---|---|---|---|---|
| B. R. Hartland lbw b de Silva | 57 | – not out | 28 |
| D. J. Boyle c Hathurusinghe b Wijegunawardene | 36 | – not out | 20 |
| J. G. Boyle lbw b Wijegunawardene | 47 | | |
| R. T. Latham c Wijegunawardene b Ranatunga | 8 | | |
| P. G. Kennedy st Tillekeratne b de Silva | 0 | | |
| D. J. Murray not out | 50 | | |
| M. W. Priest lbw b Labrooy | 31 | | |
| *†L. K. Germon not out | 34 | | |
| B 8, l-b 10, w 1, n-b 15 | 34 | L-b 2, n-b 1 | 3 |

1/105 2/116 3/139　　　　(6 wkts dec.) 297　　　　(no wkt) 51
4/142 5/187 6/241

R. M. Ford, S. J. Roberts and M. F. Sharpe did not bat.

Bowling: *First Innings*—Labrooy 23–3–83–1; Wijegunawardene 22–2–61–2; Warnaweera 17–5–50–0; de Silva 28–9–67–2; Ranatunga 4–1–12–1; Jayasuriya 1–0–3–0; Hathurusinghe 1–0–3–0. *Second Innings*—Wijegunawardene 8–0–23–0; Warnaweera 4.4–2–7–0; Jayasuriya 2–2–0–0; Hathurusinghe 4–2–6–0; Gurusinha 6–2–13–0.

## Sri Lankans

| | | | |
|---|---|---|---|
| C. P. Senanayake c Germon b Roberts | 21 | K. I. W. Wijegunawardene not out | 5 |
| U. C. Hathurusinghe c sub b D. J. Boyle | 45 | K. P. J. Warnaweera c Germon b Sharpe | 1 |
| A. P. Gurusinha c Germon b Roberts | 87 | L-b 1, w 1, n-b 2 | 4 |
| S. T. Jayasuriya b Priest | 17 | | |
| *A. Ranatunga c Priest b D. J. Boyle | 43 | 1/31 2/120 3/155　　(8 wkts dec.) 289 | |
| R. S. Kaluwitharana b Roberts | 62 | 4/180 5/246 6/271 | |
| E. A. R. de Silva c Murray b Roberts | 4 | 7/288 8/289 | |

†H. P. Tillekeratne and G. F. Labrooy did not bat.

Bowling: Roberts 22–4–83–4; Ford 22–7–54–0; Sharpe 15.3–3–46–1; Latham 12–6–25–0; Priest 19–2–60–1; D. J. Boyle 5–0–20–2.

Umpires: B. L. Aldridge and D. M. Quested.

## NEW ZEALAND v SRI LANKA

### Second Test Match

At Hamilton, February 22, 23, 24, 25, 26. Drawn. Toss: Sri Lanka. New Zealand's sixth Test venue offered a pleasant ground, good weather and attendances, an almost perfect pitch and a closely contested draw. Jones and Gurusinha scored centuries in each innings to match the feat of D. C. S. Compton and A. R. Morris, who scored twin centuries for England and Australia at Adelaide in 1946-47; Wright completed his set of hundreds against all six current Test-playing countries; and Smith held seven catches in an innings to equal the Test record, with eight in all to match New Zealand's Test record.

Though the Sri Lankans bowled too wide and short on a grassy pitch, the first morning was an anxious one for the New Zealand openers, who had put on 40 when they departed either side of lunch. The pitch still contained some life in the afternoon, but Jones and Crowe countered the seam movement and occasional lift in masterly fashion while adding 85 in 96 minutes. Jones, driving and hooking with confidence, went on to his fourth Test hundred, in 234 minutes from 173 balls, with Thomson a sturdy partner for three hours.

The second day belonged to Ratnayake, who seemed a distant cousin of the previous day's bowler, and Gurusinha. Ratnayake took five of New Zealand's last six wickets for 26 runs, becoming Sri Lanka's leading wicket-taker in Tests, and later Gurusinha held his team's innings together after four wickets fell cheaply. Aravinda de Silva seemed to believe an early boundary was essential, and skied the ball off a hasty hook to Smith. In a day of injuries, Rutherford had to go off after failing to hold a hard slip catch (New Zealand missed several in the slips and gully, which may have cost them the game), Crowe twisted his right ankle, and Ranatunga injured his back while bowling. Smith and Aravinda de Silva captained in the field on the last three days.

Gurusinha duly completed his century next morning, from 216 balls, but in spite of his six-hour effort (261 balls, one six, seventeen fours) Sri Lanka conceded a deficit of 43. After lunch, Morrison was all pace and persistence, and Watson bowled accurately. Wright now came in to play one of his finest innings. He attacked vigorously in the final session, scoring 68 out of 78 after tea and reaching his eleventh Test hundred, with his fourteenth four, in 178 minutes and 138 balls; it was a sparkling display of strokes. On the fourth afternoon Jones and Thomson provided one of the highlights of the match, adding 105 off 133 balls in 88 minutes. Thomson, with some rippling drives, reached a maiden Test fifty in 60 balls, with six fours, and Jones swept his way to a second hundred, off 172 balls with eight fours, before New Zealand's declaration left Sri Lanka a target of 418 in a minimum of 125 overs. They were 109 from 35 overs at the close, including a first-class career-best 64 by Senanayake, with ten fours and some fine cuts and hooks.

On the final day, the Test newcomer, Hathurusinghe, proved an excellent foil for the left-handed Gurusinha. Sri Lanka added 78 before lunch, and the third hour yielded 54. A first Test win over New Zealand was on the cards when Aravinda de Silva came in, after the third-wicket pair had added 117 off 235 balls, but again his mind did not seem to be firmly on the job; he gave Patel a return catch from a full toss. At tea, 140 runs were required, with six wickets and 31 overs in hand; but with Jayasuriya injured, as well as himself, Ranatunga chose not to take the gamble. Gurusinha's second hundred of the match occupied five hours eleven minutes (239 balls) and contained a six and nine fours.

*Men of the Match:* A. P. Gurusinha, A. H. Jones and I. D. S. Smith.

*Close of play:* First day, New Zealand 221-4 (A. H. Jones 109*, S. A. Thomson 32*); Second day, Sri Lanka 180-5 (A. P. Gurusinha 81*, C. P. H. Ramanayake 13*); Third day, New Zealand 170-2 (T. J. Franklin 56*, A. H. Jones 2*); Fourth day, Sri Lanka 109-1 (U. C. Hathurusinghe 30*, C. P. H. Ramanayake 11*).

## New Zealand

| | | | | |
|---|---|---|---|---|
| T. J. Franklin c P. A. de Silva b Gurusinha | ... | 15 | – b Ratnayake | 69 |
| J. G. Wright c Hathurusinghe b Labrooy | ... | 21 | – c Tillekeratne b Ramanayake | 101 |
| A. H. Jones c Tillekeratne b Ratnayake | ...... | 122 | – (4) not out | 100 |
| *M. D. Crowe c Tillekeratne b Ranatunga | ... | 36 | | |
| K. R. Rutherford c Tillekeratne b Ramanayake | . | 0 | – b E. A. R. de Silva | 6 |
| S. A. Thomson b Ramanayake | ... | 36 | – c Tillekeratne b E. A. R. de Silva | 55 |
| D. N. Patel not out | ... | 26 | – b Labrooy | 9 |
| †I. D. S. Smith c Senanayake b Ratnayake | ... | 7 | – not out | 6 |
| D. K. Morrison c Tillekeratne b Ratnayake | ... | 0 | – (3) c Jayasuriya b Ramanayake | 0 |
| C. Pringle b Ratnayake | ... | 9 | | |
| W. Watson c Tillekeratne b Ratnayake | ... | 4 | | |
| B 4, l-b 12, n-b 4 | ... | 20 | B 3, l-b 9, w 2, n-b 14 | 28 |
| | | **296** | (6 wkts dec.) | **374** |

1/40 2/40 3/125 4/126 5/239     296     1/161 2/162 3/209   (6 wkts dec.) 374
6/239 7/258 8/270 9/288                  4/222 5/327 6/359

Bowling: *First Innings*—Ratnayake 30.4-10-77-5; Labrooy 22-6-46-1; Ramanayake 27-9-52-2; Gurusinha 14.2-3-36-1; E. A. R. de Silva 14-2-35-0; Ranatunga 13.4-1-34-1. *Second Innings*—Ratnayake 27-4-70-1; Labrooy 20-2-65-1; Ramanayake 26-5-97-2; Gurusinha 4-1-12-0; E. A. R. de Silva 24-6-89-2; Hathurusinghe 2-0-15-0; P. A. de Silva 2-0-14-0.

## Sri Lanka

| | | | | |
|---|---|---|---|---|
| C. P. Senanayake c Smith b Pringle | ... | 5 | – c Jones b Watson | 64 |
| U. C. Hathurusinghe c Smith b Morrison | ... | 23 | – c sub (M. J. Greatbatch) b Thomson | 81 |
| A. P. Gurusinha c Thomson b Morrison | ...... | 119 | – (4) c Smith b Morrison | 102 |
| P. A. de Silva c Smith b Watson | ... | 1 | – (5) c and b Patel | 6 |
| †H. P. Tillekeratne c Smith b Pringle | ... | 12 | – (6) c sub (G. E. Bradburn) b Patel | 26 |
| S. T. Jayasuriya lbw b Patel | ... | 35 | | |
| C. P. H. Ramanayake run out | ... | 13 | – (3) c sub (M. J. Greatbatch) b Watson | 11 |
| *A. Ranatunga c Smith b Morrison | ... | 21 | – (7) not out | 20 |
| E. A. R. de Silva c Smith b Watson | ... | 0 | – (8) not out | 11 |
| G. F. Labrooy c Smith b Watson | ... | 6 | | |
| R. J. Ratnayake not out | ... | 1 | | |
| L-b 4, n-b 13 | ... | 17 | B 4, l-b 11, n-b 8 | 23 |
| | | **253** | (6 wkts) | **344** |

1/8 2/38 3/41 4/83 5/163     253     1/95 2/121 3/238   (6 wkts) 344
6/185 7/240 8/246 9/246                 4/245 5/300 6/320

Bowling: *First Innings*—Morrison 26-6-77-3; Pringle 20-5-64-2; Watson 26.4-8-65-3; Patel 15-4-33-1; Thomson 6-1-10-0. *Second Innings*—Morrison 25-4-85-1; Pringle 12-2-46-0; Watson 37-8-75-2; Patel 39-13-90-2; Thomson 8-3-18-1; Jones 4-1-15-0.

Umpires: B. L. Aldridge and R. S. Dunne.

## NEW ZEALAND v SRI LANKA

### Third Test Match

At Auckland, March 1, 2, 3, 4, 5. Drawn. Toss: New Zealand. Sri Lanka had the whip-hand for most of the final Test, and set a target of 383 runs in at least 101 overs. The loss of four wickets for 117 dampened New Zealand's ardour, and with the tourists setting defensive fields the game seemed doomed to a draw from mid-afternoon. However, the Sri Lankans emerged as – slightly – the moral victors of the Test series.

There was jubilation in the New Zealand camp when Smith, deputising for the injured Crowe, won the toss, for the pitch looked to favour seam bowlers. But despite frequent playing and missing, Sri Lanka were in command at the end of a day in which they scored at 3.6 runs an over. Only the pace and bounce of Cairns worried them. Gurusinha had been his calm and collected self until Cairns's fine spell before lunch had him all at sea, and early in the afternoon he was lbw to a yorker. Cairns took four of the first five wickets, but Aravinda de Silva savaged him unmercifully, hitting two fours and two sixes in an over costing 21 runs. His 96 included another twelve fours, and after taking 94 balls for his fifty, he needed only 47 for the next 46. His cover drives were sometimes hit over the top, but his hooking was lethal, as at Wellington.

The day ended with a stand of 52 in 32 minutes from Tillekeratne and Labrooy, who hit 16 off his first three balls, was 41 overnight, and reached his fifty from a record thirteen scoring strokes; his unbeaten 70 came from 80 balls, with two sixes and twelve fours. It was scary stuff for the fielders. By the close of the second day, New Zealand had slipped from 139 for one to 194 for five, despite another fine innings from Wright. Rain cut 114 minutes from the third day, when Greatbatch, though lacking his usual confidence, rescued the innings with Patel, who played some exquisite strokes. The Sri Lankans bowled with particular accuracy, and then batted handsomely on a placid pitch for most of the fourth day. Again Cairns had the better of the top order, and this time de Silva took no liberties with him. However, he attacked the other bowlers with gusto, reaching his fifty in 66 balls and adding 145 off 281 balls for the third wicket with Hathurusinghe. Sri Lanka scored 119 in the session before lunch, and were 276 when de Silva was fourth out, just before tea, with five sixes and six fours to his name in an innings of 123 from 193 balls (261 minutes). The remaining wickets fell for 43 runs.

On the final day New Zealand lost ground, chiefly through the efforts of Labrooy. Wright was handicapped by a calf muscle injury, but Jones and Thomson, who showed a touch of real class in his off-side strokeplay, denied the Sri Lankans with a stand of 100 from 214 balls.

*Man of the Match:* P. A. de Silva.

*Close of play:* First day, Sri Lanka 325-8 (G. F. Labrooy 41*); Second day, New Zealand 194-5 (M. J. Greatbatch 18*, D.N. Patel 9*); Third day, Sri Lanka 64-2 (U. C. Hathurusinghe 16*, P. A. de Silva 5*); Fourth day, New Zealand 18-0 (T. J. Franklin 5*, J. G. Wright 12*).

## Sri Lanka

| | | |
|---|---|---|
| C. P. Senanayake c Smith b Cairns | 20 | – c Greatbatch b Cairns ......... 8 |
| U. C. Hathurusinghe b Watson | 13 | – c Smith b Cairns ............ 74 |
| A. P. Gurusinha lbw b Cairns | 50 | – c and b Cairns ............. 29 |
| P. A. de Silva c Smith b Cairns | 96 | – c Morrison b Thomson ......123 |
| *A. Ranatunga c Smith b Cairns | 34 | – c Thomson b Cairns ......... 30 |
| †H. P. Tillekeratne lbw b Morrison | 31 | – c Cairns b Thomson ......... 3 |
| S. T. Jayasuriya c Smith b Watson | 18 | – not out ................. 12 |
| E. A. R. de Silva c Jones b Patel | 2 | – (9) c Greatbatch b Thomson ... 0 |
| G. F. Labrooy not out | 70 | – (8) c Morrison b Cairns ...... 1 |
| R. J. Ratnayake c Greatbatch b Watson | 18 | – c Greatbatch b Morrison ..... 20 |
| C. P. H. Ramanayake c Smith b Morrison | 1 | – b Morrison ............... 0 |
| B 2, l-b 15, w 1, n-b 9 | 27 | B 1, l-b 5, n-b 13 ....... 19 |

1/34 2/61 3/132 4/223 5/234       380     1/9 2/56 3/201 4/276 5/282    319
6/255 7/273 8/325 9/356                  6/282 7/285 8/288 9/319

Bowling: *First Innings*—Morrison 21-5-87-2; Cairns 32-5-136-4; Watson 31.5-11-81-3; Thomson 12.1-6-22-0; Patel 8-2-37-1. *Second Innings*—Morrison 20-2-74-2; Cairns 27-6-75-5; Watson 9-1-23-0; Thomson 19-5-63-3; Patel 23-6-78-0.

## New Zealand

| | | |
|---|---|---|
| T. J. Franklin lbw b Ratnayake | 13 | – c Tillekeratne b Labrooy ... 31 |
| J. G. Wright c Ranatunga b Ramanayake | 84 | – c Tillekeratne b Ramanayake ... 20 |
| A. H. Jones c Ratnayake b E. A. R. de Silva | 27 | – lbw b Labrooy ............ 73 |
| M. J. Greatbatch lbw b Labrooy | 65 | – b Labrooy ................. 7 |
| K. R. Rutherford c Gurusinha b E. A. R. de Silva | 15 | – lbw b Labrooy ............. 6 |
| S. A. Thomson lbw b Ratnayake | 1 | – not out ................. 80 |
| D. N. Patel c Labrooy b Ramanayake | 41 | – not out ................. 16 |
| *H. D. S. Smith b Ratnayake | 3 | |
| C. L. Cairns c P. A. de Silva b Labrooy | 17 | |
| D. K. Morrison b Labrooy | 7 | |
| W. Watson not out | 5 | |
| B 1, l-b 7, n-b 31 | 39 | B 1, l-b 9, n-b 18 ....... 28 |

1/63 2/139 3/140 4/170 5/172      317    1/39 2/80 3/95      (5 wkts) 261
6/247 7/257 8/299 9/304                   4/117 5/217

Bowling: *First Innings*—Labrooy 21.3-6-48-3; Ramanayake 26-7-96-2; Ratnayake 33-3-83-3; E. A. R. de Silva 29-8-67-2; Gurusinha 6-2-15-0. *Second Innings*—Ratnayake 21-3-44-0; Ramanayake 19-4-62-1; E. A. R. de Silva 25-4-61-0; Labrooy 19-6-42-4; Ranatunga 7-1-23-0; Jayasuriya 6-1-18-0; Gurusinha 1-1-0.

Umpires: B. L. Aldridge and R. L. McHarg.

# THE AUSTRALIANS IN THE WEST INDIES, 1990-91

### By TONY COZIER

Australia's sixth tour of the West Indies began with exalted expectations of an epic contest between arguably the two strongest teams in the game. That in the event such hopes were unrealised was due to several factors. First of all, unseasonal rain – combined in Jamaica with inefficient covering of the square – reduced the First and Third Tests by at least a day and a half each, leaving them as the only two draws of the series. And secondly, in reasserting their long-held paramouncy in Test cricket, West Indies won the Second and Fourth Tests by irrefutable margins, so deciding the rubber before the final match in Antigua, where Australia gained belated consolation with their first Test victory in the Caribbean since April 1978. However, West Indies' victory in the Second Test was somewhat devalued by the bizarre and incorrect run-out decision against the Australian batsman, Dean Jones, following a no-ball.

Above all else, what should have been a compelling advertisement for cricket was ruined by the obvious acrimony between the teams. This manifested itself time and again in verbal altercations on the field, and the rancour was accentuated by the television cameras which, for the first time, were transmitting live, ball-by-ball coverage back to Australia from the Caribbean. After the final Test, the umpires were moved to report to the West Indies Board on the abusive language used in the middle by certain players, and even the two Boards became involved in a succession of verbal exchanges, conducted through press releases, after comments by the West Indies captain, Vivian Richards, which were critical of the Australian team coach, Bob Simpson, himself a former Test captain.

At the final presentation ceremony, the president of the West Indies Board, Clyde Walcott, a great player in his time, referred to the soured relations, and it seemed appropriate that the Frank Worrell Trophy was nowhere to be found. It transpired that it had been lost since the West Indians' tour of Australia in 1984-85. Given that it was inaugurated to honour the late West Indies captain of the unforgettable 1960-61 series in Australia, its presence in such circumstances would have been incongruous.

West Indies owed their retention of the Frank Worrell Trophy to their experience, their self-confidence and their positive approach. They also revealed a strong sense of pride, for after the 4-1 defeat in the one-day internationals, their first such reversal at home, there was concerted pressure from the press and public to change several of the great, but aging, players, whose records were on the wane. The selectors refused to be panicked and stuck to the same eleven throughout the five Tests, a policy thoroughly vindicated by the outcome.

The West Indians' spirit was repeatedly in evidence as they fought their way out of seemingly impossible positions time and again. On the first day of the series they were 75 for six, with one of their three injured batsmen in hospital and Nos. 7 and 9 together, yet they still recovered to reach 264. When Australia appeared to be heading for a huge lead on the third day, West Indies captured their last five wickets for 14 runs. In the Second Test, Australia batted through the first day and a half for a respectable 348 but were beaten by ten wickets with ample time to spare; in the truncated Third Test, they were through the top order, only to be thwarted by West Indies' eighth-wicket pair. At Bridgetown, Australia despatched West Indies for their lowest total in a home Test for eighteen years in the first innings, and proceeded to lose by the humiliating margin of 343 runs. Such West Indian resilience undermined Australia's spirit, although when West Indies dropped their guard and seemed to relax in the final Test, Australia seized their chance.

The main difference between the teams was in attitude. The Australians consistently erred on the side of caution; the West Indians, especially in adversity, chose the option of counter-attack. The contrast was best seen in the Second Test, which was the turning-point in the series. After Australia had taken 116.4 overs to total 348 on a true pitch and a fast, small outfield, Desmond Haynes and Richie Richardson promptly seized the initiative with a partnership of 297 in 70 overs. Richardson's 182, an exhilarating exhibition of strokeplay, was enough on its own to earn him the Man of the Series award, without account being taken of his second-innings century in the First Test and his scintillating 99 in the Fourth. Australia's reticence was also clear in the decision to load their batting in the Third and Fourth Tests, limiting the attack to three specialist bowlers, even though they were behind in the series.

There were other distinctions as well. While West Indies could rely on each of their four fast bowlers – so that the absence of Ian Bishop, with a stress fracture of the lower vertebrae, was scarcely felt – Australia's main bowler, Craig McDermott, lacked consistent support. Fast, straight and aggressive, with a telling yorker complemented by a superbly disguised slower ball, McDermott took 24 wickets at 23.50 and rarely had a bad spell. But Merv Hughes, interspersing the good with the bad, paid dearly for his inconsistency, his nineteen wickets costing 31 apiece, while the lack of form, fitness and, more pertinently, confidence which limited the tall left-hander, Bruce Reid, to five wickets in two Tests, proved a crucial handicap for Australia. There was another significant difference, too, between the fast bowlers – their batting. In 24 combined innings, the Australians contributed 62 runs; in 27, the West Indian bowlers at the end of the order totalled 322. It usually meant a swift final collapse on the one hand, and an essential late rally on the other.

The batting of both teams was spasmodic and disappointing. Haynes and Richardson carried West Indies, even though Gordon Greenidge regained his old touch with a masterful double-century in the Fourth Test. The middle order remained unreliable, with the result that Jeffrey Dujon, who enjoyed a fine series in front of and behind the stumps, had to mount recoveries in partnership with Curtly Ambrose in the First and Third Tests. For Australia, only the elegant Mark Waugh, who on his first tour looked a class cricketer through and through, and the solid left-handed opener, Mark Taylor, did themselves justice. Allan Border and Dean Jones passed 50 only once each in nine Test innings, and Geoff Marsh fell away badly after scoring heavily in the one-day internationals.

The series was almost certainly the last at home for several of those cricketers who had featured prominently in West Indies' prolonged dominance of the international game. If Richards had the disappointment of a miserable time with the bat, concluded with scores of 0 and 2 in the final Test in his native Antigua, this was counter-balanced by the knowledge that he remained the only West Indian captain not to lose a rubber. By the time the countries meet again in a full series in Australia in 1992-93, the personnel in the teams is likely to have changed, and it is to be hoped that the relationship between the players will have changed also.

## AUSTRALIAN TOUR RESULTS

*Test matches* – Played 5: Won 1, Lost 2, Drawn 2.
*First-class matches* – Played 10: Won 2, Lost 2, Drawn 6.
*Wins* – West Indies, Jamaica.
*Losses* – West Indies (2).
*Draws* – West Indies (2), WICBC President's XI, Trinidad & Tobago, West Indies Under-23 XI, West Indies Cricket Board of Control XI.
*One-day internationals* – Played 5: Won 4, Lost 1.
*Other non first-class matches* – Played 4: Won 4. *Wins* – Trinidad & Tobago, Bermuda (3).

## TEST MATCH AVERAGES

### WEST INDIES – BATTING

|  | T | I | NO | R | HI | 100s | Avge |
|---|---|---|---|---|---|---|---|
| R. B. Richardson.... | 5 | 8 | 1 | 475 | 182 | 2 | 67.85 |
| A. L. Logie........ | 5 | 7 | 2 | 261 | 77* | 0 | 52.20 |
| D. L. Haynes...... | 5 | 9 | 1 | 412 | 111 | 1 | 51.50 |
| C. G. Greenidge .... | 5 | 9 | 1 | 366 | 226 | 1 | 45.75 |
| P. J. L. Dujon ...... | 5 | 7 | 0 | 209 | 70 | 0 | 29.85 |
| C. L. Hooper ...... | 5 | 8 | 0 | 199 | 62 | 0 | 24.87 |
| I. V. A. Richards.... | 5 | 8 | 1 | 174 | 52* | 0 | 24.85 |
| M. D. Marshall .... | 5 | 7 | 1 | 145 | 51 | 0 | 24.16 |
| C. E. L. Ambrose ... | 5 | 7 | 1 | 115 | 53 | 0 | 19.16 |
| C. A. Walsh........ | 5 | 7 | 2 | 44 | 12* | 0 | 8.80 |
| B. P. Patterson..... | 5 | 7 | 2 | 33 | 15 | 0 | 6.60 |

* Signifies not out.

### BOWLING

|  | O | M | R | W | BB | 5W/i | Avge |
|---|---|---|---|---|---|---|---|
| M. D. Marshall ... | 156.2 | 24 | 437 | 21 | 3-31 | 0 | 20.80 |
| B. P. Patterson.... | 136 | 19 | 409 | 18 | 5-83 | 1 | 22.72 |
| C. A. Walsh...... | 180.4 | 33 | 426 | 17 | 4-14 | 0 | 25.05 |
| C. E. L. Ambrose . | 205.4 | 47 | 493 | 18 | 3-36 | 0 | 27.38 |
| C. L. Hooper ..... | 150 | 35 | 391 | 5 | 2-28 | 0 | 78.20 |

Also bowled: I. V. A. Richards 23-2-101-0; R. B. Richardson 1-0-2-0.

### AUSTRALIA – BATTING

|  | T | I | NO | R | HI | 100s | Avge |
|---|---|---|---|---|---|---|---|
| M. E. Waugh ...... | 5 | 8 | 2 | 367 | 139* | 1 | 61.16 |
| M. A. Taylor ...... | 5 | 9 | 0 | 441 | 144 | 1 | 49.00 |
| A. R. Border ....... | 5 | 9 | 1 | 275 | 59 | 0 | 34.37 |
| D. C. Boon ....... | 5 | 9 | 1 | 266 | 109* | 1 | 33.25 |
| D. M. Jones........ | 5 | 9 | 1 | 245 | 81 | 0 | 30.62 |
| G. R. Marsh ...... | 5 | 9 | 0 | 226 | 94 | 0 | 25.11 |
| I. A. Healy ....... | 5 | 8 | 0 | 155 | 53 | 0 | 19.37 |
| M. G. Hughes ..... | 5 | 8 | 0 | 41 | 21 | 0 | 5.12 |
| C. J. McDermott.... | 5 | 8 | 0 | 18 | 7 | 0 | 2.25 |

Played in two Tests: G. R. J. Matthews 10, 1, 16; B. A. Reid 0*, 0, 0; S. R. Waugh 26, 2, 4*; M. R. Whitney 2, 1*, 0*. Played in one Test: T. M. Alderman 0, 0*; P. L. Taylor 2, 4.

* Signifies not out.

## BOWLING

|              | O     | M  | R   | W  | BB   | 5W/i | Avge  |
|--------------|-------|----|-----|----|------|------|-------|
| M. E. Waugh ...... | 65    | 18 | 183 | 8  | 4-80 | 0    | 22.87 |
| C. J. McDermott.... | 192.5 | 38 | 564 | 24 | 5-80 | 1    | 23.50 |
| A. R. Border ...... | 74    | 21 | 188 | 7  | 5-68 | 1    | 26.85 |
| M. G. Hughes ...... | 172.3 | 33 | 589 | 19 | 4-44 | 0    | 31.00 |
| B. A. Reid ......... | 73    | 12 | 229 | 5  | 2-50 | 0    | 45.80 |

Also bowled: T. M. Alderman 22.4-4-105-1; D. M. Jones 4-1-9-0; G. R. J. Matthews 73.5-11-273-3; P. L. Taylor 21-2-79-2; S. R. Waugh 35-6-90-0; M. R. Whitney 66-11-216-0.

## AUSTRALIAN AVERAGES – FIRST-CLASS MATCHES

### BATTING

|              | M  | I  | NO | R   | HI   | 100s | Avge  |
|--------------|----|----|----|-----|------|------|-------|
| M. A. Taylor ....... | 10 | 14 | 0  | 777 | 144  | 3    | 55.50 |
| M. E. Waugh ...... | 9  | 12 | 2  | 522 | 139* | 2    | 52.20 |
| S. R. Waugh ...... | 6  | 7  | 2  | 229 | 96*  | 0    | 45.80 |
| G. R. J. Matthews .. | 4  | 4  | 1  | 122 | 95*  | 0    | 40.66 |
| A. R. Border ...... | 8  | 13 | 2  | 386 | 59   | 0    | 35.09 |
| D. C. Boon ........ | 10 | 14 | 1  | 456 | 109* | 2    | 35.07 |
| D. M. Jones........ | 9  | 12 | 1  | 358 | 81   | 0    | 32.54 |
| G. R. Marsh ...... | 8  | 13 | 0  | 264 | 94   | 0    | 20.30 |
| P. L. Taylor ...... | 5  | 6  | 1  | 89  | 33   | 0    | 17.80 |
| I. A. Healy ........ | 7  | 10 | 0  | 177 | 53   | 0    | 17.70 |
| M. R. J. Veletta ... | 4  | 4  | 0  | 28  | 14   | 0    | 7.00  |
| M. G. Hughes ...... | 10 | 13 | 1  | 77  | 21   | 0    | 6.41  |
| C. J. McDermott.... | 6  | 9  | 1  | 35  | 17*  | 0    | 4.37  |
| M. R. Whitney .... | 4  | 5  | 2  | 11  | 6    | 0    | 3.66  |
| T. M. Alderman .... | 5  | 4  | 2  | 2   | 2    | 0    | 1.00  |
| B. A. Reid ......... | 5  | 5  | 1  | 3   | 2    | 0    | 0.75  |

\* *Signifies not out.*

### BOWLING

|              | O     | M  | R     | W  | BB   | 5W/i | Avge  |
|--------------|-------|----|-------|----|------|------|-------|
| C. J. McDermott ..... | 209.5 | 40 | 608   | 28 | 5-80 | 1    | 21.71 |
| M. E. Waugh ........ | 93.2  | 21 | 271   | 12 | 4-80 | 0    | 22.58 |
| P. L. Taylor ........ | 158   | 45 | 382   | 15 | 5-37 | 1    | 25.46 |
| A. R. Border ........ | 84    | 24 | 214   | 8  | 5-68 | 1    | 26.75 |
| M. G. Hughes ....... | 304.5 | 56 | 1,052 | 37 | 5-36 | 1    | 28.43 |
| M. R. Whitney ...... | 150   | 28 | 445   | 14 | 6-42 | 2    | 31.78 |
| B. A. Reid .......... | 160.1 | 28 | 527   | 16 | 4-76 | 0    | 32.93 |
| T. M. Alderman ..... | 117.4 | 22 | 346   | 9  | 5-40 | 1    | 38.44 |
| G. R. J. Matthews.... | 106.5 | 21 | 370   | 8  | 4-57 | 0    | 46.25 |

Also bowled: D. M. Jones 4-1-9-0; S. R. Waugh 78-17-234-3.

## FIELDING

15 – I. A. Healy; 13 – M. E. Waugh; 10 – M. R. J. Veletta (9 ct, 1 st); 7 – D. M. Jones; 6 – D. C. Boon, G. R. Marsh, M. A. Taylor; 5 – T. M. Alderman, M. G. Hughes; 4 – P. L. Taylor; 2 – C. J. McDermott; 1 – A. R. Border, G. R. J. Matthews, B. A. Reid, S. R. Waugh, Substitute (G. R. J. Matthews).

## WICBC PRESIDENT'S XI v AUSTRALIANS

At Basseterre, St Kitts, February 16, 17, 18, 19. Drawn. Toss: Australians. Confronting what was virtually a West Indies reserve team, the Australians were hard pressed to avoid defeat on a pitch that became progressively more uneven in bounce. The President's XI first innings was built around a third-wicket partnership of 91 in 110 minutes between Simmons, who hit twelve fours before he was the second of Whitney's five victims, and the left-handed Arthurton, who announced his intentions with a second-ball six over extra cover off Peter Taylor's off-spin. When Whitney followed Simmons's dismissal by removing Best and Holder in the space of 4 runs, the lower order contributed important runs. Only the Waugh twins batted with any confidence when the Australians replied. Steve, who offered chances at 24 and 81, was 4 short of a century when the ninth wicket fell, but was denied the chance of reaching it because Alderman was ill and unable to bat. Behind by 99, the Australians bowled with spirit, with the result that their target on the final day was 247 off 82 overs, which rain reduced to 79. However, batting was not easy. Several balls shot through low, and the run-outs of Border and Mark Waugh kept the possibility of victory in sight until, with the score 163, he was caught at mid-on off a mistimed drive. But when Steve Waugh followed in the next over, sweeping to deep backward square, and Veletta was bowled round his legs by Patterson at 174, the Australians were content to hold on for a draw. Taylor's chanceless 101 lasted just over four hours and included nine boundaries.

*Close of play:* First day, WICBC President's XI 287-8 (A. H. Gray 33*, K. C. G. Benjamin 1*); Second day, Australians 173-6 (S. R. Waugh 58*, P. L. Taylor 9*); Third day, WICBC President's XI 120-6 (D. Williams 2*, R. C. Haynes 9*).

### WICBC President's XI

| | | | | | | |
|---|---|---|---|---|---|---|
| P. V. Simmons lbw b Whitney | 71 | – | c sub b Whitney | 20 |
| D. A. Joseph c Boon b Whitney | 2 | – | lbw b Hughes | 2 |
| *R. B. Richardson b P. L. Taylor | 14 | – | b P. L. Taylor | 8 |
| K. L. T. Arthurton c Boon b Hughes | 93 | – | lbw b P. L. Taylor | 45 |
| C. A. Best c Alderman b Whitney | 22 | – | b M. E. Waugh | 22 |
| R. I. C. Holder b Whitney | 3 | – | c Veletta b M. E. Waugh | 1 |
| †D. Williams c Alderman b Hughes | 20 | – | c M. E. Waugh b Hughes | 9 |
| R. C. Haynes c M. E. Waugh b Whitney | 39 | – | c P. L. Taylor b Hughes | 14 |
| A. H. Gray c Veletta b Hughes | 58 | – | lbw b Hughes | 2 |
| K. C. G. Benjamin c M. E. Waugh b Hughes | 11 | – | not out | 2 |
| B. P. Patterson not out | 10 | – | c Veletta b Hughes | 20 |
| B 1, l-b 1, n-b 2 | 4 | | B 14, l-b 2, n-b 4 | 20 |

1/26 2/53 3/144 4/144 5/148      332    1/9 2/30 3/54 4/105 5/107    147
6/202 7/220 8/280 9/313               6/110 7/125 8/138 9/139

Bowling: *First Innings*—Alderman 17-3-44-0; Whitney 32-7-114-5; P. L. Taylor 26-9-69-1; Hughes 20-2-80-4; S. R. Waugh 8-3-23-0. *Second Innings*—Hughes 11.5-1-36-5; Whitney 16-4-37-1; P. L. Taylor 15-5-30-2; M. E. Waugh 10-1-28-2.

### Australians

| | | | | | | |
|---|---|---|---|---|---|---|
| G. R. Marsh lbw b Patterson | 1 | – | (2) b Simmons | 1 |
| M. A. Taylor b Benjamin | 16 | – | (1) c Richardson b Simmons | 101 |
| D. C. Boon c Williams b Gray | 25 | – | c Joseph b Haynes | 1 |
| M. E. Waugh c Best b Patterson | 41 | – | (5) run out | 15 |
| S. R. Waugh not out | 96 | – | (6) c Gray b Haynes | 15 |
| †M. R. J. Veletta run out | 4 | – | (7) b Patterson | 6 |
| *A. R. Border c Williams b Benjamin | 4 | – | (4) run out | 26 |
| P. L. Taylor b Patterson | 16 | – | not out | 23 |
| M. G. Hughes c Holder b Patterson | 6 | – | not out | 10 |
| M. R. Whitney lbw b Benjamin | 6 | | | |
| T. M. Alderman absent ill | | | | |
| B 1, l-b 3, w 1, n-b 13 | 18 | | B 2, l-b 4, w 1, n-b 4 | 11 |

1/7 2/38 3/63 4/122 5/146      233    1/32 2/43 3/102 4/111    (7 wkts) 204
6/159 7/195 8/213 9/233                5/163 6/163 7/174

Bowling: *First Innings*—Patterson 25–4–62–4; Gray 16–1–52–1; Benjamin 16.2–4–40–3; Haynes 21–0–75–0. *Second Innings*—Patterson 17–4–34–1; Gray 15–2–47–0; Simmons 24–7–57–2; Haynes 20–4–52–2; Arthurton 2–1–3–0; Best 1–0–5–0.

Umpires: A. E. Weekes and P. C. White.

## JAMAICA v AUSTRALIANS

At Kingston, February 21, 22, 23. Australians won by an innings and 137 runs. Toss: Jamaica. After reaching 103 for one at lunch on the opening day, Jamaica disintegrated and went on to suffer a humiliating defeat inside three of the scheduled four days. They lost their last nine first-innings wickets for 55, four to McDermott and five to Whitney, who was playing only because Reid was still unavailable with a back complaint. The Australians began badly, but a miss by Morgan at slip, off Daley, allowed Boon to escape when he was 10, and he revived the innings with a solid 105, hitting a six and nine fours. Walsh upset the momentum of the innings with a fiery spell with the second new ball in which he struck Waugh on the ear flap of the helmet, causing him to retire hurt at 31, had Healy caught behind with a fearful bouncer, and inflicted a cut above McDermott's right eye as the batsman missed an intended hook. McDermott's wound required nine stitches, and when the attack prompted a warning for intimidation from umpire Gaynor, Walsh ended the over with an off-break and then took himself off. Waugh returned to complete his century, which included a six and ten fours, and the dogged Matthews was 5 short of his when Haynes took the last two wickets. Whitney and Hughes made early inroads into the home team's batting, after which only the left-handed Adams, who remained unbeaten after 191 minutes, showed any inclination to delay the defeat.

*Close of play:* First day, Australians 86–2 (D. C. Boon 43*, A. R. Border 27*); Second day, Australians 412–6 (M. E. Waugh 99*, G. R. J. Matthews 60*).

## Jamaica

| | | | |
|---|---|---|---|
| D. S. Morgan c Healy b Whitney | 42 | – c Marsh b Hughes | 16 |
| R. G. Samuels b Whitney | 12 | – c Healy b Whitney | 14 |
| P. J. L. Dujon c Taylor b McDermott | 40 | – c Marsh b Hughes | 7 |
| †J. C. Adams b Whitney | 0 | – not out | 69 |
| C. A. Davidson lbw b McDermott | 6 | – lbw b Whitney | 15 |
| O. W. Cruickshank lbw b Whitney | 0 | – (7) c Jones b Matthews | 16 |
| R. C. Haynes c Matthews b Whitney | 17 | – (6) b Matthews | 2 |
| A. G. Daley c Boon b Whitney | 0 | – b Waugh | 4 |
| *C. A. Walsh b McDermott | 1 | – b Matthews | 1 |
| E. L. Wilson b McDermott | 4 | – c Healy b Matthews | 9 |
| R. A. Taylor not out | 0 | – run out | 0 |
| B 13, l-b 9, w 4, n-b 10 | 36 | B 13, n-b 8 | 21 |
| | **158** | | **174** |

1/29 2/107 3/107 4/115 5/124    158    1/31 2/35 3/41 4/78 5/85    174
6/128 7/133 8/134 9/158                 6/125 7/129 8/130 9/171

Bowling: *First Innings*—McDermott 17–2–44–4; Whitney 20–5–42–6; Hughes 6–0–23–0; Waugh 5–1–11–0; Matthews 3–1–16–0. *Second Innings*—Whitney 16–1–36–2; Hughes 16.3–5–47–2; Matthews 20–5–57–4; Waugh 7–1–21–1.

## Australians

| | | | |
|---|---|---|---|
| G. R. Marsh b Taylor | 2 | C. J. McDermott retired hurt | 17 |
| M. A. Taylor b Walsh | 5 | M. G. Hughes b Haynes | 3 |
| D. C. Boon c Davidson b Haynes | 105 | M. R. Whitney c Morgan b Haynes | 2 |
| *A. R. Border lbw b Taylor | 43 | | |
| D. M. Jones c Haynes b Wilson | 33 | B 16, l-b 15, w 1, n-b 22 | 54 |
| M. E. Waugh b Taylor | 108 | | |
| G. R. J. Matthews not out | 95 | 1/4 2/14 3/121 4/208 5/215 | 469 |
| †I. A. Healy c Adams b Walsh | 2 | 6/281 7/440 8/459 9/469 | |

*M. E. Waugh, when 31, retired hurt at 271 and resumed at 306, when C. J. McDermott retired hurt.*

Bowling: Taylor 35–7–86–3; Walsh 24–2–86–2; Daley 22–2–78–0; Haynes 30–3–92–3; Wilson 24–5–79–1; Cruickshank 4–0–17–0.

Umpires: L. U. Bell and A. J. Gaynor.

## WEST INDIES v AUSTRALIA

### First One-day International

At Kingston, Jamaica, February 26. Australia won by 35 runs. Toss: Australia. West Indies lost their last six wickets for 19 runs after Richardson and Logie, each scoring at a run a ball, had given them renewed hope with a partnership of 95. Logie was caught at square leg, having hit seven fours, Marshall was run out at the non-striker's end from a bowler's deflection, and McDermott then struck the decisive blows by dismissing Richardson (one six, five fours), Dujon and Gray. Australia's total was almost entirely due to the improvised strokes, expert placement and alert running between the wickets of Jones and Mark Waugh, who added 136 in 23 overs for the fourth wicket against some indisciplined bowling and fielding. Jones's unbeaten 88 was made from 105 balls, with six fours, and Waugh hit seven fours in his run-a-ball 67. It was West Indies' first home defeat in eighteen one-day internationals since they lost to England off the last ball at Port-of-Spain in March 1986.

*Man of the Match*: D. M. Jones.

### Australia

| | | | | |
|---|---|---|---|---|
| D. C. Boon b Walsh | 34 | S. R. Waugh not out | | 6 |
| G. R. Marsh run out | 26 | L-b 7, w 3, n-b 5 | | 15 |
| D. M. Jones not out | 88 | | | — |
| *A. R. Border b Hooper | 8 | 1/59 (1) 2/73 (2) | (4 wkts, 50 overs) | 244 |
| M. E. Waugh b Ambrose | 67 | 3/98 (4) 4/234 (5) | | |

†I. A. Healy, P. L. Taylor, C. J. McDermott, M. R. Whitney and B. A. Reid did not bat.

Bowling: Ambrose 9-1-46-1; Gray 10-0-53-0; Marshall 6-0-27-0; Walsh 7-1-30-1; Hooper 10-1-44-1; Richards 8-0-37-0.

### West Indies

| | | | | |
|---|---|---|---|---|
| C. G. Greenidge b S. R. Waugh | 19 | A. H. Gray c Healy b McDermott | | 2 |
| D. L. Haynes c Healy b McDermott | 17 | C. E. L. Ambrose lbw b Taylor | | 0 |
| R. B. Richardson c Jones b McDermott | 64 | C. A. Walsh not out | | 1 |
| C. L. Hooper lbw b S. R. Waugh | 6 | B 2, l-b 6, w 3, n-b 4 | | 15 |
| *I. V. A. Richards b Taylor | 18 | | | |
| A. L. Logie c S. R. Waugh | | 1/33 (2) 2/48 (1) 3/68 (4) | (45.5 overs) | 209 |
| b M. E. Waugh | 65 | 4/95 (5) 5/190 (6) 6/191 (7) | | |
| M. D. Marshall run out | 1 | 7/206 (3) 8/206 (8) | | |
| †P. J. L. Dujon c Border b McDermott | 1 | 9/207 (10) 10/209 (9) | | |

Bowling: Reid 7-2-33-0; McDermott 8.5-0-34-4; Whitney 7-1-16-0; S. R. Waugh 7-1-32-2; Taylor 9-1-48-2; M. E. Waugh 7-0-38-1.

Umpires: D. M. Archer and S. U. Bucknor.

## WEST INDIES v AUSTRALIA

### First Test Match

At Kingston, Jamaica, March 1, 2, 3, 5, 6. Drawn. Toss: West Indies. An engrossing match, with exciting possibilities over the final two days, was spoiled by the loss of the fourth day and the first session of the fifth. The frustration at having such great expectations dashed was compounded by the reason – the inadequacy of the flat, tarpaulin covers and the incompetence of the ground authority which allowed the heavy rain on the rest day to leak on to a critical portion of the pitch at the northern end, and to turn the bowler's approach at the same end into a quagmire. The embarrassment of the Jamaica Cricket Association was matched by the fury of the local media, especially as it was the lack of proper equipment which had caused the abandonment of the fourth day of the Test against England a year earlier. When stumps were drawn on the third afternoon, West Indies had recovered three times from desperate situations to be 80 ahead with eight second-innings wickets standing.

Their initial problems had been caused by the speed, accuracy and hostility of McDermott, staunchly supported by Hughes, which left them 75 for six midway through the first day. At that point, one of their main batsmen, Logie, was having seven stitches inserted to a cut above his right eye, inflicted, in spite of the grille on his helmet, when he missed a hook against McDermott, who had earlier caused the retirement of Haynes, from a blow on the toe, and required Greenidge to receive on-field treatment for a knock on the shoulder blade. This subsequently prevented Greenidge from fielding. Having baited Richards into hooking a catch to long leg, McDermott was recalled after lunch to remove Greenidge, the returning Haynes, and Marshall; but Australia's advance was halted by a partnership of 69 between Dujon and Ambrose, which had the added value of allowing Logie to recover in time to resume his innings when Ambrose provided Waugh with his first Test wicket. Seemingly unperturbed by his injury, Logie moved from 9 to 77 with dazzling strokeplay, his innings, from just 110 balls, containing twelve fours. Dujon, who spent three and a half hours in making his highest score in his last 26 Test innings, was similarly essential to the West Indian recovery.

The pitch was at its best on the second day, and Marsh and Taylor spent the first half of it consolidating Australia's position with a stand of 139. When they were out within 20 runs of each other, and Border and Jones later departed in successive overs, the dogged Boon denied West Indies a complete breakthrough. Having put on 68 with Border, he added 101 with Waugh as Australia went ahead, but the loss of the last six wickets for 42 in fifteen overs, four to Patterson's telling accuracy, limited Australia's lead. The collapse left Boon unbeaten after 6 hours 25 minutes with his tenth Test century (nine fours), his resolve unshaken either by the wickets tumbling around him or a cut on the chin from a Patterson bouncer when he was 95.

Greenidge and Haynes, the latter in particular, responded to the deficit of 107 with a stroke-filled assault that took the Australians by surprise. The pair's fifteenth century partnership in Tests put West Indies ahead before McDermott applied the brakes with an outstanding spell of thirteen overs, in which he dismissed both within the space of 16 runs. Haynes had fourteen fours in his 84. The Australians were convinced that Richardson had the better of an appeal for a leg-side catch by Healy off Waugh just before the end of the third day, but this became irrelevant when the remainder of the match was reduced to scarcely more than a meaningless half day. Richardson did go on to record his sixth century against Australia – his eleventh overall in Tests – while Richards became West Indies' highest scorer in Test cricket, overtaking Sir Garfield Sobers's 8,032 when he was 32. Border went past 9,000 runs in Tests and Haynes 6,000, and McDermott took his 100th wicket in his 27th Test.

*Men of the Match*: D. C. Boon and A. L. Logie.

*Close of play*: First day, Australia 4-0 (G. R. Marsh 0*, M. A. Taylor 2*); Second day, Australia 296-4 (D. C. Boon 71*, M. E. Waugh 22*); Third day, West Indies 187-2 (R. B. Richardson 33*, C. L. Hooper 11*); Fourth day, No play.

## West Indies

| | | | |
|---|---|---|---|
| C. G. Greenidge c and b McDermott | 27 | – c Healy b McDermott | 35 |
| D. L. Haynes b McDermott | 8 | – c Healy b McDermott | 84 |
| R. B. Richardson c Healy b Hughes | 15 | – not out | 104 |
| C. L. Hooper c Marsh b Hughes | 0 | – b McDermott | 31 |
| *I. V. A. Richards c Hughes b McDermott | 11 | – not out | 52 |
| A. L. Logie not out | 77 | | |
| †P. J. L. Dujon c Marsh b Hughes | 59 | | |
| M. D. Marshall lbw b McDermott | 0 | | |
| C. E. L. Ambrose c and b Waugh | 33 | | |
| C. A. Walsh lbw b McDermott | 10 | | |
| B. P. Patterson b Hughes | 4 | | |
| L-b 6, w 1, n-b 13 | 20 | B 15, l-b 6, w 1, n-b 6 | 28 |

1/33 (3) 2/37 (4) 3/57 (5) 4/69 (1)      264      1/118 (1) 2/134 (2) (3 wkts dec.) 334
5/75 (2) 6/75 (8) 7/144 (9) 8/166 (10)      3/216 (4)
9/234 (7) 10/264 (11)

*In the first innings D. L. Haynes, when 4, retired hurt at 9 and resumed at 69-4, when A. L. Logie, 9, retired hurt; Logie resumed at 166.*

Bowling: *First Innings*—McDermott 23-3-80-5; Whitney 21-4-58-0; Hughes 21.3-4-67-4; Matthews 11-3-28-0; Waugh 6-1-25-1. *Second Innings*—McDermott 24-10-48-3; Whitney 17-3-55-0; Hughes 22-5-79-0; Matthews 25-2-90-0; Border 10-3-21-0; Waugh 13-6-20-0.

## Australia

| | | |
|---|---|---|
| G. R. Marsh c Dujon b Ambrose | 69 | |
| M. A. Taylor c Hooper b Patterson | 58 | |
| D. C. Boon not out | 109 | |
| *A. R. Border c Dujon b Ambrose | 31 | |
| D. M. Jones c and b Hooper | 0 | |
| M. E. Waugh lbw b Marshall | 39 | |
| G. R. J. Matthews c Dujon | | |
| b Patterson | 10 | |
| †I. A. Healy lbw b Walsh | 1 | |

C. J. McDermott b Patterson ......... 1
M. G. Hughes c Hooper b Patterson ... 0
M. R. Whitney b Patterson .......... 2
B 4, l-b 23, w 4, n-b 21 ...... 52

371

1/139 (1) 2/159 (2) 3/227 (4)
4/228 (5) 5/329 (6) 6/357 (7)
7/358 (8) 8/365 (9)
9/365 (10) 10/371 (11)

Bowling: Ambrose 30-3-94-2; Patterson 24-1-83-5; Marshall 22-3-57-1; Walsh 23-4-73-1; Hooper 21-7-37-1.

*Umpires: D. M. Archer and S. U. Bucknor.*

# †WEST INDIES v AUSTRALIA

## Second One-day International

At Port-of-Spain, Trinidad, March 9. Australia won by 45 runs. Toss: West Indies. After the match had been reduced to 42 overs an innings by rain, Jones assured Australia of a challenging total from the 34 overs that the West Indians bowled, hitting nine fours in the 85 balls faced for his 64. Gray's six wickets, which earned him the Man of the Match award, included Border first ball, but he was also expensive. Haynes led West Indies' effort with seven fours in 45 off 62 balls, but Australia, supporting steady bowling with flawless fielding, never let the situation get out of control. Once Richards was caught at deep mid-wicket, trying for a second six off Whitney, the last four wickets added just 15.

*Man of the Match:* A. H. Gray.

## Australia

| | | |
|---|---|---|
| D. C. Boon c Hooper b Moseley | 5 | |
| G. R. Marsh c Hooper b Gray | 23 | |
| D. M. Jones b Gray | 64 | |
| *A. R. Border c Dujon b Gray | 0 | |
| M. E. Waugh b Simmons | 16 | |
| S. R. Waugh b Gray | 26 | |
| †I. A. Healy not out | 13 | |
| P. L. Taylor c and b Gray | 1 | |
| C. J. McDermott b Ambrose | 1 | |

M. R. Whitney c Hooper b Gray ..... 0
B 2, l-b 7, w 7, n-b 7 ........ 23

(9 wkts, 34 overs) 172

1/9 (1) 2/84 (2)
3/84 (4) 4/106 (5)
5/141 (3) 6/161 (6)
7/167 (8) 8/168 (9)
9/172 (10)

B. A. Reid did not bat.

Bowling: Ambrose 8-2-17-1; Moseley 5-0-22-1; Marshall 6-0-37-0; Gray 9-0-50-6; Hooper 3-0-18-0; Richards 1-0-4-0; Simmons 2-0-15-1.

## West Indies

| | | |
|---|---|---|
| P. V. Simmons c Healy b Reid | 13 | |
| D. L. Haynes c Healy b Whitney | 45 | |
| R. B. Richardson c S. R. Waugh | | |
| b McDermott | 5 | |
| C. L. Hooper c Healy b Whitney | 3 | |
| *I. V. A. Richards c Marsh b Whitney | 27 | |
| A. L. Logie run out | 7 | |
| †P. J. L. Dujon b McDermott | 7 | |
| M. D. Marshall c Boon b McDermott | 5 | |
| E. A. Moseley c Taylor b M. E. Waugh | 2 | |

C. E. L. Ambrose c Taylor
b M. E. Waugh . 7
A. H. Gray not out ............... 0
L-b 2, n-b 4 ............... 6

(31.1 overs) 127

1/14 (1) 2/47 (3) 3/52 (4)
4/78 (2) 5/90 (6) 6/112 (5)
7/113 (7) 8/116 (9)
9/126 (10) 10/127 (8)

Bowling: Reid 5-0-25-1; McDermott 7.1-0-29-3; Whitney 9-0-41-3; S. R. Waugh 8-0-24-0; M. E. Waugh 2-0-6-2.

*Umpires: L. H. Barker and C. E. Cumberbatch.*

## †WEST INDIES v AUSTRALIA

### Third One-day International

At Port-of-Spain, Trinidad, March 10. West Indies won by seven wickets after their target had been reduced to 181 off 36 overs because of rain between innings. Toss: Australia. Marsh, who had eight fours in 81 off 118 balls, provided the foundation to the Australian innings, with Jones, whose 36 off 49 balls contained a six and four fours, helping him add 69 in fifteen overs for the second wicket. Steve Waugh and Healy were responsible for 54 coming off the last six overs, Healy's unbeaten 33 being made from only 23 balls. The reduction of their target was to West Indies' advantage, and Richardson, first with Haynes and then with Greenidge, kept them on course. When he skied a pull to square leg, having hit fourteen fours in 90 off 94 balls, West Indies needed 49 off 7.5 overs. Amidst scenes of great excitement in a crowd of almost 20,000, Logie, hitting five fours in an unbeaten 24 off 21 balls, propelled them to victory.

*Man of the Match:* R. B. Richardson.

## Australia

| | | | | |
|---|---|---|---|---|
| G. R. Marsh b Gray | 81 | P. L. Taylor b Ambrose | | 2 |
| M. A. Taylor c Haynes b Ambrose | 3 | C. J. McDermott not out | | 3 |
| D. M. Jones c Richards b Gray | 36 | B 2, l-b 10, w 9, n-b 4 | | 25 |
| M. E. Waugh b Simmons | 17 | | | |
| *A. R. Border c Dujon b Patterson | 22 | 1/13 (2) 2/82 (3) | (7 wkts, 49 overs) | 245 |
| S. R. Waugh b Ambrose | 23 | 3/116 (4) 4/165 (5) | | |
| †I. A. Healy not out | 33 | 5/191 (1) 6/225 (6) | | |
| | | 7/239 (8) | | |

M. R. Whitney and B. A. Reid did not bat.

Bowling: Ambrose 10-1-37-3; Patterson 9-0-52-1; Gray 10-0-59-2; Simmons 10-0-35-1; Hooper 10-0-50-0.

## West Indies

| | | | | |
|---|---|---|---|---|
| P. V. Simmons c Healy b Reid | 0 | A. L. Logie not out | | 24 |
| D. L. Haynes b S. R. Waugh | 16 | B 1, l-b 5, w 3, n-b 2 | | 11 |
| R. B. Richardson c Border | | | | |
| b M. E. Waugh | 90 | 1/3 (1) 2/72 (2) | (3 wkts, 33.3 overs) | 181 |
| C. G. Greenidge not out | 40 | 3/132 (3) | | |

*I. V. A. Richards, C. L. Hooper, †P. J. L. Dujon, C. E. L. Ambrose, A. H. Gray and B. P. Patterson did not bat.

Bowling: Reid 7-0-28-1; McDermott 5-0-21-0; S. R. Waugh 7-0-39-1; P. L. Taylor 2-0-17-0; Whitney 7-0-38-0; M. E. Waugh 5.3-0-32-1.

Umpires: L. H. Barker and C. E. Cumberbatch.

## †WEST INDIES v AUSTRALIA

### Fourth One-day International

At Bridgetown, Barbados, March 13. Australia won by 37 runs. Toss: Australia. Batting first for the fourth successive time, the Australians took advantage of an exceptionally true pitch, and West Indies' tactic of choosing only three specialist bowlers, to amass their highest total in their 57 one-day internationals against West Indies. Two partnerships involving Marsh built Australia's innings after Mark Taylor and Jones were out cheaply. He added 146 in 25 overs with Border, and 87 in twelve with Mark Waugh, hitting three sixes and eight fours in his 113 off 140 balls, his eighth century in this form of the game. The Australians took 37 off Marshall's last three overs and in all hit seven sixes and nineteen fours. West Indian wickets fell steadily as the Australians fielded and caught brilliantly, and with Australia securing the series 3-1, with a game to play, West Indies incurred their first loss in a one-day rubber at home.

*Man of the Match:* G. R. Marsh.

## Australia

| | | | |
|---|---|---|---|
| M. A. Taylor c Dujon b Ambrose | 5 | C. J. McDermott not out | 1 |
| G. R. Marsh b Ambrose | 113 | | |
| D. M. Jones c Walsh b Marshall | 7 | B 2, l-b 7, w 4, n-b 5 | 18 |
| *A. R. Border c Ambrose b Hooper | 79 | | — |
| M. E. Waugh run out | 49 | 1/19 (1) 2/27 (3)　(6 wkts, 50 overs) | 283 |
| S. R. Waugh lbw b Ambrose | 5 | 3/173 (4) 4/260 (5) | |
| †I. A. Healy not out | 6 | 5/271 (2) 6/276 (6) | |

P. L. Taylor, M. R. Whitney and B. A. Reid did not bat.

Bowling: Ambrose 10–1–38–3; Marshall 10–1–67–1; Walsh 10–0–46–0; Simmons 6–0–37–0; Richards 4–0–29–0; Hooper 10–0–57–1.

## West Indies

| | | | |
|---|---|---|---|
| P. V. Simmons b McDermott | 23 | M. D. Marshall c Whitney | |
| D. L. Haynes b Reid | 22 | b McDermott | 19 |
| R. B. Richardson c McDermott | | C. E. L. Ambrose not out | 12 |
| b Whitney | 25 | C. A. Walsh c and b M. E. Waugh | 4 |
| C. G. Greenidge lbw b S. R. Waugh | 17 | | |
| *I. V. A. Richards c and b S. R. Waugh | 20 | | |
| A. L. Logie c M. A. Taylor | | L-b 6, w 1, n-b 3 | 10 |
| b M. E. Waugh | 37 | | — |
| C. L. Hooper c M. E. Waugh | | 1/39 (1) 2/49 (2) 3/89 (3)　(47 overs) | 246 |
| b P. L. Taylor | 18 | 4/95 (4) 5/118 (5) 6/158 (7) | |
| †P. J. L. Dujon c P. L. Taylor | | 7/177 (6) 8/225 (9) | |
| b M. E. Waugh | 39 | 9/241 (8) 10/246 (11) | |

Bowling: Reid 7–0–52–1; McDermott 8–0–40–2; S. R. Waugh 7–0–25–2; Whitney 10–1–39–1; P. L. Taylor 8–0–50–1; M. E. Waugh 7–0–34–3.

Umpires: D. M. Archer and L. H. Barker.

## TRINIDAD & TOBAGO v AUSTRALIANS

At Pointe-à-Pierre, Trinidad, March 15, 16, 17. Drawn. Toss: Australians. Rain delayed the start, and when it washed out the second day altogether, the managements of the two teams agreed to abandon the three-day match and play a 50-overs one instead on the scheduled final day. The abandonment was a setback for the Australians, who were anxious that Reid should have time to bowl a lengthy spell in his first first-class match, the status of which was subsequently confirmed by the West Indies Cricket Board of Control. The highlight of the limited-overs match was Lara's 91, which emphasised the form that earned him a record aggregate in the preceding domestic Red Stripe Cup tournament.

*Close of play:* First day, Trinidad & Tobago 206-6 (D. Williams 11*, R. Sieuchan 15*); Second day, No play.

## Trinidad & Tobago

| | | | |
|---|---|---|---|
| P. V. Simmons c Boon b Alderman | 28 | †D. Williams not out | 11 |
| S. Ragoonath lbw b Hughes | 37 | R. Sieuchan not out | 15 |
| A. D. Rahim b Hughes | 1 | B 8, l-b 6, w 4, n-b 6 | 24 |
| B. C. Lara c Veletta b Reid | 33 | | — |
| N. Bidhesi b P. L. Taylor | 46 | 1/68 2/73 3/76　(6 wkts) | 206 |
| R. A. M. Smith c Alderman b Matthews | 11 | 4/150 5/178 6/184 | |

*R. Nanan, R. Dhanraj and E. C. Antoine did not bat.

Bowling: Reid 15–3–59–1; Alderman 12–1–32–1; S. R. Waugh 1–1–0–0; Hughes 12–2–50–2; P. L. Taylor 10–3–27–1; Matthews 10–4–24–1.

## Australians

*D. C. Boon, M. A. Taylor, †M. R. J. Veletta, D. M. Jones, M. E. Waugh, S. R. Waugh, G. R. J. Matthews, P. L. Taylor, M. G. Hughes, T. M. Alderman and B. A. Reid.

Umpires: Farooq Ali and Z. Maccum.

†At Pointe-à-Pierre, Trinidad, March 17. Australians won by 26 runs. Toss: Australians. Australians 222 for eight (50 overs) (M. A. Taylor 38, M. R. J. Veletta 33, M. E. Waugh 32); Trinidad & Tobago 196 for nine (50 overs) (R. A. M. Smith 30, B. C. Lara 91; B. A. Reid three for 22).

## †WEST INDIES v AUSTRALIA

### Fifth One-day International

At Georgetown, Guyana, March 20. Australia won by six wickets. Toss: West Indies. Haynes and Simmons put on 85 in seventeen overs, but while Richardson built on this foundation with 94 off 88 balls (one six, eleven fours), he could find no-one to stay with him after Haynes was lbw, sweeping, in the 23rd over. West Indies' last six wickets fell for 34 in the last nine overs from McDermott and Hughes. Marsh and Border shared a sizeable partnership for Australia, 124 in 24 overs with Border's 60 coming from 61 balls (two sixes, five fours), and Marsh remained to the end. His unbeaten 106, his second successive one-day international century, was made from 158 balls and included eight fours. The match ended with Patterson delivering a no-ball and 4 wides, bringing the total number in the Australian innings to 11 wides and 24 no-balls.

*Man of the Match:* G. R. Marsh.

### West Indies

| | | | |
|---|---|---|---|
| P. V. Simmons c Hughes b Taylor | 34 | A. H. Gray c Border b McDermott | 6 |
| D. L. Haynes lbw b Taylor | 58 | C. A. Walsh b Hughes | 2 |
| R. B. Richardson c Healy b Hughes | 94 | B. P. Patterson not out | 1 |
| C. G. Greenidge run out | 6 | L-b 8, w 1, n-b 2 | 11 |
| *I. V. A. Richards c Whitney b M. E. Waugh | 10 | 1/85 (1) 2/115 (2) 3/136 (4) (49.5 overs) 251 |
| A. L. Logie b McDermott | 17 | 4/155 (5) 5/217 (6) 6/237 (3) |
| C. L. Hooper c Taylor b McDermott | 10 | 7/239 (7) 8/246 (8) |
| †P. J. L. Dujon b Hughes | 2 | 9/248 (9) 10/251 (10) |

Bowling: McDermott 10-0-29-3; Hughes 9.5-0-33-3; S. R. Waugh 3-0-33-0; Whitney 9-0-46-0; Taylor 10-0-45-2; M. E. Waugh 6-0-36-1; Border 2-0-21-0.

### Australia

| | | | |
|---|---|---|---|
| G. R. Marsh not out | 106 | S. R. Waugh not out | 26 |
| D. C. Boon b Patterson | 9 | B 4, l-b 4, w 11, n-b 14 | 33 |
| D. M. Jones run out | 11 | | |
| *A. R. Border c Dujon b Walsh | 60 | 1/12 (2) 2/37 (3)    (4 wkts, 48.3 overs) 252 |
| M. E. Waugh st Dujon b Hooper | 7 | 3/161 (4) 4/181 (5) |

†I. A. Healy, C. J. McDermott, P. L. Taylor, M. G. Hughes and M. R. Whitney did not bat.

Bowling: Patterson 6.3–0–34–1; Gray 8–0–44–0; Walsh 10–0–54–1; Simmons 10–0–53–0; Hooper 10–0–45–1; Richards 4–0–14–0.

Umpires: C. E. Cumberbatch and C. R. Duncan.

## WEST INDIES v AUSTRALIA

### Second Test Match

At Georgetown, Guyana, March 23, 24, 25, 27, 28. West Indies won by ten wickets. Toss: Australia. At 328 for six at lunch on the second day, Australia had seemingly batted themselves into a comfortable, if not impregnable, position. By lunch next day, they were 5 behind and had taken only two West Indian wickets. The spectacular and sudden shift clearly stunned them, and they showed little fight thereafter, with the result that they were almost beaten by an innings.

The responsibility lay for the transformation with Richardson. Arriving at the wicket in the third over, he launched himself into an immediate and devastating assault on the bowling, encouraged by the ideal conditions offered by the ground where he had recorded his two highest Test scores. By the end of the second day he was 114 not out, having scored 106 off 41 overs after tea, and when finally he was lbw to McDermott, third ball after lunch next day, he had been batting for five and threequarter hours. In this time he received 260 balls and hit two sixes, both from hooks, and 26 fours, mostly with searing cuts and square-drives. Haynes, sensibly flowing along in his slipstream, helped him add 297, eclipsing by 130 runs their previous second-wicket record against Australia. Haynes's sixteenth Test century, containing seventeen fours in five and a quarter hours (211 balls), was ended by a catch at silly point off Border's left-arm spin, but even when Richardson was dismissed at 353, West Indies continued to build their lead at a rapid rate. Border embarrassed his principal bowlers with his five for 68 from 30 overs and, as he observed later, the main difference between the teams was the rate at which they scored their runs. While Australia managed an average of 2.98 in their first innings, West Indies maintained 3.69 over 153.5 overs, helped by five sixes and 72 fours.

In their first innings, Australia had laboured throughout the first day to end with 249 for six off 83 overs, their attitude influenced by the early loss of Taylor and Boon. Marsh, so dominant in the previous two one-day internationals, took 5 hours 25 minutes over a solid 94 before he sliced a catch to gully in the 65th over, and it needed a stand of 101 for the seventh wicket between Waugh and Healy to send Australia past 300. When they went in a second time, an hour before lunch on the fourth day with a deficit of 221, there was nothing to play for but a draw. Yet they seemed to have little fight left, and the bizarre umpiring decision that accounted for Jones proved a further psychological setback.

Taylor, Boon and Marsh had all gone cheaply when Jones was "bowled" by a no-ball from Walsh. Hearing only the rattle of the stumps behind him, but not umpire Duncan's call, Jones headed for the pavilion, in the direction of extra cover, in the mistaken belief that he was out, whereupon Hooper rushed in from the slips, picked up the ball and uprooted the middle stump, to be joined by several team-mates in an appeal for run out. Alerted to the impending danger by Border, his partner, Jones had made a vain attempt to regain his ground, only to see umpire Cumberbatch at square leg, standing in his eleventh Test, rule him out – in contravention of the unequivocal Law 38.2: "If a no-ball has been called, the striker shall not be given run out unless he attempts to run", which Jones obviously had not. It was instructive that both captains admitted afterwards that they too were ignorant of the relevant Law, but this was of no consolation to Jones or to Australia. McDermott was also "bowled" by a Walsh no-ball later in the day, though the consequence of that was simply a bye. When he was out, early next morning, Australia were still 34 in arrears with only two wickets standing, but Healy and Hughes enabled them to avoid an innings defeat with a spirited stand of 54, delaying until mid-afternoon West Indies' first Test victory on the ground since they beat Australia there in 1964-65.

*Man of the Match:* R. B. Richardson.

*Close of play:* First day, Australia 249-6 (M. E. Waugh 30\*, I. A. Healy 3\*); Second day, West Indies 226-1 (D. L. Haynes 87\*, R. B. Richardson 114\*); Third day, West Indies 532-9 (M. D. Marshall 1\*, B. P. Patterson 0\*); Fourth day, Australia 178-7 (I. A. Healy 10\*, C. J. McDermott 0\*).

## Australia

| | | | | |
|---|---|---|---|---|
| M. A. Taylor lbw b Patterson | 0 | – (2) lbw b Ambrose | 15 |
| G. R. Marsh c Hooper b Patterson | 94 | – (1) b Walsh | 22 |
| D. C. Boon c Dujon b Marshall | 7 | – c Dujon b Marshall | 2 |
| *A. R. Border b Marshall | 47 | – c Dujon b Marshall | 34 |
| D. M. Jones b Marshall | 34 | – run out | 3 |
| M. E. Waugh c Dujon b Patterson | 71 | – c Richards b Ambrose | 31 |
| G. R. J. Matthews c Dujon b Ambrose | 1 | – c Dujon b Marshall | 16 |
| †I. A. Healy run out | 53 | – run out | 47 |
| C. J. McDermott lbw b Patterson | 1 | – c Dujon b Patterson | 4 |
| M. G. Hughes b Ambrose | 0 | – c Patterson b Walsh | 21 |
| M. R. Whitney not out | 1 | – not out | 0 |
| B 6, l-b 8, w 2, n-b 23 | 39 | B 17, l-b 6, w 2, n-b 28 | 53 |

1/3 (1) 2/24 (3) 3/124 (4) 4/188 (2)     348     1/32 (2) 2/43 (3) 3/67 (1)     248
5/237 (5) 6/238 (7) 7/339 (6)     4/73 (5) 5/130 (6) 6/161 (4)
8/346 (9) 9/346 (8) 10/348 (10)     7/172 (7) 8/187 (9)
    9/241 (8) 10/248 (10)

Bowling: *First Innings*—Ambrose 31.4-9-64-2; Patterson 24-1-80-4; Walsh 24-2-81-0; Marshall 23-3-67-3; Hooper 13-3-37-0; Richards 1-0-5-0. *Second Innings*—Ambrose 24-5-45-2; Patterson 14-5-46-1; Walsh 23-4-55-2; Marshall 15-2-31-3; Hooper 18-6-35-0; Richards 4-2-13-0.

## West Indies

| | | | |
|---|---|---|---|
| C. G. Greenidge lbw b McDermott | 2 | – not out | 5 |
| D. L. Haynes c Waugh b Border | 111 | – not out | 23 |
| R. B. Richardson b McDermott | 182 | | |
| C. L. Hooper c Waugh b Matthews | 62 | | |
| *I. V. A. Richards b Matthews | 50 | | |
| A. L. Logie c Healy b Border | 54 | | |
| †P. J. L. Dujon lbw b Border | 29 | | |
| M. D. Marshall not out | 22 | | |
| C. E. L. Ambrose b Border | 0 | | |
| C. A. Walsh b Border | 1 | | |
| B. P. Patterson lbw b Matthews | 15 | | |
| B 5, l-b 13, n-b 23 | 41 | L-b 2, n-b 1 | 3 |

1/10 (1) 2/307 (2) 3/353 (3) 4/443 (4)     569     (no wkt) 31
5/444 (5) 6/529 (7) 7/530 (6)
8/530 (9) 9/532 (10) 10/569 (11)

Bowling: *First Innings*—McDermott 36-2-114-2; Whitney 28-4-103-0; Matthews 37.5-6-155-3; Hughes 20-4-93-0; Waugh 2-0-18-0; Border 30-11-68-5. *Second Innings*—McDermott 4-1-10-0; Hughes 3.5-0-19-0.

Umpires: C. E. Cumberbatch and C. R. Duncan.

## WEST INDIES UNDER-23 XI v AUSTRALIANS

At Kingstown, St Vincent, March 30, 31, April 1, 2. Drawn. Toss: Australians. The young West Indians, having batted enterprisingly to be 252 for three at lunch on the second day, had a desperate struggle to save the match on the last day, when the Australians were denied victory by the left-handed Adams's doggedness in holding out for three hours, and by three missed chances. After the Under-23 XI had been put in, Wallace dominated an opening stand of 93 with Williams, who then added 109 with Eugene. When Williams was out to the second new ball, he had batted for 289 minutes and had hit twelve fours, but his dismissal prompted a disappointing decline to the innings. Mark Taylor's laboured 122 took him six hours and included a chance off Skeete when he was 71, as well as several narrow misses. Boon, Jones and Waugh were much more assured as the Australians built a lead of 144. They did not have quite enough time to convert it into victory, however.

*Close of play:* First day, West Indies Under-23 XI 179-1 (S. C. Williams 72*, J. Eugene 45*); Second day, Australians 92-1 (M. A. Taylor 48*, D. C. Boon 34*); Third day, Australians 390-6 (I. A. Healy 14*, A. R. Border 0*).

## West Indies Under-23 XI

| | | | |
|---|---|---|---|
| P. A. Wallace c Veletta b Reid | 52 | – b Reid | 0 |
| S. C. Williams c Veletta b Reid | 97 | – c Healy b P. L. Taylor | 19 |
| J. Eugene c Veletta b Reid | 55 | – lbw b P. L. Taylor | 25 |
| *B. C. Lara lbw b Alderman | 22 | – st Veletta b P. L. Taylor | 4 |
| J. C. Adams lbw b Hughes | 12 | – not out | 58 |
| †J. R. Murray lbw b Hughes | 1 | – c M. A. Taylor b P. L. Taylor | 0 |
| H. A. G. Anthony c P. L. Taylor b Reid | 33 | – b P. L. Taylor | 5 |
| N. O. Perry c and b P. L. Taylor | 7 | – lbw b Reid | 5 |
| L. A. Joseph c M. A. Taylor b P. L. Taylor | 1 | – b Hughes | 35 |
| S. M. Skeete c Hughes b P. L. Taylor | 3 | – lbw b Border | 0 |
| R. Dhanraj not out | 2 | – not out | 0 |
| B 4, l-b 4, n-b 14 | 22 | B 2, l-b 1, n-b 8 | 11 |

1/93 2/202 3/232 4/253 5/254      307    1/0 2/50 3/54      (9 wkts) 162
6/261 7/272 8/283 9/289                 4/55 5/55 6/77
                                    7/90 8/147 9/150

*Bowling: First Innings*—Alderman 27-5-63-1; Reid 29.1-6-76-4; Hughes 30-11-90-2; P. L. Taylor 21-5-54-3; Waugh 4-0-16-0. *Second Innings*—Reid 14-1-47-2; Alderman 4-0-17-0; P. L. Taylor 25-9-37-5; Hughes 12-0-32-1; Border 10-3-26-1.

## Australians

| | | | |
|---|---|---|---|
| M. A. Taylor b Anthony | 122 | M. G. Hughes c Lara b Perry | 9 |
| †M. R. J. Veletta c Wallace b Joseph | 4 | B. A. Reid c Lara b Perry | 2 |
| D. C. Boon run out | 53 | T. M. Alderman lbw b Anthony | 2 |
| D. M. Jones c Murray b Anthony | 60 | | |
| S. R. Waugh c Lara b Anthony | 85 | B 3, l-b 7, w 7, n-b 6 | 23 |
| P. L. Taylor run out | 33 | | |
| I. A. Healy c Eugene b Perry | 20 | 1/26 2/128 3/239 4/274 5/363 | 451 |
| *A. R. Border not out | 38 | 6/387 7/408 8/433 9/444 | |

*Bowling:* Skeete 30-4-109-0; Joseph 20-1-63-1; Perry 44-5-111-3; Anthony 26.2-2-75-4; Dhanraj 29-2-83-0.

Umpires: G. T. Browne and A. E. Weekes.

## WEST INDIES v AUSTRALIA

### Third Test Match

At Port-of-Spain, Trinidad, April 5, 6, 8, 9, 10. Drawn. Toss: West Indies. Torrential, unseasonal rain restricted play to 23 overs on the first day and eight on the second, when the outfield was completely under water, as deep as eight inches in places. More rain left the ground in a similar state on the scheduled third day, but the initiative of the West Indies Board, in bringing forward the rest day, and the efficiency of the drainage system allowed a prompt start the following morning. With two days virtually lost, a draw was almost inevitable, and when morning rain delayed the start of the final day by 55 minutes, costing a further thirteen overs, that result was doubly assured.

Even so, the cricket was not without its moments, and there was a period on the fourth afternoon when Australia scented the possibility of enforcing the follow-on. However, Dujon and Marshall averted that threat, and Dujon and Ambrose, with his first Test half-century, secured West Indies' position with a new eighth-wicket record for West Indies against Australia. One down in the series, Australia had every reason to try to take the initiative after they had been put in, but a sluggish pitch and accurate bowling limited them to 204 off the 90 overs of the first full day's play. Their difficulties were made manifest by Border, who needed

142 balls to score 43 without a boundary. It was not until the Waughs, creating a piece of history by being the first twins to play together in a Test, added 58 in an hour and a half that the innings was given some impetus.

When West Indies batted, McDermott yorked Haynes in the fifth over, and Reid, in his first Test of the series, had Greenidge caught at second slip in the next. After this, wickets kept falling to carefree strokes, Hughes taking four for 19 in the space of five and a half overs, but the Australians could not sustain the effort. Dujon and Ambrose put West Indian minds at rest with their level-headed partnership of 87 in two hours. Dujon, who batted for 247 minutes, was out to the second new ball on the final day, without adding to his overnight score, but by then the match had lost its purpose.

*Man of the Match:* P. J. L. Dujon.

*Close of play:* First day, Australia 55-1 (M. A. Taylor 28*, D. C. Boon 6*); Second day, Australia 75-1 (M. A. Taylor 35*, D. C. Boon 18*); Third day, Australia 279-6 (M. E. Waugh 57*, I. A. Healy 2*); Fourth day, West Indies 220-8 (P. J. L. Dujon 70*, C. A. Walsh 6*).

## Australia

| | | | |
|---|---|---|---|
| G. R. Marsh c Hooper b Ambrose | 10 | – (2) lbw b Marshall | 12 |
| M. A. Taylor c Walsh b Marshall | 61 | – (1) b Patterson | 2 |
| D. C. Boon c Logie b Patterson | 27 | – b Walsh | 29 |
| *A. R. Border run out | 43 | – (5) not out | 27 |
| D. M. Jones lbw b Patterson | 21 | – (4) not out | 39 |
| M. E. Waugh lbw b Marshall | 64 | | |
| S. R. Waugh c Dujon b Walsh | 26 | | |
| †I. A. Healy c Dujon b Marshall | 9 | | |
| C. J. McDermott c Richardson b Patterson | 0 | | |
| M. G. Hughes lbw b Patterson | 0 | | |
| B. A. Reid not out | 0 | | |
| B 6, l-b 14, n-b 13 | 33 | B 1, l-b 9, n-b 4 | 14 |

1/24 (1) 2/93 (3) 3/116 (2) 4/174 (5)     294     1/3 (1) 2/49 (2)     (3 wkts dec.) 123
5/210 (4) 6/268 (7) 7/293 (6)                       3/53 (3)
8/294 (9) 9/294 (10) 10/294 (8)

Bowling: *First Innings*—Ambrose 29-7-51-1; Patterson 26-2-50-4; Marshall 18.1-3-55-3; Walsh 30-9-45-1; Hooper 25-5-73-0. *Second Innings*—Ambrose 10-4-11-0; Patterson 7-0-27-1; Marshall 10-3-24-1; Walsh 12-6-11-1; Hooper 13-3-38-0; Richardson 1-0-2-0.

## West Indies

| | | | |
|---|---|---|---|
| C. G. Greenidge c M. E. Waugh b Reid | 12 | C. E. L. Ambrose c Border | |
| D. L. Haynes b McDermott | 1 | b M. E. Waugh . | 53 |
| R. B. Richardson c Taylor b Hughes | 30 | C. A. Walsh not out | 12 |
| C. L. Hooper lbw b Hughes | 12 | B. P. Patterson b McDermott | 0 |
| A. L. Logie c McDermott b Hughes | 1 | B 6, l-b 7, n-b 9 | 22 |
| *I. V. A. Richards c S. R. Waugh | | | |
| b Hughes . | 2 | 1/16 (2) 2/18 (1) 3/46 (4) 4/52 (5) | 227 |
| †P. J. L. Dujon lbw b McDermott | 70 | 5/56 (6) 6/86 (3) 7/110 (8) | |
| M. D. Marshall c McDermott b Border | 12 | 8/197 (9) 9/225 (7) 10/227 (11) | |

Bowling: McDermott 14.2-2-36-3; Reid 22-0-79-1; Border 19-5-28-1; Hughes 17-5-48-4; S. R. Waugh 5-0-10-0; M. E. Waugh 6-2-9-1; Jones 1-0-4-0.

Umpires: D. M. Archer and L. H. Barker.

# WEST INDIES CRICKET BOARD OF CONTROL XI v AUSTRALIANS

At Bridgetown, Barbados, April 13, 14, 15, 16. Drawn. Toss: West Indies Cricket Board of Control XI. With the West Indian team to tour England being chosen within a week, the match represented a final trial for several players. Simmons's impressive century and the bowling of Allen and Anthony were obviously influential in their eventual selection. However, the game itself was spoiled by the weather, which allowed only eight overs on the second day and ended the third 18.5 overs before schedule. Most of Simmons's 22 fours in the 206 deliveries he received were cleanly hit, lofted drives, and Lambert, who shared an opening stand of 125, also batted confidently until he fell to a stunning one-handed catch by Hughes at mid-off. Apart from Mark Taylor, who spent five minutes under five hours over 92, the Australians batted disappointingly and conceded a lead of 138.

*Close of play*: First day, West Indies Cricket Board of Control XI 314-6 (H. A. G. Anthony 0*, D. Williams 11*); Second day, West Indies Cricket Board of Control XI 345-8 dec.; Third day, Australians 195-6 (M. R. J. Veletta 12*, P. L. Taylor 11*).

## West Indies Cricket Board of Control XI

| | | | | |
|---|---|---|---|---|
| P. V. Simmons c Boon b S. R. Waugh | 122 | – (3) lbw b Reid | | 0 |
| C. B. Lambert c Hughes b Alderman | 72 | – (1) b Reid | | 12 |
| *C. A. Best c Veletta b Hughes | 30 | – (2) c Jones b Alderman | | 41 |
| B. C. Lara c Marsh b S. R. Waugh | 56 | – b Alderman | | 36 |
| K. L. T. Arthurton c Veletta b S. R. Waugh | 11 | – lbw b Alderman | | 19 |
| J. C. Adams run out | 4 | – not out | | 37 |
| H. A. G. Anthony c P. L. Taylor b Hughes | 9 | – c and b Alderman | | 0 |
| †D. Williams b Reid | 11 | – lbw b Alderman | | 0 |
| A. C. Cummins not out | 6 | – c Jones b Reid | | 14 |
| E. A. Moseley not out | 14 | – c Hughes b P. L. Taylor | | 11 |
| I. B. A. Allen (did not bat) | | – lbw b M. E. Waugh | | 4 |
| N-b 9 | 9 | B 3, l-b 6, n-b 6 | | 15 |

1/125 2/184 3/265 4/287 5/303    (8 wkts dec.) 345    1/16 2/16 3/82 4/108 5/119    189
6/303 7/320 8/324                                  6/126 7/130 8/156 9/182

Bowling: *First Innings*—Reid 19-3-89-1; Alderman 18-6-45-1; S. R. Waugh 21-4-76-3; Hughes 16-2-70-2; P. L. Taylor 20-6-43-0; M. E. Waugh 4-0-22-0. *Second Innings*—Reid 10-3-27-3; Hughes 8-0-35-0; P. L. Taylor 20-6-43-1; Alderman 17-3-40-5; S. R. Waugh 9-3-29-0; M. E. Waugh 2.2-0-6-1.

## Australians

| | | | | |
|---|---|---|---|---|
| *G. R. Marsh c Williams b Anthony | 26 | M. G. Hughes c Moseley b Allen | | 8 |
| M. A. Taylor c sub b Cummins | 92 | T. M. Alderman not out | | 0 |
| D. C. Boon c Adams b Anthony | 6 | B. A. Reid c sub b Anthony | | 1 |
| D. M. Jones lbw b Allen | 20 | | | |
| S. R. Waugh c Williams b Allen | 1 | | | |
| M. E. Waugh c Cummins b Moseley | 4 | B 3, l-b 4, w 3, n-b 14 | | 24 |
| †M. R. J. Veletta c Williams b Anthony | 14 | | | |
| P. L. Taylor b Allen | 11 | 1/57 2/75 3/139 4/141 5/150 | | 207 |
| | | 6/178 7/196 8/204 9/205 | | |

Bowling: Cummins 18-4-43-1; Allen 18-3-51-4; Moseley 17-5-37-1; Anthony 20.3-5-53-4; Simmons 4-0-13-0; Best 1-0-3-0.

Umpires: D. Holder and S. Lewis.

## WEST INDIES v AUSTRALIA

### Fourth Test Match

At Bridgetown, Barbados, April 19, 20, 21, 23, 24. West Indies won by 343 runs, their tenth successive Test victory on the ground. Toss: Australia. The Australians went against majority local opinion by choosing an unchanged team, with only three specialist bowlers, and then sending West Indies in. But they required only 61.1 overs to seize the early initiative, the West Indians being all out threequarters of an hour after tea, and paying the price for careless batting with their lowest total in a home Test since their 109 against Australia in Georgetown in 1972-73. Each batsman was caught – Greenidge and Richards hooking, Richardson at mid-wicket, Hooper at point and the last six in the arc from wicket-keeper to gully. However, West Indies had already taken two cheap wickets by the end of the day, and once Border was bowled by a shooter 35 minutes before lunch on the second morning, the Australian innings went into decline. Walsh claimed his 150th Test wicket with the third of his four victims as the West Indians restored the balance with spirited fast bowling of high quality. After that, there was only one team in it.

Eleven days short of his 40th birthday, and his place in more doubt than at any time during his lengthy career, Greenidge embarked on an innings that was to keep him centre stage for

11 hours 26 minutes while he compiled his nineteenth and highest Test century. By the time he was lbw to Hughes an hour into the fourth day, he had faced 478 deliveries, hit 31 fours, and had not given a chance, although the Australians felt him lucky to escape lbw appeals at 42 and 95. Along the way he had passed D. St E. Atkinson's 219, made on the same ground, which had stood since 1954-55 as the highest score by a West Indian against Australia. Greenidge shared partnerships of 129 with Haynes, their sixteenth of more than 100 in Tests, 199 with Richardson, who was dismissed for 99 (156 balls, fifteen fours) for the second time in Tests, and 102 with Hooper.

By now the match was well beyond Australia, yet Richards delayed his declaration until midway through the fourth day. It was seemingly unjustified caution; more so when Australia lost Marsh first ball, and then Boon and Border in successive overs from Ambrose late in the day. A daunting task lay ahead of Australia on the last day, but when they went through the first session for the solitary loss of the night-watchman, Hughes, their hopes were lifted, only to be dashed as the last six wickets fell for 18 off 12.3 overs after lunch. The collapse was initiated by Hooper, who bowled Jones off the face of his defensive bat, the ball rolling back on to his stumps, and removed Mark Waugh with a well-disguised faster ball.

*Man of the Match:* C. G. Greenidge.

*Close of play:* First day, Australia 56-2 (M. A. Taylor 23*, A. R. Border 17*); Second day, West Indies 138-1 (C. G. Greenidge 85*, M. D. Marshall 5*); Third day, West Indies 407-3 (C. G. Greenidge 209*, C. L. Hooper 25*); Fourth day, Australia 122-3 (M. A. Taylor 46*, M. G. Hughes 3*).

## West Indies

| | | | |
|---|---|---|---|
| C. G. Greenidge c Reid b McDermott | 10 | – lbw b Hughes | 226 |
| D. L. Haynes c M. E. Waugh b Hughes | 28 | – c Healy b M. E. Waugh | 40 |
| R. B. Richardson c Boon b McDermott | 1 | – (4) lbw b M. E. Waugh | 99 |
| C. L. Hooper c Jones b Hughes | 0 | – (5) c Healy b M. E. Waugh | 57 |
| *I. V. A. Richards c Hughes b McDermott | 32 | – (6) lbw b M. E. Waugh | 25 |
| A. L. Logie c Taylor b Reid | 11 | – (7) not out | 44 |
| †P. J. L. Dujon c Healy b Hughes | 10 | – (8) c M. E. Waugh b McDermott | 3 |
| M. D. Marshall c Marsh b Reid | 17 | – (3) c Healy b McDermott | 15 |
| C. E. L. Ambrose not out | 19 | – b Reid | 2 |
| C. A. Walsh c M. E. Waugh b McDermott | 10 | – c Marsh b Reid | 0 |
| B. P. Patterson c M. E. Waugh b Hughes | 1 | – not out | 4 |
| L-b 3, n-b 7 | 10 | L-b 19, n-b 12 | 31 |
| | **149** | (9 wkts dec.) | **536** |

1/17 (1) 2/21 (3) 3/22 (4) 4/72 (5) 5/89 (6) 6/96 (2) 7/103 (7) 8/125 (8) 9/148 (10) 10/149 (11)

1/129 (2) 2/153 (3) 3/352 (4) 4/454 (1) 5/470 (5) 6/512 (6) 7/522 (8) 8/525 (9) 9/525 (10)

*Bowling: First Innings*—McDermott 22-6-49-4; Reid 21-8-50-2; Hughes 16.1-2-44-4; S. R. Waugh 2-0-3-0. *Second Innings*—McDermott 37.3-8-130-2; Reid 30-4-100-2; Hughes 36-6-125-1; S. R. Waugh 28-6-77-0; M. E. Waugh 28-6-80-4; Jones 3-1-5-0.

## Australia

| | | | |
|---|---|---|---|
| M. A. Taylor lbw b Ambrose | 26 | – (2) lbw b Marshall | 76 |
| G. R. Marsh c Logie b Ambrose | 12 | – (1) lbw b Ambrose | 0 |
| D. C. Boon c Hooper b Marshall | 0 | – b Ambrose | 57 |
| *A. R. Border b Marshall | 0 | – c Dujon b Ambrose | 0 |
| D. M. Jones lbw b Marshall | 29 | – (6) b Hooper | 37 |
| M. E. Waugh not out | 22 | – (7) b Hooper | 3 |
| S. R. Waugh c Dujon b Patterson | 2 | – (8) not out | 4 |
| †I. A. Healy c Dujon b Walsh | 2 | – (9) b Marshall | 0 |
| M. G. Hughes c Logie b Walsh | 3 | – (5) c Dujon b Marshall | 3 |
| C. J. McDermott b Walsh | 2 | – c sub (R. I. C. Holder) b Walsh | 2 |
| B. A. Reid b Walsh | 0 | – b Walsh | 0 |
| L-b 2, n-b 14 | 16 | B 3, l-b 5, n-b 18 | 26 |
| | **134** | | **208** |

1/24 (2) 2/27 (3) 3/59 (1) 4/95 (4) 5/97 (5) 6/100 (7) 7/106 (8) 8/121 (9) 9/127 (10) 10/134 (11)

1/0 (1) 2/111 (3) 3/111 (4) 4/122 (5) 5/190 (6) 6/200 (7) 7/200 (2) 8/200 (9) 9/208 (10) 10/208 (11)

Bowling: *First Innings*—Ambrose 16–5–36–2; Patterson 13–6–22–1; Marshall 16–1–60–3; Walsh 5.1–1–14–4. *Second Innings*—Ambrose 19–7–36–3; Patterson 15–3–56–0; Walsh 15.3–4–37–2; Marshall 17–4–35–3; Hooper 18–4–28–2; Richards 3–0–8–0.

Umpires: D. M. Archer and L. H. Barker.

## WEST INDIES v AUSTRALIA

### Fifth Test Match

At St John's, Antigua, April 27, 28, 29, May 1. Australia won by 157 runs. Toss: Australia. More positive, and more relaxed, than at any time in the series, Australia gained consolation for their considerable earlier disappointments. The attitude was exemplified by the highest first-day total recorded in a Test in the West Indies, 355 for five off 87 overs. Taylor and Border added 116 off 35 overs, after which Jones and Mark Waugh provided the acceleration, taking advantage of 22 overs of uncomplicated off-spin from Hooper and Richards which yielded 128 runs, half of them coming from four sixes and ten fours. Their stand was worth 187 from 36 overs in 163 minutes when Jones was out, just before the close, for his highest score of the series. By then, Waugh had reached his second Test century, having survived a difficult caught and bowled chance to Richards at 97, and he was still there at the end of the innings after the last five wickets had fallen for 48. His boundaries in his unbeaten 139 from 188 balls were three sixes and eleven fours.

McDermott, bowling fast and straight, created early problems for West Indies, his three wickets including that of Richards for his first 0 in a Test at his home ground. When he returned for a second spell, McDermott also accounted for Haynes, lbw to the second toe-crushing yorker after hitting fifteen fours in a free-scoring innings of 84. With Dujon and Marshall also in a carefree mood, the West Indians avoided the possibility of a follow-on only with their ninth-wicket pair together.

When Australia batted again, Patterson's absence with a leg injury – after one over in which he dismissed the night-watchman, Healy – was the catalyst for an outstanding spell of four wickets for 46 off 21 consecutive overs by Walsh. Mark Taylor was the one batsman who stood between him and a complete breakthrough, and unperturbed by chances at 47 and 59, or the wickets falling around him, he moved on to his seventh Test hundred. He was eighth out after six and a quarter hours, having hit twelve fours in 144 from 281 deliveries. West Indies were left needing 455 to win in just over two days, and as Greenidge, on his 40th birthday, and Haynes put on 76 with a succession of punishing strokes, the possibility of an exciting finish did not appear entirely far-fetched. By lunch on the fourth day, however, both had been run out, Haynes at the non-striker's end off a deflection by Hughes from Greenidge's drive, and no other batsman looked to have the inclination to make a fight of it. Richards's disappointment at West Indies' first defeat in six Tests on the ground was heightened by his second failure in what he had announced would be his final Test in the West Indies. He presented a lobbed catch to mid-wicket off Border after making just 2.

*Man of the Match*: M. A. Taylor.    *Man of the Series*: R. B. Richardson.

*Close of play*: First day, Australia 355-5 (M. E. Waugh 117*, I. A. Healy 1*); Second day, Australia 6-1 (M. A. Taylor 2*, I. A. Healy 1*); Third day, West Indies 2-0 (C. G. Greenidge 2*, D. L. Haynes 0*).

## Australia

| | | | | |
|---|---|---|---|---|
| M. A. Taylor c Dujon b Hooper | 59 | – (2) c and b Ambrose | 144 |
| G. R. Marsh c Richards b Patterson | 6 | – (1) c Dujon b Ambrose | 1 |
| D. C. Boon c Greenidge b Ambrose | 0 | – (4) b Walsh | 35 |
| *A. R. Border c Dujon b Hooper | 59 | – (5) b Walsh | 5 |
| D. M. Jones lbw b Marshall | 81 | – (6) b Walsh | 8 |
| M. E. Waugh not out | 139 | – (7) lbw b Walsh | 0 |
| †I. A. Healy c Dujon b Marshall | 12 | – (3) c Logie b Patterson | 32 |
| P. L. Taylor c Dujon b Ambrose | 2 | – lbw b Marshall | 4 |
| M. G. Hughes b Ambrose | 1 | – c Walsh b Ambrose | 13 |
| C. J. McDermott c Dujon b Walsh | 7 | – c Dujon b Marshall | 1 |
| T. M. Alderman b Walsh | 0 | – not out | 0 |
| B 1, l-b 12, w 6, n-b 18 | 37 | B 11, l-b 7, n-b 4 | 22 |
| | **403** | | **265** |

1/10 (2) 2/13 (3) 3/129 (1) 4/156 (4)     1/4 (1) 2/49 (3) 3/142 (4)
5/343 (5) 6/370 (7) 7/381 (8)               4/168 (5) 5/184 (6) 6/184 (7)
8/385 (9) 9/403 (10) 10/403 (11)            7/237 (8) 8/258 (2)
                                             9/265 (9) 10/265 (10)

Bowling: *First Innings*—Ambrose 30–6–92–3; Patterson 12–1–44–1; Walsh 22–1–54–2; Marshall 22–1–72–2; Hooper 15–1–82–2; Richards 7–0–46–0. *Second Innings*—Ambrose 16–1–64–3; Walsh 26–2–56–4; Hooper 27–6–61–0; Patterson 1–0–1–1; Marshall 13.1–4–36–2; Richards 8–0–29–0.

## West Indies

| | | |
|---|---|---|
| C. G. Greenidge lbw b McDermott | 6 – run out | 43 |
| D. L. Haynes lbw b McDermott | 84 – run out | 33 |
| R. B. Richardson b McDermott | 3 – c Jones b Waugh | 41 |
| C. L. Hooper lbw b Hughes | 2 – c Waugh b P. L. Taylor | 35 |
| *I. V. A. Richards lbw b McDermott | 0 – c Alderman b Border | 2 |
| A. L. Logie c Jones b P. L. Taylor | 24 – lbw b Alderman | 61 |
| †P. J. L. Dujon c Jones b Hughes | 33 – lbw b McDermott | 4 |
| M. D. Marshall c Healy b Waugh | 28 – lbw b Hughes | 51 |
| C. E. L. Ambrose c M. A. Taylor b Hughes | 8 – run out | 0 |
| C. A. Walsh not out | 11 – c Healy b Hughes | 0 |
| B. P. Patterson b Hughes | 2 – not out | 7 |
| L-b 2, n-b 11 | 13     B 5, l-b 7, n-b 8 | 20 |

1/10 (1) 2/22 (3) 3/35 (4) 4/46 (5)  214   1/76 (2) 2/92 (1) 3/142 (3)  297
5/114 (6) 6/136 (2) 7/188 (7)              4/145 (5) 5/182 (4) 6/193 (7)
8/195 (8) 9/206 (9) 10/214 (11)           7/271 (8) 8/271 (9)
                                          9/271 (10) 10/297 (6)

Bowling: *First Innings*—McDermott 15–4–42–4; Alderman 7–0–42–0; Hughes 17–2–65–4; P. L. Taylor 11–2–40–1; Waugh 5–0–23–1. *Second Innings*—McDermott 17–2–55–1; Alderman 15.4–4–63–1; Hughes 19–5–49–2; P. L. Taylor 10–0–39–1; Border 15–2–71–1; Waugh 5–3–8–1.

Umpires: L. H. Barker and S. U. Bucknor.

---

†At St George's, Bermuda, May 9. Australians won by 18 runs. Toss: St George's CC. Australians 147 (36.1 overs) (I. A. Healy 39 not out; A. Braithwaite four for 35, N. Gibbons three for 31); St George's CC 129 (48.3 overs) (N. Gibbons 36).

---

†At St David's, Bermuda, May 11. Australians won by 34 runs. Toss: Australians. Australians 271 for eight (50 overs) (M. A. Taylor 44, A. R. Border 100, G. R. J. Matthews 30, I. A. Healy 33 not out); Bermuda Cricket Board President's XI 237 for nine (50 overs) (C. Smith 74, C. Marshall 32, Extras 33; G. R. J. Matthews three for 46).

---

†At Somerset Field, Bermuda, May 12. Australians won by 93 runs. Toss: Bermuda. Australians 247 (47.3 overs) (G. R. Marsh 107, D. C. Boon 51; C. Wade three for 51, A. Amory three for 23); Bermuda 154 (38 overs) (R. Hill 64, N. Gibbons 35; M. G. Hughes three for 21).

# SHARJAH CUP, 1990-91

The crisis in the Gulf cut back plans for a four-nation Sharjah Champions Trophy, as India and West Indies declined to send teams. Instead Pakistan and Sri Lanka contested the Sharjah Cup, sponsored by Instaphone. Sri Lanka, maintaining the good form which had brought them victory in their last game in India twelve days earlier, won the first match by a convincing six wickets, but Pakistan took the second and claimed the cup on superior run-rate. The beneficiaries of the Cricketers' Benefit Fund Series were Pakistan's Tauseef Ahmed and Wallis Mathias, who received US$35,000 each. Pakistan received US$20,000 and Sri Lanka US$10,000, while the Batsman and Bowler of the Tournament, Ijaz Ahmed and Rumesh Ratnayake, who also won the individual Man of the Match awards, took home US$1,000 each.

## †PAKISTAN v SRI LANKA

At Sharjah, December 20. Sri Lanka won by six wickets. Toss: Sri Lanka. Sri Lanka owed victory to a fine performance in the field – their wicket-keeper, Tillekeratne, took five catches – and the bowling of Ratnayake, who returned his best figures in one-day internationals. Unfortunately the match was overshadowed by an incident involving Imran Khan, who objected to the number of wides being called, and the Indian umpire, P. D. Reporter, who threatened to leave the field until placated by Javed Miandad. Sri Lanka's total of 172 included 26 wides. Captain Arjuna Ranatunga and Mahanama saw them to their target with an unbeaten fifth-wicket stand of 77, after Wasim Akram had dismissed both openers cheaply. Earlier Pakistan had collapsed from 46 for no wicket to 57 for four, with Ratnayake dismissing Zahid Fazal and Salim Malik in successive balls. Only Imran and Ijaz Ahmed, with a stand of 76, saved them from worse embarrassment.

*Man of the Match:* R. J. Ratnayake.

### Pakistan

| | | | |
|---|---|---|---|
| Saeed Anwar c Tillekeratne b Ratnayake | 32 | †Salim Yousuf c Tillekeratne | |
| Zahid Fazal c Mahanama b Ratnayake . | 11 | b Ratnayake . | 10 |
| Javed Miandad run out | 4 | Mushtaq Ahmed lbw b Ramanayake . . . | 4 |
| Salim Malik c Tillekeratne b Ratnayake | 0 | Waqar Younis not out | 2 |
| *Imran Khan c Tillekeratne | | Aqib Javed c Tillekeratne b Ratnayake . | 0 |
| b Warnaweera . | 43 | B 1, l-b 7, w 6, n-b 3 | 17 |
| Ijaz Ahmed c Warnaweera | | | |
| b Ramanayake . | 38 | 1/6 2/56 3/56 4/57 5/133 (43 overs) 170 | |
| Wasim Akram b Ramanayake . | 9 | 6/147 7/152 8/157 9/170 | |

Bowling: Labrooy 6–0–31–0; Ramanayake 9–0–29–3; Ratnayake 9–1–32–5; A. Ranatunga 9–0–27–0; Warnaweera 9–0–36–1; Gurusinha 1–0–7–0.

### Sri Lanka

| | | | |
|---|---|---|---|
| D. Ranatunga lbw b Wasim Akram . . . | 0 | R. S. Mahanama not out | 24 |
| †H. P. Tillekeratne lbw b Wasim Akram | 3 | L-b 6, w 26, n-b 12 | 44 |
| A. P. Gurusinha b Waqar Younis . . . | 33 | | |
| P. A. de Silva lbw b Aqib Javed | 23 | 1/2 2/27 3/63 (4 wkts, 39.5 overs) 172 | |
| *A. Ranatunga not out | 45 | 4/95 | |

S. T. Jayasuriya, G. F. Labrooy, R. J. Ratnayake, C. P. H. Ramanayake and K. P. J. Warnaweera did not bat.

Bowling: Imran Khan 8–2–33–0; Wasim Akram 9–0–40–2; Waqar Younis 9–1–35–1; Aqib Javed 6–0–27–1; Mushtaq Ahmed 5.5–0–24–0; Ijaz Ahmed 2–0–7–0.

Umpires: V. K. Ramaswamy and P. D. Reporter.

## †PAKISTAN v SRI LANKA

At Sharjah, December 21. Pakistan won by 50 runs. Toss: Sri Lanka. Pakistan restored their pride and won the Sharjah Cup in this match, which gave them an overall run-rate of 4.08 against Sri Lanka's 3.65. Their score was built around the unbeaten 54 of Ijaz Ahmed, who batted for 78 minutes after débutant Aamer Sohail and Imran had mounted a rescue from a disastrous start; Pakistan were 15 for three as Miandad and Salim Malik failed again. Four run-outs testified to Sri Lanka's continuing success in the field. Dammika Ranatunga and Senanayake, another international newcomer, gave their reply a steady start with 46, but then four wickets fell for 22 and the dismissal of de Silva by Waqar Younis effectively ended their hopes.

*Man of the Match*: Ijaz Ahmed.

## Pakistan

| | | |
|---|---|---|
| Saeed Anwar c Warnaweera b Labrooy . | 2 | Akram Raza run out .............. 1 |
| Aamer Sohail run out .............. | 32 | Mushtaq Ahmed run out ............ 10 |
| Javed Miandad lbw b Ramanayake .... | 1 | Waqar Younis not out .............. 0 |
| Salim Malik c Jayasuriya b Labrooy ... | 0 | |
| *Imran Khan c Senanayake | | B 4, l-b 10, w 18, n-b 1 ..... 33 |
| b Warnaweera . | 30 | |
| Ijaz Ahmed not out ................ | 54 | 1/9 2/13 3/15    (9 wkts, 43 overs) 181 |
| Wasim Akram b Warnaweera ........ | 4 | 4/70 5/82 6/94 |
| †Salim Yousuf run out .............. | 14 | 7/134 8/137 9/165 |

Bowling: Labrooy 9–1–40–2; Ramanayake 9–1–20–1; A. Ranatunga 7–1–24–0; Ratnayake 9–0–57–0; Warnaweera 9–2–26–2.

## Sri Lanka

| | | |
|---|---|---|
| D. Ranatunga c Salim Yousuf | | R. J. Ratnayake b Waqar Younis ..... 5 |
| b Akram Raza . | 19 | G. F. Labrooy st Salim Yousuf |
| C. P. Senanayake c Javed Miandad | | b Mushtaq Ahmed . 2 |
| b Mushtaq Ahmed . | 24 | C. P. H. Ramanayake not out ........ 6 |
| P. A. de Silva b Waqar Younis ....... | 24 | K. P. J. Warnaweera not out ........ 1 |
| *A. Ranatunga c Salim Yousuf | | |
| b Mushtaq Ahmed . | 5 | B 1, l-b 8, w 7 .............. 16 |
| A. P. Gurusinha run out ............ | 1 | |
| †H. P. Tillekeratne c Javed Ahmed | | 1/46 2/47 3/66    (9 wkts, 43 overs) 131 |
| b Wasim Akram . | 27 | 4/68 5/92 6/100 |
| S. T. Jayasuriya lbw b Waqar Younis .. | 1 | 7/102 8/122 9/129 |

Bowling: Imran Khan 8–1–21–0; Wasim Akram 9–2–19–1; Ijaz Ahmed 3–0–10–0; Akram Raza 9–0–33–1; Mushtaq Ahmed 6–1–14–3; Waqar Younis 8–0–25–3.

Umpires: V. K. Ramaswamy and P. D. Reporter.

# ASIA CUP, 1990-91

Staging the Asia Cup for the first time, India retained the trophy which they won in Bangladesh in 1988-89. It was their third triumph in three appearances in the tournament, though they withdrew from the 1985-86 competition held in Sri Lanka. On this occasion Pakistan were missing, after their request that the tournament should be postponed, because of inter-communal violence in Indian cities, was not accepted. Mr A. A. K. Abbasi, secretary of the Pakistan Board of Control, whose nephew had been killed, said he feared for his players' safety.

Despite the absence of the Pakistanis, India had to overcome significant opposition from Sri Lanka, who had defeated them in the final game of their one-day series in early December, and had just beaten Pakistan in one of two matches in Sharjah. Indeed, Sri Lanka finished on top of the qualifying table, having beaten both India and Bangladesh, but India took their revenge in the final, spurred on by a hat-trick from Kapil Dev two days before his 32nd birthday.

Bangladesh could not hope to compete on equal terms with their Test-playing neighbours, but against Sri Lanka they reached their highest score and were not bowled out in either of their matches. Although their bowlers had little success, Faruq Ahmed reached a record individual score for Bangladesh in the first, only to be passed by Ather Ali Khan in the second game.

## †BANGLADESH v INDIA

At Chandigarh, December 25. India won by nine wickets. Toss: Bangladesh. India had no problem overhauling Bangladesh's 170 with 13.1 overs to spare, though their inexperienced visitors deserved some credit for surviving 50 overs for the loss of only six wickets. Sidhu's unbeaten 104, from 109 balls, included ten fours and three sixes, and he shared an opening stand of 121 with Raman. Bangladesh had recovered from a shaky start of 28 for two when Faruq Ahmed and Ather Ali Khan, both of whom were dropped off the bowling of Wassan, shared a third-wicket stand of 108. But the batsmen who followed could add only 34 in the last nine overs; it was never going to be enough.

*Man of the Match:* N. S. Sidhu.

### Bangladesh

| | | | |
|---|---|---|---|
| Azhar Hussain c Azharuddin b Wassan. | 13 | Enam-ul-Haque not out.............. | 3 |
| Nurul Abedin c Raju b Prabhakar..... | 2 | Amin-ul-Islam not out.............. | 3 |
| Faruq Ahmed c Wassan b Raju....... | 57 | B 4, l-b 9, w 10, n-b 6 ....... | 29 |
| Ather Ali Khan b Raju.............. | 44 | | |
| *Minhaz-ul-Abedin b Kapil Dev ...... | 9 | 1/8 2/28 3/136 (6 wkts, 50 overs) 170 | |
| Akram Khan lbw b Kapil Dev ....... | 10 | 4/150 5/159 6/164 | |

G. M. Nawsher, †Nasir Ahmed and Alam Talukdar did not bat.

Bowling: Kapil Dev 8-1-17-2; Prabhakar 10-2-28-1; Wassan 10-0-41-1; Mukherjee 10-2-29-0; Raju 10-0-27-2; Tendulkar 2-0-15-0.

### India

W. V. Raman lbw b Ather Ali Khan .. 44
N. S. Sidhu not out ................104
S. V. Manjrekar not out ........... 11
    L-b 3, w 7, n-b 2........... 12

1/121        (1 wkt, 36.5 overs) 171

*M. Azharuddin, S. R. Tendulkar, Kapil Dev, M. Prabhakar, †K. S. More, S. L. V. Raju, S. Mukherjee and A. S. Wassan did not bat.

Bowling: Nawsher 9-1-24-0; Alam Talukdar 3-0-16-0; Azhar Hussain 3-0-25-0; Enam-ul-Haque 5-0-26-0; Minhaz-ul-Abedin 9-0-43-0; Ather Ali Khan 6-1-23-1; Amin-ul-Islam 1.5-0-11-0.

Umpires: V. K. Ramaswamy and P. D. Reporter.

### †INDIA v SRI LANKA

At Cuttack, December 28. Sri Lanka won by 36 runs. Toss: Sri Lanka. Sri Lanka's new-found confidence in the one-day game brought them a second victory over India in three weeks. Openers Senanayake and Tillekeratne gave them a steady start, which was built on with a fourth-wicket partnership of 73 from Gurusinha and the captain, Ranatunga. Although the tail folded fairly quickly they were able to set a target of 215, to which India proved quite unequal. The fielding of Jayasuriya accounted for both Shastri and Manjrekar, and he also picked up the wicket of Azharuddin, who had made his 40 from 61 balls. India's chances of recovery were dashed when Ratnayake, who finished with three for 24, bowled Kapil Dev after he had hit a 35-ball 32.

*Man of the Match:* A. Ranatunga.

### Sri Lanka

| | | | |
|---|---|---|---|
| C. P. Senanayake b Wassan .......... 27 | C. P. H. Ramanayake b Kapil Dev.... 0 | | |
| †H. P. Tillekeratne c Raju b Wassan .. 26 | S. D. Anurasiri run out ............. 8 | | |
| A. P. Gurusinha b Wassan .......... 34 | K. P. J. Warnaweera not out ........ 0 | | |
| P. A. de Silva c More b Mukherjee.... 11 |     B 8, l-b 19, w 4, n-b 1 ....... 32 | | |
| *A. Ranatunga c and b Prabhakar .... 53 | | | |
| R. S. Mahanama run out ............. 0 | 1/51 2/62 3/86     (49.2 overs) 214 | | |
| S. T. Jayasuriya lbw b Kapil Dev ..... 23 | 4/159 5/161 6/190 | | |
| R. J. Ratnayake b Kapil Dev......... 0 | 7/191 8/191 9/210 | | |

Bowling: Kapil Dev 9.2-1-48-3; Prabhakar 10-2-39-1; Mukherjee 10-0-30-1; Wassan 10-0-28-3; Raju 10-0-42-0.

### India

| | | | |
|---|---|---|---|
| R. J. Shastri run out ................. 4 | †K. S. More b Ratnayake ............. 27 | | |
| N. S. Sidhu c Mahanama b Anurasiri .. 25 | S. L. V. Raju run out ............... 0 | | |
| S. V. Manjrekar run out ............. 26 | A. S. Wassan b Ratnayake ........... 1 | | |
| *M. Azharuddin st Tillekeratne | S. Mukherjee not out ................ 2 | | |
|     b Jayasuriya . 40 |     L-b 6, w 2, n-b 5........... 13 | | |
| S. R. Tendulkar lbw b Ranatunga ..... 4 | | | |
| Kapil Dev b Ratnayake ............. 32 | 1/24 2/37 3/81 4/95 5/111   (45.5 overs) 178 | | |
| M. Prabhakar c de Silva b Warnaweera 4 | 6/123 7/165 8/166 9/173 | | |

Bowling: Ratnayake 6.5-1-24-3; Ramanayake 5-0-12-0; Anurasiri 10-0-44-1; Ranatunga 10-0-36-1; Jayasuriya 6-0-22-1; Warnaweera 8-0-34-1.

Umpires: S. Banerjee and V. K. Ramaswamy.

## †BANGLADESH v SRI LANKA

At Calcutta, December 31. Sri Lanka won by 71 runs. Toss: Sri Lanka. Fog delayed the start of the match, which was subsequently reduced to 45 overs a side. Two batting records for Bangladesh could not prevent another easy win for Sri Lanka. The team's total of 178 passed their previous one-day international record of 177, against New Zealand in the Austral-Asia Cup in 1989-90, and Ather Ali Khan's 78 not out, which included three sixes and six fours, was their highest individual score. Their bowlers also started well, restricting Sri Lanka to 87 for three before de Silva and Ranatunga put on 139 for the fourth wicket. De Silva's 89, from 60 balls and containing two sixes and eight fours, was the basis of a total of 249 for four which was too much even for Bangladesh's best.

*Man of the Match:* Ather Ali Khan.

### Sri Lanka

| | | |
|---|---|---|
| C. P. Senanayake c Akram Khan | *A. Ranatunga not out .............. | 64 |
| b Nawsher . 0 | G. F. Labrooy not out .............. | 4 |
| †H. P. Tillekeratne st Nasir Ahmed | | |
| b Azhar Hussain . 39 | L-b 11, w 4 .............. | 15 |
| A. P. Gurusinha | | |
| lbw b Minhaz-ul-Abedin . 38 | 1/0 2/85 3/87     (4 wkts, 45 overs) | 249 |
| P. A. de Silva run out .............. 89 | 4/226 | |

R. J. Ratnayake, S. T. Jayasuriya, C. P. H. Ramanayake, S. D. Anurasiri and G. P. Wickremasinghe did not bat.

Bowling: Nawsher 9–0–46–1; Saif-ul-Islam 9–1–42–0; Ather Ali Khan 4–0–24–0; Akram Khan 4–0–25–0; Azhar Hussain 9–0–33–1; Minhaz-ul-Abedin 6–1–37–1; Enam-ul-Haque 2–0–15–0; Amin-ul-Islam 2–0–16–0.

### Bangladesh

| | | |
|---|---|---|
| Azhar Hussain run out .............. 10 | Akram Khan run out .............. | 4 |
| Nurul Abedin lbw b Ramanayake ..... 0 | Enam-ul-Haque c and b Jayasuriya .. | 5 |
| Faruq Ahmed c Tillekeratne | †Nasir Ahmed c and b de Silva ....... | 11 |
| b Wickremasinghe . 12 | G. M. Nawsher c and b Gurusinha ... | 4 |
| Ather Ali Khan not out .............. 78 | B 1, l-b 2, w 13, n-b 4 ....... | 20 |
| *Minhaz-ul-Abedin c de Silva | | |
| b Anurasiri . 33 | 1/1 2/23 3/46     (9 wkts, 45 overs) | 178 |
| Amin-ul-Islam c Tillekeratne | 4/96 5/99 6/108 | |
| b Jayasuriya . 1 | 7/123 8/168 9/178 | |

Saif-ul-Islam did not bat.

Bowling: Labrooy 5–0–19–0; Ramanayake 5–0–13–1; Wickremasinghe 6–1–23–1; Anurasiri 9–0–31–1; Jayasuriya 9–1–39–2; de Silva 8–1–37–1; Gurusinha 3–0–13–1.

Umpires: S. Banerjee and P. D. Reporter.

## QUALIFYING TABLE

| | Played | Won | Lost | Points | Run-rate |
|---|---|---|---|---|---|
| Sri Lanka ....... | 2 | 2 | 0 | 8 | 4.91 |
| India .......... | 2 | 1 | 1 | 4 | 4.22 |
| Bangladesh ..... | 2 | 0 | 2 | 0 | 3.66 |

## FINAL

### †INDIA v SRI LANKA

At Calcutta, January 4. India won by seven wickets. Toss: India. Azharuddin secured the Asia Cup and the Man of the Match award with an unbeaten 58 in a final postponed for 24 hours and then shortened by rain. The game was also notable for a hat-trick from Kapil Dev, who had Mahanama caught behind off the last ball of an over, and removed Jayasuriya and

Ratnayake with the first two balls of his next. Sri Lanka were thus reduced from 176 for five, a score owing much to the 58-run fourth-wicket stand between Gurusinha and Ranatunga (56 balls), to 181 for eight. India lost their openers cheaply, but they were rescued by a third-wicket partnership of 91 from Manjrekar, whose undefeated 71 anchored the innings, and Tendulkar.

*Man of the Match*: M. Azharuddin.

## Sri Lanka

| | | | |
|---|---|---|---|
| C. P. Senanayake run out | 25 | G. F. Labrooy c Prabhakar b Kapil Dev | 10 |
| †H. P. Tillekeratne c More b Wassan | 15 | C. P. H. Ramanayake not out | 9 |
| A. P. Gurusinha run out | 39 | K. P. J. Warnaweera not out | 0 |
| P. A. de Silva c and b Mukherjee | 26 | | |
| *A. Ranatunga run out | 49 | B 1, l-b 13, w 7 | 21 |
| R. S. Mahanama c More b Kapil Dev | 5 | | |
| S. T. Jayasuriya c Manjrekar | | 1/48 2/50 3/92    (9 wkts, 45 overs) 204 | |
| b Kapil Dev | 5 | 4/150 5/175 6/176 | |
| R. J. Ratnayake lbw b Kapil Dev | 0 | 7/181 8/181 9/202 | |

Bowling: Kapil Dev 9-0-31-4; Prabhakar 9-1-36-0; Mukherjee 9-0-39-1; Wassan 7-0-35-1; Raju 8-0-34-0; Shastri 3-0-15-0.

## India

| | | | |
|---|---|---|---|
| R. J. Shastri c Tillekeratne b Labrooy | 6 | *M. Azharuddin not out | 58 |
| N. S. Sidhu c and b Ranatunga | 15 | L-b 1, w 1 | 2 |
| S. V. Manjrekar not out | 71 | | |
| S. R. Tendulkar lbw b Ratnayake | 53 | 1/14 2/30 3/121    (3 wkts, 42.1 overs) 205 | |

Kapil Dev, M. Prabhakar, †K. S. More, S. L. V. Raju, S. Mukherjee and A. S. Wassan did not bat.

Bowling: Labrooy 8.1-1-29-1; Ramanayake 7-2-32-0; Ratnayake 8-0-34-1; Ranatunga 2-0-12-1; Warnaweera 6-0-41-0; Gurusinha 6-0-26-0; Jayasuriya 5-0-30-0.

Umpires: V. K. Ramaswamy and P. D. Reporter.

# BENSON AND HEDGES WORLD
# SERIES CUP, 1990-91

## †AUSTRALIA v NEW ZEALAND

At Sydney, November 29 (day/night). Australia won by 61 runs. Toss: New Zealand. Rain between innings reduced New Zealand's quota of overs to 40, with an adjusted target of 236. Under the competition's new regulations governing interrupted games, this had been calculated on the basis of Australia's 40 highest-scoring overs. Had it been on average runs per over throughout the innings, the target would have been 216. The New Zealanders had an early setback when Border's direct hit ran out Wright, and the Australian captain was also involved in the run-out of Greatbatch. Crowe was run out by the bowler, Rackemann, as he followed through, and it took a partnership of 61 in half an hour between Rutherford and Smith to bring the evening session to life. Australia, having lost Boon in the first over, batted consistently and were soundly placed at 94 for two from 25 overs when rain reduced their innings from 50 overs to 44. Further rain prevented the last delivery being bowled.

*Man of the Match:* A. R. Border.

### Australia

| | | | | | |
|---|---|---|---|---|---|
| D. C. Boon c Smith b Pringle | 0 | | †I. A. Healy not out | | 8 |
| G. R. Marsh c Rutherford b Harris | 46 | | C. G. Rackemann c Petrie b Watson | | 0 |
| D. M. Jones c Harris b Morrison | 36 | | | | |
| *A. R. Border b Morrison | 39 | | B 4, l-b 3, w 9, n-b 1 | | 17 |
| M. E. Waugh b Pringle | 40 | | | | |
| S. R. Waugh c Watson b Petrie | 7 | | 1/0 2/54 3/134 | (9 wkts, 43.5 overs) | 236 |
| S. P. O'Donnell c Smith b Pringle | 35 | | 4/138 5/163 6/205 | | |
| P. L. Taylor c Crowe b Watson | 8 | | 7/226 8/236 9/236 | | |

B. A. Reid did not bat.

Bowling: Pringle 9-2-39-3; Petrie 9-0-43-1; Watson 8.5-1-51-2; Morrison 9-0-49-2; Harris 6-0-36-1; Crowe 2-0-11-0.

### New Zealand

| | | | | | |
|---|---|---|---|---|---|
| J. G. Wright run out | 2 | | R. G. Petrie c Jones b Taylor | | 1 |
| A. H. Jones c M. E. Waugh | | | C. Pringle not out | | 4 |
| b Rackemann | 23 | | | | |
| *M. D. Crowe run out | 21 | | B 3, l-b 11, w 4, n-b 2 | | 20 |
| M. J. Greatbatch run out | 20 | | | | |
| K. R. Rutherford lbw b Reid | 33 | | 1/2 2/49 3/55 | (7 wkts, 40 overs) | 174 |
| †I. D. S. Smith c M. E. Waugh b Reid | 33 | | 4/80 5/141 | | |
| C. Z. Harris not out | 17 | | 6/153 7/168 | | |

W. Watson and D. K. Morrison did not bat.

Bowling: O'Donnell 8-2-18-0; Reid 8-4-18-2; Rackemann 7-1-23-1; S. R. Waugh 8-1-49-0; M. E. Waugh 3-0-20-0; Taylor 6-0-32-1.

Umpires: L. J. King and P. J. McConnell.

## †ENGLAND v NEW ZEALAND

At Adelaide, December 1. New Zealand won by 7 runs. Toss: England. A second-rate display by England in a game reduced by rain to 41 overs enabled New Zealand to win with a modest score of 199. There was an irritating start for England when umpire Thomas, standing at square leg, ruled as a no-ball a rising delivery from Malcolm off which Wright, defending his upper chest, was caught at second slip. The left-hander, using his feet beautifully to off drive Hemmings, proceeded to 67. England, however, had no excuses. Three difficult catches were dropped, their over-rate was tardy (limiting the innings to 40 overs), and when batting they lacked discipline and purpose. Gower, opening because Larkins was recuperating from dentistry, got the reply off on the wrong foot when, having hooked Pringle's second ball for six, he drove the fourth to extra cover. Smith went the same way, and Atherton and Lamb took sixteen overs to add 71. Subsequently, only Morris, with an undefeated 63 off 46 balls on his one-day international début, kept his head as the asking-rate rose.

*Man of the Match:* J. G. Wright.

## New Zealand

| | |
|---|---|
| J. G. Wright c Russell b Malcolm ..... 67 | C. Z. Harris b Fraser ............. 4 |
| A. H. Jones c Russell b Malcolm ..... 6 | |
| *M. D. Crowe c Gower b Hemmings .. 16 | L-b 12, w 5, n-b 2 ......... 19 |
| K. R. Rutherford b Small ........... 50 | |
| R. T. Latham b Small .............. 27 | 1/16  2/62  3/114     (6 wkts, 40 overs) 199 |
| †I. D. S. Smith not out ............. 10 | 4/185  5/188  6/199 |

R. G. Petrie, C. Pringle, D. K. Morrison and W. Watson did not bat.

Bowling: Fraser 8-1-33-1; Malcolm 9-0-39-2; Small 7-1-25-2; Lewis 8-0-39-0; Hemmings 8-0-51-1.

## England

| | |
|---|---|
| D. I. Gower c Crowe b Pringle ...... 6 | E. E. Hemmings b Pringle ........... 3 |
| M. A. Atherton c Smith b Morrison .. 33 | A. R. C. Fraser run out ............ 0 |
| R. A. Smith c Crowe b Pringle ...... 8 | D. E. Malcolm not out ............. 3 |
| *A. J. Lamb b Watson .............. 49 | L-b 5, w 4 ................. 9 |
| J. E. Morris not out ............... 63 | |
| †R. C. Russell b Petrie ............ 7 | 1/6  2/20  3/91      (9 wkts, 40 overs) 192 |
| C. C. Lewis c Morrison b Petrie ..... 6 | 4/106  5/126  6/158 |
| G. C. Small c Wright b Morrison ..... 5 | 7/173  8/182  9/188 |

Bowling: Pringle 8-1-36-3; Petrie 8-0-26-2; Morrison 8-0-38-2; Watson 8-1-29-1; Harris 8-0-58-0.

Umpires: A. R. Crafter and I. S. Thomas.

## †AUSTRALIA v NEW ZEALAND

At Adelaide, December 2. Australia won by six wickets. Toss: New Zealand. Australia never allowed New Zealand to mount a challenge and won comfortably with three overs to spare. Alderman (8-1-16-1) gave nothing away and Rackemann was similarly effective in keeping the New Zealanders on a tight rein. A third-wicket partnership of 84 between Crowe and Rutherford, after Wright had been run out for the second match in succession against Australia, gave their innings some substance, and Latham, Petrie and Pringle made sure at the end that the bowlers would have something to defend. However, Marsh, Boon and Jones gave Australia a good start, and Border had the large crowd singing his praises as he took three consecutive boundaries off Morrison in his 62-ball 55.

*Man of the Match:* A. R. Border.

## New Zealand

| | |
|---|---|
| J. G. Wright run out ............... 16 | R. G. Petrie b S. R. Waugh ......... 21 |
| A. H. Jones lbw b Alderman ........ 4 | C. Pringle not out ............... 12 |
| *M. D. Crowe c Jones b M. E. Waugh. 50 | L-b 4, w 11, n-b 7 ......... 22 |
| K. R. Rutherford b Rackemann ..... 40 | |
| R. T. Latham not out .............. 36 | 1/8  2/38  3/122     (7 wkts, 50 overs) 208 |
| †I. D. S. Smith c Healy b Rackemann . 6 | 4/123  5/131 |
| C. Z. Harris c Healy b M. E. Waugh .. 1 | 6/143  7/185 |

W. Watson and D. K. Morrison did not bat.

Bowling: Alderman 10-2-25-1; Rackemann 10-0-38-2; O'Donnell 10-1-45-0; S. R. Waugh 10-0-49-1; Taylor 5-0-22-0; M. E. Waugh 5-0-25-2.

## Australia

| | |
|---|---|
| G. R. Marsh c Wright b Harris ...... 45 | S. R. Waugh not out ............... 4 |
| D. C. Boon c Harris b Morrison ..... 33 | L-b 9, w 17, n-b 2 ......... 28 |
| D. M. Jones c Jones b Watson ...... 38 | |
| *A. R. Border b Pringle ............ 55 | 1/64  2/115     (4 wkts, 47 overs) 210 |
| M. E. Waugh not out .............. 7 | 3/187  4/200 |

S. P. O'Donnell, P. L. Taylor, †I. A. Healy, C. G. Rackemann and T. M. Alderman did not bat.

Bowling: Pringle 10-0-42-1; Morrison 9-0-53-1; Petrie 10-0-32-0; Watson 10-1-38-1; Harris 7-0-26-1; Crowe 1-0-10-0.

Umpires: R. J. Evans and T. A. Prue.

## †ENGLAND v NEW ZEALAND

At Perth, December 7 (day/night). England won by four wickets. Toss: New Zealand. Stewart and Small restored order to a collapsing innings to bring a win initially fashioned by the bowlers. The ball moved both in daylight and under the floodlights, and there was some uneven bounce: Smith had his right forefinger broken by a ball from Lewis during the New Zealand innings, Greatbatch taking his place behind the stumps when England batted. With luck running for Morris and Larkins, who struck nine fours, England looked to be cruising to victory, but from the seventeenth over they lost six wickets for the addition of 57 runs. As New Zealand's one chance lay in bowling England out, Crowe stayed on the offensive, supporting his seam bowlers with two slips and sometimes a silly point, but Stewart and Small kept their heads and nerve. England's two newcomers, Bicknell and Tufnell, were both impressive, especially the Middlesex left-armer, who bowled slowly and with guile.

*Man of the Match: A. J. Stewart.*

### New Zealand

| | | | | |
|---|---|---|---|---|
| J. G. Wright c Lewis b Bicknell | 6 | C. Pringle c and b Small | 2 |
| A. H. Jones run out | 26 | D. K. Morrison c Russell b Lewis | 7 |
| *M. D. Crowe c Russell b Lewis | 37 | W. Watson b Lewis | 1 |
| M. J. Greatbatch c Larkins b Small | 19 | B 4, l-b 8, w 4, n-b 4 | 20 |
| K. R. Rutherford b Fraser | 11 | | |
| †I. D. S. Smith c Lamb b Bicknell | 15 | 1/16 2/52 3/94 | (49.2 overs) 158 |
| C. Z. Harris c Russell b Tufnell | 0 | 4/99 5/126 6/126 | |
| R. G. Petrie not out | 14 | 7/126 8/128 9/154 | |

Bowling: Fraser 10-3-23-1; Bicknell 10-1-36-2; Lewis 9.2-1-26-3; Small 10-1-30-2; Tufnell 10-1-31-1.

### England

| | | | | |
|---|---|---|---|---|
| J. E. Morris c Rutherford b Morrison | 31 | C. C. Lewis c Greatbatch b Pringle | 0 |
| W. Larkins c Crowe b Morrison | 44 | G. C. Small not out | 9 |
| R. A. Smith c sub (R. T. Latham) b Watson | 0 | B 4, l-b 8, w 10, n-b 1 | 23 |
| *A. J. Lamb lbw b Watson | 20 | | |
| A. J. Stewart not out | 29 | 1/72 2/73 3/100 | (6 wkts, 43.5 overs) 161 |
| †R. C. Russell c Crowe b Pringle | 5 | 4/101 5/115 6/129 | |

A. R. C. Fraser, P. C. R. Tufnell and M. P. Bicknell did not bat.

Bowling: Pringle 10-1-45-2; Petrie 10-0-39-0; Morrison 10-1-27-2; Watson 10-1-26-2; Harris 3.5-0-12-0.

Umpires: R. J. Evans and T. A. Prue.

## †AUSTRALIA v ENGLAND

At Perth, December 9. Australia won by six wickets. Toss: England. England had the makings of a competitive score until Larkins and Lamb were out to over-ambitious strokes in the nineteenth over, Lamb to his third ball. Smith and Stewart added 66 by the 36th, but with Rackemann in the final over of a remarkably hostile and accurate spell, Smith's attempted off-glide resulted only in an edge to the wicket-keeper. Three overs later, Alderman took a rolling catch right-handed at deep gully to send back Stewart. Although Bicknell (24 balls) gave the total a semblance of respectability, with Boon and Marsh putting on 56 in fourteen overs and the 100 coming up in the 25th, Australia predictably made light of it. Jones hit an enormous straight six into the Prindiville Stand as soon as Tufnell came on, yet it was only when the spinner flattened his arc, supposedly in self-defence, that Jones (74 balls) and Border scored off him more or less at will.

*Man of the Match: D. M. Jones.*

## England

| | | | |
|---|---|---|---|
| J. E. Morris b S. R. Waugh | 7 | M. P. Bicknell not out | 31 |
| W. Larkins b O'Donnell | 38 | A. R. C. Fraser c M. E. Waugh | |
| R. A. Smith c Healy b Rackemann | 37 | b O'Donnell | 4 |
| *A. J. Lamb c Alderman b O'Donnell | 3 | B 3, l-b 3, w 2, n-b 3 | 11 |
| A. J. Stewart c Alderman b Matthews | 41 | | |
| C. C. Lewis lbw b Matthews | 2 | 1/32 2/58 3/62 | (9 wkts, 50 overs) 192 |
| †R. C. Russell c O'Donnell b Alderman | 13 | 4/128 5/136 6/139 | |
| G. C. Small c Border b O'Donnell | 5 | 7/154 8/156 9/192 | |

P. C. R. Tufnell did not bat.

Bowling: Alderman 10–0–34–1; Rackemann 10–2–19–1; S. R. Waugh 10–1–52–1; O'Donnell 10–0–45–4; Matthews 10–0–36–2.

## Australia

| | | | |
|---|---|---|---|
| D. C. Boon b Small | 38 | S. R. Waugh not out | 12 |
| G. R. Marsh c Lewis b Tufnell | 37 | L-b 8, w 10, n-b 1 | 19 |
| D. M. Jones not out | 63 | | |
| *A. R. Border c Russell b Bicknell | 24 | 1/56 2/110 | (4 wkts, 41 overs) 193 |
| M. E. Waugh c Lewis b Bicknell | 0 | 3/155 4/155 | |

S. P. O'Donnell, G. R. J. Matthews, †I. A. Healy, C. G. Rackemann and T. M. Alderman did not bat.

Bowling: Fraser 9-2-30-0; Bicknell 9-0-55-2; Small 4.3-1-14-1; Lewis 8-1-36-0; Larkins 0.3-0-1-0; Tufnell 10-1-49-1.

Umpires: R. J. Evans and P. J. McConnell.

## †AUSTRALIA v NEW ZEALAND

At Melbourne, December 11 (day/night). Australia won by 39 runs. Toss: New Zealand. Spurred on by their captain's 81 from 116 balls, New Zealand made a worthy attempt to match the highest total of the current World Series Cup. It was Crowe's 100th one-day international, and also Steve Waugh's, while at the other end of the spectrum Young, replacing the injured Smith, marked his first match at this level with an unbeaten 26. Marsh and Jones set out Australia's stall with 86 in 105 balls, and then O'Donnell and Border ruthlessly exposed New Zealand's limited attack by pounding 50 runs (in a fourth-wicket stand of 80) from 22 balls. The final stages seemed pedestrian in contrast as Australia added 61 off the last eleven overs. O'Donnell raced to 66 from 43 balls, having faced 25 for his first 17 runs, while Border's 40 came off 42 balls.

*Man of the Match*: S. P. O'Donnell.

## Australia

| | | | |
|---|---|---|---|
| G. R. Marsh b Bradburn | 51 | G. R. J. Matthews not out | 16 |
| D. C. Boon c Crowe b Petrie | 5 | †I. A. Healy not out | 6 |
| D. M. Jones run out | 54 | L-b 7, w 5 | 12 |
| S. P. O'Donnell b Morrison | 66 | | |
| *A. R. Border c Latham b Pringle | 40 | 1/16 2/102 3/122 | (7 wkts, 50 overs) 263 |
| M. E. Waugh c Crowe b Pringle | 9 | 4/202 5/232 | |
| S. R. Waugh c Crowe b Morrison | 4 | 6/237 7/244 | |

M. G. Hughes and T. M. Alderman did not bat.

Bowling: Pringle 10-1-40-2; Petrie 8-2-38-1; Morrison 10-0-45-2; Bradburn 9-1-56-1; Watson 10-0-59-0; Latham 3-0-18-0.

## New Zealand

| | | | | |
|---|---|---|---|---|
| *M. D. Crowe c Matthews | | | | |
| | b M. E. Waugh . | 81 | | |
| J. G. Wright c M. E. Waugh b Alderman | 24 | | | |
| M. J. Greatbatch c Matthews | | | | |
| | b O'Donnell . | 7 | | |
| K. R. Rutherford c Alderman | | | | |
| | b S. R. Waugh . | 37 | | |
| R. T. Latham run out | 4 | | | |
| G. E. Bradburn c Healy b S. R. Waugh | 6 | | | |

†B. A. Young not out . . . . . . . . . . . . . . 26
R. G. Petrie b M. E. Waugh . . . . . . . . 10
C. Pringle b M. E. Waugh . . . . . . . . . . 6
D. K. Morrison not out . . . . . . . . . . . . 9
    L-b 8, w 4, n-b 2 . . . . . . . . . . 14

1/52 2/59 3/142     (8 wkts, 50 overs) 224
4/146 5/167 6/181
7/195 8/205

W. Watson did not bat.

Bowling: Alderman 8–1–24–1; Hughes 8–0–40–0; O'Donnell 10–1–42–1; S. R. Waugh 10–0–39–2; Matthews 8–0–51–0; M. E. Waugh 6–0–20–3.

Umpires: L. J. King and S. G. Randell.

## †ENGLAND v NEW ZEALAND

At Sydney, December 13 (day/night). England won by 33 runs. Toss: New Zealand. Injudicious batting by New Zealand's middle order in the face of accurate spin bowling, shrewdly handled by Gooch in his first game of the series, enabled England's bowlers, with the aid of one fortunate lbw decision, to save the batsmen's faces. England's score looked a good 40 below par on an afternoon of blazing sunshine, especially when Crowe and Wright raised 50 in 13.2 overs. But at 56 Lamb held a magnificent diving slip catch to dispose of Wright. With Crowe kept away from the strike, Tufnell and Hemmings, bowling respectively to seven and six men in the circle, remorselessly pushed up the asking-rate. New Zealand still had a chance until Crowe was adjudged lbw to a ball that looked sure to clear his leg stump. His 76 from 108 balls (four fours) compared favourably with Lamb's 72 off 114 (seven fours), but the latter won the match award, despite his role in the run-outs of Morris and Stewart.
*Man of the Match:* A. J. Lamb.

## England

*G. A. Gooch c Young b Petrie . . . . . . 3
W. Larkins c Watson b Pringle . . . . . . 8
R. A. Smith c Latham b Petrie . . . . . . 4
A. J. Lamb b Morrison . . . . . . . . . . 72
J. E. Morris run out . . . . . . . . . . . . . . 19
†A. J. Stewart run out . . . . . . . . . . . . 42
C. C. Lewis c and b Bradburn . . . . . . . 4
M. P. Bicknell b Pringle . . . . . . . . . . . 8

E. E. Hemmings not out . . . . . . . . . . . 8
A. R. C. Fraser lbw b Pringle . . . . . . . 5
P. C. R. Tufnell b Pringle . . . . . . . . . . 2
    L-b 7, w 10, n-b 2 . . . . . . . . 19

1/7 2/16 3/23         (46.4 overs) 194
4/66 5/143 6/156
7/179 8/179 9/188

Bowling: Pringle 8.4–0–35–4; Petrie 8–2–25–2; Watson 10–0–38–0; Morrison 10–0–45–1; Bradburn 10–0–44–1.

## New Zealand

*M. D. Crowe lbw b Fraser . . . . . . . . . 76
J. G. Wright c Lamb b Lewis . . . . . . . 23
G. E. Bradburn b Lewis . . . . . . . . . . . 2
K. R. Rutherford b Hemmings . . . . . . 1
R. T. Latham c Smith b Hemmings . . . 10
†B. A. Young c Morris b Bicknell . . . . 25
C. Z. Harris c Stewart b Lewis . . . . . . 12
R. G. Petrie c Stewart b Lewis . . . . . . 2

C. Pringle c Hemmings b Fraser . . . . 1
D. K. Morrison not out . . . . . . . . . . . . 2
W. Watson run out . . . . . . . . . . . . . . 0
    L-b 5, w 2 . . . . . . . . . . 7

1/56 2/64 3/66         (48.1 overs) 161
4/84 5/138 6/151
7/158 8/159 9/160

Bowling: Bicknell 10–0–39–1; Fraser 9–1–21–2; Lewis 9.1–0–35–4; Tufnell 10–1–27–0; Hemmings 10–1–34–2.

Umpires: A. R. Crafter and I. S. Thomas.

## †ENGLAND v NEW ZEALAND

At Brisbane, December 15. New Zealand won by eight wickets. Toss: New Zealand. England displayed their pitiful loss of confidence with the bat for the second time in three days, and this time their bowlers could not bail them out. Taking toll of Malcolm – they helped themselves to 43 off his first six overs – Crowe and Wright insured New Zealand against a collapse like the one that cost them the Sydney match. Crowe had decided against breaking up his opening alliance with Wright, even though Jones had recovered from the finger injury suffered at Perth, and he made his third commanding half-century (eight fours) in successive games. He was in reach of the first hundred of the tournament when he tested the resilience of Gooch's hand with a stinging drive off Malcolm to mid-on. Gooch's 48, from 90 balls, was the top scorer of an England innings that passed 200 thanks only to the newly arrived DeFreitas, and because New Zealand dropped four routine catches.

*Man of the Match:* M. D. Crowe.

## England

| | | | |
|---|---|---|---|
| *G. A. Gooch b Harris | 48 | C. C. Lewis run out | 3 |
| W. Larkins c Young b Petrie | 15 | P. A. J. DeFreitas not out | 27 |
| R. A. Smith b Morrison | 41 | L-b 8, w 5 | 13 |
| A. J. Lamb run out | 10 | | |
| J. E. Morris c Young b Petrie | 16 | 1/27 2/99 3/115   (6 wkts, 50 overs) | 203 |
| †A. J. Stewart not out | 30 | 4/122 5/143 6/149 | |

A. R. C. Fraser, P. C. R. Tufnell and D. E. Malcolm did not bat.

Bowling: Pringle 10–1–36–0; Petrie 10–1–32–2; Morrison 10–2–41–1; Watson 10–0–40–0; Harris 8–0–36–1; Latham 2–0–10–0.

## New Zealand

| | |
|---|---|
| *M. D. Crowe c Gooch b Malcolm | 78 |
| J. G. Wright c Stewart b Tufnell | 54 |
| A. H. Jones not out | 41 |
| R. T. Latham not out | 17 |
| B 1, l-b 4, w 4, n-b 5 | 14 |

1/109 2/178     (2 wkts, 44.3 overs) 204

K. R. Rutherford, †B. A. Young, C. Z. Harris, R. G. Petrie, C. Pringle, D. K. Morrison and W. Watson did not bat.

Bowling: Fraser 9–2–38–0; Malcolm 8–0–56–1; DeFreitas 8–0–31–0; Lewis 9.3–1–31–0; Tufnell 10–0–43–1.

Umpires: S. G. Randell and C. D. Timmins.

## †AUSTRALIA v ENGLAND

At Brisbane, December 16. Australia won by 37 runs. Toss: Australia. Jones's seventh hundred in one-day internationals lifted his average above 50 and surpassed the previous highest for Australia, 138 not out by G. S. Chappell against New Zealand in 1980-81. He faced 136 balls, hitting four sixes and twelve fours, and his stand of 185 with Marsh (124 balls) was a record for Australia against England in the one-day game. Jones was fractionally run out at 3 when DeFreitas's throw from deep third man clipped a bail from 60 yards (umpire Crafter correctly gave him the benefit of doubt), and twice he narrowly cleared fielders with leg-side mis-hits in the early stages. But after his first six, an on-drive off Hemmings that cleared the boundary by 30 yards, he was unstoppable, driving, pulling, sweeping and cutting imperiously. Theoretically, England had a chance when Gooch and Lamb took them into three figures in the 22nd over. But in Matthews's first over Lamb was caught at mid-wicket, and in his second Gooch hit over and round a skidding quicker ball. Hope lingered until Smith and Morris imagined singles were available off firm strokes to Border at mid-wicket, twenty yards away. Stewart sent the former back, but responded to the second call and was beaten by a foot, having made 40 with exquisite timing off 35 balls. DeFreitas struck a six and four fours in his 49 (57 balls).

*Man of the Match:* D. M. Jones.

## Australia

| | | | | |
|---|---|---|---|---|
| D. C. Boon lbw b Fraser | 10 | *A. R. Border not out | | 4 |
| G. R. Marsh c Larkins b Bicknell | 82 | | | |
| D. M. Jones c Tufnell b DeFreitas | 145 | B 3, l-b 12, w 7, n-b 1 | | 23 |
| S. R. Waugh not out | 14 | | | |
| M. E. Waugh c Tufnell b DeFreitas | 5 | 1/24 2/209 3/261 | (5 wkts, 50 overs) | 283 |
| S. P. O'Donnell c Morris b DeFreitas | 0 | 4/272 5/272 | | |

G. R. J. Matthews, †I. A. Healy, C. G. Rackemann and B. A. Reid did not bat.

Bowling: Fraser 10-1-47-1; Bicknell 10-0-64-1; DeFreitas 10-0-57-3; Hemmings 10-0-57-0; Tufnell 10-0-43-0.

## England

| | | | | |
|---|---|---|---|---|
| *G. A. Gooch b Matthews | 41 | M. P. Bicknell b Rackemann | | 25 |
| W. Larkins b O'Donnell | 19 | E. E. Hemmings not out | | 3 |
| A. J. Lamb c Border b Matthews | 35 | B 1, l-b 8, w 5, n-b 1 | | 15 |
| †A. J. Stewart run out | 40 | | | |
| R. A. Smith run out | 6 | 1/26 2/104 3/121 | (7 wkts, 50 overs) | 246 |
| J. E. Morris c S. R. Waugh b Matthews | 13 | 4/141 5/151 | | |
| P. A. J. DeFreitas not out | 49 | 6/174 7/213 | | |

A. R. C. Fraser and P. C. R. Tufnell did not bat.

Bowling: Reid 10-1-41-0; O'Donnell 10-2-43-1; Rackemann 10-0-41-1; S. R. Waugh 4-0-20-0; Matthews 10-0-54-3; M. E. Waugh 4-0-23-0; Border 1-0-9-0; Jones 1-0-6-0.

Umpires: A. R. Crafter and L. J. King.

## †AUSTRALIA v NEW ZEALAND

At Hobart, December 18. New Zealand won by 1 run. Toss: Australia. New Zealand's victory, before a record crowd of 11,086, confounded the pundits and threw England into confusion: they themselves now had to beat Australia to qualify for the finals. Although Border rearranged his batting order, thinking victory assured at 93 for three in the 25th over, that was scarcely any reason for this defeat. Marsh made 61 from 98 balls, and a target of 84 from the last twenty overs, with six wickets in hand, was well within Australia's compass. However, Border repaid the New Zealanders' generosity for twice dropping him early in his innings by contributing to Jones's run out and then his own, and Alderman, sent back by Matthews, became the third victim of New Zealand's resurgent fielding. Just 2 runs were required off the final over, but Pringle bowled a maiden to Reid. New Zealand, rescued from 112 for five in the 38th over by Latham (44 balls) and Young (37 balls), could hardly have considered likely such a dramatic win.

*Man of the Match:* B. A. Young.

## New Zealand

| | | | | |
|---|---|---|---|---|
| *M. D. Crowe lbw b Alderman | 5 | †B. A. Young not out | | 41 |
| J. G. Wright c S. R. Waugh b O'Donnell | 37 | R. G. Petrie not out | | 6 |
| A. H. Jones c Reid b S. R. Waugh | 12 | L-b 3, w 2, n-b 7 | | 12 |
| K. R. Rutherford run out | 26 | | | |
| C. Z. Harris c Healy b Reid | 17 | 1/17 2/40 3/71 | (6 wkts, 50 overs) | 194 |
| R. T. Latham c Jones b O'Donnell | 38 | 4/110 5/112 6/169 | | |

C. Pringle, D. K. Morrison and W. Watson did not bat.

Bowling: Alderman 10-1-52-1; Reid 10-1-25-1; O'Donnell 10-0-50-2; Matthews 10-1-33-0; M. E. Waugh 5-0-13-0; S. R. Waugh 5-1-18-1.

## Australia

| | | | |
|---|---|---|---|
| G. R. Marsh c Latham b Harris | 61 | G. R. J. Matthews not out | 24 |
| D. C. Boon c Crowe b Pringle | 2 | T. M. Alderman run out | 5 |
| S. R. Waugh c Young b Morrison | 16 | B. A. Reid run out | 1 |
| M. E. Waugh c Young b Petrie | 14 | L-b 2, w 5, n-b 2 | 9 |
| †I. A. Healy lbw b Watson | 24 | | |
| D. M. Jones run out | 25 | 1/7 2/52 3/93 | (50 overs) 193 |
| S. P. O'Donnell lbw b Harris | 0 | 4/111 5/136 6/137 | |
| *A. R. Border run out | 12 | 7/154 8/177 9/188 | |

Bowling: Pringle 10–1–34–1; Petrie 10–1–30–1; Morrison 10–0–56–1; Watson 10–0–29–1; Harris 10–0–42–2.

Umpires: S. G. Randell and C. D. Timmins.

## †AUSTRALIA v ENGLAND

At Sydney, January 1 (day/night). Australia won by 68 runs. Toss: England. A New Year's Day crowd of 36,838 saw a performance by England's batsmen which Gooch sorrowfully rated the worst during his captaincy. In stark contrast, Australia illustrated the depth of their batting. Impetuous strokes against the spinners cost the wickets of Jones and Border, and when Steve Waugh was caught behind cutting, they were 93 for five in the 24th over. However, Mark Waugh, placing and weighting his strokes classily, and O'Donnell, driving with shattering force, added 112 in 23 overs, and England owed it to Fraser and DeFreitas that the total was kept to 221. Gooch and Larkins gave England a good start with 61 of fifteen overs, but after a thunderous on-drive Gooch was caught in two minds and bowled by O'Donnell. After that the clever variations of Taylor's off-spin ruined England's chances, and the remaining wickets added only 88 in 30 overs.

*Man of the Match*: P. L. Taylor.

## Australia

| | | | |
|---|---|---|---|
| G. R. Marsh lbw b Tufnell | 29 | †I. A. Healy c Atherton b Fraser | 4 |
| D. C. Boon lbw b Fraser | 4 | P. L. Taylor not out | 2 |
| D. M. Jones c Small b Tufnell | 25 | L-b 5, w 11, n-b 1 | 17 |
| *A. R. Border c Small b Hemmings | 4 | | |
| M. E. Waugh c Larkins b Fraser | 62 | 1/15 2/55 3/72 | (7 wkts, 50 overs) 221 |
| S. R. Waugh c Stewart b Tufnell | 3 | 4/82 5/93 | |
| S. P. O'Donnell not out | 71 | 6/205 7/218 | |

C. G. Rackemann and T. M. Alderman did not bat.

Bowling: Fraser 10–2–28–3; Small 10–1–43–0; DeFreitas 10–0–48–0; Tufnell 10–2–40–3; Hemmings 10–0–57–1.

## England

| | | | |
|---|---|---|---|
| *G. A. Gooch b O'Donnell | 37 | E. E. Hemmings run out | 1 |
| W. Larkins b Taylor | 40 | A. R. C. Fraser c Boon b Rackemann | 4 |
| M. A. Atherton c Healy b S. R. Waugh | 8 | P. C. R. Tufnell not out | 0 |
| †A. J. Stewart c S. R. Waugh b Border | 18 | B 2, l-b 7, w 1, n-b 2 | 12 |
| R. A. Smith b Taylor | 1 | | |
| J. E. Morris c M. E. Waugh b Taylor | 8 | 1/65 2/81 3/103 | (45.5 overs) 153 |
| P. A. J. DeFreitas st Healy b Border | 9 | 4/109 5/117 6/125 | |
| G. C. Small st Healy b Border | 15 | 7/135 8/136 9/153 | |

Bowling: Alderman 8–0–28–0; Rackemann 7.5–1–25–1; O'Donnell 5–0–15–1; S. R. Waugh 6–0–25–1; Taylor 10–2–27–3; Border 9–1–24–3.

Umpires: L. J. King and S. G. Randell.

## †AUSTRALIA v ENGLAND

At Melbourne, January 10 (day/night). Australia won by 3 runs. Toss: Australia. After a mid-order collapse had cost England four wickets in three overs, Bicknell, Fraser and Tufnell almost won them an undeserved entry to the finals on run-rate. Two overs from Rackemann were struck for 26 and Steve Waugh was straight driven for a majestic six by Fraser in the penultimate over. The last, from Alderman, began with England 11 from victory, and ended with Tufnell needing a boundary off the last ball. He swung at it in vain outside off stump. After 38 overs of their innings Australia had been 127 for six, but Healy, who completed a 37-ball 50 off the final delivery, and Steve Waugh added 95 in twelve overs through some inspired running. Australia's victory took them ahead of England in their one-day encounters, by 25 to 24, for the first time since the initial match on the same ground on January 5, 1971.

*Man of the Match*: I. A. Healy.

### Australia

| | | | | | |
|---|---|---|---|---|---|
| D. C. Boon c Small b DeFreitas | 42 | | S. P. O'Donnell c Bicknell b Gooch | ... | 7 |
| G. R. Marsh c Stewart b Bicknell | 7 | | †I. A. Healy not out | | 50 |
| D. M. Jones c Stewart b Bicknell | 2 | | L-b 1, w 1, n-b 1 | | 3 |
| *A. R. Border c Larkins b Small | 10 | | | | |
| M. E. Waugh run out | 36 | | 1/14 2/16 3/40 (6 wkts, 50 overs) | | 222 |
| S. R. Waugh not out | 65 | | 4/81 5/112 6/127 | | |

P. L. Taylor, T. M. Alderman and C. G. Rackemann did not bat.

Bowling: Fraser 10–2–39–0; Bicknell 9.5–0–33–2; Small 10–2–50–1; Tufnell 3–0–23–0; DeFreitas 7.1–0–37–1; Gooch 10–0–39–1.

### England

| | | | | | |
|---|---|---|---|---|---|
| *G. A. Gooch c Healy b M. E. Waugh | 37 | | M. P. Bicknell c Alderman | | |
| D. I. Gower lbw b Alderman | 26 | | b S. R. Waugh | | 23 |
| W. Larkins b Alderman | 0 | | A. R. C. Fraser not out | | 38 |
| †A. J. Stewart b Taylor | 55 | | P. C. R. Tufnell not out | | 5 |
| R. A. Smith b M. E. Waugh | 7 | | L-b 6, w 5, n-b 1 | | 12 |
| J. E. Morris c Healy b M. E. Waugh | 10 | | | | |
| P. A. J. DeFreitas c Border | | | 1/39 2/39 3/93 (9 wkts, 50 overs) | | 219 |
| b M. E. Waugh | 6 | | 4/119 5/139 6/142 | | |
| G. C. Small b Taylor | 0 | | 7/142 8/146 9/176 | | |

Bowling: Alderman 9–2–31–2; Rackemann 7–0–52–0; O'Donnell 7–0–28–0; S. R. Waugh 7–1–25–1; M. E. Waugh 10–0–37–4; Taylor 10–1–40–2.

Umpires: R. J. Evans and L. J. King.

### QUALIFYING TABLE

| | Played | Won | Lost | Points | Run-rate |
|---|---|---|---|---|---|
| Australia | 8 | 7 | 1 | 14 | 4.76 |
| New Zealand | 8 | 3 | 5 | 6 | 4.06 |
| England | 8 | 2 | 6 | 4 | 4.06 |

## †AUSTRALIA v NEW ZEALAND

### First Final Match

At Sydney, January 13 (day/night). Australia won by six wickets. Toss: New Zealand. Australia's victory was considerably more convincing than a margin of five balls to spare might suggest. Anchored by Marsh, who put on 70 in fourteen overs with Taylor for the first wicket and 100 in 25 with Jones for the second, their innings could afford to have Boon and Steve Waugh taking nine overs to score the last 24 runs. They hardly missed their captain,

Border, who was resting a groin strain. New Zealand, choosing to bat first, had also begun well. Crowe and Reid, the latter coming into the side for Greatbatch, had 50 on the board in twelve overs, but apart from Jones the later batsmen struggled to keep up the momentum. In one seven-over spell late in the innings their scoring was limited to singles. O'Donnell's dismissal of Wright was his 104th wicket in one-day internationals, a record for an Australian bowler.

*Attendance*: 37,440.

## New Zealand

| | | |
|---|---|---|
| *M. D. Crowe c M. E. Waugh | | |
| b P. L. Taylor . | 35 | |
| R. B. Reid c M. A. Taylor b Alderman | 17 | |
| J. G. Wright b O'Donnell . . . . . . . . . . | 10 | |
| A. H. Jones c S. R. Waugh | | |
| b M. E. Waugh . | 43 | |
| K. R. Rutherford c and b P. L. Taylor . | 7 | |
| †B. A. Young b M. E. Waugh . . . . . . . . | 19 | |

| | | |
|---|---|---|
| R. T. Latham not out . . . . . . . . . . . . . . | 26 |
| G. R. Larsen lbw b M. E. Waugh . . . . . | 6 |
| R. G. Petrie not out . . . . . . . . . . . . . . | 11 |
| L-b 10, w 11, n-b 4 . . . . . . . . | 25 |
| | |
| 1/55 2/69 3/101    (7 wkts, 50 overs) 199 |
| 4/126 5/136 |
| 6/159 7/170 |

C. Pringle and D. K. Morrison did not bat.

Bowling: Alderman 8–1–23–1; Reid 9–0–44–0; O'Donnell 6–0–26–1; S. R. Waugh 7–0–32–0; P. L. Taylor 10–0–35–2; M. E. Waugh 10–2–29–3.

## Australia

| | | |
|---|---|---|
| *G. R. Marsh b Pringle . . . . . . . . . . . . | 70 |
| M. A. Taylor run out . . . . . . . . . . . . . | 41 |
| D. M. Jones b Morrison . . . . . . . . . . . | 49 |
| D. C. Boon not out . . . . . . . . . . . . . . | 14 |
| M. E. Waugh lbw b Morrison . . . . . . . | 0 |

| | |
|---|---|
| S. R. Waugh not out . . . . . . . . . . . . . | 16 |
| L-b 5, w 2, n-b 5 . . . . . . . . | 12 |
| | |
| 1/70 2/170    (4 wkts, 49.1 overs) 202 |
| 3/174 4/176 |

S. P. O'Donnell, †I. A. Healy, P. L. Taylor, T. M. Alderman and B. A. Reid did not bat.

Bowling: Pringle 10–1–32–1; Petrie 10–1–41–0; Morrison 10–1–43–2; Larsen 8–1–36–0; Jones 7–0–27–0; Crowe 4.1–0–18–0.

Umpires: R. J. Evans and L. J. King.

## †AUSTRALIA v NEW ZEALAND

### Second Final Match

At Melbourne, January 15 (day/night). Australia won by seven wickets. Toss: New Zealand. Whatever hopes the New Zealanders held of taking the WSC finals to a third, deciding game faded with the early dismissal of their captain, Crowe. Reid again batted with aggression, top-scoring with 64 from 94 balls, but Jones hit only one boundary in his 89-ball half-century as once again the Australian bowlers exerted mean control. Australia in reply lost their acting-captain, Marsh, to the first ball of the second over, and any of Petrie's next three deliveries might have sent Jones back. Instead, before an appreciative home crowd, Jones (105 balls, one six, six fours) played a masterful innings which took his aggregate for the series to 513 and Australia to within 10 runs of victory. Taylor's contrapuntal 71 from 93 balls and Boon's measured 40 not out from 64 more or less completed the score.

*Man of the Finals*: M. A. Taylor.     *Attendance*: 48,957.

## New Zealand

| | | |
|---|---|---|
| *M. D. Crowe b Reid . . . . . . . . . . . . . | 6 |
| R. B. Reid c Jones b P. L. Taylor . . . . . | 64 |
| J. G. Wright c P. L. Taylor b O'Donnell | 8 |
| A. H. Jones lbw b Reid . . . . . . . . . . . . | 51 |
| K. R. Rutherford c P. L. Taylor | |
| b O'Donnell . | 37 |
| R. T. Latham not out . . . . . . . . . . . . . | 20 |

| | |
|---|---|
| †B. A. Young c Jones b O'Donnell . . . . | 11 |
| C. Pringle not out . . . . . . . . . . . . . . . . | 1 |
| | |
| L-b 8, w 1, n-b 1 . . . . . . . . . . . | 10 |
| | |
| 1/14 2/51 3/102    (6 wkts, 50 overs) 208 |
| 4/171 5/177 6/194 |

G. R. Larsen, R. G. Petrie and D. K. Morrison did not bat.

Bowling: Alderman 7–1–21–0; Reid 10–3–35–2; O'Donnell 9–0–43–3; S. R. Waugh
9–1–37–0; P. L. Taylor 9–0–40–1; M. E. Waugh 6–0–24–0.

## Australia

| | | |
|---|---|---|
| M. A. Taylor c Rutherford b Jones .... 71 | M. E. Waugh not out ................. 3 | |
| *G. R. Marsh c Young b Petrie ...... 0 | B 1, l-b 12, w 2, n-b 4 ....... 19 | |
| D. M. Jones b Pringle .............. 76 | | |
| D. C. Boon not out ................. 40 | 1/2  2/120  3/199    (3 wkts, 45.3 overs) 209 | |

S. R. Waugh, S. P. O'Donnell, †I. A. Healy, P. L. Taylor, T. M. Alderman and B. A. Reid
did not bat.

Bowling: Pringle 9.3–1–30–1; Petrie 9–0–51–1; Morrison 9–0–40–0; Larsen 10–2–32–0;
Crowe 2–0–15–0; Jones 6–0–28–1.

Umpires: A. R. Crafter and P. J. McConnell.

# THE ASHES

"In affectionate remembrance of English cricket which died at The Oval, 29th August, 1882.
Deeply lamented by a large circle of sorrowing friends and acquaintances, R.I.P. N.B. The
body will be cremated and the Ashes taken to Australia."

Australia's first victory on English soil over the full strength of England, on August 29,
1882, inspired a young London journalist, Reginald Shirley Brooks, to write this mock
"obituary". It appeared in the *Sporting Times*.

Before England's defeat at The Oval, by 7 runs, arrangements had already been made for
the Hon. Ivo Bligh, afterwards Lord Darnley, to lead a team to Australia. Three weeks later
they set out, now with the popular objective of recovering the Ashes. In the event, Australia
won the First Test by nine wickets, but with England winning the next two it became
generally accepted that they brought back the Ashes.

It was long accepted that the real Ashes – a small urn believed to contain the ashes of a bail
used in the third match – were presented to Bligh by a group of Melbourne women. At the
time of the 1982 centenary of The Oval Test match, however, evidence was produced which
suggested that these ashes were the remains of a ball and that they were given to the England
captain by Sir William Clarke, the presentation taking place before the Test matches in
Australia in 1883. The certain origin of the Ashes, therefore, is the subject of some dispute.

After Lord Darnley's death in 1927, the urn was given to MCC by Lord Darnley's
Australian-born widow, Florence. It can be seen in the cricket museum at Lord's, together
with a red and gold velvet bag, made specially for it, and the scorecard of the 1882 match.

# CRICKET IN AUSTRALIA, 1990-91

## By JOHN MACKINNON

Victoria's achievement in climbing from last in the Sheffield Shield to first in consecutive years was an inspiring one, for which players, captain, coach, selectors and officials could all enjoy a feeling of satisfaction. They could point to the fact that the end had ultimately justified the means. However, Victoria's success also drew attention to a weakness in the competition. The stronger sides were handicapped by surrendering their international representatives to Test matches, World Series Cup games and to Australia's tour of the West Indies, and in this respect the Shield final between Victoria and New South Wales was something of a misnomer. The defending champions, New South Wales, had five players in the West Indies, and while Victoria themselves had two, it was none the less a little surprising that, with home ground advantage, they made rather a meal of beating such a depleted opposition.

Before the season began, the various state associations were busy recruiting new players. Queensland looked to have made the prize capture by securing Graeme Hick, the prolific Worcestershire batsman, and Peter Taylor had moved north from New South Wales. Victoria created shockwaves over their western border by luring Adelaide's prodigy, Darren Lehmann, to Melbourne; a little too covertly, according to the South Australian Cricket Association. They also enticed the left-arm swing bowler, Alan Mullally, over from Perth. In addition to losing Lehmann, South Australia also had to bid farewell to their Cricket Academy representatives, Darren Berry going back to Melbourne and Michael Bevan and Phil Alley returning to New South Wales. This drain on resources was compensated to some degree by the arrival of the Victorian fast bowler, Dennis Hickey. With so much coming and going, the Australian Cricket Board found it necessary to tighten up the rules to prevent incidents of poaching in the future.

For all its triumphant conclusion, Victoria's Shield season began inauspiciously with a nine-wicket defeat in Brisbane, which followed some puerile behaviour in Adelaide after an FAI Cup match. This episode was roundly criticised by press and officials alike. However, a recovery was imminent, and an innings victory over New South Wales effectively silenced their critics. Simon O'Donnell's captaincy became a matter for some scrutiny, especially after his public outburst against what he considered was an inept and over-manned executive, but the matter was hastily resolved. Not surprisingly there were some wry smiles in late March.

In spite of winning the Shield, Victoria lost the patronage of their main sponsor, while on the playing side they had an urgent need for opening batsmen and a spin bowler, a rare commodity in Australian cricket. Even so, considering the number of dreadful starts, the batting measured up well enough. Jamie Siddons was very much the star turn, having set up his season with double-centuries against New South Wales and South Australia, and his century in the final demonstrated a cool nerve and an iron will. Lehmann took time to settle in, and it was his great misfortune that, having done so, he suffered a serious eye injury at practice. He was brought back into the side for the final, but possibly prematurely. Wayne Phillips, if lacking some of his colleagues' flair, showed that there was no more gutsy a fighter, and

O'Donnell played some dynamic innings, especially when disaster threatened the side. Consequently, with such substance in the middle order, Dean Jones was hardly missed: his contribution in three matches was just 86 at an average of 17. In the absence of Merv Hughes, who took 29 Shield wickets at 20, the bowling could have been a problem, but Paul Reiffel adopted the mantle of spearhead when Hughes was representing Australia and responded superbly. For someone who began the season as the state's twelfth man, in Brisbane, his improvement was spectacular, and his batting, too, was an asset. Tony Dodemaide's return for the last three games brought him twenty wickets, his brisk pace and rediscovered ability to bowl an out-swinger adding much-needed penetration, and Damien Fleming played an invaluable part with his ability to make an early breakthrough. The best of five spinners selected at various stages was the slow left-armer, Paul Jackson, while Berry confirmed his competence as a wicket-keeper. Credit is due to Les Stillman, who, in his first year back from a period in South Australia as team coach, successfully maintained a level of commitment from his players. This was never better demonstrated than when all seemed lost in the final.

New South Wales continued to be unbeatable in Sydney but were vulnerable away from home: two points in Perth was the sum total garnered from five away matches. Of all the states they were the hardest hit by international calls, and only Steve Small and wicket-keeper Phil Emery played in all eleven matches. Small's achievement in exceeding 1,000 runs was remarkable for one who mostly eschewed the leg side as a scoring option, though he hit the ball with rare power on the off. Quite the brightest talent to emerge was the left-handed Michael Bevan. At the beginning of the season he had won a place in the state's one-day side, but there was no permanent role for him in the four-day games. When the chance came, however, he reeled off five hundreds in consecutive matches against each of the states. It was not just the weight of Bevan's runs which impressed, but also his ability to adapt to different pitches and never miss the chance to put away the loose ball. Mark Taylor, Mark Waugh and Steve Waugh played only three, four and five Shield games respectively, scoring prolifically and leaving gaps in the batting that could never be filled adequately.

Wayne Holdsworth took the most wickets for New South Wales. At times his pace could be devastating, but there were other times when he was erratic and expensive. Geoff Lawson and Mike Whitney bowled steadily, Whitney well enough to earn selection for the tour of the West Indies. Greg Matthews took twenty wickets in three games, but when promoted to the Test team he began to lose form and confidence, at least with the ball. Although Adrian Tucker's leg-spin was expected to be an important element in the attack, he too failed to develop as hoped, and a wayward over at Sydney to Tom Moody, which went for 30, underlined the brittleness of his control. Greg McLay, coming into the side for the second half of the season, bowled his off-spin accurately enough, and Phil Alley's left-arm pace bowling showed that it may be an asset in years to come.

Queensland, like their southern neighbours, also found points hard to come by away from home. Their determination to win the Sheffield Shield was reflected by the recall of Trevor Hohns to captain the side and the appointment of Jeff Thomson as coach, in addition to the signing of Hick. Unfortunately, it was mid-February before Hick scored the first of his three hundreds, and although his record by ordinary standards was adequate, most Queenslanders had hoped for more. In the event the biggest impact was made by Stuart Law, one of five to play all matches. No-one in the country scored more heavily, and the umpires duly voted him Sheffield Shield Player of the Year, ahead of Bevan and Siddons. Another ever present was Peter Cantrell, whose batting overtook his bowling by a ratio of 649 runs off the bat to one wicket with the ball. His gully fielding was outstanding, and also made its mark when he came on as a substitute fieldsman in the Brisbane Test. Craig McDermott's bowling, both in his six Shield matches and for Australia, was outstanding; he won the Lord's Taverners Players' Player of the Year award. Carl Rackemann and Dirk Tazelaar gave him tremendous support, while Hohns bowled so well that the selectors tried in vain to lure the veteran leg-spinner back to Test cricket.

Western Australia began the season in style, winning the FAI Cup, nearly beating England, and winning their first two Shield matches outright. The failures of the previous season seemed little more than a memory as Graeme Wood returned to favour and Bruce Reid made a convincing recovery from his back injury. But the record partnership by the Waugh twins in Perth, against a full-strength attack, was a rude setback to the team's prospects, and from then on the old frailties re-emerged. Of the regulars, Tom Moody looked to have left his best batting in England, Wood, despite two Shield hundreds, suffered frequent failures, and Wayne Andrews never found his form. On the credit side, Ken MacLeay and Tim Zoehrer provided a prolific middle-order bulwark; but while MacLeay's all-round qualities earned him a contract with Somerset, Zoehrer could not even win the second wicket-keeper's berth on the Caribbean tour, for all his impressive form. That went to Mike Veletta on account of his substantial batting achievements. Both he and Geoff Marsh were sorely missed when required by Australia, but Mark Lavender, who came in as Veletta's replacement, hit a hundred on début in Melbourne and looked a well-organised player. Reid's 21 wickets in four Shield matches underlined both his actual and potential value, but Terry Alderman played in only three matches, and Chris Matthews's fitness was a serious mid-season concern. On his day there was no more destructive a bowler in the country, and he remained a sad example of unfulfilled talent. Moody at times bowled better than he batted, and the burly Martin McCague, plucked out of the Melbourne District competition, showed a deal of promise.

For South Australia, the problems began before a ball was bowled. Not only did they lose the redoubtable Lehmann, but the SACA relieved David Hookes of the captaincy, replacing him with Andrew Hilditch. Having just launched a twelve-month testimonial for Hookes, in recognition of his services to state cricket, the SACA's decision seemed a trifle perverse. Moreover, in spite of having the most settled team in the competition, with eight playing in all matches, South Australia enjoyed only a moderate season. Winning their last match, in Perth, merely camouflaged some serious deficiencies. With Hookes spasmodically brilliant, but more often distracted, Paul Nobes was the one batsman capable of scoring, or willing to score, his runs quickly enough to set up any sort of platform from which a win might result. Hilditch's runs were born of dedicated but laborious methods, Peter Sleep was of similar ilk, and Tim May's newly discovered batting prowess was good for resistance but not for tempo. Glenn Bishop dropped down the order after the charismatic but unproductive Wayne Phillips had failed, and his experience helped the younger players, including wicket-keeper Tim Nielsen and Joe Scuderi. It was as well that Hickey had been recruited, for the bowling resources were slim; at times he bowled decidedly fast, albeit off a very long run. May bowled the most overs, no mean feat for someone whose knees were often more hindrance than help, and fit he would still have been Australia's best off-spin prospect. Scuderi also toiled hard, but it is always easier to make runs at Adelaide than to take wickets.

Tasmania looked destined to fill the bottom position from an early stage. There were some high points, notably when Dave Gilbert and Peter McPhee bowled them to an unlikely win against a full-strength Queensland in Brisbane. And in the final match, at Hobart, Rod Tucker and Gavin Robertson batted them past a forbidding New South Wales total of 502, which could have cost the visitors a place in the final. Tucker's all-round talents developed encouragingly, and his loss would be felt were he to follow his captain, Dirk Wellham, north to Brisbane. Wellham himself passed 50 eight times but never reached three figures, and by the end of the season he appeared to be still disillusioned with the captaincy, battling always with meagre resources. Gilbert and McPhee always bowled tirelessly, but with Greg Campbell injured there was not much else. The batting, too, was fragile. David Boon achieved 104 runs in three matches and Jamie Cox failed to live up to expectations.

The Sheffield Shield table reveals that three teams were penalised for not achieving the required over-rate in certain matches. Although the Queensland and South Australian deductions in their last matches were not relevant to their final placings, Victoria's penalty for bowling two overs too few in Perth did draw attention to the shortcomings of the system. Victoria had beaten Western Australia well inside the scheduled four days, but by a mere 29 runs. Had a draw been on the cards they could have bowled their spinners and so lifted their over-rate to the desired level. But in a match in which runs were running out and the cracked pitch was conducive to pace, they felt they were victims of circumstance, and with a place in the final possibly in the balance, they appealed against the penalty. The Board, after nearly two months, decided that sixteen overs per hour was not an unfair task. As one Board director said, "It's not a great rule, but all players know of it and should respond accordingly". At least it confirmed the Board's commitment to improving over-rates at all levels of the game.

# FIRST-CLASS AVERAGES, 1990-91

## BATTING

(Qualification: 500 runs)

| | M | I | NO | R | HI | 100s | Avge |
|---|---|---|---|---|---|---|---|
| S. G. Law (*Qld*) | 11 | 20 | 4 | 1,204 | 142* | 3 | 75.25 |
| M. E. Waugh (*NSW*) | 8 | 13 | 1 | 840 | 229* | 3 | 70.00 |
| M. G. Bevan (*NSW*) | 10 | 17 | 4 | 854 | 153* | 5 | 65.69 |
| J. D. Siddons (*Vic.*) | 12 | 21 | 5 | 1,034 | 245 | 4 | 64.62 |
| S. R. Waugh (*NSW*) | 8 | 11 | 1 | 598 | 216* | 1 | 59.80 |
| D. C. Boon (*Tas.*) | 9 | 17 | 2 | 809 | 121 | 2 | 53.93 |
| M. R. J. Veletta (*WA*) | 7 | 14 | 1 | 679 | 128 | 2 | 52.23 |
| P. C. Nobes (*SA*) | 11 | 20 | 2 | 937 | 131 | 2 | 52.05 |
| S. M. Small (*NSW*) | 13 | 23 | 0 | 1,186 | 126 | 4 | 51.56 |
| K. H. MacLeay (*WA*) | 11 | 19 | 7 | 586 | 102* | 1 | 48.83 |
| W. N. Phillips (*Vic.*) | 9 | 15 | 4 | 528 | 100* | 1 | 48.00 |
| G. A. Hick (*Qld*) | 11 | 21 | 2 | 904 | 155 | 3 | 47.57 |

| | M | I | NO | R | HI | 100s | Avge |
|---|---|---|---|---|---|---|---|
| G. R. Marsh (WA) | 10 | 20 | 3 | 793 | 151 | 2 | 46.64 |
| G. A. Bishop (SA) | 11 | 19 | 1 | 787 | 159 | 3 | 43.72 |
| D. M. Wellham (Tas.) | 10 | 18 | 2 | 699 | 95 | 0 | 43.68 |
| R. J. Tucker (Tas.) | 10 | 18 | 2 | 673 | 165 | 2 | 42.06 |
| G. M. Wood (WA) | 11 | 21 | 1 | 831 | 166 | 3 | 41.55 |
| W. G. Ayres (Vic.) | 9 | 16 | 2 | 544 | 139 | 2 | 38.85 |
| A. M. J. Hilditch (SA) | 11 | 19 | 2 | 637 | 119* | 2 | 37.47 |
| D. S. Lehmann (Vic.) | 10 | 17 | 0 | 626 | 139 | 2 | 36.82 |
| D. W. Hookes (SA) | 11 | 18 | 0 | 655 | 195 | 2 | 36.38 |
| S. P. O'Donnell (Vic.) | 10 | 17 | 1 | 578 | 109 | 1 | 36.12 |
| T. M. Moody (WA) | 11 | 22 | 2 | 696 | 101* | 2 | 34.80 |
| P. E. Cantrell (Qld) | 12 | 24 | 3 | 698 | 176* | 1 | 33.23 |
| T. H. Bayliss (NSW) | 11 | 19 | 2 | 520 | 163 | 1 | 30.58 |
| G. M. Watts (Vic.) | 12 | 22 | 0 | 571 | 81 | 0 | 25.95 |
| S. Monty (Qld) | 11 | 22 | 2 | 508 | 100* | 1 | 25.40 |

* Signifies not out.

## BOWLING

### (Qualification: 20 wickets)

| | O | M | R | W | BB | 5W/i | Avge |
|---|---|---|---|---|---|---|---|
| A. I. C. Dodemaide (Vic.) | 106.1 | 37 | 245 | 20 | 5-19 | 2 | 12.25 |
| C. J. McDermott (Qld) | 400.3 | 83 | 1,304 | 67 | 8-97 | 6 | 19.46 |
| C. D. Matthews (WA) | 181 | 33 | 652 | 32 | 6-48 | 3 | 20.37 |
| B. A. Reid (WA) | 375 | 89 | 1,042 | 50 | 7-51 | 4 | 20.84 |
| M. G. Hughes (Vic.) | 395.5 | 87 | 1,055 | 48 | 6-54 | 1 | 21.97 |
| P. R. Reiffel (Vic.) | 463.5 | 128 | 1,164 | 49 | 6-57 | 3 | 23.75 |
| M. R. Whitney (NSW) | 259 | 70 | 708 | 29 | 4-32 | 0 | 24.41 |
| C. G. Rackemann (Qld) | 325.4 | 82 | 951 | 36 | 5-45 | 2 | 26.41 |
| G. F. Lawson (NSW) | 340.2 | 100 | 826 | 30 | 4-31 | 0 | 27.53 |
| T. M. Alderman (WA) | 295.3 | 70 | 880 | 31 | 6-47 | 1 | 28.38 |
| P. T. McPhee (Tas.) | 376.1 | 73 | 1,232 | 43 | 6-36 | 2 | 28.65 |
| D. R. Gilbert (Tas.) | 330.2 | 71 | 957 | 32 | 6-111 | 2 | 29.90 |
| D. W. Fleming (Vic.) | 455.2 | 139 | 1,153 | 38 | 5-50 | 1 | 30.34 |
| G. R. J. Matthews (NSW) | 458.4 | 157 | 1,016 | 33 | 5-56 | 2 | 30.78 |
| D. J. Hickey (SA) | 326.1 | 48 | 1,254 | 40 | 6-72 | 2 | 31.35 |
| W. J. Holdsworth (NSW) | 328.3 | 57 | 1,185 | 37 | 6-99 | 2 | 32.02 |
| T. V. Hohns (Qld) | 347.3 | 116 | 761 | 23 | 6-102 | 2 | 33.08 |
| T. B. A. May (SA) | 473.2 | 128 | 1,285 | 37 | 6-115 | 3 | 34.72 |
| J. C. Scuderi (SA) | 368 | 96 | 1,071 | 29 | 6-117 | 2 | 36.93 |
| D. Tazelaar (Qld) | 294.1 | 82 | 886 | 23 | 4-48 | 0 | 38.52 |
| A. E. Tucker (NSW) | 289.5 | 53 | 968 | 24 | 5-38 | 1 | 40.33 |

## SHEFFIELD SHIELD, 1990-91

| | Played | Won | Lost | Drawn | 1st Inns Pts | Pts | Quotient |
|---|---|---|---|---|---|---|---|
| Victoria | 10 | 4 | 2 | 4 | 6 | 29.8* | 1.196 |
| New South Wales | 10 | 3 | 2 | 5 | 6 | 24 | 1.233 |
| Queensland | 10 | 3 | 3 | 4 | 4 | 21.5† | 1.037 |
| Western Australia | 10 | 2 | 4 | 4 | 6 | 18 | 0.873 |
| South Australia | 10 | 2 | 1 | 7 | 4 | 15.4‡ | 0.940 |
| Tasmania | 10 | 1 | 3 | 6 | 2 | 8 | 0.802 |

* 0.2 points deducted for slow over-rates.
† 0.5 points deducted for slow over-rates.
‡ 0.6 points deducted for slow over-rates.
Outright win = 6 pts; lead on first innings in a drawn game = 2 pts.
Quotient = runs per wkt scored divided by runs per wkt conceded.

**Final:** Victoria beat New South Wales by eight wickets.

## NEW SOUTH WALES v TASMANIA

At Sydney, November 2, 3, 4, 5. New South Wales won by an innings and 20 runs. New South Wales 6 pts. Toss: Tasmania. Winning the toss proved to be of little value to the Tasmanians, who were outplayed in all departments and looked short of practice. Only Farrell and Wellham, adding 114 for the third wicket, were able to resist some outstanding bowling by Lawson and Matthews. In contrast, the New South Wales batsmen took to the Tasmanian attack, with the left-handed Small especially severe while dominating an opening stand of 165 with Taylor. Taylor, dropped by Pearce when 15, found his best form and with the Waugh twins put on 162 in the two hours before lunch on the third day. His 183 occupied just under five hours; it was his fourth consecutive century at the SCG and contained 25 fours. Lawson's declaration left his bowlers with nearly four sessions in which to bowl out Tasmania a second time, and while Matthews closed one end for nearly five hours, Tucker and Whitney successfully chipped away against some tentative batting. Wellham again sold his wicket dearly and was last man out with more than two hours left.

*Close of play:* First day, Tasmania 246-7 (K. D. Pearce 4*, G. D. Campbell 0*); Second day, New South Wales 234-2 (M. A. Taylor 110*, M. E. Waugh 18*); Third day, Tasmania 75-1 (M. G. Farrell 40*, T. C. Coyle 6*).

### Tasmania

| | | | |
|---|---|---|---|
| G. Shipperd lbw b Lawson | 3 | – c M. E. Waugh b Matthews | 21 |
| M. G. Farrell c Emery b S. R. Waugh | 83 | – c Small b Tucker | 40 |
| D. C. Boon b Lawson | 7 | – (4) c and b Tucker | 12 |
| *D. M. Wellham st Emery b Matthews | 91 | – (5) c Taylor b Tucker | 51 |
| J. Cox b Lawson | 3 | – (6) c Taylor b Tucker | 0 |
| R. J. Tucker c and b Matthews | 30 | – (7) lbw b Whitney | 13 |
| K. D. Pearce c M. E. Waugh b Matthews | 15 | – (8) c Emery b Whitney | 1 |
| †T. C. Coyle b Tucker | 2 | – (3) c Bayliss b Matthews | 8 |
| G. D. Campbell c and b Matthews | 14 | – b Whitney | 6 |
| D. R. Gilbert not out | 3 | – c Emery b Whitney | 7 |
| P. T. McPhee b Matthews | 0 | – not out | 19 |
| B 11, l-b 9, n-b 4 | 24 | B 8, l-b 2, n-b 6 | 16 |

1/11 2/31 3/145 4/152 5/230    275    1/35 2/75 3/85 4/91 5/91    194
6/243 7/246 8/258 9/275            6/121 7/125 8/139 9/157

Bowling: *First Innings*—Holdsworth 12-1-37-0; Lawson 19-9-32-3; Whitney 16-3-37-0; Matthews 32.4-12-56-5; Tucker 24-6-60-1; S. R. Waugh 10-1-33-1. *Second Innings*—Holdsworth 9-2-25-0; Lawson 6-3-12-0; Whitney 14-4-36-4; Matthews 40-25-40-2; Tucker 23.5-7-71-4.

### New South Wales

| | | | |
|---|---|---|---|
| S. M. Small lbw b Farrell | 89 | *G. F. Lawson b McPhee | 1 |
| M. A. Taylor c Boon b Campbell | 183 | M. R. Whitney b Tucker | 9 |
| T. H. Bayliss b Farrell | 12 | | |
| M. E. Waugh c Boon b Pearce | 49 | B 4, l-b 7, n-b 2 | 13 |
| S. R. Waugh c Coyle b Tucker | 83 | | |
| G. R. J. Matthews c Wellham b Tucker | 32 | 1/165 2/195 3/298 (9 wkts dec.) 489 |
| †P. A. Emery not out | 18 | 4/385 5/450 6/463 |
| A. E. Tucker lbw b Tucker | 0 | 7/463 8/464 9/489 |

W. J. Holdsworth did not bat.

Bowling: Gilbert 27-4-83-0; Campbell 24-4-96-1; McPhee 29-5-86-1; Tucker 23.5-6-69-4; Farrell 25-4-76-2; Pearce 11-0-68-1.

Umpires: D. G. Graham and I. S. Thomas.

## QUEENSLAND v SOUTH AUSTRALIA

At Brisbane, November 2, 3, 4, 5. Drawn. Queensland 2 pts. Toss: South Australia. When rain interrupted play on the third afternoon, Queensland looked odds on to take outright points. McDermott and Rackemann had destroyed the South Australian first innings and, Queensland having enforced the follow-on, were threatening similar damage in the second. Instead Hookes, ever the fiercest of competitors, took on the Queensland bowlers on the final day, flaying four sixes and 23 fours in a 261-minute stay (211 balls). A spell of nine balls from Hohns realised 29 runs, including three sixes and two fours. Hookes and Nobes put on 184 for the third wicket in three hours. Queensland's first innings was a triumph for their opening batsman, Cantrell, whose career-best 176 included 21 fours and a six, occupied seven hours and gave notice of hitherto unrevealed strokemaking prowess. Cantrell distinguished himself further with four excellent catches in the gully, but Hick's début for Queensland lasted just fifteen balls and ended with a straightforward snick to Hookes at slip. South Australia spent the last 24 minutes of the match bowling eighteen overs to avoid incurring penalty points as a result of their tardy over-rate in Queensland's first innings.

*Close of play:* First day, Queensland 193-3 (P. E. Cantrell 95*, S. G. Law 62*); Second day, South Australia 110-9 (T. J. Nielsen 14*, D. J. Hickey 2*); Third day, South Australia 74-2 (P. C. Nobes 30*, D. W. Hookes 2*).

### Queensland

| | | | |
|---|---|---|---|
| P. E. Cantrell not out | 176 | – (2) not out | 10 |
| S. Monty lbw b Miller | 15 | – (1) not out | 2 |
| G. A. Hick c Hookes b Scuderi | 1 | | |
| A. R. Border c Hickey b May | 6 | | |
| S. G. Law c Nielsen b Hickey | 62 | | |
| P. L. Taylor c May b Scuderi | 69 | | |
| †I. A. Healy not out | 2 | | |
| L-b 9, n-b 12 | 21 | B 1, w 2 | 3 |

1/42 2/53 3/68 4/193 5/347      (5 wkts. dec.) 352      (no wkt) 15

*T. V. Hohns, C. J. McDermott, C. G. Rackemann and R. W. McGhee did not bat.

*Bowling: First Innings*—Miller 31-6-106-1; Hickey 22-4-80-1; Scuderi 20-5-65-2; May 24-8-60-1; Sleep 5-0-32-0. *Second Innings*—May 9-6-8-0; Hookes 9-6-6-0.

### South Australia

| | | | |
|---|---|---|---|
| *A. M. J. Hilditch c Cantrell b McDermott | 0 | – c Healy b McGhee | 5 |
| G. A. Bishop c Cantrell b McDermott | 9 | – c Healy b Rackemann | 18 |
| P. C. Nobes c Hick b Rackemann | 9 | – lbw b McDermott | 78 |
| D. W. Hookes c Hick b McDermott | 0 | – c Border b McDermott | 195 |
| P. R. Sleep c Cantrell b McGhee | 14 | – not out | 41 |
| W. B. Phillips c Healy b Rackemann | 11 | – not out | 29 |
| J. C. Scuderi lbw b Hohns | 27 | | |
| †T. J. Nielsen c Cantrell b McDermott | 22 | | |
| T. B. A. May b McDermott | 0 | | |
| C. R. Miller c Monty b Rackemann | 4 | | |
| D. J. Hickey not out | 12 | | |
| L-b 2, n-b 20 | 22 | B 5, l-b 10, n-b 16 | 31 |

1/1 2/12 3/12 4/37 5/47      130    1/17 2/68 3/252    (4 wkts. dec.) 397
6/67 7/103 8/104 9/108                         4/341

*Bowling: First Innings*—McDermott 17.1-7-40-5; McGhee 12-4-34-1; Rackemann 14-2-41-3; Taylor 7-5-11-0; Hohns 5-3-2-1. *Second Innings*—McDermott 24-2-73-2; McGhee 22-5-73-1; Rackemann 23-5-93-1; Taylor 21-6-54-0; Hohns 22-3-89-0.

Umpires: P. D. Parker and C. D. Timmins.

## QUEENSLAND v VICTORIA

At Brisbane, November 9, 10, 11. Queensland won by nine wickets. Queensland 6 pts. Toss: Victoria. O'Donnell had no hesitation in putting Queensland in to bat on a pitch that looked tailor-made for the fast bowlers, yet by stumps on the first day only five wickets had fallen – and the Victorian bowlers had conceded 29 runs in no-balls and wides. Border, meanwhile, had become entrenched and, although Hick was unable to make his mark, Law and latterly Healy had given him good support. On the second day the Queensland bowlers showed up the shortcomings of their Victorian counterparts. McDermott, bowling off a shorter run and controlling his out-swing perfectly, took the first four wickets in the space of ten balls, after which McGhee and Rackemann ensured that there was no recovery, even though O'Donnell fought hard for his half-century in 93 minutes. The follow-on brought no relief for the Victorian batting. There was some frenetic hitting on the second evening by Lehmann, whose 81 from 63 balls (eleven fours and a six) dominated a century partnership with Jones, but the Queensland bowlers had the second innings wrapped up by lunch on the third day.

*Close of play:* First day, Queensland 252-5 (A. R. Border 70*, I. A. Healy 30*); Second day, Victoria 117-4 (D. M. Jones 12*, D. W. Fleming 1*).

## Queensland

| | | | | | |
|---|---|---|---|---|---|
| P. E. Cantrell c Berry b Hughes | 14 | – (2) not out | 0 |
| S. Monty c Jones b Mullally | 26 | – (1) c Lehmann b Siddons | 0 |
| G. A. Hick c Ayres b Hughes | 5 | – not out | 11 |
| A. R. Border c Ayres b Fleming | 79 | | |
| S. G. Law c McIntyre b Fleming | 49 | | |
| P. L. Taylor c Siddons b O'Donnell | 17 | | |
| †I. A. Healy b Hughes | 30 | | |
| *T. V. Hohns not out | 15 | | |
| C. J. McDermott run out | 19 | | |
| B 2, l-b 19, w 11, n-b 20 | 52 | L-b 1, w 1 | 2 |

1/45 2/53 3/69 4/160 5/181        (8 wkts dec.) 306      1/2          (1 wkt) 13
6/259 7/273 8/306

R. W. McGhee and C. G. Rackemann did not bat.

Bowling: *First Innings*—Hughes 26–4–71–3; Fleming 24.3–8–65–2; Mullally 23–3–63–1; O'Donnell 16–5–41–1; McIntyre 12–3–43–0; Jones 1–0–2–0. *Second Innings*—Hughes 2–2–0–0; Fleming 1–1–0–0; Siddons 1–0–8–1; Lehmann 0.3–0–4–0.

## Victoria

| | | | | | |
|---|---|---|---|---|---|
| G. M. Watts lbw b McGhee | 25 | – lbw b McDermott | 4 |
| W. G. Ayres c Healy b McDermott | 0 | – c Law b McDermott | 0 |
| J. D. Siddons b McDermott | 0 | – c Hohns b McGhee | 6 |
| D. M. Jones c Monty b McDermott | 0 | – c Healy b McGhee | 37 |
| D. S. Lehmann lbw b McDermott | 5 | – c Healy b McDermott | 81 |
| *S. P. O'Donnell c Hick b McGhee | 52 | – (7) c Healy b McGhee | 52 |
| †D. S. Berry b Rackemann | 14 | – (8) c Healy b Rackemann | 10 |
| M. G. Hughes c and b Rackemann | 1 | – (9) not out | 4 |
| D. W. Fleming c Monty b Rackemann | 10 | – (6) c Taylor b McDermott | 4 |
| P. E. McIntyre c Monty b McDermott | 8 | – c Healy b Rackemann | 3 |
| A. D. Mullally not out | 19 | – c Healy b Rackemann | 0 |
| W 1, n-b 6 | 7 | L-b 6, w 1, n-b 14 | 21 |

1/5 2/5 3/5 4/13 5/64        141      1/4 2/7 3/13 4/113 5/137        176
6/93 7/98 8/109 9/114              6/144 7/165 8/171 9/176

Bowling: *First Innings*—McDermott 13.5–2–44–5; McGhee 14–5–40–2; Rackemann 11–2–34–3; Hohns 6–0–23–0. *Second Innings*—McDermott 15–3–46–4; McGhee 21–4–83–3; Rackemann 9.2–2–20–3; Taylor 3–0–21–0.

Umpires: C. A. Bertwistle and A. J. McQuillan.

## WESTERN AUSTRALIA v TASMANIA

At Perth, November 9, 10, 11, 12. Western Australia won by two wickets. Western Australia 6 pts. Toss: Western Australia. Having dominated the game for the first three days, Western Australia almost lost it in the face of inspired bowling by McPhee and Gilbert. Coming into the fourth day needing 75 runs for victory with nine wickets left, they were held up by rain for two hours, and the threat of further interruptions led to some injudicious strokes. At 78 for eight, still 9 runs short, Reid was nearly caught by Wellham off a lofted drive, and immediately after that he survived a hotly contested run-out appeal. A slash over the slips decided the match. Marsh's decision to put Tasmania in was rewarded with Farrell's dismissal from Alderman's second ball, and although Shipperd resisted for almost four and a quarter hours, Tasmania's batsmen never came to terms with the home attack. Marsh steered his team to a big lead with an excellent hundred (sixteen fours), and his century partnership with MacLeay for the seventh wicket countered a fine burst of bowling by McPhee. Tasmania's second innings was an improvement on their first, but the left-arm pace of Matthews and Reid was eventually decisive.

*Close of play:* First day, Western Australia 35-0 (G. R. Marsh 13\*, M. R. J. Veletta 11\*); Second day, Tasmania 20-0 (M. G. Farrell 17\*, G. Shipperd 1\*); Third day, Western Australia 12-1 (G. R. Marsh 5\*).

## Tasmania

| | | | |
|---|---:|---|---:|
| M. G. Farrell c MacLeay b Alderman | 0 | c MacLeay b Matthews | 29 |
| G. Shipperd c and b Andrews | 62 | c Zoehrer b Reid | 9 |
| D. C. Boon c McPhee b Alderman | 13 | c Zoehrer b Reid | 33 |
| *D. M. Wellham c Veletta b Matthews | 9 | c and b Matthews | 6 |
| J. Cox b Zoehrer b Matthews | 5 | c Zoehrer b Moody | 59 |
| R. J. Tucker c Zoehrer b Alderman | 10 | c Reid b Matthews | 18 |
| G. R. Robertson c Zoehrer b Moody | 34 | c Zoehrer b Matthews | 2 |
| †T. C. Coyle not out | 19 | c Zoehrer b Reid | 55 |
| G. D. Campbell c Veletta b Matthews | 0 | lbw b Moody | 0 |
| D. R. Gilbert lbw b MacLeay | 16 | b Alderman | 16 |
| P. T. McPhee b MacLeay | 0 | not out | 2 |
| L-b 4, n-b 6 | 10 | B 1, l-b 11, w 1, n-b 4 | 17 |
| | **177** | | **246** |

1/0 2/18 3/41 4/47 5/74
6/129 7/145 8/146 9/167

1/35 2/55 3/79 4/84
5/144 6/147 7/186
8/186 9/233

Bowling: *First Innings*—Alderman 19-3-49-3; Reid 18-7-42-0; Matthews 16-4-42-3; MacLeay 12.3-4-22-2; Moody 5-2-4-1; Andrews 8-4-14-1. *Second Innings*—Alderman 21-6-51-1; Reid 23.2-2-76-3; Matthews 15-5-52-4; MacLeay 16-8-17-0; Moody 6-1-27-2; Andrews 10-6-11-0.

## Western Australia

| | | | |
|---|---:|---|---:|
| *G. R. Marsh c Coyle b Gilbert | 117 | (2) c Shipperd b Gilbert | 11 |
| M. R. J. Veletta c Coyle b Campbell | 34 | (1) lbw b Gilbert | 7 |
| T. M. Moody c Boon b McPhee | 20 | b McPhee | 28 |
| G. M. Wood c Cox b McPhee | 10 | c Coyle b Gilbert | 0 |
| W. S. Andrews c Coyle b Tucker | 14 | c Shipperd b McPhee | 1 |
| M. W. McPhee lbw b McPhee | 1 | c Coyle b McPhee | 0 |
| †T. J. Zoehrer c Boon b McPhee | 4 | c Cox b Gilbert | 4 |
| K. H. MacLeay c Tucker b McPhee | 72 | not out | 19 |
| C. D. Matthews not out | 24 | c Farrell b McPhee | 5 |
| B. A. Reid run out | 2 | not out | 8 |
| T. M. Alderman c Campbell b McPhee | | | |
| L-b 6, n-b 28 | 34 | B 4, l-b 1 | 5 |
| | **337** | (8 wkts) | **88** |

1/85 2/133 3/143 4/162 5/171
6/179 7/290 8/306 9/314

1/12 2/25 3/33 4/38
5/38 6/53 7/69 8/78

Bowling: *First Innings*—Gilbert 21-5-75-1; Campbell 18-3-80-1; McPhee 24-2-100-6; Tucker 12-1-35-1; Robertson 8-1-31-0; Farrell 3-0-10-0. *Second Innings*—Gilbert 16.1-2-47-4; Campbell 4-2-5-0; McPhee 12-3-31-4.

Umpires: P. J. McConnell and T. A. Prue.

## SOUTH AUSTRALIA v WESTERN AUSTRALIA

At Adelaide, November 16, 17, 18, 19. Western Australia won by four wickets. Western Australia 6 pts. Toss: South Australia. Having to overcome another second-innings stutter, Western Australia won with two hours to spare. South Australia's first innings was their undoing, for they never recovered from losing three wickets in the first eight overs. Alderman and in particular Reid bowled superbly on a pitch which held no hidden terrors, as Marsh and Veletta demonstrated while putting on an untroubled 76 on the first evening. Veletta went on to bat for five and threequarter hours before falling to Hickey, who worked up a good pace and was duly rewarded for his effort. Andrews bolstered Western Australia's middle order, and their lead of 164 was decisive. When South Australia batted again, Nobes and Hookes improved on their first-innings noughts with a hard-hitting partnership of 119 in 107 minutes, but once Nobes had departed after three hours of defiance, Reid reimposed his influence and finished with eleven wickets for the match. It was the first time he had taken ten wickets in a game and was no mean effort on the Adelaide pitch.

*Close of play:* First day, Western Australia 76-0 (G. R. Marsh 40*, M. R. J. Veletta 28*); Second day, Western Australia 332; Third day, South Australia 292-8 (T. J. Nielsen 26*, C. R. Miller 8*).

## South Australia

| | | | |
|---|---|---|---|
| *A. M. J. Hilditch b Reid | 28 | – (2) lbw b Reid | 10 |
| G. A. Bishop lbw b Alderman | 3 | – (1) lbw b Alderman | 10 |
| P. C. Nobes c McPhee b Reid | 0 | – st Zoehrer b Andrews | 77 |
| D. W. Hookes c Zoehrer b Reid | 0 | – lbw b MacLeay | 64 |
| P. R. Sleep b Reid | 42 | – lbw b Reid | 12 |
| W. B. Phillips c Alderman b MacLeay | 5 | – b Reid | 19 |
| J. C. Scuderi lbw b Alderman | 4 | – c Zoehrer b Alderman | 42 |
| †T. J. Nielsen not out | 44 | – c Zoehrer b Reid | 30 |
| T. B. A. May c Marsh b Reid | 7 | – c Marsh b Reid | 7 |
| C. R. Miller b Alderman | 23 | – not out | 29 |
| D. J. Hickey b Hogan | 4 | – b Reid | 0 |
| L-b 4, n-b 4 | 8 | B 3, l-b 5, n-b 10 | 18 |
| | **168** | | **318** |

1/11 2/12 3/14 4/60 5/69 6/82 7/97 8/129 9/157

1/24 2/28 3/147 4/179 5/189 6/217 7/268 8/279 9/318

Bowling: *First Innings*—Alderman 18-2-66-3; Reid 19-5-49-5; MacLeay 17-4-35-1; Hogan 7.3-2-14-1. *Second Innings*—Alderman 22-4-86-2; Reid 27.3-3-94-6; MacLeay 17-4-47-1; Hogan 17-2-58-0; Andrews 20-6-25-1; Brayshaw 2-2-0-0.

## Western Australia

| | | | |
|---|---|---|---|
| *G. R. Marsh c Hookes b Hickey | 45 | – (2) c Nobes b May | 39 |
| M. R. J. Veletta b Hickey | 121 | – (1) lbw b May | 7 |
| M. W. McPhee lbw b Hickey | 5 | – c Hilditch b Scuderi | 51 |
| G. M. Wood c Nielsen b Scuderi | 23 | – run out | 21 |
| W. S. Andrews c Hookes b May | 85 | – b May | 0 |
| J. A. Brayshaw c Nielsen b Hickey | 2 | – lbw b Scuderi | 0 |
| †T. J. Zoehrer c Nielsen b Hickey | 0 | – not out | 7 |
| K. H. MacLeay b Scuderi | 12 | – not out | 14 |
| T. G. Hogan b Hickey | 17 | | |
| B. A. Reid c and b Hookes | 0 | | |
| T. M. Alderman not out | 0 | | |
| B 4, l-b 14, n-b 4 | 22 | B 4, l-b 5, n-b 8 | 17 |
| | **332** | (6 wkts) | **156** |

1/87 2/101 3/171 4/238 5/250 6/250 7/298 8/330 9/331

1/46 2/59 3/115 4/119 5/120 6/133

Bowling: *First Innings*—Miller 23-6-53-0; Hickey 22.3-2-72-6; Scuderi 25-9-60-2; May 39-3-93-1; Sleep 8-2-30-0; Hookes 4-1-6-1. *Second Innings*—Miller 6-2-17-0; Hickey 10-2-38-0; Scuderi 17-5-36-2; May 21.2-7-56-3.

Umpires: A. R. Crafter and S. J. Davis.

## VICTORIA v NEW SOUTH WALES

At St Kilda, Melbourne, November 16, 17, 18, 19. Victoria won by an innings and 28 runs. Victoria 6 pts. Toss: New South Wales. The representative game in Hobart against the England touring team deprived Victoria of Lehmann and McIntyre, while New South Wales lost the services of Mark Waugh and Matthews. More crucially, Taylor had broken a finger in a country game, and the depleted New South Wales batting was soon found wanting by Victoria's fast bowlers, Fleming especially. Only Steve Waugh showed the temperament to play a major innings, and he was one of three players who fell to fine slip catching by Siddons. No doubt buoyed by these achievements, Siddons proceeded to dominate the match at a time when Victoria's batsmen were also struggling. Coming to the wicket at 41 for three, he first partnered the staunchly supportive Ayres in a stand of 173 in 177 minutes and then, with New South Wales on their knees, added 189 in 164 minutes with O'Donnell. Siddons took just under seven hours (356 balls) to record his highest score, hit 34 fours and two sixes, and impressed everyone with his commanding strokeplay and disciplined approach. Batting again, New South Wales were victims of their own impetuosity, and with Fleming and Hughes able to employ attacking fields they had capitulated by lunch on the last day. More than six thousand spectators attended on Sunday, the third day.

*Close of play:* First day, Victoria 36-2 (W. G. Ayres 11\*, D. M. Jones 7\*); Second day, Victoria 406-5 (J. D. Siddons 203\*, C. White 2\*); Third day, New South Wales 199-4 (S. R. Waugh 44\*, M. G. Bevan 10\*).

## New South Wales

| | | | |
|---|---:|---|---:|
| S. M. Small c Berry b Fleming | 5 | c Berry b Hughes | 17 |
| G. S. Milliken c Berry b Fleming | 23 | lbw b Fleming | 33 |
| T. H. Bayliss lbw b Fleming | 15 | c Fleming b Hughes | 48 |
| M. D. O'Neill c O'Donnell b Reiffel | 23 | b Reiffel | 22 |
| S. R. Waugh c Siddons b Reiffel | 42 | c Watts b Fleming | 53 |
| M. G. Bevan c and b O'Donnell | 20 | b Fleming | 40 |
| †P. A. Emery c Siddons b Fleming | 16 | lbw b Hughes | 8 |
| A. E. Tucker c and b Hughes | 21 | c Reiffel b Hughes | 10 |
| *G. F. Lawson c Siddons b Hughes | 0 | c Siddons b Fleming | 18 |
| M. R. Whitney not out | 3 | b Fleming | 0 |
| W. J. Holdsworth c Reiffel b Fleming | 0 | not out | 0 |
| L-b 6, n-b 4 | 10 | B 3, l-b 12, n-b 16 | 31 |

1/9 2/25 3/72 4/72 5/132            178      1/34 2/95 3/124 4/165 5/219        280
6/138 7/168 8/168 9/178                      6/248 7/250 8/280 9/280

Bowling: *First Innings*—Hughes 20-3-57-2; Fleming 21-6-50-5; Reiffel 14-4-38-2; O'Donnell 12-5-23-1; White 1-0-4-0. *Second Innings*—Hughes 22.1-2-79-4; Fleming 25-8-69-4; Reiffel 22-7-46-2; O'Donnell 13-3-35-0; White 12-3-36-0.

## Victoria

| | | | |
|---|---:|---|---:|
| G. M. Watts b Holdsworth | 0 | M. G. Hughes c Emery b Tucker | 9 |
| W. G. Ayres run out | 78 | P. R. Reiffel b Lawson | 1 |
| W. N. Phillips c Waugh b Whitney | 10 | D. W. Fleming not out | 5 |
| D. M. Jones b Whitney | 8 | | |
| J. D. Siddons lbw b Lawson | 245 | L-b 3, w 2, n-b 20 | 25 |
| *S. P. O'Donnell c Small b O'Neill | 84 | | |
| C. White c Milliken b Whitney | 13 | 1/4 2/25 3/41 4/214 5/403 | 486 |
| †D. S. Berry c Lawson b Tucker | 8 | 6/444 7/471 8/471 9/472 | |

Bowling: Holdsworth 18-3-78-1; Whitney 34-10-91-3; Lawson 26-4-88-2; Waugh 23-4-70-0; O'Neill 18-5-50-1; Tucker 16.3-2-84-2; Bevan 4-0-22-0.

Umpires: D. W. Holt and L. J. King.

## TASMANIA v VICTORIA

At Hobart, November 29, 30, December 1, 2. Drawn. Victoria 2 pts. Toss: Victoria. A slow, placid pitch made the game little more than a contest for first-innings points, and by the third evening this had been decided in Victoria's favour. The remaining time was well spent by Victoria's top-order batsmen, and to a lesser extent by their spinners, but the fierce spirit of combat was not so evident. Victoria were indebted for their first-innings total to their new wicket-keeper, Berry, who found an unlikely ally in Hughes. These two resisted every temptation for three and a half hours and put on a priceless 115 runs for the seventh wicket. Berry's 98 occupied 315 minutes (twelve fours) and he frustratingly missed a maiden century when Coyle held a juggling catch down the leg side. Tasmania made an inauspicious start, losing three wickets for 43. The next five hours saw them lose just one for 232. Wellham adopted his usual attritional role throughout this period and received dogged support from Tucker and Cruse. Having entered the 90s, however, he became totally becalmed, and the Victorian fast bowlers grabbed the initiative. The last six wickets fell for just 31. Ayres's second-innings hundred was personally gratifying and splendidly fashioned (171 balls, sixteen fours), but in the context of the match it was not especially significant.

*Close of play:* First day, Victoria 247-6 (D. S. Berry 49*, M. G. Hughes 29*); Second day, Tasmania 149-3 (D. M. Wellham 40*, R. J. Tucker 62*); Third day, Victoria 53-0 (G. M. Watts 27*, W. G. Ayres 23*).

### Victoria

| | | | |
|---|---|---|---|
| G. M. Watts c Cruse b Gilbert | 8 | – lbw b Tucker | 59 |
| W. G. Ayres lbw b Campbell | 10 | – not out | 131 |
| W. N. Phillips c Farrell b McPhee | 48 | | |
| D. S. Lehmann c Farrell b Gilbert | 62 | – (3) c Tucker b McPhee | 50 |
| *J. D. Siddons c Coyle b Gilbert | 17 | – (4) not out | 5 |
| C. White c Coyle b Campbell | 15 | | |
| †D. S. Berry c Coyle b Tucker | 98 | | |
| M. G. Hughes c Shipperd b McPhee | 47 | | |
| P. R. Reiffel c Coyle b Tucker | 12 | | |
| D. W. Fleming not out | 17 | | |
| P. E. McIntyre run out | 0 | | |
| L-b 3, n-b 6 | 9 | B 1, l-b 7 | 8 |
| | **343** | **(2 wkts dec.)** | **253** |

1/8 2/38 3/99 4/148 5/151      1/140 2/241
6/172 7/287 8/315 9/341

Bowling: *First Innings*—Gilbert 30-5-84-3; Campbell 37-9-96-2; McPhee 24-5-71-2; Tucker 14-3-29-2; Farrell 10-4-21-0; Robertson 21-7-39-0. *Second Innings*—Gilbert 5-2-12-0; Campbell 4-1-13-0; McPhee 26-1-113-1; Tucker 12-0-54-1; Robertson 13-2-53-0.

### Tasmania

| | | | |
|---|---|---|---|
| G. Shipperd c Reiffel b Fleming | 2 | – c Berry b Hughes | 7 |
| M. G. Farrell c Phillips b Hughes | 34 | – c Lehmann b White | 27 |
| J. Cox b Hughes | 6 | – c Siddons b McIntyre | 35 |
| *D. M. Wellham c Siddons b Hughes | 95 | – (7) not out | 22 |
| R. J. Tucker c Berry b Fleming | 70 | – (8) not out | 13 |
| B. A. Cruse c Siddons b Reiffel | 52 | – (5) c and b White | 10 |
| G. R. Robertson c Berry b Reiffel | 14 | – (4) c Siddons b McIntyre | 18 |
| †T. C. Coyle c White b Fleming | 7 | – (6) c ... ad b Lehmann | 9 |
| D. R. Gilbert c Berry b Reiffel | 0 | | |
| G. D. Campbell c Berry b Hughes | 3 | | |
| P. T. McPhee not out | 3 | | |
| B 4, l-b 11, w 1, n-b 4 | 20 | B 3, l-b 4 | 7 |
| | **306** | **(6 wkts)** | **148** |

1/9 2/42 3/43 4/157 5/275      1/14 2/73 3/73
6/281 7/295 8/295 9/299        4/89 5/103 6/129

Bowling: *First Innings*—Hughes 35.4-7-79-4; Fleming 32-9-82-3; Reiffel 32-13-51-3; McIntyre 18-2-69-0; White 2-0-10-0; Lehmann 1-1-0-0. *Second Innings*—Hughes 10-4-19-1; Fleming 4-0-19-0; Reiffel 12.5-5-21-0; McIntyre 17-6-51-2; White 12-3-20-2; Lehmann 4-2-11-1.

Umpires: B. T. Knight and S. G. Randell.

## TASMANIA v SOUTH AUSTRALIA

At Hobart, December 6, 7, 8, 9. Drawn. Toss: South Australia. Rain interfered with the first three days and there was no play on the fourth. Hilditch's decision to bowl first backfired as Cox set up Tasmania's innings with a hearty performance that occupied four and a half hours, during which he shared prolific stands with Wellham (150 in 131 minutes) and Tucker (111 in 105 minutes). Tucker continued on his merry way the next day and had reached his highest score, in 263 minutes, when Wellham declared. Tasmania's chances of upsetting the South Australian batting were thwarted by their inept catching. Hilditch, dropped before scoring, was let off four times before reaching 40, and Bishop also enjoyed two lives. Of the bowlers, Gilbert suffered most.

*Close of play:* First day, Tasmania 352-5 (R. J. Tucker 62*, T. C. Coyle 2*); Second day, South Australia 20-0 (A. M. J. Hilditch 9*, G. A. Bishop 10*), Third day, South Australia 271-3 (A. M. J. Hilditch 119*).

### Tasmania

| | | | | |
|---|---|---|---|---|
| M. G. Farrell c Hookes b Scuderi | 12 | D. R. Gilbert b George | | 0 |
| G. Shipperd b Scuderi | 32 | G. D. Campbell lbw b George | | 0 |
| J. Cox c Nielsen b Scuderi | 127 | P. T. McPhee not out | | 7 |
| *D. M. Wellham c Nielsen b Scuderi | 72 | B 3, l-b 16, n-b 18 | | 37 |
| R. J. Tucker not out | 119 | | | |
| B. A. Cruse c Nielsen b George | 12 | 1/41 2/62 3/212 | (9 wkts dec.) | 453 |
| †T. C. Coyle lbw b Scuderi | 7 | 4/323 5/346 6/375 | | |
| G. R. Robertson c Nielsen b Scuderi | 28 | 7/429 8/434 9/434 | | |

Bowling: Hickey 24-2-124-0; George 26-6-75-3; Scuderi 48-15-117-6; May 16-2-57-0; Sleep 16-4-47-0; Hookes 2-0-14-0.

### South Australia

| | | |
|---|---|---|
| *A. M. J. Hilditch not out | | 119 |
| G. A. Bishop c Coyle b McPhee | | 97 |
| †T. J. Nielsen b Gilbert | | 39 |
| P. C. Nobes c Gilbert b Campbell | | 5 |
| B 1, l-b 5, w 1, n-b 4 | | 11 |

1/178 2/264 3/271     (3 wkts) 271

D. W. Hookes, P. R. Sleep, W. B. Phillips, J. C. Scuderi, T. B. A. May, S. P. George and D. J. Hickey did not bat.

Bowling: Gilbert 21-5-71-1; Campbell 21.3-5-41-1; Tucker 19-6-35-0; McPhee 16-5-37-1; Robertson 14-4-49-0; Cruse 9-0-27-0; Farrell 7-4-5-0.

Umpires: B. T. Knight and S. G. Randell.

## SOUTH AUSTRALIA v QUEENSLAND

At Adelaide, December 14, 15, 16, 17. South Australia won by 52 runs. South Australia 6 pts. Toss: South Australia. The opening day belonged to Hookes, who complemented his captain's decision to bat with a characteristic onslaught; his 178, from 197 balls in 223 minutes, featured 21 fours and five sixes and took him past L. E. Favell's record of 9,656 runs in all first-class matches for South Australia. He partnered Phillips in a fifth-wicket stand of 108 in 92 minutes and put on 152 with Scuderi at an even more hectic pace. Queensland's reply was pedestrian, Monty's unbeaten hundred taking seven and a quarter hours (373 balls). Hohns needed thirteen stitches over his right eye after being hit by a delivery from Scuderi, and May's off-spin worried all batsmen. When Queensland declared 163 behind – Hilditch had agreed not to enforce the follow-on – South Australia batted for two and a half hours, during which they lost Hilditch second ball, and Nobes, helped by some friendly bowling, smashed sixteen fours and a six. Queensland's target was 352 from 113 overs, but Hickey, taking three wickets in nine balls on the final morning, effectively ended their challenge. Law made the most of the ideal conditions with 111 in three and a half hours (168 balls, twelve fours), but May had him caught at mid-wicket and bowled South Australia to a deserved victory.

*Close of play:* First day, South Australia 439-8 (T. B. A. May 12\*, C. R. Miller 19\*); Second day, Queensland 197-5 (S. Monty 66\*, P. W. Anderson 0\*); Third day, Queensland 43-0 (S. Monty 16\*, P. E. Cantrell 27\*).

## South Australia

| | | | | |
|---|---|---|---|---|
| G. A. Bishop b McDermott | 27 | – (2) not out | | 65 |
| *A. M. J. Hilditch c Anderson b Tazelaar | 39 | – (1) c Anderson b McDermott | | 0 |
| P. C. Nobes c Monty b Tazelaar | 7 | – not out | | 114 |
| D. W. Hookes c Hick b Tazelaar | 178 | | | |
| P. R. Sleep c Hick b McDermott | 7 | | | |
| W. B. Phillips c Cantrell b Hohns | 61 | | | |
| J. C. Scuderi run out | 49 | | | |
| †T. J. Nielsen c Cantrell b McDermott | 4 | | | |
| T. B. A. May not out | 26 | | | |
| C. R. Miller c Healy b Polzin | 28 | | | |
| D. J. Hickey c Anderson b Tazelaar | 12 | | | |
| L-b 2, w 2, n-b 34 | 38 | L-b 1, n-b 8 | | 9 |
| | 476 | 1/0 (1 wkt dec.) | | 188 |

1/46 2/78 3/103 4/136 5/244
6/396 7/403 8/416 9/451

Bowling: *First Innings*—McDermott 25-6-100-3; Tazelaar 26.1-3-150-4; Polzin 21-1-99-1; Hohns 20-4-65-1; Cantrell 9-2-23-0; Hick 4-0-37-0. *Second Innings*—McDermott 6-1-23-1; Tazelaar 9-2-35-0; Polzin 9-0-40-0; Hohns 8-0-28-0; Cantrell 9-0-50-0; Clifford 3-1-9-0; Law 1-0-2-0.

## Queensland

| | | | | |
|---|---|---|---|---|
| P. E. Cantrell c May b Hickey | 14 | – (2) c Nielsen b Hickey | | 36 |
| S. Monty not out | 100 | – (1) lbw b Hickey | | 18 |
| G. A. Hick b May | 67 | – b Hickey | | 1 |
| K. J. Healy lbw b May | 3 | – b May | | 5 |
| S. G. Law c Phillips b May | 19 | – c Bishop b May | | 111 |
| P. S. Clifford lbw b Scuderi | 40 | – lbw b May | | 22 |
| †P. W. Anderson c Scuderi b Miller | 5 | – (9) c Hilditch b Hickey | | 4 |
| *T. V. Hohns retired hurt | 31 | – (8) c Miller b May | | 27 |
| C. J. McDermott not out | | – not out | | 18 |
| M. A. Polzin (did not bat) | | – b Hickey | | 30 |
| D. Tazelaar (did not bat) | | – b Hickey | | 9 |
| L-b 3, w 1, n-b 26 | 30 | B 3, l-b 1, n-b 14 | | 18 |
| | (6 wkts dec.) 313 | | | 299 |

1/26 2/128 3/136 4/180    1/54 2/55 3/58 4/62 5/124
5/189 6/261               6/134 7/182 8/251 9/260

*In the first innings T. V. Hohns retired hurt at 279.*

Bowling: *First Innings*—Hickey 13-1-69-1; Miller 16-3-40-1; May 42-18-77-3; Scuderi 29-6-85-1; Sleep 17-4-39-0. *Second Innings*—Hickey 21.2-2-75-4; Miller 10-5-12-0; May 33-4-115-6; Scuderi 11-4-48-0; Sleep 18-4-45-0.

Umpires: S. J. Davis and D. J. Harper.

## QUEENSLAND v TASMANIA

At Brisbane, December 20, 21, 22, 23. Tasmania won by 14 runs. Tasmania 6 pts. Toss: Queensland. In football terms, this match was a home-win banker, and Queenslanders will never understand how they lost it. Needing 30 to win, with six wickets in hand and Border well set, they looked certain of victory. Then, armed with the new ball, Gilbert took four wickets in six balls. Campbell removed Border, and Queensland still needed 30 to win but now with the last pair together. Several lusty swings later and Queensland's capitulation was complete – relief for Gilbert, who had dropped Border early in his innings. Tasmania's second innings had followed a similar course, McDermott taking three wickets in an over as they slumped from 123 for five to 123 for nine, but it was their first innings which began Queensland's frustration. Thanks to a six-hour vigil by Cruse, who added 126 for the eighth wicket with Gilbert, Tasmania recovered from 103 for six to reach 335. On the third day McPhee induced a Queensland batting collapse and the follow-on was averted by just 1 run.

*Close of play:* First day, Tasmania 240-7 (B. A. Cruse 68*, D. R. Gilbert 31*); Second day, Queensland 156-5 (S. G. Law 59*, I. A. Healy 13*); Third day, Queensland 5-0 (S. Monty 1*, P. E. Cantrell 0*).

## Tasmania

| | | | |
|---|---|---|---|
| G. Shipperd c Healy b McDermott | 6 | – c Hick b Rackemann | 23 |
| M. G. Farrell c Taylor b Tazelaar | 3 | – c Cantrell b Rackemann | 17 |
| D. C. Boon c Hick b Tazelaar | 7 | – b Healy b McDermott | 32 |
| *D. M. Wellham c Hick b Tazelaar | 26 | – b Taylor | 1 |
| J. Cox lbw b McDermott | 44 | – c Cantrell b McDermott | 25 |
| R. J. Tucker b McDermott | 0 | – c Healy b McDermott | 4 |
| B. A. Cruse run out | 120 | – c Tazelaar b Taylor | 10 |
| †T. C. Coyle b McDermott | 18 | – c Healy b McDermott | 0 |
| D. R. Gilbert c Healy b Rackemann | 49 | – c Border b McDermott | 0 |
| G. D. Campbell c Healy b Taylor | 6 | – c Monty b Taylor | 0 |
| P. T. McPhee not out | 13 | – not out | 7 |
| B 5, l-b 8, n-b 30 | 43 | L-b 3, n-b 12 | 15 |
| | **335** | | **134** |

1/8 2/12 3/27 4/103 5/103      1/36 2/45 3/46 4/94 5/110
6/103 7/152 8/278 9/306      6/123 7/123 8/123 9/123

Bowling: *First Innings*—McDermott 37-7-114-4; Tazelaar 29-13-54-3; Rackemann 29-4-86-1; Hohns 25-9-42-0; Taylor 13.4-4-26-1. *Second Innings*—McDermott 15-3-36-5; Tazelaar 11-3-29-0; Rackemann 13-4-21-2; Hohns 1-1-0-0; Taylor 27.2-11-45-3.

## Queensland

| | | | |
|---|---|---|---|
| P. E. Cantrell c Boon b Tucker | 32 | – (2) c Coyle b McPhee | 38 |
| S. Monty c Farrell b McPhee | 17 | – (1) c Gilbert b Tucker | 50 |
| G. A. Hick b Campbell | 17 | – lbw b Tucker | 50 |
| A. R. Border c Farrell b Campbell | 0 | – c Coyle b Campbell | 58 |
| S. G. Law not out | 75 | – b Farrell | 28 |
| P. L. Taylor c Wellham b Tucker | 5 | – c Cruse b Gilbert | 10 |
| †I. A. Healy c Tucker b McPhee | 15 | – c Coyle b Gilbert | 0 |
| *T. V. Hohns c Wellham b McPhee | 1 | – b Gilbert | 0 |
| C. J. McDermott c and b McPhee | 6 | – not out | 10 |
| D. Tazelaar c Boon b McPhee | 2 | – b Gilbert | 0 |
| C. G. Rackemann c Cox b McPhee | 0 | – c Farrell b Campbell | 4 |
| L-b 5, w 1, n-b 10 | 16 | B 6, l-b 10, w 1, n-b 4 | 21 |
| | **186** | | **269** |

1/30 2/57 3/59 4/85 5/95      1/59 2/150 3/155 4/216 5/254
6/162 7/164 8/178 9/186      6/254 7/254 8/254 9/254

Bowling: *First Innings*—Gilbert 13-1-34-0; Campbell 22-4-68-2; McPhee 17-3-36-6; Tucker 11-0-39-2; Farrell 1-0-4-0. *Second Innings*—Gilbert 22-4-51-4; Campbell 19.3-9-40-2; McPhee 19-1-69-1; Tucker 13-1-41-2; Farrell 21-1-52-1.

Umpires: P. D. Parker and C. D. Timmins.

## WESTERN AUSTRALIA v NEW SOUTH WALES

At Perth, December 20, 21, 22, 23. Drawn. New South Wales 2 pts. Toss: Western Australia. Marsh's decision to field brought a sensational reaction from the Waugh twins, who became the first brothers in first-class cricket to score double-hundreds in the same innings. They joined forces with New South Wales struggling at 137 for four and Reid enjoying a fruitful spell of three for 25. More than a day later they were still batting, and Lawson declared immediately the scoreboard showed that they had broken every Australian partnership record. Their 464, occupying 407 minutes, was also a world record for the fifth wicket. Both

Mark (446 minutes, 343 balls, one six, 35 fours) and Steve (339 balls, 24 fours) reached their highest scores, and they so dominated the vaunted Western Australian pace attack that Zoehrer had to discard his wicket-keeping duties to bowl leg-breaks. The pitch was without blemish, but Western Australia's batsmen made little impression on bowling that was at least steady, and wickets fell regularly until late on the fourth day. It was then that MacLeay and Zoehrer, both of whom survived chances early on, put on 242 in 139 minutes, setting an eighth-wicket partnership record for Western Australia and denying New South Wales the opportunity of winning outright. Both hit nineteen fours in their unbeaten hundreds. Western Australia also owed much to Matthews, who curbed his big-hitting method to hold up New South Wales for three and a half hours.

*Close of play:* First day, New South Wales 375-4 (M. E. Waugh 128*, S. R. Waugh 112*); Second day, Western Australia 131-2 (M. R. J. Veletta 59*, G. M. Wood 15*); Third day, Western Australia 92-3 (T. M. Moody 27*, C. D. Matthews 1*).

## New South Wales

| | | | |
|---|---|---|---|
| S. M. Small c Wood b Reid | 26 | S. R. Waugh not out | .216 |
| M. A. Taylor b Reid | 57 | L-b 18, n-b 26 | 44 |
| T. H. Bayliss c Zoehrer b Reid | 20 | | |
| M. D. O'Neill c Zoehrer b MacLeay | 9 | 1/37 2/106 3/111 | (4 wkts dec.) 601 |
| M. E. Waugh not out | 229 | 4/137 | |

G. R. J. Matthews, †P. A. Emery, *G. F. Lawson, M. R. Whitney and W. J. Holdsworth did not bat.

Bowling: Alderman 30-9-91-0; Reid 33-3-147-3; Matthews 17-0-95-0; Moody 14-0-63-0; MacLeay 34.2-6-109-1; Andrews 12-2-54-0; Zoehrer 5-0-24-0.

## Western Australia

| | | | |
|---|---|---|---|
| *G. R. Marsh c Matthews b Lawson | 4 | - (2) c Matthews b S. R. Waugh | 5 |
| M. R. J. Veletta run out | 64 | - (1) b Matthews | 33 |
| T. M. Moody c Whitney b Holdsworth | 38 | - c Emery b Holdsworth | 56 |
| G. M. Wood c M. E. Waugh b Whitney | 54 | - b Matthews | 12 |
| W. S. Andrews b Whitney | 23 | - (6) c Small b Whitney | 4 |
| M. W. McPhee c O'Neill b Matthews | 11 | - (7) c Taylor b Matthews | 16 |
| †T. J. Zoehrer c Small b Matthews | 17 | - (8) not out | .133 |
| K. H. MacLeay not out | 46 | - (9) not out | .102 |
| C. D. Matthews c S. R. Waugh b Lawson | 8 | - (5) c Lawson b Holdsworth | 71 |
| B. A. Reid b Holdsworth | 2 | | |
| T. M. Alderman c M. E. Waugh b Lawson | 15 | | |
| B 5, l-b 2, w 1, n-b 24 | 32 | B 12, l-b 14, w 1, n-b 16 | 43 |
| | 314 | | (7 wkts) 475 |

1/4 2/80 3/156 4/186 5/215      314     1/21 2/62 3/88 4/134     (7 wkts) 475
6/227 7/243 8/272 9/277                      5/172 6/199 7/233

Bowling: *First Innings*—Lawson 24.1-5-71-3; S. R. Waugh 5-1-18-0; Matthews 31-6-68-2; Holdsworth 20-2-74-2; Whitney 17-4-68-2; M. E. Waugh 1-0-8-0. *Second Innings*—Lawson 16-5-43-0; S. R. Waugh 10-1-43-1; Matthews 39-8-119-3; Holdsworth 25-7-92-2; Whitney 19.5-5-70-1; M. E. Waugh 4-0-41-0; O'Neill 3-0-27-0; Small 1-0-14-0; Bayliss 1-1-0-0.

Umpires: R. J. Evans and T. A. Prue.

## QUEENSLAND v NEW SOUTH WALES

At Brisbane, January 4, 5, 6, 7. Queensland won by 110 runs. Queensland 6 pts. Toss: Queensland. Lawson's enterprising captaincy looked like being rewarded with a rare win in Brisbane until his counterpart, Hohns, took the ball with New South Wales 81 for one in pursuit of a target of 267 from 74 overs. The Queensland leg-spinner first checked the onslaught waged on his fast bowlers by Small and Bayliss and then, with McDermott in support, destroyed the New South Wales effort, the last nine wickets falling for 64. Although a number of crucial wickets fell to disputed decisions, notably Waugh's, Hohns's ability to exploit the wearing pitch was the decisive factor. Queensland's aggression in their first innings had enabled a declaration early on the second day as soon as Law's century bid had ended with a catch to slip off Emery's gloves. The New South Wales reply depended mostly on Waugh, who controlled the innings superbly until he too was dismissed when a hundred beckoned, caught at backward point. Lawson promptly declared, 146 in arrears, and with Whitney bowled outstandingly to put New South Wales back in contention.

*Close of play:* First day, Queensland 300-5 (S. G. Law 64*); Second day, New South Wales 77-3 (M. E. Waugh 11*, M. G. Bevan 3*); Third day, Queensland 76-6 (P. W. Anderson 3*, C. J. McDermott 0*).

## Queensland

| | | | |
|---|---|---|---|
| P. E. Cantrell c Emery b Whitney | 67 | – (2) lbw b Lawson | 7 |
| S. Monty b Whitney | 2 | – (1) c Lawson b Whitney | 7 |
| G. A. Hick c Emery b O'Neill | 69 | – c Small b Waugh | 8 |
| P. S. Clifford c Small b Lawson | 82 | – c Emery b Whitney | 26 |
| S. G. Law c Milliken b Holdsworth | 95 | – c Holdsworth b Waugh | 9 |
| R. W. McGhee b Whitney | 0 | – (11) not out | 8 |
| P. L. Taylor c Waugh b Lawson | 6 | – (6) lbw b Lawson | 8 |
| †P. W. Anderson not out | 34 | – (7) c Emery b Whitney | 5 |
| C. J. McDermott (did not bat) | | – (8) c Emery b Lawson | 6 |
| *T. V. Hohns (did not bat) | | – (9) b Lawson | 24 |
| D. Tazelaar (did not bat) | | – (10) c Emery b Whitney | 0 |
| B 2, l-b 9, w 1, n-b 10 | 22 | L-b 8, n-b 4 | 12 |

1/4 2/130 3/162 4/299 5/300 (7 wkts dec.) 377    1/11 2/15 3/26 4/52 5/67 120
6/307 7/377    6/75 7/81 8/89 9/98

Bowling: *First Innings*—Lawson 24–4–64–2; Whitney 22–2–76–3; Holdsworth 18.3–1–74–1; Waugh 7–2–23–0; Tucker 19–0–87–0; O'Neill 17–3–42–1. *Second Innings*—Lawson 18.2–7–31–4; Whitney 18–5–32–4; Holdsworth 8–2–34–0; Waugh 8–2–15–2.

## New South Wales

| | | | |
|---|---|---|---|
| S. M. Small c and b McGhee | 25 | – c Anderson b Hohns | 67 |
| G. S. Milliken c Anderson b McDermott | 17 | – c Cantrell b McDermott | 6 |
| T. H. Bayliss c Anderson b McDermott | 5 | – c Law b McDermott | 25 |
| M. E. Waugh c McDermott b Taylor | 97 | – c Anderson b Tazelaar | 0 |
| M. D. O'Neill retired hurt | 2 | – (8) c Clifford b Hohns | 0 |
| M. G. Bevan c Anderson b McGhee | 25 | – (5) c Cantrell b Hohns | 7 |
| †P. A. Emery not out | 27 | – c Taylor b McDermott | 10 |
| A. E. Tucker not out | 2 | – (9) not out | 15 |
| *G. F. Lawson (did not bat) | | – (6) c Clifford b Hohns | 8 |
| M. R. Whitney (did not bat) | | – lbw b Hohns | 3 |
| W. J. Holdsworth (did not bat) | | – c Anderson b McDermott | 0 |
| B 4, l-b 5, w 4, n-b 18 | 31 | L-b 2, w 1, n-b 12 | 15 |

1/53 2/59 3/61 4/139 5/229 (5 wkts dec.) 231    1/35 2/92 3/93 4/106 5/118 156
6/118 7/122 8/138 9/149

*In the first innings M. D. O'Neill retired hurt at 68.*

Bowling: *First Innings*—McDermott 29–9–65–2; McGhee 29–9–74–2; Tazelaar 17–4–59–0; Taylor 7–1–23–1; Hohns 1–0–1–0. *Second Innings*—McDermott 18.4–3–82–4; McGhee 9–1–33–0; Tazelaar 11–2–21–1; Taylor 1–1–0–0; Hohns 19–10–18–5.

Umpires: C. A. Bertwistle and C. D. Timmins.

## SOUTH AUSTRALIA v VICTORIA

At Adelaide, January 11, 12, 13, 14. Drawn. Victoria 2 pts. Toss: South Australia. Victoria were denied outright victory by a matter of inches when an involuntary snick from Hickey went through the slips to the boundary. The runs gave South Australia a lead of 3, and with nine minutes left of the match, Victoria had run out of time. South Australia's first innings, on a perfect pitch, was devoid of initiative and momentum. Hilditch meandered through the first day to reach 98 and eventually carried his bat. For Victoria, Lehmann hit his first hundred for his new state, a measured effort taking 283 minutes and including seventeen fours. Siddons, his fourth-wicket partner in a stand of 148 in just over three hours, did even better, going on to his second double-century at Adelaide and batting for five and a half hours. He hit eighteen fours and a six, and had a willing ally in Emerson, with whom he added 207 in 164 minutes. South Australia lost three second-innings wickets on the third evening and were lucky not to lose a fourth when night-watchman Nielsen survived a confident stumping appeal. He went on to bat for four and a half hours. Jackson bowled his left-arm orthodox spin with great accuracy but could not make the breakthrough as May held out for 95 minutes at the end.

*Close of play:* First day, South Australia 221-7 (A. M. J. Hilditch 98*, T. B. A. May 0*); Second day, Victoria 240-3 (D. S. Lehmann 103*, J. D. Siddons 38*); Third day, South Australia 76-3 (P. C. Nobes 27*, T. J. Nielsen 0*).

## South Australia

| | | |
|---|---|---|
| G. A. Bishop b Reiffel | 21 | – (2) c Berry b Hughes .......... 18 |
| *A. M. J. Hilditch not out .................. | 108 | – (1) c Berry b Hughes .......... 12 |
| P. C. Nobes c Siddons b Jackson | 23 | – lbw b Jackson .......... 74 |
| D. W. Hookes c Phillips b Jackson | 10 | – b Jackson .......... 11 |
| P. R. Sleep c Siddons b Hughes | 25 | – (6) c Siddons b Jackson .......... 16 |
| W. B. Phillips c Berry b Hughes | 0 | – (7) c Berry b Reiffel .......... 29 |
| J. C. Scuderi c Berry b Reiffel | 16 | – (8) lbw b Jackson .......... 23 |
| †T. J. Nielsen b Fleming | 17 | – (5) lbw b Hughes .......... 79 |
| T. B. A. May lbw b Hughes | 0 | – not out .......... 13 |
| C. R. Miller b Hughes | 0 | – c Lehmann b Reiffel .......... 3 |
| D. J. Hickey b Fleming | 2 | – not out .......... 5 |
| L-b 1, n-b 10 | 11 | B 7, l-b 7, n-b 14 ..... 28 |
| | **233** | (9 wkts) **311** |

1/25 2/70 3/82 4/144 5/150          1/26 2/33 3/70
6/180 7/205 8/224 9/224             4/165 5/205 6/261
                                    7/269 8/300 9/305

Bowling: *First Innings*—Hughes 26-4-67-4; Fleming 18.5-6-45-2; Reiffel 24-3-71-2; Jackson 26-9-39-2; Emerson 5-1-10-0; Phillips 2-2-0-0. *Second Innings*—Hughes 24-2-93-3; Fleming 22-7-52-0; Reiffel 19.1-5-41-2; Jackson 41-16-73-4; Emerson 12-1-38-0.

## Victoria

| | | |
|---|---|---|
| G. M. Watts lbw b May | 16 | M. G. Hughes b May .......... 6 |
| W. G. Ayres b Miller | 6 | †D. S. Berry not out .......... 8 |
| W. N. Phillips c Nielsen b Miller | 51 | B 9, l-b 15, w 2, n-b 12 ..... 38 |
| D. S. Lehmann lbw b Scuderi | 139 | |
| *J. D. Siddons not out | 201 | 1/23 2/29 3/151        (6 wkts dec.) **541** |
| D. A. Emerson c Sleep b May | 76 | 4/299 5/506 6/520 |

P. R. Reiffel, P. W. Jackson and D. W. Fleming did not bat.

Bowling: Hickey 17.1-3-57-0; Miller 31-6-73-2; Scuderi 28-4-77-1; May 47-3-177-3; Sleep 12-2-56-0; Hookes 15-1-77-0.

Umpires: S. J. Davis and D. J. Harper.

## WESTERN AUSTRALIA v QUEENSLAND

At Perth, January 11, 12, 13, 14. Drawn. Western Australia 2 pts. Toss: Western Australia. Queensland's first innings was founded on the composed batting of 22-year-old Law, and when survival was paramount in their second innings he continued to go for his shots, hitting sixteen fours and a six in a stay of three and a quarter hours. McDermott, who was hit on the elbow by a ball from Mack when batting on the first day, bowled tirelessly to take six of the seven wickets to fall when Western Australia batted. The highlight of their innings was a sparkling partnership of 231 between the brothers-in-law, Veletta and Wood, and Veletta was unlucky to be dismissed when his helmet rolled on to the stumps. He also joined the ranks of the wounded when he was hit on the hand during Western Australia's token second innings. Queensland's survival had been aided by injuries to Matthews and MacLeay, two key bowlers in the home state's attack.

*Close of play:* First day, Queensland 326-7 (S. G. Law 102*, C. J. McDermott 51*); Second day, Western Australia 229-2 (M. R. J. Veletta 123*, G. M. Wood 66*); Third day, Queensland 109-3 (P. E. Cantrell 55*, S. G. Law 12*).

## Queensland

| | | | |
|---|---|---|---|
| P. E. Cantrell c Wood b MacLeay | 1 | – (2) c Zoehrer b Mack | 89 |
| S. Monty c Zoehrer b Mack | 43 | – (1) lbw b Moody | 13 |
| G. A. Hick c Andrews b Moody | 36 | – c Andrews b Mack | 9 |
| P. S. Clifford c Zoehrer b Capes | 28 | – c Zoehrer b Mack | 4 |
| S. G. Law not out | 142 | – c Wood b Andrews | 105 |
| S. C. Storey run out | 0 | – c Wood b Andrews | 20 |
| †P. W. Anderson c MacLeay b Moody | 4 | – lbw b Mack | 5 |
| C. J. McDermott lbw b MacLeay | 74 | – not out | 18 |
| *T. V. Hohns b Andrews | 34 | – not out | 0 |
| A. Hammelmann c Zoehrer b Capes | 1 | | |
| D. Tazelaar b Moody | 2 | | |
| L-b 13, w 2, n-b 18 | 33 | B 2, l-b 4, n-b 16 | 22 |

| | |
|---|---|
| 1/13 2/87 3/103 4/144 5/144 | **398** |
| 6/149 7/278 8/364 9/384 | |

| |
|---|
| 1/75 2/88 3/96  (7 wkts dec.) **285** |
| 4/194 5/247 |
| 6/256 7/270 |

*In the first innings C. J. McDermott, when 33, retired hurt at 200 and resumed at 278.*

Bowling: *First Innings*—Capes 28–6–95–2; MacLeay 29–8–82–2; Matthews 10–1–34–0; Mack 23–3–97–1; Moody 21.3–6–50–3; Zoehrer 6–3–18–0; Andrews 7–2–9–1. *Second Innings*—Capes 19–4–56–0; MacLeay 6–2–22–0; Mack 22–6–72–4; Moody 31–10–97–1; Andrews 20–12–32–2.

## Western Australia

| | | | |
|---|---|---|---|
| M. W. McPhee c Storey b McDermott | 2 | – (2) not out | 31 |
| M. R. J. Veletta hit wkt b McDermott | 128 | – (1) retired hurt | 4 |
| T. M. Moody c Monty b McDermott | 5 | – not out | 52 |
| G. M. Wood c McDermott b Tazelaar | 117 | | |
| *W. S. Andrews b McDermott | 43 | | |
| J. A. Brayshaw b McDermott | 16 | | |
| †T. J. Zoehrer c Tazelaar b McDermott | 28 | | |
| K. H. MacLeay not out | 6 | | |
| C. D. Matthews not out | 10 | | |
| B 4, l-b 7, n-b 36 | 47 | L-b 3, w 1, n-b 2 | 6 |

| | |
|---|---|
| 1/16 2/26 3/257 4/318 5/350  (7 wkts dec.) **402** | |
| 6/375 7/386 | |

| |
|---|
| (no wkt) **93** |

P. A. Capes and C. D. Mack did not bat.

*In the second innings M. R. J. Veletta retired hurt at 13.*

Bowling: *First Innings*—McDermott 40–12–122–6; Tazelaar 27–8–67–1; Hammelmann 22–3–94–0; Hohns 21–3–72–0; Storey 9–0–36–0. *Second Innings*—McDermott 3–2–1–0; Tazelaar 2–0–3–0; Hammelmann 6–0–32–0; Storey 6–1–26–0; Cantrell 6–1–12–0; Hick 6–1–16–0.

Umpires: G. J. Bibby and T. A. Prue.

## NEW SOUTH WALES v SOUTH AUSTRALIA

At Sydney, January 19, 20, 21, 22. Drawn. New South Wales 2 pts. Toss: South Australia. The draw flattered the South Australians, whose batsmen, on a good pitch, showed little initiative in either innings. Even the normally aggressive Nobes took 62 minutes to get off the mark on the first day. In contrast, the New South Wales batsmen went for their shots, with the Waugh twins providing another thrilling display. Their 146 for the fourth wicket came in only two hours, and Mark Waugh's effortless hundred occupied just over three hours and included twelve fours and two sixes. May's off-spin curbed the scoring for a time, but Tucker and Whitney put on 64 in 32 minutes for the tenth wicket. Benefiting from the loss of two hours play on the third day South Australia held out until the last hour on the fourth, leaving New South Wales to score 113 from seventeen overs. Small and Taylor put them ahead of schedule with 60 off eight overs, but Miller's five-wicket spell in ten balls put paid to the run-race.

*Close of play:* First day, South Australia 220-6 (M. P. Faull 34*, T. J. Nielsen 17*); Second day, New South Wales 167-3 (M. E. Waugh 29*, S. R. Waugh 28*); Third day, South Australia 31-0 (A. M. J. Hilditch 20*, G. A. Bishop 11*).

## South Australia

| | | | |
|---|---|---|---|
| G. A. Bishop c Emery b Lawson | 0 | – (2) run out | 11 |
| *A. M. J. Hilditch run out | 32 | – (1) c and b Matthews | 39 |
| P. C. Nobes c Emery b Matthews | 84 | – lbw b O'Neill | 16 |
| D. W. Hookes c Emery b Whitney | 24 | – c Taylor b Matthews | 16 |
| M. P. Faull c Emery b Whitney | 34 | – b Matthews | 6 |
| P. R. Sleep b Matthews | 0 | – lbw b O'Neill | 24 |
| J. C. Scuderi lbw b Lawson | 20 | – c Emery b O'Neill | 44 |
| †T. J. Nielsen c Taylor b Matthews | 42 | – not out | 11 |
| T. B. A. May c Emery b S. R. Waugh | 2 | – c M. E. Waugh b Matthews | 1 |
| C. R. Miller not out | 26 | – c Lawson b Matthews | 6 |
| D. J. Hickey c Emery b Tucker | 12 | – lbw b Lawson | 10 |
| B 2, l-b 2, w 3, n-b 10 | 17 | B 8, l-b 7, n-b 4 | 19 |

1/0 2/66 3/109 4/161 5/161                                    **293**
6/190 7/221 8/251 9/257

1/31 2/66 3/72 4/93 5/96                                       **203**
6/152 7/169 8/176 9/184

Bowling: *First Innings*—Lawson 23-8-51-2; Whitney 24-10-50-2; S. R. Waugh 15-3-43-1; M. E. Waugh 3-0-17-0; Matthews 39-17-73-3; Tucker 14.4-2-39-1; O'Neill 7-5-16-0. *Second Innings*—Lawson 6-2-12-1; Whitney 13-7-9-0; Matthews 46-20-77-5; Tucker 10-1-38-0; O'Neill 29-13-52-3.

## New South Wales

| | | | |
|---|---|---|---|
| S. M. Small c Hookes b May | 38 | – c Scuderi b Miller | 24 |
| M. A. Taylor c Nielsen b Hickey | 7 | – lbw b Miller | 35 |
| T. H. Bayliss c Nobes b May | 42 | – b May | 1 |
| M. E. Waugh c Bishop b Sleep | 112 | – c Nielsen b Miller | 0 |
| S. R. Waugh c Nielsen b Miller | 60 | – c Hildditch b Miller | 4 |
| M. D. O'Neill c Nielsen b Miller | 16 | – b Miller | 1 |
| G. R. J. Matthews c Miller b May | 0 | – c Nielsen b Miller | 0 |
| †P. A. Emery c and b May | 14 | – (9) not out | 9 |
| A. E. Tucker not out | 46 | – (8) not out | 1 |
| *G. F. Lawson b Sleep b May | 0 | | |
| M. R. Whitney b Hickey | 17 | | |
| B 10, l-b 4, n-b 18 | 32 | B 2, l-b 4, n-b 2 | 8 |

1/23 2/85 3/112 4/258 5/294                                   **384**
6/301 7/305 8/320 9/320

1/60 2/68 3/68 4/69         (7 wkts) **83**
5/70 6/73 7/74

Bowling: *First Innings*—Hickey 18.3-3-85-2; Miller 15-2-57-2; May 36-7-134-5; Scuderi 19-5-47-0; Sleep 15-5-47-1. *Second Innings*—Miller 5-1-12-6; May 8-0-38-1; Scuderi 4-0-27-0.

Umpires: D. M. Graham and I. S. Thomas.

## WESTERN AUSTRALIA v VICTORIA

At Perth, January 19, 20, 21, 22. Victoria won by 29 runs. Victoria 5.8 pts. Toss: Victoria. Batting first proved a decisive advantage on a pitch which developed sizeable cracks in the hot conditions and gave erratic bounce on the last two days. Even so, Victoria's 359 looked moderate by Perth standards. Lehmann played a splendid innings, mixing fierce concentration with some exotic strokes and hitting fifteen fours and two sixes in a stay of 215 minutes. Western Australia made a confident start through Marsh and Veletta, but when Veletta retired ill with sweat aggravating a bout of conjunctivitis, Victoria's fast bowlers broke the back of the innings. Only Marsh stood firm, despite various blows to the body, batting four hours and hitting seventeen fours. Watts and Ayres gave Victoria a fine start to their second innings, but Moody exploited the conditions to earn his best bowling return, his last five wickets coming in 25 balls. Western Australia's final task of scoring 248 was never really on. Hughes was often unplayable, and Berry's six catches in the innings equalled the Victorian record.

*Close of play:* First day, Victoria 330-7 (D. S. Berry 31*, P. R. Reiffel 6*); Second day, Western Australia 236-6 (M. R. J. Veletta 44*, K. H. MacLeay 7*); Third day, Western Australia 16-0 (M. R. J. Veletta 9*, G. R. Marsh 3*).

## Victoria

| | | | | | |
|---|---|---|---|---|---|
| W. G. Ayres lbw b Reid | 0 | - (2) b MacLeay | 28 |
| G. M. Watts c Zoehrer b Reid | 57 | - (1) c Zoehrer b Moody | 68 |
| D. M. Jones b Reid | 28 | - c Martyn b Moody | 13 |
| D. S. Lehmann c Andrews b Mack | 113 | - c Marsh b Reid | 8 |
| J. D. Siddons c Zoehrer b Moody | 47 | - c Zoehrer b Moody | 8 |
| *S. P. O'Donnell c Wood b Moody | 24 | - c Zoehrer b Moody | 20 |
| †D. S. Berry c Zoehrer b MacLeay | 47 | - run out | 1 |
| M. G. Hughes c Zoehrer b Moody | 2 | - c Auty b Moody | 0 |
| P. R. Reiffel c Zoehrer b MacLeay | 13 | - not out | 0 |
| D. W. Fleming c and b MacLeay | 0 | - lbw b Moody | 6 |
| P. W. Jackson not out | 0 | - lbw b Moody | 0 |
| B 4, l-b 6, n-b 18 | 28 | B 4, l-b 2, w 4, n-b 4 | 14 |

1/0 2/65 3/134 4/232 5/290     **359**     1/74 2/98 3/109 4/119 5/144     **161**
6/293 7/303 8/354 9/354                     6/145 7/146 8/155 9/161

*Bowling: First Innings*—Reid 24-3-82-3; MacLeay 18.2-6-55-3; Mack 17-2-72-1; Moody 25-8-66-3; Auty 15-3-66-0; Andrews 3-0-8-0. *Second Innings*—Reid 15-7-19-1; MacLeay 11-1-38-1; Mack 16-5-55-0; Moody 14.5-4-43-7.

## Western Australia

| | | | | |
|---|---|---|---|---|
| *G. R. Marsh b O'Donnell | 95 | - (2) c Berry b Fleming | 11 |
| M. R. J. Veletta b Fleming | 60 | - (1) lbw b Hughes | 13 |
| T. M. Moody c Berry b Fleming | 6 | - lbw b O'Donnell | 43 |
| G. M. Wood c Berry b Reiffel | 1 | - lbw b Reiffel | 20 |
| W. S. Andrews c Siddons b Hughes | 2 | - c Berry b Hughes | 19 |
| D. R. Martyn c Jackson b Fleming | 24 | - c Berry b Hughes | 27 |
| †T. J. Zoehrer c Jones b Reiffel | 17 | - c Berry b Hughes | 7 |
| K. H. MacLeay c Fleming | 23 | - c Berry b Fleming | 13 |
| C. Auty b Hughes | 3 | - not out | 17 |
| C. D. Mack not out | 1 | - c Berry b Hughes | 3 |
| B. A. Reid (did not bat) | – | - b Hughes | 2 |
| B 14, l-b 3, n-b 24 | 41 | B 12, l-b 13, n-b 18 | 43 |

1/62 2/69 3/91 4/167 5/188    (9 wkts dec.) **273**    1/30 2/30 3/93 4/115 5/139    **218**
6/223 7/260 8/271 9/273                     6/151 7/184 8/188 9/212

*In the first innings M. R. J. Veletta, when 22, retired ill at 46 and resumed at 167.*

*Bowling: First Innings*—Hughes 21-3-67-2; Fleming 25-10-62-4; O'Donnell 16-6-53-1; Reiffel 18-4-52-2; Jackson 7-2-22-0. *Second Innings*—Hughes 23-8-54-6; Fleming 19-5-49-2; O'Donnell 16-3-43-1; Reiffel 15-3-47-1.

Umpires: R. J. Evans and P. J. McConnell.

## VICTORIA v TASMANIA

At St Kilda, Melbourne, January 26, 27, 28, 29. Victoria won by 85 runs. Victoria 6 pts. Toss: Tasmania. The match was a triumph for the Victorian fast bowler, Reiffel, whose 86 in the first innings and ten wickets in the match exceeded any previous achievements. Victoria were 124 for six when Reiffel joined O'Donnell on the first afternoon, but batting sensibly for three hours they added 126 and successfully overcame hostile bowling by Gilbert and McPhee. Last out after a four-and-a-half-hour stay, Reiffel then took the new ball and broke through Tasmania's batting, reducing them to 143 for nine at stumps on the second day. At this score Wellham declared, still 7 runs short of the follow-on, but if he hoped to be put in again, the ploy failed; O'Donnell recognised the dangers of batting last. Siddons and the resolute Watts added 144 in even time for Victoria, whose declaration left them with four sessions in which to dismiss Tasmania. Reiffel removed Farrell and Shipperd in his first two overs, and although Wellham battled hard for nearly four and a half hours, Victoria's win was achieved with two hours to spare.

*Close of play:* First day, Victoria 235-6 (S. P. O'Donnell 74*, P. R. Reiffel 53*); Second day, Tasmania 143-9 (T. C. Coyle 40*, P. T. McPhee 4*); Third day, Tasmania 91-4 (D. M. Wellham 24*, D. J. Buckingham 17*).

## Victoria

| | | | |
|---|---|---|---|
| G. M. Watts c Farrell b Gilbert | 0 | (2) c Coyle b Tucker | 72 |
| W. G. Ayres c Farrell b Campbell | 4 | (1) c Coyle b Gilbert | 0 |
| W. N. Phillips c Coyle b McPhee | 32 | c Coyle b Gilbert | 6 |
| D. S. Lehmann c Gilbert b McPhee | 28 | c Farrell b Gilbert | 0 |
| J. D. Siddons c Farrell b Gilbert | 21 | not out | 101 |
| *S. P. O'Donnell c Tucker b Gilbert | 88 | not out | 20 |
| †D. S. Berry c Buckingham b McPhee | 6 | | |
| P. R. Reiffel c Wellham b Farrell | 86 | | |
| P. W. Jackson c Buckingham b McPhee | 3 | | |
| D. W. Fleming c Buckingham b Campbell | 11 | | |
| P. E. McIntyre not out | 4 | | |
| B 1, l-b 4, w 2, n-b 10 | 17 | B 2, l-b 2, w 1, n-b 8 | 13 |

1/0 2/18 3/71 4/71 5/113       300     1/6 2/26 3/26      (4 wkts dec.) 212
6/124 7/250 8/259 9/288            4/170

Bowling: *First Innings*—Gilbert 31-10-58-3; Campbell 33-4-98-2; McPhee 37-11-95-4; Tucker 15-3-34-0; Farrell 7.1-2-10-1. *Second Innings*—Gilbert 15.1-2-60-3; Campbell 5-0-19-0; McPhee 12-2-44-0; Tucker 12-2-44-1; Farrell 8-0-41-0.

## Tasmania

| | | | |
|---|---|---|---|
| G. Shipperd c O'Donnell b Fleming | 11 | b Reiffel | 1 |
| M. G. Farrell b Reiffel | 4 | c Ayres b Reiffel | 0 |
| J. Cox c Watts b Reiffel | 5 | b Fleming | 0 |
| *D. M. Wellham c Lehmann b Reiffel | 2 | c Lehmann b O'Donnell | 77 |
| R. J. Tucker c Berry b O'Donnell | 16 | run out | 41 |
| D. J. Buckingham lbw b O'Donnell | 3 | run out | 46 |
| B. A. Cruse c Berry b Reiffel | 24 | c Siddons b Fleming | 46 |
| †T. C. Coyle not out | 40 | c Berry b Reiffel | 18 |
| D. R. Gilbert c Ayres b Reiffel | 9 | c Berry b Reiffel | 0 |
| G. D. Campbell c Siddons b Reiffel | 0 | run out | 31 |
| P. T. McPhee not out | 4 | not out | 0 |
| B 1, l-b 2, n-b 22 | 25 | B 2, l-b 8, n-b 14 | 24 |

1/9 2/19 3/21 4/27 5/45     (9 wkts dec.) 143    1/3 2/4 3/4 4/65 5/145       284
6/68 7/88 8/116 9/126            6/201 7/245 8/245 9/284

Bowling: *First Innings*—Reiffel 18-4-57-6; Fleming 18-6-39-1; O'Donnell 12-4-27-2; McIntyre 9-2-17-0; Jackson 4-4-0-0. *Second Innings*—Reiffel 25-3-79-4; Fleming 25-7-75-2; O'Donnell 19-6-40-1; McIntyre 17-6-39-0; Jackson 23.2-6-41-0.

Umpires: R. C. Bailhache and P. H. Jensen.

## NEW SOUTH WALES v WESTERN AUSTRALIA

At Sydney, January 31, February 1, 2, 3. New South Wales won by nine wickets. New South Wales 6 pts. Toss: New South Wales. The match followed a similar course to that in Perth between these teams, with the New South Wales batsmen taking full toll of an attack clearly bereft of the ability to bowl on a good pitch, albeit one which took slow turn. Bayliss made an emphatic return to form, batting all through the first day, bar the two balls of Milliken's innings, and Waugh helped him add 128 before losing his off stump having a swipe at Andrews. The dashing Bevan, partnered by a more circumspect O'Neill, cashed in on the second day, and Lawson was able to declare before tea. By stumps the Western Australian innings was in ruins. McLay and Tucker, 21-year-old club-mates, bowling off-breaks and leg-breaks respectively, complemented each other ideally, and while McLay was making a formidable début, Tucker achieved his best figures. Western Australia's second innings, a quite different matter, was given a good deal of momentum when Moody hit an over of leg-side long-hops from Tucker for 6, 4, 4, 6, 4, 6, a record for Australian cricket. Moody fell after completing a worthy hundred in three hours to O'Neill's accurate leg-breaks, which not only helped stem the flow of runs but also accounted for the dangerous Andrews. New South Wales secured the match with nine overs left.

*Close of play:* First day, New South Wales 278-3 (T. H. Bayliss 152*, M. D. O'Neill 24*); Second day, Western Australia 112-6 (D. R. Martyn 0*); Third day, Western Australia 242-5 (W. S. Andrews 20*, T. J. Zoehrer 11*).

## New South Wales

| | | | |
|---|---|---|---|
| S. M. Small c Martyn b Mack | 33 | – c Andrews b Mack | 6 |
| G. S. Milliken c McPhee b Capes | 0 | – not out | 21 |
| T. H. Bayliss lbw b MacLeay | 163 | – not out | 28 |
| S. R. Waugh b Andrews | 61 | | |
| M. D. O'Neill not out | 101 | | |
| M. G. Bevan not out | 106 | | |
| B 1, l-b 2, n-b 8 | 11 | L-b 5, n-b 2 | 7 |

1/1 2/62 3/190 4/298      (4 wkts dec.) 475    1/9      (1 wkt) 62

†P. A. Emery, A. E. Tucker, G. F. McLay, *G. F. Lawson and M. R. Whitney did not bat.

Bowling: *First Innings*—Capes 24-2-103-1; MacLeay 29.3-12-69-1; Mack 24-3-93-1; Moody 23-4-73-0; Andrews 19-6-51-1; Auty 21-4-62-0; Zoehrer 9-4-21-0. *Second Innings*—Capes 4-0-15-0; Mack 3-0-12-1; Moody 2-0-9-0; Andrews 5-2-10-0; Auty 3-0-11-0.

## Western Australia

| | | | |
|---|---|---|---|
| M. W. McPhee lbw b McLay | 22 | – (2) c Emery b Whitney | 0 |
| M. R. J. Veletta c McLay b Tucker | 61 | – (1) c Milliken b Whitney | 63 |
| G. M. Wood lbw b McLay | 0 | – run out | 10 |
| T. M. Moody c Emery b Tucker | 8 | – b O'Neill | 100 |
| *W. S. Andrews b Tucker | 8 | – b O'Neill | 81 |
| P. A. Capes c Tucker b McLay | 3 | – (10) b McLay | 6 |
| D. R. Martyn not out | 17 | – (6) st Emery b Tucker | 15 |
| †T. J. Zoehrer b McLay | 0 | – (7) c Small b Tucker | 11 |
| K. H. MacLeay c Bayliss b Tucker | 0 | – (8) st Emery b Bevan | 85 |
| C. Auty c and b Tucker | 0 | – (9) c Milliken b O'Neill | 5 |
| C. D. Mack c Tucker b McLay | 1 | – not out | 0 |
| B 7, l-b 1, n-b 2 | 10 | B 14, n-b 16 | 30 |

1/44 2/44 3/71 4/91 5/112     130    1/0 2/11 3/178 4/194 5/225    406
6/112 7/118 8/119 9/123                 6/255 7/377 8/387 9/406

Bowling: *First Innings*—Lawson 5-1-9-0; Whitney 5-2-20-0; McLay 24.5-8-55-5; Tucker 24-8-38-5. *Second Innings*—Lawson 20-7-37-0; Whitney 22-5-66-2; McLay 51-24-76-1; Tucker 27-4-130-2; O'Neill 33-21-47-3; Waugh 6-1-22-0; Bevan 6.4-2-14-1.

Umpires: D. B. Hair and G. E. Reed.

## SOUTH AUSTRALIA v NEW SOUTH WALES

At Adelaide, February 15, 16, 17, 18. Drawn. South Australia 2 pts. Toss: New South Wales. New South Wales virtually put themselves out of contention with a sterile batting performance on the first day. May was allowed to bowl 79 balls without conceding a run, and he finished the day with two for 27 off 35 overs. Next day Lawson swung his bat effectively, hitting ten fours in his 61, but while 378 was a better score than seemed likely, South Australia's batsmen had little trouble passing it. Faull and May set the innings on course with a careful 76 for the fifth wicket, and May went on to his first 50, in 70 matches, batting for four hours. By the time first-innings points had been decided, little more than a day remained; time enough nevertheless for New South Wales to lose their way to the bowling of May and Hickey. However, Bevan raced to a brilliant century in two and a half hours, and Lawson's declaration left South Australia an unlikely target of 255 in 42 overs. The early demise of Hookes effectively ended their challenge.

*Close of play:* First day, New South Wales 219-7 (P. A. Emery 21*, G. J. Rowell 0*); Second day, South Australia 142-4 (M. P. Faull 59*, T. B. A. May 1*); Third day, New South Wales 45-1 (S. M. Small 20*, T. H. Bayliss 8*).

### New South Wales

| | | | | |
|---|---:|---|---:|
| S. M. Small c Gladigau b Miller | 75 | – c Hookes b May | 31 |
| G. S. Milliken c Hilditch b Gladigau | 13 | – lbw b May | 11 |
| T. H. Bayliss c Nobes b May | 28 | – c Hickey | 8 |
| M. D. O'Neill c Nobes b May | 6 | – b Hickey | 9 |
| M. G. Bevan c Hookes b Gladigau | 20 | – c Miller b Hickey | 104 |
| B. E. McNamara c Nobes b Miller | 19 | – st Nielsen b May | 26 |
| †P. A. Emery not out | 73 | – lbw b May | 6 |
| G. F. McLay b Hickey | 30 | – c Nobes b May | 0 |
| G. J. Rowell b May | 18 | – not out | 42 |
| *G. F. Lawson c Nielsen b Hickey | 61 | – not out | 7 |
| W. J. Holdsworth c Faull b May | 21 | | |
| B 3, l-b 11 | 14 | B 1, l-b 8, n-b 4 | 13 |

1/33 2/72 3/84 4/123 5/167          378          1/36 2/49 3/59   (8 wkts dec.) 257
6/169 7/215 8/254 9/335                          4/65 5/112 6/152
                                                 7/154 8/223

Bowling: *First Innings*—Hickey 29-6-70-2; Miller 19-4-59-2; Gladigau 20-2-88-2; Scuderi 18-4-63-0; May 52-29-84-4. *Second Innings*—Hickey 15.3-2-83-3; Miller 13-1-37-0; Gladigau 6-1-23-0; Scuderi 3-0-21-0; May 27-11-84-5.

### South Australia

| | | | | |
|---|---:|---|---:|
| P. C. Nobes b Holdsworth | 23 | – c Small b Rowell | 54 |
| *A. M. J. Hilditch c Small b Lawson | 6 | – c Emery b Lawson | 8 |
| M. P. Faull c Emery b McNamara | 89 | – (8) not out | 18 |
| D. W. Hookes b Holdsworth | 38 | – (3) c Holdsworth b Lawson | 2 |
| G. A. Bishop c McNamara b McLay | 34 | – (4) c Bevan b O'Neill | 34 |
| T. B. A. May b Rowell | 73 | – not out | 39 |
| †T. J. Nielsen not out | 81 | – (5) c Lawson b O'Neill | 29 |
| J. C. Scuderi not out | 49 | – (6) st Emery b Bevan | 5 |
| C. R. Miller (did not bat) | | – (6) st Emery b Bevan | 5 |
| B 2, l-b 3, w 1, n-b 10 | 16 | B 3, l-b 5, w 1, n-b 8 | 17 |

1/19 2/37 3/108 4/137 5/213     (6 wkts dec.) 381     1/11 2/35 3/86     (6 wkts) 198
6/282                                                4/126 5/135 6/154

P. W. Gladigau and D. J. Hickey did not bat.

Bowling: *First Innings*—Lawson 24-8-54-1; Holdsworth 24-5-91-2; Rowell 16-3-50-1; McLay 33-10-83-1; Bevan 20-6-52-0; O'Neill 7-2-26-0; McNamara 6-2-20-1. *Second Innings*—Lawson 9-0-42-2; Holdsworth 8-1-28-0; Rowell 4-0-31-1; McLay 2-0-8-0; Bevan 6-0-31-1; O'Neill 13-2-50-2.

Umpires: A. R. Crafter and S. J. Davis.

## TASMANIA v QUEENSLAND

At Hobart, February 15, 16, 17, 18. Drawn. Queensland 2 pts. Toss: Tasmania. Wellham put Queensland in on a two-paced pitch, only to see Cantrell dropped when 1 and Hick when 32. Gilbert was the bowler both times, but he bowled on tirelessly and was rewarded on the second day as Queensland lost their last seven wickets for 52. Much the best batting came from Hick and Law, who put on 165 in 170 minutes for the fourth wicket, Hick at last rewarding his supporters with a hundred and Law continuing in his prolific vein with some fine strokes. Tasmania made a laboured reply, and in their second innings Queensland, although enjoying a lead of 95, also struggled for runs — until, that is, Law came to the wicket. In less than an hour he cracked a cavalier 57, enabling Hohns to declare with two sessions left. Tasmania found Rackemann and Tazelaar impossible to get away, but with Wellham defiant they avoided defeat.

*Close of play:* First day, Queensland 276-3 (G. A. Hick 88*, S. G. Law 58*); Second day, Tasmania 93-1 (R. J. Bennett 42*, J. Cox 23*); Third day, Queensland 37-2 (S. Monty 22*, D. Tazelaar 0*).

## Queensland

| | | |
|---|---|---|
| P. E. Cantrell c Coyle b McPhee | 56 | – (2) c Farrell b Gilbert ......... 4 |
| S. Monty c Farrell b Gilbert | 28 | – (1) b Tucker ......... 33 |
| T. J. Barsby c Buckingham b Gilbert | 21 | – b Bower ......... 9 |
| G. A. Hick c Farrell b Gilbert | 110 | – (6) c Farrell b McPhee ......... 27 |
| S. G. Law c Farrell b Gilbert | 82 | – (7) not out ......... 57 |
| P. J. T. Goggin c Coyle b Gilbert | 10 | – (8) not out ......... 18 |
| †P. W. Anderson c Coyle b Gilbert | 4 | – (5) b Tucker ......... 0 |
| *T. V. Hohns c Cruse b McPhee | 5 | |
| M. S. Kasprowicz c Gilbert b McPhee | 19 | |
| C. G. Rackemann c Coyle b McPhee | 2 | |
| D. Tazelaar not out | 4 | – (4) c Cox b McPhee ......... 10 |
| L-b 10, w 1, n-b 22 | 33 | B 3, l-b 9, n-b 2 ......... 14 |

1/72 2/100 3/157 4/322 5/329     374     1/17 2/34 3/51    (6 wkts dec.) 172
6/337 7/346 8/358 9/368              4/51 5/87 6/101

Bowling: *First Innings*—Gilbert 41-10-111-6; Bower 26-8-69-0; McPhee 40.1-11-122-4; Tucker 10-3-28-0; Farrell 14-2-34-0. *Second Innings*—Gilbert 20-4-67-1; Bower 10-3-18-1; McPhee 7-0-42-2; Tucker 6-1-12-2; Farrell 9-3-21-0.

## Tasmania

| | | |
|---|---|---|
| R. J. Bennett b Hohns | 51 | – c Hick b Rackemann ......... 17 |
| M. G. Farrell c and b Tazelaar | 12 | – run out ......... 10 |
| J. Cox b Hick c Kasprowicz | 54 | – c Anderson b Tazelaar ......... 15 |
| *D. M. Wellham b Barsby b Rackemann | 29 | – not out ......... 59 |
| R. J. Tucker c Cantrell b Tazelaar | 80 | – c Anderson b Hohns ......... 20 |
| D. J. Buckingham c Kasprowicz b Rackemann | 8 | – c Goggin b Hohns ......... 13 |
| B. A. Cruse lbw b Cantrell | 0 | – c Hick b Rackemann ......... 19 |
| †T. C. Coyle b Tazelaar | 13 | – c Anderson b Kasprowicz ......... 12 |
| T. D. Bower not out | 11 | – not out ......... 2 |
| D. R. Gilbert c Anderson b Tazelaar | 0 | |
| P. T. McPhee run out | 3 | |
| L-b 6, n-b 12 | 18 | L-b 7, n-b 2 ......... 9 |

1/18 2/127 3/135 4/192 5/202     279     1/24 2/42 3/46 4/74    (7 wkts) 176
6/203 7/255 8/271 9/271              5/98 6/150 7/170

Bowling: *First Innings*—Rackemann 28-11-67-2; Tazelaar 25-12-48-4; Kasprowicz 25-6-67-1; Hohns 27.3-9-61-1; Cantrell 10-2-30-1. *Second Innings*—Rackemann 20-4-46-2; Tazelaar 15-3-41-1; Kasprowicz 5-1-11-1; Hohns 14-5-37-2; Cantrell 10-2-26-0; Hick 3-1-8-0.

Umpires: B. T. Knight and S. G. Randell.

## VICTORIA v WESTERN AUSTRALIA

At St Kilda, Melbourne, February 15, 16, 17, 18. Drawn. Western Australia 2 pts. Toss: Western Australia. Of the five players making their first-class débuts, two Western Australians, Lavender and McCague, had a major impact on the game. The Indian-born Lavender batted well on the first day, adding 194 in four and a half hours with Wood and helping the visitors to an impregnable score of 256 for two. Wood battled on for 438 minutes in all before gloving a lifting ball to Berry, and during his innings he passed R. J. Inverarity's record of 7,607 runs for Western Australia, having taken 120 games to Inverarity's 119. Andrews's declaration after 151 overs met with a cautious reply from the Victorian openers, but at 168 for one the home state's prospects for first-innings points looked healthy. However, the 6ft 5in tall fast bowler, McCague, dismissed Lehmann, Siddons and O'Donnell in 24 balls, and in spite of a sensible innings by Reiffel, Victoria trailed by 76 runs. The final day was of little consequence.

*Close of play:* First day, Western Australia 256-2 (G. M. Wood 106*, M. A. Wasley 2*); Second day, Victoria 80-0 (G. M. Watts 36*, W. G. Ayres 33*); Third day, Western Australia 8-0 (M. P. Lavender 1*, M. A. Wasley 7*).

### Western Australia

| | | | | |
|---|---|---|---|---|
| J. A. Brayshaw c Berry b O'Donnell | 25 | | | |
| M. P. Lavender c Lehmann b Reiffel | 118 | – (1) b Smith | 15 | |
| G. M. Wood c Berry b Reiffel | 166 | – c Reiffel b Lehmann | 50 | |
| M. A. Wasley b Reiffel | 12 | – (2) retired hurt | 7 | |
| T. M. Moody lbw b Smith | 0 | – (4) c Fleming b Warne | 73 | |
| *W. S. Andrews run out | 15 | – (5) not out | 16 | |
| D. R. Martyn not out | 68 | – (6) c Fleming b Lehmann | 1 | |
| K. H. MacLeay not out | 1 | – (7) not out | 17 | |
| L-b 5, n-b 8 | 13 | B 5, l-b 6, w 1, n-b 6 | 18 | |

1/57 2/251 3/275 4/276 5/301    (6 wkts. dec.) 418    1/56 2/140 3/162   (4 wkts. dec.) 197
6/407                                             4/164

†T. J. Zoehrer, C. D. Mack and M. J. McCague did not bat.

*In the second innings M. A. Wasley retired hurt at 8.*

Bowling: *First Innings*—Reiffel 36-10-84-3; Fleming 35-8-89-0; O'Donnell 24-5-62-1; Smith 35-9-104-1; Warne 18-7-61-0; Lehmann 3-0-13-0. *Second Innings*—Reiffel 11-3-24-0; Fleming 8-4-16-0; O'Donnell 12-4-50-0; Smith 15-3-40-1; Warne 19-6-41-1; Lehmann 8-3-15-2.

### Victoria

| | | | | |
|---|---|---|---|---|
| G. M. Watts c Zoehrer b Andrews | 81 | – (2) c Andrews b Martyn | 7 | |
| W. G. Ayres c Lavender b McCague | 39 | – (1) not out | 30 | |
| W. N. Phillips b Wasley | 43 | – not out | 21 | |
| D. S. Lehmann lbw b McCague | 19 | | | |
| J. D. Siddons c Zoehrer b McCague | 12 | | | |
| *S. P. O'Donnell b McCague | 24 | | | |
| †D. S. Berry b Mack | 16 | | | |
| P. R. Reiffel c Zoehrer b McCague | 45 | | | |
| S. K. Warne st Zoehrer b Andrews | 20 | | | |
| D. W. Fleming not out | 1 | | | |
| P. J. Smith b Wasley | 0 | | | |
| L-b 12, w 2, n-b 28 | 42 | B 4, l-b 2 | 6 | |

1/92 2/168 3/205 4/215 5/225         342    1/12              (1 wkt) 64
6/250 7/296 8/339 9/341

Bowling: *First Innings*—McCague 35-9-105-5; MacLeay 20-5-52-0; Wasley 19.5-4-53-2; Moody 15-2-30-0; Mack 21-4-69-1; Martyn 1-1-0-0; Andrews 11-5-21-2. *Second Innings*—MacLeay 3-1-4-0; Martyn 9-2-22-1; Andrews 6-0-14-0; Lavender 6-0-13-0; Zoehrer 1-0-5-0.

Umpires: R. C. Bailhache and L. J. King.

## NEW SOUTH WALES v VICTORIA

At Sydney, February 22, 23, 24, 25. New South Wales won by eight wickets. New South Wales 6 pts. Toss: Victoria. At lunch on the first day Victoria looked a beaten side, undone by some explosive fast bowling from Holdsworth, who had taken six for 39 in a score of 106 for seven. However, O'Donnell and Reiffel took 53 off six overs after the interval, and O'Donnell went on to a stunning 109 in 147 minutes, with thirteen fours and a six. His 148-run partnership with Reiffel took only two hours. Bevan was the New South Wales batting hero, scoring his third century in four innings and showing remarkable judgment, particularly against Jackson's left-arm spin. His 153 was his highest first-class score. Victoria's bowlers did well to restrict the New South Wales lead to 60, but their batsmen again failed. Even without Lawson, who injured a rib muscle, the New South Wales bowlers were never seriously challenged, and off-spinner McLay used the conditions splendidly. New South Wales had most of the final day to score 150, and although Jackson again commanded respect, sensible batting by Small and Bayliss saw them home by tea.

*Close of play:* First day, New South Wales 31-0 (S. M. Small 17*, G. S. Milliken 14*); Second day, New South Wales 320-6 (M. G. Bevan 133*, A. E. Tucker 5*); Third day, Victoria 200-9 (P. R. Reiffel 4*, P. W. Jackson 0*).

## Victoria

| | | | | |
|---|---|---|---|---|
| G. M. Watts b Holdsworth | 3 | – (2) lbw b Holdsworth | 4 |
| W. G. Ayres c Lawson b Holdsworth | 26 | – (1) c Emery b Lawson | 0 |
| W. N. Phillips b Lawson | 3 | – c Bevan b McLay | 61 |
| D. S. Lehmann c McNamara b Holdsworth | 30 | – c Bevan b McLay | 34 |
| J. D. Siddons c Emery b Holdsworth | 2 | – c Bayliss b McLay | 35 |
| *S. P. O'Donnell c Small b Tucker | 109 | – c Emery b O'Neill | 14 |
| D. A. Emerson lbw b Holdsworth | 0 | – run out | 7 |
| †D. S. Berry b Holdsworth | 0 | – c McLay b Bevan | 25 |
| P. R. Reiffel c Emery b Bevan | 43 | – not out | 7 |
| D. W. Fleming not out | 30 | – b McLay | 0 |
| P. W. Jackson lbw b Lawson | 16 | – c Bayliss b McLay | 4 |
| B 9, l-b 2, w 4, n-b 12 | 27 | B 4, l-b 11, w 1, n-b 2 | 18 |
| | **291** | | **209** |

1/7 2/14 3/71 4/73 5/84        1/5 2/7 3/60 4/114 5/155
6/84 7/86 8/234 9/244         6/163 7/188 8/197 9/197

Bowling: *First Innings*—Lawson 12.4-4-49-2; Holdsworth 22-1-99-6; McLay 10-3-37-0; Tucker 18-4-56-1; O'Neill 6-1-15-0; McNamara 2-0-6-0; Bevan 11-5-18-1. *Second Innings*—Lawson 3.1-1-4-1; Holdsworth 12-4-30-1; McLay 41.5-20-86-5; Tucker 5-1-27-0; O'Neill 12-4-29-1; McNamara 4-1-11-0; Bevan 11-9-7-1.

## New South Wales

| | | | | |
|---|---|---|---|---|
| S. M. Small c Ayres b Jackson | 65 | – b O'Donnell | 52 |
| G. S. Milliken c Berry b Reiffel | 15 | – c Siddons b O'Donnell | 37 |
| T. H. Bayliss c Watts b Fleming | 19 | – not out | 47 |
| M. D. O'Neill c O'Donnell b Jackson | 18 | – not out | 14 |
| M. G. Bevan not out | 153 | | |
| B. E. McNamara c Fleming b Reiffel | 33 | | |
| †P. A. Emery c Siddons b Reiffel | 15 | | |
| A. E. Tucker lbw b Reiffel | 9 | | |
| G. F. McLay b Jackson | 0 | | |
| *G. F. Lawson c Berry b Reiffel | 3 | | |
| W. J. Holdsworth c O'Donnell b Reiffel | 4 | | |
| B 2, l-b 6, w 5, n-b 4 | 17 | | |
| | **351** | | **(2 wkts) 150** |

1/41 2/71 3/115 4/132 5/234       1/81 2/92
6/295 7/337 8/340 9/343

Bowling: *First Innings*—Reiffel 35-8-116-6; Fleming 17-3-74-1; Jackson 47-22-83-3; Emerson 17-5-49-0; O'Donnell 9-2-21-0. *Second Innings*—Reiffel 6-1-13-0; Fleming 3-1-10-0; Jackson 26-11-30-0; Emerson 15.3-3-53-0; O'Donnell 13-4-33-2; Phillips 5-2-11-0.

Umpires: G. E. Reed and I. S. Thomas.

## QUEENSLAND v WESTERN AUSTRALIA

At Brisbane, February 22, 23, 24, 25. Queensland won by seven wickets. Queensland 6 pts. Toss: Western Australia. After three days on which neither side showed much initiative, play became more purposeful on the fourth day and 464 runs were scored. Western Australia put on 167 in the morning session, with Lavender and Moody feasting on part-time offerings served up by Queensland. A target of 295 off 64 overs represented a fair equation for two sides desperate for points, and as it happened Law hit the winning runs with nine balls remaining, he and Hick having added 111 in 74 minutes, despite Andrews's tactic of putting nine men on the boundary. Hick's second century in as many matches took a little over three hours, while Law became the youngest Queenslander to pass 1,000 runs in a season. The earlier play was notable for a remarkable spell of bowling by Rackemann, who ended Western Australia's first innings with five wickets for 4 runs off 22 balls.

*Close of play*: First day, Western Australia 228-5 (D. R. Martyn 36*, K. H. MacLeay 31*); Second day, Queensland 188-4 (S. G. Law 52*, P. J. T. Goggin 7*); Third day, Western Australia 129-2 (M. P. Lavender 52*, T. M. Moody 3*).

### Western Australia

| | | | |
|---|---|---|---|
| D. J. Harris c Anderson b Tazelaar | 0 | – c Barsby b Hohns | 23 |
| M. P. Lavender c Anderson b Hohns | 33 | – not out | 113 |
| G. M. Wood c Tazelaar b Kasprowicz | 73 | – lbw b Rackemann | 38 |
| T. M. Moody c Hohns b Tazelaar | 30 | – not out | 101 |
| *W. S. Andrews c Barsby b Tazelaar | 14 | | |
| D. R. Martyn b Rackemann | 54 | | |
| K. H. MacLeay c Anderson b Rackemann | 46 | | |
| †T. J. Zoehrer not out | 6 | | |
| M. A. Wasley c Hohns b Rackemann | 0 | | |
| M. J. McCague b Rackemann | 0 | | |
| C. D. Mack lbw b Rackemann | 0 | | |
| B 2, l-b 1, n-b 12 | 15 | B 4, l-b 5, n-b 12 | 21 |

1/5 2/61 3/113 4/137 5/170      **271**    1/61 2/123     **(2 wkts dec.) 296**
6/258 7/267 8/271 9/271

Bowling: *First Innings*—Rackemann 25.5–12–45–5; Tazelaar 31–5–106–3; Hohns 26–10–41–1; Kasprowicz 23–6–50–1; Cantrell 4–0–26–0. *Second Innings*—Rackemann 20–9–35–1; Tazelaar 16–6–44–0; Hohns 33–13–56–1; Kasprowicz 4–1–11–0; Cantrell 13–4–38–0; Law 10–2–33–0; Monty 3–0–28–0; Barsby 6–1–33–0; Hick 2–0–9–0.

### Queensland

| | | | |
|---|---|---|---|
| P. E. Cantrell c Harris b McCague | 11 | – (3) c Zoehrer b McCague | 47 |
| S. Monty lbw b McCague | 38 | – (1) c Lavender b McCague | 21 |
| T. J. Barsby c Zoehrer b Wasley | 26 | – (2) c Lavender b McCague | 37 |
| G. A. Hick c Zoehrer b Mack | 48 | – not out | 112 |
| S. G. Law c Zoehrer b MacLeay | 59 | – not out | 61 |
| P. J. T. Goggin lbw b Mack | 30 | | |
| †P. W. Anderson not out | 27 | | |
| M. S. Kasprowicz c Lavender b MacLeay | 28 | | |
| L-b 2, n-b 4 | 6 | B 10, l-b 4, w 1, n-b 4 | 19 |

1/21 2/72 3/89 4/155 5/200    **(7 wkts dec.) 273**    1/35 2/64 3/186    **(3 wkts) 297**
6/231 7/273

*T. V. Hohns, C. G. Rackemann and D. Tazelaar did not bat.

Bowling: *First Innings*—McCague 20–3–70–2; Wasley 29–7–58–1; MacLeay 30–10–60–2; Moody 4–0–13–0; Mack 14–1–51–2; Andrews 10–3–19–0. *Second Innings*—McCague 19–1–92–3; Wasley 14–2–70–0; MacLeay 11–0–27–0; Moody 3–0–25–0; Mack 14–1–54–0; Andrews 1.3–0–15–0.

Umpires: C. A. Bertwistle and P. D. Parker.

## SOUTH AUSTRALIA v TASMANIA

At Adelaide, February 22, 23, 24, 25. Drawn. South Australia 2 pts. Toss: South Australia. The bottom sides in the Shield table waged a dreary battle of attrition for the first three days. South Australia's first innings meandered on until after tea on the second day, Bishop and May having rescued their side from a precarious 160 for six with a state-record seventh-wicket partnership of 198. Bishop's 159 occupied seven hours with sixteen fours, while May's 128, his maiden century, took six and a half hours and included nine fours and a six. South Australia's prodigal fielding helped Tasmania avoid the follow-on: Soule, in his first game of the season, had reached a maiden hundred and with Gilbert had added 101 in even time for the ninth wicket when Wellham declared on the last morning 148 behind. With Hilditch showing some initiative by sending in Scuderi to open South Australia's second innings with Nobes, runs came quickly enough to enable him, soon after lunch, to set a target of 266 from 57 overs. Wellham promoted himself in the order to lead the challenge, which was sustained until the last over, when 9 runs were needed. Tasmania could manage only 6.

*Close of play:* First day, South Australia 236-6 (G. A. Bishop 92*, T. B. A. May 26*); Second day, Tasmania 48-1 (R. J. Bennett 12*, D. J. Buckingham 21*); Third day, Tasmania 303-8 (R. E. Soule 91*, D. R. Gilbert 40*).

### South Australia

| | | | | | |
|---|---|---|---|---|---|
| P. C. Nobes c Farrell b Gilbert | 4 | – (2) c Tucker b McPhee | 15 |
| *A. M. J. Hilditch c Robertson b Bower | 25 | | |
| M. P. Faull c Buckingham b Bower | 16 | – (6) not out | 5 |
| D. W. Hookes b Robertson | 24 | – (3) b Buckingham | 43 |
| G. A. Bishop c and b Robertson | 159 | – (4) c Tucker b Bower | 1 |
| †T. J. Nielsen c Soule b McPhee | 16 | – (5) not out | 27 |
| J. C. Scuderi c Soule b Bower | 17 | – (1) b Bower | 17 |
| T. B. A. May c Bennett b Robertson | 128 | | |
| P. W. Gladigau not out | 54 | | |
| D. J. Hickey c Farrell b Buckingham | 2 | | |
| M. J. Minagall c Bennett b Buckingham | 0 | | |
| B 2, l-b 11, n-b 20 | 33 | B 2, w 1, n-b 6 | 9 |

1/14 2/45 3/46 4/103 5/140       478    1/28 2/58 3/59    (4 wkts dec.) 117
6/160 7/358 8/474 9/476                   4/99

Bowling: *First Innings*—Gilbert 31-7-89-1; Bower 25-2-85-3; McPhee 32-8-87-1; Robertson 42-9-85-3; Tucker 16-1-51-0; Farrell 11-1-41-0; Buckingham 12.5-2-27-2. *Second Innings*—Bower 8-1-40-2; McPhee 7-1-27-1; Robertson 6-1-18-0; Buckingham 4-0-23-1; Cox 1-0-7-0.

### Tasmania

| | | | | |
|---|---|---|---|---|
| R. J. Bennett lbw b May | 44 | – (6) c Bishop b May | 33 |
| J. Cox c Nielsen b Hickey | 10 | – (1) c May b Hickey | 16 |
| D. J. Buckingham c Nobes b Minagall | 38 | – lbw b May | 27 |
| *D. M. Wellham c Nielsen b Scuderi | 1 | – (2) c Hookes b Minagall | 66 |
| R. J. Tucker c May b Scuderi | 7 | – (4) c Nobes b Minagall | 13 |
| M. G. Farrell lbw b Hickey | 45 | – (5) run out | 6 |
| †R. E. Soule not out | 101 | – b May | 41 |
| G. R. Robertson c Hilditch b Scuderi | 8 | – c and b Scuderi | 34 |
| T. D. Bower c Hookes b Hickey | 0 | – (10) not out | 1 |
| D. R. Gilbert not out | 57 | – (9) not out | 9 |
| B 9, l-b 3, n-b 7 | 19 | L-b 9, n-b 8 | 17 |

1/17 2/77 3/78 4/100 5/119    (8 wkts dec.) 330    1/40 2/71 3/94 4/109    (8 wkts) 263
6/215 7/228 8/229                         5/164 6/184 7/241 8/258

P. T. McPhee did not bat.

Bowling: *First Innings*—Hickey 20.3–2–92–3; Scuderi 29–8–52–3; Gladigau 12–4–39–0; May 31–14–65–1; Minagall 30–6–70–1. *Second Innings*—Hickey 6–0–27–1; Scuderi 8–0–46–1; Gladigau 4–1–20–0; May 23–1–89–3; Minagall 16–1–72–2.

Umpires: M. P. Brien and A. R. Crafter.

## NEW SOUTH WALES v QUEENSLAND

At Sydney, March 7, 8, 9, 10. Drawn. New South Wales 2 pts. Toss: Queensland. With Lawson injured, the New South Wales bowling posed few problems on an easy-paced pitch and Hick continued his recent good form with a chanceless display. However, Holdsworth, though often erratic, took his chance with the second new ball and Queensland might have hoped for something better than 375. This was confirmed when Small and Bevan, the two left-handers, took complete control and added 184 for New South Wales's third wicket in even time. Bevan's 121 included a dazzling range of strokes off all bowlers, but Small curbed his usual impetuosity while scoring his first Shield hundred in four years. Hohns's leg-spin bowling commanded respect throughout his marathon stint. Although Holdsworth made early inroads, Queensland's second innings was scarcely threatened on the last day, when the New South Wales spinners failed for once to exploit helpful conditions. Bayliss broke his right thumb attempting a difficult catch, an unfortunate end to his first match as captain.

*Close of play:* First day, Queensland 330-7 (G. A. Hick 137*, D. Tazelaar 0*); Second day, New South Wales 270-2 (S. M. Small 85*, M. G. Bevan 87*); Third day, Queensland 76-2 (T. J. Barsby 25*, G. A. Hick 21*).

## Queensland

| | | | |
|---|---|---|---|
| P. E. Cantrell c Kenny b McNamara | 20 | – (2) c McNamara b Holdsworth | 11 |
| S. Monty b O'Neill | 27 | – (1) b Holdsworth | 0 |
| T. J. Barsby c McLay b Holdsworth | 34 | – c Rowell b Holdsworth | 108 |
| G. A. Hick b Rowell | 155 | – run out | 42 |
| S. G. Law b McLay | 47 | – run out | 28 |
| A. B. Henschell c Bayliss b Holdsworth | 25 | – c McNamara b McLay | 0 |
| †P. W. Anderson c Emery b Holdsworth | 7 | – b Rowell | 51 |
| *T. V. Hohns b Holdsworth | 1 | – b Rowell | 10 |
| D. Tazelaar c Emery b Rowell | 7 | – lbw b Rowell | 11 |
| R. W. McGhee b Rowell | 3 | – not out | 14 |
| C. G. Rackemann not out | 5 | – not out | 11 |
| B 9, l-b 7, n-b 28 | 44 | B 5, l-b 16, w 1, n-b 18 | 40 |
| | **375** | (9 wkts) | **326** |

1/52 2/81 3/110 4/225 5/292 6/312 7/330 8/361 9/370

1/1 2/34 3/124 4/177 5/177 6/270 7/274 8/294 9/309

Bowling: *First Innings*—Holdsworth 26–7–85–4; Rowell 21.4–6–81–3; McNamara 12–6–17–1; McLay 16–5–50–1; O'Neill 13–1–43–1; Tucker 11–3–48–0; Bevan 8–1–35–0. *Second Innings*—Holdsworth 20–1–74–3; Rowell 15–2–39–3; McNamara 9–4–24–0; McLay 33–15–62–1; O'Neill 13–4–29–0; Tucker 17–3–60–0; Bevan 3–0–17–0.

## New South Wales

| | | | |
|---|---|---|---|
| S. M. Small lbw b Hohns | 107 | G. F. McLay b Hohns | 42 |
| B. E. McNamara c Monty b Hohns | 50 | G. J. Rowell not out | 7 |
| *T. H. Bayliss b Henschell | 16 | W. J. Holdsworth c Anderson | |
| M. G. Bevan b Tazelaar | 121 | b Rackemann | 3 |
| J. D. Kenny c Cantrell b Henschell | 51 | B 6, l-b 7, n-b 28 | 41 |
| †P. A. Emery st Anderson b Hohns | 36 | | |
| M. D. O'Neill c Monty b Hohns | 2 | 1/100 2/137 3/321 4/349 5/391 | **476** |
| A. E. Tucker b Hohns | 0 | 6/397 7/401 8/460 9/465 | |

Bowling: Rackemann 28.5–3–117–1; McGhee 15–4–57–0; Tazelaar 16–2–80–1; Hohns 55–25–102–6; Henschell 33–11–81–2; Cantrell 11–6–26–0.

Umpires: D. B. Hair and G. E. Reed.

## TASMANIA v WESTERN AUSTRALIA

At Hobart, March 7, 8, 9, 10. Drawn. Western Australia 2 pts. Toss: Western Australia. Western Australia's need for outright points was frustrated when the third day was washed out. Their bowlers, with Matthews back from injury, had given them an excellent start on the first day, but their own batting was undermined by Gilbert's fine bowling, supported by the splendid catching of Tasmania's twenty-year-old wicket-keeper, Holyman, playing his first game. On the last day Tasmania scored 235 in three hours, thanks to some generous bowling which Buckingham made the most of to reach his highest score. When Wellham declared, Western Australia needed 281 off 45 overs, and with nothing to lose, Andrews and Zoehrer went all out for victory. They put on 77 for the first wicket, but as the later batsmen hit out, wickets fell regularly. With nine overs left and eight wickets down, Matthews and McCague had little option but to play out time.

*Close of play:* First day, Western Australia 89-2 (G. M. Wood 34*, T. M. Moody 32*); Second day, Tasmania 100-2 (D. J. Buckingham 29*, P. T. McPhee 0*); Third day, No play.

## Tasmania

| | | |
|---|---|---|
| R. J. Bennett c Wood b Matthews | 8 | – lbw b McCague .......... 42 |
| J. Cox c Zoehrer b Matthews | 19 | – lbw b Matthews .......... 12 |
| D. J. Buckingham c McCague b Matthews | 9 | – lbw b Coulson ..........167 |
| *D. M. Wellham c McCague b Matthews | 57 | – (5) c McCague b Bush ........ 27 |
| R. J. Tucker c Zoehrer b Matthews | 15 | – (6) c Andrews b Coulson .... 39 |
| M. G. Farrell c Andrews b Matthews | 0 | – (7) c and b Bush ........ 7 |
| †J. F. Holyman c Wood b Bush | 12 | – (8) st Zoehrer b Bush ...... 1 |
| G. R. Robertson c Moody b Coulson | 26 | – (9) c Zoehrer b Coulson .... 12 |
| T. D. Bower c MacLeay b Coulson | 3 | |
| D. R. Gilbert c Martyn b Bush | 19 | – not out ................ 1 |
| P. T. McPhee not out | 9 | – (4) c Coulson b Matthews .... 0 |
| B 2, l-b 10, n-b 10 | 22 | B 4, l-b 5, n-b 18 ...... 27 |

1/26 2/33 3/40 4/62 5/66       199    1/39 2/94 3/102     (9 wkts dec.) 335
6/92 7/163 8/167 9/167                  4/162 5/289 6/312
                               7/318 8/330 9/335

*Bowling: First Innings*—MacLeay 4-1-6-0; McCague 13-2-52-0; Matthews 20-6-48-6; Coulson 14-2-47-2; Bush 11-3-33-2; Andrews 1-0-1-0. *Second Innings*—MacLeay 6-1-17-0; McCague 15-6-52-1; Matthews 12-2-44-2; Coulson 13.1-2-48-3; Bush 25-3-82-3; Andrews 8-1-41-0; Martyn 5-1-22-0; Moody 3-0-20-0.

## Western Australia

| | | |
|---|---|---|
| M. P. Lavender c Holyman b Bower | 0 | – (6) lbw b Bower ........ 18 |
| *W. S. Andrews c Holyman b Gilbert | 14 | – (1) b Tucker .............. 48 |
| G. M. Wood c Holyman b Gilbert | 43 | – (4) c Buckingham b McPhee ... 22 |
| T. M. Moody c Holyman b Gilbert | 39 | – (3) c Farrell b Tucker .... 23 |
| D. R. Martyn c Holyman b Gilbert | 0 | – c Tucker b McPhee ........ 20 |
| K. H. MacLeay lbw b McPhee | 48 | – (7) b McPhee ............ 5 |
| †T. J. Zoehrer run out | 18 | – (2) c Tucker b McPhee .... 50 |
| C. D. Matthews c Holyman b Gilbert | 16 | – not out ................ 5 |
| C. E. Coulson c Bennett b Buckingham | 12 | – c Tucker b Bower ........ 0 |
| M. J. McCague not out | 15 | – not out ................ 3 |
| G. E. W. Bush c Holyman b Tucker | 27 | |
| B 8, l-b 2, n-b 12 | 22 | B 4, l-b 7 ............ 11 |

1/5 2/28 3/102 4/105 5/106    254    1/77 2/123 3/134 4/169   (8 wkts) 205
6/140 7/181 8/204 9/210                 5/182 6/197 7/199 8/199

*Bowling: First Innings*—Gilbert 23-8-58-5; Bower 13-1-42-1; McPhee 17-4-43-1; Tucker 6.4-1-32-1; Robertson 8-3-24-0; Buckingham 18-3-45-1. *Second Innings*—Gilbert 14-2-57-0; Bower 9-1-42-2; McPhee 8-1-35-4; Tucker 11-0-58-2; Robertson 1-1-0-0; Buckingham 2-1-2-0.

Umpires: D. R. Close and S. G. Randell.

## VICTORIA v SOUTH AUSTRALIA

At St Kilda, Melbourne, March 7, 8, 9, 10. Drawn. Victoria 2 pts. Toss: South Australia. O'Donnell's chivalry just before tea on the final day cost Victoria dearly. The injured South Australian batsman, Nobes, took off for a single with his runner (Hookes) and both reached the apparent safety of the bowler's end, only for Nobes to be technically run out when the bails were removed at the striker's end. O'Donnell, however, revoked the appeal and Nobes, who earlier had been scoreless for 63 minutes either side of lunch, proceeded to hold up the Victorians for another 70 minutes. South Australia hardly deserved this piece of luck. Their contribution to the game was a first innings of unrelenting tedium, 300 in 517 minutes, and a second innings of similar tempo. Victoria's first innings looked in trouble at 177 for five, but Phillips returned with a broken thumb, having been struck by a full toss from George, and he and Parker put on 130 in two and a half hours. Phillips's courageous 100 came up in 266 minutes. In their second innings, when Victoria needed 142 off seventeen overs, only Siddons with 64 in 57 minutes showed the necessary skill and urgency, and they finished 21 runs short.

*Close of play:* First day, South Australia 217-6 (J. C. Scuderi 14*); Second day, Victoria 171-4 (G. R. Parker 19*, A. I. C. Dodemaide 6*); Third day, South Australia 31-3 (A. M. J. Hilditch 20*, G. A. Bishop 3*).

## South Australia

| | | | |
|---|---|---|---|
| G. H. Armstrong c Berry b Fleming | 5 | – run out | 6 |
| *A. M. J. Hilditch c Ramshaw b Reiffel | 71 | – c Ramshaw b Fleming | 49 |
| P. C. Nobes c Dodemaide b Reiffel | 82 | – (6) not out | 49 |
| D. W. Hookes c Berry b Reiffel | 0 | – c O'Donnell b Fleming | 0 |
| G. A. Bishop c Siddons b Dodemaide | 23 | – c Fleming b O'Donnell | 15 |
| †T. J. Nielsen c Siddons b Dodemaide | 11 | – (3) b Reiffel | 0 |
| J. C. Scuderi c Parker b Dodemaide | 31 | – c Berry b Reiffel | 0 |
| T. B. A. May c Phillips b Reiffel | 33 | – lbw b O'Donnell | 17 |
| D. J. Hickey c Berry b Reiffel | 24 | – c Berry b Fleming | 3 |
| S. P. George c Berry b Reiffel | 2 | – b Reiffel | 4 |
| M. J. Minagall not out | 6 | – c Berry b Reiffel | 0 |
| B 1, l-b 2, w 1, n-b 8 | 12 | L-b 2, n-b 2 | 4 |

1/9 2/163 3/163 4/168 5/194          300     1/12 2/16 3/21 4/63 5/81     148
6/217 7/241 8/287 9/289                        6/82 7/120 8/125 9/148

Bowling: *First Innings*—Reiffel 40.2-12-99-6; Fleming 26-11-52-1; Dodemaide 25-9-53-3; O'Donnell 18-5-43-0; Jackson 23-6-50-0; Siddons 2-2-0-0. *Second Innings*—Reiffel 29.2-11-44-4; Fleming 28-9-53-3; Dodemaide 13-3-20-0; O'Donnell 14-6-20-2; Jackson 10-5-9-0.

## Victoria

| | | | |
|---|---|---|---|
| D. J. Ramshaw c Nielsen b George | 11 | – (2) run out | 15 |
| G. M. Watts b George | 26 | – (1) run out | 3 |
| W. N. Phillips not out | 100 | – (6) not out | 2 |
| J. D. Siddons c Scuderi b Hickey | 50 | – not out | 64 |
| G. R. Parker not out | 76 | – c May b Scuderi | 19 |
| *S. P. O'Donnell c Nielsen b George | 0 | – (3) b Scuderi | 4 |
| A. I. C. Dodemaide c Nielsen b Hickey | 6 | | |
| B 3, l-b 3, n-b 32 | 38 | B 5, l-b 5, n-b 4 | 14 |

1/42 2/47 3/132 4/145 5/177      (5 wkts dec.) 307     1/20 2/21 3/27 4/105     (4 wkts) 121

†D. S. Berry, P. R. Reiffel, D. W. Fleming and P. W. Jackson did not bat.

*In the first innings W. N. Phillips, when 33, retired hurt at 145-3 and resumed at 177.*

Bowling: *First Innings*—Hickey 21.4-3-97-2; Scuderi 26-7-74-0; George 19-3-66-3; May 19-5-38-0; Minagall 10-2-26-0. *Second Innings*—Hickey 9-0-57-0; Scuderi 8-0-54-2.

Umpires: R. C. Bailhache and L. J. King.

## TASMANIA v NEW SOUTH WALES

At Hobart, March 14, 15, 16, 17. Drawn. Tasmania 2 pts. Toss: Tasmania. New South Wales overcame an indifferent start in which McNamara retired hurt, having been hit in the eye by a short ball from McPhee, to rattle up 423 on the first day. Bevan continued his irresistible form with his fifth hundred in as many matches, his masterly 136 taking only four hours, and he added 235 in three hours with Small, whose robust 123 included eighteen fours in 204 minutes. Lawson and Alley put on 69 in 40 minutes before the declaration on the second morning. Tasmania made a confident start, with Bennett and Cox raising the first century opening partnership in two years, and on the third day Tucker, who survived a confident appeal for a catch behind before scoring, and Robertson overtook the New South Wales total with some positive hitting. Their 156-run partnership took just 135 minutes. Both players, each opposing his native state, reached their highest scores, and left Lawson to rue his decision to declare. When New South Wales batted a second time, McPhee and newcomer Oliver had them 42 for four, still 6 runs behind, but the later batsmen had little trouble playing out time.

*Close of play:* First day, New South Wales 423-6 (G. F. McLay 22*, G. F. Lawson 7*); Second day, Tasmania 234-3 (D. M. Wellham 8*, R. J. Tucker 25*); Third day, Tasmania 532-8 (G. R. Robertson 88*, S. B. Oliver 5*).

### New South Wales

| | | | |
|---|---|---|---|
| S. M. Small c Robertson b Bower | 123 | – c Bennett b McPhee | 7 |
| B. E. McNamara retired hurt | 1 | – lbw b Oliver | 21 |
| M. D. O'Neill c Holyman b McPhee | 0 | – c Holyman b McPhee | 0 |
| M. G. Bevan c Holyman b Buckingham | 136 | – b Oliver | 3 |
| J. D. Kenny c Holyman b Bower | 73 | – c sub b Oliver | 31 |
| R. J. Green c Buckingham b Oliver | 15 | – run out | 59 |
| †P. A. Emery b Bower | 14 | – b Robertson | 53 |
| G. F. McLay c Holyman b McPhee | 24 | – c Wellham b Buckingham | 1 |
| *G. F. Lawson not out | 52 | – not out | 24 |
| P. J. S. Alley b Buckingham | 27 | – not out | 1 |
| B 1, l-b 10, n-b 26 | 37 | B 9, l-b 6, w 2, n-b 6 | 23 |

1/12 2/247 3/303 4/356 5/384   (8 wkts dec.) 502    1/11 2/11 3/19 4/42   (8 wkts) 223
6/397 7/433 8/502      5/89 6/162 7/165 8/221

W. J. Holdsworth did not bat.

*In the first innings B. E. McNamara retired hurt at 12-0.*

Bowling: *First Innings*—Bower 21-0-95-3; McPhee 29-5-135-2; Tucker 2-0-12-0; Robertson 16-0-54-0; Oliver 17-1-112-1; Buckingham 21.5-2-83-2. *Second Innings*—McPhee 20-5-59-2; Robertson 13-3-26-1; Oliver 25-4-76-3; Buckingham 16-2-39-1; Cox 2-0-8-0.

### Tasmania

| | | | |
|---|---|---|---|
| R. J. Bennett c Emery b Alley | 76 | P. T. McPhee c Kenny b McLay | 5 |
| J. Cox c Emery b McLay | 53 | S. B. Oliver c McNamara b Alley | 8 |
| D. J. Buckingham c Emery b Alley | 56 | T. D. Bower not out | 0 |
| *D. M. Wellham run out | 8 | | |
| R. J. Tucker c Kenny b McNamara | 165 | B 5, l-b 17, w 2, n-b 19 | 43 |
| B. A. Cruse c Alley b McLay | 29 | | |
| †J. F. Holyman c McLay b Holdsworth | 8 | 1/103 2/200 3/201 4/234 5/333 | 550 |
| G. R. Robertson b Holdsworth | 99 | 6/351 7/507 8/523 9/548 | |

Bowling: Holdsworth 27.3-2-111-2; Lawson 27-6-81-0; Alley 38-10-86-3; McLay 43-10-109-3; Green 4-1-14-0; O'Neill 14-3-23-0; Bevan 21-5-66-0; McNamara 12-4-38-1.

Umpires: P. T. Clark and B. T. Knight.

## VICTORIA v QUEENSLAND

At St Kilda, Melbourne, March 14, 15, 16, 17. Victoria won by 113 runs. Victoria 6 pts, Queensland −0.5 pt. Toss: Victoria. While Victoria's win took them to the top of the Shield table, Queensland had to settle for third place. Yet there were times during the match when the initiative was theirs for the taking. At stumps on the second day they were 202 for four, thanks to a sparkling 56 from Law, and Hick was firmly established with a disciplined 59 not out. A first-innings lead seemed a formality. Instead Hick could add only 4 before becoming the first of five match victims for Ramshaw, whose catching in the gully was superb. Dodemaide made short work of the tail, and Victoria led by 30. However, any celebrations over first-innings points were soon scotched by Rackemann and Tazelaar's incisive bowling. Tazelaar bowled almost throughout the innings, and Queensland were left to get 193 with time no object. Ominously they took seven overs to score a run, by which time Cantrell had already been run out, and when Dodemaide's bowling again proved too much for the tentative Queenslanders, Victoria secured match points with three hours to spare.

*Close of play:* First day, Victoria 267-9 (A. I. C. Dodemaide 28*, J. A. Sutherland 3*); Second day, Queensland 202-4 (G. A. Hick 59*, D. Tazelaar 0*); Third day, Victoria 130-7 (A. I. C. Dodemaide 9*, P. R. Reiffel 5*).

### Victoria

| | | | |
|---|---|---|---|
| G. M. Watts c Anderson b Tazelaar | 44 | – (2) c Cantrell b Tazelaar | 23 |
| D. J. Ramshaw c Anderson b Tazelaar | 8 | – (1) c Anderson b Rackemann | 0 |
| W. N. Phillips b Law b Rackemann | 34 | – c Cantrell b Rackemann | 0 |
| J. D. Siddons b Rackemann | 25 | – b Rackemann | 8 |
| G. R. Parker lbw b Hohns | 14 | – c Monty b Tazelaar | 15 |
| *S. P. O'Donnell c Tazelaar b Hohns | 46 | – run out | 56 |
| A. I. C. Dodemaide not out | 41 | – lbw b Rackemann | 17 |
| †D. S. Berry b Muller | 0 | – c Hick b Tazelaar | 0 |
| P. R. Reiffel c Monty b Muller | 0 | – c Anderson b Rackemann | 8 |
| D. W. Fleming b Rackemann | 13 | – not out | 3 |
| J. A. Sutherland c Hick b Rackemann | 10 | – c Barsby b Hohns | 14 |
| L-b 9, w 1, n-b 44 | 54 | L-b 4, n-b 14 | 18 |
| | **289** | | **162** |

1/36 2/104 3/125 4/148 5/154　　　　　　**289**　　　1/4 2/4 3/26 4/34 5/79　　　　**162**
6/215 7/215 8/219 9/263　　　　　　　　　　　　　6/119 7/119 8/140 9/143

Bowling: *First Innings*—Rackemann 30.5-12-64-4; Tazelaar 25-4-99-2; Muller 17-2-70-2; Hohns 25-8-46-2; Monty 1-0-1-0. *Second Innings*—Rackemann 23-3-86-5; Tazelaar 34-15-50-3; Muller 7-1-15-0; Hohns 8-5-7-1.

### Queensland

| | | | |
|---|---|---|---|
| P. E. Cantrell c Berry b Fleming | 16 | – (2) run out | 0 |
| S. Monty c Berry b Dodemaide | 44 | – (1) c Siddons b Sutherland | 17 |
| T. J. Barsby c Watts b Reiffel | 19 | – c Ramshaw b Reiffel | 3 |
| G. A. Hick c Ramshaw b Reiffel | 63 | – c O'Donnell b Dodemaide | 14 |
| S. G. Law c Parker b O'Donnell | 56 | – c Ramshaw b Sutherland | 2 |
| D. Tazelaar lbw b Dodemaide | 25 | – (9) not out | 12 |
| A. B. Henschell c Ramshaw b Fleming | 1 | – (6) lbw b Dodemaide | 0 |
| †P. W. Anderson c Berry b Dodemaide | 18 | – (7) c Parker b Dodemaide | 16 |
| *T. V. Hohns c Ramshaw b Dodemaide | 5 | – (8) c Fleming b Dodemaide | 3 |
| S. A. Muller not out | 2 | – c Berry b Reiffel | 3 |
| C. G. Rackemann c Berry b Sutherland | 0 | – c Parker b Dodemaide | 3 |
| B 1, l-b 7, n-b 2 | 10 | L-b 6 | 6 |
| | **259** | | **79** |

1/17 2/52 3/116 4/199 5/208　　　　　　**259**　　　1/0 2/5 3/26 4/35 5/36　　　　**79**
6/213 7/245 8/251 9/258　　　　　　　　　　　　　6/38 7/49 8/70 9/76

Bowling: *First Innings*—Reiffel 27-6-54-2; Fleming 27-9-48-2; O'Donnell 10-5-26-1; Sutherland 25.4-3-64-1; Dodemaide 23-8-59-4. *Second Innings*—Reiffel 11-5-12-2; Fleming 8-4-19-0; Sutherland 8.5-4-19-5.

Umpires: R. C. Bailhache and L. J. King.

## WESTERN AUSTRALIA v SOUTH AUSTRALIA

At Perth, March 14, 15, 16. South Australia won by an innings and 66 runs. South Australia 5.4 pts. Toss: Western Australia. South Australia's win was their first in Perth for eleven years, and from the moment Andrews forfeited the opportunity of batting first, the match was hardly a contest. Hilditch and Nobes put on 144 for the second wicket, and Bishop and Scuderi raised the tempo with 157 in 107 minutes for the sixth wicket. Bishop went on to reach 116 in four hours with fifteen fours and a six. Led by Hickey, the South Australian fast bowlers had Western Australia out inside a day and repeated the process the next day. It was a dismal performance by the home side, who had entered the match with an outside chance of making the Shield final. Nielsen, the South Australian wicket-keeper, held eleven catches, becoming only the fourth Australian to make eleven or more dismissals in a match.

*Close of play:* First day, South Australia 376-7 (G. A. Bishop 89*, T. B. A. May 1*); Second day, Western Australia 26-0 (W. S. Andrews 18*, M. P. Lavender 4*).

### South Australia

| | | | |
|---|---|---|---|
| G. H. Armstrong c Zoehrer b MacLeay | 3 | T. B. A. May b Coulson | 28 |
| *A. M. J. Hilditch c Zoehrer b McCague | 69 | D. J. Hickey c and b Matthews | 4 |
| P. C. Nobes c Lavender b McCague | 60 | S. P. George not out | 4 |
| D. W. Hookes c Lavender b McCague | 18 | | |
| G. A. Bishop c Moody b Coulson | 116 | B 1, l-b 20, w 3, n-b 36 | 60 |
| C. J. Williamson c Lavender b Matthews | 9 | | |
| J. C. Scuderi b MacLeay | 79 | 1/5 2/149 3/185 4/188 5/202 | 450 |
| †T. J. Nielsen c Andrews b McCague | 0 | 6/359 7/371 8/436 9/444 | |

Bowling: McCague 27-7-81-4; MacLeay 29-9-61-2; Coulson 22.2-4-89-2; Matthews 21-1-112-2; Bush 13-0-69-0; Andrews 4-0-17-0.

### Western Australia

| | | | |
|---|---|---|---|
| M. P. Lavender b Hickey | 4 | (2) c Nielsen b Hickey | 50 |
| *W. S. Andrews c Nielsen b George | 28 | (1) c Nielsen b Hickey | 21 |
| G. M. Wood c Bishop b Hickey | 15 | c Williamson b Scuderi | 25 |
| T. M. Moody c Nielsen b George | 18 | c Nielsen b Scuderi | 7 |
| D. R. Martyn c Nobes b Hickey | 21 | c Nielsen b Scuderi | 11 |
| K. H. MacLeay lbw b Hickey | 11 | c Hilditch b Hickey | 3 |
| †T. J. Zoehrer b Williamson | 27 | c Nielsen b Hickey | 13 |
| C. D. Matthews c Nielsen b Williamson | 31 | lbw b Scuderi | 15 |
| C. E. Coulson c Nielsen b George | 8 | c Nielsen b Williamson | 6 |
| M. J. McCague c Nielsen b Williamson | 0 | c Armstrong b Scuderi | 10 |
| G. E. W. Bush not out | 3 | not out | 4 |
| L-b 3, w 1, n-b 24 | 28 | L-b 6, w 1, n-b 18 | 25 |
| 1/9 2/27 3/76 4/85 5/114 | 194 | 1/33 2/98 3/112 4/132 5/136 | 190 |
| 6/119 7/180 8/191 9/191 | | 6/148 7/157 8/172 9/177 | |

Bowling: *First Innings*—Hickey 14-4-52-4; Scuderi 17-2-70-0; Williamson 9-4-24-3; George 12-3-45-3. *Second Innings*—Hickey 21-2-51-4; Scuderi 21.5-8-58-5; Williamson 10-5-21-1; George 13-1-54-0.

Umpires: R. A. Emerson and P. J. McConnell.

## FINAL

## VICTORIA v NEW SOUTH WALES

At Melbourne, March 22, 23, 24, 25, 26. Victoria won by eight wickets. Toss: Victoria. After rain had delayed the start of the first state match of the season at the MCG by a day, O'Donnell put New South Wales in to bat and Fleming immediately made inroads. His pace and swing had all the batsmen in trouble except for Small who, while wickets were tumbling, cut, drove, sliced and chipped his way to 82 before he was fifth out at 103. But for the slow, wet outfield, he would surely have recorded a century. Emery and Green fashioned a modest recovery without ever dominating the bowling. A Sunday crowd of 9,000 saw Victoria's batsmen surrender the initiative and seemingly lose any chance of winning the Shield. Alley, another tall left-arm fast bowler, took two wickets in his first over, and with Holdsworth more or less on target there was no escape for Victoria. Small and McNamara extended the New South Wales lead past 150, but the dismissal of the experienced Small exposed his young team-mates to the pressures of a final. Dodemaide bowled with great control and was well supported by O'Donnell and Reiffel. Set 239 to win, Victoria made another sketchy start, but Phillips dropped anchor and Siddons went for his shots, hitting fifteen fours and a six to Phillips's four fours. Their unbroken partnership of 212 in 282 minutes provided a remarkable contrast to the first innings and was a worthy climax to Victoria's Shield victory.

*Close of play:* First day, No play; Second day, New South Wales 198-8 (P. A. Emery 51*, P. J. S. Alley 4*); Third day, New South Wales 26-0 (S. M. Small 17*, B. E. McNamara 8*); Fourth day, Victoria 102-2 (W. N. Phillips 41*, J. D. Siddons 42*).

## New South Wales

| | | | | |
|---|---|---|---|---|
| S. M. Small c b O'Donnell | 82 | – b Reiffel | | 30 |
| B. E. McNamara c Siddons b Fleming | 2 | – c Parker b Reiffel | | 24 |
| M. D. O'Neill lbw b Fleming | 0 | – (5) c Berry b Dodemaide | | 0 |
| M. G. Bevan c Berry b Fleming | 6 | – lbw b O'Donnell | | 25 |
| J. D. Kenny c Berry b Dodemaide | 3 | – (6) c Berry b Dodemaide | | 15 |
| R. J. Green c Fleming b Jackson | 4 | – (7) c and b Dodemaide | | 13 |
| †P. A. Emery c Siddons b Dodemaide | 62 | – (3) c Reiffel b Dodemaide | | 7 |
| G. F. McLay c Siddons b Fleming | 3 | – c Reiffel b O'Donnell | | 0 |
| *G. F. Lawson b O'Donnell | 0 | – c Reiffel b Dodemaide | | 8 |
| P. J. S. Alley c O'Donnell b Dodemaide | 5 | – c Parker b O'Donnell | | 6 |
| W. J. Holdsworth not out | 12 | – not out | | 0 |
| L-b 8 | 8 | B 1, l-b 5 | | 6 |

1/8 2/28 3/40 4/59 5/103     223    1/50 2/63 3/81 4/81 5/99     134
6/176 7/183 8/186 9/200                   6/113 7/120 8/126 9/133

*Bowling: First Innings*—Reiffel 18-5-64-0; Fleming 24-8-53-4; Dodemaide 19.1-3-69-3; O'Donnell 11-7-14-2; Jackson 13-6-15-1. *Second Innings*—Reiffel 18-6-40-2; Fleming 10-1-29-0; Dodemaide 17.1-10-25-5; O'Donnell 12-3-34-3.

## Victoria

| | | | | |
|---|---|---|---|---|
| G. M. Watts c Green b Alley | 1 | – (2) c Bevan b Holdsworth | | 1 |
| W. N. Phillips lbw b Lawson | 26 | – (1) not out | | 91 |
| G. R. Parker c Emery b Alley | 0 | – c Kenny b Holdsworth | | 4 |
| D. S. Lehmann c Bevan b Alley | 11 | | | |
| J. D. Siddons c Bevan b Holdsworth | 2 | – (4) not out | | 124 |
| *S. P. O'Donnell c O'Neill b McNamara | 18 | | | |
| A. I. C. Dodemaide c Emery b Holdsworth | 3 | | | |
| †D. S. Berry not out | 25 | | | |
| P. R. Reiffel c O'Neill b Holdsworth | 0 | | | |
| D. W. Fleming c Emery b Holdsworth | 2 | | | |
| P. W. Jackson c Small b Holdsworth | 4 | | | |
| L-b 6, w 5, n-b 16 | 27 | B 4, l-b 4, w 1, n-b 10 | | 19 |

1/1 2/1 3/19 4/26 5/73     119    1/17 2/27       (2 wkts) 239
6/79 7/83 8/95 9/107

*Bowling: First Innings*—Holdsworth 17.3-3-55-5; Alley 18-9-33-3; Lawson 12-3-22-1; McNamara 8-5-3-1. *Second Innings*—Holdsworth 16-5-68-2; Alley 17-4-42-0; Lawson 17-5-26-0; McNamara 14-5-35-0; O'Neill 8-1-27-0; Bevan 4-0-25-0; McLay 4-1-8-0.

*Umpires:* P. J. McConnell and S. G. Randell.

## SHEFFIELD SHIELD WINNERS

| | | | |
|---|---|---|---|
| 1892-93 | Victoria | 1946-47 | Victoria |
| 1893-94 | South Australia | 1947-48 | Western Australia |
| 1894-95 | Victoria | 1948-49 | New South Wales |
| 1895-96 | New South Wales | 1949-50 | New South Wales |
| 1896-97 | New South Wales | 1950-51 | Victoria |
| 1897-98 | Victoria | 1951-52 | New South Wales |
| 1898-99 | Victoria | 1952-53 | South Australia |
| 1899-1900 | New South Wales | 1953-54 | New South Wales |
| 1900-01 | Victoria | 1954-55 | New South Wales |
| 1901-02 | New South Wales | 1955-56 | New South Wales |
| 1902-03 | New South Wales | 1956-57 | New South Wales |
| 1903-04 | New South Wales | 1957-58 | New South Wales |
| 1904-05 | New South Wales | 1958-59 | New South Wales |
| 1905-06 | New South Wales | 1959-60 | New South Wales |
| 1906-07 | New South Wales | 1960-61 | New South Wales |
| 1907-08 | Victoria | 1961-62 | New South Wales |
| 1908-09 | New South Wales | 1962-63 | Victoria |
| 1909-10 | South Australia | 1963-64 | South Australia |
| 1910-11 | New South Wales | 1964-65 | New South Wales |
| 1911-12 | New South Wales | 1965-66 | New South Wales |
| 1912-13 | South Australia | 1966-67 | Victoria |
| 1913-14 | New South Wales | 1967-68 | Western Australia |
| 1914-15 | Victoria | 1968-69 | South Australia |
| 1915-19 | No competition | 1969-70 | Victoria |
| 1919-20 | New South Wales | 1970-71 | South Australia |
| 1920-21 | New South Wales | 1971-72 | Western Australia |
| 1921-22 | Victoria | 1972-73 | Western Australia |
| 1922-23 | New South Wales | 1973-74 | Victoria |
| 1923-24 | Victoria | 1974-75 | Western Australia |
| 1924-25 | Victoria | 1975-76 | South Australia |
| 1925-26 | New South Wales | 1976-77 | Western Australia |
| 1926-27 | South Australia | 1977-78 | Western Australia |
| 1927-28 | Victoria | 1978-79 | Victoria |
| 1928-29 | New South Wales | 1979-80 | Victoria |
| 1929-30 | Victoria | 1980-81 | Western Australia |
| 1930-31 | Victoria | 1981-82 | South Australia |
| 1931-32 | New South Wales | 1982-83 | New South Wales |
| 1932-33 | New South Wales | 1983-84 | Western Australia |
| 1933-34 | Victoria | 1984-85 | New South Wales |
| 1934-35 | Victoria | 1985-86 | New South Wales |
| 1935-36 | South Australia | 1986-87 | Western Australia |
| 1936-37 | Victoria | 1987-88 | Western Australia |
| 1937-38 | New South Wales | 1988-89 | Western Australia |
| 1938-39 | South Australia | 1989-90 | New South Wales |
| 1939-40 | New South Wales | 1990-91 | Victoria |
| 1940-46 | No competition | | |

New South Wales have won the Shield 40 times, Victoria 25, South Australia 12, Western Australia 12, Queensland 0, Tasmania 0.

## TRANS-TASMAN SHIELD CHALLENGE

### NEW SOUTH WALES v WELLINGTON

At North Sydney Oval, Sydney, November 22, 23, 24, 25. New South Wales won by 160 runs. Toss: New South Wales. The match was played between the 1989-90 Sheffield Shield champions and the winners of New Zealand's Shell Trophy.

*Close of play:* First day, New South Wales 309-7 (A. E. Tucker 21*, G. F. Lawson 4*); Second day, Wellington 218; Third day, Wellington 45-0 (J. M. Aiken 22*, G. P. Burnett 21*).

## New South Wales

| | | | |
|---|---|---|---|
| S. M. Small c Jones b Larsen | 115 | – c Jones b Cederwall | 126 |
| G. S. Milliken lbw b Hotter | 4 | – c Vance b Hotter | 6 |
| T. H. Bayliss c Larsen b Hotter | 18 | – b Davis | 3 |
| M. E. Waugh b Williams | 74 | – c McSweeney b Davis | 65 |
| M. D. O'Neill c McSweeney b Cederwall | 9 | – c Jones b Cederwall | 23 |
| M. G. Bevan st McSweeney b Williams | 15 | – not out | 17 |
| †P. A. Emery c Hotter b Davis | 12 | | |
| A. E. Tucker not out | 48 | | |
| *G. F. Lawson b Hotter | 26 | | |
| M. R. Whitney c Larsen b Davis | 0 | | |
| W. J. Holdsworth c Larsen b Davis | 11 | | |
| L-b 5, w 2, n-b 36 | 43 | B 4, l-b 4, n-b 10 | 18 |

1/16 2/72 3/209 4/247 5/261       375     1/20 2/23 3/145     (5 wkts dec.) 258
6/269 7/303 8/340 9/341                4/233 5/258

Bowling: *First Innings*—Davis 28-5-97-3; Hotter 26-5-100-3; Cederwall 20-4-88-1; Larsen 21-10-32-1; Williams 20-5-53-2. *Second Innings*—Davis 13-1-57-2; Hotter 7-0-49-1; Cederwall 10.4-1-30-2; Larsen 17-5-33-0; Williams 22-6-56-0; Jones 10-3-25-0.

## Wellington

| | | | |
|---|---|---|---|
| J. M. Aiken run out | 26 | – c Emery b Holdsworth | 30 |
| G. P. Burnett c Milliken b Tucker | 50 | – c Milliken b Holdsworth | 37 |
| R. H. Vance c and b Tucker | 5 | – c Emery b Whitney | 47 |
| A. H. Jones run out | 27 | – lbw b Lawson | 10 |
| T. D. Ritchie not out | 70 | – c Tucker b Lawson | 5 |
| G. R. Larsen b Lawson | 3 | – (7) lbw b Holdsworth | 39 |
| *†E. B. McSweeney c Bayliss b Lawson | 0 | – (6) c Milliken b Holdsworth | 33 |
| B. R Williams lbw b O'Neill | 10 | – c Milliken b Bevan | 27 |
| G. N. Cederwall b Whitney | 1 | – c Tucker b Bevan | 0 |
| S. J. Hotter b Whitney | 2 | – c Bayliss b Bevan | 6 |
| W. W. Davis b Whitney | 4 | – not out | 0 |
| L-b 6, n-b 14 | 20 | B 6, l-b 9, n-b 6 | 21 |

1/70 2/82 3/113 4/132 5/148       218     1/66 2/71 3/107 4/121 5/142     255
6/152 7/193 8/196 9/214              6/195 7/224 8/229 9/255

Bowling: *First Innings*—Lawson 15-10-16-2; Whitney 14-4-39-3; Tucker 24-1-79-2; Holdsworth 8-2-19-0; O'Neill 22-9-59-1. *Second Innings*—Lawson 14-4-36-2; Whitney 20-6-51-1; Tucker 17-2-51-0; Holdsworth 19-5-49-4; O'Neill 13-4-39-0; Bayliss 5-2-8-0; Bevan 7.4-4-6-3.

Umpires: D. B. Hair and G. E. Reed.

## †FAI CUP

At Perth, October 12. Western Australia won on faster scoring-rate after rain stopped play. Western Australia's innings had already been restricted by earlier rain to 41 overs. Toss: South Australia. Western Australia 277 for five (41 overs) (M. W. McPhee 59, G. R. Marsh 110, T. M. Moody 41, Extras 34; T. B. A. May three for 60); South Australia 115 for two (20 overs) (D. W. Hookes 52).

At Brisbane, October 13. Queensland won by 4 runs. Toss: Queensland. Queensland 241 for six (50 overs) (A. R. Border 68, S. G. Law 30, P. L. Taylor 50 not out, I. A. Healy 48); Tasmania 237 for seven (50 overs) (G. Shipperd 69, J. Cox 50, R. J. Tucker 49; C. J. McDermott four for 60).

At Brisbane, October 14. New South Wales won by four wickets. Toss: Queensland. Queensland 155 (40.4 overs) (P. E. Cantrell 41, A. R. Border 60; W. J. Holdsworth five for 28); New South Wales 156 for six (44.5 overs) (M. A. Taylor 37, M. E. Waugh 31).

At Perth, October 14. Western Australia won by three wickets. Toss: Victoria. Victoria 282 for five (50 overs) (W. G. Ayres 43, D. M. Jones 72, J. D. Siddons 72 not out, S. P. O'Donnell 70); Western Australia 284 for seven (49 overs) (M. W. McPhee 41, G. R. Marsh 53, T. M. Moody 78, W. S. Andrews 50, M. R. J. Veletta 30 not out).

At Sydney, October 16. New South Wales won by 88 runs. Toss: New South Wales. New South Wales 282 for five (50 overs) (T. H. Bayliss 92, M. E. Waugh 59, S. R. Waugh 66 not out); Tasmania 194 (46.3 overs) (G. Shipperd 35, M. G. Farrell 37, D. C. Boon 31; M. R. Whitney four for 30, G. R. J. Matthews three for 35).

At Adelaide, October 17. Victoria won by 113 runs. Toss: Victoria. Victoria 240 for six (50 overs) (G. M. Watts 53, W. G. Ayres 53, D. M. Jones 41, S. P. O'Donnell 35; D. A. Clarke three for 51); South Australia 127 (40.2 overs) (P. R. Sleep 32; P. R. Reiffel three for 23, P. W. Jackson three for 21).

## Semi-finals

At Sydney, October 20. New South Wales won by six wickets. Toss: Victoria. Victoria 160 (46.2 overs) (J. D. Siddons 63; W. J. Holdsworth three for 36, S. R. Waugh four for 32); New South Wales 162 for four (43.4 overs) (T. H. Bayliss 61, M. E. Waugh 64; M. G. Hughes three for 35).

At Perth, October 21. Western Australia won by nine wickets. Toss: Queensland. Queensland 219 for seven (50 overs) (A. R. Border 65, S. G. Law 32, P. L. Taylor 45 not out); Western Australia 220 for one (46.1 overs) (M. W. McPhee 89 not out, G. R. Marsh 82, Extras 31).

## FINAL

### WESTERN AUSTRALIA v NEW SOUTH WALES

At Perth, October 27. Western Australia won by seven wickets. Toss: Western Australia.
*Man of the Match:* G. R. Marsh.

## New South Wales

| | | | |
|---|---|---|---|
| S. M. Small run out | 47 | †P. A. Emery c and b Moody | 0 |
| M. A. Taylor c Veletta b Capes | 9 | *G. F. Lawson not out | 10 |
| T. H. Bayliss c McPhee b MacLeay | 0 | L-b 22, w 10, n-b 6 | 38 |
| M. E. Waugh b Reid | 1 | | |
| S. R. Waugh c Capes b Reid | 11 | 1/55 2/58 3/74 (7 wkts, 50 overs) | 235 |
| M. G. Bevan not out | 74 | 4/81 5/108 | |
| G. R. J. Matthews c and b Moody | 45 | 6/213 7/213 | |

M. R. Whitney and W. J. Holdsworth did not bat.

Bowling: Alderman 10–1–47–0; Capes 10–0–48–1; MacLeay 10–1–33–1; Reid 10–2–34–2; Moody 9–1–46–2; Andrews 1–0–5–0.

## Western Australia

| | | | |
|---|---|---|---|
| M. W. McPhee c Taylor b Matthews | 58 | M. R. J. Veletta not out | 61 |
| *G. R. Marsh not out | 91 | L-b 7, w 8, n-b 6 | 21 |
| T. M. Moody run out | 2 | | |
| G. M. Wood lbw b M. E. Waugh | 3 | 1/114 2/118 3/126 (3 wkts, 44.5 overs) | 236 |

W. S. Andrews, †T. J. Zoehrer, K. H. MacLeay, P. A. Capes, B. A. Reid and T. M. Alderman did not bat.

Bowling: Holdsworth 7–0–57–0; Lawson 8.5–0–42–0; Whitney 6–0–33–0; Matthews 10–2–33–1; S. R. Waugh 8–0–38–0; M. E. Waugh 5–0–26–1.

Umpires: A. R. Crafter and R. J. Evans.

# CRICKET IN SOUTH AFRICA, 1990-91

## By FRANK HEYDENRYCH

The events of a well-contested South African season were quickly over-shadowed by those off the field, which culminated in recognition of South Africa by the International Cricket Council, and the country's long-awaited return to world cricket. The road to acceptance had been a long, often stormy one, and had claimed the Test careers of some of the greatest cricketers South Africa has produced. But that road has now been travelled, and all agree with hindsight that it had to be travelled. The fact that the unification of South Africa's cricket bodies took place without the wrangling, backbiting and power plays which have held back the progress of other sports in the country was to the credit of all the parties concerned.

For those in South Africa who had pressed their noses against the shop window of international cricket for two decades, this was the most momentous moment of their sporting lives. English cricket-lovers, temporarily deprived of the services of players such as Gooch, Emburey, Gatting and Foster, would have to amplify their frustration a thousand times to get some idea of what South African cricket-lovers had borne for the past twenty years.

In addition to the political changes necessary for South Africa's return to Test cricket, other changes resulted from the coming together of the South African Cricket Union and the South African Cricket Board to form the United Cricket Board of South Africa. Foremost among these at domestic level was the restructuring of the Currie Cup, for more than a century the country's premier competition. As it had been seen as the tournament of privileged cricketers, the members of the South African Cricket Board insisted it change, and the competition will henceforth be known as the Castle Cup, to be contested over four days. Bonus points have been scrapped in favour of first-innings points. Gone, too, is the Springbok emblem – something of a blow to past Springboks and their opponents. The United Cricket Board of South Africa, in addition, granted first-class status to two new regions, Western Transvaal and Eastern Transvaal. There were those who felt that this was a diminution of first-class status, but the truth is that unification brought to the game in South Africa a vast, untapped seam of cricketers.

At club level there were some extraordinary happenings. It should never be forgotten that Coloured and black cricketers often labour under inordinate burdens, most of them caused by economic imbalances. These will not disappear overnight, and because the return on investment at grass-roots level is limited, sponsorship will not always be forthcoming. However, in a gesture that went a long way to cement relationships, the Western Province captain, Adrian Kuiper, joined one of the less-privileged clubs, Primrose, a former South African Cricket Board club based at Claremont in Cape Town. And to a man the members of the SA Cricket Board stood back to allow SA Cricket Union incumbents to run the game at provincial board level. Goodwill prevailed. It was almost too much to believe. Yet when Sam Ramsamy, president-elect of the South African National Olympic Committee and a long-time opponent of apartheid, stood next to Sir Garfield Sobers and Sunil Gavaskar in Soweto, we knew it was all happening.

On the playing fields there was much for South Africa to celebrate, not least the emergence of yet another extremely fast bowler in Steven Jack of Transvaal. Fit, strong and possessing the mean streak that separates the match-winner from the good bowler, the twenty-year-old Jack took the country by storm in his first season of Currie Cup cricket, ending with 54 wickets at 16.01 apiece from ten games. He was a force in all competitions, and the prospect of Jack and Allan Donald representing South Africa in international cricket was one to savour. Craig Matthews of Western Province, a lean, tall, fast bowler who took 47 wickets at 14.74, all but won the Currie Cup on his own for his province, while the all-round displays of his team-mate, Brian McMillan, the former Warwickshire player, put him in line for a place in the coming international side. Then there was also the hostile Tertius Bosch of Northern Transvaal, a fast bowler in the Peter Heine mould, who had his best season with 42 wickets at 26.40.

Among the batsmen, Hansie Cronje of Orange Free State was being spoken of as a future captain of his country, while Andrew Hudson of Natal and Stefan Jacobs of Transvaal featured among those whose progress suggested that the future is healthy. Even so, Northern Transvaal's Mike Haysman, an Australian, was the only batsman to average more than 50 in the Currie Cup, although this was in part influenced by the difficulties which many batsmen encountered on the "result pitches" that prevailed throughout the season in some areas.

In terms of trophies won, the season was dominated by Western Province, yet they ran into form so late that they became realistic challengers for honours only in the last month of the season. When they peaked, however, they did so spectacularly, winning three Currie Cup matches on the trot while other teams pondered the intricacies of a system which rewarded positive play. Having struck a rich vein of form, Western Province went on to win the Benson and Hedges Night Series, beating Natal at Cape Town in the final. Nevertheless, while these successes gave their delighted supporters grounds for celebration, they did not completely cover over the problems which have, and still do, beset the province.

Transvaal, with a little more luck, could have won all three trophies; instead they finished with just the Nissan Shield. An annoying innovation in this competition, incidentally, was a substitution system. Teams of fourteen were named, and while only eleven players could be on the field at any one time, up to six substitutions could be made. Clever captains, such as Eastern Province's Kepler Wessels, used the system to keep their fast bowlers fresh, but after this one season the innovation was shelved.

"Rice's Babes", as Transvaal were dubbed, dominated the 55-overs Nissan Shield competition in grand style, but talk of them finishing the season as triple champions looked premature when they were beaten by Natal in the Currie Cup at the Wanderers by six wickets. However, they continued to log bonus points impressively, and it took a tremendous effort by Western Province, beating them by 5 runs at the Wanderers, to begin the winning streak that edged Transvaal out of the Currie Cup. This was the Cape side's first victory in Johannesburg in more than three decades, and their first at the new Wanderers ground.

In the semi-finals of the Night Series, Transvaal looked to have won their away leg in Durban, only for Richard Snell to bowl a no-ball to Jonty Rhodes when 7 runs were needed off the last ball. Rhodes hit this for six into the crowd, which then swarmed on to the ground, thinking the match was over.

When order was restored and Snell could bowl the final delivery, Rhodes hit it for four to snatch a sensational victory for Natal, and he again powered Transvaal out of contention when torrential rain reduced the second leg in Johannesburg to a 25-over slog. Transvaal have been written off before, and have come storming back, but the fact that they lost three Currie Cup games was proof positive for some critics that they were a spent force.

Northern Transvaal were an enigma. Despite having three heavy-scoring batsmen and an excellent trio of fast bowlers, they were never in the running for honours. Mandy Yachad scored 994 runs, and Haysman and Mike Rindel more than 700 and 600 respectively, which should have given them a wonderful platform. Bosch, Fanie de Villiers and Steve Elworthy shared 108 wickets, with the left-arm spinner, Willie Morris, taking another 24 in support. Yet the batting collapsed at critical times, and only once were the bowlers able to dismiss their opponents twice.

Eastern Province were nigh unstoppable in the early rounds of the one-day competitions, with Wessels and Philip Amm providing a mountain of runs for their battery of seamers to defend. But they fell at the final hurdle in the Nissan Shield and in the semi-finals of the Night Series. Their humiliation at the hands of Jack, who took eight for 51 at Port Elizabeth in the last round of the Currie Cup, brought their season to an appropriately sober conclusion. Triple champions the previous season, they had now surrendered all three of their trophies.

Natal mixed glorious success with some appalling failures. They were bundled out of the Nissan Shield quarter-finals by Transvaal, yet six weeks later secured their first Currie Cup win at the Wanderers in more than two decades; they made the final of the Benson and Hedges Night Series, only to surrender in meek fashion to Western Province; they crumbled at Newlands against Western Province in the Currie Cup, only to beat Northern Transvaal at Kingsmead in an invigorating run-chase in the final round of matches. Kim Hughes was targeted as a primary reason for the province's failure, was deposed as captain and subsequently retired from the game. But the faults lay much deeper than leadership.

Orange Free State, who announced that they would be coached by Eddie Barlow in 1991-92, never looked in contention. Despite the heavy scoring of Cronje, and the often inspired all-round performances of Johan van Heerden, they lacked the spark that turns good sides into winning ones. Donald bowled in cruise mode for much of the season – his subsequent success in England for Warwickshire was the cause of much bitterness – and the rest of the attack lacked the penetration to work through entire batting orders.

In the Bowl, Border, reinforced by Peter Kirsten's batting, were much too strong, and their place in the final was soon a foregone conclusion. However, they were unable to make much headway against Western Province B and had to share the trophy for the second season in succession. Kirsten's appointment as captain, and their readmittance to senior status, should enable Border's cheerful band of players to lift their game.

Unification will have different effects on the provinces. Western Province, where the former Cricket Board held sway for a number of years, will benefit most from playing numbers, for there are literally thousands of good black and Coloured cricketers in the area. Natal and Transvaal will enjoy an infusion of talented Asian players, but initially Northern Transvaal and Orange Free State will remain much the same.

The most important gain of unification, however, is that there will now be a national team which will carry the support of all South Africa – whether or not that team is of mixed races or is all white. For the cricket-lovers of this divided country, boycott and ostracism have been borne stoically, but with deep regret. To emerge from under the rock, blinking in the sunlight, and to face a future involving Curtly Ambrose, Waqar Younis, Dean Jones, Graeme Hick, Sachin Tendulkar, Aravinda de Silva, Martin Crowe and the host of great cricketers around the world was more than South Africans could have expected several years ago. That it is now within our reach is due to Ali Bacher, Steve Tshwete, Krish Mackerdhuj, Geoff Dakin, Govan Mbeki and the unsung, unheralded legion of hard-working cricket-lovers both in South Africa and around the world.

## FIRST-CLASS AVERAGES, 1990-91

### BATTING

(Qualification: 8 innings, average 35.00)

| | M | I | NO | R | HI | 100s | Avge |
|---|---|---|---|---|---|---|---|
| L. J. Koen (*Boland*) | 4 | 8 | 1 | 393 | 177* | 1 | 56.14 |
| M. D. Haysman (*N. Transvaal*) | 10 | 18 | 4 | 744 | 136* | 3 | 53.14 |
| M. Yachad (*N. Transvaal*) | 10 | 20 | 0 | 994 | 179 | 4 | 49.70 |
| K. C. Wessels (*E. Province*) | 11 | 21 | 2 | 871 | 197 | 2 | 45.84 |
| B. M. McMillan (*W. Province*) | 10 | 17 | 3 | 632 | 127 | 1 | 45.14 |
| M. J. R. Rindel (*N. Transvaal*) | 10 | 18 | 4 | 612 | 115* | 2 | 43.71 |
| E. N. Trotman (*Border*) | 5 | 8 | 2 | 250 | 61 | 0 | 41.66 |
| A. C. Hudson (*Natal*) | 10 | 19 | 3 | 673 | 184* | 2 | 42.06 |
| V. G. Cresswell (*Transvaal/Transvaal B*) | 6 | 9 | 4 | 207 | 51 | 0 | 41.40 |
| C. R. Matthews (*W. Province*) | 11 | 14 | 7 | 284 | 105 | 1 | 40.57 |
| T. N. Lazard (*E. Province/W. Province B*) | 8 | 15 | 1 | 560 | 113 | 1 | 40.00 |
| M. Erasmus (*Boland*) | 6 | 9 | 3 | 240 | 48 | 0 | 40.00 |
| W. F. Morris (*N. Transvaal*) | 7 | 9 | 4 | 199 | 48* | 0 | 39.80 |
| W. J. Cronje (*OFS*) | 10 | 19 | 1 | 715 | 101 | 2 | 39.72 |
| P. N. Kirsten (*Border*) | 5 | 8 | 1 | 278 | 105 | 1 | 39.71 |
| G. M. Charlesworth (*Griqualand West*) | 4 | 8 | 0 | 314 | 83 | 0 | 39.25 |
| M. B. Mare (*N. Transvaal/N. Transvaal B*) | 5 | 10 | 0 | 391 | 170 | 1 | 39.10 |
| T. G. Shaw (*E. Province*) | 11 | 14 | 7 | 273 | 40 | 0 | 39.00 |
| M. J. Cann (*Griqualand West*) | 4 | 8 | 0 | 308 | 141 | 1 | 38.50 |
| M. W. Rushmere (*E. Province*) | 11 | 21 | 5 | 600 | 159 | 1 | 37.50 |
| D. J. Richardson (*E. Province*) | 11 | 17 | 5 | 436 | 68 | 0 | 36.33 |
| G. Kirsten (*W. Province*) | 11 | 21 | 1 | 724 | 189 | 2 | 36.20 |
| D. J. Cullinan (*W. Province*) | 9 | 17 | 2 | 531 | 102* | 1 | 35.40 |
| J. B. Commins (*W. Province/W. Province B*) | 6 | 12 | 2 | 352 | 110* | 1 | 35.20 |
| K. C. Jackson (*W. Province/W. Province B*) | 9 | 17 | 1 | 560 | 150 | 2 | 35.00 |

\* *Signifies not out.*

### BOWLING

(Qualification: 20 wickets)

| | O | M | R | W | BB | Avge |
|---|---|---|---|---|---|---|
| C. R. Matthews (*W. Province*) | 316 | 81 | 693 | 47 | 6-58 | 14.74 |
| S. D. Jack (*Transvaal*) | 311 | 73 | 865 | 54 | 8-51 | 16.01 |
| S. Jacobs (*Transvaal*) | 201.4 | 64 | 410 | 24 | 6-35 | 17.08 |
| B. C. Fourie (*Border*) | 168.1 | 44 | 450 | 24 | 5-28 | 18.75 |

| | O | M | R | W | BB | Avge |
|---|---|---|---|---|---|---|
| P. A. Rayment (*W. Province B*) | 221.2 | 69 | 394 | 21 | 3-33 | 18.76 |
| R. P. Snell (*Transvaal*) | 261.4 | 66 | 696 | 35 | 6-58 | 19.88 |
| P. S. de Villiers (*N. Transvaal*) | 288.1 | 82 | 670 | 33 | 6-51 | 20.30 |
| C. J. van Heerden (*OFS*) | 152.5 | 36 | 433 | 20 | 5-41 | 21.65 |
| T. G. Shaw (*E. Province*) | 392.1 | 135 | 883 | 40 | 5-33 | 22.07 |
| S. J. S. Kimber (*Natal/Natal B*) | 285.3 | 55 | 861 | 39 | 4-26 | 22.07 |
| R. K. McGlashan (*Natal/Natal B*) | 164.5 | 48 | 484 | 21 | 5-104 | 23.04 |
| R. E. Bryson (*E. Province*) | 257 | 64 | 654 | 28 | 5-32 | 23.35 |
| J. N. Maguire (*E. Province*) | 505 | 131 | 1,221 | 52 | 5-52 | 23.48 |
| C. J. P. G. van Zyl (*OFS*) | 309.4 | 71 | 800 | 32 | 4-38 | 25.00 |
| A. A. Donald (*OFS*) | 274.5 | 66 | 752 | 29 | 5-38 | 25.93 |
| B. M. McMillan (*W. Province*) | 215 | 52 | 551 | 21 | 5-45 | 26.23 |
| W. F. Morris (*N. Transvaal*) | 224.2 | 55 | 633 | 24 | 6-78 | 26.37 |
| T. Bosch (*N. Transvaal*) | 348.5 | 49 | 1,109 | 42 | 7-75 | 26.40 |
| P. W. E. Rawson (*Natal*) | 346.5 | 99 | 873 | 30 | 4-64 | 29.10 |
| R. A. Lyle (*Natal/Natal B*) | 291.2 | 74 | 737 | 25 | 5-45 | 29.48 |
| M. W. Pringle (*W. Province/W. Province B*) | 304.3 | 75 | 841 | 28 | 4-44 | 30.03 |
| B. N. Schultz (*E. Province/E. Province B*) | 273 | 54 | 799 | 25 | 4-22 | 31.96 |
| T. J. Packer (*Natal*) | 243 | 52 | 678 | 21 | 3-32 | 32.28 |
| E. O. Simons (*W. Province*) | 309 | 79 | 770 | 23 | 4-16 | 33.47 |
| S. Elworthy (*N. Transvaal*) | 297.1 | 34 | 1,131 | 33 | 5-37 | 34.27 |
| A. L. Hobson (*N. Province/W. Province B*) | 305.2 | 74 | 851 | 22 | 5-61 | 38.68 |
| N. W. Pretorius (*OFS/OFS B*) | 255 | 32 | 978 | 25 | 5-60 | 39.12 |
| O. Henry (*OFS/OFS B*) | 478.3 | 106 | 1,066 | 26 | 4-91 | 41.00 |
| D. B. Rundle (*W. Province*) | 358.2 | 92 | 985 | 21 | 3-58 | 46.90 |

## CASTLE CURRIE CUP, 1990-91

| | | | | | Bonus Points | | Total |
|---|---|---|---|---|---|---|---|
| | Played | Won | Lost | Drawn | Batting | Bowling | Pts |
| Western Province | 10 | 4 | 1 | 5 | 24 | 36 | 120 |
| Transvaal | 10 | 2 | 3 | 5 | 29 | 44 | 103 |
| Natal | 10 | 2 | 2 | 6 | 24 | 36 | 90 |
| Eastern Province | 10 | 1 | 1 | 8 | 33 | 39 | 81 |
| Northern Transvaal | 10 | 1 | 2 | 7 | 27 | 39 | 81 |
| Orange Free State | 10 | 0 | 1 | 9 | 24 | 38 | 62 |

*In the following scores, \* by the name of a team indicates that they won the toss.*

At St George's Park, Port Elizabeth, October 13, 14, 15. Drawn. Eastern Province\* 280 for six dec. (T. N. Lazard 49, K. C. Wessels 58, M. Michau 69, D. J. Callaghan 68; D. Norman three for 67); Natal 313 for seven (A. C. Hudson 63, P. P. H. Trimborn 31, K. J. Hughes 74, J. N. Rhodes 49; B. N. Schultz four for 91). *Eastern Province 6 pts, Natal 6 pts.*

At Springbok Park, Bloemfontein, October 13, 14, 15. Drawn. Western Province\* 324 for six dec. (L. Seeff 53, G. Kirsten 57, D. J. Cullinan 102 not out, E. O. Simons 45; C. J. P. G. van Zyl three for 50) and 84 for two (L. Seeff 38 not out); Orange Free State 471 (W. J. Cronje 61, L. J. Wilkinson 167, C. J. van Heerden 36, O. Henry 88, G. J. Parsons 52 not out). *Orange Free State 6 pts, Western Province 5 pts.*

At Wanderers, Johannesburg, October 13, 14, 15. Transvaal won by four wickets. Northern Transvaal 154 (M. Yachad 48; S. D. Jack five for 50) and 105 (H. A. Page three for 14, R. P. Snell three for 26, C. E. B. Rice three for 32); Transvaal\* 93 (T. Bosch four for 28, S. Elworthy four for 37) and 169 for six (N. E. Wright 68 not out; S. Elworthy three for 55). *Transvaal 20 pts, Northern Transvaal 7 pts.*

At Kingsmead, Durban, October 19, 20, 21. Western Province won by 4 runs. Western Province 91 for two dec. (L. Seeff 36 not out, D. J. Cullinan 35) and 207 for six dec. (B. M. McMillan 80 not out, D. B. Rundle 48 not out; T. J. Packer three for 35); Natal* 91 for three dec. (A. C. Hudson 35, K. D. Robinson 35) and 203 (K. J. Hughes 65, J. N. Rhodes 57; B. M. McMillan five for 45, D. B. Rundle three for 58). *Western Province 16 pts, Natal 1 pt.*

At Centurion Park, Verwoerdburg, October 19, 20, 21. Drawn. Northern Transvaal 322 for three dec. (M. D. Haysman 136 not out, L. P. Vorster 141) and 251 for five dec. (M. Yachad 118, V. F. du Preez 54, M. J. R. Rindel 40 not out; J. N. Maguire three for 93); Eastern Province* 281 for two dec. (T. N. Lazard 95, M. C. Venter 129) and 167 for five (D. J. Callaghan 84 not out, D. J. Richardson 42 not out; S. Elworthy three for 47). *Northern Transvaal 5 pts, Eastern Province 5 pts.*

At Springbok Park, Bloemfontein, October 19, 20, 21. Drawn. Orange Free State* 124 (C. J. van Heerden 46; S. D. Jack four for 17) and 480 (J. M. Arthur 94, L. J. Wilkinson 163, W. J. Cronje 95, C. J. P. G van Zyl 69; R. P. Snell three for 107); Transvaal 349 (S. J. Cook 109, P. J. Botha 71, R. F. Pienaar 39, B. McBride 43 not out; O. Henry four for 91) and 144 for eight (C. E. B. Rice 33; A. A. Donald five for 39). *Orange Free State 6 pts, Transvaal 10 pts.*

At St George's Park, Port Elizabeth, December 26, 27, 28. Drawn. Eastern Province* 300 for eight dec. (M. W. Rushmere 111, T. G. Shaw 39; C. J. P. G van Zyl three for 55) and 207 for five dec. (P. G. Amm 84, D. J. Richardson 30 not out; N. Boje three for 60); Orange Free State 287 (P. J. R. Steyn 31, W. J. Cronje 33, C. J. van Heerden 54, O. Henry 59, P. J. L. Radley 35; T. G. Shaw five for 69) and 172 for seven (P. J. R. Steyn 79; T. G. Shaw five for 61). *Eastern Province 7 pts, Orange Free State 5 pts.*

At Wanderers, Johannesburg, December 26, 27, 28. Natal won by six wickets. Transvaal 270 for six dec. (N. E. Wright 61, P. J. Botha 32, R. F. Pienaar 32, S. B. Smith 40, C. E. B. Rice 36) and 124 (T. J. Packer three for 32, R. A. Lyle three for 35, S. J. S. Kimber three for 36); Natal* 197 (R. M. Bentley 54, J. N. Rhodes 40, E. L. R. Stewart 37, Extras 37; R. P. Snell six for 58) and 199 for four (A. C. Hudson 47, R. M. Bentley 33, J. N. Rhodes 48 not out; S. D. Jack three for 56). *Natal 20 pts, Transvaal 9 pts.*

At Newlands, Cape Town, December 26, 27, 28. Drawn. Northern Transvaal* 235 (M. D. Haysman 72, L. J. Barnard 33, S. Elworthy 45; M. W. Pringle four for 55, C. R. Matthews three for 15) and 269 for six dec. (M. D. Haysman 135 not out); Western Province 276 (G. Kirsten 113, B. M. McMillan 45, C. R. Matthews 43 not out; P. S. de Villiers four for 40, W. F. Morris three for 57) and 218 for nine (G. Kirsten 31, D. J. Cullinan 52, B. M. McMillan 44; W. F. Morris three for 51). *Western Province 9 pts, Northern Transvaal 7 pts.*

At Newlands, Cape Town, December 31, January 1, 2. Drawn. Western Province* 352 for seven dec. (K. C. Jackson 113, B. M. McMillan 127, E. O. Simons 38, D. B. Rundle 35 not out; R. P. Snell three for 71) and 148 (B. M. McMillan 41; R. P. Snell four for 45); Transvaal 295 for six dec. (R. F. Pienaar 102, C. E. B. Rice 99 not out; M. W. Pringle three for 70, C. R. Matthews three for 76) and 126 for five (R. F. Pienaar 53 not out). *Western Province 7 pts, Transvaal 6 pts.*

At Kingsmead, Durban, December 31, January 1, 2. Drawn. Natal* 276 for six dec. (I. B. Hobson 40, R. M. Bentley 33, J. N. Rhodes 42 retired hurt, E. L. R. Stewart 76 not out; O. Henry three for 104) and 212 (R. M. Bentley 67, P. W. E. Rawson 41, J. N. Rhodes 58; A. A. Donald three for 67); Orange Free State 255 for seven dec. (J. M. Arthur 46, W. J. Cronje 100 not out, Extras 39) and 178 for seven (W. J. Cronje 42, L. J. Wilkinson 44, G. J. Parsons 39; P. W. E. Rawson three for 75). *Natal 6 pts, Orange Free State 7 pts.*

At St George's Park, Port Elizabeth, December 31, January 1, 2. Drawn. Eastern Province* 363 for three dec. (T. N. Lazard 113, K. C. Wessels 197) and 227 for seven dec. (T. N. Lazard 38, K. C. Wessels 37, M. W. Rushmere 68 not out, T. G. Shaw 39; S. Elworthy three for 79); Northern Transvaal 326 for eight dec. (M. Yachad 60, M. J. R. Rindel 105, S. Elworthy 30 not out; T. G. Shaw four for 77, J. N. Maguire three for 82) and 128 for three (M. Yachad 77). *Eastern Province 8 pts, Northern Transvaal 3 pts.*

At Wanderers, Johannesburg, January 5, 6, 7. Drawn. Orange Free State 254 (P. J. R. Steyn 92, C. J. P. G. van Zyl 77; S. D. Jack five for 47, C. E. Eksteen three for 55) and 245 for five dec. (P. J. R. Steyn 44, L. J. Wilkinson 76, W. J. Cronje 58, C. J. van Heerden 37 not out; S. D. Jack three for 26); Transvaal* 253 for seven dec. (N. E. Wright 44, S. J. Cook 37, R. F. Pienaar 30, C. E. B. Rice 33, H. A. Page 31 not out) and 112 for six (S. J. Cook 30). *Transvaal 9 pts, Orange Free State 6 pts.*

At Centurion Park, Verwoerdburg, January 5, 6, 7. Northern Transvaal won by eight wickets. Western Province 142 (E. O. Simons 44 not out, C. R. Matthews 30; P. S. de Villiers three for 30, T. Bosch three for 37) and 365 (K. C. Jackson 39, H. H. Gibbs 35, E. O. Simons 83, C. R. Matthews 105; T. Bosch four for 62); Northern Transvaal* 238 (M. Yachad 52, L. J. Barnard 79; C. R. Matthews six for 58, M. W. Pringle four for 67) and 273 for two (M. Yachad 115, M. J. R. Rindel 115 not out). *Northern Transvaal 23 pts, Western Province 6 pts.*

At Jan Smuts Stadium, Pietermaritzburg, January 5, 6, 7. Drawn. Eastern Province 267 for eight dec. (T. N. Lazard 97, K. C. Wessels 34, D. J. Richardson 50) and 174 for six dec. (P. G. Amm 32, M. C. Venter 51, D. J. Richardson 51 not out); Natal* 192 (I. B. Hobson 54, J. Payn 49; R. E. Bryson five for 32, T. G. Shaw four for 35) and 33 for no wkt. *Natal 5 pts, Eastern Province 8 pts.*

At Springbok Park, Bloemfontein, January 11, 12, 13. Drawn. Natal 221 (R. M. Bentley 66, K. J. Hughes 38, T. J. Packer 31 not out; C. J. P. G. van Zyl four for 38, G. J. Parsons three for 56) and 179 (E. L. R. Stewart 71; C. J. van Heerden three for 14, including a hat-trick); Orange Free State* 142 (C. J. van Heerden 56; R. A. Lyle five for 45, P. W. E. Rawson three for 37) and 220 for eight (J. M. Arthur 72, C. J. van Heerden 65 not out; P. W. E. Rawson four for 64). *Orange Free State 6 pts, Natal 8 pts.*

At Newlands, Cape Town, January 11, 12, 13. Drawn. Eastern Province 171 (D. J. Callaghan 48, D. J. Richardson 40 not out; B. M. McMillan three for 25, C. R. Matthews five for 30) and 289 for seven dec. (P. G. Amm 39, M. W. Rushmere 79, D. J. Richardson 39; E. O. Simons three for 77); Western Province* 220 (A. P. Kuiper 58; B. N. Schultz three for 51, J. N. Maguire five for 56) and 113 for seven (D. J. Cullinan 58; B. N. Schultz four for 22). *Western Province 8 pts, Eastern Province 7 pts.*

At Centurion Park, Verwoerdburg, January 11, 12, 13. Drawn. Transvaal 400 for eight dec. (S. J. Cook 44, N. E. Wright 43, S. B. Smith 40, C. E. B. Rice 48, S. Jacobs 56, D. R. Laing 101 not out, Extras 30; P. S. de Villiers three for 58, S. Elworthy three for 90) and 203 for two dec. (S. J. Cook 41, N. E. Wright 93, R. F. Pienaar 54 not out); Northern Transvaal* 252 for seven dec. (M. Yachad 65, L. P. Vorster 39, M. J. R. Rindel 57; S. Jacobs three for 41) and 61 for three. *Northern Transvaal 5 pts, Transvaal 7 pts.*

At St George's Park, Port Elizabeth, January 18, 19, 20. Drawn. Western Province 246 for eight dec. (G. Kirsten 58, K. C. Jackson 53, D. J. Cullinan 38, B. M. McMillan 32; J. N. Maguire three for 43) and 233 for seven dec. (K. C. Jackson 50, D. J. Cullinan 74, E. O. Simons 35; T. G. Shaw three for 49); Eastern Province* 251 for two dec. (P. G. Amm 90, K. C. Wessels 107) and 177 for six (P. G. Amm 90, D. J. Richardson 34). *Eastern Province 8 pts, Western Province 4 pts.*

At Kingsmead, Durban, January 18, 19, 20. Drawn. Natal 347 for seven dec. (A. C. Hudson 184 not out, I. B. Hobson 55, E. L. R. Stewart 32; S. D. Jack three for 65, C. E. Eksteen three for 96) and 214 for nine dec. (A. C. Hudson 67, J. Payn 34; C. E. Eksteen three for 83); Transvaal* 264 for eight dec. (S. J. Cook 67, S. Jacobs 101 not out, C. E. B. Rice 43; P. W. E. Rawson three for 69) and 37 for one. *Natal 8 pts, Transvaal 6 pts.*

At Springbok Park, Bloemfontein, January 18, 19, 20. Drawn. Northern Transvaal* 293 (M. D. Haysman 57, L. P. Vorster 34, L. J. Barnard 36, R. V. Jennings 31, W. F. Morris 48 not out, Extras 30; C. J. P. G. van Zyl three for 54) and 217 for eight dec. (M. Yachad 92, W. F. Morris 31 not out); Orange Free State 279 (W. J. Cronje 101, C. J. P. G. van Zyl 68, Extras 37; P. S. de Villiers six for 51, T. Bosch three for 92) and 210 for eight (J. M. Arthur 62, W. J. Cronje 40, O. Henry 33; T. Bosch four for 68, W. F. Morris four for 64). *Orange Free State 9 pts, Northern Transvaal 9 pts.*

At Centurion Park, Verwoerdburg, February 22, 23, 24. Drawn. Northern Transvaal 89 (R. J. Varner five for 28, S. J. S. Kimber four for 26) and 368 for nine dec. (M. Yachad 179, M. D. Haysman 49, M. J. R. Rindel 32, L. J. Barnard 35; R. M. Bentley three for 48, T. J. Packer three for 63); Natal* 203 (J. N. Rhodes 57, R. J. Varner 33; P. S. de Villiers five for 61, T. Bosch three for 54) and 214 for nine (A. C. Hudson 31, E. L. R. Stewart 47; W. F. Morris six for 78). *Northern Transvaal 5 pts, Natal 8 pts.*

At Springbok Park, Bloemfontein, February 22, 23, 24. Drawn. Orange Free State 249 for nine dec. (W. J. Cronje 43, C. J. van Heerden 30, C. J. P. G. van Zyl 54, O. Henry 34; J. N. Maguire five for 67) and 214 for nine dec. (J. M. Arthur 61, C. J. P. G. van Zyl 41; T. G. Shaw four for 63, J. N. Maguire three for 89); Eastern Province* 216 (P. G. Amm 39, M. C. Venter 40, K. C. Wessels 56; A. A. Donald four for 67, C. J. P. G. van Zyl three for 49) and 207 for six (P. G. Amm 52, M. W. Rushmere 57; C. J. P. G. van Zyl three for 43). *Orange Free State 8 pts, Eastern Province 8 pts.*

At Wanderers, Johannesburg, February 22, 23, 24. Western Province won by 5 runs. Western Province* 148 (S. Jacobs six for 35) and 140 (R. P. Snell five for 43, S. D. Jack four for 46); Transvaal 151 (C. R. Matthews four for 19) and 132 (C. R. Matthews four for 25, B. M. McMillan four for 28). *Western Province 21 pts, Transvaal 6 pts.*

At Newlands, Cape Town, March 1, 2, 3. Western Province won by nine wickets. Natal 147 (R. M. Bentley 39; C. R. Matthews three for 22) and 121 (J. N. Rhodes 40; E. O. Simons four for 16); Western Province* 183 (G. Kirsten 46, M. F. Voss 30, B. M. McMillan 56 not out; S. J. S. Kimber four for 51) and 86 for one (G. Kirsten 38 not out, K. C. Jackson 36 not out). *Western Province 22 pts, Natal 6 pts.*

At Centurion Park, Verwoerdburg, March 1, 2, 3. Drawn. Northern Transvaal 281 for two dec. (R. V. Jennings 119, M. D. Haysman 124 not out) and 232 for six dec. (R. V. Jennings 79 not out, M. J. R. Rindel 77); Orange Free State* 178 (J. M. Arthur 38, G. F. J. Liebenberg 40, O. Henry 35; T. Bosch seven for 75) and 244 for seven (J. M. Arthur 48, W. J. Cronje 84, L. J. Wilkinson 47; W. F. Morris three for 44). *Northern Transvaal 9 pts, Orange Free State 3 pts.*

At Wanderers, Johannesburg, March 1, 2, 3. Eastern Province won by 175 runs. Eastern Province* 311 (P. G. Amm 32, K. C. Wessels 55, D. J. Callaghan 43, D. J. Richardson 68; R. P. Snell six for 80) and 153 for eight dec. (R. E. Veenstra 42; S. Jacobs three for 33, S. D. Jack three for 51); Transvaal 179 (S. J. Cook 32, N. E. Wright 37, S. B. Smith 38; J. N. Maguire five for 70) and 110 (T. G. Shaw three for 8, R. E. Bryson three for 33, J. N. Maguire three for 57). *Eastern Province 24 pts, Transvaal 7 pts.*

At St George's Park, Port Elizabeth, March 8, 9, 10. Transvaal won by 230 runs. Transvaal 227 (S. B. Smith 41, S. Jacobs 36, D. R. Laing 46 not out; R. E. Bryson five for 59, J. N. Maguire four for 88) and 245 (S. J. Cook 53, N. E. Wright 107; J. N. Maguire four for 52, R. E. Bryson three for 78); Eastern Province* 136 (S. Jacobs three for 25, S. D. Jack three for 27) and 106 (S. D. Jack eight for 51). *Transvaal 23 pts, Eastern Province 6 pts.*

At Kingsmead, Durban, March 8, 9, 10. Natal won by three wickets. Northern Transvaal* 270 for eight dec. (M. Yachad 100, M. J. R. Rindel 31, S. Elworthy 38 not out; R. K. McGlashan four for 105) and 222 for six dec. (R. V. Jennings 68, L. P. Vorster 53, M. J. R. Rindel 51 not out); Natal 245 (R. M. Bentley 73, S. J. S. Kimber 41, R. K. McGlashan 47 not out; S. Elworthy five for 37) and 248 for seven (A. C. Hudson 116 not out, I. B. Hobson 44, P. W. E. Rawson 31, Extras 37). *Natal 22 pts, Northern Transvaal 8 pts.*

At Newlands, Cape Town, March 8, 9, 10. Western Province won by 15 runs. Western Province* 199 (G. Kirsten 50, D. J. Cullinan 32; A. A. Donald three for 51, C. J. van Heerden five for 41) and 199 for eight dec. (G. Kirsten 35, E. O. Simons 30 not out, D. B. Rundle 39; N. W. Pretorius five for 60); Orange Free State 115 (O. Henry 36; C. R. Matthews four for 30) and 268 (P. J. R. Steyn 30, J. M. Arthur 35, C. J. van Heerden 57, O. Henry 31, A. A. Donald 46 not out; C. R. Matthews five for 48, D. B. Rundle three for 60). *Western Province 22 pts, Orange Free State 6 pts.*

## CURRIE CUP WINNERS

| | | | |
|---|---|---|---|
| 1889-90 | Transvaal | 1958-59 | Transvaal |
| 1890-91 | Griqualand West | 1959-60 | Natal |
| 1892-93 | Western Province | 1960-61 | Natal |
| 1893-94 | Western Province | 1962-63 | Natal |
| 1894-95 | Transvaal | 1963-64 | Natal |
| 1896-97 | Western Province | 1965-66 | Natal/Transvaal (Tied) |
| 1897-98 | Western Province | 1966-67 | Natal |
| 1902-03 | Transvaal | 1967-68 | Natal |
| 1903-04 | Transvaal | 1968-69 | Transvaal |
| 1904-05 | Transvaal | 1969-70 | Transvaal/W. Province (Tied) |
| 1906-07 | Transvaal | 1970-71 | Transvaal |
| 1908-09 | Western Province | 1971-72 | Transvaal |
| 1910-11 | Natal | 1972-73 | Transvaal |
| 1912-13 | Natal | 1973-74 | Natal |
| 1920-21 | Western Province | 1974-75 | Western Province |
| 1921-22 | Transvaal/Natal/W. Prov. (Tied) | 1975-76 | Natal |
| 1923-24 | Transvaal | 1976-77 | Natal |
| 1925-26 | Transvaal | 1977-78 | Western Province |
| 1926-27 | Transvaal | 1978-79 | Transvaal |
| 1929-30 | Transvaal | 1979-80 | Transvaal |
| 1931-32 | Western Province | 1980-81 | Natal |
| 1933-34 | Natal | 1981-82 | Western Province |
| 1934-35 | Transvaal | 1982-83 | Transvaal |
| 1936-37 | Natal | 1983-84 | Transvaal |
| 1937-38 | Natal/Transvaal (Tied) | 1984-85 | Transvaal |
| 1946-47 | Natal | 1985-86 | Western Province |
| 1947-48 | Natal | 1986-87 | Transvaal |
| 1950-51 | Transvaal | 1987-88 | Transvaal |
| 1951-52 | Natal | 1988-89 | Eastern Province |
| 1952-53 | Western Province | 1989-90 | E. Province/W. Province (Drawn) |
| 1954-55 | Natal | | |
| 1955-56 | Western Province | 1990-91 | Western Province |

## THE BOWL, 1990-91

| Section One | Played | Won | Lost | Drawn | Bonus Points Batting | Bonus Points Bowling | Total Pts |
|---|---|---|---|---|---|---|---|
| Western Province B ..... | 5 | 3 | 0 | 2 | 15 | 22 | 82 |
| Natal B .............. | 5 | 2 | 1 | 2 | 15 | 20 | 65 |
| Transvaal B ........... | 5 | 2 | 1 | 2 | 10 | 19 | 59 |
| Eastern Province B ...... | 5 | 1 | 1 | 3 | 14 | 19 | 48 |
| Orange Free State B ..... | 5 | 0 | 2 | 3 | 13 | 21 | 34 |
| Northern Transvaal B.... | 5 | 0 | 3 | 2 | 13 | 18 | 31 |

| Section Two | Played | Won | Lost | Drawn | Bonus Points Batting | Bonus Points Bowling | Total Pts |
|---|---|---|---|---|---|---|---|
| Border ................ | 4 | 2 | 0 | 2 | 15 | 20 | 65 |
| Boland ................ | 4 | 1 | 2 | 1 | 10 | 15 | 40 |
| Griqualand West........ | 4 | 1 | 2 | 1 | 7 | 13 | 35 |

*Final*: Border and Western Province B drew to share the Bowl.

At Durban, November 23, 24, 25. Western Province B won by ten wickets. Natal B* 204 (I. B. Hobson 32, E. L. R. Stewart 40; S. T. Jefferies six for 42) and 158 (J. Payn 35; A. L. Hobson five for 61); Western Province B 334 for eight dec. (P. W. Martin 40, F. B. Touzel 85, K. C. Jackson 150; D. N. Crookes five for 117) and 29 for no wkt. *Western Province B 23 pts, Natal B 5 pts.*

At Kimberley, November 30, December 1, 2. Boland won by three wickets. Griqualand West* 286 (W. E. Schonegevel 87, G. M. Charlesworth 51, D. G. Mills 74; C. W. Henderson four for 53, P. A. Koen three for 52) and 99 (C. W. Henderson four for 33, P. A. Koen three for 17, M. Erasmus three for 18); Boland 152 for seven dec. (R. Marais 43; I. M. Kidson six for 58) and 234 for seven (N. M. Snyman 37, M. S. van der Merwe 48, K. J. Bridgens 48, R. Marais 52; M. J. Cann three for 70, I. M. Kidson three for 86). *Boland 21 pts, Griqualand West 5 pts.*

At East London, December 7, 8, 9. Border won by an innings and 108 runs. Griqualand West* 130 (G. M. Charlesworth 62; B. C. Fourie five for 28) and 179 (G. F. J. Liebenberg 33, H. F. Wilson 55 not out; H. C. Lindenberg four for 53); Border 417 for five dec. (B. W. Lones 47, B. M. Osborne 50, P. N. Kirsten 74, E. N. Trotman 41, G. L. Long 91, D. H. Howell 57 not out, Extras 43). *Border 24 pts, Griqualand West 3 pts.*

At Port Elizabeth, December 10, 11, 12. Eastern Province B won by nine wickets. Northern Transvaal B* 191 (J. Groenewald 39, I. A. Hoffmann 45, A. M. Ferreira 32, Extras 33; R. E. Veenstra four for 34, J. R. Meyer three for 33) and 196 (M. B. Mare 55, D. O. Nosworthy 42; C. Roelofse five for 41, D. J. Ferrant four for 83); Eastern Province B 295 (M. C. Venter 42, G. C. Victor 93, D. J. Ferrant 40; D. W. McCosh five for 78) and 93 for one (M. C. Venter 42 not out, H. H. Donachie 37). *Eastern Province B 22 pts, Northern Transvaal B 7 pts.*

At Cape Town, December 10, 11, 12. Drawn. Western Province B* 339 for four dec. (F. B. Touzel 49, H. H. Gibbs 77, J. B. Commins 110 not out, T. J. Mitchell 30 not out; Extras 39) and 174 for nine dec. (L. F. Bleekers 75, T. J. Mitchell 39; N. E. Wright three for 58); Transvaal B 278 for six dec. (B. M. White 92, J. J. Strydom 97, Extras 35; D. G. Payne three for 36) and 140 for five (J. J. Strydom 55 not out, V. G. Cresswell 44 not out). *Western Province B 5 pts, Transvaal B 4 pts.*

At Pietermaritzburg, December 11, 12, 13. Natal B won by three wickets. Orange Free State B* 267 (E. J. Venter 55, J. M. Truter 51, N. Boje 44 retired hurt; R. K. McGlashan five for 104) and 175 (F. J. C. Cronje 52; S. J. S. Kimber three for 39, R. K. McGlashan three for 64); Natal B 297 (C. M. Casalis 44, J. Nel 43, J. Payn 89, A. Forde 44; N. Boje six for 100) and 146 for seven (J. Nel 55, J. Payn 36; F. J. C. Cronje three for 28). *Natal B 24 pts, Orange Free State B 8 pts.*

At Johannesburg, December 20, 21, 22. Drawn. Orange Free State B 275 (R. E. Cullinan 58, J. M. Truter 70, M. I. Gidley 37, Extras 33; G. D. Stevenson three for 57) and 220 for seven dec. (F. J. C. Cronje 48; J. D. du Toit three for 35); Transvaal B* 216 for seven dec. (B. M. White 35, P. J. Botha 33, D. R. Laing 31, V. G. Cresswell 51, C. M. Lister-James 33 not out; N. W. Pretorius three for 57) and 187 for five (P. L. Selsick 64, B. M. White 34, D. R. Laing 31). *Transvaal B 7 pts, Orange Free State B 6 pts.*

At Cape Town, December 20, 21, 22. Drawn. Eastern Province B* 234 (G. C. Victor 97, S. J. Palframan 33; S. T. Jefferies three for 59) and 258 for seven dec. (M. C. Venter 36, D. J. Ferrant 44, C. B. Rhodes 68 not out, Extras 36; P. A. Rayment three for 33); Western Province B 296 (F. B. Touzel 92, M. F. Voss 68; J. R. Meyer three for 48, R. E. Veenstra three for 56, C. Roelofse three for 80) and 193 for seven (F. B. Touzel 62, J. B. Commins 35). *Western Province B 8 pts, Eastern Province B 5 pts.*

At Verwoerdburg, December 20, 21, 22. Drawn. Northern Transvaal B 346 (M. B. Mare 170, I. A. Hoffmann 32; R. A. Lyle three for 82, S. J. S. Kimber three for 106) and 206 for six dec. (D. O. Nosworthy 85, A. M. Ferreira 33; D. N. Crookes three for 53); Natal B* 290 for seven dec. (C. M. Casalis 61, R. M. Bentley 62, J. Payn 34, D. N. Crookes 30, S. J. S. Kimber 35 not out, A. G. Small 38 not out; C. van Noordwyk three for 58) and 229 for seven (C. M. Casalis 36, J. Payn 32, A. J. Forde 84). *Northern Transvaal B 6 pts, Natal B 6 pts.*

At Bloemfontein, January 5, 6, 7. Drawn. Eastern Province B* 244 for nine dec. (H. H. Donachie 94, P. A. Amm 46; N Boje three for 55) and 149 for four (N. C. Johnson 58 not out, Extras 35); Orange Free State B 230 (O. Henry 65, N. Boje 77; J. R. Meyer three for 36). *Orange Free State B 8 pts, Eastern Province B 8 pts.*

At Constantia, January 5, 6, 7. Western Province B won by seven wickets. Western Province B* 289 for seven dec. (P. W. Martin 44, M. P. Stonier 31, P. A. H. Upton 100, T. J. Mitchell 57) and 108 for three (L. F. Bleekers 46, M. P. Stonier 34 not out); Northern Transvaal B 129 (B. J. Sommerville 35; A. J. McClement seven for 51) and 264 (M. B. Mare 88, I. A. Hoffmann 30, P. A. Tullis 37 not out; A. J. McClement six for 86). *Western Province B 24 pts, Northern Transvaal B 4 pts.*

At East London, January 5, 6, 7. Border won by an innings and 34 runs. Boland* 237 (W. S. Truter 55, N. M. Snyman 35, R. Marais 45, M. Erasmus 43; H. C. Lindenberg four for 43, I. L. Howell three for 48) and 192 (N. M. Snyman 51, M. S. van der Merwe 42; H. C. Lindenberg six for 35); Border 463 for seven dec. (B. M. Osborne 42, E. N. Trotman 61, G. L. Long 195, I. L. Howell 82, S. J. Base 47 not out). *Border 25 pts, Boland 5 pts.*

At Kimberley, January 19, 20, 21. Drawn. Griqualand West 162 (W. E. Schonegevel 42; P. N. Kirsten five for 40, I. L. Howell three for 18) and 158 (M. J. Cann 42, C. S. N. Marais 31; B. C. Fourie five for 41); Border* 179 (P. N. Kirsten 30, I. L. Howell 36; P. McLaren three for 60, I. M. Kidson five for 90) and 20 for two. *Griqualand West 7 pts, Border 7 pts.*

At Verwoerdburg, January 25, 26, 27. Drawn. Orange Free State B 285 for nine dec. (G. F. J. Liebenberg 50, R. E. Cullinan 37, J. M. Truter 42, C. F. Craven 44; G. W. Symmonds four for 67, I. A. Hoffmann three for 59) and 199 (E. J. Venter 33, M. I. Gidley 47, C. F. Craven 37; A. Geringer three for 37); Northern Transvaal B* 370 (P. H. Barnard 68, D. O. Nosworthy 81, A. Geringer 54, A. M. Ferreira 54; M. J. Karsten three for 62) and 99 for eight (D. O. Nosworthy 34; M. J. Karsten three for 22). *Northern Transvaal B 10 pts, Orange Free State B 6 pts.*

At Durban, January 25, 26. Natal B won by an innings and 52 runs. Natal B* 321 (C. M. Casalis 45, J. Payn 65, A. J. Forde 31, R. J. Varner 80; J. D. du Toit three for 31, S. A. Lurie three for 52); Transvaal B 97 (D. N. Crookes four for 18, S. J. S. Kimber three for 20, R. K. McGlashan three for 29) and 172 (M. J. Mitchley 35; R. K. McGlashan four for 66, S. J. S. Kimber three for 36). *Natal B 23 pts, Transvaal B 4 pts.*

At Vereeniging, February 8, 9, 10. Transvaal B won by five wickets. Northern Transvaal B 163 for eight dec. (P. H. Barnard 46, M. Ferreira 37; P. J. Botha three for 37, P. E. Smith three for 41) and 157 for six dec. (M. B. Mare 36, J. Groenewald 34; L. C. R. Jordaan four for 28); Transvaal B* 152 for four dec. (H. Engelbrecht 38, J. J. Strydom 48, M. J. Mitchley 39 not out) and 170 for five (J. J. Strydom 56, V. G. Cresswell 46 not out). *Transvaal B 21 pts, Northern Transvaal B 4 pts.*

At Bloemfontein, February 8, 9, 10. Western Province B won by 11 runs. Western Province B 169 (M. F. Voss 70; C. F. Craven six for 25) and 261 for eight dec. (F. B. Touzel 47, L. F. Bleekers 66, H. H. Gibbs 54; M. I. Gidley three for 51, M. J. Karsten three for 60); Orange Free State B* 136 (J. M. Truter 41; M. W. Pringle four for 44, A. L. Hobson three for 44) and 283 (R. A. Brown 55, G. F. J. Liebenberg 61, M. I. Gidley 57 not out, N. W. Pretorius 33; P. A. Rayment three for 44). *Western Province B 22 pts, Orange Free State B 6 pts.*

At Stellenbosch, February 9, 10, 11. Drawn. Border* 271 (B. W. Lones 118, E. N. Trotman 59; H. Barnard four for 64) and 238 (P. N. Kirsten 105, D. H. Howell 36; D. Smith four for 59, M. Erasmus three for 33); Boland 206 (N. M. Snyman 54, L. J. Koen 59, M. Erasmus 32 not out; P. N. Kirsten four for 7, B. C. Fourie three for 56) and 98 for six (W. S. Truter 42; I. L. Howell four for 29). *Boland 7 pts, Border 9 pts.*

At Port Elizabeth, February 15, 16, 17. Drawn. Natal B 161 (K. A. Forde 33, R. J. Thompson 41; R. E. Veenstra three for 36, K. G. Bauermeister three for 42) and 186 (A. J. Forde 44, D. N. Crookes 31; R. E. Veenstra four for 39, K. G. Bauermeister three for 57); Eastern Province B* 203 (M. Michau 36, P. C. Strydom 34, K. G. Bauermeister 40, R. E. Veenstra 36 not out; S. J. S. Kimber four for 39, R. J. Varner four for 62) and 139 for eight (P. A. Amm 46 not out; D. J. Pryke three for 43, S. J. S. Kimber three for 57). *Eastern Province B 8 pts, Natal B 7 pts.*

At Stellenbosch, February 22, 23, 24. Griqualand West won by five wickets. Boland* 332 for eight dec. (L. J. Koen 59, K. J. Bridgens 105, M. Erasmus 48, P. A. Koen 52; P. McLaren three for 42) and 247 for four dec. (L. J. Koen 177 not out, including a hundred before lunch); Griqualand West 289 for nine dec. (M. J. Cann 80, G. M. Charlesworth 83) and 293 for five (M. J. Cann 141, W. E. Schonegevel 48, G. M. Charlesworth 57; C. W. Henderson four for 108). *Griqualand West 20 pts, Boland 7 pts.*

At Port Elizabeth, March 1, 2, 3. Transvaal B won by ten wickets. Eastern Province B* 192 (N. C. Johnson 46, G. Victor 67; P. J. Botha three for 29) and 148 (J. P. Heath 35; T. C. Webster four for 38); Transvaal B 301 (P. J. Botha 39, J. J. Strydom 38, M. J. Mitchley 72, V. G. Cresswell 36, T. C. Webster 42 not out; K. G. Bauermeister three for 46) and 40 for no wkt. *Transvaal B 23 pts, Eastern Province B 5 pts.*

## Final

At East London, March 8, 9, 10, 11. Drawn. Border and Western Province B shared the Bowl. Western Province B 327 (T. N. Lazard 58, P. W. Martin 48, L. F. Bleekers 31, H. H. Gibbs 56, Extras 43; S. J. Base four for 84, B. C. Fourie three for 80) and 237 for eight dec. (J. B. Commins 104 not out, H. H. Gibbs 51; B. C. Fourie four for 75); Border* 200 (P. N. Kirsten 41, E. N. Trotman 44, D. H. Howell 55; D. G. Payne seven for 63) and 53 for two.

## OTHER FIRST-CLASS MATCHES

At Robertson, September 20, 21, 22. Eastern Province won by 156 runs. Eastern Province* 314 for four dec. (K. C. Wessels 96, M. W. Rushmere 88, M. Michau 51 not out, D. J. Callaghan 53 not out; J. G. de Villiers four for 64) and 181 for four dec. (M. C. Venter 34, D. J. Richardson 37, T. G. Shaw 40, K. C. Wessels 55 not out; P. A. Koen three for 37); Boland 181 (L. J. Koen 42, J. G. de Villiers 36; T. G. Shaw five for 33) and 158 (R. E. Bryson four for 40, T. G. Shaw three for 50, including a hat-trick).

At Worcester, October 5, 6, 7. Drawn. Western Province* 332 for eight dec. (G. Kirsten 189, D. J. Cullinan 42, R. J. Ryall 40 not out; P. A. Koen four for three dec. and 176 for three dec. (L. Seeff 30, D. J. Cullinan 36, B. M. McMillan 69 not out, E. O. Simons 33 not out); Boland 211 (M. Erasmus 47; E. O. Simons four for 19, C. R. Matthews three for 20) and 244 for six (W. S. Truter 56, R. Marais 32 not out, P. A. Koen 41 not out; A. L. Hobson three for 84).

## †NISSAN SHIELD

*(55 overs a side.)*

At King William's Town, October 27. Natal won by 145 runs. Natal* 363 for three (K. D. Robinson 151 not out, K. J. Hughes 119); Border Country Districts 218 for eight (K. Brown 32, J. J. Pearson 42, D. S Knott 32 not out).

At Kimberley, October 27. Boland won by two wickets. Griqualand West 222 for nine (G. F. J. Liebenberg 47, K. C. Dugmore 31; C. A. Lowe four for 62); Boland* 224 for eight (W. S. Truter 87, K. J. Bridgens 30; I. M. Kidson three for 38).

At Potchefstroom, October 27. Northern Transvaal won by eight wickets. Western Transvaal 218 for seven (J. Scholtz 100, H. P. Prinsloo 52); Northern Transvaal* 222 for two (M. Yachad 72, M. D. Haysman 66 not out, L. P. Vorster 54 not out).

At Empangeni, October 27. Eastern Province won by 269 runs. Eastern Province* 315 for three (K. C. Wessels 122, P. G. Amm 146); Natal Country Districts 46 (J. N. Maguire three for 7, R. J. McCurdy three for 12).

At Cradock, October 27. Western Province won by 167 runs. Western Province* 240 for seven (G. Kirsten 54, D. J. Cullinan 68; C. D. Handley three for 48); Eastern Province Country Districts 73 (E. O. Simons six for 8).

At Pietersburg, October 27. Transvaal won by 121 runs. Transvaal* 300 for two (S. J. Cook 140, P. J. Botha 105); Northern Transvaal Country Districts 179 for six (M. Dada 46, F. Kirsten 39, P. Lourens 44 not out; S. Jacobs three for 32).

At Vereeniging, October 27. Orange Free State won by 89 runs. Orange Free State 265 for six (J. M. Arthur 37, J. M. Truter 32, W. J. Cronje 57 not out, L. J. Wilkinson 32, O. Henry 32); Southern Transvaal Country Districts* 176 for nine (G. P. Bouwer 46, B. W. Marais 36, W. Engelbrecht 32; G. J. Parsons three for 33).

At Oudtshoorn, October 27. Border won by 141 runs. Border 260 for nine (B. W. Lones 113, G. L. Long 35; E. Kitching three for 56); Southern Cape* 119 (W. K. Watson three for 6).

## Quarter-finals

*First leg*: At Cape Town, November 3. Western Province won by six wickets. Boland 125 (E. O. Simons five for 20); Western Province* 129 for four (J. B. Commins 56 not out, A. P. Kuiper 40).

*First leg*: At Durban, November 4. Transvaal won by six wickets. Natal 105 (S. D. Jack three for 13, C. E. Eksteen three for 31); Transvaal* 106 for four (P. J. Botha 34, S. B. Smith 30).

*Second leg*: At Stellenbosch, November 10. Western Province won by 172 runs. Western Province* 235 for six (G. Kirsten 41, J. B. Commins 36, B. M. McMillan 40); Boland 63 (C. R. Matthews five for 11, M. W. Pringle three for 22).

*Second leg*: At Johannesburg, November 10. Natal won by 67 runs. Natal 211 for seven (J. N. Rhodes 59, P. W. E. Rawson 47 not out; H. A. Page three for 58); Transvaal* 144 (J. D. du Toit 41; P. W. E. Rawson three for 24).

*Third leg*: At Johannesburg, November 11. Transvaal won by 85 runs. Transvaal 236 for six (P. J. Botha 33, R. F. Pienaar 49, S. B. Smith 56, C. E. B. Rice 32); Natal* 151 (K. J. Hughes 31, J. N. Rhodes 34; H. A. Page three for 39, C. E. Eksteen three for 44).

*First leg*: At Port Elizabeth, November 17. Eastern Province won by 54 runs. Eastern Province* 247 for four (K. C. Wessels 146, P. G. Amm 45); Border 193 for seven (B. W. Lones 41, B. M. Osborne 55; R. E. Bryson three for 39).

*First leg*: At Verwoerdburg, November 18. Orange Free State won by three wickets. Northern Transvaal* 185 for nine (M. D. Haysman 56, M. J. R. Rindel 43; G. J. Parsons three for 33); Orange Free State 186 for seven (W. J. Cronje 78, C. J. van Heerden 51 not out; L. J. Barnard three for 10).

*Second leg*: At Bloemfontein, November 24. Orange Free State won by nine wickets. Northern Transvaal* 149 for nine (M. Yachad 34, M. D. Haysman 35; A. A. Donald three for 18); Orange Free State 153 for one (P. J. R. Steyn 72 not out, J. M. Arthur 51).

*Second leg*: At East London, November 24. Eastern Province won by 22 runs. Eastern Province* 222 for seven (P. G. Amm 30, K. C. Wessels 40, M. Michau 67); Border 200 (B. W. Lones 33, G. L. Long 65; R. J. McCurdy four for 49, J. N. Maguire three for 27).

## Semi-finals

*First leg*: At Bloemfontein, November 28. Transvaal won by seven wickets. Orange Free State 244 for nine (P. J. R. Steyn 94, W. J. Cronje 32, L. J. Wilkinson 31; C. E. B. Rice three for 47); Transvaal* 245 for three (S. J. Cook 124 not out, S. B. Smith 86 not out).

*First leg*: At Port Elizabeth, November 28. Western Province won on faster scoring-rate after rain ended play. Eastern Province* 234 for eight (K. C. Wessels 47, P. G. Amm 89, M. W. Rushmere 38; E. O. Simons four for 44); Western Province 172 for six (A. P. Kuiper 43 not out).

*Second leg*: At Johannesburg, December 1. Transvaal won by 54 runs. Transvaal* 191 (S. Jacobs 46, C. E. B. Rice 41; C. J. P. G. van Zyl four for 40); Orange Free State 137 (W. J. Cronje 40).

*Second leg*: At Cape Town, December 1. Eastern Province won by five wickets. Western Province 206 for nine (L. Seeff 36, D. J. Cullinan 61; B. N. Schultz three for 41); Eastern Province* 207 for five (P. G. Amm 101, D. J. Richardson 49 not out).

*Third leg*: At Cape Town, December 2. Eastern Province won by five wickets. Western Province* 204 for nine (A. P. Kuiper 36, J. J. E. Hardy 32, E. O. Simons 45; T. G. Shaw three for 31); Eastern Province 206 for five (M. W. Rushmere 79 not out, D. J. Richardson 47 not out).

# Final

At Port Elizabeth, December 15. Transvaal won by seven wickets. Eastern Province 180 for nine (K. C. Wessels 52, M. W. Rushmere 39; C. E. Eksteen three for 36); Transvaal* 183 for three (R. F. Pienaar 78 not out, S. B. Smith 53 not out).

# †BENSON AND HEDGES NIGHT SERIES

*(Day/night matches of 45 overs a side.)*

At Johannesburg, October 24. Transvaal won by six wickets. Natal 180 (A. C. Hudson 53; R. P. Snell four for 28); Transvaal* 184 for four (P. J. Botha 59, S. B. Smith 42, C. E. B. Rice 33 not out).

At Verwoerdburg, October 25. Northern Transvaal won by 55 runs. Northern Transvaal* 196 for six (M. J. R. Rindel 133 not out); Border 141 (T. Bosch three for 21, W. F. Morris three for 36).

At Port Elizabeth, October 31. Eastern Province won by 77 runs. Eastern Province* 168 for seven (P. G. Amm 55, M. W. Rushmere 46; M. W. Pringle four for 23); Western Province 91 (E. O. Simons 30; T. G. Shaw three for 8).

At Johannesburg, November 1. Transvaal won by seven wickets. Impalas* 160 for nine (W. S. Truter 35; S. D. Jack five for 20); Transvaal 162 for three (P. J. Botha 49, S. J. Cook 46).

At Durban, November 7. Western Province won by four wickets. Natal* 120 for nine (D. Norman 31 not out); Western Province 121 for six (L. Seeff 48).

At Virginia, November 8. Orange Free State won by seven wickets. Impalas* 208 for eight (M. J. Cann 53, L. J. Koen 54, G. C. Abbott 36 not out; C. J. P. G van Zyl three for 46); Orange Free State 211 for three (P. J. R. Steyn 84, L. J. Wilkinson 71 not out).

At Port Elizabeth, November 14. Eastern Province won by 13 runs. Eastern Province* 201 for three (K. C. Wessels 86, M. W. Rushmere 50, M. Michau 37 not out); Orange Free State 188 for six (P. J. R. Steyn 58, L. J. Wilkinson 48, B. T. Player 34 not out).

At Verwoerdburg, November 15. Northern Transvaal won by 53 runs. Northern Transvaal 223 for six (M. Yachad 40, M. D. Haysman 103 not out, L. J. Barnard 50); Impalas* 170 for six (G. M. Charlesworth 61, G. C. Abbott 56; T. Bosch three for 31).

At Cape Town, November 21. Western Province won by 58 runs. Western Province* 149 for eight (B. M. McMillan 56; P. S. de Villiers three for 37); Northern Transvaal 91 (M. W. Pringle three for 24).

At East London, November 22. Impalas won by 8 runs. Impalas* 195 for three (W. S. Truter 60, G. M. Charlesworth 94 not out); Border 187 for seven (B. W. Lones 43, P. N. Kirsten 98 not out).

At Verwoerdburg, December 10. Eastern Province won by nine wickets. Northern Transvaal* 209 for three (M. Yachad 104 not out, L. P. Vorster 56); Eastern Province 210 for one (K. C. Wessels 109 not out, P. G. Amm 61, M. W. Rushmere 31 not out).

At Bloemfontein, December 11. Natal won by five wickets. Orange Free State 131 for eight (J. M. Arthur 42); Natal* 134 for five (A. C. Hudson 54, J. N. Rhodes 32 not out).

At Johannesburg, December 12. Transvaal won by three wickets after rain had reduced their target to 212 off 39 overs. Western Province 244 for six (L. Seeff 48, K. C. Jackson 41, A. P. Kuiper 39, D. J. Cullinan 35); Transvaal* 215 for seven (C. E. B. Rice 68, R. F. Pienaar 37, S. Jacobs 33, R. P. Snell 32 not out; B. M. McMillan three for 27).

At East London, December 18. Transvaal won by eight wickets. Border 215 for three (B. M. Osborne 106, P. N. Kirsten 82); Transvaal* 216 for two (S. J. Cook 80, N. E. Wright 80, R. F. Pienaar 33 not out).

At Cape Town, December 19. Orange Free State won by two wickets. Western Province* 194 for eight (A. P. Kuiper 58); Orange Free State 195 for eight (P. J. R. Steyn 33, J. M. Arthur 73; P. A. Rayment four for 25, including a hat-trick).

At Port Elizabeth, December 20. Eastern Province won by four wickets. Border* 189 for eight (P. N. Kirsten 35, E. N. Trotman 53, G. L. Long 51; R. E. Bryson four for 37, R. J. McCurdy three for 34); Eastern Province 191 for six (P. G. Amm 33, K. C. Wessels 58, M. W. Rushmere 53 not out).

At Durban, December 21. Natal won by three wickets. Northern Transvaal* 178 for eight (L. P. Vorster 53, A. Geringer 57 not out, M. J. R. Rindel 35; P. W. E. Rawson three for 28, D. Norman three for 43); Natal 182 for seven (J. N. Rhodes 71).

At Johannesburg, January 25. Transvaal won by two wickets. Eastern Province 158 for eight (K. C. Wessels 59); Transvaal* 159 for eight (R. F. Pienaar 59).

At Bloemfontein, January 30. No result, rain having stopped play. Orange Free State 51 for one (P. J. R. Steyn 33 not out) v Northern Transvaal*.

At Durban, January 31. Natal won by eight wickets. Impalas 197 for seven (M. J. Cann 48, G. C. Abbott 40; T. J. Packer four for 32); Natal* 198 for two (A. C. Hudson 45, R. M. Bentley 72 not out, J. N. Rhodes 61 not out).

At East London, February 1. No result, rain having stopped play. Orange Free State 137 for five (P. J. R. Steyn 34, J. M. Arthur 36; W. K. Watson three for 47) v Border*.

At Cape Town, February 6. Western Province won by six wickets. Border* 194 for four (B. M. Osborne 30, E. N. Trotman 50 not out, C. S. Stirk 43 not out); Western Province 195 for four (G. Kirsten 49, D. J. Cullinan 47, A. P. Kuiper 48).

At Port Elizabeth, February 7. Eastern Province won by 40 runs. Eastern Province* 239 for four (M. W. Rushmere 98, D. J. Callaghan 86); Impalas 199 for seven (G. M. Charlesworth 100 not out, K. J. Bridgens 41).

At Verwoerdburg, February 8. Northern Transvaal won by 134 runs. Northern Transvaal 256 for eight (M. Yachad 104, L. J. Barnard 84; H. A. Page five for 45, S. D. Jack three for 27); Transvaal* 122 (H. A. Page 41; I. A. Hoffmann three for 20, W. F. Morris three for 46).

At Durban, February 13. Natal won by 16 runs. Natal* 189 for nine (A. C. Hudson 83, R. M. Bentley 33; R. E. Bryson four for 40); Eastern Province 173 (M. W. Rushmere 30, D. J. Callaghan 38; R. E. Bryson 38; D. N. Crookes three for 27).

At Cape Town, February 14. Western Province won by nine wickets. Impalas* 86 (B. M. McMillan three for 18); Western Province 87 for one (G. Kirsten 41 not out).

At Bloemfontein, February 15. No result, rain having stopped play. Transvaal 180 for eight (N. E. Wright 56, S. J. Cook 55); Orange Free State* 21 for two.

At East London, February 20. Border won by 40 runs. Border 173 for seven (B. M. Osborne 72 not out, E. N. Trotman 51); Natal* 133 (E. L. R. Stewart 42; B. M. Osborne five for 25).

## Semi-finals

*First leg:* At Durban, March 13. Natal won by three wickets. Transvaal 225 for three (S. J. Cook 71, R. F. Pienaar 106 not out); Natal* 229 for seven (A. C. Hudson 71, J. N. Rhodes 86 not out; S. D. Jack three for 40).

*First leg:* At Cape Town, March 20. Eastern Province won on run-rate, after rain had reduced Western Province's target to 156 off 42 overs. Eastern Province 167 for eight (K. C. Wessels 40, D. J. Callaghan 38; A. P. Kuiper three for 18); Western Province* 152 (A. P. Kuiper 79; T. G. Shaw three for 20).

*Second leg:* At Johannesburg, March 15. Natal won by six wickets in a match reduced by rain to 25 overs a side. Transvaal 158 for five (R. F. Pienaar 43, S. Jacobs 47); Natal* 161 for four (I. B. Hobson 32, R. M. Bentley 33, J. N. Rhodes 38).

*Second leg:* At Port Elizabeth, March 22. Western Province won by 6 runs. Western Province* 215 for six (K. C. Jackson 36, D. J. Cullinan 77, A. P. Kuiper 32); Eastern Province 209 for seven (K. C. Wessels 79, P. G. Amm 49).

*Third leg:* At Port Elizabeth, March 23. Western Province won by 16 runs. Western Province* 193 for eight (K. C. Jackson 36, D. J. Cullinan 32, M. F. Voss 33; R. J. McCurdy four for 48); Eastern Province 177 (M. W. Rushmere 72; E. O. Simons four for 32).

## Final

At Cape Town, March 27. Western Province won by six wickets. Natal 164 for eight (E. L. R. Stewart 49; E. O. Simons three for 27); Western Province* 168 for four (K. C. Jackson 58, A. P. Kuiper 43 not out).

---

## INTERNATIONAL YOUTH TOURNAMENT, 1991

The ninth International Youth Tournament was staged in Winnipeg, Canada, from July 8 to 16, 1991. For the first time England entered only one team, and to fit in with the Development of Excellence programme, it was decided to send an Under-18 side, even though the tournament was for cricketers aged under nineteen on January 1, 1991. Although they lost narrowly to The Netherlands, by 11 runs, and Bermuda had the same number of points in the final table, England retained the trophy won by England South in 1989 because they had beaten Bermuda, by 181 runs, earlier in the tournament. The matches, of 50 overs a side, were played on artificial pitches in high temperatures.

### Final Table

|                  | P | W | L | Pts |
|------------------|---|---|---|-----|
| England          | 5 | 4 | 1 | 8   |
| Bermuda          | 5 | 4 | 1 | 8   |
| The Netherlands  | 5 | 3 | 2 | 6   |
| Ireland          | 5 | 2 | 3 | 4   |
| Canada           | 5 | 1 | 4 | 2   |
| Denmark          | 5 | 1 | 4 | 2   |

The England party was: B. J. Aspital (*manager*), G. J. Saville (*assistant manager/coach*), J. N. Snape (Staffordshire, *captain*), W. P. C. Weston (Worcestershire, *vice-captain*), M. Bainbridge (Surrey), D. A. Blenkiron (Durham), M. Broadhurst (Yorkshire), G. Chapple (Lancashire), A. C. Cottam (Somerset), A. F. Haye (Leicestershire), R. A. Kettleborough (Yorkshire), J. S. Laney (Wiltshire), M. B. Loye (Northamptonshire), D. J. Robinson (Essex) and R. J. Rollins (Essex).

# CRICKET IN THE WEST INDIES, 1990-91

### By TONY COZIER

In winning the Red Stripe Cup for the first time since its inception in 1987-88, Barbados dominated the West Indian championship as they used to when it was contested as the Shell Shield. In its 21 years, Barbados were Shield champions twelve times, more than all the other teams put together, but it had been five years since their last title. However, the reversal of the unaccustomed trend was conclusive. Barbados won four of their five matches outright – by margins of eight wickets over Guyana, 258 runs over the 1990 champions, Leeward Islands, nine wickets over Trinidad & Tobago, and 222 runs over Jamaica – and finished 35 points clear of second-placed Trinidad & Tobago. But for crucial dropped catches on the last day of the drawn match against Windward Islands, they would most likely have emulated the Leewards' 100 per cent record of the previous season.

The success enjoyed by Barbados was a personal triumph for their captain, Desmond Haynes, who became the first batsman to score four centuries in one championship season, and established a record aggregate for the competition of 654 runs at an average of 109.00 in the five matches. He went on, in the matches against the touring Australians, to take his aggregate of first-class runs for the season past 1,000. The record had been held, for exactly a week, by Brian Lara, the 21-year-old left-hander from Trinidad & Tobago, whose consistency had brought him seven scores over 60 in his ten innings, including one century, and 627 runs, which surpassed the 572 scored in the 1983-84 Shell Shield by Ralston Otto of Leeward Islands. Ironically, Otto lost not only his record but also his place in the Leewards team in 1991.

Haynes's influence on Barbados extended to the selection room, where he instigated a policy of introducing new players into a team which had carried eight men over 30 the previous season. It meant dropping such worthy stalwarts as Franklyn Stephenson, the Nottinghamshire all-rounder, Thelston Payne, the left-handed batsman and reserve wicket-keeper, who had made six tours with the West Indians, and George Linton, a leg-spinner. As it turned out, those who took their places fully vindicated the policy. Anderson Cummins, a lively 24-year-old who would hardly have played a game but for Stephenson's exclusion, was the leading fast bowler in the Cup with 23 wickets at 19 each. These included, in the space of an hour, Test batsmen Vivian Richards, Richie Richardson and Keith Arthurton on the way to the victory over the Leewards. Sam Skeete, 21, who had led West Indies' attack in the Youth World Cup in Australia in 1987-88, bowled as fast as anyone for 21 wickets in his first full season. With Malcolm Marshall, back to full fitness and clearly enthusiastic, taking 22 wickets at 15.22 each, and Ezra Moseley producing two telling returns against the Leewards and Jamaica, Barbados possessed the penetration that allowed only one team, last-placed Windward Islands, a total of more than 300.

A new, young batsman was to the fore as well. Philo Wallace, a tall, powerfully built twenty-year-old opener, showed exciting promise with 135 off 191 balls against the Leewards, the first of Barbados's eight centuries, and finished with an average of 37.14 from 260 runs. The wicket-keeping of Courtney Browne, also twenty and in his first season, gave added weight to an overdue optimism about Barbados cricket. It had gone through lean times in recent years, to the extent that it failed to place a single player in the West Indian B team to Zimbabwe in 1989. Further evidence of a revival came later, in August 1991, when the Barbados youth team emulated the seniors by winning the annual Northern Telecom youth championships in Jamaica.

Preceding the important home series against Australia, and the later tour to England in the summer, the Red Stripe Cup matches offered an ideal chance to those challenging for places in the West Indies team. But familiar names dominated the averages. Haynes, who had led the West Indians on the tour of Pakistan in Richards's enforced absence a few weeks earlier, and Lara, who had replaced Richards in the batting order there, set new standards of run-scoring. No-one else, however, could pass 400, and those with more than 300 runs were all West Indies' representatives at one level or another. Carl Hooper of Guyana (362), Richie Richardson of the Leewards (337), Gus Logie of Trinidad & Tobago (335) and Phil Simmons of Trinidad & Tobago (344) were Test players; Clayton Lambert of Guyana (383) and Jimmy Adams of Jamaica (357), both left-handers, were B team representatives.

Although Marshall and his two young accomplices, Cummins and Skeete, collected more than twenty wickets each for Barbados, the only others to attain that standard were three well-established campaigners. Clyde Butts, Guyana's consistent off-spinner, was the highest wicket-taker with 26, and became the second bowler to pass 200 wickets in regional cricket, the other being the Trinidad & Tobago off-spinner, Ranjie Nanan. Curtly Ambrose of the Leewards and Patrick Patterson of Jamaica, both to play significant roles in the Tests against Australia, each had twenty Red Stripe wickets.

Although the Windwards – for whom the St Vincent-born Neil Williams of England was their only Test player – finished bottom of the table, were the only side to deny Barbados victory. In their second innings of that match John Eugene, an exciting twenty-year-old right-hander, scored a maiden century. Trinidad & Tobago were revived after several poor seasons, mainly by the batting of Lara but also by the captaincy, for the first time, of Logie. He instilled a new self-confidence in his team which helped them overcome the absence, after one match, of their West Indies fast bowler, Ian Bishop. Bishop suffered a back injury which kept him out of the series against Australia and the tour of England.

Jamaica, so badly let down by their batting that there was not one century in their five Cup matches, and no total higher than 268, were just above the Windwards in the Cup standings. But they did have the consolation of winning the Geddes Grant Shield in the one-day tournament, beating the Leewards in a thrilling final in front of a packed crowd at Sabina Park. Richards's throw from cover, attempting a run-out off the fifth ball of the final over, produced four overthrows that settled the result.

New ground was broken in August 1990 with the first tour of the Caribbean by an official Australian youth team. There were three "Tests", in Jamaica, Barbados and Guyana, and the Australians also had matches against Jamaica, Leeward Islands, Barbados and Guyana. Unbeaten throughout, the Australians were stronger, more mature and better prepared than their West Indian counterparts, although they were favoured by a variance in the age limit. While the Australian captain, Jamie Cox, was 21 and some of his players were over 20, the West Indians observed an under-20 limit.

## FIRST-CLASS AVERAGES, 1990-91

### BATTING

(Qualification: 250 runs)

| | M | I | NO | R | HI | 100s | Avge |
|---|---|---|---|---|---|---|---|
| D. L. Haynes (*Barbados*) | 10 | 18 | 4 | 1,066 | 146 | 5 | 76.14 |
| B. C. Lara (*T & T*) | 8 | 15 | 1 | 778 | 122* | 1 | 55.57 |
| J. Eugene (*Windward I.*) | 4 | 7 | 0 | 346 | 111 | 1 | 49.42 |
| R. B. Richardson (*Leeward I.*) | 11 | 18 | 1 | 834 | 182 | 2 | 49.05 |
| R. A. Harper (*Guyana*) | 5 | 8 | 2 | 289 | 94 | 0 | 48.16 |
| C. G. Greenidge (*Barbados*) | 9 | 14 | 1 | 616 | 226 | 2 | 47.38 |
| C. B. Lambert (*Guyana*) | 6 | 11 | 1 | 467 | 104 | 2 | 46.70 |
| A. L. Logie (*T & T*) | 10 | 17 | 4 | 596 | 116* | 1 | 45.84 |
| J. C. Adams (*Jamaica*) | 8 | 16 | 4 | 537 | 87 | 0 | 44.75 |
| K. L. T. Arthurton (*Leeward I.*) | 7 | 12 | 2 | 407 | 93 | 0 | 40.70 |
| P. V. Simmons (*T & T*) | 8 | 15 | 0 | 585 | 122 | 1 | 39.00 |
| C. L. Hooper (*Guyana*) | 10 | 16 | 1 | 561 | 102 | 1 | 37.40 |
| P. A. Wallace (*Barbados*) | 5 | 9 | 0 | 312 | 135 | 1 | 34.66 |
| S. C. Williams (*Leeward I.*) | 6 | 10 | 0 | 318 | 97 | 0 | 31.80 |
| C. A. Best (*Barbados*) | 7 | 13 | 2 | 347 | 119* | 1 | 31.54 |
| I. V. A. Richards (*Leeward I.*) | 10 | 15 | 2 | 405 | 112 | 1 | 31.15 |
| P. J. L. Dujon (*Jamaica*) | 10 | 17 | 2 | 467 | 77* | 0 | 31.13 |
| M. D. Marshall (*Barbados*) | 9 | 12 | 2 | 305 | 89 | 0 | 30.50 |
| S. Ragoonath (*T & T*) | 6 | 11 | 0 | 310 | 80 | 0 | 28.18 |
| D. S. Morgan (*Jamaica*) | 6 | 12 | 0 | 267 | 42 | 0 | 22.25 |
| R. C. Haynes (*Jamaica*) | 7 | 13 | 0 | 262 | 54 | 0 | 20.15 |

\* *Signifies not out.*

### BOWLING

(Qualification: 15 wickets)

| | O | M | R | W | BB | Avge |
|---|---|---|---|---|---|---|
| M. D. Marshall (*Barbados*) | 276.4 | 49 | 772 | 43 | 4-27 | 17.95 |
| A. C. Cummins (*Barbados*) | 158.5 | 26 | 480 | 24 | 4-26 | 20.00 |
| K. C. G. Benjamin (*Leeward I.*) | 148.2 | 24 | 460 | 21 | 7-51 | 21.90 |
| B. P. Patterson (*Jamaica*) | 304.3 | 46 | 954 | 43 | 5-57 | 22.18 |
| H. A. G. Anthony (*Leeward I.*) | 130.5 | 19 | 455 | 20 | 5-23 | 22.75 |
| C. G. Butts (*Guyana*) | 265.5 | 61 | 604 | 26 | 6-62 | 23.23 |
| E. A. Moseley (*Barbados*) | 141.5 | 20 | 401 | 17 | 6-52 | 23.58 |
| C. E. L. Ambrose (*Leeward I.*) | 382.5 | 90 | 920 | 38 | 6-10 | 24.21 |
| N. F. Williams (*Windward I.*) | 119 | 8 | 405 | 16 | 5-52 | 25.31 |
| S. M. Skeete (*Barbados*) | 156 | 21 | 541 | 21 | 6-44 | 25.76 |
| C. A. Walsh (*Jamaica*) | 351.2 | 57 | 893 | 34 | 4-14 | 26.26 |
| E. A. E. Baptiste (*Leeward I.*) | 188.4 | 36 | 475 | 18 | 6-68 | 26.38 |
| A. H. Gray (*T & T*) | 178 | 37 | 479 | 18 | 4-44 | 26.61 |
| I. B. A. Allen (*Windward I.*) | 168 | 17 | 522 | 18 | 7-48 | 29.00 |
| N. O. Perry (*Jamaica*) | 171 | 33 | 464 | 16 | 5-30 | 29.00 |
| R. Nanan (*T & T*) | 230 | 75 | 448 | 15 | 5-49 | 29.86 |
| C. L. Hooper (*Guyana*) | 318.5 | 69 | 787 | 18 | 4-48 | 43.72 |
| R. C. Haynes (*Jamaica*) | 263.2 | 40 | 710 | 16 | 3-92 | 44.37 |

## RED STRIPE CUP, 1990-91

| | Played | Won | Lost | Drawn | 1st-inns Points | Points |
|---|---|---|---|---|---|---|
| Barbados .......... | 5 | 4 | 0 | 1 | 4 | 72 |
| Trinidad & Tobago ... | 5 | 1 | 1 | 3 | 9 | 37 |
| Guyana ........... | 5 | 1 | 1 | 3 | 8 | 36 |
| Leeward Islands ...... | 5 | 1 | 1 | 3 | 8 | 36 |
| Jamaica ........... | 5 | 0 | 2 | 3 | 8 | 20 |
| Windward Islands .... | 5 | 0 | 2 | 3 | 0 | 12 |

Win = 16 pts; 1st-innings lead in drawn match = 8 pts; 1st-innings deficit in drawn match = 4 pts; 1st-innings lead in lost match = 5 pts.

*In the following scores, * by the name of a team indicates that they won the toss.*

At Queen's Park Oval, Port-of-Spain, Trinidad, January 4, 5, 6, 7. Drawn. Trinidad & Tobago* 269 (S. Ragoonath 47, A. L. Logie 30, D. I. Mohammed 67, D. Williams 57; E. A. E. Baptiste six for 68) and 196 (B. C. Lara 71; N. C. Guishard three for 15); Leeward Islands 308 (S. C. Williams 35, A. C. H. Walsh 31, R. B. Richardson 88, L. L. Harris 43, W. K. M. Benjamin 35 not out; A. H. Gray four for 71). *Trinidad & Tobago 4 pts, Leeward Islands 8 pts.*

At Kensington Oval, Bridgetown, Barbados, January 11, 12, 13, 14. Barbados won by eight wickets. Guyana 182 (S. Dhaniram 45, S. N. Mohammed 35; A. C. Cummins four for 64, M. D. Marshall four for 27) and 242 (S. Dhaniram 57, C. L. Hooper 102; S. M. Skeete six for 44); Barbados* 319 (C. G. Greenidge 67, R. I. C. Holder 50, M. D. Marshall 89, Extras 36; B. St A. Browne four for 105) and 106 for two (D. L. Haynes 40 not out). *Barbados 16 pts.*

At Sabina Park, Kingston, Jamaica, January 11, 12, 13, 14. Drawn. Trinidad & Tobago* 225 (B. C. Lara 122 not out; B. P. Patterson three for 47, C. A. Walsh three for 45) and 239 for four dec. (S. Ragoonath 65, B. C. Lara 87, A. L. Logie 52 not out); Jamaica 157 (D. S. Morgan 31, P. J. L. Dujon 32 not out; A. H. Gray four for 44, R. Nanan five for 49) and 157 for four (W. W. Lewis 57, J. C. Adams 35 not out). *Jamaica 4 pts, Trinidad & Tobago 8 pts.*

At Queen's Park, St George's, Grenada, January 11, 12, 13, 14. Drawn. Windward Islands 110 (D. A. Joseph 32; C. E. L. Ambrose six for 10) and 145 for six (J. D. Charles 30, J. J. Pierre 47); Leeward Islands* 214 for eight dec. (R. B. Richardson 41, I. V. A. Richards 73; C. E. Cuffy three for 79). *Windward Islands 4 pts, Leeward Islands 8 pts.*

At Sabina Park, Kingston, Jamaica, January 18, 19, 20, 21. Drawn. Jamaica 242 (J. C. Adams 35, P. J. L. Dujon 75, C. A. Davidson 30; C. G. Butts five for 81) and 249 for nine dec. (D. S. Morgan 38, P. J. L. Dujon 77 not out, Extras 31; C. G. Butts four for 70, C. L. Hooper four for 48); Guyana* 217 (M. A. Harper 57, R. A. Harper 30, Extras 31; B. P. Patterson three for 50, C. A. Walsh four for 60) and 192 for six (C. L. Hooper 36, M. A. Harper 38, R. A. Harper 35 not out). *Jamaica 8 pts, Guyana 4 pts.*

At Antigua Recreation Ground, St John's, Antigua, January 18, 19, 20, 21. Barbados won by 258 runs. Barbados 333 (P. A. Wallace 135, C. G. Greenidge 64, M. D. Marshall 48; C. E. L. Ambrose three for 88, K. C. G. Benjamin three for 80) and 252 (D. L. Haynes 122, C. O. Browne 30; E. A. E. Baptiste four for 80); Leeward Islands* 216 (K. L. T. Arthurton 52, E. A. E. Baptiste 36, Extras 30; E. A. Moseley six for 52) and 111 (A. C. Cummins four for 26). *Barbados 16 pts.*

At Guaracara Park, Pointe-à-Pierre, Trinidad, January 18, 19, 20, 21. Trinidad & Tobago won by 141 runs. Trinidad & Tobago* 377 (P. V. Simmons 80, S. Ragoonath 80, B. C. Lara 69, A. H. Gray 45; N. F. Williams three for 76) and 168 (B. C. Lara 96; I. B. A. Allen seven for 48, including a hat-trick); Windward Islands 242 (L. D. John 50, J. D. Charles 41, N. F. Williams 36, J. R. Murray 37 not out; A. H. Gray three for 51) and 162 (N. F. Williams 46; R. Nanan four for 39, P. V. Simmons five for 24). *Trinidad & Tobago 16 pts.*

At Kensington Oval, Bridgetown, Barbados, January 25, 26, 27, 28. Barbados won by nine wickets. Trinidad & Tobago 267 (P. V. Simmons 31, B. C. Lara 67, N. Bidhesi 36, A. H. Gray 30, R. Sieuchan 45; M. D. Marshall four for 76, S. M. Skeete four for 68) and 212 (P. V. Simmons 58, A. L. Logie 60; M. D. Marshall three for 54, S. M. Skeete four for 46); Barbados* 199 (P. A. Wallace 69; R. Dhanraj six for 64) and 282 for one (D. L. Haynes 125 not out, C. A. Best 119 not out). *Barbados 16 pts, Trinidad & Tobago 5 pts.*

At Bourda, Georgetown, Guyana, January 26, 27, 28, 29. Drawn. Guyana 424 (C. B. Lambert 100, P. D. Persaud 36, M. A. Harper 59, R. A. Harper 94, C. L. Hooper 44, C. G. Butts 36, Extras 32; C. E. L. Ambrose three for 92, I. V. A. Richards four for 55) and 194 for four dec. (C. B. Lambert 63, S. Dhaniram 37, C. L. Hooper 50 not out); Leeward Islands* 301 (S. C. Williams 58, K. L. T. Arthurton 31, N. C. Guishard 39, L. L. Harris 30, E. A. E. Baptiste 50; C. G. Butts three for 90, R. A. Harper three for 63, C. L. Hooper three for 43) and 219 for two (R. B. Richardson 98, S. C. Williams 45, K. L. T. Arthurton 66 not out). *Guyana 8 pts, Leeward Islands 14 pts.*

At Windsor Park, Roseau, Dominica, January 26, 27, 28, 29. Drawn. Jamaica 177 (J. C. Adams 71; I. B. A. Allen three for 60, N. F. Williams five for 52) and 221 for eight dec. (D. S. Morgan 31, R. G. Samuels 79; I. B. A. Allen three for 53, M. Durand four for 65); Windward Islands* 150 (M. A. Joseph 43; N. O. Perry five for 30) and 187 for three (L. D. John 62, L. A. Lewis 59, J. R. Murray 37). *Windward Islands 4 pts, Jamaica 8 pts.*

At Kensington Oval, Bridgetown, Barbados, February 1, 2, 3, 4. Drawn. Windward Islands 317 (L. D. John 35, D. A. Joseph 91, J. Eugene 45, J. D. Charles 32, I. B. A. Allen 35; S. M. Skeete three for 64) and 229 for eight (J. Eugene 111, Extras 37; M. D. Marshall three for 51); Barbados* 420 for five dec. (D. L. Haynes 113, C. G. Greenidge 105, R. I. C. Holder 105, Extras 47). *Barbados 8 pts, Windward Islands 4 pts.*

At Warner Park, Basseterre, St Kitts, February 1, 2, 3. Leeward Islands won by seven wickets. Jamaica 268 (D. S. Morgan 42, R. G. Samuels 35, J. C. Adams 87, R. C. Haynes 54; K. C. G. Benjamin seven for 51) and 113 (E. A. E. Baptiste four for 44, H. A. G. Anthony five for 23); Leeward Islands* 317 (R. B. Richardson 64, I. V. A. Richards 112, H. A. G. Anthony 82; B. P. Patterson five for 57) and 65 for three (K. L. T. Arthurton 32 not out). *Leeward Islands 16 pts.*

At Guaracara Park, Pointe-à-Pierre, Trinidad, February 1, 2, 3, 4. Drawn. Trinidad & Tobago* 220 (P. V. Simmons 55, A. L. Logie 55) and 355 for six (P. V. Simmons 92, B. C. Lara 61, A. L. Logie 116 not out, N. Bidhesi 44, Extras 31; G. E. Charles three for 71); Guyana 419 (G. E. Charles 101, C. L. Hooper 79, M. A. Harper 38, N. A. McKenzie 52 not out, L. A. Joseph 33, C. G. Butts 36; A. H. Gray three for 77, R. Dhanraj three for 96). *Trinidad & Tobago 4 pts, Guyana 8 pts.*

At Bourda, Georgetown, Guyana, February 8, 9, 10, 11. Guyana won by ten wickets. Windward Islands* 249 (S. L. Mahon 30, N. F. Williams 37, M. Durand 31, W. L. Thomas 33; G. E. Charles three for 52, C. G. Butts six for 62) and 280 (J. Eugene 75, J. D. Charles 39, J. R. Murray 38; G. E. Charles three for 54, C. G. Butts three for 79); Guyana 453 (C. B. Lambert 104, C. L. Hooper 44, R. A. Harper 62, N. A. McKenzie 90, S. N. Mohammed 43, Extras 34; N. F. Williams five for 100, M. Durand three for 71) and 77 for no wkt (C. B. Lambert 46 not out). *Guyana 16 pts.*

At Sabina Park, Kingston, Jamaica, February 8, 9, 10, 11. Barbados won by 222 runs. Barbados* 410 for nine dec. (D. L. Haynes 146, C. A. Best 40, R. I. C. Holder 38, H. W. D. Springer 53 not out, Extras 43; B. P. Patterson three for 52) and 127 for four dec. (D. L. Haynes 63 not out; C. A. Walsh three for 32); Jamaica 169 (C. A. Davidson 36, R. C. Haynes 51; O. D. Gibson three for 55, E. A. Moseley five for 48) and 146 (J. C. Adams 56; A. C. Cummins four for 51, E. A. Moseley three for 22). *Barbados 16 pts.*

## SHELL SHIELD AND RED STRIPE CUP WINNERS

The Shell Shield was replaced by the Red Stripe Cup after the 1986-87 season.

| | | | | |
|---|---|---|---|---|
| 1965-66 | Barbados | | 1978-79 | Barbados |
| 1966-67 | Barbados | | 1979-80 | Barbados |
| 1968-69 | Jamaica | | 1980-81 | Combined Islands |
| 1969-70 | Trinidad | | 1981-82 | Barbados |
| 1970-71 | Trinidad | | 1982-83 | Guyana |
| 1971-72 | Barbados | | 1983-84 | Barbados |
| 1972-73 | Guyana | | 1984-85 | Trinidad & Tobago |
| 1973-74 | Barbados | | 1985-86 | Barbados |
| 1974-75 | Guyana | | 1986-87 | Guyana |
| 1975-76 { | Trinidad | | 1987-88 | Jamaica |
| | Barbados | | 1988-89 | Jamaica |
| 1976-77 | Barbados | | 1989-90 | Leeward Islands |
| 1977-78 | Barbados | | 1990-91 | Barbados |

## †GEDDES GRANT SHIELD, 1990-91

### Zone A

At Bridgetown, Barbados, January 9. Barbados won on scoring-rate after Guyana failed to meet a revised target of 130 off 32 overs. Barbados 203 for eight (50 overs) (C. G. Greenidge 70, D. L. Haynes 36; L. A. Joseph three for 35); Guyana* 104 (29 overs) (M. D. Marshall five for 17).

At St John's, Antigua, January 16. Leeward Islands won by four wickets. Barbados 237 for seven (48 overs) (D. L. Haynes 65, C. A. Best 60); Leeward Islands* 238 for six (46.4 overs) (R. B. Richardson 56, K. L. T. Arthurton 43, L. L. Harris 40; S. M. Skeete three for 46).

At Georgetown, Guyana, January 24. Leeward Islands won by two wickets. Guyana 215 for eight (50 overs) (C. B. Lambert 46, R. A. Harper 36, C. L. Hooper 35; I. V. A. Richards three for 28, L. L. Weekes three for 51); Leeward Islands* 217 for eight (49.2 overs) (K. L. T. Arthurton 47, L. L. Harris 47, E. A. E. Baptiste 31).

### Zone B

At Kingston, Jamaica, January 9. Jamaica won by six wickets. Trinidad & Tobago 82 for nine (29 overs) (B. P. Patterson four for 13); Jamaica* 83 for four (27.4 overs).

At Pointe-à-Pierre, Trinidad, January 16. Windward Islands won by ten wickets. Trinidad & Tobago 95 (38.2 overs) (D. Williams 45; C. E. Cuffy three for 13); Windward Islands* 96 for no wkt (23 overs) (D. A. Joseph 46 not out, L. D. John 45 retired hurt).

At Roseau, Dominica, January 24. Jamaica won by two wickets after their target had been reduced to 54 off fifteen overs. Windward Islands 103 for six (33 overs) (N. F. Williams 37 not out, J. D. Charles 30; R. C. Haynes three for 27); Jamaica* 56 for eight (14.5 overs) (I. B. A. Allen four for 24, C. E. Cuffy four for 30).

### Final

At Kingston, Jamaica, February 13. Jamaica won by four wickets. Leeward Islands 228 for eight (50 overs) (I. V. A. Richards 68, R. B. Richardson 67; C. A. Walsh three for 43); Jamaica* 232 for six (49.5 overs) (R. G. Samuels 77, D. S. Morgan 63, P. J. L. Dujon 30 not out; K. C. G. Benjamin three for 52).

## †YOUNG WEST INDIES v YOUNG AUSTRALIA

**First "Test"**: At Kingston, Jamaica, August 9, 10, 11, 12. Young Australia won by two wickets. Young West Indies* 194 (P. D. Persaud 102 not out; D. W. Fleming three for 43, S. N. Warne three for 28) and 246 (P. D. Persaud 66, S. L. Campbell 59, U. Pope 35, S. P. D. Hewitt 35 not out; D. W. Fleming five for 60, C. White four for 54); Australia 180 (J. Young 32, J. Cox 33, M. G. Bevan 61; L. L. Weekes three for 33) and 261 for eight (J. Young 32, M. G. Bevan 46, J. E. R. Gallian 85, B. P. Julian 42; C. R. Folkes five for 51).

**Second "Test"**: At Bridgetown, Barbados, August 21, 22, 23, 24. Drawn. Young Australia 383 (C. White 79, D. R. Martyn 54, M. G. Bevan 148) and 217 (J. E. R. Gallian 53, D. R. Martyn 47; S. P. D. Hewitt four for 20); Young West Indies* 271 (P. D. Persaud 41, S. L. Campbell 71, R. G. Samuels 87; C. D. Mack three for 35) and 63 for three.

**Third "Test"**: At Georgetown, Guyana, August 31, September 1, 2. Young Australia won by an innings and 43 runs. Young West Indies* 74 (D. W. Fleming three for 38, J. E. R. Gallian three for 1) and 263 (P. D. Persaud 46, R. G. Samuels 84, U. Pope 51; D. W. Fleming three for 60, S. N. Warne three for 57); Young Australia 380 (J. E. R. Gallian 65, C. White 113, D. R. Martyn 54; L. L. Weekes three for 72).

# CRICKET IN NEW ZEALAND, 1990-91

## By C. R. BUTTERY

The 1990-91 Shell Trophy was dominated by Auckland, who took the lead in the fourth round and never looked like relinquishing it. Ably captained by Jeff Crowe, they went on to win the competition by a comfortable 20-point margin over Canterbury, runners-up for the second season in succession. On paper, Auckland looked to have a powerful side; but with up to six players often unavailable because of international commitments, they were seldom in a position to play at full strength. Fortunately, both the relatively inexperienced newcomers, called in to fill the gaps, and the established players performed up to expectation, and on occasions they turned in some outstanding efforts. Most noteworthy was Steve Brown's 209 not out in the important ninth-round match against Canterbury, which enabled Auckland to obtain first-innings points from a drawn game and go into the final round with an unassailable 24-point lead. Brown also scored 152 against Central Districts, and he ended the season with 588 runs at an average of 58.80. In the absence of Ian Smith, Adam Parore kept wicket admirably, while Dipak Patel's all-round abilities again proved invaluable. He scored 679 runs in twelve first-class matches, at an average of 52.23, and with 41 wickets, at 28.09 apiece, he was the country's leading wicket-taker.

In finishing second to Auckland, Canterbury could be well satisfied with their achievement. Although unable to make an impression on the strong Auckland side, they were nevertheless superior to the other four teams in the competition. The batting displayed considerable depth, and in seven games Canterbury led on the first innings. Their only outright loss was in the final match of the series, and that was because a generous second-innings declaration enabled Otago to pull off an unexpected victory by one wicket. Chris Cairns and Chris Harris continued to develop well. Cairns took 36 wickets in first-class cricket, including match figures of eleven for 105 against Central Districts at Napier, while Harris, although available for only five games, scored 353 runs at an average of 117.66. Against Northern Districts at Rotorua, Rod Latham scored 237 not out and Peter Kennedy 159 not out while amassing an unbeaten third-wicket partnership of 394, a Canterbury record and the fourth-highest partnership recorded in New Zealand.

Otago were fortunate to finish as high as third. Two of their three victories resulted from sporting declarations by their opponents, and they looked comfortable only when playing the weak Wellington side. Otherwise they were rarely able to produce a match-winning score. Peter Dobbs hit three centuries, and Ken Rutherford scored freely when he was available, but the rest of the batting could not be relied on to score consistently. Otago were also affected by the retirement of Stephen Boock, the province's most prolific wicket-taker, at the end of the previous season.

Northern Districts' fourth placing was also surprising, but for different reasons: their batting was sound and their bowling was more than adequate. However, they won only two games, although they did come close to winning two more. Opening batsmen Karl Wealleans and David White were in good form, and the middle order was strengthened by the recruitment for the season of the Glamorgan batsman, Matthew Maynard. He scored 592 runs at an average of 45.53. Shane Thomson, one of the previous year's promising players, cut back his bowling in order to concentrate on his batting, with results which must have satisfied him: 774 runs and an average of 59.53, which put him third in the national averages behind Andrew Jones and Martin Crowe. Richard de Groen, a medium-pace bowler, led Northern Districts' wicket-takers with 35 at 22.94, but the best figures were Simon Doull's five for 64 and six for 38 against Otago at Dunedin.

Central Districts, having lost Martin Crowe to Wellington, were further weakened by the unavailability of Mark Greatbatch for most of the season. Test match appearances and one-day internationals restricted him to just two Shell Trophy games, in January, in which he had scores of 80, against Otago, and 102 not out, against Canterbury. Central Districts took points from both these games, and Greatbatch's absence was certainly felt in their other matches, although Scott Briasco scored consistently well throughout the series. The bowlers proved to be expensive. The most successful was the medium-pacer, Michael Pawson, but his nineteen wickets in the Shell Trophy cost 37.05 runs each. Central Districts excelled only in their ninth-round match against Otago, which they won decisively by five wickets after conceding a lead of 120 runs on the first innings.

In a remarkable turnabout, the defending champions, Wellington, failed to win a single match, and led on the first innings only twice. They also suffered the indignity of being penalised four of their eight points because of their slow over-rate. Had the country's two leading batsmen, Martin Crowe and Andrew Jones, been available for the province all season, Wellington's fortunes might have improved, for both were in devastating form in the Tests against the visiting Sri Lankans. But Crowe could play only once and Jones twice in the Shell Trophy. Batting failures caused all of Wellington's four losses, but their situation was not helped by the decision to drop the West Indian fast bowler, Winston Davis, from the side after the fifth round. Davis had taken twenty wickets at a cost of 19.50 apiece and was by far the most successful Wellington bowler. The selectors' explanation was that, as the side had no chance of winning the competition, preference should be given to a local bowler, who would benefit from the experience of playing first-class cricket.

Despite their lack of success in the three-day competition, Wellington had little difficulty in winning the one-day Shell Cup tournament. Having won three of their five preliminary-round games, they beat Auckland in the semi-finals and resoundingly defeated Central Districts in the final. Much of the team's success was due to their opening batsmen, Richard Reid and Martin Crowe, who invariably saw them off to a good start. In the five games in which they were paired together, their average opening stand was 95. Crowe, who had moved up the order to partner the powerful-hitting Reid, scored 309 runs, including a memorable 109 against Auckland in their semi-final, while Reid was the country's leading one-day batsman. His 348 runs, at an average of 69.60, included scores of 89, 95 and 91 not out, and although not in the original selection, he was a member of the New Zealand team which flew back to Australia for the World Series Cup finals. Notwithstanding Reid and Crowe's dominance, the Wellington bowlers were largely responsible for the victory over Central Districts which won them the Cup. Patrick O'Rourke took three for 18 and Gavin Larsen three for 28 as Central Districts were dismissed for 140 in reply to Wellington's 214 for eight.

# FIRST-CLASS AVERAGES, 1990-91

## BATTING

(Qualification: 5 completed innings, average 35.00)

|  | M | I | NO | R | HI | 100s | Avge |
|---|---|---|---|---|---|---|---|
| A. H. Jones (*Wellington*) ....... | 6 | 11 | 2 | 766 | 186 | 4 | 85.11 |
| M. D. Crowe (*Wellington*) ...... | 4 | 6 | 0 | 491 | 299 | 2 | 81.83 |
| S. A. Thomson (*N. Districts*) ..... | 11 | 18 | 5 | 774 | 166 | 2 | 59.53 |
| S. W. Brown (*Auckland*) ....... | 10 | 14 | 4 | 588 | 209* | 2 | 58.80 |
| R. T. Latham (*Canterbury*) ..... | 7 | 10 | 1 | 519 | 237* | 1 | 57.66 |
| A. C. Parore (*Auckland*) ....... | 7 | 9 | 2 | 392 | 90 | 0 | 56.00 |
| J. G. Wright (*Auckland*) ...... | 4 | 8 | 0 | 429 | 101 | 1 | 53.62 |
| M. J. Greatbatch (*C. Districts*) ... | 4 | 8 | 2 | 319 | 102* | 1 | 53.16 |
| D. N. Patel (*Auckland*) .......... | 12 | 18 | 5 | 679 | 182* | 1 | 52.23 |
| P. W. Dobbs (*Otago*) ......... | 7 | 14 | 2 | 603 | 144* | 3 | 50.25 |
| G. E. Bradburn (*N. Districts*) ..... | 6 | 8 | 2 | 296 | 82 | 0 | 49.33 |
| B. A. Young (*N. Districts*) ...... | 6 | 8 | 3 | 235 | 91 | 0 | 47.00 |
| T. E. Blain (*C. Districts*) ...... | 11 | 18 | 4 | 644 | 108* | 2 | 46.00 |
| M. P. Maynard (*N. Districts*) ... | 9 | 14 | 1 | 592 | 153* | 1 | 45.53 |
| J. J. Crowe (*Auckland*) .......... | 10 | 16 | 1 | 667 | 114 | 1 | 44.46 |
| P. E. McEwan (*Canterbury*) ...... | 10 | 14 | 2 | 521 | 103* | 1 | 43.41 |
| S. W. Duff (*C. Districts*) ...... | 11 | 17 | 6 | 460 | 80 | 0 | 41.81 |
| P. S. Briasco (*C. Districts*) ..... | 11 | 20 | 3 | 708 | 92 | 0 | 41.64 |
| K. A. Wealleans (*N. Districts*) ... | 10 | 16 | 1 | 613 | 103 | 1 | 40.86 |
| D. J. White (*N. Districts*) ...... | 10 | 16 | 1 | 609 | 194* | 1 | 40.60 |
| A. J. Hunt (*Auckland*) .......... | 7 | 8 | 2 | 242 | 102* | 1 | 40.33 |
| B. R. Hartland (*Canterbury*) ..... | 10 | 17 | 2 | 594 | 129 | 2 | 39.60 |
| P. G. Kennedy (*Canterbury*) ..... | 10 | 15 | 3 | 475 | 159* | 1 | 39.58 |
| J. T. C. Vaughan (*Auckland*) ... | 9 | 11 | 2 | 346 | 88 | 0 | 38.44 |
| M. W. Priest (*Canterbury*) ...... | 11 | 13 | 1 | 460 | 119 | 2 | 38.33 |
| S. W. J. Wilson (*C. Districts*) .... | 3 | 6 | 1 | 191 | 112 | 1 | 38.20 |
| D. J. Boyle (*Canterbury*) ........ | 10 | 18 | 2 | 566 | 90 | 0 | 35.37 |
| N. A. Mallender (*Otago*) ....... | 10 | 14 | 5 | 315 | 73* | 0 | 35.00 |
| L. G. Howell (*Canterbury*) ...... | 6 | 10 | 4 | 210 | 65 | 0 | 35.00 |

\* *Signifies not out.*

## BOWLING

(Qualification: 20 wickets)

|  | O | M | R | W | BB | Avge |
|---|---|---|---|---|---|---|
| W. W. Davis (*Wellington*) ..... | 143.2 | 29 | 390 | 20 | 4-43 | 19.50 |
| R. M. Ford (*Canterbury*) ....... | 287.2 | 94 | 638 | 32 | 5-50 | 19.93 |
| R. P. de Groen (*N. Districts*) .... | 292.3 | 70 | 803 | 35 | 6-28 | 22.94 |
| R. P. Lefebvre (*Canterbury*) .... | 265.2 | 101 | 493 | 20 | 6-53 | 24.65 |
| P. W. O'Rourke (*Wellington*) .... | 387.3 | 105 | 915 | 37 | 7-81 | 24.72 |
| N. A. Mallender (*Otago*) ....... | 353.5 | 93 | 793 | 30 | 5-30 | 26.43 |
| C. L. Cairns (*Canterbury*) ...... | 291 | 45 | 952 | 36 | 7-39 | 26.44 |
| D. N. Patel (*Auckland*) ......... | 457 | 157 | 1,152 | 41 | 7-83 | 28.09 |
| M. L. Su'a (*Auckland*) .......... | 240.1 | 72 | 686 | 24 | 6-64 | 28.58 |
| G. J. Mackenzie (*Wellington*) ... | 242.1 | 39 | 786 | 27 | 5-101 | 29.11 |
| S. B. Doull (*N. Districts*) ...... | 217.4 | 45 | 662 | 22 | 6-38 | 30.09 |
| S. J. Roberts (*Canterbury*) ..... | 203.4 | 32 | 737 | 24 | 4-55 | 30.70 |
| M. W. Priest (*Canterbury*) ...... | 341.4 | 132 | 786 | 25 | 5-37 | 31.44 |
| D. J. Hunter (*Otago*) .......... | 226.2 | 39 | 788 | 25 | 4-111 | 31.52 |
| D. K. Morrison (*Auckland*) ..... | 199.1 | 35 | 676 | 21 | 5-153 | 32.19 |
| M. J. Pawson (*C. Districts*) ..... | 268.1 | 37 | 831 | 23 | 4-76 | 36.13 |
| S. W. Duff (*C. Districts*) ....... | 334.4 | 81 | 1,002 | 20 | 5-36 | 50.10 |

## SHELL TROPHY, 1990-91

|              | Played | Won | Lost | Drawn | 1st-inns Pts | Points |
|--------------|--------|-----|------|-------|--------------|--------|
| Auckland ......... | 10 | 5 | 1 | 4 | 36 | 96 |
| Canterbury......... | 10 | 4 | 1 | 5 | 28 | 76 |
| Otago ............ | 10 | 3 | 4 | 3 | 16 | 48* |
| Northern Districts.... | 10 | 2 | 3 | 5 | 20 | 44 |
| Central Districts ..... | 10 | 2 | 3 | 5 | 12 | 36 |
| Wellington ......... | 10 | 0 | 4 | 6 | 8 | 4* |

*Win = 12 pts; lead on first innings = 4 pts.*

\* Otago and Wellington were penalised 4 points each for failing to achieve an average of seventeen overs per hour.

*In the following scores, \* by the name of a team indicates that they won the toss.*

At Fitzherbert Park, Palmerston North. December 7, 8, 9. Drawn. Wellington 398 for six dec. (G. P. Burnett 96, R. H. Vance 111 retired hurt, G. R. Larsen 98, E. B. McSweeney 84 not out); Central Districts* 171 (P. S. Briasco 32, R. L. Glover 50; W. W. Davis four for 43) and 246 for three (C. J. Smith 42, P. S. Briasco 89 not out, M. W. Douglas 78 not out). *Wellington 4 pts.*

At Trustbank Park, Hamilton, December 7, 8, 9. Drawn. Northern Districts 149 (C. M. Kuggeleijn 32, G. W. McKenzie 40; K. J. Sunderland four for 42, S. W. Brown three for 40) and 319 for two dec. (K. A. Wealleans 30, M. P. Maynard 153 not out, S. A. Thomson 101 not out); Auckland* 189 for five dec. (T. J. Franklin 34, J. J. Crowe 46, S. W. Brown 40 not out; R. P. de Groen three for 36) and 183 for eight (D. N. Patel 50, S. W. Brown 35). *Auckland 4 pts.*

At Queen's Park, Invercargill, December 7, 8, 9. Canterbury won by 109 runs. Canterbury 246 (B. R. Hartland 38, P. E. McEwan 44, C. L. Cairns 50; M. H. Austen five for 71) and 222 for two dec. (D. J. Boyle 62, B. R. Hartland 125 not out); Otago* 124 (M. H. Austen 45; S. J. Roberts four for 55, R. P. Lefebvre three for 34) and 235 (K. J. Burns 70, W. L. Blair 41; S. J. Roberts three for 39, M. W. Priest four for 67). *Canterbury 16 pts.*

At Eden Park No. 1, Auckland, December 14, 15, 16. Auckland won by 50 runs. Auckland 380 for eight dec. (J. J. Crowe 42, S. W. Brown 152, A. C. Parore 83; P. S. Briasco three for 28) and 106 for four dec. (D. N. Patel 46); Central Districts* 143 (K. J. Sunderland three for 39, D. N. Patel three for 8) and 293 (C. J. Smith 52, P. S. Briasco 69, S. W. Duff 40 not out, M. J. Pawson 44; D. N. Patel four for 105, M. H. Richardson four for 71). *Auckland 16 pts.*

At Lancaster Park, Christchurch, December 14, 15, 16. Canterbury won by eight wickets. Northern Districts* 180 (K. A. Wealleans 36, N. A. Lloyd 33; C. L. Cairns four for 57) and 209 (M. P. Maynard 35, S. A. Thomson 39, G. W. McKenzie 47 not out; S. J. Roberts three for 39, R. M. Ford three for 47); Canterbury 358 for four dec. (B. R. Hartland 46, D. J. Boyle 90, L. G. Howell 65, P. E. McEwan 103 not out, M. W. Priest 36 not out) and 35 for two. *Canterbury 16 pts.*

At Basin Reserve, Wellington, December 14, 15, 16. Drawn. Otago 268 (M. H. Austen 67, K. B. K. Ibadulla 67, R. E. W. Mawhinney 44; L. J. Doull four for 45, E. J. Gray three for 30) and 231 for five dec. (K. B. K. Ibadulla 40, B. Z. Harris 32, K. J. Burns 71 not out, W. L. Blair 42; W. W. Davis three for 38); Wellington* 149 (R. B. Reid 30, T. D. Ritchie 38; D. J. Hunter three for 53, S. R. Tracy five for 28) and 300 for nine (J. M. Aiken 66, R. B. Reid 62, G. P. Burnett 31, L. J. Doull 41; S. R. Tracy three for 65). *Otago 4 pts.*

At Eden Park No. 2, Auckland, January 4, 6, 7. Drawn. Canterbury* 211 (D. J. Boyle 78, C. Z. Harris 38; D. K. Morrison three for 37, S. W. Brown five for 41) and 371 for seven dec. (P. G. Kennedy 51, R. T. Latham 96, P. E. McEwan 70, M. W. Priest 55, C. Z. Harris 30 not out; D. N. Patel four for 104); Auckland 225 (J. T. C. Vaughan 84, I. D. S. Smith 50; R. P. Lefebvre six for 53) and 155 for two (T. J. Franklin 36, J. G. Wright 88). *Auckland 4 pts.*

At Molyneux Park, Alexandra, January 4, 6, 7. Drawn. Otago 138 (W. L. Blair 45 not out; C. L. Auckram seven for 61) and 304 for nine dec. (M. H. Austen 35, K. J. Burns 39, N. A. Mallender 73 not out, D. J. Hunter 36; M. J. Pawson four for 84, P. S. Briasco three for 51); Central Districts* 217 (R. T. Hart 82, M. W. Douglas 62; N. A. Mallender five for 53, S. R. Tracy four for 52) and 220 for seven (M. J. Greatbatch 80, T. E. Blain 54; R. E. W. Mawhinney four for 51). *Central Districts 4 pts.*

At Basin Reserve, Wellington, January 4, 5, 7. Drawn. Wellington 211 (A. H. Jones 58, E. B. McSweeney 33; R. P. de Groen six for 28, S. B. Doull three for 81) and 250 for three (A. H. Jones 109 not out, R. H. Vance 57 not out); Northern Districts* 165 (K. A. Wealleans 40, M. P. Maynard 38, G. E. Bradburn 44 not out; W. W. Davis three for 58, G. J. Mackenzie four for 52, E. J. Gray three for 8). *Wellington 4 pts.*

At Eden Park No. 1, Auckland, January 11, 12, 13. Auckland won by ten wickets. Wellington* 139 (G. P. Burnett 35, L. J. Doull 35; K. J. Sutherland four for 68, M. L. Su'a three for 30) and 218 (R. H. Vance 43, E. B. McSweeney 74; M. L. Su'a six for 64); Auckland 323 (T. J. Franklin 53, B. A. Pocock 43, J. J. Crowe 51, P. A. Horne 76; P. W. O'Rourke three for 66, B. R. Williams three for 93) and 35 for no wkt. *Auckland 16 pts.*

At Lancaster Park, Christchurch, January 11, 12, 13. Drawn. Central Districts 323 for seven dec. (R. T. Hart 90, C. J. Smith 43, T. E. Blain 59 not out, S. W. Duff 37, Extras 37; S. J. Roberts three for 80, R. M. Ford three for 59) and 190 for four dec. (M. J. Greatbatch 102 not out, M. W. Douglas 34); Canterbury* 218 for five dec. (L. G. Howell 61 not out, P. G. Kennedy 80) and 270 for eight (P. G. Kennedy 94, P. E. McEwan 75; P. R. Lowes three for 108). *Central Districts 4 pts.*

At Trustbank Park, Hamilton, January 11, 12, 13. Drawn. Otago 357 for seven dec. (M. H. Austen 90, B. Z. Harris 141 not out, N. A. Mallender 39 not out; R. P. de Groen three for 66) and 250 for seven dec. (M. H. Austen 60, P. W. Dobbs 74; M. N. Hart five for 82); Northern Districts* 260 for nine dec. (K. A. Wealleans 31, M. P. Maynard 82, S. A. Thomson 76) and 239 for five (K. A. Wealleans 50, D. J. White 39, S. A. Thomson 70, M. D. Bailey 46; D. J. Hunter three for 44). *Otago 4 pts.*

At Eden Park No. 2, Auckland, January 15, 16, 17. Auckland won by 49 runs. Auckland 357 for eight dec. (T. J. Franklin 55, B. A. Pocock 31, D. N. Patel 33, S. W. Brown 56, J. T. C. Vaughan 31, I. D. S. Smith 72 not out) and 97 for two dec. (D. N. Patel 54 not out); Otago* 153 (B. Z. Harris 31; M. J. Stephens three for 55, D. N. Patel three for 26) and 252 (K. B. K. Ibadulla 45, K. J. Burns 34, N. A. Mallender 64 not out, D. J. Hunter 31; D. N. Patel seven for 83). *Auckland 16 pts.*

At Victoria Park, Wanganui, January 15, 16, 17. Central Districts won by five wickets. Northern Districts* 359 for four dec. (D. J. White 194 not out, S. A. Thomson 49, B. S. Oxenham 74) and second innings forfeited; Central Districts 100 for two dec. (P. S. Briasco 61 not out) and 260 for five (M. W. Douglas 38, T. E. Blain 108 not out, S. W. Duff 51 not out). *Central Districts 12 pts, Northern Districts 4 pts.*

At Basin Reserve, Wellington, January 15, 16, 17. Drawn. Canterbury 313 for eight dec. (B. R. Hartland 129, C. L. Cairns 33, G. K. MacDonald 30 not out; W. W. Davis four for 69) and 39 for two dec.; Wellington* 93 for three dec. (R. H. Vance 31 not out) and 150 for nine (E. J. Gray 63; R. M. Ford three for 29, M. W. Priest five for 37). *Canterbury 4 pts.*

At Lancaster Park, Christchurch, January 26, 27, 28. Drawn. Canterbury* 238 (D. J. Boyle 36, M. W. Priest 105, L. K. Germon 40; P. W. O'Rourke six for 77, G. J. Mackenzie four for 72) and 168 for nine dec. (J. G. Boyle 35, R. T. Latham 37; P. W. O'Rourke three for 31, E. J. Gray three for 55); Wellington 143 (R. P. Lefebvre four for 35, M. W. Priest three for 33) and 241 for seven (J. M. Aiken 30, J. D. Wells 39, R. A. Verry 63, E. J. Gray 31 not out). *Canterbury 4 pts.*

At Cobham Oval, Whangarei, January 26, 27, 28. Drawn. Northern Districts* 287 for three dec. (K. A. Wealleans 103, D. J. White 76, M. P. Maynard 50, S. A. Thomson 38 not out) and second innings forfeited; Central Districts 0 for no wkt dec. and 166 for seven (M. W. Douglas 42, M. J. Pawson 53 not out; C. W. Ross four for 54). *Northern Districts 4 pts.*

At Carisbrook, Dunedin, January 26, 27, 28. Otago won by two wickets. Auckland 352 for nine dec. (T. J. Franklin 62, P. A. Horne 42, J. T. C. Vaughan 38, A. J. Hunt 102 not out; D. J. Hunter four for 111) and 168 for four dec. (J. J. Crowe 61, A. C. Parore 90); Otago* 238 for two dec. (P. W. Dobbs 100 not out, M. J. Lamont 127) and 285 for eight (B. Z. Harris 44, P. W. Dobbs 74, M. H. Austen 78 not out, S. A. Robinson 30; D. N. Patel three for 82). *Otago 12 pts, Auckland 4 pts.*

At Pukekura Park, New Plymouth, February 1, 2, 3. Auckland won by 56 runs. Auckland* 283 for four dec. (D. N. Patel 182 not out, J. J. Crowe 55) and 174 for four dec. (B. A. Pocock 38, J. T. C. Vaughan 88); Central Districts 148 for four dec. (C. J. Smith 39, M. W. Douglas 61 not out; D. N. Patel three for 31) and 253 (C. J. Smith 72, M. W. Douglas 39, T. E. Blain 55, P. S. Briasco 33; D. N. Patel three for 71, M. H. Richardson five for 77). *Auckland 16 pts.*

At Smallbone Park, Rotorua, February 1, 2, 3. Canterbury won by 72 runs. Canterbury* 430 for two dec. (P. G. Kennedy 159 not out, R. T. Latham 237 not out) and second innings forfeited; Northern Districts 101 for two dec. (K. A. Wealleans 51 not out, B. A. Young 38 not out) and 257 (D. J. White 98, K. A. Wealleans 40, M. P. Maynard 43, M. D. Bailey 33; R. M. Ford three for 67, M. W. Priest three for 52). *Canterbury 16 pts.*

At Centennial Park, Oamaru, February 1, 2, 3. Otago won by eight wickets. Otago 299 (M. J. Lamont 30, K. J. Burns 76, S. A. Robinson 40, N. A. Mallender 49; P. W. O'Rourke three for 77, G. J. Mackenzie five for 101) and 33 for two; Wellington* 102 (R. H. Vance 44, N. A. Mallender five for 30, A. J. Gale three for 14) and 228 (G. P. Burnett 63, J. D. Wells 74; V. F. Johnson five for 54). *Otago 16 pts.*

At McLean Park, Napier, March 8, 9, 10. Canterbury won by an innings and 29 runs. Canterbury* 380 for six dec. (B. R. Hartland 60, R. T. Latham 45, C. Z. Harris 134 not out, P. E. McEwan 56; D. J. Leonard four for 57); Central Districts 149 (D. J. Leonard 52; C. L. Cairns seven for 39) and 202 (T. E. Blain 72; R. M. Ford five for 50, C. L. Cairns four for 66). *Canterbury 16 pts.*

At Carisbrook, Dunedin, March 8, 9, 10. Northern Districts won by 144 runs. Northern Districts* 257 (D. J. White 91, B. A. Young 32, M. P. Maynard 31, M. D. Bailey 36; N. A. Mallender five for 67) and 247 for three dec. (D. J. White 32, K. A. Wealleans 62, G. E. Bradburn 82, S. A. Thomson 42 not out); Otago (K. R. Rutherford 81; R. P. de Groen four for 59, S. B. Doull four for 64) and 180 (K. R. Rutherford 43, M. J. Lamont 36, K. J. Burns 30; S. B. Doull six for 38, C. W. Ross three for 41). *Northern Districts 16 pts.*

At Basin Reserve, Wellington, March 8, 9, 10. Auckland won by 106 runs. Auckland 278 (J. J. Crowe 114, D. N. Patel 46; P. W. O'Rourke five for 72) and 159 for three dec. (T. J. Franklin 67 not out, J. J. Crowe 77); Wellington* 149 (A. H. Jones 57; M. L. Su'a five for 44, C. Pringle four for 41) and 182 (G. P. Burnett 62; D. N. Patel five for 53). *Auckland 16 pts.*

At Lancaster Park, Christchurch, March 12, 13, 14. Drawn. Auckland* 485 (J. J. Crowe 30, D. N. Patel 53, S. W. Brown 209 not out, A. J. Hunt 48, A. C. Parore 52, Extras 31; C. L. Cairns three for 124); Canterbury 341 (C. Z. Harris 84, P. E. McEwan 47, M. W. Priest 51, C. L. Cairns 66, Extras 35; D. K. Morrison four for 75, C. Pringle five for 92). *Auckland 4 pts.*

At Horton Park, Blenheim, March 12, 13, 14. Central Districts won by five wickets. Otago* 387 for six dec. (P. W. Dobbs 144 not out, K. R. Rutherford 155; M. J. Pawson four for 80) and 218 (M. H. Austen 40, K. J. Burns 60; C. L. Auckram six for 64); Central Districts 267 for six dec. (C. J. Smith 116, S. W. J. Wilson 112; R. E. W. Mawhinney three for 37) and 339 for five (C. J. Smith 39, M. W. Douglas 76, P. S. Briasco 44, T. E. Blain 103 not out). *Central Districts 12 pts, Otago 4 pts.*

At Trustbank Park, Hamilton, March 12, 13, 14. Northern Districts won by 111 runs. Northern Districts 284* (M. P. Maynard 62, M. N. Hart 58, C. W. Ross 66; P. W. O'Rourke seven for 81) and 219 for four dec. (K. A. Wealleans 45, G. E. Bradburn 74, M. P. Maynard 61); Wellington 214 (J. D. Wells 76, R. P. de Groen three for 52) and 178 (R. H. Vance 39; R. P. de Groen four for 46, C. W. Ross four for 36). *Northern Districts 16 pts.*

At Eden Park No. 2, Auckland, March 16, 17, 18. Drawn. Auckland 358 (B. A. Pocock 39, J. J. Crowe 71, D. N. Patel 75, J. T. C. Vaughan 36, A. C. Parore 40, M. H. Richardson 34 not out; G. E. Bradburn four for 93) and 34 for no wkt; Northern Districts* 492 (K. A. Wealleans 89, G. E. Bradburn 59, S. A. Thomson 166, B. A. Young 91, R. P. de Groen 35; M. H. Richardson four for 97, A. J. Hunt four for 45). *Northern Districts 4 pts.*

At Lancaster Park, Christchurch, March 16, 17, 18. Otago won by one wicket. Canterbury* 330 for eight dec. (C. Z. Harris 46, M. W. Priest 119, C. L. Cairns 65, L. K. Germon 44 not out; A. J. Gale three for 94, V. F. Johnson three for 50) and 194 for three dec. (D. J. Boyle 67 not out, R. T. Latham 79); Otago 216 for seven dec. (P. W. Dobbs 110) and 310 for nine (K. J. Burns 59, R. E. W. Mawhinney 108, S. A. Robinson 67 not out; R. G. Petrie four for 72). *Otago 12 pts, Canterbury 4 pts.*

At Basin Reserve, Wellington, March 16, 17, 18. Drawn. Central Districts 237 for nine dec. (P. S. Briasco 76, S. W. Duff 52, D. J. Leonard 32; M. J. Sears five for 74) and 237 for three dec. (C. J. Smith 42, C. D. Ingham 101, P. S. Briasco 58); Wellington* 212 (G. R. Larsen 45, E. B. McSweeney 53, J. D. Wells 35 not out; S. W. Duff five for 36) and 179 for six (E. B. McSweeney 37, R. A. Verry 51 not out). *Central Districts 4 pts.*

## PLUNKET SHIELD AND SHELL TROPHY WINNERS

The Plunket Shield was replaced by the Shell Trophy after the 1974-75 season.

| | | | |
|---|---|---|---|
| 1921-22 | Auckland | 1958-59 | Auckland |
| 1922-23 | Canterbury | 1959-60 | Canterbury |
| 1923-24 | Wellington | 1960-61 | Wellington |
| 1924-25 | Otago | 1961-62 | Wellington |
| 1925-26 | Wellington | 1962-63 | Northern Districts |
| 1926-27 | Auckland | 1963-64 | Auckland |
| 1927-28 | Wellington | 1964-65 | Canterbury |
| 1928-29 | Auckland | 1965-66 | Wellington |
| 1929-30 | Wellington | 1966-67 | Central Districts |
| 1930-31 | Canterbury | 1967-68 | Central Districts |
| 1931-32 | Wellington | 1968-69 | Auckland |
| 1932-33 | Otago | 1969-70 | Otago |
| 1933-34 | Auckland | 1970-71 | Central Districts |
| 1934-35 | Canterbury | 1971-72 | Otago |
| 1935-36 | Wellington | 1972-73 | Wellington |
| 1936-37 | Auckland | 1973-74 | Wellington |
| 1937-38 | Auckland | 1974-75 | Otago |
| 1938-39 | Auckland | 1975-76 | Canterbury |
| 1939-40 | Auckland | 1976-77 | Otago |
| 1940-45 | No competition | 1977-78 | Auckland |
| 1945-46 | Canterbury | 1978-79 | Otago |
| 1946-47 | Auckland | 1979-80 | Northern Districts |
| 1947-48 | Otago | 1980-81 | Auckland |
| 1948-49 | Canterbury | 1981-82 | Wellington |
| 1949-50 | Wellington | 1982-83 | Wellington |
| 1950-51 | Otago | 1983-84 | Canterbury |
| 1951-52 | Canterbury | 1984-85 | Wellington |
| 1952-53 | Otago | 1985-86 | Otago |
| 1953-54 | Central Districts | 1986-87 | Central Districts |
| 1954-55 | Wellington | 1987-88 | Otago |
| 1955-56 | Canterbury | 1988-89 | Auckland |
| 1956-57 | Wellington | 1989-90 | Wellington |
| 1957-58 | Otago | 1990-91 | Auckland |

## †SHELL CUP, 1990-91

At Eden Park, Auckland, December 27. Otago won by one wicket. Auckland* 212 for nine (50 overs) (J. G. Wright 61); Otago 215 for nine (49.3 overs) (R. N. Hoskin 67, K. J. Burns 47).

At Mandeville Sports Centre, Rangiora, December 27. Wellington won by 19 runs. Wellington* 214 for eight (50 overs) (M. D. Crowe 33, R. B. Reid 89; M. W. Priest three for 34); Canterbury 195 for nine (50 overs) (C. Z. Harris 35; G. R. Larsen four for 27).

At Pukekura Park, New Plymouth, December 27. Northern Districts won by 98 runs. Northern Districts 253 for six (50 overs) (D. J. White 39, M. P. Maynard 47, B. A. Young 42, S. A. Thomson 70 not out); Central Districts* 155 (41.3 overs) (T. E. Blain 50; D. A. Beard five for 34).

At Lancaster Park, Christchurch, December 29. Central Districts won by six wickets. Canterbury 184 for six (50 overs) (P. G. Kennedy 55, C. Z. Harris 53); Central Districts* 188 for four (48.2 overs) (R. J. Harden 92 not out, T. E. Blain 64 not out; R. P. Lefebvre three for 20).

At Blake Park, Mount Maunganui, December 29. Northern Districts won by nine wickets. Otago* 105 (46.3 overs) (R. P. de Groen three for 15, S. A. Thomson three for 19); Northern Districts 109 for one (21.1 overs) (K. A. Wealleans 38 not out, M. P. Maynard 48 not out).

At Basin Reserve, Wellington, December 29. Wellington won by 69 runs. Wellington 255 for seven (50 overs) (M. D. Crowe 69, R. B. Reid 95; D. N. Patel three for 35); Auckland* 186 (45 overs) (J. G. Wright 65; L. J. Doull three for 28).

At Fitzherbert Park, Palmerston North, December 31. Auckland won by 96 runs. Auckland 220 for six (50 overs) (J. G. Wright 30, S. W. Brown 38, P. A. Horne 59 not out, D. N. Patel 42; S. P. Robertson three for 61); Central Districts* 124 (40 overs) (R. L. Glover 48 not out; C. Pringle three for 22, S. W. Brown three for 26).

At Tauranga Domain, Tauranga, December 31. Northern Districts won by seven wickets. Canterbury 154 for seven (50 overs) (C. Z. Harris 41 not out); Northern Districts* 155 for three (31.5 overs) (K. A. Wealleans 66 not out; M. P. Maynard 45).

At Molyneux Park, Alexandra, December 31. Otago won by three wickets. Wellington* 185 for seven (50 overs) (G. P. Burnett 42; S. R. Tracy three for 42, K. B. K. Ibadulla three for 32); Otago 186 for seven (49.2 overs) (K. R. Rutherford 30, K. J. Burns 54 not out; W. W. Davis three for 25).

At Lancaster Park, Christchurch, January 2. Canterbury won by five wickets. Otago* 174 for six (50 overs) (M. H. Austen 61); Canterbury 175 for five (45.2 overs) (B. R. Hartland 35, R. T. Latham 45, P. G. Kennedy 38 not out; R. E. W. Mawhinney three for 29).

At Levin Domain, Levin, January 2. Central Districts won by 79 runs. Central Districts* 244 for nine (50 overs) (R. J. Harden 97, R. L. Glover 37); Wellington 165 (43.1 overs) (G. P. Burnett 57; S. W. Duff three for 38).

At Trustbank Park, Hamilton, January 2. Auckland won by 54 runs. Auckland 239 for eight (50 overs) (S. W. Brown 100, I. D. S. Smith 31; S. A. Thomson four for 45); Northern Districts* 185 (41.4 overs) (M. P. Maynard 101 not out; D. N. Patel four for 22).

At Eden Park, Auckland, January 5. Auckland won by five wickets. Canterbury 215 for seven (50 overs) (B. R. Hartland 30, D. J. Boyle 60, C. Z. Harris 44; C. Pringle three for 43); Auckland* 216 for five (46.4 overs) (J. J. Crowe 94, S. W. Brown 50).

At Molyneux Park, Alexandra, January 5. Central Districts won by 54 runs. Central Districts 245 for six (50 overs) (S. W. Duff 77, R. J. Harden 66, T. E. Blain 33 not out); Otago* 191 (46.2 overs) (R. N. Hoskin 39, K. R. Rutherford 53; D. J. Leonard three for 32).

At Basin Reserve, Wellington, January 6. Wellington won by nine wickets. Northern Districts 165 (49.3 overs) (B. A. Young 33, S. A. Thomson 50; W. W. Davis three for 26, M. D. Crowe three for 30); Wellington* 169 for one (24.3 overs) (M. D. Crowe 65, R. B. Reid 91 not out).

## Semi-finals

At Trustbank Park, Hamilton, January 9. Central Districts won by 105 runs. Central Districts* 245 for eight (50 overs) (M. W. Douglas 40, M. J. Greatbatch 55, R. J. Harden 46, R. L. Glover 32; C. M. Kuggeleijn three for 50); Northern Districts 140 (40.2 overs).

At Basin Reserve, Wellington, January 9. Wellington won on faster scoring-rate after rain ended play. Wellington* 253 for eight (50 overs) (M. D. Crowe 109, A. H. Jones 37, G. P. Burnett 40; C. Pringle three for 45, D. K. Morrison three for 44); Auckland 155 for four (36.4 overs) (I. D. S. Smith 40 not out).

## Final

At Basin Reserve, Wellington, January 19. Wellington won by 74 runs. Wellington* 214 for eight (50 overs) (M. D. Crowe 33, R. B. Reid 47; S. P. Robertson four for 51); Central Districts 140 (42.4 overs) (S. P. Robertson 39; P. W. O'Rourke three for 18, G. R. Larsen three for 28).

## ENGLAND YOUNG CRICKETERS IN NEW ZEALAND, 1990-91

England Young Cricketers played twelve matches on a six-week tour of New Zealand early in 1991, including three four-day "Test" matches and two one-day "internationals". They lost two of the "Tests", with the other drawn, and both the one-day "internationals". Crawley, the captain, had an outstanding tour, scoring 879 runs for an average of 62.78, with three hundreds.

The team comprised: J. P. Crawley (Lancashire, *captain*), S. Bartle (Yorkshire), M. Broadhurst (Yorkshire), M. A. Butcher (Surrey), G. Chapple (Lancashire), A. Habib (Middlesex), C. J. Hawkes (Leicestershire), J. Hodgson (Berkshire), M. J. Lowrey (Cambridge University), T. A. Radford (Middlesex), A. D. Shaw (Glamorgan), B. F. Smith (Leicestershire), M. J. Thursfield (MCC) and R. J. Warren (Northamptonshire).

*First Under-19 "Test":* at Napier, February 5, 6, 7, 8. New Zealand Young Cricketers won by nine wickets. Toss: England Young Cricketers. England Young Cricketers 144 (W. P. C. Weston 30 not out, Extras 34; R. K. Brown three for 41) and 232 (J. P. Crawley 94; J. M. B. Furlong three for 14, G. Stead four for 47); New Zealand Young Cricketers 354 for nine dec. (S. Blackmore 37, L. G. Howell 100, S. Fleming 47, G. Stead 53, Extras 44; M. Broadhurst three for 61) and 23 for one.

*Second Under-19 "Test":* at New Plymouth, February 13, 14, 15, 16. Drawn. Toss: New Zealand Young Cricketers. New Zealand Young Cricketers 343 for nine dec. (S. Blackmore 94, G. Stead 32, J. M. B. Furlong 52 not out; W. P. C. Weston three for 75) and 355 for seven (S. Fleming 96, N. Astle 54, J. M. B. Furlong 73 not out, D. Nash 77 not out); England Young Cricketers 389 (T. A. Radford 68, J. P. Crawley 112, A. Habib 41, W. P. C. Weston 48, M. J. Lowrey 38; G. Stead four for 114).

*Third Under-19 "Test":* at Auckland, February 19, 20, 21, 22. New Zealand Young Cricketers won by nine wickets. Toss: New Zealand Young Cricketers. England Young Cricketers 182 (T. A. Radford 79; J. Paul six for 56) and 177 (B. F. Smith 44, A. Habib 48; M. N. Hart three for 33); New Zealand Young Cricketers 336 (S. Blackmore 33, M. N. Hart 119, N. Astle 48, J. Wilson 51, Extras 34; M. Broadhurst three for 67) and 25 for one.

# CRICKET IN INDIA, 1990-91

By R. MOHAN and SUDHIR VAIDYA

While modern batsmen may need more than a wand of willow to protect themselves on the field of play, a degree in law may become a prerequisite for informed cricket journalism in India. To see the game being dragged to the courts was not a unique experience, but the sight of a bowler uprooting a stump to assault a batsman certainly was. Such an extraordinary incident, in the final of the nation's premier tournament, the Duleep Trophy, was the worst instance of the deterioration in standards of behaviour.

The violent action, senseless yet far from unprovoked, of Rashid Patel of West Zone, who went after Raman Lamba of North Zone, stump in hand, will be remembered as the most shameful moment in the history of Indian cricket. It occurred on the final afternoon of the five-day match in Jamshedpur, after Patel had come down the pitch to aim a head-high full toss at the batsman, Lamba. Nor was it the only controversy of a game in which senior players questioned the umpires' decisions and berated officials. Yet in the end, the Board of Control for Cricket in India seemed to draw a veil over the acrimony which found its final expression in the beamer attack, for none of the players was disciplined except for Patel and Lamba, who were banned for thirteen and ten months respectively. The sequel to the violence on the pitch was a riot in the crowd, which resulted in the covers and anything else suitable being set alight, bringing the match to a premature conclusion.

As if the ill temper of the players from two of the best sides in Indian cricket was not enough, there was a stand-off between the administrators of two teams in the North Zone of the Ranji Trophy. It arose after the host team, Delhi, had brought in an umpire after lunch on the opening day of their match against Punjab at the beginning of January, the second official not having turned up. In the morning the former Test off-spinner, Srinivasaraghavan Venkataraghavan, now a national umpire, had stood at both ends, while a scorer stood at square leg. However, as the new umpire belonged to Delhi, Punjab lodged a protest, which led to immense complications.

First, the Ranji Trophy committee decided to penalise Delhi and promote Punjab to the knockout phase of the competition. When Delhi appealed, the Working Committee of the Board was deadlocked; a draw of lots by the president, Madhavrao Scindia, was in favour of a rematch, but Punjab refused to settle the issue on the field. Instead they went to a magistrate's court in their home territory of Patiala, to obtain a stay order, and once the matter was *sub judice*, the Ranji Trophy stood suspended until the last quarter-finalists were known. The resort to the judiciary to settle a cricket dispute was a clear sign of the divisions within the Board, during a year in which its president had been elected by a margin of one vote. Summer was fast approaching when the Punjab CA had a change of heart, withdrew the suit, and also abandoned any claim to play in the remainder of the tournament. With peace restored, the other two quarter-finals could be played – it was now mid-April – and the final took place in the first week of May, six weeks late.

The saving grace of this season gone awry was a grandstand finish as Bombay, after conceding a first-innings lead of 112, made a glorious yet vain bid to win the final outright and so secure a 31st championship. Over five days, 1,526 runs were scored, and only 2 runs separated the teams at the close, with Haryana winning the Ranji Trophy for the first time. They had given up the privilege of hosting the final because the Bombay CA was celebrating its diamond jubilee. Much of the credit for Haryana's win went to Kapil Dev, too seldom available for his state in busy international seasons. He kept admirably cool as Bombay, needing an unlikely 355 at 5.22 an over, launched their run-chase on the final afternoon. The assault was triggered by a splendidly struck 96 from Sachin Tendulkar, and after he tired and was dismissed by Kapil Dev, Dilip Vengsarkar, who had enjoyed a very good season, kept Bombay in the hunt. When the last man, Abhay Kuruvilla, came to the wicket, Bombay required 50 runs from six overs, and they were just 3 runs from an amazing win when a mix-up between Kuruvilla and the injured Vengsarkar's runner, Pandit, left the former stranded in mid-pitch. A disconsolate Vengsarkar, undefeated on 139, burst into tears as the Haryana men danced a jig of delight to celebrate their hard-won victory.

The keenest contest of the knockout phase was, ironically, the quarter-final between Delhi and Bombay, a match which might not have taken place had the legal processes been pursued. Bombay gained a first-innings lead of 1 run, which was enough to earn them a semi-final against Hyderabad, and there was some talk of Bombay not having run out one of Delhi's last-wicket pair because they, Bombay, were marginally behind the over-rate at the time. This touch of the absurd was a consequence of the rule which penalised teams 12 runs (previously 4) for every over they fell short of the stipulated average of fifteen overs an hour. Had a Delhi batsman got himself out a ball or two earlier, the penalty runs would have given his team the first-innings lead, generally vital in winning matches on pitches filled with runs for batsmen and despair for bowlers.

The ridiculous nature of the penalty rule was never more obvious than in the zonal match between Andhra and Hyderabad, in which the former gave away 120 runs as penalties. In a bid to bowl out Hyderabad and win outright, Andhra's captain, Vankenna Chamundeswaranath, ended up losing a match he could have drawn comfortably – and he was sacked for his pains. Too often the rule encouraged blatant ploys to hold up the bowling team. Haryana took extra care in their semi-final clash with Bengal, knowing that the title-holders had won the trophy in 1990 – and more recently their quarter-final against Karnataka – with the help of both penalty runs and the quotient rule. This runs per over calculation is used to separate teams when the first innings remain incomplete, even after five days' play – a common enough occurrence on docile pitches.

The season was a double triumph for Kapil Dev, who also equalled I. T. Botham's tally of 376 Test wickets in the solitary Test against Sri Lanka. Before "Kapil and ten others", as Haryana were known, won the Ranji Trophy, the Indian all-rounder had led North Zone to victory in the Duleep Trophy. A first-innings lead of 168 had already decided a typical Indian "batathon" before the clash between Lamba and Patel brought about the sudden end of play. Tendulkar, the teenage phenomenon, made two hundreds in successive matches in the tournament, but failed in the final. West Zone and Bombay, both led by Ravi Shastri, won the limited-overs Deodhar Trophy and Wills Trophy in the early part of the season.

The cancellation of Pakistan's proposed tour of the country released all the major players for domestic cricket, which added interest to many contests. As many as 34 hundreds were recorded in the eight knockout matches leading up to the Ranji Trophy final, though there were only two, from Deepak Sharma and Vengsarkar, at the summit. Sanjay Manjrekar scored the only triple-century of the season. His 377 against Hyderabad was the highest innings ever for Bombay, and the second highest in India, next only to B. B. Nimbalkar's unbeaten 443 for Maharashtra against Kathiawar at Pune in 1948-49. Ten Test batsmen passed 500 runs in first-class cricket, but the number of fresh faces to take 30 or more wickets could be counted on the fingertips of one hand. – R.M.

## FIRST-CLASS AVERAGES, 1990-91

### BATTING

(Qualification: 500 runs)

|  | M | I | NO | R | HI | 100s | Avge |
|---|---|---|---|---|---|---|---|
| M. D. Gunjal (*Maharashtra*) . . . . . | 5 | 7 | 3 | 533 | 204 | 2 | 133.25 |
| Ajay Sharma (*Delhi*) . . . . . . . . . . . | 6 | 6 | 1 | 614 | 216 | 3 | 122.80 |
| C. S. Pandit (*Bombay*) . . . . . . . . . | 8 | 14 | 7 | 784 | 100* | 2 | 112.00 |
| R. J. Shastri (*Bombay*) . . . . . . . . . . | 6 | 6 | 0 | 623 | 217 | 3 | 103.83 |
| D. B. Vengsarkar (*Bombay*) . . . . . . . | 11 | 15 | 3 | 1,193 | 258* | 4 | 99.41 |
| V. A. Raja (*Karnataka*) . . . . . . . . . | 7 | 11 | 2 | 842 | 267 | 2 | 93.55 |
| Arun Lal (*Bengal*) . . . . . . . . . . . . | 8 | 11 | 2 | 798 | 183 | 4 | 88.66 |
| S. V. Manjrekar (*Bombay*) . . . . . . . | 8 | 11 | 0 | 970 | 377 | 4 | 88.18 |
| K. A. Jeshwant (*Karnataka*) . . . . . . | 7 | 10 | 2 | 688 | 259* | 3 | 86.00 |
| A. Kaypee (*Haryana*) . . . . . . . . . . | 8 | 12 | 1 | 940 | 173 | 5 | 85.45 |
| M. H. Parmar (*Gujarat*) . . . . . . . . | 6 | 11 | 2 | 743 | 196 | 4 | 82.55 |
| Saurav Ganguly (*Bengal*) . . . . . . . . | 8 | 12 | 5 | 570 | 124* | 1 | 81.42 |
| N. R. Mongia (*Baroda*) . . . . . . . . . | 5 | 9 | 2 | 555 | 165 | 2 | 79.28 |
| Zakir Hussain (*Hyderabad*) . . . . . . | 7 | 9 | 2 | 541 | 200* | 2 | 77.28 |
| S. R. Tendulkar (*Bombay*) . . . . . . . | 8 | 12 | 0 | 911 | 159 | 3 | 75.91 |
| C. Saldanha (*Karnataka*) . . . . . . . . | 7 | 11 | 2 | 671 | 138* | 3 | 74.55 |
| K. Azad (*Delhi*) . . . . . . . . . . . . . | 7 | 8 | 1 | 509 | 141 | 3 | 72.71 |
| V. G. Kambli (*Bombay*) . . . . . . . . | 11 | 17 | 2 | 1,087 | 127 | 4 | 72.46 |
| S. V. Jedhe (*Maharashtra*) . . . . . . . | 6 | 9 | 0 | 638 | 182 | 3 | 70.88 |
| Snehashish Ganguly (*Bengal*) . . . . . | 8 | 10 | 1 | 562 | 158 | 2 | 62.44 |
| S. M. H. Kirmani (*Karnataka*) . . . . | 8 | 10 | 0 | 596 | 161 | 3 | 59.60 |
| Ajay Jadeja (*Haryana*) . . . . . . . . . | 10 | 15 | 2 | 657 | 94 | 0 | 50.53 |
| Deepak Sharma (*Haryana*) . . . . . . . | 8 | 13 | 1 | 591 | 199 | 1 | 49.25 |
| R. V. Sapru (*Uttar Pradesh*) . . . . . . | 6 | 12 | 0 | 559 | 98 | 0 | 46.58 |
| S. S. Khandkar (*Uttar Pradesh*) . . . . | 6 | 12 | 1 | 512 | 182* | 1 | 46.54 |
| L. S. Rajput (*Bombay*) . . . . . . . . . | 10 | 17 | 1 | 711 | 192 | 1 | 44.43 |

\* *Signifies not out.*

### BOWLING

(Qualification: 20 wickets)

|  | O | M | R | W | BB | Avge |
|---|---|---|---|---|---|---|
| Kapil Dev (*Haryana*) . . . . . . . . . . . | 282.5 | 73 | 671 | 36 | 5-69 | 18.63 |
| P. Sushil Kumar (*Orissa*) . . . . . . . . | 233 | 55 | 563 | 28 | 9-52 | 20.10 |
| D. K. Nilosey (*Madhya Pradesh*) . . . . | 143 | 22 | 466 | 21 | 4-33 | 22.19 |
| A. R. Bhat (*Karnataka*) . . . . . . . . | 231.5 | 59 | 501 | 22 | 5-69 | 22.77 |
| H. S. Sodhi (*Madhya Pradesh*) . . . . . . | 133 | 25 | 457 | 20 | 6-59 | 22.85 |
| Maninder Singh (*Delhi*) . . . . . . . . . | 361.4 | 94 | 940 | 41 | 7-55 | 22.92 |

|  | O | M | R | W | BB | Avge |
|---|---|---|---|---|---|---|
| N. D. Hirwani (*Madhya Pradesh*) ... | 218.2 | 54 | 525 | 22 | 6-85 | 23.86 |
| Chetan Sharma (*Haryana*) ......... | 342.2 | 66 | 979 | 41 | 7-72 | 23.87 |
| S. L. V. Raju (*Hyderabad*) ........ | 382 | 94 | 837 | 35 | 6-12 | 23.91 |
| A. Kumble (*Karnataka*) ........... | 300.3 | 62 | 874 | 35 | 6-75 | 24.97 |
| K. N. A. Padmanabhan (*Kerala*).... | 263.5 | 41 | 758 | 30 | 6-102 | 25.26 |
| S. Sensharma (*Bengal*) ........... | 207.4 | 39 | 645 | 25 | 6-66 | 25.80 |
| S. S. Patil (*Bombay*) ............. | 360.2 | 92 | 861 | 32 | 5-109 | 26.90 |
| J. Srinath (*Karnataka*) ........... | 187.1 | 30 | 618 | 22 | 7-93 | 28.09 |
| Arshad Ayub (*Hyderabad*) ........ | 318.5 | 69 | 900 | 29 | 8-89 | 31.03 |
| D. Mukherjee (*Bengal*) ........... | 269.5 | 51 | 819 | 24 | 5-76 | 34.12 |
| R. G. M. Patel (*Baroda*) .......... | 289.1 | 44 | 1,003 | 28 | 6-93 | 35.82 |
| Saurav Ganguly (*Bengal*) ......... | 196.3 | 22 | 766 | 20 | 3-38 | 38.30 |
| R. R. Kulkarni (*Bombay*) ......... | 287.3 | 28 | 1,115 | 24 | 4-106 | 46.45 |

*In the following scores, * by the name of a team indicates that they won the toss. When the fielding side failed to meet the required rate of fifteen overs an hour, 12 penalty runs were added to the innings total for every over short.*

## RANJI TROPHY, 1990-91

### Central Zone

At BHEL Sports Complex Ground, Bhopal, November 20, 21, 22, 23. Drawn. Madhya Pradesh* 266 (S. M. Patil 82, D. K. Nilosey 42, R. K. Chauhan 43; Parminder Singh three for 43, P. K. Krishnakumar four for 91) and 260 for four dec. (A. V. Vijayvargiya 76, M. S. Sahni 64 not out; Parminder Singh three for 54); Rajasthan 210 (S. V. Mudkavi 97 not out, D. Jain 33; H. S. Sodhi six for 59) and 148 for seven (A. V. Mudkavi 41 not out, D. Jain 32; D. K. Nilosey four for 39). *Madhya Pradesh 13 pts, Rajasthan 9 pts.*

At VCA Ground, Nagpur, November 20, 21, 22, 23. Drawn. Uttar Pradesh* 312 (R. Bharadwaj 51, R. P. Singh 141, A. W. Zaidi 32; B. B. Thakre seven for 129) and 364 for three dec. (S. S. Khandkar 182 not out, R. V. Sapru 39, S. Chaturvedi 116); Vidarbha 504 for eight dec. (U. S. Phate 33, P. B. Hingnikar 88, P. P. Pandit 65, S. J. Phadkar 89, H. R. Wasu 100 not out, R. P. Gawande 66) and 91 for four (U. I. Gani 35; R. P. Singh three for 52). *Vidarbha 13 pts, Uttar Pradesh 14 pts.*

At Karnail Singh Stadium, New Delhi, November 27, 28, 29, 30. Madhya Pradesh won by six wickets. Railways* 129 (D. K. Nilosey four for 33, S. Ansari four for 9) and 364 (Yusuf Ali Khan 127, K. Bharatan 32, R. Venkatesh 31, S. M. Kharge 67, S. Srinivasan 39; D. K. Nilosey three for 69, H. S. Sodhi three for 53); Madhya Pradesh 441 (A. V. Vijayvargiya 31, K. K. Patel 111, S. M. Patil 65, M. S. Sahni 48, D. K. Nilosey 68; D. Mishra three for 78) and 79 for four (Penalty 24). *Madhya Pradesh 16 pts, Railways 5 pts.*

At Bhilai Steel Plant Ground, Bhilai, December 4, 5, 6, 7. Madhya Pradesh won by nine wickets. Madhya Pradesh* 506 (A. V. Vijayvargiya 59, K. K. Patel 197, A. R. Khurasia 70, S. M. Patil 95; H. R. Wasu four for 161, P. V. Gandhe six for 146) and 32 for one; Vidarbha 201 (P. B. Hingnikar 56, S. J. Phadkar 37; H. S. Sodhi four for 78) and 333 (A. M. Kane 32, P. B. Hingnikar 55, H. R. Wasu 46, R. P. Gawande 76 not out, P. S. Vaidya 60; N. D. Hirwani six for 85). *Madhya Pradesh 19 pts, Vidarbha 2 pts.*

At K. D. Singh "Babu" Stadium, Lucknow, December 4, 5, 6, 7. Drawn. Uttar Pradesh 304 (S. S. Khandkar 50, A. Gautam 53, R. P. Singh 38; K. Bharatan three for 49, Ratan Singh three for 51) and 270 for six (S. S. Khandkar 52, V. S. Vats 63, R. V. Sapru 82; R. Venkatesh three for 59); Railways* 565 for seven (Yusuf Ali Khan 66, A. S. Negi 117, Durga Prasad 94, S. M. Kharge 140 not out). *Uttar Pradesh 9 pts, Railways 12 pts.*

At Karnail Singh Stadium, New Delhi, December 11, 12, 13, 14. Railways won by 59 runs. Railways* 263 (U. R. Radhakrishnan 35, K. B. Kala 44, Durga Prasad 71 not out; H. R. Wasu five for 61) and 338 for six dec. (Yusuf Ali Khan 104, U. R. Radhakrishnan 105, K. B. Kala 32, R. Venkatesh 56; H. R. Wasu four for 130); Vidarbha 244 (P. B. Hingnikar 34, H. R. Wasu 89; R Venkatesh five for 63) and 298 (M. G. Gogte 30, U. S. Phate 34, S. J. Phadkar 97, U. I. Gani 30, H. R. Wasu 33; Ratan Singh three for 60). *Railways 20 pts, Vidarbha 8 pts.*

At VCA Ground, Nagpur, December 27, 28, 29, 30. Rajasthan won by ten wickets. Vidarbha* 213 (M. G. Gogte 30, P. B. Hingnikar 39, S. J. Phadkar 42; Mohammad Aslam four for 59) and 307 (M. G. Gogte 37, P. B. Hingnikar 38, S. J. Phadkar 40, H. R. Wasu 86, P. V. Gandhe 41; Mohammad Aslam three for 97, N. P. Jain four for 79); Rajasthan 404 (V. S. Yadav 42, J. D. Mathur 190, Padam Shastri 61, Mohammad Aslam 39; P. V. Gandhe three for 127) and 119 for no wkt (A. K. Sinha 63 not out, V. S. Yadav 50 not out). *Rajasthan 19 pts, Vidarbha 5 pts.*

At Modi Stadium, Green Park, Kanpur, January 1, 2, 3, 4. Drawn. Uttar Pradesh* 196 (V. S. Vats 63, R. V. Sapru 67; D. K. Nilosey four for 49, N. D. Hirwani five for 52) and 236 for six dec. (S. S. Khandkar 41, V. S. Vats 32, S. Chaturvedi 62 not out, R. P. Singh 41, Extras 30; R. K. Chauhan three for 72); Madhya Pradesh 239 (K. K. Patel 55, D. K. Nilosey 42, S. M. Patil 33, Extras 34; M. A. Ansari six for 51) and 125 for five (K. K. Patel 36, A. R. Khurasia 35). *Uttar Pradesh 10 pts, Madhya Pradesh 12 pts.*

At MB College Ground, Udaipur, January 3, 4, 5, 6. Drawn. Railways* 484 (Yusuf Ali Khan 90, K. B. Kala 86, R. Venkatesh 58, Durga Prasad 51, K. Bharatan 32, F. Heaton 58 not out, S. Srinivasan 32, D. Mishra 30; P. Sunderam three for 61, N. P. Jain three for 104) and 21 for no wkt dec.; Rajasthan 456 (A. K. Sinha 32, V. S. Yadav 33, S. V. Mudkavi 163, L. Chaturvedi 53, D. Jain 68, Extras 52; R. Venkatesh four for 87) and 11 for no wkt. *Rajasthan 5 pts, Railways 9 pts.*

At Barkatullah Khan Stadium, Jodhpur, January 9, 10, 11, 12. Uttar Pradesh won by six wickets. Rajasthan 210 (J. D. Mathur 30, V. S. Yadav 33, P. K. Amre 51, P. Sunderam 33; M. A. Ansari four for 53, Gopal Sharma four for 39) and 102 (R. P. Singh five for 34, Ubaid Kamal four for 39); Uttar Pradesh* 229 (R. V. Sapru 80; Mohammad Aslam four for 65, S. V. Mudkavi three for 55) and 84 for four. *Uttar Pradesh 17 pts, Rajasthan 6 pts.*

Madhya Pradesh 60 pts, Uttar Pradesh 50 pts, Railways 46 pts, Rajasthan 39 pts, Vidarbha 28 pts. Madhya Pradesh and Uttar Pradesh qualified for the knockout stage.

## East Zone

At PTI Ground, Agartala, November 23, 24, 25. Orissa won by an innings and 197 runs. Tripura* 119 (R. Deb-Burman 44; P. Sushil Kumar six for 37, R. B. Biswal three for 29) and 144 (R. R. Chowdhary 40; P. Sushil Kumar nine for 52); Orissa 460 (S. Chowdhary 42, B. Mohanty 39, A. Roy 51, R. B. Biswal 160, A. Jayaprakasham 47, Extras 42; R. Deb-Burman three for 63). *Orissa 23 pts, Tripura 2 pts.*

At Maligaon Railway Stadium, Guwahati, November 23, 24, 25, 26. Drawn. Assam* 305 (D. Das 72, Rajinder Singh 68, R. Bora 57, P. Dutta 31; Dhananjay Singh five for 76, A. R. Prasad four for 66) and 255 for three dec. (D. Das 70, Rajinder Singh 115 not out); Bihar 165 (H. Gidwani 41; Rajinder Singh four for 43) and 130 for five (Sunil Singh 39 not out, S. R. Sinha 33 not out; H. Barua three for 30). *Assam 14 pts, Bihar 8 pts.*

At Maligaon Railway Stadium, Guwahati, November 30, December 1, 2, 3. Drawn. Assam* 246 (Zahir Alam 30, R. Bora 39; P. Sushil Kumar six for 80) and 250 (Zahir Alam 54, Rajinder Singh 44, G. Dutta 46 not out; S. Mohapatra five for 93, P. Sushil Kumar four for 90); Orissa 230 for six dec. (Sritam Das 33, R. B. Biswal 91, A. Khatua 32, H. B. Praharaj 31; H. Barua three for 70) and 227 for eight (S. Chowdhary 41, A. Jayaprakasham 50 not out, H. B. Praharaj 59; H. Barua four for 54, S. Chakraborty three for 80). *Assam 11 pts, Orissa 9 pts.*

At Eden Gardens, Calcutta, November 30, December 1, 2, 3. Drawn. Bengal 394 (Arun Lal 36, Snehashish Ganguly 66, A. Malhotra 47, Saurav Ganguly 72, Rajinder Singh 90; S. T. Banerjee five for 96, A. R. Prasad three for 84) and 265 for four dec. (M. Das 51, Arun Lal 111 not out, A. Malhotra 31); Bihar 291* (P. Khanna 52, B. S. Gossain 40, S. T. Banerjee 66, A. R. Prasad 30; D. Mukherjee four for 105, S. Sensharma three for 65) and 108 for four (Saurav Ganguly three for 38). *Bengal 18 pts, Bihar 10 pts.*

At Eden Gardens, Calcutta, December 6, 7, 8, 9. Bengal won by an innings and 76 runs. Orissa* 188 (D. Lenka 37, A. Roy 45, Penalty 36; D. Mukherjee three for 41, Satinder Singh four for 66) and 344 (D. Lenka 89, R. B. Biswal 108, A. Roy 54, A. Jayaprakasham 33; D. Mukherjee three for 68, Satinder Singh four for 59); Bengal 608 for four dec. (Pranab Roy 38, M. Das 186, Arun Lal 183, A. Malhotra 76 not out, Saurav Ganguly 78 not out; S. Mohapatra three for 162). *Bengal 22 pts, Orissa 4 pts.*

At PTI Ground, Agartala, December 7, 8, 9. Assam won by 363 runs. Assam* 166 (S. Banerjee three for 35, C. Dey six for 39) and 435 for six dec. (Rajinder Singh 128, R. Bora 161, P. Dutta 59, V. Tiwari 31; C. Dey three for 125); Tripura 141 (R. R. Chowdhary 36; Rajinder Singh three for 22, S. Chakraborty three for 42, P. Dutta three for 22) and 97 (Rajinder Singh six for 33, S. Chakraborty four for 33). *Assam 21 pts, Tripura 6 pts.*

At Mecon, Ranchi, December 24, 25, 26, 27. Drawn. Orissa 233 (D. Lenka 31, A. Jayaprakasham 80, Rajesh Singh 49; A. R. Prasad three for 43) and 343 for five (P. Mohapatra 157 not out, A. Jayaprakasham 108, Extras 30); Bihar* 492 (S. Das 71, B. S. Gossain 52, S. S. Karim 234; S. Mohapatra three for 142, H. B. Praharaj three for 110). *Bihar 13 pts, Orissa 6 pts.*

At Maligaon Railway Stadium, Guwahati, December 25, 26, 27, 28. Drawn. Assam 259 (Zahir Alam 56, K. K. Barua 66; S. Sensharma six for 66) and 342 for nine dec. (Zahir Alam 53, V. Tiwari 72, K. K. Barua 59, B. Majumdar 40, H. Barua 32 not out; Satinder Singh three for 48, S. Sensharma three for 110); Bengal* 376 (Pranab Roy 80, M. Das 68, Saurav Ganguly 87, S. Sensharma 38, Penalty 36; S. Chakraborty four for 77, P. Dutta three for 112) and 67 for seven. *Assam 9 pts, Bengal 14 pts.*

At Keenan Stadium, Jamshedpur, December 30, 31, January 1, 2. Bihar won by an innings and 231 runs. Bihar 513 (S. Das 92, H. Gidwani 149, S. Chatterjee 101, Abinash Kumar 36, V. Venkatram 36; C. Dey five for 125); Tripura* 146 (S. Lahiri 51; V. Venkatram three for 32) and 136 (R. R. Chowdhary 62, S. Lahiri 45; V. Venkatram six for 42, including a hat-trick). *Bihar 25 pts, Tripura 2 pts.*

At Eden Gardens, Calcutta, January 6, 7, 8, 9. Bengal won by an innings and 316 runs. Tripura 172 (S. Lahiri 42, R. Deb-Burman 38, Penalty 48; S. Sensharma three for 19, Saurav Ganguly three for 56) and 270 (R. R. Chowdhary 54, J. K. Deb-Burman 51, S. Lahiri 41; D. Mukherjee three for 76, Saurav Ganguly three for 79); Bengal* 758 for seven dec. (Pranab Roy 60, M. Das 64, Snehashish Ganguly 158, A. Malhotra 214, Saurav Ganguly 31, Rajinder Singh 63, U. Chatterjee 37 not out, Extras 35, Penalty 60). *Bengal 25 pts, Tripura 6 pts.*

Bengal 79 pts, Bihar 56 pts, Assam 55 pts, Orissa 42 pts, Tripura 16 pts. Bengal and Bihar qualified for the knockout stage.

## North Zone

At Indira Gandhi Stadium, Una, November 21, 22, 23, 24. Drawn. Jammu and Kashmir* 208 (Nirmal Singh 52, Sanjay Sharma 39 not out; A. Sen three for 60, Jaswant Rai four for 33) and 205 (Nirmal Singh 40, S. Chowdhary 44, Sanjay Sharma 57; A. Sen seven for 57); Himachal Pradesh 226 for five dec. (R. Nayyar 81; Abdul Qayyum six for 59) and 74 for four. *Himachal Pradesh 13 pts, Jammu and Kashmir 9 pts.*

At Kangda Police Stadium, Dharamsala, November 25, 26, 27. Haryana won by an innings and 115 runs. Haryana* 551 for six dec. (Deepak Sharma 85, N. R. Goel 99, A. Kaypee 168, R. Puri 110 not out, Chetan Sharma 41, Extras 32; Jaswant Rai five for 140); Himachal Pradesh 194 (A. Vij 63, Jaswant Rai 32, Shambu Sharma 43; P. Jain four for 45, S. Joshi five for 86) and 242 (R. Nayyar 33, Shakti Singh 128; Chetan Sharma six for 51). *Haryana 25 pts, Himachal Pradesh 5 pts.*

At Bikram Park, Udhampur, November 25, 26, 27, 28. Punjab won by an innings and 47 runs. Punjab 468 (Ajay Mehra 116, V. Rathore 63, Gursharan Singh 115, Bhupinder Singh, jun. 51, M. Arora 32; Sanjay Sharma three for 83, A. Gupta four for 108); Jammu and Kashmir* 166 (S. Parvez 50; Bhupinder Singh, sen. three for 47, M. I. Singh five for 55) and 255 (Kamaljit Singh 106, Sanjay Sharma 77 not out; M. Arora four for 60). *Punjab 22 pts, Jammu and Kashmir 2 pts.*

At Ferozshah Kotla Ground, Delhi, December 1, 2, 3, 4. Delhi won by an innings and 152 runs. Delhi* 534 for five dec. (R. Lamba 57, Ajay Sharma 216, K. Bhaskar Pillai 95, K. Azad 100 not out); Services 139 (Chinmoy Sharma 62; Maninder Singh seven for 55) and 243 (G. S. Thapa 40, K. M. Roshan 43, Chinmoy Sharma 47, K. Ashok Raj 43, M. Subramaniam 42; Maninder Singh three for 50, K. Azad four for 93). *Delhi 23 pts, Services 1 pt.*

At Indira Gandhi Stadium, Una, December 1, 2, 3, 4. Punjab won by an innings and 128 runs. Himachal Pradesh 131 for eight dec. (R. Nayyar 52; M. I. Singh four for 34, M. Arora four for 41) and 242 (A. Vij 72, Brijinder Sharma 63; M. Arora six for 60); Punjab* 501 for nine dec. (D. M. Pandove 45, V. Rathore 51, A. Kapoor 31, Bhupinder Singh, jun. 74, Krishna Mohan 110, Arun Sharma 31, M. Arora 50 not out; Shakti Singh five for 130). *Punjab 22 pts, Himachal Pradesh 3 pts.*

At Maulana Azad Stadium, Jammu, December 1. The pitch, on the second morning, was seen to have been tampered with. As the Haryana captain did not agree to move to a different one, the match was abandoned without further play. Outright victory was awarded to the visiting side, Haryana. Jammu and Kashmir 145 (P. Jain five for 40, Deepak Sharma three for 36); Haryana* 72 for three. *Haryana 16 pts, Jammu and Kashmir 1 pt.*

At Bikram Park, Udhampur, December 7, 8, 9. Services won by 71 runs. Services* 213 (G. S. Thapa 106 not out, K. M. Roshan 35; Abdul Qayyum three for 46, S. Parvez three for 15, A. Gupta three for 42) and 207 (Chinmoy Sharma 34, M. Subramaniam 62; Abdul Qayyum four for 58, A. Gupta five for 65); Jammu and Kashmir 199 (Ranjit Bali 42; M. Subramaniam five for 45) and 150 (M. Subramaniam five for 60, N. K. Gupta three for 41). *Services 18 pts, Jammu and Kashmir 9 pts.*

At Punjab Agricultural University Ground, Ludhiana, December 7, 8, 9, 10. Drawn. Punjab* 399 (D. M. Pandove 76, Gursharan Singh 77, Bhupinder Singh, jun. 140, Dilraj Singh 35 not out; Chetan Sharma three for 77) and 72 for one dec. (V. Rathore 32 not out); Haryana 415 (Deepak Sharma 73, Dhanraj Singh 44, N. R. Goel 30, A. Kaypee 41, Ajay Jadeja 31, R. Puri 105; M. I. Singh six for 121) and 11 for no wkt. *Punjab 7 pts, Haryana 9 pts.*

At Ferozshah Kotla Ground, Delhi, December 7, 8, 9. Delhi won by an innings and 214 runs. Himachal Pradesh 104 (Maninder Singh three for 27, K. Azad three for 18) and 205 (R. Nayyar 54, Shambu Sharma 48; Maninder Singh five for 35); Delhi* 523 for five dec. (M. Nayyar 55, R. Lamba 135, K. Bhaskar Pillai 65, Ajay Sharma 163 not out, Maninder Singh 50 not out). *Delhi 25 pts, Himachal Pradesh 4 pts.*

At Model Sports Complex, Palam, Delhi, December 31, January 1, 2, 3. Himachal Pradesh won by one wicket. Services* 266 (K. M. Roshan 38, G. S. Thapa 46, S. C. Sadangi 40, M. Subramaniam 56, S. K. Dutt 30; Shakti Singh three for 60, A. Sen three for 53) and 263 (G. S. Thapa 103, N. K. Gupta 60; Shakti Singh seven for 53); Himachal Pradesh 193 (R. Nayyar 83 not out, Brijinder Sharma 57, Shakti Singh 33; S. C. Sadangi three for 27, N. K. Gupta five for 66) and 337 for nine (R. Nayyar 81, Shambu Sharma 50, Brijinder Sharma 108 not out, Shakti Singh 42; M. V. Rao four for 92, N. K. Gupta three for 69). *Himachal Pradesh 16 pts, Services 9 pts.*

At Nehru Stadium, Gurgaon, January 7, 8, 9, 10. Drawn. Delhi* 316 (M. Nayyar 125, K. Bhaskar Pillai 35, Maninder Singh 46; Chetan Sharma five for 104, Kapil Dev three for 48) and 252 for seven dec. (Bantoo Singh 57, K. Azad 86); Haryana 321 (Deepak Sharma 86, N. R. Goel 35, V. Yadav 38, Chetan Sharma 47; Maninder Singh three for 51) and 128 for three (Ajay Jadeja 60 not out). *Haryana 14 pts, Delhi 11 pts*

At Services Sports Complex, Delhi, January 7, 8, 9, 10. Punjab won by an innings and 59 runs. Punjab* 504 for eight dec. (V. Rathore 124, Bhupinder Singh, jun. 103, Krishna Mohan 123, M. Arora 75); Services 137 (Bhupinder Singh, sen. six for 82) and 308 (H. Dutta 122, S. K. Tripathy 93, K. D. Pandey 31; Bhupinder Singh, sen. three for 74, Dilraj Singh four for 35). *Punjab 22 pts, Services 3 pts.*

At Air Force Ground, Palam, Delhi, January 12, 13, 14. Haryana won by an innings and 172 runs. Services 102 (S. Dutta 34; Chetan Sharma three for 39, Kapil Dev four for 38) and 215 (H. Dutta 38, K. D. Pandey 56, K. Ashok Raj 34, Extras 38; Chetan Sharma four for 94, Kapil Dev five for 69); Haryana* 489 (Deepak Sharma 33, A. Kaypee 127, Ajay Jadeja 46, R. Puri 172, Chetan Sharma 50 not out; H. P. Sharma three for 125, N. K. Gupta three for 94). *Haryana 23 pts, Services 5 pts.*

At Ferozshah Kotla Ground, Delhi, January 12, 13, 14, 15. Delhi won by nine wickets. Delhi* 535 for eight dec. (M. Nayyar 54, M. Prabhakar 72, Ajay Sharma 130, K. Bhaskar Pillai 56, K. Azad 101, Bantoo Singh 35) and 68 for one; Punjab 350 (D. M. Pandove 32, Arun Sharma 59, Krishna Mohan 77, M. Arora 39, M. I. Singh 42; Maninder Singh four for 102) and 252 (M. Arora 60; M. Prabhakar three for 70, Maninder Singh three for 78). *Delhi 20 pts, Punjab 8 pts.*

At Bikram Park, Udhampur, January 27, 28, 29, 30. Drawn. Jammu and Kashmir 272 (A. Gupta 32, V. Bhaskar 31, S. Chowdhary 36, Ram Swarup 46, Vivek Kumar 72; Sanjeev Sharma seven for 95) and 126 for six dec.; Delhi* 298 (Sanjay Sharma 41, Abhay Sharma 31, Harpreet Singh 63, S. S. Saini 53; Sanjay Sharma three for 96) and 24 for no wkt. *Jammu and Kashmir 8 pts, Delhi 13 pts.*

Delhi 92 pts, Haryana 87 pts, Punjab 81 pts, Himachal Pradesh 41 pts, Services 36 pts, Jammu and Kashmir 29 pts. Delhi and Haryana qualified for the knockout stage.

## South Zone

At Arlem Ground, Margao, October 23, 24, 25, 26. Drawn. Goa* 154 (H. B. P. Angle 49 not out, J. R. Shetty 34; V. Razdan three for 53, D. Vasu four for 55); Tamil Nadu 54 for one. *Goa 5 pts, Tamil Nadu 7 pts.*

At Municipal Stadium, Vishakhapatnam, November 9, 10, 11, 12. Kerala won by nine wickets. Andhra 420 (O. Vinod Kumar 92, M. F. Rehman 46, M. S. Kumar 43, V. Vinay Kumar 101, V. Vijayasarathy 50, Extras 32; K. G. Jayakumar three for 93, S. Santosh three for 73) and second innings forfeited; Kerala* 346 (V. Narayan Kutty 53, P. G. Sunder 125, F. V. Rasheed 55, B. Ramaprakash 53; B. S. Mangesh three for 69) and 76 for one (B. Ramaprakash 36 not out). *Kerala 11 pts, Andhra 4 pts.*

At Panji Gymkhana, Panji, November 10, 11, 12, 13. Drawn. Karnataka 170 for eight dec. (P. V. Shashikanth 64, A. R. Bhat 31; A. Shetty four for 31) and 208 for six dec. (C. Saldanha 102 not out, S. M. H. Kirmani 33; A. Shetty three for 61); Goa* 96 (A. R. Bhat three for 7, R. Ananth three for 3) and 100 for seven (P. A. Amonkar 52; A. R. Bhat four for 31). *Goa 10 pts, Karnataka 14 pts.*

At Gymkhana Ground, Secunderabad, November 16, 17, 18, 19. Hyderabad won by an innings and 237 runs. Kerala* 183 (V. Narayan Kutty 44, P. V. Ranganathan 53; S. L. V. Raju three for 32, Arshad Ayub three for 40) and 148 (P. V. Ranganathan 37; N. R. Yadav five for 62); Hyderabad 568 for five dec. (Abdul Azeem 90, M. V. Sridhar 44, V. Jaisimha 117, Zakir Hussain 200 not out, Extras 39; P. T. Subramaniam three for 95). *Hyderabad 24 pts, Kerala 1 pt.*

At Arlem Ground, Margao, November 17, 18, 19, 20. Drawn. Andhra 287 (A. Pathak 65, K. V. S. D. Kamaraju 54, V. Vinay Kumar 46, V. Vijayasarathy 48 not out; J. R. Shetty three for 68, U. S. Naik four for 51); Goa* 117 for two (P. R. Pradhan 60 not out, A. Gaikwad 30 not out). *Goa 6 pts, Andhra 3 pts.*

At Gymkhana Ground, Secunderabad, November 24, 25, 26, 27. Drawn. Tamil Nadu 548 for eight dec. (V. B. Chandrasekhar 86, Arjan Kripal Singh 46, N. Gautam 101, Robin Singh 123, D. Vasu 101 not out, V. Razdan 38 not out; Arshad Ayub four for 193); Hyderabad* 377 (C. Jaikumar 169, Ehtesham Ali 51, M. V. Ramanamurthy 53; S. Subramaniam four for 69) and 88 for no wkt (Abdul Azeem 30 not out, C. Jaikumar 42 retired hurt). *Hyderabad 6 pts, Tamil Nadu 10 pts.*

At Municipal Stadium, Davangere, November 24, 25, 26, 27. Karnataka won by an innings and 33 runs. Andhra* 207 (A. Pathak 42, M. F. Rehman 62, R. Krishnamohan 30; A. Kumble five for 71) and 296 (A. Pathak 47, M. S. Kumar 63, V. Chamundeswaranath 52, R. Krishnamohan 34 not out; A. R. Bhat five for 69); Karnataka 536 (P. V. Shashikanth 160, S. Ramesh Rao 90, V. A. Raja 69, S. M. H. Kirmani 39, K. A. Jeshwant 84, K. G. Sekhar 31; B. S. Mangesh five for 165). *Karnataka 23 pts, Andhra 5 pts.*

At Municipal Stadium, Cuddapah, December 1, 2, 3, 4. Hyderabad won by three wickets. Andhra* 334 (M. F. Rehman 116, V. Vijayasarathy 117; S. L. V. Raju three for 72, Kanwaljit Singh three for 87) and 334 (O. Vinod Kumar 73, M. F. Rehman 85, Extras 31; S. L. V. Raju three for 62, Kanwaljit Singh four for 134); Hyderabad 414 (Abdul Azeem 138, M. V. Sridhar 109, Zakir Hussain 37, Ehtesham Ali 35; K. Chakradhar Rao four for 108, D. Sudhakar Reddy five for 196) and 270 for seven (N. R. Yadav 39, Penalty 120; S. Krishnamohan four for 63). *Hyderabad 22 pts, Andhra 9 pts.*

At Agricultural Research Institute's Ground, Coimbatore, December 2, 3, 4, 5. Drawn. Karnataka* 716 (C. Saldanha 77, V. A. Raja 138, S. M. H. Kirmani 161, K. A. Jeshwant 259 not out, Extras 43; S. Subramaniam three for 171); Tamil Nadu 96 for four. *Tamil Nadu 3 pts, Karnataka 6 pts.*

At Victoria College Ground, Palghat, December 8, 9, 10, 11. Tamil Nadu won by 99 runs. Tamil Nadu* 394 (V. B. Chandrasekhar 40, K. Srikkanth 69, M. Mujib-ur-Rehman 37, Arjan Kripal Singh 38, Robin Singh 40, D. Vasu 59, A. R. Kapoor 73; K. N. A. Padmanabhan five for 114) and 232 (V. B. Chandrasekhar 31, K. Srikkanth 51, N. Gautam 44 not out, D. Vasu 36; K. N. A. Padmanabhan five for 49, B. Ramaprakash three for 99); Kerala 231 (B. Ramaprakash 62, P. T. Subramaniam 39; D. Vasu three for 49, A. R. Kapoor four for 40) and 296 (P. G. Sunder 89, B. Ramaprakash 68, F. V. Rasheed 55; A. R. Kapoor seven for 74). *Tamil Nadu 20 pts, Kerala 11 pts.*

At Gymkhana Ground, Secunderabad, December 11, 12, 13. Hyderabad won by an innings and 211 runs. Goa 122 (P. R. Pradhan 38, S. Mahadevan 32; M. V. Ramanamurthy three for 14, S. L. V. Raju five for 37) and 170 (Penalty 72; N. R. Yadav four for 70, M. V. Ramanamurthy five for 27); Hyderabad* 503 (Abdul Azeem 52, C. Jaikumar 67, R. A. Swarup 132, Zakir Hussain 155). *Hyderabad 25 pts, Goa 2 pts.*

At Agricultural College Ground, Thiruvananthapuram (formerly Trivandrum), December 20, 21, 22. Kerala won by 35 runs. Kerala* 110 (J. R. Shetty six for 44) and 296 (V. Narayan Kutty 105, K. N. Balasubramaniam 38, P. G. Sunder 46, P. V. Nandakumar 37, P. T. Subramaniam 35; S. Harmalkar three for 21, A. Shetty four for 76); Goa 153 (P. Rivonkar 45; K. N. A. Padmanabhan four for 26) and 218 (N. P. Parikkar 62, S. Harmalkar 42; K. N. A. Padmanabhan four for 55). *Kerala 16 pts, Goa 6 pts.*

At R. N. Shetty Stadium, Dharwar, December 23, 24, 25. Karnataka won by 76 runs. Karnataka* 225 (C. Saldanha 37, P. V. Shashikanth 53, S. M. H. Kirmani 65; Arshad Ayub six for 70, R. A. Swarup four for 15) and 204 (C. Saldanha 37, V. A. Raja 83 not out; Arshad Ayub eight for 89); Hyderabad 117 for six dec. (Abdul Azeem 31, Zakir Hussain 40; A. R. Bhat three for 39, A. Kumble three for 34) and 236 (Abdul Azeem 46, V. Jaisimha 60, Zakir Hussain 48, Arshad Ayub 33; A. Kumble five for 84). *Karnataka 13 pts, Hyderabad 8 pts.*

At Chidambaram Stadium, Madras, January 2, 3. Tamil Nadu won by ten wickets. Andhra 165 (M. F. Rehman 33, V. Vijayasarathy 32; D. Vasu three for 62, A. R. Kapoor five for 34) and 102 (D. Vasu three for 28, Robin Singh six for 31); Tamil Nadu* 257 for six dec. (Robin Singh 50, D. Vasu 35, A. R. Kapoor 70; H. Ramakishen four for 80, D. Sudhakar Reddy three for 35) and 11 for no wkt. *Tamil Nadu 18 pts, Andhra 4 pts.*

At Municipal Stadium, Thalassery (formerly Tellichery), January 5, 6, 7, 8. Karnataka won by 252 runs. Karnataka* 410 (C. Saldanha 121, P. V. Shashikanth 79, V. A. Raja 72, S. M. H. Kirmani 30, Extras 32; K. N. A. Padmanabhan six for 102) and 332 for five dec. (C. Saldanha 58, V. A. Raja 58 not out, S. Ramesh Rao 78, A. Kumble 100 not out); Kerala 244 for six dec. (P. G. Sunder 86, B. Ramaprakash 32, K. N. A. Padmanabhan 33; A. Kumble six for 75) and 246 (K. N. Balasubramaniam 34, R. V. Nandakumar 35, Penalty 60; A. Kumble five for 28). *Karnataka 21 pts, Kerala 7 pts.*

Hyderabad 85 pts, Karnataka 77 pts, Tamil Nadu 58 pts, Kerala 46 pts, Goa 29 pts, Andhra 25 pts. Hyderabad and Karnataka qualified for the knockout stage.

## West Zone

At Corporation Stadium, Rajkot, November 23, 24, 25, 26. Drawn. Saurashtra* 553 (B. S. Pujara 47, S. S. Tanna 160, B. M. Jadeja 101, A. N. Pandya 82, A. Karia 67, R. M. Mehta 35; S. J. Jadhav four for 122) and 176 for four dec. (B. S. Pujara 40, S. S. Tanna 71 not out); Maharashtra 628 for eight dec. (S. V. Jedhe 151, S. S. Sugwekar 211, N. H. Phadnis 30, S. J. Jadhav 57, S. C. Gudge 57 not out, S. V. Ranjane 56 not out; C. C. Mankad four for 160) and 5 for no wkt. *Saurashtra 10 pts, Maharashtra 12 pts.*

At Sardar Patel Stadium, Valsad, November 23, 24, 25, 26. Drawn. Gujarat 501 (N. S. Seth 31, M. H. Parmar 196, N. A. Patel 57, B. K. Patel 51, U. Belsare 60, Extras 40; R. G. M. Patel three for 95) and 282 for eight dec. (B. H. Mistry 72 not out, D. Thakkar 32 not out, Penalty 96; R. G. M. Patel four for 66); Baroda* 630 for seven dec. (N. R. Mongia 165, S. F. Dukanwala 121, A. D. Gaekwad 140, M. S. Narula 46, Extras 38) and 14 for one. *Gujarat 14 pts, Baroda 15 pts.*

At Wankhede Stadium, Bombay, November 30, December 1, 2, 3. Bombay won by ten wickets. Gujarat 231 (M. H. Parmar 111 not out, B. K. Patel 45; S. S. Patil three for 40) and 400 (M. H. Parmar 119, P. H. Bhatt 75, B. H. Mistry 101 not out; R. R. Kulkarni three for 130, P. A. Desai three for 62, S. S. Patil four for 95); Bombay* 608 for four dec. (J. B. Jadhav 46, S. S. Dighe 107, D. B. Vengsarkar 258 not out, C. S. Pandit 63, V. G. Kambli 111 not out) and 24 for no wkt. *Bombay 17 pts, Gujarat 3 pts.*

At Motibaug Palace Ground, Baroda, November 30, December 1, 2, 3. Drawn. Maharashtra* 443 for nine dec. (S. V. Jedhe 52, M. D. Gunjal 156 not out, N. H. Phadnis 36, S. J. Jadhav 69, Penalty 60; M. S. Narula three for 83) and 255 for three dec. (A. P. Deshpande 46, S. V. Jedhe 36, S. S. Sugwekar 76 not out, M. D. Gunjal 47 not out); Baroda 302 (N. R. Mongia 100, A. D. Gaekwad 94; S. V. Ranjane three for 68, R. T. Yerwadekar four for 81) and 111 for two (K. S. Chavan 51). *Baroda 11 pts, Maharashtra 17 pts.*

At Corporation Stadium, Rajkot, December 6, 7, 8, 9. Drawn. Saurashtra* 400 (B. S. Pujara 65, B. M. Jadeja 53, A. N. Pandya 44, B. Dutta 68, R. M. Mehta 83, C. C. Mankad 43; S. S. Patil three for 132) and 157 for nine (B. Dutta 67); Bombay 538 for six dec. (L. S. Rajput 49, S. S. Dighe 153, D. B. Vengsarkar 89, V. G. Kambli 103, C. S. Pandit 69, Iqbal Khan 30 not out; G. Tank three for 156). *Saurashtra 7 pts, Bombay 14 pts.*

At Poona Club, Pune, December 6, 7, 8, 9. Drawn. Maharashtra 602 for eight dec. (A. P. Deshpande 35, S. V. Jedhe 182, S. S. Sugwekar 57, M. D. Gunjal 42, Abhijit Deshpande 60, N. H. Phadnis 100 not out, V. V. Oka 44, Y. S. Kadam 34 not out; D. T. Patel three for 111) and 249 for three dec. (S. S. Bhave 104 not out, S. V. Jedhe 78, S. S. Sugwekar 45); Gujarat* 251 (M. H. Parmar 46, B. H. Mistry 37, N. A. Patel 40; R. T. Yerwadekar four for 77, Y. S. Kadam five for 55) and 262 for seven (M. H. Parmar 121 not out, B. H. Mistry 77). *Maharashtra 20 pts, Gujarat 10 pts.*

At Wankhede Stadium, Bombay, December 23, 24, 25, 26. Drawn. Baroda 215 (R. B. Parikh 36, N. R. Mongia 46, A. D. Gaekwad 56; L. S. Rajput five for 32) and 483 for nine dec. (K. S. Chavan 177 not out, N. R. Mongia 77, A. C. Bedade 64, A. D. Gaekwad 32, K. D. Amin 53; S. A. Ankola three for 74); Bombay* 377 (C. S. Pandit 78, V. G. Kambli 50, Iqbal Khan 81, Extras 40, Penalty 36; R. G. M. Patel six for 93) and 281 for five (L. S. Rajput 55, C. S. Pandit 73 not out, V. G. Kambli 64, Penalty 36). *Bombay 17 pts, Baroda 10 pts.*

At Gujarat Stadium, Motera, Ahmedabad, December 23, 24, 25, 26. Drawn. Gujarat* 329 (S. D. Pathak 111, Z. H. Jariwala 31, B. K. Patel 51, N. Y. Laliwala 42; H. Joshi four for 66) and 217 for three (M. H. Parmar 63, P. H. Bhatt 107 not out); Saurashtra 449 for six dec. (B. S. Pujara 85, S. S. Tanna 100, B. M. Jadeja 82, N. R. Odedra 130 not out; B. H. Mistry four for 115). *Gujarat 6 pts, Saurashtra 11 pts.*

At Motibaug Palace Ground, Baroda, December 29, 30, 31, January 1. Baroda won by three wickets. Saurashtra 294 (B. M. Jadeja 30, A. N. Pandya 35, B. Dutta 108, C. C. Mankad 57; R. G. M. Patel four for 71, S. A. Doshi three for 48) and 267 (B. S. Pujara 45, A. N. Pandya 62, Extras 42, Penalty 36; M. S. Narula four for 53, S. A. Doshi three for 11); Baroda* 284 (A. C. Bedade 112, R. Naik 42, N. R. Mongia 31; B. M. Radia six for 54) and 305 for seven (R. B. Parikh 35, K. S. Chavan 61, N. R. Mongia 44, M. S. Narula 52 not out, Penalty 72). *Baroda 20 pts, Saurashtra 9 pts.*

At Nehru Stadium, Pune, December 29, 30, 31, January 1. Drawn. Bombay* 515 (L. S. Rajput 35, S. S. Dighe 35, J. B. Jadhav 96, C. S. Pandit 98, V. G. Kambli 71, S. A. Ankola 36, S. Krishnan 35; R. T. Yerwadekar three for 132) and 239 for four (S. S. Dighe 95, D. B. Vengsarkar 56, V. G. Kambli 51 not out); Maharashtra 525 (S. S. Bhave 189, S. S. Sugwekar 31, M. D. Gunjal 204, Abhijit Deshpande 44, N. H. Phadnis 32; P. A. Desai three for 122, P. N. Soneji three for 110). *Maharashtra 15 pts, Bombay 10 pts.*

Maharashtra 64 pts, Bombay 58 pts, Baroda 56 pts, Saurashtra 37 pts, Gujarat 33 pts. Maharashtra and Bombay qualified for the knockout stage.

## Pre-quarter-finals

At Nehru Stadium, Indore, February 2, 3, 4, 5. Bombay won by ten wickets. Madhya Pradesh* 377 (P. K. Dwivedi 96, S. M. Patil 54, R. K. Chauhan 100 not out; S. A. Ankola three for 70, K. D. Mokashi three for 89, S. S. Patil three for 114) and 165 (R. J. Shastri five for 61, S. S. Patil four for 60); Bombay 493 (R. J. Shastri 158, S. V. Manjrekar 51, V. G. Kambli 36, S. R. Tendulkar 69, D. B. Vengsarkar 69, R. R. Kulkarni 52; N. D. Hirwani three for 125) and 50 for no wkt.

At Nehru Stadium, Pune, February 2, 3, 4, 5, 6. Drawn. Karnataka were declared winners by virtue of their first-innings lead. Karnataka* 638 (C. Saldanha 74, V. A. Raja 30, K. A. Jeshwant 175, R. S. Dravid 82, A. Kumble 111 not out, J. Srinath 59, Extras 32; Y. S. Kadam three for 104) and 307 for two (C. Saldanha 138 not out, P. V. Shashikanth 58, V. A. Raja 78); Maharashtra 311 (M. M. More 85, M. D. Gunjal 57, Penalty 60; J. Srinath seven for 93) and 268 for two (S. S. Bhave 113 not out, S. V. Jedhe 111).

## Quarter-finals

At Eden Gardens, Calcutta, February 16, 17, 18, 19, 20. Drawn. Bengal were declared winners by virtue of their quotient of 3.26 compared with Karnataka's quotient of 3.17. Karnataka* 791 for six dec. (P. V. Shashikanth 35, V. A. Raja 267, S. M. H. Kirmani 112, R. S. Dravid 134, K. A. Jeshwant 119 not out, A. Kumble 68 not out, Extras 32; S. Sensharma three for 161); Bengal 652 for nine (M. Das 41, S. J. Kalyani 260, Saurav Ganguly 74, Snehashish Ganguly 116 not out, Penalty 60; J. Srinath four for 98, V. Prasad three for 119).

At Mecon Stadium, Ranchi, February 16, 17, 18, 19, 20. Drawn. Hyderabad were declared winners by virtue of their first-innings lead. There was no play on the last three days. Bihar* 203 (H. Gidwani 46, S. Chatterjee 38, D. K. Singh 36; Kanwaljit Singh five for 44); Hyderabad 298 for six (Abdul Azeem 78, M. V. Sridhar 112 not out, M. V. Ramanamurthy 33 not out; Abinash Kumar three for 130).

At Ferozshah Kotla Ground, Delhi, April 16, 17, 18, 19, 20. Drawn. Bombay were declared winners by virtue of their first-innings lead. Bombay 390 (S. V. Manjrekar 47, S. R. Tendulkar 82, V. G. Kambli 54, C. S. Pandit 74, S. S. Patil 44; A. S. Wassan six for 117) and 719 for eight dec. (S. S. Hattangadi 137, S. V. Manjrekar 156, D. B. Vengsarkar 88, S. R. Tendulkar 125, C. S. Pandit 100 retired hurt; A. S. Wassan four for 170); Delhi* 389 (Bantoo Singh 111, Sanjay Sharma 48, Ajay Sharma 54, Sanjeev Sharma 32, A. S. Wassan 32, Extras 34; R. R. Kulkarni three for 109, S. S. Patil five for 109) and 371 for four (M. Nayyar 101 not out, Extras 32, Penalty 180).

At Nahar Singh Stadium, Faridabad, April 16, 17, 18, 19, 20. Drawn. Haryana were declared winners by virtue of their first-innings lead. Haryana* 339 (A. Kaypee 152, Kapil Dev 66, P. Jain 38; A. W. Zaidi eight for 119) and 429 for nine dec. (A. Kaypee 173, Ajay Jadeja 87, R. Puri 60, Extras 33; A. W. Zaidi six for 152); Uttar Pradesh 295 (S. S. Khandkar 69, R. V. Sapru 98, G. K. Pande 47 not out; Ajay Jadeja four for 37) and 221 for seven (R. V. Sapru 71, G. K. Pande 52, R. P. Singh 44 not out; Chetan Sharma seven for 72).

## Semi-finals

At Wankhede Stadium, Bombay, April 24, 25, 26, 27, 28. Drawn. Bombay were declared winners by virtue of their first-innings lead. Bombay* 855 for six dec. (S. V. Manjrekar 377, D. B. Vengsarkar 121, S. R. Tendulkar 70, V. G. Kambli 126, C. S. Pandit 36 not out, R. R. Kulkarni 34 not out, Extras 30, Penalty 48; N. R. Yadav three for 111) and 446 for four dec. (L. S. Rajput 50, S. S. Hattangadi 73, S. R. Tendulkar 88, V. G. Kambli 127, C. S. Pandit 100 not out); Hyderabad 498 (R. A. Swarup 123, M. V. Sridhar 184, V. Jaisimha 71, S. L. V. Raju 54, Penalty 36; R. R. Kulkarni four for 113, S. S. Patil four for 71) and 36 for no wkt.

At Eden Gardens, Calcutta, April 24, 25, 26, 27, 28. Drawn. Haryana were declared winners by virtue of their first-innings lead. Haryana 605 (Deepak Sharma 54, Ajay Jadeja 59, A. Kaypee 78, Kapil Dev 141, A. Banerjee 111, V. Yadav 106; D. Mukherjee four for 100, S. Sensharma three for 99) and 274 for five (Ajay Jadeja 85, A. Kaypee 102, Penalty 48; S. Sensharma four for 74); Bengal* 440 (Pranab Roy 45, Arun Lal 136, Snehashish Ganguly 41, U. Chatterjee 64, S. Mukherjee 50; Chetan Sharma three for 65, Kapil Dev five for 85).

## Final

At Wankhede Stadium, Bombay, May 3, 4, 5, 6, 7. Haryana won by 2 runs. Haryana* 522 (Deepak Sharma 199, Ajay Jadeja 94, A. Kaypee 52, A. Kuruvilla four for 128, S. A. Ankola three for 77) and 242 (Dhanraj Singh 33, A. Banerjee 60, Kapil Dev 41; S. A. Ankola three for 39, S. S. Patil three for 65); Bombay 410 (L. S. Rajput 74, S. S. Patil 85, S. V. Manjrekar 37, D. B. Vengsarkar 38, S. R. Tendulkar 47, C. S. Pandit 40 not out, S. A. Ankola 31; Kapil Dev three for 54, Y. Bhandari five for 118) and 352 (D. B. Vengsarkar 139 not out, S. R. Tendulkar 96, V. G. Kambli 45).

## RANJI TROPHY WINNERS

| | | | | | |
|---|---|---|---|---|---|
| 1934-35 | Bombay | 1953-54 | Bombay | 1972-73 | Bombay |
| 1935-36 | Bombay | 1954-55 | Madras | 1973-74 | Karnataka |
| 1936-37 | Nawanagar | 1955-56 | Bombay | 1974-75 | Bombay |
| 1937-38 | Hyderabad | 1956-57 | Bombay | 1975-76 | Bombay |
| 1938-39 | Bengal | 1957-58 | Baroda | 1976-77 | Bombay |
| 1939-40 | Maharashtra | 1958-59 | Bombay | 1977-78 | Karnataka |
| 1940-41 | Maharashtra | 1959-60 | Bombay | 1978-79 | Delhi |
| 1941-42 | Bombay | 1960-61 | Bombay | 1979-80 | Delhi |
| 1942-43 | Baroda | 1961-62 | Bombay | 1980-81 | Bombay |
| 1943-44 | Western India | 1962-63 | Bombay | 1981-82 | Delhi |
| 1944-45 | Bombay | 1963-64 | Bombay | 1982-83 | Karnataka |
| 1945-46 | Holkar | 1964-65 | Bombay | 1983-84 | Bombay |
| 1946-47 | Baroda | 1965-66 | Bombay | 1984-85 | Bombay |
| 1947-48 | Holkar | 1966-67 | Bombay | 1985-86 | Delhi |
| 1948-49 | Bombay | 1967-68 | Bombay | 1986-87 | Hyderabad |
| 1949-50 | Baroda | 1968-69 | Bombay | 1987-88 | Tamil Nadu |
| 1950-51 | Holkar | 1969-70 | Bombay | 1988-89 | Delhi |
| 1951-52 | Bombay | 1970-71 | Bombay | 1989-90 | Bengal |
| 1952-53 | Holkar | 1971-72 | Bombay | 1990-91 | Haryana |

## IRANI CUP, 1990-91

### Ranji Trophy Champions (Bengal) v Rest of India

At M. Chinnaswamy Stadium, Bangalore, November 2, 3, 4, 5, 6. Drawn. Rest of India 737 for seven dec. (R. J. Shastri 217, W. V. Raman 41, P. K. Amre 246, N. R. Mongia 92, S. L. V. Raju 34, Extras 49; D. Mukherjee three for 129); Bengal* 262 (Arun Lal 68, Saurav Ganguly 37, Extras 35; S. L. V. Raju four for 57) and 373 for eight (Arun Lal 164 not out, Snehashish Ganguly 76, Extras 36).

## DULEEP TROPHY, 1990-91

At Nehru Stadium, Guwahati, January 11, 12, 13, 14, 15. Drawn. West Zone were declared winners by virtue of their first-innings lead. West Zone* 604 (R. J. Shastri 35, L. S. Rajput 82, S. V. Manjrekar 122, D. B. Vengsarkar 72, S. R. Tendulkar 159, K. S. More 48; Abinash Kumar five for 172, Saurav Ganguly four for 117) and 231 for six dec. (L. S. Rajput 46, D. B. Vengsarkar 37, V. G. Kambli 87; Abinash Kumar five for 94); East Zone 317 (S. S. Karim 32, A. Malhotra 31, Saurav Ganguly 124 not out; R. R. Kulkarni four for 106, R. J. Shastri three for 80) and 136 for four (Rajinder Singh 44, Abinash Kumar 52).

## Semi-finals

At Ispat Stadium, Rourkela, January 18, 19, 20, 21, 22. Drawn. West Zone were declared winners by virtue of their first-innings lead. South Zone 515 (K. Srikkanth 58, W. V. Raman 150, Robin Singh 34, M. Azharuddin 65, S. M. H. Kirmani 110; S. R. Tendulkar three for 60) and 409 for five (K. Srikkanth 53, Robin Singh 123 not out, M. Azharuddin 87 not out, Extras 30, Penalty 72); West Zone* 747 (L. S. Rajput 192, D. B. Vengsarkar 94, S. R. Tendulkar 131, R. J. Shastri 53, V. G. Kambli 96, R. R. Kulkarni 69, Extras 60; A. Kumble three for 153).

At Moin-ul-Haque Stadium, Patna, January 18, 19, 20, 21, 22. North Zone won by ten wickets. Central Zone* 277 (Yusuf Ali Khan 72, S. S. Khandkar 37, R. V. Sapru 55; A. S. Wassan four for 57) and 206 (P. K. Amre 103; Kapil Dev three for 47, Maninder Singh five for 84); North Zone 452 (Ajay Jadeja 61, Ajay Sharma 40, K. Azad 141, M. Prabhakar 66, Kapil Dev 69; P. S. Vaidya six for 128, N. D. Hirwani three for 117) and 32 for no wkt.

## Final

At Keenan Stadium, Jamshedpur, January 25, 26, 27, 28, 29. Drawn. North Zone were declared winners by virtue of their first-innings lead. North Zone* 729 for nine dec. (Ajay Jadeja 54, R. Lamba 180, M. Prabhakar 143, K. Bhaskar Pillai 96, K. Azad 38, Kapil Dev 119, Chetan Sharma 50, Extras 33; C. C. Mankad three for 111) and 59 for no wkt; West Zone 561 (R. J. Shastri 152, L. S. Rajput 33, S. V. Manjrekar 105, D. B. Vengsarkar 114, K. S. More 50, Extras 46).

# CRICKET IN PAKISTAN, 1990-91

## By ABID ALI KAZI

For reasons outside the control of the country's cricket authorities, Pakistan's 1990-91 domestic programme enjoyed more or less uninterrupted progress, owing to the cancellation or postponement of international tours to or by Pakistan. First of all, the tour by Pakistan Under-23 to Sri Lanka in August was cancelled at the last moment – the players were in the middle of their pre-tour practice camp – owing to the troubled political situation in the host country. Then, at the end of the year, the senior team not only opted out of the Asia Cup tournament in India but also put off their projected tour there, in early January, because of the political tension between the neighbouring countries. It was in January, too, that the visit to Pakistan by England A was abandoned after three matches, the Foreign Offices of both countries advising against the team remaining in the country while anti-West sentiments were running high as a result of the war in the Gulf. As in the instance of the Pakistan teams going abroad, it was felt that the safety of the players could not be ensured.

The season got under way with the now-customary National Under-19 Championship, with twenty teams participating in two divisions at twelve centres. The Grade I tournament was won by Lahore City A, who defeated their traditional rivals, Karachi Whites, while Quetta were relegated to Grade II, from which Karachi Blues won promotion as their reward for defeating Lahore City B in the final.

The Wills Cup one-day tournament, which in recent years had generated interest and produced some good cricket, was a low-key affair, the only surprises being the defeats of Karachi Blues and ADBP at the hands of Bahawalpur and Multan respectively. As in the previous season, however, there was some wrangling over the transfer of a player, with United Bank criticising the Board of Control for Cricket in Pakistan (BCCP) for allowing Saeed Anwar to play for ADBP without obtaining a "No Objection" certificate from them. The Board rebutted the criticism, claiming that, as Saeed Anwar had not been named on United Bank's list of 25 players, they were not prepared to let a Pakistan team member go without match practice before the forthcoming tour by New Zealand. The final of the Wills Cup, between United Bank and Habib Bank, was played for the first time in Gujranwala and attracted a capacity crowd. Well beaten by 56 runs, United Bank had to be satisfied with the role of runner-up for the fifth time in the past ten finals.

The rules and the structure of the first-class competitions, the Patron's Trophy and the Quaid-e-Azam Trophy, were once again changed, as seems to have become the common practice. This time, however, the changes implemented by the Board were constructive. The old bonus-points system was abolished, and under the new system an outright win carried ten points, while the lead on first innings in a drawn game was worth five points. Matches in which a first-innings lead was not gained brought no points; nor did one in which the scores were level on first innings. The Board's strategy was to discourage teams from playing with the sole objective of gaining bonus points. To make the country's major first-class cricket regional, the Board decided that the Quaid-e-Azam Trophy competition would be for city, regional and divisional teams, while the Patron's Trophy would become the championship for commercial departments and professional organisations. In addition to these changes, the Pentangular Trophy was revived after a lapse of five years, to be contested by the top five teams in the Patron's Trophy.

United Bank headed the Patron's Trophy table with 55 points, followed by ADBP, who secured 40 points, and fittingly these two went on to contest the final. United Bank beat National Bank by ten wickets in their semi-final, but the other semi-final, between Habib Bank and ADBP, was decided on first-innings lead owing to rain and a damp pitch. The final was decided similarly, ADBP outplaying United Bank at the National Stadium in Karachi. HBFC were relegated to Grade II, the non first-class tournament, for 1991-92, while the Pakistan Automobile Corporation (PACO) qualified for the first-class section by defeating WAPDA by an innings and 79 runs in the Grade II final. HBFC's relegation was of their own making, for, having been refused a change of venue for their games against PNSC and Combined Universities, they conceded walkovers to these opponents. The Board then scratched them from the tournament, only to change its mind; not that this helped HBFC, who failed to score any points from the fixtures they played. Karachi Whites defeated Bahawalpur by an innings and 163 runs to win the Quaid-e-Azam, while Lahore City defeated Karachi Greens on first innings to win the Grade II final and gain promotion at the expense of Multan. The revived Pentangular Trophy was won by United Bank.

Shoaib Mohammad headed the batting averages for the season with 943 runs at 85.72 from eight games, his aggregate boosted by the 675 runs he scored in his seven innings against the touring New Zealanders for Pakistan and PIA. Sajid Ali, of National Bank and Karachi Whites, had the highest aggregate, 1,460 runs at 48.66 including four hundreds, and with eighteen catches in eighteen games he was also the leading fieldsman. Four other players reached 1,000 runs: Saeed Azad (National Bank and Karachi Blues) 1,291, Inzamam-ul-Haq (United Bank and Multan) 1,207, Mansoor Rana (ADBP) 1,035, and Zahoor Elahi (ADBP and Multan) 1,019.

The United Bank and Multan international pair, Waqar Younis and Masood Anwar, shared the honour of taking most wickets, with 70 apiece at 15.97 and 19.02 respectively. Aamer Hanif of Karachi Whites claimed pride of place atop the national averages, his seventeen wickets costing just 11.23 each and including a hat-trick against Bahawalpur in the Quaid-e-Azam final. The season's other hat-trick was performed by Shahid Ali Khan, for Combined Universities against PNSC in the Patron's Trophy. Munir Shaukat of Faisalabad also made his way into the record books when he dismissed Sargodha's Mohammad Hasnain with his first ball in first-class cricket. Sajjad Akbar, of Sargodha and PNSC, turned in the best all-round figures, scoring 628 runs, capturing 52 wickets and holding fourteen catches, while Bilal Ahmed, of ADBP and Faisalabad, effected 59 dismissals, including eight stumpings, in nineteen games to head the wicket-keepers' list.

## FIRST-CLASS AVERAGES, 1990-91

### BATTING

(Qualification: 500 runs, average 30.00)

| | M | I | NO | R | HI | 100s | Avge |
|---|---|---|---|---|---|---|---|
| Shoaib Mohammad (*PIA*) | 8 | 15 | 4 | 943 | 203* | 4 | 85.72 |
| Mansoor Rana (*ADBP*) | 11 | 19 | 4 | 1,035 | 157* | 4 | 69.00 |
| Shafiq Ahmad (*United Bank*) | 11 | 17 | 5 | 796 | 103* | 1 | 66.33 |
| Asif Mujtaba (*PIA/Karachi Whites*) | 9 | 12 | 3 | 580 | 189 | 3 | 64.44 |
| Inzamam-ul-Haq (*United Bank/Multan*) | 16 | 25 | 6 | 1,207 | 163* | 4 | 63.52 |
| Salim Malik (*Habib Bank*) | 10 | 17 | 2 | 949 | 138 | 4 | 63.26 |
| Pervez Shah (*United Bank*) | 11 | 15 | 5 | 580 | 116* | 3 | 58.00 |
| Sajid Ali (*National Bank/Karachi Whites*) | 18 | 33 | 3 | 1,459 | 202* | 4 | 48.63 |
| Zahoor Elahi (*ADBP/Multan*) | 13 | 25 | 3 | 1,019 | 159 | 3 | 46.31 |
| Shahid Tanvir (*National Bank*) | 11 | 21 | 6 | 648 | 113* | 1 | 43.20 |
| Ameer Akbar (*National Bank*) | 11 | 21 | 4 | 719 | 101* | 2 | 42.29 |
| Aamer Sohail (*Habib Bank/Sargodha*) | 12 | 19 | 0 | 795 | 133 | 2 | 41.84 |
| Saeed Azad (*National Bank/Karachi Blues*) | 17 | 32 | 1 | 1,291 | 178 | 2 | 41.64 |
| Sher Ali (*United Bank/Peshawar*) | 9 | 16 | 0 | 666 | 133 | 2 | 41.62 |
| Saifullah (*United Bank*) | 11 | 20 | 4 | 641 | 120 | 1 | 40.06 |
| Raees Ahmed (*United Bank*) | 12 | 21 | 3 | 718 | 125 | 3 | 39.88 |
| Ghaffar Kazmi (*ADBP*) | 9 | 17 | 1 | 596 | 108 | 1 | 37.25 |
| Sajjad Akbar (*PNSC/Sargodha*) | 16 | 22 | 5 | 628 | 104* | 1 | 36.94 |
| Mahmood Hamid (*PNSC/Karachi Whites*) | 10 | 17 | 3 | 514 | 82 | 0 | 36.71 |
| Wasim Hyder (*PIA/Faisalabad*) | 14 | 19 | 3 | 544 | 76* | 0 | 34.00 |
| Mansoor Akhtar (*United Bank/Karachi Whites*) | 18 | 27 | 1 | 874 | 121 | 2 | 33.61 |
| Atif Rauf (*ADBP*) | 11 | 21 | 0 | 699 | 153 | 2 | 33.28 |
| Shaukat Mirza (*Habib Bank*) | 12 | 22 | 2 | 627 | 100 | 1 | 31.35 |
| Iqbal Imam (*United Bank/Karachi Blues*) | 12 | 18 | 1 | 532 | 158 | 1 | 31.29 |

\* *Signifies not out.*

### BOWLING

(Qualification: 25 wickets)

| | O | M | R | W | BB | Avge |
|---|---|---|---|---|---|---|
| Wasim Akram (*Pakistan*) | 184.5 | 36 | 460 | 31 | 5-28 | 14.83 |
| Haaris Khan (*Karachi Blues*) | 359 | 88 | 855 | 56 | 7-44 | 15.26 |
| Athar Laeeq (*Karachi Whites*) | 201.3 | 37 | 669 | 42 | 7-23 | 15.92 |
| Waqar Younis (*United Bank/Multan*) | 382.3 | 89 | 1,118 | 70 | 7-64 | 15.97 |
| Mohammad Zahid (*Bahawalpur*) | 255.1 | 81 | 551 | 34 | 6-20 | 16.20 |
| Mushtaq Ahmed (*United Bank/Multan*) | 214.4 | 36 | 623 | 35 | 9-93 | 17.80 |
| Zakir Khan (*ADBP/Peshawar*) | 402.5 | 88 | 1,117 | 60 | 7-47 | 18.61 |
| Shahid Mahboob (*Karachi Whites*) | 279.5 | 52 | 880 | 47 | 8-62 | 18.72 |
| Rashid Khan (*PIA*) | 168.3 | 31 | 528 | 28 | 7-69 | 18.85 |
| Masood Anwar (*United Bank/Multan*) | 582.2 | 165 | 1,332 | 70 | 6-44 | 19.02 |
| Saleem Jaffer (*United Bank*) | 200.5 | 35 | 626 | 31 | 5-56 | 20.19 |
| Tanvir Mehdi (*United Bank*) | 217.4 | 24 | 735 | 36 | 6-52 | 20.41 |
| Amanullah (*United Bank/Sargodha*) | 226 | 46 | 708 | 34 | 5-42 | 20.82 |
| Wasim Hyder (*PIA/Faisalabad*) | 410 | 81 | 1,162 | 55 | 6-46 | 21.12 |

| | O | M | R | W | BB | Avge |
|---|---|---|---|---|---|---|
| Aziz-ur-Rehman (*Combined Universities/Sargodha*) | 341.3 | 84 | 832 | 39 | 6-81 | 21.33 |
| Saadat Gul (*Faisalabad*) | 156.2 | 29 | 535 | 25 | 6-67 | 21.40 |
| Raja Afaq (*ADBP/Rawalpindi*) | 455 | 104 | 1,180 | 55 | 5-51 | 21.45 |
| Murtaza Hussain (*Bahawalpur*) | 228 | 37 | 596 | 26 | 4-52 | 22.92 |
| Akram Raza (*Habib Bank*) | 372.1 | 88 | 1,066 | 43 | 5-57 | 24.79 |
| Barkatullah (*National Bank/Karachi Blues*) | 317.4 | 54 | 1,097 | 44 | 6-18 | 24.93 |
| Amin Lakhani (*PNSC/Karachi Blues*) | 628 | 137 | 1,549 | 61 | 5-48 | 25.39 |
| Iqbal Sikandar (*PIA/Karachi Whites*) | 461.3 | 124 | 1,147 | 39 | 4-15 | 29.41 |
| Mohammad Asif (*ADBP*) | 427.5 | 93 | 1,035 | 33 | 6-102 | 31.36 |
| Iqbal Qasim (*National Bank*) | 312.3 | 50 | 892 | 28 | 5-31 | 31.85 |
| Sajjad Akbar (*PNSC/Sargodha*) | 631.4 | 122 | 1,728 | 52 | 5-40 | 33.23 |
| Nadeem Ghauri (*Habib Bank*) | 501.4 | 140 | 1,359 | 40 | 6-57 | 33.97 |

*In the following scores,* * *by the name of a team indicates that they won the toss.*

## BCCP PATRON'S TROPHY, 1990-91

| | Played | Won | Lost | Drawn | 1st-inns lead in drawn match | Points |
|---|---|---|---|---|---|---|
| United Bank | 7 | 4 | 0 | 3 | 3 | 55 |
| ADBP | 7 | 3 | 1 | 3 | 2 | 40 |
| Habib Bank | 7 | 3 | 2 | 2 | 1 | 35 |
| National Bank | 7 | 3 | 2 | 2 | 1 | 35 |
| PNSC | 7 | 3 | 3 | 1 | 0 | 30 |
| PIA | 7 | 2 | 2 | 3 | 1 | 25 |
| Combined Universities | 7 | 2 | 5 | 0 | 0 | 20 |
| HBFC | 7 | 0 | 5 | 2 | 0 | 0 |

*Win = 10 pts; 1st-innings lead in drawn match = 5 pts.*

**Semi-finals**: *United Bank beat National Bank by ten wickets; ADBP beat Habib Bank by virtue of their first-innings lead.*
**Final**: *ADBP beat United Bank by virtue of their first-innings lead.*

*Note:* First innings closed at 85 overs in the group matches.

At Defence Housing Authority Stadium, Karachi, September 30, October 1, 2, 3. PIA won by seven wickets. HBFC* 248 for six (Fazal Qureshi 85, Munir-ul-Haq 97, Tariq Alam 32; Iqbal Sikandar three for 82) and 162 (Zulfiqar Butt 49; Wasim Hyder three for 47, Tanvir Ali four for 50); PIA 284 for nine (Shoaib Mohammad 45, Aamer Malik 48, Zahid Ahmed 56, Asif Mohammad 56, Wasim Hyder 41 not out) and 128 for three (Shoaib Mohammad 34, Aamer Malik 37 not out). *PIA 10 pts.*

At Defence Housing Authority Stadium, Karachi, October 6, 7, 8, 9. Habib Bank won by 174 runs. Habib Bank* 112 (Mohammad Javed four for 32, Amin Lakhani four for 45) and 349 for nine dec. (Arshad Pervez 126, Anwar Miandad 99, Shaukat Mirza 46; Amin Lakhani three for 154); PNSC 180 for nine (Nasir Wasti 71; Akram Raza four for 48) and 107 (Naved Anjum four for 32). *Habib Bank 10 pts.*

At Punjab University Ground, Lahore, October 6, 7, 8, 9. United Bank won by seven wickets. United Bank 291 for nine (Saifullah 39, Inzamam-ul-Haq 104, Raees Ahmed 42, Masood Anwar 48; Sajjad Ali four for 66) and 150 for three (Shafiq Ahmad 71 not out); Combined Universities* 133 (Rizwan Qazi 30; Amanullah three for 37, Masood Anwar four for 18) and 303 (Ahmad Munir 37, Sajjad Ali 87, Kashif Khan 62; Amanullah four for 33, Masood Anwar four for 57). *United Bank 10 pts.*

At Arbab Niaz Stadium, Peshawar, October 6, 7, 8, 9. ADBP won by 125 runs. ADBP* 264 (Ghaffar Kazmi 91, Bilal Ahmed 45, Raja Afaq 33 not out; Barkatullah three for 25, Iqbal Qasim four for 52) and 362 for seven dec. (Zahoor Elahi 159, Bilal Ahmed 60 not out, Javed Hayat 31 not out); National Bank 163 (Ameer Akbar 46; Manzoor Elahi four for 56) and 338 (Sajid Ali 144, Siddiq Patni 53, Ameer Akbar 69; Mohammad Asif six for 102). *ADBP 10 pts.*

At Niaz Stadium, Hyderabad, October 13, 14, 15. PNSC won by 91 runs. PNSC* 135 (Sohail Jaffer 68; Rashid Khan five for 59, Zahid Ahmed four for 12) and 171 (Sohail Jaffer 82; Rashid Khan seven for 69, Wasim Hyder three for 49); PIA 68 (Mohsin Kamal four for 27, Amin Lakhani three for 4) and 147 (Zahid Ahmed 36; Mohsin Kamal three for 68, Mohammad Javed five for 37). *PNSC 10 pts.*

At Defence Housing Authority Stadium, Karachi, October 13, 14, 15, 16. Habib Bank won by five wickets. HBFC 156 (Nadeem Ghauri five for 37) and 128 (Sarfraz Azeem 36; Akram Raza four for 42, Nadeem Ghauri four for 53); Habib Bank* 158 (Akram Raza 36, Azhar Khan 34; Mohinder Kumar eight for 84) and 131 for five (Arshad Pervez 57 not out; Mohinder Kumar four for 64). *Habib Bank 10 pts.*

At Punjab University Ground, Lahore, October 13, 14, 15, 16. National Bank won by nine wickets. National Bank* 272 for seven (Sajid Ali 84, Ameer Akbar 38, Shahid Tanvir 52 not out) and 66 for one (Sajid Ali 44 not out); Combined Universities 98 (Iqbal Qasim five for 31, Hafeez-ur-Rehman five for 37) and 239 (Ahmad Munir 53, Kashif Khan 44, Rizwan Qazi 50, Zain-ul-Abideen 38; Iqbal Qasim three for 50, Shahid Tanvir three for 40). *National Bank 10 pts.*

At Arbab Niaz Stadium, Peshawar, October 13, 14, 15, 16. United Bank won by 164 runs. United Bank 279 (Saifullah 86, Sher Ali 38, Shafiq Ahmad 47, Pervez Shah 43 not out; Zakir Khan four for 82, Raja Afaq four for 67) and 192 (Raees Ahmed 33, Pervez Shah 45, Mansoor Akhtar 35; Zakir Khan four for 35); ADBP* 216 (Mansoor Rana 55, Bilal Ahmed 37 not out; Amanullah five for 42, Tanvir Mehdi three for 42) and 91 (Tanvir Mehdi six for 52, Masood Anwar three for 17). *United Bank 10 pts.*

At National Stadium, Karachi, October 20, 21, 22. PIA won by nine wickets. PIA 392 for seven (Aamer Malik 161, Sagheer Abbas 53, Wasim Hyder 44 not out) and 82 for one (Aamer Malik 41); Habib Bank* 204 (Anwar Miandad 63, Akram Raza 32; Rashid Khan four for 78, Asif Mohammad three for 24) and 268 (Agha Zahid 46, Shaukat Mirza 100, Tahir Rasheed 31; Rashid Khan three for 75, Wasim Hyder six for 100). *PIA 10 pts.*

At Montgomery Biscuit Factory Ground, Sahiwal, October 20, 21, 22, 23. PNSC were awarded a walkover when HBFC failed to appear. *PNSC 10 pts.*

At Punjab University Ground, Lahore, October 20, 21, 22, 23. ADBP won by six wickets. Combined Universities* 259 (Ahmad Munir 38, Babar Zaman 59, Kamran Khan 57; Raja Afaq four for 76, Khatib Rizwan three for 80) and 238 (Rizwan Qazi 89, Mohammad Riaz 37; Zakir Khan seven for 47, Raja Afaq three for 79); ADBP 274 for six (Atif Rauf 109, Mansoor Rana 87) and 224 for four (Saeed Anwar 52, Mansoor Rana 80 not out, Ghaffar Kazmi 51 not out). *ADBP 10 pts.*

At LCCA Ground, Lahore, October 20, 21, 22, 23. United Bank won by eight wickets. National Bank* 208 (Tahir Shah 33, Sajid Ali 102; Masood Anwar four for 53, Mushtaq Ahmed five for 48) and 208 (Sajid Ali 51, Saeed Azad 43, Extras 34; Tanvir Mehdi five for 33, Masood Anwar three for 42); United Bank 246 (Raees Ahmed 31, Iqbal Imam 34, Shafiq Ahmad 53, Mansoor Akhtar 54; Shakil Sajjad three for 35) and 172 for two (Saifullah 57 not out, Shafiq Ahmad 66 not out). *United Bank 10 pts.*

At Bagh-e-Jinnah Ground, Lahore, October 28, 29, 30, 31. Drawn. National Bank* 303 for nine (Tahir Shah 103, Ameer Akbar 76, Wasim Arif 34 not out; Amin Lakhani four for 108) and 444 for seven dec. (Sajid Ali 80, Saeed Azad 65, Ameer Akbar 78, Shahid Tanvir 113 not out, Wasim Arif 47; Amin Lakhani three for 151); PNSC 296 (Sohail Jaffer 78, Nasir Wasti 55, Mahmood Hamid 69, Sajjad Akbar 40; Barkatullah three for 41, Shahid Tanvir three for 64) and 106 for four (Aamer Ishaq 36). *National Bank 5 pts.*

At Punjab University Ground, Lahore, October 28, 29, 30, 31. Combined Universities were awarded a walkover when HBFC failed to appear. *Combined Universities 10 pts.*

At KRL Cricket Ground, Rawalpindi, October 28, 29, 30, 31. Drawn. United Bank* 293 for five (Saifullah 41, Mansoor Akhtar 71, Shafiq Ahmad 34, Inzamam-ul-Haq 101 not out) and 320 (Shafiq Ahmad 36, Inzamam-ul-Haq 71, Pervez Shah 106, Masood Anwar 47; Wasim Hyder three for 55, Zahid Ahmed four for 92); PIA 246 (Nasir Khan 33, Sagheer Abbas 57, Zahid Ahmed 32, Asif Mohammad 38; Masood Anwar five for 72) and 291 for nine (Nasir Khan 39, Sagheer Abbas 30, Zahid Ahmed 38, Wasim Hyder 76 not out; Masood Anwar five for 94). *United Bank 5 pts.*

At LCCA Ground, Lahore, October 28, 29, 30, 31. Drawn. Habib Bank* 286 (Aamer Sohail 133, Agha Zahid 78, Shahid Javed 36; Zakir Khan four for 48, Javed Hayat four for 78) and 312 (Aamer Sohail 59, Agha Zahid 86, Shahid Javed 38, Akram Raza 38, Nadeem Ghauri 32 not out; Zakir Khan five for 86, Sabih Azhar three for 60); ADBP 241 for nine (Sabih Azhar 32, Saeed Anwar 70, Mansoor Rana 50, Ghaffar Kazmi 31; Nadeem Ghauri four for 58) and 218 for nine (Saeed Anwar 57, Sabih Azhar 61, Mansoor Rana 54; Akram Raza four for 57, Nadeem Ghauri five for 59). *Habib Bank 5 pts.*

At Municipal Stadium, Gujranwala, November 3, 4, 5, 6. National Bank won by six wickets. Habib Bank 288 for nine (Aamer Sohail 59, Moin-ul-Atiq 35, Shaukat Mirza 39, Shahid Javed 65; Shakil Sajjad four for 72, Tahir Shah four for 74) and 205 (Aamer Sohail 46, Shaukat Mirza 56; Habib Baloch seven for 98); National Bank* 333 for three (Saeed Azad 167, Ameer Akbar 100 not out) and 163 for four (Sajid Ali 102 not out). *National Bank 10 pts.*

At LCCA Ground, Lahore, November 3, 4, 5, 6. ADBP won by two wickets. PNSC* 250 (Mahmood Hamid 82, Sajjad Akbar 34; Mohammad Asif four for 77, Raja Afaq five for 75) and 198 (Sohail Miandad 57; Raja Afaq four for 25, Javed Hayat three for 43); ADBP 191 (Atif Rauf 46; Sajjad Akbar four for 50) and 260 for eight (Bilal Ahmed 45, Mansoor Rana 74 not out, Ghaffar Kazmi 64; Mohsin Kamal three for 58, Amin Lakhani four for 66). *ADBP 10 pts.*

At Punjab University Ground, Lahore, November 3, 4, 5, 6. Combined Universities won by 29 runs. Combined Universities* 250 for eight (Aziz-ur-Rehman 55, Kamran Khan 50, Kashif Khan 40 not out, Sajjad Ali 33; Zahid Ahmed five for 83) and 165 (Kamran Khan 34, Rizwan Qazi 44, Kashif Khan 42; Asif Mohammad four for 25); PIA 199 (Asif Mohammad 35, Feroze Mehdi 47, Extras 32; Shahid Ali Khan three for 38) and 187 (Zahid Ahmed 43; Aziz-ur-Rehman four for 38, Rizwan Qazi three for 32). *Combined Universities 10 pts.*

At Iqbal Stadium, Faisalabad, November 3, 4, 5, 6. Drawn. HBFC 308 for nine (Aamer Khurshid 45, Tariq Alam 71, Mohinder Kumar 55 not out; Masood Anwar four for 76) and 307 for eight dec. (Monis Qadri 31, Fazal Qureshi 61, Munir-ul-Haq 107, Wasim Ali 31, Extras 35; Tanvir Mehdi three for 73); United Bank* 312 for eight (Saifullah 49, Inzamam-ul-Haq 163 not out) and 301 for four (Raees Ahmed 125, Mansoor Akhtar 75, Inzamam-ul-Haq 45 not out; Rafat Alam three for 83). *United Bank 5 pts.*

At Punjab University Ground, Lahore, November 10, 11, 12, 13. Habib Bank won by 27 runs. Habib Bank* 211 (Moin-ul-Atiq 48, Shaukat Mirza 83 not out; Sajjad Ali five for 56) and 190 (Moin-ul-Atiq 48, Anwar Miandad 41; Rizwan Qazi four for 40); Combined Universities 208 (Munir Shah 56, Rizwan Qazi 51 not out; Waheed Niazi three for 74, Nadeem Ghauri six for 28) and 166 (Aziz-ur-Rehman 40, Kashif Khan 43; Nadeem Ghauri six for 57). *Habib Bank 10 pts.*

At Municipal Stadium, Gujranwala, November 10, 11, 12, 13. United Bank won by ten wickets. PNSC 261 (Sohail Miandad 51, Sajjad Akbar 89; Amanullah five for 54) and 107 (Tanvir Mehdi five for 50); United Bank* 307 for four (Saifullah 41, Raees Ahmed 117, Shafiq Ahmad 53 not out, Inzamam-ul-Haq 45) and 65 for no wkt (Raees Ahmed 41 not out). *United Bank 10 pts.*

At KRL Cricket Ground, Rawalpindi, November 10, 11, 12, 13. Drawn. ADBP* 302 for nine (Tanvir Ahmed 31, Mansoor Rana 102, Ghaffar Kazmi 62, Javed Hayat 52; Wasim Hyder three for 71) and 204 (Ghaffar Kazmi 108, Bilal Ahmed 38; Rashid Khan three for 47, Tanvir Ali four for 34); PIA 287 (Rizwan-uz-Zaman 32, Sagheer Abbas 78, Asif Mohammad 42, Wasim Hyder 32; Mohammad Asif five for 67, Raja Afaq three for 56) and 171 for nine (Nasir Khan 44, Rizwan-uz-Zaman 62; Zakir Khan five for 58, Mohammad Asif three for 43). *ADBP 5 pts.*

At Arbab Niaz Stadium, Peshawar, November 10, 11, 12, 13. National Bank won by seven wickets. HBFC* 196 (Aamer Kurshid 47, Munir-ul-Haq 37; Habib Baloch five for 70) and 349 for eight dec. (Aamer Kurshid 164, Monis Qadri 42, Saleem Taj 42, Rafat Alam 33; Barkatullah four for 60, Iqbal Qasim three for 110); National Bank 277 for nine (Sajid Ali 90, Mohammad Jamil 43, Wasim Arif 53; Zulfiqar Butt seven for 107) and 270 for three (Mohammad Jamil 102 not out, Saeed Azad 48, Shahid Tanvir 83). *National Bank 10 pts.*

At Punjab University Ground, Lahore, November 17, 18, 19, 20. PNSC won by an innings and 8 runs. Combined Universities* 89 (Mohsin Kamal three for 42, Amin Lakhani four for 18) and 173 (Ahmad Munir 56, Munir Shah 38; Amin Lakhani five for 48, Sajjad Akbar three for 63); PNSC 270 (Qaiser Rasheed 37, Sohail Miandad 41, Sohail Jaffer 39, Sajjad Akbar 33, Mahmoud Hamid 43, Extras 43; Shahid Ali Khan seven for 79, including a hat-trick). *PNSC 10 pts.*

At Municipal Stadium, Gujranwala, November 17, 18, 19, 20. Drawn. Habib Bank 204 (Aamer Sohail 30, Nadeem Ghauri 38; Pervez Shah three for 45, Masood Anwar five for 71) and 513 for six (Aamer Sohail 74, Agha Zahid 33, Arshad Pervez 118, Shahid Javed 161 not out, Tahir Rasheed 66); United Bank* 257 for two (Raees Ahmed 109 not out, Mansoor Akhtar 36, Shafiq Ahmad 103 not out). *United Bank 5 pts.*

At KRL Cricket Ground, Rawalpindi, November 17, 18, 19, 20. Drawn. National Bank* 184 (Mohammad Jamil 38, Tahir Shah 36, Saeed Azad 52; Asif Mujtaba four for 54, Iqbal Sikandar three for 47) and 129 for two (Sajid Ali 68); PIA 290 for five (Aamer Malik 30, Asif Mujtaba 115 not out, Zahid Ahmed 65). *PIA 5 pts.*

At Arbab Niaz Stadium, Peshawar, November 17, 18, 19, 20. Drawn. ADBP* 306 (Mansoor Rana 122, Extras 33) and 432 for three dec. (Sabih Azhar 53, Atif Rauf 153, Mansoor Rana 157 not out, Zahoor Elahi 37 not out); HBFC 272 (Munir-ul-Haq 116, Wasim Ali 63, Tariq Alam 56 not out; Zakir Khan four for 81) and 40 for five (Zakir Khan three for 19). *ADBP 5 pts.*

## Semi-finals

At National Stadium, Karachi, November 23, 24, 25. United Bank won by ten wickets. National Bank 128 (Saleem Jaffer three for 51, Pervez Shah four for 33, Tanvir Mehdi three for 27) and 207 (Sajid Ali 37, Shakil Sajjad 43, Extras 32; Saleem Jaffer four for 46, Tanvir Mehdi four for 68); United Bank* 323 (Basit Ali 45, Inzamam-ul-Haq 112, Iqbal Imam 85, Extras 33; Barkatullah six for 71, Habib Baloch four for 77) and 15 for no wkt.

At Bagh-e-Jinnah Ground, Lahore, November 24, 25, 26, 27. Drawn, ADBP were declared winners by virtue of their first-innings lead. Habib Bank 155 (Aamer Sohail 35, Arshad Pervez 34, Shaukat Mirza 42; Zakir Khan four for 60); ADBP* 243 for five (Mansoor Rana 104 not out, Zahoor Elahi 78; Naved Anjum four for 45).

## Final

At National Stadium, Karachi, December 1, 2, 3, 4, 5. Drawn, ADBP were declared winners by virtue of their first-innings lead. ADBP* 314 (Zahoor Elahi 62, Bilal Ahmed 46, Raja Afaq 50, Mohammad Asif 30 not out; Masood Anwar four for 52, Pervez Shah three for 38) and 308 (Zahoor Elahi 128, Ghaffar Kazmi 36, Manzoor Elahi 50, Extras 44; Saleem Jaffer four for 60, Pervez Shah three for 44, Masood Anwar three for 53); United Bank 217 (Raees Ahmed 35, Shafiq Ahmad 67; Zakir Khan five for 60) and 256 for eight (Pervez Shah 101, Shafiq Ahmad 53, Tauseef Ahmed 42).

## QUAID-E-AZAM TROPHY, 1990-91

| | Played | Won | Lost | Drawn | Abandoned | 1st-inns lead in drawn match | Points |
|---|---|---|---|---|---|---|---|
| Karachi Whites .... | 7 | 6 | 1 | 0 | 0 | 0 | 60 |
| Karachi Blues ..... | 6 | 3 | 1 | 2 | 1 | 0 | 30 |
| Faisalabad ........ | 7 | 2 | 2 | 3 | 0 | 2 | 30 |
| Bahawalpur ....... | 6 | 2 | 2 | 2 | 1 | 1 | 25 |
| Sargodha ......... | 7 | 2 | 2 | 3 | 0 | 0 | 20 |
| Peshawar ........ | 7 | 1 | 3 | 3 | 0 | 2 | 20 |
| Rawalpindi ....... | 5 | 1 | 2 | 2 | 2 | 1 | 15 |
| Multan............ | 7 | 1 | 5 | 1 | 0 | 1 | 15 |

*Win = 10 pts; 1st-innings lead in drawn match = 5 pts.*

**Semi-finals:** *Karachi Whites beat Faisalabad by virtue of their first-innings lead; Bahawalpur beat Karachi Blues by 28 runs.*
**Final:** *Karachi Whites beat Bahawalpur by an innings and 163 runs.*

*Note:* First innings closed at 85 overs in the group matches.

At National Stadium, Karachi, December 8, 9, 10. Karachi Whites won by nine wickets. Faisalabad 185 (Saadat Gul 62, Tanvir Afzal 38; Shahid Mahboob four for 49) and 156 (Wasim Hyder 55; Athar Laeeq three for 52); Karachi Whites* 229 (Ghulam Ali 58, Ijaz Faqih 40, Extras 37; Wasim Hyder three for 74, Saadat Gul four for 82, Nadeem Afzal three for 39) and 113 for one (Ghulam Ali 62 not out, Mansoor Akhtar 46 not out). *Karachi Whites 10 pts.*

At Bahawal Stadium, Bahawalpur, December 8, 9, 10. Bahawalpur won by six wickets. Multan 192 (Arshad Hayat 37, Inzamam-ul-Haq 59; Mohammad Altaf three for 56, Mohammad Zahid three for 45, Murtaza Hussain four for 52) and 141 (Mohammad Zahid six for 53, Murtaza Hussain three for 22); Bahawalpur* 264 (Shakeel Ahmed 31, Shahid Anwar 63, Shahzad Arshad 57, Murtaza Hussain 33 not out; Saleem Sajjad three for 20) and 70 for four (Bilal Rana three for 12). *Bahawalpur 10 pts.*

At Sargodha Stadium, Sargodha, December 8, 9, 10, 11. Sargodha won by 115 runs. Sargodha 263 (Mohammad Hasnain 40, Aamer Sohail 84, Aziz-ur-Rehman 41, Extras 33; Haaris Khan five for 77) and 252 (Mohammad Hasnain 66, Aamer Sohail 102; Haaris Khan five for 70, Nadeem Khan four for 68); Karachi Blues* 158 (Zafar Ahmed 67 not out; Wasim Khan four for 25, Sajjad Akbar three for 45) and 242 (Saeed Azad 59, Rashid Mahmood 34, Nadeem Khan 40, Baqar Rizvi 45; Wasim Khan six for 57). *Sargodha 10 pts.*

At Arbab Niaz Stadium, Peshawar, December 8, 9, 10, 11. Peshawar won by two wickets. Rawalpindi 125 (Arif Butt 40; Shahid Hussain five for 44, Farrukh Zaman four for 38) and 194 (Naseer Ahmed 37, Saleem Taj 41; Zakir Khan four for 57, Farrukh Zaman three for 38); Peshawar* 134 (Wasim Yousufi 34; Shakeel Ahmed three for 35, Raja Afaq four for 28) and 186 for eight (Sher Ali 65, Shahid Hussain 32 not out; Zahir Shah five for 66). *Peshawar 10 pts.*

At National Stadium, Karachi, December 15, 16, 17. Karachi Whites won by an innings and 77 runs. Multan 164 (Atiq Khan 79; Athar Laeeq six for 54) and 161 (Imtiaz Rasool 36 not out; Athar Laeeq three for 64; Aamer Hanif six for 54); Karachi Whites* 402 for four (Sajid Ali 202 not out, Ameer-ud-Din 51, Mansoor Akhtar 121). *Karachi Whites 10 pts.*

At Iqbal Stadium, Faisalabad, December 15, 16, 17, 18. Drawn. Faisalabad 212 for eight (Shahid Nawaz 51, Bilal Ahmed 39, Nadeem Afzal 37 not out; Mohammad Zahid three for 55, Murtaza Hussain four for 60) and 262 for six dec. (Nadeem Arshad 55, Shahid Nawaz 58, Saadat Gul 43 not out, Nadeem Afzal 36); Bahawalpur* 267 for nine (Shakeel Ahmed 42, Shahid Anwar 51, Shahzad Arshad 52, Murtaza Hussain 32; Rashid Wali three for 24) and 180 for six (Shakeel Ahmed 63, Imran Zia 41). *Bahawalpur 5 pts.*

At KRL Cricket Ground, Rawalpindi, December 15, 16, 17, 18. Rawalpindi v Karachi Blues. Abandoned without a ball bowled, owing to rain.

At Sargodha Stadium, Sargodha, December 15, 16, 17, 18. Drawn. Peshawar 167 for six (Sher Ali 69, Zafar Sarfraz 38; Aziz-ur-Rehman three for 28) v Sargodha*.

At Bahawal Stadium, Bahawalpur, December 22, 23, 24. Karachi Whites won by two wickets. Bahawalpur 196 (Naeem Taj 36, Murtaza Hussain 37; Asif Mujtaba six for 60) and 47 (Asif Mujtaba four for 14, Sohail Mehdi five for 30); Karachi Whites* 88 (Mohammad Zahid five for 22, Murtaza Hussain three for 16) and 156 for eight (Sajid Ali 43, Asif Mujtaba 45 not out; Mohammad Altaf six for 34). *Karachi Whites 10 pts.*

At Iqbal Stadium, Faisalabad, December 22, 23, 24, 25. Faisalabad won by ten wickets. Multan 120 (Inzamam-ul-Haq 52 not out; Saadat Gul six for 67, Wasim Hyder four for 32) and 255 (Aamer Bashir 48, Masood Anwar 33, Sibte Hasan 34; Wasim Hyder three for 75); Faisalabad* 304 for six (Mohammad Ashraf 113 not out, Shahid Nawaz 62, Bilal Ahmed 40; Faisal Hayat three for 95) and 72 for no wkt (Ijaz Ahmed 35 not out). *Faisalabad 10 pts.*

At KRL Cricket Ground, Rawalpindi, December 22, 23, 24, 25. Drawn. Sargodha* 188 (Sajjad Akbar 54 not out; Mohammad Riaz three for 86, Raja Afaq five for 67); Rawalpindi 213 for nine (Mohammad Iqbal 54, Naseer Ahmed 35, Raja Afaq 36, Mohammad Riaz 30; Aziz-ur-Rehman six for 81). *Rawalpindi 5 pts.*

At Arbab Niaz Stadium, Peshawar, December 22, 23, 24, 25. Drawn. Karachi Blues* 202 (Saeed Azad 51, Zafar Ahmed 39, Shakil Sajjad 40; Wahid Khan three for 32, Farrukh Zaman three for 41); Peshawar 214 for five (Sher Ali 84, Faisal Rasheed 42). *Peshawar 5 pts.*

At National Stadium, Karachi, December 29, 30, 31, January 1. Karachi Whites won by 171 runs. Karachi Whites 238 (Ghulam Ali 59, Ijaz Faqih 62; Naeem Khan four for 92, Amanullah three for 53) and 227 for nine dec. (Sajid Ali 70, Mahmood Hamid 52 not out; Amanullah four for 62, Aziz-ur-Rehman three for 49); Sargodha* 106 (Athar Laeeq seven for 23) and 188 (Aziz-ur-Rehman 54, Maqsood Ahmed 37; Shahid Mahboob four for 28, Iqbal Sikandar three for 36). *Karachi Whites 10 pts.*

At Qasim Bagh Stadium, Multan, December 29, 30, 31, January 1. Karachi Blues won by 63 runs. Karachi Blues* 296 (Iqbal Saleem 30, Saeed Azad 142, Zafar Ahmed 52; Mian Fayyaz five for 115, Masood Anwar three for 126) and 172 (Iqbal Saleem 30, Zafar Ahmed 43; Faisal Hayat three for 83, Mian Fayyaz six for 44); Multan 251 (Aamer Baig 56, Zakir Hussain 50, Sanaullah 61, Extras 33; Haaris Khan six for 89) and 154 (Mohammad Javed 40, Rizwan Sattar 32, Sanaullah 33; Baqar Rizvi three for 44, Nadeem Khan four for 30). *Karachi Blues 10 pts.*

At Iqbal Stadium, Faisalabad, December 29, 30, 31, January 1. Faisalabad won by an innings and 1 run. Peshawar 124 (Wasim Yousufi 36; Naved Nazir three for 28, Wasim Hyder six for 46) and 153 (Javed Khan 31; Saadat Gul five for 59, Wasim Hyder four for 48); Faisalabad* 278 for nine (Shahid Nawaz 92, Wasim Hyder 63, Naseer Shaukat 35; Kabir Khan three for 86). *Faisalabad 10 pts.*

At KRL Cricket Ground, Rawalpindi, December 29, 30, 31, January 1. Rawalpindi v Bahawalpur. Abandoned without a ball bowled, owing to rain.

At National Stadium, Karachi, January 5, 6, 7, 8. Karachi Whites won by an innings and 20 runs. Karachi Whites 309 for six (Ghulam Ali 55, Ameer-ud-Din 36, Aamer Hanif 79, Ishtiaq Ahmed 34 not out, Moin Khan 35; Kabir Khan four for 91); Peshawar* 155 (Sher Ali 46, Sajid Afridi 33; Shahid Mahboob eight for 62) and 134 (Wasim Yousufi 31, Sher Afgan 32; Athar Laeeq six for 50, Iqbal Sikandar four for 15). *Karachi Whites 10 pts.*

At Bahawal Stadium, Bahawalpur, January 5, 6, 7, 8. Bahawalpur were awarded the match after Sargodha had refused to continue on the first day following an umpiring dispute. Sargodha* 112 for three (Mohammad Hasnain 39, Aamer Sohail 33). *Bahawalpur 10 pts.*

At Montgomery Biscuit Factory Ground, Sahiwal, January 5, 6, 7, 8. Drawn. Multan 237 (Inzamam-ul-Haq 75; Raja Afaq four for 61, Zahir Shah four for 53) and 153 for four (Atiq-ur-Rehman 54, Inzamam-ul-Haq 55; Naeemullah three for 49); Rawalpindi* 191 (Zulfiqar Shahid 46, Shahid Javed 50; Bilal Rana four for 53, Mushtaq Ahmed four for 60). *Multan 5 pts.*

At Iqbal Stadium, Faisalabad, January 5, 6, 7, 8. Drawn. Karachi Blues* 44 (Saadat Gul four for 26, Naseer Shaukat four for 11) and 361 for nine dec. (Shoaib Siddiqi 37, Iqbal Imam 158, Nadeem Khan 76, Extras 33, Saadat Gul three for 104); Faisalabad 180 (Mohammad Ramzan 57; Haaris Khan seven for 63) and 105 for four (Mohammad Ashraf 42). *Faisalabad 5 pts.*

At Bahawal Stadium, Bahawalpur, January 12, 13, 14, 15. Karachi Blues won by four wickets. Bahawalpur* 133 (Aamer Sohail 30; Amin Lakhani four for 49, Haaris Khan three for 47) and 168 (Javed Rana 30, Tanvir Razzaq 31; Haaris Khan seven for 44, Iqbal Imam three for 13); Karachi Blues 96 (Mohammad Zahid six for 20) and 206 for six (Kamran Hussain 76, Haaris Khan 65 not out). *Karachi Blues 10 pts.*

At Montgomery Biscuit Factory Ground, Sahiwal, January 12, 13, 14, 15. Multan won by ten wickets. Multan 363 for four (Zahoor Elahi 59, Masroor Hussain 107, Tariq Mahboob 129 not out) and 135 for no wkt (Zahoor Elahi 78 not out, Masroor Hussain 52 not out); Peshawar* 173 (Zafar Sarfraz 67; Waqar Younis four for 66, Mushtaq Ahmed five for 37) and 321 (Wasim Yousufi 30, Sher Ali 133, Zafar Sarfraz 34, Extras 35; Mushtaq Ahmed nine for 93). *Multan 10 pts.*

At Sargodha Stadium, Sargodha, January 12, 13, 14, 15. Drawn. Sargodha 188 (Asad Mahmood 32, Maqsood Ahmed 35, Sajjad Akbar 50; Naseer Shaukat four for 22, Naved Nazir four for 55) and 245 for nine (Azhar Sultan 33, Maqsood Ahmed 34, Sajjad Akbar 104 not out, Abdul Shakoor 33); Faisalabad* 243 for eight (Wasim Hyder 35, Mohammad Ashraf 48, Shahid Nawaz 94; Sajjad Akbar four for 80). *Faisalabad 5 pts.*

At National Stadium, Karachi, January 12, 13, 14, 15. Karachi Whites won by four wickets. Rawalpindi 227 (Saleem Taj 115, Nadeem Abbasi 46; Shahid Mahboob five for 84) and 231 (Naseer Ahmed 53, Masood Anwar 63, Nasim Akhtar 47; Shahid Mahboob four for 87, Aamer Hanif three for 36); Karachi Whites* 286 for seven (Asif Mujtaba 35, Tahir Mahmood 90, Moin Khan 31, Jawwad Ali 48 not out; Aftab Abbasi three for 80) and 176 for six (Ishtiaq Ahmed 45, Aamer Hanif 33; Zahir Shah three for 64). *Karachi Whites 10 pts.*

At National Stadium, Karachi, January 19, 20, 21. Karachi Blues won by five wickets. Karachi Whites 145 (Azam Khan 65; Barkatullah six for 18, Haaris Khan four for 49) and 322 (Azam Khan 50, Sarwat Ali 39, Shahid Mahboob 60, Iftikhar Ahmed 81; Haaris Khan four for 92, Mohsin Mirza three for 71); Karachi Blues* 337 (Kamran Hussain 93, Iqbal Imam 42, Shoaib Siddiqi 107) and 131 for five (Kamran Hussain 49, Iqbal Imam 52; Shahid Mahboob four for 19). *Karachi Blues 10 pts.*

At Sargodha Stadium, Sargodha, January 19, 20, 21, 22. Sargodha won by six wickets. Multan 121 (Manzoor Elahi 44; Sajjad Akbar five for 40, Aziz-ur-Rehman five for 46) and 197 (Zahoor Elahi 63, Manzoor Elahi 57; Aziz-ur-Rehman five for 61); Sargodha* 179 (Mohammad Hasnain 33, Aziz-ur-Rehman 55, Sajjad Akbar 37; Waqar Younis four for 57, Bilal Rana three for 38) and 140 for four (Maqsood Ahmed 59 not out, Extras 33; Mushtaq Ahmed three for 42). *Sargodha 10 pts.*

At Arbab Niaz Stadium, Peshawar, January 19, 20, 21, 22. Drawn. Peshawar* 281 for nine (Sher Afgan 51, Sher Ali 103, Zafar Sarfraz 40 not out; Mohammad Altaf four for 95) and 214 for five (Sher Afgan 48, Sher Ali 64, Zafar Sarfraz 51 not out; Shahid Anwar three for 41); Bahawalpur 279 (Imran Zia 30, Shahid Anwar 101, Tanvir Razzaq 31, Naeem Taj 63; Shahid Hussain four for 54). *Peshawar 5 pts.*

At KRL Cricket Ground, Rawalpindi, January 25, 26, 27. Rawalpindi won by seven wickets. Faisalabad 96 (Mohammad Ramzan 52; Mohammad Riaz four for 29, Raja Afaq five for 51) and 135 (Mohammad Ashraf 53 not out; Mohammad Riaz four for 31, Raja Afaq four for 39); Rawalpindi* 211 (Arif Butt 30, Saleem Taj 41, Shahid Javed 51, Masood Anwar 32; Naved Nazir four for 55, Tanvir Afzal four for 63) and 21 for three. *Rawalpindi 10 pts.*

## Semi-finals

At Iqbal Stadium, Faisalabad, January 31, February 1, 2, 3. Drawn. Karachi Whites were declared winners by virtue of their first-innings lead. Karachi Whites* 261 for nine (Ghulam Ali 63, Mansoor Akhtar 36, Aamer Hanif 76, Mahmood Hamid 33; Naved Nazir three for 110, Tanvir Afzal three for 96) and 354 for eight (Sajid Ali 46, Mansoor Akhtar 50, Asif Mujtaba 104, Aamer Hanif 44, Iqbal Sikandar 48); Faisalabad 160 (Wasim Hyder 57, Mohammad Ashraf 36; Shahid Mahboob four for 40, Athar Laeeq five for 53).

At National Stadium, Karachi, February 2, 3, 4, 5, 6. Bahawalpur won by 28 runs. Bahawalpur 267 for nine (Shakeel Ahmed 73, Imran Zia 53, Umar Rasheed 55; Haaris Khan six for 63) and 219 (Shakeel Ahmed 92, Shahid Anwar 56; Zafar Ahmed four for 18); Karachi Blues* 186 (Iqbal Imam 33; Umar Rasheed four for 36, Mohammad Zahid three for 37) and 272 (Zafar Ahmed 73, Rashid Latif 38, Baqar Rizvi 33, Extras 35; Imran Adil four for 71, Shahzad Arshad three for 49).

## Final

At National Stadium, Karachi, February 11, 12, 13, 14. Karachi Whites won by an innings and 163 runs. Karachi Whites 399 (Asif Mujtaba 189, Moin Khan 52, Iqbal Sikandar 58; Umar Rasheed three for 58); Bahawalpur* 83 (Imran Zia 32; Athar Laeeq four for 36, Aamer Hanif three for 5, including a hat-trick) and 153 (Shahid Anwar 32, Umar Rasheed 35; Jawwad Ali three for 13, Iqbal Sikandar four for 16).

## QUAID-E-AZAM TROPHY WINNERS

| | | | |
|---|---|---|---|
| 1953-54 | Bahawalpur | 1975-76 | National Bank |
| 1954-55 | Karachi | 1976-77 | United Bank |
| 1956-57 | Punjab | 1977-78 | Habib Bank |
| 1957-58 | Bahawalpur | 1978-79 | National Bank |
| 1958-59 | Karachi | 1979-80 | PIA |
| 1959-60 | Karachi | 1980-81 | United Bank |
| 1961-62 | Karachi Blues | 1981-82 | National Bank |
| 1962-63 | Karachi A | 1982-83 | United Bank |
| 1963-64 | Karachi Blues | 1983-84 | National Bank |
| 1964-65 | Karachi Blues | 1984-85 | United Bank |
| 1966-67 | Karachi | 1985-86 | Karachi |
| 1968-69 | Lahore | 1986-87 | National Bank |
| 1969-70 | PIA | 1987-88 | PIA |
| 1970-71 | Karachi Blues | 1988-89 | ADBP |
| 1972-73 | Railways | 1989-90 | PIA |
| 1973-74 | Railways | 1990-91 | Karachi Whites |
| 1974-75 | Punjab A | | |

## WILLS PENTANGULAR LEAGUE, 1990-91

| | Played | Won | Lost | Drawn | Abandoned | 1st-inns lead in drawn match | Points |
|---|---|---|---|---|---|---|---|
| United Bank . . . . . . . | 3 | 2 | 0 | 1 | 1 | 1 | 25 |
| National Bank . . . . . | 3 | 1 | 1 | 1 | 1 | 1 | 15 |
| Habib Bank . . . . . . . . | 4 | 1 | 1 | 2 | 0 | 0 | 10 |
| PNSC . . . . . . . . . . . | 3 | 0 | 1 | 2 | 1 | 1 | 5 |
| ADBP . . . . . . . . . . . | 3 | 0 | 1 | 2 | 1 | 0 | 0 |

*Win = 10 pts; 1st-innings lead in a drawn match = 5 pts.*

*Note:* First innings closed at 85 overs in all matches.

At Gaddafi Stadium, Lahore, February 18, 19, 20, 21. National Bank won by five wickets. Habib Bank 410 for six (Agha Zahid 32, Aamer Sohail 61, Ijaz Ahmed 46, Salim Malik 138, Anwar Miandad 56, Tahir Rasheed 35 not out; Hafeez-ur-Rehman three for 104) and 266 (Agha Zahid 31, Ijaz Ahmed 32, Salim Malik 133, Akram Raza 34; Barkatullah five for 62, Shakil Sajjad three for 20); National Bank* 275 (Saeed Azad 42, Shahid Tanvir 71, Shakil Sajjad 65 not out; Akram Raza four for 106, Salim Malik three for 10) and 402 for five (Mohammad Jamil 31, Saeed Azad 138, Ameer Akbar 101 not out, Extras 32). *National Bank 10 pts.*

At LCCA Ground, Lahore, February 18, 19, 20, 21. United Bank won by an innings and 26 runs. ADBP 133 (Mansoor Rana 42; Waqar Younis three for 46, Saleem Jaffer five for 56) and 181 (Manzoor Elahi 32; Waqar Younis seven for 64); United Bank* 340 for seven (Saifullah 120, Mansoor Akhtar 32, Shafiq Ahmad 86 not out, Rashid Latif 36; Saeed Anwar three for 83). *United Bank 10 pts.*

At LCCA Ground, Lahore, February 23, 24, 25, 26. ADBP v National Bank. Abandoned without a ball bowled, owing to rain.

At Gaddafi Stadium, Lahore, February 23, 24, 25, 26. United Bank v PNSC. Abandoned without a ball bowled, owing to rain.

At Gaddafi Stadium, Lahore, February 28, March 1, 2, 3. Drawn. United Bank 304 for seven (Saifullah 53, Raees Ahmed 69, Inzamam-ul-Haq 31, Mansoor Akhtar 37, Rashid Latif 50 not out; Akram Raza four for 71) and 217 for six (Shafiq Ahmad 35, Pervez Shah 50 not out, Masood Anwar 57 not out; Naved Anjum three for 93); Habib Bank* 156 (Salim Malik 47; Waqar Younis three for 52, Masood Anwar three for 30). *United Bank 5 pts.*

At LCCA Ground, Lahore, February 28, March 1, 2, 3. Drawn. ADBP 268 (Sabih Azhar 32, Atif Rauf 44, Mansoor Rana 50, Saeed Anwar 63, Manzoor Elahi 37; Sajjad Akbar five for 100, Amin Lakhani four for 78) and 214 for two (Zahoor Elahi 118 not out, Atif Rauf 72); PNSC* 275 for five (Ramiz Raja 69, Sohail Jaffer 43, Mohammad Javed 48, Nasir Wasti 56; Mohammad Asif three for 85). *PNSC 5 pts.*

At Gaddafi Stadium, Lahore, March 5, 6, 7, 8. United Bank won by nine wickets. National Bank 259 (Ameer Akbar 35, Mohammad Jamil 39, Shahid Tanvir 56, Extras 35; Masood Anwar four for 70) and 234 (Sajid Ali 55, Wasim Arif 30, Shakil Sajjad 53; Waqar Younis three for 61, Tauseef Ahmed four for 61); United Bank* 370 for six (Inzamam-ul-Haq 72, Shafiq Ahmad 59, Pervez Shah 116 not out, Rashid Latif 52) and 124 for one (Saifullah 51 not out, Inzamam-ul-Haq 59 not out). *United Bank 10 pts.*

At LCCA Ground, Lahore, March 5, 6, 7, 8. Habib Bank won by 66 runs. Habib Bank 283 (Anwar Miandad 123, Salim Malik 71; Amin Lakhani three for 81) and 255 (Moin-ul-Atiq 30, Shaukat Mirza 61, Javed Miandad 55, Akram Raza 44; Amin Lakhani four for 97); PNSC* 208 (Mohammad Javed 74, Mahmood Hamid 53; Shakil Khan six for 59) and 264 (Sohail Miandad 43, Sohail Jaffer 51, Mohammad Javed 52; Shakil Khan three for 72, Akram Raza five for 64). *Habib Bank 10 pts.*

At Gaddafi Stadium, Lahore, March 10, 11, 12, 13. Drawn. ADBP* 325 (Atif Rauf 51, Saeed Anwar 48, Bilal Ahmed 36, Ghaffar Kazmi 50, Ghayyur Qureshi 30; Waheed Niazi four for 78, Akram Raza three for 71) and 222 for nine (Zahoor Elahi 38, Atif Rauf 38, Saeed Anwar 45, Bilal Ahmed 48 not out; Liaqat Ali three for 47); Habib Bank 325 (Moin-ul-Atiq 64, Salim Malik 115, Ijaz Ahmed 59, Extras 33; Zakir Khan three for 93).

At LCCA Ground, Lahore, March 10, 11, 12, 13. Drawn. National Bank* 336 (Saeed Azad 178, Shahid Tanvir 39, Wasim Arif 34; Amin Lakhani three for 108) and 309 for seven (Mohammad Jamil 36, Sajid Ali 58, Saeed Azad 57, Ameer Akbar 32, Shahid Tanvir 75 not out; Amin Lakhani four for 112, Sajjad Akbar three for 136); PNSC 289 for nine (Sohail Miandad 123, Mahmood Hamid 34, Sajjad Akbar 35 not out; Hafeez-ur-Rehman six for 114, Iqbal Qasim three for 124). *National Bank 5 pts.*

# THE DELOITTE RATINGS

Introduced in 1987, the Deloitte Ratings rank Test cricketers on a scale from 0 to 1,000 according to their performances in Test matches since 1981. The ratings are calculated by computer and take into account playing conditions, the quality of the opposition and the result of the matches. The value of a player's performance is assessed in relation to the Deloitte Ratings of the opposing players and it also reflects his ability to score match-winning runs or take match-winning wickets. Updated after every Test match, with a player's most recent performances carrying more weight than his earlier ones, the Deloitte Ratings endeavour to provide a current assessment of a Test cricketer's form and his place among his peers. A player cannot get a full rating until he has played 15 innings or taken 40 wickets in Test matches.

The leading 30 batsmen and bowlers in the Ratings after the 1991 series between England and West Indies and England and Sri Lanka were:

| | Batsmen | Rating | Bowlers | Rating |
|---|---|---|---|---|
| 1. | G. A. Gooch (*Eng.*) | 894 | M. D. Marshall (*WI*) | 877 |
| 2. | R. A. Smith (*Eng.*) | 872 | Waqar Younis (*Pak.*) | 852 |
| 3. | R. B. Richardson (*WI*) | 829 | C. E. L. Ambrose (*WI*) | 764 |
| 4. | Shoaib Mohammad (*Pak.*) | 773 | Imran Khan (*Pak.*) | 761 |
| 5. | M. A. Taylor (*Aust.*) | 742 | I. R. Bishop (*WI*) | 749 |
| 6. | Imran Khan (*Pak.*) | 740 | Wasim Akram (*Pak.*) | 747 |
| 7. | Salim Malik (*Pak.*) | 739 | C. J. McDermott (*Aust.*) | 727 |
| 8. | D. L. Haynes (*WI*) | 722 | B. A. Reid (*Aust.*) | 686 |
| 9. | M. D. Crowe (*NZ*) | 721 | A. R. C. Fraser (*Eng.*) | 676 |
| 10. | M. Azharuddin (*India*) | 710 | M. G. Hughes (*Aust.*) | 658 |
| 11. | M. E. Waugh (*Aust.*) | 686* | Kapil Dev (*India*) | 646 |
| 12. | A. R. Border (*Aust.*) | 683 | T. M. Alderman (*Aust.*) | 633 |
| 13. | Javed Miandad (*Pak.*) | 672 | P. A. J. DeFreitas (*Eng.*) | 600 |
| 14. | I. V. A. Richards (*WI*) | 653 | C. A. Walsh (*WI*) | 586 |
| 15. | A. H. Jones (*NZ*) | 649 | S. L. V. Raju (*India*) | 543† |
| 16. | J. G. Wright (*NZ*) | 632 | N. D. Hirwani (*India*) | 474 |
| 17. | A. L. Logie (*WI*) | 615 | B. P. Patterson (*WI*) | 468 |
| 18. | C. G. Greenidge (*WI*) | 604 | D. E. Malcolm (*Eng.*) | 459 |
| 19. | D. B. Vengsarkar (*India*) | 603 | Abdul Qadir (*Pak.*) | 450 |
| 20. | D. C. Boon (*Aust.*) | 595 | Tauseef Ahmed (*Pak.*) | 445 |
| 21. | S. V. Manjrekar (*India*) | 589 | Saleem Jaffer (*Pak.*) | 443† |
| 22. | D. M. Jones (*Aust.*) | 588 | D. K. Morrison (*NZ*) | 440 |
| 23. | A. Ranatunga (*SL*) | 572 | R. J. Ratnayake (*SL*) | 432 |
| 24. | P. A. de Silva (*SL*) | 570 | R. J. Shastri (*India*) | 429 |
| 25. | R. J. Shastri (*India*) | 568 | J. G. Bracewell (*NZ*) | 428 |
| 26. | D. I. Gower (*Eng.*) | 559 | G. C. Small (*Eng.*) | 406 |
| 27. | A. J. Stewart (*Eng.*) | 513 | E. E. Hemmings (*Eng.*) | 388 |
| 28. | C. L. Hooper (*WI*) | 506 | P. C. R. Tufnell (*Eng.*) | 376† |
| 29. | S. R. Waugh (*Aust.*) | 501 | G. F. Labrooy (*SL*) | 374† |
| 30. | A. P. Gurusinha (*SL*) | 496 | M. Prabhakar (*India*) | 367† |

\* Signifies the batsman has played fewer than 15 Test innings.
† Signifies the bowler has taken fewer than 40 Test wickets.

# CRICKET IN SRI LANKA, 1990-91

By GERRY VAIDYASEKERA and IHITHISHAM KAMARDEEN

Never before in the history of the game in Sri Lanka had there been such a fiesta of cricket as there was in 1990-91, with the visits of teams from England and Australia and a full programme of domestic first-class matches. The Sri Lankan Board's national cricket calendar fixed a total of 156 playing days, spread over a period of eight months from August 1990 to March 1991, and the Board saw the visits by the Australian Academy and England A teams as an opportunity for testing those young, promising Sri Lankan cricketers who stood on the brink of Test cricket. Interspersed were the schools matches, in which an astonishingly high standard of cricket was seen, with new records being established.

The Board's premier inter-club championship, the Division I tournament, was run in three stages, with 30 teams entering the preliminary round. These matches were two-day fixtures. The top twelve teams from this round then contested the final round, for the P. Saravanamuttu Trophy, with the matches being played over three days and having first-class status. The teams were divided into two groups, with the winners of each group meeting in the final. Group A comprised Sinhalese SC, Panadura SC, Tamil Union Cricket and Athletic Club, Colombo CC, Singha CC and Sebastianites Cricket and Athletic Club. In Group B were Nondescript CC, Galle CC, Moors SC, Moratuwa SC, Colts CC and Saracens SC. Sinhalese Sports Club retained the Division I title by defeating their traditional rivals, Nondescript, on bonus points in the rain-affected final. Nondescript were led in this match by 23-year-old Sanjeeva Weerasinghe, the youngest player to captain the club, but he will remember his first experience in this role with mixed feelings. Having won the toss, he put SSC in to bat and saw them run up 269 for seven before declaring. When the game ended, Nondescript were 193 for eight and the advantage, as well as the greater number of bonus points, lay with SSC.

The eighteen teams which did not qualify for the first-class round played for the Delmege Trophy in Section B of the Division I tournament. They were in four groups, and the group leaders then met in a semi-final round. In the final, Bloomfield Cricket and Athletic Club, captained by Sri Lanka's first Test captain, Bandula Warnapura, outplayed Nomads Sports Club by 226 runs. The final of the Delmege Trophy was contested over three days and raised to first-class status, which gave Warnapura the opportunity of appearing in first-class cricket for the first time since the removal of the ban, for touring South Africa, which had prevented him from playing cricket in Sri Lanka. Winning the Delmege Trophy was the first major honour for Bloomfield since the ban was imposed on Warnapura, and the runners-up, Nomads, also returned to the fore after several years out of the limelight.

Two teams from the south of the island contested the final of the 26-team Division II tournament, Matara Sports Club beating Ambalangoda Rio Sports Club, and Liberty won the Division III title, under the captaincy of Asger Dawoodbhoy. His father, Ibrahim Dawoodbhoy, led the same club to the same championship title in 1975-76.

The inter-provincial tournament was sponsored in 1990-91 by Singer Sri Lanka (Ltd) for a record sum of Rs625,000, more than double the sponsorship money they offered the previous season, making it the richest tournament in

Sri Lankan cricket. The matches, recognised as first-class by the Board of Control, were played over four days on a league basis. Western Province (City), led by Roy Dias, the former vice-captain of Sri Lanka, and winning all their four games, were the Singer tournament champions, while Western Province (Suburbs) filled the runners-up position. Kumara Dharmasena of Western Province (City) won the Most Promising Player award, and Chandika Hathurusinghe of North-Western Province was the Man of the Tournament. In the Western Province (Suburbs) match against Central Province, Nishantha Fernando and Samantha Sooriyarachchi added 272 for the Suburbs' second wicket, a record partnership for any Sri Lankan wicket, and as the Suburbs bowled out Central Province for 55 in their first innings D. Dias captured four wickets with four successive balls.

The Under-23 limited-overs tournament for the GTE (General Telephone Electronics) Trophy was won by Old Anandians, eleven teenagers from Ananda College, the previous year's school champions, who beat the experienced Colombo Cricket Club by 40 runs in the final. Marvan Ataputtu, the captain, won the Man of the Match and the Best Batsman awards. As expected, the two Colombo teams contested the final of the inter-district tournament, with Colombo City taking the title from Colombo Suburbs by virtue of their first-innings lead. Sinhalese Sports Club won the Hatna Trophy limited-overs tournament, beating Moors in the final. With 24 teams in contention, this competition was played in four groups.

In Wanganui, New Zealand, the Sri Lanka Islanders, led by the former Sri Lankan all-rounder, Anuruddha Polonowita, retained the World Masters Games title. They won all three matches in their group and, averaging 5.76 runs per over, won the tournament with a superior run-rate to that of the seven other competing countries.

Nearly 100 schools teams from all over the country took part in the Pure Beverages Under-19 Championship, conducted in two divisions by the Sri Lanka Schools Cricket Association. Age-group tournaments were also played at Under-13, Under-15 and Under-17 levels. St Anthony's College, Kandy, with six outright wins in the league, became the first holders of the Coca-Cola Bottlers' Trophy, while Ananda College were second, with four wins. Ananda College, however, won the knockout title for a record fourth year, beating St Anthony's in the final. De Mazenod College, Kandana, the Under-19 Division II league winners, equalled the Sri Lankan record for the most wins in a season when they became the first outstation school to record nine outright wins.

The outstanding cricketer of the season was the spin sensation of St Anthony's College, Muttiah Muralitharan, who became the first schoolboy to take 100 wickets in two successive seasons and, with a tally of 127 wickets, the highest wicket-taker in a single schools season. A match haul of eight wickets against the Australian Academy, six wickets against England A, and ten in the inter-provincial tournament increased his total for the 1990-91 season to 151 and earned him a place in the side that toured England later in the year.

The Australian Institute of Sport Cricket Academy team spent three weeks in Sri Lanka in January and February, the fifteen-member team including thirteen cricketers with experience of playing for Australian Under-19 sides. Of their six matches the young Australians won four and lost two, though they won only one of their three-day matches. It was to their credit that all their fixtures reached a positive conclusion.

During the season, Don Oslear, the English umpire, spent three weeks on the island as a guest of the Board of Control, conducting seminars for Sri Lankan umpires and officiating in the inter-provincial matches. On the coaching front, Bruce Yardley, the former Australian off-spinner, had three weeks working with the island's spin bowlers, and Frank Tyson, the former England fast bowler, spent the best part of a month coaching young fast bowlers. Ravi Ratnayeke, Sri Lanka's Test all-rounder, left with his family to take up permanent residence in Australia, and several farewell matches were played for him prior to his departure.

## SINGER INTER-PROVINCIAL TOURNAMENT AVERAGES, 1990-91

### BATTING

(Qualification: 150 runs)

|  | M | I | NO | R | HI | 100s | Avge |
|---|---|---|---|---|---|---|---|
| U. N. K. Fernando (*WP Suburbs*).... | 2 | 3 | 1 | 168 | 160 | 1 | 84.00 |
| U. C. Hathurusinghe (*NWP*)........ | 4 | 7 | 1 | 329 | 117 | 1 | 54.83 |
| U. Kodituwakku (*CP*)............. | 4 | 6 | 0 | 315 | 116 | 1 | 52.50 |
| C. P. H. Ramanayake (*SP*)......... | 3 | 4 | 0 | 190 | 69 | 0 | 47.50 |
| W. M. J. Kumudu (*SP*)............ | 3 | 5 | 1 | 178 | 87 | 0 | 44.50 |
| S. Sooriyarachchi (*WP Suburbs*).... | 4 | 6 | 0 | 256 | 148 | 1 | 42.66 |
| W. A. Wasantha (*WP Suburbs*)...... | 4 | 6 | 0 | 255 | 113 | 1 | 42.50 |
| H. Premasiri (*SP*)............... | 4 | 7 | 1 | 237 | 96 | 0 | 39.50 |
| H. P. Tillekeratne (*WP City*)...... | 4 | 5 | 0 | 182 | 100 | 1 | 36.40 |
| S. T. Jayasuriya (*SP*)............ | 3 | 5 | 0 | 179 | 64 | 0 | 35.80 |
| R. Soysa (*WP Suburbs*)........... | 4 | 6 | 0 | 205 | 97 | 0 | 34.16 |
| B. P. de Silva (*WP Suburbs*) ....... | 4 | 6 | 0 | 205 | 63 | 0 | 34.16 |
| M. S. Atapattu (*SP*)............. | 3 | 5 | 0 | 167 | 103 | 1 | 33.40 |
| D. C. Wickremasinghe (*SP*)........ | 4 | 6 | 0 | 189 | 79 | 0 | 31.50 |
| B. R. Jurangpathy (*WP City*) ....... | 4 | 7 | 1 | 169 | 69 | 0 | 28.16 |
| D. Ranatunga (*WP City*)........... | 4 | 7 | 1 | 154 | 55 | 0 | 25.66 |

### BOWLING

(Qualification: 10 wickets)

|  | O | M | R | W | BB | Avge |
|---|---|---|---|---|---|---|
| B. R. Jurangpathy (*WP City*)....... | 101 | 35 | 193 | 16 | 4-10 | 12.06 |
| E. A. R. de Silva (*WP City*)........ | 124 | 39 | 226 | 18 | 6-54 | 12.55 |
| M. P. A. Cooray (*WP Suburbs*) ..... | 92 | 15 | 260 | 17 | 5-78 | 15.29 |
| A. W. Ekanayake (*NWP*).......... | 178.3 | 50 | 415 | 25 | 8-39 | 16.60 |
| K. Dharmasena (*WP City*)......... | 162.5 | 46 | 390 | 23 | 6-23 | 16.95 |
| G. P. Wickremasinghe (*SP*)........ | 107 | 24 | 246 | 14 | 4-48 | 17.57 |
| M. Muralitharan (*CP*)............ | 102 | 28 | 193 | 10 | 5-81 | 19.30 |
| K. P. J. Warnaweera (*SP*)......... | 118 | 30 | 309 | 15 | 5-82 | 20.60 |
| K. G. Priyantha (*WP Suburbs*)..... | 132 | 28 | 361 | 17 | 4-30 | 21.23 |
| C. M. Wickremasinghe (*WP Suburbs*) | 105 | 27 | 258 | 10 | 3-39 | 25.80 |
| R. S. Kalpage (*CP*) ............. | 189.2 | 45 | 483 | 13 | 4-80 | 37.15 |

## SINGER INTER-PROVINCIAL TOURNAMENT, 1990-91

|  | Played | Won | Lost | Drawn | Points |
|---|---|---|---|---|---|
| Western Province (City) ...... | 4 | 4 | 0 | 0 | 60.30 |
| Western Province (Suburbs) .... | 4 | 2 | 1 | 1 | 34.80 |
| North-Western Province ....... | 4 | 1 | 2 | 1 | 26.50 |
| Southern Province ........... | 4 | 0 | 1 | 3 | 17.50 |
| Central Province............. | 4 | 0 | 3 | 1 | 5.00 |

At Welagedera Stadium, Kurunegala, March 14, 15, 16, 17. Western Province (Suburbs) won by 373 runs. Western Province (Suburbs) 338 (S. Sooriyarachchi 49, W. A. Wasantha 113, R. Soysa 31; A. W. Ekanayake five for 88) and 323 (R. S. Kaluwitharana 50, B. P. de Silva 63, K. Perera 52 not out; A. W. Ekanayake three for 97); North-Western Province 192 (T. M. Wijesinghe 62; M. P. A. Cooray four for 38, C. Mahesh three for 39) and 96 (M. P. A. Cooray four for 21, K. G. Priyantha three for 34).

At Maitland Place, Colombo (NCC), March 14, 15, 16, 17. Western Province (City) won by one wicket. Southern Province 383 (H. Premasiri 96, M. A. R. Samarasekera 66, S. T. Jayasuriya 64, I. de Seram 60, M. S. Atapattu 30; B. R. Jurangpathy four for 87, K. Dharmasena three for 121) and 117 (S. T. Jayasuriya 37; D. Wijesekera three for 12, K. I. W. Wijegunawardene three for 37); Western Province (City) 335 (H. P. Tillekeratne 100, A. G. D. Wickremasinghe 41, R. L. Dias 44; K. P. J. Warnaweera five for 82) and 166 for nine (A. H. Wickremaratne 65 not out, A. G. D. Wickremasinghe 37; G. P. Wickremasinghe four for 64, K. P. J. Warnaweera four for 45).

At Maitland Place, Colombo (NCC), March 21, 22, 23, 24. Western Province (Suburbs) won by an innings and 248 runs. Western Province (Suburbs) 462 (U. N. K. Fernando 160, S. Sooriyarachchi 148, R. Soysa 42, W. A. Wasantha 35; T. Kodikara three for 43, P. K. Wijetunge three for 122, R. S. Kalpage three for 254); Central Province 55 (K. G. Priyantha four for 30, D. Dias four for 18, including four wickets in four balls) and 159 (R. S. Kalpage 37, U. Kodituwakku 33).

At Maitland Crescent, Colombo, March 21, 22, 23, 24. Western Province (City) won by nine wickets. North-Western Province 143 (U. C. Hathurusinghe 45; B. R. Jurangpathy four for 10, K. Dharmasena three for 44) and 160 (U. C. Hathurusinghe 57; K. Dharmasena five for 49, B. R. Jurangpathy three for 36); Western Province (City) 269 (D. Ranatunga 45, B. R. Jurangpathy 69, R. L. Dias 51, C. P. Senanayake 30; R. Amunugama three for 33, A. W. R. Madurasinghe three for 61) and 35 for one.

At University Ground, Peradeniya, March 28, 29, 30, 31. Western Province (City) won by an innings and 30 runs. Western Province (City) 235 (P. A. de Silva 41, H. P. Tillekeratne 51, K. Dharmasena 39, M. Muralitharan five for 81, R. S. Kalpage four for 80); Central Province 65 (K. Dharmasena six for 23, E. A. R. de Silva four for 21) and 140 (U. Kodituwakku 56; E. A. R. de Silva five for 58).

At Welagedera Stadium, Kurunegala, March 28, 29, 30, 31. Drawn. North-Western Province 290 (A. W. R. Madurasinghe 65, J. A. W. Kumara 42, U. C. Hathurusinghe 32; G. P. Wickremasinghe four for 48); Southern Province 133 (D. C. Wickremasinghe 66 not out, carrying his bat; A. W. Ekanayake eight for 39) and 22 for no wkt.

At Galle Esplanade, Galle, April 4, 5, 6, 7. Drawn. Southern Province 401 for nine dec. (H. Premasiri 50, M. S. Atapattu 103, C. P. H. Ramanayake 68, M. A. R. Samarasekera 35, D. C. Wickremasinghe 31, W. M. J. Kumudu 31; R. S. Kalpage three for 147); Central Province 126 for four (T. Kodikara 54 not out, N. Sawali 34; K. P. J. Warnaweera three for 52).

At Maitland Place, Colombo (SSC), April 4, 5, 6, 7. Western Province (City) won by eight wickets. Western Province (Suburbs) 301 (R. Soysa 97, R. S. Kaluwitharana 38, D. Dias 35, R. S. Jayawardene 32; K. I. W. Wijegunawardene three for 88) and 182 (R. S. Kaluwitharana 36, W. A. Wasantha 35, B. P. de Silva 34; E. A. R. de Silva six for 54); Western Province (City) 447 (D. Ranatunga 55, B. R. Jurangpathy 58, P. A. de Silva 69, A. Ranatunga 63, R. L. Dias 41 not out, A. G. D. Wickremasinghe 36, E. A. R. de Silva 30) and 40 for two.

At Uyanwatte Stadium, Matara, April 18, 19, 20, 21. Drawn. Southern Province 387 (W. M. J. Kumudu 87, D. C. Wickremasinghe 79, S. T. Jayasuriya 70, C. P. H. Ramanayake 43 not out; M. P. A. Cooray three for 54, K. G. Priyantha three for 92) and 229 for eight dec. (W. M. J. Kumudu 59, C. P. H. Ramanayake 69, I. de Seram 45; M. P. A. Cooray five for 78); Western Province (Suburbs) 254 (W. A. Wasantha 51, B. P. de Silva 55, M. P. A. Cooray 37, S. Sooriyarachchi 35; S. M. Faumi four for 78, C. P. H. Ramanayake three for 53) and 0 for no wkt.

At Asgiriya Stadium, Kandy, April 18, 19, 20, 21. North-Western Province won by nine wickets. Central Province 226 (D. N. Nadarajah 42, U. Kodituwakku 67, C. Rajapakse 36 not out; A. W. Ekanayake four for 70) and 205 (U. Kodituwakku 116; A. W. Ekanayake four for 47); North-Western Province 319 (U. C. Hathurusinghe 117, A. W. Ekanayake 55; M. Muralitharan four for 90, R. S. Kalpage three for 95) and 116 for one (R. S. Mahanama 55, U. C. Hathurusinghe 50 not out).

## P. SARAVANAMUTTU TROPHY, 1990-91

At Maitland Crescent, Colombo, December 14, 15, 16. Colombo CC won by nine wickets. Toss: Colombo CC. Sebastianites C and AC 154 (K. Anton 67; K. I. W. Wijegunawardene three for 22, G. F. Labrooy three for 44) and 136 (S. Peiris 50; K. I. W. Wijegunawardene five for 51); Colombo CC 180 for four dec. (C. P. Senanayake 83, R. L. Dias 36, R. S. Mahanama 40 not out) and 111 for one (C. P. Senanayake 34 not out, M. A. R. Samarasekera 69).

At Havelock Park, Colombo, December 14, 15, 16. Drawn. Toss: Colts CC. Colts CC 337 for nine dec. (D. S. G. Bulankulame 113, I. Ekanayake 43, S. Wijesekera 76, Z. Muthalib 36, Extras 31; K. P. J. Warnaweera five for 116, G. S. Pitigala three for 60); Galle CC 253 for nine (S. Kodituwakku 69, H. Munasinghe 41 not out, G. S. Pitigala 48).

At Braybrook Place, Colombo, December 14, 15, 16. Drawn. Toss: Nondescript CC 223 (S. Weerasinghe 90, P. Perera 39; W. S. Silva three for 83, M. Zanhar four for 31) and 123 for four dec. (S. Weerasinghe 68 not out); Moors SC 128 (I. Shabdeen 30; A. Weerakkody three for 47, E. A. R. de Silva four for 49) and 109 for seven (W. Fernando 43 not out; A. Weerakkody three for 35).

At Tyronne Fernando Stadium, Moratuwa, December 14, 15, 16. Drawn. Toss: Moratuwa SC. Saracens SC 278 (C. I. Dunusinghe 79, S. S. K. Gallage 45, U. Sumathipala 44, Extras 42; M. P. A. Cooray four for 45, C. M. Wickremasinghe four for 60); Moratuwa SC 115 (S. Soysa 48; B. P. Nilan four for 52) and 124 for seven (P. T. S. Fernando three for 21).

At Panadura Esplanade, Panadura, December 14, 15, 16. Drawn. Toss: Panadura SC. Sinhalese SC 353 for six dec. (U. N. K. Fernando 130, A. Ranatunga 105, M. S. Atapattu 39 not out) and 93 for two (D. Ranatunga 53 not out); Panadura SC 210 (M. V. Deshapriya 50, R. Wickremaratne 34; F. S. Ahangama four for 31, P. K. Wijetunge three for 75).

At P. Saravanamuttu Stadium, Colombo, December 14, 15, 16. Drawn. Toss: Singha SC. Singha SC 167 (H. Premasiri 50, M. Nishan 37 not out; S. Dharmasena four for 32, U. C. Hathurusinghe three for 30); Tamil Union C and AC 350 for six (T. M. Wijesinghe 105, D. C. Wickremasinghe 58, U. C. Hathurusinghe 108; W. K. Jayalath three for 94).

At Maitland Crescent, Colombo, December 21, 22, 23. Drawn. Toss: Panadura SC. Colombo CC 355 for eight dec. (M. A. R. Samarasekera 71, B. R. Jurangpathy 47, R. L. Dias 58, V. Waragoda 48, C. R. Theunuwara 71 not out; R. Wickremeratne four for 105, M. de Mel three for 96); Panadura SC 119 (R. Wickremaratne 33; K. I. W. Wijegunawardene six for 46) and 214 for six (A. K. D. S. Kumara 36, S. Sooriyarachchi 40, K. P. J. A. de Silva 71, R. Soysa 37 not out).

At Maitland Place, Colombo (NCC), December 21, 22, 23. Drawn. Nondescript CC 180 (P. Perera 36; S. Kodituwakku six for 73) and 244 for eight (A. G. D. Wickremasinghe 55, R. S. Kalpage 112; G. S. Pitigala four for 55); Galle CC 145 (S. M. Faumi 32; R. S. Kalpage three for 15, N. Saranasekera three for 16) and 130 for seven (A. K. Kuruppuarachchi three for 38).

At Maitland Place, Colombo (SSC), December 21, 22, 23. Drawn. Toss: Sinhalese SC. Singha SC 187 (W. M. J. Kumudu 36, T. A. de Silva 31; M. B. Halangoda four for 49, C. N. Fernando three for 42) and 241 for six (H. Premasiri 54, H. W. Kumara 36, H. M. N. C. Dhanasinghe 45, T. A. de Silva 70); Sinhalese SC 350 (A. H. Wickremaratne 109, M. B. Halangoda 36, C. N. Fernando 58, F. S. Ahangama 51; P. Milton three for 86, A. D. B. Ranjith three for 78).

At Havelock Park, Colombo, December 21, 22, 23. Drawn. Toss: Colts CC. Colts CC 302 (V. Perera 75, I. Ekanayake 61 not out, S. Wijesekera 36; M. Fernando three for 76, U. S. C. Perera three for 60) and 81 for four; Saracens SC 260 (C. I. Dunusinghe 37, P. T. S. Fernando 40, T. H. Wijewardene 52, B. P. Nilan 43, Extras 33; Z. Muthalib four for 69, H. de Silva three for 40).

At Tyronne Fernando Stadium, Moratuwa, December 21, 22, 23. Tamil Union C and AC won by an innings and 48 runs. Toss: Sebastianites C and AC. Sebastianites C and AC 94 (R. K. B. Amunugama four for 31) and 133 (S. de Mel 43; R. K. B. Amunugama eight for 60); Tamil Union C and AC 275 for eight dec. (D. C. Wickremasinghe 108, C. Wijemanne 43, W. M. J. P. Weerasinghe 53 not out; D. Dias three for 44, A. Jabar three for 78).

At P. Saravanamuttu Stadium, Colombo, December 22, 23, 24. Drawn. Toss: Moors SC. Moors SC 181 (W. Fernando 36, S. H. U. Karnain 78; K. G. Perera four for 47, C. M. Wickremasinghe four for 61) and 61 for one (L. K. de Alwis 30); Moratuwa SC 266 (A. Wasantha 59, S. Soysa 76, A. D. N. R. de Alwis 44; M. Zanhar four for 71, S. Dharmasena three for 49).

At Maitland Crescent, Colombo, December 28, 29, 30. Drawn. Toss: Colombo CC. Colombo CC 266 (A. M. de Silva 33, R. L. Dias 144; U. C. Hathurusinghe five for 44) and 123 for four (N. de Silva 30, A. M. de Silva 49 not out); Tamil Union C and AC 197 (S. Dharmasena 70, R. K. B. Amunugama 32 not out; C. D. C. Edirimanne four for 55).

At Galle Esplanade, Galle, December 28, 29, 30. Drawn. Galle CC 171 (P. Wanasinghe 43; P. Senanayake three for 23, U. S. C. Perera three for 29); Saracens SC 16 for no wkt.

At Braybrook Place, Colombo, December 28, 29, 30. Drawn. Toss: Colts CC. Colts CC 160 (L. A. Liyanage 49; S. H. U. Karnain five for 26) and 134 for nine (M. Perera 55 not out); Moors SC 236 (L. K. de Alwis 32, M. R. D. Hameem 50, S. M. Irfan 31 not out; L. A. Liyanage three for 33).

At Maitland Place, Colombo (NCC), December 28, 29, 30. Drawn. Toss: Moratuwa SC. Moratuwa SC 180 (R. Weerawardene 48; E. A. R. de Silva four for 62) and 124 for seven (S. Soysa 36; A. K. Kuruppuarachchi five for 46); Nondescript CC 310 (S. Weerasinghe 57, R. S. Kalpage 117, L. R. Fernando 48; C. M. Wickremasinghe five for 43).

At Panadura Esplanade, Panadura, December 28, 29, 30. Panadura SC won by eight wickets. Toss: Singha SC. Singha SC 175 (P. Milton 36; M. de Mel three for 34, M. V. Deshapriya three for 58) and 109 (K. S. Asoka 31; M. V. Deshapriya seven for 41); Panadura SC 211 (S. Thenuwara 36, S. Sooriyarachchi 35, M. de Mel 59; P. Milton four for 42, W. K. Jayalath four for 62) and 75 for two.

At Maitland Place, Colombo (SSC), December 28, 29, 30. Sinhalese SC won by 573 runs. Toss: Sebastianites C and AC. Sinhalese SC 395 for seven dec. (A. A. W. Gunawardene 37, U. N. K. Fernando 63, A. H. Wickremaratne 88, M. S. Atapattu 110 not out, M. B. Halangoda 34; K. Perera five for 129) and 350 for two dec. (A. A. W. Gunawardene 133 not out, U. N. K. Fernando 160); Sebastianites C and AC 63 (M. B. Halangoda six for 16) and 109 (M. B. Halangoda three for 26, B. E. A. Rajadurai four for 18).

At Maitland Crescent, Colombo, January 4, 5, 6. Colombo CC won by an innings and 95 runs. Toss: Singha SC. Singha SC 59 (K. I. W. Wijegunawardene four for 15, C. D. C. Edirimanne five for 16) and 197 (H. W. Kumara 45, A. D. B. Ranjith 60; C. J. Jayakody seven for 99); Colombo CC 351 for six dec. (M. A. R. Samarasekera 76, N. de Silva 60, A. Senanayake 56, R. L. Dias 35, C. R. Thenuwara 49, C. J. Jayakody 36 not out, Extras 31).

At Braybrook Place, Colombo, January 4, 5, 6. Drawn. Toss: Saracens SC. Saracens SC 300 (S. Bulankulame 39, P. Senanayake 64, C. I. Dunusinghe 72, S. S. K. Gallage 40; W. S. Silva three for 76) and 182 for seven dec. (S. Bulankulame 37, S. S. K. Gallage 35, M. U. C. P. Mendis 49; M. Zanhar four for 56); Moors SC 269 (S. Dharmasena 37, L. K. de Alwis 127; T. H. Wijewardene four for 78) and 2 for no wkt.

At Tyronne Fernando Stadium, Moratuwa, January 4, 5, 6. Drawn. Toss: Galle CC. Galle CC 159 (P. Wanasinghe 60, S. Kulatunga 33; M. Fernando five for 40) and 107 for six; Moratuwa SC 172 for nine dec. (C. M. Wickremasinghe 57 not out; S. M. Faumi five for 67).

At Maitland Place, Colombo (NCC), January 4, 5, 6. Nondescript CC won by eight wickets. Toss: Colts CC. Colts CC 140 (R. Fonseka 38; R. S. Kalpage three for 50, E. A. R. de Silva four for 45) and 127 (B. W. Wijetunge 31; A. Weerakkody four for 52, R. S. Kalpage three for 23); Nondescript CC 205 (S. Weerasinghe 34, P. Perera 30, A. G. D. Wickremasinghe 36; M. Perera four for 56, E. Jayatillake three for 56) and 63 for two (S. Weerasinghe 32 not out).

At Panadura Esplanade, Panadura, January 4, 5, 6. Panadura SC won by an innings and 185 runs. Toss: Sebastianites C and AC. Panadura SC 430 for eight dec. (S. Jayawardene 31, M. Jayasena 46, R. Soysa 109, M. V. Deshapriya 46, H. Jayasena 32 not out, R. Wickremaratne 60 not out; S. C. Silva three for 75); Sebastianites C and AC 91 (A. Silva 50; R. Wickremaratne five for 22) and 154 (K. Perera 50 not out; R. Wickremaratne three for 38, M. V. Deshapriya four for 58).

At P. Saravanamuttu Stadium, Colombo, January 4, 5, 6. Sinhalese SC won by nine wickets. Toss: Tamil Union C and AC. Tamil Union C and AC 81 (M. B. Halangoda seven for 22) and 141 (U. C. Hathurusinghe 37; M. B. Halangoda six for 37); Sinhalese SC 192 (U. N. K. Fernando 46, L. R. D. Mendis 30; U. C. Hathurusinghe four for 47, P. L. A. W. N. Alwis four for 26) and 32 for one.

At Colts Ground, Havelock Park, Colombo, January 11, 12, 13. Drawn. Toss: Colts CC. Colts CC 256 (R. Wickremaratne 98, O. Wanigasekera 62; M. Fernando four for 82, M. P. A. Cooray three for 50) and 218 for six (D. S. G. Bulankulame 102 not out, M. Perera 77); Moratuwa SC 263 (P. Fernando 46, A. Wasantha 67, M. P. A. Cooray 32 not out; O. Wanigasekera four for 92).

At Galle Esplanade, Galle, January 11, 12, 13. Drawn. Toss: Galle CC. Moors SC 258 (W. S. Silva 38, W. Fernando 55, B. Jayawardene 48, M. Zanhar 34, Extras 33; S. M. Faumi three for 44, U. Wijesuriya three for 58) and 90 for four; Galle CC 143 (S. Kodituwakku 47, H. Munasinghe 44; W. S. Silva five for 27).

At Maitland Place, Colombo (NCC), January 11, 12, 13. Nondescript CC won by an innings and 2 runs. Toss: Saracens SC. Saracens SC 119 (P. T. S. Fernando 50; S. Sirimanne three for 60, K. Jayasinghe four for 22) and 122 (P. Senanayake 37; R. S. Kalpage five for 29, N. Saranasekera three for 38); Nondescript CC 243 (A. G. D. Wickremasinghe 34, R. S. Kalpage 42, K. Jayasinghe 42, S. Nizar 61; B. P. Nilan three for 57, U. S. C. Perera three for 40).

At Tyronne Fernando Stadium, Moratuwa, January 11, 12, 13. Drawn. Toss: Singha SC. Sebastianites C and AC 180 (A. Silva 47, N. Abeyratne 55; P. Milton four for 49) and 219 (K. Perera 74, A. Silva 61; P. Milton five for 65, A. D. B. Ranjith three for 47); Singha SC 252 (H. Premasiri 132, A. D. B. Ranjith 69 not out; K. Perera five for 78, A. Jabar four for 59) and 70 for one (A. D. B. Ranjith 32).

At Maitland Place, Colombo (SSC), January 11, 12, 13. Sinhalese SC won by four wickets. Toss: Sinhalese SC. Colombo CC 168 (M. A. R. Samarasekera 46; F. S. Ahangama five for 50) and 150 (V. Waragoda 33, A. M. de Silva 37; F. S. Ahangama five for 44, M. B. Halangoda five for 45); Sinhalese SC 145 (M. S. Atapattu 32, M. B. Halangoda 36; C. D. C. Edirimanne six for 62, J. Jayaratne three for 26) and 174 for six (A. H. Wickremaratne 39, M. S. Atapattu 40, M. B. Halangoda 33 not out; C. D. C. Edirimanne three for 69).

At P. Saravanamuttu Stadium, Colombo, January 11, 12, 13. Drawn. Toss: Panadura SC. Panadura SC 132 (K. P. J. A. de Silva 54 not out; S. Samaratunga three for 31, S. Dharmasena three for 25, P. L. A. W. N. Alwis three for 31) and 275 for six (H. Jayasena 75, K. P. J. A. de Silva 119 not out; S. Samaratunga three for 50); Tamil Union C and AC 291 (D. N. Nadarajah 64, U. C. Hathurusinghe 63, S. Dharmasena 65, D. C. Wickremasinghe 39; M. de Mel six for 72).

## Final

At P. Saravanamuttu Stadium, Colombo, January 18, 19, 20. Drawn; Sinhalese SC won the P. Saravanamuttu Trophy on bonus points. Toss: Nondescript CC. Sinhalese SC 269 for seven dec. (A. A. W. Gunawardene 49, U. N. K. Fernando 43, A. H. Wickremaratne 51, M. S. Atapattu 70; A. Weerakkody four for 86); Nondescript CC 193 for eight (S. Weerasinghe 95, R. S. Kalpage 34; F. S. Ahangama four for 32).

# LORDS AND COMMONS RESULTS, 1991

*Matches 12: Won 4, Lost 6, Drawn 1. No result 1.*

At Civil Service Ground, Chiswick, May 22. Lords and Commons won by 41 runs. Lords and Commons 128 (C. F. Horne 42); ACAS 87 (B. Mustill four for 14, C. F. Horne three for 37).

At Bank of England Ground, Roehampton, June 5. Mandarins won by 98 runs. Mandarins 180 for six (35 overs); Lords and Commons 82.

At Roehampton CC, June 18. No result. Conservative Agents 239 for six (30 overs); Lords and Commons 198 for five (C. Colville 109, D. Dover 45).

At Brook, June 28. Lords and Commons won by one wicket. Bümenhof 156 (D. Robson five for 43, G. Allen four for 71); Lords and Commons 160 for nine (P. Sterner 35, D. Harrison 32).

At Betchworth, June 29. Lords and Commons won by two wickets. Bümenhof 180 for seven dec. (R. Heller three for 41); Lords and Commons 185 for eight (D. Bingham 56, W. Wilton 43).

At St Paul's School, July 4. MCC won by 142 runs. MCC 271 for two dec.; Lords and Commons 129 (S. Yorke 74).

At Tunbridge Wells, July 12. Fleet Street won by seven wickets. Lords and Commons 192 for five dec. (C. Macgregor 52, S. Yorke 45); Fleet Street 195 for three.

At Burton Court, July 16. Eton Ramblers won by six wicket. Lords and Commons 290 for five dec. (Hon. M. Rawlinson 166, C. R. Peerless 54); Eton Ramblers 294 for four.

At Burton Court, August 7. Drawn. Lords and Commons 244 for eight dec. (R. Lee 77, C. Whitmore 60 not out); Guards 41 for four.

At Old Emanuels, New Malden, August 21. Law Society won.

At Harrow School, September 6. Harrow Wanderers won by three wickets. Lords and Commons 173 (Hon. M. Rawlinson 32, I. Riaz 31, D. Barbour 31); Harrow Wanderers 174 for seven (Hon. E. Brassey six for 62).

At Highclere, September 8. Lords and Commons won by 102 runs. Lords and Commons 264 for eight dec. (Hon. T. M. Lamb 84, Hon. J. Deedes 64, Hon. M. Greenway 33); Earl of Carnarvon's XI 162 (Hon. T. M. Lamb three for 30, Hon. M. Rawlinson three for 74).

# CRICKET IN ZIMBABWE, 1990-91

## FIRST-CLASS MATCHES, 1990-91

### Pakistan B in Zimbabwe

At Harare South, October 3, 4, 5. Pakistan B won by ten wickets. Toss: Zimbabwe B. Zimbabwe B 145 (C. N. Evans 39; Ayaz Jilani three for 52, Shahid Hussain five for 48) and 262 (W. R. James 61, E. A. Essop-Adam 36, G. J. Crocker 62 not out, M. G. Burmeister 31; Shakeel Khan three for 88, Asif Mujtaba four for 27); Pakistan B 375 for four dec. (Mujahid Jamshed 196, Zahid Fazal 115, Asif Mujtaba 55 not out) and 36 for no wkt.

At Bulawayo, October 8, 9, 10, 12, 13. Zimbabwe won by eight wickets. Toss: Pakistan B. Zimbabwe 436 (K. J. Arnott 121, A. Flower 50, A. D. R. Campbell 32, D. L. Houghton 115, A. C. Waller 30; Shahid Hussain three for 120, Asif Mujtaba five for 71) and 65 for two (A. H. Shah 31); Pakistan B 204 (Aamer Hanif 94, Moin Khan 38; M. P. Jarvis five for 74) and 295 (Shahid Saeed 43, Zahid Fazal 109, Asif Mujtaba 38; M. P. Jarvis seven for 86).

At Harare, October 22, 23, 24, 26. Pakistan B won by an innings and 25 runs. Toss: Zimbabwe. Zimbabwe 252 (K. J. Arnott 53, A. J. Pycroft 85; Shakeel Khan three for 66, Athar Laeeq three for 57) and 144 (A. J. Pycroft 60; Shakeel Khan three for 32, Fakhruddin Baloch four for 57); Pakistan B 421 (Shahid Saeed 92, Basit Ali 115, Shahid Nawaz 45, Zahid Fazal 113; A. J. Traicos three for 92).

## ZIMBABWE v GLAMORGAN

At Bulawayo, April 2, 3, 4. Zimbabwe won by two wickets. Toss: Glamorgan.

### Glamorgan

| | | |
|---|---|---|
| *A. R. Butcher c Jarvis b Peall | 40 | – (6) c Houghton b Huckle ...... 53 |
| S. P. James c Brandes b Huckle | 58 | – (1) lbw b Jarvis ............. 4 |
| A. Dale c James b Huckle | 102 | – (7) not out ................. 16 |
| P. A. Cottey lbw b G. W. Flower | 56 | – (5) c Shah b G. W. Flower .... 53 |
| I. Smith c Peall b G. W. Flower | 1 | – (3) c Huckle b Jarvis ........ 48 |
| R. D. B. Croft c Campbell b Jarvis | 39 | – (4) lbw b Huckle ............ 28 |
| J. Derrick not out | 14 | – (8) not out ................. 0 |
| †M. L. Roberts not out | 1 | – (2) lbw b Jarvis ............ 6 |
| L-b 7, n-b 2 | 9 | B 11, l-b 3, w 1, n-b 2 ... 17 |

1/55 2/183 3/238 4/239     (6 wkts dec.) 320    1/5 2/44 3/61     (6 wkts dec.) 225
5/267 6/318     4/117 5/173 6/224

S. L. Watkin, S. Bastien and M. Frost did not bat.

Bowling: *First Innings*—Brandes 14-3-34-0; Jarvis 23-6-73-1; Shah 19-6-43-0; Peall 20-4-65-1; Huckle 20-3-92-2; G. W. Flower 5-2-6-2. *Second Innings*—Brandes 10-1-47-0; Jarvis 15-5-29-3; Shah 4-0-20-0; Peall 10-1-17-0; Huckle 17-1-72-2; G. W. Flower 6-0-26-1.

## Zimbabwe

| | | |
|---|---|---|
| G. W. Flower c Smith b Bastien ............ | 15 | – c Butcher b Watkin ............ 13 |
| K. J. Arnott c Dale b Watkin ............ | 8 | – run out ............ 67 |
| A. D. R. Campbell not out ............ | 100 | – c Roberts b Watkin ............ 63 |
| †A. Flower st Roberts b Croft ............ | 16 | – c and b Croft ............ 4 |
| W. R. James lbw b Bastien ............ | 5 | – c sub b Butcher ............ 30 |
| *D. L. Houghton b Bastien ............ | 0 | – c Croft b Butcher ............ 44 |
| A. H. Shah b Bastien ............ | 0 | – c and b Croft ............ 16 |
| E. A. Brandes c Bastien b Derrick ............ | 94 | – b Watkin ............ 33 |
| S. G. Peall run out ............ | 1 | – not out ............ 16 |
| M. P. Jarvis not out ............ | 4 | – not out ............ 9 |
| L-b 4, n-b 6 ............ | 10 | L-b 1 ............ 1 |

1/12 2/24 3/53 4/59 5/59       (8 wkts dec.) 253    1/18 2/128 3/135 4/173    (8 wkts) 296
6/65 7/212 8/240                              5/185 6/238 7/238 8/281

A. G. Huckle did not bat.

Bowling: *First Innings*—Frost 14-5-44-0; Watkin 16-7-43-1; Bastien 16.1-6-44-4; Croft 21-6-85-1; Derrick 7-1-33-1. *Second Innings*—Frost 7-1-28-0; Watkin 15.3-1-56-3; Bastien 3-0-16-0; Croft 26-1-134-2; Derrick 2-0-17-0; Butcher 7-0-44-2.

Umpires: K. Kanjee and I. D. Robinson.

---

## ZIMBABWE v WORCESTERSHIRE

At Harare, April 8, 9, 10. Drawn. Toss: Worcestershire.

### Worcestershire

| | | |
|---|---|---|
| T. S. Curtis c Houghton b Brandes .... | 58 | I. T. Botham not out ............ 33 |
| G. J. Lord c Flower b Shah ......... | 40 | B 4, l-b 4, n-b 8 ............ 16 |
| G. A. Hick lbw b Huckle ......... | 81 | |
| D. B. D'Oliveira c Brandes b Peall .... | 81 | 1/76 2/164 |
| *P. A. Neale not out ............... | 68 | 3/200 4/335     (4 wkts dec.) 377 |

†S. J. Rhodes, R. K. Illingworth, S. R. Lampitt, C. M. Tolley and N. V. Radford did not bat.

Bowling: Brandes 15-3-50-1; Jarvis 15-2-48-0; Shah 16-2-81-1; Huckle 24-3-106-1; Peall 14-0-84-1.

### Zimbabwe

| | | |
|---|---|---|
| W. R. James c Rhodes b Lampitt ............ | 25 | – lbw b Botham ............ 40 |
| G. J. Whittal c Rhodes b Lampitt ............ | 31 | – c Tolley b Botham ............ 20 |
| A. D. R. Campbell not out ............ | 45 | – c Neale b Lampitt ............ 1 |
| †A. Flower c Rhodes b Hick ............ | 22 | – (5) b Illingworth ............ 63 |
| *D. L. Houghton c Tolley b Hick ............ | 6 | – (6) c Lord b Radford ............ 1 |
| G. A. Paterson b Illingworth ............ | 0 | – (7) c Hick b D'Oliveira ............ 42 |
| A. H. Shah b Hick ............ | 8 | – (8) not out ............ 43 |
| E. A. Brandes c Lampitt b Illingworth ............ | 5 | – (4) b Illingworth ............ 28 |
| S. G. Peall b Illingworth ............ | 5 | – not out ............ 31 |
| M. P. Jarvis st Rhodes b Illingworth ............ | 5 | |
| A. G. Huckle c Neale b Illingworth ............ | 1 | |
| L-b 3, n-b 3 ............ | 6 | L-b 1, w 1, n-b 5 ............ 7 |

1/55 2/59 3/100 4/108 5/109        157    1/43 2/57 3/66 4/100    (7 wkts) 276
6/126 7/133 8/141 9/145                            5/101 6/174 7/219

Bowling: *First Innings*—Radford 9-2-19-0; Tolley 8-2-16-0; Illingworth 25.5-13-22-5; Botham 9-2-21-0; Lampitt 8-2-23-2; Hick 24-7-53-3. *Second Innings*—Radford 20-3-62-1; Tolley 8-2-22-0; Botham 8-2-17-2; Lampitt 12-2-40-1; Illingworth 35-10-61-2; Hick 21-9-41-0; D'Oliveira 9-0-27-1; Curtis 1-0-5-0.

Umpires: I. D. Robinson and R. Suchet.

# CRICKET IN DENMARK, 1991

### By PETER S. HARGREAVES

If the 1991 Danish cricket season were to be remembered for one particular feature, it would have to be the number of times that the country's faster bowlers became injured, either intermittently or for the greater part of the season. It was not without significance that the only one of their four international matches which resulted in a Danish victory was the only one in which their best bowler, Søren Henriksen, was able to send down his full ration of overs without mishap.

Two of the losses were incurred in what is intended to be an annual series of one-day matches against The Netherlands. Played in May, at Esbjerg and on the new ground of the Husum club at Hattstedt, in Schleswig, these encounters could have gone either way. In mid-September, the Australian Under-19 team played matches against Danish national sides at Hjørring and Aalborg, in North Jutland, with the first providing an unexpected defeat for the highly rated visitors, against a team whose average age was 24. With the Danish team going through a period of rebuilding, these were fairly satisfying results, although certain tactical errors were obvious in the loss to the Australians at Aalborg under the new captain, From. Nevertheless he had had his triumph the previous day.

In senior cricket, on the domestic front, Svanholm beat Chang early in the season in a well-fought final of the nationwide knockout cup. As the season developed, Glostrup opened a lead in the first division championship, only to see it closed by their West Copenhagen rivals, Svanholm, in the later stages. Both teams finished with equal points, but Svanholm took the title on their higher average of runs per wicket, thereby completing the double. AB, who began well and then had a bad lapse in mid-season, filled third place after recovering towards the finish. At the foot of the table Slagelse, who had come up from the second division in 1990, had to go down again in exchange for the club they had replaced, Nykøbing Mors, but KB, second from bottom in the first division, easily staved off a challenge from the second division runners-up, Aarhus. From the second division, Frem and Esbjerg II went down and were replaced by the two third division zone winners, Chang II and the newly formed club, Odense. The latter resulted from the merger of the B.1909 and B.1913 clubs of that city.

No batsman was outstanding, but Allan From Hansen, Søren Henriksen and Carsten Strandvig were the most consistent. Henriksen was the leading wicket-taker, with 49, and the nigh-veteran Australian fast bowler, Ross McLellan, was again successful. However, he was well headed in the averages by Glostrup's change bowler, Benny B. Nielsen, who had a remarkable strike-rate, with 42 wickets off 142 overs at 9.54. It was pleasing to note that several spinners finished high in the averages.

In the youth divisions the Junior (under 18) title went to Glostrup, who beat Esbjerg, and Svanholm beat Esbjerg for the Boys (under 15) title. In the Lilleputs (under 13), Husum, of Schleswig, claimed their first outdoor Danish championship when they beat Køge. If any feature was noticeable here, it might have been the lack of success this time for any of the three Pakistani clubs from Copenhagen, although the senior Nørrebro side succeeded in remaining in the first division after their 1990 promotion. The national under-19 side had their moments in the International Youth Tournament at Winnipeg, Canada, but their batting did not measure up to their bowling strength.

The national women's side came out of the European Championships in The Netherlands well enough, with a first-time victory over Ireland and loss to the host country by only 4 runs. This could have an effect on Denmark's seeding in the 1993 Women's World Cup. At home, as in 1990 there was a cliffhanger final, with Glostrup edging out the playing-through champions, Nykøbing Mors, mainly through an outstanding innings by the young batting hope, Mette Frost. Batting tended to dominate the women's play-off series, which has not always been the case.

Among visitors to the country were two, from The Netherlands and England, for the veteran Forty Clubs' twentieth triangular contest, held at Slagelse in July, where a surprisingly strong home side finished top. Bancroft's School, from Woodford in Essex, again came to Denmark, this time with the former England bowler, John Lever, in the party. And in early July a representative team from Sweden played two matches in Copenhagen, only the second instance of such an event. Within days of these games, Denmark proposed Germany as an affiliate member of the ICC at the annual meeting at Lord's, and is prepared to do the same for its northern neighbour as a contribution towards furthering the game in Europe.

Finally, on the last weekend of September, the members of the old students' club, Soranerne, of the Sorø Akademi, played a commemorative match at the famous Zealand school to mark the 125th anniversary of the two historic, official matches played there in 1866.

# CRICKET IN THE NETHERLANDS

## By DAVID HARDY

August 15, 1991 will rank in Dutch cricket alongside August 16, 1989 and August 29, 1964 as a day on which The Netherlands' national team toppled a Test country. In 1989 it was England A; in 1964 it was Australia. This time it was the mighty West Indians, visiting Holland for the first time since 1957, who were unpleasantly surprised by the ever-improving Dutch team. Without Richards, Marshall and Ambrose, the tourists were beaten by five wickets in the first of two one-day games during the inaugural International Haarlem Cricket Week. The Netherlands' third and newest county professional, eighteen-year-old fast bowler André van Troost, captured three early West Indian wickets, after which Caribbean casualness did the rest. As the Dutch chased a target of 130, there was some particularly solid batting from the openers, Robert van Oosterom and Albert van Nierop, and later from the veteran Guyanese, Rupert Gomes, top-scorer with 28 not out, and Somerset's Roland Lefebvre. The second match was comfortably won by the West Indians, despite 68 and three for 15 from Tim de Leede, but history had already been made.

The Dutch team had achieved another first earlier in the season, making a pre-season tour in April of three English counties – Warwickshire, Leicestershire and Essex. However, they were at less than full strength and proved to be no match for the counties. It was a different story in the two one-day internationals against Denmark in May, one of which, curiously, was played in Germany, at the Husum club in Schleswig. The other was at Esbjerg in Denmark. An excellent all-round performance of 65 and four for 36 by de Leede was instrumental in the Dutch winning the first match, while in the second, 43-year-old Nolan Clarke hit a whirlwind 125 to give them victory in both matches. De Leede has a good chance of following his countrymen, Bakker, Lefebvre and van Troost, into county cricket in England.

The national league and cup competitions produced two new winners, providing a clear indication that Dutch cricket has more strength in depth than ever. Excelsior, from Schiedam, an area of greater Rotterdam which is renowned for its enthusiastic cricketers, became league champions for the first time, winning thirteen of their eighteen matches in the Hoofdklasse. Player-coach Tim Zoehrer, the Western Australia wicket-keeper, took 36 wickets with his leg-spinners, and Emmerson Trotman, a Barbadian who had been playing in The Netherlands since 1978, topped Excelsior's and the league's batting averages with 870 runs at 62.14. André van Troost, one of many talented young cricketers to develop at Excelsior, played a large part in his club's early-season successes, capturing sixteen wickets at 13.18 before linking up with Somerset. Voorburg CC, from The Hague area, crowned their steady rise up the leagues during the past few seasons by winning the 40-overs Telegraaf Knockout Cup.

The leading run-scorer in the Premier League was Nolan Clarke, with 1,135 runs at 59.73 for Excelsior's neighbours, Hermes DVS, and the leading wicket-taker was Richard Petrie, VOC Rotterdam's player-coach, with 45. The Olivetti Top Performance Trophy, for points awarded per match by the umpires, went to Peter Kennedy, player-coach of Koninklijke UD, who scored 870 runs at an average of 58.00.

Youth cricket continued to flourish under the watchful eye of Steven Lubbers, the national youth coach. The Colts can never have had a better chance of winning the biennial International Youth Tournament than they had at Winnipeg, Canada, in 1991. They beat England Under-18 by 11 runs, and to win the tournament they had only to beat Denmark, who were experiencing a very disappointing week. However, the old continental enemy was not going to allow that to happen; the Danes won the last match by 100 runs and the Dutch had to settle for third place behind England and Bermuda. Once again the national teams in the 12-14 and 14-16 age groups enjoyed exchanges with county teams from south-west England.

Other notable occasions during the season were the women's European Championships, staged at Haarlem in July, the visit of the powerful Australian Under-19 team, and the De Flamingo's tournament. The last mentioned celebrated 75 years of the "Dutch MCC", and among clubs taking part were, from England, MCC, Eton Ramblers and the Privateers.

## THE NETHERLANDS v WEST INDIANS

†At Rood en Wit CC, Haarlem, August 15. The Netherlands won by five wickets. West Indians 129 (45 overs) (D. Williams 31; A. P. van Troost three for 27); The Netherlands 130 for five (44.1 overs).

†At Rood en Wit CC, Haarlem, August 16. West Indians won by 88 runs. West Indians 230 for eight (55 overs) (R. B. Richardson 68, M. D. Marshall 60; T. de Leede three for 15); The Netherlands 142 (50.5 overs) (T. de Leede 68).

# WOMEN'S CRICKET, 1991

## By CAROL SALMON

As the traditional roots of cricket are increasingly undermined, the women's game in England is finding it harder and harder to keep its head above water. The 1993 World Cup, to be staged in England, will be a severe test of the character and resilience of the Women's Cricket Association, and of its unceasing efforts to obtain sponsorship and extract the maximum exposure to attract the necessary new members. Those English players who toured New Zealand earlier in 1992 will have looked with envy at their counterparts there. Australia and New Zealand play regularly for the Shell Cup in a fully sponsored environment, and the New Zealand authorities have substantial backing for their national side. As part of the Shell involvement in cricket in Australasia, England were asked to take part in a three-way competition for the Shell Cup during the New Zealand tour. This added extra one-day matches to the itinerary, but it was readily agreed on as supporting the cause of the host nation. In addition, and to make use of further sponsorship opportunities, England travelled to Sydney after the New Zealand tour to play the first five-day Test.

In 1991, the England selectors opted once again for change, with Helen Plimmer of Yorkshire becoming England's third captain since they were runners-up to Australia in the 1988-89 World Cup. Jane Powell, who led England in Australia then, captained the side to successive European Cup wins in 1989 and 1990, and Karen Smithies replaced her for the short tour to Ireland in 1990. Plimmer took over for the 1991 European Cup campaign in The Netherlands, where she sealed a fine performance as captain with a half-century in the final against Denmark, and she retained the job when the tour party to New Zealand was announced.

The England party for the European Cup contained three new caps – Marie Moralee, Sarah-Jane Cook and Janet Godman. The team was: Helen Plimmer (*captain*), Sue Metcalfe and Debbie Maybury (Yorkshire), Marie Moralee (Kent), Janet Godman (Thames Valley), Suzie Kitson (East Anglia), Lisa Nye and Gill Smith (Middlesex), Jo Chamberlain, Karen Smithies and Wendy Watson (East Midlands), Sarah-Jane Cook (Sussex) and Carole Hodges (Lancashire and Cheshire). Two further new internationals, Debbie Stock and Jane Smit, were in the fourteen-strong party for New Zealand. The full team was: Plimmer (*captain*), Metcalfe, Maybury and Janet Aspinall (Yorkshire), Janette Brittin (*vice-captain*, Surrey), Godman and Stock (Thames Valley), Kitson (East Anglia), Nye (Middlesex), Chamberlain, Smithies, Watson and Smit (East Midlands) and Hodges (Lancashire and Cheshire). The manager was Norma Izard (Kent) and the coach Ruth Prideaux (Sussex). Brittin was selected again after being unavailable for England since the World Cup in Australia, although neither she nor Chamberlain was available for the Australian part of the tour. Even more unfortunately, two of England's better bowlers in recent times, Gill Smith and Yorkshire's Clare Taylor, were unavailable to tour. Taylor, having carved out a successful career with the England women's soccer team, joined the lengthy list of double internationals.

After the many changes to the domestic programme in recent seasons, it was surprising that the England selectors found it necessary to reinstitute a final trial, at Collingham and Linton in Yorkshire on September 21, 22, before naming the New Zealand tour party. A county championship in a tournament format and a territorial weekend were introduced for players to perform in a competitive environment, and to insist on a trial match added further financial pressure on the players, not to mention the additional requirement on their time. However, it is worth repeating that, despite few if any expenses being forthcoming for matches and training weekends, few players drop out of women's cricket because of financial considerations.

East Midlands retained the area championship at Cambridge on July 27 to 31, beating Yorkshire, the only other unbeaten team until then, by seven wickets in the final. Yorkshire were dismissed for 147, and Wendy Watson (69) and Jane Smit (39 not out) steered East Midlands home. The other eight areas taking part were Lancashire and Cheshire, Kent, Thames Valley, Surrey, East Anglia, Middlesex, the West, and Sussex. Two centuries were recorded: Jo Chamberlain hit 105 for East Midlands against Thames Valley, and Carole Hodges of Lancashire and Cheshire made 123 not out against the West. The best bowling performances were Clare Whichcord's five for 17 off 9.1 overs for Kent against Sussex, and Gill Smith's five for 23 off eleven overs for Middlesex against the West.

Four teams were then named for the territorial tournament in Oxford, where two three-day matches took place from August 24 to 26. The North drew with the South, the former finishing 41 runs short of their target of 200, with Sue Metcalfe (North) producing the top score of the match with 71 not out. Janette Brittin (South) had innings of 60 and 48, and Carole Hodges (North) took seven for 35 in the South's second innings. In the other match, the Mid-West beat the East by ten wickets. The Mid-West's Jo Chamberlain captured six wickets in each innings to return match figures of twelve for 54, and for the East, Suzie Kitson took four wickets in the Mid-West's first innings, in addition to scoring 76 and 24.

Wolverhampton won the National League final, beating Vagabonds by eight wickets with 5.3 overs to spare, and North Riding were equally convincing winners of the National Club Knockout. Wolverhampton's captain, Barbara Daniels, hit an undefeated 77 from 78 deliveries as her side scored 146 for two in reply to Vagabonds' 142 for five off their allotted 40 overs. In the Knockout final, also a 40-overs-a-side match, Redoutables could manage only 101, with Janette Brittin top-scoring with 27, and North Riding, replying with 105 for four, won with 4.3 overs to spare.

During April the death occurred of Sylvia Swinburne, OBE. President of the Surrey club, Redoutables, for 25 years, she first played for the county in 1934. She was vice-chairman of the Women's Cricket Association from 1965 to 1971 and chairman from 1971 to 1977, and it was through her initiative that England played Australia at Lord's for the first time, in a one-day international, during the WCA Jubilee in 1976.

## EUROPEAN CUP, 1991

The third European Cup tournament was held in The Netherlands, at the Rood de Wit Cricket Club in Haarlem, from July 16 to 20; and as in Denmark in 1989 and England in 1990 England emerged as comfortable winners. Helen Plimmer opened her first campaign as England captain by sharing in a match-winning first-wicket stand of 59 with Debbie Maybury against Ireland. For the Irish, runners-up in 1990, the tournament proved to be a disappointment. Beaten by Denmark as well, they found themselves in a three-way tie with Denmark and The Netherlands, with the right to meet England in the final being decided on run-rate. In the event it was the Danes who went through, though if The Netherlands had scored just 16 more runs in their 25-run defeat by Ireland, they would have qualified ahead of Denmark and Ireland. The Dutch and the Danes had earlier featured in the most exciting match of the tournament, with the former scoring 126 from 54.5 overs and Denmark replying with 122 off 54.2 overs. Unfortunately, the weather interfered with some of the games – no play was possible on July 18 – and there was some criticism of the condition of the matting pitches and also of the length of the grass on the outfield.

The decision to hold the European Cup every two years, instead of annually, meant that this was the last tournament for several years. In 1993, when the next tournament would have been staged, England host the World Cup, and with all the European nations being invited to enter, it was agreed to cancel that year's European Cup.

## Results

July 16. England won by 75 runs. England 177 for eight (55 overs) (D. Maybury 36); Ireland 102 (54.2 overs) (J. M. Chamberlain three for 16, S. J. Kitson three for 26).

July 16. The Netherlands won by 4 runs. The Netherlands 126 (54.5 overs) (N. Payne 41); Denmark 122 (54.2 overs) (L. Hansen 45; J. Noortwijk three for 13).

July 17. England won by 90 runs. England 178 for eight (55 overs) (D. Maybury 47, J. M. Chamberlain 32); The Netherlands 88 for nine (55 overs) (M. Moralee three for 6).

July 17. Denmark won by 42 runs. Denmark 132 for seven (55 overs) (J. Jønsson 33, M. Frost 31; J. Herbison three for 29); Ireland 90 (49 overs) (T. Christiansen three for 17).

July 19. England won by nine wickets. Denmark 47 (29 overs) (J. M. Chamberlain seven for 8); England 48 for one (20 overs).

July 19. Ireland won by 25 runs. Ireland 97 (44.3 overs) (A. Venturini four for 17); The Netherlands 72 (41 overs) (M.-P. Moore three for 16).

### Final

July 20. England won by 179 runs. England 225 for five (55 overs) (H. Plimmer 50, W. A. Watson 69); Denmark 46 (35 overs) (C. A. Hodges four for 14).

# BIRTHS AND DEATHS OF CRICKETERS

The qualifications are as follows:

1. All players who have appeared in a Test match or a one-day international for a Test-match playing country.

2. English county players who have appeared in 50 or more first-class matches during their careers and, if dead, were still living ten years ago.

3. Players who appeared in fifteen or more first-class matches in the 1991 English season.

4. English county captains, county caps and captains of Oxford and Cambridge Universities who, if dead, were still living ten years ago.

5. All players chosen as *Wisden* Cricketers of the Year, including the Public Schoolboys chosen for the 1918 and 1919 Almanacks. Cricketers of the Year are identified by the italic notation *CY* and year of appearance. A list of the Cricketers of the Year from 1889 to 1988 appeared in *Wisden* 1989.

6. Players or personalities not otherwise qualified who are thought to be of sufficient interest to merit inclusion.

## Key to abbreviations and symbols

CUCC – Cambridge University, OUCC – Oxford University.

*Australian states*: NSW – New South Wales, Qld – Queensland, S. Aust. – South Australia, Tas. – Tasmania, Vic. – Victoria, W. Aust. – Western Australia.

*Indian teams*: Guj. – Gujarat, H'bad – Hyderabad, Ind. Rlwys – Indian Railways, Ind. Serv. – Indian Services, J/K – Jammu and Kashmir, Karn. – Karnataka (Mysore to 1972-73), M. Pradesh – Madhya Pradesh (Central India [C. Ind.] to 1939-40, Holkar to 1954-55, Madhya Bharat to 1956-57), M'tra – Maharashtra, Naw. – Nawanagar, Raja. – Rajasthan, S'tra – Saurashtra (West India [W. Ind.] to 1945-46, Kathiawar to 1949-50), S. Punjab – Southern Punjab (Patiala to 1958-59, Punjab since 1968-69), TC – Travancore-Cochin (Kerala since 1956-57), TN – Tamil Nadu (Madras to 1959-60), U. Pradesh – Uttar Pradesh (United Provinces [U. Prov.] to 1948-49), Vidarbha (CP & Berar to 1949-50, Madhya Pradesh to 1956-57).

*New Zealand provinces*: Auck. – Auckland, Cant. – Canterbury, C. Dist. – Central Districts, N. Dist. – Northern Districts, Wgtn – Wellington.

*Pakistani teams*: ADBP – Agricultural Development Bank of Pakistan, B'pur – Bahawalpur, HBFC – House Building Finance Corporation, HBL – Habib Bank Ltd, IDBP – Industrial Development Bank of Pakistan, Kar. – Karachi, MCB – Muslim Commercial Bank, NBP – National Bank of Pakistan, NWFP – North-West Frontier Province, PACO – Pakistan Automobile Corporation, Pak. Rlwys – Pakistan Railways, Pak. Us – Pakistan Universities, PIA – Pakistan International Airlines, PNSC – Pakistan National Shipping Corporation, PWD – Public Works Department, R'pindi – Rawalpindi, UBL – United Bank Ltd, WAPDA – Water and Power Development Authority.

*South African provinces*: E. Prov. – Eastern Province, Griq. W. – Griqualand West, N. Tvl – Northern Transvaal, NE Tvl – North-Eastern Transvaal, OFS – Orange Free State, Rhod. – Rhodesia, Tvl – Transvaal, W. Prov. – Western Province.

*Sri Lankan teams*: BRC – Burgher Recreation Club, CCC – Colombo Cricket Club, Mor. – Moratuwa Sports Club, NCC – Nondescripts Cricket Club, Pan. – Panadura Sports Club, SLAF – Air Force, SSC – Sinhalese Sports Club, TU – Tamil Union Cricket and Athletic Club.

*West Indies islands*: B'dos – Barbados, BG – British Guiana (Guyana since 1966), Comb. Is. – Combined Islands, Jam. – Jamaica, T/T – Trinidad & Tobago.

\* *Denotes Test player.* \*\* *Denotes appeared for two countries. There is a list of Test players country by country from page 85.*

† *Denotes also played for team under its previous name.*

Aamer Hameed (Pak. Us, Lahore, Punjab & OUCC) b Oct. 18, 1954

*Aamer Malik (ADBP) b Jan. 3, 1963

Aamer Sohail (HBL) b Sept. 14, 1966

Abberley, R. N. (Warwicks.) b April 22, 1944

*a'Beckett, E. L. (Vic.) b Aug. 11, 1907, d June 2, 1989

*Abdul Kadir (Kar. & NBP) b May 10, 1944

*Abdul Qadir (HBL, Lahore & Punjab) b Sept. 15, 1955

*Abel, R. (Surrey; *CY 1890*) b Nov. 30, 1857, d Dec. 10, 1936

Abell, Sir G. E. B. (OUCC, Worcs. & N. Ind.) b June 22, 1904, d Jan. 11, 1989

Aberdare, 3rd Lord (*see* Bruce, Hon. C. N.)

*Abid Ali, S. (H'bad) b Sept. 9, 1941

Abrahams, J. (Lancs.) b July 21, 1952

*Absolom, C. A. (CUCC & Kent) b June 7, 1846, d July 30, 1889

Acfield, D. L. (CUCC & Essex) b July 24, 1947

*Achong, E. (T/T) b Feb. 16, 1904, d Aug. 29, 1986

Ackerman, H. M. (Border, NE Tvl, Northants, Natal & W. Prov.) b April 28, 1947

A'Court, D. G. (Glos.) b July 27, 1937

Adam, Sir Ronald, 2nd Bt (Pres. MCC 1946-47) b Oct. 30, 1885, d Dec. 26, 1982

Adams, C. J. (Derbys.) b May 6, 1970

Adams, P. W. (Cheltenham & Sussex; *CY 1919*) b 1900, d Feb. 28, 1962

*Adcock, N. A. T. (Tvl & Natal; *CY 1961*) b March 8, 1931

*Adhikari, H. R. (Guj., Baroda & Ind. Serv.) b July 31, 1919

*Afaq Hussain (Kar., Pak. Us, PIA & PWD) b Dec. 31, 1939

Afford, J. A. (Notts.) b May 12, 1964

*Aftab Baloch (PWD, Kar., Sind, NBP & PIA) b April 1, 1953

*Aftab Gul (Punjab U., Pak. Us & Lahore) b March 31, 1946

*Agha Saadat Ali (Pak. Us, Punjab, B'pur & Lahore) b June 21, 1929

*Agha Zahid (Pak. Us, Punjab, Lahore & HBL) b Jan. 7, 1953

*Agnew, J. P. (Leics; *CY 1988*) b April 4, 1960

Ahangama, F. S. (SSC) b Sept. 14, 1959

Aird, R. (CUCC & Hants; Sec. MCC 1953-62, Pres. MCC 1968-69) b May 4, 1902, d Aug. 16, 1986

Aitchison, Rev. J. K. (Scotland) b May 26, 1920

*Akram Raza (Sargodha & HBL) b Nov. 22, 1964

Alabaster, G. D. (Cant., N. Dist. & Otago) b Dec. 10, 1933

*Alabaster, J. C. (Otago) b July 11, 1930

Alcock, C. W. (Sec. Surrey CCC 1872-1907, Editor *Cricket* 1882-1907) b Dec. 2, 1842, d Feb. 26, 1907

Alderman, A. E. (Derbys.) b Oct. 30, 1907, d June 4, 1990

*Alderman, T. M. (W. Aust., Kent & Glos.; *CY 1982*) b June 12, 1956

Aldridge, K. J. (Worcs & Tas.) b March 13, 1935

Alexander of Tunis, 1st Lord (Pres. MCC 1955-56) b Dec. 10, 1891, d June 16, 1969

*Alexander, F. C. M. (CUCC & Jam.) b Nov. 2, 1928

*Alexander, G. (Vic.) b April 22, 1851, d Nov. 6, 1930

*Alexander, H. H. (Vic.) b June 9, 1905

Alikhan, R. I. (Sussex, PIA & Surrey) b Dec. 28, 1962

*Alim-ud-Din (Rajputana, Guj., Sind, B'pur, Kar. & PWD) b Dec. 15, 1930

*Allan, D. W. (B'dos) b Nov. 5, 1937

*Allan, F. E. (Vic.) b Dec. 2, 1849, d Feb. 9, 1917

Allan, J. M. (OUCC, Kent, Warwicks. & Scotland) b April 2, 1932

*Allan, P. J. (Qld) b Dec. 31, 1935

Allcott, C. F. W. (Auck.) b Oct. 7, 1896, d Nov. 19, 1973

Allen, A. W. (CUCC & Northants) b Dec. 22, 1912

Allen, B. O. (CUCC & Glos.) b Oct. 13, 1911, d May 1, 1981

*Allen, D. A. (Glos.) b Oct. 29, 1935

*Allen, Sir G. O. B. (CUCC & Middx; Pres. MCC 1963-64; *special portrait 1987*) b July 31, 1902, d Nov. 29, 1989

*Allen, I. B. A. (Windwards) b Oct. 6, 1965

Allen, M. H. J. (Northants & Derbys.) b Jan. 7, 1933

*Allen, R. C. (NSW) b July 2, 1858, d May 2, 1952

Alletson, E. B. (Notts.) b March 6, 1884, d July 5, 1963

Alley, W. E. (NSW & Som.; *CY 1962*) b Feb. 3, 1919

Alleyne, H. L. (B'dos, Worcs., Natal & Kent) b Feb. 28, 1957

Alleyne, M. W. (Glos.) b May 23, 1968

*Allom, M. J. C. (CUCC & Surrey; Pres. MCC 1969-70) b March 23, 1906

*Allott, P. J. W. (Lancs. & Wgtn) b Sept. 14, 1956

Altham, H. S. (OUCC, Surrey & Hants; Pres. MCC 1959-60) b Nov. 30, 1888, d March 11, 1965

*Amalean, K. N. (SL) b April 7, 1965

*Amarnath, Lala (N. Ind., S. Punjab, Guj., Patiala, U. Pradesh & Ind. Rlwys) b Sept. 11, 1911

*Amarnath, M. (Punjab & Delhi; *CY 1984*) b Sept. 24, 1950

*Amarnath, S. (Punjab & Delhi) b Dec. 30, 1948

\*Amar Singh, L. (Patiala, W. Ind. & Naw.) b Dec. 4, 1910, d May 20, 1940

\*Ambrose, C. E. L. (Leewards & Northants; *CY 1992*) b Sept. 21, 1963

Amerasinghe, A. M. J. G. (Nomads) b Feb. 2, 1954

\*Ames, L. E. G. (Kent; *CY 1929*) b Dec. 3, 1905, d Feb. 26, 1990

\*\*Amir Elahi (Baroda, N. Ind., S. Punjab & B'pur) b Sept. 1, 1908, d Dec. 28, 1980

\*Amiss, D. L. (Warwicks.; *CY 1975*) b April 7, 1943

Anderson, I. S. (Derbys. & Boland) b April 24, 1960

Anderson, J. H. (W. Prov.) b April 26, 1874, d March 11, 1926

\*Anderson, R. W. (Cant., N. Dist., Otago & C. Dist.) b Oct. 2, 1948

\*Anderson, W. McD. (Otago, C. Dist. & Cant.) b Oct. 8, 1919, d Dec. 21, 1979

Andrew, C. R. (CUCC) b Feb. 18, 1963

\*Andrew, K. V. (Northants) b Dec. 15, 1929

Andrew, S. J. W. (Hants & Essex) b Jan. 27, 1966

\*Andrews, B. (Cant., C. Dist. & Otago) b April 4, 1945

\*Andrews, T. J. E. (NSW) b Aug. 26, 1890, d Jan. 28, 1970

Andrews, W. H. R. (Som.) b April 14, 1908, d Jan. 9, 1989

Angell, F. L. (Som.) b June 29, 1922

\*Anil Dalpat (Kar. & PIA) b Sept. 20, 1963

\*Ankola, S. A. (M'tra & Bombay) b March 1, 1968

Anurasiri, S. D. (Pan.) b Feb. 25, 1966

\*Anwar Hussain (N. Ind., Bombay, Sind & Kar.) b July 16, 1920

\*Anwar Khan (Kar., Sind & NBP) b Dec. 24, 1955

\*Appleyard, R. (Yorks.; *CY 1952*) b June 27, 1924

\*Apte, A. L. (Ind. Us, Bombay & Raja.) b Oct. 24, 1934

\*Apte, M. L. (Bombay & Bengal) b Oct. 5, 1932

\*Aqib Javed (PACO & Hants) b Aug. 5, 1972

\*Archer, A. G. (Worcs.) b Dec. 6, 1871, d July 15, 1935

\*Archer, K. A. (Qld) b Jan. 17, 1928

\*Archer, R. G. (Qld) b Oct. 25, 1933

\*Arif Butt (Lahore & Pak. Rlwys) b May 17, 1944

Arlott, John (Writer & Broadcaster) b Feb. 25, 1914, d Dec. 14, 1991

\*Armitage, T. (Yorks.) b April 25, 1848, d Sept. 21, 1922

Armstrong, N. F. (Leics.) b Dec. 22, 1892, d Jan. 19, 1990

Armstrong, T. R. (Derbys.) b Oct. 13, 1909

\*Armstrong, W. W. (Vic.; *CY 1903*) b May 22, 1879, d July 13, 1947

Arnold, A. P. (Cant. & Northants) b Oct. 16, 1926

\*Arnold, E. G. (Worcs.) b Nov. 7, 1876, d Oct. 25, 1942

\*Arnold, G. G. (Surrey & Sussex; *CY 1972*) b Sept. 3, 1944

\*Arnold, J. (Hants) b Nov. 30, 1907, d April 4, 1984

Arshad Ayub (H'bad) b Aug. 2, 1958

Arshad Pervez (Sargodha, Lahore, Pak. Us, Servis Ind., HBL & Punjab) b Oct. 1, 1952

\*Arthurton, K. L. T. (Leewards) b Feb. 21, 1965

\*Arun, B. (TN) b Dec. 14, 1962

Arun Lal (Delhi & Bengal) b Aug. 1, 1955

Asgarali, N. (T/T) b Dec. 28, 1920

Ashdown, W. H. (Kent) b Dec. 27, 1898, d Sept. 15, 1979

\*Ashley, W. H. (W. Prov.) b Feb. 10, 1862, d July 14, 1930

\*Ashraf Ali (Lahore, Income Tax, Pak Us, Pak Rlwys & UBL) b April 22, 1958

\*Ashton, C. T. (CUCC & Essex) b Feb. 19, 1901, d Oct. 31, 1942

Ashton, G. (CUCC & Worcs.) b Sept. 27, 1896, d Feb. 6, 1981

Ashton, Sir H. (CUCC & Essex; *CY 1922*; Pres. MCC 1960-61) b Feb. 13, 1898, d June 17, 1979

Asif Din, M. (Warwicks.) b Sept. 21, 1960

\*Asif Iqbal (H'bad, Kar., Kent, PIA & NBP; *CY 1968*) b June 6, 1943

\*Asif Masood (Lahore, Punjab U. & PIA) b Jan. 23, 1946

\*Asif Mujtaba (Kar. & PIA) b Nov. 4, 1967

Aslett, D. G. (Kent) b Feb. 12, 1958

Aspinall, R. (Yorks.) b Nov. 27, 1918

\*Astill, W. E. (Leics.; *CY 1933*) b March 1, 1888, d Feb. 10, 1948

Atapattu, M. S. (SSC) b Nov. 22, 1972

\*Atherton, M. A. (CUCC & Lancs.; *CY 1991*) b March 23, 1968

Athey, C. W. J. (Yorks. & Glos.) b Sept. 27, 1957

Atkinson, C. R. M. (Som.) b July 23, 1931, d June 25, 1991

\*Atkinson, D. St E. (B'dos & T/T) b Aug. 9, 1926

\*Atkinson, E. St E. (B'dos) b Nov. 6, 1927

Atkinson, G. (Som. & Lancs.) b March 29, 1938

Atkinson, J. C. M. (Som. & CUCC) b July 10, 1968

Atkinson, T. (Notts.) b Sept. 27, 1930, d Sept. 2, 1990

Attenborough, G. R. (S. Aust.) b Jan. 17, 1951

\*Attewell, W. (Notts.; *CY 1892*) b June 12, 1861, d June 11, 1927

Austin, Sir H. B. G. (B'dos) b July 15, 1877, d July 27, 1943

*Austin, R. A. (Jam.) b Sept. 5, 1954

Avery, A. V. (Essex) b Dec. 19, 1914

Aworth, C. J. (CUCC & Surrey) b Feb. 19, 1953

Ayling, J. R. (Hants) b June 13, 1967

Aylward, J. (Hants & All-England) b 1741, d Dec. 27, 1827

Aymes, A. N. (Hants) b June 4, 1964

*Azad, K. (Delhi) b Jan. 2, 1959

*Azeem Hafeez (Kar., Allied Bank & PIA) b July 29, 1963

*Azhar Khan (Lahore, Punjab, Pak. Us., PIA & HBL) b Sept. 7, 1955

*Azharuddin, M. (H'bad & Derbys.; *CY 1991*) b Feb. 8, 1963

*Azmat Rana (B'pur, PIA, Punjab, Lahore & MCB) b Nov. 3, 1951

Babington, A. M. (Sussex & Glos.) b July 22, 1963

*Bacchus, S. F. A. F. (Guyana, W. Prov. & Border) b Jan. 31, 1954

*Bacher, Dr A (Tvl) b May 24, 1942

*Badcock, C. L. (Tas. & S. Aust.) b April 10, 1914, d Dec. 13, 1982

*Badcock, F. T. (Wgtn & Otago) b Aug. 9, 1895, d Sept. 19, 1982

Baichan, L. (Guyana) b May 12, 1946

*Baig, A. A. (H'bad, OUCC & Som.) b March 19, 1939

Bailey, Sir D. T. L. (Glos.) b Aug. 5, 1918

Bailey, J. (Hants) b April 6, 1908, d Feb. 9, 1988

Bailey, J. A. (Essex & OUCC; Sec. MCC 1974-87) b June 22, 1930

*Bailey, R. J. (Northants) b Oct. 28, 1963

*Bailey, T. E. (Essex & CUCC; *CY 1950*) b Dec. 3, 1923

Baillie, A. W. (Sec. MCC 1858-63) b June 22, 1830, d May 10, 1867

Bainbridge, P. (Glos.; *CY 1986*) b April 16, 1958

*Bairstow, D. L. (Yorks. & Griq. W.) b Sept. 1, 1951

Baker, R. P. (Surrey) b April 9, 1954

*Bakewell, A. H. (Northants; *CY 1934*) b Nov. 2, 1908, d Jan. 23, 1983

Bakker, P. J. (Hants) b Aug. 19, 1957

*Balaskas, X. C. (Griq. W., Border, W. Prov., Tvl & NE Tvl) b Oct. 15, 1910

*Balderstone, J. C. (Yorks. & Leics.) b Nov. 16, 1940

Baldry, D. O. (Middx & Hants) b Dec. 26, 1931

*Banerjee, S. A. (Bengal & Bihar) b Nov. 1, 1919

*Banerjee, S. N. (Bengal, Naw., Bihar & M. Pradesh) b Oct. 3, 1911, d Oct. 14, 1980

*Bannerman, A. C. (NSW) b March 21, 1854, d Sept. 19, 1924

*Bannerman, Charles (NSW) b July 23, 1851, d Aug. 20, 1930

Bannister, J. D. (Warwicks.) b Aug. 23, 1930

*Baptiste, E. A. E. (Kent, Leewards & Northants) b March 12, 1960

*Baqa Jilani, M. (N. Ind.) b July 20, 1911, d July 2, 1941

Barber, A. T. (OUCC & Yorks.) b June 17, 1905, d March 10, 1985

*Barber, R. T. (Wgtn & C. Dist.) b June 23, 1925

*Barber, R. W. (Lancs., CUCC & Warwicks; *CY 1967*) b Sept. 26, 1935

*Barber, W. (Yorks.) b April 18, 1901, d Sept. 10, 1968

Barclay, J. R. T. (Sussex & OFS) b Jan. 22, 1954

*Bardsley, W. (NSW; *CY 1910*) b Dec. 7, 1882, d Jan. 20, 1954

Baring, A. E. G. (Hants) b Jan. 21, 1910, d Aug. 29, 1986

Barker, G. (Essex) b July 6, 1931

Barling, T. H. (Surrey) b Sept. 1, 1906

Barlow, A. (Lancs.) b Aug. 31, 1915, d May 9, 1983

*Barlow, E. J. (Tvl, E. Prov., W. Prov., Derbys. & Boland) b Aug. 12, 1940

*Barlow, G. D. (Middx) b March 26, 1950

*Barlow, R. G. (Lancs.) b May 28, 1851, d July 31, 1919

Barnard, H. M. (Hants) b July 18, 1933

Barnes, A. R. (Sec. Aust. Cricket Board 1960-81) b Sept. 12, 1916, d March 14, 1989

*Barnes, S. F. (Warwicks. & Lancs.; *CY 1910*) b April 19, 1873, d Dec. 26, 1967

*Barnes, S. G. (NSW) b June 5, 1916, d Dec. 16, 1973

*Barnes, W. (Notts.; *CY 1890*) b May 27, 1852, d March 24, 1899

*Barnett, B. A. (Vic.) b March 23, 1908, d June 29, 1979

*Barnett, C. J. (Glos.; *CY 1937*) b July 3, 1910

*Barnett, K. J. (Derbys. & Boland; *CY 1989*) b July 17, 1960

Barnwell, C. J. P. (Som.) b June 23, 1914

Baroda, Maharaja of (Manager, Ind. in Eng., 1959) b April 2, 1930, d Sept. 1, 1988

*Barratt, F. (Notts.) b April 12, 1894, d Jan. 29, 1947

Barratt, R. J. (Leics.) b May 3, 1942

*Barrett, A. G. (Jam.) b April 5, 1942

Barrett, B. J. (Auck., C. Dist., Worcs. & N. Dist.) b Nov. 16, 1966

*Barrett, J. E. (Vic.) b Oct. 15, 1866, d Feb. 9, 1916

Barrick, D. W. (Northants) b April 28, 1926

*Barrington, K. F. (Surrey; *CY 1960*) b Nov. 24, 1930, d March 14, 1981

Barron, W. (Lancs. & Northants) b Oct. 26, 1917

Barrow, I. (Jam.) b Jan. 6, 1911, d April 2, 1979

*Bartlett, E. L. (B'dos) b March 18, 1906, d Dec. 21, 1976

*Bartlett, G. A. (C. Dist. & Cant.) b Feb. 3, 1941

Bartlett, H. T. (CUCC, Surrey & Sussex; *CY 1939*) b Oct. 7, 1914, d June 26, 1988

Bartley, T. J. (Umpire) b March 19, 1908, d April 2, 1964

Barton, M. R. (OUCC & Surrey) b Oct. 14, 1914

*Barton, P. T. (Wgtn) b Oct. 9, 1935

*Barton, V. A. (Kent & Hants) b Oct. 6, 1867, d March 23, 1906

Barwick, S. R. (Glam.) b Sept. 6, 1960

Base, S. J. (W. Prov., Glam., Derbys., Boland & Border) b Jan. 2, 1960

Bates, D. L. (Sussex) b May 10, 1933

*Bates, W. (Yorks.) b Nov. 19, 1855, d Jan. 8, 1900

Batty, J. D. (Yorks.) b May 15, 1971

*Baumgartner, H. V. (OFS & Tvl) b Nov. 17, 1883, d April 8, 1938

Baxter, A. D. (Devon, Lancs., Middx & Scotland) b Jan. 20, 1910, d Jan. 28, 1986

*Bean, G. (Notts & Sussex) b March 7, 1864, d March 16, 1923

Bear, M. J. (Essex & Cant.) b Feb. 23, 1934

*Beard, D. D. (C. Dist. & N. Dist.) b Jan. 14, 1920, d July 15, 1982

*Beard, G. R. (NSW) b Aug. 19, 1950

Beauclerk, Lord Frederick (Middx, Surrey & MCC) b May 8, 1773, d April 22, 1850

Beaufort, 10th Duke of (Pres. MCC 1952-53) b April 4, 1900, d Feb. 5, 1984

*Beaumont, R. (Tvl) b Feb. 4, 1884, d May 25, 1958

Beck, J. E. F. (Wgtn) b Aug. 1, 1934

Becker, G. C. (W. Aust.) b March 13, 1936

*Bedi, B. S. (N. Punjab, Delhi & Northants) b Sept. 25, 1946

*Bedser, A. V. (Surrey; *CY 1947*) b July 4, 1918

Bedser, E. A. (Surrey) b July 4, 1918

Beet, G. (Derbys.; Umpire) b April 24, 1886, d Dec. 13, 1946

*Begbie, D. W. (Tvl) b Dec. 12, 1914

Beldham, W. (Hambledon & Surrey) b Feb. 5, 1766, d Feb. 20, 1862

*Bell, A. J. (W. Prov. & Rhod.) b April 15, 1906, d Aug. 2, 1985

Bell, R. V. (Middx & Sussex) b Jan. 7, 1931, d Oct. 26, 1989

*Bell, W. (Cant.) b Sept. 5, 1931

Bellamy, B. W. (Northants) b April 22, 1891, d Dec. 20, 1985

*Benaud, J. (NSW) b May 11, 1944

*Benaud, R. (NSW; *CY 1962*) b Oct. 6, 1930

*Benjamin, W. K. M. (Leewards & Leics.) b Dec. 31, 1964

Bennett, D. (Middx) b Dec. 18, 1933

Bennett, G. M. (Som.) b Dec. 17, 1909, d July 26, 1982

*Bennett, M. J. (NSW) b Oct. 16, 1956

Bennett, N. H. (Surrey) b Sept. 23, 1912

Bennett, R. (Lancs.) b June 16, 1940

*Benson, M. R. (Kent) b July 6, 1958

Bernard, J. R. (CUCC & Glos.) b Dec. 7, 1938

Berry, L. G. (Leics.) b April 28, 1906, d Feb. 5, 1985

*Berry, R. (Lancs., Worcs. & Derbys.) b Jan. 29, 1926

Bessant, J. G. (Glos.) b Nov. 11, 1892, d Jan. 18, 1982

*Best, C. A. (B'dos) b May 14, 1959

*Betancourt, N. (T/T) b June 4, 1887, d Oct. 12, 1947

Bhalekar, R. B. (M'tra) b Feb. 17, 1952

*Bhandari, P. (Delhi & Bengal) b Nov. 27, 1935

*Bhat, A. R. (Karn.) b April 16, 1958

Bick, D. A. (Middx) b Feb. 22, 1936

Bicknell, D. J. (Surrey) b June 24, 1967

Bicknell, M. P. (Surrey) b Jan. 14, 1969

Biddulph, K. D. (Som.) b May 29, 1932

Biggs, A. L. (E. Prov.) b April 26, 1946

*Bilby, G. P. (Wgtn) b May 7, 1941

*Binks, J. G. (Yorks.; *CY 1969*) b Oct. 5, 1935

*Binns, A. P. (Jam.) b July 24, 1929

*Binny, R. M. H. (Karn.) b July 19, 1955

Birch, J. D. (Notts.) b June 18, 1955

Bird, H. D. (Yorks. & Leics.; Umpire) b April 19, 1933

*Bird, M. C. (Lancs. & Surrey) b March 25, 1888, d Dec. 9, 1933

Bird, R. E. (Worcs.) b April 4, 1915, d Feb. 20, 1985

*Birkenshaw, J. (Yorks., Leics. & Worcs.) b Nov. 13, 1940

*Birkett, L. S. (B'dos, BG & T/T) b April 14, 1904

Birrell, H. B. (E. Prov., Rhod. & OUCC) b Dec. 1, 1927

Bishop, G. A. (S. Aust.) b Feb. 25, 1960

*Bishop, I. R. (T/T & Derbys.) b Oct. 24, 1967

*Bisset, Sir Murray (W. Prov.) b April 14, 1876, d Oct. 24, 1931

*Bissett, G. F. (Griq. W., W. Prov. & Tvl) b Nov. 5, 1905, d Nov. 14, 1965

Bissex, M. (Glos.) b Sept. 28, 1944

*Blackham, J. McC. (Vic.; *CY 1891*) b May 11, 1854, d Dec. 28, 1932

*Blackie, D. D. (Vic.) b April 5, 1882, d April 18, 1955

Blackledge, J. F. (Lancs.) b April 15, 1928

*Blain, T. E. (C. Dist.) b Feb. 17, 1962

Blair, B. R. (Otago) b Dec. 27, 1957

*Blair, R. W. (Wgtn & C. Dist.) b June 23, 1932

Blake, D. E. (Hants) b April 27, 1925

Blake, Rev. P. D. S. (OUCC & Sussex) b May 23, 1927

Blakey, R. J. (Yorks.) b Jan. 15, 1967

*Blanckenberg, J. M. (W. Prov. & Natal) b Dec. 31, 1893, 'presumed dead'

*Bland, K. C. (Rhod., E. Prov. & OFS; *CY 1966*) b April 5, 1938

Blenkiron, W. (Warwicks.) b July 21, 1942

Bligh, Hon. Ivo (*see* 8th Earl of Darnley)

Blofeld, H. C. (CUCC) b Sept. 23, 1939

Blundell, Sir E. D. (CUCC & NZ) b May 29, 1907, d Sept. 24, 1984

*Blunt, R. C. (Cant. & Otago; *CY 1928*) b Nov. 3, 1900, d June 22, 1966

*Blythe, C. (Kent; *CY 1904*) b May 30, 1879, d Nov. 8, 1917

*Board, J. H. (Glos.) b Feb. 23, 1867, d April 16, 1924

*Bock, E. G. (Griq. W., Tvl & W. Prov.) b Sept. 17, 1908, d Sept. 5, 1961

Bodkin, P. E. (CUCC) b Sept. 15, 1924

*Bolton, B. A. (Cant. & Wgtn) b May 31, 1935

*Bolus, J. B. (Yorks., Notts. & Derbys.) b Jan. 31, 1934

*Bond, G. E. (W. Prov.) b April 5, 1909, d Aug. 27, 1965

Bond, J. D. (Lancs. & Notts.; *CY 1971*) b May 6, 1932

*Bonnor, G. J. (Vic. & NSW) b Feb. 25, 1855, d June 27, 1912

*Boock, S. L. (Otago & Cant.) b Sept. 20, 1951

*Boon, D. C. (Tas.) b Dec. 29, 1960

Boon, T. J. (Leics.) b Nov. 1, 1961

*Booth, B. C. (NSW) b Oct. 19, 1933

Booth, B. J. (Lancs. & Leics.) b Dec. 3, 1935

*Booth, M. W. (Yorks.; *CY 1914*) b Dec. 10, 1886, d July 1, 1916

Booth, P. (Leics.) b Nov. 2, 1952

Booth, R. (Yorks. & Worcs.) b Oct. 1, 1926

*Borde, C. G. (Baroda & M'tra) b July 21, 1934

*Border, A. R. (NSW, Glos, Qld & Essex; *CY 1982*) b July 27, 1955

Bore, M. K. (Yorks. & Notts.) b June 2, 1947

Borrington, A. J. (Derbys.) b Dec. 8, 1948

*Bosanquet, B. J. T. (OUCC & Middx; *CY 1905*) b Oct. 13, 1877, d Oct. 12, 1936

Bose, G. (Bengal) b May 20, 1947

Boshier, B. S. (Leics.) b March 6, 1932

*Botham, I. T. (Som., Worcs. & Qld; *CY 1978*) b Nov. 24, 1955

*Botten, J. T. (NE Tvl & N. Tvl) b June 21, 1938

Boucher, J. C. (Ireland) b Dec. 22, 1910

Bourne, W. A. (B'dos & Warwicks.) b Nov. 15, 1952

*Bowden, M. P. (Surrey & Tvl) b Nov. 1, 1865, d Feb. 19, 1892

*Bowes, W. E. (Yorks.; *CY 1932*) b July 25, 1908, d Sept. 5, 1987

Bowler, P. D. (Leics., Tas. & Derbys.) b July 30, 1963

*Bowley, E. H. (Sussex & Auck.; *CY 1930*) b June 6, 1890, d July 9, 1974

Bowley, F. L. (Worcs.) b Nov. 9, 1873, d May 31, 1943

Bowman, R. (OUCC & Lancs.) b Jan. 26, 1934

Box, T. (Sussex) b Feb. 7, 1808, d July 12, 1876

*Boyce, K. D. (B'dos & Essex; *CY 1974*) b Oct. 11, 1943

*Boycott, G. (Yorks. & N. Tvl; *CY 1965*) b Oct. 21, 1940

Boyd-Moss, R. J. (CUCC & Northants) b Dec. 16, 1959

Boyes, G. S. (Hants) b March 31, 1899, d Feb. 11, 1973

*Boyle, H. F. (Vic.) b Dec. 10, 1847, d Nov. 21, 1907

*Bracewell, B. P. (C. Dist., Otago & N. Dist.) b Sept. 14, 1959

*Bracewell, J. G. (Otago & Auck.) b April 15, 1958

*Bradburn, G. E. (N. Dist.) b May 26, 1966

*Bradburn, W. P. (N. Dist.) b Nov. 24, 1938

*Bradley, W. M. (Kent) b Jan. 2, 1875, d June 19, 1944

*Bradman, Sir D. G. (NSW & S. Aust.; *CY 1931*) b Aug. 27, 1908

Bradshaw, J. C. (Leics.) b Jan. 25, 1902, d Nov. 8, 1904

Brain, B. M. (Worcs. & Glos.) b Sept. 13, 1940

Bramall, Field-Marshal The Lord (Pres. MCC 1988-89) b Dec. 18, 1923

*Brann, W. H. (E. Prov.) b April 4, 1899, d Sept. 22, 1953

Brassington, A. J. (Glos.) b Aug. 9, 1954

*Braund, L. C. (Surrey & Som.; *CY 1902*) b Oct. 18, 1875, d Dec. 23, 1955

Bray, C. (Essex) b April 6, 1898

Brayshaw, I. J. (W. Aust.) b Jan. 14, 1942

Brazier, A. F. (Surrey & Kent) b Dec. 7, 1924

Breakwell, D. (Northants & Som.) b July 2, 1948

*Brearley, J. M. (CUCC & Middx; *CY 1977*) b April 28, 1942

*Brearley, W. (Lancs.; *CY 1909*) b March 11, 1876, d Jan. 13, 1937

*Brennan, D. V. (Yorks.) b Feb. 10, 1920, d Jan. 9, 1985

Bridge, W. B. (Warwicks.) b May 29, 1938

Bridger, Rev. J. R. (Hants) b April 8, 1920, d July 14, 1986

Brierley, T. L. (Glam., Lancs. & Canada) b June 15, 1910, d Jan. 7, 1989

Briers, N. E. (Leics.) b Jan. 15, 1955

*Briggs, John (Lancs.; *CY 1889*) b Oct. 3, 1862, d Jan. 11, 1902

*Bright, R. J. (Vic.) b July 13, 1954

*Briscoe, A. W. (Tvl) b Feb. 6, 1911, d April 22, 1941

*Broad, B. C. (Glos. & Notts.) b Sept. 29, 1957

Broadbent, R. G. (Worcs.) b June 21, 1924

Brocklehurst, B. G. (Som.) b Feb. 18, 1922

*Brockwell, W. (Kimberley & Surrey; *CY 1895*) b Jan. 21, 1865, d June 30, 1935

Broderick, V. (Northants) b Aug. 17, 1920

Brodhurst, A. H. (CUCC & Glos.) b July 21, 1916

*Bromfield, H. D. (W. Prov.) b June 26, 1932

*Bromley, E. H. (W. Aust. & Vic.) b Sept. 2, 1912, d Feb. 1, 1967

*Bromley-Davenport, H. R. (CUCC, Bombay Eur. & Middx) b Aug. 18, 1870, d May 23, 1954

*Brookes, D. (Northants; *CY 1957*) b Oct. 29, 1915

Brookes, W. H. (Editor of *Wisden* 1936-39) b Dec. 5, 1894, d May 28, 1955

Brooks, R. A. (OUCC & Som.) b June 14, 1943

*Brown, A. (Kent) b Oct. 17, 1935

Brown, A. S. (Glos.) b June 24, 1936

*Brown, D. J. (Warwicks.) b Jan. 30, 1942

Brown, D. W. J. (Glos.) b Feb. 26, 1942

*Brown, F. R. (CUCC, Surrey & Northants; *CY 1933*; Pres. MCC 1971-72) b Dec. 16, 1910, d July 24, 1991

*Brown, G. (Hants) b Oct. 6, 1887, d Dec. 3, 1964

Brown, J. (Scotland) b Sept. 24, 1931

*Brown, J. T. (Yorks.; *CY 1895*) b Aug. 20, 1869, d Nov. 4, 1904

Brown, K. R. (Middx) b March 18, 1963

*Brown, L. S. (Tvl, NE Tvl & Rhod.) b Nov. 24, 1910, d Sept. 1, 1983

Brown, R. D. (Zimb.) b March 11, 1951

Brown, S. M. (Middx) b Dec. 8, 1917, d Dec. 28, 1987

*Brown, V. R. (Cant. & Auck.) b Nov. 3, 1959

*Brown, W. A. (NSW & Qld; *CY 1939*) b July 31, 1912

Brown, W. C. (Northants) b Nov. 13, 1900, d Jan. 20, 1986

*Browne, C. R. (B'dos & BG) b Oct. 8, 1890, d Jan. 12, 1964

Bruce, Hon. C. N. (3rd Lord Aberdare) (OUCC & Middx) b Aug. 2, 1885, d Oct. 4, 1957

Bruce, S. D. (W. Prov. & OFS) b Jan. 11, 1954

*Bruce, W. (Vic.) b May 22, 1864, d Aug. 3, 1925

Bruyns, A. (W. Prov. & Natal) b Sept. 19, 1946

Bryan, G. J. (Kent) b Dec. 29, 1902, d April 4, 1991

*Bryan, J. L. (CUCC & Kent; *CY 1922*) b May 26, 1896, d April 23, 1985

Bryan, R. T. (Kent) b July 30, 1898, d July 27, 1970

*Buckenham, C. P. (Essex) b Jan. 16, 1876, d Feb. 23, 1937

Buckingham, J. (Warwicks.) b Jan. 21, 1903, d Jan. 25, 1987

Budd, E. H. (Middx & All-England) b Feb. 23, 1785, d March 29, 1875

Budd, W. L. (Hants) b Oct. 25, 1913, d Aug. 23, 1986

Bull, F. G. (Essex; *CY 1898*) b April 2, 1875, d Sept. 16, 1910

Buller, J. S. (Yorks. & Worcs.; Umpire) b Aug. 23, 1909, d Aug. 7, 1970

Burden, M. D. (Hants) b Oct. 4, 1930, d Nov. 9, 1987

*Burge, P. J. (Qld; *CY 1965*) b May 17, 1932

*Burger, C. G. de V. (Natal) b July 12, 1935

Burgess, G. I. (Som.) b May 5, 1943

*Burgess, M. G. (Auck.) b July 17, 1944

*Burke, C. (Auck.) b March 22, 1914

*Burke, J. W. (NSW; *CY 1957*) b June 12, 1930, d Feb. 2, 1979

*Burke, S. F. (NE Tvl & OFS) b March 11, 1934

*Burki, Javed (Pak. Us, OUCC, Punjab, Lahore, Kar., R'pindi & NWFP) b May 8, 1938

*Burn, E. J. K. (K. E.) (Tas.) b Sept. 17, 1862, d July 20, 1956

Burnet, J. R. (Yorks.) b Oct. 11, 1918

Burns, N. D. (Essex, W. Prov. & Som.) b Sept. 19, 1965

*Burnup, C. J. (CUCC & Kent; *CY 1903*) b Nov. 21, 1875, d April 5, 1960

Burrough, H. D. (Som.) b Feb. 6, 1909

*Burton, F. J. (Vic. & NSW) b Aug. 25, 1929

*Burtt, T. B. (Cant.) b Jan. 22, 1915, d May 24, 1988

Buse, H. T. F. (Som.) b Aug. 5, 1910

Bushby, M. H. (CUCC) b July 29, 1931

Buss, A. (Sussex) b Sept. 1, 1939

Buss, M. A. (Sussex & OFS) b Jan. 24, 1944

Buswell, J. E. (Northants) b July 3, 1909

*Butcher, A. R. (Surrey & Glam.; *CY 1991*) b Jan. 7, 1954

*Butcher, B. F. (Guyana; *CY 1970*) b Sept. 3, 1933

Butcher, I. P. (Leics. & Glos.) b July 1, 1962

*Butcher, R. O. (Middx, B'dos & Tas.) b Oct. 14, 1953

*Butler, H. J. (Notts.) b March 12, 1913, d July 17, 1991

*Butler, L. S. (T/T) b Feb. 9, 1929

*Butt, H. R. (Sussex) b Dec. 27, 1865, d Dec. 21, 1928

Butterfield, L. A. (Cant.) b Aug. 29, 1913

*Butts, C. G. (Guyana) b July 8, 1957

Buxton, I. R. (Derbys.) b April 17, 1938

*Buys, I. D. (W. Prov.) b Feb. 3, 1895, dead

Byas, D. (Yorks.) b Aug. 26, 1963

*Bynoe, M. R. (B'dos) b Feb. 23, 1941

Caccia, Lord (Pres. MCC 1973-74) b Dec. 21, 1905, d Oct. 31, 1990

Caesar, Julius (Surrey & All-England) b March 25, 1830, d March 6, 1878

Caffyn, W. (Surrey & NSW) b Feb. 2, 1828, d Aug. 28, 1919

Caine, C. Stewart (Editor of *Wisden* 1926-33) b Oct. 28, 1861, d April 15, 1933

*Cairns, B. L. (C. Dist., Otago & N. Dist.) b Oct. 10, 1949

*Cairns, C. L. (N. Dist., Notts. & Cant.) b June 13, 1970

Calder, H. L. (Cranleigh; *CY 1918*) b 1900

*Callaway, S. T. (NSW & Cant.) b Feb. 6, 1868, d Nov. 25, 1923

*Callen, I. W. (Vic. & Boland) b May 2, 1955

*Calthorpe, Hon. F. S. Gough- (CUCC, Sussex & Warwicks.) b May 27, 1892, d Nov. 19, 1935

*Camacho, G. S. (Guyana) b Oct. 15, 1945

*Cameron, F. J. (Jam.) b June 22, 1923

*Cameron, F. J. (Otago) b June 1, 1932

*Cameron, H. B. (Tvl, E. Prov. & W. Prov.; *CY 1936*) b July 5, 1905, d Nov. 2, 1935

*Cameron, J. H. (CUCC, Jam. & Som.) b April 8, 1914

*Campbell, G. D. (Tas.) b March 10, 1964

*Campbell, T. (Tvl) b Feb. 9, 1882, d Oct. 5, 1924

Cannings, V. H. D. (Warwicks. & Hants) b April 3, 1919

*Capel, D. J. (Northants & E. Prov.) b Feb. 6, 1963

Caple, R. G. (Middx & Hants) b Dec. 8, 1939

Cardus, Sir Neville (Cricket Writer) b April 3, 1888, d Feb. 27, 1975

*Carew, G. McD. (B'dos) b June 4, 1910, d Dec. 9, 1974

*Carew, M. C. (T/T) b Sept. 15, 1937

*Carkeek, W. (Vic.) b Oct. 17, 1878, d Feb. 20, 1937

*Carlson, P. H. (Qld) b Aug. 8, 1951

*Carlstein, P. R. (OFS, Tvl, Natal & Rhod.) b Oct. 28, 1938

Carmody, D. K. (NSW & W. Aust.) b Feb. 16, 1919, d Oct. 21, 1977

Carpenter, D. (Glos.) b Sept. 12, 1935

Carpenter, R. (Cambs. & Utd England XI) b Nov. 18, 1830, d July 13, 1901

*Carr, A. W. (Notts.; *CY 1923*) b May 21, 1893, d Feb. 7, 1963

*Carr, D. B. (OUCC & Derbys.; *CY 1960*; Sec. TCCB 1974-86) b Dec. 28, 1926

*Carr, D. W. (Kent; *CY 1910*) b March 17, 1872, d March 23, 1950

Carr, J. D. (OUCC & Middx) b June 15, 1963

Carrick, P. (Yorks. & E. Prov.) b July 16, 1952

Carrigan, A. H. (Qld) b Aug. 26, 1917

Carrington, E. (Derbys.) b March 25, 1914

Carse, J. A. (Rhod., W. Prov., E. Prov. & Northants) b Dec. 13, 1958

*Carter, C. P. (Natal & Tvl) b April 23, 1881, d Nov. 8, 1952

*Carter, H. (NSW) b Halifax, Yorks. March 15, 1878, d June 8, 1948

Carter, R. G. (Warwicks.) b April 14, 1933

Carter, R. G. M. (Worcs.) b July 11, 1937

Carter, R. M. (Northants & Cant.) b May 25, 1960

Cartwright, H. (Derbys.) b May 12, 1951

*Cartwright, T. W. (Warwicks., Som. & Glam.) b July 22, 1935

Carty, R. A. (Hants) b July 28, 1922, d March 31, 1984

Cass, G. R. (Essex, Worcs. & Tas.) b April 23, 1940

Castell, A. T. (Hants) b Aug. 6, 1943

Castle, F. (Som.) b April 9, 1909

Catt, A. W. (Kent & W. Prov.) b Oct. 2, 1933

*Catterall, R. H. (Tvl, Rhod., Natal & OFS; *CY 1925*) b July 10, 1900, d Jan. 2, 1961

Cave, H. B. (Wgtn & C. Dist.) b Oct. 10, 1922, d Sept. 15, 1989

Chalk, F. G. H. (OUCC & Kent) b Sept. 7, 1910, d Feb. 17, 1943

*Challenor, G. (B'dos) b June 28, 1888, d July 30, 1947

*Chandrasekhar, B. S. (†Karn.; *CY 1972*) b May 17, 1945

Chandrasekhar, V. B. (TN) b Aug. 21, 1961

*Chang, H. S. (Jam.) b July 22, 1952

*Chapman, A. P. F. (Uppingham, OUCC & Kent; *CY 1919*) b Sept. 3, 1900, d Sept. 16, 1961

Chapman, H. W. (Natal) b June 30, 1890, d Dec. 1, 1941

*Chappell, G. S. (S. Aust., Som. & Qld; *CY 1973*) b Aug. 7, 1948

*Chappell, I. M. (S. Aust. & Lancs.; *CY 1976*) b Sept. 26, 1943

*Chappell, T. M. (S. Aust., W. Aust. & NSW) b Oct. 21, 1952

Chapple, M. E. (Cant. & C. Dist.) b July 25, 1930, d July 31, 1985

*Charlton, P. C. (NSW) b April 9, 1867, d Sept. 30, 1954

*Charlwood, H. R. J. (Sussex) b Dec. 19, 1846, d June 6, 1888

*Chatfield, E. J. (Wgtn) b July 3, 1950

*Chatterton, W. (Derbys.) b Dec. 27, 1861, d March 19, 1913

*Chauhan, C. P. S. (M'tra & Delhi) b July 21, 1947

Cheatle, R. G. L. (Sussex & Surrey) b July 31, 1953

*Cheetham, J. E. (W. Prov.) b May 26, 1920, d Aug. 21, 1980

Chester, F. (Worcs.; Umpire) b Jan. 20, 1895, d April 8, 1957

Chesterton, G. H. (OUCC & Worcs.) b July 15, 1922

*Chevalier, G. A. (W. Prov.) b March 9, 1937

*Childs, J. H. (Glos. & Essex; *CY 1987*) b Aug. 15, 1951

*Chipperfield, A. G. (NSW) b Nov. 17, 1905, d July 29, 1987

Chisholm, R. H. E. (Scotland) b May 22, 1927

*Chowdhury, N. R. (Bihar & Bengal) b May 23, 1923, d Dec. 14, 1979

*Christiani, C. M. (BG) b Oct. 28, 1913, d April 4, 1938

*Christiani, R. J. (BG) b July 19, 1920

*Christopherson, S. (Kent; Pres. MCC 1939-45) b Nov. 11, 1861, d April 6, 1949

*Christy, J. A. J. (Tvl & Qld) b Dec. 12, 1904, d Feb. 1, 1971

*Chubb, G. W. A. (Border & Tvl) b April 12, 1911, d Aug. 28, 1982

Clark, D. G. (Kent; Pres. MCC 1977-78) b Jan. 27, 1919

Clark, E. A. (Middx) b April 15, 1937

*Clark, E. W. (Northants) b Aug. 9, 1902, d April 28, 1982

Clark, L. S. (Essex) b March 6, 1914

*Clark, W. M. (W. Aust.) b Sept. 19, 1953

*Clarke, Dr C. B. (B'dos, Northants & Essex) b April 7, 1918

*Clarke, S. T. (B'dos, Surrey, Tvl, OFS & N. Tvl) b Dec. 11, 1954

Clarke, William (Notts.; founded All-England XI & Trent Bridge ground) b Dec. 24, 1798, d Aug. 25, 1856

Clarkson, A. (Yorks. & Som.) b Sept. 5, 1939

Claughton, J. A. (OUCC & Warwicks.) b Sept. 17, 1956

*Clay, J. C. (Glam.) b March 18, 1898, d Aug. 12, 1973

Clay, J. D. (Notts.) b Oct. 15, 1924

Clayton, G. (Lancs. & Som.) b Feb. 3, 1938

Clements, S. M. (OUCC) b April 19, 1956

*Cleverley, D. C. (Auck.) b Dec. 23, 1909

Clift, Patrick B. (Rhod., Leics. & Natal) b July 14, 1953

Clift, Philip B. (Glam.) b Sept. 3, 1918

Clinton, G. S. (Kent, Surrey & Zimb.-Rhod.) b May 5, 1953

*Close, D. B. (Yorks. & Som.; *CY 1964*) b Feb. 24, 1931

Cobb, R. A. (Leics. & Natal) b May 18, 1961

Cobham, 9th Visct (Worcs.) b Oct. 23, 1881, d July 31, 1949

Cobham, 10th Visct (Hon. C. J. Lyttelton) (Worcs.; Pres. MCC 1954) b Aug. 8, 1909, d March 20, 1977

*Cochrane, J. A. K. (Tvl & Griq. W.) b July 15, 1909, d June 15, 1987

*Coen, S. K. (OFS, W. Prov., Tvl & Border) b Oct. 14, 1902, d Jan. 28, 1967

*Colah, S. M. H. (Bombay, W. Ind. & Naw.) b Sept. 22, 1902, d Sept. 11, 1950

Colchin, Robert ("Long Robin") (Kent & All-England) b Nov. 1713, d April 1750

*Coldwell, L. J. (Worcs.) b Jan. 10, 1933

*Colley, D. J. (NSW) b March 15, 1947

Collin, T. (Warwicks.) b April 7, 1911

*Collinge, R. O. (C. Dist., Wgtn & N. Dist.) b April 2, 1946

Collins, H. L. (NSW) b Jan. 21, 1889, d May 28, 1959

Collins, R. (Lancs.) b March 10, 1934

Colquhoun, I. A. (C. Dist.) b June 8, 1924

Coman, P. G. (Cant.) b April 13, 1943

*Commaille, J. M. M. (W. Prov., Natal, OFS & Griq. W.) b Feb. 21, 1883, d July 27, 1956

*Compton, D. C. S. (Middx & Holkar; *CY 1939*) b May 23, 1918

Compton, L. H. (Middx) b Sept. 12, 1912, d Dec. 27, 1984

*Coney, J. V. (Wgtn; *CY 1984*) b June 21, 1952

*Congdon, B. E. (C. Dist., Wgtn, Otago & Cant.; *CY 1974*) b Feb. 11, 1938

*Coningham, A. (NSW & Qld) b July 14, 1863, d June 13, 1939

*Connolly, A. N. (Vic. & Middx) b June 29, 1939

Connor, C. A. (Hants) b March 24, 1961

Constable, B. (Surrey) b Feb. 19, 1921

Constant, D. J. (Kent & Leics.; Umpire) b Nov. 9, 1941

*Constantine, Lord L. N. (T/T & B'dos; *CY 1940*) b Sept. 21, 1902, d July 1, 1971

Constantine, L. S. (T/T) b May 25, 1874, d Jan. 5, 1942

*Contractor, N. J. (Guj. & Ind. Rlwys) b March 7, 1934

*Conyngham, D. P. (Natal, Tvl & W. Prov.) b May 10, 1897, d July 7, 1979

*Cook, C. (Glos.) b Aug. 23, 1921

*Cook, F. J. (E. Prov.) b 1870, dead

*Cook, G. (Northants & E. Prov.) b Oct. 9, 1951

*Cook, N. G. B. (Leics. & Northants) b June 17, 1956

Cook, S. J. (Tvl & Som.; *CY 1990*) b July 31, 1953

Cook, T. E. (Sussex) b Feb. 5, 1901, d Jan. 15, 1950

*Cooper, A. H. C. (Tvl) b Sept 2, 1893, d July 18, 1963

*Cooper, B. B. (Middx, Kent & Vic.) b March 15, 1844, d Aug. 7, 1914

Cooper, F. S. Ashley- (Cricket Historian) b March 17, 1877, d Jan. 31, 1932

Cooper, G. C. (Sussex) b Sept. 2, 1936

Cooper, H. P. (Yorks. & N. Tvl) b April 17, 1949

Cooper, K. E. (Notts.) b Dec. 27, 1957

*Cooper, W. H. (Vic.) b Sept. 11, 1849, d April 5, 1939

*Cope, G. A. (Yorks.) b Feb. 23, 1947

Copson, W. H. (Derbys.; *CY 1937*) b April 27, 1908, d Sept. 14, 1971

Cordle, A. E. (Glam.) b Sept. 21, 1940

Cork, D. G. (Derbys.) b Aug. 7, 1971

Corling, G. E. (NSW) b July 13, 1941

Cornford, J. H. (Sussex) b Dec. 9, 1911, d June 17, 1985

*Cornford, W. L. (Sussex) b Dec. 25, 1900, d Feb. 6, 1964

Cornwallis, Capt. Hon. W. S. (2nd Lord Cornwallis) (Kent) b March 14, 1892, d Jan. 4, 1982

Corrall, P. (Leics.) b July 16, 1906

Corran, A. J. (OUCC & Notts.) b Nov. 25, 1936

*Cosier, G. J. (Vic., S. Aust. & Qld) b April 25, 1953

*Cottam, J. T. (NSW) b Sept. 5, 1867, d Jan. 30, 1897

*Cottam, R. M. H. (Hants & Northants) b Oct. 16, 1944

*Cotter, A. (NSW) b Dec. 3, 1884, d Oct. 31, 1917

Cottey, P. A. (Glam.) b June 2, 1966

Cotton, J. (Notts. & Leics.) b Nov. 7, 1940

Cottrell, G. A. (CUCC) b March 23, 1945

*Coulthard, G. (Vic.) b Aug. 1, 1856, d Oct. 22, 1883

*Coventry, Hon. C. J. (Worcs.) b Feb. 26, 1867, d June 2, 1929

Coverdale, S. P. (CUCC, Yorks., & Northants) b Nov. 20, 1954

Cowan, M. J. (Yorks.) b June 10, 1933

*Cowans, N. G. (Middx) b April 17, 1961

*Cowdrey, C. S. (Kent) b Oct. 20, 1957

Cowdrey, G. R. (Kent) b June 27, 1964

*Cowdrey, Sir M. C. (OUCC & Kent; *CY 1956*; Pres. MCC 1986-87) b Dec. 24, 1932

*Cowie, J. (Auck.) b March 30, 1912

Cowley, N. G. (Hants & Glam.) b March 1, 1953

*Cowper, R. M. (Vic. & W. Aust.) b Oct. 5, 1940

Cox, A. L. (Northants) b July 22, 1907, d Nov. 1986

Cox, G., jun. (Sussex) b Aug. 23, 1911, d March 30, 1985

Cox, G. R. (Sussex) b Nov. 29, 1873, d March 24, 1949

*Cox, J. L. (Natal) b June 28, 1886, d July 4, 1971

*Coxon, A. (Yorks.) b Jan. 18, 1916

Crabtree, H. P. (Essex) b April 30, 1906, d May 28, 1982

Craig, E. J. (CUCC & Lancs.) b March 26, 1942

*Craig, I. D. (NSW) b June 12, 1935

Cranfield, L. M. (Glos.) b Aug. 29, 1909

Cranmer, P. (Warwicks.) b Sept. 10, 1914

*Cranston, J. (Glos.) b Jan. 9, 1859, d Dec. 10, 1904

Cranston, K. (Lancs.) b Oct. 20, 1917

Crapp, J. F. (Glos.) b Oct. 14, 1912, d Feb. 15, 1981

*Crawford, J. N. (Surrey, S. Aust., Wgtn & Otago; *CY 1907*) b Dec. 1, 1886, d May 2, 1963

*Crawford, P. (NSW) b Aug. 3, 1933

Crawley, A. M. (OUCC & Kent; Pres. MCC 1972-73) b April 10, 1908

Crawley, J. P. (Lancs. & CUCC) b Sept. 21, 1971

Crawley, M. A. (OUCC, Lancs. & Notts.) b Dec. 16, 1967

Cray, S. J. (Essex) b May 29, 1921

*Cresswell, G. F. (Wgtn & C. Dist.) b March 22, 1915, d Jan. 10, 1966

*Cripps, G. (W. Prov.) b Oct. 19, 1865, d July 27, 1943

*Crisp, R. J. (Rhod., W. Prov. & Worcs.) b May 28, 1911

*Croft, C. E. H. (Guyana & Lancs.) b March 15, 1953

Croft, R. D. B. (Glam.) b May 25, 1970

*Cromb, I. B. (Cant.) b June 25, 1905, d March 6, 1984

Crookes, N. S. (Natal) b Nov. 15, 1935

Cross, G. F. (Leics.) b Nov. 15, 1943

*Crowe, J. J. (S. Aust. & Auck.) b Sept. 14, 1958

*Crowe, M. D. (Auck., C. Dist., Som. & Wgtn; *CY 1985*) b Sept. 22, 1962

Crump, B. S. (Northants) b April 25, 1938

Crush, E. (Kent) b April 25, 1917

Cumbes, J. (Lancs., Surrey, Worcs. & Warwicks.) b May 4, 1944

*Cunis, R. S. (Auck. & N. Dist.) b Jan. 5, 1941

*Curnow, S. H. (Tvl) b Dec. 16, 1907, d July 28, 1986

Curran, K. M. (Glos., Zimb. & Natal) b Sept. 7, 1959

*Curtis, T. S. (Worcs. & CUCC) b Jan. 15, 1960

Cuthbertson, G. B. (Middx, Sussex & Northants) b March 23, 1901

Cutmore, J. A. (Essex) b Dec. 28, 1898, d Nov. 30, 1985

*Cuttell, W. R. (Lancs.; *CY 1898*) b Sept. 13, 1864, d Dec. 9, 1929

*Da Costa, O. C. (Jam.) b Sept. 11, 1907, d Oct. 1, 1936

Dacre, C. C. (Auck. & Glos.) b May 15, 1899, d Nov. 2, 1975

Daft, Richard (Notts. & All-England) b Nov. 2, 1835, d July 18, 1900

Dakin, G. F. (E. Prov.) b Aug. 13, 1935

Dale, A. (Glam.) b Oct. 24, 1968

Dalmeny, Lord (6th Earl of Rosebery) (Middx & Surrey) b Jan. 8, 1882, d May 30, 1974

*Dalton, E. L. (Natal) b Dec. 2, 1906, d June 3, 1981

Dani, H. T. (M'tra & Ind. Serv.) b May 24, 1933

*Daniel, W. W. (B'dos, Middx & W. Aust.) b Jan. 16, 1956

*D'Arcy, J. W. (Cant., Wgtn & Otago) b April 23, 1936

Dare, R. (Hants) b Nov. 26, 1921

*Darling, J. (S. Aust.; *CY 1900*) b Nov. 21, 1870, d Jan. 2, 1946

*Darling, L. S. (Vic.) b Aug. 14, 1909

*Darling, W. M. (S. Aust.) b May 1, 1957

*Darnley, 8th Earl of (Hon. Ivo Bligh) (CUCC & Kent; Pres. MCC 1900) b March 13, 1859, d April 10, 1927

Davey, J. (Glos.) b Sept. 4, 1944

*Davidson, A. K. (NSW; *CY 1962*) b June 14, 1929

Davies, Dai (Glam.) b Aug. 26, 1896, d July 16, 1976

Davies, Emrys (Glam.) b June 27, 1904, d Nov. 10, 1975

*Davies, E. Q. (E. Prov., Tvl & NE Tvl) b Aug. 26, 1909, d Nov. 11, 1976

Davies, H. D. (Glam.) b July 23, 1932

Davies, H. G. (Glam.) b April 23, 1913

Davies, J. G. W. (CUCC & Kent; Pres. MCC 1985-86) b Sept. 10, 1911

Davies, T. (Glam.) b Oct. 25, 1960

*Davis, B. A. (T/T & Glam.) b May 2, 1940

*Davis, C. A. (T/T) b Jan. 1, 1944

Davis, E. (Northants) b March 8, 1922

*Davis, I. C. (NSW & Qld) b June 25, 1953

Davis, M. R. (Som.) b Feb. 26, 1962

Davis, P. C. (Northants) b May 24, 1915

Davis, R. C. (Glam.) b Jan. 1, 1946

Davis, R. P. (Kent) b March 18, 1966

*Davis, S. P. (Vic.) b Nov. 8, 1959

*Davis, W. W. (Windwards, Glam., Tas., Northants & Wgtn) b Sept. 18, 1958

Davison, B. F. (Rhod., Leics, Tas. & Glos.) b Dec. 21, 1946

Davison, I. (Notts.) b Oct. 4, 1937

Dawkes, G. O. (Leics. & Derbys.) b July 19, 1920

*Dawson, E. W. (CUCC & Leics.) b Feb. 13, 1904, d June 4, 1979

*Dawson, O. C. (Natal & Border) b Sept. 1, 1919

Day, A. P. (Kent; *CY 1910*) b April 10, 1885, d Jan. 22, 1969

*de Alwis, R. G. (SSC) b Feb. 15, 1959

*Dean, H. (Lancs.) b Aug. 13, 1884, d March 12, 1957

Deane, H. G. (Natal & Tvl) b July 21, 1895, d Oct. 21, 1939

*De Caires, F. I. (BG) b May 12, 1909, d Feb. 2, 1959

*De Courcy, J. H. (NSW) b April 18, 1927

*DeFreitas, P. A. J. (Leics. & Lancs.; *CY 1992*) b Feb. 18, 1966

Delisle, G. P. S. (OUCC & Middx) b Dec. 25, 1934

*Dell, A. R. (Qld) b Aug. 6, 1947

*de Mel, A. L. F. (SL) b May 9, 1959

*Dempster, C. S. (Wgtn, Leics., Scotland & Warwicks.; *CY 1932*) b Nov. 15, 1903, d Feb. 14, 1974

*Dempster, E. W. (Wgtn) b Jan. 25, 1925

*Denness, M. H. (Scotland, Kent & Essex; *CY 1975*) b Dec. 1, 1940

Dennett, E. G. (Glos.) b April 27, 1880, d Sept. 14, 1937

Denning, P. W. (Som.) b Dec. 16, 1949

Dennis, F. (Yorks.) b June 11, 1907

Dennis, S. J. (Yorks., OFS & Glam.) b Oct. 18, 1960

*Denton, D. (Yorks.; *CY 1906*) b July 4, 1874, d Feb. 16, 1950

Deodhar, D. B. (M'tra; oldest living Ranji Trophy player) b Jan. 14, 1892

*Depeiza, C. C. (B'dos) b Oct. 10, 1927

Derrick, J. (Glam.) b Jan. 15, 1963

*Desai, R. B. (Bombay) b June 20, 1939

De Saram, F. C. (OUCC & Ceylon) b Sept. 5, 1912, d April 11, 1983

de Silva, A. M. (CCC) b Dec. 3, 1963

de Silva, D. L. S. (SL) b Nov. 17, 1956, d April 12, 1980

*de Silva, D. S. (SL) b June 11, 1942

*de Silva, E. A. R. (NCC) b March 28, 1956

de Silva, G. N. (SL) b March 12, 1955

*de Silva, G. R. A. (SL) b Dec. 12, 1952

*de Silva, P. A. (NCC) b Oct. 17, 1965

de Smidt, R. W. (W. Prov.) b Nov. 24, 1883, d Aug. 3, 1986

Devereux, L. N. (Middx, Worcs. & Glam.) b Oct. 20, 1931

de Villiers, P. S. (N. Tvl & Kent) b Oct. 13, 1964

Dewdney, C. T. (Jam.) b Oct. 23, 1933

*Dewes, J. G. (CUCC & Middx) b Oct. 11, 1926

Dews, G. (Worcs.) b June 5, 1921

*Dexter, E. R. (CUCC & Sussex; *CY 1961*) b May 15, 1935

*Dias, R. L. (CCC) b Oct. 18, 1952

Dibbs, A. H. A. (Pres. MCC 1983-84) b Dec. 9, 1918, d Nov. 28, 1985

*Dick, A. E. (Otago & Wgtn) b Oct. 10, 1936

*Dickinson, G. R. (Otago) b March 11, 1903, d March 17, 1978

*Dilley, G. R. (Kent, Natal & Worcs.) b May 18, 1959

Diment, R. A. (Glos. & Leics.) b Feb. 9, 1927

*Dipper, A. E. (Glos.) b Nov. 9, 1885, d Nov. 7, 1945

*Divecha, R. V. (Bombay, OUCC, Northants, Vidarbha & S'tra) b Oct. 18, 1927

Diver, A. J. D. (Cambs., Middx, Notts. & All-England) b June 6, 1824, d March 25, 1876

Dixon, A. L. (Kent) b Nov. 27, 1933

*Dixon, C. D. (Tvl) b Feb. 12, 1891, d Sept. 9, 1969

Dodds, T. C. (Essex) b May 29, 1919

*Dodemaide, A. I. C. (Vic. & Sussex) b Oct. 5, 1963

Doggart, A. G. (CUCC, Durham & Middx) b June 2, 1897, d June 7, 1963

*Doggart, G. H. G. (CUCC & Sussex; Pres. MCC 1981-82) b July 18, 1925

*D'Oliveira, B. L. (Worcs.; *CY 1967*) b Oct. 4, 1931

D'Oliveira, D. B. (Worcs.) b Oct. 19, 1960

*Dollery, H. E. (Warwicks. & Wgtn; *CY 1952*) b Oct. 14, 1914, d Jan. 20, 1987

Dollery, K. R. (Qld, Auck., Tas. & Warwicks.) b Dec. 9, 1924

*Dolphin, A. (Yorks.) b Dec. 24, 1885, d Oct. 23, 1942

Donald, A. A. (OFS & Warwicks.; *CY 1992*) b Oct. 20, 1966

*Donnan, H. (NSW) b Nov. 12, 1864, d Aug. 13, 1956

*Donnelly, M. P. (Wgtn, Cant., Middx, Warwicks. & OUCC; *CY 1948*) b Oct. 17, 1917

*Dooland, B. (S. Aust. & Notts.; *CY 1955*) b Nov. 1, 1923, d Sept. 8, 1980

Dorrinton, W. (Kent & All-England) b April 29, 1809, d Nov. 8, 1848

Dorset, 3rd Duke of (Kent) b March 24, 1745, d July 19, 1799

*Doshi, D. R. (Bengal, Notts., Warwicks. & S'tra) b Dec. 22, 1947

*Douglas, J. W. H. T. (Essex; *CY 1915*) b Sept. 3, 1882, d Dec. 19, 1930

Dowding, A. L. (OUCC) b April 4, 1929

*Dowe, U. G. (Jam.) b March 29, 1949

*Dower, R. R. (E. Prov.) b June 4, 1876, d Sept. 15, 1964

*Dowling, G. T. (Cant.) b March 4, 1937

*Downton, P. R. (Kent & Middx) b April 4, 1957

Draper, E. J. (E. Prov. & Griq. W.) b Sept. 27, 1934

*Draper, R. G. (E. Prov. & Griq. W.) b Dec. 24, 1926

Dredge, C. H. (Som.) b Aug. 4, 1954

*Druce, N. F. (CUCC & Surrey; *CY 1898*) b Jan. 1, 1875, d Oct. 27, 1954

Drybrough, C. D. (OUCC & Middx) b Aug. 31, 1938

*D'Souza, A. (Kar., Peshawar & PIA) b Jan. 17, 1939

*Ducat, A. (Surrey; *CY 1920*) b Feb. 16, 1886, d July 23, 1942

*Duckworth, C. A. R. (Natal & Rhod.) b March 22, 1933

*Duckworth, G. (Lancs.; *CY 1929*) b May 9, 1901, d Jan. 5, 1966

Dudleston, B. (Leics., Glos. & Rhod.) b July 16, 1945

*Duff, R. A. (NSW) b Aug. 17, 1878, d Dec. 13, 1911

*Dujon, P. J. L. (Jam.; *CY 1989*) b May 28, 1956

*Duleepsinhji, K. S. (CUCC & Sussex; *CY 1930*) b June 13, 1905, d Dec. 5, 1959

*Dumbrill, R. (Natal & Tvl) b Nov. 19, 1938

*Duminy, J. P. (OUCC, W. Prov. & Tvl) b Dec. 16, 1897, d Jan. 31, 1980

*Duncan, J. R. F. (Qld & Vic.) b March 25, 1944

Dunell, O. R. (E. Prov.) b July 15, 1856, d Oct. 21, 1929

*Dunning, J. A. (Otago & OUCC) b Feb. 6, 1903, d June 24, 1971

*Du Preez, J. H. (Rhod. & Zimb.) b Nov. 14, 1942

*Durani, S. A. (S'tra, Guj. & Raja.) b Dec. 11, 1934

Durose, A. J. (Northants) b Oct. 10, 1944

*Durston, F. J. (Middx) b July 11, 1893, d April 8, 1965

*Du Toit, J. F. (SA) b April 5, 1868, d July 10, 1909

Dye, J. C. J. (Kent, Northants & E. Prov.) b July 24, 1942

Dyer, D. D. (Natal & Tvl) b Dec. 3, 1946

*Dyer, D. V. (Natal) b May 2, 1914, d June 18, 1990

*Dyer, G. C. (NSW) b March 16, 1959

Dyer, R. I. H. B. (Warwicks.) b Dec. 22, 1958

*Dymock, G. (Qld) b July 21, 1945

Dyson, A. H. (Glam.) b July 10, 1905, d June 7, 1978

Dyson, J. (Lancs.) b July 8, 1934

*Dyson, John (NSW) b June 11, 1954

*Eady, C. J. (Tas.) b Oct. 29, 1870, d Dec. 20, 1945

*Eagar, E. D. R. (OUCC, Glos. & Hants) b Dec. 8, 1917, d Sept. 13, 1977

Eagar, M. A. (OUCC & Glos.) b March 20, 1934

Eaglestone, J. T. (Middx & Glam.) b July 24, 1923

Ealham, A. G. E. (Kent) b Aug. 30, 1944

East, D. E. (Essex) b July 27, 1959

East, R. E. (Essex) b June 20, 1947

Eastman, G. F. (Essex) b April 7, 1903, d March 15, 1991

Eastman, L. C. (Essex & Otago) b June 3, 1897, d April 17, 1941

*Eastwood, K. H. (Vic.) b Nov. 23, 1935

*Ebeling, H. I. (Vic.) b Jan. 1, 1905, d Jan. 12, 1980

Eckersley, P. T. (Lancs.) b July 2, 1904, d Aug. 13, 1940

*Edgar, B. A. (Wgtn) b Nov. 23, 1956

Edinburgh, HRH Duke of (Pres. MCC 1948-49, 1974-75) b June 10, 1921

Edmeades, B. E. A. (Essex) b Sept. 17, 1941

*Edmonds, P. H. (CUCC, Middx & E. Prov.) b March 8, 1951

Edmonds, R. B. (Warwicks.) b March 2, 1941

Edrich, B. R. (Kent & Glam.) b Aug. 18, 1922

Edrich, E. H. (Lancs.) b March 27, 1914

Edrich, G. A. (Lancs.) b July 13, 1918

*Edrich, J. H. (Surrey; *CY 1966*) b June 21, 1937

*Edrich, W. J. (Middx; *CY 1940*) b March 26, 1916, d April 24, 1986

*Edwards, G. N. (C. Dist.) b May 27, 1955

*Edwards, J. D. (Vic.) b June 12, 1862, d July 31, 1911

Edwards, M. J. (CUCC & Surrey) b March 1, 1940

*Edwards, R. (W. Aust. & NSW) b Dec. 1, 1942

*Edwards, R. M. (B'dos) b June 3, 1940

*Edwards, W. J. (W. Aust.) b Dec. 23, 1949

Eele, P. J. (Som.) b Jan. 27, 1935

Eggar, J. D. (OUCC, Hants & Derbys.) b Dec. 1, 1916, d May 3, 1983

*Ehtesham-ud-Din (Peshawar, Punjab, PIA, NBP & UBL) b Sept. 4, 1950

*Elgie, M. K. (Natal) b March 6, 1933

Ellcock, R. M. (Worcs., B'dos & Middx) b June 17, 1965

Elliott, C. S. (Derbys.) b April 24, 1912

*Elliott, H. (Derbys.) b Nov. 2, 1891, d Feb. 2, 1976

Elliott, Harold (Lancs.; Umpire) b June 15, 1904, d April 15, 1969

Ellis, G. P. (Glam.) b May 24, 1950

Ellis, J. L. (Vic.) b May 9, 1890, d July 26, 1974

Ellis, R. G. P. (OUCC & Middx) b Oct. 20 1960

*Ellison, R. M. (Kent & Tas.; *CY 1986*) b Sept. 21, 1959

Elms, R. B. (Kent & Hants) b April 5, 1949

*Emburey, J. E. (Middx & W. Prov.; *CY 1984*) b Aug. 20, 1952

*Emery, R. W. G. (Auck. & Cant.) b March 28, 1915, d Dec. 18, 1982

*Emery, S. H. (NSW) b Oct. 16, 1885, d Jan. 7, 1967

*Emmett, G. M. (Glos.) b Dec. 2, 1912, d Dec. 18, 1976

*Emmett, T. (Yorks.) b Sept. 3, 1841, d June 30, 1904

*Endean, W. R. (Tvl) b May 31, 1924

*Engineer, F. M. (Bombay & Lancs.) b Feb. 25, 1938

*Evans, A. J. (OUCC, Hants & Kent) b May 1, 1889, d Sept. 18, 1960

Evans, D. G. L. (Glam.; Umpire) b July 27, 1933, d March 25, 1990

Evans, E. (NSW) b March 6, 1849, d July 2, 1921

Evans, G. (OUCC, Glam. & Leics.) b Aug. 13, 1915

Evans, J. B. (Glam.) b Nov. 9, 1936

Evans, K. P. (Notts.) b Sept. 10, 1963

*Evans, T. G. (Kent; *CY 1951*) b Aug. 18, 1920

Every, T. (Glam.) b Dec. 19, 1909, d Jan. 20, 1990

Eyre, T. J. P. (Derbys.) b Oct. 17, 1939

Faber, M. J. J. (OUCC & Sussex) b Aug. 15, 1950, d Dec. 10, 1991

*Fagg, A. E. (Kent) b June 18, 1915, d Sept. 13, 1977

Fairbairn, A. (Middx) b Jan. 25, 1923

*Fairbrother, N. H. (Lancs.) b Sept. 9, 1963

*Fairfax, A. G. (NSW) b June 16, 1906, d May 17, 1955

Fairservice, C. (Kent & Middx) b Aug. 21, 1909

*Fane, F. L. (OUCC & Essex) b April 27, 1875, d Nov. 27, 1960

Fantham, W. E. (Warwicks.) b May 14, 1918

Farbrace, P. (Kent & Middx) b July 7, 1967

*Farnes, K. (CUCC & Essex; *CY 1939*) b July 8, 1911, d Oct. 20, 1941

Farooq Hamid (Lahore & PIA) b March 3, 1945

*Farrer, W. S. (Border) b Dec. 8, 1936

*Farrimond, W. (Lancs.) b May 23, 1903, d Nov. 14, 1979

Farrukh Zaman (Peshawar, NWFP, Punjab & MCB) b April 2, 1956

*Faulkner, G. A. (Tvl) b Dec. 17, 1881, d Sept. 10, 1930

*Favell, L. E. (S. Aust.) b Oct. 6, 1929, d June 14, 1987

*Fazal Mahmood (N. Ind., Punjab & Lahore; *CY 1955*) b Feb. 18, 1927

Fearnley, C. D. (Worcs.) b April 12, 1940

Featherstone, N. G. (Tvl, N. Tvl, Middx & Glam.) b Aug. 20, 1949

'Felix', N. (Wanostrocht) (Kent, Surrey & All-England) b Oct. 4, 1804, d Sept. 3, 1876

*Fellows-Smith, J. P. (OUCC, Tvl & Northants) b Feb. 3, 1932

Feltham, M. A. (Surrey) b June 26, 1963

Felton, N. A. (Som. & Northants) b Oct. 24, 1960

*Fender, P. G. H. (Sussex & Surrey; *CY 1915*) b Aug. 22, 1892, d June 15, 1985

*Ferguson, W. (T/T) b Dec. 14, 1917, d Feb. 23, 1961

*Fernandes, M. P. (BG) b Aug. 12, 1897, d May 8, 1981

Fernando, E. R. (SL) b Feb. 22, 1944

*Fernando, E. R. N. S. (SLAF) b Dec. 19, 1955

Fernando, T. L. (Colts) b Dec. 27, 1962

Ferreira, A. M. (N. Tvl & Warwicks.) b April 13, 1955

Ferris, G. J. F. (Leics. & Leewards) b Oct. 18, 1964

**Ferris, J. J. (NSW, Glos. & S. Aust.; *CY 1889*) b May 21, 1867, d Nov. 21, 1900

*Fichardt, C. G. (OFS) b March 20, 1870, d May 30, 1923

Fiddling, K. (Yorks. & Northants) b Oct. 13, 1917

*Fielder, A. (Kent; *CY 1907*) b July 19, 1877, d Aug. 30, 1949

Findlay, T. M. (Comb. Is. & Windwards) b Oct. 19, 1943

Findlay, W. (OUCC & Lancs.; Sec. Surrey CCC, Sec. MCC 1926-36) b June 22, 1880, d June 19, 1953

*Fingleton, J. H. (NSW) b April 28, 1908, d Nov. 22, 1981

*Finlason, C. E. (Tvl & Griq. W.) b Feb. 19, 1860, d July 31, 1917

Finney, R. J. (Derbys.) b Aug. 2, 1960

Firth, Rev. Canon J. D'E. E. (Winchester, OUCC & Notts.; *CY 1918*) b Jan. 21, 1900, d Sept. 21, 1957

Fisher, F. E. (Wgtn & C. Dist.) b July 28, 1924

Fisher, P. B. (OUCC, Middx & Worcs.) b Dec. 19, 1954

*Fishlock, L. B. (Surrey; *CY 1947*) b Jan. 2, 1907, d June 26, 1986

Fitzgerald, R. A. (CUCC & Middx; Sec. MCC 1863-76) b Oct. 1, 1834, d Oct. 28, 1881

*Flavell, J. A. (Worcs.; *CY 1965*) b May 15, 1929

*Fleetwood-Smith, L. O'B. (Vic.) b March 30, 1910, d March 16, 1971

Fleming, M. V. (Kent) b Dec. 12, 1964

Fletcher, D. A. G. (Rhod. & Zimb.) b Sept. 27, 1948

Fletcher, D. G. W. (Surrey) b July 6, 1924

*Fletcher, K. W. R. (Essex; *CY 1974*) b May 20, 1944

Fletcher, S. D. (Yorks.) b June 8, 1964

*Floquet, C. E. (Tvl) b Nov. 3, 1884, d Nov. 22, 1963

*Flowers, W. (Notts.) b Dec. 7, 1856, d Nov. 1, 1926

Foat, J. C. (Glos.) b Nov. 21, 1952

*Foley, H. (Wgtn) b Jan. 28, 1906, d Oct. 16, 1948

Folley, I. (Lancs. & Derbys.) b Jan. 9, 1963

Foord, C. W. (Yorks.) b June 11, 1924

Forbes, C. (Notts.) b Aug. 9, 1936

*Ford, F. G. J. (CUCC & Middx) b Dec. 14, 1866, d Feb. 7, 1940

Ford, N. M. (OUCC, Derbys. & Middx) b Nov. 18, 1906

Fordham, A. (Northants) b Nov. 9, 1964

Foreman, D. J. (W. Prov. & Sussex) b Feb. 1, 1933

Fosh, M. K. (CUCC & Essex) b Sept. 26, 1957

*Foster, F. R. (Warwicks.; *CY 1912*) b Jan. 31, 1889, d May 3, 1958

Foster, G. N. (OUCC, Worcs. & Kent) b Oct. 16, 1884, d Aug. 11, 1971

*Foster, H. K. (OUCC & Worcs.; *CY 1911*) b Oct. 30, 1873, d June 23, 1950

Foster, M. K. (Worcs.) b Jan. 1, 1889, d Dec. 3, 1940

*Foster, M. L. C. (Jam.) b May 9, 1943

*Foster, N. A. (Essex; *CY 1988*) b May 6, 1962

Foster, P. G. (Kent) b Oct. 9, 1916

*Foster, R. E. (OUCC & Worcs.; *CY 1901*) b April 16, 1878, d May 13, 1914

*Fothergill, A. J. (Som.) b Aug. 26, 1854, d Aug. 1, 1932

Fotheringham, H. R. (Natal & Tvl) b April 4, 1953

*Fowler, G. (Lancs.) b April 20, 1957

Fowler, W. P. (Derbys., N. Dist. & Auck.) b March 13, 1959

*Francis, B. C. (NSW & Essex) b Feb. 18, 1948

Francis, D. A. (Glam.) b Nov. 29, 1953

*Francis, G. N. (B'dos) b Dec. 7, 1897, d Jan. 12, 1942

*Francis, H. H. (Glos. & W. Prov.) b May 26, 1868, d Jan. 7, 1936

Francke, F. M. (SL & Qld) b March 29, 1941

*Francois, C. M. (Griq. W.) b June 20, 1897, d May 26, 1944

*Frank, C. N. (Tvl) b Jan. 27, 1891, d Dec. 26, 1961

*Frank, W. H. B. (SA) b Nov. 23, 1872, d Feb. 16, 1945

Franklin, H. W. F. (OUCC, Surrey & Essex) b June 30, 1901, d May 25, 1985

Franklin, T. J. (Auck.) b March 18, 1962

*Fraser, A. R. C. (Middx) b Aug. 8, 1965

*Frederick, M. C. (B'dos, Derbys. & Jam.) b May 6, 1927

*Fredericks, R. C. (†Guyana & Glam.; *CY 1974*) b Nov. 11, 1942

*Freeman, A. P. (Kent; *CY 1923*) b May 17, 1888, d Jan. 28, 1965

*Freeman, D. L. (Wgtn) b Sept. 8, 1914

*Freeman, E. W. (S. Aust.) b July 13, 1944

*Freer, F. W. (Vic.) b Dec. 4, 1915

*French, B. N. (Notts.) b Aug. 13, 1959

Frost, G. (Notts.) b Jan. 15, 1947

Frost, M. (Surrey & Glam.) b Oct. 21, 1962

Fry, C. A. (OUCC, Hants & Northants) b Jan. 14, 1940

*Fry, C. B. (OUCC, Sussex & Hants; *CY 1895*) b April 25, 1872, d Sept. 7, 1956

*Fuller, E. R. H. (W. Prov.) b Aug. 2, 1931

*Fuller, R. L. (Jam.) b Jan. 30, 1913, d May 3, 1987

*Fullerton, G. M. (Tvl) b Dec. 8, 1922

Funston, G. K. (NE Tvl & Griq. W.) b Nov. 21, 1948

*Funston, K. J. (NE Tvl, OFS & Tvl) b Dec. 3, 1925

*Furlonge, H. A. (T/T) b June 19, 1934

Gabriel, R. S. (T/T) b June 5, 1952

*Gadkari, C. V. (M'tra & Ind. Serv.) b Feb. 3, 1928

*Gaekwad, A. D. (Baroda) b Sept. 23, 1952

*Gaekwad, D. K. (Baroda) b Oct. 27, 1928

*Gaekwad, H. G. (†M. Pradesh) b Aug. 29, 1923

Gale, R. A. (Middx) b Dec. 10, 1933

*Gallichan, N. (Wgtn) b June 3, 1906, d March 25, 1969

*Gamsy, D. (Natal) b Feb. 17, 1940

*Gandotra, A. (Delhi & Bengal) b Nov. 24, 1948

*Gannon, J. B. (W. Aust.) b Feb. 8, 1947

*Ganteaume, A. G. (T/T) b Jan. 22, 1921

Gard, T. (Som.) b June 2, 1957

Gardner, L. R. (Leics.) b Feb. 23, 1934

Garland-Wells, H. M. (OUCC & Surrey) b Nov. 14, 1907

Garlick, R. G. (Lancs. & Northants) b April 11, 1917, d May 16, 1988

*Garner, J. (B'dos, Som. & S. Aust.; *CY 1980*) b Dec. 16, 1952

Garnham, M. A. (Glos., Leics. & Essex) b Aug. 20, 1960

*Garrett, T. W. (NSW) b July 26, 1858, d Aug. 6, 1943

*Gaskin, B. B. MacG. (BG) b March 21, 1908, d May 1, 1979

*Gatting, M. W. (Middx; *CY 1984*) b June 6, 1957

*Gaunt, R. A. (W. Aust. & Vic.) b Feb. 26, 1934

*Gavaskar, S. M. (Bombay & Som.; *CY 1980*) b July 10, 1949

*Gay, L. H. (CUCC, Hants & Som.) b March 24, 1871, d Nov. 1, 1949

Geary, A. C. T. (Surrey) b Sept. 11, 1900, d Jan. 23, 1989

*Geary, G. (Leics.; *CY 1927*) b July 9, 1893, d March 6, 1981

*Gedye, S. G. (Auck.) b May 2, 1929

*Gehrs, D. R. A. (S. Aust.) b Nov. 29, 1880, d June 25, 1953

Ghai, R. S. (Punjab) b June 12, 1960

*Ghavri, K. D. (S'tra & Bombay) b Feb. 28, 1951

*Ghazali, M. E. Z. (M'tra & Pak. Serv.) b June 15, 1924

*Ghorpade, J. M. (Baroda) b Oct. 2, 1930, d March 29, 1978

*Ghulam Abbas (Kar., NBP & PIA) b May 1, 1947

Ghulam Ahmed (H'bad) b July 4, 1922

*Gibb, P. A. (OUCC, Scotland, Yorks. & Essex) b July 11, 1913, d Dec. 7, 1977

Gibbons, H. H. (Worcs.) b Oct. 10, 1904, d Feb. 16, 1973

*Gibbs, G. L. (BG) b Dec. 27, 1925, d Feb. 21, 1979

*Gibbs, L. R. (†Guyana, S. Aust. & Warwicks.; *CY 1972*) b Sept. 29, 1934

Gibbs, P. J. K. (OUCC & Derbys.) b Aug. 17, 1944

Gibson, C. H. (Eton, CUCC & Sussex; *CY 1918*) b Aug. 23, 1900, d Dec. 31, 1976

Gibson, D. (Surrey) b May 1, 1936

*Giffen, G. (S. Aust.; *CY 1894*) b March 27, 1859, d Nov. 29, 1927

*Giffen, W. F. (S. Aust.) b Sept. 20, 1861, d June 29, 1949

*Gifford, N. (Worcs. & Warwicks.; *CY 1975*) b March 30, 1940

*Gilbert, D. R. (NSW, Tas. & Glos.) b Dec. 29, 1960

*Gilchrist, R. (Jam. & H'bad) b June 28, 1934

Giles, R. J. (Notts.) b Oct. 17, 1919

Gilhouley, K. (Yorks. & Notts.) b Aug. 8, 1934

Gill, A. (Notts.) b Aug. 4, 1940

*Gillespie, S. R. (Auck.) b March 2, 1957

Gilliat, R. M. C. (OUCC & Hants) b May 20, 1944

*Gilligan, A. E. R. (CUCC, Surrey & Sussex; *CY 1924*; Pres. MCC 1967-68) b Dec. 23, 1894, d Sept. 5, 1976

*Gilligan, A. H. H. (Sussex) b June 29, 1896, d May 5, 1978

Gilligan, F. W. (OUCC & Essex) b Sept. 20, 1893, d May 4, 1960

*Gilmour, G. J. (NSW) b June 26, 1951

*Gimblett, H. (Som.; *CY 1953*) b Oct. 19, 1914, d March 30, 1978

Gladstone, G. (*see* Marais, G. G.)

Gladwin, Chris (Essex & Derbys.) b May 10, 1962

*Gladwin, Cliff (Derbys.) b April 3, 1916, d April 10, 1988

*Gleeson, J. W. (NSW & E. Prov.) b March 14, 1938

*Gleeson, R. A. (E. Prov.) b Dec. 6, 1873, d Sept. 27, 1919

*Glover, G. K. (Kimberley & Griq. W.) b May 13, 1870, d Nov. 15, 1938

Glover, T. R. (OUCC) b Nov. 26, 1951

Goddard, G. F. (Scotland) b May 19, 1938

*Goddard, J. D. C. (B'dos) b April 21, 1919, d Aug. 26, 1987

*Goddard, T. L. (Natal & NE Tvl) b Aug. 1, 1931

*Goddard, T. W. (Glos.; *CY 1938*) b Oct. 1, 1900, d May 22, 1966

Goel, R. (Patiala & Haryana) b Sept. 29, 1942

Goldsmith, S. C. (Kent & Derbys.) b Dec. 19, 1964

Goldstein, F. S. (OUCC, Northants, Tvl & W. Prov.) b Oct. 14, 1944

*Gomes, H. A. (T/T & Middx; *CY 1985*) b July 13, 1953

Gomes, S. A. (T/T) b Oct. 18, 1950

Gomez, G. E. (T/T) b Oct. 10, 1919

*Gooch, G. A. (Essex & W. Prov.; *CY 1980*) b July 23, 1953

Goodway, C. C. (Warwicks.) b July 10, 1909, d May 22, 1991

Goodwin, K. (Lancs.) b June 25, 1938

Goodwin, T. J. (Leics.) b Jan. 22, 1929

Goonatillake, F. R. M. de S. (SL) b. Aug. 15, 1951

*Goonatillake, H. M. (SL) b Aug. 16, 1952

Goonesena, G. (Ceylon, Notts., CUCC & NSW) b Feb. 16, 1931

*Gopalan, M. J. (Madras) b June 6, 1909

Gopinath, C. D. (Madras) b March 1, 1930

*Gordon, N. (Tvl) b Aug. 6, 1911

Gore, H. E. (Eton & Army; *CY 1919*) b May 14, 1900, d June 7, 1990

Gould, I. J. (Middx, Auck. & Sussex) b Aug. 19, 1957

*Gover, A. R. (Surrey; *CY 1937*) b Feb. 29, 1908

*Gower, D. I. (Leics. & Hants; *CY 1979*) b April 1, 1957

Gower, G. M. (Border) b July 10, 1952

Gowrie, 1st Lord (Pres. MCC 1948-49) b July 6, 1872, d May 2, 1955

Grace, Dr Alfred b May 17, 1840, d May 24, 1916

Grace, Dr Alfred H. (Glos.) b March 10, 1866, d Sept. 16, 1929

Grace, C. B. (Clifton) b March 1882, d June 6, 1938

*Grace, Dr E. M. (Glos.) b Nov. 28, 1841, d May 20, 1911

Grace, Dr Edgar M. (MCC) (son of E. M. Grace) b Oct. 6, 1886, d Nov. 24, 1974

*Grace, G. F. (Glos.) b Dec. 13, 1850, d Sept. 22, 1880

Grace, Dr Henry (Glos.) b Jan. 31, 1833, d Nov. 15, 1895

Grace, Dr H. M. (father of W. G., E. M. and G. F.) b Feb. 21, 1808, d Dec. 23, 1871

Grace, Mrs H. M. (mother of W. G., E. M. and G. F.) b July 18, 1812, d July 25, 1884

*Grace, Dr W. G. (Glos.; *CY 1896*) b July 18, 1848, d Oct. 23, 1915

Grace, W. G., jun. (CUCC & Glos.) b July 6, 1874, d March 2, 1905

Graf, S. F. (Vic., W. Aust. & Hants) b May 19, 1957

*Graham, H. (Vic. & Otago) b Nov. 22, 1870, d Feb. 7, 1911

Graham, J. N. (Kent) b May 8, 1943

*Graham, R. (W. Prov.) b Sept. 16, 1877, d April 21, 1946

*Grant, G. C. (CUCC, T/T & Rhod.) b May 9, 1907, d Oct. 26, 1978

*Grant, R. S. (CUCC & T/T) b Dec. 15, 1909, d Oct. 18, 1977

Graveney, D. A. (Glos. & Som.) b Jan. 2, 1953

Graveney, J. K. (Glos.) b Dec. 16, 1924

*Graveney, T. W. (Glos., Worcs. & Qld; *CY 1953*) b June 16, 1927

Graves, P. J. (Sussex & OFS) b May 19, 1946

*Gray, A. H. (T/T & Surrey) b May 23, 1963

*Gray, E. J. (Wgtn) b Nov. 18, 1954

Gray, J. R. (Hants) b May 19, 1926

Gray, L. H. (Middx) b Dec. 16, 1915, d Jan. 3, 1983

Greasley, D. G. (Northants) b Jan. 20, 1926

*Greatbatch, M. J. (C. Dist.) b Dec. 11, 1963

Green, A. M. (Sussex & OFS) b May 28, 1960

Green, D. J. (Derbys. & CUCC) b Dec. 18, 1935

Green, D. M. (OUCC, Lancs. & Glos.; *CY 1969*) b Nov. 10, 1939

Green, Brig. M. A. (Glos. & Essex) b Oct. 3, 1891, d Dec. 28, 1971

*Greenough, T. (Lancs.) b Nov. 9, 1931

*Greenidge, A. E. (B'dos) b Aug. 20, 1956

*Greenidge, C. G. (Hants & B'dos; *CY 1977*) b May 1, 1951

*Greenidge, G. A. (B'dos & Sussex) b May 26, 1948

Greensmith, W. T. (Essex) b Aug. 16, 1930

*Greenwood, A. (Yorks.) b Aug. 20, 1847, d Feb. 12, 1889

Greenwood, P. (Lancs.) b Sept. 11, 1924

Greetham, C. (Som.) b Aug. 28, 1936

*Gregory, David W. (NSW; first Australian captain) b April 15, 1845, d Aug. 4, 1919

*Gregory, E. J. (NSW) b May 29, 1839, d April 22, 1899

*Gregory, J. M. (NSW; *CY 1922*) b Aug. 14, 1895, d Aug. 7, 1973
*Gregory, R. G. (Vic.) b Feb. 26, 1916, d June 10, 1942
*Gregory, S. E. (NSW; *CY 1897*) b April 14, 1870, d August 1, 1929
*Greig, A. W. (Border, E. Prov. & Sussex; *CY 1975*) b Oct. 6, 1946
*Greig, I. A. (CUCC, Border, Sussex & Surrey) b Dec. 8, 1955
*Grell, M. G. (T/T) b Dec. 18, 1899, d Jan. 11, 1976
*Grieve, B. A. F. (Eng.) b May 28, 1864, d Nov. 19, 1917
Grieves, K. J. (NSW & Lancs.) b Aug. 27, 1925, d Jan. 3, 1992
*Grieveson, R. E. (Tvl) b Aug. 24, 1909
*Griffin, G. M. (Natal & Rhod.) b June 12, 1939
*Griffith, C. C. (B'dos; *CY 1964*) b Dec. 14, 1938
Griffith, G. ("Ben") (Surrey & Utd England XI) b Dec. 20, 1833, d May 3, 1879
*Griffith, H. C. (B'dos) b Dec. 1, 1893, d March 18, 1980
Griffith, K. (Worcs.) b Jan. 17, 1950
Griffith, M. G. (CUCC & Sussex) b Nov. 25, 1943
*Griffith, S. C. (CUCC, Surrey & Sussex; Sec. MCC 1962-74; Pres. MCC 1979-80) b June 16, 1914
Griffiths, B. J. (Northants) b June 13, 1949
Griffiths, Rt Hon. The Lord (W. H.) (CUCC & Glam.; Pres. MCC 1990-91) b Sept. 26, 1923
*Grimmett, C. V. (Wgtn, Vic. & S. Aust.; *CY 1931*) b Dec. 25, 1891, d May 2, 1980
Grimshaw, N. (Northants) b May 5, 1911
*Groube, T. U. (Vic.) b Sept. 2, 1857, d Aug. 5, 1927
*Grout, A. T. W. (Qld) b March 30, 1927, d Nov. 9, 1968
Grove, C. W. (Warwicks. & Worcs.) b Dec. 16, 1912, d Feb. 15, 1982
Grover, J. N. (OUCC) b Oct. 15, 1915, d Dec. 17, 1990
Groves, M. G. M. (OUCC, Som. & W. Prov.) b Jan. 14, 1943
Grundy, J. (Notts. & Utd England XI) b March 5, 1824, d Nov. 24, 1873
*Guard, G. M. (Bombay & Guj.) b Dec. 12, 1925, d March 13, 1978
*Guest, C. E. J. (Vic. & W. Aust.) b Oct. 7, 1937
*Guha, S. (Bengal) b Jan. 31, 1946
**Guillen, S. C. (T/T & Cant.) b Sept. 24, 1924
Guise, J. L. (OUCC & Middx) b Nov. 25, 1903, d June 29, 1991
*Gunasekera, Y. (SL) b Nov. 8, 1957

**Gul Mahomed (N. Ind., Baroda, H'bad, Punjab & Lahore) b Oct. 15, 1921
*Guneratne, R. P. W. (Nomads) b Jan. 26, 1962
*Gunn, G. (Notts.; *CY 1914*) b June 13, 1879, d June 29, 1958
Gunn, G. V. (Notts.) b June 21, 1905, d Oct. 14, 1957
*Gunn, J. (Notts.; *CY 1904*) b July 19, 1876, d Aug. 21, 1963
Gunn, T. (Sussex) b Sept. 27, 1935
*Gunn, William (Notts.; *CY 1890*) b Dec. 4, 1858, d Jan. 29, 1921
*Gupte, B. P. (Bombay, Bengal & Ind. Rlwys) b Aug. 30, 1934
*Gupte, S. P. (Bombay, Bengal, Raja. & T/T) b Dec. 11, 1929
Gurr, D. R. (OUCC & Som.) b March 27, 1956
*Gursharan Singh (Punjab) b March 8, 1963
*Gurusinha, A. P. (SSC) b Sept. 16, 1966
*Guy, J. W. (C. Dist., Wgtn, Northants, Cant., Otago & N. Dist.) b Aug. 29, 1934

Haafiz Shahid (WAPDA) b May 10, 1963
Hacker, P. J. (Notts., Derbys. & OFS) b July 16, 1952
Hadlee, B. G. (Cant.) b Dec. 14, 1941
*Hadlee, D. R. (Cant.) b Jan. 6, 1948
*Hadlee, Sir R. J. (Cant., Notts. & Tas.; *CY 1982*) b July 3, 1951
*Hadlee, W. A. (Cant. & Otago) b June 4, 1915
Hafeez, A. (*see* Kardar)
Hagan, D. A. (OUCC) b June 25, 1966
*Haig, N. E. (Middx) b Dec. 12, 1887, d Oct. 27, 1966
*Haigh, S. (Yorks.; *CY 1901*) b March 19, 1871, d Feb. 27, 1921
Halfyard, D. J. (Kent & Notts.) b April 3, 1931
*Hall, A. E. (Tvl & Lancs.) b Jan. 23, 1896, d Jan. 1, 1964
*Hall, G. G. (NE Tvl & E. Prov.) b May 24, 1938, d June 26, 1987
Hall, I. W. (Derbys.) b Dec. 27, 1939
Hall, J. W. (Sussex) b March 30, 1968
Hall, Louis (Yorks.; *CY 1890*) b Nov. 1, 1852, d Nov. 19, 1915
Hall, T. A. (Derbys. & Som.) b Aug. 19, 1930, d April 21, 1984
*Hall, W. W. (B'dos, T/T & Qld) b Sept. 12, 1937
Hallam, A. W. (Lancs. & Notts.; *CY 1908*) b Nov. 12, 1869, d July 24, 1940
Hallam, M. R. (Leics.) b Sept. 10, 1931
*Halliwell, E. A. (Tvl & Middx; *CY 1905*) b Sept. 7, 1864, d Oct. 2, 1919
*Hallows, C. (Lancs.; *CY 1928*) b April 4, 1895, d Nov. 10, 1972
*Hallows, J. (Lancs.; *CY 1905*) b Nov. 14, 1873, d May 20, 1910

*Halse, C. G. (Natal) b Feb. 28, 1935

*Hamence, R. A. (S. Aust.) b Nov. 25, 1915

Hamer, A. (Yorks. & Derbys.) b Dec. 8, 1916

Hammond, H. E. (Sussex) b Nov. 7, 1907, d June 16, 1985

*Hammond, J. R. (S. Aust.) b April 19, 1950

*Hammond, W. R. (Glos.; *CY 1928*) b June 19, 1903, d July 1, 1965

Hampshire, J. H. (Yorks., Derbys. & Tas.; Umpire) b Feb. 10, 1941

*Hands, P. A. M. (W. Prov.) b March 18, 1890, d April 27, 1951

*Hands, R. H. M. (W. Prov.) b July 26, 1888, d April 20, 1918

*Hanif Mohammad (B'pur, Kar. & PIA; *CY 1968*) b Dec. 21, 1934

*Hanley, M. A. (Border & W. Prov.) b Nov. 10, 1918

Hanley, R. W. (E. Prov., OFS, Tvl & Northants) b Jan. 29, 1952

*Hanumant Singh (M. Pradesh & Raja.) b March 29, 1939

Harbord, W. E. (Yorks. & OUCC) b Dec. 15, 1908

Harden, R. J. (Som. & C. Dist.) b Aug. 16, 1965

Hardie, B. R. (Scotland & Essex) b Jan. 14, 1950

Hardikar, M. S. (Bombay) b Feb. 8, 1936

*Hardinge, H. T. W. (Kent; *CY 1915*) b Feb. 25, 1886, d May 8, 1965

Hardstaff, J. (Notts.) b Nov. 9, 1882, d April 2, 1947

*Hardstaff, J., jun. (Notts. & Auck.; *CY 1938*) b July 3, 1911, d Jan. 1, 1990

Hardy, J. J. E. (Hants, Som., W. Prov. & Glos.) b Oct. 2, 1960

Harfield, L. (Hants) b Aug. 16, 1905, d Nov. 19, 1985

*Harford, N. S. (C. Dist. & Auck.) b Aug. 30, 1930, d March 30, 1981

*Harford, R. I. (Auck.) b May 30, 1936

Harman, R. (Surrey) b Dec. 28, 1941

*Haroon Rashid (Kar., Sind, NBP, PIA & UBL) b March 25, 1953

*Harper, R. A. (Guyana & Northants) b March 17, 1963

*Harris, 4th Lord (OUCC & Kent; Pres. MCC 1895) b Feb. 3, 1851, d March 24, 1932

Harris, C. Z. (Cant.) b Nov. 20, 1969

Harris, David (Hants & All-England) b 1755, d May 19, 1803

Harris, M. J. (Middx, Notts., E. Prov. & Wgtn) b May 25, 1944

*Harris, P. G. Z. (Cant.) b July 18, 1927, d Nov. 30, 1991

*Harris, R. M. (Auck.) b July 27, 1933

*Harris, T. A. (Griq. W. & Tvl) b Aug. 27, 1916

Harrison, L. (Hants) b June 8, 1922

*Harry, J. (Vic.) b Aug. 1, 1857, d Oct. 27, 1919

Hart, G. E. (Middx) b Jan. 13, 1902, d April 11, 1987

Hart, R. T. (C. Dist.) b Nov. 7, 1961

*Hartigan, G. P. D. (Border) b Dec. 30, 1884, d Jan. 7, 1955

*Hartigan, R. J. (NSW & Qld) b Dec. 12, 1879, d June 7, 1958

*Hartkopf, A. E. V. (Vic.) b Dec. 28, 1889, d May 20, 1968

Hartley, A. (Lancs.; *CY 1911*) b April 11, 1879, d Oct. 9, 1918

*Hartley, J. C. (OUCC & Sussex) b Nov. 15, 1874, d March 8, 1963

Hartley, P. J. (Warwicks. & Yorks.) b April 18, 1960

Hartley, S. N. (Yorks. & OFS) b March 18, 1956

Harvey, J. F. (Derbys.) b Sept. 27, 1939

*Harvey, M. R. (Vic.) b April 29, 1918

Harvey, P. F. (Notts.) b Jan. 15, 1923

*Harvey, R. L. (Natal) b Sept. 14, 1911

*Harvey, R. N. (Vic. & NSW; *CY 1954*) b Oct. 8, 1928

Harvey-Walker, A. J. (Derbys.) b July 21, 1944

Hasan Jamil (Kalat, Kar., Pak. Us & PIA) b July 25, 1952

*Haseeb Ahsan (Peshawar, Pak. Us, Kar. & PIA) b July 15, 1939

Hassan, B. (Notts.) b March 24, 1944

*Hassett, A. L. (Vic.; *CY 1949*) b Aug. 28, 1913

*Hastings, B. F. (Wgtn, C. Dist. & Cant.) b March 23, 1940

*Hathorn, C. M. H. (Tvl) b April 7, 1878, d May 17, 1920

Hathurusinghe, U. C. (TU) b Sept. 13, 1968

*Hawke, 7th Lord (CUCC & Yorks.; *CY 1909*; Pres. MCC 1914-18) b Aug. 16, 1860, d Oct. 10, 1938

*Hawke, N. J. N. (W. Aust., S. Aust. & Tas.) b June 27, 1939

Hawker, Sir Cyril (Essex; Pres. MCC 1970-71) b July 21, 1900, d Feb. 22, 1991

Hawkins, D. G. (Glos.) b May 18, 1935

*Hayes, E. G. (Surrey & Leics.; *CY 1907*) b Nov. 6, 1876, d Dec. 2, 1953

*Hayes, F. C. (Lancs.) b Dec. 6, 1946

*Hayes, J. A. (Auck. & Cant.) b Jan. 11, 1927

Hayes, K. A. (OUCC & Lancs.) b Sept. 26, 1962

Haygarth, A. (Sussex; Historian) b Aug. 4, 1825, d May 1, 1903

Hayhurst, A. N. (Lancs. & Som.) b Nov. 23, 1962

*Haynes, D. L. (B'dos & Middx; *CY 1991*) b Feb. 15, 1956

Haynes, R. C. (Jam.) b Nov. 11, 1964

Haysman, M. D. (S. Aust., Leics. & N. Tvl) b April 22, 1961

Hayward, T. (Cambs. & All-England) b March 21, 1835, d July 21, 1876

*Hayward, T. W. (Surrey; *CY 1895*) b March 29, 1871, d July 19, 1939

Haywood, P. R. (Leics.) b March 30, 1947

Hazare, V. S. (M'tra, C. Ind. & Baroda) b March 11, 1915

Hazell, H. L. (Som.) b Sept. 30, 1909, d March 31, 1990

Hazlerigg, Lord, formerly Hon. A. G. (CUCC & Leics.) b Feb. 24, 1910

*Hazlitt, G. R. (Vic. & NSW) b Sept. 4, 1888, d Oct. 30, 1915

*Headley, G. A. (Jam.; *CY 1934*) b May 30, 1909, d Nov. 30, 1983

*Headley, R. G. A. (Worcs. & Jam.) b June 29, 1939

Healy, I. A. (Qld) b April 30, 1964

*Hearn, P. (Kent) b Nov. 18, 1925

*Hearne, Alec (Kent; *CY 1894*) b July 22, 1863, d May 16, 1952

**Hearne, Frank (Kent & W. Prov.) b Nov. 23, 1858, d July 14, 1949

*Hearne, G. A. L. (W. Prov.) b March 27, 1888, d Nov. 13, 1978

*Hearne, George G. (Kent) b July 7, 1856, d Feb. 13, 1932

*Hearne, J. T. (Middx; *CY 1892*) b May 3, 1867, d April 17, 1944

*Hearne, J. W. (Middx; *CY 1912*) b Feb. 11, 1891, d Sept. 14, 1965

Hearne, Thos. (Middx) b Sept. 4, 1826, d May 13, 1900

Hearne, Thos., jun. (Lord's Ground Superintendent) b Dec. 29, 1849, d Jan. 29, 1910

Heath, G. E. M. (Hants) b Feb. 20, 1913

Heath, M. (Hants) b March 9, 1934

Hedges, B. (Glam.) b Nov. 10, 1927

Hedges, L. P. (Tonbridge, OUCC, Kent & Glos.; *CY 1919*) b July 13, 1900, d Jan. 12, 1933

Hegg, W. K. (Lancs.) b Feb. 23, 1968

*Heine, P. S. (NE Tvl, OFS & Tvl) b June 28, 1928

*Hemmings, E. E. (Warwicks. & Notts.) b Feb. 20, 1949

Hemsley, E. J. O. (Worcs.) b Sept. 1, 1943

*Henderson, M. (Wgtn) b Aug. 2, 1895, d June 17, 1970

Henderson, R. (Surrey; *CY 1890*) b March 30, 1865, d Jan. 29, 1931

Henderson, S. P. (CUCC, Worcs. & Glam.) b Sept. 24, 1958

*Hendren, E. H. (Middx; *CY 1920*) b Feb. 5, 1889, d Oct. 4, 1962

*Hendrick, M. (Derbys. & Notts.; *CY 1978*) b Oct. 22, 1948

*Hendriks, J. L. (Jam.) b Dec. 21, 1933

*Hendry, H. S. T. L. (NSW & Vic.) b May 24, 1895, d Dec. 16, 1988

Henry, O. (W. Prov., Boland, OFS & Scotland) b Jan. 23, 1952

Hepworth, P. N. (Leics.) b May 4, 1967

Herman, O. W. (Hants) b Sept. 18, 1907, d June 24, 1987

Herman, R. S. (Middx, Border, Griq. W. & Hants) b Nov. 30, 1946

Heron, J. G. (Zimb.) b Nov. 8, 1948

*Heseltine, C. (Hants) b Nov. 26, 1869, d June 13, 1944

Hever, N. G. (Middx & Glam.) b Dec. 17, 1924, d Sept. 11, 1987

Hewett, H. T. (OUCC & Som.; *CY 1893*) b May 25, 1864, d March 4, 1921

Heyn, P. D. (SL) b June 26, 1945

Hibbert, P. A. (Vic.) b July 23, 1952

*Hick, G. A. (Worcs., Zimb., N. Dist. & Qld; *CY 1987*) b May 23, 1966

*Higgs, J. D. (Vic.) b July 11, 1950

*Higgs, K. (Lancs. & Leics.; *CY 1968*) b Jan. 14, 1937

Hignell, A. J. (CUCC & Glos.) b Sept. 4, 1955

*Hilditch, A. M. J. (NSW & S. Aust.) b May 20, 1956

Hill, Alan (Derbys. & OFS) b June 29, 1950

*Hill, Allen (Yorks.) b Nov. 14, 1843, d Aug. 29, 1910

*Hill, A. J. L. (CUCC & Hants) b July 26, 1871, d Sept. 6, 1950

*Hill, C. (S. Aust.; *CY 1900*) b March 18, 1877, d Sept. 5, 1945

Hill, E. (Som.) b July 9, 1923

Hill, G. (Hants) b April 15, 1913

*Hill, J. C. (Vic.) b June 25, 1923, d Aug. 11, 1974

Hill, L. W. (Glam.) b April 14, 1942

Hill, M. (Notts., Derbys & Som.) b Sept. 14, 1935

Hill, N. W. (Notts.) b Aug. 22, 1935

Hill, W. A. (Warwicks.) b April 27, 1910

Hills, J. J. (Glam.; Umpire) b Oct. 14, 1897, d Sept. 21, 1969

Hills, R. W. (Kent) b Jan. 8, 1951

Hill-Wood, C. K. (OUCC & Derbys.) b June 5, 1907, d Sept. 21, 1988

Hilton, C. (Lancs. & Essex) b Sept. 26, 1937

Hilton, J. (Lancs. & Som.) b Dec. 29, 1930

*Hilton, M. J. (Lancs.; *CY 1957*) b Aug. 2, 1928, d July 8, 1990

*Hime, C. F. W. (Natal) b Oct. 24, 1869, d Dec. 6, 1940

*Hindlekar, D. D. (Bombay) b Jan. 1, 1909, d March 30, 1949

Hinks, S. G. (Kent) b Oct. 12, 1960

*Hirst, G. H. (Yorks.; *CY 1901*) b Sept. 7, 1871, d May 10, 1954

*Hirwani, N. D. (M. Pradesh) b Oct. 18, 1968

*Hitch, J. W. (Surrey; *CY 1914*) b May 7, 1886, d July 7, 1965

Hitchcock, R. E. (Cant. & Warwicks.) b Nov. 28, 1929

*Hoad, E. L. G. (B'dos) b Jan. 29, 1896, d March 5, 1986

Hoare, D. E. (W. Aust.) b Oct. 19, 1934

*Hobbs, Sir J. B. (Surrey; *CY 1909, special portrait 1926*) b Dec. 16, 1882, d Dec. 21, 1963

Hobbs, R. N. S. (Essex & Glam.) b May 8, 1942

Hobson, D. L. (E. Prov. & W. Prov.) b Sept. 3, 1951

Hodges, J. H. (Vic.) b July 31, 1856, d Jan. 17, 1933

Hodgkinson, G. F. (Derbys.) b Feb. 19, 1914, d Jan. 7, 1987

Hodgson, A. (Northants) b Oct. 27, 1951

Hodgson, G. D. (Glos.) b Oct. 22, 1966

Hofmeyr, M. B. (OUCC & NE Tvl) b Dec. 9, 1925

*Hogan, T. G. (W. Aust.) b Sept. 23, 1956

*Hogg, R. M. (S. Aust.) b March 5, 1951

Hogg, W. (Lancs. & Warwicks.) b July 12, 1955

*Hohns, T. V. (Qld) b Jan. 23, 1954

Holder, J. W. (Hants; Umpire) b March 19, 1945

*Holder, V. A. (B'dos, Worcs. & OFS) b Oct. 8, 1945

Holding, M. A. (Jam., Lancs., Derbys., Tas. & Cant.; *CY 1977*) b Feb. 16, 1954

*Hole, G. B. (NSW & S. Aust.) b Jan. 6, 1931, d Feb. 14, 1990

*Holford, D. A. J. (B'dos & T/T) b April 16, 1940

*Holland, R. G. (NSW & Wgtn) b Oct. 19, 1946

*Hollies, W. E. (Warwicks.; *CY 1955*) b June 5, 1912, d April 16, 1981

Hollingdale, R. A. (Sussex) b March 6, 1906, d Aug. 1989

Holmes, Gp Capt. A. J. (Sussex) b June 30, 1899, d May 21, 1950

*Holmes, E. R. T. (OUCC & Surrey; *CY 1936*) b Aug. 21, 1905, d Aug. 16, 1960

Holmes, G. C. (Glam.) b Sept. 16, 1958

*Holmes, P. (Yorks.; *CY 1920*) b Nov. 25, 1886, d Sept. 3, 1971

Holt, A. G. (Hants) b April 8, 1911

*Holt, J. K., jun. (Jam.) b Aug. 12, 1923

Home of the Hirsel, Lord (Middx; Pres. MCC 1966-67) b July 2, 1903

*Hone, L. (MCC) b Jan. 30, 1853, d Dec. 31, 1896

Hooker, J. E. H. (NSW) b March 6, 1898, d Feb. 12, 1982

Hooker, R. W. (Middx) b Feb. 22, 1935

*Hookes, D. W. (S. Aust.) b May 3, 1955

*Hooper, C. L. (Guyana) b Dec. 15, 1966

*Hopkins, A. J. Y. (NSW) b May 3, 1874, d April 25, 1931

Hopkins, J. A. (Glam. & E. Prov.) b June 16, 1953

Hopkins, V. (Glos.) b Jan. 21, 1911, d Aug. 6, 1984

*Hopwood, J. L. (Lancs.) b Oct. 30, 1903, d June 15, 1985

*Horan, T. P. (Vic.) b March 8, 1854, d April 16, 1916

*Hordern, H. V. (NSW & Philadelphia) b Feb. 10, 1883, d June 17, 1938

*Hornby, A. N. (Lancs.) b Feb. 10, 1847, d Dec. 17, 1925

*Horne, P. A. (Auck.) b Jan. 21, 1960

Horner, N. F. (Yorks. & Warwicks.) b May 10, 1926

*Hornibrook, P. M. (Qld) b July 27, 1899, d Aug. 25, 1976

Horsfall, R. (Essex & Glam.) b June 26, 1920, d Aug. 25, 1981

Horton, H. (Worcs. & Hants) b April 18, 1923

Horton, J. (Worcs.) b Aug. 12, 1916

*Horton, M. J. (Worcs. & N. Dist.) b April 21, 1934

Hossell, J. J. (Warwicks.) b May 25, 1914

*Hough, K. W. (Auck.) b Oct. 24, 1928

Howland, C. B. (CUCC, Sussex & Kent) b Feb. 6, 1936

Howard, A. B. (B'dos) b Aug. 27, 1946

Howard, A. H. (Glam.) b Dec. 11, 1910

Howard, B. J. (Lancs.) b May 21, 1926

Howard, K. (Lancs.) b June 29, 1941

*Howard, N. D. (Lancs.) b May 18, 1925, d May 31, 1979

Howard, Major R. (Lancs.; MCC Team Manager) b April 17, 1890, d Sept. 10, 1967

*Howarth, G. P. (Auck., Surrey & N. Dist.) b March 29, 1951

*Howarth, H. J. (Auck.) b Dec. 25, 1943

*Howell, H. (Warwicks.) b Nov. 29, 1890, d July 9, 1932

*Howell, W. P. (NSW) b Dec. 29, 1869, d July 14, 1940

Howland, C. B. (CUCC, Sussex & Kent) b Feb. 6, 1936

*Howorth, R. (Worcs.) b April 26, 1909, d April 2, 1980

Hughes, D. P. (Lancs. & Tas.; *CY 1988*) b May 13, 1947

*Hughes, K. J. (W. Aust. & Natal; *CY 1981*) b Jan. 26, 1954

*Hughes, M. G. (Vic. & Essex) b Nov. 23, 1961

Hughes, S. P. (Middx & N. Tvl) b Dec. 20, 1959

Huish, F. H. (Kent) b Nov. 15, 1869, d March 16, 1957

Hulme, J. H. A. (Middx) b Aug. 26, 1904, d Sept. 26, 1991

Human, J. H. (CUCC & Middx) b Jan. 13, 1912, d July 22, 1991

Humpage, G. W. (Warwicks. & OFS; *CY 1985*) b April 24, 1954

Humphries, D. J. (Leics. & Worcs.) b Aug. 6, 1953

*Humphries, J. (Derbys.) b May 19, 1876, d May 7, 1946

Hunt, A. V. (Scotland & Bermuda) b Oct. 1, 1910

*Hunt, W. A. (NSW) b Aug. 26, 1908, d Dec. 31, 1983

*Hunte, C. C. (B'dos; *CY 1964*) b May 9, 1932

*Hunte, E. A. C. (T/T) b Oct. 3, 1905, d June 26, 1967

Hunter, David (Yorks.) b Feb. 23, 1860, d Jan. 11, 1927

*Hunter, Joseph (Yorks.) b Aug. 3, 1855, d Jan. 4, 1891

Hurd, A. (CUCC & Essex) b Sept. 7, 1937

*Hurst, A. G. (Vic.) b July 15, 1950

Hurst, R. J. (Middx) b Dec. 29, 1933

*Hurwood, A. (Qld) b June 17, 1902, d Sept. 26, 1982

Hussain, M. Dilawar (C. Ind. & U. Prov.) b March 19, 1907, d Aug. 26, 1967

*Hussain, N. (Essex) b March 28, 1968

*Hutchings, K. L. (Kent; *CY 1907*) b Dec. 7, 1882, d Sept. 3, 1916

Hutchinson, J. M. (Derbys.) b Nov. 29, 1896

*Hutchinson, P. (SA) b Jan. 26, 1862, d Sept. 30, 1925

*Hutton, Sir Leonard (Yorks.; *CY 1938*) b June 23, 1916, d Sept. 6, 1990

*Hutton, R. A. (CUCC, Yorks. & Tvl) b Sept. 6, 1942

*Hylton, L. G. (Jam.) b March 29, 1905, d May 17, 1955

*Ibadulla, K. (Punjab, Warwicks., Tas. & Otago) b Dec. 20, 1935

*Ibrahim, K. C. (Bombay) b Jan. 26, 1919

*Iddon, J. (Lancs.) b Jan. 8, 1902, d April 17, 1946

*Igglesden, A. P. (Kent & W. Prov.) b Oct. 8, 1964

*Ijaz Ahmed (Gujranwala, PACO & HBL) b Sept. 20, 1968

*Ijaz Butt (Pak. Us, Punjab, Lahore, R'pindi & Multan) b March 10, 1938

*Ijaz Faqih (Kar., Sind, PWD & MCB) b March 24, 1956

*Ikin, J. T. (Lancs.) b March 7, 1918, d Sept. 15, 1984

*Illingworth, R. (Yorks. & Leics.; *CY 1960*) b June 8, 1932

*Illingworth, R. K. (Worcs. & Natal) b Aug. 23, 1963

*Imran Khan (Lahore, Dawood, Worcs., OUCC, PIA, Sussex & NSW; *CY 1983*) b Nov. 25, 1952

*Imtiaz Ahmed (N. Ind., Comb. Us, NWFP, Pak. Serv., Peshawar & PAF) b Jan. 5, 1928

*Imtiaz Ali (T/T) b July 28, 1954

Inchmore, J. D. (Worcs. & N. Tvl) b Feb. 22, 1949

*Indrajitsinhji, K. S. (S'tra & Delhi) b June 15, 1937

Ingle, R. A. (Som.) b Nov. 5, 1903

Ingleby-Mackenzie, A. C. D. (Hants) b Sept. 15, 1933

Inman, C. C. (Ceylon & Leics.) b Jan. 29, 1936

Innes, G. A. S. (W. Prov. & Tvl) b Nov. 16, 1931, d July 19, 1982

*Inshan Ali (T/T) b Sept. 25, 1949

*Insole, D. J. (CUCC & Essex; *CY 1956*) b April 18, 1926

*Intikhab Alam (Kar., PIA, Surrey, PWD, Sind & Punjab) b Dec. 28, 1941

*Inverarity, R. J. (W. Aust. & S. Aust.) b Jan. 31, 1944

*Iqbal Qasim (Kar., Sind & NBP) b Aug. 6, 1953

*Irani, J. K. (Sind) b Aug. 18, 1923, d Feb. 25, 1982

Iredale, F. A. (NSW) b June 19, 1867, d April 15, 1926

Iremonger, J. (Notts.; *CY 1903*) b March 5, 1876, d March 25, 1956

*Ironmonger, H. (Qld & Vic.) b April 7, 1882, d June 1, 1971

*Ironside, D. E. J. (Tvl) b May 2, 1925

*Irvine, B. L. (W. Prov., Natal, Essex & Tvl) b March 9, 1944

*Israr Ali (S. Punjab, B'pur & Multan) b May 1, 1927

*Iverson, J. B. (Vic.) b July 27, 1915, d Oct. 24, 1973

*Jackman, R. D. (Surrey, W. Prov. & Rhod.; *CY 1981*) b Aug. 13, 1945

*Jackson, A. (NSW) b Sept. 5, 1909, d Feb. 16, 1933

Jackson, A. B. (Derbys.) b Aug. 21, 1933

Jackson, Sir A. H. M. (Derbys.) b Nov. 9, 1899, d Oct. 11, 1983

*Jackson, Rt Hon. Sir F. S. (CUCC & Yorks.; *CY 1894*; Pres. MCC 1921) b Nov. 21, 1870, d March 9, 1947

Jackson, G. R. (Derbys.) b June 23, 1896, d Feb. 21, 1966

*Jackson, H. L. (Derbys.; *CY 1959*) b April 5, 1921

Jackson, John (Notts. & All-England) b May 21, 1833, d Nov. 4, 1901

Jackson, P. F. (Worcs.) b May 11, 1911

Jacques, T. A. (Yorks.) b Feb. 19, 1905

*Jahangir Khan (N. Ind. & CUCC) b Feb. 1, 1910, d July 23, 1988

*Jai, L. P. (Bombay) b April 1, 1902, d Jan. 29, 1968

*Jaisimha, M. L. (H'bad) b March 3, 1939

Jakeman, F. (Yorks. & Northants) b Jan. 10, 1920, d May 18, 1986

*Jalal-ud-Din (PWD, Kar., IDBP & Allied Bank) b June 12, 1959

James, A. E. (Sussex) b Aug. 7, 1924

*James, K. C. (Wgtn & Northants) b March 12, 1904, d Aug. 21, 1976

James, K. D. (Middx, Hants & Wgtn) b March 18, 1961

James, R. M. (CUCC & Wgtn) b Oct. 2, 1934

James, S. P. (Glam. & CUCC) b Sept. 7, 1967

*Jameson, J. A. (Warwicks.) b June 30, 1941

*Jamshedji, R. J. D. (Bombay) b Nov. 18, 1892, d April 5, 1976

*Jardine, D. R. (OUCC & Surrey; *CY 1928*) b Oct. 23, 1900, d June 18, 1958

Jardine, M. R. (OUCC & Middx) b June 8, 1869, d Jan. 16, 1947

*Jarman, B. N. (S. Aust.) b Feb. 17, 1936

Jarrett, D. W. (OUCC & CUCC) b April 19, 1952

*Jarvis, A. H. (S. Aust.) b Oct. 19, 1860, d Nov. 15, 1933

Jarvis, K. B. S. (Kent & Glos.) b April 23, 1953

*Jarvis, P. W. (Yorks.) b June 29, 1965

*Jarvis, T. W. (Auck. & Cant.) b July 29, 1944

*Javed Akhtar (R'pindi & Pak. Serv.) b Nov. 21, 1940

*Javed Miandad (Kar., Sind, Sussex, HBL & Glam.; *CY 1982*) b June 12, 1957

*Jayantilal, K. (H'bad) b Jan. 13, 1948

*Jayasekera, R. S. A. (SL) b Dec. 7, 1957

Jayasinghe, S. (Ceylon & Leics.) b Jan. 19, 1931

Jayasinghe, A. S. (SL) b July 15, 1955

*Jayasuriya, S. T. (CCC) b June 30, 1969

Jean-Jacques, M. (Derbys.) b July 2, 1960

Jefferies, S. T. (W. Prov., Derbys., Lancs. & Hants) b Dec. 8, 1959

Jefferson, R. I. (CUCC & Surrey) b Aug. 15, 1941

*Jeganathan, S. (SL) b July 11, 1951

*Jenkins, R. O. (Worcs.; *CY 1950*) b Nov. 24, 1918

Jenkins, V. G. J. (OUCC & Glam.) b Nov. 2, 1911

*Jenner, T. J. (W. Aust. & S. Aust.) b Sept. 8, 1944

*Jennings, C. B. (S. Aust.) b June 5, 1884, d June 20, 1950

Jennings, K. F. (Som.) b Oct. 5, 1953

Jennings, R. V. (Tvl & N. Tvl) b Aug. 9, 1954

Jepson, A. (Notts.) b July 12, 1915

*Jessop, G. L. (CUCC & Glos.; *CY 1898*) b May 19, 1874, d May 11, 1955

Jesty, T. E. (Hants., Border, Griq. W., Cant., Surrey & Lancs.; *CY 1983*) b June 2, 1948

*John, V. B. (SL) b May 27, 1960

Johnson, C. (Yorks.) b Sept. 5, 1947

*Johnson, C. L. (Tvl) b 1871, d May 31, 1908

Johnson, G. W. (Kent & Tvl) b Nov. 8, 1946

*Johnson, H. H. H. (Jam.) b July 17, 1910, d June 24, 1987

Johnson, H. L. (Derbys.) b Nov. 8, 1927

*Johnson, I. W. (Vic.) b Dec. 8, 1918

Johnson, L. A. (Northants) b Aug. 12, 1936

*Johnson, L. J. (Qld) b March 18, 1919, d April 20, 1977

Johnson, P. (Notts.) b April 24, 1965

Johnson, P. D. (CUCC & Notts.) b Nov. 12, 1949

*Johnson, T. F. (T/T) b Jan. 10, 1917, d April 5, 1985

Johnston, B. A. (Broadcaster) b June 24, 1912

*Johnston, W. A. (Vic.; *CY 1949*) b Feb. 26, 1922

*Jones, A. (Glam., W. Aust., N. Tvl & Natal; *CY 1978*) b Nov. 4, 1938

Jones, A. A. (Sussex, Som., Middx, Glam., N. Tvl & OFS) b Dec. 9, 1947

*Jones, A. H. (Wgtn) b May 9, 1959

Jones, A. L. (Glam.) b June 1, 1957

Jones, A. N. (Sussex, Border & Som.) b July 22, 1961

*Jones, A. O. (Notts. & CUCC; *CY 1900*) b Aug. 16, 1872, d Dec. 21, 1914

Jones, B. J. R. (Worcs.) b Nov. 2, 1955

*Jones, C. M. (C. E. L.) (BG) b Nov. 3, 1902, d Dec. 10, 1959

*Jones, D. M. (Vic.; *CY 1990*) b March 24, 1961

*Jones, Ernest (S. Aust. & W. Aust.) b Sept. 30, 1869, d Nov. 23, 1943

Jones, E. C. (Glam.) b Dec. 14, 1912, d April 14, 1989

Jones, E. W. (Glam.) b June 25, 1942

*Jones, I. J. (Glam.) b Dec. 10, 1941

Jones, K. V. (Middx) b March 28, 1942

*Jones, P. E. (T/T) b June 6, 1917, d Nov. 21, 1991

Jones, P. H. (Kent) b June 19, 1935

*Jones, S. P. (NSW, Qld & Auck.) b Aug. 1, 1861, d July 14, 1951

Jones, W. E. (Glam.) b Oct. 31, 1916

Jordan, J. M. (Lancs.) b Feb. 7, 1932

Jorden, A. M. (CUCC & Essex) b Jan. 28, 1947

Jordon, R. C. (Vic.) b Feb. 17, 1937

*Joshi, P. G. (M'tra) b Oct. 27, 1926, d Jan. 8, 1987

Joshi, U. C. (S'tra, Ind. Rlwys, Guj. & Sussex) b Dec. 23, 1944

*Joslin, L. R. (Vic.) b Dec. 13, 1947

Jowett, D. C. P. R. (OUCC) b Jan. 24, 1931

Judd, A. K. (CUCC & Hants) b Jan. 1, 1904, d Feb. 15, 1988

Judge, P. F. (Middx, Glam. & Bengal) b May 23, 1916

Julian, R. (Leics.) b Aug. 23, 1936

*Julien, B. D. (T/T & Kent) b March 13, 1950

*Jumadeen, R. R. (T/T) b April 12, 1948

*Jupp, H. (Surrey) b Nov. 19, 1841, d April 8, 1889

*Jupp, V. W. C. (Sussex & Northants; *CY 1928*) b March 27, 1891, d July 9, 1960

*Jurangpathy, B. R. (CCC) b June 25, 1967

*Kallicharran, A. I. (Guyana, Warwicks., Qld, Tvl & OFS; *CY 1983*) b March 21, 1949

*Kaluperuma, L. W. (SL) b May 25, 1949

*Kaluperuma, S. M. S. (SL) b Oct. 22, 1961

Kaluwitharana, R. S. (SL) b Nov. 24, 1969

*Kanhai, R. B. (†Guyana, T/T, W. Aust., Warwicks. & Tas.; *CY 1964*) b Dec. 26, 1935

*Kanitkar, H. S. (M'tra) b Dec. 8, 1942

*Kapil Dev (Haryana, Northants & Worcs.; *CY 1983*) b Jan. 6, 1959

**Kardar, A. H. (formerly Abdul Hafeez) (N. Ind., OUCC, Warwicks. & Pak. Serv.) b Jan. 17, 1925

Karnain, S. H. U. (NCC) b Aug. 11, 1962

Keech, M. (Middx) b Oct. 21, 1970

*Keeton, W. W. (Notts.; *CY 1940*) b April 30, 1905, d Oct. 10, 1980

Keighley, W. G. (OUCC & Yorks.) b Jan. 10, 1925

*Keith, H. J. (Natal) b Oct. 25, 1927

Kelleher, H. R. A. (Surrey & Northants) b March 3, 1929

Kellett, S. A. (Yorks.) b Oct. 16, 1967

*Kelleway, C. (NSW) b April 25, 1886, d Nov. 16, 1944

Kelly, J. (Notts.) b Sept. 15, 1930

*Kelly, J. J. (NSW; *CY 1903*) b May 10, 1867, d Aug. 14, 1938

*Kelly, T. J. D. (Vic.) b May 3, 1844, d July 20, 1893

*Kempis, G. A. (Natal) b Aug. 4, 1865, d May 19, 1890

*Kendall, T. (Vic. & Tas.) b Aug. 24, 1851, d Aug. 17, 1924

Kennedy, A. (Lancs.) b Nov. 4, 1949

*Kennedy, A. S. (Hants; *CY 1933*) b Jan. 24, 1891, d Nov. 15, 1959

*Kenny, R. B. (Bombay & Bengal) b Sept. 29, 1930, d Nov. 21, 1985

*Kent, M. F. (Qld) b Nov. 23, 1953

*Kentish, E. S. M. (Jam. & OUCC) b Nov. 21, 1916

*Kenyon, D. (Worcs.; *CY 1963*) b May 15, 1924

*Kerr, J. L. (Cant.) b Dec. 28, 1910

Kerr, K. J. (Tvl & Warwicks.) b Sept. 11, 1961

*Kerr, R. B. (Qld) b June 16, 1961

Kerslake, R. C. (CUCC & Som.) b Dec. 26, 1942

Kettle, M. K. (Northants) b March 18, 1944

*Khalid Hassan (Punjab & Lahore) b July 14, 1937

*Khalid Wazir (Pak.) b April 27, 1936

*Khan Mohammad (N. Ind., Pak. Us, Som., B'pur, Sind, Kar. & Lahore) b Jan. 1, 1928

Khanna, S. C. (Delhi) b June 3, 1956

Kidd, E. L. (CUCC & Middx) b Oct. 18, 1889, d July 2, 1984

Kilborn, M. J. (OUCC) b Sept. 20, 1962

*Killick, Rev. E. T. (CUCC & Middx) b May 9, 1907, d May 18, 1953

Kilner, Norman (Yorks. & Warwicks.) b July 21, 1895, d April 28, 1979

*Kilner, Roy (Yorks.; *CY 1924*) b Oct. 17, 1890, d April 5, 1928

Kimpton, R. C. M. (OUCC & Worcs.) b Sept. 21, 1916

*King, C. L. (B'dos, Glam., Worcs. & Natal) b June 11, 1951

*King, F. McD. (B'dos) b Dec. 14, 1926, d Dec. 23, 1990

King, I. M. (Warwicks. & Essex) b Nov. 10, 1931

King, J. B. (Philadelphia) b Oct. 19, 1873, d Oct. 17, 1965

*King, J. H. (Leics.) b April 16, 1871, d Nov. 18, 1946

*King, L. A. (Jam. & Bengal) b Feb. 27, 1939

Kingsley, Sir P. G. T. (OUCC) b May 26, 1908

*Kinneir, S. P. (Warwicks.; *CY 1912*) b May 13, 1871, d Oct. 16, 1928

*Kippax, A. F. (NSW) b May 25, 1897, d Sept. 4, 1972

Kirby, D. (CUCC & Leics.) b Jan. 18, 1939

*Kirmani, S. M. H. (†Karn.) b Dec. 29, 1949

Kirsten, P. N. (W. Prov., Sussex, Derbys. & Border) b May 14, 1955

*Kischenchand, G. (W. Ind., Guj. & Baroda) b April 14, 1925

Kitchen, M. J. (Som.; Umpire) b Aug. 1, 1940

*Kline, L. F. (Vic.) b Sept. 29, 1934

*Knight, A. E. (Leics.; *CY 1904*) b Oct. 8, 1872, d April 25, 1946

*Knight, B. R. (Essex & Leics.) b Feb. 18, 1938

*Knight, D. J. (OUCC & Surrey; *CY 1915*) b May 12, 1894, d Jan. 5, 1960

Knight, R. D. V. (CUCC, Surrey, Glos. & Sussex) b Sept. 6, 1946

Knight, W. H. (Editor of *Wisden* 1870-79) b Nov. 29, 1812, d Aug. 16, 1879

*Knott, A. P. E. (Kent & Tas.; *CY 1970*) b April 9, 1946

Knott, C. H. (OUCC & Kent) b March 20, 1901, d June 18, 1988

Knott, C. J. (Hants) b Nov. 26, 1914

Knowles, J. (Notts.) b March 25, 1910

Knox, G. K. (Lancs.) b April 22, 1937

*Knox, N. A. (Surrey; *CY 1907*) b Oct. 10, 1884, d March 3, 1935

Kortright, C. J. (Essex) b Jan. 9, 1871, d Dec. 12, 1952

*Kotze, J. J. (Tvl & W. Prov.) b Aug. 7, 1879, d July 7, 1931

Kourie, A. J. (Tvl) b July 30, 1951

Krikken, K. M. (Derbys.) b April 9, 1969

*Kripal Singh, A. G. (Madras & H'bad) b Aug. 6, 1933, d July 23, 1987

Krishnamurthy, P. (H'bad) b July 12, 1947

Kuggeleijn, C. M. (N. Dist.) b May 10, 1956

Kuiper, A. P. (W. Prov. & Derbys.) b Aug. 24, 1959

*Kulkarni, R. R. (Bombay) b Sept. 25, 1962

*Kulkarni, U. N. (Bombay) b March 7, 1942

*Kumar, V. V. (†TN) b June 22, 1935

*Kumble, A. (Karn.) b Oct. 17, 1970

*Kunderan, B. K. (Ind. Rlwys & Mysore) b Oct. 2, 1939

*Kuruppu, D. S. B. P. (BRC) b Jan. 5, 1962

*Kuruppuarachchi, A. K. (SL) b Nov. 1, 1964

*Kuys, F. (W. Prov.) b March 21, 1870, d Sept. 12, 1953

Kynaston, R. (Middx; Sec. MCC 1846-58) b Nov. 5, 1805, d June 21, 1874

*Labrooy, G. F. (CCC) b June 7, 1964

Lacey, Sir F. E. (CUCC & 'lants; Sec MCC 1898-1926) b Oct. 19, 1859, d May 26, 1946

*Laird, B. M. (W. Aust.) b Nov. 21, 1950

*Laker, J. C. (Surrey, Auck. & Essex; *CY 1952*) b Feb. 9, 1922, d April 23, 1986

*Lall Singh (S. Punjab) b Dec. 16, 1909, d Nov. 19, 1985

*Lamb, A. J. (W. Prov., Northants & OFS; *CY 1981*) b June 20, 1954

Lamb, T. M. (OUCC, Middx & Northants) b March 24, 1953

*Lamba, R. (Delhi) b Jan. 2, 1958

*Lambert, C. B. (Guyana) b Feb. 2, 1962

Lambert, G. E. E. (Glos. & Som.) b May 11, 1918, d Oct. 31, 1991

Lambert, R. H. (Ireland) b July 18, 1874, d March 24, 1956

Lambert, Wm (Surrey) b 1779, d April 19, 1851

Lampard, A. W. (Vic. & AIF) b July 3, 1885, d Jan. 11, 1984

Lampitt, S. R. (Worcs.) b July 29, 1966

*Lance, H. R. (NE Tvl & Tvl) b June 6, 1940

Langdale, G. R. (Derbys. & Som.) b March 11, 1916

Langford, B. A. (Som.) b Dec. 17, 1935

*Langley, G. R. A. (S. Aust.; *CY 1957*) b Sept. 14, 1919

*Langridge, James (Sussex; *CY 1932*) b July 10, 1906, d Sept. 10, 1966

Langridge, J. G. (John) (Sussex; *CY 1950*) b Feb. 10, 1910

Langridge, R. J. (Sussex) b April 13, 1939

*Langton, A. B. C. (Tvl) b March 2, 1912, d Nov. 27, 1942

*Lara, B. C. (T/T) b May 2, 1969

*Larkins, W. (Northants & E. Prov.) b Nov. 22, 1953

Larsen, G. R. (Wgtn) b Sept. 27, 1962

*Larter, J. D. F. (Northants) b April 24, 1940

*Larwood, H. (Notts.; *CY 1927*) b Nov. 14, 1904

Lashley, P. D. (B'dos) b Feb. 11, 1937

Latchman, H. C. [A. H.] (Middx & Notts.) b July 26, 1943

Latham, R. T. (Cant.) b June 12, 1961

*Laughlin, T. J. (Vic.) b Jan. 30, 1951

*Laver, F. (Vic.) b Dec. 7, 1869, d Sept. 24, 1919

Lawrence, D. V. (Glos.) b Jan. 28, 1964

*Lawrence, G. B. (Rhod. & Natal) b March 31, 1932

Lawrence, J. (Som.) b March 29, 1914, d Dec. 10, 1988

*Lawry, W. M. (Vic.; *CY 1962*) b Feb. 11, 1937

*Lawson, G. F. (NSW & Lancs.) b Dec. 7, 1957

Leadbeater, B. (Yorks.) b Aug. 14, 1943

*Leadbeater, E. (Yorks. & Warwicks.) b Aug. 15, 1927

Leary, S. E. (Kent) b April 30, 1933, d Aug. 21, 1988

Lee, C. (Yorks. & Derbys.) b March 17, 1924

Lee, F. S. (Middx & Som.) b July 24, 1905, d March 30, 1982

*Lee, H. W. (Middx) b Oct. 26, 1890, d April 21, 1981

Lee, J. W. (Middx & Som.) b Feb. 1, 1904, d June 20, 1944

Lee, P. G. (Northants & Lancs.; *CY 1976*) b Aug. 27, 1945

*Lee, P. K. (S. Aust.) b Sept. 14, 1904, d Aug. 9, 1980

*Lees, W. K. (Otago) b March 19, 1952

*Lees, W. S. (Surrey; *CY 1906*) b Dec. 25, 1875, d Sept. 10, 1924

Leese, Sir Oliver, Bt (Pres. MCC 1965-66) b Oct. 27, 1894, d Jan. 20, 1978

Lefebvre, R. P. (Som. & Cant.) b Feb. 7, 1963

*Legall, R. A. (B'dos & T/T) b Dec. 1, 1925

Legard, E. (Warwicks.) b Aug. 23, 1935

*Leggat, I. B. (C. Dist.) b June 7, 1930

*Leggat, J. G. (Cant.) b May 27, 1926, d March 8, 1973

*Legge, G. B. (OUCC & Kent) b Jan. 26, 1903, d Nov. 21, 1940

Lenham, L. J. (Sussex) b May 24, 1936

Lenham, N. J. (Sussex) b Dec. 17, 1965

*le Roux, F. L. (Tvl & E. Prov.) b Feb. 5, 1882, d Sept. 22, 1963

le Roux, G. S. (W. Prov. & Sussex) b Sept. 4, 1955

*Leslie, C. F. H. (OUCC & Middx) b Dec. 8, 1861, d Feb. 12, 1921

Lester, E. (Yorks.) b Feb. 18, 1923

Lester, G. (Leics.) b Dec. 27, 1915

Lester, Dr J. A. (Philadelphia) b Aug. 1, 1871, d Sept. 3, 1969

Lethbridge, C. (Warwicks.) b June 23, 1961

*Lever, J. K. (Essex & Natal; *CY 1979*) b Feb. 24, 1949

*Lever, P. (Lancs. & Tas.) b Sept. 17, 1940

*Leveson Gower, Sir H. D. G. (OUCC & Surrey) b May 8, 1873, d Feb. 1, 1954

*Levett, W. H. V. (Kent) b Jan. 25, 1908

Lewington, P. J. (Warwicks.) b Jan. 30, 1950

*Lewis, A. R. (CUCC & Glam.) b July 6, 1938

Lewis, C. (Kent) b July 27, 1908

*Lewis, C. C. (Leics.) b Feb. 14, 1968

Lewis, D. J. (OUCC & Rhod.) b July 27, 1927

*Lewis, D. M. (Jam.) b Feb. 21, 1946

Lewis, E. B. (Warwicks.) b Jan. 5, 1918, d Oct. 19, 1983

Lewis, E. J. (Glam. & Sussex) b Jan. 31, 1942

*Lewis, P. T. (W. Prov.) b Oct. 2, 1884, d Jan. 30, 1976

Lewis, R. V. (Hants) b Aug. 6, 1947

*Leyland, M. (Yorks.; *CY 1929*) b July 20, 1900, d Jan. 1, 1967

*Liaqat Ali (Kar., Sind, HBL & PIA) b May 21, 1955

Liddicutt, A. E. (Vic.) b Oct. 17, 1891, d April 8, 1983

Lightfoot, A. (Northants) b Jan. 8, 1936

Lill, J. C. (S. Aust.) b Dec. 7, 1933

*Lillee, D. K. (W. Aust., Tas. & Northants; *CY 1973*) b July 18, 1949

*Lilley, A. A. (Warwicks.; *CY 1897*) b Nov. 28, 1866, d Nov. 17, 1929

Lilley, A. W. (Essex) b May 8, 1959

Lilley, B. (Notts.) b Feb. 11, 1895, d Aug. 4, 1950

Lillywhite, Fred (Sussex; Editor of *Lillywhite's Guide to Cricketers*) b July 23, 1829, d Sept. 15, 1866

Lillywhite, F. W. ("William") (Sussex) b June 13, 1792, d Aug. 21, 1854

*Lillywhite, James, jun. (Sussex) b Feb. 23, 1842, d Oct. 25, 1929

*Lindsay, D. T. (NE Tvl, N. Tvl & Tvl) b Sept 4, 1939

*Lindsay, J. D. (Tvl & NE Tvl) b Sept. 8, 1909, d Aug. 31, 1990

*Lindsay, N. V. (Tvl & OFS) b July 30, 1886, d Feb. 2, 1976

*Lindwall, R. R. (NSW & Qld; *CY 1949*) b Oct. 3, 1921

*Ling, W. V. S. (Griq. W. & E. Prov.) b Oct. 3, 1891, d Sept. 26, 1960

*Lissette, A. F. (Auck. & N. Dist.) b Nov. 6, 1919, d Jan. 24, 1973

Lister, J. (Yorks. & Worcs.) b May 14, 1930, d Jan. 28, 1991

Lister, W. H. L. (Lancs.) b Oct. 7, 1911

Livingston, L. (NSW & Northants) b May 3, 1920

Livingstone, D. A. (Hants) b Sept. 21, 1933, d Sept. 8, 1988

*Llewellyn, C. B. (Natal & Hants; *CY 1911*) b Sept. 26, 1876, d June 7, 1964

Llewellyn, M. J. (Glam.) b Nov. 27, 1953

Lloyd, B. J. (Glam.) b Sept. 6, 1953

*Lloyd, C. H. (†Guyana & Lancs.; *CY 1971*) b Aug. 31, 1944

*Lloyd, D. (Lancs.) b March 18, 1947

Lloyd, G. D. (Lancs.) b July 1, 1969

*Lloyd, T. A. (Warwicks. & OFS) b Nov. 5, 1956

Lloyds, J. W. (Som., OFS & Glos.) b Nov. 17, 1954

*Loader, P. J. (Surrey and W. Aust.; *CY 1958*) b Oct. 25, 1929

Lobb, B. (Warwicks. & Som.) b Jan. 11, 1931

*Lock, G. A. R. (Surrey, Leics. & W. Aust.; *CY 1954*) b July 5, 1929

Lockwood, Ephraim (Yorks.) b April 4, 1845, d Dec. 19, 1921

*Lockwood, W. H. (Notts. & Surrey; *CY 1899*) b March 25, 1868, d April 26, 1932

Lockyer, T. (Surrey & All-England) b Nov. 1, 1826, d Dec. 22, 1869

*Logan, J. D. (SA) b June 24, 1880, d Jan. 3, 1960

*Logie, A. L. (T/T) b Sept. 28, 1960

*Lohmann, G. A. (Surrey, W. Prov. & Tvl; *CY 1889*) b June 2, 1865, d Dec. 1, 1901

Lomax, J. G. (Lancs. & Som.) b May 5, 1925

Long, A. (Surrey & Sussex) b Dec. 18, 1940

Lord, G. J. (Warwicks. & Worcs.) b April 25, 1961

Lord, Thomas (Middx; founder of Lord's) b Nov. 23, 1755, d Jan. 13, 1832

*Love, H. S. B. (NSW & Vic.) b Aug. 10, 1895, d July 22, 1969

Love, J. D. (Yorks.) b April 22, 1955

Lowndes, W. G. L. F. (OUCC & Hants) b Jan. 24, 1898, d May 23, 1982

*Lowry, T. C. (Wgtn, CUCC & Som.) b Feb. 17, 1898, d July 20, 1976

*Lowson, F. A. (Yorks.) b July 1, 1925, d Sept. 8, 1984

Loxton, S. J. E. (Vic.) b March 29, 1921

*Lucas, A. P. (CUCC, Surrey, Middx & Essex) b Feb. 20, 1857, d Oct. 12, 1923

Luckes, W. T. (Som.) b Jan. 1, 1901, d Oct. 27, 1982

*Luckhurst, B. W. (Kent; *CY 1971*) b Feb. 5, 1939

Lumb, R. G. (Yorks.) b Feb. 27, 1950

*Lundie, E. B. (E. Prov., W. Prov. & Tvl) b March 15, 1888, d Sept. 12, 1917

Lynch, M. A. (Surrey & Guyana) b May 21, 1958

Lyon, B. H. (OUCC & Glos.; *CY 1931*) b Jan. 19, 1902, d June 22, 1970

Lyon, J. (Lancs.) b May 17, 1951

Lyon, M. D. (CUCC & Som.) b April 22, 1898, d Feb. 17, 1964

*Lyons, J. J. (S. Aust.) b May 21, 1863, d July 21, 1927

Lyons, K. J. (Glam.) b Dec. 18, 1946

*Lyttelton, Rt Hon. Alfred (CUCC & Middx; Pres. MCC 1898) b Feb. 7, 1857, d July 5, 1913

Lyttelton, Rt Rev. Hon. A. T. (MCC) b Jan. 7, 1852, d Feb. 19, 1903

Lyttelton, Rev. Hon. C. F. (CUCC & Worcs.) b Jan. 26, 1887, d Oct. 3, 1931

Lyttelton, Hon. C. G. (CUCC) b Oct. 27, 1842, d June 9, 1922

Lyttelton, Hon. C. J. (*see* 10th Visct Cobham)

Lyttelton, Rev. Hon. E. (CUCC & Middx) b July 23, 1855, d Jan. 26, 1942

Lyttelton, Hon. G. W. S. (CUCC) b June 12, 1847, d Dec. 5, 1913

Lyttelton, Hon. R. H. (MCC) b Jan. 18, 1854, d Nov. 7, 1939

*McAlister, P. A. (Vic.) b July 11, 1869, d May 10, 1938

*Macartney, C. G. (NSW & Otago; *CY 1922*) b June 27, 1886, d Sept. 9, 1958

*Macaulay, G. G. (Yorks.; *CY 1924*) b Dec. 7, 1897, d Dec. 13, 1940

*Macaulay, M. J. (Tvl, W. Prov., OFS, NE Tvl & E. Prov.) b April 19, 1939

*MacBryan, J. C. W. (CUCC & Som.; *CY 1925*) b July 22, 1892, d July 14, 1983

*McCabe, S. J. (NSW; *CY 1935*) b July 16, 1910, d Aug. 25, 1968

McCanlis, M. A. (OUCC, Surrey & Glos.) b June 17, 1906, d Sept. 27, 1991

*McCarthy, C. N. (Natal & CUCC) b March 24, 1929

*McConnon, J. E. (Glam.) b June 21, 1922

*McCool, C. L. (NSW, Qld & Som.) b Dec. 9, 1915, d April 5, 1986

McCorkell, N. T. (Hants) b March 23, 1912

*McCormick, E. L. (Vic.) b May 16, 1906, d June 28, 1991

*McCosker, R. B. (NSW; *CY 1976*) b Dec. 11, 1946

McCurdy, R. J. (Vic., Derbys., S. Aust. & E. Prov.) b Dec. 30, 1959

*McDermott, C. J. (Qld; *CY 1986*) b April 14, 1965

*McDonald, C. C. (Vic.) b Nov. 17, 1928

*McDonald, E. A. (Tas., Vic. & Lancs.; *CY 1922*) b Jan. 6, 1891, d July 22, 1937

*McDonnell, P. S. (Vic., NSW & Qld) b Nov. 13, 1858, d Sept. 24, 1896

McEvoy, M. S. A. (Essex & Worcs.) b Jan. 25, 1956

McEwan, K. S. (E. Prov., W. Prov., Essex & W. Aust; *CY 1978*) b July 16, 1952

*McEwan, P. E. (Cant.) b Dec. 19, 1953

McEwan, S. M. (Worcs.) b May 5, 1962

McFarlane, L. L. (Northants, Lancs. & Glam.) b Aug. 19, 1952

*McGahey, C. P. (Essex; *CY 1902*) b Feb. 12, 1871, d Jan. 10, 1935

MacGibbon, A. R. (Cant.) b Aug. 28, 1924

*McGirr, H. M. (Wgtn) b Nov. 5, 1891, d April 14, 1964

*McGlew, D. J. (Natal; *CY 1956*) b March 11, 1929

*MacGregor, G. (CUCC & Middx; *CY 1891*) b Aug. 31, 1869, d Aug. 20, 1919

*McGregor, S. N. (Otago) b Dec. 18, 1931

McHugh, F. P. (Yorks. & Glos.) b Nov. 15, 1925

*McIlwraith, J. (Vic.) b Sept. 7, 1857, d July 5, 1938

Macindoe, D. H. (OUCC) b Sept. 1, 1917, d March 3, 1986

*McIntyre, A. J. W. (Surrey; *CY 1958*) b May 14, 1918

McIntyre, J. M. (Auck. & Cant.) b July 4, 1944

*Mackay, K. D. (Qld) b Oct. 24, 1925, d June 13, 1982

McKay-Coghill, D. (Tvl) b Nov. 4, 1941

McKechnie, B. J. (Otago) b Nov. 6, 1953

*McKenzie, G. D. (W. Aust. & Leics.; *CY 1965*) b June 24, 1941

McKenzie, K. A. (NE Tvl & Tvl) b July 16, 1948

*McKibbin, T. R. (NSW) b Dec. 10, 1870, d Dec. 15, 1939

*McKinnon, A. H. (E. Prov. & Tvl) b Aug. 20, 1932, d Dec. 2, 1983

*MacKinnon, F. A. (CUCC & Kent) b April 9, 1848, d Feb. 27, 1947

McLachlan, I. M. (CUCC & S. Aust.) b Oct. 2, 1936

*MacLaren, A. C. (Lancs.; *CY 1895*) b Dec. 1, 1871, d Nov. 17, 1944

*McLaren, J. W. (Qld) b Dec. 24, 1887, d Nov. 17, 1921

*Maclean, J. A. (Qld) b April 27, 1946

Maclean, J. F. (Worcs. & Glos.) b March 1, 1901, d March 9, 1986

*McLean, R. A. (Natal; *CY 1961*) b July 9, 1930
MacLeay, K. H. (W. Aust. & Som.) b April 2, 1959
*McLeod, C. E. (Vic.) b Oct. 24, 1869, d Nov. 26, 1918
*McLeod, E. G. (Auck. & Wgtn) b Oct. 14, 1900, d Sept. 14, 1989
*McLeod, R. W. (Vic.) b Jan. 19, 1868, d June 14, 1907
McMahon, J. W. (Surrey & Som.) b Dec. 28, 1919
*McMahon, T. G. (Wgtn) b Nov. 8, 1929
*McMaster, J. E. P. (Eng.) b March 16, 1861, d June 7, 1929
McMillan, B. M. (Tvl, W. Prov. & Warwicks.) b Dec. 22, 1963
*McMillan, Q. (Tvl) b June 23, 1904, d July 3, 1948
*McMorris, E. D. A. (Jam.) b April 4, 1935
*McRae, D. A. N. (Cant.) b Dec. 25, 1912
*McShane, P. G. (Vic.) b 1857, d Dec. 11, 1903
McSweeney, E. B. (C. Dist. & Wgtn) b March 8, 1957
McVicker, N. M. (Warwicks. & Leics.) b Nov. 4, 1940
*McWatt, C. A. (BG) b Feb. 1, 1922
*Madan Lal (Punjab & Delhi) b March 20, 1951
*Maddocks, L. V. (Vic. & Tas.) b May 24, 1926
Madray, I. S. (BG) b July 2, 1934
*Madugalle, R. S. (NCC) b April 22, 1959
*Madurasinghe, A. W. R. (SL) b Jan. 30, 1961
*Maguire, J. N. (Qld, E. Prov. & Leics.) b Sept. 15, 1956
*Mahanama, R. S. (CCC) b May 31, 1966
Maher, B. J. M. (Derbys.) b Feb. 11, 1958
*Mahmood Hussain (Pak. Us, Punjab, Kar., E. Pak. & NTB) b April 2, 1932, d Dec. 25, 1991
*Mailey, A. A. (NSW) b Jan. 3, 1886, d Dec. 31, 1967
*Majid Khan (Lahore, Pak. Us, CUCC, Glam., PIA, Qld & Punjab; *CY 1970*) b Sept. 28, 1946
*Maka, E. S. (Bombay) b March 5, 1922
*Makepeace, J. W. H. (Lancs.) b Aug. 22, 1881, d Dec. 19, 1952
*Malcolm, D. E. (Derbys.) b Feb. 22, 1963
*Malhotra, A. (Haryana & Bengal) b Jan. 26, 1957
Mallender, N. A. (Northants, Otago & Som.) b Aug. 13, 1961
*Mallett, A. A. (S. Aust.) b July 13, 1945
Mallett, A. W. H. (OUCC & Kent) b Aug. 29, 1924
*Malone, M. F. (W. Aust. & Lancs.) b Oct. 9, 1950
Malone, S. J. (Essex, Hants & Glam.) b Oct. 19, 1953

*Maninder Singh (Delhi) b June 13, 1965
*Manjrekar, S. V. (Bombay) b July 12, 1965
*Manjrekar, V. L. (Bombay, Bengal, Andhra, U. Pradesh, Raja. & M'tra) b Sept. 26, 1931, d Oct. 18, 1983
*Mankad, A. V. (Bombay) b Oct. 12, 1946
*Mankad, V. (M. H.) (W. Ind., Naw., M'tra, Guj., Bengal, Bombay & Raja.; *CY 1947*) b April 12, 1917, d Aug. 21, 1978
*Mann, A. L. (W. Aust.) b Nov. 8, 1945
*Mann, F. G. (CUCC & Middx; Pres. MCC 1984-85) b Sept. 6, 1917
*Mann, F. T. (CUCC & Middx) b March 3, 1888, d Oct. 6, 1964
Mann, J. P. (Middx) b June 13, 1919
*Mann, N. B. F. (Natal & E. Prov.) b Dec. 28, 1920, d July 31, 1952
Manning, J. S. (S. Aust. & Northants) b June 11, 1924, d May 5, 1988
*Mansell, P. N. F. (Rhod.) b March 16, 1920
*Mansoor Akhtar (Kar., UBL & Sind) b Dec. 25, 1956
Mansoor Rana (ADBP) b Dec. 27, 1962
*Mantri, M. K. (Bombay & M'tra) b Sept. 1, 1921
*Manzoor Elahi (Multan, Pak. Rlwys & IDBP) b April 15, 1963
*Maqsood Ahmed (S. Punjab, R'pindi & Kar.) b March 26, 1925
Maqsood Rana (Lahore) b Aug. 1, 1972
*Marais, G. G. ("G. Gladstone") (Jam.) b Jan. 14, 1901, d May 19, 1978
Marie, G. V. (OUCC) b Feb. 17, 1945
*Markham, L. A. (Natal) b Sept. 12, 1924
*Marks, V. J. (OUCC, Som. & W. Aust.) b June 25, 1955
Marlar, R. G. (CUCC & Sussex) b Jan. 2, 1931
Marner, P. T. (Lancs. & Leics.) b March 31, 1936
*Marr, A. P. (NSW) b March 28, 1862, d March 15, 1940
*Marriott, C. S. (CUCC, Lancs. & Kent) b Sept. 14, 1895, d Oct. 13, 1966
Marsden, Tom (Eng.) b 1805, d Feb. 27, 1843
Marsh, F. E. (Derbys.) b July 7, 1920
*Marsh, G. R. (W. Aust.) b Dec. 31, 1958
*Marsh, R. W. (W. Aust.; *CY 1982*) b Nov. 4, 1947
Marsh, S. A. (Kent) b Jan. 27, 1961
Marshal, Alan (Qld & Surrey; *CY 1909*) b June 12, 1883, d July 23, 1915
Marshall, J. M. A. (Warwicks.) b Oct. 26, 1916
*Marshall, M. D. (B'dos & Hants; *CY 1983*) b April 18, 1958
*Marshall, N. E. (B'dos & T/T) b Feb. 27, 1924
*Marshall, R. E. (B'dos & Hants; *CY 1959*) b April 25, 1930
Martin, E. J. (Notts.) b Aug. 17, 1925

*Martin, F. (Kent; *CY 1892*) b Oct. 12, 1861, d Dec. 13, 1921

*Martin, F. R. (Jam.) b Oct. 12, 1893, d Nov. 23, 1967

Martin, J. D. (OUCC & Som.) b Dec. 23, 1941

*Martin, J. W. (NSW & S. Aust.) b July 28, 1931

*Martin, J. W. (Kent) b Feb. 16, 1917, d Jan. 4, 1987

Martin, P. J. (Lancs.) b Nov. 15, 1968

Martin, S. H. (Worcs., Natal & Rhod.) b Jan. 11, 1909, d Feb. 1988

Martindale, D. J. R. (Notts.) b Dec 13, 1963

*Martindale, E. A. (B'dos) b Nov. 25, 1909, d March 17, 1972

Maru, R. J. (Middx & Hants) b Oct. 28, 1962

Marx, W. F. E. (Tvl) b July 4, 1895, d June 2, 1974

*Mason, J. R. (Kent; *CY 1898*) b March 26, 1874, d Oct. 15, 1958

*Masood Anwar (UBL) b Dec. 12, 1967

Masood Iqbal (Lahore, Punjab U., Pak. Us & HBL) b April 17, 1952

*Massie, H. H. (NSW) b April 11, 1854, d Oct. 12, 1938

*Massie, R. A. L. (W. Aust.; *CY 1973*) b April 14, 1947

*Matheson, A. M. (Auck.) b Feb. 27, 1906, d Dec. 31, 1985

*Mathias, Wallis (Sind, Kar. & NBP) b Feb. 4, 1935

*Matthews, A. D. G. (Northants & Glam.) b May 3, 1904, d July 29, 1977

*Matthews, C. D. (W. Aust. & Lancs.) b Sept. 22, 1962

Matthews, C. S. (Notts.) b Oct. 17, 1929

*Matthews, G. R. J. (NSW) b Dec. 15, 1959

*Matthews, T. J. (Vic.) b April 3, 1884, d Oct. 14, 1943

Mattis, E. H. (Jam.) b April 11, 1957

*May, P. B. H. (CUCC & Surrey; *CY 1952*; Pres. MCC 1980-81) b Dec. 31, 1929

*May, T. B. A. (S. Aust.) b Jan. 26, 1962

Mayer, J. H. (Warwicks.) b March 2, 1902, d Sept. 6, 1981

Mayes, R. (Kent) b Oct. 7, 1921

*Maynard, C. (Warwicks. & Lancs.) b April 8, 1958

*Maynard, M. P. (Glam. & N. Dist.) b March 21, 1966

*Mayne, E. R. (S. Aust. & Vic.) b July 2, 1882, d Oct. 26, 1961

*Mayne, L. C. (W. Aust.) b Jan. 23, 1942

*Mead, C. P. (Hants; *CY 1912*) b March 9, 1887, d March 26, 1958

*Mead, W. (Essex; *CY 1904*) b March 25, 1868, d March 18, 1954

Meads, E. A. (Notts.) b Aug. 17, 1916

*Meale, T. (Wgtn) b Nov. 11, 1928

*Meckiff, I. (Vic.) b Jan. 6, 1935

Medlycott, K. T. (Surrey & N. Tvl) b May 12, 1965

*Meher-Homji, K. R. (W. Ind. & Bombay) b Aug. 9, 1911, d Feb. 10, 1982

*Mehra, V. L. (E. Punjab, Ind. Rlwys & Delhi) b March 12, 1938

Meintjes, D. J. (Tvl) b June 9, 1890, d July 17, 1979

*Melle, M. G. (Tvl & W. Prov.) b June 3, 1930

Melluish, M. E. L. (CUCC & Middx; Pres. MCC 1991-92) b June 13, 1932

*Melville, A. (OUCC, Sussex, Natal & Tvl; *CY 1948*) b May 19, 1910, d April 18, 1983

Mence, M. D. (Warwicks. & Glos.) b April 13, 1944

Mendis, G. D. (Sussex & Lancs.) b April 20, 1955

*Mendis, L. R. D. (SSC) b Aug. 25, 1952

*Mendonca, I. L. (BG) b July 13, 1934

Mercer, J. (Sussex, Glam. & Northants; *CY 1927*) b April 22, 1895, d Aug. 31, 1987

*Merchant, V. M. (Bombay; *CY 1937*) b Oct. 12, 1911, d Oct. 27, 1987

Merrick, T. A. (Leewards, Warwicks. & Kent) b June 10, 1963

*Merritt, W. E. (Cant. & Northants) b Aug. 18, 1908, d June 9, 1977

*Merry, C. A. (T/T) b Jan. 20, 1911, d April 19, 1964

Metcalfe, A. A. (Yorks. & OFS) b Dec. 25, 1963

Metson, C. P. (Middx & Glam.) b July 2, 1963

*Meuleman, K. D. (Vic. & W. Aust.) b Sept. 5, 1923

Meuli, E. M. (C. Dist.) b Feb. 20, 1926

Meyer, B. J. (Glos.; Umpire) b Aug. 21, 1932

Meyer, R. J. O. (CUCC, Som. & W. Ind.) b March 15, 1905, d March 9, 1991

Mian Mohammad Saaed (N. Ind. Patiala & S. Punjab; Pak.'s first captain) b Aug. 31, 1910, d Aug. 23, 1979

*Middleton, J. (W. Prov.) b Sept. 30, 1865, d Dec. 23, 1913

Middleton, T. C. (Hants) b Feb. 1, 1964

**Midwinter, W. E. (Vic. & Glos.) b June 19, 1851, d Dec. 3, 1890

Milburn, B. D. (Otago) b Nov. 24, 1943

*Milburn, C. (Northants & W. Aust.; *CY 1967*) b Oct. 23, 1941, d Feb. 28, 1990

*Milkha Singh, A. G. (Madras) b Dec. 31, 1941

Miller, A. J. T. (OUCC & Middx) b May 30, 1963

*Miller, A. M. (Eng.) b Oct. 19, 1869, d June 26, 1959

*Miller, G. (Derbys., Natal & Essex) b Sept. 8, 1952

*Miller, K. R. (Vic., NSW & Notts.; *CY 1954*) b Nov. 28, 1919

*Miller, L. S. M. (C. Dist. & Wgtn) b March 31, 1923

Miller, R. (Warwicks.) b Jan. 6, 1941

*Miller, R. C. (Jam.) b Dec. 24, 1924

*Milligan, F. W. (Yorks.) b March 19, 1870, d March 31, 1900

*Millman, G. (Notts.) b Oct. 2, 1934

Millmow, J. P. (Wgtn) b Sept. 22, 1967

Millns, D. J. (Notts. & Leics.) b Feb. 27, 1965

*Mills, C. H. (Surrey, Kimberley & W. Prov.) b Nov. 26, 1867, d July 26, 1948

*Mills, J. E. (Auck.) b Sept. 3, 1905, d Dec. 11, 1972

Mills, J. M. (CUCC & Warwicks.) b July 27, 1921

Mills, J. P. C. (CUCC & Northants.) b Dec. 6, 1958

Milner, J. (Essex) b Aug. 22, 1937

*Milton, C. A. (Glos.; *CY 1959*) b March 10, 1928

*Milton, W. H. (W. Prov.) b Dec. 3, 1854, d March 6, 1930

*Minnett, R. B. (NSW) b June 13, 1888, d Oct. 21, 1955

"Minshull", John (scorer of first recorded century) b *circa* 1741, d Oct. 1793

*Miran Bux (Pak. Serv., Punjab & R'pindi) b April 20, 1907, d Feb. 8, 1991

*Misson, F. M. (NSW) b Nov. 19, 1938

*Mitchell, A. (Yorks.) b Sept. 13, 1902, d Dec. 25, 1976

*Mitchell, B. (Tvl; *CY 1936*) b Jan. 8, 1909

Mitchell, C. G. (Som.) b Jan. 27, 1929

**Mitchell, F. (CUCC, Yorks. & Tvl; *CY 1902*) b Aug. 13, 1872, d Oct. 11, 1935

*Mitchell, T. B. (Derbys.) b Sept. 4, 1902

*Mitchell-Innes, N. S. (OUCC & Som.) b Sept. 7, 1914

Mobey, G. S. (Surrey) b March 5, 1904, d March 2, 1979

Modi, R. S. (Bombay) b Nov. 11, 1924

*Mohammad Aslam (N. Ind. & Pak. Rlwys) b Jan. 5, 1920

*Mohammad Farooq (Kar.) b April 8, 1938

*Mohammad Ilyas (Lahore & PIA) b March 19, 1946

*Mohammad Munaf (Sind, E. Pak., Kar. & PIA) b Nov. 2, 1935

*Mohammad Nazir (Pak. Rlwys) b March 8, 1946

*Mohsin Kamal (Lahore, Allied Bank & PNSC) b June 16, 1963

*Mohsin Khan (Pak. Rlwys, Kar., Sind., Pak. Us & HBL) b March 15, 1955

*Moin Khan (Karachi) b Sept. 23, 1971

Moin-ul-Atiq (UBL & Karachi) b Aug. 5, 1964

*Moir, A. McK. (Otago) b July 17, 1919

Moir, D. G. (Derbys. & Scotland) b April 13, 1957

*Mold, A. W. (Lancs.; *CY 1892*) b May 27, 1863, d April 29, 1921

Moles, A. J. (Warwicks. & Griq. W.) b Feb. 12, 1961

*Moloney, D. A. R. (Wgtn, Otago & Cant.) b Aug. 11, 1910, d July 15, 1942

Monckton of Brenchley, 1st Lord (Pres. MCC 1956-57) b Jan. 17, 1891, d Jan. 9, 1965

Mongia, N. R. (Baroda) b Dec. 19, 1969

Monkhouse, G. (Surrey) b April 26, 1954

*Moodie, G. H. (Jam.) b Nov. 25, 1915

*Moody, T. M. (W. Aust., Warwicks. & Worcs.) b Oct. 2, 1965

*Moon, L. J. (CUCC & Middx) b Feb. 9, 1878, d Nov. 23, 1916

*Mooney, F. L. H. (Wgtn) b May 26, 1921

Moore, D. N. (OUCC & Glos.) b Sept. 26, 1910

Moore, H. I. (Notts.) b Feb. 28, 1941

Moore, R. H. (Hants) b Nov. 14, 1913

Moores, P. (Worcs., Sussex & OFS) b Dec. 18, 1962

*More, K. S. (Baroda) b Sept. 4, 1962

Morgan, D. C. (Derbys.) b Feb. 26, 1929

Morgan, M. (Notts.) b May 21, 1936

*Morgan, R. W. (Auck.) b Feb. 12, 1941

*Morkel, D. P. B. (W. Prov.) b Jan. 25, 1906, d Oct. 6, 1980

*Morley, F. (Notts.) b Dec. 16, 1850, d Sept. 28, 1884

Morley, J. D. (Sussex) b Oct. 20, 1950

*Moroney, J. (NSW) b July 24, 1917

*Morris, A. R. (NSW; *CY 1949*) b Jan. 19, 1922

*Morris, H. (Glam.) b Oct. 5, 1963

Morris, H. M. (CUCC & Essex) b April 16, 1898, d Nov. 18, 1984

*Morris, J. E. (Derbys. & Griq. W.) b April 1, 1964

Morris, R. E. (OUCC) b June 8, 1967

*Morris, S. (Vic.) b June 22, 1855, d Sept. 20, 1931

*Morrison, B. D. (Wgtn) b Dec. 17, 1933

*Morrison, D. K. (Auck.) b Feb. 3, 1966

*Morrison, J. F. M. (C. Dist. & Wgtn) b Aug. 27, 1947

Mortensen, O. H. (Denmark & Derbys.) b Jan. 29, 1958

*Mortimore, J. B. (Glos.) b May 14, 1933

Mortlock, W. (Surrey & Utd Eng. XI) b July 18, 1832, d Jan. 23, 1884

*Moseley, E. A. (B'dos, Glam. & E. Prov.) b Jan. 5, 1958

Moseley, H. R. (B'dos & Som.) b May 28, 1948

*Moses, H. (NSW) b Feb. 13, 1858, d Dec. 7, 1938

*Moss, A. E. (Middx) b Nov. 14, 1930

*Moss, J. K. (Vic.) b June 29, 1947

*Motz, R. C. (Cant.; *CY 1966*) b Jan. 12, 1940

Moulding, R. P. (OUCC & Middx) b Jan. 3, 1958

*Moule, W. H. (Vic.) b Jan. 31, 1858, d Aug. 24, 1939

*Moxon, M. D. (Yorks. & Griq. W.) b May 4, 1960

Mudassar Nazar (Lahore, Punjab, Pak. Us, HBL, PIA & UBL) b April 6, 1956

*Muddiah, V. M. (Mysore & Ind. Serv.) b June 8, 1929

Mufasir-ul-Haq (Kar., Dacca, PWD, E. Pak. & NBP) b Aug. 16, 1944, d July 27, 1983

Mukherjee, S. P. (Bengal) b Oct. 5, 1964

Mullally, A. D. (W. Aust., Hants & Leics.) b July 12, 1969

Muncer, B. L. (Middx & Glam.) b Oct. 23, 1913, d Jan. 18, 1982

Munden, V. S. (Leics.) b Jan. 2, 1928

*Munir Malik (Punjab, R'pindi, Pak. Serv. & Kar.) b July 10, 1934

Munton, T. A. (Warwicks.) b July 30, 1965

**Murdoch, W. L. (NSW & Sussex) b Oct. 18, 1854, d Feb. 18, 1911

Murphy, A. J. (Lancs. & Surrey) b Aug. 6, 1962

*Murray, A. R. A. (E. Prov.) b April 30, 1922

*Murray, B. A. G. (Wgtn) b Sept. 18, 1940

*Murray, D. A. (B'dos) b Sept. 29, 1950

*Murray, D. L. (T/T, CUCC, Notts. & Warwicks.) b May 20, 1943

*Murray, J. T. (Middx; *CY 1967*) b April 1, 1935

Murray-Willis, P. E. (Worcs. & Northants) b July 14, 1910

Murrell, H. R. (Kent & Middx) b Nov. 19, 1879, d Aug. 15, 1952

Murrills, T. J. (CUCC) b Dec. 22, 1953

*Musgrove, H. (Vic.) b Nov. 27, 1860, d Nov. 2, 1931

*Mushtaq Ahmed (UBL & Multan) b June 28, 1970

*Mushtaq Ali, S. (C. Ind., Guj., †M. Pradesh & U. Pradesh) b Dec. 17, 1914

*Mushtaq Mohammad (Kar., Northants & PIA; *CY 1963*) b Nov. 22, 1943

Mynn, Alfred (Kent & All-Eng.) b Jan. 19, 1807, d Oct. 31, 1861

*Nadkarni, R. G. (M'tra & Bombay) b April 4, 1932

*Nadeem Abbasi (R'pindi) b April 15, 1964

*Nadeem Ghauri (HBL) b Oct 12, 1962

Naeem Ahmed (Kar., Pak. Us, NBP, UBL & PIA) b Sept. 20, 1952

Naeem Ahmed (Sargodha) b April 14, 1971

*Nagel, L. E. (Vic.) b March 6, 1905, d Nov. 23, 1971

*Naik, S. S. (Bombay) b Feb. 21, 1945

*Nanan, R. (T/T) b May 29, 1953

*Naoomal Jaoomal, M. (N. Ind. & Sind) b April 17, 1904, d July 18, 1980

*Narasimha Rao, M. V. (H'bad) b Aug. 11, 1954

Naseer Malik (Khairpair & NBP) b Feb. 1, 1950

Nash, J. E. (S. Aust.) b April 16, 1950

*Nash, L. J. (Tas. & Vic.) b May 2, 1910, d July 24, 1986

Nash, M. A. (Glam.) b May 9, 1945

*Nasim-ul-Ghani (Kar., Pak. Us, Dacca, E. Pak., PWD & NBP) b May 14, 1941

*Naushad Ali (Kar., E. Pak., R'pindi, Peshawar, NWFP, Punjab & Pak. Serv.) b Oct. 1, 1943

*Naved Anjum (Lahore, UBL & HBL) b July 27, 1963

*Navle, J. G. (Rajputna, C. Ind., Holkar & Gwalior) b Dec. 7, 1902, d Sept. 7, 1979

*Nayak, S. V. (Bombay) b Oct. 20, 1954

*Nayudu, Col. C. K. (C. Ind., Andhra, U. Pradesh & Holkar; *CY 1933*) b Oct. 31, 1895, d Nov. 14, 1967

*Nayudu, C. S. (C. Ind., Holkar, Baroda, Bengal, Andhra & U. Pradesh) b April 18, 1914

*Nazar Mohammad (N. Ind. & Punjab) b March 5, 1921

*Nazir Ali, S. (S. Punjab & Sussex) b June 8, 1906, d Feb. 18, 1975

Neale, P. A. (Worcs.; *CY 1989*) b June 5, 1954

*Neblett, J. M. (B'dos & BG) b Nov. 13, 1901, d March 28, 1959

Needham, A. (Surrey & Middx) b March 23, 1957

*Nel, J. D. (W. Prov.) b July 10, 1928

Nevell, W. T. (Middx, Surrey & Northants) b June 13, 1916

*Newberry, C. (Tvl) b 1889, d Aug. 1, 1916

Newell, M. (Notts.) b Feb. 25, 1965

*Newham, W. (Sussex) b Dec 12, 1860, d June 26, 1944

Newland, Richard (Sussex) b *circa* 1718, d May 29, 1791

Newman, G. C. (OUCC & Middx) b April 26, 1904, d Oct. 13, 1982

*Newman, Sir J. (Wgtn & Cant.) b July 3, 1902

Newman, J. A. (Hants & Cant.) b Nov. 12, 1884, d Dec. 21, 1973

Newman, P. G. (Derbys.) b Jan. 10, 1959

*Newport, P. J. (Worcs. & Boland) b Oct. 11, 1962

*Newson, E. S. (Tvl & Rhod.) b Dec. 2, 1910, d April 24, 1988

Newstead, J. T. (Yorks.; *CY 1909*) b Sept. 8, 1877, d March 25, 1952

*Niaz Ahmed (Dacca, PWD, E. Pak. & Pak. Rlwys) b Nov. 11, 1945

Nicholas, M. C. J. (Hants) b Sept. 29, 1957

Nicholls, D. (Kent) b Dec. 8, 1943

Nicholls, R. B. (Glos.) b Dec. 4, 1933

*Nichols, M. S. (Essex; *CY 1934*) b Oct. 6, 1900, d Jan. 26, 1961

Nicholson, A. G. (Yorks.) b June 25, 1938, d Nov. 4, 1985

*Nicholson, F. (OFS) b Sept. 17, 1909, d July 30, 1982

*Nicolson, J. F. W. (Natal & OUCC) b July 19, 1899, d Dec. 13, 1935

*Nissar, Mahomed (Patiala, S. Punjab & U. Pradesh) b Aug. 1, 1910, d March 11, 1963

*Nitschke, H. C. (S. Aust.) b April 14, 1905, d Sept. 29, 1982

*Noble, M. A. (NSW; *CY 1900*) b Jan. 28, 1873, d June 22, 1940

*Noblet, G. (S. Aust.) b Sept. 14, 1916

*Noreiga, J. M. (T/T) b April 15, 1936

Norfolk, 16th Duke of (Pres. MCC 1957-58) b May 30, 1908, d Jan. 31, 1975

Norman, M. E. J. C. (Northants & Leics.) b Jan. 19, 1933

*Norton, N. O. (W. Prov. & Border) b May 11, 1881, d June 27, 1968

*Nothling, O. E. (NSW & Qld) b Aug. 1, 1900, d Sept. 26, 1965

*Nourse, A. D. ("Dudley") (Natal; *CY 1948*) b Nov. 12, 1910, d Aug. 14, 1981

*Nourse, A. W. ("Dave") (Natal, Tvl & W. Prov.) b Jan. 26, 1878, d July 8, 1948

Nugent, 1st Lord (Pres. MCC 1962-63) b Aug. 11, 1895, d April 27, 1973

*Nunes, R. K. (Jam.) b June 7, 1894, d July 22, 1958

*Nupen, E. P. (Tvl) b Jan. 1, 1902, d Jan. 29, 1977

*Nurse, S. M. (B'dos; *CY 1967*) b Nov. 10, 1933

Nutter, A. E. (Lancs. & Northants) b June 28, 1913

*Nyalchand, S. (W. Ind., Kathiawar, Guj. & S'tra) b Sept. 14, 1919

Nye, J. K. (Sussex) b May 23, 1914

Nyren, John (Hants) b Dec. 15, 1764, d June 28, 1837

Nyren, Richard (Hants & Sussex) b 1734, d April 25, 1797

Oakes, C. (Sussex) b Aug. 10, 1912

Oakes, J. (Sussex) b March 3, 1916

*Oakman, A. S. M. (Sussex) b April 20, 1930

Oates, T. W. (Notts.) b Aug. 9, 1875, d June 18, 1949

Oates, W. F. (Yorks. & Derbys.) b June 11, 1929

O'Brien, F. P. (Cant. & Northants) b Feb. 11, 1911, d Oct. 22, 1991

*O'Brien, L. P. (Vic.) b July 2, 1907

*O'Brien, Sir T. C. (OUCC & Middx) b Nov. 5, 1861, d Dec. 9, 1948

*Ochse, A. E. (Tvl) b March 11, 1870, d April 11, 1918

*Ochse, A. L. (E. Prov.) b Oct. 11, 1899, d May 6, 1949

*O'Connor, J. (Essex) b Nov. 6, 1897, d Feb. 22, 1977

*O'Connor, J. D. A. (NSW & S. Aust.) b Sept. 9, 1875, d Aug. 23, 1941

Odendaal, A. (CUCC & Boland) b May 4, 1954

*O'Donnell, S. P. (Vic.) b Jan. 26, 1963

*Ogilvie, A. D. (Qld) b June 3, 1951

O'Gorman, T. J. G. (Derbys.) b May 15, 1967

*O'Keeffe, K. J. (NSW & Som.) b Nov. 25, 1949

*Old, C. M. (Yorks., Warwicks. & N. Tvl; *CY 1979*) b Dec. 22, 1948

*Oldfield, N. (Lancs. & Northants) b April 30, 1911

*Oldfield, W. A. (NSW; *CY 1927*) b Sept. 9, 1894, d Aug. 10, 1976

Oldham, S. (Yorks. & Derbys.) b July 26, 1948

*Oldroyd, E. (Yorks.) b Oct. 1, 1888, d Dec. 27, 1964

*O'Linn, S. (Kent, W. Prov. & Tvl) b May 5, 1927

Oliver, P. R. (Warwicks.) b May 9, 1956

O'Neill, M. D. (NSW) b March 5, 1959

*O'Neill, N. C. (NSW; *CY 1962*) b Feb. 19, 1937

Ontong, R. C. (Border, Tvl, N. Tvl & Glam.) b Sept. 9, 1955

Opatha, A. R. M. (SL) b Aug. 5, 1947

Ord, J. S. (Warwicks.) b July 12, 1912

*O'Reilly, W. J. (NSW; *CY 1935*) b Dec. 20, 1905

O'Riordan, A. J. (Ireland) b July 20, 1940

Ormrod, J. A. (Worcs. & Lancs.) b Dec. 22, 1942

O'Shaughnessy, S. J. (Lancs. & Worcs.) b Sept. 9, 1961

Oslear, D. O. (Umpire) b March 3, 1929

Ostler, D. P. (Warwicks.) b July 15, 1970

*O'Sullivan, D. R. (C. Dist. & Hants) b Nov. 16, 1944

Outschoorn, L. (Worcs.) b Sept. 26, 1918

*Overton, G. W. F. (Otago) b June 8, 1919

*Owen-Smith, H. G. O. (W. Prov., OUCC & Middx; *CY 1930*) b Feb. 18, 1909, d Feb. 28, 1990

Owen-Thomas, D. R. (CUCC & Surrey) b Sept. 20, 1948

*Oxenham, R. K. (Qld) b July 28, 1891, d Aug. 16, 1939

*Padgett, D. E. V. (Yorks.) b July 20, 1934

*Padmore, A. L. (B'dos) b Dec. 17, 1946

Page, H. A. (Tvl & Essex) b July 3, 1962

Page, J. C. T. (Kent) b May 20, 1930, d Dec. 14, 1990

Page, M. H. (Derbys.) b June 17, 1941

*Page, M. L. (Cant.) b May 8, 1902, d Feb. 13, 1987

Pai, A. M. (Bombay) b April 28, 1945

Paine, G. A. E. (Middx & Warwicks.; *CY 1935*) b June 11, 1908, d March 30, 1978

Pairaudeau, B. H. (BG & N. Dist.) b April 14, 1931

*Palairet, L. C. H. (OUCC & Som.; *CY 1893*) b May 27, 1870, d March 27, 1933

Palairet, R. C. N. (OUCC & Som.; Joint-Manager MCC in Australia 1932-33) b June 25, 1871, d Feb. 11, 1955

Palia, P. E. (Madras, U. Prov., Bombay, Mysore & Bengal) b Sept. 5, 1910, d Sept. 9, 1981

*Palm, A. W. (W. Prov.) b June 8, 1901, d Aug. 17, 1966

*Palmer, C. H. (Worcs. & Leics.; Pres. MCC 1978-79) b May 15, 1919

*Palmer, G. E. (Vic. & Tas.) b Feb. 22, 1860, d Aug. 22, 1910

Palmer, G. V. (Som.) b Nov. 1, 1965

*Palmer, K. E. (Som.; Umpire) b April 22, 1937

Palmer, R. (Som.) b July 12, 1942

*Pandit, C. S. (Bombay) b Sept. 30, 1961

Pardon, Charles Frederick (Editor of *Wisden* 1887-90) b March 28, 1850, d April 18, 1890

Pardon, Sydney H. (Editor of *Wisden* 1891-1925) b Sept. 23, 1855, d Nov. 20, 1925

*Parfitt, P. H. (Middx; *CY 1963*) b Dec. 8, 1936

Paris, C. G. A. (Hants; Pres. MCC 1975-76) b Aug. 20, 1911

Parish, R. J. (Aust. Administrator) b May 7, 1916

*Park, R. L. (Vic.) b July 30, 1892, d Jan. 23, 1947

*Parkar, G. A. (Bombay) b Oct. 24, 1955

Parkar, R. D. (Bombay) b Oct. 31, 1946

Parkar, Z. (Bombay) b Nov. 22, 1957

*Parker, C. W. L. (Glos.; *CY 1923*) b Oct. 14, 1882, d July 11, 1959

*Parker, G. M. (SA) b May 27, 1899, d May 1, 1969

Parker, G. W. (CUCC & Glos.) b Feb. 11, 1912

Parker, J. F. (Surrey) b April 23, 1913, d Jan. 27, 1983

*Parker, J. M. (N. Dist. & Worcs.) b Feb. 21, 1951

Parker, J. P. (Hants) b Nov. 29, 1902, d Aug. 9, 1984

*Parker, N. M. (Otago & Cant.) b Aug. 28, 1948

*Parker, P. W. G. (CUCC, Sussex & Natal) b Jan. 15, 1956

Parkhouse, W. G. A. (Glam.) b Oct. 12, 1925

*Parkin, C. H. (Yorks. & Lancs.; *CY 1924*) b Feb. 18, 1886, d June 15, 1943

*Parkin, D. C. (E. Prov., Tvl & Griq. W.) b Feb. 18, 1870, d March 20, 1936

Parks, H. W. (Sussex) b July 18, 1906, d May 7, 1984

*Parks, J. H. (Sussex & Cant.; *CY 1938*) b May 12, 1903, d Nov. 21, 1980

*Parks, J. M. (Sussex & Som.; *CY 1968*) b Oct. 21, 1931

Parks, R. J. (Hants) b June 15, 1959

*Parore, A. C. (Auck.) b Jan. 23, 1971

Parr, F. D. (Lancs.) b June 1, 1928

Parr, George (Notts. & All-England) b May 22, 1826, d June 23, 1891

*Parry, D. R. (Comb. Is. & Leewards) b Dec. 22, 1954

*Parsana, D. D. (S'tra, Ind. Rlwys & Guj.) b Dec. 2, 1947

Parsons, A. B. D. (CUCC & Surrey) b Sept. 20, 1933

Parsons, A. E. W. (Auck. & Sussex) b Jan. 9, 1949

Parsons, G. J. (Leics., Warwicks., Boland, Griq. W. & OFS) b Oct. 17, 1959

Parsons, Canon J. H. (Warwicks.) b May 30, 1890, d Feb. 2, 1981

*Partridge, J. T. (Rhod.) b Dec. 9, 1932, d June 7, 1988

*Partridge, N. E. (Malvern, CUCC & Warwicks.; *CY 1919*) b Aug. 10, 1900, d March 10, 1982

Partridge, R. J. (Northants) b Feb. 11, 1912

Parvez Mir (R'pindi, Lahore, Punjab, Pak. Us, Derbys., HBL & Glam.) b Sept. 24, 1953

*Pascoe, L. S. (NSW) b Feb. 13, 1950

Pasqual, S. P. (SL) b Oct. 15, 1961

Passailaigue, C. C. (Jam.) b Aug. 1902, d Jan. 7, 1972

*Patankar, C. T. (Bombay) b Nov. 24, 1930

*Pataudi, Iftikhar Ali, Nawab of (OUCC, Worcs., Patiala, N. Ind. & S. Punjab; *CY 1932*) b March 16, 1910, d Jan. 5, 1952

*Pataudi, Mansur Ali, Nawab of (Sussex, OUCC, Delhi & H'bad; *CY 1968*) b Jan. 5, 1941

Patel, A. (S'tra) b March 6, 1957

*Patel, B. P. (Karn.) b Nov. 24, 1952

*Patel, D. N. (Worcs. & Auck.) b Oct. 25, 1958

*Patel, J. M. (Guj.) b Nov. 26, 1924

*Patel, R. (Baroda) b June 1, 1964

Pathmanathan, G. (OUCC, CUCC & SL) b Jan. 23, 1954

*Patiala, Maharaja of (N. Ind., Patiala & S. Punjab) b Jan. 17, 1913, d June 17, 1974

*Patil, S. M. (Bombay & M. Pradesh) b Aug. 18, 1956

*Patil, S. R. (M'tra) b Oct. 10, 1933

*Patterson, B. P. (Jam., Tas. & Lancs.) b Sept. 15, 1961

Pauline, D. B. (Surrey & Glam.) b Dec. 15, 1960

Pawson, A. G. (OUCC & Worcs.) b May 30, 1888, d Feb. 25, 1986

Pawson, H. A. (OUCC & Kent) b Aug. 22, 1921

Payn, L. W. (Natal) b May 6, 1915

*Payne, T. R. O. (B'dos) b Feb. 13, 1957

*Paynter, E. (Lancs.; *CY 1938*) b Nov. 5, 1901, d Feb. 5, 1979

Payton, W. R. D. (Notts.) b Feb. 13, 1882, d May 2, 1943

Pearce, G. (Sussex) b Oct. 27, 1908, d June 16, 1986

Pearce, T. A. (Kent) b Dec. 18, 1910, d Aug. 11, 1982

Pearce, T. N. (Essex) b Nov. 3, 1905

*Pearse, C. O. C. (Natal) b Oct. 10, 1884, d May 7, 1953

Pearson, D. B. (Worcs.) b March 29, 1937

*Peate, E. (Yorks.) b March 2, 1856, d March 11, 1900

Peck, I. G. (CUCC & Northants) b Oct. 18, 1957

*Peebles, I. A. R. (OUCC, Middx & Scotland; *CY 1931*) b Jan. 20, 1908, d Feb. 28, 1980

*Peel, R. (Yorks.; *CY 1889*) b Feb. 12, 1857, d Aug. 12, 1941

*Pegler, S. J. (Tvl) b July 28, 1888, d Sept. 10, 1972

*Pellew, C. E. (S. Aust.) b Sept. 21, 1893, d May 9, 1981

Penn, C. (Kent) b June 19, 1963

Penn, F. (Kent) b March 7, 1851, d Dec. 26, 1916

Pepper, C. G. (NSW and Aust. Serv.; Umpire) b Sept. 15, 1918

Perera, K. G. (Mor.) b May 22, 1964

Perkins, C. G. (Northants) b June 4, 1911

Perkins, H. (CUCC & Cambs.; Sec. MCC 1876-97) b Dec. 10, 1832, d May 6, 1916

*Perks, R. T. D. (Worcs.) b Oct. 4, 1911, d Nov. 22, 1977

Perrin, P. A. (Essex; *CY 1905*) b May 26, 1876, d Nov. 20, 1945

Perryman, S. P. (Warwicks. & Worcs.) b Oct. 22, 1955

*Pervez Sajjad (Lahore, PIA & Kar.) b Aug. 30, 1942

*Petherick, P. J. (Otago & Wgtn) b Sept. 25, 1942

Petrie, E. C. (Auck. & N. Dist.) b May 22, 1927

Petrie, R. G. (Cant.) b Aug. 23, 1967

*Phadkar, D. G. (M'tra, Bombay, Bengal & Ind. Rlwys) b Dec. 10, 1925, d March 17, 1985

Phebey, A. H. (Kent) b Oct. 1, 1924

Phelan, P. J. (Essex) b Feb. 9, 1938

*Philipson, H. (OUCC & Middx) b June 8, 1866, d Dec. 4, 1935

*Phillip, N. (Comb. Is., Windwards & Essex) b June 12, 1948

Phillips, R. B. (NSW & Qld) b May 23, 1954

*Phillips, W. B. (S. Aust.) b March 1, 1958

Phillipson, C. P. (Sussex) b Feb. 10, 1952

Phillipson, W. E. (Lancs.) b Dec. 3, 1910, d Aug. 24, 1991

*Philpott, P. I. (NSW) b March 21, 1934

Piachaud, J. D. (OUCC, Hants & Ceylon) b March 1, 1937

Pick, R. A. (Notts. & Wgtn) b Nov. 19, 1963

Pickles, C. S. (Yorks.) b Jan. 30, 1966

Pickles, L. (Som.) b Sept. 17, 1932

Pienaar, R. F. (Tvl, W. Prov., N. Tvl & Kent) b July 17, 1961

Pieris, H. S. M. (SL) b Feb. 16, 1946

*Pierre, L. R. (T/T) b June 5, 1921, d April 14, 1989

Pierson, A. R. K. (Warwicks.) b July 21, 1963

*Pigott, A. C. S. (Sussex & Wgtn) b June 4, 1958

Pilch, Fuller (Norfolk & Kent) b March 17, 1804, d May 1, 1870

Pilling, H. (Lancs.) b Feb. 23, 1943

*Pilling, R. (Lancs.; *CY 1891*) b July 5, 1855, d March 28, 1891

*Pithey, A. J. (Rhod. & W. Prov.) b July 17, 1933

*Pithey, D. B. (Rhod., OUCC, Northants, W. Prov., Natal & Tvl) b Oct. 4, 1936

Pitman, R. W. C. (Hants) b Feb. 21, 1933

*Place, W. (Lancs.) b Dec 7, 1914

Platt, R. K. (Yorks. & Northants) b Dec. 21, 1932

*Playle, W. R. (Auck. & W. Aust.) b Dec. 1, 1938

Pleass, J. E. (Glam.) b May 21, 1923

*Plimsoll, J. B. (W. Prov. & Natal) b Oct. 27, 1917

Pocock, N. E. J. (Hants) b Dec. 15, 1951

*Pocock, P. I. (Surrey & N. Tvl) b Sept. 24, 1946

Pollard, P. R. (Notts.) b Sept. 24, 1968

*Pollard, R. (Lancs.) b June 19, 1912, d Dec. 16, 1985

*Pollard, V. (C. Dist. & Cant.) b Burnley Sept. 7, 1945

Pollock, A. J. (CUCC) b April 19, 1962

*Pollock, P. M. (E. Prov.; *CY 1966*) b June 30, 1941

*Pollock, R. G. (E. Prov. & Tvl; *CY 1966*) b Feb. 27, 1944

*Ponsford, W. H. (Vic.; *CY 1935*) b Oct. 19, 1900, d April 6, 1991

Pont, K. R. (Essex) b Jan. 16, 1953

*Poole, C. J. (Notts.) b March 13, 1921

Pooley, E. (Surrey & first England tour) b Feb. 13, 1838, d July 18, 1907

*Poore, M. B. (Cant.) b June 1, 1930

*Poore, Brig-Gen. R. M. (Hants & SA; *CY 1900*) b March 20, 1866, d July 14, 1938

Pope, A. V. (Derbys.) b Aug. 15, 1909

*Pope, G. H. (Derbys.) b Jan. 27, 1911

*Pope, R. J. (NSW) b Feb. 18, 1864, d July 27, 1952

Popplewell, N. F. M. (CUCC & Som.) b Aug. 8, 1957

Portal of Hungerford, 1st Lord (Pres. MCC 1958-59) b May 21, 1893, d April 22, 1971

Porter, A. (Glam.) b March 25, 1914

Porter, G. D. (W. Aust.) b March 18, 1955

Pothecary, A. E. (Hants) b March 1, 1906, d May 21, 1991

*Pothecary, J. E. (W. Prov.) b Dec. 6, 1933

Potter, G. (Sussex) b Oct. 26, 1931

Potter, J. (Vic.) b April 13, 1938

Potter, L. (Kent, Griq. W., Leics. & OFS) b Nov. 7, 1962

*Pougher, A. D. (Leics.) b April 19, 1865, d May 20, 1926

Pountain, F. R. (Sussex) b April 23, 1941

Powell, A. G. (CUCC & Essex) b Aug. 17, 1912, d June 7, 1982

*Powell, A. W. (Griq. W.) b July 18, 1873, d Sept. 11, 1948

*Prabhakar, M. (Delhi) b April 15, 1963

*Prasanna, E. A. S. (†Karn.) b May 22, 1940

Pratt, R. L. (Leics.) b Nov. 15, 1938

Pressdee, J. S. (Glam. & NE Tvl) b June 19, 1933

Preston, Hubert (Editor of *Wisden* 1944-51) b Dec. 16, 1868, d Aug. 6, 1960

Preston, K. C. (Essex) b Aug. 22, 1925

Preston, Norman (Editor of *Wisden* 1951-80) b March 18, 1903, d March 6, 1980

Pretlove, J. F. (CUCC & Kent) b Nov. 23, 1932

Price, D. G. (CUCC) b Feb. 7, 1965

Price, E. J. (Lancs. & Essex) b Oct. 27, 1918

*Price, J. S. E. (Middx) b July 22, 1937

*Price, W. F. F. (Middx) b April 25, 1902, d Jan. 13, 1969

Prichard, P. J. (Essex) b Jan. 7, 1965

*Prideaux, R. M. (CUCC, Kent, Northants, Sussex & OFS) b July 31, 1939

Pridgeon, A. P. (Worcs.) b Feb. 22, 1954

Priest, M. W. (Cant.) b Aug. 12, 1961

*Prince, C. F. H. (W. Prov., Border & E. Prov.) b Sept. 11, 1874, d March 5, 1948

Pringle, C. (Auck.) b Jan. 26, 1968

*Pringle, D. R. (CUCC & Essex) b Sept. 18, 1958

Pritchard, T. L. (Wgtn, Warwicks. & Kent) b March 10, 1917

*Procter, M. J. (Glos., Natal, W. Prov., Rhod. & OFS; *CY 1970*) b Sept. 15, 1946

Prodger, J. M. (Kent) b Sept. 1, 1935

*Promnitz, H. L. E. (Border, Griq. W. & OFS) b March 23, 1904, d Sept. 7, 1983

Prouton, R. O. (Hants) b March 1, 1926

Puckett, C. W. (W. Aust.) b Feb. 21, 1911

Pugh, C. T. M. (Glos.) b March 13, 1937

Pullan, D. A. (Notts.) b May 1, 1944

*Pullar, G. (Lancs. & Glos.; *CY 1960*) b Aug. 1, 1935

Pullinger, G. R. (Essex) b March 14, 1920, d Aug. 4, 1982

*Puna, N. (N. Dist.) b Oct. 28, 1929

*Punjabi, P. H. (Sind & Guj.) b Sept. 20, 1921

Pycroft, A. J. (Zimb.) b June 6, 1956

Pydanna, M. (Guyana) b Jan. 27, 1950

*Qasim Omar (Kar. & MCB) b Feb. 9, 1957

Quaife, B. W. (Warwicks. & Worcs.) b Nov. 24, 1899, d Nov. 28, 1984

*Quaife, William (W. G.) (Warwicks. & Griq. W.; *CY 1902*) b March 17, 1872, d Oct. 13, 1951

Quick, I. W. (Vic.) b Nov. 5, 1933

*Quinn, N. A. (Griq. W. & Tvl) b Feb. 21, 1908, d Aug. 5, 1934

*Rabone, G. O. (Wgtn & Auck.) b Nov. 6, 1921

*Rackemann, C. G. (Qld) b June 3, 1960

*Radford, N. V. (Lancs., Tvl & Worcs.; *CY 1986*) b June 7, 1957

*Radley, C. T. (Middx; *CY 1979*) b May 13, 1944

Rae, A. F. (Jam.) b Sept. 30, 1922

Raees Mohammad (Kar.) b Dec. 24, 1932

*Rai Singh, K. (S. Punjab & Ind. Serv.) b Feb. 24, 1922

Rait Kerr, Col. R. S. (Sec. MCC 1936-52) b April 13, 1891, d April 2, 1961

Rajadurai, B. E. A. (SSC) b Aug. 24, 1965

*Rajindernath, V. (N. Ind., U. Prov., S. Punjab, Bihar & E. Punjab) b Jan. 7, 1928, d Nov. 22, 1989

*Rajinder Pal (Delhi, S. Punjab & Punjab) b Nov. 18, 1937

*Rajput, L. S. (Bombay) b Dec. 18, 1961

*Raju, S. L. V. (H'bad) b July 9, 1969

Ralph, L. H. R. (Essex) b May 22, 1920

*Ramadhin, S. (T/T & Lancs.; *CY 1951*) b May 1, 1929

*Raman, W. V. (TN) b May 23, 1965

*Ramanayake, C. P. H. (TU) b Jan. 8, 1965

*Ramaswami, C. (Madras) b June 18, 1896

*Ramchand, G. S. (Sind, Bombay & Raja.) b July 26, 1927

*Ramiz Raja (Lahore, Allied Bank & PNSC) b July 14, 1962

*Ramji, L. (W. Ind.) b 1900, d Dec. 20, 1948

*Ramprakash, M. R. (Middx) b Sept. 5, 1969

Ramsamooj, D. (T/T & Northants) b July 5, 1932

*Ranasinghe, A. N. (BRC) b Oct. 13, 1956

Ranasinghe, S. K. (SL) b July 4, 1962

*Ranatunga, A. (SSC) b Dec. 1, 1963

*Ranatunga, D. (SSC) b Oct. 12, 1962
*Randall, D. W. (Notts.; *CY 1980*) b Feb. 24, 1951
Randhir Singh (Orissa & Bihar) b Aug. 16, 1957
*Rangachari, C. R. (Madras) b April 14, 1916
*Rangnekar, K. M. (M'tra, Bombay & †M. Pradesh) b June 27, 1917, d Oct. 11, 1984
*Ranjane, V. B. (M'tra & Ind. Rlwys) b July 22, 1937
*Ranjitsinhji, K. S., afterwards H. H. the Jam Sahib of Nawanagar (CUCC & Sussex; *CY 1897*) b Sept. 10, 1872, d April 2, 1933
*Ransford, V. S. (Vic.; *CY 1910*) b March 20, 1885, d March 19, 1958
Ransom, V. J. (Hants & Surrey) b March 17, 1918
*Rashid Khan (PWD, Kar. & PIA) b Dec. 15, 1959
Ratcliffe, J. D. (Warwicks.) b June 19, 1969
Ratcliffe, R. M. (Lancs.) b Oct. 29, 1951
Ratnayake, N. L. K. (SSC) b Nov. 22, 1968
*Ratnayake, R. J. (NCC) b Jan. 2, 1964
*Ratnayeke, J. R. (NCC) b May 2, 1960
Rawson, P. W. E. (Zimb. & Natal) b May 25, 1957
Rayment, A. W. H. (Hants) b May 29, 1928
Raymer, V. N. (Qld) b May 4, 1918
*Razdan, A. (Delhi) b Aug. 25, 1969
*Read, H. D. (Surrey & Essex) b Jan. 28, 1910
*Read, J. M. (Surrey; *CY 1890*) b Feb. 9, 1859, d Feb. 17, 1929
*Read, W. W. (Surrey; *CY 1893*) b Nov. 23, 1855, d Jan. 6, 1907
Reddick, T. B. (Middx, Notts. & W. Prov.) b Feb. 17, 1912, d June 1, 1982
*Reddy, B. (TN) b Nov. 12, 1954
*Redmond, R. E. (Wgtn & Auck.) b Dec. 29, 1944
*Redpath, I. R. (Vic.) b May 11, 1941
Reed, B. L. (Hants) b Sept. 17, 1937
*Reedman, J. C. (S. Aust.) b Oct. 9, 1865, d March 25, 1924
Rees, A. (Glam.) b Feb. 17, 1938
Reeve, D. A. (Sussex & Warwicks.) b April 2, 1963
Reeves, W. (Essex; Umpire) b Jan. 22, 1875, d March 22, 1944
*Rege, M. R. (M'tra) b March 18, 1924
*Rehman, S. F. (Punjab, Pak. Us & Lahore) b June 11, 1935
*Reid, B. A. (W. Aust.) b March 14, 1963
*Reid, J. F. (Auck.) b March 3, 1956
*Reid, J. R. (Wgtn & Otago; *CY 1959*) b June 3, 1928
Reid, K. P. (E. Prov. & Northants) b July 24, 1951
*Reid, N. (W. Prov.) b Dec. 26, 1890, d June 6, 1947

Reid, R. B. (Wgtn & Auck.) b Dec. 3, 1958
Reidy, B. W. (Lancs.) b Sept. 18, 1953
*Relf, A. E. (Sussex & Auck.; *CY 1914*) b June 26, 1874, d March 26, 1937
*Renneburg, D. A. (NSW) b Sept. 23, 1942
Revill, A. C. (Derbys. & Leics.) b March 27, 1923
Reynolds, B. L. (Northants) b June 10, 1932
Rhodes, A. E. G. (Derbys.) b Oct. 10, 1916, d Oct. 18, 1983
*Rhodes, H. J. (Derbys.) b July 22, 1936
Rhodes, S. D. (Notts.) b March 24, 1910, d Jan. 7, 1989
Rhodes, S. J. (Yorks. & Worcs.) b June 17, 1964
*Rhodes, W. (Yorks.; *CY 1899*) b Oct. 29, 1877, d July 8, 1973
Rice, C. E. B. (Tvl & Notts.; *CY 1981*) b July 23, 1949
Rice, J. M. (Hants) b Oct. 23, 1949
*Richards, A. R. (W. Prov.) b 1868, d Jan. 9, 1904
*Richards, B. A. (Natal, Glos., Hants & S. Aust.; *CY 1969*) b July 21, 1945
*Richards, C. J. (Surrey & OFS) b Aug. 10, 1958
Richards, G. (Glam.) b Nov. 29, 1951
*Richards, I. V. A. (Comb. Is., Leewards, Som., Qld & Glam.; *CY 1977*) b March 7, 1952
*Richards, W. H. M. (SA) b Aug. 1862, d Jan. 4, 1903
*Richardson, A. J. (S. Aust.) b July 24, 1888, d Dec. 23, 1973
Richardson, A. W. (Derbys.) b March 4, 1907, d July 29, 1983
Richardson, D. J. (E. Prov. & N. Tvl) b Sept. 16, 1959
*Richardson, D. W. (Worcs.) b Nov. 3, 1934
Richardson, G. W. (Derbys.) b April 26, 1938
*Richardson, P. E. (Worcs. & Kent; *CY 1957*) b July 4, 1931
*Richardson, R. B. (Leewards; *CY 1992*) b Jan. 12, 1962
*Richardson, T. (Surrey & Som.; *CY 1897*) b Aug. 11, 1870, d July 2, 1912
*Richardson, V. Y. (S. Aust.) b Sept. 7, 1894, d Oct. 29, 1969
*Richmond, T. L. (Notts.) b June 23, 1890, d Dec. 29, 1957
*Rickards, K. R. (Jam. & Essex) b Aug. 23, 1923
Riddington, A. (Leics.) b Dec. 22, 1911
*Ridgway, F. (Kent) b Aug. 10, 1923
Ridings, P. L. (S. Aust.) b Oct. 2, 1917
*Rigg, K. E. (Vic.) b May 21, 1906
Riley, H. (Leics.) b Oct. 3, 1902, d Jan. 24, 1989
*Ring, D. T. (Vic.) b Oct. 14, 1918
Ripley, D. (Northants) b Sept. 13, 1966

Rist, F. H. (Essex) b March 30, 1914

*Ritchie, G. M. (Qld) b Jan. 23, 1960

*Rixon, S. J. (NSW) b Feb. 25, 1954

*Rizwan-uz-Zaman (Kar. & PIA) b Sept. 4, 1962

*Roach, C. A. (T/T) b March 13, 1904, d April 16, 1988

*Roberts, A. D. G. (N. Dist.) b May 6, 1947, d Oct. 26, 1989

*Roberts, A. M. E. (Comb. Is., Leewards, Hants, NSW & Leics.; *CY 1975*) b Jan. 29, 1951

*Roberts, A. T. (Windwards) b Sept. 18, 1937

*Roberts, A. W. (Cant. & Otago) b Aug. 20, 1909, d May 13, 1978

Roberts, B. (Tvl & Derbys.) b May 30, 1962

Roberts, The Hon. Sir Denys (Pres. MCC 1989-90) b Jan. 19, 1923

Roberts, Pascall (T/T) b Dec 15, 1937

Roberts, W. S. J. (Cant.) b March 22, 1965

Roberts, W. B. (Lancs. & Victory Tests) b Sept. 27, 1914, d Aug. 24, 1951

*Robertson, G. K. (C. Dist.) b July 15, 1960

*Robertson, J. B. (W. Prov.) b June 5, 1906, d July 5, 1985

*Robertson, J. D. (Middx; *CY 1948*) b Feb. 22, 1917

*Robertson, W. R. (Vic.) b Oct. 6, 1861, d June 24, 1938

Robertson-Glasgow, R. C. (OUCC & Som.) b July 15, 1901, d March 4, 1965

Robins, D. H. (Warwicks.) b June 26, 1914

Robins, R. V. C. (Middx) b March 13, 1935

*Robins, R. W. V. (CUCC & Middx; *CY 1930*) b June 3, 1906, d Dec. 12, 1968

Robinson, A. L. (Yorks.) b Aug. 17, 1946

Robinson, Emmott (Yorks.) b Nov. 16, 1883, d Nov. 17, 1969

Robinson, Ellis P. (Yorks. & Som.) b Aug. 10, 1911

Robinson, H. B. (OUCC & Canada) b March 3, 1919

Robinson, M. (Glam., Warwicks., H'bad & Madras) b July 16, 1921

Robinson, M. A. (Northants & Yorks.) b Nov. 23, 1966

Robinson, P. E. (Yorks.) b Aug. 3, 1963

Robinson, P. J. (Worcs. & Som.) b Feb. 9, 1943

Robinson, Ray (Writer) b July 8, 1908, d July 6, 1982

*Robinson, R. D. (Vic.) b June 8, 1946

*Robinson, R. H. (NSW, S. Aust. & Otago) b March 26, 1914, d Aug. 10, 1965

*Robinson, R. T. (Notts.; *CY 1986*) b Nov. 21, 1958

Robson, E. (Som.) b May 1, 1870, d May 23, 1924

Rochford, P. (Glos.) b Aug. 27, 1928

*Rodriguez, W. V. (T/T) b June 25, 1934

Roe, B. (Som.) b Jan. 27, 1939

Roebuck, P. M. (CUCC & Som.; *CY 1988*) b March 6, 1956

Rogers, N. H. (Hants) b March 9, 1918

Rogers, R. E. (Qld) b Aug. 24, 1916

Romaines, P. W. (Northants, Glos. & Griq. W.) b Dec. 25, 1955

*Roope, G. R. J. (Surrey & Griq. W.) b July 12, 1946

*Root, C. F. (Derbys. & Worcs.) b April 16, 1890, d Jan. 20, 1954

*Rorke, G. F. (NSW) b June 27, 1938

*Rose, B. C. (Som.; *CY 1980*) b June 4, 1950

Rose, G. D. (Middx & Som.) b April 12, 1964

Roseberry, M. A. (Middx) b Nov. 28, 1966

Rosebery, 6th Earl of (*see* Dalmeny, Lord)

*Rose-Innes, A. (Kimberley & Tvl) b Feb. 16, 1868, d Nov. 22, 1946

Ross, C. J. (Wgtn & OUCC) b June 24, 1954

Rotherham, G. A. (Rugby, CUCC, Warwicks. & Wgtn; *CY 1918*) b May 28, 1899, d Jan. 31, 1985

Rouse, S. J. (Warwicks.) b Jan. 20, 1949

Routledge, R. (Middx) b July 7, 1920

*Routledge, T. W. (W. Prov. & Tvl) b April 18, 1867, d May 9, 1927

*Rowan, A. M. B. (Tvl) b Feb. 7, 1921

*Rowan, E. A. B. (Tvl; *CY 1952*) b July 20, 1909

*Rowe, C. G. (Wgtn & C. Dist.) b June 30, 1915

Rowe, C. J. C. (Kent & Glam.) b May 5, 1953

Rowe, E. J. (Notts.) b July 21, 1920, d Dec. 17, 1989

*Rowe, G. A. (W. Prov.) b June 15, 1874, d Jan. 8, 1950

*Rowe, L. G. (Jam. & Derbys.) b Jan. 8, 1949

*Roy, A. (Bengal) b June 5, 1945

*Roy, Pankaj (Bengal) b May 31, 1928

*Roy, Pranab (Bengal) b Feb. 10, 1957

*Royle, Rev. V. P. F. A. (OUCC & Lancs.) b Jan. 29, 1854, d May 21, 1929

*Rumsey, F. E. (Worcs., Som. & Derbys.) b Dec. 4, 1935

Rushmere, M. W. (E. Prov.) b Jan. 7, 1965

*Russell, A. C. [C. A. G.] (Essex; *CY 1923*) b Oct. 7, 1887, d March 23, 1961

Russell, P. E. (Derbys.) b May 9, 1944

*Russell, R. C. (Glos.; *CY 1990*) b Aug. 15, 1963

Russell, S. E. (Middx & Glos.) b Oct. 4, 1937

*Russell, W. E. (Middx) b July 3, 1936

Russom, N. (CUCC & Som.) b Dec. 3, 1958

Rutherford, I. A. (Worcs. & Otago) b June 30, 1957

*Rutherford, J. W. (W. Aust.) b Sept. 25, 1929

*Rutherford, K. R. (Otago) b Oct. 26, 1965
Ryan, M. (Yorks.) b June 23, 1933
*Ryder, J. (Vic.) b Aug. 8, 1889, d April 3, 1977

Saadat Ali (Lahore, UBL & HBFC) b Feb. 6, 1955
*Sadiq Mohammad (Kar., PIA, Tas., Essex, Glos. & UBP) b May 3, 1945
Sadler, W. C. H. (Surrey) b Sept. 24, 1896, d Feb. 12, 1981
*Saeed Ahmed (Punjab, Pak. Us, Lahore, PIA, Kar., PWD & Sind) b Oct. 1, 1937
*Saeed Anwar (UBL & ADBP) b Sept. 6, 1968
*Saggers, R. A. (NSW) b May 15, 1917, d March 1987
Sainsbury, G. E. (Essex & Glos.) b Jan. 17, 1958
Sainsbury, P. J. (Hants; *CY 1974*) b June 13, 1934
*St Hill, E. L. (T/T) b March 9, 1904, d May 21, 1957
*St Hill, W. H. (T/T) b July 6, 1893, d 1957
Sajid Ali (Kar. & NBP) b July 1, 1963
Sajjad Akbar (PNSC & Sargodha) b March 1, 1961
*Salah-ud-Din (Kar., PIA & Pak. Us) b Feb. 14, 1947
Sale, R., jun. (OUCC, Warwicks. & Derbys.) b Oct. 4, 1919, d Feb. 3, 1987
*Saleem Altaf (Lahore & PIA) b April 19, 1944
*Saleem Jaffer (Kar. & UBL) b Nov. 19, 1962
*Salim Malik (Lahore, HBL & Essex; *CY 1988*) b April 16, 1963
Salim Pervez (NBP) b Sept. 9, 1947
*Salim Yousuf (Sind, Kar., IDBP, Allied Bank & Customs) b Dec. 7, 1959
Salisbury, I. D. K. (Sussex) b Jan. 21, 1970
Samaranayake, A. D. A. (SL) b Feb. 25, 1962
*Samarasekera, M. A. R. (CCC) b Aug. 5, 1961
Sampson, H. (Yorks. & All-England) b March 13, 1813, d March 29, 1885
Samuelson, S. V. (Natal) b Nov. 21, 1883, d Nov. 18, 1958
*Sandham, A. (Surrey; *CY 1923*) b July 6, 1890, d April 20, 1982
*Sandhu, B. S. (Bombay) b Aug. 3, 1956
*Sardesai, D. N. (Bombay) b Aug. 8, 1940
*Sarfraz Nawaz (Lahore, Punjab, Northants, Pak. Rlwys & UBL) b Dec. 1, 1948
Sargeant, N. F. (Surrey) b Nov. 8, 1965
*Sarwate, C. T. (CP & B, M'tra, Bombay & †M. Pradesh) b June 22, 1920
*Saunders, J. V. (Vic. & Wgtn) b Feb. 3, 1876, d Dec. 21, 1927
Savage, J. S. (Leics. & Lancs.) b March 3, 1929

Savage, R. Le Q. (OUCC & Warwicks.) b Dec. 10, 1955
Savill, L. A. (Essex) b June 30, 1935
Saville, G. J. (Essex) b Feb. 5, 1944
Saxelby, K. (Notts.) b Feb. 23, 1959
*Saxena, R. C. (Delhi & Bihar) b Sept. 20, 1944
Sayer, D. M. (OUCC & Kent) b Sept. 19, 1936
*Scarlett, R. O. (Jam.) b Aug. 15, 1934
Schofield, R. M. (C. Dist.) b Nov. 6, 1939
*Schultz, S. S. (CUCC & Lancs.) b Aug. 29, 1857, d Dec. 18, 1937
*Schwarz, R. O. (Middx & Natal; *CY 1908*) b May 4, 1875, d Nov. 18, 1918
*Scott, A. P. H. (Jam.) b July 29, 1934
Scott, Christopher J. (Lancs.) b Sept. 16, 1959
Scott, Colin J. (Glos.) b May 1, 1919
Scott, C. W. (Notts.) b Jan. 23, 1964
*Scott, H. J. H. (Vic.) b Dec. 26, 1858, d Sept. 23, 1910
Scott, M. E. (Northants) b May 8, 1936
*Scott, O. C. (Jam.) b Aug. 25, 1893, d June 16, 1961
*Scott, R. H. (Cant.) b March 6, 1917
Scott, R. J. (Hants & Glos.) b Nov. 2, 1963
Scott, S. W. (Middx; *CY 1893*) b March 24, 1854, d Dec. 8, 1933
*Scott, V. J. (Auck.) b July 31, 1916, d Aug. 2, 1980
*Scotton, W. H. (Notts.) b Jan. 15, 1856, d July 9, 1893
*Sealey, B. J. (T/T) b Aug. 12, 1899, d Sept. 12, 1963
*Sealy, J. E. D. (B'dos & T/T) b Sept. 11, 1912, d Jan. 3, 1982
Seamer, J. W. (Som. & OUCC) b June 23, 1913
*Seccull, A. W. (Kimberley, W. Prov. & Tvl) b Sept. 14, 1868, d July 20, 1945
Seeff, L. (W. Prov.) b May 1, 1959
*Sekar, T. A. P. (TN) b March 28, 1955
*Selby, J. (Notts.) b July 1, 1849, d March 11, 1894
Sellers, A. B. (Yorks.; *CY 1940*) b March 5, 1907, d Feb. 20, 1981
*Sellers, R. H. D. (S. Aust.) b Aug. 20, 1940
*Selvey, M. W. W. (CUCC, Surrey, Middx, Glam. & OFS) b April 25, 1948
*Sen, P. (Bengal) b May 31, 1926, d Jan. 27, 1970
*Sen Gupta, A. K. (Ind. Serv.) b Aug. 3, 1939
*Senanayake, C. P. (CCC) b Dec. 19, 1962
*Serjeant, C. S. (W. Aust.) b Nov. 1, 1951
Seymour, James (Kent) b Oct. 25, 1879, d Sept. 30, 1930
*Seymour, M. A. (W. Prov.) b June 5, 1936
*Shackleton, D. (Hants.; *CY 1959*) b Aug. 12, 1924

*Shafiq Ahmad (Lahore, Punjab, NBP & UBL) b March 28, 1949

*Shafqat Rana (Lahore & PIA) b Aug. 10, 1943

*Shahid Israr (Kar. & Sind) b March 1, 1950

*Shahid Mahboob (Karachi, Quetta & PACO) b Aug. 25, 1962

*Shahid Mahmoud (Kar., Pak. Us & PWD) b March 17, 1939

*Shahid Saeed (HBFC) b Jan. 6, 1966

Shakil Khan (WAPDA & HBL) b May 28, 1968

*Shalders, W. A. (Griq. W. & Tvl) b Feb. 12, 1880, d March 18, 1917

*Sharma, Ajay (Delhi) b April 3, 1964

*Sharma, Chetan (Haryana) b Jan. 3, 1966

*Sharma, Gopal (U. Pradesh) b Aug. 3, 1960

*Sharma, P. (Raja.) b Jan. 5, 1948

Sharma, R. (Derbys.) b June 27, 1962

Sharma, Sanjeev (Delhi) b Aug. 25, 1965

Sharp, G. (Northants) b March 12, 1950

Sharp, H. P. (Middx) b Oct. 6, 1917

*Sharp, J. (Lancs.) b Feb. 15, 1878, d Jan. 28, 1938

Sharp, K. (Yorks. & Griq. W.) b April 6, 1959

*Sharpe, D. (Punjab, Pak. Rlwys, Lahore & S. Aust.) b Aug. 3, 1937

*Sharpe, J. W. (Surrey & Notts.; *CY 1892*) b Dec. 9, 1866, d June 19, 1936

*Sharpe, P. J. (Yorks. & Derbys.; *CY 1963*) b Dec. 27, 1936

*Shastri, R. J. (Bombay & Glam.) b May 27, 1962

*Shaw, Alfred (Notts. & Sussex) b Aug. 29, 1842, d Jan. 16, 1907

Shaw, C. (Yorks.) b Feb. 17, 1964

*Sheahan, A. P. (Vic.) b Sept. 30, 1946

Sheffield, J. R. (Essex & Wgtn) b Nov. 19, 1906

Shepherd, B. K. (W. Aust.) b April 23, 1937

Shepherd, D. J. (Glam.; *CY 1970*) b Aug. 12, 1927

Shepherd, D. R. (Glos.; Umpire) b Dec. 27, 1940

*Shepherd, J. N. (B'dos, Kent, Rhod. & Glos.; *CY 1979*) b Nov. 9, 1943

Shepherd, T. F. (Surrey) b Dec. 5, 1889, d Feb. 13, 1957

*Sheppard, Rt Rev. D. S. (Bishop of Liverpool) (CUCC & Sussex; *CY 1953*) b March 6, 1929

*Shepstone, G. H. (Tvl) b April 8, 1876, d July 3, 1940

*Sherwell, P. W. (Tvl) b Aug. 17, 1880, d April 17, 1948

*Sherwin, M. (Notts.; *CY 1891*) b Feb. 26, 1851, d July 3, 1910

*Shillingford, G. C. (Comb. Is. & Windwards) b Sept. 25, 1944

*Shillingford, I. T. (Comb. Is. & Windwards) b April 18, 1944

*Shinde, S. G. (Baroda, M'tra & Bombay) b Aug. 18, 1923, d June 22, 1955

Shine, K. J. (Hants) b Feb. 22, 1969

Shirreff, A. C. (CUCC, Hants, Kent & Som.) b Feb. 12, 1919

*Shivnarine, S. (Guyana) b May 13, 1952

*Shoaib Mohammad (Kar. & PIA) b Jan. 8, 1962

*Shodhan, R. H. (Guj. & Baroda) b Oct. 18, 1928

Short, A. M. (Natal) b Sept. 27, 1947

*Shrewsbury, Arthur (Notts.; *CY 1890*) b April 11, 1856, d May 19, 1903

*Shrimpton, M. J. F. (C. Dist. & N. Dist.) b June 23, 1940

*Shuja-ud-Din, Col. (N. Ind., Pak. Us, Pak. Serv., B'pur & R'pindi) b April 10, 1930

*Shukla, R. C. (Bihar & Delhi) b Feb. 4, 1948

*Shuter, J. (Kent & Surrey) b Feb. 9, 1855, d July 5, 1920

*Shuttleworth, K. (Lancs. & Leics.) b Nov. 13, 1944

Siddons, J. D. (Vic.) b April 25, 1964

*Sidebottom, A. (Yorks. & OFS) b April 1, 1954

*Sidhu, N. S. (Punjab) b Oct. 20, 1963

*Siedle, I. J. (Natal) b Jan. 11, 1903, d Aug. 24, 1982

*Sievers, M. W. (Vic.) b April 13, 1912, d May 10, 1968

*Sikander Bakht (PWD, PIA, Sind, Kar. & UBL) b Aug. 25, 1957

Silk, D. R. W. (CUCC & Som.) b Oct. 8, 1931

*Silva, S. A. R. (NCC) b Dec. 12, 1960

Sime, W. A. (Notts.) b Feb. 8, 1909, d May 5, 1982

Simmons, J. (Lancs. & Tas.; *CY 1985*) b March 28, 1941

*Simmons, P. V. (T/T) b April 18, 1963

*Simpson, R. B. (NSW & W. Aust.; *CY 1965*) b Feb. 3, 1936

*Simpson, R. T. (Notts. & Sind; *CY 1950*) b Feb. 27, 1920

Simpson-Hayward, G. H. (Worcs.) b June 7, 1875, d Oct. 2, 1936

Sims, Sir Arthur (Cant.) b July 22, 1877, d April 27, 1969

*Sims, J. M. (Middx) b May 13, 1903, d April 27, 1973

Sinclair, B. W. (Wgtn) b Oct. 23, 1936

*Sinclair, I. McK. (Cant.) b June 1, 1933

*Sinclair, J. H. (Tvl) b Oct. 16, 1876, d Feb. 23, 1913

Sincock, D. J. (S. Aust.) b Feb. 1, 1942

*Sinfield, R. A. (Glos.) b Dec. 24, 1900, d March 17, 1988

*Singh, Charan K. (T/T) b 1938

Singh, "Robin" [R. R.] (TN) b Sept. 14, 1963

Singh, R. P. (U. Pradesh) b Jan. 6, 1963

Singh, Swaranjit (CUCC, Warwicks., E. Punjab & Bengal) b July 18, 1931

Singleton, A. P. (OUCC, Worcs. & Rhod.) b Aug. 5, 1914

*Sivaramakrishnan, L. (TN) b Dec. 31, 1965

Skelding, Alec (Leics.) b Sept. 5, 1886, d April 17, 1960

Skinner, A. F. (Derbys. & Northants) b April 22, 1913, d Feb. 28, 1982

Skinner, D. A. (Derbys.) b March 22, 1920

Skinner, L. E. (Surrey & Guyana) b Sept. 7, 1950

*Slack, W. N. (Middx & Windwards) b Dec. 12, 1954, d Jan. 15, 1989

Slade, D. N. F. (Worcs.) b Aug. 24, 1940

Slade, W. D. (Glam.) b Sept. 27, 1941

*Slater, K. N. (W. Aust.) b March 12, 1935

Sleep, P. R. (S. Aust.) b May 4, 1957

*Slight, J. (Vic.) b Oct. 20, 1855, d Dec. 9, 1930

Slocombe, P. A. (Som.) b Sept. 6, 1954

*Smailes, T. F. (Yorks.) b March 27, 1910, d Dec. 1, 1970

Smales, K. (Yorks. & Notts.) b Sept. 15, 1927

*Small, G. C. (Warwicks. & S. Aust.) b Oct. 18, 1961

Small, John, sen. (Hants & All-England) b April 19, 1737, d Dec. 31, 1826

*Small, J. A. (T/T) b Nov. 3, 1892, d April 26, 1958

*Small, M. A. (B'dos) b Feb. 12, 1964

Smedley, M. J. (Notts.) b Oct. 28, 1941

*Smith, A. C. (OUCC & Warwicks.; Chief Exec. TCCB 1987-  ) b Oct. 25, 1936

Smith, B. F. (Leics.) b April 3, 1972

*Smith, Sir C. Aubrey (CUCC, Sussex & Tvl) b July 21, 1863, d Dec. 20, 1948

*Smith, C. I. J. (Middx; *CY 1935*) b Aug. 25, 1906, d Feb. 9, 1979

*Smith, C. J. E. (Tvl) b Dec. 25, 1872, d March 27, 1947

*Smith, C. L. (Natal, Glam. & Hants; *CY 1984*) b Oct. 15, 1958

Smith, C. S. (CUCC & Lancs.) b Oct. 1, 1932

*Smith, C. W. (B'dos) b July 29, 1933

*Smith, Denis (Derbys.; *CY 1936*) b Jan. 24, 1907, d Sept. 12, 1979

*Smith, D. B. M. (Vic.) b Sept. 14, 1884, d July 29, 1963

Smith, D. H. K. (Derbys. & OFS) b June 29, 1940

*Smith, D. M. (Surrey, Worcs. & Sussex) b Jan. 9, 1956

*Smith, D. R. (Glos.) b Oct. 5, 1934

*Smith, D. V. (Sussex) b June 14, 1923

Smith, Edwin (Derbys.) b Jan. 2, 1934

*Smith, E. J. (Warwicks.) b Feb. 6, 1886, d Aug. 31, 1979

*Smith, F. B. (Cant.) b March 13, 1922

*Smith, F. W. (Tvl) No details of birth or death known

Smith, G. (Kent) b Nov. 30, 1925

Smith, G. J. (Essex) b April 2, 1935

*Smith, Harry (Glos.) b May 21, 1890, d Nov. 12, 1937

*Smith, H. D. (Otago & Cant.) b Jan. 8, 1913, d Jan. 25, 1986

Smith, I. (Glam.) b March 11, 1967

*Smith, I. D. S. (C. Dist. & Auck.) b Feb. 28, 1957

Smith, K. D. (Warwicks.) b July 9, 1956

Smith, M. J. (Middx) b Jan. 4, 1942

*Smith, M. J. K. (OUCC, Leics. & Warwicks.; *CY 1960*) b June 30, 1933

Smith, N. (Yorks. & Essex) b April 1, 1949

*Smith, O. G. (Jam.; *CY 1958*) b May 5, 1933, d Sept. 9, 1959

Smith, P. A. (Warwicks.) b April 5, 1964

Smith, Ray (Essex) b Aug. 10, 1914

Smith, Roy (Som.) b April 14, 1930

*Smith, R. A. (Natal & Hants; *CY 1990*) b Sept. 13, 1963

Smith, R. C. (Leics.) b Aug. 3, 1935

*Smith, S. B. (NSW & Tvl) b Oct. 18, 1961

Smith, S. G. (T/T, Northants & Auck.; *CY 1915*) b Jan. 15, 1881, d Oct. 25, 1963

*Smith, T. P. B. (Essex; *CY 1947*) b Oct. 30, 1908, d Aug. 4, 1967

*Smith, V. I. (Natal) b Feb. 23, 1925

Smith, W. A. (Surrey) b Sept. 15, 1937

Smith, W. C. (Surrey; *CY 1911*) b Oct. 4, 1877, d July 16, 1946

*Smithson, G. A. (Yorks. & Leics.) b Nov. 1, 1926, d Sept. 6, 1970

*Snedden, C. A. (Auck.) b Jan. 7, 1918

*Snedden, M. C. (Auck.) b Nov. 23, 1958

Snellgrove, K. L. (Lancs.) b Nov. 12, 1941

*Snooke, S. D. (W. Prov. & Tvl) b Nov. 11, 1878, d April 4, 1959

*Snooke, S. J. (Border, W. Prov. & Tvl) b Feb. 1, 1881, d Aug. 14, 1966

*Snow, J. A. (Sussex; *CY 1973*) b Oct. 13, 1941

Snowden, W. (CUCC) b Sept. 27, 1952

*Sobers, Sir G. S. (B'dos, S. Aust. & Notts.; *CY 1964*) b July 28, 1936

Sohail Fazal (Lahore) b Nov. 11, 1967

*Sohoni, S. W. (M'tra, Baroda & Bombay) b March 5, 1918

Solanky, J. W. (E. Africa & Glam.) b June 30, 1942

*Solkar, E. D. (Bombay & Sussex) b March 18, 1948

*Solomon, J. S. (BG) b Aug. 26, 1930

*Solomon, W. R. T. (Tvl & E. Prov.) b April 23, 1872, d July 12, 1964

*Sood, M. M. (Delhi) b July 6, 1939

Southern, J. W. (Hants) b Sept. 2, 1952

*Southerton, James (Surrey, Hants & Sussex) b Nov. 16, 1827, d June 16, 1880

Southerton, S. J. (Editor of *Wisden* 1934-35) b July 7, 1874, d March 12, 1935

Speak, N. J. (Lancs.) b Nov. 21, 1966

Speight, M. P. (Sussex & Wgtn) b Oct. 24, 1967

Spencer, C. T. (Leics.) b Aug. 18, 1931

Spencer, J. (CUCC & Sussex) b Oct. 6, 1949

Spencer, T. W. (Kent) b March 22, 1914

Sperry, J. (Leics.) b March 19, 1910

*Spofforth, F. R. (NSW & Vic.) b Sept. 9, 1853, d June 4, 1926

*Spooner, R. H. (Lancs.; *CY 1905*) b Oct. 21, 1880, d Oct. 2, 1961

*Spooner, R. T. (Warwicks.) b Dec. 30, 1919

Springall, J. D. (Notts.) b Sept. 19, 1932

*Srikkanth, K. (TN) b Dec. 21, 1959

*Srinivasan, T. E. (TN) b Oct. 26, 1950

*Stackpole, K. R. (Vic.; *CY 1973*) b July 10, 1940

Standen, H. A. (Worcs.) b May 30, 1935

Standing, D. K. (Sussex) b Oct. 21, 1963

Stanworth, J. (Lancs.) b Sept. 30, 1960

*Stanyforth, Lt-Col. R. T. (Yorks.) b May 30, 1892, d Feb. 20, 1964

*Staples, S. J. (Notts.; *CY 1929*) b Sept. 18, 1892, d June 4, 1950

Starkie, S. (Northants) b April 4, 1926

*Statham, J. B. (Lancs.; *CY 1955*) b June 17, 1930

*Stayers, S. C. (†Guyana & Bombay) b June 9, 1937

*Steel, A. G. (CUCC & Lancs.; Pres. MCC 1902) b Sept. 24, 1858, d June 15, 1914

*Steele, D. S. (Northants & Derbys.; *CY 1976*) b Sept. 29, 1941

Steele, J. F. (Leics., Natal & Glam.) b July 23, 1946

Stephens, E. J. (Glos.) b March 23, 1910

Stephenson, F. D. (B'dos, Glos., Tas. & Notts.; *CY 1989*) b April 8, 1959

Stephenson, G. R. (Derbys. & Hants) b Nov. 19, 1942

Stephenson, H. H. (Surrey & All-England) b May 3, 1832, d Dec. 17, 1896

Stephenson, H. W. (Som.) b July 18, 1920

*Stephenson, J. P. (Essex & Boland) b March 14, 1965

Stephenson, Lt-Col. J. R. (Sec. MCC 1987- ) b Feb. 25, 1931

Stephenson, Lt-Col. J. W. A. (Essex & Worcs.) b Aug. 1, 1907, d May 20, 1982

Stevens, Edward ("Lumpy") (Hants) b circa 1735, d Sept. 7, 1819

*Stevens, G. B. (S. Aust.) b Feb. 29, 1932

*Stevens, G. T. S. (UCS, OUCC & Middx; *CY 1918*) b Jan. 7, 1901, d Sept. 19, 1970

*Stevenson, G. B. (Yorks. & Northants) b Dec. 16, 1955

Stevenson, K. (Derbys. & Hants) b Oct. 6, 1950

Stevenson, M. H. (CUCC & Derbys.) b June 13, 1927

*Stewart, A. J. (Surrey) b April 8, 1963

*Stewart, M. J. (Surrey; *CY 1958*) b Sept. 16, 1932

*Stewart, R. B. (SA) b Sept. 3, 1856, d Sept. 12, 1913

Stewart, R. W. (Glos. & Middx) b Feb. 28, 1945

Stewart, W. J. (Warwicks. & Northants) b Oct. 31, 1934

Stirling, D. A. (C. Dist.) b Oct. 5, 1961

Stocks, F. W. (Notts.) b Nov. 6, 1917

*Stoddart, A. E. (Middx; *CY 1893*) b March 11, 1863, d April 4, 1915

*Stollmeyer, J. B. (T/T) b April 11, 1921, d Sept. 10, 1989

*Stollmeyer, V. H. (T/T) b Jan. 24, 1916

*Storer, W. (Derbys.; *CY 1899*) b Jan. 25, 1867, d Feb. 28, 1912

Storey, S. J. (Surrey & Sussex) b Jan. 6, 1941

Stott, L. W. (Auck.) b Dec. 8, 1946

Stott, W. B. (Yorks.) b July 18, 1934

Stovold, A. W. (Glos. & OFS) b March 19, 1953

*Street, G. B. (Sussex) b Dec. 6, 1889, d April 24, 1924

*Stricker, L. A. (Tvl) b May 26, 1884, d Feb. 5, 1960

Stringer, P. M. (Yorks. & Leics.) b Feb. 23, 1943

*Strudwick, H. (Surrey; *CY 1912*) b Jan. 28, 1880, d Feb. 14, 1970

Strydom, W. T. (OFS) b March 21, 1942

*Studd, C. T. (CUCC & Middx) b Dec. 2, 1860, d July 16, 1931

*Studd, G. B. (CUCC & Middx) b Oct. 20, 1859, d Feb. 13, 1945

Studd, Sir Peter M. (CUCC) b Sept. 15, 1916

Sturt, M. O. C. (Middx) b Sept. 12, 1940

*Subba Row, R. (CUCC, Surrey & Northants; *CY 1961*) b Jan. 29, 1932

*Subramanya, V. (Mysore) b July 16, 1936

Such, P. M. (Notts., Leics. & Essex) b June 12, 1964

Sudhakar Rao, R. (Karn.) b Aug. 8, 1952

Sueter, T. (Hants & Surrey) b circa 1749, d Feb. 17, 1827

*Sugg, F. H. (Yorks., Derbys. & Lancs.; *CY 1890*) b Jan. 11, 1862, d May 29, 1933

Sullivan, J. (Lancs.) b Feb. 5, 1945

Sully, H. (Som. & Northants) b Nov. 1, 1939

*Sunderram, G. R. (Bombay & Raja.) b March 29, 1930

Sunnucks, P. R. (Kent) b June 22, 1916

*Surendranath, R. (Ind. Serv.) b Jan. 4, 1937

*Surridge, W. S. (Surrey; *CY 1953*) b Sept. 3, 1917

*Surti, R. F. (Guj., Raja. & Qld) b May 25, 1936

*Susskind, M. J. (CUCC, Middx & Tvl) b June 8, 1891, d July 9, 1957

*Sutcliffe, B. (Auck., Otago & N. Dist.; *CY 1950*) b Nov. 17, 1923

*Sutcliffe, H. (Yorks.; *CY 1920*) b Nov. 24, 1894, d Jan. 22, 1978

Sutcliffe, S. P. (OUCC & Warwicks.) b May 22, 1960

Sutcliffe, W. H. H. (Yorks.) b Oct. 10, 1926

Suttle, K. G. (Sussex) b Aug. 25, 1928

Swallow, I. G. (Yorks. & Som.) b Dec. 18, 1962

*Swamy, V. N. (Ind. Serv.) b May 23, 1924, d May 1, 1983

Swanton, E. W. (Middx; Writer) b Feb. 11, 1907

Swarbrook, F. W. (Derbys., Griq. W. & OFS) b Dec. 17, 1950

Swart, P. D. (Rhod., W. Prov., Glam. & Boland) b April 27, 1946

*Swetman, R. (Surrey, Notts & Glos.) b Oct. 25, 1933

Sydenham, D. A. D. (Surrey) b April 6, 1934

Symington, S. J. (Leics.) b Sept. 16, 1926

*Taber, H. B. (NSW) b April 29, 1940

*Taberer, H. M. (OUCC & Natal) b Oct. 7, 1870, d June 5, 1932

Tahir Naqqash (Servis Ind., MCB, Punjab & Lahore) b July 6, 1959

Tait, A. (Northants & Glos.) b Dec. 27, 1953

*Talat Ali (Lahore, PIA & UBL) b May 29, 1950

Talbot, R. O. (Cant. & Otago) b Nov. 26, 1903, d Jan. 5, 1983

*Tallon, D. (Qld; *CY 1949*) b Feb. 17, 1916, d Sept. 7, 1984

*Tamhane, N. S. (Bombay) b Aug. 4, 1931

*Tancred, A. B. (Kimberley, Griq. W. & Tvl) b Aug. 20, 1865, d Nov. 23, 1911

*Tancred, L. J. (Tvl) b Oct. 7, 1876, d July 28, 1934

*Tancred, V. M. (Tvl) b July 7, 1875, d June 3, 1904

Tang Choon, R. P. (T/T) b 1914, d Sept. 5, 1985

*Tapscott, G. L. (Griq. W.) b Nov. 7, 1889, d Dec. 13, 1940

*Tapscott, L. E. (Griq. W.) b March 18, 1894, d July 7, 1934

*Tarapore, K. K. (Bombay) b Dec. 17, 1910, d June 15, 1986

Tarrant, F. A. (Vic., Middx & Patiala; *CY 1908*) b Dec. 11, 1880, d Jan. 29, 1951

Tarrant, George F. (Cambs. & All-England) b Dec. 7, 1838, d July 2, 1870

*Taslim Arif (Kar., Sind & NBP) b May 1, 1954

*Tate, F. W. (Sussex) b July 24, 1867, d Feb. 24, 1943

*Tate, M. W. (Sussex; *CY 1924*) b May 30, 1895, d May 18, 1956

*Tattersall, R. (Lancs.) b Aug. 17, 1922

*Tauseef Ahmed (PWD, UBL & Kar.) b May 10, 1958

*Tavaré, C. J. (OUCC, Kent & Som.) b Oct. 27, 1954

Tayfield, A. (Natal, Tvl & NE Tvl) b June 21, 1931

*Tayfield, H. J. (Natal, Rhod. & Tvl; *CY 1956*) b Jan. 30, 1929

*Taylor, A. I. (Tvl) b July 25, 1925

Taylor, B. (Essex; *CY 1972*) b June 19, 1932

*Taylor, B. R. (Cant. & Wgtn) b July 12, 1943

*Taylor, Daniel (Natal) b Jan. 9, 1887, d Jan. 24, 1957

*Taylor, D. D. (Auck. & Warwicks.) b March 2, 1923, d Dec. 5, 1980

Taylor, D. J. S. (Surrey, Som. & Griq. W.) b Nov. 12, 1942

Taylor, G. R. (Hants) b Nov. 25, 1909, d Oct. 31, 1986

*Taylor, H. W. (Natal, Tvl & W. Prov.; *CY 1925*) b May 5, 1889, d Feb. 8, 1973

*Taylor, J. M. (NSW) b Oct. 10, 1895, d May 12, 1971

*Taylor, J. O. (T/T) b Jan. 3, 1932

*Taylor, K. (Yorks. & Auck.) b Aug. 21, 1935

Taylor, K. A. (Warwicks.) b Sept. 29, 1916

*Taylor, L. B. (Leics. & Natal) b Oct. 25, 1953

*Taylor, M. A. (NSW; *CY 1990*) b Oct 27, 1964

Taylor, M. N. S. (Notts. & Hants) b Nov. 12, 1942

Taylor, N. R. (Kent) b July 21, 1959

*Taylor, P. L. (NSW & Qld) b Aug. 22, 1956

Taylor, R. M. (Essex) b Nov. 30, 1909, d Jan. 1984

*Taylor, R. W. (Derbys.; *CY 1977*) b July 17, 1941

Taylor, T. L. (CUCC & Yorks.; *CY 1901*) b May 25, 1878, d March 16, 1960

Taylor, W. (Notts.) b Jan. 24, 1947

Tedstone, G. A. (Warwicks. & Glos.) b Jan. 19, 1961

Tendulkar, S. R. (Bombay) b April 24, 1973

Tennekoon, A. P. B. (SL) b Oct. 29, 1946

*Tennyson, 3rd Lord (Hon. L. H.) (Hants; *CY 1914*) b Nov. 7, 1889, d June 6, 1951

Terry, V. P. (Hants) b Jan. 14, 1959

*Theunissen, N. H. (W. Prov.) b May 4, 1867, d Nov. 9, 1929

Thomas, D. J. (Surrey, N. Tvl & Glos.) b June 30, 1959

*Thomas, G. (NSW) b March 21, 1938

*Thomas, J. G. (Glam., Border, E. Prov. & Northants) b Aug. 12, 1960

Thompson, A. W. (Middx) b April 17, 1916
*Thompson, G. J. (Northants; *CY 1906*) b Oct. 27, 1877, d March 3, 1943
Thompson, J. R. (CUCC & Warwicks.) b May 10, 1918
*Thompson, Nathaniel (NSW) b April 21, 1838, d Sept. 2, 1896
Thompson, R. G. (Warwicks.) b Sept. 26, 1932
*Thoms, G. R. (Vic.) b March 22, 1927
*Thomson, A. L. (Vic.) b Dec. 2, 1945
*Thomson, J. R. (NSW, Qld & Middx) b Aug. 16, 1950
*Thomson, K. (Cant.) b Feb. 26, 1941
*Thomson, N. I. (Sussex) b Jan. 23, 1929
*Thomson, S. A. (N. Dist.) b Jan. 27, 1969
Thorne, D. A. (Warwicks & OUCC) b Dec. 12, 1964
Thornton, C. I. (CUCC, Kent & Middx) b March 20, 1850, d Dec. 10, 1929
*Thornton, P. G. (Yorks., Middx & SA) b Dec. 24, 1867, d Jan. 31, 1939
Thorpe, G. P. (Surrey) b Aug. 1, 1969
*Thurlow, H. M. (Qld) b Jan. 10, 1903, d Dec. 3, 1975
*Tillekeratne, H. P. (NCC) b July 14, 1967
Tilly, H. W. (Middx) b May 25, 1932
Timms, B. S. V. (Hants & Warwicks.) b Dec. 17, 1940
Timms, J. E. (Northants) b Nov. 3, 1906, d May 18, 1980
Timms, W. W. (Northants) b Sept. 28, 1902, d Sept. 30, 1986
Tindall, M. (CUCC & Middx) b March 31, 1914
Tindall, R. A. E. (Surrey) b Sept. 23, 1935
*Tindill, E. W. T. (Wgtn) b Dec. 18, 1910
Tissera, M. H. (SL) b March 23, 1939
*Titmus, F. J. (Middx, Surrey & OFS; *CY 1963*) b Nov. 24, 1932
Todd, L. J. (Kent) b June 19, 1907, d Aug. 20, 1967
Todd, P. A. (Notts. & Glam.) b March 12, 1953
Tolchard, J. G. (Leics.) b March 17, 1944
*Tolchard, R. W. (Leics.) b June 15, 1946
Tomlins, K. P. (Middx & Glos.) b Oct. 23, 1957
*Tomlinson, D. S. (Rhod. & Border) b Sept. 4, 1910
Tompkin, M. (Leics.) b Feb. 17, 1919, d Sept. 27, 1956
Toogood, G. J. (OUCC) b Nov. 19, 1961
*Toohey, P. M. (NSW) b April 20, 1954
Tooley, C. D. M. (OUCC) b April 19, 1964
Topley, T. D. (Surrey, Essex & Griq. W.) b Feb. 25, 1964
Tordoff, G. G. (CUCC & Som.) b Dec. 6, 1929
*Toshack, E. R. H. (NSW) b Dec. 15, 1914
Townsend, A. (Warwicks.) b Aug. 26, 1921

Townsend, A. F. (Derbys.) b March 29, 1912
*Townsend, C. L. (Glos.; *CY 1899*) b Nov. 7, 1876, d Oct. 17, 1958
*Townsend, D. C. H. (OUCC) b April 20, 1912
*Townsend, L. F. (Derbys. & Auck.; *CY 1934*) b June 8, 1903
*Traicos, A. J. (Rhod. & Zimb.) b May 17, 1947
Travers, J. P. F. (S. Aust.) b Jan. 10, 1871, d Sept. 15, 1942
*Tremlett, M. F. (Som. & C. Dist.) b July 5, 1923, d July 30, 1984
Tremlett, T. M. (Hants) b July 26, 1956
*Tribe, G. E. (Vic. & Northants; *CY 1955*) b Oct. 4, 1920
*Trim, J. (BG) b Jan. 24, 1915, d Nov. 12, 1960
Trimble, G. S. (Qld) b Jan. 1, 1963
Trimble, S. C. (Qld) b Aug. 16, 1934
*Trimborn, P. H. J. (Natal) b May 18, 1940
**Trott, A. E. (Vic., Middx & Hawkes Bay; *CY 1899*) b Feb. 6, 1873, d July 30, 1914
*Trott, G. H. S. (Vic.; *CY 1894*) b Aug. 5, 1866, d Nov. 10, 1917
*Troup, G. B. (Auck.) b Oct. 3, 1952
*Trueman, F. S. (Yorks.; *CY 1953*) b Feb. 6, 1931
*Trumble, H. (Vic.; *CY 1897*) b May 12, 1867, d Aug. 14, 1938
*Trumble, J. W. (Vic.) b Sept. 16, 1863, d Aug. 17, 1944
Trump, H. R. J. (Som.) b Oct. 11, 1968
*Trumper, V. T. (NSW; *CY 1903*) b Nov. 2, 1877, d June 28, 1915
Truscott, P. B. (Wgtn) b Aug. 14, 1941
*Tuckett, L. (OFS) b Feb. 6, 1919
*Tuckett, L. R. (Natal & OFS) b April 19, 1885, d April 8, 1963
*Tufnell, N. C. (CUCC & Surrey) b June 13, 1887, d Aug. 3, 1951
*Tufnell, P. C. R. (Middx) b April 29, 1966
Tuke, Sir Anthony (Pres. MCC 1982-83) b Aug. 22, 1920
Tunnicliffe, C. J. (Derbys.) b Aug. 11, 1951
Tunnicliffe, H. T. (Notts.) b March 4, 1950
*Tunnicliffe, J. (Yorks.; *CY 1901*) b Aug. 26, 1866, d July 11, 1948
*Turnbull, M. J. (CUCC & Glam.; *CY 1931*) b March 16, 1906, d Aug. 5, 1944
Turner, A. (NSW) b July 23, 1950
*Turner, C. T. B. (NSW; *CY 1889*) b Nov. 16, 1862, d Jan. 1, 1944
Turner, D. R. (Hants & W. Prov.) b Feb. 5, 1949
Turner, F. M. (Leics.) b Aug. 8, 1934
Turner, G. J. (W. Prov., N. Tvl & OUCC) b Aug. 5, 1964
*Turner, G. M. (Otago, N. Dist. & Worcs.; *CY 1971*) b May 26, 1947

Turner, R. J. (CUCC & Som.) b Nov. 25, 1967

Turner, S. (Essex & Natal) b July 18, 1943

*Twentyman-Jones, P. S. (W. Prov.) b Sept. 13, 1876, d March 8, 1954

Twining, R. H. (OUCC & Middx; Pres. MCC 1964-65) b Nov. 3, 1889, d Jan. 3, 1979

*Tyldesley, E. (Lancs.; *CY 1920*) b Feb. 5, 1889, d May 5, 1962

*Tyldesley, J. T. (Lancs.; *CY 1902*) b Nov. 22, 1873, d Nov. 27, 1930

*Tyldesley, R. K. (Lancs.; *CY 1925*) b March 11, 1897, d Sept. 17, 1943

*Tylecote, E. F. S. (OUCC & Kent) b June 23, 1849, d March 15, 1938

*Tyler, E. J. (Som.) b Oct. 13, 1864, d Jan. 25, 1917

*Tyson, F. H. (Northants; *CY 1956*) b June 6, 1930

Ufton, D. G. (Kent) b May 31, 1928

*Ulyett, G. (Yorks.) b Oct. 21, 1851, d June 18, 1898

*Umrigar, P. R. (Bombay & Guj.) b March 28, 1926

*Underwood, D. L. (Kent; *CY 1969*) b June 8, 1945

Unwin, F. St G. (Essex) b April 23, 1911, d Oct. 4, 1990

*Valentine, A. L. (Jam.; *CY 1951*) b April 29, 1930

*Valentine, B. H. (CUCC & Kent) b Jan. 17, 1908, d Feb. 2, 1983

*Valentine, V. A. (Jam.) b April 4, 1908, d July 6, 1972

*Vance, R. H. (Wgtn) b March 31, 1955

*van der Bijl, P. G. (W. Prov. & OUCC) b Oct. 21, 1907, d Feb. 16, 1973

van der Bijl, V. A. P. (Natal, Middx & Tvl; *CY 1981*) b March 19, 1948

Van der Gucht, P. I. (Glos. & Bengal) b Nov. 2, 1911

*Van der Merwe, E. A. (Tvl) b Nov. 9, 1904, d Feb. 28, 1971

*Van der Merwe, P. L. (W. Prov. & E. Prov.) b March 14, 1937

van Geloven, J. (Yorks. & Leics.) b Jan. 4, 1934

*Van Ryneveld, C. B. (W. Prov. & OUCC) b March 19, 1928

van Zyl, C. J. P. G. (OFS & Glam.) b Oct. 1, 1961

Varachia, R. (First Pres. SA Cricket Union) b Oct. 12, 1915, d Dec. 11, 1981

Varey, D. W. (CUCC & Lancs.) b Oct. 15, 1961

*Varnals, G. D. (E. Prov., Tvl & Natal) b July 24, 1935

Vaulkhard, P. (Notts. & Derbys.) b Sept. 15, 1911

*Veivers, T. R. (Qld) b April 6, 1937

*Veletta, M. R. J. (W. Aust.) b Oct. 30, 1963

*Vengsarkar, D. B. (Bombay; *CY 1987*) b April 6, 1956

*Venkataraghavan, S. (†TN & Derbys.) b April 21, 1946

*Venkataramana, M. (TN) b April 24, 1966

*Verity, H. (Yorks.; *CY 1932*) b May 18, 1905, d July 31, 1943

*Vernon, G. F. (Middx) b June 20, 1856, d Aug. 10, 1902

Vernon, M. T. (W. Aust.) b Feb. 9, 1937

Vigar, F. H. (Essex) b July 7, 1917

*Viljoen, K. G. (Griq. W., OFS & Tvl) b May 14, 1910, d Jan. 21, 1974

*Vincent, C. L. (Tvl) b Feb. 16, 1902, d Aug. 24, 1968

Vine, J. (Sussex; *CY 1906*) b May 15, 1875, d April 25, 1946

*Vintcent, C. H. (Tvl & Griq. W.) b Sept. 2, 1866, d Sept. 28, 1943

Virgin, R. T. (Som., Northants & W. Prov.; *CY 1971*) b Aug. 26, 1939

*Viswanath, G. R. (†Karn.) b Feb. 12, 1949

*Viswanath, S. (Karn.) b Nov. 29, 1962

*Vivian, G. E. (Auck.) b Feb. 28, 1946

*Vivian, H. G. (Auck.) b Nov. 4, 1912, d Aug. 12, 1983

*Vizianagram, Maharaj Kumar of, Sir Vijay A. (U. Prov.) b Dec. 28, 1905, d Dec. 2, 1965

*Voce, W. (Notts.; *CY 1933*) b Aug. 8, 1909, d June 6, 1984

*Vogler, A. E. E. (Middx, Natal, Tvl & E. Prov.; *CY 1908*) b Nov. 28, 1876, d Aug. 9, 1946

Vonhagt, D. M. (Moors) b March 31, 1965

*Waddington, A. (Yorks.) b Feb. 4, 1893, d Oct. 28, 1959

Waddington, J. E. (Griq. W.) b Dec. 30, 1918, d Nov. 24, 1985

*Wade, H. F. (Natal) b Sept. 14, 1905, d Nov. 22, 1980

Wade, T. H. (Essex) b Nov. 24, 1910, d July 25, 1987

*Wade, W. W. (Natal) b June 18, 1914

*Wadekar, A. L. (Bombay) b April 1, 1941

*Wadsworth, K. J. (C. Dist. & Cant.) b Nov. 30, 1946, d Aug. 19, 1976

*Wainwright, E. (Yorks.; *CY 1894*) b April 8, 1865, d Oct. 28, 1919

*Waite, J. H. B. (E. Prov. & Tvl) b Jan. 19, 1930

*Waite, M. G. (S. Aust.) b Jan. 7, 1911, d Dec. 16, 1985

*Walcott, C. L. (B'dos & BG; *CY 1958*) b Jan. 17, 1926

*Walcott, L. A. (B'dos) b Jan. 18, 1894, d Feb. 27, 1984

Walden, F. I. (Northants; Umpire) b March 1, 1888, d May 3, 1949

Walford, M. M. (OUCC & Som.) b Nov. 27, 1915

Walker, A. (Northants) b July 7, 1962

Walker, A. K. (NSW & Notts.) b Oct. 4, 1925

Walker, C. (Yorks. & Hants) b June 27, 1920

Walker, C. W. (S. Aust.) b Feb. 19, 1909, d Dec. 21, 1942

Walker, I. D. (Middx) b Jan. 8, 1844, d July 6, 1898

*Walker, M. H. N. (Vic.) b Sept. 12, 1948

*Walker, P. M. (Glam., Tvl & W. Prov.) b Feb. 17, 1936

Walker, W. (Notts.) b Nov. 24, 1892, d Dec. 3, 1991

*Wall, T. W. (S. Aust.) b May 13, 1904, d March 25, 1981

*Wallace, W. M. (Auck.) b Dec. 19, 1916

Waller, C. E. (Surrey & Sussex) b Oct. 3, 1948

*Walsh, C. A. (Jam. & Glos.; *CY 1987*) b Oct. 30, 1962

Walsh, J. E. (NSW & Leics.) b Dec. 4, 1912, d May 20, 1980

*Walter, K. A. (Tvl) b Nov. 5, 1939

*Walters, C. F. (Glam. & Worcs.; *CY 1934*) b Aug. 28, 1905

*Walters, F. H. (Vic. & NSW) b Feb. 9, 1860, d June 1, 1922

Walters, J. (Derbys.) b Aug. 7, 1949

*Walters, K. D. (NSW) b Dec. 21, 1945

Walton, A. C. (OUCC & Middx) b Sept. 26, 1933

*Waqar Hassan (Pak. Us, Punjab, Pak. Serv. & Kar.) b Sept. 12, 1932

*Waqar Younis (Multan, UBL & Surrey; *CY 1992*) b Nov. 16, 1971

*Ward, Alan (Derbys., Leics. & Border) b Aug. 10, 1947

*Ward, Albert (Yorks. & Lancs.; *CY 1890*) b Nov. 21, 1865, d Jan. 6, 1939

Ward, B. (Essex) b Feb. 28, 1944

Ward, D. (Glam.) b Aug. 30, 1934

Ward, D. M. (Surrey) b Feb. 10, 1961

*Ward, F. A. (S. Aust.) b Feb. 23, 1909, d March 25, 1974

*Ward, J. T. (Cant.) b March 11, 1937

*Ward, T. A. (Tvl) b Aug. 2, 1887, d Feb. 16, 1936

Ward, T. R. (Kent) b Jan. 18, 1968

Ward, William (MCC & Hants) b July 24, 1787, d June 30, 1849

*Wardle, J. H. (Yorks.; *CY 1954*) b Jan. 8, 1923, d July 23, 1985

*Warnapura, B. (SL) b March 1, 1953

*Warnaweera, K. P. J. (Galle) b Nov. 23, 1960

Warne, F. B. (Worcs., Vic. & Tvl) b Oct. 3, 1906

Warner, A. E. (Worcs. & Derbys.) b May 12, 1959

*Warner, Sir P. F. (OUCC & Middx; *CY 1904, special portrait 1921*; Pres. MCC 1950-51) b Oct. 2, 1873, d Jan. 30, 1963

*Warr, J. J. (CUCC & Middx; Pres. MCC 1987-88) b July 16, 1927

*Warren, A. R. (Derbys.) b April 2, 1875, d Sept. 3, 1951

*Washbrook, C. (Lancs.; *CY 1947*) b Dec. 6, 1914

*Wasim Akram (Lahore, PACO, PNSC & Lancs.) b June 3, 1966

*Wasim Bari (Kar., PIA & Sind) b March 23, 1948

*Wasim Raja (Lahore, Sargodha, Pak. Us, PIA, Punjab & NBP) b July 3, 1952

Wass, T. G. (Notts.; *CY 1908*) b Dec. 26, 1873, d Oct. 27, 1953

*Wassan, A. S. (Delhi) b March 23, 1968

Wassell, A. (Hants) b April 15, 1940

*Watkin, S. L. (Glam.) b Sept. 15, 1964

*Watkins, A. J. (Glam.) b April 21, 1922

*Watkins, J. C. (Natal) b April 10, 1923

*Watkins, J. R. (NSW) b April 16, 1943

Watkinson, M. (Lancs.) b Aug. 1, 1961

*Watson, C. (Jam. & Delhi) b July 1, 1938

Watson, F. B. (Lancs.) b Sept. 17, 1898, d Feb. 1, 1976

*Watson, G. D. (Vic., W. Aust. & NSW) b March 8, 1945

Watson, G. G. (NSW, W. Aust. & Worcs.) b Jan. 29, 1955

*Watson, W. (Yorks. & Leics.; *CY 1954*) b March 7, 1920

*Watson, W. (Auck.) b Aug. 31, 1965

*Watson, W. J. (NSW) b Jan. 31, 1931

Watson, W. K. (Border, N. Tvl, E. Prov. & Notts.) b May 21, 1955

*Watt, L. (Otago) b Sept. 17, 1924

Watts, E. A. (Surrey) b Aug. 1, 1911, d May 2, 1982

Watts, H. E. (CUCC & Som.) b March 4, 1922

Watts, P. D. (Northants & Notts.) b March 31, 1938

Watts, P. J. (Northants) b June 16, 1940

*Waugh, M. E. (NSW & Essex; *CY 1991*) b June 2, 1965

*Waugh, S. R. (NSW & Som.; *CY 1989*) b June 2, 1965

*Wazir Ali, S. (C. Ind., S. Punjab & Patiala) b Sept. 15, 1903, d June 17, 1950

*Wazir Mohammad (B'pur & Kar.) b Dec. 22, 1929

Weale, S. D. (OUCC) b Sept. 16, 1967

*Webb, M. G. (Otago & Cant.) b June 22, 1947

*Webb, P. N. (Auck.) b July 14, 1957

Webb, R. J. (Otago) b Sept. 15, 1952

Webb, R. T. (Sussex) b July 11, 1922

Webb, S. G. (Manager Australians in England 1961) b Jan. 31, 1900, d Aug. 5, 1976

*Webbe, A. J. (OUCC & Middx) b Jan. 16, 1855, d Feb. 19, 1941

Webster, J. (CUCC & Northants) b Oct. 28, 1917

Webster, Dr R. V. (Warwicks. & Otago) b June 10, 1939

Webster, W. H. (CUCC & Middx; Pres. MCC 1976-77) b Feb. 22, 1910, d June 19, 1986

*Weekes, E. D. (B'dos; *CY 1951*) b Feb. 26, 1925

*Weekes, K. H. (Jam.) b Jan. 24, 1912

Weeks, R. T. (Warwicks.) b April 30, 1930

*Weerasinghe, C. D. U. S. (TU) b March 1, 1968

Weir, G. L. (Auck.) b June 2, 1908

*Wellard, A. W. (Som.; *CY 1936*) b April 8, 1902, d Dec. 31, 1980

*Wellham, D. M. (NSW & Tas.) b March 13, 1959

Wellings, E. M. (OUCC & Surrey) b April 6, 1909

Wells, A. P. (Sussex & Border) b Oct. 2, 1961

Wells, B. D. (Glos. & Notts.) b July 27, 1930

Wells, C. M. (Sussex, Border & W. Prov.) b March 3, 1960

Wenman, E. G. (Kent & England) b Aug. 18, 1803, d Dec. 31, 1879

Wensley, A. F. (Sussex) b May 23, 1898, d June 17, 1970

*Wesley, C. (Natal) b Sept. 5, 1937

*Wessels, K. C. (OFS, W. Prov., N. Tvl, Sussex, Qld & E. Prov.) b Sept. 14, 1957

West, G. H. (Editor of *Wisden* 1880-86) b 1851, d Oct. 6, 1896

*Westcott, R. J. (W. Prov.) b Sept. 19, 1927

Weston, A. J. (Worcs.) b April 8, 1959

*Wettimuny, M. D. (SL) b June 11, 1951

*Wettimuny, S. (SL; *CY 1985*) b Aug. 12, 1956

Wettimuny, S. R. de S. (SL) b Feb. 7, 1949

*Wharton, A. (Lancs. & Leics.) b April 30, 1923

*Whatmore, D. F. (Vic.) b March 16, 1954

Wheatley, K. J. (Hants) b Jan. 20, 1946

Wheatley, O. S. (CUCC, Warwicks. & Glam.; *CY 1969*) b May 28, 1935

Whitaker, Haddon (Editor of *Wisden* 1940-43) b Aug. 30, 1908, d Jan. 5, 1982

*Whitaker, J. J. (Leics.; *CY 1987*) b May 5, 1962

Whitcombe, P. A. (OUCC & Middx) b April 23, 1923

White, A. F. T. (CUCC, Warwicks. & Worcs.) b Sept. 5, 1915

*White, D. J. (N. Dist.) b June 26, 1961

*White, D. W. (Hants & Glam.) b Dec. 14, 1935

White, E. C. S. (NSW) b July 14, 1913

*White, G. C. (Tvl) b Feb. 5, 1882, d Oct. 17, 1918

*White, J. C. (Som.; *CY 1929*) b Feb. 19, 1891, d May 2, 1961

White, Hon. L. R. (5th Lord Annaly) (Middx & Victory Test) b March 15, 1927, d Sept. 30, 1990

White, R. A. (Middx & Notts.) b Oct. 6, 1936

White, R. C. (CUCC, Glos. & Tvl) b Jan. 29, 1941

*White, W. A. (B'dos) b Nov. 20, 1938

Whitehead, J. P. (Yorks. & Worcs.) b Sept. 3, 1925

Whitehouse, J. (Warwicks.) b April 8, 1949

*Whitelaw, P. E. (Auck.) b Feb. 10, 1910, d Aug. 28, 1988

Whitfield, B. J. (Natal) b March 14, 1959

Whitfield, E. W. (Surrey & Northants) b May 31, 1911

Whiting, N. H. (Worcs.) b Oct. 2, 1920

Whitington, R. S. (S. Aust. & Victory Tests; Writer) b June 30, 1912, d March 13, 1984

*Whitney, M. R. (NSW & Glos.) b Feb. 24, 1959

Whittaker, G. J. (Surrey) b May 29, 1916

Whitticase, P. (Leics.) b March 15, 1965

Whittingham, N. B. (Notts.) b Oct. 22, 1940

*Whitty, W. J. (S. Aust.) b Aug. 15, 1886, d Jan. 30, 1974

*Whysall, W. W. (Notts.; *CY 1925*) b Oct. 31, 1887, d Nov. 11, 1930

*Wickremasinghe, A. G. D. (NCC) b Dec. 27, 1965

Wickremasinghe, G. P. (BRC) b Aug. 14, 1971

Wiener, J. M. (Vic.) b May 1, 1955

*Wight, C. V. (BG) b July 28, 1902, d Oct. 4, 1969

*Wight, G. L. (BG) b May 28, 1929

Wight, P. B. (BG, Som., & Cant.) b June 25, 1930

*Wijegunawardene, K. I. W. (CCC) b Nov. 23, 1964

*Wijesuriya, R. G. C. E. (Mor.) b Feb. 18, 1960

Wild, D. J. (Northants) b Nov. 28, 1962

*Wiles, C. A. (B'dos & T/T) b Aug. 11, 1892, d Nov. 4, 1957

Wilkins, A. H. (Glam., Glos. & N. Tvl) b Aug. 22, 1953

Wilkins, C. P. (Derbys., Border, E. Prov. & Natal) b July 31, 1944

*Wilkinson, L. L. (Lancs.) b Nov. 5, 1916

Wilkinson, P. A. (Notts.) b Aug. 23, 1951

Wilkinson, Col. W. A. C. (OUCC) b Dec. 6, 1892, d Sept. 19, 1983

Willatt, G. L. (CUCC, Notts. & Derbys.) b May 7, 1918

*Willett, E. T. (Comb. Is. & Leewards) b
May 1, 1953
Willett, M. D. (Surrey) b April 21, 1933
*Willey, P. (Northants, E. Prov. & Leics.) b
Dec. 6, 1949
*Williams, A. B. (Jam.) b Nov. 21, 1949
Williams, C. B. (B'dos) b March 8, 1926
Williams, C. C. P. (Lord Williams of Elvet)
(OUCC & Essex) b Feb. 9, 1933
Williams, D. (T/T) b Nov. 4, 1963
Williams, D. L. (Glam.) b Nov. 20, 1946
*Williams, E. A. V. (B'dos) b April 10, 1914
*Williams, N. F. (Middx, Windwards &
Tas.) b July 2, 1962
Williams, R. G. (Northants) b Aug. 10,
1957
*Williams, R. J. (Natal) b April 12, 1912, d
May 14, 1984
Williamson, J. G. (Northants) b April 4,
1936
*Willis, R. G. D. (Surrey, Warwicks. & N.
Tvl; *CY 1978*) b May 30, 1949
*Willoughby, J. T. (SA) b Nov. 7, 1874, d
*circa* 1955
Willsher, E. (Kent & All-England) b Nov.
22, 1828, d Oct. 7, 1885
Wilmot, K. (Warwicks.) b April 3, 1911
Wilson, A. (Lancs.) b April 24, 1921
Wilson, A. E. (Middx & Glos.) b May 18,
1910
*Wilson, Rev. C. E. M. (CUCC & Yorks.) b
May 15, 1875, d Feb. 8, 1944
*Wilson, D. (Yorks. & MCC) b Aug. 7, 1937
*Wilson, E. R. (CUCC & Yorks.) b March
25, 1879, d July 21, 1957
Wilson, J. V. (Yorks.; *CY 1961*) b Jan. 17,
1921
*Wilson, J. W. (Vic. & S. Aust.) b Aug. 20,
1921, d Oct. 13, 1985
Wilson, P. H. L. (Surrey, Som. & N. Tvl) b
Aug. 17, 1958
Wilson, S. C. (Kent) b Feb. 18, 1928
*Wimble, C. S. (Tvl) b Jan. 9, 1864, d Jan.
28, 1930
Windows, A. R. (Glos. & CUCC) b Sept.
25, 1942
Winfield, H. M. (Notts) b June 13, 1933
Wingfield Digby, Rev. A. R. (OUCC) b
July 25, 1950
Winn, C. E. (OUCC & Sussex) b Nov. 13,
1926
*Winslow, P. L. (Sussex, Tvl & Rhod.) b
May 21, 1929
Wisden, John (Sussex; founder John
Wisden and Co. and *Wisden's Cricketers'
Almanack*) b Sept. 5, 1826, d April 5,
1884
*Wishart, K. L. (BG) b Nov. 28, 1908, d
Oct. 18, 1972
Wolton, A. V. G. (Warwicks.) b June 12,
1919, d Sept. 9, 1990

*Wood, A. (Yorks.; *CY 1939*) b Aug. 25,
1898, d April 1, 1973
*Wood, B. (Yorks., Lancs., Derbys. & E.
Prov.) b Dec. 26, 1942
Wood, C. J. B. (Leics.) b Nov. 21, 1875, d
June 5, 1960
Wood, D. J. (Sussex) b May 19, 1914, d
March 12, 1989
*Wood, G. E. C. (CUCC & Kent) b Aug. 22,
1893, d March 18, 1971
*Wood, G. M. (W. Aust.) b Nov. 6, 1956
*Wood, H. (Kent & Surrey; *CY 1891*) b Dec.
14, 1854, d April 30, 1919
*Wood, R. (Lancs. & Vic.) b March 7, 1860,
d Jan. 6, 1915
*Woodcock, A. J. (S. Aust.) b Feb. 27, 1948
Woodcock, John C. (Editor of *Wisden* 1980-
86) b Aug. 7, 1926
*Woodfull, W. M. (Vic.; *CY 1927*) b Aug.
22, 1897, d Aug. 11, 1965
Woodhead, F. G. (Notts) b Oct. 30, 1912,
d May 24, 1991
Woodhouse, G. E. S. (Som.) b Feb. 15,
1924, d Jan. 19, 1988
**Woods, S. M. J. (CUCC & Som.; *CY
1889*) b April 13, 1867, d April 30, 1931
*Wookey, S. M. (CUCC & OUCC) b Sept.
2, 1954
Wooler, C. R. D. (Leics. & Rhod.) b June
30, 1930
Wooller, W. (CUCC & Glam.) b Nov. 20,
1912
Woolley, C. N. (Glos. & Northants) b May
5, 1886, d Nov. 3, 1962
*Woolley, F. E. (Kent; *CY 1911*) b May 27,
1887, d Oct. 18, 1978
*Woolley, R. D. (Tas.) b Sept. 16, 1954
*Woolmer, R. A. (Kent, Natal & W. Prov.;
*CY 1976*) b May 14, 1948
*Worrall, J. (Vic.) b May 12, 1863, d Nov.
17, 1937
*Worrell, Sir F. M. M. (B'dos & Jam.; *CY
1951*) b Aug. 1, 1924, d March 13, 1967
Worsley, D. R. (OUCC & Lancs.) b July
18, 1941
Worsley, Sir W. A. 4th Bt (Yorks.; Pres.
MCC 1961-62) b April 5, 1890, d Dec. 4,
1973
*Worthington, T. S. (Derbys.; *CY 1937*) b
Aug. 21, 1905, d Aug. 31, 1973
Wright, A. (Warwicks.) b Aug. 25, 1941
Wright, A. J. (Glos.) b July 27, 1962
*Wright, C. W. (CUCC & Notts.) b May 27,
1863, d Jan. 10, 1936
*Wright, D. V. P. (Kent; *CY 1940*) b Aug.
21, 1914
*Wright, J. G. (N. Dist., Derbys., Cant. &
Auck.) b July 5, 1954
*Wright, K. J. (W. Aust. & S. Aust.) b Dec.
27, 1953
Wright, L. G. (Derbys.; *CY 1906*) b June
15, 1862, d Jan. 11, 1953

Wyatt, J. G. (Som.) b June 19, 1963
*Wyatt, R. E. S. (Warwicks. & Worcs.; *CY 1930*) b May 2, 1901
*Wynne, O. E. (Tvl & W. Prov.) b June 1, 1919, d July 13, 1975
*Wynyard, E. G. (Hants) b April 1, 1861, d Oct. 30, 1936

Yachad, M. (N. Tvl & Tvl) b Nov. 17, 1960
*Yadav, N. S. (H'bad) b Jan. 26, 1957
*Yajurvindra Singh (M'tra & S'tra) b Aug. 1, 1952
Yallop, G. N. (Vic.) b Oct. 7, 1952
*Yardley, B. (W. Aust.) b Sept. 5, 1947
*Yardley, N. W. D. (CUCC & Yorks.; *CY 1948*) b March 19, 1915, d Oct. 4, 1989
Yardley, T. J. (Worcs. & Northants) b Oct. 27, 1946
Yarnold, H. (Worcs.) b July 6, 1917, d Aug. 13, 1974
*Yashpal Sharma (Punjab) b Aug. 11, 1954
Yates, G. (Lancs.) b Sept. 20, 1967
Yawar Saeed (Som. & Punjab) b Jan. 22, 1935
*Yograj Singh (Haryana & Punjab) b March 25, 1958
Young, B. A. (N. Dist.) b Nov. 3, 1964

Young, D. M. (Worcs. & Glos.) b April 15, 1924
*Young, H. I. (Essex) b Feb. 5, 1876, d Dec. 12, 1964
*Young, J. A. (Middx) b Oct. 14, 1912
*Young, R. A. (CUCC & Sussex) b Sept. 16, 1885, d July 1, 1968
*Younis Ahmed (Lahore, Kar., Surrey, PIA, S. Aust., Worcs. & Glam.) b Oct. 20, 1947
*Yuile, B. W. (C. Dist.) b Oct. 29, 1941

*Zaheer Abbas (Kar., Glos., PWD, Dawood Indust., Sind & PIA; *CY 1972*) b July 24, 1947
Zahid Ahmed (PIA) b Nov. 15, 1961
*Zahid Fazal (PACO) b Nov. 10, 1973
*Zakir Khan (Sind, Peshawar & ADBP) b April 3, 1963
Zesers, A. K. (S. Aust.) b March 11, 1967
*Zoehrer, T. J. (W. Aust.) b Sept. 25, 1961
*Zulch, J. W. (Tvl) b Jan. 2, 1886, d May 19, 1924
*Zulfiqar Ahmed (B'pur & PIA) b Nov. 22, 1926
*Zulqarnain (Pak. Rlwys & Lahore) b May 25, 1962

# OBITUARIES

ALVA, SRIDHA, who died in Mangalore on November 6, 1991, at the age of 60, played some Ranji Trophy cricket for Mysore (now Karnataka) and Orissa. After retirement he turned his attention to coaching.

ARLOTT, LESLIE THOMAS JOHN, OBE, died at his home on Alderney on December 14, 1991, at the age of 77. Few men who have concentrated the interests of a lifetime on cricket have commanded as wide and thorough a knowledge of the game as John Arlott. When he was doing commentary, or composing a portrait of a Tate or a Trueman, or writing a match report for the *Guardian*, he was at or near the centre of affairs. But he was equally an expert on interests connected with the game: its vast literature, extensive history and collection of artifacts were all within his purview. To fuel his activities he had great energy, the ability to work at speed, and the charm to elicit information from whatever source he was investigating. Add in the fact that he was a poet of some stature and that he enjoyed the laughter and company of friends, whom he loved to entertain in the most civilised way, and you have a man of deep humanity.

J.A., as he perhaps over-modestly referred to himself in his autobiography, went to his first school in Basingstoke in 1920 when he was six. He soon located the cricket ground, and seeing mysterious white figures parading before him demanded to know what it was all about. His father, a patient, careful man, was pestered into providing rudimentary equipment. (Despite his early start he never became much of a player.) Six years later he made his way to his first big match, England v Australia at The Oval, where he saw Hobbs for the first time and recognised his genius. He was later to found a dining club in honour of the Master. That was his ration for the year, but it made an enormous impression on him. In 1927 he saw the whole of Sussex v Lancashire at Eastbourne, and soon he was reading anything he could lay his hands on about cricket. Cardus the reporter and Cardus the author were greedily digested. *Good Days* and *Australian Summer*, masterpieces both, were woven into the very fabric of his being. But where was this first love leading? How was he, a humble copper when war broke out in 1939, to fashion a career out of cricket?

Arlott's prospects of achieving a breakthrough into the magic circle were enhanced by an extraordinary chain of events which happened to unite his several talents with his love of cricket. In 1945 he was a police sergeant, in Southampton, but the broadcast address he made to His Majesty on VE Day on behalf of the police was the catalyst. By "sheer luck", as he himself admitted, he was introduced to all the right people behind the scenes at the BBC, and the offer of a permanent post followed. In time he was asked if he would like to do commentary on the first two matches of the Indian tour in 1946, provided they would not interfere with his job as Overseas Literary Producer. His broadcasts from Worcester and Oxford went down very well in India, and to his delight he was given the chance to cover the whole tour, including the Test matches. At Lord's, where the First Test was played, he was given the cold shoulder by his colleagues in the commentary box, resentful of the upstart who in their eyes had made off with the top job. But he survived and earned a grudging respect. Moreover, the public had begun to take note of a new and utterly individual voice coming over the air describing cricket. In the war the voice of Churchill had been a symbol of defiance, rousing ordinary folk to great deeds. Now the voice of Arlott brought comfort and reassurance as they adjusted to the ways of peace. His commentary technique was strongly influenced by his poetic sense. With the economy of a poet he could describe a piece of play without fuss or over-elaboration, being always conscious of its rhythm and mindful of its background. He was never repetitive or monotonous, except for effect. The listener's imagination was given free rein. From 1946 till the end of the 1980 season he covered every single home Test match. The voice may have dropped an octave as the years rolled by, but the level of commentary never faltered.

When the editor asked Arlott to write an appreciation of Neville Cardus for the 1965 edition of *Wisden*, he chose wisely, for Arlott was a natural disciple of the man who was 25 years his senior. The two men had much in common: they were both incurable romantics; they both combined a love of cricket with a love for the arts (music and poetry); each had a favourite county; they were both largely self-educated and had frequented libraries in their youth. From humble beginnings they both enjoyed the turn of fortune's wheel at a critical stage of their development. Arlott's debt to Cardus was immense. He saw that Cardus's cricketers were no mere cardboard figures performing complicated routines on a distant stage, but real, live human beings with hearts and minds and feelings. Cardus got close to his Lancastrians, but Arlott got even closer to his men from Hampshire and wrote about them with deep affection. He liked a character, especially the honest toiler who laboured often with little reward. His portrait of Vic Cannings is a typical example. But his study of Trueman, written in a fortnight during the postal strike in 1971, shows what he could do when his batteries were fully charged. As a piece of descriptive writing, this extract is hard to beat:

> Trueman's body swung round so completely that the batsman saw his left shoulder blade: the broad left foot was, for an infinitesimal period of time, poised to hammer the ground. He was a cocked trigger, left arm pointed high, head steady, eyes glaring at the batsman as that great stride widened: the arm slashed down and as the ball was fired down the pitch, his body was thrown hungrily after it, the right toe raking the ground closely beside the wicket as he swept on. Coming in almost from behind the umpire threw his left shoulder up and helped him to deliver from so near the stumps that sometimes he brushed the umpire. Indeed once, when Sam Pothecary was standing at Taunton, Trueman felled him, as he passed, with a blow of his steel right toe-cap on the ankle so savage as to leave that mildest of umpires limping for a fortnight.

It sounds like an express train thundering past, all pistons firing – steam of course.

Arlott was no great traveller; he preferred to stay at home in winter and watch some soccer. He covered the 1948-49 MCC tour to South Africa and was appalled by what he saw under the surface. He became a fervent opponent of apartheid and was responsible for Basil D'Oliveira's coming to England to play. His one visit to Australia was in 1954-55, when the Ashes were retained under Hutton. Apart from these two ventures, his main journalistic job was to be the *Guardian's* chief cricket correspondent from 1968 to 1980. In addition to all his other services to cricket, he was one of the leading authorities on its past. He was both archivist and historian. In 1963 he was commissioned to write a review of the "Cricket Literature of the Wisden Century". It was wide-ranging and is still a useful guide. In the *Barclays World of Cricket* he contributed two major articles, on Art and Histories. Both serve to illustrate the amazing comprehensiveness of his knowledge. From the 1950 edition of *Wisden* until this one, except for 1979 and 1980, he provided a comprehensive review of books published in the preceding year.

Arlott, the Liberal politician, always had the interests of the English county player at heart. The strong bond between them was cemented when he became president of the newly formed Cricketers' Association in 1968, at a time when cricket seemed to be in danger of disappearing as a major spectator sport. Salaries had failed to keep pace with the cost of living and morale was at rock bottom.

Arlott's democratic views and wise counsel earned him much respect in the cricket world and among the players. His moderation and tact helped in some tight corners, notably at the time of the Packer Affair, when he strove to keep the Cricketers' Association neutral.

Of all John Arlott's talents, it is his unique gift for cricket commentary which will bring him lasting fame. And nothing became him more than the manner in which he quietly slipped away from the scene at the end of his final commentary at Lord's while the crowd stood and, along with the players of England and Australia, applauded. A humble and generous man, he was appointed OBE in 1970 and had Honorary Life Membership of MCC bestowed upon him when he retired in 1980.

ATKINSON, COLIN RONALD MICHAEL, CBE, who died at Glastonbury on June 25, 1991, aged 59, became associated with Somerset in 1960, the attraction of a job at Millfield and the prospect of first-class cricket having persuaded him that his future lay in the south-west. A Yorkshireman, he had played for Northumberland and Durham with marked success, and reports of his gritty batting and accurate leg-spin bowling had reached H. W. Stephenson, the newly appointed Somerset captain, who hailed from Co. Durham. As McCool, the Australian, was retiring, there was a possible place for Atkinson in the senior side. He had already made his first-class début in 1959, for the Minor Counties against the Indians, and in 1960 he made a workmanlike start in his fifteen matches for Somerset, getting runs when they were most needed and picking up useful wickets. Not a natural player, he earned his successes by hard graft and determination, and he made himself into an energetic and menacing fielder. His next two seasons brought more than 1,200 Championship runs and 105 wickets in all, but in 1963 and 1964 his county cricket was confined almost exclusively to the Second Eleven. When he returned to the first team in 1965, it was as captain, his headmaster at Millfield, R. J. O. Meyer, himself a former Somerset captain, having agreed to release him from his duties at the school.

To start with he was cautious, but gradually he assumed full command and led the side capably into seventh place in the Championship. Arthritis in his right hand prevented him from bowling leg-spin, but at medium pace he took useful wickets at an economical cost to supplement his runs. Next year he appeared much more relaxed and confident in the field, and his good form soon communicated itself to his side. Somerset finished third, equalling their highest placing, with thirteen matches won, seven drawn and seven lost. Atkinson had by far his best season with the bat, scoring 1,120 runs at 26.04. Somerset also reached the semi-finals of the Gillette Cup, losing to Warwickshire at Birmingham, and although they fell back to eighth in the Championship in 1967, they compensated by getting to the Gillette Cup final at Lord's. There they lost by 32 runs to Kent in what was considered the best of the five finals so far played. Atkinson fielded like a tiger and impressed everyone with his control as Kent, 129 for one at lunch, were bowled out for 193. It was, however, his swan-song. He retired at the end of the season, to resume full-time teaching, having made 3,796 first-class runs for an average of 19.07 and taken 192 wickets at 31.15 in 164 matches. His highest score, an innings of 97 in a partnership of 176 for the sixth wicket with Roy Virgin, was made against Warwickshire at Birmingham in 1967. Always setting a fine example in the field, he held 75 catches.

Atkinson became headmaster of Millfield in 1971, but this in no way curtailed his interest in the county club, where he was successively cricket chairman, club chairman and then president. In the last role he was called upon to exercise all his diplomatic skills in 1986, when Richards, Garner and Botham departed amid controversy and spite. The new pavilion on the county ground at Taunton stands as a monument to his enterprise and energy as a fund-raiser. For some years he had been chairman of the PR and Marketing sub-committee of the TCCB.

ATKINSON, THOMAS, who died on September 2, 1990, aged 59, was one of several young professionals engaged by Nottinghamshire in the late 1950s, the intention being to give them a three-year trial under a youth scheme. A right-arm medium-pace bowler and a useful batsman in the lower order, he made his Championship début against Sussex at Worthing in 1957, and was stranded on 21 as Nottinghamshire failed by 24 runs to reach their target. Serious work began in 1958, and he found it hard going; his 23 wickets cost him more than 48 runs apiece and he had the unenviable distinction of propping up the national averages. On the other hand, he made his highest score of 48. In 1959, he batted profitably, with an aggregate of 341, but his 38 wickets cost 46.42 apiece. Clearly a major effort was called for if he was going to make the grade. In 1960 his wickets increased to 53, at a lower cost, and match figures of ten for 100 against Derbyshire at Ilkeston were his best performance. With the bat he totalled 467 runs, often scoring usefully when others failed, but despite this improvement he was not retained. In his 64 games he made 1,127 runs at 13.25 and took 116 wickets at 44.46 apiece.

AUGUST, GEORGE LAWRENCE BAGLEY, who was born at Mymensingh, India, died at his home in Bedford on October 13, 1991, aged 74. He was very much a Bedfordshire man, remaining loyal to his county when he might have been tempted to try his hand at a higher level. He was educated at Bedford School, where he developed into an opening or middle-order bat, and he made his début in the Minor County Championship in 1936. In 1947 he surpassed all his previous efforts with an innings of 201 against Oxfordshire on the Bedford School ground, sharing in a record opening partnership of 225 with J. A. R. Oliver. Bedfordshire's total of 539 for seven declared was their highest ever. August's form with the bat showed no sign of falling off until 1957, the year before his retirement. He made thirteen hundreds in his career and twice represented Minor Counties against first-class opposition. In 1950 against MCC at Lord's, he made 27 and 11, his dour defence playing its part as the Counties went ahead in the first innings with five wickets in hand. In 1953 Hassett's Australians crushed the Counties by an innings and 171 runs, the match being chiefly notable for Lindwall obtaining the best figures of his career, with seven for 20 in the second innings. August was unable to stem the tide as he contrived to be run out without scoring. He gave further service to Bedfordshire after he stopped playing, being their secretary from 1969 to 1984, and he was chairman of the Minor Counties Cricket Association from 1982 to 1989. He also served on the Test and County Cricket Board for several years.

BADDILEY, JOHN WILLIAM (JACK), who died in hospital at Worksop on December 16, 1990, aged 74, will be remembered with affection by visitors to Trent Bridge for the warmth of his welcome and his generous hospitality. His loss will be felt by the players and other members of the staff, to whom he had become a fatherly figure and true friend. He was elected president of Nottinghamshire in 1985, a position he held till his death, and he had served on the committee for 32 years, finally standing down at the start of 1990. During this long period, he was influential in effecting many improvements at Trent Bridge. The ground itself was largely restored and developed to meet the demands of a major cricket centre, and Baddiley was also influential in streamlining the administrative structure. It is interesting to note that, when he became a member of the committee in 1957, the fortunes of the club on the field were at rock bottom. The registration in the early 1950s of Dooland and Goonesena, with their high-class leg-spin, had brought temporary relief, and in 1968 the genius of the newly recruited Sobers pulled them up to fourth place in the Championship. But it was not until the arrival of Rice and Hadlee in the 1970s that the glories of what had become a distant past returned to Trent Bridge. Baddiley worked hard behind the scenes for the triumphs of 1981 and 1987. The experience of captaining the Second Eleven, in

1959 and 1960, at a time when the cupboard was practically bare, had led him to set in motion a wider and more efficient search for higher standards, and in the end he enjoyed his just reward.

BROWN, FREDERICK RICHARD, CBE, who died on July 24, 1991, aged 80, was an all-rounder of exceptional skill and achievement who will always be remembered for the courage and determination of his leadership of England in the 1950-51 Test series in Australia. Few visiting captains have been received with so much acclaim by the crowds of Melbourne and Sydney. Although England lost the series by four matches to one, it was soon appreciated that the 40-year-old Brown had almost single-handedly, and against every forecast, done a huge amount to revitalise English cricket, which had been humbled in turn by Australian speed and West Indian spin. What is in many ways a romantic story started when Brown was offered the captaincy of Northamptonshire early in 1949. He called his new charges back for three weeks training before the season began and went on to lead them to sixth place in the Championship – after two years at the bottom of the table. In addition, he was invited to captain England in the last two Tests against New Zealand and, crucially, a year later, the Gentlemen at Lord's. A sudden first-innings collapse, the presence of the selectors, and his sense of the occasion put Brown on his mettle. In a wonderful innings of 122, made in 110 minutes, he hit a six and sixteen fours, scoring all but 9 of the runs put on while he was at the wicket. The selectors had no need to look further for the man they wanted in Australia, and he was recalled to lead England at The Oval in the last Test against West Indies.

Indifferent form against the states did little to suggest that England would make a fight of it in the Tests; but they defied the critics by bowling out Australia for 228 on the opening day of the First Test at Brisbane. Although torrential overnight rain subsequently turned a losing score into a winning one, it was generally felt that England were superbly led and had played the better cricket. At Melbourne England lost by 28 runs: Brown's 62 in the first innings and four for 26 in Australia's second helped to make him the most popular player of the series. And so to Sydney, two down. Injuries to Bailey and Wright on the second day ruined the match as a contest, but made it memorable by compelling the feat of Bedser, Brown (bowling mostly seamers) and Warr, who sent down 123 eight-ball overs in scorching heat between 3.30 p.m. on the Saturday and lunch on Tuesday. When Brown's innings of 79 is taken into account, his contribution assumes heroic proportions. It is better to draw a veil over Adelaide, apart from Hutton's 156 not out, and go on to Melbourne, with England four down and thoroughly dejected. The captain, however, sounded the rallying call and seized the initiative by taking five of Australia's first-innings wickets after the home team had won the toss on the first morning. After that, victory by eight wickets was left in the capable hands of Hutton and Simpson. The whole picture had changed and spirits were high once more. As a postscript to Brown's main achievement, there was an immediate victory over New Zealand in Wellington, a 3-1 series win against South Africa at home in 1951, and a solitary appearance at Lord's in 1953 against Australia, at the special request of his fellow-selectors. It should also be noted that the youthful Brown had played in five Tests against New Zealand in three separate series before the war and in one against India in 1932 at Lord's.

Brown's career fell into two distinct halves. When he took over at Northampton in 1949 he had had virtually no first-class cricket for nine years, but by 1953, when he finally called it a day in county cricket, he had made 4,331 runs for them and taken 391 wickets. Before the war, he played for Surrey from 1931 to 1939, and although available for less than half their matches he delighted Oval regulars with his refreshing energy and enthusiasm. He greatly enjoyed the captaincy and the company of Percy Fender, Errol Holmes and Monty Garland-Wells in those years, and from Fender he learned that there was pace enough in the pre-war Oval pitches to reward top-class leg-spin. He had his best and most spectacular season in 1932, and events at The Oval in early August highlight the damage he was liable to inflict on suffering bowlers. Middlesex, having won the toss, collapsed for 141, and in reply Surrey were 195 for five. At this point Brown, "in a glorious display of fearless hitting", made 212 in 200 minutes, hitting seven sixes (two out of the ground) and fifteen fours. Kent and Middlesex (at Lord's in the return match) felt the full force of his explosive power before the season was over, and his double of 1,135 runs and 120 wickets was rewarded with a place on the boat to Australia with Jardine's side. He was one of the Five Cricketers of the Year in the 1933 *Wisden*.

Freddie Brown was born at Lima, Peru, where his father, no mean cricketer himself, was in business. The boy's left-handedness at everything met with paternal disapproval, and he was forced to change over, fortunately with no damage to his natural co-ordination. At his prep school, St Pirans, he made rapid strides under the tutorage of Aubrey Faulkner, who was on the staff, so that when he moved on to The Leys, he had four years of unbroken success, with more than 2,000 runs and nearly 200 wickets for the XI. Before his first season at Cambridge, he was advised by Faulkner to concentrate on leg-breaks and googlies as his main weapons in first-class cricket, keeping his medium-pace swingers up his sleeve as a variation. That he was able to carry this out is a tribute to his adaptability. In his two seasons at Cambridge, 1930 and 1931, he exceeded 1,000 runs in 25 matches and took exactly 100 wickets. In his first University Match he played two useful innings, and in 1931, when the Nawab of Pataudi made his record 238 not out for Oxford, he sustained an accurate and probing attack with five for 153 in 43.5 overs.

In an appendix to his book, *Cricket Musketeer*, published in 1954, no fewer than 27 instances of fast scoring involving Brown are cited, and it is estimated that he scored at 64 runs per hour in his longer innings, usually with shirt billowing and with a white kerchief ever present. In a career stretching from 1930 to 1961, he made 13,325 runs at 27.36, including 22 hundreds, took 1,221 wickets at 26.21 apiece, and held 212 catches. He performed the double again in 1949, and in 1952 he missed a third by a single wicket. He passed 1,000 runs four times. His best bowling figures were eight for 34 against Somerset at Weston-super-Mare in 1939. In his 22 Tests, fifteen as captain, Brown made 734 runs for an average of 25.31 and took 45 wickets at 31.06. He was chairman of selectors in 1953, and later in the decade he managed the MCC sides in South Africa and Australia. He was President of MCC in 1971-72 and also of the NCA and ESCA.

BRYAN, BRIGADIER GODFREY JAMES, CBE, who died at Canterbury on April 4, 1991, aged 88, was the youngest of three cricketing brothers, all of whom played for Kent. G.J. was possibly the most talented, a tall, strong, dashing left-hander with a fine array of attacking strokes, but he gave himself less chance of reaching the top than his brothers by choosing an Army career. Of the other two, J.L. was a member of A. E. R. Gilligan's MCC team in Australia in 1924-25 and R.T. captained Kent in 1937. They were both schoolmasters.

G.J. showed unusual precocity in his last two years at Wellington, where his deeds caused quite a stir in 1919 and 1920. As a sixteen-year-old in 1919 he made an unbeaten 102 against Westminster in a home fixture and went on, with the help of three not outs, to average 74.75 with an aggregate of 598 runs. A year later his figures were 8-2-699-148*-116.50, with hundreds against Bradfield, Westminster, Haileybury, Charterhouse and Free Foresters. Referred to by *Wisden* as the crack Public School batsman of the year, he played in the Schools Week at Lord's and hit a fifty. This was child's play. Picked for Kent against Nottinghamshire at Trent Bridge in the last match of the season, he made a memorable début by hitting 124 in the second innings as Kent followed on, putting on 187 for the first wicket with A. F. Bickmore. In 1921 he made 179 against Hampshire at Canterbury, hitting three sixes and 26 fours and with L. P. Hedges adding 208 in only two hours. When the South Africans were over in 1924, he seized upon the occasion to hit 229 against them for the Combined Services at Portsmouth, getting 116 of his runs in boundaries in four hours at the crease. Against Warwickshire at Birmingham he made 124 for his county, going in first and being sixth out with the score 174. In 1925, Kent had a notable triumph over Lancashire at Dover, winning by two wickets in a match of moderate scores, and all three Bryan brothers played. J.L. made 77, and G.J. saw Kent through the crisis at the end with a sterling innings of 39 not out.

Although his opportunities for county cricket were limited, Army cricket kept him in touch with the first-class game. He returned to Lord's year after year for the Army, and hardly ever failed to give the Navy bowlers a drubbing. In 1926 he hit 82 in an hour with three sixes and ten fours, an innings which turned the match decisively in the Army's favour, and in 1928 Bryan (93) and E. S. B. Williams (228) added 258 for the third wicket in only two hours; the Army went on to declare at 589 for five. Bryan's two remaining hundreds were both for the Army, against Oxford and Cambridge Universities, and on each occasion he displayed his customary brilliance. His 112 at Fenner's in 1925 was made out of a total of 196, the next highest score being 27. In all, he appeared in 70 first-class matches, 51 of them for Kent, and made 3,192 runs at 30.11, hitting six hundreds. As an occasional slow left-arm bowler, his best performance was five for 148 for Kent in an Australian total of 676 at Canterbury in 1921. He took 35 wickets in all at 50.08 apiece, and made 46 catches.

BURROWS, BRIGADIER JAMES THOMAS, CBE, DSO, who died at Christchurch, New Zealand, on June 10, 1991, aged 86, played nine first-class matches for Canterbury as a right-arm fast-medium bowler between 1926-27 and 1932-33. He took 31 wickets at 22.06, a useful return, and had an extraordinary batting record, going to the wicket twelve times in his accustomed position at No. 11 without ever being dismissed. These visits produced a grand total of 36 runs. In 1930 he took part in a famous match between Canterbury and Auckland, when Canterbury were set to score 473 runs in 400 minutes and made them with three minutes and four wickets to spare. In Auckland's second innings of 537, Burrows put the brake on by taking two for 89 in 43.4 overs in fearful heat, an important contribution. He also excelled at boxing and rugby, and in 1928 he was selected as a forward for the All Blacks' tour of South Africa.

BUTLER, HAROLD JAMES, died in Nottingham on July 17, 1991, aged 78, while on holiday there as a guest of the county club for which he had played in 306 matches between 1933 and 1954. Taken on at Trent Bridge as a right-arm fast-medium bowler, he was introduced to first-class cricket at twenty when Larwood broke down on his return from Australia. Among several promising performances that season was his five for 36 in 24 overs at Trent Bridge against Yorkshire, at a time when they were running away with the Championship. Yorkshire's total of 155 left them behind on first innings for the first time in county matches since the start of the season. However, it was another four years before he really caused a stir, routing Surrey at Trent Bridge with a career-best eight for 15 in fourteen overs, including a hat-trick. Within a month he had performed the feat a second time, against Leicestershire at Worksop. With Larwood in the toils and Voce incapacitated with a twisted knee, Butler's 78 wickets that season at 24.39 made him the most successful bowler in the team.

Appendicitis in June 1938 put him out for the rest of the Australian summer, just when he was heading the national averages with 39 wickets at 16.61, but a determined comeback in 1939 brought him 105 wickets at 22.96, including a third hat-trick in his return of five for 23 against Hampshire. His batting was improving, too, and with more than 400 runs he averaged around 18. Three sixes and six fours contributed to his 62, the highest score of his career, in a last-wicket stand of 68 in half an hour against Glamorgan at Swansea.

If perhaps unfortunate not to get a Test before the war, he finally caught the selectors' attention in 1947, when he took 106 wickets at 22.55. Lively and intelligent bowling for the Players at Lord's in mid-July led to a place in the England side for the Fourth Test against South Africa at Leeds. He had a good match, with seven for 66 all told, and the tourists scored painfully slowly off him in both innings. But injury kept him out of the final Test, at The Oval, and misfortune continued to dog him in the Caribbean, where it was intended he would be G. O. B. Allen's main strike bowler. A calf injury ruled him out of the First Test, and an attack of malaria prevented him from playing in the last two. In between, at Port-of-Spain, he took five wickets in the drawn Second Test, bowling well in adverse conditions. However, there was no place for him in 1948, when Edrich, Coxon, Pollard, Cranston and Watkins all shared the new ball against Australia with Bedser.

A crowd of 20,000 attended the first day of his benefit match against Yorkshire in 1950, a fine tribute to a great servant of the club, and that season, at the age of 37, he just failed to take 100 wickets for the third time. He kept going, often with little help from the other end, until 1954, when he retired on doctor's advice. Bowling on the quick side of medium, Butler had throughout his career been economical in terms of runs per over, always keeping a tidy line and adjusting his length skilfully according to the conditions. In 319 matches in all, he took 952 wickets at 24.44, while his hard hitting brought him 2,962 runs for an average of 10.54. In his two Tests – he deserved to have played in more – he took twelve wickets at 17.91.

CACCIA, LORD, GCMG, GCVO (HAROLD ANTHONY), who died on October 31, 1990, aged 84, won his colours at Eton in 1924 and played at Lord's as a bowler, taking two wickets in Harrow's second innings, which effectively halted their pursuit of victory. He was nominated President of MCC for 1973-74 by Aidan Crawley, and it was felt that his diplomatic skills would be invaluable in reconciling the differences in world cricket that followed in the wake of the D'Oliveira affair. In the Asian countries, for example, there was an opinion that MCC should not remain the game's governing body.

CHINNASWAMY, MANGALAM, died in Bangalore after a long illness on October 31, 1991. He was 91. A traditionalist, who sacrificed a career at the Bar in order to devote himself to cricket, he was a founder member of the Karnataka Cricket Association and the moving force behind the development of the stadium at Bangalore, which now bears his name. In 1967, as secretary to the Board of Control for Cricket in India, he accompanied the touring side to England. He later became president of the BCCI and was active in preventing Indian Test cricketers from being lured into World Series Cricket.

COCKBURN, JAMES SYDNEY DAVID, who died at Brisbane on November 13, 1990, aged 74, was an all-rounder who played for Queensland in two first-class matches in 1936-37 when he was only twenty. The first was against G. O. B. Allen's MCC tourists at Brisbane immediately before the First Test: given the new ball, he failed to take a wicket in either innings, and he had little success with the bat. In the New Year, when Queensland were made to follow on 320 behind by Victoria at Brisbane, Cockburn contributed a valuable 35 to their 447 in the second innings. His solitary success with the ball was the dismissal of the Test player, Keith Rigg. Cockburn also played for a Queensland Country XI at Ipswich against Allen's team, making 33 when the home side collapsed in the second innings and taking two wickets, and ten years later he scored 12 and 41 in the equivalent fixture at Gympie against Hammond's MCC side. In his two first-class matches he made 43 runs, average 10.75, and his one wicket cost 148 runs.

CROUCH, HENRY RUSSELL (KIM), who died on April 17, 1991, aged 76, appeared in three first-class matches, two for Minor Counties representative teams in 1935 and one for Surrey against the Combined Services in 1946. His first match, at Oxford, was ruined by rain, and he failed to do himself justice in his second, against the South Africans at Skegness. Three years in the XI at Tonbridge, from 1930 to 1932, he scored 1,274 runs and took 75 wickets, and in his last year, when he captained Tonbridge, he was chosen for the Lord's Schools against The Rest.

CUNLIFFE, CAPTAIN ROBERT LIONEL BROOKE, RN, CBE, who died in December 1990, aged 95, was for a time the second oldest survivor from first-class cricket before the 1914-18 war, Willis Walker of Nottinghamshire being the other. He made his début for the Navy against the Army in the second of two matches celebrating the centenary of the Lord's ground in 1914. A vigorous lower-order batsman with some pretensions to leg-spin, Cunliffe enjoyed an excellent match with the ball, taking eight for 155, including five for 78 in the second innings. He was captain of the Navy in 1927, leading them to an overdue victory over the Army, whose batting was very strong in the 1920s, and his maiden first-class fifty also came that year, with 50 against the New Zealanders at Portsmouth. He improved on this in 1928, making 64 at Lord's as the Navy sank with all hands against their old rivals, and a year later he hit 87, his highest score, for the Navy and Marines against MCC at Chatham in the follow-on, helping to effect a "magnificent" recovery. In ten first-class matches Cunliffe made 335 runs for an average of 23.92, while his sixteen wickets cost 36.37 apiece.

CURRIE, JOHN DAVID, who died at Leicester on December 8, 1990, aged 58, had played one first-class game, for Somerset against Leicestershire at Bath in 1953, when in 1956 he was given a trial by Oxford. A powerfully built right-hander, who that winter had played rugby for England at lock forward, he achieved little of note in his five games, or in the four he played the following year. His best effort was an innings of 38 in 1957 – easily the highest score in Oxford's total of 95 against Yorkshire. In his ten first-class matches he scored 283 runs for an average of 14.89. Currie was capped 25 times by England at rugby.

DAY, FREDERICK GORDON KENNETH, who died at Whitchurch, Bristol, on December 9, 1991, aged 72, played seven times for Somerset in first-class matches, scoring 201 runs for an average of 18.27 and effecting fifteen dismissals, eight of which were stumpings. Four of those stumpings came in his first game, off Lawrence and Hazell in a friendly against Glamorgan at Swansea in 1950. In May 1956 he was called on by the county when Stephenson was injured, and in his six games he deputised with marked efficiency. Indeed, with 168 runs and a highest score of 56 not out, at Old Trafford, he was a useful addition to the lower middle order. Day was a stalwart of the Knowle club, for which he scored some 30 hundreds in as many years.

DENHAM, HON. EVAN HORRELL, who died at Christchurch, New Zealand, on June 16, 1991, aged 78, was born in Brisbane but soon after was taken to New Zealand. His speciality was slow leg-spin, and in his solitary Plunket Shield match, for Canterbury against Wellington, he dismissed the New Zealand wicket-keeper, F. L. H. Mooney. This one wicket cost him 28 runs in eleven overs.

DE VIGNE, STANLEY PIERRE, died at Kenilworth, Cape Town on January 17, 1991, aged 71. A right-handed opening batsman, he played in nine matches for North-Eastern Transvaal, making his début in 1950-51 against Western Province at Cape Town. His highest score, and only fifty, was an innings of 55 against Border at Queenstown that season. In all he made 300 runs for an average of 17.64 and held fourteen catches, seven of which were taken in one match at Benoni against Orange Free State. This was a record for catches in a match by a fielder in South Africa until it was equalled in 1982-83 by Alan Barrow for Transvaal B against Northern Transvaal B.

DOLMAN, FRANK, MBE, who died on October 31, 1990, at the age of 87, spent a lifetime in the service of cricket. He was elected an executive officer of the Club Cricket Conference as long ago as 1930 and held the post without a break for 61 years. In 1960 he became its chairman, serving until retirement in 1977. The indefatigable Dolman was at one time president of the National Cricket Club Association, and having been a founder member of the Cricket Umpires' Association he was its chairman from 1971 to 1981.

DYSON, JOHN HUMPHREY, who died at Exeter in 1990 at the age of 76, won his Blue for Oxford in 1936 as a slow left-arm bowler. A Yorkshireman by birth, he was two years in the XI at Charterhouse, captaining them in 1932, when he took 54 wickets at 13.59 and played for The Rest against the Lord's Schools. In 1933, his first season at Oxford, he maintained his reputation in the Freshmen's Match, but after managing only one wicket in each innings of his first-class début, against the Free Foresters, he was not given another match. The next year started well, only to end in disappointment when the Oxford captain, F. G. H. Chalk, perturbed by Dyson's loss of form, replaced him in the side for Lord's at the last possible moment. Dyson must have wondered how on earth he had taken 23 wickets for Oxford in The Parks, including Sutcliffe, Leyland and Hutton in the match against his native county. In 1935 he received a mauling from the youthful Washbrook, who made 228, and that was that. But he bowled so well in 1936, finishing with 34 wickets for the University at 22.88, that finally he was awarded his Blue. Against Cambridge, who made more than 400, he was the most economical of the regular bowlers, with his three for 94 accounting for leading batsmen. Dyson played in 26 first-class matches in all, mostly for Oxford, and took 68 wickets at 31.51. His batting brought him 211 runs at 7.53, with a top score of 35.

EASTMAN, GEORGE FREDERICK, who died at Eastbourne on March 15, 1991, aged 87, was the younger brother of the better-known L. C. Eastman, the Essex all-rounder. George kept wicket soundly for the county in 22 Championship matches in 1927, but his batting at No. 10 or No. 11 was a negligible factor, and this was to count against him. He had fewer opportunities in 1928, although his batting was a little more effective, and it was the same story in 1929, by which time Sheffield and Wade, both much better bats, were queueing up to take the gloves. However, he produced a defiant flourish against Sussex at Horsham. After Sussex had been disposed of for 248, Essex struggled until M. C. Raison and Eastman joined forces in a last-wicket partnership of 69, which brought Essex right back into the game. His share was 34 not out. Eastman played 48 times for Essex, taking 29 catches and effecting 21 stumpings, and he managed to put together 265 runs for an average of 6.97. He also played soccer for Clapton Orient.

EVANS, GEORGE HERBERT DAVID, who died at Weston-super-Mare in June 1991, aged 62, was one of several amateurs called upon by Somerset in 1953 in an attempt, albeit unsuccessful, to solve their team problems. Evans, a right-handed middle-order batsman, must have aroused some hopes when he made 34 and 56 in a three-day match against an RAF attack which contained Trueman. But his eight Championship games which followed produced only 180 runs for an average of 12.85. Although a highest score of 42, against Essex at Weston-super-Mare, came as some relief after three successive noughts, it was also his last innings for the county.

FABER, MARK JAMES JULIAN, died suddenly in hospital on December 10, 1991, aged 41, after an operation, when complications had set in. A grandson of Harold Macmillan, he graced the playing fields of Eton with elegant and powerful strokeplay in the late 1960s, making most of his runs at No. 3 or No. 4. In 1967 he was consistency itself, topping the averages at 43.22, and the next year, when the season was for the most part chill and damp, he was in irresistible form with 751 runs for an average of 83.44. His crowning achievement was 100 at Lord's against Harrow, the last hundred to date by an Etonian in the traditional match. His innings contained fourteen fours, and he shared in a splendid partnership of 126 for the third wicket with V. A. Cazalet after the opening pair had been dismissed without scoring at the start of the match. All seemed to be set fair as Faber made his début for Oxford in The Parks in 1970. Instead he had a wretched experience, struggling to make runs in a desperately weak batting side. There were simply no senior players capable of giving a lead and affording protection. He was discarded too soon. A year later, despite his maiden first-class fifty, the rest was all disappointment, and it says much for his character that he tried for his Blue once again in 1972. This time he was successful, but the events at Lord's were too one-sided to make his University Match enjoyable. From 1973 to 1976 he played for Sussex with limited success, except for 1975 when, finding freedom enough to use his strokes to telling effect, he made 1,060 runs for an average of 30.28. Of his three hundreds, the first – 112 not out against Middlesex at Hove in 1974 – was the most meritorious: it came with a six off the 101st ball he received and contained 21 fours in an hour and a half. The other two, after he had played very well early on, were devalued towards the end by "declaration" bowling. Halfway through 1976 he dropped out of the Sussex Championship side and played no more first-class cricket, disenchanted with the spirit and manner in which the game was being played. Perhaps he would have been more at home in the 1930s; as it was, in a utilitarian age he eked out an existence with 3,009 runs in 78 first-class matches, averaging 22.12. He held 42 catches.

FOSTER, LEON NEVILLE, died in Auckland on April 19, 1991. A neat right-hand batsman, he played in a single first-class match for Barbados in 1935-36, hitting 43 in the first innings.

FREARSON, RAYMOND ERIC, who died at Skegness on February 22, 1991, aged 87, made something of a name for himself by scoring more than 1,300 runs for Lincolnshire in the Minor Counties Championship in 1925 and 1926, and he was subsequently called up for three first-class representative matches. The first was in 1927 for East of England against the New Zealanders at Wisbech, where opening the innings he made 4 and 2. Playing for Minor Counties against the same opponents in 1931, he scored 13, batting at No. 7. He had had no opportunity to bat for Minor Counties against Lancashire in 1929 because rain washed out play after the first day. A right-handed batsman and leg-spinner, Frearson had distinguished himself as a schoolboy cricketer at Eastbourne College from 1920 to 1922. A double-century in 1925 for Lincolnshire against Cambridgeshire at Grantham, followed by 140 and 63, both unbeaten, against Yorkshire Second Eleven at Bridlington, were his best performances.

GAEKWAD, COLONEL KHANDARAO SHIVAJIRAO, who died on October 26, 1991 in Bombay, aged 75, played in five first-class matches for Gujarat and Baroda in the early days of the Ranji Trophy in the 1930s. He made 52 runs, with a highest score of 23, and took ten wickets at 45.70.

GAJRAJ SINGH, who died on October 28, 1991 in Sentokhba, Jaipur, aged 35, took 40 wickets bowling left-arm spin for Rajasthan from 1980-81 to 1985-86.

GOODWAY, CYRIL CLEMENT, who died on May 22, 1991, aged 81, was more responsible than any other for the excellence of the modern Edgbaston ground. From 1929, when the South Africans were the visitors, until 1957, the year of the May-Cowdrey stand of 411 against West Indies, no Test match was staged there, and for much of that period the ground wore a distinctly seedy look. In some respects the club, though not so much the players, needed a good shake-up, and in Goodway it found just the man. He was elected to the committee in 1945 and soon became a member of the house and ground committee, his business experience, allied to his vision and enthusiasm, enabling him to make the most of this power base. By the end of the 1940s, building and reconstruction were well under way, and equipped with a new pavilion, stands and scorebox, Edgbaston won back its Test status. In 1959 Goodway became chairman of the house and ground committee, a position he held for twenty years, supervising further developments, and he was chairman of the club from 1972 to 1983.

Goodway's success as an administrator was enhanced by his standing as a player. A wicket-keeper of high class, he first appeared for his native Staffordshire in 1932, when S. F. Barnes was still playing, and his work in 1934, 1935 and 1936 was singled out in *Wisden* for special praise. He made his first-class début for Warwickshire in 1937, against Worcestershire at Edgbaston, and in 1946, with Buckingham no longer available, Goodway enjoyed his only full season of first-class cricket. In 40 appearances for Warwickshire he effected 65 dismissals, including 22 stumpings, mostly with the co-operation of Hollies. He batted near the bottom of the order and could make a useful score, his highest being 37 not out against Glamorgan at Birmingham in 1946. Altogether he made 434 runs for an average of 8.03.

Perhaps Goodway's happiest inspiration was to found the Warwickshire Old Cricketers Association in 1958. He knew that there is generally nothing retired players enjoy more than the opportunity to renew the acquaintance of old colleagues, and each year he would be the driving force behind a well-organised programme of social events. Other counties followed suit.

GROVER, JOHN NELSON, who died in Dorset on December 17, 1990, aged 75, won his Blue at Oxford in 1936 and went on to captain the University in 1938. He had made a considerable impression at Winchester in 1933 with his aggressive batting, and a year later he earned praise for his efficiency behind the stumps and for his judgment and perception as captain. He lost no time making his mark at Oxford, hitting an unbeaten 71 in the Freshmen's Match of 1935, but received no further trial. Dashing cricket in the Seniors' Match in his second year, followed by a splendid 119 against Lancashire in The Parks in only his second first-class match, marked by driving of tremendous power, set him up for his place in the side at Lord's. He was well below his best for much of the 1937 season, but a hundred against the Minor Counties, which included four sixes and nine fours, sent him to Lord's in the right frame of mind. There, playing with much freedom, he hit a hundred before lunch on the second day, going from 14 overnight to 121 before being dismissed in the last over of the morning session. Oxford won by seven wickets. In his year as captain, little went right for him and his team. Grover played in 33 first-class matches, all for Oxford, making 1,188 runs for an average of 23.96, and later he appeared for his native Northumberland.

GUISE, JOHN LINDSAY, who died at Eastbourne on June 29, 1991, aged 87, belonged to the select few who have achieved fame through one big performance. In Guise's case it was his innings of 278 for Winchester against Eton on Agar's Plough in 1921, the largest score in a public schools match. Winchester had been bowled out for 57 in their first innings on a rain-affected pitch, and Eton, benefiting from the improving conditions, had taken a lead of 198. By the close of play, Guise, who had opened the batting, was 86 not out and the score 130 for three; next day he took complete charge, farming the bowling "like a veteran" before being run out with the score 381. He had batted throughout the innings, had hit 45 fours, and given one possible chance. Eton, needing 184 to win, made light of their task, getting home by eight wickets.

Though no great stylist, Guise possessed all the solid virtues, watching the ball right on to the bat and playing very late. His leg-side play was said to be superior to that of all his contemporaries, and one good judge suggested that his "ring-craft" was his main asset. He had already shown his promise by making a hundred against Harrow in 1920, and in 1921, helped by his great innings, he made 924 runs for an average of 54.35. He was also a bowler of no little skill, sending down slow-medium deliveries of beguiling innocence which floated gently either way and, like the sirens, lured batsmen to destruction. He picked up 63 wickets in his last two years at school. His commanding form in 1922 made him an automatic choice for the representative matches in Schools Week at Lord's.

No Freshman could have had a more disheartening time at Oxford than Guise had in 1923. He missed the whole of May through illness and, after hitting 120 against the West Indian tourists, he was prevented from playing against Cambridge by a last-minute injury. However, he played for Middlesex in a few matches, none more remarkable than that against Kent during Canterbury Week. At the beginning of Kent's second innings, he dismissed four of their first five batsmen at a personal coast of 9 runs, his victims being J. L. Bryan, Seymour, Woolley and Ashdown, and although Woolley had made 270 (c Allen b Guise) in the first innings, Kent were beaten by seven wickets. In 1924 Guise showed splendid form, averaging 38.18 for Oxford and playing a quite superb innings of 154 not out against Surrey at The Oval. At Lord's, his unusual bowling brought him four for 19 in the University Match, and later, in the Championship, his second-innings hundred helped Middlesex to a 27-run win at Trent Bridge after they had followed on more than 200 runs behind. He captained Oxford in 1925, batting solidly and much better than an average of 24 would suggest. His innings of 58 was his second half-century in the University Match. After going down from Oxford, he went to India, but back in England in 1929 he played in twelve matches for Middlesex. Thereafter, having returned to Winchester to teach, he could play in only a handful of matches each year, and his last first-class appearance was in 1934. In 94 matches, 57 of them for Middlesex, Guise made 3,775 runs at 26.21, took 68 wickets at a cost of 28.11, and held 53 catches.

HAMMOND, COMMANDER REGINALD JOSEPH LESLIE, OBE, RN, who died at Chichester on January 3, 1991, aged 81, represented the Navy at cricket, squash and rugby. A right-handed batsman, something of a utility player who could open in an emergency, and an efficient wicket-keeper, he played in six first-class matches and several others of importance between 1948 and 1951. His first-class cricket was for the Combined Services, beginning in 1948 with their victory over the eventual champions, Glamorgan, at Cardiff. He had every reason to be pleased with his 52 runs and four dismissals in the match. At Lord's in 1950, he had a ring-side seat when Colin Cowdrey scored 126 not out and 55 for the Public Schools against the Combined Services, having a week earlier hit an unbeaten hundred there himself in an unbroken partnership of 279 for the Navy against the RAF. He made 80 against the Army, also at Lord's, that year, and at Chelmsford, for the Services against Essex, he scored 46 as he and J. H. G. Deighton put on 118 for the last wicket. Against the South Africans at Portsmouth in 1951, he conceded only one bye in a total of 499 for five declared. Altogether, Hammond made 199 runs in first-class cricket for an average of 18.09, took six catches and made three stumpings.

HARDING, HIS HONOUR W. ROWE, who died on February 10, 1991, aged 89, was chairman of Glamorgan from 1959 to 1976 and president of the club from 1979 until the time of his death. He had taken over as chairman following a period of internal dispute which led to the resignation of the previous chairman, Colonel J. M. Bevan, and ten of his committee. The old committee had tried to dispense with the services of Glamorgan's captain/secretary, Wilf Wooller, as secretary on a permanent basis, and when the matter was put to the members in a referendum, the answer was a decisive vote of no confidence in the committee. It was greatly due to Harding's good sense that the affair was soon largely forgotten. A well-known figure in South Wales legal circles, he was a circuit judge for 22 years. In the 1920s he played seventeen times for Wales as a wing-threequarter and was a member of the 1924 British Lions in South Africa.

HARRIS, PARKE GERALD ZINZAN (ZIN), who died on November 30, 1991, aged 62, played in nine Test matches for New Zealand between 1955 and 1965. A useful, aggressive right-handed batsman and an occasional purveyor of slow off-breaks, he was among the most popular of New Zealand cricketers, with a breezy personality and an infectious smile. He first appeared for Canterbury in March 1950, scoring 49 in his début innings against an Australian attack consisting of Davidson, Len Johnson, Ring and Iverson. Early on, his best season was 1953-54, when he made 274 runs in the Plunket Shield for an average of 39.14, and two years later, in 1955-56, he went on his first overseas tour, to Pakistan and India. This was very much a pioneering tour for the New Zealanders, who had had no previous experience of the heat, dust and general discomfort of travel on the subcontinent, not to mention gastric problems. Harris was as much a victim as the rest of his colleagues, and only in an innings of 95 against the Indian Universities at Nagpur in January, in the last match of the tour, did he really show his ability. Back in October he had made his Test début against Pakistan at Karachi, the first match of the three-Test series, and he also played in the Second Test, at Lahore, and against India in the Bombay Test. In ten games in both countries he managed 361 runs at 22.56.

In 1960-61, MCC sent the equivalent of a modern England A team to New Zealand, captained by Dennis Silk, and after a painstaking 108 for Canterbury against the tourists Harris was chosen for all three representative matches between New Zealand and MCC. He made his mark in the first two, top-scoring at Dunedin with 78 in the first innings, and in the second match, at Wellington, making 34 and helping the hard-hitting Motz in a sixth-wicket stand of 89 in 70 minutes after the first five wickets had gone for 43. Next season, 1961-62, he was the oldest member of the team which toured South Africa under J. R. Reid and shared the series at two matches each. Harris, playing in all five Tests, came second to Reid in the Test averages with 284 runs at 31.55. His major triumph was in the Third Test at Cape Town in the New Year, when he made 101 in the first innings and helped lay the foundation of a 72-run victory. He and Chapple put on 148 for the fifth wicket after a thunderous 92 by Reid. Harris was also in the picture in the First and Fourth Tests, and he finished the tour with 638 runs for an average of 26.58. His international career had seemed over when he was resurrected for the Second Test against Pakistan at Auckland in January 1965, without even a Plunket Shield innings under his belt, but with scores of 1 and 0 the experiment was not a success. His career record was 3,122 runs, average 28.11, in 69 matches and he also took 21 wickets at 30.80 apiece. Two of his sons have played first-class cricket – Ben for Canterbury and Otago, and Chris, the New Zealand international, for Canterbury – while Tim, a wicket-keeper, trained with the New Zealand development squad. All three excelled in the field, as their father had.

HAWKER, SIR FRANK CYRIL, who died on February 22, 1991, aged 90, was President of MCC for 1970-71. A member of the City of London School XI from 1917 to 1919, he became a talented club cricketer, playing mostly for Southgate, but also turning out for such clubs as Free Foresters and the Gentlemen of Essex. In 1937 he appeared in his only first-class match, for Essex against a powerful Lancashire side at Old Trafford, and batting at No. 8 he made 16 and 10. Like everything else in the match, his efforts were dwarfed by Paynter's magnificent 266.

HAWKEY, RICHARD BLADWORTH, died on March 19, 1991, aged 67. A right-hand bat and fast-medium bowler, he had distinguished himself in the Merchant Taylors', Northwood XI of 1941 by taking 40 wickets at 11.67, concentrating his attack mainly on the leg stump. After war service he went up to Cambridge, and while there he played in three first-class matches. His début was in 1948 for the Free Foresters against the University at Fenner's, his contribution being 13 and 4, batting at No. 2. Next year he played twice for the University. Against the New Zealanders he shared the new ball with J. J. Warr, but did not take a wicket, and a week later he opened both the batting and bowling against Warwickshire without doing anything to suggest he warranted an extended trial. In all, he made 42 runs for an average of 7.00, and his one wicket cost 139 runs. He was an international squash player.

HILLARY, ANTHONY AYLMER, who died at Truro on June 20, 1991, aged 64, played in one match for Cambridge University at Fenner's in May 1951, Sussex being the opposition. After three men were out for 41, he helped May rescue the innings, scoring a good-looking 49 in a fourth-wicket partnership of 107. However, with Sheppard returning to the side in June and Subba Row, a Freshman, showing encouraging form, he was not given another opportunity. Between 1955 and 1962 he appeared regularly for Berkshire with some success.

HILL-SMITH, WYNDHAM, OBE, who died at Angaston, South Australia, on October 25, 1990, aged 81, played in nine first-class games from 1931-32 to 1933-34, eight of them for Western Australia. Opening the innings for the state against the South Africans in the last match of their 1931-32 tour, the left-handed Hill-Smith scored 56 in 75 minutes to provide about the only cheer in a disappointing total of 183. Seven months later, he played in the first two matches of Jardine's MCC tour, scoring 26 for the state and 17 and 32 for an Australian XI. The presence of Richardson, Fingleton, Bradman and McCabe in the top five could not save the combined side from following on after MCC had declared at 583 for seven, but Hill-Smith's stubborn batting on the last day, on a rain-affected pitch, helped save the match. In all, he averaged 28.07 from an aggregate of 393 runs, his highest score being 68 against Victoria on Western Australia's tour of the Eastern states in 1933-34. In later life he became famous for the liberal hospitality which he extended to touring teams at his Yalumba vineyard in South Australia.

**HULME, JOSEPH HAROLD ANTHONY**, who died at Winchmore Hill, North London on September 26, 1991, aged 87, was a regular professional member of the Middlesex side from 1929 to 1939. Throughout the 1920s, and ever since their entry into the Championship, Middlesex had looked to amateurs for their runs, and then all at once what had been an unbroken succession was reduced to a trickle. Their chief professional stalwarts – Hearne, Harry Lee, Durston and (to a lesser extent) Hendren – were ageing, and it was no surprise to find them bumping along in the lower reaches of the Championship early in the 1930s. With Hendren, Hulme played an important part in bridging the gap until the arrival of Edrich, Compton, Robertson and Brown. A right-handed middle-order batsman with aggressive instincts, he was also a brilliant deep field and a useful medium-fast bowler.

After a modest start in 1929, he played so well in 1930 that he was awarded his cap. His first hundred, against Warwickshire at Edgbaston, came after half the Middlesex side were out for 109; in the end he took out his bat for 117, made in three and a half hours. By 1932 he was expected to take on more responsibility, and in passing 1,000 runs for the first time he raised his average above 30. A faultless 106 against Gloucestershire at Lord's turned the match in the home side's favour, and against Yorkshire at Sheffield Hulme (114 not out) and Sims saved the game with a partnership of 149. His 1,258 runs in 1934 included four hundreds, all in the Championship, and the 1,233 runs he made in the damp, depressing summer of 1936 were worth far more than their face value in so miserable a season. Hulme's 101 against Essex at Colchester was one of his best innings: Middlesex lost five men for 27 before Hulme and Compton put on 132 with resolute batting against Farnes and Nichols, who were exploiting a pitch of varying pace and bounce.

Hulme's speed round the boundary, as he cut off certain-looking fours, was an extension of his dazzling pace on the right wing for England and the Arsenal, with whom he won three Championship and two FA Cup winners' medals. Just as remarkable was his speed between the wickets; Hulme and Hendren together were a delight to watch. In 225 matches he made 8,103 runs for an average of 26.56, the highest of his twelve hundreds being 143 against Gloucestershire at Bristol. His bowling brought him 89 wickets at 36.40, and he held 110 catches.

**HUMAN, JOHN HANBURY**, who died in Sydney on July 22, 1991, aged 79, was an outstanding natural games-player; a brilliant attacking middle-order batsman as well as a useful leg-spinner. Good judges at Repton, where he was in the XI for five years, maintained that John Human, younger brother of Roger, played better cricket in school matches than had been seen there for many years. In 1929, his third year, he shared in a great partnership of 253 with C. C. Clarke against the Pilgrims, his 136 being his first century for the school. Appointed captain for the following year, he was in devastating form, making 704 runs for an average of 78.22 and obtaining three centuries and four fifties by bold, aggressive strokeplay. Keeping up his reputation in 1931 with three consecutive hundreds for Repton, and some useful innings in Schools Week at Lord's, he was expected to enjoy a smooth passage into the first-class game when he went up to Cambridge. Events, however, were to follow a strange course. Human played well enough for his 39 in the Freshmen's Match, but his claim for a further trial was disregarded by the captain, A. G. Hazlerigg, until the tour was well under way – and then only by chance. During the University's match with Surrey at The Oval, a member of the team noticed in a newspaper that Human had made 231 for Berkshire against Hertfordshire in the Minor Counties Championship. He was summoned by wire to Eastbourne for the next match, against H. D. G. Leveson Gower's XI, and an innings of 158 not out, even if not against the strongest of attacks, was good enough for him to be invited to play against Oxford with no more ado. He justified his selection with scores of 35 and 28 at Lord's. Yet none of this would have happened if the Hertfordshire mid-on had not dropped him off a sitter early in his double-century innings.

In 1933 Human finished top of the Cambridge averages, making 812 runs at 45.11 with two separate hundreds (110 and 122) to his credit against Surrey at The Oval. This was also his best season with the ball, and in taking 29 wickets at 32.37 he showed greater control over his leg-spin than hitherto. Against Lancashire at Fenner's he took seven for 133 in a total of more than 400, and the following year he improved on these figures with seven for 119 at Cardiff. In 1933-34 he toured India with MCC under D. R. Jardine, only to suffer early on from an attack of malaria. However, he had fully recovered in time for the 1934 season, when he captained Cambridge and in all first-class matches made 1,399 runs for an average of 53.80, including five centuries. His best was an unbeaten 146 at Worcester, where the University squeezed home by three wickets.

In 1935, the year of the "leather-jackets" that made the Lord's square a graveyard for batsmen, Human played a full season for Middlesex. Little went right for him until August, when he scored two hundreds in successive innings as he shared in two splendid partnerships with Hendren: 285 at The Oval and 189 at Trent Bridge, facing Larwood and Voce. That winter he was a member of E. R. T. Holmes's side which toured Australia and New Zealand, and helped by 87 at Adelaide, 118 against Queensland at Brisbane, and 97 in an unofficial "Test" against New Zealand in Dunedin, he averaged just over 30. Back home he graced the 1936 season with 115 for MCC against the Indians in his only first-class innings, reaching three figures with a six into the Pavilion, and the following year he occasionally captained Middlesex when Robins was on Test duty. In 1938 he struck such good form in his several games for the county that his absences were a matter for general regret. By now, however, he had married the daughter of the mayor of Sydney and had decided to settle in Australia. In 105 first-class matches, Human's forceful methods brought him 5,246 runs for an average of 35.68, including fifteen hundreds, and he twice reached 1,000 runs in a season. His leg-breaks earned him 73 wickets at 34.23 apiece and he held 66 catches, being a magnificent fielder in any position.

JOHNSTON, CLIVE WILLIAM (SAILOR), who died on May 12, 1991, aged 66, played eleven times for New South Wales between 1949-50 and 1957-58, usually batting in the middle order and occasionally acting as captain when senior players were unavailable. His two best efforts with the bat were 65 against South Australia at Sydney in 1952-53, in a rain-ruined match, and 68 at Brisbane in 1956-57. Altogether he hit 418 runs for an average of 23.22.

JONES, PRIOR ERSKINE, died on November 21, 1991 in Port-of-Spain at the age of 74. A fast bowler with a splendid physique, delivering right-arm with a slinging type of action, he was 22 in 1939 and running into his physical prime when the outbreak of war brought an end to Test cricket for six years. Jones had captained Trinidad at soccer well before he had the chance to play in a Test match for West Indies. During the war years the islands kept in touch by arranging first-class friendlies, but while these were few in number, and in most the scoring was colossal, Jones and the bespectacled Lance Pierre, also from Trinidad, became talked about as the best fast-bowling combination in the Caribbean since Constantine and Martindale. When in 1947-48 an under-strength England, captained by G. O. B. Allen, arrived for a four-match Test series, the 30-year-old Jones was chosen for the First Test. His four for 54 at Bridgetown suggested that he was on course for a successful series, but this was his only appearance. The evidence strongly suggests that he was injured soon after in the first MCC v Trinidad match.

Jones was picked to tour India in West Indies' first venture to the subcontinent, in 1948-49, and while the awesome power of their batting bemused their hosts, the bowling attracted less attention. Even so, Jones was continually to the fore, taking seventeen wickets in the series in 191 overs at 28.17. In the Fourth Test at Madras, he took six wickets for 58, including four for 30 in the second innings as India were routed for 144. In *Wisden* we find that "Jones bowled with more fire and devil than at any other time in the tour . . . and if [he] came in for barracking none could deny the merit of his performance". At Bombay in the final Test, with West Indies one up, Jones prevented India from squaring the series with a remarkably well-sustained spell of fast bowling. Pegged back by his leg-stump attack in their pursuit of 361, they were 6 runs short with two wickets in hand at the finish. Jones's full analysis was 41–8–85–5, with Hazare, a crucial wicket, bowled for 122. Before returning home he wrought havoc at Colombo against Ceylon with match figures of ten for 62 as the tourists won the first of two games by an innings and 22 runs. And with 51 wickets at 18.54, he headed the tour averages, a distinction he richly deserved.

Jones was never quite the same after these exertions, though with his easy temperament he remained a splendid tourist and team member. In England in 1950 he played in two of the four Tests but did not get enough bowling to run into form. Ramadhin and Valentine had taken over the attack and the rest had walk-on parts. He took 33 wickets at 29.69 on the full tour. If England in 1950 was an anticlimax, Australia in 1951-52 was even more so. He played at Sydney in the Second Test, taking three for 68 in Australia's 517, but it was to be his final Test. Still, some relief came when he made 46 against Tasmania at Launceston. Throughout his career he had batted conscientiously amongst the lower order with limited success. In his nine Tests he made 47 runs at 5.22 and took 25 wickets at 30.04, while in 61 matches his first-class record was 775 runs at 14.09 and 169 wickets at 26.81. He held 33 catches.

**KING, FRANK McDONALD,** who died at Bescot, near Walsall, on December 23, 1990, aged 64, was possibly the best fast bowler produced by the West Indies during the long period between the enforced retirement of Constantine in 1939 and the advent in 1959 of Wesley Hall. In his account of the Fifth Test between West Indies and England at Kingston, Jamaica, in 1953-54, E. W. Swanton commented: "King has real pace and he brings down the ball from the very top. He is 6ft 2in, slender in build and with long arms. His spell this morning was the fastest I have seen in West Indies. It contained a number of balls outside the leg stump, which the presence of leg-slips made it dangerous to glide, and a generous assortment of bumpers. Once there were three bumpers in four balls . . ." England's makeshift opener, Bailey, received a sickening crack on the side of the head, and later Compton was toppled on to his wicket by a flying ball. According to *Wisden*, in an effort to pull the game round after his team had been dismissed for 139, Stollmeyer had called on King for a maximum effort. His response was an analysis on the second day of 21–11–31–2, but its legacy was a strained leg muscle, and he did not bowl again in the innings. As King was virtually the only strike bowler available at the time, it is hardly surprising that he became increasingly prone to muscular injuries.

He first appeared on the scene for Barbados against MCC in 1947-48, and by 1952-53 he was ready for Test cricket, playing in all five Tests against the first Indian Test team to visit the Caribbean. Against much stubborn batting he took seventeen wickets at 28.23 in 238.1 overs, including his best Test figures, five for 74, in the Third Test in Trinidad, when he ripped through the middle order, sending back Umrigar, Manjrekar and Mankad. A year later he missed two Tests against Hutton's side, but was hostile and lively in the other three. His analysis in England's first innings at Port-of-Spain in the Fourth Test, 48.2–16–97–3, stands as a monument to his hard work and persistence. In 1954-55 Australia, smarting from their failure to regain the Ashes, played devastating cricket, and King, along with everyone else, received heavy punishment at the hands of a team which made twelve hundreds in the series. Injury ruined his tour of New Zealand in 1955-56, but he was fit and looking forward to the 1957 tour of England. When Gilchrist gained the selectors' vote, King gave up first-class cricket there and then, emigrated to England and settled in the Midlands, where he played with distinction for West Bromwich Dartmouth in the Birmingham League. In 31 first-class matches he took 90 wickets at a cost of 28.75, with five for 35 against Jamaica at Bridgetown in 1951-52 as his best return. Batting usually at No. 10 or No. 11, he made 237 runs for an average of 9.11, with a highest score of 30 not out against Trinidad at Georgetown in 1956-57. In his fourteen Tests he took 29 wickets at 39.96 apiece and scored 116 runs for an average of 8.28.

LAMBERT, GEORGE ERNEST EDWARD, who died at his home in Bristol on October 31, 1991, aged 72, was, as a fast-medium right-arm bowler, effectively the spearhead of Gloucestershire's attack from 1939 to 1957, when he retired with 917 wickets to his credit at 28.56 apiece. A more than useful lower-order batsman, capable of protecting what for much of his time was one of the longest tails in the Championship, he made 6,375 runs with an average of 14.89. He also held 194 catches. He was not a true all-rounder, however; rather a quick bowler who batted better than most, to which his 21 fifties bear ample testimony. He is well remembered by his contemporaries for his beautiful sideways action, which enabled him naturally to move the ball away from a right-handed opponent, and Andy Wilson, who stood to him for several seasons, asserted that he could move the ball both ways. An analysis of his career shows significantly that a high percentage of his wickets were from the top five of the opposition batting order. There was a period between 1948 and 1951 when he was decidedly quick for six or seven overs with the new ball and was regarded by many on the county circuit as the fastest bowler in England. He might have come under closer scrutiny from the selectors for the 1950-51 tour of Australia if he had come from a more fashionable county, and indeed Charles Parker, always a champion of the underprivileged, was overheard arguing Lambert's claims forcefully in conversation with Gubby Allen. Lambert had a sunnier disposition than most of his kind, and his sense of humour endeared him to his colleagues.

A Londoner by birth, he was on the groundstaff at Lord's before moving to Gloucestershire in 1937. The following year he made his first-class début, against Lancashire at Old Trafford, and in 1939 he bowled with such life and accuracy that he took 74 wickets at 26 apiece and was awarded his cap. His eight for 82 against Essex at Gloucester was largely responsible for a win by an innings and 93 runs; and when Yorkshire came to Bristol he took four for 58 in their first innings, dismissing Hutton, Leyland and Barber and paving the way for victory over the champions by seven wickets. The Second World War deprived him of six fruitful years, and several seasons passed before he clicked into top gear. This was partly due to Goddard and Cook being used as the main strike-force on the well-sanded Bristol wicket, but when the retirement of Goddard put greater responsibility on Lambert's shoulders, he responded magnificently. In 1950 he took 95 wickets and bowled nearly 900 overs. His ten for 172 in the match against Kent at Bristol in May was the most influential factor in a thrilling game which could have gone either way and ended in a draw. A year later his record was much the same, and his five for 78 against the South Africans at Bristol, in a total of 388 for nine declared, was impressive work, especially as he dismissed Waite, Endean and Cheetham.

In 1952 Lambert reached his peak with 105 wickets in the Championship and 113 in all matches at 22.75. His seven for 123 against Yorkshire at Bristol contained four of the first five wickets in the first innings and the first three in the second. He dismissed Hutton, whose wicket was at that time the most prized, in each innings. Among a crop of splendid match figures, nine for 93 against Warwickshire at Cheltenham and eight for 100 at Hove stand out. Next year a return of 86 wickets, plus a higher average, marked a slight falling off, but he more than made up for this by hitting 719 runs for an average of 18.92. In 1954 he missed some matches through injury, but came back in 1955, his benefit season, with a resilient all-round performance. Playing as many as 56 innings, he reached his highest aggregate, 861 runs at 17.93, and took 80 wickets. He distinguished himself against Surrey at Cheltenham by removing the top five in the visitors' order, with the fifth wicket falling at 39, and at Worcester he made 100 not out, the only hundred of his career. As he neared retirement he occasionally showed some of his old fire, and in June 1956 his career-best eight for 35 in Yorkshire's first innings at Bristol set up victory by ten wickets, Gloucestershire's first over Yorkshire since 1948. Against Leicestershire he made 67 and shared in a seventh-wicket stand of 189 with Graveney (190), the next highest score being 12. Lambert retired at the end of the 1957 season, by which time he was approaching 38, and in 1960 he took up an appointment as Somerset's coach, captaining the Second Eleven in some matches and appearing three times in the County Championship side.

LEATHER, THOMAS WILLIAM, who was born in Rutherglen, Glasgow, died in Victoria, Australia on May 10, 1991, aged 80. A fast-medium right-arm opening bowler, he played four times for Victoria in the mid-1930s against Western Australia and Tasmania but was never selected for a Sheffield Shield match. In 1935-36, while the Australian team was in South Africa, Jack Ryder captained a side to India consisting of veterans such as Macartney, Hendry and "Dainty" Ironmonger, plus one or two younger men to do the hard work. Leather was one of the lucky ones and proved an excellent choice, in all first-class matches taking 47 wickets at 17.11, including 22 at 12.91 in the four matches against All-India. The following October he was chosen to play in Sydney in a testimonial match for W. Bardsley and J. M. Gregory, a great honour as there were eighteen Test players on view, and given first use of the new ball in each innings he took two wickets. In nineteen first-class matches he scored 219 runs at 13.68 and took 63 wickets for an average of 20.19.

LINDSAY, JOHN DIXON, died at Benoni on August 31, 1990, when a few days short of his 81st birthday. A wicket-keeper who was capable of useful runs or stubborn resistance down the order, he made his Currie Cup début for Transvaal at Johannesburg in December 1933, but his next appearance, in 1936-37, was also his last for the full province of Transvaal. Next season he was elected captain of the newly formed North-Eastern Transvaal and led them to third place in the competition. In the first post-war Currie Cup season, 1946-47, he made his highest score, 51, batting at No. 8 against Rhodesia at Brakpan, and he was the first-choice wicket-keeper in the South African side which toured England under Alan Melville in 1947. According to *Wisden*, ". . . though he always gave the impression of much natural skill, he began shakily on the wet wickets and seemed to lose confidence so that Fullerton, a much better batsman, displaced him in the last two Tests". Certainly he received a nasty blow over the eye keeping to Athol Rowan at Worcester in the first match of the tour, but before the end of May the sun was shining and his keeping in the first three Tests received high praise, especially when he conceded only two byes in England's 554 for eight declared at Lord's. On the tour he held eighteen catches and made seven stumpings.

Lindsay later played for Natal and retired from first-class cricket in 1954-55, having made 55 dismissals in 29 matches, sixteen of them stumpings. He also scored 346 runs for an average of 11.16, being not out fourteen times. In 1960 he became a national selector, and he was later president of Northern Transvaal. His son, Denis, a wicket-keeper also, played nineteen times for South Africa before their exclusion from Test cricket.

LISTER, JOSEPH, who died at Harrogate on January 28, 1991, aged 60, had been Yorkshire's secretary since 1971. A dark cloud hung over Yorkshire CCC during his period of office, but throughout all the bitterness and intrigue he remained firmly at the helm. In 1948, after three years in the Cheltenham XI, he showed excellent form against Haileybury at Lord's and was picked for the Rest against the Southern Schools. A spirited innings of 75, made in 80 minutes, created a fine impression. National Service followed, and with it his first-class début, in 1951, for the Combined Services against Glamorgan at Pontypridd. In 1953 he averaged 64.16 for Yorkshire Second Eleven, but halfway through the following season, after two matches for the senior side, he took up the position of assistant-secretary to Worcestershire, for whom he also appeared that year. A right-handed middle-order batsman, he was never averse to opening, however, and in 1955 he shared in a first-wicket stand of 100 with Kenyon against Nottinghamshire at Kidderminster. Against Kent at Worcester he missed a century by 1 run, losing his leg stump to a slow full toss from Page. Other useful scores brought him more than 500 runs. In 1956, as well as becoming joint-secretary, he took on the captaincy of the Second Eleven, and he went on to lead them to their championship in 1962 and 1963, missing a hat-trick by a whisker in 1964. Worcestershire's two Championships in 1964 and 1965 owed much to the development of the Second Eleven under Lister. In his 24 first-class matches, he made 796 runs for an average of 20.41.

McALPINE, ALFRED JAMES (JIMMIE), who died on November 6, 1991, at the age of 83, was a patron of cricket in the old style, even to the extent of engaging, at one time, his own professional. Although sufficiently energetic a cricketer to have won his colours at Repton in 1926, and to captain Denbighshire in the 1930s, when they propped up the Minor Counties Championship, he was more in his element running his own side on the charming private ground at Marchwiel Hall, the family estate near Wrexham. This was country house cricket at its best, in which the play was keen, the standard very good and the hospitality as generous as it was jovial. The Free Foresters, the Cheshire Gentlemen and the Northern Nomads had regular fixtures there. It is also the ground from which Marchwiel won the National Village Championship in 1980 and 1984.

McCALL, BARNEY ERNEST WILFORD, who died in hospital at Cardiff on March 31, 1991, aged 77, was one of the best cricketers produced by Weymouth College between the wars. A left-handed bat and slow left-arm bowler, he was a member of the XI for five years from 1927 to 1931, with 636 runs (average 45.42) and 31 wickets at 19.54 in 1930 representing his best all-round season. In 1931, when Weymouth's matches were practically all ruined by the monsoon which hit the country at regular intervals, and run-making was an unrewarding pastime, he led his side from the front with his bowling and finished with the remarkable figures of 102.1–21–283–40–7.07. The choice of an Army career largely put paid to any chance he may have had to establish himself in senior cricket, and he was restricted to three first-class games, all for different teams. In 1936 he turned out for the Army against the University at Fenner's. Cambridge, batting first, scrambled home by 5 runs, and McCall's 31 in the fourth innings contributed in no small measure to the close result. Having made a successful début for Dorset the same year, he represented the Minor Counties against the University at Oxford in 1937, claiming three well-taken catches at short leg in the second innings, and in

1948 he was in the Combined Services side that played Worcestershire at New Road. He made 56 first-class runs all told at 9.33 and took one wicket for 35 runs. A prominent rugby footballer, he was capped three times for Wales in 1935-36.

McCANLIS, MAURICE ALFRED, who died on September 27, 1991, at the age of 85, played cricket with distinction for Cranleigh before going up to Oxford in the autumn of 1924. He was primarily a right-arm fast-medium bowler, able to swing the ball away from the right-hander, but he could bat well enough to make a hundred for his school in 1923, when he hit 371 runs for an average of 33.72. His bowling that year was devastating, bringing 36 wickets at 5.11 in 119 overs, and if he had to work harder for success in 1924, his 35 wickets nevertheless were reasonable at 13.65. He made little impact in the Freshmen's Match in 1925 and must have been surprised at his selection to play against Leicestershire a fortnight later. Going in last he helped to put on 59 in less than an hour with J. W. Greenstock, ending unbeaten on 30, and with three for 32 in 21 overs in the county's first innings he might have felt he warranted a further trial. None came. In 1926, however, he was one of the mainstays of the attack, with 31 wickets at 29.70, and won his Blue with no trouble. In the University Match he produced a sensational opening spell, sending back E. W. Dawson, F. J. Seabrook and K. S. Duleepsinhji without conceding a run. All three were lured by perfectly pitched out-swingers and caught at second slip by G. B. Legge. McCanlis finished with five for 59, and was 15 not out when Oxford lost by 34 runs. His 33 wickets the following season were obtained at a reduced cost of 22.93, and also with a much improved striking-rate. At Lord's, when Cambridge cut loose in their second innings and were able to declare at 349 for nine, he alone escaped punishment with an economical four for 47 in 23.4 overs.

Captain in 1928, he missed almost the whole of the home programme in The Parks because of illness and injury, and he was only just beginning to find some sort of form by the time of the University Match. He managed five wickets, but probably had greater satisfaction from masterminding a rearguard action from the dressing-room, as his tailenders fought tooth and nail to ward off defeat. The last pair were unparted for 25 minutes, and saved McCanlis from a hat-trick of defeats. That was virtually the end of his first-class career. He had made two appearances for Surrey while at Oxford, and played for Gloucestershire once in 1929. He also played for Rajputana in 1938-39 and 1939-40, when he was teaching in India. Apart from that spell, he taught at Cheltenham from 1932 to 1966. McCanlis made 493 runs in first-class cricket at 15.40, and his 82 wickets were obtained at a cost of 32.21. A threequarter at rugby, he played twice for Oxford at Twickenham and won two England caps in 1930-31.

McCORMICK, ERNEST LESLIE, who died at Tweed Heads, New South Wales on June 28, 1991, aged 85, toured England in 1938 as the lone spearhead of an Australian attack based on spin in the persons of O'Reilly, Fleetwood-Smith and Frank Ward. He had a fearsome reputation for high pace, which Bradman himself gently encouraged before the team arrived, but the tour was not over before some expressed the view that he was the most overrated bowler to visit England. McCormick had been wreaking havoc in Melbourne grade cricket when he was given his first state game, against Tasmania in 1929-30. He took only one wicket, and on the second day he was involved in a controversial incident when the ball slipped from his hand as he was about to bowl. Not only did the umpire signal a wide, but the batsmen took a run without the ball being hit, and what should have been a dead ball seems to have found its way into the scorebooks as two wides. Two seasons later, in 1931-32, he came well to the fore with 22 wickets, twice taking five in an innings; but with Alexander blocking his path it was 1934-35 before he really established himself, capturing 22 wickets in Shield matches at

29.81 and winning a place in the team to South Africa under V. Y. Richardson in 1935-36. There, in a series dominated by Grimmett and O'Reilly, he took fifteen wickets at a cost of 27.86, and in all first-class matches 49 at 18.06. When MCC visited Australia in 1936-37, he started the series explosively, extracting life and lift from the Brisbane pitch to remove Worthington with the first ball of the match and have England 20 for three when he sent back Fagg and Hammond with successive deliveries. But three overs later he was virtually put out of the match by an attack of lumbago, which also ruled him out of the Third Test. However, he played his part at Adelaide and Melbourne in Australia's recovery, and at the end of the season he delivered eleven overs of blistering pace at Adelaide to take the first nine wickets for 40 in South Australia's second innings. This left Victoria to score 49 runs to win the Sheffield Shield. That return and his match figures of twelve for 96 were career bests for McCormick.

Rarely has a touring cricketer had such a humiliating or frustrating experience as befell McCormick at Worcester in the opening match of the 1938 tour: he was no-balled nineteen times in his first three overs, and 35 times in the match. He regained enough control to produce a dangerous spell on the first day at Lord's in the Second Test, sending back Hutton, Edrich and Barnett with only 31 on the board. But this time Hammond remained to score a magnificent 240. His ten wickets in the series cost him 34.50, and in eighteen first-class matches on the tour he took 34 wickets at an average of 33.41. Back home he took 24 wickets at 35.70 as Victoria chased South Australia for the Sheffield Shield, but the war brought his first-class cricket to an end. In a career lasting nine and a quarter years he captured 241 wickets, many from the top places in the batting order, at a cost of 27.74, while in twelve Tests he took 36 wickets at 29.97. He was a left-handed bat of no great pretensions, but he could look back on one occasion at Melbourne in 1934-35 when he and Fleetwood-Smith made 98 for the last wicket against Queensland. They swiped at everything, and no-one could be absolutely sure how many times they were dropped before the pantomime was over. According to McCormick, who was undefeated on 77 (his highest score), it was thirteen. In 85 matches he scored 582 runs for an average of 8.68 and held 46 catches. An instrument-maker and jeweller, he made the Frank Worrell Trophy, contested in Australia–West Indies series.

MELSOME, BRIGADIER ROBERT GEORGE WILLIAM (BOB), MBE, died at Gloucester on November 3, 1991, aged 85. As a boy at Lancing he developed into a middle-order right-hand bat and a slow off-break bowler of considerable potential and tight control, and he took 25 wickets at 11.20 in 1924, the year he captained the XI. The great triumph of the season was victory over Tonbridge by 61 runs. In 1925 he was given a trial of eight home matches as a batsman by Gloucestershire, the spin bowling at that time being in the capable hands of Parker, Sinfield and Percy Mills, and he nearly made a success of it with 172 runs at 15.72. But after his 47 against Middlesex at Bristol, when he helped Bloodworth put on 94 in 95 minutes for the sixth wicket, he managed only 25 runs in his last five innings. By 1926 he was playing representative cricket for the Army, and he had a memorable week early in June when he upset each University in turn. At Oxford he claimed eight for 103, which included a spell of four for 11, and at Fenner's his analyses were 17–4–38–5 and 20–6–35–3, his "appreciable" break and accuracy being duly noted. A month later he was in great form at Lord's in the needle match against the Navy, taking six for 44 in the second innings to earn another mention in dispatches. After several years abroad with his regiment, he reappeared in the Inter-Services match in 1931; and he turned out regularly in these games almost until the war, making useful runs and taking wickets. Against the Public Schools at Lord's, in August 1938, he made a robust 74 and took five for 52 with his probing spin, thus emphasising his genuine all-round ability. However, he failed to impress the Australians a fortnight later in a two-day match at Aldershot, the wicket of Fingleton costing him 23 runs in four overs. In his 27 first-class matches, Melsome made exactly 500 runs, for an average of 13.15, and captured 45 wickets at 24.40 apiece.

MEYER, ROLLO JOHN OLIVER (JACK), OBE, who died in hospital at Bristol on March 9, 1991, just six days before his 86th birthday, was the founder of Millfield School and for many years its headmaster. Most people who knew little or nothing about the way he ran it were aware that it produced a succession of high-class games-players, including cricketers. It was Meyer's all-round ability at games, and his firm belief in their character-forming importance, which prompted him to make the necessary arrangements to support the promising youngster during his time at Millfield. He went to Haileybury himself and won his colours at sixteen, emerging as a somewhat mercurial forcing batsman and a bowler who delivered just about everything under the sun at slow-medium to medium pace. He became a compulsive experimenter, ceaselessly plotting and planning; subtle variations of pace, spin and swerve based on correct line and length were his main weapons. His flair for the big occasion, already evident in 1921, enabled him to put the shackles on Cheltenham in the following year, when he took four of their top five wickets for 39 in 26 overs. As captain in 1923 he got through an immense amount of bowling, sending down 333.3 overs for 59 wickets at 16.17, and still found the energy to make 360 runs. H. S. Altham, writing on public schools cricket in the 1924 edition of *Wisden*, remarked that: "Meyer got through more work with the ball than any other school bowler ... but in spite of this he very rarely lost his length, and even at the end of term at Lord's there was a lissomness and nip about his bowling which suggested a certain class. He was, as a captain should be, at his best in the school games . . . having a real field day against Uppingham – eight for 75 in the first innings and five for 39 in the second."

A tall, wiry, tense, restless figure, he went up to Cambridge in 1923 and did not disappoint his supporters the following season, taking nine wickets in the Freshmen's trial. Adapting easily to the demands of the first-class game, he produced consistently good figures in match after match, and he was rewarded with selection for a Gentlemen v Players match at Blackpool at the end of the season. In the Players' first innings his full analysis was 21.1–5–38–8. He won his Blue in all three years, and in May 1926 he attracted special notice when he took six for 65 in 45.5 overs for Cambridge against the Australians at Fenner's, his victims including Collins, Macartney, Ponsford and Andrews. When the Australians went in a second time, needing 59 to win in twenty minutes, Meyer took two for 5 in three overs and the match was drawn. Yet just when he was looking like a possible Test player, he was lost to English cricket for ten years, going to India to try his hand at cotton broking. Not that he neglected his cricket: in 1926-27 he played in four matches against A. E. R. Gilligan's MCC team, and a year later he secured the best bowling figures of his career, with nine for 160 (sixteen for 188 in the match) for the Europeans against the Muslims at Bombay.

In 1936 Meyer, throwing in his lot with Somerset on his return from India, proved to be a vastly improved batsman. Indeed, statistics show that he was twice as good. He announced himself with 202 not out at Taunton when Somerset were forced to follow on after Lancashire had made 423, hitting one six and 26 fours, mainly through beautifully timed drives. This commanding show hoisted him to thirteenth place in the general averages, and in 1937 he made 543 Championship runs for an average of 38.78, without the help of a single not out. Twelve years after his first triumph against the Australians, he excelled himself in 1938 – this time at Lord's, with five for 66 in 26.2 overs for the Gentlemen of England in the Australians' first innings of 397. Fingleton, Brown and Bradman were among his victims. After war service with the RAFVR he played in ten matches in 1946, his excellent form with the bat including two free innings of 52 and 94 against Essex at Taunton, where he drove a ball from Peter Smith over the pavilion into the churchyard, and in 1947 he was entrusted with the captaincy of Somerset. Perhaps results did not come up to expectations, but the professionals, if bemused by the eccentricity of his stratagems, appreciated his concern for their well-being. He had to put up with the discomforts of lumbago for much of the season, but even so he managed a typical flourish in August, with innings of 88 and 65 against Glamorgan at Weston-super-Mare. Meyer, whose cricket was at times not without a touch of genius, played in 127 first-class matches, including 65 for Somerset to 1949, and made 4,621 runs for an average of 23.69, with two hundreds. His bowling earned him 408 wickets at 25.31, and he held 85 catches.

MILLETT, FREDERICK WILLIAM, who died, aged 63, in Macclesfield Hospital on April 30, 1991 from a heart attack, following a car accident, really put Cheshire as a minor county on the map. He did it both through his work behind the scenes on committees and other bodies and, more importantly, by his skill and enthusiasm on the field. His tactical enterprise when he was captain, from 1960 to 1970, and his knowledge of the workings of the two-day, two-innings game, came to be appreciated by all concerned. Cheshire, hitherto ill-considered opponents, were soon rated among the most popular counties to play, and in 1967 they carried off the Minor Counties Championship. Millett first played for them in 1949, and soon settled into the role of opening batsman. When he stood down at the end of the 1972 season, he had made 8,432 runs for them in 210 championship appearances, as well as taking 300 wickets. Midway through his career, he had discovered the art of bowling off-breaks. His contribution in the championship year was 300 runs and 41 wickets at 11.24.

Millett played seven times in first-class fixtures for Minor Counties representative teams, and with 312 runs for an average of 31.20 in these games he demonstrated that he could have stepped up a gear into first-class cricket. In 1969 he had the double honour of captaining the Minor Counties against the West Indians and, batting at No. 6, making 102 not out against them. In addition to his work for Cheshire, he was a member of the MCC committee, serving for a time on the Club's influential Grounds and Fixtures sub-committee, and in 1982 he was player/manager on the MCC tour in the United States, captained by A. R. Lewis.

MILLINGTON, ERROL, who died in his native Barbados on April 29, 1991, aged 75, was a tall, slim, left-arm fast-medium bowler. He made his début in Jamaica in 1946-47, and in 1950-51 he appeared twice against Trinidad in the Quadrangular Tournament used by the West Indies selectors to help them choose the side to tour Australia in 1950-51. His three matches brought him five wickets at 40.80 each.

MIRAN BUX (MALIK MIRANBAKSH), who died at Dhok Rata, Rawalpindi old town, on February 8, 1991, in his 84th year, was the oldest cricketer to make his Test début in the twentieth century. Summoned to play for Pakistan in the Third Test against India at Lahore, when the match began on January 29, 1955, he was 47 years and 284 days old. Only James Southerton, who played for England at Melbourne in the first of all Test matches in 1877, made his début at a more advanced age (49 years 119 days). And only four others have played Test cricket at a greater age: Wilfred Rhodes, "Dainty" Ironmonger, W. G. Grace and George Gunn. A tall man, with large hands, Miran Bux worked for a number of years at the Rawalpindi Club as coach and groundsman, and there he perfected the art of off-spin bowling, with its attendant variations. Recognition came in 1948-49, when he appeared for the Commander-in-Chief's XI against the West Indians at Rawalpindi, and he seized his chance by taking five for 62, including

Headley and Walcott, in the first innings. When a Commonwealth XI were the visitors in the corresponding fixture a year later, his match figures were ten for 82. Among others he had the Australian Test spinner, George Tribe, in all kinds of trouble before trapping him lbw, and in old age Miran still remembered Tribe's sporting acknowledgment of his skill with a pat of his bat as he left the wicket. In his first Test for Pakistan he had the Indian batsmen at full stretch, especially Umrigar, who was dropped off him early on; his figures were 48–20–82–2 in India's first innings of 251, but he did not bowl in the second innings. At Peshawar in the Fourth Test he was allowed only ten overs, and that was that.

By now Pakistan's domestic cricket was beginning to take shape. The main competition was for the Quaid-e-Azam Trophy, the format varying from year to year, and in 1956-57 Miran achieved his best performance of his career: six for 15 for Services at Dacca against East Pakistan (Whites), who were all out for 33. In his last season, two years later, he had match figures of nine for 72 for Rawalpindi against Services. In fifteen first-class matches he took 48 wickets at 19.43 apiece.

**MOBEY, GERALD SPENCER (GEORGE)**, died on March 2, 1979, three days before his 75th birthday. His death had gone unrecorded; and it is thanks to the perceptive enquiries of David T. Smith that it has come to light. Mobey was afflicted by bronchitis and emphysema towards the end of his life and seems to have become something of a recluse. This may well have caused his death to go unnoticed. A high-class wicket-keeper and useful right-hand batsman, he made his first-class début for Surrey in 1930 against Cambridge University at The Oval, hitting 48 not out; but condemned to the relative obscurity of the Minor Counties Championship by the efficiency of Ted Brooks, he was not able to command a regular place in the first team until halfway through 1939. That same season he had kept brilliantly for Minor Counties against the West Indians at Lord's. A more ambitious man than Mobey might have looked elsewhere for employment, but he seems to have been content with his role as understudy. Indeed, Mobey's experience was not dissimilar to that of Farrimond of Lancashire, who in spite of two MCC tours and four matches for England could not displace Duckworth behind the stumps in the county side. Mobey was chosen for MCC's projected tour of India in 1939-40 and, but for the war, could well have been a Test player himself. He had strengthened the Surrey batting in 1939 by some sound displays, and in making 66 not out at The Oval against Gloucestershire had shared in a last-wicket partnership of 88 with Gover. In 1946 he had his only full season without a rival in sight and performed admirably at the age of 42. Arthur McIntyre, already on the staff, became the first-choice wicket-keeper in 1947 and Mobey quietly withdrew from the scene, finding employment as coach at Tonbridge for two years. Surrey called him back for four matches in 1948 when McIntyre was injured at the end of July. From 1950 to 1955 he was on the first-class umpires' list. In 81 first-class games he made 1,684 runs for an average of 18.10, and his dismissals numbered 141, eleven of which were stumped.

**MOON, DOMINIC JAMES TIMOTHY**, who died on November 26, 1991, aged eighteen, in hospital at Canterbury following a motor accident, had been twelfth man for Kent against Gloucestershire earlier in the year. A promising left-handed opening batsman, he was captain of the Kent College XI in 1991, making three significant hundreds to lead his side to victory, and he went on to mark his second eleven début for Kent with a top score of 63 in their first innings against Nottinghamshire. He had represented Kent Schools since the age of ten and England Schools (South) at Under-15 and Under-19. In December he was due to attend the Bull Under-18 Development of Excellence coaching at Lilleshall.

MUMFORD, LAURENCE (LAURIE), who died at Havering-Atte-Bower on May 22, 1991, aged 72, succeeded E. M. Wellings as the chief cricket correspondent of the London *Evening News*. He covered England's tour to the West Indies in 1973-74 and went to Australia three times with England teams.

O'BRIEN, FRANCIS PATRICK, who died on October 22, 1991, aged 80, had an excellent record in his 23 matches for Canterbury from 1932-33 to 1945-46, scoring 1,317 runs at 35.59 with four hundreds and six fifties. A hard-hitting right-hand middle-order batsman, tall, elegant and a powerful driver, he engaged in a memorable partnership with Walter Hadlee in 1939-40 against Otago, the pair winning the match by hitting 210 in 82 minutes after their side had been left to score 303 in 160 minutes. O'Brien came near to international honours, being twelfth man for his country on one occasion. In 1938 he was taken on by Northamptonshire in an effort to climb off the foot of the Championship table, and while neither he nor the county had much to reflect on with pleasure that season, a year later O'Brien made 784 runs at 21.18, despite the generally wet conditions. With K. C. James and W. E. Merritt also at Northampton, he was the "third useful Colonial" in the team, and on one jolly occasion, against Warwickshire at Northampton, the three contributed to the total as follows: James (No. 7) 50, O'Brien (No. 8) 48 and Merritt (No. 9) 53 not out. They couldn't win that match, but at least they helped R. P. Nelson, an inspiring captain, to pass on the wooden spoon to Leicestershire. In 66 first-class matches on opposite sides of the globe O'Brien made 2,649 runs for an average of 24.52, and if his occasional right-arm medium-pace bowling was expensive at 46.78 a wicket, his fourteen victims included such notable scalps as Herbert Sutcliffe, Hutton, Hassett, Constantine, Compton and Edrich. He held 34 catches.

PAGE, JOHN COLIN THEODORE, who died, aged 60, on December 14, 1990 when driving home from the Sevenoaks indoor school, had been manager of Kent from 1975 to 1981, taking over from Leslie Ames, and was director of youth coaching for the county until shortly before his death. He was originally offered terms in 1949 as a keen, promising fast-medium bowler, and he made his Championship début in 1950. However, it soon became clear that he would fall short of the required standard in this role, and in 1952 he began to experiment with off-spin, at once looking a much more likely prospect. Thereafter progress was steady, and he had some excellent figures, among them a match return of twelve for 169 at Northampton in 1954 and, making skilful use of a rain-damaged pitch, six for 33 as Middlesex were bowled out for 118 at Lord's in 1955. He was capped in 1957, when he took 69 wickets at 18.34, including a career-best eight for 117 in a Warwickshire total of 443 at Birmingham, but while there were 86 wickets in 1958 and 72 in 1959, it seemed that he had reached his ceiling. The turning-point in Page's career came in 1960 with his appointment as captain of the Second Eleven. His brief was to build up a body of players who would go on to win something in the 1970s, and just how well he succeeded is shown by the names of those players who formed the nucleus of the Championship side of 1970: Knott, Underwood, Denness, Luckhurst and Ealham. Of these, the first four played for England with distinction. Along the way his young men won the Second Eleven Championship in 1961, 1969 and 1970, and under his guidance Kent completed a marvellous decade by taking the County Championship in 1977 (jointly) and 1978, as well as excelling in the one-day competitions. Page played in 198 matches for Kent, taking 521 wickets at 28.72. As a batsman he had no pretensions to anything other than being a tailender and made 818 runs for an average of 5.48. He held 74 catches.

PASSMORE, JOHN, who died in August 1991 at Cape Town, aged 80, would have rejoiced greatly at South Africa's return to the fold. He was a true cricketing pioneer in that for a long time he was the only member of the cricket establishment to take the game to the black townships. An example of his single-minded devotion was the setting up of the John Passmore Week, annually organised at national level to focus attention on burgeoning black schoolboy talent. In years to come, when the South African national squad contains black cricketers, they will surely look back on John Passmore's devoted work in introducing them to the game. In a tribute to him, Dr Ali Bacher wrote: "His example symbolises the spirit of our new cricket, and history will accord him a very special place in South African cricket's Hall of Fame."

PAWLE, SHAFTO GERALD STRACHAN, who died in Cornwall on July 26, 1991, aged 77, was a widely experienced journalist, who made a return to cricket reporting after a long absence when he wrote for the *Daily Telegraph* for some fifteen years up to the mid-1980s. He had joined the *Yorkshire Post* before he was eighteen and witnessed at close range one of the great periods of Yorkshire cricket, when they earned seven Championships between 1931 and 1939. After the war he spent several years at the *Sunday Times*. His biography of his friend and neighbour, entitled *R. E. S. Wyatt – fighting cricketer*, published in 1985, threw new light on several controversial issues, including the genesis of bodyline. An England squash international, Pawle qualified as a playing member of MCC, his sponsors being Sir Pelham Warner and Sir Henry Leveson Gower.

PHILLIPSON, WILLIAM EDWARD (EDDIE), who died on August 24, 1991 in Trafford General Hospital, aged 80, was a valuable member of the Lancashire side before and immediately after the Second World War. A genuine all-rounder, he was a right-arm fast-medium opening bowler and a solid, reliable middle-order batsman. He made a notable first-class début in 1933 against Sussex at Old Trafford: going in last, he played with such good sense and judgment that he helped his captain, P. T. Eckersley, put on 102. His own contribution was 27. In 1934, although his opportunities were limited, he registered a career-best eight for 100 against Kent at Dover, and a year later 71 wickets at 22.00, and more than 400 runs, signalled an impressive advance. By 1937 he was fully into his stride and came within striking distance of the double. His total of 131 wickets was bettered only by eleven others, and against Nottinghamshire at Old Trafford he hit his maiden hundred. Lancashire were 78 for five before Paynter (132) and Phillipson (105) put on 176 for the sixth wicket. He had another fine season with the ball in 1939, claiming 133 wickets at 22.33 and three times finishing with seven in an innings. At Gloucester, where he "combined length, swing and pace off the pitch" as the home team were hustled out for 79, Phillipson's figures were seven for 18 from 11.6 eight-ball overs. That summer also produced his highest score – 113 at Preston when Glamorgan were the visitors.

In August 1945, after war service in the RAF, Phillipson appeared in the fifth and final Victory "Test", at Old Trafford, enjoying notable success with nine wickets in the match, including six in the second innings. He bowled very straight, drawing most of the Australians into the stroke against their will, and only Miller and Cristofani played him with any confidence. He was also chosen to play for England against the Dominions at Lord's three days later. Although in 1946 he picked up the threads so well that he made 855 runs and took 80 wickets at 24.12, he was now in his 36th year, and two years later he felt compelled to retire. In 162 matches he had scored 4,096 runs for an average of 25.76, taken 555 wickets at 24.72, and held 82 catches. Subsequently he played for Northumberland, and from 1956 to 1978 he was on the first-class umpires' list. During that time he stood in twelve Tests.

PONSFORD, WILLIAM HAROLD, died at Kyneton, Victoria, on April 6, 1991; at 90, he was Australia's oldest living Test cricketer and the sole survivor of H. L. Collins's 1926 team in England. He made 162 in his second first-class game, for Victoria against Tasmania at Launceston in February 1922, but did not play for the state again until selected against the same opposition a year later in Melbourne. Then, in what was only his fourth innings, he created a sensation by hitting 429 in 477 minutes: it was the world's highest first-class score until he bettered it five years later. Furthermore, Victoria's 1,059 was the first four-figure total in any first-class match, and Ponsford, who was captaining his side, stayed until he made the 1,000th run himself, having gone in at 200 for three.

He was soon to prove that his 429 was something more than money for old rope against moderate bowling, as some would have it. The previous record-holder, A. C. MacLaren, had protested peevishly at the status of the match. Four centuries for Victoria in 1923-24, including 248 out of 456 with Edgar Mayne for the first wicket against Queensland – still an Australian record – sounded a warning note of what was in store for bowlers. The next season he played in all five Tests against England and scored 110 and 128 in the first two, an unprecedented achievement. His tour of England in 1926 was less successful, but early in December a veritable torrent of runs began to flow from his bat. Never before had anyone strung together such a series of colossal scores as Ponsford did in 1926-27 and 1927-28. In 1926-27, his innings were 214 and 54, 151, 352, 108 and 84, 12 and 116, 131 and 7, producing an aggregate of 1,229 runs at 122.90; in 1927-28 he scored 133, 437, 202 and 38, 336, 6 and 2, and 63 – an aggregate of 1,217 at 152.12. His 336 against South Australia in January 1928 was his eleventh first-class hundred in consecutive matches in Australia.

Only phenomenal powers of concentration, a high degree of physical fitness and an insatiable appetite for runs could have sustained him through so many hours at the crease. Over Christmas in 1926, Ponsford was especially devastating form. On the second day of Victoria's match against New South Wales at Melbourne, he dominated an opening partnership of 375 with Woodfull, and his 352, of which 334 were made in a day, contained 36 fours. It was the foundation of Victoria's 1,107, still the record first-class total. But in reviewing 1927-28 the gods must have deemed Ponsford guilty of hubris, after he had had the temerity to amass 1,013 runs in only four innings. Nemesis was soon to follow: his new world-record score of 437, made in 621 minutes against Queensland at Melbourne, was eclipsed two years later by the young Bradman's 452 not out.

Ponsford, who was born in the Melbourne suburb of North Fitzroy, showed an unusual aptitude for cricket from his earliest years, taking as his model Les Cody, the state player, whose strokeplay he greatly admired. Pennant cricket for the St Kilda club led on to his first-class début for Victoria in 1920-21, against Douglas's MCC side. A baseball batter's strength of forearm and wrist enabled him to wield a very heavy bat, and if never exactly a stylist, Ponsford soon developed into a formidable all-round batsman, with great strength on the on side. He was a fierce driver in front of the wicket and always worked hard to keep up the momentum of an innings; his two quadruple centuries each contained 42 fours. He was second to none as a player of spin bowling, and O'Reilly reckoned him to be an even tougher opponent than Bradman to bowl at. Against high pace he was less secure, and when facing left-armers like Voce and Quinn, the South African, he at times showed a tendency to move too far across his wicket.

The difference between Ponsford's career and Test averages is 17 runs. In his first and last series, those of 1924-25 and 1934 against England, he made nearly half of his total of Test runs for an average of 64.81, whereas in his other six series he made his runs at under 40. This calls for an explanation. Although a member of the supporting cast in England in 1930, Ponsford played two fine innings – 81 at Lord's and 110 at The Oval; and in 1930-31 he took heavy toll of the West Indies attack, just pipping Bradman in the averages. But in his other three series against England, the rhythm and progress of his Test career was disrupted by illness, injury and bodyline. In 1926, his first tour of England was ruined by an attack of tonsillitis, which kept him out of action for the whole of June. He played in the last two Tests without success. Two years later, in 1928-29, a ball from Larwood broke a bone in his hand in the Second Test, at Sydney, after the same bowler had dismissed him for 2 and 6 at Brisbane. In 1932-33 he never flinched when under fire, and staying in line he absorbed a lot of punishment in putting together a brave and skilful 85 at Adelaide in the Third Test.

By the time he arrived in England on his third tour, in 1934, Ponsford was due for a change of fortune. Unbeaten double-hundreds at Cambridge and Lord's suggested that the gods might be relenting at last, and when Ponsford and Bradman joined forces at Headingley in the Fourth Test, putting on 388 for the fourth wicket, Ponsford's play was seen to be not one whit inferior to Bradman's. Neville Cardus, rhapsodising in characteristic fashion, saw the two champions as soloists in some grand double concerto. England were overwhelmed, but the damage done to them at The Oval was even worse. In a partnership surpassed in Tests only two months before Ponsford's death, by A. H. Jones and M. D. Crowe, he and Bradman added 451 for the second wicket in a mere 316 minutes. Ponsford's personal contributions in those two Tests were 181 and 266. He topped the Test averages with 569 runs at 94.83 and was one of *Wisden*'s Five Cricketers of the Year. Above all, he had shown the English public what he could do, whereupon he deemed it appropriate to retire from first-class cricket when still only 34.

Ponsford is the only player to have exceeded 400 twice. He and Hammond, apart from Bradman who made six, are the only players to have hit four triple-hundreds, and his 281 not out against MCC at Lord's in 1934 is the highest score by an Australian on the ground. He shared in five partnerships of 375 or more; with Woodfull, whose career record so closely matched his own, he put together 23 three-figure partnerships, eighteen of them for the first wicket and twelve over 150. In 162 first-class matches, he scored 13,819 runs at 65.18, an average only Bradman and Merchant have bettered among batsmen with more than 10,000 runs, and he hit 47 hundreds. In the Sheffield Shield his runs totalled 5,413 at 83.27, and in 29 Tests he made 2,122 runs for an average of 48.22. A superb out-fielder in any position, he had 71 catches to his credit – although, when examined for war service, he was found to be red-green colour-blind. "Ponny" was a man of few words outside the dressing-room: shy, modest and shunning publicity at all costs. When he was "postered" in Sydney in 1928 after his extraordinary four-innings sequence, it must have given him nightmares; the flow of runs suddenly stopped. Few, however, have been more eloquent with the bat than the great Victorian.

POTHECARY, ARTHUR ERNEST (SAM), who died at Iver on May 21, 1991, aged 85, occupied most places in the middle order for Hampshire during a career which extended from 1927 to 1946. A left-handed batsman, he was also an occasional slow left-arm bowler with a pleasing style which, early on, had suggested real class. Towards the end of the 1920s, Hampshire were looking to bring in replacements for such stalwarts as Mead, Brown, Newman and Kennedy, and Pothecary was one of a number of young professionals tried. On his début, against Surrey at The Oval in 1927, he went in last, making 24, and took four second-innings wickets, including those of Hobbs and Sandham, a performance which led to exaggerated hopes for his future progress. As it was, he had to serve a long apprenticeship before finally producing some consistent form in 1932. In 1933 he made his thousand runs for the first of four times, and his maiden hundred, 101 at Southampton, helped Hampshire avoid defeat after a big Surrey score. His best years were 1936 to 1938. Not many centuries are made at No. 9, but Pothecary performed this feat against Northamptonshire at Portsmouth in 1936. In all he made nine hundreds, with the highest, 130, coming against the New Zealand tourists at Bournemouth in 1937. In 1938 he enjoyed his best season with 1,357 runs at 27.14. Pothecary played in just three matches after the war, and in his 271 first-class games, all for Hampshire, he totalled 9,477 runs for an average of 23.34. Although his bowling never fulfilled its early promise, he picked up 52 wickets at 41.15; in the field, he often shone at cover-point and he held 46 catches. He was appointed to the first-class umpires' list in 1949, and later took charge of the RAF ground at Uxbridge.

**POWYS-MAURICE, CANON LIONEL SELWYN**, who died at Buckden, Huntingdonshire, on January 1, 1991, aged 91, showed exceptional promise as a schoolboy batsman. As L. S. P. Maurice, he had a highly successful season for Haileybury in 1917, going in first and scoring 398 runs in twelve innings; his 140 against Uppingham, made in two hours with scarcely a mistake, was the XI's highest score. However, he made little impression as a Freshman at Oxford, and a trial in the Seniors' Match of 1922 went no further. Northamptonshire took an interest in him that summer, and after a splendid innings of 65 against Worcestershire at Northampton on his début, scoring all round the wicket and hitting one six and seven fours, he was given an extended run and recalled in 1923. As it turned out, he failed to play another innings of note, and his eleven matches produced just 156 runs for an average of 8.21.

**PUCKETT, MAXWELL CHARLES**, who died in Adelaide on August 25, 1991, at the age of 56, played in one inter-state match for South Australia, against Western Australia at Adelaide in 1964-65. A right-arm fast-medium bowler, he was called up because David Sincock, South Australia's left-arm wrist-spinner, was playing for Australia against Pakistan in Melbourne. Puckett bowled first and then second change, taking a wicket in each innings at a reasonable cost. His father, C. W. Puckett, had played for Western Australia against South Australia in 1939-40, also taking two wickets.

**RIMBAULT, BRIGADIER GEOFFREY ACWORTH, CBE, DSO, MC, DL**, died on October 20, 1991 at Bovey Tracey, aged 83. From 1924 to 1926 he played with distinction for the Dulwich XI, being described at sixteen as an attractive type of player and being commended for his part in a great stand in the match with MCC. In 1925 he had an excellent record, making 644 runs for an average of more than 50, and H. S. Altham, writing in *Wisden*, called him an outstanding cricketer. ". . . he started rather shakily, but played some splendid innings and in power and variety of stroke was clearly in a class by himself. His 209 not out against Incogniti was a really brilliant piece of batting, while he took toll of the Authentics bowling to the tune of another century, and met with consistent success for the Young Surrey Amateurs in August. A fine field at mid-off, he should be a tower of strength to whom he captains in the coming season." He was indeed that tower of strength in 1926, for in addition to making 500 runs he showed leadership qualities quite out of the ordinary. That August, he played for a Public Schools XV against the Australians at Lord's, a match not to be repeated on subsequent tours, and going in early he was bowled by Everett for 3. Having shown all the attributes for successful leadership, Rimbault was earmarked by Surrey for this role in the future, but he chose a military career instead and closed the door on a life in first-class cricket. In India he played for the Europeans in 1933-34, and in 1938 he made 16 in the Army's only innings against the University at Cambridge.

SCHOKMAN, VERNON C. (PUG), who died in Australia in 1991, aged 86, was a prominent figure in Ceylon cricket between the wars. A useful middle-order batsman, he was an outstanding wicket-keeper, notable for his quiet efficiency. As a schoolboy he made four hundreds for Trinity College, Kandy, between 1920-21 and 1923-24, the highest being 142 against Royal College, as he added 260 for the fourth wicket with Roy Gibson – still a record in Sri Lankan schools cricket. He captained the team in his last two years. Later he played for the Ceylon Police Force. He was first-choice wicket-keeper on Ceylon's first official tour of India in 1932-33, when he scored usefully, and also appeared for All Ceylon and the combined India and Ceylon team when Jardine brought MCC to Colombo in February 1934. In the second match he had reached 39, much the highest score in a first-innings total of 104, when a rising ball from E. W. Clark struck him on the head and he fell on his wicket. The crowd, familiar with the controversy of the bodyline tour of Australia the previous year, were in uproar and booed the visitors, who won by only 8 runs. Schokman's two catches and a stumping had helped to dismiss them for 78 in the second innings. He continued to represent the island until the visit of the 1938 Australians under Bradman.

SERRURIER, LOUIS ROY, died at Hermanus, Cape Province, on January 16, 1991, aged 85. An all-rounder who opened the batting, and the bowling if needed, he was educated at Cape Town and went up to Oxford in October 1924. Ten for 72 in the Freshmen's Match earned him a place in the University side, but he lost his form and dropped out of the running for a Blue in 1925. Given a golden opportunity to prove his worth the following year when he was sent in first against the Australians, he failed to get a start in either innings. In his last year, he was most unfortunate not to get the final place for the Lord's match, especially as he had taken fourteen wickets at 25.71 and a further five for the Harlequins against the University. Later in 1927, however, he played in seven games for Worcestershire, bringing some solidity to the side and heading the averages. He was at his best against Gloucestershire at Bristol, making 110 and 59 with little support in either innings. After his return to South Africa, Serrurier distinguished himself in February 1928 by carrying his bat for Western Province against MCC. His 74, made out of 162, was a determined effort against a varied attack including Hammond, Wyatt, Freeman and Astill. In the trial matches of 1928-29 which preceded the tour to England, he registered 59, 51 and 171, the highest score of his career, and with his knowledge of English conditions he must have been considered for a place. However, the vote went against him. He had a successful Currie Cup in 1929-30, making 105 against Natal and averaging 39.85, but that was his last full season. In 1931-32 he made one appearance for Transvaal, scoring 56 at Durban in his only innings to increase his first-class aggregate, from 30 games, to 1,281 runs for an average of 33.71. His bowling earned him 42 wickets at 26.83 apiece, and he took seventeen catches.

SMITH, PETER WILLOUGHBY, who died in London following a heart attack on December 6, 1991, aged 55, had since 1989 been the Public Relations Manager at the Test and County Cricket Board. This was a new appointment, and he soon came to grips with the many complex problems involving the first-class game's relations with the media. In his short period in office there was a noticeable improvement in communication and mutual understanding. After the best possible grounding as a sports writer with Hayter's, from 1974 to 1979 he was cricket and rugby correspondent for the *News of the World*, and then cricket correspondent of the *Daily Mail* until 1988. He was chairman of the Cricket Writers Club from 1982 to 1985.

STOCKLEY, ANTHONY JOHN, who died in Adelaide on May 29, 1991, aged 51, was a prominent off-break bowler in Surrey club cricket when the county called him up for three first-class games in 1968 as cover for Pocock. Tried against three different types of opposition – Cambridge University, W. M. Lawry's Australians and Kent (in the Championship) – he came through with flying colours and showed admirable temperament and control in collecting ten wickets for 194 runs. He was a towering figure, 6ft 8in tall, and the steepness of his flight and lift from the pitch clearly made him an awkward proposition. His analysis against the Australians, 37–14–74–4, points to the respect with which he was treated. Stockley toured Australia in 1974 with the Club Cricket Conference and emigrated two years later, settling in Adelaide, where he performed well enough to be included in the South Australian state squad, though he was not selected for a Sheffield Shield match.

TELANG, BHALACHANDRA (BABU), who died at Varanasi on July 22, 1991, aged 75, played for Uttar Pradesh in the Ranji Trophy, making his début in the Trophy's first season, 1934-35, when the team was known as United Provinces. Captain in 1951-52, his last season, he was a right-hand batsman with a highest score of 176 against Assam at Dehra Dun in 1950-51, when he shared in a partnership of 241 with M. Shukla. In twelve first-class matches he scored 448 runs for an average of 22.40, while his one wicket cost 166 runs.

TUCKER, WILLIAM ELDON, CVO, MBE, TD, FRCS, who died at his home in Bermuda on August 4, 1991, aged 87, was a distinguished orthopaedic surgeon, who chose to specialise in sporting injuries. The cricket-loving public and especial admirers of Denis Compton may not have realised that the extension of his career beyond 1949 until 1957 was entirely due to Tucker, who performed a series of operations on the most celebrated knee in the land. Tucker himself was a sportsman, who played rugby for England, winning three caps.

TURNER, KENNETH CHARLES (KEN), who died at Northampton on September 24, 1991, aged 71, was one of the most successful county administrators of his time. After service with the Army in the British Zone of Occupation in Germany, he was appointed assistant secretary at Northamptonshire in 1949, and if this was a leap in the dark, for Turner had had little, if any, experience of cricket, it was not the only inspired move made by the committee. That same year they had persuaded F. R. Brown to take charge on the field. The rehabilitation of Northamptonshire's cricket was under way. In 1958 Turner became secretary, and with his formidable and dominating personality he was until his retirement in 1985 a powerful influence behind the scenes. His fund-raising in his early days was legendary. Largely by means of a football pool, and then by promoting rock concerts in the Indoor School, large sums were collected, out of which the playing staff was greatly strengthened. For a layman, he possessed an uncanny skill for spotting potential in young players, who were nurtured with great care and attention. He was always looking for the hard-working, solid sort of player and had no time for *prima donna* types.

The achievements of the club during his long tenure of office were considerable once the spectre of continuous failure had been banished. The Gillette Cup and Benson and Hedges Cup were won in 1976 and 1980 respectively, and twice, in 1979 and 1981, Northamptonshire were the losing finalists at Lord's in the 60-over final. Downright in expressing his opinion and not noted for his tact, he will be remembered with respect as an important figure in the development of Northamptonshire cricket.

**WAHID, MOHAMMED ABDUL,** who died in 1991 as the result of a motor accident, aged 80, was one of the leading all-rounders in Ceylon cricket from 1930 to 1950. A dual-purpose left-arm bowler, he toured India in 1940-41 with the national team, and though the hard Indian pitches did not suit his kind of bowling, he proved his worth as a patient opening batsman. His 52 against All-India at Baroda occupied more than three hours. For many years he captained the Moors club and frequently claimed 100 wickets a season in club cricket.

**WALKER, WILLIS,** who died on December 3, 1991 in a nursing-home at Keighley, Yorkshire, having just embarked on his 100th year, had for some years been recognised as the oldest living county cricketer. A right-handed batsman and an elegant strokeplayer, he was for much of the time between 1913 and 1937 Nottinghamshire's No. 3, and as such he was an integral part of the side which won the Championship in 1929, having so nearly taken the honours two years before. He was born at Gosforth in Northumberland on November 24, 1892.

Walker's father was employed as a clerk on the estate of Sir Joseph Laycock, which lay between Retford and Bawtry, near Nottingham, and was equipped with its own cricket ground, where two all-day games a week were staged. Thus the boy, shy and retiring by nature, enjoyed the privilege of growing up and learning his cricket in gracious surroundings. Promise was fulfilled when he was taken on to the Nottinghamshire groundstaff in 1911, and two years later, at twenty, he made his first-class début at Dewsbury against the powerful Yorkshire side. A few more opportunities came his way before the war caused a break, but after serving as a PT instructor at the Royal Navy Depot at Crystal Palace, he prudently chose to rebuild his game by playing for Keighley in the Bradford League. Not until four seasons had passed did he rejoin Nottinghamshire, in 1923. His captain, A. W. Carr, enabled him to get his maiden hundred that year, against Essex, by delaying the declaration, and 1924 saw a further advance. When the breakthrough came in 1925, with the retirement of the elder Hardstaff, the pattern of Walker's career was already becoming apparent. He made 1,384 runs at 33.75 that summer, an average very near his career figure of 32.37, and for the following ten seasons, except 1934 when illness interfered, his performance stayed on a highish plateau with little or no variation. In 1933 he made 1,730 runs at 39.31, having a year earlier had his best average of 42.05, but 1936 and 1937 brought a gentle decline, and when the time came he was pleased to retire, having scored in all 18,259 runs and passed 1,000 runs on ten occasions. His fielding in the deep was exemplary, as might be expected from a former Football League goalkeeper, and he held 110 catches. He was always immaculately turned out.

Walker's career was highlighted by 31 hundreds, the biggest coming at Lord's in 1930 against Middlesex. He batted through the first day for 165 not out, revealing off-side strokes of the highest class, with the occasional exquisite late cut, and on the other side of the wicket a nice selection of placements off his legs. His skill on treacherous turf was superbly illustrated by his undefeated 133 at Coventry against Warwickshire in 1929, Nottinghamshire's Championship year. Their team was a blend of solid, near-veteran batting and youthful, vigorous fast bowling, and Walker held a pivotal position in the batting line-up, with George Gunn, Whysall, Payton and Carr before and aft. At one time or another he shared in large partnerships with all these players, most notably with Gunn when the pair added 265 in only three hours for the second wicket against Hampshire at Bournemouth in 1928. He was also the batting link in the inevitable period of transition, most unfortunately aggravated by the sudden death of Whysall in November 1930, calmly settling things down as the new generation of Keeton, Charlie Harris, Joe Hardstaff Junior and G. V. Gunn gradually took over.

Walker, a shy and self-effacing man, was never a dominating player, hungry for runs. The limit of his ambition was to serve his county as well as he possibly could.

It is not surprising that he and Hobbs became firm friends, with a high regard for each other. They were much the same: quiet, gentlemanly, honest and upright. And they both made a success of small sports businesses which flourished under careful stewardship.

WEAVER, MAJOR PHILIP HUMPHREY PETER, who died on June 28, 1991, aged 79, made nearly 2,500 runs for King's School, Bruton, from 1927 to 1930. Dyslexia had prevented his being admitted to one of the more fashionable cricketing schools. In successive years his highest innings were 168 not out, 155 not out and 154, and in 1930 his aggregate was 982 with an average of 75.53; but no invitation came to play in the Schools Week at Lord's. A hard-working opening bowler, he also took 89 wickets for the XI. In spite of these achievements, he had played no big cricket when he appeared twice for Hampshire in 1938: against Glamorgan at Cardiff, where he made 17 and 1, and Cambridge at Southampton, when he got 37. In the Second World War he served with the SAS.

WEBB, DARREN, who was killed by a fall from a train in Zimbabwe on March 12, 1991, aged twenty, while coaching there, seemed to be on the threshold of a county career. A member of the Horsham club, he made impressive progress through Sussex Young Cricketers' grades and in 1990 was in the National Association of Young Cricketers' squad to play the MCC Schools at Lord's. He missed final selection there, but an unbeaten century in the Esso/NAYC Festival earned him the batting award at Cambridge. Prior to his death he had been awarded the Crole-Rees bursary, which in effect would have maintained him as a full-time member of the Sussex staff.

WHITMAN, ERIC IOAN EMLYN, who died on December 5, 1990, aged 81, appeared in two matches for Glamorgan in 1932. Given the new ball at Leicester he produced the respectable analysis of 10-1-27-1 in the second innings, and in the following match, at Edgbaston, he toiled away throughout Warwickshire's innings of 463 for five declared, sending down 34 overs for 113 runs. His two wickets were the good ones of Len Bates and Jack Parsons. He would seem to have earned further opportunities, but an average cost of 57.33 for his three wickets may have persuaded the club otherwise. His batting low down the order brought him 27 runs for an average of 9.00, with a highest score of 16. Whitman also played Minor Counties cricket for Cambridgeshire.

WIGNALL, ERIC WILLIAM EDWARD, who died at Oxhey, Hertfordshire, on January 2, 1991, aged 58, played in three matches for Gloucestershire in 1952 and 1953. A right-handed batsman and leg-break bowler, he had previously been on the groundstaff at Lord's. When Gloucestershire met the Combined Services at Bristol in 1953, after an interesting struggle the Services were set 339 to win. They were going well and looking like winners until Wignall chipped in with two vital wickets: he caught and bowled the redoubtable A. C. Shirreff for 77 and dismissed J. E. Manners when he was 34. In the end, the Services fell 33 runs short of their target. Wignall had made 24 runs, average 8.00, and taken two wickets at 31.50 apiece when injury forced him to give up any further ideas of first-class cricket.

WOODHEAD, FRANCIS GERALD, who died in Nottingham on May 24, 1991, aged 78, was a fast-medium right-arm bowler who played for Nottinghamshire on either side of the Second World War, making his début in 1934 and playing his last match early in 1950. He was on the staff at Trent Bridge at a difficult time. It was hoped that he and Harold Butler would fill at least some of the gap left by the retirement of Larwood and the gradual waning of Voce's powers, but both men were prone to injury and the pitches at Trent Bridge favoured batsmen much too much for the health of the county's cricket. Woodhead made a good impression with his return of four for 60 in more than 30 overs against Sussex at Trent Bridge in 1934, his victims including John Langridge, George Cox and Harry Parks, and in 1935 he was given more of a run in the Championship side. His 22 wickets at 20.63 contained a splendid performance, six for 28, against Warwickshire in the home match, but the next two seasons were disappointing. He was accurate, able to move the ball sharply from a perfect length, and hard to get away, but throughout his career he found wickets elusive. His best season was 1938, when he took 69 wickets at 25.04. At Trent Bridge towards the end of August he exploited the moisture left by a heavy dew to claim seven for 24 as Worcestershire were bundled out for 73, and this remained the best bowling of his career.

In the first post-war season Woodhead was worked hard, sending down more than 650 overs at a cost of little more than two and a half runs per over; with seven for 41 in 18.2 overs in Gloucestershire's first innings at Nottingham he did not deserve to be on the losing side. The highlight of an otherwise barren season in 1948 was his dismissal of Bradman, Hassett and Miller, all bowled, when the tourists came to Nottingham. His career figures show that he took 320 wickets at 32.96 apiece, but he was a better bowler than that. He was not much of a batsman, but sometimes he connected to good effect, as when he made 38 not out against all-conquering Yorkshire at Trent Bridge in 1938. He hit three sixes and took part in a last-wicket stand of 56, which increased the Nottinghamshire lead to 83. In 141 first-class matches, Woodhead made 1,100 runs for an average of 8.46, with a highest score of 52 not out against Hampshire in 1936, and he held 80 catches. Throughout the 1950s and till 1965 he was the cricket professional at Nottingham High School, and in 1970 he returned to Trent Bridge, where he became a highly respected and successful coach. He was awarded a testimonial in 1979 to mark his final retirement.

WYKES, NIGEL GORDON (TIGER), who died in December 1991, aged 85, played 30 matches for his native county, Essex, and won a Blue at Cambridge in 1928. An opening or middle-order left-handed bat, he had shown distinct promise at Oundle, where in 1923 he was the soundest batsman of a good side, scoring 110, 79 not out and 80 in consecutive innings towards an aggregate of 489 and an average of 54.30. Next year, despite slightly inferior figures, he was "thought to be on an equal to any batsman Oundle has turned out." His century against Pembroke was a grand innings." In 1925 he made his first-class début for Essex against Leicestershire at Southend, at the tail-end of the season, and a year later he played just once for Cambridge in his quest for a Blue. This turned out to be an "ordeal by fire", for he encountered the young Larwood at his fastest. In 1927 he made his two centuries – 145 not out at Fenner's against the Army and 162 for Essex against Kent at Leyton, "batting finely for more than four hours and a half" – but he won his Blue in 1928 as much for his fielding as his batting, having dropped down the order to No. 9. Still, he made two useful contributions at Lord's, with 27 and 19 not out. Wykes spent his working life teaching at Eton, eventually becoming a housemaster, and until 1936 he found time to play one or two matches a year for Essex after the end of term. In all he made 1,277 runs for an average of 23.64.

# THE LAWS OF CRICKET

## (1980 CODE)

*World copyright of MCC and reprinted by permission of MCC. Copies of the "Laws of Cricket" may be obtained from Lord's Cricket Ground.*

## INDEX TO THE LAWS

## LAW 1.  THE PLAYERS

### 1. Number of Players and Captain

A match is played between two sides each of eleven players, one of whom shall be captain. In the event of the captain not being available at any time, a deputy shall act for him.

### 2. Nomination of Players

Before the toss for innings, the captain shall nominate his players, who may not thereafter be changed without the consent of the opposing captain.

*Note*

**(a) More or Less than Eleven Players a Side**
A match may be played by agreement between sides of more or less than eleven players, but not more than eleven players may field.

## LAW 2.  SUBSTITUTES AND RUNNERS: BATSMAN OR FIELDSMAN LEAVING THE FIELD: BATSMAN RETIRING: BATSMAN COMMENCING INNINGS

### 1. Substitutes

In normal circumstances, a substitute shall be allowed to field only for a player who satisfies the umpire that he has become injured or become ill during the match. However, in very exceptional circumstances, the umpires may use their discretion to allow a substitute for a player who has to leave the field or does not take the field for other wholly acceptable reasons, subject to consent being given by the opposing captain. If a player wishes to change his shirt, boots, etc., he may leave the field to do so (no changing on the field), but no substitute will be allowed.

### 2. Objection to Substitutes

The opposing captain shall have no right of objection to any player acting as substitute in the field, nor as to where he shall field, although he may object to the substitute acting as wicket-keeper.

*Experimental Law: The opposing captain shall have no right of objection to any player acting as substitute on the field, nor as to where he shall field; however no substitute shall act as wicket-keeper. (It has been recommended that this Experimental Law should apply in all levels of cricket from April 1, 1989).*

### 3. Substitute not to Bat or Bowl

A substitute shall not be allowed to bat or bowl.

### 4. A Player for whom a Substitute has Acted

A player may bat, bowl or field even though a substitute has acted for him.

### 5. Runner

A runner shall be allowed for a batsman who, during the match, is incapacitated by illness or injury. The person acting as runner shall be a member of the batting side and shall, if possible, have already batted in that innings.

## 6. Runner's Equipment

The player acting as runner for an injured batsman shall wear the same external protective equipment as the injured batsman.

## 7. Transgression of the Laws by an Injured Batsman or Runner

An injured batsman may be out should his runner break any one of Laws 33 (Handled the Ball), 37 (Obstructing the Field) or 38 (Run Out). As striker he remains himself subject to the Laws. Furthermore, should he be out of his ground for any purpose and the wicket at the wicket-keeper's end be put down he shall be out under Law 38 (Run Out) or Law 39 (Stumped), irrespective of the position of the other batsman or the runner, and no runs shall be scored.

When not the striker, the injured batsman is out of the game and shall stand where he does not interfere with the play. Should he bring himself into the game in any way, then he shall suffer the penalties that any transgression of the Laws demands.

## 8. Fieldsman Leaving the Field

No fieldsman shall leave the field or return during a session of play without the consent of the umpire at the bowler's end. The umpire's consent is also necessary if a substitute is required for a fieldsman, when his side returns to the field after an interval. If a member of the fielding side leaves the field or fails to return after an interval and is absent from the field for longer than fifteen minutes, he shall not be permitted to bowl after his return until he has been on the field for at least that length of playing time for which he was absent. This restriction shall not apply at the start of a new day's play.

## 9. Batsman Leaving the Field or Retiring

A batsman may leave the field or retire at any time owing to illness, injury or other unavoidable cause, having previously notified the umpire at the bowler's end. He may resume his innings at the fall of a wicket, which for the purposes of this Law shall include the retirement of another batsman.

If he leaves the field or retires for any other reason he may resume his innings only with the consent of the opposing captain.

When a batsman has left the field or retired and is unable to return owing to illness, injury or other unavoidable cause, his innings is to be recorded as "retired, not out". Otherwise it is to be recorded as "retired, out".

## 10. Commencement of a Batsman's Innings

A batsman shall be considered to have commenced his innings once he has stepped on to the field of play.

*Note*

    **(a) Substitutes and Runners**
    For the purpose of these Laws, allowable illnesses or injuries are those which occur at any time after the nomination by the captains of their teams.

## LAW 3.   THE UMPIRES

## 1. Appointment

Before the toss for innings, two umpires shall be appointed, one for each end, to control the game with absolute impartiality as required by the Laws.

## 2. Change of Umpires

No umpire shall be changed during a match without the consent of both captains.

### 3. Special Conditions

Before the toss for innings, the umpires shall agree with both captains on any special conditions affecting the conduct of the match.

### 4. The Wickets

The umpires shall satisfy themselves before the start of the match that the wickets are properly pitched.

### 5. Clock or Watch

The umpires shall agree between themselves and inform both captains before the start of the match on the watch or clock to be followed during the match.

### 6. Conduct and Implements

Before and during a match the umpires shall ensure that the conduct of the game and the implements used are strictly in accordance with the Laws.

### 7. Fair and Unfair Play

The umpires shall be the sole judges of fair and unfair play.

### 8. Fitness of Ground, Weather and Light

(a) The umpires shall be the sole judges of the fitness of the ground, weather and light for play.
　(i) However, before deciding to suspend play, or not to start play, or not to resume play after an interval or stoppage, the umpires shall establish whether both captains (the batsmen at the wicket may deputise for their captain) wish to commence or to continue in the prevailing conditions; if so, their wishes shall be met.
　(ii) In addition, if during play the umpires decide that the light is unfit, only the batting side shall have the option of continuing play. After agreeing to continue to play in unfit light conditions, the captain of the batting side (or a batsman at the wicket) may appeal against the light to the umpires, who shall uphold the appeal only if, in their opinion, the light has deteriorated since the agreement to continue was made.

(b) After any suspension of play, the umpires, unaccompanied by any of the players or officials, shall, on their own initiative, carry out an inspection immediately the conditions improve and shall continue to inspect at intervals. Immediately the umpires decide that play is possible they shall call upon the players to resume the game.

### 9. Exceptional Circumstances

In exceptional circumstances, other than those of weather, ground or light, the umpires may decide to suspend or abandon play. Before making such a decision the umpires shall establish, if the circumstances allow, whether both captains (the batsmen at the wicket may deputise for their captain) wish to continue in the prevailing conditions; if so, their wishes shall be met.

### 10. Position of Umpires

The umpires shall stand where they can best see any act upon which their decision may be required.

Subject to this over-riding consideration, the umpire at the bowler's end shall stand where he does not interfere with either the bowler's run-up or the striker's view.

The umpire at the striker's end may elect to stand on the off instead of the leg side of the pitch, provided he informs the captain of the fielding side and the striker of his intention to do so.

## 11. Umpires Changing Ends

The umpires shall change ends after each side has had one innings.

## 12. Disputes

All disputes shall be determined by the umpires, and if they disagree the actual state of things shall continue.

## 13. Signals

The following code of signals shall be used by umpires who will wait until a signal has been answered by a scorer before allowing the game to proceed.

| | |
|---|---|
| Boundary | – by waving the arm from side to side. |
| Boundary 6 | – by raising both arms above the head. |
| Bye | – by raising an open hand above the head. |
| Dead Ball | – by crossing and re-crossing the wrists below the waist. |
| Leg-bye | – by touching a raised knee with the hand. |
| No-ball | – by extending one arm horizontally. |
| Out | – by raising the index finger above the head. If not out, the umpire shall call "not out". |
| Short run | – by bending the arm upwards and by touching the nearer shoulder with the tips of the fingers. |
| Wide | – by extending both arms horizontally. |

## 14. Correctness of Scores

The umpires shall be responsible for satisfying themselves on the correctness of the scores throughout and at the conclusion of the match. See Law 21.6 (Correctness of Result).

*Notes*

**(a) Attendance of Umpires**
The umpires should be present on the ground and report to the ground executive or the equivalent at least thirty minutes before the start of a day's play.

**(b) Consultation between Umpires and Scorers**
Consultation between umpires and scorers over doubtful points is essential.

**(c) Fitness of Ground**
The umpires shall consider the ground as unfit for play when it is so wet or slippery as to deprive the bowlers of a reasonable foothold, the fieldsmen, other than the deep-fielders, of the power of free movement, or the batsmen of the ability to play their strokes or to run between the wickets. Play should not be suspended merely because the grass and the ball are wet and slippery.

**(d) Fitness of Weather and Light**
The umpires should suspend play only when they consider that the conditions are so bad that it is unreasonable or dangerous to continue.

# LAW 4.   THE SCORERS

## 1. Recording Runs

All runs scored shall be recorded by scorers appointed for the purpose. Where there are two scorers they shall frequently check to ensure that the score-sheets agree.

## 2. Acknowledging Signals

The scorers shall accept and immediately acknowledge all instructions and signals given to them by the umpires.

## LAW 5.  THE BALL

### 1. Weight and Size

The ball, when new, shall weigh not less than $5\frac{1}{2}$ ounces/155.9g, nor more than $5\frac{3}{4}$ ounces/163g; and shall measure not less than $8\frac{13}{16}$ inches/22.4cm, nor more than 9 inches/22.9cm in circumference.

### 2. Approval of Balls

All balls used in matches shall be approved by the umpires and captains before the start of the match.

### 3. New Ball

Subject to agreement to the contrary, having been made before the toss, either captain may demand a new ball at the start of each innings.

### 4. New Ball in Match of Three or More Days' Duration

In a match of three or more days' duration, the captain of the fielding side may demand a new ball after the prescribed number of overs has been bowled with the old one. The governing body for cricket in the country concerned shall decide the number of overs applicable in that country, which shall be not less than 75 six-ball overs (55 eight-ball overs).

### 5. Ball Lost or Becoming Unfit for Play

In the event of a ball during play being lost or, in the opinion of the umpires, becoming unfit for play, the umpires shall allow it to be replaced by one that in their opinion has had a similar amount of wear. If a ball is to be replaced, the umpires shall inform the batsman.

*Note*

    **(a) Specifications**
    The specifications, as described in 1 above, shall apply to top-grade balls only. The following degrees of tolerance will be acceptable for other grades of ball.

    (i) *Men's Grades 2–4*
        Weight: $5\frac{5}{16}$ ounces/150g to $5\frac{13}{16}$ ounces/165g.
        Size: $8\frac{11}{16}$ inches/22.0cm to $9\frac{1}{16}$ inches/23.0cm.

    (ii) *Women's*
        Weight: $4\frac{15}{16}$ ounces/140g to $5\frac{5}{16}$ ounces/150g.
        Size: $8\frac{1}{4}$ inches/21.0cm to $8\frac{7}{8}$ inches/22.5cm.

    (iii) *Junior*
        Weight: $4\frac{5}{16}$ ounces/133g to $5\frac{1}{16}$ ounces/143g.
        Size: $8\frac{1}{16}$ inches/20.5cm to $8\frac{11}{16}$ inches/22.0cm.

## LAW 6.  THE BAT

### 1. Width and Length

The bat overall shall not be more than 38 inches/96.5cm in length; the blade of the bat shall be made of wood and shall not exceed $4\frac{1}{4}$ inches/10.8cm at the widest part.

*Note*

    (a) The blade of the bat may be covered with material for protection, strengthening or repair. Such material shall not exceed $\frac{1}{16}$ inch/1.56mm in thickness.

## LAW 7.  THE PITCH

### 1. Area of Pitch

The pitch is the area between the bowling creases – see Law 9 (The Bowling and Popping Creases). It shall measure 5 feet/1.52m in width on either side of a line joining the centre of the middle stumps of the wickets – see Law 8 (The Wickets).

## 2. Selection and Preparation

Before the toss for innings, the executive of the ground shall be responsible for the selection and preparation of the pitch; thereafter the umpires shall control its use and maintenance.

## 3. Changing Pitch

The pitch shall not be changed during a match unless it becomes unfit for play, and then only with the consent of both captains.

## 4. Non-Turf Pitches

In the event of a non-turf pitch being used, the following shall apply:

(a) Length: That of the playing surface to a minimum of 58 feet/17.68m.

(b) Width: That of the playing surface to a minimum of 6 feet/1.83m.

See Law 10 (Rolling, Sweeping, Mowing, Watering the Pitch and Re-marking of Creases) Note (a).

# LAW 8. THE WICKETS

## 1. Width and Pitching

Two sets of wickets, each 9 inches/22.86cm wide, and consisting of three wooden stumps with two wooden bails upon the top, shall be pitched opposite and parallel to each other at a distance of 22 yards/20.12m between the centres of the two middle stumps.

## 2. Size of Stumps

The stumps shall be of equal and sufficient size to prevent the ball from passing between them. Their tops shall be 28 inches/71.1cm above the ground, and shall be dome-shaped except for the bail grooves.

## 3. Size of Bails

The bails shall be each $4\frac{3}{8}$ inches/11.1cm in length and when in position on the top of the stumps shall not project more than $\frac{1}{2}$ inch/1.3cm above them.

*Notes*

**(a) Dispensing with Bails**

In a high wind the umpires may decide to dispense with the use of bails.

**(b) Junior Cricket**

For junior cricket, as defined by the local governing body, the following measurements for the wickets shall apply:

Width – 8 inches/20.32cm.
Pitched – 21 yards/19.20m.
Height – 27 inches/68.58cm.
Bails – each $3\frac{7}{8}$ inches/9.84cm in length and should not project more than $\frac{1}{2}$ inch/1.3cm above the stumps.

# LAW 9. THE BOWLING, POPPING AND RETURN CREASES

## 1. The Bowling Crease

The bowling crease shall be marked in line with the stumps at each end and shall be 8 feet 8 inches/2.64m in length, with the stumps in the centre.

## 2. The Popping Crease

The popping crease, which is the back edge of the crease marking, shall be in front of and parallel with the bowling crease. It shall have the back edge of the crease marking 4 feet/1.22m from the centre of the stumps and shall extend to a minimum of 6 feet/1.83m on either side of the line of the wicket.

The popping crease shall be considered to be unlimited in length.

### 3. The Return Crease

The return crease marking, of which the inside edge is the crease, shall be at each end of the bowling crease and at right angles to it. The return crease shall be marked to a minimum of 4 feet/1.22m behind the wicket and shall be considered to be unlimited in length. A forward extension shall be marked to the popping crease.

## LAW 10.  ROLLING, SWEEPING, MOWING, WATERING THE PITCH AND RE-MARKING OF CREASES

### 1. Rolling

During the match the pitch may be rolled at the request of the captain of the batting side, for a period of not more than seven minutes before the start of each innings, other than the first innings of the match, and before the start of each day's play. In addition, if, after the toss and before the first innings of the match, the start is delayed, the captain of the batting side shall have the right to have the pitch rolled for not more than seven minutes.

The pitch shall not otherwise be rolled during the match.

The seven minutes' rolling permitted before the start of a day's play shall take place not earlier than half an hour before the start of play and the captain of the batting side may delay such rolling until ten minutes before the start of play should he so desire.

If a captain declares an innings closed less than fifteen minutes before the resumption of play, and the other captain is thereby prevented from exercising his option of seven minutes' rolling or if he is so prevented for any other reason, the time for rolling shall be taken out of the normal playing time.

### 2. Sweeping

Such sweeping of the pitch as is necessary during the match shall be done so that the seven minutes allowed for rolling the pitch, provided for in 1 above, is not affected.

### 3. Mowing

**(a) Responsibilities of Ground Authority and of Umpires**
All mowings which are carried out before the toss for innings shall be the responsibility of the ground authority; thereafter they shall be carried out under the supervision of the umpires. See Law 7.2 (Selection and Preparation).

**(b) Initial Mowing**
The pitch shall be mown before play begins on the day the match is scheduled to start, or in the case of a delayed start on the day the match is expected to start. See 3(a) above (Responsibilities of Ground Authority and of Umpires).

**(c) Subsequent Mowings in a Match of Two or More Days' Duration**
In a match of two or more days' duration, the pitch shall be mown daily before play begins. Should this mowing not take place because of weather conditions, rest days or other reasons, the pitch shall be mown on the first day on which the match is resumed.

**(d) Mowing of the Outfield in a Match of Two or More Days' Duration**
In order to ensure that conditions are as similar as possible for both sides, the outfield shall normally be mown before the commencement of play on each day of the match, if ground and weather conditions allow. See Note (b) to this Law.

### 4. Watering

The pitch shall not be watered during a match.

### 5. Re-marking Creases

Whenever possible the creases shall be re-marked.

### 6. Maintenance of Foot-holes

In wet weather, the umpires shall ensure that the holes made by the bowlers and batsmen are cleaned out and dried whenever necessary to facilitate play. In matches of two or more days' duration, the umpires shall allow, if necessary, the re-turfing of foot-holes made by the bowler in his delivery stride, or the use of quick-setting fillings for the same purpose, before the start of each day's play.

## 7. Securing of Footholds and Maintenance of Pitch

During play, the umpires shall allow either batsman to beat the pitch with his bat and players to secure their footholds by the use of sawdust, provided that no damage to the pitch is so caused, and Law 42 (Unfair Play) is not contravened.

*Notes*

### (a) Non-turf Pitches

The above Law 10 applies to turf pitches.

The game is played on non-turf pitches in many countries at various levels. Whilst the conduct of the game on these surfaces should always be in accordance with the Laws of Cricket, it is recognised that it may sometimes be necessary for governing bodies to lay down special playing conditions to suit the type of non-turf pitch used in their country.

In matches played against touring teams, any special playing conditions should be agreed in advance by both parties.

### (b) Mowing of the Outfield in a Match of Two or More Days' Duration

If, for reasons other than ground and weather conditions, daily and complete mowing is not possible, the ground authority shall notify the captains and umpires, before the toss for innings, of the procedure to be adopted for such mowing during the match.

### (c) Choice of Roller

If there is more than one roller available, the captain of the batting side shall have a choice.

## LAW 11.  COVERING THE PITCH

### 1. Before the Start of a Match

Before the start of a match, complete covering of the pitch shall be allowed.

### 2. During a Match

The pitch shall not be completely covered during a match unless prior arrangement or regulations so provide.

### 3. Covering Bowlers' Run-up

Whenever possible, the bowlers' run-up shall be covered, but the covers so used shall not extend further than 4 feet/1.22m in front of the popping crease.

*Note*

### (a) Removal of Covers

The covers should be removed as promptly as possible whenever the weather permits.

## LAW 12.  INNINGS

### 1. Number of Innings

A match shall be of one or two innings of each side according to agreement reached before the start of play.

### 2. Alternate Innings

In a two-innings match each side shall take their innings alternately except in the case provided for in Law 13 (The Follow-on).

### 3. The Toss

The captains shall toss for the choice of innings on the field of play not later than fifteen minutes before the time scheduled for the match to start, or before the time agreed upon for play to start.

## 4. Choice of Innings

The winner of the toss shall notify his decision to bat or to field to the opposing captain not later than ten minutes before the time scheduled for the match to start, or before the time agreed upon for play to start. The decision shall not thereafter be altered.

## 5. Continuation after One Innings of Each Side

Despite the terms of 1 above, in a one-innings match, when a result has been reached on the first innings, the captains may agree to the continuation of play if, in their opinion, there is a prospect of carrying the game to a further issue in the time left. See Law 21 (Result).

*Notes*

**(a) Limited Innings – One-innings Match**
In a one-innings match, each innings may, by agreement, be limited by a number of overs or by a period of time.

**(b) Limited Innings – Two-innings Match**
In a two-innings match, the first innings of each side may, by agreement, be limited to a number of overs or by a period of time.

## LAW 13.   THE FOLLOW-ON

### 1. Lead on First Innings

In a two-innings match the side which bats first and leads by 200 runs in a match of five days or more, by 150 runs in a three-day or four-day match, by 100 runs in a two-day match, or by 75 runs in a one-day match, shall have the option of requiring the other side to follow their innings.

### 2. Day's Play Lost

If no play takes place on the first day of a match of two or more days' duration, 1 above shall apply in accordance with the number of days' play remaining from the actual start of the match.

## LAW 14.   DECLARATIONS

### 1. Time of Declaration

The captain of the batting side may declare an innings closed at any time during a match, irrespective of its duration.

### 2. Forfeiture of Second Innings

A captain may forfeit his second innings, provided his decision to do so is notified to the opposing captain and umpires in sufficient time to allow seven minutes' rolling of the pitch. See Law 10 (Rolling, Sweeping, Mowing, Watering the Pitch and Re-marking of Creases). The normal ten-minute interval between innings shall be applied.

## LAW 15.   START OF PLAY

### 1. Call of Play

At the start of each innings and of each day's play, and on the resumption of play after any interval or interruption, the umpire at the bowler's end shall call "play".

### 2. Practice on the Field

At no time on any day of the match shall there be any bowling or batting practice on the pitch.

No practice may take place on the field if, in the opinion of the umpires, it could result in a waste of time.

## 3. Trial Run-up

No bowler shall have a trial run-up after "play" has been called in any session of play, except at the fall of a wicket when an umpire may allow such a trial run-up if he is satisfied that it will not cause any waste of time.

# LAW 16.  INTERVALS

## 1. Length

The umpire shall allow such intervals as have been agreed upon for meals, and ten minutes between each innings.

## 2. Luncheon Interval – Innings Ending or Stoppage within Ten Minutes of Interval

If an innings ends or there is a stoppage caused by weather or bad light within ten minutes of the agreed time for the luncheon interval, the interval shall be taken immediately.

The time remaining in the session of play shall be added to the agreed length of the interval but no extra allowance shall be made for the ten-minute interval between innings.

## 3. Tea Interval – Innings Ending or Stoppage within Thirty Minutes of Interval

If an innings ends or there is a stoppage caused by weather or bad light within thirty minutes of the agreed time for the tea interval, the interval shall be taken immediately.

The interval shall be of the agreed length and, if applicable, shall include the ten-minute interval between innings.

## 4. Tea Interval – Continuation of Play

If, at the agreed time for the tea interval, nine wickets are down, play shall continue for a period not exceeding thirty minutes or until the innings is concluded.

## 5. Tea Interval – Agreement to Forgo

At any time during the match, the captains may agree to forgo a tea interval.

## 6. Intervals for Drinks

If both captains agree before the start of a match that intervals for drinks may be taken, the option to take such intervals shall be available to either side. These intervals shall be restricted to one per session, shall be kept as short as possible, shall not be taken in the last hour of the match, and in any case shall not exceed five minutes.

The agreed times for these intervals shall be strictly adhered to, except that if a wicket falls within five minutes of the agreed time then drinks shall be taken out immediately.

If an innings ends or there is a stoppage caused by weather or bad light within thirty minutes of the agreed time for a drinks interval, there will be no interval for drinks in that session.

At any time during the match the captains may agree to forgo any such drinks interval.

*Notes*

### (a) Tea Interval – One-day Match
In a one-day match, a specific time for the tea interval need not necessarily be arranged, and it may be agreed to take this interval between the innings of a one-innings match.

### (b) Changing the Agreed Time of Intervals
In the event of the ground, weather or light conditions causing a suspension of play, the umpires, after consultation with the captains, may decide in the interests of time-saving to bring forward the time of the luncheon or tea interval.

## LAW 17.   CESSATION OF PLAY

### 1. Call of Time

The umpire at the bowler's end shall call "time" on the cessation of play before any interval or interruption of play, at the end of each day's play, and at the conclusion of the match. See Law 27 (Appeals).

### 2. Removal of Bails

After the call of "time", the umpires shall remove the bails from both wickets.

### 3. Starting a Last Over

The last over before an interval or the close of play shall be started provided the umpire, after walking at his normal pace, has arrived at his position behind the stumps at the bowler's end before time has been reached.

### 4. Completion of the Last Over of a Session

The last over before an interval or the close of play shall be completed unless a batsman is out or retires during that over within two minutes of the interval or the close of play or unless the players have occasion to leave the field.

### 5. Completion of the Last Over of a Match

An over in progress at the close of play on the final day of a match shall be completed at the request of either captain, even if a wicket falls after time has been reached.

If, during the last over, the players have occasion to leave the field, the umpires shall call "time" and there shall be no resumption of play and the match shall be at an end.

### 6. Last Hour of Match – Number of Overs

The umpires shall indicate when one hour of playing time of the match remains according to the agreed hours of play. The next over after that moment shall be the first of a minimum of twenty six-ball overs (fifteen eight-ball overs), provided a result is not reached earlier or there is no interval or interruption of play.

### 7. Last Hour of Match – Intervals between Innings and Interruptions of Play

If, at the commencement of the last hour of the match, an interval or interruption of play is in progress or if, during the last hour, there is an interval between innings or an interruption of play, the minimum number of overs to be bowled on the resumption of play shall be reduced in proportion to the duration, within the last hour of the match, of any such interval or interruption.

The minimum number of overs to be bowled after the resumption of play shall be calculated as follows:

(a) In the case of an interval or interruption of play being in progress at the commencement of the last hour of the match, or in the case of a first interval or interruption, a deduction shall be made from the minimum of twenty six-ball overs (or fifteen eight-ball overs).

(b) If there is a later interval or interruption, a further deduction shall be made from the minimum number of overs which should have been bowled following the last resumption of play.

(c) These deductions shall be based on the following factors:

   (i) The number of overs already bowled in the last hour of the match or, in the case of a later interval or interruption, in the last session of play.

   (ii) The number of overs lost as a result of the interval or interruption allowing one six-ball over for every full three minutes (or one eight-ball over for every full four minutes) of interval or interruption.

   (iii) Any over left uncompleted at the end of an innings to be excluded from these calculations.

(iv) Any over left uncompleted at the start of an interruption of play to be completed when play is resumed and to count as one over bowled.

(v) An interval to start with the end of an innings and to end ten minutes later; an interruption to start on the call of "time" and to end on the call of "play".

(d) In the event of an innings being completed and a new innings commencing during the last hour of the match, the number of overs to be bowled in the new innings shall be calculated on the basis of one six-ball over for every three minutes or part thereof remaining for play (or one eight-ball over for every four minutes or part thereof remaining for play); or alternatively on the basis that sufficient overs be bowled to enable the full minimum quota of overs to be completed under circumstances governed by (a), (b) and (c) above. In all such cases the alternative which allows the greater number of overs shall be employed.

## 8. Bowler Unable to Complete an Over during Last Hour of the Match

If, for any reason, a bowler is unable to complete an over during the period of play referred to in 6 above, Law 22.7 (Bowler Incapacitated or Suspended during an Over) shall apply.

# LAW 18. SCORING

## 1. A Run

The score shall be reckoned by runs. A run is scored:

(a) So often as the batsmen, after a hit or at any time while the ball is in play, shall have crossed and made good their ground from end to end.

(b) When a boundary is scored. See Law 19 (Boundaries).

(c) When penalty runs are awarded. See 6 below.

## 2. Short Runs

(a) If either batsman runs a short run, the umpire shall call and signal "one short" as soon as the ball becomes dead and that run shall not be scored. A run is short if a batsman fails to make good his ground on turning for a further run.

(b) Although a short run shortens the succeeding one, the latter, if completed, shall count.

(c) If either or both batsmen deliberately run short the umpire shall, as soon as he sees that the fielding side have no chance of dismissing either batsman, call and signal "dead ball" and disallow any runs attempted or previously scored. The batsmen shall return to their original ends.

(d) If both batsmen run short in one and the same run, only 1 run shall be deducted.

(e) Only if 3 or more runs are attempted can more than one be short and then, subject to (c) and (d) above, all runs so called shall be disallowed. If there has been more than one short run the umpires shall instruct the scorers as to the number of runs disallowed.

## 3. Striker Caught

If the striker is caught, no run shall be scored.

## 4. Batsman Run Out

If a batsman is run out, only that run which was being attempted shall not be scored. If, however, an injured striker himself is run out, no runs shall be scored. See Law 2.7 (Transgression of the Laws by an Injured Batsman or Runner).

## 5. Batsman Obstructing the Field

If a batsman is out Obstructing the Field, any runs completed before the obstruction occurs shall be scored unless such obstruction prevents a catch being made, in which case no runs shall be scored.

## 6. Runs Scored for Penalties

Runs shall be scored for penalties under Laws 20 (Lost Ball), 24 (No-ball), 25 (Wide-ball), 41.1 (Fielding the Ball) and for boundary allowances under Law 19 (Boundaries).

## 7. Batsman Returning to Wicket he has Left

If, while the ball is in play, the batsmen have crossed in running, neither shall return to the wicket he has left, even though a short run has been called or no run has been scored as in the case of a catch. Batsmen, however, shall return to the wickets they originally left in the cases of a boundary and of any disallowance of runs and of an injured batsman being, himself, run out. See Law 2.7 (Transgression by an Injured Batsman or Runner).

*Note*

### (a) Short Run
A striker taking stance in front of his popping crease may run from that point without penalty.

# LAW 19.   BOUNDARIES

## 1. The Boundary of the Playing Area

Before the toss for innings, the umpires shall agree with both captains on the boundary of the playing area. The boundary shall, if possible, be marked by a white line, a rope laid on the ground, or a fence. If flags or posts only are used to mark a boundary, the imaginary line joining such points shall be regarded as the boundary. An obstacle, or person, within the playing area shall not be regarded as a boundary unless so decided by the umpires before the toss for innings. Sightscreens within, or partially within, the playing area shall be regarded as the boundary and when the ball strikes or passes within or under or directly over any part of the screen, a boundary shall be scored.

## 2. Runs Scored for Boundaries

Before the toss for innings, the umpires shall agree with both captains the runs to be allowed for boundaries, and in deciding the allowance for them, the umpires and captains shall be guided by the prevailing custom of the ground. The allowance for a boundary shall normally be 4 runs, and 6 runs for all hits pitching over and clear of the boundary line or fence, even though the ball has been previously touched by a fieldsman. 6 runs shall also be scored if a fieldsman, after catching a ball, carries it over the boundary. See Law 32 (Caught) Note (a). 6 runs shall not be scored when a ball struck by the striker hits a sightscreen full pitch if the screen is within, or partially within, the playing area, but if the ball is struck directly over a sightscreen so situated, 6 runs shall be scored.

## 3. A Boundary

A boundary shall be scored and signalled by the umpire at the bowler's end whenever, in his opinion:

(a) A ball in play touches or crosses the boundary, however marked.

(b) A fieldsman with ball in hand touches or grounds any part of his person on or over a boundary line.

(c) A fieldsman with ball in hand grounds any part of his person over a boundary fence or board. This allows the fieldsman to touch or lean on or over a boundary fence or board in preventing a boundary.

## 4. Runs Exceeding Boundary Allowance

The runs completed at the instant the ball reaches the boundary shall count if they exceed the boundary allowance.

## 5. Overthrows or Wilful Act of a Fieldsman

If the boundary results from an overthrow or from the wilful act of a fieldsman, any runs already completed and the allowance shall be added to the score. The run in progress shall count provided that the batsmen have crossed at the instant of the throw or act.

*Note*

### (a) Position of Sightscreens
Sightscreens should, if possible, be positioned wholly outside the playing area, as near as possible to the boundary line.

## LAW 20.  LOST BALL

### 1. Runs Scored

If a ball in play cannot be found or recovered, any fieldsman may call "lost ball" when 6 runs shall be added to the score; but if more than 6 have been run before "lost ball" is called, as many runs as have been completed shall be scored. The run in progress shall count provided that the batsmen have crossed at the instant of the call of "lost ball".

### 2. How Scored

The runs shall be added to the score of the striker if the ball has been struck, but otherwise to the score of byes, leg-byes, no-balls or wides as the case may be.

## LAW 21.  THE RESULT

### 1. A Win – Two-innings Matches

The side which has scored a total of runs in excess of that scored by the opposing side in its two completed innings shall be the winner.

### 2. A Win – One-innings Matches

(a)  One-innings matches, unless played out as in 1 above, shall be decided on the first innings, but see Law 12.5 (Continuation after One Innings of Each Side).

(b)  If the captains agree to continue play after the completion of one innings of each side in accordance with Law 12.5 (Continuation after One Innings of Each Side) and a result is not achieved on the second innings, the first innings result shall stand.

### 3. Umpires Awarding a Match

(a)  A match shall be lost by a side which, during the match, (i) refuses to play, or (ii) concedes defeat, and the umpires shall award the match to the other side.

(b)  Should both batsmen at the wickets or the fielding side leave the field at any time without the agreement of the umpires, this shall constitute a refusal to play and, on appeal, the umpires shall award the match to the other side in accordance with (a) above.

### 4. A Tie

The result of a match shall be a tie when the scores are equal at the conclusion of play, but only if the side batting last has completed its innings.

If the scores of the completed first innings of a one-day match are equal, it shall be a tie but only if the match has not been played out to a further conclusion.

### 5. A Draw

A match not determined in any of the ways as in 1, 2, 3 and 4 above shall count as a draw.

### 6. Correctness of Result

Any decision as to the correctness of the scores shall be the responsibility of the umpires. See Law 3.14 (Correctness of Scores).

If, after the umpires and players have left the field in the belief that the match has been concluded, the umpires decide that a mistake in scoring has occurred, which affects the result, and provided time has not been reached, they shall order play to resume and to continue until the agreed finishing time unless a result is reached earlier.

If the umpires decide that a mistake has occurred and time has been reached, the umpires shall immediately inform both captains of the necessary corrections to the scores and, if applicable, to the result.

## 7. Acceptance of Result

In accepting the scores as notified by the scorers and agreed by the umpires, the captains of both sides thereby accept the result.

*Notes*

**(a) Statement of Results**
The result of a finished match is stated as a win by runs, except in the case of a win by the side batting last when it is by the number of wickets still then to fall.

**(b) Winning Hit or Extras**
As soon as the side has won, see 1 and 2 above, the umpire shall call "time", the match is finished, and nothing that happens thereafter other than as a result of a mistake in scoring (see 6 above) shall be regarded as part of the match.

However, if a boundary constitutes the winning hit – or extras – and the boundary allowance exceeds the number of runs required to win the match, such runs scored shall be credited to the side's total and, in the case of a hit, to the striker's score.

## LAW 22.  THE OVER

### 1. Number of Balls

The ball shall be bowled from each wicket alternately in overs of either six or eight balls according to agreement before the match.

### 2. Call of "Over"

When the agreed number of balls has been bowled, and as the ball becomes dead or when it becomes clear to the umpire at the bowler's end that both the fielding side and the batsmen at the wicket have ceased to regard the ball as in play, the umpire shall call "over" before leaving the wicket.

### 3. No-ball or Wide-ball

Neither a no-ball nor a wide-ball shall be reckoned as one of the over.

### 4. Umpire Miscounting

If an umpire miscounts the number of balls, the over as counted by the umpire shall stand.

### 5. Bowler Changing Ends

A bowler shall be allowed to change ends as often as desired, provided only that he does not bowl two overs consecutively in an innings.

### 6. The Bowler Finishing an Over

A bowler shall finish an over in progress unless he be incapacitated or be suspended under Law 42.8 (The Bowling of Fast Short-pitched Balls), 9 (The Bowling of Fast High Full Pitches), 10 (Time Wasting) and 11 (Players Damaging the Pitch). If an over is left incomplete for any reason at the start of an interval or interruption of play, it shall be finished on the resumption of play.

### 7. Bowler Incapacitated or Suspended during an Over

If, for any reason, a bowler is incapacitated while running up to bowl the first ball of an over, or is incapacitated or suspended during an over, the umpire shall call and signal "dead ball" and another bowler shall be allowed to bowl or complete the over from the same end, provided only that he shall not bowl two overs, or part thereof, consecutively in one innings.

### 8. Position of Non-striker

The batsman at the bowler's end shall normally stand on the opposite side of the wicket to that from which the ball is being delivered, unless a request to do otherwise is granted by the umpire.

## LAW 23.  DEAD BALL

### 1. The Ball Becomes Dead
When:

(a) It is finally settled in the hands of the wicket-keeper or the bowler.

(b) It reaches or pitches over the boundary.

(c) A batsman is out.

(d) Whether played or not, it lodges in the clothing or equipment of a batsman or the clothing of an umpire.

(e) A ball lodges in a protective helmet worn by a member of the fielding side.

(f) A penalty is awarded under Law 20 (Lost Ball) or Law 41.1 (Fielding the Ball).

(g) The umpire calls "over" or "time".

### 2. Either Umpire Shall Call and Signal "Dead Ball"
When:

(a) He intervenes in a case of unfair play.

(b) A serious injury to a player or umpire occurs.

(c) He is satisfied that, for an adequate reason, the striker is not ready to receive the ball and makes no attempt to play it.

(d) The bowler drops the ball accidentally before delivery, or the ball does not leave his hand for any reason.

(e) One or both bails fall from the striker's wicket before he receives delivery.

(f) He leaves his normal position for consultation.

(g) He is required to do so under Law 26.3 (Disallowance of Leg-byes).

### 3. The Ball Ceases to be Dead
When:

(a) The bowler starts his run-up or bowling action.

### 4. The Ball is Not Dead
When:

(a) It strikes an umpire (unless it lodges in his dress).

(b) The wicket is broken or struck down (unless a batsman is out thereby).

(c) An unsuccessful appeal is made.

(d) The wicket is broken accidentally either by the bowler during his delivery or by a batsman in running.

(e) The umpire has called "no-ball" or "wide".

*Notes*

**(a) Ball Finally Settled**
Whether the ball is finally settled or not – see 1(a) above – must be a question for the umpires alone to decide.

**(b) Action on Call of "Dead Ball"**
 (i) If "dead ball" is called prior to the striker receiving a delivery, the bowler shall be allowed an additional ball.
 (ii) If "dead ball" is called after the striker receives a delivery, the bowler shall not be allowed an additional ball, unless a "no-ball" or "wide" has been called.

## LAW 24. NO-BALL

### 1. Mode of Delivery

The umpire shall indicate to the striker whether the bowler intends to bowl over or round the wicket, overarm or underarm, right- or left-handed. Failure on the part of the bowler to indicate in advance a change in his mode of delivery is unfair and the umpire shall call and signal "no-ball".

### 2. Fair Delivery – The Arm

For a delivery to be fair the ball must be bowled, not thrown – see Note (a) below. If either umpire is not entirely satisfied with the absolute fairness of a delivery in this respect he shall call and signal "no-ball" instantly upon delivery.

### 3. Fair Delivery – The Feet

The umpire at the bowler's wicket shall call and signal "no-ball" if he is not satisfied that in the delivery stride:

    (a) The bowler's back foot has landed within and not touching the return crease or its forward extension; or

    (b) Some part of the front foot whether grounded or raised was behind the popping crease.

### 4. Bowler Throwing at Striker's Wicket before Delivery

If the bowler, before delivering the ball, throws it at the striker's wicket in an attempt to run him out, the umpire shall call and signal "no-ball". See Law 42.12 (Batsman Unfairly Stealing a Run) and Law 38 (Run Out).

### 5. Bowler Attempting to Run Out Non-striker before Delivery

If the bowler, before delivering the ball, attempts to run out the non-striker, any runs which result shall be allowed and shall be scored as no-balls. Such an attempt shall not count as a ball in the over. The umpire shall not call "no-ball". See Law 42.12 (Batsman Unfairly Stealing a Run).

### 6. Infringement of Laws by a Wicket-keeper or a Fieldsman

The umpire shall call and signal "no-ball" in the event of the wicket-keeper infringing Law 40.1 (Position of Wicket-keeper) or a fieldsman infringing Law 41.2 (Limitation of On-side Fieldsmen) or Law 41.3 (Position of Fieldsmen).

### 7. Revoking a Call

An umpire shall revoke the call "no-ball" if the ball does not leave the bowler's hand for any reason. See Law 23.2 (Either Umpire Shall Call and Signal "Dead Ball").

### 8. Penalty

A penalty of 1 run for a no-ball shall be scored if no runs are made otherwise.

### 9. Runs from a No-ball

The striker may hit a no-ball and whatever runs result shall be added to his score. Runs made otherwise from a no-ball shall be scored no-balls.

### 10. Out from a No-ball

The striker shall be out from a no-ball if he breaks Law 34 (Hit the Ball Twice) and either batsman may be run out or shall be given out if either breaks Law 33 (Handled the Ball) or Law 37 (Obstructing the Field).

### 11. Batsman Given Out off a No-ball

Should a batsman be given out off a no-ball the penalty for bowling it shall stand unless runs are otherwise scored.

*Notes*

(a) **Definition of a Throw**

A ball shall be deemed to have been thrown if, in the opinion of either umpire, the process of straightening the bowling arm, whether it be partial or complete, takes place during that part of the delivery swing which directly precedes the ball leaving the hand. This definition shall not debar a bowler from the use of the wrist in the delivery swing.

(b) **No-ball Not Counting in Over**

A no-ball shall not be reckoned as one of the over. See Law 22.3 (No-ball or Wide-ball).

# LAW 25. WIDE-BALL

## 1. Judging a Wide

If the bowler bowls the ball so high over or so wide of the wicket that, in the opinion of the umpire, it passes out of the reach of the striker, standing in a normal guard position, the umpire shall call and signal "wide-ball" as soon as it has passed the line of the striker's wicket.

The umpire shall not adjudge a ball as being wide if:

(a) The striker, by moving from his guard position, causes the ball to pass out of his reach.

(b) The striker moves and thus brings the ball within his reach.

## 2. Penalty

A penalty of 1 run for a wide shall be scored if no runs are made otherwise.

## 3. Ball Coming to Rest in Front of the Striker

If a ball which the umpire considers to have been delivered comes to rest in front of the line of the striker's wicket, "wide" shall not be called. The striker has a right, without interference from the fielding side, to make one attempt to hit the ball. If the fielding side interfere, the umpire shall replace the ball where it came to rest and shall order the fieldsmen to resume the places they occupied in the field before the ball was delivered.

The umpire shall call and signal "dead ball" as soon as it is clear that the striker does not intend to hit the ball, or after the striker has made an unsuccessful attempt to hit the ball.

## 4. Revoking a Call

The umpire shall revoke the call if the striker hits a ball which has been called "wide".

## 5. Ball Not Dead

The ball does not become dead on the call of "wide-ball" – see Law 23.4 (The Ball is Not Dead).

## 6. Runs Resulting from a Wide

All runs which are run or result from a wide-ball which is not a no-ball shall be scored wide-balls, or if no runs are made 1 shall be scored.

## 7. Out from a Wide

The striker shall be out from a wide-ball if he breaks Law 35 (Hit Wicket), or Law 39 (Stumped). Either batsman may be run out and shall be out if he breaks Law 33 (Handled the Ball), or Law 37 (Obstructing the Field).

## 8. Batsman Given Out off a Wide

Should a batsman be given out off a wide, the penalty for bowling it shall stand unless runs are otherwise made.

*Note*

(a) **Wide-ball Not Counting in Over**

A wide-ball shall not be reckoned as one of the over – see Law 22.3 (No-ball or Wide-ball).

## LAW 26. BYE AND LEG-BYE

### 1. Byes

If the ball, not having been called "wide" or "no-ball", passes the striker without touching his bat or person, and any runs are obtained, the umpire shall signal "bye" and the run or runs shall be credited as such to the batting side.

### 2. Leg-byes

If the ball, not having been called "wide" or "no-ball", is unintentionally deflected by the striker's dress or person, except a hand holding the bat, and any runs are obtained the umpire shall signal "leg-bye" and the run or runs so scored shall be credited as such to the batting side.

Such leg-byes shall be scored only if, in the opinion of the umpire, the striker has:

    (a) Attempted to play the ball with his bat; or

    (b) Tried to avoid being hit by the ball.

### 3. Disallowance of Leg-byes

In the case of a deflection by the striker's person, other than in 2(a) and (b) above, the umpire shall call and signal "dead ball" as soon as 1 run has been completed or when it is clear that a run is not being attempted, or the ball has reached the boundary.

On the call and signal of "dead ball" the batsmen shall return to their original ends and no runs shall be allowed.

## LAW 27. APPEALS

### 1. Time of Appeals

The umpires shall not give a batsman out unless appealed to by the other side which shall be done prior to the bowler beginning his run-up or bowling action to deliver the next ball. Under Law 23.1 (g) (The Ball Becomes Dead), the ball is dead on "over" being called; this does not, however, invalidate an appeal made prior to the first ball of the following over provided "time" has not been called – see Law 17.1 (Call of Time).

### 2. An Appeal "How's That?"

An appeal "How's That?" shall cover all ways of being out.

### 3. Answering Appeals

The umpire at the bowler's wicket shall answer appeals before the other umpire in all cases except those arising out of Law 35 (Hit Wicket) or Law 39 (Stumped) or Law 38 (Run Out) when this occurs at the striker's wicket.

When either umpire has given a batsman not out, the other umpire shall, within his jurisdiction, answer the appeal or a further appeal, provided it is made in time in accordance with 1 above (Time of Appeals).

### 4. Consultation by Umpires

An umpire may consult with the other umpire on a point of fact which the latter may have been in a better position to see and shall then give his decision. If, after consultation, there is still doubt remaining the decision shall be in favour of the batsman.

### 5. Batsman Leaving his Wicket under a Misapprehension

The umpires shall intervene if satisfied that a batsman, not having been given out, has left his wicket under a misapprehension that he has been dismissed.

### 6. Umpire's Decision

The umpire's decision is final. He may alter his decision, provided that such alteration is made promptly.

### 7. Withdrawal of an Appeal

In exceptional circumstances the captain of the fielding side may seek permission of the umpire to withdraw an appeal provided the outgoing batsman has not left the playing area. If this is allowed, the umpire shall cancel his decision.

## LAW 28. THE WICKET IS DOWN

### 1. Wicket Down

The wicket is down if:

    (a) Either the ball or the striker's bat or person completely removes either bail from the top of the stumps. A disturbance of a bail, whether temporary or not, shall not constitute a complete removal, but the wicket is down if a bail in falling lodges between two of the stumps.

    (b) Any player completely removes with his hand or arm a bail from the top of the stumps, provided that the ball is held in that hand or in the hand of the arm so used.

    (c) When both bails are off, a stump is struck out of the ground by the ball, or a player strikes or pulls a stump out of the ground, provided that the ball is held in the hand(s) or in the hand of the arm so used.

### 2. One Bail Off

If one bail is off, it shall be sufficient for the purpose of putting the wicket down to remove the remaining bail, or to strike or pull any of the three stumps out of the ground in any of the ways stated in 1 above.

### 3. All the Stumps Out of the Ground

If all the stumps are out of the ground, the fielding side shall be allowed to put back one or more stumps in order to have an opportunity of putting the wicket down.

### 4. Dispensing with Bails

If owing to the strength of the wind, it has been agreed to dispense with the bails in accordance with Law 8, Note (a) (Dispensing with Bails), the decision as to when the wicket is down is one for the umpires to decide on the facts before them. In such circumstances and if the umpires so decide, the wicket shall be held to be down even though a stump has not been struck out of the ground.

*Note*

    **(a) Remaking the Wicket**
    If the wicket is broken while the ball is in play, it is not the umpire's duty to remake the wicket until the ball has become dead – see Law 23 (Dead Ball). A member of the fielding side, however, may remake the wicket in such circumstances.

## LAW 29. BATSMAN OUT OF HIS GROUND

### 1. When out of his Ground

A batsman shall be considered to be out of his ground unless some part of his bat in his hand or of his person is grounded behind the line of the popping crease.

## LAW 30. BOWLED

### 1. Out Bowled

The striker shall be out *Bowled* if:

    (a) His wicket is bowled down, even if the ball first touches his bat or person.

    (b) He breaks his wicket by hitting or kicking the ball on to it before the completion of a stroke, or as a result of attempting to guard his wicket. See Law 34.1 (Out Hit the Ball Twice).

*Note*

    **(a) Out Bowled – Not lbw**
    The striker is out bowled if the ball is deflected on to his wicket even though a decision against him would be justified under Law 36 (lbw).

## LAW 31. TIMED OUT

### 1. Out Timed Out

An incoming batsman shall be out *Timed Out* if he wilfully takes more than two minutes to come in – the two minutes being timed from the moment a wicket falls until the new batsman steps on to the field of play.

If this is not complied with and if the umpire is satisfied that the delay was wilful and if an appeal is made, the new batsman shall be given out by the umpire at the bowler's end.

### 2. Time to be Added

The time taken by the umpires to investigate the cause of the delay shall be added at the normal close of play.

*Notes*

   **(a) Entry in Scorebook**
   The correct entry in the scorebook when a batsman is given out under this Law is "timed out", and the bowler does not get credit for the wicket.

   **(b) Batsmen Crossing on the Field of Play**
   It is an essential duty of the captains to ensure that the in-going batsman passes the out-going one before the latter leaves the field of play.

## LAW 32. CAUGHT

### 1. Out Caught

The striker shall be out *Caught* if the ball touches his bat or if it touches below the wrist his hand or glove, holding the bat, and is subsequently held by a fieldsman before it touches the ground.

### 2. A Fair Catch

A catch shall be considered to have been fairly made if:

   (a) The fieldsman is within the field of play throughout the act of making the catch.

   (i) The act of making the catch shall start from the time when the fieldsman first handles the ball and shall end when he both retains complete control over the further disposal of the ball and remains within the field of play.

   (ii) In order to be within the field of play, the fieldsman may not touch or ground any part of his person on or over a boundary line. When the boundary is marked by a fence or board the fieldsman may not ground any part of his person over the boundary fence or board, but may touch or lean over the boundary fence or board in completing the catch.

   (b) The ball is hugged to the body of the catcher or accidentally lodges in his dress or, in the case of the wicket-keeper, in his pads. However, a striker may not be caught if a ball lodges in a protective helmet worn by a fieldsman, in which case the umpire shall call and signal "dead ball". See Law 23 (Dead Ball).

   (c) The ball does not touch the ground even though a hand holding it does so in effecting the catch.

   (d) A fieldsman catches the ball, after it has been lawfully played a second time by the striker, but only if the ball has not touched the ground since being first struck.

   (e) A fieldsman catches the ball after it has touched an umpire, another fieldsman or the other batsman. However, a striker may not be caught if a ball has touched a protective helmet worn by a fieldsman.

   (f) The ball is caught off an obstruction within the boundary provided it has not previously been agreed to regard the obstruction as a boundary.

### 3. Scoring of Runs

If a striker is caught, no run shall be scored.

*Notes*

**(a) Scoring from an Attempted Catch**
When a fieldsman carrying the ball touches or grounds any part of his person on or over a boundary marked by a line, 6 runs shall be scored.

**(b) Ball Still in Play**
If a fieldsman releases the ball before he crosses the boundary, the ball will be considered to be still in play and it may be caught by another fieldsman. However, if the original fieldsman returns to the field of play and handles the ball, a catch may not be made.

## LAW 33. HANDLED THE BALL

### 1. Out Handled the Ball

Either batsman on appeal shall be out *Handled the Ball* if he wilfully touches the ball while in play with the hand not holding the bat unless he does so with the consent of the opposite side.

*Note*

**(a) Entry in Scorebook**
The correct entry in the scorebook when a batsman is given out under this Law is "handled the ball", and the bowler does not get credit for the wicket.

## LAW 34. HIT THE BALL TWICE

### 1. Out Hit the Ball Twice

The striker, on appeal, shall be out *Hit the Ball Twice* if, after the ball is struck or is stopped by any part of his person, he wilfully strikes it again with his bat or person except for the sole purpose of guarding his wicket: this he may do with his bat or any part of his person other than his hands, but see Law 37.2 (Obstructing a Ball From Being Caught).

For the purpose of this Law, a hand holding the bat shall be regarded as part of the bat.

### 2. Returning the Ball to a Fieldsman

The striker, on appeal, shall be out under this Law if, without the consent of the opposite side, he uses his bat or person to return the ball to any of the fielding side.

### 3. Runs from Ball Lawfully Struck Twice

No runs except those which result from an overthrow or penalty – see Law 41 (The Fieldsman) – shall be scored from a ball lawfully struck twice.

*Notes*

**(a) Entry in Scorebook**
The correct entry in the scorebook when the striker is given out under this Law is "hit the ball twice", and the bowler does not get credit for the wicket.

**(b) Runs Credited to the Batsman**
Any runs awarded under 3 above as a result of an overthrow or penalty shall be credited to the striker, provided the ball in the first instance has touched the bat, or, if otherwise, as extras.

## LAW 35. HIT WICKET

### 1. Out Hit Wicket

The striker shall be out *Hit Wicket* if, while the ball is in play:

(a) His wicket is broken with any part of his person, dress, or equipment as a result of any action taken by him in preparing to receive or in receiving a delivery, or in setting off for his first run, immediately after playing, or playing at, the ball.

(b) He hits down his wicket whilst lawfully making a second stroke for the purpose of guarding his wicket within the provisions of Law 34.1 (Out Hit the Ball Twice).

*Notes*

**(a) Not Out Hit Wicket**

A batsman is not out under this Law should his wicket be broken in any of the ways referred to in 1(a) above if:

    (i) It occurs while he is in the act of running, other than in setting off for his first run immediately after playing at the ball, or while he is avoiding being run out or stumped.

    (ii) The bowler after starting his run-up or bowling action does not deliver the ball; in which case the umpire shall immediately call and signal "dead ball".

    (iii) It occurs whilst he is avoiding a throw-in at any time.

# LAW 36.  LEG BEFORE WICKET

## 1. Out lbw

The striker shall be out *lbw* in the circumstances set out below:

**(a) Striker Attempting to Play the Ball**

The striker shall be out lbw if he first intercepts with any part of his person, dress or equipment a fair ball which would have hit the wicket and which has not previously touched his bat or a hand holding the bat, provided that:

    (i) The ball pitched in a straight line between wicket and wicket or on the off side of the striker's wicket, or in the case of a ball intercepted full pitch would have pitched in a straight line between wicket and wicket; and

    (ii) The point of impact is in a straight line between wicket and wicket, even if above the level of the bails.

**(b) Striker Making No Attempt to Play the Ball**

The striker shall be out lbw even if the ball is intercepted outside the line of the off stump if, in the opinion of the umpire, he has made no genuine attempt to play the ball with his bat, but has intercepted the ball with some part of his person and if the circumstances set out in (a) above apply.

# LAW 37.  OBSTRUCTING THE FIELD

## 1. Wilful Obstruction

Either batsman, on appeal, shall be out *Obstructing the Field* if he wilfully obstructs the opposite side by word or action.

## 2. Obstructing a Ball From Being Caught

The striker, on appeal, shall be out should wilful obstruction by either batsman prevent a catch being made.

This shall apply even though the striker causes the obstruction in lawfully guarding his wicket under the provisions of Law 34. See Law 34.1 (Out Hit the Ball Twice).

*Notes*

**(a) Accidental Obstruction**

The umpires must decide whether the obstruction was wilful or not. The accidental interception of a throw-in by a batsman while running does not break this Law.

**(b) Entry in Scorebook**

The correct entry in the scorebook when a batsman is given out under this Law is "obstructing the field", and the bowler does not get credit for the wicket.

## LAW 38. RUN OUT

### 1. Out Run Out

Either batsman shall be out *Run Out* if in running or at any time while the ball is in play – except in the circumstances described in Law 39 (Stumped) – he is out of his ground and his wicket is put down by the opposite side. If, however, a batsman in running makes good his ground he shall not be out run out if he subsequently leaves his ground, in order to avoid injury, and the wicket is put down.

### 2. "No-ball" Called

If a no-ball has been called, the striker shall not be given run out unless he attempts to run.

### 3. Which Batsman Is Out

If the batsmen have crossed in running, he who runs for the wicket which is put down shall be out; if they have not crossed, he who has left the wicket which is put down shall be out. If a batsman remains in his ground or returns to his ground and the other batsman joins him there, the latter shall be out if his wicket is put down.

### 4. Scoring of Runs

If a batsman is run out, only that run which is being attempted shall not be scored. If, however, an injured striker himself is run out, no runs shall be scored. See Law 2.7 (Transgression of the Laws by an Injured Batsman or Runner).

*Notes*

**(a) Ball Played on to Opposite Wicket**
If the ball is played on to the opposite wicket, neither batsman is liable to be run out unless the ball has been touched by a fieldsman before the wicket is broken.

**(b) Entry in Scorebook**
The correct entry in the scorebook when a batsman is given out under this Law is "run out", and the bowler does not get credit for the wicket.

## LAW 39. STUMPED

### 1. Out Stumped

The striker shall be out *Stumped* if, in receiving the ball, not being a no-ball, he is out of his ground otherwise than in attempting a run and the wicket is put down by the wicket-keeper without the intervention of another fieldsman.

### 2. Action by the Wicket-keeper

The wicket-keeper may take the ball in front of the wicket in an attempt to stump the striker only if the ball has touched the bat or person of the striker.

*Note*

**(a) Ball Rebounding from Wicket-keeper's Person**
The striker may be out stumped if, in the circumstances stated in 1 above, the wicket is broken by a ball rebounding from the wicket-keeper's person or equipment or is kicked or thrown by the wicket-keeper on to the wicket.

## LAW 40. THE WICKET-KEEPER

### 1. Position of Wicket-keeper

The wicket-keeper shall remain wholly behind the wicket until a ball delivered by the bowler touches the bat or person of the striker, or passes the wicket, or until the striker attempts a run.

In the event of the wicket-keeper contravening this Law, the umpire at the striker's end shall call and signal "no-ball" at the instant of delivery or as soon as possible thereafter.

## 2. Restriction on Actions of the Wicket-keeper

If the wicket-keeper interferes with the striker's right to play the ball and to guard his wicket, the striker shall not be out except under Laws 33 (Handled the Ball), 34 (Hit the Ball Twice), 37 (Obstructing the Field), 38 (Run Out).

## 3. Interference with the Wicket-keeper by the Striker

If in the legitimate defence of his wicket, the striker interferes with the wicket-keeper, he shall not be out, except as provided for in Law 37.2 (Obstructing a Ball From Being Caught).

# LAW 41. THE FIELDSMAN

## 1. Fielding the Ball

The fieldsman may stop the ball with any part of his person, but if he wilfully stops it otherwise, 5 runs shall be added to the run or runs already scored; if no run has been scored 5 penalty runs shall be awarded. The run in progress shall count provided that the batsmen have crossed at the instant of the act. If the ball has been struck, the penalty shall be added to the score of the striker, but otherwise to the scores of byes, leg-byes, no-balls or wides as the case may be.

## 2. Limitation of On-side Fieldsmen

The number of on-side fieldsmen behind the popping crease at the instant of the bowler's delivery shall not exceed two. In the event of infringement by the fielding side the umpire at the striker's end shall call and signal "no-ball" at the instant of delivery or as soon as possible thereafter.

## 3. Position of Fieldsmen

Whilst the ball is in play and until the ball has made contact with the bat or the striker's person or has passed his bat, no fieldsman, other than the bowler, may stand on or have any part of his person extended over the pitch (measuring 22 yards/20.12m × 10 feet/3.05m). In the event of a fieldsman contravening this Law, the umpire at the bowler's end shall call and signal "no-ball" at the instant of delivery or as soon as possible thereafter. See Law 40.1 (Position of Wicket-keeper).

## 4. Fieldsmen's Protective Helmets

Protective helmets, when not in use by members of the fielding side, shall be placed, if above the surface, only on the ground behind the wicket-keeper. In the event of the ball, when in play, striking a helmet whilst in this position, 5 penalty runs shall be awarded as laid down in Law 41.1 and Note (a).

*Note*

> **(a) Batsmen Changing Ends**
> The 5 runs referred to in 1 and 4 above are a penalty and the batsmen do not change ends solely by reason of this penalty.

# LAW 42. UNFAIR PLAY

## 1. Responsibility of Captains

The captains are responsible at all times for ensuring that play is conducted within the spirit of the game as well as within the Laws.

## 2. Responsibility of Umpires

The umpires are the sole judges of fair and unfair play.

## 3. Intervention by the Umpire

The umpires shall intervene without appeal by calling and signalling "dead ball" in the case of unfair play, but should not otherwise interfere with the progress of the game except as required to do so by the Laws.

## 4. Lifting the Seam

A player shall not lift the seam of the ball for any reason. Should this be done, the umpires shall change the ball for one of similar condition to that in use prior to the contravention. See Note (a).

## 5. Changing the Condition of the Ball

Any member of the fielding side may polish the ball provided that such polishing wastes no time and that no artificial substance is used. No-one shall rub the ball on the ground or use any artificial substance or take any other action to alter the condition of the ball.

In the event of a contravention of this Law, the umpires, after consultation, shall change the ball for one of similar condition to that in use prior to the contravention.

This Law does not prevent a member of the fielding side from drying a wet ball, or removing mud from the ball. See Note (b).

## 6. Incommoding the Striker

An umpire is justified in intervening under this Law and shall call and signal "dead ball" if, in his opinion, any player of the fielding side incommodes the striker by any noise or action while he is receiving the ball.

## 7. Obstruction of a Batsman in Running

It shall be considered unfair if any fieldsman wilfully obstructs a batsman in running. In these circumstances the umpire shall call and signal "dead ball" and allow any completed runs and the run in progress, or alternatively any boundary scored.

## 8. The Bowling of Fast Short-pitched Balls

The bowling of fast short-pitched balls is unfair if, in the opinion of the umpire at the bowler's end, it constitutes an attempt to intimidate the striker. See Note (d).

Umpires shall consider intimidation to be the deliberate bowling of fast short-pitched balls which by their length, height and direction are intended or likely to inflict physical injury on the striker. The relative skill of the striker shall also be taken into consideration.

In the event of such unfair bowling, the umpire at the bowler's end shall adopt the following procedure:

(a) In the first instance the umpire shall call and signal "no-ball", caution the bowler and inform the other umpire, the captain of the fielding side and the batsmen of what has occurred.

(b) If this caution is ineffective, he shall repeat the above procedure and indicate to the bowler that this is a final warning.

(c) Both the above caution and final warning shall continue to apply even though the bowler may later change ends.

(d) Should the above warnings prove ineffective the umpire at the bowler's end shall:

   (i) At the first repetition call and signal "no-ball" and when the ball is dead direct the captain to take the bowler off forthwith and to complete the over with another bowler, provided that the bowler does not bowl two overs or part thereof consecutively. See Law 22.7 (Bowler Incapacitated or Suspended during an Over).

   (ii) Not allow the bowler, thus taken off, to bowl again in the same innings.

   (iii) Report the occurrence to the captain of the batting side as soon as the players leave the field for an interval.

   (iv) Report the occurrence to the executive of the fielding side and to any governing body responsible for the match, who shall take any further action which is considered to be appropriate against the bowler concerned.

## 9. The Bowling of Fast High Full Pitches

The bowling of fast high full pitches is unfair. See Note (e).

In the event of such unfair bowling the umpire at the bowler's end shall adopt the procedures of caution, final warnings, action against the bowler and reporting as set out in 8 above.

## 10. Time Wasting

Any form of time wasting is unfair.

(a) In the event of the captain of the fielding side wasting time or allowing any member of his side to waste time, the umpire at the bowler's end shall adopt the following procedure:

(i) In the first instance he shall caution the captain of the fielding side and inform the other umpire of what has occurred.

(ii) If this caution is ineffective he shall repeat the above procedure and indicate to the captain that this is a final warning.

(iii) The umpire shall report the occurrence to the captain of the batting side as soon as the players leave the field for an interval.

(iv) Should the above procedure prove ineffective the umpire shall report the occurrence to the executive of the fielding side and to any governing body responsible for that match, who shall take appropriate action against the captain and the players concerned.

(b) In the event of a bowler taking unnecessarily long to bowl an over the umpire at the bowler's end shall adopt the procedures, other than the calling of "no-ball", of caution, final warning, action against the bowler and reporting.

(c) In the event of a batsman wasting time (See Note (f)) other than in the manner described in Law 31 (Timed Out), the umpire at the bowler's end shall adopt the following procedure:

(i) In the first instance he shall caution the batsman and inform the other umpire at once, and the captain of the batting side, as soon as the players leave the field for an interval, of what has occurred.

(ii) If this proves ineffective, he shall repeat the caution, indicate to the batsman that this is a final warning and inform the other umpire.

(iii) The umpire shall report the occurrence to both captains as soon as the players leave the field for an interval.

(iv) Should the above procedure prove ineffective, the umpire shall report the occurrence to the executive of the batting side and to any governing body responsible for that match, who shall take appropriate action against the player concerned.

## 11. Players Damaging the Pitch

The umpires shall intervene and prevent players from causing damage to the pitch which may assist the bowlers of either side. See Note (c).

(a) In the event of any member of the fielding side damaging the pitch, the umpire shall follow the procedure of caution, final warning, and reporting as set out in 10(a) above.

(b) In the event of a bowler contravening this Law by running down the pitch after delivering the ball, the umpire at the bowler's end shall first caution the bowler. If this caution is ineffective the umpire shall adopt the procedures, as set out in 8 above other than the calling and signalling of "no-ball".

(c) In the event of a batsman damaging the pitch the umpire at the bowler's end shall follow the procedures of caution, final warning and reporting as set out in 10(c) above.

## 12. Batsman Unfairly Stealing a Run

Any attempt by the batsman to steal a run during the bowler's run-up is unfair. Unless the bowler attempts to run out either batsman – see Law 24.4 (Bowler Throwing at Striker's Wicket before Delivery) and Law 24.5 (Bowler Attempting to Run Out Non-striker before Delivery) – the umpire shall call and signal "dead ball" as soon as the batsmen cross in any such attempt to run. The batsmen shall then return to their original wickets.

## 13. Player's Conduct

In the event of a player failing to comply with the instructions of an umpire, criticising his decisions by word or action, or showing dissent, or generally behaving in a manner which might bring the game into disrepute, the umpire concerned shall, in the first place, report the matter to the other umpire and to the player's captain requesting the latter to take action. If this proves ineffective, the umpire shall report the incident as soon as possible to the executive of the player's team and to any governing body responsible for the match, who shall take any further action which is considered appropriate against the player or players concerned.

*Notes*

### (a) The Condition of the Ball
Umpires shall make frequent and irregular inspections of the condition of the ball.

### (b) Drying of a Wet Ball
A wet ball may be dried on a towel or with sawdust.

### (c) Danger Area
The danger area on the pitch, which must be protected from damage by a bowler, shall be regarded by the umpires as the area contained by an imaginary line 4 feet/1.22m from the popping crease, and parallel to it, and within two imaginary and parallel lines drawn down the pitch from points on that line 1 foot/30.48cm on either side of the middle stump.

### (d) Fast Short-pitched Balls
As a guide, a fast short-pitched ball is one which pitches short and passes, or would have passed, above the shoulder height of the striker standing in a normal batting stance at the crease.

### (e) The Bowling of Fast Full Pitches
The bowling of one fast, high full pitch shall be considered to be unfair if, in the opinion of the umpire, it is deliberate, bowled at the striker, and if it passes or would have passed above the shoulder height of the striker when standing in a normal batting stance at the crease.

### (f) Time Wasting by Batsmen
Other than in exceptional circumstances, the batsman should always be ready to take strike when the bowler is ready to start his run-up.

---

# ADDRESSES OF REPRESENTATIVE BODIES

INTERNATIONAL CRICKET COUNCIL: Lt-Col. J. R. Stephenson, OBE, Lord's Ground, London NW8 8QN.

AUSTRALIA: Australian Cricket Board, D. L. Richards, 90 Jolimont Street, Jolimont, Victoria 3002.

ENGLAND: Cricket Council, A. C. Smith, Lord's Ground, London NW8 8QN.

INDIA: Board of Control for Cricket in India, C. Nagaraj, Chinnaswamy Stadium, Mahatma Gandhi Road, Bangalore 560 001.

NEW ZEALAND: New Zealand Cricket Inc., G. T. Dowling, OBE, PO Box 958, 109 Cambridge Terrace, Christchurch.

PAKISTAN: Board of Control for Cricket in Pakistan, Shahid Rafi, Gaddafi Stadium, Lahore.

SOUTH AFRICA: United Cricket Board of South Africa, Dr A. Bacher, PO Box 55009, Northlands 2116, Transvaal.

SRI LANKA: Board of Control for Cricket in Sri Lanka, N. Perera, 35 Maitland Place, Colombo 7.

WEST INDIES: West Indies Cricket Board of Control, G. S. Camacho, Kensington Oval, Fontabelle, St Michael, Barbados.

ARGENTINA: Argentine Cricket Association, C. M. Gibson, c/o The English Club, 25 de Mayo 586, 1002 Buenos Aires.

BAHAMAS: Bahamas Cricket Association, Mrs J. M. Forbes, PO Box N-10101, Nassau.

BANGLADESH: Bangladesh Cricket Board of Control, M. Aminul Huq Mani, The Stadium, Dhaka 1,000.

BELGIUM: Belgian Cricket Federation, C. Wolfe, Rue de l'Eglise, St Martin 12, B-1390, BIEZ.

BERMUDA: Bermuda Cricket Board of Control, W. Smith, PO Box 992, Hamilton.

CANADA: Canadian Cricket Association, K. R. Bullock, PO Box 1364, Brockville, Ontario, K6V 5Y6.

DENMARK: Danish Cricket Association, J. Holmen, Idraettens Hus, Brøndby, DK 2605.

EAST AND CENTRAL AFRICA: East and Central African Cricket Conference, S. Patel, PO Box 7377, Ndola, Zambia.

FIJI: Fiji Cricket Association, P. I. Knight, PO Box 300, Suva.

FRANCE: Fédération Française du Cricket, O. Dubaut, 73 Rue Curial, 75019 Paris.

GERMANY: Deutscher Cricket Bund, R. Schwiete, Adalbert-Stifter-Strasse 6d, 6450 Hanau.

GIBRALTAR: Gibraltar Cricket Association, T. J. Finlayson, 21 Sandpits House, Withams Road.

HONG KONG: Hong Kong Cricket Association, J. A. Cribbin, University of Hong Kong, Extra-Mural Studies, Pokfulam Road.

ISRAEL: Israel Cricket Association, N. Davidson, PO Box 93, Ben-Gurion Airport 70100.

ITALY: Associazione Italiana Cricket, S. Gambino, Via S. Ignazio 9, 00186 Rome.

JAPAN: Japan Cricket Association, R. G. Martineau, Shizuoko City, Chiyoda 736, Yamadai Corp. 305, Japan 420.

KENYA: Kenya Cricket Association, B. Mauladad, PO Box 45870, Nairobi.

MALAYSIA: Malaysian Cricket Association, Lt-Cdr K. Selvaratnam (Retd), c/o Delcom Services Sdn Bhd, No. 42 Jalan 1/82B, Bangsar Utama, Bangsar, 59000 Kuala Lumpur.

NEPAL: Cricket Association of Nepal, Jaikumar H. Shah, PO Box 925, Kathmandu.

NETHERLANDS: Royal Netherlands Cricket Board, A. de la Mar, Neuiwe Kalfjeslaan 1182 AA Amstelveen.

PAPUA NEW GUINEA: Papua New Guinea Cricket Board of Control, W. Satchell, PO Box 1105, Boroko.

SINGAPORE: Singapore Cricket Association, R. Sivasubramaniam, 5000-D Marine Parade Road 22-16, Laguna Park.

SWITZERLAND: Swiss Cricket Association, P. Nixon, Spitzackerstrasse 32, 4103 Bottmingen.

UNITED ARAB EMIRATES: Emirates Cricket Board, Abdul Rahman Bukhatir, Sharjah Cricket Stadium, PO Box 88, Sharjah.

USA: United States of America Cricket Association, Naseeruddin Khan, 2361 Hickory Road, Plymouth Meeting, Pennsylvania 19462.

WEST AFRICA: West Africa Cricket Conference, O. Akinlotan, National Sports Commission, National Stadium, PO Box 145, Surulere, Lagos, Nigeria.

ZIMBABWE: Zimbabwe Cricket Union, D. A. Ellman-Brown, PO Box 702, Harare.

BRITISH UNIVERSITIES SPORTS FEDERATION: 28 Woburn Square, London WC1.

CLUB CRICKET CONFERENCE: A. E. F. Stevens, 353 West Barnes Lane, New Malden, Surrey, KT3 6JF.

ENGLAND SCHOOLS' CRICKET ASSOCIATION: C. J. Cooper, 68 Hatherley Road, Winchester, Hampshire SO22 6RR.

IRISH CRICKET UNION: D. Scott, 45 Foxrock Park, Foxrock, Dublin 18, Ireland.

MINOR COUNTIES CRICKET ASSOCIATION: D. J. M. Armstrong, Thorpe Cottage, Mill Common, Ridlington, North Walsham, NR28 9TY.

NATIONAL CRICKET ASSOCIATION: B. J. Aspital, Lord's Ground, London NW8 8QN.

SCARBOROUGH CRICKET FESTIVAL: Colin T. Adamson, Cricket Ground, North Marine Road, Scarborough, North Yorkshire, YO12 7TJ.

SCOTTISH CRICKET UNION: R. W. Barclay, Caledonia House, South Gyle, Edinburgh, EH12 9DQ.

COMBINED SERVICES: Lt-Col. K. Hitchcock, c/o Army Sport Control Board, Clayton Barracks, Aldershot, Hampshire GU11 2BG.

THE SPORTS COUNCIL: Director-General, 16 Upper Woburn Place, London WC1 0QP.

ASSOCIATION OF CRICKET UMPIRES: L. J. Cheeseman, 16 Ruden Way, Epsom Downs, Surrey, KT17 3LN.

WOMEN'S CRICKET ASSOCIATION: J. Featherstone, 41 St Michael's Lane, Headingley, Leeds LS6 3BR.

*The addresses of MCC, the First-Class Counties, and Minor Counties are given at the head of each separate section.*

# INTERNATIONAL CRICKET COUNCIL

On June 15, 1909, representatives of cricket in England, Australia and South Africa met at Lord's and founded the Imperial Cricket Conference. Membership was confined to the governing bodies of cricket in countries within the British Commonwealth where Test cricket was played. India, New Zealand and West Indies were elected as members on May 31, 1926, Pakistan on July 28, 1952, and Sri Lanka on July 21, 1981. South Africa ceased to be a member of ICC on leaving the British Commonwealth in May, 1961, but was elected as a Full Member in 1991.

On July 15, 1965, the Conference was renamed the International Cricket Conference and new rules were adopted to permit the election of countries from outside the British Commonwealth. This led to the growth of the Conference, with the admission of Associate Members, who were entitled to one vote, while the Foundation and Full Members were each entitled to two votes, on ICC resolutions. On July 12, 13, 1989, the Conference was renamed the International Cricket Council and revised rules were adopted.

## CONSTITUTION

**Chairman:** The nominee of the President of MCC, with the confirmation of the members at the annual conference. Prior to making his nomination, the President of MCC shall have appropriate consultations, including with all Foundation and Full Members. The term of office is for one year, commencing October 1, but subject to the proviso that no Chairman shall remain continuously in office for more than four years, the Chairman may offer himself for re-nomination for a further year.

**Secretary:** To be appointed by members at the annual conference. Normally the office will be filled by the Secretary of MCC.

**Administrator:** Appointed for such periods as determined by members at the annual conference.

**Foundation Members:** Australia and United Kingdom.

**Full Members:** India, New Zealand, Pakistan, South Africa, Sri Lanka and West Indies.

**Associate Members\*:** Argentina (1974), Bangladesh (1977), Bermuda (1966), Canada (1968), Denmark (1966), East and Central Africa (1966), Fiji (1965), Gibraltar (1969), Hong Kong (1969), Israel (1974), Kenya (1981), Malaysia (1967), Netherlands (1966), Papua New Guinea (1973), Singapore (1974), United Arab Emirates (1990), USA (1965), West Africa (1976) and Zimbabwe (1981).

**Affiliate Members\*:** Bahamas (1987), Belgium (1991), France (1987), Germany (1991), Italy (1984), Japan (1989), Nepal (1988) and Switzerland (1985).

*\* Year of election shown in parentheses.*

## MEMBERSHIP

The following governing bodies for cricket shall be eligible for election.

**Foundation Members:** The governing bodies for cricket in the United Kingdom and Australia are known as Foundation Members (while also being Full Members of ICC) and have certain additional rights as set out in the Rules of the Council.

**Full Members:** The governing body for cricket recognised by ICC of a country, or countries associated for cricket purposes, or geographical area, from which representative teams are qualified to play official Test matches.

**Associate Members:** The governing body for cricket recognised by ICC of a country, or countries associated for cricket purposes, or a geographical area, which does not qualify as a Full Member but where cricket is firmly established and organised.

**Affiliate Members:** The governing body for cricket recognised by ICC of a country, or countries associated for cricket purposes, or a geographical area (which is not part of one of those already constituted as a Full or Associate Member) where ICC recognises that cricket is played in accordance with the Laws of Cricket. Affiliate Members have no right to vote or to propose or second resolutions at ICC meetings.

# TEST MATCHES

## 1. Duration of Test Matches

Within a maximum of 30 hours' playing time, the duration of Test matches shall be a matter for negotiation and agreement between the two countries in any particular series of Test matches.

When agreeing the Playing Conditions prior to the commencement of a Test series, the participating countries may:

(a) Extend the playing hours of the last Test beyond the limit of 30 hours, in a series in which, at the conclusion of the penultimate match, one side does not hold a lead of more than one match.

(b) In the event of play being suspended for any reason other than normal intervals, extend the playing time on that day by the amount of time lost up to a maximum of one hour, except in the last hour of the match.

(c) Play on the rest day, conditions and circumstances permitting, should a full day's play be lost on either the second or third scheduled days of play.

(d) Make up time lost in excess of five minutes in each day's play owing to circumstances outside the game, other than acts of God.

*Note.* The umpires shall determine when such time shall be made up. This could, if conditions and circumstances permit, include the following day.

## 2. Qualification Rules

A cricketer can be qualified to play in a Test match and one-day international either by birth or by residence.

(a) Qualification by birth. A cricketer, unless debarred by ICC, is always eligible to play for the country of his birth.

(b) Qualification by residence. A cricketer, unless debarred by ICC, shall be eligible to play for any country in which he is residing and has been residing during the four immediately preceding years, provided that he has not played for the country of his birth during that period.

*Notes*

(a) Notwithstanding anything hereinbefore contained, any player who has once played in a Test match or one-day international for any country shall not afterwards be eligible to play in a Test match or one-day international against that country, without the consent of its governing body.

(b) Members shall be responsible for submitting, in reasonable time for the approval of ICC, the names of any cricketers whose qualifications are in doubt, and furnishing their qualifications.

(c) ICC in conjunction with the governing body of any country may impose more stringent qualification rules for that country.

## 3. The Appointment of Umpires

The following rules for the selection and appointment of Test match umpires shall be followed as far as is practicable to do so:

(a) The home authority shall appoint a committee for the purpose of nominating umpires to officiate in all Test matches.

(b) Test match umpires will be nominated by this committee from those umpires officiating in first-class matches during the current season.

(c) Wherever possible, umpires likely to be nominated by this committee shall officiate in matches against the visiting team, thus giving the visiting captain an opportunity to judge the umpires to be nominated. As long as possible before each Test match, the manager of the touring team and the secretary of the home authority will be informed of the names of the umpires nominated for the particular Test match. Any objection against either umpire must be lodged within three days of the notice being received or at least seven days before the match, whichever is the later, and will be dealt with by the committee as set up in (a), or by a special committee appointed by the home authority, whose decision shall be final. The names of the umpires shall not be given to the media until after this time has elapsed.

(d) While a captain is entitled to submit objections to a particular umpire nominated for a Test match, he may not ask for a particular umpire to be given precedence for appointment over any other. If either captain raises what is considered by the committee (or by the special committee appointed by the home authority) to be a definite and reasonable objection to any particular umpire, his wishes shall be met.

(e) The sole authority for handling media enquiries shall be the official representative appointed by the home authority for the purpose, and not the captains or any of the players.

# CODE OF CONDUCT

1. The captains are responsible at all times for ensuring that play is conducted within the spirit of the game as well as within the Laws.

2. Players and team officials shall not at any time engage in conduct unbecoming to an international player or team official which could bring them or the game into disrepute.

3. Players and team officials must at all times accept the umpire's decision. Players must not show dissent at the umpire's decision.

4. Players and team officials shall not intimidate, assault or attempt to intimidate or assault an umpire, another player or a spectator.

5. Players and team officials shall not use crude or abusive language (known as "sledging") nor make offensive gestures.

6. Players and team officials shall not use or in any way be concerned in the use or distribution of illegal drugs.

7. Players and team officials shall not disclose or comment upon any alleged breach of the Code or upon any hearing, report or decision arising from such breach.

8. Players and team officials shall not make any public pronouncement or media comment which is detrimental either to the game in general; or to a particular tour in which they are involved; or about any tour between other countries which is taking place; or to relations between the Boards of the competing teams.

## Application, Interpretation and Enforcement of the Code

1. The Code shall apply:

   (a) To players and, where applicable, to team officials of both teams for all Test matches and limited-overs international matches;

   (b) To players and, where applicable, to team officials of official touring teams for all matches, other than Test matches and limited-overs internationals ("other matches") with such modifications as ICC shall consider necessary in the absence of a match referee for other matches.

2. Breaches of the Code shall be deemed also to include a breach of any ICC Regulation in force from time to time, including (without limitation) those relating to advertising on cricket clothing and equipment, and, in Test matches, those relating to minimum over-rates.

3. The Code, breach of which may render a player or team official liable to disciplinary action, shall be enforced:

   (a) In the case of Test matches and limited-overs internationals in accordance with procedures and guidelines laid down for the match referee; and

   (b) In the case of other matches, in such manner as ICC shall consider appropriate at the time when the incident occurs. This shall, so far as is practicable, follow the procedures and guidelines laid down for the match referee.

## ICC MATCH REFEREE

### 1. Objective

To act on behalf of ICC to:

   (a) see that the full implications of Law 42.1 are properly understood and upheld; and

   (b) to ensure that the spirit of the game is observed and the conduct of the game maintained during Test matches and limited-overs internationals by players, umpires and team officials, either on or off the field, his responsibility being confined to the precincts of the ground.

### 2. Terms of Reference

   (a) To be the independent representative of ICC (appointed by the Chairman or, in his absence, the Secretary, after consultation with the Boards concerned), at all Test matches and limited-overs internationals, respecting the authority of the host country which is promoting a series, or the ground authority which is administering a match or series of matches.

   (b) To liaise with the appointed umpires, but not in any way to interfere with their traditional role.

   (c) To carry out the following duties:

   (i) Observe and adjudicate upon breaches of the Code of Conduct.

   (ii) Impose penalties for failure to maintain the minimum over-rate as set by ICC (presently fifteen overs per hour).

   (iii) Impose penalties for deliberate acts of unfair play; e.g. the deliberate slowing-down of over-rates and the deliberate speeding-up of overs to make up for any shortfall during a day's play.

   (iv) Impose penalties for infringements of the ICC Regulation relating to advertising on cricket clothing and equipment.

   (v) Impose penalties incurred under any other ICC Regulation which may be passed from time to time and which falls within the Terms of Reference.

   (vi) Ensure the conduct of the game is upheld by the umpires in accordance with the Laws of Cricket and the Playing Conditions as agreed by the two Boards concerned in a series, and to give support to the umpires in this regard if required.

### 3. Method of Operation

The match referee must be present on all days of the match or matches assigned to him from the time the players arrive within the precincts of the ground until a reasonable time after close of play, bearing in mind that reports can be submitted up to one hour after the end of the day's play. He must ensure, in conjunction with the ground authority, that he has a good view of the match and has access to a television monitor and video equipment.

## 4. Penalties

The referee may in his absolute discretion impose any penalty by way of reprimand and/or fine and/or suspension.

(a) Maximum fine to be imposed for breaches of the Code of Conduct and other ICC Regulations (excluding over-rates) – 75 per cent of a player's match fee.

When a player is on tour, the fine shall be calculated on the last match fee paid to that player in his previous domestic season. If a player did not participate in an international match during his previous domestic season, that player shall be fined on the basis which would have applied had he played in an international match in his previous domestic season.

(b) Maximum suspension to be imposed for breaches of the Code of Conduct and other ICC Regulations – three Test matches.

If any matches of international standard take place between Test matches, the ban will also include these. This ban may well carry over into a future series. A player's participation in his own domestic cricket during the period of any ban imposed by the ICC match referee will be up to his own Board to determine.

(c) Penalties for slow over-rates

(i) **Test Matches**

Over-rates shall be assessed on fifteen overs per hour; i.e. a minimum of 90 overs in a six-hour day, subject to the following deductions:

Two minutes per wicket taken;
Four minutes for drinks breaks in excess of one per session;
Actual time where treatment by authorised medical personnel is required on the ground, and also for a player leaving the field owing to serious injury.

Overs will be calculated at the end of the match. For each over short of the target number, five per cent of each player's match fee in the fielding side is to be deducted.

(ii) **Limited-overs Internationals**

The target over-rate is to be fifteen overs per hour. In the event of the target over-rate not being reached, for each over short of the number required to be bowled in the scheduled time, the fielding side will be fined an amount equal to five per cent of each player's match fee for the match.

For touring teams where a tour fee is paid, the match fee will be taken to be the match fee paid by the touring team's country in its previous domestic season. A penalty may be reviewed by the match referee if, after consultation with the umpires, he is of the opinion that events beyond the control of the fielding side, including time-wasting by the batting side, prevented that team from bowling the required number of overs.

## 5. Payment of Fines

Fines must be paid within one calendar month by the player(s) to his (their) Board who will, in turn, forward such fine(s) to the Secretary of ICC. Any player(s) failing to meet this requirement will be rendered unavailable for selection in any fixture under the control of his (their) own Board.

# THE BOWLING OF FAST, SHORT-PITCHED BALLS: LAW 42.8

Experimental Regulation for Test matches only for three years
with effect from October 1, 1991

A bowler shall be limited to one fast, short-pitched ball per over per batsman. If this limit is exceeded, the following procedure shall be applied:

(a) If a bowler delivers a second fast, short-pitched ball in an over to the same batsman, the umpire shall call and signal "no-ball" and indicate the reason to the bowler, to the captain of the fielding side and to the other umpire.

(b) If a bowler is no-balled a second time in the innings for the same offence, the umpire shall warn the bowler, indicate to him that this is a final warning, and inform the captain of the fielding side and the other umpire of what has occurred.

(c) If the bowler is no-balled a third time in the same innings for the same offence, the umpire shall:

    (i) As soon as the ball is dead, direct the captain of the fielding side to take the bowler off forthwith and to complete the over with another bowler, provided that the bowler does not bowl two overs, or part thereof, consecutively;

    (ii) Not allow the bowler, thus taken off, to bowl in the same innings;

    (iii) Report the occurrence to the captain of the batting side as soon as the players leave the field for an interval;

    (iv) Report the occurrence immediately after the day's play to the management of the fielding side and to the governing body responsible for the match, who shall take any further action which is considered to be appropriate against the bowler concerned.

**Definition**

A fast, short-pitched ball shall be defined as a ball which passes, or would have passed, above the shoulder of the batsman standing upright at the crease.

# THE BOWLING OF FAST, HIGH FULL PITCHES: LAW 42.9

The bowling of fast, high full pitches is unfair.

In Test matches and limited-overs internationals played by Test match countries, Law 42.9 shall be replaced by the following:

A fast, high full-pitched ball shall be defined as a ball that passes, or would have passed, on the full above the shoulder height of a batsman standing upright at the crease. Should a bowler bowl a fast, high-pitched ball, either umpire shall call and signal "no-ball".

In the event of such unfair bowling, the umpire at the bowler's end shall adopt the procedures of caution, final warning, action against the bowler and reporting as set out in Law 42.8 of the Laws of Cricket.

# MEETINGS IN 1991

## INTERNATIONAL CRICKET COUNCIL

At a Special Meeting of the International Cricket Council on January 9, 10 in Melbourne, Australia – the first formal meeting of ICC to be held away from Lord's – it was agreed that independent match referees would be appointed for Test matches and one-day internationals, to enforce the forthcoming ICC Code of Conduct and to oversee the imposition of fines for slow over-rates. The meeting approved in principle independent umpires from a third country standing in all international matches, but with costs estimated at £500,000 a year, the setting-up of such a panel was not considered possible without sponsorship. It was indicated, however, that individual countries could, if they wished, appoint independent umpires at their own expense. A letter from South Africa, advising of a proposed new and single ruling body for the country's cricket, was noted.

## TCCB SPRING MEETING

At its Spring Meeting, held at Lord's on March 5, 6, the Test and County Cricket Board accepted, almost unanimously, the recommendation of its Executive Committee that it reappoint the England Committee under the chairmanship of E. R. Dexter for a further twelve months. The Board also endorsed the policy of selecting a team of observers to assist the England Committee. Nevertheless, reservations were expressed about the performances of the three representative teams which England sent abroad during the winter: the senior team to Australia and New Zealand, the A side to Pakistan and Sri Lanka, and the Under-19s to New Zealand. Areas of concern included the fitness of players, given the occurrence of injuries on the tour of Australia, the standard of fielding in English cricket, and, again with regard to Australia, the itinerary. Mr Dexter said that specific attention would be given to a number of matters, including media relations and the roles of particular individual officers to ensure that there was a clear definition of jobs.

With regard to the County Championship, the Board agreed that from 1992, when the inclusion of Durham would mean each county playing five opponents twice, counties would be able to nominate one county they wanted to play twice, so that traditional fixtures could be maintained; the other four matches would be decided by random selection. At the request of the Cricketers' Association it was agreed also that, in calculating over-rates in the County Championship, three minutes rather than the statutory two would be allowed after the fall of a wicket. The Board stressed that it did not want to see a return to green, over-grassed pitches for Championship matches following the decision at the 1990 Winter Meeting to remove references to colour from the guidelines on pitches.

Approval was given to the Marketing Committee to carry out further experiments with regard to the use of advertising logos on the outfield, but a decision on the introduction of coloured clothing for Sunday League cricket was deferred.

## TCCB SPECIAL MEETING

At a Special Meeting at Lord's on May 14, the Test and County Cricket Board rejected, by thirteen votes to six, proposals to reform the Sunday League by dividing it into two divisions of eight teams each, so reducing the amount of 40-overs cricket. Only four counties, Kent, Leicestershire, Middlesex and Surrey, plus MCC and the Minor Counties, supported the proposals. Instead the meeting voted for the introduction of coloured clothing and the use of a white ball in the Sunday competition in 1992.

## INTERNATIONAL CRICKET COUNCIL

At its Annual Meeting at Lord's on July 10, the International Cricket Council admitted South Africa to full membership. A founder member of the Imperial Cricket Conference, South Africa had ceased to be a member of ICC on leaving the British Commonwealth in May 1961 and had last played Test cricket in March 1970. Their return, under the auspices of the non-racial United Cricket Board of South Africa, was proposed by India and seconded by Australia, although West Indies had expressed reservations about the resolution being voted on, because it was not on the agenda for the meeting. However, the chairman, M. C. Cowdrey, ruled that South Africa's application should be heard. It was announced after the meeting that South Africa "should not" take part in the World Cup in 1992.

In addition, the meeting brought in an eight-point Code of Conduct and an average minimum over-rate of fifteen overs per hour for Test matches and one-day internationals, both to be enforced by an ICC referee, plus experimental Laws governing the bowling of fast, short-pitched deliveries and beamers. Full details of these may be found in the International Cricket Council section of this Almanack.

## TCCB SUMMER MEETING

At its Summer Meeting, held at Lord's on August 15, the Test and County Cricket Board agreed to set up a working party, under the chairmanship of M. P. Murray of Middlesex, to investigate the state of the domestic first-class game in England. It was expected that the working party's investigation, which would also be aimed at improving standards at international level, would take twelve months, and that its recommendations would be implemented by 1994 if so decided by the Board. The meeting also voted to allow sponsors' logos to be painted on the outfield at matches in England. This followed a two-year experiment.

## TCCB WINTER MEETING

At its Winter Meeting, held at Lord's on December 11, 12, the Test and County Cricket Board approved, from 1992, a sliding scale of fines for counties which failed to bowl sixteen overs an hour in the limited-overs competitions, and ruled that in all county cricket no player would be allowed to remove a helmet from the field until the next interval. These measures reflected the Board's concern at the pace at which county cricket had been played in recent years. The Board heard that its decision at the Special Meeting in May, concerning the introduction of coloured clothing and white balls in the Sunday League, would not be implemented in 1992 in the absence of a new sponsor for the League. Since that meeting, Refuge Assurance, sponsors of the Sunday League from 1987, had announced that they would not be renewing their contract after 1991.

It was agreed that the ICC regulation concerning one fast, short-pitched delivery per over per batsman would apply in county cricket from 1992. The meeting gave a vote of confidence to the England Committee, while at the same time augmenting it by an additional selector, to be chosen at the 1992 Spring Meeting, who would strengthen liaison with the counties and sustain continuity from year to year.

---

## ERRATA

### WISDEN, 1977

Page 965     G. J. Gilmour scored 32*, not 134, for Wanderers v South African Invitation XI at Johannesburg.

### WISDEN, 1979

Page 680     The Sussex total was 61, not 60, extras being 10, not 9 (n-b 2).
Page 919     In the Young New Zealand second innings, G. Miller bowled seventeen overs, not seven.

## WISDEN, 1980

Page 328    The last line of the fifth paragraph should read "... Mankad's 184 in 1952", not 1932.

## WISDEN, 1991

Page 275    The list of batsmen scoring 100 before lunch should include S. J. Cook, 120*, Somerset v Warwickshire at Taunton (3rd day).

Page 276    The entry for Most Sixes off Successive Balls should include the three sixes hit by P. A. J. DeFreitas (off G. J. Turner) for Lancashire v Oxford University at Oxford.

Page 349    In Surrey v Sri Lankans, D. S. B. P. Kuruppu kept wicket for the Sri Lankans, not H. P. Tillekeratne.

Pages 545 and 546    M. W. Alleyne (22 years 93 days) did not become Gloucestershire's youngest double-centurion in the Championship, as stated. W. R. Hammond was aged 22 years 61 days when he scored 250* for Gloucestershire v Lancashire at Manchester in 1925.

Page 723    In Hampshire's innings v Northamptonshire, R. J. Maru scored 10 and C. A. Connor 7*; not as stated.

Page 734    N. V. Radford did not bowl a maiden over v Warwickshire.
            G. R. Cowdrey, not R. P. Davis, was in Kent's team v Gloucestershire.

Page 736    C. M. Wells bowled 1 maiden, not 0, v Derbyshire.

Page 737    P. W. G. Parker scored 85* and I. J. Gould 16* v Minor Counties; not as stated.

Page 751    Subsequent to the 1991 *Wisden* going to press, the TCCB ruled that the scores in the abandoned match between Essex and Leicestershire would stand for the purposes of players' statistics. The scorecard was as follows:

## Leicestershire

| | | | | |
|---|---|---|---|---|
| T. J. Boon c Gooch b Foster | 24 | G. J. Parsons b Pringle | | 0 |
| *N. E. Briers b Foster | 15 | M. I. Gidley not out | | 1 |
| J. J. Whitaker lbw b Topley | 18 | L-b 2 | | 2 |
| L. Potter not out | 46 | | | |
| C. C. Lewis run out | 28 | 1/36 2/43 3/64 | (6 wkts, 45 overs) | 162 |
| †P. Whitticase c Stephenson b Topley | 28 | 4/116 5/153 6/155 | | |

J. P. Agnew, A. D. Mullally and L. B. Taylor did not bat.

Bowling: Foster 8–2–29–2; Ilott 7–1–22–0; Pringle 9–1–31–1; Topley 9–1–27–2; Childs 7–0–32–0; Stephenson 5–0–19–0.

## Essex

*G. A. Gooch, B. R. Hardie, J. P. Stephenson, M. E. Waugh, P. J. Prichard, D. R. Pringle, †M. A. Garnham, N. A. Foster, T. D. Topley, J. H. Childs and M. C. Ilott.

Page 752    D. Cowan, not A. Bee, was b Taylor 3; Bee did not bat.

Page 772    M. Frost did not bat v Leicestershire; he was not 0*. A. D. Mullally bowled 1 maiden, not 0, v Glamorgan.

Pages 779 and 780    A. P. Wells of Sussex was st Russell, not caught. C. M. Wells bowled 1 maiden, not 0, v Gloucestershire.

Page 783    N. G. Cowley bowled 1 maiden, not 0, v Glamorgan.

Page 811    F. D. Stephenson did not bowl a maiden over v Lancashire.

Page 822    In the match v Derbyshire, A. J. Murphy conceded 37 runs, not 26, and A. G. Robson conceded 26 runs, not 37.

Page 831    A. P. Igglesden of Kent was b Reeve, not caught as stated.

Page 1008    In Pakistan's innings in the Third Test, K. Srikkanth conceded 19 runs, not 18, and R. J. Shastri conceded 104 runs, not 105.

Page 1271    In the summary of Sir Leonard Hutton's career, the statement, "He reached 100 centuries in 619 innings, the lowest ratio by an Englishman", should read "... at the time the lowest ratio by an Englishman".

# CRICKET BOOKS, 1991

## By JOHN ARLOTT

The 68 titles submitted for review this year represent, in the opinion of this reviewer, the most uniformly high-standard output of any year in modern times.

*Cricket in Many Lands* (Hodder & Stoughton; £14.99), by Tony Lewis, is a 238-page octavo with a brief but valuable appendix of Test scores. It stirs echoes of C. L. R. James's text, "What do they know of cricket who only cricket know?" Mr Lewis was a Test match captain who became a writer and broadcaster on the game. Here he deals not only with cricket facts, opinions and ideas, but with cricketers and their ways. However, it underestimates him to describe him as a cricket writer: he is so much more than that, and here some 70-odd essays roam the range of his interest. At one moment he raises a debatable point, next he clarifies another; here he conjures up a player, there he analyses his technique. He constantly engages the interest with the breadth of his ideas, for he does not confine himself to bowling a ball or wielding a bat, but to the entire realm of cricket.

*The Wisden Illustrated History of Cricket* (Macdonald/Queen Anne Press; £16.95), by Vic Marks, with records by Bill Frindall, is an attractive, well-illustrated 256-page quarto. It is a sensitively written history, with a good literary background. Mr Marks avoids the usual clichés and achieves such neat condensation as, "In May 1977 the Packer affair appeared cataclysmic, but by 1987 it was a dim memory". The major events are laid out neatly enough, and it is important that the author is genuinely in touch with his subject and the dressing-rooms. He is by no means without humour and has not neglected that aspect in his illustration. Essentially, however, this is a mature, balanced look at cricket history, well written and generously illustrated in black-and-white and colour.

*The Wisden Papers 1969-1990: Mixed Fortunes* (Stanley Paul; £16.99), edited by Benny Green, is described by the editor as the final volume of the series and as covering "The sadly modern, sulphurous age of cricket". However, Mr Green, an industrious and sensitive anthologist, has, as usual, come up with an outstanding collection of writings. His authors range over Michael Melford, Jack Fingleton, John Kay, Irving Rosenwater, Andrew Sandham, Sir Compton Mackenzie, Philip Snow and Ian Peebles. The subjects range as widely as Compton's Record Season, F. R. Foster, Tales of W. G. Grace, G. O. Allen, The Cricket Rhymester, MCC and South Africa, The Lawrence Awards and the little gem in "We Already Knew He Could Bat" (Graeme Hick) by Peter Roebuck. The selection has been made with perception and a genuine feeling for the essential qualities of *Wisden*.

*From Sammy to Jimmy* (Partridge Press; £16.99), by Peter Roebuck, is "The Official History of Somerset County Cricket Club". The Sammy in the title is S. M. J. Woods (Australia, England and Somerset), the Jimmy is S. J. Cook (South Africa and Somerset), thus justifying, unusually lightly, the fact that the book is published "To coincide with the Centenary of Somerset CCC's birth as a first-class county". A thorough and readable 443-page account, with a few relevant statistics, it is concerned mainly with the county's growth, change and personalities. Mr Roebuck is serious indeed, as when he ends a chapter on the season of 1982 with such a sentence as: "This Benson and Hedges Cup was the last of those days of wine and roses: for a time, hereafter, enough games were won to disguise deterioration but ever more it was obvious that a spirit had been lost as Somerset fragmented." There are some black-and-white illustrations revealing players and times, including one of S. M. J. Woods epitomising the Somerset cricketing ideal.

*Brylcreem Summer* (Kingswood Press; £14.99), by Eric Midwinter, will be for those of appropriate age a nostalgic account of 1947, which for many was the first genuinely post-war season. It was, of course, the year in which Denis Compton and Bill Edrich made their vast mountains of runs which overcame South Africa. The South Africans, in their turn, put forward Alan Melville, Bruce Mitchell, Dudley Nourse and Athol Rowan. It was, however, the two Middlesex players who became national figures with their record-breaking aggregates. Middlesex, captained by R. W. V. Robins, won the County Championship, and in the county game Doug Wright, Joe Hardstaff, Len Hutton and Charlie Barnett, with the veterans, John Clay and Tom Goddard, made their marks. All these names are wonderful material for those who recall that season with happiness. For others, too, Mr Midwinter's story has intriguing and attractive angles. A perfect gift for cricket followers of that certain age, it is a 184-page octavo with photographic illustrations.

*The Ashes: England in Australia 1990-91* (Heinemann Australia; no price given) is an account, by Mark Ray and Alan Lee, of England's tour in Australia. It is a 160-page quarto with generous illustration, some of it in colour. Much of it appears in first-person quotations, and the whole atmosphere of the book is companionable, even though the series was not one of success for England.

*West Indies in England: The Great Post-War Tours* (Kingswood Press; £14.99), by John Figueroa, is a 225-page octavo account of ten striking tours, with photographic illustrations and ample statistical appendices. John Figueroa was constantly with all of those West Indian sides, watched them at close quarters, was friendly with many of the players, broadcast about them, and generally studied their development. His is a most knowledgeable story, and he ends by posing the question, "Which was the greatest West Indies team?" He goes at least so far as to select a representative team from tours between 1950 and 1988. His side is Greenidge, Rae, Richards, Worrell, Sobers, Weekes, Marshall, Holding, Hendriks, Garner and Gibbs. That, of course, immediately starts discussion. Where is Walcott? What of Ramadhin and Valentine? And Hall? And so we are back in the collection of outstanding players West Indies sent to England in that period. It is, in other words, not merely an account but also a series of posed questions; all in all, it is a display of quite remarkably gifted players who contributed to the greatness of West Indian cricket in those years.

*A History of the County Cricket Championship* (Guinness Publishing; £11.99), by Robert Brooke, is a well-documented history with ample photographic illustrations throughout its 192 octavo pages. Mr Brooke is a considerable member of the Association of Cricket Statisticians and lays out his facts in most orderly fashion. The whole parade compels many comparisons, and while it is hard to call a collection of records readable, this one compels not only reference but a reading through of facts from the gigantic to the normal.

*Cricket's Champion Counties* (Breedon Books; £14.95), by David Lemmon, covers most of the same ground as Mr Brooke's book, but it does so quite differently, concentrating on the most successful teams. A 255-page octavo, it is illustrated with good black-and-white photographs and runs through Amateurs and Professionals, Birth of the County Championship, The Flowering of the White Rose, The Wars of the Roses, The Yorkshire of Brian Sellers, Surrey and Stuart Surridge, The Kings of One-day Cricket, Kent's Vintage Years, Middlesex, and Vintage Essex. The prolific Mr Lemmon has written with his usual enthusiasm and well-read background.

*The Complete Record of West Indian Test Cricketers* (ACL & Polar Publishing; £17.95), by Bridgette Lawrence and Ray Goble, with a foreword by Sir Garfield Sobers, is a 384-page quarto, with generous black-and-white illustrations. The biographical descriptions run from Ellis "Puss" Achong to Sir Frank Worrell, "the first black man to be appointed captain of the West Indies for more than one match"; they are followed by quite voluminous statistics, giving the season by season and series by series records of every individual West Indian Test player.

*By His Own Hand: A Study of Cricket's Suicides* (Stanley Paul; £15.99), by David Frith, is a 264-page octavo with black-and-white illustrations. It is a compelling piece of research. Mr Frith's first sentences are: "Self-destruction is fairly commonplace on the cricket field. 'Unplayable' balls, in the strictly scientific sense, are extremely rare." Even in a book review it is painful to rehearse the names of those cricketers – great or small – who took their own lives, but in truth it does seem that some of them were so inclined. One can recall instances of cricketers who seemed depressed beyond measure at some incident, usually a dismissal, but one had usually observed a depression, quite unattached to cricket, in the player beforehand. Mr Frith's study does hold the reader and is well worth reading – provided there is some cheer at hand.

*The Joy of a Lifetime: India's Tour of England 1990* (Marine Sports; Rs30), by Harsha Bhogle, is a 195-page small paperbound octavo. It is enthusiastically and readably written, and at points is extremely revealing to the non-Indian cricket watcher. Some may be baffled by the word printed in large letters across the cover, "Sachincredible!" But all is explained in a passage from the chapter of the same title, giving an account of the Old Trafford Test between England and India on that tour. "Sachin Tendulkar will score many, many more hundreds for India, but the freshness of this one will never fade." The whole book, indeed, has an air of freshness and deserves to be read.

*Cricket Beyond The Bazaar* (Allen & Unwin; $A24.95), by Mike Coward, is a 178-page octavo, illustrated chiefly by two four-page clutches of photographs. It is primarily a story of the last ten years of cricket by Australia on the Indian subcontinent, notably the Madras tied Test of 1986-87, the 1987 World Cup, which the Australians won, and the Australian team's threatened walk-out of Pakistan in 1988-89. However, Mr Coward provides plenty of background material, there are friendly forewords by Sunil Gavaskar and Imran Khan, and the whole work bespeaks a painstaking study of the subject. This is a fresh and worthwhile view of the game in Asia, seen through Western eyes without condescension or loftiness. It should be required reading for every Western writer who prepares to write on the game as it is played in the East. As an inside view of a matter invariably written about from the outside, it should for that reason be on every cricket student's shelf.

*Testing Times* (Robson Books; £9.95), by Graham Gooch, is a paperbound 244-page octavo in which the England captain deals thoroughly with five series and one Test played by England under his captaincy. There is also a

38-page appendix of statistics. The author is at pains to point out his own shortcomings as well as his merits, stating his case with such passages as, "Once I'm in, I try to eliminate mistakes. That doesn't mean I block, but I don't step outside the bounds of my normal rhythm of play. There's a difference between making a century and scoring one; I'm talking not about being slow, but about being patient, prepared to graft for your runs, and not making mistakes." The book is full of similar good common sense, and among the match accounts there are some absorbing pieces about the England–West Indies series of 1991. Graham Gooch finishes with these words: "Leading the Test team has been a great honour, all the more special because I got a second chance that I never thought possible. Having lost it once, I was and am determined to give it my best shot in every way – that is what I expect from those cricketers who play with me."

*The Wisden Book of Test Captains* (Stanley Paul; £15.99), by Ted Corbett and Joanne King, is a 256-page octavo, with some black-and-white illustrations. Yet another in the rash of cricket books in recent years which have incorporated in their titles the name of *Wisden*, it is a most meticulous list of the Test captains of all eight Test-playing countries, providing their results, biographical notes, and their playing performances as captains. This is thorough and painstaking and has some nice touches of character. It also contains such unexpected information as that about H. M. Taberer, who, in addition to captaining South Africa in his only Test, "once won a bet that he could throw a cricket ball 100 yards whilst standing in a tub".

*The Wisden Book of Test Cricket: Volume I 1877-1977, Volume II 1977-1989* (Macdonald/Queen Anne Press; £25 each), by Bill Frindall, extends this invaluable series of Test match scores and records to the end of the 1989 Ashes series between England and Australia. An addition to this, the third edition, is the inclusion of the close of play and not out batsmen's scores for every day of Test cricket.

*England versus West Indies* (Crowood Press; £19.95), is by Gerry Cotter, is a 320-page small quarto, most generously illustrated in black-and-white and colour. Sub-titled "A History of the Tests and Other Matches", it starts in 1895 and ends, in time, with 1973-90. It has been written with considerable care and study by an author most fully grounded in his subject. Indeed, it is difficult to think of anyone else presently equipped to cover so much ground so thoroughly. For instance, he closes a passage on Lance Gibbs's becoming his country's leading wicket-taker: "Towards the end, the knuckle on the index finger of his right hand became greatly swollen, and although at the age of forty he had two good performances in India – 6 for 76 and 7 for 98 – there was a feeling, prevalent especially in Yorkshire, that he was kept in the Test team primarily to overtake Trueman and become the first West Indian to lead the wicket-takers. He was forty-one when he achieved it and, even if he had bowled nearly 12,000 more balls than Trueman, he had earned his place in the sun by sheer hard work." This must become the standard work on its subject.

The limited edition of the year is *Gooch's Golden Summer* (Boundary Books; £33), by Bill Frindall, with an appreciation by Trevor Bailey and photography by Patrick Eagar. Signed by all three, it is an 86-page octavo limited to 333 copies, the number reached by Gooch in his innings against India at Lord's. With a pleasing binding – the first ten are in a *de luxe* edition bound in full leather – it contains text by Mr Frindall and reproductions of his actual score-

sheets. It is a luxury volume which will undoubtedly become a collector's item.

*Early Cricket in Sydney 1803 to 1856* (New South Wales Cricket Association, Sydney; $A29.95), by James Scott, edited by Richard Cashman and Stephen Gibbs, is a 243-page quarto with reproductions of photographs. It is, in fact, one of two consecutive volumes by Mr Scott – the other was completed in 1935 – and is a remarkable piece of preservation: one of seven bound volumes amounting to 1,030 pages donated to the New South Wales Cricket Association by the author's daughter, Miss Florence Scott. This is, unquestionably, a most important cricket work, affording a magnificent record of cricket in Sydney, and indeed in Australia in general. Messrs Cashman and Gibbs have edited with care and sympathy, realising that they were handling an item of considerable national value. It shows the earliest references to cricket in Australia, and some of the illustrations are of immense interest to the researcher, as all is to the historian.

*W.G.'s Birthday Party* (Chatto & Windus; £13.99), by David Kynaston, is an outstanding reconstruction of the cricket match of which *Wisden* wrote in the following year (1899), "When the fixtures for 1898 were being arranged, the Committee of the MCC had the happy inspiration to fix the Gentlemen and Players match for the 18th July – Mr W. G. Grace's fiftieth birthday. More than that, they secured at the Secretaries' meeting in December a perfectly clear date for the fixture and thus made themselves certain of getting representative elevens." Mr Kynaston is by profession a historian; his only misfortune here is the fact that, as he points out in referring to the drawing of stumps on the dismissal of Haigh at 6.30 p.m. on that first day: "As soon as Haigh was given out, the umpires pulled up the stumps and WG led his men off the field, even though the official card stated that stumps would be drawn at seven o'clock . . . The likeliest explanation for this early cessation – no official reason was given – was that MCC were honouring WG that evening with a banquet in the Pavilion for which preparations needed to be made. This banquet was very much a private affair, and no reports of it would appear in the press." Otherwise, all is immaculately arranged in this 154-page octavo: the events of the match, biographical details of the players, and, in the final chapter, the path they followed to the grave.

*The Narrow Line* (Kingswood Press; £13.99), by Geoff Cook and Neville Scott, is an outstanding 182-page octavo sub-titled "An Anatomy of Professional Cricket". This is no happy-ending games-playing account. As Mike Brearley says in his foreword – and the very fact of his writing it is guarantee of the book's quality – "It has few anecdotes or match descriptions. It is self-effacing and does not rely on the heroics of star players." It is, indeed, one of the most thoughtful studies of the profession yet published. Geoff Cook was for twenty years an opening batsman, latterly captain of Northamptonshire and seven times capped for England; for some years he was chairman, and is now secretary, of the Cricketers' Association. He was appointed director of cricket for Durham as that county prepared for entry into first-class cricket in 1992. Neville Scott has been a Shakespearian researcher, a teacher at Cardiff University, and a reporter for Cricketcall, the *Daily Telegraph* and the BBC World Service. Diverting and illuminating, this book should be compulsory reading, not only for the bar-room critics, but for every county cricket committee member.

*A Who's Who of Lancashire County Cricket Club 1865-1990* (Breedon Books; £14.95), by Robert Brooke and David Goodyear, is a well-made, black-and-white illustrated 251-page octavo. It is extremely inclusive, recalling several players who played only one match for the county and that without scoring or bowling. Of those who did more, there are some concentrated, accurate biographical notes, giving dates of birth (and death), education, number of matches and full first-class record, as well as other relevant information.

*Fifty Years of Irish Cricket 1940 to 1990* (Lindis, Roundhay Road, Bridlington; £10.95), by William West, is a 144-page octavo, containing twenty pages of text and "A number of scoresheets". Mr West, a barrister, "More at home in the pavilion than at the crease", also includes best batting and bowling averages which, incidentally, are headed by N. W. D. Yardley and H. Verity.

*Players on Parade: A History of Bath Cricket Club* (Good Books; £4.99), by John Ruddick, is an 86-page octavo with an attractive paper binding of the painting of the ground by Roy Perry. The club's most impressive riverside ground is called North Parade, and the list of their players also impresses. Three of Bath's players were chosen for England: the great Tom Richardson, who also, of course, played for Surrey, Len Braund, and J. C. W. MacBryan, who was picked once against South Africa for a match almost washed out by rain. He did not bat, bowl or take a catch, and was never picked again: a unique case. The list shows also that 42 other of the club's players appeared for Somerset or other counties. It is an attractive story of a club which was founded as the Bath Association Club in 1859 and became the Bath Cricket Club in 1913.

*One Hundred Years of Cricket at Blaydon* (Blaydon Cricket Club, 4 East Acres, Blaydon, Tyneside; £4), with a history by Jack Chapman, is a 118-page paperbound quarto which celebrates the centenary of the club. The text effectively combines club cricket history with much shrewd observation and no little humour, while the whole is decorated with many black-and-white photographs.

*1666 And All That . . . 325 Years of Cricket in Richmond* (Richmond CC, Old Deer Park, 187 Kew Road, Richmond, Surrey; no price given), a 40-page oblong quarto edited by Norman Harris, is a celebratory publication of the Richmond club in Surrey. It contains some pleasing illustrations and text concerning the club, which played against New Zealand in 1927, two years before that country achieved Test status, and which has in its time offered a stage for a number of famous players, some of whose photographs appear here.

*Cricket Grounds* (The Sports Turf Research Institute, Bingley, West Yorkshire BD16 1AU; £23, plus £2.50 p. & p.), sub-titled "The Evolution, Maintenance and Construction of Natural Turf Cricket Tables and Outfields", by R. D. C. Evans, is a relevantly illustrated, workmanlike publication, technically informed and going into the last details of its subject. Certainly its 279 quarto pages appear to leave no aspect unexamined, and while this is not light entertainment, it is most valuably informative and essential for a working groundsman or ground supervisor. As an example of its thoroughness, it cites 26 weeds likely to be found on cricket grounds and gives their botanical names and their susceptibility to herbicides. Indication of its treatment is implicit in the following paragraph: "Ideally a ball pitching on a good length, two or three yards in front of the stumps, should rise half to full stump height by the time it reaches the bowling crease. If the wicket surface slopes away from the bowler it will lower the bounce. Conversely, a pitch sloping up from the bowling end gives a higher bounce. Check therefore that surface levels are within the limits laid down in the previous chapter. The question of both general slopes over the table surface as a whole, or smaller-scale undulations in the surface of an individual wicket, should be considered – remember that the latter can be checked using strings or straight-edges."

*The Terms of the Game: A Dictionary of Cricket* (Houghton Mifflin/ Gollancz; £5.99), by Frank Tyson, is a 186-page paperbound octavo with a few technical line illustrations where required. This is a most scholarly work on the language of cricket, defining and describing in genuinely illuminating fashion its subject, not only for the beginner but also for many active players who may not be as precisely informed as the author.

*The Field Book of Cricket from 1853 to the Present* (Pelham Books; £16.99), edited by David Rayvern Allen, contains probably the least-known material collected on that period. *The Field* is not by any means a "popular" periodical among cricket readers. This, however, is a highly readable collection of cricket material from a publication which, under the editorship of no less a personality than Robert Smith Surtees, the creator of Jorrocks, preceded the appearance of *Wisden* in 1864. It had been substantially a periodical for the country gentleman, covering his activities and, by no means exclusively in its cricket section, the first-class game. A substantial 275-page octavo, illustrated by some reproductions of black-and-white drawings from the magazine, Mr Rayvern Allen's anthology is immensely enjoyable, essentially unfamiliar and at times even surprising – as when a writer to the magazine, "Fitzbob", suggests in the Correspondents File: "When a bowler bowls over the wicket, the batsman generally suffers disadvantage through the umpire standing behind the bowler's arm. Why should not the umpire be compelled to wear a white jacket instead of the conventional dark coat of his species?" By no means all the contributors are letter-writers: they include F. S. Ashley-Cooper, and Lord Tennyson on "The best innings I ever played". As this is the cricketer, not the Laureate, it emerges as his half-century against the Australians at Leeds in 1921. Other sections include Period Clothes, A Girdle Around the Globe, Curiouser and Curiouser – a most absorbing collection – Out in the Sticks, Hasty Departures [Obituaries], At School and with Club, and Bookish Cricket, in which the value of a set of *Wisdens* in 1923 is put at £25. It is, all in all, a remarkable collection of material which takes much well-spent time to read.

*The Pavilion Book of Pavilions* (Pavilion; £14.99), by Jonathan Rice, is a quite delightful, informed and varied study of its subject, from the huge building at Swansea to the little hut at Saltwood. It is 112 pages of superb illustration, both colour and black-and-white, and amusing text. Mr Rice's touch has humour as well as knowledge of and a genuine sympathy for his subject. Some of Paul Barker's photographs are sheer delight and the final product is simply outstanding.

*The Longest Game* (Kingswood Press; £16.99) is a 440-page octavo collection of more than 70 pieces, edited by Alex Buzo and Jamie Grant, who describe it as the best cricket writing from Alexander to Zavos: from the Gabba to the Yabba. The pieces vary in length, and many will be new to their readers. Few, for instance, will be familiar with the opening, "What has

52 legs, sunburn and squeals?" The answer is to be found on page 327 of this diverting book.

*Ashes: True Tales from Cricket's Greatest Stars* (Angus & Robertson; £6.99) is a 208-page octavo of short reminiscences by famous players. Many of the stories will be new to the readers, and almost every piece is decorated with a special cartoon of the player, umpire, commentator or whoever made the contribution. The whole makes a light and cheerful book.

*Padwick's Bibliography of Cricket: Volume 2* (Library Association, published for the Cricket Society; £39.50), compiled by Stephen Eley and Peter Griffiths, continues where Volume 1 finished, which was at item 8,294, and it adds a further 4,023. The method is as scholarly as ever, with all the items in classified groups, and a full alphabetical index. Its coverage is world-wide and it includes all available references up to the end of 1989, including those published between 1980 and 1989 which were not included in the basic volume. The editors undertake that amendments will appear in a future consolidated edition. Mr Padwick can hardly have known what he was undertaking when he began this bibliography. The books about cricket are numerous – much more so than most people might imagine – and this was the first thorough attempt to bring them all together. It is a staggering list, and will continue to grow from discoveries, quite apart from natural growth with time. "According to Padwick" will become a term of reference, and this work is not likely to be superseded. Indeed, the attempt would awe anyone who faced it.

*Sussex Cricketers 1815-1990* (Association of Cricket Statisticians; £2.50), by Philip Bailey and Philip Thorn, is a 48-page octavo, paper bound, and is, to the obvious delight of the officers of the Association, "The seventeenth and final County booklet". As usual, there is a detailed list of every player, his first and last appearance, matches, innings, runs, highest score, average, and bowling figures. A complete set of "county cricketers" now affords valuable reference, for all that every year it is, of course, rendered out of date.

*Herbert Sutcliffe: Cricket Maestro* (Simon & Schuster; £14.99), by Alan Hill, is a 280-page octavo, generously illustrated in black-and-white. It is another of this author's distinguished biographies, right in subject, treatment and content. Mr Hill's style is both balanced and unfussy; he knows when to state and when to quote, and he builds Sutcliffe's contemporaries into the picture so that they fit it. Thus he quotes Leslie Ames: "Yorkshire would often need only one innings for victory and this restricted Herbert's chances. The opposite would be true of Hammond, playing for a less dominant county. He would play many more innings for Gloucestershire and thus have more opportunities to increase his tally of centuries." In such a fashion he constantly leads the reader to think, thus heightening both his concentration and his interest.

*Anandji Dossa – A Birthday Tribute* (The Association of Cricket Statisticians and Scorers of India, 10-2B Madhav Wadi, MMG Road, Dadar, Bombay 400 014; no price given) is a 13-page octavo pamphlet saluting Anandji Dossa, the Indian statistician who "works for hours every day collecting bits and pieces which when put together will make an encyclopaedia of Indian cricket, his finest tribute to the game he loves".

*Spring, Summer, Autumn* (Kingswood Press; £14.99), by Rob Steen, is subtitled "Three Cricketers, One Season". The dust-wrapper of this 230-page octavo names the three as Nadeem Shahid, Adrian Jones and David Hughes. The season concerned is 1990, when Shahid, "Spring", spent his first full term with Essex, Jones, "Summer", already a mature player, ended his contract with Somerset, and Hughes, "Autumn", at 43 continued his captaincy of Lancashire. Mr Steen follows them in his own, very personal style: "Would you Adam 'n' Eve it. The opening day of the Championship season at Old Trafford and the rain is not on some soggy plain in Spain, but here." He is constantly close to his characters, which must have involved him in some quite elaborate travelling arrangements, and he stays with them to the end of the summer, when Shahid has topped his thousand runs, Jones has taken more Championship wickets – 52 – than anyone else for Somerset, and Lancashire under Hughes have won the NatWest Bank Trophy and the Benson and Hedges Cup, been runners-up in the Refuge Assurance League and finished sixth in the Britannic Assurance Championship. That one finds oneself in constant sympathy with these three is the measure of Mr Steen's success in choosing and tracing them.

*The Cricketing Greigs* (Breedon Books; £14.95), by David Lemmon, is a 234-page octavo with some black-and-white illustrations. It deals not only with Tony and Ian – both of whom played Test cricket for England – but also with their father, Sandy Greig, a Scot who was awarded the DSO for his work in Bomber Command during the Second World War, and who loved and coached in both rugby and cricket. The industrious Mr Lemmon supposes that "His proudest moments were the fact that his two sons played Test cricket, both for England". The main part of the book, though, is concerned with Tony, Ian and "The Packer Affair". It is an account which may correct some opinions.

*Fred: Then and Now* (Kingswood Press; £14.99), by Don Mosey, is a 196-page octavo, with black-and-white illustrations. It is a biography of the author's friend and constant colleague, and is consciously divided into two parts: "The Player" and "The Man". That latter section, best part of half the content, deals with Trueman's career since he gave up playing cricket for Yorkshire 23 years ago. In that period he has made a fresh reputation as cricket broadcaster and TV personality. In addition, a whole series of legends has grown up around him: most of them probably true, some clearly not. They all add up, however, to make an extremely readable book, written with great enthusiasm by an obvious Trueman admirer.

*Hitting Across the Line* (Headline; £14.95) is the 288-page octavo autobiography of Viv Richards, with photographic illustrations in two sequences of sixteen and numerous reproductions of scorecards. The author is by no means content to deal with the details of batting, bowling and fielding. Although one section, in particular, deals with the playing side, this is essentially a book of Viv Richards's beliefs, cricket philosophy and personal feelings. He is very consciously and proudly an Antiguan, with much to say in the early stages about his father, a sports enthusiast who was acting-superintendent of the local prison in St John's; and he goes on to his great admiration for Clive Lloyd, his friendship with Ian Botham, his disagreement with Somerset and his move to Glamorgan. He is downright in his statement of opinions, utterly loyal to the people who commanded his loyalty, and, in his conviction of his duty to cricket, concerned that he discharges it. He acknowledges and thanks Mick Middles "who helped to record my thoughts and memories, adding his own observations along the way". The arrangement works well. The book continues into 52 pages of statistics, and even these produce surprises: Richards's first three innings for West Indies were 4, 3, and 192 not out.

*My Early Life* (Macmillan; £15.99), by Graeme Hick, is a 178-page octavo, illustrated in black-and-white, which says quite early in its text: "One thing I am proud of, though: no cricket team that I played in at Prince Edward's ever lost a game. That still means more to me than averaging 216 at the age of thirteen." That comes from a cricketer who scored his first century at the age of six and played for his country, Zimbabwe, while still at school. He is only the second batsman since the Second World War to score 1,000 runs before the end of May, and his score of 405 not out that season, 1988, is the highest individual score in England this century. However, there is much more to the book than a recital of such remarkable feats, and although Hick has still to redeem his total promise, this is a valuable account of the early days of one who, surely, must end up high in the list of all batsmen. The reader will await with some eagerness the next volume in the story.

*The Alderman's Tale* (Weidenfeld; £14.95) is a 200-page autobiography by Don Mosey, the commentator and cricket writer. Mr Mosey has been around – his experience is wide on many subjects apart from cricket – and he does not mince his words or pull his punches. He has much to say that is interesting and rewarding to read, but the overall impression is not one of goodwill towards all with whom he has worked. There is, nevertheless, much to be learned from this story for those who follow cricket and its broadcasting and reporting.

*On the Edge of my Seat* (Stanley Paul; £12.99), by Henry Blofeld, is a 177-page octavo of reminiscences, with a few black-and-white illustrations. The dedication, "For my wife, Bitten, who gritted her teeth with true Swedish phlegm when I wrote the first two chapters on our honeymoon", strikes the personal note of humour which pervades the entire book. As the collection takes in Test matches played in various parts of the world from Lord's to Leeds, Adelaide to Georgetown, the first reaction of any reader must be one of envy at such a width of Test-watching experience. To read it, however, is to share an immense wealth of enjoyment of good cricket. Mr Blofeld writes with not only humour but an enthusiasm which does not fade with the years.

*Forty-Five Summers* (Pelham Books; £16.99), by Brian Johnston, is a 176-page quarto so generously illustrated as to seem more black-and-white pictures than text. That text is gentle and friendly, full of cheerful anecdotes and kindly comments as it deals with the period from 1946 to 1990: the book is sub-titled, "Personal memories of 264 Test Matches seen from the commentary box". It is pure Johnston in its generosity and determination to enjoy the cricket as it comes. Players are relished and so is play. The cover illustration is a characteristically grinning portrait of the author against the background of play at Lord's.

*Coming of Age* (Stanley Paul; £14.99), by Eddie Hemmings, with Graham Otway, is a 148-page octavo autobiography of the Warwickshire, Nottinghamshire and England off-spinner. It is, as one would expect from its author, a straightforward, sensible account, with good cricket stories and much good advice for the ordinary cricketer.

*There's Life After Cheltenham* (The Coach House, Ponsonby, Seascale, Cumbria CA20 1BX; £4.95), by Nico Craven, is the author-publisher's 24th cricket booklet and, or so he claims, the last until Gloucestershire win the Championship. As usual, it is full of the pleasure he takes in Gloucestershire cricket.

*The Village Cricket Tour* (Chilton Designs; £9.95), by Vernon Coleman, is a 173-page octavo by an extremely prolific author, whose third cricket book

this is. It deals with the West Country tour of the fictitious Midland Parks Peripatetics team. It is true to type and the reader familiar with such a trip will recognise many of the situations and characters. "'To next year's tour,' said Arthur, draining his whisky flask. We all drank to that."

*The Guinness Book of Cricket Facts and Feats* (Guinness Publishing; £14.99), by Bill Frindall, is in its third edition and is characteristically thorough and orderly. Mr Frindall knows his cricket and how to use statistics; he has observed the game as well as the record book, and here colour illustrations, as well as black-and-white, strengthen his arm. Essentially, however, he is concerned with facts, their availability and reference.

*First-class Cricket: A Complete Record 1939* (Breedon Books; £14.95), edited by Jim Ledbetter, with Peter Wynne-Thomas, researched by the Association of Cricket Statisticians, is a nine-and-a-half-inch-square 255-page record book. It includes the 1939 first-class season in England, MCC in South Africa, 1938-39, and the first-class seasons in New Zealand, Australia, the West Indies and India, 1938-39, plus a thorough index. There is plenty of detail, some hitherto unpublished, with ample black-and-white photographic illustration, and while the editors do not intrude, they are sensitive in their provision of information. The team photographs are thorough, and a portrait of Wally Hammond is splendid. The publishers announce that this is the first in a series.

*Figures of Cricket* (Marine Sports; available from Sportspages, Caxton Walk, 94-96 Charing Cross Road, London WC2H 0JG; £9.95, plus £1.75 p. & p.), by Sudhir Vaidya, is a striking example of the type of cricket book India does so well. Painstaking in its detail, bound in boards, it consists of 424 pages of closely printed statistics, covering all the Test-playing countries in sections relating to batting, bowling, wicket-keeping, fielding, all-rounders, captains, teams, players' records, summaries of Tests, Test centres, and umpires. In every case it goes back as far as first-class records exist. It has little illustration, but it is well laid-out and, so far as can be ascertained, it is accurate. It has no elaboration except, some may feel, that it goes to the uttermost limit of records.

The County Yearbooks, notices of which follow, may be assumed to include the counties' match scores of the previous season for first and second elevens, chairmen's reports, and biographical notes on players. Only additions to that generalisation are mentioned.

*Derbyshire County Cricket Year Book 1991* (Derbyshire CCC; £3.50) has a survey by Kim Barnett, a Farewell by Gerald Mortimer, a poem by John Hollinshead, a profile of Guy Willatt, Cricket Ties of Derbyshire by William Powell, and other features by "An Old Supporter" and Ian Hall.

*Essex County Cricket Club 1991 Yearbook* (Essex CCC; £5) contains feature articles by Graham Gooch, Keith Fletcher, John Lever, Doug Insole, Trevor Bailey, Godfrey Evans, Derek Randall, David Acfield, Frank Keating and Peter Smith. It is a 288-page octavo, paper bound.

*Glamorgan County Cricket Club 1991 Yearbook* (Glamorgan CCC; £4), a 160-page octavo, has contributions by Tony Lewis, Alan Butcher, Brian Murgatroyd, Graham Clutton, Matthew Engel and Mike Fatkin.

*Hampshire Yearbook 1991* (Hampshire CCC; £4.50) is a 200-page octavo, with pieces by John Hughes, Patrick Symes, David Foot and Alan Edwards, as well as a poem by Imogen Grosberg.

produced by The Association of Cricket Statisticians and Scorers of India. It runs to 486 pages, in which can be found full scores of first-class matches in India, international tours and tournaments, and of some domestic limited-overs competitions. There is a useful Who's Who incorporating the season's first-class averages, statistical notes and highlights, and a record section for Indian cricket. The Cricketer of the Year is Sachin Tendulkar, and there are articles on J. G. Greig, a pioneer of Indian cricket, and Indians in English county and university cricket.

*Spin Punch* (Rupa; available from Turbomaster Ltd, 22 Repton Road, Kenton, Middlesex HA3 9QD; £8.95, plus £1.50 p. & p.), by Dilip Doshi, is the autobiography of that Indian left-arm spinner who made his Test début when he was 31 and was discarded at 35. In that time, as Sir Garfield Sobers writes in his foreword, "he took 114 wickets in his 33 Tests and it should be remembered that he, then, carried the Indian spin attack almost on his own". Doshi also took 101 wickets in 1980 for Warwickshire, for whom he had two seasons after six with Nottinghamshire. He is a thoughtful man, a quality often found in spin bowlers and regarded with suspicion by administrators and selectors; given his dealings with them, there must have been times when he wondered if it was worth continuing. Yet, as his writing reveals, he has never ceased to love and enjoy cricket.

*First-Class Cricket in Australia: Vol. 1 1850-51 to 1941-42* (published by and available from Ray Webster, PO Box 1074, Glen Waverley, Victoria 3150, Australia; $A80, plus $A10 p. & p.), compiled by Ray Webster and edited by Allan Miller, is limited to 1,500 numbered and signed editions and is the culmination of 25 years of studious part-time research by Mr Webster. It is the first of a planned three-volume series covering all first-class cricket in Australia. But more than that, it sets a standard for all record books of this kind to follow. One sees in it Mr Miller's intellectual approach to recording cricket, as well as Mr Webster's industry, for instead of providing the obvious, this 1,068-page volume presents what is required. So, in addition to the full scores of 964 first-class games, the reader is also given second-innings batting and bowling orders, débuts, the twelfth men, close of play scores, attendances and receipts, and a report of each match providing relevant statistical and historical details. To cap it all, an Index of Players gives full biographical details of every cricketer who appears in the preceding scorecards, including the number of the match or matches in which he appears. The whole is admirably produced, casebound in green cloth, with endpapers illustrated by oval portraits of 100 Australian cricketers of the time.

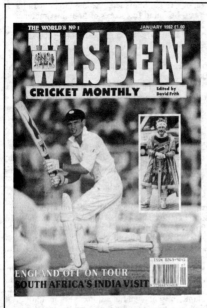

# FIXTURES, 1992

*\* Indicates Sunday play.*   *† Not first-class.*

*4d = Play over 4 days; where not indicated, first-class matches are of 3 days' duration.*

### Monday, April 13

| | |
|---|---|
| Lord's (4d) | England A v Essex |

### Tuesday, April 14

| | |
|---|---|
| Cambridge | Cambridge U. v Leics. |
| Oxford | Oxford U. v Durham |

### Friday, April 17

| | |
|---|---|
| Cambridge | Cambridge U. v Middx |
| Oxford | Oxford U. v Worcs. |

### Tuesday, April 21

#### †Benson and Hedges Cup (1 day)

| | |
|---|---|
| Durham | Durham v Glam. |
| Chelmsford | Essex v Lancs. |
| Cheltenham (Dowty Arle Court) | Glos. v Leics. |
| Canterbury | Kent v Somerset |
| Lord's | Middx v Minor Counties |
| Forfar | Scotland v Northants |
| Hove | Sussex v Surrey |
| Birmingham | Warwicks. v Yorks. |
| Worcester | Worcs. v Derbys. |
| | |
| Leeds (4d) | †Yorks. 2nd XI v England Under-19 |

### Thursday, April 23

#### †Benson and Hedges Cup (1 day)

| | |
|---|---|
| Oxford | Combined Universities v Worcs. |
| Derby | Derbys. v Glam. |
| Cheltenham (Dowty Arle Court) | Glos. v Minor Counties |
| Southampton | Hants v Essex |
| Manchester | Lancs. v Scotland |
| Leicester | Leics. v Sussex |
| Nottingham | Notts. v Kent |
| Taunton | Somerset v Yorks. |
| The Oval | Surrey v Middx |

### Saturday, April 25

| | |
|---|---|
| Durham (4d) | Durham v Leics. |
| Southampton (4d) | Hants v Sussex |
| Manchester* (4d) | Lancs. v Kent |
| Lord's (4d) | Middx v Glam. |
| Nottingham* (4d) | Notts. v Warwicks. |
| Taunton* (4d) | Somerset v Glos. |
| The Oval (4d) | Surrey v Yorks. |
| Worcester (4d) | Worcs. v Northants |
| Cambridge | Cambridge U. v Essex |

### Thursday, April 30

#### †Benson and Hedges Cup (1 day)

| | |
|---|---|
| Derby | Derbys. v Combined Universities |
| Chelmsford | Essex v Scotland |
| Southampton | Hants v Northants |
| Leicester | Leics. v Surrey |
| Lord's | Middx v Glos. |
| Marlow | Minor Counties v Sussex |
| Birmingham | Warwicks. v Notts. |
| Worcester | Worcs. v Durham |
| Leeds | Yorks. v Kent |

### Saturday, May 2

#### †Benson and Hedges Cup (1 day)

| | |
|---|---|
| Cambridge‡ | Combined Universities v Durham |
| Cardiff | Glam. v Worcs. |
| Manchester | Lancs. v Hants |
| Leicester | Leics. v Middx |
| Northampton | Northants v Essex |
| Taunton | Somerset v Warwicks. |
| The Oval‡ | Surrey v Minor Counties |
| Hove | Sussex v Glos. |
| Leeds | Yorks. v Notts. |

*‡ Reserve day, Sunday.*

### Sunday, May 3

| | |
|---|---|
| Arundel | †Lavinia, Duchess of Norfolk's XI v Pakistanis (1 day) |

### Monday, May 4

| | |
|---|---|
| Canterbury | †Kent v Pakistanis (1 day) |

## Tuesday, May 5

### †Benson and Hedges Cup (1 day)

| | |
|---|---|
| Jesmond | Durham v Derbys. |
| Cardiff | Glam. v Combined Universities |
| Glasgow (Hamilton Crescent) | Scotland v Hants |
| Canterbury | Kent v Warwicks. |
| Stone | Minor Counties v Leics. |
| Northampton | Northants v Lancs. |
| Nottingham | Notts. v Somerset |
| The Oval | Surrey v Glos. |
| Hove | Sussex v Middx |

## Wednesday, May 6

| | |
|---|---|
| Worcester | Worcestershire v Pakistanis |

## Thursday, May 7

| | |
|---|---|
| Chelmsford (4d) | Essex v Leics. |
| Canterbury (4d) | Kent v Durham |
| Lord's* (4d) | Middx v Lancs. |
| Northampton (4d) | Northants v Surrey |
| Hove (4d) | Sussex v Somerset |
| Birmingham (4d) | Warwicks. v Derbys. |
| Leeds (4d) | Yorks. v Hants |
| Oxford | Oxford U. v Notts. |

## Saturday, May 9

| | |
|---|---|
| Cardiff* | Glam. v Pakistanis |

## Tuesday, May 12

| | |
|---|---|
| Cambridge | Cambridge U. v Warwicks. |
| Oxford | Oxford U. v Middx |

## Wednesday, May 13

| | |
|---|---|
| Taunton | Somerset v Pakistanis |

## Thursday, May 14

| | |
|---|---|
| Derby (4d) | Derbys. v Worcs. |
| Chelmsford (4d) | Essex v Kent |
| Cardiff* (4d) | Glam. v Durham |
| Leicester (4d) | Leics. v Lancs. |
| Northampton (4d) | Northants v Notts. |
| Leeds* (4d) | Yorks. v Glos. |

## Friday, May 15

| | |
|---|---|
| Cambridge | Cambridge U. v Surrey |
| Oxford | Oxford U. v Hants |

## Saturday, May 16

| | |
|---|---|
| Hove | †Sussex v Pakistanis (1 day) |

## Sunday, May 17

| | |
|---|---|
| Hove | †Sussex v Pakistanis (1 day) |

## Tuesday, May 19

| | |
|---|---|
| Gloucester (4d) | Glos. v Worcs. |
| Southampton (4d) | Hants v Surrey |
| Leicester (4d) | Leics. v Middx |

## Wednesday, May 20

| | |
|---|---|
| Lord's | †ENGLAND v PAKISTAN (1st 1-day Texaco Trophy) |
| Swansea | Glam. v Warwicks. |
| Canterbury | Kent v Yorks. |
| Blackpool | Lancs. v Derbys. |
| Nottingham | Notts. v Sussex |
| Taunton | Somerset v Essex |

## Friday, May 22

| | |
|---|---|
| The Oval | †ENGLAND v PAKISTAN (2nd 1-day Texaco Trophy) |

## Saturday, May 23

| | |
|---|---|
| Leicester* | Leicestershire v Pakistanis |
| Derby | Derbys. v Notts. |
| Stockton-on-Tees | Durham v Northants |
| Gloucester | Glos. v Somerset |
| Manchester | Lancs. v Hants |
| Lord's | Middx v Surrey |
| Hove | Sussex v Kent |
| Birmingham | Warwicks. v Worcs. |

## Wednesday, May 27

### †Benson and Hedges Cup – Quarter-finals (1 day)

| | |
|---|---|
| Luton | England Amateur XI v Pakistanis (2 days) |

## Friday, May 29

| | |
|---|---|
| Swansea | Glam. v Leics. |
| Southampton | Hants v Durham |
| Manchester | Lancs. v Somerset |
| Northampton | Northants v Derbys. |
| The Oval | Surrey v Sussex |
| Worcester | Worcs. v Glos. |
| Oxford | Oxford U. v Yorks. |

**Saturday, May 30**

| | |
|---|---|
| Lord's* | Middx v Pakistanis |

**Tuesday, June 2**

| | |
|---|---|
| Darlington | Durham v Somerset |
| Chelmsford | Essex v Glam. |
| Basingstoke | Hants v Yorks. |
| Tunbridge Wells | Kent v Worcs. |
| Northampton | Northants v Leics. |
| Nottingham | Notts. v Middx |
| The Oval | Surrey v Derbys. |
| Hove | Sussex v Warwicks. |
| Oxford | Oxford U. v Lancs. |

**Thursday, June 4**

| | |
|---|---|
| Birmingham* | ENGLAND v PAKISTAN (1st Cornhill Test, 5 days) |

**Friday, June 5**

| | |
|---|---|
| Chesterfield | Derbys. v Durham |
| Tunbridge Wells | Kent v Essex |
| Manchester | Lancs. v Glos. |
| Lord's | Middx v Leics. |
| Middlesbrough | Yorks. v Somerset |

**Tuesday, June 9**

| | |
|---|---|
| Harrogate | †Tilcon Trophy (3 days) |

**Wednesday, June 10**

**†Benson and Hedges Cup – Semi-finals**
(1 day)

| | |
|---|---|
| Nottingham or Canterbury | Notts. or Kent v Pakistanis |

**Friday, June 12**

| | |
|---|---|
| Hartlepool | Durham v Essex |
| Colwyn Bay | Glam. v Lancs. |
| Leicester | Leics. v Sussex |
| The Oval | Surrey v Worcs. |
| Birmingham | Warwicks. v Hants |
| Harrogate | Yorks. v Derbys. |

**Saturday, June 13**

| | |
|---|---|
| Northampton* | Northants v Pakistanis |

**Tuesday, June 16**

| | |
|---|---|
| Bristol | Glos. v Kent |
| Leicester | Leics. v Hants |
| Nottingham | Notts. v Lancs. |
| Bath | Somerset v Northants |

| | |
|---|---|
| Coventry & North Warwicks | Warwicks. v Middx |
| Worcester | Worcs. v Glam. |
| Leeds | Yorks. v Essex |
| Cambridge | Cambridge U. v Derbys. |

**Thursday, June 18**

| | |
|---|---|
| Lord's* | ENGLAND v PAKISTAN (2nd Cornhill Test, 5 days) |

**Friday, June 19**

| | |
|---|---|
| Bristol | Glos. v Warwicks. |
| Bournemouth | Hants v Essex |
| Manchester | Lancs. v Middx |
| Nottingham | Notts. v Northants |
| Bath | Somerset v Surrey |
| Horsham | Sussex v Durham |
| Worcester | Worcs. v Yorks. |
| Cambridge* | Cambridge U. v Kent |
| Oxford | Oxford U. v Glam. |

**Saturday, June 20**

| | |
|---|---|
| Dundee (Broughty Ferry)* | Scotland v Ireland |

**Wednesday, June 24**

**†NatWest Bank Trophy – First Round**
(1 day)

| | |
|---|---|
| Beaconsfield | Bucks. v Sussex |
| Derby | Derbys. v Berks. |
| Chelmsford | Essex v Cumb. |
| Swansea | Glam. v Surrey |
| Bristol | Glos. v Cheshire |
| Southampton | Hants v Dorset |
| Dublin (Castle Avenue) | Ireland v Durham |
| Canterbury | Kent v Devon |
| Leicester | Leics. v Norfolk |
| Northampton | Northants v Cambs. |
| Nottingham | Notts. v Worcs. |
| Oxford (Christ Church) | Oxon. v Lancs. |
| Telford (St Georges) | Salop v Middx |
| Taunton | Somerset v Scotland |
| Birmingham | Warwicks. v Staffs. |
| Leeds | Yorks. v Northumb. |
| Cambridge | Oxford & Camb. Univs v Pakistanis |
| Lord's | †Eton v Harrow |

### Friday, June 26

| | |
|---|---|
| Derby | Derbys. v Warwicks. |
| Ilford | Essex v Lancs. |
| Bristol | Glos. v Surrey |
| Lord's | Middx v Somerset |
| Luton | Northants v Glam. |
| Worcester | Worcs. v Sussex |

### Saturday, June 27

| | |
|---|---|
| Southampton* | Hants v Pakistanis |
| Gateshead Fell* | Durham v Kent |
| Nottingham* | Notts. v Cambridge U. |

### Tuesday, June 30

| | |
|---|---|
| Derby | Derbys. v Glos. |
| Ilford | Essex v Middx |
| Maidstone | Kent v Notts. |
| Leicester | Leics. v Worcs. |
| The Oval | Surrey v Northants |
| Arundel | Sussex v Hants |
| Lord's | Oxford U. v Cambridge U. |

### Thursday, July 2

| | |
|---|---|
| Manchester | ENGLAND v PAKISTAN (3rd Cornhill Test, 5 days) |

### Friday, July 3

| | |
|---|---|
| Stockton-on-Tees | Durham v Glos. |
| Neath | Glam. v Surrey |
| Southampton | Hants v Notts. |
| Maidstone | Kent v Lancs. |
| Northampton | Northants v Sussex |
| Taunton | Somerset v Derbys. |
| Birmingham | Warwicks. v Essex |
| Sheffield | Yorks. v Leics. |

### Thursday, July 9

†NatWest Bank Trophy – Second Round
(1 day)

| | |
|---|---|
| Derby or Finchampstead | Derbys. or Berks. v Leics. or Norfolk |
| Chelmsford or Netherfield | Essex or Cumb. v Oxon. or Lancs. |
| Southampton or Bournemouth | Hants or Dorset v Kent or Devon |
| Northampton or March | Northants or Cambs. v Yorks. or Northumb. |
| Nottingham or Worcester | Notts. or Worcs. v Glam. or Surrey |
| Telford (St Georges) or Uxbridge | Salop or Middx v Ireland or Durham |

| | |
|---|---|
| Taunton or Glasgow (Hamilton Crescent) | Somerset or Scotland v Glos. or Cheshire |
| Birmingham or Stone | Warwicks. or Staffs. v Bucks. or Sussex |
| Haslingden | †League Cricket Conference v Pakistanis (1 day) |

### Friday, July 10

| | |
|---|---|
| Oxford | †MCC Schools Festival (4 days) |

### Saturday, July 11

| | |
|---|---|
| Lord's | †BENSON AND HEDGES CUP FINAL (1 day) |
| Glasgow (Titwood) | †Scotland v Pakistanis (1 day) |

### Sunday, July 12

| | |
|---|---|
| Glasgow (Titwood) | †Scotland v Pakistanis (1 day) |

### Tuesday, July 14

| | |
|---|---|
| Chester-le-Street | Durham v Pakistanis |
| Southend | Essex v Glos. |
| Portsmouth | Hants v Derbys. |
| Southport | Lancs. v Leics. |
| Uxbridge | Middx v Northants |
| Nottingham | Notts. v Worcs. |
| Guildford | Surrey v Kent |
| Sheffield | Yorks. v Warwicks. |
| Lord's | †MCC v MCC Schools (1 day) |

### Wednesday, July 15

| | |
|---|---|
| Lord's | †MCC Schools v NAYC (1 day) |

### Thursday, July 16

| | |
|---|---|
| Lord's | †NCA Young Cricketers v Combined Services (1 day) |

### Friday, July 17

| | |
|---|---|
| Southend | Essex v Sussex |
| Cheltenham Coll. | Glos. v Yorks. |
| Portsmouth | Hants v Glam. |
| Leicester | Leics. v Somerset |
| Uxbridge | Middx v Worcs. |
| Northampton | Northants v Lancs. |
| Nottingham | Notts. v Durham |
| Guildford | Surrey v Warwicks. |

### Saturday, July 18

| | |
|---|---|
| Derby* | Derbys. v Pakistanis |

### Monday, July 20

| | |
|---|---|
| Lord's | †MCC v Scotland |

### Tuesday, July 21

| | |
|---|---|
| Derby | Derbys. v Middx |
| Cardiff | Glam. v Yorks. |
| Cheltenham Coll. | Glos. v Hants |
| Canterbury | Kent v Somerset |
| Leicester | Leics. v Durham |
| Northampton | Northants v Warwicks. |
| The Oval | Surrey v Notts. |
| Hove | Sussex v Lancs. |
| Kidderminster | Worcs. v Essex |

### Thursday, July 23

| | |
|---|---|
| Leeds* | ENGLAND v PAKISTAN (4th Cornhill Test, 5 days) |

### Friday, July 24

| | |
|---|---|
| Abergavenny | Glam. v Somerset |
| Cheltenham Coll. | Glos. v Sussex |
| Leicester | Leics. v Essex |
| Lord's | Middx v Durham |
| Birmingham | Warwicks. v Notts. |
| Worcester | Worcs. v Derbys. |

### Wednesday, July 29

**†NatWest Bank Trophy – Quarter-finals (1 day)**

| | |
|---|---|
| Marlow | †Minor Counties v Pakistanis (2 days) |
| Jesmond | †England XI v Rest of the World XI (1 day) |

### Thursday, July 30

| | |
|---|---|
| Jesmond | †England XI v Rest of the World XI (1 day) |

### Friday, July 31

| | |
|---|---|
| Durham | Durham v Surrey |
| Swansea | Glam. v Kent |
| Taunton* | Somerset v Sussex |
| Birmingham | Warwicks. v Leics. |
| Leeds | Yorks. v Lancs. |

### Saturday, August 1

| | |
|---|---|
| Chelmsford* | Essex v Pakistanis |

### Tuesday, August 4

| | |
|---|---|
| Ilkeston | Derbys. v Leics. |
| Durham | Durham v Yorks. |
| Chelmsford | Essex v Northants |
| Canterbury | Kent v Middx |
| Lytham | Lancs. v Surrey |
| Worksop | Notts. v Glos. |
| Taunton | Somerset v Warwicks. |
| Eastbourne | Sussex v Glam. |
| Worcester | Worcs. v Hants |

### Thursday, August 6

| | |
|---|---|
| The Oval* | ENGLAND v PAKISTAN (5th Cornhill Test, 5 days) |

### Friday, August 7

| | |
|---|---|
| Canterbury | Kent v Hants |
| Manchester | Lancs. v Worcs. |
| Lord's | Middx v Glos. |
| Northampton | Northants v Yorks. |
| Nottingham | Notts. v Glam. |
| Eastbourne | Sussex v Derbys. |
| Birmingham | Warwicks. v Durham |

### Monday, August 10

†Bain Clarkson Trophy Semi-finals (1 day)

### Tuesday, August 11

†Bain Clarkson Trophy Semi-finals (1 day) (if not played on August 10)

### Wednesday, August 12

**†NatWest Bank Trophy – Semi-finals (1 day)**

| | |
|---|---|
| Birmingham‡ | †Warwicks. v Pakistanis (1 day) |

### Thursday, August 13

| | |
|---|---|
| Birmingham‡ | †Warwicks. v Pakistanis (1 day) |

‡ *Or another first-class county if Warwicks. in NWB Trophy semi-finals.*

### Friday, August 14

| | |
|---|---|
| Chesterfield | Derbys. v Kent |
| Hartlepool | Durham v Glam. |
| Colchester | Essex v Notts. |
| Bournemouth | Hants v Northants |
| Uxbridge | Middx v Yorks. |
| The Oval | Surrey v Leics. |
| Leeds* | †England Under-19 v Sri Lanka Under-19 (1st "Test") (4 days) |

### Saturday, August 15

| | |
|---|---|
| Bristol* | Glos. v Pakistanis |

### Tuesday, August 18

| | |
|---|---|
| Chesterfield | Derbys. v Glam. |
| Colchester | Essex v Surrey |
| Bristol | Glos. v Northants |
| Bournemouth | Hants v Middx |
| Leicester | Leics. v Kent |
| Weston-super-Mare | Somerset v Worcs. |
| Birmingham | Warwicks. v Lancs. |
| Scarborough | Yorks. v Notts. |

### Thursday, August 20

| | |
|---|---|
| Nottingham | †ENGLAND v PAKISTAN (3rd 1-day Texaco Trophy) |

### Friday, August 21

| | |
|---|---|
| Swansea | Glam. v Glos. |
| Leicester | Leics. v Notts. |
| Northampton | Northants v Kent |
| Weston-super-Mare | Somerset v Hants |
| Hove | Sussex v Middx |
| Worcester | Worcs. v Durham |
| Bradford | Yorks. v Surrey |

### Saturday, August 22

| | |
|---|---|
| Lord's | †ENGLAND v PAKISTAN (4th 1-day Texaco Trophy) |

### Monday, August 24

| | |
|---|---|
| Manchester | †ENGLAND v PAKISTAN (5th 1-day Texaco Trophy) |

### Tuesday, August 25

| | |
|---|---|
| Taunton | †England Under-19 v Sri Lanka Under-19 (2nd "Test") (4 days) |

### Wednesday, August 26

| | |
|---|---|
| Scarborough | World XI v Pakistanis |
| Derby (4d) | Derbys. v Somerset |
| Darlington (4d) | Durham v Hants |
| Canterbury (4d) | Kent v Glos. |
| Manchester (4d) | Lancs. v Yorks. |
| Northampton (4d) | Northants v Middx |
| Hove (4d) | Sussex v Essex |
| Birmingham (4d) | Warwicks. v Glam. |
| Worcester (4d) | Worcs. v Notts. |
| Lord's | †Minor Counties Knockout Final (1 day) |

### Saturday, August 29

| | |
|---|---|
| Lord's | †National Club Championship Final |
| Scarborough | †World XI v Eastern Province (1 day) |

### Sunday, August 30

| | |
|---|---|
| Lord's | †National Village Championship Final |
| Scarborough | †World XI v Eastern Province (1 day) |

### Monday, August 31

| | |
|---|---|
| Chelmsford (4d) | Essex v Hants |
| Cardiff (4d) | Glam. v Sussex |
| Bristol (4d) | Glos. v Leics. |
| Nottingham (4d) | Notts. v Derbys. |
| The Oval (4d) | Surrey v Somerset |
| Worcester (4d) | Worcs. v Warwicks. |
| Scarborough (4d) | Yorks. v Northants |

### Friday, September 4

| | |
|---|---|
| Scarborough | †Joshua Tetley Festival Trophy (3 days) |

### Saturday, September 5

| | |
|---|---|
| Lord's | †NATWEST BANK TROPHY FINAL (1 day) |

### Monday, September 7

| | |
|---|---|
| Derby (4d) | Derbys. v Essex |
| Canterbury (4d) | Kent v Glam. |
| Manchester (4d) | Lancs. v Sussex |
| Nottingham (4d) | Notts. v Surrey |
| Taunton (4d) | Somerset v Durham |

*Matches involving NWB Trophy finalists to be played on September 8-11.*

| | |
|---|---|
| Worcester | England Under-19 v Sri Lanka Under-19 (3rd "Test") (4 days) |

†Bain Clarkson Trophy Final (1 day)

### Tuesday, September 8

| | |
|---|---|
| Lord's (4d) | Middx v Warwicks. |

### Saturday, September 12

| | |
|---|---|
| Gateshead Fell* (4d) | Durham v Lancs. |
| Cardiff* (4d) | Glam. v Derbys. |
| Bristol* (4d) | Glos. v Essex |
| Southampton* (4d) | Hants v Worcs. |
| Leicester* (4d) | Leics. v Northants |
| Taunton* (4d) | Somerset v Notts. |
| The Oval* (4d) | Surrey v Middx |
| Hove* (4d) | Sussex v Yorks. |
| Birmingham* (4d) | Warwicks. v Kent |

## PAKISTANI TOUR, 1992

### MAY

| | | |
|---|---|---|
| 3 | Arundel | †v Lavinia, Duchess of Norfolk's XI (1 day) |
| 4 | Canterbury | †v Kent (1 day) |
| 6 | Worcester | v Worcs. |
| 9 | Cardiff* | v Glam. |
| 13 | Taunton | v Somerset |
| 16 | Hove | †v Sussex (1 day) |
| 17 | Hove | †v Sussex (1 day) |
| 20 | Lord's | †v ENGLAND (1st 1-day Texaco Trophy) |
| 22 | The Oval | †v ENGLAND (2nd 1-day Texaco Trophy) |
| 23 | Leicester* | v Leics. |
| 27 | Luton | †v England Amateur XI (2 days) |
| 30 | Lord's* | v Middx |

### JUNE

| | | |
|---|---|---|
| 4 | Birmingham* | v ENGLAND (1st Cornhill Test, 5 days) |
| 10 | Nottingham or Canterbury | v Notts. or Kent |
| 13 | Northampton* | v Northants |
| 18 | Lord's* | v ENGLAND (2nd Cornhill Test, 5 days) |
| 24 | Cambridge | v Oxford & Camb. Univs |
| 27 | Southampton* | v Hants |

### JULY

| | | |
|---|---|---|
| 2 | Manchester | v ENGLAND (3rd Cornhill Test, 5 days) |
| 9 | Haslingden | †v League Cricket Conference (1 day) |
| 11 | Glasgow (Titwood) | †v Scotland (1 day) |
| 12 | Glasgow (Titwood) | †v Scotland (1 day) |
| 14 | Chester-le-Street | v Durham |
| 18 | Derby* | v Derbys. |
| 23 | Leeds* | v ENGLAND (4th Cornhill Test, 5 days) |
| 29 | Marlow | †v Minor Counties (2 days) |

### AUGUST

| | | |
|---|---|---|
| 1 | Chelmsford* | v Essex |
| 6 | The Oval* | v ENGLAND (5th Cornhill Test, 5 days) |
| 12 | Birmingham‡ | †v Warwicks. (1 day) |
| 13 | Birmingham‡ | †v Warwicks. (1 day) |

‡ *Or another first-class county if Warwicks. in NWB Trophy semi-finals.*

| | | |
|---|---|---|
| 15 | Bristol* | v Glos. |
| 20 | Nottingham | †v ENGLAND (3rd 1-day Texaco Trophy) |
| 22 | Lord's | †v ENGLAND (4th 1-day Texaco Trophy) |
| 24 | Manchester | †v ENGLAND (5th 1-day Texaco Trophy) |
| 26 | Scarborough | v World XI |

## †SUNDAY LEAGUE, 1992

### APRIL

19–Derbys. v Essex (Derby); Durham v Lancs. (Durham); Hants v Glos. (Southampton); Kent v Somerset (Canterbury); Leics. v Middx (Leicester); Notts. v Sussex (Nottingham); Surrey v Northants (The Oval); Warwicks. v Glam. (Birmingham); Worcs. v Yorks. (Worcester).

26–Durham v Leics. (Gateshead Fell); Essex v Surrey (Chelmsford); Middx v Glam. (Lord's); Sussex v Yorks. (Hove); Worcs. v Northants (Worcester).

### MAY

3–Glam. v Worcs. (Cardiff); Lancs. v Hants (Manchester); Leics. v Essex (Leicester); Middx v Glos. (Lord's); Northants v Kent (Northampton); Somerset v Warwicks. (Taunton); Yorks. v Notts. (Leeds).

10–Derbys. v Glos. (Derby); Essex v Northants (Chelmsford); Kent v Durham (Canterbury); Notts. v Surrey (Nottingham); Sussex v Somerset (Hove); Worcs. v Warwicks. (Worcester).

17–Derbys. v Worcs. (Derby); Northants v Lancs. (Northampton); Notts. v Middx (Nottingham); Somerset v Hants (Taunton); Surrey v Kent (The Oval); Warwicks. v Leics. (Birmingham).

24–Derbys. v Notts. (Derby); Durham v Northants (Stockton-on-Tees); Essex v Glam. (Chelmsford); Glos. v Somerset (Gloucester); Kent v Sussex (Canterbury); Surrey v Sussex (The Oval); Warwicks. v Lancs. (Birmingham); Yorks. v Hants (Leeds).

31–Glam. v Leics. (Swansea); Hants v Durham (Southampton); Kent v Yorks. (Canterbury); Lancs. v Somerset (Manchester); Northants v Derbys. (Northampton); Notts. v Glos. (Nottingham); Sussex v Warwicks. (Hove); Worcs. v Essex (Worcester).

## JUNE

7–Derbys. v Durham (Chesterfield); Essex v Kent (Chelmsford); Hants v Surrey (Basingstoke); Lancs. v Glos. (Manchester); Middx v Warwicks. (Lord's); Sussex v Glam. (Hove); Yorks. v Somerset (Middlesbrough).

14–Durham v Essex (Hartlepool); Glam. v Lancs. (Colwyn Bay); Glos. v Kent (Swindon); Leics. v Sussex (Leicester); Somerset v Notts. (Bath); Surrey v Worcs. (The Oval); Warwicks. v Hants (Birmingham); Yorks. v Derbys. (Leeds).

21–Derbys. v Middx (Derby); Glam. v Yorks. (Ebbw Vale); Glos. v Warwicks. (Bristol); Hants v Essex (Bournemouth); Lancs. v Leics. (Manchester); Notts. v Northants (Nottingham); Somerset v Surrey (Bath); Sussex v Durham (Horsham).

28–Derbys. v Leics. (Derby); Essex v Lancs. (Ilford); Glos. v Surrey (Bristol); Middx v Somerset (Lord's); Northants v Glam. (Luton); Worcs. v Sussex (Worcester); Yorks. v Warwicks. (Scarborough).

## JULY

5–Durham v Glos. (Stockton-on-Tees); Glam. v Surrey (Llanelli); Hants v Notts. (Southampton); Kent v Lancs. (Maidstone); Middx v Worcs. (Lord's); Northants v Sussex (Tring); Somerset v Derbys. (Taunton); Warwicks. v Essex (Birmingham); Yorks. v Leics. (Sheffield).

12–Glos. v Northants (Moreton-in-Marsh); Kent v Notts. (Canterbury); Lancs. v Middx (Manchester); Leics. v Worcs.

(Leicester); Somerset v Durham (Taunton); Surrey v Derbys. (The Oval); Sussex v Hants (Hove); Yorks. v Essex (Scarborough). *Note: Matches involving the Benson and Hedges Cup finalists to be rearranged.*

19–Essex v Sussex (Southend); Glos. v Yorks. (Cheltenham Coll.); Hants v Glam. (Portsmouth); Kent v Worcs. (Canterbury); Leics. v Somerset (Leicester); Northants v Middx (Northampton); Notts. v Durham (Nottingham); Surrey v Warwicks. (The Oval).

26–Glam. v Derbys. (Pontypridd); Glos. v Sussex (Cheltenham Coll.); Lancs. v Surrey (Manchester); Leics. v Kent (Leicester); Middx v Durham (Lord's); Somerset v Northants (Taunton); Warwicks. v Notts. (Birmingham); Worcs. v Hants (Worcester).

## AUGUST

2–Derbys. v Warwicks. (Leek); Durham v Surrey (Durham); Glam. v Kent (Swansea); Hants v Middx (Southampton); Notts. v Leics. (Nottingham); Worcs. v Glos. (Worcester); Yorks. v Lancs. (Leeds).

9–Glos. v Leics. (Bristol); Kent v Hants (Canterbury); Lancs. v Worcs. (Manchester); Middx v Essex (Lord's); Northants v Yorks. (Northampton); Notts. v Glam. (Nottingham); Sussex v Derbys. (Eastbourne); Warwicks. v Durham (Birmingham).

16–Derbys. v Kent (Chesterfield); Durham v Glam. (Hartlepool); Essex v Notts. (Colchester); Hants v Northants (Bournemouth); Middx v Yorks. (Uxbridge); Somerset v Worcs. (Taunton); Surrey v Leics. (The Oval); Sussex v Lancs. (Hove).

23–Glos. v Glam. (Bristol or Lydney); Hants v Derbys. (Southampton); Leics. v Northants (Leicester); Notts. v Lancs. (Nottingham); Somerset v Essex (Weston-super-Mare); Sussex v Middx (Hove); Warwicks. v Kent (Birmingham); Worcs. v Durham (Worcester); Yorks. v Surrey (Scarborough).

30–Durham v Yorks. (Darlington); Essex v Glos. (Chelmsford); Glam. v Somerset (Cardiff); Kent v Sussex (Canterbury); Lancs. v Derbys. (Manchester); Leics. v Hants (Leicester); Northants v Warwicks. (Northampton); Surrey v Middx (The Oval); Worcs. v Notts. (Worcester).

# †RAPID CRICKETLINE SECOND ELEVEN CHAMPIONSHIP, 1992

*All matches are of three days' duration.*

## APRIL

**21**–Lancs. v Derbys. (Liverpool); Somerset v Kent (King's College, Taunton).

**27**–Hants v Somerset (Portsmouth); Kent v Lancs. (Canterbury); Leics. v Durham (Leicester); Sussex v Worcs. (Hove); Yorks. v Surrey (Leeds).

**28**–Derbys. v Glos. (Shipley Hall, Ilkeston).

## MAY

**5**–Glos. v Somerset (Bristol); Middx v Yorks. (Uxbridge).

**6**–Durham v Sussex (Sunderland); Leics. v Lancs. (Leicester); Warwicks. v Derbys. (Knowle & Dorridge).

**11**–Essex v Notts. (Colchester).

**12**–Lancs. v Yorks. (Manchester); Middx v Kent (Harrow); Surrey v Durham (The Oval); Sussex v Derbys. (Horsham); Worcs. v Hants (Old Hill CC).

**13**–Somerset v Northants (North Perrott).

**19**–Durham v Derbys. (Felling); Glos. v Leics. (Dowty Arle Court, Cheltenham); Yorks. v Notts. (Harrogate).

**20**–Essex v Kent (Chelmsford); Hants v Warwicks. (Bournemouth); Lancs. v Middx (Manchester); Northants v Glam. (Northampton); Worcs. v Surrey (Worcester).

**26**–Hants v Sussex (Bournemouth); Leics. v Somerset (Kibworth); Northants v Warwicks. (Oundle School); Notts. v Lancs. (Worthington Simpson); Yorks. v Glos. (Todmorden).

**27**–Durham v Essex (Boldon); Kent v Glam. (Maidstone); Middx v Surrey (Uxbridge).

## JUNE

**2**–Glam. v Essex (Ammanford); Glos. v Lancs. (Bristol); Kent v Surrey (Canterbury); Leics. v Derbys. (Loughborough GS); Notts. v Durham (Steetley, Shireoaks); Warwicks. v Sussex (Stratford-upon-Avon); Yorks. v Hants (York).

**3**–Northants v Middx (Oundle School).

**9**–Durham v Lancs. (Chester-le-Street); Glam. v Middx (Abergavenny); Kent v Glos. (Sittingbourne); Northants v Leics. (Old Northamptonians CC); Somerset v Derbys. (Glastonbury); Surrey v Sussex (Banstead); Warwicks. v Essex (Griff & Coton, Nuneaton); Worcs. v Notts. (Barnt Green).

**16**–Essex v Yorks. (Southend); Glam. v Derbys. (Cardiff); Kent v Leics. (Dartford); Lancs. v Worcs. (Manchester); Middx v Warwicks. (RAF Vine Lane, Uxbridge); Northants v Durham (Northampton); Somerset v Surrey (Taunton); Sussex v Notts. (Hastings).

**23**–Derbys. v Kent (Abbotsholme School, Rocester); Durham v Warwicks. (Shildon); Essex v Hants (Leigh-on-Sea); Glam. v Surrey (Pontarddulais); Middx v Worcs. (Harrow); Yorks. v Leics. (Park Avenue, Bradford).

**24**–Notts. v Northants (Worksop CC); Surrey v Glos. (The Oval).

**30**–Durham v Somerset (Eppleton); Hants v Glam. (Bournemouth); Middx v Derbys. (Southgate); Northants v Lancs. (Oundle School); Notts. v Glos. (Nottingham); Sussex v Essex (Hove); Warwicks. v Kent (Studley); Worcs. v Yorks. (Worcester).

## JULY

**6**–Leics. v Warwicks. (Oakham).

**7**–Derbys. v Yorks. (Chesterfield); Glos. v Hants (Bristol); Lancs. v Somerset (Northern CC, Crosby); Surrey v Notts. (The Oval); Sussex v Kent (Hove); Worcs. v Northants (Kidderminster).

**14**–Glam. v Somerset (Ebbw Vale); Kent v Durham (Maidstone); Leics. v Middx (Hinckley); Northants v Sussex (Bedford School); Notts. v Hants (Collingham); Warwicks. v Yorks. (Leamington Spa); Worcs. v Glos. (Worcester).

**21**–Durham v Middx (Seaton Carew); Essex v Glos. (Chelmsford); Northants v Hants (Wellingborough School); Notts. v Glam. (Worksop College); Warwicks. v Surrey (Mitchells & Butlers); Worcs. v Kent (Flagge Meadow, Worcester).

**28**–Derbys. v Worcs. (Belper Meadow); Essex v Surrey (Southend); Glam. v Leics. (Cardiff); Glos. v Middx (Kings School, Gloucester); Kent v Hants (Folkestone); Lancs. v Sussex (Liverpool); Somerset v Notts. (Clevedon); Yorks. v Northants (Marske-by-Sea).

## AUGUST

**4**–Derbys. v Surrey (Derby); Glos. v Glam. (Bristol); Hants v Durham (Southampton); Lancs. v Essex (Manchester); Leics. v Worcs. (Leicester); Middx v Somerset (Southgate); Notts. v Warwicks. (Nottingham); Sussex v Yorks. (Hove).

**12**–Derbys. v Notts. (Shipley Hall, Ilkeston); Middx v Essex (Enfield); Surrey v Northants (Guildford); Warwicks. v Somerset (Walmley); Worcs. v Glam. (Halesowen); Yorks. v Kent (Elland).

**17**–Northants v Glos. (Northampton).

**18**–Derbys. v Essex (Heanor); Durham v Yorks. (Boldon); Hants v Middx (Southampton); Lancs. v Warwicks. (Blackpool); Leics. v Sussex (Market Harborough); Somerset v Worcs. (Taunton); Surrey v Glam. (The Oval).

**22**–Glam. v Durham (BP Llandarcy); Hants v Leics. (Bournemouth).

**25**–Glos. v Durham (Dowty Arle Court, Cheltenham); Kent v Northants (Folkestone); Surrey v Leics. (The Oval).

**26**–Essex v Worcs. (Colchester); Glam. v Warwicks. (Usk); Hants v Lancs. (Southampton); Notts. v Middx (Nottingham); Sussex v Somerset (Eastbourne).

## SEPTEMBER

**1**–Derbys. v Northants (Chesterfield); Glam. v Lancs. (Pontymister); Glos. v Sussex (Cheltenham Town CC); Kent v Notts. (Canterbury); Leics. v Essex (Leicester); Somerset v Yorks. (Taunton); Surrey v Hants (Guildford).

**2**–Warwicks. v Worcs. (Moseley).

**9**–Durham v Worcs. (Seaton Carew); Essex v Northants (Chelmsford); Glos. v Warwicks. (Bristol); Hants v Derbys. (Southampton); Notts. v Leics. (Steetley, Shireoaks); Surrey v Lancs. (The Oval); Sussex v Middx (Horsham); Yorks. v Glam. (Park Avenue, Bradford).

**16**–Somerset v Essex (Taunton).

# †BAIN CLARKSON TROPHY, 1992

*All matches are of one day's duration.*

## APRIL

**20**–Lancs. v Derbys. (Manchester).

**24**–MCC Young Cricketers v Middx (Birkbeck College, Greenford).

**30**–Kent v Middx (Canterbury); Leics. v Durham (Uppingham School).

## MAY

**1**–Derbys. v Durham (Chesterfield); Glos. v Worcs. (Bristol); Kent v MCC Young Cricketers (Canterbury); Yorks. v Lancs. (Bingley).

**4**–Durham v Notts (Norton CC); Glos. v Somerset (Bristol); Sussex v Middx (Hove).

**5**–Derbys. v Notts. (Chesterfield); Leics. v Lancs. (Leicester).

**8**–Somerset v Hants (Taunton); Surrey v Kent (The Oval).

**11**–Derbys. v Leics. (Chesterfield); Glos. v Warwicks. (Bristol); Lancs. v Yorks. (Manchester); Surrey v Middx (The Oval); Worcs. v Hants (Worcester).

**12**–Glos. v Glam. (Bristol); Leics. v Northants (Leicester).

**14**–Notts. v Leics. (Nottingham).

**15**–Middx v Kent (Harrow).

**18**–Essex v Middx (Wickford); Glam. v Glos. (Bridgend); MCC Young Cricketers v Sussex (Norbury); Worcs. v Somerset (Worcester); Yorks. v Notts. (Bingley).

**19**–Essex v Kent (Chelmsford); Hants v Warwicks. (Bournemouth).

**22**–Durham v Derbys. (Philadelphia CC).

**25**–Notts. v Lancs. (Nottingham); Yorks. v Derbys. (Bawtry Road, Sheffield).

**26**–Middx v Surrey (Ealing).

**29**–Leics. v Notts. (Leicester); Warwicks. v Somerset (Solihull).

## JUNE

**1**–Kent v Surrey (Canterbury); Lancs. v Northants (Wigan); Leics. v Derbys. (Leicester); Middx v Sussex (RAF Vine Lane, Uxbridge); Notts. v Durham (Farnsfield); Somerset v Glos. (Taunton).

**5**–Somerset v Glam. (Winscombe); Surrey v MCC Young Cricketers (The Oval); Worcs. v Warwicks. (Worcester).

**8**–Hants v Somerset (Southampton); Lancs. v Notts. (Lancaster); Surrey v Sussex (The Oval); Yorks. v Durham (Abbeydale Park, Sheffield).

**12**–Durham v Lancs. (Bishop Auckland); Sussex v MCC Young Cricketers (Eastbourne); Warwicks. v Glos. (Old Edwardians).

**15**–Hants v Glos. (Southampton); Kent v Essex (Maidstone); Middx v MCC Young Cricketers (Uxbridge); Notts. v Yorks. (Worksop College).

**19**–Derbys. v Lancs. (Checkley); Northants v Durham (Northampton); Warwicks. v Worcs. (Birmingham).

**21**–Worcs. v Glos. (Worcester).

**22**–Notts. v Derbys. (Worthington Simpson); Surrey v Essex (The Oval); Yorks. v Leics. (Park Avenue, Bradford).

**26**–Durham v Leics. (Durham City CC); Glam. v Somerset (Panteg); Hants v Worcs. (Bournemouth).

**29**–Leics. v Yorks. (Leicester); Northants v Lancs. (Northampton); Sussex v Essex (Hove).

### JULY

**3**–Derbys. v Northants (Knypersley); Hants v Glam. (Bournemouth); MCC Young Cricketers v Surrey (Norbury).

**6**–Derbys. v Yorks. (Chesterfield); MCC Young Cricketers v Kent (Norbury); Notts. v Northants (Nottingham); Sussex v Surrey (Hove); Worcs. v Glam. (Worcester).

**9**–MCC Young Cricketers v Essex (Birkbeck College, Greenford).

**10**–Glam. v Warwicks. (Cardiff); Glos. v Hants (Bristol); Middx v Essex (Harrow); Sussex v Kent (Lewes Priory).

**13**–Essex v Sussex (Newbury Park); Glam. v Hants (Cardiff); Northants v Leics. (Northampton).

**17**–Kent v Sussex (Maidstone); Northants v Yorks. (Bedford Modern School); Somerset v Warwicks. (Taunton).

**20**–Durham v Yorks. (Durham School); Essex v MCC Young Cricketers (Newbury Park); Lancs. v Leics. (Manchester); Northants v Notts. (Banbury); Warwicks. v Glam. (Birmingham).

**24**–Northants v Derbys. (Northampton); Somerset v Worcs. (Taunton); Warwicks. v Hants (Coventry & North Warwicks.).

**27**–Durham v Northants (Durham School); Essex v Surrey (Southend); Glam. v Worcs. (Swansea).

**31**–Lancs. v Durham (Northern CC, Crosby); Yorks. v Northants (Marske-by-Sea).

**Semi-finals** to be played on August 10 or August 11.

**Final** to be played on September 7 (reserve day September 8).

## †MINOR COUNTIES CHAMPIONSHIP, 1992

*All matches are of two days' duration.*

### MAY

**24**–Berks. v Oxon. (Falkland CC, Newbury); Herefords. v Wales (Brockhampton CC); Lincs. v Beds. (Sleaford).

**25**–Dorset v Salop (Sherborne School).

**26**–Cumb. v Suffolk (Carlisle).

**28**–Staffs. v Suffolk (Meir Heath).

### JUNE

**3**–Cambs. v Staffs. (March).

**7**–Beds. v Norfolk (Bedford School); Berks. v Herefords. (Kidmore End CC); Oxon. v Wales (Pressed Steel, Oxford); Salop v Wilts. (St Georges, Telford); Herts. v Bucks. (St Albans); Lincs. v Northumb. (Burghley Park).

**8**–Cornwall v Cheshire (Redruth).

**10**–Cambs. v Suffolk (Wisbech); Devon v Cheshire (Torquay).

**16**–Northumb. v Herts. (Jesmond); Staffs. v Bucks. (Brewood).

**18**–Cumb. v Herts. (Millom).

21—Beds. v Northumb. (Henlow); Cheshire v Wales (Neston); Cornwall v Devon (Camborne); Lincs. v Cambs. (Bourne); Salop v Herefords. (Shrewsbury); Wilts. v Oxon. (BR Swindon).

28—Herefords. v Devon (Hereford City SC); Wilts. v Berks. (Trowbridge).

*Unless either side is playing in the Holt Cup semi-finals.*

29—Cumb. v Norfolk (Penrith).

## JULY

1—Staffs. v Norfolk (Norton).

5—Cornwall v Wilts. (Truro); Devon v Dorset (Sidmouth); Herts. v Lincs. (Stevenage); Northumb. v Bucks. (Jesmond); Wales v Salop (Colwyn Bay).

7—Cumb. v Bucks. (Barrow).

12—Cheshire v Salop (Warrington); Herefords. v Dorset (Brockhampton).

13—Northumb. v Staffs. (Ashington).

15—Cambs. v Bucks. (Cambridge); Cumb. v Staffs. (Netherfield); Suffolk v Lincs. (Mildenhall).

19—Berks. v Devon (Reading CC); Dorset v Oxon. (Weymouth); Lincs. v Cumb. (Cleethorpes); Wales v Cornwall (Penarth); Wilts. v Cheshire (Trowbridge).

21—Dorset v Cheshire (Dorchester); Herefords. v Cornwall (Dales CC, Leominster).

22—Beds. v Herts. (Luton); Cambs. v Northumb. (Cambridge).

26—Devon v Wilts. (Exmouth); Norfolk v Lincs. (Lakenham); Staffs. v Herts. (Leek).

27—Oxon. v Cornwall (Christ Church, Oxford).

28—Suffolk v Beds. (Ipswich School).

29—Berks. v Cornwall (Reading CC); Norfolk v Cambs. (Lakenham).

## AUGUST

2—Beds. v Cumb. (Bedford Town CC); Bucks. v Lincs. (Slough); Cheshire v Herefords. (Stalybridge); Dorset v Berks. (Dorchester); Norfolk v Herts. (Lakenham); Suffolk v Northumb. (Bury St Edmunds); Wilts. v Wales (Marlborough College).

3—Cornwall v Salop (Falmouth).

4—Cambs. v Cumb. (March); Norfolk v Northumb. (Lakenham).

5—Devon v Salop (Bovey Tracey).

9—Berks. v Wales (Finchampstead CC); Cheshire v Oxon. (Bowdon); Herts. v Cambs. (Hertford); Lincs. v Staffs. (Lincoln Lindum); Wilts. v Dorset (Devizes).

11—Bucks. v Norfolk (Beaconsfield); Salop v Oxon. (Oswestry).

16—Cheshire v Berks. (Toft); Cornwall v Dorset (St Austell); Herts. v Suffolk (Letchworth); Northumb. v Cumb. (Jesmond); Oxon. v Herefords. (Aston Rowant); Staffs. v Beds. (Stone); Wales v Devon (Ebbw Vale).

18—Beds. v Cambs. (Leighton Buzzard); Salop v Berks. (Wellington).

23—Bucks. v Suffolk (Marlow); Oxon. v Devon (Banbury XX).

30—Bucks. v Beds. (Amersham); Suffolk v Norfolk (Copdock, Ipswich); Wales v Dorset (Pontarddulais).

31—Herefords. v Wilts. (Hereford City SC).

## SEPTEMBER

13—Final at Worcester.

# †HOLT CUP KNOCKOUT COMPETITION, 1992

*All matches are of one day's duration.*

### Qualifying Round

**May 17** Cheshire v Northumb. (Chester Boughton Hall); Cumb. v Lincs. (Barrow); Salop v Herefords. (Perkins, Shrewsbury); Wales v Staffs. (Northop Hall).

### First Round

**May 31** Bucks. v Berks. (Aylesbury); Cambs. v Norfolk (The Ley's School); Cornwall v Devon (Truro); Cumb. or Lincs. v Cheshire or Northumb. (Burneside or Sleaford); Oxon. v Herts. (Christ Church, Oxford); Suffolk v Beds. (Framlingham College); Wales or Staffs. v Salop or Herefords. (Neath or Longton); Wilts. v Dorset (Devizes).

**Quarter-finals** to be played on June 14.

**Semi-finals** to be played on June 28.

**Final** to be played on August 26 at Lord's.